June 11–16, 2012
Beijing, China

Association for Computing Machinery

Advancing Computing as a Science & Profession

PLDI'12

Proceedings of the 2012 ACM SIGPLAN Conference on
Programming Language Design and Implementation

Sponsored by:

ACM SIGPLAN

Supported by:

Adobe, Facebook, Google, HP Labs, Huawei, IBM Research, Intel, LogicBlox, Microsoft Research, Oracle, Qualcomm Innovation Center, Samsung, and VMWare

Association for
Computing Machinery

Advancing Computing as a Science & Profession

The Association for Computing Machinery
2 Penn Plaza, Suite 701
New York, New York 10121-0701

ISBN: 978-1-4503-1205-9

Additional copies may be ordered prepaid from:

ACM Order Department
PO Box 30777
New York, NY 10087-0777, USA

Phone: 1-800-342-6626 (USA and Canada)
+1-212-626-0500 (Global)
Fax: +1-212-944-1318
E-mail: acmhelp@acm.org
Hours of Operation: 8:30 am – 4:30 pm ET

ACM Order Number: 548120

Printed in the USA

Message from the Chairs

It is our great pleasure to welcome you to Beijing for PLDI 2012, the 33rd ACM SIGPLAN Conference on Programming Language Design and Implementation. PLDI is the leading research conference about programming languages and their implementations. The PLDI 2012 program includes research papers, keynotes, a Student Research Competition, and several workshops, tutorials, and other colocated events.

This year's conference received a record 255 submissions. These submissions were reviewed in two phases. Each paper received 3 initial reviews in phase 1, after which authors were given an opportunity to respond to these reviews. Based on the initial reviews and author responses, additional reviews were solicited for approximately 70% of the submissions in a second phase of reviewing. Of these papers that made it to phase 2, 88 were discussed during the PC meeting, which took place from January 28-29, in Philadelphia.

More than 1000 reviews were written, of which most (62.9%) came from the thirty-one member Program Committee (PC). The forty-seven member External Review Committee (ERC) contributed with most of the other evaluations (32.1%). However, 92 other reviewers also participated in the evaluation process and provided expertise in some highly specialized areas. Papers submitted by Program Committee members were evaluated by the External Review Committee and the decisions on these papers was made by consensus. After careful evaluation, 48 papers were accepted for presentation at the conference. As a result, PLDI'12 will once again have a dual-track program.

Putting together PLDI 2012 was a team effort. First of all, we would like to thank the authors and workshop and tutorial organizers for providing the contents of the program. We are very grateful to the members of the Program Committee and External Committee, and to the many additional reviewers for evaluating many submissions on a tight schedule. We also owe a debt of gratitude to Coordination Chair Xiaobing Feng, Workshop Chairs Xiangyu Zhang and Chengyong Wu, Tutorial Chair Matthew Flatt, Publicity Chairs Matthew Might and Charles Zhang, Student Research Competition Chair Armando Solar-Lezama, Finance and Sponsorship Chair Iulian Neamtiu, and Webmaster Lei Zhao for their assistance with various aspects of organizing PLDI 2012. We gratefully acknowledge our sponsor ACM SIGPLAN, and corporate supporters (Adobe, Facebook, Google, HP Labs, Huawei, IBM Research, Intel, LogicBlox, Microsoft, Oracle, Qualcomm, Samsung, and VMware) for their generous contributions. Finally, we want to thank all of the conference attendees for contributing to making the conference a success. We hope that you will find the PLDI 2012 program interesting, thought-provoking, and inspiring, and that the conference will give you valuable opportunities to share ideas with members of our vibrant programming languages community.

Jan Vitek
PLDI 2012 Conference co-Chair
Purdue University

Haibo Lin
PLDI 2012 Conference co-Chair
Microsoft China

Frank Tip
PLDI 2012 Program Chair
IBM T.J. Watson Research Center

Table of Contents

Session 3A: Parallelism

Session Chair: Dan Grossman *(University of Washington)*

Session 3B: Reasoning, Inference, and Symbolic Execution

Session Chair: Eran Yahav *(Technion)*

Session 4A: Program Analysis I

Session Chair: Anders Møller *(Aarhus University)*

Session 4B: Web Applications

Session Chair: Robby Findler *(Northwestern University)*

Session 5A: Type-Based Techniques

Session Chair: Ben Liblit *(University of Wisconsin-Madison)*

Session 5B: C and C++

Session Chair: Hans-J. Boehm *(HP Labs)*

Session 6A: Optimization

Session Chair: Laurie Hendren *(McGill University)*

Session 6B: Verification

Session Chair: Eran Yahav *(Technion)*

Session 7A: Synthesis

Session Chair: Zhendong Su *(University of California, Davis)*

Session 7B: Program Analysis II

Session Chair: Susan Eisenbach *(Imperial College)*

PLDI 2012 Conference Organization

Conference Co-Chairs: Jan Vitek, *Purdue University*
Haibo Lin, *Microsoft China*

Program Chair: Frank Tip, *IBM T.J. Watson Research Center*

Coordination Chair: Xiaobing Feng, *ICT, Chinese Academy of Sciences*

Workshop Chairs: Xiangyu Zhang, *Purdue University*
Chengyong Wu, *ICT, Chinese Academy of Sciences*

Tutorial Chair: Matthew Flatt, *University of Utah*

Publicity Chair: Matthew Might, *University of Utah*

Pacific Publicity Chair: Charles Zhang, *The Hongkong University of Science and Technology*

Student Research Competition Chair: Armando Solar-Lezama, *MIT*

Finance and Sponsorship Chair: Iulian Neamtiu, *University of California, Riverside*

Webmaster: Lei Zhao, *Purdue University*

Steering Committee Chair: Jack Davidson, *University of Virginia*

Steering Committee: Kathleen Fisher, *Tufts University*
Philip Wadler, *University of Edinburgh*
Chandra Krintz, *University of Calfornia, Santa Barbara*
Graham Hutton, *University of Nottingham*
Jan Vitek, *Purdue University*
Frank Tip, *IBM T.J. Watson Research Center*
Mary Hall, *University of Utah*
David Padua, *University of Illinois at Urbana-Champaign*
Ben Zorn, *Microsoft Research*
Alex Aiken, *Stanford University*

Program Committee: Hans-J. Boehm, *HP Labs*
Wenguang Chen, *Tsinghua University*
Jong-Deok Choi, *Samsung Electronics*
Cliff Click, *Azul Systems*
Byron Cook, *Microsoft Research and QM, Univ. of London*
Amer Diwan, *Google*
Sophia Drossopoulou, *Imperial College London*
Susan Eisenbach, *Imperial College London*
Robby Findler, *Northwestern University*
Stephen Fink, *IBM T. J. Watson Research Center*
Cormac Flanagan, *University of California, Santa Cruz*

Program Committee (continued):

Stephen Freund, *Williams College*
Patrice Godefroid, *Microsoft Research*
Dan Grossman, *University of Washington*
Samuel Guyer, *Tufts University*
Laurie Hendren, *McGill University*
Tony Hosking, *Purdue University*
Jaakko Järvi, *Texas A&M University*
Ondrej Lhotak, *University of Waterloo*
Ben Liblit, *University of Wisconsin-Madison*
Calvin Lin, *The University of Texas at Austin*
Margaret Martonosi, *Princeton University*
Todd Millstein, *University of California, Los Angeles*
Anders Møller, *Aarhus University*
Nathaniel Nystrom, *University of Lugano, Switzerland*
David Padua, *University of Illinois*
Barbara Ryder, *Virginia Tech*
Zhendong Su, *University of California, Davis*
Emina Torlak, *University of California, Berkeley*
Chenggang Wu, *ICT, Chinese Academy of Sciences*
Eran Yahav, *Technion, Israel*

External Review Committee:

J. Nelson Amaral, *University of Alberta*
Matthew Arnold, *IBM T. J. Watson Research Center*
Steve Blackburn, *Australian National University*
Guy Blelloch, *Carnegie-Mellon University*
Kim Bruce, *Pomona College*
Luis Ceze, *University of Washington*
Dhruva Chakrabarti, *HP Labs*
Satish Chandra, *IBM India Research*
Bor-Yuh Evan Chang, *University of Colorado at Boulder*
Swarat Chaudhuri, *Rice University*
Chen Ding, *University of Rochester*
Erik Ernst, *Aarhus University*
Azadeh Farzan, *University of Toronto*
Matthew Flatt, *University of Utah*
Jeffrey S. Foster, *University of Maryland, College Park*
Ronald Garcia, *University of British Columbia*
Robert Grimm, *New York University*
Aarti Gupta, *NEC Labs*
Ben Hardekopf, *University of California, Santa Barbara*
Chris Hawblitzel, *Microsoft Research*
Görel Hedin, *Lund University*
Robert Hundt, *Google*
Richard Jones, *University of Kent*
Roy Ju, *AMD*
Shriram Krishnamurthi, *Brown University*
Martha Kim, *Columbia University*
Jens Knoop, *Vienna University of Technology*
Ulrich Kremer, *Rutgers*

External Review Committee (continued):

Doug Lea, *State University of New York at Oswego*
Jenq-Kuen Lee, *National Tsing Hua University*
Sorin Lerner, *University of California, San Diego*
Kathryn S. McKinley, *The University of Texas at Austin*
Matthew Might, *University of Utah*
Hanspeter Mössenböck, *Johannes Kepler University Linz*
Satish Narayanasamy, *University of Michigan*
James Noble, *Victoria University of Wellington*
Shaz Qadeer, *Microsoft Research*
G. Ramalingam, *Microsoft Research India*
John Regehr, *University of Utah*
Max Schaefer, *IBM T. J. Watson Research Center*
Manu Sridharan, *IBM T. J. Watson Research Center*
Christoph von Praun, *Georg-Simon-Ohm Hochschule Nürnberg*
Mandana Vaziri, *IBM T. J. Watson Research Center*
Adam Welc, *Adobe*
Youfeng Wu, *Intel*
Steve Zdancewic, *University of Pennsylvania*
Xiangyu Zhang, *Purdue University*

Student Research Selection Committee:

Isil Dillig, *College of William & Mary*
Kathleen Fisher, *Tufts University*
Sriram Rajamani, *Microsoft Research*
Andrey Rybalchenko, *Technische Universität Mnchen*
Armando Solar-Lezama, *MIT*
Martin Vechev, *ETH Zürich*

Additional Reviewers:

Saman Amarasinghe
Shay Artzi
Pavel Avgustinov
Cedric Bastoul
Tom Bergan
Lars Bergstrom
Armin Biere
Michael Carbin
Walter Chang
Xiao-Wen Chang
Pablo Chico
Mike Chu
Silvio Ricardo Cordeiro
Eva Darulova
Dibyendu Das
Joe Devietti
Julian Dolby
Eelco Dolstra
Gabriel Dos Reis
Curtis Dunham
David Eberly
Michael Ernst
Yaoqing Gao
Rahul Garg
Matthew Gaudet
Dan Ghica
Alexey Gotsman
Eric Goubault
Sumit Gulwani
Mary Hall
Wentao Han
Jiangzhou He
Manuel Hermenegildo
Yuan-Shin Hwang
Suresh Jagannathan
Akanksha Jain
Doug Kimelman
Viktor Kuncak

Additional Reviewers (continued):

Michael Lai
Julia Lawall
Jianjun Li
Jin Li
Percy Liang
Chu-cheow Lim
Kun Ling
Brandon Lucia
Sharad Malik
Jincheng Miao
Kevin Millikin
Piramanayagam Arumuga Nainar
Joe Near
Flemming Nielson
Donald Nguyen
Robert O'Callahan
Valeria de Paiva
David Pichardie
Keshav Pingali
Marco Pistoia
Tristan Ravitch
Lakshminarayanan Renganarayana
Cindy Rubio González
Claudio Russo
Hesam Samimi
Adrian Sampson
Karu Sankaralingam
Vijay Saraswat
Jeremy Siek
Satnam Singh
Jeffrey Mark Siskind
Armando Solar-Lezama
Kathryn Stolee
Tijs van der Storm
Nikhil Swamy
Peter Sweeney
Olivier Tardieu
Bill Thies
Sid Touati-Ali
Martin Vechev
Clark Verbrugge
Jurgen Vinju
Eelco Visser
Wenwen Wang
Zhenjiang Wang
Shiyi Wei
Jason Wilkins
Benjamin Wood
Tian Xiao
Di Xu
Xiang Yuan
Carlo Zaniolo
Dingfei Zhang
Hongjuan Zhang

PLDI'12 Sponsor & Supporters

Sponsor:

Supporters:

Compiling a High-Level Language for GPUs

(via Language Support for Architectures and Compilers)

Christophe Dubach[1,2] Perry Cheng[2] Rodric Rabbah[2] David F. Bacon[2] Stephen J. Fink[2]

[1]University of Edinburgh [2]IBM Research

christophe.dubach@ed.ac.uk {perry,rabbah,dfb,sjfink}@us.ibm.com

Abstract

Languages such as OpenCL and CUDA offer a standard interface for general-purpose programming of GPUs. However, with these languages, programmers must explicitly manage numerous low-level details involving communication and synchronization. This burden makes programming GPUs difficult and error-prone, rendering these powerful devices inaccessible to most programmers.

We desire a higher-level programming model that makes GPUs more accessible while also effectively exploiting their computational power. This paper presents features of Lime, a new Java-compatible language targeting heterogeneous systems, that allow an optimizing compiler to generate high quality GPU code. The key insight is that the language type system enforces isolation and immutability invariants that allow the compiler to optimize for a GPU without heroic compiler analysis.

Our compiler attains GPU speedups between 75% and 140% of the performance of native OpenCL code.

Categories and Subject Descriptors D.3.3 [*Programming Languages*]: Language Constructs and Features

General Terms Design, Languages, Performance

Keywords GPU, OpenCL, Java, Lime, Streaming, Map, Reduce

1. Introduction

In response to increasing challenges with frequency scaling, hardware designers have turned to architectures with increasing degrees of explicit parallelism. Today's hardware offerings range from general purpose chips with a few cores (*e.g.*, Intel Core i7), to specialized distributed-memory multiple-SIMD platforms (*e.g.*, IBM Cell), to graphics processors (GPUs) that support large-scale data parallel computations. Additionally, several efforts underway attempt to exploit reconfigurable hardware (FPGAs), with massively bit-parallel execution, for general-purpose computation.

OpenCL [ ] and CUDA [ ] have emerged as mainstream languages for programming GPUs and multicore systems. These popular languages provide APIs that expose low-level details of the device architecture. The programmer must manually tune low-level code for a specific device in order to fully exploit its processing resources. For example, a sub-optimal mapping of data to a GPU's non-uniform memory hierarchy may degrade performance by a factor of ten or more.

Experience shows that programming in a high-level language is more productive, portable, and less error-prone. Ideally, a programmer should express a program using high-level constructs that are architecture independent, and have the compiler automatically generate device-specific code that is competitive with low-level hand-written code. Indeed, programmers have enjoyed these benefits with general purpose programming languages on general purpose CPUs for several decades. In this paper, we address challenges in delivering similar benefits for programs running with GPUs.

This paper presents details of a GPU programming model in a new programming language called Lime. As presented earlier [ ], Lime is a Java-compatible object-oriented language which targets heterogeneous systems with general purpose processors, FPGAs, and GPUs. The Lime methodology allows a programmer to gently refactor a suitable Java program into a pattern amenable for heterogeneous parallel devices. We present the design and evaluation of the Lime compiler and runtime subsystems specific to GPUs.

The Lime language exposes parallelism and computation explicitly with high level abstractions [ ]. Notably, the type system for these abstractions enforces key invariants regarding isolation and immutability. The optimizing compiler leverages these invariants to generate efficient parallel code for multicores and GPUs, without relying on deep program analysis.

This paper shows how a Lime programmer can exploit a GPU without writing complex low-level code required with mainstream approaches (OpenCL or CUDA). The compiler and runtime system coordinate to automatically orchestrate communication and computation, map data to the GPU memory hierarchy, and tune the kernel code to deliver robust end-to-end performance. The contributions of this paper are:

- A design and implementation of an optimizing compiler to generate high quality GPU code from high-level language abstractions including isolated parallel tasks, communication operators, value types to express immutable data structures, and fine-grained map-and-reduce operations (Sections 3-4).
- A set of automatic optimizations for GPU architectures that may be applied without sophisticated alias analysis or data dependence analysis. These include memory optimizations that improve locality, reduce bank conflicts, and permit vectorization (Section 4.2).
- A detailed empirical performance evaluation comparing the generated code to hand-tuned OpenCL programs. The performance of the generated code lies between 75% to 140% of hand-written and tuned native OpenCL code (Section 5).

The performance results show that across a suite of 9 benchmarks, our compiler delivers a speedup ranging from $12x - 430x$ for the NVidia GeForce GTX580 architecture (Fermi) and $12x -$

PLDI'12, June 11–16, Beijing, China.

416x for the AMD Radeon HD5970. Further, using the OpenCL multicore runtime, we report a performance gain between $4.8x$ – $32.5x$ for the Intel Core i7 architecture.

2. OpenCL Background

OpenCL and CUDA represent the *de facto* standards for general purpose programming on GPUs. OpenCL, in particular, was designed to provide an industry-standard API for systems with heterogeneous devices.

Although OpenCL provides a portable API, the API presents a low-level interface to the underlying hardware. The OpenCL programmer must explicitly manage many low-level details to map data to appropriate address spaces, enable vectorization, schedule data transfers between the host and device, and manage synchronization among queues connecting the host and devices.

In this section, we briefly review the structure of a small OpenCL N-Body application. This example motivates the need for high-level abstractions and introduces tuning issues germane to GPU performance.

Figure 1 illustrates an N-Body simulation expressed using a common OpenCL programming pattern. Lines 1-16 embody a data-parallel kernel that represents a n^2 force calculation. The kernel may run on a GPU or a multicore CPU.

Address Space Qualifiers The kernel declaration (line 1) includes address space qualifiers that map the respective data to the GPU memory hierarchy. OpenCL presents a non-uniform memory hierarchy with five types of memories: `private`, `local`, `global`, `constant` and `image`. The `private` memory represents a fast, small memory private to each computational thread. The `local` memory represents a shared memory, used to coherently share data between a small group of related threads called a *work group*. The `global` memory provides a shared address space for all threads on a device, with no implicit coherency guarantees across work groups. The `constant` and `image` memories represent specialized read-only storage. The former, typically a small space, usually holds constants referenced by a computational kernel. Graphics applications typically store texture objects for rendering a scene in the image memory. We inspected a number of OpenCL benchmarks and found that the kernels often use private, constant, and global qualifiers in the kernel signatures.

Vectorization The kernel code features the use of the OpenCL `float4` data type (lines 5, 6, 12). The code represents the forces as an array of tuple elements each consisting of four floating-point values, even though each force value has only three components. This decision allows the device to vectorize the memory accesses. OpenCL 1.0 only supports vectors of size 2, 4, 8, and 16.

Kernel Tuning The force calculation illustrates a typical data parallel pattern where multiple instances (*work items*) of the same kernel operate on disjoint data sets. Lines 2-4 show some manual calculations to determine the working set for a running work item. The working set depends on the number of concurrent kernel instances, a user-determined property that is typically determined through trial and error to suit the computational power of the target device. For N-Body, each working set represents the subset of particles for which the work item computes forces. The loop at lines 8-15 iterates through the kernel working set and computes the forces for the corresponding particles. Lines 9, 10, and 15 access local memory and perform synchronizations between kernel instances to ensure correct access to local memory.

Orchestrating Execution The second half of Figure 1 shows a fraction of the host code necessary to orchestrate the execution of the kernel code. A typical execution pattern applies the following steps: (1) discover and initialize the device and compile the kernel code, (2) create a command queue, (3) create the kernel, (4) create read and write buffers, (5) enqueue commands to transfer the read buffer, invoke kernel, and transfer the write buffer. The programmer is responsible for scheduling the data transfers and overlapping these with kernel computation. This process uses at least a dozen OpenCL procedures based on our inspection of several hand-tuned OpenCL programs. We omitted an additional 182 lines of code which deal with step (1) alone.

3. Lime Programming Language

The previous example shows that OpenCL allows fine-grain control of the host and kernel code, but the low-level details impose a significant burden on the programmer. Similar points hold for CUDA. In contrast, Lime [ ] provides a high-level object-oriented language offering task, data, and pipeline parallelism. It extends Java with several constructs designed for programming heterogeneous architectures with GPU and FPGA accelerators. Here, we briefly review the Lime constructs which the compiler relies on to efficiently offload computation to a GPU.

Figure 2 represents a Lime implementation of the N-Body example. Since the language is Java-compatible and interoperable, it provides a gentle migration path from Java. The figure illustrates this process with white and black squares: white squares prefix original Java code and black ones prefix new Lime code.

Line 3 sets up the main computation, as embodied in a *task graph* data structure. A task graph is a directed graph of computations, where values flow between tasks over edges in the graph. The `nbody` task graph from line 3 is illustrated in the figure below.

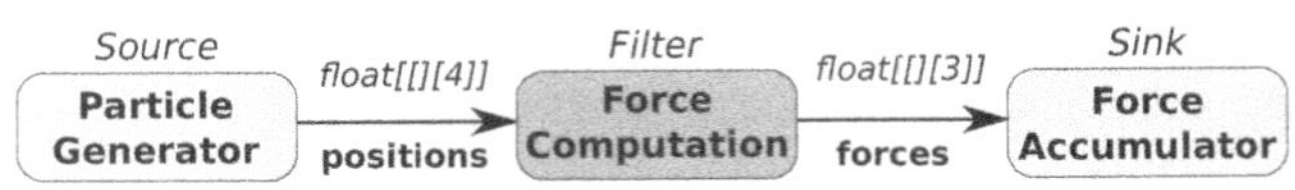

A particle generator task emits an initial set of particles, stored as an array of 4-element tuples: three elements for the position and one for the mass. A force computation task computes the force acting on each particle using a simple n^2 algorithm. This task produces an array of 3-element tuples representing the forces acting on each particle. The force accumulator task consumes these forces, and computes a new position for each particle.

The task graph just described represents a single simulation step. Typically the algorithm runs for a large number of simulation steps.

Two noteworthy Lime operators appear on line 3. First is the `task` operator, which creates a computational unit equivalent to an OpenCL kernel. Second is the `=>` (connect) operator, which represents the flow of data between tasks. The `finish` on line 4 initiates the computation and forces completion. This is necessary since Lime decouples the creation of task graphs from their execution.

3.1 Task and Connect

The `task` operator is used to create tasks (line 3). A task repeatedly applies a *worker* method as long as input data is presented to the task via an input port, and enqueues its output (the result of the method application) to an output stream. The operator binds the method specified after the dot to the task worker method. The worker method may be static (`NBody.computeForces`) or an instance method (*e.g.*, `NBody().particleGen`). In the latter, the task operator creates an instance of the type `NBody` and binds its instance method to the worker. The distinction between the two cases is that static worker methods are essentially pure functions and the instance methods may be stateful. Methods in lime are task-agnostic, meaning they may be invoked as conventional static or in-

```
1  ■ kernel void calcForceKernel(global float4* positions, global float4* forces, local float4* localPos) {
2  ■     int gi = get_global_id(0);     int ti = get_local_id(0);
3  ■     int gs = get_global_size(0);   int ls = get_local_size(0);
4  ■     int blks = gs / ls;
5  ■     float4 pi = positions[gi];
6  ■     float4 force = {0,0,0,0};
7  ■     int baseIndex = 0;
8  ■     for (int b=0; b<blks; b++) {
9  ■       localPos[ti] = positions[baseIndex+ti];
10 ■       barrier(CLK_LOCAL_MEM_FENCE);
11 ■       for (int j=0; j<ls; j++) {
12 ■         float4 pj = localPos[j];
13 ■         ... update force based on pi and pj ... }
14 ■       baseIndex += ls;
15 ■       barrier(CLK_LOCAL_MEM_FENCE); }
16 ■     forces[gi] = acc; }
17
18 ░ void runKernel(int N /*num particles*/, cl_float4* positions /*initial state*/) {
19 ░   cl_float4* forces = calloc(N, sizeof(cl_float4));
20 ░   // create the input and output buffers using helper functions
21 ░   cl_mem input  = clCreateBuffer(context, CL_MEM_READ_ONLY,  sizeof(cl_float4)*N, NULL, NULL);
22 ░   cl_mem output = clCreateBuffer(context, CL_MEM_WRITE_ONLY, sizeof(cl_float4)*N, NULL, NULL);
23 ░   // lock-step iteration
24 ░   while(true) {
25 ░     // send the input data to the device (non-blocking)
26 ░     clEnqueueWriteBuffer(queue, input, CL_FALSE, 0, sizeof(cl_float4) * N, positions, 0, NULL, NULL);
27 ░     // pass the arguments to the kernel
28 ░     clSetKernelArg(calcForceKernel, 0, sizeof(cl_mem), &input);
29 ░     clSetKernelArg(calcForceKernel, 1, sizeof(cl_mem), &output);
30 ░     clSetKernelArg(calcForceKernel, 2, maxWorkGroupSize * sizeof(cl_float4), NULL);
31 ░     // start the one-dimensional kernel with N threads (force computation)
32 ░     clEnqueueNDRangeKernel(queue, calcForceKernel, 1, NULL, &N, NULL, 0, NULL, NULL);
33 ░     // read back the data from the device (blocking)
34 ░     clEnqueueReadBuffer(queue, output, CL_TRUE, 0, sizeof(cl_float4) * N, forces, 0, NULL, NULL );
35 ░     // update state based on the acceleration computed (force accumulator)
36 ░     update_position(positions, forces); } }
```

Figure 1. Parts of the OpenCL kernel ■ and host code ░ for N-Body

stance methods and only become worker methods by applying the task operator.

The language runtime repeatedly invokes the worker method as long as data items are available on the input port. A special case is the source task (lines 6-8) that emits data until interrupted by an `Underflow Exception` that can be thrown by any task to notify that the computation is finished.

Tasks in Lime are either *isolated* or *non-isolated*. An isolated task, also known as a *filter*, has its own address space and may not access mutable global state (*e.g.*, non-final statics fields in Java). Lime achieves isolation using a combination of *local* methods, and *value* types.

The worker method of an isolated task must be declared `local` (lines 10 and 13). A local method may only call other local methods, and may not access global mutable fields. The worker methods input immutable (value types) arguments (if any) and must return values (if any). This ensures that data exchanged between tasks does not mutate in flight, and provides the compiler and runtime greater opportunities for optimizing communication between tasks without imposing undue burden on the compiler to infer invariants involving aliasing.

A value type represents a deeply immutable object type (*e.g.*, data structure or array) declared using the *value* modifier on a type. A value array is indicated using double brackets, so for example `float[[][4]]` is a two dimensional array of floats, where the outer dimension is unbounded, the inner dimension is bounded to size four, and the entire array is immutable. Value arrays must be initialized at construction time (lines 8 and 17).

The `task` operator encapsulates computation whereas the `=>` (connect) operator encapsulates communication between tasks (line 3). This operator is used to connect two tasks when the output type of the upstream task (left of the operator) matches the input type of the downstream task (right of the operator). Lime exposes the communication between tasks explicitly using the connect operator so that the compiler and runtime can optimize the I/O and synchronization between tasks automatically and without programmer intervention, in contrast to OpenCL (see Figure 1 lines 20-35).

3.2 Map and Reduce

Lime also offers a *map* and *reduce* model for fine-grained data parallelism. This model suits the thread-level parallelism available in GPUs, and also short-vector SIMD instructions available in many general purpose ISAs.

A map operation applies a (logical) function to each element of some aggregate data structure, producing another aggregate data structure. The reduce operation combines values from an aggregate data structure using a combinator function. These abstractions are well-known in traditional functional languages.

The map operator is represented by the `@` token; see line 11 of Figure 2. It applies the function `computeParticleForces` to each element of the `particles` array, and returns the resultant array. Each application of the map function computes the force interactions between a particle `p` and all other `particles` (lines 13-17). The example omits the core force computation since it is similar in all implementations (OpenCL, Java and Lime).

```
□ public class NBody {
□   public static void simulate() {
■     Task nbody = task NBody().particleGen => task NBody.computeForces => task NBody().forceAccumulator;
□     nbody.finish(); }

■   private float[[][4]] particleGen() {
□     float[][4] theParticles = ...;  // initial state of the particles
■     return new float[[][4]](theParticles); }

■   private static local float[[][3]] computeForces(float[[][4]] particles) {
■     return NBody @ computeParticleForces(particles, particles); }

■   private static local float[[3]] computeParticleForces(float[[4]] p, float[[][4]] particles) {
□     float fx = 0, fy = 0, fz = 0;
□     for (int j=0; j<particles.length; j++) {
□       ... } // scalar computation to update fx, fy, and fz based on p and particles[j]
■     return new float[[]] { fx, fy, fz }; }

■   private void forceAccumulator(float[[][3]] particles) {
□     ... } // update the state of the particles for next iteration
□ }
```

Figure 2. Lime version of force calculation of NBody. The code marked with □ is original Java Source.

A reduction in Lime is expressed using an operator or method followed by ! to indicate the operator or method should be treated as a combinator. The language permits instance or static methods as well as certain arithmetic operators to serve as reduction operators as long as they apply to two arguments of the same type and produce a result of that type.

4. Compilation Methodology

The explicit separation of computation and communication in Lime via the task and connect operators relieves the programmer from the burden of orchestrating the execution of tasks between host and device. This responsibility now falls onto the Lime compiler and runtime. Similarly, because Lime programs do not force the programmer to make an explicit distinction between the kernel and host codes, the compiler must determine a partitioning of the program between host (CPU) and device (GPU).

Our compilation methodology is illustrated in Figure 3. The compiler partitions the source code into host and device code, and compiles each partition to native code. The Lime compiler generates a mix of Java bytecodes and OpenCL. The bytecodes run in an unmodified Java virtual machine. The generated OpenCL code encompasses both the compiler-tuned kernels and the coordination and scheduling code for managing the buffers, scheduling data transfers and executing the kernels.

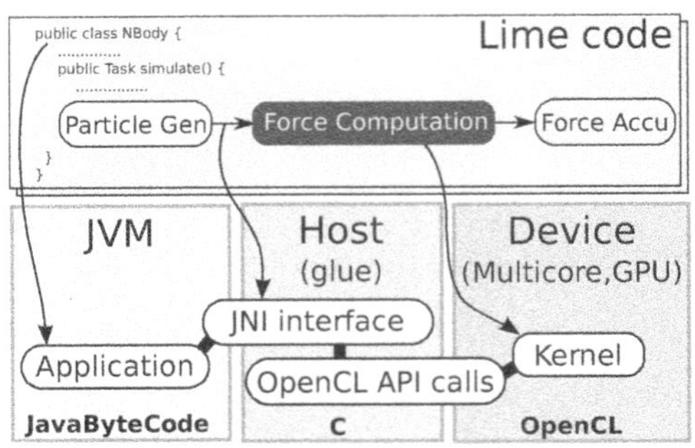

Figure 3. Starting from a Lime program, our compiler produces the application code that runs in the JVM, the C code that handle data exchange and the calls to the OpenCL API and finally the OpenCL kernel code.

4.1 Kernel Identification

In the N-Body example, the main computation workload lies in the n^2 force calculation. Thus, a natural partition of the N-Body example runs the `particleGen` and `forceAccumulator` tasks on the host and the `computeForces` task on the GPU.

To allow offloading, the compiler requires the `computeForces` task to be an *isolated* task, also known as a filter. The language semantics for a filter guarantee that it does not perform globally side-effecting operations because it is isolated (*i.e.*, local) and its arguments are immutable (*i.e.*, values). As a result, our compiler recognizes filter task creations, and treats each filter as the unit of computation to offload. Note that the system may freely move filters between device and host without concern for data-races and non-determinism.

Within each filter, the compiler scans for map and reduce operations to identify opportunities for kernel-level data-parallelism. The compiler detects data-parallel maps and generates corresponding parallel implementations without deep dependence analysis. Instead, it checks for the following invariants on map expressions: (a) the map function is static and local, and (b) the map function arguments are value types (includes primitive types). The type system guarantees that a static local method does not access globally mutable data, and because the value arguments are immutable, the map function is pure and side-effect free. In a similar way, the compiler may infer a parallel reduction.

Following kernel identification, the compiler performs kernel optimization (Section 4.2) with an emphasis on the GPU memory hierarchy. Lastly, the compiler generates appropriate glue code to orchestrate both the data transfers and the kernel invocations (Section 4.3). The glue code is implied by the connect operator which identifies the communication required between host and device.

Table 1 summarizes the differences between programming in OpenCL and compiling Lime code for GPUs. The salient observation is that Lime provides a much higher level of abstraction and does not expose low-level architectural details.

Table 1. GPU programming in OpenCL vs. Lime.

	OpenCL	Lime
offload unit	kernel	filter
communication	API	=> operator
data parallelism	manual	map & reduce
memory qualifiers	manual	compiler
synchronization	manual	compiler
scheduling	manual	compiler

4.2 Kernel Optimizations

The mechanics of optimizing and generating an OpenCL kernel from a Lime filter center on the exploitation of map and reduce operations for thread and SIMD parallelism, and applying a set of locality enhancing optimizations that take advantage of the OpenCL memory organization when applicable (*e.g.*, a GPU).

Figure 4 shows the code generated by the Lime compiler for the Lime code snippet shown earlier. The compiler takes advantages of the semantic information available at the source level to determine that the map operation (Figure 2 line 11) is data-parallel, and it exploits the immutable and bounded-size nature of individual particles to perform memory optimizations and vectorization. The generated kernel code will adapt to any number of threads started by the Lime runtime or as requested by the user. In Figure 4 line 9, the kernel loop iterates over the array of particles with each thread assigned an element `i` at line 10. This generated code is more robust than the hand-written OpenCL kernels we inspected because it executes correctly independent of the number of threads.

In addition to the obvious kernel input and output arguments, the compiler also generates a structure to contain runtime bookkeeping information and data values needed by the kernel code (see Figure 4(b)). Examples of the latter include array lengths that are used explicitly at line 15 and implicitly at line 11. This record is passed to the kernel as a parameter on line 2.

4.2.1 Memory Optimizations

Once the kernel is identified, a key optimization maps non-scalar (*e.g.*, array) data to the different memory structures in the device. This section describes how the compiler optimizes memory accesses for the OpenCL memory hierarchy (common to GPUs). The compiler permits for any of the optimizations to be enabled and disabled so that it is possible to perform an automated exploration of the memory mapping and layout.

The compiler drives memory optimizations using a relatively simple *pattern matching* algorithm. It scans the intermediate representation for common memory access idioms and applies the corresponding transformation when a pattern is encountered. In contrast to much previous work, our memory optimizer does not require sophisticated alias analysis or data dependence analysis. Instead, our compiler exploits the strong type system in Lime to infer necessary invariants without deep analysis. For example, immutable value types in the source language provide the key invariants that memory locations are read only and cannot be reassigned.

We claim that enabling a relatively simple memory optimizer is a strength of our approach, as compared to more unconstrained input languages that necessitate heroic program analysis.

Figure 5 illustrates some of the idioms recognized by the Lime compiler. In the figure and the text that follows, a *parallel loop* corresponds to a data-parallel map operator that the compiler has already inferred.

Global Memory Mapping data to the global memory is the default behavior of the optimizer when no other mapping is possible.

```
1  kernel void computeForces(
2    constant runtime_info_t* ri,
3    global float4* particles,
4    global float* result)
5  {
6     int gi = get_global_id(0);
7     int gs = get_global_size(0);
8     int len = ri->particles_length;
9     for (int it=0; it<len; it+=gs) {
10        int i=it+gs;
11        if (i<len) {
12           float fx=0;
13           float fy=0;
14           float fz=0;
15           float4 pi = particles[gi];
16           for (int j=0; j<len; j++) {
17              float4 pj = particles[j];
18              ... computation to update fx, fy
19              ... and fz based on pi and pj
20           }
21           result[gi*3+0] = fx;
22           result[gi*3+1] = fy;
23           result[gi*3+2] = fz;
24  }  }  }
```

(a) Generated OpenCL code

```
typedef struct {
   int particles_length;
} runtime_info_t;
```

(b) Generated structure for runtime information

Figure 4. Lime to OpenCL code generation

Private Memory The compiler attempts to map all the arrays that are not shared across threads to the fast private memory. Due to the extremely small capacity of this type of memory, the compiler only considers arrays whose size can be determined statically and does not exceed a certain threshold value. An array is not shared when it is allocated within the inner most parallel loop since each thread will execute its own instance of the loop body. Figure 5(a-b) show a simple example where an array variable `arr` is mapped to the private memory in OpenCL.

Local Memory In most OpenCL application, the local memory is used as a type of scratch pad for shared data. This memory is the second fastest type of memory. It is typically used when the data is reused among several threads running on the same core. A typical example where this happens is in the case of a double nested loop as shown in Figures 5(c-d). The parallel inner most loop reuses the value `v`. Since this inner loop is parallelized into many threads, it is possible to store parts of the `arg` array in the local memory and thus increase data reuse. The compiler performs a code transformation similar to loop tiling. When the size of the local memory cannot be determined statically our system dynamically allocates memory at runtime depending on the number of parallel threads.

The local memory is typically organized in different banks, with consecutive words assigned to different banks. Once the optimizer has decided to map an array into the local memory it determines whether padding is necessary in order to avoid bank conflicts. This is a common optimization although often done manually [ ] in OpenCL or CUDA kernels. In Lime, it is relatively easier to automatically apply this optimization using the type information available and the fact that the code is virtually free from pointers as opposed to lower-level pointer-rich programs. The Lime compiler

```
float[] doWork(...) {
  Parallel loop {
    T[] arr = new T[10];
  } ...
```

(a) Private memory candidate (allocation within parallel region)

```
kernel doWork(...) {
  ...
  private int arr[10];
  ...
```

(b) OpenCL using private array allocation

```
float[] doWork(float[] arg) {
  ...
  Parallel loop (i) {
    float v = arg[i];
    Parallel loop {
      v;
    } } ...
```

(c) Local memory candidate (nested loop with data reuse)

```
kernel doWork(global float* arg,
              local float* local_mem) {
  ...
  if (local_id(1) == 0)
    local_mem[local_id(0)] = arg[global_id(0)];
  float v = local_mem[local_id(0)];
  ...
```

(d) OpenCL using local memory (synchronization omitted)

```
float[] doWork(float[][4] arg) {
  ...
  Parallel loop {
    float[4] v = arg[x];
    v[2];
  } ...
```

(e) Image memory candidate (accesses to v static)

```
kernel doWork(read_only image_2d_f arg) {
  ...
  ...
  float4 v = read_imagef(arg, {x,0});
  v.s2;
  ...
```

(f) OpenCL using image memory

```
float[] doWork(float[] arg) {   ...
    Parallel loop {
      arg[x];
  } ...
```

(g) Constant memory candidate (x invariant in the loop)

```
kernel doWork(constant float* arg) {
  ...
  arg[x];
  ...
```

(h) OpenCL using constant memory

Figure 5. Example of code patterns that our optimizer is looking for and the corresponding generated OpenCL in pseudo-code. Readers familiar with writing OpenCL code may recognize here some typical code pattern often encountered in OpenCL kernels.

detects the size of the array elements and adds padding accordingly. This ensures that each consecutive thread reads data from a different bank, thus increasing memory throughput.

Image Memory The compiler tries to map read-only arrays into the image memory. Since OpenCL 1.0 only supports access to the image memory by groups of 4 words, the compiler limits the scope to arrays whose last dimension is either 2 or 4. The compiler adopts a packed representation in the case where the last array dimension is of length 2. In addition, it prevents the optimizer from assigning to image memory arrays whose last dimensions elements are not accessed contemporaneously, in order to ensure good performance. Figure 5(e-f) shows a typical candidate (`arg`) for this optimization. The Lime array access expressions are converted into the appropriate OpenCL image access functions. Since the OpenCL does not support 1D images, the compiler maps the index x to the 2D coordinate `(x,0)` [1].

Constant Memory The constant memory is reserved for values that are *broadcast* to all the threads. That is, all the threads read the same address. In this case, the compiler identifies array accesses within a parallel loop that are accessed using a loop-invariant index as shown in Figure 5(g-h).

[1] The compiler implementation is more complex since the compiler may perform modulo operations when the index is greater than the maximum width supported by the image format.

4.2.2 Vectorization

Following the memory optimizations, the compiler vectorizes memory accesses for multidimensional arrays. An innermost array dimension is a vectorization candidate if it is of length 2, 4, 8 or 16. This optimization is only applied for arrays that are read-only and whose access to the last dimension is known statically. Vectorizing the memory accesses usually reduces the total number of memory accesses and thus improves bandwidth utilization and performance. This optimization is applied for data mapped to the global, local or constant memory (the image memory optimization is intrinsically already vectorized). Once again, the benefit of using a high-level language that allows for pointer-free programming makes this type of analysis simple.

4.3 Orchestrating Communication

Although the data and code isolation of Lime tasks makes computation offloading possible, the runtime system must still efficiently transfer data to and from the main system memory to the device. Because Lime targets devices that include GPUs and FPGAs, the runtime implementation adopts a universal "wire" format that relies only on sending a byte stream as shown in Figure 6.

The communication steps between the host JVM and the native device entail (1) serializing a Lime value to a byte array, (2) crossing the JNI boundary, and (3) converting this byte array into a C-style value. The particular representation of a value for use in OpenCL is specific to our code generator; the C deserializer does not necessarily convert to a standard C format. The return path is a mirror image in which we convert the OpenCL data structure to a

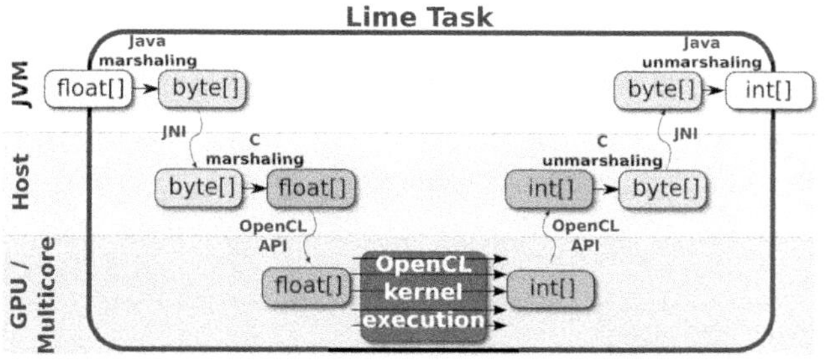

Figure 6. Data transfer between Java and the OpenCL device. This example shows a task that takes a float array as input and returns an int array.

byte array, return from the JNI call, and then deserialize from the byte array back into a heap-resident Lime value.

If not optimized, high communication costs can cancel out any performance gains from exploiting a GPU. Our initial implementation was simple and used Lime's internal runtime type information to serialize and deserialize. Unfortunately, the performance was so poor that more than 90% of the time was spent marshaling data to or from a byte array. Performance was greatly improved by writing custom serialization routines for the most common types–primitives and (nested) arrays of primitives. During the initialization process of migrating a task to a native device, the runtime will find a custom serializer based on the data type. Because the default marshaller is written recursively, we modified it to use a specialized marshaller recursively when available. For instance, if the data type is a tuple of integer arrays, then although there is no specialization at the tuple level, the lowest level integer arrays (where most of the data actually is) will still be optimized. Finally, because Lime arrays can express bounds (e.g., sub-rectangular arrays are possible), the runtime system can sometimes determine the exact size of the target byte array up-front.

Marshaling on the C side is similar but more specialized. Because our OpenCL backend only handles rectangular arrays of primitives, the data is generally densely packed. The layout must take alignment and vectorization into consideration, making the marshaller more specialized though less comprehensive. Because the serialization is primarily memory-bound, we simply use malloc/free rather than implement our own memory manager to lower costs.

Our current communication implementation could be further optimized since it entails repeated serialization in the same address space. However, our current design affords a common format as a starting point for a communication subsystem that supports heterogeneous devices. One might further optimize the protocol by creating specific communication channels so that the sender and receiver are aware of the data format the other party desires. Going even further, one might be able to avoid a low-level memory copy by pinning memory pages and managing memory explicitly. However, these changes come at the cost of OS and JVM portability.

5. Evaluation

We present an empirical evaluation of the Lime system to answer three questions:

1. **End-to-end Speedup.** Can the Lime programmer effectively exploit a GPU to improve performance? That is, can the system deliver high performance, including all communication costs and runtime overhead?
2. **Comparison to hand-tuned OpenCL.** What is the quality of the OpenCL code generated by the Lime compiler as compared to hand-tuned native OpenCL implementations?
3. **Computation vs. Communication.** How much overhead does the system introduce to communicate between the host and device?

Table 3 reports the set of benchmarks used in this study. The set includes three benchmarks from Parboil [ ] and two benchmarks from JavaGrande (JG) [ ]; we selected the benchmarks that were easiest to port to Lime. We expect other benchmarks which can be expressed using task graphs and map and reduce to benefit in the same way. In addition we include two benchmarks, N-Body and Mosaic, that we wrote from scratch. Previous sections reviewed N-Body in detail. Mosaic features a map-and-reduce algorithm to compare tiles from a reference image to tiles from an image library to find the best-matched tiles using a scoring function.

Some of the benchmarks predominantly exercise floating-point arithmetic. ALUs in modern processors perform floating-point arithmetic in at least double-precision, whereas GPU ALU building blocks are single-precision. For GPUs, single-precision operations run faster than double-precision ones. Because this paper focuses on compilation rather than numerical stability issues, we present results for both single- and double-precision variants in cases where precision strongly affects performance.

Table 2 lists the hardware platforms evaluated. We measure performance on four platforms. In each case, Lime tasks are compiled to OpenCL and run natively using the OpenCL runtime, while the remaining application code runs in bytecode. The Intel Core i7 system runs 64-bit Ubuntu Linux 10.10 with the 2.6.35-28 kernel. The NVidia cards represent two generations of GPU architectures: a recent GeForce GTX580 (Fermi) and a 2006 GeForce GTX8800. The latter is used to compare the Parboil benchmarks since they are specifically hand-optimized for this card [ ]. The GeForce architecture evolved substantially between these generations. Notably, the Fermi architecture adds caches in addition to the local memory. The NVidia GPUs use CUDA 4.0.13 with device driver version 270.40. The AMD GPU uses driver version 11.9 and AMD OpenCL SDK 2.5-RC2.

5.1 End-to-end Speedup

Figure 7 shows the bottom-line, end-to-end performance results including all system overheads. The figure represents performance results of the Lime code compiled to OpenCL, running partially in bytecode and partially in the native OpenCL runtime for the CPU (top) and the GPU (bottom). The figure reports speedup based on wall-clock execution times, measured after a preliminary warmup phase to ensure JIT optimizations occur. The figure normalizes speed as compared to Lime code running entirely in bytecode.

The baseline Lime bytecode performance achieves 95-98% of the performance of the original pure Java implementations for N-Body, Mosaic and JG-Series. In the worst case, the performance of JG-Crypt is half as fast when running Lime compiled to bytecode, as compared to the original Java. This slowdown is an artifact of our methodology in porting from Java, since we only ported the dominant computational kernels to Lime. As a result, the Java to Lime interoperability introduces some overhead with respect to array conversion, and further the cost of byte-array accesses in Lime are more expensive than in Java. However, note that the acceleration gained by compiling the kernels to OpenCL more than compensates for the slowdown due to this interoperation.

Since the end-to-end measurements include both computation and communication costs, we only show the results for the Core i7, the faster NVidia GTX580, and the AMD HD5970. This is because the overheads are proportionately larger with greater acceleration.

Table 2. Evaluation platforms. Note, the number of GPU cores represents the number of Streaming Multiprocessors.

Type	Model	Cores	FP units per core	Const. mem	Local mem	L1 cache	L2 cache	L3 cache
CPU	Intel Core i7-990X	6	4 single (4 double)			6x64KB	6x256KB	12MB
GPU	NVidia GeForce GTX 8800	16	8 single	64KB	16x16KB			
GPU	NVidia GeForce GTX 580	16	32 single (16 double)	64KB	16x48KB	16x16KB	768KB	
GPU	AMD Radeon HD 5970	20	80 single	64KB	20x32KB			

Table 3. Benchmarks used in the evaluation.

Name	Description	Input size	Output size	Data Type
N-Body	N-Body simulation	64KB / 128KB	48KB / 128KB	Float / Double
Mosaic	Mosaic image application	600KB	5MB	Integer
Parboil-CP	Coulombic Potential	62KB	1MB	Float
Parboil-MRIQ	Magnetic Resonance Imaging	432KB	256KB	Float
Parboil-RPES	Rys Polynomial Equation Solver	13MB	4MB	Float
JG-Crypt	IDEA encryption	3MB	3MB	Byte
JG-Series	Fourier coefficient analysis	780KB / 1560KB	780KB / 1560KB	Float / Double

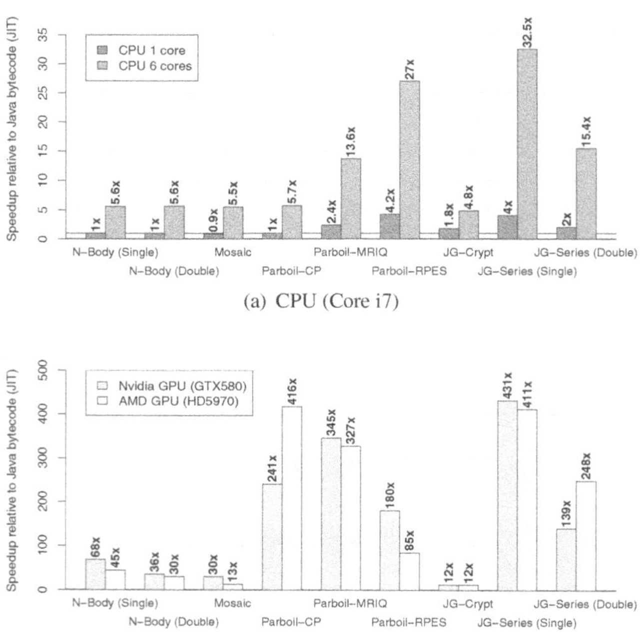

(a) CPU (Core i7)

(b) GPU

Figure 7. End-to-end speedup (includes overhead).

Figure 7(a) shows the speedups (higher is better) when running on 1 or 6 cores. Since the CPU supports hyperthreading, running on a single core runs two threads, one each for the JVM and OpenCL kernel. The 1-core performance is generally the same as the baseline, with a 10% degradation in the worst case because of high marshaling costs (see Figure 9). The gains for Parboil-MRIQ, Parboil-RPES, and JG-Series result from a faster implementation of the transcendental functions in OpenCL compared to Java.

The performance scales as the number of cores is increased, with five benchmarks showing a speedup of $4.8 - 5.7x$. The four remaining benchmarks show super-linear speedups of $13.6-32.5x$ using 6-cores. This is attributed to hyper-threading (permitting two OpenCL threads to run per core) and cache effects.

Figure 7(b) shows the speedups resulting from co-execution between the JVM and the GPU. The speedups vary significantly depending on the benchmark and platform, ranging from 12x to 431x. The benchmarks which do not use floating-point (JG-Crypt and Mosaic), or which use simple floating-point operations (N-Body) see the lowest end-to-end speedups. These benchmarks also have high communication to computation ratios, as shown in later results. The largest performance gains manifest for applications using transcendental functions.

The results also show that double-precision computation on the GTX580 is approximately $2-3x$ slower than single-precision, and $\approx 1.5x$ slower on the HD5970.

Overall, the results demonstrate that the Lime system delivers substantial end-to-end speedups as compared to the original Java programs, for all the benchmarks and platforms considered.

5.2 Comparison to hand-tuned OpenCL

Next, we evaluate the code quality of the generated OpenCL code, as well as the different memory optimizations described earlier. For this purpose, we wrote and hand-tuned OpenCL versions of N-Body and Mosaic, and converted three existing Parboil benchmarks originally written in CUDA to OpenCL. We made our best effort to optimize N-Body and Mosaic for the GTX580 GPU. We also include results for the GTX8800 GPU because the Parboil benchmarks were optimized specifically for this card by another research group [ ].

OpenCL requires the programmer to select the number of threads to run and how these threads map to cores. These tuning parameters can have a strong impact on performance. To control for these variables, we conducted an exhaustive systematic offline exploration of the tuning parameters and use the best settings for each experiment. For example, the hand-tuned versions of the Parboil benchmarks are optimized for the GTX8800, but those settings are not competitive on the GTX580. A system could perform this auto-tuning automatically ahead of time or at runtime, but such tuning falls outside the scope of this paper.

To evaluate code quality, we measure only time spent in computational kernels on the GPU, and exclude time spent on the host and time spent in explicit communication between host and GPU. Figure 8 shows the relative performance of computational kernels for compiled Lime code as compared to hand-tuned OpenCL. A speedup greater than one indicates performance better than hand-tuned code. A speedup less than one indicates a slow down and an opportunity for further improvements in the Lime compiler.

For each benchmark, the Figure shows results using the various memory optimizations applied by the Lime compiler including

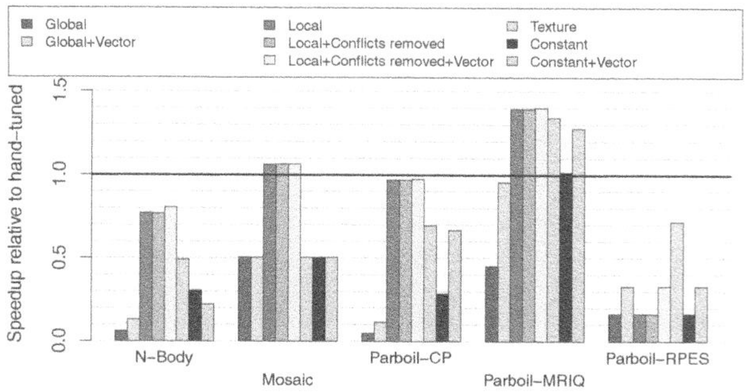

(a) NVidia GTX8800

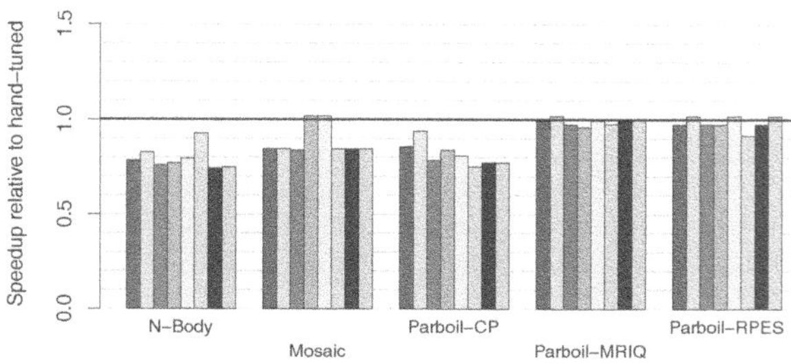

(b) NVidia GTX580 (Fermi)

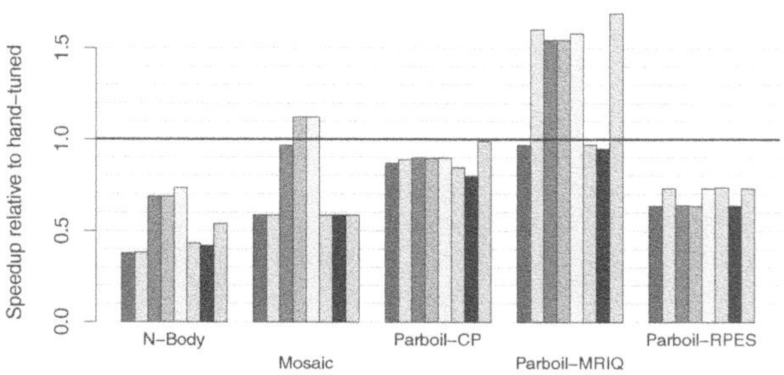

(c) AMD Radeon HD5970

Figure 8. Lime vs. hand-tuned OpenCL kernel-times and effects of optimizations.

vectorization. The Figure shows 8 bars per benchmark, representing each of the memory optimizations covered in Sections 4.2.

Overall, the results show that with the best optimization choices, the Lime compiler delivers competitive performance, attaining between 75% and 140% of the hand-coded performance. Exceeding hand-coded performance indicates cases where the human programmer was imperfect – we discuss specific issues below.

The results show that using the global memory generally yields the worst performance, even when using vectorization. In the worse cases, the slowdown is up to $10x$ compared to hand-tuned for the GTX8800, up to 60% for the HD5970, and 20% for the GTX580.

On the other hand, the compiler can often use the local memories effectively. Note in particular that the compiled code surprisingly outperforms the hand-tuned versions for the Mosaic benchmark. After further investigation, we discovered that the compiled code is more effective at reducing memory bank conflicts. The compiler-generated code for Parboil-MRIQ also slightly outperforms the hand-tuned kernel, when using constant memory. The Parboil-RPES benchmark benefits significantly from the use of texture memory on the GTX8800 because it is equipped with a hardware cache, and this benchmark exhibits good spatial locality.

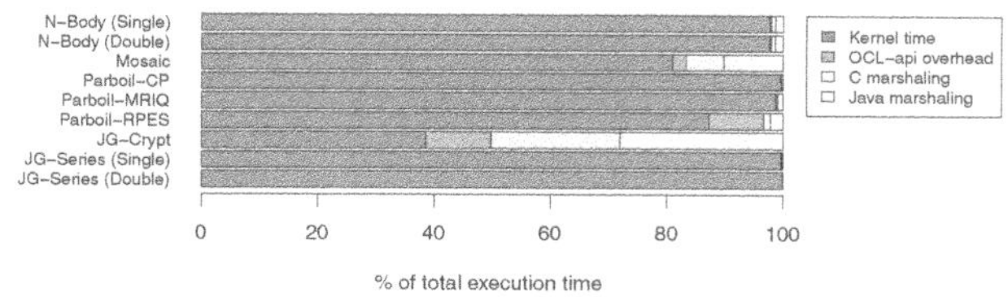

(a) CPU (Core i7)

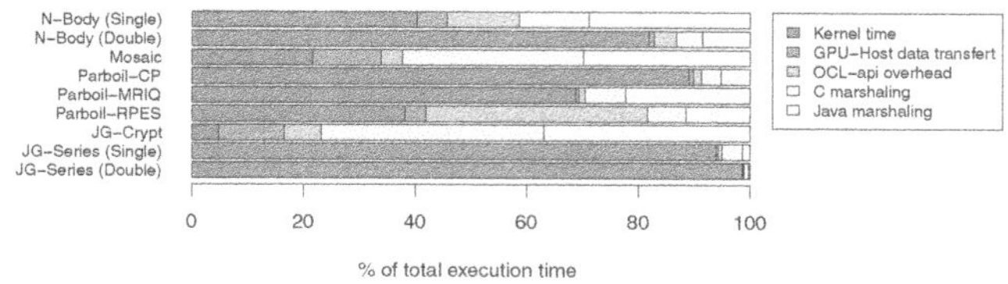

(b) GPU (GTX580)

Figure 9. Computation and communication costs.

The GTX580 architecture differs from the other GPUs by placing a cache between the device memory and the cores. As a direct consequence, the performance is less sensitive to memory optimizations, as shown in Figure 8(b). Using global memory delivers performance relatively close to the hand-tuned version, however, optimizations are necessary to recover the last 10-20% of performance in some benchmarks.

We conclude that it is possible for a Lime compiler to achieve performance competitive with typical hand-tuned code for the platforms and benchmarks considered. The results also demonstrate the sensitivity of performance to the GPU memory architecture. We claim these results further demonstrate the need to lift the level of programming abstraction away from low-level GPU details. Clearly, writing a portable, high-performance OpenCL code for multiple devices imposes a substantial burden on a human programmer.

5.3 Communication vs. Computation

The end-to-end speedups shown earlier include all runtime overhead, including communication between host and device. In our system, offloading the computation involves moving the data from Java to C and also from C back to Java (refer to Figure 6). In addition, there are costs attributed to the OpenCL API, and PCIe transfer costs to move data from the host to the device.

Figure 9 shows the breakdown of computation (kernel time) and communication costs (everything else). When running on a multicore, shared memory obviates the need for memory transfers; as a rule, computation dominates the execution time (Figure 9(a)). JG-Crypt provides an exception to the rule, since its computation ratio per byte is particularly low.

In contrast, the communication costs on a GPU are relatively higher due to its greater computational power. We show the results for the GTX580 in Figure 9(b); the computation to communication ratios are comparable for the other GPUs.

Most of the overhead (30%) comes from data marshaling (both Java and C). Marshaling objects in Java suffers from significant overheads due to arrays bounds checking and object allocation. Setting up OpenCL data structures is relatively fast (typically 5%), except for JG-RPES (40%). We are investigating the cause of this anomaly.

The raw data transfer from host memory to device memory does not play a major role in communication costs. We expect this trend to continue with PCIe3.0 and tighter integration of GPU and CPU.

Overall, the combined overhead due to all communication averages 40%. Although this overhead is high, the tremendous computational power of the GPU still allows impressive end-to-end speedups.

We conclude that communication costs, while not yet crippling, leave much room for improvement. In future work, we plan to pursue various strategies to reduce communication overhead. To avoid extraneous copying, the Java marshaling code should marshal directly to a format as required for device memory. This would approximately halve the marshaling overhead. More generally, the communication costs can be hidden by well-known pipelining techniques that overlap communication and computation; these techniques lie beyond the scope of this paper.

6. Related Work

Recent years have seen many projects targeting general purpose languages to exploit multicores and GPUs. The closest related work is Sponge [ ], a compiler which generates CUDA code from the StreamIt [ ] programming language. Udupa et al. [ ] also target StreamIt for GPUs. This work focuses on the problem of scheduling the tasks to the GPUs. Similar to our work, Sponge schedules different tasks onto GPUs and optimizes the mapping to the different type of memory. In contrast to Sponge, our system generates OpenCL code which can target multicore platforms as well as GPUs. Sponge supports only coarse-grained parallelism, whereas Lime includes constructs that support fine-grained data parallel as well. Data parallel operations make it easier to exploit thousands of threads on a GPU. Further, the StreamIt programming model is much simpler compared to Lime as it does not permit object allocation or unbounded arrays, requires the task graph to be fully resolved at compile time, and does not support object-oriented programming features. Lime on the other hand does not have any of these limitations. Further, because Lime is Java-compatible, it permits a gentle migration of existing Java code.

6.1 GPU Programming and Optimization

There are many other task-oriented languages that are suitable for GPU programming. Cg [ ] was among the first languages to be developed to program GPUs. Then Brook [ ] was introduced featuring the use of a streaming programming model. Accelerator [ ] was later developed as a C# API library that uses a data-parallel model based on parallel array to program GPUs. Today, general purpose computations on GPUs is dominated by OpenCL [ ] and CUDA [ ]. Some researchers are investigating automatically translating OpenMP source code to CUDA [ ] while others apply directives to sequential C code to convert them into CUDA programs with the hiCUDA [ ] framework. Earlier parts of this paper address the primary differences between Lime and OpenCL. These advantages are the same compared to CUDA.

Another related new language is the IBM X10 language. It provides abstractions for programming distributed memory parallel computers (*e.g.*, clusters) with a globally shared, partitioned address space. X10 considers the GPU as a shared-memory parallel computer (X10 "place"), where threads ("activities") communicate and synchronize through shared memory. Their work [ ] to incorporate CUDA abstractions does not describe compiler optimizations to map data structures to the GPU memory hierarchy. Instead it provides language constructs for the programmer to manage this mapping explicitly.

Yang et al. [ ] contribute a compiler framework to optimize GPU code. This compiler takes a simple unoptimized kernel as input and applies optimizations as discussed in [ ]. Similarly, CUDA-Lite [ ] coalesces memory accesses of existing kernels. A compiler for a high level language (HLL) can apply similar optimizations after translating to a low level representation. However, a HLL compiler can perform more aggressive transformations by exploiting higher-level semantic information embodied in the source code. We demonstrated several techniques whereby the Lime compiler exploits high-level information exposed by the type system to realize aggressive parallelization, prove isolation, and optimize the mapping to the memory hierarchy. It is unclear whether a low-level approach can in general recover this level of semantic information, due to difficulties inherent to sound whole program static analysis of object-oriented languages.

6.2 Multicores Programming

Gordon et al. [ ] developed a compiler that maps the StreamIt language to multicore architectures. Intel's array building block (ArBB) [ ] consists of a virtual machine and a C++ API that defines new parallel types such as collections. These collections are treated like values and the JIT optimizes these and extract thread and vector (SIMD) parallelism. Our work differs in that we start directly with a streaming computational model, making it easier to decompose programs for heterogeneous platforms. In contrast to ArBB, where the programmer has to deal specifically with data transformation between the C data types and the parallel collections (using the bind function), the programmer simply uses the standard array types provided by Lime. Finally, our system works with GPUs as well as multicores without changes to the program.

6.3 Runtime for Heterogeneous Platforms

SoCC [ ] is an extension to C that allows the programmer to manage distributed memory, express pipeline parallelism and map the different tasks to resources. EXOCHI [ ] is an effort from Intel that focuses on providing a runtime for integrating accelerators with general purpose processor. It provides shared memory and dynamic mapping of tasks to accelerators. The Quilin [ ] system is composed of a C API that is used to write parallel programs and an adaptable runtime that dynamically maps computations to processing elements in a CPU+GPU system. Jablin et al. [ ] proposed a new runtime management system that frees the programmer from explicitly managing data movement between the CPU and GPU on the host side. It determines which data are required by a GPU kernel and also copies the data to the GPU memory. The Lime model intrinsically provides this functionality via the task graph, and our compilation methodology leverages the language semantics and type system to automatically partition the code between host and device, generate the corresponding code, and coordinate the overall execution without programmer intervention.

7. Conclusion

This paper reviewed how a compiler for Lime, a high-level Java-compatible language, can exploit computational resources on a GPU. Exploiting invariants enforced by the type system, the compiler and runtime system implement transformations to exploit massively parallel GPU devices with non-uniform memory hierarchies. Benefiting from language and compiler co-design, the system achieves these goals without ambitious program analysis. Experimental results show that for the cases considered, the system delivers impressive speedups as compared to a Java implementation, and generates code quality in the same ballpark as hand-tuned code.

Although this paper has focused on GPUs, Lime supports a variety of architectures including specialized multicores and FPGAs. The results from this paper indicate that the Lime approach remains promising for GPUs, as part of a larger vision for programming heterogeneous system. We remain encouraged that this language-based approach may help bring the computational power of heterogeneous architectures to mainstream programmers.

Acknowledgments

We thank Joshua Auerbach and the members of the Liquid Metal team who contributed infrastructure and a stimulating working environment. Christophe Dubach was partially supported by the Royal Academy of Engineering and EPSRC.

References

[1] Parboil Benchmark Suite. http://impact.crhc.illinois.edu/parboil.php, 2011.

[2] J. Auerbach, D. F. Bacon, P. Cheng, and R. Rabbah. Lime: a Java-compatible and synthesizable language for heterogeneous architectures. In *OOPSLA*, 2010.

[3] I. Buck, T. Foley, D. Horn, J. Sugerman, K. Fatahalian, M. Houston, and P. Hanrahan. Brook for GPUs: stream computing on graphics hardware. In *SIGGRAPH*, 2004.

[4] D. Cunningham, R. Bordewekar, and V. Saraswat. GPU programming in a high level language: Compiling X10 to CUDA. In *X10 Worksop*, 2011.

[5] M. I. Gordon, W. Thies, and S. Amarasinghe. Exploiting coarse-grained task, data, and pipeline parallelism in stream programs. In *ASPLOS*, 2006.

[6] T. D. Han and T. S. Abdelrahman. hiCUDA: High-level GPGPU programming. *IEEE Trans. Parallel Distrib. Syst.*, 22, Jan 2011.

[7] A. H. Hormati, M. Samadi, M. Woh, T. Mudge, and S. Mahlke. Sponge: portable stream programming on graphics engines. In *ASPLOS*, 2011.

[8] T. B. Jablin, P. Prabhu, J. A. Jablin, N. P. Johnson, S. R. Beard, and D. I. August. Automatic CPU-GPU communication management and optimization. In *PLDI*, 2011.

[9] Khronos OpenCL Working Group. *The OpenCL Specification.*

[10] S. Lee, S.-J. Min, and R. Eigenmann. OpenMP to GPGPU: a compiler framework for automatic translation and optimization. In *PPoPP*, 2009.

[11] C.-K. Luk, S. Hong, and H. Kim. Qilin: exploiting parallelism on heterogeneous multiprocessors with adaptive mapping. In *MICRO*, 2009.

[12] W. R. Mark, R. S. Glanville, K. Akeley, and M. J. Kilgard. Cg: a system for programming graphics hardware in a C-like language. In *SIGGRAPH*, 2003.

[13] J. A. Mathew, P. D. Coddington, and K. A. Hawick. Analysis and development of Java Grande benchmarks. In *Proceedings of the ACM 1999 conference on Java Grande*, JAVA '99, pp. 72–80, New York, NY, USA, 1999. ACM.

[14] C. Newburn, B. So, Z. Liu, M. McCool, A. Ghuloum, S. Toit, Z. G. Wang, Z. H. Du, Y. Chen, G. Wu, P. Guo, Z. Liu, and D. Zhang. Intel's Array Building Blocks: A retargetable, dynamic compiler and embedded language. In *CGO*, 2011.

[15] NVIDIA Corporation. *The CUDA Specification.*

[16] A. D. Reid, K. Flautner, E. Grimley-Evans, and Y. Lin. SoC-C: efficient programming abstractions for heterogeneous multicore systems on chip. In *CASES*, 2008.

[17] S. Ryoo, C. I. Rodrigues, S. S. Baghsorkhi, S. S. Stone, D. B. Kirk, and W.-m. W. Hwu. Optimization principles and application performance evaluation of a multithreaded GPU using CUDA. In *PPoPP*, 2008.

[18] D. Tarditi, S. Puri, and J. Oglesby. Accelerator: using data parallelism to program GPUs for general-purpose uses. In *ASPLOS*, 2006.

[19] W. Thies, M. Karczmarek, and S. P. Amarasinghe. StreamIt: A language for streaming applications. In *CC*, 2002.

[20] A. Udupa, R. Govindarajan, and M. J. Thazhuthaveetil. Software pipelined execution of stream programs on GPUs. In *CGO*, 2009.

[21] S.-Z. Ueng, M. Lathara, S. S. Baghsorkhi, and W.-M. W. Hwu. Languages and compilers for parallel computing. In *LCPC*, 2008.

[22] P. H. Wang, J. D. Collins, G. N. Chinya, H. Jiang, X. Tian, M. Girkar, N. Y. Yang, G.-Y. Lueh, and H. Wang. EXOCHI: architecture and programming environment for a heterogeneous multi-core multithreaded system. In *PLDI*, 2007.

[23] Y. Yang, P. Xiang, J. Kong, and H. Zhou. A GPGPU compiler for memory optimization and parallelism management. In *PLDI*, 2010.

Adaptive Input-aware Compilation for Graphics Engines

Mehrzad Samadi
University of Michigan, Ann Arbor
mehrzads@umich.edu

Amir Hormati
Microsoft Research, Redmond
amir.hormati@microsoft.com

Mojtaba Mehrara
NVIDIA Research, Santa Clara
mmehrara@nvidia.com

Janghaeng Lee
University of Michigan, Ann Arbor
jhaeng@umich.edu

Scott Mahlke
University of Michigan, Ann Arbor
mahlke@umich.edu

Abstract

While graphics processing units (GPUs) provide low-cost and efficient platforms for accelerating high performance computations, the tedious process of performance tuning required to optimize applications is an obstacle to wider adoption of GPUs. In addition to the programmability challenges posed by GPU's complex memory hierarchy and parallelism model, a well-known application design problem is target portability across different GPUs. However, even for a single GPU target, changing a program's input characteristics can make an already-optimized implementation of a program perform poorly. In this work, we propose Adaptic, an adaptive input-aware compilation system to tackle this important, yet overlooked, input portability problem. Using this system, programmers develop their applications in a high-level streaming language and let Adaptic undertake the difficult task of input portable optimizations and code generation. Several input-aware optimizations are introduced to make efficient use of the memory hierarchy and customize thread composition. At runtime, a properly optimized version of the application is executed based on the actual program input. We perform a head-to-head comparison between the Adaptic generated and hand-optimized CUDA programs. The results show that Adaptic is capable of generating codes that can perform on par with their hand-optimized counterparts over certain input ranges and outperform them when the input falls out of the hand-optimized programs' "comfort zone". Furthermore, we show that input-aware results are sustainable across different GPU targets making it possible to write and optimize applications once and run them anywhere.

Categories and Subject Descriptors D.3.4 [*Programming Languages*]: Processors—Compilers

General Terms Design, Languages, Performance

Keywords Streaming, Compiler, GPU, Optimization, Portability

1. Introduction

GPUs are specialized hardware accelerators capable of rendering graphics much faster than conventional general-purpose processors. They are widely used in personal computers, tablets, mobile phones, and game consoles. Modern GPUs are not only efficient at manipulating computer graphics, but also are more effective than CPUs for algorithms where processing of large data blocks is done in parallel. This is mainly due to their highly parallel architecture. Recent works have shown that in optimistic cases, speedups of 100-300x [20], and in pessimistic cases, speedups of 2.5x [15], are achievable using modern GPUs compared to the latest CPUs.

PLDI'12, June 11–16, 2012, Beijing, China.

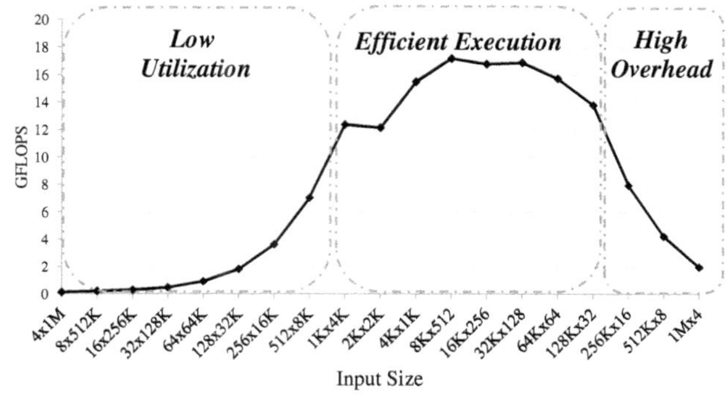

Figure 1: *Performance of the transposed matrix vector multiplication benchmark from the CUBLAS library on an NVIDIA Tesla C2050. The X-axis shows the input dimensions in number of rows x number of columns format.*

While GPUs provide inexpensive, highly parallel hardware for accelerating parallel workloads, the programming complexity remains a significant challenge for application developers. Developing programs to effectively utilize GPU's massive compute power and memory bandwidth requires a thorough understanding of the application and details of the underlying architecture. Graphics chip manufacturers, such as NVIDIA and AMD, have tried to alleviate part of the complexity by introducing new programming models, such as CUDA and OpenCL. Although these models abstract the underlying GPU architecture by providing unified processing interfaces, developers still need to deal with many problems such as managing the amount of on-chip memory used per thread, total number of threads per multiprocessor, and the off-chip memory access pattern in order to maximize GPU utilization and application performance [24]. Therefore, programmers must manually perform a tedious cycle of performance tuning to achieve the desired performance.

Many prior efforts have tried to address this programmability challenge mainly along three interrelated angles. The works in [2, 3, 12, 14] provide high-level abstractions at the language level to enable easier expression of algorithms. These abstractions are later used by the compiler to generate efficient binaries for GPUs. Adding annotations to current models (CUDA or OpenCL) or popular languages (C or Fortran) to guide compiler optimizations is another method used in [8, 31, 34]. Finally, works in [1, 25, 33] try to automatically generate optimized code from a basic, possibly poorly performing, parallel or sequential implementation of an application.

The hard problem of finding the optimal implementation of an algorithm on a single GPU target is further complicated when attempting to create software that can be run efficiently on multiple GPU architectures. For example, NVIDIA GPUs have different architectural parameters, such as number of registers and size of shared memory, that can make an implementation which is optimal for one architecture sub-optimal for another. The situation is even worse if the goal is to have an optimal implementation for GPUs across multiple vendors. We call this issue the *target portability* problem.

The portability issue is not specific to moving applications across different GPU targets. Even for a fixed GPU target, changing the problem size and dimensions can make a specific implementation of an algorithm sub-optimal, resulting in poor performance portability. Figure 1 illustrates this issue for the transposed matrix vector multiplication (TMV) benchmark from the CUBLAS library . All input matrices have the same number of elements but arranged in different shapes. The benchmark performs consistently between 12 and 17 GFLOPs over the input dimension range of 1Kx4K to 128Kx32 on an NVIDIA Tesla C2050 GPU. However, when input dimensions fall out of this range, the performance degrades rapidly by up to a factor of more than 20x. The main reason for this effect is that the number of blocks and threads in the application are set based on the number of rows and columns in the input matrix. Therefore, this benchmark works efficiently for a certain range of these values and for other input dimensions, either there is not enough blocks to run in parallel and hide memory latency (towards the left end of X-axis in the figure), or the data chunk that each block is operating on is too small to amortize the overhead of parallel block execution (towards the right end of X-axis in the figure). We call this the *input portability* problem.

There are various reasons for this problem in GPUs such as unbalanced workload across processors, excessive number of threads, and inefficient usage of local or off-chip memory bandwidth. Unbalanced workloads occur when a kernel has a small number of blocks causing several processors to be idle during execution, which leads to under-utilization of GPU resources and poor performance. Excessive number of threads result in sequential thread execution due to lack of enough resources in the GPU to run all threads in parallel. Finally, inefficient memory bandwidth usage can be due to the pattern of memory accesses which are determined based on the size or dimensions of the input data in some programs. Therefore, memory optimizations must be adapted based on the input to efficiently utilize the memory bandwidth.

One solution to the input portability problem is to have the programmer design and develop different algorithms for each input range and size. However, this would impose a considerable implementation and verification overhead as applications become larger, more complex, and need to work across a wide range of inputs. For instance, as shown later, five distinct kernel implementations are needed to efficiently utilize the processing power of a GPU across the complete input spectrum in the TMV benchmark. Multi-kernel applications complicate matters even more as programmers must deal with the cross-product of choices for each kernel as the input is varied. Clearly, automatic tools will become essential to guarantee high performance across various input dimensions.

In this work, we focus on tackling the input portability problem while providing GPU target portability. We employ a high-level streaming programming model to express target algorithms. This model provides explicit communication between various program kernels and its structured and constrained memory access lets the compiler make intelligent optimization decisions without having to worry about dependencies between kernels. An *adaptive input-aware compilation system*, called *Adaptic*, is proposed that is capable of automatically generating optimized CUDA code for a wide range of input sizes and dimensions from a high-level algorithm description. Adaptic decomposes the problem space based on the input size into discrete scenarios and creates a customized implementation for each scenario. Decomposition and customization are accomplished through a suite of optimizations that include a set of memory optimizations to coalesce memory access patterns employed by the high-level streaming model and to efficiently execute algorithms that access several neighboring memory locations at the same time. In addition, a group of optimizations are introduced to effectively break up the work in large program segments for efficient execution across many threads and blocks. Finally, two optimizations are introduced to combine the work of two segments so that execution overhead can be reduced.

An enhanced version of the performance model introduced in [10] is employed to predict application behavior for each range of input size and dimensions. Based on these predictions, optimizations are applied selectively by the compiler. At runtime, based on the provided input to the program, the best version of the generated code is selected and executed to maximize performance. This method frees application developers from the tedious task of fine-tuning and possibly changing the algorithm for each input range.

The specific contributions offered by this work are as follows:

- We propose a system that treats input portability as a first class programmability challenge for GPUs and provide means to solve it.
- We propose input-aware optimizations to overcome memory related performance deficiencies and break up the work fairly between working units based on the input size and dimensions.
- We develop an adaptive compilation and runtime system that optimizes performance for various input ranges by conforming to the user input and identifying and adjusting required optimizations.

2. Background

Exposed communication and an abundance of parallelism are the key features making stream programming a flexible and architecture-independent solution for parallel programming. In this paper, we employ a stream programming model based on Synchronous Data Flow (SDF) model. In SDF, computation is performed by *actors*, which are independent and isolated computational units, communicating only through data-flow buffers such as FIFOs. SDF, and its many variants, expose input and output processing rates of actors. This provides many optimization opportunities that can lead to efficient scheduling decisions for assignment of actors to cores, and allocation of buffers in local memories.

One way of writing streaming programs is to include all the computation performed in an actor inside a *work* method. This method runs repeatedly as long as the actor has data to consume on its input port. The amount of data that the work method consumes is called the *pop* rate. Similarly, the amount of data each work invocation produces is called the *push* rate. Some streaming languages, including StreamIt [27], also provide non-destructive reads, called *peek*, that do not alter the state of the input buffer. In this work, we use the StreamIt programming language to implement streaming programs. StreamIt is an architecture-independent streaming language based on SDF and allows the programmer to algorithmically describe the computational graph. In StreamIt, actors can be organized hierarchically into *pipelines* (i.e., sequential composition), *split-joins* (i.e., parallel composition), and *feedback loops* (i.e., cyclic composition).

To ensure correct functionality in StreamIt programs, it is important to create a steady state schedule which involves rate-matching of the stream graph. There is a buffer between each two consecutive actors and its size is determined based on the program's input size and pop and push rates of previous actors. Rate-matching assigns a repetition number to each actor. In a StreamIt schedule, an actor is enclosed by a *for-loop* that iterates as many times as this repetition number.

Finally, since StreamIt programs are incognizant of input size and dimensions, Adaptic's input code is the same for all inputs but the output implementation will be different for various input sizes. The techniques that we propose in this paper are evaluated on StreamIt but are applicable to other streaming languages as well.

3. Adaptic Overview

The Adaptic compiler takes a platform-independent StreamIt program, ranges of its possible input size and dimension values, and the target GPU as input, and generates optimized CUDA code based on those ranges and the target. A StreamIt program consists of several actors that can be described as fine-grained jobs executed by each thread. Each actor in the stream graph is converted to a CUDA kernel with a number of threads and blocks. By performing

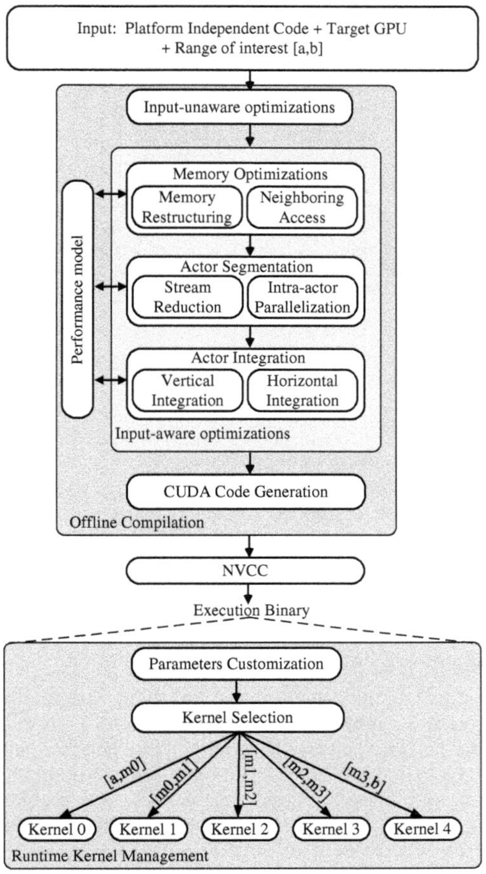

Figure 2: *Compilation Flow in Adaptic.*

input-aware stream compilation, Adaptic decides how many threads and blocks to assign to the CUDA kernel generated for each actor. Figure 2 shows the Adaptic's compilation flow which consists of four main components: baseline input-unaware optimizations, performance model, input-aware optimizations, and CUDA code generation. In addition, a matching runtime system selects appropriate kernels and sets their input parameters according to the program input at execution time. This section gives an overview of these four components as well as the runtime kernel management, while Section 4 details our proposed input-aware optimizations.

Input-unaware Optimizations: This step performs a set of input-unaware optimizations on the program and decides whether each actor should be executed on the CPU or GPU. This decision may be changed later by input-aware optimizations. Input-unaware optimizations are similar to those introduced in [12]. They include optimizations such as loop unrolling, data prefetching, and memory transfer acceleration. They can be used to generate CUDA code that is reasonably optimized and works for all input sizes, but its performance peaks for certain ranges of input and is suboptimal outside those ranges.

Performance Model: Adaptic relies on a high-level performance model to estimate the execution time of each kernel and to decide on using different optimizations for various problem sizes and GPU targets. This model is similar to the one described in [10], and classifies CUDA kernels into three categories of memory-bound, computation-bound, and latency-bound.

Memory-bound kernels have enough warps to efficiently hide the computation latency. Execution time of each warp is dominated by memory accesses. In computation-bound kernels, since most of the time is spent on computation, the execution time can be estimated as the total computation time. It should be noted that in these kernels, a large number of active warps is also assumed so that the scheduler would be able to hide memory access latencies with computation.

The last category, latency-bound kernels, are those that do not have enough active warps on each streaming multiprocessor (SM), and the scheduler cannot hide the latency of the computation or memory by switching between warps. Execution time of these latency-bound kernels is estimated by adding up the computation and memory access times. A kernel is latency-bound if there are not enough active warps for hiding the latency. There are two situations that lead to a small number of active warps: not enough data parallelism in the kernel or high shared resource consumption in each thread block.

In order to determine the type of each kernel, Adaptic counts the number of active warps on each SM. Based on this number and the target GPU, it determines whether the kernel is latency-bound or not. If not, Adaptic treats that kernel as both memory-bound and computation-bound and calculates the corresponding execution cycles based on the number of coalesced and non-coalesced memory accesses, computation instructions and the number of synchronization points, all of which are dependent on the input and can be computed at compile time as a function of input size and dimensions. The maximum of these two numbers determines the final kernel category.

Based on these categories, The performance model estimates the execution time of a kernel both before and after applying each optimization as a function of input dimensions. The performance break-even points determine the dimensions at which the corresponding optimization should be enabled or disabled.

Input-aware Optimizations: During each input-aware optimization phase, its potential performance impact for all input ranges is estimated using the model. These input ranges are provided by previous input-aware phases. If the optimization is beneficial, it is added to the optimization list for the whole range. However, if the optimization is only suitable for a subset of that range, Adaptic divides the range into smaller subranges, and populates optimization lists for each new subrange accordingly. In other words, Adaptic divides up operating input ranges to subranges if necessary, and applies different optimizations to each subrange. Therefore, separate kernels should be later generated for these subranges.

Code Generation: At the end of the compilation flow, the code generation stage generates optimized CUDA kernels for each input range based on optimization lists constructed by the optimization phase and the performance model. Since the performance model uses the target specifications to make optimization decisions, code generation is different for different targets. In addition, necessary code for runtime kernel management is also generated by the code generation unit based on the kernels and their operating input ranges. All these codes are later translated to a binary using the native CUDA compiler.

Runtime Kernel Management: A runtime kernel management unit is developed to dynamically select a properly optimized kernel at runtime based on the program input. This unit also determines the values of parameters that should be passed to each kernel at launch time including the number of blocks, number of threads per block, and the size of allocated shared memory. In order to remove kernel management overhead at runtime, this unit is completely executed on the CPU during the initial data transfer from CPU to GPU.

4. Input-aware Optimizations

As mentioned in Section 1, several factors such as inefficient use of memory bandwidth, unbalanced workload across processors, and excessive number of threads lead to ineffectiveness of input-unaware optimizations in achieving high performance across different inputs. The goal of input-aware optimizations in this work is to deal with these inefficiencies.

Two *memory optimizations* are introduced in Section 4.1 to solve inefficient use of local or off-chip memory bandwidth. In addition, two other sets of optimizations, namely *actor segmentation* and *actor integration* are detailed in Sections 4.2 and 4.3 respectively to tackle both unbalanced processor workload and excessive number of threads in the context of streaming.

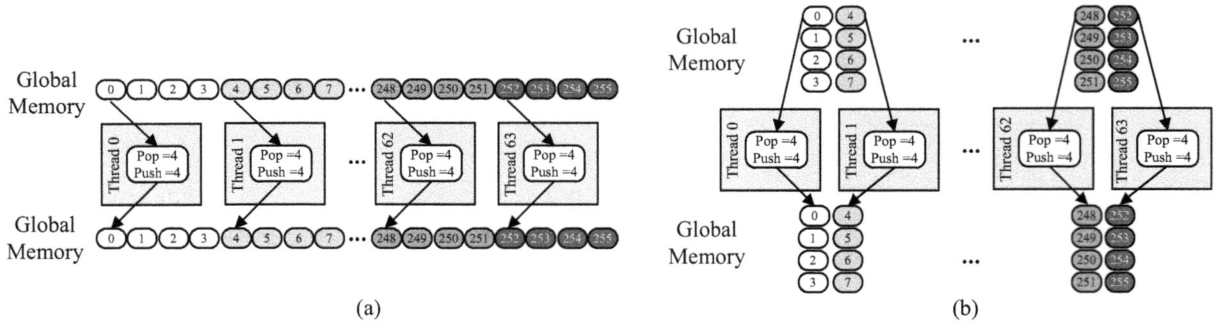

Figure 3: *Memory restructuring optimization. (a) Global memory access pattern of an actor with four pops and four pushes. Accesses are not coalesced because accessed addresses are not adjacent. (b) Access patterns after memory restructuring. Accessed addresses are adjacent at each point in time and accesses are all coalesced.*

4.1 Memory Optimizations

In this section, two memory optimizations, *memory restructuring* and *neighboring access optimization* are explained. These optimizations are useful for several classes of applications that are suitable for GPUs.

4.1.1 Memory Restructuring

One of the most effective ways to increase the performance of GPU applications is coalescing off-chip memory accesses. When all memory accesses of one warp are in a single cache line, the memory controller is able to coalesce all accesses into a single global memory access. Figure 3a illustrates how an actor with four pops and four pushes accesses global memory. In this example, each actor in each thread accesses four consecutive memory words. The first pop operations in threads 0 to 64 access memory word locations 0, 4, 8,..., 252, second pop operations access locations 1, 5, 9,..., 253, etc. Since these locations are not consecutive in memory, non-coalesced global memory accesses occur, leading to poor performance.

There are two ways to coalesce these memory accesses. One way is to transfer all data to the shared memory in a coalesced manner and since shared memory is accessible by all threads in a block, each thread can work on its own data. In this method, each thread fetches other threads' data from global memory as well as part of its own data. The same method can be applied for write-backs to global memory as well. All threads write their output to shared memory and then they transfer all data in a coalesced pattern to the global memory. Although using shared memory for coalescing accesses can improve performance, it has two shortcomings: number of threads is limited by the size of shared memory and the total number of instructions is increased due to address computations.

We use another method for coalescing accesses and that is to restructure the input array in a way that each pop access in all threads accesses consecutive elements of one row of the input in global memory. Figure 3b shows how this restructuring coalesces all memory accesses without using shared memory. This method has the advantage of minimizing the number of additional instructions and does not limit the number of threads by the size of shared memory. In addition, since this optimization is not using shared memory to coalesce off-chip memory accesses, shared memory can be utilized to store real shared data.

This optimization is not applicable when there are two or more actors with mismatching push and pop rates in the program. In those cases, rate matched buffers between kernels also have to be restructured, which involves extra write and reads from global memory, leading to poor performance.

However, as the work in [26] shows, since most consecutive actors in streaming benchmarks have matching rates, using memory restructuring would be beneficial. The CPU can restructure data at generation time and transfer it to the global memory of the GPU. The GPU launches kernels and when all of them are finished, the CPU reads back the output data. Due to the dependency of pop and push rates of some of the actors are on input size, this optimization can have different effects for various sizes.

In addition to coalescing global memory accesses, memory restructuring can also be applied to shared memory to remove bank conflicts. After applying this optimization, all threads access consecutive addresses in shared memory. Since adjacent addresses in shared memory belong to different shared memory banks, there would be no bank conflicts.

4.1.2 Neighboring Access Optimization

A common pattern in many applications is to access a point and its neighboring locations to calculate the data for that point. These benchmarks are very common in simulation benchmarks, for instance, the temperature of each point on a surface is computed based on the temperature of its neighbors. In streaming programs, non-destructive reads (peek) are used to read the neighbors' data while the address of the main point increases linearly in each iteration. Figure 4a shows an example StreamIt code for a *five-point stencil* actor that has neighboring access pattern and Figure 4b illustrates the access pattern for this code. In this example, each element is dependent on its top, bottom, right, and left elements. Each thread first reads all top elements, which are consecutive, leading to coalesced memory accesses. The same pattern holds for bottom, right, left and center elements. However, the main problem with this class of actors is excessive global memory accesses. For instance, accessing all top, bottom, left, right and center elements in each thread simply means accessing the whole input five times.

An efficient way to alleviate this problem is to use shared memory such that each block brings in one tile of data to shared memory and works on that. Since the data close to tile edges is needed for both neighboring tiles, tiles should be overlapping. These overlapping regions, called *halo*, are brought in for each tile at all four edges. Since branch divergence occurs only within a warp, both tile and halo widths should be multiples of warp size to make all accesses of each warp coalesced and prevent control flow divergence for address calculations.

Since halo regions are fetched for each tile, they should be as small as possible to minimize extra memory accesses. In order to decrease the overhead of extra memory accesses, Adaptic uses *super tiles*. In such a tile, the ratio of the halo size to the main tile size is decreased by merging several simple tiles. Each super tile is assigned to one block and each thread computes several output elements in different tiles. In this case, each block brings in a super tile from global memory to shared memory, performs the computation, and writes back the super tile to global memory.

Figure 5 shows a super tile assigned to a block in our example. Dark gray elements construct the main tiles while the light gray elements are halo parts. The number in each element indicates the thread index reading that element's address. In this example, warp size is set to 2 and there are 8 threads in each block. Each tile is 4x2 and by merging four tiles together, one super tile with 4x8 elements is formed. Since all width values should be multiples of warp size to maintain memory coalescing, the width of right and left halo parts in this example are set to 2. As a result, One of the halo values on each

```
5-Point Stencil(pop,peek:size, push:size)
  for (index=0; index<size; index++)
    if (not on edge)
      Top    = peek(index - width)
      Bottom = peek(index + width)
      Right  = peek(index + 1)
      Left   = peek(index - 1)
      Center = peek(index - 1)
    push(func(Top,Bottom,Right,Left,center))
```

(a)

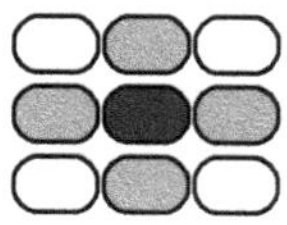

(b)

Figure 4: *(a) An example StreamIt code of a five-point stencil actor. (b) Memory access pattern of this actor.*

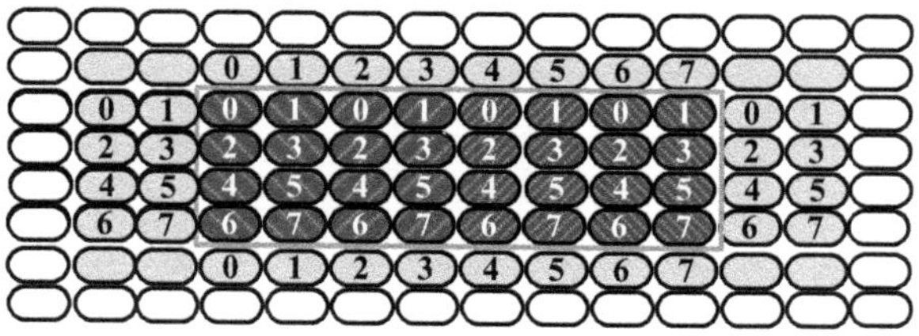

Figure 5: *A super tile assigned to one block. Dark gray addresses are main part and light gray parts are halo parts. Numbers in each small box indicates which thread reads this address.*

side (left and right) are not used in the computations for this super tile.

Increasing the size of super tiles leads to an increase in the allocated shared memory for each block, which in turn, could result in lower number of concurrent blocks executed on each GPU SM. Since this issue may change the type of kernel from computation-bound or memory-bound to latency-bound, the data size processed by each block should be chosen carefully.

For each application, Adaptic has to calculate the size and shape of a super tile. In general, the size of each super tile should not be more than the maximum shared memory per block, which is a constant value based on the target GPU. The super tile's size is dependent on the input size. For small input sizes it is beneficial to use smaller super tiles in order to have more blocks. Large super tiles are advantageous for large input sizes to reduce excessive memory accesses. Using the performance model and the input size, Adaptic can calculate the size for each super tile. Then, given the size, Adaptic needs to find the shape (width and height) of a super tile. For this purpose, Adaptic uses a reuse metric to maximize the number of served memory accesses while minimizing the size of extra halo regions. Adaptic uses the following reuse metric to find the optimal shape and size for each tile:

$$Reuse\_Metric = \frac{\sum_{Tile} Element\_Accesses}{Halo\_Size}$$

In this formula, $Element\_Accesses$ is the number of times each element in the shared memory is accessed during the computation of the whole output matrix, and the summation is taken over all elements in the tile. Since the best tile is the one with small halo region that can compute a large chunk of output, Adaptic chooses rectangular tiles with maximum possible $Reuse\_Metrics$.

Once the size and shape of super tiles and halo regions are determined, the output CUDA code will be similar to the code shown in Figure 6. First, the kernel reads in the super tile and all its halos to the shared memory, after which synchronization makes shared memory visible to all threads. Subsequently, each block starts working on its own data residing in the shared memory to perform the computation and output the results.

4.2 Actor Segmentation

Optimizations in this category attempt to divide the job of one large actor between several threads/blocks to increase the performance. In order to have balanced workload across processors with efficient number of threads, this segmentation should be done based on the input size.

The two main optimizations in this category are *stream reduction* and *intra-actor parallelization*. Reduction is one of the important algorithms used in many GPU applications. The goal of *stream*

```
Neighboring-access Kernel <<<Blocks, threads>>>
  Top halo      →  shared memory
  Bottom halo   →  shared memory
  Right halo    →  shared memory
  Left halo     →  shared memory
  for tile in super tile
    tile → shared memory
  sync();
  Do computations and write results
```

Figure 6: *A generic neighboring access CUDA code. First, different halo parts and the super tile are moved from global to shared memory. Subsequently, computations are performed on the shared memory data.*

reduction optimization is to efficiently translate reduction operations to CUDA in streaming programs. *Intra-actor parallelization*'s goal is to break the dependency between iterations of large loops and make them more amenable to execution on GPUs.

4.2.1 Stream Reduction

A reduction operation generally takes a large array as input, performs computations on it, and generates a single element as output. This operation is usually parallelized on GPUs using a tree-based approach, such that each level in the computation tree consumes the outputs from the previous level and produces the input for the next level. In uniform reduction, each tree level reduces the number of elements by a fixed factor and the last level outputs one element as the final result. The only condition for using this method is that the reduction operation needs to be associative and commutative.

A naive way of implementing the tree-based approach in a stream graph is to represent each tree node as an individual actor with small pop/push rates. Executing one kernel for each small actor would make the kernel launching overhead significant and degrade the performance dramatically. Another method of representing reduction is by using one filter that pops the whole input array and pushes the final result as shown in Figure 7a. The actor can not be translated to an efficient kernel due to the limited number of possible in-flight threads.

On the other hand, Adaptic automatically detects reduction operations in its streaming graph input using pattern matching. After this detection phase, it replaces the reduction actor with a highly optimized kernel in its output CUDA code based on the input size and the target GPU. This reduction kernel receives N_{arrays} different arrays with $N_{elements}$ elements each as input, and produces one element per array as output. Data is initially read from global memory, reduced and written to shared memory, and read again from shared memory and reduced to the final result for each array. In this work, we introduce two approaches for translating reduction actors to CUDA kernels.

When the array input size, $N_{elements}$, is small compared to the total number of input arrays (N_{arrays}) Adaptic produces a single reduction kernel in which each block computes the reduction output for one input array (Figure 7b). Thus, this kernel should be launched with N_{arrays} blocks. This approach is beneficial for large array counts so that Adaptic can launch enough blocks to fill up the resources during execution.

However, when the array input size ($N_{elements}$), is large compared to total number of input arrays (N_{arrays}), the reduction output for each array is computed individually by two kernels (Figure 7c). The first kernel, called the initial reduction kernel, chunks up the input array and lets each block reduce a different data chunk. The number of these blocks, $N_{initial\_blocks}$ is dependent on the value of $N_{elements}$ and the target GPU. Since there is no global synchronization between threads of different blocks, results of these blocks ($N_{initial\_blocks} * N_{arrays}$ elements) are written back to global memory. Subsequently, another kernel, called the merge kernel, is launched to merge the outputs from different blocks of the initial reduction kernel down to N_{arrays} elements. In the merge kernel, each block is used to compute the reduction output of one input array. Therefore, this kernel should be launched with N_{arrays} blocks.

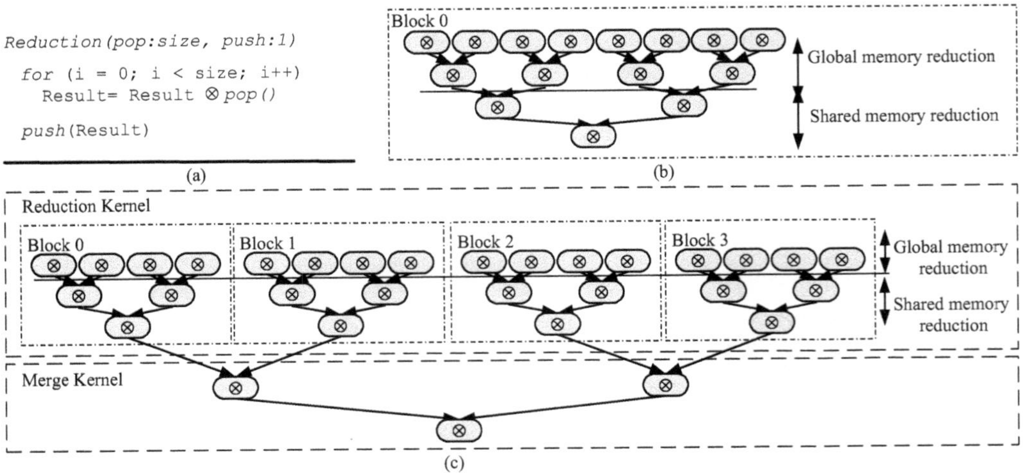

Figure 7: *Stream reduction technique. (a) StreamIt code for a reduction actor. (b) Each block is responsible for computing output for one chunk of data in two phases. In the first phase, each thread reads from global memory and writes reduction output to the shared memory and in the second phase, shared memory data is reduced to one output element. (c) In the two kernel approach, different blocks of the first kernel work on different chunks of data and the second kernel reads all reduction kernel's output and compute final result.*

```
Initial Kernel Reduction<<<reductionBlocks, threads>>>
      /* Global memory reduction phase */
  Result = 0;
  numberOfThreads = BlockDim * gridDim;
  for ( index=tid; index<size; index+= numberOfThreads)
     Result = Result ⊗ Input[Index];

    SharedData[tid] = Result;

       /* Shared memory reduction phase */
  activeThreads = blockDim;
  while (activeThreads > WARP_SIZE){
    if (tid <activethreads)
L1    activeThreads /=2;
      sync();
      SharedData[tid] ⊗= SharedData[tid+activeThreads];
    }
  Stride = WARP_SIZE;
  if (tid < WARP_SIZE)
    while (stride > 1){
      sync();
L2    SharedData[tid] ⊗= SharedData[tid + stride];
      stride /=2;}
   if tid = 0
     Output[bid] = SharedData[0];
```

Figure 8: *The initial reduction kernel's CUDA code.*

Figure 8 shows Adaptic's resulting CUDA code for the initial reduction kernel. In the first phase, the input array in global memory is divided into chunks of data. Each thread computes the output for each chunk, and copies it to shared memory. The amount of shared memory usage in each block is equal to $Threads\_per\_Block * Element\_Size$. As discussed in Section 4.1.1, all global memory accesses are coalesced as a result of memory restructuring and there would be no bank conflicts in shared memory in this phase.

In the next phase, the results stored in shared memory are reduced in multiple steps to form the input to the merge kernel. At each step of this phase, the number of active threads performing reduction are reduced by half. Loop L1 in Figure 8 represents these steps. They continue until the number of active threads equals the number of threads in a single warp. At this point, reducing the number of threads any further would cause control-flow divergence and inferior performance. Therefore, we keep the number of active threads constant and just have some threads doing unnecessary computation (Loop L2 in Figure 8). It should be noted that after each step, synchronization is necessary to make shared memory changes visible to other threads. Finally, the thread with $tid = 0$ computes the final reduction result and writes it back to the global memory.

4.2.2 Intra-actor Parallelization

The goal of intra-actor parallelization is to find data parallelism in large actors. As mentioned before, it is difficult to generate optimized CUDA code for actors with large pop or push rates, consisting of loops with high trip counts. This optimization breaks these actors into individual iterations which are later efficiently mapped to the GPU. Using data flow analysis, Adaptic detects cross-iteration dependencies. If no dependency is found, Adaptic simply assigns each iteration to one thread and executes all iterations in parallel. It also replaces all induction variable uses with their correct value based on the thread index.

In some cases, Adaptic breaks the dependence between different iterations by eliminating recurrences. One common source of recurrence is accumulator variables. This happens when a loop contains an accumulator variable $count$ incremented by a constant C in every iteration ($count = count + C$). This accumulation causes cross-iteration dependencies in the loop, making thread assignment as described impossible. However, intra-actor parallelization technique breaks this dependence by changing the original accumulation construct to $count = initial\_value + induction\_variable * C$ and making all iterations independent.

In general, this optimization is able to remove all linear recurrence constructs and replace them by independent induction variable-based counterparts. This is similar to the induction variable substitution optimization that parallelizing compilers perform to break these recurrences and exploit loop level parallelism on CPUs.

4.3 Actor Integration

This optimization merges several actors or threads together to balance threads' workloads based on the input size in order to get the best performance. Two types of actor integration optimization are introduced in this paper. Vertical integration technique reduces off-chip memory traffic by storing intermediate results in the shared rather than global memory. Horizontal integration technique reduces off chip memory accesses and synchronization overhead and also lets the merged actors share instructions.

4.3.1 Vertical Integration

During this optimization, Adaptic vertically integrates some actors to improve performance by reducing memory accesses, removing kernel call overhead, and increasing instruction overlap. The reason for its effectiveness is that integrated actors can communicate through shared memory and there is no need to write back to the global off-chip memory. Also, integrating all actors together results in one kernel and global memory accesses of this one kernel are coalesced by the memory restructuring optimization. However, since input and output buffers of the middle actors in the integrated kernel are allocated in the shared memory, the number of active threads executing these actors are limited by the size of shared memory. This limitation often prevents Adaptic from integrating all actors together. Based on the performance model, Adaptic finds the best candidates for this optimizations. Since push and pop rates of some actors can be dependant on the input size, this optimization is beneficial for some ranges of input size.

Another optimization made possible after actor integration is replacing *transfer actors* with index translation. Transfer actors are the ones that do not perform any computation and only reorganize input buffer's data and write it to the output buffer. Since input and output buffers of the middle actors in integrated kernels are both allocated in the shared memory, there is no need to read the data from input buffer, shuffle it, and write it to the output buffer. This task can be done by index translation. Index translation gets thread indexes based on the transfer pattern, generates the new index pattern, and passes it to the next actor.

4.3.2 Horizontal Integration

The goal of horizontal integration is removing excessive computations or synchronizations by merging several threads or actors that can run in parallel. There are two kinds of horizontal integration techniques: horizontal actor integration and horizontal thread integration. In streaming languages, we use a duplicate splitter to allow different actors to work on the same data. In this case, instead of launching one kernel for each actor, one kernel is launched to do the job of all the actors working on the same data. Therefore, in addition to reducing kernel overheads, memory access and synchronization overheads are also reduced. For example, assume there is a program that needs maximum and summation of all elements in an array. Instead of running two kernels to compute these values, Adaptic launches one kernel to compute both. In this case, off-chip memory accesses and synchronizations only happen once instead of twice.

Horizontal thread integration merges several consecutive threads working on consecutive memory locations in one kernel. This method reduces the number of threads and blocks used by the kernel. Merged threads can share part of the computation that had to be done independently in each of the original threads and decrease the number of issued instructions. When the number of thread blocks is high, it is beneficial to use horizontal thread integration to reduce the number of threads and blocks and allow them to run in parallel. Otherwise it is better not to integrate threads and have more threads with less work to increase the possibility hiding memory latency by switching between threads.

5. Experiments

A set of benchmarks from the NVIDIA CUDA SDK and the CUBLAS library 3.2 are used to evaluate Adaptic. We developed StreamIt versions of these benchmarks, compiled them with Adaptic, and compared their performance with the original hand-optimized benchmarks. We also present three case studies to better demonstrate and explain the effectiveness of Adaptic's compilation algorithms. The first case study is performed on a CUBLAS benchmark to investigate the effect of our optimizations over a wide range of inputs. Then, we present two more case studies on real world applications, biconjugate gradient stabilized method and support vector machine [4], executed on two different GPUs, to demonstrate how Adaptic performs on larger programs with many actors and on different GPU targets. Adaptic compilation phases are implemented in the backend of the StreamIt compiler [27] and its C code generator is modified to generate CUDA code. Both Adaptic's output codes and the original benchmarks are compiled for execution on the GPU using NVIDIA nvcc 3.2. GCC 4.1 is used to generate the x86 binary for execution on the host processor. The target system has an Intel Xeon X5650 CPU and an NVIDIA Tesla C2050 GPU with 3GB GDDR5 global memory with NVIDIA driver 260.04. The other system used for experiments in Sections 5.2.2 and 5.2.3 has an Intel Core 2 Extreme CPU and an NVIDIA GeForce GTX 285 GPU with 2GB GDDR2 global memory.

5.1 Input Portability

In order to show how Adaptic handles portability across different input problem sizes, we set up seven different input sizes for each benchmark and compared their performance with the original CUDA code running with the same input sizes. It should be noted that these seven input sizes are chosen from the working range of the CUDA benchmarks because there are many sizes for which the SDK benchmarks would not operate correctly.

Figure 9 shows the results for eight CUDA benchmarks that were sensitive to changes in the input size, while results for input-insensitive benchmarks are discussed in Section 5.3. As can be seen, Adaptic-generated code is better than the hand-optimized CUDA code for all problem sizes in *Scalar Product*, *MonteCarlo*, *Ocean FFT*, and *Convolution Separable* from the SDK, and *Isamax/Isamin*, *Snrm2*, *Sasum*, and *Sdot* from CUBLAS. A combination of actor segmentation and actor integration were used to optimize all CUBLAS benchmarks. In addition to these optimizations, memory restructuring was applied to *Sdot*.

Sdot is computing the dot product of two vectors. For large vectors, using the two kernel reduction is beneficial, but for small sizes, in order to reduce kernel launch overhead, Adaptic uses the one kernel reduction. Using input-aware optimizations leads to upto 4.5x speedup in this benchmark compared to the original program. *Convolution Separable* has two actors, and processes data row-wise in one and column-wise in the other. Memory optimizations are effective for this benchmark as both of these two actors have neighboring memory access pattern. Therefore, as the input becomes smaller, Adaptic reduces the super tile sizes adaptively to retain the high number of blocks and, therefore, achieves better performance than the baseline hand-optimized code. *OceanFFT* also has a neighboring access actor and Adaptic uses different tile sizes to improve performance over the hand-optimized code. *Scalar Product* computes scalar products of pairs of vectors. The original benchmark uses the single kernel reduction, and it achieves good performance when there are many pairs of vectors in the input. However, for fewer pairs of vectors, it is better to use the whole GPU to compute the result for each pair. Using the two kernel reduction for those inputs, Adaptic is able to achieve upto 6x speedup compared to the original hand-optimized version.

MonteCarlo performs about the same as the original hand-optimized version. The reason is that the original benchmark already has two kernels performing the same task, but optimized for different ranges of input problem sizes. In other words, *MonteCarlo* has originally been developed in an input portable way. Therefore, the output of Adaptic is similar to the original version and the performance is the same for all sizes but it is generated automatically by the compiler.

Since Adaptic generates different kernels for some actors in the streaming program, the output binary size could be larger than the original binary optimized for one specific range. In our experiments including the case studies, Adaptic's output binaries were on average 1.4x and upto 2.5x larger than their input-unaware counterparts, which is quite reasonable considering the fact that some kernels could have upto five different versions for various input ranges. However, because each program also has kernels with one versions, the combination leads to this moderate code size increase.

These results further show the fact that our approach in Adaptic is able to adaptively generate optimized CUDA code for different problem sizes without any source code modifications.

5.2 Case studies

5.2.1 Transposed Matrix Vector multiplication

In this section, we look into the effects of our optimizations on the performance of the transposed matrix vector multiplication benchmark from CUBLAS over a wide range of input sizes and dimensions. As was mentioned in Section 1, the original benchmark cannot provide sustainable performance gains for different input dimensions. However, with the aid of input-aware optimizations, Adaptic is able to generate five different kernels with different structures, where each kernel is parametrized to get better performance for a

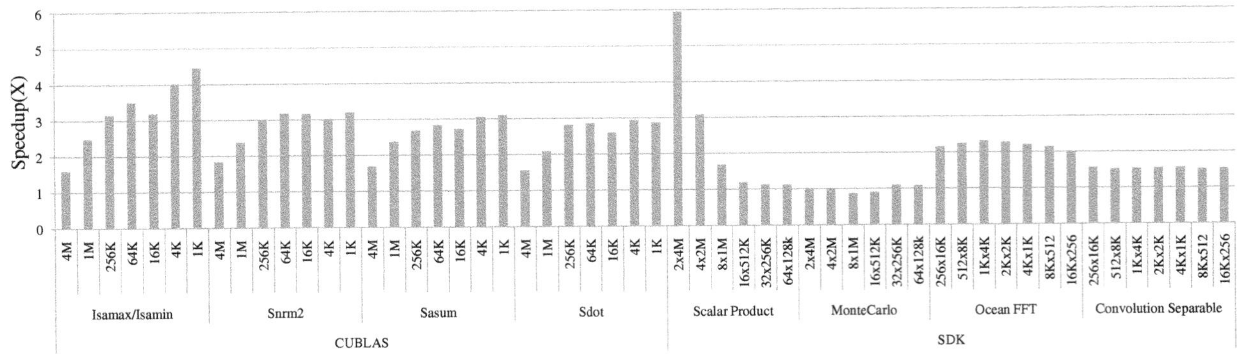

Figure 9: *Adaptic-generated code speedups normalized to the hand-optimized CUDA code for 7 different input sizes.*

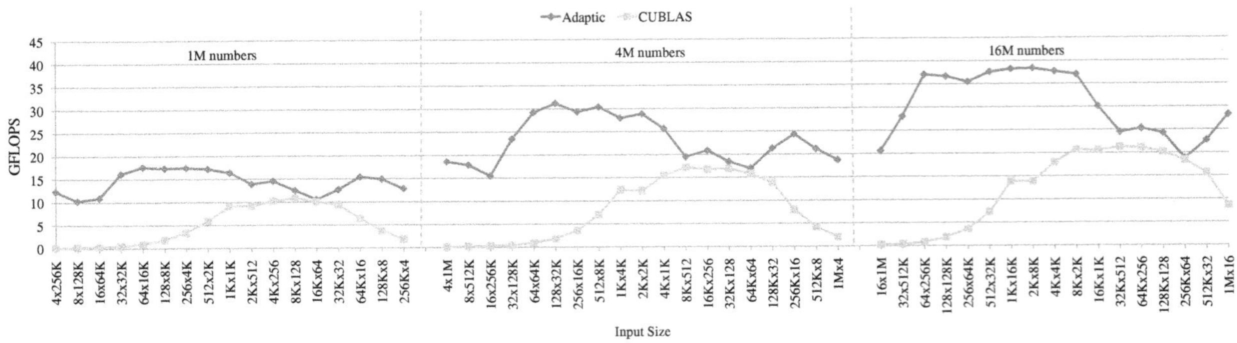

Figure 10: *Transposed matrix vector multiplication performance comparison of CUBLAS and Adaptic.*

specific range of input dimensions. At runtime the proper kernel is launched based on the program input.

In the first kernel, which is beneficial for matrices with many columns and few rows, Adaptic uses the two kernel version of reduction. For each row, one kernel is launched and the whole GPU is used to compute the dot product of one row with the input vector. The second kernel is a single-kernel reduction function where each block is responsible for one row. This kernel achieves its best performance for square matrices. In the third kernel, in addition to the single-kernel reduction function, by using horizontal thread integration, Adaptic adaptively merges several rows and each block is responsible for computing several dot products instead of one. This kernel is beneficial for matrices with more rows than columns. The fourth kernel is also similar to the single-kernel reduction, except that in its shared memory reduction phase, each thread is responsible for computing one output. The last kernel generated by Adaptic achieves its best performance for matrices with many rows and few columns. In this case, the size of each row is small and the corresponding actor has small pop rates. For this kind of actor, our baseline optimizations are effective in generating efficient code. Therefore, Adaptic does not need to add optimization to that. In this kernel, each thread is responsible for computing the dot product of a single row and the input vector.

Figure 10 compares the performance of this benchmark with Adaptic-generated code for three different matrix sizes over a range of matrix dimensions. As it can be seen, although for some input dimensions Adaptic's performance is really close to CUBLAS, for most of them Adaptic outperforms CUBLAS by a large margin.

5.2.2 Biconjugate gradient stabilized method

The biconjugate gradient stabilized method (BiCGSTAB) is an iterative method used for finding the numeral solution of nonsymmetric linear systems such as $Ax=B$ for x where A is a square matrix. This method has 11 linear steps that can be written easily with the CUBLAS library for GPUs. We wrote this program both in StreamIt and CUDA with CUBLAS functions and measured the performance of the two for different sizes of A. Figure 11 shows an in-depth comparison and breakdown of the effects of Adaptic's individual optimizations on this benchmark for different input sizes across two GPU targets - NVIDIA Tesla C2050 and GTX285. The baseline in this figure is the generated code after only applying size-unaware optimizations. The Sgemv, Sdot, Sscal and Saxpy CUBLAS functions were used to implement the CUDA version of this benchmark. The problem of using the CUBLAS library is that the programmer should split each step into several sub-steps to be able to use CUBLAS functions. Execution of these sub-steps leads to more memory accesses and kernel launch overhead.

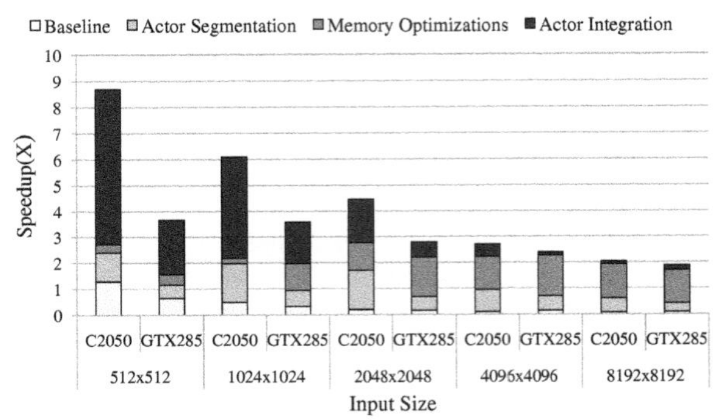

Figure 11: *Performance of the Adaptic-generated Biconjugate gradient stabilized method benchmark normalized to the CUBLAS implementation on two different GPU targets.*

On the other hand, Adaptic merges all these sub-steps together and launches a single kernel for one step. As shown in Figure 11, most of the speedup for small sizes comes from the integration optimization. Since most of the execution time is spent in matrix vector multiplication for large sizes such as 8192x8192, the effect of integration is not as high for these sizes. However, actor segmentation that generates smaller actors and increases parallelism, and memory restructuring play more important roles in achieving better performance for larger sizes.

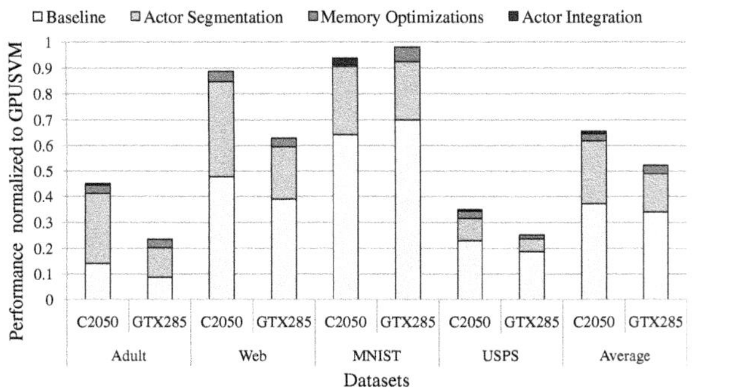

Figure 12: *Performance of the Adaptic-generated SVM training benchmark compared to the hand-optimized CUDA code in the GPUSVM implementation on two different GPU targets.*

5.2.3 Nonlinear Support Vector Machine Training

Support Vector Machines (SVMs) are used for analyzing and recognizing patterns in the input data. The standard two class SVM takes a set of input data and for each input predicts which class it belongs to among the two possible classes. This classification is based on a model, which is generated after training with a set of example inputs. Support vector machine training and classification are both very computationally intensive.

We implemented a StreamIt version of this algorithm based on the implementation in [4]. Figure 12 shows the performance of the Adaptic-generated code compared to the GPUSVM [4] hand-optimized CUDA code in this benchmark for four different input datasets. On average, Adaptic achieves 65% of the performance of the GPUSVM implementation. The reason for the large performance gap in Adult and USPS datasets is that GPUSVM performs an application-specific optimization where it utilizes unused regions of the GPU memory to cache the results of some heavy computations. In case those computations have to be performed again, it simply reads the results in from the memory. Therefore, for input sets which cause a lot of duplicate computations, including *Adult* and *USPS*, GPUSVM performs better than Adaptic-generated code.

In this program, unlike the previous example, actor integration is not very effective and most of the performance improvement comes from actor segmentation. On average, actor segmentation, memory restructuring, and actor integration improve the performance by 37%, 4%, and 1%, respectively.

5.3 Performance of Input Insensitive Applications

Although the main goal of Adaptic compiler is to maintain good performance across a wide range of inputs, it also performs well on the benchmarks that are not sensitive to input. Our experiments show that a combination of Adaptic optimizations makes the average performance of our compiler-generated code on par with the hand-optimized benchmarks, while writing StreamIt applications as the input to Adaptic involves much less effort by the programmer compared to the hand-optimized programs.

We ran Adaptic on a set of benchmarks from CUBLAS and the SDK (*BlackScholes*, *VectorAdd*, *Saxpy*, *Scopy*, *Sscal*, *Sswap*, and *Srot*, *DCT*, *QuasiRandomGenerator*, and *Histogram*), and on average the performance of Adaptic's output is within 5% of the original CUDA versions. This shows that Adaptic does not cause slowdowns for applications that are not sensitive to input size.

6. Related Work

The most common languages GPU programmers use to write GPU code are CUDA and OpenCL. Although these new languages partially alleviate the complexity of GPU programming, they do not provide an architecture-independent solution. There is an extensive literature investigating many alternative methods to support target portability.

Works in [2, 3, 7, 9, 12, 14, 21, 30] focus on generating optimized CUDA code from higher levels of abstraction. The Sponge compiler [12] compiles StreamIt programs and generates optimized CUDA to provide portability between different GPU targets. The work in [30] compiles stream programs for GPUs using software pipelining techniques. The work in [5] compiles Python programs for graphic processors. Copperhead [3] provides a nested set of parallel abstractions expressed in the Python programming language. Their compiler gets Python code as input and generates optimized CUDA code. It uses built-in functions of Python such as sort, scan, and reduce to abstract common CUDA program constructs. The work in [14] automatically generates optimized CUDA programs from OpenMP programs. MapCG [9] uses MapReduce framework to run high level programs on both multi-core CPUs and GPUs. Brook for GPUs [2] is one of the first papers about compilation for GPUs, which extends the C language to include simple data-parallel constructs. Compiling Matlab file to CUDA is also investigated in [21]. CnC_CUDA [7] use Intel's Concurrent Collections programming model to generate optimized CUDA code. All these works look into improving the programmability of GPUs, and in some cases, provide target portability. However, Adaptic provides portability across different inputs as well as GPU targets. In addition, Adaptic employs various input-aware optimizations and its output performance is comparable to hand written CUDA code.

Several other works have focused on automatically optimizing CUDA kernels [10, 33, 34]. The work in [33] performs GPU code compilation with a focus on memory optimizations and parallelism management. The input to this compiler is a naive GPU kernel function and their compiler analyzes the code and generates optimized CUDA code for various GPU targets. CUDA-Lite [34] is another compilation framework that takes naive GPU kernel functions as input and tries to coalesce all memory accesses by using shared memory. Hong et al. [10] propose an analytical performance model for GPUs that compilers can use to predict the behavior of their generated code. None of these works provide means to address the input portability problem.

The problem of input-aware optimizations has been studied in several previous works [17, 18, 28, 29]. The only work that tackles the input portability problem in the context of GPUs is introduced in [18]. In this work, programmers should provide optimizations' pragmas for the compiler and then compiler generates different programs with different optimizations based on those pragmas. Their approach is to run all these different versions of one program for different inputs and save all the results into a database. For each input, they check this database and find the best version and run it on the GPU.

There are other works that have focused on generating CUDA code from sequential input [1, 8, 16, 25, 31]. hiCUDA [8] is a high-level directive-based compiler framework for CUDA programming where programmers need to insert directives into sequential C code to define the boundaries of kernel functions. The work in [1] is an automatic code transformation system that generates CUDA code from input sequential C code without annotations for affine programs. In [31], by using C pragma preprocessor directives, programmers help compiler to generate efficient CUDA code. In [25], programmers use C# language and a library to write their programs and let the compiler generate efficient GPU code.The work in [16] proposes an extension to a Java JIT compiler that executes program on the GPU.

Gordon et al. [6] perform stream-graph refinements to statically determine the best mapping of a StreamIt program to a multi-core CPU. Researchers have also proposed ways to map and optimize synchronous data-flow languages to SIMD engines [11], distributed shared memory systems [13]. In a recent work [26], the authors talk about the usefulness of different features of StreamIt to a wide range of streaming applications.

Works in [22, 23, 32] map reduction to heterogeneous systems with GPUs. Mapping stencil loops to GPUs and tiling size tradeoff are also studied by [1] and [19]. However, Adaptic applies input-aware optimizations adaptively and more generally on streaming applications to provide input portability

7. Conclusion

GPUs provide an attractive platform for accelerating parallel workloads. However, their programming complexity poses a significant challenge to application developers. In addition, they have to deal with portability problems across both different targets and various inputs. While target portability has received a great deal of attention in the research community, the input portability problem has not been investigated before. This problem arises when a program optimized for a certain range of inputs, shows poor performance along different input ranges.

In this work, we proposed Adaptic, an adaptive input-aware compiler for GPUs. Using this compiler, programmers can implement their algorithms once using the high-level constructs of a streaming language and compile them to CUDA code for all possible input sizes and various GPUs targets. Adaptic, with the help of its input-aware optimizations, can generate highly-optimized GPU kernels to maintain high performance across different problem sizes. At runtime, Adaptic's runtime kernel management chooses the best performing kernel based on the input. Our results show that Adaptic's generated code has similar performance to the hand-optimized CUDA code over the original program's input comfort zone, while achieving upto 6x speedup when the input falls out of this range.

Acknowledgement

Much gratitude goes to the anonymous referees who provided excellent feedback on this work. This research was supported by ARM Ltd., the Gigascale Systems Research Center, and the National Science Foundation under grant CNS-0964478.

References

[1] M. M. Baskaran, J. Ramanujam, and P. Sadayappan. Automatic C-to-CUDA code generation for affine programs. In *Proc. of the 19th International Conference on Compiler Construction*, pages 244–263, 2010.

[2] I. Buck et al. Brook for GPUs: Stream computing on graphics hardware. *ACM Transactions on Graphics*, 23(3):777–786, Aug. 2004.

[3] B. Catanzaro, M. Garland, and K. Keutzer. Copperhead: compiling an embedded data parallel language. In *Proc. of the 16th ACM SIGPLAN Symposium on Principles and Practice of Parallel Programming*, pages 47–56, 2011.

[4] B. Catanzaro, N. Sundaram, and K. Keutzer. Fast support vector machine training and classification on graphics processors. In *Proc. of the 25th International Conference on Machine learning*, pages 104–111, 2008.

[5] R. Garg and J. N. Amaral. Compiling python to a hybrid execution environment. In *Proc. of the 3rd Workshop on General Purpose Processing on Graphics Processing Units*, pages 19–30, 2010.

[6] M. I. Gordon, W. Thies, and S. Amarasinghe. Exploiting coarse-grained task, data, and pipeline parallelism in stream programs. In *14th International Conference on Architectural Support for Programming Languages and Operating Systems*, pages 151–162, 2006.

[7] M. Grossman, A. Simion, Z. Budimli, and V. Sarkar. CnC-CUDA: Declarative Programming for GPUs. In *Proc. of the 23rd Workshop on Languages and Compilers for Parallel Computing*, pages 230–245, 2010.

[8] T. Han and T. Abdelrahman. hiCUDA: High-level GPGPU programming. *IEEE Transactions on Parallel and Distributed Systems*, 22(1):52–61, 2010.

[9] C. Hong, D. Chen, W. Chen, W. Zheng, and H. Lin. Mapcg: writing parallel program portable between CPU and GPU. In *Proc. of the 19th International Conference on Parallel Architectures and Compilation Techniques*, pages 217–226, 2010.

[10] S. Hong and H. Kim. An analytical model for a GPU architecture with memory-level and thread-level parallelism awareness. In *Proc. of the 36th Annual International Symposium on Computer Architecture*, pages 152–163, 2009.

[11] A. Hormati, Y. Choi, M. Woh, M. Kudlur, R. Rabbah, T. Mudge, and S. Mahlke. Macross: Macro-simdization of streaming applications. In *18th International Conference on Architectural Support for Programming Languages and Operating Systems*, pages 285–296, 2010.

[12] A. H. Hormati, M. Samadi, M. Woh, T. Mudge, and S. Mahlke. Sponge: portable stream programming on graphics engines. In *19th International Conference on Architectural Support for Programming Languages and Operating Systems*, pages 381–392, 2011.

[13] M. Kudlur and S. Mahlke. Orchestrating the execution of stream programs on multicore platforms. In *Proc. of the '08 Conference on Programming Language Design and Implementation*, pages 114–124, June 2008.

[14] S. Lee, S.-J. Min, and R. Eigenmann. OpenMP to GPGPU: a compiler framework for automatic translation and optimization. In *Proc. of the 14th ACM SIGPLAN Symposium on Principles and Practice of Parallel Programming*, pages 101–110, 2009.

[15] V. W. Lee, C. Kim, J. Chhugani, M. Deisher, D. Kim, A. D. Nguyen, N. Satish, M. Smelyanskiy, S. Chennupaty, P. Hammarlund, R. Singhal, and P. Dubey. Debunking the 100x GPU vs. CPU myth: an evaluation of throughput computing on CPU and GPU. In *Proc. of the 37th Annual International Symposium on Computer Architecture*, pages 451–460, 2010.

[16] A. Leung, O. Lhoták, and G. Lashari. Automatic parallelization for graphics processing units. In *Proc. of the 7th International Conference on Principles and Practice of Programming in Java*, pages 91–100, 2009.

[17] X. Li, M. J. Garzarán, and D. Padua. A dynamically tuned sorting library. In *Proc. of the 2004 International Symposium on Code Generation and Optimization*, pages 111–, 2004.

[18] Y. Liu, E. Z. Zhang, and X. Shen. A cross-input adaptive framework for GPU program optimizations. In *2009 IEEE International Symposium on Parallel and Distributed Processing*, pages 1–10, 2009.

[19] J. Meng and K. Skadron. Performance modeling and automatic ghost zone optimization for iterative stencil loops on GPUs. In *Proc. of the 2009 International Conference on Supercomputing*, pages 256–265, 2009.

[20] NVIDIA. GPUs Are Only Up To 14 Times Faster than CPUs says Intel, 2010. http://blogs.nvidia.com/ntersect/2010/06/gpus-are-only-up-to-14-times-faster-than-cpus-says-intel.html.

[21] A. Prasad, J. Anantpur, and R. Govindarajan. Automatic compilation of MATLAB programs for synergistic execution on heterogeneous processors. In *Proc. of the '11 Conference on Programming Language Design and Implementation*, pages 152–163, 2011.

[22] V. T. Ravi, W. Ma, D. Chiu, and G. Agrawal. Compiler and runtime support for enabling generalized reduction computations on heterogeneous parallel configurations. In *Proc. of the 2010 International Conference on Supercomputing*, pages 137–146, 2010.

[23] D. Roger, U. Assarsson, and N. Holzschuch. Efficient stream reduction on the GPU. In *Proc. of the 1st Workshop on General Purpose Processing on Graphics Processing Units*, pages 1–4, 2007.

[24] S. Ryoo, C. I. Rodrigues, S. S. Baghsorkhi, S. S. Stone, D. B. Kirk, and W. mei W. Hwu. Optimization principles and application performance evaluation of a multithreaded GPU using CUDA. In *Proc. of the 13th ACM SIGPLAN Symposium on Principles and Practice of Parallel Programming*, pages 73–82, 2008.

[25] D. Tarditi, S. Puri, and J. Oglesby. Accelerator: using data parallelism to program GPUs for general-purpose uses. In *14th International Conference on Architectural Support for Programming Languages and Operating Systems*, pages 325–335, 2006.

[26] W. Thies and S. Amarasinghe. An empirical characterization of stream programs and its implications for language and compiler design. In *Proc. of the 19th International Conference on Parallel Architectures and Compilation Techniques*, pages 365–376, 2010.

[27] W. Thies, M. Karczmarek, and S. P. Amarasinghe. StreamIt: A language for streaming applications. In *Proc. of the 2002 International Conference on Compiler Construction*, pages 179–196, 2002.

[28] N. Thomas, G. Tanase, O. Tkachyshyn, J. Perdue, N. M. Amato, and L. Rauchwerger. A framework for adaptive algorithm selection in stapl. In *Proc. of the 10th ACM SIGPLAN Symposium on Principles and Practice of Parallel Programming*, pages 277–288, 2005.

[29] K. Tian, Y. Jiang, E. Z. Zhang, and X. Shen. An input-centric paradigm for program dynamic optimizations. In *Proceedings of the OOPSLA'10*, pages 125–139, 2010.

[30] A. Udupa, R. Govindarajan, and M. J. Thazhuthaveetil. Software pipelined execution of stream programs on GPUs. In *Proc. of the 2009 International Symposium on Code Generation and Optimization*, pages 200–209, 2009.

[31] M. Wolfe. Implementing the PGI accelerator model. In *Proc. of the 3rd Workshop on General Purpose Processing on Graphics Processing Units*, pages 43–50, 2010.

[32] X.-L. Wu, N. Obeid, and W.-M. Hwu. Exploiting more parallelism from applications having generalized reductions on GPU architectures. In *Proc. of the 2010 10th International Conference on Computers and Information Technology*, pages 1175–1180, 2010.

[33] Y. Yang, P. Xiang, J. Kong, and H. Zhou. A GPGPU compiler for memory optimization and parallelism management. In *Proc. of the '10 Conference on Programming Language Design and Implementation*, pages 86–97, 2010.

[34] S. zee Ueng, M. Lathara, S. S. Baghsorkhi, and W. mei W. Hwu. CUDA-Lite: Reducing GPU programming complexity. In *Proc. of the 21st Workshop on Languages and Compilers for Parallel Computing*, pages 1–15, 2008.

And Then There Were None:

A Stall-Free Real-Time Garbage Collector for Reconfigurable Hardware

David F. Bacon   Perry Cheng   Sunil Shukla

IBM Research

{dfb,perry,skshukla}@us.ibm.com

Abstract

Programmers are turning to radical architectures such as reconfigurable hardware (FPGAs) to achieve performance. But such systems, programmed at a very low level in languages with impoverished abstractions, are orders of magnitude more complex to use than conventional CPUs. The continued exponential increase in transistors, combined with the desire to implement ever more sophisticated algorithms, makes it imperative that such systems be programmed at much higher levels of abstraction. One of the fundamental high-level language features is automatic memory management in the form of garbage collection.

We present the first implementation of a complete garbage collector in hardware (as opposed to previous "hardware-assist" techniques), using an FPGA and its on-chip memory. Using a completely concurrent snapshot algorithm, it provides single-cycle access to the heap, and never stalls the mutator for even a single cycle, achieving a deterministic mutator utilization (MMU) of 100%.

We have synthesized the collector to hardware and show that it never consumes more than 1% of the logic resources of a high-end FPGA. For comparison we also implemented explicit (malloc/free) memory management, and show that real-time collection is about 4% to 17% slower than malloc, with comparable energy consumption. Surprisingly, in hardware real-time collection is superior to stop-the-world collection on every performance axis, and even for stressful micro-benchmarks can achieve 100% MMU with heaps as small as 1.01 to 1.4 times the absolute minimum.

Categories and Subject Descriptors B.3.3 [*Memory Structures*]: Worst-case analysis; B.5.1 [*Register-Transfer-Level Implementation*]: Memory design; B.7.1 [*Integrated Circuits*]: Gate arrays; C.3 [*Special-Purpose and Application-Based Systems*]: Real-time and embedded systems; D.3.3 [*Programming Languages*]: Language Constructs and Features; D.3.4 [*Programming Languages*]: Memory management (garbage collection)

General Terms Design, Languages, Experimentation, Performance

Keywords Block RAM, FPGA, High Level Synthesis, Garbage Collection, Real Time

PLDI'12, June 11–16, 2012, Beijing, China.

1. Introduction

The end of frequency scaling has driven architects and developers to parallelism in search of performance. However, general-purpose MIMD parallelism is inefficient and power-hungry, with power rapidly becoming the limiting factor. This has led the search for performance to non-traditional chip architectures like GPUs and other more radical architectures. The most radical general-purpose computing platform of all is reconfigurable hardware, in the form of Field-Programmable Gate Arrays (FPGAs).

FPGAs are now available with over 1 million programmable logic cells and 8 MB of on-chip "block RAM", providing a massive amount of bit-level parallelism combined with single-cycle access to the memory capacity of a VAX-11/780. Furthermore, because that memory is distributed throughout the chip in 18 Kbit units, algorithms with huge data bandwidth can also be implemented.

However, programming methodology for FPGAs has lagged far behind their capacity, which in turn has greatly reduced their application to general-purpose computing. The most common languages for FPGA programming are still hardware description languages (VHDL and Verilog) in which the only abstractions are bits, arrays of bits, registers, wires, and so on. The entire approach to programming them is oriented around the synthesis of a chip that happens to be reconfigurable, as opposed to programming a general-purpose device.

Recent research has focused on raising the level of abstraction and programmability to that of high-level software-based programming languages, in particular, the Kiwi project [14] which uses C#, and the Liquid Metal project, which has developed the Lime language [4] based on Java.

However, up until now, whether programmers are writing in low-level HDLs or high-level languages like Kiwi and Lime, use of dynamic memory management has only just begun to be explored [11, 25], and use of garbage collection has been nonexistent.

In this paper we present a garbage collector synthesized entirely into hardware, capable of collecting a heap of *uniform* objects completely concurrently. We call such a heap of uniform objects a *miniheap*. By uniform we mean that the shape of the objects (the size of the data fields and the location of pointers) is fixed. Thus we trade a degree of flexibility in the memory layout for large gains in collector performance.

In the FPGA domain this makes sense: due to the distributed nature of the memory it is common to build pipelined designs where each stage of the pipeline maintains its own internal data structures that are able to access their local block RAM in parallel with other pipeline stages. Furthermore, fixed data layouts can provide order-of-magnitude better performance because they allow designs which deterministically process one operation per clock cycle.

For instance, the Lime language provides the capability to map a graph of compute tasks, each with its own private heap memory, onto the FPGA. Thus it is more important to handle many small heaps with a high degree of efficiency, than to handle a high degree of heterogeneity in the data layout.

Historically, it is also interesting to note that McCarthy's invention of garbage collection for LISP [18] was in the context of an IBM 704 with only 4K 36-bit words, essentially used as a fixed-format heap of S-expressions.

Algorithmically, our collector is a fairly straightforward Yuasa-style snapshot-at-the-beginning concurrent collector [35], with a linear sweep phase. However, by taking advantage of hardware structures like dual-ported memories, the ability to simultaneously read and write a register in a single cycle, and to atomically distribute a control signal across the entire system, we are able to develop a collector that *never* interferes with the mutator.

Furthermore, the mutator has single-cycle access to memory, and the design can actually support multiple simultaneous memory operations per cycle. Arbitration circuits delay some collector operations by one cycle in favor of mutator operations, but the collector can keep up with a mutator even when it performs a memory operation every cycle (allocations are limited to one every other cycle).

The collector we describe can be used either directly with programs hand-written in hardware description languages (which we explore this paper) or as part of a hardware "run-time system" targeted by a compiler for a C-to-gates [11, 25] or high-level language [4, 14] system including dynamic memory allocation. The latter is left to future work, and we concentrate in this paper on exploring the design, analysis, and limits of the hardware collector.

The contributions of this paper are:

- the first implementation of an entire garbage collector in hardware (as opposed to hardware-assist or microcode), including both stop-the-world and fully concurrent variants;
- the first garbage collector to entirely eliminate mutator interference by the collector (by even a single cycle), thereby achieving minimum mutator utilization (MMU [7]) of 100%;
- an implementation of the collector in Verilog along with demanding hardware-based client applications performing up to one memory allocation every 14 cycles;
- a performance evaluation showing the cost of garbage collection in absolute terms and relative to malloc/free, including dynamic measurement of throughput and energy;
- analytic closed-form worst-case bounds (in cycles) for collection time and minimum heap size required for 0-stall real-time behavior, along with experimental evidence of safety, and tightness within 2-6% for time and 3% for space; and
- an exploration of the design space showing that in hardware, real-time collection simultaneously achieves higher throughput, and lower latency, memory usage, and energy consumption than stop-the-world collection.

2. FPGA Background

Field Programmable Gate Arrays (FPGAs) are programmable logic devices consisting of 4- or 6-input look-up tables (LUTs) which can be used to implement combinational logic, and flip-flops which can be used to implement sequential logic. On the Xilinx FPGAs which we use in this work, several LUTs and flip-flops are combined together to form a unit called a *slice*, which is the standard unit in which resource consumption is reported for FPGAs (Altera FPGAs use a slightly different architecture).

FPGAs also include a clock distribution network for propagating a globally synchronized clock to allow for the use of conventional clocked digital logic. Our collector takes advantage of this global clock in a number of ways, in particular to implement an efficient single-cycle atomic root snapshot.

The FPGA also contains a large amount of configurable routing resources for connecting the slices, based on the data flow in the hardware description language program. The routing resources are used by the place-and-route (PAR) tool during hardware synthesis.

2.1 Memory Structures on FPGAs

Particularly important to this work are the memories available on the FPGA. Block RAMs (BRAMs) are specialized memory structures embedded within the FPGA for resource-efficient implementation of large random- and sequential-access memories.

The Xilinx Virtex-5 LX330T [32] device that we use in this paper (one of the largest in that family) has a BRAM capacity of 1.5 MB; the latest generation of Xilinx devices, the Virtex-7, have as much as 8 MB of BRAM.

A single BRAM in a Virtex-5 FPGA can store up to 36 Kilobits (Kb) of memory. An important feature of BRAM is that it can be organized in various form factors (analogous to word sizes on a CPU). On the Virtex-5, form factors of 1, 2, 4, 9, 18, 36, 72, and so on are supported. A 36 Kb BRAM can also be used as two logically separate 18 Kb BRAMs. Moreover, a larger memory structure can be built by cascading multiple BRAMs horizontally, vertically or in a hybrid manner. Any memory structure in the design which is smaller than 18 Kb would lead to quantization (or, in memory system parlance, "fragmentation").

The quantization effect can be considerable depending on the logical memory structure in the design (and is explored in Section 7). A BRAM can be used as a true dual ported (TDP) RAM providing two fully independent read-write ports. Furthermore, each port supports either read, write, read-before-write, or read-after-write operations. Our collector makes significant use of read-before-write for things like the Yuasa-style write barrier [35].

BRAMs can also be configured for use as FIFO queues rather than as random access memories; we make use of this feature for implementing the mark queues in the tracing phase of the collector.

FPGAs are typically packaged on boards with dedicated off-chip DRAM and/or SRAM which can be accessed via a memory controller synthesized for the FPGA. Such memory could be used to implement much larger heap structures. However, we do not consider use of DRAM or SRAM in this paper because we are focusing on high-performance designs with highly deterministic (single cycle) behavior.

3. Memory Architecture

The memory architecture — that is, the way in which object fields are laid out in memory, and the free list is maintained — is common to our support of both malloc/free and garbage-collected abstractions. In this section we describe our memory architecture as well as some of the alternatives, and discuss the tradeoffs qualitatively. Some tradeoffs are explored quantitatively in Section 7.

Since memory structures within an FPGA are typically and of necessity far more uniform than in a conventional software heap, we organize memory into one or more *miniheaps*, in which objects have a fixed size and "shape" in terms of division between pointer and data fields. This is essentially the same design as the "big bag of pages" (BIBOP) style in conventional software memory allocator design, in which the metadata for the objects is implicit in the page in which they reside [28].

The fixed shape of the miniheaps is a natural match to the FPGA, which must use fixed-width data paths to transmit the objects and fields across the routing network to achieve high performance.

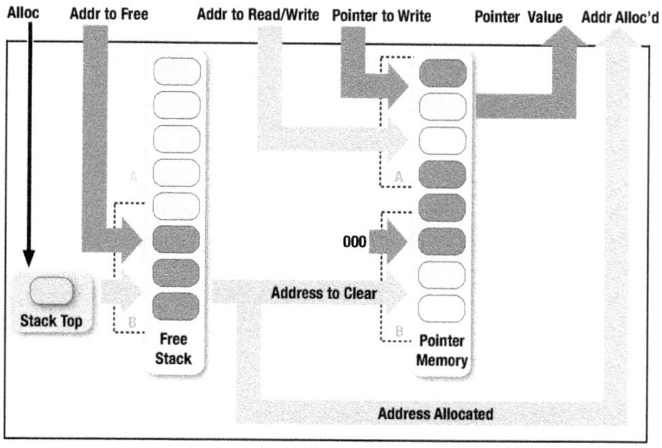

Figure 1. Memory module design for malloc/free interface, showing a single field of pointer type (for heap size $N = 8$ and pointer width $\log N = 3$). Block RAMs are in yellow, with the dual ports (A/B) shown. For each port, the data line is above and the address select line is below. Ovals designate 3-bit wide pointer fields; those in blue are in use.

3.1 Miniheap Interface

Each miniheap has an interface allowing objects to be allocated (and freed when using explicit memory management), and operations allowing individual data fields to be read or written.

In this paper we will consider miniheaps with one or two pointer fields and one or two data fields. This is sufficient for implementing many stack, list, queue, and tree data structures, as well as S-expressions. FPGA modules for common applications like packet processing, compression, etc. are covered by such structures.

Our design allows an arbitrary number of data fields. Increasing the number of pointer fields is straightforward for malloc-style memory. However, for garbage collected memory, the extension would require additional logic. We believe this is relatively straightforward to implement (and include details below) but the experimental results in this paper are confined to one- and two-pointer objects.

3.2 Miniheap with Malloc/Free

There are many ways in which the interface in Section 3.1 can be implemented. Fundamentally, these represent a time/space (and sometimes power) trade-off between the number of available parallel operations, and the amount of hardware resources consumed.

For FPGAs, one specifies a logical memory block with a desired data width and number of entries, and the synthesis tools attempt to allocate the required number of individual Block RAMs as efficiently as possible, using various packing strategies. We refer to the BRAMs for such a logical memory block as a *BRAM set*.

In our design we use one BRAM set for each field in the object. For example, if there are two pointer fields and one data field, then there are three BRAM sets.

The non-pointer field has a natural width associated with its data type (for instance 32 bits). However, for a miniheap of size N, the pointer fields must only be $\lceil \log_2 N \rceil$ bits wide. Because data widths on the FPGA are completely customizable, we use precisely the required number of bits. Thus a larger miniheap will increase in size not only because of the number of entries, but because the pointer fields themselves become larger.

As in software, the pointer value 0 is reserved to mean "`null`", so a miniheap of size N can really only store $N - 1$ objects.

A high-level block diagram of the memory manager is shown in Figure 1. It shows the primary data and control fields of the memory module, although many of the signals have been elided to simplify the diagram. For clarity of presentation it shows a single object field, of pointer type (Pointer Memory), which is stored in a single BRAM set. A second BRAM set (Free Stack) is used to store a stack of free objects.

For an object with f fields, there would be f BRAM sets with associated interfaces for the write and read values (but *not* an additional address port). And of course there is only a single free stack, regardless of how many fields the object has.

The *Alloc* signal is a one-bit signal used to implement the `malloc` operation. A register is used to hold the value of the stack top. Assuming it is non-zero, it is decremented and then presented on port B of the Free Stack BRAM set, in *read* mode. The resulting pointer to a free field is then returned (*Addr Alloc'd*), but is also fed to port B of the Pointer Memory, in *write* mode with the write value hard-wired to `000` (or "`null`").

To free an object, the pointer is presented to the memory manager (*Addr to Free*). The Stack Top register is used as the address for the Free Stack BRAM set on port B, in write mode, with the data value *Addr to Free*. Then the Stack Top register is incremented. This causes the pointer to the freed object to be pushed onto the Free Stack.

In order to read or write a field in the Pointer Memory, the *Addr to Read/Write* is presented, and, if writing, a *Pointer to Write*. This uses port A of the BRAM set in either read or write mode, returning a value on the *Pointer Value* port in the former case.

Note that this design, by taking advantage of dual-porting the BRAMs, can allow a read or write to proceed in parallel with an allocate or free.

3.3 Fragmentation and Other Trade-Offs

The BRAM quantization described in Section 2.1 can play a significant role in the efficiency of BRAM utilization. For instance, for a miniheap of size $N = 256$, pointers are 8 bits wide, so a single 18 Kb BRAM configured as 9 bits wide would be used. This wastes 1 bit per entry, but also wastes 1.75K entries, since only 256 (0.25K) entries are needed. The 1 bit wasted per field is a form of *internal fragmentation* and the 1.75K wasted fields are a form of *external fragmentation*.

To reduce external fragmentation, multiple fields of the same size could be implemented with a single BRAM set. However, since BRAMs are dual-ported, supporting more than two fields would result in a loss of parallelism in terms of field access. Furthermore, since we use one BRAM port for initialization of fields when they are allocated, this effect comes into play even with two fields.

The opposite approach is also possible: multiple fields can be implemented with a single BRAM set, resulting in a wider data width. In principle this can reduce internal fragmentation. However, in practice we find that this can actually result in poorer resource allocation. A wider data width also means that updates to individual fields must be performed with a read/modify/write sequence, which requires two cycles. Furthermore, the read/modify/write can not be pipelined, so in addition to higher latency, throughput can be halved.

Threaded Free List. A common software optimization would be to represent the free objects not as a stack of pointers, but as a linked list threaded through the unused objects (that is, a linked list through the first pointer field). Since the set of allocated and free objects are mutually exclusive, this optimization is essentially free modulo cache locality effects.

However, in hardware, this causes resource contention on the BRAM set containing the first pointer (since it is doing double duty). Thus parallelism is reduced: read or write operations on the first pointer can not be performed in the same cycle as `malloc` or `free`, and the latter require two cycles rather than one.

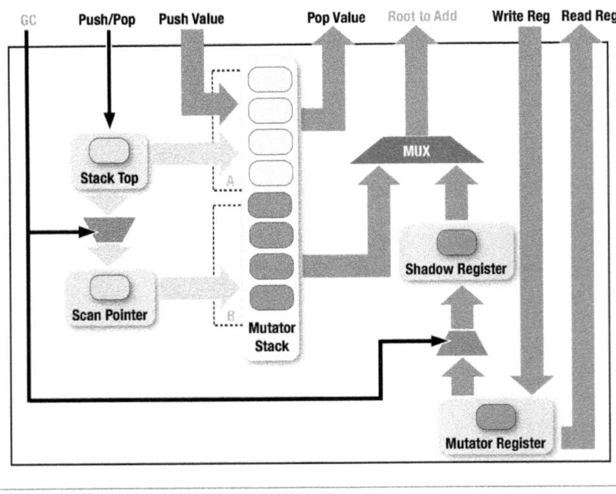

Figure 2. Single-Cycle Atomic Root Snapshot Engine

4. Garbage Collector Design

We now describe the implementation of both a stop-the-world and a fully concurrent collector in hardware. In software, the architecture of these two styles of collector are radically different. In hardware, the differences are much smaller, as the same fundamental structures and interfaces are used.

The concurrent collector has a few extra data structures (implemented with BRAMs) and also requires more careful allocation of BRAM ports to avoid contention, but these features do not negatively affect the use of the design in the stop-the-world collector. Therefore, we will present the concurrent collector design, and merely mention here that the stop-the-world variant omits the shadow register(s) from the root engine, the write barrier register and logic from the trace engine, and the used map and logic from the sweep engine.

Our collector comprises three separate components, which handle the atomic root snapshot, tracing, and sweeping.

4.1 Background: Yuasa's Snapshot Algorithm

Before delving into the details of our implementation, we describe Yuasa's snapshot algorithm [35] which is the basis of our implementation. While the mechanics in hardware are quite different, it is interesting to note that implementing in hardware allows us to achieve a higher degree of concurrency and determinism than state-of-the-art software algorithms, but without incorporating more sophisticated algorithmic techniques developed in the interim.

The fundamental principle of the snapshot algorithm is that when collection is initiated, a *logical* snapshot of the heap is taken. The collector then runs in this logical snapshot, and collects everything that was garbage at snapshot time.

In Yuasa's original algorithm, the snapshot consisted of the registers, stacks, and global variables. This set of pointers was gathered synchronously (since then, much research has been devoted to avoiding the need for any global synchronization at snapshot time or during phase transitions [3, 22]).

Once the roots have been gathered, the mutator is allowed to proceed and the collector runs concurrently, marking the transitive closure of the roots.

If the mutator concurrently modifies the heap, its only obligation is to make sure that the collector can still find all of the objects that existed in the heap at snapshot time. This is accomplished by the use of a *write barrier*: before any pointer is over-written, it is recorded in a buffer and treated as a root for the purposes of collection.

Objects that are freshly allocated during a collection are not eligible for collection (they are "allocated black" in the parlance of collector literature).

The advantage of the snapshot algorithm is its simplicity and determinism. Since it operates in a logical snapshot at an instant in time, the invariants are easy to describe. In addition, termination is simple and deterministic, since the amount of work is bounded at the instant that collection begins.

This is in contrast to the "incremental update" style algorithms of Steele [27] and Dijkstra [12] (and numerous successors), which attempt to "chase" objects that are freshly allocated during collection.

4.2 Root Snapshot

The concurrent collector uses the snapshot-at-the-beginning algorithm described above. Yuasa's original algorithm required a global pause while the snapshot was taken by recording the roots; since then real-time collectors have endeavored to reduce the pause required by the root snapshot. In hardware, we are able to completely eliminate the snapshot pause by taking advantage of the parallelism and synchronization available in the hardware.

The snapshot must take two types of roots into account: those in registers, and those on the stack. Figure 2 shows the root snapshot module, simplified to show a single stack and a single register.

The snapshot is controlled by the *GC* input signal, which goes high for one clock cycle at the beginning of collection. The snapshot is defined as the state of the memory at the beginning of the *next cycle* after the *GC* signal goes high. This allows some setup time and reduces synchronization requirements.

The register snapshot is obtained by using a shadow register. In the cycle after the *GC* signal goes high, the value of the register is copied into the shadow register. This can happen even if the register is also written by the mutator in the same cycle, since the new value will not be latched until the end of the cycle.

The stack snapshot is obtained by having another register in addition to the Stack Top register, called the Scan Pointer. In the same cycle that the *GC* signal goes high, the value of the Stack Top pointer minus one is written into the Scan Pointer (because the Stack Top points to the entry above the actual top value). Beginning in the following cycle, the Scan Pointer is used as the source address to port B of the BRAM set containing the stack, and the pointer is read out, going through the MUX and emerging on the *Root to Add* port from the snapshot module. The Scan Pointer is also decremented in preparation for the following cycle.

Note that the mutator can continue to use the stack via port A of the BRAM set, while the snapshot uses port B. And since the mutator can not pop values off the stack faster than the collector can read them out, the property is preserved that the snapshot contains *exactly* those roots that existed in the cycle following the *GC* signal.

A detail omitted from the diagram is that a state machine is required to sequence the values from the stack and the shadow register(s) through the MUX to the *Root to Add* port. Note that the values from the stack must be processed first, because the stack snapshot technique relies on staying ahead of the mutator without any explicit synchronization.

If multiple stacks were desired, then a "shadow" stack would be required to hold values as they were read out before the mutator could overwrite them, which could then be sequenced onto the *Root to Add* port.

As will be seen in Section 4.4, collection is triggered (only) by an allocation that causes free space to drop below a threshold. Therefore the generation of root snapshot logic only needs to consider those hardware states in which this might occur. Any register or stack not live in those states can be safely ignored.

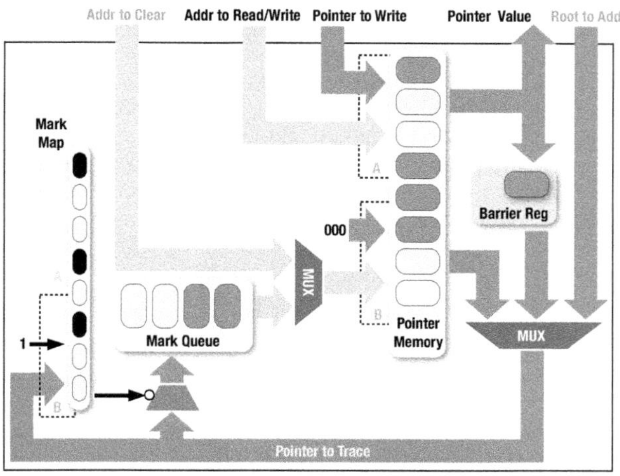

Figure 3. Tracing Engine and a Single Pointer Memory

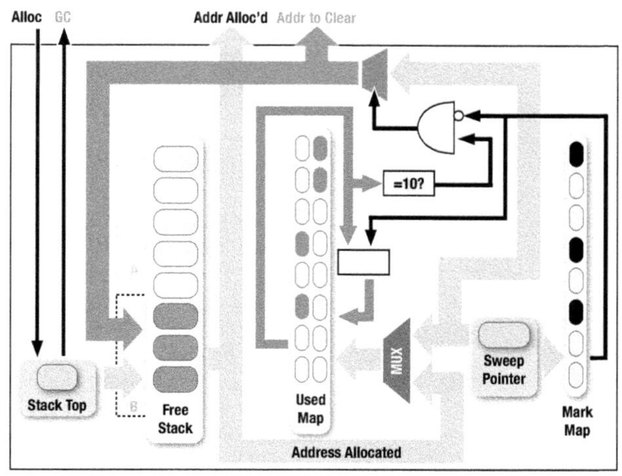

Figure 4. Free Stack and Sweeping Engine

4.3 Tracing

The tracing engine, along with a single pointer memory (corresponding to a single pointer field in an object) is shown in Figure 3. It provides the same mutator interface as the malloc/free style memory manager of Figure 1: *Addr to Read/Write*, *Pointer to Write*, and *Pointer Value* – except that the external interface *Addr to Free* is replaced by the internal interface (denoted in red) *Addr to Clear*, which is generated by the Sweep module (described in Section 4.4).

The only additional interface is the *Root to Add* port which takes its inputs from the output port of the same name of the Root Engine in Figure 2.

As it executes, there are three sources of pointers for the engine to trace: externally added roots from the snapshot, internally traced roots from the pointer memory, and over-written pointers from the pointer memory (captured with a Yuasa-style barrier to maintain the snapshot property). The different pointer sources flow through a MUX, and on each cycle a pointer can be presented to the Mark Map, which contains one bit for each of the N memory locations.

Using the BRAM read-before-write mode, the old mark value is read, and then the mark value is unconditionally set to 1. If the old mark value is 0, this pointer has not yet been traversed, so the negation of the old mark value (indicated by the bubble) is used to control whether the pointer is added to the Mark Queue (note that this means that all values in the Mark Queue have been filtered, so at most $N - 1$ values can flow through the queue). The Mark Queue is a BRAM used in FIFO (rather than random access) mode.

Pointers from the Mark Queue are presented as a read address on port B of the Pointer Memory, and if the fetched values are non-null are fed through the MUX and thence to the marking step.

The write barrier is implemented by using port A of the Pointer Memory BRAM in read-before-write mode. When the mutator writes a pointer, the old value is read out first and placed into the Barrier Reg. This is subsequently fed through the MUX and marked (the timing and arbitration is discussed below).

Given the three BRAMs involved in the marking process, processing one pointer requires 3 cycles. However, the marking engine is implemented as a *3-stage pipeline*, so it is able to sustain a throughput of one pointer per cycle.

4.3.1 Trace Engine Pairing

For objects with two pointers, two trace engines are paired together to maximize resource usage (this is not shown in the figure). Since each trace engine only uses one port of the mark map, both engines can mark concurrently.

Furthermore, the two mark queues are MUXed together and the next item to mark is always taken from the longer queue. When there is only one item to enqueue, it is placed on the shorter queue. Using this design, we provision each of the 2 queues to be of size $3N/8 + R$ (where R is the maximum number of roots), which guarantees that the queues will never overflow. For a formal argument, see Appendix A.

On each cycle, one pointer is removed from the queues, and the two pointers in the object retrieved are examined and potentially marked and enqueued.

The final optimization is that since there are now two write barrier registers and two mark queues, the write barrier values are not processed until there are two of them. This means that the mark engines can make progress every other cycle even if the application is performing one write per cycle.

4.3.2 Trace Termination and WCET Effects

The termination protocol for marking is simple: once the last item from the mark queues is popped (both mark queues become empty), it takes 2 or 3 cycles for the trace engine to finish the current pipeline. If the two pointers returned by the heap are null, then the mark process is terminated in the second cycle as there is no need to read the mark bits in this case. Otherwise the mark bit for the non-null pointers are read to ensure that both pointers are marked, in which case the mark phase is terminated in the third cycle.

Write barrier values arriving after the first cycle of termination can be ignored, since by the snapshot property they would either have to be newly allocated or else discovered by tracing the heap.

However, note that some (realistic) data structures, in particular linked lists, will cause a pathological behavior, in which a pointer is marked, removed from the queue, which will appear empty, and then 2 cycles later the next pointer from the linked list will be enqueued. So while the pipeline can sustain marking one object per cycle, pipeline bubbles will occur which reduce that throughput.

We are currently investigating speculative "pointer forwarding" optimizations but they have not been implemented so we merely note that it may be possible to remove at least one if not both of these bubbles at a modest cost in additional logic.

4.4 Sweeping

Once tracing is complete, the sweep phase begins, in which memory is reclaimed. The high-level design is shown in Figure 4. The sweep engine also handles allocation requests and maintains the stack of pointers to free memory (Free Stack). The Mark Map here is the same Mark Map as in Figure 3.

When an *Alloc* request arrives from the mutator, the Stack Top register is used to remove a pointer to a free object from the Free Stack, and the stack pointer is decremented. If the stack pointer falls below a certain level (we typically use 25%), then a garbage collection is triggered by raising the *GC* signal which is connected to the root snapshot engine (Figure 2).

The address popped from the Free Stack is returned to the mutator on the *Addr Alloc'd* port. It is also used to set the object's entry in the Used Map, to `01`, meaning "freshly allocated" (and thus "black"). A value of `00` means "free", in which case the object is on the Free Stack.

When tracing is completed, sweeping begins in the next machine cycle. Sweeping is a simple linear scan. The Sweep Pointer is initialized to 1 (since slot 0 is reserved for `null`), and on every cycle (except when pre-empted by allocation) the sweep pointer is presented to both the Mark Map and the Used Map.

If an object is marked, its Used Map entry is set to `10`. If an object is not marked and its used map entry is `10` (the *and* gate in the figure) then the used map entry is reset to `00`. Although only 3 states are used, the particular choice of bit pattern is based on avoiding unneeded logic. The resulting signal is also used to control whether the current Sweep Pointer address is going to be freed. If so, it is pushed onto the Free Stack and also output on the *Addr to Clear* port, which is connected to the mark engine so that the data values being freed are zeroed out.

Note that since clearing only occurs during sweeping, there is no contention for the Pointer Memory port in the trace engine between clearing and marking. Furthermore, an allocation and a free may happen in the same cycle: the top-of-stack is accessed using read-before-write mode and returned as the *Addr Alloc'd*, and then the newly freed object is pushed back.

When an object is allocated, its entry in the Mark Map is *not* set (otherwise an extra interlock would be required). This means that the tracing engine may encounter newly allocated objects in its marking pipeline (via newly installed pointers in the heap), albeit at most once since they will then be marked. This also affects WCET analysis, as we will see in the next section.

5. Analysis of Real-Time Behavior

First of all, we note that since the design of our real-time collector allows mutation and collection to occur unconditionally together in a single cycle, the minimum mutator utilization (or MMU [7]), is 100% unless insufficient resources are dedicated to the heap.

Furthermore, unlike software-based collectors [5, 16], the system is fully deterministic because we can analyze the worst case behavior down to the (machine) cycle.

Given R is the maximum number of roots, N is the size of the heap, then the worst-case time (in cycles) for garbage collection is

$$T = T_R + T_M + T_W + T_X + T_S + T_A \tag{1}$$

where T_R is the time to snapshot the roots, T_M is the time (in cycles) to mark, T_S is the time to sweep, and T_W is the time lost to write barriers during marking, T_X is the time lost to blackening newly allocated objects during marking, and T_A is time lost to allocations during sweeping.

In the worst case, without any knowledge of the application,

$$T_R = R + 2 \quad T_M = 3N + 3 \quad T_W = 0 \quad T_X = 0 \quad T_S = N$$

The reasoning for these quantities follows. During the snapshot phase, we can place one root into the mark queue every cycle, plus one cycle to start and finish the phase, accounting for $R+2$. During marking, there could be N objects in the heap, configured as a linked list which caused the mark pipeline to stall for two cycles on each object, plus 3 cycles to terminate. Sweeping is unaffected by application characteristics, and always takes N cycles. Pre-emption of the collector by mutator write barriers (T_W) does not factor into the worst-case analysis because the write barrier work is overlapped with the collector stalls. Extra mark operations to blacken newly allocated objects (T_X) also simply fill stall cycles.

Our design allows an allocation operation *in every cycle*, but allocation pre-empts the sweep phase, meaning that such an allocation rate can only be sustained in short bursts. The largest sustainable allocation rate is 0.5 – otherwise the heap would be exhausted before sweeping completed. Thus $T_A = N$ and

$$T_{\text{worst}} = R + 5N + 5 \tag{2}$$

5.1 Application-Specific Analysis

Real-time analysis typically takes advantage of at least some application-specific knowledge. This is likely to be particularly true of hardware-based systems. Fortunately, the structure of such systems makes it more likely that such factors can be quantified to a high degree of precision, e.g. by looking at operations per clock cycle in the synthesized design.

Let μ be the average number of mutations per cycle ($\mu \leq 1$), α be the average number of allocations per cycle ($\alpha < 0.5$), and m be the maximum number of live data objects in the heap at any one time ($m < N$). Then we can more precisely estimate

$$T'_M = 3m + 3 \quad T'_X = \alpha T'_M \quad T'_W = \frac{\mu}{2-\mu} m \quad T'_A = \frac{\alpha}{1-\alpha} N$$

Note that both α and μ can only be averaged over a *time window* guaranteed to be less than or equal to the phases which they influence; m is a safe window size.

The largest inaccuracy is still due to pipeline stalls during marking, for which worst- and average-case behavior can be very different. We therefore let B be the number of pipeline stalls ($0 \leq B \leq 2m$), so an even more precise bound on marking is $T''_M = m + B + 3$ (and also improving $T''_X = \alpha T''_M$).

For a linked list, $B = 2m$; for three linked lists each with its own root, $B = 0$. We hypothesize that for the heap considered as a forest without back-edges, B is bounded by the number of levels of width 1 plus the number of levels of width 2 (when the width is 3 or greater, there is enough parallelism to keep the 3-stage pipeline full and avoid stalls).

Using these application-specific estimates, we then are able to bound the worst-case execution time (WCET) of collection as

$$T_{\max} = \left(\frac{1}{1-\alpha}\right)\left(R + B + 5 + \frac{2}{2-\mu} m + \frac{N}{1-\alpha}\right) \tag{3}$$

5.2 Minimum Heap Size

Once the worst-case execution time for collection is known, we can solve for the minimum heap size in which the collector can run with real-time behavior (zero stalls). Obviously m objects must be available for the live data. While a collection taking time $T_{\max}$ takes place, another $\alpha T_{\max}$ objects can be allocated. However, there may also be $\alpha T_{\max}$ floating garbage from the previous cycle when a collection starts. Thus the minimum heap size is

$$N_{\min} = m + 2\alpha T_{\max} \tag{4}$$

and if we denote the non-size-dependent portion of $T_{\max}$ from equation (3) by

$$K = \left(\frac{1}{1-\alpha}\right)\left(R + B + 5 + \frac{2}{2-\mu} m\right)$$

then we can solve for

$$
\begin{aligned}
N_{\min} &= m + 2\alpha T_{\max} \\
&= m + 2\alpha \left(K + \frac{N_{\min}}{(1-\alpha)^2} \right) \\
N_{\min} &= \frac{(1-\alpha)^2 (m + 2\alpha K)}{1 - 4\alpha + \alpha^2}
\end{aligned} \tag{5}
$$

6. Experimental Methodology

Since we have implemented the first collector of this kind, we can not simply use a standard set of benchmarks to evaluate it. Therefore, we have implemented two micro-benchmarks intended to be representative of the types of structures that might be used in an FPGA: a doubly-ended queue (deque), which is common in packet processing, and a binary tree, which is common for algorithms like compression.

It is important to note that because of the very high degree of determinism in the hardware, and in our collector implementation, such micro-benchmarks can provide a far more accurate picture of performance than in typical evaluations of CPU-based collectors running in software. There are no cache effects, no time-slicing, and no interrupts. Because there are no higher order effects, the performance behavior presented to the mutator by the collector and vice versa is completely captured by the memory management API at a cycle-accurate level. We validate this experimentally by showing that the estimates for collection time and minimum real-time heap size (from Section 5.1) are highly accurate.

A given micro-benchmark can be paired with one of the three memory management implementations (Malloc, stop-the-world GC, and real-time GC). Furthermore, these are parameterized by the size of the miniheap, and for the collectors, the trigger at which to start collection (although for most purposes, we simply trigger when free space falls below 25%). We call these *design points*.

There are many FPGA product lines and many different configurations within each line. Our experiments are performed using a Xilinx Virtex-5 LX330T [32], which is the largest chip within the Virtex5 LXT product line (that is now two generations old). Given that the motivation to use dynamic memory management will go up with complexity, and complexity will go up with larger chips, we believe that this is a good representative design.

The LX330T has 51,840 slices and 11,664 Kb (1.4 MB) of Block RAM. Fabricated in 65nm technology, the chip is theoretically capable of being clocked at up to 550 MHz, but realistic designs generally run between 100 and 300 MHz.

For each design point, we perform complete synthesis, including place-and-route (PAR), for the LX330T chip. PAR is the final physical synthesis stage and it reports the highest clock frequency the design can be clocked at, as well as the device resource utilization such as slices and BRAM. We used Xilinx ISE 13.4 tool for synthesis.

6.1 Description of Benchmarks

Our first benchmark is a binary search tree which is standard member of a family of binary tree data structures including variants like red-black trees, splay trees, and heaps. Though all the standard operations are implemented, the benchmark, for simplicity, exports only three operations: insert, delete, and traverse. The benchmark can be run against a workload containing a sequence of such operations. Our workload generator is configured to keep the maximum number of live nodes to 8192 while bursts of inserts and deletes can cause the instantaneous amount of live nodes to fall to 7/8 of that. The burstiness of the benchmark necessitates measuring the allocation rate dynamically through instrumentation but provides a more realistic and challenging test for our collector. Traversal operations are included to confirm that our collector is not corrupting any data as the heap size is reduced. The allocation rate of the binary tree is proportional to the tree depth and could be characterized as intermediate for micro-benchmarks. In the context of a complete program, the final allocation rate is potentially even lower. As far as pipeline stalls, there will only be $B = 3$ stalls since the fanout of the tree fills the pipeline after the first two levels have been processed.

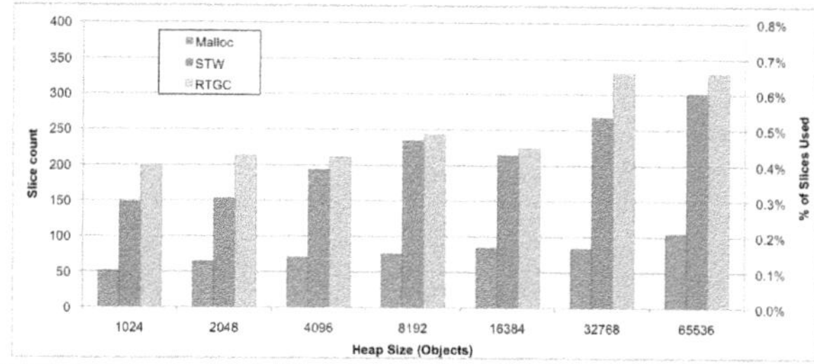

Figure 5. FPGA Logic Resource (slice) Usage

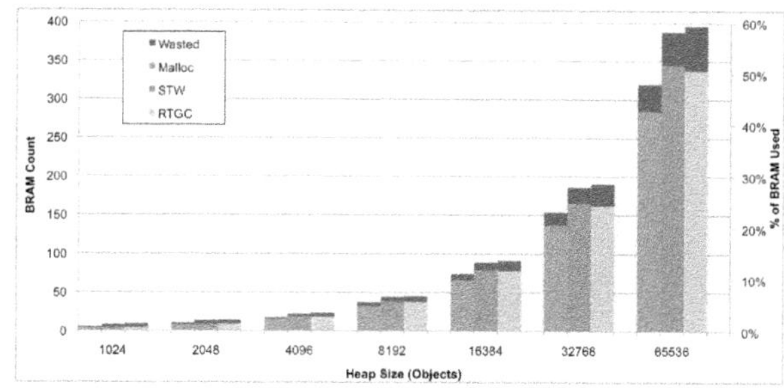

Figure 6. Block RAM Usage, including fragmentation wastage

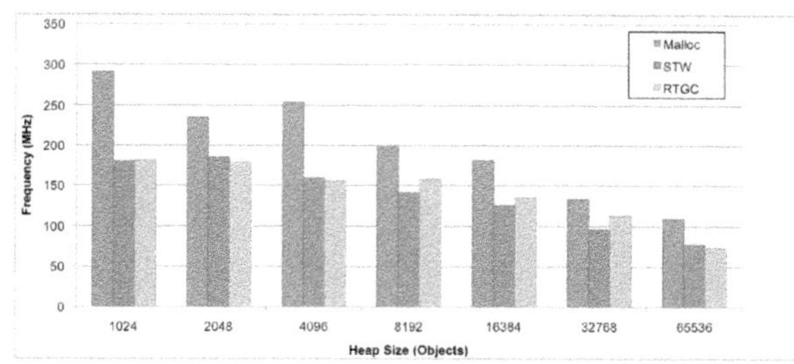

Figure 7. Synthesized Clock Frequency

The second benchmark is a deque (double-ended queue). The doubly-linked list can be modified by pushes and pops to either the front or back. As before, our workload consists of a random sequence of such operations while keeping the maximum amount of live data to 8192. To contrast with the previous benchmark, there are no deliberate bursts which makes the allocation rate more consistent but also keeps the amount of live data always quite close to the maximum. Because there is no traversal or computation, the allocation rate is much higher and stresses the collector much more. As far as traversal, a doubly-linked list is equivalent to two singly-linked lists each of half the length. Thus, there will be $B = m/2$ stalls in the marking pipeline.

7. Evaluation

We begin by examining the cost, in terms of static resources, of the 3 memory managers – malloc/free ("Malloc") , stop-the-world collection ("STW"), and real-time concurrent collection ("RTGC").

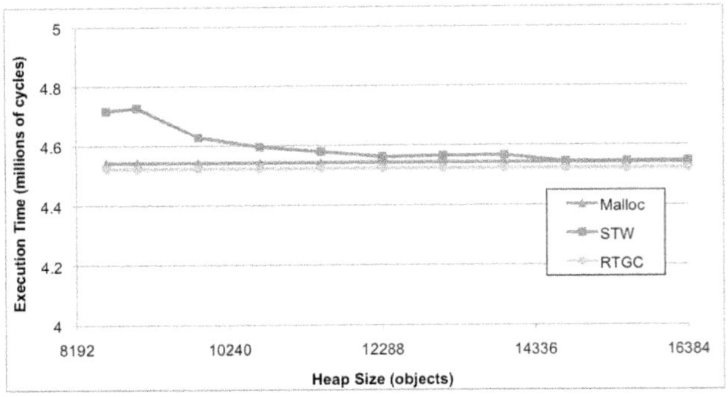

(a) Execution duration in cycles of Binary Tree

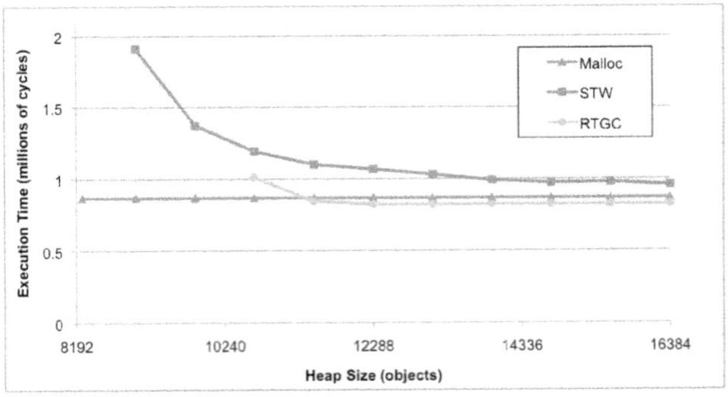

(b) Execution duration in cycles of Deque

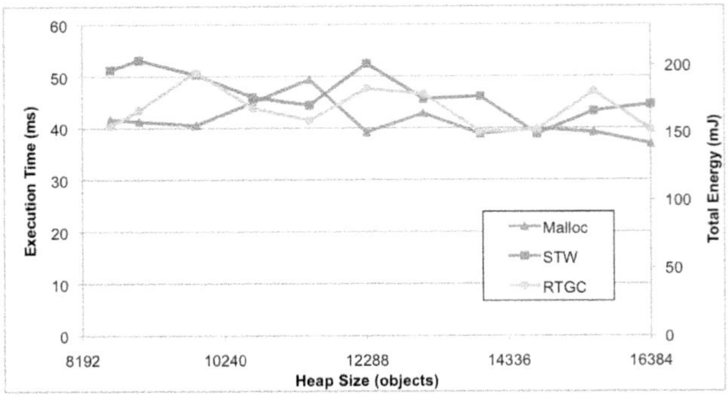

(c) Execution time in milliseconds of Binary Tree

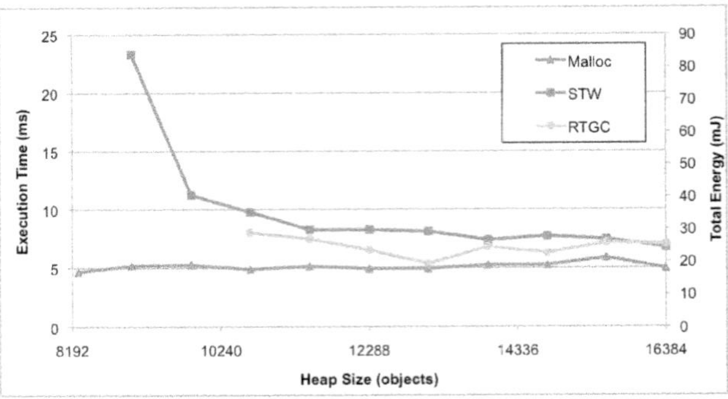

(d) Execution time in milliseconds of Deque

Figure 8. Throughput measurements for the Binary Tree and Deque Microbenchmarks. Because energy consumption is dominated by static power, which is virtually constant, graphs (c) and (d) also show energy in millijoules; the curves are identical.

For these purposes we synthesize the memory manager in the absence of any application. This provides insight into the cost of the memory management itself, and also provides an upper bound on the performance of actual applications (since they can only use more resources or cause the clock frequency to decline).

We evaluate design points at heap sizes (in objects) from 1K to 64K in powers of 2. For these purposes we use an object layout of two pointers and one 32-bit data field. The results are shown in Figures 5 to 7. Figure 5 shows the utilization of non-memory logic resources (in slices). As expected, garbage collection requires more logic than Malloc. Between the two collectors, RTGC requires between 4% to 39% more slices than STW. While RTGC consumes up to 4 times more slices than Malloc in relative terms, in absolute terms it uses less than 0.7% of the total slices even for the largest heap size so logic consumption for all 3 schemes is effectively a non-issue.

Figure 6 shows BRAM consumption. Because we have chosen powers of 2 for heap sizes, the largest heap size only uses 60% of the BRAM resources (one is of course free to choose other sizes). At the smaller heap sizes, garbage collectors consume up to 80% more BRAMs than Malloc. However, at realistic heap sizes, the figure drops to 24%. In addition, RTGC requires about 2-12% more memory than STW since it requires the additional 2-bit wide Used Map to cope with concurrent allocation. Fragmentation is noticeable but not a major factor, ranging from 11-31% for Malloc and 11-53% for garbage collection. As before, at larger heap sizes, the fragmentation decreases. Some wastage can be avoided by choosing heap sizes more carefully, not necessarily a power of 2, by noting that BRAMs are available in 18Kb blocks. However, some fragmentation loss is inherent in the quantization of BRAMs as they are chained together to form larger memories.

Finally, Figure 7 shows the synthesized clock frequency at different design points. Here we see a significant effect from the more complex logic for garbage collection: even though it consumes relatively little area, clock frequency for garbage collection is noticeably slower (15-39%) than Malloc across all design points. On the other hand, the difference between STW and RTGC is small with RTGC often faster. Regardless of the form of memory management, clock frequency declines as the heap becomes larger. However, the overall clock rate may very well be constrained by the application logic rather than the collector logic, as we will see below.

7.1 Dynamic Measurements

So far we have discussed the costs of memory management in the absence of applications; we now consider what happens when the memory manager is "linked" to the microbenchmarks from Section 6.1. Unlike the previous section, where we concentrated on the effects of a wide range of memory sizes on static chip resources, here we focus on a smaller range of sizes using a trace with a single maximum live data set of $m = 8192$ as described previously. We then vary the heap size N from m to $2m$ at fractional increments of $m/10$. As we make memory scarce, the resolution is also increased to $m/100$ to show how the system behaves at very tight conditions. Each design point requires a full synthesis of the hardware design which can affect the frequency, power, and execution time.

7.1.1 Throughput

Figure 8 shows the throughput of the benchmarks as the heap size varies for all 3 schemes. To understand the interaction of various effects, we not only examine the throughput both in cycle

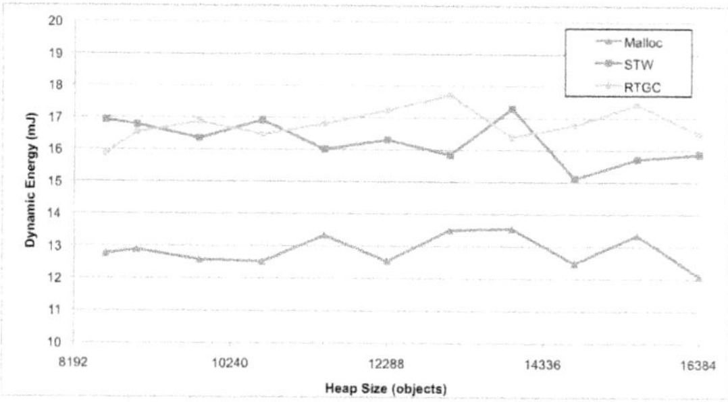

(a) Dynamic Energy in milli-joules of Binary Tree

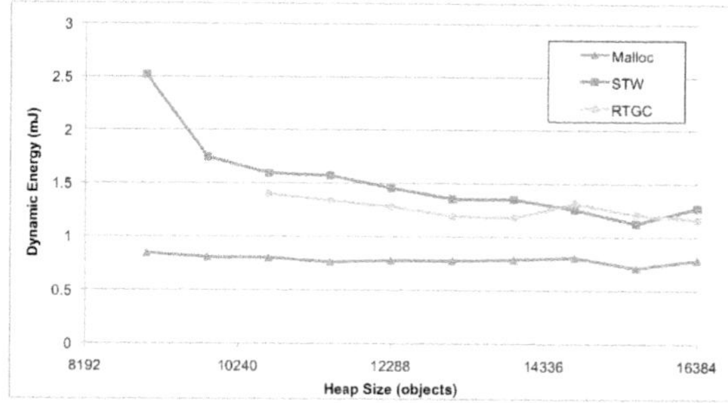

(b) Dynamic Energy in milli-joules of Deque

Figure 9. Dynamic Energy

duration (graphs (a) and (b)), but also, since the synthesizable clock frequencies vary, in physical time (graphs (c) and (d)).

The Binary Tree benchmark goes through phases that are allocation- and mutation-intensive, and those that are not. As a result its allocation rate α is 0.009 objects/cycle, and its mutation rate μ is 0.02 pointer writes/cycle, when considered over a window size of m cycles. Because of these relatively low rates, the duration in cycles in Figure 8(a) of both Malloc and RTGC stays constant from $2m$ all the way down to $1.1m$. RTGC actually consumes slightly fewer cycles since it does not need to issue explicit `free` operations. Because STW pauses the mutator, each collection increases the total number of cycles required. As the heap gets tight, the duration in cycles for STW rises quickly.

However, when we obtain the physical time by dividing total duration in cycles by synthesized clock frequency, as shown in Figure 8(c), things become less cut and dried. Although Malloc alone can be synthesized at considerably higher frequencies than STW or RTGC (Figure 7), it is often the application rather than the memory manager that becomes the limiting factor on clock speed. Therefore, though the differences between the three memory managers is small, there are many chaotic variations. These are primarily explained by expected random variations in the synthesis tool which uses simulated annealing to achieve a good placement and routing. To maintain fairness, we have used same settings for all the synthesis jobs and avoided explicit manual optimizations.

The Deque benchmark shows a different behavior. With much higher allocation and mutation rates ($\alpha = 0.07$ and $\mu = 0.13$), it is much more sensitive to collector activity. As seen in Figure 8(b), even at heap size $N = 2m$, STW consumes noticeably more cycles, rising to almost double the cycles at $N = 1.1m$. By contrast RTGC consumes slightly fewer cycles than Malloc until it begins to experience stall cycles (non-real-time behavior) at $N = 1.4m$ because it cannot keep up with the mutator.

The Deque benchmark is considerably simpler than Binary Tree in terms of logic, so it has a correspondingly lower impact on synthesized clock frequency. The effect is seen clearly in Figure 8(d): Malloc synthesizes at a higher frequency, allowing it to make up RTGC's slight advantage in cycles and consume 25% less time on an average. STW suffers even more from the combined effect of a lower clock frequency and additional cycles due to synchronous collection. On average, RTGC is faster than STW by 14% and of course does not interrupt the application at all.

These measurements reveal some surprising trends that are completely contrary to the expected trade-offs for software collectors: RTGC is actually *faster, more deterministic, and requires less heap space* than STW! There seems to be no reason to use STW because the natural advantage of implementing concurrency in hardware completely supersedes the traditional latency versus bandwidth tradeoff in software.

Furthermore, RTGC allows applications to run at far lower multiples of the maximum live set m than possible for either real-time or stop-the-world collectors in software. RTGC is also only moderately slower than Malloc, meaning that the cost of abstraction is considerably more palatable. As predicted, this performance gap only decreases with more complex applications.

7.1.2 Energy

The *energy* (or power-delay product) is the product of average power dissipation and physical time. It is a better metric than power alone since it takes into the account the actual time needed to finish a given workload. For example, dynamic power consumption can be reduced by lowering the clock frequency but it does not mean that the energy consumed to finish the workload is also reduced. To calculate the energy we need to have knowledge of the power consumption and the total time taken to finish the workload. We calculated the power, which is a sum of static and dynamic power, using the Xpower tool from Xilinx [33]. The Xpower tool provides an approximate estimate of the power consumed by a design, for a particular FPGA device, by taking several factors into account such as simulation data, clock frequency, supply voltages, ambient and junction temperature. The accuracy of the result depends most importantly on the simulation data which is a representative of the target application. Based on the switching activity of the nets embedded in the simulation data, the dynamic power can be calculated very accurately. Static power consumption (the power consumed by the chip simply when it is on) for an FPGA chip is independent of the design. We have found that the static power contributes more than 90% of the total power for all the cases we investigated.

We synthesized the Binary Tree and Deque benchmarks for each heap sizes shown in Figure 8 to get the clock frequency and generate a fully placed-and-routed netlist. Then we simulated each design using the ModelSim simulator to generate the toggle activity of each net in the design and the result is stored in the VCD format [19]. We fed the synthesized netlist, the VCD file and the clock frequency constraint to the Xpower tool which provides detailed information about the static and dynamic power consumption. The power consumption is then multiplied by the execution time (in seconds) to calculate the total energy consumption.

The total energy consumption for Binary Tree and Deque is shown in Figure 8(c) and Figure 8(d) respectively (using the secondary right-hand axis). Because static power is so much larger than the dynamic power, the total power tracks the execution time within 1% and it is shown on the same graph. To demonstrate the differences in energy due to the design and benchmarks, the dynamic energy consumption for the Binary Tree and Deque benchmarks is shown in Figure 9.

For the Binary Tree benchmark, the average energy consumption (averaged over all the design points) for RTGC is lower than

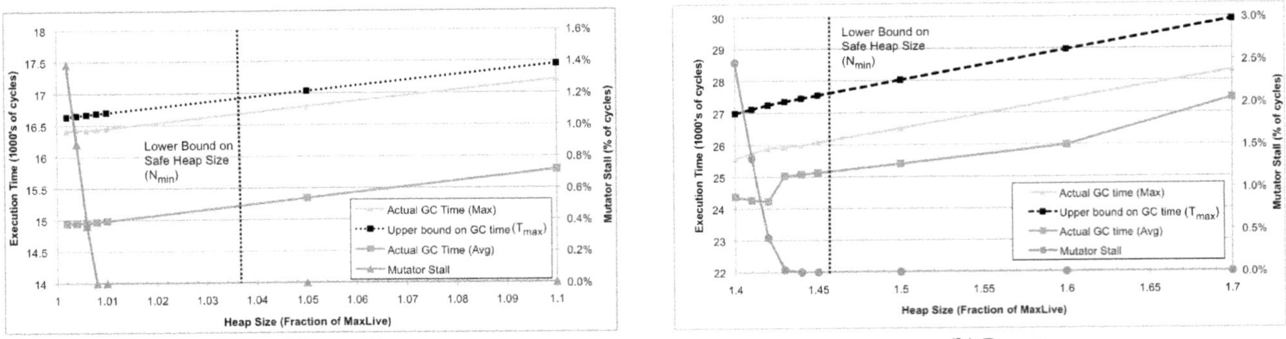

(a) Binary Tree **(b) Deque**

Figure 10. Comparison of analytic worst-case duration (in cycles) and heap space for RTGC compared to measured values

STW by 6% and higher than Malloc by 8%. For the Deque benchmark, on average RTGC consumes 14% less and 34% more energy than STW and Malloc respectively. The dynamic energy provides additional insight into the nature of benchmarks. For Binary Tree, RTGC consumes 3% and 30% more dynamic energy than STW and Malloc respectively. For Deque, RTGC consumes 8% less and 63% more dynamic energy than STW and Malloc respectively.

The analysis shows that the energy consumption is highly application-dependent. For both the benchmarks we considered it is safe to say that RTGC is a better choice than STW as far as energy consumption is considered. The average total energy consumption of Malloc is smaller than RTGC for both the benchmarks. However, as the complexity and size of benchmark increases the energy consumption gap between RTGC and Malloc diminishes.

7.2 Validation of Real-time Bounds

Because the design and analysis of our concurrent collector is intended to be cycle-accurate, we can validate the time and space bounds of the collector with expectation that they will be fully met. Figure 10 shows the actual time spent in garbage collection and the analytic upper bound (T_{max} from equation 3). Note that we show both average as well as the maximum time spent in garbage collections. The heap size is chosen to be much tighter than in earlier graphs as our focus here is how the collector behaves when it is under stress (near $N_{\min}$ from equation 4). For convenience, we express heap size as a fraction (N/m) of the maximum amount of live data since our bounds are almost linear when considered in terms of m and N.

Average time spent in collection is always less than the predicted worst case with an actual difference of about 10% for both programs. We also show the amount of stalls experienced by the benchmark as a fraction of total time. At larger heap sizes, there are no stalls. As the heap size is reduced, there will come a point when the collector cannot keep up and the mutator's allocation request will be blocked. For Binary Tree this occurs when the heap is a mere $1.01 \times m$ while the more allocation-intensive Deque fails at $1.43 \times m$. Our predicted N_{min} values of 1.037 and 1.457 are correctly above the actual failure points.

Because the average collection time includes multiple phases of a program, it can be significantly lower than the maximum collection time. We see that the gap between T_{max} and collection time shrinks from 10% to about 2% and 6% when one considers maximum rather than average collection time. For space, N_{min} has only a worst-case flavor as there is adequate heap space only if the heap is sufficient at every collection. The space bound is within 3% of when stalls begin. Our time and space bounds are not only empirically validated but are tight.

In general, time spent for a single collection falls as the heap size is decreased since the sweep phase will take less time. It may seem surprising that this happens even when the heap size is taken below N_{min}. However, falling below this safe point causes mutator stalls but does not penalize the collector at all. In fact, because the mutator is stalled, it can no longer interfere with the collector which will additionally, though very slightly, speed up collection. Of course, since the overall goal is to avoid mutator stalls, operating in this regime is inadvisable.

8. Related Work

There has been very little work on supporting high-level memory abstractions in reconfigurable hardware, and none on garbage collection. Simsa, Singh, et al. [11, 25] have explored compilation of C subprograms that use malloc/free into VHDL or Bluespec for synthesis to FPGAs.

LEAP scratchpads [1] provide an expandable memory abstraction which presents a BRAM interface, but uses off-chip RAM if the structure is too large to fit, and transparently uses the on-chip BRAM as a cache. Such a system could be coupled with ours in order to provide a larger, virtualized memory, albeit at the expense of determinism and throughput.

Faes et al. [13] have built an "FPGA-aware" collector, with a completely different goal from ours: allowing the FPGA to maintain references into the CPU's main program heap. This facilitates co-processing by the FPGA.

8.1 Micro-coded Collectors

Meyer [20] has built a special-purpose processor and an associated garbage collection co-processor (using Baker's semi-space algorithm [6]), and realized them on an Altera APEX FPGA. However, the design and the goals were very different. Meyer's collector is for a general-purpose heap allocated in DRAM, and for a program operating on what is for the most part a conventional CPU. The collector is implemented with a microcoded co-processor, and the CPU is modified with a special pointer register set, and pointer operations include support for read and write barriers. Some of the control logic also runs in software on the main CPU. By contrast, we have created fully custom logic that is much more tightly integrated with the memory, for "programs" that are also synthesized into hardware, and with deterministic single-cycle memory access.

Maximum collector pauses in Meyer's system are 500 cycles (2.5 μs at 200 MHz), due to root scanning. Read barriers and interlocks also cause pauses up to 200 cycles. By contrast our collector pauses for 0 clock cycles. Meyer's collector also requires heaps of 2 times the maximum live data in order to avoid non-real-time behavior, considerably more than our collector. Of course, our performance comes at a cost in flexibility: Meyer's collector handles arbitrary heap shapes and larger memories.

The Intel iAPX 432, the apotheosis of CISC architecture, did not provide explicit frees, and microcoded the marking portion of Dijkstra's on-the-fly collector (the rest was implemented in the iMAX-432 operating system). The system object table contained bits for the tri-color marking abstraction [31].

Schmidt and Nilsen [23] studied the design (using the DLX simulator) of a *garbage collected memory module* (GCMM), in which a memory module plugged into a conventional bus included paired DRAMs (for the collector semispaces) and an extra processor that ran Baker's algorithm [6]. The interface to the CPU for operations like allocation, root descriptors, and so on are implemented as memory mapped ports. They report delays of 0.5 ms to initiate a collection and 1 μs for allocate, fetch, and store.

8.2 Hardware-assisted Collection

Most hardware support for garbage collection has been in the form of specialized memory barriers (particularly read barriers) because of their high throughput cost. The Symbolics Lisp Machine [21] introduced this kind of hardware barrier to implement Baker's algorithm [6]. Both the Lisp Machine and SOAR [30] also introduced hardware support for generational write barriers.

Frustration with the availability and acceptance of custom processor designs to support garbage collection gave rise to a "stock hardware" line of research, using conventional CPU features to support collector operations [2, 8]. The pendulum swung back with the the Azul Vega processor and its associated collector [10]. Hardware support for read barriers, fast user-mode trap handlers (4-10 cycles), cooperative pre-emption, and special TLB support enabled a collector capable of handling very large heaps and large numbers of processors. The collector achieved an MMU of 21% at 50 ms (the authors hypothesize due largely to read barrier trap storms), and 52% at 200 ms. Ironically, the Azul collector has recently been ported to a "stock hardware" x86 platform running on a Linux kernel augmented with page remapping operations [29].

Hardware support has also been proposed for reference counting. Joao et al. [17] describe a processor extended with a "reference count coalescing buffer" which is able to filter over 96% of reference count traffic. Srisa-an and Lo [26] propose a co-processor that performs saturating reference counting (using 2- or 3-bit counts) backed by a conventional tracing collector. Yu [34] proposes a system with a reference-counted nursery and an incrementally traced mature space, using hardware support for allocation and write barriers and a specialized cache architecture.

Heil and Smith [15] apply hardware support for profiling to the garbage collection problem, by treating it as a form of instrumentation of store operations. The instrumented operations are then handled by service threads, and there is an additional thread to perform marking and sweeping.

Schoeberl [24] extends the JOP Java processor with hardware support for non-blocking object copies in the memory controller. This allows compaction operations to be pre-empted at the granularity of a single write.

9. Conclusion

We have described our design, implementation, and evaluation of the first garbage collectors to be completely synthesized into hardware. The real-time version causes *zero* cycles of interference with the mutator, achieving for the first time a minimum mutator utilization of 100%.

Careful implementation allows a closed-form analytic solution for worst-case execution time (WCET) of the collector, and a lower bound on heap size to achieve real-time behavior. These bounds are also cycle-accurate.

In software there are large trade-offs between stop-the-world and real-time collection in terms of throughput, latency, and space. Our measurements show that in hardware the real-time collector is faster, has lower (zero) latency, and can run effectively in less space. In addition, it consumes less overall energy because it can run to completion faster.

This performance and determinism is not without cost: our collector only supports a single fixed object layout. Supporting larger objects with more pointers is a relatively straightforward extension to our design; supporting multiple object layouts is more challenging but we believe can be achieved without sacrificing the fundamental advantages.

Compared to explicit memory management, hardware garbage collection still sacrifices some throughput in exchange for a higher level of abstraction. It may be possible to narrow this gap through more aggressive pipelining. However, the gap in space needed to achieve good performance is substantially smaller than in software.

For the first time, garbage collection of programs synthesized to hardware is practical and realizable.

A. Proof of Overflow Freedom

As described in Section 4.3.1, the queues for a pair of trace engines are each sized to have $3N/8 + R$ entries. Here we prove that neither queue will overflow. We begin by reviewing various GC operations that affect the queue. During the root phase, R roots are inserted into queue 0 while write barrier entries are inserted into queue 1. Thus, queue 1 can have up to R entries at the start of the tracing phase. Each trace step in the tracing phase pops from the fuller queue and then inserts up to 2 pointers (one in each queue). Interleaved with the traced steps are write barrier insertions which can also insert up to 2 pointers (one in each queue). If the write barrier step inserts only one pointer, then it will insert into the emptier queue.

We note that the operations in the mark phase are symmetric with respect to the two queues. Specifically, there is no bias in either the pushes and pops nor in the graph traversal since the role of left and right pointers are interchangeable. However, there is a difference in the root phase in that queue 0 is always equally or more full than queue 1. Thus, if there were to be overflow at all, it would occur in queue 0.

At the end of the root phase, the queues have up to R items so we must show that the queue will not grow by more than $3N/8$ during the tracing phase. The tracing phase can be considered to be a sequence of tracing steps and write barrier insertions. Tracing steps always pop an item and can push 0, 1, or 2 items. Write barrier insertions perform no pops but can push 0, 1, or 2 items. A write barrier operation that pushes 0 items does not change the state at all and need not be considered. However, a trace step that pushes 0 items cannot be so easily dismissed since the total number of trace steps is bounded by N. Thus, limiting any type of trace steps potentially affects the overall outcome.

We take full advantage of the balanced push and pop by noting that no operation increases queue imbalance beyond a difference of 1 between the queues since both the trace step pops from the fuller queue and the write barrier pushes onto the emptier queue for the case when it pushes only one item. If there were a pathological sequence of operations that causes either queue to overflow, then in the step just prior, the soon-to-overflow queue must be full and the other queue must be nearly full. Further, we need not consider write barrier operations that perform a single-push as we can conceptually rearrange them into half as many double-push operations which run faster. If there were to be an overflow, they would occur even faster with this rearrangement. Thus, we need only bound the total queue growth to $N/2$. We label the 3 types of tracing steps T_0, T_1, and T_2 based on the number of pushes they perform. Note that the net effect on the queue size is one less than the index. Similarly, we have W_2 which stands for the number of 2-push write barrier operations.

We are trying to maximize total occupancy which is given by

$$-T_0 + T_2 + 2W_2$$

subject to the usual non-negativity constraints as well as 3 additional constraints. The first constraint expresses the fact that we schedule at most one write barrier operation for each tracing operation. The second and third constraints require that the total number of pushes and pops cannot exceed the total number of objects.

$$\begin{aligned} T_0 + T_1 + T_2 &\geq W_2 \\ T_1 + 2T_2 + 2W_2 &\leq N \\ T_0 + T_1 + T_2 &\leq N \end{aligned}$$

With a slight rearrangement, these equations can be put in the "standard form" of a linear programming problem [9]. Although the quantities are constrained to be integral (making this in reality an integer linear programming problem), we are safe in droppping the integrality constraints as that only increases the feasible region. The over-approximation of the objective is not a soundness issue since we are establishing an upper bound. Conversely, the bound is also rather tight by noting the total size of the coefficients in the objective function.

The problem is easily solved with the simplex method and standard tableau techniques show that the problem is feasible and bounded with the objective maximized at $3N/4$ and the free variables T_0 and T_1 at zero while T_2 and W_2 are at $N/4$. Since the queues always maintain balance, we arrive at the final individual queue size by halving the $3N/4$ and including the capacity needed for the root phase to arrive at $3N/8 + R$.

We omit the actual tableaus as they are uninteresting and shed less insight than by examining a few key points in the space. From the objective function, it is intuitively desirable to maximize W_2. If we allow only W_2 and T_0 to be non-zero, then we will have both at $N/2$ with a total occupancy of $N/2$. Similarly, allowing only W_2 and T_1 into play at $N/3$ will achieve $2N/3$. Finally, W_2 and T_2 both at $N/4$ achieves the maximum of $3N/4$. If we were to leave out W_2 entirely, T_2 increases to $N/2$ but the objective actually decreases to $N/2$. The changes in these values confirm our intutition that trace operations that perform no pushes do not stress the queues and that maximizing the write barrier operations will cause the greatest occupancy.

Acknowledgments

We thank the members of the Liquid Metal team at IBM Research who contributed insights, infrastructure, and a stimulating working environment: Joshua Auerbach, Stephen Fink, and Rodric Rabbah. We also thank team members and the reviewers for their corrections and insightful comments which helped to improve the paper.

References

[1] M. Adler et al. Leap scratchpads: automatic memory and cache management for reconfigurable logic. In *FPGA*, pp. 25–28, 2011.

[2] A. W. Appel, J. R. Ellis, and K. Li. Real-time concurrent collection on stock multiprocessors. In *PLDI*, pp. 11–20, June 1988.

[3] J. Auerbach, D. F. Bacon, P. Cheng, D. Grove, B. Biron, C. Gracie, B. McCloskey, A. Micic, and R. Sciampacone. Tax-and-spend: democratic scheduling for real-time garbage collection. In *EMSOFT*, pp. 245–254, 2008.

[4] J. Auerbach, D. F. Bacon, P. Cheng, and R. Rabbah. Lime: a Java-compatible and synthesizable language for heterogeneous architectures. In *OOPSLA*, pp. 89–108, Oct. 2010.

[5] D. F. Bacon, P. Cheng, and V. T. Rajan. A real-time garbage collector with low overhead and consistent utilization. In *POPL*, pp. 285–298, Jan. 2003.

[6] H. G. Baker. List processing in real-time on a serial computer. *Commun. ACM*, 21(4):280–294, Apr. 1978.

[7] G. E. Blelloch and P. Cheng. On bounding time and space for multiprocessor garbage collection. In *PLDI*, pp. 104–117, June 1999.

[8] R. A. Brooks. Trading data space for reduced time and code space in real-time garbage collection on stock hardware. In *LFP*, pp. 256–262, Aug. 1984.

[9] V. Chvatal. *Linear Programming*. W. H. Freeman and Company, 1983.

[10] C. Click, G. Tene, and M. Wolf. The pauseless GC algorithm. In *VEE*, pp. 46–56, 2005.

[11] B. Cook et al. Finding heap-bounds for hardware synthesis. In *FMCAD*, pp. 205 -212, Nov. 2009.

[12] E. W. Dijkstra, L. Lamport, A. J. Martin, C. S. Scholten, and E. F. M. Steffens. On-the-fly garbage collection: an exercise in cooperation. *Commun. ACM*, 21(11):966–975, 1978.

[13] P. Faes, M. Christiaens, D. Buytaert, and D. Stroobandt. FPGA- aware garbage collection in Java. In *FPL*, pp. 675–680, 2005.

[14] D. Greaves and S. Singh. Kiwi: Synthesis of FPGA circuits from parallel programs. In *FCCM*, 2008.

[15] T. H. Heil and J. E. Smith. Concurrent garbage collection using hardware-assisted profiling. In *ISMM*, pp. 80–93, 2000.

[16] R. Henriksson. *Scheduling Garbage Collection in Embedded Systems*. PhD thesis, Lund Institute of Technology, July 1998.

[17] J. A. Joao, O. Mutlu, and Y. N. Patt. Flexible reference-counting-based hardware acceleration for garbage collection. In *ISCA*, pp. 418–428, 2009.

[18] J. McCarthy. Recursive functions of symbolic expressions and their computation by machine. *Commun. ACM*, 3(4):184–195, 1960.

[19] Mentor Graphics. *ModelSim SE Users Manual*. Version 10.0c.

[20] M. Meyer. An on-chip garbage collection coprocessor for embedded real-time systems. In *RTCSA*, pp. 517–524, 2005.

[21] D. A. Moon. Garbage collection in a large LISP system. In *LFP*, Aug. 1984.

[22] F. Pizlo, D. Frampton, E. Petrank, and B. Steensgaard. Stopless: a real-time garbage collector for multiprocessors. In *ISMM*, pp. 159–172, 2007.

[23] W. J. Schmidt and K. D. Nilsen. Performance of a hardware-assisted real-time garbage collector. In *ASPLOS*, pp. 76–85, 1994.

[24] M. Schoeberl and W. Puffitsch. Nonblocking real-time garbage collection. *ACM Trans. Embedded Comput. Sys.*, 10:1–28, 2010.

[25] J. Simsa and S. Singh. Designing hardware with dynamic memory abstraction. In *FPGA*, pp. 69–72, 2010.

[26] W. Srisa-an, C.-T. D. Lo, and J. M. Chang. Active memory processor: A hardware garbage collector for real-time Java embedded devices. *IEEE Trans. Mob. Comput.*, 2(2):89–101, 2003.

[27] G. L. Steele, Jr. Multiprocessing compactifying garbage collection. *Commun. ACM*, 18(9):495–508, Sept. 1975.

[28] G. L. Steele, Jr. Data representation in PDP-10 MACLISP. Tech. rep., MIT, 1977. AI Memo 420.

[29] G. Tene, B. Iyengar, and M. Wolf. C4: the continuously concurrent compacting collector. In *ISMM*, pp. 79–88, 2011.

[30] D. Ungar et al. Architecture of SOAR: Smalltalk on a RISC. In *ISCA*, pp. 188–197, 1984.

[31] Wikipedia. Intel iAPX 432, Nov. 2011.

[32] Xilinx. Virtex-5 family overview. Tech. Rep. DS100, Feb. 2009.

[33] Xilinx. Power methodology guide. Tech. Rep. DS786, Mar. 2011.

[34] W. S. Yu. Hardware concurrent garbage collection for object-oriented processor. Master's thesis, City University of Hong Kong, 2005.

[35] T. Yuasa. Real-time garbage collection on general-purpose machines. *J. Systems and Software*, 11(3):181–198, Mar. 1990.

The Implicit Calculus

A New Foundation for Generic Programming

Bruno C. d. S. Oliveira
Seoul National University
bruno@ropas.snu.ac.kr

Tom Schrijvers
Universiteit Gent
tom.schrijvers@ugent.be

Wontae Choi
Seoul National University
wtchoi@ropas.snu.ac.kr

Wonchan Lee
Seoul National University
wclee@ropas.snu.ac.kr

Kwangkeun Yi
Seoul National University
kwang@ropas.snu.ac.kr

Abstract

Generic programming (GP) is an increasingly important trend in programming languages. Well-known GP mechanisms, such as type classes and the C++0x concepts proposal, usually combine two features: 1) a special type of interfaces; and 2) *implicit instantiation* of implementations of those interfaces.

Scala *implicits* are a GP language mechanism, inspired by type classes, that break with the tradition of coupling implicit instantiation with a special type of interface. Instead, implicits provide only implicit instantiation, which is generalized to work for *any types*. This turns out to be quite powerful and useful to address many limitations that show up in other GP mechanisms.

This paper synthesizes the key ideas of implicits formally in a minimal and general core calculus called the implicit calculus ($\lambda_{\Rightarrow}$), and it shows how to build source languages supporting implicit instantiation on top of it. A novelty of the calculus is its support for *partial resolution* and *higher-order rules* (a feature that has been proposed before, but was never formalized or implemented). Ultimately, the implicit calculus provides a formal model of implicits, which can be used by language designers to study and inform implementations of similar mechanisms in their own languages.

Categories and Subject Descriptors D.3.2 [*Programming Languages*]: Language Classifications—Functional Languages, Object-Oriented Languages; F.3.3 [*Logics and Meanings of Programs*]: Studies of Program Constructs

General Terms Languages

Keywords Implicit parameters, type classes, C++ concepts, generic programming, Haskell, Scala.

1. Introduction

Generic programming (GP) [23] is a programming style that decouples algorithms from the concrete types on which they operate. Decoupling is achieved through parametrization. Typical forms of parametrization include parametrization by type (for example: *parametric polymorphism*, *generics* or *templates*) or parametrization by algebraic structures (such as a monoid or a group).

A central idea in generic programming is *implicit instantiation* of generic parameters. Implicit instantiation means that, when generic algorithms are called with concrete arguments, the generic arguments (concrete types, algebraic structures, or some other form of generic parameters) are automatically determined by the compiler. The benefit is that generic algorithms become as easy to use as specialized algorithms. To illustrate implicit instantiation and its benefits consider a *polymorphic* sorting function:

$$sort\,[\alpha] : (\alpha \to \alpha \to \mathit{Bool}) \to \mathit{List}\ \alpha \to \mathit{List}\ \alpha$$

with 3 parameters: the type of the elements in the list (α); the comparison operator; and the list to be compared. Instantiating all 3 parameters explicitly at every use of $sort$ would be quite tedious. It is likely that, for a given type, the sorting function is called with the same, explicitly passed, comparison function over and over again. Moreover it is easy to infer the type parameter α. GP greatly simplifies such calls by making the type argument and the comparison operator implicit.

$$isort : \forall \alpha.(\alpha \to \alpha \to \mathit{Bool}) \Rightarrow \mathit{List}\ \alpha \to \mathit{List}\ \alpha$$

The function $isort$ declares that the comparison function is implicit by using $\Rightarrow$ instead of $\to$. It is used as:

$$\mathbf{implicit}\ \{\mathit{cmpInt} : \mathit{Int} \to \mathit{Int} \to \mathit{Bool}\}\ \mathbf{in}$$
$$(isort\,[2,1,3], isort\,[5,9,3])$$

The two calls of $isort$ each take only one explicit argument: the list to be sorted. Both the concrete type of the elements (*Int*) and the comparison operator (cmpInt) are *implicitly* instantiated.

The element type is automatically inferred from the type of the list. More interestingly, the implicit comparison operator is automatically determined in a process called *resolution*. Resolution is a type-directed process that uses a set of *rules*, the *implicit* (or *rule*) environment, to find a value that matches the type required by the function call. The **implicit** construct extends the implicit environment with new rules. In other words, **implicit** is a *scoping* construct for rules similar to a conventional **let**-binding. Thus, in the subexpression $(isort\,[2,1,3], isort\,[5,9,3])$, cmpInt is in the local scope and available for resolution.

1.1 Existing Approaches to Generic Programming

The two main strongholds of GP are the C++ and the functional programming (FP) communities. Many of the pillars of GP are

PLDI'12, June 11–16, Beijing, China.

based on the ideas promoted by Musser and Stepanov [23]. These ideas were used in C++ libraries such as the Standard Template Library [24] and Boost [1]. In the FP community, Haskell *type classes* [42] have proven to be an excellent mechanism for GP, although their original design did not have that purpose. As years passed the FP community created its own forms of GP [14, 10, 21].

Garcia et al.'s [9] comparative study of programming language support for GP was an important milestone for both communities. According to that study many languages provide some support for GP. However, Haskell did particularly well, largely due to type classes. A direct consequence of that work was to bring the two main lines of work on GP closer together and promote cross-pollination of ideas. Haskell adopted *associated types* [4, 3], which was the only weak point found in the original comparison. For the C++ community, type classes presented an inspiration for developing language support for *concepts* [23, 11, 35].

Several researchers started working on various approaches to concepts (see Siek's work [34] for a historical overview). Some researchers focused on integrating concepts into C++ [7, 11], while others focused on developing new languages with GP in mind. The work on System F^G [35, 36] is an example of the latter approach: Building on the experience from the C++ generic programming community and some of the ideas of type classes, Siek and Lumsdaine developed a simple core calculus based on System F which integrates concepts and improves on type classes in several respects. In particular, System F^G supports *scoping* of rules[1].

During the same period Scala emerged as new contender in the area of generic programming. Much like Haskell, Scala was not originally developed with generic programming in mind. However Scala included an alternative to type classes: *implicits*. Implicits were initially viewed as *a poor man's type classes* [26]. Yet, ultimately, they proved to be quite flexible and in some ways superior to type classes. In fact Scala turns out to have very good support for generic programming [28, 29].

A distinguishing feature of Scala implicits, and a reason for their power, is that resolution works for *any type*. This allows Scala to simply reuse standard OO interfaces/classes (which are regular types) to model concepts, and avoids introducing another type of interface in the language. In contrast, with type classes, or the various concept proposals, resolution is tightly coupled with the type class or concept-like interfaces.

1.2 Limitations of Existing Mechanisms

Twenty years of programming experience with type classes gave the FP community insights about the limitations of type classes. Some of these limitations were addressed by concept proposals. Other limitations were solved by implicits. However, as far as we know, no existing language or language proposal overcomes all limitations. We discuss these limitations next.

Global scoping: In Haskell, rules[2] are global and there can be only a single rule for any given type [18, 2, 6, 8]. Locally scoped rules are not available. Several researchers have already proposed to fix this issue: with named rules [18] or locally scoped ones [2, 6, 8]. However none of those proposals have been adopted.

Both proposals for concepts and Scala implicits offer scoping of rules and as such do not suffer from this limitation.

Second class interfaces: Haskell type classes are second-class constructs compared to regular types: in Haskell, it is not possible to abstract over a type class [13]. Yet, the need for first-class type classes is real in practice. For example, Lämmel and Peyton Jones [21] desire the following type class for their GP approach:

$$\textbf{class}\ (\mathit{Typeable}\ \alpha, \mathit{cxt}\ \alpha) \Rightarrow \mathit{Data}\ \mathit{cxt}\ \alpha\ \textbf{where}$$
$$\quad \mathit{gmapQ} :: (\forall \beta. \mathit{Data}\ \mathit{cxt}\ \beta \Rightarrow \beta \rightarrow r) \rightarrow \alpha \rightarrow [r]$$

In this type class, the intention is that the ctx variable abstracts over a concrete type class. Unfortunately, Haskell does not support type class abstraction. Proposals for concepts inherit this limitation from type classes. Concepts and type classes are usually interpreted as predicates on types rather than types, and cannot be abstracted over as regular types. In contrast, because in Scala concepts are modeled with types, it is possible to abstract over concepts. Oliveira and Gibbons [28] show how to encode this example in Scala.

No higher-order rules: Finally type classes do not support higher-order rules. As noted by Hinze and Peyton Jones [12], non-regular Haskell datatypes like:

$$\textbf{data}\ \mathit{Perfect}\ f\ \alpha = \mathit{Nil} \mid \mathit{Cons}\ \alpha\ (\mathit{Perfect}\ f\ (f\ \alpha))$$

require type class instances such as:

$$\textbf{instance}\ (\forall \beta. \mathit{Show}\ \beta \Rightarrow \mathit{Show}\ (f\ \beta), \mathit{Show}\ \alpha) \Rightarrow$$
$$\quad \mathit{Show}\ (\mathit{Perfect}\ f\ \alpha)$$

which Haskell does not support, as it restricts instances (or rules) to be first-order. This rule is *higher-order* because it assumes another rule, $\forall \beta. \mathit{Show}\ \beta \Rightarrow \mathit{Show}\ (f\ \beta)$, that contains an assumption itself. Also note that this assumed rule is polymorphic in β.

Both concept proposals and Scala implicits inherit the limitation of first-order rules.

1.3 Contributions

This paper presents $\lambda_{\Rightarrow}$, a minimal and general core calculus for implicits and it shows how to build a source language supporting implicit instantiation on top of it. Perhaps surprisingly the core calculus itself does not provide implicit instantiation: instantiation of generic arguments is explicit. Instead $\lambda_{\Rightarrow}$ provides two key mechanisms for generic programming: 1) a type-directed resolution mechanism and 2) scoping constructs for rules. Implicit instantiation is then built as a convenience mechanism on top of $\lambda_{\Rightarrow}$ by combining type-directed resolution with conventional type-inference. We illustrate this on a simple, but quite expressive source language.

The calculus is inspired by Scala implicits and it synthesizes core ideas of that mechanism formally. In particular, like Scala implicits, a key idea is that resolution and implicit instantiation work for any type. This allows those mechanisms to be more widely useful and applicable, since they can be used with other types in the language. The calculus is also closely related to System F^G, and like System F^G, rules available in the implicit environment are lexically scoped and scopes can be nested.

A novelty of our calculus is its support for partial resolution and higher-order rules. Although Hinze and Peyton Jones [12] have discussed higher-order rules informally and several other researchers noted their usefulness [40, 31, 28], no existing language or calculus provides support for them. Higher-order rules are just the analogue of higher-order functions in the implicits world. They arise naturally once we take the view that resolution should work for any type. Partial resolution adds additional expressive power and it is especially useful in the presence of higher-order rules.

From the GP perspective $\lambda_{\Rightarrow}$ offers a new foundation for generic programming. The relation between the implicit calculus and Scala implicits is comparable to the relation between System F^G and various concept proposals; or the relation between formal calculi of type classes and Haskell type classes: The implicit calculus is a minimal and general model of implicits useful for language designers wishing to study and inform implementations of similar GP mechanisms in their own languages.

[1] In the context of C++ rules correspond to *models* or *concept_maps*.

[2] In the context of Haskell rules correspond to *type-class instances*.

In summary, our contributions are as follows.

- Our *implicit calculus* $\lambda_{\Rightarrow}$ provides a simple, expressive and general formal model for implicits. Despite its expressiveness, the calculus is minimal and provides an ideal setting for the formal study of implicits and GP.
- Of particular interest is our resolution mechanism, which is significantly more expressive than existing mechanisms in the literature. It is based on a simple (logic-programming style) query language, works for any type, and it supports partial resolution as well as higher-order rules.
- The calculus has a polymorphic type system and an elaboration semantics to System F. This also provides an effective implementation of our calculus. The elaboration semantics is proved to be type-preserving, ensuring the soundness of the calculus.
- We present a small, but realistic source language, built on top of $\lambda_{\Rightarrow}$ via a type-directed encoding. This language features implicit instantiation and a simple type of interface, which can be used to model simple forms of concepts. This source language also supports higher-order rules.
- Finally, both $\lambda_{\Rightarrow}$ and the source language have been implemented and the source code for their implementation is available at `http://ropas.snu.ac.kr/~bruno/implicit`.

Organization Section 2 presents an informal overview of our calculus. Section 3 shows a polymorphic type system that statically excludes ill-behaved programs. Section 4 shows the elaboration semantics of our calculus into System F and correctness results. Section 5 presents the source language and its encoding into $\lambda_{\Rightarrow}$. Section 6 discusses comparisons and related work. Section 7 concludes. The companion technical report [30] provides additional technical material and proofs.

2. Overview of the Implicit Calculus $\lambda_{\Rightarrow}$

Our calculus $\lambda_{\Rightarrow}$ combines standard scoping mechanisms (abstractions and applications) and types à la System F, with a logic-programming-style query language. At the heart of the language is a threefold interpretation of types:

$$types \cong propositions \cong rules$$

Firstly, types have their traditional meaning of classifying terms. Secondly, via the Curry-Howard isomorphism, types can also be interpreted as propositions – in the context of GP, the type proposition denotes the availability in the implicit environment of a value of the corresponding type. Thirdly, a type is interpreted as a logic-programming style rule, i.e., a Prolog rule or Horn clause [19]. Resolution [20] connects rules and propositions: it is the means to show (the evidence) that a proposition is entailed by a set of rules.

Next we present the key features of $\lambda_{\Rightarrow}$ and how these features are used for GP. For readability purposes we sometimes omit redundant type annotations and slightly simplify the syntax.

Fetching values by types: A central construct in $\lambda_{\Rightarrow}$ is a query. Queries allow values to be fetched by type, not by name. For example, in the following function call

$$foo\ ?Int$$

the query $?Int$ looks up a value of type Int in the implicit environment, to serve as an actual argument.

Constructing values with type-directed rules: $\lambda_{\Rightarrow}$ constructs values, using programmer-defined, type-directed rules (similar to functions). A rule (or rule abstraction) defines how to compute, from implicit arguments, a value of a particular type. For example, here is a rule that computes an $Int \times Bool$ pair from implicit Int and $Bool$ values:

$$(\!|(?Int+1, \neg\, ?Bool) : \{Int, Bool\} \Rightarrow Int \times Bool|\!)$$

The rule abstraction syntax resembles a type-annotated expression: the expression $(?Int+1, \neg\, ?Bool)$ to the left of the colon is the *rule body*, and to the right is the *rule type* $\{Int, Bool\} \Rightarrow Int \times Bool$. A rule abstraction abstracts over a set of implicit values (here $\{Int, Bool\}$), or, more generally, over rules to build values.

Hence, when a value of type $Int \times Bool$ is needed (expressed by the query $?(Int \times Bool)$), the above rule can be used, provided that an integer and a boolean value are available in the implicit environment. In such an environment, the rule returns a pair of the incremented Int value and negated $Bool$ value.

The implicit environment is extended through rule application (analogous to extending the environment with function applications). Rule application is expressed as, for example:

$$(\!|(?Int+1, \neg\, ?Bool) : \{Int, Bool\} \Rightarrow Int \times Bool|\!)\ \textbf{with}\ \{1, True\}$$

With syntactic sugar similar to a **let**-expression, a rule abstraction-application combination is denoted more compactly as:

$$\textbf{implicit}\ \{1, True\}\ \textbf{in}\ (?Int+1, \neg\, ?Bool)$$

which returns $(2, False)$.

Higher-order rules: $\lambda_{\Rightarrow}$ supports higher-order rules. For example, the rule

$$(\!|?(Int \times Int) : \{Int, \{Int\} \Rightarrow Int \times Int\} \Rightarrow Int \times Int|\!),$$

when applied, will compute an integer pair given an integer and a rule to compute an integer pair from an integer. Hence, the following rule application returns $(3, 4)$:

$$\textbf{implicit}\ \{3, (\!|(?Int, ?Int+1) : \{Int\} \Rightarrow Int \times Int|\!)\}\ \textbf{in}\ ?(Int \times Int)$$

Recursive resolution: Note that resolving the query $?(Int \times Int)$ involves applying multiple rules. The current environment does not contain the required integer pair. It does however contain the integer 3 and a rule $(\!|(?Int, ?Int+1) : \{Int\} \Rightarrow Int \times Int|\!)$ to compute a pair from an integer. Hence, the query is resolved with $(3, 4)$, the result of applying the pair-producing rule to 3.

Polymorphic rules and queries: $\lambda_{\Rightarrow}$ allows polymorphic rules. For example, the rule

$$(\!|(?\alpha, ?\alpha) : \forall\alpha.\{\alpha\} \Rightarrow \alpha \times \alpha|\!)$$

can be instantiated to multiple rules of monomorphic types

$$\{Int\} \Rightarrow Int \times Int, \{Bool\} \Rightarrow Bool \times Bool, \ldots$$

Multiple monomorphic queries can be resolved by the same rule. The following expression returns $((3,3), (True, True))$:

$$\textbf{implicit}\ \{3, True, (\!|(?\alpha, ?\alpha) : \forall\alpha.\{\alpha\} \Rightarrow \alpha \times \alpha|\!)\}\ \textbf{in}\ (?(Int \times Int), ?(Bool \times Bool))$$

Polymorphic rules can also be used to resolve polymorphic queries:

$$\textbf{implicit}\ \{(\!|(?\alpha, ?\alpha) : \forall\alpha.\{\alpha\} \Rightarrow \alpha \times \alpha|\!)\}\ \textbf{in}\ ?(\forall\alpha.\{\alpha\} \Rightarrow \alpha \times \alpha)$$

Combining higher-order and polymorphic rules: The rule

$$(\!|?((Int \times Int) \times (Int \times Int)) : \{Int, \forall\alpha.\{\alpha\} \Rightarrow \alpha \times \alpha\} \Rightarrow (Int \times Int) \times (Int \times Int)|\!)$$

prescribes how to build a pair of integer pairs, inductively from an integer value, by consecutively applying the rule of type

$$\forall\alpha.\{\alpha\} \Rightarrow \alpha \times \alpha$$

twice: first to an integer, and again to the result (an integer pair). For example, the following expression returns $((3,3),(3,3))$:

$$\textbf{implicit}\ \{3, (\!|(?\alpha, ?\alpha) : \forall\alpha.\{\alpha\} \Rightarrow \alpha\times\alpha|\!)\}\ \textbf{in}\\ ?((\mathit{Int}\times \mathit{Int})\times(\mathit{Int}\times \mathit{Int}))$$

Locally and lexically scoped rules: Rules can be nested and resolution respects the lexical scope of rules. Consider the following program:

$$\textbf{implicit}\ \{1\}\ \textbf{in}\\ \quad\textbf{implicit}\ \{\mathit{True}, (\!|\ \textbf{if}\ ?\mathit{Bool}\ \textbf{then}\ 2 : \{\mathit{Bool}\} \Rightarrow \mathit{Int}|\!)\}\\ \quad\textbf{in}\ ?\mathit{Int}$$

The query $?\mathit{Int}$ is not resolved with the integer value 1. Instead the rule that returns an integer from a boolean is applied to the boolean True, because those two rules can provide an integer value and they are nearer to the query. So, the program returns 2 and not 1.

Overlapping rules: Two rules overlap if their return types intersect, i.e., when they can both be used to resolve the same query. Overlapping rules are allowed in $\lambda_{\Rightarrow}$ through nested scoping. The nearest matching rule takes priority over other matching rules. For example consider the following program:

$$\textbf{implicit}\ \{\lambda x.x : \forall\alpha.\alpha \to \alpha\}\ \textbf{in}\\ \quad\textbf{implicit}\ \{\lambda n.n+1 : \mathit{Int} \to \mathit{Int}\}\ \textbf{in}\\ \qquad ?(\mathit{Int} \to \mathit{Int})\ 1$$

In this case $\lambda n.n+1 : \mathit{Int} \to \mathit{Int}$ is the lexically nearest match in the implicit environment and evaluating this program results in 2. However, if we have the following program instead:

$$\textbf{implicit}\ \{\lambda n.n+1 : \mathit{Int} \to \mathit{Int}\}\ \textbf{in}\\ \quad\textbf{implicit}\ \{\lambda x.x : \forall\alpha.\alpha \to \alpha\}\ \textbf{in}\\ \qquad ?(\mathit{Int} \to \mathit{Int})\ 1$$

Then the lexically nearest match is $\lambda x.x{:}\forall\alpha.\alpha \to \alpha$ and evaluating this program results in 1.

3. The $\lambda_{\Rightarrow}$ Calculus

This section formalizes the syntax and type system of $\lambda_{\Rightarrow}$.

3.1 Syntax

This is the syntax of the calculus:

$$\begin{array}{llll} \text{(Simple) Types} & \tau & ::= & \alpha \mid \mathit{Int} \mid \tau_1 \to \tau_2 \mid \rho \\ \text{Rule Types} & \rho & ::= & \forall\vec{\alpha}.\bar{\rho} \Rightarrow \tau \\ \text{Expressions} & e & ::= & n \mid x \mid \lambda x : \tau.e \mid e_1\, e_2 \\ & & \mid & ?\rho \mid (\!|e : \rho|\!) \mid e[\vec{\tau}] \mid e\ \textbf{with}\ \overline{e : \rho} \end{array}$$

Types τ are either type variables α, the integer type Int, function types $\tau_1 \to \tau_2$ or rule types ρ. A *rule type* $\rho = \forall\vec{\alpha}.\bar{\rho} \Rightarrow \tau$ is a type scheme with universally quantified variables $\vec{\alpha}$ and an (implicit) *context* $\bar{\rho}$. This *context* summarizes the assumed implicit environment. Note that we use $\vec{o}$ to denote an ordered sequence $o_1, \ldots, o_n$ of entities and $\bar{o}$ to denote a set $\{o_1, \ldots, o_n\}$. Such ordered sequences and sets can be empty, and we often omit empty universal quantifiers and empty contexts from a rule type. The base case of rule types is when $\bar{\rho}$ is the empty set (that is $\forall\vec{\alpha}.\{\} \Rightarrow \tau$ or, more compactly, $\forall\vec{\alpha}.\tau$).

Expressions include integer constants n and the three basic typed λ-calculus expressions (variables, lambda binders and applications). A *query* $?\rho$ queries the implicit environment for a value of type ρ. A *rule abstraction* $(\!|e : \forall\vec{\alpha}.\bar{\rho} \Rightarrow \tau|\!)$ builds a rule whose type is $\forall\vec{\alpha}.\bar{\rho} \Rightarrow \tau$ and whose body is e.

Without loss of generality we assume that all variables x and type variables α in binders are distinct. If not, they can be easily renamed apart to be so.

Note that, unlike System F, our calculus does not have a separate Λ binder for type variables. Instead rule abstractions play a dual role in the binding structure: 1) the universal quantification of type variables (which binds types), and 2) the context (which binds a rule set). Therefore, a Λ binder can be encoded using a rule with an empty context:

$$\Lambda\vec{\alpha}.(e : \tau) \stackrel{\text{def}}{=} (\!|e : \forall\vec{\alpha}.\tau|\!)$$

The design choice of making rules double binders is due to our interpretation of rules as logic programming rules[3]. After all, in the matching process of resolution, a rule is applied as a unit. Hence, separating rules into more primitive binders (à la System F's type and value binders) would only complicate the definition of resolution unnecessarily. However, elimination can be modularized into two constructs: *type application* $e[\vec{\tau}]$ and *rule application* e **with** $\overline{e : \rho}$.

Using rule abstractions and applications we can build the **implicit** sugar that we have used in Sections 1 and 2.

$$\textbf{implicit}\ \overline{e : \rho}\ \textbf{in}\ e_1 : \tau \stackrel{\text{def}}{=} (\!|e_1 : \bar{\rho} \Rightarrow \tau|\!)\ \textbf{with}\ \overline{e : \rho}$$

For readability purposes, when we use **implicit** we omit the type annotation τ. As we shall see in Section 5 this annotation can be automatically inferred.

For brevity and simplicity reasons, we have kept $\lambda_{\Rightarrow}$ small. In examples we may use additional syntax such as built-in integer operators and boolean literals and types.

3.2 Type System

Figure 1 presents the static type system of $\lambda_{\Rightarrow}$. The typing judgment $\Gamma \mid \Delta \vdash e : \tau$ means that expression e has type τ under type environment Γ and implicit environment Δ. The auxiliary resolution judgment $\Delta \vdash_r \rho$ expresses that type ρ is resolvable with respect to Δ. Here, Γ is the conventional type environment that captures type variables; Δ is the *implicit environment*, defined as a stack of contexts. Figure 1 also presents lookup in the implicit environment ($\Delta\langle\tau\rangle$) and in contexts ($\bar{\rho}\langle\tau\rangle$).

We will not discuss the first four rules ((TyInt), (TyVar), (TyAbs) and (TyApp)) because they are entirely standard. For now we also ignore the gray-shaded conditions in the other rules; they are explained in Section 3.3.

Rule (TyRule) checks a rule abstraction $(\!|e : \forall\vec{\alpha}.\bar{\rho} \Rightarrow \tau|\!)$ by checking whether the rule's body e actually has the type τ under the assumed implicit type context $\bar{\rho}$. Rule (TyInst) instantiates a rule type's type variables $\vec{\alpha}$ with the given types $\vec{\tau}$, and rule (TyRApp) instantiates the type context $\bar{\rho}$ with expressions of the required rule types $\overline{e : \rho}$. Finally, rule (TyQuery) delegates queries directly to the resolution rule (TyRes).

Resolution Principle The underlying principle of resolution in $\lambda_{\Rightarrow}$ originates from resolution in logic. Following the Curry-Howard correspondence, we assign to each type a corresponding logical interpretation with the $(\cdot)^{\dagger}$ function:

Definition 3.1 (Logical Interpretation)**.**

$$\begin{array}{rcl} \alpha^{\dagger} & = & \alpha^{\dagger} \\ \mathit{Int}^{\dagger} & = & \mathit{Int}^{\dagger} \\ (\tau_1 \to \tau_2)^{\dagger} & = & \tau_1^{\dagger} \to^{\dagger} \tau_2^{\dagger} \\ (\forall\vec{\alpha}.\bar{\rho} \Rightarrow \tau)^{\dagger} & = & \forall\vec{\alpha}^{\dagger}. \bigwedge_{\rho\in\bar{\rho}} \rho^{\dagger} \Rightarrow \tau^{\dagger} \end{array}$$

Here, type variables α map to propositional variables $\alpha^{\dagger}$ and the primitive type Int maps to the propositional constant $\mathit{Int}^{\dagger}$. Unlike

[3] In Prolog these are not separated either.

Type Environments	Γ	$::=$	$\cdot \mid \Gamma; x : \tau$
Implicit Environments	Δ	$::=$	$\cdot \mid \Delta; \bar{\rho}$

$\boxed{\Gamma \mid \Delta \vdash e : \tau}$

(TyInt) $$\Gamma \mid \Delta \vdash n : Int$$

(TyVar) $$\frac{(x : \tau) \in \Gamma}{\Gamma \mid \Delta \vdash x : \tau}$$

(TyAbs) $$\frac{\Gamma; x : \tau_1 \mid \Delta \vdash e : \tau_2}{\Gamma \mid \Delta \vdash \lambda x : \tau_1 . e : \tau_1 \to \tau_2}$$

(TyApp) $$\frac{\Gamma \mid \Delta \vdash e_1 : \tau_2 \to \tau_1 \qquad \Gamma \mid \Delta \vdash e_2 : \tau_2}{\Gamma \mid \Delta \vdash e_1\, e_2 : \tau_1}$$

(TyRule) $$\frac{\rho = \forall \vec{\alpha}.\bar{\rho} \Rightarrow \tau \quad \mathsf{unambiguous}(\rho) \qquad \Gamma \mid \Delta; \bar{\rho} \vdash e : \tau \quad \vec{\alpha} \cap ftv(\Gamma, \Delta) = \emptyset}{\Gamma \mid \Delta \vdash (\!| e : \rho |\!) : \rho}$$

(TyInst) $$\frac{\Gamma \mid \Delta \vdash e : \forall \vec{\alpha}.\bar{\rho} \Rightarrow \tau}{\Gamma \mid \Delta \vdash e[\vec{\tau}] : [\vec{\alpha} \mapsto \vec{\tau}](\bar{\rho} \Rightarrow \tau)}$$

(TyRApp) $$\frac{\Gamma \mid \Delta \vdash e : \bar{\rho} \Rightarrow \tau \qquad \Gamma \mid \Delta \vdash e_i : \rho_i \quad (\forall e_i : \rho_i \in \overline{e : \rho})}{\Gamma \mid \Delta \vdash (e \,\mathbf{with}\, \overline{e : \rho}) : \tau}$$

(TyQuery) $$\frac{\Delta \vdash_r \rho \quad \mathsf{unambiguous}(\rho)}{\Gamma \mid \Delta \vdash ?\rho : \rho}$$

$\boxed{\Delta \vdash_r \rho}$

(TyRes) $$\frac{\Delta\langle\tau\rangle = \bar{\rho}' \Rightarrow \tau \qquad \Delta \vdash_r \rho_i \quad (\forall \rho_i \in \bar{\rho}' - \bar{\rho})}{\Delta \vdash_r \forall \vec{\alpha}.\bar{\rho} \Rightarrow \tau}$$

$\boxed{\Delta\langle\tau\rangle = \rho}$

$$\frac{\bar{\rho}\langle\tau\rangle = \rho \qquad \mathsf{no\_overlap}(\bar{\rho}, \tau)}{(\Delta; \bar{\rho})\langle\tau\rangle = \rho}$$

$$\frac{\bar{\rho}\langle\tau\rangle = \bot \quad \Delta\langle\tau\rangle = \rho}{(\Delta; \bar{\rho})\langle\tau\rangle = \rho}$$

$\boxed{\bar{\rho}\langle\tau\rangle = \rho}$

$$\frac{\rho \in \bar{\rho} \qquad \rho = \forall \vec{\alpha}'.\bar{\rho}' \Rightarrow \tau' \qquad \theta\tau' = \tau}{\bar{\rho}\langle\tau\rangle = \theta\bar{\rho}' \Rightarrow \tau}$$

Figure 1. Type System

Curry-Howard, we do not map function types to logical implications; we deliberately restrict our implicational reasoning to rule types. So, instead we also map the function arrow to an uninterpreted higher-order predicate $\to^\dagger$. Finally, as already indicated, we map rule types to logical implications.

Resolution in $\lambda_\Rightarrow$ then corresponds to checking entailment of the logical interpretation. We postulate this property as a theorem that constrains the design of resolution.

Theorem 3.1 (Resolution Specification)**.**

If $\Delta \vdash_r \rho$, *then* $\Delta^\dagger \models \rho^\dagger$.

Resolution for Simple Types The step from the logical interpretation to the (TyRes) rule in Figure 1 is non-trivial. So, let us first look at a simpler incarnation. What does resolution look like for simple types τ like *Int*?

(SimpleRes) $$\frac{\Delta\langle\tau\rangle = \bar{\rho}' \Rightarrow \tau \qquad \Delta \vdash_r \rho_i \quad (\forall \rho_i \in \bar{\rho}')}{\Delta \vdash_r \tau}$$

First, it looks up a *matching* rule type in the implicit environment by means of the lookup function $\Delta\langle\tau\rangle$ defined in Fig. 1. This partial function respects the nested scopes: it first looks in the topmost context of the implicit environment, and, only if it does not find a matching rule, does it descend. Within an environment context, the lookup function looks for a rule type whose right-hand side τ' can be instantiated to the queried τ using a matching unifier θ. This rule type is then returned in instantiated form.

The matching expresses that the looked-up rule produces a value of the required type. To do so, the looked-up rule may itself require other implicit values. This requirement is captured in the context $\bar{\rho}'$, which must be resolved recursively. Hence, the resolution rule is itself a recursive rule. When the context $\bar{\rho}'$ of the looked-up rule is empty, a base case of the recursion has been reached.

Example Consider this query for a tuple of integers:

$$Int; \forall\alpha.\{\alpha\} \Rightarrow \alpha \times \alpha \vdash_r Int \times Int$$

Lookup yields the second rule, which produces a tuple, instantiated to $\{Int\} \Rightarrow Int \times Int$ with matching substitution $\theta = [\alpha \mapsto Int]$. In order to produce a tuple, the rule requires a value of the component type. Hence, resolution proceeds by recursively querying for *Int*. Now lookup yields the first rule, which produces an integer, with empty matching substitution and no further requirements.

Resolution for Rule Types So far, so good. Apart from allowing any types, recursive querying for simple types is quite similar to recursive type class resolution, and $\lambda_\Rightarrow$ carefully captures the expected behavior. However, what is distinctly novel in $\lambda_\Rightarrow$, is that it also provides *resolution of rule types*, which requires a markedly different treatment.

(RuleRes) $$\frac{\Delta\langle\tau\rangle = \bar{\rho} \Rightarrow \tau}{\Delta \vdash_r \forall \vec{\alpha}.\bar{\rho} \Rightarrow \tau}$$

Here we retrieve a whole rule from the environment, including its context. Resolution again performs a lookup based on a matching right-hand side τ, but subsequently also matches the context with the one that is queried. No recursive resolution takes place.

Example Consider a variant of the above query:

$$Int; \forall\alpha.\{\alpha\} \Rightarrow \alpha \times \alpha \vdash_r \{Int\} \Rightarrow Int \times Int$$

Again lookup yields the second rule, instantiated to $\{Int\} \Rightarrow Int \times Int$. The context $\{Int\}$ of this rule matches the context of the queried rule. Hence, the query is resolved without recursive resolution.

Unified Resolution The feat that our actual resolution rule (TyRes) accomplishes is to unify these seemingly disparate forms of resolution into one single inference rule. In fact, both (SimpleRes) and (RuleRes) are special cases of (TyRes), which provides some additional expressiveness in the form of *partial resolution* (explained below).

The first hurdle for (TyRes) is that types τ and rule types ρ are different syntactic categories. Judging from its definition, (TyRes) only covers rule types. How do we get it to treat simple types then? Just promote the simple type τ to its corresponding rule type $\forall.\{\} \Rightarrow \tau$ and (TyRes) will do what we expect for simple types, including recursive resolution. At the same time, it still matches proper rule types exactly, without recursion, when that is appropriate.

Choosing the right treatment for the context is the second hurdle. This part is managed by recursively resolving $\bar{\rho}' - \bar{\rho}$. In the case of promoted simple types, $\bar{\rho}$ is empty, and the whole of $\bar{\rho}'$ is recursively solved; which is exactly what we want. In the case $\bar{\rho}'$ matches $\bar{\rho}$, no recursive resolution takes place. Again this perfectly corresponds to what we have set out above for proper rule types. However, there is a third case, where $\bar{\rho}' - \bar{\rho}$ is a non-empty proper subset of $\bar{\rho}'$. We call this situation, where part of the retrieved rule's context is recursively resolved and part is not, *partial resolution*.

Example Here is another query variant:

$$Bool; \forall\alpha.\{Bool, \alpha\} \Rightarrow \alpha \times \alpha \vdash_r \{Int\} \Rightarrow Int \times Int$$

The first lookup yields the second rule, instantiated to $\{Bool, Int\} \Rightarrow Int \times Int$, which almost matches the queried rule type. Only $Bool$ in the context is unwelcome, so it is eliminated through a recursive resolution step. Fortunately, the first rule in the environment is available for that.

3.3 Additional Type System Conditions

The gray-shaded conditions in the type system are to check lookup errors (no_overlap) and ambiguous instantiations (unambiguous).

Avoiding Lookup Errors To prevent lookup failures, we have to check for two situations:

- A lookup has no matching rule in the environment.
- A lookup has multiple matching rules which have different rule types but can yield values of the same type (overlapping rules).

The former condition is directly captured in the definition of lookup among a set of rule types. The latter condition is captured in the no_overlap property, which is defined as:

$$\begin{array}{lllll} \multicolumn{5}{l}{\mathsf{no\_overlap}(\{\rho_1, \ldots, \rho_n\}, \tau) \stackrel{\mathsf{def}}{=}} \\ \forall i, j. & & \rho_i = \forall \vec{\alpha_i}.\bar{\rho}_i \Rightarrow \tau_i & \wedge & \exists \theta_i.\theta_i \tau_i = \tau \\ & \wedge & \rho_j = \forall \vec{\alpha_j}.\bar{\rho}_j \Rightarrow \tau_j & \wedge & \exists \theta_j.\theta_j \tau_j = \tau \\ & \Longrightarrow & i = j & & \end{array}$$

Avoiding Ambiguous Instantiations We avoid ambiguous instantiations in the same way as Haskell does: all quantified type variables ($\vec{\alpha}$) in a rule type ($\forall\vec{\alpha}.\bar{\rho} \Rightarrow \tau$) must occur in τ. We use the unambiguous condition to check in (TyRule) and (TyQuery):

$$\begin{array}{l} \mathsf{unambiguous}(\forall\vec{\alpha}.\bar{\rho} \Rightarrow \tau) = \vec{\alpha} \subseteq ftv(\tau) \\ \qquad\qquad\qquad\qquad \wedge\, \forall \rho_i \in \bar{\rho}.\mathsf{unambiguous}(\rho_i). \end{array}$$

If there is a quantified type variable not in type τ, the type may yield ambiguous instantiations (e.g. $\forall\alpha.\{\alpha\} \Rightarrow Int$).

4. Type-Directed Translation to System F

In this section we define the dynamic semantics of $\lambda_{\Rightarrow}$ in terms of System F's dynamic semantics, by means of a type directed translation. This translation turns implicit contexts into explicit parameters and statically resolves all queries, much like Wadler and Blott's dictionary passing translation for type classes [42]. The advantage of this approach is that we simultaneously provide a meaning to well-typed $\lambda_{\Rightarrow}$ programs and an effective implementation that resolves all queries statically.

4.1 Type-Directed Translation

Figure 2 presents the translation rules that convert $\lambda_{\Rightarrow}$ expressions into ones of System F extended with the integer and unit types. This figure essentially extends Figure 1 with the necessary information for the translation, but for readability we have omitted the earlier gray-shaded conditions.

The syntax of System F is as follows:

$$\begin{array}{lll} \text{Types} & T & ::= \alpha \mid T \rightarrow T \mid \forall\alpha.T \mid Int \mid () \\ \text{Expressions} & E & ::= x \mid \lambda(x : T).E \mid E\ E \mid \Lambda\alpha.E \mid E\ T \mid n \mid () \end{array}$$

$$\begin{array}{llll} \text{Type Environments} & \Gamma & ::= & \cdot \mid \Gamma; x : \tau \\ \text{Translation Environments} & \Delta & ::= & \cdot \mid \Delta; \overline{\rho : x} \end{array}$$

$$\boxed{\Gamma \mid \Delta \vdash e : \tau \rightsquigarrow E}$$

$$\texttt{(TrInt)} \quad \Gamma \mid \Delta \vdash n : Int \rightsquigarrow n$$

$$\texttt{(TrVar)} \quad \frac{(x : \tau) \in \Gamma}{\Gamma \mid \Delta \vdash x : \tau \rightsquigarrow x}$$

$$\texttt{(TrAbs)} \quad \frac{\Gamma; x : \tau_1 \mid \Delta \vdash e : \tau_2 \rightsquigarrow E}{\Gamma \mid \Delta \vdash \lambda x : \tau_1.e : \tau_1 \rightarrow \tau_2 \rightsquigarrow \lambda x : |\tau_1|.E}$$

$$\texttt{(TrApp)} \quad \frac{\begin{array}{c}\Gamma \mid \Delta \vdash e_1 : \tau_2 \rightarrow \tau_1 \rightsquigarrow E_1 \\ \Gamma \mid \Delta \vdash e_2 : \tau_2 \rightsquigarrow E_2\end{array}}{\Gamma \mid \Delta \vdash e_1\, e_2 : \tau_1 \rightsquigarrow E_1\, E_2}$$

$$\texttt{(TrQuery)} \quad \frac{\Delta \vdash_r \rho \rightsquigarrow E}{\Gamma \mid \Delta \vdash ?\rho : \rho \rightsquigarrow E}$$

$$\texttt{(TrRule)} \quad \frac{\begin{array}{c}\rho = \forall\vec{\alpha}.\bar{\rho} \Rightarrow \tau \quad \vec{\alpha} \cap ftv(\Gamma, \Delta) = \emptyset \\ \Gamma \mid \Delta; \overline{\rho : x} \vdash e : \tau \rightsquigarrow E \qquad \bar{x}\ \text{fresh}\end{array}}{\Gamma \mid \Delta \vdash (\!| e : \rho |\!) : \rho \rightsquigarrow \Lambda\vec{\alpha}.\lambda(\vec{x} : |\vec{\rho}|).E}$$

$$\texttt{(TrInst)} \quad \frac{\Gamma \mid \Delta \vdash e : \forall\vec{\alpha}.\bar{\rho} \Rightarrow \tau \rightsquigarrow E}{\Gamma \mid \Delta \vdash e[\vec{\tau}] : [\vec{\alpha} \mapsto \vec{\tau}](\bar{\rho} \Rightarrow \tau) \rightsquigarrow E\, |\vec{\tau}|}$$

$$\texttt{(TrRApp)} \quad \frac{\begin{array}{c}\Gamma \mid \Delta \vdash e : \bar{\rho} \Rightarrow \tau \rightsquigarrow E \\ \Gamma \mid \Delta \vdash e_i : \rho_i \rightsquigarrow E_i \quad (\forall e_i : \rho_i \in \overline{e : \rho})\end{array}}{\Gamma \mid \Delta \vdash (e\ \mathbf{with}\ \overline{e : \rho}) : \tau \rightsquigarrow E\, \vec{E}}$$

$$\boxed{\Delta \vdash_r \rho \rightsquigarrow E}$$

$$\texttt{(TrRes)} \quad \frac{\begin{array}{c}\Delta(\tau) = \bar{\rho}' \Rightarrow \tau : E \qquad \bar{x}\ \text{fresh} \\ \forall \rho_i \in \bar{\rho}' : \begin{cases} \Delta \vdash_r \rho_i \rightsquigarrow E_i & , \rho_i \notin \bar{\rho} \\ E_i = x_i & , \rho_i \in \bar{\rho} \end{cases}\end{array}}{\Delta \vdash_r \forall\vec{\alpha}.\bar{\rho} \Rightarrow \tau \rightsquigarrow \Lambda\vec{\alpha}.\lambda(\vec{x} : |\vec{\rho}|).(E\, \vec{E})}$$

$$\boxed{\Delta\langle\tau\rangle = \rho : E} \qquad \frac{\overline{\rho : x}\langle\tau\rangle = \rho : E}{(\Delta; \overline{\rho : x})\langle\tau\rangle = \rho : E}$$

$$\frac{\overline{\rho : x}\langle\tau\rangle = \bot \quad \Delta\langle\tau\rangle = \rho}{(\Delta; \overline{\rho : x})\langle\tau\rangle = \rho}$$

$$\boxed{\overline{\rho : x}\langle\tau\rangle = \rho : E} \qquad \frac{\begin{array}{c}(\rho : x) \in \overline{\rho : x} \qquad \rho = \forall\vec{\alpha}'.\bar{\rho}' \Rightarrow \tau' \\ \theta\tau' = \tau \qquad \theta = [\vec{\alpha}' \mapsto \vec{\tau}]\end{array}}{\overline{\rho : x}\langle\tau\rangle = \theta\bar{\rho}' \Rightarrow \tau : x\, |\vec{\tau}|}$$

$$\begin{array}{rcl} |\alpha| & = & \alpha \\ |Int| & = & Int \\ |\tau_1 \rightarrow \tau_2| & = & |\tau_1| \rightarrow |\tau_2| \\ |\forall\vec{\alpha}.\{\rho_1, \cdots, \rho_n\} \Rightarrow \tau| & = & \forall\vec{\alpha}.|\rho_1| \rightarrow \cdots \rightarrow |\rho_n| \rightarrow |\tau| \\ |\Gamma| & = & \{(x : |\tau|) \mid (x : \tau) \in \Gamma\} \\ |\Delta| & = & \{(x : |\rho|) \mid (\rho : x) \in \Delta\} \end{array}$$

Figure 2. Type-directed Translation to System F

The main translation judgment is

$$\Gamma \mid \Delta \vdash e : \tau \rightsquigarrow E,$$

which states that the translation of $\lambda_{\Rightarrow}$ expression e with type τ is System F expression E, with respect to type environment Γ and translation environment Δ. The translation environment Δ relates each rule type in the earlier implicit environment to a System F variable x; this variable serves as value-level explicit evidence for the implicit rule. Lookup in the translation environment is defined similarly to lookup in the type environment, except that the lookup now returns a pair of a rule type and an evidence variable.

Figure 2 also defines the type translation function $|\cdot|$ from $\lambda_{\Rightarrow}$ types τ to System F types T. In order to obtain a unique translation of types, we assume that the types in a context are lexicographically ordered.

Variables, lambda abstractions and applications are translated straightforwardly. Queries are translated by rule (TrQuery) using the auxiliary resolution judgment $\vdash_r$, defined by rule (TrRes). Note that rule (TrRes) performs the same process that rule (TyRes) performs in the type system except that it additionally collects evidence variables.

Rule (TrRule) translates rule abstractions to explicit type and value abstractions in System F, and rule (TrInst) translates instantiation to type application. Finally, rule (TrRApp) translates rule application to application in System F.

Example We have that:

$$\cdot \mid \cdot \vdash (\!|(?\alpha, ?\alpha) : \forall\alpha.\{\alpha\} \Rightarrow \alpha \times \alpha|\!) \rightsquigarrow \Lambda\alpha.\lambda(x:\alpha).(x,x)$$

and also:

$$(Int : x_1), (\forall\alpha.\{\alpha\} \Rightarrow \alpha \times \alpha : x_2) \vdash_r Int \times Int \rightsquigarrow x_2\ Int\ x_1$$

For brevity, Figure 2 omits the case where the context of a rule type is empty. To properly handle empty contexts, the translation of rule type should include $|\{\} \Rightarrow \tau| = () \rightarrow |\tau|$ and the translation rules (TrRule), (TrRApp) and (TrRes) should be extended in the obvious way.

Theorem 4.1 (Type-preserving translation). *Let e be a $\lambda_{\Rightarrow}$ expression, τ be a type and E be a System F expression. If $\cdot \mid \cdot \vdash e : \tau \rightsquigarrow E$, then $\cdot \vdash E : |\tau|$.*

Proof. (Sketch) We first prove[4] the more general lemma "if $\Gamma \mid \Delta \vdash e : \tau \rightsquigarrow E$, then $|\Gamma|, |\Delta| \vdash E : |\tau|$" by induction on the derivation of translation. Then, the theorem trivially follows. □

4.2 Dynamic Semantics

Finally, we define the dynamic semantics of $\lambda_{\Rightarrow}$ as the composition of the type-directed translation and System F's dynamic semantics. Following Siek's notation [35], this dynamic semantics is:

$$eval(e) = V \qquad where \cdot \mid \cdot \vdash e : \tau \rightsquigarrow E \; and \; E \rightarrow^* V$$

with $\rightarrow^*$ the reflexive, transitive closure of System F's standard single-step call-by-value reduction relation.

Now we can state the conventional type safety theorem for $\lambda_{\Rightarrow}$:

Theorem 4.2 (Type Safety). *If $\cdot \mid \cdot \vdash e : \tau$, then $eval(e) = V$ for some System F value V.*

The proof follows trivially from Theorem 4.1.

[4] in the technical report

```
interface Eq α = {eq : α → α → Bool}
let (≡) : ∀α. {Eq α} ⇒ α → α → Bool = eq ? in
let eqInt1 : Eq Int = Eq {eq = primEqInt} in
let eqInt2 : Eq Int = Eq {eq = λx y.isEven x ∧ isEven y} in
let eqBool : Eq Bool = Eq {eq = primEqBool} in
let eqPair : ∀α β. {Eq α, Eq β} ⇒ Eq (α, β) =
      Eq {eq = λx y.fst x ≡ fst y ∧ snd x ≡ snd y} in
let p1 : (Int, Bool) = (4, True) in
let p2 : (Int, Bool) = (8, True) in
implicit {eqInt1, eqBool, eqPair} in
(p1 ≡ p2, implicit {eqInt2} in p1 ≡ p2)
```

Figure 3. Encoding the Equality Type Class

Interface Declarations

interface $I\ \vec{\alpha} = \overline{u : T}$

Types

T	::=	α	Type Variables
	|	Int	Integer Type
	|	$I\ \vec{T}$	Interface Type
	|	$T \rightarrow T$	Function
σ	::=	$\forall\overline{\alpha}.\ \overline{\sigma} \Rightarrow T$	Rule Type

Expressions

E	::=	n	Integer Literal
	|	x	Lambda Variable
	|	$\lambda x.E$	Abstraction
	|	$E_1\ E_2$	Application
	|	u	Let Variable
	|	**let** $u : \sigma = E_1$ **in** E_2	Let
	|	**implicit** $\overline{u}$ **in** E_2	Implicit Scoping
	|	$?$	Implicit Lookup
	|	$I\ \overline{u = E}$	Interface Implementation

Figure 4. Syntax of Source Language

5. Source Languages and Implicit Instantiation

Languages like Haskell and Scala provide a lot more programmer convenience than $\lambda_{\Rightarrow}$ (which is a low level core language) because of higher-level GP constructs, interfaces and implicit instantiation. This section illustrates how to build a simple source language on top of $\lambda_{\Rightarrow}$ to add the expected convenience. We should note that unlike Haskell this language supports local and nested scoping, and unlike both Haskell and Scala it supports higher-order rules. We present the type-directed translation from the source to $\lambda_{\Rightarrow}$.

5.1 Type-directed Translation to $\lambda_{\Rightarrow}$

The full syntax of the source language is presented in Figure 4. Its use is illustrated in the program of Figure 3, which comprises an encoding of Haskell's equality type class Eq. The example shows that the source language features a simple type of interface $I\ \vec{T}$ (basically records), which are used to encode simple forms of type classes. Note that we follow Haskell's conventions for records: field names u are unique and they are modeled as regular functions taking a record as the first argument. So a field u with type T in an interface declaration $I\ \vec{\alpha}$ actually has type $\forall\vec{\alpha}.\{\} \Rightarrow I\ \vec{\alpha} \rightarrow T$. There are also other conventional programming constructs (such as **let** expressions, lambdas and primitive types).

Unlike the core language, we strongly differentiate between simple types T and type schemes σ in order to facilitate type inference. Moreover, as the source language provides implicit rather than explicit type instantiation, the order of type variables in a

Type Environments $\quad G \quad ::= \quad \cdot \mid G, u : \sigma \mid G, x : T$

$\boxed{G \vdash E : T \rightsquigarrow e}$

(TyIntL) $$G \vdash n : \mathit{Int} \rightsquigarrow n$$

(TyVar) $$\frac{G(x) = T}{G \vdash x : T \rightsquigarrow x}$$

(TyAbs) $$\frac{G, x : T_1 \vdash E \rightsquigarrow e}{G \vdash \lambda x.E : T_1 \to T_2 \rightsquigarrow \lambda x : [\![T_1]\!].e}$$

(TyApp) $$\frac{G \vdash E_1 : T_1 \to T_2 \rightsquigarrow e_1 \qquad G \vdash E_2 : T_1 \rightsquigarrow e_2}{G \vdash E_1\ E_2 : T_2 \rightsquigarrow e_1\ e_2}$$

(TyLVar) $$\frac{G(u) = \forall \bar{\alpha}.\, \bar{\sigma} \Rightarrow T' \qquad \theta = [\bar{\alpha} \mapsto \vec{T}] \quad T = \theta T' \qquad q_i = (?[\![\theta\sigma_i]\!]) : [\![\theta\sigma_i]\!] \quad (\forall \sigma_i \in \bar{\sigma})}{G \vdash u : T \rightsquigarrow u[[\![\vec{T}]\!]]\ \textbf{with}\ \bar{q}}$$

(TyLet) $$\frac{\sigma = \forall \bar{\alpha}.\bar{\sigma} \Rightarrow T_1 \qquad G \vdash E_1 : T_1 \rightsquigarrow e_1 \qquad G, u : \sigma \vdash E_2 : T_2 \rightsquigarrow e_2}{G \vdash\ \textbf{let}\ u : \sigma = E_1\ \textbf{in}\ E_2 : T_2 \rightsquigarrow (\lambda u : [\![\sigma]\!].e_2)\ (\!| e_1 : [\![\sigma]\!] |\!)}$$

(TyImp) $$\frac{G \vdash E : T \rightsquigarrow e \qquad G(u_i) = \sigma_i \quad q_i = u_i : [\![\sigma_i]\!] \quad (\forall u_i \in \bar{u})}{G \vdash\ \textbf{implicit}\ \bar{u}\ \textbf{in}\ E : T \rightsquigarrow (\!| e : [\![\bar{\sigma}]\!] \Rightarrow [\![T]\!] |\!)\ \textbf{with}\ \bar{q}}$$

(TyIVar) $$G \vdash ? : T \rightsquigarrow ?(\{\} \Rightarrow [\![T]\!])\ \textbf{with}\ \{\}$$

(TyRec) $$\frac{\forall i : \begin{cases} G(u_i) = \forall \bar{\alpha}.\{\} \Rightarrow I\ \vec{\alpha} \to T_i \\ G \vdash E_i : \theta T_i \rightsquigarrow e \quad \theta = [\vec{\alpha} \mapsto \vec{T}] \end{cases}}{G \vdash I\ \overline{u = E} : I\ \vec{T} \rightsquigarrow I\ \overline{u = e}}$$

$$\begin{aligned} [\![\alpha]\!] &= \alpha \\ [\![\mathit{Int}]\!] &= \mathit{Int} \\ [\![T_1 \to T_2]\!] &= [\![T_1]\!] \to [\![T_2]\!] \\ [\![I\ \vec{T}]\!] &= I\ [\![\vec{T}]\!] \\ [\![\forall \bar{\alpha}.\bar{\sigma} \Rightarrow T]\!] &= \forall [\![\vec{\alpha}]\!].[\![\bar{\sigma}]\!] \Rightarrow [\![T]\!] \end{aligned}$$

Figure 5. Type-directed Encoding of Source Language in $\lambda_\Rightarrow$

quantifier is no longer relevant. Hence, they are represented by a set ($\forall \bar{\alpha}$). We also distinguish simply typed variables x from let-bound variables u with polymorphic type σ.

Figure 5 presents the type-directed translation $G \vdash E : T \rightsquigarrow e$ of source language expressions E of type T to core expressions e, with respect to type environment G. The type environment collects both simply and polymorphic variable typings. The connection between source types T and σ on the one hand and core types τ and ρ on the other hand is captured in the auxiliary function $[\![\cdot]\!]$. Note that this function imposes a canonical ordering $\vec{\alpha}$ on the set of quantifier variables $\bar{\alpha}$ (based on their precedence in the left-to-right prefix traversal of the quantified type term). For the translation of records, we assume that $\lambda_\Rightarrow$ is extended likewise with records.

let and let-bound variables The rule (`TyLet`) in Figure 5 shows the type-directed translation for **let** expressions. This translation binds the variable u using a regular lambda abstraction in an expression e_2, which is the result of the translation of the body of the **let** construct (E_2). Then it applies that abstraction to a rule whose rule type is just the corresponding (translated) type of the definition (σ_1), and whose body is the translation of the expression E_1.

The source language provides convenience to the user by inferring type arguments and implicit values automatically. This inference happens in rule (**TyLVar**), i.e., the use of **let**-bound variables. That rule recovers the type scheme of variable u from the environment G. Then it instantiates the type scheme and fires the necessary queries to resolve the context.

Queries The source language also includes a query operator (?). Unlike $\lambda_\Rightarrow$ this query operator does not explicitly state the type; that information is provided implicitly through type inference. For example, instead of using $p_1 \equiv p_2$ in Figure 5, we could have directly used the field *eq* as follows:

$$eq\ ?\ p_1\ p_2$$

When used in this way, the query acts like a Coq placeholder (_), which similarly instructs Coq to automatically infer a value.

The translation of source language queries, given by the rule (**TyIVar**), is fairly straightforward. To simplify type-inference, the query is limited to types, and does not support partial resolution. In the translated code the query is combined with a rule instantiation and application in order to eliminate the empty rule set.

Implicit scoping The **implicit** construct is the core scoping construct of the source language. It is first used in our example to make $eqInt_1$, *eqBool* and *eqPair* available for resolution at the expression

$$(p_1 \equiv p_2, \textbf{implicit}\ \{eqInt_2\}\ \textbf{in}\ p_1 \equiv p_2)$$

Within this expression there is a second occurrence of **implicit**, which introduces an overlapping rule ($eqInt_2$) that takes priority over $eqInt_1$ for the subexpression $p_1 \equiv p_2$.

The translation rule (**TyImp**) of **implicit** into $\lambda_\Rightarrow$ also exploits type-information to avoid redundant type annotations. It is not necessary to annotate the **let**-bound variables used in the rule set $\bar{u}$ since that information is recovered from the environment G.

Higher-order rules and implicit instantiation for any type The following example illustrates higher-order rules and implicit instantiation working for any type in the source language.

$$\begin{aligned} &\textbf{let}\ show : \forall \alpha.\ \{\alpha \to String\} \Rightarrow \alpha \to String = \ ?\ \textbf{in} \\ &\textbf{let}\ showInt : Int \to String = \ldots\ \textbf{in} \\ &\textbf{let}\ comma : \forall \alpha.\ \{\alpha \to String\} \Rightarrow [\alpha] \to String = \ldots\ \textbf{in} \\ &\textbf{let}\ space : \forall \alpha.\ \{\alpha \to String\} \Rightarrow [\alpha] \to String = \ldots\ \textbf{in} \\ &\textbf{let}\ o : \{Int \to String, \{Int \to String\} \Rightarrow [Int] \to String\} \\ &\qquad \Rightarrow String = show\,[1,2,3]\ \textbf{in} \\ &\textbf{implicit}\ showInt\ \textbf{in} \\ &(\textbf{implicit}\ comma\ \textbf{in}\ o, \textbf{implicit}\ space\ \textbf{in}\ o) \end{aligned}$$

For brevity, we have omitted the implementations of *showInt*, *comma* and *space*; but *showInt* renders an *Int* as a *String* in the conventional way, while *comma* and *space* provide two ways for rendering lists. Evaluation of the expression yields (`"1,2,3"`, `"1 2 3"`). Thanks to the implicit rule parameters, the contexts of the two calls to o control how the lists are rendered.

This example differs from that in Figure 3 in that instead of using a *nominal* interface type like *Eq*, it uses standard functions to model a simple concept for pretty printing values. The use of functions as implicit values is similar to *structural* matching of concepts, since only the type of the function matters for resolution.

5.2 Extensions

The goal of our work is to present a minimal and general framework for implicits. As such we have avoided making assumptions about extensions that would be useful for some languages, but not others.

In this section we briefly discuss some extensions that would be useful in the context of particular languages and the implications that they would have in our framework.

Full-blown Concepts The most noticeable feature that was not discussed is a full-blown notion of concepts. One reason not to commit to a particular notion of concepts is that there is no general agreement on what the right notion of concepts is. For example, following Haskell type classes, the C++0x concept proposal [11] is based on a *nominal* approach with *explicit* concept refinement, while Stroustrup favors a *structural* approach with *implicit* concept refinement because that would be more familiar to C++ programmers [38]. Moreover, various other proposals for GP mechanisms have their own notion of interface: Scala uses standard OO hierarchies; Dreyer et al. use ML-modules [8]; and in dependently typed systems (dependent) record types are used [37, 5].

An advantage of $\lambda_{\Rightarrow}$ is that no particular notion of interface is imposed on source language designers. Instead, language designers are free to use the one they prefer. In our source language, for simplicity, we opted to add a very simple (and limited) type of interface. But existing language designs [29, 8, 37, 5] offer evidence that more sophisticated types of interfaces, including some form of refinement or associated types, can be built on top of $\lambda_{\Rightarrow}$.

Type Constructor Polymorphism and Higher-order Rules Type constructor polymorphism is an advanced, but highly powerful GP feature available in Haskell and Scala, among others. It allows abstracting container types like $List$ and $Tree$ with a type variable f; and applying the abstracted container type to different element types, e.g., $f\ Int$ and $f\ Bool$.

This type constructor polymorhism leads to a need for higher-order rules: rules for containers of elements that depend on rules for the elements. The instance for showing values of type $Perfect\ f\ \alpha$ in Section 1, is a typical example of this need.

Extending $\lambda_{\Rightarrow}$ with type constructor polymorphism is not hard. Basically, we need to add a kind system and move from a System F like language to a System F_ω like language.

Subtyping Languages like Scala or C++ have subtyping. Subtyping would require significant adaptations to $\lambda_{\Rightarrow}$. Essentially, instead of targetting System F, we would have to target a version of System F with subtyping. In addition, the notion of matching in the lookup function $\Delta\langle\tau\rangle$ would have to be adjusted, as well as the *no_overlap* condition. While subtyping is a useful feature, some language designs do not support it because it makes the system more complex and interferes with type-inference.

Type-inference Languages without subtyping (like Haskell or ML) make it easier to support better type-inference. Since we do not use subtyping, it is possible to improve support for type-inference in our source language. In particular, we currently require a type annotation for **let** expressions, but it should be possible to make that annotation optional, by building on existing work for the GHC Haskell compiler [33, 41].

6. Related Work

Throughout the paper we have already discussed a lot of related work. In what follows, we offer a more detailed technical comparison of $\lambda_{\Rightarrow}$ versus System F^G and Scala implicits, which are the closest to our work. Then we discuss the relation with other work in the literature.

System F^G Generally speaking our calculus is more primitive and general than System F^G. In contrast to $\lambda_{\Rightarrow}$, System F^G has both a notion of concepts and implicit instantiation of concepts[5].

[5] Note that instantiation of type variables is still explicit.

This has the advantage that language designers can just reuse that infrastructure, instead of having to implement it. The language G [36] is based on System F^G and it makes good use of these built-in mechanisms. However, System F^G also imposes important design choices. Firstly it forces the language designer to use the notion of concepts that is built-in to System F^G. In contrast $\lambda_{\Rightarrow}$ offers a freedom of choice (see also the discussion in Section 5.2). Secondly, fixing implicit instantiation in the core prevents useful alternatives. For example, Scala and several other systems do provide implicit instantiation by default, but also offer the option of explicit instantiation, which is useful to resolve ambiguities [29, 18, 6, 8]. This cannot be modeled on top of System F^G, because explicit instantiation is not available. In contrast, by taking explicit instantiation (rule application) as a core feature, $\lambda_{\Rightarrow}$ can serve as a target for languages that offer both styles of instantiation.

There are also important differences in terms of scoping and resolution of rules. System F^G only formalizes a very simple type of resolution, which does not support recursive resolution. Furthermore, scoping is less fine-grained than in $\lambda_{\Rightarrow}$. For example, System F^G requires a built-in construct for **model** expressions, but in $\lambda_{\Rightarrow}$ **implicit** (which plays a similar role) is just syntactic sugar on top of more primitive constructs.

Scala Implicits Scala implicits are integrated in a full-blown language, but they have only been informally described in the literature [29, 27]. Our calculus aims at providing a formal model of implicits, but there are some noteworthy differences between $\lambda_{\Rightarrow}$ and Scala implicits. In contrast to $\lambda_{\Rightarrow}$, Scala has subtyping. As discussed in Section 5.2 subtyping would require some adaptations to our calculus. In Scala, nested scoping can only happen through subclassing and the rules for resolution in the presence of overlapping instances are quite ad-hoc. Furthermore, Scala has no (first-class) rule abstractions. Rather, implicit arguments can only be used in definitions. In contrast $\lambda_{\Rightarrow}$ provides a more general and disciplined account of scoping for rules.

Type Classes Obviously, the original work on type classes [42] and the framework of *qualified types* [15] around it has greatly influenced our own work, as well as that of System F^G and Scala.

There is a lot of work on Haskell type classes in the literature. Notably, there have been some proposals for addressing the limitations that arise from global scoping [18, 6]. However in those designs, type classes are still second-class and resolution only works for type classes. The GHC Haskell compiler supports overlapping instances [17], that live in the same global scope. This allows some relief for the lack of local scoping. A lot of recent work on type classes is focused on increasingly more powerful "type class" interfaces. *Functional dependencies* [16], *associated types* [4, 3] and *type families* [32] are all examples of this trend. This line of work is orthogonal to our work.

Other Languages and Systems *Modular type classes* [8] are a language design that uses ML-modules to model type classes. The main novelty of this design is that, in addition to explicit instantiation of modules, implicit instantiation is also supported. In contrast to $\lambda_{\Rightarrow}$, implicit instantiation is limited to modules and, although local scoping is allowed, it cannot be nested.

Instance arguments [5] are an Agda extension that is closely related to implicits. However, unlike most GP mechanisms, implicit rules are not declared explicitly. Furthermore resolution is limited in its expressive power, to avoid introducing a different computational model in Agda. This design differs significantly from $\lambda_{\Rightarrow}$, where resolution is very expressive and the scoping mechanisms allow explicit rule declarations.

Implicit parameters [22] are a Haskell extension that allows *named* arguments to be passed implicitly. Implicit parameters are resolved by name, not by type and there is no recursive resolution.

GP and Logic Programming The connection between Haskell type classes and Prolog is folklore. Neubauer et. al. [25] also explore the connection with *Functional Logic Programming* and consider different evaluation strategies to deal with overlapping rules. With *Constraint Handling Rules*, Stuckey and Sulzmann [39] use *Constraint Logic Programming* to implement type classes.

7. Conclusion

Our main contribution is the development of the implicit calculus $\lambda_{\Rightarrow}$. This calculus isolates and formalizes the key ideas of Scala implicits and provides a simple model for language designers interested in developing similar mechanisms for their own languages. In addition, $\lambda_{\Rightarrow}$ supports higher-order rules and partial resolution, which add considerable expressiveness to the calculus.

Implicits provide an interesting alternative to conventional GP mechanisms like type classes or concepts. By decoupling resolution from a particular type of interfaces, implicits make resolution more powerful and general. Furthermore, this decoupling has other benefits too. For example, by modeling concept interfaces as conventional types, those interfaces can be abstracted as any other types, avoiding the issue of second class interfaces that arise with type classes or concepts.

Ultimately, all the expressiveness offered by $\lambda_{\Rightarrow}$ offers a wide-range of possibilities for new generic programming applications.

Acknowledgements We are grateful to Ben Delaware, Derek Dreyer, Jeremy Gibbons, Scott Kilpatrick, Phil Wadler, Beta Ziliani, the members of ROPAS and the anonymous reviewers for their comments and suggestions. This work was partially supported by Korea Ministry of Education, Science and Technology/Korea Science and Enginering Foundation's ERC grant R11-2008-007-01002-0, Brain Korea 21, Mid-career Research Program 2010-0022061, and by Singapore Ministry of Education research grant MOE2010-T2-2-073.

References

[1] The Boost C++ libraries. http://www.boost.org/, 2010.

[2] C. Camarão and L. Figueiredo. Type inference for overloading without restrictions, declarations or annotations. In *FLOPS*, 1999.

[3] M. Chakravarty, G. Keller, and S. L. Peyton Jones. Associated type synonyms. In *ICFP*, 2005.

[4] M. Chakravarty, G. Keller, S. L. Peyton Jones, and S. Marlow. Associated types with class. In *POPL*, 2005.

[5] D. Devriese and F. Piessens. On the bright side of type classes: Instance arguments in agda. In *ICFP*, 2011.

[6] A. Dijkstra and S. D. Swierstra. Making implicit parameters explicit. Technical report, Utrecht University, 2005.

[7] G. Dos Reis and B. Stroustrup. Specifying C++ concepts. In *POPL '06*, pages 295–308, 2006.

[8] D. Dreyer, R. Harper, M. Chakravarty, and G. Keller. Modular type classes. In *POPL*, 2007.

[9] R. Garcia, J. Jarvi, A. Lumsdaine, Jeremy Siek, and J. Willcock. A comparative study of language support for generic programming. In *OOPSLA*, 2003.

[10] J. Gibbons. Patterns in datatype-generic programming. In *The Fun of Programming, Cornerstones in Computing*. Palgrave, 2003.

[11] D. Gregor, J. Järvi, J. G. Siek, B. Stroustrup, G. Dos Reis, and A. Lumsdaine. Concepts: linguistic support for generic programming in c++. In *OOPSLA*, 2006.

[12] R. Hinze and S. L. Peyton Jones. Derivable type classes. *Electronic Notes in Theoretical Computer Science*, 41(1):5 – 35, 2001.

[13] J. Hughes. Restricted data types in Haskell. In *Haskell*, 1999.

[14] P. Jansson and J. Jeuring. Polytypic programming. In *AFP*. Springer-Verlag, 1996.

[15] M. P. Jones. Simplifying and improving qualified types. In *FPCA*, 1995.

[16] M. P. Jones. Type classes with functional dependencies. In *ESOP*, 2000.

[17] S. L. Peyton Jones, M. P. Jones, and E. Meijer. Type classes: exploring the design space. In *Haskell Workshop*, 1997.

[18] W. Kahl and J. Scheffczyk. Named instances for Haskell type classes. In *Haskell Workshop*, 2001.

[19] R. Kowalski. Predicate logic as a programming language. In *Proceedings of IFIP Congress*, 1974.

[20] R. Kowalski, Donald, and Kuehner. Linear resolution with selection function. *Artificial Intelligence*, 2, 1971.

[21] R. Lämmel and S. L. Peyton Jones. Scrap your boilerplate with class: extensible generic functions. In *ICFP*, 2005.

[22] J. Lewis, J. Launchbury, E. Meijer, and M. Shields. Implicit parameters: dynamic scoping with static types. In *POPL*, 2000.

[23] D. Musser and A. Stepanov. Generic programming. In *Symbolic and algebraic computation: ISSAC 88*, pages 13–25. Springer, 1988.

[24] D. R. Musser and A. Saini. *The STL Tutorial and Reference Guide: C++ Programming with the Standard Template Library*. Addison Wesley Longman Publishing Co., Inc., 1995.

[25] M. Neubauer, P. Thiemann, M. Gasbichler, and M. Sperber. Functional logic overloading. In *POPL*, 2002.

[26] M. Odersky. Poor man's type classes. `http://lamp.epfl.ch/~odersky/talks/wg2.8-boston06.pdf`, July 2006.

[27] M. Odersky. The Scala language specification, version 2.8, 2010.

[28] B. C. d. S. Oliveira and J. Gibbons. Scala for generic programmers. *Journal of Functional Programming*, 20, 2010.

[29] B. C. d. S. Oliveira, A. Moors, and M. Odersky. Type classes as objects and implicits. In *OOPSLA*, 2010.

[30] B. C. d. S. Oliveira, T. Schrijvers, W. Choi, W. Lee, and K. Yi. Extended report: The implicit calculus. `http://arxiv.org/abs/1203.4499`, 2012.

[31] A. Rodriguez, J. Jeuring, P. Jansson, A. Gerdes, O. Kiselyov, and B. C. d. S. Oliveira. Comparing libraries for generic programming in haskell. In *Haskell*, 2008.

[32] T. Schrijvers, S. L. Peyton Jones, M. Chakravarty, and M. Sulzmann. Type checking with open type functions. In *ICFP*, 2008.

[33] T. Schrijvers, S. L. Peyton Jones, M. Sulzmann, and D. Vytiniotis. Complete and decidable type inference for GADTs. In *ICFP*, 2009.

[34] J. Siek. The C++0x Concepts Effort. `http://ecee.colorado.edu/~siek/concepts_effort.pdf`, 2011.

[35] J. G. Siek and A. Lumsdaine. Essential language support for generic programming. In *PLDI*, 2005.

[36] J. G. Siek and A. Lumsdaine. A language for generic programming in the large. *Science of Computer Programming*, 76(5), 2011.

[37] M. Sozeau and N. Oury. First-class type classes. In *TPHOLs*, 2008.

[38] B. Stroustrup. Simplifying the use of concepts. Technical report, Technical Report N2906, ISO/IEC JTC 1 SC22 WG21, 2009.

[39] P. J. Stuckey and M. Sulzmann. A theory of overloading. In *ICFP*, 2002.

[40] V. Trifonov. Simulating quantified class constraints. In *Haskell*, 2003.

[41] D. Vytiniotis, S. L. Peyton Jones, T. Schrijvers, and M. Sulzmann. OUTSIDEIN(X): Modular type inference with local assumptions. *Journal of Functional Programming*, 21(4–5):333–412, 2011.

[42] P. L. Wadler and S. Blott. How to make ad-hoc polymorphism less ad hoc. In *POPL*, 1989.

Deterministic Parallelism via Liquid Effects *

Ming Kawaguchi Patrick Rondon Alexander Bakst Ranjit Jhala
University of California, San Diego
{mwookawa,prondon,abakst,jhala}@cs.ucsd.edu

Abstract

Shared memory multithreading is a popular approach to parallel programming, but also fiendishly hard to get right. We present *Liquid Effects*, a type-and-effect system based on refinement types which allows for fine-grained, low-level, shared memory multithreading while statically guaranteeing that a program is deterministic. Liquid Effects records the effect of an expression as a formula in first-order logic, making our type-and-effect system highly expressive. Further, effects like Read and Write are recorded in Liquid Effects as ordinary uninterpreted predicates, leaving the effect system open to extension by the user. By building our system as an extension to an existing dependent refinement type system, our system gains precise value- and branch-sensitive reasoning about effects. Finally, our system exploits the Liquid Types refinement type inference technique to automatically infer refinement types and effects. We have implemented our type-and-effect checking techniques in CSOLVE, a refinement type inference system for C programs. We demonstrate how CSOLVE uses Liquid Effects to prove the determinism of a variety of benchmarks.

Categories and Subject Descriptors D.2.4 [*Software Engineering*]: Software/Program Verification – Validation; D.1.3 [*Programming Techniques*]: Concurrent Programming – Parallel Programming

General Terms Languages, Reliability, Verification

Keywords Liquid Types, Type Inference, Dependent Types, C, Safe Parallel Programming, Determinism

1. Introduction

How do we program multi-core hardware? While many models have been proposed, the model of multiple sequential threads concurrently executing over a single shared memory remains popular due to its efficiency, its universal support in mainstream programming languages and its conceptual simplicity. Unfortunately, shared memory multithreading is fiendishly hard to get right, due to the inherent non-determinism of thread scheduling. Unless the programmer is exceptionally vigilant, concurrent accesses to shared data can result in non-deterministic behaviors in the program, potentially yielding difficult-to-reproduce "heisenbugs" whose appearance depends on obscurities in the bowels of the operation system's scheduler and are hence notoriously hard to isolate and fix.

Determinism By Default. One way forward is to make parallel programs "deterministic by default" [2] such that, no matter how threads are scheduled, program behavior remains the same, eliminating unruly heisenbugs and allowing the programmer to reason about their parallel programs as if they were sequential. In recent years, many static and dynamic approaches have been proposed for ensuring determinism in parallel programs. While dynamic approaches allow arbitrary data sharing patterns, they also impose non-trivial run-time overheads and hence are best in situations where there is relatively little sharing [5]. In contrast, while static approaches have nearly no run-time overhead, they have been limited to high-level languages like Haskell [7] and Java [2] and require that shared structures be refactored into specific types or classes for which deterministic compilation strategies exist, thereby restricting the scope of sharing patterns.

Liquid Effects. In this paper, we present *Liquid Effects*, a type-and-effect system based on refinement type inference which uses recent advances in SMT solvers to provide the best of both worlds: it allows for fine-grained shared memory multithreading in low-level languages with program-specific data access patterns, and yet statically guarantees that programs are deterministic.

Any system that meets these goals must satisfy several criteria. First, the system must support *precise and expressive effect specifications*. To precisely characterize the effect of program statements, it must precisely reason about complex heap access patterns, including patterns not foreseen by the system's designers, and it must be able to reason about relations between program values like loop bounds and array segment sizes. Second, the system must be *extensible* with user-defined effects to track effects which are domain-specific and thus could not be foreseen by the system's designers. Finally, the system must support *effect inference*, so that the programmer is not overwhelmed by the burden of providing effect annotations.

1. Precise and Expressive Effect Specifications. Our Liquid Effects type-and-effect system expresses the effect of a statement on the heap as a formula in first-order logic that classifies which addresses in the heap are accessed and with what effect they were accessed — for example, whether the data was read or written. Expressing effects as first-order formulas makes our type-and-effect system highly expressive: for example, using the decidable theory of linear arithmetic, it is simple to express heap access patterns like processing chunks of an array in parallel or performing strided accesses in a number of separate threads. Using first-order formulas for effects ensures that our system can express complex access patterns not foreseen by the system's designers, and allows us to incorporate powerful off-the-shelf SMT solvers in our system for reasoning about effects. Further, by building our type-and-effect system as

* This work was supported by NSF grants CCF-0644361, CNS-0720802, CCF-0702603, and a gift from Microsoft Research.

PLDI'12, June 11–16, 2012, Beijing, China.

```
void sumBlock (char *a, int i, int len) {
  if (len <= 1) return;

  int hl = len / 2;
  cobegin {
    sumBlock (a, i, hl);
    sumBlock (a, i + hl, len - hl);
  }

  a[i] += a[i + hl];
}

int sum1 (char *a, int len) {
  sumBlock (a, 0, len);

  return a[0];
}
```

Figure 1. Parallel Array Summation With Contiguous Partitions

an extension to an existing dependent refinement type system and allowing effect formulas to reference program variables, our system gains precise value and branch-sensitive reasoning about effects.

2. Extensibility. Our effect formulas specify how locations on the heap are affected using *effect labeling predicates* like Read and Write. These effect labeling predicates are ordinary uninterpreted predicates in first-order logic; our system does not treat effect labeling predicates specially. Thus, we are able to provide extensibility by parameterizing our system over a set of user-defined effect labeling predicates. Further, we allow the user to give *commutativity declarations* specifying which pairs of effects have benign interactions when they simultaneously occur in separate threads of execution. This enables users to track domain-specific effects not envisioned by the designers of the type-and-effect system.

3. Effect Inference. Our type rules can be easily recast as an algorithm for generating constraints over unknown refinement types and effect formulas; these constraints can then be solved using the Liquid Types technique for invariant inference, thus yielding a highly-automatic type-based method for proving determinism.

To illustrate the utility of Liquid Effects, we have implemented our type-and-effect checking techniques in CSOLVE, a refinement type inference system for C programs based on Liquid Types. We demonstrate how CSOLVE uses Liquid Effects to prove the determinism of a variety of benchmarks from the literature requiring precise, value-aware tracking of both built-in and user-defined heap effects while imposing a low annotation burden on the user. As a result, CSOLVE opens the door to efficient, deterministic programming in mainstream languages like C.

2. Overview

We start with a high-level overview of our approach. Figures 1 and 2 show two functions, `sum1` and `sum2` respectively, which add up the elements of an array of size 2^k *in-place* by dividing the work up into independent sub-computations that can be executed in parallel. At the end of both procedures, the first element of the array contains the final sum. In this section, we demonstrate how our system seamlessly combines path-sensitive reasoning using refinement types, heap effect tracking, and SMT-based reasoning to prove that `sum1` and `sum2` are deterministic.

2.1 Contiguous Partitions

The function `sum1` sums array `a` of length `len` using the auxiliary function `sumBlock`, which sums the elements of the contiguous segment of array `a` consisting of `len`-many elements and beginning at index `i`. Given an array segment of length `len`, `sumBlock` computes the sum of the segment's elements by dividing it into two contiguous subsegments which are recursively summed using `sumBlock`. The recursive calls place the sum of each subsegment in the first element of the segment; `sumBlock` computes its final result by summing the first element of each subsegment and stores it in the first element of the entire array segment.

Cobegin Blocks. To improve performance, we can perform the two recursive calls inside `sumBlock` in parallel. This is accomplished using the `cobegin` construct, which evaluates each statement in a block in parallel. Note that the recursive calls both read and write to the array passed to `sumBlock`; thus, to prove that the program is deterministic, we have to show that the part of the array that is written by each call does not overlap with the portion of the array that is read by the other. In the following, we demonstrate how our system is able to show that the recursive calls access disjoint parts of the array and thus that the function `sumBlock` is deterministic.

Effect Formulas. We compute the region of the array accessed by `sumBlock` as an *effect formula* that describes which pointers into the array are accessed by a call to `sumBlock` with parameters `i` and `len`. We note that the final line of `sumBlock` writes element `i` of `a`. We state the effect of this write as the formula [1]

$$\Sigma_{\mathtt{a[i]}} \doteq \nu = \mathtt{a} + \mathtt{i}.$$

We interpret the above formula, $\Sigma_{\mathtt{a[i]}}$, as "the pointer ν accessed by the expression `a[i]` is equal to the pointer obtained by incrementing pointer `a` by `i`." The final line of `sumBlock` also reads element $\mathtt{i} + \mathtt{hl}$ of `a`. The effect of this read is stated as a similar formula:

$$\Sigma_{\mathtt{a[i+hl]}} \doteq \nu = \mathtt{a} + \mathtt{i} + \mathtt{hl}.$$

The total effect of the final line of `sumBlock` stating which portion of the heap it accesses is then given by the disjunction of the two effect formulas:

$$\Sigma_{\mathtt{a[i]}} \oplus \Sigma_{\mathtt{a[i+hl]}} \doteq \nu = \mathtt{a} + \mathtt{i} \lor \nu = \mathtt{a} + \mathtt{i} + \mathtt{hl}.$$

The above formula says that the heap locations accessed in the final line of `sumBlock` are exactly the locations corresponding to `a[i]` and $\mathtt{a}[\mathtt{i} + \mathtt{hl}]$. Having determined the effect of the final line of `sumBlock` as a formula over the local variables `a`, `i`, and `hl`, we make two observations to determine the effect of the entire `sumBlock` function as a formula over its arguments `a`, `i`, and `len`. First, we observe that, in the case where $\mathtt{len} = 2$,

$$\mathtt{a}[\mathtt{i} + \mathtt{hl}] = \mathtt{a}[\mathtt{i} + \mathtt{len} - 1].$$

From this, we can see inductively that a call to `sumBlock` with index `i` and length `len` will access elements `a[i]` to $\mathtt{a}[\mathtt{i} + \mathtt{len} - 1]$. Thus, we can soundly ascribe `sumBlock` the effect

$$\Sigma_{\mathtt{sumBlock}} \doteq \mathtt{a} + \mathtt{i} \leq \nu \land \nu < \mathtt{a} + \mathtt{i} + \mathtt{len}.$$

That is, `sumBlock` will access all elements in the given array segment.

Determinism via Effect Disjointness. We are now ready to prove that the recursive calls within `sumBlock` access disjoint regions of the heap and thus that `sumBlock` behaves deterministically when the calls are executed in parallel. We determine the effect of the first recursive call by *instantiating* `sumBlock`'s effect, *i.e.*, by replacing formals `a`, `i`, and `len` with actuals `a`, `i`, and `hl`, respectively:

$$\Sigma_{\text{Call 1}} \doteq \mathtt{a} + \mathtt{i} \leq \nu \land \nu < \mathtt{a} + \mathtt{i} + \mathtt{hl}.$$

[1] Here we associate effects with program expressions like `a[i]`. However, in the technical development and our implementation, effects are associated with heap locations in order to soundly account for aliasing (section 4).

```
declare effect Accumulate;
declare Accumulate commutes with Accumulate;

void accumLog (char *l, int j)
  effect
   (&l[j], Accumulate(v) && !Read(v) && !Write(v));

void sumStride (char *a, int stride, char *log) {
  foreach (i, 0, THREADS) {
    for (int j = i; j < stride; j += THREADS) {
        a[j] += a[j + stride];
        accumLog (log, j);
    }
  }
}

int sum2 (char *a, int len) {
  log = (char *) malloc (len);

  for (int stride = len/2; stride > 0; stride /= 2)
    sumStride (a, stride, log);

  return a[0];
}
```

Figure 2. Parallel Array Summation With Strided Partitions

The resulting effect states that the first recursive call only accesses array elements $\mathtt{a}[\mathtt{i}]$ through $\mathtt{a}[\mathtt{i}+\mathtt{hl}-1]$. We determine the effect of the second recursive call with a similar instantiation of `sumBlock`'s effect:

$$\Sigma_{\text{Call 2}} \doteq \mathtt{a}+\mathtt{i}+\mathtt{hl} \leq \nu \wedge \nu < \mathtt{a}+\mathtt{i}+\mathtt{len}-\mathtt{hl}.$$

All that remains is to show that the effects $\Sigma_{\text{Call 1}}$ and $\Sigma_{\text{Call 2}}$ are disjoint. We do so by asking an SMT solver to prove the unsatisfiability of the conjoined *access intersection* formula

$$\Sigma_{\text{Unsafe}} = \Sigma_{\text{Call 1}} \wedge \Sigma_{\text{Call 2}},$$

whose inconsistency establishes that the intersection of the sets of pointers ν accessed by both recursive calls is empty.

2.2 Complex Partitions

In the previous example, function `sum1` computed the sum of an array's elements by recursively subdividing the array into halves and operating on each half separately before combining the results. We were able to demonstrate that `sum1` is deterministic by showing that the concurrent recursive calls to `sumBlock` operate on disjoint contiguous segments of the array. We now show that our system is capable of proving determinism even when the array access patterns are significantly more complex.

Function `sum2` uses the auxiliary function `sumStride`, which sums an array's elements using the following strategy: First, the array is divided into two contiguous segments. Each element in the first half is added to the corresponding element in the second half, and the element in the first half is replaced with the result. The problem is now reduced to summing only the first half of the array, which proceeds in the same fashion, until we can reduce the problem no further, at which point the sum of all the array elements is contained in the first element of the array.

Foreach Blocks. To increase performance, the pairwise additions between corresponding elements in the first and second halves of the array are performed in parallel, with the level of parallelism determined by a compile-time constant `THREADS`. The parallel threads are spawned using the `foreach` construct. The statement

```
foreach (i, l, u) s;
```

executes statement `s` once with each possible binding of `i` in the range $[\mathtt{l}, \mathtt{u})$. Further, all executions of statement `s` are performed in parallel. The `foreach` loop within `sumStride` spawns `THREADS` many threads. Thread `i` processes elements $\mathtt{i}, \mathtt{i}+\mathtt{THREADS}, \mathtt{i}+2*\mathtt{THREADS}$, *etc.*, of array `a`. While this strided decomposition may appear contrived, it is commonly used in GPU programming to maximize memory bandwidth by enabling "adjacent" threads to access adjacent array cells via *memory coalescing* [1].

To prove that the `foreach` loop within `sumStride` is deterministic, we must show that no location that is written in one iteration is either read from or written to in another iteration. (We ignore the effect of the call to the function `accumLog` for now and return to it later.) Note that this differs from the situation with `sum1`: in order to demonstrate that `sum1` is deterministic, it was not necessary to consider read and write effects separately; it was enough to know that recursive calls to `sumBlock` operated on disjoint portions of the heap. However, the access pattern of a single iteration of the `foreach` loop in `sumStride` is considerably more complicated, and reasoning about noninterference between loop iterations will require tracking not only which locations are affected but precisely how they are affected — that is, whether they are read from or written to.

Labeled Effect Formulas. We begin by computing the effect of each iteration of the loop on the heap, tracking which locations are accessed as well as which effects are performed at each location. We first compute the effect of each iteration of the inner `for` loop, which adds the value of $\mathtt{a}[\mathtt{j}+\mathtt{stride}]$ to $\mathtt{a}[\mathtt{j}]$. We will use the unary *effect labeling predicates* $\text{Read}(\nu)$ and $\text{Write}(\nu)$ to record the fact that a location in the heap has or has not been read from or written to, respectively. We capture the effect of the read of $\mathtt{a}[\mathtt{j}+\mathtt{stride}]$ with the effect formula

$$\Sigma_1 \doteq \text{Read}(\nu) \wedge \neg\text{Write}(\nu) \wedge \nu = \mathtt{a}+\mathtt{j}+\mathtt{stride}.$$

Note that we have used the effect label predicates Read and Write to record not only that we have accessed $\mathtt{a}[\mathtt{j}+\mathtt{stride}]$ but also that this location was only read from, not written to. We record the effect of the write to $\mathtt{a}[\mathtt{j}]$ with a similar formula:

$$\Sigma_2 \doteq \text{Write}(\nu) \wedge \neg\text{Read}(\nu) \wedge \nu = \mathtt{a}+\mathtt{j}$$

As before, the overall effect of these two operations performed sequentially, and thus the effect of a single iteration of the inner `for` loop is the disjunction of the two effect formulas above:

$$\Sigma_{\mathtt{j}} \doteq \Sigma_1 \vee \Sigma_2$$

Iteration Effect Formulas. Having computed the effect of a single iteration of `sumStride`'s inner `for` loop, the next step in proving that `sumStride` is deterministic is to compute the effect of each iteration of the outer `foreach` loop, with our goal being to show that the effects of any two distinct iterations must be disjoint. We begin by generalizing the effect formula we computed to describe the effect of a single iteration of the inner `for` loop to an effect formula describing the effect of the entire `for` loop. The effect formula describing the effect of the entire `for` is an effect formula that does not reference the loop induction variable `j`, but is implied by the conjunction of the loop body's single-iteration effect and any loop invariants that apply to the loop induction variable `j`.

Note that the induction variable `j` enjoys the loop invariant

$$\mathtt{j} < \mathtt{stride} \wedge \mathtt{j} \equiv \mathtt{i} \bmod \mathtt{THREADS}.$$

Given this invariant for `j`, we can now summarize the effect of the `for` loop as an effect formula which does not reference the loop induction variable `j` but is implied by the conjunction of the above invariant on j and the single-iteration effect formula Σ_j:

$$\Sigma_{\texttt{for}} \doteq (\text{Write}(\nu) \Rightarrow (\nu - \texttt{a}) \equiv \texttt{i} \bmod \texttt{THREADS})$$
$$\wedge (\text{Write}(\nu) \Rightarrow \nu < \texttt{a} + \texttt{stride})$$
$$\wedge (\text{Read}(\nu) \Rightarrow \nu \geq \texttt{a} + \texttt{stride}) \quad (1)$$

We have now computed the effect of `sumStride`'s inner `for` loop, and thus the effect of a single iteration of `sumStride`'s outer `foreach` loop.

Effect Projection. We define an effect projection operator $\pi(\Sigma, E)$ which returns the restriction of the effect formula Σ to the effect label E. In essence, the effect projection is the formula implied by the conjunction of Σ and $E(\nu)$. For example, the projection of the Write effect of iteration i of the `foreach` loop represents the addresses written by thread i.

Determinism via Iteration Effect Disjointness. To prove that the `foreach` loop is deterministic, we must show that values that are written in one iteration are not read or overwritten in another. First, we show that no two `foreach` iterations (*i.e.,* threads) write to the same location, or, in other words, that distinct iterations write through disjoint sets of pointers. We establish this fact by asking the SMT solver to prove the unsatisfiability of the *write-write intersection* formula:

$$\Sigma_{\mathsf{Unsafe}} = \pi(\Sigma_{\texttt{for}}, \text{Write}) \wedge \pi(\Sigma_{\texttt{for}}, \text{Write})[\texttt{i} \mapsto \texttt{i}']$$
$$\wedge\, \texttt{i} \neq \texttt{i}' \wedge 0 \leq \texttt{i}, \texttt{i}' < \texttt{THREADS}.$$

The formula is indeed unsatisfiable as, from Equation 1,

$$\pi(\Sigma_{\texttt{for}}, \text{Write}) \doteq (\nu - \texttt{a}) \equiv \texttt{i} \bmod \texttt{THREADS}$$
$$\wedge\, \nu < \texttt{a} + \texttt{stride} \quad (2)$$

and so, after substituting $\texttt{i}'$ the query formula is

$$(\nu - \texttt{a}) \equiv \texttt{i} \bmod \texttt{THREADS} \wedge (\nu - \texttt{a}) \equiv \texttt{i}' \bmod \texttt{THREADS}$$

which is unsatisfiable when $\texttt{i} \neq \texttt{i}'$.

Next, we prove that no heap location is read in one iteration (*i.e.,* thread) and written in another. As before, we verify that the intersection of the pointers read in one iteration with those written in another iteration is empty. Concretely, we ask the SMT solver to prove the unsatisfiability of the *write-read intersection* formula

$$\Sigma_{\mathsf{Unsafe}} = \pi(\Sigma_{\texttt{for}}, \text{Write}) \wedge \pi(\Sigma_{\texttt{for}}, \text{Read})[\texttt{i} \mapsto \texttt{i}'] \wedge \texttt{i} \neq \texttt{i}'$$

where, from Equation 1, the locations *read* in a single iteration of the `foreach` loop are described by the Read projection

$$\pi(\Sigma_{\texttt{for}}, \text{Read}) \doteq \nu \geq \texttt{a} + \texttt{stride}.$$

After substituting the the write effect from Equation 2, we can see that the write-read-intersection formula is unsatisfiable as

$$\nu < \texttt{a} + \texttt{stride} \wedge \nu \geq \texttt{a} + \texttt{stride}$$

is inconsistent. Thus, by proving the disjointness of the write-write and write-read effects, we have proved that the `foreach` loop inside `sumStride` is deterministic.

2.3 User-Defined Effects

By expressing our effect labeling predicates as ordinary uninterpreted predicates in first-order logic, we open the door to allowing the user to define their own effects. Such user-defined effects are first-class: we reason about them using the same mechanisms as the built-in predicates Read and Write, and effect formulas over user-defined predicates are equally as expressive as those over the built-in predicates.

We return to the `sumStride` function to demonstrate the use of user-defined effects. The `for` loop in `sumStride` tracks how many times the entry a[j] is written by incrementing the j-th value in the counter array `log` using the externally-defined function `accumLog`. We assume that the `accumLog` function is implemented so that its operation is atomic. Thus, using `accumLog` to increment the count of the same element in two distinct iterations of the `foreach` loop does not cause non-determinism.

Specifying Effects. We create a new user-defined effect predicate to track the effect of the `accumLog` function using the statement

```
declare effect Accumulate;
```

This extends the set of effect predicates that our system tracks to

$$\mathbb{E} \doteq \{\text{Read}, \text{Write}, \text{Accumulate}\}.$$

We then annotate the prototype of the `accumLog` function to specify `accumLog` causes the Accumulate effect to occur on the j-th entry of its parameter array l:

```
void accumLog (char *l, int j)
  effect
    (&l[j], Accumulate(v) && !Read(v) && !Write(v));
```

Specifying Commutativity. We specify that our user effect Accumulate does not cause nondeterminism even when it occurs on the same location in two separate threads using the *commutativity annotation*

```
declare Accumulate commutes with Accumulate;
```

This annotation extends the set of pairs of effects that commute with each other — that is, which can occur in either order without affecting the result of the computation. In particular, the commutativity annotation above extends the set of commutable pairs to

$$\mathbb{C} \doteq \{(\text{Read}, \text{Read}), (\text{Accumulate}, \text{Accumulate})\}.$$

The extended set formally specifies that in addition to pairs of Read effects (included by default), pairs of of Accumulate effects also commute, and hence may be allowed to occur simultaneously.

Generalized Effect Disjointness. Finally, we generalize our method for ensuring determinism. We check the disjointness of two effect formulas Σ_1 and Σ_2 by asking the SMT solver to prove the unsatisfiability of the *effect intersection* formula:

$$\Sigma_{\mathsf{Unsafe}} = \exists (E_1, E_2) \in (\mathbb{E} \times \mathbb{E} \setminus \mathbb{C}).\pi(\Sigma_1, E_1) \wedge \pi(\Sigma_2, E_2).$$

That is, for each possible combination of effect predicates that have not been explicitly declared to commute, we check that the two effect sets are disjoint when projected on those effects.

Thus, by declaring an Accumulate effect which is commutative, we are able to verify the determinism of `sum2`.

Effect Inference. In the preceding, we gave explicit loop invariants and heap effects where necessary. Later in this paper, we explain how we use Liquid Type inference [28] to reduce the annotation burden on the programmer by automatically inferring the loop invariants and heap effects given above.

Outline. The remainder of this paper is organized as follows: In section 3, we give the syntax of LC_E programs, informally explain their semantics, and give the syntax of LC_E's types. We define the type system of LC_E in section 4. In section 5, we give an overview of the results of applying an implementation of a typechecker for LC_E to a series of examples from the literature. We review related work in section 6.

3. Syntax and Semantics

In this section, we present the syntax of LC_E programs, informally discuss their semantics, and give the syntax of LC_E types.

v	$::=$		**Values**
	$\mid$	x	variable
	$\mid$	n	integer
	$\mid$	$\&n$	pointer
a	$::=$		**Pure Expressions**
	$\mid$	v	value
	$\mid$	$a_1 \circ a_2$	arithmetic operation
	$\mid$	$a_1 +_p a_2$	pointer arithmetic
	$\mid$	$a_1 \sim a_2$	comparison
e	$::=$		**Expressions**
	$\mid$	a	pure expression
	$\mid$	$*v$	heap read
	$\mid$	$*v_1 := v_2$	heap write
	$\mid$	**if** v **then** e_1 **else** e_2	if-then-else
	$\mid$	$f(\overline{v})$	function call
	$\mid$	**malloc**(v)	memory allocation
	$\mid$	**let** $x = e_1$ **in** e_2	let binding
	$\mid$	**letu** $x =$ **unfold** v **in** e	location unfold
	$\mid$	**fold** l	location fold
	$\mid$	$e_1 \parallel e_2$	parallel composition
	$\mid$	**for each** x **in** v_1 **to** v_2 $\{e\}$	parallel iteration
F	$::=$	$f\ (\overline{x_i})\ \{\ e\ \}$	**Function Declarations**
P	$::=$	$\overline{F}\ e$	**Programs**

Figure 3. Syntax of LC_E programs

b	$::=$		**Base Types**
	$\mid$	$\mathtt{int}(i)$	integer
	$\mid$	$\mathtt{ref}(l, i)$	pointer
p	$::=$	$\phi(\overline{v})$	**Refinement Formulas**
τ	$::=$	$\{\nu : b \mid p\}$	**Refinement Types**
i	$::=$		**Indices**
	$\mid$	n	constant
	$\mid$	n^{+m}	sequence
c	$::=$	$\overline{i : \tau}$	**Blocks**
l	$::=$		**Heap Locations**
	$\mid$	$\tilde{l}$	abstract location
	$\mid$	l_j	concrete location
h	$::=$		**Heap Types**
	$\mid$	ε	empty heap
	$\mid$	$h * l \mapsto c$	extended heap
Σ	$::=$		**Heap Effects**
	$\mid$	ε	empty effect
	$\mid$	$\Sigma * \tilde{l} \mapsto p$	extended effect
σ	$::=$	$(\overline{x_i : \tau_i})/h_1 \rightarrow \tau/h_2/\Sigma$	**Function Schemes**

Figure 4. Syntax of LC_E types

3.1 Programs

The syntax of LC_E programs is shown in Figure 3. Most of the expression forms for expressing sequential computation are standard or covered extensively in previous work [28]; the expression forms for parallel computation are new to this work.

Values. The set of LC_E values v includes program variables, integer constants n, and constant pointer values $\&n$ representing addresses in the heap. With the exception of the null pointer value &0, constant pointer values do not appear in source programs.

Expressions. The set of pure LC_E expressions a includes values v, integer arithmetic expressions $a_1 \circ a_2$, where $\circ$ is one of the standard arithmetic operators $+$, $-$, $*$, *etc.*, pointer arithmetic expressions $a_1 +_p a_2$, and comparisons $a_1 \sim a_2$ where $\sim$ is one of the comparison operators $=$, $<$, $>$, *etc.* Following standard practice, zero and non-zero values represent falsity and truth, respectively.

The set of LC_E expressions e includes the pure expressions a as well as all side-effecting operations. The expression forms for pointer read and write, if-then-else, function call, memory allocation, and let binding are all standard. The location unfold and fold expressions are used to support type-based reasoning about the heap using strong updates As they have no effect on the dynamic semantics of LC_E programs, we defer discussion of location unfold and fold expressions to section 4.

Parallel Expressions. The set of LC_E expressions includes two forms for expressing parallel computations. The first, parallel composition $e_1 \parallel e_2$, evaluates expressions e_1 and e_2 in parallel and returns when both subexpressions have evaluated to values.

The second parallel expression form is the parallel iteration expression form **for each** x **in** v_1 **to** v_2 $\{e\}$, where v_1 and v_2 are integer values. A parallel iteration expression is evaluated by evaluating the body expression e once for each possible binding of variable x to an integer in the range $[v_1, v_2)$. All iterations are evaluated in parallel, and the parallel iteration expression returns when all iterations have finished evaluating. Both forms of parallel expressions are evaluated solely for their side effects.

Functions and Programs. A function declaration $f\ (\overline{x_i})\ \{\ e\ \}$ declares a function f with arguments x_i whose body is the expression e. The return value of the function is the value of the expression. An LC_E program consists of a sequence of function declarations F followed by an expression e which is evaluated in the environment containing the previously-declared functions.

3.2 Types

The syntax of LC_E types is shown in Figure 4.

Base Types. The base types b of LC_E include integer types $\mathtt{int}(i)$ and pointer types $\mathtt{ref}(l, i)$. The integer type $\mathtt{int}(i)$ describes an integer whose value is in the set described by the index i; the set of indices is described below. The pointer type $\mathtt{ref}(l, i)$ describes a pointer value to the heap location l whose offset from the beginning of location l is an integer belonging to the set described by index i.

Indices. The language of LC_E base types uses *indices* i to approximate the values of integers and the offsets of pointers from the starts of the heap locations where they point. There are two forms of indices. The first, the singleton index n, describes the set of integers $\{n\}$. The second, the sequence index n^{+m}, represents the sequence of offsets $\{n + lm\}_{l=0}^{\infty}$.

Refinement Types. The LC_E refinement types τ are formed by joining a base type b with a refinement formula p to form the refinement type $\{\nu : b \mid p\}$. The distinguished *value variable* ν refers to the value described by this type. The *refinement formula* p is a logical formula $\phi(\nu, \overline{v})$ over LC_E values $\overline{v}$ and the value variable ν. The type $\{\nu : b \mid p\}$ describes all values v of base type b that satisfy the formula $p[\nu \mapsto v]$. Our refinements are first-order formulas with equality, uninterpreted functions, and linear arithmetic.

When it is unambiguous from the context, we use b to abbreviate $\{\nu : b \mid \text{true}\}$.

Blocks. A block c describes the contents of a heap location as a sequence of bindings from indices i to refinement types τ. Each binding $i : \tau$ states that a value of type τ is contained in the block at each offset n from the start of the block which is described by the index i. Bindings of the form $m : \tau$, where types are bound to singleton indices, refer to exactly one element within the block; as such, we allow the refinement formulas within the same block to refer to the value at offset m using the syntax $@m$. We require all indices in a block to be disjoint.

Heap Types. Heap types h statically describe the contents of run-time heaps as sets of bindings from heap locations l to blocks c. A heap type is either the empty heap ε or a heap h extended with a binding from location l to block c, written $h * l \mapsto c$. The location l is either an *abstract location* $\tilde{l}$, which corresponds to arbitrarily many run-time heap locations, or a *concrete location* l_j, which corresponds to exactly one run-time heap location. The distinction between abstract and concrete locations is used to implement a form of sound strong updates on heap types in the presence of aliasing, unbounded collections, and concurrency; we defer detailed discussion to section 4. Locations may be bound at most once in a heap.

Heap Effects. A heap effect Σ describes the effect of an expression on a set of heap locations as a set of bindings from heap locations l to effect formulas p. A heap effect is either the empty effect ε or an effect Σ extended with a binding from location $\tilde{l}$ to an *effect formula* p over the in-scope program variables and the value variable ν, written $\Sigma * \tilde{l} \mapsto p$. Intuitively, an effect binding $\tilde{l} \mapsto p$ describes the effect of an expression on location $\tilde{l}$ as the set of pointers v such that the formula $p[\nu \mapsto v]$ is valid. Note that we only bind abstract locations in heap effects.

Effect Formulas. The formula portion of an effect binding can describe the effect of an expression with varying degrees of precision, from simply describing whether the expression accesses the location at all, to describing which offsets into a location are accessed, to describing which offsets into a location are accessed and how they are accessed (*e.g.* whether they are read or written).

For example, if we use the function $\mathrm{BB}(\nu)$ to refer to the beginning of the block where ν points, we can record the fact that expression e accesses the first ten items in the block at location $\tilde{l}$ (for either reading or writing) with the effect binding

$$\tilde{l} \mapsto \mathrm{BB}(\nu) \leq \nu \wedge \nu < \mathrm{BB}(\nu) + 10,$$

i.e., by stating that all pointers used by e to accesses location $\tilde{l}$ satisfy the above formula. To record that an expression does not access location $\tilde{l}$ at all, we ascribe it the effect formula false.

We add further expressiveness to our language of effect formulas by enriching it with effect-specific predicates used to describe the particular effects that occurred within a location. We use the unary predicates $\mathrm{Read}(v)$ and $\mathrm{Write}(v)$ to indicate that pointer v was read from or written to, respectively. Using these predicates, we can precisely state how an expression depends upon or affects the contents of a heap location.

For example, we can specify that an expression does not write to a location $\tilde{l}$ using the effect binding

$$\tilde{l} \mapsto \neg\mathrm{Write}(\nu).$$

On the other hand, we may specify precisely which offsets into $\tilde{l}$ are written by using Write to guard a predicate describing a set of pointers into $\tilde{l}$. For example, the effect binding

$$\tilde{l} \mapsto \mathrm{Write}(\nu) \Rightarrow (\mathrm{BB}(\nu) \leq \nu \wedge \nu < \mathrm{BB}(\nu) + 10)$$

describes an expression which writes to the first ten elements of the block at $\tilde{l}$.

Effect predicates like Read and Write may only appear in heap effect bindings; they may not appear in type refinements.

Function Schemes. A LC_E *function scheme*

$$(\overline{x_i : \tau_i})/h_1 \ \rightarrow \ \tau/h_2/\Sigma$$

is the type of functions which take arguments x_i of corresponding types τ_i in a heap of type h_1, return values of type τ in a heap of type h_2, and incur side-effects described by the heap effect Σ. The types of function parameters may depend on the other function parameters, and the type of the input heap may depend on the parameters. The types of the return value, output heap, and heap effect may depend on the types of the parameters. We implicitly quantify over all the location names appearing in a function scheme.

4. Type System

In this section, we present the typing rules of LC_E. We begin with a discussion of LC_E's type environments. We then discuss LC_E's expression typing rules, paying particular attention to how the rules carefully track side effects. Finally, we describe how we use tracked effects to ensure determinism.

Type Environments. Our typing rules make use of three types of environments. A *local environment*, Γ, is a sequence of *type bindings* of the form $x : \tau$ recording the types of in-scope variables and *guard formulas* p recording any branch conditions under which an expression is evaluated. A global environment, Φ, is a sequence of function type bindings of the form $f : S$ which maps functions to their refined type signatures. Finally, an effect environment Π is a pair $(\mathbb{E}, \mathbb{C})$. The first component in the pair, $\mathbb{E}$, is a set of effect label predicates. The second component in the pair, $\mathbb{C}$, is a set of pairs of effect label predicates such that $(E_1, E_2) \in \mathbb{C}$ states that effect E_1 *commutes* with E_2. By default, $\mathbb{E}$ includes the built-in effects, Read and Write, and $\mathbb{C}$ includes the pair (Read, Read), which states that competing reads to the same address in different threads produce a result that is independent of their ordering. In our typing rules, we implicitly assume a single global effect environment Π.

Local environments are well-formed if each bound type or guard formula is well-formed in the environment that precedes it. An effect environment $(\mathbb{E}, \mathbb{C})$ is well-formed as long as $\mathbb{C}$ is symmetric and only references effects in the set $\mathbb{E}$, *i.e.*, $\mathbb{C} \subseteq \mathbb{E} \times \mathbb{E}$, and $(E_1, E_2) \in \mathbb{C}$ iff $(E_2, E_1) \in \mathbb{C}$.

$$\begin{array}{llr}
\Gamma & ::= \epsilon \mid x : \tau ; \Gamma \mid p ; \Gamma & \text{(Local Environment)} \\
\Phi & ::= \epsilon \mid \mathtt{f} : \sigma ; \Phi & \text{(Global Environment)} \\
\mathbb{E} & ::= \{\mathrm{Read}, \mathrm{Write}\} \mid E ; \mathbb{E} & \\
\mathbb{C} & ::= (\mathrm{Read}, \mathrm{Read}) \mid (E, E) ; \mathbb{C} & \\
\Pi & ::= (\mathbb{E}, \mathbb{C}) & \text{(Effect Environment)}
\end{array}$$

4.1 Typing Judgments

We now discuss the rules for ensuring type well-formedness, subtyping, and typing expressions. Due to space constraints, we only present the formal definitions of the most pertinent rules, and defer the remainder to the accompanying technical report [16].

Subtyping Judgments. The rules for subtyping refinement types are straightforward: type τ_1 is a subtype of τ_2 in environment Γ, written $\Gamma \vdash \tau_1 <: \tau_2$, if 1) τ_1's refinement implies τ_2 under the assumptions recorded as refinement types and guard predicates in Γ and 2) τ_1's index is included in τ_2's when both are interpreted as sets.

Heap type h_1 is a subtype of h_2 in environment Γ, written $\Gamma \vdash h_1 <: h_2$, if both heaps share the same domain and, for each location l, the block bound to l in h_1 is a subtype of the block bound to l in h_2. Subtyping between blocks is pairwise subtyping between the types bound to each index in each block; we use substitutions to place bindings to offsets $@i$ in the environment.

Because effect formulas are first-order formulas, subtyping between effects is simply subtyping between refinement types: an effect Σ_1 is a subtype of Σ_2 in environment Γ, written $\Gamma \vdash \Sigma_1 <:$

Σ_2, if each effect formula bound to a location in Σ_1 implies the formula bound to the same location in Σ_2 using the assumptions in Γ.

Type Well-Formedness. The type well-formedness rules of LC_E ensure that all refinement and effect formulas are well-scoped and that heap types and heap effects are well-defined maps over locations. These rules are straightforward; we briefly discuss them below, deferring their formal definitions [16].

A heap effect Σ is well-formed with respect to environment Γ and heap h, written $\Gamma, h \vdash \Sigma$, if it binds only abstract locations which are bound in h, binds a location at most once, and binds locations to effect formulas which are well-scoped in Γ. Further, an effect formula p is well-formed in an effect environment $(\mathbb{E}, \mathbb{C})$ if all effect names in p are present in $\mathbb{E}$.

A refinement type τ is well-formed with respect to Γ, written $\Gamma \vdash \tau$, if its refinement predicate references only variables contained in Γ. A heap type h is well-formed in environment Γ, written $\Gamma \vdash h$, if it binds any location at most once, binds a corresponding abstract location for each concrete location it binds, and contains only well-formed refinement types.

A "world" consisting of a refinement type, heap type, and heap effect is well-formed with respect to environment Γ, written $\Gamma \vdash \tau/h/\Sigma$, if, with respect to the environment Γ, the type and heap type are well-formed and the heap effect Σ is well-formed with respect to the heap h.

The rule for determining the well-formedness of function type schemes is standard.

Pure Expression Typing. The rules for typing a pure expression a in an environment Γ, written $\Gamma \vdash a : \tau$, are straightforward, and are deferred to [16]. These rules assign each pure expression a refinement type that records the exact value of the expression.

Expression Typing and Effect Tracking. Figure 5 shows the rules for typing expressions which explicitly manipulate heap effects to track or compose side-effects. Each expression is typed with a refinement type, a refinement heap assigning types to the heap's contents after evaluating the expression, and an effect which records how the expression accesses each heap location as a mapping from locations to effect formulas. We use the abbreviation `void` to indicate the type $\{\nu : \texttt{int}(0) \mid \text{true}\}$.

Pointer dereference expressions $*v$ are typed by the rule [T-READ]. The value v is typed to find the location and index into which it points in the heap; the type of the expression is the type at this location and index. The rule records the read's effect in the heap by creating a new binding to v's abstract location, $\tilde{l}$, and uses the auxiliary function *logEffect* to create an effect formula which states that the only location that is accessed by this dereference is exactly that pointed to by v (*i.e.,* $\nu = v$), that the location is read (*i.e.,* $\text{Read}(\nu)$), and that no other effect occurs.

The rules for typing heap-mutating expressions of the form $*v_1 := v_2$, [T-SUPD] and [T-WUPD], are similar to [T-READ]. The two rules for mutation differ only in whether they perform a strong update on the type of the heap, *i.e.,* writing through a pointer with a singleton index strongly updates the type of the heap, while writing through a pointer with a sequence index does not.

Expressions are sequenced using the **let** construct, typed by rule [T-LET]. The majority of the rule is standard; we discuss only the portion concerning effects. The rule types expressions e_1 and e_2 to yield their respective effects Σ_1 and Σ_2. The effect of the entire **let** expression is the composition of the two effects, $\Sigma_1 \oplus \Sigma_2$, defined in Figure 5. We check that Σ_2 is well-formed in the initial environment to ensure that the variable x does not escape its scope.

Rule [T-PAR] types the parallel composition expression $e_1 \parallel e_2$. Expressions e_1 and e_2 are typed to obtain their effects Σ_1 and Σ_2. We then use the OK judgment, defined in Figure 5, to verify that effects Σ_1 and Σ_2 commute, *i.e.,* that the program remains deterministic regardless of the interleaving of the two concurrently-executing expressions. We give $e_1 \parallel e_2$ the effect $\Sigma_1 \oplus \Sigma_2$. We require that the input heap for a parallel composition expression must be *abstract*, that is, contain only bindings for parallel compositions; this forces the expressions which are run in parallel to unfold any locations they access, which in turn enforces

Typing Rules $\boxed{\Phi, \Gamma, h \vdash e : \tau/h_2/\Sigma}$

$$\frac{\Gamma \vdash v : \texttt{ref}(l_j, i) \qquad h = h_1 * l_j \mapsto \ldots, i{:}\tau, \ldots}{\Phi, \Gamma, h \vdash *v : \tau/h/\tilde{l} \mapsto \mathit{logEffect}(v, \text{Read})} \text{[T-READ]}$$

$$\frac{\begin{array}{c} h = h_1 * l_j \mapsto \ldots, n{:}b, \ldots \\ \Gamma \vdash v_1 : \texttt{ref}(l_j, n) \qquad \Gamma \vdash v_2 : b \\ h' = h_1 * l_j \mapsto \ldots, n{:}\{\nu : b \mid \nu = v_2\}, \ldots \end{array}}{\Phi, \Gamma, h \vdash *v_1 := v_2 : \texttt{void}/h'/\tilde{l} \mapsto \mathit{logEffect}(v_1, \text{Write})} \text{[T-SUPD]}$$

$$\frac{\begin{array}{c} \Gamma \vdash v_1 : \texttt{ref}(l_j, n^{+m}) \\ \Gamma \vdash v_2 : \hat{\tau} \qquad h = h_1 * l_j \mapsto \ldots, n^{+m}{:}\hat{\tau}, \ldots \end{array}}{\Phi, \Gamma, h \vdash *v_1 := v_2 : \texttt{void}/h/\tilde{l} \mapsto \mathit{logEffect}(v_1, \text{Write})} \text{[T-WUPD]}$$

$$\frac{\begin{array}{c} \Phi, \Gamma, h \vdash e_1 : \tau_1/h_1/\Sigma_1 \\ \Phi, \Gamma; x{:}\tau_1, h_1 \vdash e_2 : \hat{\tau}_2/\hat{h}_2/\hat{\Sigma}_2 \qquad \Gamma \vdash \hat{\tau}_2/\hat{h}_2/\hat{\Sigma}_2 \end{array}}{\Phi, \Gamma, h \vdash \textbf{let } x = e_1 \textbf{ in } e_2 : \hat{\tau}_2/\hat{h}_2/\Sigma_1 \oplus \hat{\Sigma}_2} \text{[T-LET]}$$

$$\frac{\begin{array}{c} \Phi, \Gamma, h \vdash e_1 : \tau_1/\hat{h}'/\hat{\Sigma}_1 \qquad \Phi, \Gamma, h \vdash e_2 : \tau_2/\hat{h}'/\hat{\Sigma}_2 \\ \Phi, \Gamma, \hat{h}' \vdash \hat{\Sigma}_{\{1,2\}} \qquad \Phi, \Gamma \vdash OK(\hat{\Sigma}_1, \hat{\Sigma}_2) \qquad h \text{ abstract} \end{array}}{\Phi, \Gamma, h \vdash e_1 \parallel e_2 : \texttt{void}/\hat{h}'/\hat{\Sigma}_1 \oplus \hat{\Sigma}_2} \text{[T-PAR]}$$

$$\frac{\begin{array}{c} \Gamma \vdash v_1 : \texttt{int}(i) \qquad \Gamma \vdash v_2 : \texttt{int}(i) \\ \Gamma_1 = \Gamma; x{:}\{\nu : \texttt{int}(i) \mid v_1 \leq \nu < v_2\} \\ \Phi, \Gamma_1, h \vdash e : \tau/h/\Sigma \qquad y \text{ fresh} \\ \Gamma_2 = \Gamma_1; y{:}\{\nu : \texttt{int}(i) \mid v_1 \leq \nu < v_2 \wedge \nu \neq x\} \\ \Phi, \Gamma_2 \vdash OK(\Sigma, \Sigma[x \mapsto y]) \\ \Phi, \Gamma, h \vdash \tau/h/\hat{\Sigma}' \qquad \Gamma_1 \vdash \Sigma <: \hat{\Sigma}' \qquad h \text{ abstract} \end{array}}{\Phi, \Gamma, h \vdash \textbf{for each } x \textbf{ in } v_1 \textbf{ to } v_2\ \{e\} : \texttt{void}/h/\hat{\Sigma}'} \text{[T-FOREACH]}$$

$$\frac{\begin{array}{c} \Gamma \vdash v : \{\nu : \texttt{ref}(\tilde{l}, i_y) \mid \nu \neq 0\} \\ h = h_0 * \tilde{l} \mapsto \overline{n_k : \tau_k}, \overline{i^+ : \tau^+} \\ \theta = [\overline{@n_k \mapsto x_k}] \qquad \overline{x_k} \text{ fresh} \qquad \Gamma_1 = \Gamma; \overline{x_k : \theta\tau_k} \\ l_j \text{ fresh} \qquad h_1 = h * l_j \mapsto \overline{n_k : \{\nu = x_k\}}, \overline{i^+ : \theta\tau^+} \\ \Phi, \Gamma_1; x{:}\{\nu : \texttt{ref}(l_j, i_y) \mid \nu = v\}, h_1 \vdash e : \hat{\tau}_2/\hat{h}_2/\hat{\Sigma} \\ \Gamma_1 \vdash h_1 \qquad \Gamma \vdash \hat{\tau}_2/\hat{h}_2/\hat{\Sigma} \\ \Sigma = \hat{\Sigma} \oplus \{(\tilde{l} \mapsto \mathit{logEffect}(\text{BB}(\nu) + n_k, \text{Read}))\}_{n_k} \end{array}}{\Phi, \Gamma, h \vdash \textbf{letu } x = \textbf{unfold } v \textbf{ in } e : \hat{\tau}_2/\hat{h}_2/\Sigma} \text{[T-UNFOLD]}$$

$$\frac{h = h_0 * \tilde{l} \mapsto \hat{c}_1 * l_j \mapsto c_2 \qquad \Gamma \vdash c_2 <: \hat{c}_1}{\Phi, \Gamma, h \vdash \textbf{fold } L : \texttt{void}/h_0 * \tilde{l} \mapsto \hat{c}_1/\varepsilon} \text{[T-FOLD]}$$

Effects Checking $\boxed{\Gamma \vdash OK(\Sigma_1, \Sigma_2)}$

$$\frac{\begin{array}{c} \Psi(E_1, E_2) = \pi(p_1, E_1) \wedge \pi(p_2, E_2) \\ \forall (E_1, E_2) \in (\mathbb{E} \times \mathbb{E}) \setminus \mathbb{C}.\mathsf{Unsat}([\![\Gamma]\!] \wedge \Psi(E_1, E_2)) \end{array}}{\Gamma \vdash OK(p_1, p_2)}$$

$$\frac{\forall l \in \mathit{Dom}(\Sigma_1 \oplus \Sigma_2). \Gamma \vdash OK(\text{LU}(\Sigma_1, l), \text{LU}(\Sigma_2, l))}{\Gamma \vdash OK(\Sigma_1, \Sigma_2)}$$

Effects Operations

$$\Sigma_1 \oplus \Sigma_2 \doteq \{l \mapsto \text{LU}(\Sigma_1, l) \vee \text{LU}(\Sigma_2, l)\}_{l \in \bigcup \mathit{Dom}(\Sigma_{1,2})}$$

$$\text{LU}(\Sigma, l) \doteq \begin{cases} \Sigma(l) & l \in \mathit{Dom}(\Sigma) \\ \text{false} & \text{o.w.} \end{cases}$$

$$\pi(p, E) \doteq p[E \mapsto \text{Check}] \wedge \text{Check}(\nu)$$

$$\mathit{logEffect}(v, E) \doteq E(\nu) \wedge \nu = v \wedge_{E' \in \mathbb{E} \setminus \{E\}} \neg E'(\nu)$$

Figure 5. Typing Rules

several invariants that will prevent the type system from unsoundly assuming invariants in one thread which may be broken by the heap writes performed in another. We elaborate on this below.

Rule [T-FOREACH] types the **foreach** parallel loop expression. The loop induction variable i ranges over values between v_1 and v_2, exclusive; we type the body expression e in the environment enriched with an appropriate binding for i and compute the resulting heap and per-iteration effect Σ. We require that the heap is loop-invariant. To ensure that the behavior of the **foreach** loop is deterministic, we must check that the effects of distinct iterations do not interfere. Hence, we check non-interference at two arbitrary, distinct iterations by adding a binding for a fresh name j to the environment with the invariant that $i \neq j$, and verifying with OK that the effect at an iteration i, Σ, commutes with the effect at a distinct iteration j, $\Sigma[i \mapsto j]$. We return Σ', which subsumes Σ but is well-formed in the original environment, ensuring that the loop induction variable i does not escape its scope. As with [T-PAR], we require that the input heap is abstract, for the same reasons.

Strong Updates and Concurrency. The rules [T-UNFOLD] and [T-FOLD] are used to implement a local non-aliasing discipline for performing strong updates on the types of heap locations when only one pointer to the location is accessed at a time. The mechanism is similar to freeze/thaw and adopt/focus [34, 10]. These rules are treated in previous work [28]; we now discuss how these rules handle effects and briefly recap their handling of strong updates.

Rule [T-UNFOLD] types the **letu** construct for unfolding a pointer to an abstract location, $\tilde{l}$, to obtain a pointer to a corresponding concrete location, l_j, bound to the variable x. [T-UNFOLD] constructs the block bound to l_j by creating a skolem variable x_j for each binding of a singleton index n_j to a type τ_j; the binding is a singleton index in a concrete location, so it corresponds to exactly one datum on the heap. We apply an appropriate substitution to the elements within the block, then typecheck the body expression e with respect to the extended heap and enriched environment. Well-formedness constraints ensure that an abstract location is never unfolded twice in the same scope and that x does not escape its scope.

We allow two concurrently-executing expressions to unfold, and thus simultaneously access, the same abstract location. When a location is unfolded, our type system records the refinement types bound to each of its singleton indices in the environment. If we do not take care, the refinement types bound to singleton indices and recorded in the environment may be invalidated by an effect (*e.g.* a write) occurring in a simultaneously-executing expression.Thus, an expression which unfolds a location *implicitly* depends on the data whose invariants are recorded in its environment at the time of unfolding. To capture these implicit dependencies, when a pointer v is unfolded, we conservatively record a pseudo-read [33] at each singleton offset n_k within the block into which v points by recording in the heap effect that the pointer $\text{BB}(v)+n_k$ is read, where $\text{BB}(v)$ is the beginning of the memory block where v points. Then, the invariant recorded in the environment at the unfolding is preserved, as any violating writes would get caught by the determinism check.

Rule [T-FOLD] removes a concrete location from the heap so that a different pointer to the same abstract location may be unfolded. The rule ensures that the currently-unfolded concrete location's block is a subtype of the corresponding abstract location's so that we can be sure that the abstract location's invariant holds when it is unfolded later. The **fold** expression has no heap effect.

Program Typing. The remaining expression forms do not manipulate heap effects; as their typing judgments are straightforward and covered in previous work [28], we defer their definition [16]. We note that the rule for typing **if** expressions records the value of the branch condition in the environment when typing each branch. The judgments for typing function declarations and programs in LC_E are straightforward and are deferred to [16].

Program	LOC	Quals	Annot	Changes	T (s)
Reduce	39	7	7	N/A	8.8
SumReduce	39	1	3	0	1.8
QuickSort	73	3	4	N/A	5.9
MergeSort	95	6	7	0	32.4
IDEA	222	7	5	3	59.7
K-Means	458	7	10	16	63.7

Table 1. (LOC) is the number of source code lines as reported by *sloccount*, (Quals) is the number of logical qualifiers required to prove memory safety and determinism, (Annot) is the number of annotated function signatures plus the number of effect and commutativity declarations. (Changes) is the number of program modifications, (T) is the time in seconds taken for verification.

4.2 Handling Effects

We now describe the auxiliary definitions used by the typing rules of subsection 4.1 for checking effect noninterference.

Combining Effects. In Figure 5, we define the $\oplus$ operator for combining effects. Our decision to encode effects as formulas in first-order logic makes the definition of this operator especially simple: for each location l, the combined effect of Σ_1 and Σ_2 on location l is the disjunction of of the effects on l recorded in Σ_1 and Σ_2. We use the auxiliary function $\text{LU}(\Sigma, l)$ to look up the effect formula for location l in Σ; if there is no binding for l in Σ, the false formula, indicating no effect, is returned instead.

Effects Checking. We check the noninterference of heap effects Σ_1, Σ_2 using the OK judgment, defined in Figure 5. The effects are noninterfering if the formulas bound to locations in both heap effects are pairwise noninterfering. Two effect formulas p_1 and p_2 are noninterfering as follows. For each pair of non-commuting effects E_1 and E_2 in the set $\mathbb{E}$, we project the set of pointers in p_1 (resp., p_2) which are accessed with effect E_1 (resp., E_2) using the effect projection operator π. Now, if the conjunction of the projected formulas is unsatisfiable, the effect formulas are noninterfering.

User-Defined Effects and Commutativity. We allow our set of effects $\mathbb{E}$ to be extended with additional effect label predicates by the user. To specify how these effects interact, commutativity annotations can be provided that indicate which effects do not result in nondeterministic behavior when run simultaneously. Then, the user may override the effect of any function by providing an effect Σ as an annotation, allowing additional flexibility to specify domain-specific effects or override the effect system if needed.

5. Evaluation

We have implemented the techniques in this paper as an extension to CSOLVE, a refinement type-based verifier for C. CSOLVE takes as input a C program and a set of logical qualifiers, or formulas over the value variable ν, to use in refinement and effect inference. CSOLVE then checks the program both for memory safety errors (*e.g.* out-of-bounds array accesses, null pointer dereferences) and non-determinism. If CSOLVE determines that the program is free from such errors, it outputs an annotation file containing the types of program variables, heaps, functions, and heap effects. If CSOLVE cannot determine that the program is safe, it outputs an error message with the line number of the potential error and the inferred types of the program variables in scope at that location.

Type and Effect Inference. CSOLVE infers refinement types and effect formulas using the predicate abstraction-based Liquid Types [28] technique; we give a high-level overview here. We note that there are expressions whose refinement types and heap effects cannot be constructed from the types and heap effects of subexpressions or from bindings in the heap and environment but instead

```
<region r1,r2,r3 | r1:* # r3:*, r2:* # r3:*> void
merge(DPJArrayInt<r1> a, DPJArrayInt<r2> b, DPJArrayInt<r3> c)
  reads r1:*, r2:* writes r3:* {
  if (a.length <= merge_size)
    seq_merge(a, b, c);
  else {
    int ha=a.length/2, sb=split(a.get(ha),b);
    final DPJPartitionInt<r1> a_split=new DPJPartitionInt<r1>(a,hd);
    final DPJPartitionInt<r2> a_split=new DPJPartitionInt<r2>(b,sb);
    final DPJPartitionInt<r3> c_split=new DPJPartitionInt<r3>(c,ha+sb);
    cobegin { merge(a_split.get(0),b_split.get(0),c_split.get(0));
              merge(a_split.get(1),b_split.get(1),c_split.get(1)); }}}
```

Figure 6. DPJ merge function

```
qualif Q(V: ptr) : &&[_ <= V; V {<, >=} (_ + _ + _)]

void merge(int* ARRAY LOC(L) a,
           int* ARRAY LOC(L) b,
           int la, int lb, int* ARRAY c) {
  if (la <= merge_size){
    seq_merge(a, b, la, lb, c);
  } else {
    int ha = la / 2, sb = split(a[ha],b,lb);
    cobegin {
      merge(a,b,ha,sb,c);
      merge(a+ha,b+sb,la-ha,lb-sb,c+ha+sb); }}}
```

Figure 7. CSolve merge function

must be *synthesized*. For example, the function typing rule requires us to synthesize types, heaps, and heap effects for functions. This is comparable to inferring pre- and post-conditions for functions (and similarly, loop invariants), which reduces to determining appropriate formulas for refinement types and effects. To make inference tractable, we require that formulas contained in synthesized types, heaps, and heap effects are *liquid, i.e.,* conjunctions of *logical qualifier* formulas provided by the user. These qualifiers are templates for predicates that may appear in types or effects. We read our inference rules as an algorithm for constructing subtyping constraints which, when solved, yield a refinement typing for the program.

Methodology. To evaluate our approach, we drew from the set of Deterministic Parallel Java (DPJ) benchmarks reported in [2]. For those which were parallelized using the methods we support, namely heap effects and commutativity annotations, we verified determinism and memory safety using our system. Our goals for the evaluation were to show that our system was as expressive as DPJ's for these benchmarks while requiring less program restructuring.

Results. The results of running CSolve on the following benchmarks are presented in Table 1. `Reduce` is the program given in section 2. `SumReduce` initializes an array using parallel iteration, then sums the results using a parallel divide-and-conquer strategy. `MergeSort` divides an array into quarters, recursively sorting each in parallel. It then merges pairs of sorted quarters in parallel, and finally merges the two sorted halves to yield a single sorted array. The final merges are performed recursively in parallel. `QuickSort` is a standard in-place quicksort adapted from a sequential version included with DPJ. We parallelized the algorithm by partitioning the input array around its median, then recursively sorting each partition in parallel. `K-Means` was adapted from the STAMP benchmarks [23], the C implementation that was ported for DPJ. `IDEA` is an encryption/decryption kernel ported to C from DPJ.

Changes. Some benchmarks required modifications in order to conform to the current implementation of CSolve; this does not indicate inherent limitations in the technique. These include: multi-dimensionalizing flattened arrays, writing stubs for matrix **malloc**, expanding structure fields (`K-Means`), and soundly abstracting non-linear operations and `#define`-ing configuration parameters to constants to work around a bug in the SMT solver (`IDEA`).

Annotations. CSolve requires two classes of annotations to compute base types for the program. First, the annotation `ARRAY` is required to distinguish between pointers to singletons and pointers to arrays. Second, as base type inference is intraprocedural, we must additionally specify which pointer parameters may be aliased by annotating them with a location parameter of the form `LOC(L)`.

Qualitative Comparison. Since the annotations used by CSolve and DPJ are very different, a quantitative comparison between them is not meaningful. Instead, we illustrate the kinds of annotations used by each tool and qualitatively compare them. Figures 6, 7 contain DPJ, and CSolve code, resp., implementing the recursive `Merge` routine from `MergeSort`, including region annotations and required wrapper classes. In the latter, `Merge` takes two arrays `a` and `b` and recursively splits them, sequentially merging them into array `c` at a target size. In particular, each statement in the cobegin writes to a different contiguous interval of `c`.

In DPJ, verifying this invariant requires: First, wrapping all arrays with an API class `DPJArrayInt`, and then wrapping each contiguous subarray with another class `DPJArrayPartitionInt`. This must be done because DPJ does not support precise effects over partitions of native Java arrays. Second, the method must be explicitly declared to be polymorphic over named regions `r1`, `r2`, and `r3`, corresponding to the memory locations in which the formals reside. Finally, `Merge` must be explicitly annotated with the appropriate effects, *i.e.,* it reads `r1` and `r2` and writes `r3`.

In CSolve, verifying this invariant requires: First, specifying that `a` and `b` are potentially aliased arrays (the annotation `LOC(L) ARRAY`). Second, we specify the qualifiers used to synthesize refinement types and heap effects via the line starting with `qualif`. This specification says that a predicate of the given form may appear in a type or effect, with the wildcard _ replaced by any program identifier in scope for that type or effect. Using the given qualifier, CSolve infers that `a` and `b`'s location is only read, and that `c`'s location is only written at indices described by the formula $c \leq \nu < c + la + lb$, which suffices to prove determinism.

Unlike DPJ, CSolve does not require invasive changes to code (*e.g.* explicit array partitioning), and hence supports domain- and program-specific sharing patterns (*e.g.* memory coalescing from Figure 2). However, this comes at the cost of providing qualifiers. In future work, abstract interpretation may help lessen this burden.

6. Related Work

We limit our discussion to static mechanisms for checking and enforcing determinism, in particular the literature that pertains to reasoning about heap disjointness: type-and-effect systems, semantic determinism checking, and other closely related techniques.

Named Regions. Region-based approaches assign references (or objects) to distinct segments of the heap, which are explicitly named and manipulated by the programmer. This approach was introduced in the context of adding impure computations to a functional language, and developed as a means of controlling the side-effects incurred by segments of code in sequential programs [20, 21]. Effects were also investigated in the context of safe, programmer-controlled memory management [31, 15, 19]. Ideas from this work led to the notion of abstract heap locations [34, 13, 10] and our notion of fold and unfold.

Ownership Types. In the OO setting, regions are closely related to *ownership types* which use the class hierarchy of the program to separate the heap into disjoint, nested regions [9, 29]. In addition to isolation, ownership types can be used to track effects [8], and to reason about data races and deadlocks [6, 4, 22].

Such techniques can be used to enforce determinism [30], but regions and ownership relations are not enough to enforce fine-grained separation. Instead, we must precisely track relations between program variables. We are inspired by DPJ [2], which shows how some sharing patterns can be captured in a dependent region system. However, we show the full expressiveness of refinement type inference and SMT solvers can be brought to bear to enable complex, low-level sharing with static determinism guarantees.

Checking Properties of Multithreaded Programs. Several authors have looked into type-and-effect systems for checking other properties of multithreaded programs. For example, [11, 24] show how types can be used to prevent races, [12] describes an effect discipline that encodes Lipton's Reduction method for proving atomicity. Our work focuses on the higher-level semantic property of determinism. Nevertheless, it would be useful to understand how race-freedom and atomicity could be used to establish determinism. Others [27, 3] have looked at proving that different blocks of operations *commute*. In future work, we could use these to automatically generate effect labels and commutativity constraints.

Program Logics and Abstract Interpretation. There is a vast literature on the use of logic (and abstract interpretation) to reason about sets of addresses (*i.e.,* the heap). The literature on logically reasoning about the heap includes the pioneering work in TVLA [35], separation logic [26], and the direct encoding of heaps in first-order logic [17, 18], or with explicit sets of addresses called dynamic frames [14]. These logics have also been applied to reason about concurrency and parallelism: [25] looks at using separation logic to obtain (deterministic) parallel programs, and [35] uses abstract interpretation to find loop invariants for multithreaded, heap-manipulating Java programs. The above look at analyzing disjointness for linked data structures. The most closely related to our work is [32], which uses intra-procedural numeric abstract interpretation to determine the set of array indices used by different threads, and then checks disjointness over the domains.

Our work differs in that we show how to consolidate all the above lines of work into a uniform location-based heap abstraction (for separation logic-style disjoint structures) with type refinements that track finer-grained invariants. Unlike [25], we can verify access patterns that require sophisticated arithmetic reasoning, and unlike [32] we can check separation between disjoint structures, and even indices drawn from compound structures like arrays, lists and so on. Our type system allows "context-sensitive" reasoning about (recursive) procedures. Further, first-order refinements allow us to verify domain-specific sharing patterns via first class effect labels [21].

References

[1] Nvidia cuda programming guide.

[2] S. V. Adve, S. Heumann, R. Komuravelli, J. Overbey, P. Simmons, H. Sung, and M. Vakilian. A type and effect system for deterministic parallel java. In *OOPSLA*, 2009.

[3] F. Aleen and N. Clark. Commutativity analysis for software parallelization: letting program transformations see the big picture. In *ASPLOS*, 2009.

[4] Z. R. Anderson, D. Gay, R. Ennals, and E. A. Brewer. Sharc: checking data sharing strategies for multithreaded c. In *PLDI*, 2008.

[5] A. Aviram, S.-C. Weng, S. Hu, and B. Ford. Efficient system-enforced deterministic parallelism. In *OSDI*, 2010.

[6] C. Boyapati, R. Lee, and M. C. Rinard. Ownership types for safe programming: preventing data races and deadlocks. In *OOPSLA*, 2002.

[7] M. Chakravarty, G. Keller, R. Lechtchinsky, and W. Pfannenstiel. Nepal: Nested data parallelism in haskell. In *Euro-Par*, 2001.

[8] D. G. Clarke and S. Drossopoulou. Ownership, encapsulation and the disjointness of type and effect. In *OOPSLA*, 2002.

[9] D. G. Clarke, J. Noble, and J. M. Potter. Simple ownership types for object containment. In *ECOOP*, 2001.

[10] R. DeLine and M. Fähndrich. Enforcing high-level protocols in low-level software. In *PLDI*, 2001.

[11] C. Flanagan and S. N. Freund. Type-based race detection for java. In *PLDI*, pages 219–232, 2000.

[12] C. Flanagan and S. Qadeer. A type and effect system for atomicity. In *PLDI*, 2003.

[13] J. Foster, T. Terauchi, and A. Aiken. Flow-sensitive type qualifiers. In *PLDI*, 2002.

[14] B. Jacobs, F. Piessens, J. Smans, K. R. M. Leino, and W. Schulte. A programming model for concurrent object-oriented programs. *TOPLAS*, 2008.

[15] T. Jim, J. G. Morrisett, D. Grossman, M. W. Hicks, J. Cheney, and Y. Wang. Cyclone: A safe dialect of c. In *USENIX*, 2002.

[16] M. Kawaguchi, P. Rondon, A. Bakst, and R. Jhala. Liquid effects: Technical report. `http://goto.ucsd.edu/~rjhala/liquid`.

[17] S. K. Lahiri and S. Qadeer. Back to the future: revisiting precise program verification using smt solvers. In *POPL*, 2008.

[18] S. K. Lahiri, S. Qadeer, and D. Walker. Linear maps. In *PLPV*, 2011.

[19] C. Lattner and V. S. Adve. Automatic pool allocation: improving performance by controlling data structure layout in the heap. In *PLDI*, 2005.

[20] K. R. M. Leino, A. Poetzsch-Heffter, and Y. Zhou. Using data groups to specify and check side effects, 2002.

[21] D. Marino and T. D. Millstein. A generic type-and-effect system. In A. Kennedy and A. Ahmed, editors, *TLDI*, pages 39–50. ACM, 2009.

[22] J.-P. Martin, M. Hicks, M. Costa, P. Akritidis, and M. Castro. Dynamically checking ownership policies in concurrent c/c++ programs. In *POPL*, pages 457–470, 2010.

[23] C. C. Minh, J. Chung, C. Kozyrakis, and K. Olukotun. Stamp: Stanford transactional applications for multi-processing. In *IISWC*, 2008.

[24] P. Pratikakis, J. S. Foster, and M. W. Hicks. Locksmith: context-sensitive correlation analysis for race detection. In *PLDI*, 2006.

[25] M. Raza, C. Calcagno, and P. Gardner. Automatic parallelization with separation logic. In *ESOP*, pages 348–362, 2009.

[26] J. C. Reynolds. Separation logic: A logic for shared mutable data structures. In *LICS*, pages 55–74, 2002.

[27] M. C. Rinard and P. C. Diniz. Commutativity analysis: A new analysis technique for parallelizing compilers. *TOPLAS*, 19(6), 1997.

[28] P. Rondon, M. Kawaguchi, and R. Jhala. Low-level liquid types. In *POPL*, 2010.

[29] M. Smith. Towards an effects system for ownership domains. In *In ECOOP Workshop - FTfJP 2005*, 2005.

[30] T. Terauchi and A. Aiken. A capability calculus for concurrency and determinism. *TOPLAS*, 30, 2008.

[31] M. Tofte and J.-P. Talpin. A theory of stack allocation in polymorphically typed languages, 1993.

[32] M. T. Vechev, E. Yahav, R. Raman, and V. Sarkar. Automatic verification of determinism for structured parallel programs. In *SAS*, 2010.

[33] J. Voung, R. Chugh, R. Jhala, and S. Lerner. Dataflow analysis for concurrent programs using data race detection. In *PLDI*, 2008.

[34] D. Walker and J. Morrisett. Alias types for recursive data structures. 2000.

[35] E. Yahav and M. Sagiv. Verifying safety properties of concurrent heap-manipulating programs. *TOPLAS*, 32(5), 2010.

Speculative Linearizability

Rachid Guerraoui Viktor Kuncak Giuliano Losa

School of Computer and Communication Sciences
Swiss Federal Institute of Technology Lausanne (EPFL)
rachid.guerraoui@epfl.ch viktor.kuncak@epfl.ch giuliano.losa@epfl.ch

Abstract

Linearizability is a key design methodology for reasoning about implementations of concurrent abstract data types in both shared memory and message passing systems. It provides the illusion that operations execute sequentially and fault-free, despite the asynchrony and faults inherent to a concurrent system, especially a distributed one. A key property of linearizability is inter-object composability: a system composed of linearizable objects is itself linearizable. However, devising linearizable objects is very difficult, requiring complex algorithms to work correctly under general circumstances, and often resulting in bad average-case behavior. Concurrent algorithm designers therefore resort to speculation: optimizing algorithms to handle common scenarios more efficiently. The outcome are even more complex protocols, for which it is no longer tractable to prove their correctness.

To simplify the design of efficient yet robust linearizable protocols, we propose a new notion: *speculative linearizability*. This property is as general as linearizability, yet it allows intra-object composability: the correctness of independent protocol phases implies the correctness of their composition. In particular, it allows the designer to focus solely on the proof of an optimization and derive the correctness of the overall protocol from the correctness of the existing, non-optimized one.

Our notion of protocol phases allows processes to independently switch from one phase to another, without requiring them to reach agreement to determine the change of a phase. To illustrate the applicability of our methodology, we show how examples of speculative algorithms for shared memory and asynchronous message passing naturally fit into our framework.

We rigorously define speculative linearizability and prove our intra-object composition theorem in a trace-based as well as an automaton-based model. To obtain a further degree of confidence, we also formalize and mechanically check the theorem in the automaton-based model, using the I/O automata framework within the Isabelle interactive proof assistant. We expect our framework to enable, for the first time, scalable specifications and mechanical proofs of speculative implementations of linearizable objects.

Categories and Subject Descriptors D.1.3 [*Software*]: Concurrent Programming

Keywords Speculation, Distributed Systems, Modularity

PLDI'12, June 11–16, 2012, Beijing, China.

1. Introduction

The correctness of a system of processes communicating through linearizable objects [12, 17, 18] reduces to the correctness of the sequential executions of that system. In other words, linearizability reduces the difficult problem of reasoning about concurrent data types to that of reasoning about sequential ones. In this sense, the use of linearizable objects greatly simplifies the construction of concurrent systems. At first glance, the design and implementation of linearizable objects themselves looks also simple. One can focus on each object independently, design the underlying linearizable algorithm, implement and test it, and then compose it with algorithms ensuring the linearizability of the other objects of the system. In short, linearizability is preserved by *inter-object composition*: a set of objects is linearizable if and only if each object is linearizable when considered independently of the others.

However, it is extremely difficult to devise efficient and robust implementations of a linearizable object, even when considered independently from the others. The difficulty stems from the following dilemma. On the one hand, achieving robustness in a concurrent system requires assuming that the scheduling of processes, communication, and faults is completely nondeterministic. The object does not know which execution is going to unfold but needs to deliver a response to each of its method invocations no matter the execution. The object has to prepare for all scenarios, using up its resources for that task. This *conservative* approach typically yields *wait-free* [11] but inefficient strategies. On the other hand, achieving efficiency requires *speculating* that only a small subset of executions is likely to occur [23]. This is practically appealing because a real system typically spends most of its time in a common case and seldom experiences periods of alternative executions. Should the object focus on a very small subset of executions, it would save resources by preparing only for that restricted subset. Typically, the common cases that are usually considered in practice are those where the system is synchronous, there is no failure, contention is not very high, a specific conditional branch is to be considered, etc. At a high level, a speculative system repeats the following steps:

1. Speculate about the likelihood of certain executions and choose a corresponding algorithm.
2. Initialize the chosen algorithm.
3. Monitor the algorithm to estimate if the speculation was accurate. If not, abort the algorithm and recover a consistent state.

Examples of speculation include the Ethernet protocol, where processes speculatively occupy a single-user communication medium before backing off if collision is detected, or branch prediction in microprocessors, where the processor speculates that a particular branch in the code will be taken before discarding its computation if this is not the case. More recent instances of speculation include optimistic replication [15] or adaptive mutual exclusion [14]. In fact, most practical concurrent systems are speculative. In general, speculative systems may choose between many different options, or *speculation phases*, in order to closely match a changing common case.

To illustrate the challenges addressed in this work, consider a speculative algorithm that may switch between any two of n speculation phases in a safe manner. That is, recovering a consistent state of the first phase and then initializing the second. Doing so in an ad-hoc manner poses two major *scalability* problems to the design process. First, there are $O(n^2)$ different switching cases that need to be carefully handled in order to preserve linearizability. Second, adding a new phase to an object composed of n phases built ad-hoc may require deep changes to all of the n existing phases.

The case of State Machine Replication [16] (abbreviated SMR), used to build robust linearizable object implementations, illustrates those problems. Non-speculative SMR algorithms like Paxos [7] or PBFT [6] are notoriously hard to understand. The formal correctness proof of Disk Paxos [13] took about 7000 lines. Only an informal proof, 35 pages long, of a simplified version of PBFT is known to the authors [5]. Speculative SMR protocols are even harder. For instance, the Zyzzyva [15] protocol combines PBFT with a fast path implemented by a simple agreement protocol. The fast path is more efficient than PBFT when there are no failures. In the advent of failures, the fast path cannot make progress and Zyzzyva falls back to executing PBFT. The ad-hoc composition of the fast path with PBFT required deep changes to both algorithms and resulted in an entanglement that is hardly understandable. Although PBFT had previously been widely tested [5], Zyzzyva suffered from fragile implementations and no correctness proof has ever been proposed. In fact, Zyzzyva, being restricted to two phases, is very fragile [24]. If the common case is not what is expected by the fast path one falls-back to PBFT, making the optimization useless. An adversary can easily weaken the system by always making it abort the fast path and go through the slow one. Introducing a new dimension of speculation might make the protocol more robust but would require a new ad-hoc composition, including an alternative fast-path, at a cost comparable to the effort needed to build Zyzzyva from scratch, namely a Dantean effort. Given the diversity of situations encountered in practice, we are convinced that this ad-hoc approach is simply intractable.

Contributions. We propose in this paper a framework for devising, reasoning about, and mechanically verifying effective and robust linearizable implementations of concurrent data types in a scalable way. In short, we show how speculative implementations of linearizable objects can be devised and analyzed in an *incremental* manner. One can focus on each dimension of speculation independently of the others. For example, a programmer can first devise an algorithm with no speculation, implement, test, and prove it correct, then augment it later with an optimization that speculates that a certain subset of executions is more likely to occur (say there is no failure). This optimization sub-algorithm is composed with the original one as is. Later, another programmer can consider other dimensions of speculations (say there is no contention or asynchrony) and add new phases, still without modifying the original implementation and proofs.

At the heart of our framework lies our new notion, *speculative linearizability*. Speculative linearizability encompasses the notion of *switch actions*, which makes it significantly richer than linearizability, yet it reduces to linearizability if these actions are ignored. Speculative linearizability augments classical linearizability with a new aspect of composition. Not only a system of concurrent objects can be considered correct if each of them is correct (*inter-object composition*), but a set of algorithms implementing different speculation phases of the *same* object is correct if each of them is correct (*intra-object composition*). We express this new aspect

```
//Shared Register V, Initially ⊥
Function propose(val):
if V = ⊥ then
    V ← val
    return val
else
    return V
end if
```

Figure 1. Consensus Specification

through a new composition theorem which we state and prove. Intuitively, speculative linearizability captures the idea of *safe* and *live abortability*. An implementation can abort if the assumptions behind speculation reveals wrong. When it does abort, it does so in a safe manner, by preserving the consistency (linearizability) of the object state. Moreover, the abort is also performed in a live manner, because a new protocol phase can resume and make progress. Processes can switch independently from one phase to another, without the need to reach agreement. Our notion of speculative linearizability is itself based on a new definition of linearizability. This definition is interesting in its own right because it enables a more local form of reasoning than the original definition and it allows for repeated events, which are the norm in practice. We have proved that our new definition of linearizability is equivalent to the classical definition.

The generality of our framework and its Isabelle/HOL formalization [10] sets our work apart from state of the art in the area [1, 2, 8]: we enable for the first time scalable mechanically-checked development of linearizable objects of arbitrary abstract data types.

Additional proofs and formalizations are available in [9, 10], as well as at `http://lara.epfl.ch/w/slin`.

2. Putting Speculative Linearizability to Work

In this section we provide intuition for speculative linearizability and its key property: intra-object composability. Our goal is to motivate correct-by-construction design of objects based on speculation phases. As an illustration, we present two speculative implementations of a consensus object. Each is composed of two speculation phases. The first applies to the message-passing computation model and the other to the shared-memory model. We analyze each phase of those speculative implementations in isolation and conclude, using the intra-object composition theorem, that their compositions are correct implementations of consensus.

2.1 Message-Passing Consensus

Our first example is a consensus implementation in a system composed of client and server processes which communicate by asynchronous message passing and which may crash at any point. Our goal is to implement consensus among the clients. Notable use cases of consensus in message-passing systems include Google's Chubby distributed lock service [4] and the Gaios reliable data store [3].

Consensus allows a set of clients to agree on a common value. Clients each propose a value and should receive a common decision value taken among their proposals. We consider implementations that offer an invocation function *propose*($value$) to each of its clients. The invocation *propose*(val) returns another value indicating the common decision. When a process returns from *propose*($value$) with a value d, we say the it *decides* value d. An algorithm is linearizable with respect to the consensus data type if all calls to *propose*(val) appear as if they executed atomically the algorithm in Figure 1 at some point after their invocation (we assume that proposal are different from $\perp$).

In an asynchronous message-passing system where processes may crash, there is no component which can reliably hold state. Hence, some crucial data may become unavailable due to the failure of a process. For example, a process may decide some value and then crash before informing any other process of its decision. In this case other processes have no way to know which value the crashed process decided and they cannot decide without risking to violate consensus.

Paxos [7] is an algorithm that implements consensus if less than half of the servers may fail. Paxos has a minimum latency of 3 message delays. However, suppose that executions are fault free and contention free (i.e. the time intervals delimited by corresponding invocations and responses do not overlap). Under this assumption, very simple algorithms can solve consensus much faster than Paxos, which still has a minimum latency of 3 message delays.

We would like to optimize Paxos for the fault-free and contention-free case. This could be done ad-hoc by adding a fast path inside Paxos. However, Paxos is a very intricate algorithm: the proof of Disk Paxos [7], a variant of Paxos, is 7000 lines long [13]. Adding a fast path to Paxos would require re-examining the correctness of the entire algorithm, because the fast path is interleaved with executions of the others parts. The entire proof would, in principle, need to be rewritten.

Our framework allows us to optimize Paxos without directly modifying the original algorithm, and enables reasoning about the correctness of the optimization independently of the basic Paxos itself. To use our framework, we wrap Paxos in a simple interface that allows composition with other speculation phases. This requires adding a trivial level of indirection and makes Paxos a speculation phase in its own right. Speculative linearizability ensures that any speculatively linearizable speculation phase can be composed with the Paxos speculation phase to form a correct implementation of consensus. Moreover, speculative linearizability, instantiated for consensus, is a property independent of Paxos. Therefore, from the point of view of algorithm designers, speculative linearizability hides the internal complexity of Paxos.

In this example we compose Paxos with the *Quorum* speculation phase, inspired from [8]. Quorum manages to decide on the value in only 2 message delays, whenever there is neither contention nor faults. If faults or contention happen, Quorum cannot decide and instead passes control to Paxos. In this case, we say that Quorum *switches* to Paxos. From then on, Paxos takes over the execution and can decide as long as less than half of the processes are faulty. To highlight that Paxos is used as a backup when optimization by Quorum is not possible, we call the Paxos speculation phase Backup. Using speculative linearizability, we will prove that the composition of Quorum and Backup is linearizable by reasoning about Quorum in isolation and by reusing an existing proof of Paxos.

By combining Quorum and Backup we obtain a system that is optimized for contention-free and fault-free loads while still remaining correct in all other conditions under which the Backup is correct. Such an approach has proved empirically successful in recent work [8]; the present paper provides the underlying theoretical foundations for such approaches.

We now describe more precisely the Quorum and Backup speculation phases. Their interface is that of a consensus object, as defined above, augmented with a *switch-to-backup*(sv) call. The *switch-to-backup*(sv) call is used by a client to switch from the Quorum phase to Backup, i.e. *switch-to-backup*(sv) is a procedure of Backup which may be called by a client executing Quorum. The sv parameter is called a *switch value*. A client calling *switch-to-backup*(sv) transfer its pending invocation to Backup and provides sv as an indication to Backup on how to take over Quorum's execution.

Informally, the Quorum algorithm works as follows:

- Upon *propose*(v), a client c broadcasts its proposal to all server processes and waits for accept messages. It also stores v in local variable *proposal*$_c$ of its memory and starts a local timer t_c.
- When a server process receives a proposal v from a client c:
  - If it has not sent any accept message, it sends an accept message $accept(v)$ to c.
  - If it has already sent an accept message $accept(v')$, it sends $accept(v')$ to c.
- If a client receives two different accept messages, it switches to Backup by calling and returning *switch-to-backup*(*proposal*$_c$).
- If a client receives the same accept messages $accept(v)$ from all the servers, then it decides v.
- If timer t_c expires, then c waits for at least one message $accept(v')$ from a server, or selects one v' if it has some messages of the form $accept(v')$ already. It then switches to Backup by calling *switch-to-backup*(v').

The Backup phase is Lamport's Paxos algorithm where clients have the role of proposers and learners, while servers have the role of acceptors. Backup treats the switch calls from Quorum as regular proposals. In other words, upon a call *switch-to-backup*(v), a client process proposes the value v to the Paxos algorithm.

By composing Quorum and Backup we obtain a linearizable implementation of consensus that is optimized for crash-free and contention-free workloads. This new optimized implementation of consensus was obtained by composing a black-box implementation of Paxos with a much simpler protocol, Quorum, which makes progress only under particular conditions.

We next uncover the principles behind this approach and we will show the correctness of our optimized protocol by reasoning about each speculation phase in isolation, independently of each other. Thanks to our modular approach, we will be able to rely the existing proof of Paxos [13] to show the correctness of Backup with minor effort.

2.2 Linearizability

Before explaining *speculative* linearizability, we briefly review linearizability itself: we provide both its classical definition and our new formalization.

We consider a set of concurrent clients accessing an object through *invocation* procedures whose execution ends by returning a *response*, as in the consensus examples above. We assume that each client is sequential. In other words, a client does not invoke the object before having returned from its preceding invocation.

An object is accessed *sequentially* if every response to an invocation immediately follows the invocation. There must be no other response or invocation in between them. For example, the specification of a consensus object states that all processes return the same decision value and that this value must have been proposed by some process before it can be returned. Hence, in a sequential execution, the first proposed value must be returned to every process. Note that this corresponds to executing sequentially the algorithm in Figure 1: The first process executing will impose its value to all others.

We consider only deterministic objects. Therefore, in the sequential case, the response to a given invocation is determined by the sequence of past invocations that the object received. Therefore, we represent a sequential execution by its subsequence containing only and all invocations in the execution. We call such sequences of invocations *histories*.

When accessed concurrently, invocations and responses of different processes may be arbitrarily interleaved. The sequences of invocations and responses that may be observed at the interface of an object that is accessed concurrently are called *traces*. The occurrence of an invocation or a response in a trace is called an *event*, or *action*.

Linearizability is defined with respect to a sequential specification, which is a description of the allowed behaviors of the object when it is accessed sequentially. Intuitively, a trace is linearizable if each invocation appears to take effect at a single point in time after the invocation call and before the corresponding response. This intuitive definition can be restated as follows: A trace t is linearizable if we can associate, to each response r returned by a client c, a history h (called *commit history*) such that:

1. The response r is the response obtained in the sequential execution represented by history h.
2. All invocations in the history h are invoked in the trace t before the response r is returned.
3. The history h ends with the last invocation of client c.
4. For all commit histories h_1 and h_2, either h_1 is a prefix of h_2 or h_2 is a prefix of h_1.

This definition of linearizability is stated precisely in Section 4. In the terminology of Section 4, condition 1 above says that history h *explains* response r. Condition 1 is specific to a particular abstract data type. Conditions 2 and 3 correspond to *Validity*, and 4 to *Commit Order*. They do not depend on the particular ADT considered. We have proved [9] that this definition is equivalent to the original definition of linearizability [12].

As an example, consider a trace of a consensus object such that client c_1 proposes value v_1, then client c_2 proposes value v_2, then client c_2 returns v_2, and finally client c_1 returns v_2. This execution is linearizable because the returned values are as if the invocation of client c_2 was executed atomically before the invocation of client c_1. To show this, associate the history $[propose(v_2)]$ to the response of c_2 and the history $[propose(v_2), propose(v_1)]$ to the response of c_1. It is easy to check that all four conditions above are satisfied. Notably, when applied sequentially to a consensus object, both histories lead to response v_2. By the definition above, the trace is linearizable. Examples of traces that are *not* linearizable include:

$[c_1$ proposes v_1, c_2 proposes v_2, c_1 decides v_1, c_2 decides $v_2]$, as well as:

$[c_1$ proposes v_1, c_1 decides v_2, c_2 proposes v_2, c_2 decides $v_2]$.

2.3 Speculative Linearizability

We now consider modular implementations composed of two speculation phases (the definition generalizes to any number of phases). As in the composition of the Quorum and Backup algorithms, each client process starts by executing the first phase and may *switch* to the second phase using a procedure call, providing an argument that we call a *switch value* along with its pending invocation. In the examples of this section we omit the pending invocation from switch calls for the sake of conciseness.

We would like to reason about each speculation phase in isolation. For this purpose, we require that the switch values provided by the clients when changing phase be the only information passed from one speculation phase to the other. No side effects are permitted across speculation phases. Speculation phases are thus separated by a clear interface: a call to the phase's switch procedure with a switch value and a pending invocation as arguments.

Speculative linearizability is a property of speculation phases that relates the switch events and the invocations received by the speculation phase to the responses and switch events produced by the same phase. Moreover, no assumption other that trivial well-formedness conditions is made on the received switch events and invocations. This allows us to check that a phase is speculatively linearizable by reasoning about the phase independently of other phases it might be composed with.

Speculative linearizability is an extension of linearizability to traces that contain switch calls. In the definition of linearizability stated above, we associated to each response returned by a client a history of inputs with certain properties. In the same spirit, in addition to associating histories to responses returned, we now associate to each switch call in the trace a history of inputs. With respect to the first phase, we call these histories *abort histories*. With respect to the second phase, we call them *init histories*.

Such histories associated to switch calls represent possible linearizations of the execution of the first speculation phase. The idea is that, with the knowledge of how the execution of the first phase was linearized, the second phase can continue execution without violating linearizability. In order for a speculation phase to deduce a possible current linearization from a switch value, we suppose that all speculation phases agree on a common mapping from switch values to histories. We denote this mapping by r_{init}.

Depending on the particular data type being implemented, there are some sets of histories whose members all bring the system in the same logical state. In other words, the response to a new invocation is independent of which history of such a set was executed before. We call histories in such sets *equivalent* with respect to the data type. Consider our consensus example. Any set of histories whose members start with the same proposal is a set of equivalent histories: because the first proposal is the decision value, any new invocation will return the first proposed value. Processes invoking the object at a point after such a history has been executed cannot tell which history in the set actually happened. Because of this observation, we require that speculation phases agree on a mapping from switch values to *sets* of equivalent histories, as opposed to a single history. This allows us to use a compact representation of histories while ensuring that enough information is available for the second phase to take over the execution.

Two other principles, fault tolerance and avoidance of unnecessary synchronization, influenced our definition. For fault tolerance, we do not rely on just one client passing a single switch value. For efficiency reasons, we avoid the requirement that all clients switch with the same value because it would imply solving a potentially expensive agreement problem. Hence, the switch values of different clients may be different and no single switch call determines the execution of the second phase.

Applied to the first phase, speculative linearizability requires that the first phase be linearizable. Moreover, for all traces of the first phase, it must be possible to associate histories to the switch events so that each such history is a possible linearization of the trace up to the considered event and each association from switch event to history respects the common mapping that phases agree on. Finally, the longest common prefix of all abort histories must be a full linearization of the trace of the first phase. The last two requirements correspond to the *Abort Order* property of Section 5.

Applied to the second phase, speculative linearizability says that for all traces t of the second phase, for all possible associations of histories to switch values that respect the common mapping agreed on, by concatenating t to the trace represented by the longest common prefix of all init histories and by replacing switch calls with the pending invocation they contain, one should obtain a linearizable trace. This corresponds to the *Init Order* property of Section 5.

Having defined the new concept of speculative linearizability, we will show that the composition of any number of speculatively linearizable phases is a linearizable algorithm. This result is a corollary of our intra-object composition theorem, which states that the composition of two speculation phases is itself a speculation phase.

2.4 Applying Speculative Linearizability to Quorum+Backup

We next show that our message-passing speculation phases, Quorum and Backup, satisfy speculative linearizability. As explained above, we view the values passed when switching from Quorum to Backup as representing sets of histories equivalent to some linearization of Quorum's execution. To this end we assumed that speculation phases agreed on a common mapping from switch events to sets of histories. In this example, the mapping of a switch event of client c with switch value v is the set of all histories starting with invocation *propose*(v) from a client $c' \neq c$ and containing only invocations from clients other than c. Hence, a client switching to Backup with switch value v indicates to Backup that any history in the set mapped to v is a possible linearization of Quorum's execution.

Quorum is speculatively linearizable. We prove that Quorum is speculatively linearizable in two steps. First, we show that Quorum satisfies the following three invariants. Then we show that those invariants imply speculative linearizability.

I1: If some client c decides value v then all clients that switch, either before or after c decides, do so with value v.

I2: If some client c decides value v then all clients that decide do so with value v.

I3: All clients that switch or decide do so with a value that was proposed before they switch or decide.

In Quorum, if there are no faults nor contention, a client broadcasting a proposal will receive identical accept messages from all server processes and will return the value contained in the accept messages. However, if contention causes proposals from different clients to be received in different orders at different servers, or if a server fails or messages are lost, clients will switch to Backup because different accept messages will be received or not enough messages will be received before the timers expire.

Observe that if a client returns a value v in Quorum then all servers will reply with *accept*(v) to all the other clients. This is because a client only returns value v if all servers send it accept messages with value v, and a server always responds with the same accept message. Hence, if some client decided, all the other clients will either return the same value v or will switch to Backup with the initialization value v in case message loss or server crashes cause their timers to expire. From these observation we can conclude that the invariants I1 and I2 are satisfied by any trace of Quorum.

Moreover, as servers respond with an accept message containing the first proposal received, client processes return or switch with a value that was proposed before. Hence, the invariant I3 holds.

We now prove that any trace satisfying I1, I2, and I3 satisfies speculative linearizability. Consider a trace t of Quorum that satisfies I1, I2, and I3.

According to the definition of speculative linearizability for the first phase, we begin by showing that t is linearizable. If no client decides then the trace t is trivially linearizable. Therefore assume that some clients decide. The invariant I2 implies that all decisions in the trace are the same. Let v be the common decision. The invariant I3 implies that some client, noted *winner*, proposed v before any client decided v. Let the history h be such that h starts with *winner*'s proposal and the sub-sequence of h starting at position 2 is equal to the subsequence of t containing all the proposals of the clients that decide and that are not *winner*. The history h represents a linearization of trace t. We satisfy our definition of linearizability by associating to each decision from a client c the history h truncated just after the proposal of c. The linearizability of Quorum follows.

To prove speculative linearizability, it remains to show that we can associate appropriate histories to each switch event in t. We consider two cases.

First, assume that some clients decided. Then, by invariant I1 we know that clients decide or switch with the same value v. Let history h be as defined above. To each switch event in t we associate h. By definition of h, h starts with the common decision v and all clients that switch do so with value v. Moreover the clients that switch do not decide; their invocations thus do not appear in h. Hence, the association from switch events to histories respects the common mapping. Moreover, h is a linearization of trace t. Therefore, each history associated to a switch event is a linearization of t. Finally, the longest common prefix of all histories associated to switch events is obviously h itself, and h is a linearization of trace t. We conclude that t satisfies speculative linearizability.

Now assume that no client decides. In this case the trace is trivially linearizable. Moreover, it is easy to associate histories to switch events, so that the longest common prefix of all such histories is empty. We thus trivially have that t satisfies speculative linearizability.

Note that a client that does not fail returns or switches at the latest when its timer expires. Quorum is thus wait-free.

Backup is speculatively linearizable. As for Quorum, we proceed by first abstracting Backup using simple invariants and then proving that those invariants imply speculative linearizability. Since Paxos has been proved correct in the past [13], we can trivially abstract Backup using the following two invariants:

I4 All clients decide the same value.

I5 All clients decide a switch value previously submitted by some client.

Consider a trace t satisfying invariants I4 and I5. We consider two cases. First assume that all switch values are the same and equal to v. Then, by definition of the common mapping from switch events to histories, for all associations of histories to switch events respecting the common mapping, the longest common prefix h of the histories associated to switch values is such that h starts with an invocation *propose*(v) from a client c that doesn't execute in t and contains only invocations by clients that don't execute in t. Let t_h be the trace represented by history h. By invariants I4 and I5 we know that all clients decide value v in t. Let t' be the trace t where switch calls are replaced by the pending invocation they contain. Consider the concatenation $t_h@t'$ of t_h and t'. Let the history h' be the concatenation of h and some ordering of the proposals in t'. Because h represents t_h and because all clients decide v in t, we have that h' is a linearization of $t_h@t'$. Hence, t satisfies speculative linearizability.

Now suppose that at least two switch values are different. Then for any association of histories to switch events respecting the common mapping, the longest common prefix of the histories associated to switch events is the empty history. From invariants I4 and I5 we have that all processes decide on one of the switch values submitted before any decision. Hence, t is linearizable, and so is the concatenation of the empty history and t. Therefore, t satisfies speculative linearizability.

We have proved that Quorum and Backup satisfy speculative linearizability. Therefore, using the intra-object composition theorem that we will prove below, we conclude that the composition of Quorum and Backup is a linearizable implementation of consensus.

Using speculative linearizability, we have optimized the Paxos algorithm to obtain an algorithm that has a latency of two message delays in the absence of faults and contention. Implementing this optimization by modifying the Paxos algorithm would have meant modifying a notoriously intricate distributed algorithm. Instead, by using our framework, we were able to optimize Paxos without modifying it. Moreover, thanks to the intra-object composition theorem, we easily proved the optimized protocol correct just by proving the optimization speculatively linearizable and by relying on the correctness of Paxos.

2.5 Shared-Memory Consensus

To illustrate the broad applicability of our framework we now apply it to an algorithm in the shared-memory model. We consider a consensus implementation in an asynchronous shared-memory system.

Consensus can be implemented on modern microprocessors using the wait-free compare-and-swap (CAS) instruction, but this instruction may be slower than an atomic register access. It has been proved [11] that wait-free consensus cannot be implemented with registers.

However, assuming that all executions are contention free (i.e. sequential), Figure 1 implements consensus using only registers. Hence the following question: is it possible to devise an object that uses only registers in contention-free executions but that always executes correctly? We obtain such an object by composing a register-based speculation phase called *RCons*, shown in Figure 2, and a CAS-based speculation phase called *CASCons*, shown in Figure 3. The CAS-based speculation phase is a straightforward implementation of consensus using the CAS operation. Both speculation phase are inspired by [25]. It turns out that these speculation phases, like many other speculation-based objects, are instances of our framework.

The register-based consensus uses a wait-free splitter algorithm [19]. The splitter guarantees that at most one process returns with true and all others return with false. Moreover, it guarantees that, in the absence of contention, exactly one process returns with true. A splitter can be implemented using only registers, as in our example implementation in Figure 2.

A client invokes the register-based speculation phase using the function *propose*(val), where val is the value that it proposes. To simplify the notation, we assume that, at the time of the call, the caller identifier is stored in the special variable *c*. The register-based speculation phase, *RCons*, can return the content of register V, or it can switch to the CAS-based speculation phase, *CASCons*, by invoking the function *switch-to-CASCons*(V) and returning its result. In the latter case, we say that a client *switches* with value v, where v is the content of register V when it was last read. Such switching is the basic mechanism of composing speculation phases in our framework.

As for Quorum and Backup, we will show that the composition of the phases *RCons* and *CASCons* form a linearizable implementation of consensus by a modular reasoning. Thanks to the intra-object composition theorem, we will get the correctness of the composition of *RCons* and *CASCons* by analyzing each in isolation.

Let us now show that the *RCons* and *CASCons* algorithms are speculatively linearizable.

As for Quorum and Backup, we will first consider *RCons* in isolation and, given an arbitrary execution of *RCons*, we will show that we can associate appropriate histories to the responses returned and to the switch calls. We will then consider *CASCons* in isolation and show that, given an arbitrary execution of *CASCons* and an arbitrary association of histories to the switch calls of *CASCons* (respecting the common mapping), we can associate appropriate histories to the responses appearing in the trace.

We first show that the invariants I1, I2, and I3 defined for Quorum also hold of the traces of *RCons*. To establish these invariants, we first observe the following: By property of the splitter, at most one client executes lines 15 to 18. Moreover, if one client *c* does so and returns, it makes sure that other clients will either return with

```
1: Object RCons
2: //Shared Register V, Initially ⊥; and D, Initially ⊥
3: //Shared Register Contention ∈ {true, false}, Initially false
4: //Shared Registers: Y ∈ {true, false}, Initially false; and X
5: //Local Variable v; local constant c denoting the caller's identifier
6: Function propose(val):
7: v ← val
8: if D ≠ ⊥ then
9:     return D
10: end if
11: if splitter() = true then
12:     V ← v
13:     if ¬Contention then
14:         D ← v
15:         return v
16:     else
17:         return switch-to-CASCons(v)
18:     end if
19: else
20:     Contention = true
21:     if V ≠ ⊥ then
22:         v ← V
23:     end if
24:     return switch-to-CASCons(v)
25: end if
26: Function splitter():
27: X ← c //Remember that c is the caller's identifier
28: if Y = true then
29:     return false
30: end if
31: Y ← true
32: if X = c then
33:     return true
34: else
35:     return false
36: end if
```

Figure 2. Register-Based Speculative Consensus

```
1: Object CASCons
2: //Shared Register D Initially ⊥
3: Function switch-to-CASCons(val):
4: return CAS(D, ⊥, val)
5: Function propose(val):
6: //Since processes have to call switch-to-CASCons first, we know that
   the consensus has already been won, hence just return D.
7: return D
```

Figure 3. CAS-Based Speculative Consensus

its value at line 12 or switch with its value at line 27. Indeed, if the variable *Contention* is false at line 16, it means that no process got past line 23. Therefore, all processes that switch will find *c*'s value in variable *V* at line 25. We conclude that the invariants I1 and I2 hold on all executions of *RCons*. If some client *c* returns value v then all clients that switch, either before or after *c* returns, do so with value v and if some client *c* returns value v then all clients that return do so with value v. Next, observe that all clients return or switch with their own value or with the content of register V, which can only contain proposed values. Consequently, the invariant I3 is also an invariant on all executions of *RCons*: All clients that switch do so with a value that was proposed before they switch.

Similarly, the *CASCons* phase can be abstracted by the same invariants that we used to abstract the Backup speculation phase: All clients return the same value and all clients return a switch value previously submitted by some client.

When we proved that Quorum and Backup are speculatively linearizable, we showed that the invariants I1, I2, and I3 imply speculative linearizability of the first phase and that the invariants I4 and I5 imply the speculative linearizability of the second phase.

Since we established that the traces of *RCons* satisfy I1, I2, and I3 and that the traces of *CASCons* satisfy I4 and I5 we can conclude that *RCons* and *CASCons* satisfy speculative linearizability.

We will now formally define speculative linearizability.

3. Trace Properties

In this section we define trace properties and the operations they support. Trace properties are our model of distributed systems.

A trace property is a set of finite sequences of events. We use trace properties to describe the set of all finite sequences that a system can generate, as well as the desired properties of systems, such as linearizability with respect to a given abstract data type. We restrict ourselves to finite sequences because our work deals with safety properties only.

Sequences. We write $[1..n]$ for the set $\{1, 2, \ldots, n\}$. A *sequence* s of length n with elements from a set E is a function $s : [1..n] \rightarrow E$. We denote n by $|s|$. We write E^* for the set of all sequences of elements in E. We write $[e_1, e_2, \ldots, e_n]$ for the sequence s such that $s(1) = e_1$, $s(2) = e_2$, ..., and $s(n) = e_n$. If $s = [e_1, e_2, \ldots, e_n]$ then $s{::}e_{n+1}$ is the sequence $[e_1, e_2, \ldots, e_n, e_{n+1}]$. If $s = [e_1, e_2, \ldots, e_n]$ and $s' = [e'_1, e'_2, \ldots, e'_n]$ then $s{:::}s' = [e_1, \ldots, e_n, e'_1, \ldots, e'_n]$ and, if $m < |s|$, we write $s_{|m}$ for the the sequence $[e_1, e_2, \ldots, e_m]$. We say that a sequence s is a *prefix* of a sequence s' iff there exists a sequence s'' such that $s' = s{:::}s''$. We say s is a *strict prefix* of s' iff the s'' is non-empty. Given a set of sequences P, the longest common prefix of set P is the longest among the sequences s' such that for all sequence $s \in P$, s' is a prefix of s.

Multisets. We represent multisets of elements of set E by a multiplicity function $E \rightarrow \mathbb{N}$. Given two multisets m_1 and m_2 and $e \in E$, we define $(m_1 \cup m_2)(e) = max(m_1(e), m_2(e))$ and $(m_1 \uplus m_2)(e) = m_1(e) + m_2(e)$. Moreover $m_1 \subseteq m_2$ iff for all $e \in E$, $m_1(e) \leq m_2(e)$. Let $elems : E^* \rightarrow (E \rightarrow \mathbb{N})$ be a function that given a sequence returns a multiset representing all the elements found in the sequence and their number of occurences. Given a sequence s we write $e \in s$ iff $elems(s)(e) > 0$.

Trace Properties. A trace is a sequence of *actions* which represents *events* happening at the interface between a system and its environment. An event occurs at some point in time and has no duration. We can approximate invoking a method and starting to execute it as one action. The execution of a method from start to finish, however, is typically not an action because it has a positive duration in time. We would represent it with an invocation action and a return action.

We classify actions into input and output actions. This classification is especially important to define composition of systems, because we need to know which actions of a component affect another component. The classification is described by a *signature*. A signature *sig* is a pair (in, out) where in is a set of input actions and out is a disjoint set of output actions. We require in and out to be disjoint. We denote by *acts*(*sig*) the set of all actions in signature *sig*. When all the actions of a trace t belong to *acts*(*sig*) we say that t is a trace in *sig*.

Definition 1. *A* trace property *is a pair $P = (sig, Traces)$ where sig is a signature and Traces is a set of traces in acts(sig).*

We denote *sig* by *sig*(P) and *Traces* by *Traces*(P). We allow to write $in(P)$ instead of $in(sig(P))$ and similarly for the other sets of actions defined above.

We say that a trace property Q satisfies a trace property P, denoted $Q \models P$, if Q's signature is equal to P's signature and the set of trace of Q is a subset of the set of traces of P:

$$Q \models P \Leftrightarrow \quad (sig(Q) = sig(P) \wedge Traces(Q) \subseteq Traces(P))\,.$$

Composition of Trace Properties. Trace properties may be composed only if their signatures are *compatible*. Signatures sig_1 and sig_2 are compatible if and only if they have no output actions in common, that is $out(sig_1)$ is disjoint from $out(sig_2)$. As a result, $out(sig_1) \cap acts(sig_2) \subseteq in(sig_2)$ and vice versa. We define the *projection* $proj(t, A)$ of a trace t onto a set A of actions as the sequence obtained by removing all actions of t that are not in A. For example, $proj([x, y, x', z, y', z, y, z, y], \{x', y'\}) = [x', y']$.

Definition 2. *If sig_1 is compatible with sig_2 then the composition $P = P_1 || P_2$ is such that:*

- *The signature $sig(P)$ is such that $in(P) = (in(P_1) \cup in(P_2)) \setminus (out(P_1) \cup out(P_2))$ and $out(P) = out(P_1) \cup out(P_2)$.*
- *The set of traces $Traces(P)$ is the largest set of traces in $acts(P)$ such that if $t \in Traces(P)$ then $proj(t, acts(P_1)) \in Traces(P_1)$ and $proj(t, acts(P_2)) \in Traces(P_2)$*

Intuitively, composition requires components to execute at the same time the actions that appear as input of one component and output of the other. Actions that appear in a unique component are executed asynchronously from the other components. Composition has the following property:

Property 1. *If $Q_1 \models P_1$ and $Q_2 \models P_2$ then $Q_1 || Q_2 \models P_1 || P_2$.*

Projection of Trace Properties.

Definition 3. *Given a trace property P we define its projection $proj(P, A)$ onto a set of actions A such that $sig(proj(P, A)) = (in(P) \cap A, out(P) \cap A)$ and $Traces(proj(P, A)) = \{t \mid \exists t' \in Traces(P).t = proj(t', A)\}$*

Applying the *proj* operator to a trace property P amounts to removing all the actions not in A from P's interface.

4. Linearizability

Our notion of speculative linearizability is itself based on a new definition of linearizability. This definition is interesting in its own right because it enables a more local form of reasoning than the original definition. Moreover, it allows for repeated events, which are the norm in practice. The technical report [9] contains a proof that our new definition of linearizability is equivalent to the classical definition.

4.1 Abstract Data Types

Abstract Data Types (ADTs) formalize our intuitive understanding of how sequential objects may behave.

In order to simplify our discussion in the rest of the paper, we deviate from the usual, state-machine based, definition of abstract data types. However we do so without loss of generality. Traditionally, the allowed behaviors are described using an ad-hoc state machine that given a state and an input transitions to a new state and produces an output. Instead, we determine outputs from the input history seen so far using an *output function*. Computation of the output function amounts to replaying the execution of the state-machine description.

Definition 4. *An ADT T is a tuple $T = (I_T, O_T, f_T)$ where I_T is a non-empty set, whose members we call* inputs, *O_T is a disjoint non-empty set whose members we call* outputs, *and $f_T : I_T^* \rightarrow O_T$ is an output function.*

In the rest of the paper, we consider objects of some fixed ADT $T = (I_T, O_T, f_T)$.

Example 1. *We consider a consensus object with operations of the form $(p(v), d(v'))$ with v and v' belonging to some set V_{Cons}. $p(v)$ is a shorthand for "propose(v)" and $d(v)$ for "decide(v)". The consensus object must guarantee that a unique value v may be decided and that at any point a decided value has been pro-*

posed before. Hence, because we are considering sequential executions, the first proposed value must be decided in all subsequent operations. Formally, we define the ADT Cons such that $I_{Cons} = \{p(v) \mid v \in V_{Cons}\}$, $O_{Cons} = \{d(v) \mid v \in V_{Cons}\}$, $f_{Cons}([p(v_1), p(v_2), \ldots, p(v_n)]) = d(v_1)$

4.2 A Trace Model of Concurrent Objects

We consider a set C of asynchronous sequential processes called clients. Clients use a concurrent object of ADT T by calling the object's invocation function with one of the ADT's inputs, and the invocation function returns one of the ADT's outputs. We denote a sequence of interaction between clients and object as follows. Suppose that the following sequence of interactions between clients and object is observed: Client c_1 invokes input in_1; Client c_2 invokes input in_2; Client c_2 returns with output out_2; Finally client c_1 returns with output out_1. This sequence of interactions is denoted by the sequence of actions

$$[inv(c_1, in_1), inv(c_2, in_2), res(c_2, in_2, out_2), res(c_1, in_1, out_1)]$$

Signature of a Concurrent Object Formally, a sequence of interactions between a concurrent object and its clients is a trace of actions in the signature sig_T, where the inputs $in(sig_T)$, called invocation actions, are of the form $inv(c, n, in)$ and the outputs $out(sig_T)$, called response actions, are of the form $res(c, n, in, out)$ for some client c, natural number n, $in \in I_T$, and $out \in O_T$.

The reader will notice that the second parameter of the actions is not present in our preceding example. It will be used in Subsection 5 to define the signature of a speculation phase.

In Section 4 we define the trace property Lin_T such that a concurrent object described by a trace property O is linearizable w.r.t. T if and only if $O \subseteq Lin_T$.

Underscore Notation. Throughout the paper we will use the underscore symbol "_" in mathematical expressions. Each occurrence of this symbol is to be replaced by a fixed fresh variable. For example, we might say an action a is an invocation action if $a = inv(\_, \_, \_)$, or equivalently, that if $a = inv(c, n, in)$ for some c, n, and in, then a is an invocation action.

4.3 A New Definition of Classical Linearizability

In this section we define a trace property called linearizability, and noted Lin_T. Informally, a trace in sig_T is said to be linearizable iff its actions may be reordered to form a *sequential trace* that:

1. Respects the semantics of the ADT T.
2. Preserves the order of non-overlapping operations.

Property 1 implies that clients accessing a linearizable object cannot tell whether the object produces sequential or concurrent traces. This is a crucial property because it hides concurrency from the view of application developers. Property 2 makes linearizability a *local* property. In other words, a system composed of linearizable objects is itself linearizable. We refer the reader to [12] for an in-depth discussion about linearizability.

Instead of using the definition above we propose a new definition of linearizability that will simplify our task when we define speculation phases. It directly establishes a relationship between the linearizable traces and the ADT, without the intermediary of sequential traces.

Note that some definitions of linearizability [12] assume more or less explicitly that all inputs submitted are unique. This seems unwarranted as many algorithms qualified as implementing a linearizable object are deemed correct without requiring this assumption. Our definition does not rely on this assumption and it coincides with the other definitions on traces satisfying the assumption.

Consider a trace t in sig_T.

Definition 5. *Trace t is linearizable iff it is* well-formed *and it admits a* linearization function $g : [1..|t|] \rightarrow I_T^*$.

We define linearization functions and well-formed traces below.

To ensure that our definition corresponds to the usual one, in the technical report [9] we also formalize the usual definition of linearizability [12], by defining when a trace is linearizable*, even in case of repeated events. We then prove the equivalence between the two definitions.

Theorem 1. *A trace in sig_T is linearizable if and only if it is linearizable*.*

4.4 Linearization Functions

In the rest of the paper we call sequences of inputs histories. A linearization function maps the indices of t to histories which must satisfy two properties:

First, applying the ADT's output function to the history associated with a response index must yield the output contained in the response. Hence a linearization function may be seen as giving an explanation of the outputs observed, in term of the ADT's semantics.

Second, the history associated to a response index must only contain inputs invoked before index i and for all pairs of histories corresponding to response indices, one is a strict prefix of the other. This second condition gives us a total order on the response indices of t (the prefix order on histories) which corresponds to the reordering needed in the original definition.

A history corresponding to some response index i in a trace t according to a linearization function is said to be a linearization of the (concurrent) trace $t_{|i}$.

We now state this definition formally:

Definition 6. ***Linearization Function.*** *A function g is a linearization function for t iff*

- *Function g* explains *trace t.*
- *Function g and trace t satisfy the* validity*(t,g) and* commit-order*(t,g) predicates.*

Definition 7. ***Explains.*** *We say that function g explains trace t iff for all index $i \in [1..|t|]$, if $t(i) = res(\_, \_, \_, out)$ then $out = f_T(g(i))$.*

Consider a function $g : [1..n] \rightarrow I_T^*$ that explains trace t.

Definition 8. ***Commit Index and Commit Histories.*** *If $i \in [1..n]$ is such that $t(i) = res(\_, \_, \_, \_)$ then we say that i is a* commit index *and that $g(i)$ is a (t, g)-commit history.*

Definition 9. ***Sequence of Previous Inputs.*** *We define the sequence of previous inputs at i in t, $inputs(t, i)$, as the sequence of all inputs submitted before index i in trace t. Formally, for all $i \in [1..|t|]$, $|inputs(t, i)| = |proj(t_{|i}, in(sig_T)|$, and for all $j \in [1..|inputs(t, i)|]$, $proj(t_{|i}, in(sig_T))(j) = inv(\_, \_, inputs(t, i)(j))$.*

Definition 10. ***Valid Commit Index*** *For all index $i \in [1..|t|]$ such that $t(i) = res(\_, \_, in, \_)$, we say that i is (t, g)-valid iff $elems(g(i)) \subseteq elems(inputs(t, i))$ and the input in is the last element of the history $g(i)$.*

In other words, if $t(i) = res(\_, \_, in, \_)$ then $g(i)$ is a permutation of the sequence of previous inputs at i and ends with the input in.

We now define validity and commit-order:

Definition 11. ***Validity**(t,g). All commit indices in t are (t, g)-valid.*

Definition 12. ***Commit Order**(t,g): For all pairs of distinct commit indices (i, j), either $g(i)$ is a strict prefix of $g(j)$ or $g(j)$ is a strict prefix of $g(i)$.*

Example 2. *Consider the following trace t:*

$[inv(c, in_1), inv(c', in_2), res(c', in_2, f_T([in_2])), res(c, in_1, f_T([in_2, in_1]))]$.

Consider a function g such that $g(3) = [in_2]$ and $g(4) = [in_2, in_1]$. The function g explains t. Moreover t and g satisfy validity and commit-order. Hence g is a linearization function for t.

4.5 Well-Formed Traces

The well-formedness of traces is a basic requirement. For example, it states that a response should be given to a client only if it previously issued an invocation.

Given a client c, let $Act_T(c)$ be the union of the sets $\{inv(c, \_, in) | in \in I_T\}$ and $\{res(c, \_, in, out) | in \in I_T \wedge out \in O_T\}$.

Definition 13. ***Client sub-trace.*** *The client sub-trace $sub(t, c)$ of trace t in sig_T is the trace $sub(t, c) = proj(t, Act_T(c))$.*

Definition 14. ***Well-formed client sub-trace.*** *A client sub-trace t is well-formed iff $t(1)$ is such that $t(1) = inv(\_, \_, \_)$ and for all $i \in [1..|t| - 1]$, if $t(i) = inv(\_, \_, in)$, then $t(i+1) = res(\_, \_, in, \_)$.*

Definition 15. ***Well-formed traces.*** *We say that trace t in sig_T is* well-formed *if and only if all its client sub-traces are well-formed.*

Note that invocations with no corresponding response may appear in a well-formed trace. We say that those invocations are pending.

4.6 The Lin_T Trace Property

We define the trace property Lin_T such that the signature $sig(Lin_T)$ is sig_T and the set $Traces(Lin_T)$ is the set of all traces satisfying linearizability.

Finally, consider a system S whose behavior is denoted by a trace property P. We say that the system S implements the ADT T if and only if $proj(S, sig_T) \models Lin_T$.

5. Speculative Linearizability

We next present our main results: a precise definition of speculative linearizability, and the proof that a composition of implementations that are speculatively linearizable implementations is itself speculatively linearizable. This section presents a trace-based formalization. We summarize an alternative, automata-based, formalization in Section 6.

5.1 Speculation Phases

We now consider concurrent objects implemented by several speculation phases. Clients use a speculation phase by calling the object's invocation functions and the invocation functions return outputs to the clients. However, a speculation phase also accepts initialization calls from clients and it may switch to another speculation phase.

Moreover, each speculation phases is identified by a natural number and a speculation phase identified by n may only switch to a speculation phase identified by $n + 1$. Clients start by accessing speculation phase 1 and continue to do so as long as they return in the phase 1. However, speculation phase 1 may switch to phase 2. In this case it passes an initialization value and its pending input to phase 2. A client which returns in phase 2 stops accessing speculation phase 1 and instead uses phase 2 for its next invocations.

Let S_1 and S_2 be two consecutive speculation phases. Suppose that client c_1 invokes input in_1 on S_1; client c_2 invokes input in_2 on S_1; client c_2 switches from S_1 to S_2 providing initialization value v; client c_1 returns response out_1 from S_1; finally client c_2 returns response out_2 from S_2. This sequence of interactions is denoted by this sequence of events, from now on called actions:

$$[inv(c_1, 1, in_1), inv(c_2, 1, in_2), swi(c_2, 2, in_2, v),$$
$$res(c_1, 1, in_1, out_1), res(c_2, 2, in_2, out_2)]$$

Instead of formalizing the signature of a single speculation phase identified by a natural number we generalize to the signature of a composition of speculation phases. We now assume that a speculation phase may be composed of several other speculation phases.

Let $\mathbb{N}^2_< = \{(m, n) \mid (m, n) \in \mathbb{N}^2 \wedge m < n\}$. We denote a speculation phase by an element of $\mathbb{N}^2_<$. A speculation phase $(m, n) \in \mathbb{N}^2_<$ describes the possible behaviors of the composition of speculation phases from m to n.

We now explain why we make this generalization.

We would like to define a property $P(n)$ of speculation phase n, for $n \in \mathbb{N}$, such that for all $m \in \mathbb{N}$ the composition $P(1)||P(2)|| \dots ||P(m)$ implements Lin_T. To prove that

$$P(1)||P(2)|| \dots ||P(m) \models Lin_T$$

we generalize $P(n)$ to $P(m, n)$ in order to use induction.

We would like $P(m, n)$ to be such that:

$$\text{For all natural number } n > 1,\ P(1, n) \models Lin_T \quad (1)$$

$$\text{For all } (m, n) \in \mathbb{N}^2_< \text{ and } (n, o) \in \mathbb{N}^2_<,$$
$$P(m, n)||P(n, o) \models P(m, o) \quad (2)$$

Using induction and equation 2 we have that for all $n > 1$,

$$P(1, 2)||P(2, 3)|| \dots ||P(n - 1, n) \models P(1, n).$$

Thus, with equation 1, we have that for all $n > 1$,

$$P(1, 2)||P(2, 3)|| \dots ||P(n - 1, n) \models Lin_T \quad (3)$$

Now suppose that we have a family of trace properties $Q_1, Q_2, \dots, Q_n$, representing implementations of speculation phases, such that $Q_i \models P(i, i + 1)$ for all $i \in [1..n]$. Let $Comp = Q_1||Q_2|| \dots ||Q_n$. By property 1 and equation 3, we have that $Comp \models Lin_T$.

Signature of a Speculation Phase We now define a signature $sig_T(m, n, Init)$ which models the interface of a speculation phase (m, n) that uses initialization values from the set *Init*. For all $m \in \mathbb{N}$ and any arbitrary non-empty set *Init* of initialization values, we define the set of *switch actions* as formed of all actions of the form $swi(c, m, in, v)$ where c is a client, $m \in \mathbb{N}$, $in \in I_T$, and $v \in Init$.

Definition 16. ***Signature of a speculation phase.*** *For all $(m, n) \in \mathbb{N}^2_<$ and any non-empty set Init of initialization values we define the signature $sig_T(m, n, Init)$ as the union of the sets of all invocation actions $inv(\_, o, \_)$, of all response actions $res(\_, o, \_, \_)$, and of all switch actions $swi(\_, o, \_, \_)$, where $o \in [m..n]$.*

5.2 Specification of a Speculation Phase

In this section we propose a specification for speculation phases. We consider a set of initialization values *Init*, and a relation $r_{init} \in Init \times I_T^*$ such that r_{init}^{-1} is a total onto function. The relation r_{init} associates a set of input sequences to any value in *Init*. Remember that the init values convey information about the execution of one phase to the next phase. We think of this information in terms of input histories which represent possible linearizations of the concurrent trace of a phase. We say the set of input sequences associated by r_{init} with a value is the value's possible interpretations.

We will now define a trace property $SLin_T(m, n)$, such that

- For all natural number m, $proj(SLin_T(1, m), acts(sig_T)) \models Lin_T$.
- For all $(m, n) \in \mathbb{N}^2_<$ and $(n, o) \in \mathbb{N}^2_<$, $SLin_T(m, n)||SLin_T(n, o) \models SLin_T(m, o)$.

We define the property $SLin_T(m, n)$ in the same vein as Lin_T. Consider a trace t in $sig_T(m, n, Init)$.

Definition 17. ***Interpretation of Init Actions.*** *We say that a function $f : [1..|t|] \to I^*$ is an interpretation of the init actions of t iff for all index $i \in [1..|t|]$, if $t(i) = swi(\_, m, \_, v)$ then $(v, f(i)) \in r_{\mathit{init}}$.*

Definition 18. ***Interpretation of Abort Actions.*** *We say that a function $f : [1..|t|] \to I^*$ is an interpretation of the abort actions of t iff for all index $i \in [1..|t|]$, if $t(i) = swi(\_, n, \_, v)$ then $(v, f(i)) \in r_{\mathit{init}}$.*

Definition 19. ***Speculatively Linearizable.*** *We say that trace t is (m, n)-speculatively linearizable iff trace t is (m, n)-well-formed and for all interpretation f_{init} of the init actions of t, there exists two functions $g : [1..|t|] \to I_T^*$ and $f_{\mathit{abort}} : [1..|t|] \to I_T^*$ such that:*

- *f_{abort} is an interpretation of the abort actions of t.*
- *g is an $(f_{\mathit{init}}, f_{\mathit{abort}}, m, n)$-speculative linearization function for t.*

5.3 Speculative Linearization Functions

Intuition Behind the Definitions. Consider a speculation phase S_1 whose clients switch to speculation phase S_2. We require clients to switch with a value whose set of possible interpretations includes a possible linearization of the concurrent trace at the point where the client switches. Note that every history (1) of which all commit histories are prefix and (2) that contains only values that have been invoked is a possible linearization. This is the intuition behind the definition of Abort-Order property (Definition 32).

To ensure that phase S_2 continues executing consistently with what phase S_1 did, we require all its commit histories to have as a prefix one of the possible linearizations of S_1's trace. This is the intuition behind the Init Order property (Definition 31). However S_2 receives switch values that represent sets of histories, and cannot determine which history in this set is a possible linearization. Hence the quantifier alternation in Definition 19: for all possible interpretations of the init values, phase S_2 needs to ensure the existence of a proper linearization function.

Definition 20. ***Speculative linearization function.*** *A function $g : [1..|t|] \to I_T^*$ is a $(f_{\mathit{init}}, f_{\mathit{abort}}, m, n)$-speculative linearization function for t iff:*

- *The function g explains trace t.*
- *The predicates Validity$(t, g, f_{\mathit{init}}, f_{\mathit{abort}})$, Commit-Order$(t, g)$, Init-Order$(t, g, f_{\mathit{init}}, f_{\mathit{abort}})$, and Abort-Order$(t, g, f_{\mathit{abort}})$ hold.*

Definition 21. ***Explains.*** *We say that the function g explains trace t iff for all index $i \in [1..|t|]$, if $t(i) = res(\_, \_, \_, out)$ then $out = f_T(g(i))$*

Consider a function $g : [1..|t|] \to I_T^*$ that explains trace t and consider two functions $f_{\mathit{init}} \subseteq r_{\mathit{init}}$ and $f_{\mathit{abort}} \subseteq r_{\mathit{init}}$. In order to define validity, commit-order, init-order, and abort-order we need the definitions 22 to 28 below.

Definition 22. ***Commit Indices and Commit Histories.*** *If $i \in [1..n]$ is such that $t(i) = res(\_, \_, \_, \_)$ then we say that i is a (t, m, n)-*commit index *and that $g(i)$ is a (t, g)-*commit history.

Definition 23. ***Init Indices and Init Histories.*** *If $i \in [1..n]$ is such that $t(i) = swi(\_, m, \_, v)$ we say that i is a (t, m, n)-*init index *and that $f_{\mathit{init}}(i)$ is a $(t, m, n, f_{\mathit{init}})$-*init history.

Definition 24. ***Abort Indices and Abort Histories.*** *If $i \in [1..n]$ is such that $t(i) = swi(\_, n, \_, v)$ we say that i is a (t, m, n)-*abort index *and that $f_{\mathit{abort}}(i)$ is a $(t, m, n, f_{\mathit{abort}})$-*abort history.

The multiset $ivi(m, t, f_{\mathit{init}}, i)$ contains all the inputs known to to have been invoked in phases (k, l), where $l \leq m$:

Definition 25. ***Initially Valid Inputs.***

$$ivi(m, t, f_{\mathit{init}}, i) =$$
$$\biguplus \{elems(f_{\mathit{init}}(v)) \cup \{in\} \mid \exists j < i.t(i) = swi(\_, m, in, v)\}.$$

Note that, in the previous definition, $\biguplus$ is the multiset union (defined in Section 3) and corresponds to pointwise maximum of representation functions.

Now recall that *inputs*(t, i) is the sequence of inputs that were invoked before i in t.

Definition 26. ***Valid Inputs.*** *We define*

$$vi(m, t, f_{\mathit{init}}, i) = ivi(m, t, f_{\mathit{init}}, i) \uplus elems(\mathit{inputs}(t, i))$$

Definition 27. ***Valid Commit Index.*** *For all index i such that $t(i) = res(\_, \_, in, \_)$, we say that i is $(t, g, f_{\mathit{init}})$-*valid *if and only if $elems(g(i)) \subseteq vi(m, t, f_{\mathit{init}}, i)$ and the input in is the last element of history $g(i)$.*

Definition 28. ***Valid Abort Index.*** *For all index i such that $t(i) = swi(\_, n, in, v)$, we say that i is $(t, f_{\mathit{init}}, f_{\mathit{abort}})$-*valid *if and only if $elems(f_{\mathit{abort}}(v)) \cup \{in\} \subseteq vi(m, t, f_{\mathit{init}}, i)$.*

We now define validity, commit-order, init-order, and abort-order:

Definition 29. ***Validity**$(t, g, f_{\mathit{init}}, f_{\mathit{abort}})$: All (t, m, n)-commit indices are $(t, g, f_{\mathit{init}})$-valid and all (t, m, n)-abort indices are $(t, f_{\mathit{init}}, f_{\mathit{abort}})$-valid.*

Definition 30. ***Commit Order**(t,g): For all pair of distinct commit indices i, j, either $g(j)$ is a strict prefix of $g(i)$ or $g(i)$ is a strict prefix of $g(j)$.*

Definition 31. ***Init Order**$(t, g, f_{\mathit{init}}, f_{\mathit{abort}})$: The longest common prefix of all $(t, m, n, f_{\mathit{init}})$-init histories is a strict prefix of all (t, g)-commit histories and of all $(t, m, n, f_{\mathit{abort}})$-abort histories.*

We assume that the longest common prefix of an empty set of histories is the empty history.

Definition 32. ***Abort Order**$(t, g, f_{\mathit{abort}})$: All (t, g)-commit histories are prefix of all $(t, m, n, f_{\mathit{abort}})$-abort histories.*

Note that if $m = 1$, then t has no init histories. Hence Init Order does not constrain commit and abort histories.

5.4 Well-Formed Traces

The well-formedness condition defines basic requirements on traces of a concurrent object.

Given a client c let $Act_T(c, m, n)$ be the set of actions such that

$$\begin{aligned} Act_T(c, m, n) = &\{inv(c, o, in) | o \in [m..n] \wedge in \in I_T\} \\ &\cup \{res(c, o, in, r) | o \in [m..n] \wedge in \in I_T \wedge r \in O_T\} \\ &\cup \{swi(c, o, in, v) | o \in \{m, n\} \wedge in \in I_T \wedge r \in O_T \wedge v \in Init\} \end{aligned}$$

Note that the switch actions whose second parameter is not m or n are projected away.

Definition 33. ***Client sub-trace.*** *The (m, n)-client-sub-trace of the trace t is the trace $sub(t, m, n, c) = proj(t, Act_T(c, m, n))$.*

Definition 34. ***Well-formed client sub-trace.*** *A (m, n)-client sub-trace t_c is well-formed iff it is empty or:*

- *For all $i \in [1..|t_c| - 1]$, if $t(i) = inv(\_, \_, in)$ or $t(i) = swi(\_, m, in, \_)$, then $t(i + 1) = res(\_, \_, in, \_)$ or $t(i + 1) = swi(\_, n, in, \_)$.*
- *If t_c contains an abort action then it is the last element of t_c.*
- *If $m \neq 1$ then $t_c(1)$ is an init action and there are no other init actions in t_c.*
- *If $m = 1$ then $t_c(1)$ is an invocation and there are no init actions in t_c.*

Definition 35. ***Well-formed traces.*** *We say that the trace t is (m,n)-well-formed if and only if all its (m,n)-client sub-traces are well-formed.*

5.5 The $SLin_T$ Trace Property

We define the trace property $SLin_T(m,n)$ as follows:

Definition 36. *The $SLin_T(m,n)$ is such that the signature $sig(SLin_T(m,n))$ is $sig_T(m,n,Init)$ and the set $Traces(SLin_T(m,n))$ is the set of all traces satisfying (m,n)-speculative linearizability.*

Finally, consider a system S whose behavior is denoted by a trace property P. We say that the system S is a (m,n)-speculation phase if and only if $proj(P, sig(m,n)) \models ALin(m,n)$.

Theorem 2. *For all natural number m, any initialization set Init, and any initialization relation r_{init},*

$$proj(SLin_T(1,m), acts(sig_T)) = Lin_T$$

Proof. Compared to linearizability, speculative linearizability only adds constraints on the actions that are not in the signature sig_T. □

5.6 Intra-Object Composition Theorem

Our main theorem states that the composition of two speculation phases is also a speculation phase.

Theorem 3. *Suppose that $S_1 \models SLin_T(m,n)$ and $S_2 \models SLin_T(n,o)$, then $proj(S_1||S_2, sig_T(m,o,Init)) \models SLin_T(m,o)$.*

The proof of this result in the technical report [9]. It consists of two pages in the current format. Among the key steps is the construction of a speculative linearization function g that explains the traces of the composition of two phases. The function is constructed by merging two speculative linearization functions. To show that it is indeed a speculative linearization function we use a form of transitive reasoning to relate commit histories between different phases through abort histories. Among the properties of speculative linearizability, Validity is the most difficult to show, in part because it is sensitive to the fact that we allow duplicate events in our traces (something that even most existing developments of classic linearizability ignore).

6. Automata Specification of Speculative Linearizability and Isabelle/HOL Proof

We have also formalized in Isabelle/HOL an executable version of the specification of speculative linearizability. Our formalization is based on the theory of I/O-automata [21], which is formalized in Isabelle's IOA framework [22]. Our specification automaton corresponds to speculative linearizability instantiated for State Machine Replication [16] protocols (abbreviated SMR protocols). We wrote a mechanically-checked proof of the intra-object composition theorem for the automata specification. Thanks to this proof, it is now possible to obtain mechanically-checked proofs of speculative SMR protocols from the mechanically-checked proofs of its speculation phases taken in isolation. Moreover, our proof of the intra-object composition theorem shows that refinement proofs in our framework are practical.

The speculative approach to SMR protocols has been shown to yield some of the most efficient SMR protocols in practice [8]. Therefore, our formalization and the proof of the intra-object composition theorem enable for the first time scalable mechanically-checked proofs of practical SMR protocols. A proof document and the corresponding Isabelle theories are available at the Archive of Formal Proofs [10].

Informal Description of the Automata Specification. The automata specification is a formalization of speculative linearizability for an ADT that we call the universal ADT. The output function of the universal ADT is the identity function. In other words, this ADT responds to an invocation with its full trace, in the form of a history. The universal ADT can be used as an abstraction for generic SMR protocols [8] because, given a linearizable implementation, it suffices to apply the output function of another ADT A to the responses in order obtain an implementation of A. We formalize the case where histories of inputs are used as initialization values and where the relation r_{init} maps a history h to the singleton set $\{h\}$. The specification automaton can be seen as an implementation of speculative linearizability in which all clients reside on a unique, centralized, process.

The automaton receives invocations and switch calls as inputs and produces responses and switch call outputs.

The specification automaton maintains a state with the following components:

- A history *hist*, representing the longest linearization made visible to a client (i.e. the longest commit history);
- for each client c, a phase $phase(c) \in \{$ Sleep, Pending, Ready, or Aborted $\}$;
- for each client c, $pending(c)$, the last input submitted by c;
- a set *InitHists* containing the init histories received;
- two booleans: *aborted* and *initialized*.

We say that an input is pending if it is the last submitted input of a client c whose phase is "Pending" and if it is not present in *hist*.

The automaton starts in a state where *hist* is the empty history, *InitHists* is the empty set, *aborted* and *initialized* are set to *false*, and for all clients c, $phase(c) =$ "Sleep".

We now describe how the automaton reacts to the inputs it receives, namely invocations and switch calls from the previous phase. When receiving a switch call from the previous phase by client c, if $phase(c)$ equals "Sleep" then the automaton adds the provided init history to the set *InitHists* and sets $pending(c)$ to the provided input. When receiving a new invocation by client c, if $phase(c)$ equals "Ready", the automaton sets $pending(c)$ to the input received. In both cases $phase(c)$ is then set to "Pending". This denotes the fact that client c is waiting for a response to input $pending(c)$.

Moreover, the automaton nondeterministically performs one of the following actions:

A1 If *initialized* $=$ *false* and if there is at least one client c such that $phase(c)$ is not "Sleep", then the automaton computes the longest common prefix of the histories in *InitHists*, assigns it to *hist*, and sets *initialized* to *true*.

A2 It selects a pending input, say from client c, appends it to *hist*, emits an output for client c containing the new value of *hist* as response, and sets $phase(c)$ to "Ready".

A3 It sets *aborted* to *true*.

A4 If *aborted* $=$ *true* then a client c such that $phase(c)$ is not "Aborted" is selected is $phase(c)$ is set to "Aborted". Moreover, the automaton emits a switch action containing an abort value h' such that *hist* is a prefix of h' and the inputs of h' which are not in *hist* are pending.

The precise definition of our specification automaton is available in the ALM entry [10] of the Archive of Formal Proofs.

Relation to the Trace Based Specification. The trace-based specification requires associating histories to responses (commit histories) and switch actions (init and abort histories). Because our ADT's output function is the identity and because $r_{init}(h) = \{h\}$, we have no choice but to associate to a response or switch action the very history it contains (remember that outputs and switch values are histories in this section). Hence commit histories are obtained by truncating *hist* at a pending request. Since *hist* grows by appending to it, we have that Commit Order is satisfied. Moreover, abort histories are obtained by appending some pending requests to *hist*, and at this point *hist* does not grow anymore. Hence Abort Order holds. Since *hist* is initialized with the longest common prefix of the init histories seen, Init Order also holds. Finally, *hist* grows by appending pending requests to it, Validity is also satisfied.

To gain more insight into speculative linearizability, one may also observe that any extension of history *hist* with some pending requests is a linearization of the current trace. Thanks to this observation, step A2 may be interpreted as selecting a possible linearization and producing an output that realizes it. Step A4 can be seen as passing one of the possible linearizations to the next speculation phase. Finally, in step A1, the automaton computes the weakest (given the init histories it received) under-approximation of the set of possible linearizations of the previous phase and selects one of them to initialize its execution.

Proof of the Intra-Object Composition Theorem. To prove the intra-object composition theorem in this formulation, we construct a refinement mapping [20] between the composition of two speculation phases and a single speculation phase. We prove the refinement mapping correct with the help of 15 state invariants about the composed automaton. Using the meta-theorem about refinement mappings (included in the IOA theory packaged with Isabelle/HOL), we conclude that the set of traces of the composition of two speculation phases is included in the set of traces of a single speculation phase. The proof is written in the structured proof language Isar [26] and consists of roughly of 500 proof steps. With the specification, it forms a total of 1600 lines of Isabelle/HOL code.

Our automata specification can be used as the basis for mechanically-checked refinement proofs of distributed protocols. Our proof of the composition is a good example of such a refinement proof and shows the practicality of the approach.

7. Concluding Remarks

We have presented speculative linearizability, an extension of the theory of linearizability. Our extension allows us to implement linearizable objects by composing independently devised speculation phases that are optimized for different situations. This form of intra-object composition complements the classical concept of inter-object composition, inherent to linearizability in its traditional form. We propose a formalized framework that enables, for the first time, scalable mechanically-checked development of linearizable objects of arbitrary abstract data types.

Our work can be viewed as generalization of [1] and [2]. The former work focused on contention-free executions and did not address composition: a protocol that aborts simply stops executing with no possibility of switching. In the latter work, a classification of the trace properties that are switchable is proposed. A global synchronization is required for switching. In contrast, our notion of speculative linearizability does not require the switching protocols to solve agreement and is, in that sense, much more general. Our work can also be viewed as a formalization of a generalized form of *Abortable State Machine Replication (Abstract)*, an abstraction presented in an intuitive form in [8] to allow the construction of speculative Byzantine Fault Tolerant SMR protocols by composing independently designed speculation phases. Compared to [8] , our work concerns arbitrary abstract data types, including one-shot ones, and generalizes the idea to linearizability. Being strictly more general, our framework can be used to reason about the fault-tolerant algorithms developed following those approaches [1, 2, 8].

References

[1] M. K. Aguilera, S. Frolund, V. Hadzilacos, S. L. Horn, and S. Toueg. Abortable and query-abortable objects and their efficient implementation. In *PODC*, 2007.

[2] M. Bickford, C. Kreitz, R. v. Renesse, and X. Liu. Proving hybrid protocols correct. In *TPHOLs '01*, 2001.

[3] W. J. Bolosky, D. Bradshaw, R. B. Haagens, N. P. Kusters, and P. Li. Paxos replicated state machines as the basis of a high-performance data store. In *Proc. NSDI*. USENIX Assoc., 2011.

[4] M. Burrows. The Chubby lock service for loosely-coupled distributed systems. In *Proc. OSDI*. USENIX Assoc., 2006.

[5] M. Castro and B. Liskov. A correctness proof for a practical byzantine-fault-tolerant replication algorithm. Technical report, MIT, 1999.

[6] M. Castro and B. Liskov. Practical Byzantine fault tolerance. In *OSDI*, 1999.

[7] E. Gafni and L. Lamport. Disk paxos. *Distributed Computing*, 16(1):1–20, 2003.

[8] R. Guerraoui, N. Knezevic, V. Quema, and M. Vukolic. The Next 700 BFT Protocols. In *EUROSYS*, 2010.

[9] R. Guerraoui, V. Kuncak, and G. Losa. Speculative Linearizability. Technical Report 170038, EPFL, 2011.

[10] R. Guerraoui, V. Kuncak, and G. Losa. Abortable linearizable modules. In G. Klein, T. Nipkow, and L. Paulson, editors, *The Archive of Formal Proofs*. `http://afp.sf.net/entries/Abortable_Linearizable_Modules.shtml`, March 2012. Formal proof development.

[11] M. Herlihy. Wait-free synchronization. *ACM Trans. Program. Lang. Syst.*, 13:124–149, January 1991.

[12] M. P. Herlihy and J. M. Wing. Linearizability: a correctness condition for concurrent objects. *ACM Trans. Program. Lang. Syst.*, 12(3):463–492, 1990.

[13] M. Jaskelioff and S. Merz. Proving the correctness of Disk Paxos. In G. Klein, T. Nipkow, and L. Paulson, editors, *The Archive of Formal Proofs*. `http://afp.sf.net/entries/DiskPaxos.shtml`, June 2005. Formal proof development.

[14] P. Jayanti. Adaptive and efficient abortable mutual exclusion. In *PODC*, 2003.

[15] R. Kotla, L. Alvisi, M. Dahlin, A. Clement, and E. Wong. Zyzzyva: speculative Byzantine fault tolerance. In *SOSP*, 2007.

[16] L. Lamport. The implementation of reliable distributed multiprocess systems. *Computer Networks*, 2:95–114, 1978.

[17] L. Lamport. On interprocess communication. part I: Basic formalism. *Distributed Computing*, 1(2):77–85, 1986.

[18] L. Lamport. On interprocess communication. part II: Algorithms. *Distributed Computing*, 1(2):86–101, 1986.

[19] L. Lamport. A fast mutual exclusion algorithm. *ACM Trans. Comput. Syst.*, 5(1):1–11, 1987.

[20] N. Lynch and F. Vaandrager. Forward and backward simulations I: untimed systems. *Inf. Comput.*, 121:214–233, September 1995.

[21] N. A. Lynch and M. R. Tuttle. An introduction to input/output automata. *CWI Quarterly*, 2:219–246, 1989.

[22] O. Müller. I/O automata and beyond: Temporal logic and abstraction in Isabelle. In *TPHOLs*, pages 331–348, 1998.

[23] F. Pedone. Boosting system performance with optimistic distributed protocols. *Computer*, 34(12):80–86, 2001.

[24] A. Singh, T. Das, P. Maniatis, P. Druschel, and T. Roscoe. BFT protocols under fire. In *NSDI*, 2008.

[25] M. M. V. Luchangco and N. Shavit. On the uncontended complexity of consensus. In *ICDCS*, pages 45–59, 2003.

[26] M. Wenzel. Isar - a generic interpretative approach to readable formal proof documents. In *TPHOLs*, pages 167–184, 1999.

Algorithmic Profiling

Dmitrijs Zaparanuks
University of Lugano
Dmitrijs.Zaparanuks@usi.ch

Matthias Hauswirth
University of Lugano
Matthias.Hauswirth@usi.ch

Abstract

Traditional profilers identify where a program spends most of its resources. They do not provide information about *why* the program spends those resources or about how resource consumption *would change* for different program inputs. In this paper we introduce the idea of *algorithmic profiling*. While a traditional profiler determines a set of measured cost *values*, an algorithmic profiler determines a cost *function*. It does that by automatically determining the "inputs" of a program, by measuring the program's "cost" for any given input, and by inferring an empirical cost function.

Categories and Subject Descriptors C.4 [*Performance of Systems*]: Measurement techniques; D.2.8 [*Software Engineering*]: Metrics—Performance measures

General Terms Performance, Measurement

Keywords Algorithmic Profiling, Algorithmic Complexity

1. Introduction

When developers need to understand and optimize the performance of their code, they use traditional profilers. Since the introduction of gprof [5], profilers have been focused on finding the locations in software that are responsible for excessive resource consumption, be that execution time, memory allocation, usage, or leaks, cache performance, various forms of contention, or even energy consumption. One commonality of such profiling approaches is that they only provide information about a specific program run. Different runs, with different inputs, may lead to different profiles. A profile created by a traditional profiler does not enable the developer to predict how the program might scale to larger inputs, and it provides only limited information for the reasons of the observed resource consumption.

The resource consumption of a software system is affected by three main factors, (1) the *algorithm* used, (2) the *problem size* (the program input), and (3) the *implementation* of that algorithm in a programming language running on a concrete execution platform. Traditional profilers provide measures of resource consumption that conflate all three factors: they only report the overall cost. They do not help in understanding how the cost was affected by the algorithm, the program input, and the underlying implementation.

Our new profiling approach, *Algorithmic Profiling*, addresses this limitation. Instead of providing a single number representing the cost of a given run, we provide a *cost function* that relates program input to algorithmic steps.

Algorithms researchers and advanced practitioners use cost functions when analyzing the complexity of their algorithms. They usually perform asymptotic analysis to bound cost. In contrast, our algorithmic profiling approach automatically determines approximate cost functions based on multiple program runs. Our cost functions are approximations, not bounds. They thus provide no guarantees, but they have the advantage that they represent the *expected* realistic cost, not a possibly loose worst case bound or an idealized, potentially unrealistic, average case cost.

The program in **Listing 1** shows an implementation of the insertion sort algorithm for a linked list. If we run this program under a traditional hotness profiler, we learn that most of the execution time is spent in method `sort`. A finer grained profile would tell us in which lines, statements, or bytecode instructions we spent most time. However, the profile would not provide any information about the algorithmic complexity of the program. An algorithmic profiler, on the other hand, would automatically produce results such as the ones shown in **Figure 1**. The figure shows three examples. In all three examples the program was run on a set of inputs that are representative of the expected application usage. In the top plot (a), that usage corresponds to sorting random lists, in the middle plot (b), it corresponds to sorting lists that are already sorted, while in the bottom plot (c), it correspond to sorting lists that are already sorted in reverse order. The x-axis in each plot shows the input size (corresponding to the length of the list), and the y-axis shows the number of algorithmic steps (corresponding to overall iteration counts). Each dot represents a program run with a different input, and the curves represent the approximate cost functions of the program expected for the given type of inputs.

These plots may look simple, and indeed, they are what a programmer would produce when manually determining the empirical cost function of an algorithm. The programmer would study the code to (1) locate the algorithm, to (2) determine the algorithm's essential operations (e.g., the comparisons or the swaps in the insertion sort), to (3) determine what the input of the algorithm could be (e.g., the linked list passed as an argument to the sort function), and to (4) determine how to quantify the input's size (e.g., by traversing the linked lists to count the number of nodes). He would then (5) instrument the program to count these operations and to measure the input's size. Our algorithmic profiling approach performs all the above steps *automatically* for arbitrary programs. It only needs the original program and a set of representative program executions to produce graphs like those in Figure 1.

These graphs of cost functions provide the developer with much deeper insight into program performance than a simple hotness profile. A hotness profile provides a single number (or a number for each code region). An algorithmic profile uncovers the relationship of execution cost and program input. It provides the programmer with scalability information by pointing out algorithms with high complexity, and it uncovers which inputs are the causes of long

PLDI'12, June 11–16, 2012, Beijing, China.

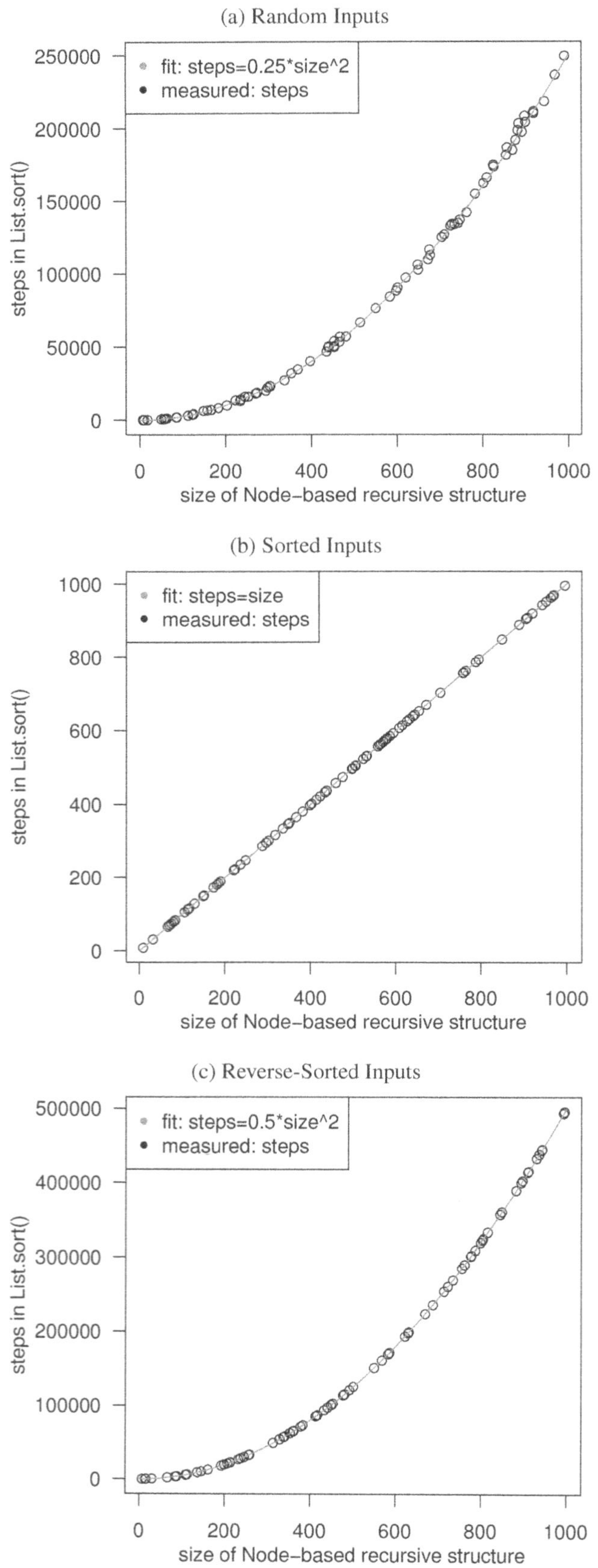

Figure 1. Cost Function of Insertion Sort

Listing 1. Insertion Sort

```
public class List {
 private Node head, tail;
 public void sort() {
  if (head==null || head.next==null) return;
  Node firstUnsorted = head.next;
  while (firstUnsorted!=null) {
   Node target = firstUnsorted;
   Node nextUnsorted = firstUnsorted.next;
   while (target.prev!=null &&
          target.prev.value>target.value) {
    final Node candidate = target.prev;
    final Node pred = candidate.prev;
    final Node succ = target.next;
    if (pred!=null) {
     pred.next = target;
    } else {
     head = target;
    }
    target.prev = pred;
    if (succ!=null) {
     succ.prev = candidate;
    } else {
     tail = candidate;
    }
    candidate.next = succ;
    target.next = candidate;
    candidate.prev = target;
   }
   firstUnsorted = nextUnsorted;
  }
 }
 public void append(int value) {
  final Node node = new Node(value);
  if (tail==null) {
   tail = node;
   head = tail;
  } else {
   tail.next = node;
   node.prev = tail;
   tail = tail.next;
  }
 }
}
```

running times. Moreover, by combining an algorithmic profile with a traditional hotness profile, the developer can understand all three factors (problem size, algorithmic complexity, and implementation cost) affecting the overall performance of the program.

This paper makes the following contributions:

1. We introduce *Algorithmic Profiling*, an approach to automatically infer approximations of the *expected algorithmic cost functions* of algorithm implementations. An algorithmic profiler requires no human intervention or code annotations. It simply analyzes program executions on a set of representative inputs.
2. We discuss different approaches to automatically determine the *input* of an algorithm and its size (the domain of the cost function). Traditionally, a human analyst has to define the concrete meaning of the abstract notion of “input size” (e.g., the size of this array, the number of nodes in this tree) for a given algorithm implementation.
3. We discuss different approaches to automatically determine the *cost* of an algorithm (the range of the cost function). Traditionally, a human analyst has to specify how to measure the cost of

Listing 2. Example Program

```java
public class Main {
 public static void main(String[] args) {
  measure();
 }
 private static void measure() {
  for (int size=0; size<1000; size++) {
   for (int i=0; i<10; i++) {
    final List list = new List();
    constructRandom(list, size);
    sort(list);
   }
  }
 }
 private static void constructRandom(
     List list, int size) {
  final Random r = new Random();
  for (int i=0; i<size; i++) {
   list.append(r.nextInt(size));
  }
 }
 private static void sort(List list) {
  list.sort();
 }
}

public class Node {
 public Node prev;
 public Node next;
 public final int value;
 public Node(int value) {
  this.value = value;
 }
}
```

an algorithm (e.g., the number of comparisons, or the number of swaps).

4. We present an approach to automatically *partition a program into multiple algorithms*. Any realistic program involves many different algorithms, and the boundaries between algorithms are difficult to define. We introduce an intuitive heuristic to identify boundaries between different algorithms in a program.
5. We describe AlgoProf, our prototype implementation of an Algorithmic Profiler for Java programs, and we demonstrate it in several small case studies.

The remainder of this paper is structured as follows. Section 2 presents our approach, Section 3 describes our implementation, Section 4 demonstrates the approach, Section 5 discusses limitations and future work, Section 6 presents related work, and Section 7 concludes.

2. Approach

This section describes the idea of Algorithmic Profiling on a conceptual level. The next section will describe our prototype, AlgoProf, which implements some, but not all, of the key aspects of this approach. We explain our approach based on a running example, which consists of the full program (**Listing 2**) containing the insertion sort algorithm shown in Listing 1. The program constructs an unsorted linked list of `Nodes` in `Main.constructRandom()` and sorts that list in `Main.sort()`. This process is repeated for lists of length 0 to 999, ten times for each length, in `Main.measure()`.

Most traditional profilers attach execution cost to syntactic constructs (e.g., methods or statements) of the program. **Figure 2** illustrates an example of such a profile, showing the calling context

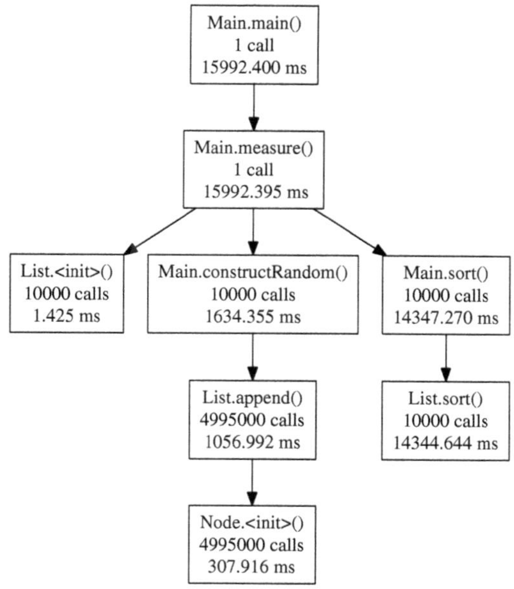

Figure 2. Traditional Profile: Calling Context Tree

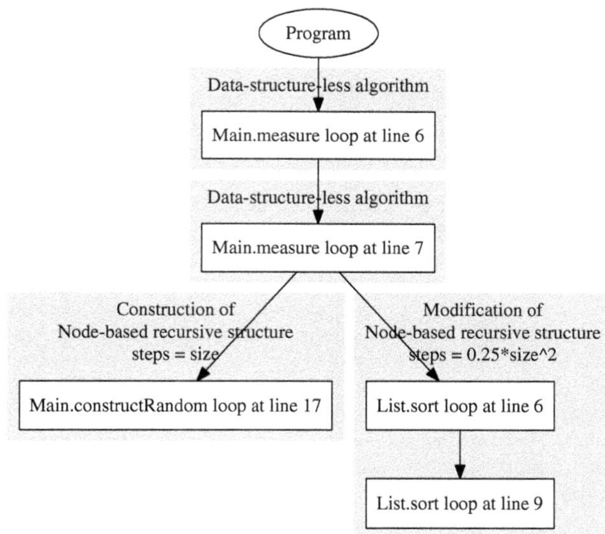

Figure 3. Algorithmic Profile: Repetition Tree

tree of our running example. Each method (or, more precisely, each calling context) is annotated with the number of times it was called and the total time spent in it (its hotness). The profile shows that `List.append` and the `Node` constructor are the most frequently called methods, and that `List.sort` is the hottest method (in terms of exclusive time). The profile does not provide any information for the cause of the hotness (why the method takes so much time), and it does not allow the developer to predict how different inputs would affect the hotness. These two aspects are important for understanding and improving program performance.

Our algorithmic profiles provide this missing information. They focus on *repetitions*, which are the essential ingredients of any algorithm [21]. We identify all *loops* in control-flow graphs and all *recursions* in the program's call graph. Instead of attributing execution cost to a calling context tree, we attribute execution cost and inputs to a "repetition tree" (a dynamic loop and recursion nesting tree). **Figure 3** shows the repetition tree for our running example. It shows that our program contains five loops, and it shows their dynamic nesting. Instead of using cost metrics such as invocation counts, wall-clock time, or instruction counts, we use higher-level cost metrics such as repetition counts and data structure access counts. Moreover, unlike traditional profilers, we also determine the algorithm input and the size of that input. Given a set of program runs, each providing an input size and a cost, we then produce plots mapping input size to cost (like those in Figure 1) and we infer cost functions (like `steps = 0.25*size^2` in Figure 3).

For our running example, the annotation in the bottom right gray box in Figure 3 shows that our profiler automatically identified an algorithm that *modifies* a `Node`-based recursive structure (a data structure consisting of objects of class `Node`). This tells us that the algorithm does not just traverse the structure, but that it modifies it, without creating new `Nodes`. It also shows that, given a structure of *size* `Nodes`, this algorithm takes 0.25*size^2 algorithmic steps. This information represents a high-level summary of the algorithm's performance. A developer can retrieve the data from which that cost function was inferred (the plot in Figure 1 (a)), and get summary statistics (such as the number of times the algorithm was called, or the range of input sizes it encountered). Given this information – that the algorithm's expected complexity is quadratic, and that the sizes of the inputs are not negligible – the developer can decide to constrain the size of the input, or to replace the algorithm with a more efficient one.

2.1 Construct Repetition Tree

The repetition tree is our basic structure for representing a set of program executions. Figure 3 shows a repetition tree for a program without recursion. To construct repetition trees of recursive programs, we collapse recursive call chains, and we represent the header method of the recursive chain as a node in the repetition tree. The repetition tree thus consists of loop nodes and recursion header nodes. Each node represents a repetitive computation. It keeps track of each invocation of that computation (entrance to the loop, and entry call of the recursion header method). For each invocation of a repetitive computation, we gather the number of repetitions (counting loop back edge traversals, and counting subsequent calls to the recursion header method).

An *algorithm* corresponds to a connected subgraph of the repetition tree. It has a root node, to which we attribute cost and input size. It may also contain descendants of the root node, if they are deemed to be part of the same algorithm (see Section 2.5 for how we group repetition nodes into algorithms). Figure 3 represents each algorithm with a gray rectangle, annotated with information about its input and with an empirical cost function.

2.2 Measure Cost

Computational complexity theory uses *models of computation* that define the set of primitive operations used in the computation and their respective costs. These models, and their primitive operations, are chosen by the person performing the analysis. A commonly used model is the *random access machine model*, where the primitive operations are memory reads and writes, and where these operations have unit cost.

Our algorithmic profiling approach also admits multiple possible cost models. Our models are defined by their primitive operations. We abstract away from the underlying platform and focus on operations that are meaningful to the developer at the source code level:

Algorithmic Steps. An algorithmic step corresponds to one iteration of a loop or recursion. An algorithmic step is a generic operation that abstracts away from the specific operations performed in each repetition. It thus allows the comparison of the cost of arbitrary repetitions using a single measure.

Structure Reads. A structure read corresponds to a read of a reference in a recursive data type or a load of an element in an array. It allows us to distinguish between read-only traversals of structures and modifications of structures.

Structure Writes. Analog to a structure read, a structure write corresponds to an update of a reference in a recursive data type or a store of an element in an array.

Structure Element Creations. A structure element creation corresponds to the allocation of a new object of a recursive data type. It allows us to distinguish between modifications and constructions of a data structure.

Input Reads. An input read corresponds to a read operation of data from outside the program (e.g., a read from a file or network socket). Some algorithms may not operate on in-memory structures, but they may consume input from outside the program.

Output Writes. An output write corresponds to a write operation of data to the outside world (e.g., a write to a file or network socket).

2.3 Determine Inputs

To determine the inputs of an algorithm, an algorithmic profiler determines which data structures or external files the algorithm accesses.

Recursive Data Structures. To find the recursive data structures related to an algorithm, the profiler tracks accesses to field references within all recursive data structures (`Node.next` and `Node.prev` in our running example), and whenever an access occurs at runtime, it determines the current node in the repetition tree (the innermost loop or recursion), and it associates that data structure with the corresponding repetition node.

Arrays. To find arrays related to an algorithm, the profiler tracks all array loads and stores and associates the corresponding arrays with the current repetition tree node.

Program Inputs/Outputs. To find program inputs and outputs related to an algorithm, the profiler tracks all reads and writes to the external world, and associates the corresponding streams or file handles to the current repetition tree node.

Given our approach, an algorithm can be related to multiple inputs. For example, an algorithm may traverse a graph-like data structure and serialize it into a file, it may traverse a given data structure and produce a "translation" in the form of a different structure (e.g., convert a linked list into an array), or it may process information from two independent data structures (e.g., compute the dot product of two vectors). An algorithmic profiler will keep track of all the inputs it encounters.

Some algorithms (for example mathematical algorithms) do not operate on data *structures* and do not read or write external data, but they encode data in primitive types (e.g., in variables of type `int`). For such algorithms, determining the "input" (and input size) is difficult. For example, the input size n for multiplication (with a complexity of $O(n^2)$ when using the schoolbook long multiplication algorithm) is defined by the *number of digits* in the factors, while the input size m for the factorial algorithm (with a complexity of $O(m^2 \log m)$ when using bottom-up multiplication) is the *value* of the argument. Note that for arbitrary precision arithmetic, the algorithms will have to use either recursive types or arrays to represent their numbers, and thus our approach will be able to compute some measure of the input size.

2.4 Measure Input Size

To measure the input size, we traverse the recursive data structure, we count the array's elements, or we measure the size of the external file. In an executing program, structures are dynamic: they shrink and grow. Many algorithms do not just traverse a structure, but they modify it throughout their execution. There thus is no single size of a structure, and we have to measure the size of a structure every time an algorithm accesses that structure. To find a single number representing the size (needed to compute a cost function relating structure size to execution cost) we use the *maximum* size of the structure throughout the algorithm's operation. Using the maximum is reasonable as it produces intuitive results for the many common algorithms that *create* a structure (size is 0 at the beginning and N at the end), or algorithms that *destroy* a structure.

If we repeatedly want to measure the size of a continuously *changing* structure, we need to address the issue of identity. How do we know whether two structures that are not identical should be considered the same? Is a structure with one less element still the same structure? We answer these questions as follows. Each time a structure is accessed, we take a snapshot of that structure by traversing it. A snapshot of a structure I corresponds to the set S of all elements in that structure at that time. We use one of the following *equivalence criteria* to determine whether two snapshots represent the *same* structure.

All Elements Equivalent. Two snapshots S_1 and S_2 are equivalent if all elements of the two snapshots are equivalent ($S_1 \equiv S_2$).

Some Elements Equivalent. Two snapshots S_1 and S_2 are equivalent if some of the elements of the two snapshots are equivalent ($S_1 \cap S_2 \neq \emptyset$). This less strict equivalence criterion is not only useful because data structures evolve, but also because the traversals capturing the two snapshots may have started from different elements, and thus the two snapshots may not see all the elements of the entire structure (if the structure instance is not strongly connected).

Same Array. This equivalence criterion only works for arrays. Array elements are contained in an array object, and thus two snapshots that correspond to identical arrays ($I_1 \equiv I_2$) can be considered equivalent.

Same Type. Two snapshots are equivalent if they have the same type ($t(S_1) \equiv t(S_2)$). This criterion considers two entirely disconnected structure instances equivalent.

2.5 Group Repetition Nodes into Algorithms

Given a realistic program, does that program implement one big algorithm, or does it implement a collection of multiple algorithms? We argue that both answers are valid, and that algorithms can invoke other algorithms just like methods can invoke other methods. While a program could be described as one large algorithm, the computational constructs programmers usually call "algorithm" are more limited in focus. In our motivating example, sorting the list represents a traditional algorithm, and constructing the list represents another algorithm. The loop nest in the `measure` method is more difficult to classify: it could be considered yet another algorithm, each of its two loops could be considered an independent algorithm, or the two loops could be considered too trivial for being called an algorithm at all. To approximate an intuitive notion of algorithm, we partition the repetition tree of an entire program run into connected subgraphs using one of several possible strategies. Moreover, given an interactive visualization tool for the repetition tree, developers could group nodes into algorithms according to their own intuition.

Listing 3. Combining Costs

```
for (int o=0; o<3; o++) {
  ...
  for (int i=0; i<o; i++) {
    ...
  }
  ...
}
```

Our profiling approach uses an automatic strategy for grouping repetition tree nodes into algorithms. The general idea is to group parent and child repetitions that access at least one common input into a single algorithm. We use the equivalence criteria defined in the previous section to determine whether the two structure snapshots from the two repetitions represent the same structure. In our running example, the two loops in the sort method intuitively form a single algorithm. For this example, all of the applicable equivalence criteria (*Same Array* is not applicable for a recursive data structure) would lead to this intuitive grouping of repetition nodes. One could envision other strategies, such as the grouping of loops located in the same method (which would work for the sort algorithm in the running example).

2.6 Combine Costs

When two repetition tree nodes are grouped into an algorithm, the child's cost is added to the parent's cost. In particular, for a given invocation of the parent, the parent's overall cost is equal to the parent's cost (e.g., algorithmic steps) plus the sum of the child's costs across all invocations of the child inside that parent invocation.

In the example of **Listing 3**, the cost of an invocation of the outer loop would be 3 outer loop iterations plus (0+1+2) inner loop iterations, leading to a total of 6 algorithmic steps. By also counting the outer loop's iterations, this approach accounts for outer loop iterations even when the inner loop does not execute.

2.7 Infer Cost Function

Given a set of <input size, cost> tuples, an algorithmic profiler should produce plots like those in Figure 1. Those plots show the raw data and a cost function. The step of automatically inferring a cost function or estimating an upper bound asymptotic complexity from the raw data is the subject of study in the area of *empirical algorithmics* [8, 9, 14], which investigates the use of regression approaches and heuristics for this purpose. In this paper we do not discuss this step, and in our algorithmic profiling prototype we currently fit cost functions by hand.

2.8 Classify Algorithms

Besides inferring a cost function for an algorithm, an algorithmic profiler can provide additional information that helps in understanding the algorithm. In particular, given the information about the algorithm's input, the profiler can distinguish between several different kinds of algorithms:

Traversal. A traversal algorithm performs a read-only traversal of a recursive data structure or an array. It performs *Structure Reads*, but does not perform any *Structure Writes* or *Structure Element Creations*.

Modification. A modification algorithm modifies the links of a recursive data structure or the contents of an array. It performs *Structure Writes*, but does not perform any *Structure Element Creations*. As Figure 3 shows, the loop nest in `List.sort` is considered a "Modification of a `Node`-based recursive structure".

Construction. A construction algorithm performs *Structure Element Creations*, that is, it allocates objects of recursive types. As Figure 3 shows, the loop in `List.constructRandom` is considered a "Construction of a `Node`-based recursive structure".

Input. An input algorithm performs *Input Reads*, that is, it consumes external input.

Output. An output algorithm performs *Output Writes*, that is, it produces external output.

Data-structure-less algorithm. Any algorithm that does not fall into any of the above categories is considered data-structure-less. The absence of a measurable input also means that we are unable to infer the input size and cost function. As Figure 3 shows, the two loops in `Main.measure` are considered "Data structure-less algorithms".

Traversal, modification, and construction are mutually exclusive with respect to a given data structure. That is, if an algorithm constructs a specific data structure (e.g., the `constructRandom` loop in the running example creates a `Node`-based structure), it is classified as a construction of that data structure, but not as a modification or traversal of that data structure. This mutual exclusion is limited to operations on the same data structure, e.g., the same algorithm may traverse one data structure and construct a different data structure.

3. Implementation

To evaluate our algorithmic profiling approach we built AlgoProf, an algorithmic profiler for Java. AlgoProf analyzes and instruments Java bytecode.

3.1 Instrumentation

AlgoProf uses dynamic binary instrumentation to instrument the following constructs in the application code:

Loop entry and loop exit. These drive the construction of the loop nodes in the repetition tree.

Loop back edges. These support counting algorithmic steps.

Method entries and exits. These enable the construction of the recursion nodes in the repetition tree. Moreover, they enable the counting of algorithmic steps in recursive algorithms. By using a static analysis to determine headers in recursive method cycles [21], AlgoProf can limit this instrumentation to only those methods that are recursion headers.

Array and reference instance field accesses. These *ALOAD and *ASTORE as well as PUTFIELD and GETFIELD bytecode instructions enable the detection and measurement of input data and the counting of read or write-based costs. By using a static analysis to determine recursive data structures [22], AlgoProf can limit field access instrumentation to accesses of fields participating in a recursive cycle (e.g., `Node.next` and `Node.prev`, but not `Node.payload`).

Object allocations. These NEW bytecode instructions enable the counting of allocation-based costs. Static analysis can limit this instrumentation to allocations of instances of classes that are part of a recursive type (e.g., `Node`).

AlgoProf currently does not track external program input and output operations. Support for this could be added by instrumenting the Java I/O classes.

3.2 Dynamic Analysis

At runtime, AlgoProf is called from the instrumented code. It collects all the information necessary for producing an algorithmic profile. Most importantly, it incrementally builds a repetition tree for each thread executing in the program. The tree already folds recursive calls, so on any given path to the root, a given method can only occur once. To support the unwinding of recursive calls, AlgoProf also maintains an unfolded shadow stack (`stack`). Each stack element represents a loop or recursion and points to the corresponding repetition tree node. At any given time, AlgoProf maintains a reference to the current repetition tree node (`tn`). The element at the top of the shadow stack (`stack.top()`) usually points to the same repetition tree node pointed to by `tn`. AlgoProf handles calls from the instrumented code in the following ways:

Loop entry.
```
tn = tn.getOrCreateChild(loop)
stack.push(tn)
```

Loop exit.
```
remeasureInputs()
finalizeRepetition(tn)
tn = stack.pop()
```

Loop back edge.
```
tn.cost{STEP}++
```

Method entry.
```
header = tree.findOnPathToRoot(tn, method)
if (header!=null) {
  tn = header
  tn.cost{STEP}++
} else {
  tn = tn.getOrCreateChild(method)
}
tn.recursionDepth++
stack.push(tn)
```

Method exits.
```
tn.recursionDepth—
if (tn.recursionDepth==0) {
  remeasureInputs()
  finalizeRepetition(tn)
}
tn = stack.pop()
```

Array access.
```
tn.cost{type(array), LOAD/STORE}++
identifyAndMeasureArray(array, tn)
```

Reference instance field access.
```
if (partOfRecursiveType(type(object))) {
  tn.cost{id(object), GET/PUT}++
  tn.cost{id(object), type(object), GET/PUT}++
  identifyAndMeasureStructure(object, tn)
}
```

Object allocation.
```
if (partOfRecursiveType(type(object))) {
  tn.cost{type(object), NEW}++
}
```

Note that AlgoProf correctly handles exceptional control flow, i.e., when exceptions cause control to exit a loop or a method, AlgoProf performs the corresponding *Loop exit* or *Method exit* operation.

3.3 Measuring Cost

The `cost` field in the repetition tree nodes represents a map from specific primitive operations (on specific inputs) to their execution counts.

Algorithmic step. `cost{STEP}` $\rightarrow$ `15` means that the repetition performed 15 algorithmic steps.

Array access. `cost{input#1, LOAD}` $\rightarrow$ `10` means that the repetition performed 10 LOAD operations on an array known as input with ID 1.

Recursive structure access. `cost{input#3, PUT}` $\rightarrow$ `99` means that the repetition performed 99 PUT operations on the recursive structure known as input with ID 3.

Recursive structure access (by element type). `cost{input#3, Vertex, PUT}` $\rightarrow$ `33` means that the repetition performed 33 PUT operations on fields of type `Vertex` in the recursive structure known as input with ID 3 (e.g., a recursive structure modeling a graph as `Edge` and `Vertex` objects).

Recursive structure element creation. `cost{ListNode, NEW}` $\rightarrow$ `9` means that the repetition allocated 9 `ListNode` instances (a class that is part of a recursive structure).

The analysis calls `finalizeRepetition` whenever a repetition terminates (at a loop exit or at a return from the outermost call of a recursive method). This finalization of the repetition adds the contents of the `cost` field to the history of invocations of this repetition tree node. This means that each node in the repetition tree contains historical information (data structure sizes and operation counts) for each and every invocation of that repetition. While this can lead to large memory requirements for our profiler, keeping historic input size and cost information is necessary to infer cost functions. To reduce this overhead, an optimized version of a profiler could try to infer the cost function online, and discard the individual data points, or it could try to sample a subset of invocations for frequently invoked repetitions.

3.4 Measuring Input Size

To identify an input and to determine its size, we traverse the corresponding array or recursive structure. We measure input sizes in three possible situations:

`IdentifyAndMeasureArray` is called due to an array access. For array identification, out of the strategies described in Section 2.5, AlgoProf implements the *Some Elements Identical* strategy, because it is effective for algorithms that "resize" arrays by reallocation[1].

AlgoProf supports two strategies for measuring the size of an array: the *capacity* strategy uses the array's capacity (the number of elements the array can store), while the *unique element count* strategy traverses all elements of the array (for reference arrays, all non-null elements), and computes the size of the set of unique elements. This second strategy is useful to approximate the amount of space used in an array by algorithms that allocate an array but only use a small fraction of its capacity. However, it has the drawback that it does not count duplicate elements. This is particularly problematic for arrays of small primitive types (e.g., booleans or bytes).

AlgoProf treats multi-dimensional arrays analog to algorithmic steps. That is, it counts all elements of the top-level array and all elements of the lower-level arrays. For example, the 2-dimensional triangular array `new int[][] {new int[0], new int[1], new int[2]}` has a size of $3 + (0 + 1 + 2)$ elements, which is exactly the same as the number of algorithmic steps in the analog loop nest in Listing 3.

`IdentifyAndMeasureStructure` is called due to a recursive reference field access. For recursive data structure identification, out of the strategies described in Section 2.5, AlgoProf implements the *Some Elements Identical* strategy.

A recursive data structure can consist of multiple Java classes. For example, a graph can be modeled as a recursive structure involving a `Vertex` and an `Edge` class. AlgoProf provides a total object count (i.e., the total number of objects involved in a graph), and it provides separate counts of objects for each specific type (i.e., the number of `Vertex` objects involved in the graph, and the number of `Edge` objects involved in that graph). Many recursive structures also involve arrays. For example, a tree may consist of a `Node` class that has a `Node[]` field containing references to all its children. When traversing a recursive structure, we also traverse these arrays. In addition to object counts, AlgoProf also provides the counts of non-null array elements traversed in this way. Analog to object counts, AlgoProf provides a total reference count as well as separate reference counts by types. For example, for a graph modeled with a `Vertex` class that has a `Vertex[]` field containing references to all its incident vertices, the graph's edges are implicit and correspond to the references in the `Vertex[]`.

`IdentifyAndMeasureStructure` receives an object reference. It starts traversing the structure at that reference. If the structure is not strongly connected, then it will not reach all objects that might be deemed part of that structure (had the traversal started from a different object reference). This is one reason for why AlgoProf uses the *Some Elements Identical* strategy to determine the equivalence of two recursive structure snapshots.

`RemeasureInputs` is called when control exits the repetition (exit from a loop or recursive call chain). It enables an optimization: instead of taking a structure snapshot at every access to a structure, we only take two snapshots: first at the repetition's first accesses of the structure (starting from the first reference accessed), and a second time when the repetition exits (starting from the last reference accessed in that repetition). This way, if a repetition is a *Construction*, such as in one of the examples in **Listing 4**, we can still traverse and measure the completely constructed input in the end, but we do not need to traverse the structure at every access. We only need to memorize the one accessed reference at every access, so we know where to start our traversal from at the exit of the repetition.

3.5 Using AlgoProf

AlgoProf produces an algorithmic profile consisting of a repetition tree similar to the one shown in Figure 3. For each algorithm, it produces multiple plots of its complexity, based on the combinations of their inputs (sizes of all their accessed structures) and cost measures (algorithmic steps, the various structure access counts, and element allocation counts). Figure 1 (a) shows an example of such a plot for the sort algorithm in Figure 3, with the number of `Node` objects in the `Node`-based recursive structure as input size and algorithmic steps as the cost measure. AlgoProf currently does not automatically fit a cost function onto the measured data points, but we manually fit those functions using a statistics package. Given that we have several cost measures, and given that some algorithms access multiple inputs, the number of cost functions for each algorithm can become large. We use simple heuristics to automatically

[1] Implementations of resizable arrays allocate a new, larger, array when the current backing-array gets full. Treating the original (small) and the newly allocated (grown) array as the same input is essential when reasoning about an algorithm operating on such a dynamically resizable array.

Listing 4. First access in Constructions cannot see whole structure

```
Node constructListWithLoop(int size) {
  Node list;
  for (int i=0; i<size; i++) {
    Node head = new Node();
    // first PUTFIELD: reachable structure size 1
    head.next = list;
    list = head;
  }
  return head;
}
Node constructListWithRecursion(int size) {
  if (size==0) return null;
  else {
    Node list = constructList(size-1);
    Node head = new Node();
    // first PUTFIELD: reachable structure size 1
    head.next = list;
    return head;
  }
}
void constructPartiallyUsedArray() {
  int[] values = new int[1000];
  for (int i=0; i<10; i++) {
    // first IASTORE: array "size" 1
    values[i] = i*2;
  }
}
```

highlight useful ones: we focus on algorithmic steps as a cost, and we exclude those cost functions of inputs that never change in size or that cause constant cost.

Moreover, for realistic applications, we use traditional CCT hotness profiles (gathered with Java's built-in hprof profiler) to focus algorithmic profiling on hot regions of code.

4. Demonstration

We now summarize the behavior of AlgoProf on several examples representing creations and traversals of various data structure implementations, and we present two small, illustrative examples.

4.1 Handling Different Kinds of Data Structures

Table 1 provides an overview over 18 illustrative example programs we profiled with AlgoProf. Those programs essentially implement traversals of various data structure implementations. Each example focuses on one kind of data structure but implements several algorithms (e.g., building the structure, traversing the structure iteratively, and traversing the structure recursively).

The examples involve naked arrays, lists, trees, and graphs (column "Struct"). Column "Impl." shows how this structure is implemented (as an "array", or as a "linked" (recursive) data structure). Column "Linkage" shows how the elements of the structure are linked. Column "T" describes how one can define the structure's payload type (the type of the information stored inside the elements): the type of the payload is hard-coded (B), the structure uses inheritance to allow subclasses to define the payload type (I), or the structure uses generics (G) to allow defining the payload type. Column "Rem." contains further remarks: For arrays it specifies whether they are one or multi-dimensional, for dynamically resized array-based lists it describes how they grow (grow by one, or double in size), and for trees it describes their arity (binary or N-ary).

The remaining three columns summarize the results. Column "I" states whether all the inputs we as programmers considered inputs were detected (x) or not (-). For all these examples, AlgoProf detected the inputs as expected. Column "S" shows that AlgoProf correctly measured the size of each input. Column "G" describes whether the loops we consider to be part of one algorithm were indeed grouped together (x) or not (-). In this column, a (*) means that we ended up with a correct grouping, but that a slight change in the algorithm's implementation could lead to an incorrect grouping. The way AlgoProf groups repetitions into algorithms does not work well for array-based systems. The reason is that in repetition nests that implement an algorithm, such as the one in **Listing 5**, sometimes only the innermost repetition actually accesses the array. That is, outside the innermost loop, the outer loop contains no *ALOAD or *ASTORE instructions that would access the array. Thus, AlgoProf does not merge the two loops into one algorithm, but it creates two separate algorithms instead: the innermost loop which is accessing the array, and the outer loop as a data-structure-less algorithm.

Listing 5. Repetition nest not grouped by AlgoProf

```
int[][] array = ...;

for (int i=0; i<array.length; i++)
  // no access to array[i] here
  for (int j=0; j<array[i].length; j++)
    array[i][j] = ...;
```

We believe that this limitation could be overcome with a data-flow analysis that determines which loops increment the indices used in the array accesses. For Listing 5, the outer loop increments variable i, which is then used in the array access in the inner loop. Such an approach could be considered the dual to the way we handle recursive structures: we look at the accesses of the recursive links (e.g., the `next` field in a linked list node), not at the accesses of the payload (e.g., the `value` field in a linked list node; or the element in an array).

Struct	Impl.	Linkage	T	Rem.	I	S	G
array	array	NA	B	1d	x	x	*
array	array	NA	B	2d	x	x	-
list	array	NA	B	double	x	x	*
list	array	NA	B	grow by 1	x	x	*
list	array	NA	G	grow by 1	x	x	*
list	array	NA	I	grow by 1	x	x	*
list	linked	directed	B		x	x	x
list	linked	directed	G		x	x	x
list	linked	directed	I		x	x	x
tree	array	NA	B	binary	x	x	*
tree	linked	directed	B	binary	x	x	x
tree	linked	bidi	B	binary	x	x	x
tree	linked	directed	B	n-ary	x	x	x
tree	linked	bidi	B	n-ary	x	x	x
graph	array	directed	B	2d	x	x	-
graph	linked	directed	B		x	x	x
graph	linked	bidi	B		x	x	x
graph	linked	unidirected	B		x	x	x

Table 1. Data Structure Examples

4.2 Uncovering Algorithmic Inefficiencies

Listing 6 shows an implementation of a dynamically-growing array-backed list. Given that Java's arrays cannot grow, such a list needs to allocate a new, larger array when it runs out of space in the current array. A naive developer will grow the array by one element (or by a constant number of elements) which will lead to quadratic cost. By changing one line in the code (grow the array by doubling its size), the cost can be made linear.

Listing 6. Growing an array-backed list

```
final ArrayList list = new ArrayList();
for (int i=0; i<size; i++) {
  list.append("n"+i);
}
...
public void append(final String value) {
  growIfFull();
  array[size++] = value;
}
private void grow() {
  if (size==array.length) {
    final String[] newArray =
      new String[array.length+1]; // naive
      new String[array.length*2]; // ideal
    for (int i=0; i<array.length; i++)
      newArray[i] = array[i];
    array = newArray;
  }
}
```

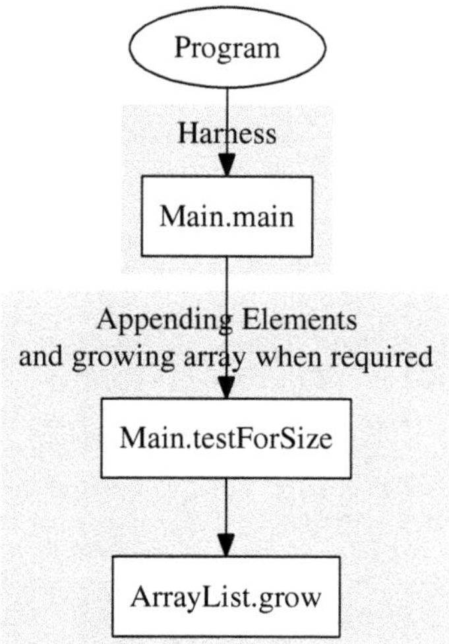

Figure 4. Repetition tree for growing an array-backed list

Figure 4 shows the program's repetition tree, indicating three repetition nodes grouped into two algorithms. The top algorithm consists of the harness running `testForSize` with various sizes. The lower algorithm consists of the loop calling `list.append()` and the inner loop that grows the list. Given that the two loops are grouped together, we see the total cost of appending *size* elements. **Figure 5** shows the corresponding cost function. For the naive developer's implementation, the cost grows quadratically in the size of the list. For the ideal implementation, the cost grows linearly.

4.3 Being Agnostic to Programming Paradigm

The insertion sort implementation in Listing 1 is imperative, iterative, and uses a mutable data structure. Does AlgoProf produce the same profile for an insertion sort implementation that is functional, recursive, and uses an immutable data structure? We found that the profile was almost identical[2]. The repetition tree contains the same repetitions as the tree in Figure 1, and the repetitions are grouped into the same algorithms with the same complexities. This demonstrates one of the key points about algorithmic profiling: the implementations may look entirely different, but their automatically generated algorithmic profiles agree.

[2] `http://sape.inf.usi.ch/algorithmic-profiling`

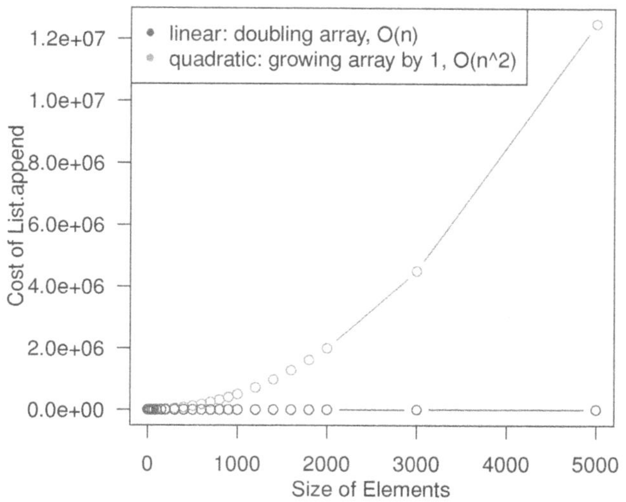

Figure 5. Cost functions for growing array by 1 and doubling array

5. Limitations and Future Work

AlgoProf is based on heuristics. Its grouping of repetitions into algorithms and its notion of "input" (the way it identifies the data an algorithm is tied to) may not always match the developer's intuition. Moreover, AlgoProf can only infer a cost function for algorithms that operate on data structures, because it cannot infer any input size for algorithms that operate on primitive data types. Finally, its cost functions only represent approximations. However, we believe that the repetition tree, the (partial) grouping of repetition tree nodes into algorithms based on the data they access, the classification of these algorithms (into construction, modification, traversal, input, and output), and the approximations of their cost functions, provide useful information to a developer. We are not aware of any other profiling approach that can produce such information automatically.

The probably most severe limitation of AlgoProf is its overhead, both in terms of space and time. Realistic benchmarks execute several orders of magnitude slower under AlgoProf. However, AlgoProf only represents an initial prototype, without any significant optimizations. There is a clear need – and we believe a great potential – for optimizations. For example, taking complete snapshots of structures at ever access, or even at every start and end of a repetition, and storing the complete snapshots in memory, is wasteful, and incremental approaches, together with more powerful static analyses, could probably drastically reduce the overhead of our current prototype. Similar gains might be possible by piggybacking data structure size measurements on the heap traversals performed by the garbage collector

While AlgoProf correctly deals with multiple threads, our approach specifically targets sequential algorithms. AlgoProf produces a repetition tree for each thread, and it completely ignores any communication between threads.

Besides investigating possible optimizations for our approach, we also would like to perform a more thorough evaluation. AlgoProf cannot possibly be "correct" in what it deems an algorithm, that algorithm's input, and a useful measure of cost. All it can do is match a human developer's intuition. Thus, it would be interesting to explore how algorithmic profiles help developers to detect and fix performance bugs, and which of its strategies and heuristics are most effective for this purpose.

6. Related Work

Goldsmith et al. [4] had a similar goal to ours: they ran a program given several inputs, measured cost and fitted a curve. However, except for the cost, which was automatically determined by counting basic block invocations, the other aspects (e.g., algorithm identification and input size determination) had to be performed manually. Later work [3] proposed to switch the cost metric from basic block counts to loop iterations, but it ignored recursions, and it still required all the former manual interventions. Related work in empirical algorithmics [8, 9, 14] discusses the difficulties in inferring algorithmic cost functions and asymptotic complexity from experimental data. And further research analyzes program executions to extract performance models other than cost functions, for example models in the form of layered queueing networks [6].

Jump [7] introduces dynamic shape analysis, focusing on the shapes and sizes of recursive structures in the heap. Prior research [13, 15] performed shape analysis statically. We traverse recursive heap structures at runtime, when identifying inputs, and we measure their sizes. We do not, however, try to infer any shape properties. We possibly might benefit from understanding their shape properties, for example to incrementalize our approach to measuring structure sizes.

Further work on analyzing data structures at runtime includes approaches to find costly data structures [10], to measure object lifetimes [2], to track data structures for post-mortem analysis [16], to profile the use of recursive data structures [11, 12], to perform "copy profiling" [19], to find "low-utility data structures" [20], to perform "container profiling" [17] and to find "inefficiently used containers" [18]. It would be interesting to try to combine those approaches with algorithmic profiling.

Recently, Bergel et al. presented domain-specific profiling [1], an approach that also produces higher-level profiles. That work takes almost the opposite direction as ours: algorithmic profiling is a domain-*independent* profiling approach that strives to achieve a level of abstraction without requiring any developer involvement.

7. Conclusions

Algorithmic profiling is an automatic approach to infer the computational cost of the algorithms embodied in a program. Given a program and a set of representative program executions, an algorithmic profiler identifies algorithms and inputs to those algorithms, measures meaningful notions of cost, and infers a cost function for each algorithm that relates cost to input size. The profiler presents the programmer with a repetition tree, in which it highlights the algorithms. It annotates each algorithm with the kind of operations it performs (e.g., construct, modify, traverse), the kind of data structures it processes, and an estimated cost function.

Developers can use algorithmic profiles to identify algorithms with high computational complexity, or to better understand program regions with high measured execution times. Given an algorithmic profile, programmers can further estimate how a program scales, that is, how a program's running time would be affected by further increases in input size.

We believe that *algorithmic profiling* relates to *algorithmic complexity analysis* like *software testing* relates to *formal verification*: it does not provide any guarantees, but can be effective in finding and fixing real-world problems.

References

[1] A. Bergel, O. Nierstrasz, L. Renggli, and J. Ressia. Domain-specific profiling. In J. Bishop and A. Vallecillo, editors, *Objects, Models, Components, Patterns*, volume 6705 of *Lecture Notes in Computer Science*, pages 68–82. Springer, 2011.

[2] B. Dufour, B. G. Ryder, and G. Sevitsky. Blended analysis for performance understanding of framework-based applications. In *Proceedings of the 2007 international symposium on Software testing and analysis*, ISSTA '07, pages 118–128. ACM, 2007.

[3] S. F. Goldsmith. *Measuring Empirical Computational Complexity*. PhD thesis, University of California, Berkeley, 2009.

[4] S. F. Goldsmith, A. S. Aiken, and D. S. Wilkerson. Measuring empirical computational complexity. In *Proceedings of the the 6th joint meeting of the FSE*, ESEC-FSE '07, pages 395–404. ACM, 2007.

[5] S. L. Graham, P. B. Kessler, and M. K. McKusick. gprof: a call graph execution profiler. *SIGPLAN Not.*, 39(4):49–57, 2004.

[6] T. Israr, M. Woodside, and G. Franks. Interaction tree algorithms to extract effective architecture and layered performance models from traces. *J. Syst. Softw.*, 80:474–492, April 2007.

[7] M. Jump and K. S. McKinley. Dynamic shape analysis via degree metrics. In *Proceedings of the 2009 international symposium on Memory management*, ISMM '09, pages 119–128. ACM, 2009.

[8] C. McGeoch, P. Sanders, R. Fleischer, P. R. Cohen, and D. Precup. *Experimental algorithmics*, chapter Using finite experiments to study asymptotic performance. Springer, 2002.

[9] C. C. Mcgeoch. *Experimental analysis of algorithms*. PhD thesis, Carnegie Mellon University, Pittsburgh, PA, USA, 1986.

[10] N. Mitchell, E. Schonberg, and G. Sevitsky. Making sense of large heaps. In *Proceedings of the 23rd European Conference on ECOOP 2009*, Genoa, pages 77–97. Springer, 2009.

[11] S. Pheng and C. Verbrugge. Dynamic data structure analysis for java programs. In *Program Comprehension, 2006. ICPC 2006. 14th IEEE International Conference on*, pages 191 –201, 2006.

[12] E. Raman and D. I. August. Recursive data structure profiling. In *Proceedings of the 2005 workshop on Memory system performance*, MSP '05, pages 5–14. ACM, 2005.

[13] M. Sagiv, T. Reps, and R. Wilhelm. Solving shape-analysis problems in languages with destructive updating. *ACM Trans. Program. Lang. Syst.*, 20:1–50, January 1998.

[14] P. Sanders and R. Fleischer. Asymptotic complexity from experiments? a case study for randomized algorithms. In *WAE '00: Proceedings of the 4th International Workshop on Algorithm Engineering*, pages 135–146. Springer, 2001.

[15] R. Wilhelm, S. Sagiv, and T. W. Reps. Shape analysis. In *Proceedings of the 9th International Conference on Compiler Construction*, CC '00, pages 1–17. Springer, 2000.

[16] X. Xiao, J. Zhou, and C. Zhang. Tracking data structures for post-mortem analysis. In *ICSE 2011 NIER Track*, 2011.

[17] G. Xu and A. Rountev. Precise memory leak detection for java software using container profiling. In *Proceedings of the 30th international conference on Software engineering*, ICSE '08, pages 151–160. ACM, 2008.

[18] G. Xu and A. Rountev. Detecting inefficiently-used containers to avoid bloat. In *Proceedings of the 2010 ACM SIGPLAN conference on Programming language design and implementation*, PLDI '10, pages 160–173, New York, NY, USA, 2010. ACM.

[19] G. Xu, M. Arnold, N. Mitchell, A. Rountev, and G. Sevitsky. Go with the flow: profiling copies to find runtime bloat. In *Proceedings of the 2009 ACM SIGPLAN conference on Programming language design and implementation*, PLDI '09, pages 419–430. ACM, 2009.

[20] G. Xu, N. Mitchell, M. Arnold, A. Rountev, E. Schonberg, and G. Sevitsky. Finding low-utility data structures. In *Proceedings of the 2010 ACM SIGPLAN conference on Programming language design and implementation*, PLDI '10, pages 174–186. ACM, 2010.

[21] D. Zaparanuks and M. Hauswirth. The beauty and the beast: Separating design from algorithm. In *Proceedings of the European Conference on Object-Oriented Programming (ECOOP'11)*, 2011.

[22] D. Zaparanuks and M. Hauswirth. Vision paper: The essence of structural models. In J. Whittle, T. Clark, and T. Kühne, editors, *Model Driven Engineering Languages and Systems*, volume 6981 of *Lecture Notes in Computer Science*, pages 470–479. Springer, 2011.

Understanding and Detecting Real-World Performance Bugs

Guoliang Jin Linhai Song Xiaoming Shi Joel Scherpelz * Shan Lu
University of Wisconsin–Madison
{aliang, songlh, xiaoming, shanlu}@cs.wisc.edu joel.scherpelz@gmail.com

Abstract

Developers frequently use inefficient code sequences that could be fixed by simple patches. These inefficient code sequences can cause significant performance degradation and resource waste, referred to as performance bugs. Meager increases in single threaded performance in the multi-core era and increasing emphasis on energy efficiency call for more effort in tackling performance bugs.

This paper conducts a comprehensive study of 109 real-world performance bugs that are randomly sampled from five representative software suites (Apache, Chrome, GCC, Mozilla, and MySQL). The findings of this study provide guidance for future work to avoid, expose, detect, and fix performance bugs.

Guided by our characteristics study, efficiency rules are extracted from 25 patches and are used to detect performance bugs. 332 previously unknown performance problems are found in the latest versions of MySQL, Apache, and Mozilla applications, including 219 performance problems found by applying rules across applications.

Categories and Subject Descriptors D.2.5 [*Software Engineering*]: Testing and Debugging; D.4.8 [*Operating Systems*]: Performance

General Terms Languages, Measurement, Performance, Reliability

Keywords performance bugs, characteristics study, rule-based bug detection

1. Introduction

1.1 Motivation

Slow and inefficient software can easily frustrate users and cause financial losses. Although researchers have devoted decades to transparently improving software performance, *performance bugs* continue to pervasively degrade performance and waste computation resources in the field [40]. Meanwhile, current support for combating performance bugs is preliminary due to the poor understanding of real-world performance bugs.

Following the convention of developers and researchers on this topic [5, 26, 40, 50], we refer to performance bugs as software defects where relatively simple *source-code* changes can significantly speed up software, while preserving functionality. These defects can**not** be optimized away by state-of-practice compilers, thus bothering end users. Figure 1 shows an example of a real-world performance bug. Apache HTTPD developers forgot to change a parameter of API apr_stat after an API upgrade. This mistake caused more than ten times slowdown in Apache servers.

Patch for Apache Bug 45464	**What is this bug**
modules/dav/fs/repos.c	An Apache-API upgrade causes **apr_stat** to retrieve more information from the file system and take longer time.
status = apr_stat (fscontext->info, - APR_DEFAULT); + APR_TYPE);	Now, APR_TYPE retrieves exactly what developers originally needed through APR_DEFAULT.
Impact: causes httpd server **10+ times slower** in file listing	

Figure 1: A performance bug from Apache-HTTPD ('+' and '-' denote the code added and deleted to fix this bug)

Performance bugs exist widely in released software. For example, Mozilla developers have fixed 5–60 performance bugs reported by users *every month* over the past 10 years. The prevalence of performance bugs is inevitable because little work has been done to help developers avoid performance-related mistakes. In addition, performance testing mainly relies on ineffective black-box random testing and manual input design, which allows the majority of performance bugs to escape [40].

Performance bugs lead to reduced throughput, increased latency, and wasted resources in the field. In the past, they have caused several highly publicized failures, causing hundred-million dollar software projects to be abandoned [41, 45].

Worse still, performance problems are costly to diagnose due to their non fail-stop symptoms. Software companies may need several months of effort by experts to find a couple of performance bugs that cause a few hundred-millisecond delay in the 99th percentile latency of their service [49].

The following trends will make the performance-bug problem more critical in the future:

Hardware: For many years, Moore's law ensured that hardware would make software faster over time with no software development effort. In the multi-core era, when each core is unlikely to become faster, performance bugs are particularly harmful.

Software: The increasing complexity of software systems and rapidly changing workloads provide new opportunities for performance waste and new challenges in diagnosis [11].

Energy efficiency: Increasing energy costs provide a powerful economic argument for avoiding performance bugs. When one is willing to sacrifice the service quality to reduce energy consumption [3, 31], ignoring performance bugs is unforgivable. For exam-

* This work was done when the author was a graduate student at University of Wisconsin. Currently the author is working in NVIDIA.

PLDI'12, June 11–16, 2012, Beijing, China.

ple, by fixing bugs that have doubled the execution time, one may potentially halve the carbon footprint of buying and operating computers.

Performance bugs may not have been reported as often as functional bugs, because they do not cause fail-stop failures. However, considering the preliminary support for combating performance bugs, it is time to pay more attention to them when we enter a new resource-constrained computing world.

1.2 Contribution 1: Characteristics Study

Many empirical studies [7, 34, 43, 46, 53] have been conducted for traditional bugs that lead to incorrect software functionality, referred to as *functional bugs*. These studies have successfully guided the design of functional software testing, functional bug detection, and failure diagnosis.

Poor understanding of performance bugs and wrong perceptions, such as *"performance is taken care of by compilers and hardware"*, are partly the causes of today's performance-bug problem [12]. The lack of empirical studies on topics like "how performance bugs are introduced", "what input conditions are necessary to expose performance bugs", "what the common root causes of real-world performance bugs are", and "how performance bugs are fixed by developers", have severely limited the design of performance-bug avoidance, testing, detection, and fixing tools.

This paper makes the first, to the best of our knowledge, comprehensive study of real-world performance bugs based on 109 bugs randomly collected from the bug databases of five representative open-source software suites (Apache, Chrome, GCC, Mozilla, and MySQL). Our study has made the following findings.

Guidance for bug avoidance. Two thirds of the studied bugs are introduced by developers' wrong understanding of workload or API performance features. More than one quarter of the bugs arise from previously correct code due to workload or API changes. To avoid performance bugs, developers need performance-oriented annotation systems and change-impact analysis. (Section 4.2).

Guidance for performance testing. Almost half of the studied bugs require inputs with **both** special features and large scales to manifest. New performance-testing schemes that combine the input-generation techniques used by functional testing [4, 17] with a consideration towards large scales will significantly improve the state of the art (Section 4.3).

Guidance for bug detection. Recent works [5, 11, 26, 47, 57, 58] have demonstrated the potential of performance-bug detection. Our study found common root-cause and structural patterns of real-world performance bugs that can help improve the coverage and accuracy of performance-bug detection (Sections 4.1 and 4.5).

Guidance for bug fixing and detection. Almost half of the examined bug patches include reusable efficiency rules that can help detect and fix performance bugs (Section 4.4).

Comparison with functional bugs. Performance bugs tend to hide for much longer time in software than functional bugs (Section 4.5). Unlike functional bugs, performance bugs cannot all be modeled as rare events, because a non-negligible portion of them can be triggered by almost all inputs (Section 4.3).

General motivation (1) Many performance-bug patches are small. The fact that we can achieve significant performance improvement through a few lines of code change motivates researchers to pay more attention to performance bugs (Section 4.4). (2) A non-negligible portion of performance bugs in multi-threaded software are related to synchronization. Developers need tool support to avoid over-synchronization traps (Section 4.3).

1.3 Contribution 2: Bug Detection

Rule-based bug detection is effective for detecting functional bugs [6, 21, 30, 42]. Following our characteristics study, we hypothesize that (1) efficiency-related rules exist; (2) we can extract rules from performance-bug patches; and (3) we can use the extracted rules to discover previously unknown performance bugs.

To test these hypotheses, we collected rules from 25 Apache, Mozilla, and MySQL bug patches and built static checkers to find violations to these rules.

Our checkers automatically found 125 *potential performance problems* (*PPPs*) in the original buggy versions of Apache, Mozilla, and MySQL. Programmers failed to fix them together with the original 25 bugs where the rules came from.

Our checkers also found 332 previously unknown PPPs in the latest versions of Apache, Mozilla, and MySQL. These include 219 PPPs found by checking an application using rules extracted from a *different* application.

Our thorough code reviews and unit testings confirm that each PPP runs significantly slower than its functionality-preserving alternate suggested by the checker. Some of these PPPs are already confirmed by developers and fixed based on our report.

The main contribution of our bug-detection work is that it confirms the existence and value of efficiency rules: efficiency rules in our study are usually violated at more than one place, by more than one developer, and sometimes in more than one program. Our experience motivates future work to automatically generate efficiency rules, through new patch languages [43], automated patch analysis [36], source code analysis, or performance-oriented annotations. Future work can also improve the accuracy of performance-bug detection by combining static checking with dynamic analysis and workload monitoring.

2. Methodology

2.1 Applications

Application Suite Description (language)	# Bugs
Apache Suite HTTPD: Web Server (C) TomCat: Web Application Server (Java) Ant: Build management utility (Java)	25
Chromium Suite Google Chrome browser (C/C++)	10
GCC Suite GCC & G++ Compiler (C/C++)	10
Mozilla Suite Firefox: Web Browser (C++, JavaScript) Thunderbird: Email Client (C++, JavaScript)	36
MySQL Suite Server: Database Server (C/C++) Connector: DB Client Libraries (C/C++/Java/.Net)	28
Total	109

Table 1: Applications and bugs used in the study

We chose five open-source software suites to examine: Apache, Chrome, GCC, Mozilla, and MySQL. These popular, award-winning software suites [22] are all large-scale and mature, with millions of lines of source code and well maintained bug databases.

As shown in Table 1, these five suites provide a good coverage of various types of software, such as interactive GUI applications, server software, command-line utilities, compilers, and libraries. They are primarily written in C/C++ and Java. Although they are all open-source software, Chrome is backed up by Google and MySQL was acquired by Sun/Oracle in 2008. Furthermore, the Chrome browser was first released in 2008, while the other four have had 10–15 years of bug reporting history. From these applications, we can observe both traditions and new software trends such as web applications.

2.2 Bug Collection

GCC, Mozilla, and MySQL developers *explicitly* mark certain reports in their bug databases as performance bugs using special tags, which are *compile-time-hog*, *perf*, and *S5* respectively. Apache and Chrome developers do not use any special tag to mark performance bugs. Therefore, we searched their bug databases using a set of performance-related keywords ('slow', 'performance', 'latency', 'throughput', etc.).

From these sources, we *randomly* sampled 109 fixed bugs that have sufficient documentation. The details are shown in Table 1.

Among these bugs, 44 were reported after 2008, 38 were reported between 2004 and 2007, and 27 were reported before 2004. 41 bugs came from server applications and 68 bugs came from client applications.

2.3 Caveats

Our findings need to be taken with the methodology in mind. The applications in our study cover representative and important software categories, workload, development background, and programming languages. Of course, there are still uncovered categories, such as scientific computing software and distributed systems.

The bugs in our study are collected from five bug databases without bias. We have followed the decisions made by developers about what are performance bugs, and have not intentionally ignored any aspect of performance problems in bug databases. Of course, some performance problems may never be reported to the bug databases and some reported problems may never be fixed by developers. Unfortunately, there is no conceivable way to study these unreported or unfixed performance problems. We believe the bugs in our study provide a representative sample of the reported and fixed performance bugs in these representative applications.

We have spent more than one year to study all sources of information related to each bug, including forum discussions, patches, source code repositories, and others. Each bug is studied by at least two people and the whole process consists of several rounds of bug (re-)study, bug (re-)categorization, cross checking, etc.

Finally, we do not emphasize any quantitative characteristic results, and most of the characteristics we found are consistent across all examined applications.

3. Case Studies

The goal of our study is to improve software efficiency by inspiring better techniques to avoid, expose, detect, and fix performance bugs. This section uses four motivating examples from our bug set to demonstrate the feasibility and potential of our study. Particularly, we will answer the following questions using these examples: (1) Are performance bugs too different from traditional bugs to study along the traditional bug-fighting process (i.e., bug avoidance, testing, detection, and fixing)? (2) If they are not too different, are they too similar to be worthy of a study? (3) If developers were more careful, do we still need research and tool support to combat performance bugs?

Transparent Draw (Figure 2) Mozilla developers implemented a procedure nsImage::Draw for figure scaling, compositing, and rendering, which is a waste of time for transparent figures. This problem did not catch developers' attention until two years later when 1 pixel by 1 pixel transparent GIFs became general purpose spacers widely used by Web developers to work around certain idiosyncrasies in HTML 4. The patch of this bug skips nsImage::Draw when the function input is a transparent figure.

Intensive GC (Figure 3) Users reported that Firefox cost 10 times more CPU than Safari on some popular Web pages, such as gmail.com. Lengthy profiling and code investigation revealed that Firefox conducted an expensive garbage collection process GC at the end of *every* XMLHttpRequest, which is too frequent. A developer then recalled that GC was added there five years ago when XHRs were infrequent and each XHR replaced substantial portions of the DOM in JavaScript. However, things have changed

Mozilla Bug 66461 & Patch	What is this bug

nsImage::Draw(...) {
...
+ if(mIsTransparent) return;
...
//render the input image
} *nsImageGTK.cpp*
	When the input is a transparent image, all the computation in *Draw* is useless.
	Mozilla developers did not expect that transparent images are commonly used by web developers to help layout.
	The patch conditionally skips *Draw*.

Figure 2: A Mozilla bug drawing transparent figures

Mozilla Bug 515287 & Patch	What is this bug

XMLHttpRequest::OnStop(){
//at the end of each XHR
...
-- *mScriptContext->GC();*
} *nsXMLHttpRequest.cpp*
	This was not a bug until Web 2.0, where doing garbage collection (*GC*) after every XMLHttpRequest (XHR) is too frequent.
	It causes Firefox to consume **10X more CPU** at idle GMail pages than Safari.

Figure 3: A Mozilla bug doing intensive GCs

Mozilla Bug 490742 & Patch	What is this bug

for (i = 0; i < tabs.length; i++) {
...
- tabs[i].doTransact();
}
+ doAggregateTransact(tabs);
nsPlacesTransactionsService.js
	doTransact saves one tab into 'bookmark' SQLite Database.
	Firefox hangs @ 'bookmark all (tabs)'.
	The patch adds a new API to aggregate DB transactions.

Figure 4: A Mozilla bug with un-batched DB operations

MySQL Bug 38941 & Patch	What is this bug
int fastmutex_lock (fmutex_t *mp){ ... - maxdelay += (double) **random**(); + maxdelay += (double) **park_rng**(); ... } *thr_mutex.c*	random() is a serialized global-mutex-protected glibc function. Using it inside '*fastmutex*' causes **40X slowdown** in users' experiments.

Figure 5: A MySQL bug with over synchronization

in modern Web pages. As a primary feature enabling web 2.0, XHRs are much more common than five years ago. This bug is fixed by removing the call to GC.

Bookmark All (Figure 4) Users reported that Firefox hung when they clicked 'bookmark all (tabs)' with 20 open tabs. Investigation revealed that Firefox used *N* database transactions to bookmark *N* tabs, which is very time consuming comparing with batching all bookmark tasks into a single transaction. Discussion among developers revealed that the database service library of Firefox did not provide interface for aggregating tasks into one transaction, because there was almost no batchable database task in Firefox a few years back. The addition of batchable functionalities such as 'bookmark all (tabs)' exposed this inefficiency problem. After replacing *N* invocations of doTransact with a single doAggregateTransact, the hang disappears. During patch review, developers found two more places with similar problems and fixed them by doAggregateTransact.

Slow Fast-Lock (Figure 5) MySQL synchronization-library developers implemented a fastmutex_lock for fast locking. Unfortunately, users' unit test showed that fastmutex_lock could be 40 times slower than normal locks. It turns out that library function random() actually contains a lock. This lock serializes every threads that invoke random(). Developers fixed this bug by replacing random() with a non-synchronized random number generator.

These four bugs can help us answer the questions asked earlier.

(1) They have similarity with traditional bugs. For example, they are all related to usage rules of functions/APIs, a topic well studied by previous work on detecting functional bugs [30, 33].

(2) They also have interesting differences compared to traditional bugs. For example, the code snippets in Figure 2–4 turned buggy (or buggier) long after they were written, which is rare for functional bugs. As another example, testing designed for functional bugs cannot effectively expose bugs like *Bookmark All*. Once the program has tried the 'bookmark all' button with one or two open tabs, bookmarking more tabs will not improve the statement or branch coverage and will be skipped by functional testing.

(3) Developers cannot fight these bugs by themselves. They cannot predict future workload or code changes to avoid bugs like *Transparent Draw*, *Intensive GC*, and *Bookmark All*. Even experts who implemented synchronization libraries could not avoid bugs like *Slow Fast-Lock*, given opaque APIs with unexpected performance features. Research and tool support are needed here.

Of course, it is premature to draw any conclusion based on four bugs. Next, we will comprehensively study 109 performance bugs.

4. Characteristics Study

We will study the following aspects of real-world performance bugs, following their life stages and different ways to combat them.

1. What are the root causes of performance bugs? This study will provide a basic understanding of real-world performance bugs and give guidance to bug detection research.

2. How are performance bugs introduced? This study will shed light on how to avoid introducing performance bugs.

3. How can performance bugs manifest? This study can help design effective testing techniques to expose performance bugs after they are introduced into software.

4. How are performance bugs fixed? Answers to this question will help improve the patching process.

The result of this study is shown in Table 2.

4.1 Root Causes of Performance Bugs

There are a large variety of potential root causes for inefficient code, such as poorly designed algorithms, non-optimal data structures, cache-unfriendly data layouts, etc. Our goal here is **not** to discover previously unheard-of root causes, but to check whether there are common root-cause patterns among real-world performance bugs that bug detection can focus on.

Our study shows that the majority of real-world performance bugs in our study are covered by only a couple of root-cause categories. Common patterns do exist and performance is mostly lost at call sites and function boundaries, as follows.

Uncoordinated Functions More than a third of the performance bugs in our study are caused by inefficient function-call combinations composed of efficient individual functions. This occurs to the *Bookmark All* example shown in Figure 4. Using doTransact to bookmark one URL in one database transaction is efficient. However, bookmarking *N* URLs using *N* separate transactions is less efficient than calling doAggregateTransact to batch all URL bookmarkings in one transaction.

Skippable Function More than a quarter of bugs are caused by calling functions that conduct unnecessary work given the calling context, such as calling nsImage::Draw for transparent figures in the *Transparent Draw* bug (Figure 2) and calling unnecessary GCs in the *Intensive GC* bug (Figure 3).

Synchronization Issues Unnecessary synchronization that intensifies thread competition is also a common cause of performance loss, as shown in the *Slow Fast-Lock* bug (Figure 5). These bugs are especially common in server applications, contributing to 4 out of 15 Apache server bugs and 5 out of 26 MySQL server bugs.

Others The remaining 23 bugs are caused by a variety of reasons. Some use wrong data structures. Some are related to hardware architecture issues. Some are caused by high-level design/algorithm issues, with long propagation chains. For example, MySQL39295 occurs when MySQL mistakenly invalidates the query cache for read-only queries. This operation itself does not take time, but it causes cache misses and performance losses later. This type of root cause is especially common in GCC.

4.2 How Performance Bugs Are Introduced

We have studied the discussion among developers in bug databases and checked the source code of different software versions to understand how bugs are introduced. Our study has particularly focused on the challenges faced by developers in writing efficient software, and features of modern software that affect the introduction of performance bugs.

Our study shows that developers are in a great need of tools that can help them avoid the following mistakes.

Workload Mismatch Performance bugs are most frequently introduced when developers' workload understanding does not match with the reality.

Our further investigation shows that the following challenges are responsible for most workload mismatches.

Firstly, the input paradigm could shift *after* code implementation. For example, the HTML standard change and new trends in web-page content led to *Transparent Draw* and *Intensive GC*, shown in Figure 2 and Figure 3.

Secondly, software workload has become much more diverse and complex than before. A single program, such as Mozilla, may face various types of workload issues: the popularity of transparent figures on web pages led to *Transparent Draw* in Figure 2; the high frequency of XMLHttpRequest led to *Intensive GC* in Figure 3; users' habit of not changing the default configuration setting led to Mozilla Bug110555.

The increasingly dynamic and diverse workload of modern software will lead to more performance bugs in the future.

API Misunderstanding The second most common reason is that developers misunderstand the performance feature of certain functions. This occurs for 31 bugs in our study.

Sometimes, the performance of a function is sensitive to the value of a particular parameter, and developers happen to use performance-hurting values.

Sometimes, developers use a function to perform task i, and are unaware of an irrelevant task j conducted by this function that hurts performance but not functionality. For example, MySQL developers did not know the synchronization inside random and introduced the *Slow Fast-Lock* bug shown in Figure 5.

Code encapsulation in modern software leads to many APIs with poorly documented performance features. We have seen developers explicitly complain about this issue [51]. It will lead to more performance bugs in the future.

Others Apart from workload issues and API issues, there are also other reasons behind performance bugs. Interestingly, some performance bugs are side-effects of functional bugs. For example, in Mozilla196994, developers forgot to reset a busy-flag. This semantic bug causes an event handler to be constantly busy. As a result, a performance loss is the only externally visible symptom of this bug.

When a bug was not buggy An interesting trend is that 29 out of 109 bugs were not born buggy. They became inefficient long after they were written due to workload shift, such as that in *Transparent Draw* and *Intensive GC* (Figures 2 and 3), and code changes in other part of the software, such as that in Figure 1.

	Apache	Chrome	GCC	Mozilla	MySQL	Total
Number of bugs studied	25	10	10	36	28	109
Root Causes of Performance Bugs						
Uncoordinated Functions: function calls take a detour to generate results	12	4	2	15	9	42
Skippable Function: a function call with un-used results	6	4	3	14	7	34
Synchronization Issues: inefficient synchronization among threads	5	1	0	1	5	12
Others: all the bugs not belonging to the above three categories	3	1	5	6	8	23
How Performance Bugs Are Introduced						
Workload Issues: developers' workload assumption is wrong or out-dated	13	2	5	14	7	41
API Issues: misunderstand performance features of functions/APIs	6	3	1	13	8	31
Others: all the bugs not belonging to the above two categories	6	5	4	10	13	38
How Performance Bugs Are Exposed						
Always Active: almost every input on every platform can trigger this bug	2	3	0	6	4	15
Special Feature: need special-value inputs to cover specific code regions	19	6	10	22	18	75
Special Scale: need large-scale inputs to execute a code region many times	17	2	10	23	19	71
Feature+Scale: the intersection of Special Feature and Special Scale	13	1	10	15	13	52
How Performance Bugs Are Fixed						
Change Call Sequence: a sequence of function calls reorganized/replaced	10	2	3	20	12	47
Change Condition: a condition added or modified to skip certain code	2	7	6	10	10	35
Change A Parameter: changing one function/configuration parameter	5	0	1	4	3	13
Others: all the bugs not belonging to the above three categories	9	3	0	4	7	23

Table 2: Categorization for Sections 4.1 – 4.4 (most categories in each section are not exclusive)

In Chrome70153, when GPU accelerator became available, some software rendering code became inefficient. Many of these bugs went through regression testing without being caught.

4.3 How Performance Bugs Are Exposed

We define *exposing a performance bug* as causing a *perceivably* negative performance impact, following the convention used in most bug reports.

Our study demonstrates several unique challenges for performance testing.

Always Active Bugs A non-negligible portion of performance bugs are almost always active. They are located at the start-up phase, shutdown phase, or other places that are exercised by almost all inputs. They could be very harmful in the long term, because they waste performance at every deployment site during every run of a program. Many of these bugs were caught during comparison with other software (e.g., Chrome vs. Mozilla vs. Safari).

Judging whether performance bugs have manifested is a unique challenge in performance testing.

Input Feature & Scale Conditions About two thirds of performance bugs need inputs with special features to manifest. Otherwise, the buggy code units cannot be touched. Unfortunately, this is not what black-box testing is good at. Much manual effort will be needed to design test inputs, a problem well studied by past research in functional testing [4, 5].

About two thirds of performance bugs need large-scale inputs to manifest in a perceivable way. These bugs cannot be effectively exposed if software testing executes each buggy code unit only once, which unfortunately is the goal of most functional testing.

Almost half of the bugs need inputs that have special features **and** large scales to manifest. For example, to trigger the bug shown in Figure 4, the user has to click 'bookmark all' (i.e., special feature), with many open tabs (i.e., large scale).

4.4 How Performance Bugs Are Fixed

We have manually checked the final patches to answer two questions. Are there common strategies for fixing performance bugs? How complicated are performance patches?

The result of our study is opposite to the intuition that performance patches must be complicated and lack common patterns.

Fixing strategies There are three common strategies in fixing performance bugs, as shown in Table 2.

The most common one is to change a function-call sequence, referred to as *Change Call Sequence*. It is used to fix 47 bugs. Many bugs with uncoordinated function calls are fixed by this strategy (e.g., *Bookmark All* in Figure 4). Some bugs with skippable function calls are also fixed by this strategy, where buggy function calls are removed or relocated (e.g. *Intensive GC* in Figure 3).

The second most common strategy is *Change Condition*. It is used in 35 patches, where code units that do not always generate useful results are conditionally skipped. For example, `Draw` is conditionally skipped to fix *Transparent Draw* (Figure 2).

Finally, 13 bugs are fixed by simply changing a parameter in the program. For example, the Apache bug shown in Figure 1 is fixed by changing a parameter of `apr_stat`; MySQL45475 is fixed by changing the configuration parameter `TABLE_OPEN_CACHE_MIN` from 64 to 400.

Are patches complicated? Most performance bugs in our study can be fixed through simple changes. In fact, 42 out of 109 bug patches contain five or fewer lines of code changes. The median patch size for all examined bugs is 8 lines of code.

The small patch size is a result of the above fixing strategies. *Change A Parameter* mostly requires just one line of code change. 33 out of the 47 *Change Call Sequence* patches involve only existing functions, with no need to implement new functions. Many *Change Condition* patches are also small.

4.5 Other Characteristics

Life Time We chose Mozilla to investigate the life time of performance bugs, due to its convenient CVS query interface. We consider a bug's life to have started when its buggy code was first written. The 36 Mozilla bugs in our study took 935 days on average to get discovered, and another 140 days on average to be fixed. For comparison, we randomly sampled 36 functional bugs from Mozilla. These bugs took 252 days on average to be discovered, which is much shorter than that of performance bugs in Mozilla.

These bugs took another 117 days on average to be fixed, which is a similar amount of time with those performance bugs.

Location For each bug, we studied the location of its minimum unit of inefficiency. We found that over three quarters of bugs are located inside either an input-dependent loop or an input-event handler. For example, the buggy code in Figure 3 is executed at every XHR completion. The bug in Figure 2 wastes performance for every transparent image on a web page. About 40% of buggy code units contain a loop whose number of iterations scales with input. For example, the buggy code unit in Figure 4 contains a loop that iterates as many times as the number of open tabs in the browser. In addition, about half performance bugs involve I/Os or other time-consuming system calls. There are a few bugs whose buggy code units only execute once or twice during each program execution. For example, the Mozilla110555 bug wastes performance while processing exactly two fixed-size default configuration files, userChrome.css and userContent.css, during the startup of a browser.

Correlation Among Categories Following previous empirical studies [29], we use a statistical metric *lift* to study the correlation among characteristic categories. The *lift* of category A and category B, denoted as *lift(AB)*, is calculated as $\frac{P(AB)}{P(A)P(B)}$, where P(AB) is the probability of a bug belonging to both categories A and B. When *lift(AB)* equals 1, category A and category B are independent with each other. When *lift(AB)* is greater than 1, categories A and B are positively correlated: when a bug belongs to A, it likely also belongs to B. The larger the *lift* is, the more positively A and B are correlated. When *lift(AB)* is smaller than 1, A and B are negatively correlated: when a bug belongs to A, it likely does not belong to B. The smaller the *lift* is, the more negatively A and B are correlated.

Among all categories, the *Skippable Function* root cause and the *Change Condition* bug-fix strategy are the most positively correlated with a 2.02 lift. The *Workload Issues* bug-introducing reason is strongly correlated with the *Change-A-Parameter* bug-fix strategy with a 1.84 lift. The *Uncoordinated Functions* root cause and the *API Issues* bug-introducing reason are the third most positively correlated pair with a 1.76 lift. On the other hand, the *Synchronization Issues* root cause and the *Change Condition* fix strategy are the most negatively correlated categories of different characteristic aspects[1]. Their lift is only 0.26.

Server Bugs vs. Client Bugs Our study includes 41 bugs from server applications and 68 bugs from client applications. To understand whether these two types of bugs have different characteristics, we apply chi-square test [56] to each category listed in Table 2. We choose 0.01 as the significance level of our chi-square test. Under this setting, if we conclude that server and client bugs have different probabilities of falling into a particular characteristic category, this conclusion only has 1% probability to be wrong.

We find that, among all the categories listed in Table 2, only the *Synchronization Issues* category is significantly different between server bugs and client bugs — *Synchronization Issues* have caused 22% of server bugs and only 4.4% of client bugs.

5. Lessons from Our Study

Comparison with Functional Bugs There are several interesting comparisons between performance and functional bugs. (1) The distribution of performance-failure rates over software life time follows neither the bathtub model of hardware errors nor the gradually maturing model of functional bugs, because performance bugs have long hiding periods (Section 4.5) and can emerge from non-buggy places when software evolves (Section 4.2). (2) Unlike functional bugs, performance bugs cannot always be modeled as rare events, because some of them are always active (Section 4.3). (3) The percentage of synchronization problems among performance bugs in our study is higher than the percentage of synchronization problems among functional bugs in a previous study for a similar set of applications [29] (Section 4.1).

Bug Detection Our study motivates future research in performance-bug detection: performance bugs cannot be easily avoided (Section 4.2); and, they can escape testing even when the buggy code is exercised (Section 4.3).

Our study provides future bug detectors with common root cause and location patterns (Section 4.1 and Section 4.5).

Rule-based bug detection [13, 21, 30, 33] are promising for detecting performance bugs. It will be discussed in Section 6 in detail. Invariant-based bug detection and delta debugging [14, 60] are also promising. Our study shows that the majority of performance bugs require special inputs to manifest (Section 4.3). In addition, the same piece of code may behave buggy and non-buggy in different software versions (Section 4.2). This provides opportunities for invariant extraction and violation checking.

Annotation Systems Annotation systems are used in many software development environments [37, 54]. Unfortunately, they mainly communicate functionality information.

Our study calls for performance-aware annotation systems [44, 55] that help developers maintain and communicate APIs' performance features and workload assumptions (Section 4.2). Simple support such as warning about the existence of locks in a library function, specifying the complexity of a function, and indicating the desired range of a performance-sensitive parameter can go a long way in avoiding performance bugs. Recent work that automatically calculates function complexity is also promising [18].

Testing Regression testing and change-impact analysis have to consider workload changes and performance impacts, because new performance bugs may emerge from old code (Section 4.2).

Performance testing can be improved if its input design combines smart input-generation techniques used in functional testing [4, 17] with an emphasis on large scale (Section 4.3).

Expressing performance oracles and judging whether performance bugs have occurred are critical challenges in performance testing (Section 4.3). Techniques that can smartly compare performance numbers across inputs and automatically discover the existence of performance problems are desired.

Diagnosis Profiling is frequently used to bootstrap performance diagnosis. Our root-cause study shows that extra analysis is needed to help diagnose performance bugs. It is difficult to use profiling alone to locate the root cause of a performance bug that has a long propagation chain or wastes computation time at function boundaries, which is very common (Section 4.1).

Future Directions One might argue that performance sometimes needs to be sacrificed for better productivity and functional correctness. However, the fact that we can often achieve significant performance improvement through only a few lines of code change motivates future research to pay more attention to performance bugs (Section 4.4). Our study suggests that the workload trend and API features of modern software will lead to more performance bugs in the future (Section 4.2). In addition, our study observes a significant portion of synchronization-related performance bugs in multi-threaded software. There will be more bugs of this type in the multi-core era.

Finally, our observations have been consistent across old software and new software (Chrome), old bugs (27 pre-2004 bugs) and new bugs (44 post-2008 bugs). Therefore, we are confident that these lessons will be useful at least for the near future.

[1] Two categories of the same aspect, such as the *Skippable Function* root cause and the *Uncoordinated Functions* root cause, usually have a highly negative correlation.

6. Rule-Based Performance-Bug Detection

6.1 Overview

Rule-based detection approach is effective for discovering functional bugs and security vulnerabilities [6, 15, 21, 30, 42]. Many functional bugs can be identified by comparing against certain function-call sequences that have to be followed in a program for functional correctness and security.

We hypothesize that rule-based bug detection is useful for detecting performance bugs based on our characteristics study:

Efficiency rules should exist. Those inefficient function-call sequences studied in Section 4.1 could all become rules. For example, random() should not be used by concurrent threads, and doTransact() in loops should be replaced by aggregateTransact().

Efficiency rules can be easily collected from patches, as most patches are small and follow regular fixing strategies (Section 4.4).

Efficiency rules could be widely applicable, as a misunderstanding of an API or workload could affect many places and lead to many bugs, considering how bugs are introduced (Section 4.2).

This section will test our hypothesis and provide guidance for future work on combating performance bugs.

6.2 Efficiency Rules in Patches

Terminology *Efficiency rules*, or *rules*, include two components: a *transformation* and a *condition* for applying the transformation. Once a code region satisfies the condition, the transformation can be applied to improve performance and preserve functionality.

We have manually checked all the 109 performance-bug patches. 50 out of these 109 patches contain efficiency rules, coming from all five applications. The other 59 do not contain rules, because they either target too specific program contexts or are too general to be useful for rule-based bug detection.

Call Sequence Conditions
function C::f() is invoked
function f1 is always followed by f2
function f1 is called once in each iteration of a loop
Parameter/Return Conditions
*n*th parameter of f1 equals K (constant)
*n*th parameter of f1 is the same variable as the return of f2
a param. of f1 and a param. of f2 point to the same object
the return of f1 is not used later
the parameter of f1 is not modified within certain scope
the input is a long string
Calling Context Conditions
function f1 is only called by one thread
function f1 can be called simultaneously by multiple threads
function f1 is called many times during the execution

Table 3: Typical conditions in function rules

Most of these 50 rules, according to the *lift* correlation metric, are related to the *Uncoordinated Functions* root cause and the *Change Call Sequence* fix strategy. The conditions for applying these rules are composed of conditions on function-call sequences, parameter/return variables, and calling contexts, as shown in Table 3. For example, to apply the *Bookmark All* patch in Figure 4 elsewhere, one needs to find places that call doTransact inside a loop; to apply the patch in Figure 1 elsewhere, one needs to ensure that certain fields of the object pointed by the first parameter of apr_stat is not used afterward. There are also non-function rules, usually containing *Change Condition* transformation and other miscellaneous algorithm improvements.

6.3 Building Rule Checkers

Selecting Statically Checkable Rules Some rules' applying conditions are statically checkable, such as function f1 inside a loop; some are dynamically checkable, such as function f1 called by multiple threads at the same time; some are related to workload, such as having many large input files.

We check three largest application suites in our study: Apache, MySQL, and Mozilla. We find that 40 bug patches from them contain rules. 25 out of these 40 have applying conditions that are mostly statically checkable. Therefore, we have built checkers based on these **25** efficiency rules.

Checker Implementation We build 25 checkers in total. 14 of them are built using LLVM compiler infrastructure [27] for rules from C/C++ applications. LLVM works well for C++ software that troubles many other static analysis infrastructure [43]. It also provides sufficient data type, data flow, and control flow analysis support for our checking. The other 11 checkers are written in Python for 11 rules from Java, JavaScript, and C# applications.

The checker implementation is mostly straightforward. Each checker goes through software bitcode, in case of LLVM checkers, or source code, in case of Python checkers, looking for places that satisfy the patch-applying condition. We briefly discuss how our checkers examine typical conditions for function rules in the following.

Checking call-sequence conditions, exemplified in Table 3, involve mainly three tasks: (1) Differentiating functions with the same name but different classes; (2) Collecting loop information (loop-head, loop-exit conditions, loop-body boundaries, etc.); (3) Control flow analysis. LLVM provides sufficient support for all these tasks. Checkers written in Python struggle from time to time.

Checking parameter/return conditions, exemplified in Table 3, typically rely on data-flow analysis. In our current prototype, LLVM checkers conduct intra-procedural data-flow analysis. This analysis is scalable, but may lead to false positives and negatives. In practice, it works well as shown by our experimental results. Our current Python checkers can extract parameters of particular function calls, but can only do preliminary data-flow analysis.

6.4 Rule-Checking Methodology

We conduct all the experiments on an 8-core Intel Xeon machine running Linux version 2.6.18.

We apply every checker to the following software:

(1) The exact version of the software that the original patch was applied to, which is referred to as *original version*;

(2) The latest version of the software that the original patch was applied to, which is referred to as *original software*;

(3) The latest versions of software applications that are **different** from the one that the original patch was applied to, which is referred to as *different software*. This was applied to 13 checkers, whose rules are about *glibc* library functions, Java library functions, and some general algorithm tricks. We will refer to this as *cross-application checking*. For example, a C/C++ checker from MySQL will be applied to Mozilla and Apache HTTPD for cross-application checking; a Java checker from Apache TomCat server will be applied to the 65 other Java applications in the Apache software suite[2].

The checking results are categorized into three types: *PPPs*, *bad practices*, and *false positives*. As discussed in Section 1.3, a PPP is an inefficient code region that runs slower than its functionality-preserving alternate implied by the efficiency rule. A bad practice is a region prone to becoming inefficient in the future. We reported some PPPs to developers. Among those reported, 14 PPPs detected by 6 different checkers have been confirmed and fixed by the

[2] Development teams behind different Apache applications are different

developers. Other reported PPPs are put on hold due to lack of bug-triggering input information, which is unfortunately out of the scope of this work.

Finally, we have also changed each checker slightly to report code regions that follow each efficiency rule. We refer to these regions as *good practices*, the opposite of PPPs.

6.5 Rule-Checking Results

Overall Results As shown in Table 4, 125 PPPs are found in the *original version* of software. Programmers missed them and failed to fix them together with the original bugs.

113 previously unknown PPPs are found in the latest versions of the *original software*, including bugs inherited from the original version and bugs newly introduced. Figure 6 shows an example.

219 previously unknown PPPs are found in the latest versions of *different software*. An example is shown in Figure 6.

14 PPPs in the latest versions of Apache, Mozilla, and MySQL are already confirmed and fixed by developers based on our report.

These results confirm that performance bugs widely exist. Efficiency rules exist and are useful for finding performance problems.

PPPs In Original Versions 17 out of 25 checkers found new PPPs, 125 in total, in the original versions of the buggy software.

Some developers clearly tried to find all similar bugs when fixing one bug, but did not succeed. For example, in MySQL14637, after two buggy code regions were reported, developers found three more places that were similarly inefficient and fixed them altogether. Unfortunately, there were another 50 code regions that violated the same efficiency rule and skipped developers' checking, as shown in Table 4. Similarly, MySQL developers found and fixed 3 places that had the inefficiency pattern shown in Figure 6, but missed the other 15 places.

113 out of these 125 PPPs exist in different files or even different modules where the original bugs exist, which is probably why they were missed by developers. These PPPs end up in several ways: (1) 4 of them were fixed in later versions, which took 14–31 months; (2) 20 eventually disappeared, because the functions containing these PPPs were removed or re-implemented; (3) 101 still exist in the latest versions of the software, wasting computation resources 12–89 months after the original bugs were fixed.

Lesson The above results show that developers do need support to systematically and automatically find similar performance bugs and fix them all at once.

PPPs In The Latest Versions 2 of the 25 checkers are no longer applicable in the latest versions, because the functions involved in these checkers have been removed. The remaining 23 checkers are applied to the latest versions of corresponding software and find 113 PPPs. Among them, 101 PPPs were inherited from the original buggy versions. The other 12 were introduced later.

Lesson Developers cannot completely avoid the mistakes they made and corrected before, which is understandable considering the large number of bugs in software. Specification systems and automated checkers can prevent developers from introducing old bugs into new code.

PPPs In Different Software Applications An exciting result is that 8 out of 13 cross-application checkers have successfully found previously unknown PPPs in the latest versions of applications that are different from where the rules came from.

Most of these checkers reflect common pitfalls in using library functions. For example, Figure 6 shows a pitfall of using String::indexof(). Apache-Ant developers made this mistake, and we found Apache-Struts developers also made a similar mistake.

Apache32546 checker presents an interesting case. In the original bug report, developers from Apache-Slide recognized that a small buffer size would severely hurt the performance of java.io.InputStream.read (byte buffer[]) for reasonably large input (e.g., larger than 50KB). Replacing their original 2KB buffer with a 200KB buffer achieved **80 times** throughput improvement in WebDav server. We first confirmed that this rule is still valid. Our checker then found 135 places in the latest versions of 36 software applications where similar mistakes were made. These places use small buffers (1KB – 4KB) to read images or data files from disk or web, and are doomed to performance losses.

Some checkers reflect algorithm improvements and are also applicable to many applications. For example, algorithm improvements for string operations proposed by MySQL developers (MySQL14637 and MySQL49491) also apply for Mozilla and Apache HTTPD.

Cross-application checking also helps validate efficiency rules. For example, by comparing how java.util.zip.Deflater.deflate() is used across applications, we found that Ant developers' understanding of this API, reflected by their discussion, was wrong. They fixed Apache45396 by coincidence.

Lesson The above results show that there exist general inefficiency patterns that go beyond one application, just like that for functional bugs [21]. Maintaining specifications and checkers for these general patterns can significantly save developers' effort, and allow them to learn from other developers and other software. We can even discover performance bugs in a software where no performance patch has ever been filed.

Bad Practices Other than PPPs, some code regions identified by the checkers are categorized as bad practices. For example, there are code regions very similar to the MySQL PPP shown in Figure 6, except that the calculation of end is not completely useless as end is used in places other than the invocation of ismbchar. Clearly this practice is more likely to cause performance problems in the future than directly using mysqlcs→mbmaxlen as the parameter for ismbchar function.

Good Practices Code regions that have well followed the efficiency rules are also identified by slightly changed checkers. For example, we found that in 13 places of various applications developers do use InputStream.read (byte buffer[]) in a performance efficient way: buffer has a configurable size or a large size that suits the workload (e.g., 64K in some Hadoop code).

Lesson Violations to efficiency rules are not always rare comparing with good practices. Previous techniques that use statistical analysis to infer functional rules [13, 30] may not work for efficiency rules.

False Positives Our PPP detection is accurate. On average, the false-positive-vs-PPP rate is 1:4. The false positives mainly come from three sources.

First, Python checkers have no object-type information. Therefore, some rules are applied to functions with right function names but wrong classes (e.g., Mozilla490742 and Apache32546). This is not a problem in LLVM checkers.

Second, some non-function rules are difficult to accurately express and check, which leads to false positives in MySQL14637.

Third, accurately checking some efficiency rules requires runtime and/or workload information, which inevitably leads to false positives in our static checkers. False positives in Apache44408 and Apache48778 mostly belong to this category. These false positives can be largely eliminated by run-time checkers.

Performance Results Our checkers are efficient. Each Python checker finishes checking 10 million lines of code within 90 seconds. Our LLVM checkers are mainly applied to MySQL, Mozilla Firefox, and Apache HTTPD. It takes 4 – 1270 seconds for one LLVM checker to process one application.

We tried unit testing on PPPs. The performance difference is significant. For example, for programs that read images and files

ID	Orig. Buggy Version				Lastest Version of Same Softw.				Latest Version of Diff. Softw.				
	PPP	BadPr	F.P.	GoodPr	*PPP*	BadPr	F.P.	GoodPr	*PPP*	BadPr	F.P.	GoodPr	
Mozilla 35294	*5*	0	10	/	-	-	-	/	-	-	-	/	C++
Mozilla103330	*2*	0	0	117	*0*	0	0	7	-	-	-	-	C++
Mozilla258793	*1*	0	2	0	*0*	1	1	2	-	-	-	-	C++
Mozilla267506	*6*	0	0	9	*3*	0	0	19	-	-	-	-	C++
Mozilla311566	*26*	0	7	0	*25*	0	8	2	-	-	-	-	C++
Mozilla104962	*0*	0	0	1	*3*	0	0	12	*0*	0	0	0	C#
Mozilla124686	*0*	1	0	14	*0*	0	0	1	*0*	0	0	0	C#
Mozilla490742	*1*	0	3	5	*0*	0	0	4	-	-	-	-	JS
MySQL14637	*50*	0	11	/	*49*	0	11	/	*46*	0	31	/	C/C++
MySQL15811	*15*	20	5	5	*16*	20	7	7	-	-	-	-	C++
MySQL38769	*0*	0	1	5	-	-	-	-	-	-	-	-	C++
MySQL38941	*1*	4	0	2	*1*	4	0	2	*3*	5	2	0	C/C++
MySQL38968	*3*	0	1	38	*2*	0	2	43	-	-	-	-	C/C++
MySQL39268	*7*	0	0	4	*7*	0	0	18	-	-	-	-	C++
MySQL49491	*1*	0	0	0	*1*	0	0	2	*3*	0	0	0	C/C++
MySQL26152	*0*	0	0	0	*0*	0	0	0	*0*	0	1	4	C#
MySQL45699	*0*	2	0	0	*0*	0	0	0	*9*	0	0	45	C#/Java
Apache33605	*0*	2	0	/	*0*	2	0	/	*0*	5	0	/	C
Apache45464	*3*	0	0	47	*3*	0	0	67	-	-	-	-	C
Apache19101	*1*	0	0	1	*1*	0	0	0	-	-	-	-	Java
Apache32546	*1*	0	0	0	*1*	0	0	0	*135*	24	9	13	Java
Apache34464	*0*	0	0	3	*0*	0	0	2	*1*	0	0	12	Java
Apache44408	*1*	0	1	1	*0*	0	1	2	*3*	1	2	2	Java
Apache45396	*0*	0	0	0	*0*	0	0	1	*0*	0	0	1	Java
Apache48778	*1*	0	0	0	*1*	0	0	0	*19*	14	1	17	Java
Total	*125*	29	41	252	*113*	27	30	191	*219*	49	46	94	

Table 4: Checking results (BadPr: bad practice; F.P.: false positives; GoodPr: good practices. More detailed definitions are presented in Section 6.4. '-': not applicable. '/': good-practice checker does not exist.)

Patch for MySQL Bug 15811 (MySQL v5.0.23)

```
- char *end=str+strlen(str);
- if (ismbchar(cs, str, end))
+ if (ismbchar(cs, str, str + cs->mbmaxlen))
                                   strings/ctype-mb.c
```

What is this bug

ismbchar checks whether a string (2nd param.) is coded by a specific character-set (1st param).

Since *ismbchar* only checks the first CHARSET::mbmaxlen characters of a string, calculating the exact length & range of a string is unnecessary.

A PPP we found in the latest version of MySQL

```
  /* 'end' is only used in the ismbchar checking*/
- for (end=s; *end ; end++) ;
- if (ismbchar(mysqlcs, s, end) )
+ if (ismbchar(mysqlcs, s, s+mysqlcs→mbmaxlen)
                                   libmysql/libmysql.c
```

Patch for Apache-Ant Bug 34464 (Ant v1.6.2)

```
+ int i = -k.length();
- while (s.indexOf(k) == -1) {
+ while (i++<0 || s.substring(i).indexOf(k)==-1)
    {s.append (nextchar());}
```

What is this bug

String::indexOf(String *sub*) looks for sub-string *sub* from the beginning of a string s.

If program has already compared the first N characters of *s* with *sub*, it is better not to repeat this.

The Struts PPP is already confirmed and patched by Struts developers based on our report

A PPP we found in the latest version of Struts

```
while (1) {
-  n = s.indexOf("%\\>");
+  n = s.substring(n+2).indexOf("%\\>");
   if (n < 0) break;
   ... // replace "%\\>" by "%>" and continue
}
```

Figure 6: PPPs we found in latest versions of *original* and *different* software (the gray area shows how these two PPPs should be fixed)

using InputStream.read(byte buffer[]) with a 4KB-buffer parameter, we can stably get 3 times throughput improvement through a 40K-buffer parameter. When we feed the unit test with a 50MB file, which is a quite common image-file workload these days, the file operation time decreases from 0.87 second to 0.26 second, a definitely perceivable difference. As another example, the Struts code shown in Figure 6 is from a utility function used for processing JSP files. Our unit testing with a 15K JSP file shows that the simple patch can decrease latency by 0.1 second, a perceivable difference in interactive web applications.

Whole system testing turns out to be difficult, as suggested by our characteristics study (Section 4.3). No PPP detected by our checkers belongs to the always-active category. Future performance-oriented input-generation tools will significantly help performance testing and identify truly severe PPPs. Execution frequency information can also help future static performance-bug detectors to rank the severity of PPPs.

6.6 Discussions

Effectiveness of rule-based performance-bug detection

Effort saving Rule-based detection not only identifies problems, but also suggests alternative implementations with better efficiency. These alternative implementations often have small sizes and regular patterns, as shown in Figure 6, making PPP validation and fixing easy. It is also conceivable to enhance our checkers for automated PPP fixing.

Improving performance These PPPs showed significant performance improvement than their alternative implementations in our unit testing. Without fixing these PPPs, these unit-level performance losses could aggregate into intolerable performance problems that are difficult to diagnose. This is especially significant considering that many performance bugs are difficult to catch using other approaches.

Maintaining code readability Like those 109 patches studied earlier, most PPPs detected by us can be fixed through changes to a few lines of code, as shown in Figure 6. Even for the few complicated PPPs, wrapper-functions or macros can easily address the patch-readability issue.

Other usage Rules and checkers can serve as performance specifications for future software development. They can aid in code maintenance when software evolves. Developers can also save PPPs to an inefficiency list for future performance diagnosis.

Of course, this is only a starting point for rule-based performance-bug detection. We expect our experience to motivate future work on automatically generating rules, checkers, or even patches.

Can these problems be detected by other tools?

Copy-paste detectors Most PPPs that we found are **not** from copy-paste code regions and cannot be detected by text-matching tools [16, 28], as we can see in Figure 6. Rule violations are not rare. When developers misunderstand an API, they tend to make mistakes whenever they use this API. As a result, these mistakes usually go beyond copy-paste code regions.

Compiler optimization None of the bugs that provided the efficiency rules could be optimized away by compilers used in Apache, MySQL, and Mozilla. Many PPPs involve library functions and algorithmic inefficiency, and are almost impossible for a compiler to optimize (Figure 6). Even for the few cases where compiler optimization might help (Figure 1), the required inter-procedural and points-to analyses are not scalable for real-world large software.

General rule-based bug detectors Ideas for detecting functional bugs can greatly benefit and inspire future research on performance bug detection. However, many approaches cannot be directly applied. Tools that automatically infer functional correctness rules [13, 30, 33] may not be suitable for efficiency rules, because rule violations are not rare, as shown in Table 4. In addition, many efficiency rules either involve only one function or discourage multiple functions to be used together, making them unsuitable for tools that focus on function correlations.

7. Related Work

High performance computing (HPC) Performance is a central topic in the HPC community. Many tools for performance profiling and visualization have been developed [20, 23, 35, 38]. However, the performance issues encountered there differ from those in mainstream software. For example, the inputs of HPC are more regular; it is relatively easy to achieve high code coverage in testing HPC programs; load balancing and parallelism are much more important in HPC world.

Performance diagnosis A lot of progress has been made on profiling-based performance diagnosis [10, 19, 25, 39]. A better understanding of the common root causes, hidden locations, and propagation patterns of performance bugs can help profiling research to save manual effort in performance diagnosis and bug fixing.

Performance debugging in distributed systems has also received much attention. Many previous works tried to isolate bottlenecks in (semi-) blackbox systems [1], correlate system metrics with performance behaviors [8, 48], avoid performance problems at runtime [52], and diagnose problems through logs [59]. In distributed systems, a performance problem in a single node could spread into the entire system. Of course, there are also many performance problems unique to distributed environment.

Performance testing Performance testing includes load tests, stress tests, and soak tests. Most existing performance-testing tools [24] treat software as a blackbox. They mostly rely on developers to manually design test cases and interpret results, or simply conduct stress testing by increasing the number of concurrent users and requests. Consequently, testing is costly and ineffective [9]. It is widely acknowledged in the industry that better performance testing techniques are needed [40].

Tools for functional correctness Many ideas used for fighting functional bugs would also work for fighting performance bugs. The semantic patch project [43] provides a special language for developers to write patches in and automatically pushes each patch to multiple locations. We, however, cannot directly use semantic patches for this work, because the existing semantic patch framework does not provide sufficient data-type information and data-flow analysis support for our checkers. It also only works for C programs at this point. Of course, it is conceivable to extend the idea of semantic patches to cover performance bugs, which coincides with the goal of our work. We want to demonstrate the significance of performance bugs, and explore the challenges and opportunities faced when tackling performance bugs.

Our work only looks at one side of performance problems. It complements works on other critical issues, such as code optimization, architecture design, system resource management, mitigating false sharing [32], and configuration problems [2]. We omit further discussion due to the space constraints.

8. Conclusions

Performance bugs have largely been ignored in previous research on software defects. Facing the increasing significance of performance bugs, this paper provides one of the first studies on real-world performance bugs based on 109 bugs collected from five representative software suites. The study covers a wide spectrum of characteristics, and provides guidance for future research on performance-bug avoidance, performance testing, bug detection, etc. Guided by this study, we further explore rule-based performance-bug detection using efficiency rules implied by patches, and find many previously unknown performance problems. This work is only a starting point for understanding and fighting performance bugs. We expect it to deepen our understanding of performance bugs and bring more attention to performance bugs. More information of this work is available at `https://www.cs.wisc.edu/users/shanlu/performance-bugs`.

Acknowledgments

We would like to thank the anonymous reviewers for their invaluable feedback. We thank Andrea Arpaci-Dusseau, Remzi Arpaci-Dusseau, Mark Hill, Ben Liblit, Barton Miller, and Michael Swift for many helpful discussions and suggestions. Shan Lu is supported by a Claire Boothe Luce faculty fellowship, and her research group is supported by NSF under grants CCF-1018180 and CCF-1054616.

References

[1] M. K. Aguilera, J. C. Mogul, J. L. Wiener, P. Reynolds, and A. Muthitacharoen. Performance debugging for distributed systems of black boxes. In *SOSP*, 2003.

[2] M. Attariyan and J. Flinn. Automating configuration troubleshooting with dynamic information flow analysis. In *OSDI*, 2010.

[3] W. Baek and T. M. Chilimbi. Green: a framework for supporting energy-conscious programming using controlled approximation. In *PLDI*, 2010.

[4] C. Cadar, D. Dunbar, and D. Engler. Klee: Unassisted and automatic generation of high-coverage tests for complex systems programs. In *OSDI*, 2008.

[5] V. Chipounov, V. Kuznetsov, and G. Candea. S2E: a platform for in-vivo multi-path analysis of software systems. In *ASPLOS*, 2011.

[6] A. Chou, B. Chelf, D. Engler, and M. Heinrich. Using meta-level compilation to check FLASH protocol code. In *ASPLOS*, 2000.

[7] A. Chou, J. Yang, B. Chelf, S. Hallem, and D. R. Engler. An empirical study of operating system errors. In *SOSP*, 2001.

[8] I. Cohen, M. Goldszmidt, T. Kelly, J. Symons, and J. S. Chase. Correlating instrumentation data to system states: a building block for automated diagnosis and control. In *OSDI*, 2004.

[9] M. Corporation. *Performance Testing Guidance for Web Applications*. Microsoft Press, 2007.

[10] A. Diwan, M. Hauswirth, T. Mytkowicz, and P. F. Sweeney. Trace-analyzer: a system for processing performance traces. *Softw. Pract. Exper.*, March 2011.

[11] B. Dufour, B. G. Ryder, and G. Sevitsky. A scalable technique for characterizing the usage of temporaries in framework-intensive java applications. In *FSE*, 2008.

[12] R. F. Dugan. Performance lies my professor told me: the case for teaching software performance engineering to undergraduates. In *WOSP*, 2004.

[13] D. Engler, D. Y. Chen, S. Hallem, A. Chou, and B. Chelf. Bugs as deviant behavior: A general approach to inferring errors in systems code. In *SOSP*, 2001.

[14] M. Ernst, A. Czeisler, W. G. Griswold, and D. Notkin. Quickly detecting relevant program invariants. In *ICSE*, 2000.

[15] Fortify. HP Fortify Static Code Analyzer (SCA). https://www.fortify.com/products/hpfssc/source-code-analyzer.html.

[16] M. Gabel, J. Yang, Y. Yu, M. Goldszmidt, and Z. Su. Scalable and systematic detection of buggy inconsistencies in source code. In *OOPSLA*, 2010.

[17] P. Godefroid, N. Klarlund, and K. Sen. Dart: directed automated random testing. In *PLDI*, 2005.

[18] S. Gulwani, K. K. Mehra, and T. Chilimbi. Speed: precise and efficient static estimation of program computational complexity. In *POPL*, 2009.

[19] M. Hauswirth, A. Diwan, P. F. Sweeney, and M. C. Mozer. Automating vertical profiling. In *OOPSLA*, 2005.

[20] J. K. Hollingsworth, R. B. Irvin, and B. P. Miller. The integration of application and system based metrics in a parallel program performance tool. In *PPOPP*, 1991.

[21] D. Hovemeyer and W. Pugh. Finding bugs is easy. In *OOPSLA*, 2004.

[22] InfoWorld. Top 10 open source hall of famers. http://www.infoworld.com/d/open-source/top-10-open-source-hall-famers-848.

[23] R. B. Irvin and B. P. Miller. Mapping performance data for high-level and data views of parallel program performance. In *ICS*, 1996.

[24] JMeter. Java desktop application designed for load tests. http://jakarta.apache.org/jmeter.

[25] M. Jovic, A. Adamoli, and M. Hauswirth. Catch me if you can: performance bug detection in the wild. In *OOPSLA*, 2011.

[26] C. Killian, K. Nagaraj, S. Pervez, R. Braud, J. W. Anderson, and R. Jhala. Finding latent performance bugs in systems implementations. In *FSE*, 2010.

[27] C. Lattner and V. Adve. LLVM: A compilation framework for lifelong program analysis & transformation. In *CGO*, 2004.

[28] Z. Li, S. Lu, S. Myagmar, and Y. Zhou. CP-Miner: A Tool for Finding Copy-paste and Related Bugs in Operating System Code. In *OSDI*, 2004.

[29] Z. Li, L. Tan, X. Wang, Y. Zhou, and C. Zhai. Have things changed now?: an empirical study of bug characteristics in modern open source software. In *ASID*, 2006.

[30] Z. Li and Y. Zhou. PR-Miner: Automatically extracting implicit programming rules and detecting violations in large software code. In *FSE*, Sept 2005.

[31] S. Liu, K. Pattabiraman, T. Moscibroda, and B. G. Zorn. Flikker: saving DRAM refresh-power through critical data partitioning. In *ASPLOS*, 2011.

[32] T. Liu and E. D. Berger. Precise detection and automatic mitigation of false sharing. In *OOPSLA*, 2011.

[33] V. B. Livshits and T. Zimmermann. Dynamine: Finding common error patterns by mining software revision histories. In *FSE*, 2005.

[34] S. Lu, S. Park, E. Seo, and Y. Zhou. Learning from mistakes – a comprehensive study of real world concurrency bug characteristics. In *ASPLOS*, 2008.

[35] J. Mellor-Crummey, R. J. Fowler, G. Marin, and N. Tallent. Hpcview: A tool for top-down analysis of node performance. *J. Supercomput.*, 23(1):81–104, 2002.

[36] N. Meng, M. Kim, and K. S. McKinley. Systematic editing: generating program transformations from an example. In *PLDI*, 2011.

[37] Microsoft. MSDN SAL annotations. http://msdn2.microsoft.com/en-us/library/ms235402.aspx.

[38] B. P. Miller, M. D. Callaghan, J. M. Cargille, J. K. Hollingsworth, R. B. Irvin, K. L. Karavanic, K. Kunchithapadam, and T. Newhall. The paradyn parallel performance measurement tool. *Computer*, 28(11), 1995.

[39] N. Mitchell. The diary of a datum: an approach to modeling runtime complexity in framework-based applications. In *ECOOP*, 2006.

[40] I. Molyneaux. *The Art of Application Performance Testing: Help for Programmers and Quality Assurance*. O'Reilly Media, 2009.

[41] G. E. Morris. Lessons from the colorado benefits management system disaster. www.ad-mkt-review.com/publichtml/air/ai200411.html, 2004.

[42] G. Muller, Y. Padioleau, J. L. Lawall, and R. R. Hansen. Semantic patches considered helpful. *Operating Systems Review*, 40(3):90–92, 2006.

[43] N. Palix, G. Thomas, S. Saha, C. Calvès, J. Lawall, and G. Muller. Faults in linux: ten years later. In *ASPLOS*, 2011.

[44] S. E. Perl and W. E. Weihl. Performance assertion checking. In *SOSP*, 1993.

[45] T. Richardson. 1901 census site still down after six months. http://www.theregister.co.uk/2002/07/03/1901_census_site_still_down/.

[46] C. J. Rossbach, O. S. Hofmann, and E. Witchel. Is transactional programming actually easier? In *PPoPP*, 2010.

[47] A. Shankar, M. Arnold, and R. Bodik. Jolt: lightweight dynamic analysis and removal of object churn. In *OOPSLA*, 2008.

[48] K. Shen, C. Stewart, C. Li, and X. Li. Reference-driven performance anomaly identification. In *SIGMETRICS*, 2009.

[49] R. L. Sites. Identifying dark latency.

[50] C. U. Smith and L. G. Williams. Software performance antipatterns. In *Proceedings of the 2nd international workshop on Software and performance*, 2000.

[51] Stefan Bodewig. Bug 45396: There is no hint in the javadocs. https://issues.apache.org/ bugzilla/show_bug.cgi?id=45396#c4.

[52] C. Stewart, K. Shen, A. Iyengar, and J. Yin. Entomomodel: Understanding and avoiding performance anomaly manifestations. In *MASCOTS*, 2010.

[53] M. Sullivan and R. Chillarege. A comparison of software defects in database management systems and operating systems. In *FTCS*, 1992.

[54] L. Torvalds. Sparse - a semantic parser for c. http://www.kernel.org/pub/software/devel/sparse/.

[55] J. S. Vetter and P. H. Worley. Asserting performance expectations. In *Supercomputing*, 2002.

[56] wikipedia. Chi-squared test. http://en.wikipedia.org/wiki/Chi-squared_test.

[57] G. Xu, M. Arnold, N. Mitchell, A. Rountev, and G. Sevitsky. Go with the flow: profiling copies to find runtime bloat. In *PLDI '09*, 2009.

[58] G. Xu, N. Mitchell, M. Arnold, A. Rountev, E. Schonberg, and G. Sevitsky. Finding low-utility data structures. In *PLDI*, 2010.

[59] W. Xu, L. Huang, A. Fox, D. Patterson, and M. I. Jordan. Detecting large-scale system problems by mining console logs. In *SOSP*, 2009.

[60] A. Zeller. Isolating cause-effect chains from computer programs. In *FSE*, 2002.

Input-Sensitive Profiling

Emilio Coppa
Dept. of Computer and System Sciences
Sapienza University of Rome
ercoppa@gmail.com

Camil Demetrescu
Dept. of Computer and System Sciences
Sapienza University of Rome
demetres@dis.uniroma1.it

Irene Finocchi
Dept. of Computer Science
Sapienza University of Rome
finocchi@di.uniroma1.it

Abstract

In this paper we present a profiling methodology and toolkit for helping developers discover hidden asymptotic inefficiencies in the code. From one or more runs of a program, our profiler automatically measures how the performance of individual routines scales as a function of the input size, yielding clues to their growth rate. The output of the profiler is, for each executed routine of the program, a set of tuples that aggregate performance costs by input size. The collected profiles can be used to produce performance plots and derive trend functions by statistical curve fitting or bounding techniques. A key feature of our method is the ability to automatically measure the size of the input given to a generic code fragment: to this aim, we propose an effective metric for estimating the input size of a routine and show how to compute it efficiently. We discuss several case studies, showing that our approach can reveal asymptotic bottlenecks that other profilers may fail to detect and characterize the workload and behavior of individual routines in the context of real applications. To prove the feasibility of our techniques, we implemented a Valgrind tool called `aprof` and performed an extensive experimental evaluation on the SPEC CPU2006 benchmarks. Our experiments show that `aprof` delivers comparable performance to other prominent Valgrind tools, and can generate informative plots even from single runs on typical workloads for most algorithmically-critical routines.

Categories and Subject Descriptors D.2.8 [*Software Engineering*]: Metrics—performance measures

General Terms Algorithms, Measurement, Performance.

Keywords Performance profiling, asymptotic analysis, dynamic program analysis, instrumentation.

1. Introduction

Performance profiling plays a crucial role in software development, allowing programmers to test the efficiency of an application and discover possible performance bottlenecks. Traditional profilers associate performance metrics to nodes or paths of the control flow or call graph by collecting runtime information on specific workloads [2, 19, 27, 39]. These approaches provide valuable information for studying the dynamic behavior of a program and guiding optimizations to portions of the code that take most resources on the considered inputs. However, they may fail to characterize how the performance of a program scales as a function of the input size, which is crucial for the efficiency and reliability of software. Seemingly benign fragments of code may be fast on some testing workloads, passing unnoticed in traditional profilers, while all of a sudden they can become major performance bottlenecks when deployed on larger inputs. As an anecdotal example, we report a story [8] related to the COSMOS circuit simulator, originally developed by Randal E. Bryant and his colleagues at CMU [10]. When the project was adopted by a major semiconductor manufacturer, it underwent a major performance tuning phase, including a modification to a function in charge of mapping signal names to electrical nodes, which appeared to be especially time-consuming: by just hashing on bounded-length name prefixes rather than on entire names, the simulator became faster on all benchmarks. However, when circuits later grew larger and adopted hierarchical naming schemes, many signal names ended up sharing long common prefixes, and thus hashed to the same buckets. As a result, the simulator startup time became intolerable, taking hours for what should have required a few minutes. Identifying the problem - introduced several years before in an effort to optimize the program - required several days of analysis. There are many other examples of large software projects where this sort of problems occurred [9].

The problem of empirically studying the asymptotic behavior of a program has been the target of extensive research in experimental algorithmics [14, 25, 30, 33]. Individual portions of algorithmic code are typically analyzed on ad-hoc test harnesses, which reproduce real-world scenarios by performing multiple runs with different and determinable input parameters, collecting experimental data for comparing the actual relative performance of algorithms and studying their amenability for use in specific applications. While this approach provides valuable information for complementing theoretical analyses, it has several drawbacks as a performance evaluation method in actual software development. Firstly, it is typically difficult and time-consuming to manually extract portions of code from an application and analyze them separately on different input sizes to determine their performance growth rate. Furthermore, asymptotic inefficiencies may be introduced by programming errors in unexpected locations, whose detection requires automated and systematic profiling methodologies, especially on large-scale systems. As another point, by studying performance-critical routines out of their context, we miss how they interact with the overall application in which they are deployed, including cache effects and branch mispredictions. We also notice that it may be hard to collect real data about typical usage scenarios to be reproduced in experiments, in particular when the workloads of interest are generated by intermediate steps of a computation.

Our contributions. Motivated by the observation that critical algorithmic routines should be analyzed within the actual context of the software projects in which they are deployed, this paper makes

PLDI'12, June 11–16, 2012, Beijing, China.

a first step towards bridging the gap between the profiling practice and the methodologies used in experimental algorithmics. As a main contribution, we devise a new automated profiling technique for helping developers discover hidden asymptotic inefficiencies in the code. To prove the effectiveness of our approach, we developed a Valgrind [34] tool called `aprof`: from one or more runs of a program, `aprof` automatically measures how the performance of individual routines scales as a function of the input size. Using statistical curve fitting [11] and curve bounding [31] techniques on the collected profiles, developers can derive closed form expressions that describe mathematical cost functions for program routines, yielding clues to their growth rate. We discuss several case studies, showing that our approach can reveal asymptotic bottlenecks that other profilers may fail to detect and characterize the workload and behavior of individual routines in the context of real applications. In particular, we focus on applications included in prominent Linux distributions as well as in the SPEC CPU2006 suite. A distinguishing feature of our approach is the ability to automatically measure the size of the input given to a generic routine. This allows us to explore a novel dimension in interprocedural context-sensitive profiling where costs are associated to distinct input sizes of a routine, rather than to paths in the call graph as in traditional contextual profiling [2, 16, 46]. To support this approach, which we call *input-sensitive profiling*, we propose an effective metric for estimating the input size of a routine by counting the number of distinct memory cells first accessed by the routine with a read operation, and show how to compute it efficiently. An extensive experimental evaluation on the SPEC CPU2006 benchmarks reveals that `aprof` is as efficient as other prominent Valgrind tools, and can generate informative plots even from single runs on typical workloads for most algorithmically-critical routines. The tool is available at `http://code.google.com/p/aprof/`.

The remainder of this paper is organized as follows. In Section 2 we introduce our profiling methodology, discussing relevant properties of our approach. In Section 3 we present case studies that demonstrate the utility of input-sensitive profiling. Section 4 proposes an efficient profiling algorithm, Section 5 describes the most relevant aspect of the implementation of `aprof`, and Section 6 presents our experimental results. Related work is discussed in Section 7 and concluding remarks are given in Section 8.

2. Input-Sensitive Profiling

In this section we introduce our input-sensitive profiling methodology. Differently from the classical analysis of algorithms based on theoretical cost models, where the input size of a procedure is a parameter known a priori and clear from the abstract description of the underlying algorithm, a key challenge of an automated approach is the ability to automatically infer the size of the input data on which a function operates. We first propose a solution to this basic problem.

2.1 Read Memory Size

We introduce a metric, which we call *read memory size*, for estimating the input size of a routine invocation:

Definition 1. *The* read memory size (RMS) *of the execution of a routine f is the number of distinct memory cells first accessed by f, or by a descendant of f in the call tree, with a read operation.*

The main idea is that cells that are accessed by a function for the first time with a read operation contain the input values of the routine. Conversely, if a cell is first written and then read by the routine, the read value is not part of the input as it was determined by the routine itself. We notice that the RMS definition, which is based on tracing low-level memory accesses made by the program, supports memory dereferencing and pointers in a natural way.

Example 1. Consider the following trace of operations.

```
1.  call f
2.    read x
3.    write y
4.    call g
5.      read x
6.      read y
7.      read z
8.      write w
9.      return
10.   read w
11.   return
```

Function `g` performs three first-read operations (lines 5 – 7) and its RMS is thus 3. Function `f` performs five read operations, three of which through its subroutine `g`. However, its RMS is only 2: the **`read`** operations at line 5, line 6, and line 10 are not first-reads with respect to `f`. Indeed, `x` has been already read at line 2 and `y` and `w` are written at lines 3 and 8, respectively, before being read. Hence, only the read operations at lines 2 and 7 contribute to the computation of the read memory size of function `f`.

In Section 4 we will propose an efficient algorithm for computing the RMS of each routine invocation from a program execution trace.

2.2 Profiling Methodology

For each routine f, we determine the set $N_f = \{n_1, n_2, \ldots\}$ of distinct RMS values on which f is called during the execution of a program. For each $n_i \in N_f$, which is an estimate of an input size, we collect a tuple $\langle n_i, c_i, max_i, min_i, sum_i, sq_i \rangle$, where:

- c_i is the number of times the routine is called on input size n_i;
- max_i and min_i are the maximum and minimum costs required by any execution of f on input size n_i, respectively;
- sum_i and sq_i are the sum of the costs required by the executions of f on input size n_i and the sum of the costs' squares, respectively.

We use the generic term *cost* to refer to any performance metric, e.g., time, number of executed basic blocks, etc. The cost of a routine execution is intended as a *cumulative cost*, i.e., it includes the costs of all the routine's descendants in the call tree.

Analysis metrics. The value $avg_i = sum_i/c_i$ is the average cost per invocation on input size n_i, while sq_i is used for computing the cost variance var_i. The sets of points $\langle n_i, max_i \rangle$, $\langle n_i, min_i \rangle$, and $\langle n_i, avg_i \rangle$ estimate how the worst-case, best-case, and average-case costs of a routine grow as a function of the input size (see Figure 1a for an example generated with our technique). The total cost per input size, the variance between execution costs, and the frequency distribution of the input sizes are given by points $\langle n_i, sum_i \rangle$, $\langle n_i, var_i \rangle$, and $\langle n_i, c_i \rangle$, respectively (see Figures 1b, 1c, and 1d).

Example 2. To exemplify our profiling methodology, we analyze the simple C code fragment on the left. Any execution of `get` has RMS 3. This accounts for the addresses of lvalues `v`, `i`, and `v[i]`, which contain the input values of the function. Routine `mid` reads 3 distinct addresses as well: `v` and `n` directly at line 5, and `v[n/2]` indirectly via a call to `get`. Variable `m` is not counted in the RMS of `mid` as it is first accessed by a write operation at line 5. In this example, an input-sensitive profiler would just collect one performance tuple for `get` and one for `mid`, i.e., $|N_{\texttt{get}}| = |N_{\texttt{mid}}| = 1$.

```
1: int get(int v[], int i) {
2:     return v[i];
3: }

4: int mid(int v[], int n) {
5:     int m = get(v, n/2);
6:     return m;
7: }
```

Example 3. Our next example illustrates the case where the size of the input may vary at each call:

```
int count_zero(int v[], int n) {
    int i, count = 0;
    for (i=0; i<n; i++) count += (v[i]==0 ? 1:0);
    return count;
}
```

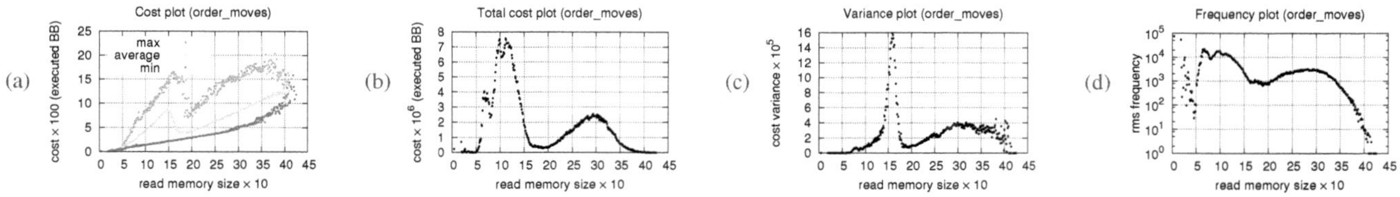

Figure 1. Input-sensitive plots automatically computed by `aprof`. All plots are related to function `order_moves()` of the `sjeng` chess playing program included in the SPEC CPU2006 benchmarks [23], executed on a single reference workload.

The function, which counts the number of 0's in the input array `v`, has RMS $\texttt{n}+2$: it reads variables `v` and `n`, and the first `n` cells of the array pointed to by `v`. An input-sensitive profiler would collect one performance tuple for each distinct value of `n` on which `count_zero` is called during the execution of the program. In this case, the number of tuples $|N_{\texttt{count\_zero}}|$ cannot exceed the number of distinct calls of the function.

Example 4. We now show that even a *single* invocation of a function made by a program can yield several performance tuples. Consider a recursive variant of the `count_zero` function:

```
int count_zero(int v[], int n) {
    if (n<1) return 0;
    return (v[n-1]==0 ? 1:0) + count_zero(v, n-1);
}
```

Observe that, just like the iterative version, the first invocation of function `count_zero` has RMS $n_1 = \texttt{n} + 2$. However, calling `count_zero` on parameter `n` also results in `n` additional recursive activations of the function for all size values ranging from $\texttt{n} - 1$ down to 0. Therefore, we collect $\texttt{n} + 1$ performance tuples from just one starting activation, i.e., $|N_{\texttt{count\_zero}}| = \texttt{n} + 1$. The read memory size corresponding to the i-th invocation is $n_i = \texttt{n} - i + 3$, for each $i \in [1, \texttt{n} + 1]$.

2.3 Characterizing Asymptotic Behavior

The examples presented in Section 2.2 show that our profiling approach allows a tool to automatically collect performance tuples from an execution run, relating cost measures to the input size of a routine. As exemplified in Figure 1, collected profiles can be used to produce performance plots, providing effective visualizations of the behavior of a program. A natural question we address in this section is to which extent this methodology can help developers assess the asymptotic cost of a piece of code.

Asymptotics vs. finite experiments. The ultimate goal of the complexity analysis of algorithms is to find closed form expressions for the running time or other measures of resource consumption (e.g., space usage, cache misses, or number of transmitted bits). Since this may be too difficult, it is common to estimate the theoretical complexity in an asymptotic sense, i.e., for arbitrarily large inputs. To get insights on the asymptotic behavior from finite experiments, it would be necessary to extrapolate trend data beyond the range of experimentation. Unfortunately, no data analysis method for inferring asymptotic trends can be guaranteed to be correct for all data sets: as observed in [31], for any finite vector of problem sizes there are functions of arbitrarily high degree that are indistinguishable from the constant function at those sizes. Throughout this paper we will exploit two main techniques: curve fitting and curve bounding. Statistical curve fitting [11] is the process of constructing a mathematical function that has the best fit to a series of data points. Regression analysis techniques are widely used for this kind of predictions: in our examples, we used the curve fitting tools provided by `gnuplot` [45]. Given a set of data points (X_i, Y_i) obtained from an experiment such that $Y_i = f(X_i)$ for some unknown function f, curve bounding [31] makes it possible to estimate complexity classes $O(g_1)$ and $\Omega(g_2)$ such that $f \in O(g_1)$ and $f \in \Omega(g_2)$. In this paper we will perform curve bounding by "guess ratio", which works by considering a guess function h and analyzing the trend of ratio $f(n)/h(n)$: the ratio stabilizes to a nonnegative constant if $f \in O(h)$, while it (eventually) increases if $f \notin O(h)$.

Number of collected tuples. The number of collected tuples plays a fundamental role in characterizing the behavior of a routine. This number depends on several factors, including the structure of the routine, how it is used in the context of the program, and ultimately the workload on which the program is tested. We have seen that recursive functions allow it to collect several tuples with just one initial call. In Section 6 we will provide a quantitative evaluation of the number of distinct tuples that can be collected for each routine in a variety of applications on typical workloads. As we will discuss in Section 3, variety of input patterns in test workloads is more important than their sheer size: small workloads can yield large amounts of information, while large repetitive inputs may be of little help. We also observe that profiles of the same program collected from different runs can be naturally merged together to generate profiles with a larger number of tuples.

Accuracy of the* RMS *metric. For functions that read their input entirely at least once, the read memory size approximates within constant factors the actual input size n: hence, if RMS $= \Omega(n)$, the input-sensitive profile of a function f correctly estimates the theoretical cost $T_f(n)$ of the algorithm implemented by f. This is not the case for sublinear functions. For instance, consider a binary search over a sorted array, which reads only $O(\log n)$ cells of the input array: in this case RMS $= O(\log n)$, so our approach estimates $T(\log n)$ rather than $T(n)$. Sublinear functions, however, are unlikely to represent performance bottlenecks and are therefore the less interesting from a profiling perspective.

We remark that the RMS is a measure of distinct accessed memory cells. Hence, it fails to characterize computations whose running time is determined by the value of some variable: e.g., the RMS of the naive algorithm for computing the factorial of a number n would be constant, regardless of the value of n. Aggregating performance measurements by distinct values of function arguments is an alternative approach that is explored, e.g., in [28].

Parameters passed in registers, which should be regarded as part of a function's input, are also not counted in the RMS. However, they only account for small additive constants, and are therefore negligible for estimating growth rates for sufficiently large inputs. For instance, if parameters `v` and `n` of function `count_zero` discussed in Section 2.2 are held by the compiler in registers rather than on stack, the RMS would be exactly `n` rather than `n+2`.

3. Case Studies

In this section we describe scenarios where input-sensitive profiling can provide valuable information to the programmer. Our examples are based on the `aprof` tool described in Section 5 and use basic block (BB) counts as performance metric.

	index	% time	self	children	name
	[1]	99.9	2.00	16.23	main [1]
(a)	[2]	52.2	5.82	3.70	addword [2]
	[3]	31.3	2.81	2.90	str_tolower [3]
	[4]	20.3	3.70	0.00	hash [4]
	[1]	100.0	0.21	4.61	main [1]
(b)	[2]	61.8	0.98	2.00	str_tolower [2]
	[3]	41.4	2.00	0.00	wf_tolower [3]
	[4]	32.6	0.07	1.50	addword [4]

Figure 2. Output of `gprof` for application `wf` on two different texts: (a) Anna Karenina; (b) protein sequences.

Discovering hidden inefficiencies. As a first example, we show that input-sensitive profiling makes it possible to discover performance bottlenecks that may not be revealed by standard profiling methods. Our discussion is based on `wf-0.41` [15], a simple word frequency counter included in the current development head of Linux Fedora (Fedora 17–Beefy Miracle): `wf` scans a text file and counts the frequency of words in the text. To efficiently count repetitions, it adds words to a hash table using a function called `addword`, and reimplements a variety of ad-hoc string utility functions to handle the ISO Latin-1 representation, including a function (`str_tolower`) to convert all characters to lower case.

We analyzed `wf` with both `gprof` [19] and `aprof` on a text corpus taken from the *Gutenberg Project* [22], considering several books from classical literature. On all test sets, `gprof` ranked `addword` as the hottest function. For instance, on Tolstoj's "Anna Karenina", `addword` took roughly 52% of the total time, as shown in Figure 2a. This was not surprising, as it appears to be algorithmically more complex than all other basic text management functions. We also profiled `wf` with `gprof` on larger and larger input texts from [22] to study how the performance of individual routines scales as a function of the size of the program's input. Collected profiles confirmed that `addword` is consistently more expensive than all other functions. Figure 3–left reports the performance trends of `addword` and `str_tolower`, obtained by extracting performance figures from 11 different `gprof` reports for input files of different size derived from texts in [22]. Both curves seem to grow linearly as a function of `wf`'s input size. The tests we made with `gprof` did not provide any evidence of asymptotic bottlenecks in `wf`.

In contrast, `aprof` discovered a rather different scenario already on the smaller workload, pinpointing a serious inefficiency in a seemingly benign function: surprisingly, the cost of `str_tolower` turned out to grow quadratically with the length of the input string (see Figure 3–middle). Conversely, `aprof` showed that `addword` scales linearly (see Figure 3–right). By analyzing the source code of `str_tolower`:

```
void str_tolower(char *str) {
    int i;
    for (i=0; i < strlen(str); i++)
        str[i] = wf_tolower(str[i]);
}
```

we noticed that `strlen` is redundantly called at each iteration, resulting in a quadratic running time. Once we discovered the inefficiency using `aprof`, we made a second set of experiments on carefully selected inputs with very long words, where the inefficiency in `str_tolower` is most likely to impact significantly the overall running time. In particular, we considered a data set containing long protein sequences taken from the *Genomics-96* data set of the Genome Informatics Research Lab [17]. Indeed, on this data set `gprof` showed that `str_tolower` accounts for 61.8% of the total time, while `addword` drops to 32.6% (Figure 2b).

The inefficiency found by `aprof` in `wf` is rather common [9] and was very easy to fix by loop-invariant code motion. To complete our investigation, we compared the wall-clock time required by the original `wf-0.41` code included in the Fedora RPM, and a new version where `strlen(str)` was moved out of the loop: fixing the code improved the total running time of `wf` by 6% on Anna Karenina and by 30% on protein sequences.

Discussion. The `wf` example shows that repeating classic `gprof`-style profiling at scale to assess the computational complexity of individual routines can yield misleading results: `gprof` failed to reveal the quadratic trend of `str_tolower`, even making several tests on workloads of different size, because the input of `str_tolower` are *single* words of the input text, not the *entire* document given as input to the application. In general, the input of a routine is often produced by other routines (e.g., `wf`'s text tokenizer feeds strings to `str_tolower`) and may be unpredictably related to the input of the overall application. Hence, setting up a collection of test workloads for an application to expose the asymptotic behavior of individual routines can be rather difficult with traditional profilers. Also, different input families may be needed to characterize different routines, making this approach largely impractical. Since a typical text contains words of different lengths and `aprof` collects separate performance measurements for each distinct input size, it could correctly pinpoint the quadratic trend of `str_tolower`'s cost function even on a single run on a small input.

Workload characterization. The most realistic program executions are on deployed systems. A benefit of our profiling methodology is that it can give insights on the typical workloads on which a function is called in the context of real applications. This information might be very useful not only for code optimization, but also for algorithmic improvements, even theoretical, in specific scenarios. For instance, routing algorithms for GPS navigation systems are specifically designed to take advantage of the sparsity of the input road networks on which they are deployed. Similarly, if an application always needs to sort arrays with less than 16 items, it may be convenient to use a non-optimal sorting algorithm with runtime n^2 instead of an asymptotically optimal one with runtime $4n \log n$.

Figure 4 provides a concrete example where the workload of a function can be rather different depending on the specific application scenario and data set, showing that our profiler can highlight such differences. In particular, we ran the word frequency counter `wf` discussed above on two different inputs (Anna Karenina and protein sequences), and analyzed the `strlen` function used by `wf`. Notice that the read memory size of `strlen` is an indirect measure of the length of the strings on which it is invoked: the maximum RMS is about 20 for Anna Karenina and larger than 900 for protein sequences, highlighting the structural difference between these two data sets. Even more significant is the fact that the frequency curves shown on the left of Figure 4 have opposite trends: decreasing on Anna Karenina, as we would expect for a natural language text, and increasing on protein sequences. Since long protein sequences tend to be very frequent, on this data set `strlen` will likely have a tangible impact on the execution cost.

Exposing empirical asymptotics. Input-sensitive profiles can characterize the empirical asymptotic behavior of program routines in realistic execution scenarios, often yielding more precise results than theoretical cost models. For instance, the `gg_sort` routine included in SPEC CPU2006 component `gobmk` [23] implements the combsort algorithm [1], a variant of bubblesort that compares items at distance larger than 1. Combsort is known to have at least quadratic running time in the worst case, but can rival fast algorithms like quicksort in many practical cases. This is confirmed by the guess ratio plot of `gg_sort`, which stabilizes to a constant value when divided by the guess function $n \log n$, as

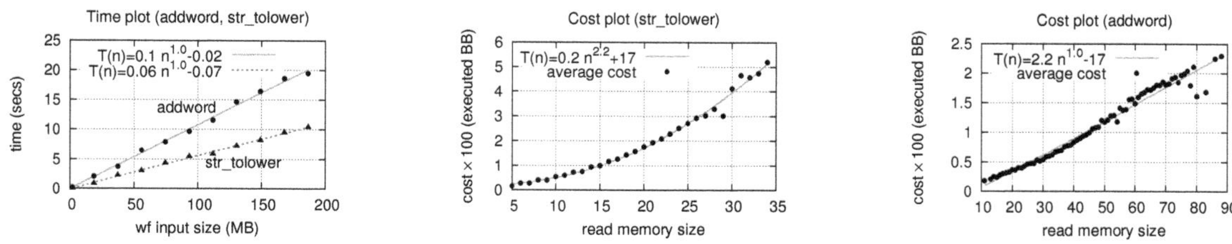

Figure 3. Profiling of `wf`'s functions `addword` and `str_tolower` on texts from classical literature: cost trends derived from the profiles produced by 11 runs of `gprof` on input files of different size (left); cost trends derived by a single run of `aprof` on the smallest workload (middle and right). Regression curves are obtained by least-squares fitting.

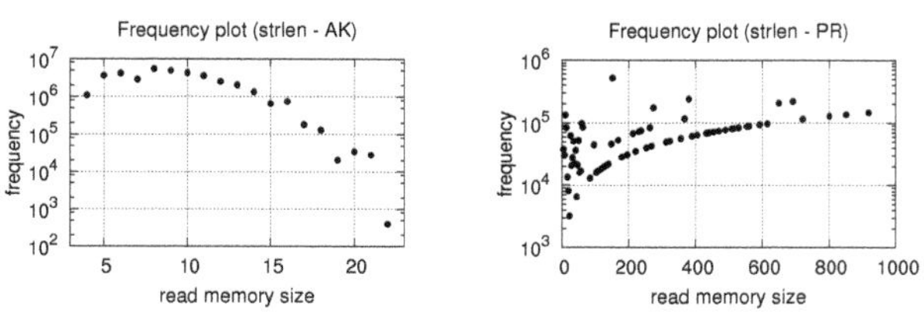

Figure 4. Workload characterization of function `strlen` used by application `wf` on two different texts: Anna Karenina (AK) and protein sequences (PR).

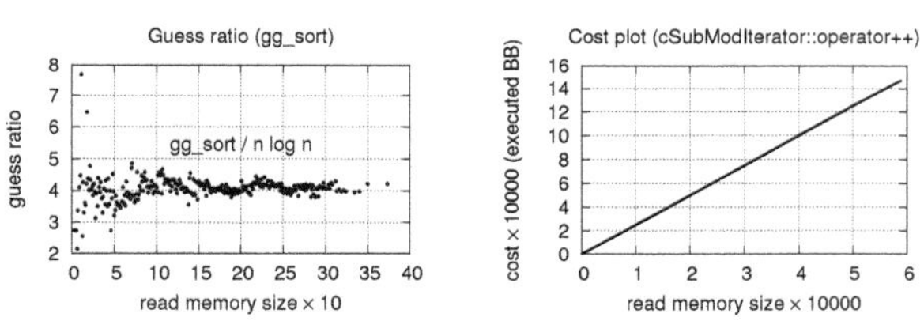

(a) (b)

Figure 5. Input-sensitive profiles excerpted from two SPEC CPU2006 benchmarks: (a) routine `gg_sort` from the SPEC component `gobmk` (curve bounding is based on guess function $n \log n$); (b) routine `cSubModIterator::operator++` from the SPEC component `omnetpp`.

shown in Figure 5(a). In other cases, the asymptotic trends empirically observed by `aprof` can direct the programmer's attention to critical routines that may otherwise pass unnoticed. As an example, the chart in Figure 5(b) shows that the cost trend of routine `cSubModIterator::operator++` defined in SPEC benchmark `omnetpp` [23] is linear, differently from what one might expect from a ++ operator. Actually, after profiling `omnetpp` with `aprof`, we found in `cSubModIterator`'s source code the comment: "this should be replaced with something faster".

4. Algorithms

In this section we describe an efficient algorithm for computing the read memory size and the input-sensitive profile of a routine. An input-sensitive profiler is given as input a trace of program operations, including routine activations (`call`), routine completions (`return`), and `read`/`write` memory accesses (see Example 1 in Section 2.1). Additional operations might be traced, depending on the specific performance metrics to be computed. For each operation, the profiler must update RMS and cost information. Before describing our algorithm, we discuss a simple-minded approach as a warm-up for the reader.

4.1 A Simple-Minded Approach

Each activation of a routine f has its own read memory size, which is part of the set N_f of input sizes on which f is invoked during the execution of the program (see Section 2.2). Computing the RMS of an activation of f requires to monitor the set of locations that are read during that activation (not only by f itself, but also by its descendants in the call tree) before being written. A simple-minded approach is to maintain a list A_f of all memory locations accessed (both read and written) during the activation of f. Immediately after entering f, this list is empty and the RMS is equal to 0. When f accesses a location w for the first time, then w is added to A_f and, if the access is a `read` operation, the RMS is increased by 1. The same check and update must be performed for all pending routine activations in the call stack, which are implicitly accessing location w through their descendant f. If we start from the most recent activations, it is possible to stop stack-walking when the first routine h is encountered such that w already belongs to A_h. However, h may be the program root in the worst case, making updates based on stack-walking prohibitively time-consuming. The space usage of this approach is also quite demanding: in the worst case, each distinct memory location could be stored in all lists A_h of pending routine activations, and in that case the space would be proportional to the memory size times the maximum stack depth.

4.2 The Latest-Access Algorithm

We now describe a more space- and time-efficient algorithm, sketched in Figure 6. The main idea is to avoid maintaining explicitly the RMS and the lists A_f of accessed locations, but to store only partial information that can be updated quickly during the computation and from which the RMS can be easily derived upon the completion of a routine. In more detail, for each pending activation of a routine f, we store the set L_f of locations whose *latest* access was done by f (either directly or by its completed subroutines). It is not difficult to see that each memory location is stored in exactly one set, i.e., at any time during the execution of the program the sets L_f partition the locations accessed so far. The sets L_f of latest accesses are stored implicitly by associating timestamps to routines and memory locations, as described below.

Data structures. The algorithm uses a shadow run-time stack S, whose top is indexed by variable *top*. For each $i \in [1, top]$, the i-th stack entry $S[i]$ stores:

- The id $S[i].rtn$ of the i-th pending routine activation.
- The timestamp $S[i].ts$ of the i-th pending activation, i.e., the time at which the routine was entered.
- The cumulative cost $S[i].cost$ of the activation.

procedure `call`(r):
1: $count$++
2: top++
3: $S[top].rtn \leftarrow r$
4: $S[top].ts \leftarrow count$
5: $S[top].rms \leftarrow 0$
6: $S[top].cost \leftarrow$ `get_cost()`

procedure `return`():
1: `collect`$(S[top].rtn,$
$\quad S[top].rms,$
$\quad$ `get_cost()` $- S[top].cost)$
2: $S[top-1].rms$ += $S[top].rms$
3: top− −

procedure `read`(w):
1: **if** $ts[w] < S[top].ts$ **then**
2: $\quad S[top].rms$++
3: $\quad$ **if** $ts[w] \neq 0$ **then**
4: $\quad\quad$ let i be the max index in S such that $S[i].ts \leq ts[w]$
5: $\quad\quad S[i].rms$− −
6: $\quad$ **end if**
7: **end if**
8: $ts[w] \leftarrow count$

procedure `write`(w):
1: $ts[w] \leftarrow count$

Figure 6. Algorithm for RMS computation and input-sensitive profiling: procedures for processing execution trace events.

- The *partial read memory size* $S[i].rms$ of the activation, defined so that the following invariant property holds throughout the execution:

$$\forall i,\ 1 \leq i \leq top: \qquad \text{RMS}(i) = \sum_{j=i}^{top} S[j].rms \qquad (1)$$

  where $\text{RMS}(i)$ denotes the current RMS value of the i-th pending activation on the portion of the execution trace already seen.

It can be proved that Invariant 1 is equivalent to the following equality:

$$S[i].rms = \text{RMS}(i) - \text{RMS}(i+1)$$

i.e., that the partial read memory size maintained by our algorithm is the difference between the RMS of an activation and the RMS of its pending child (if any). Moreover, it follows from Invariant 1 that the RMS and the partial RMS of the topmost routine coincide:

$$\text{RMS}(top) = S[top].rms \qquad (2)$$

In particular, this is true upon completion of a routine, and guarantees that any algorithm able to maintain Invariant 1 will correctly compute the RMS of any routine activation.

Besides the shadow stack S, our algorithm also maintains, for each memory location w, a timestamp $ts[w]$ containing the time of the latest access (read or write) to w. Memory timestamps are initialized to 0 and time is measured by a global counter $count$, that maintains the total number of routine activations.

Algorithm and analysis. The partial read memory size can be maintained more efficiently than the RMS, as shown in Figure 6. To prove the correctness of our approach, in the following we show that all procedures correctly preserve Invariant 1.

When a routine r is invoked (see procedure `call`(r)), the time counter is incremented by 1 and a new shadow stack entry associated with r is appropriately initialized. Upon completion of the routine, its partial RMS is added to the partial RMS of its parent (see line 2 of procedure `return`). It is not difficult to see that this operation preserves Invariant 1. Performance metrics of the completed routine are also collected (line 1): these metrics are associated with the RMS value $S[top].rms$, which at this point coincides with the true RMS (see Equation 2).

Memory access operations on a location w update the timestamp $ts[w]$ with the current counter value (line 1 of procedure `write` and line 8 of procedure `read`). The read operation might also update the partial memory sizes of two distinct routine activations (lines 2 and 5). Namely, if location w has never been accessed by the topmost routine or by any of its completed descendants (condition tested in line 1), then the current access is a first read to w with respect to the topmost routine, whose partial RMS is increased by 1. We have now two cases:

- If the timestamp of location w is still 0 (test at line 3), this is the first access to w in the entire execution of the program, and no other counter needs to be changed. Notice that Invariant 1 is maintained by the execution of line 2, since in this case the RMS of all pending routines increases by 1.
- If the timestamp of location w is not 0, location w has been accessed before during the execution and, in view of the inequality in line 1, the last access happened in some ancestor v of the topmost routine (or in one of v's completed descendants). In this case, the algorithm finds the deepest ancestor that has accessed w (line 4) and decreases its partial RMS by 1: this restores Invariant 1 for all pending activations j such that $1 \leq j \leq i$, whose RMS must not be affected by the current read operation.

The running time of all operations is constant, except for line 4 of procedure `read`. Since the timestamps $S[i].ts$ of routine activations on any call path are increasing, line 4 can be implemented with a binary search and requires $O(\log d)$ time in the worst case, where d is the maximum stack depth during the execution of the program.

We also designed and implemented an asymptotically faster algorithm based on disjoint-sets data structures [40], but in our experiments it was slower and required more space than the solution we presented in this section.

5. Implementation

In this section we discuss our implementation of `aprof` based on the Valgrind [34] framework. Valgrind provides a dynamic instrumentation infrastructure that translates the binary code into an architecture-neutral intermediate representation (VEX). Analysis tools provide callbacks for events generated by the stream of VEX executed instructions.

Instrumentation. While tracing memory accesses is relatively simple in Valgrind, reliably instrumenting function calls and returns is instead rather complex. `aprof` uses a similar approach as the `callgrind` profiling tool [42]: we maintain a shadow runtime stack and cover a wide range of exotic cases to detect function entry/exit events, including jumps to different ELF sections/objects, special handling for dynamically linked functions via `_dl_runtime_resolve`, etc. Our tool takes advantage of the flexible infrastructure of Valgrind and provides full support for multithreaded applications by generating separate profiles for each thread.

Shadow memory. To maintain the timestamps ts of memory cells needed for computing the RMS values, we shadow each memory location accessed by the program with a 32-bit counter. Similarly to the `memcheck` tool [38], we use a two-levels lookup table. The address space is divided in 64 K chunks of 64 KB each (on 64-bit machines, we extend address space coverage to 256 GB). So, the primary table indexes all 64 KB chunks. When an address is referenced by a program, if not already done, we allocate a new secondary table for covering that chunk and we update the primary table for future references. The secondary table contains the set of 32-bit timestamps of addresses covered by the chunk.

Memory tracing resolution: space-accuracy tradeoffs. To reduce the space needed by the lookup table, `aprof` allows users to configure the resolution of distinct observable memory objects, trading space for accuracy. This can potentially impact the number of distinct RMS values observed by `aprof`, and therefore the number of collected performance tuples. We denote by k the size in bytes of the smallest observable objects, which we assume to be aligned to addresses multiple of k. For $k = 1$, we have the finest resolution, shadowing the addresses of all accessed individual memory bytes. For $k = 2$, we trace accesses to 2-bytes words aligned at 16-bit

	TIME					SPACE				
	secs	slowdown				MB	overhead			
	native	mem check	callgrind base	callgrind cache	aprof	native	mem check	callgrind base	callgrind cache	aprof
perlbench	585	34.8	98	178.3	55.4	757	2.1	1.1	1.1	2.1
bzip2	852	11.0	32	90.1	28.7	959	1.3	1.1	1.1	2.0
gcc	523	17.5	47	97.5	33.8	488	2.7	2.1	2.3	3.9
mcf	504	5.8	15	35.1	12.2	1,785	1.3	1.0	1.0	2.0
gobmk	645	28.2	72	135.7	44.8	138	1.8	1.5	1.6	2.1
hmmer	1,153	10.8	23	90.7	27.6	137	1.9	1.4	1.5	1.9
sjeng	798	28.4	94	149.3	45.8	279	1.4	1.2	1.2	1.9
libquantum	790	8.0	31	80.2	21.3	171	1.7	1.5	1.6	2.5
h264ref	903	28.4	85	193.5	67.5	173	1.7	1.4	1.4	2.0
omnetpp	517	16.1	45	82.9	28.8	280	2.8	1.3	1.2	2.0
astar	698	11.8	26	67.1	22.8	444	1.5	1.2	1.2	2.0
xalancbmk	341	35.0	95	171.3	78.3	536	1.8	1.2	1.2	2.3
bwaves	1,239	15.7	17.2	79.1	24.3	982	1.3	1.1	1.1	2.0
gamess	1,161	28.3	42.1	147.4	40.9	748	1.1	1.1	1.1	1.1
milc	520	13.8	12.3	60.9	18.5	795	1.3	1.1	1.1	2.0
gromacs	727	21.1	14.0	76.0	21.5	153	1.5	1.2	1.3	1.5
cactusADM	1.934	14.2	6.4	52.7	17.4	1,111	1.2	1.1	1.1	1.6
leslie3d	745	16.4	12.9	83.2	24.3	231	1.5	1.3	1.3	1.9
namd	640	20.3	15.7	89.5	21.5	161	1.8	1.4	1.4	1.8
soplex	355	11.1	25.6	73.4	26.3	738	1.3	1.2	1.2	2.2
povray	298	41.3	81.0	166.0	55.2	118	2.7	1.6	1.6	1.8
calculix	1,880	24.1	22.1	104.3	27.0	232	1.6	1.9	1.9	2.5
GemsFDTD	610	20.3	10.4	86.8	26.1	937	1.3	1.1	1.1	2.0
tonto	770	31.0	48.1	136.7	42.3	147	2.0	1.5	1.6	2.0
lbm	452	25.4	10.4	85.2	26.6	517	1.3	1.1	1.1	2.0
wrf	996	24.6	27.9	108.4	29.9	809	1.6	1.2	1.2	2.1
sphinx3	800	30.8	39.6	109.5	38.7	159	2.0	1.4	1.4	2.1
geometric mean		19.1	29.4	97.3	30.6		1.6	1.3	1.3	2.0

Table 1. Performance comparison of aprof and other Valgrind tools on the SPEC CPU2006 benchmarks.

boundaries, halving the universe of timestamps. The larger k, the smaller the RMS accuracy for routines working on small objects (e.g., strings of characters) and the smaller the size of the shadow memory. By default, $k = 4$ in aprof.

Optimizations. aprof performs several optimizations at instrumentation time. For instance, we reduce the number of traced memory accesses by coalescing into a single event each pair of load/store events (caused by the same guest instruction) operating on the same object. We also discard all other events related to objects already referenced within the same basic block.

A performance-critical operation is the timestamp search of line 4 in the read procedure of Figure 6. As we observed in Section 4.2, implementing this operation with a binary search on the shadow stack guarantees a worst-case bound of $O(\log d)$, where d is the current depth of the stack. However, our experiments revealed that a sequential scan tends to be faster in practice, as on average it performs a very small number of iterations.

Performance metric. We count basic blocks as performance measure: we observed that, compared to running time measurements, this adds a light burden to the analysis time overhead, and improves accuracy in characterizing asymptotic behavior even on small workloads. The choice of counting basic blocks rather than measuring time for studying asymptotic trends has several other advantages, very well motivated in [18].

Other issues. We noticed that calls to dynamically linked libraries made via _dl_runtime_resolve generate spurious memory accesses that may introduce some noise in the collected performance tuples. To improve reliability of RMS computations, we handled _dl_runtime_resolve as a special case by disabling its cost and RMS propagation to the ancestors.

Finally, to handle overflows of the main routine activations counter ($count$) in long-running applications, aprof performs a periodical global renumbering of timestamps in its data structures.

6. Experimental Evaluation

In this section we discuss the results of an extensive experimental evaluation of aprof on the CPU2006 benchmarks of the Standard Performance Evaluation Corporation [23]. Our experiments aim both at studying the resources required by our tool compared to other prominent heavyweight dynamic program analysis tools, and at analyzing relevant properties of the input-sensitive profiles generated for the considered benchmarks.

6.1 Experimental Setup

Benchmarks. Our experiments are mainly based on the SPEC CPU2006 v1.1 suite, considering both integer (CINT) and floating-point (CFP) components. All of them were run on the SPEC reference workloads in 64-bit mode. For CINT, we successfully tested all 12 components. In the case of CFP, we omitted zeusmp due to a known Valgrind issue, and dealII as it failed to terminate on all evaluated tools. We could successfully test all remaining 15 components. For the sake of completeness, we also included in our tests the wf-0.41 [15] word frequency counter discussed in Section 3 on a 117 MB input text file consisting of the concatenation of several copies of Anna Karenina [22] and protein sequences [17].

Platform. Experiments were performed on a cluster machine with two nodes, each equipped with eight 64-bit Intel Xeon CPU E5520 at 2.27 GHz, with 48 GB of RAM running Linux kernel 2.6.18 with gcc 4.1.2 and Valgrind 3.7.0 – SVN rev. 12129.

Evaluation metrics. We collected running times reported by specrun, the execution engine of the CPU2006 test harness, and the peak virtual memory space required over all tested workloads for each benchmark. We also collected all the profiling reports generated by aprof on the CPU2006 suite, measuring relevant parameters such as the number of collected tuples for each routine. Profiled functions covered both the executable binary and all dynamically linked libraries.

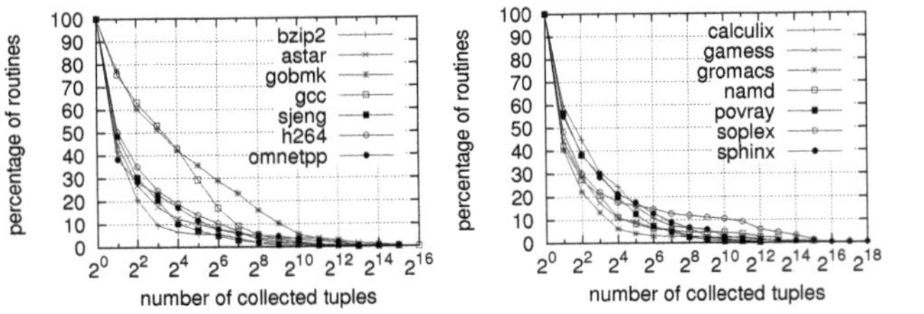

(a) integer benchmarks (b) floating-point benchmarks

Figure 7. Percentage of routines for which aprof collected at least a given number of performance tuples for a representative set of SPEC CPU2006 benchmarks.

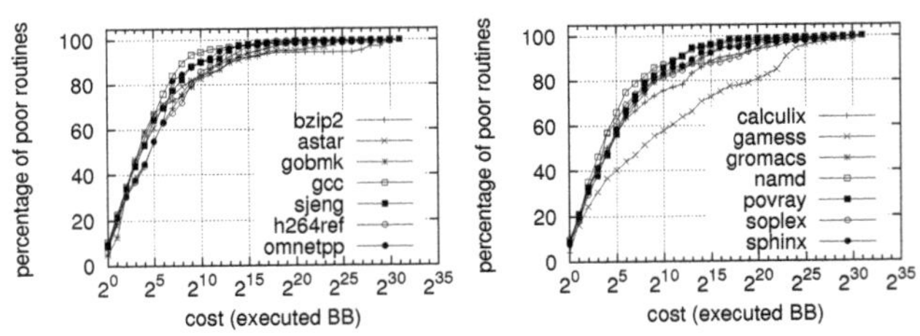

(a) integer benchmarks (b) floating-point benchmarks

Figure 8. Percentage of routines with less than 10 collected tuples and at least a given maximum cost for a representative set of SPEC CPU2006 benchmarks.

Evaluated tools. We compared the performance of `aprof` to two prominent and widely used Valgrind tools: `memcheck` [38], a tool for detecting memory-related errors, and `callgrind` [42], a call-graph generating cache and branch prediction profiler. We considered two settings for `callgrind`: the basic call-graph generating tool and the tool extended with cache simulation, calling them `callgrind-base` and `callgrind-cache`, respectively. Although the considered tools solve different analysis problems, all of them share the same instrumentation infrastructure provided by Valgrind, which accounts for a significant fraction of the execution times: `memcheck` does not trace function calls/returns and mainly relies on memory read/write events; `callgrind-base` instruments function calls/returns, but not memory accesses, while `callgrind-cache` traces both kinds of events like `aprof`. In our experiments with `aprof`, we also considered different values of the memory tracing resolution k discussed in Section 5. Unless otherwise stated, we used `aprof` with $k = 4$.

6.2 Experimental Results

Performance results. Performance figures of our evaluated tools on the SPEC CPU2006 benchmarks are summarized in Table 1. Compared to native execution, `aprof`'s mean slowdown factor is $30.6\times$ ($31.9\times$ on CINT and $27.9\times$ on CFP), with a peak slowdown of $78.3\times$ for `xalancbmk`, an XSLT engine for XML processing. `callgrind-cache`, which is most similar to `aprof` from a tracing perspective, is up to $4.2\times$ slower than `aprof`, with a mean slowdown of $3.2\times$. `callgrind-base` is $1.5\times$ slower than `aprof` on CINT and $1.4\times$ faster on CFP: overall, the two tools deliver comparable performance, even if `callgrind-base` does not trace memory accesses. Compared to `memcheck`, which is the less heavyweight of all considered tools, `aprof` is about $1.6\times$ slower. However, `memcheck` does not trace function calls/returns, which account for a significant fraction of `aprof`'s performance.

The mean memory requirements of `aprof` are within a factor of 2 of native execution, with a peak of $3.9\times$ for `gcc`. This is needed for shadowing accessed memory cells with 32-bit timestamps and for maintaining the performance tuples. Compared to `memcheck`, which also uses a memory shadowing approach, `aprof` requires about 20% more space. However, the current version of `aprof` does not use any shadow memory compression scheme as `memcheck` does, and the amount of generated profile data is higher. Both versions of `callgrind`, which do not use shadow values, require less space than `aprof` and `memcheck` (30% overhead compared to native execution). Performance figures on `wf-0.41` are similar, with a slowdown of $43.1\times$ and a space overhead of $1.9\times$.

Analysis of input-sensitive profiles. Our second set of experiments aims at evaluating some relevant properties of the profiling data generated by `aprof` on the SPEC CPU2006 benchmarks. A first natural question is how many performance tuples can be automatically collected for each routine from a *single* run of a program on a typical workload. Charts in Figure 7 plot the percentage of routines that have at least a given number of tuples for a representative set of programs and workloads from both the integer and floating-point suites. The experiment shows that the results can significantly vary across different benchmarks, ranging from programs where the fraction of routines drops quickly with the number of collected tuples such as `bzip2`, which does most of the work in a handful of hot routines, to larger-scale programs containing a wealth of algorithmic-intensive functions such as `gcc`, with several rich routines having many tuples. For instance, the fraction of routines with at least 10 tuples ranges from a minimum of 7.8% for `bzip2` to a maximum of 49.1% for `gcc`, with an average value of 18.1% for all benchmarks. This observation draws an interesting parallel with the well-known Pareto principle, which accounts most of a program's cost to a small fraction of the routines. Notice that for some functions `aprof` collected hundreds of thousands of tuples. To assess the potential relevance of "poor" routines, for which we may not have enough tuples to produce informative plots, we studied their cost distribution, reported in Figure 8. The chart shows that the *maximum* cost per invocation of most poor functions with less than 10 tuples is small (e.g., 70% of poor functions *never* execute more than 100 basic blocks per invocation), and therefore they are unlikely to be of any asymptotic interest in the context of the application in which they are deployed.

Space-accuracy tradeoffs. As a final experiment, we analyzed the impact of the memory tracing resolution k (see Section 5) on the performance of `aprof` and on the profiles it generated on a representative subset of CINT and CFP benchmarks. Our tests, reported in Figure 9, show that the mean running time for the considered benchmarks is barely affected by varying k, while space usage decreases with k as expected. We also studied how the percentage of routines with at least 10 tuples varies with k, showing that the loss of accuracy for lower resolutions is small compared to the space savings, hence it is reasonable to use $k > 1$.

7. Related Work

Performance profiling. Performance profiling has been the subject of extensive research since the early 70's [27]. In early profilers, performance measurements were associated to isolated syntactic units of a program, such as procedures or statements. The importance of contextual information was recognized early and pioneered by gprof's call graph profiles [19]. Since a single level of context sensitivity may be inaccurate [36, 39], Ammons, Ball, and Larus introduced the calling context tree (CCT), a compact data structure to associate performance metrics with entire paths through a program's call graph [2]. A variety of techniques have later been proposed to reduce the slowdown incurred by CCT-based profilers that work by exhaustive instrumentation, including sampling [16, 21, 43] and bursting [3, 24, 46]. Since the CCT can be

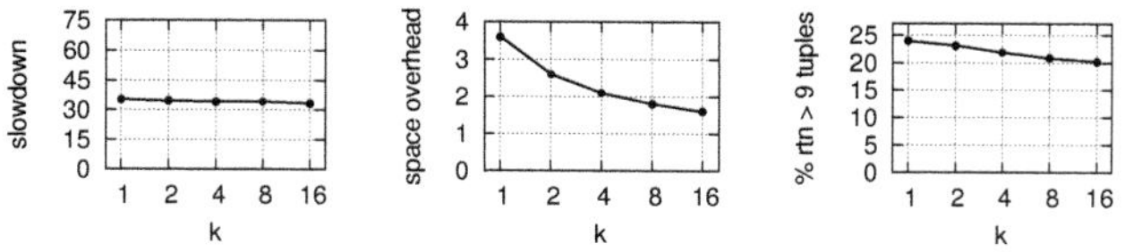

Figure 9. Impact of memory tracing resolution k on time, space and accuracy, as geometric mean computed over SPEC CPU2006 benchmarks `bzip2`, `gobmk`, `astar`, `gcc`, `sphinx3`, and `gamess`.

very large and difficult to analyze, a different set of works targets space issues in context-sensitive profiling [7, 13, 20].

At the intraprocedural level, context information is encoded by path profiles [4], that determine how many times each path in the control flow graph executes. The seminal work of Ball and Larus [4] has spawned much research on flow-sensitive profiling: see, e.g., [2, 5, 6, 26, 32, 37, 41].

All these works on context-sensitive profiling aim at associating performance metrics to distinct paths traversed either in the call graph or in the control flow graph during a program's execution, but do not explore input-sensitivity issues that are the target of this paper. Context- and input-sensitivity represent two orthogonal aspects of program profiles and can be naturally combined. The method proposed by Goldsmith, Aiken, and Wilkerson [18] allows it measure the empirical computational complexity of a program and is much closer in spirit to our work: the program is run on different workloads (possibly spanning several orders of magnitude in size), the performance of its routines is measured, and all the observations are fit to a model that predicts performance as a function of the workload size. Differently from `aprof`, however, the workload size of the program's routines is not computed automatically, but numerical features characterizing the different workloads must be explicitly specified by the user.

Performance prediction. Performance prediction provides means to estimate the running time of a program on different platforms. Profile-based prediction tools, which are most closely related to our work, first run benchmark programs once under lightweight instrumentation tools in order to generate average statistics for a program run, and then feed these statistics to analysis tools that compute an estimate of the run time on a specific machine. While the instrumentation phase runs the entire program, the analysis phase runs in a time roughly proportional to the number of static instructions, which is typically several orders of magnitude smaller than the number of instructions actually executed. It has been shown in [35] that this technique can accurately predict the performance of a detailed out-of-order issue processor model, largely improving over earlier static analysis methods. Differently from our work, the goal in [35] is to predict the performance of the same benchmark on different platform models, and not how the performance scales with the input size: repeated runs of the instrumentation phase on different inputs are necessary to pinpoint scalability issues.

The problem of understanding how an application's performance scales given different problem sizes is addressed in [29], describing a methodology for constructing semi-automatically models of an application's characteristics parameterized by problem size. In [29], data from multiple runs with different and determinable input parameters are first collected and then used to compute a curve parameterized by a parameter related to the problem size. This is quite different from our approach, where the input size of each routine activation is automatically computed by the profiler and the analysis of data extracted from a single program run may be sufficient to determine the growth rate of the routines' performance: with our methodology, we cannot predict how an entire program will scale with different problem sizes, but we can rather automatically discover hidden asymptotic inefficiencies of different program's components.

WCET (Worst-Case Execution Time) analysis tools [44] used in the development of real-time systems also address the problem of estimating execution times depending on the input data. In particular, measurement-based methods need to direct input-data generation in search for worst-case or long program execution times. This is fundamentally different from input-sensitive profiling, which does not aim at identifying worst-case instances, but rather at understanding how the execution cost scales on specific workloads as the input size grows.

Experimental algorithmics. Although worst-case asymptotic analysis provides a strong mathematical framework for the analysis of algorithms, predicting the actual behavior of an algorithmic code may still be a very difficult task [14, 30, 33], since general theoretical models and techniques do not directly fit to actual existing machines and to real-world problem instances. Experimental algorithmics complements and reinforces theoretical analyses with empirical studies aimed at discovering easy and hard instances for a problem and measuring practical indicators (implementation constant factors, locality of references, cache and communication complexity effects) that may be difficult to predict theoretically. The problem of inferring asymptotic bounds from experimental data is rather difficult and there is no sound and generally accepted solution. Some researchers have nevertheless proposed heuristics for the "empirical curve bounding" problem, showing their effectiveness for several synthetic and real datasets [31].

Performance profilers are especially useful in the experimental analysis of algorithmic code. In particular, input-sensitive profiling conjugates asymptotic algorithmic theory with profiling practice, and we believe that it may represent a useful tool in this domain, providing valuable hints to experimenters about asymptotic inefficiencies and typical usage scenarios of critical subroutines. Moreover, papers in experimental algorithmics only rarely analyze algorithms *in situ*, i.e., within the actual context of applications they are deployed in. Our approach makes *in situ* analysis viable (and easy), thus exposing possible performance effects (e.g., a larger number of cache misses) due to the interaction with the overall application.

8. Conclusions

We have proposed a novel approach to performance profiling inspired by asymptotic cost models. The running time of an algorithm is typically estimated by theoretical means as a function relating the size of the input to the number of steps of the algorithm. On the other side, profilers collect runtime information on a single run on a specific input: this kind of information, although useful, does not provide insights on code scalability with respect to the input size. Our profiler relates the measured cost required by the execution of each code fragment to the size of the processed input data. In this way, it can induce an estimated growth rate of the running time, pinpointing scalability problems more precisely than traditional code profiling. We have shown that our approach is both methodologically sound and practical.

Measuring automatically the size of the input given to a generic code fragment raises a variety of interesting questions. Namely, the RMS metric is a measure of distinct accessed memory cells, but does not consider data that are not stored in the process memory at the beginning of a function's execution. For instance, data received on-line (e.g., reads from external devices such as the network, keyboard, or timer) or non-deterministic input values read from I/Os (e.g., input items read in a loop over a file iterator) are not counted in the input size. A possible solution to these issues could hinge upon the techniques for logging non-determinism described in [12]. We regard extending our model towards this direction as an interesting open issue.

Acknowledgements

We would like to thank Randal Bryant and David O'Hallaron for their feedback on the difficulty of discovering asymptotic inefficiencies in large software applications, and to Matthew Hammer for many useful discussions. We are also indebted to Umberto Ferraro Petrillo for hosting our experiments on the Intel Xeon cluster machine described in Section 6.1 and to Bruno Aleandri for developing an earlier version of `aprof`.

This work was supported in part by the Italian Ministry of Education, University, and Research (MIUR) under PRIN 2008TFBWL4 national research project "AlgoDEEP: Algorithmic Challenges for Data-Intensive Processing on Emerging Computing Platforms".

References

[1] An efficient variation of bubble sort. *Information Processing Letters*, 11(1):5 – 6, 1980.

[2] G. Ammons, T. Ball, and J. R. Larus. Exploiting hardware performance counters with flow and context sensitive profiling. *SIGPLAN Not.*, 32(5):85–96, 1997.

[3] M. Arnold and B. Ryder. A framework for reducing the cost of instrumented code. In *PLDI*, pages 168–179. ACM, 2001.

[4] T. Ball and J. R. Larus. Efficient path profiling. In *MICRO 29: Proceedings of the 29th annual ACM/IEEE international symposium on Microarchitecture*, pages 46–57, 1996.

[5] T. Ball, P. Mataga, and M. Sagiv. Edge profiling versus path profiling: the showdown. In *POPL*, pages 134–148. ACM, 1998.

[6] M. D. Bond and K. S. McKinley. Practical path profiling for dynamic optimizers. In *CGO*, pages 205–216. IEEE Computer Society, 2005.

[7] M. D. Bond and K. S. McKinley. Probabilistic calling context. *SIGPLAN Not. (Proc. OOPSLA 2007)*, 42(10):97–112, 2007.

[8] R. E. Bryant. Personal communication, September 2011.

[9] R. E. Bryant and D. R. O'Hallaron. *Computer Systems: A Programmer's Perspective*. Pearson Education, 2010.

[10] R. E. Bryant, D. L. Beatty, K. S. Brace, K. Cho, and T. J. Sheffler. COSMOS: A Compiled Simulator for MOS Circuits. In *DAC*, pages 9–16, 1987.

[11] J. M. Chambers, W. S. Cleveland, B. Kleiner, and P. A. Tukey. *Graphical Methods for Data Analysis*. Chapman and Hall, New York, 1983.

[12] J. Chow, T. Garfinkel, and P. M. Chen. Decoupling dynamic program analysis from execution in virtual environments. In *USENIX 2008 Annual Technical Conference*, pages 1–14, 2008.

[13] D. C. D'Elia, C. Demetrescu, and I. Finocchi. Mining hot calling contexts in small space. In M. W. Hall and D. A. Padua, editors, *PLDI*, pages 516–527. ACM, 2011.

[14] C. Demetrescu, I. Finocchi, and G. F. Italiano. Algorithm engineering. *Bulletin of the EATCS (algorithmics column)*, 79:48–63, 2003.

[15] Fedora Project. `wf`: simple word frequency counter. `http://rpmfind.net//linux/RPM/fedora/devel/rawhide/src/w/wf-0.41-6.fc17.src.html`.

[16] N. Froyd, J. Mellor-Crummey, and R. Fowler. Low-overhead call path profiling of unmodified, optimized code. In *Proc. 19th Annual International Conf. on Supercomputing*, pages 81–90. ACM, 2005.

[17] Genome bioinformatics research laboratory. Resources and datasets. `http://genome.crg.es/main/databases.html`.

[18] S. Goldsmith, A. Aiken, and D. S. Wilkerson. Measuring empirical computational complexity. In *ESEC/SIGSOFT FSE*, pages 395–404, 2007.

[19] S. L. Graham, P. B. Kessler, and M. K. McKusick. gprof: a call graph execution profiler (with retrospective). In K. S. McKinley, editor, *Best of PLDI*, pages 49–57. ACM, 1982.

[20] R. J. Hall. Call path refinement profiles. *IEEE Trans. Softw. Eng.*, 21 (6):481–496, 1995.

[21] R. J. Hall and A. J. Goldberg. Call path profiling of monotonic program resources in UNIX. In *Proc. Summer 1993 USENIX Technical Conference*, pages 1–19. USENIX Association, 1993.

[22] M. Hart. Gutenberg Project. `http://www.gutenberg.org/`.

[23] J. L. Henning. Spec cpu2006 benchmark descriptions. *SIGARCH Comput. Archit. News*, 34:1–17, 2006.

[24] M. Hirzel and T. Chilimbi. Bursty tracing: A framework for low-overhead temporal profiling. In *Proc. 4th ACM Workshop on Feedback-Directed and Dynamic Optimization*, 2001.

[25] D. Johnson. A theoretician's guide to the experimental analysis of algorithms. In *Data Structures, Near Neighbor Searches, and Methodology*, pages 215–250. American Mathematical Society, 2002.

[26] R. Joshi, M. D. Bond, and C. Zilles. Targeted path profiling: Lower overhead path profiling for staged dynamic optimization systems. In *CGO*, pages 239–250. IEEE Computer Society, 2004.

[27] D. E. Knuth and F. R. Stevenson. Optimal measurement points for program frequency counts. *BIT*, 13:313–322, 1973.

[28] T. Küstner, J. Weidendorfer, and T. Weinzierl. Argument controlled profiling. In *Euro-Par'09*, pages 177–184, 2010.

[29] G. Marin and J. M. Mellor-Crummey. Cross-architecture performance predictions for scientific applications using parameterized models. In *Proc. SIGMETRICS 2004*, pages 2–13, 2004.

[30] C. C. McGeoch. Experimental algorithmics. *Communications of the ACM*, 50(11):27–31, 2007.

[31] C. C. McGeoch, P. Sanders, R. Fleischer, P. R. Cohen, and D. Precup. Using finite experiments to study asymptotic performance. In *Experimental Algorithmics*, LNCS 2547, pages 93–126, 2002.

[32] D. Melski and T. W. Reps. Interprocedural path profiling. In *Proc. 8th Int. Conf. on Compiler Construction*, LNCS 1575, pages 47–62, 1999.

[33] B. M. E. Moret. Towards a discipline of experimental algorithmics. In *Data Structures, Near Neighbor Searches, and Methodology*, pages 197–250. American Mathematical Society, 2002.

[34] N. Nethercote and J. Seward. Valgrind: a framework for heavyweight dynamic binary instrumentation. In *PLDI*, pages 89–100, 2007.

[35] D. Ofelt and J. L. Hennessy. Efficient performance prediction for modern microprocessors. In *SIGMETRICS*, pages 229–239, 2000.

[36] C. Ponder and R. J. Fateman. Inaccuracies in program profilers. *Softw., Pract. Exper.*, 18(5):459–467, 1988.

[37] S. Roy and Y. N. Srikant. Profiling k-iteration paths: A generalization of the ball-larus profiling algorithm. In *CGO*, pages 70–80, 2009.

[38] J. Seward and N. Nethercote. Using Valgrind to detect undefined value errors with bit-precision. In *USENIX Annual Technical Conference*, pages 17–30. USENIX, 2005.

[39] J. M. Spivey. Fast, accurate call graph profiling. *Softw., Pract. Exper.*, 34(3):249–264, 2004.

[40] R. E. Tarjan. Efficiency of a good but not linear set union algorithm. *J. ACM*, 22(2):215–225, 1975.

[41] K. Vaswani, A. V. Nori, and T. M. Chilimbi. Preferential path profiling: compactly numbering interesting paths. In *POPL*, pages 351–362. ACM, 2007.

[42] J. Weidendorfer, M. Kowarschik, and C. Trinitis. A tool suite for simulation based analysis of memory access behavior. In *Int. Conf. on Computational Science*, LNCS 3038, pages 440–447, 2004.

[43] J. Whaley. A portable sampling-based profiler for Java virtual machines. In *Proc. ACM 2000 Conf. on Java Grande*, pages 78–87, 2000.

[44] R. Wilhelm, J. Engblom, A. Ermedahl, N. Holsti, S. Thesing, D. B. Whalley, G. Bernat, C. Ferdinand, R. Heckmann, T. Mitra, F. Mueller, I. Puaut, P. P. Puschner, J. Staschulat, and P. Stenström. The worst-case execution-time problem - overview of methods and survey of tools. *ACM Trans. Embedded Comput. Syst.*, 7(3), 2008.

[45] T. Williams and C. Kelley. Gnuplot: command-driven interactive function plotting program. `http://www.gnuplot.info/`.

[46] X. Zhuang, M. J. Serrano, H. W. Cain, and J.-D. Choi. Accurate, efficient, and adaptive calling context profiling. In *PLDI*, pages 263–271, 2006.

Language-Based Control and Mitigation of Timing Channels

Danfeng Zhang
Department of Computer Science
Cornell University
Ithaca, NY 14853
zhangdf@cs.cornell.edu

Aslan Askarov *
School of Engineering and Computer Science, Harvard University
Cambridge, MA 02138
aslan@seas.harvard.edu

Andrew C. Myers
Department of Computer Science
Cornell University
Ithaca, NY 14853
andru@cs.cornell.edu

Abstract

We propose a new language-based approach to mitigating timing channels. In this language, well-typed programs provably leak only a bounded amount of information over time through external timing channels. By incorporating mechanisms for predictive mitigation of timing channels, this approach also permits a more expressive programming model. Timing channels arising from interaction with underlying hardware features such as instruction caches are controlled. Assumptions about the underlying hardware are explicitly formalized, supporting the design of hardware that efficiently controls timing channels. One such hardware design is modeled and used to show that timing channels can be controlled in some simple programs of real-world significance.

Categories and Subject Descriptors D.2.4 [*Software/Program Verification*]: Formal Methods; D.4.6 [*Security and protection*]: Information Flow Controls

General Terms Languages, Security

Keywords Timing channels, mitigation, information flow

1. Introduction

Timing channels have long been a difficult and important problem for computer security. They can be used by adversaries as side channels or as covert channels to learn private information, including cryptographic keys and passwords [8, 13, 14, 18, 22, 24, 29, 36].

Timing channels can be categorized as internal or external [28]. *Internal timing channels* exist when timing channels are converted to storage channels within a system and affect the results computed. *External timing channels* exist when the adversary can learn something from the time at which the system interacts with the outside world. In either case, confidential information transmitted through timing channels constitutes *timing leakage*.

Internal timing channels that exploit races between threads have been addressed by enforcing low determinism [16, 37] and by constraining thread scheduling [26, 28]. The focus of this paper is instead on controlling *external* timing channels, for which current methods are less satisfactory. Starting with Agat [3], program transformations have been proposed to remove external timing channels. However, these methods restrict expressiveness: for example, loop guards can depend only on public information. Further, they do not handle some realistic hardware features. External mitigation is another approach to control external timing channels, by quantitatively limiting how much information leaks via the timing of external interactions [5, 20, 38]. Since external mitigation treats computation as a black box, it cannot distinguish between benign timing variations and variations that leak information. When most timing variation is benign, this leads to a significant performance penalty.

This work introduces a more complete and effective language-based method for controlling external timing channels, with provably bounded leakage. Broadly, the new method improves control of external timing channels in three ways:

- Unlike methods based on code transformation [3], this method supports more realistic programs and hardware. For example, it can be implemented on hardware with an instruction cache.
- Another difference from code-transformation approaches is that it offers a fully expressive programming model; in particular, loops with high (confidential) guards are permitted.
- The method does not need to be as conservative as external timing mitigation because a program analysis can distinguish between benign timing variations and those carrying confidential information, and can distinguish between multiple distinct security levels. This fine-grained reasoning about timing channels improves the tradeoff between security and performance.

Timing channels arise in general from the interaction of programs with the underlying implementation of the language in which the programs are written. This language implementation includes not only the compiler or interpreter used, but also the underlying hardware. Reasoning accurately about timing channels purely at the source language level is essentially impossible because language semantics, by design, prevent precise reasoning about time.

An important contribution of this paper is therefore a system of simple, static annotations that provides just enough information about the underlying language implementation to enable accurate reasoning about timing channels. These annotations form a contract between the software (language) level and the hardware implementation.

A second contribution of this paper is a formalization of this contract. Using this formal contract, implementers may verify that their compiler and architecture designs control timing channels. We illustrate this by sketching the design of a simple memory cache architecture that avoids timing channels.

A third contribution is a new language mechanism that improves expressive power achievable while controlling timing channels. It uses *predictive timing mitigation* [5] to bound the amount of information that leaks through timing. With this mechanism, algorithms whose timing behavior *does* depend on confidential information can be implemented securely; predictive mitigation ensures that total timing leakage is bounded by a programmer-specified function.

* This work was done while the author was at Cornell University.

PLDI'12, June 11–16, 2012, Beijing, China.

To evaluate the correctness and effectiveness of our approach, we simulated hardware satisfying the hardware side of the software–hardware contract. We evaluate the use of our approach on two applications vulnerable to timing attacks. The results suggest that the combination of language-based mitigation and secure hardware works well, with only modest slowdown.

We proceed as follows. Section 2 discusses the problem of controlling timing channels on modern computer hardware, and gives an overview of the new method. Section 3 introduces a programming language designed to permit precise reasoning about timing channels. Its semantics formalize several constraints that must be satisfied by a secure implementation. Section 4 sketches how these constraints can be satisfied by both stock and specialized hardware implementations. A type system for the language that soundly controls timing channels is presented in Section 5; its novel multilevel quantitative security guarantees are explored in Section 6. Predictive mitigation of timing channels is discussed in Section 7. Section 8 presents performance results from a simulated implementation of language-based predictive mitigation. Related work is covered in Section 9, and Section 10 concludes.

2. Language-level timing mitigation

Controlling timing channels is difficult because confidential information can affect timing in many ways, and yet we want to be able to analyze these timing dependencies at the source level. However, language semantics do not and should not define timing precisely.

2.1 Timing dependencies

We call timing channels visible at the source-language level *direct timing dependencies*. In this example, control flow affects timing.

```
1  if (h)
2     sleep(1);
3  else
4     sleep(10);
5  sleep(h);
```

Assume `h` holds confidential data and that `sleep` (e) suspends execution of the program for the amount of time specified by e. Since line 4 takes longer to execute than line 2, one bit of `h` is leaked through timing. Attacks on RSA have also used control-flow-related timing channels [8, 18]. Another source of direct timing dependencies is operations whose execution time depends on parameter values, such as the `sleep` command at line 5.

Modern hardware also creates *indirect timing dependencies* in which execution time depends on hardware state that has no source-level representation. The following code shows that the data cache is one source of indirect dependencies.

```
1  if (h1)
2     h2:=l1;
3  else
4     h2:=l2;
5  l3:=l1;
```

Suppose only `h1` and `h2` are confidential and that neither `l1` nor `l2` are cached initially. Even though both branches have the same instructions and similar memory access patterns, executing this code fragment is likely to take less time when `h1` is not zero: because `l1` is cached at line 2, line 5 runs faster, and the value of `h1` leaks through timing.

Some timing attacks [14, 24] also exploit data cache timing dependencies to infer AES encryption keys, but indirect dependencies arising from other hardware components have also been exploited to construct attacks: instruction and data caches [1], branch predictors and branch target buffers [2], and shared functional units [34].

We use the term *machine environment* to refer to all hardware state that is invisible at the language level but that is needed to predict timing. Timing channels relying on indirect dependencies are at best difficult to reason about at language level—the semantics of languages and even of instruction set architectures (ISAs) hide information about execution time by abstracting away low-level implementation details. For instance, we do not know that the timing of line 5 depends on `h1` without knowing how the data cache works in the example above.

It is worth noting that we assume a strong adversary that is particularly interesting with the rise of cloud computing: an adversary coresident on the system, controlling concurrent threads that can read low memory locations. The adversary can therefore time when low memory locations change. Further, the adversary can probe timing using the shared cache. This is a more powerful adversary than that considered in much previous work on timing channels, including prior attempts to control decryption side channels [5, 20, 38]. The prior methods are not effective against this adversary, who can efficiently learn secret keys using timing side channels [24].

2.2 Representing indirect timing dependencies abstractly

Recent work in the architecture community has aimed for a hardware-based solution to timing channels. Their hardware designs implicitly rely on assumptions about how software uses the hardware, but these assumptions have not been rigorously defined. For example, the cache design by Wang and Lee [35] works only under the assumption that the AES lookup table is preloaded into cache and that the load time is not observable to the adversary [19].

Timing channels cannot be controlled effectively purely at the source code or the hardware level. Hardware mechanisms can help, but do a poor job of controlling language-level leaks such as implicit flows. The question, then, is how to usefully and accurately characterize the timing semantics of code at the source level. Our insight is to combine the language-level and hardware-level approaches, by representing the machine environment abstractly at source level.

As is standard in information flow type systems [27], we associate all information with a *security label* that in this case describes the confidentiality of the information. Labels ℓ_1 and ℓ_2 are ordered, written $\ell_1 \sqsubseteq \ell_2$, if ℓ_2 describes a confidentiality requirement that is at least as strong as that of ℓ_1. It is secure for information to flow from label ℓ_1 to label ℓ_2. We assume there are at least two distinct labels L (low) and H (high) such that $L \sqsubseteq H \not\sqsubseteq L$. The label of public information is L; that of secret is H. As is standard, we denote by $\top$ the most restrictive label, and by $\bot$, the least restrictive one.

We assume that different components of the machine environment have security labels as well. For example, different partitions in a partitioned cache [35] can be associated with different labels.

To track how information flows into the machine environment, but without concretely representing the hardware state, we associate two labels with each command in the program. The first of these labels is the command's *read label* ℓ_r. The read label is an upper bound on the label of hardware state that affects the run time of the command. For example, the run time of a command with $\ell_r = L$ depends only on hardware state with label L or below. The second of these labels is the command's *write label* ℓ_w. The write label is a lower bound on the label of hardware state that the command can modify. It ensures that the labels of hardware state reflect the confidentiality of information that has flowed into that state.

For example, suppose that there is only one (low) data cache, which to be conservative means that anyone can learn from timing whether a given memory location is cached. Therefore both the read and write label of every command must be L. The previous example is then annotated as follows, where the first label in brackets is the read label, and the second, the write label.

```
1  if (h1)[L,L]
2     h2:=l1;[L,L]
3  else
4     h2:=l2;[L,L]
5  l3:=l1;[L,L]
```

The example on the left is insecure because execution of lines 2 and 4 is conditioned on the high variable `h1`. Therefore these lines are in a *high context*, one in which the program counter label [11] is high. If lines 2 and 4 update cache state in the usual way, the low write label permits low hardware state to be affected by `h1`. This insecure information flow is a form of *implicit flow* [11], but one in which hardware state with no language-level representation is being updated.

Since lines 2 and 4 occur in a high context, the write label of these commands must be H for this program to be secure. Consequently, the hardware may not update low parts of the machine environment. One way to avoid modifying the cache is to deactivate it in high contexts. A generalization of this idea is to partition the cache into two partitions, low and high. Cache misses in a high context then cause only the high cache partition to be updated.

With ℓ_r and ℓ_w abstracting the timing behavior of hardware, timing channel security can be statically checked at the language level, according to the type system described in Sec. 5. Moreover, these timing labels could be inferred automatically according to the type system, reducing the burden on programmers.

2.3 Language-level mitigation of timing channels

Strictly disallowing all timing leakage can be done as sketched thus far, but results in an impractically restrictive programming language because execution time is not permitted to depend on confidential information in any way.

To increase expressiveness, we introduce a new command `mitigate` to the language. Command `mitigate` (e,ℓ) c executes the command c while ensuring that timing leakage is bounded. The expression e computes an initial prediction for the execution time of c. The label ℓ bounds what information that can learned by observing the timing leakage c. That is, no information at level ℓ' such that $\ell' \not\sqsubseteq \ell$ can be learned from c's execution time. This property is enforced by the type system of Sec. 5. Moreover, the type system ensures that timing leakage can be bounded using the variation in the execution time of `mitigate` commands.

To provide a strict bound on the execution time of `mitigate` commands while providing practical performance, we introduce the use of predictive timing mitigation [5, 38] as a language-level mechanism. The idea is that given a prediction of how long executing c will take (the e in `mitigate` command), the `mitigate` command ensures that at least that much time is consumed by simply waiting if necessary. In the case of a misprediction (that is, when the estimate is too low), a larger prediction is generated , and the execution time is padded accordingly. Mispredictions also inflate the predictions generated by subsequent uses of `mitigate`.

For example, we can use `mitigate` to limit timing leakage from the command `sleep(h)`, as in this program:

```
mitigate(1,H){sleep(h)[H,H]}
```

The possible execution times of this program will not be arbitrary; they might, for example, be forced by `mitigate` to be the powers of 2. Limiting the possible execution times bounds the timing leakage from `sleep`. We explore the details of the mitigation mechanism more fully in Sec. 7 and evaluate its performance in Sec. 8.

Previous work has shown that predictive timing mitigation can bound timing leakage to a function that is sublinear (in fact, polylogarithmic) in time. But this is the first work that provides similar, quantitative bounds on timing leakage at the language level.

3. A language for controlling timing channels

Fig. 1 gives the syntax for a simple imperative language extended with our mechanism. All the novel elements—read and write labels, and the `mitigate` and `sleep` commands—have already been introduced. Notice that the sequential composition command itself needs no timing labels. As a technical convenience, each `mitigate` in the source has a unique identifier η. These identifiers are mainly used in Sec. 6; they are omitted where they are not essential.

We present our semantics in a series of modular steps. We start with a *core semantics*, a largely standard semantics for a while-language, which ignores timing. Next, we develop an *abstracted full semantics* that describes the timing semantics of the language more accurately while abstracting away parameters that depend on the language implementation, including the hardware and the compiler.

$$
\begin{aligned}
e &::= n \mid x \mid e\ op\ e \\
c &::= \mathtt{skip}_{[\ell_r,\ell_w]} \mid (x := e)_{[\ell_r,\ell_w]} \mid c;c \mid (\mathtt{while}\ e\ \mathtt{do}\ c)_{[\ell_r,\ell_w]} \\
&\quad \mid (\mathtt{if}\ e\ \mathtt{then}\ c_1\ \mathtt{else}\ c_2)_{[\ell_r,\ell_w]} \\
&\quad \mid (\mathtt{mitigate}_\eta\ (e,\ell)\ c)_{[\ell_r,\ell_w]} \mid (\mathtt{sleep}\ e)_{[\ell_r,\ell_w]}
\end{aligned}
$$

Figure 1: Syntax of the language

$$\langle \mathtt{skip}_{[\ell_r,\ell_w]}, m\rangle \to \langle \mathtt{stop}, m\rangle \qquad \langle (\mathtt{sleep}\ e)_{[\ell_r,\ell_w]}, m\rangle \to \langle \mathtt{stop}, m\rangle$$

$$\langle (\mathtt{mitigate}\ (e,\ell)\ c)_{[\ell_r,\ell_w]}, m\rangle \to \langle c, m\rangle$$

$$\frac{\langle c_1,m\rangle \to \langle \mathtt{stop},m'\rangle}{\langle c_1;c_2,m\rangle \to \langle c_2,m'\rangle} \qquad \frac{\langle c_1,m\rangle \to \langle c_1',m'\rangle \quad c_1' \neq \mathtt{stop}}{\langle c_1;c_2,m\rangle \to \langle c_1';c_2,m'\rangle}$$

$$\frac{\langle e,m\rangle \Downarrow v}{\langle (x:=e)_{[\ell_r,\ell_w]},m\rangle \to \langle \mathtt{stop}, m[x\mapsto v]\rangle}$$

$$\frac{\langle e,m\rangle \Downarrow n \quad n\neq 0 \implies i=1 \quad n=0 \implies i=2}{\langle (\mathtt{if}\ e\ \mathtt{then}\ c_1\ \mathtt{else}\ c_2)_{[\ell_r,\ell_w]},m\rangle \to \langle c_i,m\rangle}$$

$$\frac{\langle e,m\rangle \Downarrow n \qquad n\neq 0}{\langle (\mathtt{while}\ e\ \mathtt{do}\ c)_{[\ell_r,\ell_w]},m\rangle \to \langle c;(\mathtt{while}\ e\ \mathtt{do}\ c)_{[\ell_r,\ell_w]},m\rangle}$$

$$\frac{\langle e,m\rangle \Downarrow n \qquad n=0}{\langle (\mathtt{while}\ e\ \mathtt{do}\ c)_{[\ell_r,\ell_w]},m\rangle \to \langle \mathtt{stop},m\rangle}$$

Figure 2: Core semantics of commands (unmitigated)

3.1 Core semantics

For expressions we use a standard big-step evaluation $\langle e,m\rangle \Downarrow v$ when expression e in memory m evaluates to value v. For commands (Fig. 2), we write $\langle c,m\rangle \to \langle c',m'\rangle$ for the transition of command c in memory m to command c' in memory m'. Note that read and write labels are not used in these rules. The rules use `stop` as a syntactic marker of the end of computation. We distinguish `stop` from the command $\mathtt{skip}_{[\ell_r,\ell_w]}$ because `skip` is a real command that may consume some measurable time (e.g., reading from the instruction cache), whereas `stop` is purely syntactic and takes no time at all. For `mitigate` we give an identity semantics for now: `mitigate` (e,ℓ) c simply evaluates to c. Since time is not part of the core semantics, `sleep` behaves like `skip`.

3.2 Abstracted full language semantics

The core semantics ignores timing; the job of the full language semantics is to supply a complete description of timing so that timing channels can be precisely identified.

Writing down a full semantics as a set of transition rules would define the complete timing behavior of the language. But this would be useful only for a particular language implementation on particular hardware. Instead, we permit *any* full semantics that satisfies a certain set of properties yet to be described. What is presented here is therefore a kind of abstracted full semantics in which only the key properties are fixed. This approach makes the results more general.

These key properties fall into two categories, which we call faithfulness requirements and security requirements. The faithfulness requirements (Sec. 3.5) are straightforward; the security requirements (Sec. 3.6) are more subtle.

3.3 Configurations

Configurations in the full semantics have the form $\langle c, m, E, G\rangle$. As in the core semantics, c and m are the current program and memory. Component E is the machine environment, and G is the global clock. In general G can be measured in any units of time, but we interpret it as machine clock cycles hereafter. We write $\langle c, m, E, G\rangle \rightarrow \langle c', m', E', G'\rangle$ for evaluation transitions.

The full semantics of expression evaluation obviously also needs to be small-step, but we choose a presentation style that elides the details of expression evaluation.

As before, the machine environment E represents hardware state that may affect timing but that is not needed by the core semantics. Hardware components captured by E include the data cache and instruction cache, the branch prediction buffer, the translation lookaside buffer (TLB), and other low-level components. The machine environment might also include hidden state added by the compiler for performance optimization.

For example, if one considers only the timing effects of data cache and instruction caches, denoted by D and I respectively, E could be a configuration of the form $E = \langle D, I\rangle$.

Note that while both the memory m and the machine environment E can affect timing, only the memory affects program control flow. This is the reason to distinguish them in the semantics. The environment E can be completely abstract as long as the properties for the full semantics are satisfied. This separation also ensures that the core semantics is completely standard.

The separation of m and E also clarifies possibilities for hardware design. For instance, it is possible for confidential data to be stored securely in a public partition of E, but not in public memory (cf. Sec. 4.1).

3.4 Threat model

To evaluate whether the programming language achieves its security goals, we need to describe the power of the adversary in terms of the semantics. We associate an adversary with a security level ℓ_A bounding what information the adversary can observe directly. To represent the confidentiality of memory, we assume that an environment Γ maps variable names to security levels. If a memory location (variable) has security level ℓ that flows to ℓ_A (that is, $\ell \sqsubseteq \ell_A$), the adversary is able to see the contents of that memory location. Recall that we are defending against a strong, coresident adversary. Therefore, by monitoring such a memory location for changes, the adversary can also measure the times at which the location is updated.

Two memories m_1 and m_2 are *ℓ-equivalent*, denoted $m_1 \sim_\ell m_2$, when they agree on the contents of locations at level ℓ and below:

$$m_1 \sim_\ell m_2 \triangleq \forall x \,.\, \Gamma(x) \sqsubseteq \ell \,.\, m_1(x) = m_2(x)$$

Intuitively, ℓ-equivalence of two memories means that an observer at level ℓ cannot distinguish these two memories.

Projected equivalence. We define *projected equivalence* on memories to require equivalence of variables with *exactly* level ℓ:

$$m_1 \simeq_\ell m_2 \triangleq \forall x \,.\, \Gamma(x) = \ell \,.\, m_1(x) = m_2(x)$$

We assume there is a corresponding projected equivalence relation on machine environments. If two machine environments E_1 and E_2 have equivalent ℓ-projections, denoted $E_1 \simeq_\ell E_2$, then ℓ-level information that is stored in these environments is indistinguishable. The precise definition of projected equivalence depends on the hardware and perhaps the language implementation. For example, for a two-level partitioned cache containing some entries at level L and some at level H, two caches have equivalent H-projections if they contain the same cache entries in the H portion, regardless of the L entries.

Using projected equivalence it is straightforward to define ℓ-equivalence on machine environments:

$$E_1 \sim_\ell E_2 \triangleq \forall \ell' \sqsubseteq \ell \,.\, E_1 \simeq_{\ell'} E_2$$

3.5 Faithfulness requirements for the full semantics

The faithfulness requirements for the full semantics comprise four properties: adequacy, deterministic execution, sequential composition, and accurate sleep duration.

Adequacy specifies that the core semantics and the full semantics describe the same executions: for any transition in the core semantics there is a matching transition in the full semantics and vice versa.

PROPERTY 1 (Adequacy of core semantics). $\forall m, c, c', E, G\,.$

$$(\exists E', G' \,.\, \langle c, m, E, G\rangle \rightarrow \langle c', m', E', G'\rangle) \Leftrightarrow \langle c, m\rangle \rightarrow \langle c', m'\rangle$$

We also require that the full semantics be deterministic, which means that the machine environment E completely captures the possible influences on timing.

PROPERTY 2 (Deterministic execution). $\forall m, c, E, G\,.$

$$\langle c, m, E, G\rangle \rightarrow \langle c_1, m_1, E_1, G_1\rangle \wedge \langle c, m, E, G\rangle \rightarrow \langle c_2, m_2, E_2, G_2\rangle \implies E_1 = E_2 \wedge G_1 = G_2$$

Since the core semantics is already deterministic, determinism of the machine environment and time components suffices.

Sequential composition must correctly accumulate time and propagate the machine environment.

PROPERTY 3 (Sequential composition).

1. $\forall c_1, c_2, m, E, G\,.$

$$\langle c_1, m, E, G\rangle \rightarrow \langle \texttt{stop}, m', E', G'\rangle \Leftrightarrow \langle c_1; c_2, m, E, G\rangle \rightarrow \langle c_2, m', E', G'\rangle$$

2. $\forall c_1, c_2, c_1', m, E, G$ *such that* $c_1' \neq \texttt{stop}\,.$

$$\langle c_1, m, E, G\rangle \rightarrow \langle c_1', m', E', G'\rangle \Leftrightarrow \langle c_1; c_2, m, E, G\rangle \rightarrow \langle c_1'; c_2, m', E', G'\rangle$$

Finally, the `sleep` command must take the correct amount of time because it is used for timing mitigation. When its argument is negative, it is assumed to take no time.

PROPERTY 4 (Accurate sleep duration). $\forall n, m, E, G, \ell_r, \ell_w\,.$

$$\langle (\texttt{sleep}\, n)_{[\ell_r, \ell_w]}, m, E, G\rangle \rightarrow \langle \texttt{stop}, m, E', G'\rangle \Rightarrow G' = G + \max(n, 0)$$

Discussion. The faithfulness requirements are mostly straightforward. The assumption of determinacy might sound unrealistic for concurrent execution. But if information leaks through timing because some other thread preempts this one, the problem is in the scheduler or in the other thread, not in the current thread. Deterministic time is realistic if we interpret G as the number of clock cycles the current thread has used.

3.6 Security requirements for the full semantics

For security, the full semantics also must satisfy certain properties to ensure that read and write labels accurately describe timing. These properties are specified as constraints on the full semantic configurations that must hold after each evaluation step. In the formalization of these properties, we quantify over labeled commands with the form $c_{[\ell_r, \ell_w]}$: that is, all commands except sequential composition.

Write labels. The write label ℓ_w is the lower bound on the parts of the machine environment that a single evaluation step modifies. Property 5 in Fig. 3 formalizes the requirements on the machine environment: executing a labeled command $c_{[\ell_r, \ell_w]}$ cannot modify parts of the environment at levels to which ℓ_w does not flow.

Example. Consider program $\texttt{sleep}(h)_{[\ell_r, H]}$ under the two-level security lattice $L \sqsubseteq H$. This command is annotated with the write label H. The only level ℓ such that $\ell_w \not\sqsubseteq \ell$ is $\ell = L$. In this case, Property 5 requires that an execution of $\texttt{sleep}(h)_{[\ell_r, H]}$ does not modify L parts of the machine environment.

Consider program $\texttt{sleep}(h)_{[\ell_r, L]}$ which has write label L. Because there is no security level ℓ such that $L \not\sqsubseteq \ell$, Property 5 does not constrain the machine environment for this command.

PROPERTY 5 (Write label). *Given a labeled command $c_{[\ell_r,\ell_w]}$, and a level ℓ such that $\ell_w \not\sqsubseteq \ell$*

$$\forall m, E, G\ .\ \langle c_{[\ell_r,\ell_w]}, m, E, G\rangle \to \langle c', m', E', G'\rangle \implies E \simeq_\ell E'$$

PROPERTY 6 (Read label). *Given any command $c_{[\ell_r,\ell_w]}$,*

$$\begin{aligned}\forall m_1, m_2, E_1, E_2, G\ .\ (\forall x \in vars_1(c_{[\ell_r,\ell_w]})\ .\ m_1(x) = m_2(x))\\ \wedge E_1 \sim_{\ell_r} E_2\\ \wedge \langle c_{[\ell_r,\ell_w]}, m_1, E_1, G\rangle \to \langle c_1, m_1', E_1', G_1\rangle\\ \wedge \langle c_{[\ell_r,\ell_w]}, m_2, E_2, G\rangle \to \langle c_2, m_2', E_2', G_2\rangle \implies G_1 = G_2\end{aligned}$$

PROPERTY 7 (Single-step machine-environment noninterference). *Given any labeled command $c_{[\ell_r,\ell_w]}$, and any level ℓ,*

$$\begin{aligned}\forall m_1, m_2, E_1, E_2, G_1, G_2\ .\ m_1 \sim_\ell m_2 \wedge E_1 \sim_\ell E_2\\ \wedge \langle c_{[\ell_r,\ell_w]}, m_1, E_1, G_1\rangle \to \langle c_1, m_1', E_1', G_1'\rangle\\ \wedge \langle c_{[\ell_r,\ell_w]}, m_2, E_2, G_2\rangle \to \langle c_2, m_2', E_2', G_2'\rangle \implies E_1' \sim_\ell E_2'\end{aligned}$$

Figure 3: Security requirements

Read labels. The read label ℓ_r of a command specifies which parts of the machine environment may affect the time necessary to perform the single next evaluation step. For a compound command such as `if`, `while`, or `mitigate`, this time does not include time spent in subcommands.

Property 6 in Fig. 3 formalizes the requirement that read labels accurately capture the influences of the machine environment. This formalization uses the $vars_1$ function, which identifies the part of memory that may affect the timing of the next evaluation step—that is, a set of variables. We need $vars_1$ because parts of the memory can also affect timing, such as e in `sleep` (e). A simple syntactic definition of $vars_1$ conservatively approximates the timing influences of memory, but a more precise definition might depend on particularities of the hardware implementation. For `skip`, this set is empty; for $x := e$ and `sleep` (e), the set consists of x and all variables in expression e; for `if` e `then` c_1 `else` c_2, `while` e `do` c, and `mitigate` (e, ℓ) c, it contains only variables in e and excludes those in subcommands, since only e is evaluated during the next step.

In the definition in Fig. 3, equality of G_1 and G_2 means that a single step takes exactly the same time. Both configurations take the same time, because m_1 and m_2 must agree on all variables x that are evaluated in this step. This expresses our assumption that values of variables other than those explicitly evaluated in a single step cannot influence its timing. Machine environments E_1 and E_2 are required to be ℓ_r-equivalent, to ensure that parts of the machine environment other than those at ℓ_r and below also cannot influence its timing.

Consider command `sleep` $(h)_{[L,\ell_w]}$ with read-label $\ell_r = L$, with respect to all possible pairs of memories m_1, m_2 and machine environments E_1, E_2. Whenever $m_1(h)$ and $m_2(h)$ have different values, Property 6 places no restrictions on the timing of this command regardless of E_1, E_2. When $m_1(h) = m_2(h)$, we require that if E_1 and E_2 are L-equivalent, the resulting time must be the same. To satisfy such a property, the H parts of the machine environment cannot affect the evaluation time.

Single-step noninterference. Property 5 specifies which parts of the machine environment can be modified. However, it does not say anything more about the nature of the modifications. For example, consider a three-level security lattice $L \sqsubseteq M \sqsubseteq H$, and a command $(x := y)_{[M,M]}$, where both the read label and write label are M. Property 5 requires that no modifications to L parts of the environment are allowed, but modifications to the M level are not restricted. This creates possibilities for insecure modifications of machine environments when H-parts of the machine environment propagate into the M-parts. To control such propagation, we introduce Property 7 in Fig. 3. Note that here level ℓ is independent of read or write labels.

4. A sketch of secure hardware

To illustrate how the requirements for the full language semantics enable secure hardware design, we sketch two possible ways for a design of cache and TLB to realize Properties 5–7. For simplicity, we assume the two-point label lattice $L \sqsubseteq H$ throughout this section.

We start with a standard single-partition data cache similar to current commodity cache designs and then explore a more sophisticated partitioned cache similar to that in [35].

4.1 Choosing machine environments

The machine environment does not need to include all hardware state. It should be precise enough to ensure that equivalent commands always take the same time in equal environments, and no more precise. Including state that has no effect on timing leads to overly conservative security enforcement that hurts performance.

For example, consider a data cache, usually structured as a set of cache lines. Each cache line contains a tag, a data block and a valid bit. Let us compare two possible ways to describe this as a machine environment: a more precise modeling of all three fields—a set of triples $\langle$tag, data block, valid bit$\rangle$—versus a coarser modeling of only the tags and valid bits—a set of pairs $\langle$tag, valid bit$\rangle$.

The coarse-grained abstraction of data cache state is adequate to predict execution time, since for most cache implementations, the contents of data blocks do not affect access time. The fine-grained abstraction does not work as well. For example, consider the command `h := h'` occurring in a low context. That is, variables `h` and `h'` are confidential, but the fact that the assignment is happening is not. With the fine-grained abstraction, the low part of the cache cannot record the value of `h` if Property 7 is to hold, because the low-equivalent memories m_1 and m_2 appearing in its definition may differ on the value of `h'`. With the coarse-grained abstraction, the location `h` can be stored in low cache, because Property 7 holds without making the value of `h'` part of the machine environment.

The coarse-grained abstraction shows that high variables can reside in low cache without hurting security in at least some circumstances. This is quite different from the treatment of memory, because public memory cannot hold confidential data. Without the formalization of Property 7, it would be difficult to reason about it. Yet this insight is important for performance: otherwise, code with a low timing label cannot access high variables using cache.

4.2 Realization on standard hardware

At least some standard CPUs can satisfy the security requirements (Properties 5–7). Intel's family of Pentium and Xeon processors has a "no-fill" mode in which accesses are served directly from memory on cache misses, with no evictions from nor filling of the data cache.

Our approach can be implemented by treating the whole cache as low, and therefore disallowing cache writes from high contexts. For each block of instructions with $\ell_w = H$, the compiler inserts a no-fill start instruction before, and a no-fill exit instruction after.

It is easy to verify that Properties 5–7 hold, as follows:

Property 5. For commands with $\ell_w = L$, this property is vacuously true since there is no ℓ such that $L \not\sqsubseteq \ell$. Commands with $\ell_w = H$ are executed in "no-fill" mode, so the result is trivial.

Property 6. Since there is only one (L) partition, $E_1 \sim_{\ell_r} E_2$ is equivalent to $E_1 = E_2$. The property can be verified for each command. For instance, consider command `sleep` $(e)_{[\ell_r,\ell_w]}$. The condition $\forall x \in vars_1(c_{[\ell_r,\ell_w]}).m_1(x) = m_2(x)$ ensures that $m_1(e) = m_2(e)$. Thus, this command is suspended for the same time. Moreover, since $E_1 = E_2$, cache access time must be the same according to Property 2. So, we have $G_1 = G_2$.

Property 7. We only need to check the L partition, which can be verified for each command. For instance, consider command `sleep` $(e)_{[\ell_r,\ell_w]}$. When $\ell_w = H$, the result is true simply because the cache is not modified. Otherwise, the same addresses (variables) are accessed. Since initial cache states are equivalent, identical accesses yields equivalent cache states.

4.3 A more efficient realization

A more efficient hardware design might partition both the cache(s) and the TLB according to security labels. Let us assume both the cache and TLB are equally, statically partitioned into two parts: L and H. The hardware accesses different parts as directed by a timing label that is provided from the software level. As discussed in Sec. 8, we have implemented a simulation of this design; here we focus on the correctness of hardware design.

One subtle issue is consistency, since data can be stored in both the L and the H partitions. We avoid inconsistency by keeping only one copy in the cache and TLB. In any CPU pipeline stage that accesses memory when the timing label is H, both H and L partitions are searched. If there is a cache miss, data is installed in the H partition. When the timing label is L, only the L partition is searched. However, to preserve consistency, instead of fetching the data from next level or memory, the controller moves the data from H partition if it already exists there. To satisfy Property 6, the hardware ensures this process takes the same time as a cache miss.

We can informally verify Properties 5–7 for this design as well:

Property 5. When the write label is L, this property holds trivially because there is no label such that $L \not\sqsubseteq \ell$. When the write label is H, a new entry is installed only in the H partition, so $E \sim_L E'$.

Property 6. The premise of Property 6 ensures that all variables evaluated in a single step have identical values, so any variation in execution time is due to the machine environment. When the read label is H, $E_1 \sim_H E_2$ ensures that the machine environments are identical; therefore, the access time is also identical. When the read label is L, the access time depends only on the existence of the entry in L cache/TLB. Even if the data is in the H partition, the load time is the same as if there were an L-partition miss.

Property 7. This requirement requires noninterference for a single step. Contents of the H partition can affect the L part in the next step only when data is stored in the H partition and the access has a timing label L. Since data is installed into the L part regardless of the state of the H partition, this property is still satisfied.

Discussion on formal proof and multilevel security. We have discussed efficient hardware for a two-level label system. Verification of multilevel security hardware is more challenging. One realization exists in Caisson [21], which enforces a version of noninterference that is both memory and timing-sensitive. Property 7 requires only timing-*insensitive* noninterference, so Caisson arguably tackles an unnecessarily difficult problem. A similar implementation that satisfies Property 7 more exactly might be more efficient.

5. A type system for controlling timing channels

Next, we present the security type system for our language. This section focuses on the non-quantitative guarantees that the type system provides, assuming Properties 1–7 hold. We show that the type system isolates the places where timing needs to be controlled externally. These places are where `mitigate` commands are needed.

5.1 Security type system

Typing rules for expressions have form $\Gamma \vdash e : \ell$ where Γ is the security environment (a map from variables to security labels), e is the expression, and ℓ is the type of the expression. The rules are standard [27] and we omit them here. Typing rules for commands, in Fig. 4, have the form $\Gamma, pc, \tau \vdash c : \tau'$. Here pc is the usual program-counter label [27], τ is the timing *start-label*, and τ' is the timing *end-label*. The timing start- and end-labels bound the level of information that flows into timing before and after executing c, respectively. We write $\Gamma \vdash c$ to denote $\Gamma, \bot, \bot \vdash c : \tau'$ for some τ'.

All rules enforce the constraint $\tau \sqsubseteq \tau'$ because timing dependencies accumulate as the program executes. Every rule except (T-MTG) also propagates the timing end-labels of subcommands. This can be seen most clearly in the rule for sequential composition (T-SEQ): the end-label from c_1 is the start-label for c_2.

All remaining rules require $pc \sqsubseteq \ell_w$. This restriction, together with Property 5, ensures that no confidential information about control flow leaks to the low parts of the machine environment. We do not require $\tau \sqsubseteq \ell_w$ because we assume the adversary cannot directly observe the timing of updates to the machine environment. This assumption is reasonable since the ISA gives no way to check whether a given location is in cache.

Rule (T-SKIP) takes the read label ℓ_r into account in its timing end-label. The intuition is that reading from confidential parts of the machine environment should be reflected in the timing end-label.

Rule (T-ASGN) for assignments $x := e$ requires $\ell \sqcup pc \sqcup \tau \sqcup \ell_r \sqsubseteq \Gamma(x)$, where ℓ is the level of the expression. The condition $\ell \sqcup pc \sqsubseteq \Gamma(x)$ is standard. We also require $\tau \sqcup \ell_r \sqsubseteq \Gamma(x)$, to prevent information from leaking via the timing of the update, from either the current time or the machine environment. The timing end-label is set to $\Gamma(x)$, bounding all sources of timing leaks.

Notice that the write label ℓ_w is independent of the label on x. The reason is that ℓ_w is the interface for software to tell hardware which state may be modified. A low write label on an assignment to a high variable permits the variable to be stored in low cache.

Because `sleep` has no memory side effects, rule (T-SLEEP) is slightly simpler than that for assignments; the timing end-label conservatively includes all sources of timing information leaks.

Rule (T-IF) restricts the environment in which branches c_1 and c_2 are type-checked. As is standard, the program-counter label is raised to $\ell \sqcup pc$. The timing start-labels are also restricted to reflect the effect of reading from the ℓ_r-parts of the machine environment and of the branching expression. Rule (T-WHILE) imposes similar conditions on end-label τ', except that τ' can also be used as both start- and end-labels for type-checking the loop body.

The most interesting rule is (T-MTG). The end-label τ' from command c is bounded by mitigation label ℓ', but τ' does not propagate to the end-label of the `mitigate`. Instead, the end-label of the `mitigate` command only accounts for the timing of evaluating expression e. This is because the predictive mitigation mechanism used at run time controls how c's timing leaks information.

We have seen that for security, the write label of a command must be higher than the label of the program counter. There is no corresponding restriction on the read label of a command. The hardware may be able to provide better performance if a higher read label is chosen. For instance, in most cache designs, reading from the cache changes its state. The cache can only be used when $\ell_r = \ell_w$, so this condition should be satisfied for best performance.

5.2 Machine-environment noninterference

An important property of the type system is that it guarantees machine environment noninterference. This requires execution to preserve low-equivalence of memory and machine environments.

THEOREM 1 (Memory and machine-environment noninterference).

$$\begin{aligned}
&\forall E_1, E_2, m_1, m_2, G, c, \ell \,.\, \Gamma \vdash c \wedge m_1 \sim_\ell m_2 \wedge E_1 \sim_\ell E_2 \\
&\quad \wedge \langle c, m_1, E_1, G\rangle \to^* \langle \texttt{stop}, m_1', E_1', G_1\rangle \\
&\quad \wedge \langle c, m_2, E_2, G\rangle \to^* \langle \texttt{stop}, m_2', E_2', G_2\rangle \\
&\qquad \Longrightarrow m_1' \sim_\ell m_2' \wedge E_1' \sim_\ell E_2'
\end{aligned}$$

$$\frac{pc \sqsubseteq \ell_w}{\Gamma, pc, \tau \vdash \texttt{skip}_{[\ell_r,\ell_w]} : \tau \sqcup \ell_r}\ \text{T-SKIP} \qquad \frac{\Gamma \vdash e : \ell \quad pc \sqsubseteq \ell_w \quad \ell \sqcup pc \sqcup \tau \sqcup \ell_r \sqsubseteq \Gamma(x)}{\Gamma, pc, \tau \vdash x := e_{[\ell_r,\ell_w]} : \Gamma(x)}\ \text{T-ASGN} \qquad \frac{\Gamma \vdash e : \ell \quad pc \sqsubseteq \ell_w}{\Gamma, pc, \tau \vdash (\texttt{sleep}\ (e))_{[\ell_r,\ell_w]} : \tau \sqcup \ell \sqcup \ell_r}\ \text{T-SLEEP}$$

$$\frac{\Gamma \vdash e : \ell \quad pc \sqsubseteq \ell_w \quad \Gamma, \ell \sqcup pc, \ell \sqcup \tau \sqcup \ell_r \vdash c_i : \tau_i \quad i = 1,2}{\Gamma, pc, \tau \vdash (\texttt{if}\ e\ \texttt{then}\ c_1\ \texttt{else}\ c_2)_{[\ell_r,\ell_w]} : \tau_1 \sqcup \tau_2}\ \text{T-IF} \qquad \frac{\Gamma \vdash e : \ell \quad pc \sqsubseteq \ell_w \quad \ell \sqcup \tau \sqcup \ell_r \sqsubseteq \tau' \quad \Gamma, \ell \sqcup pc, \tau' \vdash c : \tau'}{\Gamma, pc, \tau \vdash (\texttt{while}\ e\ \texttt{do}\ c)_{[\ell_r,\ell_w]} : \tau'}\ \text{T-WHILE}$$

$$\frac{\Gamma, pc, \tau \vdash c_1 : \tau_1 \quad \Gamma, pc, \tau_1 \vdash c_2 : \tau_2}{\Gamma, pc, \tau \vdash c_1 ; c_2 : \tau_2}\ \text{T-SEQ} \qquad \frac{\Gamma \vdash e : \ell \quad pc \sqsubseteq \ell_w \quad \Gamma, pc, \tau \sqcup \ell \sqcup \ell_r \vdash c : \tau' \quad \tau' \sqsubseteq \ell'}{\Gamma, pc, \tau \vdash (\texttt{mitigate}\ (e, \ell')\ c)_{[\ell_r,\ell_w]} : \ell \sqcup \tau \sqcup \ell_r}\ \text{T-MTG}$$

Figure 4: Typing rules: commands

Theorem 1 guarantees the adversary obtains no information by observing public parts of the memory and machine environments. Any confidential information the adversary obtains must be via timing. The proof is provided in the corresponding technical report [39].

Theorem 1 does *not* guarantee that information is not leaked through timing, that is, by observation of G. However, such a guarantee holds if the program contains no `mitigate` commands. This stronger guarantee is not proved here because it is a corollary of more general results presented in the next section.

A note on termination. The definition of memory and machine noninterference in Theorem 1 is presented in the batch-style termination-insensitive form [4]. Such definitions are simple but ordinarily limit one's results to programs that eventually terminate. Because termination channels are a special case of timing channels, using a batch-style definition is not fundamentally limiting here.

6. Quantitative properties of the type system

The type system identifies potential timing channels in the program. We now introduce a quantitative measure of leakage for multilevel systems, and show that the type system quantitatively bounds leakage through both timing and storage channels. The main result of this section is that information leakage can be bounded in the terms of the variation in the execution time of `mitigate` commands alone.

6.1 Adversary observations

As discussed earlier in Sec. 3.4, an adversary at level ℓ_A observes memory, including timing of updates to memory, at levels up to ℓ_A. The adversary does not directly observe the time of termination of the program, but this is easily simulated by adding a final low assignment to the program. To formally define adversary observations, we refine our presentation of the language semantics with *observable assignment events*.

Observable assignment events. Let $\alpha \in \{(x,v,t), \varepsilon\}$ range over observable events, which can be either an assignment to variable x of value v at time t, or an empty event ε. An event (x,v,G') is generated by assignment transitions $\langle x := e, m, E, G\rangle \to \langle \texttt{stop}, m', E', G'\rangle$, where $\langle m, e\rangle \Downarrow v$, and by all transitions whose derivation includes a subderivation of such a transition.

We write $\langle c,m,E,G\rangle \Rrightarrow (\mathbf{x},\mathbf{v},\mathbf{t})$ if configuration $\langle c,m,E,G\rangle$ produces a sequence of events $(\mathbf{x},\mathbf{v},\mathbf{t}) = (x_1,v_1,t_1)\ldots(x_n,v_n,t_n)$ and reaches a final configuration $\langle \texttt{stop}, m', E', G'\rangle$ for some m', E', G'.

ℓ_A-observable events. An event (x,v,t) is observable to the adversary at level ℓ_A when $\Gamma(x) \sqsubseteq \ell_A$. Given a configuration $\langle c,m,E,G\rangle$ such that $\langle c,m,E,G\rangle \Rrightarrow (\mathbf{x},\mathbf{v},\mathbf{t})$, we write $\langle c,m,E,G\rangle \Rrightarrow_{\ell_A} (\mathbf{x}',\mathbf{v}',\mathbf{t}')$ for the longest subsequence of $(\mathbf{x},\mathbf{v},\mathbf{t})$ such that for all events (x_i,v_i,t_i) in $(\mathbf{x}',\mathbf{v}',\mathbf{t}')$ it holds that $\Gamma(x_i) \sqsubseteq \ell_A$.

For example, for program $l_1 := l_2; h_1 := l_1$, the H-adversary observes two assignments: $\langle c,m,E,G\rangle \Rrightarrow_H (l_1,v_1,t_1),(h_1,v_2,t_2)$ for some v_1,t_1,v_2 and t_2. For the L-adversary, we have $\langle c,m,E,G\rangle \Rrightarrow_L (l_1,v_1,t_1)$, which does not include the assignment to h_1.

6.2 Measuring leakage in a multilevel environment

Using ℓ_A-observable events, we can define a novel information-theoretic measure of leakage: leakage from a set of security levels $\mathscr{L}$ to an adversary level ℓ_A. We start with an observation on our adversary model and the corresponding auxiliary definition.

Because an adversary observes all levels up to ℓ_A, we can exclude these security levels from the ones that give new information. Let $\mathscr{L}_{\ell_A}$ be the subset of $\mathscr{L}$ that excludes all levels observable to ℓ_A, that is $\mathscr{L}_{\ell_A} \triangleq \{\ell' \mid \ell' \in \mathscr{L} \wedge \ell' \not\sqsubseteq \ell_A\}$. For example, for a three-level lattice $L \sqsubseteq M \sqsubseteq H$, with $\ell_A = M$, if $\mathscr{L} = \{M,H\}$ then $\mathscr{L}_{\ell_A} = \{H\}$.

Fig. 5a illustrates a general form of this definition. The adversary level ℓ_A is represented by the white point; the levels observable to the adversary correspond to the small rectangular area under the point ℓ_A. The set of security levels $\mathscr{L}$ is represented by the dashed rectangle (though in general this set does not have to be contiguous). The gray area corresponds to the security levels that are in $\mathscr{L}_{\ell_A}$.

Leakage from $\mathscr{L}$ to ℓ_A. We measure the quantitative leakage as the logarithm (base 2) of the number of distinguishable observations of the adversary—the possible $(\mathbf{x},\mathbf{v},\mathbf{t})$ sequences—from indistinguishable memory and machine environments. As shown in [38], this measure bounds those of Shannon entropy and min-entropy, used in the literature [11, 22, 31].

DEFINITION 1 (Quantitative leakage from $\mathscr{L}$ to ℓ_A). *Given any ℓ_A, m, and E, the leakage of program c from levels $\mathscr{L}$ to level ℓ_A, denoted by $\mathsf{Q}(\mathscr{L},\ell_A,c,m,E)$ is defined as follows*

$$\mathsf{Q}(\mathscr{L},\ell_A,c,m,E) \triangleq \log(|\ \{(\mathbf{x},\mathbf{v},\mathbf{t}) \mid \exists m',E' \,.\, (\forall \ell' \,.\, \ell' \notin \mathscr{L}_{\ell_A} \,.\, m \simeq_{\ell'} m' \wedge E \simeq_{\ell'} E') \wedge \langle c,m',E',0\rangle \Rrightarrow_{\ell_A} (\mathbf{x},\mathbf{v},\mathbf{t})\}\ |)$$

This definition uses $\mathscr{L}_{\ell_A}$ to restrict the quantification of the memory and machine environments so that we allow variations only in $\mathscr{L}_{\ell_A}$ parts of memory and machine environments. This is expressed by requiring projected equivalence (on the second line of the definition) for all levels ℓ' not in $\mathscr{L}_{\ell_A}$. Visually, using Fig. 5a, this captures the flows from the gray area to the lower rectangle.

Note that the definition distinguishes flows between different levels. For example, in a three-level security lattice $L \sqsubseteq M \sqsubseteq H$ and a program `sleep` (h) where h has level H, the leakage from $\{M\}$ to L is zero even though flow from $\{H\}$ to L is not.

6.3 Guarantees of the type system

The type system provides an important property: leakage from $\mathscr{L}$ to ℓ_A is bounded by the timing variation of the `mitigate` commands whose mitigation level ℓ' is in the *upward closure* of $\mathscr{L}_{\ell_A}$.

Upward closure. In order to correctly approximate leakage from levels in $\mathscr{L}_{\ell_A}$, we need to account for all levels that are as restrictive as the ones in $\mathscr{L}_{\ell_A}$. For example, in a three-level lattice $L \sqsubseteq M \sqsubseteq H$, let $\mathscr{L}$ be the set $\{M\}$, and let $\ell_A = L$; then $\mathscr{L}_{\ell_A} = \{M\}$. Information from M can flow to H, so in order to account conservatively for leakage from $\{M\}$, we must also account for leakage from H. Our definitions therefore use the upward closure of $\mathscr{L}_{\ell_A}$, written as

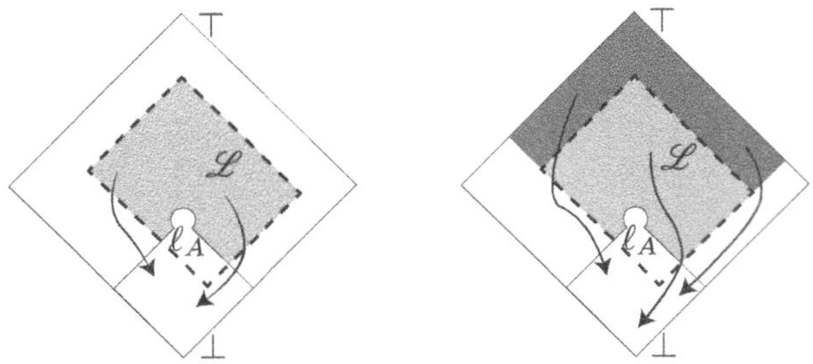

(a) Leakage from $\mathscr{L}$ to ℓ_A *(b)* Variations with $\mathscr{L}_{\ell_A}^{\sqsubseteq}$

Figure 5: Quantitative leakage

$\mathscr{L}_{\ell_A}\!\uparrow \triangleq \{\ell' \mid \exists \ell \in \mathscr{L}_{\ell_A} \wedge \ell \sqsubseteq \ell'\}$. In this example, $\mathscr{L}_{\ell_A}\!\uparrow = \{M, H\}$. Fig. 5b illustrates the relationship between $\mathscr{L}_{\ell_A}$ and its upper closure, where $\mathscr{L}_{\ell_A}\!\uparrow$ includes both shades of gray.

Trace and projection of mitigate commands. Next, we focus on the amount of time a `mitigate` command takes to execute. Recall from Sec. 3 that each `mitigate` in a program source has an η-identifier. For brevity, we refer to the command $\texttt{mitigate}_\eta$ as M_η. Consider trace $\langle c, m, E, G\rangle \to^* \langle \texttt{stop}, m', E', G'\rangle$. We overload the notation for $\Rrightarrow$, by writing $\langle c, m, E, G\rangle \Rrightarrow (\mathbf{M}, \mathbf{t})$, where $(\mathbf{M}, \mathbf{t})$ is a vector of `mitigate` commands executed in the above trace. The vector consists of the individual tuples $(\mathbf{M}, \mathbf{t}) = (M_{\eta_1}, t_1) \ldots (M_{\eta_n}, t_n)$ where (M_{η_i}, t_i) are ordered by the time of completion, and each (M_{η_i}, t_i) corresponds to a $\texttt{mitigate}_{\eta_i}$ taking time t_i to execute.

Further, define the *projection* of mitigate commands $(\mathbf{M}, \mathbf{t}) \upharpoonright^{\mathsf{f}}$ as the longest subsequence of $(\mathbf{M}, \mathbf{t})$ such that each (M_η, t) in the subsequence satisfies predicate f.

Low-determinism of `mitigate` commands. Consider the following well-typed program that uses `mitigate` twice.

```
mitigate₁(1,H) {
  if (high)
  then mitigate₂(1, H) { h:=h+1 }
  else skip; }
```

Let us write $pc(M_\eta)$ for the value of the pc-label at program point η. It is easy to see that $pc(M_1) = L$, and $pc(M_2) = H$. Because M_2 is nested within M_1, the timing of M_2 is accumulated in the timing of M_1. Therefore, when reasoning about the timing of the whole program, it is sufficient to only reason about the timing of M_1. In general, given a set of levels $\mathscr{L}$, an adversary level ℓ_A, and a vector $(\mathbf{M}, \mathbf{t})$, we filter high `mitigate` commands by the projection $(\mathbf{M}, \mathbf{t}) \upharpoonright^{pc(M_\eta) \notin \mathscr{L}_{\ell_A}\uparrow}$. This projection consists of all the `mitigate` commands whose pc-label is in the white area in Fig. 5b.

Filtering out high `mitigate` commands rules out unrelated variations in the `mitigate` commands. It turns out that in well-typed programs, the occurrence of the remaining low `mitigate` commands is deterministic (we call these commands *low-deterministic*). This result, formalized in the following lemma, is used in the derivation of leakage bounds in Sec. 7.

LEMMA 1. *(Low-determinism of* `mitigate` *commands). For all programs c such that $\Gamma \vdash c$, adversary levels ℓ_A, sets of security levels $\mathscr{L}$, and memories and environments E_1, E_2, m_1, m_2 such that $(\forall \ell' \notin \mathscr{L}_{\ell_A}\!\uparrow . \, E_1 \simeq_{\ell'} E_2 \wedge m_1 \simeq_{\ell'} m_2)$, we have*

$$\langle c, m_1, E_1, 0\rangle \Rrightarrow (\mathbf{M_1}, \mathbf{t_1}) \wedge \langle c, m_2, E_2, 0\rangle \Rrightarrow (\mathbf{M_2}, \mathbf{t_2})$$
$$\Longrightarrow \mathbf{M_1} \upharpoonright^{pc(M_\eta) \notin \mathscr{L}_{\ell_A}\uparrow} = \mathbf{M_2} \upharpoonright^{pc(M_\eta) \notin \mathscr{L}_{\ell_A}\uparrow}$$

Note that there are no constraints on time components $\mathbf{t_1}$ and $\mathbf{t_2}$. That is, the same `mitigate` commands may take different times to execute in different traces. The proof is contained in the corresponding technical report [39].

Mitigation levels. Per Sec. 3, the argument ℓ in $\texttt{mitigate}_\eta\ (e, \ell)\ c$ is an upper bound on the timing leakage of command c. Let $lev(M_\eta)$ be the label argument of $\texttt{mitigate}_\eta$ command. We call this the *mitigation level* of M_η. Note that $lev(M_\eta)$ is unrelated to $pc(M_\eta)$. For instance, in the example above, $pc(M_1) = L$, because M_1 appears in the L-context, but $lev(M_1) = H$.

Mitigation levels are connected to how much information an adversary at level ℓ_A may learn. For example, information at level ℓ can leak to adversary at level ℓ_A ($\ell \not\sqsubseteq \ell_A$) by a command M_η only when $\ell \sqsubseteq lev(M_\eta)$. In general, information from a set of levels $\mathscr{L}$ can be leaked by `mitigate` commands such that $lev(M_\eta) \in \mathscr{L}_{\ell_A}\!\uparrow$.

This leads to the definition of *timing variations*.

DEFINITION 2 (Timing variations of `mitigate` commands). *Given a set of security levels $\mathscr{L}$, an adversary level ℓ_A, program c, memory m, and a machine environment E, let V be the* timing variations *of* `mitigate` *commands:*

$$\mathsf{V}(\mathscr{L}, \ell_A, c, m, E) \triangleq \{\mathbf{t'} \mid \exists\, m', E' \,.$$
$$(\forall \ell' \notin \mathscr{L}_{\ell_A}\!\uparrow . \, m \simeq_{\ell'} m' \wedge E \simeq_{\ell'} E') \wedge \langle c, m', E', 0\rangle \Rrightarrow (\mathbf{M}, \mathbf{t})$$
$$\wedge\, (\mathbf{M'}, \mathbf{t'}) = (\mathbf{M}, \mathbf{t}) \upharpoonright^{pc(M_\eta) \notin \mathscr{L}_{\ell_A}\uparrow \wedge lev(M_\eta) \in \mathscr{L}_{\ell_A}\uparrow}\}$$

An interesting component of this definition is the predicate used to project $(\mathbf{M}, \mathbf{t})$. In essence, we only focus on the `mitigate` commands that appear in low contexts and have high mitigation levels, such as the first `mitigate` in the example earlier. Also notice that this set counts only the distinct timing components of the `mitigate` command projection, ignoring the $\mathbf{M'}$ component. This is sufficient because for well-typed programs the $\mathbf{M'}$ components of the vectors $(\mathbf{M'}, \mathbf{t'})$ are low-deterministic by Lemma 1.

In this definition, memory and machine environments are quantified differently from Definition 1, by considering variations with respect to a larger set of security levels $\mathscr{L}_{\ell_A}\!\uparrow$. In Fig. 5b, this corresponds to flows from both gray areas to the area observable by the adversary.

Leakage bounds guaranteed by the type system. The type system ensures that only the execution time of `mitigate` commands within certain projections may leak information.

THEOREM 2 (Bound on leakage via variations). *Given a command c, such that $\Gamma \vdash c$, and an adversary level ℓ_A, we have that for all m, E and $\mathscr{L}$ it holds that*

$$\mathsf{Q}(\mathscr{L}, \ell_A, c, m, E) \leq \log |\mathsf{V}(\mathscr{L}, \ell_A, c, m, E)|$$

The proof is included in the corresponding technical report [39]. An interesting corollary of the theorem is that leakage is zero whenever a program c contains no `mitigate` command, or more generally, when all `mitigate` commands take fixed time since there is only one timing variation of `mitigate` commands in this special case.

7. Predictive mitigation

Predictive mitigation [5, 38] removes confidential information from timing of public events by delaying them according to predefined schedules. We build upon this prior work [5, 38], but unlike the earlier work, our results improve precision for multilevel security, enabling better tradeoffs between security and performance.

Instead of delaying public assignments themselves, we delay the completions of `mitigate` commands that may potentially precede public events. This is sufficient for well-typed programs, because according to Theorem 2, only timing variations of `mitigate` commands carry sensitive information. The idea is that as long as the execution time of the `mitigate` command is no greater than predicted, little information is leaked. Upon a misprediction (when actual execution time is longer than predicted), a new schedule is chosen in such a way that future mispredictions are rarer.

$$\langle \texttt{update}(n,\ell),m,E,G\rangle \to \langle(\texttt{while}\ (\texttt{time} - s_\eta \geq \texttt{predict}(n,\ell))\ \texttt{do}\ (\texttt{Miss}[\ell] := \texttt{Miss}[\ell]+1;)_{[\bot,\bot]})_{[\bot,\bot]},m,E,G\rangle \quad \text{(S-UPDATE)}$$

$$\langle \texttt{mitigate}_\eta\ (n,\ell)\ c,m,E,G\rangle \to \langle s_\eta := \texttt{time}_{[\bot,\bot]};c;\texttt{update}(n,\ell);(\texttt{sleep}\ (\texttt{predict}(n,\ell) - \texttt{time} + s_\eta))_{[\bot,\bot]},m,E,G\rangle \quad \text{(S-MTGPRED)}$$

Figure 6: Predictive semantics for `mitigate`

Name	# of sets	issue	block size	latency
L1 Data Cache	128	4-way	32 byte	1 cycle
L2 Data Cache	1024	4-way	64 byte	6 cycles
L1 Inst. Cache	512	1-way	32 byte	1 cycle
L2 Inst. Cache	1024	4-way	64 byte	6 cycles
Data TLB	16	4-way	4KB	30 cycles
Instruction TLB	32	4-way	4KB	30 cycles

Table 1: Machine environment parameters

Mitigating semantics. Fig. 6 shows the fragment of small-step semantics that implements predictive mitigation. We record mispredictions in a special array `Miss`, assuming `Miss` is initialized to zeros and is otherwise unreferenced in programs. Expression `time` provides the current value of the global clock. Expression $\texttt{predict}(n,\ell) = \max(n,1)\cdot 2^{\texttt{Miss}[\ell]}$ returns the current prediction for level ℓ with initial estimate n. This prediction is the *fast doubling scheme* [5] with the *local penalty policy* [38] ; other schemes and penalty policies are possible [5, 38], but are not considered here.

In rule (S-MTGPRED), `mitigate` transitions to a code fragment that penalizes and delays the execution time of c. Variable s_η records the time when mitigation has started. If execution of `c` takes less time ($\texttt{time} - s_\eta$) than predicted, command `update` does nothing; the execution idles until the predicted time. If executing `c` takes longer than predicted, `update` increments `Miss[ℓ]` until the new prediction is greater than the time that c has consumed.

Leakage analysis of the mitigating semantics. Note that all auxiliary commands in Fig. 6 have labels $[\bot,\bot]$, ensuring no confidential information about machine environments is leaked when executing these commands. Moreover, the execution time of the whole mitigated block is at least $\texttt{predict}(n,\ell)$. Thus, the timing variation of a single `mitigate` command is controlled by the variation of possible values of $\texttt{predict}(n,\ell)$.

We can show that leakage is at most $|\mathscr{L}_{\ell_A}\!\uparrow|\cdot\log(K+1)\cdot(1+\log T)$. Here T is the elapsed time and K is the number of relevant `mitigate` statements in the trace: the ones satisfying $pc(M_\eta) \notin \mathscr{L}_{\ell_A}\!\uparrow \wedge lev(M_\eta) \in \mathscr{L}_{\ell_A}\!\uparrow$. When `mitigate` is not used, $K=0$, so no timing leakage occurs. When K is unknown, it can be conservatively bounded by T, yielding an $O(\log^2 T)$ leakage bound. Note that the bound is proportional to the size of the set $\mathscr{L}_{\ell_A}\!\uparrow$. A detailed analysis and derivation can be found in the technical report [39].

8. Implementation

We implemented a simulation of the partitioned cache design described in Sec. 4.3 so we could evaluate our approach on real C programs. As case studies, we chose two applications previously shown to be vulnerable to timing attacks. The results suggest the new mechanism is sound and has reasonable performance.

8.1 Hardware implementation

We developed a detailed, dynamically scheduled processor model supporting two-level data and instruction caches, data and instruction TLBs, and speculative execution. Table 1 summarizes the features of the machine environment. We implemented this processor design by modifying the SimpleScalar simulator, v.3.0e [9].

A new register is added as an interface to communicate the timing label from the software to the hardware. Simply encoding the timing labels into instructions does not work, since labels may be required before the instruction is fetched and decoded: for example, to guide instruction cache behavior. Labels are also propagated along the pipeline to restrict the behavior of hardware.

As discussed in Sec. 5.1, commodity cache designs require $\ell_r = \ell_w$. In our implementation, we treat this requirement as an extra side condition in the type system.

8.2 Compilation

We use the `gcc` compiler in the SimpleScalar tool set to run C applications on the simulator. Sensitive data in applications are labeled, and timing labels are then inferred as the least restrictive labels satisfying the typing rules from Fig. 4 (transferring the rules from Sec. 5 to C is straightforward). To inform the hardware of the current timing label, assembly code setting the timing-label register is inserted before and after command blocks.

Selecting the initial prediction. With the doubling policy, the slowdown of mitigation is at most twice the worst-case time. To improve performance, we can sample the running time of mitigated commands, setting the initial prediction to be a little higher than the average. In the experiments, we used 110% of average running time, measured with randomly generated secrets, as the initial prediction.

8.3 Web login case study

Web applications have been shown vulnerable to timing channel attacks. For example, Bortz and Boneh [7] have shown that adversaries can probe for valid usernames using a timing channel in the login process. This is unfortunate since usernames can be abused for spam, advertising, and phishing.

The pseudo-code for a simple web-application login procedure is on the right. The variable `response` and user inputs `user`, `pass` are public to users. Contents of the preloaded hashmap `m` (MD5 digests of valid usernames and corresponding passwords), password digest `hash` and the login status `state` are secrets. The final assignment to public variable `response` is always 1 on purpose in order to avoid the storage channel arising from the response. However, the timing of this assignment might create a timing channel.

```
1   Hashmap m:=loadusers()
2   while true
3     (user, pass):=input()
4     uhash:=MD5(user)
5     if uhash in m
6       hash:=m.get(uhash)
7       phash:=MD5(pass)
8       if phash=hash
9         state:=success
10    state:=fail
11    response:=1
```

The leakage is explicit when all confidential data (`m`, `hash` and `state`) are labeled `H`. The type system forces line 1 and line 5–10 to have high timing labels, so without a `mitigate` command, type checking fails at line 11. We secure this code by separately mitigating both line 1 and lines 5–10. The code then type-checks.

Correctness. In each of our experiments, we measured the time needed to perform a login attempt using 100 different usernames. Since valid usernames (the hashmap `m`) are secrets in this case study, we varied the number of these usernames that were valid among 10, 50, and 100. The resulting measurements are shown as three curves in the upper part of Fig. 7. The horizontal axis shows which login attempt was measured and the vertical axis is time.

The data for 10 and 50 valid usernames show that an adversary can easily distinguish invalid and valid usernames using login time. There is also measurable variation in timing even among different valid usernames. It is not clear what a clever adversary could learn from this, but since passwords are used in the computation, it seems likely that something about them is leaked too.

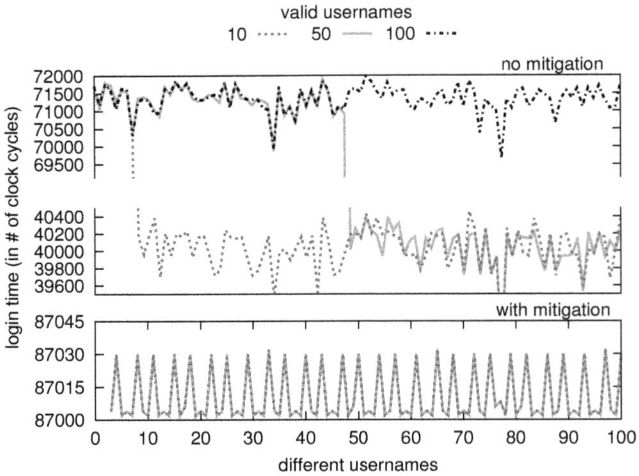

Figure 7: Login time with various secrets

	nopar	moff	mon
ave. time (valid)	70618	78610	86132
ave. time (invalid)	39593	43756	86147
overhead (valid)	1	1.11	1.22

Table 2: Login time with various usernames and options (in clock cycles)

The lower part of the figure shows the timing of the same experiments with timing channel mitigation in use. With mitigation enabled, execution time does not depend on secrets, and therefore all three curves coincide. This result validates the soundness of our approach. The roughly 30-cycle timing difference between different requests does not represent a security vulnerability because it is unaffected by secrets; it is influenced only by public information such as the position in the request sequence.

Performance. Table 2 shows the execution time of the main loop with various options, including both valid and invalid usernames, hardware with no partitions (nopar), and secure hardware both without (moff) and with (mon) mitigation.

As in Fig. 7, for unmitigated logins, valid and invalid usernames can be easily distinguished, but mitigation prevents this (we also verified that the tiny difference is unaffected by secrets). Table 2 shows that partitioned hardware is slower by about 11%. On valid usernames, language-based mitigation adds 10% slowdown; slowdown with combined software/hardware mitigation is about 22%.

8.4 RSA case study

The timing of efficient RSA implementations depends on the private key, creating a vulnerability to timing attacks [8, 18]. Using the RSA reference implementation, we demonstrate that its timing channels can be mitigated when decrypting a multi-block message.

```
1  text:=readText()
2  for each block b in text
3      ...preprocess...
4      compute (p:=b^key mod n)
5      ...postprocess...
6      write(output, plain)
```

In the pseudo-code on the left, only line 4 uses confidential data. Therefore, source code corresponding to this line is labeled as high. Both "preprocess" and "postprocess" include low assignments whose timing is observable to the adversary.

Correctness. We use 100 encrypted messages and two different private keys to measure whether secrets affect timing. The upper plot in Fig. 8 shows that different private keys have different decryption times, so decryption time does leak information about the private key. The lower plot shows that mitigated time is exactly 32,001,922 cycles regardless of the private key. Timing channel leakage is successfully mitigated.

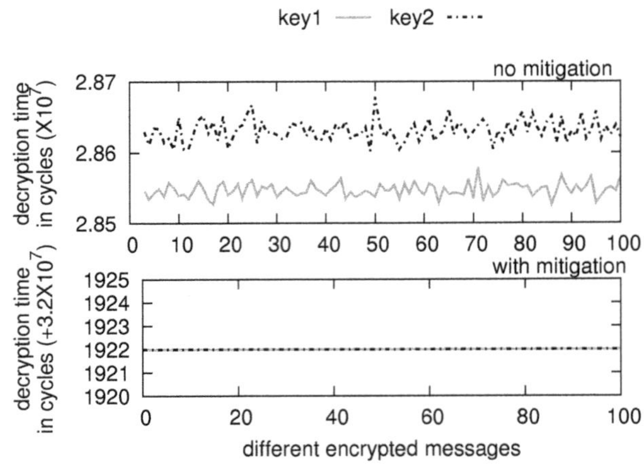

Figure 8: Decryption time with various secrets

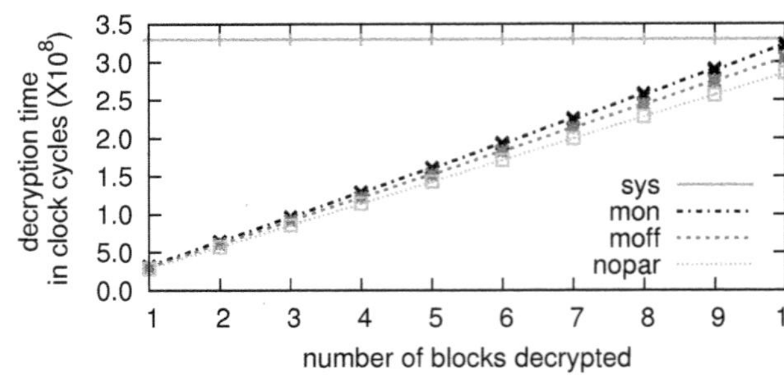

Figure 9: Language-level vs. system-level mitigation

Performance. To evaluate how mitigation affects decryption time, we use 10 encrypted secret messages whose size ranges from 1 to 10 blocks; the size is treated as public. We also compared the performance of language-level mitigation with system-level predictive mitigation [5], even though system-level mitigation is not effective against the strong, coresident attacker. To simulate system-level mitigation, the entire code body was wrapped in a single `mitigate` command. The results in Fig. 9 show that fine-grained language-based mitigation is faster because it does not try to mitigate the timing variation due to the number of decrypted blocks.

9. Related work

Control of internal timing channels has been studied from different perspectives, and several papers have explored a language-based approach. Low observational determinism [16, 37] can control these channels by eliminating dangerous races.

External timing channels are harder to control. Much prior language-based work on external timing channels uses simple, implicit models of timing, and no previous work fully addresses indirect dependencies. Type systems have been proposed to prevent timing channels [33], but are very restrictive. Often (e.g., [28, 30, 32, 33]) timing behavior of the program is assumed to be accurately described by the number of steps taken in an operational semantics. This assumption does not hold even at the machine-language level, unless we fully model the hardware implementation in the operational semantics and verify the entire software and hardware stack together. Our approach adds a layer of abstraction so software and hardware can be designed and verified independently.

Some previous work uses program transformation to remove indirect dependencies, though only those arising from data cache. The main idea is to equalize the execution time of different branches, but a price is paid in expressiveness, since these languages either rule out loops with confidential guards (as in [3, 6, 15]), or limit the number of loop iterations [10, 23]. These methods do not handle all indirect timing dependencies; for example, the instruction cache is not handled, so verified programs remain vulnerable to other indirect timing attacks [1, 2, 34].

Secure multi-execution [12, 17] provides timing-sensitive noninterference yet is probably less restrictive than the prior approaches discussed above. The security guarantee is weaker than in our approach: that the number of instructions executed, rather than the time, leaks no information for incomparable levels. Extra computational work is also required per security level, hurting performance, and no quantitative bound on leakage is obtained.

Though security cannot be enforced purely at the hardware level, hardware techniques have been proposed to mitigate timing channels. Targeting cache-based timing attacks, both static [25] and dynamic [35] mechanisms, based on the idea of partitioned cache, have been proposed. Such designs are ad hoc and hard to verify against other attacks. For example, Kong et al. [19] show vulnerabilities in Wang's cache design [35]. Recent work by Li et al. [21] introduces a statically verifiable hardware description language for building hardware that is information-flow secure by construction. This work could complement our own.

10. Conclusions

Timing channels have long been considered one of the toughest challenges in computer security. They have become more of a concern as different computing systems are more tightly intermeshed and code from different trust domains is executed on the same hardware (e.g., cloud computing servers and web browsers).

Solving the timing channel problem requires work at both the hardware level and the software level. Neither level has enough information to allow accurate reasoning about timing channels, because timing is a property that crosses abstraction boundaries.

The new abstraction of read and write labels makes a useful step toward allowing timing channels to be controlled effectively at the language level. The corresponding security properties help guide the design of hardware secure against timing attacks.

For programs where timing channels cannot be blocked entirely, predictive mitigation can be incorporated at the language level. The security guarantees of this language-level enforcement have been proved formally; the performance characteristics of the enforcement mechanism have been studied experimentally and appear promising.

Acknowledgments

We thank Owen Arden, Dan Ports, and Nate Foster for their helpful suggestions. This work has been supported by a grant from the Office of Naval Research (ONR N000140910652), by two grants from the NSF: 0424422 (the TRUST center), and 0964409, and by MURI grant FA9550-12-1-0400, administered by the US Air Force. This research is also sponsored by the Air Force Research Laboratory.

References

[1] O. Acıiçmez. Yet another microarchitectural attack: Exploiting I-cache. In *Proceedings of the ACM Workshop on Computer Security Architecture (CSAW '07)*, pages 11–18, 2007.

[2] O. Acıiçmez, C. Koç, and J. Seifert. On the power of simple branch prediction analysis. In *ASIACCS*, pages 312–320, 2007.

[3] J. Agat. Transforming out timing leaks. In *Proc. 27th ACM Symp. on Principles of Programming Languages (POPL)*, pages 40–53, Boston, MA, January 2000.

[4] A. Askarov, S. Hunt, A. Sabelfeld, and D. Sands. Termination-insensitive noninterference leaks more than just a bit. In *ESORICS*, pages 333–348, October 2008.

[5] A. Askarov, D. Zhang, and A. C. Myers. Predictive black-box mitigation of timing channels. In *ACM Conf. on Computer and Communications Security (CCS)*, pages 297–307, October 2010.

[6] G. Barthe, T. Rezk, and M. Warnier. Preventing timing leaks through transactional branching instructions. *Electronic Notes in Theoretical Computer Science*, 153(2):33–55, 2006.

[7] A. Bortz and D. Boneh. Exposing private information by timing web applications. In *Proc. 16th Int'l World-Wide Web Conf.*, May 2007.

[8] D. Brumley and D. Boneh. Remote timing attacks are practical. *Computer Networks*, January 2005.

[9] D. C. Burger and T. M. Austin. The SimpleScalar tool set, version 3.0. Technical Report CS-TR-97-1342, University of Wisconsin, Madison, June 1997.

[10] B. Coppens, I. Verbauwhede, K. D. Bosschere, and B. D. Sutter. Practical mitigations for timing-based side-channel attacks on modern x86 processors. *IEEE Symposium on Security and Privacy*, pages 45–60, 2009.

[11] D. E. Denning. *Cryptography and Data Security*. Addison-Wesley, Reading, Massachusetts, 1982.

[12] D. Devriese and F. Piessens. Noninterference through secure multi-execution. In *IEEE Symposium on Security and Privacy*, pages 109–124, May 2010.

[13] J. Giffin, R. Greenstadt, P. Litwack, and R. Tibbetts. Covert messaging through TCP timestamps. *Privacy Enhancing Technologies, Lecture Notes in Computer Science*, 2482(2003):189–193, 2003.

[14] D. Gullasch, E. Bangerter, and S. Krenn. Cache games—bringing access-based cache attacks on AES to practice. In *IEEE Symposium on Security and Privacy*, pages 490–505, 2011.

[15] D. Hedin and D. Sands. Timing aware information flow security for a JavaCard-like bytecode. *Electronic Notes in Theoretical Computer Science*, 141(1):163–182, 2005.

[16] M. Huisman, P. Worah, and K. Sunesen. A temporal logic characterisation of observational determinism. In *Proc. 19th IEEE Computer Security Foundations Workshop*, 2006.

[17] V. Kashyap, B. Wiedermann, and B. Hardekopf. Timing- and termination-sensitive secure information flow: Exploring a new approach. In *IEEE Symposium on Security and Privacy*, pages 413–430, May 2011.

[18] P. Kocher. Timing attacks on implementations of Diffie–Hellman, RSA, DSS, and other systems. In *Advances in Cryptology—CRYPTO'96*, August 1996.

[19] J. Kong, O. Acıiçmez, J.-P. Seifert, and H. Zhou. Deconstructing new cache designs for thwarting software cache-based side channel attacks. In *Proceedings of the 2nd ACM Workshop on Computer Security Architectures*, pages 25–34, 2008.

[20] B. Köpf and M. Dürmuth. A provably secure and efficient countermeasure against timing attacks. In *2009 IEEE Computer Security Foundations*, July 2009.

[21] X. Li, M. Tiwari, J. Oberg, V. Kashyap, F. Chong, T. Sherwood, and B. Hardekopf. Caisson: a hardware description language for secure information flow. In *ACM SIGPLAN Conference on Programming Language Design and Implementation*, pages 109–120, 2011.

[22] J. K. Millen. Covert channel capacity. In *Proc. IEEE Symposium on Security and Privacy*, Oakland, CA, April 1987.

[23] D. Molnar, M. Piotrowski, D. Schultz, and D. Wagner. The program counter security model: automatic detection and removal of control-flow side channel attacks. *Cryptology ePrint archive: report 2005/368*, 2005.

[24] D. Osvik, A. Shamir, and E. Tromer. Cache attacks and countermeasures: the case of AES. *Topics in Cryptology–CT-RSA 2006*, January 2006.

[25] D. Page. Partitioned cache architecture as a side-channel defense mechanism. In *Cryptology ePrint Archive, Report 2005/280*, 2005.

[26] A. Russo and A. Sabelfeld. Securing interaction between threads and the scheduler. In *Proc. 19th IEEE Computer Security Foundations Workshop*, 2006.

[27] A. Sabelfeld and A. C. Myers. Language-based information-flow security. *IEEE Journal on Selected Areas in Communications*, 21(1):5–19, January 2003.

[28] A. Sabelfeld and D. Sands. Probabilistic noninterference for multi-threaded programs. In *Proc. 13th IEEE Computer Security Foundations Workshop*, pages 200–214. IEEE Computer Society Press, July 2000.

[29] S. Sellke, C. Wang, and S. Bagchi. TCP/IP timing channels: Theory to implementation. In *Proc. INFOCOM 2009*, pages 2204–2212, January 2009.

[30] G. Smith. A new type system for secure information flow. In *Proc. 14th IEEE Computer Security Foundations Workshop*, pages 115–125, June 2001.

[31] G. Smith. On the foundations of quantitative information flow. *Foundations of Software Science and Computational Structures*, 5504:288–302, 2009.

[32] G. Smith and D. Volpano. Secure information flow in a multi-threaded imperative language. In *Proc. 25th ACM Symp. on Principles of Programming Languages (POPL)*, pages 355–364, January 1998.

[33] D. Volpano and G. Smith. Eliminating covert flows with minimum typings. In *Proc. 10th IEEE Computer Security Foundations Workshop*, pages 156–168, 1997.

[34] Z. Wang and R. Lee. Covert and side channels due to processor architecture. In *ACSAC '06*, pages 473–482, 2006.

[35] Z. Wang and R. Lee. New cache designs for thwarting software cache-based side channel attacks. In *Proceedings of the 34th annual international symposium on computer architecture (ISCA '07)*, pages 494–505, 2007.

[36] J. C. Wray. An analysis of covert timing channels. In *Proc. IEEE Symposium on Security and Privacy*, pages 2–7, 1991.

[37] S. Zdancewic and A. C. Myers. Observational determinism for concurrent program security. In *Proc. 16th IEEE Computer Security Foundations Workshop*, pages 29–43, June 2003.

[38] D. Zhang, A. Askarov, and A. C. Myers. Predictive mitigation of timing channels in interactive systems. In *ACM Conf. on Computer and Communications Security (CCS)*, pages 563–574, October 2011.

[39] D. Zhang, A. Askarov, and A. C. Myers. Language mechanisms for controlling and mitigating timing channels. Technical report, Cornell University, March 2012. `http://hdl.handle.net/1813/28635`.

Diderot: A Parallel DSL for Image Analysis and Visualization

Charisee Chiw Gordon Kindlmann John Reppy Lamont Samuels Nick Seltzer
University of Chicago
{cchiw,glk,jhr,lamonts,nseltzer}@cs.uchicago.edu

Abstract

Research scientists and medical professionals use imaging technology, such as *computed tomography* (CT) and *magnetic resonance imaging* (MRI) to measure a wide variety of biological and physical objects. The increasing sophistication of imaging technology creates demand for equally sophisticated computational techniques to analyze and visualize the image data. Analysis and visualization codes are often crafted for a specific experiment or set of images, thus imaging scientists need support for quickly developing codes that are reliable, robust, and efficient.

In this paper, we present the design and implementation of Diderot, which is a parallel domain-specific language for biomedical image analysis and visualization. Diderot supports a high-level model of computation that is based on continuous tensor fields. These tensor fields are reconstructed from discrete image data using separable convolution kernels, but may also be defined by applying higher-order operations, such as differentiation (∇). Early experiments demonstrate that Diderot provides both a high-level concise notation for image analysis and visualization algorithms, as well as high sequential and parallel performance.

Categories and Subject Descriptors D.3.2 [*Programming Languages*]: Language classifications — Very high-level languages; D.3.2 [*Programming Languages*]: Language Classifications—Concurrent, distributed, and parallel languages; D.3.4 [*Programming Languages*]: Processors—Compilers

Keywords Domain Specific Languages, Image Analysis, Scientific Visualization, Parallelism

1. Introduction

Biomedical researchers use multi-dimensional imaging to study structure and function of biological systems with a variety of imaging modalities, including *confocal microscopy*, *computed tomography* (CT), and *magnetic resonance imaging* (MRI). Recent advances in imaging hardware have increased their speed, resolution, and flexibility. For example, synchrotron radiation microCT produces scalar-valued volume images with 2048^3 samples (as compared to 512^3 for clinical CT), and routine MRI scans include images of vectors (for blood flow in heart) and tensors (for diffusion anisostropy in brain tissue). Besides increasing the biomedical value of imaging, the quantities and types of data from modern imaging hardware also strain the capabilities of established tools for image processing. Scientists working with the new imaging techniques and applications are the best positioned to create and evaluate methods of image data processing, but they do not have the programming background to create the efficient parallel implementations required to handle the quantity of data involved.

In this paper, we present a domain-specific language (DSL), called Diderot, that simplifies the portable implementation of parallel methods of biomedical image analysis and visualization. *Image analysis* extracts quantitative or geometric descriptions of the image structure in order to characterize specific properties of the underlying organ or tissue. An example is extracting ridge lines and valley lines to find blood vessels and airways, respectively, from a CT lung scan. *Visualization* combines measurements of local image data properties with elements of computer graphics in order to qualitatively depict structures via rendered images. An example is using direct volume rendering to illustrate the over-all shape and inter-relationship of tissue boundaries.

Diderot supports a high-level model of computation that is based on continuous tensor fields. Throughout, we use *tensors* to refer collectively to scalars, vectors, and matrices, which encompasses the types of values produced by the imaging modalities mentioned above, as well as values produced by taking spatial derivatives of images. Diderot permits programmers to express algorithms directly in terms of tensors, tensor fields, and tensor field operations, using the same mathematical notation that would be used in vector and tensor calculus (such as ∇ for the gradient). We intend for Diderot to be useful for prototyping image analysis and visualization methods in contexts where a meaningful evaluation of the methods requires its application to real image data, but the real data volumes are of a size that requires efficient parallel computation. With its support for high-level mathematical notation, Diderot will also be useful in educational contexts where the conceptual transparency of the implementation is of primary importance.

This paper makes several contributions. First, we introduce a novel DSL that directly supports higher-order operations on continuous tensor fields. Diderot's type system tracks properties, such as continuity, which helps ensure sensible numerical results. We also describe how principles of tensor calculus may be applied to address the challenges of compiling a very-high-level language like Diderot. Lastly, we demonstrate the benefits of Diderot relative to hand-coded algorithms for parallel computing performance.

The paper is organized as follows. In the next section, we review the mathematical foundations of image processing on which Diderot is based. We then present Diderot's design in Section 3 and illustrate its features with several examples in Section 4. We then describe important aspects of our implementation, including the implementation of tensor fields. Section 6 presents performance results, followed by a discussion of related work. We describe future plans for the system in Section 8 and then summarize our results in Section 9.

PLDI'12, June 11–16, Beijing, China

2. Background

A review of background mathematics will simplify later description of the mathematical elements supported by Diderot, and will provide the context for our description of the domain of computation for which Diderot is specialized.

We adopt tensors as a concrete type in Diderot to provide a general way of representing the values stored in images and produced by operations on images. 0-order tensors, or scalars, capture real-valued samples from scans typically shown in grayscale (*e.g.*, CT). 1-order tensors, or vectors, describe directional quantities such as velocity and spatial derivatives of scalar fields. 2-order tensors, represented as matrices, describe linear transforms on vectors, first derivatives of vector fields, and second derivatives of scalar fields.

Measured image data is discretely sampled on a regular grid (regardless of the modality or image type), but the underlying objects being scanned exist in a continuous space, which we call *world space*. Signal processing provides the machinery for reconstructing (or *probing*) continuous signals from discrete data via convolution at arbitrary positions [20]. Convolving one-dimensional discrete data $V[i]$ with a continuous reconstruction kernel $h(x)$ produces a continuous signal $(V \circledast h)(x)$. *Separable* convolution uses a single one-dimensional kernel $h(x)$ to create a multi-dimensional kernel, for example in three dimensions $H(x, y, z) = h(x)h(y)h(z)$. Convolution also provides the means of measuring derivatives in fields. The partial derivatives of $F = V \circledast H$ are found by convolution with separable product of kernels and their derivatives, *e.g.*, $\frac{\partial F}{\partial y}$ is found by convolution with $\frac{\partial H}{\partial y} = h(x)h'(y)h(z)$. Kernels can be chosen according to the needed level of differentiability, while balancing the quality of reconstruction with the computational cost of having larger support (*i.e.* needing a larger neighborhood of image values to compute the convolution sum).

Diderot is specialized for highly parallel analysis and visualization of continuously differentiable tensor fields arising from multidimensional imaging. The continuity of fields is important because relevant features in the image data tend to lie in between pixels and at arbitrary orientations. Simplifying how programmers can express computations within world space helps prevent the results from needlessly reflecting the discrete image grid. The differentiability of fields is required because many structures of interest are defined in terms of spatial derivatives. Extracting the network of blood vessels from a CT scan is a good example of the need for continuity and differentiability. Accurate results depend on tracing the centers of vessel pathways in between pixel locations, where gradients and Hessians (first and second derivatives) are computed to locate the *ridge line* image features that coincide with the vessels [2, 11]. Tensors may also originate in the image data, as with second-order diffusion tensors measured via MRI, for which a common task is tracing paths along the tensor principal eigenvector to model brain connectivity [4]. Diderot simplifies the rapid exploration and implementation of these types of algorithms by naturally supporting the mathematical ingredients with which they are expressed: vectors, tensors, eigensystems, kernels, fields, and derivatives.

We have chosen to develop a new domain-specific language because of weaknesses with existing languages, libraries, and tools. Established high-level array-processing languages commonly used for image processing, including Matlab [18], IDL [15] and Python/Numpy [25], facilitate operations on entire image arrays or their sub-arrays. The computational cost is distributed uniformly over the image, and parallelization according to memory layout is straightforward. An early example of this approach is the *image algebra* formulation of gray-scale image-to-image computation developed by Ritter and Gader [24]. For our intended applications, however, it is not convenient to express the computation in terms of discrete sets of image data values. The transparent implementation of the blood vessel extraction and fiber tractography mentioned above, for example, hinges on a notion of continuous fields, a fundamental abstraction available in Diderot. Also, the parallelism we intend to capture is not structured according to the underlying image data array, but by the output of the visualization or analysis, *i.e.*, rendered pixels in volume rendering, tractography pathways curving through space, and points along ridge feature lines. Third, array-processing languages are often optimized for uniform access rather than irregular or sparse access patterns, so techniques that work adequately for two-dimensional images do not scale well to memory-intensive three-dimensional images, especially when the algorithmic output (as with blood vessel extraction) occupies only a small fraction of the volume data.

Another strategy for creating image analysis and visualization tools is to use a specialized library that already encapsulates many of the useful operations and constructs. A good example is the Insight Toolkit (ITK) [14], a large C++ image processing framework. The drawbacks here, relative to a domain-specific language, relate to program conciseness and simplicity. ITK relies heavily on C++ templates to achieve generality with respect to image type and dimension, so the code can be challenging to understand and debug. In ITK, as with array-processing languages, it is easiest to parallelize algorithms that compute over whole image arrays, since this is the structure of the image registration and segmentation routines for which ITK was originally designed.

3. Language design

The class of applications that Diderot targets are characterized as consisting of many largely independent subcomputations. For example, the rays in a volume renderer, the paths from fiber tractography, and the particles in a particle system. In Diderot, these mostly independent computations are modeled as *strands*, which execute in a *bulk synchronous* fashion [26, 31]. Diderot uses a C-like syntax for its computational notation, but this notation is extended with mathematical types and operators.

3.1 Types and values

Diderot is a monomorphic, statically-typed, language with a fairly small collection of types. The basic concrete values include strings, booleans, integers, and tensors. We have five types of concrete values: booleans, integers, strings, tensors, and fixed-size sequences of values. The type **`tensor`**`[`σ`]` is a tensor with *shape* $\sigma \in \{i \mid 1 < i\}^*$. The number of dimensions in σ (*i.e.*, the length of σ) is the *order* of the tensor. For example, **`tensor`**`[]` is a 0-order tensor and is the type of scalars, while **`tensor`**`[3]` is a 1-order tensor that is the type of 3D vectors. We define type synonyms for common tensor types, including **`real`** and **`vec3`**.

In addition to concrete values, Diderot defines three forms of abstract type: images, kernels, and fields. Images are multidimensional arrays of tensor data. The type **`image`**`(`d`) [`σ`]` is the abstract type of image data, where $d \in \{1, 2, 3\}$ specifies the dimension of the data and σ specifies the shape of the tensor values at each image sample. We do not program directly with image data. Instead we use convolution kernels to define a continuous reconstruction of the discrete data. The type **`kernel#`**k is the type of a C^k kernel (*i.e.*, it has k continuous derivatives). Diderot provides a number of useful built-in kernels, including the C^0 `tent` for linear interpolation (so named because of its shape), the C^1 interpolating Catmull-Rom cubic spline `ctmr`, and the C^2 (non-interpolating) uniform cubic B-spline basis function `bspln3` [3]. Finally, continuous tensor fields have type **`field#`**k`(`d`) [`σ`]`, where k is the number of continuous derivatives, d is the dimension of the field's domain, and σ is the shape of its range. A field is a function from d-dimensional space to tensors with the shape σ.

```
1  input real stepSz = 0.1; // size of steps
2  input vec3 eye;          // eye location
3  input vec3 orig;         // pixel (0,0) location
4  input vec3 cVec;         // vector between columns
5  input vec3 rVec;         // vector between rows
6  input real opacMin;      // value with opacity 0.0
7  input real opacMax;      // value with opacity 1.0
8  image(3)[] img = load ("hand.nrrd");
9  field#2(3)[] F = img ⊛ bspln3;
10
11 strand RayCast (int r, int c) {
12   vec3 pos = orig + real(r)*rVec + real(c)*cVec;
13   vec3 dir = normalize(pos - eye);
14   real t = 0.0;
15   real transp = 1.0;
16   output real gray = 0.0;
17
18   update {
19     pos = pos + stepSz*dir;
20     t = t + stepSz;
21     if (inside (pos, F)) {
22       real val = F(pos);
23       if (val > opacMin) {
24         real opac = 1.0 if (val > opacMax)
25                 else (val - opacMin)/(opacMax - opacMin);
26         vec3 norm = -normalize(∇F(pos));
27         gray += transp*opac*max(0.0, -dir • norm);
28         transp *= 1.0 - opac;
29       }
30     }
31     if (t > 40.0) stabilize;
32   }
33 }
34
35 initially [
36   RayCast(ui, vi) | vi in 0 .. imgResV-1,
37                     ui in 0 .. imgResU-1
38 ];
```

Figure 1. Simple direct volume rendering code

3.2 Tensor and field expressions

A key feature of Diderot is that it supports mathematical notation for computing with tensors and fields. Diderot syntax uses Unicode characters to represent mathematical constants (π) and a rich set of operations on tensors. In addition to standard arithmetic operations, these include dot product (`u•v`), cross product (`u×v`), tensor product (`u⊗v`), and vector norm (`|u|`).

Computing with continuous tensor fields is one of the unique characteristics of Diderot. Field values are constructed by convolving image data with kernels (`img⊛bspln3`), but they can also be defined by using higher-order operations, such as addition, subtraction, and scaling of fields. Most importantly, Diderot supports differentiation of fields using the operators ∇ (for scalar fields) and $\nabla\otimes$ (for higher-order tensor fields). Two operations on fields are testing whether a point `x` lies within the domain of a field `F` (`inside(x, F)`) and *probing* a field `F` at a point `x` (`F(x)`). As we show in the examples below, probing and differentiating are fundamental to extracting geometric information from fields.

3.3 Program structure

A Diderot program is organized into three sections: global definitions, which include program inputs; strand definitions, which define the computational core of the algorithm; and initialization, which defines the initial set of strands. To illustrate this structure and the features of Diderot, we use the simple direct volume renderer shown in Figure 1 as a running example. This computation requires probing both the scalar field to determine its opacity and the its gradient to determine the surface normal.

3.3.1 Global definitions

Lines 1–9 of Figure 1 define the global variables of our example. Global variables in Diderot are immutable. The first six of these are marked as **`input`** variables, which means that they can be set outside the program (they may also have a default value, as in the case of `stepSz`). The Diderot compiler synthesizes glue code that allows command-line setting of input variables. Line 8 loads image file `"hand.nrrd"` and binds variable `img` to it. The type of `img` is a 3D scalar image, which is checked when the image is loaded. The `load` function may only be used in global part of the program. Note that we do not specify the representation of the image values on disk; *i.e.*, they could be signed ints, floats, *etc.* The compiler generates code that maps image values to reals. Line 9 defines a scalar field `F`, reconstructed by convolution with the `bspln3` kernel, providing the C^2 continuity reflected in the type of `F`.

3.3.2 Strands

Much like a kernel function in CUDA [22] or OpenCL [16], a strand in Diderot encapsulates the computational core of the application. Each strand has parameters (*e.g.*, `r` and `c` on line 11), a *state* (lines 12–13) and an **`update`** method (lines 18–33). The strand state variables are initialized when the strand is created; some variables may be annotated as **`output`** variables, which define the part of the strand state that is reported in the program's output. Unlike globals, strand state variables are mutable, but we avoid features, such as pointers, that would make analysis difficult. In addition, strand methods may define local variables (the scoping rules are essentially the same as C's).

The **`update`** method of the `RayCast` strand starts by advancing the strand's position along a ray (lines 20 and 21). It then tests to see if the position lies within the field `F` domain (line 22). If the strand's position is inside the domain, we *probe* the field `F` and compare the field's value to our lower opacity threshold. By changing the opacity range, we can pick out different features of the image (*e.g.*, skin or bone). In lines 27–29, we find the contribution of the current position to the image using the gradient field to compute diffuse lighting. Note that we use Python's syntax for conditional expressions (lines 25 and 26). In line 32, we check to see if the ray has gone beyond a distance limit, in which case we *stabilize* the strand, which means that it ceases to be updated. As we will see in later examples, a strand may also have a **`stabilize`** method that is invoked when the strand stabilizes.

3.3.3 Initialization

The last part of a Diderot program is the initialization section, which specifies the initial set of strands in the computation.[1] Diderot uses a comprehension syntax, similar those of Haskell or Python, to define the initial set of strands. For example, the volume renderer specifies a grid of initial ray positions in lines 35–38. When the strands are initialized as a grid, it implies that the strands will all stabilize (*i.e.*, they do not die). The grid structure is then preserved in the output. For example, the grid of initial strands created above will produce a grid of pixel values, one per ray.

Diderot also allows one to specify an initial *collection* of strands by using "{ }" as the brackets around the comprehension (instead of "[ ]"). In this case, the program's output will be a one-dimension array of values; one for each stable strand.

3.4 Diderot's type system

Diderot has a monomorphic type system that captures the important mathematical properties of the program, such as the continuity of

[1] In the current version of the language, described in this paper, strands are only created at startup. Eventually, we plan to support dynamic strand creation (see Section 8).

$$\frac{\Gamma \vdash V : \mathtt{image}(d)[\sigma] \qquad \Gamma \vdash h : \mathtt{kernel\#}k}{\Gamma \vdash V \circledast h : \mathtt{field\#}k(d)[\sigma]}$$

$$\frac{\Gamma \vdash F : \mathtt{field\#}k(d)[\,] \qquad k > 0 \qquad k' = k - 1}{\Gamma \vdash \nabla F : \mathtt{field\#}k'(d)[d]}$$

$$\frac{\Gamma \vdash F : \mathtt{field\#}k(d)[\sigma,\, d'] \qquad k > 0 \qquad k' = k - 1}{\Gamma \vdash \nabla\!\otimes F : \mathtt{field\#}k'(d)[\sigma,\, d',\, d]}$$

$$\frac{\Gamma \vdash F : \mathtt{field\#}k(d)[\sigma] \qquad \Gamma \vdash p : \mathtt{tensor}[d]}{\Gamma \vdash F(p) : \mathtt{tensor}[\sigma]}$$

Figure 2. Key typing judgments for Diderot

fields. Figure 2 presents the most important rules in the type system. The first rule shows how the properties of the image data and convolution kernel determine the type of resulting field. The next two rules capture the fact that differentiation reduces the continuity of the field, but increases its order. Lastly, the typing rule for probe is similar to function application (as one would expect).

4. Examples

Diderot's language design and computational model support a range of visualization and analysis methods. In this section, we illustrate the language's expressiveness with several examples of computations typical of visualization and analysis algorithms.

4.1 Implicit Surface Curvature

One physical property of interest is the *curvature* of implicit surfaces within the image. Just as the gradient of a field is used to find the implicit surface normal, the second derivative of the field, the Hessian, determines curvature (*i.e.*, the change in normal due to motion along the surface). The principal curvatures κ_1 and κ_2 can be computed from the tensor $\mathbf{G}$ defined by [17]

$$\begin{aligned} \mathbf{G} &= \frac{-\mathbf{PHP}}{|\nabla F|} \\ \text{where} & \\ \mathbf{P} &= \mathbf{I} - \mathbf{n} \otimes \mathbf{n}^T \\ \mathbf{n} &= \frac{\nabla F}{|\nabla F|} \\ \mathbf{H} &= \nabla \otimes \nabla F \end{aligned}$$

The eigenvalues of $\mathbf{G}$ are 0, κ_1, and κ_2, so the principal curvatures appear in the tensor invariants of $\mathbf{G}$

$$\begin{aligned} \mathrm{trace}(\mathbf{G}) &= \kappa_1 + \kappa_2 \\ |\mathbf{G}| &= \sqrt{\kappa_1^2 + \kappa_2^2} \end{aligned}$$

where $|\mathbf{G}|$ is the Frobenius norm of $\mathbf{G}$. With some algebra, we get

$$\begin{aligned} \kappa_1 &= \frac{\mathrm{trace}(\mathbf{G}) + d}{2} \\ \kappa_2 &= \frac{\mathrm{trace}(\mathbf{G}) - d}{2} \\ \text{where} & \\ d &= \sqrt{2|\mathbf{G}|^2 - \mathrm{trace}(\mathbf{G})^2} \end{aligned}$$

To visualize surface shape in a volume rendering, we can use a bivariate function of κ_1 and κ_2 to assign color based on local curvature. Diderot code that implements this is shown in Figure 3. Notice that the mathematical specification given above translates directly into Diderot; one can easily see that the code is an implementation of the method that one might derive on the whiteboard. This example also illustrates the use of a field to implement a color assignment function (*i.e.*, the `RGB` field). We sample this field using bilinear interpolation, which is provided by the `tent` kernel. The resulting image from applying this technique to a synthetic data set is shown in Figure 4 (this figure also includes an image of the bivariate colormap function).

```
// RGB colormap of (kappa1,kapp2)
field#0(2)[3] RGB = tent ⊛ load(xfer);
...
  update {
    ...
    vec3 grad = -∇F(pos);
    vec3 norm = normalize(grad);
    tensor[3,3] H = ∇ ⊗ ∇F(pos);
    tensor[3,3] P = identity[3] - norm⊗norm;
    tensor[3,3] G = -(P•H•P)/|grad|;
    real disc = sqrt(2.0*|G|^2 - trace(G)^2);
    real k1 = (trace(G) + disc)/2.0;
    real k2 = (trace(G) - disc)/2.0;
    // find material RGBA
    vec3 matRGB =
        RGB([max(-1.0, min(1.0, 6.0*k1)),
             max(-1.0, min(1.0, 6.0*k2))]);
    ...
  }
```

Figure 3. Computing the surface color based on implicit surface curvatures

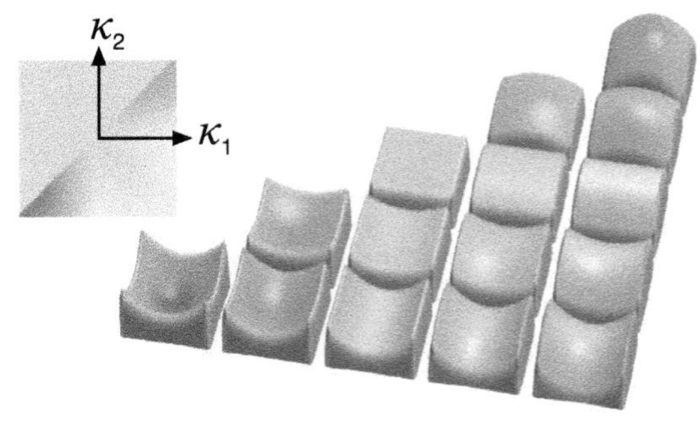

Figure 4. Volume rendering with color determined by implicit surface curvatures (κ_1, κ_2)

4.2 Line Integral Convolution (LIC)

Line integral convolution (LIC) is a vector field visualization method that can be concisely expressed in Diderot. LIC visualizes a vector field by blurring an underlying noise texture (a scalar field) along vector field streamlines [7]. Streamlines are paths everywhere tangent to the vector field, computed by numerical integration; in our benchmark we use the midpoint method (a second-order Runge-Kutta method). For each pixel in the output, we define a strand that computes a streamline. The pixel value is the average of noise texture samples taken along all computed vertices of the streamline seeded at that pixel. The Diderot implementation in Figure 5 simultaneously computes downstream (`forw`) and upstream (`back`) segments of the streamlines of the `vectors` synthetic vector field, sampling the `rand` scalar field at each step, and stopping each after `stepNum` steps. The output graylevel contrast is modulated by the the vector field velocity at the seedpoint `|V(pos0)|`, creating the LIC result shown in Figure 6.

4.3 Particle-based feature sampling

One class of applications that Diderot targets is the use of *particles* to detect and sample image features, such as isocontours [21]. As a simple example, we consider detecting isocontours in a 2D grayscale image. Figure 7 gives the strand definition for this pro-

```
field#1(2)[2] V = load("vectors.nrrd") ⊛ ctmr;
field#0(2)[] R = load("rand.nrrd") ⊛ tent;

strand LIC (vec2 pos0) {
  vec2 forw = pos0;
  vec2 back = pos0;
  output real sum = R(pos0);
  int step = 0;

  update {
    forw += h*V(forw + 0.5*h*V(forw));
    back += h*V(back - 0.5*h*V(back));
    sum += R(forw) + R(back);
    step += 1;
    if (step == stepNum) {
      sum *= |V(pos0)| / real(1 + 2*stepNum);
      stabilize;
    }
  }
}
```

Figure 5. Line Integral Convolution (LIC)

Figure 6. Line Integral Convolution (LIC) on synthetic data

gram. This program defines an initial collection of strands that are positioned in a 2D grid pattern. The image value at a strand's initial position determines the isovalue f_0 that it will search for. The strand's update method uses Newton-Raphson iteration to find the root of $F(\mathbf{x}) = f(\mathbf{x}) - f_0$ by motion along the normalized gradient $\nabla F / |\nabla F|$. The strand's search can terminate in one of two ways: if the length of the position update `|delta|` falls below `epsilon`, then the strand stabilizes — its position will be the output. Otherwise, if the strand wanders outside the field domain or takes too many steps, then the strand dies and produces no output. Since some strands die during execution, the final collection of stable strands will be a subset of the initial collection. Figure 8 shows a visualization of running this algorithm on a grayscale version of a portrait of Denis Diderot by Louis-Michel van Loo. The final positions of the stable strands are rendered as green dots. Note that the image is depicted with nearest-neighbor interpolation to show its individual pixels as squares, while the continuous interpolation (afforded by convolution with the Catmull-Rom cubic spline `ctmr`) creates isocontours that smoothly trace between pixels.

5. Implementation

Compiling a very-high-level language like Diderot requires a mix of traditional compiler techniques with domain-specific transformations and optimizations. In this section, we give an overview of our language implementation and describe the techniques that we have developed for compiling the higher-order field operations. We also provide a brief description of our runtime system.

```
field#1(2)[] f = ctmr ⊛ load("ddro.nrrd");

strand sample (int ui, int vi) {
  output vec2 pos = ···;
  // set isovalue to closest of 50, 30, or 10
  real f0 = 50.0 if f(pos) >= 40.0
            else 30.0 if f(pos) >= 20.0
            else 10.0;
  int steps = 0;
  update {
    if (!inside(pos, f) || steps > stepsMax)
      die;
    vec2 grad = ∇f(pos);
    vec2 delta = // the Newton-Raphson step
      normalize(grad) * (f(pos) - f0)/|grad|;
    if (|delta| < epsilon)
      stabilize;
    pos -= delta;
    steps += 1;
  }
}
```

Figure 7. Detecting isocontours

Figure 8. Isocontour detection in a grayscale image

5.1 Compiler overview

The Diderot compiler comprises roughly 19,000 lines of Standard ML code, which is organized into three main phases: the front-end, optimization and lowering, and code generation.

The front-end consists of parsing, type checking, and simplification. Although Diderot is a monomorphic language, most of its operators have instances at multiple types. For example, addition works on integers, tensors of all shapes, and fields. Since having to type check each operator as a special case would be prohibitively complicated, we use a mix of *ad hoc* overloading and polymorphism in the type checker. The internal representation of types includes kinded type variables, shape variables, and dimension variables. The type checking process introduces constraints between the variables, which are solved by unification. Once a program is type checked, the operator instances are instantiated at specific monotypes. The typed AST is then converted into a simplified representation, where temporaries are introduced for intermediate values and operator are applied only to variables. At this point we also duplicate code, as necessary, to ensure that fields are statically determined. For example, if the source program contained the line

```
real y = (F1 if b else F2)(x);
```

the simplified representation is transformed to code that is equivalent to

```
real y = F1(x) if b else F2(x);
```

This transformation is necessary because of the way we compile probe operations. While it could result in exponential code growth, we believe that in practice code growth will not be significant.

The optimization and lowering occurs over a series of three intermediate representations (IRs) based on Static Single Assignment (SSA) form [9]. These IRs share a common control-flow graph representation, but differ in their types and operations.

HighIR is essentially a desugared version of the source language with source-level types and operations.

MidIR supports vectors, transforms between coordinate spaces, loading image data, and kernel evaluations. At this stage, fields and probes have been compiled away into lower-level code.

LowIR supports basic operations on vectors, scalars, and memory objects.

The translations between these representations replaces higher-level operations with their equivalent lower-level operations. For example, field probes in the HighIR are expanded into the convolution of image samples and kernel evaluations in the MidIR. We discuss this particular expansion in more detail below.

The final phase is code generation. We have separate backends for different targets: sequential C code with vector extensions [12], parallel C code, OpenCL [16], and CUDA [22] (planned). Because these targets are all block-structured languages, our first step in code generation is to convert the LowIR SSA representation into a block-structured AST. The target-specific backends translate this representation into the appropriate representation and augment the code with type definitions and runtime support. The output is then passed to the host system's compiler.

5.2 Implementing field operations

Diderot's fields are abstract values that represent continuous functions. As such, we use a symbolic representation of field values in the compiler that is used to generate code for the `inside` test and for probing a field. In the simplest case, code that probes a tensor field is translated into code that maps the world-space position to image space and then convolves the image values from the neighborhood of the position using a kernel. This translation occurs when the program is converted from HighIR to MidIR; we then expand kernel evaluations into vectorized arithmetic when we convert from MidIR to LowIR.

While the case of probing a field that is defined directly by convolving an image with a kernel is straightforward, in general the problem is more complicated, since fields can be defined by higher-order operations such as scaling, addition, and differentiation. Thus, before we can translate HighIR to MidIR, we must normalize the field computations. Effectively, this process lowers higher-order operations that work on fields to operations that work on tensors. We call this process *field normalization.*

We can formalize field normalization as a translation from a language of field expressions to a normalized language of field probes and tensor operations. Figure 9 gives the grammars of these two languages; we have simplified the presentation by omitting many operators available in Diderot. In the source language (Figure 9a), we have tensor-valued expressions (denoted by e) and field-valued

$$
\begin{array}{rcl}
(f_1 + f_2)(x) & \Rightarrow & f_1(x) + f_2(x) \\
(e * f)(x) & \Rightarrow & e * f(x) \\
\nabla(f_1 + f_2) & \Rightarrow & \nabla f_1 + \nabla f_2 \\
\nabla(e * f) & \Rightarrow & e * \nabla f \\
\nabla(V \circledast h) & \Rightarrow & V \circledast \nabla h \\
\nabla(V \circledast \nabla^i h) & \Rightarrow & V \circledast \nabla^{i+1} h
\end{array}
$$

Figure 10. Rewriting rules for field normalization

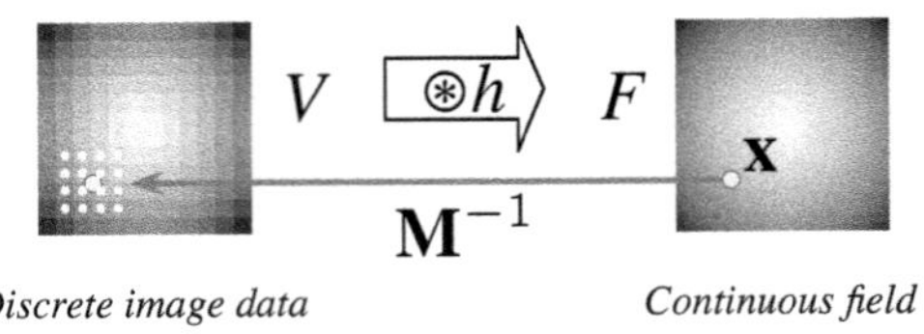

Figure 11. Probing a 2D field $F = V \circledast h$ at $\mathbf{x}$, where $\mathbf{M}$ is the mapping from world coordinates to image-space coordinates

expressions (denoted by f). Using the rewrite rules given in Figure 10, we can transform source-language expressions into the normalized language of Figure 9b. The normalized language enforces three key invariants on the structure of the computation:

1. All differentiation operations have been pushed down to the kernels in convolutions. We add a superscript to the ∇ operator to specify the level of differentiation. ∇^2 should not be confused with the standard notation for the Laplacian.
2. The fields involved in probe operations are defined directly as convolutions.
3. Arithmetic operations on fields have been lowered to operations on tensors.

These properties are key to being able to synthesize code for the probe operations, as is described in the next section.

5.3 Synthesizing probe operations

Once we have normalized the field operations as described above, we must still synthesize code to implement field probes. These operations get compiled down into code that maps the world-space coordinates to image space and then convolves the image values in the neighborhood of the position, as is illustrated by Figure 11. As discussed in Section 2, we use separable kernels to reconstruct the value of a field at a specific point. For example, if $F = V \circledast h$ is a 2-dimensional scalar field, then probing F at the location $\mathbf{x}$ is defined by the equation

$$F(\mathbf{x}) = \sum_{i=1-s}^{s} \sum_{j=1-s}^{s} V[\mathbf{n} + \langle i, j \rangle] h(\mathbf{f}_x - i) h(\mathbf{f}_y - j)$$

where s is the support of h, $\mathbf{n} = \lfloor \mathbf{M}^{-1}\mathbf{x} \rfloor$ and $\mathbf{f} = \mathbf{M}^{-1}\mathbf{x} - \mathbf{n}$.

One of the main challenges of synthesizing code for probe operations is that the shape of the result and the nesting of summations can be arbitrarily complicated. For example, assume that F is a 2D scalar field of type **field#**$k(2)[\,]$ and G is a 2D vector field of type **field#**$k(2)[2]$. Then the probe expressions $\nabla \otimes G(\mathbf{x})$ and $\nabla \otimes \nabla F(\mathbf{x})$ both have type **tensor**$[2, 2]$, but the code required to implement the two probes is very different. Tensor calculus provides the notational tools to manage this process, in that the differentiation operator (∇) can be treated as a vector of partial-

$$\begin{array}{rcll} e & ::= & f(x) & \text{field probe} \\ & | & \cdots & \\ f & ::= & V \circledast h & \text{convolution} \\ & | & \nabla f & \text{differentiation} \\ & | & f + f & \text{field addition} \\ & | & e * f & \text{field scaling} \end{array}$$

(a) source language

$$\begin{array}{rcll} \hat{e} & ::= & \hat{f}(x) & \text{field probe} \\ & | & \hat{e} + \hat{e} & \text{tensor addition} \\ & | & \hat{e} * \hat{e} & \text{tensor scaling} \\ & | & \cdots & \\ \hat{f} & ::= & V \circledast \hat{h} & \text{convolution} \\ \hat{h} & ::= & \nabla^i h & \text{kernel with } i \geq 0 \text{ levels of differentiation} \end{array}$$

(b) normalized language

Figure 9. The source and target languages of field normalization, where V denotes images and h denotes kernels

differentiation operators. For example, in 2D we have

$$\nabla = \begin{bmatrix} \frac{\partial}{\partial x} \\ \frac{\partial}{\partial y} \end{bmatrix}$$

We can use this representation to handle the probing of the gradient of a scalar field F

$$\begin{aligned} \nabla F(\mathbf{x}) &= (V \circledast \nabla h)(\mathbf{x}) \\ &= \left(V \circledast \begin{bmatrix} \frac{\partial}{\partial x} h \\ \frac{\partial}{\partial y} h \end{bmatrix} \right)(\mathbf{x}) \\ &= \begin{bmatrix} \sum_i \sum_j V[\mathbf{n} + \langle i, j \rangle] h'(\mathbf{f}_x - i) h(\mathbf{f}_y - j) \\ \sum_i \sum_j V[\mathbf{n} + \langle i, j \rangle] h(\mathbf{f}_x - i) h'(\mathbf{f}_y - j) \end{bmatrix} \end{aligned}$$

Note that the partial-differentiation operators tell us where to use h and where to use the first derivative h' in the reconstruction.

This approach generalizes to multiple levels of differentiation in a natural way. For example, the Hessian of F is defined as $\nabla \otimes \nabla F$, which is normalized to $V \circledast \nabla^2 h$, which can be written as $V \circledast \nabla \otimes \nabla h$. Thus we have

$$\nabla \otimes \nabla h = \begin{bmatrix} \frac{\partial^2}{\partial x^2} & \frac{\partial^2}{\partial xy} \\ \frac{\partial^2}{\partial xy} & \frac{\partial^2}{\partial y^2} \end{bmatrix} h = \begin{bmatrix} \frac{\partial^2}{\partial x^2} h & \frac{\partial^2}{\partial xy} h \\ \frac{\partial^2}{\partial xy} h & \frac{\partial^2}{\partial y^2} h \end{bmatrix}$$

The resulting $x \times 2$ matrix defines the structure of the result of probing the Hessian of F.

When the image data is not scalar (*e.g.*, the 2D vector field G mentioned above), we have further outer iteration over the shape of the image's range. For example, if $G = V \circledast h$ is a 2D vector field, then the probe $G(\mathbf{x})$ will be expressed as

$$\begin{aligned} G(\mathbf{x}) &= (V \circledast h)(\mathbf{x}) \\ &= \begin{bmatrix} V_1 \circledast h \\ V_2 \circledast h \end{bmatrix}(\mathbf{x}) \\ &= \begin{bmatrix} \sum_i \sum_j V_1[\mathbf{n} + \langle i, j \rangle] h(\mathbf{f}_x - i) h(\mathbf{f}_y - j) \\ \sum_i \sum_j V_2[\mathbf{n} + \langle i, j \rangle] h(\mathbf{f}_x - i) h(\mathbf{f}_y - j) \end{bmatrix} \end{aligned}$$

Note that while the result of this probe has the same type as $\nabla F(\mathbf{x})$, the underlying computation is different.

Our implementation must also correctly handle mapping between coordinate spaces. An image dataset comes with orientation information that can be represented as a transform $\mathbf{M}$ mapping from position in the image's index space to position in world space. We use the inverse mapping $\mathbf{M}^{-1}$ to convert the position of a probe, which is in world space, back to image space, but we also have to consider the mapping of the probe's result back to world space. Gradients are measured in image space by convolution with kernel derivatives (as described above). Being a *covariant* quantity, gradients are converted to world space by $\mathbf{M}^{-T}$, the inverse transpose of the transform $\mathbf{M}$ for converting positions (a *contravariant* quantity) to world space [27]. On the other hand, when probing a vector field created by convolution of a vector-valued image dataset, the vectors are assumed to be already represented in world space, and hence need no post-probe transformation.

The final step in generating executable code for field probes is to expand the kernel evaluations. This expansion takes place as part of the translation from MidIR to LowIR. The kernels that Diderot supports are all piecewise polynomial, so it straightforward to symbolically differentiate them. The process described in this section results in code that is easily vectorized (in fact the MidIR and LowIRs support vectorized operations).

5.4 Domain-specific optimizations

In addition to the transformations required to support the operations on fields that we have described above, the Diderot compiler performs a number of other optimizations. Specifically, we implement an extended form of constant folding and dead-code elimination that shrinks (or contracts) the program [1] and we eliminate redundant computations using value numbering [5]. While these are optimizations that are found in many compilers, when they are combined with the domain-specific operators in our IR, they produce domain-specific optimizations that a general-purpose compiler would be unlikely to achieve. For example, if a program probes both a field F and the gradient field ∇F at the same position, there are redundant convolution computations that can be detected and eliminated. Another example is the symmetry of the Hessian, which is also detected by our value-numbering pass.

5.5 Runtime support

The Diderot runtime is comprised of common code for loading image data from Nrrd files [29] and writing the program's output to either a text or Nrrd file.[2] The common part of the runtime also provides support for initializing input variables.

In addition to the common code, there is target-specific code for managing strands. Recall that Diderot uses a bulk-synchronous parallelism model [26, 31]. In this model, execution is divided into *super steps*; during a super-step each strand's update method is evaluated once. The program executes until all of the strands are either stabilized or dead. For the sequential target, the runtime implements this model as a loop nest, with the outer loop iterating once per super-step and the inner loop iterating once per strand.

The parallel version of the runtime is implemented using POSIX threads. The system creates a collection of worker threads (the default is one per hardware core/processor) and manages a work-list of strands. To keep synchronization overhead low, the strands in the work-list are organized into blocks of strands (currently 4096 strands per block). During a super-step, each worker grabs and updates strands until the work-list is empty. Barrier synchronization is used to coordinate the threads at the end of a super step.

[2] The Nrrd file format is designed for multi-dimensional image data and includes metadata for the image's coordinate system and axes.

6. Performance evaluation

In addition to providing a very-high-level programming model, we are also interested in providing high-performance; especially on modern multicore systems. In this section we present results from four benchmark programs that represent typical workloads for image analysis, including parallel scaling results for the Diderot implementations. We also compare Diderot's performance with hand-written C programs that use the Teem library [30]. Teem includes convolution-based reconstruction of values and derivatives from discretely sampled fields, which closely matches the mathematical abstraction of a field supported by Diderot, but with a less convenient API, as described in Section 7.

6.1 Experimental method

Our test machine is an 8-core MacPro with 2.93 GHz Xeon X5570 processors and 12Gb of memory running Mac OS X 10.7.2. We used the Apple `clang` C compiler (version 3.0) to compile the Teem version of the benchmarks and as a backend to the Diderot compiler. In both cases, code was compiled with optimization level `-O3`. For each benchmark, we report the average of 40 runs on a lightly-loaded machine; the standard deviations for these experiments were typically less than 0.1 seconds.

6.2 Benchmarks

We present results from four benchmark programs, which are summarized in Table 1. In the table we give the lines of code of both the Teem version (written in C) and the Diderot version. We further split out the lines of code in the computational core of the benchmark. For the Teem version, this number is the loop-nest that performs the computation, while for the Diderot program it is the **`update`** method.[3] From this table it can be seen that Diderot provides a significant advantage in conciseness over using the Teem library, which, itself is a big advantage over writing the code directly in C. The lines-of-code numbers do not include comments, blank lines, or timing code. The table also includes the number of initial strands for each program.

These benchmark programs, which were chosen to be representative of the kinds of applications for which Diderot has been designed, are described in more detail below.

vr-lite: A simple volume renderer that displays surfaces using Phong shading, which depends on the gradient in the scalar field. This simple program is typical of one that might be used in an educational context.

illust-vr: A more complex volume renderer that produces illustrative (or non-photo-realistic) renderings, using various curvature computations based on the gradient and Hessian. This example showcases the tensor calculations that are awkward to express in other languages.

lic2d: Computes a line integral convolution [7] visualization of a vector field, in which a noise texture is blurred along vector field streamlines. This program highlights convolution and differentiation in a vector field.

ridge3d: An initial uniform distribution of points within a portion of CT scan of a lung is moved iteratively towards the centers of blood vessels, using Newton optimization to compute ridge lines [11]. This program computes the eigenvalues and eigenvectors of the Hessian, and permits the implementation to closely resemble the mathematical definition of a ridge line.

[3] For the Teem versions of the benchmark, the computational core does *not* include the setup code used to specify the field properties that are being probed.

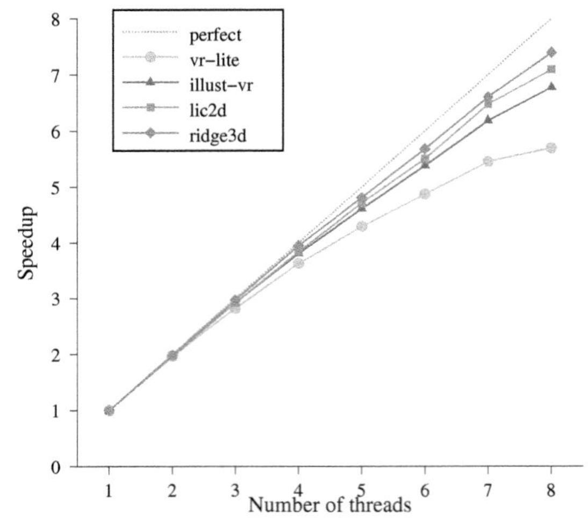

Figure 12. Parallel speedup

6.3 Measurements

For each benchmark program, we measured the wall-clock time it took to execute the computation kernel. This measurement excludes the initial loading of the image data, other initialization, and the writing of the result. Typically, the excluded time was on the order of 0.2 seconds. Table 2 presents the results of our experiments. For each benchmark program, we present the execution time for the Teem version, the sequential Diderot version, and the parallel version on 1, 2, and 8 processors. The Teem programs use a mix of single and double-precision arithmetic in their implementation (the Teem Library uses doubles internally). When compiling a Diderot program, on the other hand, the user must decide if reals are represented as single or double-precision floats. To verify that the difference in precision is not reason that Diderot is faster, we measured both the single and double-precision versions of the Diderot programs. From Table 2, it can be seen that while using double-precision arithmetic does result in a significant slow-down, it does not wholly explain the difference. We have done some detailed profiling of the Teem versions of several of the benchmarks, and we believe that a major part of the difference is Teem's use of callbacks to implement field probes. Diderot's use of vector operations (*i.e.*, SSE) may also account for some of the difference. Thus, compared to Teem, Diderot provides a more concise programming notation, better performance, and easier support for parallel computation.

6.4 SMP performance

The Diderot execution model is designed for both simplicity and efficient execution on parallel hardware. Since strands execute independently, we expect efficient scaling on parallel hardware. In Figure 12, we present the parallel speedup curves for the single-precision version of our benchmarks. We use the sequential version of these programs without the overhead of scheduling (*i.e.*, the **Seq.** column from Table 1). As we expect, all of the benchmarks scale well. For vr-lite, we see some tailing-off at eight threads, which we believe is because of lack of work (notice from Table 1 that vr-lite has the fewest strands). With some experimentation, we found that the biggest limitation to parallelism was the lock that controls access to the work-list. With smaller blocks of strands (recall that we use 4,096 strands per block), we saw a significant reduction in parallel scaling. Other than adjusting the strand-block size, we have

Program	LOC (total:core) Teem	Diderot	# strands	Description
vr-lite	223:44	68:26	165,600	Simple volume-renderer with Phong shading running on CT scan of hand
illust-vr	324:61	83:39	307,200	Fancy volume-renderer with cartoon shading running on CT scan of hand
lic2d	260:66	53:32	572,220	Line Integral Convolution in 2D running on synthetic data
ridge3d	360:55	44:24	1,728,000	Particle-based ridge detection running on lung data

Table 1. The benchmark programs

Program	Teem	Diderot single-precision				Diderot double-precision			
		Seq.	1P	2P	8P	Seq.	1P	2P	8P
vr-lite	26.77	14.92	14.95	7.59	2.62	16.52	16.44	8.35	2.92
illust-vr	132.85	54.17	54.40	27.55	8.00	80.63	82.16	41.18	11.86
lic2d	3.22	2.02	2.03	1.02	0.30	2.47	2.47	1.24	0.37
ridge3d	11.18	8.40	8.36	4.22	1.14	9.34	10.27	5.16	1.39

Table 2. Average performance results over 40 runs (times in seconds)

not done any performance tuning of the runtime, so we expect that we will be able to improve performance and scaling.

7. Related work

There are a variety of domain-specific languages and frameworks that provide similar features supported in Diderot. Many of these are examples of using the power of DSLs to provide programers with high-level parallel programming models.

Teem is a collection of libraries that support image analysis and visualization algorithms [30]. Teem provides support for convolution-based measurements via kernels, but as a C library, the programming model is much less direct. A Diderot programmer can declare a scalar field `F` and then use `F(pos)` and `∇F(pos)` for the field value and gradient at some point `pos`. A Teem programmer would have to create a probing context in which image data and kernels are set, specify the list of all quantities that are to be computed for every probe, and then update the probe context to allocate buffers to store probe results. After calling the probe function at a particular location `pos`, the programmer then copies the value and gradient out of the probe buffer.

Shadie is a DSL for direct-volume rendering applications that is targeted at GPUs [13]. The framework is based on the notion of shaders, which are functions that define what happens along a given ray for the entire visualization. Similar to Diderot, shaders support the ability to perform computations on continuous fields and their derivatives. But Shadie is limited to direct-volume rendering applications, whereas Diderot supports other visualization applications such as LIC, fiber tractography, and particle systems. Furthermore, Shadie's support for field operations is restricted to a set of built-in functions (*e.g.* `cubic_query_3d` for probing the gradient field reconstructed using a cubic spline), whereas Diderot provides a collection of orthogonal operations on fields.

Scout is a high-level DSL for image visualization and analysis [19]. Scout supports a data-parallel programming model based on the concept of *shapes*, which are regions of voxels in the image data. Scout is designed for a different class of algorithms than Diderot. Specifically, algorithms that are defined in terms of computations over discrete voxels, such as stencil algorithms, rather than over a continuous tensor fields.

Spiral is a DSL for digital signal processing algorithms [23]. Its implementation encapsulates significant mathematical knowledge of the various complex algorithms in digital signal processing, which allows Spiral to generate fine-tuned code for a given platform. This notion of developing a high-level mathematical programming model is also emphasized in Diderot. As with Spiral, Diderot allows its users to focus more on the mathematics and allowing the system to generate high-performance code for their platform. Although Spiral provides a powerful mathematical model, it targeted at the somewhat different domain of signal processing.

Delite is an ongoing project to support the development of embedded parallel DSLs [6, 8] and was the inspiration for the Diderot project. The framework aids in decreasing the burden of parallelizing DSL programs (*e.g.*, scheduling) and has been used for machine learning [28] and mesh-based PDEs [10]. While the Delite project and Diderot project share the idea that parallel DSLs are an effective way to provide portable parallelism, they differ in the way that the DSL is presented to the user. Delite embeds the DSL in Scala, which limits the notational flexibility of the design, whereas Diderot's syntax is designed to fit its application domain. Furthermore, Diderot's runtime has been designed to allow Diderot programs to be embedded as libraries in any host language that supports calling C code, whereas Delite applications must be written in Scala, which is not a common language in the visualization community.

8. Future work

While the current version of Diderot is sufficient to implement many interesting visualization algorithms, we have plans to extend the language design, add additional targets, and otherwise improve the system. These plans include obvious extensions, such as adding functions and simple data structures, as well as extensions targeted at image analysis algorithms. We describe some of the latter plans here.

8.1 Portable parallelism

One implementation challenge of Diderot is to extract maximum performance across a wide range of different parallel architectures. Diderot already includes an efficient multicore parallel implementation. We also have an OpenCL backend that is targeted at GPUs, but we plan to extend our implementation to support clusters, including GPU clusters.

8.2 Richer concurrency model

The current design of Diderot limits strand creation to initialization time and does not provide any mechanism for strand communication. While the number of active strands can dynamically vary, because of **`die`**, it only monotonically decreases. For algorithms, such as particle systems, where strands are used to explore the image space, it is useful to be able to dynamically create new strands on the fly. But it only makes sense to create new strands when there is a region that is relatively empty of strands. Therefore, we plan to extend the programming model with three mechanisms: a mechanism for creating new strands, a mechanism for reading the state of nearby strands, and a mechanism for global computations (*i.e.*, reductions) over the whole set of active and stable strands. Keeping with our bulk-synchronous semantics, these mechanisms will be tied to the super steps. New strands will come into existence at the end of the super step, strands will only be able to read the state of other strands as it was at the beginning of the super step, and the global computations will occur at the end of the super step.

8.3 More tensor math

We plan to extend our implementation to support larger set of tensor and field operations, such as divergence ($\nabla\bullet$) and curl ($\nabla\times$). To support this richer set of operators, however, we will have to make changes in our internal representation. Specifically, we are exploring the use of Einstein notation as a compact way to represent tensor computations.

9. Conclusion

We have presented Diderot, a parallel domain-specific language for image analysis and visualization algorithms. Diderot provides the programmer with a very-high-level programming model based on the concepts and notations of tensor calculus, which allows the algorithms to be expressed in their natural mathematical notation. We have described the techniques that we use to implement this high-level model and have presented performance data the demonstrates that we can have both high-level notation and high-performance in the same system.

Acknowledgments

We thank the NVIDIA Corporation for their generous donation of both hardware and financial support. This material is based upon work performed in part while John Reppy was serving at the National Science Foundation.

References

[1] A. W. Appel and T. Jim. Shrinking lambda expressions in linear time. *JFP*, 7:515–540, Sept. 1997.

[2] S. R. Aylward and E. Bullitt. Initialization, noise, singularities, and scale in height ridge traversal for tubular object centerline extraction. *IEEE TMI*, 21(2):61–75, Feb 2002.

[3] R. Bartels, J. Beatty, and B. Barsky. *An Introduction to Splines for Use in Computer Graphics and Geometric Modeling*. Morgan Kaufmann Publishers, New York, NY, 1987.

[4] P. J. Basser, S. Pajevic, C. Pierpaoli, J. Duda, and A. Aldroubi. In vivo fiber tractograpy using DT-MRI data. *Magnetic Resonance in Medicine*, 44:625–632, 2000.

[5] P. Briggs, K. D. Cooper, , and L. T. Simpson. Value numbering. *SP&E*, 27(6):701–724, June 1997.

[6] K. J. Brown, A. K. Sujeeth, H. Lee, T. Rompf, H. Chafi, M. Odersky, and K. Olukotun. A heterogeneous parallel framework for domain-specific languages. In *PACT '11*, Oct. 2011.

[7] B. Cabral and L. C. Leedom. Imaging vector fields using line integral convolution. In *SIGGRAPH '93*, pages 263–270, New York, NY, Aug. 1993. ACM.

[8] H. Chafi, Z. Devito, A. Moors, T. Rompf, A. K. Sujeeth, P. Hanrahan, M. Odersky, and K. Olukotun. Language virtualization for heterogeneous parallel computing. In *OOPSLA '10*, pages 835–847, Oct. 2010. Part of the Onward! 2010 Conference.

[9] R. Cytron, J. Ferrante, B. K. Rosen, M. N. Wegman, and F. K. Zadeck. Efficiently computing static single assignment form and the control dependence graph. *ACM TOPLAS*, 13(4):451–490, Oct 1991.

[10] Z. DeVito, N. Joubert, F. Palacios, S. Oakley, M. Medina, M. Barrientos, E. Elsen, F. Ham, A. Aiken, K. Duraisamy, E. Darve, J. Alonso, and P. Hanrahan. Liszt: A domain specific language for building portable mesh-based PDE solvers. In *SC '11*, pages 1–12, Nov. 2011.

[11] D. Eberly. *Ridges in Image and Data Analysis*. Kluwer Academic Publishers, Boston, MA, 1996.

[12] *Using vector instructions through built-in functions*. Free Software Foundation. URL `http://gcc.gnu.org/onlinedocs/gcc/Vector-Extensions.html`.

[13] M. Hašan, J. Wolfgang, G. Chen, and H. Pfister. Shadie: A domain-specific language for volume visualization. Draft paper; available at `http://miloshasan.net/Shadie/shadie.pdf`, 2010.

[14] L. Ibanez and W. Schroeder. *The ITK Software Guide*. Kitware Inc., 2005.

[15] *IDL: Interactive Data Language*. ITT Visual Information Solutions. `http://www.ittvis.com/ProductServices/IDL.aspx`.

[16] *The OpenCL Specification (Version 1.1)*. Khronos OpenCL Working Group, 2010. Available from `http://www.khronos.org/opencl`.

[17] G. Kindlmann, R. Whitaker, T. Tasdizen, and T. Moller. Curvature-based transfer functions for direct volume rendering: Methods and applications. In *VIZ '03*, pages 67–74, Los Alamitos, CA, Oct. 2003. IEEE Computer Society Press.

[18] *MATLAB — The language of technical computing*. The Mathworks, Inc. `http://www.mathworks.com/products/matlab`.

[19] P. McCormick, J. Inman, J. Ahrens, J. Mohd-Yusof, G. Roth, and S. Cummins. Scout: A data-parallel programming language for graphics processors. *Journal of Parallel Computing*, 33:648–662, Nov. 2007. ISSN 0167-8191.

[20] E. H. W. Meijering, W. J. Niessen, and M. A. Viergever. Quantitative evaluation of convolution-based methods for medical image interpolation. *Medical Image Analysis*, 5(2):111–126, June 2001.

[21] M. D. Meyer, P. Georgel, and R. T. Whitaker. Robust particle systems for curvature dependent sampling of implicit surfaces. In *SMI '05*, pages 124–133, June 2005.

[22] *NVIDIA CUDA C Programming Guide (Version 4.0)*. NVIDIA, May 2011. Available from `http://developer.nvidia.com/category/zone/cuda-zone`.

[23] M. Puschel, J. Moura, J. Johnson, D. Padua, M. Veloso, B. Singer, J. Xiong, F. Franchetti, A. Gacic, Y. Voronenko, K. Chen, R. Johnson, and N. Rizzolo. SPIRAL: Code generation for DSP transforms. *Proc. of the IEEE*, 93(2):232–275, Feb. 2005.

[24] G. X. Ritter and P. D. Gader. Image algebra techniques for parallel image processing. *JPDC*, 4(1):7–44, Feb. 1987.

[25] *NumPy: Numerical Python*. Scientific Tools for Python. `http://numpy.scipy.org`.

[26] D. Skillicorn, J. M. Hill, and W. McColl. Questions and answers about BSP. *Scientific Programming*, 6(3):249–274, 1997.

[27] B. Spain. *Tensor Calculus: A Concise Course*. Dover, Mineola, NY, 2003.

[28] A. K. Sujeeth, H. Lee, K. J. Brown, T. Rompf, H. Chafi, M. Wu, A. R. Atreya, M. Odersky, and K. Olukotun. Optiml: An implicitly parallel domain-specific language for machine learning. In *ICML '11*, June 2011.

[29] *NRRD: Nearly Raw Raster Data*. Teem Library, . `http://teem.sf.net/nrrd`.

[30] *Teem website at* `http://teem.sf.net`. Teem Library, .

[31] L. G. Valiant. A bridging model for parallel computation. *CACM*, 33 (8):103–111, Aug. 1990.

Synthesising Graphics Card Programs from DSLs

Luke Cartey
University of Oxford
luke.cartey@cs.ox.ac.uk

Rune Lyngsoe
University of Oxford
lyngsoe@stats.ox.ac.uk

Oege de Moor
University of Oxford
oege.de.moor@cs.ox.ac.uk

Abstract

Over the last five years, graphics cards have become a tempting target for scientific computing, thanks to unrivaled peak performance, often producing a runtime speed-up of x10 to x25 over comparable CPU solutions.

However, this increase can be difficult to achieve, and doing so often requires a fundamental rethink. This is especially problematic in scientific computing, where experts do not want to learn yet another architecture.

In this paper we develop a method for automatically parallelising recursive functions of the sort found in scientific papers. Using a static analysis of the function dependencies we identify sets — partitions — of independent elements, which we use to synthesise an efficient GPU implementation using polyhedral code generation techniques. We then augment our language with DSL extensions to support a wider variety of applications, and demonstrate the effectiveness of this with three case studies, showing significant performance improvement over equivalent CPU methods, and similar efficiency to hand-tuned GPU implementations.

Categories and Subject Descriptors I.2.2 [*Automatic Programming*]: Program Synthesis; D.1.3 [*Concurrent Programming*]: Parallel Programming

General Terms Language, Performance

Keywords gpu, scientific applications, program synthesis, dynamic programming

1. Introduction

Recent advances in graphics card design have embraced the rapid pace of change predicted by Moore's law to unlock a mass market massively-parallel architecture, with phenomenally high potential peak performance. Unfortunately, this great power also comes at a cost: an architecture that is often difficult to program effectively and efficiently.

The problem is twofold — we must identify a suitable parallel algorithm and we must use the resources of the device efficiently. Whilst we have a comprehensive understanding of how to map graphical problems to massively-parallel devices, for many other classes of problems it is less clear what parallel algorithm might be suitable. Much of the work so far has pragmatically focused on data-parallelism; applying the same problem to a large data-set by assigning a single problem to each thread. We want to focus on those problems which require a more nuanced algorithm to achieve peak performance on the GPU.

With the area in an embryonic stage, language support has often been aimed at extending existing languages with parallel primitive operations. However, a growing number of people are approaching from a different angle — by providing high-level languages or specifications which are automatically parallelised (Liszt & OptiML[2], FLAME[15], Nikola[18] and Obsidian[7])

In this paper we propose a system for synthesising graphics card programs from recursion equations. We develop a simple language for describing such recursions, then augment those equations with domain-specific notations. This allows us to support a wide-range of recursive problems in many different domains. We build on existing work to develop an automatically parallelising end-to-end compiler that generates appropriate target code for NVIDIA GPUs.

1.1 Graphics Cards

Modern graphics cards are powered by massively parallel processors. These typically consist of a large number of cores — hundreds to thousands — arranged in a series of multi-processors. Each multi-processor contains a number of cores that work synchronously to achieve parallelisation, and each multi-processor acts independently of any other — there are no global synchronisation mechanisms. Indeed, this is a deliberate design decision to reduce the complexity of the hardware.

In practice, this forces us to use the GPU in one of two ways: an *inter-task* parallel system where each thread solves one problem, and so all threads on a multiprocessor compute the same instruction for different problems in sync, and an *intra-task* parallel system, where blocks of threads work co-operatively on the same problem. Inter-parallel systems tend to be more straight forward, and focused on data-parallelism. We will focus on problems suited to intra-parallel solutions in this paper.

1.2 Domain Specific Languages

Domain Specific Languages (DSLs) differ from general-purpose languages in that they may restrict the language or make assumptions about the input, in order to produce optimised output code[19]. We can use the knowledge derived from the concise input to provide both static and dynamic optimisations. Domain users also gain benefits from such a language — an interface for describing their problems in the way they understand them, which will often lead to better code and more opportunities for reuse. Our approach in this paper is to allow scientists to describe their problems in the same way they describe them in papers and other literature.

1.3 Scientific Problems

Some of the most demanding users of high-performance hardware are from the scientific community. In this paper, we will use case studies from bioinformatics to motivate our approach. It is an ideal match — typical problems require features with obvious parallel

PLDI'12, June 11–16, 2012, Beijing, China.

potential, such as large data-sets and extensive search spaces. Common applications include sequence alignment[3], gene finding[10], homology search[3] and structure prediction applications. Almost every practical application listed uses a form of recursive equation to define and describe the problem, often with an associated data model, such as a matrix, Hidden Markov Model or graph structure.

Our choice of bioinformatics as a case study does not represent a fundamental limit to our approach, and we expect that our framework could support many problems in other scientific domains and beyond.

1.4 Contributions

In this paper we develop a minimal language for describing recursive functions that can then be automatically parallelised. Furthermore, we show how we can fulfill this promise by adding domain specific extensions. Our contributions are:

- We design a simple host language for recursive problems (Section 4). One of our main contributions is to describe how this simple, but nonetheless expressive, language can be used to automatically synthesise a program targeting a massively parallel processor such as a GPU. The synthesis takes the following form:
  - We use existing techniques[9, 11] to frame the parallelisation problem as one of partitioning the call-graph into an ordered list of groups, where all members of a group are independent. We use a *scheduling* function which determines, for each call, to which partition it belongs (Section 4.4).
  - We show how the scheduling function can be used to synthesise a graphics card program using a polyhedral code-generation tool, CLooG[1](Section 4.3).
  - We define what criteria a scheduling function must satisfy in order to be valid for a given recursive equation. This is used as the foundation for an analysis that will verify user-provided schedules (Section 4.5).
  - A recursive equation will usually be amenable to multiple partition schemes. We use the identified criteria to frame the search for a schedule. We develop a technique for automatically finding valid and minimal schedules (Section 4.6).
- Many scientific problems can be written as recursive problems over complex data structures. We show how limited extensions to our host language can be made, and, importantly, what domain specific extensions can be made without losing the advantages of the automatic parallelisation (Section 5).
- We evaluate our approach for a variety of applications in our target domain, comparing against standard CPU approaches as well as hand-optimized GPU solutions (Section 6).

2. Anatomy of a scientific recursive problem

The *edit-distance* problem is a straight-forward example of a recursive problem. It asks us to compare two strings to find the minimum cost of making a series of edit or match operations to transform one string to another. It is one that is relevant in scientific domains such as bioinformatics, where the *Smith-Waterman* algorithm is an edit distance algorithm for aligning two biological sequences.

The *Principle of Optimality* allows us to frame the problem as a combination of a series of sub-problems, and so we can provide a recursive definition to determine the solution. For the edit-distance algorithm, as for many optimisation algorithms, this provides a natural and intuitive way of describing the solution (see Figure 1).

This form of declaration has an implicit method of evaluation, a recursive function, which is most naturally solved in a serial fashion, one call at a time. However, for many problems, this is not the most efficient solution. For example, we may repeat computations unnecessarily when two different calls depend on the same computed value. *Dynamic programming* permits us to store those repeated computations, or even tabulate the result bottom up—$d(0, 0)$ first, followed by dependent computations.

$$d(x,y) = \begin{cases} x & \text{if } y = 0 \\ y & \text{if } x = 0 \\ d(x-1, y-1) & \text{if } s[x] = t[y] \\ min\begin{pmatrix} d(x-1,y), \\ d(x,y-1), \\ d(x-1,y-1) \end{pmatrix} + 1 & \text{otherwise} \end{cases}$$

Figure 1. The edit distance recursion on strings s and t.

This leads to another example of redundancy in the edit-distance problem — once we have computed $d(0, 0)$, it does not matter whether we compute $d(1, 0)$ or $d(0, 1)$ as they are *independent* — that is, they do not depend on each others values. This opens up the possibility of concurrently executing both $d(1, 0)$ and $d(0, 1)$. Similarly, we can observe that any set of cells on an $x + y$ diagonal line are independent, and can be computed concurrently provided that all prior dependencies are solved.

The edit-distance problem illustrates how recursive problems often have a useful form of concurrency, and whilst edit-distance problems have frequently been parallelised in this way, many similar recursive problems have not, and new ones constantly emerge. Given that these problems — specifically in bioinformatics — are often large or long running, it would be ideal if we could exploit any available concurrency using massively-parallel processors of the sort available in graphics cards.

The question is, can we develop a technique for mapping a recursive definition to a parallel environment? Such an approach would permit us to use recursions as a *host language* for describing parallel problems. This paper seeks to answer that question.

2.1 Dependent computations

For this, and further sections, we will assume that we have a single recursive problem that is to be computed in a bottom-up fashion using dynamic programming.

The first step to answering our question is to acknowledge that it is the recursive dependencies that will determine what, if any, form of concurrency will be available to us. Any parallel scheme we choose will need to respect the dependencies in the problem.

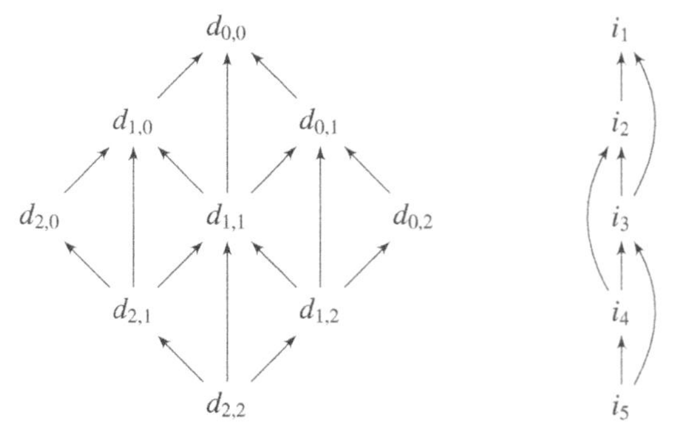

(a) Edit distance (b) Fibonacci

Figure 2. An example of the difference between a linear (2b) and a wide dependency graph (2a)

.

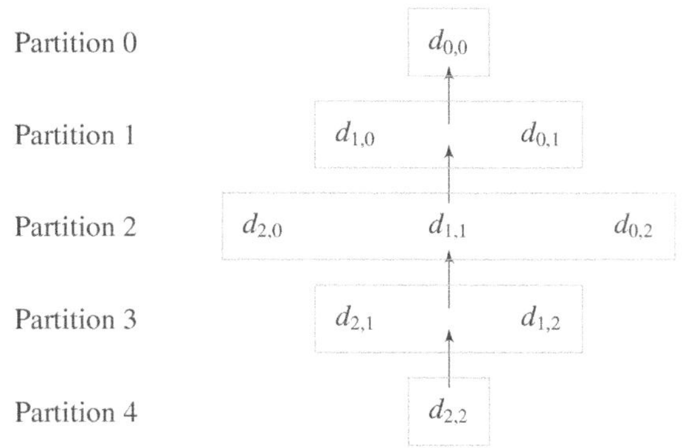

Figure 3. A valid diagonal schedule for the 3x3 edit distance problem. This schedule has five partitions.

Figure 2 contains the contrasting *dependency graphs* for the edit distance algorithm on a 3x3 problem and a straight-forward recursive definition of the Fibonacci sequence for *fib*(5). It is clear that the Fibonacci recursion permits no parallel solution — analysing each sub-problem only unlocks one other sub-problem. In comparison, sub-problems in the edit distance recursion can clearly unlock multiple other sub-problems — once we compute $d_{0,0}$, we can compute either $d_{1,0}$ or $d_{0,1}$. We say that the computation of $d_{1,0}$ is *independent* of $d_{0,1}$, and therefore the problem provides no constraints on the order of evaluation between the two. Consequently, we can evaluate them one after another, or even evaluate them simultaneously. It is this independence property within problems that we hope to exploit when identifying a parallel solution.

2.2 Scheduling partitions

Any form of concurrency requires that we identify a number of computations that can be executed simultaneously. This is especially important when we are developing an intra-multiprocessor application for a graphics card, where all threads must work in sync with each other.

In a finite recursive problem, such as the edit distance problem, we might think of this as dividing the elements in the domain — that is, the recursive calls in the dependency graph — into sets of computations that can be concurrently executed. Our intuitive understanding of "can be concurrently executed" here should be that the computations are independent, that is, the elements in the set should not depend on any other elements in the set, either directly or indirectly.

It is clear that a single problem may permit many different partitions, and that partitions may even overlap. Each partition may also require some dependencies to have been computed before the partition itself can be evaluated.

To this end we define a *schedule*, a group of partitions that together cover the entire domain and do not overlap. As implied by the term schedule, this defines a total order between partitions in the domain, providing a fixed sequence of execution and simplifying the dependency graph. Figure 3 illustrates a valid scheduling of the 3x3 edit distance problem. We can think of each partition as a *time-step* of the computation.

Typically a schedule for a function f is defined as a mapping or function from the original domain to the partitions of the schedule[9]. We denote this schedule as S_f — the *scheduling function* for f.

For example, if we have two sets of arguments to f, $\bar{x}$ and $\bar{y}$, then if $S_f(\bar{x}) = S_f(\bar{y})$ we know that we can independently evaluate the results $f(\bar{x})$ and $f(\bar{y})$. In our edit distance example, if $S_d(0,1) = S_d(1,0)$ then we can deduce that $d(0,1)$ and $d(1,0)$ can be computed independently of each other.

We note that any technique that defines S_f explicitly as a direct enumeration of the cells of each partition is doomed to fail — to do so would be both memory intensive and difficult to determine efficiently a priori on problems of varying sizes.

Instead, we make the analysis tractable and the implementation possible by restricting the schedule to be an affine function. Affine functions allow us to describe a wide-variety of *regular* partitions of the dependency graph with a single function, which can then be used to synthesise a parallel solution.

In the edit distance example (Figure 3) it is clear that an appropriate scheduling function is $S_d = x + y$ — the parallel lines which represent independent values are described by the equation $x + y = c$, where c is the current partition. Figure 4 illustrates some schedules commonly found in scientific problems.

2.3 Choosing a schedule

It is clear that not all schedules are created equal. We must therefore define some criteria for choosing an appropriate schedule such that it is both *valid* and *efficient*.

As we previously observed, the validity of a schedule is determined by the dependencies described in the recursive function. In other words, a valid schedule is one that ensures that any dependency between two elements is fulfilled by executing the dependent before the dependee. We can do this in an inductive fashion, by proving any direct dependencies of an element are fulfilled before evaluating that element. What are the dependencies of f? The recursive calls of f; each different set of arguments to a recursive call constitutes a potential dependency.

We will formalise this choice by identifying from each recursive call a *criterion* on valid schedules. The key condition which we wish to maintain is that the partition — e.g time-step — of the recursive call is less than that of the current call. Take, for example, the edit distance algorithm in Figure 1. It has three recursive calls $d(x-1,y)$, $d(x,y-1)$ and $d(x-1,y-1)$. We will therefore need to prove that the following equations hold:

$$S_d(x,y) > S_d(x-1,y),$$
$$S_d(x,y) > S_d(x,y-1)$$
$$S_d(x,y) > S_d(x-1,y-1)$$

If, as before, we select $S_d(x,y) = x + y$, it is clear that all three are true, therefore this is a valid schedule.

An efficient schedule is one which will make best use of the resources available. In an ideal world, we would take in to consideration the exact configuration of the hardware available — including the number of cores and their purpose. However, it may not be practical to determine this precisely. We will instead aim to minimise the number of partitions we need to evaluate, as that will provide a reasonable proxy for an efficient solution. This maximises the average size of each partition.

Again, if we consider the edit distance example, an equally valid schedule would be $S_d(x,y) = 2x + y$, however this results in more partitions and would therefore be considered a less efficient schedule. There are very few occasions where a schedule with more partitions will be more efficient. These arguments are further developed in Section 4.

3. A hosted language environment for massively parallel architectures

In the previous section we have outlined how we might identify a parallel solution for a language that is sufficient to describe recursively defined problems at a high-level. However, the majority

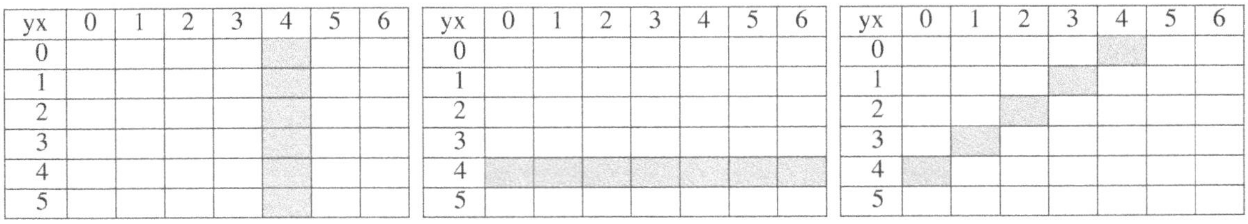

(a) $S_f = x$ (b) $S_f = y$ (c) $S_f = x + y$

Figure 4. An example of three parallel strategies for the two dimensional case. Each case highlights the partition where $S_f = 4$.

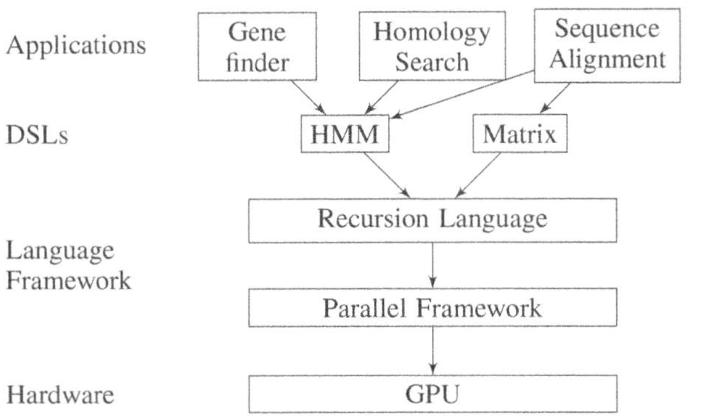

Figure 5. The levels of a hosted language environment for massively parallel architectures

of problems require more than a pure recursive function to describe. In bioinformatics, problems often refer to models, data matrices or other structures or systems. In addition, a simple recursive language may not provide the necessary terseness or clarity in the language to aid the domain-focused user.

To this end, we will integrate our simple recursive language into a wider framework for hosting domain specific languages targeting GPUs. Our system will be designed to match, as closely as is practical, the descriptions of algorithms that scientists typically provide in papers. Figure 5 describes the architecture of our system. Each DSL can be written as an extension to our base language, which is a DSL in itself for describing parallel computations..

This approach has a number of benefits. It takes the common elements from many domains, and uses a unified language to describe them. Our work in effectively parallelising this host language is therefore shared amongst many different domains, and provides a common language based on how these problems are typically described. At the same time, the extensions we write for specific domains allows implementors to concentrate on how to parallelise the elements unique to that domain, such as how to layout a particular model in memory. We later (Section 5) show how our base language can permit a wide range of extensions without breaking the parallelisation rules.

Our language is designed to mimic the style of a scripting language, providing basic operations — in this case recursive functions — and allowing users to potentially combine different DSLs. We will provide statements in the language for function definition, file loading, printing and function execution, including a map primitive, allowing us to map a function to a sequence of arguments. This map primitive supports the high-level inter-multiprocessor parallelisation.

```
Func ::= funcname varname* Expr
Expr ::= Expr + Expr | Expr − Expr | Expr × Expr | Expr/Expr
       | Expr < Expr | Expr > Expr | Expr = Expr | Expr! = Expr
       | Expr min Expr | Expr max Expr
       | (Expr)
       | Var[Expr]
       | Var
       | funcname(Expr*)
       | integer
       | if Expr then Expr else Expr
Var  ::= varname
```

Figure 6. The grammar for the domain specific language describing the permitted operations

3.1 Function definition

We provide the function definition section of our grammar in Figure 6. An example of a function for the edit-distance problem is given in Figure 7. We have based it on pure function definitions, with common arithmetic operations and recursive calls. The recursive function calls are only to named functions — no higher order or first class functions are allowed, and so no pointer analysis is required. This is a key restriction for a tractable analysis. In addition, we only support single recursive functions, as the analysis of mutually recursive functions is significantly more difficult.

Recursive calls are also restricted by limiting the *descent functions* — that is, the function that is applied to the original arguments to get the recursive arguments. Like the scheduling function, and for similar reasons, we will enforce that the descent functions are affine functions on the parameters. Without restriction, it will be difficult to enforce that the recursive calls only refer to partitions of a lower value.

The majority of applications in bioinformatics are based on analysis of sequences of characters, and so we provide a *sequence* primitive which can be queried by index. No further operations are provided on sequences — sequences are immutable. In particular, recursion on sub-sequences is only supported through indices.

The only conditional operation we will allow is a branching *if* expression. To allow branching to occur, we must allow conditional operators, which will consist of the numerical comparison operators, and an equality comparison for characters. Although the base language provides no looping construct, it is an operation that we could add with a domain extension — e.g looping over a data model.

By constraining the allowed functions we permit a tractable analysis — we do not preclude an analysis of a more comprehensive definition. We simply take a pragmatic approach to support the most commonly found forms for scientific applications.

3.2 Type System

Our base language has a simple type system which includes the following primitive types: integers, characters, sequences, indices on sequences, floats, probabilities, booleans and alphabets. We justify the introduction of a probability type as well as a general floating point type by the frequency with which bioinformatics applications use probabilities. By introducing a high-level type, we can determine an appropriate low-level representation. For example, a frequent problem is underflow when dealing with multiplying small probabilities using floating points. We can counter this by converting probabilities to log space, where we can use addition instead of multiplication. Alternatively, we could introduce a custom extended exponent implementation.

Alphabets define a set of characters; sequence and character types are specified with reference to a particular alphabet. In the edit distance example (Figure 7), sequence s and t refer to the English alphabet, denoted by *en*. Indices specify the sequence to which they belong; this is necessary so we can determine the dimensions of the recursive problem for analysis and tabulation. In the edit distance example, index i references string s in this way, as does j with string t.

To support recursive functions with some invariant parameters, we introduce two classifications — calling and recursive. These classifications are baked in to the compiler — with each type belonging to either, neither or both. For a type to occur in the parameter declaration of a function, it must be either a calling or recursive type. The classifications are:

- *Calling* type — a type is a calling type when it must be instantiated before the problem can begin, and remains *constant* over a single recursive run.
- *Recursive* type — a type is a recursive type when it must be specified each time we recurse - it is therefore *varying*. The prototype for a recursive call is simply all the parameters whose types are annotated as recursive.

Sequences are a calling type, so in the edit distance example the strings (the sequences) s and t are defined once and remain constant over a single recursion, while we vary the indices i and j.

We have included two types in the framework that can act as recursive parameters — integers and explicit indices on sequences. Types may be both calling and recursive — for example, integer types, where the initial value determines the size of the domain. This is because the domain of all parameters must be finite for the method to be applicable, so we must specify an initial value for the integer domain. In the case of indices, they are naturally bound by the size of the sequence they reference.

We use this finite nature to our advantage to state that all recursive types must define a mapping between elements in their domain and the natural numbers. We can therefore assume in our analysis that parameters can be considered as natural numbers.

3.3 Intermediate Representation

The target of our high-level framework is a low-level intermediate representation we have devised to abstract away the details of a particular massively-parallel environment. This allows us to separate out the construction of the overall parallel framework from the exact environment. We only target NVIDIA CUDA graphics cards at this stage, but in principle our abstract representation would allow us to support other vendors in the future.

```
int d(seq[en] s, index[s] i, seq[en] t, index[t] j) =
  if i == 0 then
    j
  else if j == 0 then
    i
  else if s[i - 1] == t[j - 1] then
    d(i - 1, j - 1)
  else
    (d(i - 1, j) min d(i, j - 1) min d(i - 1, j - 1)) + 1
```

Figure 7. The source code of a simple edit distance recursion

```
parfor threads t in 0..tn
  for p in 0..max_partition:
    for elements of p assigned to t
      x0,...,xn = I(p, t)
      farr[x0,...,xn] = f(x0,...,xn)
    sync
```

Figure 8. The program synthesis template

4. Parallelising Recursive Functions

4.1 Overview

In this section we describe our process for synthesising a graphics card program from a recursive definition. Our method takes the following steps:

1. We first encode the dependencies of the recursion as a series of criteria on the scheduling function (Section 4.5).
2. We use these criteria and a suitable goal function to automatically find, using a constraint solver, the coefficients of a valid scheduling function, which is optimal with respect to the number of partitions required (Section 4.6).
3. Given a scheduling function, we synthesise a massively parallel program using a polyhedral code generation tool, CLooG[1] (Section 4.3).
4. Finally, we discuss the issue of evaluating multiple problems on the same GPU (Section 4.7).

4.2 Scheduling Functions

Thus far we have only described the scheduling function informally. It maps the elements in the domain of our function f — the possible calls to f — to partitions. A partition is an integer value, thus providing a total ordering over partitions. There may be many valid schedules for each function; different schemes of parallelising the problem are described by different schedules.

We will define a schedule for function f to be an affine function, named S_f with integer coefficients:

$$S_f = a_1 x_1 + \ldots + a_n x_n$$

Where $a_1, \ldots, a_n \in \mathbb{Z}$ and the *recursive* or *source* domain of f is defined as $X = X_1, \ldots, X_n$, where $\bar{x} \in X$ when $\bar{x} = (x_0, \ldots, x_n)$ and $x_i \in X_i$. The constraints on the function ensure that the analysis is tractable and the implementation efficient; they are not, however, fundamental limits and the extent to which they can be lifted will be discussed later in the section.

4.3 Program Synthesis

Scheduling functions provide a succinct way to describe the dependencies of a problem. However, to have any practical utility, we must be able to use it to synthesise a practical and efficient program. We start by tying this knot as a way to motivate and guide the search for a schedule.

Figure 8 outlines our approach: we will loop over the time-step partitions of the schedule in the domain, computing each partition entirely before synchronising and continuing on. Each thread will be allocated a number of elements to compute. For each partition, each thread will loop over all assigned elements.

The computation of each element proceeds by calling some function I to determine the indices of x associated with the current

```
for (p=0;p<=m+n;p++) {
 for (i=max(0,p-m);i<=min(n,p);i++) {
   S1(i,p-i);
 }
}
```

Figure 9. CLooG output for the edit distance problem with a scheduling (scattering) function of $S_d(x, y) = x + y$.

```
parfor threads t in 0..tn {
 for (p=0;p<=m+n;p++) {
  for (i=t+max(0,p-m);i<=min(n,p);i+=tn) {
    x0,x1 = i, (p - i);
    farr[x0,x1] = f(x0,x1);
  }
  sync
 }
}
```

Figure 10. Our conversion of the CLooG loop.

partition, thread and thread-step. We can then calculate the value and store it in the dynamic programming array, possibly for future use.

To formalise our approach, we will use the *polyhedral model*[12]. We can consider the original domain of our recursive function a polyhedron — a convex polyhedron representing the elements of $X_1, \ldots, X_n$ that the recursion can visits Our scheduling function then becomes an *affine transformation* of that source polyhedron to a target polyhedron, and I is the inverse of that transformation. The polyhedral model has been extensively researched in relation to loop parallelisation, however the principal is the same for recursions.

Using a scheduling function alone as an affine transformation creates a mapping from the recursive domain to a single dimension — the time-step. We still need iterate through all elements in the domain, assigning them to threads — a set of *space* dimensions.

CLooG[1] is a code-generation tool that can determine iterations over dimensions in this way. It takes, as input, the source polyhedron and the schedule — or *scattering function*, as it is described in CLooG. The output of this is a series of nested loops that iterate over the entire domain. In our case, the first, outer, loop will be over our partition time-steps. Each further nested loop represents a new space dimension of the target polyhedron, and the collection of all those inner nested loops iterates over all elements in the partition. This transformation should ensure that each element of the source — recursive — domain has an equivalent element in the target domain. Typically the number of dimensions in the target polyhedron will match that of the source polyhedron.

The code generated by CLooG will be a set of nested loops for a single thread. We must take one of the space dimension loops to use to map to our threads. We choose the outer loop. Given *tn* threads, with the thread designated by *t*, we can convert this loop:

```
for (int v = <start>; v < <end>; v+=<inc>)
```

by computing the entire range in groups of *tn* threads, like so:

```
for (int v = <start> + t; v < <end>; v+=(<inc>+tn))
```

Consider the edit distance example, where $S_f(x, y) = x + y$. Figure 9 describes the output given by CLooG. Figure 10 gives our parallel version of the loop.

4.4 Formalising function dependencies

The derivation of a suitable schedule is the first step in our compilation process. For that, we will first need to formalise the description of the dependencies between function calls.

Recall that f is a pure function, so we know that the result of the function is dependent only on the arguments in the domain. We can therefore define a call, c, as the list of the arguments, $y_0, \ldots y_n$, to the function f, where each y_i is a value in the domain of the equivalent parameter of f.

Let $G(C, E)$ be the call graph for f, where C is the set of possible calls and E is a set of edge pairs (c_1, c_2). The edge (c_1, c_2) represents the case when c_1 *may* call c_2. We do no branch analysis based on conditionals — instead, we consider all recursive calls in the function to be part of E. We will say $c_1 \to c_2$ when $(c_1, c_2) \in E$.

Using E we can define the relation $\leadsto$ — the transitive closure of E. We can think of this as the transitive closure of the dependency graph. Validation of S_f can then be defined in terms of the transitive closure:

$$c_1 \leadsto c_2 \Rightarrow S_f(c_1) > S_f(c_2) \tag{1}$$

This is the *partition ordering* condition. The definition encompasses two important properties. The first is that there is an implicit ordering over partitions, such that if we evaluate the lowest time-step partition followed by the next time-step partition and so on, we are guaranteed to maintain the order of dependencies required by $\leadsto$.

The second is that two elements in a single partition must be *independent*. A pair of calls, c_1, c_2, are then described as *independent* iff there is no call path between them, that is $c_1 \not\leadsto c_2$. If two calls are independent, they can be computed without reference to each other, and therefore can be computed synchronously. The partition ordering condition implies just that:

$$S_f(c_1) = S_f(c_2) \Rightarrow c_1 \not\leadsto c_2 \tag{2}$$

By finding integer coefficients $a_1, \ldots, a_n$ of $S_f = a_1x_1 + \ldots + a_nx_n$ such that it adheres to 1, we will use this implication of independence to generate a parallel implementation.

4.5 Validity of a schedule

We have now defined the properties of a valid schedule. However, as formulated in (1), it is difficult to efficiently apply directly to a schedule. In this section, we derive a set of *criteria* that valid schedules adhere to.

This has two practical consequences — firstly, users can specify a schedule that we can then verify. Secondly, we will use the validity criteria to automatically determine a schedule (Section 4.6).

For a S_f to be valid, it must adhere to the implication in (1). We will show this inductively, by considering the direct dependencies of the call. Recall that $\leadsto$ is the transitive closure of $\to$ ($c_1 \leadsto c_2 \Rightarrow c_1 \to^\star c_2$). We can thus satisfy our condition by proving that for all $c_1 \to c_2$ the following holds:

$$c_1 \to c_2 \Rightarrow S_f(c_1) > S_f(c_2) \tag{3}$$

So far we have simply stated that $\to$ is the set of all direct dependencies of calls. We will need to define $\to$ in terms of the recursive calls of the function.

For a function $f(x_1, \ldots, x_n)$, a recursive call will consist of $f(xr_1, \ldots, xr_n)$, where xr_i are linear combinations of the initial parameters, e.g $xr_i = b_{i,1}x_1 + \ldots + b_{i,n}x_n + c_i$. These xr are the *descent functions* of the recursive call.

Each recursive call therefore represents a *set* of dependencies, described by:

$$\{(x_1, \ldots, x_n) \to (xr_1, \ldots, xr_n) | \forall x_1, \ldots, x_n\}$$

For each recursive call site, we will need to verify that this set satisfies (3). Substituting in our S_f equations:

$$S_f(x_1, \ldots, x_n) - S_f(xr_1, \ldots, xr_n) > 0, \forall x_1, \ldots, x_n$$

Recalling our pre-condition that S_f is affine, and evaluating by variable substitution, this is equivalent to the following condition:

$$a_1(x_1 - xr_1) + \ldots + a_n(x_n - xr_n) > 0, \forall x_1, \ldots, x_n$$

This equation denotes the *criteria* on a valid schedule. We derive one criterion for each recursive call in the function, and confirm that a S_f is valid by confirming it satisfies all the criteria.

When the descent function xr_i is uniform (e.g of the form $x_i + c_i$) — the majority of practical cases — this equation will simplify to $(-a_1c_1) + \ldots + (-a_nc_n) > 0$, which is straight-forward to analyse. For any descent function that is affine (e.g of the form $A\bar{x} + \bar{c}$), the criteria will require the runtime range of x to determine the validity.

4.6 Automatically determining a schedule

In the previous section, we derived a series of criteria which we used to verify a pre-existing schedule, perhaps provided by a user. In this section, we will use the same criteria to derive a schedule on behalf of the user. This is fully automatic — no further user input beyond the recursion is required. In this way, we can support both automatic and user-specified parallelisation schemes.

Our aim is to describe a Constraint Satisfaction Problem (CSP) that combines the criteria of the previous section — which will enforce the validity of the scheduling function — with a selection measure which will help choose an efficient schedule. We can then pass these conditions and goal into a suitable CSP solver to find the coefficients $a_1, \ldots, a_n$ of a solution S_f.

By necessity, the selection measure will need to be a heuristic — the various factors that affect the execution time are difficult to predict prior to execution, and may include which memory operations occur and when, the number of instructions, the size of the problem and the exact hardware used.

As such, the heuristic we have chosen is the number of partitions required to evaluate the entire table. By minimising the number of partitions, we are maximising the average size of a partition, and therefore maximising the ideal amount of parallelisation provided by an "ideal device" with infinite synchronous cores. In practice, we have a fixed number of cores, so we will have to evaluate partitions in blocks, regardless of the size of the partition.

If we have a schedule, $S_f(\bar{x}) = a_1x_1 + \ldots + a_nx_n$, where $\bar{x} = x_1, \ldots, x_n$, then we can compute the minimum number of partitions by minimising the difference between the largest and the smallest partition in the range, using the following formula:

$$min_{a_1,\ldots,a_n}(max_{\bar{x}}(S_f(\bar{x})) - min_{\bar{x}}(S_f(\bar{x}))) \quad (4)$$

Our intention is to construct this as a CSP over $a_1, \ldots, a_n$. However, it is clear that equation (4) is not a linear problem — we are trying to solve for both a and x. How can we encode this as a CSP problem if it is not linear?

The solution to this apparent problem comes from the observation that S_f is linear, and therefore the maximum value of S_f occurs when each component of S_f is maximised. How do we maximise a_ix_i? As we run our algorithm at runtime, we allow ourselves the luxury of knowing the range of x_i, e.g $0 \leq x_i < n_i$. We can therefore maximise the component by maximising x_i, if a_i is positive, and minimising x_i if a_i is negative. We can do the reverse to minimise the component, and thus find the minimum expression

With this approach we will need to evaluate up to 2^n different constraint problems to find the solution. This is practical for two reasons: the majority of applications are between two or three dimensions, and in most of cases, the criteria may predispose us to eliminate a subset of these problems — for example, if we already know $a_i > 0$ then $x_i = n_i - 1$, as it is the largest value in the range.

For each constraint problem, we specify the maximum and minimum values of $x_1, \ldots, x_n$, use equation (4) as the goal we wish to minimise, and add a criteria for each recursive call, as discussed in the previous section. If a result is found, we store the minimum goal value found, and the first set of solution coefficients, and continue to the next problem, until we have checked or eliminated all dimensions.

4.7 Multiple problems

Our technique so far discusses how to map a single problem to a single multiprocessor — rather than employing all multiprocessors in a GPU. Typically a single problem is *tiled* across the multiprocessors, however bioinformatics often deals with large numbers of small problems. The compilation algorithm above makes use of the precise bounds of each domain to determine the best S_f and a_f. Different problem sizes may therefore require different schedules to run efficiently. What we want is to evaluate the problems simultaneously on different multiprocessors, so we must synthesise a solution that can apply different schedules to each problem.

To this end, we have developed a *conditional* parallelisation technique, where we adapt the CSP to derive multiple valid schedules. Considering all selected schedules, we then derive conditions under which each particular schedule is *minimal*, which we then evaluate at runtime on a problem-by-problem basis to determine which generated parallelisation code to use. For example, given a function $f(x, y) = \ldots f(x-1, y-1)\ldots$, the minimal schedule depends on the length — when $n_x < n_y$ then $S_f(x, y) = x$ otherwise $S_f(x, y) = y$.

Our solution proceeds by adapting the CSP for the schedule to remove the goal value. Instead of deriving a single, minimal, solution, we instead propagate the constraints to derive the valid range of each variable. The descent functions must be uniform, as we can no longer consider runtime ranges.

Given the ranges of values found by the CSP, we could loop over all the possible coefficients for the scheduling function. However, we would identify many schedules that are valid but never minimal for any value in the domain. e.g, in our previous example we might find the following non-minimal schedules (2, 1),(2, 2),(3, 3), when it is clear that the only minimal schedules are (1, 0) and (0, 1). Formally, a schedule is *minimal* iff the coefficients a of the schedule satisfy $\exists\bar{x} \in X : \forall\bar{b} \in P : \bar{a}\bar{x} < \bar{b}\bar{x}$, where P is the set of valid schedules.

Identifying the complete set of minimal schedules a priori is tricky. Instead, we determine a subset of the minimal schedules with positive coefficients using the following method:

1. Create all $n!$ permutations of the domains e.g in two dimensions 1, 2 and 2, 1
2. For each permutation, we minimise each dimension in turn, propagating the constraints until we find a solution which we add to the set. We therefore find the first lexicographical solution with respect to the permutation of dimensions. Each defined solution is minimal for some $\bar{x}$. We note that in practice the majority of problems have a single schedule, so the set size is far smaller than $n!$.

It may seem that this method is potentially expensive. To limit this effect, we restrict the coefficients to a small fixed number (10) that is customisable by the end user and note that n is usually small. Additionally, unlike the runtime analysis described for single problems, this analysis can be performed during compile time.

For each schedule found, we find use CLooG to generate the appropriate set of nested loops to iterate over the space. We use the conditions to determine which of the generated code paths to take. This does not lead to any unnecessary code branching on the GPU, as a single problem will be alllocated to a single multiprocessor, and each thread on that multiprocessor will choose the same schedule.

4.8 Sliding window optimisation

In a traditional dynamic programming algorithm all prior results are stored until the computation is complete. One of the benefits of partitioning the dependency graph is that we can determine the range of previous results required, with respect to the number of partitions. We define this as the *sliding window* over the domain.

When the recursive descent functions are uniform, we can use the precise value of each criteria to determine the size of the sliding window, in terms of the number of previous partitions required. When the descent functions are affine, this is not possible. This optimisation is especially relevant for a GPU, since it will allow us to store a much smaller table for the intermediate values. This smaller table will typically fit in a cache that is much closer to the processor, such as shared memory on a NVIDIA GPU, almost eliminating the significant latency to global memory.

4.9 Limitations of the Approach

We have made it clear that we are only considering affine scheduling and descent functions — that is, linear combinations of the coefficients. We justify this limitation in three ways:

1. Goods solvers are available which can determine solutions in linear cases — if the recursive parameters or the scheduling function were not linear, we would not be able to use CSP or linear programming techniques.
2. We can synthesise good target code in the linear case; it is not clear how a non-linear function would be synthesised because it would be difficult to find the inverse transformation.
3. Problems in bioinformatics, our target domain, infrequently require non-linear cases.

In addition, for our technique in Section 4.7, we require uniform descent functions. This restriction is necessary as an affine descent would require knowledge of the runtime range to evaluate.

Our approach is optimal with respect to the number of partitions we evaluate. However, this does not guarantee a minimal execution time. In particular, we will typically evaluate a partition in *blocks* of threads. Doing so can lead to wasted execution on the GPU, where a theoretically worse schedule might, in fact do better.

5. Domain Extensions

In Section 3, we described our proposed architecture in which our simple base language can be expanded by domain specific extensions. The intention of such DSLs is not that they relax any of the limitations set out in the paper, but instead be used to extend the data-structure and traversal operations to support specific applications. The following features can be defined as language extensions without modification to the described compilation algorithm:

- The introduction of any branching expression;
- Create new "recursive" data-types on the condition there is a defined mapping to the natural numbers;
- Create new looping expressions, where the extension can define the range of the loops at runtime, and can therefore derive solvable criteria on recursions within the loop.

New extensions should cover areas with wide applicability, so that the cost of a cross-specialist developing the extension is amortised across a wide array of applications. For the purpose of our evaluation, we have produced two such extensions — "Hidden Markov Models" and "Substitution Matrices". Both are widely used in bioinformatics, and extend our interesting, but neutered, language to something which can tackle real problems in that domain.

5.1 Substitution Matrices

Substitution Matrices represent a simple data-extension to our language. They allow the user to describe the cost of substituting one character in an alphabet for another. We introduce a new statement to our language for defining the matrix with a straight-forward table. This is represented by a new type, matrix, that can be passed to functions, and a new expression to load the substition value.

$$Expr \quad ::= \quad \ldots \mid Var[Expr, Expr]$$

The introduction of this expression has no affect on the recursion analysis. The generated load code for this expression will depend where we locate the table; in shared memory for small tables or global memory for large.

5.2 Hidden Markov Models

A Hidden Markov Model (HMM) is a statistical model for random stochastic processes, constructed as a probabilistic finite automata. Models consist of a set of states, where transitions between states are associated with a probability. Each transition only depends on the current state - the *markov* property. The *hidden* part of the name derives from the fact that we cannot observe the states - instead each state contains a distribution over some *emission alphabet*.

As with the substitution matrix, we introduce a new statement to our language for defining the HMM model. This allows the user to define states, transitions and emissions. With it we introduce some new types - a HMM calling type, to pass the model to the function, and state and transitions as recursive types. To be able to tabulate recursions using states or transitions we provide an arbitrary total ordering over each one, providing a mapping to the natural numbers (see Section 3.2). The ordering is arbitrary because no recursion depends on the position of the states.

We add the following new expressions for exploring the model:

$$\begin{array}{lll} Expr & ::= & \ldots \\ & \mid & Var.start \\ & \mid & Var.end \\ & \mid & Var.isstart \\ & \mid & Var.isend \\ & \mid & Var.emission[Expr] \\ & \mid & Var.transitionsto \\ & \mid & Var.transitionsfrom \\ & \mid & sum(var\ in\ Expr\ :\ Expr) \end{array}$$

`start` and `end` load the states associated with a transition. `isstart` and `isend` determine whether the state is the last or the first. `emission[Expr]` is the probability of a state emitting the Expr value.

The final expressions `transitionsto` and `transitionsfrom` are for identifying the sets of transitions to and from a state. We provide a summation statement (amongst others such as max and min), which can iterate over these sets of transitions.

Figure 11 compares the mathematical description of one of the canonical HMM algorithms to the implementation in our language. We recurse over s, the states in the HMM, and i, the indices into the sequence x.

The only new expression that affects the recursion analysis is the summation expression. The expression evaluated for each element may include a recursive call that depends on the newly created variable. For example, the forward algorithm has a recursive call using the start state of the transition within the sum (Line 8). For the

$F(0,0) = 1$
$F(s,0) = 0 \; for \; s > 0$
$F(s,i) = e_{s,x[i]} \sum_{p:t_{p,s}>0} t_{p,s} F(p, i-1)$

(a) The recursive equation, where $F(s,i)$ is the likelihood we are in state s at position i in the sequence x. $t_{s,p}$ is the probability of transitioning from state s to state p

```
prob forward(hmm h, state[h] s, seq[*] x, index[x] i) =
    if i == 0 then
        if s.isstart then 1.0 else 0.0
    else
        // The end state is silent
        (if s.isend then 1.0 else s.emission[x[i-1]])
        * sum(t in s.transitionsto :
              t.prob * forward(t.start, i - 1))
```

(b) The implementation in our extension

Figure 11. The forward algorithm, mathematical description compared to the implementation

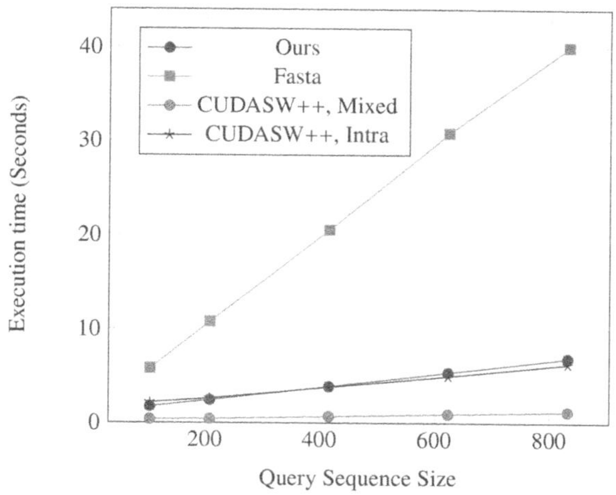

Figure 12. Smith-Waterman performance on varying query sequence sizes for a database of 75,000 sequences.

purpose of the analysis, we assume that the newly created variable - in this case t - can vary over all possible values and thus t.start, in this case, varies over any state. We conclude that our schedule can only be $S_{forward}(s,i) = i$.

6. Evaluation

There are two factors that will influence performance using our framework. The first is the choice of schedule, the second is the low-level implementation. In this paper, we have concentrated on selecting the former. We have chosen our schedule to be minimal with respect to the number of partitions. This choice was justified in Section 4.6, however we will note, for those that desire something more practical, that quantitative justification would be hard to achieve beyond the observation that in the given examples — edit distance, HMM algorithms — it produces the expected result.

As this paper has described the construction of a DSL *framework* our aim in this section is to demonstrate that we can use it to build efficient DSLs. For this reason we choose to analyse a number of DSLs rather than a specific DSL in detail. Each of our three case studies uses the base language described here, plus an extension, and is compared to existing CPU and, where possible, GPU applications to show that our framework is up to scratch.

These case studies are real applications in bioinformatics, using real genome data on existing models to provide a realistic comparison. In all cases our framework automatically derived the parallelisation schemes — no schedules were specified by the user. In each case we compare against a hand-coded GPU application, our tool has succesfully derived the same parallel strategy as the hand-coded application.

All quoted results are inclusive of setup time, such as memory allocation and copying to/from device. Our framework provides a runtime environment. Consequently, the times for our software are inclusive of scanning and parsing the input files. We have not, however, included the code generation time - we cache the compiled code for each function. The code generation overhead is typically around 1 second, primarily due to inefficiencys in the way in which we call ClooG from Java. We expect to be able to reduce this overhead drastically in future releases. We note that programs written in DSLs of this type are rarely large enough to increase this compilation overhead.

Results were obtained on a NVIDIA GTX 480 with 1.5GB of RAM, and CPU results using Intel Xeon E5520 CPU with 4GB of RAM. Each test was performed three times, and the results averaged. Results across runs were observed to be regular, and so we have not provided error bars.

6.1 Smith-Waterman

The Smith-Waterman algorithm is an implementation of the local edit distance problem, used for sequence alignment. The typical application will compare one *query* sequence against a database of other sequences, to identify high-scoring alignments. We implement the Smith-Waterman algorithm using the substitution matrix extension to determine the cost of substituting characters. The expected parallelisation is along the diagonal $x + y$, as with other edit distance algorithms.

For comparison, we use CUDASW++ 2.0[13] a GPU implementation of Smith-Waterman using the NVIDIA CUDA framework and the ssearch tool in Fasta[16], compiled without SSE2 vector instructions. CUDASW++ 2.0 provides two methods of parallelisation — intra-task parallelisation, which uses parallel diagonals across the table in the same way as our recursion, and an inter-task parallelisation, with a database sequence allocated per thread. Best performance is achieved by a hybrid approach, where smaller sequences are computed with inter-task and larger with intra-task. We provide both the hybrid and the intra-task results for CUDASW++ for comparison.

Our results (Figure 12) are very similar to the intra-task CUDASW++, and comfortably beat Fasta, demonstrating that we are reaching similar performance to the hand-coded, hand-tuned CUDASW++ for this type of parallelisation. As expected, the best overall performance is achieved by using the hybrid parallelisation approach. For this paper we have deliberately focused on automatic parallelisation in an intra-task manner. This is because inter-task parallelisation is algorithmically trivial. Although we have not covered the techniques in this paper, generation of a sequence-per-thread kernel as well as a intra-task kernel is straight-forward from our DSL code, and we would expect to achieve results on par with the hybrid CUDASW++.

6.2 Gene-finding Hidden Markov Models

Gene finding or gene prediction is the process of identifying genes in regions of DNA. They are often described using Hidden Markov Models, which are trained to recognise statistical features of genes, and used for likelihood estimation and prediction.

We build a simple gene-finder using our HMM extension language. We compare our results against HMMoC 1.3[14], a code-

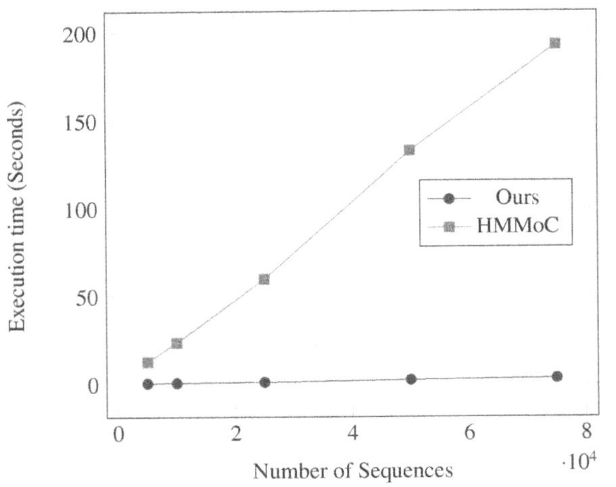

Figure 13. Gene-finding performance on varying sequence sizes.

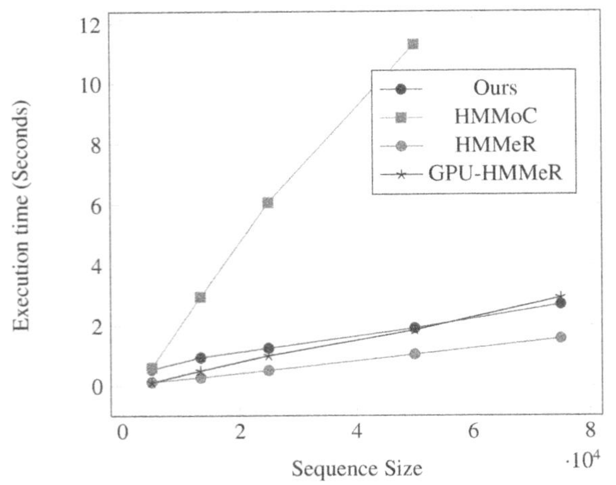

Figure 14. Performance on the TK model of 10 positions, with varying numbers of sequences.

generation tool for HMMs on CPUs. Our results (Figure 13) show a significant performance increase in line with the expected results over a CPU technique on this application — at larger database sizes, when we are using the GPU to its full extent, the performance increase is about x60. HMMoC is single-threaded application; considering the relative strengths of the CPU and GPU this speed-up is in line with what we might expect. As far as we are aware, there are no existing equivalent tools for GPUs.

6.3 Profile Hidden Markov Models

Profile HMMs are a type of HMM designed for representing a family of sequences. Typical applications include training models and database searching, where we apply a database of sequences to the profile model in order to determine new sequences that belong to a given family. We perform a database search using the forward algorithm on various sequence and profile models. Once again, we provide comparison to HMMoC, as a general purpose HMM tool, as well as to HMMeR[4], a special purpose tool for profile HMMs. In addition, we compare to a GPU port of HMMeR 2.0, GPU-HMMeR[21].

HMMeR is a high-performance, widely used tool — hand-coded and hand-tuned over 15 years to provide optimal performance on profile models. The latest version, HMMeR 3.0, uses

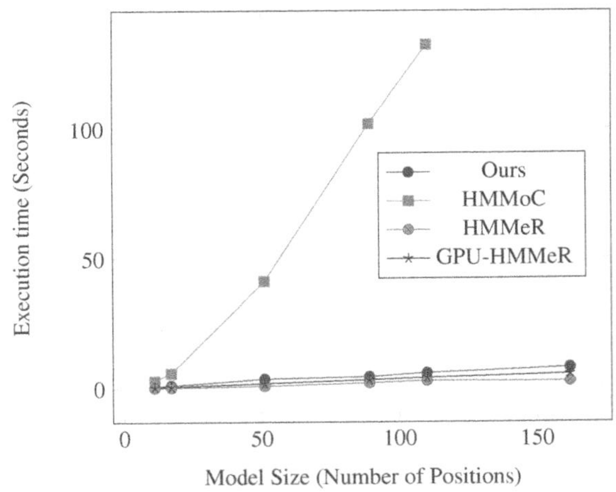

Figure 15. Performance on a dataset of 13,355 sequences, on models of a varying size.

a series of filters to remove low-scoring sequences at low cost by evaluating simplified models and algorithms, such as the MSV (Multiple Segment Viterbi), before bringing the full forward algorithm to bear on a much smaller set of problems. Whilst it would be both viable and beneficial to translate such techniques into our language, it would be a significant undertaking. To that end, we set the "–max" flag to turn off all such filtering and provide a fair comparison between a best of breed full forward algorithm for profile HMMs on the CPU to our GPU implementation.

Our results (Figures 14 and 15) show an expected large increase in performance over HMMoC for the GPU techniques. Our runtime performance is on par with GHMMeR. Any difference in performance is primarily due to the overhead of our runtime framework, and is smoothed out on larger sequence sets. However, all three are beaten by the most recently released version of HMMeR, 3.0.

Whilst it may at first this might be surprising, it must be remembered that HMMeR can make a number of assumptions about the nature of the problem that we are unable to do in a general HMM tool. HMMeR is also well optimised, using multiple threads and vectorised code on the CPU to maximise performance. However, this was a significant undertaking for the developers — what we provide is access to this type of performance across a much wider range of problems without the need to put in 15 years of optimisation into each one.

7. Related Work

Schedules were first proposed as a means of parallel analysis of recursive functions in the seminal paper by Karp et. al. [9], and further developed in [20]. Much of the further work in this area has been focused on loop parallelization[11], and in particular the *polyhedral* model[12] where it has been profitably used for code generation[1] for loop schedules.

There is a wealth of literature on parallel implementations of fully fledged functional programming languages, and a recent tutorial in the context of Haskell is [8]. We have consciously restricted our input language to enable more aggressive optimisations. Elliott [5] shows how functional programs can be used to generate efficient code for graphics operations on graphics processors. There is an overlap with this paper in that we use a restricted functional input language, but Elliott does not address the problem of mapping complex dynamic programming recursions to a GPU architecture.

DSLs are a growing trend in the graphics card world. Our approach of using a host language with extensions is very similar to the concept of "Language Virtualization" provided by the Delite framework[2]. Where our approaches differ is that we develop a host language that provides automatic parallelisation, where they make use of the use of the DSL capabilities of Scala to support the creation of extension which can provide parallelisation. Examples include *Liszt* for physics simulations and *OptiML* for machine learning. Other examples of graphics card DSLs include *Nikola*[15] and Obisidian[18], both embedded DSLs for array computations and FLAME[7] a DSL for dense linear algebra.

Algebraic Dynamic Programming[6] is an example of a DSL designed specifically for Dynamic Programming problems in bioinformatics using strings, and has recently been extended to GPUs[17]. Whilst similar to our approach, it is currently deals only in diagonal parallelisation with one input sequence per problem.

8. Conclusion

In this paper we have shown that scientists can automatically synthesise efficient GPU code from specifications that read like the algorithm descriptions in their papers. Our preliminary results show that performance of the synthesised code is on a par with hand-tuned code for several important real world examples. However, the advantage of our system is that it can support domains far beyond these single application hand-tuned implementations.

Our technique is to partition the domain of a recursion into sets of values that can be computed concurrently. We adopt the construction of scheduling functions to achieve this, and have described how we can select such a function and subsequently derive a graphics card implementation. We apply insights from loop parallelisation using polyhedra to recursively defined problems on modern synchronous processors.

We have shown that such an approach can produce efficient and effective results, with minimal work on the part of the domain-focused user, and without needing to know the architectural complexities of the graphics card — bringing high-level language approaches close to hand-optimised CPU and GPU performance.

9. Further Work

We would like to extend our work to support mutually recursive functions, by deriving multiple scheduling functions, one for each function, whose partition time-step values are compatible. The same principle holds as for a single scheduling function; if $S_f(\bar{x}) < S_g(\bar{y})$ then $f(\bar{x})$ must be computed before $g(\bar{y})$. This would allow us to support more complicated applications, such as RNA secondary structure prediction.

In Section 3.2 we provided a simplified view of the translation of complex parameters — the need for them to map to natural numbers. In practice, the ordering of the model elements may be important to achieve high performance — different orderings may permit or restrict the available schedules.

References

[1] C. Bastoul. Code generation in the polyhedral model is easier than you think. In *PACT'13 IEEE International Conference on Parallel Architecture and Compilation Techniques*, pages 7–16, Juan-les-Pins, France, September 2004.

[2] H. Chafi, Z. DeVito, A. Moors, T. Rompf, A. K. Sujeeth, P. Hanrahan, M. Odersky, and K. Olukotun. Language virtualization for heterogeneous parallel computing. In *OOPSLA '10: Proceedings of the ACM international conference on Object oriented programming systems languages and applications*, pages 835–847, New York, NY, USA, 2010. ACM. ISBN 978-1-4503-0203-6.

[3] R. Durbin, S. R. Eddy, A. Krogh, and G. Mitchison. *Biological Sequence Analysis: Probabilistic Models of Proteins and Nucleic Acids*. Cambridge University Press, July 1999. ISBN 0521629713.

[4] S. Eddy. HMMer Website, including User Manual. http://hmmer.wustl.edu.

[5] C. Elliott. Programming graphics processors functionally. In *Proceedings of the 2004 ACM SIGPLAN workshop on Haskell*, Haskell '04, pages 45–56, New York, NY, USA, 2004. ACM. ISBN 1-58113-850-4. doi: http://doi.acm.org/10.1145/1017472.1017482.

[6] R. Giegerich and C. Meyer. Algebraic dynamic programming. In *AMAST '02: Proceedings of the 9th International Conference on Algebraic Methodology and Software Technology*, pages 349–364, London, UK, 2002. Springer-Verlag. ISBN 3-540-44144-1.

[7] J. A. Gunnels, F. G. Gustavson, G. M. Henry, and R. A. van de Geijn. FLAME: Formal Linear Algebra Methods Environment. *ACM Transactions on Mathematical Software*, 27(4):422–455, Dec. 2001. ISSN 0098-3500. URL `http://doi.acm.org/10.1145/504210.504213`.

[8] S. L. P. Jones and S. Singh. A tutorial on parallel and concurrent programming in haskell. In P. W. M. Koopman, R. Plasmeijer, and S. D. Swierstra, editors, *Advanced Functional Programming*, volume 5832 of *Lecture Notes in Computer Science*, pages 267–305. Springer, 2008. ISBN 978-3-642-04651-3.

[9] R. M. Karp and M. Held. Finite-state processes and dynamic programming. *SIAM Journal on Applied Mathematics*, 15(3):693–718, 1967. doi: 10.1137/0115060.

[10] A. Krogh, I. S. Mian, and D. Haussler. A hidden markov model that finds genes in e.coli dna. *Nucleic Acids Research*, 22(22):4768–4778, 1994. doi: 10.1093/nar/22.22.4768.

[11] L. Lamport. The parallel execution of do loops. *Communications of The ACM*, 17:83–93, February 1974. doi: 10.1145/360827.360844.

[12] C. Lengauer. Loop parallelization in the polytope model. In *CONCUR '93, Lecture Notes in Computer Science 715*, pages 398–416. Springer-Verlag, 1993.

[13] Y. Liu, B. Schmidt, and D. Maskell. Cudasw++2.0: enhanced smith-waterman protein database search on cuda-enabled gpus based on simt and virtualized simd abstractions. *BMC Research Notes*, 3(1): 93, 2010. ISSN 1756-0500. doi: 10.1186/1756-0500-3-93.

[14] G. Lunter. HMMoC a compiler for hidden Markov models. *Bioinformatics*, 23(18):2485–2487, September 2007. doi: 10.1093/bioinformatics/btm350.

[15] G. Mainland and G. Morrisett. Nikola: embedding compiled gpu functions in haskell. In *Haskell '10: Proceedings of the third ACM Haskell symposium on Haskell*, pages 67–78, New York, NY, USA, 2010. ACM. ISBN 978-1-4503-0252-4.

[16] W. R. Pearson and D. J. Lipman. Improved tools for biological sequence comparison. *Proceedings of The National Academy of Sciences*, 85:2444–2448, 1988.

[17] P. Steffen, R. Giegerich, and M. Giraud. Gpu parallelization of algebraic dynamic programming. 2009. URL `HAL:http://hal.archives-ouvertes.fr/inria-00438219/en/`.

[18] J. Svensson, K. Claessen, and M. Sheeran. Gpgpu kernel implementation and refinement using obsidian. *Procedia Computer Science*, 1(1):2065 – 2074, 2010. ISSN 1877-0509. doi: DOI: 10.1016/j.procs.2010.04.231. ICCS 2010.

[19] A. van Deursen, P. Klint, and J. Visser. Domain-specific languages: an annotated bibliography. *SIGPLAN Not.*, 35:26–36, June 2000.

[20] H. Verge, C. Mauras, and P. Quinton. The alpha language and its use for the design of systolic arrays. *The Journal of VLSI Signal Processing*, 3:173–182, 1991. ISSN 0922-5773. URL `http://dx.doi.org/10.1007/BF00925828`. 10.1007/BF00925828.

[21] J. P. Walters, V. Balu, S. Kompalli, and V. Chaudhary. Evaluating the use of gpus in liver image segmentation and hmmer database searches. In *IPDPS '09: Proceedings of the 2009 IEEE International Symposium on Parallel&Distributed Processing*, pages 1–12, Washington, DC, USA, 2009. IEEE Computer Society. ISBN 978-1-4244-3751-1.

Parcae: A System for Flexible Parallel Execution

Arun Raman
Intel Research
Santa Clara, CA, USA
arun.a.raman@intel.com

Ayal Zaks
Intel Corporation
Haifa, Israel
ayal.zaks@intel.com

Jae W. Lee
Sungkyunkwan University
Suwon, Korea
jaewlee@skku.edu

David I. August
Princeton University
Princeton, NJ, USA
august@princeton.edu

Abstract

Workload, platform, and available resources constitute a parallel program's execution environment. Most parallelization efforts statically target an anticipated range of environments, but performance generally degrades outside that range. Existing approaches address this problem with dynamic tuning but do not optimize a multiprogrammed system holistically. Further, they either require manual programming effort or are limited to array-based data-parallel programs.

This paper presents Parcae, a generally applicable automatic system for platform-wide dynamic tuning. Parcae includes (i) the Nona compiler, which creates *flexible parallel programs* whose tasks can be efficiently reconfigured during execution; (ii) the Decima monitor, which measures resource availability and system performance to detect change in the environment; and (iii) the Morta executor, which cuts short the life of executing tasks, replacing them with other functionally equivalent tasks better suited to the current environment. Parallel programs made flexible by Parcae outperform original parallel implementations in many interesting scenarios.

Categories and Subject Descriptors D.1.3 [*Software*]: Concurrent Programming—Parallel Programming; D.3.4 [*Programming Languages*]: Processors—Compilers, Run-time environments

General Terms Design, Performance

Keywords automatic parallelization, code generation, compiler, flexible, multicore, parallel, performance portability, run-time, adaptivity, tuning

1. Introduction

The emergence of general-purpose multicore processors has resulted in a spurt of activity in parallel programming models. Justifiably, the primary focus of these programming models has been parallelism extraction. However, parallelism extraction is just one part of the problem of synthesizing well-performing programs which execute efficiently in a variety of execution environments. The other, equally important part is the tuning of the extracted parallelism [29, 30]. In the absence of intelligent tuning, a parallel program may perform worse than the original sequential program [23, 40].

PLDI'12, June 11–16, 2012, Beijing, China.

Parallel program performance depends on several environmental *run-time* factors. Synchronization and communication overheads are often difficult to predict and may erode the benefits of parallelism [40]. Parallel resources available to the program may vary, including number of cores and memory bandwidth [9, 23]. In addition, application workload can change during execution. Most parallel programs are produced by programmers or compilers with a single static parallelism configuration encoded at development or compile time. Any single program configuration is likely to become suboptimal with changes in the execution environment [33, 40].

Libraries such as OpenMP and Intel Threading Building Blocks allow programmers to encode multiple program configurations implicitly, and have an appropriate configuration chosen at run-time based on the execution environment [33, 40]. These libraries, however, require programmers to expend considerable efforts (re-) writing the parallel program. Furthermore, the run-time systems of these libraries optimize the execution of individual programs, without exploring platform-wide implications and opportunities.

Ideally, compilers should automatically generate flexible parallel programs which adapt to changes in their execution environment. Existing compiler and run-time systems tune parameters such as the degree of parallelism of data-parallel (DOALL) loops and block size of loops, either statically or dynamically, to match the execution environment [3, 5, 14, 17, 41, 44]. These systems are limited to optimizing array-based programs with communication-free data-parallelism, where the performance impact of those parameters can be relatively easily modeled. However, for general-purpose programs with complex dependency patterns, parallelism is typically non-uniform and involves explicit synchronization or communication. This significantly complicates performance modeling, often resulting in a large space of possibly effective parallelism configurations. Existing compiler-based parallelization algorithms for such general-purpose programs select a single configuration, typically one deemed most suitable for an unloaded platform [34, 43, 47].

This paper presents Parcae, a compiler and run-time software system that delivers performance portability for both array-based programs and general-purpose programs, extending the applicability of prior work. The Parcae compiler, Nona, creates flexible parallel programs by (i) extracting multiple types of parallelism from a program region; (ii) creating code to efficiently pause, reconfigure, and resume its execution; and (iii) inserting profiling hooks for a run-time system to monitor its performance. The Parcae run-time system, comprising the Decima monitor and the Morta executor, maximizes overall system performance by (i) monitoring program performance and system events, such as launches of new programs, to detect change in the execution environment, and (ii) determining the best configurations of all flexible parallel programs executing concurrently for the new environment.

We evaluate Parcae on two real platforms with 8 and 24 cores. Flexible parallel execution enabled by Parcae is compared with conventional parallel execution of programs generated by a compiler applying high quality parallelizing transforms: PS-DSWP [34, 43] and DOANY [31, 46], targeting 8 and 24 threads with OS load balancing. Across seven benchmarks, Parcae reduces execution time by -1.4% (a small slowdown) to 41.9% with concomitant estimated processor energy savings of 23.9% to 83.9%. Platform-wide, Parcae reduces execution time of an entire workload by 12.8% to 53.5% with concomitant estimated processor energy savings of 22.4% to 76.3%.

In summary, the main contributions of this work are:

1. a compilation framework that is sufficiently powerful to automatically transform both array-based and general-purpose sequential programs into flexible parallel programs (Section 3),
2. a lightweight monitoring and execution framework to determine and enforce platform-wide optimal parallelism configurations of multiple concurrently executing programs (Section 4), and
3. a prototype implementation and its evaluation on seven benchmarks demonstrating its effectiveness in delivering robust portable performance (Section 6).

2. Run-time Variability and Implications

During program execution, the workload processed by the program may change phase or the parallel resources available to the program may vary. As an example, consider the problem of determining an ideal program configuration while the number of cores allocated to a program by the OS varies. This is a common scenario in platforms that are shared by multiple programs. Figure 1 shows optimized performance of the `blackscholes` option pricing benchmark from the PARSEC benchmark suite [7]. The compiler parallelized the outermost loop using a three-stage pipeline parallelization scheme (sequential-parallel-sequential). The program was executed on two different platforms, processing three different reference inputs, and making use of different number of cores. Observe that:

- On both platforms, the parallel version performs worse than sequential if three cores or fewer are employed.
- On Platform 1, the parallel version scales to 8 cores on Input 1, plateaus at 6 cores on Input 2, and is only slightly better than sequential on Input 3.
- On Platform 2, the parallel version scales to 10 cores but degrades afterwards on Input 1, plateaus at 4 cores on Input 2 (with 34% speedup), and performs worse than sequential on Input 3.

The reason for poor performance on Input 3 is the significantly greater communication bandwidth requirement, which overwhelms the benefits of parallelization. From the example, we infer that:

- The optimal configuration depends in general on both platform and workload characteristics.
- Employing more cores may not result in better performance, and may even degrade it. Moreover, parallel versions may even be slower than the sequential version.
- If an optimal configuration uses fewer cores than the total available, energy can be saved by switching off unused cores.
- The range of scenarios and varying concerns lay undue burden on programmers to ensure performance portability.

This work presents a system that optimizes and executes programs in a way that flexibly adapts them to new execution environments. Based on the above inferences, the proposed system:

1. prepares multiple parallel versions for each parallel region, as well as a sequential baseline version;
2. optimizes thread-level-parallelism leveraging both data- and pipeline-parallelism schemes;
3. generates parallel code that can be efficiently tuned and replaced online as the parallel region executes;
4. periodically optimizes and tunes multiple simultaneously executing programs for the duration of their execution; and

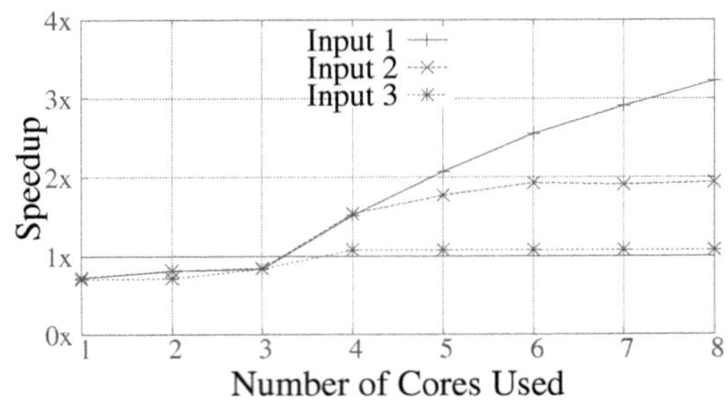

(a) Platform 1: 8-core, 8 GB RAM

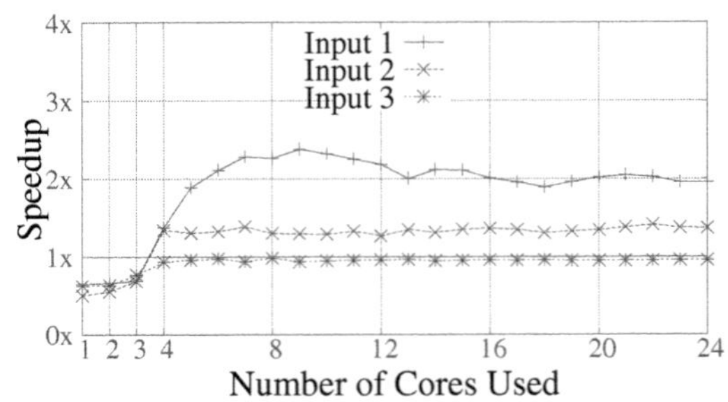

(b) Platform 2: 24-core, 24 GB RAM

Figure 1. Performance variability running `blackscholes` option pricing across 3 workloads and 2 parallel platforms.

5. performs all of the above automatically, easing the burden on the programmer.

Figure 2 shows an example of the proposed execution model on a hypothetical five-core machine. Each parallel region consists of a set of concurrently executing tasks. (The inscription inside each box indicates the task and iteration number of a region; e.g., $M5$ represents the fifth iteration of task M.) At time t_0, program P_1 is launched with a pipeline parallel configuration (PS-DSWP[1]) having three stages corresponding to tasks A, B, and C. A and C are executed sequentially whereas B is executed in parallel by 3 cores as determined by the run-time system. At time t_1, another program P_2 is launched on the same machine. In response, the run-time system signals P_1 to pause at the end of its current iteration (iteration 5). The core receiving this signal (Core 1) acknowledges the signal at time t_2 and propagates the pause signal to the other cores. At time t_3, P_1 reaches a known consistent state, following which the run-time system determines a new allocation of resources to programs P_1 and P_2, say 2 cores to P_1 and 3 cores to P_2. At time t_4, the run-time system launches DOANY[2] execution of both programs P_1 and P_2. For P_1, task K and the synchronization block implement the same functionality as tasks A, B, and C.

3. Compilation for Flexible Parallel Execution

The Nona compiler identifies parallelizable regions in a sequential program and applies multiple parallelizing transforms to each region, generating multiple versions of *flexible code*. The generated flexible code can be paused during its sequential or parallel execution, reconfigured, and efficiently resumed by the Morta task executor. Nona also inserts profiling hooks into the generated code for the Decima monitor to observe program behavior. The parallelizing

[1] The PS-DSWP transformation splits a loop body across stages and schedules them for concurrent execution. It enforces dependencies through inter-stage communication channels.

[2] The DOANY transformation schedules loop iterations for parallel execution while synchronizing shared data accesses by means of critical sections.

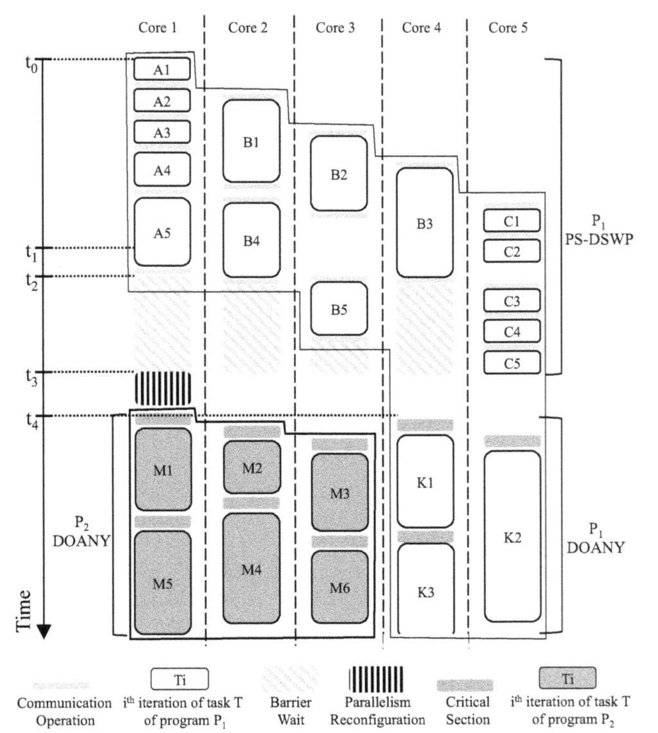

Figure 2. Parcae execution model: (t_0) program P_1 is launched; (t_1) program P_2 is launched; (t_2) P_1 acknowledges signal to pause; (t_3) P_1 reaches a known consistent state; (t_4) new resource allocation is determined and parallel execution of P_2 begins while P_1 switches to a parallelization that is better for two cores.

transforms which we focus on in this work target loop nests as their candidate regions. We therefore describe the generation of flexible code at this level, implemented in the following three steps.

3.1 Parallelism Discovery and PDG Building

In the first step, Nona discovers parallelism by building a Program Dependence Graph (PDG) of the hottest outermost loop nest [1]. Some data dependency edges in the PDG can be relaxed and their corresponding nodes allowed to execute in parallel by applying special techniques such as privatization and re-association of reduction operations. Nona automatically identifies min, max, and sum reductions [1]. Other dependency edges might be relaxed, allowing the corresponding nodes to execute in either order, but not concurrently; Nona processes commutativity annotations provided by the programmer for this purpose [31, 43]. As Figure 3 shows, Nona propagates these annotations from the source code to the PDG, relaxes dependencies between commutative operations, and synthesizes the appropriate synchronization to ensure atomicity.

3.2 Multiple Parallelizations

In the second step, Nona applies multiple parallelizing transforms to the PDG of a loop nest. In this work, we employ a data-parallel transform with critical sections (DOANY [31, 46]) and a pipeline transform (PS-DSWP [34, 43]). The framework can accommodate additional, new transforms. Each transform extracts a distinct form of thread-level parallelism encapsulated in code packages called *tasks*. The original, sequential version of the loop is also maintained as a task.

Each task essentially contains the body of a loop, whose iterations must either execute sequentially or may execute in parallel. A task is labeled as either *sequential* or *parallel* accordingly. Note that parallel execution may involve communication or synchronization. A dynamic *instance* of a task refers to any single iteration of the loop contained in the task. Dynamic instances of a sequential task cannot execute concurrently with each other, whereas dynamic instances of a parallel task can.

DOANY tests the PDG with commutativity relaxations produced in the first step for absence of loop-carried dependencies to determine applicability. If there are no loop-carried dependencies, DOANY extracts the loop body into a parallel task, marshals all loop live-ins into the task via the heap, and inserts appropriate synchronization operations to ensure atomicity of all commutative operations. Iterations of the loop thus constructed may be executed concurrently by multiple threads without violating program semantics.

PS-DSWP is a widely applicable parallelization technique that partitions the loop into "stages", with each stage comprised of groups of instructions that are cyclically dependent on each other. Each stage essentially corresponds to a loop containing part of the original loop's body. These stages are constructed by building the strongly connected components (SCCs) of the PDG and partitioning the induced SCC graph. Inter-stage dependencies are satisfied via appropriate communication. A stage is sequential or parallel depending on whether the intra-stage dependencies are carried by the transformed loop's backedge or not. Iterations of a parallel stage may be executed concurrently by multiple threads.

The tasks extracted by each parallelizing transform are initially generated by the Multi-Threaded Code Generation algorithm (MTCG) [34]. MTCG operates in four steps (see Figure 4(a)). First, for each task, MTCG generates a new control flow graph (CFG) containing the relevant basic blocks. Second, MTCG inserts instructions corresponding to each basic block in the newly created CFG for that task. Third, MTCG inserts inter-task communication instructions (*send* and *recv* in case of PS-DSWP) and synchronization instructions (*lock* and *unlock* in case of DOANY). Fourth, MTCG replicates branch instructions into the newly created CFGs as necessary to match the original CFG.

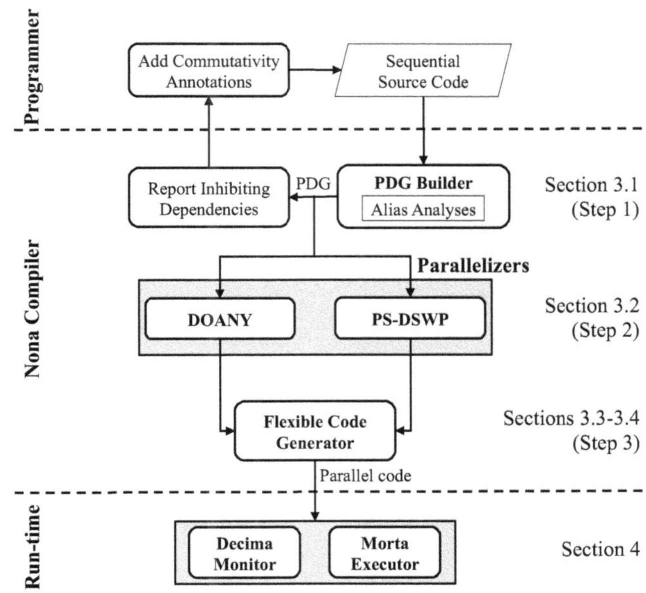

Figure 3. Parcae Architecture and Parallelization Workflow

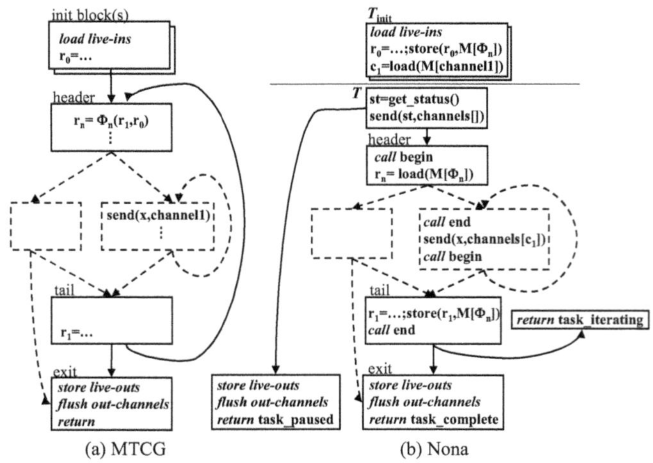

Figure 4. Original and transformed task code produced by MTCG and Nona, respectively. Dashed blocks/arcs represent arbitrary control flow within the loop.

3.3 Flexible Code Generation

In the third step, Nona adapts the code generated by MTCG for flexible execution. Originally, the code generated by MTCG targets a fixed number of statically bound threads for each task. However, flexible parallel execution entails dynamic scheduling of task instances across different threads, execution of parallel tasks by a varying number of threads, and pausing a set of tasks followed by resumption of a possibly different set of tasks. Flexible parallel execution is hindered by:

1. Dependencies through private storage: A thread's registers and stack are private. Consequently, cross-iteration dependencies (between one task instance and another) carried by registers and the stack inhibit executing instances across multiple threads.
2. Inter-task communication: MTCG constructs point-to-point communication channels between threads executing tasks, and communicates dependencies in round-robin order across threads. If the number of threads executing each task varies at run-time, the dependencies across the communicating tasks may be reordered, violating sequential semantics.
3. Cross-iteration dependencies: These also inhibit the pausing of executing tasks and relaying of work remaining in the parallel region to a new set of tasks.

To facilitate flexible execution, Nona applies the following changes:

1. Upon completing each iteration, every task yields to the runtime system that determines whether the task should pause or may resume execution on the same thread or a different thread.
2. Registers and stack variables that are live across iterations of sequential tasks are saved and reloaded on the heap at the end and beginning of each iteration, respectively.
3. Parallel tasks avoid having local state across iterations, by sharing cross-iteration data in global memory .
4. When pipelined tasks pause, they flush their communication channels, sending all pending items down the pipeline.
5. Upon resumption, tasks execute an initialization sequence to reload invariant live-in data, and the run-time system resets the communication channels.

3.3.1 Changes to Task Control Flow

Consider the control flow graph CFG_T of an arbitrary task T, as generated by MTCG (Figure 4(a)). CFG_T represents a single-entry-single-exit code region containing a loop with a single `tail`→`header` backedge. There is a single entry edge reaching `header` block from outside the loop; there may be multiple exits from the loop, but all reach a single `exit` block which cannot be reached from outside the loop.

Nona modifies CFG_T to support migration (see Figure 4(b)). The backedge is redirected from `tail` to a new exit block which returns `task_iterating` (instead of reaching the `header`). The original `exit` block now returns `task_complete`. Section 3.3.4 discusses the third (and last) exit block which is reached from a new pre-header block and returns `task_paused`.

The control logic to execute task instances is extracted into a separate loop, shown in Algorithm 1. The Morta executor sets up every worker thread to execute this loop. Upon receiving `task_iterating`, the thread increments a counter that tracks the number of iterations per task. Upon completing or pausing a task, the thread waits for other tasks of the region to complete or pause by means of a barrier, before starting to execute a new task.

Algorithm 1: Control logic for executing task instances

```
// getTaskInstance() blocks until reconfiguration ends or until next
   region begins. It returns NULL when program ends.
while instance ← runtime.getTaskInstance() do
    retVal ← invoke(instance.function, instance.args);
    if retVal == task_iterating then
        taskIterCount[instance.getTaskID()]++;
    else
        // retVal == task_paused or task_complete
        instance.flushOutChannels();
        region ← instance.getRegion();
        region.waitOnBarrier();
        if retVal == task_complete then
            region.terminate()
```

3.3.2 Saving and Restoring State

Sequential tasks may have cross-iteration dependencies that flow through registers and variables on the stack, which are local to a thread. To facilitate lightweight migration to another thread, Nona inserts code to copy such variables to the heap at the end of each iteration and reload them at the beginning of each iteration. Note that the amount of information that needs to be copied through the heap is typically much smaller when applied between iterations, than at arbitrary locations as in general context switches or checkpoints.

Nona uses Static Single Assignment form (SSA) to represent code. In SSA form, loop-carried register dependencies are captured by ϕ nodes in the loop `header`. Figure 4 shows how flows through registers are converted into flows through the heap. Note that a register value need only be stored to the heap at the end of an iteration, not on every write to the register. This minimizes the cost of saving register state. A similar treatment addresses stack variables. The figure also shows how blocks preceding the loop header are extracted into a separate function (T_{init}). This function includes the loading of loop-invariant live-in values, and will be executed at every task activation and resumption.

3.3.3 Inter-task Communication

In PS-DSWP parallelizations, dependencies between tasks executing different stages need to be enforced. MTCG communicates such dependencies by inserting instructions for *send-receive* operations over point-to-point communication channels [34].

Communication between two sequential tasks is straightforward; communication between a sequential task (S) and a parallel task (P) involves data arbitration and merge. Consider a dependency edge $u \to v$ where $u \in S$ and $v \in P$. Let p be the (varying) number of threads that execute P. The value produced by the thread executing S flows to each of the threads executing P in a round-robin fashion: on the ith instance of S, the value is communicated through the $(i \bmod p)^{th}$ channel. MTCG uses the induction variable (i), which is incremented once per instance of S, to identify the channel for a value that flows over the dependency edge. This holds analogously for dependency edges from a parallel task to a sequential task.

In MTCG, the number of threads p that execute a parallel task P is fixed at compile-time. This is not the case for Nona because the value of p may be changed by Mortaduring execution. Still, the above communication mechanism suffices provided p and the communication channels are maintained as run-time parameters, and that task instances are made *relayable*.

3.3.4 Relayable Task Instances

As described in Section 3.3.2, parallel tasks are constructed to have no local cross-iteration dependencies, and sequential tasks have all their cross-iteration data placed in the global heap between iterations. Thus, every task instance can halt after finishing or before starting an iteration, leaving the program in a known consistent state. Once instances halt, the system can be reconfigured safely and subsequent instances will continue to execute according to the new set of tasks and their thread allocation.

At the beginning of each iteration, every instance checks for a pause signal (see `get_status()` in Figure 4(b)), received either directly from Morta or from another instance. If an instance receives a pause signal, it propagates the signal and yields to Morta by returning `task_paused`. These signals are initiated and propagated as follows.

Initiating pause signals: When Morta chooses to reconfigure the program, it sends a pause signal to designated *master* tasks. In the DOANY and sequential versions, the single task is the master task, and in the case of PS-DSWP, only the task executing the first stage is designated as master. The master tasks are designed to query Morta for pause signals at the beginning of each instance, to which Morta responds with either `continue` or `pause`.

Propagating pause signals across pipelined tasks: The master task of a pipeline-parallel region relays the `continue` or `pause` notification to all other tasks in the region, following the structure of the pipeline. This is achieved by placing *send* instructions to all directly connected tasks in the loop header of the master task (before any other instruction, see `send(st,channels[])` in Figure 4(b)), and matching *receive* instructions (via `get_status()`) in the corresponding location of each of the connected tasks. Subsequent send-receive messages are placed analogously down the stages of the pipeline. This ensures that all parts of an iteration, scattered across pipeline stages, pause appropriately.

All send-receive operations occur over the same point-to-point communication channels used for dependency flows. Upon receiving a `pause` signal, a task explicitly flushes all outgoing channels, transmitting all pending items down the pipeline. This mechanism ensures that all channels are drained properly, relying on the property that at the end of a flushed iteration, all relevant incoming data has been received and processed.

Pausing process: Upon receiving a `pause` signal, a task exits the parallel region by jumping to an exit block which returns `task_paused`. Exiting a parallel region on a pause is identical to exiting the region upon reaching the end of the loop. Indeed, the block returning `task_paused` contains the same instructions as the block returning `task_complete`. These instructions include flushing outgoing channels (see Figure 4(b)). After exiting the iteration, the thread waits on a barrier for other threads executing the parallel region to exit as well (see Algorithm 1).

To resume execution, Morta launches the set of tasks determined to be optimal for the new execution environment. Each task first executes T_{init} when launched (the task initialization function, see Figure 4(b)). Section 5 discusses the overhead of pause and resume as well as the means to alleviate it.

3.4 Hooks for Autonomous Monitoring

An important aspect of Parcae is task execution time monitoring by Decima. Decima distinguishes between the time a task spends computing and the time it spends waiting for communication, possibly across multiple parallel instances. Morta relies on this information to optimize program configurations. To enable such monitoring, Nona inserts `begin` and `end` hooks into the code of each task. These hooks obtain timestamps using the `rdtsc` instruction on x86 platforms (whose overhead is presented in Section 6.5). Nona inserts `end` immediately before each *send* and *receive* instruction, and `begin` immediately after each *send* and *receive* instruction. Nona also inserts `begin` into the entry block of a task and `end` into the `task_executing` exit block.

The `begin` and `end` hooks help calculate the total compute-time of an instance by accumulating local time intervals (between consecutive {`begin`, `end`} pairs). These local compute-times of each instance then update a global compute-time counter per task, which feeds Decima (described in Section 4), requiring no inter-thread synchronization. Note that the total execute-time of an instance can easily be reported too, as the time elapsed between the first `begin` and the last `end`, from which the communication overhead can be derived. The latter may be important for affinity and allocation optimization purposes; however, these effects were found to be insignificant on our evaluation platforms and experiments.

4. Online Monitoring and Optimization

The goal of the Morta run-time system is to rapidly find parallelism configurations that are optimal for the execution environment. This work focuses on the following optimization objective: minimize total execution time, and subject to that, minimize energy consumption. Morta achieves this objective by maximizing iteration throughput (number of iterations processed per second) and saving idle threads, as explained in this section. The system design allows additional goals, as desired.

A parallelism configuration consists of: (1) a Parallelization Scheme (prepared by Nona, see Section 3), which maps each loop to one of the following: $\mathcal{S} = \{\text{DOANY}, \text{PS-DSWP}, \text{SEQ}\}$; and (2) a Degree of Parallelism (DoP) D, the varying number of threads allocated to every parallel task of DOANY or PS-DSWP schemes. A configuration also contains an assignment of threads to cores, but this aspect was not significant on our evaluation platforms.

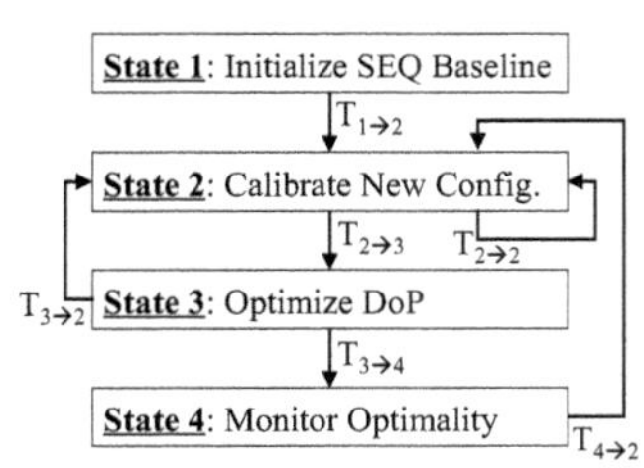

(a) Finite State Machine Structure

$T_{1\to2}$	Measured SEQ baseline, reconfigure to parallel scheme.
$T_{2\to3}$	Feed configuration profile.
$T_{3\to2}$	Reconfigure to next scheme.
$T_{3\to4}$	Reconfigure to optimal DoP.
$T_{4\to2}$	Detected change in workload, re-calibrate configuration.
$T_{2\to2}$ $T_{3\to2}$ $T_{4\to2}$	Detected change in resource allocation, re-calibrate configuration.

(b) Description of Transitions

Figure 5. Run-time Controller

Morta uses the following schema to identify optimal configurations: establish a baseline performance metric; identify an optimal configuration by repeatedly searching for a better configuration, pausing execution to change configurations, and measuring the performance of the new configuration relative to the baseline; monitor optimality of current configuration and trigger a new search if the dynamic execution environment changes. The finite state machine shown in Figure 5 implements the above schema.

State 1: Initialize Sequential Baseline. When a program enters a parallel region, Morta selects the sequential scheme ($S' =$ SEQ, $D' = \{1\}$) and monitors its execution to establish a baseline throughput T_{seq}. After completing a fixed number of N_{seq} iterations (set to 10 in the current implementation), Morta reconfigures the program to execute in an initial parallel scheme $S' = S_{\text{par}}$ and default DoP $D' = D_{\text{par}}$, and transitions to State 2. (In our current implementation, $S_{\text{par}} =$ PS-DSWP and D_{par} is determined as described later in Section 4.1.) Note that D' is a vector, every element of which represents the DoP of a single task. Also, the initial value of D' need not be 1 (explained in Section 4.1).

State 2: Calibrate New Configuration. In State 2, Morta treats the current parallel configuration with its scheme and DoP (S', D') as being new. It gathers initial timing information for scheme S' while repeatedly reconfiguring the system to $D' \pm 1$ and executing each configuration for a number of iterations N_{par}[3]. This is done to establish a direction for the search for an optimum DoP in the next state. After completing the calibration iterations, Morta restores the original (S', D') configuration and moves to State 3.

State 3: Optimize Degree of Parallelism (DoP). Based on the information collected in State 2, Morta performs a local monotonic search for an optimal DoP for each task, repeatedly reconfiguring the system to different values of DoP and executing a number of N_{par} iterations to measure its performance. Specifically, it uses a finite difference gradient ascent control law [15, 39], as described in detail in Section 4.1. This process converges to an optimal DoP (D'') for the given scheme S', with associated throughput T''. If T'' is better than the best throughput T^* achieved so far for the region, Morta updates T^* with T'' and records S', D''. ($T^* = T_{\text{seq}}$ initially.) Morta then selects the next scheme S' from $\mathcal{S}$, resets DoP to its default $D' = D_{\text{par}}$, reconfigures the system accordingly, and returns to State 2. If all schemes in $\mathcal{S}$ have been explored, Morta retrieves the configuration S', D'' that achieved the best throughput T^*, reconfigures the system accordingly, and moves to State 4.

State 4: Monitor Configuration Optimality. In this state, the Decima monitor performs a passive monitoring of the system (i.e., no reconfigurations) to detect changes in either the resources allocated to the program or in the workload of the program itself. For the former, Decima interacts with the platform-wide run-time system (described in Section 4.2). For the latter, Decima monitors the throughput of the parallel region; if the throughput changes by more than a preset threshold, the workload is deemed to have changed. If any such change is detected, the configuration is suspected to have become suboptimal, and control returns to State 2 retaining the current scheme. If the change corresponds to an increase in resources, the current DoP is retained (hopefully as a good starting point); otherwise, if resources decreased or the throughput of the workload itself decreased, the DoP is reset to its initial value D_{par}.

Note that all reconfigurations that modify the DoP while keeping the scheme intact (such as those carried out by State 2, State 3, and potentially upon transitions $T_{3\to4}$ and $T_{4\to2}$) do not require changing the code distributed among the worker threads. Reconfigurations that do modify the parallelization scheme, upon transitions $T_{1\to2}$ and $T_{3\to2}$, do involve replacing this code.

[3] The number of iterations N_{par} is dynamically set to $\max(N_{\text{seq}}, 2 \cdot d_P)$, where d_P is the current DoP of the parallel task being optimized.

Algorithm 2: Optimizing multiple DoPs in a region

```
Input: Calibrated parallel region, thread budget N
Output: Optimized DoP for region (≤ N)
totalDoP ← computeTotalDoP(region.parallelTasks())
foreach P_i ∈ region.parallelTasks() do
    P_i.opt ← false; P_i.sat ← false
repeat
    optimize_a_task ← false
    𝒫 ← sortInAscendingThroughput(region.parallelTasks())
    for P_i ∈ 𝒫 while ¬optimize_a_task do
        overline(d_{P_i}) ← N − totalDoP + d_{P_i}
        if (¬P_i.opt) ∨ ((d_{P_i} < overline(d_{P_i})) ∧ (¬P_i.sat)) then
            d_{P_i} ← gradientAscent(P_i, d_{P_i}, overline(d_{P_i}))
            P_i.opt ← true; P_i.sat ← (d_{P_i} < overline(d_{P_i}))
            totalDoP ← updateTotalDoP(totalDoP, d_{P_i})
            optimize_a_task ← true
until ¬optimize_a_task
if parThroughput(region) > (0.9*totalDoP)*seqThroughput(region) then
    return totalDoP        // current parallel scheme profitable, keep it
else if bumpToNextScheme(region) then
    return calibrateAndOptimize(region) // try next scheme recursively
else return 1 // no parallel scheme is profitable, revert to sequential
```

4.1 Optimizing the Degrees of Parallelism

A given parallelization scheme may comprise both sequential $\{S_1, S_2, \ldots, S_m\}$ and parallel tasks $\{P_1, P_2, \ldots, P_n\}$. The degree of parallelism d_{S_i} for every sequential task is inherently 1. The objective of optimizing DoP (State 3 of Figure 5(a)) is therefore to find a degree of parallelism d_{P_i} for each parallel task that maximizes the overall performance of the region. The problem can be formulated as follows:

Maximize overall throughput: $T = f(d_{P_1}, d_{P_2}, \ldots, d_{P_n})$

$$\text{subject to: } d_{P_i} \geq 1 \ \forall i, \quad \sum_{i=1}^{n} d_{P_i} \leq N$$

where N denotes the total number of threads available to the program minus those used by its sequential tasks (m). Morta optimizes each d_{P_i} separately, in turn, according to the relative throughputs of the tasks in ascending order (see Algorithm 2). This is done in order to prioritize slower tasks, which are typically bottlenecks in pipelined networks of sequential-parallel tasks.

Morta computes the optimal DoP d_{P_i} for a parallel task P_i by using a fast iterative gradient ascent technique [39], based on the assumption that function f is unimodal with a single (local) optimum. Section 6.4 discusses the impact of this assumption. On each iteration of the optimization routine, the current throughput is compared with the previous throughput[4], and this difference either establishes the gradient of the change to the next DoP or concludes the search. First, an upper bound $\overline{d_{P_i}}$ on the allowed DoP is calculated, which is equal to the maximum number of threads currently available for P_i. Initially, every parallel task is assigned half of its fair share of threads: $\frac{N}{2n}$. Thus, $\overline{d_{P_i}} = N - \sum_{j \neq i} \frac{N}{2n} = \frac{(n+1)N}{2n}$. The search for an optimal $d_{P_i} \in [1, 2, \ldots, \overline{d_{P_i}}]$ starts at the midpoint of this range: $d_{P_i}(0) = D_{\text{par}} = \frac{1}{2}\overline{d_{P_i}}$. Morta then sets $d_{P_i}(1) = d_{P_i}(0) \pm 1$ according to whichever achieves greater throughput. We call the search *increasing* or *decreasing*, respectively.

[4] Throughput is measured directly as the number of iterations executed in a certain amount of time, rather than computed analytically by relying on some model of the throughput function f.

Next, the gradient between the current $(k+1)$ solution and the previous (k) solution is calculated, starting from $k=0$:

$$\delta(k+1) = T(d_{P_i}(k+1)) - T(d_{P_i}(k)). \quad (1)$$

If $\delta(k+1) < 0$, the optimal solution has been passed and Morta terminates the search taking $d_{P_i}(k)$ to be the solution. Recall that we seek to maximize the throughput, and subject to that, minimize the number of threads (thereby saving energy). The case $\delta(k+1) = 0$ is treated similar to case $\delta(k+1) < 0$ above if the search is increasing, and similar to case $\delta(k+1) > 0$ below if the search is decreasing. If $\delta(k+1) > 0$, the next solution is calculated according to the gradient ascent formula:

$$d_{P_i}(k+2) = d_{P_i}(k+1) + \alpha\delta(k+1) \quad (2)$$

where α is positive if the search is increasing, and negative if the search is decreasing. The search continues by incrementing k and evaluating Equation 1 and Equation 2, repeatedly.

After optimizing d_{P_i}, the process repeats by sorting the tasks according to their throughputs, and selecting the next task P_j to optimize. The process terminates after all d_{P_i}'s have been optimized, possibly more than once, and cannot be further improved.

Once the search terminates at an optimal DoP, Morta measures the overall throughput of the region $T = f(d_{P_1}, \ldots, d_{P_n})$ and compares it with the baseline sequential throughput T_{seq} measured in State 1. The parallel configuration is deemed profitable only if its efficiency is significantly better than that of the sequential configuration. Otherwise, Morta repeats the optimization process considering an alternative parallel scheme exposed by Nona, if any (corresponding to transition $T_{3\to 2}$ in Figure 5). When all available schemes have been considered, Morta chooses the most efficient scheme (possibly even SEQ) for execution, and enters State 4. To accelerate the optimization process, Morta caches previously optimized configurations and reuses them, if feasible, as initial configurations upon future entry into a parallel region.

4.2 Platform-wide Control

The description of the Morta run-time system in Section 4.1 applies to a single program executing a parallel region. However, the same control system used to optimize the parallel execution of one program easily extends and generalizes to multiple programs running concurrently, thereby achieving platform-wide execution optimization. Indeed, each executing program p can be considered as a collection of parallel and sequential tasks, executed in parallel and independent of other co-scheduled programs, as if all programs belong to one parallel region with multiple parallel tasks. At this outer level, Morta must decide how to partition the total number of threads $\mathcal{N}$ available in the system across the different co-scheduled programs: $\mathcal{N} = \sum_p N_p$, such that a specified optimization goal is met. Given its budget of threads N_p, a program is optimized and monitored by its dedicated controller. Algorithm 3 summarizes the platform-wide control logic to minimize the overall execution time of a batch of co-scheduled programs.

The platform-wide Morta run-time system is implemented as a daemon, launched upon system boot. When a flexible parallel program p is launched, its controller registers itself with the daemon and acquires its fair share of resources N_p; initially $N_p = \mathcal{N}/\mathcal{P}$ where $\mathcal{P}$ is the number of flexible parallel programs. Each controller proceeds to initialize, optimize, and monitor its program, as explained (through States 1,2,3 and 4), and reports its optimal amount of resources $N'_p \leq N_p$ to the daemon (upon transition $T_{3\to 4}$).

On receiving optimization results N'_p from the controllers, the daemon distributes slack resources $\mathcal{N} - \sum_p N'_p$ if any, among controllers with $N'_p = N_p$. Finally, the daemon monitors changes in system resources (launch and termination of programs) and repartitions resources across executing programs when they occur.

Algorithm 3: Platform-wide Optimization

```
Input: platform-wide thread budget 𝒩
Output: Optimized DoP for platform (≤ 𝒩)
slack ← 𝒩
activePrograms ← platform.programs
while slack > 0 do
    foreach P ∈ activePrograms do
        N_P_slack ← slack/activePrograms.size
        slack ← slack - N_P_slack
        N_P ← N_P_new + N_P_slack        // N_P_new ← 0 initially
        N_P_new ← P.optimizeDoP(P.region, N_P)
        if N_P_new < N_P then
            slack ← slack + (N_P - N_P_new)
            activePrograms.extract(P)
```

5. Reducing Run-time Overheads

The Morta run-time system's overheads include:

1. Task Migratability: consisting of (i) Task Activation, yielding to and returning from the task activation loop; and (ii) Data Management, loading and saving cross-iteration dependency data; both occurring per iteration.
2. Pause-Resume: on receiving a pause signal, all threads synchronize by means of a barrier; threads which reach the barrier early waste cycles waiting for the slower threads to catch up (shown as Barrier Wait in Figure 2). Tasks must be re-started on threads on resumption.
3. Parallelism Reconfiguration: time spent executing core optimization routine to determine new parallelism configurations (shown as Parallelism Reconfiguration in Figure 2).
4. Status Query: querying Morta whether the program should pause, after each iteration.
5. Monitoring: recording timestamps for execution time statistics.

On our evaluation platforms, the last two were barely noticeable. The remaining overheads (measured and reported in Section 6.5) can be significantly reduced in the common case:

1. Task Migratability: Rather than returning to the task activation loop every iteration as in Figure 4, an optimized (yet non-migratable) version may retain the original loop backedge. This makes it possible to hoist the load out of the loop header into the preheader, and to push the corresponding store into the pause exit block (see Figure 4). Note that this only constrains the migration of sequential tasks in between parallelism reconfigurations since sequential tasks have dependencies flowing across task instances.
2. Parallelism Reconfiguration: The thread executing the master task is the first to receive the pause signal, directly from Morta. This thread can immediately start executing the optimization routine to determine the next parallelism configuration, rather than waiting for other threads. This overlaps the time spent executing the optimization routine with the gap between the last and first threads to reach the barrier.
3. Pause-Resume: During gradient ascent, which performs most reconfigurations, the degree of parallelism (DoP) of a parallel task is increased or decreased. Recall that a parallel task is explicitly constructed such that it either does not have any loop-carried dependencies or updates global memory with appropriate synchronization. Consequently, additional threads may start executing the parallel task without violating program consistency, eliminating the need for a full barrier wait. In the pres-

ence of communication with other tasks, however, actions appropriate to the communication policy must be taken. As described in Section 3, a sequential task sends (receives) dependencies in round-robin order to (from) each of the threads executing the parallel task. The sequential task must process all tokens up to the iteration at which the parallel region was paused, before changing the width of the communication channel between itself and the parallel task whose DoP is being optimized. The optimized Morta run-time system can ensure this by leveraging the iteration counts of each task.

6. Evaluation

Table 2 describes the two **real** platforms used to evaluate Parcae. The Nona compiler is built on LLVM [19] revision 129859. Nona generates optimized assembly which is then assembled and linked by GCC version 4.4.1. Parcae is compared with an LLVM compiler also built on revision 129859, applying fixed high-quality parallelization schemes (PS-DSWP [34, 43] and DOANY [31, 46]) targeting an unloaded parallel platform, and using a standard threadpool with load balancing by the Linux scheduler [31, 43]. The Morta run-time system is implemented on top of the same threadpool, facilitating fair comparison.

As a second point of comparison, the optimal program configuration is determined for each workload by enumerating all possible static parallelism configurations of the program and picking the best performing one. The performance of Parcae is then compared against that of the optimal configuration. The execution time of the sequential program produced by the same set of optimizations excluding the parallelization transformations serves as the baseline for speedup computation of all parallel runs. All execution times used to compute speedups in Table 1 are averages over N runs, where $N \geq 3$ is the minimum number of runs required for a standard deviation of less than 5% of the geomean execution time.

Processors will have interfaces to turn cores on or off at fine time granularities [8]. To evaluate energy savings that Parcae could deliver by leveraging such capabilities, we measured the power consumption characteristic of each platform by executing a power-virus that maintains 100% CPU utilization of each core to measure power draw when a number of cores are busy, and by leaving the system unused to measure power draw when those cores are idle. The processor's dynamic power range is then the difference between active and idle power. Active processor power consumption as a fraction of whole platform power consumption is 18.0% for Platform 1 and 26.7% for Platform 2. Processor energy is then computed as the integral of the piece-wise product of time spent actively using a number of cores and the average power draw of those many active cores. Recent work uses a similar methodology [8].

Table 1 describes the benchmarks selected to evaluate Parcae. These include benchmarks parallelized by the baseline state-of-the-art compiler [31, 43], allowing direct comparison. The last three columns of the table provide a summary of the execution time and energy improvements delivered by Parcae. These improvements are discussed in detail below. In the interest of space, we present case studies using one application for three interesting scenarios, each highlighting a different aspect of Parcae.

6.1 Parcae Adapts Execution to Workload Change

`blackscholes` calculates the prices for a portfolio of European options using the Black-Scholes partial differential equation [7]. To study workload variation, the source code is modified to enable pricing of two different portfolios. Nona is able to apply the PS-DSWP parallelization scheme, in addition to SEQ. Figure 6(b) shows Morta and Decima in action. Morta starts in State 1 to initialize the sequential baseline. It then enters State 2 to set the initial configuration and determine the direction for gradient ascent.

Feature	Platform 1	Platform 2
Brand Name	Intel Xeon® E5310	Intel Xeon® X7460
Processor	Intel Core®, 64-bit	Intel Core®, 64-bit
Clock Speed	1.60 GHz	2.66 GHz
Total # Cores	8	24
Total L2 Cache	16 MB	36 MB
Total L3 Cache	-	64 MB
Total RAM	8 GB	24 GB
OS	Linux 2.6.32	Linux 2.6.31

Table 2. Hardware Platforms Used for Evaluation

In State 3, it performs gradient ascent until peak throughput is achieved, at which point ($t = 5.0s$) it enters State 4 to monitor the execution of this configuration. During the optimization phase, the re-configuration interval constantly varies according to the optimization logic; this results in compute throughput measurements that are accurate relative to each other, but are less accurate with respect to the baseline throughput. Hence, once the peak is reached, the system stabilizes for additional iterations to obtain a more accurate throughput measurement. Decima's workload change detection logic kicks in after this throughput measurement. At $t = 56.6s$, Decima detects workload change via drop in throughput, and signals Morta to re-optimize in response. In State 3, Morta reduces DoP by performing decreasing gradient ascent, finally to reach State 4 at $t = 79.9s$; Decima monitors the remaining execution. Parcae achieves performance within 1.4% of optimal (due to overheads) while consuming 45.4% less energy.

6.2 Parcae Optimizes Across Multiple Parallelization Schemes

`geti` is a data mining program that computes a list of frequent itemsets using a vertical database. The set semantics of the output operations enables order relaxation via commutativity, which is expressed using 11 annotations in 889 lines of source code [31]. The resulting dependence graph is then amenable to PS-DSWP and DOANY parallelization schemes (in addition to SEQ). Figure 6(c) shows the execution trace. As with `blackscholes`, Morta starts in State 1 to initialize the sequential baseline. In State 2, it calibrates an initial configuration of the PS-DSWP scheme, and starts an increasing gradient ascent in State 3. Morta determines an optimal configuration for the PS-DSWP scheme (at $t = 14.0s$), and compares throughput with that of the SEQ scheme. As the comparison is below the preset threshold, Morta returns to State 2 in order to evaluate the next parallel scheme: DOANY. Optimizing the DoP for DOANY then takes place in State 3 (from $t = 16.8s$ until $t = 26.0s$). The optimal DOANY configuration is found to be of adequate throughput, so Morta moves to State 4 and Decima monitors the remaining execution. Parcae improves performance over the baseline by 12.6%, and achieves performance within 18.6% of optimal. Parcae reduces energy consumption by 23.9%.

6.3 Parcae Adapts Execution to Resource Availability Change

Figures 6(d) and 6(e) illustrate Morta's platform-wide control capability, with the former highlighting control of programs with homogeneous characteristics while the latter heterogeneous. In both cases, the controller primarily aims to minimize the overall execution time of the batch of programs. Simultaneously, by virtue of fair allocation of slack resources to all active programs on each round of optimization in Algorithm 3, the platform-wide controller also seeks to avoid adversely impacting any one program.

Homogeneous characteristics: Eight copies of `blackscholes` processing the same input are launched in succession on Platform 2 having 24 cores. For brevity, the execution of only one copy P_0 is shown (labeled *Program* P_0). The figure also shows platform-wide

Program	Origin	Main Loop	Parallel Coverage	Total number of		Parcae Improvement relative to		
				Invocations	Iterations	Baseline [31, 43] Exec. Time	Baseline [31, 43] Energy	Optimal Exec. Time
blackscholes	Seq. version from PARSEC [7]	`worker`	92.94%	1	1000	-1.39%	45.35%	-1.39%
geti	MineBench [26]	`FindSomeETIs`	99.99%	24	12242	12.55%	23.90%	-18.56%
kmeans	STAMP [25]	`work`	99.30%	501	131334144	41.94%	83.89%	-62.98%
ks	LLVM Test Suite [21]	`FindMaxGpAndSwap`	99.97%	7750	488250	3.78%	35.11%	-0.83%
md5sum	Open Source [4]	`main`	99.99%	1	384	34.41%	58.51%	-3.55%
potrace	Open Source [38]	`main`	100.00%	1	200	9.95%	42.67%	-2.97%
url	NetBench [24]	`main`	100.00%	1	40000	-0.18%	36.22%	-2.40%

Table 1. Sequential programs transformed, their origin, transformed loop, fraction of total execution time spent in parallelized loop, number of invocations and iterations of the parallelized loop, and improvements in execution time and energy delivered by Parcae. The improvements are on a single input on Platform 2, and are relative to baseline parallel and optimal parallel versions of these programs. Optimal versions are determined via offline exhaustive search. Positive numbers indicate improvement.

INIT State 1: Initialize
CAL State 2: Calibrate
OPT State 3: Optimize
MON State 4: Monitor

(S) Sequential Scheme
(S,Px,S) PS-DSWP Scheme with DoP = x
(Px) DOANY Scheme with DoP = x

Running Throughput
Running Energy
Program Degree of Parallelism
System Degree of Parallelism

(a) Legend

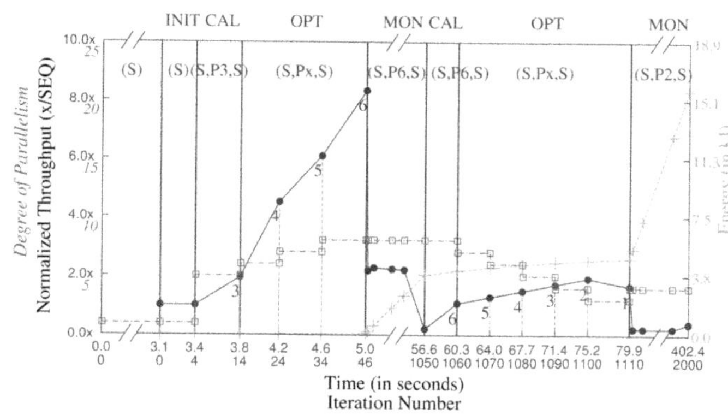

(b) `blackscholes`: Controller re-optimizes when workload changes

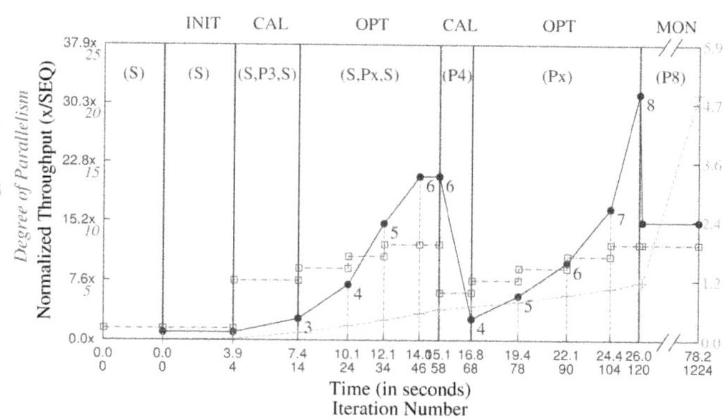

(c) `geti`: Controller determines optimal execution scheme from many

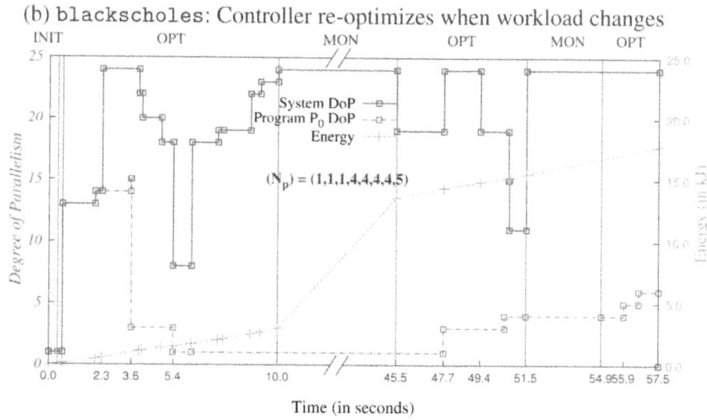

(d) Controller optimizes eight homogeneous programs simultaneously

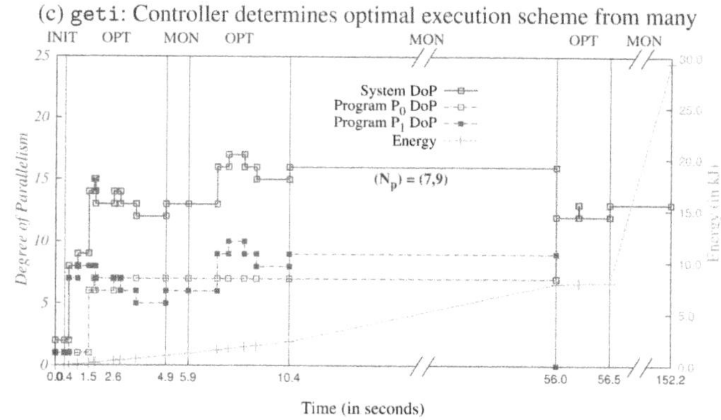

(e) Controller optimizes two heterogeneous programs simultaneously

Figure 6. Parcae run-time control. Solid vertical lines indicate state transition times. All throughput values are normalized to the throughput measured in the INIT state. In (b) and (c), the state transitions shown at the top of each figure are those of an individual program's controller, whereas in (d) and (e), they are the transitions of the platform-wide Morta daemon.

dynamic thread utilization as determined by the platform-wide daemon (labeled *System*). P_0 begins execution on an unloaded machine, so following the initialization of State 1, State 2 calibrates the parallel task of the PS-DSWP scheme starting from a DoP of $d_{P_0} = \frac{1}{2}\overline{d_{P_0}} = 11$. (There are two additional sequential tasks resulting in a whole program DoP of 13.) P_0's controller then transitions to State 3 and performs an increasing gradient ascent. By $t = 3.6s$, all eight program copies have launched, and the daemon reallocates threads across them: each copy is assigned a DoP of 3. In response, P_0's controller transitions to State 2 and measures the parallel performance of configuration (S,P1,S), which is now the only feasible parallel configuration. It then computes the configuration's efficiency and compares the efficiency with that of sequential execution, determining at time $t = 5.4s$ that sequential execution is preferred, and returning 2 threads back to the daemon. Spare threads are redistributed by the daemon among the copies repeatedly. By $t = 10.0s$, the platform-wide optimization algorithm converges (at $\{N_p\} = \{1, 1, 1, 4, 4, 4, 4, 5\}$), all copies enter their stable configurations, and the controllers enter State 4 (the monitoring state). At $t = 45.5s$, the fastest copy terminates, yielding its (5) threads back to the daemon, which in turn initiates another round of optimization. The figure shows how, barring the short optimization phases, Parcae enables full use of all threads on the platform. Compared to OS scheduling of the eight copies of the baseline 24-thread parallel version, Parcae reduces total execution time of the workload by 12.8%, and energy consumption by 29.1%.

Interestingly, the benefit in execution time using Parcae increases as the number of concurrently executing programs increases. With sixteen copies, execution time and energy improve by 18.3% and 52.7%, respectively. With twenty four copies, improvements reach 22.4% and 22.4%, respectively. The co-operative release and acquisition of resources by Parcae reduces contention among concurrently executing programs. Scheduling and memory contention significantly overwhelm the benefits of parallel execution when copies of the baseline parallelized programs execute each with 24 threads.

Heterogeneous characteristics: One copy each of `kmeans` (labeled *Program* P_0) and `blackscholes` (labeled *Program* P_1) are launched in succession on Platform 2 having 24 cores. `kmeans` is a DOANY parallel loop with a single parallel task whereas `blackscholes` is a PS-DSWP parallel loop with two sequential tasks and one parallel task. Additionally, the two programs differ in parallelization scalability, average time per iteration, and total execution time. The platform-wide daemon initiates a round of optimization at $t = 0.4s$ when both programs have launched, and assigns each program its fair share DoP of 12. It then optimizes each program in turn starting with P_0. In response, P_0's optimizer performs gradient ascent to determine optimal use of the assigned threads. At $t = 2.6s$, P_0 determines that (P7) is the optimal parallelism configuration and returns 5 threads back to the daemon. In the meantime, P_1's controller performs gradient ascent to determine that the optimal parallelism configuration is (S,P4,S) and returns 6 threads back to the daemon at $t = 4.9s$. The daemon then initiates another round of optimization at $t = 5.9s$ by assigning the slack threads to P_1 via a DoP assignment of 17. P_1's controller performs gradient ascent again to settle at (S,P7,S). By $t = 10.4s$, the platform-wide optimization algorithm has converged (at $\{N_p\} = \{7, 9\}$), and the individual controllers of both programs are in the monitoring state. At $t = 56.0s$, program P_1 finishes and yields its threads back to the daemon, which in turn initiates another round of optimization by allocating those threads to P_0. P_0's controller performs gradient ascent and determines that (P13) is the ideal parallelism configuration and enters the monitoring state. It stays in that state until P_0 finishes at $t = 152.2s$.

Operation	Overhead		
	Platform 1	Platform 2	Unit
Task Migratability			
- Task Activation	11	7	nanoseconds per task instance
- Data Management	3	2	nanoseconds per dependency per task instance
Status Query	8	5	nanoseconds per query
Monitoring	44	15	nanoseconds per timestamp
Pause-Resume	33	4	milliseconds per pause-resume
Parallelism Reconfiguration	35	2	milliseconds per reconfiguration

Table 3. Recurring run-time overheads

Compared to OS scheduling of the baseline 24-thread parallel versions of the two benchmarks, Parcae reduces total execution time of the workload by 53.5%, and energy consumption by 76.3% by virtue of reducing the total execution time and using fewer cores. Parcae improves the execution time of each benchmark as well: `kmeans` improves by 53.5% and `blackscholes` by 36.7%. Recall that on a platform with no contention from other programs, the Parcae version of `blackscholes` took longer to execute than the baseline version (Table 1). Parcae's benefits manifest when the same program is executed on the same platform but with contention from other programs.

6.4 Optimality: A Closer Look

While Parcae delivers significant performance improvements, its achievements are still short of optimal execution determined via offline exhaustive search (see Table 1) for two main reasons. For `blackscholes`, `geti`, `md5sum`, and `potrace`, Parcae identifies the optimal configuration, but converges to that solution after first spending multiple iterations in SEQ and other sub-optimal schemes. In addition to the above overhead, for `kmeans`, `ks`, and `url`, the assumption about unimodal performance characteristic with increasing DoP (discussed in Section 4.1) does not hold; Parcae identifies a local optimum, which is worse than the global optimum. The Parcae gradient ascent algorithm can be enhanced to escape from local optima. We leave this to future work.

6.5 Morta and Decima Overheads

The execution time improvements reported in Table 1 account for all overheads of the system. Table 3 shows each overhead independently. The first three overheads are recurring (incurred on each instance of each task). To quantify them, we executed microbenchmarks designed to exercise each overhead independently. All aspects of the run-time control system are implemented in shared memory, thus making the run-time operations extremely lightweight. In the common case, task instances are executed on the same core, resulting in low-latency access to cross-iteration dependency data. Timestamp acquisitions are not serializing instructions; their latencies may be masked naturally via hardware exploiting instruction-level parallelism. By comparison to the geomean time per iteration across all benchmarks (1552.30 microseconds), the recurring overheads incurred on each iteration (or task instance) are orders of magnitude lower. "Pause-Resume" and "Parallelism Reconfiguration" overheads are application-specific and DoP-specific. The overheads shown in these two categories are for `blackscholes` with maximum DoP.

7. Related Work

Auto-parallelization: Most work on auto-parallelization at compile-time (e.g., [34, 43, 47]) or run-time (e.g., [18, 30, 35, 37]) is primarily concerned with parallelism discovery and extraction. Parcae addresses the complementary problem of parallelism tuning and optimization. Parcae tunes parallelism dynamically, and is designed to work with multiple automatic parallelization passes.

Flexible Parallel Execution: Adaptive Thread Management throttles the number of threads allocated to DOALL loops during execution, as their measured speedup exceeds or falls short of an expected speedup [13, 14]. Dynamic feedback has been used to determine the best synchronization policy from among those exposed by the compiler [12]. The ADAPT optimizer applies loop optimizations at run-time to create new variants of code [44]. Parcae employs multiple parallelization schemes prepared at compile-time to support efficient optimization at run-time, and optimizes multiple programs co-scheduled on a system. A key novelty over prior work is the mechanism for efficient pausing of one set of communicating tasks, followed by the resumption of the parallel region's execution by a different set of communicating tasks.

Auto-tuning: Auto-tuning is used to optimize parameters that impact performance. The optimal number of threads in an application's thread-pool can be determined across multiple application runs [16, 45]. For linear algebra codes, optimal loop tiling factors can be determined at compile-time for each platform [3, 5, 32]. However, not all important architectural variables can be handled by such parameterized adaptation; some choices require changing the underlying source code. This type of adaptation involves generating distinct implementations for the same operation [3]. The PetaBricks [2] and Elastin [27] frameworks leverage alternative code implementations exposed by programmers. Parcae automatically generates multiple versions for each parallel region from standard source code, and selects and tunes them at run-time based on performance feedback.

Parallelization Libraries: Numerous interfaces and enabling run-time systems have been proposed to adapt parallel program execution to run-time variability [10, 11, 22, 33, 40]. These systems burden the programmer with the task of extracting parallelism and with the task of expressing parallelism such that it can be optimized. Parcae minimizes the burden on the programmer as far as parallelism extraction is concerned, and fully automates the task of rewriting the parallel program for flexible execution. The run-time systems in those works either require the programmer to specify the degree of parallelism thus limiting performance portability (e.g. Cilk++ [20]), or are not adaptive (e.g. the TBB Auto Partitioner [36]), or handle only counted DOALL parallel loops (e.g. the Lazy Splitting scheduler [42]), or only optimize a single program in isolation; Parcae optimizes multiple programs running concurrently, handles counted and uncounted loops with different forms of parallelism, adapts parallelism configurations to changes in the environment, and delivers portable performance.

Operating Systems: Future operating systems for multicores will need tighter integration between parallel application run-time systems and operating system schedulers [6, 9, 28]. Parcae demonstrates the benefits of such an integration. Parcae's monitoring and resource management services could be integrated with operating systems for manycore processors such as Barrelfish [6].

8. Conclusion

This paper presented Parcae, a system that automatically generates flexible parallel programs and that monitors and optimizes the execution of multiple flexible programs running on a shared parallel platform. Compared to conventional parallel execution of seven benchmarks, Parcae reduced execution time by -1.4% (a small slowdown) to 41.9% with concomitant estimated processor energy savings of 23.9% to 83.9%. While Parcae was evaluated in the context of two parallelizing transforms, it can be extended to support additional, new ones. Parcae can improve the performance of flexible parallel programs even when co-scheduled with conventional, inflexible programs. With promising advances in auto-parallelization and increasing diversity in execution environments, a holistic, automatic, dynamic, and generally applicable parallelism tuning system will only become more relevant.

Acknowledgments

We thank the members of the Liberty Research Group for their support and feedback. We thank Carole-Jean Wu and Lennart Beringer for feedback on an early draft of this paper. We thank the anonymous reviewers for their insightful comments. This material is based on work supported by National Science Foundation Grant 1047879. Jae W. Lee was partly supported by the Korean IT R&D program of MKE/KEIT KI001810041244. This work was carried out while Arun Raman was a graduate student at Princeton University, and while Ayal Zaks was visiting Princeton University, supported by the HiPEAC network of excellence, and on leave from IBM Haifa Research Lab.

References

[1] R. Allen and K. Kennedy. *Optimizing Compilers for Modern Architectures: A Dependence-based Approach*. Morgan Kaufmann Publishers Inc., 2002.

[2] J. Ansel, C. Chan, Y. L. Wong, M. Olszewski, Q. Zhao, A. Edelman, and S. Amarasinghe. PetaBricks: A language and compiler for algorithmic choice. In *Proceedings of the 30th ACM SIGPLAN Conference on Programming Language Design and Implementation (PLDI)*, 2009.

[3] C. W. Antoine, A. Petitet, and J. J. Dongarra. Automated empirical optimization of software and the ATLAS project. *Parallel Computing*, 27:2001, 2000.

[4] Apple Open Source. md5sum: Message Digest 5 computation. http://www.opensource.apple.com/darwinsource.

[5] M. M. Baskaran, N. Vydyanathan, U. K. R. Bondhugula, J. Ramanujam, A. Rountev, and P. Sadayappan. Compiler-assisted dynamic scheduling for effective parallelization of loop nests on multicore processors. In *Proceedings of the 14th ACM SIGPLAN Symposium on Principles and Practice of Parallel Programming (PPoPP)*, pages 219–228, 2009.

[6] A. Baumann, P. Barham, P.-E. Dagand, T. Harris, R. Isaacs, S. Peter, T. Roscoe, A. Schüpbach, and A. Singhania. The multikernel: A new OS architecture for scalable multicore systems. In *Proceedings of the ACM SIGOPS 22nd Symposium on Operating Systems Principles (SOSP)*, pages 29–44, 2009.

[7] C. Bienia, S. Kumar, J. P. Singh, and K. Li. The PARSEC benchmark suite: Characterization and architectural implications. In *Proceedings of the 17th International Conference on Parallel Architectures and Compilation Techniques (PACT)*, 2008.

[8] O. Bilgir, M. Martonosi, and Q. Wu. Exploring the potential of CMP core count management on data center energy savings. In *Proceedings of the 3rd Workshop on Energy Efficient Design (WEED)*, 2011.

[9] S. L. Bird and B. J. Smith. PACORA: Performance aware convex optimization for resource allocation. In *Proceedings of the 3rd USENIX Workshop on Hot Topics in Parallelism (HotPar: Posters)*, 2011.

[10] F. Blagojevic, D. S. Nikolopoulos, A. Stamatakis, C. D. Antonopoulos, and M. Curtis-Maury. Runtime scheduling of dynamic parallelism on accelerator-based multi-core systems. *Parallel Computing*, 33(10-11):700–719, 2007.

[11] Y. Ding, M. Kandemir, P. Raghavan, and M. J. Irwin. Adapting application execution in CMPs using helper threads. *Journal of Parallel and Distributed Computing*, 69(9):790 – 806, 2009.

[12] P. Diniz and M. Rinard. Dynamic feedback: An effective technique for adaptive computing. In *Proceedings of the 18th ACM SIGPLAN Conference on Programming Language Design and Implementation (PLDI)*, 1997.

[13] G. Edjlali, G. Agrawal, A. Sussman, J. Humphries, and J. Saltz. Compiler and runtime support for programming in adaptive parallel environments. In *Scientific Programming*, pages 215–227, 1995.

[14] M. W. Hall and M. Martonosi. Adaptive parallelism in compiler-parallelized code. In *Proceedings of the 2nd SUIF Compiler Workshop*, 1997.

[15] J. L. Hellerstein, V. Morrison, and E. Eilebrecht. Applying control theory in the real world: Experience with building a controller for the .NET thread pool. *Performance Evaluation Review*, 37:38–42, 2010.

[16] T. Karcher and V. Pankratius. Run-time automatic performance tuning for multicore applications. In *Proceedings of the International Euro-Par Conference on Parallel Processing (Euro-Par)*, pages 3–14, 2011.

[17] A. Kejariwal, A. Nicolau, A. V. Veidenbaum, U. Banerjee, and C. D. Polychronopoulos. Efficient scheduling of nested parallel loops on multi-core systems. In *Proceedings of the 2009 International Conference on Parallel Processing (ICPP)*, pages 74–83, 2009.

[18] M. Kulkarni, K. Pingali, B. Walter, G. Ramanarayanan, K. Bala, and L. P. Chew. Optimistic parallelism requires abstractions. In *Proceedings of the 28th ACM SIGPLAN Conference on Programming Language Design and Implementation (PLDI)*, pages 211–222, 2007.

[19] C. Lattner and V. Adve. LLVM: A compilation framework for lifelong program analysis & transformation. In *Proceedings of the Annual International Symposium on Code Generation and Optimization (CGO)*, pages 75–86, 2004.

[20] C. E. Leiserson. The Cilk++ concurrency platform. In *Proceedings of the 46th ACM/IEEE Design Automation Conference (DAC)*, pages 522–527, 2009.

[21] LLVM Test Suite Guide. http://llvm.org/docs/TestingGuide.html.

[22] C.-K. Luk, S. Hong, and H. Kim. Qilin: Exploiting parallelism on heterogeneous multiprocessors with adaptive mapping. In *Proceedings of the 42nd Annual IEEE/ACM International Symposium on Microarchitecture (MICRO)*, pages 45–55, 2009.

[23] J. Mars, N. Vachharajani, M. L. Soffa, and R. Hundt. Contention aware execution: Online contention detection and response. In *Proceedings of the Annual International Symposium on Code Generation and Optimization (CGO)*, Toronto, Canada, 2010.

[24] G. Memik, W. H. Mangione-Smith, and W. Hu. NetBench: A benchmarking suite for network processors. In *Proceedings of the 2001 IEEE/ACM International Conference on Computer-Aided Design (ICCAD)*, 2001.

[25] C. C. Minh, J. Chung, C. Kozyrakis, and K. Olukotun. STAMP: Stanford Transactional Applications for Multi-Processing. In *Proceedings of the IEEE International Symposium on Workload Characterization (IISWC)*, 2008.

[26] R. Narayanan, B. Ozisikyilmaz, J. Zambreno, G. Memik, and A. Choudhary. Minebench: A benchmark suite for data mining workloads. 2006.

[27] I. Neamtiu. Elastic executions from inelastic programs. In *Proceedings of the 6th International Symposium on Software Engineering for Adaptive and Self-Managing Systems (SEAMS)*, 2011.

[28] H. Pan, B. Hindman, and K. Asanović. Composing parallel software efficiently with Lithe. In *Proceedings of the 31st ACM SIGPLAN Conference on Programming Language Design and Implementation (PLDI)*, pages 376–387, 2010.

[29] D. A. Penry. Multicore diversity: A software developer's nightmare. *ACM SIGOPS Operating Systems Review*, 43:100–101, 2009.

[30] C. D. Polychronopoulos. The hierarchical task graph and its use in auto-scheduling. In *Proceedings of the 5th International Conference on Supercomputing (ICS)*, pages 252–263, 1991.

[31] P. Prabhu, S. Ghosh, Y. Zhang, N. P. Johnson, and D. I. August. Commutative set: A language extension for implicit parallel programming. In *Proceedings of the 32nd ACM SIGPLAN Conference on Programming Language Design and Implementation (PLDI)*, 2011.

[32] M. Püschel, F. Franchetti, and Y. Voronenko. *Encyclopedia of Parallel Computing*, chapter Spiral. Springer, 2011.

[33] A. Raman, H. Kim, T. Oh, J. W. Lee, and D. I. August. Parallelism orchestration using DoPE: the degree of parallelism executive. In *Proceedings of the 32nd ACM SIGPLAN Conference on Programming Language Design and Implementation (PLDI)*, 2011.

[34] E. Raman, G. Ottoni, A. Raman, M. Bridges, and D. I. August. Parallel-stage decoupled software pipelining. In *Proceedings of the Annual International Symposium on Code Generation and Optimization (CGO)*, 2008.

[35] L. Rauchwerger, N. M. Amato, and D. A. Padua. A scalable method for run-time loop parallelization. *International Journal of Parallel Programming (IJPP)*, 26:537–576, 1995.

[36] A. Robison, M. Voss, and A. Kukanov. Optimization via reflection on work stealing in TBB. In *Proceedings of the 22nd International Parallel and Distributed Processing Symposium (IPDPS)*, pages 1–8, 2008.

[37] J. Saltz, R. Mirchandaney, and R. Crowley. Run-time parallelization and scheduling of loops. *IEEE Transactions on Computers*, 40, 1991.

[38] P. Selinger. potrace: Transforming bitmaps into vector graphics. http://potrace.sourceforge.net.

[39] J. C. Spall. *Introduction to Stochastic Search and Optimization*. Wiley-Interscience, 2003.

[40] M. A. Suleman, M. K. Qureshi, Khubaib, and Y. N. Patt. Feedback-directed pipeline parallelism. In *Proceedings of the 19th International Conference on Parallel Architecture and Compilation Techniques (PACT)*, pages 147–156, 2010.

[41] A. Tiwari and J. K. Hollingsworth. Online adaptive code generation and tuning. In *Proceedings of the 25th International Parallel and Distributed Processing Symposium (IPDPS)*, 2011.

[42] A. Tzannes, G. C. Caragea, R. Barua, and U. Vishkin. Lazy binary-splitting: A run-time adaptive work-stealing scheduler. In *Proceedings of the 15th ACM SIGPLAN Symposium on Principles and Practice of Parallel Programming (PPoPP)*, pages 179–190, 2010.

[43] H. Vandierendonck, S. Rul, and K. De Bosschere. The Paralax infrastructure: Automatic parallelization with a helping hand. In *Proceedings of the 19th International Conference on Parallel Architecture and Compilation Techniques (PACT)*, pages 389–400, 2010.

[44] M. J. Voss and R. Eigenmann. ADAPT: Automated de-coupled adaptive program transformation. In *Proceedings of the 1999 International Conference on Parallel Processing (ICPP)*, pages 163–170, 1999.

[45] Z. Wang and M. F. O'Boyle. Mapping parallelism to multi-cores: A machine learning based approach. In *Proceedings of the 14th ACM SIGPLAN Symposium on Principles and Practice of Parallel Programming (PPoPP)*, pages 75–84, 2009.

[46] M. Wolfe. DOANY: Not just another parallel loop. In *Proceedings of the 4th International Workshop on Languages and Compilers for Parallel Computing (LCPC)*, 1992.

[47] H. Zhong, M. Mehrara, S. Lieberman, and S. Mahlke. Uncovering hidden loop level parallelism in sequential applications. In *Proceedings of the 14th International Symposium on High-Performance Computer Architecture (HPCA)*, 2008.

JANUS: Exploiting Parallelism via Hindsight

Omer Tripp
Tel Aviv University
omertrip@post.tau.ac.il

Roman Manevich
The University of Texas at Austin
roman@ices.utexas.edu

John Field
Google
jfield@google.com

Mooly Sagiv
Tel Aviv University
msagiv@post.tau.ac.il

Abstract

This paper addresses the problem of reducing unnecessary conflicts in optimistic synchronization. Optimistic synchronization must ensure that any two concurrently executing transactions that commit are properly synchronized. Conflict detection is an approximate check for this condition. For efficiency, the traditional approach to conflict detection conservatively checks that the memory locations mutually accessed by two concurrent transactions are accessed only for reading.

We present JANUS, a parallelization system that performs conflict detection by considering sequences of operations and their composite effect on the system's state. This is done efficiently, such that the runtime overhead due to conflict detection is on a par with that of write-conflict-based detection. In certain common scenarios, this mode of refinement dramatically improves the precision of conflict detection, thereby reducing the number of false conflicts.

Our empirical evaluation of JANUS shows that this precision gain reduces the abort rate by an order of magnitude (22x on average), and achieves a speedup of up to 2.5x, on a suite of real-world benchmarks where no parallelism is exploited by the standard approach.

Categories and Subject Descriptors D.1.3 [*Programming Techniques*]: Concurrent Programming

General Terms Experimentation, Measurement, Performance

Keywords speculative execution, concurrency, conflict detection, transactional memory

1. Introduction

Optimistic synchronization enables synchronizing parallel and distributed computations without the use of blocking. If such optimism causes improper synchronization, then the mis-synchronized work is undone and the entire system is restored to a consistent state.

Optimistic synchronization is a promising approach to parallelizing software. It offers ease of use (compared to writing explicitly concurrent programs) and clear correctness guarantees; namely: atomicity, whereby the changes made by a transaction become visible to other transactions only at commit time; serializability, whereby committed transactions appear to execute in some serial order; and deadlock avoidance. Thanks to these strong guarantees, embodiments of this approach—in particular, software transactional memory [ ] (STM)—have received much attention.

```
int work = 0;
/* parallel */ foreach (item in items)
   process(item, work);

process(Item item, int work) {
   work += weightOf(item);
   Result result = processItem(item);
   if (result.isSuccessful()) // item processed successfully?
      work -= weightOf(item);
   foreach (Item sitem in item.subitems)
      process(sitem, work); } // recursive call
```

Figure 1. Program with available parallelism that is hard to exploit

Optimistic synchronization is speculative in nature. Typically, when a conflict is detected between two concurrent transactions, one of the transactions is aborted, resulting in wasted work. Conflict detection is commonly carried out by checking whether the concurrent transactions access a mutual memory location, where at least one of them writes it. This is known as the *write-set* approach.

The write-set approach is efficient, but at the same time, overly conservative in ensuring serializability when the concurrent transactions—in their entirety—commute. Replacing the write-set approach for conflict detection, which tests every pair of operations performed by the concurrent transactions for commutativity, with a more refined detection algorithm, which considers a broader view of the concurrent histories in its commutativity judgments, can potentially reduce unnecessary aborts, thereby increasing the level of concurrency.

Illustrative Example Consider the program in Figure 1, inspired by the JFileSync application [ ] (which we later discuss), where a collection of items is processed, and pending work (corresponding to items whose processing wasn't successful) is accumulated into variable `work`. Assuming that `processItem` is a pure function (i.e., free of side effects) and `processItem` calls are largely successful, the above loop admits a high degree of available parallelism. As long as updates to `work` are performed atomically, distinct items can be processed concurrently. Since most iterations restore `work` to its value at the beginning of the iteration, speculation is preferable to locking in ensuring the atomicity of accesses to `work`: If each iteration is executed as a transaction, then in most cases, concurrent transactions are not in conflict having acted as the identity function on the shared state (`work`).

Using the write-set conflict-detection approach, however, conflicts would be detected between any pair of transactions whose executions interleave, causing (at least) one of the transactions to abort. In effect, the execution of all transactions will be serialized, resulting in slowdown (compared to sequential execution of the loop). In contrast, with more accurate detection, which considers *sequences* of memory accesses rather than single operations, the synchronization algorithm can exploit the observation that most transactions preserve the original value of `work`, which enables a high level of concurrency and a potential speedup (depending on the cost of internal bookkeeping and load balancing).

Current Approaches Recent techniques that we are aware of for improving speculative parallelization are challenged by this example. Transactional checkpointing [ ], dependence-aware transactional memory [ ] and elastic transactions [ ] are all effective in reducing the cost and magnitude of aborts, yet these techniques cannot utilize the available parallelism in the above loop, which can only be appreciated by considering the (dynamic) interplay between increments and decrements of variable `work`.

Abstract locking [, ,] would also be futile in this case. Even if an abstraction specification is provided, transactions would conflict at the semantic level when attempting to increment and decrement variable `work` concurrently. Other forms of user specification, such as early release [ ] or the annotations supported by the Alter system [ ], are also of limited value here, because there is no particular conflict kind that can be universally suppressed without changing the semantics of the program.

Contributions Straightforward enforcement of sequence-based conflict detection is prohibitively expensive, especially relative to write-set-based detection. This paper describes an efficient technique for accomplishing such refined judgments while keeping runtime overhead on a par with that of the write-set-based approach.

The key to our technique is a *training phase* (Section 5.1), where sequences of operations that are likely to appear in conflict queries during parallel execution of the client application are extracted from single-threaded, synchronization-free, training runs of the application, and symbolic commutativity conditions are computed offline for pairs of such sequences.

For the information learned during training to generalize to new runs, our technique uses *generalization* (Section 5.2). This is done by mapping a concrete sequence (observed during training) to a regular abstraction of that sequence, such that commutativity conditions involving the original sequence remain valid for its abstraction.

For the information learned during training to be of practical value, our technique uses *projection* (Section 5.3), a commutativity testing algorithm ensuring that the dynamic context needed—during parallel execution—to check if a cached evaluation (learned during training) can be used for a commutativity query is essentially the same as in write-set detection: Only the read and write sets of operations are recorded. This also allows falling back to the write-set approach if the query cannot be answered from the cache.

We have implemented our sequence-based detection approach in JANUS, a parametric parallelization system based on optimistic synchronization (Section 4). The JANUS algorithm is abstract enough to encompass both memory-level statements and operations on abstract data types (ADTs), which enable further boosting of the detection algorithm's accuracy. In the latter case, the programmer specifies a representation function mapping a concrete data type to its abstract state, as well as the semantic interpretation of operations over the ADT.

Our evaluation of JANUS on a suite of five real-world benchmarks (Section 7) highlights the importance of sequence-based detection: JANUS achieved speedups of up to 2.5x, with few aborts, where its counterpart using write-set detection did not utilize any of the available parallelism in the benchmarks, and suffered from 22x more aborts.

The paper provides proof sketches for the correctness of the algorithms comprising our system. We defer full formal proofs to an accompanying technical report [ ].

2. Motivation

The simple example of Figure 1 illustrates one of several semantic patterns appearing in real-world applications (cf. Table 5) that motivate refined, "sequence-based" reasoning about commutativity between histories. Below is a *non-exhaustive* list of such patterns, which we next illustrate using popular open-source applications:

Identity The transaction manipulates the shared state, but upon termination, restores it to its configuration prior to its execution.

Reduction A sequence of values is reduced to a single value by an associative and commutative operator.

Shared-as-local Shared memory is used as a "scratch pad". The transaction overwrites values set by other transactions, and only reads values written by its own execution. Programmers typically use this pattern as an optimization for reducing allocation overhead.

Equal-writes Distinct transactions assign the same value to a shared memory location. This pattern is useful when the condition enabling two (concurrent) transactions to write equal values can be checked efficiently at runtime.

Spurious-reads A read memory location cannot influence the transaction's observable effect (cf. [ ]).

JFileSync The identity pattern is exemplified by Figure 2, where (a simplified version of) the JFileSync [ ] file-synchronization utility is presented. The main loop of JFileSync iterates over pairs of files or directories recursively, and computes file synchronization metadata for each pair via the `compareFiles` call. Each iteration updates the number of items left to handle, as well as the overall "weight" of pending items, when a new work item is encountered (fields `itemsStarted` and `itemsWeight` of `monitor`, respectively). These values are popped once processing of that item completes.

Compile-time parallelization of this loop is impaired by data dependencies between iterations due to `monitor` and its fields. Moreover, even if the compiler is able to assert that `monitor` can be privatized, the shared `progress` object—responsible for interacting with "observers" of the computation (via calls to `fireUpdate`)—must remain shared for cancelation requests to apply to all active transactions. This mandates careful synchronization of concurrent accesses to `monitor`, which presents a challenge not only for the compiler, but also for developers attempting manual parallelization of this code. Speculative parallelization is thus appealing, but the write-set approach is too conservative.

JGraphT-1 Figure 3, showing the code of the JGraphT greedy graph-coloring algorithm, illustrates the spurious-reads pattern: Two transactions that execute in parallel starting from the same valuation of `maxColor` can only conflict if both assign new (and different) values to `maxColor`. If one (or both) of the transactions merely reads this variable, then there is no threat of conflict, and so read–write conflicts can safely be suppressed.

A compiler would fail to parallelize this algorithm because of loop-carried dependencies involving not only `maxColor`, but also the

```
/* parallel */ for (JFSDirectoryPair pair : pairs) {
  monitor.itemsStarted.add(2);
  monitor.itemsWeight.add(1);
  monitor.rootUriSrc = pair.getSrc();
  monitor.rootUriTgt = pair.getTgt();
  if (!progress.isCanceled()) { ...; weight = ...;
    monitor.itemsStarted.add(srcDirs.length+tgtDirs.length);
    monitor.itemsWeight.add(weight);
    progress.fireUpdate(); ...;
    /* compareFiles is recursive, also making "balanced" add-remove calls */
    compareFiles(...);
    monitor.itemsStarted.remove(monitor.itemsStarted.size()-1);
    monitor.itemsWeight.remove(monitor.itemsWeight.size()-1); }
  monitor.itemsStarted.remove(monitor.itemsStarted.size()-1);
  monitor.itemsWeight.remove(monitor.itemsWeight.size()-1);
  progress.fireUpdate(); }
```

Figure 2. JFileSync: *identity* (monitor.{itemsStarted,itemsWeight}) and *shared-as-local* (monitor.{rootUriSrc,rootUriTgt})

```
RuleSets rs = ruleSetFactory.createRuleSets(rulesets);
/* parallel */ for (DataSource dataSource : files) {
  String niceFileName = dataSource.getNiceFileName(...); ...;
  ctx.sourceCodeFilename = niceFileName;
  ctx.sourceCodeFile = new File(niceFileName); ...;
  rs.start(ctx); ...;
  rs.end(ctx); ...; }

/* in GenericClassCounterRule.java; called transitively by rs.start */
@Override
public void start(RuleContext ctx) {
  ctx.setAttribute(COUNTER_LABEL, new AtomicLong());
  super.start(ctx); }
```

Figure 4. PMD: *shared-as-local* (ctx)

shared color and usedColors arrays, where usedColors follows the shared-as-local pattern. These would also impair speculation based on the write-set approach. Manual parallelization of the code (e.g., using map reduction) is also not immediate, because the greedy algorithm mandates ordered traversal over the nodes of the graph.

PMD A near match for the shared-as-local pattern appears in PMD, a popular code scanner for Java whose main loop is shown in Figure 4. Most of the fields of the shared RuleContext instance, ctx, are treated as local by the loop's iterations. For example, each iteration first writes sourceCodeFile and sourceCodeFilename, and only later reads these fields. However, sharing between iterations is enabled via attributes stored in ctx (by calling {set,get}Attribute). This means that ctx cannot be privatized.

Compile-time parallelization of the PMD loop is thus inhibited. Manual transformation is also subtle: Calls to {set,get}Attribute occur deep in the call stack from the main loop, and are thus hard to track and observe. Sound handling of the persistent attributes further requires manual transformation of the RuleContext class, such that the fields that are amenable to privatization become separate from those that must remain global. Synchronization must then be added to mediate accesses to the global RuleContext state. Finally, write-set-based speculation will perform poorly because all iterations update the "local" sourceCodeFile and sourceCodeFilename fields.

Weka Last, Figure 5 presents code from the Weka data-mining library that is responsible for rendering a graph to a display device. This algorithm illustrates the equal-writes pattern in that distinct iterations accessing the same pixel do not conflict if they have set the Graphics object to the same color.

Since the iterations are not invariantly independent, a compiler cannot statically parallelize this code, nor is it clear which manual transformations can be applied in this case. Speculative parallelization of the loop that is oblivious to pixel colors and only considers the accessed pixels is also overly pessimistic, but accounting for

```
int[] order = ...; // permutation of nodes fixing traversal order
int[] color = new int[neighbors.length];
int maxColor = 1;
BitSet usedColors = new BitSet(neighbors.length);
/* parallel */ for (int i = 0; i < neighbors.length; i++) {
  int v = order[i];
  usedColors.clear();
  for (int j = 0; j < neighbors[v].length; j++) {
    int nb = neighbors[v][j];
    if (color[nb] > 0) {
      usedColors.set(color[nb]); } }
  color[v] = 1;
  while (usedColors.get(color[v])) {
    color[v]++; }
  if (color[v] > maxColor) {
    maxColor = color[v]; } }
```

Figure 3. JGraphT-1: *shared-as-local* (usedColors) and *spurious-reads* (maxColor)

```
Graphics2D g = ...;
/* parallel */ for (int index=0; index<nodes.size(); index++) {
  GraphNode n = (GraphNode) nodes.elementAt(index);
  if (n.nodeType == NORMAL) {
    g.setColor(this.getBackground().darker().darker());
    g.fillOval(x+n.x+...,y+n.y,nodeWidth, nodeHeight);
    g.setColor(Color.White); ...;
    g.drawString(n.lbl,x+n.x+...,y+n.y+nodeHeight/2+...); ...;
    g.setColor(Color.black);
  } else {
    g.drawLine(x+n.x+...,y+n.y,x+n.x+...,y+n.y+nodeHeight); }
  int x1, y1, x2, y2; ...;
  g.drawLine(x+x1, y+y1, x+x2, y+y2); ...; }
```

Figure 5. Weka: *equal-writes* (graphics)

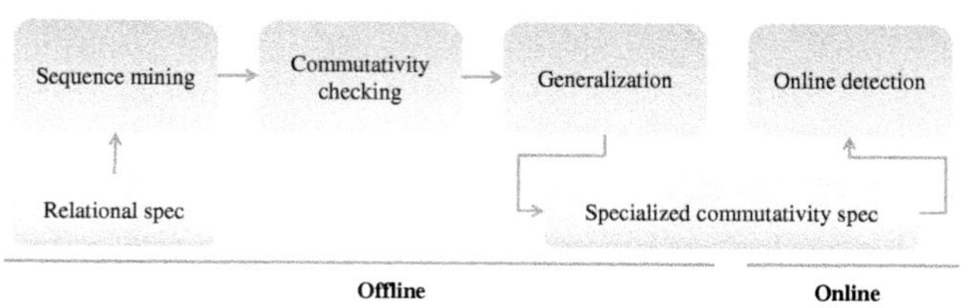

Figure 6. Outline of the JANUS architecture

pixel values entails customization of the detection algorithm and may further lead to prohibitive instrumentation overhead.

3. Overview

The examples of Section 2 motivate more accurate conflict detection. However, boosting the accuracy of the detection algorithm comes at the cost of degrading performance. The write-set heuristic, employed in many realistic parallelization systems (e.g., [, , ,]), tracks the read and write sets of a transaction, such that conflict detection reduces to a check whether there is a memory location that one of the concurrent transactions writes and the other accesses (either reading from it or writing to it).

Moving beyond the write-set approach, toward more accurate detection algorithms, involves two potential performance penalties: First, if the algorithm bases its judgment on information that is beyond read and write sets (e.g., the commutativity policies in [ ]), then further instrumentation overhead—for collecting this additional information—is incurred. Second, the complexity of the detection algorithm itself may be prohibitive. This rules out naïve realization of sequence-based commutativity.

On the other hand, the codes in Figures 2–5—all real-world applications—illustrate several common scenarios where sequence-based reasoning provides significant value over the write-set approach. This remains true in the presence of state abstraction [,], where conflicts are tracked atop the semantic state of data structures implementing ADTs. Though the (likely impractical) solution of instrumenting the program's state to record arbitrary trace information is theoretically possible, doing so does not only degrade performance, but also involves manual user intervention in deciding which information to record.

Our Approach In this paper, we present an automated technique for performing conflict detection over (potentially long) sequences, such that (i) there is no instrumentation overhead beyond that of the write-set approach, and (ii) the complexity of the detection algorithm is also comparable to write-set-based detection. Our technique, based on a preliminary learning phase, favors applications where learning holds promise, in that the effect of transactions on the shared state remains similar across different inputs. For other applications, where this is not the case, our approach will behave analogously to the write-set approach.

The flow of our solution is illustrated in Figure 6. The key aspect of our approach is offline learning of commutativity information: The application is profiled using training data, and commutativity conditions are evaluated for sequences arising during training that are expected to occur (frequently) in production mode. These candidate sequences essentially comprise dependent operations within the trace. During parallel execution, the conditions that were learned offline are used to test commutativity over sequences that are "similar" to the ones identified in training.

To ensure that the runtime overhead of our system is comparable to that of the write-set heuristic, the offline commutativity information we compute relates to sequences of operations over *individual* memory locations (Section 5.3). At runtime, this enables reconstruction of single-location-based sequences from the read and write sets of operations, and thus the dynamic context needed for sequence-based detection does not impose any instrumentation cost beyond that of the write-set approach.

The process prescribed by our approach consists of the following stages:

1. The input to our system is a user specification mapping concrete data structures to their (abstract) relational representation. The semantic state of a data structure is specified as a set of relations, and operations over the data structure are expressed using relational primitives. The `BitSet` class used in Figure 3, for instance, can be encoded as a 2-ary relation mapping integral values to boolean values. A relational description of the `get` operation is then specified as a `select` query, and similarly, setting the bit at index n to value x translates into removing the (unique) tuple whose first component is n and then inserting $\langle n, x\rangle$. The primary reason for the relational specification is that it facilitates reasoning about commutativity between sequences of operations.
2. Next, the subject application is exercised in "sequential" (i.e., single-threaded) mode using training inputs, such that no synchronization is required. In these runs, sequential dependencies are tracked between trace operations, and sequences of dependent operations that belong in different transactions are considered. In the example of Figure 3, for instance, two such sequences may be { `work+=2; work-=2; work+=1; work-=1;` } and { `work+=3; work-=3;` }.
3. Commutativity conditions—in the form of designated input states—are then computed for each pair of such sequences, where concrete values are substituted by symbolic values (e.g., { `work+=`x`; work-=`x`;` } for the second sequence). Generalization from concrete observations to arbitrary sequences is done using a theorem prover to ensure soundness.
4. To lift the learned commutativity information to new runs of the application, the sequences recorded during training are generalized into an abstract regular form by allowing arbitrarily many occurrences of idempotent subsequences within the generalized sequence (Section 5.2). The abstraction of { `work+=`x`; work-=`x`;` }, for example, is { `work+=`x`; work-=`x`;` }$^+$ (where $+$ denotes the Kleene-cross operator).
5. Finally, in production mode, a commutativity query is answered positively based on the cached information if the sequences in the query match a cached pair of sequences, and the input state belongs in the designated input states for the matched pair. If no match is found in the cache, then our technique falls back to the write-set approach.

4. The JANUS Parallelization Protocol

In this section, we define the protocol enforced by our parallelization system, where we leave the conflict-detection algorithm unspecified (until Section 5, which defines sequence-based conflict detection). We refer the reader to [ ] for a formal description of the transition system underlying our protocol.

4.1 Parallelization Protocol

JANUS accepts as input (i) an initial configuration of the shared state, (ii) a list of tasks, each consisting of a program **prog** to be run and initial data values ($o \rightarrow \nu$), and (iii) a specification whether to commit the tasks in the order in which they were given. JANUS maintains two state variables: an atomic integer (*Clock*) implementing the versioning of the shared state, and a read-write lock (*lock*) for synchronizing concurrent activities. (In Figure 7, we denote use of the read (write) lock provided by *lock* when invoking an operation via the "with *lock.r* (*lock.w*)" syntax.)

JANUS repeatedly tries to execute the input tasks asynchronously, in parallel, until its task pool is drained (DOPARALLEL). Each execution attempt (RUNTASK call) encloses the argument task in a transaction, where the task's identifier and the time of creation of the transaction are recorded (CREATETRANSACTION). CREATETRANSACTION copies the global state (*Sh*), as well as the task-specific data ($o \rightarrow \nu$), into the local state of the freshly defined transaction. (Note that CREATETRANSACTION requires only a read lock, which enables multiple simultaneous transaction initializations.)

Next, RUNTASK executes the transaction sequentially (RUNSEQUENTIAL). In the case of in-order execution, the transaction can try to commit (after sequential execution) only once all its preceding transactions (ordered by task identifiers) have committed. As soon as this happens, or if the *ordered* flag is not set, the transaction repeatedly attempts to commit until it either succeeds or fails. This is done by retrieving the sequence of operations committed between the time of start of the transaction (*t.Begin*) and the present time (*now*), and checking for conflicts between this portion of the system's history (ops^c) and the operations performed by the transaction (*t.Log*). (Note that no lock is acquired for conflict detection, which we later compensate for in COMMIT.)

If conflicts are detected between the histories, then the transaction aborts and RUNTASK will be called again from scratch. Otherwise, COMMIT is called. (Note that this is the only call that is governed by a write lock.) COMMIT first checks whether the considered system history has evolved between the point where DETECTCONFLICT was invoked and the present time (using the $now \neq tcheck$ test). If the history is valid (i.e., it hasn't evolved), then (i) *clock* is incremented, and (ii) all the operations the transaction performed on privatized copies of global objects are replayed on their counterparts in global memory (REPLAYLOGGEDOPERATIONS). Otherwise, conflict detection is re-attempted.

Versioning To reduce the cost of state privatization, which is a key aspect of the JANUS algorithm, (fully) persistent data structures [ ] can be used. A persistent data structure preserves the pre-

```
The JANUS Parallelization Protocol

Types:
  Transaction = Record {
    tid                : integer   // transaction identifier
    Begin              : integer   // transaction begin time
    Loc                : state     // transaction-local state
    SharedPrivatized   : state     // privatized shared state
    SharedSnapshot     : state     // snapshot of shared state at Begin
    Log                : list      // history of operations }
Inputs:
  ⟨⟨prog_1, o_1 → ν_1⟩, ..., ⟨prog_m, o_m → ν_m⟩⟩: tasks
  Sh_0: initial global (i.e., shared) state
  ordered: in-order execution flag

Variables:
  Clock: atomic integer initialized to 1
  lock: read-write lock with read lock r and write lock w

DOPARALLEL:
  for i := 1 ... m
    do asynchronously r := RUNTASK(prog_i, o_i → ν_i, i) while ¬r

RUNTASK(prog, o → ν, i):
  t := CREATETRANSACTION(o → ν, i) with lock.r
  RUNSEQUENTIAL(prog, t) // manipulates t.{Loc, SharedPrivatized, Log}
  if ordered wait until t.tid = GET(Clock)
  do while true
    now := GET(Clock) with lock.r
    ops^c := GETCOMMITTEDHISTORY(t.Begin, now)
    if DETECTCONFLICTS(t.SharedSnapshot, t.Log, ops^c)
      return false // abort
    if COMMIT(t, now) with lock.w
      return true

CREATETRANSACTION(o → ν, i):
  t := FRESHTRANSACTION (
    tid := i
    Begin := GET(Clock)
    Loc := (o → ν)
    SharedPrivatized := Sh
    SharedSnapshot := Sh
    Log := ε )

COMMIT(t, tcheck):
  now := GET(Clock)
  if now ≠ tcheck
    return false // abort
  INCREMENT(Clock)
  REPLAYLOGGEDOPERATIONS(t.Log, Sh)
  return true
```

Figure 7. Pseudo-code of the parallelization protocol enforced by JANUS, where the conflict-detection algorithm is unspecified

vious version of itself when modified; a data structure is *fully* persistent if every version can be both accessed and modified, which—in our case—permits concurrent modification of the shared state by multiple simultaneous transactions.

Conflict Detection The ideal test for conflicts is an explicit commutativity check. Assume that transaction t started running at time t_0, in state σ_0, and is performing a conflict test at time t_k. We denote by $\overline{b} = \langle b_1, \ldots, b_n \rangle$ the sequence of operations corresponding to transaction t. We refer to the operations corresponding to transactions that committed within time interval $[t_0, t_k]$, denoted by $\overline{a} = \langle a_1, \ldots, a_m \rangle$, as the *conflict history* of transaction t. Then t is in conflict with its conflict history iff

$$[\![\overline{a} \cdot \overline{b}]\!](\sigma_0) \neq [\![\overline{b} \cdot \overline{a}]\!](\sigma_0).$$

We say that a conflict-detection algorithm is *sound* if it does not permit a transaction that does not commute with its conflict history to commit. We say that a conflict-detection algorithm is *valid* if it does not prevent a transaction with an empty conflict history from committing.

Theorem 4.1. *Assume that the protocol of Figure 7 is instantiated with a sound and valid conflict-detection algorithm. Then*

1. *(**termination**) every run of the protocol is guaranteed to terminate if the sequential execution of all tasks (operation* RUNSEQUENTIAL*) terminates; and*
2. *(**serializability**) assuming termination, (i) every ordered run of the protocol is guaranteed to terminate in the same final state as its sequential counterpart, and (ii) every unordered run of the protocol is guaranteed to terminate in the same final state as a sequential execution of the tasks where their order of execution corresponds to the commit order in the concurrent run.*

Proof Sketch. For termination, observe that a RUNTASK call by task t can fail iff there is another task, t', whose RUNTASK call succeeds. Further observe that failure due to successful RUNTASK calls of other tasks can only occur finitely many times, since the number of tasks scheduled for execution is fixed and known in advance, which guarantees that a scheduled task will eventually commit.

For correctness, we rely on the soundness of the conflict-detection algorithm. In-order execution is enforced by preventing a transaction from attempting a commit until the global counter matches its identifier, which implies that all preceding tasks have committed already. □

5. Conflict Detection with Hindsight

The focus of this section is on the sequence-based conflict-detection algorithm employed by JANUS. The techniques enabling this algorithm are discussed in turn in the following subsections.

5.1 The Training Phase

The purpose of training is to specialize the detection algorithm in advance of parallel execution by building a cache of commutativity conditions relating to sequences of operations. In production mode, this cache saves the (expensive) work of performing sequence-based commutativity checking. Instead, the cache is searched for a match for the concurrent sequences in their input state. If no match is found, then the detection algorithm defaults to write-set-based detection.

Values and Dependencies. In support of dependence-analysis techniques that we introduce later in this paper, we make the assumption that the values assigned to objects are separable into subvalues. Formally, we assume a subvalue lattice with a partial ordering $v' \preceq v$, a join operation $\sqcup$, a meet operator $\sqcap$, and a subtraction operator defined for two ordered values $v' \preceq v$ by $v - v' \stackrel{\text{def}}{=} \min\{w \mid w \sqcup v' = v\}$.

Let *op* be an operation, such that the invocation of *op* in state σ yields state σ': $[\![op]\!](\sigma) = \sigma'$. Further, let $\langle o, v \rangle$ be an object-value pair in state σ, and $\langle o, v' \rangle$ its corresponding object-value pair in σ'. We denote the invocation of *op* in state σ by op_σ. The *frame* of op_σ's restriction to o, denoted as $op^f_\sigma(o)$, is the maximal unchanged subvalue of o: $v^f = v \sqcap v'$. The *written* subvalue of op_σ's restriction to o is defined as $op^w_\sigma(o) = (v - v^f) \sqcup (v' - v^f)$. Finally, the *read* subvalue of op_σ's restriction to o, given by $op^r_\sigma(o)$, is the minimal subvalue $v^r \preceq v^f$, such that $[\![op]\!](\sigma) = [\![op]\!](\sigma[o \rightarrow (v \setminus v^f) \sqcup v^r])$. Intuitively, v^r is the portion of the frame that determines the outcome of *op* in state σ.

A dependency arises between two operation instances, op_{σ_1} and $\widetilde{op}_{\sigma_2}$, if there exists an object $o \in dom(\sigma_1) \cap dom(\sigma_2)$, such that

$$(op^w_{\sigma_1}(o) \sqcup op^r_{\sigma_1}(o)) \sqcap (\widetilde{op}^w_{\sigma_2}(o) \sqcup \widetilde{op}^r_{\sigma_2}(o)) \neq \bot. \quad (1)$$

That is, op_{σ_1} and $\widetilde{op}_{\sigma_2}$ both access a common subvalue of v, either for reading or for writing. (Input dependencies are subsumed by this definition.) We note that our definition of a dependency, inspired by [ ], is general enough to apply both in a concrete semantics and in an abstract semantics induced by state coarsening.

Mining Sequences. We begin by explaining how the sequences are obtained. For a specific training payload, the training algorithm tracks dependencies between operations, within as well as across tasks, according to Equation 1. This results in a global dependence graph, $G = \langle V, E \rangle$, where the nodes of G are the operation instances from the run, and edge $v_1 \xrightarrow{l} v_2 \in E$ denotes that v_1 depends on v_2 over location l.

Next, for each location l accessed during the run, the (unique) maximal dependence path corresponding to l in G is retrieved. The path is then partitioned according to task boundaries. This yields a collection of subpaths, each corresponding to the operations involving l within a single task. These subpaths capture dependent sequences of operations that may participate, during parallel execution, in conflict queries.

We then compute commutativity conditions for each pair of such sequences. The conditions refer to the input state in which the sequences are evaluated. Our current prototype has limited symbolic capabilities, which we continuously evolve on demand. We presently account for equality and inequality tests appearing in the sequence, and further support certain useful distinctions that are particular to container ADTs (such as the presence of a key in a `Map` object).

5.2 Generalization via Sequence Abstraction

Concrete sequences of operations on shared locations often vary dynamically as a function of the input. For example, the add–subtract sequences induced by `work` in Figure 2 are length-wise proportional to the complexity of the input items. Caching commutativity information that holds for particular concrete sequences (those mined from sequential runs of the concurrent system) is thus of restricted value, as these sequences are tightly coupled to the training payloads.

To address this, we exploit the observation that distinct concrete sequences having the same "regular" description are, under certain conditions, conflict-wise equivalent. For instance, sequence `{ work+=1;work-=1; }`—arising for the program in Figure 1— induces the same conflicts as `{ work+=1;work-=1;work+=1;work-=1 }`, and more generally, as any sequence in the language of regular expression (`{ work+=1;work-=1 }`)$^+$.

This is stated formally in the following claim, which relies on the notion of idempotence to assert a sufficient condition for conflict-wise equivalence between concrete sequences exhibiting the same regularity.

Lemma 5.1. *Let $s := s_1 \cdot s_2 \cdot s_3$ be a concrete sequence of operations, and assume that s_2 is an idempotent subsequence of s. Then operation* CONFLICT *from Figure 8 cannot distinguish between s and sequence $s' := s_1 \cdot s_2 \cdot s_2 \cdot s_3$. That is, given sequence $\overline{s}$, s conflicts with $\overline{s}$ in input state σ according to* CONFLICT *iff s' conflicts with $\overline{s}$ in this state.*

Proof Sketch. Let σ' be the intermediate state after evaluating s_2 within s starting at entry state σ. Then if we evaluate s' at state σ, then the intermediate state *before* the second evaluation of s_2, as well as *after* it, is σ'. This implies that (i) the final states following evaluation of both s and s' at state σ are identical, and moreover, (ii) read operations within the first and second occurrences of s_2 within s' yield identical results. □

Sequence-based Conflict Detection Using Projection

Inputs:
$\langle op^t_1, \ldots, op^t_m \rangle$: operations performed by current transaction
$\langle op^c_1, \ldots, op^c_n \rangle$: committed operations
G: entry state of current transaction

DETECTCONFLICTS:
$m^t :=$ DECOMPOSE($\langle op^t_1, \ldots, op^t_m \rangle$)
$m^c :=$ DECOMPOSE($\langle op^c_1, \ldots, op^c_n \rangle$)
for $loc \in$ DOM(m^t) $\cap$ DOM(m^c)
  if CONFLICT($G, loc, m^t(loc), m^c(loc)$) return **true**
return **false**

DECOMPOSE($\langle op_1, \ldots, op_k \rangle$):
$subseqs := \emptyset$
for $i := 1 \ldots k$
  $\{loc_1, \ldots, loc_l\} :=$ GETACCESSEDLOCATIONS(op_k)
  for $j := 1 \ldots l$
    $subseqs := subseqs[loc_j \to subseqs(loc_j) \cdot op_k]$
return $subseqs$

CONFLICT($\sigma, l, \langle op_1, \ldots, op_k \rangle, \langle \overline{op}_1, \ldots, \overline{op}_w \rangle$):
$r_1 :=$ GETREADSUBSEQUENCES($\langle op_1, \ldots, op_k \rangle$)
$r_2 :=$ GETREADSUBSEQUENCES($\langle \overline{op}_1, \ldots, \overline{op}_w \rangle$)
for $rsubseq \in r_1$
  if $\neg$SAMEREAD($\sigma, rsubseq, \langle \overline{op}_1, \ldots, \overline{op}_w \rangle$) return **true**
for $rsubseq \in r_2$
  if $\neg$SAMEREAD($\sigma, rsubseq, \langle op_1, \ldots, op_k \rangle$) return **true**
if $\neg$COMMUTE($\sigma, l, \langle op_1, \ldots, op_k \rangle, \langle \overline{op}_1, \ldots, \overline{op}_w \rangle$) return **true**
return **false**

SAMEREAD($\sigma, l, \langle op_1, \ldots, op_k \rangle, \langle \overline{op}_1, \ldots, \overline{op}_w \rangle$):
$\sigma'_1 := \langle op_1, \ldots, op_k \rangle (\sigma)$
$\sigma'_2 := \langle \overline{op}_1, \ldots, \overline{op}_w \rangle \cdot \langle op_1, \ldots, op_k \rangle (\sigma)$
$v_1 := \sigma'_1(l)$
$v_2 := \sigma'_2(l)$
return $v_1 = v_2$

GETREADSUBSEQUENCES($\langle op_1, \ldots, op_k \rangle$):
$rsubseqs := \emptyset$
for $i := 1 \ldots k$
  if ISREAD(op_i) $rsubseqs := rsubseqs \cup \{\langle op_1, \ldots, op_i \rangle\}$
return $rsubseqs$

Figure 8. Algorithm for conflict detection using projection

Generalization mitigates the problem of cache misses, and further allows use of "small" (yet sufficiently representative) inputs during training to accelerate cache population. Instead of relating commutativity conditions to concrete sequences, which mandates an exact match for a commutativity query arising at runtime, JANUS relates commutativity conditions to abstract sequences. These are computed offline, during the training phase, based on the concrete sequences due to the sequential runs. JANUS iteratively searches—in a bottom-up fashion—for idempotent subsequences within the concrete sequence, and applies the Kleene-cross abstraction to these subsequences.

5.3 Conflict Detection Using Projection

Figure 8 presents an "idealized" version of JANUS' projection-based algorithm for conflict-detection. The algorithm checks whether the operations $\langle op^t_i \rangle^m_{i=1}$ of the current transaction, t, conflict with operations $\langle op^c_i \rangle^n_{i=1}$, which were committed by other transactions while t was running.

DETECTCONFLICTS first decomposes sequences $\langle op_i^t \rangle_{i=1}^m$ and $\langle op_i^c \rangle_{i=1}^n$ into multiple subsequences, such that every subsequence consists of the dependent operations accessing a single location. This is enabled by recording the read and write sets of each operations. Next, the sequences corresponding to shared locations (per the $loc \in \text{DOM}(m^t) \cap \text{DOM}(m^c)$ restriction) are analyzed for conflicts (in CONFLICT). Importantly, private locations—and the sequences of operations applied to them—are safely ignored, which for many realistic benchmarks is a dramatic saving.

A conflict is flagged between location-centric subsequences s_1 and s_2 induced by location l in one of two cases: Either (i) the value resulting from a read operation within s_1 (s_2) is influenced by whether s_2 (s_1) is performed before s_1 (s_2) or not (the SAMEREAD tests), or (ii) s_1 and s_2 do not commute over l.

The algorithm in Figure 8 is idealized in that in practice, CONFLICT consults its cache—populated during the training phase—instead of directly executing the SAMEREAD and COMMUTE checks. These are executed offline over the sequences due to training. If a miss is registered, then JANUS' default behavior is to fall back to write-set-based detection. Alternatively, JANUS can be configured to perform the sequence-based check online, which is unlikely to be acceptable in performance (though memoization can be used to support "online training").

Correctness While the location-wise commutativity check is natural, the SAMEREAD tests are less obvious. Lemma 5.2 affirms that together, these two checks pose as a sound transaction-wide commutativity judgment. The following example (in Java syntax) demonstrates that COMMUTE alone does not suffice:

```
x = 0, y = 0;
{ b = x==0; if (b) y = 1; x = 1; }     /* 1st transaction */
{ x = 1; }                             /* 2nd transaction */
```

In this program, the subsequences corresponding to both `x` and `y` commute. (`{ b = x==0; x = 1; }` commutes with `{ x = 1; }`, and `{ y = 1; }` trivially commutes with ϵ.) Yet the two transactions do not commute. This is because the (control) dependence between `x` and `y` is (incorrectly) ignored. The requirement that intermediate reads be unaffected by the order of execution of the concurrent transactions is a conservative approximation of the flow (through local state) between shared locations.

Lemma 5.2. *Let t_1 and t_2 be two transactions, such that t_1 commits during the execution of t_2. Further let $ops_1 = \langle op_1^i \rangle_{i=1}^m$ and $ops_2 = \langle op_2^i \rangle_{i=1}^n$ be the histories corresponding to t_1 and t_2, respectively, and σ the system state when t_2 begins execution. We denote by $\{ops_1^l : l \in L_1\}$ ($\{ops_2^l : l \in L_2\}$) the location-centric subsequences induced by ops_1 (ops_2), where L_1 (L_2) denotes the locations accessed by ops_1 (ops_2). Then t_1 and t_2 commute in σ if the following two conditions hold for every $l \in L_1 \cap L_2$:*

1. *(**commutativity**) ops_1^l and ops_2^l commute with respect to l: $([\![ops_1^l \cdot ops_2^l]\!](\sigma))(l) = ([\![ops_2^l \cdot ops_1^l]\!](\sigma))(l)$.*
2. *(**intermediate reads**) every read of l within ops_1^l (ops_2^l) results in the same value regardless of whether ops_1^l (ops_2^l) is evaluated in state σ or in state $[\![ops_2^l]\!](\sigma)$ ($[\![ops_1^l]\!](\sigma)$).*

Proof Sketch. We assume that the two conditions above hold, and prove for an arbitrary shared location l that its value is the same in both orders of execution of t_1 and t_2. First, we observe that control flow within t_1 (t_2) remains the same regardless of whether t_2 (t_1) is executed before t_1 (t_2). This is guaranteed by the invariance of intermediate reads from the shared state under the order of execution of t_1 and t_2, and these—assuming that the transactions are deterministic—are the only way of influencing the flow of a transaction. The projection of t_1's (t_2's) history on l therefore remains sequence ops_1^l (ops_2^l) regardless of the order of execution of t_1 and t_2. This, together with our assumption that ops_1^l and ops_2^l commute with respect to l in starting state σ, yields the conclusion that l's value is invariant under the order of execution of t_1 and t_2. □

The above claim, as well as its proof, extend naturally to the case where multiple transactions commit during the execution of a concurrent transaction.

Relaxed Consistency Beyond the baseline checks, and similarly to [ ], JANUS supports a user-provided specification of consistency relaxations for data structures of choice. The user may specify that updates to (instances of) a data structure be committed in the presence of read-after-write (RAW) and/or write-after-write (WAW) conflicts involving the data structure's state.

The specification that RAW conflicts are tolerable for a data structure translates into dropping the SAMEREAD checks for shared locations defined by that data structure during conflict detection (cf. Figure 3). Analogously, tolerance of WAW conflicts is handled by dropping the final COMMUTE test (cf. Figure 4).

JANUS also performs limited automatic inference of relaxation specifications. For example, if out-of-order parallelization is permitted, then JANUS ignores WAW dependencies chaining two transactions, because these imply (under transitive reduction) that the transactions access the shared locations in conflict by first defining them and only then (potentially) reading them, and the final value of the shared locations is immaterial (as indicated by the out-of-order specification). This pattern is exemplified in Figure 4.

6. Relational Instantiation

In this section, we present a relational realization of the techniques described in Section 5. Representing object states and operations in relational form provides a natural way of computing the composite effect of a sequence of operations.

The relational instantiation is also general enough to encompass both standard (memory-level) transactions, whose executions consist of a sequence of statements, and transactions where certain data structures are equipped with abstraction specifications. These specifications enable treating method invocations atomically by considering their effect over abstract states.

The latter setting is similar in spirit to [ ] and [ ], where ADT semantics are taken into account in conflict detection to reduce the rate of spurious conflicts.

6.1 Preliminaries

Relations, Tuples and Dependencies We instantiate the definitions from 5.1 to the domain of relations. Assume a set v of untyped values drawn from a universe $\mathbb{V}$, which includes the integers: $\mathbb{Z} \subseteq \mathbb{V}$. A *tuple* $t = \langle c_1 : v_1, \ldots, c_k : v_k \rangle$ maps a set of columns (c_i) to values from $\mathbb{V}$. We use $t\ c$ to denote the valuation of tuple t on column c. A *relation* is a set of tuples over identical columns. We define a partial ordering on relations $r' \preceq r \overset{\text{def}}{=} r' \subseteq r$ by the subset relation, join by set union, meet by set intersection, and subtraction by set subtraction.

We write $t \models \phi$ if tuple t satisfies formula ϕ, where ϕ is in the language of the grammar in Table 1. For any t, $t \models \mathbf{true}$, and similarly, $t \not\models \mathbf{false}$. Finally, $t \models c = v$ iff $t\ c = v$.

A relation r has a functional dependency (FD) $\delta := C_1 \to C_2$ if any pair of tuples in r that are equal on columns C_1 are also equal on columns C_2. We refer to C_1 (C_2) as the *domain* (*range*) of δ. We say that tuples t and t' *match* in relation r, and denote this by $t \sim_r t'$, if (i) r defines an FD c, such that t and t' are equal on all the columns in the domain of c, or (ii) r does not define any FD and t and t' are equal on all common columns.

States and State Transformers In the relational representation, the value of an object comprises one or more relations: $o \mapsto$

ϕ	$:=$ **true** | **false** | $c = v$ |	**(atomic)**
	$\neg\phi$ |	**(negation)**
	$\phi \land \phi$ | $\phi \lor \phi$	**(binary)**

Table 1. Production rules for formulas

Operation	Effect
`insert` $r\ t$	$r' = (r \setminus \{t' : t \sim_r t'\}) \cup \{t\}$
`remove` $r\ t$	$r' = r \setminus \{t\}$
$w :=$ `select` $r\ \phi$	$r' = r,\ w = \{t \in r : t \models \phi\}$

Table 2. Primitive relational operations and their meaning

$\{r_i\}_{i=1}^{k}$. Each relation r_i is assumed to have at most one FD, where moreover, the domain and range of the FD partition the relation's columns. Intuitively, this specializes the relation as a function mapping "locations" to their associated "values".

The effect of primitive relational operations is listed in Table 2. `insert` first removes the tuples matching its argument tuple from its argument relation, and then adds that tuple to the relation. `remove` ensures that its argument tuple is not in the relation. Finally, `select` defines a relation containing the tuples from its argument relation that match the selection criterion, expressed as a propositional formula over the grammar of Table 1.

State transformers—both concrete and abstract—are expressed as sequences over the primitive relational operations. JANUS allows specifying different transformers for invocations of the same operation with different arguments.

6.2 Sequence-based Conflict Detection

We now explain how the techniques described in Section 5 are realized using the relational representation.

Tracking Dependencies The footprint of primitive relational operations is defined in Table 3. For sound tracking of dependencies between operations, we consider tuple t as belonging in the read set of operation `remove` $r\ t$ if r does not contain t [ ].

The footprint of a transformer, $\tau = \langle r_1, \ldots, r_k \rangle$, is the cumulative footprint of the relational operations it consists of:

$$write(\tau) = \bigcup_{1 \le i \le k} write(r_i)$$
$$read(\tau) = \bigcup_{1 \le i \le k} read(r_i)$$

These definitions support the projection algorithm by enabling dependence-based decomposition of histories, as performed by the DECOMPOSE operation in Figure 8.

Equivalence Testing Both SAMEREAD and COMMUTE test for equivalence between different views of an object's value. COMMUTE considers the entire state of the object, whereas SAMEREAD considers only the relation defined by a read operation, which captures part of the object's state.

To perform equivalence judgments, we rely on a logical representation of the content of a relation, as specified in Table 4: The content of a relation is expressed as a restriction—formulated as a propositional formula—on the values from $\mathbb{V}$ contained in the relation. Thus, the removal of (the tuples in) relation w from relation r is reflected in the formula describing the content of r (ϕ^r) by conjoining it with the negation of the formula corresponding to w. Similarly, adding w to r is reflected as a disjunction from the formula describing the content of w.

The update rules corresponding to primitive operations are slightly more complex. For example, the rule for `insert` prescribes that first the tuples matching the tuple t to be inserted are removed. This is accomplished by conjoining formula $\bigvee_{c \in C_{dom}} c \neq t\ c$ with ϕ^r. Next, to express that t is then added to the relation, formula $\bigwedge_{c \in C} c = t\ c$ is disjoined from the intermediate formula.

Operation	Read Set	Write Set
`insert` $r\ t$	$\emptyset$	$\{t\} \cup \{t' \in r : t' \sim_r t\}$
`remove` $r\ t$	$t \in r\ ?\ \emptyset : \{t\}$	$t \in r\ ?\ \{t\} : \emptyset$
`select` $r\ \phi$	$\{t \in r : t \models \phi\}$	$\emptyset$

Table 3. The footprint of primitive relational operations

Operation	Formula
$r' = r \setminus w$	$\phi^{r'} = \phi^r \land \neg\phi^w$
$r' = r \cup w$	$\phi^{r'} = \phi^r \lor \phi^w$
$r' = r \cap w$	$\phi^{r'} = \phi^r \land \phi^w$
`insert` $r\ t$	$\phi^{r'} = (\phi^r \land \bigvee_{c \in C_{dom}} c \neq t\ c) \lor \bigwedge_{c \in C} c = t\ c$
`remove` $r\ t$	$\phi^{r'} = \phi^r \land \bigvee_{c \in C} c \neq t\ c$
$w :=$ `select` $r\ \psi$	$\phi^w = \phi^r \land \psi$

Table 4. Logical representation of transformations on a relation

Describing the content of a relation in propositional form allows implementing (symbolic) equivalence tests as calls to a SAT solver. Given two representations ϕ^r and ψ^r of the content of relation r, JANUS checks for equivalence between ϕ^r and ψ^r by asking the SAT solver for a satisfying assignment for $\neg(\phi^r \Leftrightarrow \psi^r)$. If the solver fails to find such an assignment (without timing out), then ϕ^r and ψ^r are confirmed to be equivalent.

7. Empirical Evaluation

In this section, we describe our prototype implementation of JANUS, as well as its experimental evaluation on a suite of five real-world benchmarks, where we tested (i) the gain from sequence-based conflict detection (compared to standard detection), and (ii) the significance of basing this mode of detection on offline training (with and without sequence abstraction).

7.1 Preliminaries

Prototype Implementation JANUS is implemented as a (static) Java library that exposes an interface for running client-provided tasks in parallel (via the `run`, `runInOrder` and `runOutOfOrder` methods), as well as for controlling various aspects of the execution (e.g., enabling profiling, configuring the profiling policy, setting the number of threads, modifying the thread management policy, etc).

For logging purposes, JANUS automatically inserts instrumentation hooks into its client application at runtime. For this, we reused functionality from Chord [ ], a framework for transforming and analyzing Java bytecode based on the Joeq compiler infrastructure [ ] and the Javassist bytecode-instrumentation library [ ]. JANUS also uses the Sat4j SAT solver [ ] for resolving equivalence queries (cf. Section 6.2).

The current JANUS prototype does not automatically identify candidate loops for parallelization. Instead, the user decides where to apply JANUSby manually transforming a loop structure into a JANUScall. (This decision can be guided by automated tools, such as [ ], which we are planning to integrate into JANUS.)

JANUS accepts user-provided abstraction specifications as extensions of its core algorithm written in Java. When an instance o of a specified data structure is created, JANUS maps it to a fresh set of relations (per the specification). Later, when an operation is invoked on o, JANUS applies the model associated with the operation to the (abstract) relational state of the object, thereby accounting for the effect of the operation. The binding between concrete execution events and the user specification is handled automatically (via instrumentation).

Benchmarks We used five real-world benchmarks, all taken from the SourceForge code repository [ ], for our experiments. These are listed in Table 5. All the benchmarks are sequential (though

PMD has an execution mode where certain subcomputations are run in parallel), and their core functionality involves processing a collection of items in a loop. (This obviated the need to select which loop to parallelize.)

In JGraphT, we considered two distinct algorithms within the `GreedyColoring` entry point: (i) an optimized version of the greedy algorithm for graph coloring (`color`), and (ii) an implementation of the saturation-degree heuristic for node ordering for the greedy coloring algorithm (`largestSaturationFirstOrder`). In JFileSync, we used the `JFSComparison` entry point, which computes the differences (at all hierarchies) between pairs of directories. In PMD, we considered the main entry point (`PMD`), which iterates over a collection of Java source files and analyzes them (intraprocedurally) for correctness and quality problems. Finally, in Weka we used the `GraphVisualizer` entry point, which renders a graph to a display device by traversing its nodes.

For each of the benchmarks, we manually transformed the relevant loop by casting its iterations into task objects and replacing the loop construct by a call to JANUS to run the tasks in parallel. These transformations proved straightforward, being purely syntactic, and can be automated with relative ease.

Experimental Setup Our experimental design consists of two sets of experiements. In the first, we compared between two versions of JANUS whose sole difference lies in whether or not sequence-wide reasoning is used in terms of overall performance and retry rate. The *write-set-based* version checks for conflicts using the standard approach of breaking the concurrent histories into their constituent operations and testing each of the resulting operation pairs for conflicts. The *sequence-based* version instead embodies the detection algorithm of Section 5. We stress that the *write-set-based* algorithm is implemented as a subset of its *sequence-based* counterpart, which cancels out differences due to implementation choices (e.g., code optimizations).

The second experiment is concerned with the significance of offline training, and measures the fraction of misses in sequence-based conflict queries as an indication of how well JANUS generalizes from training runs. For pair $\langle s_1, s_2 \rangle$ of sequences, a miss occurs (during a production run) if there is no matching entry in the commutativity specification built during offline training. In our measurements, we count only unique queries (and thus multiple hits/misses for the same query are counted as one). Our evaluation comprises two modes of detection: with and without sequence abstraction (Section 5.2), which provides insight into the value of this technique.

In our experiments, we ran JANUS 5 times in training mode and 10 times in production mode. All the measurements prsented in this section are based on averages over all production runs excluding the first (cold) run. Inputs for the training and production runs were based on available clients of the benchmarks (mainly unit tests). A characterization of the inputs appears in Table 6. For scalability, we authored abstraction specifications for shared data structures. To identify these data structures, we used the Hawkeye tool [ ].

We conducted our experiments using an IBM J9 V1.6.0 VM running on a Linux machine with an Intel Core i7 920 (Nehalem) processor that has four 2.67GHz cores, each multiplexing 2 hardware threads, for a total of 8 threads.

7.2 Performance Results

Figure 9 presents the speedup results for each of the benchmarks using 1–8 threads with both versions of JANUS. The ratio of overall retries to the number of transactions is shown in Figure 10. Results on cache misses in the 8-threads configuration appear in Figure 11.

Speedup and Retries The performance results shown in Figure 9 demonstrate the dramatic effect of sequence-based reasoning: The sequence-based version of JANUS achieves an average speedup of 1.5x on 8 threads, where JFileSync enjoys a speedup of close to 2.5x. Conversely, the write-set-based version degrades performance with an average slowdown of 1.66x (or, equivalently, speedup of 0.6x) on 8 threads. These trends hold not only on average, but also for each of the benchmarks individually.

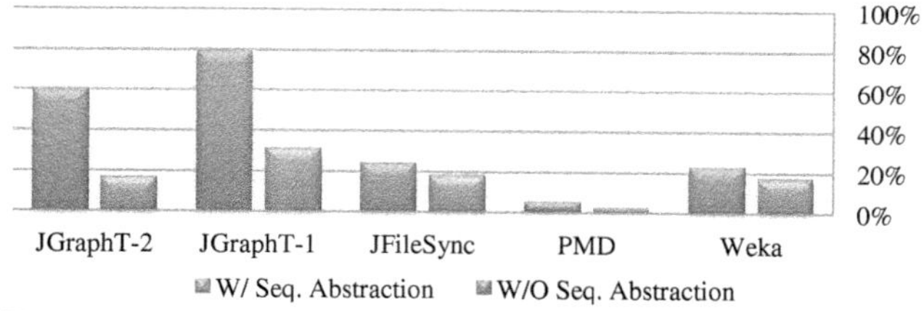

Figure 11. Misses: the ratio of misses to queries with and without the sequence-abstraction technique of Section 5.2

JGraphT-2 is the only benchmark where speedup under sequence-based detection is negligible. Our analysis indicates that this is because the transactions in this benchmark make intensive access to shared memory (comprising 6 data containers) all across their execution. Sequence-based detection is highly effective for this benchmark, as Figure 10 clearly indicates, but the JANUS protocol is geared toward transactions that make infrequent access to shared memory, such that the costs of privatization and fusion are amortized by the local work performed by the transaction.

The speedup data is compatible with the retry statistics presented in Figure 10. For all benchmarks, the number of retries under write-set-based detection is prohibitive: For PMD and JGraphT-2, the number of retries is directly proportional to the number of tasks, regardless of the number of threads. For the remaining benchmarks, the number of retries increases with the number of threads, the most extreme case being JGraphT-1 where the average number of retries per task is 4 with 8 threads.

In contrast, sequence-based detection yields a very low retries-to-transactions ratio, the average being 0.07 compared to 1.51 with write-set-based detection, which is a 22x improvement. A partial explanation for this significant gap between the detection algorithms is the commutative patterns exhibited by the benchmarks, which are listed in Table 5.

Misses The data on misses in Figure 11 indicates that (i) the commutativity specification due to the training runs generalizes well to production runs under sequence abstraction, but (ii) without sequence abstraction, generalization deteriorates significantly. More concretely, the average miss rate is less than 17% with sequence abstraction, with no more than 30% misses for all benchmarks (the worst being JGraphT-1), and 38% without applying abstraction to the sequences observed in training, where JGraphT-1 exhibits approximately 80% misses in this configuration. Sequence abstraction enables a 2.24x improvement in generalization from training runs, which points to the significance of this heuristic.

Sequence abstraction is most useful for the JGraphT benchamrks. For the other benchmarks, generalization is already robust even without this heuristic ($\leq$24% misses), which leaves little room for improvment. Indeed, access patterns to shared memory are highly dynamic in the JGraphT algorithms (e.g., the calls to `usedColors.set` inside an inner loop of variable length in Figure 3), making sequence abstraction significant for these benchmarks.

Discussion Manual or static identification of commutative patterns in the benchmarks we've considered can be challenging, if not impossible: First, these benchmarks are all of real-world scale (well beyond 100K LOC). They comprise multiple abstraction lay-

Name	Version	Description	Prevalent Patterns
JFileSync [ ]	2.2	Utility for synchronizing pairs of directories	Identity
JGraphT [ ]	0.8.1	(1) Greedy graph-coloring algorithm	Shared-as-local, spurious-reads
		(2) Saturation-degree node-ordering algorithm for heuristic graph coloring	Shared-as-local, equal-writes
PMD [ ]	4.2	Java source code analyzer	Shared-as-local, reduction
Weka [ ]	3.6.4	Machine-learning library for data-mining tasks	Equal-writes

Table 5. Benchmark characteristics

Benchmark	Input Description	Training Data	Production Data
JFileSync [ ]	List of directory pairs	Random lists of length 5	Random lists of length 25
JGraphT [ ]	Parameters for creation of random simple graph	100 nodes; average degree of 5	1000 nodes; average degree of 5
PMD [ ]	List of Java source files	Random lists of length 10	Random lists of length 100
Weka [ ]	Parameters for creation of random Bayesian network	100 nodes; average degree of 10	1000 nodes; average degree of 10

Table 6. Inputs for training and production runs

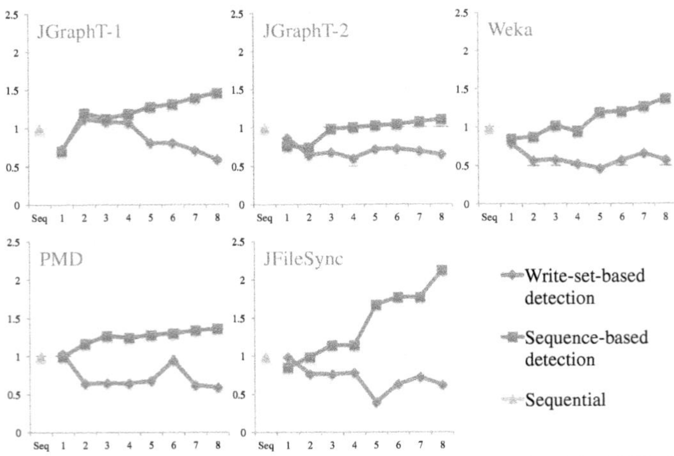

Figure 9. Speedup: the ratio of sequential to parallel execution times as a function of the number of threads (1–8)

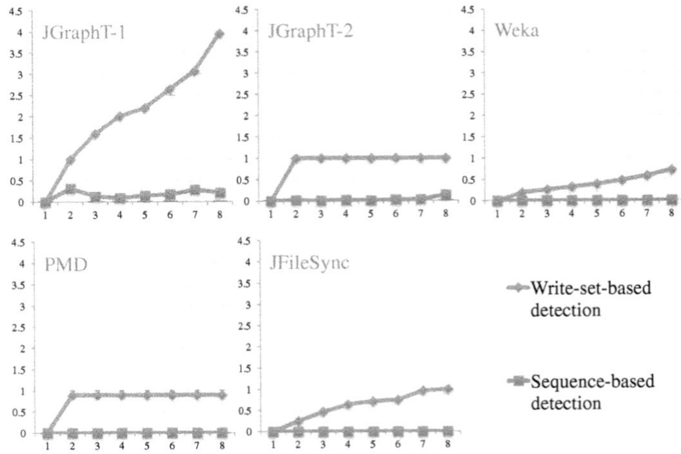

Figure 10. Retries: the ratio of overall retries to the number of scheduled tasks as a function of the number of threads (1–8)

ers, and the behaviors that induce commutative patterns typically span nontrivial interprocedural control flows (cf. Figure 4).

Moreover, in some cases the patterns do not hold invariantly, or hold only for some of the conflicted memory locations. This is the case, e.g., with JGraphT-2, where the ordering algorithm manipulates several shared arrays whose access patterns are determined dynamically, according to the input graph. JANUS exploits the available parallelism, which cannot be identified statically or captured concisely via a pattern, but can be effectively leveraged based on data from training runs (only 16% misses for JGraphT-2).

Though the speedup for JGraphT-2 in specific is modest, we are encouraged by our overall performance results. While the speedups we've obtained are not directly proportional to the number of threads, we have managed to considerably improve the performance of four out of the five *real-world* benchmarks we experimented with (by 1.6x or more) via automatic parallelization.

We also believe that these results can be further improved: First, our prototype implementation of JANUS can benefit from more careful engineering. For example, our current implementation doesn't reclaim the logs of garbage transactions whose concurrent transactions have also terminated, and implements privatization transformations in a naïve fashion, instead of using full persistency. Second, the hardware we used does not enable full 8-thread parallelization: The 8 available hardware threads are supported by only 4 cores, each multiplexing 2 threads.

8. Related Work

There is an extensive body of research on synchronization in general, and optimistic synchronization in specific, that dates back to Bernstein's work from the 1960s on the use of commutativity in concurrency control [ ]. Due to space constraints, we restrict our discussion to closely related research.

Use of Abstraction Herlihy and Koskinen [ ] develop *transactional boosting*, a methodology for transforming linearizable objects into transactional objects. Boosting leverages ADT semantics for more accurate conflict detection by avoiding spurious conflicts due to the ADT's concrete realization. The *Galois* parallelization system [ ], designed to exploit available parallelism in irregular applications, embodies a similar approach.

In [ ], Koskinen et al. define a unified framework for describing both memory-level transactions and transactional boosting. Their framework allows conflict detection both at the concrete level, where simple statements are tested for commutativity, and at the abstract level, where the abstract effect of ADT operations is considered. Similarly, Tripp et al. [ ] describe a unified framework for simultaneously tracking both concrete and abstract dependencies in sequential executions of a program, where concrete dependencies involve simple statements and abstract dependencies are due to a semantic conflict between ADT operations. The goal of this analysis is to uncover dataflow impediments to parallelization, where abstraction is used to reduce the rate of false impediments.

JANUS also enables state abstraction being parameterized in the state representation: It can track conflicts atop concrete program states, but the user can also apply abstraction specifications for shared data structures. A unique feature of JANUS, beyond state abstraction, is sequence-wide reasoning: JANUS is able to account for complete histories of operations during conflict detection.

Sequence-based detection is expressible in the (general) *gatekeeping* [ ] conflict-detection paradigm, where the gatekeeper keeps track of all the actions performed by a transaction to enable state rollback, as well as to evaluate commutativity conditions that refer to the history of the computation. JANUS can be seen as the first (automated) realization of the gatekeeping scheme, which is—in general—nontrivial to implement, as the user is required to write explicitly concurrent (and highly optimized) synchronization code.

Concrete STM Various techniques have been proposed for avoiding false aborts and/or reducing their cost in standard STM. We mention some of these techniques below.

Dependence-aware transactional management [ ] delays the decision whether to abort a conflicted transaction until any of the concurrent transactions in conflict with it commits. This is done by maintaining the dependency relation between transactions, such that if the conflicted transaction depends only on transactions that have aborted, then it need not abort.

Transaction checkpointing [ ] reduces the cost of aborts by taking snapshots of intermediate (local and global) states during the execution of a transaction. Similarly, an *elastic* transaction [ ] is able to respond to a conflict situation by dropping its work thus far into a transaction that immediately commits and initiating a new transaction (which might itself be elastic).

Closed and abstract nested transactions [,] mitigate the cost of benign conflicts by restructuring large transactions, such that operations that are likely to suffer from such conflicts are moved into smaller, nested transactions. Nested transactions can then be rerun without re-executing their enclosing transaction.

The above techniques are all orthogonal to our approach. We expect that their incorporation into our synchronization algorithm should be seamless. We leave such integrations for future research.

User Annotations Udupa et al. [ ] build a a parallelization system, which—based on programmer annotations—violates certain dependencies while preserving overall program functionality. This enables reordering of loop iterations, as well as tolerance of stale reads. The system can also infer which annotations are likely to improve performance through use of a test-driven framework.

The *early-release* [ ] technique, developed by Herlihy et al., allows the programmer to specify object-specific semantics that the transaction can then utilize to shrink its read set in certain computation flows. An example of this is Figure 3.

Similarly to these works, JANUS has facilities for expressing consistency relaxations. The specification can either be granular and refer to specific shared objects, or it can be coarse and hold simultaneously for all the shared objects. JANUS also supports limited inference capabilities (cf. Section 5.3). The inferred annotations are sound, and cannot result in incorrect parallelization. This is in contrast to user-provided annotations, which both JANUS and the works above assume—rather than verify—to be correct.

9. Conclusion

We have presented JANUS, a speculative parallelization system that performs accurate conflict detection by testing entire sequences of operations—rather than individual operations—for conflicts. A key feature of JANUS is offline training: JANUS utilizes profiling data to build a specialized, sequence-based commutativity specification that can be queried efficiently at runtime.

Our evaluation of JANUS on five real-world benchmarks indicates that sequence-based detection is effective. JANUS achieves a speedup of up to 2.5x, where its instantiation with write-set-based detection fails to exploit the available parallelism, and even degrades performance, with 22x more false conflicts.

Acknowledgments

We thank Adam Morrison, Guy Gueta and the anonymous referees for their insightful feedback on earlier versions of the paper.

References

[1] The chord analysis framework. `http://code.google.com/p/jchord/`.

[2] The jfilesync utility. `http://jfilesync.sourceforge.net`.

[3] The jgrapht java graph library. `http://www.jgrapht.org`.

[4] Pmd java source code scanner. `http://pmd.sourceforge.net`.

[5] The sat4j sat solver. `http://www.sat4j.org/`.

[6] The sourceforge code repository. `http://sourceforge.net/`.

[7] The weka machine-learning library. `http://weka.sourceforge.net`.

[8] A. Bernstein. Analysis of programs for parallel processing. *IEEE Transactions on Electronic Computers*, pages 757–762, 1966.

[9] S. Chiba and M. Nishizawa. An easy-to-use toolkit for efficient java bytecode translators. In *Proceedings of the 2nd international conference on Generative programming and component engineering*, pages 364–376, 2003.

[10] J. R. Driscoll, N. Sarnak, D. D. Sleator, and R. E. Tarjan. Making data structures persistent. *J. Comput. Syst. Sci.*, 38:86–124, 1989.

[11] P. Felber, V. Gramoli, and R. Guerraoui. Elastic transactions. In *DISC*, pages 93–107, 2009.

[12] T. Harris, S. Marlow, S. Peyton-Jones, and M. Herlihy. Composable memory transactions. In *Proceedings of the tenth ACM SIGPLAN symposium on Principles and practice of parallel programming*, pages 48–60, 2005.

[13] T. Harris and S. Stipic. Abstract nested transactions. The 2nd ACM SIGPLAN Workshop on Transactional Computing, 2007.

[14] M. Herlihy and E. Koskinen. Transactional boosting: a methodology for highly-concurrent transactional objects. In *PPoPP*. ACM, 2008.

[15] M. Herlihy, V. Luchangco, P. A. Martin, and M. Moir. Nonblocking memory management support for dynamic-sized data structures. *ACM Trans. Comput. Syst.*, 23(2):146–196, 2005.

[16] M. Herlihy and J.E.B. Moss. Transactional memory: Architectural support for lock-free data structures. In *ISCA*, 1993.

[17] E. Koskinen and M. Herlihy. Checkpoints and continuations instead of nested transactions. In *SPAA*, pages 160–168, 2008.

[18] E. Koskinen, M. J. Parkinson, and M. Herlihy. Coarse-grained transactions. In *POPL*, pages 19–30, 2010.

[19] M. Kulkarni, D. Nguyen, D. Prountzos, X. Sui, and K. Pingali. Exploiting the commutativity lattice. In *PLDI*, 2011.

[20] M. Kulkarni, K. Pingali, B. Walter, G. Ramanarayanan, K. Bala, and L. P. Chew. Optimistic parallelism requires abstractions. In *PLDI*, 2007.

[21] H. E. Ramadan, I. Roy, M. Herlihy, and E. Witchel. Committing conflicting transactions in an stm. In *PPOPP*, pages 163–172, 2009.

[22] O. Tripp, R. Manevich, J. Field, and M. Sagiv. JANUS: Exploiting parallelism via hindsight. Technical report, Tel Aviv University, 2012.

[23] O. Tripp, G. Yorsh, J. Field, and M. Sagiv. Hawkeye: effective discovery of dataflow impediments to parallelization. In *OOPSLA*, pages 207–224, 2011.

[24] A. Udupa, K. Rajan, and W. Thies. Alter: exploiting breakable dependences for parallelization. In *Proceedings of the 32nd ACM SIGPLAN conference on Programming language design and implementation*, pages 480–491, 2011.

[25] J. Whaley. Joeq: A virtual machine and compiler infrastructure. *Sci. Comput. Program.*, 57:339–356, 2005.

Reagents: Expressing and Composing Fine-grained Concurrency

Aaron Turon
Northeastern University
turon@ccs.neu.edu

Abstract

Efficient communication and synchronization is crucial for fine-grained parallelism. Libraries providing such features, while indispensable, are difficult to write, and often cannot be tailored or composed to meet the needs of specific users. We introduce *reagents*, a set of combinators for concisely expressing concurrency algorithms. Reagents scale as well as their hand-coded counterparts, while providing the composability existing libraries lack.

Categories and Subject Descriptors D.1.3 [*Programming techniques*]: Concurrent programming; D.3.3 [*Language constructs and features*]: Concurrent programming structures

General Terms Design, Algorithms, Languages, Performance

Keywords fine-grained concurrency, nonblocking algorithms, monads, arrows, compositional concurrency

1. Introduction

Programs are what happens between cache misses.

The problem

Amdahl's law tells us that sequential bottlenecks fundamentally limit our profit from parallelism. In practice, the effect is amplified by another factor: interprocessor communication, often in the form of cache coherence. When one thread waits on another, the program pays the cost of lost parallelism *and* an extra cache miss. The extra misses can easily accumulate to yield parallel *slowdown*, more than negating the benefits of the remaining parallelism.

Cache, as ever, is king.

The easy answer is: avoid communication. In other words, parallelize at a coarse grain, giving threads large chunks of independent work. But some work doesn't easily factor into large chunks, or equal-size chunks. Fine-grained parallelism is easier to find, and easier to sprinkle throughout existing sequential code.

Another answer is: communicate efficiently. The past two decades have produced a sizable collection of algorithms for synchronization, communication, and shared storage which minimize the use of memory bandwidth and avoid unnecessary waiting. This research effort has led to industrial-strength libraries—`java.util.concurrent` (JUC) the most prominent—offering a wide range of primitives appropriate for fine-grained parallelism.

PLDI'12, June 11–16, 2012, Beijing, China.

Such libraries are an enormous undertaking—and one that must be repeated for new platforms. They tend to be conservative, implementing only those data structures and primitives likely to fulfill common needs, and it is generally not possible to safely combine the facilities of the library. For example, JUC provides queues, sets and maps, but not stacks or bags. Its queues come in both blocking and nonblocking forms, while its sets and maps are nonblocking only. Although the queues provide atomic (thread-safe) dequeuing and sets provide atomic insertion, it is not possible to combine these into a single atomic operation that moves an element from a queue into a set.

In short, libraries for fine-grained concurrency are indispensable, but hard to write, hard to extend by composition, and hard to tailor to the needs of particular users.

Our contribution

We have developed *reagents*, which abstractly represent fine-grained concurrent operations. Reagents are *expressive* and *composable*, but when invoked retain the scalability and performance of existing algorithms:

Expressive Reagents provide a basic set of building blocks for writing concurrent data structures and synchronizers. The building blocks include isolated atomic updates to shared state, and interactive synchronous communication through message passing. This blend of isolation and interaction is essential for expressing the full range of fine-grained concurrent algorithms (§3.3). The building blocks also bake in many common concurrency patterns, like optimistic retry loops, backoff schemes, and blocking and signaling. Using reagents, it is possible to express sophisticated concurrency algorithms at a higher level of abstraction, while retaining the performance and scalability of direct, hand-written implementations.

Composable Reagents also provide a set of composition operators, including choice, sequencing and pairing. Using these operators, clients can extend and tailor concurrency primitives without knowledge of the underlying algorithms. For example, if a reagent provides only a nonblocking version of an operation like `dequeue`, a user can easily tailor it to a version that blocks if the queue is empty; this extension will work regardless of how `dequeue` is defined, and will continue to work even if the `dequeue` implementation is changed. Similarly, clients of reagent libraries can sequence operations together to provide atomic move operations between arbitrary concurrent collections—again, without access to or knowledge of the implementations. Compositionality is also useful to algorithm designers, since many sophisticated algorithms can be understood as compositions of simpler ones (§3.3, §3.4).

We begin in §2 by illustrating, through examples, some of the common patterns, tradeoffs and concerns in designing fine-grained concurrent algorithms. The two subsequent sections contain our core technical contributions:

- The **design** of the reagent combinators is given in §3. Each combinator is motivated by specific needs and patterns in concurrent algorithms; the section shows in particular how to write all of the algorithms described in §2 concisely and at a higher-than-usual level of abstraction.
- The **implementation** of reagents is detailed in §5, via both high-level discussion and excerpts from our code in Scala. It reveals the extent to which reagents turn patterns of fine-grained concurrency into a general algorithmic framework. It also shows how certain choices in the design of reagents enable important optimizations in their implementation.

Reagents have a clear cost model that provides an important guarantee: they do not impose extra overhead on the atomic updates performed by individual concurrent algorithms. That is, a reagent-based algorithm manipulates shared memory in exactly the same way as its hand-written counterpart, even if it reads and writes many disparate locations. This is a guarantee not generally provided by concurrency abstractions like software transactional memory (STM), which employ redo or undo logs or other mechanisms to support composable atomicity. Reagents only impose overheads when *multiple* algorithms are sequenced into a large atomic block, *e.g.* in an atomic transfer between collections.

In principle, then, reagents offer a strictly better situation than with current libraries: when used to express the algorithms provided by current libraries, reagents provide a higher level of abstraction yet impose negligible overhead; nothing is lost. But unlike with current libraries, the algorithms can then be extended, tailored, and combined. Extra costs are only paid when the new atomic compositions are used.

We test this principle empirically in §6 by comparing multiple reagent-based collections to their hand-written counterparts, as well as to lock-based and STM-based implementations. The benchmarks include both single operations used in isolation (where little overhead for reagents is expected) and combined atomic transfers. We compare at both high and low levels of contention. Reagents perform universally better than the lock- and STM-based implementations, and are indeed competitive with hand-written lock-free implementations.

Finally, it is worth noting in passing that reagents generalize both Concurrent ML [22] and Transactional Events [4], yielding the first lock-free implementation for both. We give a thorough discussion of this and other related work—especially STM—in §7.

A prototype implementation of reagents, together with the benchmarks and benchmarking harness we used, can be found at

`https://github.com/aturon/ChemistrySet`

2. Background

Broadly, we are interested in data structures and algorithms for communication, synchronization, or both. This section gives a brief survey of the most important techniques for communication and synchronization in a fine-grained setting—exactly the techniques that reagents abstract and generalize. Readers already familiar with Treiber stacks [28], elimination-backoff stacks [9], dual stacks [24], and MCS locks [19] can safely skip to §3.

Given our target of cache-coherent, shared-memory architectures, the most direct way of communicating between threads is modifying shared memory. The challenge is to provide both *atomicity* and *scalability*: communications must happen concurrently both without corruption and without clogging the limited memory bandwidth, even when many cores are communicating. A simple way to provide atomicity is to associate a lock with each shared data structure, acquiring the lock before performing any operation.

```
class TreiberStack[A] {
  private val head = new AtomicReference[List[A]](Nil)
  def push(a: A) {
    val backoff = new Backoff
    while (true) {
      val cur = head.get()
      if (head.cas(cur, a :: cur)) return
      backoff.once()
    }
  }
  def tryPop(): Option[A] = {
    val backoff = new Backoff
    while (true) {
      val cur = head.get()
      cur match {
        case Nil      ⇒ return None
        case a :: tail ⇒
          if (head.cas(cur, tail)) return Some(a)
      }
      backoff.once()
    }
  }
}
```

Figure 1. Treiber's stack (in Scala)

The prevailing wisdom[1] is that such *coarse-grained* locking is inherently unscalable:

- It forces operations on the data structure to be serialized, even when they could be performed in parallel.
- It adds extra cache-coherence traffic, since each core must acquire the same lock's cache line in exclusive mode before operating. For fine-grained communication, that means at least one cache miss per operation.
- It is susceptible to preemptions or stalls of a thread holding a lock, which prevents other threads from making progress.

To achieve scalability, data structures employ finer-grained locking, or eschew locking altogether. Fine-grained locking associates locks with small, independent parts of a data structure, allowing those parts to be manipulated in parallel. Lockless (or *nonblocking*) data structures instead perform updates directly, using hardware-level operations (like compare-and-set) to ensure atomicity. Doing the updates directly means that there is no extra communication or contention for locks, but it also generally means that the entire update must consist of changing a single word of memory—a constraint which is often quite challenging to meet.

Fig. 1 gives a classic example of a fine-grained concurrent data structure: Treiber's lock-free stack [28]. The stack is represented as an *immutable* linked list. Mutation occurs solely through the head pointer, represented here as an AtomicReference. The head is mutated using compareAndSet (here abbreviated as cas), which takes an expected value and a new value, and atomically updates the reference if it has the expected value. It returns **true** iff the update was successful.

A word about Scala: the syntax

exp **match** { **case** pat1 ⇒ body1 ... **case** patN ⇒ bodyN }

denotes pattern matching, where the value of exp is matched in order against pat1 up to patN. In Fig. 1, we use the two list constructors Nil and :: (an inline cons) in patterns.

[1] With some dissenting opinions, as in the recent work on *flat combining* [10].

The push and tryPop operations are implemented in a typical *optimistic* style: they take a snapshot of the head, perform some local computation with it, and then attempt to update it accordingly. The computation is optimistic because it is performed without holding a lock. The head might concurrently change, invalidating the cas intended to update it. To account for possible interference, the snapshot-compute-update code executes within a retry loop. While the loop may retry forever, it can only do so by repeatedly failing to cas, which in turn means that an unlimited number of other operations on the stack are succeeding. In other words, push and tryPop are formally lock free.

To successfully cas, a core must acquire the relevant cache line in exclusive mode, or something conceptually equivalent. When several cores attempt to cas a common reference, they must coordinate at the hardware level, using precious memory bandwidth and wasting processor cycles. A failed cas is evidence that there is *contention* over a common location. To increase the cas success rate and conserve memory bandwidth, fine-grained concurrent algorithms employ a *backoff* scheme, which here we have abstracted into a lightweight Backoff class. The class encapsulates the simplest scheme: busy-wait for a random amount of time that grows exponentially each time once is invoked.

Treiber's stack scales better than a lock-based stack mainly because it decreases the amount of shared data that must be updated per operation: instead of acquiring a shared lock, altering a shared stack pointer, and releasing the shared lock, Treiber's stack does a single CAS to update the shared pointer directly. However, that pointer is still a centralized source of contention. While exponential backoff helps relieve the contention, we can do better by parallelizing stack operations—which is counterintuitive, given that they all involve modifying the top of the stack.

Parallelization requires a change of perspective. Normally, we view concurrent operations on the same part of a data structure as competing to atomically update that data structure; we want the operations to be isolated. On the other hand, sometimes operations can "help" each other: a push and a tryPop effectively cancel each other out. This insight leads to a scheme called *elimination backoff* [9, 26]. Operations first try the usual cas-based code. If the cas fails, rather than busy-waiting, the operations advertise their presence on a side-channel, reducing the contention for the head pointer. If a push and tryPop detect their mutual presence, the push can pass its argument directly to tryPop through the side-channel, and no change to the head pointer is necessary. Atomicity is not violated, because had the push and pop executed in sequence, the head pointer would have been returned to its original value anyway. On the other hand, if no dual operation is detected during backoff, the operation withdraws its offer and tries once more to cas the head.

Both push and tryPop are *total* operations: they can succeed no matter what state the stack is in, and fail (and retry) only due to active interference from concurrent threads. A true pop operation, on the other hand, is *partial*: it is undefined when the stack is empty. Often this is taken to mean that the operation should block until another thread moves the stack into a state on which the operation is defined. Partial operations introduce considerable complexity, because *all* operations on the data structure must potentially signal blocked threads, depending on the changes being performed. In some cases, it is possible to cleverly treat signaling in essentially the same way as atomic updates [24].

Synchronization and signaling is also subject to cache and memory bandwidth concerns, but it would take us too far afield to discuss these in depth. Mellor-Crummey and Scott pioneered the now-common techniques for grappling with these concerns [19], and we apply their techniques in implementing the blocking and signaling protocols for reagents (§5).

```
// Shared state
upd:  Ref[A] ⇒ (A × B ⇀ A × C) ⇒ Reagent[B,C]

// Message passing
swap: Endpoint[A,B] ⇒ Reagent[A,B]

// Composition
+ :   Reagent[A,B] × Reagent[A,B] ⇒ Reagent[A,B]
>> :  Reagent[A,B] × Reagent[B,C] ⇒ Reagent[A,C]
* :   Reagent[A,B] × Reagent[A,C] ⇒ Reagent[A, B × C]

// Post−commit actions
postCommit: (A ⇒ Unit) ⇒ Reagent[A,A]
```

Figure 2. The core reagent combinators

3. Reagents: the core combinators

Reagents are a new instance of an old idea: representing computations as data. The computations being represented are fine-grained concurrent operations, so a value of type Reagent[A,B] represents a function from A to B that internally interacts with a concurrent data structure through mutation, synchronization, or both. Because the computations are data, however, they can be combined in ways that go beyond simple function composition. Each way of combining reagents corresponds to a way of combining their internal interactions with concurrent data structures. Existing reagents—for example, those built by a concurrency expert—can be composed by library users, without those users knowing their internal implementation. This way of balancing *abstraction* and *composition* was pioneered with Concurrent ML [22], and is now associated with *monads* [30] and *arrows* [14]. Our contribution is giving a set of combinators appropriate for expressing and composing fine-grained concurrent algorithms, with a clear cost semantics and implementation story (§5).

The reagent combinators encompass a blend of duals:

Shared state *versus* Message passing

Given the goal of using reagents to express algorithms like Treiber's stack (§2), it is not surprising that reagents include primitives from shared-state concurrency. But what about message passing? Underlying the shared state/message passing duality is a deeper one:

Isolation *versus* Interaction

Operations on shared state are generally required to be atomic, which means in particular that they are isolated from one another; concurrent shared-state operations appear to be *linearizable* [13] into a series of nonoverlapping, sequential operations. Synchronous message passing is just the opposite: rather than appearing to not overlap, sends and receives are *required* to overlap. Fine-grained concurrent operations straddle these two extremes, appearing to be isolated while internally tolerating (or exploiting) interaction. Elimination backoff (§2) provides a striking example of this phenomenon, and reagents can capture it concisely (§3.3).

There is also duality in reagent composition:

Disjunction *versus* Conjunction

In particular, we can combine two reagents by requiring exactly one of them to take effect (choice), or by requiring both of them to take effect in a single atomic step (join).

Finally, reagents, like functions, are inert. To be useful, they must be invoked. Reagents offer two means of invocation:

Active (reactants) *versus* Passive (catalysts)

In chemistry, a reagent is a participant in a reaction, and reagents are subdivided into *reactants*, which are consumed during reaction, and *catalysts*, which enable reactions but are not consumed by them. Similarly for us. Invoking a reagent as a reactant is akin to calling it as a function: its internal operations are performed once, yielding a result or blocking until it is possible to do so. Invoking it as a catalyst instead makes it passively available as a participant in reactions. Because catalysts are not "used up," they can participate in many reactions in parallel.

In the rest of this section, we introduce the core reagent combinators and use them to build a series of increasingly complex concurrent algorithms. By the end, we will have seen how to implement all of the algorithms described in §2, and several more besides.

3.1 Atomic updates on Refs

Memory is shared between reagents using the type Ref[A] of atomically-updatable references. The upd combinator (Fig. 2) represents atomic updates to references. It takes an *update function*, which tells how to transform a snapshot of the reference cell and some input into an updated value for the cell and some output. Using upd, we can rewrite TreiberStack in a more readable and concise way:

```
class TreiberStack [A] {
  private val head = new Ref[List[A]]( Nil )
  val push: Reagent[A, Unit] = upd(head) {
    case (xs, x) ⇒ (x::xs, ())
  }
  val tryPop: Reagent[Unit, Option[A]] = upd(head) {
    case (x :: xs, ()) ⇒ (xs, Some(x))
    case ( Nil ,   ()) ⇒ (Nil, None)
  }
}
```

In Scala, anonymous partial functions are written as a series of cases enclosed in braces. For push and tryPop, the case analyses are exhaustive, so the update functions are in fact total. Unit is akin to void: it is a type with a single member, written ().

Being reagents, push and tryPop are inert values. They can be invoked as reactants using the ! method, which is pronounced "react." For a Reagent[A,B] the ! method takes an A and returns a B. Scala permits infix notation for methods, so we can use a TreiberStack s by writing s.push ! 42. The key point is that when we invoke these reagents, we are executing *exactly* the same algorithms written by hand in §2, including the retry loop with exponential backoff; reagents systematize and internalize common patterns of fine-grained concurrency. By exposing push and tryPop as reagents rather than methods, we allow further composition and tailoring by a user of the data structure (§3.3, §3.4).

While tryPop handles both empty and nonempty stacks, we can write a variant that drops the empty case:

```
val pop: Reagent[Unit, A] =
  upd(head) { case (x :: xs, ()) ⇒ (xs, x) }
```

Now our update function is partial. An invocation s.pop ! () will block the calling thread unless or until the stack is nonempty.

In general, there are two ways a reagent can fail to react: *transiently* or *permanently*. Transient failures arise when a reagent loses a race to CAS a location; they can only be caused by *active interference* from another thread. A reagent that has failed transiently should retry, rather than block, following the concurrency patterns laid out in §2. Permanent failures arise when a reagent places requirements on its environment—such as the requirement, with pop above, that the head reference yield a nonempty list. Such failures are permanent in the sense that only activity by another thread can enable the reagent to proceed. When faced with a permanent failure, a reagent should block until signaled that the underlying state has changed. Blocking and signaling are entirely handled by the reagent implementation; there is therefore no risk of lost wakeups.

The reagent upd(f) reagent can fail permanently only for those inputs on which f is undefined.

3.2 Synchronization: how reagents react

With reagents, updates to shared memory are isolated, so they cannot be used for interaction in which the parties are mutually aware. Reagents interact instead through *synchronous swap channels*, which consist of two complementary *endpoints*. The method mkChan[A,B] returns a pair of type

(Endpoint[A,B], Endpoint[B,A])

The combinator for communication is swap (see Fig. 2), which lifts an Endpoint[A,B] to a Reagent[A,B]. When two reagents communicate on opposite endpoints, they provide messages of complementary type (A and B, for example) and receive each other's messages. We call a successful communication a *reaction* between reagents. On the other hand, if no complementary message is available, swap will block until a reaction can take place—a permanent failure.

3.3 Disjunction of reagents: choice

If r and s are two reagents of the same type, their *choice* r + s will behave like one of them, nondeterministically, when invoked. The most straightforward use of choice is waiting on several signals simultaneously, while consuming only one of them. For example, if c and d are endpoints of the same type, swap(c) + swap(d) is a reagent that will accept exactly one message, either from c or from d. If neither endpoint has a message available, the reagent will block until one of them does.

A more interesting use of choice is adding backoff strategies (of the kind described in §2). For example, we can build an elimination backoff stack as follows:

```
class EliminationStack [A] {
  private val s = new TreiberStack[A]
  private val (elimPop, elimPush) = mkChan[Unit,A]
  val push: Reagent[A,Unit] = s.push + swap(elimPush)
  val pop:  Reagent[Unit,A] = s.pop  + swap(elimPop)
}
```

Choice is left-biased, so when push is invoked, it will first attempt to push onto the underlying Treiber stack. If the underlying push fails (due to a lost CAS race), push will attempt to send a message along elimPush, *i.e.*, to synchronize with a concurrent popper. If it succeeds, the push reagent completes without ever having modified its underlying stack.

For choice, failure depends on the underlying reagents. A choice fails permanently only when *both* of its underlying reagents have failed permanently. If either fails transiently, the choice reagent has failed transiently and should therefore retry. Reasoning along these lines, we deduce that push never blocks, since the underlying s.push can only fail transiently. On the other hand, pop can block because s.pop can fail permanently on an empty stack and swap(elimPop) can fail permanently if there are no offers from pushers.

When push or pop retry, they will *spinwait* briefly for another thread to accept their message along elimPush or elimPop; the length of the wait grows exponentially, as part of the exponential backoff logic. Once the waiting time is up, the communication attempt is canceled, and the whole reagent is retried. This protocol is elaborated in §5.

3.4 Conjunction of reagents: sequencing and pairing

Choice offers a kind of disjunction on reagents. There are also two ways of *conjoining* two reagents, so that the composed reagent has the effect of both underlying reagents:

- End-to-end composition, via *sequencing*: if r: Reagent[A,B] and s: Reagent[B,C] then r >> s: Reagent[A,C].
- Side-by-side composition, via *pairing*: if r: Reagent[A,B] and s: Reagent[A,C] then r * s: Reagent[A,(B,C)].

These combinators differ only in information flow. Each guarantees that the atomic actions of both underlying reagents become a single atomic action for the composition. For example, if s1 and s2 are both stacks, then s1.pop >> s2.push is a reagent that will atomically transfer an element from the top of one to the top of the other. The reagent will block if s1 is empty. Similarly, s1.pop * s2.pop will pop, in one atomic action, the top elements of both stacks, or block if either is empty.

Here we begin to see the benefits of the reagent abstraction. Both of the example combinations work regardless of how the underlying stacks are implemented. If both stacks use elimination backoff, the conjoined operations will potentially use elimination on both simultaneously. This behavior is entirely emergent; it does not require any code on the part of the stack author, and it does not require the stack user to know anything about the implementation. Reagents can be composed in unanticipated ways.

Conjunctions provide a solution to the Dining Philosophers problem: to consume two resources atomically, one simply conjoins two reagents that each consume a single resource. For example, if c and d are endpoints of type Unit to A and B respectively, then swap(c) * swap(d) is a reagent that receives messages on both endpoints simultaneously and atomically. There is no risk of introducing a deadlock through inconsistent acquisition ordering, because the reagents implementation is responsible for the ultimately acquisition order, and will ensure that this order is globally consistent.

The failure behavior of conjunctions is dual to that of disjunctions: if *either* conjunct fails permanently, the entire conjunction fails permanently.

The implementation details for conjunctions are discussed later (§5), but a key point is that the performance cost is *pay as you go*. Single atomic reagents like push and pop execute a single CAS—just like the standard nonblocking algorithms they are meant to implement—even though these operations can be combined into larger atomic operations. The cost of conjunction is only incurred when a conjoined reagent is actually used. This is a crucial difference from STM, which generally incurs overheads regardless of the size of the atomic blocks; see §7 for more discussion.

3.5 Catalysts: persistent reagents

The ! operator invokes a reagent as a reactant: the invocation lasts for a single reaction, and any messages sent by the reagent are consumed by the reaction. But sometimes it is useful for reagent invocations to persist beyond a single reaction, *i.e.*, to act as catalysts. For example, the following function creates a catalyst that merges input from two endpoints and sends the resulting pairs to another endpoint:

```
def zip(in1: Endpoint[Unit, A], in2: Endpoint[Unit, B],
        out: Endpoint[(A,B), Unit]) =
  dissolve ((swap(in1) * swap(in2)) >> swap(out))
```

The dissolve function takes a Reagent[Unit, Unit] and introduces it as a catalyst.[2] Operationally, in this example, that just means sending messages along in1 and in2 that are marked as catalyzing messages, and hence are not consumed during reaction. The upshot is that senders along in1 will see the catalyzing messages, look for messages along in2 to pair with, and ultimately send messages along out (and similarly in the other order).

Catalysts could instead be expressed using a thread that repeatedly invokes a reagent as a reactant. Allowing direct expression through dissolve is more efficient (since it does not tie up a thread) and allows greater parallelism (since, as with the zip example above, multiple reagents can react with it in parallel).

Catalysts are not limited to message passing. The zip example above could be rephrased in terms of arbitrary reagents rather than just endpoints.

[2] For simplicity, we have not given a way to cancel catalysts after they have been introduced, but cancellation is easy to add.

3.6 Post-commit actions

Reagents support "post commit actions", which comprise code to be run after a reaction has successfully taken place, *e.g.* for signaling or spawning another thread after an operation completes. The postCommit combinator (Fig. 2) takes a function from A to Unit and produces a Reagent[A,A]. The post-commit action will be recorded along with the input of type A, which is passed along unchanged. Once the reaction completes, the action will be invoked on the stored input. The combinator is meant to be used in sequence with other combinators that will produce the appropriate input. For example, the reagent pop >> postCommit(println) will print the popped element from a stack after the pop has completed.

3.7 Case study: the join calculus

Fournet and Gonthier's *join calculus* [6] provides an interesting example of the expressive power of reagents. The join calculus is based on message passing, but instead of a simple "receive" primitive on channels, programmers write *join patterns*. The join patterns for a set of channels say, once and for all, how to react to messages along those channels. Each pattern $c_1(x_1) \& \cdots \& c_n(x_n) \triangleright b$ consists of a sequence of channels c_i with names x_i for the messages along those channels, and a body b in which the names x_i are bound. A join pattern *matches* if messages are available on each of the listed channels, and it *fires* by atomically consuming *all* of the messages and then running the body. Since several patterns may be given for the same channels, the choice of which pattern to fire may be nondeterministic.

The join pattern $c_1(x_1) \ \& \ \cdots \ \& \ c_n(x_n) \triangleright b$ can be interpreted directly as a catalyst. The join operator & is interpreted as a conjunction *, the channel names as appropriate swap instances, and the body b as a post-commit action. Altogether, the reagent corresponding to the pattern is

$$(\mathsf{swap}(c_1) * \cdots * \mathsf{swap}(c_n)) \gg \mathsf{postCommit}(b)$$

A set of join patterns governing a set of channels can all be written in this way and dissolved as catalysts, which is equivalent to dissolving the choice of all the patterns. Thus, reagents provide a scalable implementation of the join calculus, along the lines of the one developed in previous work with Russo [29].

3.8 Atomicity guarantees

Because conjunction distributes over disjunction, every reagent built using the core combinators (Fig. 2) can be viewed as a disjunction of conjunctions, where each conjunction contains some combination of updates and swaps. For such a reagent, reactions atomically execute all of the conjuncts within exactly one of the disjuncts. This STM-like guarantee is too strong for algorithms which read shared memory without requiring the reads to be "visible" (*i.e.*, to participate in an atomic transaction). The next section will introduce *computed* reagents which allow invisible reads and writes, trading weaker guarantees for better performance.

```
// Low-level shared state combinators
read: Ref[A] ⇒ Reagent[Unit, A]
cas:  Ref[A] × A × A ⇒ Reagent[Unit, Unit]

// Computational combinators
ret:       A ⇒ Reagent[Unit,A]
computed: (A ⇀ Reagent[Unit, B]) ⇒ Reagent[A,B]
```

Figure 3. The low-level and computational combinators

When reagents interact through message passing, their atomicity becomes intertwined: they must react together in a single atomic step. This requirement raises an important but subtle question: what should happen when isolation and interaction conflict? Consider two reagents that interact over a channel, but also each update the *same* shared reference. The atomicity semantics demands that both reagents involved in the reaction atomically commit, but the isolation on references demands that the updates be performed in separate atomic steps.

For both simplicity and performance, we consider such situations to be *illegal*, and throw an exception in such cases. Ideally, the static types of reagents would somehow track the necessary information to determine whether compositions are safe, but we leave such a type discipline for future work. In practice, this rules out only compositions of certain operations within the *same* data structure, which are much less common than compositions across data structures. It is also straightforward to adopt an alternative approach, *e.g.* the one taken by Communicating Transactions (§7), which treats isolation/interaction conflicts as transient failures.

4. Low-level and computational combinators

4.1 Computed reagents

The combinators introduced in §3 are powerful, but they impose a strict phase separation: reagents are constructed prior to, and independently from, the data that flows through them. Phase separation is useful, because it allows reagent execution to be optimized based on complete knowledge of the computation to be performed (see §5). But in many cases the choice of computation to be performed depends on the input or other dynamic data. The computed combinator (Fig. 3) expresses such cases. It takes a partial function from A to Reagent[Unit,B] and yields a Reagent[A,B]. When the reagent computed(f) is invoked, it is given an argument value of type A, to which it applies the function f. If f is not defined for that input, the computed reagent issues a permanent (blocking) failure, similarly to the upd function. Otherwise, the application of f will yield another, dynamically-computed reagent, which is then invoked with (), the unit value.

In functional programming terms, the core reagent combinators of §3 can be viewed in terms of *arrows* [14], which are abstract, composable computations whose structure is statically determined. With the addition of computed, reagents can also be viewed in terms of *monads* [30], which extend arrows with dynamic determination of computational structure.

In the remainder of this section, we introduce a handful of lower-level combinators which are useful in connection with computed reagents. We close with a case study: Michael and Scott's lock-free queue [20].

4.2 Shared state: read and cas

Although the upd combinator is convenient, it is sometimes necessary to work with shared state with a greater degree of control. To this end, we include two combinators, read and cas (see Fig. 2), for working directly on Ref values. Together with the computed combinator described in §4.1, read and cas suffice to *build* upd.

The read combinator is straightforward: if r has type Ref[A], then read(r) has type Reagent[Unit, A] and, when invoked, returns a snapshot of r. The cas combinator takes a Ref[A] and two A arguments, giving the expected and updated values, respectively. Unlike its counterpart for AtomicReference, a cas reagent does *not* yield a boolean result. A failure to CAS is transient, and therefore results in a retry.

4.3 Constant and tentative reagents

The ret combinator (Fig. 2) always succeeds, immediately returning the given value.

Because choice is left-biased, it can be used together with the remaining combinators to express *tentative* reagents: if r is a Reagent[A,B] then r? is a Reagent[A,Option[B]] that first tries r (wrapping its output with Some) and then tries ret(None), which always succeeds. This allows a reaction to be attempted, without retrying it when it fails.

```
class MSQueue[A] {
  private case class Node(data: A, next: Ref[Node])
  private val head = new Ref(new Node(null)) // sentinel
  private val tail  = new Ref(read(head) ! ()) // sentinel
  val tryDeq: Reagent[Unit, Option[A]] = upd(head) {
    case (Node(_, Ref(n@Node(x, _))), ()) ⇒ (n, Some(x))
    case (emp,                          ()) ⇒ (emp, None)
  }
  private def findAndEnq(n: Node): Reagent[Unit,Unit] =
    read( tail ) ! () match {
      case ov@Node(_, r@Ref(null)) ⇒ // found true tail
        cas(r, null, n) >>
        postCommit { cas(tail, ov, n)? ! () }
      case ov@Node(_, Ref(nv)) ⇒ // not the true tail
        cas( tail, ov, nv)? ! (); // catch up tail ref
        findAndEnq(n)
    }
  val enq: Reagent[A, Unit] = computed {
    (x: A) ⇒ findAndEnq(new Node(x, new Ref(null)))
  }
}
```

Figure 4. The Michael-Scott queue, using reagents

4.4 Case study: the Michael-Scott queue

To illustrate the use of computed, we now show how to implement the classic Michael-Scott lock-free queue [20]. Unlike a stack, in which all activity focuses on the head, queues have two loci of updates. That means, in particular, that the Refs used by its reagents may vary depending on the current state of the queue. The strategy we employ to implement it readily scales to more complicated examples, such as concurrent skiplists or the lazy, lock-free set algorithm [11]. With any of these examples, we reap the usual benefits: a concise, composable and extensible exposition of the algorithm.

Here is a brief overview of the Michael-Scott algorithm. The queue is represented as a *mutable* linked list, with a sentinel node at the head (front) of the queue. The head pointer always points to the current sentinel node; nodes are dequeued by a CAS to this pointer, just like Treiber stacks (but lagged by one node). The true tail of the queue is the unique node, reachable from the head pointer, with a null next pointer; thanks to the sentinel, such a node is guaranteed to exist. If the queue is empty, the same node will be the head (sentinel) and tail. Finally, as an optimization for enqueing, a tail pointer is maintained with the invariant that the true tail node is always reachable from it. The tail pointer may lag behind the true tail node, however, which allows the algorithm to work using only single-word CAS instructions.

Our reagent-based implementation of the Michael-Scott queue is shown in Fig. 4. The node representation is given as an inner *case* class. In Scala, case classes provide two features we take advantage of. First, the parameters to their constructors (here data and next) are automatically added as final fields to the class, which are initialized to the constructor argument values. Second, they extend pattern matching through **case** so that instances can be *deconstructed*. A pattern like **case** Node(d, n) matches any instance of the node class, binding d to its data field and n to its next field.

The head and tail references of the queue are initialized to the same sentinel node. Here we use the read combinator (§4.2) to extract the sentinel value from the head when constructing the tail. The read reagent in tail 's initializing expression is immediately executed during construction of an MSQueue instance.

The tryDeq reagent is very similar to the tryPop reagent in TreiberStack, modulo the sentinel node. The reagent pattern matches on the sentinel node, ignoring its data field by using _, the wildcard. The next field is then matched to a nested pattern, Ref(n@Node(x, _)). This pattern immediately reads the current value of the reference stored in next, binds that value to n, and then matches the pattern Node(x,_) against n. If the pattern matches—which it will any time the next field of the sentinel is non-null—the node n becomes the new head (and hence the new sentinel).

Since the location of the tail node is determined dynamically by the data in the queue, the enq reagent must itself be determined dynamically. For enq, we compute a dynamic reagent by first taking the given input x, creating a node with that data, and then calling a private function findAndEnq that will locate the tail of the queue and yield a reagent to update it to the new node. Since findAndEnq is private and tail-recursive, Scala will compile it to a loop.

The findAndEnq function searches for the *true* tail node (whose next field is null) starting from the tail pointer, which may lag. To perform the search, findAndEnq must read the tail pointer, which it does using the read combinator. *There is a subtle but important point here: this read occurs while the final reagent is being computed.* That means, in particular, that the read is *not* part of the computed reagent; it is a side-effect of computing the reagent. The distinction is important: such a read is effectively "invisible" to the outer reagent being computed, and thus is not guaranteed to happen atomically with it. Invisible reads and writes are useful for avoiding compound atomic updates, but must be employed carefully to ensure that the computed reagent provides appropriate atomicity guarantees.

Once the tail pointer has been read, its value is pattern-matched to determine whether it points to the true tail. If it does, findAndEnq yields a cas reagent (§4.2) that will update the next field of the tail node from null to the new node. The attached post-commit action attempts to catch up the tail pointer through a cas. Since the cas fails only if further nodes have been enqueued by other concurrent threads, we perform it tentatively (§4.3); it is not necessary or desirable to retry on failure.

If, on the other hand, the tail pointer is lagging, findAndEnq performs an invisible cas to update it. Since it may be racing with other enqueuers to catch up the tail, a failure to CAS is ignored here. Regardless of the outcome of the cas, the findAndEnq function will restart from a freshly-read tail pointer. Notice that in this case, an entire iteration of findAndEnq is executed with no visible impact or record on the final computed reagent—there is no extended redo log or compound atomic transaction.

5. Implementation

Having seen the design and application of reagents, we now turn to their implementation. We begin with a high-level overview (§5.1) introducing the key techniques and data structures we use. We then delve into the core code of our Scala implementation, beginning with the primary entry point (the ! method, §5.4) and continuing with the key combinators. For space reasons, we do not discuss the implementation of catalysts, which is fairly straightforward.

5.1 The basic approach

When invoked, reagents attempt to *react*, which is *conceptually* a two phase process: first, the desired reaction is built up; second, the reaction is atomically committed. We emphasize "conceptually" because, as discussed in the introduction, reagents are designed to avoid this kind of overhead in the common case. We first discuss the general case (which imposes overhead) but return momentarily to the common (no overhead) case.

An attempt to react can fail during either phase. A failure during the first phase, *i.e.* a failure to build up the desired reaction, is always a permanent failure (§3.3). Permanent failures indicate that the reagent cannot proceed given current conditions, and should therefore block until another thread intervenes and causes conditions to change. On the other hand, a failure during the second phase, *i.e.* a failure to commit, is always a transient failure (§3.3). Transient failures indicate that the reagent should retry, since the reaction was halted due to active interference from another thread. In general, a reaction encompasses three lists: the CASes to be performed, the messages to be consumed, and the actions to be performed after committing. It thus resembles the redo log used in some STM implementations [15].

In the common case that a reagent performs only one visible (§4.1) CAS or message swap, those components of the reaction are not necessary and hence are not used. Instead, the CAS or swap is performed immediately, compressing the two phases of reaction. Aside from avoiding extra allocations, this key optimization means that in the common case a cas or upd in a reagent leads to exactly one executed CAS during reaction, with no extra overhead. When a reaction encompasses multiple visible CASes, a costlier *k*CAS protocol must be used to ensure atomicity. We discuss the *k*CAS protocol in §5.5, and the common case single CAS in §5.6.

In the implementation, Reagent[A,B] is an abstract class all of whose subclasses are hidden. The subclasses roughly correspond to the combinator functions (which are responsible for instantiating them), and instances of the subclasses store the arguments given to their corresponding combinator. Each subclass provides an implementation of the tryReact method, which is an abstract method of Reagent[A,B] with the following signature:

```
def tryReact(a: A, rx: Reaction, offer: Offer[B]): Any
```

The Any type in Scala lies at the top of the subtyping hierarchy, akin to Object in Java. Here we are using Any to represent a union of the type B with the type Failure, where the latter has just two singleton instances, Block and Retry, corresponding to permanent and transient failures.

In other words, tryReact takes the input (type A) to the reagent and the reaction built up so far, and either completes the reaction, returning a result (type B), or fails, returning one of the failure singletons (Block or Retry). The remaining argument, offer, is used for synchronization and communication between reagents, which we explain next.

5.2 Offers

Message passing between reagents is synchronous, meaning that both reagents take part in a single, common reaction. In the implementation, this works by one reagent placing an *offer* to react

```
def !(a: A): B = {
  val backoff = new Backoff
  def withoutOffer(): B =
    tryReact(a, empty, null) match {
      case Block ⇒ withOffer()
      case Retry ⇒
        backoff.once()
        if (maySync) withOffer() else withoutOffer()
      case ans   ⇒ ans.asInstanceOf[B]
    }
  def withOffer(): B = {
    val offer = new Offer[B]
    tryReact(a, empty, offer) match {
      case (f: Failure) ⇒
        if (f == Block) park() else backoff.once(offer)
        if (offer.rescind) withOffer() else offer.answer
      case ans ⇒ ans.asInstanceOf[B]
    }
  }
  withoutOffer()
}
```

Figure 5. The ! method, defined in Reagent[A,B]

in a location visible to the other. The reagent making the offer either spinwaits or blocks until the offer is fulfilled; if it spinwaits, it may later decide to withdraw the offer. The reagent accepting the offer combines the accumulated reactions of both reagents, and attempts to commit them together. Fulfilling the offer means, in particular, providing a final "answer" value that should be returned by the reagent that made the offer. Each offer includes a status field, which is either Pending, Rescinded, or a final answer. Hence, the Offer class is parameterized by the answer type; a Reagent[A,B] will use Offer[B]. When fulfilling an offer, a reagent CASes its status from Pending to the desired final answer.

In addition to providing a basic means of synchronization, the offer data structure is used to resolve external choices. For example, the reagent swap(ep1) + swap(ep2) may resolve its choices internally by fulfilling an existing offer on ep1 or ep2; but if no offers are available, the reagent will post a *single* offer to *both* endpoints, allowing the choice to be resolved externally. Reagents attempting to consume that offer will race to change a single, shared status field, thereby ensuring that such choices are resolved atomically.

Offers are made as part of the same tryReact process that builds and commits reactions. The offer argument to tryReact is non-null whenever an offer is to be made.

5.3 Continuations

For implementing backtracking choice and message passing, it is necessary for each reagent to know and have control over the reagents that are sequenced after it. Thus we do not represent the reagent sequencing combinator >> with its own class. Instead, each reagent records its own *continuation*, which is another reagent. Thus, for example, while the cas combinator produces a reagent of type Reagent[Unit,Unit], the CAS class has a parameter k of type Reagent[Unit,R], and CAS extends Reagent[Unit,R] rather than Reagent[Unit,Unit]. The R stands for (final) result.

The combinator functions are responsible for mapping from the user-facing API, which does not use continuations, to the internal reagent subclasses, which do. Each reagent initially begins with the empty continuation, called Commit, the behavior of which is explained in §5.5. The sequencing combinator then merely plumbs together the continuation arguments of its parameters.

5.4 The entry point: reacting

The code for performing a reaction is given in the ! method definition for Reagent[A,B], shown in Fig. 5. This method provides two generalized versions of the optimistic retry loops we described in §2. The retry loops are written as a local, tail-recursive functions, which Scala compiles down to loops.

The first retry loop, withoutOffer, attempts to perform the reaction without making visible offers to other reagents. It may, however, find and consume offers from other reagents as necessary for message passing. To initiate the reaction, withoutOffer calls the abstract tryReact method with the input a, an empty reaction to start with, and no offer. If the reaction fails in the first phase (a permanent failure, represented by Block), the next attempt must be made with an offer, to set up the blocking/signaling protocol. If the reaction fails in the second phase (a transient failure, represented by Retry), there is likely contention over shared data. To reduce the contention, withoutOffer performs one cycle of exponential backoff before retrying. If the reagent includes communication attempts, the retry is performed with an offer, since doing so increases chances of elimination (§3.3) without further contention. Finally, if both phases of the reaction succeed, the final answer is returned.

The second retry loop, withOffer, is similar, but begins by allocating an Offer object to make visible to other reagents. Once the offer had been made, the reagent can actually block when faced with a permanent failure; the offer will ensure that the attempted reaction is visible to other reagents, which may complete it. Blocking is performed by the park method provided by Java's LockSupport class. On a transient failure, the reagent spinwaits, checking the offer's status. In either case, once the reagent has finished waiting it attempts to rescind the offer, which will fail if another reagent has fulfilled the offer.[3]

Initially, the reaction is attempted using withoutOffer, representing optimism that the reaction can be completed without making a visible offer.

5.5 The exit point: committing

As mentioned in §5.2, the initial continuation for reagents is the Commit continuation, shown in Fig. 6. The tryReact method of Commit makes the transition from building up a Reaction object to actually committing it.

If the reagent has made an offer, but has also completed the first phase of reaction, the offer must be rescinded before the commit phase is attempted—otherwise, the reaction could complete twice. As with the ! method, the attempt to rescind the offer is in a race with other reagents that may be completing the offer. If Commit loses the race, it returns the answer provided by the offer. Otherwise, it attempts to commit the reaction, and if successful simply returns its input, which is the final answer for the reaction.

Committing a reaction requires a kCAS operation: k compare and sets must be performed atomically. This operation, which forms the basis of STM, is in general expensive and not available through hardware. There are several software implementations that provide nonblocking progress guarantees [1, 7, 18]. Reagents that perform a multiword CAS will inherit the progress properties of the chosen implementation.

For our prototype implementation, we have opted to use an extremely simple implementation that replaces each location to be CASed with a sentinel value, essentially locking the location. As the Reaction object is assembled, locations are kept in address order, which guarantees a consistent global order and hence avoids dead- and live-lock within the kCAS implementation. The advan-

[3] Even if the reagent had blocked, it is still necessary to check the status of its offer, because park allows spurious wakeups.

```
class Commit[A] extends Reagent[A,A] {
  def tryReact(a: A, rx: Reaction, offer: Offer[A]) =
    if (offer != null && !offer.rescind) offer.answer
    else if (rx.commit) a
    else Retry
}
```

```
class CAS[A,R](ref: Ref[A], ov: A, nv: A, k: Reagent[A,R])
  extends Reagent[Unit,R] {
  def tryReact(u: Unit, rx: Reaction, offer: Offer[R]) =
    if (!rx.hasCAS && !k.hasCAS)
      if (ref.cas(ov, nv)) k.tryReact((), rx, offer)
      else Retry
    else
      k.tryReact((), rx.withCAS(ref, ov, nv), offer)
}
```

```
class Choice[A,B](r1: Reagent[A,B], r2: Reagent[A,B])
  extends Reagent[A,B] {
  def tryReact(a: A, rx: Reaction, offer: Offer[B]) =
    r1.tryReact(a, rx, offer) match {
      case Retry ⇒ r2.tryReact(a, rx, offer) match {
        case (_: Failure) ⇒ Retry // must retry r1
        case ans          ⇒ ans
      }
      case Block ⇒ r2.tryReact(a, rx, offer)
      case ans   ⇒ ans
    }
}
```

```
class Computed[A,B](c: A ⇀ Reagent[Unit,B])
  extends Reagent[A,B] {
  def tryReact(a: A, rx: Reaction, offer: Offer[B]) =
    if (c.isDefinedAt(a)) c(a).tryReact((), rx, offer)
    else Block
}
```

```
class Swap[A,B,R](ep: Endpoint[A,B], k: Reagent[B, R])
  extends Reagent[A,R] {
  // NB: this code glosses over some important details
  //     discussed in the Channels subsection
  def tryReact(a: A, rx: Reaction, offer: Offer[R]) = {
    if (offer != null) // send message if so requested
      ep.put(new Message(a, rx, k, offer))
    def tryFrom(cur: Cursor, failMode: Failure): Any =
      cur.getNext match {
        case Some(msg, next) ⇒
          msg.exchange(k).tryReact(a, rx, offer) match {
            case Retry ⇒ tryFrom(next, Retry)
            case Block ⇒ tryFrom(next, failMode)
            case ans   ⇒ ans
          }
        case None ⇒ failMode
      }
    tryFrom(ep.dual.cursor, Retry) // attempt reaction
  }
```

Figure 6. Excerpts from the reagent subclasses

tage of this implementation, other than its simplicity, is that is has no impact on the performance of single-word CASes to references, which we expect to be the common case; such CASes can be performed directly, without any awareness of the kCAS protocol. Our experimental results in §6 indicate that even this simple kCAS implementation provides reasonable performance—much better than STM or coarse-grained locking—but a more sophisticated kCAS would likely do even better.

5.6 Shared state

The implementation of the cas combinator is given by the CAS class, shown in Fig. 6. Its tryReact method is fairly simple, but it illustrates a key optimization we have mentioned several times: if neither the reaction so far nor the continuation of the cas are performing a CAS, then the entire reagent is performing a single CAS, and can thus attempt the CAS immediately. This optimization eliminates the overhead of creating a new Reaction object and employing the kCAS protocol, and it means that lock-free algorithms like TreiberStack and MSQueue behave just like their hand-written counterparts. If, on the other hand, the reagent may perform a kCAS, then the current cas is recorded into a new Reaction object, which is passed to the continuation. In either case, the continuation is invoked with the unit value as its argument.

5.7 Choice

The implementation of choice (Fig. 6) is pleasantly simple. It attempts a reaction with either arm of the choice, going in left to right order. As explained in §3.3, a permanent failure of choice can only result from a permanent failure of *both* arms. Also, note that the right arm is tried even if the left arm has only failed transiently.

5.8 Computed reagents

The implementation of computed reagents (Fig. 6) is exactly as described in §4.1: attempt to execute the stored computation c on the argument a to the reagent, and invoke the resulting reagent with a unit value. If c is not defined at a, the computed reagent issues a permanent failure. The implementation makes clear that the invisible reads and writes performed within the computation c do not even have access to the Reaction object, and so cannot enlarge the atomic update performed when it is committed.

5.9 Channels

We represent each endpoint of a channel as a lock-free bag (which can itself be built using reagents). The lock-freedom allows multiple reagents to interact with the bag in parallel; the fact that it is a bag rather than a queue trades a weaker ordering guarantee for increased parallelism, but any lock-free collection would suffice.

The endpoint bags store messages, which wrap offers with additional data from the sender:

```
case class Message[A,B,C](
  payload: A,              // sender's actual message data
  senderRx: Reaction,      // sender's checkpointed reaction
  senderK: Reagent[B,C],   // sender's reagent continuation
  offer: Offer[C])         // sender's offer
```

Each message is essentially a checkpoint of a reaction in progress, where the reaction is blocked until the payload (of type A) can be swapped for a dual payload (of type B). Hence the stored sender continuation takes a B for input; it returns a C, which matches the final answer type of the sender's offer.

The core implementation of swap is shown in the Swap class in Fig. 6. If an offer is being made, it must be posted in a new message on the endpoint before any attempt is made to react with existing offers. This ordering guarantees that there are no lost wakeups: each reagent is responsible only for those messages posted prior to it posting its own message.[4]

Once the offer (if any) is posted, tryReact peruses messages on the dual endpoint using the tail-recursive loop, tryFrom. The

[4] Our earlier work [29] with Russo on scalable join patterns gives a more detailed explanation of this protocol and its liveness properties.

loop navigates through the dual endpoint's bag using a simple cursor, which will reveal at least those messages present prior to the reagent's own message being posted to its endpoint. If a message is found, tryFrom attempts to complete the reaction; the exchange method combines the reaction and continuation of the located message with those of the reagent executing it, and actually performs the payload swap. If the reaction is successful, the final result is returned (and the result for the other reagent is separately written to its offer status). If the reaction fails, tryFrom continues to look for other messages. If no messages remain, swap behaves as if it were a disjunction: it fails permanently only if *all* messages it encountered led to permanent failures.

The code sketch we have given for channels glosses over several details of the real implementation, including avoiding fulfilling one's own offer or a single offer multiple times, and allowing multiple interactions between two reagents within a single reaction.

6. Performance

Fine-grained concurrent data structures are usually evaluated by targeted microbenchmarking, with focus on contention effects and fine-grained parallel speedup [2, 7, 9, 10, 12, 19, 20, 24]. In addition to those basic aims, we wish to evaluate (1) the extent to which reagent-based algorithms can compete with their hand-built counterparts and (2) whether reagent composition is a plausible approach for scalable atomic transfers. To this end, we designed a series of benchmarks focusing on simple lock-free collections, where overhead from reagents is easy to gauge. Each benchmark consists of n threads running a loop, where in each iteration they apply one or more atomic operations on a shared data structure and then simulate a workload by spinning for a short time. For a high contention simulation, the spinning lasts for $0.25\mu s$ on average, while for a low contention simulation, we spin for $2.5\mu s$.

In the "PushPop" benchmark, all of the threads alternate pushing and popping data to a single, shared stack. In the "StackTransfer" benchmark, there are two shared stacks, and each thread pushes to one stack, atomically transfers an element from that stack to the other stack, and then pops an element from the second stack; the direction of movement is chosen randomly. The "EnqDeq" and "QueueTransfer" benchmarks are analogous, but work with queues instead. The stack benchmarks compare our reagent-based TreiberStack to (1) a hand-built Treiber stack, (2) a mutable stack protected by a single lock, and (3) a stack using STM. The queue benchmarks compare our reagent-based MSQueue to (1) a hand-built Michael-Scott queue, (2) a mutable queue protected by a lock, and (3) a queue using STM. For the transfer benchmarks, the hand-built data structures are dropped, since they do not support atomic transfer; for the lock-based data structures, we acquire both locks in a fixed order before performing the transfer.

We used the Multiverse STM, a sophisticated open-source implementation of Transaction Locking II [3] which is distributed as part of the Akka package for Scala.[5] Our benchmarks were run on a 3.46Ghz Intel Xeon X5677 (Westmere) with 32GB RAM and 12MB of shared L3 cache. The machine has two physical processors with four hyperthreaded cores each, for a total of 16 hardware threads. L1 and L2 caches are per-core. The software environment includes Ubuntu 10.04.3 and the Hotspot JVM 6u27.

The results are shown in Fig. 7; the x-axes show thread counts, while the y-axes show throughput (iterations/μs, so larger numbers are better). The reagent-based data structures perform universally better than the lock- or STM-based data structures. The results show that reagents can plausibly compete with hand-built concurrent data structures, while providing scalable composed operations that are rarely provided for such data structures.

[5] Although TL2 is intended for more complex data structures than the ones tested here, it is by far the most readily available production STM in the Java/Scala ecosystem.

7. Related work

7.1 Concurrent ML

Concurrent ML [22] was designed to resolve an apparent tension between abstraction and choice: if protocols are represented abstractly as functions, it is impossible to express the choice of two abstract protocols. The solution is *higher-order concurrency*, a code-as-data approach in which synchronous message-passing protocols are represented abstractly as *events*. CML's events are built up from combinators, including a choice combinator, communication combinators, and combinators for arbitrary computations not involving communication. Reagents are clearly influenced by the design of CML's events, and include variants of CML's core event combinators (communication and choice). But where CML is aimed squarely at capturing synchronous communication protocols, reagents are designed for writing and tailoring fine-grained concurrent data structures and synchronization primitives. This difference in motivation led us to include a number of additional combinators, including those dealing directly with shared state.

Originally, CML was focused on managing concurrency rather than profiting from parallelism, and this focus was reflected in its implementation. More recently, a parallel implementation of CML was proposed [23]. The key challenge is resolving uses of choice both consistently and scalably. It is addressed by *sharing*: an event making a choice is enrolled as offering a communication corresponding to each possible choice, and when a communication is accepted, the (single, shared) event is atomically marked as consumed. We follow a similar strategy in dealing with message passing, but where Parallel CML uses lock-based queues to store messages, we show how to use lock-free bags for increased parallelism (§5). We also show how to incorporate choice resolution with shared-state updates and our conjunction combinators.

7.2 Software transactional memory

Software transactional memory was originally intended "to provide a general highly concurrent method for translating sequential object implementations into non-blocking ones" [25]. This ambitious goal has led to a remarkable research literature, which has been summarized in textbook form [15]. Much of the research is devoted to achieving scalability on multiprocessors or multicores, sometimes by relaxing consistency guarantees or only providing obstruction-freedom rather than lock-freemdom [12].

Reagents, on the other hand, are aimed at a less ambitious goal: enabling the concise expression, user tailoring, and composition of fine-grained concurrent algorithms. That is, unlike STM, reagents do not attempt to provide a *universal* fine-grained concurrent algorithm. Instead, they assist in writing and using specific algorithms.

There is a clear tradeoff. Using STM, one can implement a concurrent stack or queue by simply wrapping a sequential version in an atomic block, which requires no algorithmic insight and is simpler than the stack or queue we give in §3. But even with a very clever STM, these implementations are unlikely to scale as well as our elimination stack or Michael-Scott queue; some evidence for that is shown in §6.

Reagents carve out a middle ground between completely hand-written algorithms and the completely automatic atomic blocks of STM. When used in isolation, reagents are *guaranteed* to perform only the CASes that the hand-written algorithm would, so they introduce no overhead on shared-memory operations; by recoding an algorithm use reagents, you lose nothing. Yet unlike hand-written algorithms, reagents can be composed using choice, tailored with new blocking behavior, or combined into larger atomic blocks.

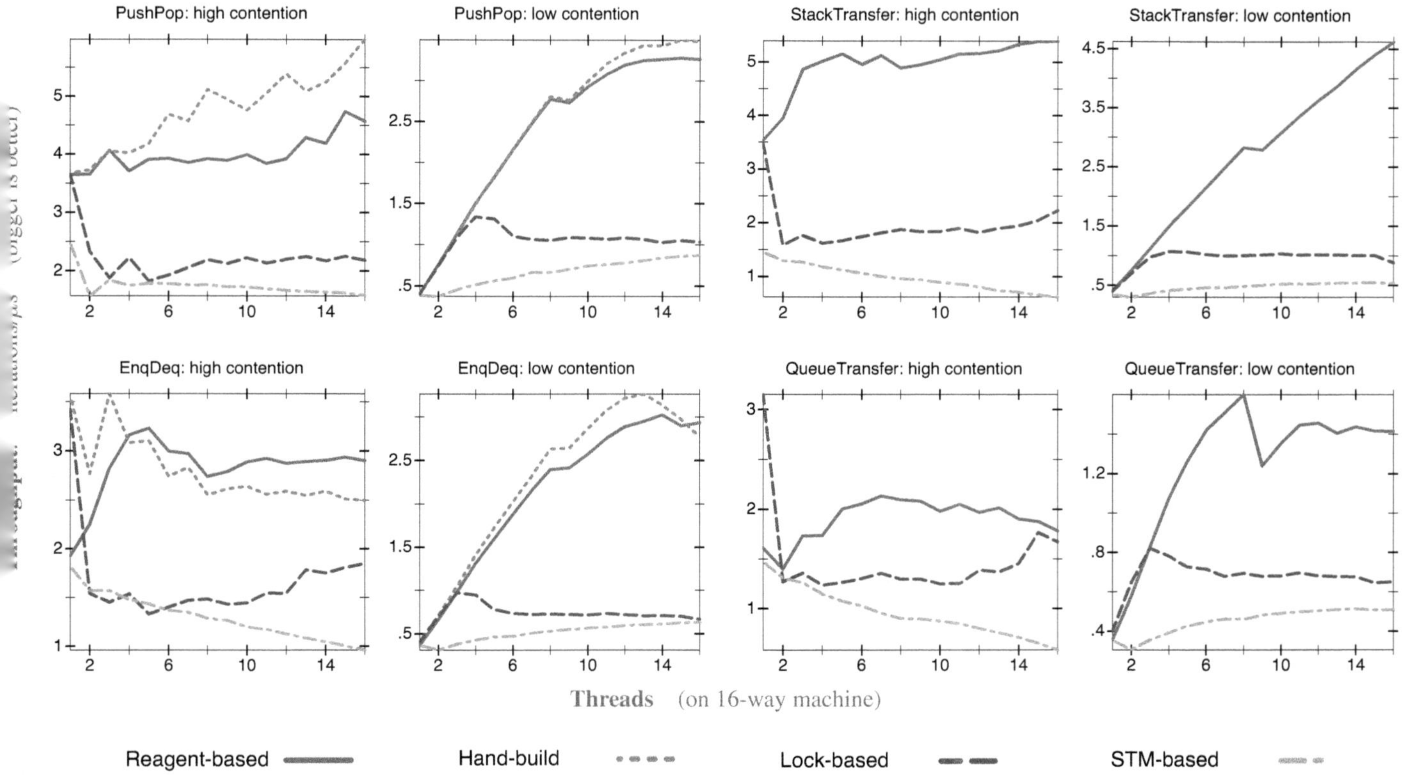

Figure 7. Benchmarking results

Haskell's STM [8] was inspirational in showing that transactions can be represented via monads [21], explicitly composed, and combined with blocking and choice operators. Reagents also form a monad, but we have chosen an interface closer to *arrows* [14], to encourage static reagent layout wherever possible (§4.1). Like orElse in Haskell's STM, our choice operator is left-biased. But unlike orElse, our choice operator will attempt the right-hand side even when the left-hand side has only failed transiently (rather than permanently).[6] While the distinction appears technical, it is crucial for supporting examples like the elimination backoff stack (§3.3).

7.3 Transactions that communicate

A central tenet of transactions is *isolation*: transactions should not be aware of concurrent changes to memory from other transactions. But sometimes it is desirable for concurrent transactions to coordinate or otherwise communicate while executing. Recent papers have proposed mechanisms for incorporating communication with STM, in the form of Communicating Transactions [16], Transaction Communicators [17], and Transactions with Isolation and Cooperation (TIC, [27]). A key question in this line of work is how the expected isolation of shared memory can safely coexist with concurrent communication. Communicating Transactions use explicit, asynchronous message passing to communicate; the mechanism is entirely separate from shared memory, which retains isolation. On the other hand, Transaction Communicators and TIC allow isolation to be weakened in a controlled way.

Our mixture of message-passing and shared-state combinators most closely resembles the work on Communicating Transactions. Of course, the most important difference is in the way we deal with shared state discussed in §7.2. We also believe that *synchronous* communication is better for expressing patterns like elimination (§3.3), since they rely on participants being mutually-aware.

There has also been work treating pure message-passing in a transactional way. Transactional Events [4] combines CML with an atomic sequencing operator. Previously, Transactional Events were implemented on top of Haskell's STM, relied on search threads[7] for matching communications, and used an STM-based representation of channels. However, Transactional Events are expressible using reagents, through the combination of swap and the conjunction combinators. Doing so yields a new implementation that does not require search threads, performs parallel matching for communication, and represents channels as lock-free bags. We are not in a position to do a head-to-head comparison, but based on the results in §6, we expect the reagent-based implementation to scale better on fine-grained workloads.

Another message-passing system with a transactional flavor is the Join Calculus [6], discussed in §3.7. The treatment of conjunction, message passing, and catalysis is essentially inherited from our previous work giving a scalable implementation of the join calculus [29].

7.4 Composing fine-grained concurrent data structures

Most of the literature on fine-grained concurrent data structures is focused on "within-object" atomicity, for example developing algorithms for inserting or removing elements into a collection atomically. However, there has been some recent work studying the problem of transferring data atomically between such fine-grained data structures [2]. The basic approach relies on a kCAS operation in much the same way that reagent sequencing does. The transfer methods must be defined manually, in advance, and with access to

[6] Note that retry in Haskell's STM signals a *permanent* failure, rather than an optimistic retry.

[7] The implementation can be made to work with a single search thread at the cost of lost parallelism.

the internals of the relevant data structures, whereas reagents allow arbitrary new compositions, without manual definition, and without access to the code or internals of the involved data structures. Nevertheless, the implementation of reagent composition yields an algorithm very similar to the manually-written transfer methods.

It is also possible to go in the other direction: start from STM, which provides composition, and add an "escape hatch" for writing arbitrary fine-grained concurrent algorithms within the scope of a transaction. The escape hatch can be provided through unlogged reads and/or writes to memory locations being used by transactions, as in early release [12] or elastic transactions [5]. As we discussed above (§7.2), we favor an approach where the focus is foremost on writing fine-grained algorithms, with *guarantees* about the performance and shared-memory semantics of those algorithms. Providing such guarantees via an escape hatch mechanism may be difficult or impossible, depending on the details of the STM implementation. As we showed in §3, it is also very useful to have combinators for choice, message-passing, and blocking, if one wishes to capture the full range of fine-grained concurrent algorithms.

8. Conclusion and planned work

Reagents blend together message passing and shared state concurrency to provide an abstract, compositional way of writing fine-grained concurrent algorithms. We see this work as serving the needs of two distinct groups: concurrency experts and concurrency users. Using reagents, experts can write libraries more easily, because common patterns are expressible as abstractions and many are built-in. Users can then extend, tailor and compose the resulting library without detailed knowledge of the algorithms involved.

There is significant remaining work for elucidating both the theory and practice of reagents. On the theoretical side, developing a formal operational semantics would help to clarify the interactions possible between shared state and message passing, as well as the atomicity guarantees that reagents provide. On the practical side, developing a serious concurrency library using reagents would go a long way toward demonstrating their usability. In future work, we plan to pursue both of these goals. In addition, we plan to expand the scope of reagents to include fine-grained locking as well as non-blocking data structures.

Acknowledgments

Thanks to Claudio Russo, Vincent St-Amour, Sam Tobin-Hochstadt, Jesse Tov and Mitchell Wand for insightful discussions during the development of this work. Pete Manolios provided access to benchmarking equipment. Thanks go to Neil Toronto for the development of the new Racket plot library. The anonymous reviewers provided thorough reviews which led to several improvements to the presentation. Finally, I greatly appreciate the generous financial support of Microsoft Research.

References

[1] H. Attiya and E. Hillel. Highly-concurrent multi-word synchronization. In *ICDCN*, 2008.

[2] D. Cederman and P. Tsigas. Supporting lock-free composition of concurrent data objects. In *CF*, 2010.

[3] D. Dice, O. Shalev, and N. Shavit. Transactional locking II. *DISC*, 2006.

[4] K. Donnelly and M. Fluet. Transactional events. *JFP*, 18(5 & 6):649 – 706, Oct. 2008.

[5] P. Felber, V. Gramoli, and R. Guerraoui. Elastic transactions. In *DISC*, 2009.

[6] C. Fournet and G. Gonthier. The reflexive chemical abstract machine and the join-calculus. In *POPL*, 1996.

[7] K. Fraser and T. Harris. Concurrent programming without locks. *TOCS*, 25(2), May 2007.

[8] T. Harris, S. Marlow, S. Peyton-Jones, and M. Herlihy. Composable memory transactions. In *PPOPP*, Aug. 2005.

[9] D. Hendler, N. Shavit, and L. Yerushalmi. A scalable lock-free stack algorithm. In *SPAA*, Jan. 2004.

[10] D. Hendler, I. Incze, N. Shavit, and M. Tzafrir. Flat combining and the synchronization-parallelism tradeoff. In *SPAA*, 2010.

[11] M. Herlihy and N. Shavit. *The Art of Multiprocessor Programming*. Morgan Kaufmann, 2008.

[12] M. Herlihy, V. Luchangco, M. Moir, and W. Scherer III. Software transactional memory for dynamic-sized data structures. In *PODC*, 2003. ISBN 1581137087.

[13] M. P. Herlihy and J. M. Wing. Linearizability: a correctness condition for concurrent objects. *TOPLAS*, 12(3):463–492, 1990.

[14] J. Hughes. Generalising monads to arrows. *Science of computer programming*, 37(1-3):67–111, May 2000.

[15] J. Larus and R. Rajwar. *Transactional memory*. Morgan and Claypool, 2006.

[16] M. Lesani and J. Palsberg. Communicating memory transactions. In *PPOPP*, 2011.

[17] V. Luchangco and V. Marathe. Transaction communicators: enabling cooperation among concurrent transactions. In *PPOPP*, 2011.

[18] V. Luchangco, M. Moir, and N. Shavit. Nonblocking k-compare-single-swap. In *SPAA*, Dec. 2003.

[19] J. Mellor-Crummey and M. Scott. Algorithms for scalable synchronization on shared-memory multiprocessors. *TOCS*, 9(1):21–65, 1991.

[20] M. M. Michael and M. L. Scott. Simple, fast, and practical non-blocking and blocking concurrent queue algorithms. In *PODC*, 1996.

[21] S. Peyton Jones and P. Wadler. Imperative functional programming. In *POPL*, 1993.

[22] J. Reppy. CML: a higher order concurrent language. In *PLDI*, 1991.

[23] J. Reppy, C. Russo, and Y. Xiao. Parallel concurrent ML. In *ICFP*, Aug. 2009.

[24] W. Scherer III and M. Scott. Nonblocking concurrent data structures with condition synchronization. In *DISC*. Springer, 2004.

[25] N. Shavit and D. Touitou. Software transactional memory. *Distributed Computing*, 10(2):99–116, Feb. 1997.

[26] N. Shavit and D. Touitou. Elimination trees and the construction of pools and stacks. *Theory of Computing Systems*, 30:645–670, 1997.

[27] Y. Smaragdakis, A. Kay, R. Behrends, and M. Young. Transactions with isolation and cooperation. In *OOPSLA*, 2007.

[28] R. Treiber. Systems programming: Coping with parallelism. Technical report, IBM Almaden Research Center, 1986.

[29] A. Turon and C. V. Russo. Scalable Join Patterns. In *OOPSLA*, 2011.

[30] P. Wadler. The essence of functional programming. In *POPL*, 1992.

Proving Acceptability Properties of Relaxed Nondeterministic Approximate Programs

Michael Carbin Deokhwan Kim Sasa Misailovic Martin C. Rinard
MIT CSAIL
{mcarbin, dkim, misailo, rinard}@csail.mit.edu

Abstract

Approximate program transformations such as skipping tasks [29, 30], loop perforation [21, 22, 35], reduction sampling [38], multiple selectable implementations [3, 4, 16, 38], dynamic knobs [16], synchronization elimination [20, 32], approximate function memoization [11], and approximate data types [34] produce programs that can execute at a variety of points in an underlying performance versus accuracy tradeoff space. These transformed programs have the ability to trade accuracy of their results for increased performance by dynamically and nondeterministically modifying variables that control their execution.

We call such transformed programs *relaxed* programs because they have been extended with additional nondeterminism to relax their semantics and enable greater flexibility in their execution.

We present language constructs for developing and specifying relaxed programs. We also present proof rules for reasoning about *acceptability properties* [28], which the program must satisfy to be acceptable. Our proof rules work with two kinds of acceptability properties: *relational* acceptability properties, which characterize desired relationships between the values of variables in the original and relaxed programs, and *unary* acceptability properties, which involve values only from a single (original or relaxed) program. The proof rules support a *staged* reasoning approach in which the majority of the reasoning effort works with the original program. Exploiting the common structure that the original and relaxed programs share, relational reasoning transfers reasoning effort from the original program to prove properties of the relaxed program.

We have formalized the dynamic semantics of our target programming language and the proof rules in Coq and verified that the proof rules are sound with respect to the dynamic semantics. Our Coq implementation enables developers to obtain fully machine-checked verifications of their relaxed programs.

Categories and Subject Descriptors D.3.2 [*Programming Languages*]: Language Classifications—Nondeterministic languages; F.3.1 [*Logics and Meanings of Programs*]: Specifying and Verifying and Reasoning about Programs; F.3.2 [*Logics and Meanings of Programs*]: Semantics of Programming Languages

General Terms Languages, Performance, Theory, Verification

Keywords Coq, Acceptability, Relaxed Programs, Relational Hoare Logic

1. Introduction

In recent years researchers have developed a range of mechanisms for dynamically varying application behavior. Typical goals include maximizing performance subject to an accuracy constraint, maximizing accuracy subject to a performance constraint, or dynamically adjusting program behavior to adapt to changes in the characteristics of the underlying hardware platform (such as varying load or clock rate) [16, 17]. Specific mechanisms include skipping tasks [29, 30], loop perforation (skipping iterations of time-consuming loops) [21, 22, 35], sampling reduction inputs [38], multiple selectable implementations of a given component or components [3, 4, 16, 38], dynamic knobs (configuration parameters that can be changed as the program executes) [16], synchronization elimination (forgoing synchronization not required to produce an acceptably accurate result) [20, 32], approximate function memoization (returning a previously computed value when the arguments of a function call are close to the arguments of a previous call) [11], and approximate data types [32, 34].

All of these mechanisms can produce a *relaxed program* — a program that may adjust its execution by changing one or more variables subject to a specified *relaxation predicate*. For example, a perforated program may dynamically choose to skip loop iterations each time it enters a given loop. A relaxed program is therefore a nondeterministic program, with each execution a variant of the original execution. The different executions typically share a common global structure, with local differences at only those parts of the computation affected by the modified variables.

1.1 Acceptability

To use these relaxation mechanisms, a developer must ensure that the resulting relaxed program is acceptable. We formalize acceptability as *acceptability properties* that the program must satisfy to be acceptable. Acceptability properties include *integrity properties* that the program must satisfy to successfully produce a result and *accuracy properties* that characterize how accurate the produced result must be. For example, an integrity property might state that a function must return a value greater than zero (otherwise the program might crash), while an accuracy property might state that the relaxed program must (potentially only with high probability) produce a result that differs by at most a specified percentage from the result that the original program produces [21, 38].

1.2 Reasoning About Relaxed Programs

We present language constructs for developing relaxed programs and stating acceptability properties. We also present proof rules for verifying the stated acceptability properties. Our language and proof rules support a staged approach in which the developer first develops a standard program and uses standard approaches to reason about this program to determine that it satisfies desired acceptability properties. We refer to the dynamic semantics of the program at this stage as the *original semantics* of the program.

Either the developer or an automated system (such as a compiler that implements loop perforation) then *relaxes* the program to enable additional nondeterministic executions. We refer to the dynamic semantics of the program at this stage as the *relaxed semantics* of the program.

Finally, the developer uses *relational reasoning* to verify that the relaxation maintains the desired acceptability properties. Specifically, the developer specifies and verifies additional *relational assertions* that characterize the relationship between the original and relaxed semantics. These relational assertions facilitate the overall verification of the relaxed program. This approach is designed to reduce the overall reasoning effort by exploiting the common structure that the original and relaxed programs share. With this approach the majority of the reasoning effort works with the original program and is then transferred via relational reasoning to verify the nondeterministic relaxed program.

1.3 Relaxed Programming Constructs

Basic relaxed programming constructs include nondeterministic variable assignments (via the `relax` statement), relational assertions that relate the relaxed semantics to the original semantics (via the `relate` statement), unary assertions (via the `assert` statement), and unary assumptions (via the `assume` statement).

The Relax Statement. The `relax (X) st (P)` statement specifies a nondeterministic assignment to the set of variables `X`. Specifically, the `relax` statement can assign the variables in `X` to any set of values that satisfies the relaxation predicate `P`. When added to the program, the `relax` statement affects only the relaxed semantics of the program; in the original semantics it has no effect.

The Relate Statement. The `relate P` statement asserts that the predicate `P` must hold at the program point where the statement appears. The predicate `P` is a *relational predicate* — it may reference values from both the original and relaxed executions. So, for example, the statement might require the value of a variable `x` in relaxed executions to be greater than or equal to the value of `x` in the original execution.

The Assert Statement. The `assert P` statement states that `P` must hold at the point where the statement appears. In contrast to the `relate` statement, `P` is a *unary predicate* — it only references values from a single execution (original or relaxed) as in a standard assertion. In the original semantics, our proof rules generate an obligation to prove that an `assert` statement holds for all executions. To ensure that the `assert` statement remains valid in the relaxed semantics, our proof rule in the relaxed semantics generates an obligation to prove that if the assertion is valid in the original semantics, then the current relation between the original and relaxed semantics establishes that the assertion is valid in the relaxed semantics. For example, it may be possible to prove that all the variables referenced in an assertion have the same values in the original and relaxed semantics — i.e., the relaxation does not interfere with the assertion. In this way, relational reasoning serves as a bridge to transfer properties of the original program over to the relaxed program.

The Assume Statement. The `assume P` statement states that the unary predicate `P` holds at the point where the statement appears. In the original semantics the `assume` statement does not generate any proof obligations — the proof system simply accepts that `P` holds. To verify that the relaxation does not interfere with the reasoning behind the assumption, the proof rules for the relaxed semantics generate an obligation to prove that if the assumption `P` holds in all original executions, then it holds in all relaxed executions. The proofs work in much the same way as for the `assert` statement except that the proof rules do not generate an obligation to verify that `P` holds in the original semantics.

1.4 Key Properties of Acceptable Relaxed Programs

Our approach makes it possible to formalize key properties that are critical to the development and deployment of acceptable relaxed programs.

Integrity and Noninterference. Essentially all programs have basic integrity properties that must hold for all executions of the program. Examples include the absence of out of bounds array accesses or null pointer dereferences. Developers typically use either `assert` or `assume` statements to formalize these integrity properties. Because successful relaxations do not typically interfere with the basic integrity of the original program, the reasoning that establishes the validity of the integrity properties typically transfers directly from the original program over to the relaxed program. Relational assertions that establish the equality of values of variables in the original and relaxed executions (i.e., *noninterference*) often form the bridge that enables this direct transfer (see Section 5).

Accuracy. Relaxed programs exploit the freedom of the computation to, within limits, produce a range of different outputs. Accuracy properties formalize how accurate the outputs must be to stay within the acceptable range. For example, a perforatable loop may produce a range of acceptable results, with (typically depending on the amount of perforation) some more accurate than others. Because it is often convenient to express accuracy requirements by bounding the difference between results from the original and relaxed executions, developers can use `relate` statements to express accuracy properties (see Section 5).

Debuggability. The `assume` statement provides developers with the ability to state (formally unverified) assumptions that they believe to be true in the original program. But if an assumption is not valid, the program may fail or exhibit unintended behaviors.

Relaxation without verification can therefore complicate debugging — it may cause the relaxed program to violate assumptions that are valid in the original program (and therefore to exhibit unintended behaviors that are not possible in the original program). Our proof rules, by ensuring that if the assumption is valid in the original program, then it remains valid in the relaxed program, simplify debugging by eliminating this potential source of unintended behaviors.

Note that our proof rules can work together effectively to prove important acceptability properties. For example, the developer may use a `relate` statement to establish a relationship between values in variables in the original and relaxed executions, then use this relationship to prove that the property specified by an `assert` or `assume` statement holds in all relaxed executions.

1.5 Proof Rules and Formal Properties

We structure our proof rules as a set of Hoare logics:

- **Axiomatic Original Semantics:** The *original* Hoare-style semantics models the original execution of the program wherein `relax` statements have no effect.
- **Axiomatic Relaxed Semantics:** The *relational* Hoare-style semantics relates executions in the relaxed semantics to executions in the original semantics. The predicates of the judgment are given in a relational logic that enables us to express properties over the values of variables in both the original and relaxed executions of the program. A proof with the axiomatic relaxed semantics relates the two semantics of the program in lockstep and, therefore, supports the transfer of reasoning about the original semantics to the relaxed semantics by enabling, for example, noninterference proofs.

One key aspect of the axiomatic relaxed semantics is that it must also give an appropriate semantics for relaxed programs in which the original and relaxed executions may branch in different directions at a control flow construct (at this point the two executions are no longer in lockstep). In particular, we do not support relational reasoning for program points at which the executions are no longer in lockstep (`relate` statements do not have a natural semantics at such program points). Our relaxed semantics therefore incorporates a nonrelational axiomatic *intermediate semantics* that captures the desired behavior of the relaxed execution as it executes without a corresponding original execution. We also appropriately restrict the location of `relate` statements to program points at which the original and relaxed programs execute in lockstep.

Our proof rules are sound and establish the following semantic properties of verified relaxed programs:

- **Original Progress Modulo Assumptions:** If the program verifies under the axiomatic original semantics, then no execution of the program in the dynamic original semantics violates an assertion. By design, a program may still terminate in error if a specified `assume` statement is not valid.
- **Soundness of Relational Assertions:** If the program verifies under the axiomatic relaxed semantics, then all pairs of executions in the dynamic original and relaxed semantics satisfy the `relate` statements in the program.
- **Relative Relaxed Progress:** If the program verifies under the axiomatic relaxed semantics and no executions in the dynamic original semantics violate an assertion or an assumption, then no execution in the dynamic relaxed semantics violates an assertion or an assumption.
- **Relaxed Progress:** If the program verifies under both the original and relaxed axiomatic semantics and no execution in the dynamic original semantics violates an assumption, then no execution in the dynamic relaxed semantics violates an assertion or an assumption.
- **Relaxed Progress Modulo Original Assumptions:** If the program verifies under both the original and relaxed axiomatic semantics, then if an execution in the dynamic relaxed semantics violates an assertion or an assumption, then an execution in the dynamic original semantics violates an assumption.

These properties assure developers that verified relaxation produces a program that satisfies the stated acceptability properties. Our design supports a development process in which developers can use the full range of standard techniques (verification, testing, code reviews) to validate properties that they believe to be true of the original program. They can then use `assume` statements to formally state these properties and incorporate them (via relational reasoning) into the verification of the relaxed program. This verification ensures that if the relaxed program fails because of a violated assumption, then the developer can reproduce the violated assumption in the original program.

1.6 Coq Verification Framework

We have formalized the dynamic original and relaxed semantics with the Coq proof assistant [1]. We have also used Coq to formalize our proof rules and obtain a fully machine-checked proof that the rules are sound with respect to the dynamic semantics and provide the stated semantic properties. Our Coq formalization makes it possible to develop fully machine-checked verifications of relaxed programs. We have used our framework to develop and verify several small relaxed programs.

Our Coq implementation contains approximately 8000 lines of code and proof scripts, with 1300 lines devoted to the original semantics and its soundness proofs and 1900 additional lines devoted to the relaxed semantics and its soundness proofs. A large portion (approximately 3500 lines) is devoted to formalizing the semantics of our relational assertion logic and its soundness with respect to operations such as substitution.

1.7 Contributions

This paper makes the following contributions:

- **Relaxed Programming:** It identifies the concept of relaxed programming as a way to specify nondeterministic variants of an original program. The variants often occupy a range of points in an underlying performance versus accuracy trade-off space. Current techniques that can produce relaxed programs include skipping tasks [29, 30], loop perforation [21, 22, 35], reduction sampling [38], multiple selectable implementations [3, 4, 16, 38], dynamic knobs [16], synchronization elimination [20, 32], approximate function memoization [11], and approximate data types [34].
- **Relational Reasoning and Proof Rules:** It presents a basic reasoning approach and proof rules for verifying acceptability properties of relaxed programs. With this approach, the majority of the reasoning effort works with the original program and is transferred to the relaxed program through relational reasoning.
- **Coq Formalization and Soundness Results:** It presents a formalization of the dynamic semantics and proof rules in Coq. We have used this formalization to prove that the proof rules are sound with respect to the dynamic original and relaxed semantics. We note that our Coq formalization contains a reusable implementation of our relational assertion logic that is, in principle, suitable for other uses such as verifying traditional compiler transformations [7, 31, 36, 39].
- **Verified Programs:** It presents several relaxed programs for which we have used the Coq formalization to develop fully machine-checked verifications.

Relaxed programs can deliver substantial flexibility, performance, and resource consumption benefits. But to successfully deploy relaxed programs, developers need to have confidence that the relaxation satisfies important acceptability properties. This paper presents a foundational formal reasoning system that leverages the structure and relationships that the original and relaxed executions share to enable the verification of these properties.

2. Language Syntax and Dynamic Semantics

Figure 1 presents a simple imperative language with integer variables, integer arithmetic expressions, boolean expressions, conditional statements, while loops, and sequential composition. For generality, we support nondeterminism in the original semantics via the `havoc` (X) `st` (B) statement which nondeterministically assigns the variables in `X` to values that satisfy B. The `relax` (X) `st` (B) statement supports nondeterministic relaxation — in the original semantics it has no effect; in the relaxed semantics it nondeterministically assigns the variables in `X` to values that satisfy B. The language also supports the standard `assume` and `assert` statements.

A main point of departure from standard languages is the addition of *relational integer expressions* (E^*) and *relational boolean expressions* (B^*). Unlike standard expressions, which involve values from only the current execution, relational expressions can reference values from both the original ($x\langle o\rangle$) and

$$
\begin{aligned}
\texttt{iop} &::= + \mid - \mid * \mid / \mid \ldots \\
\texttt{cmp} &::= < \mid > \mid = \mid \ldots \\
\texttt{lop} &::= \wedge \mid \vee \mid \ldots \\
X &::= \texttt{x} \mid \texttt{x}, X \\
E &::= \texttt{n} \mid \texttt{x} \mid E \ \texttt{iop} \ E \\
E^* &::= \texttt{n} \mid \texttt{x}\langle\texttt{o}\rangle \mid \texttt{x}\langle\texttt{r}\rangle \mid E^* \ \texttt{iop} \ E^* \\
B &::= \texttt{true} \mid \texttt{false} \mid E \ \texttt{cmp} \ E \mid B \ \texttt{lop} \ B \mid \neg B \\
B^* &::= \texttt{true} \mid \texttt{false} \mid E^* \ \texttt{cmp} \ E^* \mid B^* \ \texttt{lop} \ B^* \mid \neg B^* \\
S &::= \texttt{skip} \mid \texttt{x = } E \mid \texttt{havoc} \ (X) \ \texttt{st} \ (B) \mid \texttt{relax} \ (X) \ \texttt{st} \ (B) \\
&\mid \texttt{if} \ (B) \ \{S_1\} \ \texttt{else} \ \{S_2\} \mid \texttt{while} \ (B) \ \{S\} \\
&\mid \texttt{assume} \ B \mid \texttt{assert} \ B \mid \texttt{relate l} : \ B^* \\
&\mid S \ ; \ S
\end{aligned}
$$

Figure 1. Language Syntax

$$
\begin{aligned}
&[\![E]\!] \in \Sigma \to \mathbb{Z} \\
&[\![\texttt{n}]\!](\sigma) = n \\
&[\![\texttt{x}]\!](\sigma) = \sigma(x) \\
&[\![E_1 \ \texttt{iop} \ E_2]\!](\sigma) = [\![E_1]\!](\sigma) \ iop \ [\![E_2]\!](\sigma)
\end{aligned}
$$

$$
\begin{aligned}
&[\![E^*]\!] \in \Sigma \times \Sigma \to \mathbb{Z} \\
&[\![\texttt{n}]\!](\sigma_1, \sigma_2) = n \\
&[\![\texttt{x}\langle\texttt{o}\rangle]\!](\sigma_1, \sigma_2) = \sigma_1(x) \quad [\![\texttt{x}\langle\texttt{r}\rangle]\!](\sigma_1, \sigma_2) = \sigma_2(x) \\
&[\![E_1^* \ \texttt{iop} \ E_2^*]\!](\sigma_1, \sigma_2) = [\![E_1^*]\!](\sigma_1, \sigma_2) \ iop \ [\![E_2^*]\!](\sigma_1, \sigma_2)
\end{aligned}
$$

$$
\begin{aligned}
&[\![B]\!] \in \Sigma \to \mathbb{B} \\
&[\![\texttt{true}]\!](\sigma) = \mathit{true} \quad [\![\texttt{false}]\!](\sigma) = \mathit{false} \\
&[\![E_1 \ \texttt{cmp} \ E_2]\!](\sigma) = [\![E_1]\!](\sigma) \ cmp \ [\![E_2]\!](\sigma) \\
&[\![B_1 \ \texttt{lop} \ B_2]\!](\sigma) = [\![B_1]\!](\sigma) \ lop \ [\![B_2]\!](\sigma) \\
&[\![\neg B]\!](\sigma) = \begin{cases} \mathit{true}, & [\![B]\!](\sigma) = \mathit{false} \\ \mathit{false}, & [\![B]\!](\sigma) = \mathit{true} \end{cases}
\end{aligned}
$$

$$
\begin{aligned}
&[\![B^*]\!] \in \Sigma \times \Sigma \to \mathbb{B} \\
&[\![\texttt{true}]\!](\sigma_1, \sigma_2) = \mathit{true} \quad [\![\texttt{false}]\!](\sigma_1, \sigma_2) = \mathit{false} \\
&[\![E_1^* \ \texttt{cmp} \ E_2^*]\!](\sigma_1, \sigma_2) = [\![E_1^*]\!](\sigma_1, \sigma_2) \ cmp \ [\![E_2^*]\!](\sigma_1, \sigma_2) \\
&[\![B_1^* \ \texttt{lop} \ B_2^*]\!](\sigma_1, \sigma_2) = [\![B_1^*]\!](\sigma_1, \sigma_2) \ lop \ [\![B_2^*]\!](\sigma_1, \sigma_2) \\
&[\![\neg B^*]\!](\sigma_1, \sigma_2) = \begin{cases} \mathit{true}, & [\![B^*]\!](\sigma_1, \sigma_2) = \mathit{false} \\ \mathit{false}, & [\![B^*]\!](\sigma_1, \sigma_2) = \mathit{true} \end{cases}
\end{aligned}
$$

$$
\text{expr}\frac{[\![e]\!](\sigma) = n}{\langle e \ , \ \sigma \rangle \Downarrow_E n} \qquad \text{bexp}\frac{[\![b]\!](\sigma) = v}{\langle b \ , \ \sigma \rangle \Downarrow_B v}
$$

Figure 2. Semantics of Expressions

relaxed ($\texttt{x}\langle\texttt{r}\rangle$) executions. These relational expressions enable `relate` statements to specify relationships that must hold between the original and relaxed executions. For example, the statement `relate l :` $\texttt{x}\langle\texttt{o}\rangle = \texttt{x}\langle\texttt{r}\rangle$ asserts that at the current program point (with label `l`), `x` must have the same value in both executions.

2.1 Semantics of Expressions

Figure 2 presents the semantics of expressions in the language. The denotations of expressions are functions mapping a state or pair of states to either an integer ($\mathbb{Z}$) or boolean value ($\mathbb{B}$). A state (σ) is a finite map from program variables, *Vars*, to integers, $\mathbb{Z}$, and is an element of the domain $\Sigma = \mathit{Vars} \overset{\mathit{fin}}{\to} \mathbb{Z}$, which is the set of all finite maps from variables to integers.

The semantic function $[\![E]\!]$ defines the semantics for integer expressions, which are composed of the standard integer operations (e.g., $+, -, *, /, \ldots$) on integer operands. The semantic function $[\![B]\!]$ defines the semantics of boolean expressions, which are composed of the standard comparison operators on integers (e.g., $<, =, >, \ldots$) and the standard boolean operators (e.g., $\wedge, \vee, \ldots$).

The semantic function $[\![E^*]\!]$ defines the semantics for relational integer expressions as a function mapping a pair of states (σ_1, σ_2) to an integer number. Our convention is to have the first component of the state pair be a state from the original semantics and the second component a state from the relaxed semantics. Therefore, a reference to a variable in the original semantics, $\texttt{x}\langle\texttt{o}\rangle$, is equivalent to $\sigma_1(x)$ whereas a reference to a variable, $\texttt{x}\langle\texttt{r}\rangle$, in the relaxed semantics is equivalent to $\sigma_2(x)$.

The semantic function $[\![B^*]\!]$ likewise extends the semantics for boolean expressions with the capability to express boolean properties over relational integer expressions.

2.2 Dynamic Original Semantics

Figure 3 presents the dynamic original semantics of the program in a big-step operational style. The evaluation relation $\langle s, \ \sigma\rangle \Downarrow_o \phi$ denotes that evaluating the statement s in the state σ yields the output configuration ϕ. An output configuration is an element in the domain $\Phi = \{ba\} \cup \{wr\} \cup (\Sigma \times \Psi)$.

The distinguished element *ba* ("bad assume") denotes that the program has failed at an `assume` statement in the program. The distinguished element wr ("wrong") denotes that the program has failed due to another error, such as an unsatisfied `assert` statement.

An element in the domain $\Sigma \times \Psi$ indicates that the program has terminated successfully, yielding a final state σ and an *observation list*, $\psi \in \Psi$, which is the sequence of *observations* emitted by `relate` statements during the execution of the program.

An observation (l, σ) is an element in the domain $L \times \Sigma$. L is the finite domain consisting of all the labels specified in `relate` statements in the program — the execution of each `relate` statement emits an observation consisting of its label along with the current state of the program.

The structure of an observation list is given by the standard constructors for lists: $\Psi = \emptyset \mid (l, \sigma) :: \Psi$. We also use the notation $\psi_1.\psi_2$ to denote the result of appending two lists.

Evaluation Rules

The rules for `skip`, assignment, `if`, sequential composition, and `while` statements follow the standard semantics for these constructs. The semantics for nonstandard constructs are as follows:

Havoc. The `havoc` (X) `st` (e) statement nondeterministically assigns values to the set of variables in X such that their values satisfy the statement's predicate e. All variables not specified in X retain their previous values. If there does not exist an assignment of values to X that satisfy e, then the statement evaluates to wr.

Assert. The `assert` e statement checks that the state satisfies its predicate e. If e evaluates to *true*, then execution continues; otherwise, the statement evaluates to wr.

Assume. The `assume` e statement checks that the state satisfies its predicate e. If e evaluates to *true*, then execution continues; otherwise, the statement evaluates to ba.

Relax. The `relax` (X) `st` (e) statement does not modify the state of the program in the original semantics. Because we require the

$$\boxed{\langle s,\ \sigma\rangle \Downarrow_o \phi}$$

$$\text{skip}\ \frac{}{\langle \texttt{skip},\ \sigma\rangle \Downarrow_o \langle \sigma,\ \emptyset\rangle} \qquad \text{assign}\ \frac{\langle e\ ,\ \sigma\rangle \Downarrow_E n}{\langle x \texttt{ = } e,\ \sigma\rangle \Downarrow_o \langle \sigma[x \mapsto n],\ \emptyset\rangle}$$

$$\text{havoc-t}\ \frac{\langle e\ ,\ \sigma'\rangle \Downarrow_B \mathit{true} \quad \forall_{x \notin X} \cdot \sigma(x) = \sigma'(x)}{\langle \texttt{havoc}\ (X)\ \texttt{st}\ (e),\ \sigma\rangle \Downarrow_o \langle \sigma',\ \emptyset\rangle} \qquad \text{havoc-f}\ \frac{\neg\exists_{\sigma'} \cdot (\langle e\ ,\ \sigma'\rangle \Downarrow_B \mathit{true} \wedge \forall_{x \notin X} \cdot \sigma(x) = \sigma'(x))}{\langle \texttt{havoc}\ (X)\ \texttt{st}\ (e),\ \sigma\rangle \Downarrow_o wr}$$

$$\text{assert-t}\ \frac{\langle e\ ,\ \sigma\rangle \Downarrow_B \mathit{true}}{\langle \texttt{assert}\ e,\ \sigma\rangle \Downarrow_o \langle \sigma,\ \emptyset\rangle} \qquad \text{assert-f}\ \frac{\langle e\ ,\ \sigma\rangle \Downarrow_B \mathit{false}}{\langle \texttt{assert}\ e,\ \sigma\rangle \Downarrow_o wr} \qquad \text{assume-t}\ \frac{\langle e\ ,\ \sigma\rangle \Downarrow_B \mathit{true}}{\langle \texttt{assume}\ e,\ \sigma\rangle \Downarrow_o \langle \sigma,\ \emptyset\rangle}$$

$$\text{assume-f}\ \frac{\langle e\ ,\ \sigma\rangle \Downarrow_B \mathit{false}}{\langle \texttt{assume}\ e,\ \sigma\rangle \Downarrow_o ba} \qquad \text{relax}\ \frac{\langle \texttt{assert}\ e,\ \sigma\rangle \Downarrow_o \phi}{\langle \texttt{relax}\ (X)\ \texttt{st}\ (e),\ \sigma\rangle \Downarrow_o \phi} \qquad \text{relate}\ \frac{}{\langle \texttt{relate}\ l:\ \ e^*,\ \sigma\rangle \Downarrow_o \langle \sigma,\ (l, \sigma)\rangle}$$

$$\text{if-t}\ \frac{\langle b\ ,\ \sigma\rangle \Downarrow_B \mathit{true} \quad \langle s_1,\ \sigma\rangle \Downarrow_o \phi}{\langle \texttt{if}\ (b)\ \{s_1\}\ \texttt{else}\ \{s_2\},\ \sigma\rangle \Downarrow_o \phi} \qquad \text{if-f}\ \frac{\langle b\ ,\ \sigma\rangle \Downarrow_B \mathit{false} \quad \langle s_2,\ \sigma\rangle \Downarrow_o \phi}{\langle \texttt{if}\ (b)\ \{s_1\}\ \texttt{else}\ \{s_2\},\ \sigma\rangle \Downarrow_o \phi} \qquad \text{seq}\ \frac{\langle s_1,\ \sigma\rangle \Downarrow_o \langle \sigma',\ \psi_1\rangle \quad \langle s_2,\ \sigma'\rangle \Downarrow_o \langle \sigma'',\ \psi_2\rangle}{\langle s_1\ ;\ s_2,\ \sigma\rangle \Downarrow_o \langle \sigma'',\ \psi_2.\psi_1\rangle}$$

$$\text{while-f}\ \frac{\langle b\ ,\ \sigma\rangle \Downarrow_B \mathit{false}}{\langle \texttt{while}\ (b)\ \{s\},\ \sigma\rangle \Downarrow_o \langle \sigma,\ \emptyset\rangle} \qquad \text{while-t}\ \frac{\langle b\ ,\ \sigma\rangle \Downarrow_B \mathit{true} \quad \langle s,\ \sigma\rangle \Downarrow_o \langle \sigma',\ \psi_1\rangle \quad \langle \texttt{while}\ (b)\ \{s\},\ \sigma'\rangle \Downarrow_o \langle \sigma'',\ \psi_2\rangle}{\langle \texttt{while}\ (b)\ \{s\},\ \sigma\rangle \Downarrow_o \langle \sigma'',\ \psi_2.\psi_1\rangle}$$

Figure 3. Dynamic Original Semantics

$$\boxed{\langle s,\ \sigma\rangle \Downarrow_r \phi} \qquad \text{relax}\ \frac{\langle \texttt{havoc}\ (X)\ \texttt{st}\ (e),\ \sigma\rangle \Downarrow_r \phi}{\langle \texttt{relax}\ (X)\ \texttt{st}\ (e),\ \sigma\rangle \Downarrow_r \phi}$$

Figure 4. Dynamic Relaxed Semantics

original execution to be one of the relaxed executions, the dynamic original semantics requires the relaxation predicate e to hold in the original execution.

Relate. The `relate` $l:\ e^*$ statement is a relational assertion over original and relaxed executions of the program. The dynamic semantics emits an observation consisting of the statement's label l along with the current state of the program. This semantics enables us to define and verify a relation on the observation lists emitted by the original and relaxed programs (see Section 4).

We omit the standard rules for propagating errors (ba and wr) through the program. However, the reader can refer to our previous technical report for further details [9].

2.3 Dynamic Relaxed Semantics

Figure 4 presents an abbreviated version of the dynamic relaxed semantics. The relation $\langle s,\ \sigma\rangle \Downarrow_r \phi$ denotes that evaluating the statement s in the state σ yields the output configuration ϕ.

The dynamic relaxed semantics builds upon the original semantics. It differs only in that `relax` statements modify the state of the program. We therefore omit the presentation of all the rules that are either reused (`skip`, assignment, `havoc`, `assert`, and `assume`) or adapted to refer to the relaxed dynamic semantics in their premises (i.e., sequential composition, `if`, and `while`).

Relax. The `relax` (X) `st` (e) statement nondeterministically modifies the state of the program in the relaxed semantics so that it satisfies the statement's predicate e. The rule implements the modification by reusing the rule for `havoc` statements.

3. Axiomatic Semantics

We next present axiomatic semantics for relaxed programs.

- **Axiomatic Original Semantics.** The proof rules model the dynamic original semantics of the program. If the program verifies with these rules, then no execution of the program in the dynamic original semantics violates an assertion (i.e., evaluates to wr). However, the program may dynamically violate an assumption (i.e., evaluate to ba).

$$P ::= \texttt{true} \mid \texttt{false} \mid E\ \texttt{cmp}\ E \mid P\ \texttt{lop}\ P \mid \neg P \mid \exists \texttt{x} \cdot P$$

$$P^* ::= \texttt{true} \mid \texttt{false} \mid E^*\ \texttt{cmp}\ E^* \mid P^*\ \texttt{lop}\ P^* \mid \neg P^* \mid \exists \texttt{x}\langle\texttt{o}\rangle \cdot P^* \mid \exists \texttt{x}\langle\texttt{r}\rangle \cdot P^*$$

Figure 5. Relational Assertion Logic Syntax

$$\begin{aligned}
[\![P]\!] &\in \mathcal{P}(\Sigma) \\
[\![\texttt{true}]\!] &= \Sigma \qquad [\![\texttt{false}]\!] = \emptyset \\
[\![E_1\ \texttt{cmp}\ E_2]\!] &= \{\sigma \mid [\![E_1]\!](\sigma)\ \mathit{cmp}\ [\![E_2]\!](\sigma)\} \\
[\![P_1\ \texttt{lop}\ P_2\ ]\!] &= \{\sigma \mid \sigma \in [\![P_1]\!]\ \mathit{lop}\ \sigma \in [\![P_2]\!]\} \\
[\![\neg P]\!] &= [\![\texttt{true}]\!] \setminus [\![P]\!] \\
[\![\exists \texttt{x} \cdot P]\!] &= \{\sigma \mid n \in \mathbb{Z},\ \sigma \in [\![P[n/x]]\!]\}
\end{aligned}$$

$$\begin{aligned}
[\![P^*]\!] &\in \mathcal{P}(\Sigma \times \Sigma) \\
[\![\texttt{true}]\!] &= \Sigma \times \Sigma \qquad [\![\texttt{false}]\!] = \emptyset \\
[\![E_1^*\ \texttt{cmp}\ E_2^*]\!] &= \{(\sigma_1, \sigma_2) \mid [\![E_1^*]\!](\sigma_1, \sigma_2)\ \mathit{cmp}\ [\![E_2^*]\!](\sigma_1, \sigma_2)\} \\
[\![P_1^*\ \texttt{lop}\ P_2^*]\!] &= \{(\sigma_1, \sigma_2) \mid (\sigma_1, \sigma_2) \in [\![P_1^*]\!]\ \mathit{lop}\ (\sigma_1, \sigma_2) \in [\![P_2^*]\!]\} \\
[\![\neg P^*]\!] &= [\![\texttt{true}]\!] \setminus [\![P^*]\!] \\
[\![\exists \texttt{x}\langle\texttt{o}\rangle \cdot P^*]\!] &= \{(\sigma_1, \sigma_2) \mid n \in \mathbb{Z},\ (\sigma_1, \sigma_2) \in [\![P^*[n/x\langle\texttt{o}\rangle]]\!]\} \\
[\![\exists \texttt{x}\langle\texttt{r}\rangle \cdot P^*]\!] &= \{(\sigma_1, \sigma_2) \mid n \in \mathbb{Z},\ (\sigma_1, \sigma_2) \in [\![P^*[n/x\langle\texttt{r}\rangle]]\!]\}
\end{aligned}$$

Figure 6. Relational Assertion Logic Semantics

- **Axiomatic Relaxed Semantics.** The proof rules model pairs of executions of the program in the dynamic original and dynamic relaxed semantics. If the program verifies with these rules, then if all executions in the original semantics execute without error (i.e., do not evaluate to wr or ba), then all executions in the relaxed semantics execute without error. A proof with these rules also guarantees that pairs of original and relaxed executions satisfy all of the `relate` statements in the program.

3.1 Relational Assertion Logic

Figure 5 presents the concrete syntax of our *relational* assertion logic. This logic extends a nonrelational assertion logic with relational formulas, which then allows us to reason about the validity of relational boolean expressions in `relate` statements. Its presentation follows the style of Benton's Relational Hoare Logic [7].

$$\boxed{\vdash_o \{P\}\ s\ \{Q\}} \qquad \text{skip}\ \frac{}{\vdash_o \{P\}\ \texttt{skip}\ \{P\}} \qquad \text{seq}\ \frac{\vdash_o \{P\}\ s_1\ \{R\} \quad \vdash_o \{R\}\ s_2\ \{Q\}}{\vdash_o \{P\}\ s_1; s_2\ \{Q\}} \qquad \text{assign}\ \frac{}{\vdash_o \{Q[e/x]\}\ \texttt{x = } e\ \{Q\}}$$

$$\text{havoc}\ \frac{[\![(\exists_{X'} \cdot P[X'/X]) \wedge e]\!] \neq \emptyset \quad \mathit{fresh}(X')}{\vdash_o \{P\}\ \texttt{havoc}\ (X)\ \texttt{st}\ (e)\ \{(\exists_{X'} \cdot P[X'/X]) \wedge e\}} \qquad \text{assert}\ \frac{}{\vdash_o \{P \wedge e\}\ \texttt{assert}\ e\ \{P \wedge e\}}$$

$$\text{assume}\ \frac{}{\vdash_o \{P\}\ \texttt{assume}\ e\ \{P \wedge e\}} \qquad \text{relax}\ \frac{\vdash_o \{P\}\ \texttt{assert}\ e\ \{Q\}}{\vdash_o \{P\}\ \texttt{relax}\ (X)\ \texttt{st}\ (e)\ \{Q\}} \qquad \text{if}\ \frac{\vdash_o \{P \wedge b\}\ s_1\ \{Q\} \quad \vdash_o \{P \wedge \neg b\}\ s_2\ \{Q\}}{\vdash_o \{P\}\ \texttt{if}\ (b)\ \{s_1\}\ \texttt{else}\ \{s_2\}\ \{Q\}}$$

$$\text{relate}\ \frac{}{\vdash_o \{P\}\ \texttt{relate}\ l:\ \ e^*\ \{P\}} \qquad \text{while}\ \frac{\vdash_o \{P \wedge b\}\ s\ \{P\}}{\vdash_o \{P\}\ \texttt{while}\ (b)\ \{s\}\ \{P \wedge \neg b\}} \qquad \text{conseq}\ \frac{\models P \Rightarrow P' \quad \vdash_o \{P'\}\ s\ \{Q'\} \quad \models Q' \Rightarrow Q}{\vdash_o \{P\}\ s\ \{Q\}}$$

Figure 7. Axiomatic Original Semantics

3.1.1 Syntax

The syntactic category P gives the syntax for formulas in first-order logic with integer expressions and existential quantification. The syntactic category P^* gives corresponding syntax for writing relational formulas. P^* extends P by allowing formulas to refer to relational integer expressions.

3.1.2 Semantics

Figure 6 presents the semantics of formulas in the logic. The denotation of a nonrelational formula $[\![P]\!]$ is the set of states that satisfy the formula. $[\![P]\!]$ reuses the semantic definitions for integer expressions from Figure 2 to construct a definition for each formula. The denotation of a relational formula $[\![P^*]\!]$ closely follows that of nonrelational formulas: it is the set of pairs of states that satisfy the relation. References to the original semantics (e.g., $\texttt{x}\langle\texttt{o}\rangle$) refer to the first component of the pair and references to the relaxed semantics (e.g., $\texttt{x}\langle\texttt{r}\rangle$) refer to the second component.

Injections. We define injection functions $inj_o(P)$ and $inj_r(P)$, which construct a relational formula in P^* from a nonrelational formula in P. Conceptually, $inj_o(P)$ constructs a relational formula where P holds for the original semantics by replacing variables (e.g., $\texttt{x}$) in P with the relational original variables (e.g., $\texttt{x}\langle\texttt{o}\rangle$); $inj_r(P)$ does the same with the relational relaxed variables such that P holds for the relaxed semantics. This means that $inj_o(P)$ (resp. $inj_r(P)$) creates a formula representing all state pairs where the first (resp. second) component satisfies P:

$$[\![inj_o(P)]\!] = \{(\sigma_1, \sigma_2) \mid \sigma_1 \in [\![P]\!]\}$$
$$[\![inj_r(P)]\!] = \{(\sigma_1, \sigma_2) \mid \sigma_2 \in [\![P]\!]\}$$

We also define the notation $\langle P_1 \cdot P_2 \rangle$ for combining a predicate P_1 over the original semantics with a predicate P_2 over the relaxed:

$$\langle P_1 \cdot P_2 \rangle \equiv inj_o(P_1) \wedge inj_r(P_2)$$

Projections. We define two semantic functions $prj_o(P^*)$ and $prj_r(P^*)$. Each function projects a relational formula in P^* to the set of states corresponding to either the first (prj_o) or second (prj_r) component of each state pair in the denotation of the formula:

$$prj_o(P^*) \equiv \{\sigma_1 \mid (\sigma_1, \sigma_2) \in [\![P^*]\!]\}$$
$$prj_r(P^*) \equiv \{\sigma_2 \mid (\sigma_1, \sigma_2) \in [\![P^*]\!]\}$$

The projection functions allow us to decompose a relational formula over the original and relaxed semantics into the set of states that satisfy the relation for either the original or relaxed semantics individually. We use projection to define the following relations between relational and nonrelational formulas:

$$P^* \models_o P \equiv prj_o(P^*) \subseteq [\![P]\!]$$
$$P^* \models_r P \equiv prj_r(P^*) \subseteq [\![P]\!]$$

Fresh Variables and Substitution. The predicate $\mathit{fresh}(x)$, denoting that x is a fresh variable in the context of an inference rule, is true if $x \in \mathit{Vars}$ and x does not appear in the rule's premises or consequent. Our proof rules also use the standard capture-avoiding substitution $P[e/x]$. We denote multiple substitution $P[e_1/x_1] \cdots [e_n/x_n]$ as $P[e_1, \cdots, e_n/x_1, \cdots, x_n]$. We define substitution over P^* similarly.

Auxiliary Notations. We also define the following judgments for later use in both the rules of our program logics and the discussion of their semantics:

$$\sigma \models P \equiv \sigma \in [\![P]\!] \qquad (\sigma_1, \sigma_2) \models P^* \equiv (\sigma_1, \sigma_2) \in [\![P^*]\!]$$
$$\models P_1 \Rightarrow P_2 \equiv [\![P_1]\!] \subseteq [\![P_2]\!] \qquad \models P_1^* \Rightarrow P_2^* \equiv [\![P_1^*]\!] \subseteq [\![P_2]\!]$$

3.2 Original Semantics

Figure 7 presents a manual translation of our Coq formalization of the axiomatic original semantics of the program. The Hoare-style judgment $\vdash_o \{P\}\ s\ \{Q\}$ models the original execution of the program wherein relax statements have no effect. The intended meaning of the semantic judgment $\models_o \{P\}\ s\ \{Q\}$ is: for all states σ, if $\sigma \models P$ and $\langle s,\ \sigma \rangle \Downarrow_o \langle \sigma',\ \psi \rangle$, then $\sigma' \models Q$. In other words, if σ satisfies P and an original execution of s from σ yields a new state σ', then σ' satisfies Q. We note that this definition asserts only partial correctness and not total correctness.

We have elided a discussion of the rules for standard constructs (i.e., `skip`, assign, sequential composition, `if`, `while`, and consequence) because their definitions are the same as in standard presentations (e.g., Floyd [14] and Hoare [15]). We define the nonstandard rules as follows:

The havoc rule requires in its premise that e must be satisfiable by adjusting only the variables in X while retaining the values of other variables. A `havoc` statement evaluates to wr only if there is no way to transform the current state into a new state satisfying e just by changing the variables in X.

The assert rule requires the predicate e to hold in the precondition. The rule therefore requires a proof of e.

The assume rule differs from the assert rule in that it assumes the validity of e and then makes e part of the postcondition. Because there is no obligation to prove e for an `assume` statement, e may not hold for all states that satisfy P and, as a result, the `assume` may evaluate to ba. However, by design, we allow `assume` statements to fail in the dynamic original semantics.

The relax rule specifies that a `relax` statement is a no-op that does not change the program's state in the original semantics. Our definition of relaxation, however, requires that the original execution must still satisfy e. To enforce this constraint, the rule reuses the rule for the `assert` statement.

$$\boxed{\vdash_r \{P^*\}\ s\ \{Q^*\}}$$

$$\text{diverge}\ \frac{P^* \models_o P_o \quad P^* \models_r P_r \quad \vdash_o \{P_o\}\ s\ \{Q_o\} \quad \vdash_i \{P_r\}\ s\ \{Q_r\} \quad \mathit{no\_rel}(s)}{\vdash_r \{P^*\}\ s\ \{\langle Q_o \cdot Q_r\rangle\}}$$

$$\text{relax}\ \frac{[\![(\exists_{X'\langle \mathtt{r}\rangle} \cdot P^*[X'\langle \mathtt{r}\rangle/X\langle \mathtt{r}\rangle]) \wedge inj_r(e)]\!] \neq \emptyset \quad \mathit{fresh}(X')}{\vdash_r \{P^*\}\ \texttt{relax}\ (X)\ \texttt{st}\ (e)\ \{(\exists_{X'\langle \mathtt{r}\rangle} \cdot P^*[X'\langle \mathtt{r}\rangle/X\langle \mathtt{r}\rangle]) \wedge \langle e \cdot e\rangle\}}$$

$$\text{relate}\ \frac{}{\vdash_r \{P^* \wedge e^*\}\ \texttt{relate}\ l:\ e^*\ \{P^* \wedge e^*\}}$$

$$\text{assert}\ \frac{\models P^* \wedge inj_o(e) \Rightarrow inj_r(e)}{\vdash_r \{P^*\}\ \texttt{assert}\ e\ \{P^* \wedge \langle e \cdot e\rangle\}}$$

$$\text{if}\ \frac{\models P^* \Rightarrow \langle b \cdot b\rangle \vee \langle \neg b \cdot \neg b\rangle \quad \vdash_r \{P^* \wedge \langle b \cdot b\rangle\}\ s_1\ \{Q^*\} \quad \vdash_r \{P^* \wedge \langle \neg b \cdot \neg b\rangle\}\ s_2\ \{Q^*\}}{\vdash_r \{P^*\}\ \texttt{if}\ (b)\ \{s_1\}\ \texttt{else}\ \{s_2\}\ \{Q^*\}}$$

$$\text{assume}\ \frac{\models P^* \wedge inj_o(e) \Rightarrow inj_r(e)}{\vdash_r \{P^*\}\ \texttt{assume}\ e\ \{P^* \wedge \langle e \cdot e\rangle\}}$$

$$\text{while}\ \frac{\models P^* \Rightarrow \langle b \cdot b\rangle \vee \langle \neg b \cdot \neg b\rangle \quad \vdash_r \{P^* \wedge \langle b \cdot b\rangle\}\ s\ \{P^*\}}{\vdash_r \{P^*\}\ \texttt{while}\ (b)\ \{s\}\ \{P^* \wedge \langle \neg b \cdot \neg b\rangle\}}$$

Figure 8. Axiomatic Relaxed Semantics

The relate rule gives `relate` statements the same semantics as `skip` because, unlike the axiomatic relaxed semantics (see Section 3.3), the axiomatic original semantics references only a single execution of the program and does not use relational reasoning.

3.3 Relaxed Semantics

Figure 8 presents a manual translation of our Coq formalization of the axiomatic relaxed semantics of the program. The proof rules for the relaxed semantics are relational in that they relate executions of the program under the dynamic relaxed semantics to executions under the dynamic original semantics. The intended meaning of each judgment $\models_r \{P^*\}\ s\ \{Q^*\}$ is the partial correctness assertion: if $(\sigma_o, \sigma_r) \models P^*$, $\langle s,\ \sigma_o\rangle \Downarrow_o \langle \sigma_o',\ \psi_1\rangle$, and $\langle s,\ \sigma_r\rangle \Downarrow_r \langle \sigma_r',\ \psi_2\rangle$, then $(\sigma_o', \sigma_r') \models Q^*$.

The rules are designed to transfer the reasoning from the axiomatic original semantics to prove properties about the axiomatic relaxed semantics. Specifically, the axiomatic relaxed semantics need not re-prove properties about the dynamic original semantics (e.g., the validity of `assert` statements). It can instead simply assume that these properties are established by the axiomatic original semantics and then transfer their validity to the relaxed semantics via relational reasoning. We have elided discussions of most of the standard rules. The nonstandard rules operate as follows:

The relax rule distinguishes the semantics of relaxation in the original and relaxed semantics of the program. The rule is similar to the havoc rule in the axiomatic original semantics except that 1) it deals with a relational formula and 2) the rule only modifies (i.e., substitutes) relaxed variables, such as $\mathtt{x}\langle\mathtt{r}\rangle$, whereas variables over the original semantics $\mathtt{x}\langle\mathtt{o}\rangle$ are not modified. We use a shorthand $X\langle\mathtt{r}\rangle \equiv \{x\langle\mathtt{r}\rangle \mid x \in X\}$ to denote the syntactic extension of a set of variables in X to relaxed variables.

The relate rule enables us to reason about `relate` statements in the program. Similar to a nonrelational assertion, the rule requires e^* to hold in the precondition. This ensures that e^* holds for all pairs of original and relaxed executions that reach the statement.

The assert rule demonstrates how we can use relational reasoning to prove assertions in the relaxed semantics. Specifically, we can first assume that the assertion is true in the original semantics (i.e., $inj_o(e)$) because it has been verified with the axiomatic original semantics. If $P^* \wedge inj_o(e)$ implies $inj_r(e)$, we can then conclude that the assertion is true in the relaxed semantics (i.e., $inj_r(e)$).

For example, if the precondition of the statement `assert` e requires all of the free variables in e to be the same in both semantics (i.e., for all $\mathtt{x} \in \mathit{free}(e)$, $\mathtt{x}\langle\mathtt{o}\rangle$ `==` $\mathtt{x}\langle\mathtt{r}\rangle$), then because the axiomatic original semantics proves that the assertion is true in the dynamic original semantics, we can conclude that the assertion is also true in the dynamic relaxed semantics.

The assume rule demonstrates how relational reasoning allows us to use relations between the original and relaxed semantics of the program to reason about assumptions in the relaxed semantics in the same way as we do for assertions — i.e., if the assumption is true in the original semantics of the program, then it is also true in the relaxed semantics.

$$\boxed{\vdash_i \{P\}\ s\ \{Q\}} \qquad \text{relax}\ \frac{\vdash_i \{P\}\ \texttt{havoc}\ (X)\ \texttt{st}\ (e)\ \{Q\}}{\vdash_i \{P\}\ \texttt{relax}\ (X)\ \texttt{st}\ (e)\ \{Q\}}$$

$$\text{assume}\ \frac{}{\vdash_i \{P \wedge e\}\ \texttt{assume}\ e\ \{P \wedge e\}}$$

Figure 9. Axiomatic Intermediate Semantics

Convergent and Divergent Control Flow. An important aspect of relaxed programs is that the original and relaxed executions of a program may branch in different directions at a control flow construct. Specifically, if two executions branch in the same direction, then we can continue to reason about them relationally in lockstep. However, if the two executions diverge, then the executions execute different statements and, as a result, we lose our relational reasoning power. We note that it is possible for two executions to diverge at a control flow construct and then converge again at the end of the construct, allowing us to regain our relational reasoning power.

The relaxed axiomatic semantics captures this property via a set of proof rules for *convergent control flow* constructs (i.e., the original and relaxed executions always branch in the same direction) and another set for *divergent control flow* constructs. [1]

3.3.1 Convergent Control Flow

The `if` rule allows us to continue to use relational reasoning inside an `if` statement if it has convergent control flow. We establish this convergence by checking that for all σ_1, σ_2, if $(\sigma_1, \sigma_2) \models P^*$ then the conditional's boolean expression either evaluates to *true* in both the original and relaxed semantics or it evaluates to *false* in both semantics. If so, then in all cases, the original and relaxed semantics take the same branch together. Otherwise control flow may diverge and the rule cannot be applied.

The `while` rule is similar in form to the `if` rule in that it requires that control flow be convergent to allow us to continue to use relational reasoning within the body of a `while` statement.

3.3.2 Divergent Control Flow

The *diverge* rule enables a proof to proceed if the original and relaxed semantics diverge at a control flow construct. The rule establishes the postcondition of the statement by independently establishing that $\vdash_o \{P_o\}\ s\ \{Q_o\}$ for the original semantics and that $\vdash_i \{P_r\}\ s\ \{Q_r\}$ for the relaxed semantics, where P_o and P_r are left and right projections of P^*. The judgment $\vdash_i \{P_r\}\ s\ \{Q_r\}$

[1] We provide a detailed formalization of convergent control flow in the supplementary material of this paper on the ACM Digital Library.

is a set of proof rules for the axiomatic *intermediate* semantics of the program. Figure 9 gives an abbreviated presentation of the program logic for the intermediate semantics of the program.

The axiomatic intermediate semantics is a nonrelational characterization of the dynamic relaxed semantics and is very similar to the axiomatic original semantics. The intended meaning of the judgment $\models_i \{P\}\ s\ \{Q\}$ is: for all states σ, if $\sigma \models P$ and $\langle s,\ \sigma\rangle \Downarrow_r \langle \sigma',\ \psi\rangle$, then $\sigma' \models Q$. This semantics differs from the axiomatic original semantics in two ways:

- **The relax rule** specifies that `relax` (X) `st` (e) may apply any modification to the variables in X as long as the new values satisfy e. In the axiomatic original semantics the `relax` statement is a no-op.
- **The assume rule** requires (just as for `assert` statements) a proof that e holds in relaxed executions. The goal is to ensure that the relaxation does not invalidate the reasoning used to establish that e holds in the original program. In the axiomatic original semantics there is no such proof obligation — e is simply assumed to be valid.

We conclude the presentation of the diverge rule by noting that it is also guarded by the predicate *no_rel*(s), which evaluates to *true* if no `relate` statements appear within s. This predicate therefore prevents `relate` statements from appearing in divergent control flow statements where we are unable to use relational reasoning to establish that the `relate` statement is satisfied.

We also note that the use of projections by $\models_o$ and $\models_r$ in this rule means that all relationships between the two semantics are lost and must be reestablished at the end of the statement. Relationships that are not modified by the statement, however, can be preserved via a relational frame rule.

4. Properties

We now present the technical definitions, lemmas, and theorems that establish the semantic properties of programs in the language.

The key property of our language and proof rules is Relative Relaxed Progress (Section 4.3), which states that our proof rules guarantee that if the original program executes without error, then the relaxed program executes without error. This property enables a developer to combine a proof in the axiomatic original semantics with formally unverified assumptions to demonstrate that the original program is error free. The developer can then augment this reasoning with a proof in the axiomatic relaxed semantics to therefore show that the relaxed program is error free. An important consequence of this formulation is that if a formally unverified assumption is not valid and produces unintended behaviors in the program, then these behaviors can be reproduced and debugged in the original program.

In our formalization, we restrict ourselves to terminating relaxed programs. Also, while we only present brief proof sketches, the full sources of our Coq formalization and proofs are available online at

`http://groups.csail.mit.edu/pac/acceptability`

4.1 Original Semantics

Our axiomatic definition for the original semantics is sound and can be used to establish a *weak* form of the traditional progress theorem for programs. Specifically, if you can write a proof in the axiomatic original semantics and an execution in the original semantics terminates, then the resulting state is not wr. This differs from a *strong* form of progress that establishes the same for all programs (including nonterminating programs), which would require a small-step or coinductive formalization of our dynamic semantics.

Lemma 1 (Soundness).

$$\textit{If } \vdash_o \{P\}\ s\ \{Q\},\ \textit{then} \models_o \{P\}\ s\ \{Q\}$$

This lemma establishes that our axiomatic definition is sound with respect to the dynamic original semantics of the program. More specifically, given a proof $\vdash_o \{P\}\ s\ \{Q\}$, it is the case that for all states $\sigma \models P$, if $\langle s,\ \sigma\rangle \Downarrow_o \langle \sigma',\ \psi\rangle$, then $\sigma' \models Q$.

Proof Sketch. This proof proceeds by induction on the rules of $\vdash_o \{P\}\ s\ \{Q\}$. A large portion of the proof effort involves proving the semantics of substitution in the case of the assignment rule and the `havoc` rule. The case of the `havoc` rule also requires mutual induction on the lists of modified and fresh variables to establish that the post-condition holds. The cases for structural rules (`if` and sequential composition) follow from induction and the case for the `while` statement proceeds by nested induction on derivations of the evaluation relation. □

Lemma 2 (Original Progress Modulo Assumptions).

$$\textit{If } \vdash_o \{P\}\ s\ \{Q\},\ \textit{and } \sigma \models P\ ,\ \textit{and } \langle s,\ \sigma\rangle \Downarrow_o \phi\ ,\ \textit{then } \phi \neq wr$$

This lemma establishes the progress property that we desire for the original semantics. Specifically, given a proof in the original axiomatic semantics, then for all states that satisfy P, if execution terminates, then the execution does not yield wr. By design, the judgment does not preclude the program from evaluating to ba (indicating that it has violated an assumption).

Proof Sketch. This proof proceeds by induction on the rules of $\vdash_o \{P\}\ s\ \{Q\}$. We only need to consider three primitive statements where the program may evaluate to wr: `havoc` (the satisfiability check in the premise guards against this), `assert` e (the fact that e must hold in the precondition guards against this), and `relax` (follows by induction because execution of a `relax` statement reduces to execution of an `assert` statement). □

4.2 Intermediate Semantics

The axiomatic relaxed semantics establishes several progress properties about the relaxed execution of the program. However, to prove progress for the axiomatic relaxed semantics, we need to first prove the same for the axiomatic intermediate semantics.

The definition for the axiomatic intermediate semantics is sound and, also, establishes a form of progress for the relaxed semantics of the program. Specifically, the intermediate semantics models the behavior of a relaxed execution after it has branched at a control flow construct in a different direction than an original execution. When this happens, the relaxed execution must not violate assertions (evaluate to wr) or violate assumptions (evaluate to ba).

Lemma 3 (Soundness).

$$\textit{If } \vdash_i \{P\}\ s\ \{Q\},\ \textit{then} \models_i \{P\}\ s\ \{Q\}$$

This lemma establishes that our axiomatic definition is sound with respect to the dynamic relaxed semantics: given a proof $\vdash_i \{P\}\ s\ \{Q\}$, it is the case that for all states $\sigma \models P$, if $\langle s,\ \sigma\rangle \Downarrow_r \langle \sigma',\ \psi\rangle$, then $\sigma' \models Q$.

Proof Sketch. This proof proceeds by induction on the rules of $\vdash_i \{P\}\ s\ \{Q\}$. Because the axiomatic intermediate semantics reuses a large portion of the axiomatic original semantics, and the definition of the dynamic relaxed semantics is very similar to that of the dynamic original semantics, the vast majority of the proof follows from the proofs in Lemma 1. □

Lemma 4 (Progress).

$$\textit{If } \vdash_i \{P\}\ s\ \{Q\}, \textit{ and } \sigma \models P, \textit{ and } \langle s,\ \sigma\rangle\ \Downarrow_r\ \phi, \\ \textit{then } \neg err(\phi) \\ \textit{where } err(\phi) \equiv \phi = wr \lor \phi = ba$$

This lemma establishes the progress property that we desire for the axiomatic intermediate semantics. Specifically, given a proof $\vdash_i \{P\}\ s\ \{Q\}$, it is the case that for all states that satisfy P, if execution terminates, then the execution does not yield an error. Note that this guarantee is stronger than that for the axiomatic original semantics in that it does not allow a relaxed execution to violate an assumption whereas an original execution may do so.

Proof Sketch. The proof proceeds by induction on the rules of $\vdash_i \{P\}\ s\ \{Q\}$. As in the proof of soundness (Lemma 3), the vast majority of the proof follows from our proofs about the axiomatic original semantics; in this case most of the proof follows directly from Lemma 2 (Original Progress Modulo Assumptions). The proof differs for two statements: `relax` (the proof follows by induction because execution of a `relax` statement reduces to the execution of a `havoc`) and `assume` (the proof also follows by induction as execution of an `assume` reduces to an `assert`). □

4.3 Relaxed Semantics

Lemma 5 (Soundness).

$$\textit{If } \vdash_r \{P^*\}\ s\ \{Q^*\}, \textit{ then } \models_r \{P^*\}\ s\ \{Q^*\}$$

This lemma establishes that our axiomatic definition is sound with respect to the original and relaxed semantics of the program. Specifically, given a proof $\vdash_r \{P^*\}\ s\ \{Q^*\}$, it is the case that for all states $(\sigma_o, \sigma_r) \models P^*$, if $\langle s,\ \sigma_o\rangle\ \Downarrow_o\ \langle\sigma_o',\ \psi_1\rangle$ and $\langle s,\ \sigma_r\rangle\ \Downarrow_r\ \langle\sigma_r',\ \psi_2\rangle$, then $(\sigma_o', \sigma_r') \models Q^*$.

Proof Sketch. The proof proceeds by induction on the rules of $\vdash_r \{P^*\}\ s\ \{Q^*\}$. The proof is largely similar to that for the original axiomatic semantics in that much of the work lies in proving the semantics of substitution for the `relax` statement, which has a proof that is similar to `havoc` in the original axiomatic semantics. The cases for structural rules (`if` and sequential composition) follow from induction and the case for the `while` statement proceeds by nested mutual induction on derivations of the original and relaxed execution of the statement. The most distinct case is the rule for diverge: this proof uses the soundness of the original axiomatic semantics (Lemma 1) and the soundness of the intermediate axiomatic semantics (Lemma 3) to establish the soundness of the rule for executions in which the original and relaxed executions branch in different directions at a control flow construct. □

Theorem 6 (Soundness of Relational Assertions).

$$\textit{If } \vdash_r \{P^*\}\ s\ \{Q^*\}, \textit{ and } (\sigma_o, \sigma_r) \models P^*, \\ \textit{and } \langle s,\ \sigma_o\rangle\ \Downarrow_o\ \langle\sigma_o',\ \psi_1\rangle, \textit{ and } \langle s,\ \sigma_r\rangle\ \Downarrow_r\ \langle\sigma_r',\ \psi_2\rangle, \\ \textit{then } \Gamma \vdash \psi_1 \sim \psi_2$$

This theorem establishes that given a proof in the relaxed axiomatic semantics, if the original execution of the program terminates successfully and the relaxed execution of the program terminates successfully, then the observation lists generated by the executions (ψ_1 and ψ_2, respectively) satisfy the observational compatibility relation $\Gamma \vdash \psi_1 \sim \psi_2$. Observational compatibility implies that the original and relaxed executions of the program satisfy all executed `relate` statements; we define the relation as follows:

$$\frac{}{\Gamma \vdash \emptyset \sim \emptyset} \qquad \frac{[\![\Gamma(l)]\!](\sigma_1, \sigma_2) = \textit{true} \quad \Gamma \vdash \psi_1 \sim \psi_2}{\Gamma \vdash (l, \sigma_1) :: \psi_1 \sim (l, \sigma_2) :: \psi_2}$$

The symbol Γ represents a finite map from `relate` labels to relational boolean expressions (i.e, $\Gamma \in L \to B^*$). We define this map by structural induction on the syntax of the program, where the label of each `relate` statement in the program maps to its relational boolean expression. We require that `relate` statements in well-formed programs be uniquely labeled.

The rules specify that if two observations lists are empty, then they are compatible. Otherwise, any two lists are compatible if 1) the labels in the head are the same (indicating that they are generated by the same `relate` statement), 2) the relational boolean expression for the label evaluates to *true* for the states in the head, and 3) the tails of the two lists are also compatible.

Proof Sketch. This proof proceeds by induction on the rules of $\vdash_r \{P^*\}\ s\ \{Q^*\}$. The two interesting cases are the *diverge* rule and the rule for `relate` statements. For the diverge rule, we use the fact that the rule requires *no_rel*(s) (which requires that no `relate` statements appear inside s). We can therefore conclude that the observation list for the statement is empty and, therefore, original and relaxed executions of the statement are trivially compatible. In the case of the relate rule, the proof uses the rule's precondition to establish that the two emitted observations satisfy the `relate` statement's condition. □

Theorem 7 (Relative Relaxed Progress).

$$\textit{If } \vdash_r \{P^*\}\ s\ \{Q^*\}, \textit{ and } (\sigma_o, \sigma_r) \models P^*, \textit{ and } \langle s,\ \sigma_o\rangle\ \Downarrow_o\ \phi_o, \\ \textit{and } \neg err(\phi_o), \textit{ and } \langle s,\ \sigma_r\rangle\ \Downarrow_r\ \phi_r, \textit{ then } \neg err(\phi_r)$$

This theorem establishes the relative progress guarantee for the relaxed semantics of the program. Specifically, given a proof $\vdash_r \{P^*\}\ s\ \{Q^*\}$, it is the case that for all pairs of states (σ_o, σ_r) that satisfy P^*, if an original execution terminates and does not produce an error, then if a relaxed execution terminates, it also does not produce an error.

Proof Sketch. This proof proceeds by induction on the rules of $\vdash_r \{P^*\}\ s\ \{Q^*\}$. The most important cases are the `assert` and `assume` statements and the *diverge* rule. The proofs for `assert` and `assume` are similar in that the premise ensures that if the original execution evaluates to *true*, then the condition also evaluates to *true* in the relaxed execution. We do not have to consider the case where the original execution evaluates to *false* because this would imply that $\phi_o = wr \lor \phi_o = ba$, which is inconsistent with the assumption that $\neg err(\phi_o)$.

The diverge rule demonstrates the utility of our design of the axiomatic intermediate semantics. For this rule, we can no longer use facts about the original execution to prove facts about the relaxed execution. Therefore, the relaxed execution must be inherently error free. The proof uses the progress guarantee of the axiomatic intermediate semantics (Lemma 4) to establish exactly that. □

Theorem 8 (Relaxed Progress).

$$\textit{If } \vdash_o \{P\}\ s\ \{Q\}, \textit{ and } \vdash_r \{P^*\}\ s\ \{Q^*\}, \textit{ and } P^* \models_o P_o, \\ \textit{and } (\sigma_o, \sigma_r) \models P^*, \textit{ and } \langle s,\ \sigma_o\rangle\ \Downarrow_o\ \phi_o, \textit{ and } \phi_o \neq ba, \\ \textit{and } \langle s,\ \sigma_r\rangle\ \Downarrow_r\ \phi_r, \textit{ then } \neg err(\phi_r).$$

This theorem combines the multiple proofs and assumptions in our programming model to establish the main progress guarantee for relaxed programs: given 1) a proof in the original axiomatic semantics, 2) a proof in the relaxed axiomatic semantics, and 3) that executions in the original semantics terminate and do not violate an assumption, then if a relaxed execution terminates, it does not produce an error.

Proof Sketch. This proof follows directly from our assumptions, Lemma 2 (Original Progress Modulo Assumptions), and Theorem 7 (Relative Progress). Our assumptions and Lemma 2 establish that if an original execution terminates, then it does not terminate in error. By Theorem 7, we can conclude that if a relaxed execution terminates, it does not produce an error. □

Corollary 9 (Relaxed Progress Modulo Original Assumptions).

If $\vdash_o \{P\}\ s\ \{Q\}$, *and* $\vdash_r \{P^*\}\ s\ \{Q^*\}$, *and* $P^* \models_o P_o$, *and* $(\sigma_o, \sigma_r) \models P^*$, *and* $\langle s,\ \sigma_r\rangle \Downarrow_r \phi_r$, *and* $err(\phi_r)$, *If* $\langle s,\ \sigma_o\rangle \Downarrow_o \phi_o$, *then* $\phi_o = ba$

This corollary of Theorem 8 captures an important aspect of how our programming model incorporates assumptions, which may cause errors in both original and relaxed executions. Given proofs in the original and relaxed axiomatic semantics, if an error occurs in a relaxed execution and the original execution terminates, the original execution must violate an assumption. Errors in the relaxed program therefore correspond to invalid assumptions in the original program. To debug an error in a relaxed execution, a developer should therefore look for invalid assumptions in the original program.

5. Example Relaxed Programs

Inspired by programs that researchers have successfully relaxed in prior work, we developed several example programs designed to capture the core aspects of the successful relaxations. We then formalized key acceptability properties of the relaxations and used our Coq formalization to prove these properties.

5.1 Dynamic Knobs

Swish++ is an open-source search engine. We work with a successful relaxation that uses Dynamic Knobs to reduce the number of search results that Swish++ presents to the user when the server is under heavy load [16]. The rationale for this relaxation is that 1) users are typically only interested in the top search results and 2) users are very sensitive to how quickly the results are presented — even a short delay can significantly reduce advertisement revenue.

Relaxation. The transformation targets a loop that formats and presents the search query results. The loop keeps track of the number of search results, which we denote by N. The loop also has a control variable max_r which is a threshold on the number of elements that should be presented to the user: if N is smaller than max_r, then all results will be presented; otherwise, only the first max_r results will be presented.

A relaxed program can nondeterministically change max_r to reduce the number of iterations of this loop while still returning the most important results:

```
original_max_r = max_r;
relax (max_r) st
  (original_max_r <= 10 && max_r == original_max_r)
  || (10 < original_max_r && 10 <= max_r);
```

This code first saves the original value of the control variable max_r in original_max_r. It then relaxes max_r. There are two cases: if the original value of this control variable was less than or equal to 10, then the relaxed execution should be the same as the original execution — it presents the same number of results, since the value of max_r does not change. If, on the other hand, the original value was greater than 10, the only constraint is that the value of max_r is not smaller than 10, meaning that it should return at least the top 10 results when available. The relax statement nondeterministically changes max_r subject to these constraints.

Acceptability. One acceptability property is that the relaxed execution must present either all of the search results from the original execution to the user (if the number of search results in the original execution is less than or equal to 10), or at least the first 10 results (if the number of results in the original execution is greater than 10). The following relate statement captures these constraints:

```
relate (num_r<o> < 10 && num_r<o> == num_r<r>) ||
       (10 <= num_r<o> && 10 <= num_r<r>);
```

The loop that formats and presents the search results maintains a count num_r of the number of formatted and presented results. This statement therefore uses the value of num_r in the original program (denoted num_r<o>) to determine how many search results the original execution presents. The relate statement uses num_r<o> and the (potentially different) value of num_r in the relaxed execution (num_r<r>) to formalize the desired relationship between the two executions.

Verification. The proof of the relate statement involves 330 lines of Coq proof scripts. Because the relaxation changes the number of loop iterations, the proof uses the divergent control flow rule to reason about the loop in the original semantics and relaxed semantics separately. The key proof steps establish that the condition of the relax statement holds before entering the loop and that original_max_r<o> == original_max_r<r> and N<o> == N<r>. The loop invariant in both the original and relaxed execution is num_r <= max_r && num_r <= N.

Once control flow converges after the loop, the relate statement's precondition can be deduced via a proof by cases or, as in our proof environment, verified by an automated theorem prover.

5.2 Statistical Automatic Parallelization

Our next example is drawn from a parallelization of the Water computation [8] with statistical accuracy bounds [20]. In this computation a control variable determines whether to execute a loop sequentially or in parallel. To maximize performance, the parallelization eliminates lock operations that make updates to an array RS execute atomically. The resulting race conditions produce a parallel computation whose result may vary nondeterministically (because of CPU scheduling variations) within acceptable accuracy bounds.

Relaxation. We model the relaxation nondeterminism by relaxing each element in RS with no constraints:[2]

```
relax (RS) st (true);
```

In a loop that executes after the parallel loop, the Water computation compares RS[K] to a cutoff variable gCUT2 and, if it is less than the cutoff, uses RS[K] to update an array FF (here EXP(RS[K]) is an expression involving RS):

```
while (K < N) {
  if (RS[K] < gCUT2) { FF[K] = EXP(RS[K]); }
  K = K + 1;
}
```

Acceptability. A key acceptability property is that K stays within the bounds of the array FF.[3] The array bounds are stored in the variable len_FF. We assume that the developer establishes, via some standard reasoning process, that the original execution does not violate the array bounds and therefore inserts the statement assume (K < len_FF) inside the if statement just before the assignment to FF[K].

[2] Although we do not present our treatment of arrays in this paper, our Coq formalization supports reasoning about arrays, which is a straightforward extension of our presented framework.

[3] We note that K must also be within the bounds of RS; the proof is similar.

Verification. Recall that the verification of the relaxed program must verify that the condition in each assume statement holds in the relaxed execution. One approach is noninterference — verify that relaxation does not affect the values of the variables in the predicate. However, this is a relational property and because the assume statement appears at a divergent control flow point (it depends on the value of the relaxed variable RS), this approach does not work.

The developer therefore inserts another assume statement, assume (K < len_FF), just before the if statement. It is possible to verify this statement using noninterference, then propagate the condition through the if statement to verify the second assume statement.

The Coq verification of this program consists of approximately 310 lines of proof script. The key proof step verifies the relational loop invariants K<o> == K<r> and len_FF<o> == len_FF<r>. These invariants enable us to prove that the relaxation does not interfere with the assumption.

5.3 Approximate Memory and Data Types

Our third example is drawn from the LU decomposition algorithm implemented in the SciMark2 benchmark suite [2]. Researchers have demonstrated that lower-power, approximate memories and CPU compute units can be used to lower the energy consumption of this computation at the expense of a small loss in accuracy [18, 34].

We focus on the part of the computation that computes the pivot row p for each column j in a matrix A. The pivot row is the row that contains the maximum element in the column.

```
i = j + 1;
while ( i < N ) {
  a = A[i][j];
  if (a > max) { max = a; p = i; }
  i = i + 1;
}
```

Relaxation. Following the assumptions on errors in approximate memories described in [25], if A is stored in approximate memory, then we can model the range of errors when reading a value from A with a relaxation that nondeterministically adds a bounded error e to the result:

```
original_a = a;
relax (a) st (original_a - e <= a &&
              a <= original_a + e);
```

Acceptability. One acceptability property for this computation is that the value in the selected pivot row (max) in the relaxed execution does not differ from the result in an original execution by more than e. We can specify this with a relate statement:

```
relate max<o> - max<r> <= e && max<r> - max<o> <= e
```

We note that this relate statement asserts the *Lipschitz-continuity* of the computation: small changes in the inputs lead to proportionally small changes in the output.

Verification. The Coq verification of this program consists of approximately 315 lines of proof script. The key proof step verifies that max<o> - max<r> <= e && max<r> - max<o> <= e (the relation specified by the relate statement) is loop invariant.

6. Future Work

Termination. Our proof rules are designed to support the verification of acceptability properties that can be described with assert statements—which must hold independently for both original and relaxed executions—and relate statements, which relate original and relaxed executions. While such properties establish a partial correctness guarantee (as in standard Hoare logic), other acceptability properties may also prescribe total correctness: proofs of termination as well as partial correctness.

Because relaxed programs may contain additional nondeterministic and dynamically varying control flow, proving termination for a relaxed program may be more challenging than proving nontermination for the original program. One approach is to use relational reasoning to transfer the termination proof from the original program to the relaxed program (in much the same way as for our current set of acceptability properties). And while our proof machinery is not designed to support termination proofs, the rules in our axiomatic relaxed semantics do establish a relative termination guarantee for convergent while loops (whose termination conditions are proved to be equivalent in the original and relaxed semantics). Relative termination for such convergent loops ensures that if the loop terminates in the original program then it also terminates in the relaxed program. We anticipate that such a notion of relative termination (akin to our relative progress) will be a fruitful direction for future work.

Completeness. We have omitted a formal statement of the completeness of the logic because we believe that there are additional acceptability properties of relaxed programs that interact with termination, divergent control flow, and the semantics of errant executions in which the original or relaxed semantics can evaluate to ba or wr. We intend to explore the meaning of completeness and its interactions with these properties in future work.

7. Related Work

Executable Specifications. Executable specifications, via techniques such as refinement and constraint solving, produce concrete outputs that satisfy the specification [13, 19, 23, 27, 33, 37]. Applications include recovering from errors in existing code and providing alternate implementations for code that may be difficult to develop using standard techniques.

The research in this paper differs in that it promotes nondeterministic relaxation to obtain semantically different but still acceptable variants of the original program. Our focus is therefore on enabling developers to specify and prove acceptability requirements that involve relational properties between the original and relaxed programs.

Unreliable Memory and Critical Data. Researchers have proposed techniques for enabling programs to distinguish data that can be stored in unreliable low-power memory from critical data whose values must be stored reliably [10, 18, 34]. These systems focus on data values (such as the values of pixels in an image) that can, in principle, legally take on *any* value. While the techniques presented in this paper support the verification of this class of programs, they also support the verification of a more general class of programs whose legal data values are constrained by relaxation predicates.

Relational Program Logics. Our program logic for the relaxed semantics of the program builds on previous work on the Relational Hoare Logic (RHL) [7]. RHL itself was inspired by Credible Compilation [31] and Translation Validation [26] and and has since inspired other forms of relational reasoning. Researchers have also defined relational separation logic [5, 36], probabilistic Hoare logic [6], and have used relational reasoning to verify the correctness of semantics-preserving compiler transformations [12, 31, 39], Lipschitz-continuity [12], access control policies [24], and differential privacy mechanisms [6].

While the majority of previous research has focused on proving that transformed programs retain the semantics of the original program, our goal is different — specifically, to prove that relaxed executions (which typically have different semantics) preserve important acceptability properties. We adapt RHL to prove properties that relate the original and relaxed executions and extend RHL to reason about assertions (which reference only the current execution) and assumptions (which are assumed to hold in original executions but must be shown to hold in relaxed executions).

8. Conclusion

The additional nondeterminism in relaxed programs enables programs to operate at a variety of points with different combinations of accuracy, performance, and resource consumption characteristics. It is possible to exploit this flexibility to satisfy a variety of goals, including trading off accuracy for enhanced performance or reduced energy consumption [3, 4, 11, 16–18, 20–22, 29, 30, 32, 34, 35, 38] or responding to load spikes or other fluctuations in the characteristics of the underlying computational platform [16, 17, 29, 34].

We present formal reasoning techniques that make it possible to verify important acceptability properties of relaxed programs. Standard verification techniques reference only the current execution of the current program under verification. Our techniques, in contrast, aim to reduce the verification effort by taking a relational approach that exploits the close relationship between the original and relaxed executions. Our goal is to give developers the verified acceptability properties they need to confidently deploy relaxed programs and exploit the substantial flexibility, performance, and resource consumption advantages that relaxed programs offer.

Acknowledgments

We would like to thank Fan Long and our anonymous reviewers for their insightful comments. We also note our earlier technical report on reasoning about relaxed programs [9]. This research was supported in part by the National Science Foundation (Grants CCF-0811397, CCF-0905244, CCF-1036241, and IIS-0835652), DARPA (Grants FA8650-11-C-7192 and FA8750-12-2-0110), and the United States Department of Energy (Grant DE-SC0005288).

References

[1] The Coq Proof Assistant. http://coq.inria.fr.

[2] Scimark 2.0. http://math.nist.gov/scimark2.

[3] J. Ansel, C. Chan, Y. L. Wong, M. Olszewski, Q. Zhao, A. Edelman, and S. Amarasinghe. Petabricks: a language and compiler for algorithmic choice. PLDI, 2009.

[4] W. Baek and T. M. Chilimbi. Green: a framework for supporting energy-conscious programming using controlled approximation. PLDI, 2010.

[5] G. Barthe, J. Crespo, and C. Kunz. Relational verification using product programs. FM, 2011.

[6] G. Barthe, B. Köpf, F. Olmedo, and S. Zanella Béguelin. Probabilistic reasoning for differential privacy. POPL, 2012.

[7] N. Benton. Simple relational correctness proofs for static analyses and program transformations. POPL, 2004.

[8] W. Blume and R. Eigenmann. Performance analysis of parallelizing compilers on the Perfect Benchmarks programs. *Transactions on Parallel and Distributed Systems*, 3(6), 1992.

[9] M. Carbin, D. Kim, S. Misailovic, and M. Rinard. Reasoning about Relaxed Programs. Technical Report MIT-CSAIL-TR-2011-050, MIT, 2011.

[10] M. Carbin and M. Rinard. Automatically Identifying Critical Input Regions and Code in Applications. ISSTA, 2010.

[11] S. Chaudhuri, S. Gulwani, R. Lublinerman, and S. Navidpour. Proving Programs Robust. FSE, 2011.

[12] J.M. Crespo and C. Kunz. A machine-checked framework for relational separation logic. SEFM, 2011.

[13] B. Demsky and M. Rinard. Data structure repair using goal-directed reasoning. ICSE, 2005.

[14] R. W. Floyd. Assigning meanings to programs. *Mathematical aspects of computer science*, 19(19-32), 1967.

[15] C. A. R. Hoare. An axiomatic basis for computer programming. *Commun. ACM*, 12(10), October 1969.

[16] H. Hoffman, S. Sidiroglou, M. Carbin, S. Misailovic, A. Agarwal, and M. Rinard. Dynamic knobs for responsive power-aware computing. ASPLOS, 2011.

[17] H. Hoffmann, S. Misailovic, S. Sidiroglou, A. Agarwal, and M. Rinard. Using Code Perforation to Improve Performance, Reduce Energy Consumption, and Respond to Failures . Technical Report MIT-CSAIL-TR-2009-042, MIT, 2009.

[18] S. Liu, K. Pattabiraman, T. Moscibroda, and B. Zorn. Flikker: Saving dram refresh-power through critical data partitioning. ASPLOS, 2011.

[19] A. Milicevic, D. Rayside, K. Yessenov, and D. Jackson. Unifying execution of imperative and declarative code. ICSE, 2011.

[20] S. Misailovic, D. Kim, and M. Rinard. Parallelizing sequential programs with statistical accuracy tests. Technical Report MIT-CSAIL-TR-2010-038, MIT, 2010.

[21] S. Misailovic, D. Roy, and M. Rinard. Probabilistically Accurate Program Transformations. SAS, 2011.

[22] S. Misailovic, S. Sidiroglou, H. Hoffmann, and M. Rinard. Quality of service profiling. ICSE, 2010.

[23] C. Morgan. The specification statement. *Transactions on Programming Languages and Systems*, 10(3), 1988.

[24] A. Nanevski, A. Banerjee, and D. Garg. Verification of information flow and access control policies with dependent types. SP, 2011.

[25] J. Nelson, A. Sampson, and L. Ceze. Dense approximate storage in phase-change memory. ASPLOS-WACI, 2011.

[26] A. Pnueli, M. Siegel, and E. Singerman. Translation validation. TACAS, 1998.

[27] D. Rayside, A. Milicevic, K. Yessenov, G. Dennis, and D. Jackson. Agile specifications. OOPSLA, 2009.

[28] M. Rinard. Acceptability-oriented computing. OOPSLA Onwards '03.

[29] M. Rinard. Probabilistic accuracy bounds for fault-tolerant computations that discard tasks. ICS, 2006.

[30] M. Rinard. Using early phase termination to eliminate load imbalances at barrier synchronization points. OOPSLA, 2007.

[31] M. C. Rinard and D. Marinov. Credible compilation with pointers. RTRV, 1999.

[32] Martin Rinard. A lossy, synchronization-free, race-full, but still acceptably accurate parallel space-subdivision tree construction algorithm. Technical Report MIT-CSAIL-TR-2012-005, MIT, 2012.

[33] H. Samimi, E. Aung, and T. Millstein. Falling back on executable specifications. ECOOP, 2010.

[34] A. Sampson, W. Dietl, E. Fortuna, D. Gnanapragasam, L. Ceze, and D. Grossman. Enerj: approximate data types for safe and general low-power computation. PLDI, 2011.

[35] S. Sidiroglou, S. Misailovic, H. Hoffmann, and M. Rinard. Managing Performance vs. Accuracy Trade-offs With Loop Perforation. FSE '11.

[36] H Yang. Relational separation logic. *Theoretical Computer Science*, 375(1-3), May 2007.

[37] J. Yang, K. Yessenov, and A. Solar-Lezama. A language for automatically enforcing privacy policies. POPL, 2012.

[38] Z. Zhu, S. Misailovic, J. Kelner, and M. Rinard. Randomized accuracy-aware program transformations for efficient approximate computations. POPL, 2012.

[39] L. Zuck, A. Pnueli, and R. Leviathan. Validation of optimizing compilers. Technical report, Weizmann Institute of Science, 2001.

Automated Error Diagnosis Using Abductive Inference *

Isil Dillig
Department of Computer Science
College of William & Mary
idillig@cs.wm.edu

Thomas Dillig
Department of Computer Science
College of William & Mary
tdillig@cs.wm.edu

Alex Aiken
Department of Computer Science
Stanford University
aiken@cs.stanford.edu

Abstract

When program verification tools fail to verify a program, either the program is buggy or the report is a false alarm. In this situation, the burden is on the user to manually classify the report, but this task is time-consuming, error-prone, and does not utilize facts already proven by the analysis. We present a new technique for assisting users in classifying error reports. Our technique computes small, relevant queries presented to a user that capture exactly the information the analysis is missing to either discharge or validate the error. Our insight is that identifying these missing facts is an instance of the *abductive inference problem* in logic, and we present a new algorithm for computing the smallest and most general abductions in this setting. We perform the first user study to rigorously evaluate the accuracy and effort involved in manual classification of error reports. Our study demonstrates that our new technique is very useful for improving both the speed and accuracy of error report classification. Specifically, our approach improves classification accuracy from 33% to 90% and reduces the time programmers take to classify error reports from approximately 5 minutes to under 1 minute.

Categories and Subject Descriptors F.3.1 [*Logics and Meaning of Programs*]: Specifying and Verifying and Reasoning about Programs

General Terms Languages, Verification, Algorithms, Experimentation

Keywords Error diagnosis, abductive inference, static analysis

1. Introduction

Automated software verification systems perform sophisticated reasoning to prove the correctness of program properties, such as validity of assertions, memory safety, and lack of run-time exceptions. If the tool concludes that the program satisfies the property, then all is well. On the other hand, if the tool claims that the program may violate the property, there are two possibilities:

- either the program is indeed buggy, or
- the report generated by the tool is a false alarm

* This work was supported by NSF grants CCF-0915766 and CCF-0702681.

PLDI'12, June 11–16, 2012, Beijing, China.
Copyright © 2012 ACM 978-1-4503-1205-9/12/06... $10.00

Since program verification is, in general, undecidable, false alarms are inevitable no matter how sophisticated the reasoning performed by the analysis tool. Thus, when a static analysis fails to verify the correctness of a program, the burden is on the user to decide whether the report generated by the tool is a genuine bug or a false alarm. This situation is undesirable for multiple reasons:

- Manual report classification is a very time-consuming task that requires expertise, patience, and understanding of the program.
- Even if the cause of the report is very simple (e.g., the analysis could not establish a single, local fact), there is no bound on the amount of work the user must do to discover this cause. Effectively, the user must repeat all of the successful reasoning the tool performed just to discover where it became stuck.
- Manual classification of error reports is error-prone: As corroborated by our experimental results, users often misclassify false alarms as genuine bugs, or much more problematically, genuine bugs as false alarms.

We believe that the difficulty of manual report classification is a major remaining impediment to the wide-spread adoption of even the most precise and state-of-the-art static analysis tools. As reported in a recent article by Bessey et al., the overwhelming experience in the field is that users who do not understand error reports become frustrated and ignore those reports [1].

In this paper, we propose a new technique for assisting users in classifying error reports when automated static analyses fail to verify a program. Our technique allows verification tools to interact with users by computing small, relevant queries that capture exactly the facts that the analysis is missing to either verify the program or prove the existence of a real error. These queries are then presented to a user who decides whether the answer to the query is yes or no.

The first kind of query we compute is a *proof obligation query*, which asks the user whether a property P is a program invariant. These queries have the key characteristic that, if P is indeed an invariant, then the program is error-free. Furthermore, proof obligation queries are as simple and as general as possible: they capture exactly, and only, the information the analysis is missing to verify the program. Our analysis also computes a second kind of query, called a *failure witness query*, which asks the user whether a property P can arise in some execution. The key feature of a witness query is that, if P can indeed occur in some execution, the program must have an error. Furthermore, our technique computes simplest and most general failure witness queries: they capture precisely the facts the analysis is missing to be certain that the program is buggy.

Our approach to error report classification is semi-automatic: It computes simple and relevant queries to resolve the error report, but trusts a user to correctly answer them. Since this technique is only useful when an automated analysis has been unable to verify the program, it is inevitable to ask the user for some help. In fact, the current best practice asks the user to do all the work, as manual report classification is 100% trusted user information. Our approach minimizes -in a precise sense- the amount of trusted information the user must supply, both simplifying and speeding up her job while also increasing the accuracy of the classification.

There are four salient features underlying our approach:

- We describe a static analysis algorithm that makes explicit all possible sources of incompleteness in static analyzers and uses facts inferred by any other program analysis technique.
- This representation allows the analysis to not only prove the absence of errors but also to prove their presence, i.e., in some cases, the analysis can decide that the program must be buggy.
- When the analysis can neither discharge nor validate a potential error, it computes small, relevant queries to be presented to the user, called proof obligations and failure witnesses, that ultimately allow the analysis to discharge or validate an error.
- If the user's answer to a proof obligation query is "yes", the analysis can discharge the potential error. Similarly, if the user's answer to a failure witness query is "yes", the analysis can prove the existence of an error. Otherwise, our technique computes new proof obligation and failure witness queries, until the error can either be discharged or validated. Queries are posed to the user in order of increasing cost, meaning that the user is asked the questions that should be the easiest to answer first. Since state-of-the-art static analyzers typically lose information in few places, it is easier for the user to answer simple queries about a handful of missing analysis facts than to manually inspect and understand an entire program.

1.1 Informal Overview

We illustrate key features of our approach with a simple example:

```
void foo(int flag, unsigned int n)
{
1:   int k = 1;
2:   if(flag) k = n*n;

3:   int i = 0, j = 0;
4:   while(i <= n) {
5:       i++;
6:       j+=i;
7:   }
8:  int z = k + i + j;
9:  assert(z > 2*n);
}
```

This code snippet contains an assertion at line 9 which is guaranteed to hold [1]. Assume that a static analysis fails to verify this program and reports a potential assertion failure for line 9. Of course, just because the tool reports a false alarm does not mean it has inferred no useful information about the program. For instance, the analysis may have inferred that k's value after line 2 is at least 0 (as **n*n** is always non-negative), and that the value of i after the loop is at least 0 and greater than **n**. Our goal is to utilize these facts inferred by the analysis to assist the user in classifying this report.

The first key idea underlying our technique is to model potential sources of incompleteness in static analyses using *abstraction variables*. In this example, since the exact values of i and j are unknown after the loop, our technique introduces abstraction variables α_i and α_j to model the unknown values of i and j at line 7. Similarly, assuming the analysis does not reason precisely about non-linear arithmetic, our technique introduces abstraction variable α_{n*n} to model the unknown result of the multiplication at line 2.

Next, our technique utilizes invariants obtained by any static analysis to infer restrictions on abstraction variables. For example, since an existing static analyzer has inferred that **n*n** is always non-negative, we have the side condition:

$$\alpha_{n*n} \geq 0$$

Similarly, since we know that the value of i after the loop is greater than n and at least 0, the abstraction variable α_i must satisfy:

$$\alpha_i \geq 0 \ \wedge \alpha_i > n$$

Thus, for line 9, our technique obtains the following invariant $\mathcal{I}$:

$$\mathcal{I} = (\alpha_{n*n} \geq 0 \ \wedge \ \alpha_i \geq 0 \ \wedge \ \alpha_i > n \ \wedge \ n \geq 0)$$

Here, the first three predicates in $\mathcal{I}$ express invariants obtained from an existing static analysis, and the last predicate $n \geq 0$ expresses that unsigned variables are non-negative.

Now that we can explicitly name each potential source of imprecision, our technique computes an exact symbolic value set for each expression in the program. For instance, the value of variable k at line 2 is represented by the symbolic value set:

$$\{(1, \neg\text{flag}), (\alpha_{n*n}, \text{flag})\}$$

meaning that k has value 1 under constraint ¬flag and the unknown value represented by α_{n*n} under condition flag. Similarly, the values of variables i and j at line 7 after the loop are represented by the singleton value sets $\{(\alpha_i, \textit{true})\}$ and $\{(\alpha_j, \textit{true})\}$. Since **z** is obtained by adding **k**, **i**, and **j**, we can use symbolic value sets of **k**, **i**, and **j** to compute the symbolic value of **z**, given by:

$$\{(1 + \alpha_i + \alpha_j, \neg\text{flag}), (\alpha_{n*n} + \alpha_i + \alpha_j, \text{flag})\}$$

Since the assertion at line 9 succeeds if the value of **z** is greater than **2*n**, we can use the symbolic value set for **z** to compute the condition ϕ under which the assertion holds:

$$\phi \ = \ (1{+}\alpha_i{+}\alpha_j > 2{*}n \wedge \neg\text{flag}) \vee (\alpha_{n*n}{+}\alpha_i{+}\alpha_j > 2{*}n \wedge \text{flag})$$

Observe that the assertion is verified if the invariants $\mathcal{I}$ entail the success condition ϕ of the assertion, i.e.,:

$$\mathcal{I} \models \phi$$

Similarly, we know that the assertion is guaranteed to fail if:

$$\mathcal{I} \models \neg\phi$$

In this example, since neither $\mathcal{I} \models \phi$ nor $\mathcal{I} \models \neg\phi$, the analysis cannot discharge or validate the potential assertion failure.

Thus, our goal is to identify the possible facts the analysis is missing to either discharge or validate the error and ask the user whether these facts indeed hold. Our insight is that this problem is an instance of the *abductive inference* problem in logic, where the goal is to find an explanatory hypothesis for a desired outcome. Formally, given known facts F and a desired outcome O, an abductive inference problem is to find an explanation E such that:

$$F \wedge E \models O \text{ and } \text{SAT}(F \wedge E)$$

In other words, the abduction E is consistent with known facts F, and together with F, is sufficient to explain O.

In our setting, the desired outcome is to either prove the absence of an error or to validate its existence. Thus, we solve two abductive inference problems, one to infer the missing information necessary to verify the program, and one to find the missing facts to validate the presence of an error. Specifically, to prove the absence of an error, we compute a *proof obligation* Γ by solving the following abductive inference problem:

$$\mathcal{I} \wedge \Gamma \models \phi \text{ and } \text{SAT}(\mathcal{I} \wedge \Gamma)$$

In other words, a proof obligation Γ is consistent with program invariants $\mathcal{I}$ and, along with $\mathcal{I}$, is sufficient to discharge the error. Furthermore, we are not interested in just any solution to the abductive inference problem; what we want is a *weakest minimum proof*

[1] In this example, we assume there are no integer overflows.

obligation so that the queries presented to the user are as small and as general as possible. In this example, using the techniques of Section 4, we compute a weakest minimum proof obligation as:

$$\alpha_j \geq n$$

Thus, if the user can show that `j >= n` always holds at line 7, the analysis can discharge the potential error.

Dually, to prove the presence of an error, we compute a *failure witness* Υ by solving a second abductive inference problem:

$$\mathcal{I} \wedge \Upsilon \models \neg\phi \text{ and } \text{SAT}(\mathcal{I} \wedge \Upsilon)$$

In other words, a failure witness is also consistent with program invariants, and if Υ holds in *some* execution, we know that the program must have an error. Again, we are not interested in any solution to the abductive inference problem; instead, we want to find a *weakest minimum failure witness* to ensure that the queries we compute are as small and as general as possible. For our running example, techniques described in Section 4 yield the following weakest minimum failure witness:

$$\neg\text{flag} \wedge \alpha_i + \alpha_j < 0$$

Thus, if the user can show that `i+j < 0` is possible at line 7 in an execution where `!flag` holds, the analysis can validate the error.

After computing weakest minimum proof obligations and failure witnesses, our technique then decides whether it is more promising to try to discharge the error or to validate it by comparing the costs of the proof obligation and failure witness. In this example, our technique decides that it is more promising to try to discharge the error and therefore queries the user whether `j>=n` is a program invariant at line 7.

Since it is easy to show that `j >= n` always holds at line 7, the analysis can immediately discharge the error. Observe that, although the assertion condition in this example requires reasoning about values of multiple variables `i`, `j`, `k`, and `z`, our technique can take advantage of facts already established by the analysis to compute a simple and intuitive query involving only variable `j`.

1.2 Organization and Contributions

The rest of this paper is organized as follows: Section 2 defines a simple language in which we formalize our technique. Section 3 describes a static analysis that makes explicit potential sources of imprecision and performs symbolic value propagation. Section 4 defines weakest minimum proof obligations and failure witnesses, describes a technique for computing them, and presents an iterative algorithm for validating or discharging error reports. Section 5 describes our implementation; Section 6 presents experimental results. Finally, Section 7 surveys related work, and Section 8 concludes. In summary, this paper makes the following contributions:

- We present a new technique for semi-automatic report classification when static analyzers are unable to verify the program.
- We define weakest minimum proof obligations and failure witnesses as a technical characterization of simple, relevant facts useful for resolving error reports.
- We present the problem of computing proof obligations and failure witnesses as an abductive inference problem and give a new algorithm for computing abductions in this setting.
- We show how proof obligations and failure witnesses can be used to interact with users until a potential error is resolved.
- We perform a user study to evaluate our technique. Our results show that the new technique is very useful both for improving the time required to classify error reports as well as for dramatically improving the accuracy of report classification. Specifically, our approach improves classification accuracy from 33% to 90% and reduces the time programmers take to classify error reports from approximately 5 minutes to under 1 minute.

$$\frac{}{S \vdash v : S(v)} \qquad \frac{}{S \vdash c : c} \qquad \frac{\oplus \in \{+,-,*\} \quad S \vdash e_1 : c_1 \quad S \vdash e_2 : c_2}{S \vdash e_1 \oplus e_2 : c_1 \oplus c_2}$$

$$\frac{S \vdash e_1 : c_1 \quad S \vdash e_2 : c_2 \quad b = \begin{cases} \text{true} & \text{if } c_1 \oslash c_2 \\ \text{false} & \text{otherwise} \end{cases}}{S \vdash e_1 \oslash e_2 : b} \qquad \frac{\text{lop} \in \{\wedge, \vee\} \quad S \vdash p_1 : b_1 \quad S \vdash p_2 : b_2}{S \vdash p_1 \text{ lop } p_2 : b_1 \text{ lop } b_2}$$

$$\frac{S \vdash p : b}{S \vdash \neg p : \neg b} \qquad \frac{S \vdash e : c}{S \vdash v = e : S[c/v]} \qquad \frac{}{S \vdash \texttt{skip} : S}$$

$$\frac{S \vdash p : \text{true} \quad S \vdash s_1 : S_1}{S \vdash \texttt{if}(p)\ \texttt{then}\ s_1\ \texttt{else}\ s_2 : S_1} \qquad \frac{S \vdash p : \text{false} \quad S \vdash s_2 : S_2}{S \vdash \texttt{if}(p)\ \texttt{then}\ s_1\ \texttt{else}\ s_2 : S_2}$$

$$\frac{S \vdash s_1 : S_1 \quad S_1 \vdash s_2 : S_2}{S \vdash s_1; s_2 : S_2} \qquad \frac{S \vdash p : \text{true} \quad S \vdash s : S' \quad S' \vdash \text{loop}^{\rho}(p)\{s\} : S''}{S \vdash \text{loop}^{\rho}(p)\{s\} : S''}$$

$$\frac{S \vdash \text{loop}^{\rho}(p)\{s\} : S' \quad S' \vdash p' : \text{true}}{S \vdash \texttt{while}^{\rho}(p)\{s\}[@p'] : S'} \qquad \frac{S \vdash p : \text{false}}{S \vdash \text{loop}^{\rho}(p)\{s\} : S}$$

$$\frac{S = [c_1/a_1, \ldots, c_k/a_k][0/v_1, \ldots, 0/v_n] \quad S \vdash s : S' \quad S' \vdash p : b}{\vdash \lambda\vec{a}.(\texttt{let}\ \vec{v}\ \texttt{in}\ (s; \texttt{check}(p)))(c_1, \ldots c_k) : b}$$

Figure 1. Operational semantics of the language from Section 2

2. Language

In this section, we present a simple programming language that we use to formalize our technique:

Program P	:=	$\lambda\vec{a}.\ (\texttt{let}\ \vec{v}\ \texttt{in}\ (s; \texttt{check}(p)))$
Statement s	:=	$v = e \mid \texttt{skip} \mid s_1; s_2$
		$\mid \texttt{if}(p)\ \texttt{then}\ s_1\ \texttt{else}\ s_2$
		$\mid \texttt{while}^{\rho}(p)\{s\}[@p']?$
Expression e	:=	$v \mid c \mid c * e \mid e_1 \oplus e_2 \ (\oplus \in \{+,-\})$
Predicate p	:=	$e_1 \oslash e_2 \ (\oslash \in \{<,>,=\})$
		$\mid p_1 \wedge p_2 \mid p_1 \vee p_2 \mid \neg p$

In this language, a program with inputs $\vec{a}$ and local variables $\vec{v}$ consists of a statement s and a `check`(p) statement, which checks whether predicate p evaluates to *true*. The program evaluates to *true* if predicate p holds, and to *false* otherwise. We say that an execution of a program P is *error-free* if P evaluates to *true* in this execution, and *buggy* otherwise. Similarly, we say that program P is error-free if P evaluates to *true* in *all* possible executions, and buggy if P evaluates to *false* in some execution.

Statements in this language consist of assignments ($v = e$, where v is bound in the `let` statement) , `skip` statements, sequencing ($s_1; s_2$), `if` statements, and `while` loops labeled with unique identifiers ρ. Observe that `while` loops can be optionally tagged with annotations of the form $@p'$, where predicate p' corresponds to invariants that hold after the loop. For the purposes of this paper, these invariants may be obtained from any automatic sound static analysis technique, such as abstract interpretation or predicate abstraction. We say that a program P is *analyzed* if all while loops are annotated with sound post-conditions using a static analyzer.

Expressions include integer variables v, integer constants c, and arithmetic operations. This language has an expressive family of predicates which include comparisons between expressions, as well as conjunction, disjunction, and negation. The operational semantics is given in Figure 1. We omit function calls from this

$$\frac{\begin{array}{c}\theta_1 = \{(\pi_1, \phi_1), \ldots, (\pi_k, \phi_k)\} \\ \theta_2 = \{(\pi'_1, \phi'_1), \ldots, (\pi'_n, \phi'_n)\} \\ \theta = \bigcup_{ij}((\pi_i \oplus \pi'_j), (\phi_i \wedge \phi'_j))\end{array}}{\vdash \theta_1 \oplus \theta_2 : \theta}$$

$$\frac{\begin{array}{c}\theta_1 = \{(\pi_1, \phi_1), \ldots, (\pi_k, \phi_k)\} \\ \theta_2 = \{(\pi'_1, \phi'_1), \ldots, (\pi'_n, \phi'_n)\} \\ \phi = \bigvee_{ij}((\pi_i \oslash \pi'_j) \wedge \phi_i \wedge \phi'_j)\end{array}}{\vdash \theta_1 \oslash \theta_2 : \phi}$$

$$\frac{\theta' = \bigcup_{(\pi_i, \phi_i) \in \theta} (\pi_i, (\phi_i \wedge \phi))}{\vdash \theta \wedge \phi : \theta'}$$

Figure 2. Operations on symbolic value sets

$$\frac{}{\mathbb{S} \vdash v : \mathbb{S}(v)} \quad \frac{}{\mathbb{S} \vdash c : (c, \mathit{true})} \quad \frac{\begin{array}{c}\oplus \in \{+, -, *\} \\ \mathbb{S} \vdash e_1 : \theta_1 \quad \mathbb{S} \vdash e_2 : \theta_2\end{array}}{\mathbb{S} \vdash e_1 \oplus e_2 : \theta_1 \oplus \theta_2}$$

Figure 3. Symbolic evaluation rules for expressions

language, as the issues raised by function calls are orthogonal and not necessary for understanding our technique. However, our implementation is an interprocedural analysis (see Section 5).

3. Analysis

In this section, we describe a static analysis that is performed after a verification tool already analyzed the program, inferring the $@p'$ annotations on `while` loops and reporting a potential error. Our analysis, which is a prerequisite for computing relevant queries to classify the error report, has the following key characteristics:

- Values of program variables are represented by symbolic expressions consisting of constants and *analysis variables*.
- There are two kinds of analysis variables: *input variables* ν represent unknown values of program inputs, and *abstraction variables* α model unknown values of variables due to an imprecision in the analysis. For instance, abstraction variables represent values that may be unknown after loops.
- The analysis uses facts inferred by other analyzers, which are annotated using the $@p'$ construct on loops. These invariants are used to constrain values of abstraction variables.
- The only source of imprecision in this analysis is loops; it performs exact symbolic value propagation on loop-free code.

Our static analysis is described in Figures 2, 3, 4, and 5. Values of program variables are represented as symbolic expressions π:

$$\pi := \nu \mid \alpha \mid c \mid \pi_1 + \pi_2 \mid \pi_1 - \pi_2 \mid c * \pi$$

Besides input variables ν and abstraction variables α, symbolic expressions are integer constants c, addition or subtraction of symbolic expressions, and linear multiplication. Since the only imprecision of the static analysis for the simple language from Section 2 is due to loops, abstraction variables are only used to model the (potentially) unknown values of program variables after loops.

In the analysis, environment $\mathbb{S}$ maps program variables to *symbolic value sets* θ:

$$\theta := 2^{(\pi, \phi)}$$

where π is a symbolic expression and ϕ is a constraint. Since variables may have different symbolic values on different program paths, the constraint ϕ allows the analysis to keep values on different paths separate. For concreteness, constraints in this paper are in the theory of of linear arithmetic over integers.

$$\frac{\begin{array}{c}\mathbb{S} \vdash e_1 : \theta_1 \\ \mathbb{S} \vdash e_2 : \theta_2\end{array}}{\mathbb{S} \vdash e_1 \oslash e_2 : \theta_1 \oslash \theta_2} \quad \frac{\begin{array}{c}\text{lop} \in \{\wedge, \vee\} \\ \mathbb{S} \vdash p_1 : \phi_1 \\ \mathbb{S} \vdash p_2 : \phi_2\end{array}}{\mathbb{S} \vdash p_1 \text{ lop } p_2 : \phi_1 \text{ lop } \phi_2} \quad \frac{\mathbb{S} \vdash p : \phi}{\mathbb{S} \vdash \neg p : \neg \phi}$$

Figure 4. Symbolic evaluation rules for predicates

$$\frac{\begin{array}{c}\mathbb{S} \vdash e : \theta \\ \mathbb{S}' = \mathbb{S}[\theta / v]\end{array}}{\mathbb{S}, \mathcal{I} \vdash v = e : \mathbb{S}', \mathcal{I}} \quad \frac{}{\mathbb{S}, \mathcal{I} \vdash \texttt{skip} : \mathbb{S}, \mathcal{I}} \quad \frac{\begin{array}{c}\mathbb{S}, \mathcal{I} \vdash s_1 : \mathbb{S}_1, \mathcal{I}_1 \\ \mathbb{S}_1, \mathcal{I}_1 \vdash s_2 : \mathbb{S}_2, \mathcal{I}_2\end{array}}{\mathbb{S}, \mathcal{I} \vdash s_1; s_2 : \mathbb{S}_2, \mathcal{I}_2}$$

$$\frac{\begin{array}{c}\mathbb{S} \vdash p : \phi \\ \mathbb{S}, \mathcal{I} \vdash s_1 : \mathbb{S}_1, \mathcal{I}_1 \quad \mathbb{S}, \mathcal{I} \vdash s_2 : \mathbb{S}_2, \mathcal{I}_2 \\ \mathbb{S}' = (\mathbb{S}_1 \wedge \phi) \sqcup (\mathbb{S}_2 \wedge \neg \phi) \\ \mathcal{I}' = ((\phi \Rightarrow \mathcal{I}_1) \wedge (\neg \phi \Rightarrow \mathcal{I}_2))\end{array}}{\mathbb{S}, \mathcal{I} \vdash \texttt{if}(p) \texttt{ then } s_1 \texttt{ else } s_2 : \mathbb{S}', \mathcal{I}'}$$

$$\frac{\mathbb{S}' = \mathbb{S}[(\alpha_1^\rho, \mathit{true})/v_1, \ldots, (\alpha_k^\rho, \mathit{true})/v_k])(\vec{v} \text{ modified in } s)}{\mathbb{S}, \mathcal{I} \vdash \text{loop}^\rho(p)\{s\} : \mathbb{S}', \mathcal{I}}$$

$$\frac{\mathbb{S}, \mathcal{I} \vdash \text{loop}^\rho(p)\{s\} : \mathbb{S}', \mathcal{I} \quad \mathbb{S}' \vdash p' : \phi}{\mathbb{S}, \mathcal{I} \vdash \texttt{while}^\rho(p)\{s\}[@p'] : \mathbb{S}', \mathcal{I} \wedge \phi}$$

$$\frac{\begin{array}{c}\mathbb{S} = [(\nu_1, \mathit{true})/a_1, \ldots, (\nu_k, \mathit{true})/a_k] \\ \mathbb{S}' = \mathbb{S}[(0, \mathit{true})/v_1, \ldots, (0, \mathit{true})/v_n] \\ \mathbb{S}', \mathit{true} \vdash s : \mathbb{S}'', \mathcal{I} \quad \mathbb{S}'' \vdash p : \phi\end{array}}{\vdash \lambda \vec{a}.(\texttt{let } \vec{v} \texttt{ in } (s; \texttt{check}(p))) : \mathcal{I}, \phi}$$

Figure 5. Transformers for the static analysis

Figure 2 defines some useful operations on symbolic value sets. The first rule $\theta_1 \oplus \theta_2$ describes how to perform arithmetic operations on symbolic value sets, where $\oplus$ ranges over $+, -, *$ and where θ is the symbolic value set representing the result of the arithmetic operation. The second rule $\theta_1 \oslash \theta_2$ (where $\oslash$ is $<, >$, or $=$) describes how to compare value sets θ_1 and θ_2. The result is a constraint ϕ, which describes the condition under which θ_1 is less than, greater than, or equal to θ_2. Finally, the last rule in this figure defines what it means to conjoin a constraint ϕ with a value set θ.

Figures 3 and 4 describe symbolic evaluation of expressions and predicates, and are direct analogues of the corresponding operational semantics rules in Figure 1, with integer constants replaced by symbolic value sets and boolean constants with constraints.

The first six rules in Figure 5 describe the transformers for statements and derive judgements of the form:

$$\mathbb{S}, \mathcal{I} \vdash s : \mathbb{S}', \mathcal{I}'$$

Since statements may modify values of program variables, each statement may modify $\mathbb{S}$ and produce a new symbolic store $\mathbb{S}'$. The constraints $\mathcal{I}$ and $\mathcal{I}'$ describe invariants about abstraction variables obtained from annotations on `while` loops.

The first three rules in Figure 5 are self-explanatory and are straightforward analogues of their concrete counterparts from Figure 1. In the rule for `if` statements, facts that are obtained by analyzing the `then` branch s_1 (resp. `else` branch s_2) only hold under the conditional p (resp. $\neg p$). Therefore, we first compute the symbolic evaluation of conditional p as ϕ and conjoin ϕ to all facts obtained in the `then` branch and $\neg \phi$ to facts obtained in the `else` branch. In this rule, conjunction on symbolic stores is defined as:

$$\forall v \in \mathit{dom}(\mathbb{S}).\ (\mathbb{S} \wedge \phi)(v) = \{(\pi_j, \phi_j \wedge \phi) \mid (\pi_j, \phi_j) \in \mathbb{S}(v)\}$$

This rule also uses an (exact) join operation $\sqcup$ on symbolic stores, defined as:

$$(\pi, \phi) \in \mathbb{S}_1(v) \wedge (\pi, \phi') \in \mathbb{S}_2(v) \Rightarrow (\pi, \phi \vee \phi') \in (\mathbb{S}_1 \sqcup \mathbb{S}_2)(v)$$
$$(\pi, \phi) \in \mathbb{S}_i(v) \wedge (\pi, \_) \notin \mathbb{S}_j(v) \Rightarrow (\pi, \phi) \in (\mathbb{S}_1 \sqcup \mathbb{S}_2)(v)$$

Thus, in the rule for `if` statements, the symbolic store $\mathbb{S}'$ is obtained by conjoining ϕ to all bindings in $\mathbb{S}_1$, $\neg\phi$ to all bindings in $\mathbb{S}_2$, and then combining the resulting symbolic stores. Similarly, observe that a new invariant $\mathcal{I}'$ is obtained as:

$$(\phi \Rightarrow \mathcal{I}_1) \wedge (\neg\phi \Rightarrow \mathcal{I}_2)$$

because invariants obtained from the `then` branch only hold under ϕ, while invariants obtained in the `else` branch hold under $\neg\phi$.

The rule for `while` loops does not infer any loop invariants, but instead uses loop postconditions already inferred by other analyses annotated using the $@p'$ construct. For this reason, we first bind the values of all variables $v_1, \ldots, v_k$ modified in the loop body to fresh abstraction variables $\alpha_1^\rho, \ldots, \alpha_k^\rho$ in the $\text{loop}^\rho(p)\{s\}$ helper rule. Now, to utilize any known invariants on the values of $v_1, \ldots, v_k$, we symbolically evaluate the annotated invariant $@p'$ as constraint ϕ and obtain a new invariant $\mathcal{I} \wedge \phi$ after analyzing the `while` loop. Observe that since the annotation $@p'$ is symbolically evaluated under store $\mathbb{S}'$ and since loop modified variables are bound to their corresponding abstraction variables α in $\mathbb{S}'$, the new invariant ϕ constrains values of abstraction variables introduced in this loop.

The last rule in Figure 5 describes the analysis of the whole program. The initial store is obtained by binding the arguments $a_1, \ldots, a_k$ to analysis variables $\nu_1, \ldots, \nu_k$ and initializing local variables to 0, as specified by the concrete semantics. The result of the analysis is a pair of constraints $\mathcal{I}, \phi$ where $\mathcal{I}$ represents all known invariants on the abstraction variables and ϕ represents the condition under which the program evaluates to *true*.

LEMMA 1. *Let P be any program such that $\vdash P : \mathcal{I}, \phi$. If $\mathcal{I} \models \phi$, then P is error-free (i.e., evaluates to* true *in all executions).*

PROOF 1. *Given in the extended version of this paper [2].*

LEMMA 2. *Let P be any program such that $\vdash P : \mathcal{I}, \phi$. If $\mathcal{I} \models \neg\phi$, then P must be buggy.*

PROOF 2. *Given in the extended version of this paper [2].*

At first glance, the condition in Lemma 2 may seem too strong as the satisfiability of the formula $\mathcal{I} \wedge \neg\phi$ is sufficient to establish that the program *may* be buggy. However, here, we are interested in proving that the program *must* be buggy, which we can only guarantee if $\mathcal{I} \models \neg\phi$.

EXAMPLE 1. *Consider the following program with annotated invariants obtained from a static analysis:*

```
λa1, a2.(let k, i, j, z in (
  if(a2 > 0) then k = a2 else k = 1;
  while¹(i < a2 + 1){
    i = i + 1;
    j = j + i;
  }@[i > -1 ∧ i > a2]
  if(a1 > 0) then z = k + i + j else z = 2 * a2 + 1;
  check(z > 2 * a2)
))
```

Applying the analysis rules described in this section, we obtain:

$$\mathcal{I} = \alpha_i^1 \geq 0 \wedge \alpha_i^1 > \nu_2$$

and success condition ϕ:

$$\begin{array}{rl} & (\nu_2 + \alpha_i^1 + \alpha_j^1 > 2\nu_2 \wedge \nu_2 > 0 \wedge \nu_1 > 0) \\ \vee & (1 + \alpha_i^1 + \alpha_j^1 > 2\nu_2 \wedge \nu_2 \leq 0 \wedge \nu_1 > 0) \\ \vee & (2\nu_2 + 1 > 2\nu_2 \wedge \nu_1 \leq 0) \end{array}$$

Since neither $\mathcal{I} \models \phi$ nor $\mathcal{I} \models \neg\phi$, the potential error can neither be discharged nor validated.

4. Query Guided Error Diagnosis

As Lemmas 1 and 2 from Section 3 show, our analysis can sometimes prove that a program is error-free or definitely buggy. Unfortunately, in many cases, the outcome of the analysis is not definite: It can neither discharge the potential error nor prove that the program is buggy. In this case, the error report must be inspected by a human who classifies the report as a genuine bug or false alarm. As mentioned in Section 1, this situation is problematic because manual classification is time-consuming, difficult, and error-prone.

In this section, we describe a novel technique for computing small, relevant queries that systematically allow definite classification of error reports. More technically, our goal is to identify relevant facts such that, along with these facts, either Lemma 1 applies (in which case, the report is definitely a false alarm) or Lemma 2 holds (in which case the report is confirmed to be a genuine bug).

4.1 Weakest Minimum Queries to Discharge Error

Suppose that, for a given program P, the analysis from Section 3 derives the judgment

$$\vdash P : \mathcal{I}, \phi$$

but neither Lemma 1 nor Lemma 2 applies. To be able to discharge the error, what we need to do is to find a formula Γ such that, along with $\mathcal{I}$, Γ implies the success condition ϕ. Specifically, we need to solve the following abductive inference problem:

DEFINITION 1. **(Proof Obligation)** *Given known facts $\mathcal{I}$ and success condition ϕ, a* proof obligation *is a formula Γ such that:*

$$\Gamma \wedge \mathcal{I} \models \phi \quad \textit{and} \quad \textit{SAT}(\Gamma \wedge \mathcal{I})$$

Thus, a proof obligation Γ is consistent with known program invariants $\mathcal{I}$, and together with $\mathcal{I}$ allows us to prove the success condition ϕ. Observe that there is always a trivial proof obligation, namely $\Gamma = \phi$. In other words, a trivial way to discharge the error is simply to ask the user to show the success condition ϕ itself! Therefore, we are not interested in just any proof obligation, but simple, intuitive proof obligations that are local and easy for the user to decide. To make precise what we mean by simple proof obligations, it is necessary to assign a cost to each formula Γ. In this paper, we assign costs to proof obligations as follows:

DEFINITION 2. **(Cost of Proof Obligation)** *Let Γ be a proof obligation query for $\mathcal{I}, \phi$, and let Π_p be a mapping from variables to costs such that $\Pi_p(\alpha) = 1$ for abstraction variable α and $\Pi_p(\nu) = |\textit{Vars}(\phi) \cup \textit{Vars}(\mathcal{I})|$ for input variable ν. Then:*

$$\textit{Cost}(\Gamma) = \sum_{v \in \textit{Vars}(\Gamma)} \Pi_p(v)$$

The above cost function assigns cost 1 to each abstraction variable α and cost $|\text{Vars}(\phi) \cup \text{Vars}(\mathcal{I})|$ to each input variable ν. Of course, it is impossible to exactly capture the intuitiveness of a program fact with a mathematical formula, and any definition of query cost necessarily approximates the human effort required to decide that query. We choose to approximate the simplicity of a query as given by Definition 2 because it captures the following intuitions:

- Local facts are generally easier to decide for humans: Our cost function assigns a lower cost to formulas with fewer abstraction variables, because queries involving fewer variables require the user to reason about fewer sources of analysis imprecision.
- In general, it is undesirable to make assumptions about the program's execution environment (i.e., inputs in our language): For this reason, the cost function assigns a higher cost to formulas containing input variables ν. In fact, the intuition behind assigning cost $|\text{Vars}(\phi) \cup \text{Vars}(\mathcal{I})|$ to input variables ν is to ensure that it is more expensive to constrain a single input vs. all sources

of imprecision. In other words, if there is any way to discharge the error without constraining the program's execution environment, the analysis will ask those queries first.

While this cost definition could be refined, we found it to capture simplicity well in practice (see Section 6). Furthermore, the techniques we describe are agnostic to the definition of query cost; we only require that cost is a function of variables in the formula. Given a function that assigns costs to queries, we can now define a special kind of proof obligation that we are interested in computing:

DEFINITION 3. **(Weakest Minimum Proof Obligation)** *Given facts $\mathcal{I}$ and success condition ϕ, a* weakest minimum proof obligation *is a formula Γ such that:*

1. $\Gamma \wedge \mathcal{I} \models \phi$ *and* $SAT(\Gamma \wedge \mathcal{I})$
2. *For any other Γ' that satisfies (1), either $Cost(\Gamma) < Cost(\Gamma')$ or $Cost(\Gamma) = Cost(\Gamma') \wedge (\Gamma \not\Rightarrow \Gamma' \vee \Gamma \Leftrightarrow \Gamma')$*

Thus, a weakest minimum proof obligation Γ has cost less than or equal to any other proof obligation, and Γ is no stronger than other proof obligations with the same minimum cost as Γ. As argued earlier, the condition of minimality captures the intuitive notion of simplicity. Furthermore, the requirement that Γ is no stronger than other proof obligations with the same cost expresses generality. In particular, we do not want to ask the user about invariants that are stronger than necessary to discharge the error.

4.1.1 Computing Weakest Minimum Proof Obligations

We now turn to the problem of how to compute weakest minimum proof obligations. First, observe that we can rewrite $\Gamma \wedge \mathcal{I} \models \phi$ as:

$$\Gamma \models \mathcal{I} \Rightarrow \phi$$

Thus, Γ is a formula with minimum cost that entails $\mathcal{I} \Rightarrow \phi$. Our insight is that we can make use of a *minimum partial satisfying assignment* of $\mathcal{I} \Rightarrow \phi$ to compute the weakest Γ with minimum cost.

DEFINITION 4. **(Cost of Partial Assignment)** *Let σ be a partial assignment for a formula ϕ and let Π be a mapping from variables in ϕ to non-negative integers. The cost of partial assignment σ, written $Cost(\sigma)$ is $\sum_{v \in Vars(\sigma)} \Pi(v)$*

DEFINITION 5. **(Minimum Satisfying Assignment)** *Given mapping Π from variables to costs, a minimum satisfying assignment of formula φ is a partial assignment σ to a subset of the variables in φ such that:*

- $\sigma(\varphi) \equiv$ true
- $\forall \sigma'$ *such that* $\sigma'(\varphi) \equiv$ true, $Cost(\sigma) \leq Cost(\sigma')$

In this paper, we do not address the problem of computing minimum satisfying assignments for formulas. An algorithm for computing minimum satisfying assignments in theories that admit quantifier elimination is described in [3]. Since the theory of linear arithmetic over integers used in this paper admits quantifier elimination, the algorithm of [3] is directly applicable.

Minimum satisfying assignments are useful because they allow us to determine the minimum set of variables that any proof obligation Γ must contain. However, we are not interested in *any* minimum satisfying assignment to $\mathcal{I} \Rightarrow \phi$ since some minimum satisfying assignments make $\mathcal{I} \Rightarrow \phi$ true by falsifying $\mathcal{I}$. Such assignments are not interesting in this context because they violate known invariants $\mathcal{I}$ about the program. Thus, what we want is a minimum satisfying assignment to $\mathcal{I} \Rightarrow \phi$ that is consistent with $\mathcal{I}$.

DEFINITION 6. **(Consistent Minimum Satisfying Assignment)** *A minimum satisfying assignment σ of φ is consistent with φ' if $\sigma(\varphi')$ is satisfiable.*

Suppose σ is a minimum satisfying assignment of $\mathcal{I} \Rightarrow \phi$ consistent with $\mathcal{I}$. Now, if we interpret σ as a logical formula F_σ (i.e., a conjunction of equalities between variables and constants), F_σ is in fact a proof obligation, since, by definition:

$$F_\sigma \models \mathcal{I} \Rightarrow \phi \text{ and } \mathrm{SAT}(F_\sigma \wedge \mathcal{I})$$

Furthermore, F_σ also has minimum cost, but, it is not the weakest proof obligation. More specifically, since F_σ assigns each variable to a concrete value, it is in fact a *strongest* proof obligation with minimum cost and is not very likely to be a valid program invariant.

What we are really after, then, is a formula Γ containing only the variables in σ but that is also the weakest formula containing these variables that still entails $\mathcal{I} \Rightarrow \phi$. In other words, what we want is the *weakest sufficient condition* of $\mathcal{I} \Rightarrow \phi$ containing only the variables in σ.

LEMMA 3. *Let V be the set of variables in a minimum satisfying assignment of $\mathcal{I} \Rightarrow \phi$ consistent with $\mathcal{I}$, and let $\overline{V}$ be the set of variables in $\mathcal{I} \Rightarrow \phi$ but not in V. We can obtain a weakest minimum proof obligation by eliminating the quantifiers from the formula:*

$$\forall \overline{V}.\ (\mathcal{I} \Rightarrow \phi)$$

PROOF 3. *The fact that this formula is a minimum proof obligation follows from Definition 6. The fact that this formula is the weakest such one follows from the well-known result that the weakest sufficient condition of a formula ϕ containing only variables $\overline{V}$ is given by $\forall \overline{V}.\phi$ and from the fact that linear integer arithmetic admits quantifier elimination.*

Remark: While the formula computed as described in Lemma 3 yields a weakest minimum proof obligation, this formula may be redundant. In other words, parts of this formula may already be implied by the known invariants $\mathcal{I}$. Thus, to avoid unnecessary queries, we simplify the formula computed as in Lemma 3 with respect to $\mathcal{I}$. This can be achieved, for instance, by using the simplification algorithm of [4], with $\mathcal{I}$ as the initial critical constraint.

EXAMPLE 2. *We now illustrate the computation of the proof obligation Γ on Example 1, where we already computed $\mathcal{I}$ and ϕ. Here, a minimum satisfying assignment to $\mathcal{I} \Rightarrow \phi$ that is consistent with $\mathcal{I}$ is $\alpha_j^1 = 0$. Now, we eliminate the quantifiers from the formula:*

$$\forall \nu_1, \nu_2, \alpha_i^1.\ (\mathcal{I} \Rightarrow \phi)$$

which, after simplification, yields $\alpha_j^1 \geq 0$. Thus, the assertion in Example 1 can be proven if the user shows that $\mathtt{j} \geq 0$ *after the loop, which is indeed the case. Observe that the query we pose to the user is much simpler compared to ϕ.*

4.1.2 Deciding Proof Obligation Queries

As discussed earlier, a proof obligation Γ is a query presented to a user, and, if true, proves the absence of an error in the program. Formally, we define a valid answer to a proof obligation query:

DEFINITION 7. **(Valid Answer to Proof Obligation Query)** *We say that the answer to a proof obligation query Γ is valid iff:*

- *The answer is either yes or no*
- *If the answer if yes, then Γ holds on* all *program executions (i.e., Γ is a program invariant)*
- *If the answer is no, then there is at least one execution in which Γ is violated*

In practice, a user may not always be able to give a definite yes/no answer to a proof obligation query; thus it is reasonable to accept "I don't know" as an answer. We discuss how to extend our technique to handle "I don't know" answers to queries in Section 5.

In this paper, we do not address the problem of verifying that the user's answer to a query is correct. Since our technique only applies in cases where automated verification fails, it is difficult, and sometimes even impossible, to completely eliminate trusted user information. Thus, our goal is to minimize the amount of trusted user information required to verify the program, making the job of the user much easier and improving classification accuracy.

LEMMA 4. *Let Γ be a proof obligation query, and suppose "yes" is a valid answer to this query. Then, the program is error-free.*

PROOF 4. *This follows immediately from the definition of proof obligation and validity of answer to the query.*

4.2 Weakest Minimum Queries to Validate An Error

In this section, we now turn to the complementary problem of validating the *existence* of a real error in the program. Recall from Lemma 2 that the condition

$$\mathcal{I} \models \neg\phi$$

guarantees that the program must contain a real error.

Now, to validate the existence of an error, we need to solve the same kind of abductive inference problem we considered in the previous section. More specifically, we need to find a formula Υ, called a *failure witness*, defined as follows:

DEFINITION 8. **(Failure Witness)** *Given facts $\mathcal{I}$ and success condition ϕ of a program, a* failure witness *is a formula Υ such that:*

$$\mathcal{I} \wedge \Upsilon \models \neg\phi \quad \textit{and} \quad \textit{SAT}(\Upsilon \wedge \mathcal{I})$$

As in the case of proof obligations, we are not interested in *any* failure witness, as some witnesses may be more complicated than necessary or overly restrictive. Thus, to be able to ask the user simple and general witness queries, we want to obtain a *weakest minimum failure witness*. For this purpose, we define cost of failure witnesses as follows:

DEFINITION 9. **(Cost of Failure Witness)** *Let Υ be a failure witness for $\mathcal{I}, \phi$, and let Π_w be a mapping from variables to costs such that $\Pi_w(\nu) = 1$ for input variable ν and $\Pi_w(\alpha) = |\textit{Vars}(\phi) \cup \textit{Vars}(\mathcal{I})|$ for abstraction variable α. Then:*

$$\textit{Cost}(\Upsilon) = \sum_{v \in \textit{Vars}(\Upsilon)} \Pi_w(v)$$

Similar to that for proof obligations, this cost function is biased in favor of queries involving local facts, as it penalizes witness queries involving more abstraction variables. But in contrast to proof obligations, we prefer witness queries involving only inputs to those involving abstraction variables. Since it is in general undesirable to make assumptions about the program's inputs, it is likely that witness queries involving input variables are easy to answer affirmatively, and are thus assigned a lower cost. While this cost definition merely approximates the simplicity and usefulness of a witness query, we found it to work well in practice.

We can now define *weakest minimum failure witness*:

DEFINITION 10. **(Weakest Minimum Failure Witness)** *Given known facts $\mathcal{I}$ about a program P and success condition ϕ, a* weakest minimum failure witness *of P is a formula Υ such that:*

1. *$\Upsilon \wedge \mathcal{I} \models \neg\phi$ and $\textit{SAT}(\Upsilon \wedge \mathcal{I})$*
2. *For any other Υ' that satisfies (1), either $\textit{Cost}(\Upsilon) < \textit{Cost}(\Upsilon')$ or $\textit{Cost}(\Upsilon) = \textit{Cost}(\Upsilon') \wedge (\Upsilon \not\Rightarrow \Upsilon' \vee \Upsilon \Leftrightarrow \Upsilon')$ where Cost is defined according to Definition 9.*

The computation of weakest minimum failure witnesses is analogous to the computation of weakest minimum proof obligations:

LEMMA 5. *Let V be the set of variables in a minimum satisfying assignment of $\mathcal{I} \Rightarrow \neg\phi$ consistent with $\mathcal{I}$, and let $\overline{V}$ be the set of variables in $\mathcal{I} \Rightarrow \neg\phi$ but not in V. Then, a weakest minimum failure witness is obtained by eliminating the quantifiers from the formula:*

$$\forall \overline{V}.\ (\mathcal{I} \Rightarrow \neg\phi)$$

4.2.1 Deciding Failure Witness Queries

A failure witness is a query such that if the user answers "yes", then there exists at least one execution in which the program fails. Thus, a *valid answer* to a witness query is defined as follows:

DEFINITION 11. **(Valid Answer to Witness Query)** *We say that the answer to a failure witness query Υ is valid iff:*

- *The answer is either yes or no*
- *If the answer is yes, then there exists at least one program execution where Υ holds*
- *If the answer is no, then there is no execution in which Υ holds, i.e. $\neg\Upsilon$ is a program invariant.*

Observe that answering "yes" to a witness query has very different semantics than answering "yes" to a proof obligation query: In the former case, Υ needs to hold in only one execution (existential semantics), whereas in the latter case, Γ must hold in all executions (universal semantics). Furthermore, observe that answering "no" to a witness query Υ is equivalent to answering "yes" to a proof obligation query $\neg\Upsilon$. Similarly, answering "no" to a proof obligation query Γ is equivalent to answering "yes" to a witness query $\neg\Gamma$.

LEMMA 6. *Let Υ be a failure witness query, and suppose "yes" is a valid answer to this query. Then, the program exhibits an error in at least one execution.*

PROOF 5. *This follows from the definition of failure witness and validity of answer to the witness query.*

4.3 The Full Algorithm

We now describe the algorithm, presented in Figure 6, for systematically generating a sequence of queries until the error report is resolved. This algorithm takes as input the known program invariants $\mathcal{I}$ and the success condition ϕ. The set W is a set of witnesses, i.e., conditions known to hold in some execution of the program.

In lines 5-6 of the algorithm, we first compute proof obligation Γ as described in Section 4.1. Here, $\texttt{compute\_msa}(\varphi, S, \Pi_p)$ computes the set of variables in the minimum satisfying assignment of φ consistent with the set of formulas given by S with respect to cost mapping Π_p (recall Definition 2). As discussed in Section 4.1, the minimum satisfying assignment needs to be consistent with $\mathcal{I}$, since we do not want to issue queries about facts that violate known program invariants. Furthermore, we want the minimum satisfying assignment to be consistent with all learned witnesses in W, since we do not want to ask the user queries about facts for whose violation we already have witnesses. In line 4, the notation $\overline{V_1}$ denotes the set of variables that are in $\mathcal{I} \Rightarrow \phi$ but that are not part of the minimum satisfying assignment. As stated by Lemma 3, we can compute the weakest minimum proof obligation Γ by eliminating the universal quantifiers from the formula $\forall \overline{V_1}.\, \mathcal{I} \Rightarrow \phi$.

Dually, lines 7-8 compute a weakest minimum failure witness Υ as described in Section 4.2: We first compute the minimum satisfying assignment of $\mathcal{I} \Rightarrow \neg\phi$ consistent with $\mathcal{I}$ with respect to cost function Π_w (recall Definition 9). Again, it is important that the minimum satisfying assignment is consistent with $\mathcal{I}$, as we do not want to ask queries that we know cannot hold in any execution. However, in this case, it is not necessary that the assignment is consistent with W since the failure witness needs to hold for only `function diagnose_error(`$\mathcal{I}, \phi$`) :`

1 : `set` $W = \emptyset$;

2 : `while(true){`

3 : `if(`VALID($\mathcal{I} \Rightarrow \phi$)`) return` ERROR_DISCHARGED
4 : `if(`$\exists \psi \in W$. UNSAT($\mathcal{I} \wedge \psi \wedge \phi$)`) return` ERROR_VALIDATED

5 : $V_1 =$ `compute_msa(`$\mathcal{I} \Rightarrow \phi, W \cup \mathcal{I}, \Pi_p$`)`
6 : $\Gamma =$ `elim_quantifier(`$\forall \overline{V_1}.(\mathcal{I} \Rightarrow \phi)$`)`

7 : $V_2 =$ `compute_msa(`$\mathcal{I} \Rightarrow \neg\phi, \mathcal{I}, \Pi_w$`)`
8 : $\Upsilon =$ `elim_quantifier(`$\forall \overline{V_2}.(\mathcal{I} \Rightarrow \neg\phi)$`)`

9 : `if(`Cost(Γ) $\leq$ Cost(Υ)`){`
10 : $Q_1 =$ `form_invariant_query(`Γ`)`
11 : `if(answer to` $Q_1=$ YES`) return` ERROR_DISCHARGED
12 : $W := W \cup (\neg\Gamma)$
13 : `}`

14 : `else{`
15 : $Q_2 =$ `form_witness_query(`Υ`)`
16 : `if(answer to` $Q_2=$ YES`) return` ERROR_VALIDATED
17 : $\mathcal{I} := \mathcal{I} \wedge (\neg\Upsilon)$
18 : `}`
19 : `}`

Figure 6. Algorithm for Diagnosing Error Reports

one, rather than for all, executions. Finally, as shown by Lemma 5, we compute the weakest minimum failure witness by eliminating quantifiers from the formula $\forall \overline{V_2}.\ \mathcal{I} \Rightarrow \neg\phi$, where $\overline{V_2}$ is the set of variables in $\mathcal{I} \Rightarrow \neg\phi$, but not in V_2.

At line 9, we compare the costs of the proof obligation Γ and the failure witness Υ to decide whether it is more promising to try to discharge the error or to validate it. If the cost of Γ is cheaper, then at line 10, we formulate the proof obligation Γ as an invariant query (discussed further in Section 4.4). If the user answers the invariant query positively, we have discharged the error. On the other hand, if the user decides that Γ is not an invariant, then we have learned a new witness: We now know there exists at least one execution where Γ is violated; thus we add $\neg\Gamma$ to the set of witness formulas.

On the other hand, if the error validation strategy has lower cost than the error discharge strategy (lines 14-18), we formulate Υ as a witness query (again, see Section 4.4). If the answer to this query is "yes", we have validated the error. On the other hand, if the answer to the witness query is "no", this means there is no execution in which Υ holds. In this case, we have learned that $\neg\Upsilon$ is an invariant, and we conjoin it with the existing invariants $\mathcal{I}$.

Observe that at lines 3-4, we check whether the error can be discharged or validated with the current invariants $\mathcal{I}$ and witnesses W. This check is necessary because even when the user answers "no" to a query, we still learn additional facts as a result.

Also, observe that the queries computed by our algorithm may increasingly become more difficult over time. As the analysis progresses, $\mathcal{I}$ becomes stronger and more witnesses are acquired; thus, the minimum satisfying assignment needs to be consistent with more facts and may therefore contain more variables. In fact, in the unlikely case where the user answers "no" to all queries, the final query may degenerate into the success condition itself.

4.4 From Formulas to Queries

So far, we focused on computing small, relevant formulas that are useful for classifying error reports. We now discuss how to present these formulas in a way that can be easily understood by humans.

The first challenge is to translate analysis variables into program expressions that can be understood without knowledge of internal analysis details. This problem is easily solved in our representation since there is a straightforward mapping between analysis variables and program expressions: Input variables ν_i used in the analysis represent values of program inputs a_i, and abstraction variables α_i^ρ represent values of program variables v_i at program point ρ.

The second challenge is that query formulas presented to the user may be arbitrary boolean combinations of program expressions. Since it is unrealistic to expect programmers not well-versed in logic to easily reason about complicated boolean expressions, we need to decompose queries with complex boolean structure to a series of simpler queries. To achieve this goal, we observe that invariant queries distribute over conjuncts, while witness queries distribute over disjuncts. More specifically, if $\phi_1 \wedge \phi_2$ is an invariant, it is necessary that ϕ_1 and ϕ_2 are independently also invariants. Similarly, if $\phi_1 \vee \phi_2$ is a witness, it is necessary that ϕ_1 is possible in some execution or ϕ_2 is possible in some execution. Thus, we first convert invariant queries to conjunctive normal form (CNF) and treat each clause as a separate, independent query. Dually, we convert witness queries to disjunctive normal form (DNF) and reason about each clause independently.

We also further decompose clauses into simpler queries. For witness queries, observe that if ϕ_1 and ϕ_2 are individually witnesses, this does not mean $\phi_1 \wedge \phi_2$ is also a witness, since ϕ_1 and ϕ_2 may be possible in distinct executions, but never possible in the same execution. In this case, we decompose a conjunct $\phi_1 \wedge \phi_2$ by first querying whether ϕ_1 is possible in some execution and then ask whether ϕ_2 is also possible in an execution where ϕ_1 holds.

For invariant queries, clauses contain disjunctions, which humans typically find difficult to reason about. Thus, for an invariant query $\phi_1 \vee \phi_2$, we first ask whether either ϕ_1 or ϕ_2 are independently invariants, which is often the case. In cases where a truly disjunctive invariant is required, observe that for $\phi_1 \vee \phi_2$ to be an invariant, $\neg\phi_1 \wedge \neg\phi_2$ should *not* be a witness. Thus, to avoid disjunctions, we convert the invariant query $\phi_1 \vee \phi_2$ into the witness query $\neg\phi_1 \wedge \neg\phi_2$ and use the same technique described in the previous paragraph to decompose conjunctive witness queries.

In addition to making queries more understandable, decomposing queries into simpler, independent subqueries also has another advantage: We can learn additional facts for every subquery even when the entire query may not be shown. For example, although $\phi_1 \wedge \phi_2$ is not an invariant, ϕ_1 could still be an invariant. It is easy to integrate this additional information learned from subqueries into the algorithm, and our implementation uses this optimization.

5. Implementation

We have implemented the proposed technique on top of the Compass analysis framework for C programs [5–7]. While the simple language from Section 2 contains only integer variables and no function calls, our implementation extends the technique to deal with other features of the C language supported in Compass, such as pointers, arrays, and function calls. In particular, Compass reasons about heap objects and arrays using the techniques described in [5, 6] and uses a summary-based technique for interprocedural analysis [7]. Besides imprecise loop invariants, Compass also has other sources of imprecision, such as non-linear arithmetic or inline assembly, which are also modeled using abstraction variables. In addition, side effects of library functions that we choose not to analyze or whose source code is unavailable are also modeled using abstraction variables.

In the algorithm from Section 4.3, we require users to give only yes/no answers to queries, but, in practice, this requirement is unrealistic, as programmers cannot always answer a query. Thus, we allow users to answer "I don't know" and extend the algorithm

				Manual classification				New technique			
	LOC	Kind	Classification	% correct	% wrong	% ?	Avg. time	% correct	% wrong	% ?	Avg. time
Problem 1	88	synthetic	false alarm	43.5 %	34.8 %	21.7%	297 s	92.3 %	3.9%	3.9 %	57 s
Problem 2	352	real	false alarm	30.8 %	50.0 %	19.2 %	269 s	87.0 %	8.7%	4.4 %	40 s
Problem 3	66	synthetic	false alarm	46.2 %	38.5 %	15.4 %	266 s	79.2 %	20.8%	0.0%	58 s
Problem 4	278	real	real bug	37.5 %	45.8 %	16.7 %	265 s	92.3 %	7.7 %	0.0%	53 s
Problem 5	363	real	false alarm	32.0 %	48.0 %	20.0 %	289 s	100.0 %	0.0 %	0.0 %	46 s
Problem 6	173	real	false alarm	25.0%	54.2 %	20.8%	339 s	92.0 %	8.0 %	0.0 %	54 s
Problem 7	326	real	real bug	40.0 %	56.0 %	4.0%	233 s	79.2 %	8.3 %	12.5 %	55 s
Problem 8	97	synthetic	false alarm	16.7 %	70.8 %	12.5 %	271 s	92.0%	8.0%	0.0%	58 s
Problem 9	116	synthetic	real bug	25.0 %	58.3 %	16.7 %	308 s	92.0 %	4.0%	4.0%	62 s
Problem 10	72	synthetic	real bug	24.0 %	60.0 %	16.0 %	455 s	95.8 %	4.2%	0.0 %	68 s
Problem 11	118	synthetic	real bug	41.7 %	45.8%	12.5%	235 s	84.0 %	16.0%	0.0%	50 s
Average	186	n/a	n/a	32.9 %	51.1 %	16.0 %	293 s	89.6 %	7.3 %	2.3 %	55 s

Figure 7. Results from our user study

from Section 4.3 to deal with such uncertainty. Specifically, our algorithm maintains a set of *potential witnesses* and *potential invariants*. If Γ is an invariant query that the user cannot answer, we add Γ as a potential invariant and $\neg\Gamma$ as a potential witness. Similarly, if Υ is a witness query that the user cannot decide, we add Υ as a potential witness and $\neg\Upsilon$ as a potential invariant. To avoid repeating the same queries, these potential witnesses and invariants are taken into account when computing minimum satisfying assignments: Minimum satisfying assignments in the proof obligation case must be consistent with potential invariants and witnesses, while the minimum satisfying assignments for the witness case must be consistent with potential invariants.

Our technique utilizes minimum satisfying assignments for computing abductions, but no off-the-shelf SMT solver we know of provides this functionality. Thus, we have integrated the required functionality for providing minimum satisfying assignments into our own Mistral SMT solver; the algorithm we implemented for this purpose is described in [3].

6. Experiments

To evaluate the proposed technique, we performed a user study in which we asked professional programmers to classify error reports as genuine bugs or false alarms. Our study consists of 11 problems, five of which are code fragments taken directly or slightly modified from real open source C programs (e.g., Unix coreutils, OpenSSH), and six of which are benchmarks from our program analysis test suite. These benchmarks are available from http://www.cs.wm.edu/~tdillig/pldi12-benchmarks.tar.gz. All benchmarks contain between 66-363 lines of code and one assertion. For examples drawn from real applications, we only included those parts of the code that are relevant to deciding the validity of the assertion (i.e., a manual slice). Five of our benchmark problems contain real errors while the remaining six are error-free. The analysis we performed initially reports potential, but not certain, errors on all eleven benchmarks. The causes of these uncertain error reports are diverse, including imprecise loop invariants, missing annotations on library functions, non-linear arithmetic, and missing facts about the program's execution environment (e.g., relationship between `argc` and `argv`).

For a given problem, each participant was randomly assigned to classify an error report either manually or using the proposed technique. Therefore, each participant classified approximately half the benchmarks manually and half of them using the new technique. In the manual classification case, the participants were asked to decide whether the report is a false alarm, a real bug, or whether they cannot decide. When using our new technique, the participants were asked to give a "Yes", "No", or "I don't know" answer to a series of questions generated by our tool, ranging from one to three questions on these benchmarks. The time for query computation is negligible; in all cases, the computation time is below 0.1s.

For our user study, we recruited 56 professional programmers through ODesk and paid them $40 each for participating in the study. Each participant was required to have at least one year of C programming experience and to have ODesk's "systems programming certification". In addition to our eleven benchmark problems, the study also included three simple diagnostic questions that were not identified as such to the participants. We excluded participants who gave the wrong answer to any of the diagnostic questions, resulting in 49 valid participants for our study. Thus, each benchmark problem was classified manually by about 24 people and classified using our technique by approximately the same number of people.

Figure 7 summarizes the results of our user study. The first three columns in the table give details about each benchmark. The column labeled "LOC" gives the lines of code presented to participants; the column "Kind" identifies whether the benchmark is taken from a real application or from our program analysis test suite (i.e., synthetic). Finally, the column "Classification" indicates the correct classification of the report (false alarm or real bug).

The next four columns in the table ("Manual classification") give statistics about accuracy and speed of manual classification. The column "% correct" indicates the percentage of participants who correctly classified the report; the column "% wrong" gives the percentage of participants who chose the wrong classification. The column labeled "% ?" gives the percentage of participants who answered "I don't know". Finally, the column "Avg. time" shows the average time participants took to classify the report.

The next four columns in the table (marked "New Technique") give the same statistics about accuracy of classification and timing using the new technique presented in this paper.

As the results in Figure 7 demonstrate, the average accuracy of manual report classification is surprisingly low: On average, 32.9% of the participants are able to classify an error report correctly, while 51.1% of the participants incorrectly classify a real bug as a false alarm or a false alarm as a real bug. Also, observe that 16% of participants are unable to classify the error report despite spending significant time. (Our instructions specifically mentioned that participants should only choose "I don't know" after spending at least 8 minutes on each benchmark.) Finally, observe that programmers take an average of approximately 5 minutes to manually classify error reports despite the fact that their classification is often wrong.

These results indicate that manual classification is extremely unreliable and time-consuming even on our small benchmark examples. In fact, the group of programmers who participated in our study do not seem to outperform randomly assigning a classification to each report. We believe this is strong evidence that the usefulness of static analysis techniques can be greatly improved by assisting programmers in classifying and understanding error reports.

As the results in Figure 7 also demonstrate, the accuracy and speed of report classification dramatically improve when programmers use our new technique. While only 32.9% of participants correctly classify an error report using manual classification, 89.6% of participants give the correct answer using our technique. Similarly, the percentage of participants who give the wrong answer drops from 51.1% to 7.3%. In addition to dramatically improving classification accuracy, our technique also substantially reduces the time programmers need to classify reports: The average classification time drops from approximately 5 minutes to under 1 minute.

As standard in user studies, we performed a t-test to evaluate the statistical significance of our results. The p-value of a two-tailed t-test (assuming potentially unequal variance) comparing manual classification accuracy vs. our technique is 5×10^{-8}. This means the probability that our technique has no influence on classification accuracy is less than 1 in 10,000,000. Similarly, the p-value for a t-test comparing classification times is 1.2×10^{-28}, indicating our results are statistically significant.

To give the reader a flavor of how our technique makes report classification much easier, we briefly describe the reasoning required to classify Problem 6, based on the `chroot` utility from the Unix coreutils. In this program, the value of variable `optind` is correlated with four different return values of function `getopt_long`. To prove the assertion in this example, we have to remember all four return values of `getopt_long` along with the intricate path conditions associated with each of these return points and mentally evaluate several conditionals, all of which are relevant to proving the assertion. In fact, an author of this submission spent approximately half an hour to decide that the report is indeed a false alarm. In contrast, if we use the technique proposed in this paper, the user only needs to answer one simple query asking whether the value of `optind` is always greater than zero after a `while` loop. This query is easy to decide by inspecting only three lines of code immediately preceding the program point associated with the query.

7. Related Work

Explaining Error Traces in Model Checking Several papers focus on explaining error traces identified by model checkers [8–13]. Ball et al. describe an algorithm for localizing the likely cause of an error given a trace produced by a model checker [8]. Groce et al. present an error localization technique that computes the minimum distance between an error trace and a successful execution [9]. Ravi and Somenzi present an algorithm for giving succinct explanations for error traces, and like our technique, they employ minimum satisfying assignments to derive these explanations [13]. Jose and Majumdar give an algorithm for fault localization using maximum satisfiability [10]. This technique computes the maximum satisfiable set of clauses in an extended trace formula, and the complement of this set is identified as a potential cause of the error. In this work, we share the goal of making error reports easier to understand for programmers. However, our technique does not require a counterexample produced by model checkers and can be gainfully combined with any static analysis. Furthermore, our technique is useful for classifying and understanding false alarms, which are not addressed by these techniques.

Counterexample-Guided Abstraction Refinement (CEGAR) Our technique is similar to CEGAR in that both approaches infer relevant conditions that are useful for eliminating false alarms [14–16]. The main difference is that CEGAR-based approaches learn new predicates from one concrete counterexample trace. Thus, while the learned predicate may be sufficient to prevent this *particular* counterexample trace, it may not be sufficient to eliminate other spurious traces reaching the same error. In contrast, proof obligations we compute are, if valid, guaranteed to rule out the false alarm entirely. Furthermore, while CEGAR-based approaches have the advantage of being fully automatic and not requiring assistance from the user, they are not guaranteed to terminate.

Techniques for Error Report Understanding Manevich at al. present a post-mortem backwards dataflow analysis for constructing failing execution traces from a failure point [17]. This technique can sometimes show that the report is a false alarm. Le and Soffa describe a fault correlation technique that can be helpful for diagnosing error reports [18]. Their technique groups error reports according to their root cause, which may aid in understanding these reports. The approach of [19] computes a *patch*, which is a modified version of the program not containing the error, and this patch is included in the bug report. While these techniques may sometimes be insightful for understanding a report, they do not allow the classification of an error report as a real bug or false alarm.

Program slicing [20–22] is useful for identifying statements in the source code that may be relevant to the potential failure. However, program slices are typically large and do not take advantage of facts already shown by the analysis. Unlike our technique, a slice also does not provide any semantic clues about whether the report corresponds to a genuine bug or false alarm.

Explaining Type Errors There has been much work on explaining errors that arise in type inference [23–26]. Since errors during polymorphic type checking result from unification failure, the location associated with a report is often not useful for understanding its cause. The techniques of [23–25] augment type inference with information useful for explaining the chain of inferences that led to the error. The algorithm described in [26] does not modify the original compiler, but searches for a program close to the original one that does type check. We share the goal of making static reasoning transparent to users; however, the afore-mentioned approaches specialize in explaining type inference errors while our technique assists users in classifying reports generated by verification tools.

Combining May and Must Information There has been recent work on combining may and must information to prove both the presence and absence of errors. Must information has been harvested both from dynamic analysis [27–29] and computed purely statically [30]. While these approaches are useful for showing the presence of errors, they do not help when errors can neither be discharged nor proven, which is our focus. However, we believe must information obtained from dynamic analysis could be useful for automatically deciding some of our failure witness queries.

8. Conclusion and Future Work

We have presented a new technique for assisting users with classifying error reports generated by static analyses. Our technique can be gainfully combined with any static analysis to make their results more understandable for users. We have evaluated this technique with a user study; our results indicate that the new technique improves both the time and accuracy of report classification.

We believe that the approach described in this paper can be further improved by making use of underapproximations. In particular, the analysis described in Section 3 can only prove the program is buggy if $\mathcal{I} \models \neg\phi$. However, since $\mathcal{I}$ is an invariant (i.e., an overapproximation of program behavior), $\mathcal{I} \models \neg\phi$ indicates that every execution of the program must be buggy. By making use of underapproximations obtained through static or dynamic techniques, the analysis can prove that *some* executions of the program must be buggy without requiring the user's help. We believe dynamic analysis could also be very useful for automatically discharging some of the failure witness queries.

References

[1] Bessey, A., Block, K., Chelf, B., Chou, A., Fulton, B., Hallem, S., Henri-Gros, C., Kamsky, A., McPeak, S., Engler, D.: A few billion lines of code later: using static analysis to find bugs in the real world. Communications of the ACM **53**(2) (2010) 66–75

[2] Dillig, I., Dillig, T., Aiken, A.: Automated error diagnosis using abductive inference (extended version). http://www.cs.wm.edu/~idillig/pldi12-extended.pdf

[3] Dillig, I., Dillig, T., McMillan, K., Aiken, A.: Minimum satisfying assignments for SMT. In: To appear in CAV. (2012)

[4] Dillig, I., Dillig, T., Aiken, A.: Small formulas for large programs: On-line constraint simplification in scalable static analysis. Static Analysis Symposium (SAS) (2010) 236–252

[5] Dillig, I., Dillig, T., Aiken, A.: Fluid updates: Beyond strong vs. weak updates. ESOP (2010) 246–266

[6] Dillig, I., Dillig, T., Aiken, A.: Precise reasoning for programs using containers. POPL (2011) 187–200

[7] Dillig, I., Dillig, T., Aiken, A., Sagiv, M.: Precise and compact modular procedure summaries for heap manipulating programs. In: PLDI. (2011) 567–577

[8] Ball, T., Naik, M., Rajamani, S.: From symptom to cause: localizing errors in counterexample traces. POPL **38**(1) (2003) 97–105

[9] Groce, A.: Error explanation with distance metrics. TACAS (2004) 108–122

[10] Jose, M., Majumdar, R.: Cause clue clauses: error localization using maximum satisfiability. In: PLDI, ACM (2011) 437–446

[11] Griesmayer, A., Staber, S., Bloem, R.: Automated fault localization for c programs. Theoretical Computer Science **174**(4) (2007) 95–111

[12] Renieres, M., Reiss, S.: Fault localization with nearest neighbor queries. In: ASE. (2003) 30–39

[13] Ravi, K., Somenzi, F.: Minimal assignments for bounded model checking. TACAS (2004) 31–45

[14] Henzinger, T., Jhala, R., Majumdar, R., Sutre, G.: Software verification with blast. Model Checking Software (2003) 624–624

[15] Ball, T., Rajamani, S.: The SLAM project: debugging system software via static analysis. In: POPL, NY, USA (2002) 1–3

[16] Henzinger, T., Jhala, R., Majumdar, R., McMillan, K.: Abstractions from proofs. POPL **39**(1) (2004) 232–244

[17] Manevich, R., Sridharan, M., Adams, S., Das, M., Yang, Z.: PSE: explaining program failures via postmortem static analysis. In: FSE. Volume 29., ACM (2004) 63–72

[18] Le, W., Soffa, M.: Path-based fault correlations. In: FSE. (2010) 307–316

[19] Weimer, W.: Patches as better bug reports. In: GPCE. (2006) 181–190

[20] Weiser, M.: Program slicing. In: ICSE, IEEE Press (1981) 439–449

[21] Korel, B., Laski, J.: Dynamic program slicing. Information Processing Letters **29**(3) (1988) 155–163

[22] Sridharan, M., Fink, S., Bodik, R.: Thin slicing. In: PLDI, ACM (2007) 112–122

[23] Beaven, M., Stansifer, R.: Explaining type errors in polymorphic languages. LOPLAS **2**(1-4) (1993) 17–30

[24] Haack, C., Wells, J.: Type error slicing in implicitly typed higher-order languages. Programming Languages and Systems (2003) 284–301

[25] Yang, J.: Explaining type errors by finding the source of a type conflict. Trends in Functional Programming (1999) 49–57

[26] Lerner, B., Flower, M., Grossman, D., Chambers, C.: Searching for type-error messages. In: PLDI, ACM (2007) 425–434

[27] Nori, A., Rajamani, S., Tetali, S., Thakur, A.: The yogi project: Software property checking via static analysis and testing. TACAS (2009) 178–181

[28] Godefroid, P., Nori, A., Rajamani, S., Tetali, S.: Compositional may-must program analysis: unleashing the power of alternation. In: POPL. Volume 45., ACM (2010) 43–56

[29] Yorsh, G., Ball, T., Sagiv, M.: Testing, abstraction, theorem proving: better together! In: ISSTA, ACM (2006) 145–156

[30] Dillig, I., Dillig, T., Aiken, A.: Sound, complete and scalable path-sensitive analysis. In: PLDI, ACM (2008) 270–280

Efficient State Merging in Symbolic Execution

Volodymyr Kuznetsov Johannes Kinder Stefan Bucur George Candea
School of Computer and Communication Sciences
École Polytechnique Fédérale de Lausanne (EPFL), Switzerland
{vova.kuznetsov,johannes.kinder,stefan.bucur,george.candea}@epfl.ch

Abstract

Symbolic execution has proven to be a practical technique for building automated test case generation and bug finding tools. Nevertheless, due to state explosion, these tools still struggle to achieve scalability. Given a program, one way to reduce the number of states that the tools need to explore is to merge states obtained on different paths. Alas, doing so increases the size of symbolic path conditions (thereby stressing the underlying constraint solver) and interferes with optimizations of the exploration process (also referred to as search strategies). The net effect is that state merging may actually lower performance rather than increase it.

We present a way to automatically choose when and how to merge states such that the performance of symbolic execution is significantly increased. First, we present *query count estimation*, a method for statically estimating the impact that each symbolic variable has on solver queries that follow a potential merge point; states are then merged only when doing so promises to be advantageous. Second, we present *dynamic state merging*, a technique for merging states that interacts favorably with search strategies in automated test case generation and bug finding tools.

Experiments on the 96 GNU COREUTILS show that our approach consistently achieves several orders of magnitude speedup over previously published results. Our code and experimental data are publicly available at `http://cloud9.epfl.ch`.

Categories and Subject Descriptors D.2.4 [*Software Engineering*]: Software/Program Verification; D.2.5 [*Software Engineering*]: Testing and Debugging – Symbolic Execution, Testing Tools; F.3.1 [*Logics and Meanings of Programs*]: Specifying and Verifying and Reasoning about Programs

Keywords Testing, Symbolic Execution, Verification, Bounded Software Model Checking, State Merging

1. Introduction

Recent tools [5–7, 18, 19] have applied symbolic execution to automated test case generation and bug finding with impressive results—they demonstrate that symbolic execution brings unique practical advantages. First, such tools perform dynamic analysis, in that they actually execute a target program and can directly execute any calls to external libraries or the operating system by concretizing arguments; this broadens their applicability to many real-world programs. Second, these tools share with static analysis the ability to simultaneously reason about multiple program behaviors, which improves the degree of completeness they achieve. Third, symbolic execution does not use abstraction but is fully precise with respect to predicate transformer semantics [11]; it generates "per-path verification conditions" whose satisfiability implies the reachability of a particular statement, so it generally does not have false positives. Fourth, recent advances in SAT and SMT (SAT Modulo Theory) solving [10, 12, 15] have made tools based on symbolic execution significantly faster. Overall, symbolic execution promises to help solve many important, practical program analysis problems.

Nevertheless, today's symbolic execution engines still struggle to achieve scalability, because of path explosion: the number of possible paths in a program is generally exponential in its size. States in symbolic execution encode the history of branch decisions (the *path condition*) and precisely characterize the value of each variable in terms of input values (the *symbolic store*), so path explosion becomes synonymous with state explosion. Alas, the benefit of not having false positives in bug finding (save for over-approximate environment assumptions) comes at the cost of having to analyze an exponential number of states.

One way to reduce the number of states is to merge states that correspond to different paths. This is standard in classic static analysis, where the resulting merged state over-approximates the individual states that were merged. Several techniques, such as ESP [9] and trace partitioning [27], reduce but do not eliminate the resulting imprecision (which can be a source of false positives) by associating separate abstract domain elements to some sets of execution paths. In symbolic execution, as a matter of principle, a merged state would have to precisely represent the information from *all* execution paths *without any* over-approximation. Consider, for example, the program *if (x<0) {x=0;} else {x=5;}* with input X assigned to x. We denote with (pc, s) a state that is reachable for inputs obeying path condition pc and in which the symbolic store $s = [v_0 = e_0, \ldots, v_n = e_n]$ maps variable v_i to expression e_i, respectively. In this case, the two states $(X < 0, [x = 0])$ and $(X \geq 0, [x = 5])$, which correspond to the two feasible paths, can be merged into one state $(\text{true}, [x = \text{ite}(X < 0, 0, 5)])$. Here, $\text{ite}(c, p, q)$ denotes the if-then-else operator that evaluates to p if c is true, and to q otherwise. If states were merged this way for every branch of a program, symbolic execution would become similar to verification condition generation or bounded model checking, where the entire problem instance is encoded in one monolithic formula that is passed in full to a solver.

State merging effectively decreases the number of paths that have to be explored [16, 20], but also increases the size of the symbolic expressions describing variables. Merging introduces disjunctions, which are notoriously difficult for SMT solvers, particularly for those using eager translation to SAT [15]. Merging also converts differing concrete values into symbolic expressions, as in the example above: the value of x was concrete in the two separate states, but symbolic $(\text{ite}(X < 0, 0, 5))$ in the merged state. If x were to ap-

PLDI'12, June 11–16, Beijing, China.

pear in branch conditions or array indices later in the execution, the choice of merging the states may lead to more solver invocations than without merging. This combination of larger symbolic expressions and extra solver invocations can drown out the benefit of having fewer states to analyze, leading to an actual *decrease* in the overall performance of symbolic execution [20].

Furthermore, state merging conflicts with important optimizations in symbolic execution: search-based symbolic execution engines, like the ones used in test case generators and bug finding tools, employ *search strategies* to prioritize searching of "interesting" paths over "less interesting" ones, e.g., with respect to maximizing line coverage given a fixed time budget. To maximize the opportunities for state merging, however, the engine would have to traverse the control flow graph in topological order, which typically contradicts the strategy's path prioritization policy.

Contributions. In this paper, we describe a solution to these two challenges that yields a net benefit in practice. We combine the state space reduction benefits of merged exploration with the constraint solving benefits of individual exploration, while mitigating the ensuing drawbacks. Experiments on the GNU COREUTILS show that employing our approach in a symbolic execution engine achieves speedups over the state of the art that are exponential in the size of symbolic input. Our contributions are:

- We present *query count estimation*, a way to statically approximate the number of times each variable will appear in future solver queries after a potential merge point. We then selectively merge two states only when we expect differing variables to appear infrequently in later solver queries. Since this selective merging merely groups paths instead of pruning them, inaccuracies in the estimation do not hurt soundness or completeness.
- We present *dynamic state merging*, a merging algorithm specifically designed to interact favorably with search strategies. The algorithm explores paths independently of each other and uses a similarity metric to identify on-the-fly opportunities for merging, while preserving the search strategy's privilege of dictating exploration priorities.

Organization. In §2, we characterize the design space of precise symbolic analysis using a generic algorithm. With bounded model checking on one end of the spectrum and symbolic execution on the other, we analyze middle-ground approaches (such as function summaries [16]) and argue for an opportunistic, dynamic approach to navigating this design space based on cost estimates. In this context, we introduce query count estimation (§3) and dynamic state merging (§4). We then describe our implementation in the KLEE symbolic execution engine and present a systematic evaluation of the individual and combined effects of the two proposed methods (§5). We review related work in §6 and conclude with §7.

2. Trade-offs in Symbolic Program Analysis

Test generation by symbolic execution is just one of a multitude of precise symbolic program analyses that are facilitated by SAT or SMT solvers. Tools such as CBMC [8], Saturn [31], and Calysto [2] have shown that exact, abstraction-free path sensitive local reasoning is feasible and can be fully outsourced to an external solver. With the help of a generic worklist algorithm (§2.1), we illustrate the relationship among precise symbolic program analyses and explain the trade-offs in the resulting solver queries (§2.2). We conclude that state merging critically affects all types of precise symbolic program analysis. Motivated by this insight, we give a brief overview of our proposed approach to state merging (§2.3).

2.1 General Symbolic Exploration

Precise symbolic program analyses essentially perform forward expression substitution starting from a set of input variables. The resulting formulae are then used to falsify assertions and find bugs, or to generate input assignments and generate test cases. Algorithm 1 is a generic algorithm for symbolic program analysis that can be used to implement different analysis flavors. For illustration purposes, we consider only a simple input language with assignments, conditional goto statements, assertions, and halt statements.

Input: Choice function *pickNext*, similarity relation $\sim$, branch checker *follow*, and initial location ℓ_0.
Data: Worklist w and set of successor states S.

1 $w := \{(\ell_0, \text{true}, \lambda v.v)\}$;
2 **while** $w \neq \varnothing$ **do**
3 $\quad (\ell, pc, s) := pickNext(w)$; $S := \varnothing$;
$\quad$ // Symbolically execute the next instruction
4 $\quad$ **switch** $instr(\ell)$ **do**
5 $\quad\quad$ **case** $v := e$ // assignment
6 $\quad\quad\quad S := \{(succ(\ell), pc, s[v \mapsto \textbf{eval}(s,e)])\}$;
7 $\quad\quad$ **case** $\mathsf{if}(e)\ \mathsf{goto}\ \ell'$ // conditional jump
8 $\quad\quad\quad$ **if** $follow(pc \wedge s \wedge e)$ **then**
9 $\quad\quad\quad\quad S := \{(\ell', pc \wedge e, s)\}$;
10 $\quad\quad\quad$ **if** $follow(pc \wedge s \wedge \neg e)$ **then**
11 $\quad\quad\quad\quad S := S \cup \{(succ(\ell), pc \wedge \neg e, s)\}$;
12 $\quad\quad$ **case** $\mathsf{assert}(e)$ // assertion
13 $\quad\quad\quad$ **if** $isSatisfiable(pc \wedge s \wedge \neg e)$ **then** abort;
14 $\quad\quad\quad$ **else** $S := \{(succ(\ell), pc, s)\}$;
15 $\quad\quad$ **case** halt // program halt
16 $\quad\quad\quad$ **print** pc;
$\quad$ // Merge new states with matching ones in w
17 $\quad$ **forall** $(\ell'', pc', s') \in S$ **do**
18 $\quad\quad$ **if** $\exists (\ell'', pc'', s'') \in w : (\ell'', pc'', s'') \sim (\ell'', pc', s')$ **then**
19 $\quad\quad\quad w := w \setminus \{(\ell'', pc'', s'')\}$;
20 $\quad\quad\quad w := w \cup \{(\ell'', pc' \vee pc'', \lambda v.\text{ite}(pc', s'[v], s''[v]))\}$;
21 $\quad\quad$ **else**
22 $\quad\quad\quad w := w \cup \{(\ell'', pc', s')\}$;
23 **print** "no errors";

Algorithm 1. Generic symbolic exploration.

The algorithm is parameterized by a function *pickNext* for choosing the next state in the worklist, a function *follow* that returns a decision on whether to follow a branch, and a relation $\sim$ that controls whether states should be merged. We now extend the notation for states used in §1 to triples (ℓ, pc, s), consisting of a program location ℓ, the path condition pc, and the symbolic store s that maps each variable to either a concrete value or an expression over input variables. In line 1, the worklist w of the algorithm is initialized with a state whose symbolic store maps each variable to itself (for simplicity, we exclude named constants). Here, $\lambda x.e$ denotes the function mapping parameter x to an expression e (we will use $\lambda(x_1, \ldots x_n).e$ for multiple parameters). In each iteration, the algorithm picks a new state from the worklist (line 3).

On encountering an assignment $v := e$ (lines 5-6), the algorithm creates a successor state at the fall-through successor location $succ(\ell)$ of ℓ by updating the symbolic store s with a mapping from v to a new symbolic expression obtained by evaluating e in the context of s, and adds the new state to the set S. At every branch (lines 7-11), the algorithm first checks whether to follow either path and, if so, adds the corresponding condition to the successor state, which in turn is added to S. Analyses can decide to not follow a branch if the branch is infeasible or would exceed a limit on loop unrolling. For assertions (line 12-14), the path condition, the symbolic store, and the negated assertion are put in conjunction and checked for satisfiability. Since the algorithm does not over-approximate, this check has no false positives. Halt statements terminate the analyzed program, so the algorithm just outputs the path condition, a satisfying assignment of which can be used to generate a test case for the execution leading to the halt.

In lines 17-22, the new states in S are then merged with any matching states in the worklist before being added to the worklist themselves. Two states match if they share the same location and are similar according to $\sim$. Merging creates a disjunction of the two path conditions (which can be simplified by factoring out common prefixes) and builds the merged symbolic store from ite expressions that assert one or the other original value, depending on the path taken (line 20). The ite expressions that assert an identical value in both cases (because it was equal in both symbolic stores) can be simplified to that value.

2.2 The Design Space of Symbolic Program Analysis

The differences between various implementations of precise symbolic analysis lie in the following aspects:

1. the handling of loops and/or recursion;
2. whether and how the feasibility of individual branches is checked to avoid encoding infeasible paths;
3. whether and how states from different paths are merged;
4. compositionality, i.e., the use of function summaries.

Loops affect soundness and completeness, while the other aspects are trade-offs that critically affect analysis performance. We now illustrate these different aspects using Algorithm 1.

Loops and Recursion. Bounded model checkers [8] and extended static checkers [2, 13, 31] unroll loops up to a certain bound, which can be iteratively increased if an injected unwinding assertion fails. Such unrolling is usually performed by statically rewriting the CFG, but can be fit into Algorithm 1 by defining *follow* to return false for branches that would unroll a loop beyond the bound. Symbolic execution explores loops as long as it cannot prove the infeasibility of the loop condition. A search strategy, implemented in the function *pickNext*, can bias the analysis against states that perform many repetitions of the same loop. For example, a search strategy optimized for line coverage selects states close to unexplored code and avoids states in deep loop unrollings [6].

Dynamic test generation as implemented in DART [18] starts with an arbitrary initial unrolling of the loop and explores different unrollings in subsequent tests. That is, DART implements *pickNext* to follow concrete executions, postponing branch alternatives until they are covered by a subsequent concrete execution.

All these approaches essentially perform loop unrolling and are generally incomplete for finite analysis times. Loop invariants are rarely used (though [17] is an exception) since weak invariants can introduce false positives, which these precise analyses are specifically designed to avoid. Weakest precondition-based program verification engines such as Boogie [26] and Havoc [24], which also interface with external solvers, rely on the user to supply sufficiently strong invariants for proving all properties of interest.

Feasibility Checking. While performing expression substitution along individual paths, certain combinations of conditional branches can turn out to be infeasible. Not propagating states that represent infeasible paths helps to reduce path explosion by investing solving time earlier in the execution. Intermediate feasibility checks are usually performed only by symbolic execution engines that follow a single path at a time (when reasoning about groups of paths, branches are less likely to be infeasible), in which case *follow* simply invokes the constraint solver.

State Merging. When states meet at the same control location, there are two general possibilities for combining their information: either the states are maintained separately, or the states are merged into a single state. In precise symbolic analysis, merging is not allowed to introduce abstraction. From a conceptual viewpoint, state merging therefore only changes the shape of a formula that characterizes a set of execution paths: if states are kept separate, a set of paths is described by their disjunction; if states are merged, there is only one formula with disjunctions in the path condition and ite expressions in the symbolic store that guard the values of the variables depending on the path taken.

In general, we distinguish two extremes: (i) complete separation of paths, as implemented by *search-based symbolic execution* (e.g., [4–6, 18, 19, 23]), and (ii) complete *static state merging*, as implemented by verification condition generators (e.g., [2, 8, 21, 31]). Static state merging combines states at join points after completely encoding all subpaths, i.e., it defines *pickNext* to explore all subpaths leading to a join point before picking any states at the join point, and it defines $\sim$ to contain all pairs of states. In search-based symbolic execution engines, *pickNext* can be chosen freely according to the search goal, and $\sim$ is empty. Thus, they can, for example, choose to explore just the successors of a specific state and delay exploration of additional loop iterations.

Some approaches adopt intermediate merging strategies. In the context of bounded model checking (BMC), Ganai and Gupta [14] investigate splitting the verification condition along subsets of paths. This moves BMC a step into the direction of symbolic execution, and corresponds to partitioning the $\sim$ relation. Hansen et al. [20] describe an implementation of static state merging in which they modify the exploration strategy to effectively traverse the CFG in topological order and merge all states that share the same program location. For two of their three tested examples, the total solving time increases with this strategy thus showing this approach to be sub-optimal. Another prominent example of state merging is the use of function summaries in symbolic execution, which we explain below.

Compositionality. For precise interprocedural symbolic execution, the simplest and most common approach is function inlining. This causes functions to be re-analyzed at every call site, which could be avoided using function summaries. Summaries that do not introduce abstraction and are thus suitable for symbolic execution can be implemented by computing an intraprocedural path condition in terms of function inputs, and then merging all states at the function exit.

Alas, applying such a function summary is essentially as expensive as re-analyzing the function, if the translation effort from the programming logic into the representation logic is negligible. Using a summary instead of inlining avoids only the feasibility checks for intraprocedural paths that are infeasible regardless of the function input. The cost of the other feasibility checks that a non-compositional symbolic execution would perform is not eliminated by function summaries. Instead, the branch conditions are contained in the ite expressions of the summary and will increase the complexity of later SMT queries.

For dynamic test generation, Godefroid [16] suggests to collect summaries as disjunctions of pairs of input and output constraints. In further work [1], this is extended to record summaries one path at a time and to apply partial summaries whenever they match the input preconditions. Dynamic test generation re-executes the full program (with heavy instrumentation) for each branch of which the alternate case is to be analyzed. Due to re-execution, analyzing all branches in functions would come at an especially high cost, so the savings outweigh the additional solving costs for the merged summary states.

For simplicity, Algorithm 1 is just intraprocedural, supporting function calls by inlining. It can generate precise symbolic function summaries, if invoked per procedure and with a similarity relation that merges all states when the function terminates.

2.3 Our Approach: Dynamically Navigate the Design Space

Precise symbolic analyses are roughly equivalent in their treatment of loops, but all other design choices (merging at control points, feasibility checking, and function summaries) boil down to choosing which paths to analyze separately vs. which ones to combine into common formulae. In other words, all analyses lie along a spectrum, with search-based symbolic execution (no state merging) at one extreme and whole-program verification condition generation (static state merging) at the other extreme. Instead of making a static design choice of where to be in this spectrum, our approach is to enable a symbolic analysis to choose dynamically the most advantageous point and merge states according to the expected benefit of such a merge.

On the one hand, merging reduces the number of states, but on the other hand, the remaining states become more expensive to explore. In the merged state, each variable that had distinct values in the original states must be constrained by an input-dependent ite expression, which increases the time required to solve future queries involving such variables. If the distinct values were concrete, merging would cause additional solver invocations where expressions could have been evaluated concretely in separate states.

Furthermore, there is an inherent incompatibility between partial searches using coverage-guided search strategies (as is often done in test generation) and static state merging at control flow join points: merging can be maximized by exploring the CFG in topological order, so that a combined state can be computed from its syntactic predecessors. A coverage-guided search strategy, however, will dynamically deprioritize some states (e.g., defer for later the exploration of additional iterations of a loop), which prevents using a topological order.

Therefore, to make state merging practical, we must solve two problems: (1) Automatically identify an advantageous balance between exploring fewer complex states vs. more simpler states, and merge states only when this promises to reduce exploration time; and (2) Efficiently combine state merging with search strategies that deprioritize "non-interesting" execution paths.

To solve the first problem, we developed *query count estimation* (QCE), a way to estimate how variables that are different in two potentially mergeable states will be used in the future. We preprocess the program using a lightweight static analysis to identify how often each variable is used in branch conditions past any given point in the CFG, and use this as a heuristic estimate of how many subsequent solver queries that variable is likely to be part of. Using this heuristic, we check whether two states are sufficiently similar that merging them would yield a net benefit. That is, the additional cost of solving more and harder SMT queries is outweighed by the savings from exploring fewer paths. The results of this static analysis affect only the completion time of the symbolic analysis—not its soundness or completeness.

To solve the second problem, we introduce *dynamic state merging* (DSM), a way to dynamically identify opportunities for merging regardless of the exploration order imposed by the search strategy. Without any restrictions on the search strategy, only states that meet at the same location by chance could ever be merged. To increase the opportunities for merging, we maintain a bounded history of the predecessors of the states in the worklist. When picking the next state to process from the worklist, we check whether some state a_1 is similar to a predecessor a_2' of another state a_2 in the worklist. If yes, then state a_1, which is in some sense lagging behind a_2, is prioritized over the others. This causes it to be temporarily *fast-forwarded*, until its own successor matches up with the candidate-for-merging state a_2. If the state diverges, i.e., one of a_1's successors is no longer sufficiently similar to a predecessor of a_2, the merge attempt is abandoned. Thus, while the search strategy is still in control, DSM identifies merge opportunities dynamically within a fixed distance and only briefly takes over control to attempt the merge. After the merge attempt, the search strategy continues as before. Like QCE, DSM does not affect soundness or completeness of the symbolic analysis.

We combine the solutions to these two problems by using QCE (explained in detail in §3) to compute the similarity relation used by DSM (§4). Even though we initially developed these techniques to improve the performance of search-based symbolic execution engines for test generation, we believe our analysis and the insights into building efficiently solvable symbolic formulae from programs are applicable to other symbolic program analyses as well.

```
1  void main(int argc, char **argv) {
2    int r = 1, arg = 1;
3    if (arg < argc)
4      if (strcmp(argv[arg], "-n") == 0) {
5        r = 0; ++arg;
6      }
7    for (; arg < argc; ++arg)
8      for (int i = 0; argv[arg][i] != 0; ++i)
9        putchar(argv[arg][i]);
10   if (r)
11     putchar('\n');
12 }
```

Figure 1. Simplified version of the echo program.

3. Query Count Estimation

We now illustrate the need for estimating the expected benefit of merging using an example (§3.1), show how to compute the query count estimates (§3.2), and then justify our decisions (§3.3).

3.1 Motivating Example

Consider the example program in Figure 1, a simplified version of the UNIX `echo` utility that prints all its arguments to standard output, except for argument 0, which holds the program name. If the first regular argument is "-n", no newline character is appended. We analyze this program using Algorithm 1, assuming bounded input. Specifically, we assume that $\texttt{argc} = N+1$ for some constant $N \geq 1$, and that each of the N command-line arguments, pointed to by the corresponding element of `argv`, is a zero-terminated string of up to L characters. For simplicity, we assume that `strcmp` and `putchar` do not split paths. Under these preconditions, the total number of feasible program paths is $L^N + L^{N-1}$, and the branch condition at line 3 is always true.

The execution paths first split at line 4 on the condition C that $argv[1]$ points to the string "-n". Line 6 is then reached by the two states $(6, C, [\texttt{r} = 0, \texttt{arg} = 2])$ and $(6, \neg C, [\texttt{r} = 1, \texttt{arg} = 1])$. These two can be merged into the single (but fully precise) state $(6, \text{true}, [\texttt{r} = \text{ite}(C, 0, 1), \texttt{arg} = \text{ite}(C, 2, 1)])$. Consider now the loop condition $\texttt{arg} < \texttt{argc}$ in line 7. If the states were kept separate, this condition could be evaluated concretely in both states, as $1 < N+1$ and $2 < N+1$, respectively. In the merged state, however, the condition would become the disjunctive expression $\text{ite}(C, 2, 1) < N+1$, which now requires a solver invocation where it was not previously necessary. The consequences of having merged at line 6 become even worse later in the execution, for the condition at line 8. The array index is no longer concrete, so the SMT solver is required to reason about symbolic memory accesses in the theory of arrays on every iteration of the nested loop. In this example, merging reduces the total number of states, but the merged state is more expensive to reason about. Our experiments confirm that the total time required to fully explore all feasible paths in this program is significantly shorter if the paths are *not* merged on line 6.

Now consider the branching point in the inner loop header at line 8. Since this loop may be executed up to L times, each state that enters the loop creates L successor states, one for each loop exit possibility. For example, a state exiting after the second iteration is $(8, \ldots \wedge \texttt{argv}[1][0] \neq 0 \wedge \texttt{argv}[1][1] = 0, [\ldots, \texttt{i} = 1])$. On the next iteration of the outer loop (line 7), each of these L states again spawns L successors. At the end of the N outer loop iterations, there is a total of L^N states. However, all of the states created in the loop at line 8 during the same iteration of the outer loop differ only in the value of the temporary variable `i`, which is never used again in the program. Therefore, merging these states does not increase the cost of subsequent feasibility checks, yet it cuts the number of states after the outer loop down to the number of states before the loop (2 in our example). Note that, while the path condition of the merged state is created as a disjunction, here it can be simplified to the common prefix of all path conditions.

There is another, less obvious, opportunity for merging states. Looking back at the first feasible branch at line 4, consider the state $(7, C, [\texttt{r} = 0, \texttt{arg} = 1])$, which corresponds to the path through the "then" branch, and the state $(7, \neg C, [\texttt{r} = 1, \texttt{arg} = 1])$, which corresponds to the path through the "else" branch and one first iteration over the outer loop. Merging these two states yields the state $(7, \text{true}, [\texttt{r} = \text{ite}(C, 0, 1), \texttt{arg} = 1])$, which introduces a disjunction for the symbolic expression representing the value of the variable `r`. Unlike the `arg` variable we discussed above, `r` is used only once on line 10, just before the program terminates. Therefore, the time saved by exploring the loops at lines 7-9 with fewer states can outweigh the cost of testing the more complex branch condition on line 10 in the merged state.

This example demonstrates that the net benefit of merging two states depends heavily on how often variables whose values differ between two states affect later branch conditions. This is the key insight behind QCE, which we explain next.

3.2 Computing the Heuristic

To make an exact merging decision, one would have to compute the cumulative solving times for both the merged and unmerged cases. But this is impractical, so the query count estimation heuristic (QCE) makes several simplifications that allow it to be largely precomputed before symbolic execution begins. QCE can be calibrated using a number of parameters, which we denote using the Greek letters α, β, and κ.

At each program location ℓ, QCE pre-computes a set $H(\ell)$ of "hot variables" that are likely to cause many queries to the solver if they were to contain symbolic values. The heuristic is to avoid introducing new symbolic values for these "hot variables". Specifically, states should be merged only if every hot variable either has the same concrete value in both states or is already symbolic in at least one of the states. Formally, QCE is implemented by defining the similarity relation $\sim$ of Algorithm 1 as

$$(\ell, pc_1, s_1) \sim_{qce} (\ell, pc_2, s_2) \iff \forall v \in H(\ell) : s_1[v] = s_2[v] \vee I \blacktriangleleft s_1[v] \vee I \blacktriangleleft s_2[v], \quad (1)$$

where $I \blacktriangleleft s[v]$ denotes that variable v has a symbolic value in the symbolic store s (i.e., it depends on the set of symbolic inputs I).

In order to check whether a variable v is hot at location ℓ, QCE estimates the number of additional queries $Q_{add}(\ell, v)$ that would be executed after reaching ℓ if variable v were to be made symbolic. Variable v is determined to be hot if this number is larger than a fixed fraction α of the total number of queries $Q_t(\ell)$ that will be executed after reaching ℓ:

$$H(\ell) = \{v \in V \mid Q_{add}(\ell, v) > \alpha \cdot Q_t(\ell)\} \quad (2)$$

To estimate these numbers of queries efficiently, we assume that every executed conditional branch leads to a solver query with a fixed probability (which could be taken into account by suitably adjusting the value of α), and that each branch is feasible with a fixed probability β. Consider function q that descends recursively into the control flow graph counting the number of queries that are selected by a function c:

$$q(\ell', c) = \quad (3)$$
$$\begin{cases} \beta \cdot q(succ(\ell'), c) + \beta \cdot q(\ell'', c) + c(\ell', e) & instr(\ell') = \mathsf{if}(e)\,\mathsf{goto}\,\ell'' \\ 0 & instr(\ell') = \mathsf{halt} \\ q(succ(\ell'), c) & \text{otherwise} \end{cases}$$

Then $Q_{add}(\ell, v)$ and $Q_t(\ell)$ can be computed recursively as follows:

$$Q_{add}(\ell, v) = q\big(\ell, \lambda(\ell', e).\,\text{ite}\big((\ell, v) \lhd (\ell', e), 1, 0\big)\big)$$
$$Q_t(\ell) = q\big(\ell, \lambda(\ell', e).\,1\big), \quad (4)$$

where $(\ell, v) \lhd (\ell', e)$ denotes the fact that expression e at location ℓ' may depend on the value of variable v at location ℓ. For the sake of simplicity, we assume all program loops to be unrolled and all function calls to be inlined. For loops (and recursive function calls) whose number of iterations cannot be determined statically, QCE assumes a fixed maximum number of iterations κ.

Note that the implementation of QCE is limited to estimating the number of additional queries without taking into account the fact that queries may become more expensive due to ite expressions. Our evaluation shows that this suffices in most cases, but we also found a few cases in which lifting this limitation would improve our results. The justification of QCE in §3.3 describes how to integrate the cost of ite expressions in the computation.

Interprocedural QCE. In our implementation, we avoid the assumption of inlined functions by computing $Q_{add}(\ell, v)$ and $Q_t(\ell)$ for all function entry points ℓ as function summaries. We do this compositionally, by computing per-function *local* query counts in a bottom-up fashion. The local query counts for a function `F` include all queries issued inside `F` and all functions called by `F`. To compute these, we extend Equation (3) to handle function calls. At every call site, the local query counts are incremented by the local query counts at the entry point of the callee. Since the local query counts do not include queries issued after the function returns to the caller (this would require context-sensitive local query counts), we perform the last step of the computation dynamically during symbolic execution. We obtain the global query counts by adding the local query counts at the location of the current state to the sum of the local query counts of all return locations in the call stack.

Parameters. In our implementation, QCE is parametrized by α, β, and the loop bound κ. Optimal values for these parameters are difficult to compute analytically. For a given program, one can empirically find good parameter values using a simple hill-climbing method. In our experiments, we determined the parameter values this way using four programs and then used these values for the other programs, with good results (see §5.1).

Illustrating Example. Consider again the program in Figure 1 with the same input constraints we described in §3.1. We now illustrate how QCE can be used to decide whether to merge states at lines 6 and 7. We use the heuristic parameters $\alpha = 0.5$, $\beta = 0.6$ and, to keep the example brief, we set $\kappa = 1$. First, we pre-compute $Q_t(7)$ and $Q_{add}(7, v)$ for $v \in \{\texttt{r}, \texttt{arg}\}$ using Equation (4). For brevity, we omit the computation of Q_{add} for `argc`, `argv`, and array contents referenced by `argv`. For $Q_{add}(7, \texttt{arg})$, we get

$$\begin{aligned} Q_{add}&(7, \texttt{arg}) = q(7, c) \\ &= \beta q(8, c) + \beta q(10, c) + c(7, \texttt{arg} < \texttt{argc}) = \beta q(8, c) + 1 \\ &= \beta(\beta q(9, c) + \beta q(10, c) + c(8, \texttt{argv[arg][i]} \neq 0)) + 1 \\ &= \beta(\beta q(9, c) + 1) + 1 = \beta(\beta q(10, c) + 1) + 1 = \beta + 1 = 1.6, \end{aligned}$$

where $c = \lambda(\ell', e).\,\text{ite}((7, \texttt{arg}) \lhd (\ell', e), 1, 0)$. Similarly, we compute that $Q_{add}(7, \texttt{r}) = \beta + 2\beta^2 = 1.32$ and $Q_t(7) = 1 + 2\beta + 2\beta^2 = 2.92$ and, according to Equation (2), $H(7) = \{\texttt{arg}\}$. As there are no branches between lines 6 and 7, we have $H(6) = H(7) = \{\texttt{arg}\}$. Hence, in this example, the QCE similarity relation (1) allows the states at line 6 or 7 to be merged if the values of arg in the two states are either equal or symbolic. This is consistent with the results of our manual analysis in §3.1.

3.3 Justification

We now link our design of QCE to a cost model through the successive application of five key simplifying assumptions. Since QCE is merely a heuristic and not a precise computation, the following only provides a justification for the reasoning behind it, but not a formal derivation. Here we explain a full variant of QCE that includes an estimate of the cost for introducing ite expressions, even though it is not currently implemented in our prototype.

As mentioned above, an optimal heuristic for the similarity relation would compute whether the cumulative solving time T_m for all descendants of the merged state is guaranteed to be less than the combined respective times T_1 and T_2 for the two individual states, i.e., whether $T_m < T_1 + T_2$. In the ideal case of merging two identical states, we would have $T_m = T_1 = T_2$. Thus, merging just two states could theoretically cut the remaining exploration time in half. This is why, in principle, repeated merging can reduce the cumulative solving time by an exponential factor.

Precisely predicting the time required for solving a formula without actually solving it is generally impossible, therefore we apply a first simplification:

Simplifying Assumption 1. *A query takes one time unit to solve. Introducing new* ite *expressions into the query increases the cost to $\zeta > 1$ time units, where ζ is a parameter of the heuristic.*

Thus, we assume the estimated solving time to be linear in the number of queries of each type. In a further simplification, we treat the number of queries that each one of two merge candidates would *individually* cause in the future as equal:

Simplifying Assumption 2. *Two states at the same program location that are candidates for merging will cause the same number Q_t of queries if they are explored separately.*

This simplification is a prerequisite for statically computing query counts for a location in a way that is independent of the actual states during symbolic execution. The merged state then will also invoke these Q_t queries, but some queries will take longer to solve due to introduced ite expressions, and some additional queries become necessary. We denote the number of queries into which merging introduces ite expressions by Q_{ite} (with $Q_{ite} \leq Q_t$). The total cumulative cost of solving these queries is $\zeta \cdot Q_{ite}$, as per our first simplification. Additionally, the merged state can require extra solver invocations for queries corresponding to branch conditions that depend on constant but different values in the individual states (as in the loop conditions on lines 9 and 10 of Figure 1). This number of additional queries is Q_{add}.

Note that we ignore the possible cost of introducing disjunctions into the path condition. In many common cases, the different conjuncts of the two path conditions are just negations of each other, and thus the disjunctive path condition can be simplified to the common prefix of the two individual path conditions.

With these simplifications, the total cost of solver queries in the merged state is $1 \cdot (Q_t - Q_{ite})$ for the remaining regular queries plus $\zeta \cdot Q_{ite}$ for queries involving new ite expressions, plus $1 \cdot Q_{add}$ for the additional queries. We can thus formulate the criterion for performing a single merge as $Q_t - Q_{ite} + \zeta \cdot Q_{ite} + Q_{add} < 2 \cdot Q_t$, which simplifies to

$$(\zeta - 1)Q_{ite} + Q_{add} < Q_t. \tag{5}$$

The values for Q_t, Q_{ite}, and Q_{add} must be computed over the set of all feasible executions of the merged state. To statically estimate the feasibility of future paths, we add the following simplification:

Simplifying Assumption 3. *Each branch of a conditional statement is feasible with probability $0.5 < \beta < 1$, independently of the other branch.*

We can now estimate the query counts recursively. In the following definition, which is restated from (3), function $c(\ell', e)$ can be instantiated for Q_t, Q_{ite}, and Q_{add} individually to return 1 if checking the feasibility of a branch condition e at location ℓ' causes a query of the specific type (regular, involving ite expressions, or additional), or 0 otherwise:[1]

$$q(\ell', c) = \tag{6}$$

$$\begin{cases} \beta \cdot q(succ(\ell'), c) + \beta \cdot q(\ell'', c) + c(\ell', e) & instr(\ell') = \mathsf{if}(e)\,\mathsf{goto}\,\ell'' \\ 0 & instr(\ell') = \mathsf{halt} \\ q(succ(\ell'), c) & \text{otherwise} \end{cases}$$

For this definition, loop unrolling ensures that conditional statements in loops are counted as many times as the loop can execute. Loops and recursive calls with bounds that are not statically known are unrolled up to a fixed depth, given by the heuristic parameter κ.

The symbolic execution engine issues a query whenever a state (ℓ, pc, s) encounters a branch with a conditional expression e that depends on program input, i.e., e evaluates to an expression $s[e]$ containing variables from the set of inputs I. We denote this by $I \blacktriangleleft s[e]$. To ease notation, we add the following shorthands: we use $s_1[v] \neq_s s_2[v] \overset{def}{\Leftrightarrow} (I \blacktriangleleft s_1[v] \vee I \blacktriangleleft s_2[v]) \wedge s_1[v] \neq s_2[v]$ for the condition causing ite expressions, i.e., symbolic but non-equal variables in two states, and we use $s_1[v] \neq_c s_2[v] \overset{def}{\Leftrightarrow} \neg(I \blacktriangleleft s_1[v] \vee I \blacktriangleleft s_2[v]) \wedge s_1[v] \neq s_2[v]$ for the condition causing additional queries, i.e., concrete and non-equal variables in two states.

To define a function $c(\ell', e)$ for the different types of query counts, we need a method to check whether the branch condition e depends on inputs when reached from one of the individual states. We approximate this statically using a path-insensitive data dependence analysis, and write $(\ell, v) \lhd (\ell', e)$ if expression e at location ℓ' may depend on the value of variable v at location ℓ. Thus, we can define the query counts as follows:

$$Q_t((\ell, pc_1, s_1), (\ell, pc_2, s_2)) = q\big(\ell, \lambda(\ell', e).\; \text{ite}(\exists v\colon (I \blacktriangleleft s_1[v] \vee I \blacktriangleleft s_2[v]) \wedge (\ell, v) \lhd (\ell', e)), 1, 0\big)$$

$$Q_{ite}((\ell, pc_1, s_1), (\ell, pc_2, s_2)) = q\big(\ell, \lambda(\ell', e).\; \text{ite}(\exists v : s_1[v] \neq_s s_2[v] \wedge (\ell, v) \lhd (\ell', e)), 1, 0\big)$$

$$Q_{add}((\ell, pc_1, s_1), (\ell, pc_2, s_2)) = q\big(\ell, \lambda(\ell', e).\; \text{ite}(\exists v : s_1[v] \neq_c s_2[v] \wedge (\ell, v) \lhd (\ell', e), 1, 0\big)$$

Computing this recursive relation is expensive, and it cannot be pre-computed before symbolic execution because it requires determining which variables depend on program inputs in the states considered for merging. We therefore assume a fixed probability of input dependence:

Simplifying Assumption 4. *The number of branches whose conditions are dependent on inputs is a fixed fraction φ of the total number of conditional branches.*

[1] Note that, for simplicity of exposition, we only refer to branch conditions here. In practice, other instructions, such as assertion checks or memory accesses with input-dependent offsets, will also trigger solver queries. Our implementation extends the definition of c to account for these queries.

This enables us to eliminate all variable dependencies from Q_t and simplify it to $Q_t(\ell) = \varphi \cdot q(\ell, \lambda(\ell', e).1)$. Now, Q_t depends only on the program location and can thus be statically pre-computed.

Q_{ite} and Q_{add} count queries for which specific variable pairs are not equal in the two merge candidates. Therefore, we would need to statically pre-compute Q_{ite} and Q_{add} for each subset of variables that could be symbolic in either state during symbolic execution. To eliminate this dependency on the combination of specific variables, we compute query counts for individual variables. The *per-variable query counts* $Q_{ite}(\ell, v)$ and $Q_{add}(\ell, v)$ are defined as the value of $Q_{ite}(\ell)$ and $Q_{add}(\ell)$, respectively, computed as if v was the only variable that differs between the merge candidates. The per-variable query counts can be computed as $Q_{ite}(\ell, v) = Q_{add}(\ell, v) = q(\ell, \lambda(\ell', e).\,\mathrm{ite}((\ell, v) \lhd (\ell', e), 1, 0))$.

Summing the per-variable query counts for all variables that differ between the merge candidates will grossly over-estimate the actual values of Q_{ite} and Q_{add}, since conditional expressions often depend on more than just one variable, and many queries would thus be counted multiple times. Similarly, using just the maximum per-variable query count would cause an under-estimation. In fact,

$$\max_{\{v \in V | s_1[v] \neq_c s_2[v]\}} Q_{add}(\ell, v) \leq Q_{add}(\ell) \leq \sum_{\{v \in V | s_1[v] \neq_c s_2[v]\}} Q_{add}(\ell, v)$$

and analogously for Q_{ite}. We therefore make a final simplification:

Simplifying Assumption 5. *Total query counts are equal to the maximum per-variable query counts for an individual variable times some factor* σ, *i.e.,*

$$Q_{ite}(\ell) \approx \sigma \cdot \max_{\{v \in V | s_1[v] \neq_s s_2[v]\}} Q_{ite}(\ell, v)$$

$$Q_{add}(\ell) \approx \sigma \cdot \max_{\{v \in V | s_1[v] \neq_c s_2[v]\}} Q_{add}(\ell, v).$$

The intuition behind this assumption is that the number of independent variables correlates with the input size and not with the total number of variables. Applying this substitution to Equation (5) we can now define the similarity relation $\sim_{qce}$ as

$$(\ell, pc_1, s_1) \sim_{qce} (\ell, pc_2, s_2) \overset{def}{\iff} \quad (7)$$

$$(\zeta - 1) \max_{\{v \in V | s_1[v] \neq_s s_2[v]\}} Q_{ite}(\ell, v) + \max_{\{v \in V | s_1[v] \neq_c s_2[v]\}} Q_{add}(\ell, v) < \frac{Q_t}{\sigma}$$

with

$$Q_{ite}(\ell, v) = Q_{add}(\ell, v) = q\big(\ell, \lambda(\ell', e).\,\mathrm{ite}\big((\ell, v) \lhd (\ell', e), 1, 0\big)\big),$$

$$Q_t(\ell) = \varphi \cdot q\big(\ell, \lambda(\ell', e).\,1\big),$$

and the recursively descending q as defined in Equation (6). For convenience, we rename $\frac{\varphi}{\sigma}$ to the unified parameter α. Thus, α, β, ζ and the unrolling bound κ remain as the only parameters to QCE. The variant of QCE implemented in our prototype is derived from Equation (7) by removing Q_{ite} from the criterion, to arrive at

$$\max_{\{v \in V | s_1[v] \neq_c s_2[v]\}} Q_{add}(\ell, v) < \alpha Q_t,$$

which is equivalent to

$$\forall v \in V : s_1[v] \neq_c s_2[v] \rightarrow Q_{add}(\ell, v) < \alpha Q_t.$$

To facilitate an efficient implementation in combination with dynamic state merging, as discussed in the next section, we collect a set of variables that exceed the threshold $H_{add}(\ell) = \{v \in V \mid Q_{add}(v) > \alpha Q_t\}$ and can state the similarity relation as (1).

This motivates the use of QCE for estimating the similarity of states. We show that QCE is effective in practice in §5.

4. Dynamic State Merging

We now explain the challenges for applying state merging in fully automated, precise, but incomplete symbolic program analysis (§4.1). To overcome these problems, we motivate (§4.2) and introduce (§4.3) the dynamic state merging algorithm.

```
1 if (logPacketHash) {
2   hash = computeHash(pkt);
3   log("Packet: %s, hash: %s", pkt->name, hash);
4 } else {
5   log("Packet: %s", pkt->name);
6 }
7 handlePacket(pkt);
```

Figure 2. Example code illustrating how static state merging can interfere with search heuristics.

4.1 Static Merging and Incomplete Exploration

A symbolic program analysis using static state merging traverses the CFG in topological order and attempts to merge states at every joint point. This allows to perform exhaustive exploration with state merging in the fewest possible steps. To ensure termination, the analysis has to stop loop unrolling at a certain depth, unless loops can be summarized by loop invariants. This method is optimal for verification condition generators that encode full programs with bounded or summarized loops. Search-based symbolic execution engines, however, which typically perform incomplete explorations, do not bound loops but are guided by search strategies that prioritize exploring new code over unrolling additional loop iterations. An exploration in strict topological order would override such strategies and stall the engine by requiring it to fully unroll the possibly infinitely many iterations of a loop before proceeding.

This is a problem even for loops that symbolic execution could, in principle, explore exhaustively. Coverage-oriented search strategies are designed to quickly maximize metrics such as statement coverage. The restriction to topological order interferes with such strategies, reducing their performance or even completely stopping them from achieving any progress towards their goal. We support this argument with experimental evidence in §5.5.

Consider the example code in Figure 2. Depending on the flag `logPacketHash`, the program writes to a log either just the name of a packet or both the name and a hash value. The code then processes the packet. In this example, exploring the "else" branch of the conditional statement on line 1 is fast, while exploring the "then" branch is expensive due to the `computeHash` function processing the entire input packet. A coverage-oriented search strategy will likely choose to explore the "else" branch first to quickly reach `handlePacket`, or switch to the "else" branch after not making progress towards its coverage goal being stuck unrolling loops inside the `computeHash` function. With static state merging, the symbolic execution engine has to merge all states at line 7, which requires all execution paths to be explored exhaustively up to that location. Therefore, no code in the `handlePacket` function can be reached before exploring every path in the `computeHash` function, thus being in conflict with the coverage-oriented search heuristic. This conflict could be solved by allowing the merge of only those states that, according to the chosen search strategy, would reach the same point in a program at about the same time. In our example, the state that takes the "else" branch should not be merged with any state that takes the "then" branch, allowing the search strategy to prioritize it independently.

4.2 Rationale Behind Dynamic State Merging

To solve the problems of static state merging, we propose *dynamic state merging* (DSM). DSM does not require states to share the same program location in order to be considered for merging. The rationale behind dynamic state merging is the following: consider two abstract states $a_1 = (\ell_1, pc_1, s_1)$ and $a_2 = (\ell_2, pc_2, s_2)$, with $\ell_1 \neq \ell_2$, that are both in the worklist. Assume that a_1', one of the transitive successors of a_1 (which have not been computed yet)

Input: Worklist w, choice functions $pickNext_D$ and $pickNext_F$, similarity relation $\sim$, trace function $pred$, threshold δ
Data: Forwarding set F.
Result: The next state to execute.

```
// Determine the forwarding set
F := {a ∈ w | ∃a' ∈ w : ∃a'' ∈ pred(a', δ) : a ~ a''};
if F ≠ ∅ then          // Choose a state from the forwarding set
  | return pickNext_F(F)
else                   // Choose a state using the driving heuristic
  | return pickNext_D(w)
```

Algorithm 2. The *pickNext* method for dynamic state merging.

will reach location ℓ_2. Provided that the number of steps required to reach ℓ_2 from a_1 is small, and the expected similarity of a'_1 and a_2 is high, enough that merging them will be beneficial, it is worth overriding a coverage-oriented search strategy to compute a'_1 next and to then merge it with a_2. We refer to this override as *fast-forwarding*, because a_1 is forwarded to a_2's location with temporary priority before resuming the regular search strategy.

To check whether a_1 can be expected to be similar to a_2 in the near future, we check whether a_1 could have been merged with a predecessor a'_2 of a_2, i.e., whether $a_1 \sim a'_2$. The underlying expectation, which our experiments confirm, is that if two states are similar, then their two respective successors after a few steps of execution are also likely (but not guaranteed) to be similar.

Note that fast-forwarding deals with special cases automatically: if a state forks while being fast-forwarded, all children that are still similar to a recent predecessor of a state in the worklist are fast-forwarded. If a state leaves the path taken by the state it is similar to, i.e., fast-forwarding diverges, the state is no longer similar to any predecessor and is thus no longer prioritized.

4.3 The Dynamic State Merging Algorithm

The DSM algorithm is an instance of Algorithm 1 with a *pickNext* function as defined in Algorithm 2. DSM relies on an external "driving" heuristic (given as a function $pickNext_D$), such as a traditional coverage-oriented heuristic, to select the next state. However, when the algorithm detects that some states, computed as a set F, are likely to be mergeable after at most δ steps of execution, DSM overrides the driving heuristic and picks the next state to execute from F according to another external search heuristic $pickNext_F$.

The algorithm uses a function $pred(a, \delta)$ to compute the set of predecessors of a within a distance of δ. The function can be defined as $pred(a, \delta) = \{a' \mid \exists n \leq \delta : a \in post^n(a')\}$, where $post(a')$ denotes the set of immediate successor states computed by Algorithm 1 for a state a'. Keeping a precise history of reached states can incur prohibitive space costs, but we reduce the space requirements as follows: states from the history are only used for comparisons with respect to $\sim$, hence it is only required to store the parts of the state that are relevant to the relation. Moreover, if the $\sim$ relation is only sensitive to equality, the implementation can store and compare hash values of the relevant information from past states. In this case, checking whether the state belongs to F is implemented as a simple hash table lookup. Hash collisions do not pose a problem, because a full check of the similarity relation is still performed when fast-forwarding finishes and the states are about to be merged. Moreover, the set F is rebuilt after each execution step, so, if a state was added to F due to a collision, it is unlikely to be added again to F in the next step, as a second collision for two different hash values has low probability.

The relation $\sim_{qce}$, defined in Equation (1) in §3.3, can be modified to check for equality only, as required for using hashing in the implementation. We express the condition for variables to be either symbolic or equal in Equation (1) by $h(s_1[v]) = h(s_2[v])$, where $h(v) = \text{ite}(I \blacktriangleleft v, \star, v)$ filters out symbolic variables by mapping them to a unique special value. The implementation can thus store just the hash value of $\bigcup_{v \in H(\ell)} h(v)$ for a state. Then $\sim_{qce}$ can be checked by comparing the hash values of the two states (modulo hash collisions).

The function $pickNext_F$ determines the execution order among the states selected for fast-forwarding. In our implementation, we pick the first state from F according to the topological order of the CFG. Thus, states that lie behind with respect to the topological order first catch up and are merged with later states.

5. Experimental Evaluation

We now show that, in practice, our approach attains exponential speedup compared to base symbolic execution (Figure 5). We first introduce our prototype implementation (§5.1) and present our evaluation metrics (§5.2). We then evaluate how DSM combined with QCE improves the thoroughness of program exploration in a time-bounded scenario (§5.3). We then show that QCE lies at a sweet spot between single-path exploration and static merging (§5.4). Finally, we demonstrate that DSM is essential for combining state merging with coverage-oriented search strategies in incomplete exploration (§5.5).

5.1 Prototype

We built our prototype on top of the KLEE symbolic execution engine [6]. It takes as input a program in LLVM bitcode [25] and a specification of which program inputs should be marked as symbolic for the analysis: command-line arguments or file contents. KLEE implements precise non-compositional symbolic execution with feasibility checks performed at every conditional branch. It uses search strategies to guide exploration; the stock strategies include random search and a strategy biased toward covering previously unexplored program statements.

To support QCE, we extended KLEE to perform a static analysis of the LLVM bitcode to compute local query count estimates as explained in §3.2. The analysis is executed before the path exploration and annotates each program location with the corresponding query count estimates $Q_t(\ell)$ and $Q_{add}(\ell, v)$ as defined in §3.2. The pass is implemented as an LLVM per-function bottom-up call graph traversal (with bounded recursion) and performs the analysis compositionally. When analyzing each function, the pass attempts to statically determine trip counts (number of iterations) for loops. If it cannot, it approximates them with the loop bound parameter κ. The QCE analysis tracks the query count for local variables, function arguments, and in-memory variables indexed by a constant offset and pointed to by either a local variable, a function argument, or a global variable. We check data dependencies between variables by traversing the program in SSA form. As LLVM's SSA form handles only local variables, we do not track dependencies between in-memory variables except when loading them to locals. We modified KLEE to compute interprocedural query counts and sets of hot variables $H(\ell)$ dynamically during symbolic execution, following §3.2.

We implemented DSM as defined by Algorithm 2 in the form of a search strategy layer in KLEE's stacked strategy system plus an execution tracking system that incrementally computes state hashes (see §4.3). Each strategy uses its own logic to select a state from the worklist, but can rely on an underlying strategy whenever it has to make a choice among a set of equally important states. In our case, the DSM strategy returns a state from the fast-forwarding set of states ($pickNext_F$), or, if this set is empty, it resorts to the underlying driving heuristic to select a state from the general worklist ($pickNext_D$). Depending on the purpose of each experiment, we employ different driving heuristics: for complete

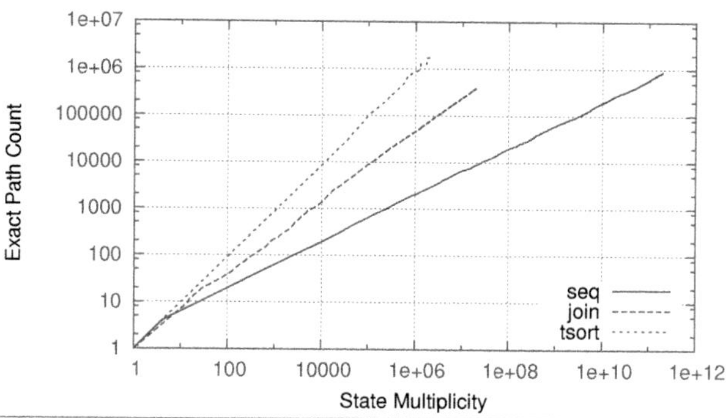

Figure 3. The exact number of paths as a function of state multiplicity for 3 COREUTILS tools. Both axes are logarithmic.

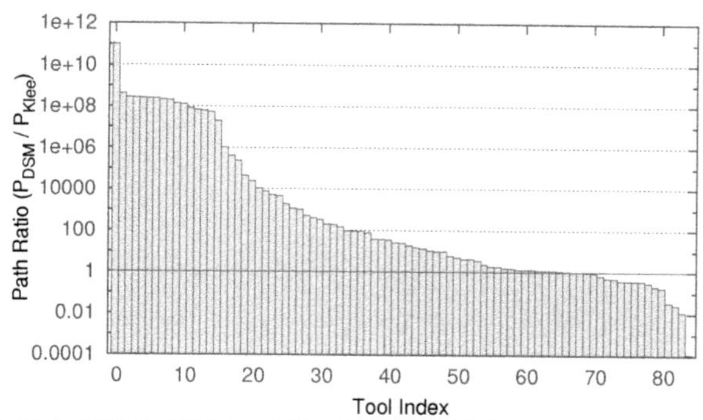

Figure 4. Relative increase in explored paths for DSM + QCE vs. regular KLEE (1h time budget). Each bar represents a COREUTIL.

explorations, we used random search, while for partial explorations aimed at obtaining statement coverage, we employed the coverage-oriented search heuristics in [6].

Evaluation Targets. We performed all our experiments on the COREUTILS suite of widely used UNIX command-line utilities, ranging from file manipulation (`cp`, `mv`, etc.) to text processing (`cut`, `sort`, etc.) and shell control flow (e.g., `test`). The total size of the COREUTILS code is 72.1 KLOC, as measured by SLOCCOUNT [30]. We tested these tools using symbolic command line arguments and `stdin` as input. In some cases, the symbolic input size is small enough for KLEE to complete the exploration in less than 5 minutes. We discarded these data points from our evaluation, since such a short period of time is dominated by the constant overhead of our static analysis, whereas we are interested in evaluating the prototype's asymptotic behavior.

5.2 Evaluation Metrics

We evaluate our prototype by comparing it to non-merging search-based symbolic execution as implemented in KLEE. We perform the comparison according to (1) the *amount of exploration* performed given a fixed time budget, and (2) the *time* necessary to complete a fixed exploration task, i.e., the exhaustive search of a set of paths determined by a given symbolic input.

Estimating Number of Paths in Merged States. A direct comparison of the amount of exploration between merge-based and regular symbolic execution is difficult, because counting the feasible paths that have been explored with state merging requires checking the feasibility of each path individually. This is as hard as repeating the exploration without merging, so it is impractical in the cases where symbolic execution without merging times out.

We therefore estimate the path count in a merged state with the help of *state multiplicity*: the multiplicity of a single-path state is 1; when two states merge, the multiplicity of the resulting state is the sum of their multiplicities. State multiplicity over-estimates the path count because, when the state is split at later branches, state multiplicity carries over to both child states, effectively doubling the counted number of paths at each branch (assuming that, as long as a branch is feasible for the merged state, it is also feasible for all the paths represented by it).

For our estimation, we made the assumption that "path explosion" can be modeled as an exponential function $a \cdot 2^{b \cdot n}$, where a and b are program-specific constants, and the growth parameter n indicates the progress of unrolling the program CFG along the paths of interest. Both the path count p and state multiplicity m are then based on this formula, each with different values for the constants a and b. Since n depends on the behavior of the search strategy, it cannot be easily determined. However, we can avoid computing n because, at any point in time, both the exact path count and the state multiplicity have the same growth parameter n corresponding to the current exploration progress. Hence, we can take the two model equations $m = a_m \cdot 2^{b_m \cdot n}$ and $p = a_p \cdot 2^{b_p \cdot n}$ and obtain n from the first equation and substitute it in the second. This yields a relation between p and m of the form $\log p \approx c_1 + c_2 \log m$, where c_1 and c_2 are program-dependent coefficients.

To empirically validate this relation, we extended our prototype to accurately track the number of feasible paths by maintaining all the original single-path states along with the merged states. We counted the exact number of paths and the state multiplicity for 1 hour and confirmed a linear relation between the logarithms of the two values. Figure 3 illustrates the dependency between m and p with representative measurements of c_2 for 3 COREUTILS.

In the experiments reported in the rest of this section, we approximated the number of paths for state merging as follows. First, we ran the experiments for 1 hour, while accurately tracking the number of feasible paths as explained above (if exploration with merging was 1000× faster, this 1 hour would correspond to ~4 seconds of exploration). From this data, we computed the values of c_1 and c_2. Second, we ran the full experiments, while tracking only the state multiplicity for merged states, which does not incur a significant overhead. Using c_1 and c_2, we then converted the state multiplicity values into the estimation of the feasible path count.

5.3 Faster Path Exploration with DSM and QCE

We were first concerned with how much DSM and QCE, when combined, speed up symbolic execution. We let both our prototype and KLEE run for 1 hour on each of the COREUTILS, and we measured the number of paths explored by each tool. The size of the symbolic inputs passed to each utility was large enough to keep each tool busy for the duration of each run.

Figure 4 shows, for each of the tested COREUTILS, a bar representing the ratio between the number of program paths explored by our prototype and KLEE, respectively. The results indicate that our technique explores up to 11 orders of magnitude more paths than plain symbolic execution in the same amount of time. On 14 utilities, our prototype explored fewer paths, which we believe to be due to ignoring ite expressions (see §3.3) and limitations of our prototype (see §5.1). Our prototype crashed on 5 utilities, which we do not include in our results. We show a single representative for every tool aliased by multiple names (e.g., `ls`, `dir`, and `vdir`).

5.4 Achieving Exponential Speedup with QCE

We now answer the question of how much faster can our technique exhaustively explore a program for a fixed input size. In exhaustive exploration, a coverage-oriented search strategy is not necessary, therefore we focused on the effects of QCE alone. We used it in implementing a selective form of static state merging instead of DSM. Static state merging (SSM) chooses states from the worklist

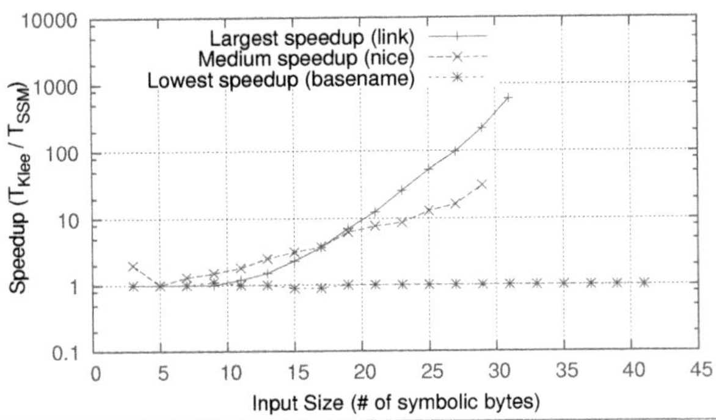

Figure 5. Speedup of QCE versus input size for exhaustive exploration of three representative COREUTILS.

in topological order and attempts to merge them at control flow join points. Selective SSM uses query count estimation to keep some states separate. Intuitively (and confirmed experimentally in §5.5), SSM performs better than DSM in exhaustive exploration, since it avoids unnecessary computation. However, for incomplete exploration, SSM performs worse than DSM.

We evaluate QCE from two perspectives. First, we look at how much QCE speeds up state merging for complete path exploration tasks. Second, we look at how the QCE heuristic parameters influence performance. We collected our measurements by running each of the COREUTILS for 2 hours, using plain KLEE, and QCE with SSM. For each configuration, we ran experiments with multiple values of symbolic input size, and we measured the corresponding completion time.

Exhaustive Exploration. Figure 5 shows the evolution of the completion time ratio (speedup) between SSM using QCE and plain KLEE for three representative COREUTILS programs, as we increase the symbolic input size. One of them achieved the highest speedup, another shows an average speedup, while the last does not show any improvement. This graph illustrates that our prototype completed the exploration goal exponentially faster as the symbolic input size increased. Figure 5 also shows that applying QCE does not always lead to speedup. However, Figure 6 shows this is actually an infrequent case. The scatter plot illustrates how the execution time of SSM using QCE compares to KLEE when aggregating over the entire set of experiments. The black dots correspond to experiment instances where both our prototype and KLEE finished on time, while the triangles on the right side correspond to situations where KLEE timed out after 2 hours (and thus indicate a lower bound on the actual speedup). The gray disks indicate the relative size of the symbolic inputs used in each experiment instance. Since, in the majority of cases, KLEE times out without completing the exploration, we only show on this graph the timeout points of the smallest input size for each tool, which give a loose lower bound on the speedup. We notice that most of the points in Figure 6 are located in the lower-right part of the graph, which correspond to higher speedup values. Moreover, in the cases where both KLEE and our prototype finish on time, large speedups (the lower-right part of the graph) tend to correspond to larger sizes of the symbolic input (larger gray circles). This re-confirms the fact that our speedup is proportional to the size of program input, i.e., the very source of the exponential growth of paths that bottlenecks KLEE.

To get a better understanding of the behavior of QCE, we took a deeper look at the execution of several COREUTILS tools: some that exhibit high speedup, and some for which the performance of our prototype is worse than KLEE's. We extended our prototype to explore states in both merged and unmerged forms. For every solver query in a merged state, we matched all the queries during the same execution step in all the corresponding unmerged states. We then

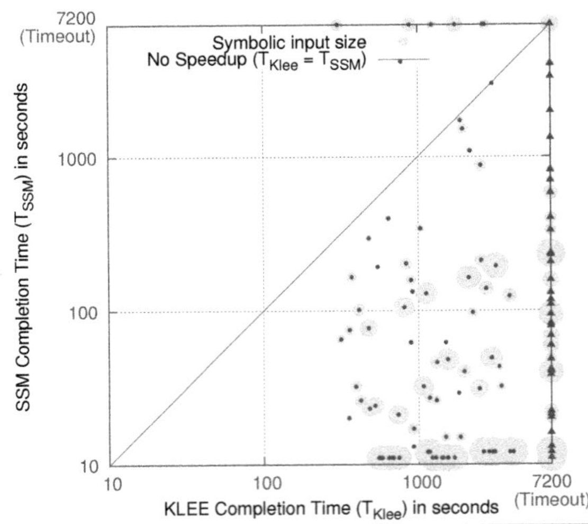

Figure 6. QCE + SSM vs. plain KLEE with varying input sizes (shown as gray disk size). Triangles denote that KLEE timed out after 2h and are thus *lower* bounds on the actual speedup.

compared query times in the merged and unmerged versions and identified those that became slower due to state merging.

We discovered that, even for tools that exhibited high overall speedup, some queries are more expensive in the merged state than the corresponding queries for the unmerged states combined. In these cases, however, the slowdown was amortized by the reduction in the total number of states to explore, and hence the total number of queries to solve. A typical example is the `sleep` utility, which reads a list of integers from the command line and sums their value in the variable `seconds`. It then validates the resulting value and performs the actual sleep operation. Here, QCE does not identify `seconds` as a hot variable, and all states forked during parsing are merged into a single state, avoiding the exponential increase in paths for each additional integer parsed. Since the value of `seconds` depends on the parsing result, it becomes a complex symbolic expression in the merged state, leading to several complex solver queries in the validation code. Nevertheless, these queries are amortized by the substantial reduction in the number of states to analyze. This example shows that QCE does allow merging of states that differ in live variables, so it is strictly more general than methods based on live variable analysis [3].

In cases where our prototype performed worse than plain KLEE, we observed a large number of queries that were more expensive in the merged state. These queries commonly contained ite expressions and disjunctive path conditions introduced by state merging. The former case shows that our QCE prototype can be improved by including the estimation of ite expressions introduced by state merging, as described in §3.3. The latter suggests using a constraint solver that can handle disjunctions more efficiently.

Influence of Heuristic Parameters. The values of the QCE parameters α, β, and κ affect the exploration time of each program. We determined optimal values for α and β experimentally, using hill-climbing over four COREUTILS chosen at random, and obtained $\alpha = 10^{-12}$ and $\beta = 0.8$. We then reused the same values for all other experiments in our evaluation and found that these values perform well in practice. Regarding the loop bound κ, we noticed that many of the loops with an input-dependent number of iterations actually iterate over program inputs. Hence, we chose $\kappa = 10$ corresponding to the average input size in our experiments.

We observed that, among these parameters, the value of α has the highest impact on the running time. In essence, α controls how aggressively the engine tries to merge. When α is ∞, no variables

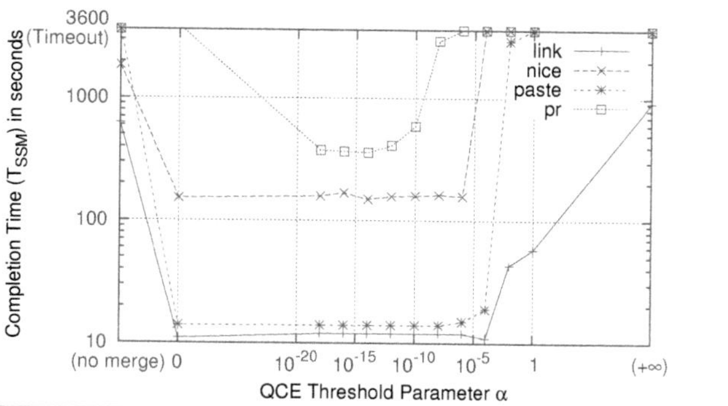

Figure 7. Impact on performance of the threshold parameter α.

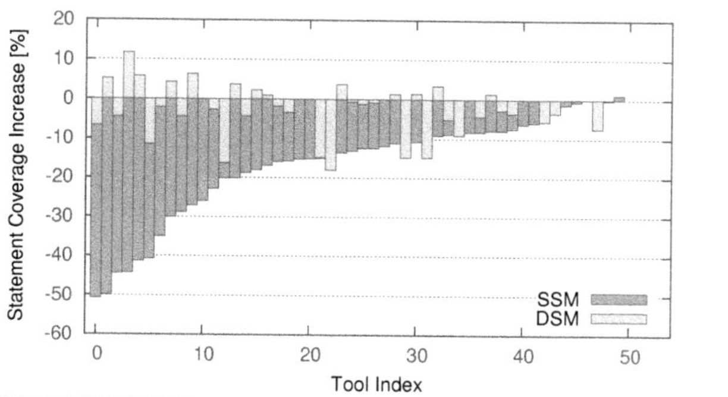

Figure 8. Change in statement coverage of DSM and SSM vs. regular KLEE for a coverage-oriented, incomplete exploration.

are determined to be hot, and QCE allows all states to be merged. When α is 0, states that contain variables with different concrete values are never merged. Due to this property, we call α the QCE *threshold parameter*. To illustrate this dependency, we randomly chose four COREUTILS (`link`, `nice`, `paste`, `pr`) and ran them using SSM for up to 1 hour with different values of α. Figure 7 shows, for each target program, the dependency of the completion time on the threshold parameter. The special point "(no merge)" on the x-axis corresponds to executions with state merging disabled. Note that here we did not cut execution times below 5 minutes.

5.5 Reaching an Exploration Goal with DSM

We now verify whether DSM allows the underlying driving heuristic to reach the goal while still merging states according to QCE. To isolate the effects of DSM, we compare DSM to our SSM implementation, with both using QCE in making merge decisions.

First, we use the coverage-oriented search heuristic from [6] with DSM, and look at how much statement coverage it can achieve in an incomplete setting (1 hour timeout and large search space). The value of the fast-forwarding distance δ was chosen experimentally to equal 8 basic blocks. Figure 8 compares the increase in statement coverage obtained by DSM and SSM over base KLEE on those COREUTILS for which the exploration remained incomplete after 1 hour. SSM consistently obtains worse coverage values, confirming its inability to adapt to the exploration goal. However, DSM roughly matches the coverage values of the underlying driving heuristic. Thus, the experiment confirms that DSM's merging avoids interfering with the logic of the driving heuristic, while traversing orders of magnitude more paths (§5.3). Even though these additional paths do not necessarily increase statement coverage, they can increase other coverage metrics and ultimately offer higher confidence in the resulting tests. We measured that, on average, 69% of the states selected for fast-forwarding were successfully merged with another state. Hence, the DSM approach to predict state similarity (§4.3) works well in practice.

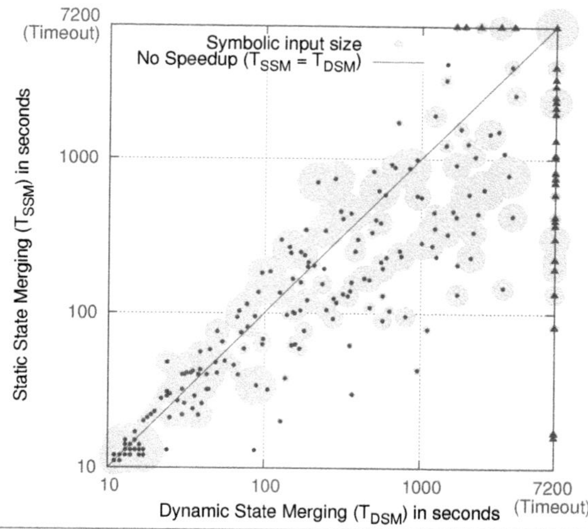

Figure 9. Comparison between the time needed to achieve exhaustive exploration for SSM and DSM.

Second, we evaluated the penalty of DSM compared to SSM in *exhaustive* exploration (see §5.4). For this experiment, we ran both techniques with varying input sizes. Figure 9 aggregates the results in a scatter plot. Most data points are grouped around the diagonal, indicating that the performance of both techniques is comparable, even though DSM is slower than SSM by 15% on average.

We conclude that DSM, while being slightly less efficient than SSM in exhaustive exploration, meets its purpose of allowing the driving heuristic to follow the exploration goal.

Overall, the combination of DSM and QCE offers exponential speedups over KLEE, which suggests that these are two important steps towards improving the performance of symbolic execution.

6. Related Work

We discussed the most closely related work in §2, where we focused on what we called precise symbolic program analysis. In this section, we look a bit further into alternative approaches that are similar in that they build symbolic expressions and rely on SAT or SMT solving, but use other techniques for improving scalability.

A first class of techniques focuses on pruning redundant states in symbolic execution. Boonstoppel et al. [3] dynamically determine variable liveness during symbolic execution. Their analysis considers the already explored paths through the current statement and determines the variables that are dead on all paths. It then uses the rest of the variables to check whether a state is equivalent to a previously explored one and can be safely pruned. In a sense, this is a special case of QCE, where no merging is performed unless the differing variables never used again. In our approach, we do not actually prune paths but still represent them in the merged state. If the differing variables are never used, this is equivalent to pruning one of the paths. This allows us to use imprecise static analysis and to merge in cases where variables are not dead but just rarely used.

McMillan [28] introduces lazy annotation in symbolic execution to build summaries on the fly and generalize them by Craig interpolation. This generalization goes beyond regular symbolic summaries, but is also computationally more expensive; we would like to measure the net effectiveness of this technique in future work.

A proven effective way to scale up symbolic program analysis is to forgo precision and introduce abstraction. Saturn [31] uses a symbolic exploration algorithm to build verification conditions for specific properties. It is specifically designed to find bugs in large system software and therefore sacrifices precision at several points. Loops are unrolled just once, and functions are aggressively summarized. Similarly, Calysto [2] relies on structural abstraction to initially represent function effects as fresh variables. False positives are iteratively eliminated by replacing these variables with precise function summaries.

The bounded model checker in the Varvel/F-Soft verification platform uses lightweight static analysis to infer over-approximate function summaries that are only applied below a configurable depth in the call graph [21, 22]. Therefore, it introduces abstraction only at deeper levels, in an effort to reduce false positives. Sery et al. [29] describe the use of over-approximate summaries in bounded model checking. Whenever assertion violations are found, their method falls back to inlining, to avoid false positives. Therefore, speedups are only attainable for successful verification runs.

Abstraction-based analyses could scale significantly better than symbolic execution. However, they are prone to false positives and, perhaps more importantly, are harder to deploy. Symbolic execution engines do not require hand-written stubs for external functions or system calls, but can instead simply execute the call by concretizing its parameters. This sacrifices the theoretical guarantee of eventually achieving complete path coverage, but is a significant advantage for test case generation and bug finding.

7. Conclusions

In symbolic execution, state merging reduces the number of states that have to be explored, but increases the burden on the constraint solver. We introduced two techniques for reaping practical benefits from state merging: query count estimation and dynamic state merging. With this combination of techniques, state merging becomes completely dynamic and benefit-driven, unlike static strategies such as static merging or precise function summaries. We experimentally confirmed that our approach can significantly improve exploration time and coverage. This suggests that we have indeed come close to a sweet spot in balancing the simplicity of exploring single paths vs. the reduction of redundancy in exploring multiple paths in a merged state.

Other types of precise symbolic program analysis face similar design choices for grouping paths, but approach the sweet spot from a different angle. Therefore, we believe that our results generalize beyond just symbolic execution and that, for example, query count estimation can serve as a partitioning strategy for verification conditions in bounded model checking.

Acknowledgments

We would like to thank Péter Bokor, Aarti Gupta, Rupak Majumdar, Raimondas Sasnauskas, Jonas Wagner, and Cristian Zamfir for their valuable feedback on earlier drafts of this paper. We are grateful to Google and Microsoft for generously supporting our work.

References

[1] S. Anand, P. Godefroid, and N. Tillmann. Demand-driven compositional symbolic execution. In *Intl. Conf. on Tools and Algorithms for the Construction and Analysis of Systems (TACAS)*, 2008.

[2] D. Babic and A. J. Hu. Calysto: scalable and precise extended static checking. In *Intl. Conf. on Software Engineering (ICSE)*, 2008.

[3] P. Boonstoppel, C. Cadar, and D. R. Engler. RWset: Attacking path explosion in constraint-based test generation. In *Intl. Conf. on Tools and Algorithms for the Construction and Analysis of Systems (TACAS)*, 2008.

[4] R. S. Boyer, B. Elspas, and K. N. Levitt. SELECT – a formal system for testing and debugging programs by symbolic execution. In *Intl. Conf. on Reliable Software (ICRS)*, 1975.

[5] C. Cadar, V. Ganesh, P. M. Pawlowski, D. L. Dill, and D. R. Engler. EXE: Automatically generating inputs of death. In *Conf. on Computer and Communications Security (CCS)*, 2006.

[6] C. Cadar, D. Dunbar, and D. R. Engler. KLEE: Unassisted and automatic generation of high-coverage tests for complex systems programs. In *Symp. on Operating Systems Design and Implementation (SOSP)*, 2008.

[7] V. Chipounov, V. Kuznetsov, and G. Candea. S2E: A platform for in-vivo multi-path analysis of software systems. In *Intl. Conf. on Architectural Support for Programming Languages and Operating Systems (ASPLOS)*, 2011.

[8] E. Clarke, D. Kroening, and F. Lerda. A tool for checking ANSI-C programs. In *Intl. Conf. on Tools and Algorithms for the Construction and Analysis of Systems (TACAS)*, 2004.

[9] M. Das, S. Lerner, and M. Seigle. ESP: Path-sensitive program verification in polynomial time. In *Intl. Conf. on Programming Language Design and Implem. (PLDI)*, 2002.

[10] L. M. de Moura and N. Bjørner. Z3: An efficient SMT solver. In *Intl. Conf. on Tools and Algorithms for the Construction and Analysis of Systems (TACAS)*, 2008.

[11] E. W. Dijkstra. Guarded commands, nondeterminacy and formal derivation of programs. *Commun. ACM*, 18(8):453–457, 1975.

[12] N. Eén and N. Sörensson. An extensible SAT-solver. In *Intl. Conf. on Theory and Applications of Satisfiability Testing (SAT)*, 2003.

[13] C. Flanagan, K. R. M. Leino, M. Lillibridge, G. Nelson, J. B. Saxe, and R. Stata. Extended static checking for Java. In *Intl. Conf. on Programming Language Design and Implem. (PLDI)*, 2002.

[14] M. K. Ganai and A. Gupta. Tunneling and slicing: towards scalable BMC. In *Design Automation Conf. (DAC)*, 2008.

[15] V. Ganesh and D. L. Dill. A decision procedure for bit-vectors and arrays. In *Intl. Conf. on Computer Aided Verification (CAV)*, 2007.

[16] P. Godefroid. Compositional dynamic test generation. In *Symp. on Principles of Programming Languages (POPL)*, 2007.

[17] P. Godefroid and D. Luchaup. Automatic partial loop summarization in dynamic test generation. In *Intl. Symp. on Software Testing and Analysis (ISSTA)*, 2011.

[18] P. Godefroid, N. Klarlund, and K. Sen. DART: Directed automated random testing. In *Intl. Conf. on Programming Language Design and Implem. (PLDI)*, 2005.

[19] P. Godefroid, M. Y. Levin, and D. Molnar. Automated whitebox fuzz testing. In *Network and Distributed System Security Symp. (NDSS)*, 2008.

[20] T. Hansen, P. Schachte, and H. Sondergaard. State joining and splitting for the symbolic execution of binaries. In *Intl. Conf. on Runtime Verification (RV)*, 2009.

[21] F. Ivancic, Z. Yang, M. K. Ganai, A. Gupta, I. Shlyakhter, and P. Ashar. F-soft: Software verification platform. In *Intl. Conf. on Computer Aided Verification (CAV)*, 2005.

[22] F. Ivancic, G. Balakrishnan, A. Gupta, S. Sankaranarayanan, N. Maeda, H. Tokuoka, T. Imoto, and Y. Miyazaki. DC2: A framework for scalable, scope-bounded software verification. In *Intl. Conf. on Automated Software Engineering (ASE)*, 2011.

[23] J. C. King. A new approach to program testing. In *Intl. Conf. on Reliable Software (ICRS)*, 1975.

[24] S. K. Lahiri and S. Qadeer. Back to the future: revisiting precise program verification using SMT solvers. In *Symp. on Principles of Programming Languages (POPL)*, 2008.

[25] C. Lattner and V. Adve. LLVM: A compilation framework for lifelong program analysis and transformation. In *Intl. Symp. on Code Generation and Optimization (CGO)*, 2004.

[26] K. R. M. Leino and P. Rümmer. A polymorphic intermediate verification language: Design and logical encoding. In *Intl. Conf. on Tools and Algorithms for the Construction and Analysis of Systems (TACAS)*, 2010.

[27] L. Mauborgne and X. Rival. Trace partitioning in abstract interpretation based static analyzers. In *European Symp. on Programming (ESOP)*, 2005.

[28] K. L. McMillan. Lazy annotation for program testing and verification. In *Intl. Conf. on Computer Aided Verification (CAV)*, 2010.

[29] O. Sery, G. Fedyukovich, and N. Sharygina. Interpolation-based function summaries in bounded model checking. In *Haifa Verification Conf. (HVC)*, 2011.

[30] D. Wheeler. SLOCCount. http://www.dwheeler.com/sloccount/, 2010.

[31] Y. Xie and A. Aiken. Scalable error detection using boolean satisfiability. In *Symp. on Principles of Programming Languages (POPL)*, 2005.

Sound and Precise Analysis of Parallel Programs through Schedule Specialization

Jingyue Wu Yang Tang Gang Hu Heming Cui Junfeng Yang
Columbia University
{jingyue,ty,ganghu,heming,junfeng}@cs.columbia.edu

Abstract

Parallel programs are known to be difficult to analyze. A key reason is that they typically have an enormous number of execution interleavings, or *schedules*. Static analysis over all schedules requires over-approximations, resulting in poor precision; dynamic analysis rarely covers more than a tiny fraction of all schedules. We propose an approach called *schedule specialization* to analyze a parallel program over only a small set of schedules for precision, and then enforce these schedules at runtime for soundness of the static analysis results. We build a schedule specialization framework for C/C++ multithreaded programs that use Pthreads. Our framework avoids the need to modify every analysis to be schedule-aware by specializing a program into a simpler program based on a schedule, so that the resultant program can be analyzed with stock analyses for improved precision. Moreover, our framework provides a precise *schedule-aware* def-use analysis on memory locations, enabling us to build three highly precise analyses: an alias analyzer, a data-race detector, and a path slicer. Evaluation on 17 programs, including 2 real-world programs and 15 popular benchmarks, shows that analyses using our framework reduced may-aliases by 61.9%, false race reports by 69%, and path slices by 48.7%; and detected 7 unknown bugs in well-checked programs.

Categories and Subject Descriptors D.2.4 [*Software Engineering*]: Software/Program Verification; D.4.5 [*Operating Systems*]: Threads

General Terms Algorithms, Design, Reliability, Verification

Keywords Specialization, parallel programs, multithreading, control-flow analysis, data-flow analysis, constraint solving

1. Introduction

The computational power provided by multicore hardware and demanded by the massive number of cloud services has made parallel programs increasingly pervasive and critical. Yet, these programs are known to be difficult to get right; they are often plagued with concurrency errors [25], some of which have caused critical failures [23, 30, 37].

A key reason for these bugs is that parallel programs are difficult to analyze using automated tools. These programs typically have an enormous—asymptotically exponential in the total execution lengths—number of execution interleavings, or *schedules*, presumably to react to various timing factors for performance. Static analysis over all these schedules requires over-approximations, resulting in poor precision and many false positives. Dynamic analysis can precisely analyze the schedules that occur, but it rarely covers more than a tiny fraction of all possible schedules, and the next execution may well run into an unchecked schedule with errors.

Our first contribution is a new approach we call *schedule specialization* that combines the soundness of static analysis and the precision of dynamic analysis. Our insight is that not all of the exponentially many schedules are necessary for good performance. A small set often suffices, as illustrated by recent work on efficient deterministic multithreading [16, 17, 24, 28]. Based on this insight, our approach statically analyzes a parallel program over a small set of schedules, then dynamically enforces these schedules. By focusing on only a small set of schedules, we vastly improve the precision of static analysis; by enforcing the analyzed schedules dynamically, we guarantee soundness of the analysis results. Our approach is loosely analogous to previous approaches that combine static analysis and dynamic checking for memory safety (*e.g.*, [26]), but ours aims at parallel programs and schedules.

Schedule specialization may be implemented in many ways for many parallel programming models such as message passing and multithreading; this paper presents one such implementation for C/C++ programs using Pthreads [34]. We represent a schedule as a total order of synchronizations such as lock operations,[1] which can be efficiently enforced [16, 28, 32]. To ensure that schedules are feasible, we collect them from real executions. To enforce schedules, we leverage our PEREGRINE [17] deterministic multithreading system which can enforce a small set of schedules on a wide range of inputs. For instance, it can use about a hundred schedules to cover over 90% of requests in a real HTTP trace for `Apache` [7]. By reusing schedules, we not only make program behaviors repeatable across inputs, but also amortize the static analysis cost in schedule specialization.[2]

A key challenge we face in implementing schedule specialization is how to statically analyze a program w.r.t. a schedule. A naïve method is to make every analysis involved aware of the schedule, but this method would be quite labor-intensive and error-prone. It may also be fragile: if a crucial analysis, such as alias analysis, is unaware of the schedule, it may easily pollute other analyses.

Solving this challenge leads to our second contribution, a program analysis framework with a set of sound and precise algorithms to *specialize* a program according to a schedule. The resultant program has simpler control and data flow than the original program, and can be analyzed with stock analyses, such as constant folding and dead code elimination, for improved precision. In addition, our framework provides a precise def-use analysis that computes *schedule-aware*, *must*-def-use results on memory locations, which can be the foundation of many other powerful analyses (§7).

To specialize a program toward a schedule, our framework works in two steps. It first specializes the control flow by rewriting the program to map each synchronization in the schedule to a

[1] Users can customize the schedule granularity by selecting which synchronizations go into the schedules (§3).

[2] A set of previously collected schedules may not cover all inputs. If soundness is required on inputs not covered, we may use dynamic analysis (§3).

PLDI'12, June 11–16, 2012, Beijing, China.

unique statement. It then specializes the data flow according to the schedule through a series of analyses and rewrites. For instance, if the program loops `N` (a program variable) times to spawn worker threads and the schedule dictates three worker threads, our framework specializes `N`, as well as the other variables where the value of `N` flows to, to be three. The simplified control and data flow can then greatly improve analysis precision.

Our framework has broad applications. For instance, we can build precise static verifiers (*e.g.*, to verify error-freedom) because our verifiers need only verify a program w.r.t. the schedules enforced. Stock compiler optimizations automatically become more effective on a specialized program because it has simpler control and data flow. Our framework can also benefit "read-only" analyses which do not require enforcing schedules at runtime. For instance, we can build precise error detectors that check a program against a set of common schedules to detect errors more likely to occur, while drastically reducing false positive rates. We can perform precise, automated post-mortem analysis of a failure by analyzing only the schedule recorded in a system log to trim down possible causes.

To demonstrate the usefulness of schedule specialization, we have built three powerful applications with high precision, which form our third contribution of this paper. We create a schedule-aware alias analyzer that can distinguish array elements, leveraging the def-use analysis provided by our framework. Moreover, we create a precise static race detector to detect only the data races that may occur when a given schedule is enforced, thus yielding few false positives. Lastly, we create a schedule-aware path slicer [21] to remove irrelevant statements from an execution trace. This slicer can be applied, for instance, to pinpoint the root cause of a failure or generate filters of bad inputs [15].

We have implemented our framework within the LLVM compiler [1] and evaluated it on 17 multithreaded programs, including 2 real programs such as a popular parallel compression utility `PBZip2` [3] and 15 widely used parallel benchmarks from SPLASH2 [4] and PARSEC [2]. Our results show that schedule specialization greatly improves precision: on average, it reduced may aliases by 61.9%, false race reports by 69%, and path slices by 48.7%. The improved precision also helped detect 7 unknown bugs in well-checked [19, 25, 29, 38, 39] programs.

This paper is organized as follows. We first present relevant background on PEREGRINE (§2) and an overview our framework (§3), then present the key algorithms using an example (§4) and detailed descriptions (§5). We then discuss implementation issues (§6), describe the analyses (§7) we build on top of our framework, and show the evaluation results (§8). We finally discuss related work (§9) and conclude (§10).

2. Background: The PEREGRINE System

Our framework leverages PEREGRINE [17] to collect and enforce schedules. This section briefly describes the relevant mechanisms in PEREGRINE; for details of PEREGRINE, please refer to [16, 17].

Collecting schedules. To ensure that schedules are feasible, we collect them from real executions. To do so, we first replace all synchronizations in a program with calls to our synchronization wrappers. At runtime, when a synchronization wrapper is invoked, it appends an entry to a central log file, then calls the underlying synchronization. The synchronization wrappers are properly synchronized so that only one wrapper may run at any time, ensuring that all synchronizations are totally ordered. After the execution finishes, the log contains a schedule. To collect a set of schedules, we repeatedly run a program against representative workloads, and record the schedule in each execution. Although one could use clever heuristics to select schedules, such as iterating through many schedules to pick the fastest one, we currently do not do so.

Enforcing schedules. Given a schedule, we first compute the *preconditions* required for reusing the schedule on later inputs (explained in the next few paragraphs). Then, if an input meeting these preconditions arrives, we enforce the schedule. Specifically, we make all threads call synchronization wrappers following the total order specified in the schedule, and these wrappers are again properly synchronized so that no two are concurrent. Prior results [16, 17, 24, 28] including ours [16, 17] show that enforcing a synchronization order is efficient because most code is not synchronization and can still run in parallel. For instance, this overhead in PEREGRINE ranges from 68.7% faster to 46.6% slower on a diverse set of 18 programs, including the `Apache` [7].

To compute preconditions for a schedule, we first record a detailed execution trace when recording a schedule. We then perform a modified version [17] of *path slicing* [21] on the trace to remove statement instances that do not affect the feasibility of the schedule, *i.e.*, the reachability of all synchronizations in the schedule. Our version of path slicing correctly tracks dependencies (*e.g.*, shared data accesses) *across* threads. Once we compute a path slice for each thread, we *symbolically* execute each slice, tracking the constraints on input data, such as command line arguments and data read from a file or socket. We then use the conjunction of the constraints from each thread as the preconditions of the schedule.

These preconditions have three properties. First, they do not guarantee program termination because we want to sidestep the difficult problem of statically establishing termination. This property is inherited from path slicing [21]. Second, since computing weakest preconditions is undecidable, the preconditions PEREGRINE computes stay on the sound side: if an input satisfies these preconditions, it can be processed by the corresponding schedule (modulo termination). However, these preconditions may preclude inputs that can indeed be processed by the schedule. Third, these preconditions avoid data races, which may cause an execution to diverge, preventing PEREGRINE from enforcing a given schedule. When computing preconditions, PEREGRINE detects potential races that did not occur in a recorded trace, but may occur if we reuse the schedule on different inputs. It computes preconditions sufficient to avoid these races. PEREGRINE makes the races that occurred in the recorded trace deterministic using dynamic instrumentation.

Our PEREGRINE results show that a small number of schedules can cover a wide range of workloads for half of the 18 evaluated programs. We observe that the synchronizations in these programs depend mostly on "meta" properties such as the number of processor cores, and tend to be loosely coupled with the inputs. For these programs, the coverage of a schedule can be extremely high. For instance, consider `PBZip2` which divides an input file evenly among multiple threads to compress. Two schedules are sufficient to compress any file for `PBZip2` as long as the number of worker threads remains the same. (`PBZip2` needs one schedule if the file size can be evenly divided and another otherwise.) Another data point: about a hundred schedules are sufficient to cover over 90% of requests in a real HTTP trace for `Apache` [7]. This *stability* [16] not only makes program behaviors repeatable across inputs, but also reduces the runtime overhead of our framework (§3).

3. Framework Overview

This section presents an overview of our schedule specialization framework by presenting its key definitions and properties.

We assign each statement in a program P a unique static label l_j. An *execution trace*, or a *trace*, of P, denoted by T, is a potentially infinite sequence of dynamic statement instances $i_0, i_1, \ldots$ where each i_j is a tuple $\langle t, l \rangle$, indicating that i_j is an instance of statement l executed by thread t; and if i_j was completed before the start of i_n, then $j < n$ (concurrently executed statements can be ordered either way). Given $i = \langle t, l \rangle$, we use $i.label$ to access l.

A *schedule*, denoted by S, is a sequence of synchronizations $s_0, s_1, \ldots, s_N$ where each s_j is a dynamic statement instance $\langle t, l \rangle$ and l is a synchronization statement. While we anticipate our approach will work well with many parallel programming models, our current framework targets C/C++ programs that use Pthreads. It includes three types of synchronizations in the schedules: (1) Pthread synchronizations such as `pthread_create` and `pthread_mutex_lock` operations; (2) entries and exits of thread functions (functions passed to `pthread_create`) and `main` because these events are natural synchronization points; and (3) additional function calls to resolve ambiguity when a synchronization may be invoked in different calling contexts (explained in §5.1). We call the first two classes *true synchronizations* and the last class *derived synchronizations*. Unless otherwise specified, we use synchronizations to refer to both true and derived synchronizations.

To ensure that schedules are feasible, we collect them from terminating execution traces. A schedule includes only totally ordered synchronizations because our runtime ensures that synchronizations are never concurrent (§2). It need not contain all synchronizations from a trace, enabling flexible tradeoffs between precision and analysis time (see the end of this section).

Different traces may map to the same schedule because traces are more fine-grained than schedules. We use $run(P)$ to denote the set of all traces of program P, including non-terminating ones. These traces cover all possible inputs to P. We use $runs_S(P)$ to denote the subset of traces in $run(P)$ with schedule S enforced. Traces in $runs_S(P)$ cover only inputs meeting the preconditions of S. Even though S is collected from a terminating trace, another trace with S enforced may still be non-terminating because the preconditions PEREGRINE computes do not guarantee termination (§2). Thus, $runs_S(P)$ may include non-terminating traces with a prefix of S enforced.

Without schedule specialization, a static analysis has to consider conceptually all traces in $run(P)$ for soundness. With schedule specialization, a static analysis need consider only traces in $runs_S(P)$ for each enforced schedule S, potentially computing much more precise results. One method to use this potential is to modify every analysis to be aware of the schedule and consider a set of executions closer to $runs_S(P)$, but this method has the drawbacks discussed in §1.

To avoid modifying every analysis to be aware of schedules, our framework rewrites P into a specialized program P_S for each schedule S so that $run(P_S)$ is close to $runs_S(P)$. P_S can then be analyzed with many stock analyses for improved precision. To analyze P over a set of schedules, we can generate a specialized program for each schedule, then merge the analysis results. In addition, our framework provides a constraint-based def-use analysis on P_S that computes precise must-def-use chains on memory locations allowed only by the schedule S. By querying this def-use analysis, stock or slightly modified advanced analyses such as alias analysis can then compute schedule-aware results.

Precision. Ideally for full precision, our framework should make $run(P_S) = runs_S(P)$, so that static analysis of P_S considers only traces in $runs_S(P)$. In our current framework, $run(P_S)$ may still include traces not in $runs_S(P)$ because, without enforcing S with PEREGRINE, an execution of P_S may use a different schedule. Nonetheless, since $run(P_S)$ is much smaller than $run(P)$, stock analyses on P_S should still yield more precise results than on P. Our def-use analysis excludes def-use chains forbidden by the total order in S. That is, it considers traces in $runs_S(P_S)$, which our specialization algorithms (§5) guarantee to be $runs_S(P)$. The def-use results provided by our framework are thus much more precise than what a stock def-use analysis can compute on P_S.

Soundness. Our framework guarantees that static analysis results on P_S hold for all traces in $runs_S(P)$, *i.e.*, whenever schedule S is enforced on program P, because (1) the results from a static analysis on P_S should hold for all traces in $run(P_S)$; and (2) our specialization algorithms guarantee $run(P_S) \supseteq runs_S(P)$. In addition, our framework guarantees that the def-use results it provides hold for $runs_S(P_S)$, which is $runs_S(P)$.

Assumptions and non-assumptions. In our current framework, the soundness of static analysis results is conditioned on that one of the analyzed schedules is enforced. A finite set of schedules collected by PEREGRINE, however, may not cover all inputs. If an input cannot be processed by any of the schedules (or it can but our framework cannot determine this fact), the static analysis results may no longer hold for the execution on this input. If users want to retain soundness on such inputs, they may use dynamic analysis. For instance, if the analysis goal is to verify race freedom, they may use dynamic data race detection on such inputs. If dynamic analysis is used, the overall runtime overhead of our framework may depend on the actual workload, or how frequently it can enforce an analyzed schedule. Fortunately, our PEREGRINE results show that, for many programs, a small set of schedules can cover a wide range of the workloads (§2). For these programs and workloads, our framework rarely needs to use dynamic analysis.

Moreover, even if we cannot use a small set of schedules to cover a wide range of workloads, schedule specialization is still useful for many applications. These applications include all read-only applications such as error detection and post-mortem analysis which do not require soundness on the inputs not covered by analyzed schedules. They also include optimizations because we can simply run the original program on the inputs not covered.

At the algorithmic level, we do not assume data-race-free programs because we intend to keep our framework general and applicable to not just optimizations, but other applications, such as verification and error detection. In particular, data races cannot prevent us from enforcing a schedule (§2). Nonetheless, if optimization is the only goal, we can easily modify our algorithms to exploit this assumption for better results. At the implementation level, our current framework leverages the LLVM compiler, which may indeed assume race freedom. This assumption may be removed by re-implementing the LLVM components we leverage.

Our framework does not require that a schedule collected from a trace includes all synchronizations in the trace. Instead, users can customize the schedule granularity, or which synchronizations go into the schedules, by blacklisting certain synchronization statements. This design enables users to make flexible three-way tradeoffs between precision, analysis time, and schedule reuse-rate. In general, fine-grained schedules have lower reuse-rates and lead to larger specialized programs and longer analysis time, but make the analysis results more precise. One exception is that users should typically blacklist synchronizations hidden behind an abstraction boundary, such as a memory allocator interface, because these synchronizations rarely improve precision but worsen analysis time and reuse-rate. For instance, we blacklisted the lock operations in the custom memory allocator in `cholesky` (§6). An interesting research question is how to optimally make this three-way tradeoff, which we leave for future work.

4. An Example and Algorithm Overview

This section illustrates how our framework operates using an example based on two programs in our evaluation benchmarks: `aget`, a parallel `wget`-like utility; and `fft`, a parallel scientific benchmark.

Figure 1 shows the example program. As can be seen from the code, each thread accesses a disjoint partition of `results`. Suppose we want to build a precise alias analysis to compute this fact, so that we can for example avoid wrongly flagging accesses to `results`

```
1 : int results[MAX];
2 : struct {int first; int last;} ranges[MAX];
3 : int global_id = 0;
4 : int main(int argc, char *argv[]) {
5 :   int i;
6 :   int p = atoi(argv[1]), n = atoi(argv[2]);
7 :   for (i = 0; i < p; ++i) {
8 :     ranges[i].first = n * i / p;
9 :     ranges[i].last = n * (i + 1) / p;
10:   }
11:   for (i = 0; i < p; ++i)
12:     pthread_create(&child[i], 0, worker, 0);
13:   for (i = 0; i < p; ++i)
14:     pthread_join(child[i], 0);
15:   return 0;
16: }
17: void *worker(void *arg) {
18:   pthread_mutex_lock(&global_id_lock);
19:   int my_id = global_id++;
20:   pthread_mutex_unlock(&global_id_lock);
21:   for (int i = ranges[my_id].first; i < ranges[my_id].last; ++i)
22:     results[i] = compute(i);
23:   return 0;
24: }
```

Figure 1: *An example showing how schedule specialization works.* Variable n and p are two inputs that specify the size of the global array `results` and the number of worker threads, respectively. The code first partitions `results` evenly by the number of worker threads p and saves the range of each thread to `ranges` (lines 7–10); it then starts p worker threads to process the partitions (lines 11–12). Each worker enters a critical section to set its instance of `my_id` and increment `global_id` (lines 18–20), and then computes and saves the results to its partition (lines 21–22).

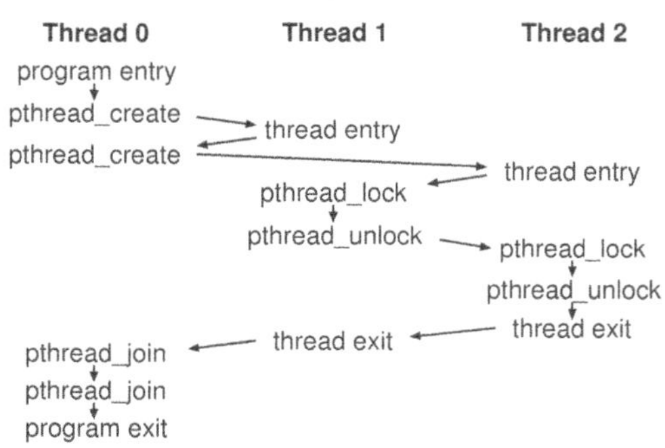

Figure 2: *A possible schedule of the example in Figure 1 when* p *is 2.*

as races for a static race detector. Unfortunately, doing so requires solving a variety of difficult problems. For instance, since p, the number of threads, is determined at runtime, static analysis often has to approximate these dynamic threads as one or two abstract thread instances. It may thus collapse distinct accesses to `results` from different threads as one access, computing imprecise alias results. Even if an analysis can (1) distinguish the accesses to `results` by different threads and (2) infer bounds on integers such as array indices using range analysis [33], it may still fail to compute that these accesses are disjoint. The reason is that the array partition each worker accesses depends on its instance of `my_id`, which further depends on the schedule (or the order in which worker threads enter the critical section at lines 18–20). In short, if a static analysis has to consider all possible schedules of this program, it would be very difficult to compute precise results.

Fortunately, these difficult problems are greatly simplified by schedule specialization. Suppose whenever p is 2, we always enforce the schedule shown in Figure 2. Since the number of threads is fixed, distinguishing them becomes easy. In addition, since the

```
... // same global declarations as in Figure 1
int main(int argc, char *argv[]) {
  int i;
  int p = atoi(argv[1]), n = atoi(argv[2]);
  for (i = 0; i < p; ++i) {
    ranges[i].first = n * i / p;
    ranges[i].last = n * (i + 1) / p;
  }
  i = 0; assume(i < p);
  pthread_create(&child[i], 0, worker_CLONE1, 0);
  ++i; assume(i < p);
  pthread_create(&child[i], 0, worker_CLONE2, 0);
  ++i; assume(i >= p);
  i = 0; assume(i < p);
  pthread_join(child[i], 0);
  ++i; assume(i < p);
  pthread_join(child[i], 0);
  ++i; assume(i >= p);
  return 0;
}
void *worker_CLONE1(void *arg) {
  pthread_mutex_lock(&global_id_lock);
  int my_id = global_id++;
  pthread_mutex_unlock(&global_id_lock);
  for (int i = ranges[my_id].first; i < ranges[my_id].last; ++i)
    results[i] = compute(i);
  return 0;
}
void *worker_CLONE2(void *arg) {
  pthread_mutex_lock(&global_id_lock);
  int my_id = global_id++;
  pthread_mutex_unlock(&global_id_lock);
  for (int i = ranges[my_id].first; i < ranges[my_id].last; ++i)
    results[i] = compute(i);
  return 0;
}
```

Figure 3: *The resultant program after control-flow specialization.* The loops at lines 11–12 and lines 13–14 in Figure 1 are unrolled because they contain synchronizations in the schedule, while the other loops are not. Thread function `worker` is cloned twice, making it easy for an analysis to distinguish the two worker threads. The algorithm adds special `assume` calls to pass constraints on variables to the data-flow specialization step.

order in which threads enter the critical section at lines 18–20 is fixed, each worker thread always gets a fixed `my_id` and thus accesses a fixed partition of `results`.

To practically take advantage of these observations, our framework specializes a program toward a schedule. It does so in two steps. In the first step, it specializes the control flow of the program by "straightening" the program so that each synchronization in the schedule maps to a unique statement, and the synchronizations within each thread are control-equivalent. Specifically, it first constructs a super control flow graph (CFG) of the program, which includes function call and return edges. It then iterates through each pair of consecutive synchronizations (s_1, s_2) in a thread, and clones the statements between s_1 and s_2 in the CFG. Figure 3 shows the result after specializing control flow. Loops containing synchronizations such as `pthread_create` are unrolled, and thread functions are cloned, making it easy for an analysis to distinguish threads. Note that such cloning and unrolling are selectively done only to functions that may do synchronizations, so they would not explode the size of a specialized program.

In the second step, our framework specializes the data flow through a series of analyses. For instance, it constructs an advanced def-use graph for variables and memory locations according to the schedule, and replaces variables with constant values when it can.

```
... // same global declarations as in Figure 1
int main(int argc, char *argv[]) {
  int p = atoi(argv[1]), n = atoi(argv[2]);
  ranges[0].first = 0;
  ranges[0].last = n / 2;
  ranges[1].first = n / 2;
  ranges[1].last = n;
  pthread_create(&child[0], 0, worker_CLONE1, 0);
  pthread_create(&child[1], 0, worker_CLONE2, 0);
  pthread_join(child[0], 0);
  pthread_join(child[1], 0);
  return 0;
}
void *worker_CLONE1(void *arg) {
  pthread_mutex_lock(&global_id_lock);
  global_id = 1;
  pthread_mutex_unlock(&global_id_lock);
  for (int i = 0; i < ranges[0].last; ++i)
    results[i] = compute(i);
  return 0;
}
void *worker_CLONE2(void *arg) {
  pthread_mutex_lock(&global_id_lock);
  global_id = 2;
  pthread_mutex_unlock(&global_id_lock);
  for (int i = ranges[1].first; i < ranges[1].last; ++i)
    results[i] = compute(i);
  return 0;
}
```

Figure 4: *The resultant program after data-flow specialization.* Variable p and my_id are replaced with constants, the loop at lines 5–8 in Figure 3 is unrolled, and some dead code is removed.

It does these analyses by collecting constraints from the program and querying a constraint solver. For instance, from lines 9, 11, and 13 in Figure 3, it infers that p must be 2, so it replaces p with 2. Similarly, it computes a precise def-use chain for the accesses to global_id, and infers that each my_id instance has a constant value. Once variables are replaced with constants, we can apply techniques such as constant folding, dead code elimination, and loop unrolling to further specialize the program. Moreover, these stock techniques and our analyses can run iteratively, until the program cannot be specialized any more. Figure 4 shows the result of specializing data flow.

Benefits of schedule specialization. The specialized program in Figure 4 has much simpler control and data flow than the original program in Figure 1, enabling stock analyses to compute more precise results. For instance, range analysis can now compute thread-sensitive results because the worker function is cloned; it can also compute precise bounds for the loop index i in the worker clones because the indice to ranges are now constant, not my_id which can have a large range if no schedule is enforced.

Our framework guarantees that static analysis results on Figure 4 hold for the set of all traces with the schedule in Figure 2 enforced. This set is fairly large because this schedule can be enforced as long as the number of threads p is 2, regardless of the data size n or the contents of other input data. A small set of such schedules, including one for each number of threads, can practically cover all inputs because (1) most parallel programs we evaluate achieve peak performance when the number of worker threads is identical or close to the number of processor cores and (2) the number of cores a machine has is typically small (*e.g.*, smaller than 100). This example illustrates the best case of our approach: by analyzing only a small set of schedules, we enjoy both precision and soundness for practically all inputs.

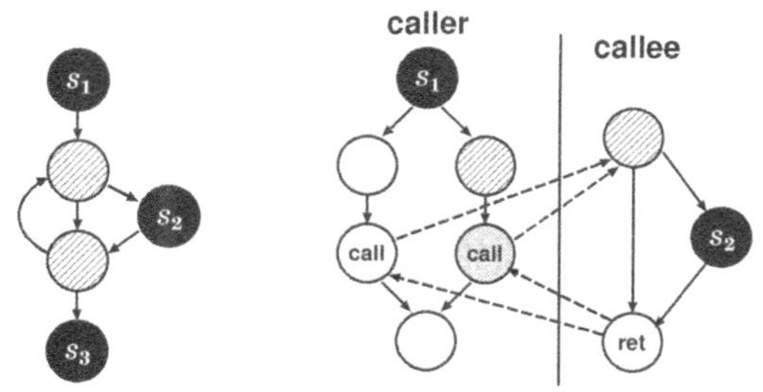

(a) *Intra-procedural ambiguity* (b) *Inter-procedural ambiguity*

Figure 5: *Two types of ambiguity.* The black nodes are synchronizations. The hatched nodes are the statements between s_1 and s_2 computed by the reachability analysis. The gray "call" node is a derived synchronization marked to resolve inter-procedural ambiguity.

5. Algorithms

This section describes our algorithms to specialize the control flow (§5.1) and data flow (§5.2) of a program toward a schedule.

5.1 Specializing Control Flow

To ease the description of our algorithms, we define a *segment*, denoted by G, as the maximal portion of the CFG between two synchronization statements l_1 and l_2 that is free of other synchronization statements. A segment between l_1 and l_2 includes any statement s.t. (1) l_1 can reach this statement in the CFG without reaching any other synchronization statements and (2) this statement can reach l_2 without reaching any other synchronization statements. We denote the set of statements in G by $G.L$, and the set of control-flow edges in G by $G.E$.

To specialize the control flow, we clone the segment between every two consecutive synchronizations within a thread, and then join all cloned segments together to form the specialized program. One difficulty to find all statements between two consecutive synchronizations is *ambiguity*: there may be multiple ways from one synchronization to another. For instance, Figure 5a shows an ambiguous case caused by multiple paths in the CFG. The loop body shown has two paths, only one of which contains synchronization s_2. This loop has to be transformed so that s_1 and s_2 become control-equivalent. Our algorithm to specialize control flow automatically handles this case, described later in this subsection.

Figure 5b shows another ambiguous case caused by multiple paths in the call graph. From s_1 to s_2, we can go through either call. To resolve call-stack ambiguity, we instrument calls to functions that may transitively do synchronizations, and include these *derived synchronizations* in the schedule as well. The result is that we can compute exactly one call stack for each synchronization in a schedule. Our evaluation shows that the number of derived synchronizations is small, and they incur negligible overhead (§8.2).

Algorithm 1 shows how we specialize the control flow of a program. We first explain the helper function SpecializeControlFlowThread, which takes the original program P, a schedule S, and a thread t, and outputs a subprogram P'_t specialized according to t's synchronizations in S. For every two consecutive synchronizations of t, this function does a forward and a backward depth-first search to find the segment between the two synchronizations. It then clones the segment, copying and renaming functions as necessary, and appends the segment clone to P'_t.

Function DFS traverses the CFG from statement l_1 to l_2 and saves the visited portion of the CFG to output parameter G_{out}. It backtracks whenever it meets a synchronization. During the traversal, it maintains the current call stack in cs so that it can compute where to return (l_{ret}). When it reaches l_2, it saves the call stack to output parameter cs_{out}, which SpecializeControlFlowThread will pass to BackwardDFS (in the same iteration) and DFS (in the next iteration). If there are multiple paths from l_1 to l_2, DFS may reach

Algorithm 1: Control-Flow Specialization

Input : the original program P and a schedule S
Output: the specialized program
SpecializeControlFlow(P, S)
  foreach thread t **do**
    $P'_t \leftarrow$ SpecializeControlFlowThread(P, S, t)
  foreach P'_t **do**
    foreach statement l in P'_t **do**
      if l is a `pthread_create` **then**
        $ct \leftarrow$ child thread created by l
        set thread function of l to P'_{ct}
  return $\cup_t P'_t$
SpecializeControlFlowThread(P, S, t)
  $P'_t \leftarrow \emptyset$ // the specialized subprogram for thread t
  $cs \leftarrow \emptyset$ // the call stack of the current synchronization
  $S_t \leftarrow$ the sub-schedule of S for thread t
  for (s_i, s_{i+1}) in S_t **do**
    $G \leftarrow (\{s_i.label\}, \emptyset)$ // segment between s_i & s_{i+1}
    // G and the second cs below are output parameters.
    DFS(cs, $s_i.label$, $s_{i+1}.label$, cs, G)
    BackwardDFS(cs, $s_{i+1}.label$, $s_i.label$, G)
    $P'_t \leftarrow P'_t \cup$ Clone(G)
  return P'_t
DFS(cs, l_1, l_2, cs_{out}, G_{out})   // l_1 and l_2 may be the same
  if l_1 is a derived synchronization **then**
    $l \leftarrow$ entry of l_1's callee function
    TryDFS($cs + l_1$, l_1, l, l_2, cs_{out}, G_{out})
  else if l_1 is a return statement **then**
    $l_{ret} \leftarrow$ the top of cs
    $l \leftarrow l_{ret}$'s intra-procedural successor
    TryDFS($cs - l_{ret}$, l_1, l, l_2, cs_{out}, G_{out})
  else
    foreach intra-procedural successor l of l_1 **do**
      TryDFS(cs, l_1, l, l_2, cs_{out}, G_{out})
TryDFS(cs, l_1, l, l_2, cs_{out}, G_{out})
  $G_{out}.E \leftarrow G_{out}.E \cup \{(l_1, l)\}$
  if $l = l_2$ **then**
    $cs_{out} \leftarrow cs$
  if $l \notin G_{out}.L$ **then**
    $G_{out}.L \leftarrow G_{out}.L \cup \{l\}$
    if l is not a synchronization **then**
      DFS(cs, l, l_2, cs_{out}, G_{out})

l_2 multiple times in one traversal, but each time the call stack must always be identical because call-stack ambiguity is resolved.

The results of DFS may include statements and CFG edges that cannot reach $s_{i+1}.label$. BackwardDFS prunes these statements and edges by traversing G, not the full CFG, backward from $s_{i+1}.label$ to $s_i.label$. It is similar to DFS except it is backward and need not output a call stack, so we omit it from Algorithm 1.

We now explain the main function of this algorithm, SpecializeControlFlow. It first invokes SpecializeControlFlowThread to compute a specialized program based on the synchronizations of each thread. It then replaces the thread function in each `pthread_create` callsite with the cloned thread function. It finally merges all the specialized programs together.

Discussion. We note three subtleties of Algorithm 1. First, it automatically handles the ambiguity in Figure 5a. Suppose the schedule is $s_1 s_2 s_3$. We do not know the loop bound because one path in the loop body calls s_2 and the other does not. However, our algorithm can still specialize the CFG into Figure 6. This feature is critical

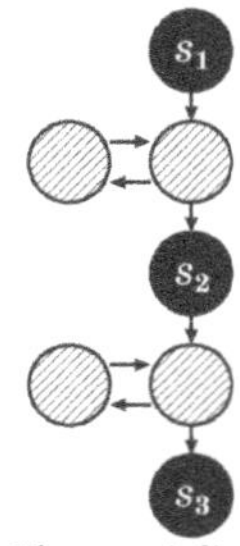

Figure 6: *The specialized CFG of Figure 5a with schedule $s_1 s_2 s_3$.*

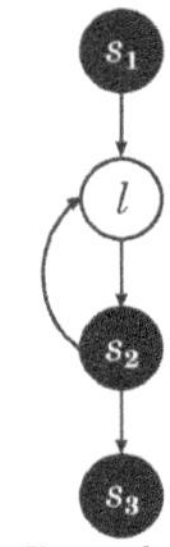

Figure 7: *Example illustrating the need to traverse CFG edges.*

in some cases. For example, if s_2 is `pthread_create`, this feature clones the thread functions, providing thread-sensitivity.

Second, *DFS* traverses into the body of a function only when the call to this function is a derived synchronization, *i.e.*, this function may transitively do synchronization. Thus, the G_{out} it computes includes only CFG portions from such functions, and is not a full segment. The effect is that only these CFG portions are cloned, possibly multiple times, and each clone is *unique* to a segment in the resultant program; other functions are copied verbatim to the resultant program. By doing so, we capture the information from the schedule without exploding the size of a specialized program.

Lastly, to compute a segment, we cannot simply compute only the statements in the segment and copy all edges from the original CFG. To illustrate, consider Figure 7. Suppose the schedule is $s_1 s_2 s_3$. The segment between s_1 and s_2 should include statements s_1, s_2, and l, but exclude the CFG edge from s_2 to l.

5.2 Specializing Data Flow

Given a control-flow-specialized program, we specialize its data flow using a series of constraint-based analyses leveraging the STP [5] integer constraint solver. We collect constraints on two types of program constructs: the LLVM virtual registers and memory locations. LLVM virtual registers are already in static-single-assignment (SSA) form, so collecting constraints on them is relatively straightforward. Table 1 lists how we collect constraints for some LLVM instructions; the remaining instructions are similar and omitted for space. We handle loops by exploiting LLVM's loop structure: most of the loops in our evaluated programs are canonicalized by LLVM so that we can easily collect range constraints on the loop indices.

Our algorithm to collect constraints on memory locations mimics classic def-use analysis. It collects two forms of constraints on memory locations: (1) the value loaded by an LLVM load instruction is the same as the value stored by a store instruction and (2) the value loaded by a load is the same as the value loaded by another load. That is, we treat an LLVM load instruction as a "use" and an LLVM *load or store* instruction as a "def." Treating loads as defs shortens the def-use chains and reduces analysis time.

Collecting precise def-use constraints on memory locations is challenging for multithreaded programs. Fortunately, schedule specialization enables two key refinements over classic def-use analysis so that our algorithm can collect more precise constraints. First, we compute def-use chains spanning across threads because multiple threads may indeed access the same shared memory location. Without schedule specialization, it would be hopeless to track precise inter-thread def-use chains because the defs and uses may pair up in numerous ways depending on the schedules.

Second, we compute *must*-def-use, instead of may-def-use, results. Our insight is that by fixing the schedule, we often fix the def-use chains of key shared data, such as the `global_id` in Figure 1. It is thus most cost-effective to focus on these must-def-use chains because (1) they essentially capture the information (and hence the precision; see results in §8.1) from the schedule and (2)

Instruction type	LLVM instruction	STP constraint	Note
binary	$a = b$ op c	$a = b$ op c	"op" is a binary operator
integer comparison	a = icmp pred, b, c	$a = (b$ pred $c)$	"pred" is an integer comparison predicate such as $<$ and $\neq$
pointer arithmetic	a = gep $b, i_1, \ldots, i_k$	$a = b + i_1 \times$ sizeof(*b) + the offset of i_k-th field of i_{k-1}-th field of ... of i_2-th field of b	"gep" calculates the location of a specific field in an array/structure
select instruction	a = select b, v_1, v_2	$b = 0 \rightarrow a = v_1$ $b = 1 \rightarrow a = v_2$	If $b = 0$, $a = v_1$; otherwise $a = v_2$
Φ instruction	$a = \Phi(v_1, \ldots, v_k)$	$a = v_1$ or ... or $a = v_k$	a may have any incoming value
call and return	$a = \text{func}(b_1, \ldots, b_k)$ $\text{func}(f_1, \ldots, f_k)$ {return r;}	$b_1 = f_1, \ldots, b_k = f_k$ $a = r$	Capture the equalities between the actual and formal parameters/return values

Table 1: Collecting constraints from LLVM instructions on virtual registers.

there are typically much fewer must-def-use constraints than may-def-use constraints, so the constraint-solving cost is low.

To practically implement these refinements, we compute def-use chains only on the instructions unique to each segment. In addition, we look for defs of a use only from its *inter-thread dominators* which always execute before the use once the schedule is enforced. These dominators are dominators on the CFG augmented with edges representing the total order of synchronizations in a schedule. We explain our algorithm as well as these refinements in the next few paragraphs.

Algorithm 2 shows the pseudo code to collect def-use constraints for memory locations. It operates on a control-flow specialized program with each synchronization in the schedule mapped to a unique instruction. It references several symbols defined on the instructions and segments (§5.1) in this program:

- $value(l)$: the value loaded if l is a load instruction, or the value stored if l is a store;
- $loc(l)$: the memory location accessed by instruction l;
- $segment(l)$: the unique (explained in the next paragraph) segment containing instruction l, or $None$;
- $thread(G)$: the thread containing segment G;
- $begin(G)$: the synchronization at the beginning of segment G;
- $end(G)$: the synchronization at the end of segment G;
- $reach(l_1, l_2)$: the set of instructions on all *simple paths* from l_1 to l_2 in the CFG. A simple path has no repeated instructions.

Each segment has some unique instructions cloned by Algorithm 1; $segment(l)$ returns the containing segment for these instructions, or $None$ otherwise. We define a *partial order* over these instructions as follows: l_1 *happens-before* l_2, or $l_1 \prec l_2$, if (1) both l_1 and l_2 are synchronizations, and l_1 comes earlier than l_2 in the schedule; (2) $segment(l_1) = segment(l_2)$, and l_1 comes earlier in the segment; or (3) $\exists l_3$, s.t. $l_1 \prec l_3$ and $l_3 \prec l_2$. We say $G_1 \prec G_2$ if $end(G_1) \prec begin(G_2)$. Two instructions (segments) are concurrent if there is no happens-before between them.

At the top level, Algorithm 2 is similar to classic def-use analysis. CaptureConstraints takes a use u, calls PotentialDefs to get a set of potential defs, and, for each *live* def not killed, adds an equality constraint between the value used and the live def.

PotentialDefs illustrates how we implement the refinements enabled by schedule specialization. It processes a use u only if $segment(u)$ is not $None$, *i.e.*, u is unique to a segment. It searches for defs only in the instructions unique to each segment. To account for shared data access, it searches each thread t_d for a def of u. If t_d is the thread containing u, we search backwards from u for the latest dominator in CFG that accesses the same location. Otherwise, we search backwards from the latest synchronization s in t_d that happens-before u, and locate the latest dominator of s in CFG that accesses the same location. This dominator of s is essentially an inter-thread dominator of u. The result of PotentialDefs contains at most one def from each thread. In addition, it contains at most one store and possibly many loads (because we treat loads as defs).

Algorithm 2: Capture Constraints on Memory Locations

```
CaptureConstraints(u)
    foreach d ∈ PotentialDefs(u) do
        if not MayBeKilled(d, u) then
            AddConstraint("value(u) = value(d)")
PotentialDefs(u)
    defs ← ∅
    G_u ← segment(u)
    p ← loc(u)
    if G_u ≠ None then
        foreach thread t_d do
            if thread(G_u) = t_d then
                defs ← defs ∪ LatestDef(u, p)
            else
                G_d ← latest segment of t_d s.t. G_d ≺ G_u
                defs ← defs ∪ LatestDef(end(G_d), p)
    return defs
LatestDef(l, p)        // returns the latest intra-thread definition
    d ← l
    repeat
        d ← ImmediateDominator(d);
    until d = None or MustAlias(p, loc(d))
    if d ≠ None then return {d}
    else return ∅
MayBeKilled(d, u)
    G_d ← segment(d)
    G_u ← segment(u)
    if G_d = G_u then
        return MayStore(reach(d, u), u)
    foreach segment G s.t. begin(G) ≺ end(G_u) and
    begin(G_d) ≺ end(G) and G ≠ G_d and G ≠ G_u do
        if MayStore(G, u) then return true
    return MayStore(reach(d, end(G_d)), u) or
    MayStore(reach(begin(G_u), u), u)
MayStore(L, u)
    foreach store l ∈ L do
        if MayAlias(loc(l), loc(u)) then return true
    return false
```

Function MayBeKilled checks whether def d is killed by any instruction that may store to $loc(u)$ and execute after d and before u. It considers all instructions, not just the unique ones, for soundness. If d and u are in the same segment, *MayBeKilled* simply checks the instructions between d and u in the CFG. Otherwise, it checks instructions in any segment that may (1) begin no later than the end of u's segment G_u and (2) end no earlier than the begin of d's segment G_d. Note that these segments include not only the ones concurrent to G_u or G_d, but also any segment G s.t. $G_d \prec G \prec G_u$.

The above algorithm to collect constraints on memory locations needs alias analysis to determine whether two pointers must or may alias. We answer these queries again using STP. The question "whether v_1 and v_2 may alias" is rephrased as "whether $v_1 = v_2$ is satisfiable," and "whether v_1 and v_2 must alias" is rephrased as "whether $v_1 = v_2$ is provable." Since constraint solving may take time, we also ported `bddbddb` [36], a faster but less precise alias analysis to our framework, by writing an LLVM front end to collect program facts into the format `bddbddb` expects. We always query `bddbddb` first before STP.

Once constraints are captured, we perform a series of analyses based on these constraints. One analysis infers which LLVM virtual register has constant values (recall that these registers are in SSA form). It first queries STP for an assignment of value v_j to each variable a_j. For each a_j, it then adds $a_j = v_j$ to the current constraints, and checks whether STP can prove the new constraints. If so, it replaces a_j with v_j, such as replacing variable `p` in Figure 1 with constant 2. Once variables are replaced with constants, we perform stock LLVM analyses, such as constant folding, dead code elimination, and loop unrolling, which automatically gain precision due to schedule specialization. These analyses may further simplify a program, so we iteratively run data-flow specialization and these stock analyses until the specialized program converges.

6. Implementation

We implement our framework within LLVM [1]. The specialization algorithms described in the previous section are implemented as an LLVM pass that specializes the LLVM bitcode representation of an original program into a new bitcode program. These passes are of 11,754 lines of C/C++ code, with 2,586 lines for control-flow specialization and 9,168 lines for data-flow specialization. The remaining of this section discusses several implementation issues.

6.1 Constructing Call Graph

For clarity, Algorithm 1 assumes a simple call graph where each function call has a unique callee and unique return address. However, the programs we analyze do use function pointers and exceptions, invalidating this assumption. To resolve a call to a function pointer, we query our alias analysis and call *TryDFS* on each possible callee. To handle exceptions, we pair up the LLVM instruction that unwinds the stack (`UnwindInst`) with the call instruction that sets an exception handler (`InvokeInst`).

6.2 Optimizing Constraint Solving

Data-flow specialization (§5.2) frequently queries STP, and these queries can be quite expensive. We thus create four optimizations to speed up constraint solving. First, when identifying which variables are constants, we avoid querying STP for each variable. Specifically, when we query STP to prove that a variable is constant, we remember the value assignment STP returns even if STP cannot prove the query. If a variable has two different values in these assignments, then this variable cannot be constant, so we do not need to query STP whether this variable is constant. This optimization alone speeds up our framework by over 10 times.

Second, we cache extensively. Recall that data-flow specialization runs Algorithm 2 and other analyses iteratively. Within each iteration, we cache all alias results to avoid redundantly querying STP. Across iterations, we cache "must" and "must-not" alias results and the def-use results because each iteration only adds more constraints and does not invalidate these precise results.

Third, we use a union-find algorithm to speed up equality constraints solving. The def-use constraints we collect are all equality constraints. When the number of STP variables involved in these constraints increases, the STP queries tend to run slower. To reduce the number of STP variables, we put program variables that must be equal in one equivalent class represented by a union-find data structure, and assign only one STP variable to each class.

Lastly, we parallelize constraint solving. The STP queries issued by our framework are mostly independent. Specifically, each run of Algorithm 2 on a use is completely independent of another. In addition, checking whether one variable is constant is often independent of checking another. We have built a parallel version of STP that speeds up our framework by roughly 3x when running on a quad-core machine.

6.3 Manual Annotations

Our framework supports three types of annotations to increase precision and reduce analysis time. First, users can provide a blacklist of synchronization statements to customize which synchronizations go into the schedules (§3). Second, users can write regular assertions to enable our framework to collect more precise constraints. For instance, they can write "`assert(lower_bound <= index && index <= upper_bound)`" to inform our framework the range constraints on `index`. Third, users can provide function summaries to reduce analysis time. Some functions in the evaluated programs are quite complex and contain many load and store instructions, causing our framework to collect a large set of constraints. However, these functions often have simple shared memory access patterns which users can easily summarize to speed up constraint solving. These summaries can be quite coarse-grained, such as "function `foo` writes an unconstrained value to variable `x`." Users write summaries by writing fake functions, which our framework analyzes instead of the original functions. By supporting annotations in forms of assertions and fake functions, we avoid the need to support an annotation language.

Of the 17 programs evaluated, we annotated only 4 programs. We blacklisted the lock operations in the custom memory allocator in `cholesky`. We annotated two loops in `raytrace` with assertions because they are not in LLVM-canonical form. (Currently our framework handles only canonical loops.) We summarized five functions: `image_segment` and `image_extract_helper` in `ferret`, `TraverseBVH_with_StandardMesh` and `TraverseBVH_with_DirectMesh` in `raytrace`, and `LogLikelihood` in `bodytrack`. These summaries range from 8 to 18 lines.

7. Applications

To demonstrate the precision of our framework, we build three powerful analyses. The first is a precise schedule-aware alias analyzer, built on top of our def-use analysis (§5.2). We chose to build an alias analyzer because alias analysis is crucial to many program analyses and optimizations. Our analyzer provides a standard MayAlias(p, q) query interface, making it effortless to switch existing analyses to our our alias analyzer. Under the hood, MayAlias first queries a coarse-grained, existing alias analysis; if this coarse-grained analysis returns true, MayAlias then queries our def-use analysis for precise answers. The existing alias analysis we used is the C version[3] of `bddbddb` ported to LLVM.

The second tool is a precise static race detector that detects races that may occur only when a schedule is enforced. The detection logic appears identical to classic race detectors: two memory accesses are a race if (1) they may alias, (2) at least one of the accesses is a store, and (3) they are concurrent. There are two key differences. First, ours uses schedule-aware alias analysis. Second, ours detects concurrent accesses w.r.t. a total synchronization order (§5.2), more stringent than the execution order constraints dictated by the synchronizations. These two differences enable our detector to emit no or extremely few false positives (§8.1). Multiple races

[3] The alias analysis we use makes several assumptions about the C programs it analyzes for soundness; these assumptions are described in [9].

flagged on a specialized program may map to the same race in the original program because control-flow specialization clones statements. Our race detector emits only one report in this case.

The third tool is a thread-sensitive path slicer. Intuitively, given a program path, *path slicing* removes from the path the statements irrelevant to reach a given target statement [21]. The algorithm for doing so tracks control- and data-dependencies between statements, and removes statements that the target does not control- or data-depend upon. As previous work describes, path slicing can be applied to many problems, such as post-mortem analysis [21], counter-example generation [21], and malicious-input filtering [15]. Our path slicer improves upon existing path slicing work [21] by tracking dependencies across threads. Dependencies may arise across threads due to data or control flow. For example, if thread t_0 stores to pointer p, and t_1 then loads from q which may alias p, then the load in t_1 data-depends on the store in t_0. Similarly, if different branches of a branch statement in t_0 may cause t_1 to load different values from a shared variable, then the load in t_1 control-depends on the branch statement in t_0. Our path slicer correctly tracks these dependencies by leveraging our precise alias analyzer. Another feature of our path slicer is that it can slice toward multiple targets.

8. Evaluation

We evaluated our schedule specialization framework on a diverse set of 17 programs, including `PBZip2` 1.1.5, a parallel compression utility; `aget` 0.4.1, a parallel `wget`-like utility; parallel implementations of 15 computation-intensive algorithms, 8 in SPLASH2 and 7 in PARSEC. We excluded 4 programs from SPLASH2 and 6 from PARSEC because we cannot compile them down to LLVM bitcode code, they use OpenMP [13] instead of Pthreads [34], data-flow specialization runs out of time on them, the compiled code does not run correctly in 64-bit environment, or our current prototype cannot handle them due to an implementation bug. All of the programs were widely used in previous studies [19, 25, 29, 38, 39].

We generated schedules for the programs evaluated using the following workloads: for SPLASH2 programs, we used the default arguments except that we ran them with four threads. These programs finish within 100 ms. For `PBZip2`, we compressed a 10 MB randomly generated text file. For `aget`, we downloaded a file of 1 MB from the internet. Unless otherwise specified, we ran all programs using four threads. This machine is a 2.8GHz Intel 12-core machine with 64 GB memory running 64-bit Linux 2.6.38. We compiled all programs using Clang and LLVM 2.9 with the default optimization level (often `-O2` or `-O3`) of each program.

In the remainder of this section, we first focus on two evaluation questions: (1) how much more precise the analyses become with schedule specialization (§8.1); and (2) what the overhead of our framework is (§8.2). We then present the bugs we detected with the precision provided by schedule specialization (§8.3).

8.1 Precision

We measured how our framework can improve the precision on the three analyses we built, the alias analyzer, the race detector, and the path slicer (§7). Our methodology is to apply these analyses on an original program, the control-flow specialized program, and the data-flow specialized program, and then compare the results.

Alias analysis precision. We quantified alias analysis precision by measuring *alias percentage*, the percentage of alias queries that return "may", instead of "must" and "must-not", responses because the latter two responses are precise. We selected the two pointers in each query from different threads to stress-test our alias analyzer because these pointers may appear to point to the same global array or the "same" thread-private heap or stack location, but are actually not aliases because most programs we evaluated access distinct

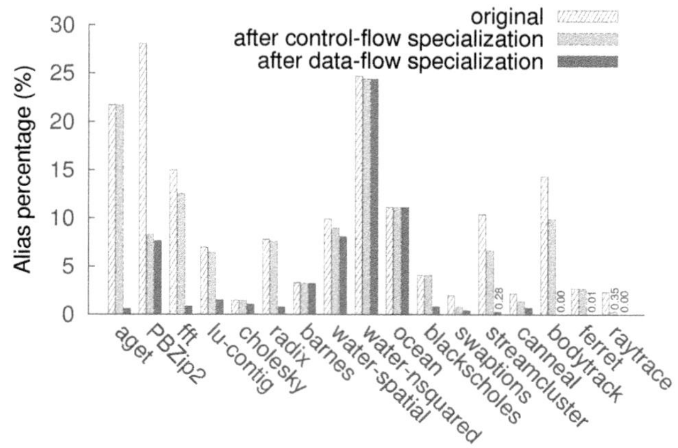

Figure 8: *Precision of the schedule-aware alias analysis.* Y axis represents the percentage of alias queries that return "may" responses. Lower bars mean more precise results. Each cluster in the figure corresponds to the results from one program. The three columns in a cluster represent the alias percentage when applying our analysis on the original program, the control-flow specialized program, and the data-flow specialized program.

memory locations in different threads. The total number of such queries can be large for programs that do many memory accesses, so we sampled some percentage of the queries to bound the total query time. The sampling ratio for `aget`, `PBZip2` and `fft` is $\frac{1}{50}$; for `water-spatial`, $\frac{1}{5000}$; and for `barnes`, `water-nsquared`, and `ocean`, $\frac{1}{50000}$. For all other programs, we processed all queries.

Figure 8 shows the alias precision results. For 12 programs (`aget`, `PBZip2`, `fft`, `lu-contig`, `radix`, `blackscholes`, `swaptions`, `streamcluster`, `canneal`, `bodytrack`, `ferret`, and `raytrace`), control-flow and data-flow specialization combined greatly improved precision. For instance, they reduced the alias percentage down to below 0.1% for `aget`. For 7 (`PBZip2`, `fft`, `swaptions`, `streamcluster`, `canneal`, `bodytrack`, and `raytrace`) of these 12 programs, control-flow specialization improved the alias analysis precision significantly. For instance, it reduced the alias percentage of `PBZip2` from 28.04% to 8.30%, a 70.4% reduction. The reason is that these programs allocate a fair amount of thread-private heap or stack data. Since the control-flow specialization clones thread functions and thus automatically provides thread sensitivity, our alias analyzer distinguishes accesses from different threads, achieving high precision. Although control-flow specialization alone did not significantly improve precision for the other 6 programs (`aget`, `PBZip2`, `lu-contig`, `radix`, `blackscholes`, and `ferret`) of the 12 programs, it created opportunities for data-flow specialization to improve precision. For the remaining 5 programs (`cholesky`, `barnes`, `water-spatial`, `water-nsquared`, and `ocean`), the reduction was not significant. This small reduction could be caused by the imprecision in our analyzer (*e.g.*, it is not path-sensitive), or real bugs in the original programs (§8.3). The mean reduction over all programs is 61.9%.

Race detection precision. We report the precision of our race detector here, and describe the detected bugs in §8.3. To evaluate its precision, we compared the number of false positives it emitted to a baseline race detector we built. This baseline detector uses the same definition of concurrent accesses (§7), except that it queries our `bddbddb` port instead of our alias analysis because our precise alias results can only be computed assuming a given schedule will be enforced. Since the total number of concurrent memory access pairs may be large, we used sampling for some benchmarks. The sampling ratio was $\frac{1}{50}$ for `PBZip2`, `fft`, `barnes`, `water-spatial`, and `ocean`; and $\frac{1}{5000}$ for `water-nsquared`. For all other programs, we checked all concurrent access pairs.

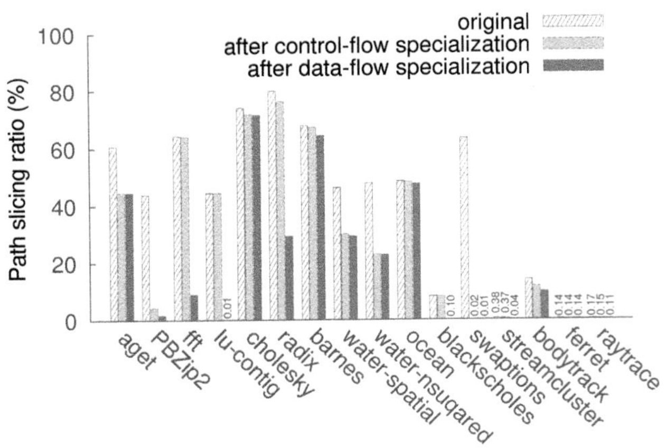

Figure 9: *Path slicing ratio on the original program, after control-flow specialization, and after data-flow specialization.*

Program	FP_{ours}	$FP_{baseline}$	$Races$
aget	0	72	1
PBZip2	0	125	32
fft	0	96	0
lu-contig	18	18	0
cholesky	7	31	0
radix	14	53	0
barnes *	369	370	n/a
water-spatial *	1799	2447	n/a
water-nsquared *	333	354	n/a
ocean *	292	331	n/a
blackscholes	0	3	0
swaptions	0	165	0
streamcluster	0	4	0
canneal	0	21	0
bodytrack	0	4	0
ferret	0	6	0
raytrace	0	215	0

Table 2: *Precision of the race detector.* FP_{ours} and $FP_{baseline}$ show the number of false positives for our detector and the baseline, respectively. $Races$ show the true races detected. The four starred programs have a larger number of reports, so we conservatively treated all reports as false positives.

We counted the number of false positives for our detector, denoted by FP_{ours}, by inspecting its reports. Since the number of reports for **barnes**, **water-spatial**, **water-nsquared**, and **ocean** is large, we inspected a random selection of 20 reports, and found that they were all false positives. We thus conservatively treated all reports from these programs as false positives. We counted the number of false positives for the baseline detector, denoted by $FP_{baseline}$, by computing $R_{baseline} - R_{ours} + FP_{ours}$ where R is the number of reports. This formula works because our detector is more precise than the baseline detector, and a report flagged only by the baseline detector must be a false positive.

Table 2 shows the false positive comparison results for all 17 programs. For 10 of them, the precision of framework enabled our detector to reduce the number of false positives to 0. The reduction for **cholesky** and **radix** is also large. For **lu-contig**, **barnes**, **water-nsquared**, **water-spatial**, and **ocean**, our race detector reported slightly fewer races than the baseline; some of these results are expected based on our alias precision results. The mean reduction over all programs is 69.0%.

Table 2 also shows the number of true but benign races detected. (We present the harmful races in §8.3.) Our detector found 1 race on variable **bwritten** in **aget** and 32 races on variable **AllDone**, **NumBlocks**, and **OutputBuffer** in PBZip2. Without the precision of our framework, users may have to inspect hundreds of reports before finding the true races.

Program	LOC	Sched	Cons	Use	CF (s)	DF (s)
aget	866	219	2667	720	1.4	1551.7
PBZip2	9869	158	1382	480	3.1	973.1
fft	877	98	1122	277	1.5	113.8
lu-contig	904	48	824	229	1.4	65.0
cholesky	3962	42	1550	1302	2.3	1967.9
radix	919	112	1016	330	1.5	42.5
barnes	2234	5555	1605	19280	5.4	1968.1
water-spatial	1958	1037	14572	5008	2.8	313.4
water-nsquared	1620	4768	48023	14530	4.1	468.8
ocean	2958	5709	66253	18580	6.8	1795.0
blackscholes	1264	51	482	130	1.2	38.3
swaptions	1094	15	215	105	1.3	9.7
streamcluster	1765	90	840	216	1.5	834.6
canneal	2794	31	535	311	5.4	96.9
bodytrack	7696	381	998	240	1.7	20.9
ferret	10765	153	439	118	1.0	35.3
raytrace	13226	87	13468	417	1.4	5397.8

Table 3: *Specialization time.* **LOC** shows the lines of code in each program. The LOC of PBZip2 includes the bzip2 compression library. We show the time spent in specializing control flow (**CF**) and data flow (**DF**). Since specialization time are affected by the schedule, constraints, and queries, we also show the schedule length (**Sched**), the number of constraints (**Cons**), and the number of uses in the def-use analysis (**Use**).

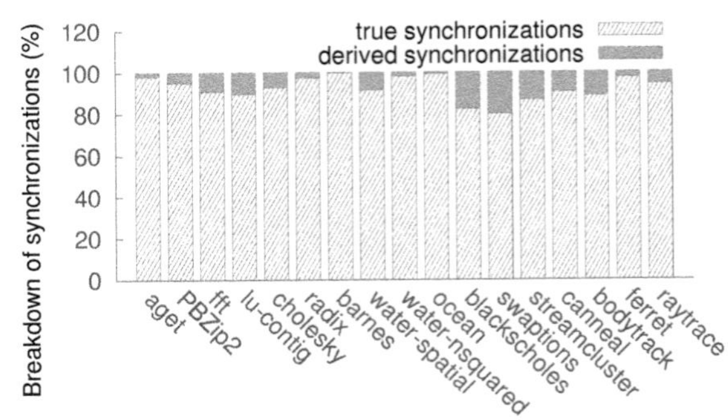

Figure 10: *True vs. derived synchronizations in schedules.*

Path slicer precision. To quantify the precision of our path slicer, we measured *slicing ratio*, the percentage of statements that remain in an execution trace. Figure 9 compares the precision of path slicing on the original programs and the specialized programs.[4] Control-flow specialization largely reduced the slicing ratio for **PBZip2**, **aget**, **swaptions**, **water-spatial**, and **water-nsquared**. For instance, it reduced the slicing ratio for PBZip2 from 43.84% to 4.40%, a 89.97% reduction. Data-flow specialization further reduced the ratio for **PBZip2**, **swaptions**, **blackscholes**, **streamcluster**, **fft**, **lu-contig** and **radix**. For instance, it reduced the slicing ratio for **fft** from 64.25% to 8.95%, a 86.08% reduction. The ratio reduction for **cholesky**, **barnes**, and **ocean** was relatively small because our alias analysis sometimes reports may-alias for pointers accessed in different threads, causing more instructions than necessary to be included in the slices. The mean reduction over all programs is 48.7%.

8.2 Overhead

Table 3 shows the time specializing the control and data flow for each program. Control-flow specialization is much faster than data-flow specialization because it does not require expensive constraint-based analysis. Data-flow specialization typically finishes within minutes or hours. This time is correlated with the size of the schedule, the number of constraints collected, and the number of constraint-solving queries.

We also measured the number of derived synchronizations, *i.e.*, the calls to functions may transitively do synchronizations to re-

[4] We obtained the slicing results from an earlier prototype of our framework.

Program	Position	Bug	Effect
`aget`	Download.c: 87-95	`rbuf` may not have the byte sequence `\r\n\r\n`. `aget` needs an extra bound check.	race, program crash, or large data corruption
`aget`	Download.c: 98-99	The bound check should be `td->offset + dr - i > foffset`, not `dr - i > foffset`. The size passed to `pwrite` should be `foffset - td->offset`, not `foffset - i`.	race, or program crash
`aget`	Download.c: 99,101,113,115	`aget` should check the return value of `pwrite`.	race, program crash, or small data corruption
`aget`	Download.c:111	`aget` should check the return value of `recv`.	race, program crash, or small data corruption
`radix`	radix.C:148	`radix` should check variable `radix` against its upper bound 4096.	race, program crash.
`radix`	radix.C:159	`radix` should check `num_keys` against its upper bound 262144.	race, or program crash
`fft`	fft.C:162	`fft` should check `log2_line_size` against its upper bound 4.	program crash (before a race may occur)

Table 4: *Bugs found.*

solve call-stack ambiguity (§5.1). If this number is large, the overhead to record schedules and specialize programs may increase. Figure 10 shows that, for every program evaluated, the majority of the synchronizations in the schedule are still true synchronizations. Therefore, including derived synchronizations in the schedules does not incur significant overhead.

8.3 Bugs Found

The precision of our framework helped detect 7 previously unknown bugs in the evaluated programs. This result is particularly interesting considering that the evaluated programs have been well checked in previous work [19, 25, 29, 38, 39].

These bugs were typically detected as follows. Our analyses flagged two memory accesses from different threads as potential aliases or races, even though they should not be. We initially thought these "false positives" were due to the imprecision of our analyses and inspected them. Specifically, we queried STP for a solution to make the two pointers accessed identical.

Surprisingly, many of these "false positives" turned to be real bugs. A common cause is that an input variable is used as an array index without being checked against the upper or lower bounds of the array or the partition of the array assigned to a thread. Such off-bound accesses may indeed cause different threads to race, and our analyses thus flagged them. We detected 7 such bugs in `aget`, `radix`, and `fft`, which are shown in Table 4. These bugs may cause races, program crashes, or, worse, file data corruption. We manually verified these effects by running the buggy benchmarks on the bug-inducing inputs generated by STP. (The results presented in the previous two subsections are from the patched programs because we do not want these bugs to pollute our evaluation.)

9. Related Work

Slicing. Slicing techniques can remove irrelevant statements or instructions. Program slicing [35] does so on programs, dynamic slicing [6, 40] on dynamic execution traces, and path slicing [21] on (potentially infeasible) paths. Precondition slicing [15] is similar to path slicing with improved precision by incorporating dynamic information into the analysis.

Our technique to specialize a program toward a schedule differs from these slicing techniques because it takes as input both a program and a schedule, and outputs a specialized program that can actually run. Moreover, our technique does not merely remove statements; instead, it may transform a program by cloning statements when specializing the control flow of the program, replacing variables with constants when specializing the data flow, *etc.*

Deterministic multithreading. Several recent systems [8, 10–12, 16–18, 24, 28] eliminate nondeterminism due to thread interleaving; our TERN [16] and PEREGRINE [17] further reduce input nondeterminism. These DMT systems are not designed to facilitate static analysis. For instance, all existing DMT systems except TERN and PEREGRINE compute schedules online without storing them explicitly, making it difficult to analyze a program w.r.t. these implicit schedules. Moreover, although several DMT systems constrain a program to always use the same schedule for the same input, they may force the program to use a different schedule when the input changes slightly. This *instability* [16] not only aggravates input nondeterminism, but also largely prevents amortizing the static analysis cost in schedule specialization.

Nonetheless, our framework may use one of these systems to enforce schedules. Indeed, our framework leverages our PEREGRINE system, which explicitly stores and reuses schedules. Although PEREGRINE used a technique similar to the specialization algorithms described in §5, our PEREGRINE paper [17] described the technique mainly from a user's perspective, and presented no schedule specialization framework nor detailed algorithms.

Program specialization. Program specialization can specialize a program according to various goals [14, 20, 22, 27, 31]. For instance, it can specialize according to common inputs [14, 27]. The specialized programs can then be better optimized. Unlike previous work, our framework specializes a program toward a set of schedules, thus allowing stock analyses and optimizations to run on the specialized programs. To the best of our knowledge, we are the first to specialize a program toward schedules.

10. Conclusion and Future Work

We have presented *schedule specialization*, an approach to analyze a multithreaded program over a small set of schedules for precision, and then enforce these schedules at runtime for soundness. We have built a framework that specializes a program into a simpler program based on a schedule, so that the resultant program can be analyzed with stock analyses. Our framework provides a precise schedule-aware def-use analysis, enabling many powerful applications. Our results show that our framework can drastically improve the precision of alias analysis, path slicing, and race detection.

In our future work, we plan to leverage the precision provided by our framework to build precise error detectors, post-mortem analyzers, verifiers, and optimizers for multithreaded programs. In addition, we believe a similar specialization approach can improve analysis precision for sequential programs, too. In general, static analysis over all possible executions may be imprecise. To improve precision, we may perform static analysis over only a small set of executions (*e.g.*, the most common executions) and, if necessary, resort to dynamic analyses for the other executions. We believe this direction will face many interesting precision, soundness, and overhead tradeoffs, which we will investigate.

Acknowledgement

Alex Aiken, Stephen Edwards, Roxana Geambasu, Martha Kim, Eric Powders, and the anonymous reviewers provided many helpful comments, which have substantially improved the content and presentation of this paper. We thank Huayang Guo for LaTeX help. This work was supported in part by AFRL FA8650-11-C-7190, FA8650-10-C-7024 and FA8750-10-2-0253; and NSF CNS-1117805, CNS-1054906 (CAREER), CNS-1012633, and CNS-0905246.

References

[1] The LLVM compiler framework. http://llvm.org.

[2] The Princeton application repository for shared-memory computers (PARSEC). http://parsec.cs.princeton.edu/.

[3] Parallel BZIP2 (PBZIP2). http://compression.ca/pbzip2/.

[4] Stanford parallel applications for shared memory (SPLASH). http://www-flash.stanford.edu/apps/SPLASH/.

[5] STP Constraint Solver. https://sites.google.com/site/stpfastprover/.

[6] H. Agrawal and J. R. Horgan. Dynamic program slicing. In *Proceedings of the ACM SIGPLAN '90 Conference on Programming Language Design and Implementation (PLDI '90)*, pages 246–256, 1990.

[7] Apache Web Server. http://www.apache.org.

[8] A. Aviram, S.-C. Weng, S. Hu, and B. Ford. Efficient system-enforced deterministic parallelism. In *Proceedings of the Ninth Symposium on Operating Systems Design and Implementation (OSDI '10)*, Oct. 2010.

[9] D. Avots, M. Dalton, V. B. Livshits, and M. S. Lam. Improving software security with a C pointer analysis. In *Proceedings of the 27th International Conference on Software Engineering (ICSE '05)*, pages 332–341, May 2005.

[10] T. Bergan, O. Anderson, J. Devietti, L. Ceze, and D. Grossman. CoreDet: a compiler and runtime system for deterministic multithreaded execution. In *Fifteenth International Conference on Architecture Support for Programming Languages and Operating Systems (ASPLOS '10)*, pages 53–64, Mar. 2010.

[11] T. Bergan, N. Hunt, L. Ceze, and S. D. Gribble. Deterministic process groups in dOS. In *Proceedings of the Ninth Symposium on Operating Systems Design and Implementation (OSDI '10)*, pages 1–16, Oct. 2010.

[12] E. Berger, T. Yang, T. Liu, D. Krishnan, and A. Novark. Grace: safe and efficient concurrent programming. In *Conference on Object-Oriented Programming Systems, Languages, and Applications (OOPSLA '09)*, pages 81–96, Oct. 2009.

[13] O. A. R. Board. OpenMP application program interface version 3.0, May 2008.

[14] C. Consel and O. Danvy. Tutorial notes on partial evaluation. In *Proceedings of the 20th Annual Symposium on Principles of Programming Languages (POPL '93)*, pages 493–501, 1993.

[15] M. Costa, M. Castro, L. Zhou, L. Zhang, and M. Peinado. Bouncer: securing software by blocking bad input. In *Proceedings of the 21st ACM Symposium on Operating Systems Principles (SOSP '07)*, pages 117–130, Oct. 2007.

[16] H. Cui, J. Wu, C.-C. Tsai, and J. Yang. Stable deterministic multithreading through schedule memoization. In *Proceedings of the Ninth Symposium on Operating Systems Design and Implementation (OSDI '10)*, Oct. 2010.

[17] H. Cui, J. Wu, J. Gallagher, H. Guo, and J. Yang. Efficient deterministic multithreading through schedule relaxation. In *Proceedings of the 23rd ACM Symposium on Operating Systems Principles (SOSP '11)*, Oct. 2011.

[18] J. Devietti, B. Lucia, L. Ceze, and M. Oskin. DMP: deterministic shared memory multiprocessing. In *Fourteenth International Conference on Architecture Support for Programming Languages and Operating Systems (ASPLOS '09)*, pages 85–96, Mar. 2009.

[19] Q. Gao, W. Zhang, Z. Chen, M. Zheng, and F. Qin. 2ndStrike: towards manifesting hidden concurrency typestate bugs. In *Sixteenth International Conference on Architecture Support for Programming Languages and Operating Systems (ASPLOS '11)*, pages 239–250, Mar. 2011.

[20] R. Glück and J. Jørgensen. Efficient multi-level generating extensions for program specialization. In *Proceedings of the 7th International Symposium on Programming Languages: Implementations, Logics and Programs*, pages 259–278, 1995.

[21] R. Jhala and R. Majumdar. Path slicing. In *Proceedings of the ACM SIGPLAN 2005 Conference on Programming Language Design and Implementation (PLDI '05)*, pages 38–47, 2005.

[22] J. Jørgensen. Generating a compiler for a lazy language by partial evaluation. In *Proceedings of the 19th Annual Symposium on Principles of Programming Languages (POPL '92)*, pages 258–268, 1992.

[23] N. G. Leveson and C. S. Turner. An investigation of the therac-25 accidents. *Computer*, 26(7):18–41, 1993.

[24] T. Liu, C. Curtsinger, and E. D. Berger. DTHREADS: efficient deterministic multithreading. In *Proceedings of the 23rd ACM Symposium on Operating Systems Principles (SOSP '11)*, Oct. 2011.

[25] S. Lu, S. Park, E. Seo, and Y. Zhou. Learning from mistakes: a comprehensive study on real world concurrency bug characteristics. In *Thirteenth International Conference on Architecture Support for Programming Languages and Operating Systems (ASPLOS '08)*, pages 329–339, Mar. 2008.

[26] G. C. Necula, S. McPeak, and W. Weimer. CCured: type-safe retrofitting of legacy code. In *Proceedings of the 29th Annual Symposium on Principles of Programming Languages (POPL '02)*, pages 128–139, 2002.

[27] V. Nirkhe and W. Pugh. Partial evaluation of high-level imperative programming languages with applications in hard real-time systems. In *Proceedings of the 19th Annual Symposium on Principles of Programming Languages (POPL '92)*, pages 269–280, 1992.

[28] M. Olszewski, J. Ansel, and S. Amarasinghe. Kendo: efficient deterministic multithreading in software. In *Fourteenth International Conference on Architecture Support for Programming Languages and Operating Systems (ASPLOS '09)*, pages 97–108, Mar. 2009.

[29] S. Park, S. Lu, and Y. Zhou. CTrigger: exposing atomicity violation bugs from their hiding places. In *Fourteenth International Conference on Architecture Support for Programming Languages and Operating Systems (ASPLOS '09)*, pages 25–36, Mar. 2009.

[30] K. Poulsen. Software bug contributed to blackout. http://www.securityfocus.com/news/8016, Feb. 2004.

[31] T. Reps and T. Turnidge. Program specialization via program slicing. In *Proceedings of the Dagstuhl Seminar on Partial Evaluation*, volume 1101, pages 409–429. Springer-Verlag, 1996.

[32] M. Ronsse and K. De Bosschere. Recplay: a fully integrated practical record/replay system. *ACM Trans. Comput. Syst.*, 17(2):133–152, 1999.

[33] R. Rugina and M. Rinard. Symbolic bounds analysis of pointers, array indices, and accessed memory regions. In *Proceedings of the ACM SIGPLAN 2000 Conference on Programming Language Design and Implementation (PLDI '00)*, pages 182–195, June 2000.

[34] The Open Group and the IEEE. POSIX.1-2008. http://pubs.opengroup.org/onlinepubs/9699919799/, 2008.

[35] M. D. Weiser. *Program slices: formal, psychological, and practical investigations of an automatic program abstraction method.* PhD thesis, 1979.

[36] J. Whaley and M. S. Lam. Cloning-based context-sensitive pointer alias analysis using binary decision diagrams. In *Proceedings of the ACM SIGPLAN 2004 Conference on Programming Language Design and Implementation (PLDI '04)*, pages 131–144, June 2004.

[37] J. Yang, A. Cui, J. Gallagher, S. Stolfo, and S. Sethumadhavan. Concurrency attacks. Technical Report CUCS-028-11, Columbia University.

[38] W. Zhang, C. Sun, and S. Lu. ConMem: detecting severe concurrency bugs through an effect-oriented approach. In *Fifteenth International Conference on Architecture Support for Programming Languages and Operating Systems (ASPLOS '10)*, pages 179–192, Mar. 2010.

[39] W. Zhang, J. Lim, R. Olichandran, J. Scherpelz, G. Jin, S. Lu, and T. Reps. ConSeq: detecting concurrency bugs through sequential errors. In *Sixteenth International Conference on Architecture Support for Programming Languages and Operating Systems (ASPLOS '11)*, pages 251–264, Mar. 2011.

[40] X. Zhang and R. Gupta. Cost effective dynamic program slicing. In *Proceedings of the ACM SIGPLAN 2004 Conference on Programming Language Design and Implementation (PLDI '04)*, pages 94–106, 2004.

Parallelizing Top-Down Interprocedural Analyses

Aws Albarghouthi *
University of Toronto
aws@cs.toronto.edu

Rahul Kumar
Microsoft Corporation
rahulku@microsoft.com

Aditya V. Nori
Microsoft Research India
adityan@microsoft.com

Sriram K. Rajamani
Microsoft Research India
sriram@microsoft.com

Abstract

Modularity is a central theme in any scalable program analysis. The core idea in a modular analysis is to build summaries at procedure boundaries, and use the summary of a procedure to analyze the effect of calling it at its calling context. There are two ways to perform a modular program analysis: (1) top-down and (2) bottom-up. A bottom-up analysis proceeds upwards from the leaves of the call graph, and analyzes each procedure in the most general calling context and builds its summary. In contrast, a top-down analysis starts from the root of the call graph, and proceeds downward, analyzing each procedure in its calling context. Top-down analyses have several applications in verification and software model checking. However, traditionally, bottom-up analyses have been easier to scale and parallelize than top-down analyses.

In this paper, we propose a generic framework, BOLT, which uses MapReduce style parallelism to scale top-down analyses. In particular, we consider top-down analyses that are demand driven, such as the ones used for software model checking. In such analyses, each intraprocedural analysis happens in the context of a reachability query. A query Q over a procedure P results in query tree that consists of sub-queries over the procedures called by P. The key insight in BOLT is that the query tree can be explored in parallel using MapReduce style parallelism – the map stage can be used to run a set of enabled queries in parallel, and the reduce stage can be used to manage inter-dependencies between queries. Iterating the map and reduce stages alternately, we can exploit the parallelism inherent in top-down analyses. Another unique feature of BOLT is that it is parameterized by the algorithm used for intraprocedural analysis. Several kinds of analyses, including may-analyses, must-analyses, and may-must-analyses can be parallelized using BOLT.

We have implemented the BOLT framework and instantiated the intraprocedural parameter with a may-must-analysis. We have run BOLT on a test suite consisting of 45 Microsoft Windows device drivers and 150 safety properties. Our results demonstrate an average speedup of 3.71x and a maximum speedup of 7.4x (with 8 cores) over a sequential analysis. Moreover, in several checks where a sequential analysis fails, BOLT is able to successfully complete its analysis.

* This author performed the work reported here during a summer internship at Microsoft Research India.

PLDI'12, June 11–16, 2012, Beijing, China.

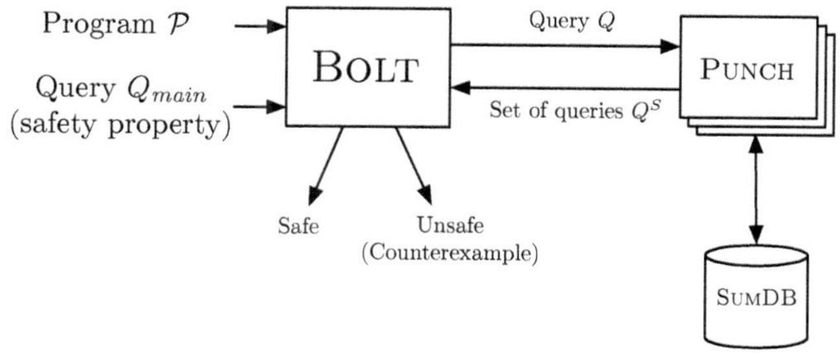

Figure 1. Black box view of the BOLT framework.

Categories and Subject Descriptors D.2.4 [*Software Engineering*]: Software/Program Verification– assertion checkers, correctness proofs, formal methods, model checking; D.2.5 [*Software Engineering*]: Testing and Debugging– symbolic execution, testing tools; F.3.1 [*Logics and Meanings of Programs*]: Specifying and Verifying and Reasoning about Programs– assertions, pre- and post-conditions

General Terms Parallelism, Testing, Verification

Keywords Abstraction refinement; Interprocedural analysis; Software model checking

1. Introduction

Scalable program analyses work by exploiting the modular structure of programs. Almost every interprocedural analysis builds summaries at procedure boundaries, and uses the summary of a procedure at its calling contexts, in order to scale to large programs. Broadly, interprocedural analyses can be classified as either top-down or bottom-up, depending on whether the analysis proceeds from callers to callees or vice-versa.

Bottom-up analyses have been traditionally easier to scale. They work by processing the call graph of the program upwards from the leaves. In a bottom-up analysis, before a procedure P_i is analyzed, all the procedures P_j that are called by P_i are analyzed, and for each P_j its summary S_{P_j} is computed, typically without considering the calling contexts of P_j. Then, during the analysis of P_i the summary S_{P_j} is used to calculate the effects of calling P_j, instead of the body of P_j. One of the significant advantages of bottom-up analyses is their decoupling between callers of a procedure P and the analysis of the body of P, which enables parallelization. For instance, the designers of the SATURN tool [1], a scalable bottom-up analysis, say that "*another advantage of analyzing procedures separately is that the process is easily parallelized, with parallelism limited only by analysis dependencies between different procedures. We use compute clusters of 40-100 cores to run Saturn analyses in parallel and normally achieve 80-90% efficiency*".

In contrast, a top-down analysis starts from the root of the call graph and proceeds downward, analyzing each procedure in its calling context. Top-down analyses have several applications in verification and software model checking [2, 3, 19], as well as dynamic test generation [16, 30]. However, top-down analyses have been more challenging to scale and parallelize. During a top-down analysis, the analysis of a procedure P_i is done separately for each calling context, leading to repeated analysis of each procedure, and fine grained dependencies between analysis instances. Hence, top-down analyses are harder to scale. However, top-down analyses do have precision advantages. Since each analysis of a procedure P_i is done with respect to a calling context, the summary built for that context can be more precise. Thus, software model checkers such as SLAM [4] and BLAST [10], which employ a top-down analysis, are able to be very precise, and have very low false error rates, but only scale to programs of size 100K lines of code [7].

Thus, it is natural to ask if we can parallelize and scale top-down analyses. In particular, we consider top-down analyses that are demand driven, such as the ones used for software model checking. In such analyses, each intraprocedural analysis happens in the context of a query. A query Q over a procedure P results in sub-queries over procedures called by P. The query Q is in a "blocked" state (that is, it cannot make progress) until at least one of these sub-queries can be answered using a summary. When such a summary is available for one or more of the sub-queries, the parent query Q transitions to a "ready" state where it can continue to execute, and may produce new sub-queries and get "blocked" again. When the analysis of a query Q is conclusive, it moves to a "done" state. It is important to note that (this will be illustrated later) a query Q can move to a "done" state, even before all of its sub-queries are done. Therefore, in this situation, the remaining (transitive) sub-queries of q can be stopped and garbage collected. Thus, the dependencies between query instances are more intricate and detailed during a top-down analysis.

In this paper, we propose a generic framework, BOLT, which uses MapReduce [13] style parallelism to scale top-down analyses. The key insight in BOLT is that the query tree can be explored in parallel as follows:

- The *map stage* is used to run a set of "ready" queries in parallel, which can potentially result in a new set of sub-queries, and
- the *reduce stage* is used to manage interdependencies between queries, assess which parent queries can be moved to the "ready" state from the "blocked" state, and which queries can be garbage collected because they are no longer necessary for the parents that originated these queries.

By iterating the map and reduce stages alternately, BOLT can exploit the parallelism inherent in any top-down analysis.

BOLT is parameterized by an intraprocedural analysis algorithm, which we shall henceforth call PUNCH, used to analyze a single procedure. BOLT initially receives a program $\mathcal{P}$ and a reachability query Q_{main} over the main procedure *main* of $\mathcal{P}$ and it employs PUNCH to process Q_{main}. PUNCH explores paths in *main* either forward or backward, or using combination of both. It can use an overapproximate analysis, an underapproximate analysis, or a combination of both. Whenever it encounters a method call P_i, PUNCH formulates a sub-query Q_i for P_i, which it needs to know about P_i in order to answer the query it was asked, namely Q_{main}. We say that Q_i is a *child* of the *parent* query Q_{main}. PUNCH first looks for a summary which can answer Q_i in a database of summaries SUMDB. If a suitable summary is found, it answers Q_i using that summary and moves on. If not, PUNCH sets the query Q_i to the ready state and adds it to the set of queries it will return, and explores other paths in *main*, repeating the same strategy to handle any procedure calls it encounters on these paths. The PUNCH call on the query Q_{main} finishes when PUNCH cannot perform any further analysis in *main* without getting answers to queries it has made to callees of *main*. At this point, it returns all the sub-queries it has generated (which are all in the ready state), and Q_{main} itself, which it sets to blocked state. The next map stage applies PUNCH to all the queries that are in the ready state in parallel, and the subsequent reduce stage then processes the answers produced by the map stage, removing completed and redundant queries, and informing parent queries when their children have produced answers. This process continues until Q_{main} returns an answer. Figure 1 shows an overview of the BOLT framework which uses multiple instances of PUNCH in parallel and a database of procedure summaries SUMDB that stores results produced by PUNCH to avoid recomputing similar queries over the same procedure.

In our exposition of BOLT, we provide a formal specification of the parameter PUNCH that any correct instantiation of BOLT should respect. PUNCH can be instantiated to capture different kinds of analyses. An instantiation of PUNCH to a "may-analysis" or an overapproximation-based analysis, using "may" summaries, can parallelize analyses such as SLAM [4] and BLAST [10]. An instantiation of PUNCH to a "must-analysis" or an underapproximation-based analysis, using "must" summaries, can parallelize analyses such as DART [17] and CUTE [35]. We present an instantiation of PUNCH that uses a "may-must-analysis", combining overapproximations and underapproximations, to parallelize algorithms in the family of DASH [9, 19].

Our contributions are summarized as follows.

– BOLT: a generic framework for parallelizing top-down interprocedural analyses. In particular, the framework targets demand driven analyses such as the ones used in software model checkers.

– An instantiation of the BOLT framework with an intraprocedural analysis algorithm that uses a "may-must" analysis combining testing (in the style of DART and CUTE) and abstraction (in the style of SLAM and BLAST).

– A modular implementation of BOLT, where different intraprocedural algorithms can be plugged-in and parallelized seamlessly; and an extensive experimental evaluation of BOLT, using our may-must-analysis on a number of Microsoft Windows device drivers and safety properties, that demonstrates an average speedup of 3.71x and a maximum speedup of 7.4x using 8 cores (in comparison with a sequential analysis). Using BOLT, we have been able to analyze several driver-property pairs that sequential analyses have been unable to analyze previously.

The rest of the paper is organized as follows: Section 2 provides an overview of BOLT and motivates its style of parallelism. Section 3 is a formal description of the BOLT framework. Section 4 discusses the various instantiations of the intraprocedural parameter PUNCH. Section 5 discusses our implementation and evaluation of BOLT. Section 6 compares BOLT with related work. Finally, Section 7 concludes the paper and outlines directions for future research.

```
int foo(int p_foo);
int bar(int p_bar);
int baz(int p_baz);

main(int i, int j){
  int x, y;
  if (j > 0)
    x = foo(i);
  else if (j > -10)
    x = bar(i);
  else
    x = baz(j);

  y = x + 5;
  assert(y > 0);
}
```

(a)

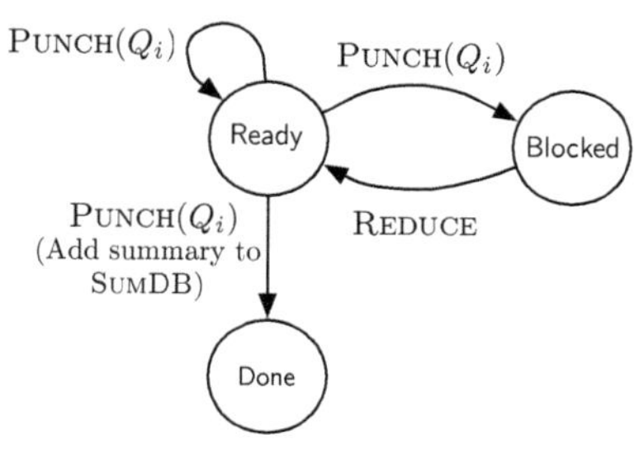

(b)

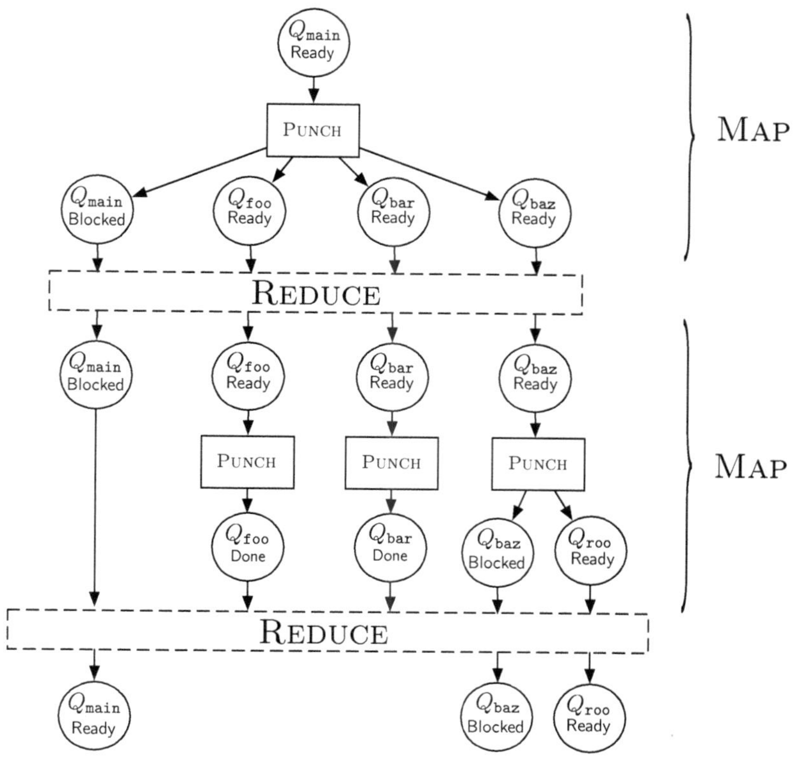

(c)

Figure 2. (a) Procedure `main` of example program, (b) State machine of a query Q_i, and (c) Illustration of BOLT on (a).

2. Motivation

In this section, we illustrate the operation of BOLT on a toy program and also motivate BOLT's style of parallelism by examining a real-world application.

2.1 Illustration of BOLT on a Toy Program

Consider the program shown in Figure 2(a) with main procedure `main`. Procedure `main` invokes three other procedures, `bar`, `foo`, and `baz`, which only have their signatures shown. Our goal is to check if there exists some input to `main` that violates the assertion "`assert(y > 0)`" at the end of the procedure. This check is encoded as the following query (formally defined in Section 3) over the procedure `main` .

$$Q_{\texttt{main}} = \langle \mathit{true} \overset{?}{\Longrightarrow}_{\texttt{main}} \texttt{y <= 0} \rangle \qquad (1)$$

This query asks the question if there is an execution through the procedure `main` starting in any input state (denoted by the precondition true) and ending in a state satisfying the error condition `y <= 0`.

As shown in Figure 2(c), BOLT alternates between the map and reduce stages in the style of the MapReduce framework [13]. Specifically, BOLT operates on this example as follows.

The first stage is the map stage where BOLT applies PUNCH to the main query $Q_{\texttt{main}}$, which is initially in the Ready state, i.e., ready to be processed (the state machine for a lifespan of a query is shown in Figure 2(b)). This results in the new queries $Q_{\texttt{foo}}$, $Q_{\texttt{bar}}$ and $Q_{\texttt{baz}}$, which are children of $Q_{\texttt{main}}$, all of which are in the Ready state:

$$Q_{\texttt{foo}} = \langle \mathit{true} \overset{?}{\Longrightarrow}_{\texttt{foo}} \texttt{ret <= -5} \rangle \qquad (2)$$

$$Q_{\texttt{bar}} = \langle \mathit{true} \overset{?}{\Longrightarrow}_{\texttt{bar}} \texttt{ret <= -5} \rangle \qquad (3)$$

$$Q_{\texttt{baz}} = \langle \texttt{p\_baz <= -10} \overset{?}{\Longrightarrow}_{\texttt{baz}} \texttt{ret <= -5} \rangle \qquad (4)$$

Here, we assume that the intraprocedural analysis instantiated by PUNCH is able to ascertain that the assertion "`assert(y > 0)`" in the procedure `main` holds if and only if each of the procedures `foo`, `bar`, and `baz`, return a value greater than -5. Note that $Q_{\texttt{baz}}$ has the precondition `p_baz <= -10`, since `baz` is only called with inputs less than or equal to -10.

The query $Q_{\texttt{main}}$ is now in the Blocked state, because it needs an answer from at least one of its child sub-queries before it can make progress. The reduce stage analyzes if any interdependencies between the queries have been resolved, and in this case, none are resolved, so all the queries remain in their respective states (the first reduce stage is essentially a no-op).

The second map stage applies PUNCH, *in parallel*, to each of the Ready queries $Q_{\texttt{foo}}$, $Q_{\texttt{bar}}$, and $Q_{\texttt{baz}}$. We assume that the first two queries, $Q_{\texttt{foo}}$ and $Q_{\texttt{bar}}$, complete at this stage (perhaps due to `foo` and `bar` being leaves in the call-graph) and therefore move to the Done state, and $Q_{\texttt{baz}}$ moves to the Blocked state and generates a new query $Q_{\texttt{roo}}$. The Done state implies that the analysis of the query is complete. BOLT stores the results of Done queries as procedure summaries in a summary database SUMDB, in order to avoid recomputing them. A summary can be either a *must* summary, representing an underapproximation of the procedure and containing a path to error states, or a *not-may* summary, representing an overapproximation of the procedure and excluding paths to error states [19].

Since $Q_{\texttt{foo}}$ and $Q_{\texttt{bar}}$ have moved to a Done state, the reduce stage now sets $Q_{\texttt{main}}$ to a Ready state, and thus enables it to be processed by PUNCH in the next map stage, now that some of its

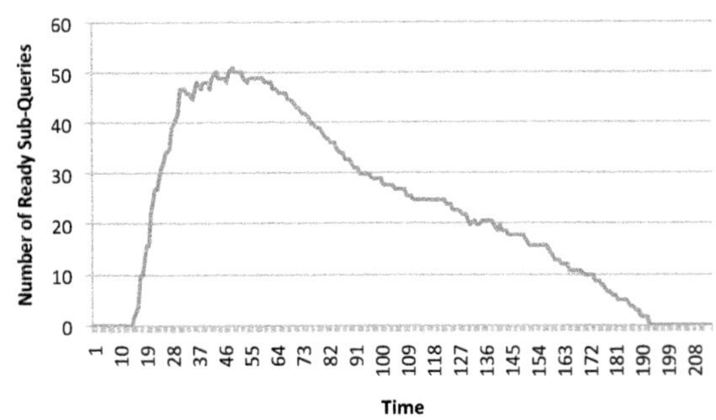

Figure 3. Potential of parallelism illustrated on a device driver.

child sub-queries have returned results (summaries). The reduce stage also deletes all Done queries (and their descendants). In this case, it deletes $Q_{\texttt{bar}}$ and $Q_{\texttt{foo}}$.

In subsequent stages (not shown in the figure), it may so happen that $Q_{\texttt{main}}$ completes due to the answers it gets from the sub-queries $Q_{\texttt{foo}}$ and $Q_{\texttt{bar}}$. If that happens, the next reduce stage will garbage collect the remaining queries such as $Q_{\texttt{baz}}$ and $Q_{\texttt{roo}}$, since their answers are no longer required (i.e., we have been able to answer $Q_{\texttt{main}}$ even without requiring the answers to these sub-queries).

To summarize, BOLT alternates between two phases: the parallel map stage, which applies PUNCH in parallel to verification queries, and the reduce stage, which performs housekeeping, getting rid of unnecessary queries and reactivating blocked ones. The process continues until the main query $Q_{\texttt{main}}$ is answered.

2.2 Opportunity for Parallelism

Since our goal is to parallelize top-down analyses, it is important to ascertain the amount of parallelism available in the query tree induced by a top-down analysis for real-world programs. Thus, for these programs, it is useful to know the number of Ready queries in each successive stage of the MapReduce process in order to understand the level of parallelism that is available.

To get a rough idea of the amount of parallelism available in analyzing device drivers, which are our target application, we instrumented a sequential top-down analysis and recorded the total number of Ready sub-queries over the lifetime of a query for a dispatch routine (the *main* procedure) in a device driver. Figure 3 shows this number plotted against time, for a typical device driver. At its peak, the query has around 50 Ready sub-queries. On this driver, a sequential top-down analysis would analyze each of these Ready sub-queries one at a time. In contrast, BOLT exploits the fact that these Ready queries can be analyzed independently, and, therefore, parallelizes execution of these sub-queries on the available processor cores. Once these sub-queries run in parallel, they will in turn generate more sub-queries with more opportunity for exploiting parallelism. Ultimately, the speedup obtained by BOLT depends on several other factors (see Section 5.1 for a thorough evaluation), but the above methodology is useful to understand the amount of parallelism inherently available in any top-down analysis, and the gains we can expect out of parallelizing the analysis using BOLT.

3. The BOLT Framework

In this section, we describe the BOLT framework together with its intraprocedural parameter PUNCH for solving reachability queries.

3.1 Preliminaries

Programs A program $\mathcal{P}$ is a set of procedures $\{P_0, \ldots, P_n\}$, where P_0 is the main procedure (entry point). A procedure P_i is a tuple $(V_i, N_i, E_i, n_i^0, n_i^x, \lambda_i)$, where

- V_i is the disjoint union of the set of local variables V_i^L of P_i and the set of global variables V_G of $\mathcal{P}$.
- N_i is the set of control nodes (locations).
- $E_i : N_i \times N_i$ is the set of edges between control nodes.
- $n_i^0, n_i^x \in N_i$ are the entry and exit locations, respectively.
- $\lambda_i : E_i \longrightarrow \mathsf{Stmt}$ is a labeling function, where Stmt is the set of program statements over V_i. Statements in Stmt are either *simple statements* or *call statements*. A simple statement in a procedure P_i is an assignment statement `x = ` E or an assume statement `assume`(Q), where `x` is a variable in V_i, E is an expression over the variables V_i, and Q is a Boolean expression over the variables V_i. A call statement to procedure P_j is of the form `call` P_j.

We assume, w.l.o.g., that communication between procedures is performed via the global variables V_G, and for each procedure P_i, there does not exist a node $n \in N_i$ such that $(n_i^x, n) \in E_i$.

Program Model A *configuration* of a procedure P_i is a pair (n, σ), where $n \in N_i$ and the *state* σ is a valuation of variables V_i of P_i. The set of all states of P_i is denoted by Σ_{P_i}. Every edge $e \in E_i$ is a relation $\Gamma_e \subseteq \Sigma_{P_i} \times \Sigma_{P_i}$ defined by the standard semantics of the statement $\lambda_i(e)$.

The initial configurations of a procedure P_i are $\{(n_i^0, \sigma) \mid \sigma \in \Sigma_{P_i}\}$. From a configuration (n, σ), P_i can execute a statement by traversing some edge $e = (n, n') \in E_i$ and reaching a configuration (n', σ'), where $(\sigma, \sigma') \in \Gamma_e$. We say that a configuration (n, σ) can *reach* another configuration (n', σ'), where $n, n' \in N_i$ if and only if there exists a sequence of edges in $(n, n_1), (n_1, n_2), \ldots, (n_m, n') \in E_i$ which if executed from state σ leads to state σ'.

Procedure Summaries For any procedure P_i, let φ_1 and φ_2 be formulae representing sets of states in $2^{\Sigma_{P_i}}$. Then, we have two types of summaries for P_i, *must summaries* and *not-may summaries* defined as follows [19].

- *Must Summary*: $\langle \varphi_1 \overset{must}{\Longrightarrow}_{P_i} \varphi_2 \rangle$ is a must summary for P_i if and only if every exit configuration (n_i^x, σ'), where $\sigma' \in \varphi_2$, is reachable from some initial configuration (n_i^0, σ), where $\sigma \in \varphi_1$.
- *Not-may Summary*: $\langle \varphi \overset{\neg may}{\Longrightarrow}_{P_j} \varphi_2 \rangle$ is a not-may summary for P_i if and only if every initial configuration (n_i^0, σ), where $\sigma \in \varphi_1$, cannot reach any exit configuration (n_i^x, σ'), where $\sigma' \in \varphi_2$.

Queries A *query* Q_i over some procedure P_j is defined as a 4-tuple $(q_i, s_i, p_i, \mathcal{O}_i)$, where

- q_i is a *reachability question* of the form $\langle \varphi_1 \overset{?}{\Longrightarrow}_{P_j} \varphi_2 \rangle$, asking if a procedure P_j starting in a configuration in $\{(n_j^0, \sigma) \mid \sigma \in \varphi_1\}$ can reach a configuration in $\{(n_j^x, \sigma) \mid \sigma \in \varphi_2\}$.
- $s_i \in \{\mathsf{Ready}, \mathsf{Blocked}, \mathsf{Done}\}$ is the *query state*.
- p_i is the index of the parent query Q_{p_i} of Q_i.
- $\mathcal{O}_i$ is a *verification object* that maintains the internal state of a query. The exact nature of this object depends on the kind of analysis being performed by BOLT (may-analysis/must-analysis/may-must-analysis). We will formally describe this in Section 4.

A procedure summary $\mathcal{S}$ can be used to *answer* a reachability question $\langle \varphi_1 \overset{?}{\Longrightarrow}_{P_j} \varphi_2 \rangle$ in either of the following ways:

- *Answer* = *"yes"*, if $\mathcal{S} = \langle \hat{\varphi}_1 \overset{must}{\Longrightarrow}_{P_j} \hat{\varphi}_2 \rangle$, where $\hat{\varphi}_1 \subseteq \varphi_1$ and $\varphi_2 \cap \hat{\varphi}_2 \neq \emptyset$,
- *Answer* = *"no"*, if $\mathcal{S} = \langle \hat{\varphi}_1 \overset{\neg may}{\Longrightarrow}_{P_j} \hat{\varphi}_2 \rangle$, where $\varphi_1 \subseteq \hat{\varphi}_1$ and $\varphi_2 \subseteq \hat{\varphi}_2$.

Intuitively, a must-summary $\mathcal{S}$ answers a reachability question $\langle \varphi_1 \overset{?}{\Longrightarrow}_{P_j} \varphi_2 \rangle$ with a *"yes, there is an execution from a state in φ_1 to a state in φ_2 through P_j"*. On the other hand, if $\mathcal{S}$ is a not-may summary, then it answers the reachability question with a *"no, there are no executions through P_j from any state in φ_1 to any state in φ_2"*.

A *verification question* for a program $\mathcal{P}$ is a query $Q_0 = (q_0, s_0, p_0, \mathcal{O}_0)$ over its main procedure P_0, where $q_0 = \langle \varphi_1 \overset{?}{\Longrightarrow}_{P_0} \varphi_2 \rangle$, φ_2 describes undesirable (error) states, and p_0 is undefined, since the initial query Q_0 does not have any parent queries.

3.2 PUNCH: The Intraprocedural Parameter

BOLT is parameterized by an intraprocedural analysis algorithm PUNCH for manipulating queries. PUNCH takes a query Q_i in the Ready state, and the goal is to either compute a summary that answers the reachability question of Q_i or produce new queries required to answer Q_i. PUNCH stores procedure summaries that it computes in a database SUMDB. PUNCH also queries SUMDB for procedure summaries in order to avoid recomputing answers to queries. The formal specification of PUNCH is described below.

Input: $Q_i = (q_i, s_i, p_i, \mathcal{O}_i)$.

Output: Set of queries R.

Precondition: $s_i = \textsf{Ready}$.

Postcondition: $R = \{Q_i'\} \cup C$, where $Q_i' = (q_i, s_i', p_i, \mathcal{O}')$ and

1. $(s_i' = \textsf{Done}) \implies (C = \emptyset)$, and
2. $(s_i' \in \{\textsf{Blocked}, \textsf{Ready}\}) \implies$ $\forall (q_j, s_j, p_j, \mathcal{O}_j) \in C \cdot p_j = i \wedge s_j = \textsf{Ready}$

PUNCH takes a query $Q_i = (q_i, s_i, p_i, \mathcal{O}_i)$ as input and returns a set of queries R. If PUNCH successfully analyzes Q_i, it returns a copy Q_i' of Q_i in a Done state (formula 1 of the above postcondition), and *adds a summary that answers q_i to* SUMDB, as a side effect. Otherwise, it returns a copy Q_i' of Q_i that is Ready or Blocked, and a set of child sub-queries C of Q_i' (formula 2 of the above postcondition). Every child sub-query $Q_j = (q_j, s_j, p_j, \mathcal{O}_j) \in C$ is uniquely identified by its index j. If a query Q_i is in the Blocked state, PUNCH cannot make any progress with Q_i and can only continue when one of its children has an answer (i.e., the child reaches Done state and adds a summary to SUMDB). If Q_i is in the Ready state, PUNCH can perform more processing on Q_i. Note that the only side-effect of PUNCH is the addition of summaries to SUMDB.

BOLT expects PUNCH to operate as follows. First, PUNCH attempts to answer a query Q_i on some procedure P_j by analyzing P_j using the summaries of the procedures P_j calls that are stored in SUMDB. If it fails to find appropriate summaries for those procedures, it moves Q_i to a Blocked state and produces a number of new sub-queries C. The query Q_i remains Blocked until one of its sub-queries is Done (and, therefore, has a summary in SUMDB). Alternatively, PUNCH may decide to preempt an ongoing analysis of Q_i and return Q_i in a Ready state. In Section 4, we present several instantiations of PUNCH.

```
 1: function BOLT(Program 𝒫, Query Q0 = (q0, s0, p0, 𝒪0))
 2:     QSet = {Q0}
 3:     while ¬∃(qi, si, pi, 𝒪i) ∈ QSet · si = Done ∧ qi = q0 do
        MAP:
 4:         QSet′ ← ⊎{PUNCH(Qi) | Qi ∈ QSet ∧ si = Ready}
 5:         QSet ← QSet′ ∪ {Qi | Qi ∈ QSet ∧ si ≠ Ready}
        REDUCE:
 6:         for all Qi = (qi, si, pi, 𝒪i) ∈ QSet do
 7:             if si = Done then
 8:                 if s_pi = Blocked then set s_pi to Ready
 9:                 (* remove subtree rooted at Qi from QSet *)
10:                 QSet ← QSet \ Descendants(Qi)
11:     if there exists a must summary for q0 in SUMDB then
12:         return "Error Reachable"
13:     else
14:         return "Program is Safe"
```

Figure 4. BOLT algorithm

3.3 BOLT: The Parallel Top-Down Verification Framework

BOLT uses MapReduce [13] and is formally described in Figure 4. BOLT takes as input a program $\mathcal{P}$ and a verification question Q_0 over the main procedure P_0 of $\mathcal{P}$. The algorithm starts with a set of queries QSet that is initialized to the verification question (line 2). Each iteration (lines 3 – 10) is divided into two stages:

1. The MAP stage (lines 4 – 5): Applies PUNCH, *in parallel*, to each query $Q_i \in$ QSet that is in Ready state. QSet′ is then assigned the union of all of the results returned by all calls to PUNCH. This is denoted by parallel union symbol $\uplus$. The only resource shared by parallel instances of PUNCH is the summary database SUMDB.
2. The REDUCE stage (lines 6 – 10): Removes redundant and Done queries from QSet. The function *Descendants*(Q_i) is used to denote the image of the transitive closure of the parent-child relation starting from Q_i. For every query Q_i s.t. $s_i =$ Done, all descendants of Q_i, including Q_i, are removed from QSet, since they were added to QSet to help answer Q_i, and now that $s_i =$ Done, they are no longer required. Additionally, the REDUCE stage sets parents of Done queries to Ready state, as new results about their child queries have been added to SUMDB by PUNCH, potentially enabling parent queries to be Done in the next MAP stage.

The algorithm keeps iterating and executing the MAP and REDUCE stages until q_0 is answered. For a query Q_i, when $s_i =$ Done, SUMDB either contains a must summary or a not-may summary that answers q_i (by definition of PUNCH). Therefore, when BOLT exits the loop at line 3, we know that there exists a summary that answers the reachability question q_0. If q_0 is answered by a must summary, then BOLT returns "Error Reachable", as there is an execution to the error states defined in q_0. On the other hand, if q_0 is answered by a not-may summary, then BOLT returns "Program is Safe", since the not-may summary precludes any execution to an error state in q_0.

Example 1. Recall the example from Section 2.1. In the second iteration of BOLT, the MAP stage applies PUNCH to the Ready queries in QSet: $Q_{\texttt{foo}}$, $Q_{\texttt{bar}}$ and $Q_{\texttt{baz}}$. That is, in the second iteration, QSet is assigned as follows:

$$\textsf{QSet}' \leftarrow \text{PUNCH}(Q_{\texttt{foo}}) \cup \text{PUNCH}(Q_{\texttt{bar}}) \cup \text{PUNCH}(Q_{\texttt{baz}})$$

$$= \{Q_{\texttt{foo}}'\} \cup \{Q_{\texttt{bar}}'\} \cup \{Q_{\texttt{roo}}, Q_{\texttt{baz}}'\}, \text{ and}$$

$$\textsf{QSet} \leftarrow \textsf{QSet}' \cup Q_{\texttt{main}}$$

Note that PUNCH($Q_{\texttt{foo}}$), PUNCH($Q_{\texttt{bar}}$), and PUNCH($Q_{\texttt{baz}}$), are computed in parallel. Subsequently, the REDUCE stage realizes that $Q'_{\texttt{foo}}$ and $Q'_{\texttt{bar}}$ are Done and, therefore, sets $Q_{\texttt{main}}$ to a Ready state and removes $Q'_{\texttt{foo}}$ and $Q'_{\texttt{bar}}$ from QSet.

4. Instantiations of PUNCH

In this section, we will describe how any must-analysis, may-analysis, and may-must-analysis can be suitably modified to meet the specification of PUNCH given in Section 3.2. For a detailed exposition of must-, may-, and may-must-analyses, the reader is referred to [19].

Assume that PUNCH, is given a query $Q_m = (q_m, s_m, p_m, \mathcal{O}_m)$, where $q_m = \langle \varphi_1 \overset{?}{\Longrightarrow}_{P_i} \varphi_2 \rangle$ and $s_m =$ Ready. We start by defining a *must-map* and a *may-map* over procedure P_i as follows:

- **Must-map**: A must-map $\Omega : N_i \to 2^{\Sigma_{P_i}}$ maps locations $n \in N_i$ of P_i to sets of states, representing an underapproximation of the set of reachable states at that location from states in φ_1 at n_i^0. For each node $n \in N_i$, we use Ω_n to denote $\Omega(n)$. Initially, $\Omega_{n_i^0} = \varphi_1$, and for all $n \in N_i \setminus \{n_i^0\}, \Omega_n = \emptyset$.
- **May-map**: A may-map $\Pi : N_i \to 2^{2^{\Sigma_{P_i}}}$ maps locations $n \in N_i$ of P_i to sets of sets of states (*partitions*), which together represent an overapproximation of the set of states that can reach φ_2 at that location. For each node $n \in N_i$, we use Π_n to denote $\Pi(n)$. Initially, $\Pi_{n_i^x} = \{\varphi_2, \Sigma_{P_i} \setminus \varphi_2\}$, and for every $n \in N_i \setminus \{n_i^x\}, \Pi_n = \{\Sigma_{P_i}\}$.

For a node $n \in N_i$, we treat sets of states Ω_n and $\varphi_n \in \Pi_n$ as formulas and use the notation Ω_n^G and φ_n^G to denote versions of Ω_n and φ_n where all local variables are existentially quantified.

In what follows, we sketch how different analyses populate these maps to answer the reachability question q_m.

Must-Analysis A must-analysis explores a subset of the behaviors, or an underapproximation, of a given program, and is therefore useful for proving the presence of errors. For example, DART [16] and CUTE [35] use a combination of symbolic and concrete executions to explore an underapproximation of a program.

In a must-analysis, PUNCH progressively propagates sets of reachable states along edges of the procedure P_i. If at any point $\Omega_{n_i^x} \cap \varphi_2 \neq \emptyset$, then the postcondition φ_2 of q_m is reachable from a state in φ_1, and, therefore, a must-summary that answers q_m can be generated and stored in SUMDB. The verification object $\mathcal{O}_m$ for a must-analysis is the must-map Ω.

The main difference from a typical must-analysis is the way in which PUNCH propagates reachable states over call statements. Given an edge $e = (n, n') \in E_i$ such that $\lambda_i(e)$ is a call statement `call` P_j, PUNCH encodes reachability over this call as the reachability question $\langle \Omega_n^G \overset{?}{\Longrightarrow}_{P_j} \Sigma_{P_j} \rangle$, and first checks whether a must-summary that answers this question is available in SUMDB. If such a must-summary exists in SUMDB, it uses the summary to update the set of reachable states $\Omega_{n'}$ at location n', the destination location of the call-edge e. On the other hand, if a must-summary is unavailable, PUNCH creates a child query Q_k, where $q_k = \langle \Omega_n^G \overset{?}{\Longrightarrow}_{P_j} \Sigma_{P_j} \rangle$, and adds it to R (the set of sub-queries that PUNCH returns, which contains an updated copy of Q_m). In contrast, a regular must-analysis would analyze the procedure P_j and compute reachability information.

If PUNCH successfully computes all reachable states, then it terminates analysis of Q_m. But since a must-analysis is not guaranteed to converge, PUNCH continues to analyze Q_m up to some time limit or an upper-bound on the number of explored paths before it stops analysis and returns a set of child sub-queries R of Q_m. This is to ensure that the MAP stage always terminates. When PUNCH stops its analysis of Q_m, the state of PUNCH, which is the must-map Ω, is saved in $\mathcal{O}_m$, so that the next time Q_m is processed by PUNCH, it can continue exploration from the saved state $\mathcal{O}_m$.

May-Analysis A may-analysis explores an overapproximation of a program's behaviors, and is therefore used to prove absence of errors. For example, software model checkers such as SLAM [5] and BLAST [10] overapproximate the set of states reachable in a program using predicate abstraction [20].

In our case, the goal of a may-analysis is to prove that no execution can reach a state in φ_2 at n_i^x from a state in φ_1 at n_i^0. For every edge $e = (n, n') \in E_i$, we assume that there exists an *abstract edge* between every $\psi_n \in \Pi_n$ and every $\psi_{n'} \in \Pi_{n'}$ (denoted by $\psi_n \to_e \psi_{n'}$). The may-analysis proceeds by eliminating infeasible abstract edges in order to prove that φ_2 is unreachable. Eliminated abstract edges are stored in the set $\bar{E}$, which is initially empty.

Suppose that for edge $e = (n, n')$, $\lambda_i(e)$ is a simple statement, and that there exists an abstract edge $\psi_1 \to_e \psi_2$. A may-analysis checks if ψ_1 can reach a state in ψ_2 by taking edge e. In case it cannot, ψ_1 is split into two partitions: $\psi_1 \wedge \theta$ and $\psi_1 \wedge \neg\theta$, where $pre(\lambda_i(e), \psi_2) \subseteq \theta$ and $pre(\lambda_i(e), \psi_2)$ is the preimage of the set of states ψ_2 w.r.t the statement $\lambda_i(e)$. Since no state in $\psi_1 \wedge \neg\theta$ can reach ψ_2, $\bar{E}$ is updated with the edge $(\psi_1 \wedge \neg\theta, \psi_2)$. Intuitively, the partition ψ_1 is refined into a partition that may reach ψ_2, and another one that may not.

Now suppose that $\lambda_i(e)$ is a call statement to some procedure P_j. Then, PUNCH encodes the reachability question $\langle \psi_1^G \overset{?}{\Longrightarrow}_{P_j} \psi_2^G \rangle$. If there exists exists a not-may summary $\langle \widehat{\psi_1} \overset{\neg may}{\Longrightarrow}_{P_j} \widehat{\psi_2} \rangle$ that answers this reachability question, then we know that there are no executions from ψ_1 to ψ_2. Therefore, PUNCH splits ψ_1 into $\psi_1 \wedge \theta$ and $\psi_1 \wedge \neg\theta$, where $\theta \subseteq \widehat{\varphi_1}$, and adds $(\psi_1 \wedge \theta, \psi_2)$ to the set $\bar{E}$. Otherwise, if there does not exist such a summary, PUNCH adds a child query Q_k, where $q_k = \langle \psi_1^G \overset{?}{\Longrightarrow}_{P_j} \psi_2^G \rangle$, to the set R.

As discussed, a may-analysis maintains the map Π and the set of eliminated edges $\bar{E}$. Therefore, when PUNCH returns Q_m in a Ready or Blocked state, $\mathcal{O}_m$ is set to $(\Pi, \bar{E})$. A may-analysis sets the query Q_m to Done when all partitions of n_i^0 intersecting with φ_1 cannot reach a partition of n_i^x intersecting with φ_2, where reachability is defined via abstract edges. As with a must-analysis, for fairness, PUNCH may decide to terminate analysis prematurely and store the state of the analysis in $\mathcal{O}_m$.

May-Must-Analysis Finally, may-must-analyses combine a must-analysis with a may-analysis in order to efficiently find errors as well as prove their absence. The SYNERGY [22] and DASH [9] algorithms are examples of may-must-analyses. Both use testing, symbolic execution and abstraction to check properties of programs. Interpolation-based software model checking algorithms, such as [2, 24, 31], can also be seen as may-must-analyses. Such algorithms also use symbolic executions to error locations to find bugs and, in case of infeasible executions, use interpolants derived from refutation proofs to create an abstraction that eliminates a large number of potential counterexamples.

For the query Q_m, a may-must-analysis maintains Π, Ω, and $\bar{E}$. That is, if PUNCH returns Q_m in a Ready or Blocked state, it sets $\mathcal{O}_m$ to $(\Pi, \Omega, \bar{E})$.

A may-must-analysis only analyzes an abstract transition $\psi_1 \to_e \psi_2$, where $e = (n, n') \in E_i$ and $\lambda_i(e)$ is a call to some procedure P_j, if $\Omega_n \cap \psi_1 \neq \emptyset$ and $\Omega_{n'} \cap \psi_2 = \emptyset$. That is, only abstract transitions which have been reached by the must analysis, but not taken, are analyzed. These transitions are called "frontiers" in [9, 22].

A may-must-analysis handles such abstract transitions as follows:

```
let bolt () =
  while (Q_0.isNotDone()) do
    QSet := Async.AsParallel
      [for Q_i in QSet -> async {return punch Q_i}];
    reduce ();
  done;
  ...
```

Figure 5. F# implementation of BOLT's main function `bolt`.

1. If there exists a must summary $\langle \widehat{\psi_1} \stackrel{must}{\Longrightarrow}_{P_i} \widehat{\psi_2} \rangle$ that answers the query $\langle \Omega_n^G \stackrel{?}{\Longrightarrow}_{P_j} \psi_2^G \rangle$, then we know that there exists an execution from Ω_n to ψ_2 through P_j, and, therefore, PUNCH updates $\Omega_{n'}$ to be $\Omega_{n'} \cup \theta$, where $\theta \subseteq \widehat{\psi_2}$ and $\theta \cap \psi_2 \neq \emptyset$.
2. If there exists a not-may summary $\langle \widehat{\psi_1} \stackrel{\neg may}{\Longrightarrow}_{P_i} \widehat{\psi_2} \rangle$ that answers the query $\langle \Omega_n^G \stackrel{?}{\Longrightarrow}_{P_j} \psi_2^G \rangle$, then we know that there are no executions from Ω_n to ψ_2, and, therefore, PUNCH splits region ψ_1 into $\psi_1 \wedge \neg\theta$ and $\psi_1 \wedge \theta$, where $\theta \subseteq \widehat{\varphi_1}$ and $\neg\theta \cap \Omega_n = \emptyset$. Thus, the edge $(\psi_1 \wedge \theta, \psi_2)$ is added to $\bar{E}$.
3. Finally, if neither kind of summaries exist, then a child query Q_k, where $q_k = \langle (\Omega_n \wedge \psi_1)^G \stackrel{?}{\Longrightarrow}_{P_i} \psi_2^G \rangle$, is added to R.

In a may-must-analysis, PUNCH continues processing a query Q_m until a must summary is produced, a not-may summary is produced, or all abstract edges have been analyzed and child queries have to be answered to continue processing. Similar to may- and must-analysis, PUNCH may decide to terminate analysis prematurely.

In summary, we have shown how PUNCH can be instantiated with various classes of analyses, which encompass a large number of already published algorithms from the literature. In the following section, we discuss a may-must implementation of PUNCH, based on DASH [9], and describe our empirical evaluation of BOLT on a number of Microsoft Windows device drivers.

5. Implementation and Evaluation

We have implemented BOLT in the F# programming language and integrated it with the Static Driver Verifier toolkit (SDV) [6] for Microsoft Windows device drivers. Our implementation adopts a pluggable architecture, where different instantiations of PUNCH that adhere to the specification in Section 3.2 can be easily integrated into our tool. The main function `bolt` of our implementation is partially shown in Figure 5. Our implementation assumes that `punch` is a pure function (except for its communication with SUMDB) that takes a query as input and returns a set of queries. As a result, the only resource shared between different threads of execution is the summary database SUMDB. This provides a natural framework where program analysis designers can plug in their intraprocedural analyses and automatically produce parallelized interprocedural analyses, without having to be faced with the intricacies of parallelizing individual analyses.

The instance of PUNCH that we have implemented is a variant of the may-must DASH algorithm [9] as described in Section 4. Our implementation of PUNCH uses the Z3 SMT solver [12] for satisfiability checking and can handle C programs with primitive datatypes, structured types, pointers, and function pointers. Checking if a summary answers a query is done via a call to the SMT solver.

5.1 Experiments

We now present our experimental setup and results for the BOLT algorithm.

Statistic	
Total time taken (sequential)	26 hours
Total time taken (parallel)	7 hours
Average observed speedup	3.71x
Maximum observed speedup	7.41x

Table 2. Cumulative results for BOLT on 50 checks (#threads=64, #cores=8).

Experimental Setup Our goal is to study the scalability of BOLT. We do this by measuring the speedup of BOLT over a sequential may-must top-down analysis. To precisely measure and study the scalability of the algorithm, we introduce an artificial throttle that allows us to limit the number of threads that can perform queries in parallel. The artificial throttle has the effect of limiting the total number of physical cores available to the algorithm, when the number of maximum threads is less than the total physical cores available, which also imposes a bound on the number of Ready queries processed by PUNCH in the MAP stage. In cases where the number of allowed maximum threads is greater than the number of physical cores available, the .NET environment (since BOLT is implemented using F#), thread scheduling, and contention play an important part in determining the final overall speedup. It should be noted that the theoretical limit of the speedup that can be achieved on a given test machine is N, where N is the total number of available physical cores, unless super linear speedup can be achieved by the parallel algorithm eliminating work that the sequential algorithm must perform.

We ran our experiments on an HP workstation with 8 Intel Xeon 2.66 GHz cores and 8 GB of memory. We set our initial number of maximum concurrent threads to be 1 (representing a sequential analysis) and doubled it for every subsequent run. The upper limit for the maximum number of concurrent threads is 128. All the experiments were run with resource limitations of 3000 seconds (wall clock time) and 1800 MB of memory.

Our evaluation of BOLT was over a test suite consisting of 45 Microsoft Windows device drivers and 150 safety properties[1]. For the purposes of reporting results, we select all checks (that is, driver-property pairs) where the sequential version of BOLT requires at least 1000 seconds to generate a proof. These are interesting checks (total of 50 checks) where a lot of computation is required and, in some cases, the sequential analysis is unable to produce a result. Therefore, they serve as challenge problems for BOLT. It turns out that all these checks were cases where the program satisfies the property (and thus a proof is reported by BOLT). For a study of effects of may-must summaries on the efficiency of the analysis, we refer the reader to [19, 33].

Results The cumulative results are presented in Table 2. For the 50 checks, where the sequential algorithm takes at least 1000 seconds for generating a proof, the average observed speedup using BOLT was 3.71x. The maximum observed speedup was 7.41x. These results were obtained using 8 cores, and a maximum of 64 threads.

We now analyze a sample of the 50 checks in greater detail. Table 1 shows the detailed results for 6 checks. Each row represents a single check and the time/speedup observed for different configurations of the maximum number of concurrent threads allowed. The speedup is calculated as the ratio of the time taken by the parallel version of BOLT (with 2 threads, 4 threads, etc.) to that of the sequential version of BOLT (with 1 thread).

[1] A subset of our benchmarks is available as part of the SDV-RP toolkit: `http://research.microsoft.com/en-us/projects/slam`.

Property / Max. Number of Threads	1	2		4		8		16		32		64		128	
	Time	Time	Speedup	Time	Speedup	Time	Speedup	Time	Speedup	Time	Speedup	Time	Speedup	Time	Speedup
Driver: `toastmon` (25KLOC)															
`PendedCompletedRequest`	1006	328	3.07	345	2.91	373	2.70	297	3.39	221	4.55	219	4.59	223	4.51
`PnpIrpCompletion`	2224	929	2.39	827	2.69	1041	2.14	599	3.71	300	7.41	300	7.41	300	7.41
Driver: `parport` (2KLOC)															
`MarkPowerDown`	1821	688	2.65	573	3.18	543	3.35	460	3.96	313	5.82	326	5.58	328	5.55
`PowerDownFail`	1916	673	2.85	566	3.38	524	3.65	398	4.81	305	6.28	315	6.08	318	6.03
`PowerUpFail`	2040	718	2.84	691	2.95	689	2.96	565	3.61	306	6.67	315	6.48	300	6.80
`RemoveLockMnSurpriseRemove`	1794	678	2.65	576	3.11	538	3.33	405	4.43	311	5.77	315	5.69	315	5.69

Table 1. Average observed time (in seconds) and speedup of parallel BOLT compared to sequential BOLT for varying number of maximum concurrent threads (#cores=8).

Driver	Property	Result		Time
		Seq	Parallel	
`daytona`	`IoAllocateFree`	TO	Proof	2800
`mouser`	`NsRemoveLockMnRemove`	TO	Proof	2743
`featured1`	`ForwardedAtBadIrql`	TO	Proof	2966
`incomplete2`	`RemoveLockForwardDeviceControl`	TO	Proof	1205
`selsusp`	`IrqlExAllocatePool`	TO	Proof	1951

Table 3. Driver and property combinations where BOLT was able to produce a proof (#cores = 8) and the sequential (Seq) version ran out of time (TO).

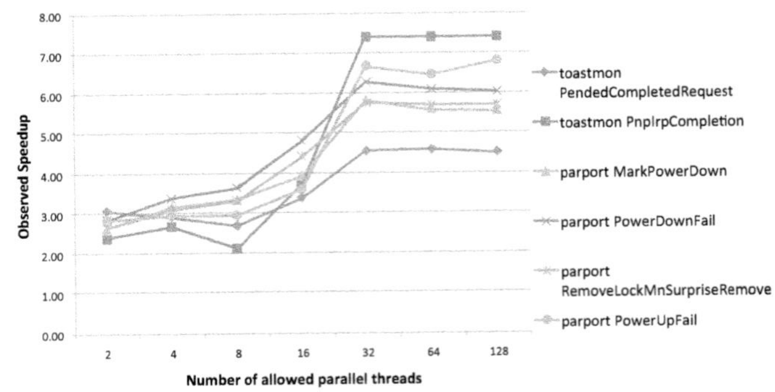

Figure 6. Measured speedup of the BOLT algorithm relative to the sequential version (#cores=8).

For the `toastmon` driver and the `PnpIrpCompletion`[2] property, we see that the speedup achieved with a maximum of 2 concurrent threads is 2.39. As the number of threads is increased to 128, the observed speedup of 7.41 reaches close to the theoretical maximum speedup achievable on the test machine (8 cores). For other checks in the table, we see that, in general, the observed speedup increases as the number of maximum concurrent threads is increased. Figure 6 illustrates the speedups reported in Table 1. The super linear speedup observed in some cases is related to the query processing order, which is discussed in the latter part of this section. In general, we find that the BOLT algorithm always achieves speedup, with the possibility of providing super linear speedup in some cases.

Table 3 shows checks where BOLT successfully produces a proof, whereas the sequential analysis runs out of resources. As can be seen from the table, in many cases, the time taken by BOLT is very close to the timeout limit of 3000 seconds, indicating the degree of difficulty and high amount of computation that is necessary to successfully complete the verification. In general, the speedups achieved by BOLT are due to parallelism, as well as the scheduling of queries. That is, sequential implementations tend to have a fixed deterministic exploration strategy of the query tree and are therefore unable to discover invariants in many cases. On the other hand, BOLT, due to its inherent parallel exploration, may compute invariants that the sequential version cannot discover.

In-depth Analysis To further understand the behavior of BOLT, we make the following measurements in our experiments.

- *The number of queries that are processed as verification progresses.* Figure 7 shows the number of queries processed in parallel for varying numbers of maximum threads (2 – 128) on the `PnpIrpCompletion` property of the `toastmon` driver. Note that, in Figure 7(f), there are two lines present on the chart, but due to the fact that they are exactly equivalent, it appears as only a single line.

  From the graphs, we see that when the number of maximum concurrent threads is less than 16, there is always a constant amount of work that is to be performed and all the threads are always close to 100% utilization. When the number of maximum threads is increased to more than 16, depending on the nature of the input program, mostly, an insufficient number of queries are produced. This results in only a few threads being utilized in an efficient and maximal manner, which explains the lower than expected observed speedup. Figures 7(e) and (f) clearly illustrate this fact. We can see that the number of queries processed in parallel is very inconsistent and never reaches the allowed maximum of 64 or 128. In particular, since a small number of queries need to be made, the graph for 64 and 128 is exactly the same.

- *Total number of queries that have to be performed when varying the degree of allowed concurrency/parallelism.* As the number of maximum concurrent threads is increased, the order of the queries performed changes. This can have two possible outcomes. First, the order of the queries may impact the verification positively, since an important fact can be learned earlier in the verification, which in turn reduces the number of queries that have to be performed. The net effect is that in some cases super linear speedup is observed (as seen in Table 1). Second, the order of the queries may result in an increased number of queries (due to redundancy), which elongates the verification task and reduces the observed speedup relative to the maximum theoretical speedup. Table 4 shows the total number of queries made for different numbers of maximum concurrent threads allowed for the two properties listed for the `toastmon` driver. As we can see in the the case of the `PnpIrpCompletion` property, the algorithm performs only 1.2 times as many queries for 128 threads as it did for 2 threads. But for the `PendedCompletedRequest` property, the algorithm performs 3.5 times as many queries. This fact directly relates to the lower observed speedup for the `PendedCompletedRequest` check, in comparison with the `PnpIrpCompletion` check (shown in Table 1).

[2] Visit http://msdn.microsoft.com/en-us/library/ff551714.aspx for a list of properties.

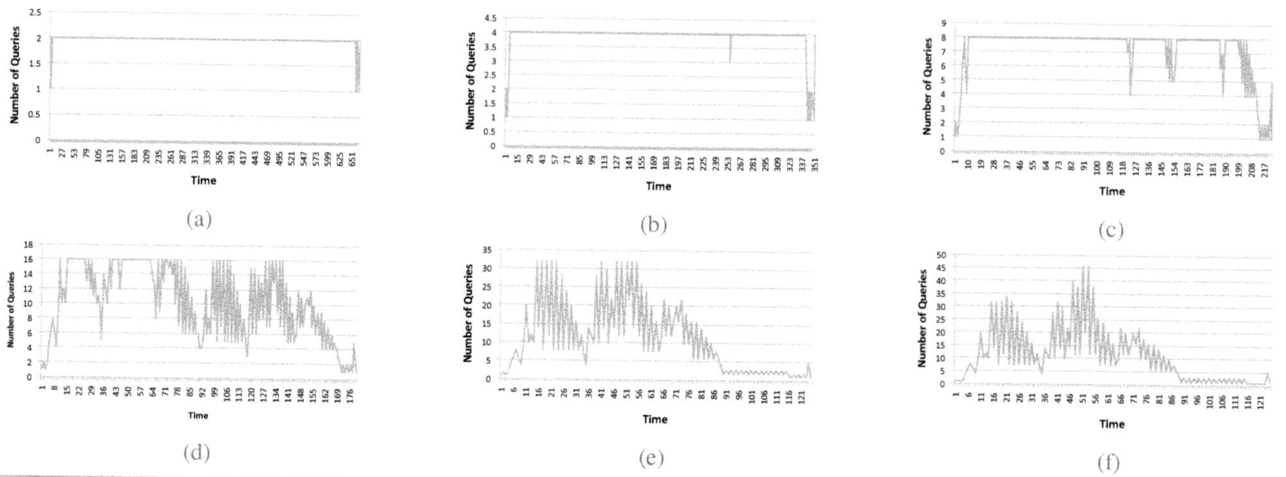

Figure 7. Number of concurrent queries performed over time for the driver `toastmon` and the property `PnpIrpCompletion` (#cores=8). Maximum number of threads for subfigures (a), (b), (c), (d) , (e) and (f) are 2, 4, 8, 16, 32, and 64 respectively. For 128 threads, the results are identical to 64 threads.

	Maximum Number of Threads						
Property	2	4	8	16	32	64	128
`PendedCompletedRequest`	873	1374	2213	2479	2529	3005	3078
`PnpIrpCompletion`	1198	1369	1614	1854	1383	1429	1429

Table 4. Total number of queries performed during verification for various degrees of parallelism on the `toastmon` driver (#cores=8).

Discussion. Our implementation and experiments shows that for may-must-analysis BOLT provides an average speedup of 3.7x and maximum speedup of 7.4x with 8 cores. This has enabled us to complete verification runs that sequential analyses have been unable to analyze previously. In particular, we have been able to complete every driver-property benchmark we have with BOLT, several of which we have previously found impossible to complete. Furthermore, each run of PUNCH needs to load only the procedure under analysis into memory, except for whole program information such as alias analysis, which can be stored in the database. Thus, we get significant advantages in memory savings, in addition to savings in time.

Our detailed investigation into the amount of parallelism available showed that, for the current set of benchmarks we have, increasing thread-level parallelism stops speeding up the analysis after 64 threads, since each MAP stage analyzes small number of queries. To this end, we see two avenues for efficiently utilizing a larger number of cores: (1) getting larger benchmarks with potential for even larger parallelism; and (2) designing a speculative extension to BOLT, where we can speculate on potential queries that will be made and analyze them even before the queries are actually created, thereby, generating more parallelism using speculation. We leave these directions for future work.

6. Related Work

Parallel and distributed algorithms for static analysis and testing is an active area of research [15, 29, 32, 34]. The unique feature of the BOLT framework is that it parallelizes interprocedural analyses that work in a top-down and demand-driven manner. Also, in contrast to earlier efforts to parallelize static and dynamic analysis, BOLT offers a pluggable architecture which inherits the nature of its underlying intraprocedural analysis (as described in Section 4). In this section, we place BOLT in the context of related work. Specifically, we compare BOLT with other parallel static analyses, as well as parallel finite state verification (model checking) and exploration techniques.

Parallel/Distributed Static Analysis Techniques As discussed in Section 1, bottom-up interprocedural analyses are amenable to parallelization due to the decoupling between callers and callees. For example, the SATURN software analysis tool [1] employs a bottom-up analysis and has been shown to scale to the entire Linux kernel, both in the interprocedurally path-insensitive [37] and path-sensitive settings [14]. In comparison, BOLT targets demand-driven top-down analyses, and is parameterized by the algorithm used for intraprocedural analysis. Therefore, BOLT can be easily applied to parallelizing existing software model checking and dynamic test generation techniques, for example, as we have shown with our instantiation of PUNCH to a DASH-like [9, 19] may-must algorithm.

Microsoft's Static Driver Verifier toolkit uses manually created harnesses [7], which specify a set of independent device driver entry points in order to create an embarrassingly parallel workload. On the other hand, BOLT is automatically able to exploit parallelism that occurs at finer levels of granularity. We believe that both techniques complement each other and their combination has the potential for greater scalability.

Lopes et al. [29] propose a distributed tree-based [25] software model checking algorithm based on the CEGAR [11] framework. The tree unrolling of the control flow graph of a program, consisting of a single procedure, is distributed amongst multiple machines. We summarize the differences between [29] and BOLT as follows: (1) [29] is intraprocedural and does not reuse procedure summaries as BOLT does. (2) BOLT is not restricted to a specific intraprocedural analysis. In fact, we believe that the distributed algorithm of [29] can be easily adapted to be an implementation of the intraprocedural parameter PUNCH. (3) The instantiation of PUNCH we present here does not use predicate abstraction and, therefore, skips the expensive step of computing an abstract post transformer required in [29].

In [32], Monniaux describes a parallel implementation of the Astrée abstract interpretation-based static analyzer. At certain branching locations (dispatch points), instead of analyzing program paths in sequence, they are analyzed in parallel. On three embedded software applications, the experiments showed around 2x speedup on 5 processors.

Several other parallel static analysis techniques have been recently proposed. One prominent example is EigenCFA [34], where

GPUs are used to parallelize higher-order control-flow analysis. The authors report up to 72x speedup, when compared to other sequential techniques.

Parallel/Distributed Exploration Techniques In the finite state verification arena, several parallel/distributed model checking algorithms have been proposed, e.g., [8, 21, 36]. At a high level, the methodology adopted by these techniques involves partitioning the state space and distributing the search to several threads or processors. Both [8] and [36], propose distribution strategies for explicit state model checking, where each node is responsible for exploring a partition of the state space. The authors of [27] propose a load balancing strategy to improve the performance of the state space partitioning algorithms to achieve higher speedup. Similarly, the technique in [21] partitions BDDs in symbolic model checking and distributes them to several threads. In [26], a multi-core algorithm along with load balancing techniques geared towards shared memory systems is proposed. In [15], a method is proposed for distributed randomized state space search in the context of Java Path Finder (JPF) [23]. In contrast to the above techniques, BOLT exploits a program's procedural decomposition in order to efficiently parallelize top-down demand-driven analyses.

7. Conclusion and Future Work

Modularity plays a central role in most scalable program analyses. Modular analyses are either top-down, where analysis starts at the main procedure and descends through the call-graph, or bottom-up, where analysis starts with the leaves of the call-graph and goes upwards to the main procedure. Top-down analyses are extensively used in software model checking and test generation. However, unlike their bottom-up counterparts, they are hard to parallelize due to the fine-grained interactions between analysis instances (queries).

In this paper, we have presented BOLT: a parameterized framework for parallelizing top-down interprocedural analyses. BOLT adopts a MapReduce-like strategy for parallelizing processing of reachability queries over multiple procedures in a top-down analysis. We have shown how a number of may-, must-, and may-must-analyses can be parallelized using BOLT. We have also demonstrated the strength of BOLT by parallelizing a may-must analysis. Our experimental results on device drivers showed that BOLT scales well on an 8-core machine, and is able to verify several checks where the sequential version runs out of resources.

We see a number of opportunities for continuing research in this direction:

- **Distributed BOLT**: BOLT's MapReduce architecture permits it to be easily implemented as a distributed application using programming models for large scale distributed systems [38]. As noted in [1], the limiting factor for scaling any analysis to very large programs is memory and not time, and this forms the primary motivation for performing a bottom-up analysis. Indeed, our experience with BOLT also indicates that its memory usage is significantly smaller than that the corresponding sequential top-down analysis. Therefore, we believe that we can distribute the parallelism that BOLT exposes across large-scale clusters of machines and, thereby, scale top-down analysis to very large programs.
- **Deriving value out of larger number of cores**: Our investigation showed that, on our set of benchmarks, increasing thread-level parallelism stops speeding up the analysis beyond 64 threads, due to limitations in the number of queries available for the MAP stage. Thus, we see two directions for efficiently utilizing a larger number of cores and, potentially, distributing the analysis: (1) getting larger benchmarks with potential for even larger parallelism, and (2) designing a speculative extension to BOLT, where we can predict what queries will be made and analyze them even before the queries are actually created, thereby, generating more parallelism using speculation.
- **Other instantiations of BOLT**: We would also like to experiment with other instantiations of PUNCH. For example, it would be interesting to apply BOLT for fuzz testing large scale systems in the style of SAGE [18]. Another interesting application for BOLT is the verification of concurrent programs. Recent research on reducing concurrent analysis to a sequential analysis [28] makes it possible to instantiate PUNCH so that BOLT is able to verify properties of concurrent programs.

Acknowledgments

We thank Tony Hoare, Vlad Levin, Jakob Lichtenberg and Robert Simmons for many useful discussions that shaped our work and the anonymous reviewers for their insightful comments and suggestions.

References

[1] A. Aiken, S. Bugrara, I. Dillig, T. Dillig, B. Hackett, and P. Hawkins. An overview of the Saturn project. In *Program Analysis for Software Tools and Engineering (PASTE 2007)*, pages 43–48, 2007.

[2] A. Albarghouthi, A. Gurfinkel, and M. Chechik. Whale: An interpolation-based algorithm for interprocedural verification. In *Verification, Model Checking, and Abstract Interpretation (VMCAI 2012)*, 2012.

[3] T. Ball and S. K. Rajamani. Bebop: A symbolic model checker for boolean programs. In *SPIN Workshop on Model Checking of Software (SPIN 2000)*, pages 113–130, 2000.

[4] T. Ball and S. K. Rajamani. The SLAM toolkit. In *Computer Aided Verification (CAV 2001)*, pages 260–264, 2001.

[5] T. Ball, R. Majumdar, T. D. Millstein, and S. K. Rajamani. Automatic Predicate Abstraction of C Programs. In *Programming language design and implementation (PLDI'01)*, pages 203–213. ACM, 2001.

[6] T. Ball, B. Cook, V. Levin, and S. K. Rajamani. SLAM and Static Driver Verifier: Technology transfer of formal methods inside Microsoft. In *Integrated Formal Methods (IFM 2004)*, pages 1–20, 2004.

[7] T. Ball, V. Levin, and S. K. Rajamani. A decade of software model checking with SLAM. *Communications of the ACM*, 54:68–76, July 2011.

[8] J. Barnat, L. Brim, and J. Stribrna. Distributed LTL model-checking in SPIN. In *SPIN Workshop on Model Checking of Software (SPIN 2001)*, pages 200–216, 2001.

[9] N. E. Beckman, A. V. Nori, S. K. Rajamani, and R. J. Simmons. Proofs from tests. In *International Symposium on Software Testing and Analysis (ISSTA 2008)*, pages 3–14, 2008.

[10] D. Beyer, T. A. Henzinger, R. Jhala, and R. Majumdar. "The Software Model Checker BLAST". *STTT: International Journal on Software Tools for Technology Transfer*, 9(5-6):505–525, 2007.

[11] E. Clarke, O. Grumberg, S. Jha, Y. Lu, and H. Veith. Counterexample-Guided Abstraction Refinement. In *Computer Aided Verification (CAV 2000)*, pages 154–169, 2000.

[12] L. de Moura and N. Bjørner. Z3: An efficient SMT solver. In *Tools and Algorithms for the Construction and Analysis of Systems (TACAS 2008)*, pages 337–340, 2008.

[13] J. Dean and S. Ghemawat. MapReduce: Simplified data processing on large clusters. In *Operating Systems Design and Implementation (OSDI 2004)*, pages 137–150, 2004.

[14] I. Dillig, T. Dillig, and A. Aiken. Sound, complete and scalable path-sensitive analysis. In *Programming Language Design and Implementation (PLDI 2008)*, pages 270–280, 2008.

[15] M. B. Dwyer, S. G. Elbaum, S. Person, and R. Purandare. Parallel randomized state-space search. In *International Conference on Software Engineering (ICSE 2007)*, pages 3–12, 2007.

[16] P. Godefroid. Compositional dynamic test generation. In *Principles of Programming Languages (POPL 2007)*, pages 47–54, 2007.

[17] P. Godefroid, N. Klarlund, and K. Sen. DART: Directed automated random testing. In *Programming Language Design and Implementation (PLDI 2005)*, pages 213–223, 2005.

[18] P. Godefroid, M. Y. Levin, and D. A. Molnar. Automated whitebox fuzz testing. In *Network and Distributed System Security Symposium (NDSS 2008)*, 2008.

[19] P. Godefroid, A. Nori, S. Rajamani, and S. Tetali. Compositional may-must program analysis: Unleashing the power of alternation. In *Principles of Programming Languages (POPL 2010)*, pages 43–56, 2010.

[20] S. Graf and H. Saïdi. Construction of abstract state graphs with PVS. In *Computer Aided Verification (CAV 1997)*, pages 72–83, 1997.

[21] O. Grumberg, T. Heyman, N. Ifergan, and A. Schuster. Achieving speedups in distributed symbolic reachability analysis through asynchronous computation. In *Correct Hardware Design and Verification Methods (CHARME 1995)*, pages 129–145, 2005.

[22] B. Gulavani, T. Henzinger, Y. Kannan, A. V. Nori, and S. K. Rajamani. SYNERGY: A new algorithm for property checking. In *Foundations of Software Engineering (FSE 2006)*, pages 117–127, 2006.

[23] K. Havelund and T. Pressburger. Model Checking Java Programs Using Java Pathfinder. *International Journal on Software Tools for Technology Transfer*, 1999.

[24] M. Heizmann, J. Hoenicke, and A. Podelski. Nested interpolants. In *Principles of Programming Languages (POPL 2010)*, pages 471–482, 2010.

[25] T. Henzinger, R. Jhala, R. Majumdar, and G. Sutre. Lazy abstraction. In *Principles of Programming Languages (POPL 2002)*, pages 58–70, 2002.

[26] G. J. Holzmann and D. Bosnacki. The design of a multicore extension of the SPIN model checker. *IEEE Transactions on Software Engineering*, 33:659–674, October 2007.

[27] R. Kumar and E. G. Mercer. Load balancing parallel explicit state model checking. *Electronic Notes in Theoretical Computer Science*, 128:19–34, 2005.

[28] A. Lal and T. W. Reps. Reducing concurrent analysis under a context bound to sequential analysis. *Formal Methods in System Design (FMSD)*, 35(1):73–97, 2009.

[29] N. P. Lopes and A. Rybalchenko. Distributed and predictable software model checking. In *Verification, Model Checking, and Abstract Interpretation (VMCAI 2011)*, pages 340–355, 2011.

[30] K. McMillan. Lazy annotation for program testing and verification. In *Computer Aided Verification (CAV 2010)*, pages 104–118, 2010.

[31] K. L. McMillan. Lazy abstraction with interpolants. In *Computer Aided Verification (CAV 2006)*, pages 123–136, 2006.

[32] D. Monniaux. The parallel implementation of the astrée static analyzer. In K. Yi, editor, *APLAS*, volume 3780 of *Lecture Notes in Computer Science*, pages 86–96. Springer, 2005. ISBN 3-540-29735-9.

[33] A. V. Nori and S. K. Rajamani. An empirical study of optimizations in Yogi. In *International Conference on Software Engineering (ICSE 2010)*, pages 355–364, 2010.

[34] T. Prabhu, S. Ramalingam, M. Might, and M. Hall. EigenCFA: accelerating flow analysis with GPUs. In *Principles of Programming Languages (POPL 2011)*, pages 511–522, 2011.

[35] K. Sen, D. Marinov, and G. Agha. CUTE: A concolic unit testing engine for C. In *Foundations of Software Engineering (ESEC-FSE 2005)*, pages 263–272, 2005.

[36] U. Stern and D. L. Dill. Parallelizing the Murphi Verifier. In *Computer Aided Verification (CAV 1997)*, pages 256–278, 1997.

[37] Y. Xie and A. Aiken. Scalable error detection using Boolean satisfiability. In *Principles of Programming Languages (POPL 2005)*, pages 351–363, 2005.

[38] Y. Yu, M. Isard, D. Fetterly, M. Budiu, U. Erlingsson, P. K. Gunda, and J. Currey. DryadLINQ: a system for general-purpose distributed data-parallel computing using a high-level language. In *Operating Systems Design and Implementation (OSDI 2008)*, pages 1–14, 2008.

Design and Implementation of Sparse Global Analyses for C-like Languages

Hakjoo Oh Kihong Heo Wonchan Lee Woosuk Lee Kwangkeun Yi
Seoul National University
{pronto,khheo,wclee,wslee,kwang}@ropas.snu.ac.kr

Abstract

In this article we present a general method for achieving global static analyzers that are precise, sound, yet also scalable. Our method generalizes the sparse analysis techniques on top of the abstract interpretation framework to support relational as well as non-relational semantics properties for C-like languages. We first use the abstract interpretation framework to have a global static analyzer whose scalability is unattended. Upon this underlying sound static analyzer, we add our generalized sparse analysis techniques to improve its scalability while preserving the precision of the underlying analysis. Our framework determines what to prove to guarantee that the resulting sparse version should preserve the precision of the underlying analyzer.

We formally present our framework; we present that existing sparse analyses are all restricted instances of our framework; we show more semantically elaborate design examples of sparse non-relational and relational static analyses; we present their implementation results that scale to analyze up to one million lines of C programs. We also show a set of implementation techniques that turn out to be critical to economically support the sparse analysis process.

Categories and Subject Descriptors F.3.2 [*Semantics of Programming Languages*]: Program Analysis

Keywords Static analysis, abstract interpretation, sparse analysis

1. Introduction

Precise, sound, scalable yet global static analyzers have been unachievable in general. Other than almost syntactic properties, once the target property becomes slightly deep in semantics it's been a daunting challenge to achieve the four goals in a single static analyzer. This situation explains why, for example, in the static error detection tools for full C, there exists a clear dichotomy: either "bug-finders" that risk being unsound yet scalable or "verifiers" that risk being unscalable yet sound. No such tools are scalable to globally analyze million lines of C code while being sound and precise enough for practical use.

In this article we present a general method for achieving global static analyzers that are precise, sound, yet also scalable. Our approach generalizes the sparse analysis ideas on top of the abstract interpretation framework. Since the abstract interpretation framework [9, 11] guides us to design sound yet arbitrarily precise static analyzers for any target language, we first use the framework to have a global static analyzer whose scalability is unattended. Upon this underlying sound static analyzer, we add our generalized sparse analysis techniques to improve its scalability while preserving the precision of the underlying analysis. Our framework determines what to prove to guarantee that the resulting sparse version should preserve the precision of the underlying analyzer.

Our framework bridges the gap between the two existing technologies – abstract interpretation and sparse analysis – towards the design of sound, yet scalable global static analyzers. Note that while abstract interpretation framework provides a theoretical knob to control the analysis precision without violating its correctness, the framework does not provide a knob to control the resulting analyzer's scalability preserving its precision. On the other hand, existing sparse analysis techniques [6, 14, 15, 19, 20, 24, 40, 42, 44] achieve scalability, but they are mostly algorithmic and tightly coupled with particular analyses.[1] The sparse techniques are not general enough to be used for an arbitrarily complicated semantic analysis.

Contributions Our contributions are as follows.

- We propose a general framework for designing sparse static analysis. Our framework is semantics-based and precision-preserving. We prove that our framework yields a correct sparse analysis that has the same precision as the original.
- We present a new notion of data dependency, which is a key to the precision-preserving sparse analysis. Unlike conventional def-use chains, sparse analysis with our data dependency is fully precise.
- We design sparse non-relational and relational analysis which are still general as themselves. We can instantiate these designs with a particular non-relational and relational abstract domains, respectively.
- We prove the practicality of our framework by experimentally demonstrating the achieved speedup of an industrial-strength static analyzer [23, 26, 28, 35–38]. The sparse analysis can analyze programs up to 1 million lines of C code with interval domain and up to 100K lines of C code with octagon domain.

Outline Section 2 explains our sparse analysis framework. Section 3 and 4 design sparse non-relational and relational analyes, respectively, based on our framework. Section 5 discusses several issues involved in the implementations. Section 6 presents the experimental studies. Section 7 discusses related work.

[1] A few techniques [7, 39] are in general settings but instead they take coarse-grained approach to sparsity.

PLDI'12, June 11–16, 2012, Beijing, China.

2. Sparse Analysis Framework

2.1 Notation

Given function $f \in A \to B$, we write $f|_C$ for the restriction of function f to the domain $\mathsf{dom}(f) \cap C$. We write $f\backslash_C$ for the restriction of f to the domain $\mathsf{dom}(f) - C$. We abuse the notation $f|_a$ and $f\backslash_a$ for the domain restrictions on singleton set $\{a\}$. We write $f[a \mapsto b]$ for the function got from function f by changing the value for a to b. We write $f[a_1 \mapsto b_1, \cdots, a_n \mapsto b_n]$ for $f[a_1 \mapsto b_1] \cdots [a_n \mapsto b_n]$. We write $f[\{a_1, \cdots, a_n\} \overset{w}{\mapsto} b]$ for $f[a_1 \mapsto f(a_1) \sqcup b, \cdots, a_n \mapsto f(a_n) \sqcup b]$ (weak update).

2.2 Program

A program is a tuple $\langle \mathbb{C}, \hookrightarrow \rangle$ where $\mathbb{C}$ is a finite set of control points and $\hookrightarrow \subseteq \mathbb{C} \times \mathbb{C}$ is a relation that denotes control flows of the program; $c' \hookrightarrow c$ indicates that c is a next control point of c'. Each control point is associated with a command, denoted $\mathsf{cmd}(c)$. A path $p = p_0 p_1 \ldots p_n$ is a sequence of control points such that $p_0 \hookrightarrow p_1 \hookrightarrow \cdots \hookrightarrow p_n$. We write $\mathsf{Paths} = \mathbf{lfp}\lambda P.\{c_0 c_1 \mid c_0 \hookrightarrow c_1\} \cup \{p_0 \ldots p_n c \mid p \in P \wedge p_n \hookrightarrow c\}$ for the set of all paths in the program.

Collecting Semantics Collecting semantics of program P is an invariant $[\![P]\!] \in \mathbb{C} \to 2^{\mathbb{S}}$ that represents a set of reachable states at each control point, where the concrete domain of states, $\mathbb{S} = \mathbb{L} \to \mathbb{V}$, maps concrete locations ($\mathbb{L}$) to concrete values ($\mathbb{V}$). The collecting semantics is characterized by the least fixpoint of semantic function $F \in (\mathbb{C} \to 2^{\mathbb{S}}) \to (\mathbb{C} \to 2^{\mathbb{S}})$ such that,

$$F(X) = \lambda c \in \mathbb{C}.f_c(\bigcup_{c' \hookrightarrow c} X(c')). \tag{1}$$

where $f_c \in 2^{\mathbb{S}} \to 2^{\mathbb{S}}$ is a semantic function at control point c. Because our framework is independent from target languages, we leave out the definition of the concrete semantic function f_c.

2.3 Baseline Abstraction

We abstract the collecting semantics of program P by the following Galois connection

$$\mathbb{C} \to 2^{\mathbb{S}} \underset{\alpha}{\overset{\gamma}{\leftrightarrows}} \mathbb{C} \to \hat{\mathbb{S}} \tag{2}$$

where α and γ are pointwise liftings of abstract and concretization function $\alpha_{\mathbb{S}}$ and $\gamma_{\mathbb{S}}$ (such that $2^{\mathbb{S}} \underset{\alpha_{\mathbb{S}}}{\overset{\gamma_{\mathbb{S}}}{\leftrightarrows}} \hat{\mathbb{S}}$), respectively.

We consider a particular, yet general, family of abstract domains where abstract state $\hat{\mathbb{S}}$ is map $\hat{\mathbb{L}} \to \hat{\mathbb{V}}$ where $\hat{\mathbb{L}}$ is a finite set of abstract locations, and $\hat{\mathbb{V}}$ is a (potentially infinite) set of abstract values. All non-relational abstract domains, such as intervals [9], are members of this family. Furthermore, the family covers some numerical, relational domains. Practical relational analyses exploit *packed* relationality [4, 13, 34, 43]; the abstract domain is of form *Packs* $\to \hat{\mathbb{R}}$ where *Packs* is a set of variable groups selected to be related together. $\hat{\mathbb{R}}$ denotes numerical constraints among variables in those groups. In such *packed* relational analysis, each variable pack is treated as an abstract location ($\hat{\mathbb{L}}$) and numerical constraints amount to abstract values ($\hat{\mathbb{V}}$). Examples of the numerical constraints are domain of octagons [34] and polyhedrons [12]. In practice, relational analyses are necessarily packed relational [4, 13] because of otherwise unacceptable costs.

Abstract semantics is characterized as a least fixpoint of abstract semantic function $\hat{F} \in (\mathbb{C} \to \hat{\mathbb{S}}) \to (\mathbb{C} \to \hat{\mathbb{S}})$ defined as,

$$\hat{F}(\hat{X}) = \lambda c \in \mathbb{C}.\hat{f}_c(\bigsqcup_{c' \hookrightarrow c} \hat{X}(c')). \tag{3}$$

where $\hat{f}_c \in \hat{\mathbb{S}} \to \hat{\mathbb{S}}$ is a monotone abstract semantic function for control point c. We assume that $\hat{F}$ is sound with respect to F, i.e., $\alpha \circ F \sqsubseteq \hat{F} \circ \alpha$, then the soundness of abstract semantics is followed by the fixpoint transfer theorem [11].

2.4 Sparse Analysis by Eliminating Unnecessary Propagation

The abstract semantic function given in (3) propagates some abstract values unnecessarily. For example, suppose that we analyze statement $x := y$ using a non-relational domain, like interval domain [9]. We know for sure that the abstract semantic function for the statement *defines* a new abstract value only at variable x and *uses* only the abstract value of variable y. Thus, it is unnecessary to propagate the whole abstract states. However, the function given in (3) blindly propagates the whole abstract states of all predecessors c' to control point c.

To make the analysis sparse, we need to eliminate this unnecessary propagation by making the semantic function propagate abstract values along data dependency, not control flows; that is, we make the semantic function propagate only the abstract values newly computed at one control point to the other where they are actually used. In the rest of this section, we explain how to make abstract semantic function (3) sparse while preserving its precision and soundness.

2.5 Definition and Use Set

We first need to precisely define what are "definitions" and "uses". They are defined in terms of abstract semantics, i.e., abstract semantic function $\hat{f}_c$, not concrete semantics.

Definition 1 (Definition set). *Let S be the least fixpoint $\mathbf{lfp}\hat{F}$ of the original semantic function $\hat{F}$. Definition set $\mathsf{D}(c)$ at control point c is a set of abstract locations that are assigned a new abstract value by abstract semantic function $\hat{f}_c$, i.e.*

$$\mathsf{D}(c) \triangleq \{l \in \hat{\mathbb{L}} \mid \exists \hat{s} \sqsubseteq \bigsqcup_{c' \hookrightarrow c} S(c').\hat{f}_c(\hat{s})(l) \neq \hat{s}(l)\}.$$

Definition 2 (Use set). *Let S be the least fixpoint $\mathbf{lfp}\hat{F}$ of the original semantic function $\hat{F}$. Use set $\mathsf{U}(c)$ at control point c is a set of abstract locations that are used by abstract semantic function $\hat{f}_c$, i.e.*

$$\mathsf{U}(c) \triangleq \{l \in \hat{\mathbb{L}} \mid \exists \hat{s} \sqsubseteq \bigsqcup_{c' \hookrightarrow c} S(c').\hat{f}_c(\hat{s})|_{\mathsf{D}(c)} \neq \hat{f}_c(\hat{s}\backslash_l)|_{\mathsf{D}(c)}\}.$$

Example 1. *Consider the following simple subset of C:*

$$\begin{array}{rcl} cmd & \to & x := e \mid *x := e \\ e & \to & x \mid \&x \mid *x. \end{array}$$

The meaning of each statement and each expression is fairly standard. We design a pointer analysis for this as follows:

$$\begin{array}{rcl} \hat{s} \in \hat{\mathbb{S}} & = & Var \to 2^{Var} \\ \hat{f}_c(\hat{s}) & = & \begin{cases} \hat{s}[x \mapsto \hat{\mathcal{E}}(e)(\hat{s})] & \mathsf{cmd}(c) = x := e \\ \hat{s}[y \mapsto \hat{\mathcal{E}}(e)(\hat{s})] & \mathsf{cmd}(c) = *x := e \\ & \text{and } \hat{s}(x) = \{y\} \\ \hat{s}[\hat{s}(x) \overset{w}{\mapsto} \hat{\mathcal{E}}(e)(\hat{s})] & \mathsf{cmd}(c) = *x := e \end{cases} \\ \hat{\mathcal{E}}(e)(\hat{s}) & = & \begin{cases} \hat{s}(x) & e = x \\ \{x\} & e = \&x \\ \bigcup_{y \in \hat{s}(x)} \hat{s}(y) & e = *x \end{cases} \end{array}$$

Now suppose that we analyze program ⑩$x := \&y;$ ⑪$*p := \&z;$ ⑫$y := x;$ *(superscripts are control points). Suppose that points-to set of pointer p is $\{x, y\}$ at control point* ⑪ *according to the fixpoint. Definition set and use set at each control point are as follows.*

$$\begin{array}{rclrcl} \mathsf{D}(⑩) & = & \{x\} & \mathsf{U}(⑩) & = & \varnothing \\ \mathsf{D}(⑪) & = & \{x, y\} & \mathsf{U}(⑪) & = & \{p, x, y\} \\ \mathsf{D}(⑫) & = & \{y\} & \mathsf{U}(⑫) & = & \{x\} \end{array}$$

Note that $\mathsf{U}(⑪)$ *contains* $\mathsf{D}(⑪)$ *because of the weak update* ($\overset{w}{\mapsto}$)*: the semantics of weak update* $\hat{s}[l \overset{w}{\mapsto} v] = \hat{s}[l \mapsto \hat{s}(l) \sqcup v]$ *is defined to use the target location l. This implicit use information, which does not explicitly appear in the program text, is naturally captured by following the semantics.*

2.6 Data Dependencies

Once identifying definition and use sets at each control point, we can discover data dependencies of abstract semantic function $\hat{F}$ between two control points. Intuitively, if the abstract value of abstract location l defined at control point c_0 is used at control point c_n, there is a data dependency between c_0 and c_n on l. Formal definition of data dependency is given below:

Definition 3 (Data dependency). *Data dependency is ternary relation* $\rightsquigarrow \subseteq \mathbb{C} \times \hat{\mathbb{L}} \times \mathbb{C}$ *defined as follows:*

$$c_0 \overset{l}{\rightsquigarrow} c_n \triangleq \exists c_0 \dots c_n \in \mathsf{Paths}, l \in \hat{\mathbb{L}}. \quad l \in \mathsf{D}(c_0) \cap \mathsf{U}(c_n) \wedge \forall i \in (0,n). l \notin \mathsf{D}(c_i)$$

The definition means that if there exists a path from control point c_0 to c_n, a value of abstract location l can be defined at c_0 and used at c_n, and there is no intermediate control point c_i that may change the value of l, then a data dependency exists between control points c_0 and c_n on location l. One might wonder why the data dependency excludes not only a path that always kills the definition but also a path that might, but not always, kill the definition. In the latter case, the definition that might be killed is, by Definition 2, included in the use set of the definition point.

Example 2. *In the program presented in Example 1, we can find two data dependencies,* $⑩ \overset{x}{\rightsquigarrow} ⑪$ *and* $⑪ \overset{x}{\rightsquigarrow} ⑫$.

Comparison with Def-use Chains Our notion of data dependency is different from the conventional notion of def-use chains. If we want to conservatively collect all the possible def-use chains, we should exclude only the paths from definition points to use points when there exists a point that always kills the definition. We can slightly modify Definition 3 to express def-use chain relation $\rightsquigarrow_{\mathsf{du}}$ as follows:

$$c_0 \overset{l}{\rightsquigarrow}_{\mathsf{du}} c_n \triangleq \exists c_0 \dots c_n \in \mathsf{Paths}, l \in \hat{\mathbb{L}}. \quad l \in \mathsf{D}(c_0) \cap \mathsf{U}(c_n) \wedge \forall i \in (0,n). l \notin \mathsf{D}_{\mathsf{always}}(c_i)$$

where $\mathsf{D}_{\mathsf{always}}(c)$ denotes the set of abstract locations that are always killed at control point c.

Example 3. *We can find three def-use chains,* $⑩ \overset{x}{\rightsquigarrow}_{\mathsf{du}} ⑪$, $⑩ \overset{x}{\rightsquigarrow}_{\mathsf{du}} ⑫$, *and* $⑪ \overset{x}{\rightsquigarrow}_{\mathsf{du}} ⑫$ *in Example 1.*

The reason why we use our notion of data dependencies instead of def-use chains is that our data dependencies preserve the precision of the analysis even when approximations are involved. On the other hand, sparse analysis with approximated def-use chains may lose precision, which becomes evident in Section 2.8.

2.7 Sparse Abstract Semantic Function

Using data dependency, we can make abstract semantic function sparse, which propagates between control points only the abstract values that participate in the fixpoint computation. Sparse abstract function $\hat{F}_s$, whose definition is given below, is the same as the original except that it propagates abstract values along to the data dependency, not along to control flows:

$$\hat{F}_s(\hat{X}) = \lambda c \in \mathbb{C}. \hat{f}_c\Big(\bigsqcup_{c_d \overset{l}{\rightsquigarrow} c} \hat{X}(c_d)|_l\Big).$$

As this definition is only different in that it is defined over data dependency ($\rightsquigarrow$), we can reuse abstract semantic function $\hat{f}_c$, and its soundness result, from the original analysis design.

The following lemma states that the analysis result with sparse abstract semantic function is the same as the one of original analysis.

Lemma 1 (Correctness). *Let* $\mathcal{S}$ *and* $\mathcal{S}_s$ *be* $\mathbf{lfp}\hat{F}$ *and* $\mathbf{lfp}\hat{F}_s$*. Then,*

$$\forall c \in \mathbb{C}. \forall l \in \mathsf{D}(c). \mathcal{S}_s(c)(l) = \mathcal{S}(c)(l).$$

The lemma guarantees that the sparse analysis result is identical to the original result only up to the entries that are defined in every control point. This is fair since the sparse analysis result does not contain the entries unnecessary for its computation.

2.8 Sparse Analysis with Approximated Data Dependency

Sparse analysis designed until Section 2.7 might not be practical since we can decide definition set D and use set U only with the original fixpoint $\mathbf{lfp}\hat{F}$ computed.

To design a practical sparse analysis, we can approximate data dependency using approximated definition set $\hat{\mathsf{D}}$ and use set $\hat{\mathsf{U}}$ ($\hat{\mathsf{D}}$ and $\hat{\mathsf{U}}$ are arbitrary sets that respect some properties in Definition 5).

Definition 4 (Approximated Data Dependency). *Approximated data dependency is ternary relation* $\rightsquigarrow_a \subseteq \mathbb{C} \times \hat{\mathbb{L}} \times \mathbb{C}$ *defined as follows:*

$$c_0 \overset{l}{\rightsquigarrow}_a c_n \triangleq \exists c_0 \dots c_n \in \mathsf{Paths}, l \in \hat{\mathbb{L}}. \quad l \in \hat{\mathsf{D}}(c_0) \cap \hat{\mathsf{U}}(c_n) \wedge \forall i \in (0,n). l \notin \hat{\mathsf{D}}(c_i)$$

The definition is the same except that it is defined over $\hat{\mathsf{D}}$ and $\hat{\mathsf{U}}$. The derived sparse analysis is to compute the fixpoint of the following abstract semantic function:

$$\hat{F}_a(\hat{X}) = \lambda c \in \mathbb{C}. \hat{f}_c\Big(\bigsqcup_{c_d \overset{l}{\rightsquigarrow}_a c} \hat{X}(c_d)|_l\Big).$$

One thing to note is that not all $\hat{\mathsf{D}}$ and $\hat{\mathsf{U}}$ make the derived sparse analysis compute the same result as the original. First, both $\hat{\mathsf{D}}(c)$ and $\hat{\mathsf{U}}(c)$ at each control point should be an over-approximation of $\mathsf{D}(c)$ and $\mathsf{U}(c)$, respectively (we can easily show that the analysis computes different result if one of them is an under-approximation). Next, all spurious definitions that are included in $\hat{\mathsf{D}}$ but not in D should be also included in $\hat{\mathsf{U}}$. The following example illustrates what happens when there exists an abstract location which is a spurious definition but is not included in the approximated use set.

Example 4. *Consider the same program presented in Example 1, except that we now suppose the points-to set of pointer* p *being* $\{y\}$*. Then, definition set and use set at each control point are as follows:*

$$\begin{array}{lllllll} \mathsf{D}(⑩) & = & \{x\} & \mathsf{U}(⑩) & = & \varnothing \\ \mathsf{D}(⑪) & = & \{y\} & \mathsf{U}(⑪) & = & \{p\} \\ \mathsf{D}(⑫) & = & \{y\} & \mathsf{U}(⑫) & = & \{x\}. \end{array}$$

Note that $\mathsf{U}(11)$ *does not contain* $\mathsf{D}(11)$ *because of strong update. The following is one example of unsafe approximation.*

$$\begin{array}{lllllll} \hat{\mathsf{D}}(⑩) & = & \{x\} & \hat{\mathsf{U}}(⑩) & = & \varnothing \\ \hat{\mathsf{D}}(⑪) & = & \{x,y\} & \hat{\mathsf{U}}(⑪) & = & \{p\} \\ \hat{\mathsf{D}}(⑫) & = & \{y\} & \hat{\mathsf{U}}(⑫) & = & \{x\}. \end{array}$$

This approximation is unsafe because spurious definition $\{x\}$ *at control point ⑪ is not included in approximated use set* $\hat{\mathsf{U}}(⑪)$*. With this approximation, abstract value of* x *at ⑩ is not propagated to ⑫, while it is propagated in the original analysis* ($⑩ \overset{x}{\rightsquigarrow} ⑫$, *but* $⑩ \overset{x}{\not\rightsquigarrow}_a ⑫$)*. However, if* $\{x\} \subseteq \hat{\mathsf{U}}(⑪)$*, then the abstract value* *will be propagated through two data dependencies,* ⑩ $\overset{x}{\rightsquigarrow}_a$ ⑪ *and* ⑪ $\overset{x}{\rightsquigarrow}_a$ ⑫*. Note that x is not defined at* ⑪*, thus the propagated abstract value for x is not modified at* ⑪*.*

We can formally define safe approximations of definition set and use set as follows:

Definition 5. *Set $\hat{\mathsf{D}}(c)$ and $\hat{\mathsf{U}}(c)$ are a safe approximation of definition set $\mathsf{D}(c)$ and use set $\mathsf{U}(c)$, respectively, if and only if*

(1) $\hat{\mathsf{D}}(c) \supseteq \mathsf{D}(c) \wedge \hat{\mathsf{U}}(c) \supseteq \mathsf{U}(c)$*; and*
(2) $\hat{\mathsf{D}}(c) - \mathsf{D}(c) \subseteq \hat{\mathsf{U}}(c)$.

The remaining things is to prove that the safe approximation $\hat{\mathsf{D}}$ and $\hat{\mathsf{U}}$ yields the correct sparse analysis, which the following lemma states:

Lemma 2 (Correctness of Safe Approximation). *Suppose sparse abstract semantic function $\hat{F}_a$ is derived by the safe approximation $\hat{\mathsf{D}}$ and $\hat{\mathsf{U}}$. Let $\mathcal{S}$ and $\mathcal{S}_a$ be* $\mathbf{lfp}\hat{F}$ *and* $\mathbf{lfp}\hat{F}_a$*. Then,*

$$\forall c \in \mathbb{C}.\forall l \in \hat{\mathsf{D}}(c).\mathcal{S}_a(c)(l) = \mathcal{S}(c)(l).$$

Precision Loss with Conservative Def-use Chains While approximated data dependency does not degrade the precision of an analysis, conservative def-use chains from approximated definition set and use set make the analysis less precise even if the approximation is safe. The following example illustrates the case of imprecision.

Example 5. *Consider the program in Example 1, assuming the points-to set of* p *being $\{x\}$. The following approximated definition and use sets*

$$\begin{array}{lcllcl} \hat{\mathsf{D}}(⑩) & = & \{x\} & \hat{\mathsf{U}}(⑩) & = & \varnothing \\ \hat{\mathsf{D}}(⑪) & = & \{x, y\} & \hat{\mathsf{U}}(⑪) & = & \{p, y\} \\ \hat{\mathsf{D}}(⑫) & = & \{y\} & \hat{\mathsf{U}}(⑫) & = & \{x\}. \end{array}$$

establish the following two def-use chains: ⑪ $\overset{x}{\rightsquigarrow}_{\mathsf{du}}$ ⑫*, and* ⑩ $\overset{x}{\rightsquigarrow}_{\mathsf{du}}$ ⑫ *(we assume here that relation $\rightsquigarrow_{\mathsf{du}}$ is similarly modified as in Definition 4). With these conservative def-use chains, the points-to set of x propagated to control point* ⑫ *is $\{y\} \cup \{z\}$, which is bigger set than $\{z\}$, the one that appears in the original analysis.*

2.9 Designing Sparse Analysis Steps in the Framework

In summary, the design of sparse analysis within our framework is done in the following two steps:

(1) Design a static analysis based on abstract interpretation framework [9]. Note that the abstract domain should be a member of the family explained in Section 2.3.

(2) Design a method to find a safe approximation $\hat{\mathsf{D}}$ and $\hat{\mathsf{U}}$ of definition set D and use set U (Definition 5).

3. Designing Sparse Non-Relational Analysis

As a concrete example, we show how to design sparse non-relational analyses within our framework. Following Section 2.9, we proceed in two steps: (1) We design a conventional non-relational analysis based on abstract interpretation. Relying on the abstract interpretation framework [9, 10], we can flexibly design a static analysis of our interest with soundness guaranteed. (2) We design a method to find $\hat{\mathsf{D}}$ and $\hat{\mathsf{U}}$ and prove that they are safe approximations (Definition 5). The sparse analysis designed in this section is the core of our interval domain-based static analyzer, $\mathsf{Interval}_{\mathsf{sparse}}$, which will be evaluated in Section 6.

For brevity, we restrict our presentation to the following simple subset of C, where a variable has either an integer value or a pointer (i.e. $\mathbb{V} = \mathbb{Z} + \mathbb{L}$):

$$\begin{array}{l} cmd \to x := e \mid *x := e \mid \{\!\!\{x < n\}\!\!\} \\ \quad \text{where } e \to n \mid x \mid \&x \mid *x \mid e{+}e \end{array}$$

Assignment $x := e$ corresponds to assigning the value of expression e to variable x. Store $*x := e$ performs indirect assignments; the value of e is assigned to the location that x points to. An assume command $\{\!\!\{x < n\}\!\!\}$ makes the program continue only when the condition evaluates to true.

3.1 Step 1: Designing Non-sparse Analysis

Abstract Domain From the baseline abstraction (in Section 2.3), we consider a family of state abstractions $2^{\mathbb{S}} \underset{\alpha_{\mathbb{S}}}{\overset{\gamma_{\mathbb{S}}}{\leftrightarrows}} \hat{\mathbb{S}}$ such that, (Because it is standard, we omit the definition of $\alpha_{\mathbb{S}}$.)

$$\hat{\mathbb{S}} = \hat{\mathbb{L}} \to \hat{\mathbb{V}} \qquad \hat{\mathbb{L}} = Var \qquad \hat{\mathbb{V}} = \hat{\mathbb{Z}} \times \hat{\mathbb{P}} \qquad \hat{\mathbb{P}} = 2^{\hat{\mathbb{L}}}$$

An abstract location is a program variable. An abstract value is a pair of an abstract integer $\hat{\mathbb{Z}}$ and an abstract pointer $\hat{\mathbb{P}}$. A set of integers is abstracted to an abstract integer ($2^{\mathbb{Z}} \underset{\alpha_{\mathbb{Z}}}{\overset{\gamma_{\mathbb{Z}}}{\leftrightarrows}} \hat{\mathbb{Z}}$). Note that the abstraction is generic so we can choose any non-relational numeric domains of our interest, such as intervals ($\hat{\mathbb{Z}} = \{[l, u] \mid l, u \in \mathbb{Z} \cup \{-\infty, +\infty\} \wedge l \leq u\} \cup \{\bot\}$). For simplicity, we do not abstract pointers (because they are finite): pointer values are kept by a points-to set ($\hat{\mathbb{P}} = 2^{\hat{\mathbb{L}}}$). Other pointer abstractions are also orthogonally applicable.

Abstract Semantics The abstract semantics is defined by the least fixpoint of semantic function (3), $\hat{F}$, where the abstract semantic function $\hat{f}_c \in \hat{\mathbb{S}} \to \hat{\mathbb{S}}$ is defined as follows:

$$\hat{f}_c(\hat{s}) = \begin{cases} \hat{s}[x \mapsto \hat{\mathcal{E}}(e)(\hat{s})] & \mathsf{cmd}(c) = x := e \\ \hat{s}[\hat{s}(x).\hat{\mathbb{P}} \overset{w}{\mapsto} \hat{\mathcal{E}}(e)(\hat{s})] & \mathsf{cmd}(c) = *x := e \\ \hat{s}[x \mapsto \langle \hat{s}(x).\hat{\mathbb{Z}} \sqcap_{\hat{\mathbb{Z}}} \alpha_{\mathbb{Z}}(\{z \in \mathbb{Z} | z < n\}), \hat{s}(x).\hat{\mathbb{P}}\rangle] & \mathsf{cmd}(c) = \{\!\!\{x < n\}\!\!\} \end{cases}$$

Auxiliary function $\hat{\mathcal{E}}(e)(\hat{s})$ computes abstract value of e under $\hat{s}$. Assignment $x := e$ updates the value of x. Store $*x := e$ weakly[2] updates the value of abstract locations that $*x$ denotes. $\{\!\!\{x < n\}\!\!\}$ confines the interval value of x according to the condition. $\hat{\mathcal{E}} \in e \to \hat{\mathbb{S}} \to \hat{\mathbb{V}}$ is defined as follows:

$$\begin{array}{rcl} \hat{\mathcal{E}}(n)(\hat{s}) & = & \langle \alpha_{\mathbb{Z}}(\{n\}), \bot \rangle \\ \hat{\mathcal{E}}(x)(\hat{s}) & = & \hat{s}(x) \\ \hat{\mathcal{E}}(\&x)(\hat{s}) & = & \langle \bot, \{x\} \rangle \\ \hat{\mathcal{E}}(*x)(\hat{s}) & = & \bigsqcup\{\hat{s}(a) \mid a \in \hat{s}(x).\hat{\mathbb{P}}\} \\ \hat{\mathcal{E}}(e_1{+}e_2)(\hat{s}) & = & \langle v_1.\hat{\mathbb{Z}} \hat{+}_{\hat{\mathbb{Z}}} v_2.\hat{\mathbb{Z}}, v_1.\hat{\mathbb{P}} \cup v_2.\hat{\mathbb{P}} \rangle \\ & & \text{where } v_1 = \hat{\mathcal{E}}(e_1)(\hat{s}), v_2 = \hat{\mathcal{E}}(e_2)(\hat{s}) \end{array}$$

Note that the above analysis is parameterized by an abstract numeric domain $\hat{\mathbb{Z}}$ and sound operators $\hat{+}_{\hat{\mathbb{Z}}}$ and $\sqcap_{\hat{\mathbb{Z}}}$.

3.2 Step 2: Finding Definitions and Uses

The second step is to find safe approximations of definitions and uses. The framework provides a mathematical definitions regarding correctness but does not provide how to find safe $\hat{\mathsf{D}}$ and $\hat{\mathsf{U}}$. In the rest part of this section, we present a semantics-based, systematic way to find them.

We propose to find $\hat{\mathsf{D}}$ and $\hat{\mathsf{U}}$ from a conservative approximation of $\hat{F}$. We call the approximated analysis by pre-analysis. Let $\hat{\mathbb{D}}_{pre}$ and $\hat{F}_{pre}$ be the domain and semantic function of such a pre-

[2] For brevity, we consider only weak updates. Applying strong update is orthogonal to our sparse analysis design.

analysis, which satisfies the following two conditions.

$$\mathbb{C} \to \hat{\mathbb{S}} \xleftarrow[\alpha_{pre}]{\gamma_{pre}} \hat{\mathbb{D}}_{pre} \qquad \alpha_{pre} \circ \hat{F} \sqsubseteq \hat{F}_{pre} \circ \alpha_{pre}$$

By abstract interpretation framework [9, 10], such a pre-analysis is guaranteed to be conservative, i.e., $\alpha_{pre}(\mathbf{lfp}\hat{F}) \sqsubseteq \mathbf{lfp}\hat{F}_{pre}$. As an example, in experiments (Section 6), we use a simple abstraction as follows:

$$\mathbb{C} \to \hat{\mathbb{S}} \xleftarrow[\alpha_{pre}]{\gamma_{pre}} \hat{\mathbb{S}} \qquad \begin{array}{rcl} \alpha_{pre} & = & \lambda \hat{X}. \bigsqcup\{\hat{X}(c) \mid c \in \mathsf{dom}(\hat{X})\} \\ \hat{F}_{pre} & = & \lambda \hat{s}. \bigsqcup_{c \in \mathbb{C}} \hat{f}_c(\hat{s}) \end{array}$$

The abstraction ignores the control flows of programs and computes a single global invariant (a.k.a., flow-insensitivity).

We now define $\hat{\mathsf{D}}$ and $\hat{\mathsf{U}}$ by using pre-analysis. Let $\hat{\mathcal{T}}_{pre} \in \mathbb{C} \to \hat{\mathbb{S}}$ be the pre-analysis result in terms of original analysis, i.e., $\hat{\mathcal{T}}_{pre} = \gamma_{pre}(\mathbf{lfp}\hat{F}_{pre})$. The definitions of $\hat{\mathsf{D}}$ and $\hat{\mathsf{U}}$ are naturally derived from the semantic definition of $\hat{f}_c$.

$$\hat{\mathsf{D}}(c) = \begin{cases} \{x\} & \mathsf{cmd}(c) = x := e \\ \hat{\mathcal{T}}_{pre}(c)(x).\hat{\mathbb{P}} & \mathsf{cmd}(c) = *x := e \\ \{x\} & \mathsf{cmd}(c) = \{\!\!\{x < n\}\!\!\} \end{cases}$$

$\hat{\mathsf{D}}$ is defined to include locations whose values are potentially defined (changed). In the definition of $\hat{f}_c$ for $x := e$ and $\{\!\!\{x < n\}\!\!\}$, we notice that abstract location x may be defined. In $*x := e$, we see that $\hat{f}_c$ may define locations $\hat{s}(x).\hat{\mathbb{P}}$ for a given input state $\hat{s}$ at program point c. Here, we use the pre-analysis: because we cannot have the input state $\hat{s}$ prior to the analysis, we instead use its conservative abstraction $\hat{\mathcal{T}}_{pre}(c)$. Such $\hat{\mathsf{D}}$ satisfies the safe approximation condition (Definition 5), because we collect all potentially defined locations, pre-analysis is conservative, and $\hat{f}$ is monotone.

Before defining $\hat{\mathsf{U}}$, we define an auxiliary function $\mathcal{U} \in e \to \hat{\mathbb{S}} \to 2^{\hat{\mathbb{L}}}$. Given expression e and state $\hat{s}$, $\mathcal{U}(e)(\hat{s})$ finds the set of abstract locations that are referenced during the evaluation of $\hat{\mathcal{E}}(e)(\hat{s})$. Thus, $\mathcal{U}$ is naturally derived from the definition of $\hat{\mathcal{E}}$.

$$\begin{array}{rcl} \mathcal{U}(n)(\hat{s}) & = & \emptyset \\ \mathcal{U}(x)(\hat{s}) & = & \{x\} \\ \mathcal{U}(\&x)(\hat{s}) & = & \emptyset \\ \mathcal{U}(*x)(\hat{s}) & = & \{x\} \cup \hat{s}(x).\hat{\mathbb{P}} \\ \mathcal{U}(e_1{+}e_2)(\hat{s}) & = & \mathcal{U}(e_1)(\hat{s}) \cup \mathcal{U}(e_2)(\hat{s}) \end{array}$$

When e is either n or $\&x$, $\hat{\mathcal{E}}$ does not refer any abstract location. Because $\hat{\mathcal{E}}(x)(\hat{s})$ references abstract location x, $\mathcal{U}(x)(\hat{s})$ is defined by $\{x\}$. $\hat{\mathcal{E}}(*x)(\hat{s})$ references location x and each location $a \in \hat{s}(x)$, thus the set of referenced locations is $\{x\} \cup \hat{s}(x).\hat{\mathbb{P}}$. $\hat{\mathsf{U}}$ is defined as follows: (For brevity, let $\hat{s}_c = \hat{\mathcal{T}}_{pre}(c)$)

$$\hat{\mathsf{U}}(c) = \begin{cases} \mathcal{U}(e)(\hat{s}_c) & \mathsf{cmd}(c) = x := e \\ \{x\} \cup \hat{s}_c(x).\hat{\mathbb{P}} \cup \mathcal{U}(e)(\hat{s}_c) & \mathsf{cmd}(c) = *x := e \\ \{x\} & \mathsf{cmd}(c) = \{\!\!\{x < n\}\!\!\} \end{cases}$$

Using $\hat{\mathcal{T}}_{pre}$ and $\mathcal{U}$, we collect abstract locations that are potentially used during the evaluation of e. Because $\hat{f}_c$ is defined to refer to abstract location x in $*x := e$ and $\{\!\!\{x < n\}\!\!\}$, $\mathcal{U}$ additionally includes x. Note that, in $*x := e$, $\hat{\mathsf{U}}(c)$ includes $\hat{s}_c(x).\hat{\mathbb{P}}$ because $\hat{f}_c$ performs weak updates.

Lemma 3. *$\hat{\mathsf{D}}$ and $\hat{\mathsf{U}}$ are safe approximations.*

Sparse Pointer Analysis as Instances We can instantiate this design of non-relational analysis to the recent two successful scalable sparse analysis presented in [19, 20].

Semi-sparse analysis [19] applies sparse analysis only for top-level variables whose addresses are never taken. We do the same thing by designing pre-analysis which computes a fixpoint $\hat{\mathcal{T}}_{pre}$ such that $\hat{\mathcal{T}}_{pre}(c)(x).\hat{\mathbb{P}} = \hat{\mathbb{L}}$ for all xs that are not top-level variables.

Staged Flow-Sensitive Analysis [20] uses auxiliary flow-insensitive pointer analysis to get an over-approximation of def-use information on pointer variables. By coincidence, our sparse non-relational analysis already does the same analysis for pointer variables except it also tracks numeric constraints of variables. We can design pre-analysis whose precision is incomparable to the original one, as in [20], although the framework cannot guarantee the correctness anymore.

4. Designing Sparse Relational Analysis

As another example, we show how to design sparse relational analyses. In Section 4.1, we define the family of relational analyses that our framework considers. In Section 4.2, we define safe $\hat{\mathsf{D}}$ and $\hat{\mathsf{U}}$ for the analysis.

We consider *packed* relational analysis [4, 34]. A pack is a semantically related set of variables. In the rest of this section, we assume a set of variable packs, $Packs \subseteq 2^{Var}$ such that $\bigcup Packs = Var$, are given by users or a pre-analysis [13, 34]. In a packed relational analysis, abstract states ($\hat{\mathbb{S}}$) map variable packs (*Packs*) to a relational domain ($\hat{\mathbb{R}}$), i.e., $\hat{\mathbb{S}} = Packs \to \hat{\mathbb{R}}$.

The distinguishing feature of sparse relational analysis is that definition sets and use sets are defined in terms of variable packs. For example, at a simple statement $x := 1$, all the variable packs that contain x may be defined and used at the same time, while only variable x may be defined and not used in non-relational analysis. As a result, data dependencies are also defined in terms of variable packs, i.e., $\rightsquigarrow \subseteq \mathbb{C} \times Packs \times \mathbb{C}$. We denote a pack of variables $x_1, \cdots, x_n$ as $\langle\!\langle x_1, \cdots, x_n \rangle\!\rangle$.

4.1 Step 1: Designing Non-sparse Analysis

For brevity, we consider the following pointer-free language: ($\mathbb{S} = Var \to \mathbb{Z}$).

$$cmd \to x := e \mid \{\!\!\{x < n\}\!\!\} \quad \text{where } e \to n \mid x \mid e{+}e$$

Including pointers in the language does not require novelty but verbosity. We focus only on the key differences between non-relational and relational sparse analysis designs.

Abstract Domain From the baseline abstraction (in Section 2.3), we consider a family of state abstractions $2^{\mathbb{S}} \xleftarrow[\alpha_{\mathbb{S}}]{\gamma_{\mathbb{S}}} \hat{\mathbb{S}}$ such that, ($\alpha_{\mathbb{S}}$ is defined using $\alpha_{\hat{\mathbb{R}}}$ such that $2^{\mathbb{S}} \xleftarrow[\alpha_{\hat{\mathbb{R}}}]{\gamma_{\hat{\mathbb{R}}}} \hat{\mathbb{R}}$.)

$$\hat{\mathbb{S}} = \hat{\mathbb{L}} \to \hat{\mathbb{V}} \qquad \hat{\mathbb{L}} = Packs \qquad \hat{\mathbb{V}} = \hat{\mathbb{R}}$$

Abstract Semantics In packed relational analysis, we sometimes need to know actual values (such as ranges) of variables. For example, suppose we analyze $a := b$ with $Packs = \{\langle\!\langle a, c\rangle\!\rangle, \langle\!\langle b, c\rangle\!\rangle\}$. Analyzing the statement amounts to updating the abstract value for pack $\langle\!\langle a, c\rangle\!\rangle$. However, because variable b is not contained in the pack, we need to obtain the value of b from the abstract value associated with $\langle\!\langle b, c\rangle\!\rangle$. Here, the value for b is obtained by projecting the relational domain elements for $\langle\!\langle b, c\rangle\!\rangle$ into a non-relational value, such as intervals. To this end, we transform the original program into an internal form that replaces such variables with their actual values: suppose the actual value of b in terms of intervals is $\langle 1, 2\rangle$ then $a := b$ is transformed into $a := \langle 1, 2\rangle$. Formally, we assume abstract semantic function $\hat{\mathcal{R}} \in cmd^{rel} \to \hat{\mathbb{R}} \to \hat{\mathbb{R}}$ for relational domain $\hat{\mathbb{R}}$ is defined over the following internal language:

$$cmd^{rel} \to x := e^{rel} \mid \{\!\!\{x < \hat{\mathbb{Z}}\}\!\!\} \text{ where } e^{rel} \to \hat{\mathbb{Z}} \mid x \mid e^{rel}{+}e^{rel}$$

where $\hat{\mathbb{Z}}$ is a (non-relational) abstract integer ($2^{\mathbb{Z}} \xleftarrow[\alpha_{\mathbb{Z}}]{\gamma_{\mathbb{Z}}} \hat{\mathbb{Z}}$). Note that this language is not for program codes, but for our semantics definition.

We now define the semantics of the packed relational analysis. The abstract semantics is defined by the least fixpoint of semantic function (3), where the abstract semantic function $\hat{f}_c$ is defined as follows:

$$\hat{f}_c(\hat{s}) = \hat{s}[p_1 \mapsto \hat{\mathcal{R}}(cmd_1)(\hat{s}(p_1)), \ldots, p_k \mapsto \hat{\mathcal{R}}(cmd_k)(\hat{s}(p_k))]$$

where

$$\begin{array}{rcl} \{p_1, \ldots, p_k\} & = & \mathsf{pack}(x) \\ cmd_i & = & \mathscr{T}(p_i)(\hat{s})(\mathsf{cmd}(c)) \end{array}$$

For variable x, $\mathsf{pack}(x)$ returns the set of packs that contains x, i.e., $\mathsf{pack}(x) = \{p \in \mathit{Packs} \mid x \in p\}$. For both $x := e$ and $\{\!\{x < n\}\!\}$, we update only the packs that include x. $\mathscr{T}$ is the function that transforms cmd into cmd^{rel}. Given a variable pack p, state $\hat{s}$, and command cmd, $\mathscr{T}(p)(\hat{s}) \in cmd \to cmd^{rel}$ returns transformed command for a given command.

$$\begin{array}{rcl} \mathscr{T}(p)(\hat{s})(x := e) & = & x := \mathscr{T}_e(p)(\hat{s})(e) \\ \mathscr{T}(p)(\hat{s})(\{\!\{x < n\}\!\}) & = & \{\!\{x < \mathscr{T}_e(p)(\hat{s})(n)\}\!\} \end{array}$$

where $\mathscr{T}_e(p)(\hat{s}) \in e \to e^{rel}$ transforms expressions:

$$\begin{array}{rcl} \mathscr{T}_e(p)(\hat{s})(n) & = & \alpha_{\mathbb{Z}}(\{n\}) \\ \mathscr{T}_e(p)(\hat{s})(x) & = & \begin{cases} x & \text{if } x \in p \\ \pi_x(\hat{s}) & \text{otherwise} \end{cases} \\ \mathscr{T}_e(p)(\hat{s})(e_1{+}e_2) & = & \mathscr{T}_e(p)(\hat{s})(e_1){+}\mathscr{T}_e(p)(\hat{s})(e_2) \end{array}$$

where $\pi_x \in \hat{\mathbb{S}} \to \hat{\mathbb{Z}}$ is a function that projects a relational domain element onto variable x to obtain its abstract integer value. To be safe, π_x should satisfies the following condition:

$$\forall \hat{s} \in \hat{\mathbb{S}}.\pi_x(\hat{s}) \sqsupseteq \alpha_{\hat{\mathbb{Z}}}(\{s(x) | s \in \gamma_{\hat{\mathbb{R}}}(\sqcap_{p \in \mathsf{pack}(x)} \hat{s}(p))\})$$

4.2 Step 2: Finding Definitions and Uses

We now approximate $\hat{\mathsf{D}}$ and $\hat{\mathsf{U}}$. In the previous section, we already presented a general, semantics-based method to safely approximate $\hat{\mathsf{D}}$ and $\hat{\mathsf{U}}$ for a given abstract semantics. Because our language in this section is pointer-free, simple syntactic method is enough for our purpose.

The distinguishing feature of sparse relational analysis is that the entities that are defined and used are variable packs, not each variable. From the definition of $\hat{f}_c$, we notice that packs $\mathsf{pack}(x)$ are potentially defined both in assignment and assume:

$$\hat{\mathsf{D}}(c) = \begin{cases} \mathsf{pack}(x) & \mathsf{cmd}(c) = x := e \\ \mathsf{pack}(x) & \mathsf{cmd}(c) = \{\!\{x < n\}\!\} \end{cases}$$

$\hat{\mathsf{U}}$ is defined depending on the definition of π_x. On the assumption that *Packs* contains singleton packs of all program variables, we may define π_x as follows:

$$\pi_x(\hat{s}) = \pi_x^{rel}(\hat{s}(\{x\}))$$

where $\pi_x^{rel} \in \hat{\mathbb{R}} \to \hat{\mathbb{Z}}$ which project a relational domain element onto variable x to obtain its abstract integer value, which is supplied by each relational domain, e.g., see [34].

Now, we define $\hat{\mathsf{U}}$ as follows:

$$\hat{\mathsf{U}}(c) = \begin{cases} \mathsf{pack}(x) \cup \{\langle\!\langle l \rangle\!\rangle \mid l \in V\} & \mathsf{cmd}(c) = x := e \\ \mathsf{pack}(x) & \mathsf{cmd}(c) = \{\!\{x < n\}\!\} \end{cases}$$

where $V = \mathcal{V}(e) - \bigcup \mathsf{pack}(x)$, and $\mathcal{V}(e)$ denotes the set of variables that appear inside an expression e.

Lemma 4. *$\hat{\mathsf{D}}$ and $\hat{\mathsf{U}}$ are safe approximations.*

5. Implementation Techniques

Implementing sparse analysis presents unique challenges regarding construction and management of data dependencies. Because data dependencies for realistic programs are very complex, it is a key to practical sparse analyzers to generate data dependencies efficiently in space and time. We describe the basic algorithm we used for data dependency generation, and discuss two issues that we experienced significant performance variations depending on different implementation choices.

Generation of Data Dependencies We use the standard SSA algorithm to generate data dependencies. Because our notion of data dependencies equals to def-use chains with $\hat{\mathsf{D}}$ and $\hat{\mathsf{U}}$ being treated as must-definitions and must-uses, any def-use chain generation algorithms (e.g., reaching definition analysis, SSA algorithm, etc) can be used. We use SSA generation because it is fast and reduces the size of def-use chains [44].

Interprocedural Extension With semantics-based approach in mind, interprocedural sparse analysis is no more difficult than its intraprocedural counterpart. Designing a method to find safe definitions and uses for semantic functions regarding procedure calls is all that we need for interprocedural extension.

However, during the implementation, we noticed that this natural extension may not be scalable in practice. The main problem was due to unexpected spurious dependencies among procedures. Consider the following code and suppose we compute data dependencies for global variable x.

```
int f() { x=0;¹ h(); a=x;² }
int h() { ... } // does not use variable x
int g() { x=1;³ h(); b=x;⁴ }
```

Data dependencies for x not only include $1 \overset{x}{\leadsto} 2$ and $3 \overset{x}{\leadsto} 4$ but also include spurious dependencies $1 \overset{x}{\leadsto} 4$ and $3 \overset{x}{\leadsto} 2$, because there are control flow paths from 1 to 4 (as well as 3 to 2) via the common procedure calls to h. In real C programs, thousands of global variables exist and procedures are called from many different call-sites, which generates overwhelming number of spurious dependencies. In our experiments, such spurious dependencies made the analysis hardly scalable. Staged pointer analysis algorithm [20] takes this approach but no performance problem was reported; we guess this is because pointer analysis typically ignores non-pointer statements (by sparse evaluation techniques [7, 39]) and number of pointer variables are just small subset of the entire variables. However, our analyzers trace all semantics of C, i.e., value flows of all types including pointers and numbers.

Thus, we generate data dependencies separately for each procedure. In this approach, we need to specially handle procedure calls: we treat a procedure call as a definition (resp., use) of all abstract locations defined (resp., used) by the callee. In addition, we treat the entry point of each procedure as definitions of all the abstract locations that are used in the body of the procedure. With these information, can we generate data dependencies of each procedure independently from other procedures. After generating dependencies of procedures, we connect inter-dependences from call statements to the entry of callee with abstract locations that are used by the callee. The advantage of this approach is that the number of spurious dependencies are reduced: variable x is not propagated to procedure h because h does not use x. However, the disadvantage of this approach is that data dependencies are not fully sparse. For example, consider a call chain $\mathtt{f} \to \mathtt{g} \to \mathtt{h}$ and suppose x is defined in procedure f and used in procedure h. Even when x is not used inside g, value of x is propagated to h only after it is first propagated to g. In our experiments, this incomplete sparseness of the analysis could not make the resulting sparse analysis scalable enough.

We solved the problem by applying the following optimization to the generated data dependencies ($\rightsquigarrow$) until convergence: suppose $a \overset{l}{\rightsquigarrow} b$, $b \overset{l}{\rightsquigarrow} c$, and that l is not defined nor used in b, then we remove those two dependencies and add $a \overset{l}{\rightsquigarrow} c$. This optimization makes the analysis more sparse, leading to a significant speed up.

For the interprocedural extension, we use the flow-insensitive analysis (defined in Section 3.2) to prior resolve function pointers. Because the pre-analysis is fairly precise[3], the precision loss caused by this approximation of the callgraph would be reasonably small in practice [33].

Using BDDs in Representing Data Dependencies The second practical issue is memory consumption of data dependencies. Analyzing real C programs must deal with hundreds of thousands of statements and abstract locations. Thus, naive representations for the data dependencies immediately makes memory problems. For example, in analyzing ghostscript-9.00 (the largest benchmark in Table 1), the data dependencies consist of 201 K abstract locations spanning over 2.8 M statements. Storing such dependency relation in a naive set-based implementation, which keeps a map ($\in \mathbb{C} \times \mathbb{C} \rightarrow 2^{\mathbb{L}}$), did not work for such large programs (It only worked for programs of moderate sizes less than 150 KLOC). Fortunately, the dependency relation is highly redundant, making it a good application of BDDs. For example, $\langle c_1, c_3, l\rangle \in (\rightsquigarrow)$ and $\langle c_2, c_3, l\rangle$ are different but share the common suffix, and $\langle c_1, c_2, l_1\rangle$ and $\langle c_1, c_2, l_2\rangle$ are different but share the common prefix. BDDs can effectively share such common suffixes and prefixes. We treat each relation $\langle c_1, c_2, l\rangle$, by bit-encoding each control point and abstract location, as a boolean function that is naturally represented by BDDs. This way of using BDDs greatly reduced memory costs. For example, for vim60 (227 KLOC), set-based representation of data dependencies required more than 24 GB of memory but BDD-implementation just required 1 GB. No particular dynamic variable ordering was necessary in our case.

6. Experiments

In this section, we evaluate sparse non-relational and relational static analyses designed in Section 3 and Section 4, respectively. The evaluation was performed on top of SPARROW [23, 25, 26, 28, 35–38], an industrial-strength static analyzer for C programs.

For the non-relational analysis, we use the interval domain [9], a representative non-relational domain that is widely used in practice [1, 2, 4, 13, 26]. For the relational analysis, we use the octagon domain [34], a representative relational domain whose effectiveness is well-known in practice [4, 13, 28, 43].

We have analyzed 16 software packages. Table 1 shows characteristics of our benchmark programs. The benchmarks are various open-source applications, and most of them are from GNU open-source projects. Standard library calls are summarized using hand-crafted function stubs. For other unknown procedure calls to external code, we assume that the procedure returns arbitrary values and has no side-effect. Procedures that are unreachable from the main procedure, such as callbacks, are made to be explicitly called from the main procedure. All experiments were done on a Linux 2.6 system running on a single core of Intel 3.07 GHz box with 24 GB of main memory.

6.1 Interval Domain-based Sparse Analysis

[3] The pointer abstraction of our pre-analysis is basically the same with inclusion-based pointer analysis, which is the most precise form of flow-insensitive pointer analysis [18]. In addition, our pre-analysis combines numeric analysis and pointer analysis, which further enhances the precision of the pointer analysis [2, 13].

Setting The baseline analyzer, $\mathsf{Interval}_{\mathsf{base}}$, is the global abstract interpretation engine of SPARROW. The abstract domain of the analysis is an extension of the one defined in Section 3 to support additional C features such as arrays and structures. The analysis abstracts an array by a set of tuples of base address, offset, and size. Abstraction of dynamically allocated array is similarly handled except that base addresses are abstracted by their allocation-sites. A structure is abstracted by a tuple of base address and set of field locations (the analysis is field-sensitive). The fixpoint is computed by a worklist algorithm using the conventional widening operator [9] for interval domain. Details of the analysis can be found in [23, 26, 28, 35–38].

The baseline analyzer is not a straw-man but much engineering effort has been put to its implementation. In particular, the analysis exploits the technique of localization [38, 41, 45], which localizes the analysis so that each code block is analyzed with only the to-be-accessed parts of the input state. We use the access-based technique [38], which was shown to be faster by up to 50x than the conventional, reachability-based localization technique [38].

From the baseline, we made $\mathsf{Interval}_{\mathsf{vanilla}}$ and $\mathsf{Interval}_{\mathsf{sparse}}$. $\mathsf{Interval}_{\mathsf{vanilla}}$ is identical to $\mathsf{Interval}_{\mathsf{base}}$ except that $\mathsf{Interval}_{\mathsf{vanilla}}$ does not perform the access-based localization. We compare the performance between $\mathsf{Interval}_{\mathsf{vanilla}}$ and $\mathsf{Interval}_{\mathsf{base}}$ just to check that our baseline analyzer is not a straw-man. $\mathsf{Interval}_{\mathsf{sparse}}$ is the sparse version derived from the baseline. The sparse analysis consists of three steps: pre-analysis (to approximate def-use sets), data dependency generation, and actual fixpoint computation. As described in Section 3, we use a flow-insensitive pre-analysis. The fixpoint of sparse abstract semantic function is computed by a worklist-based fixpoint algorithm. The analyzers are written in OCaml. We use the BuDDy library [30] for BDD implementation.

Results Table 2 gives the analysis time and peak memory consumption of the three analyzers. Because three analyzers share a common frontend, we report only the analysis time. For $\mathsf{Interval}_{\mathsf{base}}$, the time includes the pre-analysis [38]. For $\mathsf{Interval}_{\mathsf{sparse}}$, **Dep** includes times for pre-analysis and data dependency generation. **Fix** represent the time for fixpoint computation.

The results show that $\mathsf{Interval}_{\mathsf{base}}$ already has a competitive performance: it is faster than $\mathsf{Interval}_{\mathsf{vanilla}}$ by 8–55x, saving peak memory consumption by 54–85%. $\mathsf{Interval}_{\mathsf{vanilla}}$ scales to 35 KLOC before running out of time limit (24 hours). In contrast, $\mathsf{Interval}_{\mathsf{base}}$ scales to 111 KLOC.

$\mathsf{Interval}_{\mathsf{sparse}}$ is faster than $\mathsf{Interval}_{\mathsf{base}}$ by 5–110x and saves memory by 3–92%. In particular, the analysis' scalability has been remarkably improved: $\mathsf{Interval}_{\mathsf{sparse}}$ scales to 1.4M LOC, which is an order of magnitude larger than that of $\mathsf{Interval}_{\mathsf{base}}$.

There are some counterintuitive results. First, the analysis time for $\mathsf{Interval}_{\mathsf{sparse}}$ does not strictly depend on program sizes. For example, analyzing emacs-22.1 (399 KLOC) requires 10 hours, taking six times more than analyzing ghostscript-9.00 (1,363 KLOC). This is mainly because some real C programs have unexpectedly large recursive call cycles [27, 37, 46]. Column **maxSCC** in Table 1 reports the sizes of the largest strongly connected component in the callgraph. Note that some programs (such as nethack-3.3.0, vim60, and emacs-22.1) have a large cycle that contains hundreds or even thousands of procedures. Such non-trivial SCCs markedly increase analysis cost because the large cyclic dependencies among procedures make data dependencies much more complex.

Second, data dependency generation takes longer time than actual fixpoint computation. For example, data dependency generation for ghostscript-9.00 takes 14,116 s but the fixpoint is computed in 698 s. The seemingly unbalanced timing results are partly because of the uses of BDDs in dependency construction. While BDD dramatically saves memory costs, set operations for BDDs

Program	LOC	Functions	Statements	Blocks	maxSCC	AbsLocs
gzip-1.2.4a	7K	132	6,446	4,152	2	1,784
bc-1.06	13K	132	10,368	4,731	1	1,619
tar-1.13	20K	221	12,199	8,586	13	3,245
less-382	23K	382	23,367	9,207	46	3,658
make-3.76.1	27K	190	14,010	9,094	57	4,527
wget-1.9	35K	433	28,958	14,537	13	6,675
screen-4.0.2	45K	588	39,693	29,498	65	12,566
a2ps-4.14	64K	980	86,867	27,565	6	17,684
sendmail-8.13.6	130K	756	76,630	52,505	60	19,135
nethack-3.3.0	211K	2,207	237,427	157,645	997	54,989
vim60	227K	2,770	150,950	107,629	1,668	40,979
emacs-22.1	399K	3,388	204,865	161,118	1,554	66,413
python-2.5.1	435K	2,996	241,511	99,014	723	51,859
linux-3.0	710K	13,856	345,407	300,203	493	139,667
gimp-2.6	959K	11,728	1,482,230	286,588	2	190,806
ghostscript-9.00	1,363K	12,993	2,891,500	342,293	39	201,161

Table 1. Benchmarks: lines of code (**LOC**) is obtained by running `wc` on the source before preprocessing and macro expansion. **Functions** reports the number of functions in source code. **Statements** and **Blocks** report the number of statements and basic blocks in our intermediate representation of programs (after preprocessing). **maxSCC** reports the size of the largest strongly connected component in the callgraph. **AbsLocs** reports the number of abstract locations that are generated during the interval domain-based analysis .

Programs	$\mathsf{Interval}_{\mathsf{vanilla}}$		$\mathsf{Interval}_{\mathsf{base}}$		$\mathbf{Spd}\uparrow_1$	$\mathbf{Mem}\downarrow_1$	$\mathsf{Interval}_{\mathsf{sparse}}$						$\mathbf{Spd}\uparrow_2$	$\mathbf{Mem}\downarrow_2$
	Time	Mem	Time	Mem			Dep	Fix	Total	Mem	$\hat{\mathsf{D}}(c)$	$\hat{\mathsf{U}}(c)$		
gzip-1.2.4a	772	240	14	65	55 x	73 %	2	1	3	63	2.4	2.5	5 x	3 %
bc-1.06	1,270	276	96	126	13 x	54 %	4	3	7	75	4.6	4.9	14 x	40 %
tar-1.13	12,947	881	338	177	38 x	80 %	6	2	8	93	2.9	2.9	42 x	47 %
less-382	9,561	1,113	1,211	378	8 x	66 %	27	6	33	127	11.9	11.9	37 x	66 %
make-3.76.1	24,240	1,391	1,893	443	13 x	68 %	16	5	21	114	5.8	5.8	90 x	74 %
wget-1.9	44,092	2,546	1,214	378	36 x	85 %	8	3	11	85	2.4	2.4	110 x	78 %
screen-4.0.2	∞	N/A	31,324	3,996	N/A	N/A	724	43	767	303	53.0	54.0	41 x	92 %
a2ps-4.14	∞	N/A	3,200	1,392	N/A	N/A	31	9	40	353	2.6	2.8	80 x	75 %
sendmail-8.13.6	∞	N/A	∞	N/A	N/A	N/A	517	227	744	678	20.7	20.7	N/A	N/A
nethack-3.3.0	∞	N/A	∞	N/A	N/A	N/A	14,126	2,247	16,373	5,298	72.4	72.4	N/A	N/A
vim60	∞	N/A	∞	N/A	N/A	N/A	17,518	6,280	23,798	5,190	180.2	180.3	N/A	N/A
emacs-22.1	∞	N/A	∞	N/A	N/A	N/A	29,552	8,278	37,830	7,795	285.3	285.5	N/A	N/A
python-2.5.1	∞	N/A	∞	N/A	N/A	N/A	9,677	1,362	11,039	5,535	108.1	108.1	N/A	N/A
linux-3.0	∞	N/A	∞	N/A	N/A	N/A	26,669	6,949	33,618	20,529	76.2	74.8	N/A	N/A
gimp-2.6	∞	N/A	∞	N/A	N/A	N/A	3,751	123	3,874	3,602	4.1	3.9	N/A	N/A
ghostscript-9.00	∞	N/A	∞	N/A	N/A	N/A	14,116	698	14,814	6,384	9.7	9.7	N/A	N/A

Table 2. Performance of interval analysis: time (in seconds) and peak memory consumption (in megabytes) of the various versions of analyses. ∞ means the analysis ran out of time (exceeded 24 hour time limit). **Dep** and **Fix** reports the time spent during data dependency analysis and actual analysis steps, respectively, of the sparse analysis. $\mathbf{Spd}\uparrow_1$ is the speed-up of $\mathsf{Interval}_{\mathsf{base}}$ over $\mathsf{Interval}_{\mathsf{vanilla}}$. $\mathbf{Mem}\downarrow_1$ shows the memory savings of $\mathsf{Interval}_{\mathsf{base}}$ over $\mathsf{Interval}_{\mathsf{vanilla}}$. $\mathbf{Spd}\uparrow_2$ is the speed-up of $\mathsf{Interval}_{\mathsf{sparse}}$ over $\mathsf{Interval}_{\mathsf{base}}$. $\mathbf{Mem}\downarrow_2$ shows the memory savings of $\mathsf{Interval}_{\mathsf{sparse}}$ over $\mathsf{Interval}_{\mathsf{base}}$. $\hat{\mathsf{D}}(c)$ and $\hat{\mathsf{U}}(c)$ show the average size of $\hat{\mathsf{D}}(c)$ and $\hat{\mathsf{U}}(c)$, respectively.

such as addition and removal are noticeably slower than usual set operations.

6.2 Octagon Domain-based Sparse Analysis

Setting We implemented octagon domain-based static analyzers $\mathsf{Octagon}_{\mathsf{vanilla}}$, $\mathsf{Octagon}_{\mathsf{base}}$, and $\mathsf{Octagon}_{\mathsf{sparse}}$ by replacing interval domains of SPARROW with octagon domains. Non-numerical values (such as pointers, array, and structures) are handled in the same way as the interval analysis. $\mathsf{Octagon}_{\mathsf{base}}$ performs the access-based localization [38] in terms of variable packs. $\mathsf{Octagon}_{\mathsf{vanilla}}$ is the same except for the localization. $\mathsf{Octagon}_{\mathsf{sparse}}$ is the sparse version of $\mathsf{Octagon}_{\mathsf{base}}$. To represent octagon domain, we used Apron library [22].

In all experiments, we used a syntax-directed packing strategy. Our packing heuristic is similar to Miné's approach [13, 34], which groups abstract locations that have syntactic locality. For examples, abstract locations involved in the linear expressions or loops are grouped together. Scope of the locality is limited within each of syntactic C blocks. We also group abstract locations involved in actual and formal parameters, which is necessary to capture relations across procedure boundaries. Large packs whose sizes exceed a threshold (10) were split down into smaller ones.

Results While $\mathsf{Octagon}_{\mathsf{vanilla}}$ requires extremely large amount of time and memory space but $\mathsf{Octagon}_{\mathsf{base}}$ makes the analysis realistic by leveraging the access-based localization. $\mathsf{Octagon}_{\mathsf{base}}$ is able to analyze 35 KLOC within 5 hours and 10GB of memory. With the localization, analysis speed of $\mathsf{Octagon}_{\mathsf{base}}$ increases by 8x–9x and memory consumption decreases by 54%–62%. Though $\mathsf{Octagon}_{\mathsf{base}}$ saves a lot of memory, the analysis is still not scalable at all. For example, tar-1.13 requires 6 times more memory than gzip-1.2.4a. This memory consumption is not reasonable considering program size and interval analysis result.

Thanks to sparse analysis technique, $\mathsf{Octagon}_{\mathsf{sparse}}$ becomes more practical and scales to 130 KLOC within 18 hours and 29 GB of memory consumption. $\mathsf{Octagon}_{\mathsf{sparse}}$ is 13–56x faster than $\mathsf{Octagon}_{\mathsf{base}}$ and saves memory consumption by 75%–95%.

6.3 Discussion

Sparsity We discuss the relation between performance and sparsity. Column $\hat{\mathsf{D}}(c)$ and $\hat{\mathsf{U}}(c)$ in Table 2 and Table 3 show how many abstract locations are defined and used for each basic block on average. It clearly shows the key observation in sparse analysis for real programs; only a few abstract locations are defined and used in each program point. For example, the interval domain-based analy-

Programs	Octagon$_{vanilla}$		Octagon$_{base}$		Spd↑$_1$	Mem↓$_1$	Octagon$_{sparse}$						Spd↑$_2$	Mem↓$_2$
	Time	Mem	Time	Mem			Dep	Fix	Total	Mem	$\hat{D}(c)$	$\hat{U}(c)$		
gzip-1.2.4a	2,078	2,832	273	1,072	8 x	62 %	7	14	21	269	13.8	14.5	13 x	75 %
bc-1.06	9,536	6,987	1,065	3,230	9 x	54 %	20	35	55	358	25.2	31.7	19 x	89 %
tar-1.13	∞	N/A	9,566	5,963	N/A	N/A	55	133	188	526	38.3	39.3	51 x	91 %
less-382	∞	N/A	16,121	8,410	N/A	N/A	92	340	432	458	42.6	45.4	37 x	95 %
make-3.76.1	∞	N/A	17,724	12,771	N/A	N/A	91	240	331	666	51.4	55.7	53 x	95 %
wget-1.9	∞	N/A	15,998	9,363	N/A	N/A	107	181	288	646	31.9	32.9	56 x	93 %
screen-4.0.2	∞	N/A	∞	N/A	N/A	N/A	2,452	13,981	16,433	9,199	372.4	376.1	N/A	N/A
a2ps-4.14	∞	N/A	∞	N/A	N/A	N/A	296	8,271	8,566	1,996	97.7	99.0	N/A	N/A
sendmail-8.13.6	∞	N/A	∞	N/A	N/A	N/A	7,256	57,552	64,808	29,658	467.6	492.3	N/A	N/A

Table 3. Performance of octagon analysis: all columns are the same as those in Table 2

sis of a2ps-4.14 defines and uses only 0.1% of all abstract locations in one program point.

One interesting observation from the experiment results is that the analysis performance is more dependent on the sparsity than the program size. For instance, even though ghostscript-9.00 is 3.5 times bigger than emacs-22.1 in terms of LOC, ghostscript-9.00 takes 2.6 times less time to analyze. Behind this phenomenon, there is a large difference on sparsity; average $\hat{D}(c)$ size (and $\hat{U}(c)$ size) of emacs-22.1 is 30 times bigger than the one of ghostscript-9.00.

Variable Packing For maximal precision, packing strategy should be more carefully devised for each target program. However, note that our purpose of experiments is to show relative performance of Octagon$_{sparse}$ over Octagon$_{base}$, and we applied the same packing strategy for all analyzers. Though our general-purpose packing strategy is not specialized to each program, the packing strategy reasonably groups logically related variables. The average size of packs is 5–7 for our benchmarks. Domain-specific packing strategies, such as ones used in Astrée [34] or CGS [43], reports the similar results: 3–4 [34] or 5 [43].

7. Related Work

Existing sparse analysis techniques are divided into two groups:

- fine-grained sparse analyses in particular settings, e.g., [15, 19, 20, 40, 44], and
- coarse-grained sparse analyses in general settings, e.g., [7, 14, 21, 39].

In this paper, we present a method to obtain fine-grained sparse analyses in a general setting.

Sparse Pointer Analysis Sparse pointer analysis techniques [19, 20, 29] are not general enough to be used for arbitrarily complicated semantic analysis. Recently, scalability of flow-sensitive pointer analysis has been greatly improved using sparse analysis; in 2009, Hardekopf et al. [19] presented a pointer analysis algorithm that scales to large code bases (up to 474 KLOC) for the first time, and after that, flow-sensitive pointer analysis becomes scalable even to millions of lines of code via sparse analysis techniques [20, 29]. We already showed that our framework subsumes two scalable sparse pointer analyses presented in [19, 20]. In addition, the techniques are tightly coupled with pointer analysis and it is not obvious how to generalize them and prove their correctness. We provide a general framework that enables a family of abstract interpretation to be automatically turned into sparse analysis versions.

One noteworthy point is that designing a correct sparse analyses in general was easy in our case because our method is semantics-based (by abstract interpretation). For example, sparse pointer analysis [20] relies on χ and μ functions [8] to correctly model pointers, which is essentially independent of the analysis semantics. In our case, these extra techniques are unnecessary because we derive sparse analyses faithfully from the abstract semantics of the original analysis.

Sparse Dataflow Analysis Traditional sparse analysis techniques are in a simpler setting than the one postulated in our framework. Sparse analysis techniques were first pioneered for optimizing dataflow analysis [15, 40, 44]. Reif and Lewis [40] developed a sparse analysis algorithm for constant propagation and Wegman et al. [44] extended it to conditional constant propagation. Dhamdhere et al. [15] showed how to perform sparse partial redundancy elimination. These algorithms are fully sparse in that precise def-use chains are syntactically identifiable and values are always propagated along to def-use chains (in an SSA form). However, these techniques only consider the programs without pointers.

Sparse Evaluation Sparse evaluation techniques [7, 14, 21, 39] are generally applicable but have limitations in sparseness. The goal of sparse evaluation [7, 14, 21, 39] is to remove statements whose abstract semantic functions are identity function. For example, in typical pointer analyses, statements for numerical computation are considered as identity and we can remove those statements before analysis begins. Sparse evaluation techniques are not effective when the underlying analysis does not have many identity functions, which is the case for static analyses that consider "full" semantics, including numbers and pointers (our case).

Localization Localization [32, 38, 41, 45] is used in general settings but not powerful enough. When analyzing code blocks such as procedure bodies, localization attempts to remove irrelevant parts of abstract states that will not be used during the analysis. It is widely used as a key cost-reduction technique in many semantics-based static analysis, such as shape analysis [41, 45], higher-order flow analysis [32], and numeric abstract interpretation [38]. However, localization cannot avoid unnecessary propagation of abstract values along control flows.

Scalable Global Analyzers Our interval and octagon domain-based analyzers achieve higher scalability (up to 1 MLOC and 130 KLOC, respectively) than the previous general-purpose global analyzers. Zitser et al. [47] report that PolySpace C Verifier [31], a commercial tool for detection of runtime errors, cannot analyze sendmail because of scalability problem. Both our interval and octagon domain-based analyzers can analyze sendmail. Airac [26, 35], a general-purpose interval domain-based global static analyzer, scales only to 30 KLOC in global analysis. Recently, a significant progress has been reported by Oh et al. [38], but it still does not scale over 120 KLOC. Other similar (interval domain-based) analyzers are also not scalable to large code bases [1, 2]. Nevertheless, there have been scalable domain-specific static analyzers, like Astrée [4, 13] and CGS [43], which scale to hundreds of thousands lines of code. However, Astrée targets on programs that do not have recursion and backward gotos, which enables a very efficient interpretation-based analysis [13], and CGS is not fully flow-sensitive [43]. There are other summary-based approaches [16, 17] for scalable global analysis, which are independent of our abstract interpretation-based approach.

BDDs We propose a new usage of Binary Decision Diagram (BDD) [5] in program analysis. We represent data dependency relation in BDDs. Most of the previous uses are limited to compact representations of points-to sets in pointer analysis [3, 19, 20].

Acknowledgments

We thank Lucas Brutschy and Yoonseok Ko for their contributions to the implementation. We thank Deokhwan Kim, Daejun Park, and all members of Programming Research Laboratory in Seoul National University for their useful comments and suggestions. We would also like to thank the anonymous PLDI reviewers for their constructive feedback on this paper. This work was supported by the Engineering Research Center of Excellence Program of Korea Ministry of Education, Science and Technology(MEST) / National Research Foundation of Korea(NRF) (Grant 2012-0000468) and the Brain Korea 21 Project, School of Electrical Engineering and Computer Science, Seoul National University in 2011.

References

[1] X. Allamigeon, W. Godard, and C. Hymans. Static analysis of string manipulations in critical embedded C programs. In *SAS*, 2006.

[2] G. Balakrishnan and T. Reps. Analyzing memory accesses in x86 binary executables. In *CC*, 2004.

[3] M. Berndl, O. Lhoták, F. Qian, L. Hendren, and N. Umanee. Points-to analysis using bdds. In *PLDI*, 2003.

[4] B. Blanchet, P. Cousot, R. Cousot, J. Feret, L. Mauborgne, A. Miné, D. Monniaux, and X. Rival. A static analyzer for large safety-critical software. In *PLDI*, 2003.

[5] R. E. Bryant. Graph-based algorithms for boolean function manipulation. *IEEETC*, 1986.

[6] D. R. Chase, M. Wegman, and F. K. Zadeck. Analysis of pointers and structures. In *PLDI*, 1990.

[7] J.-D. Choi, R. Cytron, and J. Ferrante. Automatic construction of sparse data flow evaluation graphs. In *POPL*, 1991.

[8] F. C. Chow, S. Chan, S.-M. Liu, R. Lo, and M. Streich. Effective representation of aliases and indirect memory operations in ssa form. In *CC*, 1996.

[9] P. Cousot and R. Cousot. Abstract interpretation: A unified lattice model for static analysis of programs by construction or approximation of fixpoints. In *POPL*, 1977.

[10] P. Cousot and R. Cousot. Systematic design of program analysis frameworks. In *POPL*, 1979.

[11] P. Cousot and R. Cousot. Abstract interpretation frameworks. *J. Log. Comput.*, 1992.

[12] P. Cousot and N. Halbwachs. Automatic discovery of linear restraints among variables of a program. In *POPL*, 1978.

[13] P. Cousot, R. Cousot, J. Feret, L. Mauborgne, A. Miné, and X. Rival. Why does astrée scale up? *Formal Methods in System Design*, 2009.

[14] R. K. Cytron and J. Ferrante. Efficiently computing ϕ-nodes on-the-fly. *TOPLAS*, 1995.

[15] D. M. Dhamdhere, B. K. Rosen, and F. K. Zadeck. How to analyze large programs efficiently and informatively. In *PLDI*, 1992.

[16] I. Dillig, T. Dillig, and A. Aiken. Sound, complete and scalable path-sensitive analysis. In *PLDI*, 2008.

[17] I. Dillig, T. Dillig, and A. Aiken. Precise reasoning for programs using containers. In *POPL*, 2011.

[18] B. Hardekopf and C. Lin. The ant and the grasshopper: fast and accurate pointer analysis for millions of lines of code. In *PLDI*, 2007.

[19] B. Hardekopf and C. Lin. Semi-sparse flow-sensitive pointer analysis. In *POPL*, 2009.

[20] B. Hardekopf and C. Lin. Flow-sensitive pointer analysis for millions of lines of code. In *CGO*, 2011.

[21] M. Hind and A. Pioli. Assessing the effects of flow-sensitivity on pointer alias analyses. In *SAS*, 1998.

[22] B. Jeannet and A. Miné. Apron: A library of numerical abstract domains for static analysis. In *CAV*, 2009.

[23] Y. Jhee, M. Jin, Y. Jung, D. Kim, S. Kong, H. Lee, H. Oh, D. Park, and K. Yi. Abstract interpretation + impure catalysts: Our Sparrow experience. Presentation at the Workshop of the 30 Years of Abstract Interpretation, San Francisco, `ropas.snu.ac.kr/\char'\~kwang/paper/30yai-08.pdf`, January 2008.

[24] R. Johnson and K. Pingali. Dependence-based program analysis. In *PLDI*, 1993.

[25] Y. Jung and K. Yi. Practical memory leak detector based on parameterized procedural summaries. In *ISMM*, 2008.

[26] Y. Jung, J. Kim, J. Shin, and K. Yi. Taming false alarms from a domain-unaware C analyzer by a bayesian statistical post analysis. In *SAS*, 2005.

[27] C. Lattner, A. Lenharth, and V. Adve. Making Context-Sensitive Points-to Analysis with Heap Cloning Practical For The Real World. In *PLDI*, 2007.

[28] W. Lee, W. Lee, and K. Yi. Sound non-statistical clustering of static analysis alarms. In *VMCAI*, 2012.

[29] L. Li, C. Cifuentes, and N. Keynes. Boosting the performance of flow-sensitive points-to analysis using value flow. In *FSE*, 2011.

[30] J. Lind-Nielson. BuDDy, a binary decision diagram package.

[31] MathWorks. Polyspace embedded software verification. `http://www.mathworks.com/products/polyspace/index.html`.

[32] M. Might and O. Shivers. Improving flow analyses via ΓCFA: Abstract garbage collection and counting. In *ICFP*, 2006.

[33] A. Milanova, A. Rountev, and B. G. Ryder. Precise and efficient call graph construction for c programs with function pointers. *Journal of Automated Software Engineering*, 2004.

[34] A. Miné. The Octagon Abstract Domain. *HOSC*, 2006.

[35] H. Oh. Large spurious cycle in global static analyses and its algorithmic mitigation. In *APLAS*, 2009.

[36] H. Oh and K. Yi. An algorithmic mitigation of large spurious interprocedural cycles in static analysis. *SPE*, 2010.

[37] H. Oh and K. Yi. Access-based localization with bypassing. In *APLAS*, 2011.

[38] H. Oh, L. Brutschy, and K. Yi. Access analysis-based tight localization of abstract memories. In *VMCAI*, 2011.

[39] G. Ramalingam. On sparse evaluation representations. *Theoretical Computer Science*, 2002.

[40] J. H. Reif and H. R. Lewis. Symbolic evaluation and the global value graph. In *POPL*, 1977.

[41] N. Rinetzky, J. Bauer, T. Reps, M. Sagiv, and R. Wilhelm. A semantics for procedure local heaps and its abstractions. In *POPL*, 2005.

[42] T. B. Tok, S. Z. Guyer, and C. Lin. Efficient flow-sensitive interprocedural data-flow analysis in the presence of pointers. In *CC*, 2006.

[43] A. Venet and G. Brat. Precise and efficient static array bound checking for large embedded c programs. In *PLDI*, 2004.

[44] M. N. Wegman and F. K. Zadeck. Constant propagation with conditional branches. *TOPLAS*, 1991.

[45] H. Yang, O. Lee, J. Berdine, C. Calcagno, B. Cook, D. Distefano, and P. O'Hearn. Scalable shape analysis for systems code. In *CAV*, 2008.

[46] H. Yu, J. Xue, W. Huo, X. Feng, and Z. Zhang. Level by level: making flow- and context-sensitive pointer analysis scalable for millions of lines of code. In *CGO*, 2010.

[47] M. Zitser, D. E. S. Group, and T. Leek. Testing static analysis tools using exploitable buffer overflows from open source code. In *FSE*, 2004.

Fast and Precise Hybrid Type Inference for JavaScript

Brian Hackett Shu-yu Guo *

Mozilla

{bhackett,shu}@mozilla.com

Abstract

JavaScript performance is often bound by its dynamically typed nature. Compilers do not have access to static type information, making generation of efficient, type-specialized machine code difficult. We seek to solve this problem by inferring types. In this paper we present a hybrid type inference algorithm for JavaScript based on points-to analysis. Our algorithm is *fast*, in that it pays for itself in the optimizations it enables. Our algorithm is also *precise*, generating information that closely reflects the program's actual behavior even when analyzing polymorphic code, by augmenting static analysis with run-time type barriers.

We showcase an implementation for Mozilla Firefox's JavaScript engine, demonstrating both performance gains and viability. Through integration with the just-in-time (JIT) compiler in Firefox, we have improved performance on major benchmarks and JavaScript-heavy websites by up to 50%. Inference-enabled compilation is the default compilation mode as of Firefox 9.

Categories and Subject Descriptors D.3.4 [*Processors*]: Compilers, optimization

Keywords type inference, hybrid, just-in-time compilation

1. The Need for Hybrid Analysis

Consider the example JavaScript program in Figure 1. This program constructs an array of `Box` objects wrapping integer values, then calls a `use` function which adds up the contents of all those `Box` objects. No types are specified for any of the variables or other values used in this program, in keeping with JavaScript's dynamically-typed nature. Nevertheless, most operations in this program interact with type information, and knowledge of the involved types is needed to compile efficient code.

In particular, we are interested in the addition `res + v` on line 9. In JavaScript, addition coerces the operands into strings or numbers if necessary. String concatenation is performed for the former, and numeric addition for the latter.

Without static information about the types of `res` and `v`, a JIT compiler must emit code to handle all possible combinations of operand types. Moreover, every time values are copied around, the compiler must emit code to keep track of the types of the involved values, using either a separate type tag for the value or a specialized marshaling format. This incurs a large runtime overhead on the generated code, greatly increases the complexity of the compiler, and makes effective implementation of important optimizations like register allocation and loop invariant code motion much harder.

```
1  function Box(v) {
2    this.p = v;
3  }
4
5  function use(a) {
6    var res = 0;
7    for (var i = 0; i < 1000; i++) {
8      var v = a[i].p;
9      res = res + v;
10   }
11   return res;
12 }
13
14 function main() {
15   var a = [];
16   for (var i = 0; i < 1000; i++)
17     a[i] = new Box(10);
18   use(a);
19 }
```

Figure 1. Motivating Example

If we knew the types of `res` and `v`, we could compile code which performs an integer addition without the need to check or to track the types of `res` and `v`. With static knowledge of all types involved in the program, the compiler can in many cases generate code similar to that produced for a statically-typed language such as Java, with similar optimizations.

We can statically infer possible types for `res` and `v` by reasoning about the effect the program's assignments and operations have on values produced later. This is illustrated below. For brevity, we do not consider the possibility of `Box` and `use` being overwritten.

1. On line 17, `main` passes an integer when constructing `Box` objects. On line 2, `Box` assigns its parameter to the result's `p` property. Thus, `Box` objects can have an integer property `p`.
2. Also on line 17, `main` assigns a `Box` object to an element of `a`. On line 15, `a` is assigned an array literal, so the elements of that literal could be `Box` objects.
3. On line 18, `main` passes `a` to `use`, so `a` within `use` can refer to the array created on line 15. When `use` accesses an element of `a` on line 8, per #2 the result can be a `Box` object.
4. On line 8, property `p` of a value at `a[i]` is assigned to `v`. Per #3 `a[i]` can be a `Box` object, and per #1 the `p` property can be an integer. Thus, `v` can be an integer.

* Work partly done at the University of California, Los Angeles, Los Angeles, CA.

PLDI'12, June 11–16, 2012, Beijing, China.

5. On line 6, `res` is assigned an integer. Since `v` can be an integer, `res + v` can be an integer. When that addition is assigned to `res` on line 9, the assigned type is consistent with the known possible types of `res`.

This reasoning can be captured with inclusion constraints; we compute sets of possible types for each expression and model the flow between these sets as subset relationships. To compile correct code, we need to know not just *some* possible types for variables, but *all* possible types. In this sense, the static inference above is unsound: it does not account for all possible behaviors of the program. A few such behaviors are described below.

- The read of `a[i]` may access a *hole* in the array. Out of bounds array accesses in JavaScript produce the `undefined` value if the array's prototype does not have a matching property. Such holes can also be in the middle of an array; assigning to just `a[0]` and `a[2]` leaves a missing value at `a[1]`.
- Similarly, the read of `a[i].p` may be accessing a missing property and may produce the `undefined` value.
- The addition `res + v` may overflow. JavaScript has a single number type which does not distinguish between integers and doubles. However, it is extremely important for performance that JavaScript compilers distinguish the two and try to represent numbers as integers wherever possible. An addition of two integers may overflow and produce a number which can only be represented as a double.

In some cases these behaviors can be proven not to occur, but usually they cannot be ruled out. A standard solution is to capture these behaviors statically, but this is unfruitful. The static analysis must be sound, and to be sound in light of highly dynamic behaviors is to be conservative: many element or property accesses will be marked as possibly undefined, and many integer operations will be marked as possibly overflowing. The resulting type information would be too imprecise to be useful for optimization.

Our solution, and our key technical novelty, is to combine unsound static inference of the types of expressions and heap values with targeted dynamic type updates. Behaviors which are not accounted for statically must be caught dynamically, modifying inferred types to reflect those new behaviors if caught. If `a[i]` accesses a hole, the inferred types for the result must be marked as possibly `undefined`. If `res + v` overflows, the inferred types for the result must be marked as possibly a double.

With or without analysis, the generated code needs to test for array holes and integer overflow in order to correctly model the semantics of the language. We call dynamic type updates based on these events *semantic triggers*; they are placed on rarely taken execution paths and incur a cost to update the inferred types only the first time that path is taken.

The presence of these triggers illustrates the key invariant our analysis preserves:

> Inferred types must conservatively model all types for variables and object properties which currently exist and have existed in the past, but not those which could exist in the future.

This has important implications:

- The program can be analyzed incrementally. Code is not analyzed until it first executes, and code which does not execute need not be analyzed. This is necessary for JavaScript due to dynamic code loading and generation. It is also important for reducing analysis time on websites, which often load several megabytes of code and only execute a fraction of it.
- Assumptions about types made by the JIT compiler can be invalidated at almost any time. This affects the correctness of the JIT-compiled code, and the virtual machine must be able to recompile or discard code at any time, especially when that code is on the stack.

Dynamic checks and the key invariant are also critical to our handling of polymorphic code within a program. Suppose somewhere else in the program we have `new Box("hello!")`. Doing so will cause `Box` objects to be created which hold strings, illustrating the use of `Box` as a polymorphic structure. Our analysis does not distinguish `Box` objects created in different places, and the result of the `a[i].p` access in `use` will be regarded as potentially producing a string. Naively, solving the constraints produced by the analysis will mark `a[i].p`, `v`, `res + v`, and `res` as all producing either an integer or a string, even if `use`'s runtime behavior is actually monomorphic and only works on `Box` objects containing integers.

This problem of imprecision leaking across the program is serious: even if a program is mostly monomorphic, analysis precision can easily be poisoned by a small amount of polymorphic code.

We deal with uses of polymorphic structures and functions using runtime checks. At all element and property accesses, we keep track of both the set of types which *could* be observed for the access and the set of types which *have been* observed. The former will be a superset of the latter, and if the two are different then we insert a runtime check, a *type barrier*, to check for conformance between the resultant value and the observed type set. Mismatches lead to updates of the observed type set.

For the example program, a type barrier is required on the `a[i].p` access on line 8. The barrier will test that the value being read is an integer. If a string shows up due to a call to `use` outside of `main`, then the possible types of the `a[i].p` access will be updated, and `res` and `v` will be marked as possibly strings by resolving the analysis constraints.

Type barriers differ from the semantic triggers described earlier in that the tests they perform are not required by the language and do not need to be performed if our analysis is not being used. We are effectively betting that the required barriers pay for themselves by enabling generation of better code using more precise type information. We have found this to be the case in practice (§4.1.1, §4.2.5).

1.1 Comparison with other techniques

The reader may question, "Why not use more sophisticated static analyses that produce more precise results?" Our choice for the static analysis to not distinguish `Box` objects created in different places is deliberate. To be useful in a JIT setting, the analysis must be fast, and the time and space used by the analysis quickly degrade as complexity increases. Moreover, there is a tremendous variety of polymorphic behavior seen in JavaScript code in the wild, and to retain precision even the most sophisticated static analysis would need to fall back to dynamic checks some of the time.

Interestingly, *less* sophisticated static analyses do not fare well either. Unification-based analyses undermine the utility of dynamic checks; precision is unrecoverable despite dynamic monitoring.

More dynamic compilation strategies, such as the technique used by V8's Crankshaft JavaScript engine, generate type-specialized code based on profiling information, without static knowledge of possible argument or heap types [9, 10]. Such techniques will determine the types of expressions with similar precision to our analysis, but will always require type checks on function arguments or when reading heap values. By modeling all possible types of heap values, we only need type checks at accesses with type barriers, a difference which significantly improves performance (§4.1.1).

We believe that our partitioning of static and dynamic analysis is a sweet spot for JIT compilation of a highly dynamic language. Our main technical contribution is a hybrid inference algorithm for the entirety of JavaScript, using inclusion constraints to unsoundly infer types extended with runtime semantic triggers to generate sound type information, as well as type barriers to efficiently and precisely handle polymorphic code. Our practical contributions include both an implementation of our algorithm and a realistic evaluation. The implementation is integrated with the JIT compiler used in Firefox and is of production quality. Our evaluation has various metrics showing the effectiveness of the analysis and modified compiler on benchmarks as well as popular websites, games, and demos.

The remainder of the paper is organized as follows. In §2 we describe the static and dynamic aspects of our analysis. In §3 we outline implementation of the analysis as well as integration with the JavaScript JIT compiler inside Firefox. In §4 we present empirical results. In §5 we discuss related work, and in §6 we conclude.

2. Analysis

We present our analysis in two parts, the static "may-have-type" analysis and the dynamic "must-have-type" analysis. The algorithm is based on Andersen-style (inclusion based) pointer analysis [6]. The static analysis is intentionally unsound with respect to the semantics of JavaScript. It does not account for all possible behaviors of expressions and statements and only generates constraints that model a "may-have-type" relation. All behaviors excluded by the type constraints must be detected at runtime and their effects on types in the program dynamically recorded. The analysis runs in the browser as functions are trying to execute: code is analyzed function-at-a-time.

Inclusion based pointer analysis has a worst-case complexity of $O(n^3)$ and is very well studied. It has been shown to perform and scale well despite its cubic worst-case complexity [23]. We reaffirm this with our evaluation; even when analyzing large amounts of code the presence of runtime checks keeps type sets small and constraints easy to resolve.

We describe constraint generation and checks required for a simplified core of JavaScript expressions and statements, shown in Figure 2. We let f, x, y range over variables, p range over property names, i range over integer literals, and s range over string literals. The only control flow in the core language is `if`, which tests for definedness, and via anonymous functions `fn`.

The types over which we are trying to infer are also shown in Figure 2. The types can be primitive or an object type o.[1] The `int` type indicates a number expressible as a signed 32-bit integer and is subsumed by `number` — `int` is added to all type sets containing `number`. There is no arrow type for functions, as functions are treated as objects with special argument and return properties, as we show below. Finally, we have sets of types which the analysis computes.

2.1 Object Types

To reason about the effects of property accesses, we need type information for JavaScript objects and their properties. Each object is immutably assigned an *object type* o. When $o \in T_e$ for some expression e, then the possible values for e when it is executed include all objects with type o.

For the sake of brevity and ease of exposition, our simplified JavaScript core only contains the ability to construct `Object`-prototyped object literals via the `{}` syntax; two objects have the same type when they were allocated via the same literal.

In full JavaScript, types are assigned to objects according to their prototype: all objects with the same type have the same prototype. Additionally, objects with the same prototype have the same type, except for plain `Object`, `Array` and `Function` objects. `Object` and `Array` objects have the same type if they were allocated at the same source location, and `Function` objects have the same type if they are closures for the same script. `Object` and `Function` objects which represent builtin objects such as class prototypes, the `Math` object and native functions are given unique types, to aid later optimizations (§2.5).

[1] In full JavaScript, we also have the primitive types `bool` and `null`.

$v ::= \texttt{undefined} \mid i \mid s \mid \texttt{\{\}} \mid \texttt{fn}(x)\ s\ \texttt{ret}\ e$	values
$e ::= v \mid x \mid x+y \mid x.p \mid x[i] \mid f(x)$	expressions
$s ::= \texttt{if}(x)\ s\ \texttt{else}\ s \mid x = e \mid x.p = e \mid x[i] = e$	statements
$\tau ::= \texttt{undefined} \mid \texttt{int} \mid \texttt{number} \mid \texttt{string} \mid o$	types
$T ::= \mathscr{P}(\tau)$	type sets
$A ::= \tau \in T \mid A \wedge A \mid A \vee A$	antecedents
$C ::= T \supseteq T \mid T \supseteq_{\mathscr{B}} T \mid A \Rightarrow C \mid \forall o \in T \Rightarrow C$	constraints

Figure 2. Simplified JavaScript Core, Types, and Constraints

The type of an object is nominal: it is independent from the properties it has. Objects which are structurally identical may have different types, and objects with the same type may have different structures. This is crucial for efficient analysis. JavaScript allows addition or deletion of object properties at any time. Using structural typing would make an object's type a flow-sensitive property, making precise inference harder to achieve.

Instead, for each object type we compute the possible properties which objects of that type can have and the possible types of those properties. These are denoted as type sets $prop(o, p)$ and $index(o)$. The set $prop(o, p)$ captures the possible types of a non-integer property p for objects with type o, while $index(o)$ captures the possible types of all integer properties of all objects with type o. These sets cover the types of both "own" properties (those directly held by the object) as well as properties inherited from the object's prototype. `Function` objects have two additional type sets $arg(o)$ and $ret(o)$, denoting the possible types that the function's single parameter and return value can have.

2.2 Type Constraints

The static portion of our analysis generates constraints modeling the flow of types through the program. We assign to each expression e a type set representing the set of types it may have at runtime, denoted T_e. These constraints are unsound with respect to JavaScript semantics. Each constraint is augmented with triggers to fill in the remaining possible behaviors of the operation. For each rule, we informally describe the required triggers.

The grammar of constraints are shown in Figure 2. We have the standard subset constraint, $\supseteq$, a *barrier subset constraint*, $\supseteq_{\mathscr{B}}$, the simple conditional constraint, $\Rightarrow$, and the universal conditional constraint. For two type sets X and Y, $X \supseteq Y$ means that all types in Y are propagated to X at the time of constraint generation, i.e. during analysis. On the other hand, $X \supseteq_{\mathscr{B}} Y$ means that if Y contains types that are not in X, then a type barrier is required which updates the types in X according to values which are dynamically assigned to the location X represents (§2.3). Conditional constraints' antecedents are limited to conjunctions and disjunctions of set membership tests. For an antecendent A and a constraint C, $A \Rightarrow C$ takes on the meaning of C whenever A holds during propagation. The universal conditional constraint $\forall o \in T \Rightarrow C$ is like the simple conditional constraint, but is always universally quantified over all object types of a type set T. Constraint propagation can happen both during analysis and at runtime. Barriers may trigger propagation at runtime, and the set membership antecedent is checked

$$\mathscr{C} : (\text{expression} + \text{statement}) \rightarrow \mathscr{P}(C)$$

`undefined`	$\{\ T_{\texttt{undefined}} \supseteq \{\texttt{undefined}\}\ \}$	(UNDEF)
i	$\{\ T_i \supseteq \{\texttt{int}\}\ \}$	(INT)
s	$\{\ T_s \supseteq \{\texttt{string}\}\ \}$	(STR)
`{}`	$\{\ T_{\{\}} \supseteq \{o\}\ \}$ where o fresh	(OBJ)
$\texttt{fn}(x)\ s\ \texttt{ret}\ e$	$\left\{ \begin{array}{l} T_{\texttt{fn}(x)\ s\ \texttt{ret}\ e} \supseteq \{o\}, \\ T_x \supseteq_{\mathscr{B}} arg(o), \\ ret(o) \supseteq T_e \end{array} \right\}$ where o fresh	(FUN)
x	$\emptyset$	(VAR)
$x+y$	$\left\{ \begin{array}{l} \texttt{int} \in T_x \wedge \texttt{int} \in T_y \Rightarrow T_{x+y} \supseteq \{\texttt{int}\}, \\ \texttt{int} \in T_x \wedge \texttt{number} \in T_y \Rightarrow T_{x+y} \supseteq \{\texttt{number}\}, \\ \texttt{number} \in T_x \wedge \texttt{int} \in T_y \Rightarrow T_{x+y} \supseteq \{\texttt{number}\}, \\ \texttt{string} \in T_x \vee \texttt{string} \in T_y \Rightarrow T_{x+y} \supseteq \{\texttt{string}\} \end{array} \right\}$	(ADD)
$x.p$	$\{\ \forall o \in T_x \Rightarrow T_{x.p} \supseteq_{\mathscr{B}} prop(o,p)\ \}$	(PROP)
$x[i]$	$\{\ \forall o \in T_x \Rightarrow T_{x[i]} \supseteq_{\mathscr{B}} index(o)\ \}$	(INDEX)
$x = e$	$\{\ T_x \supseteq T_e\ \}$	(A-VAR)
$x.p = e$	$\{\ \forall o \in T_x \Rightarrow prop(o,p) \supseteq T_e\ \}$	(A-PROP)
$x[i] = e$	$\{\ \forall o \in T_x \Rightarrow index(o) \supseteq T_e\ \}$	(A-INDEX)
$f(x)$	$\left\{ \begin{array}{l} \forall o \in T_f \Rightarrow arg(o) \supseteq x, \\ \forall o \in T_f \Rightarrow T_{f(x)} \supseteq ret(o) \end{array} \right\}$	(APP)
$\texttt{if}(x)\ s_1\ \texttt{else}\ s_2$	$\mathscr{C}(s_1) \cup \mathscr{C}(s_2)$	(IF)

Figure 3. Constraint Generation Function $\mathscr{C}$

during propagation. This is a radical departure from the traditional model of generating a constraint graph then immediately solving that graph.

Rules for the constraint generation function $\mathscr{C}$ are shown in Figure 3. On the lefthand column is the expression or statement to be analyzed, and on the right hand column is the set of constraints generated. Statically analyzing a function takes the union of the results from applying $\mathscr{C}$ to every statement in the method.

The UNDEF, INT, STR, and OBJ rules for literals and the VAR rule for variables are straightforward.

The FUN rule for anonymous function literals is similar to the object literal rule, but also sets up additional constraints for its argument x and its body e. This rule may be thought of as a read out of f's argument and an assignment into f's return value. The body of the function, s, is not analyzed. Recall that we analyze functions lazily, so the body is not processed until it is about to execute.

The ADD rule is complex, as addition in JavaScript is similarly complex. It is defined for any combination of values, can perform either a numeric addition, string concatenation, or even function calls if either of its operands is an object (calling their `valueOf` or `toString` members, producing a number or string).

Using unsound modeling lets us cut through this complexity. Additions in actual programs are typically used to add two numbers or concatenate a string with something else. We statically model exactly these cases and use semantic triggers to monitor the results produced by other combinations of values, at little runtime cost. Note that even the integer addition rule we have given is unsound: the result will be marked as an integer, ignoring the possibility of overflow.

PROP accesses a named property p from the possible objects referred to by x, with the result the union of $prop(o,p)$ for all such objects. This rule is complete only in cases where the object referred to by x (or its prototype) actually has the p property. Accesses on properties which are not actually part of an object produce `undefined`. Accesses on missing properties are rare, and yet in many cases we cannot prove that an object definitely has some property. In such cases we do not dilute the resulting type sets with `undefined`. We instead use a trigger on execution paths accessing a missing property to update the result type of the access with `undefined`.

INDEX is similar to PROP, with the added problem that any property of the object could be accessed. In JavaScript, `x["p"]` is equivalent to `x.p`. If x has the object type o, an index operation can access a potentially infinite number of type sets $prop(o,p)$. Figuring out exactly which such properties are possible is generally intractable. We do not model such arbitrary accesses at all, and treat all index operations as operating on an integer, which we collapse into a single type set $index(o)$. In full JavaScript, any indexed access which is on a non-integer property, or is on an integer property which is missing from an object, must be accounted for with triggers in the same manner as PROP.

A-VAR, A-PROP and A-INDEX invert the corresponding read expressions. These rules are complete, except that A-INDEX presumes that an integer property is being accessed. Again, in full JavaScript, the effects on $prop(o,p)$ resulting from assignments to a string index `x["p"]` on some x with object type o must be accounted for with runtime checks.

APP for function applications may be thought of as an assignment into f's argument and a read out of f's body, or return value. In other words, it is analogous to FUN with the polarities reversed.

Our analysis is flow-insensitive, so the IF rule is simply the union of the constraints generated by the branches.

2.3 Type Barriers

As described in §1, type barriers are dynamic type checks inserted to improve analysis precision in the presence of polymorphic code. Propagation along an assignment $X = Y$ can be modeled statically as a subset constraint $X \supseteq Y$ or dynamically as a barrier constraint $X \supseteq_{\mathscr{B}} Y$. It is always safe to use one in place of the other; in §4.2.5 we show the effect of always using subset constraints in lieu of barrier constraints.

For a barrier constraint $X \supseteq_{\mathscr{B}} Y$, a type barrier is required whenever $X \not\supseteq Y$. The barrier dynamically checks that the type of each value flowing across the assignment is actually in X, and updates X whenever values of a new type are encountered. Thought of another way, the vanilla subset constraint propagates all types during analysis. The barrier subset constraint does not propagate types during analysis but defers with dynamic checks, propagating the types only if necessary at runtime.

Type barriers are much like dynamic type casts in Java: assignments from a more general type to a more specific type are possible as long as a dynamic test occurs for conformance. However, rather than throw an exception (as in Java) a tripped type barrier will despecialize the target of the assignment.

The presence or absence of type barriers for a given barrier constraint is not monotonic with respect to the contents of the type sets in the program. As new types are discovered, new type barriers may be required, and existing ones may become unnecessary. However, it is always safe to perform the runtime tests for a given barrier.

In the constraint generation rules in Figure 3 we present three rules which employ type barriers: PROP, INDEX, and FUN. We use barriers on function argument binding to precisely model polymorphic call sites where only certain combinations of argument types and callee functions are possible. Barriers could be used for other

$$T_{\texttt{use}} \supseteq \{Use\} \quad (1)$$

$$T_{\texttt{a}'} \supseteq_{\mathscr{B}} arg(Use) \quad (2)$$

$$ret(Use) \supseteq T_{\texttt{res}} \quad (3)$$

$$T_{\texttt{a}} \supseteq \{A\} \quad (4)$$

$$T_{\texttt{tmp}} \supseteq \{Box\} \quad (5)$$

$$\forall o \in T_{\texttt{tmp}} \Rightarrow prop(o, \texttt{p}) \supseteq \{\texttt{int}\} \quad (6)$$

$$\forall o \in T_{\texttt{a}} \Rightarrow index(o) \supseteq T_{\texttt{tmp}} \quad (7)$$

$$\forall o \in T_{\texttt{use}} \Rightarrow arg(o) \supseteq T_{\texttt{a}} \quad (8)$$

$$\forall o \in T_{\texttt{use}} \Rightarrow T_{\texttt{use(a)}} \supseteq ret(o) \quad (9)$$

$$\forall o \in T_{\texttt{a}'} \Rightarrow T_{\texttt{tmp2}} \supseteq_{\mathscr{B}} index(o) \quad (10)$$

$$\forall o \in T_{\texttt{tmp2}} \Rightarrow T_{\texttt{v}} \supseteq_{\mathscr{B}} prop(o, \texttt{p}) \quad (11)$$

Figure 4. Motivating Example Constraints

types of assignments, such as at return sites, but we do not do so. Allowing barriers in new places is unlikely to significantly change the total number of required barriers — improving precision by adding barriers in one place can make barriers in another place unnecessary.

2.4 Example Constraints

The constraint generation rules as presented are not expressive enough to process the motivating example in Figure 1 in full; we must first desugar the motivating example to look like the simplified core. In the interest of space, we will instead focus on a few interesting lines and provide the desugaring where needed. In the following walkthrough we show how the variable `v` on line 8 gets the type `int`.

At line 5, the declaration of the `use` function needs to be desugared to assigning an anonymous function to a variable named `use`.[2] This will match FUN. Let us call the fresh object type for the function *Use*. We generate (1), (2), and (3). To avoid confusion with the variable `a` used below, the argument of `use` is renamed to `a'`.

At line 15, an empty array is created. The core does not handle arrays, but for the purposes of constraint generation it is enough to treat them as objects. Thus, this will match OBJ and A-VAR. Let us call the fresh object type for this source location *A*. Combining both rules, we generate (4).

At line 17, `Box` objects are created. Though the core does not handle **new** constructions, we may desugar `a[i] = new Box(10)` to `tmp = {}; tmp.p = 10; a[i] = tmp`. The first desugared assignment matches OBJ and A-VAR. Let us call the fresh object type for this source location *Box* (this desugaring is approximate; in practice for **new** we assign object types to the new object according to the called function's prototype). We can combine the above two rules to generate (5). The second desugared assignment matches A-PROP and INT. Again, we can combine these two rules to generate the conditional (6). The third desugared assignment matches A-INDEX. We generate the conditional (7). At this point we propagate *Box* through (6) and *A* through (7), as we know those set memberships hold during analysis.

At line 18, there is a call to `use`. This matches APP and generates the constraints (8) and (9). Note that (2) employs a barrier constraint. Barrier constraints restrict propagation of types to runtime, so $T_{\texttt{a}}$ *does not* propagate to $T_{\texttt{a}'}$ even though we know statically $Use \in T_{\texttt{use}}$. And at the current time, before `use` is actually called, $T_{\texttt{a}'} \not\supseteq T_{\texttt{a}}$, which means we need to emit a dynamic check, or type barrier, that continues the propagation should new types be observed during runtime.

Until `main` is executed to the point where `use` is called, no further analysis is done. That is, we *interleave* constraint generation, propagation, and code execution. Propagation, due to barrier constraints, can happen during analysis and at runtime. Suppose then that `main` is executed and it calls `use`. First, the type barrier we inserted at the argument binding for `use` is triggered, and the types of $T_{\texttt{a}}$ are propagated to $T_{\texttt{a}'}$. That is, $T_{\texttt{a}'} \supseteq \{A\}$.

Line 8 is where we tie together our extant constraints. First it must be desugared to use a temporary: `tmp2 = a'[i]; v = tmp2.p`. The first desugared assignment matches INDEX and A-VAR. We combine the two to generate (10). The second desugared assignment matches PROP and A-VAR, so we generate (11). Both (10) and (11) emit type barriers, so no propagation occurs until line 8 executes. The type barrier required by (10) is triggered and propagates *Box* to $T_{\texttt{tmp2}}$. Now that $Box \in T_{\texttt{tmp2}}$, the type barrier for (11) triggers and propagates `int` from $prop(Box, \texttt{p})$ to $T_{\texttt{v}}$.

At this point, as we have observed all possible types of the property access `a'[i].p`, no dynamic checks are required by the barrier constraints in (10) and (11). But this removal may not be permanent. If we analyze new code which adds new types to the type set $prop(Box, \texttt{p})$, we will need to re-emit the dynamic check. For instance, if in the future we were to see `new Box("hello!")` elsewhere in the code, we would need to re-emit the type barrier.

2.5 Supplemental Analyses

Semantic triggers are generally cheap, but they nevertheless incur a cost. These checks should be eliminated in as many cases as possible. Eliminating such checks requires more detailed analysis information. Rather than build additional complexity into the type analysis itself, we use supplemental analyses which leverage type information but do not modify the set of inferred types. We describe the three most important supplemental analyses below, and our implementation contains several others.

Integer Overflow In the execution of a JavaScript program, the overall cost of doing integer overflow checks is very small. On kernels which do many additions, however, the cost can become significant. We have measured overflow check overhead at 10-20% of total execution time on microbenchmarks.

Using type information, we normally know statically where integers are being added. We use two techniques on those sites to remove overflow checks. First, for simple additions in a loop (mainly loop counters) we try to use the loop termination condition to compute a range check which can be hoisted from the loop, a standard technique which can only be performed for JavaScript with type information available. Second, integer additions which are used as inputs to bitwise operators do not need overflow checks, as bitwise operators truncate their inputs to 32 bit integers.

Packed Arrays Arrays are usually constructed by writing to their elements in ascending order, with no gaps; we call these arrays *packed*. Packed arrays do not have holes in the middle, and if an access is statically known to be on a packed array then only a bounds check is required. There are a large number of ways packed arrays can be constructed, however, which makes it difficult to statically prove an array is packed. Instead, we dynamically detect out-of-order writes on an array, and mark the type of the array object as possibly not packed. If an object type has never been marked as not packed, then all objects with that type are packed arrays.

The packed status of an object type can change dynamically due to out-of-order writes, possibly invalidating JIT code.

Definite Properties JavaScript objects are internally laid out as a map from property names to slots in an array of values. If a property

[2] We do not desugar the `Box` function in the same fashion as it is used as a constructor on line 17.

access can be resolved statically to a particular slot in the array, then the access is on a *definite* property and can be compiled as a direct lookup. This is comparable to field accesses in a language with static object layouts, such as Java or C++.

We identify definite property accesses in three ways. First, if the property access is on an object with a unique type, we know the exact JavaScript object being accessed and can use the slot in its property map. Second, object literals allocated in the same place have the same type, and definite properties can be picked up from the order the literal adds properties. Third, objects created by calling `new` on the same function will have the same prototype (unless the function's `prototype` property is overwritten), and we analyze the function's body to identify properties it definitely adds before letting the new object escape.

These techniques are sensitive to properties being deleted or reconfigured, and if such events happen then JIT code will be invalidated in the same way as by packed array or type set changes.

3. Implementation

We have implemented this analysis for SpiderMonkey, the JavaScript engine in Firefox. We have also modified the engine's JIT compiler, JaegerMonkey, to use inferred type information when generating code. Without type information, JaegerMonkey generates code in a fairly mechanical translation from the original SpiderMonkey bytecode for a script. Using type information, we were able to improve on this in several ways:

- Values with statically known types can be tracked in JIT-compiled code using an untyped representation. Encoding the type in a value requires significant memory traffic or marshaling overhead. An untyped representation stores just the data component of a value. Additionally, knowing the type of a value statically eliminates many dynamic type tests.
- Several classical compiler optimizations were added, including linear scan register allocation, loop invariant code motion, and function call inlining.

  These optimizations could be applied without having static type information. Doing so is, however, far more difficult and far less effective than in the case where types are known. For example, loop invariant code motion depends on knowing whether operations are idempotent (in general, JavaScript operations are not), and register allocation requires types to determine whether values should be stored in general purpose or floating point registers.

In §3.1 we describe how we handle dynamic recompilation in response to type changes, and in §3.2 we describe the techniques used to manage analysis memory usage.

3.1 Recompilation

As described in §1, computed type information can change as a result of runtime checks, newly analyzed code or other dynamic behavior. For compiled code to rely on this type information, we must be able to recompile the code in response to changes in types while that code is still running.

As each script is compiled, we keep track of all type information queried by the compiler. Afterwards, the dependencies are encoded and attached to the relevant type sets, and if those type sets change in the future the script is marked for recompilation. We represent the contents of type sets explicitly and eagerly resolve constraints, so that new types immediately trigger recompilation with little overhead.

When a script is marked for recompilation, we discard the JIT code for the script, and resume execution in the interpreter. We do not compile scripts until after a certain number of calls or loop back edges are taken, and these counters are reset whenever discarding JIT code. Once the script warms back up, it will be recompiled using the new type information in the same manner as its initial compilation.

3.2 Memory Management

Two major goals of JIT compilation in a web browser stand in stark contrast to one another: generate code that is as fast as possible, and use as little memory as possible. JIT code can consume a large amount of memory, and the type sets and constraints computed by our analysis consume even more. We reconcile this conflict by observing how browsers are used in practice: to surf the web. The web page being viewed, content being generated, and JavaScript code being run are constantly changing. The compiler and analysis need to not only quickly adapt to new scripts that are running, but also to quickly discard regenerable data associated with old scripts that are no longer running frequently, even if the old scripts are still reachable and not subject to garbage collection.

We do this with a simple trick: on every garbage collection, we throw away all JIT code and as much analysis information as possible. All inferred types are functionally determined from a small core of type information: type sets for the properties of objects, function arguments, and the observed type sets associated with barrier constraints and the semantic triggers that have been tripped. All type constraints and all other type sets are discarded, notably the type sets describing the intermediate expressions in a function without barriers on them. This constitutes the great majority of the memory allocated for analysis. Should the involved functions warm back up and require recompilation, they will be reanalyzed. In combination with the retained type information, the complete analysis state for the function is then recovered.

In Firefox, garbage collections typically happen every several seconds. If the user is quickly changing pages or tabs, unused JIT code and analysis information will be quickly destroyed. If the user is staying on one page, active scripts may be repeatedly recompiled and reanalyzed, but the timeframe between collections keeps this as a small portion of overall runtime. When many tabs are open (the case where memory usage is most important for the browser), analysis information typically accounts for less than 2% of the browser's overall memory usage.

4. Evaluation

We evaluate the effectiveness of our analysis in two ways. In §4.1 we compare the performance on major JavaScript benchmarks of a single compiler with and without use of analyzed type information. In §4.2 we examine the behavior of the analysis on a selection of JavaScript-heavy websites to gauge the effectiveness of the analysis in practice.

4.1 Benchmark Performance

As described in §3, we have integrated our analysis into the JaegerMonkey JIT compiler used in Firefox. We compare performance of the compiler used both without the analysis (JM) and with the analysis (JM+TI). JM+TI adds several major optimizations to JM, and requires additional compilations due to dynamic type changes (§3.1). Figure 5 shows the effect of these changes on the popular SunSpider[3] JavaScript benchmark.

The compilation sections of Figure 5 show the total amount of time spent compiling and the total number of script compilations for both versions of the compiler. For JM+TI, compilation time also includes time spent generating and solving type constraints, which is small: 4ms for the entire benchmark. JM performs 146 compilations, while JM+TI performs 224, an increase of 78. The total

[3] `http://www.webkit.org/perf/sunspider/sunspider.html`

	JM Compilation		JM+TI Compilation			×1 Times (ms)			×20 Times (ms)		
Test	Time (ms)	#	Time (ms)	#	Ratio	JM	JM+TI	Ratio	JM	JM+TI	Ratio
3d-cube	2.68	15	8.21	24	3.06	14.1	16.6	1.18	226.9	138.8	0.61
3d-morph	0.55	2	1.59	7	2.89	9.8	10.3	1.05	184.7	174.6	0.95
3d-raytrace	2.25	19	6.04	22	2.68	14.7	15.6	1.06	268.6	152.2	0.57
access-binary-trees	0.63	4	1.03	7	1.63	6.1	5.2	0.85	101.4	70.8	0.70
access-fannkuch	0.65	1	2.43	4	3.76	15.3	10.1	0.66	289.9	113.7	0.39
access-nbody	1.01	5	1.49	5	1.47	9.9	5.3	0.54	175.6	73.2	0.42
access-nsieve	0.28	1	0.63	2	2.25	6.9	4.5	0.65	143.1	90.7	0.63
bitops-3bit-bits-in-byte	0.28	2	0.58	3	2.07	1.7	0.8	0.47	29.9	10.0	0.33
bitops-bits-in-byte	0.29	2	0.54	3	1.86	7.0	4.8	0.69	139.4	85.4	0.61
bitops-bitwise-and	0.24	1	0.39	1	1.63	6.1	3.1	0.51	125.2	63.7	0.51
bitops-nsieve-bits	0.35	1	0.73	2	2.09	6.0	3.6	0.60	116.1	63.9	0.55
controlflow-recursive	0.38	3	0.65	6	1.71	2.6	2.7	1.04	49.4	42.3	0.86
crypto-aes	2.04	14	6.61	23	3.24	9.3	10.9	1.17	162.6	107.7	0.66
crypto-md5	1.81	9	3.42	13	1.89	6.1	6.0	0.98	62.0	27.1	0.44
crypto-sha1	0.88	7	2.46	11	2.80	3.1	4.0	1.29	44.2	19.4	0.44
date-format-tofte	0.93	21	2.27	24	2.44	16.4	18.3	1.12	316.6	321.8	1.02
date-format-xparb	0.88	7	1.26	6	1.43	11.6	14.8	1.28	219.4	285.1	1.30
math-cordic	0.45	3	0.94	5	2.09	7.4	3.4	0.46	141.0	50.3	0.36
math-partial-sums	0.47	1	1.03	3	2.19	14.1	12.4	0.88	278.4	232.6	0.84
math-spectral-norm	0.54	5	1.39	9	2.57	5.0	3.4	0.68	92.6	51.2	0.55
regexp-dna	0.00	0	0.00	0	0.00	16.3	16.1	0.99	254.5	268.8	1.06
string-base64	0.87	3	1.90	5	2.18	7.8	6.5	0.83	151.9	103.6	0.68
string-fasta	0.59	4	1.70	9	2.88	10.0	7.3	0.73	124.0	93.4	0.75
string-tagcloud	0.54	4	1.54	6	2.85	21.0	24.3	1.16	372.4	433.4	1.17
string-unpack-code	0.89	8	2.65	16	2.98	24.4	26.7	1.09	417.6	442.5	1.06
string-validate-input	0.58	4	1.65	8	2.84	10.2	9.5	0.93	216.6	184.1	0.85
Total	21.06	146	53.13	224	2.52	261.9	246.4	0.94	4703.6	3700.3	0.79

Figure 5. SunSpider-0.9.1 Benchmark Results

compilation time for JM+TI is 2.52 times that of JM, an increase of 32ms, due a combination of recompilations, type analysis and the extra complexity of the added optimizations.

Despite the significant extra compilation cost, the type-based optimizations performed by JM+TI quickly pay for themselves. The ×1 and ×20 sections of Figure 5 show the running times of the two versions of the compiler and generated code on the benchmark run once and modified to run twenty times, respectively. In the single run case JM+TI improves over JM by a factor of 1.06. One run of SunSpider completes in less than 250ms, which makes it difficult to get an optimization to pay for itself on this benchmark. JavaScript-heavy webpages are typically viewed for longer than 1/4 of a second, and longer execution times better show the effect of type based optimizations. When run twenty times, the speedup given by JM+TI increases to a factor of 1.27.

Figures 6 and 7 compare the performance of JM and JM+TI on two other popular benchmarks, the V8[4] and Kraken[5] suites. These suites run for several seconds each, far longer than SunSpider, and show a larger speedup. V8 scores (which are given as a rate, rather than a raw time; larger is better) improve by a factor of 1.50, and Kraken scores improve by a factor of 2.69.

Across the benchmarks, not all tests improved equally, and some regressed compared to the engine's performance without the analysis. These include the date-format-xparb and string-tagcloud tests in SunSpider, and the RayTrace and RegExp tests in the V8. These are tests which spend little time in JIT code, and perform many side effects in VM code itself. Changes to objects which happen in the VM due to, e.g., the behavior of builtin functions, must be tracked to ensure the correctness of type information for the heap. We are working to reduce the overhead incurred by such side effects.

4.1.1 Performance Cost of Barriers

The cost of using type barriers is of crucial importance for two reasons. First, if barriers are very expensive then the effectiveness of the compiler on websites which require many barriers (§4.2.2) is greatly reduced. Second, if barriers are very cheap then the time and memory spent tracking the types of heap values would be unnecessary.

To estimate this cost, we modified the compiler to artificially introduce barriers at every indexed and property access, as if the types of all values in the heap were unknown. For benchmarks, this is a great increase above the baseline barrier frequency (§4.2.2). Figure 8 gives times for the modified compiler on the tracked benchmarks. On a single run of SunSpider, performance was even with the JM compiler. In all other cases, performance was significantly better than the JM compiler and significantly worse than the JM+TI compiler.

This indicates that while the compiler will still be able to effectively optimize code in cases where types of heap values are not well known, accurately inferring such types and minimizing the barrier count is important for maximizing performance.

4.2 Website Performance

In this section we measure the precision of the analysis on a variety of websites. The impact of compiler optimizations is difficult to accurately measure on websites due to confounding issues like differences in network latency and other browser effects. Since

[4] `http://v8.googlecode.com/svn/data/benchmarks/v6/run.html`

[5] `http://krakenbenchmark.mozilla.org`

Test	JM	JM+TI	Ratio
Richards	4497	7152	1.59
DeltaBlue	3250	9087	2.80
Crypto	5205	13376	2.57
RayTrace	3733	3217	0.86
EarleyBoyer	4546	6291	1.38
RegExp	1547	1316	0.85
Splay	4775	7049	1.48
Total	3702	5555	1.50

Figure 6. V8 (version 6) Benchmark Scores (higher is better)

Test	JM (ms)	JM+TI (ms)	Ratio
ai-astar	889.4	137.8	0.15
audio-beat-detection	641.0	374.8	0.58
audio-dft	627.8	352.6	0.56
audio-fft	494.0	229.8	0.47
audio-oscillator	518.0	221.2	0.43
imaging-gaussian-blur	4351.4	730.0	0.17
imaging-darkroom	699.6	586.8	0.84
imaging-desaturate	821.2	209.2	0.25
json-parse-financial	116.6	119.2	1.02
json-stringify-tinderbox	80.0	78.8	0.99
crypto-aes	201.6	158.0	0.78
crypto-ccm	127.8	133.6	1.05
crypto-pbkdf2	454.8	350.2	0.77
crypto-sha256-iterative	153.2	106.2	0.69
Total	10176.4	3778.2	0.37

Figure 7. Kraken-1.1 Benchmark Results

Suite	Time/Score	vs. JM	vs. JM+TI
Sunspider-0.9.1 ×1	262.2	1.00	1.06
Sunspider-0.9.1 ×20	4044.3	0.86	1.09
Kraken-1.1	7948.6	0.78	2.10
V8 (version 6)	4317	1.17	0.78

Figure 8. Benchmark Results with 100% barriers

analysis precision directly ties into the quality of generated code, it makes a good surrogate for optimization effectiveness.

We modified Firefox to track several precision metrics, all of which operate at the granularity of individual operations. A brief description of the websites used is included below.

- Nine popular websites which use JavaScript extensively. Each site was used for several minutes, exercising various features.
- The membench50 suite[6], a memory testing framework which loads the front pages of 50 popular websites.
- The three benchmark suites described in §4.1.
- Seven games and demos which are bound on JavaScript performance. Each was used for several minutes or, in the case of non-interactive demos, viewed to completion.

A full description of the tested websites and methodology used for each is available in the appendix of the full version of the paper.

When developing the analysis and compiler we tuned behavior for the three covered benchmark suites, as well as various websites. Besides the benchmarks, no tuning work has been done for any of the websites described here.

We address several questions related to analysis precision, listed by section below. The answers to these sometimes differ significantly across the different categories of websites.

§4.2.1 How polymorphic are values read at access sites?

§4.2.2 How often are type barriers required?

§4.2.3 How polymorphic are performed operations?

§4.2.4 How polymorphic are the objects used at access sites?

§4.2.5 How important are type barriers for precision?

4.2.1 Access Site Polymorphism

The degree of polymorphism used in practice is of utmost importance for our analysis. The analysis is sound and will always compute a lower bound on the possible types that can appear at the various points in a program, so the precision of the generated type information is limited for access sites and operations which are polymorphic in practice. We draw the following distinction for the level of precision obtained:

Monomorphic Sites that have only ever produced a single kind of value. Two values are of the same kind if they are either primitives of the same type or both objects with possibly different object types. Access sites containing objects of multiple types can often be optimized just as well as sites containing objects of a single type, as long as all the observed object types share common attributes (§4.2.4).

Dimorphic Sites that have produced either strings or objects (but not both), and also at most one of the `undefined`, `null`, or a boolean value. Even though multiple kinds are possible at such sites, an untyped representation can still be used, as a single test on the unboxed form will determine the type. The untyped representation of objects and strings are pointers, whereas `undefined`, `null`, and booleans are either 0 or 1.

Polymorphic Sites that have produced values of multiple kinds. Compiled code must use a typed representation which keeps track of the value's kind.

The inferred precision section of Figure 9 shows the fractions of dynamic indexed element and property reads which were at a site inferred as producing monomorphic, dimorphic, or polymorphic sets of values. All these sites have type barriers on them, so the set of inferred types is equivalent to the set of observed types.

The category used for a dynamic access is determined from the types inferred at the time of the access. Since the types inferred for an access site can grow as a program executes, dynamic accesses at the same site can contribute to different columns over time.

Averaged across pages, 84.7% of reads were at monomorphic sites, and 90.2% were at monomorphic or dimorphic sites. The latter figure is 85.4% for websites, 97.3% for benchmarks, and 94.3% for games and demos; websites are more polymorphic than games and demos, but by and large behave in a monomorphic fashion.

4.2.2 Barrier Frequency

Examining the frequency with which type barriers are required gives insight to the precision of the model of the heap constructed by the analysis.

The *Barrier* column of Figure 9 shows the frequencies of indexed and property accesses on sampled pages which required a barrier. Averaged across pages, barriers were required on 41.4% of such accesses. There is a large disparity between websites and other pages. Websites were fairly homogenous, requiring barriers on be-

[6] `http://gregor-wagner.com/tmp/mem50`

Test	Inferred Precision (%)			Barrier (%)	Arithmetic (%)				Indices (%)			
	Mono	Di	Poly		Int	Double	Other	Unknown	Int	Double	Other	Unknown
gmail	78	5	17	47	62	9	7	21	44	0	47	8
googlemaps	81	7	12	36	66	26	3	5	60	6	30	4
facebook	73	11	16	42	43	0	40	16	62	0	32	6
flickr	71	19	10	74	61	1	30	8	27	0	70	3
grooveshark	64	15	21	63	65	1	13	21	28	0	56	16
meebo	78	11	10	35	66	9	18	8	17	0	34	49
reddit	71	7	22	51	64	0	29	7	22	0	71	7
youtube	83	11	6	38	50	27	19	4	33	0	38	29
280slides	79	3	19	64	48	51	1	0	6	0	91	2
membench50	76	11	13	49	65	7	18	10	44	0	47	10
sunspider	99	0	1	7	72	21	7	0	95	0	4	1
v8bench	86	7	7	26	98	1	0	0	100	0	0	0
kraken	100	0	0	3	61	37	2	0	100	0	0	0
angrybirds	97	2	1	93	22	78	0	0	88	8	0	5
gameboy	88	0	12	16	54	36	3	7	88	0	0	12
bullet	84	0	16	92	54	38	0	7	79	20	0	1
lights	97	1	2	15	34	66	0	1	95	0	4	1
FOTN	98	1	1	20	39	61	0	0	96	0	3	0
monalisa	99	1	0	4	94	3	2	0	100	0	0	0
ztype	91	1	9	52	43	41	8	8	79	9	12	0
Average	84.7	5.7	9.8	41.4	58.1	25.7	10.0	6.2	63.2	1.7	27.0	7.7

Figure 9. Website Type Profiling Results

tween 35% and 74% of accesses (averaging 50%), while benchmarks, games and demos were generally much lower, averaging 17.9% except for two outliers above 90%.

The larger proportion of barriers required for websites indicates that heap layouts and types tend to be more complicated for websites than for games and demos. Still, the presence of the type barriers themselves means that we detect as monomorphic the very large proportion of access sites which are, with only a small amount of barrier checking overhead incurred by the more complicated heaps.

The two outliers requiring a very high proportion of barriers do most of their accesses at a small number of sites; the involved objects have multiple types assigned to their properties, which leads to barriers being required. Per §4.1.1, such sites will still see significant performance improvements but will perform worse than if the barriers were not in place. We are building tools to identify hot spots and performance faults in order to help developers more easily optimize their code.

4.2.3 Operation Precision

The arithmetic and indices sections of Figure 9 show the frequency of inferred types for arithmetic operations and the index operand of indexed accesses, respectively. These are operations for which precise type information is crucial for efficient compilation, and give a sense of the precision of type information for operations which do not have associated type barriers.

In the arithmetic section, the *Int*, *Double*, *Other*, and *Unknown* columns indicate, respectively, operations on known integers which give an integer result, operations on integers or doubles which give a double result, operations on any other type of known value, and operations where at least one of the operand types is unknown. Overall, precise types were found for 93.8% of arithmetic operations, including 90.2% of operations performed by websites. Comparing websites with other pages, websites tend to do far more arithmetic on non-numeric values — 27.8% vs. 0.5% — and considerably less arithmetic on doubles — 13.1% vs. 46.1%.

Test	Indexed Acc. (%)			Property Acc. (%)		
	Packed	Array	Uk	Def	PIC	Uk
gmail	90	4	5	31	57	12
googlemaps	92	1	7	18	77	5
facebook	16	68	16	41	53	6
flickr	27	0	73	33	53	14
grooveshark	90	2	8	20	66	14
meebo	57	0	43	40	57	3
reddit	97	0	3	45	51	4
youtube	100	0	0	32	49	19
280slides	88	12	0	23	56	21
membench50	80	4	16	35	58	6
sunspider	93	6	1	81	19	0
v8bench	7	93	0	64	36	0
kraken	99	0	0	96	4	0
angrybirds	90	0	10	22	76	2
gameboy	98	0	2	6	94	0
bullet	4	96	0	32	65	3
lights	97	3	1	21	78	1
FOTN	91	6	3	46	54	0
monalisa	87	0	13	78	22	0
ztype	100	0	0	23	76	0
Average	75.2	14.8	10.1	39.4	55.1	5.5

Figure 10. Indexed/Property Access Precision

In the indices section, the *Int*, *Double*, *Other*, and *Unknown* columns indicate, respectively, that the type of the index, i.e., the type of `i` in an expression such as `a[i]`, is known to be an integer, a double, any other known type, or unknown. Websites tend to have more unknown index types than both benchmarks and games.

Test	Precision		Arithmetic	
	Poly (%)	Ratio	Unknown (%)	Ratio
gmail	46	2.7	32	1.5
googlemaps	38	3.2	23	4.6
facebook	48	3.0	20	1.3
flickr	61	6.1	39	4.9
grooveshark	58	2.8	30	1.4
meebo	36	3.6	28	3.5
reddit	37	1.7	13	1.9
youtube	40	6.7	28	7.0
280slides	76	4.0	93	—
membench50	47	3.6	29	2.9
sunspider	5	—	6	—
v8bench	18	2.6	1	—
kraken	2	—	2	—
angrybirds	90	—	93	—
gameboy	15	1.3	7	1.0
bullet	62	3.9	79	11.3
lights	37	—	63	—
FOTN	28	—	57	—
monalisa	44	—	41	—
ztype	54	6.0	63	7.9
Average	42.1	4.3	37.4	6.0

Figure 11. Type Profiles Without Barriers

4.2.4 Access Site Precision

Efficiently compiling indexed element and property accesses requires knowledge of the kind of object being accessed. This information is more specific than the monomorphic/polymorphic distinction drawn in §4.2.1. Figure 10 shows the fractions of indexed accesses on arrays and of all property accesses which were optimized based on static knowledge.

In the indexed access section, the *Packed* column shows the fraction of operations known to be on packed arrays (§2.5), while the *Array* column shows the fraction known to be on arrays not known to be packed. Indexed operations behave differently on arrays vs. other objects, and avoiding dynamic array checks achieves some speedup. The *Uk* column is the fraction of dynamic accesses on arrays which are not statically known to be on arrays.

Static detection of array operations is very good on all kinds of sites, with an average of 75.2% of accesses on known packed arrays and an additional 14.8% on known but possibly not packed arrays. A few outlier websites are responsible for the great majority of accesses in the latter category. For example, the V8 Crypto benchmark contains almost all of the benchmark's array accesses, and the arrays used are not known to be packed due to the top down order in which they are initialized. Still, speed improvements on this benchmark are very large.

In the property access section of Figure 10, the *Def* column shows the fraction of operations which were statically resolved as definite properties (§2.5), while the *PIC* column shows the fraction which were not resolved statically but were matched using a fallback mechanism, polymorphic inline caches [14]. The *Uk* column is the fraction of operations which were not resolved either statically or with a PIC and required a call into the VM; this includes accesses where objects with many different layouts are used, and accesses on rare kinds of properties such as those with scripted getters or setters.

The *Def* column gives a measurement of how many times during execution dynamic checks were avoided. Since our analysis is hybrid, we cannot (nor does it make sense to) measure how many dynamic checks are statically removed, as a site whose dynamic checks have been removed may have them re-added due to invalidation of analysis results.

An average of 39.4% of property accesses were resolved as definite properties, with a much higher average proportion on benchmarks of 80.3%. The remainder were mostly handled by PICs, with only 5.5% of accesses requiring a VM call. Together, these suggest that objects on websites are by and large constructed in a consistent fashion, but that our detection of definite properties needs to be more robust on object construction patterns seen on websites but not on benchmarks.

4.2.5 Precision Without Barriers

To test the practical effect of using type barriers to improve precision, we repeated the above website tests using a build of Firefox where subset constraints were used in place of barrier constraints, and type barriers were not used at all (semantic triggers were still used). Some of the numbers from these runs are shown in Figure 11.

The precision section shows the fraction of indexed and property accesses which were inferred as polymorphic, and the arithmetic section shows the fraction of arithmetic operations where at least one operand type was unknown. Both sections show the ratio of the given fraction to the comparable fraction with type barriers enabled, with entries struck out when the comparable fraction is near zero. Overall, with type barriers disabled 42.1% of accesses are polymorphic and 37.4% of arithmetic operations have operands of unknown type; precision is far worse than with type barriers.

Benchmarks are affected much less than other kinds of sites, which makes it difficult to measure the practical performance impact of removing barriers. These benchmarks use polymorphic structures much less than the web at large.

5. Related Work

There is an enormous literature on points-to analysis, JIT compilation, and type inference. We only compare against a few here.

The most relevant work on type inference for JavaScript to the current work is Logozzo and Venter's work on rapid atomic type analysis [16]. Like ours, their analysis is also designed to be used online in the context of JIT compilation and must be able to pay for itself. Unlike ours, their analysis is purely static and much more sophisticated, utilizing a theory of integers to better infer integral types vs. floating point types. We eschew sophistication in favor of simplicity and speed. Our evaluation shows that even a much simpler static analysis, when coupled with dynamic checks, performs very well "in the wild". Our analysis is more practical: we have improved handling of what Logozzo and Venter termed "havoc" statements, such as `eval`, which make static analysis results imprecise. As Richards et al. argued in their surveys, real-world use of `eval` is pervasive, between 50% and 82% for popular websites [20, 21].

Other works on type inference for JavaScript are more formal. The work of Anderson et al. describes a structural object type system with subtyping over an idealized subset of JavaScript [7]. As the properties held by JavaScript objects change dynamically, the structural type of an object is a flow-sensitive property. Thiemann and Jensen et al.'s typing frameworks approach this problem by using recency types [15, 24]. The work of Jensen et al. is in the context of better tooling for JavaScript, and their experiments suggest that the algorithm is not suitable for online use in a JIT compiler. Again, these analyses do not perform well in the presence of statically uncomputable builtin functions such as `eval`.

Performing static type inference on dynamic languages has been proposed at least as early as Aiken and Murphy [4]. More related in spirit to the current work are the works of the the implementors of the Self language [25]. In implementing type inference for

JavaScript, we faced many challenges similar to what they faced decades earlier [1, 26]. Agesen outlines the design space for type inference algorithms along the dimensions of efficiency and precision. We strived for an algorithm that is both fast and efficient, at the expense of requiring runtime checks when dealing with complex code.

Tracing JIT compilers [11, 12] have precise information about the types of expressions, but solely using type feedback limits the optimizations that can be performed. Reaching peak performance requires static knowledge about the possible types of heap values.

Agesen and Hölzle compared the static approach of type inference with the dynamic approach of type feedback and described the strengths and weaknesses of both [2]. Our system tries to achieve the best of both worlds. The greatest difficulty in static type inference for polymorphic dynamic languages, whether functional or object-oriented, is the need to compute both data and control flow during type inference. We solve this by using runtime information where static analyses do poorly, e.g. determining the particular field of a polymorphic receiver or the particular function bound to a variable. Our type barriers may be seen as a type cast in the context of Glew and Palsberg's work on method inlining [13].

Framing the type inference problem as a flow problem is a well-known approach [17, 18]; practical examples include Self's inferencer [3]. Aiken and Wimmers presented general results on type inference using subset constraints [5]. More recently, Rastogi et al. has described a gradual type inference algorithm for ActionScript, an optionally-typed language related to JavaScript [19]. They recognized that unlike static type systems, hybrid type systems need not guarantee that every use of a variable be safe for every definition of that variable. As such, their type inference algorithm is also encoded as a flow problem. Though their type system itself is hybrid — it admits the *dynamic* type — their analysis is static.

Other hybrid approaches to typing exist, such as Cartwright and Fagan's soft typing and Taha and Siek's gradual typing [8, 22]. They have been largely for the purposes of correctness and early error detection, though soft typing has been successfully used to eliminate runtime checks [27]. We say these approaches are at least partially *prescriptive*, in that they help enforce a typing discipline, while ours is entirely *descriptive*, in that we are inferring types only to help JIT compilation.

6. Conclusion and Future Work

We have described a hybrid type inference algorithm that is both fast and precise using constraint-based static analysis and runtime checks. Our production-quality implementation integrated with the JavaScript JIT compiler inside Firefox has demonstrated the analysis to be both effective and viable. We have presented compelling empirical results: the analysis enables generation of much faster code, and infers precise information on both benchmarks and real websites.

We hope to look more closely at type barriers in the future with the aim to reduce their frequency without degrading precision. We also hope to look at capturing more formally the hybrid nature of our algorithm.

Acknowledgements. We thank the Mozilla JavaScript team, Alex Aiken, Dave Herman, Todd Millstein, Jens Palsberg, and Sam Tobin-Hochstadt for draft reading and helpful discussion.

References

[1] O. Agesen. Constraint-Based Type Inference and Parametric Polymorphism, 1994.

[2] O. Agesen and U. Hölzle. Type feedback vs. concrete type inference: A comparison of optimization techniques for object-oriented languages. In *OOPSLA*, pages 91–107, 1995.

[3] O. Agesen, J. Palsberg, and M. I. Schwartzbach. Type Inference of Self: Analysis of Objects with Dynamic and Multiple Inheritance. In *ECOOP*, pages 247–267, 1993.

[4] A. Aiken and B. R. Murphy. Static Type Inference in a Dynamically Typed Language. In *POPL*, pages 279–290, 1991.

[5] A. Aiken and E. L. Wimmers. Type Inclusion Constraints and Type Inference. In *FPCA*, pages 31–41, 1993.

[6] L. O. Andersen. *Program Analysis and Specialization for the C Programming Language*. PhD thesis, DIKU, University of Copenhagen, 1994.

[7] C. Anderson, S. Drossopoulou, and P. Giannini. Towards Type Inference for JavaScript. In *ECOOP*, pages 428–452, 2005.

[8] R. Cartwright and M. Fagan. Soft Typing. In *PLDI*, pages 278–292, 1991.

[9] C. Chambers. *The Design and Implementation of the SELF Compiler, an Optimizing Compiler for Object-Oriented Programming Languages*. PhD thesis, Department of Computer Science, Stanford, 1992.

[10] C. Chambers and D. Ungar. Customization: Optimizing Compiler Technology for SELF, A Dynamically-Typed Object-Oriented Programming Language. In *PLDI*, 1989.

[11] M. Chang, E. W. Smith, R. Reitmaier, M. Bebenita, A. Gal, C. Wimmer, B. Eich, and M. Franz. Tracing for Web 3.0: Trace Compilation for the Next Generation Web Applications. In *VEE*, pages 71–80, 2009.

[12] A. Gal, B. Eich, M. Shaver, D. Anderson, D. Mandelin, M. R. Haghighat, B. Kaplan, G. Hoare, B. Zbarsky, J. Orendorff, J. Ruderman, E. W. Smith, R. Reitmaier, M. Bebenita, M. Chang, and M. Franz. Trace-based just-in-time type specialization for dynamic languages. In *PLDI*, pages 465–478, 2009.

[13] N. Glew and J. Palsberg. Type-Safe Method Inlining. In *ECOOP*, pages 525–544, 2002.

[14] U. Hölzle, C. Chambers, and D. Ungar. Optimizing Dynamically-Typed Object-Oriented Languages With Polymorphic Inline Caches. In *ECOOP*, pages 21–38, 1991.

[15] S. H. Jensen, A. Møller, and P. Thiemann. Type Analysis for JavaScript. In *SAS*, pages 238–255, 2009.

[16] F. Logozzo and H. Venter. RATA: Rapid Atomic Type Analysis by Abstract Interpretation. Application to JavaScript Optimization. In *CC*, pages 66–83, 2010.

[17] N. Oxhøj, J. Palsberg, and M. I. Schwartzbach. Making Type Inference Practical. In *ECOOP*, 1992.

[18] J. Palsberg and M. I. Schwartzbach. Object-Oriented Type Inference. In *OOPSLA*, 1991.

[19] A. Rastogi, A. Chaudhuri, and B. Homer. The Ins and Outs of Gradual Type Inference. In *POPL*, pages 481–494, 2012.

[20] G. Richards, S. Lebresne, B. Burg, and J. Vitek. An analysis of the dynamic behavior of JavaScript programs. In *PLDI*, pages 1–12, 2010.

[21] G. Richards, C. Hammer, B. Burg, and J. Vitek. The Eval That Men Do – A Large-Scale Study of the Use of Eval in JavaScript Applications. In *ECOOP*, pages 52–78, 2011.

[22] J. G. Siek and W. Taha. Gradual Typing for Objects. In *ECOOP*, 2007.

[23] M. Sridharan and S. J. Fink. The Complexity of Andersen's Analysis in Practice. In *SAS*, pages 205–221, 2009.

[24] P. Thiemann. Towards a Type System for Analyzing JavaScript Programs. In *ESOP*, pages 408–422, 2005.

[25] D. Ungar and R. B. Smith. Self: The Power of Simplicity. In *OOPSLA*, pages 227–242, 1987.

[26] D. Ungar, R. B. Smith, C. Chambers, and U. Hölzle. Object, Message, and Performance: How they Coexist in Self. *Computer*, 25:53–64, October 1992. ISSN 0018-9162.

[27] A. K. Wright and R. Cartwright. A Practical Soft Type System for Scheme. *ACM Trans. Program. Lang. Syst.*, 19(1):87–152, 1997.

Race Detection for Web Applications

Boris Petrov
Sofia University
boris.petrov.petrov@gmail.com

Martin Vechev
ETH Zürich
martin.vechev@inf.ethz.ch

Manu Sridharan Julian Dolby
IBM T.J. Watson Research Center
{msridhar,dolby}@us.ibm.com

Abstract

Modern web pages are becoming increasingly full-featured, and this additional functionality often requires greater use of asynchrony. Unfortunately, this asynchrony can trigger unexpected concurrency errors, even though web page scripts are executed sequentially.

We present the first formulation of a *happens-before relation* for common web platform features. Developing this relation was a non-trivial task, due to complex feature interactions and browser differences. We also present a *logical* memory access model for web applications that abstracts away browser implementation details.

Based on the above, we implemented WEBRACER, the first dynamic race detector for web applications. WEBRACER is implemented atop the production-quality WebKit engine, enabling testing of full-featured web sites. WEBRACER can also simulate certain user actions, exposing more races.

We evaluated WEBRACER by testing a large set of Fortune 100 company web sites. We discovered many harmful races, and also gained insights into how developers handle asynchrony in practice.

Categories and Subject Descriptors D.2.4 [*Software Engineering*]: Software/Program Verification—Reliability; D.2.5 [*Software Engineering*]: Testing and Debugging—Monitors,Testing tools; F.3.1 [*Logics and Meanings of Programs*]: Specifying and Verifying and Reasoning about Programs

Keywords concurrency, asynchrony, web, race detection, non-determinism

1. Introduction

Modern web pages are increasingly becoming full-featured web *applications*, with rich user interfaces and significant client-side code and state. The web platform has significant advantages for application development, including quick deployment of updates, easier portability across desktops and mobile devices, and seamless client-server integration.

Due to the increasing popularity and complexity of web applications, there is a growing need for programming tools and reasoning techniques that match those for more mature platforms. This paper presents techniques to help developers make safer use of *asynchronous constructs* in the web platform. Web applications are making greater use of these constructs as their functionality becomes richer. For example, user interactions and completion of certain network requests can be processed in an asynchronous, event-driven style. Also, sites are making increasing use of delayed or asynchronous loading of JavaScript code itself, to speed initial page rendering and increase perceived responsiveness [24].

Use of asynchrony can lead to serious concurrency errors in web applications. Since the JavaScript code in web pages runs sequentially, there is less awareness of these concurrency errors than for languages like Java that have shared-memory multi-threading. Nevertheless, such errors can arise, due to non-determinism in event dispatch, network bandwidth, CPU speed, etc. (we give concrete examples in Section 2).

Such errors have caused serious bugs in real-world web applications. Developers at Mozilla noticed that many of the non-deterministic failures in their regression test suite were due to race conditions in the unit test inputs [20], leading to documentation on how to avoid such problems [19]. The Hotmail email service was broken in the Firefox web browser for some time due to a race, with the bug causing a loss of message content.[1] Race conditions leading to data loss have been discovered in this paper and have also been reported in previous work [25].

To clarify the behavior of asynchrony in web applications, we present the first formulation of a *happens-before relation* [16] for the most commonly-used JavaScript and HTML features. While various types of web-application concurrency errors have been discussed previously [15, 19, 24, 25], we are unaware of any discussion that formulates these issues over a common model. Furthermore, while there are ongoing efforts to specify the web platform more carefully [10], defining a useful happens-before relation is still non-trivial, due to complex interactions between JavaScript and standard HTML features and browser deviations from the specification. The happens-before relation presented here was developed based on an in-depth study of relevant specifications, browser behaviors, and how constructs are used in practice.

Another key contribution of our work is a model of which *logical* memory locations are being accessed by various web platform features, necessary for building tools like a race detector. Typically, memory accesses can simply be defined as those reads and writes occurring at the machine or virtual-machine level. However, for web applications, there is no obvious definition of machine-level accesses, as operations may access JavaScript heap locations, browser-specific native data structures, or both. Our model of logical memory locations enables reasoning about these memory-access operations in a browser-independent manner.

Based on our models of the happens-before relation and logical memory locations, we implemented WEBRACER, a dynamic race detector for web applications.[2] The dynamic approach lets WEB-

PLDI'12, June 11–16, 2012, Beijing, China.

[1] `https://bugzilla.mozilla.org/show_bug.cgi?id=538892`

[2] Apart from dynamic race detection, our models are also a suitable basis for other concurrency analyses, e.g., static race detection or atomicity checking.

RACER precisely handle many complex features of web applications that would be difficult to handle with static analysis alone. The JavaScript language has many difficult-to-analyze constructs, like prototype chains and `eval`, that are used frequently in real-world applications [22]. WEBRACER can simply observe the relevant effects of these constructs, side-stepping difficult static analysis issues. Further, WEBRACER precisely handles interactions between JavaScript and HTML via the Document Object Model (DOM) data structure, a tree representation of the HTML often queried via string matching of node identifiers. WEBRACER is able to find races at the level of concrete DOM tree nodes (i.e., individual HTML elements) by observing accesses to memory addresses. WEBRACER is also able to simulate certain user interactions, exposing more races.

We implemented WEBRACER atop WebKit [3], a robust rendering engine used in many production browsers (e.g., Safari[3] and Google Chrome[4]). Using a production engine allowed for WEBRACER to be tested on full-featured, real-world web sites. In an experimental evaluation, we ran our tool on a large set of Fortune 100 company web sites and detected thousands of race conditions. A manual inspection of a subset of reported races showed that many of them reflected real bugs. We also gained insights into how web developers manage asynchrony in practice, applicable to future tools. Note that finding real bugs on deployed web sites was quite a challenging test for WEBRACER due to our unfamiliarity with the sites' code and frequent code obfuscation; we expect WEBRACER to be even more effective for a developer debugging her own site.

This paper makes the following contributions:

- We give the first formulation of a happens-before relation to capture the asynchronous behaviors of most commonly-used web platform constructs.
- We define a model of how operations in web applications access logical memory locations, independent of browser implementation details.
- We present WEBRACER, a dynamic race detector based on our models and built on the production-quality WebKit engine.
- We describe an evaluation of WEBRACER on a large set of production web sites, in which we discovered many harmful races and gained insights into how asynchronous constructs are used in practice.

This paper is organized as follows. Section 2 gives examples of web site concurrency errors. Section 3 presents our happens-before relation. Section 4 shows our logical memory access model. Section 5 describes our race detection algorithm and implementation. Section 6 presents our evaluation. Section 7 discusses limitations. Section 8 discusses related work, and Section 9 concludes.

2. Motivation

In this section, we explain in more detail how data races can arise in web applications, give several motivating examples illustrating possible types of races, and show the potential harm caused by such races. We also use the examples to illustrate the happens-before relationships and logical memory accesses that our model must include.

2.1 Sources of Races

For our purposes, the execution of a web application can be roughly seen as consisting of two types of activities: (1) conversion of HTML into a DOM tree [1] and (2) execution of scripts containing

[3] http://www.apple.com/safari/

[4] http://www.google.com/chrome

```
<script>x = 1;</script>
<iframe src="a.html" />
<iframe src="b.html" />

<!-- a.html -->
<script>x = 2;</script>

<!-- b.html -->
<script>alert(x);</script>
```

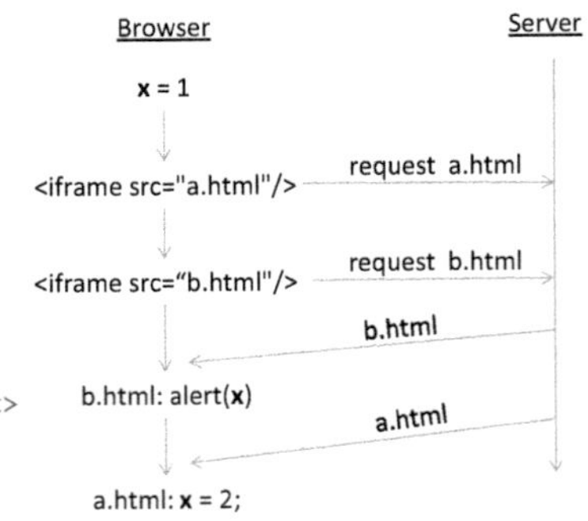

Figure 1. On the left is a simple example containing a race on **x**. On the right is an execution of the code showing the race on **x**.

JavaScript code. In most modern browsers, these activities are always interleaved in a single thread of execution, prohibiting many types of true concurrency (e.g., two distinct scripts cannot execute concurrently).[5] So, the traditional definition of a data race involving two unordered memory accesses (one of which must be a write) from distinct execution threads does not apply directly.

Instead, races in web application arise from environmental asynchrony, typically triggered via event dispatch. The web platform employs an event-based programming model to handle a variety of external events—pages may register handler code to be executed after user interactions (e.g., a mouse click) or the completion of some page loading operation, etc. Scripts may also explicitly queue functions to execute after some amount of time via the `setTimeout` or `setInterval` methods [2]. These event handler functions may execute in a non-deterministic order due to a variety of factors, e.g., variation in network bandwidth, CPU resources, or the timing of user input events.

Asynchronous events often lead to race conditions in conjunction with a web browser's rendering of a *partially-loaded* page. During the page load process, modern browsers aggressively attempt to render the HTML and JavaScript code downloaded so far, thereby improving perceived browser performance. When a partially-loaded page is rendered, user interactions may be interleaved with the remainder of the page load process in an unexpected manner, leading to race conditions. Furthermore, web application authors often exploit partial page rendering by deliberately delaying the download and execution of certain script code. In such cases, the page appears to load quickly, but some code required for user interaction may not yet be loaded, again leading to races.

We shall now illustrate these issues with examples of four types of data races. We start with standard data races on JavaScript memory locations, similar to those seen in other languages like Java. We then illustrate three types of races which are more specific to the web platform: HTML races, function races, and event dispatch races. These race types are worth distinguishing since the racing accesses do not always appear as standard memory accesses in the JavaScript code.

2.2 Variable Races

As in many other languages, web applications may have data races on program variables, i.e., JavaScript memory locations. A very simple example appears on the left side in Fig. 1. Here, a variable `x` is set to `1` in the global scope. Then, two `iframe` elements are created;

[5] The Opera web browser (`http://www.opera.com`) may execute scripts from different frames concurrently; we do not consider this case in the current work, as all other major browsers avoid such behavior.

```
<input type="text" id="depart" />
...
<script type="text/javascript">
// add a hint to the box
document.getElementById("depart").value =
  "City of Departure";
// code to remove hint when user clicks
...
</script>
```

Figure 2. Southwest: A data race on a form field value.

```
<script type="text/javascript">
function show(emailTo,EmailC) {
  ...
  EmailC.value = emailTo;
  v = $get('dw');
  v.style.display = "block";
}
</script>

....

<a href=
"javascript:show('x@x.com', a)">
    Send Email
</a>
...

<div id=dw style="display:none">
  // HTML form to send email
</div>
```

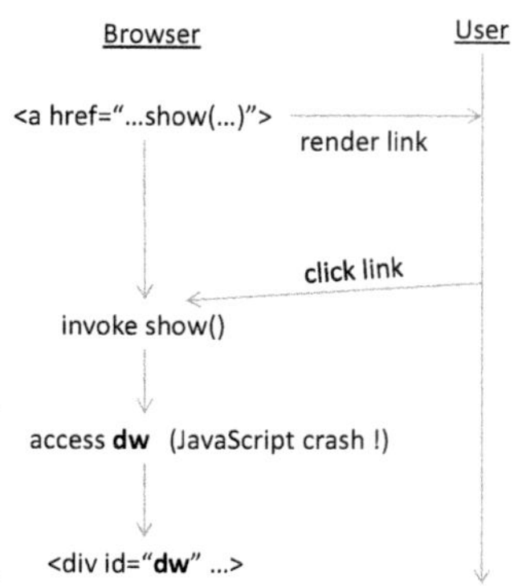

Figure 3. On the left is an example containing an HTML race on **dw**. On the right is an execution of the code showing the race on HTML element **dw** that causes a JavaScript error (crash).

an iframe contains the content of some other HTML file, loaded asynchronously. In this case, the iframes cause a.html and b.html to be loaded asynchronously. The script in b.html may display 1 or 2 depending on when the script in a.html is executed, a clear data race on variable x. The trace shown on the right in Fig. 1 illustrates the case where b.html displays 1.

Note that in Fig. 1, the first write x = 1 does *not* race with the write x = 2 in a.html, since the first script will always execute before the iframes are loaded. Our happens-before relation accurately captures such orderings between HTML element parsing and script execution.

Data races may also occur on properties of a DOM node (representing an HTML element), potentially making them more directly visible (and annoying) to the user. Consider the example of Fig. 2, a simplified version of a real bug discovered in the southwest.com web site.[6] First, an input element is created in which the user can type their departure city for a flight search. Later in the page, a script sets the value in the input box to "City of Departure", as a hint to the user, and adds code to make the hint text disappear when the user clicks in the box (not shown). Here, the non-determinism stems from partial page rendering: the user may see and interact with the input text box *before* the script loads and runs, and if this occurs, the script will simply overwrite any text that the user has entered! Our race detection tool is able to discover this type of bug *automatically* by simulating certain user interactions (details in Section 5.2.2).

2.3 HTML races

Certain web application data races are more unique to the semantics of the web platform and JavaScript. An *HTML race* occurs when an

[6] This bug appears to have been fixed in the latest version of the site.

```
<iframe id="i" src="bug413310-subframe.html"
  onload="setTimeout(doNextStep, 20)">
...
<script type="text/javascript">
...
function doNextStep() {...}
</script>
```

Figure 4. An example of a function race.

access of a DOM node representing an HTML element may occur before or after its creation. Consider the left side of Fig. 3, based on code with a race from valero.com discovered by our tool. Here, the div at the end of the example with id dw holds an HTML form for sending email, hidden by default (since the value of the style attribute is display:none). When the user clicks the "Send Email" link, the show() JavaScript function executes and the style of dw is changed, making the form appear. (The $get function employed by show() is essentially equivalent to the document.getElementById() function.)

Here, the problem arises if the user clicks the "Send Email" link *before* the dw element has loaded, as shown in the trace in the right part of Fig. 3. In this case, the show() function will attempt to set the style of a non-existent element, leading to an exception being thrown and termination of JavaScript execution. Web browsers are designed to hide many "bad" JavaScript behaviors, and in this case, the JavaScript crash will not be shown to the user—the link will simply appear to do nothing when clicked, and subsequent scripts will continue to be executed. These hidden crashes can mask more serious problems, as mutations to global JavaScript state preceding the crashes persist, possibly leaving objects in an inconsistent state. In Fig. 3, the effect of the statement EmailC.value = emailTo in show() will remain even if the subsequent statement accessing dw crashes, potentially affecting execution of subsequent scripts on the page.

Note that for this case, it is not obvious which "memory location" the operations race upon. Within a browser implementation, the concrete memory location(s) involved may depend on how exactly the DOM data structure is implemented. In our model, we define a logical HTML element location l for the dw element, with the JavaScript $get call reading l and the browser's parsing of the div node writing l. In this manner, the data race can be modeled independent of browser implementations.

2.4 Function races

Similarly to an HTML race, a *function race* occurs when an invocation of function f may occur before or after the parsing of f.[7] Fig. 4 gives an example of a function race, extracted from a Mozilla Firefox unit test that was failing non-deterministically. Here, we have an iframe whose onload handler (executed after the src HTML file is loaded) uses setTimeout() to perform a delayed invocation of doNextStep(), declared in the later script tag. The problem is that even with the 20ms delay, doNextStep() may be invoked before its declaring script is loaded if the iframe's HTML loads too fast. Invoking a non-existent function in JavaScript causes an exception, which in this case would cause the corresponding unit test to fail. In general, these exceptions may lead to the same types of problems described in Section 2.3 with HTML races, due to JavaScript code possibly being terminated in an inconsistent state. Here, the race can be fixed by moving the script element above the

[7] One site we ran WEBRACER on contained this code comment, indicating awareness of function races:
```
/* Duplicated the JS function to get rid of race condition
happening in the dashboard page. */
```
We do not endorse their solution.

```
<iframe id="i" src="a.html" />
...
<script>
document.getElementById("i").onload = function() {...}
</script>
```

Figure 5. An example of an event dispatch race.

iframe, in which case our happens-before relation would show that doNextStep() is always parsed before being invoked.

2.5 Event dispatch races

An *event dispatch race* occurs when an event may fire before or after some handler for that event is added. Fig. 5 gives a small example of such a race. Here, the onload handler for an iframe is set in a separate script, rather than directly in the iframe tag via the onload attribute. Third-party scripts often add event handlers in this way, since they cannot modify attributes in the HTML source directly. With this example, it is possible that the iframe's load event will fire even before the script executes (if the iframe loads very quickly), in which case the installed onload handler will never run.

Note that for this example, one racing "access" is the read of the iframe's onload attribute by the browser when the iframe's load event is dispatched—this read is not explicit in the HTML or JavaScript code. Our model of happens-before and logical memory can both expose this race and also show that there is no race if the iframe's onload attribute is set in the tag itself.

3. Happens-Before

In this section we formulate a happens-before relation that captures key ordering constraints for the most common web-platform features. First, we give a brief background on the relevant HTML and script constructs. Then, we define *operations* that comprise (atomic) execution. Finally, we define the *happens-before* relation between operations.

We note that defining the happens-before relation can be quite challenging because relevant specifications can be vague and sometimes browsers differ on how they implement the specification. This section represents our best effort to define a happens-before relation that agrees with both the specification [10] and how most major browsers work. In cases, where the specification was unclear or behavior differed significantly across browsers, we erred on the side of not adding happens-before edges in order to not miss races.

3.1 Background

First, we give some brief, informal background on the web platform constructs discussed in this section. Due to space constraints, we cannot give a complete treatment of all relevant features; the reader should consult online documentation and specifications for further details [10, 17].

HTML An HTML page consists of a tree of *elements*. Each element is typically delimited with an opening and a closing tag, e.g., <p>...</p> for a paragraph element. Within an HTML page, we say that element e_1 *precedes* element e_2 if e_1's opening tag appears syntactically earlier than e_2's opening tag. For instance, in the example below, element a precedes elements b and c, and element b precedes element c:

```
<div id="a">
  <div id="b"></div>
</div>
<div id="c"></div>
```

A *static* HTML element is declared syntactically in the page; elements may also be inserted by scripts, as discussed below.

Scripts and the DOM JavaScript code is added to a page via <script> elements. A static script element is *inline* if its code is declared in its body, e.g., <script>x = 10;</script>. Otherwise, a script element is *external*, and its code resides in a file specified via the src attribute, e.g., <script src="code.js"></script>. We elide a detailed description of the JavaScript programming language for space; see external resources for further details [6, 17].

The *Document Object Model (DOM) tree* [1] is a parsed representation of a page's elements that gets rendered by the web browser and possibly accessed or mutated by scripts. Each node in the DOM tree has *attributes* to hold meta-data, including attributes that mirror those seen in the corresponding HTML tag (e.g., a node representing a <script> element may have a src attribute).[8] Scripts can add or remove nodes from the DOM, leading the web browser to update its page rendering. Scripts may also insert new script nodes into the DOM to make the browser load and execute new code (possibly asynchronously); we say a script added in this manner is *script-inserted*. As with static <script> elements, a script-inserted script is *inline* if its code is present as a child node and *external* if the code location is in its src attribute.

Asynchronous and deferred scripts Both static script elements and script-inserted scripts may be declared as *asynchronous* or *deferred* via attributes. Intuitively, a deferred script should run after all static HTML elements have been parsed, while an asynchronous script may run at any time (we capture the constraints more precisely in Section 3.3). An asynchronous script has a boolean async attribute with value true, and a deferred script has a similar defer attribute, e.g.:

```
<script src="code1.js" async="true"></script>
<script src="code2.js" defer="true"></script>
```

Asynchronous and deferred scripts must be external (i.e., their src attribute must be set), and a script cannot be both asynchronous and deferred. An external script that is neither asynchronous nor deferred is a *synchronous* script.

Frames HTML pages may be embedded in *inline frames* in other pages via the <iframe> tag, e.g.:

```
<iframe src="nested.html"></iframe>
```

The HTML in an inline frame is loaded asynchronously, making iframes interesting from a happens-before perspective. The root HTML page and each (transitive) inline frame has its own *window* object, and each window has an associated *document* object, essentially the root of the corresponding DOM tree.

Events and Handlers Web applications must be written in an event-driven style, registering handler scripts to be executed when various types of events occur. Events are dispatched, e.g., for user interactions (clicks, typing, etc.) and the completion of loading various elements (images, scripts, etc.). Every event has a *target* denoting the object upon it was dispatched (e.g., for a click event, the DOM node for the button that was clicked).

Asynchronous networks requests (so-called "AJAX" requests) are made by invoking send() on some XmlHttpRequest object o. At various stages of the request (including completion), the readystate-change event is dispatched with target o.

For simplicity, we ignore two features of event dispatch in this section (though they are fully handled by our implementation):

1. Inline event dispatch, where a script explicitly fires an event via a method call.
2. Propagation of events through a DOM tree, via "capturing" and "bubbling" [5].

These features, and corresponding minor modifications to the happens-before rules, are discussed further in Appendix A.

[8] Strictly, elements have *content attributes*, while DOM nodes have *IDL attributes*; we call both attributes here.

DOM content and window load Two events of particular interest are the `DOMContentLoaded` event on a document, indicating (roughly) that the static HTML for the document has been parsed, and the `load` event on a window object, fired after resources like images and inline frames have fully loaded. Scripts very often register handlers on these events to perform additional computation once other resources have been loaded, so capturing their happens-before relationships precisely is important.

Timed execution The `setTimeout` and `setInterval` functions can be used to perform delayed execution of some script code. A call `setTimeout(f,i)` causes f to be executed i milliseconds or later. `setInterval(f,i)` is similar, but it executes f every i milliseconds. Due to their timing-dependent behavior, capturing happens-before for these functions is crucial.

3.2 Operations

Next, we define the kinds of *operations* we consider in this work. These operations will be used to specify the happens-before relation in Section 3.3. Each operation has a unique identifier taken from the set $OpId$.

Strictly speaking, we have only two types of atomic operations during web page loading: (1) parsing of HTML or (2) execution of script code. We write $parse(E)$ for the operation that parses a static HTML element E. For convenience, we separate script execution operations into several types:

- $exe(E)$: the operation executing the source in a `script` element E (either static or script-inserted).
- The execution of an event handler due to an event dispatch.
- $cb(E)$: the execution of the callback script E resulting from a `setTimeout(E, _)` call.
- $cb^i(E)$: the execution of the i'th invocation ($i \geq 0$) of a callback script E resulting from a `setInterval(E, _)` call.

We also introduce some helper functions related to operations:

- $create(E)$ denotes the operation that inserts an element E into a document (i.e., a DOM tree). If E is a static HTML element, then $create(E) = parse(E)$. Otherwise, $create(E)$ is the operation associated with the script that inserts E.
- $disp_i(E,T)$ denotes the set of operations that execute all event handlers for the ith dispatch of event E at target T.
- $ld(T)$ denotes $disp_0(\texttt{load}, T)$, if T has a `load` event.
- $dcl(D)$ denotes $disp_0(\texttt{DOMContentLoaded}, D)$ for a document D.

3.3 Building the Happens-Before

Here, we give a complete definition of our happens-before relation for the web features described in Section 3.1. As stated earlier, we developed this relation based both on studying the specifications [5, 10] and common browser behaviors, aiming to only introduce rules where all of them mostly agreed (with fewer happens-before edges, more possible races are exposed).

The happens-before relation, denoted $\prec$, is a binary relation on operation identifiers, i.e. $\prec \; \subseteq OpId \times OpId$. As a shortcut we use $A \prec B$ to mean $(A, B) \in \prec$ and $A \not\prec B$ to mean $(A, B) \notin \prec$. When we say that that two operations are in the happens-before, we mean the identifiers of these operations.

Sometimes we need to define a happens-before between an operation A and all operations found in a set B. In that case, we overload $A \prec B$ to mean $\forall(a,b) \in \{A\} \times B.\ a \prec b$. The definitions of $A \prec B$ when A is a set and B is an operation or when both A and B are sets is similar. In the rules below, only the identifiers $disp_0$, ld and dcl represent sets.

We group our rules for constructing the happens-before in roughly the same order as the order in which the corresponding features are described in Section 3.1.

Static HTML Elements in static HTML are essentially processed in syntactic order, i.e.:

1. Let E_1 and E_2 be two static HTML elements in the same document, such that E_1 precedes E_2 (see Section 3.1). Then:
   (a) $parse(E_1) \prec parse(E_2)$.
   (b) if E_1 is an inline script, $exe(E_1) \prec parse(E_2)$.
   (c) if E_1 is a synchronous script, $ld(E_1) \prec parse(E_2)$.

Script Parsing, Execution, and Loading The following basic rules govern all script elements E:

2. $create(E) \prec exe(E)$
3. $exe(E) \prec ld(E)$ (except for inline scripts, which have no `load` event).

Note that script-inserted inline scripts execute synchronously and their code does *not* execute as part of a new operation.[9]

Asynchronous and Deferred Scripts Static deferred scripts execute in syntactic order after the DOM content has been loaded, captured with the following rules.

4. Let E be any element in a document D such that $create(E) \prec dcl(D)$ and let S be a static deferred script element in D. Then $create(E) \prec exe(S)$.
5. If E_1 and E_2 are static deferred script elements, and E_1 precedes E_2, then $ld(E_1) \prec exe(E_2)$.

Asynchronous scripts and external script-inserted scripts may execute in any order. Apart from rules 2 and 3, such a script is only governed by rule 15, relating its `load` event to that of the containing window.

Inner Frames The HTML nested in an `iframe` element I loads asynchronously, with the following constraints:

6. For any element E in the nested document for I, $create(I) \prec create(E)$.
7. I's `load` event fires after the `load` event for the nested window W_I, i.e., $ld(W_I) \prec ld(I)$.

Event Handlers Some basic rules apply to event handler execution. Consider $A \in disp_i(e,T)$ for some $i \geq 0$, event e, and target T.

8. The target must have been created previously: $create(T) \prec A$.
9. For any $B \in disp_j(e,T)$, where $0 \leq j < i$, $B \prec A$.

We also have the following rule for AJAX requests:

10. Let A be the operation invoking `send()` on an `XmlHttpRequest` object T. Then, $A \prec disp_0(\texttt{readystatechange}, T)$.

DOM Content and Window Load These rules define happens-before relationships for the `DOMContentLoaded` event on a document and the `load` event on a window (in addition to rule 7). We begin with a basic rule relating the two:

11. Let D be the document of a window W. Then $dcl(D) \prec ld(W)$.

The following rules indicate which operations must happen before the `DOMContentLoaded` event for a document D:

[9] Recent browser versions adhere to this rule, but older versions of Firefox did not [23].

12. Let E be a static HTML element in D. Then $parse(E) \prec dcl(D)$.
13. Let E be a static inline script element in D. Then $exe(E) \prec dcl(D)$.
14. Let E be a static synchronous or deferred script element in D. Then $ld(E) \prec dcl(D)$.

Finally, this rule shows which events must precede the `load` event for a window W:

15. Let E be an element in the document of W s.t. $create(E) \prec ld(W)$ holds and E has a `load` event (e.g., an `img` or `script` element). Then $ld(E) \prec ld(W)$.

Note that due to rule 3, rule 15 also relates the execution of scripts and the window `load` event.

Timed Execution The following two rules govern `setTimeout` and `setInterval` executions:

16. Let A be an operation which calls `setTimeout(B, _)`. Then $A \prec cb(B)$.
17. Let A be an operation which calls `setInterval(B, _)`. Then $A \prec cb^0(B)$ and $\forall i \geq 0. cb^i(B) \prec cb^{i+1}(B)$.

Finally, we note that the happens-before relation is transitive: if $A \prec B$ and $B \prec C$, then $A \prec C$. Hence, the final relation $\prec$ is built by taking the transitive closure of all pairs given above.

4. Memory Accesses

In this section, we describe the shared *memory accesses* that an operation can perform. The notion of memory access is complicated by the fact that the web platform has no natural definition of "machine-level" accesses, as common operations manipulate both JavaScript heap locations and browser-internal data structures (e.g., DOM operations). Here, in addition to the usual JavaScript variables, we identify HTML elements in the DOM and event handlers as key *logical* locations accessed by operations. We define accesses to these locations in a browser-independent manner, easing high-level reasoning. We discuss each type of location in turn.

4.1 Accesses on Variables

Let $JSVar$ be the set of JavaScript variables that could potentially be shared among different operations. Such variables may include:

- Local variables (which could be shared between different operations via a closure).
- Object properties (instance fields and array element).
- Global variables (which are technically properties of a "global object").

By $JSVar$ we mean the set of concrete runtime memory addresses corresponding to these JavaScript variables. Reads and writes of these addresses are potential shared memory accesses.

Functions We treat a declaration of a function named F (i.e. not a lambda function) in JavaScript scope S as a write of an anonymous function with F's body to a local variable named F, where the local variable assignment is placed at the beginning of scope S, in accordance with JavaScript semantics. For example, the following:

```
{ // scope S
  some_statements A;
  function foo() { some_statements B; }
  some_statements C;
  function bar() { some_statements D; }
}
```

is treated as:

```
{ // scope S
  var foo = function() { some_statements B; };
  var bar = function() { some_statements D; };
  some_statements A;
  some_statements C;
}
```

Additional Cases The following accesses are modeled as writes to properties of DOM objects in the JavaScript heap:

- Adding/removing a child element B to/from an element A (whether statically or dynamically) is considered a write to B's `parentNode` property and a write to A's `childNodes[i]` property, where i is the index of B in the `childNodes` list.
- Modification of an HTML form element is treated as a write to the corresponding DOM node attribute. For example, the user typing into an `input` or `textbox` element is considered a write to the element's `value` attribute, clicking a `checkbox` writes its `checked` property, etc.

4.2 Accesses on HTML Elements

Let $HElem$ denotes the set of HTML elements. Then:

Write Accesses The following write to an HTML element e:

- Inserting e (either via static parsing or dynamic JavaScript insertion) into a document. Dynamic insertion of an HTML element also dynamically inserts all of its child elements. The `appendChild` and `insertBefore` functions in JavaScript are examples of ways to dynamically insert elements.
- Removing e (dynamically via JavaScript) from a document (which also removes its child elements). The `removeChild` function in JavaScript is an example of a way to dynamically remove an element.

Read Accesses JavaScript code can perform a logical read of an HTML element e via accessor methods or direct reads. Examples include:

```
document.getElementById, document.body,
document.getElementsByName, document.forms[i],
document.getElementsByTagName, document.images[i],
document.childNodes[i], document.anchors[i],
document.links[i], document.scripts[i]
```

4.3 Accesses on Event Handlers

The combination of a target element el, event e and event handler h defines a logical event handler location $(el, e, h) \in Eloc$. Note that by having h in the logical location instead of only el and e we allow accesses that manipulate disjoint handlers for the same event e to not interfere.

Write Accesses The following accesses write an event handler location:

- Parsing of an element with an event handler content attribute [10, Section 6.1.6.1], for example:
  `<img id="g" onload="doWorkA()"></img>`
- Writing the event handler attribute of an element, for example:
  `document.getElementById("g").onload = "doWorkB()"`
- Invoking the `addEventListener` function on an element
- Invoking the `removeEventListener` function on an element

Read Accesses An event handler location (el, e, h) is read when executing event handler h due to an event dispatch of event e with current target el. An event dispatch could be initiated by a user (e.g. clicking a button) or programmatically (e.g. calling `el.focus()` to dispatch a `focus` event on element `el`).

5. Race Detection

In this section, we define the notion of a data race based on our happens-before relation (Section 3) and memory access model (Section 4), describe our race detector, and finally discuss WEBRACER, our WebKit-based race detector implementation.

5.1 Race Detector

We next define what a race is, and then we present our dynamic race detector.

Definition of a Race From the definition of happens-before and memory accesses, we define a race as follows. Let $A, A' \in \{read, write\} \times OpId$ be memory accesses to some logical location m in an execution. A race exists between A and A' if:

- $op(A) \neq op(A')$ (accesses performed by different operations).
- $op(A) \not\prec op(A')$ and $op(A') \not\prec op(A)$ (the operations are not in the happens-before).
- $kind(A) = write$ or $kind(A') = write$ (one of the accesses is a write).

In the above, op gives the operation identifier for an access, and $kind$ gives the access type (read or write).

Algorithm Next, we define our race detector at the declarative level. We maintain two auxiliary maps $LastRead$ and $LastWrite$ for instrumenting read and write accesses respectively:

$$LastRead \in Loc \rightarrow Id$$

$$LastWrite \in Loc \rightarrow Id$$

Here, $Loc = HElem \cup JSVar \cup Eloc$ and $Id = \{\bot\} \cup OpId$. We use $\bot$ to denote a specially designated value used for initialization. For each location, the map maintains two fields: the first field is the identifier of the operation that last read the location, and the second is the identifier of the last operation that wrote the location. For convenience we define a function CHC to mean Can-Happen-Concurrently as:

$$CHC \in OpId \times OpId \rightarrow Bool$$

$$CHC(A, B) = A \neq \bot \wedge B \neq \bot \wedge A \not\prec B \wedge B \not\prec A$$

Intuitively, two operations A and B can happen concurrently when both are not equal to $\bot$ and (A, B) and (B, A) are not in the happens-before relation.

Our race detection algorithm works as follows: at the start, all entries in both maps are initialized: $\forall e \in Loc$, $LastRead[e] := \bot$ and $LastWrite[e] := \bot$.

Then, upon an access A to an element $e \in Loc$:

- If $kind(A) = read$:
  1. Report a race if $CHC(LastWrite[e], op(A)) = true$.
  2. $LastRead[e] := op(A)$.
- If $kind(A) = write$:
  1. Report a race if:
     $CHC(LastWrite[e], op(A)) = true$, or
     $CHC(LastRead[e], op(A)) = true$
  2. $LastWrite[e] := op(A)$.

That is, on a read, we check whether the last write (if a write occurred) can happen concurrently with the read. If this is the case, we report a read-write race. Similarly, on a write, we check whether the last read (if a read occurred) or the last write (if a write occurred) can happen concurrently with the current write, and if so, we report a read-write or a write-write race respectively.

Note that our race detector only keeps a constant amount of auxiliary information per memory location: a read or a write access will always overwrite its corresponding slot in the location. One advantage of this is that the algorithm will scale well with the number of operations.

Limitation A limitation of our race detector is that it may sometimes miss races. Consider the following example with three operations each performing a single access to location e (for convenience the operation identifier is shown next to the memory access):

$$1: read\, e \quad || \quad 2: write\, e \quad || \quad 3: read\, e$$

Assume that $1 \prec 2$, but that otherwise the operations are unrelated by $\prec$. If the following sequence of operations occurs: $3 \cdot 1 \cdot 2$, the algorithm will not report the race between 2 and 3, since when 2 executes, the detector only has information about the most recent read 1 of e. We plan to address this limitation in future work.

5.2 Implementation

Here, we describe WEBRACER, which includes an implementation of our race detector in WebKit as well as automatic exploration of functionality for simulating user interactions. We note that although we describe a particular race detector, our framework is flexible and allows us to plug in any dynamic race detector (for instance, one could implement an adapted version of FastTrack [7]).

5.2.1 Instrumentation

It was quite difficult to find all relevant instrumentation points in WebKit required to capture the happens-before and memory accesses needed for our race detector. The reason is that WebKit has no single intermediate representation (IR) where all relevant operations are exposed (this is in contrast to say JVM bytecodes, where finding the right bytecodes to be instrumented is straightforward). While WebKit's JavaScript interpreter does have an IR, our detector also requires intercepting HTML parsing, event dispatch, parsing of new JavaScript functions, and so on. Adding instrumentation required careful study of the WebKit code base. We believe that in the future, it would be useful to have a well-defined, standard instrumentation interface for browsers that analysis tools like WEBRACER could be built upon.

Our instrumentation code communicates events directly to the race detector, rather than generating a separate event trace. Internally, the race detector represents the happens-before relation rather directly as a graph structure. While this representation is simple, repeated graph traversals contribute to the high overhead of our implementation (see Section 6); we plan to employ a more efficient vector-clock representation in the future.

5.2.2 Automatic Exploration

WEBRACER allows for manual browsing and interaction with web sites to discover races. To further automate this process, we also implemented *automatic exploration*, which systematically dispatches events corresponding to user actions. Automatic exploration was quite useful for our experiments, as it avoided having to manually trigger each event on each site (a tedious process).

Automatic exploration works by generating any event of certain types for which an event handler was registered by the page. We do all automatic dispatch of events together after the window `load` event is dispatched, simplifying reasoning about WEBRACER's output (since all automatically-dispatched events are together). The events we dispatched automatically were: `mouseover`, `mousemove`, `mouseout`, `mouseup`, `mousedown`, `keydown`, `keyup`, `keypress`, `change`, `input`, `focus` and `blur`. Additionally, we also generated clicks on links which had JavaScript as protocol in their `href`'s.

We also augmented automatic exploration to expose races on the contents of text boxes and input fields (like the race in Fig. 2). Exposing such races was non-trivial, since simply typing in a text box does not modify the `value` property of the corresponding DOM object (the location that can be accessed by scripts). We solved this problem by adding a handler for the `input` event to all text boxes and input fields which effectively contained the code `this.value := this.value`. With this handler, any typing in a text box immediately updates the corresponding DOM node's `value` property. Finally, we added code to simulate typing into all text boxes.

Overall For instrumentation purposes, we changed roughly 30 `.cpp` and `.h` files in the WebKit source. The changes were not very intrusive – we were able to fairly easily port WEBRACER across several WebKit versions.[10] The total source code for WEBRACER after all modifications, including the race detector was around 2000 lines of C++ code.

5.3 Filters

We also implemented a system for easily adding post-processing filters to WEBRACER's output, to heuristically filter out certain races. Such filters can be useful, e.g., for helping to focus attention on races more likely to reflect application bugs. In running WEBRACER on production web sites written by others, we found the following two filters to be particularly useful:

Focus on form races This filter suppressed all variable races that did *not* involve the value of some HTML form field, e.g., the value in an `<input>` text box. Races on form field values have a high potential to be harmful, as they involve potential side effects of user inputs (see Fig. 2). As an additional enhancement, we further filtered out races on HTML form fields in which the operation(s) writing the form field value v had a read of v preceding the write. Such reads often check to ensure that the user has not modified the field, which makes the race harmless.

Focus on single-dispatch events This filter retained only event dispatch races involving events that dispatch at most once, e.g., the `load` event for a window. Races on such events are more likely to be harmful since once the event is dispatched, an added handler will never be run. In contrast, a `click` event on a button may dispatch multiple times, and missing one of those clicks is less likely to be a serious issue.

Note that we found these filters to be useful specifically for finding harmful races in deployed web sites (see Section 6.3). In a scenario where a developer or tester is checking her own web site for races, alternative filtering may be more suitable.

6. Evaluation

Here we describe an experimental evaluation of our prototype race detector, WEBRACER. In our evaluation, we wanted to test the hypothesis that WEBRACER could be used to find bugs in real web sites, without overwhelming the user with benign race reports. We also wanted to understand better what techniques web developers use to manage asynchronous operations in practice. After describing our experimental configuration (Section 6.1), we present both raw WEBRACER results (Section 6.2) and results with the filtering of Section 5.3 enabled (Section 6.3).

[10] The evaluated version of WEBRACER was built atop WebKit SVN 91698.

Race type	Mean	Median	Max
HTML	2.2	0.0	112
Function	0.4	0.0	6
Variable	22.4	5.5	269
Event Dispatch	22.3	7.0	198
All	47.3	27.0	278

Table 1. The mean, median, and maximum number of races of each type across our test web sites.

6.1 Experimental Configuration

We ran WEBRACER on a set of 100 web sites, comprised of home pages of Fortune 100 companies,[11] and manually inspected the output to find harmful races (to be defined shortly). We ran WEBRACER with automatic exploration enabled (see Section 5.2) to simulate user interaction with each site. This experiment was quite a challenging test, as we were attempting to find bugs in well-tested, deployed web sites whose code was unfamiliar to us.

A key issue in our evaluation was how to determine if a reported race was *harmful*, i.e., whether it indicated a web site bug. In general, making this determination requires knowing the desired semantics of the web site's code. However, we found that discovering relevant semantics by reading a site's code was often infeasible, due to use of complex JavaScript libraries and obfuscating code-compression techniques (e.g., shortening of variable and function names).[12] Given this difficulty, we conservatively classified races as harmful only when they could lead to behavior that was likely to be undesirable independent of application semantics. We defined an HTML race (see Section 2.3) as harmful if it could lead to an attempted update of a yet-to-be-created DOM node, causing a runtime exception. Similarly, a function race (Section 2.4) was harmful if it could cause an invocation of a yet-to-be-parsed function. We discuss harmful variable and event dispatch races in Section 6.3.

6.2 Raw Results

Table 1 gives the mean, median, and maximum number of races of each type reported by WEBRACER across the test web sites, without any filtering.[13] The average number of HTML and function races per site was quite low, making manual inspection manageable. (We discuss the results of that inspection in Section 6.3.) While the median number of variable and event dispatch races per site was still low, several sites had a large number of these races, raising the average number of races per site to 47.3.[14]

Via manual inspection, we found that for many variable races on these sites, the corresponding code was difficult to understand, making it hard to determine if the races were harmful. The difficulty in code understanding stemmed primarily from obfuscation and sophisticated use of asynchronous, delayed script loading, often via complex JavaScript libraries like jQuery.[15] We believe that if a developer were using WEBRACER on their own (un-obfuscated) code, inspection of these variable races would be significantly easier.

[11] At `http://www.srl.inf.ethz.ch/webracer`, we have made available the complete list of the sites that we tested.

[12] Such compression techniques are often used to speed up script downloads.

[13] Note that like many other dynamic race detectors, WEBRACER reports at most one race per location in a given run.

[14] The races reported across different runs for the same site had little variance; our numbers are taken from a typical run.

[15] `http://jquery.com/`

Website	HTML		Function		Variable		EventDisp	
Allstate	**6**	**(6)**	**2**	**(0)**	0		0	
AmericanExpress	**41**	**(1)**	0		0		0	
BankOfAmerica	**4**	**(0)**	**1**	**(1)**	0		0	
BestBuy	0		**2**	**(0)**	0		0	
CiscoSystems	0		**1**	**(0)**	0		0	
Citigroup	**3**	**(0)**	**3**	**(2)**	0		**1**	**(0)**
Comcast	0		**6**	**(1)**	0		0	
ConocoPhillips	0		**2**	**(1)**	0		0	
Costco	**3**	**(3)**	0		0		0	
FedEx	**1**	**(0)**	0		0		0	
Ford	**112**	**(0)**	0		0		0	
GeneralDynamics	0		**1**	**(0)**	0		0	
GeneralMotors	0		**1**	**(0)**	0		0	
HartfordFinancial	**1**	**(1)**	0		0		0	
HomeDepot	0		**1**	**(0)**	0		0	
Humana	0		0		0		**13**	**(13)**
IBM	**16**	**(0)**	0		**1**	**(1)**	0	
Intel	0		**3**	**(0)**	0		0	
JPMorganChase	**3**	**(3)**	**5**	**(0)**	0		0	
JohnsonControls	**1**	**(1)**	0		**1**	**(0)**	0	
Kroger	**1**	**(0)**	0		0		0	
LibertyMutual	0		**4**	**(0)**	0		**1**	**(0)**
Lowes	**1**	**(0)**	0		0		0	
Macys	0		0		**1**	**(1)**	0	
MassMutual	**1**	**(0)**	0		0		0	
MerrillLynch	**1**	**(1)**	0		0		0	
MetLife	0		0		0		**35**	**(35)**
MorganStanley	**1**	**(1)**	0		0		0	
Motorola	**1**	**(0)**	0		0		**1**	**(0)**
NewsCorporation	**1**	**(0)**	0		0		0	
Safeway	0		0		**1**	**(1)**	0	
Sunoco	**11**	**(11)**	0		0		0	
Target	**2**	**(2)**	0		**1**	**(1)**	0	
UnitedHealthGroup	0		0		0		**1**	**(0)**
UnitedTechnologies	**2**	**(1)**	0		0		0	
ValeroEnergy	**5**	**(1)**	**4**	**(1)**	**2**	**(0)**	0	
Verizon	0		**1**	**(1)**	0		0	
WalMart	0		0		**1**	**(1)**	0	
Walgreens	0		0		0		**35**	**(35)**
WaltDisney	**1**	**(0)**	0		0		0	
WellsFargo	0		0		0		**4**	**(0)**
Total	**219**	**(32)**	**37**	**(7)**	**8**	**(5)**	**91**	**(83)**

Table 2. Races reported by WEBRACER on the test web sites, after filtering (see Section 6.3). Sites with no races are elided. The number of harmful races is shown in parenthesis.

We also found that many event dispatch races arose due to deliberate delays in script loading, making those races "benign" with respect to the desired semantics. For example, consider a site s that shows a pop-up menu when the user hovers the mouse over an image i. If s delays loading of the script implementing the pop-up menu (to speed loading of the rest of the page), i may be displayed long before the pop-up menu is available. WEBRACER reports such behavior as a race, and it may indeed be annoying to a user to have degraded functionality as the page is loading (particularly over a slow connection). However, given that the developer must make a deliberate decision to delay script loading, we do not classify such races as harmful.

6.3 Results with Filtering

Table 2 shows the number of races reported by WEBRACER after the filters described in Section 5.3 were enabled, with the number of harmful races shown in parentheses. With the filters enabled, the number of variable and event dispatch races were dramatically reduced, making manual inspection more feasible.

Harmful races We discuss the discovered harmful races of each type in turn.

HTML We found 32 races on HTML elements that could lead to a runtime exception due to access of a non-existent DOM node. They were mostly similar in form to the example in Fig. 3. In some cases, the script performing the DOM node access was loaded asynchronously, making the race less obvious.

Function The seven harmful races were similar to the example of Fig. 4. However, the handler invoking a possibly-undefined function was typically attached to mouse hover or click events, rather than load events. Hence, our automatic exploration (which simulated the clicks and mouse events) was key to exposing these races.

Variable We considered a variable race to be harmful if it could cause user input to be erased, as in the example from Fig. 2. We found five such harmful races on HTML search boxes, and in each case verified that user input during page load would be deleted by a script executing later. The low false-positive rate for this race type (with filtering enabled) indicates that WEBRACER is already an effective tool for finding these high-severity bugs.

Event Dispatch We considered an event dispatch race to be harmful if due to the race, a handler attached to an event might *never* be executed, in accordance with the intuition behind the corresponding filter (see Section 5.3). All the harmful races in this category were due to use of the Gomez performance-monitoring script.[16] Gomez attempts to monitor image load time by checking for new images in the DOM every 10ms (via `setInterval`) and attaching an `onload` handler to each image as it is added. The problem is that if an image loads very quickly, Gomez may add its handler after an image's `load` event has fired. Gomez may have some separate code to compensate for this issue, but we could not tell from the obfuscated versions we were able to inspect.

Benign races The primary cause of benign race reports was synchronization between scripts via data dependence. A canonical example was the Ford site, where all the 112 benign HTML races stemmed from a single pattern, similar to the following:

```
function addPopUp() {
  if (document.getElementById("last") != null) {
    // mutate many DOM nodes
  } else {
    setTimeout(addPopUp,250);
  }
}
```

Via `setTimeout`, the code repeatedly checks if the DOM node `last` has been created, and if so, many other DOM nodes are mutated. The HTML for the page is constructed such that if `last` has been created, all the DOM nodes possibly mutated by the script must exist.

We observe that this commonly used pattern (and variants) operationally encodes a form of ordering between operations: an operation can successfully proceed only if some other operation has executed. To aid human and automated reasoning about such code, it would be very useful if the web platform had an explicit ordering construct for expressing such dependencies in a more declarative manner.

In conclusion, WEBRACER is already an effective tool for finding certain types of harmful races. Further, our data show that benign races are mostly due to either deliberate delays in adding page functionality (see Section 6.2) or synchronization via data dependencies, suggesting directions for future tool improvement. We expect that WEBRACER would be even more effective when used as part of the development process.

Performance WEBRACER was not optimized for performance; we focused instead on achieving good coverage of the many browser instrumentation points required (see Section 5.2). WebKit's just-in-time (JIT) JavaScript compiler was disabled in WEB-

[16] `http://www.gomez.com/`

RACER (as only the interpreter was instrumented), causing a significant slowdown even without instrumentation. WEBRACER's performance was sufficient for finding races in the web sites that we looked at, handling pages with tens of thousands of operations in less than a minute in most cases. However, heavy JavaScript usage incurred significant overhead—we observed a roughly 500X slowdown for the SunSpider benchmarks[17] compared to running with the JIT compiler and no instrumentation. In future work, we plan to develop an optimized implementation that employs more efficient data structures in the race detector (see Section 5.2) and that does not require disabling the JIT compiler.

7. Limitations

Although we have added instrumentation for most commonly-used web features in WEBRACER, we have not yet handled all relevant features (a difficult task, as new features are being added to the web platform rapidly). For instance, WEBRACER's instrumentation does not yet add all relevant happens-before edges corresponding to rule 10 from Section 3.3 for AJAX requests. Also, we have not instrumented calls to `clearTimeout` and `clearInterval` calls [2], which may race with the execution of handlers installed via `setTimeout` and `setInterval`. In general, missing happens-before edges may lead to false positives. Also, our instrumentation does not yet detect DOM node mutation due to application of rules from stylesheets.

In some cases, it is unclear whether certain interactions should be classified as a race. For instance, one can "move" elements with the function `appendChild` (i.e. move an element that is already in the document). If an element is accessed (e.g., via `getElementById`) in parallel with being "moved," then WEBRACER will report a race. However, it is plausible that this interaction should not be classified as a race, since the element existed in the document at all times and was only moved.

Finally, WEBRACER may report false-positive event handler races in cases where the firing of certain events is disabled. For instance, say that a button b is inserted into a document with its visibility set to hidden, disabling clicks. Later, operation 1 adds an `onclick` handler for b and makes b visible, and operation 2 represents a user clicking on b. Since our happens-before relation does not consider the visibility of buttons, we have $1 \not\preceq 2$ according to our rules, and WEBRACER will report a false-positive race. In general, detecting disabled events is non-trivial (e.g., clicks may in effect be disabled by shrinking a button), and more robust handling is left for future work.

8. Related Work

Several of the concurrency issues we address were identified informally in a position paper by Ide et al. [11], including races from asynchronous data exchange between a rich client and a Web server and from interleaved HTML parsing and event handler execution (all of which we capture). They advocate higher-level abstractions to handle these issues, but they do not implement either such abstractions or any error-checking tool.

Perhaps the closest work to our own is Zheng et al.'s work on statically detecting races caused by uses of asynchronous requests (so called "AJAX" calls) in JavaScript code [25]. Their system acquires an application's JavaScript code by extracting it from the server-side code (currently, PHP is handled). Their static technique is able to detect AJAX races without having to exercise program behaviors, unlike WEBRACER. Also, their system has special handling for *cookie* state that we have not implemented; adding such handling to WEBRACER would be straightforward. WEBRACER detects a significantly broader class of races than their system (it can catch AJAX races since separate handlers will have no happens-before edges between them). Also, since WEBRACER is implemented entirely in a browser, it works for any server-side technology and for deployed web sites; their current approach requires separate work for each server-side technology. In the future, we plan to investigate how WEBRACER could be enhanced by incorporating static analyses like theirs.

In general, precise detection of the same races found by WEBRACER would be very difficult in a purely static approach like that of Zheng et al., due to pervasive DOM usage (including mutation that may add new scripts) and hard-to-analyze JavaScript features (see discussion in Section 1). The most precise static DOM model we know of is that in Jensen et al. [13], which uses a single abstract representative for all DOM nodes with the same tag (e.g., a single representative for all `<div>` nodes). This abstraction would cause many false positives in a race detector.

There have been several other efforts to detect bugs in JavaScript programs (e.g., [8, 12, 14, 21]), but we are not aware of any previous systems aimed at detecting races besides the Zheng et al. work [25] discussed above.

Recently, a number of novel race detectors for Java-like languages have been developed. For example, FastTrack [7] is a state-of-the art race detector using vector clocks augmented with various optimizations to reduce the space overhead per memory location in the common case to a constant. In our setting, the language is more restrictive as it does not support locks (JavaScript execution is an atomic operation), enabling us to implemented a more specialized race detector. However, in the future, it may be possible to optimize our detector even further.

Our automatic exploration mode (see Section 5.2.2) is similar to the Artemis system [4], which performs feedback-directed execution of event handlers, aiming to maximizing code coverage. Our technique currently does a shallower exploration than Artemis, sufficient for exposing many races. We plan on pursuing deeper automatic exploration techniques like Artemis in the future.

Other previous work has focused on better programming models that enable developers to more easily avoid certain races. Flapjax [18] provides abstractions for reasoning about and composing *event streams* and *behaviors*, allowing for code that, e.g., handles a series of updates from a server without having to manage low-level details of `XMLHttpRequests`. The Flapjax programming model should help programmers avoid some of the data races that we describe. Mobl [9] takes a somewhat different approach by providing a more synchronous interface to creating Web applications, again abstracting away some of the race-prone features of the web platform. While these systems hold promise for future applications, they do not address the problem of finding races in existing code.

9. Conclusion

The Web platform poses a particular challenge to analyzing concurrency: there are multiple specifications and implementations defining the platform, concurrency is introduced in implicit, event-driven ways, and many different features and APIs are relevant to concurrency. In this environment, we provide the first core tools for reasoning about concurrency: a *happens-before* relation over common HTML and JavaScript constructs, and a *logical model* of memory accesses for capturing state interactions. We show the value of these tools with WEBRACER, the first dynamic race detector for Web applications. WEBRACER found numerous races across top Web sites, including harmful ones capable of causing anomalies like lost input.

Future work includes further automating the detection and possibly remediation of data races in Web applications. Also, at the level of specifications, a precise definition of what concurrent interactions are meant to be allowed would be very useful (we found

[17] `http://www.webkit.org/perf/sunspider/sunspider.html`

defining a reasonable happens-before relation to be surprisingly challenging). Such a definition must provide more clarity to developers, but also not overly restrict the concurrency that has become crucial to performant web applications.

Acknowledgements

We thank Robert O'Callahan for pointing out that concurrency issues can occur in client web applications and for suggesting Firefox test cases as candidates for analysis. We also thank Max Schäfer and the anonymous reviewers for their detailed comments.

References

[1] HTML5 DOM tree. `http://dev.w3.org/html5/spec/Overview.html#dom-trees`.

[2] `setTimeout` specification. `http://www.whatwg.org/specs/web-apps/current-work/multipage/timers.html#dom-windowtimers-settimeout`.

[3] WebKit. `http://www.webkit.org/`.

[4] Shay Artzi, Julian Dolby, Simon Holm Jensen, Anders Møller, and Frank Tip. A Framework for Automated Testing of JavaScript Web Applications. In *ICSE*, May 2011.

[5] Document Object Model (DOM) Level 3 Events Specification. `http://www.w3.org/TR/DOM-Level-3-Events/`.

[6] ECMA. ECMAScript Language Specification, 5th edition, 2009. ECMA-262.

[7] Cormac Flanagan and Stephen N. Freund. FastTrack: efficient and precise dynamic race detection. In *PLDI*, 2009.

[8] Salvatore Guarnieri and V. Benjamin Livshits. Gatekeeper: Mostly static enforcement of security and reliability policies for JavaScript code. In *USENIX Security Symposium*, pages 151–168, 2009.

[9] Zef Hemel and Eelco Visser. Declaratively programming the mobile web with Mobl. In *OOPSLA*, 2011.

[10] HTML5 specification. `http://www.w3.org/TR/html5/`.

[11] James Ide, Ratislav Bodik, and Doug Kimelman. Concurrency concerns in rich Internet applications. In *Workshop on Exploiting Concurrency Efficiently and Correctly (EC2)*, 2009.

[12] Dongseok Jang, Ranjit Jhala, Sorin Lerner, and Hovav Shacham. An empirical study of privacy-violating information flows in JavaScript web applications. In *ACM Conference on Computer and Communications Security*, pages 270–283, 2010.

[13] Simon Holm Jensen, Magnus Madsen, and Anders Møller. Modeling the HTML DOM and browser API in static analysis of JavaScript web applications. In *ESEC/FSE*, 2011.

[14] Simon Holm Jensen, Anders Møller, and Peter Thiemann. Interprocedural Analysis with Lazy Propagation. In *SAS*, 2010.

[15] Olav Junker Kjaer. Timing and synchronization in JavaScript. `http://dev.opera.com/articles/view/timing-and-synchronization-in-javascript/`. Accessed 03-November-2011.

[16] Leslie Lamport. Time, clocks, and the ordering of events in a distributed system. *Commun. ACM*, 21:558–565, July 1978.

[17] Mozilla Developer Network. `https://developer.mozilla.org/`.

[18] Leo A. Meyerovich, Arjun Guha, Jacob Baskin, Gregory H. Cooper, Michael Greenberg, Aleks Bromfield, and Shriram Krishnamurthi. Flapjax: a programming language for Ajax applications. In *OOPSLA*, 2009.

[19] Mozilla Developer Network. Avoiding intermittent oranges. `https://developer.mozilla.org/en/QA/Avoiding_intermittent_oranges`. Accessed 18-October-2011.

[20] Robert O'Callahan, December 2010. Personal communication.

[21] Joe Gibbs Politz, Spiridon Aristides Eliopoulos, Arjun Guha, and Shriram Krishnamurthi. ADsafety: Type-based verification of JavaScript sandboxing. In *USENIX Security Symposium*, 2011.

[22] Gregor Richards, Sylvain Lebresne, Brian Burg, and Jan Vitek. An analysis of the dynamic behavior of javascript programs. *SIGPLAN Not.*, 45:1–12, June 2010.

[23] Henri Sivonen. HTML5 script execution changes in Firefox 4. `http://hsivonen.iki.fi/script-execution/`. Accessed 05-November-2011.

[24] Steve Souders. *Even Faster Web Sites: Performance Best Practices for Web Developers*. O'Reilly Media, 2009.

[25] Yunhui Zheng, Tao Bao, and Xiangyu Zhang. Statically locating web application bugs caused by asynchronous calls. In *WWW*, 2011.

A. Happens-Before for Events

Here, we describe how event dispatch works in detail and give some additional (or refined) rules for handling events.

How Events Work Here we briefly sketch event firing; more details can be found in [10, 15]. Firing an event E is done on an element or object T (called a target). Some events can have different phases associated with it: *Capturing*, *At-Target*, *Bubbling* and *Default*. The *Capturing* phase goes through all targets starting at the top of the DOM tree (at the document/window object) and moving down towards the event target T. At each target, all handlers which are registered for that type of event are executed. After the *Capturing* phase, the *At-Target* phase follows, which dispatches all handlers on the event target T. Following is the *Bubbling* phase which works from the target T up towards the document/window object and dispatches the event on all targets on the way. At last, there is the default action which kicks in and dispatches on the target T. For example, on a link element, the `href` may be followed or executed if it is JavaScript code (i.e., of the form `href="javascript:..."`).

To define the happens-before, we first need some definitions. An *inline* event dispatch is the act of programmatically firing an event from JavaScript. An example would be the call `element.click()` in JavaScript code, which fires a `click` event on `element`. Anything else is considered as a *non-inline* event dispatch. An example would be the `mousemove` event firing due to the user moving her mouse, the `load` event for a `window` firing or the `readystatechange` event dispatching on an `XMLHttpRequest` object.

Splitting Happens-Before Since script execution is atomic, the browser will not preempt a script in order to execute a different script, parse more HTML, etc. However, event-handler execution could actually be triggered in the *middle* of JavaScript code due to an inline event dispatch. Let A be such a JavaScript operation that is interleaved with event-handler execution. Given an execution A, we define $A_{[i:j)}$ to mean the subsequence of A starting and including the i'th transition in A and ending with but not including the j'th transition (if $i < 0, j \geq |A|$, or $i = j$, then $A_{[i:j)} = \epsilon$). Then, given an execution A interrupted by an inline event dispatch, let the event dispatch invocation be the k'th transition in A's execution. Let B be the set of operations generated by the inline event dispatch. Then: $A_{[0:k)} \prec B$ and $B \prec A_{[k+1:|A|)}$.

When using $A_{[i:j)}$ in the happens-before, we mean that a unique operation identifier is created for this sequence of transitions. Then, in the happens-before as discussed in Section 3.3, we replace an interleaved operation A with the set $\{A_{[0:k)}, A_{[k+1:|A|)}\} \cup B$ (dealing with sets in the happens-before was already explained earlier).

Event Phasing Happens-Before We denote $hop(E, ET, P, T)_i$ as the set of all operations that are the executions of all handlers for the ith dispatch of event E dispatched on target ET in phase P with current target T. Let $A \in hop(E_1, ET_1, P_1, T_1)_i$ and $B \in hop(E_2, ET_2, P_2, T_2)_j$. If E_1 and E_2 are both non-inline events, $ET_1 = ET_2$, $E_1 = E_2$, and ($i < j$ or ($i = j$ and ($P_1 \neq P_2$ or $T_1 \neq T_2$))), then $A \prec B$.

Engage: A Deployment Management System

Jeffrey Fischer
genForma Corp, USA
jeffrey.fischer@genforma.com

Rupak Majumdar
MPI-SWS, Germany
rupak@mpi-sws.org

Shahram Esmaeilsabzali
MPI-SWS, Germany
shahram@mpi-sws.org

Abstract

Many modern applications are built by combining independently developed packages and services that are distributed over many machines with complex inter-dependencies. The assembly, installation, and management of such applications is hard, and usually performed either manually or by writing customized scripts. We present Engage, a system for configuring, installing, and managing complex application stacks. Engage consists of three components: a domain-specific model to describe component metadata and inter-component dependencies; a constraint-based algorithm that takes a partial installation specification and computes a full installation plan; and a runtime system that co-ordinates the deployment of the application across multiple machines and manages the deployed system. By explicitly modeling configuration metadata and inter-component dependencies, Engage enables static checking of application configurations and automated, constraint-driven, generation of installation plans across multiple machines. This reduces the tedious manual process of application configuration, installation, and management.

We have implemented Engage and we have used it to successfully host a number of applications. We describe our experiences in using Engage to manage a generic platform that hosts Django applications in the cloud or on premises.

Categories and Subject Descriptors D.2.9 [*Software Engineering*]: Management; K.6.2 [*Management of Computing and Information Systems*]: Installation management

General Terms Design, Languages, Management

Keywords Application deployment, declarative languages, cloud computing

1. Introduction

Many modern applications are built from components which are inter-dependent, distributed, and created independently. By combining existing components in a loosely-coupled architecture, applications delivering significant functionality in a scalable manner can be quickly created. However, the assembly, installation, and management of such systems in a consistent and effective way is currently a difficult and resource-intensive problem. Packages and services have dependencies that have to be satisfied, and misconfigurations between individual components and services can cause the application to become unstable or corrupted.

While there are tools that automate portions of this process for specific packages, e.g., package managers on Linux distributions, there are few tools that provide end-to-end functionality for the entire software stack, especially for distributed applications running on many nodes (e.g., in a private or public cloud infrastructure). In practice, large-scale software stacks are often managed using custom script-based tools and manual techniques. This process is error-prone, as upgrades to individual packages can break existing and implicit dependencies in the system. It is also labor-intensive, since the process must be performed manually by system administrators, developers, and end-users, and effort may be duplicated within the same organization. In fact, application administration overhead is mentioned as one main barrier to the adoption of free and open-source software [13].

The challenge of dependency management in software package installation is well-studied, and constraint-based tools to manage package installations on single machines have been developed [12, 17, 19]. However, none of the available tools consider additional factors that come up in managing a distributed application stack:

1. **Physical context**: Components may be distributed across multiple machines. Certain dependencies (e.g., libraries) have to be resolved within the context of a single machine (e.g., each machine running a Java component must install (possibly different versions of) the Java Runtime Environment), and certain dependencies must be resolved across machines (e.g., an application server and a back-end task processor may live on different servers but connect to the same database). Existing tools do not consider multi-machine dependencies.
2. **Configuration management**: Additionally, each component of an application may have its own collection of configuration settings. Such settings may be maintained in a configuration file or database or passed to a component through command line parameters or environment variables. These settings may determine how a component interacts with its dependencies. One must ensure that all selected components of an application have been configured to connect to each other as required by their dependency relationships. For example, an application depending on a database must be configured to connect to the host and port number on which the database is listening, and may need to know the database user's name and password. Currently, it is the user's responsibility to connect the configuration options between components (e.g., by manually setting the values in the application's configuration file).
3. **Application management**: Many application components use long-running processes (e.g. services or daemons) that need to be explicitly started, restarted, or stopped. Startup/shutdown of the full application stack can be deceptively difficult to automate due to timing issues between dependent services. If a component is started without first ensuring that all of its dependen-

PLDI'12, June 11–16, 2012, Beijing, China.

cies have completed their startup, it might intermittently fail due to connection errors. Most package management tools do not consider service startup/shutdown, and do not provide ways to express dependencies in the application stack.

We present Engage, a system for managing application stack configuration, installation, and maintenance. Engage has three components. The first is a declarative framework for specifying component metadata such as configuration parameters as well as dependencies between different components and services. The second is a constraint-based algorithm that takes a *partial installation specification* (a list of the main application components to be installed) and automatically produces a full installation specification (a list of all components to be installed). Finally, a runtime system co-ordinates the installation of components in an installation specification and manages the deployed system locally or on the cloud.

In Engage, a component, called a *resource*, is modeled using two parts: a *type* and a *driver*. A *type* for the resource describes configuration options and dependencies associated with a component. The configuration options specify required configuration parameters for the components, including input configuration options that are provided by components that the current resource depends on, and output configurations that the configured resource exports to downstream dependencies. The dependencies specify other components the current resource depends on, such as the machine in which it executes, other libraries and services that must be present on the same machine, and other services (possibly on diffferent machines) that it requires. A *driver* for the resource specifies a state machine that manages its lifecycle at runtime (e.g., installation, startup, shutdown, etc.). Together, the type and the driver specify completely the dependencies and the configurations required to install and use a resource. A subtyping mechanism ensures that each resource can be developed independently and reused in many different contexts.

A *resource instance* is a specific instantiation of a resource that is deployed, for instance, a specific server or a specific instance of a MySQL database. An application is described by compositions of resource instances (an *installation specification*), and it can be checked statically to ensure that all dependencies are met, there are no circular or conflicting dependencies, and that configuration parameters between dependent components are passed correctly. For example, we can check that, if an application component has a dependency on a database, there is a resource instance in the installation specification corresponding to a database component, and the application component gets its input configuration options for the database from the outputs of the database component. Since resources can model the physical context of a machine, we can statically reason about the physical context; for instance, checking that certain libraries exist on the same machine. Additionally, the resource drivers ensure that the runtime system has enough information to start up and shut down services according to their dependencies. Thus, the resource types enable static checking of application stacks for dependencies and conflicts, for configuration and physical context management, and the types together with the drivers enable runtime application management.

Rather than writing the entire installation specification, which can be long and tedious, Engage allows the user to only specify a *partial installation specification*, which outlines the main application components and the machines they should be installed on. A *configuration engine* takes the partial installation specification and produces a *full installation specification* by computing the transitive closure of dependencies of the components, resolving choices between components through Boolean constraint solving, and adding component dependency links to form a directed acyclic graph of resource instances.

The Engage runtime system then takes this full installation specification and deploys it (locally or on the cloud), using the dependency order on resource instances and the actions in the resource drivers to order the sequence of installations and startups. The drivers specify the order in which operations can be performed on a resource instance, and also implement each operation using an underlying programming language. The runtime system monitors the application as it runs, and can manage the application stack (e.g., to stop the application) based on the dependency order specified in the install specification. At the end of this process, the user should have a full application installed, configured, and running, potentially across multiple machines.

We have implemented the Engage system and have used Engage as the deployment and management tool for a number of case studies. The core of Engage contains about 26K lines of Python code, 6K lines of OCaml code, and about 5K lines of metadata. Engage is integrated with both Rackspace and Amazon Web Services and can deploy applications on these services. Engage has been used as the core technology behind a commercial platform-as-a-service company for application stacks written in Django and using standard components such as Python packages, databases (MySQL), key-value stores (Redis, MongoDB), message queues (RabbitMQ, Celery), and web caches (Memcached). It has efficiently managed the configuration, deployment, and upgrades of complex third-party applications. In addition, we have used Engage to configure and manage Java-based and pure Python applications.

Related Work Engage is different from an *operating-system-level package manager* (OSLPM), such as dpkg for Debian, RPM, or apt. These tools manage dependencies among packages on a single machine, but do not provide support for configuration management, application management (e.g., server startup), or multi-machine deployments. However, they form the building blocks for Engage: a driver for a resource can use an OSLPM to install the required packages on a machine. Thus, Engage is complementary to OSLPM, and uses OSLPM's to provide support for higher-level issues in application deployment and maintenance for each platform.

Constraint-based tools [11, 17–19] manage individual software packages at a single machine level, but do not provide support for configuration management, multi-machine deployments, or application management. A constraint usually specifies pre-requisites (and conflicts) for a package, but does not model configuration parameters or service startup/shutdown requirements. The constraint-based configuration in Engage is inspired by these tools, but in addition, Engage provides support for configuration and application management across multiple physical contexts (machines). The distribution editor of the EDOS project [17] provides a means to check the consistency and installability of a set of interdependent packages. However, in the distribution editor, this information is not used for analysis or for application-level installation. Model-based formalisms are used to detect compatibility and upgrade problems [10, 11], but not across physical contexts, nor targeted toward application stack management.

The input/output/configuration ports of Engage's resource types were inspired by module systems for more general purpose languages, including Units [14], nesC [15], and ArchJava [7]. Unlike these systems, the connections between modules (resources) in Engage are implicit, using dependency constraints to instantiate resources and establish connections. Engage's resource definition language provides a combination of traditional module systems (importing/exporting definitions, subtyping of individual values and structures) and constraint languages.

Engage is similar to *configuration management* systems such as Puppet [1], Chef [2], LCFG [8], and CfEngine [9], which provide a domain-specific language to model the "desired state" for a machine, e.g., files that should be present and services that should be running. These systems use a client-server model in which a server holds the model of the desired state for a machine, and the client ensures this configuration is met. Engage improves upon the design of existing configuration management systems in the following ways. First, Engage separates the declarative specification of resources (resource types) and the imperative details of their installation (instances and drivers). This enables type-checking for configurations and to detect configuration or dependency problems statically. Second, through the constraint-based configuration engine, Engage allows the compact specification of application stacks, usually over an order of magnitude smaller than the full installation specification required by other systems. In practice, we have found the combination of instance/type separation and a contraint-based dependency model result in very flexible install specifications. We can take an application and deploy it on multiple platforms (e.g. MacOSX and Linux) and in multiple configurations (e.g. development, testing, and production) without significantly more work than is required for a single configuration. This is not possible with traditional configuration management systems, which are optimized for keeping large numbers of nearly identical systems in a given standard configuraiton.

Finally, while configuration management systems can be used to support resource management over multiple servers, each client is usually managed in isolation with no coordination between servers. Engage provides a means to coordinate and configure between services across machines according to their dependencies.

SmartFrog [16] supports distributed application deployment by modeling the components of a system and providing a framework for *lifecycle managers* to manage individual components and their coordination. Engage's deployment engine uses a similar approach, with drivers in lieu of lifecycle managers. Engage additionally uses the dependency relationship information it obtains from the configuration phase to determine the sequencing of deployment actions. The use of constraint-based configuration is also novel.

2. Overview

We now describe Engage through an example. As noted before, Engage has three main components:

1. A declarative language to describe *resources*. A resource is a generic term for a software package (e.g., the Apache web server), operating system (e.g., Ubuntu 10.4), or a virtual or physical machine. Its description consists of a *type* (the configuration parameters and dependencies) and a *driver* (a state machine for managing the component).
2. A *configuration engine* that takes a database of resources and a *partial installation specification* and produces a *full installation specification* that describes how a collection of software components should look when installed and configured.
3. The Engage runtime, consisting of a *deployment engine* and runtime services that install and manage components in a deployment. It calls the drivers of each component in the full installation specification and starts services in dependency order.

OpenMRS We demonstrate how Engage can be used to install and manage OpenMRS, an open source enterprise medical records system [20]. OpenMRS is written in Java, and runs as a servlet contained within the Apache Tomcat webserver. It depends on Java, version 5 or greater. Either the Java Developer Kit (JDK) or Java Runtime Environment (JRE) may be used. The Tomcat distribution should be at least version 5.5 but before 6.0.29. OpenMRS talks to a MySQL database in the backend, where the MySQL distribution should be version 5 or greater. In a production setting, the database will run on a separate machine from the application server. OpenMRS itself does not have any specific operating system dependen-

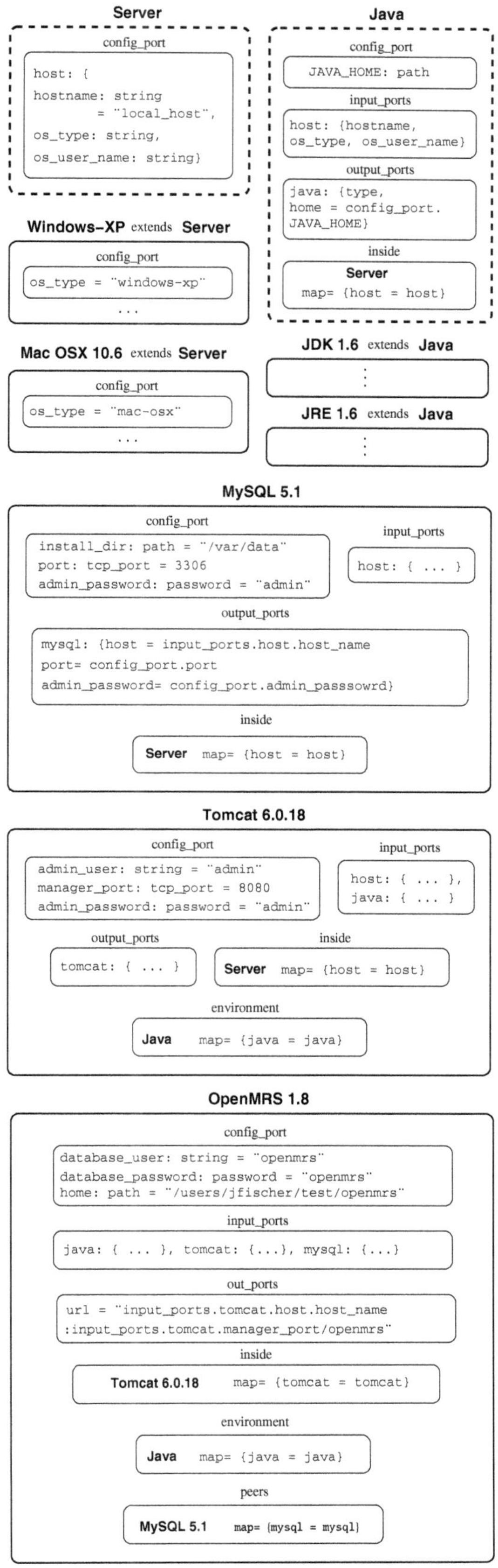

Figure 1: Resource types for OpenMRS installation

```
{ "id": "server", "key": "Mac-OSX 10.6",
  "config_port": {
    hostname="localhost", os_user_name="root"
  }
},
{ "id": "tomcat", "key": "Tomcat 6.0.18",
  "inside": { "id":"server" }
},
{ "id": "openmrs", "key": "OpenMRS 1.8"
  "inside": { "id":"tomcat" }
}
```

Figure 2: Partial installation specification for OpenMRS

cies. Thus the operating systems are limited by the availability of Java and MySQL. This includes Windows XP/Vista, Linux, Solaris, and Mac OSX. Different executables for Java and MySQL are required for each platform.

A single-machine installation for OpenMRS is described on the OpenMRS web page, and consists of a 10-page document. This document gives a list of the software components which must be installed in order to install OpenMRS, in their dependency order. It points to a different document for installing and configuring MySQL. Moreover, the document gives separate conditions for Windows and for Ubuntu (after 10.10 and before 10.10). The installation requirements and dependencies in the installation are given as comments in the document. We give two examples:

- Java must be installed before installing Tomcat.
- [When starting OpenMRS] Ensure that Tomcat is started by checking to see if icon in the tray is green (Windows install).

It is the user's responsibility to troubleshoot the installation if some of these conditions are not met. When moving from one deployment (e.g., test) to another (e.g., production), the user must manually reconstruct all the installation steps (or write ad hoc scripts to automate the steps). Moreover, the instructions are sometimes incomplete (for example, how to check if Tomcat is started on Ubuntu? How to check it programmatically?). Our intent is not to deride the OpenMRS installation document (indeed, OpenMRS has a very readable set of instructions), but to point out that these are common issues in many installation specifications.

Engage We now describe how the OpenMRS installation is managed in Engage. For simplicity, we only describe the configuration for a Mac OSX 10.6 server with Tomcat 6.0.18. Software or hardware components, called *resources*, are represented in Engage using two parts: a *resource type* describes the configuration metadata and dependencies on other resources, and a *resource driver* describes a state machine that manages the lifecycle of the resource. We assume resource types and drivers are written by the component developer, not the end user installing the application.

We first describe resource types. Figure 1 shows the resource types that are relevant to the OpenMRS installation (simplified for readability). (We omit describing a concrete syntax for resources.) Each resource description has a (unique) key identifying the resource, sets of typed configuration, input, and output ports, and dependency specifications on other components. Typically, the key consists of the name of the package and its version. The ports specify attributes (key-value pairs) internal to the component's configuration (the *configuration* ports), attributes derived from other components on which the component depends (*input* ports), and attributes that the component exports to downstream components (*output* ports). For example, the resource type for key `MySQL 5.1` (MySQL version 5.1) has a configuration port called `port` that specifies the default port (3306), and has an output port, also called `port`, that copies its value from the configuration port for downstream components connecting to it.

The dependencies come in three types. An *inside dependency* specifies the container resource in which the current resource must execute. In general, this is a physical or virtual machine, or a "container" like Tomcat which contains other packages. If a resource does not have an inside dependency, it corresponds to a virtual or physical machine. For example, the (abstract) resource `Server` and its subclasses `Mac OSX 10.6` and `Windows-XP` refer to machines. On the other hand, the resource `Tomcat 6.0.18` has an inside dependency on a `Server`, meaning that in a deployment, `Tomcat` runs inside a sub-class of resource type `Server` (since `Server` is abstract and cannot be instantiated). The resource `OpenMRS 1.8` has an inside dependency on `Tomcat 6.0.18`, since it executes as a servlet inside the `Tomcat` server.

An *environment dependency* specifies other resources that must be present (and possibly execute) on the same machine as a precondition for the installation and execution of the current resource. For example, both `Tomcat` and `OpenMRS` have environment dependencies on `Java`, which means that an instance of a subclass of resource type of `Java` must be installed on a machine before `Tomcat` or `OpenMRS` can be installed on that machine. In addition, an environment dependency also specifies how configuration options from the output ports of a resource flow into the input ports of the current resource. For example, the output port `java` in the `Java` resource type is an input to `OpenMRS 1.8`

A *peer dependency* specifies resources must be present, but not necessarily on the same machine. For example, `OpenMRS 1.8` has a peer dependency on the `MySQL 5.1` database, meaning that an instance of `MySQL 5.1` must be deployed before `OpenMRS 1.8` can be deployed, but possibly on a machine different from that of OpenMRS.

When a resource type A depends on a resource type B, the resource A can obtain the value of an output port of B by using a *port mapping*. A port mapping relates an output port of a resource type to an input port of another. For example, `OpenMRS 1.8` maps the output port `mysql` of `MySQL 5.1` into its input port that has the same name.

Well-formed sets of resource types ensure that the union of all dependency relations is acyclic, and that each input port is mapped exactly once by the set of dependencies. Given a resource, we call the set of resources that it transitively depends on its set of *upstream dependencies* and the set of resources that transitively depend on it its set of *downstream dependencies*.

Resource *types* correspond to the classes in an OO language, resource *instances* represent specific resources instantiations (e.g. a copy of `MySQL 5.1` installed on server `demotest` and listening on port 3306) and correspond to objects. An instance of a resource has a globally unique identifier, fills in concrete values for all ports, and replaces each dependency in the resource type with a concrete instance. A full installation specification provides a list of each instance required to deploy an application. For example, given *resource types* for each component required by OpenMRS, the user can write an installation specification describing all the components that are required to install OpenMRS. Engage's type system can check the installation specification to make sure all required dependencies are present in the correct physical context and that each instance is correctly configured.

Writing full installation specifications can get tedious. Engage's configuration engine allows the end user to provide *partial installation specifications*, and automatically determines what other resources must be instantiated to deploy the system. Figure 2 shows the partial installation specification written by a user for OpenMRS. It consists of three resource instances: an instance `server` for a machine running Mac OSX version 10.6, an instance `tomcat` of Tomcat running inside `server`, and an instance `openmrs` for the OpenMRS application running inside `tomcat`. In particular, the user does not have to explicitly give the other dependencies on Java and MySQL. The partial installation specification may also define values for individual configuration port properties. In our example, the `hostname` and `os_user_name` properties have been assigned values. Unassigned configuration properties will take the default values defined in the associated resource types.

The configuration engine takes this partial installation specification and expands out all the dependencies to generate a set of Boolean constraints such that the Boolean constraints are satisfiable iff there is a full installation specification which includes all of the resource instances mentioned in the partial installation specification. The atomic propositions in the Boolean constraints consist of instances of resources: the proposition is true in a satisfying assignment iff the corresponding resource instance must be deployed. For the partial installation specification of Figure 2, the configuration engine generates the following constraints:

$\texttt{server} \wedge$	from install spec
$\texttt{tomcat} \wedge$	from install spec
$\texttt{openmrs} \wedge$	from install spec
$\texttt{openmrs} \rightarrow \boxtimes\{\texttt{jdk}, \texttt{jre}\} \wedge$	env dep
$\texttt{tomcat} \rightarrow \boxtimes\{\texttt{jdk}, \texttt{jre}\} \wedge$	env dep
$\texttt{openmrs} \rightarrow \texttt{mysql} \wedge$	peer dep
$\texttt{tomcat} \rightarrow \texttt{server} \wedge$	inside dep
$\texttt{openmrs} \rightarrow \texttt{tomcat} \wedge$	inside dep
$\texttt{mysql} \rightarrow \texttt{server} \wedge$	inside dep
$\texttt{jdk} \rightarrow \texttt{server} \wedge$	inside dep
$\texttt{jre} \rightarrow \texttt{server}$	inside dep

where $\boxtimes S$ is the "exactly one" predicate that asserts that exactly one proposition from the set S is true. The first three constraints arise from the partial installation specification (each instance there must be deployed). The next three arise out of environment (and peer, for the last one) dependencies, and state that the deployment of the l.h.s. implies the deployment of the r.h.s. The final five arise out of inside dependencies. Note that the peer dependency of OpenMRS on MySQL could be resolved by "creating" a new machine instance and installing MySQL on that machine. However, our constraint generation process assumes that no new machines should be created. Thus, unless explicitly specified, a peer dependency is deployed at the same machine as the machine of its dependent.

The constraints are satisfied, e.g., by setting `server`, `jdk`, `tomcat`, `mysql`, and `openmrs` to true, and `jre` to false. This corresponds to a deployment where a Java development kit, a Tomcat server, a MySQL database instance, and the OpenMRS application are all installed on a server running Mac OSX 10.6. Given this solution, we can also "tie together" the input and output ports by traversing the resource instances in topological order of dependencies, starting with the output ports of `server`, and using the definitions of output ports of preceding resource instances to get values of input ports according to the port mappings specified in the dependencies. Valuations to the input ports then determine the configuration and output ports of the instance. In this way, we can propagate configuration options along the application stack. The result of this process is a *full installation specification*, that details the components that must be installed, their configuration parameters, and the order of their installation. The last is obtained via the partial order imposed by the dependencies of the resource instances.

Finally, the Engage deployment system takes an install specification and deploys the components in the order of dependencies. The deployment system uses the corresponding driver for each resource instance. A resource driver is a state machine with special states *uninstalled*, *active*, and *inactive* (the latter two possibly the same state), with guarded actions between states. Figure 3 shows an example resource driver for Tomcat. An action (e.g., `install`) is implemented in an underlying programming language and performs some modification of the system state. For example, the `install` action can call an OS-level package manager to download and install a package. A guard describes a precondition for the action, and is omitted if an action can be performed at any time. A guard of the form $\uparrow s$ (respectively, $\downarrow s$) states that an action can be performed only when the state machines of all upstream (respectively, downstream) dependencies are in state $s \in \{uninstalled, active, inactive\}$. The actions on the state machines are performed by the Engage runtime system. The runtime system manages the state machines of all installed components and can check the status of guards. The runtime system can also monitor a deployment and shut it down (by shutting down services in the reverse order of dependencies).

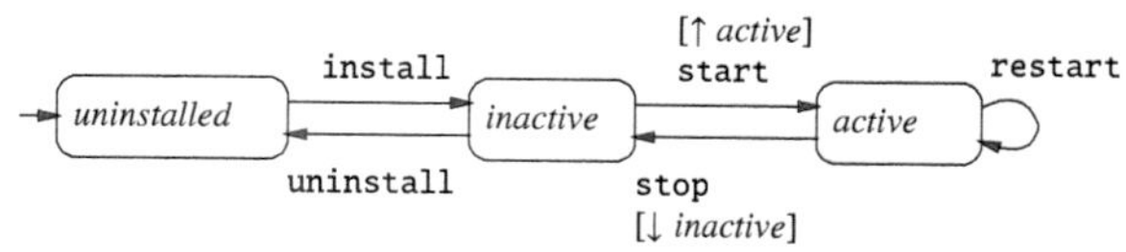

Figure 3: Resource driver for Tomcat

Engage ameliorates the problems of manual deployment in the following ways. First, dependencies among resource types ensure that required packages are installed when a resource instance is being installed (e.g., `Java` has already been installed before installing `Tomcat`). Second, the resource drivers and the runtime ensure that required services are already started when starting an application (e.g., `Tomcat` and `MySQL` daemons are already started when `OpenMRS` is started: their resource drivers are both in *active* when starting `OpenMRS`). While there is work involved in developing resource types and drivers, they are done once by the package developer, and any subsequent installation scenario involving the resource is completely automated. In contrast to ad hoc custom scripts, the declarative language enables static detection of configuration problems, e.g., cyclic dependencies between components, or unsolvable constraints in installation. In contrast to configuration management systems, the configuration engine significantly reduces user input: in our implementation, the (unsimplified) `OpenMRS` partial installation specification took 22 lines, and the full installation specification was 204 lines. Note that resource descriptions are reusable and can be used in different installations; e.g, the `MySQL` resource can be used in any deployment that requires a MySQL database.

3. Resource Types

In Engage, the fundamental abstraction for software and hardware components is a *resource*. A resource consists of a description of the metadata required to configure, install, or upgrade a component (its *resource type*) and a *driver* consisting of code that reads the metadata and manages the lifecycle of the component (installation, upgrade, rollback, etc.). We explain resource types here, and explain drivers in Section 5.

3.1 Resource Types

A *resource type* is an abstraction to model how a component may be instantiated. A *resource instance* is an instantiation of a resource type that describes how a specific resource will be (or has been) configured and installed. In analogy with object-oriented programming, a resource type is a class and a resource instance is an object of that class. Each resource type has a unique identifier (usually, name of the component and its version) in a global name space. In addition, a resource type has ports and dependency constraints.

Ports Configuration data for a component are described in *ports*. A port has a *name* and a *type*. We assume an (unspecified) set of base types. For a port p, we write p.name and p.type to refer to the name and the type, respectively. Communication of configuration data between components is performed by connecting appropriate ports of two components.

Dependencies Dependencies between resource types specify ordering constraints between components, and determine how ports of a resource get their values. Engage specifies three types of dependencies.

An *inside dependency* specifies that an instance of a resource type can exist only inside an instance of another resource type; e.g., Tomcat can exist only "inside" a Server. Each resource type has either zero inside dependencies, in which case it must represent a physical machine, or exactly one inside dependency. Inside dependencies can be nested: e.g., a servlet can be inside Tomcat, which in turn is inside a server. For any resource type, one can walk the inside dependencies to eventually reach a physical machine, and this is the machine on which the component gets installed and run.

A resource type R_1 has an *environment dependency* on a resource type R_2 if it depends on a resource of type R_2 to be installed in an enclosing resource. As an example, Tomcat requires that the Java runtime environment be installed on the machine it is installed on. (However, Tomcat is not installed "inside" Java.)

A resource type R_1 has a *peer dependency* on a resource type R_2 if it calls services provided by an instance of R_2. In this case, unlike environment constraints, an instance of R_2 need not be installed on the same machine as the instance of R_1. For example, OpenMRS has a peer dependency on MySQL, and OpenMRS can make calls to the database over TCP/IP.

Formal Model Formally, a resource type

$$R = \langle \mathsf{key}, \mathsf{InP}, \mathsf{ConfP}, \mathsf{OutP}, \mathsf{Inside}, \mathsf{Env}, \mathsf{Peer} \rangle$$

consists of a (globally unique) *key* key (usually consisting of a name and a version), three disjoint sets of *input ports* InP, *configuration ports* ConfP, and *output ports* OutP, an optional *inside dependency* Inside or `null`, a set of *environment dependencies* Env, and a set of *peer dependencies* Peer. We assume each port $p \in$ ConfP is either a *default* constant or defined as a function of the ports in InP, and each port $p \in$ OutP is either a default constant or defined as a function of the ports in InP $\cup$ ConfP. For a key key, we write $[\![\mathsf{key}]\!]$ to denote the (unique) resource type for that key. For a resource type R, we write R.key, R.InP, etc. to denote the components of the resource type.

The input ports are used to receive data from other resources. The output ports are used to affect the behavior of other resources by providing configuration data. The configuration ports are used to store resource-specific metadata used in configuration and installation. A configuration port of a resource can read from an input port of the same resource, and an output port of a resource can read from an input or config port of the resource.

Each dependency (inside, environment, or peer) is a pair $(\mathsf{key}', \mathsf{pmap})$, where key′ is a key to a resource and pmap is a partial mapping from $[\![\mathsf{key}']\!]$.OutP to R.InP.

Inside, environment, and peer dependencies induce ordering relations on resource types. Let R and R' be resource types. We write $R \preceq_i R'$ (the *inside* ordering) if $R.\mathsf{Inside} = (R'.\mathsf{key}, \cdot)$. We write $R \preceq_e R'$ (the *environment* ordering) if $(R'.\mathsf{key}, \cdot) \in R.\mathsf{Env}$. We write $R \preceq_p R'$ (the *peer* ordering) if $(R'.\mathsf{key}, \cdot) \in R.\mathsf{Peer}$.

A *machine* is a resource whose inside dependency is `null`.

Well-formedness A finite set of resource types is called *well-formed* if the following conditions hold:

1. Each key appearing in an inside, environment, or peer dependency is mapped to a resource type in the set (no pending dependencies).
2. If a resource does not have an *inside* dependency, it does not have any input ports. Such resources usually correspond to physical machines.
3. Each input port is mapped exactly once in the port mappings of the inside, environment, and peer dependencies. Each output port is assigned a value. That is, the range of port mappings in two dependencies is disjoint, and the union of ranges is the set of all input ports.
4. The ordering $\preceq_i \cup \preceq_e \cup \preceq_p$ on resource types is acyclic.

For any resource type R in a well-formed set of resource types, one can follow inside constraints to a machine. This represents the physical context in which an instance of R will be installed.

3.2 Abstract Resources and Subtyping

We extend the core language with inheritance and abstract resource types. A resource type can be marked *abstract* or *concrete*. An abstract resource type cannot be instantiated, but can be used for inheritance. For example, in Section 2, we defined an abstract resource type `Server` for a server, and subclasses for Mac OSX and Windows servers. The generic `Server` cannot be instantiated, but its subclasses specifying the OS can be instantiated. Instances of concrete resource types can be deployed. By default, we assume resource types are concrete and omit the concrete qualifier.

Sub-resource types extend base resource type definitions by adding ports and dependencies. Fields from a super-resource type are implicitly replicated in the sub-resource type, or overridden as explained below.

Figure 4 presents the subtyping rules to ensure well-formedness of the sub-resource tree. The rules define subtyping relations $\leq_{in}$, $\leq_{conf}$, and $\leq_{out}$ for input, config, and output ports, respectively, their extensions to sets of ports and port mappings, and a $\leq_{RT}$ relation that checks for subtyping between resource types by checking subtyping of the corresponding resource types of their inside, environment, and peer dependencies. We assume an (unspecified) subtyping relation $\leq$ on the base types over which ports are defined. Note that the subtyping relation on base types go on opposite directions for input ports and for config and output ports. This is related to the usual co-variance and contra-variance of method arguments. Sub-resource types extend base resource types by defining more input, config, and output ports, subtyping the inside dependency, and adding additional environment and peer dependencies.

3.3 Resource Instances

A *resource instance* is created from a resource type by assigning concrete values to its configuration ports and by replacing dependency constraints with directional links to other resource instances. In addition to the components of a resource type, each resource instance has a globally unique *resource identifier* that uniquely identifies the resource instance. The identifier helps distinguish two instances of the same resource type in a deployment, e.g., two servers both running Mac OSX 10.6.

Deployment information for an application can be provided by giving a set of resource instances obtained from corresponding resource types, such that for every instance in the set, each dependency is instantiated with a concrete link to another resource instance, and the values in the output ports and mapped input ports for the resource instances match. Such a document is referred to as an *installation specification*.

Input ports
$$\frac{p'.\mathsf{name} = p.\mathsf{name} \qquad p'.\mathsf{type} \le p.\mathsf{type}}{p' \le_{in} p}$$

Config ports
$$\frac{p'.\mathsf{name} = p.\mathsf{name} \qquad p'.\mathsf{type} \ge p.\mathsf{type}}{p' \le_{conf} p}$$

Output ports
$$\frac{p'.\mathsf{name} = p.\mathsf{name} \qquad p'.\mathsf{type} \ge p.\mathsf{type}}{p' \le_{out} p}$$

Sets of input ports
$$\frac{\forall p \in P \cdot \exists p' \in P' \cdot p' \le_{in} p}{P' \le_{IN} P}$$

Sets of config ports
$$\frac{\forall p \in P \cdot \exists p' \in P' \cdot p' \le_{out} p}{P' \le_{CONF} P}$$

Sets of output ports
$$\frac{\forall p \in P \cdot \exists p' \in P' \cdot p' \le_{out} p}{P' \le_{OUT} P}$$

Port mappings
$$\frac{\forall (p,q) \in m \cdot \exists (p',q') \in m' \cdot (p' \le_{out} p \wedge q' \le_{in} q)}{m' \le_{pm} m}$$

Refl
$$\frac{}{R \le_{RT} R}$$

Trans
$$\frac{R \le_{RT} R' \qquad R' \le_{RT} R''}{R \le_{RT} R''}$$

Resource types
$$\frac{\begin{array}{c} R'.\mathsf{InP} \le_{IN} R.\mathsf{InP} \quad R'.\mathsf{ConfP} \le_{CONF} R.\mathsf{ConfP} \quad R'.\mathsf{OutP} \le_{OUT} R.\mathsf{OutP} \\ ([\![R'.\mathsf{Inside.key'}]\!] \le_{RT} [\![R.\mathsf{Inside.key'}]\!] \vee [\![R'.\mathsf{Inside.key'}]\!] = [\![R.\mathsf{Inside.key'}]\!] = \mathsf{null}) \wedge (R'.\mathsf{Inside.pmap} \le_{pm} R.\mathsf{Inside.pmap}) \\ \forall (I,m) \in R.\mathsf{Env} \cdot \exists (I',m') \in R'.\mathsf{Env} \cdot ([\![I']\!] \le_{RT} [\![I]\!] \wedge m' \le_{pm} m) \qquad \forall (X,m) \in R.\mathsf{Peer} \cdot \exists (X',m') \in R'.\mathsf{Peer} \cdot ([\![X']\!] \le_{RT} [\![X]\!] \wedge m' \le_{pm} m) \end{array}}{R' \le_{RT} R}$$

Figure 4: The rules for subtyping between two resource types.

3.4 Syntactic Sugar and Extensions

For brevity, we introduce some syntactic sugar in the language and in our examples. We allow a port to be a structure with named fields. We allow disjunctions in the descriptions of inside dependencies, and positive Boolean combinations of resource types in environment and peer dependencies. For example, we can express that a resource type R (e.g., Tomcat) is inside either resource type R_1 (e.g., Mac-OSX 10.6) or resource type R_2 (e.g., Windows 7), and a resource type R (e.g., OpenMRS) has an environment dependency on resource type R_1 (e.g., Java) as well as one of R_2 (e.g., MySQL) or R_3 (e.g., Postgres). The use of disjunctions is a convenient shorthand, and can be simulated by defining the appropriate super-resource types and their sub-resource types. To simplify the check for well-formedness, we require the ranges of two port mappings that are disjunctively combined to be identical.

To model a common idiom in which a resource depends on one of a number of versions of a different one (e.g., OpenMRS depends on versions of Tomcat before version 6.0.29), we add syntactic sugar to allow specifying ranges of versions for the same package, which are internally expanded to disjunctions of the different versions satisfying the range.

The implementation of Engage also has some extensions that we do not model here. Each port of a resource type in our implementation has a *static* or *dynamic* binding. A static port is assigned a value at the instantiation time of a resource of that type. For example, these can be default values. A dynamic port is assigned a value at the installation time of a resource. By default, we assume all ports are dynamic (and we omit mentioning the binding explicitly). Only configuration and output ports can have the static binding. A static configuration port must be a constant. A static output port is either a constant or a function of static configuration ports. Inside, environment, and peer dependencies are extended with two port maps: in a dependency of resource R on R', one port map maps output ports of R' to the inputs of R (as before), and the other maps static output ports of R to input ports of R'. Static ports are useful to flow configuration parameters in the "reverse direction" of dependencies. For example, when installing OpenMRS, we need to pass a server configuration file back to Tomcat. In our implementation, we use static ports to achieve this. However, by the nature of static ports, all configuration values flowing in the reverse direction can be resolved statically, and these configurations will be known when installing R' even though R has not been installed yet.

4. Configuration

In practice, writing the entire set of resource instances in an installation specification can be tedious. Instead, Engage allows the user to specify a *partial* installation specification. A partial installation specification is a set of partial resource instances, that is, a set of resource instances for which only a subset of dependencies are instantiated by concrete resource instances. For example, Figure 2 shows a partial installation specification with instance `server` obtained from a resource of type Mac OSX 10.6, a resource instance `tomcat` for a resource of type Tomcat 6.0.18, and a resource instance `openmrs` for OpenMRS 1.8. An installation specification *extends* a partial installation specification if each resource instance in the partial specification is also present in the installation specification. Engage automatically generates a *full* installation specification extending the partial specification, by using the dependency relations in the resource types and automated constraint solving.

The configuration engine takes as input a collection of resource types and a partial install specification (a collection of partial resource instances) and produces as output a set of complete resource instances (called the (full) *installation specification*) such that: (1) for every resource instance, and for every inside, environment, or peer dependency of its corresponding resource type, there exists a resource instance that satisfies the inside, environment, or peer dependency, respectively, and (2) each input port of a resource instance is mapped to exactly one output port of a different resource instance.

Given a partial instantiation specification, $\mathcal{I}$, the configuration engine computes a set of Boolean constraints using the following two steps. In the following, we assume that there is a fixed, well-formed set of resource types, $\mathcal{R}$, in the system and that every resource instance in the partial install specification is an instantiation of some resource type from this set.

Hypergraph Generation The hypergraph generation phase takes a partial install specification and constructs a directed *resource instance graph* whose nodes are resource instances, and whose hyperedges represent dependencies between resource instances. Without loss of generality, we assume that for each resource instance, the inside dependency is either `null` or a disjunction of resources, and the environment and peer dependencies are a set of disjunctions of resources.

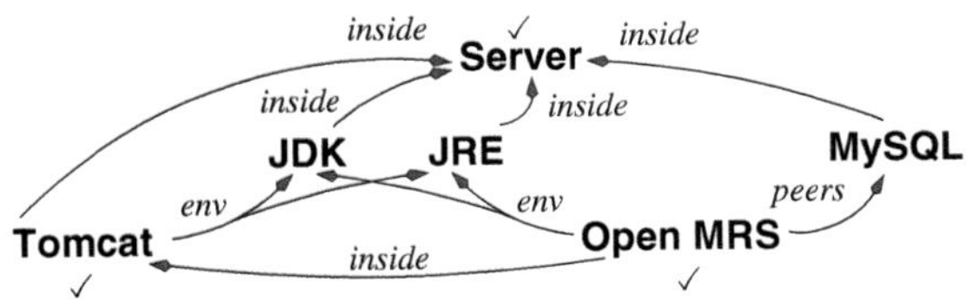

Figure 5: Hypergraph for partial installation specification in Figure 2

If a resource type has a dependency on an abstract resource r, we replace the dependency to r with a disjunction of concrete resources in the following way. We traverse the subtypes of r in the subclassing tree for r, starting at r and stopping whenever we see a concrete subtype of r. In this way, we get a "frontier" F of subtypes of r of concrete resources. We replace the dependency on r by a disjunction of the concrete resources in F. For example, if there is a dependency on the abstract resource `Java` (see Figure 1), it is replaced by the disjunction of the concrete resources `JDK 1.6` and `JRE 1.6`. After this transformation, there are no dependencies on abstract resources. (If such a frontier cannot be found, that is, if there is an abstract resource at the leaf of the subclassing tree rooted at r, we stop with an error.)

The hypergraph generation algorithm, $\mathsf{GraphGen}(\mathcal{R}, \mathcal{I})$, is a worklist-based algorithm to process instances. It proceeds as follows.

First, for every resource instance in the partial install specification, we create a node in the hypergraph and add it to the worklist. Recall that in addition to the key of the resource, each resource instance is globally uniquely identified by an additional identifier.

Second, we iteratively process partial resource instances from the worklist until the worklist is empty. Suppose we are processing resource instance r of resource R. We go through the dependencies of r.

We assume that the partial installation specification resolves inside dependencies of each resource instance in it by providing a resource instance on which r is inside-dependent (that is, the system does not generate new machines automatically). Given r, we check that there is an existing resource instance which matches the inside dependency. For each inside dependency, we create a directed edge labeled "*inside*" from the node in the graph that represents r to the node that represents its container.

Now consider environment dependencies of r. By assumption, the environment dependencies are a set of disjunctions. For each dependency in the set, we create a hyperedge with source r, and targets as follows. Suppose the dependency is a disjunction of resource keys $k_1, \ldots, k_n$, and consider the processing of key k_1. If we can already find a node r_1 in the graph with key k'_1 such that $[\![k'_1]\!] \leq_{RT} [\![k_1]\!]$ and such that r_1 is inside the same machine as r, we add the node r_1 as a target of the hyperedge. If there is no such node, we instantiate a new resource instance r_{new} with key k_1, inside the same machine as the machine of r, add the node for r_{new} to the graph as well as the worklist. (We add r_{new} to the worklist to ensure its dependencies are processed in the future.) At the end of this process, we construct a hyperedge with source r and n targets, one for each disjunct in the dependency, and label it "environment".

For peer dependencies of r, we proceed similarly. The only difference is that we look for a matching resource that is a subtype of the key, but need not be on the same machine. If we find such a node in the graph, we add it as the target of the hyperedge. If we do not find a matching resource, we add a new instance, but conservatively assume that the new instance resides in the same machine as r.

Figure 5 shows the dependencies generated when processing the partial instantiation specification of Figure 2. We have marked the resource instances that were present in the specification with a "✓".

LEMMA 1. *Let $\mathcal{R}$ be a set of well-formed resource types and $\mathcal{I}$ a partial install specification. Then procedure* $\mathsf{GraphGen}(\mathcal{R}, \mathcal{I})$ *creates a directed hypergraph $G = (V, E)$, such that: (i) for each resource instance $r \in \mathcal{I}$, we have $r \in V$, and for each resource instance $r \in V$, either $r \in \mathcal{I}$ or there is some resource instance $r' \in \mathcal{I}$ that is transitively dependent on the key of r; (ii) for each resource instance $r \in V$, if r.*Inside *is not* `null`, *then there is a resource instance $r' \in \mathcal{I}$ such that there is an inside edge from r to r'; (iii) for each resource key k such that there is an environment dependency from k to r, there is an hyperedge with source r containing a target resource instance with key k such that this resource instance is on the same machine as r; (iv) for each resource key k such that there is a peer dependency from k to r, there is an hyperedge with source r containing a target resource instance with key k.*

Intuitively, this lemma states that the generated graph correctly encodes the dependencies of all resource instances in $\mathcal{I}$.

Constraint Generation Given the directed hypergraph $\mathsf{GraphGen}(\mathcal{R}, \mathcal{I})$, we generate Boolean constraints as follows. An atomic proposition is of the form $\mathsf{rsrc}(id)$, where id is a resource instance identifier; it states that the resource instance with identifier id is installed in the machine obtained by following its inside dependencies.

We generate two kinds of constraints from the graph.

First, for each vertex in the constraint graph that represents a resource instance specified in the partial install specification, we add the constraint $\mathsf{rsrc}(m, id)$. This constraint ensures that each resource instance mentioned in the partial install specification is indeed instantiated in the deployment.

Second, we generate *dependency constraints* for each node v as follows. For each hyperedge e with source v and targets $\{v_1, \ldots, v_n\}$, we generate a constraint

$$\mathsf{rsrc}(v) \rightarrow \boxtimes\{\mathsf{rsrc}(v_1), \ldots, \mathsf{rsrc}(v_n)\} \tag{1}$$

where $\boxtimes S$ is the Boolean predicate that is true iff exactly one proposition from S is true. Formally,

$$\boxtimes S \equiv (\bigvee_{p \in S} p_i) \wedge \bigwedge_{p \in S} (p \rightarrow \bigwedge_{q \in S, q \neq p} \neg q)$$

We denote the conjunction of the set of all above predicates for a set of well-formed resource types $\mathcal{R}$ and a partial install specification $\mathcal{I}$ as $\mathsf{Generate}(\mathcal{R}, \mathcal{I})$.

THEOREM 1. *Let $\mathcal{R}$ be a set of well-formed resource types and $\mathcal{I}$ a partial install specification. There exists a full installation specification extending the partial install specification iff the formula* $\mathsf{Generate}(\mathcal{R}, \mathcal{I})$ *is satisfiable.*

A satisfying assignment to the Boolean constraints determines a full installation specification extending the partial installation specification. We can compute the values of all input, configuration, and output ports of all resource instances by a linear pass in topological order of dependencies, filling in the input ports of each resource instance based on the already-computed values of output ports.

5. Deployment

Engage's *deployment engine* takes a full installation specification and automatically deploys the application. It provides runtime support for provisioning servers, co-ordinating installations, as well as generic monitoring, shutdown, and upgrade services for applications. The deployment engine uses *drivers* for each resource to co-ordinate its actions.

5.1 Resource Drivers

In addition to a type, a resource specifies a *driver* that implements a state machine for the lifecycle management of the instances of that type. A driver state machine consists of a set of *states* and a set of *transitions* between them. Each state machine has three special states, *uninstalled*, *inactive*, and *active*, called the *basic states*. Initially, a state machine resides in its *uninstalled*.

Each transition has a *guard* and an *action*. The guard of each action is either *true* or a conjunctive condition about the basic states of all the resource instances that the driver's associated resource instance depends on (i.e., the upstream resource instances) or the resource instances that depend on the driver's resource instance (i.e., the downstream resource instances). Basic state predicates are of the form $\uparrow s$ or $\downarrow s$, where $s \in \{uninstalled, inactive, active\}$. A basic state predicate $\uparrow s$ (respectively, $\downarrow s$) is true if the state machines for all upstream (respectively, downstream) resource instances are in state s. Each guarded action is implemented in an underlying programming language (Python in our implementation).

A resource instance starts its life in its initial state, *uninstalled*, and proceeds through various states in the state machine depending on transitions invoked by the deployment engine. If the guard of a transition is *true*, then the action can be performed at any time. Otherwise, the transition blocks until the guard becomes true, at which point the action is executed and the state is updated.

Formally, the driver for a resource type R is a state machine $(Q, uninstalled, inactive, active, \mathcal{A}, \delta)$ consisting of a set of *states* Q with $\{uninstalled, inactive, active\} \subseteq Q$, a set of *actions* $\mathcal{A}$, and a (partial) transition function $\delta : Q \times (BasicStatesPred \times \mathcal{A}) \rightharpoonup Q$, where *BasicStatesPred* is a conjunction of basic state predicates.

Figure 3 shows the state machine for the Tomcat server. The server starts in the initial *uninstalled* state. The action `install` takes it to the *inactive* state. From the *inactive* state, the action `start` takes it to the *active*, and has the precondition that all upstream dependencies are active. From the *active* state, the `stop` action takes it back to the *inactive* state and has the precondition that all downstream dependencies are inactive. In the *active* state, the server can be restarted. Each guarded action carries out system changes and commands required to install, start, or stop the server, as well as additional book-keeping.

5.2 Runtime Services

Provisioning The starting point of a deployment is the set of physical or virtual servers on which the application software will be installed. Engage provides a set of runtime tools to determine properties of servers, such as hostname, IP address, operating system, CPU architecture, etc. These tools automatically create a resource instance for the server, and in practice, are used to start writing a new partial installation specification when the servers are known. In addition, Engage provides integration with cloud servers through the *libcloud* APIs [3]. If a machine resource instance in the partial installation specification does not include configuration details, and Engage is being run in a cloud environment, a new virtual server is provisioned to perform the role of that machine in the deployment. In this case, the additional host configuration details (obtained from the cloud infrastructure) are added to the installation specification before passing it to the configuration engine. Engage currently integrates with Rackspace cloud services and Amazon AWS.

Installation, Monitoring, and Shutdown Given a full installation specification, the deployment engine executes commands on the resource drivers for each resource instance in the specification such that every driver state machine is in its active state. At this point, the system is defined to be deployed.

The deployment engine orders resource instances according to dependencies. Since the dependency ordering is acyclic, this is always possible. In the beginning, the resource driver for each resource instance is in its initial state. The deployment engine executes driver transitions to bring each driver to its active state. The process can be performed in parallel, as long as the dependency ordering is met, and the precondition for each transition is satisfied. Since the deployment engine tracks the states of each resource instance, it can co-ordinate the calls.

In the multi-host case, we must coordinate the install across multiple hosts. The implementation of a multi-host install can be simplified if one can partially order the machines such that for every two machines m_1 and m_2, m_1 is before m_2 if there is some resource instance to be installed in m_2 that depends on some resource instance in m_1 but no resource instance to be installed in m_2 depends on some instance in m_1. We have found this assumption to be valid for all the systems that we have modeled thus far, and our implementation makes this simplifying assumption. In this case, we can break the overall install specification into per-node specifications and run a slave instance of Engage on each target host. The entire deployment is then coordinated from a master host, with each slave running with no awareness of the others. Slave deployments can run in parallel when the slaves have no inter-dependencies.

The runtime includes a plugin framework for the automatic integration with monitoring and management tools. For example, Engage integrates with *monit* [4], a process monitoring/restart service. The runtime system adds an instance of monit to the installation specification for each target host, ensuring that monit itself will be installed. After the deployment completes, the resource type is used by the plugin to generate a monit configuration file registered with monit. Users can view the status and resource usage of each installed service. If the process associated with a service fails, it will be automatically restarted by monit using a set of runtime services provided by Engage.

Shutting down an application goes in the reverse dependency order, and applies transitions of each resource driver to bring each state machine to an inactive state. Again, the runtime co-ordinates this activity since it knows the dependencies and tracks the states of the resource drivers.

Upgrades Initial deployment of an application stack is only one part of its lifecycle. Changes after initial deployment may incude bug fixes, enhancements, infrastructure updates, security patches, and updates to Engage itself. Given that Engage has a full description of the deployed system, multiple upgrade strategies are possible.

Currently, we require that the user (or a utility program, as in the case of Django) provide a *partial install specification* describing the desired new state of the system. This is used to compute a full install specification for the deployed system. The current system is then backed up, and any components that will be removed or that cannot be upgraded in-place are uninstalled. The new system is now deployed, per the install specification, upgrading and adding components as needed. If the upgrade fails, the partially installed components are uninstalled and the old version restored from the backup. This upgrade approach is relatively easy to implement, supports rollback in the case of errors, and can handle changes to any layer of the stack, including Engage. However, all upgrades using this approach experience the worst case upgrade time, even if there are only minor differences between the old and new configurations. We leave optimizations of the upgrade framework as future work, possibly extending [11].

App name	Description	Source	Comments
Areneae	Simple test app	Beta tester	Deployed by a third party
Buzzfire	Twitter bookmark and ranking app	Open source	Uses Redis key-value store
Codespeed	Web application performance monitor	Open source	
Django-Blog	Blogging platform	Beta tester	Deployed by a third party; Installs 18 Python package dependencies
Django-CMS	Content Management System	Open source	
FA	Manage faculty, student, and postdoc applications	Beta tester	Application used in production
Feature Collector	Gather software feature requests	Developed internally	
WebApp	Run production web site for Django hosting company	Developed internally	Application used in production

Table 1: Django applications. "Beta testers" are independent application developers who used the service.

6. Evaluation

We have implemented the Engage system and we have used it in active deployment in providing platform-as-a-service support for Django applications. The front-end for the declarative framework and the configuration engine are written in about 6K lines of Ocaml. We use the the MiniSat satisfiability solver to solve Boolean constraints. The runtime system (provisioning and deployment engine) and resource drivers are written in about 26K lines of Python. In addition, we have about 5K lines of resource types in our resource library. We allow deployments to be performed either on a given set of servers or on dynamically provisioned servers from Rackspace or Amazon Web Services (AWS). The entire system, including the resource types, is open source and (for Django applications) available through a web service.

We have installed several open source applications, including OpenMRS (described in Section 2). In the following, we give two case studies that we have performed using the system. The first (JasperReports) was used as a case study to compare times for a manual install versus the time needed to automate an installation by developing the required resource types and drivers in Engage. The second (Django applications) describes our experience hosting third party applications on the cloud.

6.1 JasperReports

The Jasper Reports Server [5] provides a web user interface and web service APIs for generating, viewing, and managing reports. It runs in a servlet container (e.g., Apache Tomcat) and requires a database (e.g., MySQL). The installation guide is 77 pages long, with 8 pages dedicated to the specific approach we used for installing Jasper.

We compared the time for installing Jasper manually with the time to automate the installation of Jasper in Engage. The manual installations were performed by one of the authors, who had not attempted to install Jasper previously. It took him 5 hours the first time, 2 hours 15 minutes the second time, and converged to around 1 hour in subsequent tries. Much of the learning curve was due to imprecise instructions that led to incorrect actions (followed by debugging sessions and rolling back), environment issues, and locating/downloading the required prerequisite software.

Engage already included resources for Tomcat and MySQL. To automate Jasper installation, we created two new resources: one for Jasper Reports Server itself and one for a MySQL JDBC connector required as a dependency for Jasper. Specifying the resource type for the JDBC connector required 40 lines. No additional Python code was required for the driver as we were able to reuse existing generic driver code for downloading and extracting archives. The resource for Jasper was 69 lines of types and 201 lines of Python code (including comments).

The automated installation of Jasper Reports Server via Engage performs environment checks (e.g., required TCP/IP ports are available), downloads required application packages, installs the components in dependency order, and starts the database, web server, and reports server. After installation, the reports server can be managed (start, stop, status check) via Engage, or automatically integrated with 3rd party management tools.

The development time for Engage support of Jasper Reports Server was 3 hours 56 minutes. This time was broken down into 47 minutes for resource type design, 81 minutes for driver development, and 108 minutes for debugging and testing.

Running the automated install of Jasper Reports Server takes 17 minutes if the required software packages are downloaded from the internet and 5 minutes if they are obtained from a local file cache. The automation of the Jasper install via Engage ensures a repeatable process, supports both local and cloud-based targets, and can be used as a part of a larger deployment (e.g., where the reports server can be used as a service to a web application). The partial installation specification for Jasper is 26 lines long. The full installation specification generated by the configuration engine is 434 lines long.

6.2 Django Applications

We implemented resources and drivers for installation and management of applications developed in Django [6], a web application framework written in Python. A goal of our Django support was to enable Django developers to deploy their existing applications on different environments (local test environments and production environments on the cloud) with little changes and no need to understand the internals of Engage. To achieve this, we built an *application packager* that validates a Django application, extracts some metadata used by Engage, and packages the application into an archive with a pre-defined layout. This application can then be deployed by Engage to the cloud or a local machine. We provide pre-defined partial installation specifications for the same application to be deployed in different configurations (e.g., debug or production, local or cloud), supporting the migration of changes through the full development lifecycle: from development to QA to staging to production.

Django support involves 37 resources, of which 14 are specific to Django applications. Engage allows the following (independent) configuration choices for Django applications:

- **OS**: MacOSX (two versions) or Ubuntu Linux (two versions)
- **Web server**: Gunicorn or Apache HTTP server
- **Database**: SQLite or MySQL
- **Optional components**: RabbitMQ/Celery (message queuing), Redis (key-value store), and memcached (caching)
- **Optional monitoring**: Monit

Thus, we currently support 256 distinct deployment configurations on a single node. Furthermore, many topologies of these components are permitted by the Engage architecture: everything deployed to the same node, a separate node for each component, multiple application nodes, etc. Finally, our Django driver supports the declarative enumeration of Python packages available from the Python package index (http://pypi.python.org) to be installed as a prerequisite to the Django application.

Evaluating installs We have evaluated Engage's Django support by testing it with Django applications developed by us, obtained as open source applications, and provided by third party beta testers. Table 1 summarizes eight of the applications we deployed. All eight applications were deployable by Engage without requiring any application-specific deployment code. Areneae and Django-Blog are particularly interesting, as they were developed and deployed by beta customers (who had no prior contact with the paper authors), using only our documentation and a few email exchanges. WebApp is the production infrastructure that runs a commercial PaaS (Platform as a Service) site. It is about 4K lines of code, and uses asynchronous messaging, cron jobs, and caching. The partial installation specification for the production site is 61 lines long and has seven resources. The full installation specification generated by the Engage configuration engine from this spec is 1,444 lines long and has 29 resources.

Evaluating upgrades To evaluate application upgrades, we took two snapshots of the FA application about four months apart. Both snapshots represented production versions of the application. Between the two snapshots, the user interface, application logic, and database schema all changed. We use South, a *database migration* framework, in the Engage Django driver to support application upgrades involving database schema changes. Using South, we were able to automatically upgrade from the old version to the new version of the application, while preserving the content in the database. If we introduce an error in the second application version that causes the upgrade to fail, Engage automatically rolls back to the prior application version.

7. Conclusion

We have presented Engage, a novel system for deployment of complex multi-component, distributed applications. Our contribution in this paper is twofold. First, we introduce a domain-specific language that provides the necessary syntax to impose a set of common structural dependencies between a set of inter-dependent resources succinctly and explicitly. Second, we present a tool suite that exploits the language: (i) to provide effective static checks to identify specification flaws and incompatibilities; (ii) to identify a full installation specification of a system from an input partial installation specification; (iii) to carry out an installation specification automatically; and (iv) to manage the life cycles of installed resources automatically.

References

[1] Puppet at Puppet Labs: http://www.puppetlabs.com/.

[2] Chef at Opscode: http://www.opscode.com/chef/.

[3] Apache Libcloud: http://libcloud.apache.org/.

[4] Monit: http://mmonit.com/monit/.

[5] JasperReports Server: http://www.jaspersoft.com/reporting-server/.

[6] Django: https://www.djangoproject.com/.

[7] J. Aldrich, C. Chambers, and D. Notkin. Architectural reasoning in ArchJava. In *ECOOP '02*, pages 334–367. Springer, 2002.

[8] P. Anderson and A. Scobie. LCFG: the next generation. In *UKUUG Winter Conference. UKUUG*, 2002.

[9] M. Burgess. A site configuration engine. *Computing Systems*, 8(2):309–337, 1995.

[10] A. Cicchetti, D. Di Ruscio, P. Pelliccione, A. Pierantonio, and S. Zacchirol. A model driven approach to upgrade package based software systems. In *Evaluation of Novel Approaches to Software Engineering*, pages 262–276. Springer, 2010.

[11] R. Di Cosmo, D. Di Ruscio, P. Pelliccione, A. Pierantonio, and S. Zacchiroli. Supporting software evolution in component-based FOSS systems. *Science of Computer Programming*, 2010.

[12] R. Di Cosmo and J. Vouillon. On software component co-installability. In *SIGSOFT FSE '11*, pages 256–266. ACM, 2011.

[13] R. Di Cosmo, P. Trezentos, and S. Zacchiroli. Package upgrades in FOSS distributions: Details and challenges. In *HotSWup '08*, 2008.

[14] M. Flatt and M. Felleisen. Units: Cool modules for HOT languages. In *PLDI '98*, pages 236–248. ACM, 1998.

[15] D. Gay, P. Levis, R. von Behren, M. Welsh, E. Brewer, and D. Culler. The nesC language: A holistic approach to networked embedded systems. In *PLDI '03*, pages 1–11. ACM, 2003.

[16] P. Goldsack, J. Guijarro, S. Loughran, A. Coles, A. Farrell, A. Lain, P. Murray, and P. Toft. The SmartFrog configuration management framework. *Operating Systems Review*, 43(1):16–25, 2009.

[17] F. Mancinelli, J. Boender, R. di Cosmo, J. Vouillon, B. Durak, X. Leroy, and R. Treinen. Managing the complexity of large free and open source package-based software distributions. In *ASE '06*, pages 199–208. IEEE Computer Society, 2006.

[18] P. Trezentos, I. Lynce, and A. L. Oliveira. Apt-pbo: solving the software dependency problem using pseudo-Boolean optimization. In *ASE '10*, pages 427–436. ACM, 2010.

[19] C. Tucker, D. Shuffelton, R. Jhala, and S. Lerner. OPIUM: Optimal package install/uninstall manager. In *ICSE '07*, pages 178–188. IEEE Computer Society, 2007.

[20] B.A. Wolfe, B.W. Mamlin, P.G. Biondich, H. Fraser, D. Jazayeri, C. Allen, J. Miranda, and W.M. Tierney. Cooking Up an Open Source EMR for Developing Countries: OpenMRS — A Recipe for Successful Collaboration. In *American Medical Informatics Association Annual Symposium*, pages 529 – 533. AMIA, 2006.

Type-Directed Completion of Partial Expressions

Daniel Perelman
University of Washington
perelman@cs.washington.edu

Sumit Gulwani Thomas Ball
Microsoft Research Redmond
{sumitg,tball}@microsoft.com

Dan Grossman
University of Washington
djg@cs.washington.edu

Abstract

Modern programming frameworks provide enormous libraries arranged in complex structures, so much so that a large part of modern programming is searching for APIs that "surely exist" somewhere in an unfamiliar part of the framework. We present a novel way of phrasing a search for an unknown API: the programmer simply writes an expression leaving holes for the parts they do not know. We call these expressions *partial expressions*. We present an efficient algorithm that produces likely completions ordered by a ranking scheme based primarily on the similarity of the types of the APIs suggested to the types of the known expressions. This gives a powerful language for both API discovery and code completion with a small impedance mismatch from writing code. In an automated experiment on mature C# projects, we show our algorithm can place the intended expression in the top 10 choices over 80% of the time.

Categories and Subject Descriptors D.2.6 [*Software Engineering*]: Programming Environments—Integrated Environments; D.2.13 [*Software Engineering*]: Reusable Software—Reuse Models; I.2.2 [*Artificial Intelligence*]: Automatic Programming—Program synthesis

General Terms Languages, Experimentation

Keywords program synthesis, partial expressions, code completion, type-based analysis, ranking

1. Introduction

Modern programming frameworks such as those found in Java and .NET consist of a huge number of classes organized into many namespaces. For example, the .NET Framework 4.0 has over 280,000 methods, 30,000 types, and 697 namespaces. Discovering the right method to achieve a particular task in this huge framework can feel like searching for a needle in a haystack. Programmers often perform searches through unfamiliar APIs using their IDE's code completion, for example Visual Studio's Intellisense, which requires the programmer to either provide a receiver or iterate through the possible receivers by brute force. Fundamentally, today's code completion tools still expect programmers to find the right method by name (something that implicitly assumes they will know the right name for the concept, which may not be true [4]) and to fill in all the arguments.

Our approach: We define a language of *partial expressions*, in which programmers can indicate in a superset of the language's concrete syntax that certain subexpressions need to be filled in or possibly reordered. We interpret a partial expression as a query that returns a ranked list of well-typed completions, where each completion is a synthesized small code snippet. This model is simple, general, and precisely specified, allowing for a variety of uses and extensions. We developed an efficient algorithm for generating completions of a partial expression. We also developed a ranking scheme primarily based on (sub)typing information to prefer more precise expressions (e.g., a method taking `AVerySpecificType` rather than `Object`).

Code-completion problems addressed: We have used our partial expression language and its implementation for finding completions to address three code-completion problems:

1. Given k arguments and without distinguishing one as the object-oriented receiver, predict a method call including these and possibly other arguments. Note that the name of the method being called is not given; the method name, along with the order of arguments to it, is the output of our system.
2. Given a method call with missing arguments, predict these arguments (with simple expressions such as variables or field and property[1] lookups of variables).
3. Given an incomplete binary expression such as an assignment statement, predict field and property lookups (i.e., given e predict $e.f$) on the left or right side of the operation.

Results: We demonstrate that our approach ranks the correct result highly most of the time and often outperforms or complements existing widely deployed technologies like Intellisense. To collect a large amount of empirical data, we have chosen to leave IDE integration and user studies to future work. Instead, we take existing codebases and run our tool after automatically replacing existing method calls, assignments, and comparisons with appropriate partial expressions. On our corpus of programs, results include:

- For over 80% of method calls (and over 90% if we know the call's return type), there are two or fewer arguments to the call such that with only those arguments, our system will rank the intended method name within the top 10.
- If a simple argument (e.g., a variable) is omitted from a method call, our system can fill it back in correctly (the top-ranked choice) 55% of the time.
- When a field or property lookup is omitted from an expression, we can use surrounding type context to rank the missing property in the top 10 over 90% of the time.

Overall, our work demonstrates that IDEs could use already-available type information to help programmers find methods they want and save keystrokes much more than they do today.

PLDI'12, June 11–16, 2012, Beijing, China.

[1] Properties are syntactic sugar for writing getters and setters like fields.

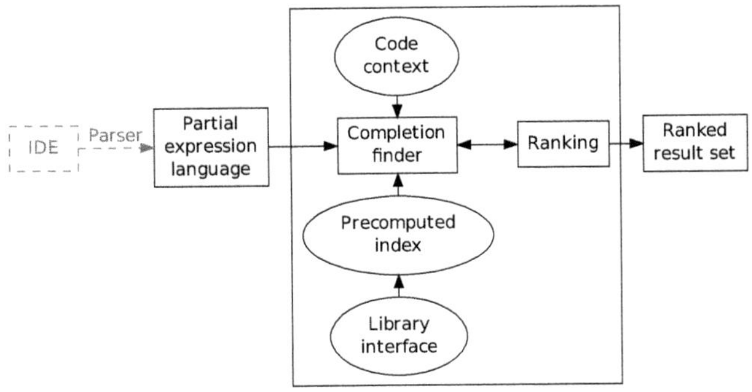

Figure 1. Workflow

Contributions This paper includes the following contributions:

- Identification of the need for a search facility based on partial expressions which we have detailed using illustrative examples in Section 2.
- Design of the partial expressions language and how partial expressions relate to complete expressions as formally defined in Section 3.
- An efficient algorithm for completing partial expressions and ranking the results described in Section 4, which integrates the ranking procedure and off-line indexing of large libraries.
- A large experimental evaluation of the quality and performance of our algorithm on real code presented in Section 5.
- An evaluation of the relative and absolute importance of each ranking feature detailed in Section 5.4.

Section 6 reviews related work and Section 7 concludes the paper.

2. Illustrative Examples

This section describes three examples that use partial expressions in our system and then considers performing the same tasks using prior work. Section 2.1 describes how our system handles these examples. Section 2.2 discusses normal code completion. Section 2.3 covers the closest related work, the Prospector tool[10].

2.1 Our system

Synthesizing Method Names

Suppose you are writing code using an image editing API (specifically, the Paint.NET image editor[2]) and want to figure out how to make an image smaller. Your first instinct may be to write `img.Shrink(size)`. Unfortunately, that API does not exist; the actual API for shrinking an image is

```
public static Document ResizeDocument(
 Document document, Size newSize,
 AnchorEdge edge, ColorBgra background)
```

We will step through how our tool handles this example, using Figure 1 which shows the workflow of our tool. For this example, you would write the query "`?({img, size})`" in the partial expression language described in Section 3. The query is passed to the algorithm represented by the large box described in Section 4 which also has access to the code context which says that `img` and `size` are local variables of types `Document` and `Size`, respectively. The first ten elements of the ranked result set are shown in Figure 2. The static `ResizeDocument` method is the first choice.

Synthesizing Method Arguments

Suppose you already know there is a method `Distance` that returns the distance between two `Point` objects, but are not sure where one of the endpoints is defined. The query "`Distance(point, ?)`" produces a list of `Point`s that could be filled in as the second argument. This includes any locals, fields, or static fields or methods or recursively any fields of those of type `Point`. For example, Figure 3 shows the results of that query in the context of the `EllipseArc` class of the DynamicGeometry library. There, `point` is the only local variable of type `Point`. In this case, the actual argument was `this.Center` which appears third in the list.

[2] http://www.getpaint.net/

```
PaintDotNet.Actions.CanvasSizeAction
    .ResizeDocument(img, size, ◇, ◇)
PaintDotNet.Functional.Func.Bind(◇, size, img)
PaintDotNet.Pair.Create(size, img)
PaintDotNet.Quadruple.Create(size, img, ◇, ◇)
PaintDotNet.Triple.Create(size, img, ◇)
PaintDotNet.PropertySystem
    .StaticListChoiceProperty
    .CreateForEnum(img, size, ◇)
System.Drawing.Size.Equals(size, img)
System.Object.ReferenceEquals(size, img)
PaintDotNet.Document.OnDeserialization(img, size)
PaintDotNet.PropertySystem.Property
    .Create(◇, size, img)
```

Figure 2. The first ten results generated and ranked by our system for the query `?({img, size})`.

```
point
this.BeginLocation
this.Center
this.EndLocation
DynamicGeometry.Math.InfinitePoint
shapeStyle.GetSampleGlyph()
.RenderTransformOrigin
this.shape.RenderTransformOrigin
this.ArcShape.Point
this.Figure.StartPoint
this.Shape.RenderTransformOrigin
```

Figure 3. The first ten results generated and ranked by our system for the `?` in the query `Distance(point, ?)`.

Synthesizing Field Lookups

For a more targeted version of the above, the search can be narrowed by specifying the base object to look under. We will consider synthesizing field lookups in the context of a comparison operator. The query "`point.?*m >= this.?*m`" includes `point` and `this` along with zero or more field lookups or zero-argument instance method calls after them. The top ten ranked completions for this query are listed in Figure 4. Note that by completing both holes simultaneously, only completions where the two sides have fields of compatible types are shown.

2.2 Code Completion

Today, programmers can use code completion such as Intellisense in Visual Studio to try to navigate unfamiliar APIs. Intellisense completes code in sections separated by periods ("`.`") by using the type of the expression to the left of the period and textually searching through the list for any string the programmer types. If there is no period, then Intellisense will list the available local variables, types, and namespaces. This often works well, particularly when the programmer has a good idea of where the API they want is or if there are relatively few choices. On the other hand, it performs poorly on our examples.

```
point.X >= this.P1.X
point.X >= this.P2.X
point.X >= this.Midpoint.X
point.X >= this.FirstValidValue().X
point.Y >= this.P1.Y
point.Y >= this.P2.Y
point.Y >= this.Midpoint.Y
point.Y >= this.FirstValidValue().Y
point.X >= this.Length
point.Y >= this.Length
```

Figure 4. The first ten results generated and ranked by our system for the query `point.?*m >= this.?*m`.

Synthesizing Method Names

Using Intellisense to find the nonexistent `Shrink` method, a programmer might type "`img.shr`", see that there is no "`Shrink`" method, and then skim through the rest of the instance methods. As that will also fail to find the desired method, the programmer might continue by typing in "`PaintDotNet.`" and use Intellisense to browse the available static methods, eventually finding `PaintDotNet.Actions.CanvasSizeAction` where the method is located. Hopefully documentation on the various classes and namespaces shown by Intellisense's tooltip will help guide the programmer to the desired method, but this is dependent on the API designer documenting their code well and the documentation using terminology and abstractions that the programmer understands. A programmer would likely search through many namespaces and classes before happening upon the right one.

Synthesizing Method Arguments

If the user has already entered "`Distance(point, `" and then triggers Intellisense, Intellisense will list of every namespace, type, variable, and instance method in context even though many choices will not type-check (as the programmer may intend to call a method or perform a property lookup on one of those objects). When the list is brought up, the most recently used local variable of type `Point`, which would be `point` in this case, will be selected. The programmer will have to read through many unrelated options to locate the other values of type `Point`.

Note that Eclipse's code completion is actually significantly different in this scenario. It will list all of the local variables valid for the argument position along with common constants like `null`. If a more complicated expression is desired, the user has to cancel out and request the normal code completion which is similar to Visual Studio's.

Synthesizing Field Lookups

Given "`point.`", Intellisense will list all fields and methods of that object. The listing will go only one level deep: if the user wants a field of a field, they have to know which field to select first.

2.3 Prospector

The Prospector tool by Mandelin et al.[10] is an API discovery tool which constructs values using mined "jungloids" which convert from one input type to one output type and are combined into longer jungloids. The tool uses a local variable to construct a value of the output type. The motivating example in this prior work is converting an `IFile` to an `ASTNode` in the Eclipse API which requires a non-obvious intermediate step involving a third type:

```
IFile file = ...;
ICompilationUnit cu =
    JavaCore.createCompilationUnitFrom(file);
ASTNode ast = AST.parseCompilationUnit(cu, false);
```

$$\text{(a)}\quad e ::= call \mid varName \mid e\texttt{.}fieldName \mid e\texttt{:=}e \mid e\texttt{<}e$$
$$call ::= methodName\texttt{(}e_1\texttt{,}\ldots\texttt{,}e_n\texttt{)}$$
$$\text{(b)}\quad \tilde{e} ::= \tilde{a} \mid \texttt{?} \mid \diamond$$
$$\tilde{a} ::= e \mid \tilde{a}\texttt{.?f} \mid \tilde{a}\texttt{.?*f} \mid \tilde{a}\texttt{.?m} \mid \tilde{a}\texttt{.?*m} \mid \widetilde{call} \mid \tilde{e}\texttt{:=}\tilde{e} \mid \tilde{e}\texttt{<}\tilde{e}$$
$$\widetilde{call} ::= \texttt{?(\{}\tilde{e}_1\texttt{,}\ldots\texttt{,}\tilde{e}_n\texttt{\})} \mid methodName\texttt{(}\tilde{e}_1\texttt{,}\ldots\texttt{,}\tilde{e}_n\texttt{)}$$

Figure 5. (a) Expression language (b) Partial expression language

The Prospector UI triggers queries only at assignments to variables, but that is a minor implementation detail.

Synthesizing Method Names

As Prospector can consider only one type as input, a programmer might query for a conversion from `Size` to `Document` or from `Document` to `Document`, which does not quite match the programmers intuition of wanting to resize the document. Prospector will return methods with arguments it cannot fill in. It prefers fewer unknown arguments, so `ResizeDocument` would likely be rather far down in the list of options for either query.

Synthesizing Method Arguments

Queried for type `Point`, Prospector would give a similar list to the one our tool creates, although it does not consider globals as possible inputs to its algorithm. Specifically, Prospector would give any locals of the proper type and recursively find any fields of the proper type. It may also find chains that involve downcasts found to work elsewhere in the codebase, which our tool would not find.

Synthesizing Field Lookups

Prospector does not take suggestions of starting points from the user, although its UI could theoretically be modified to do so. On the other hand, Prospector has only one target type and cannot make more complicated expressions like the one above with a `>=` operator. The closest corresponding use of Prospector would be to guess the type for either side of the comparison and have Prospector find fields of that type.

3. Partial expression language

Queries in our system are partial expressions. A partial expression is similar to a normal (or "complete") expression except some information may be omitted or reordered. A partial expression can have many possible completions formed by filling in the holes and reordering subexpressions in different ways.

Complete expression syntax

Before defining partial expressions, we first define a simple expression language given by the e and $call$ productions in Figure 5(a), which models features found in traditional programming languages. Our simple language has variables, field lookups, assignments, a comparison operator, and method calls. (Other operators are omitted from the formalism.) Also, the receiver of a method call is considered to be its first argument in order to simplify notation as when reordering arguments, an argument other than the first may be chosen as the receiver.

Partial expression syntax

Partial expressions are defined by the $\tilde{e}$, $\tilde{a}$, and $\widetilde{call}$ productions in Figure 5(b). Partial expressions support omitting the following classes of unknown information:

- **Entire subexpressions.** `?` gives no information about the structure of the expression, only that it is missing and should be filled in. On the other hand, $\diamond$ should not be filled in: it indicates a

$$\frac{\tilde{e} \Downarrow e}{\tilde{e}\texttt{.?} \Downarrow e} \qquad \frac{\tilde{e} \Downarrow e}{\tilde{e}\texttt{.?m} \Downarrow e.m()} \qquad \frac{\tilde{e} \Downarrow e}{\tilde{e}\texttt{.?f} \Downarrow e.f}$$

$$\frac{}{\tilde{e}\texttt{.?*f} \Downarrow \tilde{e}\texttt{.?f.?*f}} \qquad \frac{}{\tilde{e}\texttt{.?*m} \Downarrow \tilde{e}\texttt{.?m.?*m}} \qquad \frac{}{\tilde{e}\texttt{.?m} \Downarrow \tilde{e}\texttt{.?f}}$$

$$\frac{\tilde{e}_1 \Downarrow e_1 \qquad \tilde{e}_2 \Downarrow e_2}{\tilde{e}_1\texttt{:=}\tilde{e}_2 \Downarrow e_1\texttt{:=}e_2} \qquad \frac{\tilde{e}_1 \Downarrow e_1 \qquad \tilde{e}_2 \Downarrow e_2}{\tilde{e}_1\texttt{<}\tilde{e}_2 \Downarrow e_1\texttt{<}e_2}$$

$$\frac{\tilde{e}_i \Downarrow e_i}{m(\tilde{e}_1, \ldots, \tilde{e}_i, \ldots, \tilde{e}_n) \Downarrow m(\tilde{e}_1, \ldots, e_i, \ldots, \tilde{e}_n)}$$

$$\frac{\tilde{e}_i \Downarrow e_i}{\texttt{?}(\{\tilde{e}_1, \ldots, \tilde{e}_i, \ldots, \tilde{e}_n\}) \Downarrow \texttt{?}(\{\tilde{e}_1, \ldots, e_i, \ldots, \tilde{e}_n\})}$$

$$\frac{k \geq n, e_j = \diamond \text{ for } j > n \quad \sigma \in S_k}{\texttt{?}(\{e_1, \ldots, e_n\}) \Downarrow m(e_{\sigma_1}, \ldots, e_{\sigma_k})}$$

$$\frac{v \text{ is a live local or global variable}}{\texttt{?} \Downarrow v\texttt{.?*m}}$$

$$\frac{\tilde{e}_1 \Downarrow \tilde{e}_2 \qquad \tilde{e}_2 \Downarrow \tilde{e}_3}{\tilde{e}_1 \Downarrow \tilde{e}_3}$$

Figure 6. Semantics of partial expressions. The final result must type-check in the context of the query, treating ◇ as having any type.

subexpression to ignore due to being independent of the current query (so making it a ? would only add irrelevant results) or simply being a subexpression the programmer intends to fill in later, perhaps due to working left-to-right.

- **Field lookups.** The $\tilde{a}$ production defines a series of four `.?` suffixes which are slightly different ways of saying that an expression is missing one or more field lookups or the desired expression is actually the result of a method call on the expression. The '`f`' suffix is short for "field" and can be completed as a single field lookup or nothing. The `.?*` suffixes complete as the `.?` versions repeated as many times as needed.
- **Simple method calls.** The `.?m` suffix is like the `.?f` suffix. The '`m`' is short for "zero-argument method call" and can be completed as a call to an instance method with zero additional arguments or also as a field lookup or nothing.
- **Which method to call.** `?`$(\{\tilde{e}_1, \tilde{e}_2\})$ represents a call to some unknown method with two known arguments, which may themselves be partial expressions.
- **Number and ordering of arguments to a method.** For unknown methods, there may also be additional arguments missing or the arguments may be out of order, which is represented by the use of set notation for the arguments in `?`$(\{\tilde{e}_1, \tilde{e}_2\})$.

Partial expression semantics

Figure 6 gives the full semantics of the partial expression language. The $\Downarrow$ judgement nondeterministically takes a partial expression to a complete expression with the exception that any ◇ subexpressions remain. With the exception of the `.?*` rules, each rule removes or refines some hole, making the partial expression one step closer to a complete expression. The bottom rule allows for the composition of other rules. The top leftmost rule allows any of the `.?` suffixes to be omitted. For type checking, ◇ is treated as a wildcard: as long as some choice of type for the ◇ works, the expression is considered to type check. The actual algorithm implemented does not use these rules exactly, although it matches their semantics.

The partial expressions language semantics never add operations like multiplication or new method calls (other than to zero-argument methods). The idea is that any place where computation is intended should be explicitly specified, and the completions simply list specific APIs for the computations. The exception for zero-argument methods is made because they are often used in place of properties for style reasons or due to limitations of the underlying language.

Examples

The first example from Section 2, `?({img, size})`, is a method call with an unknown name and two complete expressions as arguments. It can be expanded to any method that can take those two variables in any two of its argument positions, so `Triple.Create(◇, size, img)` is a valid completion. Note that no attempt is made to fill in the extra argument. This is done to reduce the number of choices when recommending methods; for other applications fully completing the expression may be useful. The user may afterward decide to convert the ◇ to ? or some other partial expression.

Our second example from Section 2, `Distance(point, ?)` can take one step to one of

- `Distance(point, point.?*m)`,
- `Distance(point, this.?*m)`,
- `Distance(point, shapeStyle.?*m)`

or many other possibilities. Any local in scope or global (static field or zero-argument static method) could be chosen to appear before the `.?*m`. Whatever is selected is completed to some expression of type `Point`. Any `.?` suffix can be omitted when completing an expression, so `point.?*m` can be completed as `point` which is the first option in Figure 3. `this.?*m` can also become one or more lookups by going to `this.?m.?*m` in one step and the `.?m` becomes some field. For `ArcShape`, `this.ArcShape.?*m` is further completed to `this.ArcShape.Point`. Any of the completions mentioned so far would have been valid for `.?f` instead of `.?m` as well. On the other hand, for `shapeStyle.?*m`, the first `.?m` from the `.?*m` is completed with an instance method `.GetSampleGlyph()` that returns an object with a field `RenderTransformOrigin` of type `Point` which the remaining `.?*m` can complete to.

An unknown method's arguments may themselves be partial expressions. For example, `?({strBuilder.?*m,e.?*m})` could expand to `Append(strBuilder, e.StackTrace)` (which would normally be written as `strBuilder.Append(e.StackTrace)`).

The third example from Section 2, `point.?*m >= this.?*m`, also uses `.?*m`, so the completions work as above, but, as there are two of them in the expression related by the `>=`, there must be a definition of `>=` which is type compatible with the two completions. In this example, all the comparable fields have types `int` or `double`. But suppose `Point` had a field `Timestamp` of type `DateTime`; then `Point.Timestamp >= this.P1.Timestamp` would be a valid completion, but `Point.X >= this.P1.Timestamp` would not.

4. Algorithm

This section describes an algorithm (represented by the boxed section of Figure 1) for completing partial expressions. The algorithm takes a partial expression and an integer n as input and returns an ordered list of n proposed completions. The algorithm has access to static information about the surrounding code and libraries: the types of the values used in the expression, the locals in scope, and the visible library methods and fields. Bounding n is important because some partial expressions have an infinite list of completions. What constitutes a valid completion is defined by Figure 6.

The algorithm described in this section does completion finding and ranking simultaneously in order to compute the top n completions efficiently. Section 4.1 describes the ranking function. Section 4.2 describes the completion finder and the integrated algorithm whose design is informed by the ranking function.

$$
\begin{aligned}
\mathsf{score}(expr) &= \textstyle\sum_{s \in \mathsf{subexps}(expr)} \mathsf{score}(s) \\
&+ \textstyle\sum_{s \in \mathsf{subexps}(expr)} \mathsf{td}(\mathsf{type}(s), \mathsf{type}(\mathsf{param}(s))) \\
&+ 2 \cdot \mathsf{dots}(expr) \\
&+ \textstyle\sum_{s \in \mathsf{subexps}(expr)} \mathsf{abstype}(s) \\
&\qquad\qquad \neq \mathsf{abstype}(\mathsf{param}(s)) \\
\mathsf{scorec}(call) &= \mathsf{score}(call) \\
&+ (\mathsf{isInstance}(call) \vee \mathsf{isNonLocalStatic}(call)) \\
&+ \max\Big(0, 3 - (\mathsf{nsArgs}(call) \neq \mathsf{reciever}(call)) \\
&\qquad \cdot \Big|\bigcap_{s \in \mathsf{nsArgs}(call)} \mathsf{ns}(\mathsf{type}(a))\Big|\Big) \\
\mathsf{scorecmp}(expr_1, expr_2) &= \mathsf{score}(expr_1 < expr_2) \\
&+ 3 \cdot (\mathsf{name}(expr_1) \neq \mathsf{name}(expr_2))
\end{aligned}
$$

$$
\mathsf{nsArgs}(call) = \{a \in \mathsf{subexps}\,(call) \mid \mathsf{type}(a) \text{ is not primitive}\}
$$

Figure 7. The ranking function. Note that boolean values are considered 1 if true and 0 if false and that abstract types ($\mathsf{abstype}(\cdot)$) are considered not equal if both are *undefined*.

4.1 Ranking

This section defines a function that maps completed expressions that may contain ◇ subexpressions to integer scores. This function is used to rank the results returned by the completion finder in ascending order of the ranking score (i.e., a lower score is better). The function is defined such that each term is non-negative, so if any subset of the terms are known, their sum is a lower bound on the ranking score and can be used to prune the search space.

The computation is a sum of various terms summarized in Figure 7. $\mathsf{score}(\cdot)$ applies to all expressions while $\mathsf{scorec}(\cdot)$ is a specialized version with tweaks for method calls and $\mathsf{scorecmp}(\cdot,\cdot)$ is a specialized version with a tweak for comparisons. The computation is defined recursively, so for methods or operators with arguments, the sum of the scores of their arguments is added to the score. The scoring function incorporates several features we designed based on studying code examples and our own intuition. This section explains these features in detail. Section 5.4 evaluates each feature's contribution to our empirical results.

Type distance The primary feature in the ranking function is "type distance", for example from a method call argument's type to the type of the corresponding method parameter. Informally, it is the distance in the class hierarchy, extended to consider primitive types, interfaces, etc. For example, if `Rectangle` extends `Shape` which extends `Object`, $\mathsf{td}(\texttt{Rectangle}, \texttt{Shape}) = 1$ and $\mathsf{td}(\texttt{Rectangle}, \texttt{Object}) = 2$. Far away types are less likely to be used for each other, so method calls and binary operations where the arguments have a higher type distance are less likely to be what the user wanted.

Formally, the type distance from a type α usable in a position of type β to that type β, $\mathsf{td}(\alpha, \beta)$, is defined as follows:

$$
\mathsf{td}(\alpha, \beta) = \begin{cases} undefined & \text{no implicit conversion of } \alpha \text{ to } \beta \\ 0 & \text{if } \alpha = \beta \\ 1 & \text{if } \alpha \text{ and } \beta \text{ are primitive types} \\ 1 + \mathsf{td}(\mathsf{s}(\alpha), \beta) & \text{otherwise} \end{cases}
$$

$\mathsf{s}(\alpha)$ is the explicitly declared immediate supertype of α which to minimizes $\mathsf{td}(\mathsf{s}(\alpha), \beta)$. Note that $\mathsf{td}(\alpha, \beta)$ is used by the ranking function only when it is defined as that corresponds to the expression being type correct.

The type distance term is the sum of the type distances from the type of each argument arg to the type of the corresponding formal parameter $\mathsf{param}(arg)$. For method calls this is well-defined; binary operators are treated as methods with two parameters both of the more general type, so the type distance between the two arguments to the operator is used.

Depth The next term prefers expressions with fewer subexpressions. The ranking scheme prefers shorter expressions by computing the complexity of the expression which is approximated by the number of dots in the expression and multiplying that value by 2 to weight it more heavily. For example, dots("`this.foo`") $= 1$ so it would get a cost of 2 while dots("`this.bar.ToBaz()`") $= 2$ so it would get a cost of 4. To avoid double counting, any dots which are part of subexpressions are not counted here and instead are included via the subexpressions score term.

In-scope static methods Instance method calls will tend to have a type distance of zero for the receiver, so type distance has an implicit bias against static method calls. Noting that static methods of the enclosing type can be called without qualification, just like instance methods with `this` as the receiver, our ranking algorithm should similarly not disfavor such in-scope static methods. This is fixed by adding a cost of 1 if either the method is an instance method or the method is a static method that is not in scope.

Common namespace As related APIs tend to be grouped into nearby namespaces, the algorithm prefers calls where the types of all the arguments with non-primitive types and the class containing the method definition are all in the same namespace. Primitive types, including `string`, are ignored in this step because they are used with varying semantics in many different libraries. Furthermore, deeper namespaces tend to be more precise so a deep common namespace indicates the method is more likely to be related to all of the provided arguments. Specifically, the algorithm takes the set of all namespaces of non-primitive types among the arguments, treats them as lists of strings (so "`System.Collections`" is ["`System`", "`Collections`"]), finds the (often empty) common prefix, and uses its length to compute the "namespace score". To avoid this boosting the scores of instance calls with only one non-primitive argument, the similarity score is 0 in that case.

In order to have the namespace similarity term be non-negative, namespace similarities are capped at 3, and 3 minus the length of the common prefix is used as the common namespace term.

Same name Comparisons are often made between corresponding fields of different objects. Whether two fields have corresponding meanings can be approximated by checking if they have the same name. That is, `p.X` is more likely to be compared to `this.Center.X` than to `this.Center.Y`. To capture this, a 3 point penalty is assigned to comparisons where the last lookups on the two sides do not have the same name. The value is intentionally chosen to be greater than the cost of a lookup, so a slightly longer expression that ends with a field of the right name is considered better than a shorter one that does not.

Abstract type inference

We now introduce an important refinement to the basic ranking function that partitions types into "abstract types" based on usage, which is particularly important for commonly used types like `string`. Abstract types may have richer semantics than `string` such as "path" or "font family name". Our approach is based on the Lackwit tool that infers abstract types of integers in C[11].

Abstract types are computed automatically using type inference. An abstract type variable is assigned to every local variable, formal parameter, and formal return type, and a type equality constraint is added whenever a value is assigned or used as a method call argument. As all constraints are equality on atoms, the standard unification algorithm can be implemented using union-find.

In order to avoid merging every abstract type `.ToString()` or `.GetHashCode()` is called on, methods defined on `Object` are treated as being distinct methods for every type. All other methods have formal parameter and formal return type terms associated with their definition which are shared with any overriding methods. A more principled approach might involve a concept of subtyping for abstract types, but that would greatly complicate the algorithm for what would likely be minimal gain.

For example, consider the following code from Family.Show:[3]

```
string appLocation = Path.Combine(
    Environment.GetFolderPath(
        Environment.SpecialFolder.MyDocuments),
    App.ApplicationFolderName);
if (!Directory.Exists(appLocation))
    Directory.CreateDirectory(appLocation);
return Path.Combine(appLocation,
                    Const.DataFileName);
```

`Directory.Exists`, `Directory.CreateDirectory`, and `Path.Combine` take `appLocation` as their first argument, so the analysis concludes their first arguments are all the same abstract type. Furthermore, from the first statement, that must also be the abstract type of the return values of `Path.Combine` and `Environment.GetFolderPath`. On the other hand, there is no evidence that would lead the analysis to believe the second argument of `Path.Combine` is of that abstract type, instead `App.ApplicationFolderName` and `Const.DataFileName` are believed to both be of some other type. Intuitively, a programmer might call those two types "directory name" and "file name".

In the ranking function, the type distance computation is refined by adding an additional cost of 1 if the abstract types do not match.

4.2 Completion finder

This section presents a general algorithm for computing the top n ranked completions of a partial expression, first giving a naive implementation and then discussing optimizations. The main logic is Algorithm 1 which returns a generator that returns all completions of a partial expression in order by score. The **yield return** statement returns a single completion, and when the next completion is requested, execution continues on the next statement. The first n elements of `AllCompletions(`$\tilde{e}$`)` are the top n ranked completions of $\tilde{e}$.

Note that for any partial expressions containing `.?*f` or `.?*m`, this generator will usually continue producing more completions forever, but can be called only n times to get just the top n completions. It may be easier to first read the algorithm while ignoring the `score` variable, which is necessary to handle the unbounded result set for `.?*f` or `.?*m`. Then it is a simple recursive algorithm which computes every possible completion of its subexpressions and uses those completions to generate every possible completion of the entire expression (e.g. all methods that can take those arguments).

Note that `?` is interpreted as $vars$`.?*m` where $vars$ is a special subexpression whose list of completions is every local and global variable in scope.

We now discuss various useful optimizations.

Cache subexpression scores

A subexpression's score will be needed for every completion it appears in. To compute it only once, the algorithm is redefined such that it returns a set of pairs of completions and their scores.

Compute completions not in score order

In the algorithm given above, completions with a score not equal to `score` are discarded and regenerated later. To avoid that work,

[3] `http://www.vertigo.com/familyshow.aspx`

Algorithm 1: `AllCompletions(`$\tilde{e}$`)`

```
input  : ẽ: a partial expression
output : a generator of all completions in order by score
subexps ← the list of immediate subexpressions of ẽ;
Let subcomps be a map from subexps to completions;
foreach s ← subexps do
    subcomps[s] ← AllCompletions(s);
end
foreach score ← [0, ∞) do
    foreach concreteSubs ← all choices of exactly one
        completion for each subexpression from subcomps
        whose score(concreteSubs) ≤ score do
        foreach type-correct completion c of ẽ using
            subexpressions concreteSubs where
            score(c) = score do
            yield return c;
        end
    end
end
```

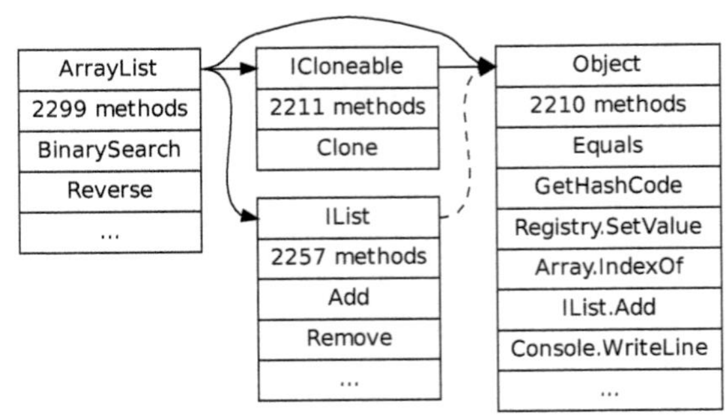

Figure 8. The method index. The supertypes of `IList` other than `Object` are omitted for brevity.

completions with a score greater than `score` can be saved to be output later. For most partial expressions, it makes sense to compute all of the completions for a given value of `concreteSubs` at once. In the case of `.?*f` and `.?*m` queries, the algorithm will never be done computing every possible completion, but `foo.?*f` can be thought of as the union of `.?f` queries first on `foo`, then on the results of `foo.?f`, etc. Then each completion set is finite and the basis for the future completions. In pseudocode, this is implemented as inserting each completion `c` into `subcomps`.

Indexing

As written, how the algorithm iterates over possible completions is unspecified. This is especially a problem for unknown methods as simply iterating over all methods in a huge framework would take too long. An index is maintained that maps every type to a set of methods for which at least one of the arguments may be of that type. Then, given a query like `?(`$\{e_1, e_2\}$`)`, each of the argument types is looked up to see how many methods would have to be considered for that type and the smallest set is chosen. That set will almost always be orders of magnitude smaller than the set of all methods.

Part of a method index is shown in Figure 8. In order to save memory, the method index is organized such that looking up a type τ gets a set of methods which have parameters of the exact type τ along with pointers to the method indexes for the immediate supertypes of τ. Due to the type distance part of the ranking algorithm explained in Section 4.1, each method index visited will give progressively worse ranked results.

Methods are a prime candidate for indexing as there are many methods and few that take a specific type. Although the current implementation does not do so, queries for multiple field lookups could also be made more efficient using an index that indicates for each type which types are reachable by a `.?*f` or `.?*m` query, how many lookups are needed, and which lookups can lead to a value of that type. For example, a `Line` type with `Point` fields `p1` and `p2` and a `GetLength()` method would have an entry denoting that the type `double` is reachable in ≥ 2 lookups using a `.?*f` query with the next lookup being one of `p1` or `p2` while it is reachable in ≥ 1 lookup using a `.?*m` query with the next lookup being one of `GetLength()`, `p1`, or `p2`.

Avoid computing type-incorrect completions

If the possible valid types for the completions were known, then the type reachability index would be more useful: otherwise results of every type have to be generated anyway for completeness. At the top level, the context will often provide a type unless the expression being completed is the initial value for a variable annotated only as `var`. On the recursive step of the algorithm, the possible types may not be known or may not be precise enough to be useful: there are methods that take multiple arguments of type `Object`, so even knowing one of the argument types does not narrow down the possibilities for the rest. On the other hand, binary operators and assignments are relatively restrictive on which pairs of types are valid, so enumerating the types of the completions for one side could significantly narrow down the possibilities for the other side.

Grouping computations by type

Which completions are valid is determined solely by the types of the expressions involved. Hence, instead of considering every completion of every subexpression separately, the completions of each subexpression can be grouped by type after grouping by score to reduce the number of times the algorithm has to check if a given type is valid in a given position. This also allows type distance computations to be done once for all subexpressions of the same types. Any remaining ranking features are computed separately for each completion as grouping by them is no faster than computing their terms of the ranking function.

5. Evaluation

We implemented the algorithm described using the Microsoft Research Common Compiler Infrastructure (CCI).[4] CCI reads .NET binaries and decompiles them into a language resembling C#. Unfortunately, we were unable to work on actual source code because at the time the experiments were performed, no tools for analyzing the source code of C# programs existed—and even if they did exist, open source C# programs are relatively rare.

We performed experiments where our tool found expressions in mature software projects, removed some information to make those expressions into partial expressions, and ran our algorithm on those partial expressions to see where the real expression ranks in the results.

All experiments were run on a virtual machine allocated one core of a Core 2 Duo E8400 3GHz processor and 1GB of RAM.

One minor issue is that any precomputation, specifically abstract type inference, would see the expression we are trying to recreate when in actual practice the expression would not yet exist. To avoid this situation, we re-run abstract type inference for each expression, eliminating the expression and all code that follows it in the enclosing method—we do consider the rest of the program.

We describe three case studies whose significance we have previously discussed in Section 2 and show that the ranking scheme is effective and the algorithm is efficient. After that, we analyze the importance of the individual ranking features in Section 5.4. Finally, we discuss threats to validity in Section 5.5.

[4] `https://cciast.codeplex.com/`

Table 1. Summary of quality of best results for each call

Program	# calls	# top 10	# top 10..20
Paint.Net[a]	3188	2288	525
WiX[b]	13192	11430	512
GNOME Do[c]	208	167	22
Banshee[d]	91	82	2
.NET[e]	2801	2345	145
Family.Show[f]	586	510	23
LiveGeometry[g]	1110	1072	3
Totals	21176	17894 (84.5%)	1232 (5.8%)

[a] `http://www.getpaint.net/`—image editor (main `.exe`)
[b] `http://wix.codeplex.com/`—Windows Installer XML
[c] `http://do.davebsd.com/`—application launcher
[d] `http://banshee.fm/`—media player
[e] .NET Framework v3.5 libraries System.Core.dll, mscorlib.dll
[f] `http://www.vertigo.com/familyshow.aspx`—WPF example application
[g] `http://livegeometry.codeplex.com/`—geometry visualizer

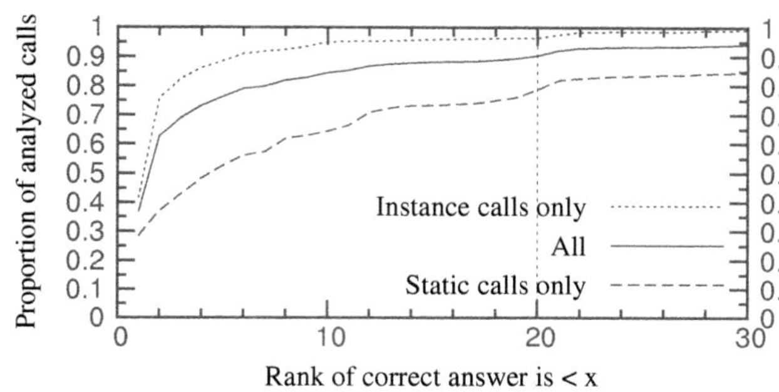

Figure 9. The proportion of calls of each type with the best rank of at least the given value

5.1 Predicting Method Names

Our first experiment shows that queries consisting of one or two arguments can effectively find methods. We ran our analysis on 21,176 calls across parts of seven C# projects listed in Table 1. We generated queries by finding all calls with ≥ 2 arguments (including the receiver, if any) and giving one or two of the call's arguments to the algorithm. We evaluated the algorithm on where in the results list the actual method appeared. While putting the correct result as the first choice is ideal, we do not consider it necessary for usefulness since users can quickly skim several plausible results.

Figure 9 shows the results overall and partitioned between static and instance calls. Almost 85% of the time, the algorithm is able to give the correct method in the top 10 choices. An additional 5% of the time, the correct method appears in the next 10 choices out of a total of hundreds of choices on average.

Notably, the algorithm fares significantly better on instance calls than static calls. This is not too surprising as the search space is much larger for static calls. This might also indicate that the current heuristics prefer instance calls more strongly than they should.

Unfortunately, we cannot algorithmically determine which argument subset a user would use as their search query. Instead, we show that usually for *some* set of no more than 2 arguments the correct method being highly ranked. Our intuition, which would need a user study to validate fully, is that evaluating our approach

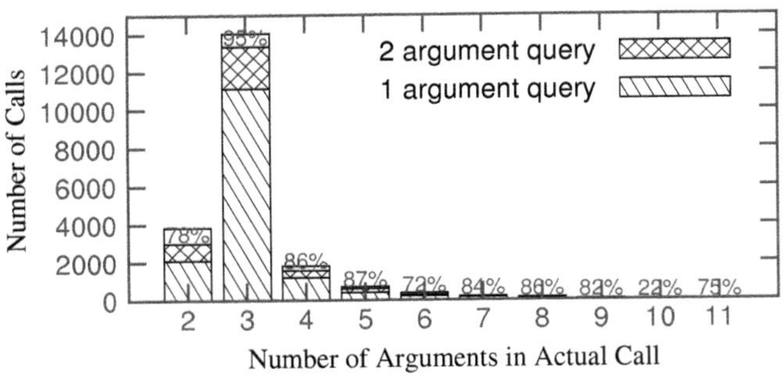

Figure 10. Each bar represents all calls analyzed with the number of arguments. The sections of the bar correspond to how many of those arguments the algorithm needed to put the original call in the top 20 results.

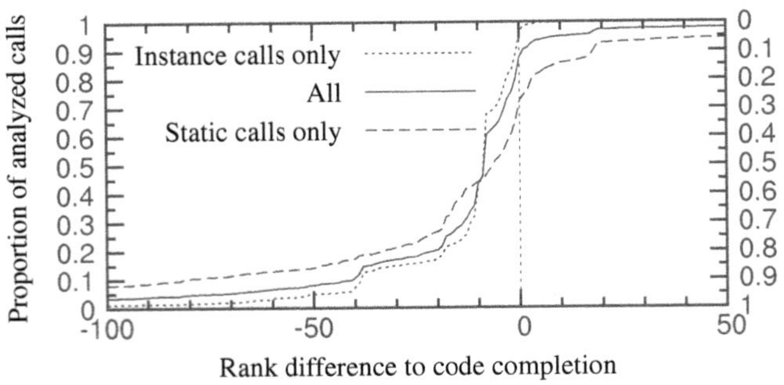

Figure 11. Difference in rank between our algorithm and Intellisense

by choosing for the best possible subset of arguments is reasonable because programmers are capable of identifying the most useful arguments (e.g., `PreciseLibraryType` instead of `string` or `Pair`).

Figure 10 shows that a single argument is often enough for the algorithm to determine which method was desired, in this case defined as putting the method in the top 20 choices. Not shown in the graph is that adding a third argument leads to only negligible improvement in these results; note that even knowing all of the arguments to a method might not be enough to place it in the top 20 choices. Above the bars is the percentage of calls the algorithm was able to guess using only two arguments, which is high for any number of arguments. The intuition is that most of the arguments are not important, although there are also more opportunities for an argument to be of a rarely used type. The low value for 10 argument calls is due to there being very few such calls and most of them being from a large family of methods which all have the same method signature.

Comparison to code completion

Figure 11 compares our ranking algorithm to Intellisense. The y-axes are read as the left side measuring the proportion of calls our system did better on and the right side measuring the proportion of calls Intellisense did better on.

We modeled Intellisense as being given the receiver (or receiver type for static calls) and listing its members in alphabetic order. Intellisense knows which argument is the receiver but is not using knowledge of the arguments. It was considered to list only instance members for instance receivers and only static members for static receivers. Given this ordering, we were able to compute the rank in the alphabetic list of the correct answer. We then subtracted that rank from the rank given by our algorithm, so negative numbers mean our algorithm gave the correct answer a higher rank.

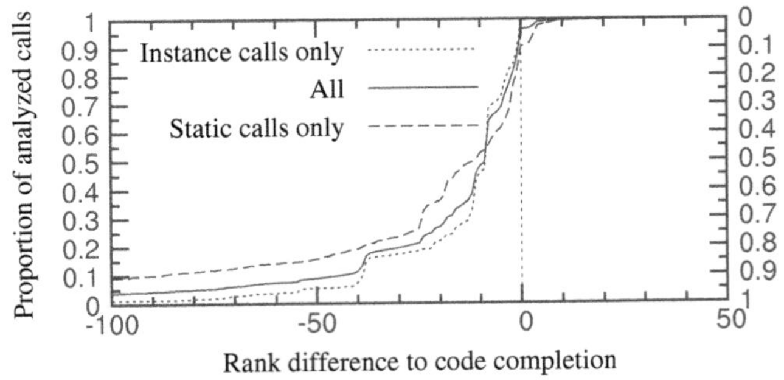

Figure 12. Difference in rank between our algorithm filtering its results for those matching the correct return type and Intellisense

About 45% of the time, our position is at least 10 higher than it is with Intellisense. Since Intellisense displays at most 10 results at a time, this means it is not initially displayed by Intellisense.

Subtracting the ranks is oversimplifying the comparison. First, the different tools have different inputs. Our tool does not require the receiver but is helped by being provided a second argument. Second, the Intellisense results are listed in alphabetic order which is likely easier to skim through than the results from our tool which will be ordered by their ranking scores. The take-away is not that our tool is "better" than Intellisense; they serve different purposes. Instead, we wanted to show that our tool is often able to greatly reduce the number of choices a user would have to sift through compared to Intellisense even if the user knew the correct receiver.

Figure 12 shows a similar comparison to the one in Figure 11 except that our algorithm additionally knew the desired return type (or `void`) and only suggested methods whose return type matched.

The assumption of a known return type is not used elsewhere both because, in the context of API discovery, the user may often not know what return type to use, and the `var` keyword in C# and equivalents in other languages allow a user to omit return types.

Speed For 98.9% of the calls analyzed, the query with the best result ran in under half a second, which is fast enough for interactive use.

As a caveat, these times do not include running the abstract type inference algorithm. That could take as long as several minutes for a large codebase but can be done incrementally in the background.

These times were measured using CCI reading binaries as opposed to getting the information from an IDE's incremental compiler. How that affects performance is unclear, but any such effects were minimized by memoizing a lot of the information from CCI, so the vast majority of the time was spent in our algorithm.

5.2 Predicting Method Arguments

Our second experiment investigated how often arguments to a method could be filled in by knowing their type.

Looking at the same method calls as the previous experiment, for each argument in each call, a query was generated with that argument replaced with `?`. There were a total of 69,927 arguments across the 21,176 calls. 23,927 were considered not guessable due to having an expression form that our partial expression completer does not generate like an array lookup or a constant value.

Figure 13 shows how well our algorithm is able to predict method arguments, with the lower line ignoring the low-hanging fruit of local variables. Over 80% of the time, the algorithm is able to suggest the intended argument as one of the top 10 choices given out of an average of hundreds of choices.

Use of expressions other than local variables in argument positions is common as shown in Figure 14. Programmers must somehow discover the proper APIs for these expressions: Intellisense

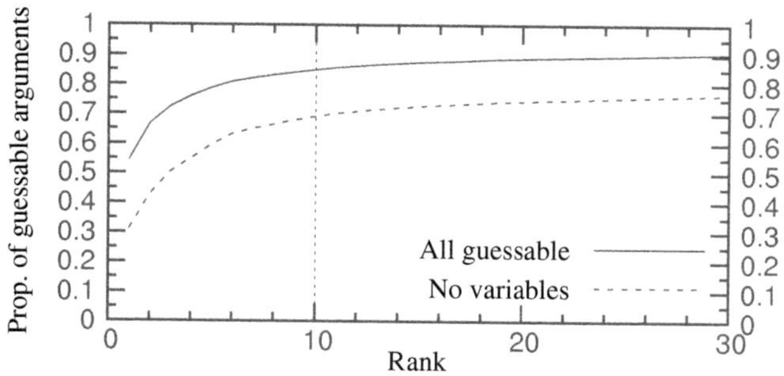

Figure 13. The proportion of guessable arguments which could be guessed with a given rank and the same ignoring arguments which are just local variable references

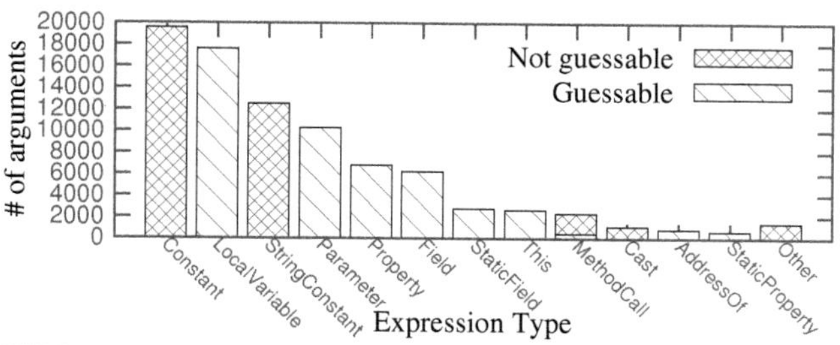

Figure 14. The types of expressions found in argument positions, showing which ones are considered guessable

only suggests local variables given an argument position. The "not guessable" expressions are those that involve constants or computation like an addition or a non-zero argument method call that could be guessed by neither our technique nor Intellisense. Our partial expression language captures more of the expressions programmers use as arguments including field/property lookups which are relatively common and require browsing to find using Intellisense.

As our experiments are on decompiled binaries and not the original source, these arguments may not be exactly what the programmer wrote. In particular, expressions might be stored in temporary variables that they did not write or temporaries they did write might be removed, putting their definition in an argument position.

Speed Our tool is capable of enumerating suggested arguments in under a tenth of a second 92% of the time and under half a second over 98% of the time, which is fast enough for an interactive tool.

5.3 Predicting Field Lookups

Our third experiment determines how often field/property lookups could be omitted in assignments and comparisons (on either side).

Our corpus includes 14,004 assignments where the target ends with a field lookup, 7,074 where the source does, and 966 where both do. For those assignments, Figure 15 shows the rank of the correct answer when our algorithm was given the assignment with the final field lookups removed and `.?m` added to the end of both sides of the assignment. The correct answer was in the top 10 choices over 90% of the time when one field lookup was removed, but only about 59% of the time when a field lookup was removed from both sides, going up to 75% when considering the top 20 choices. There were a total of dozens of choices on average.

Our corpus includes 620 comparisons where the left side ends in a lookup, 162 of which end in two lookups; 620 comparisons where the right side ends in a lookup, 174 of which end in two lookups; and 125 where both sides end in a lookup. Of those, Figure 16 shows the ranks our tool gave to the expression in the

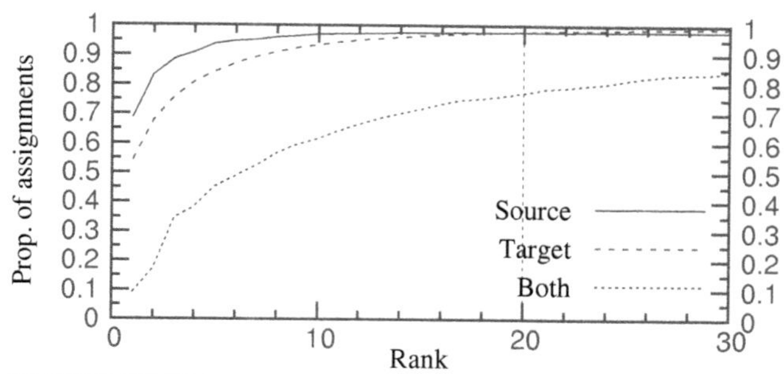

Figure 15. Proportion of assignments where a field lookup could be removed from one or both sides and guessed with a given rank

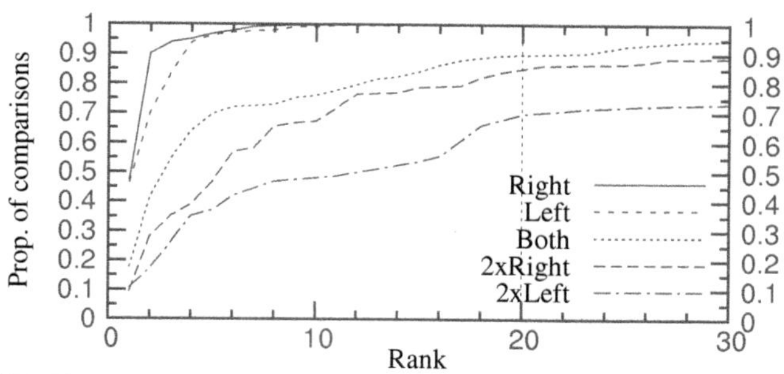

Figure 16. Proportion of comparisons where field lookups could be removed from one or both sides and guessed with a given rank

source given the query containing the original expression with the lookups removed and `.?m.?m` added to the end of both sides.

The numbers are significantly better than for assignments because there are fewer possibilities: few types support comparisons. One lookup can be placed within the top 10 for nearly every instance in our corpus. If we allow 20 choices, then two lookups where one lookup is on each side can be guessed 89% of the time while two lookups on the same side can be guessed 85% of the time if they are are on right and 69% of the time of they are on the left. The discrepancy between the latter two appears to be that comparisons against constants are usually written with the complicated expression on the left and the constant on the right, and the name matching feature is not helpful for comparisons to constants.

Speed 99.5% of these queries ran in under half a second.

5.4 Sensitivity analysis of ranking function

To see which parts of the ranking function were most important, we re-ran the experiments with various modified ranking functions. Each modified version either included only one of the terms or left out one of the terms, in addition to versions that left out and included both the type distance term and the abstract type term. Table 2 shows the data for the proportion of expressions where the correct answer was in the top 20 choices for different variants of the ranking function for each of the experiments.

Methods Type distance and abstract type distance are the only features that matter. Leaving out the namespace and in-scope static terms seems to make almost no difference. Furthermore, the two type distance terms separately are both good, with abstract type distance alone being a little better, but not quite as good as the two together, confirming that both are useful.

Arguments It seems that only the depth feature seems to matter. Leaving it out makes the results much worse while leaving any other term out has almost no effect. In fact, looking at the "+d"

	Count	All	−n	−s	−d	−m	−t	−a	−at	+n	+s	+d	+m	+t	+a	+at
Methods																
All	21176	0.90	0.90	0.90	-	-	0.85	0.84	0.43	0.43	0.43	-	-	0.84	0.85	0.90
Instance	13904	0.96	0.96	0.96	-	-	0.87	0.94	0.31	0.31	0.31	-	-	0.94	0.87	0.96
Static	7272	0.78	0.78	0.78	-	-	0.80	0.65	0.65	0.68	0.65	-	-	0.64	0.81	0.78
Arguments																
Normal	45325	0.90	0.90	-	0.72	-	0.90	0.90	0.90	0.72	-	0.90	-	0.72	0.72	0.72
No variables	14925	0.77	0.77	-	0.65	-	0.76	0.77	0.76	0.64	-	0.76	-	0.65	0.64	0.65
Assignments																
Target	14004	0.97	-	-	0.87	-	0.97	0.97	0.97	-	-	0.97	-	0.81	0.87	0.87
Source	7074	0.89	-	-	0.87	-	0.90	0.89	0.90	-	-	0.90	-	0.87	0.89	0.87
Both	966	0.75	-	-	0.76	-	0.74	0.75	0.73	-	-	0.73	-	0.75	0.75	0.76
Comparisons																
Left	620	1.00	-	-	0.23	1.00	1.00	1.00	1.00	-	-	1.00	0.65	0.25	0.68	0.25
Right	620	1.00	-	-	0.51	1.00	1.00	1.00	1.00	-	-	1.00	0.53	0.62	0.85	0.62
Both	125	0.89	-	-	0.46	0.87	0.88	0.89	0.88	-	-	0.87	0.46	0.42	0.37	0.42
2xLeft	162	0.69	-	-	0.14	0.69	0.70	0.69	0.70	-	-	0.69	0.41	0.18	0.57	0.18
2xRight	174	0.85	-	-	0.63	0.81	0.81	0.85	0.81	-	-	0.77	0.58	0.71	0.73	0.71

Table 2. Ranking function term sensitivity. Each cell is the proportion where correct answer was found in the top 20 choices with various modifications of the ranking function. "All" is the full ranking function. For the rest, − means without certain terms, + means with only certain terms: 'n'=namespaces, 's'=in-scope static, 'd'=depth, 'm'=matching name, 't'=normal type distance, and 'a'=abstract type distance.

column, using just the depth term gives almost exactly the same results as the full ranking scheme.

Assignments For just one lookup removed from either side, once again only depth matters, but when a lookup is missing from both sides, the type distance computation becomes important. In fact, in the case of a lookup missing from both sides, leaving out the depth component improves the results. This is not too surprising as there are likely many possible assignments which require adding only one lookup to either side. The interesting part is that apparently these lookups can be distinguished from the proper one by looking at more detailed type information (recall that only assignments which are type correct are even being considered).

Comparisons Depth once again seems to be most important. Except on the "2xRight" row, depth appears to be the only significant feature. The different values for that row vary little, indicating that each ranking feature is somewhat useful, but there is little gain from combining them. On average, there were hundreds of type-correct options, so the ranking function is definitely doing something to place the correct option in the top 20.

5.5 Threats to validity

As the experiments were run on decompiled code instead of actual source code, they may not apply to how programmers actually write code. Particularly, the decompiled code may have simpler expressions due to a compiler factoring out additional local variables from complex expressions. This did not appear to be the case from looking at code being analyzed as non-trivial expressions were visible like method calls and binary operations in method argument positions. On the other hand, the decompiled code looked different across projects (specifically, some projects had local variables with names like "`local0`" while others had actual names), so there may be some compiler-dependence involved.

Working on completed projects as opposed to codebases in the process of being developed means that abstract type inference algorithm may have had more information than it would have had in a real development scenario. Note that since the rest of the features work only on the current expression, they are unaffected by the maturity of the codebase. On the other hand, more development likely corresponds to more APIs existing in the codebase which could appear in the results of a query.

The subset of the arguments that got the best results was always used, not the subset of arguments that the programmer would be most likely to think of when writing a query. Naturally, the latter is difficult to determine automatically. Looking at the results, the queries generated tended to seem reasonable. The main reason this could be a problem is when one of the options to a method is a type used only as an option to a small number of methods like the `System.IO.FileMode` enum which is used only for methods that open files. Such types seemed to be rare, although no quantitative analysis was done to confirm that.

More importantly, every single expression in the analyzed codebases was used, as opposed to restricting the analysis to only the ones that the programmer would find difficult to write. Naturally, the latter is difficult to determine automatically. It seems safe to assume that the vast majority of API usages in a codebase were easy for the programmer to write, so the experiment results cannot be taken as direct evidence that our proposed tool would be effective in answering queries. Instead, the experiment results should be taken as an argument that expressions in a program tend to be well specified by a small subset of the information needed to exactly define the expression, and therefore the technique of searching for expressions using a partial expression as a query should tend to work well in practice.

The experiments worked only on C# code. We expect to obtain similar results on code written in languages with a rich type system such as Java.

6. Related Work

Prospector[10] is perhaps the closest related work. With Prospector, as discussed in Section 2.3, a user makes a query for a conversion from one type to another and gets what the authors call a "jungloid" which is a series of operations including method calls, field lookups, and downcasts from examples in the code. That paper noted that shorter jungloids tend to be more likely to be correct and also that jungloids that cross package boundaries are less likely to be correct, both of which are ideas used by our ranking function.

PARSEWeb[17] performs the same task as Prospector except it mines code examples from web searches.

InSynth[6] also produces expressions for a given point in code using the type as well as the context to build more complicated expressions using a theorem prover. InSynth's ranking algorithm is based on machine learning from examples. It, like Prospector, differs from our work in that it generates expressions from scratch with no input from the programmer to guide it. Their evaluation was on small snippets of Java example code translated to Scala which is difficult to compare to our evaluation on mature C# projects.

Typsy[1] searches for APIs by generating expressions involving any number of method and constructor calls and field lookups given a list of arguments, a return type, and a library package to search within. Typsy will only return expressions with all arguments filled in, so it will generate expressions to construct any missing arguments for methods it finds. The expressions are ranked by their size similar to the depth term in our system, although our depth term does not count the number of method and constructor calls because it will not generate new ones not specified by the programmer.

API Explorer[3] supports queries both for methods taking a given argument and for how to construct a value of a given type. When querying for methods, a keyword can also be provided, so the results are filtered to contain only methods with synonyms of that keyword in the name. The ordering of the results uses a computation similar to our type distance feature. Both types of queries can be expressed in our partial expressions language, except we do not have a way to filter by keywords, and the version used for our experiments does not generate constructor calls when asked for an unknown method.

Strathcona[7] and XSnippet[14] both use context to produce queries which may be helpful to the programmer. In a similar vein, CodeBroker[18] performs searches for APIs based on the documentation of the method currently being written in order to recommend APIs the user may not even be aware of.

Little and Miller[9] propose a system using "keyword programming" to generate method calls where the user gives keywords and the system generates a method call that includes arguments that have most or all of the keywords. Their system attempts to be closer to natural language than ours at the cost of a lower success rate.

Hou and Pletcher[8] recommend various ways of filtering and sorting APIs to show the most relevant choices first. Their system is mainly based on manual annotations of APIs as well as considering how often an API is used. Their work is complementary as it could be used to filter out irrelevant methods from our results.

Searching for functions by type has been recommended for functional programming languages[13][20]. Those proposals differ in that the type signature alone, along with modifications to, for example, handle both curried and uncurried functions, tends to be sufficient for a search. In imperative languages with subtyping, inexact matches are more likely to be meaningful and side-effects make it more likely that many options have the same type.

For discovery of entire modules at once, specification matching can search by specification[21]. Semantics-based code search[12] similarly searches based on specifications including tests and keywords but additionally may make minor modifications to the code to fit the details of the specification.

SNIFF[2] returns snippets matching natural language queries by mining multiple examples from existing code, matching them based on the documentation of the APIs they use, and combining them based on their similarities to eliminate the usage-specific parts of the snippets. Unlike our algorithm, this technique requires the API being searched to be well-documented.

MatchMaker[19] handles API discovery at a different scale: given two types, it generates the glue code to connect those two types by generalizing examples from existing code.

Program sketching[15][16] is a form of program synthesis[5] where the programmer writes a partial program with holes and provides a specification the solution must satisfy. Our technique is similar but considers only a single expression at a time and avoids the need for an explicit specification by using type information to filter the results.

7. Conclusions and Future Work

This paper has shown that type-directed completion of partial expressions can effectively fill in short code snippets that are complicated enough to be difficult to discover using code completion. Furthermore, our ranking scheme is able to sift through hundreds of options to often place the correct answer among the top results.

Future work would be to implement an IDE plug-in and perform a user study to determine if it is useful in real development situations as well as possibly seeing if developers have other ideas for how such a plugin could be used or for similar ideas for lightweight searches. Extending the algorithm to other programming languages is also future work. The features are at least partially tied to C#/Java and will need to be adapted to make sense in other languages.

Acknowledgments

This work was funded by a grant from Microsoft Research. We thank the anonymous reviewers for their valuable feedback.

References

[1] C. Bolton. Typsy: a type-based search tool for Java programmers. In C. Miller, editor, *Selected 2001 SRC Summer Intern Projects*, Technical Note 2001-004. Compaq Systems Research Center, Dec. 2001.

[2] S. Chatterjee, S. Juvekar, and K. Sen. SNIFF: A search engine for Java using free-form queries. ETAPS/FASE, 2009.

[3] E. Duala-Ekoko and M. P. Robillard. Using structure-based recommendations to facilitate discoverability in APIs. ECOOP, 2011.

[4] G. Furnas, T. Landauer, L. Gomez, and S. Dumais. The vocabulary problem in human-system communication. *CACM*, 30, Nov 1987.

[5] S. Gulwani. Dimensions in program synthesis. In *PPDP*, 2010.

[6] T. Gvero, V. Kuncak, and R. Piskac. Interactive synthesis of code snippets. In *Computer Aided Verification (CAV) Tool Demo*, 2011.

[7] R. Holmes and G. C. Murphy. Using structural context to recommend source code examples. ICSE, 2005.

[8] D. Hou and D. M. Pletcher. Towards a better code completion system by API grouping, filtering, and popularity-based ranking. RSSE, 2010.

[9] G. Little and R. C. Miller. Keyword programming in Java. ASE, 2007.

[10] D. Mandelin, L. Xu, R. Bodík, and D. Kimelman. Jungloid mining: helping to navigate the API jungle. PLDI, 2005.

[11] R. O'Callahan and D. Jackson. Lackwit: A program understanding tool based on type inference. ICSE, 1997.

[12] S. P. Reiss. Semantics-based code search. ICSE, 2009.

[13] M. Rittri and M. Rittri. Retrieving library identifiers via equational matching of types. CADE, 1992.

[14] N. Sahavechaphan and K. Claypool. XSnippet: mining for sample code. OOPSLA, 2006.

[15] A. Solar Lezama. *Program Synthesis By Sketching*. PhD thesis, EECS Department, University of California, Berkeley, Dec 2008.

[16] A. Solar-Lezama. The sketching approach to program synthesis. APLAS, 2009.

[17] S. Thummalapenta and T. Xie. PARSEWeb: a programmer assistant for reusing open source code on the web. ASE, 2007.

[18] Y. Ye and G. Fischer. Supporting reuse by delivering task-relevant and personalized information. ICSE, 2002.

[19] K. Yessenov, Z. Xu, and A. Solar-Lezama. Data-driven synthesis for object-oriented frameworks. OOPSLA, 2011.

[20] A. M. Zaremski and J. M. Wing. Signature matching: a tool for using software libraries. *ACM Trans. Softw. Eng. Methodol.*, April 1995.

[21] A. M. Zaremski and J. M. Wing. Specification matching of software components. *ACM Trans. Softw. Eng. Methodol.*, 6:333–369, 1996.

Self-Stabilizing Java

Yong hun Eom and Brian Demsky
University of California, Irvine
{yeom,bdemsky}@uci.edu

Abstract

Self-stabilizing programs automatically recover from state corruption caused by software bugs and other sources to reach the correct state. A number of applications are inherently self-stabilizing—such programs typically overwrite all non-constant data with new input data. We present a type system and static analyses that together check whether a program is self-stabilizing. We combine this with a code generation strategy that ensures that a program continues executing long enough to self-stabilize. Our experience using SJava indicates that (1) SJava annotations are easy to write once one understands a program and (2) SJava successfully checked that several benchmarks were self-stabilizing.

Categories and Subject Descriptors D.2.4 [*Software Engineering*]: Software/Program Verification—Reliability

General Terms Languages, Reliability

Keywords Self-Stabilization, Software Robustness

1. Introduction

Software bugs have long plagued software systems. Proving software systems correct remains a difficult problem. Practitioners have instead relied on extensive testing to verify that programs operate correctly in the scenarios that they are likely to be used (i.e., their comfort zones [14]). Despite extensive testing effort, it is common for unusual inputs to trigger a bug that corrupts the program's state. After a bug corrupts a program's state, the program can in general behave arbitrarily. Self-stabilizing systems, however, are guaranteed to reach the correct state after a finite number of steps [6].

This paper presents a combination of a type system and static analyses that together check that a software application is self-stabilizing with respect to rarely-triggered software bugs and certain types of transient hardware failures. The self-stabilization property checked by SJava is very powerful—it ensures that if a user returns to using a software system in the ways it was tested for, the software system will resume working correctly.

1.1 Basic Approach

SJava checks that program executions eventually transition from incorrect states to the correct state by showing that incorrect values eventually leave the execution and are replaced by correct values.

PLDI'12, June 11–16, 2012, Beijing, China.

The approach targets programs that have a main event loop that acquires new inputs at each iteration. SJava partitions both the heap and variable memory locations into abstract locations using location types. Location types form a lattice. SJava checks two properties that together ensure that a program self-stabilizes. The first property is that values only flow from higher to lower abstract locations (hence referred to as the *flow-down rule*). Like information flow [12], SJava must enforce the flow constraint on both the explicit flows caused by assignments and the implicit flows caused by branching on a value and then storing a value. SJava leverages a linear type system to prohibit aliases that could potentially subvert the flow-down rule. The second property is that values can only remain at a location for a bounded time.

Figure 1 presents a graphical depiction of the effect of these two properties on an execution whose state is corrupted by a bug. The red ×'s indicate corrupted values while the green ✓'s indicate correct values. These two properties together ensure that after a bounded time, memory locations with the highest location types have the same value in both the correct execution and the buggy execution. As the execution progresses, memory locations with lower location types have their corrupted values overwritten with correct values. Eventually, all memory locations have correct values and the buggy execution has self-stabilized into the correct state.

1.2 Error Model

SJava checks that applications self-stabilize in response to errors that occur inside the event loop. We make the assumption that the application successfully reaches the entrance to the event loop. We believe that this is a reasonable assumption; a human can often intervene for systems that fail to start up. Furthermore, we assume that all input reads are performed unconditionally in every iteration of the event loop, to eliminate the possibility of framing errors.

SJava primarily targets rarely-triggered software bugs. We assume that code is mostly correct with the possibility that rare input sequences may cause the program to behave incorrectly. We model these errors as incorrect state transitions to an incorrect state. The SJava system guarantees that if a program in a bad state is fed a

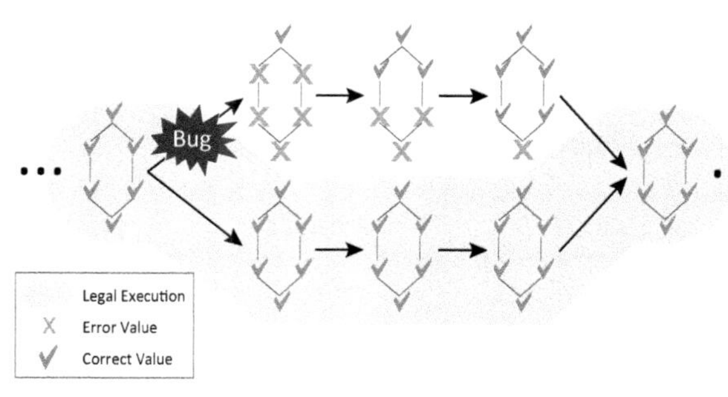

Figure 1. Trace of the Program State

previously tested input sequence longer than the self-stabilization period, the program will reach the exact state as in the test.

Our basic approach is also applicable to certain types of hardware errors. For example, SJava can guarantee self-stabilization for hardware errors that create faulty inputs to an application. In general, SJava can handle transient hardware errors if the hardware errors (1) do not affect the termination of loops, (2) do not corrupt event loop invariant values in variables or memory, (3) do not violate type safety, and (4) do not cause the execution to jump to arbitrary statements. Compiler and hardware implementations can ensure these types of guarantees thus preserving the self-stabilization property [7–9].

1.3 Usage Scenarios

We envision several usage scenarios focusing on embedded controllers and stream decoders. We describe a few scenarios in more detail below:

- **Multimedia Streaming:** Unexpected values can easily cause video and audio decoders to crash or misbehave and prevent playing the remainder of a multimedia stream. Self-stabilizing decoders might fail to decode short periods of a stream due to software bugs, but these failures will only be transient and the remainder of the stream will be correctly decoded.
- **Embedded Controllers:** Many embedded controllers are intended to operate for long periods without human intervention. Software bugs can cause these controllers to enter states where they fail to perform as intended. In some cases, it may take significant time for humans to recognize that the controller is misbehaving and reset the software systems. Self-stabilizing controllers are guaranteed to return to correct operation.
- **Safety Critical Code:** A concern with safety critical systems is that possibly undetected bugs might transition a software system to a corrupted state that prevents further operation. While self-stabilizing systems do not guarantee the absence of bugs, they bound the time frame that even undetected errors can affect the correct operation of a system. Self-stabilization is not intended to replace the rigorous validation processes that are currently used to ensure correctness, but rather to complement these processes to limit the consequences of bugs that inevitably slip through.

1.4 Contributions

This paper makes the following contributions:

- **Basic Approach:** It presents a basic approach for checking whether programs are self-stabilizing.
- **Types for Self-Stabilization:** It presents a type system that ensures that values eventually flow out of a program to return the program to the correct state.
- **Implementation:** It presents an implementation of an SJava compiler including the type system and static analyses.
- **Experience:** It presents our experiences using SJava to check that several applications are self-stabilizing.

The remainder of the paper is organized as follows. Section 2 presents an example. Section 3 presents the location type abstraction. Section 4 presents the type checking rules. Section 5 presents the static analysis that checks that corrupted values are eventually evicted. Section 6 presents our approach for ensuring that event loop iterations terminate. Section 7 presents our approach to code generation. Section 8 overviews the basic correctness argument. Section 9 evaluates our approach on several benchmark applications. Section 10 presents related work; we conclude in Section 11.

```
1  @LATTICE("DIR<TMP,TMP<BIN")
2  public class WDSensor{
3    @LOC("BIN") private WindRec windRec = new WindRec();
4    @LOC("DIR") private int dir;
5
6    @LATTICE("STR<WDOBJ,WDOBJ<IN")
7    @THISLOC("WDOBJ")
8    public void windDirection(){
9      SJAVA:
10     while(true){  // main event loop
11       @LOC("IN") int inDir = Device.readSensor();
12       // move old wind directions one step down
13       windRec.dir2 = windRec.dir1;
14       windRec.dir1 = windRec.dir0;
15       // add a new wind direction
16       windRec.dir0 = inDir;
17       @LOC("STR") String strDir = calculate();
18       broadcastChange(strDir);
19     }
20   }
21
22   @LATTICE("OUT<CAOBJ")
23   @THISLOC("CAOBJ")
24   @RETURNLOC("OUT")
25   public String calculate(){
26      @LOC("CAOBJ,TMP") int majorDir;
27      @LOC("OUT") String strDir;
28      // calculate the majority
29      ...
30      this.dir = majorDir;
31      strDir = convertToString(majorDir);
32      return strDir;
33   }
34 }
35
36 @LATTICE("DIR2<DIR1,DIR1<DIR0")
37 class WindRec{
38   @LOC("DIR0") public int dir0;
39   @LOC("DIR1") public int dir1;
40   @LOC("DIR2") public int dir2;
41 }
```

Figure 2. Wind Direction Sensor Example

2. Example

We present a Java weather station example to illustrate SJava. The weather station processes sensor inputs and broadcasts them. Figure 2 presents the main event loop for the weather station. The loop reads sensor data from a device in Line 11, adds it to the `WindRec` object that stores the most recent three directions in Line 16, and determines the wind direction by calling the `calculate()` method. To compensate for sensor errors, the `calculate()` method examines the previous three directions and computes the median to discard invalid direction values.

2.1 Self-Stabilization

Software bugs or hardware failures can corrupt an application's state, causing problems during its subsequent execution. In our example, there are many possible ways of arriving at an incorrect state. In one possible scenario, the device returns an erroneous value, which is not one of the 16 possible directions. This value is stored in and corrupts the `windRec` data structure. Next, the `convertToString()` method throws an uncaught null pointer exception due to the corrupted value in `windRec`. Finally, the program fails to show the current wind direction.

Once a bug occurs, the system potentially has undefined and possibly undesirable behavior because the program's state may contain corrupted values. Our observation is that the system will resume normal behavior if the execution eventually arrives at the correct state. In the example, after any erroneous value enters the `windRec` data structure the program would return to the correct execution after at most three iterations of the main loop. SJava only computes whether a program self-stabilizes and not when it self-stabilizes. However, it is possible to compute bounds by analyzing the lattice.

SJava analyzes programs that employ the main event loop pattern: an outer loop retrieves a new input, processes it, and produces the output. The goal is to check that all effects of a value disappear after a finite number of main event loop iterations.

To show that the program cannot remain indefinitely in incorrect states, we first establish an ordering relation on the memory locations in the program. The ordering relation forms a location hierarchy that constrains how values flow through the program. Precisely, it ensures that values flow in one direction: from higher locations to lower locations. Therefore, assignments are only allowed if the location of the left-hand side of an assignment is lower than the location of the value to be stored.

However, forbidding assignments that violate ordering constraints is not sufficient to obtain the desired property because it does not force values in the program's memory to be evicted within a finite number of steps. Therefore, the SJava compiler ensures that non-loop invariant values that are live are evicted within one loop iteration. Our analysis is designed to check eviction of memory locations within one loop iteration as checking longer eviction times is unlikely to provide significant benefits but requires more sophisticated techniques that can reason about predicates.

Even if a program does not store any values indefinitely, it may crash before it reaches a legal state. Given the guarantee that the system will return to the correct state, the developer may choose to have the program log and then ignore uncaught exceptions. SJava optionally supports ignoring uncaught exceptions to ensure that the program will execute long enough to self-stabilize.

2.2 SJava Annotations

Line 1 of Figure 2 defines the location hierarchy for the fields in the `WDSensor` class. The ordering relation, as defined by the < operator, allows values to flow from the location type that appears after the operator to the location type that appears before the operator. The example location hierarchy constrains values to only flow down from locations with the `BIN` location type to locations with the `TMP` location type to locations with the `DIR` location type (flows directly from the `BIN` location to the `DIR` location that skip the `TMP` location are allowed). We use the annotation `@LOC` to declare that the field `windRec` has the location type `BIN` in Line 3.

Line 22 defines the location hierarchy for the `calculate()` method. Local variables have composite locations, where a composite location consists of a location in the method's hierarchy followed by any number of locations from field hierarchies. The ordering of composite locations is given by comparing the elements of the two composite locations in lexical order. Line 26 declares the composite location type `LOC`⟨`CAOBJ`, `TMP`⟩ for the `majorDir` variable. This location is lower than ⟨`CAOBJ`, `BIN`⟩ and higher than ⟨`CAOBJ`, `DIR`⟩ since the field hierarchy has the ordering relations `DIR` $\sqsubset$ `TMP` and `TMP` $\sqsubset$ `BIN`. Developers must assign a location in the hierarchy to the `this` variable using the annotation `@THISLOC`. Line 23 assigns the `CAOBJ` location to the `this` variable.

The special label `SJAVA` in Line 9 specifies that the `while` loop in the next line is the main event loop. We next discuss how the compiler checks that the program statements evaluated through the iteration of the main event loop do not violate the flow constraints.

2.3 Checking Self-Stabilization

The SJava compiler checks the parts of the program that are callable from the main event loop. First, it checks that every field, variable, and parameter accessed in the main event loop has been annotated with a location type. Next, it checks that all assignments respect the ordering relation. Specifically, an assignment is only allowed if the left-hand side's location is lower than the value being assigned. For example, the assignment to `this.str` in line 30 is valid because the location type ⟨`CAOBJ`, `TMP`⟩ of the source value is higher than the location type ⟨`CAOBJ`, `DIR`⟩ of the destination.

For every call site, the compiler must check that value flows created by the callee do not violate the caller's ordering constraints. Location lattices in SJava are not global—each method instance has its own locally-scoped location lattice. SJava's method local location lattices allow a single method to be used in several different contexts in which the arguments do not have the same location types. It also makes our type system composable—the SJava location type system captures the behavior of a method and not how the method happens to be used in the overall system. SJava must ensure that the location lattice of the callee enforces the flow constraints of the caller's argument. Alternatively, this check can be viewed as verifying that the caller and callee lattices can be merged into a single combined lattice. Specifically, the compiler (1) checks that the ordering constraints of the arguments in the caller satisfy the ordering constraints required by the location types of the callee's parameters and (2) computes the highest caller location for the return value that is consistent with the callee's ordering constraints. For example, the compiler processes the location annotations for the `calculate` method to determine that its return value is lower than its receiver object, and then checks that this is consistent with the caller's lattice (i.e., that the variable `strDir` has a lower location than the `this` variable).

The SJava compiler also checks that all memory locations accessed by the event loop are either loop invariant or were overwritten in either the current or previous loop iteration. In the example, all variables and fields are obviously overwritten by each iteration of the event loop. A termination analysis (Section 6) ensures that each iteration of the event loop terminates by prohibiting recursive calls [1] and checking that inner loops terminate.

3. Location Type System

In SJava, every memory location has a location type in addition to its Java type. A location type constrains which types can be stored in the corresponding memory location. The compiler checks that every assignment moves values from memory locations with higher location types to memory locations with lower location types.

3.1 Location Types

A program execution may create a statically unbounded number of concrete memory locations. We therefore map the concrete memory locations to a finite set of location types. Location types are assigned by the developer to field declarations, variable declarations, and parameter declarations.

3.2 Location Type Lattice

The location hierarchy is defined by the lattice $\langle L_{SET}, \sqsubseteq \rangle$, where L_{SET} is the set of location types and the binary relation $\sqsubseteq$ establishes an ordering between location types. It is useful to note that we use both the reflexive partial ordering ($\sqsubseteq$) and the corresponding strict partial ordering ($\sqsubset$). We make use of the reflexive partial ordering to support the standard lattice machinery while our type checking rules rely on the strict partial ordering.

For example, `low` $\sqsubset$ `high` means that the location `high` is higher than `low`, specifying that values can legally flow from memory locations with the location type `high` to memory locations with the location type `low`. The location lattice includes the top and bottom locations. The top location $\top$ is the highest location, whose values

[1] Note that the type system and other static analyses currently handle recursive calls. The restriction against recursive calls is only due to limitations in our termination analysis.

Annotation	Role	Applied to
@LATTICE	Defines a location hierarchy	Classes and Methods
@METHODDEFAULT	Defines the class-wide default method hierarchy	Classes
@LOC	Assigns a location to a declaration	Fields, Variables, and Parameters
@THISLOC	Selects a location for the 'this' reference	Methods
@PCLOC	Selects a location for the program counter	Methods
@GLOBALLOC	Selects a location for static references	Methods
@RETURNLOC	Selects a location for a return value	Methods
@DELEGATE	Transfers ownership	Method Parameters
@TRUST	Indicates that a method was manually inspected	Methods

Figure 3. Annotations

can flow anywhere. The bottom location $\perp$ is the lowest location, any value can flow to such locations. The location lattice has the *meet* operator $\sqcap$, which computes the greatest lower bound (GLB) of any two location types in the lattice. Our GLB operation is the standard lexicographic GLB.

3.3 Method and Field Location Lattices

SJava has a separate location hierarchy for each class and method. Each class has a field hierarchy lattice that defines an ordering between fields of the same object instance. Each method has a method hierarchy lattice that is used to establish an ordering between the different variables in the method. Both the field and method hierarchies are defined as lattices. The next section discusses how the elements of method and field hierarchies are combined into a composite location that orders all memory locations in a program.

3.4 Composite Location Types

A composite location type is a sequence of location elements—the first element of the composite location is a method location from the current method's method hierarchy lattice, followed by a sequence of zero or more field locations. Consider the field access expression `foo.bar.z`. It has the composite location type ⟨FOO, Foo.BAR, Bar.Z⟩, where the local variable `foo` has the location type `FOO`, the field `bar` has the location type `BAR` in the field hierarchy of class `Foo`, and `z` has the location type `Z` in the field hierarchy of class `Bar`.

For every field access, the compiler computes the composite location that describes the position in the ordering of the field by combining the composite location type of the reference variable with the field location element. Developers have the option to declare any level of the composite location for local variables. This enables a developer to set the local variable's ordering relative to specific fields so that a local variable with a composite location can take a value from one field, and then store it back to another field in the same object.

3.4.1 Comparison

The comparison of two composite locations is based on lexicographical ordering of the location elements. The comparison begins with the first elements of the two composite locations. If the first elements are not identical, then the lattice for the first location determines the ordering relation of two locations. If the first elements are identical, the comparison continues onward to later elements in the composite location types.

The composite location with n location elements has a set of partial orders $\{\sqsubseteq_1, \sqsubseteq_2, ..., \sqsubseteq_n\}$. The partial ordering relation of the composite location is defined as follows:

$$\langle a_1, a_2, ..., a_n\rangle \sqsubseteq_C \langle b_1, b_2, ..., b_n\rangle \Leftrightarrow$$
$$\exists j \in \{1, ..., n\}.(a_j \sqsubset_j b_j \vee (j = n \wedge a_j = b_j)) \wedge \forall i < j.a_i = b_i$$

Location elements at position i come from a lattice that defines a partial ordering relation $\sqsubseteq_i$. If two field elements are from different classes, then the composite location types are incomparable.

Lexicographical ordering addresses the following issue with implicit information flows through heap paths. Consider a heap path to a primitive field (e.g., `x.f`, where `f` is a primitive field)—if a value is high enough to flow to a reference along the path to the object with field (e.g., the variable `x`), with lexicographical ordering it is also high enough to legally flow to the field (e.g., `f`). The ordering therefore simplifies the typing rules because such flows cannot violate the ordering relation.

3.5 Inheritance

As a subclass inherits fields and methods from its parent class, it must preserve the ordering hierarchy from the parent class. The compiler checks that every location defined in the parent is included in the subclass's field hierarchy. The subclass can of course declare new locations in its hierarchy. The compiler checks that the value flows allowed by the subclass are the same in the parent to prevent the ordering constraints from being subverted by an overridden method or a cast. Checking the hierarchy of an overridden method is exactly the same as the field hierarchy check with the additional constraint that the parameters must have the same declared locations.

3.6 Location Type Annotations

SJava's location type annotations are written using standard Java annotations. Figure 3 summarizes the basic types of SJava annotations. The annotation `@LATTICE` defines a location hierarchy and can be applied to both class and method declarations. Figure 4 presents the grammar for lattice declarations and location declarations. The value in the `@LATTICE` annotation consists of a series of binary relation entries that define the ordering relation. The binary relation uses the inequality notation <, `x` < `y` means that a value can flow from `y` to `x`.

latticeDecl := `@LATTICE` (*orderDecls,sharedLocDecls*)
orderDecls := *orderDecls, orderDecl* | *orderDecl*
orderDecl := *location* < *location*
sharedLocDecls := *sharedLocDecls, location** | *location**
compositeLoc := `@LOC` (*locationList*)
deltaLoc := `@DELTA` (*locationList* | *deltaLoc*)
locationList := *locationList, locElement* | *locElement*
locElement := *location* | ClassName.*location*

Figure 4. Location Declaration and Annotation Grammar

Every method must have a method hierarchy, but declaring a lattice for every method can be labor intensive. Therefore, the SJava provides a default lattice for the method. The `@METHODDEFAULT` annotation on the class declaration defines a class-wide method lattice. If a method is not annotated with a method hierarchy using the `@LATTICE` annotation, the method uses the default lattice for the class. When many methods' behaviors are similar, the default lattice can significantly reduce the annotation burden.

The developer specifies the location types of variable, field, and parameter declarations using the annotation `@LOC` followed by a parenthesized composite location. The `@THISLOC` annotation designates a location in the method hierarchy for the `this` variable. This allows the compiler to derive the proper composite location for a value accessed through the `this` variable and compute its ordering relations relative to other local variables.

Assigning a location to the static field references is done in a similar manner to the `this` variable. The `@GLOBALLOC` annotation specifies the location of static fields in the method lattice. The type checker ensures that method lattices consistently order globals relative to arguments using the checks that we use to preserve ordering between arguments. At this point, SJava does not support defining an ordering relation between static fields from different classes. Instead, we envision that static fields will be primarily used to store constants, and therefore can be assigned to a very high location. However, static fields could be supported by partitioning them into groups, using annotations to describe the locations of groups, and checking that different methods use these locations consistently.

The program counter location tracks implicit flows. If a method can be safely called when the program counter location is lower than one of the parameter locations, the developer can use the `@PCLOC` to declare the initial location for the program counter. Otherwise, the program counter has the top location.

As noted, developers can assign any composite location to local variables and parameters. For example, on Line 26 from Figure 2, the annotation `@LOC("CAOBJ,TMP") int majorDir` indicates that the variable `majorDir` has the composite location type ⟨`CAOBJ`, `TMP`⟩. For method declarations, the annotation `@LOC` specifies the location type for a parameter and the annotation `@RETURNLOC` specifies the location type of the return value.

4. Flow-down Rule

SJava's type checking is independent from the standard Java type checking, so this section will focus only on the location type checking rules. In SJava, every memory location has a location type that captures how values can flow into and out of that memory location.

We define the following notations: The symbol L represents a composite location type, which is a sequence of location elements. The symbol l represents a location element. The elements of a composite location are $\langle l_0, l_1, ..., l_{n-1} \rangle$. The function *size(L)* returns the size of the sequence representation of the location type L. The static environment Γ provides a mapping from identifiers to location types, Γ_m provides a mapping for the callee m. The *callee_init_env* function returns the initial type environment at the beginning of the method body. The notation $\Gamma(x)$ gives a mapping from the identifier x to either the location type L or the location element l bound to the field. One of the identifiers is the *program counter location* `pc` that represents the current context constraint that restricts the location type of the destination of any assignments. The purpose of the *program counter location* is to track implicit value flows.

4.1 Location Type Checking Rules

Figure 5 presents the type checking rules. There are two kinds of type judgment rules. The judgment $\Gamma \vdash e : L$ states that the expression e has the location type L in the Γ environment. The judgment $\Gamma \vdash e$ states that the expression e is well-typed with respect to the environment Γ. The notation $\Gamma[pc = v]$ represents the same environment except that the program counter pc is bound to new value v. We next describe the basic checking rules:

$$\text{(LITERAL)}\frac{true}{\Gamma \vdash literal : \top} \qquad \text{(OP)}\frac{\Gamma \vdash e_0 : L_0 \quad \Gamma \vdash e_1 : L_1 \quad L = L_0 \sqcap L_1}{\Gamma \vdash e_0 \Box e_1 : L}$$

$$\text{(ASSIGN)}\frac{\Gamma(x) = L \quad \Gamma \vdash e : L_e \quad \Gamma \vdash L \sqsubset L_e \quad \Gamma \vdash L \sqsubset \Gamma(pc)}{\Gamma \vdash x = e : L}$$

$$\text{(VAR)}\frac{\Gamma(x) = L}{\Gamma \vdash x : L} \qquad \text{(FD\_R)}\frac{\Gamma \vdash e : L_e \quad \Gamma(f) = l_f \quad L = L_e \oplus l_f}{\Gamma \vdash e.f : L}$$

$$\text{(FD\_W)}\frac{\begin{array}{c}\Gamma \vdash e_0 : L_0 \quad \Gamma(f) = l_f \quad \Gamma \vdash e_1 : L_1 \\ L = L_0 \oplus l_f \quad \Gamma \vdash L \sqsubset L_1 \quad \Gamma \vdash L \sqsubset \Gamma(pc)\end{array}}{\Gamma \vdash e_0.f = e_1 : L}$$

$$\text{(IF)}\frac{\Gamma \vdash c : L_c \quad \Gamma[pc = \Gamma(pc) \sqcap L_c] \vdash e_{i \in \{1,2\}}}{\Gamma \vdash \mathtt{if}(c)\; e_1 \;\mathtt{else}\; e_2}$$

$$\text{(WHILE)}\frac{\Gamma \vdash c : L_c \quad \Gamma[pc = \Gamma(pc) \sqcap L_c] \vdash e}{\Gamma \vdash \mathtt{while}(c)\; e}$$

$$\text{(ARRAY\_VAR)}\frac{\Gamma \vdash a : L_a \quad \Gamma \vdash i : L_i \quad L = L_a \sqcap L_i}{\Gamma \vdash a[i] : L}$$

$$\text{(ARRAY\_ASG)}\frac{\begin{array}{c}\Gamma \vdash a : L_a \quad \Gamma \vdash i : L_i \quad \Gamma \vdash e : L_e \\ \Gamma \vdash L_a \sqsubset L_i \quad \Gamma \vdash L_a \sqsubset L_e \quad \Gamma \vdash L_a \sqsubset \Gamma(pc)\end{array}}{\Gamma \vdash a[i] = e : L_a}$$

$$\text{(CALL\_SITE)}\frac{\begin{array}{c}\Gamma_m = callee\_init\_env(\mathtt{@RETURNLOC}(V_{rv})\ \mathtt{@THISLOC}(V_t)\ \mathtt{@PCLOC}(V_{pc}) \\ m(\mathtt{@LOC}(V_{p1})p_1, ..., \mathtt{@LOC}(V_{pn})p_n)) \\ \Gamma_m \vdash p_0 : L_0^m \;...\; \Gamma_m \vdash p_n : L_n^m \qquad \Gamma \vdash a_0 : L_0 \;...\; \Gamma \vdash a_n : L_n \\ \forall i, j \in \{0, ..., n\}\ \Gamma_m \vdash L_i^m \sqsubset L_j^m \;\Rightarrow\; \Gamma \vdash L_i \sqsubset L_j \\ X_i = (\mathtt{if}\,(\mathtt{sub}(L_i^m, 0, 1) = L_0^m)\ \mathtt{then}\ L_0 \oplus \mathtt{sub}(L_i^m, 1, size(L_i^m)\ \mathtt{else}\ \bot\,) \\ \forall i \in \{1, ..., n\}\ \Gamma \vdash (X_i \sqsubset L_i \vee X_i = L_i) \\ I_r = \{i \mid \forall i \in \{0, ..., n\},\ \Gamma_m \vdash (L_{rv}^m \sqsubset L_i^m \vee L_{rv}^m = L_i^m)\} \quad L_r = \bigsqcap_{i \in I_r} L_i \\ \forall i \in \{0, ..., n\} \quad L_i^m \sqsubset \Gamma_m(pc) \;\Rightarrow\; L_i \sqsubset \Gamma(pc) \\ \text{call is virtual w/ multiple targets} \;\Rightarrow\; \Gamma_m(pc) \sqsubset L_0^m\end{array}}{\Gamma \vdash a_0.m(a_1, ..., a_n) : L_r}$$

$$\langle l_0, l_1, ..., l_n \rangle \oplus l_m = \langle l_0, l_1, ..., l_n, l_m \rangle$$

$$\mathtt{sub}(\langle l_0, l_1, ..., l_n \rangle, i, j) = \langle l_i, ..., l_{j-1} \rangle$$

Figure 5. Location Type Checking Rules

Literal: Every literal value has the highest location type `TOP` in the location hierarchy, denoted by $\top$. Therefore, all constant values in a program can flow to any memory location.

Operation: The operation rule derives the location type of an arithmetic expression of the form $e_0 \Box e_1$. The derived location type is the greatest lower bound of the location types of two operands.

Variable Assignment: A variable assignment causes a value flow from its right-hand side to its left-hand side. The `ASSIGN` rule checks that the destination's location type is lower than the source's location type. The last premise tracks implicit flows by checking the context constraints due to control flow.

Field Read: For a field read expression `e.f`, a new composite location is derived by appending the location type of the field `f` to the location type of the base expression `e`. The binary operation $\oplus$ adds a new location element to the end of the composite location.

Field Assignments: The field assignment rule is similar that for variable assignments except that the composite location type of the left-hand side is derived from the field access expression.

4.2 Arrays

The naïve approach to handling arrays is to assign all the elements of an array to the same location type. This approach prohibits value flows between elements of the same array and is therefore too restrictive for most real-world applications.

SJava supports two different approaches to arrays. In the first approach, the array have a special *shared location* type that allows value flows between array elements provided that the entire array is cleared out (or lowered) at the same time at some point in each iteration of the event loop. Section 4.7 presents more details on shared locations.

Alternatively, SJava can assign unique locations to each array element. In this case, the array elements are ordered in sequence with the first element having the lowest location and the last having the highest. The SJava library then provides an `insert` method that shifts all the elements down by one index and assigns a new value to the last position. The type system assumes that this method moves all values in the array one step down. The eviction analysis ensures that the insert method is called at least once in each loop iteration.

To ensure that a value flow between an index value and an array does not violate ordering constraints, SJava has two separate rules for array expressions. The ARRAY_VAR rule checks that an array access expression has a location type that is the greatest lower bound of both the location type of the array and the location type of the index. The array assignment rule ARRAY_ASG has to consider the relative ordering of an array and the index value used for that array. The location type of the array should be lower than the location type of the index since the value of the array index affects how values flow into the array. The rule also checks that the location type of an array variable is lower than the value expression being assigned.

4.3 Implicit Flow

Conditional branches may cause implicit value flows that could violate the ordering constraints. The example code below introduces an implicit flow. The value of the variable `a` in the `if` condition statement affects the value assigned to the variable `b`. As a result, if the location type of the variable `b` is higher than the location type of the variable `a`, it is a violation of the ordering constraint since there exists a value flow between them.

```
if (a>0) b=1; else b=0;
```

To prevent implicit flows that violate ordering constraints, the IF and WHILE rules update the program counter location with the location type of the `if` condition or `while` condition, respectively. This ensures that any conditional assignments in the body of the `if` statement or loop prohibit implicit flows that are not permitted.

For the example, after evaluating an `if` statement, the `pc` is set to the location type of the condition expression $\langle A \rangle$, then the compiler checks that the left-hand side of the assignment `b` has a location type lower than `pc`'s location type.

The compiler also ensures that a method call in a conditional branch respects implicit flows. The callee's program counter location reflects the location type of the call site's context constraint.

4.4 Method Invocation

Location type annotations in method declarations impose restrictions that both the caller and the callee must respect. When arguments are passed to the parameters of the call site, the caller must respect the callee's restrictions on the relative orderings of the arguments and the return value. The callee must in turn respect the constraints its declared interface places on its internal value flows. The two sets of restrictions together guarantee that method invocation respects the ordering constraints of the caller and the callee. Alternatively, the call site checks can be viewed as checking that the collection of method lattices can be transformed into one global method lattice that is consistent with the program's value flows.

4.4.1 Call Site Checking

The parameter's location type describes how the location type of an argument in the caller is transferred into the method hierarchy

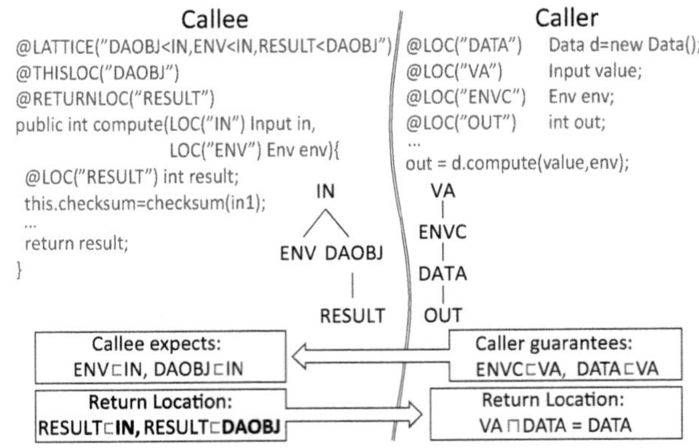

Figure 6. Method Invocation

of the callee. From the perspective of the callee, relative orderings between parameters establish ordering constraints on the location type of a value passed in, which the caller must respect when it assigns values to arguments.

Type checking the call site ensures that the caller provides arguments that respect the callee's ordering constraints, which requires the type checker to check the mapping of location types from the caller's arguments to the callee's parameters. For each call site $m_s(a_0, a_1, ..., a_n)$ to the corresponding method declaration $m(p_0, p_1, .., p_n)$, the rule CALL_SITE checks that for any two parameters p_i and p_j if the callee has the ordering relation $p_i \sqsubset p_j$ between parameters, then the caller has to have the corresponding ordering relation $a_i \sqsubset a_j$ between its arguments. If the callee does not have any ordering relation between two parameters, the caller does not need to respect any ordering constraints on the corresponding two arguments because it implies that the callee will not have a value flow between two parameters. Figure 6 illustrates how the compiler checks constraints of the caller and the callee. The callee has two ordering relations among parameters, ENV ⊏ IN and DAOBJ ⊏ IN in its hierarchy, and therefore the callee imposes two ordering constraints on the caller's arguments. The caller must guarantee that the corresponding arguments have same relation in its hierarchy, in this case ENVC ⊏ VA and DATA ⊏ VA.

If the first element of a parameter location type matches the location type of the current object `this` and a field element is in the next position, the callee establishes ordering constraints relative to the field lattice of the current object. This provides more specific constraints on the ordering relations of fields in the current object; the caller needs to satisfy constraints on not only the ordering relations between arguments, but also the ordering relations of fields given by the field hierarchy of the object referenced type of `this`. For example, suppose that the parameter has the location type ⟨IOBJ, F⟩ and the receiver object has the location type IOBJ. The corresponding argument in the caller is required to be higher than or equal to ⟨O, F⟩ if the object whose method is being invoked has the location type ⟨O⟩ in the caller.

4.4.2 Return Value Location

The call site rule uses the location types of the parameters and the return value to conservatively compute the set of flows that the callee may produce. The rule then computes a caller location type that allows all of these flows in the callee context. This check can be viewed as checking that it is possible to combine the callee and the caller lattices in a way that allows all existing information flows.

The CALL_SITE rule in Figure 5 computes the caller's return value location as follows. First, it computes the set of parameter location types that are higher than or equal to the declared return location type. Parameters that are not higher than the return location type are irrelevant because the ordering constraints prevent value flows from these parameters. In Figure 6, the `compute` method provides a set of parameter location types {`IN`,`DAOBJ`} for calculating the return value location. Next, the rule creates a set of argument location types in the caller that correspond to this set of parameters and then computes the greatest lower bound of the location types of these arguments. The caller in Figure 6 computes the greatest lower bound of `VA` and `DATA` since the callee locations `IN` and `DAOBJ` correspond to the locations `VA` and `DATA`, respectively, in the caller's hierarchy. In this case, the location type of the return value is `DATA`, which means that the caller must not return a value that is lower than the location type `DATA`. If the return value of the method is the right-hand side of an assignment, the rule `ASSIGN` then checks that the return value location is higher than the left-hand side. The last assignment in the right column of the Figure 6 satisfies the ordering constraints with the location type of the return value `DATA`.

4.5 Objects

Non-static fields are always accessed through an instance reference variable. The location types of instance reference variables provide a way to compute the relative ordering between other local instances. In the case of copying field values from one instance to another instance, the static checking checks that the location of the source instance is higher than the destination. The current implementation of SJava prohibits recursive data structures. Future work could relax this constraint. One approach is to require programs to delete all references to a recursive data structures within some loop iteration bound.

4.5.1 Aliasing

Aliasing refers to the situation in which multiple references point to the same object. In SJava, if two aliased references to the same object were allowed to have different location types, this would open the possibility of values flowing from the lower locations to higher locations through the aliased references in violation of the flow-down rule. For example, suppose that a program creates two references with different location types to the same object. The static checking as described would allow the program to use the higher reference to access a value from a field that was written to using the lower reference. One approach to ensuring that aliasing is safe is to ensure that all aliases to an object have the same location type.

SJava uses linear types to restrict aliasing. SJava's linear type system prohibits multiple heap aliases from referencing the same object. This implies that the heap that can be updated by the event loop in SJava must be a forest of objects (multiple disjoint trees). SJava allows limited aliasing from local variables and parameters—variable aliases are allowed as long as all aliases have the same location type. A side effect is that if an alias exists to any object in a tree, the location type of all objects in that tree cannot be changed.

4.5.2 Ownership Transfer

In some cases, a method may need to lower the location type of an object passed in as a parameter. SJava supports ownership transfer to allow a caller method to transfer ownership of a non-aliased reference to a callee method.

The method acquires ownership of a non-aliased reference through parameters with the `@DELEGATE` annotation. Exclusive ownership allows the method to lower the location type of a reference, to transfer its ownership to other methods, to create heap references to the object, and to remove subtrees from the heap reachable from the object. Ownership transfer guarantees that a given reference must be owned by only one method and no aliases to the object exist in other scopes. In this respect, the caller has the responsibility to pass a unique reference argument to the callee. Static checking of the caller checks that all references to the object are dead after the call site. Methods can only returned owned references. Returning aliased references could be supported with an annotation that declares that the return value is aliased and gives the parameter from which the alias was obtained.

The ownership status of a variable can be either (1) a parent method owns the tree (i.e. the object is aliased), (2) in the case of temporary variable used to traverse a locally own tree, the local variable that contains the owned reference to the tree's root, or (3) the current local variable owns the reference. We only allow changing the level of a reference if (1) the reference owns the tree and (2) no other local variables refer to objects in the same tree. We allow transferring ownership of a component object of a tree only if (1) the current method owns the tree and (2) the temporary variable used to remove the reference is the only reference other than the owning reference.

4.6 Delta Locations

Code often uses temporary variables to access data structures. Including location types for all of these temporary variables would greatly complicate both the method and field hierarchies. Instead, SJava provides a special function `delta` that takes a composite location and generates a new composite location, called a *delta location*, which is lower than the input composite location and higher than everything that is lower than the input composite location. The delta function is applied to a whole composite location. The delta function can be applied to the output of itself to generate a descending series of composite locations.

Consider a code segment that copies a value from an object field to a local variable, computes a value using the local variable, and then stores the value to a different, lower field of the same object. This value flow involves a variable, so it requires the variable to have a location between the two fields in the field hierarchy. With the delta function applied to the composite location of the source field, it is straightforward to generate a composite location for the local variable that is lower than the source field and higher than the destination field. In the example from Section 2, the composite location ⟨`CAOBJ`,`TMP`⟩ can be replaced with `delta`(⟨`CAOBJ`,`BIN`⟩) in Line 26. It generates a new location that is lower than ⟨`CAOBJ`,`BIN`⟩ and higher than all locations below ⟨`CAOBJ`,`BIN`⟩.

For correctness purposes, delta functions are syntactic sugar that introduces new elements into the hierarchy of the last component of the composite location and updates the lattice appropriately.

4.7 Shared Locations

The flow-down rule ensures that every assignment lowers the location type of the value being assigned. This constraint prohibits common computations that read from a set of memory locations, perform computation, and store the results into the same set of memory locations. This constraint also prohibits simple `for` loops, e.g., `for(int i=0;i<10;i++) ;`, as the increment operation violates the standard flow-down rule.

SJava provides shared location types for primitive types to allow developers to specify a set of memory locations with the same composite location that values can flow freely between. The developer can assign the same shared location to multiple locations, and then freely flow values between those locations. Shared location are explicitly listed in the lattice annotation with a *.

SJava must ensure that a program actually clears out all memory locations with the same shared location type and does not merely shuffle corrupted values between memory locations. A shared memory location is cleared when a value from a higher location is written and remains cleared until the program overwrites that memory location with a value with the same shared location type.

SJava checks that all memory locations with the same shared location type are simultaneously in the cleared state at least once per an event loop iteration (or before every use). Therefore, the program cannot use a shared location to store values indefinitely (and circumvent self-stabilization) even though a shared location may keep values through assignments. In the next section, we describe how SJava uses static analysis to check this constraint. Among other uses, shared locations are useful for allowing index variables in `for` loops.

5. Eviction of Values

Although the flow-down rule ensures that all value flows respect the ordering constraints, it does not ensure that values leave a memory location in a bounded time period. For example, suppose that a variable is written by one event loop iteration, and all future iterations of the event loop read that value. In this scenario, a corrupted value can remain indefinitely and the execution may never self-stabilize. This section presents a static analysis that ensures that a memory location does not store values indefinitely.

5.1 Definitely-Written Analysis

The definitely-written analysis ensures that reads inside the event loop either read (1) a value written outside of the event loop or (2) a value written by the current or the immediately preceding event loop iteration. This ensures that corrupted values cannot remain live in the same memory location indefinitely.

The analysis checks that for each memory location M that the event loop either (1) overwrites M or (2) overwrites a reference that lies on the heap path to M (thus lowering M or making it unreachable). The analysis operates in two stages. In the first stage, it computes read and write sets. In the second stage, it checks that the event loop body respects the definitely-written constraints.

5.1.1 Computing Read and Write Sets

The analysis generates the read set R^m, the may-write set OW^m, and the must-write set WT^m for the main event loop and each method m that is callable from the main event loop. Elements of these sets are represented by heap paths, which are n-tuples of references that describe the sequence of heap accesses to reach a memory location from one of the method's parameters. For example, accessing the field `f` of an expression `x` that is reachable from the parameter $\mathtt{p}_1$ through a sequence of references $r_1, ..., r_n$ generates the heap path $\langle \mathtt{p}_1, r_1, ..., r_n, \mathtt{f}\rangle$. The analysis computes a mapping HP that maps a variable to the heap path that describes the sequence of references from the parameter to the object the variable references. The analysis can safely ignore reads and writes on local variables as they will go out of scope when the method exits.

Our analysis uses a standard fixed-point algorithm. Figure 7 presents the transfer functions for computing read and write set. We define the helper function $HP(\mathtt{x})=\{hp \mid \langle \mathtt{x}, hp\rangle \in HP\}$.

Read: The set R^m contains the heap paths that must either be never written in the loop or overwritten before the method m is called in a different iteration of the event loop. The field read statement `x=y.f` generates a new heap path for `x` by appending the field `f` to the heap path $HP(\mathtt{y})$. The read statement also adds the corresponding heap path to R^m if it or a prefix may not have been overwritten since the method entry.

Write: The field write statement `x.f=y` adds the heap path through `f` to the set WT and the set OW^m. Note that it is not necessary to ensure that we update existing heap paths when creating a new heap path. The reason is that the flow-down rule ensures that reference involved in new heap paths must flow down.

Call Site: For the call site $\mathtt{c}(a_0, ..., a_n)$, the callee's read and write effects are propagated to the caller. The analysis first computes the sets OW^c_{bound}, WT^c_{bound} and R^c_{bound} for all possible callees.

st	
`x=y.f`	$HP' = HP \cup \{\langle x, p \oplus f\rangle \mid p \in HP(\mathtt{y})\}$ $R_{new} = \{p \oplus f \mid p \in HP(\mathtt{y}), \exists p' \in WT \Rightarrow \neg\mathtt{Pre}(p \oplus f, p')\}$ $R^{m'} = R^m \cup R_{new}$
`x.f=y`	$WT' = WT \cup \{HP(\mathtt{x}) \oplus f\}$ $OW^{m'} = OW^m \cup \{HP(\mathtt{x}) \oplus f\}$
`call` $\mathtt{c}(a_0, ..., a_n)$	$R^c_{bound} = \bigcup_{c \in calleeSet(c), i \in \{0,...,n\}} \{HP(\mathtt{a_i}) \odot r \mid r \in R^c \wedge \mathtt{Eq}(r, p_i)\}$ $OW^c_{bound} = \bigcup_{c \in calleeSet(c), i \in \{0,...,n\}} \{HP(\mathtt{a_i}) \odot r \mid r \in OW^c \wedge \mathtt{Eq}(r, p_i)\}$ $WT^c_{bound} = \bigcap_{c \in calleeSet(c), i \in \{0,...,n\}} \{HP(\mathtt{a_i}) \odot r \mid r \in WT^c \wedge \mathtt{Eq}(r, p_i)\}$ $R_{new} = \{p \mid p \in R^c_{bound}, \exists p' \in WT \Rightarrow \neg\mathtt{Pre}(p, p')\}$ $R^{m'} = R^m \cup R_{new}$ $OW^{m'} = OW^m \cup OW^c_{bound}$ $WT' = WT \cup WT^c_{bound}$
`merge`	$WT' = \bigcap_{i \in pred(st)} WT_i$
`exit`	$WT^m = \bigcap_{i \in pred(st)} WT_i$

Figure 7. Transfer Functions for Computing Read and Write Sets

$$\langle a_0, a_1, ..., a_n\rangle \oplus b = \langle a_0, ..., a_n, b\rangle$$

$$\langle a_0, a_1, ..., a_n\rangle \odot \langle b_0, b_1, ..., b_n\rangle = \langle a_0, ..., a_n, b_1, ..., b_n\rangle$$

$$\mathtt{Eq}(\langle a_0, ..., a_n\rangle, \langle b_0, ..., b_n\rangle) = (a_0 = b_0)$$

$$\mathtt{Pre}(\langle a_0, ..., a_n\rangle, \langle b_0, ..., b_k\rangle) = k \leq n \wedge (\langle a_0, ..., a_k\rangle = \langle b_0, ..., b_k\rangle)$$

Figure 8. Auxiliary Operators and Functions

The operator $\odot$ converts the effects of the callee to the caller by replacing a parameter reference with the corresponding argument heap path. For example, the argument has the heap path $\langle \mathtt{d}, \mathtt{g}\rangle$ that is passed as the parameter `x` to the callee c. If the callee has the two read tuples $\langle \mathtt{x}, \mathtt{y}, \mathtt{a}\rangle$ and $\langle \mathtt{x}, \mathtt{y}, \mathtt{b}\rangle$ in its set R^c, the corresponding caller context read tuples $\langle \mathtt{d}, \mathtt{g}, \mathtt{y}, \mathtt{a}\rangle$ and $\langle \mathtt{d}, \mathtt{g}, \mathtt{y}, \mathtt{b}\rangle$ are added to the set R^c_{bound}. The set R^c_{bound} and OW^c_{bound} are the union of all possible callees, and the set WT^c_{bound} is the intersection of all possible callees. Then, the set R^m of the caller gains an element of R^c_{bound} if that element or some prefix has not been written by the caller m. The set OW^m and WT also gain write effects from OW^c_{bound} and WT^c_{bound}, respectively.

Control Flow Join: The join operation of the must-write set WT is intersection because memory locations must be overwritten on all possible program paths.

Method Exit: Without loss of generality, we assume the method exit node appears after all return nodes of the method. The set WT^m is the intersection of the set WT_i for all predecessors i.

Arrays: Arrays are handled in a similar fashion to fields with special support for the array specific calls in the SJava library.

5.1.2 Checking the Main Event Loop

We next describe the operation of the definitely-written analysis on the event loop. The definitely-written analysis must ensure that all memory locations that the event loop reads are either (1) loop invariant, (2) overwritten in the current loop before the read, or (3) overwritten in every loop iteration. For reads from local variables, we check with a straightforward dataflow analysis that either (1) all reaching definitions are from outside the event loop, (2) the variable must be overwritten in the current loop before the read statement, or (3) the variable must be overwritten in every loop iteration.

For reads from the heap, we check the condition in the main event loop at each call site and each field dereference. For each newly read heap path p in the set R_{new} for the statement st, we check that either:

1. that the heap path p is never written in the event loop, i.e., $p \notin OW$,
2. that the heap path p or some prefix is overwritten in the current event loop before executing the statement st, i.e., $\exists p' \in WT_{st}, \texttt{Pre}(p, p')$, or
3. that the heap path p or some prefix is overwritten in every loop iteration, i.e., at every loop backedge statement st' $\exists p' \in WT_{st'}, \texttt{Pre}(p, p')$.

5.2 Shared Location Extension

Recall that all memory locations with the same shared location must be overwritten with values from a higher location at the same time. Our analysis for shared locations checks that one of following conditions is satisfied for all memory locations with the same shared location type at the same program point: (1) the value in the memory location was written in the current loop iteration from a higher memory location or (2) one of the references in the heap path that leads to the memory location was written in the current loop iteration.

The shared location analysis is an extension to the definitely-written analysis. The analysis computes a mapping from a shared location to a set of heap paths or variables that belong to the same shared location. When a program statement writes a shared memory location, the analysis adds the memory location to the set only if the value being assigned to is from a higher location. If the value has the same shared location type, the memory location is removed from the set.

Whenever all memory locations with the same shared location type are cleared out, the definitely-written analysis adds the shared location type to the currently cleared shared locations types set for the current program point. The analysis then uses this set to compute at each statement which shared locations must be cleared in the current loop iteration before reaching a given statement. It then uses the shared locations must be cleared set in an analogous fashion to the set WT.

6. Termination of Event Loop Iterations

SJava ensures that values flow out of a program after a bounded number of iterations of the main event loop. It is of course possible for an iteration of the main event loop to fail to terminate due to memory corruption, a software bug, or by design. In this situation, an application could fail to self-stabilize because it never finishes an iteration of the main event loop and therefore the corrupted values never leave. We must therefore assure that every loop iteration of the main event loop terminates.

The halting problem is of course known to be undecidable. The proposed termination analysis instead targets checking common terminating loop patterns. In the next section, we describe how SJava checks that the execution of inner loops terminates. SJava addresses the possibility of looping recursive calls by prohibiting recursive calls.

6.1 Loop Termination Analysis

We implemented a simple loop termination analysis. Our analysis verifies loop termination if a loop both (1) has an index variable and at each iteration the index variable is incremented by a constant value and (2) every iteration of the loop evaluates at least one inequality of the appropriate form for the increment statement and that consists of the index variable and a guard value that does not change over the iterations. The most common type of for-loop follows this pattern.

For every nested loop in the event loop, the compiler first computes the set of induction variables and then checks that every loop iteration evaluates at least one conditional loop exit that is composed of an appropriate inequality of an induction variable and an invariant value. This check guarantees that the loop terminates because at each iteration, the induction variable proceeds toward the termination condition by increasing its value.

6.2 Loop Termination Annotations

This simple analysis cannot always determine that a loop terminates. Prohibiting the remaining loops is unlikely to be practical. To support loops where the SJava compiler cannot statically reason about termination, SJava provides two loop annotations: the maximum loop annotation and the unchecked annotation.

The maximum loop annotation modifies the original loop to enforce a developer-specified loop iteration bound. When the compiler flags a possible infinite loop, the developer can simply annotate the loop with a maximum loop annotation to force the loop to terminate within a given iteration bound. The compiler then generates code to enforce this bound.

It can be difficult to specify a maximum iteration bound for certain types of loops. In this case, developers can manually analyze the loop. If the developer manually checks that the loop terminates, the developer can apply a special unchecked annotation to the loop. Unchecked loops are indicated with a Java loop label that starts with the string `TERMINATE_`. The compiler then trusts that the developer has checked that the annotated loop always terminates.

7. Code Generation for Self-Stabilization

SJava checks that if an execution continues, it will self-stabilize into the correct state. However, an uncaught exception can cause the program to terminate before it self-stabilizes. There are two different approaches for handling such errors. In many cases, it may be appropriate to simply restart the program. Even in such cases, checking that the program is self-stabilizing ensures that silent software bugs cannot leave the program in incorrect states indefinitely. In other cases, the restart time may be significant. In these cases, the developer may choose to ignore uncaught exceptions. Note that the period of incorrect behavior caused by ignoring the error is limited because SJava ensures that the execution will self-stabilize into the correct state. Our compiler therefore implements an option to eliminate uncaught exceptions—we simply generate code that logs the error and then gives the error cases defined behavior. For example, under this option dereferencing a null pointer simply produces another null pointer. Virtual method calls on null receiver objects pose a related problem—self-stabilization may rely on code inside one of the targets of the call executing. In this case, the execution would choose one of the possible method targets to execute.

8. Correctness

We next sketch the basic correctness argument for SJava.

Lemma 1 (Top Values). *If an SJava program type checks and passes the static analyses, then memory locations with the top location type have the correct values after one loop iteration.*

Proof Sketch: After one loop iteration, memory locations with the top location cannot be corrupted as they are either constants or input data for the current loop iteration.

Lemma 2 (Propagation). *If SJava type checks a program and all memory locations with location types with a maximum distance of n from the top value in the lattice have correct values at the beginning of a non-erroneous loop iteration, then all live memory locations with locations types with a maximum distance of n + 1 from the top value in the lattice must have correct values at the end of the loop iteration.*

Proof Sketch: If a memory location has a location type with a maximum distance of $n + 1$, then all memory locations that are higher than it must have correct values (they have lower maximum distances) by assumption. If a value in a memory location is live (there is a read that could read this value before it is overwritten), then SJava requires each loop iteration to overwrite the memory location. The new value must be correct as all locations higher than this memory location have correct values.

Theorem 1 (Self-Stabilization). *If an SJava program type checks and passes the static analyses, then it self-stabilizes.*

Proof Sketch: The location type lattice has a finite height, therefore by induction on Lemmas 1 and 2 all non-constant memory locations will eventually have the correct values.

9. Evaluation

We implemented a compiler for SJava and evaluated it by annotating three existing Java applications: JLayer, an MP3 decoder; LEA, an eye-tracker; and Sumo Robot, a robot controller.

We conducted experiments in which we randomly injected errors to measure the self-stabilizing behavior of each benchmark. Our compiler generated error injection code that randomly selects memory and mathematical operations, and replaces the original value with a random value.

9.1 MP3 Decoder

JLayer is an MP3 decoder and is available at `http://www.javazoom.net/javalayer/javalayer.html`. MP3 files are composed of a sequence of frames. In JLayer, every event loop iteration retrieves a `BitStream` object that corresponds to a frame. The `BitStream` object reads and returns one frame from the input audio file and maintains persistent state to store the file offset. The `BitStream` object was carefully manually designed to be self-stabilizing by resyncing to MP3 frames, and we annotated the `BitStream` object as trusted to self-stabilize.

We focused our efforts on automatically checking that the more complex decoder is self-stabilizing. The decoder is self-stabilizing because the event loop flushes out all non loop-invariant state within a bounded time. As long as the event loop retrieves new valid audio frames, it will resume the normal behavior from an arbitrary state of the non-loop invariant storage.

We modified the program to minimize interactions between trusted components and checked components. Interactions between trusted and checked components (i.e., more than one method call per loop iteration or inputs to trusted components) make manually checking trusted code more difficult. For example, if a trusted method takes parameters from the self-stabilization code, the developer must reason about the behavior of the trusted code with potentially corrupted parameter values.

We found that the last two steps in the original code, the IMDCT and the Synthesis Filter Bank, use the results from the previous frame. In the original code, the results from two different loop iterations are stored in the same array, which makes it difficult to reason about value flows. Therefore, we use two separate arrays—one to store the merged results and one to forward results from the current loop iteration to the next loop iteration.

Our experiments were designed to qualitatively evaluate how the program self-stabilizes after an error corrupts its state. We randomly injected an error during the program's execution and measured the time until the program resumes outputting the correct values. We performed 1,000 trials of the experiment and observed 466 trials with corrupted outputs. Figure 9 shows the distribution of the number of output samples from when the error is injected until the point at which JLayer returned to outputting normal values. JLayer returned to normal behavior in less than 500 output samples when an error was injected into the transformation to generate PCM samples, which is the final step of the decoding process. The large peak at 1,700 samples occurs when an error is injected into the frequency domain transformations for one of the two granules that comprise a frame. Because the frequency transformation computations involve many operations, such error injections are likely. The corrupted results of the computation then continue to affect the output for approximately 1,700 samples. In general, errors that corrupted an internal data structure, for instance the buffer index of the `BitStream`, affected more output samples. In all cases, errors affected fewer than 2,208 output samples.

Figure 10 shows a section of JLayer's decoded audio signal output from one of the trials. The normal output of JLayer is plotted in blue. The output from the execution with error injection is plotted in red. The red box is due to the signal for the error execution deviating from the normal execution by oscillating at high frequency between -32,767 and 32,767. After 1,630 samples the program behavior returned to normal until termination.

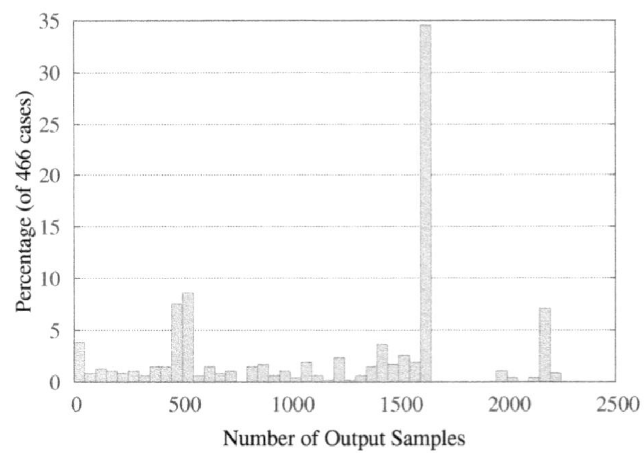

Figure 9. Distribution of the number of output samples required for the program to return to the normal behavior after an error injection.

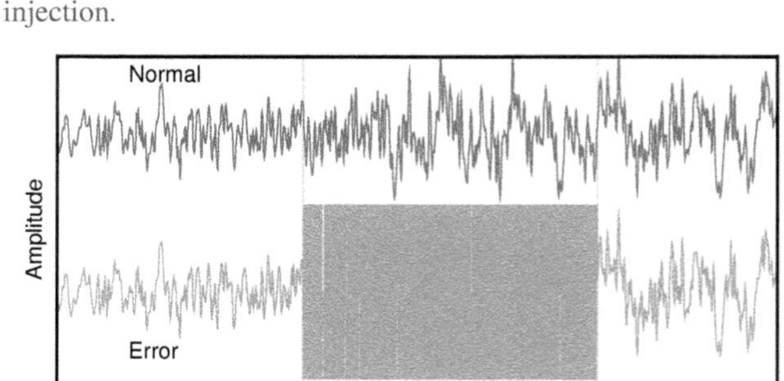

Figure 10. MP3Decoder output: normal execution (blue, top) and execution with injected error (red, bottom). After error injection, the signal oscillates rapidly until it resumes normal behavior.

Benchmark	Location	Lattice	Method Default	Lines
MP3 Decoder	690	54	24	15,634
Eye Tracking	143	33	21	4,571
Robot Control	77	15	13	3,201

Figure 11. Number and Type of Annotations

9.2 Eye Tracking

LEA is a lightweight eye tracking algorithm library and is available at `http://sourceforge.net/projects/lea-eyetracking/`. At each iteration, LEA takes an input image from a web cam, tracks eye movements, and returns relative movements in 8 directions (i.e., up, left, down, ...). The algorithm first detects a face in the input image, which allows it to localize the search region for eye detection. When an eye position is detected, LEA determines movement by computing the deviation from the last three eye positions. LEA stores the last three eye positions in the array to provide a better estimation. Every iteration inserts a new position at the beginning of the array and shifts the previous results down by one. All memory locations except the array of previous positions are overwritten in each iteration. The previous positions are not used to compute new positions while the direction result is derived from the three previous positions. Thus, the program returns the correct execution within three iterations of the event loop.

We annotated LEA and checked that it self-stabilizes. We modified the original code to convert multi-threaded code to single-threaded code. No other modifications were necessary to verify self-stabilization.

We performed 100 executions with injected errors and observed 8 executions with changed output samples. For each trial, we randomly injected errors at 10 consecutive instructions and compared eye positions and direction decisions with the correct output generated by the non-instrumented version. In our 8 trials, LEA returned to outputting correct values in the next iteration of the main event loop. While the SJava annotations imply a longer worst-case self-stabilization period, in practice it is hard to trigger this behavior through randomized error injection.

9.3 Robot Control

Sumo Robot controls robots and is available at `http://java.net/projects/sumorobots/`. The goal of a Sumo Robot is to push the opponent out of a ring while staying away from the ring edge. A robot is equipped with two types of sensors: a sonar sensor, which detects the opponent, and a line sensor, which detects the ring edge. Each iteration of the event loop reads data from the sensors, selects a movement type and speed, and then generates a motor controller command. The `StrategyMgr` object implements the analysis of the sensor input and the selection of the movement type. Once a motor control command is sent to the hardware, the command persists until another command is sent. We do not attempt to automatically analyze the motor controller because it is not stateless. We annotated the motor controller as trusted code, and modified the original code to make sure that every iteration overwrites the command arguments to the motor controller.

We evaluated the behavior of the Sumo Robot controller using simulated sensor inputs. We performed 100 error-injected executions. For each execution, we recorded the movement decisions of the strategy controller at every iteration of the event loop, and then compared the movement decisions with the output from an error-free execution. In the presence of the injected errors, we observed 54 trials with changed outputs and observed that the Sumo Robot controller resumed the normal behavior in the next iteration of the main event loop after the error occurred.

9.4 Annotation Effort

In SJava, the developer must annotate all variable, field, and method declarations accessed by the event loop. We found the location type errors from the compiler helpful in correctly annotating the code.

Figure 11 summarizes our annotation effort. For each benchmark, we list the number of location assignments using `@LOC` in the Location column, the number of lattice definitions using `@LATTICE` in the Lattice column, the number of default method lattice definitions using `@METHODDEFAULT` in the Method Default column, and lines of code including libraries. We found defining the structure of lattices to be straightforward. The default method lattice reduces the number of annotations because many methods share a similar structure and therefore we simply reused the same lattice. While the annotations do require extra developer effort, we found that this effort was small for our benchmarks, especially when compared to the effort of manually checking self-stabilization.

In our experience, SJava required minimal development effort once we understood the overall design of the program because value flows often reflect interactions between individual modules in the design specification. If a developer intends to develop a new software system for SJava, our experience leads us to believe that effort involved in annotating code will marginally exceed the amount of effort required to write Java types.

10. Related Work

Self-stabilization was initially suggested by Dijkstra in the context of robust distributed algorithms [6]. There has recently been work by Dolev et al. [7–9] that proposes techniques to ensure that the underlying layers (processor, operating system, and compiler) preserve the self-stabilizing nature of an application. Their work does not check that the actual application is self-stabilizing. Therefore, our work on SJava to check that applications self-stabilize is complementary to this work.

Language-based information flow employs type systems to check that information flows in an application do not violate the desired requirements[12, 15, 16]. Our approach is similar in some aspects. The key differences are that our approach must support much finer-grained divisions of data and must check that values only remain in a given location for a bounded time.

Linear types have been leveraged in programming languages[10, 11, 19] for various purposes including safe concurrent programming, resource management, and protocol checking. SJava uses a modified linear type system to avoid soundness problems from aliasing. Termination analysis plays an important role in verifying safety critical systems.

Even though it is not possible to have a sound and complete termination analysis, several proposed techniques are mature enough to analyze termination in many cases [1–4, 18]. If necessary, we could easily replace our termination analysis with more sophisticated approaches.

Failure-oblivious computing [13] enables programs to continue execution past memory errors by manufacturing values for reads or discarding writes. This approach works well for applications with short error propagation distances. Our work is complementary in that it can guarantee that a program has short error propagation distances. Other work detect bugs and tries re-execution in a slightly different environment [17]. Data structure repair [5] takes an interventional approach; upon detecting data structure corruption, it repairs them with respect to a specification. Data structure repair only guarantees that a program will reach some consistent state, while our work guarantees that all effects of the bug eventually disappear. Moreover, our approach does not require a specification and therefore eliminates the need to precisely define correct behavior.

11. Conclusion

Self-stabilization has long been proposed as an approach for fault tolerance. Wide scale guarantees of self-stabilization have the potential to significantly improve the safety and user experience of software systems. SJava is the first system for checking that applications are self-stabilizing. A developer simply annotates the source code to capture the flow of values. The SJava compiler then checks that incorrect values will eventually leave the program returning the program to the exact correct state. Our experience indicates that this approach can successfully check self-stabilization of our benchmark applications.

Acknowledgments

This research was supported by the National Science Foundation under grants CCF-0846195 and CCF-0725350. We would like to thank Patrick Lam, Harry Xu, Philip Reames, Philippe Suter, and the anonymous reviewers for their helpful comments. We would like to thank James Jenista for help with the experiments.

References

[1] A. Bradley, Z. Manna, and H. Sipma. Termination of polynomial programs. In *Proceedings of Verification, Model Checking, and Abstract Interpretation*, volume 3385, pages 113–129. 2005.

[2] J. Brotherston, R. Bornat, and C. Calcagno. Cyclic proofs of program termination in separation logic. pages 101–112, 2008.

[3] B. Cook, A. Podelski, and A. Rybalchenko. Termination proofs for systems code. In *Proceedings of the 2006 ACM SIGPLAN Conference on Programming Language Design and Implementation*, pages 415–426, 2006.

[4] B. Cook, A. Podelski, and A. Rybalchenko. Proving thread termination. In *Proceedings of the 2007 ACM SIGPLAN Conference on Programming Language Design and Implementation*, pages 320–330, 2007.

[5] B. Demsky and M. Rinard. Data structure repair using goal-directed reasoning. In *Proceedings of the 27th International Conference on Software Engineering*, pages 176–185, 2005.

[6] E. W. Dijkstra. Self-stabilizing systems in spite of distributed control. *Communications of the ACM*, 17:643–644, November 1974.

[7] S. Dolev, Y. Haviv, and M. Sagiv. Self-stabilization preserving compiler. *ACM Transactions on Programming Languages and Systems*, 31:22:1–22:42, August 2009.

[8] S. Dolev and Y. A. Haviv. Self-stabilizing microprocessor: Analyzing and overcoming soft errors. *IEEE Transactions on Computers*, 55:385–399, 2006.

[9] S. Dolev and R. Yagel. Toward self-stabilizing operating systems. In *Proceedings of the 15th International Conference on Database and Expert Systems Applications*, pages 684 – 688, 2004.

[10] M. Fahndrich and R. DeLine. Adoption and focus: practical linear types for imperative programming. In *Proceedings of the 2002 ACM SIGPLAN Conference on Programming Language Design and Implementation*, pages 13–24, 2002.

[11] P. Haller and M. Odersky. Capabilities for uniqueness and borrowing. In *Proceedings of the 24th European Conference on Object-Oriented Programming*, pages 354–378, 2010.

[12] A. C. Myers. JFlow: Practical mostly-static information flow control. In *Proceedings of the Symposium on Principles of Programming Languages*, pages 228–241, 1999.

[13] M. Rinard, C. Cadar, D. Dumitran, D. M. Roy, T. Leu, and W. S. Beebee, Jr. Enhancing server availability and security through failure-oblivious computing. In *Proceedings of the 6th Symposium on Operating Systems Design and Implementation*, 2004.

[14] M. C. Rinard. Living in the comfort zone. In *Proceeding of the 22nd ACM SIGPLAN Conference on Object-Oriented Programming, Systems, Languages, and Applications*, 2007.

[15] A. Sabelfeld and A. Myers. Language-based information-flow security. *IEEE Journal on Selected Areas in Communications*, 21(1):5 – 19, January 2003.

[16] A. Sampson, W. Dietl, E. Fortuna, D. Gnanapragasam, L. Ceze, and D. Grossman. EnerJ: Approximate data types for safe and general low-power computation. In *Proceedings of the 2011 ACM SIGPLAN Conference on Programming Language Design and Implementation*, pages 164–174, 2011.

[17] S. Sidiroglou, M. E. Locasto, S. W. Boyd, and A. D. Keromytis. Building a reactive immune system for software services. In *Proceedings of the USENIX Annual Technical Conference*, 2005.

[18] F. Spoto, F. Mesnard, and E. Payet. A termination analyzer for Java bytecode based on path-length. *ACM Transactions on Programming Languages and Systems*, 32:8:1–8:70, March 2010.

[19] P. Wadler. Linear types can change the world! In *Proceedings of the International Conference on Programming Concepts and Methods*, 1990.

Type-Directed Automatic Incrementalization

Yan Chen Joshua Dunfield Umut A. Acar
Max Planck Institute for Software Systems
{chenyan, joshua, umut}@mpi-sws.org

Abstract

Application data often changes slowly or incrementally over time. Since incremental changes to input often result in only small changes in output, it is often feasible to respond to such changes asymptotically more efficiently than by re-running the whole computation. Traditionally, realizing such asymptotic efficiency improvements requires designing problem-specific algorithms known as dynamic or incremental algorithms, which are often significantly more complicated than conventional algorithms to design, analyze, implement, and use. A long-standing open problem is to develop techniques that automatically transform conventional programs so that they correctly and efficiently respond to incremental changes.

In this paper, we describe a significant step towards solving the problem of automatic incrementalization: a programming language and a compiler that can, given a few type annotations describing what can change over time, compile a conventional program that assumes its data to be static (unchanging over time) to an incremental program. Based on recent advances in self-adjusting computation, including a theoretical proposal for translating purely functional programs to self-adjusting programs, we develop techniques for translating conventional Standard ML programs to self-adjusting programs. By extending the Standard ML language, we design a fully featured programming language with higher-order features, a module system, and a powerful type system, and implement a compiler for this language. The resulting programming language, LML, enables translating conventional programs decorated with simple type annotations into incremental programs that can respond to changes in their data correctly and efficiently.

We evaluate the effectiveness of our approach by considering a range of benchmarks involving lists, vectors, and matrices, as well as a ray tracer. For these benchmarks, our compiler incrementalizes existing code with only trivial amounts of annotation. The resulting programs are often asymptotically more efficient, leading to orders of magnitude speedups in practice.

Categories and Subject Descriptors F.3.3 [*Logics and Meanings of Programs*]: Studies of Program Constructs

Keywords Self-adjusting computation; incrementalization; type annotations; compiler optimization; performance

1. Introduction

Much modern software is highly dynamic: it continually receives input and responds by computing the corresponding output. This dynamic nature of computation creates both opportunities and challenges. Opportunities arise because the input data, which changes over time as a result of interactions, often changes *incrementally*—by a small amount at a time. Such incremental changes make it possible to compute the new output efficiently by reusing intermediate computations. In the common case, updating the output dynamically instead of recomputing it leads to asymptotically more efficient response times, which can dramatically improve practical efficiency. The challenges stem from the difficulty of realizing this potential: designing, analyzing, and implementing software systems that can operate efficiently on dynamically changing data.

In the algorithms and programming-languages communities, considerable work has been done on dynamic systems; for surveys, see Chiang and Tamassia [1992]; Ramalingam and Reps [1993]; Agarwal et al. [2002]; Demetrescu et al. [2005]. The algorithms community devises ad hoc dynamic algorithms for specific problems. While these algorithms can be very efficient, often achieving optimal complexity, they are generally hard to design, analyze, and implement. Dynamic algorithms are also difficult to compose in a modular fashion, limiting their applicability in large software systems. The programming-languages community develops languages for expressing dynamic programs and compilation techniques for translating these high-level programs into executables that respond efficiently to dynamic changes. This approach is often called *incremental computation.* Incremental computation can dramatically simplify developing dynamic software, but achieving optimal efficiency has remained elusive. This is perhaps unsurprising, because the problem is inherently challenging: the compiler is ultimately expected to generate code that significantly outperforms the source code, often by an asymptotically significant margin.

Recent advances in *self-adjusting computation* made important progress on the problem of incremental computation. By proposing dynamic dependency graphs, and a change propagation algorithm [Acar et al. 2006] that utilizes a particular form of memoization techniques [Acar et al. 2009, 2008], the approach enables the programmer to express dynamic computations via several language abstractions. Previous work extended existing languages including C [Hammer et al. 2009, 2011] and ML [Acar et al. 2009; Ley-Wild et al. 2008] to support self-adjusting computation. Evaluations showed that the approach can achieve asymptotically efficient updates for a reasonably broad range of benchmarks [Acar et al. 2009; Hammer et al. 2011], and even help solve major open problems in a range of domains including computational geometry [Acar et al. 2010] and machine learning [Sümer et al. 2011]. More recent work generalized the approach to support parallel computation on multicores, taking advantage of the performance benefits of parallelism and incremental computation at the same time by exploiting structural similarities between them [Burckhardt et al. 2011; Acar et al. 2011]. The approach has also been applied to large-scale MapReduce computations in distributed systems [Bhatotia et al. 2011].

PLDI'12, June 11–16, 2012, Beijing, China.

While these advances chart a viable approach to incremental computation by eliminating the need to design and implement sophisticated algorithms for dynamic problems, they still require significant programmer involvement. For example, writing a self-adjusting program in ΔML [Ley-Wild et al. 2008] requires carefully annotating the program with specific primitives that determine how to construct the dynamic dependence graph and perform change propagation.

In this paper, we design a language, LML, that allows the programmer to derive self-adjusting software from conventional programs through simple type annotations and implement a compiler for LML. Specifically, LML extends the Standard ML language, which has a range of features including higher-order functions, an advanced module system, and imperative references, with level type qualifiers, which enable marking certain data as *changeable*, that is, subject to modifications over time. For example, when programming a ray tracer, we mark the surface properties of objects as changeable. We implement a compiler for our language that generates code that can be executed with fixed input as usual, but also can automatically respond to changes by updating its output via change propagation.

Our approach to automatic incrementalization builds on recent advances in self-adjusting computation. Specifically, Chen et al. [2011] develop an algorithm for translating purely functional programs decorated with type annotations into self-adjusting programs. Their work, however, is purely theoretical; it considers only a simplified language, and provides no implementation or empirical results. We extend their algorithm for full Standard ML including a key imperative feature (mutable references), and extend the MLton compiler [MLton] for Standard ML (Section 3) to generate efficient self-adjusting executables from type annotations by using the extended translation algorithm.

Our compiler takes the user annotations and propagates them through various phases of the compiler to intermediate code, where it applies the translation algorithm. Assuming a runtime system that provides primitives for self-adjusting computation, the translation algorithm generates code by minimally inserting the self-adjusting primitives via type-directed, local rewrites. Such local rewrites, however, can lead to globally suboptimal code by inserting redundant calls to self-adjusting primitives. We therefore formulate a global rewriting system for eliminating such redundant code, and prove that the rewriting rules are terminating and confluent (Section 3.4). We implement the run-time system for self-adjusting primitives directly in SML.

We evaluate our implementation (Section 4) by considering benchmarks including various primitives on lists, sorting functions, vector operations, matrix operations, and a ray tracer. For each of these, we only need to insert some keywords into the program to specify the desired behavior. Specifically, most benchmarks require trivial decorations, often amounting to inserting type qualifiers in one or two lines of code. No changes to the structure of the types, or any part of the code itself, are necessary. The executables generated by the compilers respond automatically and efficiently to small changes to their data. We frequently observe significant asymptotic improvements in efficiency and obtain significant speedups ranging from 10% (for large changes that affect a significant portion of the output) to several orders of magnitude.

2. Overview

We illustrate our approach through a simple example. First, we describe matrix multiplication in ordinary SML. Next, we describe a self-adjusting version, which could be written by hand, that can update its output asymptotically more efficiently (by nearly a quadratic factor) than a complete re-computation. We then describe our approach, where we obtain the same code automatically by adding a single type qualifier to the code and compiling it with our compiler. In the example, we consider a particular kind of change to the input and briefly outline other possibilities in Section 2.4. In all cases, the executable generated by our compiler updates the output correctly and efficiently, leading to orders of magnitude speedups in practice (Section 4).

2.1 Matrix Multiplication in SML

The SML code in Figure 1 multiplies two matrices, where a matrix is represented as a vector of rows, and each row is a vector of integers. Omitting the annotation `$C`, this is the usual $\Theta(n^3)$ matrix-multiplication algorithm. Using the `map` function over vectors, it iterates over the rows of the first matrix and the columns of the second (transposed for faster access). By using the `map2` function, it multiplies each element of the row with the corresponding element of the column, and using `reduce`, adds these results to generate one element of the output matrix.

The function `transpose`, whose code is not shown here, transposes a matrix. The functions `map`, `map2` and `reduce` perform standard operations on vectors: Given a vector $a = \langle a_1, \ldots, a_n \rangle$ and a function f, the call `map(a,f)` returns a vector $\langle f(a_1), \ldots, f(a_n) \rangle$). Similarly, given two vectors a and b and a binary function f, the call `map2(a,b,f)` returns $\langle f(a_1, b_1), \ldots, f(a_n, b_n) \rangle$). Given a vector $a = \langle a_1, \ldots, a_n \rangle$, an identity element Z and an associative binary function $\oplus$, the call `reduce(a,Z,⊕)` returns $a_1 \oplus \cdots \oplus a_n$ if $n > 0$, and Z if $n = 0$.

2.2 Self-Adjusting Matrix Multiplication

Suppose that we are interested in changing the elements of the matrix incrementally and updating the result of multiplication. One approach would be to develop an algorithm specific to this problem. For matrices with integers or floating-point numbers, this does not seem particularly difficult: we could devise an algorithm that undoes the effect of the changed input element and updates the sum by factoring in its new value. However, such an algorithm assumes addition and multiplication are commutative and have inverses; in reality, floating-point arithmetic does not have these properties. Moreover, matrix multiplication can be used for a whole array of computations, some of which don't admit such inverses. In these cases, it is significantly more challenging to come up with an efficient incremental algorithm.

More generally, the history of research on incremental algorithms demonstrates that they can be extremely challenging to design and implement. For example, a paper on an advanced dynamic algorithm for planar convex hull exceeds 100 pages [Jakob 2002]; that algorithm appears very difficult to implement, and to the best of our knowledge, has never been implemented. In contrast, standard non-incremental algorithms for convex hull can be implemented in less than 50 lines of SML.

Writing self-adjusting matrix-multiply. Self-adjusting computation offers a way to write efficient incremental algorithms by modifying the code for the standard, non-incremental algorithm. The idea is to distinguish between *stable* and *changeable* data and insert operations that manipulate changeable data. Incremental changes can be made to the changeable parts of the input and a *change propagation* algorithm can be used to update the computation. Figure 2 shows code written in a direct style similar to previous work [Acar et al. 2009]. Stable data is handled as usual: the type of a stable integer is simply `int`. Changeable data, however, is stored in *modifiables*: a changeable integer becomes an `int mod`. We declare `matrix` as `((int mod) vector) vector`: a vector of vectors of integers, where the integer elements are wrapped by modifiables. This allows changing the individual elements of the matrix and updating the computation automatically.

```
type matrix = ((int $C) vector) vector
multiply : matrix * matrix → matrix

fun multiply (A, B) =
  let val Tb = transpose B
  in
    map (A, fn row ⇒
      map (Tb, fn col ⇒
        reduce (map2 (row,
                      col,
                      fn (a,b) ⇒ a*b),


                0,
                fn (x, res) ⇒ x+res)))

  end
```

Figure 1. Matrix multiplication in SML.

```
type matrix = ((int mod) vector) vector
multiply : matrix * matrix → matrix

fun multiply (A, B) =
  let val Tb = transpose B
  in
    map (A, fn row ⇒
      map (Tb, fn col ⇒
        reduce (map2 (row,
                      col,
                      fn (a,b) ⇒ Mod (Read a (fn a' ⇒
                                   Read b (fn b' ⇒ Write (a'*b'))))),
                Mod (Write 0),
                fn (x, res) ⇒
                  Mod (Read x (fn x' ⇒ Read res (fn res' ⇒
                    Write (x'+res')))))))
  end
```

Figure 2. Compiler-generated self-adjusting matrix multiplication.

When writing a self-adjusting program by hand, we first determine the changeable parts of the data, and then edit the code to explicitly manipulate such data through `Read`, `Write` and `Mod` primitives. This process is relatively cumbersome and error-prone: we must identify the sections of code that depend on changeable data, conforming to a modal type system. Specifically, a `Read` primitive can be used only inside a "changeable" section of code, which must be contained within the dynamic scope of a `Mod` operation, and each `Mod` operation must end with a `Write` that places a changeable value in it.

As an example, consider the function passed to `map2`, `fn (a,b) ⇒ a*b`. This function directly operates on elements of the matrix, which are changeable integers. Since they are changeable integers, they must be stored in modifiables and have type `int mod` in the self-adjusting program. Thus, the function cannot multiply `a` and `b` directly. Instead, we write a `Read` that passes the contents of the modifiable `a` to a function `fn a' ⇒ Read b ....` A second `Read` gets the contents of the modifiable `b`. The `a'` and `b'` appearing in `Write (a'*b')` have type `int`, so we can multiply them normally. Because `a'*b'` depends on changeable data (information flows from a and `b`, which are changeable), it is also changeable, and must be written to a fresh modifiable: `Mod (... Write (a'*b'))`.

In contrast, calls to `transpose`, `map`, `map2` and `reduce` need not be treated specially, because they operate on stable data (vectors); note that the elements of the vector are changeable but the vectors themselves are not. The bodies of these functions, however, still need to be modified to accommodate changes in the types: they all now operate on vectors whose elements are changeable, and in some cases, their other arguments also change (e.g., the function argument of `map2`).

Change propagation. Given the self-adjusting matrix multiplication function, we can run it in much the same way as running the standard version. Such a complete run takes asymptotically as long as the complete run but incurs some constant-factor overhead in practice.

After a complete run, we can change any or all of the changeable data and update the output by performing change propagation. As an example, consider changing one element of the first matrix and performing change propagation. This propagation will trigger execution of the n multiplication operations that use this element and the `reduce` operation that computes the new sum. When multiplying $n \times n$ matrices, it is not difficult to show that change propagation takes $O(n \log n)$ time. Since at least n entries in the output matrix must be updated, this is within a $\log n$ factor of the trivial lower bound $\Omega(n)$; in fact, it is likely that $O(n \log n)$ is tight in the general case. Consequently, change propagation is nearly quadratically faster than a complete execution, a huge gain in efficiency. In writing this self-adjusting program, we realized this efficiency without designing and implementing an incremental algorithm, but we nevertheless had to make significant changes to the code.

2.3 Type-Directed Self-Adjustment

As the description of the self-adjusting matrix multiply suggests, writing self-adjusting programs can require rather invasive changes to the code. In our approach, our compiler can derive self-adjusting programs automatically, based on simple type annotations. For example, given the code in Figure 1 and the annotation `$C` (the first line) that makes the element type `int` changeable, our compiler derives the code in Figure 2 automatically. As a result, starting with a trivial annotation to the type declarations, our compiler yields a near-quadratic-time improvement in run time.

We refer to the type annotations as *levels* and the resulting types as *level types*. Programmers need only annotate the types of changeable data with `$C`; all other types remain stable. For example:

- `int` is a stable integer;
- `int $C` is a changeable integer;
- `(int $C) vector` is a stable vector of changeable integers.

The last type may look odd—how can the vector be stable when its elements are changeable? But it simply expresses that each element is individually changeable, while the vector as a whole is not changeable: it would not be possible to replace the entire vector except by changing each element individually.

2.4 Remarks

In the above example, we allow changes to individual elements by representing matrices as stable vectors with changeable elements: `((int $C) vector) vector`. Our approach also makes it possible to use many other representations, again deriving self-adjusting code automatically. For example, if we expect entire rows of the input matrices to change at once, we could choose to represent matrices as changeable rows of stable elements, `((int) vector $C) vector`. This would track the computation only at the granularity of entire rows and result in optimal updates for full row changes of the input. Using our approach, we could derive a self-adjusting program suitable for this case by changing the type annotation, with no changes to the source code itself at all.

Similarly, it can be beneficial to use a blocked representation, where the matrix is represented with blocks, smaller matrices of size $m \times m$ for some constant m (typically between 10 and 100). This representation has superior locality, often resulting in better practical efficiency. Our compiler easily generates self-adjusting code that treats the blocks, and not individual elements, as changeable. As we show in our experimental evaluation (Section 4), this blocking technique leads to extremely time- and space-efficient self-adjusting computations.

3. Design and Implementation

To support type-directed, automatic incrementalization, we extended Standard ML with a single keyword `$C`, a type qualifier, and extended the MLton compiler [MLton] for Standard ML to generate self-adjusting executables. This extension to SML does not restrict the language in any way, allowing all its features to be used freely, including the module language.

The most important additions to the compiler are a translation phase, an optimization phase, and a run-time system. In this section, we describe the structure of our system, and discuss some of its key components in more detail.

3.1 Structure of the Compiler

The compiler pipeline is shown in Figure 3. Although the surface language has only one type annotation, `$C`, in all intermediate languages, we explicitly mark all types as stable or changeable using two type qualifiers `$S` and `$C`. We modified all of MLton's phases that come before the new translation phase (**Translate**) to propagate these type annotations. The translation phase uses type qualifiers to generate self-adjusting code in the SXML intermediate language of MLton, as discussed in the next section. The optimization phase eliminates some important redundancies of the code produced by the translation phase. For technical reasons related to MLton's dead code elimination (see Section 3.5), we stop the compiler after the optimization phase and run an unmodified version of MLton on the SXML output, producing an executable.

3.2 Pre-Translation Phases

We extended the MLton lexer and parser to handle types with `$C` annotations, producing abstract syntax in which types include level information. We systematically added levels to several typed intermediate languages (CoreML, "XML", and SXML), and modified each pre-translation phase to accept and propagate levels in types. Thus, we leverage MLton's broad scope—it accepts full Standard ML—and its various code transformations: elaboration, defunctorization, linearization (conversion to A-normal form), dead code elimination, monomorphization of ML-polymorphic code, etc.

3.3 Self-Adjusting Translation

We apply our translation on MLton's SXML intermediate language, a monomorphic subset of SML in A-normal form. SXML is suitable for the transformation to self-adjusting code because our transformation algorithm expects, and produces, monomorphic code in A-normal form.

Our translation algorithm extends the algorithm of Chen et al. [2011] to support full SML, including (recursive) data types and imperative references. The translation algorithm is relatively technical, making its presentation difficult in the context of this paper, but we give a high-level overview and briefly illustrate some of the extensions needed to handle full SML. The translation algorithm takes SXML code and transforms it into SXML code containing self-adjusting computation primitives, whose implementations will be supplied by the run-time system. The self-adjusting primitives include **mod**, **read**, and **write** functions for creating, reading from, and writing to modifiable references. At a high level, the translation rules inspect the code locally, insert **read**s where changeable data is used (according to type information), and ensure that each **read** takes place within the dynamic scope of a call to **mod**. To ensure this and other correctness properties, the rules distinguish stable and changeable modes.

$$\frac{\Gamma \vdash x : \tau \underset{\$S}{\hookrightarrow} x'}{\Gamma \vdash (\mathbf{ref}\ x) : (\tau\ \mathbf{ref}^{\$C}) \underset{\$S}{\hookrightarrow} \mathbf{mod}\ (\mathbf{write}(x'))}\ \text{(Ref)}$$

$$\frac{\Gamma \vdash x_2 : \tau'\ \mathbf{ref}^{\$C} \underset{\$S}{\hookrightarrow} x_2 \qquad \Gamma, x_1 : \tau' \vdash e : \tau \underset{\$C}{\hookrightarrow} e'}{\Gamma \vdash \mathbf{let}\ x_1 = \,!x_2\ \mathbf{in}\ e : \tau \underset{\$C}{\hookrightarrow} \mathbf{read}\ x_2\ \mathbf{as}\ x_1\ \mathbf{in}\ e'}\ \text{(Deref)}$$

$$\frac{\begin{array}{ll}\Gamma \vdash x_1 : \tau'\ \mathbf{ref}^{\$C} \underset{\$S}{\hookrightarrow} x_1 & \\ \Gamma \vdash x_2 : \tau' \underset{\$S}{\hookrightarrow} x_2' & \Gamma \vdash e : \tau \underset{\$C}{\hookrightarrow} e'\end{array}}{\Gamma \vdash \mathbf{let}\ \_ = (x_1 := x_2)\ \mathbf{in}\ e : \tau \underset{\$C}{\hookrightarrow} \mathbf{impwrite}\ x_1 := x_2'\ \mathbf{in}\ e'}\ \text{(Assign)}$$

Figure 4. Translation rules for mutable references

Figure 4 shows the translation rules for mutable references, which we translate to modifiables. The translation judgment $\Gamma \vdash e : \tau \underset{\varepsilon}{\hookrightarrow} e'$ is read "in environment Γ and mode ε, source expression e at type τ translates to e'". In stable mode `$S`, the translation produces stable code that cannot inspect changeable data or directly use changeable code; in changeable mode `$C`, the translation produces changeable code that can appear within the body of a **read** and can manipulate references. For translation of imperative references, we add another primitive **impwrite** that updates the value of a modifiable directly.

Stable functions may be called with either stable or changeable arguments. For example, the program might use the built-in SML + function on changeable integers. Our translation algorithm handles such polymorphic usage by inserting coercions, which read changeable arguments and create a modifiable from the result.

3.4 Optimization

Our translation algorithm follows a system of inductive rules, which are guided only by local information—the structure of types and terms. This locality is key to simplifying the algorithm and the implementation but it often generates code with redundant operations. For example, translating **fst** x, where $x : (\mathbf{int}^{\$C} \times \tau_2)^{\$S}$, in changeable mode generates the term **read** (**mod** (**let** r = **fst** x **in write**(r))) **as** x' **in write**(x'), which is redundant: it creates a temporary modifiable for the first projection of x and immediately reads its contents. A more efficient translation, **let** x' = **fst** x **in write**(x'), avoids the temporary modifiable.

Such redundancies turn out to be common, because of the local nature of the translation algorithm. We therefore developed a post-translation optimization phase to eliminate redundant operations. Figure 5 illustrates the rules that drive the optimization phase. Each rule eliminates three operations: reading from a modifiable, writing to a modifiable, and creating a modifiable. As we show in Section 4.8, this optimization phase reduces the execution time for self-adjusting programs by up to 60%.

Eliminating write-create-read. The left-hand side of rewrite rule (1) evaluates an expression e_1 into a new modifiable, then immediately reads the contents of the modifiable into x'. The right-hand side evaluates e_1 and binds the result to x' with no extra modifiable.

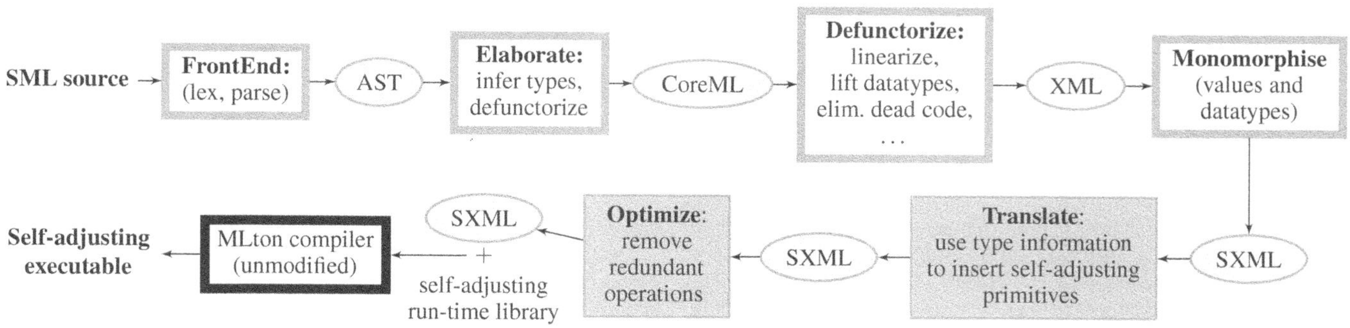

Figure 3. The structure of our compiler: new phases, modified phases, unmodified phases, intermediate languages

$$\begin{array}{lclr}\textbf{read}\ (\textbf{mod}\ (\textbf{let}\ r = e_1\ \textbf{in}\ \textbf{write}(r))) & & & \\ \qquad\qquad \textbf{as}\ x'\ \textbf{in}\ e_2 & \longrightarrow & \textbf{let}\ x' = e_1\ \textbf{in}\ e_2 & (1)\\ \textbf{read}\ (\textbf{mod}\ e)\ \textbf{as}\ x'\ \textbf{in}\ \textbf{write}(x') & \longrightarrow & e & (2)\\ \textbf{mod}\ (\textbf{read}\ e\ \textbf{as}\ x'\ \textbf{in}\ \textbf{write}(x')) & \longrightarrow & e & (3)\end{array}$$

Figure 5. Optimization rules

Eliminating create-read-write. The left-hand side of (2) evaluates e (which, since it is the body of a **mod**, must end in a **write**), creates a modifiable, reads the just-written value into x', and writes it again. The right-hand side just evaluates e.

Eliminating read-write-create. Rule (3) is similar to rule (2): the left-hand side reads some modifiable e into a variable x', and immediately writes x' back to a new modifiable; the right-hand side only evaluates e.

These rules are shrinking reduction rules guaranteed to make the program smaller [Appel and Jim 1997]. The rules are also terminating and confluent. Termination is immediate, because in each rule, the right-hand side is smaller than the left-hand side: rule (1) replaces one **let** with another and drops a **read**, a **mod** and a **write**. In rules (2) and (3), the right-hand side is a proper subterm of the left-hand side. Confluence (the property that all choices of rewrite sequences eventually yield α-equivalent terms) is not immediate, but is straightforward:

Theorem 3.1. *Rules (1)–(3) are locally confluent.*

Proof. First, the left-hand sides of rules (1) and (2) may overlap exactly: either rule can be applied to $\textbf{read}\ (\textbf{mod}\ (\textbf{let}\ r = e_1\ \textbf{in}\ \textbf{write}(r)))\ \textbf{as}\ x'\ \textbf{in}\ \textbf{write}(x')$, but the right-hand sides of (1) and (2) are $\textbf{let}\ x' = e_1\ \textbf{in}\ \textbf{write}(x')$ and $\textbf{let}\ r = e_1\ \textbf{in}\ \textbf{write}(r)$, which are α-equivalent. Rules (2) and (3) may overlap critically, but in all cases yield α-equivalent terms. One case (the other is similar) is:

$$\begin{array}{ll} & \underline{\textbf{read}\ (\textbf{mod}\ (\textbf{read}\ e_3\ \textbf{as}\ x_3'\ \textbf{in}\ x_3'))\ \textbf{as}\ x_2'\ \textbf{in}\ \textbf{write}(x_2')} \\ \xrightarrow{(2)} & \underline{\textbf{read}\ e_3\ \textbf{as}\ x_3'\ \textbf{in}\ \textbf{write}(x_3')} \end{array}$$

$$\begin{array}{ll} & \textbf{read}\ (\underline{\textbf{mod}\ (\textbf{read}\ e_3\ \textbf{as}\ x_3'\ \textbf{in}\ x_3'))}\ \textbf{as}\ x_2'\ \textbf{in}\ \textbf{write}(x_2') \\ \xrightarrow{(3)} & \textbf{read}\ \underline{e_3}\ \textbf{as}\ x_2'\ \textbf{in}\ \textbf{write}(x_2') \end{array}$$

Otherwise, redexes overlap only when an entire left-hand side is a subterm of the e in another left-hand side (possibly of the same rule). Such *non-critical overlap* cases follow as in Baader and Nipkow [1998, pp. 137–138]. □

Since the rules are terminating and locally confluent, by Newman's lemma [Newman 1942], they are globally confluent. Thus, we can safely apply them in any order, to arbitrary subterms, until no rules apply. In practice, it suffices to traverse the program only once: if we traverse it in preorder, we apply rules near the leaves of the tree first. That means the subterms of the left-hand sides have already been rewritten, so the right-hand sides will contain no more candidate subterms.

3.5 Final Stage

The translated, optimized SXML code has explicit self-adjusting computation primitives, suitable for use with a self-adjusting run-time library implementing these primitives. Our implementation of this library is written in SML, so we might expect to run the full MLton pipeline on the library and source program together to produce an executable. Since, however, no calls to the library appear in the user's source program, dead code elimination deletes the library code from the program during MLton's Defunctorize phase. Instead of re-engineering MLton's dead code elimination to specially treat library code as live, we take a simpler approach. Taking advantage of the fact that SXML is a subset of SML, we cut off the pipeline after producing optimized self-adjusting SXML, combine the SXML output of the translation phase with the library, and generate an executable by running the unmodified MLton compiler.

3.6 Runtime Environment

As described above, we compile the translated user program together with a self-adjusting run-time library. This library implements the self-adjusting primitives (`Mod`, `Read`, `Write`) used by the translated code. When executed, the library constructs a dependency graph during the complete run. The library also provides facilities for changing the input and invoking change propagation to reflect changes to the output.

4. Experiments

We present an experimental evaluation of our approach and compare it to previous work.

4.1 Benchmarks

We implemented a number of benchmarks in our LML language, including standard self-adjusting-computation benchmarks from previous work [Acar et al. 2009; Ley-Wild et al. 2008], additional benchmarks on vectors and matrices, and a ray tracer. LML makes it relatively straightforward to derive self-adjusting versions of programs. Specifically, we simply wrote the standard code for our benchmarks and changed the type declarations to allow for changes to the input data. For the ray tracer, we used an unmodified SML implementation of a sphere ray tracer [King 1998].

Our benchmarks include some standard list primitives (map, filter, split), quicksort, and mergesort (qsort, msort). These include simple iteration (map, filter, split), accumulator passing (qsort), and divide-and-conquer algorithms (qsort, msort). All of these list benchmarks operate on integers: map applies $f(i) = i \div 3 + i \div 5 + i \div 7$ to each element; filter keeps the elements when $f(i)$ is even; split partitions its input; qsort and msort implement sorting algorithms. Similarly, our vector benchmarks include vec-reduce, vec-mult (dot product), mat-vec-mult (matrix-vector multiplication), mat-add, transpose (matrix transpose), mat-mult, and block-mat-mult (matrix multiplication on matrices that use a simple blocked representation).

The vector and matrix benchmarks implement the corresponding vector or matrix algorithm with double-precision (64-bit) floating point numbers; when multiplying two doubles, we normalize the result by their sum to prevent overflows when operating on large matrices. For our matrix benchmarks, we consider two different representations of matrices: the standard representation where the elements are laid out in memory in row-major order, and the blocked representation where elements are blocked into small sub-matrices. Our final benchmark is an off-the-shelf ray tracer that supports point and directional lights, sphere and plane objects, and diffuse, specular, transparent, and reflective surface properties.

To support flexible changes to the input data, our list benchmarks permit insertion and deletion of any element from the input; in LML, this requires simply specifying the "tail" of the lists as changeable. Our vector and matrix benchmarks permit changing any element of the input; in LML, this requires simply specifying the vector and matrix elements as changeable. Our blocked matrix benchmark permits changing any block (and thus any element) of the input. Our ray tracer permits changing the surface properties of objects in the image; thus, for a fixed input scene (lights and objects) and output image size, we can render multiple images via change propagation.

The type annotations needed to enable these changes in our self-adjusting versions of the benchmarks were trivial. Each benchmark, including the ray tracer, required changes to no more than a few lines of code—in fact, never more than two lines.

For each benchmark, we evaluate a conventional implementation and four self-adjusting versions. Three of these are hand-coded versions from previous work, "CPS" [Ley-Wild et al. 2008], "CEAL" [Hammer et al. 2011] and "AFL" [Acar et al. 2009]. We use these benchmarks exactly as published, except for setting the test parameters and input data consistently to enable comparison. The last set, labeled "Type-Directed", consists of the self-adjusting programs generated by our LML compiler. Our LML list benchmarks use the same memoization strategy as the "AFL" versions of the list benchmarks; the rest of the benchmarks do not need memoization in LML.

4.2 Experimental Setup

We used a 2 GHz Intel Xeon with 64 GB memory running Linux. The machine has multiple cores but all benchmarks are sequential. We compile all our benchmarks using our LML compiler. For comparison to previous work on ΔML, we use the publicly available ΔML compiler [DeltaML]. We execute all benchmarks with the "gc-summary" option to report garbage collection statistics, but exclude garbage-collection times from our experiments to focus on the actual computation time; we separately discuss garbage collection in Section 4.10.

For our measurements, we generate all inputs and all data changes uniformly randomly and sample over all possible changes. More specifically, the inputs to our integer benchmarks are random permutations of integers from 1 to n, where n is the input size. The inputs to our floating-point benchmarks are randomly generated floating-point numbers via the SML library. To increase the coverage of our evaluation, for each measurement, we average over four different input instances, as well as all input changes over each of these inputs.

For each benchmark we measure the complete running time of the conventional and the self-adjusting versions. All reported times are in seconds or milliseconds, averaged over four independent runs. Timings exclude creation of the initial input; in change-propagation timings, we also exclude the initial, pre-processing run (construction of the test data plus the complete run). To measure efficiency in responding to small data changes, we compute the *propagation time* for responding to an incremental change. The nature of the change depends on the benchmarks. For list benchmarks, we report the average time to insert or delete an element from the input list (average over all elements). For vector and matrix benchmarks, we report the average time to change an element of the vector or matrix by replacing it with a randomly generated element (averaged over all positions in the vector or one position per row in the matrix). For the ray tracer, we consider a range of changes which we describe later when discussing the ray tracer in detail.

4.3 Experiments: Correctness

To verify that our compiler generates self-adjusting executables that can respond to changes to their data correctly, we used three approaches: type checking, manual inspection, and extensive testing. Our compiler generates self-adjusting code to a text file, which we then type-check and compile along with a stand-alone self-adjusting-computation library, which we have separately implemented. SML's type system verifies that the translated code satisfies certain invariants. Since we can inspect the translated code manually, we can also spot-check the code, which is not a foolproof method but increases confidence. We have used this facility extensively when implementing the compiler.

Additionally, we have developed a testing framework, which makes a massive number of randomly generated changes to the input data, and checks that the executable responds correctly to each such change by comparing its output with that of a "verifier" (reference implementation) that computes the given output using a straightforward, non-incremental algorithm. Using this framework, we have verified the correctness of all the self-adjusting executables generated by our compiler.

4.4 Experiments: Timings Summary

Table 1 shows a summary of the timings that we collected for our benchmarks at fixed input sizes (written in parentheses after the benchmark's name). All times are reported in seconds. The first column ("Conv. Run") shows the run time of the conventional (reference) implementation with an input of specified size. The conventional version cannot self-adjust, but does not incur the overhead of trace construction as self-adjusting versions do. The second column ("Self-Adj. Run") shows the run time of the self-adjusting version with an input of specified size. Such a self-adjusting run constructs a trace as it executes, which can then be used to respond automatically to incremental changes to data via change propagation. The third column ("Self-Adj. Avg. Prop.") shows the average time for a change propagation after a small change to the input (as described in Section 4.1, the specific nature of the changes depend on the application).

The last two columns of the table, "Overhead" and "Speedup", report the ratio of the self-adjusting run to the conventional run, and the ratio of the conventional run to change propagation. The overhead is the slowdown that a self-adjusting run incurs compared to a run of the conventional program. The speedup measures the speedup that change propagation delivers compared to re-

Application (Input size)	Conv. Run (s)	Self-Adj. Run (s)	Self-Adj. Avg. Prop. (s)	Overhead	Speedup
map(10^6)	0.05	0.83	1.1×10^{-6}	16.7	4.6×10^4
filter(10^6)	0.04	1.25	1.4×10^{-6}	27.7	3.2×10^4
split(10^6)	0.14	1.63	3.2×10^{-6}	11.6	4.4×10^4
msort(10^5)	0.30	5.83	3.5×10^{-4}	19.5	850.92
qsort(10^5)	0.05	3.40	4.9×10^{-4}	64.2	108.17
vec-reduce(10^6)	0.05	0.26	4.4×10^{-6}	5.5	1.1×10^4
vec-mult(10^6)	0.18	1.10	6.7×10^{-6}	5.9	2.8×10^4
mat-vec-mult(10^3)	0.17	0.81	1.4×10^{-5}	4.6	1.3×10^4
mat-add(10^3)	0.10	0.36	4.9×10^{-7}	3.7	2.0×10^5
transpose(10^4)	2.14	2.15	5.1×10^{-8}	1.0	4.2×10^7
mat-mult(400)	10.65	90.22	5.8×10^{-3}	8.5	1.8×10^3
block-mat-mult(10^3)	7.03	8.38	4.6×10^{-3}	1.2	1.5×10^3

Table 1. Summary of benchmark timings.

computing with the conventional version. An analysis of the data shows that the overheads are higher for simple benchmarks such as list operations (which are dominated by memory accesses), but significantly lower for other benchmarks. The overheads for `qsort` are traditionally high, commensurate with the previous work. In all benchmarks, we observe massive speedups, thanks to the asymptotic improvements delivered by change propagation. In the common case, the overhead is incurred only once: after a self-adjusting run, we can change the input data incrementally and use change propagation, with massive speedups.

4.5 Experiments: Merge Sort

Although it is not apparent from the summary in Table 1, our experiments show that for all our benchmarks, the overheads of self-adjusting versions are constant and do not depend on the input size, whereas speedups, being asymptotically significant, increase with the input size. To illustrate this property, we examine our merge sort benchmark; in Appendix A, we show the corresponding data for four more representative benchmarks.

The plot on the left in Figure 6 shows the time (in seconds) for the complete run of self-adjusting merge sort compared to the conventional version, for a range of input sizes (x axis). The figure suggests that, in both the conventional and self-adjusting versions, the complete-run time grows almost linearly, and they exhibit the same asymptotic complexity, $O(n \log n)$. The plot in the middle of Figure 6 shows the time—in milliseconds—for change propagation after inserting/deleting one element for each input size (x axis). As can be seen, the time taken by change propagation grows sublinearly as the input size increases. This is consistent with the $O(\log n)$ bound that we can show analytically. The plot on the right in Figure 6 shows the speedups for different input sizes (x axis): the time for a run of the conventional algorithm divided by the time for change propagation. The plots show that speedups increase linearly with the input size, consistent with the theoretical bound. To obtain this asymptotic improvement, we only insert one keyword in the code and use our compiler to generate the self-adjusting version.

4.6 Experiments: Matrix Multiplication

Our type-based approach gives the programmer great flexibility in specifying changeable elements in different granularity. The difference in the data representation can lead to dramatically different time and space performance. For example, `mat-mult` performs matrix multiplication using the standard matrix representation where each element of the matrix is changeable, while `block-mat-mult` considers the blocked representation where elements are blocked into groups of 20×20 submatrices. As we can see from Table 1, although the blocked version has a smaller speedup, as changing one element requires recomputing the whole submatrix, it has much less overhead compared to the standard representation. To further explore this trade-off, Figure 7 shows the time and space of blocked matrix multiplication with block sizes from 20×20 to 50×50.

Run time. In Figure 7, the leftmost plot shows the time for the complete run of self-adjusting blocked-matrix multiply with different block sizes, as well as the conventional version. The figure suggests that all benchmarks exhibit the same asymptotic complexity, $O(n^3)$. We also observe that as the block size increases, the overhead becomes smaller. This is because we treat each block as a single modifiable, reducing the number of modifiables tracked at run time. The second plot in Figure 7 shows the time for change propagation after changing a block for each input size (x axis) with different block sizes. The time taken by change propagation grows almost linearly as the input size increases, which is consistent with the $O(n \log n)$ bound that we can compute analytically. Changing any part of a block requires recomputing the whole block, so propagation is faster with smaller block sizes. The third plot in Figure 7 shows speedups for different input sizes. Speedups increase asymptotically with input size, consistent with the theoretical bound of $O(n^2/\log n)$. Smaller blocks have higher speedups. For example, for a 1000×1000 matrix, the 20×20 block enables $1200\times$ speedup, while the 50×50 block has $280\times$ speedup.

Space. The rightmost plot in Figure 7 shows the memory used by change propagation with different block sizes (the complete run never uses more memory than change propagation). As with all other approaches to self-adjusting computation, our approach exploits a trade-off between memory (space) and time (we compare the space usage of other approaches in Section 4.9). We store computation traces in memory and use them to respond to incremental data changes, resulting in an increase in memory usage and a decrease in response time. Typically, self-adjusting programs use asymptotically as much memory as the run-time of the computation. The plot shows results consistent with the theoretical bound of $O(n^3)$. Although a smaller block size leads to larger speedups, it requires more memory, because the total number of modifiables created is proportional to the number of blocks in the matrix.

As can be seen from the plot, memory consumption can be high. However, it can be reduced by programmer control over dependencies, which self-adjusting computation provides [Acar et al. 2009; Hammer et al. 2011]: The programmer can specify larger chunks of data, instead of single units, as changeable. Our approach further simplifies such control by requiring only the types to be changed. As a concrete example, our matrix-multiplication benchmark with 50×50 blocks consumes about 300 MB as we change each element of the input matrix and update the output. This is about 10 times the space needed to store the two input matrices and the result matrix, but enables a $280\times$ speedup when re-computing the output.

4.7 Experiments: Ray Tracer

Many applications are suitable for incremental computation, because making a small change to their input on average causes small changes to their output. But some applications are not. Arguably, incremental computation techniques should be avoided or used cautiously in such applications. To evaluate the effectiveness of our approach in such limiting cases, we considered ray tracing, where a small change to the input can require a large fraction of the output image to be updated. In our experiments, we rendered an input scene of 3 light sources and 19 objects with an output image size of 512×512 and then repeatedly changed the surface properties

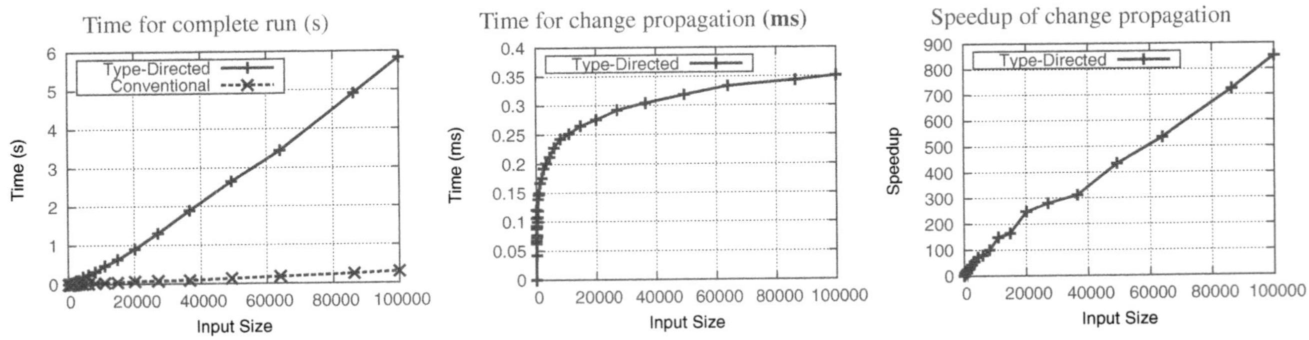

Figure 6. Time for complete run; time and speedup for change propagation for `msort`

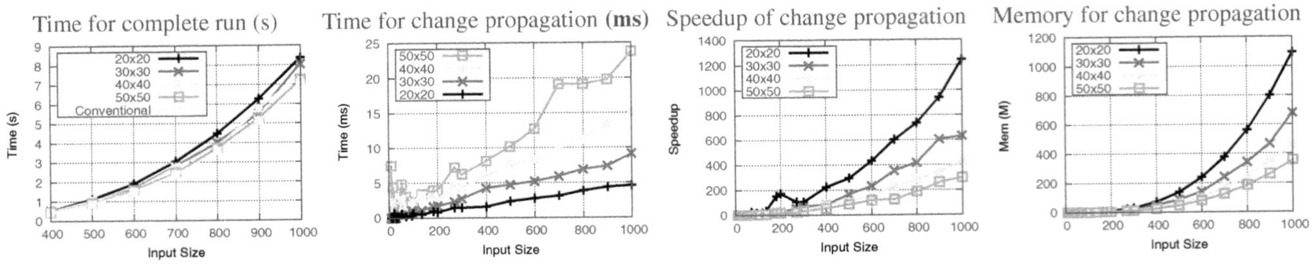

Figure 7. Time for complete run; time, speedup and memory for change propagation for blocked matrix multiply

Surface Changed	Image Diff. (% pixels)	Conv. Run (s)	Self-Adj. Run (s)	Self-Adj. Avg. Prop. (s)	Overhead	Speedup
A^D	57.22%	4.07	6.32	3.04	1.55	1.34
A^M	57.22%	1.91	5.75	8.48	3.02	0.22
B^D	8.43%	2.37	4.87	0.55	2.05	4.29
B^M	8.43%	2.44	4.42	1.00	1.81	2.44
C^D	9.20%	2.43	3.97	0.59	1.64	4.09
C^M	9.20%	2.16	3.86	1.12	1.79	1.92
D^D	1.85%	2.44	3.83	0.12	1.57	20.21
D^M	1.85%	2.19	3.85	0.20	1.76	10.74
E^D	11.64%	4.10	6.28	1.27	1.53	3.22
E^M	11.74%	2.79	5.83	1.87	2.09	1.49
F^D	19.47%	2.85	5.78	1.57	2.03	1.82
F^M	19.47%	2.83	3.92	2.97	1.38	0.95
G^D	27.37%	2.85	3.92	2.58	1.38	1.11
G^M	27.47%	2.82	5.36	4.64	1.90	0.61

Table 2. Summary of ray tracer timings.

of a single surface (which may be shared by multiple objects in the scene). We considered three kinds of changes: a change to the color of a surface, a change from a diffuse (non-reflective) surface to a mirrored surface, and a change from a mirrored to diffuse surface. We measured the time for a complete run of both the conventional and the self-adjusting versions, and the average propagation time for a single toggle of a surface property. For each change to the input, we also measured the change in the output image as a fraction of pixels. Figure 8 illustrates an example.

Table 2 shows the timings for various kinds of changes. The first column shows the percentage of pixels changed in the output. Each pair of rows corresponds to changing the surface properties of a set of objects (sets labeled A through G) to diffuse (non-reflective)

Figure 8. Two images produced by our ray tracer. To produce the right-hand image, we change the surfaces of the four green balls from diffused surfaces to mirrored surfaces. Change propagation yields about a 2× speedup over re-computing the output.

and mirror surfaces in that order, as indicated by superscripts $\cdot^D$ and $\cdot^M$ respectively. Our measurements show that even when a large fraction of the output image must change, our approach can perform better than recomputing from scratch. We also observe that since mirrors reflect light, making a surface mirrored often requires performing more work during change propagation than making the surface diffuse. Indeed, we observe that the speedups obtained for mirror changes are consistently about half of the speedups for diffuse changes.

4.8 Experiments: Compiler Optimizations

In Section 3.4 we described some key optimizations that eliminate redundancies in the code. To measure the effectiveness of these optimizations, we measured the running time for our benchmarks compiled with and without these optimizations. Since the optimizations always eliminate redundant calls, we expected them to improve efficiency consistently, and also quite significantly. As can be seen in Figure 9 by comparing the bars labeled "Unopt." (green) and "Type-Directed" (black), our experiments indeed show that the optimizations can improve the time of the complete run and the

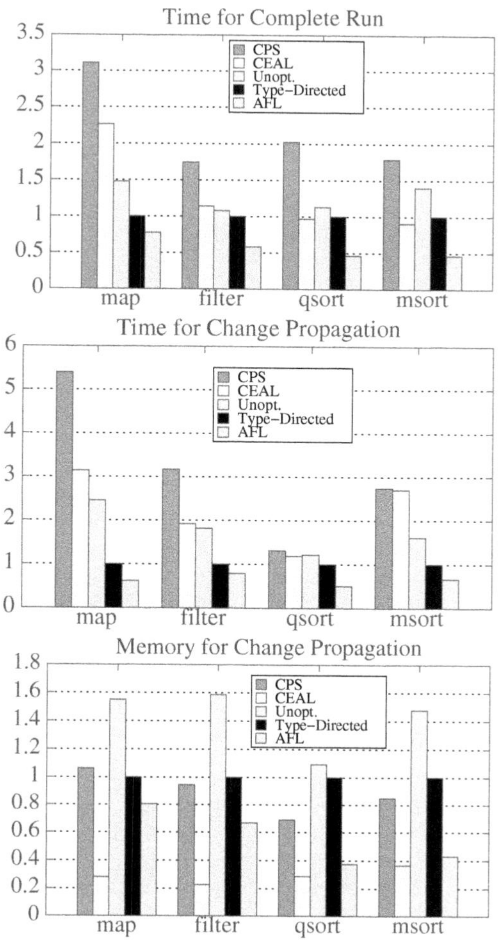

Figure 9. Time and memory for complete run and change propagation at fixed input sizes, normalized to "Type-Directed" (set to 1). We note for readability that the top-down order of the legend corresponds to the horizontal ordering of the bars.

time and space for change propagation by as much as 60%. The complete run never uses more space than change propagation does. We will discuss the rest of Figure 9 in Section 4.9.

4.9 Experiments: Comparison to Previous Work

We compare our results with previous work: the combinator library (AFL) in SML [Acar et al. 2009], the continuation-passing style (CPS) approach in SML [Ley-Wild et al. 2008], and the C-based CEAL system [Hammer et al. 2011], which is a carefully engineered and highly optimized system that can be competitive with hand-crafted algorithms [Demetrescu et al. 2004]. Figure 9 shows this comparison for the common benchmarks with fixed input sizes of 1 million keys for list operations and 100,000 keys for sorting, with results normalized to "Type-Directed" (= 1.0).

The comparison shows that, for both time and space, our approach is within a factor of two of AFL, a carefully engineered hand-written library. The principal reason for AFL's performance is its multiple interfaces to the self-adjusting primitives, which the programmer selects by hand. For example, AFL provides an unsafe interface that the quicksort benchmark uses to speed up the partition, creating half as many modifiables as with the standard interface. Our compiler does not directly support these low-level primitives, so we cannot perform the same optimizations. In AFL, programmers need to restructure programs in monadic style, explicitly

Surface Changed	Image Diff. (% pixels)	Type-Dir. Run (s)	CPS Run (s)	Speedup vs. CPS	Type-Dir. Prop (s)	CPS Prop (s)	Speedup vs. CPS
A^D	57.22%	6.32	5.88	0.93	3.04	4.36	1.43
A^M	57.22%	5.75	7.35	1.28	8.48	13.86	1.64
B^D	8.43%	4.87	8.06	1.66	0.55	1.01	1.82
B^M	8.43%	4.42	7.75	1.75	1.00	1.80	1.80
C^D	9.20%	3.97	7.97	2.01	0.59	1.15	1.93
C^M	9.20%	3.86	7.63	1.98	1.12	1.93	1.72
D^D	1.85%	3.83	7.95	2.07	0.12	0.21	1.75
D^M	1.85%	3.85	7.57	1.97	0.20	0.28	1.39
E^D	11.64%	6.28	5.88	0.94	1.27	2.52	1.98
E^M	11.74%	5.83	12.41	2.13	1.87	3.44	1.84
F^D	19.47%	5.78	11.96	2.07	1.57	3.00	1.91
F^M	19.47%	3.92	9.44	2.41	2.97	5.41	1.82
G^D	27.37%	3.92	9.64	2.46	2.58	4.69	1.82
G^M	27.47%	5.36	11.02	2.06	4.64	8.60	1.85

Table 3. Comparison of ray tracer with CPS

constructing the dependency graph. This process is similar to doing type inference and translation by hand. Our approach makes self-adjusting programs much easier to write, yet their performance is competitive with carefully-engineered self-adjusting programs.

Compared to CPS, our approach is approximately twice as fast, even though the CPS approach requires widespread changes to the program code and ours does not. The primary reason for the performance gap is likely that the CPS-based transformation relies on coarse approximations of true dependencies (based on continuations); our compiler identifies dependencies more precisely by using a type-directed translation. Additionally, we compared our ray tracer with one based on CPS, where our approach ("Type-Dir.") is approximately twice as fast as CPS (Table 3). Our approach often uses slightly more space than the CPS based approach, probably because of redundancies in the automatically generated code that can be eliminated manually in the CPS approach.

Compared to CEAL [Hammer et al. 2011], our approach is usually faster but occasionally slightly slower. We find this very interesting because the CEAL benchmarks use hand-written, potentially unsound optimizations, such as selective destination-passing and sharing of trace nodes [Hammer et al. 2011, Sections 7.2 and 8.1], that can result in incorrectly updated output. We also compared our approach to sound versions of CEAL benchmarks, which were a factor of two slower than the unsound versions. We use up to five times as much space; given that our approach uses space consistent with the other ML based approach ("CPS"), this is probably because of differences between ML, a functional, garbage-collected language, and C. When compared to sound versions of the CEAL benchmarks, which is arguably the more fair comparison, CEAL's space advantage decreases by a factor of two.

To summarize, even though our approach accepts conventional code with only a few type annotations, the generated programs perform better than most hand-written code in two programming languages, and are competitive with hand-written code in AFL. Memory usage is comparable to other ML-based approaches.

4.10 Experiments: the Effect of Garbage Collection

In our evaluation thus far, we did not include garbage-collection times because they are very sensitive to garbage collection parameters, which can be specified during run time. For example, our compiler allows us to specify a heap size when executing a program. If this heap size is sufficiently large to accommodate the live data of our benchmarks, then the timings show that essentially no time is spent in garbage collection. When we do not specify a heap size, memory is managed automatically, taking care not to over-expand the heap unnecessarily, by keeping the heap size close to the size of

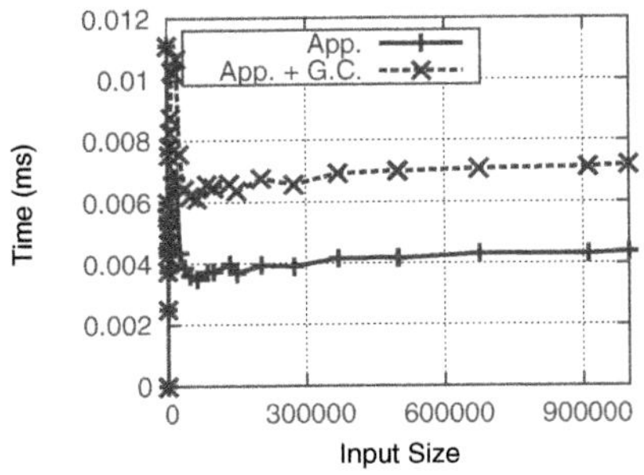

Figure 10. Propagation time for `vec-reduce` including GC time.

the live data. With this setting, our timings show that garbage collection behaves differently in the complete run and change propagation. The time can vary from negligible to moderate during complete runs of self-adjusting executables. For example, in blocked matrix multiplication, garbage collection times are less than 10%, but in vector multiplication, garbage collection takes nearly half of the total running time. Previous work on self-adjusting computation shows similar tradeoffs [Hammer and Acar 2008; Acar et al. 2009]. During change propagation, however, we observe that garbage-collection times are relatively small even when not using a fixed heap. Figure 10 shows the garbage collection time for vector reduce, which is close to the worst-case typical behavior that we obtain in our benchmarks. In some applications such as raytracing and blocked matrix multiplication, garbage collection times are negligible.

5. Related Work

The problem of enabling computation to respond efficiently to changes has been studied extensively. We briefly examine some earlier techniques for incremental computation and information flow. Detailed background can be found in several excellent surveys [Ramalingam and Reps 1993; Chiang and Tamassia 1992; Agarwal et al. 2002; Demetrescu et al. 2005; Sabelfeld and Myers 2003].

Incremental and self-adjusting computation. Earlier work on incremental computation, which took place in the '80s and '90s, was primarily based on dependence graphs and memoization. Dependence graphs record the dependencies between data in a computation and use a change-propagation algorithm to update the computation when the input is modified [Demers et al. 1981; Hoover 1987]. Dependence graphs have been effective in applications such as syntax-directed computations, but are not general-purpose because change propagation cannot update the dependence structure. As an alternative, researchers have proposed memoization (also called function caching) [Pugh and Teitelbaum 1989; Abadi et al. 1996; Heydon et al. 2000]. A classic idea [Bellman 1957; McCarthy 1963; Michie 1968], memoization applies to any purely functional program. It improves efficiency when executions of a program with similar inputs involve similar function calls, but such calls are relatively rare: small modifications to input can prevent reuse by changing the arguments to many function calls.

More recent work on self-adjusting computation proposed a particular technique for incremental computation that combines dynamic dependence graphs [Acar et al. 2006] and a form of computational memoization [Acar et al. 2009] to achieve efficient updates. Variants of self-adjusting computation have been implemented in several host languages such as C [Hammer et al. 2011], Java [Shankar and Bodik 2007], Haskell [Carlsson 2002], and SML [Ley-Wild et al. 2008]. Self-adjusting computation often achieves asymptotically efficient updates for a reasonably broad range of benchmarks [Acar et al. 2009; Hammer et al. 2011], can help verify runtime invariants [Shankar and Bodik 2007], and even help solve major open problems in many domains including computational geometry [Acar et al. 2010] and machine learning [Sümer et al. 2011]. More recent work shows that the approach can be generalized to parallel computations, taking simultaneous advantage of parallelism and incremental computation time by exploiting structural similarities between them [Hammer et al. 2007; Burckhardt et al. 2011; Acar et al. 2011], as well as large-scale distributed systems [Bhatotia et al. 2011].

Of all these previous approaches, DITTO [Shankar and Bodik 2007] and Incoop [Bhatotia et al. 2011] have the advantage of being completely transparent—they require no programmer annotations or changes to the code. But they only target specific domains—invariant checking for DITTO and large-scale MapReduce computations for Incoop—making them unsuited to general-purpose computations. Of the general approaches, library-based systems in SML and in C# [Acar et al. 2009; Burckhardt et al. 2011] require the programmer to guarantee certain invariants for correctness. These invariants are nontrivial to check statically or dynamically, and motivated the approaches taken by ΔML and CEAL.

ΔML [Ley-Wild et al. 2008] and the most recent version of the CEAL language system [Hammer et al. 2011] can ensure that self-adjusting programs respond to changes to their input correctly. As described in Section 2, ΔML requires writing self-adjusting programs in an explicit style by inserting several primitives that can require substantial changes to the code. Recent work on CEAL shows that a large fraction of annotations can be eliminated, but at the cost of tracing and recording all dependencies, which can lead to significant loss of time efficiency and space blowup.

The approach we describe in this paper uses a type-directed translation to enable selective dependency tracking, recording only the parts of the computation that can be affected by the changes. It guarantees that the output is updated correctly and efficiently under any changes to the data. The approach is based on the theoretical work of Chen et al. [2011]. That work, however, considered a minimal language and provided no implementation or practical evidence that the approach can be realized in practice. As our experimental evaluation shows, our implementation performs very well, usually outperforming ΔML and CEAL even though they require heavy programmer involvement, while our approach required only tiny changes to type declarations and no changes to the code itself. Our approach thus allows taking advantage of the benefits of self-adjusting computation without the burden of major program restructuring.

Information flow. A number of information flow type systems have been developed to check security properties, including the SLam calculus [Heintze and Riecke 1998], JFlow [Myers 1999] and a monadic system [Crary et al. 2005]. To save energy by approximating subcomputations, Sampson et al. [2011] use information flow to analyze dependencies. The type system of Chen et al. [2011] used many ideas from Pottier and Simonet [2003].

Coco [Swamy et al. 2011] transforms constructions such as effects from impure style (as in ML) to an explicit monadic style (as in Haskell). In other words, it translates effects in lightweight style into effects in a heavyweight style. But it does not support implicit self-adjusting computation: uses of effects, though lightweight compared to monadic style, must be explicit in the source program. Even such relatively lightweight constructs are pervasive in explicit self-adjusting computations and, compared to implicit self-adjusting computation, very tedious to program with.

6. Conclusion

We present the design, implementation, and evaluation of a programming language and compiler that enable programmers to write programs that respond automatically to changes to their data, using only simple type annotations. By design, our approach guarantees that the compiled programs respond to data changes correctly. Through self-adjusting-computation techniques and a carefully designed type-directed mechanism for identifying dependencies, the compiler yields executables that can respond to incremental changes efficiently. Conventional benchmarks such as matrix multiplication and ray tracers can be compiled to efficient incremental executables, with only tiny changes to their type specifications. Our language and compiler take an important step in solving the long-standing problem of creating high-level languages for developing software that can react to incremental change correctly and efficiently with minimal programmer involvement.

Acknowledgments We thank the anonymous PLDI reviewers for their very useful comments on the submitted version of this paper, and Matthew A. Hammer for help with the CEAL benchmarks.

References

M. Abadi, B. W. Lampson, and J.-J. Lévy. Analysis and caching of dependencies. In *International Conference on Functional Programming*, pages 83–91, 1996.

U. A. Acar, G. E. Blelloch, and R. Harper. Adaptive functional programming. *ACM Trans. Prog. Lang. Sys.*, 28(6):990–1034, 2006.

U. A. Acar, A. Ahmed, and M. Blume. Imperative self-adjusting computation. In *Proceedings of the 25th Annual ACM Symposium on Principles of Programming Languages*, 2008.

U. A. Acar, G. E. Blelloch, M. Blume, R. Harper, and K. Tangwongsan. An experimental analysis of self-adjusting computation. *ACM Trans. Prog. Lang. Sys.*, 32(1):3:1–53, 2009.

U. A. Acar, A. Cotter, B. Hudson, and D. Türkoğlu. Dynamic well-spaced point sets. In *Symposium on Computational Geometry*, 2010.

U. A. Acar, A. Cotter, B. Hudson, and D. Türkoğlu. Parallelism in dynamic well-spaced point sets. In *Proceedings of the 23rd ACM Symposium on Parallelism in Algorithms and Architectures*, 2011.

P. K. Agarwal, L. J. Guibas, H. Edelsbrunner, J. Erickson, M. Isard, S. Har-Peled, J. Hershberger, C. Jensen, L. Kavraki, P. Koehl, M. Lin, D. Manocha, D. Metaxas, B. Mirtich, D. Mount, S. Muthukrishnan, D. Pai, E. Sacks, J. Snoeyink, S. Suri, and O. Wolfson. Algorithmic issues in modeling motion. *ACM Comput. Surv.*, 34(4):550–572, 2002.

A. W. Appel and T. Jim. Shrinking lambda expressions in linear time. *J. Funct. Program.*, 7(5):515–540, Sept. 1997.

F. Baader and T. Nipkow. *Term rewriting and all that*. Cambridge University Press, 1998.

R. Bellman. *Dynamic Programming*. Princeton Univ. Press, 1957.

P. Bhatotia, A. Wieder, R. Rodrigues, U. A. Acar, and R. Pasquini. Incoop: MapReduce for incremental computations. In *ACM Symposium on Cloud Computing*, 2011.

S. Burckhardt, D. Leijen, C. Sadowski, J. Yi, and T. Ball. Two for the price of one: A model for parallel and incremental computation. In *ACM SIGPLAN Conference on Object-Oriented Programming, Systems, Languages, and Applications*, 2011.

M. Carlsson. Monads for incremental computing. In *International Conference on Functional Programming*, pages 26–35, 2002.

Y. Chen, J. Dunfield, M. A. Hammer, and U. A. Acar. Implicit self-adjusting computation for purely functional programs. In *Int'l Conference on Functional Programming (ICFP '11)*, pages 129–141, Sept. 2011.

Y.-J. Chiang and R. Tamassia. Dynamic algorithms in computational geometry. *Proceedings of the IEEE*, 80(9):1412–1434, 1992.

K. Crary, A. Kliger, and F. Pfenning. A monadic analysis of information flow security with mutable state. *Journal of Functional Programming*, 15(2):249–291, 2005.

DeltaML. DeltaML web site. `http://ttic.uchicago.edu/~pl/sa-sml/`.

A. Demers, T. Reps, and T. Teitelbaum. Incremental evaluation of attribute grammars with application to syntax-directed editors. In *Principles of Programming Languages*, pages 105–116, 1981.

C. Demetrescu, S. Emiliozzi, and G. F. Italiano. Experimental analysis of dynamic all pairs shortest path algorithms. In *ACM-SIAM Symposium on Discrete Algorithms (SODA)*, pages 369–378, 2004.

C. Demetrescu, I. Finocchi, and G. Italiano. *Handbook on Data Structures and Applications*, chapter 36: Dynamic Graphs. CRC Press, 2005.

M. Hammer and U. A. Acar. Memory management for self-adjusting computation. In *International Symposium on Memory Management*, pages 51–60, 2008.

M. Hammer, U. A. Acar, M. Rajagopalan, and A. Ghuloum. A proposal for parallel self-adjusting computation. In *DAMP '07: Declarative Aspects of Multicore Programming*, 2007.

M. Hammer, G. Neis, Y. Chen, and U. A. Acar. Self-adjusting stack machines. In *ACM SIGPLAN Conference on Object-Oriented Programming, Systems, Languages, and Applications (OOPSLA)*, 2011.

M. A. Hammer, U. A. Acar, and Y. Chen. CEAL: a C-based language for self-adjusting computation. In *ACM SIGPLAN Conference on Programming Language Design and Implementation*, 2009.

N. Heintze and J. G. Riecke. The SLam calculus: programming with secrecy and integrity. In *Principles of Programming Languages (POPL '98)*, pages 365–377, 1998.

A. Heydon, R. Levin, and Y. Yu. Caching function calls using precise dependencies. In *Programming Language Design and Implementation*, pages 311–320, 2000.

R. Hoover. *Incremental Graph Evaluation*. PhD thesis, Department of Computer Science, Cornell University, May 1987.

R. Jakob. *Dynamic Planar Convex Hull*. PhD thesis, Department of Computer Science, University of Aarhus, 2002.

D. J. King. A ray tracer for spheres, 1998. `http://www.cs.rice.edu/~dmp4866/darcs/nofib/spectral/sphere/`.

R. Ley-Wild, M. Fluet, and U. A. Acar. Compiling self-adjusting programs with continuations. In *Int'l Conference on Functional Programming*, 2008.

J. McCarthy. A basis for a mathematical theory of computation. In P. Braffort and D. Hirschberg, editors, *Computer Programming and Formal Systems*, pages 33–70. North-Holland, Amsterdam, 1963.

D. Michie. "Memo" functions and machine learning. *Nature*, 218:19–22, 1968.

MLton. MLton web site. `http://www.mlton.org`.

A. C. Myers. JFlow: practical mostly-static information flow control. In *Principles of Programming Languages*, pages 228–241, 1999.

M. H. A. Newman. On theories with a combinatorial definition of "equivalence". *Annals of Mathematics*, 43(2):223–243, 1942.

F. Pottier and V. Simonet. Information flow inference for ML. *ACM Trans. Prog. Lang. Sys.*, 25(1):117–158, Jan. 2003.

W. Pugh and T. Teitelbaum. Incremental computation via function caching. In *Principles of Programming Languages*, pages 315–328, 1989.

G. Ramalingam and T. Reps. A categorized bibliography on incremental computation. In *Principles of Programming Languages*, pages 502–510, 1993.

A. Sabelfeld and A. C. Myers. Language-based information-flow security. *IEEE J. Selected Areas in Communications*, 21(1), 2003.

A. Sampson, W. Dietl, E. Fortuna, D. Gnanapragasam, L. Ceze, and D. Grossman. EnerJ: Approximate data types for safe and general low-power computation. In *Programming Language Design and Implementation*, pages 164–174, 2011.

A. Shankar and R. Bodik. DITTO: Automatic incrementalization of data structure invariant checks (in Java). In *Programming Language Design and Implementation*, 2007.

O. Sümer, U. A. Acar, A. Ihler, and R. Mettu. Fast parallel and adaptive updates for dual-decomposition solvers. In *Conference on Artificial Intelligence (AAAI)*, 2011.

N. Swamy, N. Guts, D. Leijen, and M. Hicks. Lightweight monadic programming in ML. In *International Conference on Functional Programming (ICFP)*, Sept. 2011.

A. Appendix

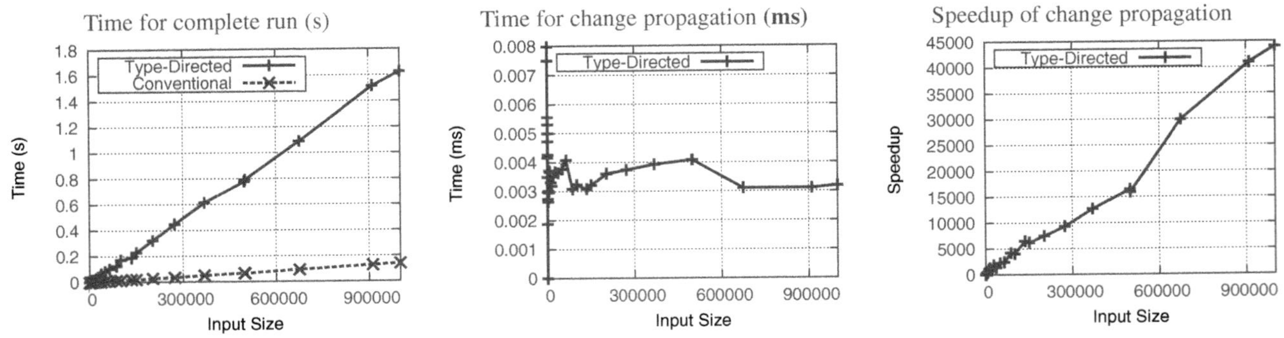

Figure 11. Time for complete run; time and speedup for change propagation for `split`

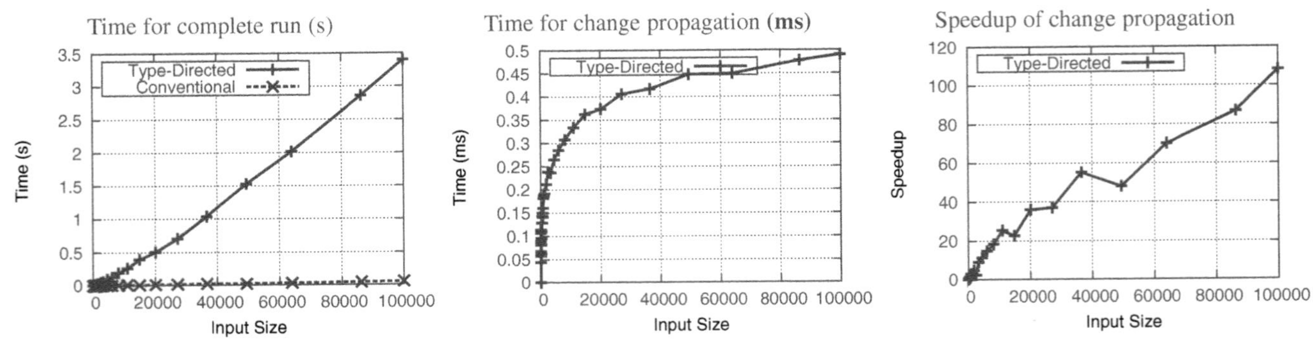

Figure 12. Time for complete run; time and speedup for change propagation for `qsort`

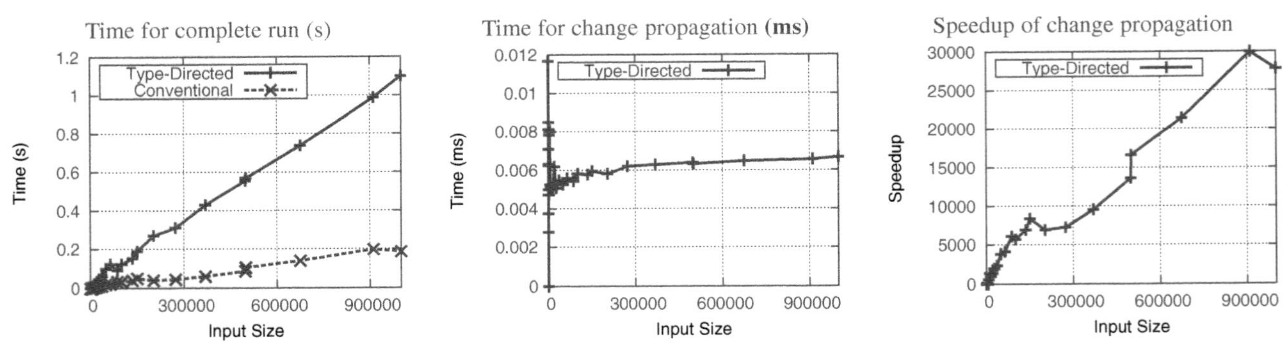

Figure 13. Time for complete run; time and speedup for change propagation for `vec-mult`

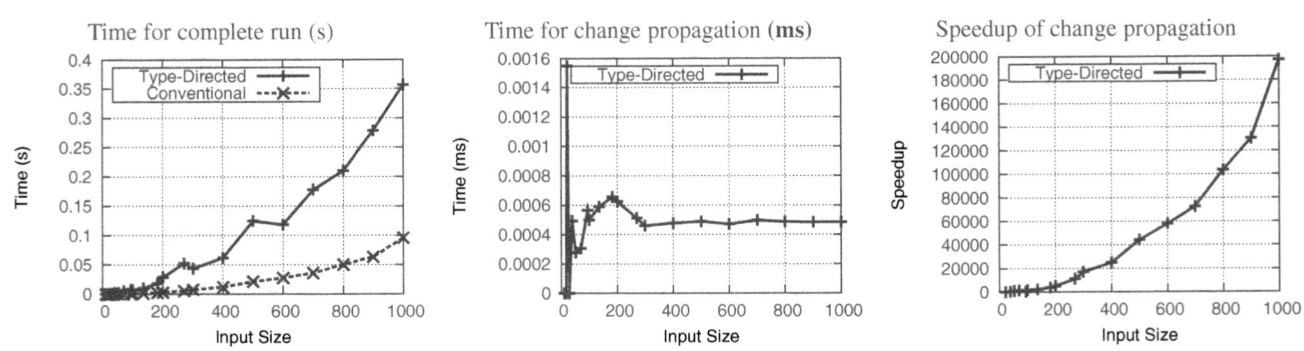

Figure 14. Time for complete run; time and speedup for change propagation for `mat-add`

Synchronising C/C++ and POWER

Susmit Sarkar[1] Kayvan Memarian[1] Scott Owens[1] Mark Batty[1] Peter Sewell[1]
Luc Maranget[2] Jade Alglave[3] Derek Williams[4]

[1]University of Cambridge, {first.last}@cl.cam.ac.uk
[2]INRIA, luc.maranget@inria.fr
[3]University of Oxford, jade.alglave@comlab.ox.ac.uk
[4]IBM Austin, striker@us.ibm.com

Abstract

Shared memory concurrency relies on synchronisation primitives: compare-and-swap, load-reserve/store-conditional (aka LL/SC), language-level mutexes, and so on. In a sequentially consistent setting, or even in the TSO setting of x86 and Sparc, these have well-understood semantics. But in the very relaxed settings of IBM® POWER®, ARM, or C/C++, it remains surprisingly unclear exactly what the programmer can depend on.

This paper studies relaxed-memory synchronisation. On the hardware side, we give a clear semantic characterisation of the load-reserve/store-conditional primitives as provided by POWER multiprocessors, for the first time since they were introduced 20 years ago; we cover their interaction with relaxed loads, stores, barriers, and dependencies. Our model, while not officially sanctioned by the vendor, is validated by extensive testing, comparing actual implementation behaviour against an oracle generated from the model, and by detailed discussion with IBM staff. We believe the ARM semantics to be similar.

On the software side, we prove sound a proposed compilation scheme of the C/C++ synchronisation constructs to POWER, including C/C++ spinlock mutexes, fences, and read-modify-write operations, together with the simpler atomic operations for which soundness is already known from our previous work; this is a first step in verifying concurrent algorithms that use load-reserve/store-conditional with respect to a realistic semantics. We also build confidence in the C/C++ model in its own terms, fixing some omissions and contributing to the C standards committee adoption of the C++11 concurrency model.

Categories and Subject Descriptors C.1.2 [*Multiple Data Stream Architectures (Multiprocessors)*]: Parallel processors; D.1.3 [*Concurrent Programming*]: Parallel programming; F.3.1 [*Specifying and Verifying and Reasoning about Programs*]

General Terms Languages, Reliability, Standardisation, Theory, Verification

Keywords Relaxed Memory Models, Semantics

1. Introduction

Synchronisation is fundamental to shared-memory concurrency, but the properties of basic real-world synchronisation primitives remain surprisingly unclear: there is a big gap between the usual descriptions of their behaviour, which presuppose a sequentially consistent (SC) [Lam79] setting, and their behaviour in actual multiprocessors and programming languages, which are not SC. Instead of interleaving operations from different threads, all with a consistent view of memory, real systems expose *relaxed memory models* to the programmer, to allow for hardware and compiler optimisations. In such a setting, even basic properties, such as locks ensuring that locations are "not concurrently accessed", become hard to understand, as one cannot reason in simple global-time terms; the semantics of synchronisation primitives are necessarily intertwined with the relaxed semantics of other code, including whatever loads, stores, and barriers are present.

This paper addresses relaxed-memory synchronisation in hardware and in software, and the relationship between the two. Our first main contribution, on the hardware side, is a usable model for the synchronisation primitives, load-reserve/store-conditional pairs, of the highly relaxed IBM® Power Architecture® (§2). While these have been present in the architecture for 20 years, their relaxed-memory behaviour have never before been clearly explained (for example, confusion on this point has led to a Linux kernel bug in the implementations of atomic operations [McK11], as we remark in §2). We do so with a novel abstraction, of a write *reaching coherence point*, with just the properties that are needed in the semantics. This removes any need for modelling the implementation detail of reservation registers, which becomes very complex in a setting with speculative and out-of-order execution.

We establish confidence in our model in multiple ways (§3), including extensive experimental testing (comparing processor behaviour against the model), detailed discussion with IBM staff, and proofs of basic properties, about the strength of load-reserve/store-conditional pairs (§3.2), and that a simple locking discipline guarantees SC for POWER programs (§5).

For our second main contribution, on the software side, we prove correctness of a mapping of the principal C/C++ synchronisation constructs to POWER (§5). We consider C/C++ locks, atomic read-modify-write (RMW) operations, fences, and atomic loads and stores, with the various possible memory-order parameters, from relaxed to SC (for locks we consider basic mutexes, not reentrant or timed, and just their lock and unlock interface, and we do not consider condition variables or futures). We take the implementation of spinlocks from the POWER documentation [Pow09, p.717,718], combining that with the POWER implementation of C/C++ RMWs, fences and atomic operations proposed by McKenney and Silvera [MS11]. Locks and RMWs both rely on the POWER load-reserve/store-conditional.

In the process of doing this proof, we identified and fixed several technical issues with the C/C++11 concurrency model and with our previous formalisation; we describe those in §4, together with a

PLDI'12, June 11–16, 2012, Beijing, China.

brief summary of the design of that model and an explanation of the C/C++ fences, to make this paper as self-contained as possible.

POWER and C/C++11 are both subtle models, though of quite different kinds, and there is an interplay between them: implementability on POWER (and the similar ARM) had a major influence on the design of C/C++11, and, conversely, the desire to support efficient language implementation imposes constraints on the architecture. Our work illuminates such choices by showing what is necessary for soundness; as we show in §2, the models are in some respects "tight" against each other.

More generally, our correctness proof for this lock implementation is a first step towards reasoning about more sophisticated concurrent algorithms (using load-reserve/store-conditional synchronisation directly, or in C/C++) with respect to a realistic semantics; and our models provide a basis for future work on compiler correctness, program analysis and verification, and tool building.

Our models and the statements of our results and key lemmas are expressed in the lightweight mechanised specification language Lem [OBZNS11]; our proofs are rigorous but non-mechanised. The details of both are available online in the supplementary material [cpp], together with the data from our experimental testing and our `ppcmem` web interface for interactively exploring the model.

Related Work There is surprisingly little directly related work. We build first on our own recent line of work, where we have developed a high-fidelity abstract-machine model of the loads, stores and barriers of the POWER architecture, without load-reserve/store-conditional (Sarkar et al. [SSA+11]). On the C/C++ front, Boehm and Adve describe the core of the C/C++11 design [BA08]. We have provided a mathematisation of the concurrency model of C/C++11 (Batty et al. [BOS+11]), which we correct and use here. There, we also proved correctness of a compilation scheme from C/C++11 nonatomic and atomic loads and stores, and fences, to x86-TSO. The strength of the target memory model (and the omission of locks and RMWs) makes that a much simpler problem than the one we address here. We previously used these two models to show correctness of compilation from C/C++11 to POWER, for the fragment of C/C++ consisting just of nonatomic and atomic stores and loads of various kinds [BMO+12]. Here our extended models and proof finally cover all of the main features of concurrency in POWER and in C/C++.

There have been, to the best of our knowledge, three previous serious attempts at realistic relaxed-memory semantics of load-reserve/store-conditional in the POWER setting, none of which are satisfactory for the current architecture. Corella, Stone, and Barton [CSB93] give an axiomatic model and show the correctness of an implementation of locks in terms of it. Their model does not cover the weaker `lwsync` barrier (which was not present in the Power Architecture of the time), and their lock implementation is therefore more conservative than the one we consider, with two `syncs`. Moreover, as Adir et al. note [AAS03], the basic model is flawed in that it permits the non-SC final state of a message-passing-with-syncs example. Adir et al. give a more elaborate model, with a view order per thread, sketching extensions for the synchronisation instructions, but this is still for the non-cumulative barriers of the time. Our previous global-time axiomatic model (Alglave et al. [AM11]) appears reasonable for load-reserve/store-conditional in isolation but too weak for the POWER `lwsync` barrier, permitting some behaviour that the C/C++11 mapping requires to be forbidden.

2. Optimistic Synchronisation on POWER: Load-reserve/Store-conditional

Load-reserve/store-conditional primitives were introduced by Jensen *et al.* [JHB87] as a RISC-architecture alternative to the compare-and-swap (CAS) instruction; they have been used in the IBM® PowerPC® architecture since 1992 and are also present in ARM, MIPS, and Alpha. They are also known as load-linked/store-conditional (LL/SC), or, on ARM, load-exclusive/store-exclusive. They provide a simple form of optimistic concurrency (very roughly, optimistic transactions on single locations).

Herlihy [Her93] uses load-reserve/store-conditional to implement various wait-free and lock-free algorithms, noting that (as for CAS, but unlike test-and-set and fetch-and-add) it is *universal* in terms of consensus number, and moreover that load-reserve/store-conditional is practically superior to CAS in that it defends against the ABA problem. These results, as for almost all other work in concurrent algorithms, use an underlying sequentially consistent (SC) semantics.

In a sequentially consistent setting, one can describe the behaviour of load-reserve/store-conditional fairly simply. A load-reserve does a load from some memory address; and a subsequent store-conditional to the same address will either succeed or fail. It will definitely fail if some other thread has written to that address in the meantime (or for some other reasons), otherwise (where the write read from by the load-reserve is still the most recent write to that address) it might succeed, performing a store. Moreover, the store-conditional sets a flag so that later instructions can determine whether or not it succeeded; load-reserve/store-conditional pairs are often repeated until success. This makes it easy to express a variety of atomic update operations, as in the following POWER assembly code for an atomic add (ARM code would be similar, with LDREX and STREX):

```
1:lwarx  r0,0,r2  \\ load-reserve from [r2] to r0
  add    r0,r1,r0 \\ add register r1 to register r0
  stwcx. r0,0,r2  \\ store-conditional r0 to [r2]
  bne-   1b       \\ ...looping until success
```

In an SC world, the store-conditional would be guaranteed to fail if some other thread writes to `[r2]` since the load-reserve; which could be achieved in hardware by monitoring whether any other thread gains write ownership of the cache line holding `[r2]` in the meantime. Note that other operations are permitted between the load-reserve and store-conditional, including memory reads and writes, though, unlike transactions, nothing is rolled back if the store-conditional fails.

However, actual POWER and ARM multiprocessors are *not* sequentially consistent, but rather have highly relaxed memory models, in which program executions are not simple interleavings of the instructions of each thread. A priori, it is unclear what it means to say that another thread has written to the relevant address *between* the load-reserve and store-conditional, as one has to understand how they interact with the thread-local out-of-order and speculative execution, and with the storage subsystem reordering, of these machines. Moreover, the vendor architecture [Pow09] does not resolve these questions as clearly as one might hope. It describes the behaviour of load-reserve/store-conditional informally in terms of *reservations*, allowing a store-conditional to succeed only if *"the storage location specified by the lwarx that established the reservation has not been stored into by another processor or mechanism since the reservation was created"*. This is simultaneously too much and too little hardware implementation detail: the *"since"* cannot refer to an SC order, but the machine execution order is not precisely specified.

We solve these problems with an abstract-machine semantics, extending the model of Sarkar et al. [SSA+11] to cover load-reserve/store-conditional. That model comprises a thread semantics, with explicit out-of-order and speculative execution of each hardware thread, composed with a storage subsystem semantics. The latter abstracts from the cache and store-buffer hierarchy and from the cache protocol: for each address it maintains just a strict partial order, the *coherence order*, of the ordering commitments that have been made among the writes to that address, and for each thread it maintains a list of the writes (and barriers) that have been propagated to that thread. For example, at a certain point in abstract-machine execution, one might have established these constraints among 5 writes (by different threads) to x:

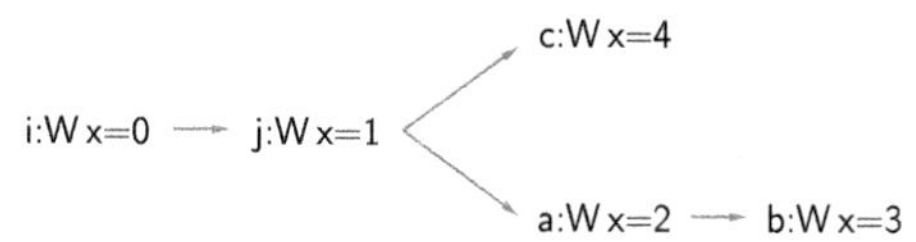

with writes [i:W x=0, a:W x=2] propagated to some arbitrary thread. In that state, a read of x by that thread would see the most recent of those two, reading 2; or write b could be propagated to that thread, appending it to that list (as it is coherence-after the writes already propagated there); or a partial coherence commitment transition could make c ordered before a, or after a but still unrelated to b, or before b but still unrelated to a, or after b. A new write by a thread is made coherence-after all writes previously propagated to that thread but initially coherence-unrelated to other writes. This machinery guarantees coherence in the normal sense, and also supports a semantics for the POWER cumulative memory barriers in its non-multi-copy-atomic setting, where writes to different addresses can propagate to other threads in different orders. The `sync` and `lwsync` barriers constrain that propagation, as we return to in §5, and a `sync` also waits until writes that have previously been propagated to its thread (the `sync`'s *Group A*), or some coherence successors thereof, have been propagated to all threads.

Looking at a successful load-reserve/store-conditional pair in these terms, we can see that for it to provide an atomic update, the write of the store-conditional must become an *immediate coherence successor* of the write read from by the load-reserve, with no other coherence-intervening write to the same address. Moreover, that property must be maintained: no other write can be allowed to become coherence-intervening later in the abstract-machine execution. To express this, the key thing we need to introduce to the model is the concept of a write *reaching coherence point*, after which its coherence-predecessors are linearly ordered and fixed (no additional write can become coherence-before it). Our main new rule describing how the storage subsystem (in state s) can process a successful store-conditional is as follows.

Accept a successful write-conditional request A write-conditional request w by a thread tid, with an accompanying $wprev$ that was read by the program-order-previous read-reserve, can be accepted and succeed if:

1. the write $wprev$ is to the same address as w;
2. $wprev$ has reached coherence point;
3. no coherence-successor of $wprev$ by another thread has reached coherence point or has been propagated to thread tid; and
4. all writes by tid to the same address as $wprev$ (in particular, all those since $wprev$ was propagated to tid) have reached coherence point.

Action:

1. add the new write w to $s.writes\_seen$, to record the new write as seen by the storage subsystem;
2. append the new write w to $s.events\_propagated\_to\ (tid)$, to record the new write as propagated to its own thread;
3. record that w has reached coherence point; and
4. update $s.coherence$ by adding edges to make write w:
   (a) coherence-after all writes to the same address that have reached coherence point (including $wprev$); and
   (b) coherence-before all writes seen (except itself) to the same address that have not yet reached coherence point.

Note that a store-conditional can succeed even if there are outstanding other writes to the same address by different threads (that might have been read from by yet different threads), but that any such other writes become coherence-later than the store-conditional itself. For example, given the coherence order above, if only i has reached coherence point, and if just i has been propagated to some thread, that thread could do an atomic add of 5 by executing a load-reserve of x=0 from i, adding 5 to that value, and doing a successful store-conditional of x=5, the latter becoming an immediate coherence successor of i, and a coherence-predecessor of all the other writes:

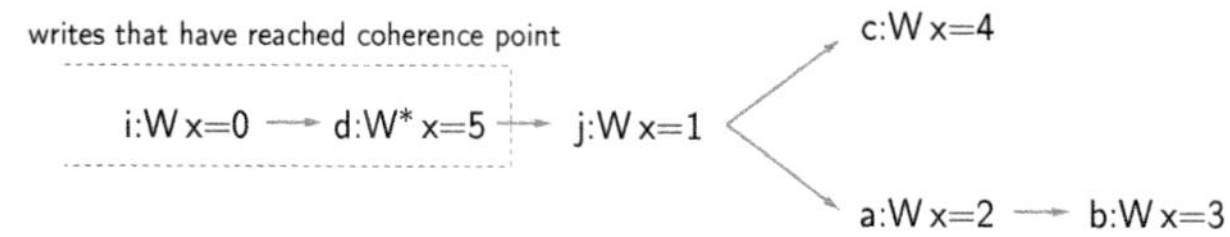

Alternatively, in another execution, a could become coherence-before c, then j and a could reach coherence point, and that load-reserve could read 2 from a and add 5, with the resulting store-conditional of 7 becoming an immediate coherence successor, coherence-before just b and c:

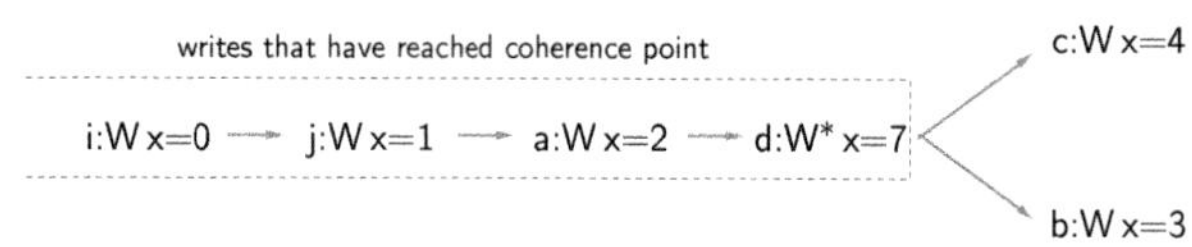

A store-conditional can nondeterministically fail at any time, modelling clearing of the reservation by various events, including writes to other addresses within the same cache line, hypervisor/OS context switches, and *'implementation-specific characteristics of the coherence mechanism [which] cause the reservation to be lost'* [Pow09] (moreover, the architecture explicitly does not include a fairness guarantee). It is believed that current implementations do provide forward progress, but the architecture text does not guarantee it; without characterising those implementation-specific details, and making assumptions on the other events, we have to assume that arbitrary store-conditional failures are possible. This effectively restricts one to reasoning about safety properties.

In this paper we do not model the architecture's *reservation granules*: the rules above consider only whether write-conditionals and load-reserves are to exactly the same address (which is the normal use-case), but in the architecture the significant fact is whether the two addresses lie in the same reservation granule (in current implementations, reservation granules are the same size as cache lines). Modelling realistic (non-single-word) reservation granules would require a store-conditional to fail if there is an intervening write to the same granule, and permit a store-conditional to succeed if the preceding load-reserve was to any address in the same granule. This could be done by modifying preconditions in the above rule, to say that no write to an address in the same granule as the store-conditional has been propagated to tid since $wprev$ was read from by the load-reserve, and to say that the write $wprev$ read from by the load-reserve was to an address in the same granule as the store-conditional.

We also have to specify exactly when a write can reach coherence point, with the rule below. Note that `sync` and `lwsync` barriers constrain the order in which writes can reach coherence point, but, apart from that, barriers and load-reserve/store-conditionals are largely independent.

Write reaches its coherence point This is an internal transition of the storage subsystem, for a write it has already seen, if:

1. the write has not yet reached its coherence point;
2. all its coherence-predecessor writes have reached their coherence points; and
3. all writes (to any address, and by any thread) propagated to the writing thread before a barrier (also by the writing thread) before this write, have reached their coherence points.

Action:

1. add this write to *s.writes_past_coherence_point*; and
2. update *s.coherence* to record that this write is coherence-before all writes seen (except itself) that are to the same address and are not past their coherence points.

Turning now to the thread semantics, load-reserve and store-conditional instructions all commit in program order relative to each other. Apart from that, load-reserves are committed just like normal loads, while store-conditionals are committed by a thread rule that synchronises with the storage-subsytem "Accept store-conditional request" rule above, the thread commit rule additionally imposing:

Commit in-flight instruction

... if this is a write-conditional instruction: send a write-conditional request mentioning the write read from by the most recent program-order-preceding load-reserve instruction without an intervening write-conditional (if there is such a load-reserve); receive the corresponding success/fail response; and set flags accordingly. If there is no such load-reserve, simply set flags as for a fail.

Despite the commit-order constraint, a load-reserve can be *satisfied* (by reading a value from the storage subsystem) exactly like a normal load, and (like a normal load) this can be done out-of-order and speculatively, long before it is committed. In contrast to normal loads, however, there is an additional restriction on load-reserve speculation, that a load-reserve cannot be satisfied until all program-order previous load-reserves and store-conditionals are committed. This models the architectural requirement of a single reservation register per thread. In the model this leads to forbidding the example execution on the left below. Consistent with this, the example is not observable on IBM® POWER® 6 and IBM® POWER® 7 implementations.

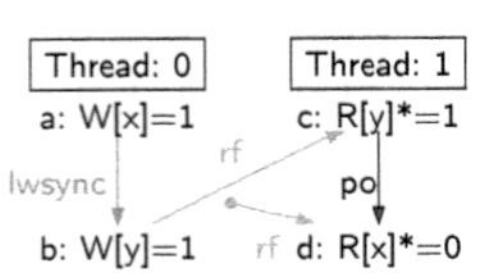

Test MP+lwsync+porr: Forbidden

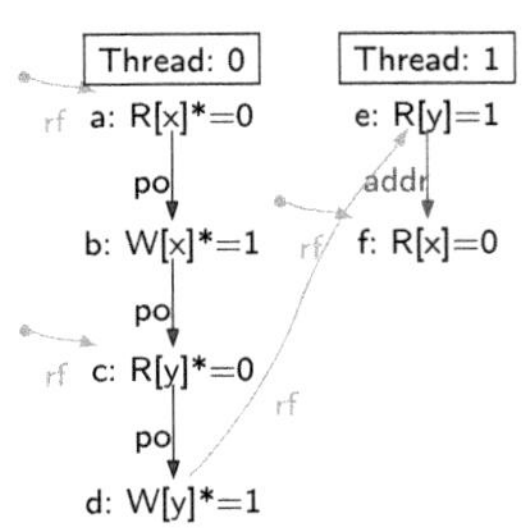

Test MP+poaa+addr: Allowed

Note also that despite the constraint on their commit order, store-conditionals to different addresses can still propagate to other threads out-of-order, as shown on the right above. This is allowed in the model and observable on POWER 6 and POWER 7.

Each diagram shows the memory read and write events of a candidate execution of an assembly program running on one or more hardware threads; the assembly source code is in the supplementary material. Events include unique ids (a, b, etc.), the addresses of reads and writes (x, y, etc.), and the values read and written. Load-reserve and store-conditional events are indicated with a star. Various edges pick out key relationships between instructions in the source, or more specifically in the particular control-flow unfolding of the source for the execution in question:

- po edges relates events from instructions in program order (in this control-flow unfolding);
- an lwsync edge indicates that there is a POWER lightweight sync barrier in program order between the instructions that gave rise to the two events;
- a sync edge indicates a POWER heavyweight sync barrier;
- an eieio edge indicates a POWER eieio barrier;
- an addr edge indicates that the address of the second event is dependent (through a dataflow path via registers and computation) on the value read by the first;
- a data edge indicates that the data written by the second event is dependent on the value read by the first;
- a ctrl edge indicates there is a dataflow path from the first read read to the test of a conditional branch that program-order-precedes the second event (branches are not shown explicitly); and
- a ctrlisync edge indicates there is such a dataflow path from the first read to the test of a conditional branch that program-order-precedes an isync instruction before the second read.

Three further relations characterise the remainder of the dynamics of the execution:

- an rf edge from a write to a read indicates that the read read-from that write (rf edges from the initial state are marked with a red dot for the source);
- a co edge between writes to the same address gives the final coherence order between them; and
- an rcp edge between writes indicates the order in which those writes reached coherence point (usually we elide these edges).

Moreover, load-reserve and store-conditional do not impose any special constraint on normal loads and stores to different addresses: they do not act like a barrier of any kind, and so loads after a load-reserve/store-conditional pair might be speculated before it. If one wants to prevent that, one needs to add surrounding barriers. Confusion on this point seems to have been responsible for a Linux kernel bug [McK11] that was recently identified by McKenney and confirmed using our model: the Linux `atomic_add_return` implementation (from which the code above is taken), is assumed there to prevent speculation, but its implementation used overly weak barriers; the same was true for other similar read-modify-write operations. The example is in the supplementary material.

One also has to consider whether writes can be observably forwarded to a load-reserve or from a store-conditional within a thread, on speculative paths before they have reached the storage subsystem. This can happen on POWER and ARM for normal loads and stores, as shown by the PPOCA example of [SSA+11]. Interestingly, we can show that allowing such forwarding in the model from a store-conditional would make the mapping of C/C++11 atomics to POWER unsound: the C/C++ candidate execution on the right (in the notation recalled in §4) is forbidden in C/C++11, but the corresponding execution in POWER would be allowed in our model if speculative forwarding from the store-conditional of the RMW were to be permitted. The architectural intent (though this is arguably not completely clear from the text) is to rule out this behaviour in a different way, allowing implementation forwarding from store-conditionals but requiring that any store-conditionals must respect an implicit data dependence to the prior load-reserve through the architected reservation register, even when no actual data dependence is present;

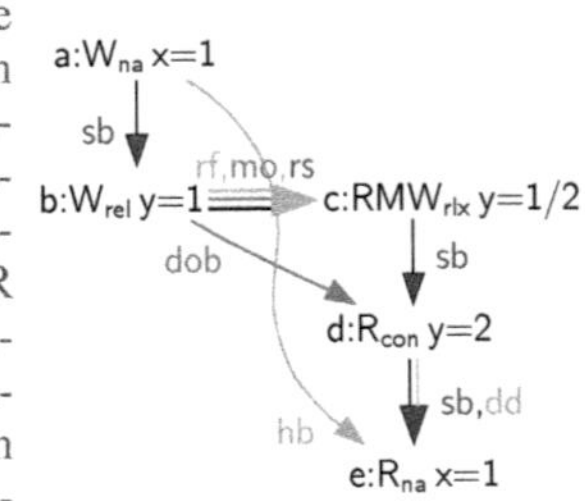

hence preventing such forwarding until the previous load-reserve has been satisfied. An implementation of such forwarding would be extremely aggressive and complex, and has not been attempted in practice.

This is a case where our POWER and C/C++11 models are tight against each other: one either has to rule out such forwarding becoming observable in the Power Architecture or permit the example in C/C++ (or change the mapping, but there is no obvious alternative that preserves the performance advantage of a consume over an acquire). It illustrates how constructing formal models at this level of detail can identify deep architectural and micro-architectural choices beyond current implementation practice, arising from the detailed interplay between the high-level language memory models and aggressively weakly ordered hardware models.

For completeness, we also include in this paper the POWER `eieio` barrier, in addition to the previously-covered `sync`, `lwsync`, and `isync`, though it is not used in the C/C++ mapping. Architecturally, `eieio` orders pairs of same-thread writes as far as all other threads are concerned (`eieio` has additional effects for Caching Inhibited memory, which we do not cover here), and the message-passing test on the left is forbidden. However, the extension on the right, with the write to x pulled out to a third thread, is allowed, notwithstanding the architectural mention of cumulativity, because `eieio` does not order reads (e.g. b) w.r.t. writes.

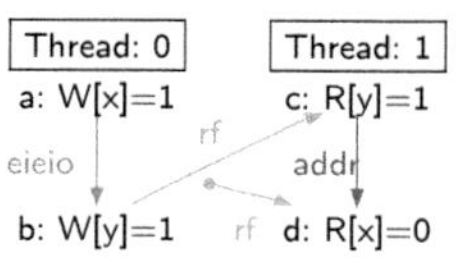

Test MP+eieio+addr: Forbidden

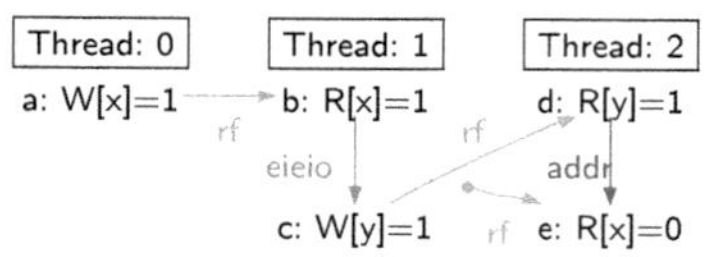

Test WRC+eieio+addr: Allowed

Adding `eieio` between b and c of the MP+poaa+addr example above suffices to rule out the non-SC behaviour there. We model `eieio` in the storage subsystem exactly like `lwsync`, together with a more relaxed thread commit rule. Preliminary testing suggests that current implementations have considerably stronger behaviour than the architecture, more like `lwsync`.

We also remark for completeness that we have made a technical change to our `lwsync` semantics: our [SSA+11] model let reads after `lwsync`s be satisfied but restarted them, whereas now they are blocked until the `lwsync` commits. This has no observable effect but is simpler to work with.

Discussion Our semantics abstracts substantially from hardware implementation detail, focussing on the essential properties of the store-conditional. The notion of a write reaching coherence point abstracts from the hardware machinery needed to maintain coherence; it captures just the minimal properties required to express the semantics. From the literature and vendor documentation, one would be tempted to build an operational model with explicit per-thread reservation flags, set and cleared as the abstract machine executes, and indeed we did so at first, but that quickly becomes very complex when one considers reservations being set or cleared on speculative execution paths that may be rolled back. The 'implicit reservation' style that we introduce here, testing just the necessary coherence properties at write-conditional commit time, is much simpler to express and to work with.

3. Validation

Our model has been validated in six distinct ways. First, it was developed in discussion with a senior IBM POWER designer/architect, who has extensive experience of the POWER load-reserve/store-conditional implementations. Second, we built a tool, with a kernel generated from the Lem code of the model, which allows us to explore the behaviour of litmus-test example programs, interactively via a web interface (available in the supplementary material) and in batch mode (calculating all model-allowed behaviour); this tool was used in the analysis of the Linux bug mentioned above. Third, using that tool for regression testing, we checked that the addition of coherence points did not affect the observable behaviour allowed by the model for as many tests that do not involve load-reserve/store-conditional as we could test. Adding coherence points enlarges the search space needed to exhaustively explore tests, but the new version of the tool terminated in manageable memory occupancy (up to 10 GB) for 299 out of the 314 *VAR3* tests [SSA+11], and also for approximately 450 new tests; for all these, the two models allow the same outcomes. Fourth, experimentally: we developed a large set of new litmus tests, as described below, ran them on generations of POWER machines (PowerPC G5, POWER 6 and POWER 7), and compared the results against those for the model (as produced by our tool). Fifth, we proved theoretical results about our POWER model on its own terms, in §3.2 below. Finally, our main theoretical result of this paper, proving that the C/C++11 synchronisation primitives can be correctly compiled to POWER, demonstrates that the model is strong enough for non-trivial usage.

3.1 Experimental Validation

First, we hand-wrote tests to exercise the basic functionalities of load-reserve and store-conditional instructions. For example, a test RSV+Fail shows that a store-conditional associated to a load-reserve will fail if there is a load-reserve to a distinct location (on actual machines, to a distinct reservation granule) in between in program order.

To systematically exercise corners of the model, we designed several series of tests, automatically generated with the diy tool [AMSS10]. The first and more important series (12499 tests) derives from the systematic tests of [SSA+11]. Assuming that mapping plain accesses to load-reserves or read-modify-write sequences might forbid some behaviours previously allowed by the model, but not the other way round, we selected the tests allowed by the [SSA+11] model (limited to 5 accesses to reduce the number of tests to run). We call these tests *plain tests*, since all accesses are plain reads and writes. Then we generated all the possible *atomic variations* of these plain tests, with a load-reserve or a load-reserve/store-conditional sequence in place of some plain accesses. For a read we use *fetch and no-op* (FNO), and for a write *fetch and store* (STA) constructs [Pow09, p.719]. Both FNO and STA read a value with a load-reserve, then the FNO writes back the same value with a store-conditional, while the STA writes a predefined different value with its store-conditional. Note that we cannot map a write to a store-conditional alone, because the store-conditional needs a program-order previous load-reserve to succeed. They are wrapped in loops, though in practice in our model tool we unroll the loops once.

The second series, "Rfi" (intra-thread, or internal, read-from), exercises the impact of atomic variations on store forwarding. To do so, we generated a restricted subset of our plain tests, namely some that exhibit a violation of SC in the form of a *critical cycle* [SS88], with at least one internal (intra-thread) read-from edge, and up to 3 threads; this gave a series of 1338 tests. We replaced the accesses along the internal read-from edges with FNO/STAs and load-reserves, as in the first series. Interestingly, many of the Rfi variations that involve only load-reserves were observed on POWER 6 but not on PowerPC G5 or POWER 7, e.g. a test 2+2W+lwsync+rfi-data. This suggests that the implementation of load-reserve is less liberal on the latter two.

The last series exercises in practice what we establish as a theorem about the model in §3.2: when *all* accesses of a test are replaced by FNO or STA, then the test only has SC behaviours. We tested this on a restricted subset of our plain tests, namely the 68 that exhibit a violation of SC *via* a critical cycle, and that have up to 4 threads. Running those tests on hardware showed no non-SC behaviour, consistent with the model's prediction as captured by the theorem.

Taking all these load-reserve/store-conditional tests together is 13963 tests. We have run all those on PowerPC G5, POWER 6 and POWER 7 machines many times — at least $5 \cdot 10^7$ each on PowerPC G5, $8.5 \cdot 10^8$ on POWER 6, and $2.3 \cdot 10^9$ on POWER 7 — and our model exploration tool terminated in less than 16GB memory for 10455 tests. We also have relatively thorough testing of `eieio`, with 235 tests run on POWER 6 and 7 and in the model. For all the above, all outcomes observable on the hardware are allowed by our model; in this sense the model is experimentally sound, modulo only the reservation granule issue described above.

Representative data is below (with the full dataset online).

	Model	Power6	Power7
MP+lwsync+porr	Forbid	Ok, 0/2.6G	Ok, 0/6.1G
MP+poaa+addr	Allow	Ok, 27k/1.1G	Ok, 56/1.4G
2+2W+rfipr-datarps	Allow	Ok, 58/545k	No, 0/4.4G Allow unseen

3.2 Restoring SC with FNOs and STAs

Despite the relaxed nature of POWER load-reserve/store-conditional (as illustrated by the first two MP examples of §2), if one replaces *all* loads and stores by FNO and STA respectively, one regains SC behaviour:

THEOREM 1. *Mapping all accesses to FNOs for loads and STAs for stores restores SC.*

Proof Outline: Note first that the successful store-conditionals (SSC) of an FNO or STA reach their coherence points as soon as they are committed. Thus there is a total order over all SSCs of a program (not just a per-location order), following the abstract-machine order in which the writes of this program reach their coherence points (we call this order rcp). Of course, this order is only over successful write-conditionals, not plain writes. Two SSCs in program order are committed in that order, thus reach their coherence point in that order, so rcp respects program order. Moreover, if all accesses are mapped to FNO and STA, we know that the threads communicate only through SSCs that are read by load-reserves and that a load-reserve before an SSC must read the (here unique) coherence-maximal value.

4. C/C++ Locks, RMWs, and Fences

Historically, the C and C++ standards did not cover concurrency, considering it to be a library issue. That is not a satisfactory position, as observed by Boehm [Boe05], and the recent ISO C11 and C++11 revisions incorporates concurrency for the first time [Bec11, ISO11].

The design, as outlined by Boehm and Adve [BA08], is based on a data-race-free (DRF) [AH90] model for normal code: for a program written using threads, mutexes and sequentially consistent *atomic*[1] operations, if it has no races in any execution then it is supposed to have SC semantics[2]; while if some execution does exhibit a race, the program's behaviour is undefined (and an implementation is entirely unconstrained). This permits a broad range of compiler optimisations [Šev11] and allows implementation on relaxed-memory multiprocessors without requiring expensive barriers or special load and store instructions for every memory access. However, implementing SC atomic operations can still be expensive, and therefore the language also includes a variety of *low-level atomics* for high-performance concurrent algorithms: atomic reads, writes, and read-modify-write operations with weaker properties that are cheaper to implement. They are annotated with a *memory order*: either *relaxed*, providing no synchronisation; *release* (for writes and RMWs), *acquire* (for reads and RMWs), or *release_acquire* (for RMWs), providing synchronisation for message-passing idioms; or *consume*, a weaker variant of read-acquire that lets programmers take advantage of the fact that POWER and ARM respect data and address dependencies at little or no cost. SC atomics also have release/acquire semantics. The language also includes release/acquire and SC *fences*.

The standard is written in prose, subject to the usual problems of ambiguity, but we have produced a formal semantics for the concurrency model [BOS+11]. In discussion with members of the ISO WG21 concurrency subgroup, we identified various issues with earlier drafts of the standard, proposing solutions that are now incorporated into the standard; there is a close correspondence between the formal semantics and the C++11 text. The C standard has followed suit: at the time of writing, the C++11 concurrency model has been partially incorporated into C11, but some of the C++11 fixes are not yet incorporated. We highlighted these (together with a simplification to the model) at a recent WG14 meeting, which has registered them as defect reports for a future Technical Corrigendum.

In this section we explain enough of the C/C++11 memory model to support our discussion and proof of how it can be implemented above POWER in §5. We recall the mathematical structure of the Batty et al. semantics and explain the lock, read-modify-write, and fence synchronisation primitives informally. The basic semantics for these is not a contribution of this paper (a version was given in [BOS+11]) but the explanation here is new, and we have had to make three significant improvements to the semantics:

- We place the responsibility for correctly using mutexes on the programmer, in accordance with intuition and with the standard. Previous work, including [BA08, BOS+11], placed it instead on the compiler, imposing unrealistic requirements, e.g. that the implementation of unlock has to check that the mutex is currently held by the unlocking thread.
- We carefully specify how lock and read-modify-write operations can block owing to store-conditional operations that can fail continually on the Power Architecture.
- We add two missing cases to the fence semantics.

We discuss these in more detail below, and the mathematically rigorous version of the improved model is available in the supplementary material.

The C/C++11 memory model is axiomatic (quite different in style to our POWER abstract machine): presuming a threadwise operational semantics that defines candidate executions consisting of the sets of memory read and write actions for threads in isolation, it defines when such a candidate is *consistent* and whether it has a race of some kind. Consistency is defined in terms of several relations, including a *happens-before (hb)* relation that embodies the language's notion of causality.

The three basic relations, *sequenced-before (sb)*, *reads-from (rf)*, and *modification order (mo)*, are closely related to our POWER abstract machine's notion of program order, reads-from, and coherence order, respectively. Sequenced-before is a threadwise partial order that does not need to be total (for example, the operands `x` and `y` of `x == y` are not related by sequenced-before). Modifica-

[1] In C/C++11 terminology, *atomic* plays a very loosely similar role to Java *volatile*: in C/C++11, for defining whether a program has undefined behaviour, atomic operations (which might be single loads, single stores, or read-modify-writes) are not deemed to have data races with other atomic operations, even if they are not separated in happens-before.

[2] In fact this is not quite true, as Batty et al. [BMO+12] observe, due to a subtlety involving atomic initialisation.

tion order is a per-location total order over the write operations to that location. A modification order is only needed for atomic locations; it can contain atomic writes with various memory orders, together with non-atomic initialisation writes.

The *synchronises-with (sw)* and happens-before relations are calculated from sequenced-before and reads-from. A write-release synchronises with a read-acquire that reads-from the write. Read-acquires can also synchronise with some (but not necessarily all) write-releases that appear in modification order before the read-from write; this is formalised by *release sequences*, which we do not detail here. Happens-before is then built as the transitive closure of synchronises-with and sequenced-before, with some exceptions relating to read-consumes which we do not detail here. Four coherence axioms require that happens-before is consistent with modification order. Synchronises-with and happens-before have no direct counterparts in POWER: the compilation of C/C++ to POWER must insert enough barriers to ensure that synchronizing write/read pairs enjoy the right ordering properties (see §5).

The *sequential consistency (sc)* relation is a total order on all of the SC reads and writes. It is required to be consistent with sequenced-before, modification-order, and happens-before.

A program has a data race if there is some consistent execution with two happens-before unrelated reads/writes on the same location, where at least one is a write, and at least one is not atomic.

4.1 Locks

To model mutexes, we use three kinds of additional actions: locks, unlocks, and blocks. In a consistent execution, a total order *lock order (lo)* (analogous to modification order) over these ensures that no mutex is acquired when already held: between any pair of locks of the same mutex, there must be an unlock of that mutex. Furthermore, lock order must be consistent with happens-before. Lastly, the lock order introduces synchronisation from each unlock to later locks of the same mutex, ensuring that the actions in each critical section happen-before the actions in subsequent ones. In the example execution here, actions a and d lock mutex m, c and f unlock it, and the non-atomic writes b and read e are inside critical sections. The synchronisation between c and d ensures that e reads from b, and that e and b do not race.

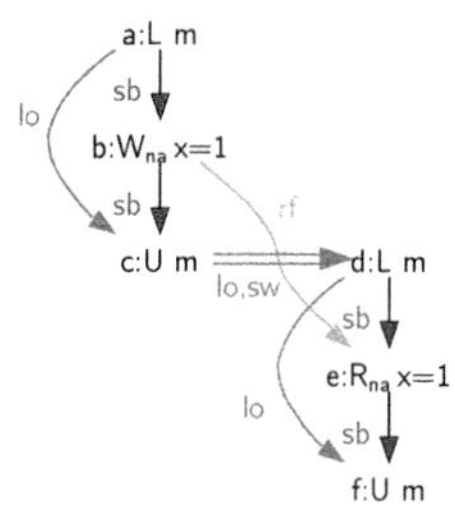

These C/C++ candidate execution diagrams are analogous to the POWER execution diagrams of §2. They pick out one candidate execution of a program (the programs are in the supplementary material), and show the memory write and read actions and the lock and unlock actions of that candidate execution. Each action is annotated by the location and value, and, for memory reads and writes, the memory order parameter. The actions are arranged in vertical columns by thread. Among these actions, we depict the key C/C++ relations:

- sb edges show sequenced-before, in this control-flow unfolding (recall that sequenced-before is not necessarily total over the events of a thread);
- rf edges from write actions to read actions show that the read reads-from that write (as before, reads from an initial state are marked with a red dot for the source);
- mo edges show modification order, relating all write actions at an atomic location;
- sc edges show the SC order, a total order over all SC actions; and
- lo edges show the lock order, a total order over all lock and unlock actions.

From these, two derived relations can be calculated:

- sw edges depict the C/C++ synchronizes-with relation; and
- hb edges depict the C/C++ happens-before relation.

In previous work [BA08, BOS$^+$11], a consistent execution also required that lock/unlock actions strictly alternate in lock order, and that the unlock of a mutex must follow the lock that acquired it in sequenced-before. Putting this requirement on consistent executions requires that the compiler or lock implementation enforce it, for example, by having each unlock call dynamically check that the mutex is held by the unlocking thread. To support efficient unlock implementations that have no such check, the C/C++11 standard places this requirement on the programmer, and so we allow consistent executions with improper calls to unlock, but give such programs undefined behavior.

Not all attempts to acquire a mutex eventually succeed: the program could be deadlocked, or a particular acquisition could be starved forever. To model this, on an attempted acquisition the threadwise operational semantics non-deterministically generates either a lock action, representing success, or a block action, representing deadlock or starvation. In the latter case, we require that the operational semantics not produce any further actions sequenced after the block. The concept of blocked mutex acquisition does not explicitly appear in the standard, or in prior work; we add it to properly separate the axiomatic memory model from the threadwise operational semantics. Because block actions appear in lock order, the memory model can place constraints on them to specify the exact fairness or liveness guarantees enjoyed by mutex acquisition. The operational semantics only needs to know whether a certain call is blocked or not. This contrasts with the typical operational treatment of mutexes in which locking and unlocking operations manipulate a piece of shared state; state which, in a relaxed memory setting, must be governed by the memory model.

As we discuss in §2, the Power Architecture allows store-conditionals to fail arbitrarily, and there is no simple guarantee ruling out repeated failure (though implementations do go to great lengths to provide forward progress). In §5, we consider an implementation of C/C++11 mutexes based on POWER load-reserve/store-conditional instructions, and in this context a mutex acquisition can block indefinitely, even in the absence of deadlock or contention, due to continual, spurious store-conditional failures. To model this possibility in C/C++11, we allow block actions to appear anywhere in the lock order, without constraint. However, if one were modelling a particular POWER implementation that guaranteed store-conditional liveness, one could use a stronger C/C++11 model: in lock order, each block is either preceded by a lock which is never unlocked (the deadlock case), or followed by an infinite number of locks (the starvation case).

To simplify our reasoning about the connection between POWER and C/C++11 mutexes in §5, we also use an alternative model that, first, uses a separate lock order for each mutex, and, second, requires that each unlock synchronise only with the next lock in that order. We have proved the equivalence of the two models (see the supplementary material); the equivalence relies on having undefined behaviour for programs that misuse locks.

4.2 RMWs

C/C++11 has three kinds of atomic RMWs: `fetch_add` and similar, `compare_exchange_strong`, and `compare_exchange_weak`. The first updates the value at a given address, the second is a traditional CAS, and the third is a traditional CAS except that it can fail spuriously. The first two are implemented on POWER with load-reserve/store-conditional pairs with loops to account for the store-conditional failing. Thus, like mutex acquisition, the operational semantics must allow them to block. The last is implemented with a simple load-reserve/store-conditional pair (which exposes the possibility of non-deterministic spurious failures).

Successful RMWs are modelled by an RMW action that both reads and writes; atomicity is guaranteed by requiring that the read reads-from the immediate predecessor of the write in modification order. Thus, in the example to the right, RMW-relaxed d must read from write-relaxed b, and not write-relaxed a.

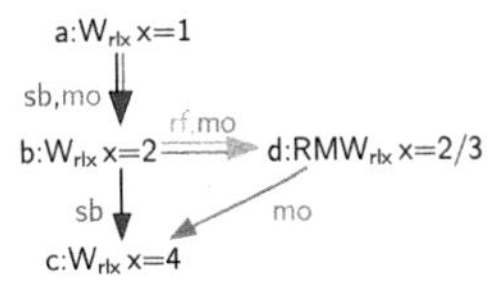

4.3 Fences

In C/C++11, fences are used to replace multiple acquire/release or SC operations with more efficient relaxed ones. There are four kinds: acquire, release, acquire/release, and SC fences.

Acquire and release fences establish synchronises-with relationships, even when the reading and writing actions are relaxed. In the message-passing example on the left below, the acquire fence g synchronises with write-release d even though the read f is relaxed; this synchronisation ensures that non-atomic write c happens before non-atomic read h. This might help performance: for example, if f were in a loop waiting to observe d's write; we only have to pay for the acquire once, rather than on each iteration. In the variation on the right, a single release fence j ensures synchronisation based on multiple relaxed writes k and l.

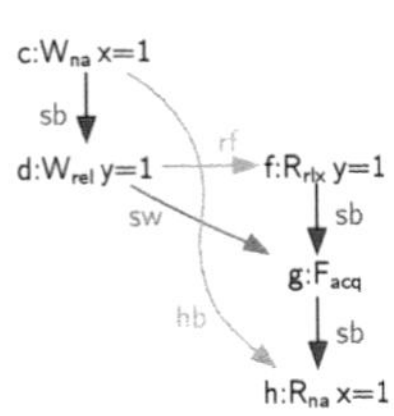

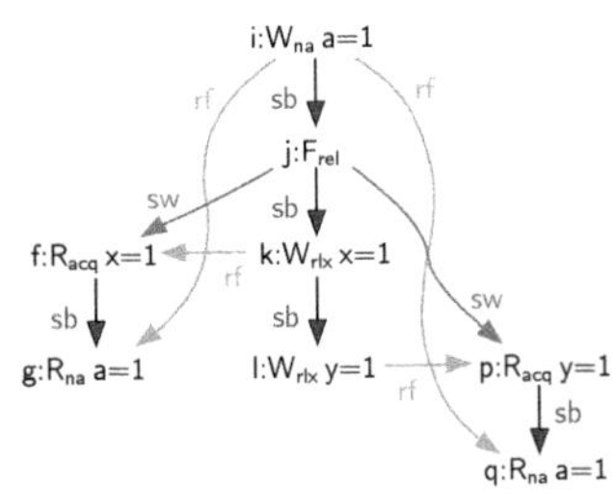

SC fences appear in the sc relation, and enforce a set of coherence-like axioms between it and modification order. In the store-buffering (or Dekker's) example on the right, SC atomic reads and writes are used to ensure that at least one of the reads d or g reads-from one of the writes c or f. We can get the same guarantee by making one thread's operations relaxed and putting an SC fence in between, or even making all four operations relaxed and using two SC fences, as below.

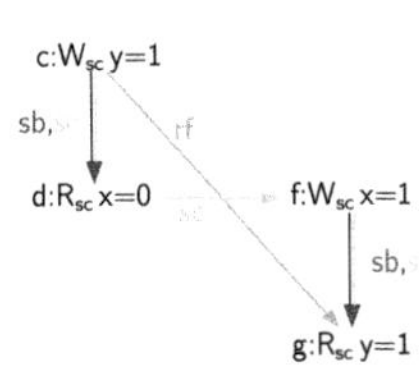

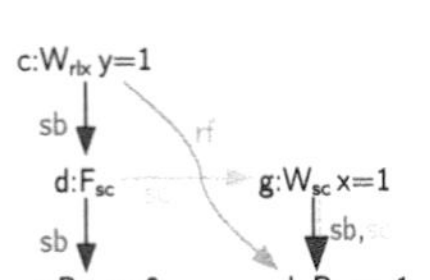

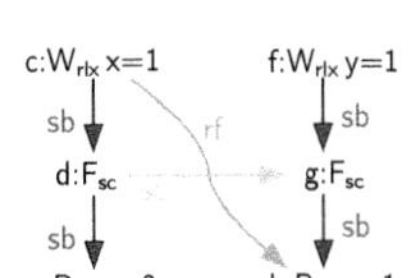

Despite their name, C/C++11 SC fences are not designed to restore sequential consistency to programs that use low-level atomics (in part because in the Itanium architecture there is no implementation fence that would do so [Int02]). For example, the IRIW litmus test from [BA08] with two SC fences is allowed in C/C++ (in the model, the 6 SC fence conditions do not impose any constraint on the *sc* order between two SC fences because of a non-SC-atomic read before one fence and a read after another).

The proof of our main result in §5, together with the preliminary results of [BMO+12], are arguably the first extensive validation of the C/C++11 model. To the best of our knowledge, large-scale software development of concurrent C/C++11 code has not yet begun, as that practical validation requires production compilers which are only just becoming available. Even when they are, and are correct, they may provide over-strong models, so at present proof is the only way to determine whether code is correct with respect to the specification rather than with respect to some particular implementation.

5. Compiling Synchronisation Primitives: from C/C++ to POWER

We now discuss our second main contribution, the correctness proof of one mapping of the principal C/C++ synchronisation constructs —locks, read-modify-writes, and fences— to POWER, using load-reserve/store-conditional and the POWER barriers. The proof can be easily adapted to show related mappings, with different barrier placement on C/C++ SC operations, or SC atomics implemented with load-reserve/store-conditional, correct as well. This subsumes the result of Batty et al. [BMO+12], which just covered C/C++ loads and stores (with their various possible memory orders).

The mapping we consider combines the scheme proposed by McKenney and Silvera [MS11] for C/C++11 atomics, fences and RMWs with the spinlock implementation given in the Power Architecture [Pow09, p.717,718]. We first give the mapping with some informal intuition about its soundness (focussing on locks) before describing the main ideas of our proof.

5.1 Compiling from C/C++ to POWER

Locks Assuming that register `r3` contains a lock location, `r4` contains the value signifying that a lock is free and `r5` the value signifying that a lock is taken, the POWER implementation of a spinlock is:

```
loop:
  lwarx r6,0,r3,1 # load-reserve lock [r3] into r6
  cmpw r4,r6      # go to wait if lock not free,
  bne- wait       #  eventually returning to loop
  stwcx. r5,0,r3  # store-cond to try to set lock
  bne- loop       # loop if lost reservation
  isync           # import barrier
```

The implementation of unlock is:

```
  lwsync          # export barrier
  stw r4,0(r3)    # normal store to release lock
```

In the lock implementation, a load-reserve/store-conditional pair works on the lock location. The load is followed by a check on the value stored at the lock location; if the lock is not free, the code branches to a waiting routine (which might be a loop doing a normal read on the lock location, or a backoff, and which will return to `loop` to try to establish a new reservation). Otherwise the code tries to set the lock with a store-conditional. As discussed in §2, this will fail if the new value cannot be made an immediate coherence successor of the write read by the load-reserve (e.g. if some other thread has taken the lock in the meantime), and in that case it again returns to `loop`, otherwise the lock has been taken successfully and atomically. The implementation of unlock has a simple store at the lock location writing the value that signifies that the lock is free.

As a result, a C/C++ unlock/lock synchronisation is, at the POWER ISA level, a store-to-load communication. For this to truly be a synchronisation, the implementation also must include additional protection. The unlock store is preceded by an `lwsync` instruction. The effect of this barrier is first to restrict the reordering of instructions in its own thread: an `lwsync` must be committed after any program-order-preceding memory-access instruction, and before any memory-access instruction following in program order is satisfied (for reads) or committed. The second effect is an ordering of the propagation of stores. For any `lwsync` barrier, our POWER model keeps track of the set of stores and barriers that have been done by or propagated to its thread before it was committed. Before the `lwsync` can be propagated to another thread *tid*, all the members of this set, called its Group A, must first be propagated to *tid*. In the context of the unlock/lock synchronisation, this guarantees that any store visible to the unlocking thread before its unlocking store (to the lock location) must also be visible to the locking thread, before the load-reserve (of the successful store-conditional/load-reserve pair) on the lock location.

The propagation ordering enforced by an `lwsync` is transitive, in the following sense. Consider a chain of unlock/lock synchronisations, with each unlock directly following a lock on the same thread, and each lock directly following an unlock on a different thread. This corresponds to a chain of thread-crossing store/load communications. In this communication, the stores come from the unlocking stores to the lock location, and the successful store-conditionals of lock acquires, while the loads correspond to the load-reserves at the lock location from the successful store-conditional/load-reserve pair of locks. For the communication to occur, each store must propagate to the thread of its associated load. If the first store of the chain is preceded by an `lwsync`, then this barrier along with its Group A must propagate to the second thread of the chain before the store it precedes. Since a load-reserve/store-conditional pair must be committed in order, the `lwsync` and its Group A stores are therefore propagated to the second thread before the store-conditional of that second thread is committed. Hence for this second thread's store-conditional to propagate to the third thread of the chain, the first thread's barrier along with its Group A must first propagate to that third thread. The argument continues to the rest of the chain.

Additionally, the last branch instruction of the lock implementation is followed by an `isync` instruction. As a result of this combination of a dependency from the result of the store-conditional to a conditional branch, followed by an `isync` (together, a kind of *ctrlisync* dependency) any program-order-following loads cannot be speculated before the store-conditional succeeds. Hence, any program-order-following loads must see the stores that were performed by the unlocking thread, before the unlock was executed.

A fully locked POWER program is SC The intuition above for locks is applicable in a wider context than C/C++. For a simple result along those lines, consider a POWER assembly program (not necessarily compiled from C/C++), which has all competing accesses (those accessing the same location, from distinct threads, at least one of them being a write) protected by locks, using a distinct lock variable per shared-memory variable (denoted below by lx, ly, etc., for locks protecting variables x, y, etc.). We assume all locations are disjoint and of the same size, and ignore the case of overlapping accesses.

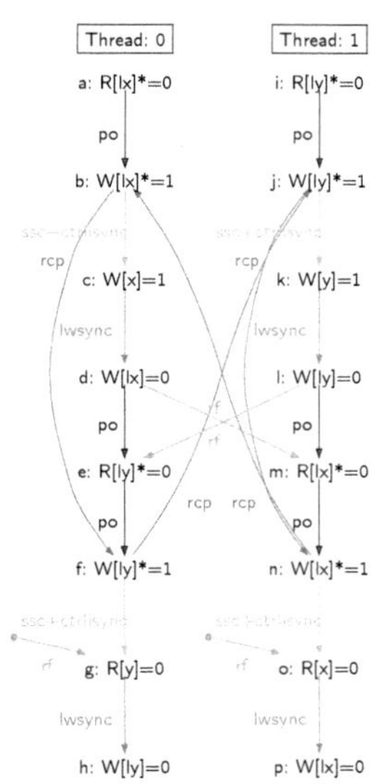

Test SB+locks: Forbidden

Using the `isync` at the end of the lock sequence and the `lwsync` at the beginning of the unlock sequence, we get that two accesses in program order guarded by locks follow the order in which the SSC of their lock primitives reach coherence point. For example in the test SB+locks on the right, the write c to x on Thread 0 is committed after the SSC b to lx reaches coherence point, as depicted by the magenta ssc+ctrlisync arrow.

The lock write to ly on Thread 0 reaches coherence point before the lock write to ly on Thread 1, as depicted by the blue arrow rcp from Thread 0 to Thread 1, thus restoring SC for this test. Fleshing out this line of reasoning proves our next theorem:

THEOREM 2. *Protecting access to each address with an associated lock restores SC, assuming the program does not use distinct overlapping locations.*

RMWs The implementation of C/C++ RMWs also relies on load-reserve/store-conditional pairs. Here, without loss of generality, we only discuss the implementation of one kind of RMW, the "fetch_add" operation with an implementation as in the first §2 example: a load-reserve/store-conditional pair surrounding an addition instruction, the whole wrapped in a loop waiting for the store-conditional to succeed. The implementations of other kinds of RMWs use different instructions between the load-reserve/store-conditional pair but have essentially the same correctness argument.

RMWs are parameterised by a memory order, and the mapping places POWER barriers at the beginning and dependencies at the end of the load-reserve/store-conditional block, in the same style as the implementations of non-RMW C/C++ atomic accesses. The implementation of a relaxed RMW has no additional barriers; the implementation of a release RMW is preceded by an `lwsync` barrier; that of an acquire RMW is followed by a ctrlisync dependency; acquire/release combines both; and that of an SC RMW is preceded by a `sync` and followed by a ctrlisync dependency.

Fences C/C++ fences are compiled to single barrier instructions: SC fences are mapped to a `sync` and all the others to `lwsync`.

non-RMW atomics For non-RMW atomic memory accesses the compilation maps each C/C++ read or write to corresponding POWER instruction together with protecting barrier instructions, as for the RMWs above but with the addition of *consume* loads, which have no barrier but require the compiler to preserve dependencies [MS11, BMO+12].

5.2 Correctness proof

Our second main result is the correctness of this compilation scheme. To focus on the concurrency issues, we abstract from the details of thread-local compilation: we consider an arbitrary non-optimising compiler (preserving memory accesses, program order and thread-local dependencies) that uses this compilation scheme for the concurrency primitives. Informally, our result is as follows; the formal statement and proof are in the supplementary material.

THEOREM 3. *Consider a non-optimising compiler that uses the mapping above. For any race-free C/C++ program, compile it to POWER and take any execution trace of our POWER abstract machine. Then there exists a C/C++ execution that is both equivalent to the POWER trace and accepted by the C/C++ memory model as a consistent execution of the original C/C++ program.*

This is in the same style as the result of Batty et al. [BMO+12] for the compilation mapping in the absence of locks, fences and RMWs. We now outline the overall proof structure, common to both works, and then show how to extend it to handle the synchronisation primitives.

The proof describes a procedure for constructing a C/C++ execution from any POWER trace that guarantees their equivalence, and then shows the consistency of that C/C++ execution. But this construction does not work for racy programs. As a straightforward example, consider a C/C++ program with two threads, the first doing a non-atomic write at a location x, the second doing a non-atomic read on x. The C/C++ memory model rules out any consistent execution with the read reading from the write, because they are unrelated in C/C++ happens-before, and thus the execution would be racy. But in the compiled POWER code, which has no direct analogue of the C/C++ happens-before, nothing prevents the corresponding store propagating to the second thread to be read by the load. For the verification of the consistency of the reconstructed C/C++ execution to succeed, the following consequence of race-freedom is required: "in the C/C++ execution, a read cannot read-from a write that it is not related to by happens-before". The proof splits on whether this condition holds. If it does hold, consistency of the reconstructed execution can be directly shown, while if it does not hold, it can be shown that the original C/C++ program must have been racy, thus leading to a contradiction.

The latter proof is technically involved because one needs to build a racy, consistent C/C++ execution that does not exactly correspond to the POWER trace. There are two areas where this part of Batty et al.'s proof could fail when adding synchronisation constructs: in the top-level case split, and in the way that POWER-level speculation complicates the construction of the racy C/C++ execution. In fact, our alternate C/C++ formalisation of locks (§4.1) removes the need for modifying the case split: the new proof has a similar case split (on whether unlocks are used properly), but it is simpler because the proof is about the C/C++ model only, not in combination with POWER. Furthermore, careful modelling of the absence of store-conditional forwarding (§2) means that the construction in the existing proof works unchanged.

Returning to showing consistency of a reconstructed execution, several properties regarding the interaction of the happens-before relation with other relations defined by the C/C++ memory model have to be verified of the constructed C/C++ execution. To directly exploit our POWER model, the statements of all these properties are translated into equivalent statements regarding the POWER trace from which the C/C++ execution was built: we define relations on the elements of POWER traces and show a correspondence between these and the C/C++ relations. For most relations, clear counterparts exist. For example, the C/C++ *sequenced-before* corresponds roughly to the POWER program order (though some care needs to be taken, as sequenced-before is a partial order while the program order is total). However, there is nothing that corresponds directly to the happens-before relation. Instead, a more complex POWER relation is built from the other POWER relations.

Using this characterisation, a *propagation lemma* states that for any pair of C/C++ actions a and b related by happens-before, the instruction corresponding to b sees any stores that the instruction corresponding to a is able to see: any store propagated to the thread of a before a is executed, is also propagated to the thread of b before b is executed (a read is executed at the latest abstract-machine transition in which it is satisfied — all previous reads having been restarted — while a write is executed when it is committed). Using this lemma in conjunction with the preconditions and actions of the POWER model transitions, the conditions required by the C/C++ memory model can be verified. For example, when the POWER storage subsystem accepts a write request, one of its actions is to update the coherence order so that the store being accepted is coherence-after any store already propagated to its thread, which is needed when verifying one of the coherence properties required by C/C++.

Finally, a total order for SC actions must be built from the POWER trace, but as for happens-before there is no direct analogue of this relation in POWER. Instead, we show that the POWER `sync` barrier associated with SC actions by the mapping ensures that we never get cyclic dependencies if we take into account all the required properties of this order (e.g., a read may not read from a write after in SC order).

Including the synchronisation primitives The addition of the synchronisation primitives affects the definition of the happens-before relation. In particular, RMWs make the definition of release-sequences more complicated, and locks and fences introduce new ways for a synchronises-with edge to appear. This in turn affects the definition of the POWER analogue to happens-before. Here is the new characterisation of the transitive part of happens-before with synchronisation primitives, using relations derived from a POWER trace:

$$\begin{aligned}&((sync_t \cup lwsync_t)^{\text{refl}};\\&coi_t^{\text{refl}};\\&rfe_t;\\&(rmw_t; rf_t)^*;\\&(ctrlisync_t \cup dd_t^{\text{refl}} \cup lwsync_t)^{\text{refl}})^+\end{aligned}$$

where semicolon denotes relational composition, and $\cdot^{\text{refl}}$ and $\cdot^+$ are respectively the reflexive and transitive closures. The full potentially non-transitive happens-before relation is obtained by taking the union with program order, but that does not present any difficulty for the proof. The $sync_t$ and $lwsync_t$ relations relate commit transitions of memory accesses corresponding to memory instructions from a single thread which are separated in program-order by, respectively, a `sync` or `lwsync`. This part of the characterisation corresponds to the barriers introduced by the compilation mapping before unlocks, and release atomic-stores, fences, and RMWs. The coi_t relation relates commit transitions of stores from the same thread which are related in the coherence order. In the absence of RMWs, this relation is the POWER analogue of the C/C++ release-sequence relation, and the rfe_t relation (relating the commit transition of a store to the commit transition of a load reading from that store from a different thread) was the next component. With RMWs, we need something more elaborate: the rmw_t relation identifies the presence of a load-reserve/store-conditional pair. The rf_t relation extends rfe_t by also allowing the store and load to be on the same thread. The composition $(rmw_t; rf_t)^+$ corresponds to a chain of RMWs ending a C/C++ release sequence. Note that they may be RMWs anywhere in a release-sequence, not only at the end, but in that case the RMW chain must come back to the thread of the release head, and then the last RMW is related to the release head by the coi_t relation. The last component of the characterisation is the union of $ctrlisync_t$ (the ctrlisync analogue of the $sync_t$ and $lwsync_t$ relations, dd_t (data dependency, for C/C++ consume atomics, included in our proof but not discussed here) and $lwsync_t$. This corresponds to the barriers or dependencies placed after acquire and consume reads or to acquire fences. The $lwsync_t$ here is added, corresponding to acquire fences.

Despite the expanded definition of the analogue of happens-before, the key abstraction of the propagation lemma still holds. Thus the proof of consistency of the reconstructed C/C++ execution extends smoothly to the addition of C/C++ locks, RMWs, and fences. There is one new condition to check for the consistency of a C/C++ execution: an RMW action must read from its last predecessor in the modification-order. In terms of the POWER implementation, this means that the load-reserve must read from the last coherence predecessor of the store-conditional — but that is just what we are guaranteed from the rules given in §2, for a successful store-conditional.

Finally, SC fences must be a part of the sc relation, and this interacts with modification order to impose 6 additional coherence-like conditions. As before, there is no obvious order in the POWER machine trace with the right properties. Instead, we build the sc relation from a POWER machine trace by directly checking that these 6 conditions are not violated. To take one example, having the sc relation between the SC fences go one way in the store-buffering example of §4 imposes a condition that at least one read-from edge cannot be from a write that is too old in modification order. Recalling that SC fences are mapped to the POWER `sync` barrier, we use a property of this barrier (that it must wait for all group A writes, or coherence successors thereof, to be propagated to all threads) to guarantee this condition. Indeed, the corresponding example in POWER is SB+syncs, which only has SC behaviour.

Discussion: C/C++ and POWER Our proof establishes a close correspondence between C/C++ executions and POWER abstract machine executions of the compiled program. Nevertheless, there are programs with different behaviours on the two models. As noted previously, IRIW with two SC fences is allowed in C/C++, whereas its compilation with `syncs` is forbidden, and sometimes the mapping imposes stronger barriers than strictly necessary. For example, consider the 2+2W test of [SSA+11]. Here the only way to regain SC behaviour in C/C++ is to either use SC fences or all SC accesses everywhere. The test maps to 2+2W+syncs, which is indeed forbidden in POWER, but in fact here `lwsyncs` would have been enough.

6. Conclusion

With this work, together with [SSA+11, BOS+11, BMO+12], we finally have a semantics for real-world concurrent programming in C/C++ and on POWER multiprocessors that is complete enough to support reasoning about real OS and VM kernel code, at least in the absence of mixed-size accesses, and that is sufficiently well validated that one can have confidence in the results.

This opens the door to future work on verification techniques and analysis tools for such code. For example, looking informally at Michael's lock-free datastructure algorithms using hazard pointers [Mic04] (one of which was verified in an SC setting using separation logic [PBO07]), one can consider verification of efficient *implementations* of those abstract concurrent algorithms, either at the POWER ISA level, where one needs the various POWER barriers and load-reserve/store-conditional, or, making use of our main result here, at the C/C++ level, where one needs to add a particular placement of C/C++ fences and RMWs (interestingly, the two appear to coincide here: the C/C++ concurrency model is sufficiently expressive that one can express exactly the low-level synchronisation needed, as one would hope. Understanding how to do such verifications, especially compositionally, is a major open problem, as is the question of how to determine the best such placement. As we have seen, our work is also identifying subtle architectural choices.

We believe that the ARM architecture is broadly similar to POWER in these respects (though it is not identical to the model we present here), and hence that it will be possible to adapt the proof to ARM. We are currently engaged in further testing and in discussion with ARM staff to establish confidence there.

Acknowledgements We acknowledge funding from EPSRC grants EP/F036345, EP/H005633, EP/H027351, and EP/G026254/1, and from ANR project WMC (ANR-11-JS02-011), and thank the anonymous reviewers for their comments.

References

[AH90] S. V. Adve and M. D. Hill. Weak ordering — a new definition. In *Proc. ISCA*, 1990.

[AM11] J. Alglave and L. Maranget. Stability in weak memory models. In *Proc. CAV*, 2011.

[AMSS10] J. Alglave, L. Maranget, S. Sarkar, and P. Sewell. Fences in weak memory models. In *Proc. CAV*, 2010.

[BA08] H.-J. Boehm and S.V. Adve. Foundations of the C++ concurrency memory model. In *Proc. PLDI*, 2008.

[Bec11] P. Becker, editor. *Programming Languages — C++*. 2011. ISO/IEC 14882:2011. A non-final but recent version is available at `http://www.open-std.org/jtc1/sc22/wg21/docs/papers/2011/n3242.pdf`.

[BMO+12] M. Batty, K. Memarian, S. Owens, S. Sarkar, and P. Sewell. Clarifying and compiling C/C++ concurrency: from C++11 to POWER. In *Proc. POPL*, 2012. `http://www.cl.cam.ac.uk/~pes20/cppppc/`.

[Boe05] H.-J. Boehm. Threads cannot be implemented as a library. In *Proc. PLDI*, 2005.

[BOS+11] M. Batty, S. Owens, S. Sarkar, P. Sewell, and T. Weber. Mathematizing C++ concurrency. In *Proc. POPL*, 2011.

[cpp] Supplementary material. `http://www.cl.cam.ac.uk/users/pes20/cppppc-supplemental`.

[CSB93] F. Corella, J. M. Stone, and C. M. Barton. A formal specification of the PowerPC shared memory architecture. Technical Report RC18638, IBM, 1993.

[Her93] M. Herlihy. A methodology for implementing highly concurrent data objects. *TOPLAS*, 15(5):745–770, Nov 1993.

[Int02] Intel. A formal specification of Intel Itanium processor family memory ordering. `http://www.intel.com/design/itanium/downloads/251429.htm`, October 2002.

[ISO11] *Programming Languages — C*. 2011. ISO/IEC 9899:2011. A non-final but recent version is available at `http://www.open-std.org/jtc1/sc22/wg14/docs/n1539.pdf`.

[JHB87] E. H. Jensen, G. W. Hagensen, and J. M. Broughton. A new approach to exclusive data access in shared memory multiprocessors. (Technical Report UCRL-97663), Nov 1987.

[Lam79] L. Lamport. How to make a multiprocessor computer that correctly executes multiprocess programs. *IEEE Trans. Comput.*, C-28(9):690–691, 1979.

[McK11] P. E. McKenney. [patch rfc tip/core/rcu 0/28] preview of rcu changes for 3.3, November 2011. `https://lkml.org/lkml/2011/11/2/363`.

[Mic04] M. M. Michael. Hazard pointers: Safe memory reclamation for lock-free objects. *IEEE Trans. Parallel Distrib. Syst.*, 15:491–504, June 2004.

[MS11] P. E. McKenney and R. Silvera. Example POWER implementation for C/C++ memory model. `http://www.rdrop.com/users/paulmck/scalability/paper/N2745r.2011.03.04a.html`, 2011.

[OBZNS11] S. Owens, P. Böhm, F. Zappa Nardelli, and P. Sewell. Lem: A lightweight tool for heavyweight semantics. In *Proc. ITP, LNCS 6898*, 2011. "Rough Diamond" section.

[PBO07] M. Parkinson, R. Bornat, and P. O'Hearn. Modular verification of a non-blocking stack. In *Proc. POPL*, 2007.

[Pow09] *Power ISA Version 2.06*. IBM, 2009.

[Šev11] J. Ševčík . Safe optimisations for shared-memory concurrent programs. In *Proc. PLDI*, 2011.

[SS88] D. Shasha and M. Snir. Efficient and correct execution of parallel programs that share memory. *TOPLAS*, 10:282–312, 1988.

[SSA+11] S. Sarkar, P. Sewell, J. Alglave, L. Maranget, and D. Williams. Understanding POWER multiprocessors. In *PLDI*, 2011.

SuperC: Parsing All of C by Taming the Preprocessor

Paul Gazzillo Robert Grimm

New York University

{gazzillo,rgrimm}@cs.nyu.edu

Abstract

C tools, such as source browsers, bug finders, and automated refactorings, need to process two languages: C itself and the preprocessor. The latter improves expressivity through file includes, macros, and static conditionals. But it operates only on tokens, making it hard to even parse both languages. This paper presents a complete, performant solution to this problem. First, a configuration-preserving preprocessor resolves includes and macros yet leaves static conditionals intact, thus preserving a program's variability. To ensure completeness, we analyze all interactions between preprocessor features and identify techniques for correctly handling them. Second, a configuration-preserving parser generates a well-formed AST with static choice nodes for conditionals. It forks new subparsers when encountering static conditionals and merges them again after the conditionals. To ensure performance, we present a simple algorithm for table-driven Fork-Merge LR parsing and four novel optimizations. We demonstrate the effectiveness of our approach on the x86 Linux kernel.

Categories and Subject Descriptors D.3.4 [*Programming Languages*]: Processors; D.2.3 [*Software Engineering*]: Coding Tools and Techniques

General Terms Languages, Algorithms

Keywords C, preprocessor, LR parsing, Fork-Merge LR parsing, SuperC

1. Introduction

Large-scale software development requires effective tool support, such as source code browsers, bug finders, and automated refactorings. This need is especially pressing for C, since it is the language of choice for critical software infrastructure, including the Linux kernel and Apache web server. However, building tools for C presents a special challenge. C is not only low-level and unsafe, but source code mixes *two* languages: the C language proper and the preprocessor. First, the preprocessor adds facilities lacking from C itself. Notably, file includes (`#include`) provide rudimentary modularity, macros (`#define`) enable code transformation with a function-like syntax, and static conditionals (`#if`, `#ifdef`, and so on) capture variability. Second, the preprocessor is oblivious to C constructs and operates only on individual tokens. Real-world C code reflects both points: preprocessor usage is widespread and often violates C syntax [14].

Existing C tools punt on the full complexity of processing both languages. They either process one configuration at a time (e.g., the Cxref source browser [8], the Astrée bug finder [9], and Xcode refactorings [10]), rely on a single, maximal configuration (e.g., the Coverity bug finder [6]), or build on incomplete heuristics (e.g., the LXR source browser [20] and Eclipse refactorings [21]). Processing one configuration at a time is infeasible for large programs such as Linux, which has over 10,000 configuration variables [38]. Maximal configurations cover only part of the source code, mainly due to static conditionals with more than one branch. For example, Linux' `allyesconfig` enables less than 80% of the code blocks contained in conditionals [37]. And heuristic algorithms prevent programmers from utilizing the full expressivity of C and its preprocessor. Most research focused on parsing the two languages does not fare better, again processing only some configurations at a time or relying on incomplete algorithms [1, 3–5, 15, 19, 29, 31, 36, 41].

Only MAPR [33] and TypeChef [25, 26] come close to solving the problem by using a two-stage approach. First, a configuration-preserving *preprocessor* resolves file includes and macros yet leaves static conditionals intact. Second, a configuration-preserving *parser* forks its state into subparsers when encountering static conditionals and then merges them again after conditionals. The parser also normalizes the conditionals so that they bracket only complete C constructs and produces a well-formed AST with embedded static choice nodes. Critically, both stages preserve a C program's full variability and thus facilitate analysis and transformation of all source code. But MAPR and TypeChef still fall short. First, the MAPR preprocessor is not documented at all, making it impossible to repeat that result, and the TypeChef preprocessor misses several interactions between preprocessor features. Second, both systems' parsers are limited. TypeChef's LL parser combinator library automates forking but has seven combinators to merge subparsers again. This means that developers not only need to reengineer their grammars with TypeChef's combinators but also have to correctly employ the various join combinators. In contrast, MAPR's table-driven LR parser engine automates both forking and merging. But its naive forking strategy results in subparsers exponential to the number of conditional branches when a constant number of subparsers suffices.

This paper significantly improves on both systems and presents a rigorous treatment of both configuration-preserving preprocessing and parsing. In exploring configuration-preserving preprocessing, we focus on completeness. We present a careful analysis of *all* interactions between preprocessor features and identify techniques for correctly handling them. Notably, we show that a configuration-preserving preprocessor needs to hoist conditionals around other

PLDI'12, June 11–16, 2012, Beijing, China.

preprocessor operations, since preprocessor operations cannot be composed with conditionals. In exploring configuration-preserving parsing, we focus on performance. We present a simple algorithm for *Fork-Merge LR* (FMLR) parsing, which not only subsumes MAPR's algorithm but also has well-defined hooks for optimization. We then introduce four such optimizations, which decrease the number of forked subparsers (the *token follow set* and *lazy shifts*), eliminate duplicate work done by subparsers (*shared reduces*), and let subparsers merge as soon as possible (*early reduces*). Our optimizations are not only applied automatically, they also subsume TypeChef's specialized join combinators. The result is compelling. SuperC, our open-source tool[1] implementing these techniques, can fully parse programs with high variability, notably the entire x86 Linux kernel. In contrast, TypeChef can only parse a constrained version and MAPR fails for most source files.

Like MAPR, our work is inspired by GLR parsing [39], which also forks and merges subparsers. But whereas GLR parsers match different productions to the same input fragment, FMLR matches the same production to different input fragments. Furthermore, unlike GLR and TypeChef, FMLR parsers can reuse existing LR grammars and parser table generators; only the parser engine is new. This markedly decreases the engineering effort necessary for adapting our work. Compared to previous work, this paper makes the following contributions:

- An analysis of the challenges involved in parsing C with arbitrary preprocessor usage and an empirical quantification for the x86 version of the Linux kernel.
- A comprehensive treatment of techniques for configuration-preserving preprocessing and parsing, including novel performance optimizations.
- SuperC, an open-source tool for parsing all of C, and its demonstration on the x86 Linux kernel.

Overall, our work solves the problem of how to completely and efficiently parse all of C, 40 years after invention of the language, and thus lays the foundation for building more powerful C analysis and transformation tools.

2. The Problem and Solution Approach

C compilers such as gcc process only one variant of the source code at a time. They pick the one branch of each static conditional that matches the *configuration variables* passed to the preprocessor, e.g., through the `-D` command line option. Different configuration variable settings, or *configurations*, result in different executables, all from the same C sources. In contrast, other C tools, such as source browsers, bug finders, and automated refactorings, need to be *configuration-preserving*. They need to process all branches of static conditionals and, for each branch, track the configurations enabling the branch, i.e., its *presence condition*. This considerably complicates C tools except compilers, starting with preprocessing and parsing.

Figure 1 illustrates SuperC's configuration-preserving preprocessing and parsing on a simple example from the x86 Linux kernel (version 2.6.33.3, which is used throughout this paper). Figure 1a shows the original source code, which utilizes the three main preprocessor facilities: an include directive on line 1, macro definitions on lines 3 and 4, and conditional directives on lines 10 and 14. The code has two configurations, one when `CONFIG_INPUT_MOUSEDEV_PSAUX` is defined and one when it is not defined. After preprocessing, shown in Figure 1b, the header file has been included (not shown) and the macros have been expanded on lines 6, 7, and 10, but the conditional directives remain

```
1  #include "major.h" // Defines MISC_MAJOR to be 10
2
3  #define MOUSEDEV_MIX 31
4  #define MOUSEDEV_MINOR_BASE 32
5
6  static int mousedev_open(struct inode *inode, struct file *file)
7  {
8    int i;
9
10 #ifdef CONFIG_INPUT_MOUSEDEV_PSAUX
11   if (imajor(inode) == MISC_MAJOR)
12     i = MOUSEDEV_MIX;
13   else
14 #endif
15     i = iminor(inode) - MOUSEDEV_MINOR_BASE;
16
17   return 0;
18 }
```

(a) The unpreprocessed source.

```
1  static int mousedev_open(struct inode *inode, struct file *file)
2  {
3    int i;
4
5  #ifdef CONFIG_INPUT_MOUSEDEV_PSAUX
6    if (imajor(inode) == 10)
7      i = 31;
8    else
9  #endif
10     i = iminor(inode) - 32;
11
12   return 0;
13 }
```

(b) The preprocessed source preserving all configurations.

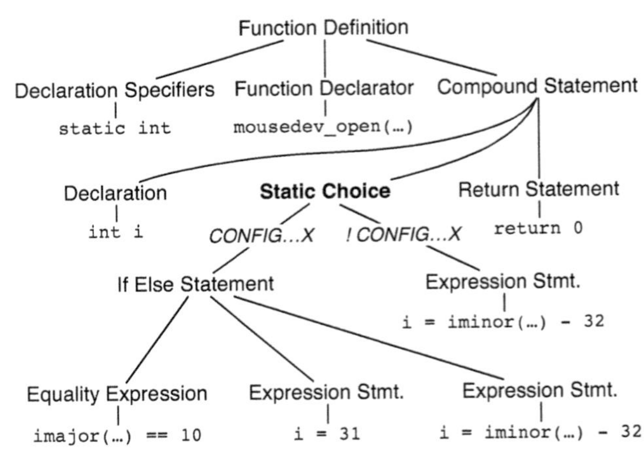

(c) Sketch of the AST containing all configurations.

Figure 1. From source code to preprocessed code to AST. The example is edited down for simplicity from drivers/input/mousedev.c.

on lines 5 and 9. Finally, in Figure 1c, the parser has generated an AST containing both configurations with a static choice node corresponding to the static conditional on lines 5–9 in Figure 1b.

2.1 Interactions Between C and the Preprocessor

The complexity of configuration-preserving C processing stems from the interaction of preprocessor features with each other and with the C language. Table 1 summarizes these interactions. Rows denote language features and are grouped by the three steps of C processing: lexing, preprocessing, and parsing. The first column names the feature and the second column describes the implementation strategy. The remaining columns capture complications arising from the interaction of features, and the corresponding table

[1] `http://cs.nyu.edu/xtc/`.

Language Construct	Implementation	Surrounded by Conditionals	Contain Conditionals	Contain Multiply-Defined Macros	Other
Lexer					
Layout	Annotate tokens				
Preprocessor					
Macro (Un)Definition	Use conditional macro table	Add multiple entries to macro table		Do not expand until invocation	Trim infeasible entries on redefinition
Object-Like Macro Invocations	Expand all definitions	Ignore infeasible definitions		Expand nested macros	Get ground truth for built-ins from compiler
Function-Like Macro Invocations	Expand all definitions	Ignore infeasible definitions	Hoist conditionals around invocations	Expand nested macros	Support differing argument numbers and variadics
Token Pasting & Stringification	Apply pasting & stringification		Hoist conditionals around token pasting & stringification		
File Includes	Include and preprocess files	Preprocess under presence conditions		Hoist conditionals around includes	Reinclude when guard macro is not false
Static Conditionals	Preprocess all branches	Conjoin presence conditions		Ignore infeasible definitions	
Conditional Expressions	Evaluate presence conditions			Hoist conditionals around expressions	Preserve order for non-boolean expressions
Error Directives	Ignore erroneous branches				
Line, Warning, & Pragma Directives	Treat as layout				
Parser					
C Constructs	Use FMLR Parser	Fork and merge subparsers			
Typedef Names	Use conditional symbol table	Add multiple entries to symbol table			Fork subparsers on ambiguous names

Table 1. Interactions between C preprocessor and language features. Gray entries in the last three columns are newly supported by SuperC.

```
#ifdef CONFIG_64BIT
#define BITS_PER_LONG 64
#else
#define BITS_PER_LONG 32
#endif
```

Figure 2. A multiply-defined macro from include/asm-generic/bitsperlong.h.

entries indicate how to overcome the complications. Blank entries indicate impossible interactions. Gray entries highlight interactions not yet supported by TypeChef. In contrast, SuperC does address all interactions—besides annotating tokens with layout and with line, warning, and pragma directives. (We have removed a buggy implementation of these annotations from SuperC for now.)

Layout. The first step is lexing. The lexer converts raw program text into tokens, stripping layout such as whitespace and comments. Since lexing is performed before preprocessing and parsing, it does not interact with the other two steps. However, automated refactorings, by definition, restructure source code and need to output program text *as originally written*, modulo any intended changes. Consequently, they need to annotate tokens with surrounding layout—plus, keep sufficient information about preprocessor operations to restore them as well.

Macro (un)definitions. The second step is preprocessing. It collects macro definitions (`#define`) and undefinitions (`#undef`) in a macro table—with definitions being either object-like

`#define` *name body*

or function-like

`#define` *name*`(`*parameters*`)` *body*

```
// In include/linux/byteorder/little_endian.h:
#define __cpu_to_le32(x) ((__force __le32)(__u32)(x))

#ifdef __KERNEL__
// Included from include/linux/byteorder/generic.h:
#define cpu_to_le32 __cpu_to_le32
#endif

// In drivers/pci/proc.c:
_put_user(cpu_to_le32(val), (__le32 __user *) buf);
```

Figure 3. A macro conditionally expanding to another macro.

Definitions and undefinitions for the same macro may appear in different branches of static conditionals, creating a *multiply-defined macro* that depends on the configuration. Figure 2 shows such a macro, `BITS_PER_LONG`, whose definition depends on the `CONFIG_64BIT` configuration variable. A configuration-preserving preprocessor records *all* definitions in its macro table, tagging each entry with the presence condition of the `#define` directive while also removing infeasible entries on each update. The preprocessor also records undefinitions, so that it can determine which macros are neither defined nor undefined and thus *free*, i.e., configuration variables. Wherever multiply-defined macros are used, they propagate an *implicit conditional*. It is as if the programmer had written an explicit conditional in the first place—an observation first made by Garrido and Johnson [19].

Macro invocations. Since macros may be nested within each other, a configuration-preserving preprocessor, just like an ordinary preprocessor, needs to recursively expand each macro. Furthermore, since C compilers have built-in object-like macros, such as `__STDC_VERSION__` to indicate the version of the C standard, the preprocessor needs to be configured with the ground truth of the targeted compiler.

```
1 #ifdef __KERNEL__
2 __cpu_to_le32
3 #else
4 cpu_to_le32
5 #endif
6 (val)
```

(a) After expansion of `cpu_to_le32`.

```
1 #ifdef __KERNEL__
2 __cpu_to_le32(val)
3 #else
4 cpu_to_le32(val)
5 #endif
```

(b) After hoisting the conditional.

```
1 #ifdef __KERNEL
2 ((__force __le32)(__u32)(val))
3 #else
4 cpu_to_le32(val)
5 #endif
```

(c) After expansion of `__cpu_to_le32`.

Figure 4. Preprocessing `cpu_to_le32(val)` in Fig. 3:10.

Beyond these straightforward issues, a configuration-preserving preprocessor needs to handle two more subtle interactions. First, a macro invocation may be surrounded by static conditionals. Consequently, the preprocessor needs to ignore macro definitions that are infeasible for the presence condition of the invocation site. Second, function-like macro invocations may contain conditionals, either explicitly in source code or implicitly through multiply-defined macros. These conditionals can alter the function-like macro invocation by changing its name or arguments, including their number and values. To preserve the function-like invocation while also allowing for differing argument numbers and variadics (a gcc extension) in different conditional branches, the preprocessor needs to *hoist* the conditionals around the invocation.

Figures 3 and 4 illustrate the hoisting of conditionals. Figure 3 contains a sequence of tokens on line 10, `cpu_to_le32(val)`, which either expands to an invocation of the function-like macro `__cpu_to_le32`, if `__KERNEL__` is defined, or denotes the invocation of the C function `cpu_to_le32`, if `__KERNEL__` is not defined. Figure 4 shows the three stages of preprocessing the sequence. First, in 4a, the preprocessor expands `cpu_to_le32`, which makes the conditional explicit but also breaks the nested macro invocation on line 2. Second, in 4b, the preprocessor hoists the conditional around the entire sequence of tokens, which duplicates `(val)` in each branch and thus restores the invocation on line 2. Third, in 4c, the preprocessor recursively expands `__cpu_to_le32` on line 2, which completes preprocessing for the sequence.

Token-pasting and stringification. Macros may contain two operators that modify tokens: The infix token-pasting operator `##` concatenates two tokens, and the prefix stringification operator `#` converts a sequence of tokens into a string literal. The preprocessor simply applies these operators, with one complication: the operators' arguments may contain conditionals, either explicitly in source code or implicitly via multiply-defined macros. As for function-like macros, a configuration-preserving preprocessor needs to hoist conditionals around these operators. Figure 5 illustrates this for token-pasting: 5a shows the source code; 5b shows the result of expanding all macros, including `BITS_PER_LONG` from Figure 2; and 5c shows the result of hoisting the conditional out of the token-pasting.

File includes. To produce complete compilation units, a configuration-preserving preprocessor recursively resolves file includes (`#include`). If the directive is nested in a static conditional, the

```
#define uintBPL_t uint(BITS_PER_LONG)
#define uint(x) xuint(x)
#define xuint(x) __le ## x

uintBPL_t *p = ... ;
```

(a) The macro definitions and invocation.

```
__le ##
#ifdef CONFIG_64BIT
64
#else
32
#endif
*p = ... ;
```

(b) After expanding the macros.

```
#ifdef CONFIG_64BIT
__le ## 64
#else
__le ## 32
#endif
*p = ... ;
```

(c) After hoisting the conditional.

Figure 5. A token-pasting example from fs/udf/balloc.c.

preprocessor needs to process the header file under the corresponding presence condition. Furthermore, if a guard macro, which is traditionally named `FILENAME_H` and protects against multiple inclusion, has been undefined, the preprocessor needs to process the same header file again. More interestingly, include directives may contain macros that provide part of the file name. If the macro in such a *computed include* is multiply-defined, the preprocessor needs to hoist the implicit conditional out of the directive, just as for macro invocations, token-pasting, and stringification.

Conditionals. Static conditionals enable multiple configurations, so both configuration-preserving preprocessor and parser need to process all branches. The preprocessor converts static conditionals' expressions into presence conditions, and when conditionals are nested within each other, conjoins nested conditionals' presence conditions. As described for macro invocations above, this lets the preprocessor ignore infeasible definitions during expansion of multiply-defined macros.

However, two issues complicate the conversion of conditional expressions into presence conditions. First, a conditional expression may contain arbitrary macros, not just configuration variables. So the preprocessor needs to expand the macros, which may be multiply-defined. When expanding a multiply-defined macro, the preprocessor needs to convert the macro's implicit conditional into logical form and hoist it around the conditional expression. For example, when converting the conditional expression

```
BITS_PER_LONG == 32
```

from kernel/sched.c into a presence condition, the preprocessor expands the definition of `BITS_PER_LONG` from Figure 2 and hoists it around the conditional expression, to arrive at

```
    defined(CONFIG_64BIT) && 64 == 32 \
 || !defined(CONFIG_64BIT) && 32 == 32
```

which makes testing for `CONFIG_64BIT` explicit with the `defined` operator and simplifies to

```
!defined(CONFIG_64BIT)
```

after constant folding.

Second, configuration variables may be non-boolean and conditional expressions may contain arbitrary arithmetic subexpressions, such as `NR_CPUS < 256` (from arch/x86/include/asm/spinlock.h).

```
static int (*check_part[])(struct parsed_partitions *) = {
#ifdef CONFIG_ACORN_PARTITION_ICS
  adfspart_check_ICS,
#endif
#ifdef CONFIG_ACORN_PARTITION_POWERTEC
  adfspart_check_POWERTEC,
#endif
#ifdef CONFIG_ACORN_PARTITION_EESOX
  adfspart_check_EESOX,
#endif
  // 15 more, similar initializers
  NULL
};
```

Figure 6. An example of a C construct containing an exponential number of unique configurations from fs/partitions/check.c.

Since there is no known efficient algorithm for comparing arbitrary polynomials [24], such subexpressions prevent the preprocessor from trimming infeasible configurations. Instead, it needs to treat non-boolean subexpressions as opaque text and preserve their branches' source code ordering, i.e., never omit or combine them and never move other branches across them.

Other preprocessor directives. The C preprocessor supports four additional directives, to issue errors (`#error`) and warnings (`#warning`), to instruct compilers (`#pragma`), and to overwrite line numbers (`#line`). A configuration-preserving preprocessor simply reports errors and warnings, and also terminates for errors appearing outside static conditionals. More importantly, it treats conditional branches containing error directives as infeasible and disables their parsing. Otherwise, it preserves such directives as token annotations to support automated refactorings.

C constructs. The third and final step is parsing. The preprocessor produces entire compilation units, which may contain static conditionals but no other preprocessor operations. The configuration-preserving parser processes all branches of each conditional by *forking* its internal state into subparsers and *merging* the subparsers again after the conditional. This way, it produces an AST containing all configurations, with static choice nodes for conditionals.

One significant complication is that static conditionals may still appear between arbitrary tokens, thus violating C syntax. However, the AST may only contain nodes representing complete C constructs. To recognize C constructs with embedded configurations, the parser may require a subparser per configuration. For example, the statement on lines 5–10 in Figure 1b has two configurations and requires two subparsers. The parser may also parse tokens shared between configurations several times. In the example, line 10 is parsed twice, once as part of the if-then-else statement and once as a stand-alone expression statement. This way, the parser hoists conditionals out of C constructs, much like the preprocessor hoists them out of preprocessor operations.

Using a subparser per embedded configuration is acceptable for most declarations, statements, and expressions. They have a small number of terminals and nonterminals and thus can contain only a limited number of configurations. However, if a C construct contains repeated nonterminals, this can lead to an exponential blow-up of configurations and therefore subparsers. For example, the array initializer in Figure 6 has 2^{18} unique configurations. Using a subparser for each configuration is clearly infeasible and avoiding it requires careful optimization of the parsing algorithm.

Typedef names. A final complication results from the fact that C syntax is context-sensitive [35]. Depending on context, names can either be typedef names, i.e., type aliases, or they can be object, function, and `enum` constant names. Furthermore, the same code snippet can have fundamentally different semantics, depending on names. For example, `T * p;` is either a *declaration* of `p` as a pointer to type `T` or an *expression statement* that multiplies the variables `T` and `p`, depending on whether `T` is a typedef name. C parsers usually employ a symbol table to disambiguate names [22, 35]. In the presence of conditionals, however, a name may be both. Consequently, a configuration-preserving parser needs to maintain configuration-dependent symbol table entries and fork subparsers when encountering an implicit conditional due to an ambiguously defined name.

Algorithm 1 Hoisting Conditionals

1: **procedure** HOIST(c, τ)
2:     ▷ Initialize a new conditional with an empty branch.
3:     $C \leftarrow [\,(c, \bullet)\,]$
4:     **for all** $a \in \tau$ **do**
5:         **if** a is a language token **then**
6:             ▷ Append a to all branches in C.
7:             $C \leftarrow [\,(c_i, \tau_i a) \mid (c_i, \tau_i) \in C\,]$
8:         **else** ▷ a is a conditional.
9:             ▷ Recursively hoist conditionals in each branch.
10:             $B \leftarrow [\,b \mid b \in \text{HOIST}(c_i, \tau_i) \text{ and } (c_i, \tau_i) \in a\,]$
11:             ▷ Combine with already hoisted conditionals.
12:             $C \leftarrow C \times B$
13:         **end if**
14:     **end for**
15:     **return** C
16: **end procedure**

3. The Configuration-Preserving Preprocessor

SuperC's configuration-preserving preprocessor accepts C files, performs all operations while preserving static conditionals, and produces compilation units. While tedious to engineer, its functionality mostly follows from the discussion in the previous section. Two features, however, require further elaboration: the hoisting of conditionals around preprocessor operations and the conversion of conditional expressions into presence conditions.

3.1 Hoisting Static Conditionals

Preprocessor directives as well as function-like macro invocations, token-pasting, and stringification may only contain ordinary language tokens. Consequently, they are ill-defined in the presence of implicit or explicit embedded static conditionals. To perform these preprocessor operations, SuperC's configuration-preserving preprocessor needs to hoist conditionals, so that only ordinary tokens appear in the branches of the innermost conditionals.

Algorithm 1 formally defines HOIST. It takes a presence condition c and a list of ordinary tokens and entire conditionals τ under the presence condition. Each static conditional C, in turn, is treated as a list of branches

$$C := [\,(c_1, \tau_1), \ldots, (c_n, \tau_n)\,]$$

with each branch having a presence condition c_i and a list of tokens and nested conditionals τ_i. Line 3 initializes the result C with an empty conditional branch. Lines 4–14 iterate over the tokens and conditionals in τ, updating C as necessary. And line 15 returns the result C. Lines 5–7 of the loop handle ordinary tokens, which are present in all embedded configurations and are appended to all branches in C, as illustrated for `(val)` in Figure 4b and for `__le ##` in Figure 5c. Lines 8–13 of the loop handle conditionals by recursively hoisting any nested conditionals in line 10 and then combining the result B with C in line 12. The cross product for conditionals in line 12 is defined as

$$C \times B := [\,(c_i \wedge c_j, \tau_i \tau_j) \mid (c_i, \tau_i) \in C \text{ and } (c_j, \tau_j) \in B\,]$$

and generalizes line 7 by combining every branch in C with every branch in B.

SuperC uses Hoist for all preprocessor operations that may contain conditionals except for function-like macro invocations. The problem with the latter is that, to call Hoist, the preprocessor needs to know which tokens and conditionals belong to an operation. But different conditional branches of a function-like macro invocation may contain different macro names and numbers of arguments, and even additional, unrelated tokens. Consequently, SuperC uses a version of Hoist for function-like macro invocations that interleaves parsing with hoisting. For each conditional branch, it tracks parentheses and commas, which change the parsing state of the invocation. Once all variations of the invocation have been recognized across all conditional branches, each invocation is separately expanded. If a variation contains an object-like or undefined macro, the argument list is left in place, as illustrated in Fig. 4c:4.

3.2 Converting Conditional Expressions

To reason about presence conditions, SuperC converts conditional expressions into Binary Decision Diagrams (BDDs) [12, 42], which are an efficient, symbolic representation of boolean functions. BDDs include support for boolean constants, boolean variables, as well as negation, conjunction, and disjunction. On top of that, BDDs are *canonical*: Two boolean functions are the same if and only if their BDD representations are the same [12]. This makes it not only possible to directly combine BDDs, e.g., when tracking the presence conditions of nested or hoisted conditionals, but also to easily compare two BDDs for equality, e.g., when testing for an infeasible configuration by evaluating $c_1 \wedge c_2 = \mathit{false}$.

Before converting a conditional expression into a BDD, SuperC expands any macros outside invocations of the `defined` operator, hoists multiply-defined macros around the expression, and performs constant folding. The resulting conditional expression uses negations, conjunctions, and disjunctions to combine four types of subexpressions: constants, free macros, arithmetic expressions, and `defined` invocations. SuperC converts each of these subexpressions into a BDD as follows and then combines the resulting BDDs with the necessary logical operations:

1. A constant translates to *false* if zero and to *true* otherwise.
2. A free macro translates to a BDD variable.
3. An arithmetic subexpression also translates to a BDD variable.
4. `defined(`M`)` translates into the disjunction of presence conditions under which M is defined. However, if M is free:
   (a) If M is a guard macro, `defined(`M`)` translates to *false*.
   (b) Otherwise, `defined(`M`)` translates to a BDD variable.

Just like gcc, Case 4a treats M as a guard macro, if a header file starts with a conditional directive that tests `!defined(`M`)` and is followed by `#define` M, and the matching `#endif` ends the file. To ensure that repeated occurrences of the same free macro, arithmetic expression, or `defined(`M`)` for free M translate to the same BDD variable, SuperC maintains a mapping between these expressions and their BDD variables. In the case of arithmetic expressions, it normalizes the text by removing whitespace and comments.

4. The Configuration-Preserving Parser

SuperC's configuration-preserving FMLR parser builds on LR parsing [2, 28], a bottom-up parsing technique. To recognize the input, LR parsers maintain an explicit parser stack, which contains terminals, i.e., tokens, and nonterminals. On each step, LR parsers perform one of four actions: (1) *shift* to copy a token from the input onto the stack and increment the parser's position in the input, (2) *reduce* to replace one or more top-most stack elements with a nonterminal, (3) *accept* to successfully complete parsing, and (4) *reject* to terminate parsing with an error. The choice of action depends on both the next token in the input and the parser stack. To ensure efficient operation, LR parsers use a deterministic finite control and store the state of the control with each stack element.

Algorithm 2 Fork-Merge LR Parsing

```
 1: procedure PARSE(a₀)
 2:     Q.init((true, a₀, s₀))  ▷ The initial subparser for a₀.
 3:     while Q ≠ ∅ do
 4:         p ← Q.pull()  ▷ Step the next subparser.
 5:         T ← FOLLOW(p.c, p.a)
 6:         if |T| = 1 then
 7:             ▷ Do an LR action and reschedule the subparser.
 8:             Q.insert(LR(T(1), p))
 9:         else  ▷ The follow-set contains several tokens.
10:             ▷ Fork subparsers and reschedule them.
11:             Q.insertAll(FORK(T, p))
12:         end if
13:         Q ← MERGE(Q)
14:     end while
15: end procedure
```

Compared to top-down parsing techniques, such as LL [34] and PEG [7, 16], LR parsers are an attractive foundation for configuration-preserving parsing for three reasons. First, LR parsers make the parsing state explicit, in form of the parser stack. Consequently, it is easy to fork the parser state on a static conditional, e.g., by representing the stack as a singly-linked list and by creating new stack elements that point to the shared remainder. Second, LR parsers are relatively straight-forward to build, since most of the complexity lies in generating the parsing tables, which determine control transitions and actions. In fact, SuperC uses LALR parsing tables [13] produced by an existing parser generator. Third, LR parsers support left-recursion in addition to right-recursion, which is helpful for writing programming language grammars.

4.1 Fork-Merge LR Parsing

Algorithm 2 formalizes FMLR parsing. It uses a queue Q of LR subparsers p. Each subparser $p := (c, a, s)$ has a presence condition c, a next token or conditional a, which is also called the *head*, and an LR parser stack s. Each subparser recognizes a distinct configuration, i.e., the different presence conditions $p.c$ are mutually exclusive, and all subparsers together recognize all configurations, i.e., the disjunction of all their presence conditions is *true*. Q is a priority queue, ordered by the position of the head $p.a$ in the input. This ensures that subparsers merge at the earliest opportunity, as no subparser can outrun the other subparsers.

Line 2 initializes the queue Q with the subparser for the initial token or conditional a_0, and lines 3–14 step individual subparsers until the queue is empty, i.e., all subparsers have accepted or rejected. On each iteration, line 4 pulls the earliest subparser p from the queue. Line 5 computes the *token follow-set* for $p.c$ and $p.a$, which contains pairs (c_i, a_i) of ordinary language tokens a_i and their presence conditions c_i. The follow-set computation is detailed in Section 4.2. Intuitively, it captures the actual variability of source code and includes the first language token on each path through static conditionals from the current input position. If the follow-set contains a single element, e.g., $p.a$ is an ordinary token and $T = \{(p.c, p.a)\}$, lines 6–8 perform an LR action on the only element $T(1)$ and the subparser p. Unless the LR action is *accept* or *reject*, line 8 also reschedules the subparser. Otherwise, the follow-set contains more than one element, e.g., $p.a$ is a conditional. Since each subparser can only perform LR actions one after another,

Algorithm 3 The Token Follow-Set

```
1: procedure FOLLOW(c, a)
2:     T ← ∅  ▷ Initialize the follow-set.
3:     procedure FIRST(c, a)
4:         loop
5:             if a is a language token then
6:                 T ← T ∪ {(c, a)}
7:                 return false
8:             else ▷ a is a conditional.
9:                 c_r ← false  ▷ Initialize remaining condition.
10:                for all (c_i, τ_i) ∈ a do
11:                    if τ_i = • then
12:                        c_r ← c_r ∨ c ∧ c_i
13:                    else
14:                        c_r ← c_r ∨ FIRST(c ∧ c_i, τ_i(1))
15:                    end if
16:                end for
17:                if c_r = false or a is last element in branch then
18:                    return c_r
19:                end if
20:                c ← c_r
21:                a ← next token or conditional after a
22:            end if
23:        end loop
24:    end procedure
25:    loop
26:        c ← FIRST(c, a)
27:        if c = false then return T end if  ▷ Done.
28:        a ← next token or conditional after a
29:    end loop
30: end procedure
```

lines 9–12 fork a subparser for each presence condition and token $(c_i, a_i) \in T$ and then reschedule the subparsers. Finally, line 13 tries to merge subparsers again. Subparsers may merge if they have the same head and LR stack, which ensures that conditionals are hoisted out of C constructs.

4.2 The Token Follow-Set

A critical challenge for configuration-preserving parsing is *which* subparsers to create. The naive strategy, employed by MAPR, forks a subparser for every branch of every static conditional. But conditionals may have empty branches and even omit branches, like the implicit else branch in Figure 1. Furthermore, they may be directly nested within conditional branches, and they may directly follow other conditionals. Consequently, the naive strategy forks a great many unnecessary subparsers and is intractable for complex C programs such as Linux. Instead, FMLR relies on the token follow-set to capture the source code's actual variability, thus limiting the number of forked subparsers.

Algorithm 3 formally defines FOLLOW. It takes a presence condition c and a token or conditional a, and it returns the follow-set T for a, which contains pairs (c_i, a_i) of ordinary tokens a_i and their presence conditions c_i. By construction, each token a_i appears exactly once in T; consequently, the follow-set is *ordered* by the tokens' positions in the input. Line 2 initializes T to the empty set. Lines 3–24 define the nested procedure FIRST. It scans well-nested conditionals and adds the first ordinary token and presence condition for each configuration to T. It then returns the presence condition of any remaining configuration, i.e., conditional branches that are empty or implicit and thus do not contain ordinary tokens. Lines 25–29 repeatedly call FIRST until all configurations have been covered, i.e., the remaining configuration is *false*. Line 28 moves on to the next token or conditional, while also stepping out of conditionals. In other words, if the token or conditional a is the last element in the branch of a conditional, which, in turn, may be the last element in the branch of another conditional (and so on), line 28 updates a with the first element after the conditionals.

FIRST does the brunt of the work. It takes a token or conditional a and presence condition c. Lines 4–23 then iterate over the elements of a conditional branch or at a compilation unit's top-level, starting with a. Lines 5–7 handle ordinary language tokens. Line 6 adds the token and presence condition to the follow-set T. Line 7 terminates the loop by returning *false*, indicating no remaining configuration. Lines 8–22 handle conditionals. Line 9 initializes the remaining configuration c_r to *false*. Lines 10–16 then iterate over the branches of the conditional a, including any implicit branch. If a branch is empty, line 12 adds the conjunction of its presence condition c_i and the overall presence condition c to the remaining configuration c_r. Otherwise, line 14 recurses over the branch, starting with the first token or conditional $\tau_i(1)$, and adds the result to the remaining configuration c_r. If, after iterating over the branches of the conditional, the remaining configuration is *false* or there are no more tokens or conditionals to process, lines 17–19 terminate FIRST's main loop by returning c_r. Finally, lines 20–21 set up the next iteration of the loop by updating c with the remaining configuration and a with the next token or conditional.

$$\textsc{Fork}(T, p) := \{\, (c, a, p.s) \mid (c, a) \in T \,\}$$
$$\textsc{Merge}(Q) := \{\, (\bigvee p.c, a, s) \mid a = p.a \text{ and } s = p.s\ \forall p \in Q \,\}$$

(a) Basic forking and merging.

$$\textsc{Fork}(T, p) := \{\, (H, p.s) \mid H \in \textsc{Lazy}(T, p) \cup \textsc{Shared}(T, p) \,\}$$
$$\textsc{Lazy}(T, p) := \{\, \bigcup \{(c, a)\} \mid \textsc{Action}(a, p.s) = \texttt{`shift'}\ \forall (c, a) \in T \,\}$$
$$\textsc{Shared}(T, p) := \{\, \bigcup \{(c, a)\} \mid \textsc{Action}(a, p.s) = \texttt{`reduce}\ n\texttt{'}\ \forall (c, a) \in T \,\}$$

(b) Optimized forking.

Figure 7. The definitions of fork and merge.

4.3 Forking and Merging

Figure 7a shows the definitions of FORK and MERGE. FORK creates new subparsers from a token follow-set T to replace a subparser p. Each new subparser has a different presence condition c and token a from the follow-set T but the same LR stack $p.s$. Consequently, it recognizes a more specific configuration than the original subparser p. MERGE has the opposite effect. It takes the priority queue Q and combines any subparsers $p \in Q$ that have the same head and LR stack. Such subparsers are redundant: they will necessarily perform the same parsing actions for the rest of the input, since FMLR, like LR, is deterministic. Each merged subparser replaces the original subparsers; its presence condition is the disjunction of the original subparsers' presence conditions. Consequently, it recognizes a more general configuration than any of the original subparsers. MERGE is similar to GLR's *local ambiguity packing* [39], which also combines equivalent subparsers, except that FMLR subparsers have presence conditions.

4.4 Optimizations

In addition to the token follow-set, FMLR relies on three more optimizations to contain the state explosion caused by static conditionals: early reduces, lazy shifts, and shared reduces. *Early reduces* are a tie-breaker for the priority queue. When subparsers have the same head a, they favor subparsers that will reduce over subparsers that will shift. Since reduces, unlike shifts, do not change a subparser's head, early reduces prevent subparsers from outrunning each other and create more opportunities for merging subparsers.

While early reduces seek to increase merge opportunities, lazy shifts and shared reduces seek to decrease the number and work of forked subparsers, respectively. First, *lazy shifts* delay the forking of subparsers that will shift. They are based on the observation that a sequence of static conditionals with empty or implicit branches, such as the array initializer in Figure 6, often results in a follow-set, whose tokens all require a shift as the next LR action. However, since FMLR steps subparsers by position of the head, the subparser for the first such token performs its shift (plus other LR actions) and can merge again *before* the subparser for the second such token can even perform its shift. Consequently, it is wasteful to eagerly fork the subparsers. Second, *shared reduces* reduce a single stack for several heads at the same time. They are based on the observation that conditionals often result in a follow-set, whose tokens all require a reduce to the same nonterminal; e.g., both tokens in the follow-set of the conditional in Figure 1b reduce the declaration on line 3. Consequently, it is wasteful to first fork the subparsers and then reduce their stacks in the same way.

Figure 7b formally defines both lazy shifts and shared reduces. Both optimizations result in *multi-headed* subparsers $p := (H, s)$, which have more than one head and presence condition

$$H := \{(c_1, a_1), \ldots, (c_n, a_n)\}$$

Just as for the follow-set, each token a_i appears exactly once in H and the set is ordered by the tokens' positions in the input. Algorithm 2 generalizes to multi-headed subparsers as follows. It prioritizes a multi-headed subparser by its earliest head a_1. Next, by definition of optimized forking, the follow-set of a multi-headed subparser (H, s) is H. However, the optimized version of the FMLR algorithm always performs an LR operation on a multi-headed subparser, i.e., treats it as if the follow-set contains a single ordinary token. If the multi-headed subparser will shift, it forks off a single-headed subparser p' for the earliest head, shifts p', and then reschedules both subparsers. If the multi-headed subparser will reduce, it reduces p and immediately recalculates $\text{FORK}(H, p)$, since the next LR action may not be the same reduce for all heads anymore. Finally, it merges multi-headed subparsers p if they have the same head $\{(\_, a_1), \ldots, (\_, a_n)\} = p.H$ and the same LR stack $s = p.s$; it computes the merged parser's presence conditions as the disjunction of the original subparser's corresponding presence conditions $c_i = \bigvee p.H(i).c$.

4.5 Putting It All Together

We are now ready to illustrate FMLR on the array initializer in Figure 6. For simplicity, we treat `NULL` as a token and ignore that the macro usually expands to `((void *)0)`. For concision, we subscript each subparser and set symbol with its current line number in Figure 6. We also use b_n to denote the boolean variable representing the conditional expression on line n, e.g.,

$$b_2 \sim \texttt{defined(CONFIG\_ACORN\_PARTITION\_ICS)}$$

Finally, we refer to one iteration through FMLR's main loop in Algorithm 2 as a *step*.

Since line 1 in Figure 6 contains only ordinary tokens, FMLR behaves like an LR parser, stepping through the tokens with a single subparser p_1. Upon reaching line 2, FMLR computes FOLLOW for the conditional on lines 2–4. To this end, FIRST iterates over the conditionals and `NULL` token in the initializer list by updating a in Alg. 3:21. On each iteration besides the last, FIRST also recurses over the branches of a conditional, including the implicit else branch. As a result, it updates the remaining configuration in Alg. 3:12 with a conjunction of negated conditional expressions, yielding the follow-set

$$\begin{aligned} T_2 = \{ &(b_2, \texttt{adfspart\_check\_ICS}), \\ &(\neg b_2 \wedge b_5, \texttt{adfspart\_check\_POWERTEC}), \\ &\ldots, (\neg b_2 \wedge \neg b_5 \wedge \neg b_8 \wedge \ldots, \texttt{NULL})\} \end{aligned}$$

Since all tokens in T_2 reduce the empty input to the *InitializerList* nonterminal, *shared reduces* turns p_2 into a multi-headed subparser with $H_2 = T_2$. FMLR then steps p_3. It reduces the subparser, which does not change the heads, i.e., $H_3 = H_2$, but modifies the stack to

$$p_3.s = \ldots \ \{ \ \textit{InitializerList}$$

It then calculates $\text{FORK}(H_3, p_3)$; since all tokens in H_3 now shift, *lazy shifts* produces the same multi-headed subparser. FMLR steps p_3 again. It forks off a single-headed subparser p'_3 and shifts the identifier token on line 3 onto its stack. Next, FMLR steps p'_3. It shifts the comma token onto the stack, which yields

$$p'_3.s = \ldots \ \{ \ \textit{InitializerList} \ \texttt{adfspart\_check\_ICS} \ ,$$

and updates the head $p'_3.a$ to the conditional on lines 5–7. FMLR steps p'_5 again, computing the subparser's follow-set as

$$\begin{aligned} T'_5 = \{ &(b_2 \wedge b_5, \texttt{adfspart\_check\_POWERTEC}), \\ &\ldots, (b_2 \wedge \neg b_5 \wedge \neg b_8 \wedge \ldots, \texttt{NULL})\} \end{aligned}$$

Since all tokens in T'_5 reduce the top three stack elements to an *InitializerList*, *shared reduces* turns p'_5 into a multi-headed subparser with $H'_5 = T'_5$. At this point, both p_6 and p'_6 are multi-headed subparsers with the same heads, though their stacks differ. Due to *early reduces*, FMLR steps p'_6. It reduces the stack, which yields the same stack as that of p_6, and calculates FORK, which does not change p'_6 due to *lazy shifts*. It then merges the two multi-headed subparsers, which disjoins b_2 with $\neg b_2$ for all presence conditions and thus eliminates b_2 from H_6. FMLR then repeats the process of forking, shifting, reducing, and merging for the remaining 17 conditionals until a single-headed subparser p completes the array initializer on lines 12–13. That way, FMLR parses 2^{18} distinct configurations with only 2 subparsers!

5. Pragmatics

Having covered the overall approach and algorithms, we now turn to the pragmatics of building a real-world tool. SuperC implements the three steps of parsing all of C—lexing, preprocessing, and parsing—in Java. We engineered both preprocessor and parser from scratch, but rely on JFlex [27] to generate the lexer and on Bison [17] to generate the LALR parser tables. Since Bison generates C headers, we wrote a small C program that converts them to Java. As inputs to JFlex and Bison, we reuse Roskind's tokenization rules and grammar for C [35], respectively; we added support for common gcc extensions. To parse conditional expressions, the preprocessor also reuses a C expression grammar distributed with the *Rats!* parser generator [22]. To facilitate future retargeting to other languages, SuperC's preprocessor accesses tokens through an interface that hides source language aspects not relevant to preprocessing. Furthermore, the preprocessor does not pass conditional directives to the parser but rather replaces each directive's tokens with a single special token that encodes the conditional operation and references the conditional expression as a BDD. Finally, the parser is not only configured with the parser tables but also with plug-ins that control AST construction (Section 5.1) and context management (Section 5.2). To support these plug-ins, each subparser stack element has a field for the current semantic value and each subparser has a field for the current context.

5.1 Building Abstract Syntax Trees

To simplify AST construction, SuperC includes an annotation facility that eliminates explicit semantic actions in most cases. Developers simply add special comments next to productions. Our AST tool then extracts these comments and generates the corresponding Java plug-in code, which is invoked when reducing a subparser's stack. By default, SuperC creates an AST node that is an instance of a generic node class, is named after the production, and has the semantic values of all terminals and nonterminals as children. Four annotations override this default. (1) `layout` omits the production's value from the AST. It is used for punctuation. (2) `passthrough` reuses a child's semantic value, if it is the only child in an alternative. It is particularly useful for expressions, whose productions tend to be deeply nested for precedence (17 levels for C). (3) `list` encodes the semantic values of a recursive production as a linear list. It is necessary because LR grammars typically represent repetitions as left-recursive productions. (4) `action` executes arbitrary Java code instead of automatically generating an AST node.

A fifth annotation, `complete`, determines which productions are complete syntactic units. SuperC merges only subparsers with the same, complete nonterminal on top of their stacks; while merging, it combines the subparsers' semantic values with a static choice node. The selection of complete syntactic units requires care. Treating too many productions as complete forces downstream tools to handle static choice nodes in too many different language constructs. Treating too few productions as complete may result in an exponential subparser number in the presence of embedded configurations, e.g., the array initializer in Figure 6. SuperC's C grammar tries to strike a balance by treating not only declarations, definitions, statements, and expressions as complete syntactic units, but also members in commonly configured lists, including function parameters, `struct` and `union` members, as well as `struct`, `union`, and array initializers.

5.2 Managing Parser Context

SuperC's context management plug-in enables the recognition of context-sensitive languages, including C, without modifying the FMLR parser. The plug-in has four callbacks: (1) `reclassify` modifies the token follow-set by changing or adding tokens. It is called after computing the follow-set, i.e., line 5 in Algorithm 2. (2) `forkContext` creates a new context and is called during forking. (3) `mayMerge` determines whether two contexts allow merging and is called while merging subparsers. (4) `mergeContexts` actually combines two contexts and is also called while merging.

SuperC's C plug-in works as follows. Its context is a symbol table that tracks which names denote values or types under which presence conditions and in which C language scopes. Productions that declare names and enter/exit C scopes update the symbol table through helper productions that are empty but have semantic actions. `reclassify` checks the name of each identifier, which is the only token generated for names by SuperC's lexer. If the name denotes a type in the current scope, `reclassify` replaces the identifier with a typedef name. If the name is ambiguously defined under the current presence condition, it instead adds the typedef name to the follow-set. This causes the FMLR parser to fork an extra subparser on such names, even though there is no explicit conditional. `forkContext` duplicates the current symbol table scope. `mayMerge` allows merging only at the same scope nesting level. Finally, `mergeContexts` combines any symbol table scopes not already shared between the two contexts.

6. Evaluation

To evaluate our work, we explore three questions. Section 6.1 examines how prevalent preprocessor usage is in real-world code. It measures preprocessor directives and feature interactions in the Linux kernel. Section 6.2 examines how effective FMLR is at containing the state explosion caused by static conditionals. It measures the number of subparsers necessary for parsing Linux and also compares to our reimplementation of MAPR. Section 6.3 examines how well SuperC performs. It measures the latency for parsing Linux and also compares to TypeChef. We focus on Linux for three reasons: (a) it is large and complex, (b) it has many developers with differing coding styles and skills, and (c) it is subject to staggering performance and variability requirements. However, since the Linux build system does not use the preprocessor for setting architecture-specific header files, we evaluate only the x86 version of the kernel. In summary, our evaluation demonstrates that Linux provides a cornucopia of preprocessor usage, that FMLR requires less than 40 subparsers for Linux whereas MAPR fails on most source files, and that SuperC performs well enough, outrunning TypeChef by more than a factor of four and out-scaling it for complex compilation units.

	Total	C Files	Headers
LoC	5,600,227	85%	15%
All Directives	532,713	34%	66%
`#define`	366,424	16%	84%
`#if`, `#ifdef`, `#ifndef`	38,198	58%	42%
`#include`	86,604	85%	15%

(a) Number of directives compared to lines of code (LoC).

Header Name	C Files That Include Header
include/linux/module.h	3,741 (49%)
include/linux/init.h	2,841 (37%)
include/linux/kernel.h	2,567 (33%)
include/linux/slab.h	1,800 (23%)
include/linux/delay.h	1,505 (20%)

(b) The top five most frequently included headers.

Table 2. A developer's view of x86 Linux preprocessor usage.

6.1 Preprocessor Usage and Interactions

Table 2 provides a *developer's view* of preprocessor usage in the x86 Linux kernel. The data was collected by running `cloc`, `grep`, and `wc` on individual C and header *files*. Table 2a compares the number of preprocessor directives to lines of code (LoC), excluding comments and empty lines. Even this simple analysis demonstrates extensive preprocessor usage: almost 10% of all LoC are preprocessor directives. Yet, when looking at C files, preprocessor usage is not nearly as evident for two reasons. First, macro invocations look like C identifiers and C function calls; they may also be nested in other macros. Consequently, they are not captured by this analysis. Second, C programs usually rely on headers for common definitions, i.e., as a poor man's module system. The data corroborates this. 66% of all directives and 84% of macro definitions are in header files. Furthermore, 15% of include directives are in header files, resulting in long chains of dependencies. Finally, some headers are directly included in thousands of C files (and preprocessed for each one). Table 2b shows the top five most frequently included headers; `module.h` alone is included in nearly half of all C files.

Table 3 provides a *tool's view* of preprocessor usage in the x86 Linux kernel. The data was collected by instrumenting SuperC and applying our tool on *compilation units*, i.e., C files plus the closure of included headers. It captures information not available in the simple counts of Table 2, including macro invocations. Table 3 loosely follows the organization of Table 1. Each row shows a preprocessor or C language construct. The first column names the construct, the second column shows its usage, and the third and fourth columns show its interactions. Each entry is the distribution in three percentiles, "50th · 90th · 100th," across compilation units. Table 3 confirms that preprocessor usage is extensive. It also confirms that most interactions identified in Section 2 occur in real-world C code.

Language Construct	Total	Interaction with Conditionals		Other Interactions	
Macro Definitions	34k · 45k · 122k	Contained in	34k · 45k · 122k	Redefinitions	23k · 33k · 111k
Macro Invocations	98k · 140k · 381k	Trimmed Hoisted	16k · 21k · 70k 154 · 292 · 876	Nested invocations Built-in macros	64k · 97k · 258k 135
Token-Pasting	4k · 6k · 22k	Hoisted	0 · 0 · 180		
Stringification	6k · 8k · 23k	Hoisted	361 · 589 · 6,082		
File Includes	1,608 · 2,160 · 5,939	Hoisted	33 · 55 · 165	Computed includes Reincluded headers	34 · 56 · 168 1,185 · 1,743 · 5,488
Static Conditionals	8k · 10k · 29k	Hoisted Max. depth	331 · 437 · 1,258 28 · 33 · 40	With non-boolean expressions	509 · 713 · 1,975
Error Directives	42 · 57 · 168				
C Declarations & Statements	34k · 49k · 127k	Containing	722 · 896 · 2,746		
Typedef Names	748 · 1,028 · 2,554	Ambiguously defined names	0 · 0 · 0		

Table 3. A tool's view of x86 Linux preprocessor usage. Entries show percentiles across compilation units: 50th · 90th · 100th.

The vast majority of measured preprocessor interactions involve macros. First, almost all macro definitions are contained in static conditionals, i.e., any difference is hidden by rounding to the nearest thousand. This is due to most definitions occurring in header files and most header files, in turn, containing a single static conditional that protects against multiple inclusion. Second, over 60% of macro invocations appear from within other macros; e.g., the median for total macro invocations is 98k, while the median for nested invocations is 64k. This makes it especially difficult to fully analyze macro invocations without running the preprocessor, e.g., by inspecting source code. While not nearly as frequent as interactions involving macros, static conditionals do appear within function-like macro invocations, token-pasting and stringification operators, file includes, as well as conditional expressions. Consequently, a configuration-preserving preprocessor must hoist such conditionals. Similarly, non-boolean expressions do appear in conditionals and the preprocessor must preserve them. However, two exceptions are notable. Computed includes are very rare and ambiguously-defined names do not occur at all, likely because both make it very hard to reason about source code.

6.2 Subparser Counts

According to Table 3, most compilation units contain thousands of static conditionals. This raises the question of whether recognizing C code across conditionals is even feasible. Two factors determine feasibility: (1) the breadth of conditionals, which forces the forking of subparsers, and (2) the incidence of partial C constructs in conditionals, which prevents the merging of subparsers. The number of subparsers per iteration of FMLR's main loop in Alg. 2:3–14 precisely captures the combined effect of these two factors.

Figure 8 shows the cumulative distribution of subparser counts per FMLR iteration for the x86 Linux kernel under different optimization levels: 8a identifies the maxima and 8b characterizes the overall shape. For comparison, the former also includes MAPR. We reimplemented MAPR by modifying SuperC to optionally fork a subparser for every conditional branch instead of using the token follow-set. We also reimplemented MAPR's tie-breaker for the priority queue, which favors the subparser with the larger stack [33]. Figure 8 demonstrates that MAPR is intractable for Linux, triggering a kill-switch at 16,000 subparsers for 98% of all compilation units. In contrast, the token follow-set alone makes FMLR feasible for the entire x86 Linux kernel. The lazy shifts, shared reduces, and early reduces optimizations further decrease subparser counts, by up to a factor of 12. They also help keep the AST smaller: fewer forked subparsers means fewer static choice nodes in the tree, and earlier merging means more tree fragments outside static choice nodes, i.e., shared between configurations.

	Subparsers	
Optimization Level	**99th %**	**Max.**
Shared, Lazy, & Early	21	39
Shared & Lazy	22	39
Shared	21	77
Lazy	32	468
Follow-Set Only	33	468
MAPR & Largest First	>16,000 on 98% of comp. units	
MAPR	>16,000 on 98% of comp. units	

(a) The maximum number across optimizations.

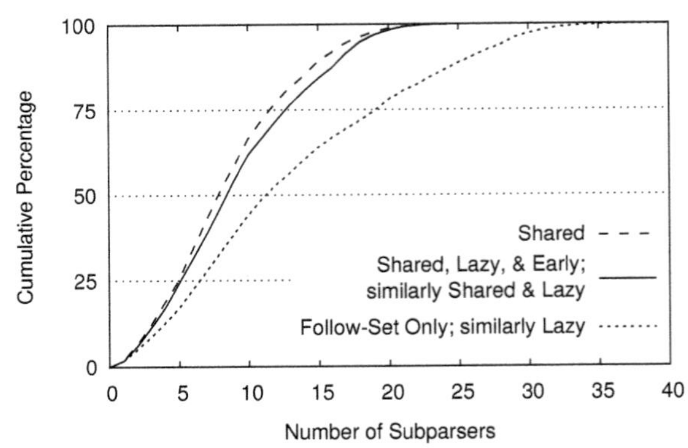

(b) The cumulative distribution across optimizations.

Figure 8. Subparser counts per main FMLR loop iteration.

6.3 Performance

Both SuperC and TypeChef run on the Java virtual machine, which enables a direct performance comparison. All of SuperC and TypeChef's preprocessor are written in Java, whereas TypeChef's parser is written in Scala. Running either tool on x86 Linux requires some preparation. (1) As discussed in Section 2, both tools need to be configured with gcc's built-in macros. SuperC automates this through its build system; TypeChef's distribution includes manually generated files for different compilers and versions. (2) Both tools require a list of C files identifying the kernel's compilation units. We reuse the list of 7,665 C files distributed with Type-

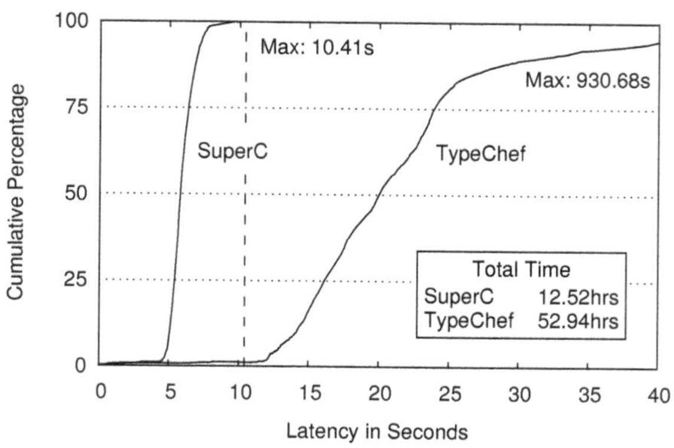

Figure 9. SuperC and TypeChef latency per compilation unit.

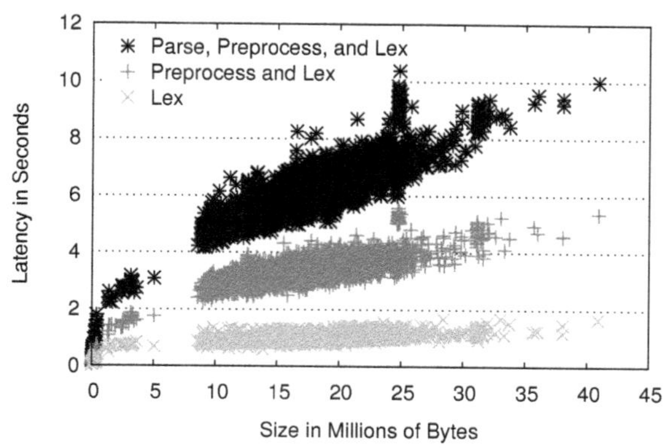

Figure 10. SuperC latency by compilation unit size.

Chef. Kästner et al. assembled it by analyzing Linux' configuration database [26]. (3) SuperC needs to be configured with four definitions of non-boolean macros. We discovered the four macros by comparing the result of running gcc's preprocessor, i.e., `gcc -E`, under the `allyesconfig` configuration on the 7,665 C files with the result of running it on the output of SuperC's configuration-preserving preprocessor for the same files. With those four definitions in place, the results are identical modulo whitespace. This comparison also provides us with high assurance that SuperC's preprocessor is correct. (SuperC's parser is less rigorously validated with hand-written regression tests.) (4) TypeChef needs to be configured with over 300 additional macro definitions. It also treats macros that are not explicitly marked as configuration variables, i.e., have the `CONFIG_` prefix, as undefined instead of free.

We refer to the experimental setup including only the first three steps as the *unconstrained* kernel and the setup including all four steps as the *constrained* kernel. As of 2/18/12, TypeChef runs only on the constrained kernel, and only on version 2.6.33.3. To ensure that results are comparable, the examples and experiments in this paper also draw on version 2.6.33.3 of Linux. At the same time, SuperC runs on both constrained and unconstrained kernels. In fact, the data presented in Table 3 for preprocessor usage and in Figure 8 for subparser counts was collected by running SuperC on the unconstrained kernel. By comparison, the constrained kernel has less variability: its 99th and 100th percentile subparser counts are 12 and 32, as opposed to 21 and 39 for the unconstrained kernel. SuperC also runs on other versions of Linux; we validated our tool on the latest stable version, 3.2.9.

Figure 9 shows the cumulative latency distribution across compilation units of the constrained kernel when running SuperC or TypeChef on an off-the-shelf PC. For each tool, it also identifies the maximum latency for a compilation unit and the total latency for the kernel. The latter number should be treated as a convenient summary, but no more: workload and tools easily parallelize across cores and machines. When considering the 50th and 80th percentiles, both tools perform reasonably well. While SuperC is between 3.4 to 3.8 times faster than TypeChef, both curves show a mostly linear increase, which is consistent with a normal distribution. However, the "knee" in TypeChef's curve at about 25 seconds and the subsequent long tail, reaching over 15 minutes, indicates a serious scalability bottleneck. The likely cause is the conversion of complex presence conditions into conjunctive normal form [25]; this representation is required by TypeChef's SAT solver, which TypeChef uses instead of BDDs.

Figure 10 plots a breakdown of SuperC latency. It demonstrates that SuperC's performance scales roughly linearly with compilation unit size. Lexing, preprocessing, and parsing each scale roughly linearly as well, with most of the total latency split between preprocessing and parsing. The spike at about 25 MB is due to fs/xfs/ containing code with a high density of macro invocations. To provide a performance baseline, we measured the cumulative latency distribution for gcc lexing, preprocessing, and parsing the 7,665 compilation units under `allyesconfig`. We rely on gcc's `-ftime-report` command line option for the timing data. The 50th, 90th, and 100th percentiles are 0.18, 0.24, and 0.87 seconds, i.e., a factor of 12 to 32 speedup compared to SuperC. It reflects that gcc does not have to preserve static conditionals and that gcc's C implementation has been carefully tuned for many years.

7. Related Work

Our work joins a good many attempts at solving the problem of parsing C with arbitrary preprocessor usage [1, 3–5, 15, 19, 25, 26, 29, 31, 33, 36, 41]. Out of these efforts, only MAPR [33] and TypeChef [25, 26] come close to solving the problem. Since we already provided a detailed comparison to MAPR and TypeChef in Sections 1, 2 and 6, we only discuss the other efforts here.

Previous, and incomplete, work on recognizing all of C can be classified into three categories. First are tools, such as Xrefactory [41], that process source code one configuration at a time, after full preprocessing. This approach is also taken by Apple's Xcode IDE [10]. However, due to the exponential explosion of the configuration space, this is only practical for small source files with little variability. Second are tools, such as CRefactory [19], that employ a fixed but incomplete algorithm. This approach is also taken by the Eclipse CDT IDE [21]. It is good enough—as long as source code does not contain idioms that break the algorithm, which is a big if for complex programs such as Linux. Third are tools, such as Yacfe [31], that provide a plug-in architecture for heuristically recognizing additional idioms. However, this approach creates an arms race between tool builders and program developers, who need to push both preprocessor and C itself to wring the last bit of flexibility and performance out of their code—as amply demonstrated by Ernst et al. [14], Tartler et al. [38], and this paper's Section 6.

Considering parsing more generally, our work is comparable to efforts that build on the basic parsing formalisms, i.e., LR [28], LL [34], and PEG [7, 16], and seek to improve expressiveness and/or performance. Notably, Elkhound [30] explores how to improve the performance of generalized LR (GLR) parsers by falling back on LALR for unambiguous productions. Both SDF2 [11, 40] and *Rats!* [22] explore how to make grammars modular by building on formalisms that are closed under composition, GLR and PEG, respectively. *Rats!* also explores how to speed up PEG implementations, which, by default, memoize intermediate results to support arbitrary back-tracking with linear performance. Finally,

ANTLR [32] explores how to provide most of the expressivity of GLR and PEG, but with better performance by supporting variable look-ahead for LL parsing.

At a finer level of detail, Fork-Merge LR parsing relies on a DAG of parser stacks, just like Elkhound, but for a substantially different reason. Elkhound forks its internal state to accept ambiguous *grammars*, while SuperC forks its internal state to accept ambiguous *inputs*. Next, like several other parser generators, SuperC relies on annotations in the grammar to control AST building. For instance, ANTLR, JavaCC/JJTree [23], *Rats!*, SableCC [18], and SDF2 provide comparable facilities. Finally, many parsers for C employ an ad-hoc technique for disambiguating typedef names from other names, termed the "lexer hack" by Roskind [35]. Instead, SuperC relies on a more general plug-in facility for context management. *Rats!* has a comparable facility, though details differ significantly due to the underlying parsing formalisms, i.e., LR for SuperC and PEG for *Rats!*.

8. Conclusion

This paper explores how to perform syntactic analysis of C code while preserving its variability, i.e., static conditionals. First, we identify all challenges posed by interactions between C preprocessor and language proper. Our anecdotal and empirical evidence from the x86 Linux kernel demonstrates that meeting these challenges is critical for processing real-world C programs. Second, we present novel algorithms for configuration-preserving preprocessing and parsing. Hoisting makes it possible to preprocess source code while preserving static conditionals. The token follow-set as well as early reduces, lazy shifts, and shared reduces make it possible to parse the result with very few LR subparsers and to generate a well-formed AST. Third, we discuss the pragmatics of building a real-world tool, SuperC, and demonstrate its effectiveness on Linux. For future work, we will extend SuperC with support for automated refactorings and explore configuration-preserving semantic analysis. We expect that the latter, much like our configuration-preserving syntactic analysis, will require incorporating presence conditions into all functionality, including by maintaining multiply-defined symbols. In summary, forty years after C's invention, we finally lay the foundation for efficiently processing *all of C*.

Acknowledgements

We thank Martin Hirzel, Christian Kästner, Julian Rosse, and the anonymous reviewers for their helpful feedback on earlier versions of this paper. We also thank Jinyang Li and Russell Power for letting us use their cluster for data collection. This work is supported by NSF CNS-0448349, CNS-0615129, and CCF-1017849.

References

[1] B. Adams et al. Can we refactor conditional compilation into aspects? In *Proc. 8th AOSD*, pp. 243–254, Mar. 2009.

[2] A. V. Aho et al. *Compilers: Principles, Techniques, and Tools*. Addison-Wesley, 2nd edition, Aug. 2006.

[3] R. L. Akers et al. Re-engineering C++ component models via automatic program transformation. In *Proc. 12th WCRE*, pp. 13–22, Nov. 2005.

[4] G. J. Badros and D. Notkin. A framework for preprocessor-aware C source code analyses. *SPE*, 30(8):907–924, July 2000.

[5] I. D. Baxter and M. Mehlich. Preprocessor conditional removal by simple partial evaluation. In *Proc. 8th WCRE*, pp. 281–290, Oct. 2001.

[6] A. Bessey et al. A few billion lines of code later: Using static analysis to find bugs in the real world. *CACM*, 53(2):66–75, Feb. 2010.

[7] A. Birman and J. D. Ullman. Parsing algorithms with backtrack. *Information and Control*, 23(1):1–34, Aug. 1973.

[8] A. M. Bishop. C cross referencing and documenting tool. `http://www.gedanken.demon.co.uk/cxref/`.

[9] B. Blanchet et al. A static analyzer for large safety-critical software. In *Proc. PLDI*, pp. 196–207, June 2003.

[10] R. Bowdidge. Performance trade-offs implementing refactoring support for Objective-C. In *Proc. 3rd WRT*, Oct. 2009.

[11] M. Bravenboer and E. Visser. Concrete syntax for objects. In *Proc. 19th OOPSLA*, pp. 365–383, Oct. 2004.

[12] R. E. Bryant. Graph-based algorithms for boolean function manipulation. *TOC*, C-35(8):677–691, Aug. 1986.

[13] F. DeRemer and T. Pennello. Efficient computation of LALR(1) look-ahead sets. *TOPLAS*, 4(4):615–649, Oct. 1982.

[14] M. D. Ernst et al. An empirical analysis of C preprocessor use. *TSE*, 28(12):1146–1170, Dec. 2002.

[15] J.-M. Favre. Understanding-in-the-large. In *Proc. 5th IWPC*, pp. 29–38, Mar. 1997.

[16] B. Ford. Parsing expression grammars: A recognition-based syntactic foundation. In *Proc. 31st POPL*, pp. 111–122, Jan. 2004.

[17] Free Software Foundation. Bison. `http://www.gnu.org/software/bison/`.

[18] É. Gagnon. SableCC, an object-oriented compiler framework. Master's thesis, McGill University, Mar. 1998.

[19] A. Garrido and R. Johnson. Analyzing multiple configurations of a C program. In *Proc. 21st ICSM*, pp. 379–388, Sept. 2005.

[20] A. G. Gleditsch and P. K. Gjermshus. The LXR project. `http://lxr.sourceforge.net/`.

[21] E. Graf et al. Refactoring support for the C++ development tooling. In *Companion 22nd OOPSLA*, pp. 781–782, Oct. 2007.

[22] R. Grimm. Better extensibility through modular syntax. In *Proc. PLDI*, pp. 38–51, June 2006.

[23] java.net. JJTree reference documentation. `http://javacc.java.net/doc/JJTree.html`.

[24] V. Kabanets and R. Impagliazzo. Derandomizing polynomial identity tests means proving circuit lower bounds. In *Proc. 35th STOC*, pp. 355–364, June 2003.

[25] C. Kästner et al. Partial preprocessing C code for variability analysis. In *Proc. 5th VaMoS*, pp. 127–136, Jan. 2011.

[26] C. Kästner et al. Variability-aware parsing in the presence of lexical macros and conditional compilation. In *Proc. 26th OOPSLA*, pp. 805–824, Oct. 2011.

[27] G. Klein et al. JFlex: The fast scanner generator for Java. `http://jflex.de/`.

[28] D. E. Knuth. On the translation of languages from left to right. *Information and Control*, 8(6):607–639, Dec. 1965.

[29] B. McCloskey and E. Brewer. ASTEC: A new approach to refactoring C. In *Proc. 10th ESEC*, pp. 21–30, Sept. 2005.

[30] S. McPeak and G. C. Necula. Elkhound: A fast, practical GLR parser generator. In *Proc. 13th CC*, vol. 2985 of *LNCS*, pp. 73–88, Mar. 2004.

[31] Y. Padioleau. Parsing C/C++ code without pre-processing. In *Proc. 18th CC*, vol. 5501 of *LNCS*, pp. 109–125, Mar. 2009.

[32] T. Parr and K. Fisher. LL(*): The foundation of the ANTLR parser generator. In *Proc. PLDI*, pp. 425–436, June 2011.

[33] M. Platoff et al. An integrated program representation and toolkit for the maintenance of C programs. In *Proc. ICSM*, pp. 129–137, Oct. 1991.

[34] D. J. Rosenkrantz and R. E. Stearns. Properties of deterministic top down grammars. In *Proc. 1st STOC*, pp. 165–180, May 1969.

[35] J. Roskind. Parsing C, the last word. The comp.compilers newgroup, Jan. 1992. `http://groups.google.com/group/comp.compilers/msg/c0797b5b668605b4`.

[36] D. Spinellis. Global analysis and transformations in preprocessed languages. *TSE*, 29(11):1019–1030, Nov. 2003.

[37] R. Tartler et al. Configuration coverage in the analysis of large-scale system software. *OSR*, 45(3):10–14, Dec. 2011.

[38] R. Tartler et al. Feature consistency in compile-time-configurable system software: Facing the Linux 10,000 feature problem. In *Proc. 6th EuroSys*, pp. 47–60, Apr. 2011.

[39] M. Tomita, ed. *Generalized LR Parsing*. Kluwer, 1991.

[40] E. Visser. *Syntax Definition for Language Prototyping*. PhD thesis, University of Amsterdam, Sept. 1997.

[41] M. Vittek. Refactoring browser with preprocessor. In *Proc. 7th CSMR*, pp. 101–110, Mar. 2003.

[42] J. Whaley. JavaBDD. `http://javabdd.sourceforge.net/`.

Test-Case Reduction for C Compiler Bugs

John Regehr
University of Utah
regehr@cs.utah.edu

Yang Chen
University of Utah
chenyang@cs.utah.edu

Pascal Cuoq
CEA LIST
pascal.cuoq@cea.fr

Eric Eide
University of Utah
eeide@cs.utah.edu

Chucky Ellison
University of Illinois
celliso2@illinois.edu

Xuejun Yang
University of Utah
jxyang@cs.utah.edu

Abstract

To report a compiler bug, one must often find a small test case that triggers the bug. The existing approach to automated test-case reduction, delta debugging, works by removing substrings of the original input; the result is a concatenation of substrings that delta cannot remove. We have found this approach less than ideal for reducing C programs because it typically yields test cases that are too large or even invalid (relying on undefined behavior). To obtain small and valid test cases consistently, we designed and implemented three new, domain-specific test-case reducers. The best of these is based on a novel framework in which a generic fixpoint computation invokes modular transformations that perform reduction operations. This reducer produces outputs that are, on average, more than 25 times smaller than those produced by our other reducers or by the existing reducer that is most commonly used by compiler developers. We conclude that effective program reduction requires more than straightforward delta debugging.

Categories and Subject Descriptors D.2.5 [*Software Engineering*]: Testing and Debugging—testing tools; D.3.2 [*Programming Languages*]: Language Classifications—C; D.3.4 [*Programming Languages*]: Processors—compilers

Keywords compiler testing, compiler defect, automated testing, random testing, bug reporting, test-case minimization

1. Introduction

Although many compiler bugs can be demonstrated by small test cases, bugs in released compilers are more typically discovered while building large projects. Before a bug can be reported, the circumstances leading to it must be narrowed down. The most important part of this process is *test-case reduction*: the construction of a small input that triggers the compiler bug.

PLDI'12, June 11–16, 2012, Beijing, China.

The importance of test-case reduction is emphasized in the GCC documentation,[1] which states that:

> Our bug reporting instructions ask for the preprocessed version of the file that triggers the bug. Often this file is very large; there are several reasons for making it as small as possible...

The instructions for submitting bug reports to the LLVM developers also highlight the importance of test-case reduction.[2] Indeed, LLVM ships with the Bugpoint tool[3] that automates reduction at the level of LLVM IR. The importance that compiler developers place on small test cases stems from the simple fact that manual test-case reduction is both difficult and time consuming. With limited time to spend fixing bugs, compiler writers require bug reporters to undertake the effort of reducing large fault-causing inputs to small ones.

Like debugging, distilling a bug-causing compiler input to its essence is often an exercise in trial and error. One must repeatedly experiment by removing or simplifying pieces of the input program, compiling and running the partially reduced program, and backtracking when a change to the input causes the compiler bug to no longer be triggered. In some cases—for example, reducing a deterministic assertion failure in the compiler—manual test-case reduction is tedious but tractable. In other cases—e.g., reducing a miscompilation bug in a large, multi-threaded application—manual test-case reduction may be so difficult as to be infeasible. Our belief is that many compiler bugs go unreported due to the high difficulty of isolating them. When confronted with a compiler bug, a reasonable compiler user might easily decide that the most economic course is to find a workaround, and not to be "sidetracked" by the significant time and effort required to produce a small test case and report the bug.

Our goal in this paper is to automate most or all of the work required to reduce bug-triggering test cases for C compilers. Our work is motivated by two problems that we have encountered in applying state-of-the-art reducers. First, these tools get stuck at local minima that are too large. This necessitates subsequent manual reduction, preventing reportable compiler bugs from being generated in an entirely automated fashion. We have developed new reducers that use domain-specific knowledge to overcome the barriers that trap previous tools. Second, existing test-case reducers often generate test cases that execute *undefined behaviors*. These test cases are useless because the C language standard guarantees

[1] `http://gcc.gnu.org/bugs/minimize.html`
`http://gcc.gnu.org/wiki/A_guide_to_testcase_reduction`

[2] `http://llvm.org/docs/HowToSubmitABug.html`

[3] `http://llvm.org/docs/Bugpoint.html`

```
int printf (const char *, ...);
union U5 {
  short f1;
  int f3:13;
};
const union U5 a = { 30155 };
int
main () {
  printf ("%d\n", a.f1);
  printf ("%d\n", a.f3);
  return 0;
}
```

Listing 1. Test case that demonstrates a bug in GCC 4.4.0

nothing about the behavior of such programs. For example, all C/C++ compiler teams we have interacted with will ignore (in the best case) any bug report that depends upon the value of an uninitialized local variable. Our new reducers confront this *test-case validity problem* directly: they avoid undefined test-case behaviors during reduction, thereby ensuring that the final reduced test cases are suitable for bug reporting.

Our work is also motivated by Csmith, a random test-case generator that has resulted in more than 400 previously unknown C compiler bugs being reported [17]. Using randomized differential testing, Csmith automates the construction of programs that trigger compiler bugs. These programs are large out of necessity: we found that bug-finding was most effective when random programs' average size was 81 KB [17, §3.3]. In this paper, we use 98 bug-inducing programs created by Csmith as the inputs to several automated program reducers, including three written by ourselves. Two of the new reducers are implemented as Csmith add-ons and can only reduce Csmith-generated programs. However, the most effective reducer (in terms of size of output) that we developed is generic: it can reduce any C program, whether generated by Csmith or not. In the great majority of cases, one or more of our reducers can distill the large (37–297 KB) test cases created by Csmith into small test cases (typically less than 0.5 KB) that preserve the bug-triggering features of the original inputs. Our reducers do this automatically and without introducing undefined behavior into the reduced test cases.

Our contributions are as follows:

1. We identify existing delta-debugging algorithms as point solutions in a more general framework. We present three new, domain-specific test-case reducers for C code that fit into this framework.
2. We identify the *test-case validity problem* as a crucial part of test-case reduction for compilers of programming languages that admit undefined and unspecified behaviors. This problem has not been acknowledged or solved in previous work. We present various solutions to the test-case validity problem.
3. We show that our best reducer produces output more than 25 times smaller than that produced by a line-based delta debugger, on average.

2. Reporting Compiler Bugs

An ideal compiler bug report is based on a small, easy-to-read, self-contained, and well-defined test program. This paper is about automatically constructing programs that meet these criteria. Other elements found in a good bug report include:

- the identification of the buggy compiler: its version, its target machine and OS, how it was built, and so on;
- instructions for reproducing the failure, including a description of how the compiler was invoked; and
- the expected and actual outputs of the compiled test program (assuming that the compiler does not fail to compile the test).

For example, the following report is informative enough that it would likely be acted upon by compiler developers:

> On x86-64, the program in Listing 1 should print:
> `30155`
> `-2613`
> However, using GCC 4.4.0 (built from scratch) and also GCC "Ubuntu 4.4.3-4ubuntu5" (the current vendor-supplied compiler on Ubuntu 10.04.3 LTS as of Nov 6 2011) on x86-64, we get:
> `$ gcc -O1 small.c`
> `$ ./a.out`
> `30155`
> `30155`

The program in Listing 1 is the verbatim output from one of our C program reducers. The underlying problem is an actual GCC bug that affects Ubuntu 10.04, a major and currently supported Linux distribution.

The program in Listing 1 is free from undefined and unspecified behaviors,[4,5] although it does involve implementation-defined behavior regarding the representations of data objects. Implementation-defined behaviors are allowed in test cases; indeed, in C, such basic things as the ranges of `int` and `char` are implementation-defined.

Although the example at hand may seem to involve the "technical minutiae" of C, it is important for compilers to get these details right. Large programs such as operating systems and virtual-machine monitors depend on subtle behaviors like those executed by Listing 1. Automated test-case reduction, when successful, allows one to obtain small test cases that cleanly present the essence of a problem.

3. Background

In this section we distinguish test-case minimization from test-case reduction. We also summarize delta debugging, an existing approach to test-case reduction.

3.1 The Test-Case Minimization Problem

Let I be the set of all valid inputs to some system under test (SUT). For $i \in I$, let $|i|$ be the size of i according to an appropriate metric such as bytes or tokens. Let $B \subseteq I$ be the set of inputs that trigger a particular failure of interest in the SUT, e.g., a crash at a particular location in the SUT. The *test-case minimization problem* for a SUT and a particular failure is to find i_{Bmin} where $i_{Bmin} \in B$ and $\forall i \in B, |i| \geq |i_{Bmin}|$. Note that i_{Bmin} may not be unique; there may be several minimum-sized inputs that result in the failure of interest. For the sake of clarity, however, we describe the search for i_{Bmin} as if it were unique.

[4] The C99 language standard [7] identifies many program behaviors that are *undefined* or *unspecified*. An example undefined behavior is dereferencing a null pointer. When a C program executes an undefined behavior, "anything can happen": the C standard places no requirements on the C implementation. Unspecified behaviors, on the other hand, permit the compiler to choose from a variety of alternatives with no requirement for consistency. An example unspecified behavior is the order in which the arguments of a function call are evaluated. Like C programs in general, good test cases for C compilers must not execute any undefined behaviors and must not depend on a particular choice for unspecified behaviors.

[5] Footnote 82 in the C99 language standard allows `a.f3` to be accessed by the second `printf()` call [7, §6.5.2.3]. This footnote, introduced in TC3, supersedes language in Annex J of the previous C99 standard which states that "the value of a union member other than the last one stored into" is unspecified. Subtle interactions between different parts of the standard—and even outright contradictions, as we see here—are not uncommon when interpreting tricky C programs.

Consider the task of finding i_{Bmin} given only an initial failing test case i_{seed}. Without knowledge of the internals of the SUT, the only information that i_{seed} provides is that it triggers the failure of interest and therefore defines a maximum value of $|i_{Bmin}|$. The reason that i_{seed} causes the failure of interest is unknown, and thus in principle, any input that is smaller than i_{seed} may also trigger the failure of interest. The only way to find i_{Bmin}, which is the absolute smallest failure-inducing input, is exhaustive search.

Let $I_{<S}$ be the set of inputs not larger than a size bound S. For realistic systems under test, one can expect that $|I_{<S}|$ is an exponential function of S. Finding i_{Bmin} requires testing increasingly large members of I until a failure-inducing input is found. Thus, it is easy to see that the test-case minimization problem is intractable unless $|i_{seed}|$ is quite small. Consequently, all test-case minimization work that we are aware of is heuristic.

An analogy can be made between test-case minimization and compiler optimization. In both situations, the problem is to find an element in a large set of programs that has a desired property while also minimizing a cost function. The major difference is that while optimization can be phrased as a relatively concise mathematical problem ("find the cheapest machine program that is semantically equivalent to the input program"), test-case minimization is conducted in the absence of an effective semantics: the minimizer lacks a model for predicting which inputs will trigger the failure of interest in the SUT. The exact program-optimization problem can be solved for small programs by encoding the meaning of the program mathematically and then passing the problem to a SAT/SMT solver [8]. In contrast, an analogous solution to the test-case minimization problem would require either a brute-force search of $I_{<|i_{seed}|}$ or else a mathematical encoding of the entire SUT.

Heuristic solutions to the test-case minimization problem start with a failure-inducing input i_{seed} and transform it. Through repeated transformation and testing, they search for ever-smaller inputs that cause the failure of interest in the SUT. We refer to this process as *test-case reduction* so as to distinguish it from absolute minimization. The goal of a reducer is to create a small test case from a large one; a reducer R_1 can be said to be better than a reducer R_2 if, over a given set of test cases, R_1 consistently produces smaller outputs than R_2 does. Our focus in this paper is on high-quality test-case reducers for C compilers, i.e., reducing C programs.

3.2 Delta Debugging

Although point solutions to the test-case reduction problem have existed for some time (see Section 8), a generic solution was not formulated until Zeller and Hildebrandt [18] developed two *delta debugging* algorithms. The *dd* algorithm seeks to minimize the difference between a failure-inducing test case and a given template; the *ddmin* algorithm is a special case of *dd* where the template is empty. Thus, *ddmin*'s goal is to minimize the size of a failure-inducing test case.

Ddmin heuristically removes contiguous regions ("chunks") of the test in order to generate a series of *variants*. *Unsuccessful variants* are those that do not trigger the sought-after behavior; all unsuccessful variants are discarded. *Successful variants*, on the other hand, are those that trigger the desired behavior. Each successful variant is used as the new basis for producing future variants; in other words, the search is greedy. When no successful variants can be generated from the current basis, the chunk size is decreased. The algorithm terminates when the chunk size cannot be further decreased and no more successful variants can be produced. The final result is the last successful variant that was produced; by the nature of the search, this is the smallest variant that produces the desired behavior. *Ddmin* can be fast even for large test cases when it is successful in removing large chunks early in its execution. If it cannot remove large input chunks, however, *ddmin* can take a long time to terminate—especially if it is expensive to discriminate between successful and unsuccessful variants.

Delta debugging was generalized to create *hierarchical delta debugging* (HDD) [13], in which chunk selection is guided by the hierarchical structure of the input. For several failure-inducing C and XSLT programs, HDD was shown to significantly reduce reduction time and also produce better results, when compared with *ddmin*.

McPeak and Wilkerson [12] implemented a variant of *ddmin*—which we refer to as "Berkeley delta" in this paper—that is both well-known and commonly used by compiler developers. Berkeley delta is generic and line-based: all variants are produced by removing one or more contiguous lines from the test input. With the help of a separate utility, called *topformflat*, Berkeley delta can be used to perform hierarchical delta debugging over program source code. The *topformflat* utility preprocesses an input test case and "flattens languages with balanced delimiters, such as most common programming languages, so that all nesting below a specified depth is on one line."[6] This is simple and effective.

4. Generalized Delta Debugging

Our observation is that algorithms such as *dd*, *ddmin*, and HDD are specific instantiations of a simple and powerful framework for reducing test cases. Most of the hard-coded aspects of these existing algorithms can be usefully generalized in order to more effectively reduce failure-inducing inputs, including the following.

Generalized transformations *ddmin* uses text-oriented chunk removal to create variants, and HDD uses an AST-oriented removal strategy. The former removes a substring with each search step, and the latter removes a subtree. However, our experience is that reducing a failure-triggering C program to a very small size requires a much richer set of transformations such as removing an argument from a function and simultaneously all its call sites, performing inline substitution of a function body, replacing an aggregate type with its constituent scalars, and so on. These transformations may operate on many scattered program points in one step, and they cannot be described as operations that simply delete a substring or subtree.

Generalized search *ddmin*'s and HDD's search strategies are greedy. This is simple and efficient but ignores a wealth of research on search that may avoid local minima by being non-greedy or improve search-termination speed by not looking at alternatives that are unlikely to be profitable. Additionally, transformations such as inlining the body of a function or splitting up a complex expression may increase code size (by adding references to temporary variables) while ultimately leading to better output. A greedy search rules out exploration of these variants, and thus tends to become stuck at a local minimum where no further substring or subtree eliminations are possible.

Addressing test-case validity *ddmin* and related algorithms ignore the *test-case validity problem*: the fact that in some use cases, some variants will be incorrect in ways that are not or cannot be detected by the system under test. This is the case when reducing C programs. For example, when a C compiler is given a program to compile, the compiler cannot in general decide if the program will dereference a null pointer or perform an out-of-bounds array access when the program is run. Both are undefined behaviors and must not happen in a valid compiler test case. Thus, for reducing compiler test cases, a delta-based reducer cannot rely on the compiler (the system under test) to detect when a variant is invalid. Sophisticated solutions are required to overcome this issue.

[6] `http://delta.tigris.org/using_delta.html`

Generalized fitness functions The goal of *ddmin*, HDD, and other delta debugging algorithms is to create a minimum-sized failure-inducing test. In general, however, any fitness function can be used to characterize preferable test cases. For example, since the eventual consumer for a reduced test case is a human being, it is undesirable to create tiny reduced programs if they are hard to understand. Consider these simple examples. First, almost any C program can be made smaller, but harder to read, by eliminating whitespace and playing preprocessor tricks. Second, our experience is that turning a union type into a struct can make a test case considerably easier to understand while also making it (at least) one byte larger.

In summary, *generalized delta debugging* refers to any iterative optimization strategy for simplifying the circumstances leading to program failure. A generalized delta debugger combines a search algorithm, a transformation operator, a validity-checking function, and a fitness function.

5. Test-Case Validity

Ensuring that variants are valid C programs was the most serious problem we faced doing this work. Beyond statically ill-formed C programs, *dynamically* invalid programs are those that execute an operation with undefined behavior or rely on unspecified behavior.

5.1 The Validity Problem

Consider this program:

```
int main (void) {
  int x;
  x = 2;
  return x + 1;
}
```

Assume that compiler A emits code that properly returns 3 while compiler B is buggy and generates code returning a different result. The goal of a test-case reducer is to create the smallest possible program triggering the bug in B. During reduction many variants will be produced, perhaps including this one where the line of code assigning a value to `x` has been removed:

```
int main (void) {
  int x;
  return x + 1;
}
```

This variant, however, is not a valid test case. Even if this variant exhibits the desired behavior—compilers A and B return different results—the divergence is potentially due to its reliance on undefined behavior: reading uninitialized storage. In fact, on a common Linux platform, GCC and Clang emit code returning different results for this variant, even when optimizations are disabled. Because delta debugging is an iterative optimization algorithm, once a test-case reduction goes wrong in this fashion, it is likely to remain stuck there, abandoning the original sense of the search. Compiler developers are typically most unhappy to receive a bug report whose test input relies on undefined or unspecified behavior. This is not a hypothetical problem—a web page for the Keil C compiler states that "Fewer than 1% of the bug reports we receive are actually bugs."[7]

In this specific case we might redefine the test-case criterion to be: "Compilers A and B generate code returning divergent results, and neither compiler warns about using an uninitialized variable." In this case, the solution would likely be successful. On the other hand, compiler warnings about uninitialized storage are typically unsound in the presence of function calls, arrays, and pointers. Furthermore, even after we solve this problem, the C99 standard describes 190 more kinds of undefined behavior that must be addressed to ensure that a test case is valid. As previously noted, not all of these behaviors are statically detectable by a compiler. Beyond undefined behavior, there are also many kinds of unspecified behavior that cause similar problems.

In reducing C programs, we have found the most problematic behaviors to be:

- use before initialization of function-scoped storage;
- pointer and array errors;
- integer overflow and shift past bitwidth;
- struct and union errors; and
- mismatches between `printf`'s arguments and format string.

Many languages including C, C++, C# (in unsafe code), and Scheme have some form of non-determinism or unspecified behavior, meaning the test-case validity problem is generally applicable in other languages. (There is current work toward cataloging problematic undefined and unspecified behaviors for many languages [14].) Providing a solution to the test-case validity problem for C, with its hundreds of undefined and unspecified behaviors, suggests that this can be done for other languages as well.

5.2 Solutions

There are two ways to avoid accepting variants that rely on undefined and unspecified behavior. First, the test-case reducer can avoid generating incorrect variants. We do not know how to implement such a reducer for general C programs. However, we have created two reducers that rely on the fact that Csmith already knows how to create conforming C programs [17]. Through extensions to Csmith, we can use Csmith to generate smaller versions of programs it has previously output. The second approach is to blindly generate a mix of valid and invalid variants and then use an external tool to detect invalid code. Sound, automatic static analyzers for C code have been available for some time, but we know of none that can give a large random program a "clean bill of health." To reliably avoid false positives, a semantics-checking C interpreter is needed. Two of these have recently become available.

5.2.1 KCC

KCC [6] is a semantics-based interpreter and analysis tool for C. In addition to interpretation, it is capable of debugging, catching undefined behaviors, state space search, and model checking. All of these modes are mechanically generated from a single formal semantics for C. KCC can catch many undefined behaviors by virtue of the semantics "getting stuck" when a program is not well defined. While KCC does not detect all undefined behavior, it is capable of catching the behaviors listed in Section 5.1.

No major changes were needed in KCC to make it useful in test-case reduction. However, we added English-language error messages for most of the common undefined behaviors, which made it easier to understand exactly how variants go wrong. Additionally, we added detectors for some previously-uncaught undefined behaviors to the tool because those behaviors were found in variants. Any errors reported by KCC are guaranteed to be real errors in the program, under the assumption that the underlying semantics accurately captures C.

5.2.2 Frama-C

Frama-C [5] is an open-source, extensible, static-analysis framework for C. It features a value-analysis plug-in [2]: an abstract interpreter roughly comparable to Polyspace [10] and Astrée [1]. The value analysis uses non-relational domains adapted to the C language; it soundly detects and warns about a sizable set of C's undefined

[7] `http://www.keil.com/support/bugreport.asp`

and unspecified behaviors. At the same time, it is designed to avoid warning about constructs that are technically undefined, but that programmers use intentionally, for example in embedded code. Conflicts between these objectives are resolved according to the following principle: if a compiler implementer would use the undefinedness of a construct as a reason to not fix a compiler bug, then the value analysis warns about the construct.

We were able to leverage the fact that programs generated by Csmith are *closed*—they take no external inputs—in order to avoid pessimism in Frama-C. By indefinitely deferring joins in the value analysis, Frama-C can effectively be as precise as a C interpreter, propagating a singleton abstract state all the way to the end of the program. This greatly increased precision comes at a cost of extended analysis time and memory consumption. We added an efficient interpreter mode to the value analysis, so as to diagnose terminating closed programs without the usual memory and time overhead caused by indefinitely postponed joins. Additionally, we fixed [4] several Frama-C bugs that interfered with the correct interpretation of Csmith-generated programs.

5.2.3 A Hybrid Solution

KCC and Frama-C are capable of detecting subtle dynamic violations of the C standard. They both assume their inputs to be compilable C programs; however, some of the delta debugging algorithms that we used to reduce C programs (e.g., Berkeley delta) produce variants are not even syntactically valid. Therefore, in practice we employ a hybrid solution for detecting invalid code. First, we compile a variant using any convenient C compiler, rapidly rejecting it if it fails to compile or generates warnings that reliably correspond to misbehavior. Second, we optionally examine the variant using Valgrind and/or the Clang static analyzer, again looking for specific warnings or errors that reliably indicate incorrect code. Finally, surviving variants are tested using KCC and/or Frama-C.

5.2.4 Validity for Compiler-Crash Inputs

Test cases for compiler-crash bugs—where the compiler process returns a non-zero status code to the operating system—may have weaker validity requirements than do the test cases for wrong-code bugs. As a matter of implementation quality, a compiler vendor will usually fix a segmentation fault or similar problem even if the crash-inducing test case, for example, uses a variable without initialization. Relaxing the correctness criterion permits crash-inducing inputs to be smaller and to be produced more rapidly. We take advantage of these facts when reducing C programs that cause compiler-crash bugs.

6. New Approaches to Test-Case Reduction

We implemented three new reducers for C programs. Two of them only work for programs generated by Csmith, while the third is general-purpose and would work in the reduction of any C program. (In fact, it can also be used to reduce C++ programs, though it has not yet been tuned for that purpose.)

All three of our reducers adopt Berkeley delta's convention of being parameterized by a test that determines whether a variant is successful or unsuccessful. The test determines if the variant triggers the compiler bug and also, if necessary, determines whether it is statically and dynamically valid C code.

6.1 Reduction in Csmith by Altering the Random Number Sequence

A program generated by Csmith is completely determined by a sequence of integers that describes a path through Csmith's decision tree. Usually this sequence comes from a pseudo-random number generator (PRNG), but it does not need to. Our *Seq-Reduce* test-case reducer bypasses the PRNG in order to generate variants. The result is guaranteed to be a valid C program, so no external validity-checking tool is required.

Seq-Reduce's implementation is split between a driver and two special-purpose Csmith modes. Together, these components act as a generalized delta-debugging loop in which Csmith produces variants and the driver determines whether they are successful or not.

First, the driver launches Csmith with a command telling it to dump the specification of the failure-inducing input to a file. Next, the driver repeatedly invokes Csmith using a command that tells it to load the saved sequence, modify it randomly, and then dump both the new program and its specification. If the new program constitutes a successful variant (i.e., it triggers the compiler failure and it is smaller than the previous smallest variant), this becomes the new program specification. Otherwise, Seq-Reduce rolls back to the previous successful variant. Seq-Reduce is the only randomized test-case reducer that we are aware of.

Seq-Reduce has several advantages. First, it has low implementation complexity, adding about 750 lines of code to Csmith; only 30 of these are at all entangled with Csmith's main logic. The driver is 300 lines of Perl. Second, Seq-Reduce is embarrassingly parallel. For example, for the experiments in Section 7, we ran it on four cores.

The main problem with Seq-Reduce is that it does not do a good job reducing programs in cases where the problematic code is generated late in Csmith's execution. Changes that appear near the start of a Csmith program specification tend to perturb Csmith's internal state in ways that prevent it from emitting desirable variants later on. Additionally, Seq-Reduce has no obvious termination criterion. In practice we use a timeout to terminate Seq-Reduce.

6.2 AST-Based Reduction in Csmith Using Run-Time Information

Our next reducer, *Fast-Reduce*, is also based on Csmith. It explores the idea that test-case reduction can benefit from run-time information. As suggested by its name, Fast-Reduce is intended to give fairly good results in as little time as possible. It is structured as an add-on to Csmith that can query not only the static structure of the generated program, but also its runtime behavior. Dynamic queries are implemented by instrumenting Csmith's generated code, resulting in machine-readable output when the test case is executed. Fast-Reduce supports a number of transformations; we describe three representative ones.

Dead-code elimination Programs generated by Csmith tend to contain a lot of dead code. In many cases, dead code can be removed without "breaking" a test case; Fast-Reduce attempts to do so early in its execution because this tends to give good results quickly. First, Fast-Reduce issues a static query to find which basic blocks are (conservatively) reachable from `main`. Next, it issues a dynamic query to discover which reachable blocks are actually executed. If removing dead code all at once results in an unsuccessful variant, Fast-Reduce rolls back the change and attempts to remove dead code piecewise.

Exploiting path divergence Some wrong-code bugs affect control flow: the miscompiled executable follows a different execution path than does a correctly compiled executable. Fast-Reduce uses differential testing to actively look for this kind of divergence while reducing programs because it provides a strong clue about the location of the critical piece of code in the test case that triggers miscompilation.

Effect inlining Removing the body of a large function is one of the biggest wins available to a C program reducer. Fast-Reduce can attempt to remove a function even when call sites to the function exist; its strategy is to render the function unnecessary by replacing each call with inline code that has the same dynamic effect as the

```
current = original_test_case
while (!fixpoint) {
    foreach t in transformations {
        state = t::new ()
        while (true) {
            variant = current
            result = t::transform (variant, state)
            if (result == stop)
                break
            /* variant has behavior of interest
               and meets validity criterion? */
            if (is_successful (variant))
                current = variant
            else
                state = t::advance (current, state)
        }
    }
}
```

Listing 2. The C-Reduce algorithm

function call. First, Fast-Reduce issues a static query to find all call sites for the target function. Second, it selects a call site and issues a dynamic query to record the values of global variables before and after each execution of that site. (This includes the values of pointer-typed variables.) If the call site is executed multiple times, an arbitrary final effect is selected. Fast-Reduce then replaces the call with its effect, generating a variant. This variant, and others generated by performing the same transformation at other call sites and other target functions, are all tested. When the body of a function finally becomes unreferenced, Fast-Reduce attempts to remove it.

The advantages of Fast-Reduce are that it requires no external validity-checking tool and it is very fast. Its primary disadvantage is that it does not always provide good results; sometimes it gets stuck quite early. Out of the 3,000 lines of C++ comprising Fast-Reduce, about 300 are significantly entangled with Csmith. Fast-Reduce also includes a driver component that orchestrates the reduction; it is about 1,700 lines of Perl.

6.3 A Modular Reducer

Our third new reducer, *C-Reduce*, exploits the insight that the transformations used to construct variants do not need to be hard-coded. C-Reduce invokes a collection of pluggable transformations until a global fixpoint is reached; pseudocode for C-Reduce is shown in Listing 2.

A transformation that plugs into C-Reduce is simply an iterator that walks through a test case performing source-to-source alterations. A transformation must implement three functions. The first, `new`, takes no parameters and returns a fresh transformation state object. The second, `transform`, takes a state object and a path to a test case; it modifies the test case in place and returns a status code that is either:

- `ok`, indicating that a transformation was performed; or
- `stop`, indicating that the transformation has run out of opportunities for the test case at hand.

The third, `advance`, takes a state object and a path to a test case; it advances the iterator to the next transformation opportunity.

As shown in Listing 2, C-Reduce calls `advance` only upon detecting an unsuccessful variant. A successful variant does not require advancing the iterator because it is assumed that an opportunity for transformation has been eliminated from the transformed test case. This means that for C-Reduce to terminate, it must be the case that (for any initial test case, and for a fresh transformation state) each transformation eventually returns `stop` under non-deterministic choice between (1) calling `advance` and leaving the current test case unchanged, and (2) not calling `advance` but changing the current test case to be the output of the transformation. Meeting this requirement has been natural for each of the 50+ transformations we have implemented so far. The order in which a transformation iterates through a test case is not specified by C-Reduce; in practice, each transformation uses a convenient ordering such as preorder for tree-based passes and line-order for line-based passes.

At present, C-Reduce calls five kinds of transformations. The first includes "peephole optimizations" that operate on a contiguous segment of the tokens within a test case. These include changing identifiers and integer constants to `0` or `1`, removing type qualifiers, removing a balanced pair of curly braces and all interior text, and removing an operator and one of its operands (e.g., changing `a+b` into `a` or `b`).

The second kind of transformation includes those that make localized but non-contiguous changes. Examples include removing balanced parentheses and curly braces without altering the text inside them, and replacing a ternary operator (C's `?:` construct) with the code from one of its branches.

The third is a C-Reduce module that closely follows Berkeley delta: it removes one or more contiguous lines of text from a test case. The number of lines to remove is initially the number of lines in the test case, and is successively halved until it reaches one line, at which point the test case is reformatted using *topformflat*. This transformation is 74 lines of Perl whereas Berkeley delta is 383 lines, showing that implementing a transformation is considerably easier than implementing an entire delta debugging loop.

Fourth, C-Reduce invokes external pretty-printing commands such as GNU indent. It is important that this kind of tool is called within the delta debugging loop, as opposed to being part of a pre- or post-processing step, because it is not unheard of for simple reformatting to turn a failure-inducing test case into one that does not trigger a compiler bug.

The final class of transformation was motivated by our observation that to create reduced failure-inducing C programs nearly as small as those produced by skilled humans, a collection of compiler-like transformations is needed. C-Reduce currently has 30 source-to-source transformations for C code including:

- performing scalar replacement of aggregates;
- removing a level of indirection from a pointer- or array-typed variable;
- factoring a function call out of a complex expression;
- combining multiple, same-typed variable definitions into a single compound definition;
- moving a function-scoped variable to global scope;
- removing a parameter from a function and all of its call sites, while adding a variable of the same name and type at function scope;
- removing an unused function or variable;
- giving a function, variable, or parameter a new, shorter name;
- changing a function to return void, and deleting all `return` statements in it;
- performing inline substitution of small function bodies;
- performing copy propagation; and
- turning unions into structs.

We implemented these using LLVM's Clang front end.

We have implemented only one performance optimization in C-Reduce: memoization of the (sometimes quite expensive) test for discriminating between successful and unsuccessful variants. Redundant tests occur when two or more peephole transformations produce the same output, and they also occur during the final iteration of the fixpoint computation—which, by necessity, performs some redundant tests. Several additional opportunities for speed-up exist, and we intend to implement speed improvements in future work. As shown by the results in Section 7, however, automated test-case reduction with C-Reduce already runs fast enough to be useful as part of an automated bug-reporting process.

7. Results

This section compares our reducers against each other and against Berkeley delta.

7.1 Toward a Corpus of C Programs Triggering Diverse Compiler Bugs

To thoroughly evaluate test-case reducers for C compiler bugs, one needs a number of test inputs that trigger compiler-crash bugs and wrong-code bugs. Moreover, these test cases should map to a diverse collection of underlying defects. We have observed that some compiler bugs (e.g., a crash while parsing a top-level pragma) lend themselves to easy reduction, whereas others (e.g., a wrong-code bug in an interprocedural transformation) are more difficult.

We assembled our test corpus by manufacturing a large number of bug-triggering programs and then selecting a subset that appear to map to diverse underlying bugs. To find bug-triggering programs, we ran Csmith for a few days on a collection of compilers that target x86-64 on Linux. The compilers we used were: LLVM/Clang 2.6–2.9, GCC 3.[2–4].0, GCC 4.[0–6].0, Intel CC 12.0.5, Open64 4.2.4, and Sun CC 5.11. From the set of bug-triggering inputs created by Csmith, we selected the members of our bug-triggering corpus by hand. For crash bugs we chose only one test case for each distinct "symptom"—a specific assertion violation or similar that a compiler prints while crashing. No obvious heuristic exists for figuring out which test cases triggering wrong-code bugs map to which underlying bugs, so we simply gathered no more than five wrong-code triggers for each compiler that we tested. In the end, we selected 98 test cases: 57 inputs that each trigger a different compiler crash, and 41 inputs that trigger incorrect code generation.

7.2 Evaluating Reducers

We ran Berkeley delta and our new reducers on our corpus of bug-triggering test inputs, using a machine with 16 GB of RAM, based on an Intel Core i7-2600 processor, running Ubuntu Linux 11.10 in 64-bit mode. For these experiments we disabled Linux's address space layout randomization (ASLR) feature, which is intended to thwart certain kinds of malware. ASLR has the side effect of causing some compiler bugs to occur non-deterministically. All test-case reducers that we are aware of (including our new ones) operate under the assumption that buggy executions can be detected deterministically.

The inputs to each reducer—Berkeley delta, Seq-Reduce, Fast-Reduce, and C-Reduce—are the test case that is to be reduced and a shell script that determines whether a variant is successful. Berkeley delta additionally requires a "level" parameter that specifies how much syntax-driven flattening of its input to perform. The web page for this tool suggests running the main delta script twice at level zero, twice at level one, twice at level two, and finally twice at level ten. That is what we did.

Tables 1 and 2 summarize the results of our reducer experiments. For each test case we measured:

- The size of the original test case, as emitted by Csmith.
- The size of the test case after being reduced by Berkeley delta, and the time taken by reduction. For wrong-code bugs, we evaluated Berkeley delta using both KCC and Frama-C as checkers for undefined behavior.

```
int printf (const char *, ...);
struct {
  int f0;
  int f1;
  int f2;
}
a, b = {
  0, 0, 1
};
void
fn1 () {
  a = b;
  a = a;
}
int
main () {
  fn1 ();
  printf ("%d\n", a.f2);
  return 0;
}
```

Listing 3. The median-sized reduced test case output by C-Reduce with Frama-C for wrong-code bugs. GCC 4.3.0 for x86-64 produces incorrect code with –Os. This is W22 in Table 1.

- The size of the test case after being reduced by Seq-Reduce with a 20-minute timeout, and the time taken by reduction. (It occasionally runs for longer than its nominal timeout when Csmith is slow.) Because Seq-Reduce is embarrassingly parallel, we ran four independent instances of it on our four-way test machine, and upon termination chose the best result.
- The size of the test case after being reduced by Fast-Reduce, and the time taken by reduction.
- The size of the test case after being reduced by C-Reduce and the time taken by reduction. For wrong-code bugs, again we used both KCC and Frama-C as checkers for undefined behavior.

Our choice of metrics—the size of the final output and the time taken to get it—is influenced by our belief that these are the primary metrics that people reporting compiler bugs care about. Because our results contain some significant outliers, we report both mean and median values at the bottom of each table.

7.3 Analysis of Wrong-Code Bug Results

As Table 1 shows, reducing a test case triggering a wrong-code bug is often fast, but in a few cases takes many hours.

Berkeley delta This tool generally fails to generate test cases that we would include in a compiler bug report as-is. The median run time of Berkeley delta when combined with Frama-C is four minutes; with KCC, the median is a little less than an hour.

Seq-Reduce On average, Seq-Reduce creates reduced output about twice as large as Berkeley delta's; more reduction would need to be performed before including these test cases in a compiler bug report. The primary value of Seq-Reduce lies in its simplicity. Also, it serves as a proof of concept for a generalized delta debugger based on randomized search.

Fast-Reduce Fast-Reduce is by far the fastest reducer. However, its final output is often too large to be included in compiler bug reports—its median output size is almost 3 KB—so further reduction must be performed by hand or by a different automated reducer.

C-Reduce C-Reduce is the only reducer we tested that consistently produces results that we would directly copy into a bug report. Listing 3 shows the median-sized reduced test case out of the 41 reduced wrong-code outputs produced by C-Reduce (for C-Reduce paired with Frama-C). It reasonably approximates the "typical"

ID	Compiler	Flags	Original Size	Berkeley delta with Frama-C Size	Berkeley delta with Frama-C Time	Berkeley delta with KCC Size	Berkeley delta with KCC Time	Seq-Reduce Size	Seq-Reduce Time	Fast-Reduce Size	Fast-Reduce Time	C-Reduce with Frama-C Size	C-Reduce with Frama-C Time	C-Reduce with KCC Size	C-Reduce with KCC Time
W1	Clang 2.7	–O2	58,753	10,745	3	10,745	40	16,556	20	49,810	0	295	6	295	64
W2	GCC 3.2.0	–O3	54,301	15,153	4	15,153	30	15,717	20	50,200	1	179	5	179	42
W3	GCC 3.2.0	–O3	62,095	6,624	4	6,624	57	13,860	20	1,230	0	214	6	214	62
W4	GCC 3.3.0	–O3	54,301	15,153	4	15,153	31	22,410	20	50,200	0	176	5	176	39
W5	GCC 3.3.0	–O3	60,010	1,379	1	1,902	54	12,948	20	55,908	0	248	5	248	41
W6	GCC 3.3.0	–O3	89,036	2,414	2	2,399	47	9,992	20	85,944	0	248	5	248	46
W7	GCC 3.4.0	–O3	39,489	9,647	2	9,647	23	4,632	20	30,525	0	184	5	184	44
W8	GCC 4.0.0	–O3	42,516	1,995	5	2,550	91	13,953	20	2,247	1	134	11	134	67
W9	GCC 4.1.0	–O1	57,079	1,775	1	1,775	27	41,209	20	586	0	178	6	178	28
W10	GCC 4.1.0	–O1	81,067	5,789	4	4,044	113	47,841	20	5,299	0	242	9	242	215
W11	GCC 4.1.0	–O3	50,081	6,559	3	6,498	44	5,730	20	47,057	0	873	11	745	69
W12	GCC 4.1.0	–O3	57,028	11,658	3	11,658	32	5,911	20	2,124	0	202	27	202	209
W13	GCC 4.1.0	–O3	61,119	10,570	7	10,570	114	20,010	20	12,321	1	221	13	221	132
W14	GCC 4.2.0	–O0	44,078	5,208	2	5,208	21	5,615	20	2,407	0	176	5	176	32
W15	GCC 4.2.0	–O0	53,922	12,418	4	12,418	33	9,636	20	3,661	3	868	22	868	81
W16	GCC 4.2.0	–O0	56,842	15,772	7	13,585	144	7,001	20	52,377	0	971	18	971	343
W17	GCC 4.2.0	–O1	41,262	8,312	3	8,312	75	5,980	20	36,647	0	205	11	205	153
W18	GCC 4.3.0	–O0	45,298	7,816	4	7,816	63	10,652	20	6,094	0	196	7	196	79
W19	GCC 4.3.0	–O0	55,727	5,975	4	5,975	190	17,089	20	903	0	182	9	182	119
W20	GCC 4.3.0	–O2	64,349	10,233	9	10,233	88	30,228	20	2,990	0	205	10	205	72
W21	GCC 4.3.0	–O2	67,227	10,396	6	10,360	209	11,097	20	1,670	0	172	6	172	134
W22	GCC 4.3.0	–Os	96,273	10,689	7	10,814	119	37,327	20	1,961	0	192	12	199	663
W23	GCC 4.4.0	–O0	43,030	859	1	859	14	1,216	20	384	0	179	1	179	11
W24	GCC 4.4.0	–O0	52,278	1,144	1	753	130	1,103	20	393	0	182	1	182	73
W25	GCC 4.4.0	–O0	65,597	1,108	1	1,108	46	1,119	20	397	0	179	1	179	14
W26	GCC 4.4.0	–O2	40,147	4,120	2	4,120	13	6,805	20	36,060	0	755	5	755	30
W27	GCC 4.4.0	–Os	86,103	3,537	2	3,537	60	7,257	20	801	0	245	4	245	53
W28	Intel CC 12.0.5	–O2	42,510	13,983	6	13,983	260	18,181	20	33,530	1	187	81	317	2,312
W29	Intel CC 12.0.5	–Os	38,232	9,756	5	9,756	55	22,635	20	3,007	0	162	12	173	59
W30	Intel CC 12.0.5	–fast	48,803	2,967	4	2,967	28	9,242	20	2,317	0	185	7	196	31
W31	Intel CC 12.0.5	–fast	81,103	6,881	8	6,881	252	56,247	20	7,353	1	119	10	130	268
W32	Open64 4.2.4	–O2	43,176	1,428	2	1,428	28	1,259	20	376	0	218	4	218	28
W33	Open64 4.2.4	–O2	43,384	6,874	3	6,874	82	5,997	20	4,802	0	207	8	207	108
W34	Open64 4.2.4	–O2	65,732	3,976	4	3,948	77	12,189	20	316	0	216	5	216	91
W35	Open64 4.2.4	–O2	79,971	2,512	5	2,687	118	11,165	20	427	0	218	6	218	127
W36	Open64 4.2.4	–O3	96,008	30,239	11	29,956	279	17,091	20	31,320	11	160	102	160	1,129
W37	Sun CC 5.11	–xO2	41,597	1,023	1	1,023	5	1,173	20	241	0	148	4	148	11
W38	Sun CC 5.11	–xO2	43,176	6,391	3	6,391	54	6,109	20	1,767	0	144	8	144	86
W39	Sun CC 5.11	–xO2	43,384	7,090	3	7,090	77	5,744	20	2,046	0	145	7	145	113
W40	Sun CC 5.11	–xO2	69,657	6,025	4	6,025	108	28,710	20	6,340	1	204	13	204	143
W41	Sun CC 5.11	–xO2	70,793	1,322	1	1,322	18	14,302	20	248	0	145	3	145	21
		Mean	58,208	7,256	4	7,174	82	14,462	20	15,470	1	258	12	259	182
		Median	55,727	6,559	4	6,498	57	11,097	20	2,990	0	192	7	199	72

Table 1. Compiler bugs used in the "wrong code" part of our evaluation. Program sizes are in bytes, and reduction times are in minutes.

C-Reduce output that might be reported to a compiler developer. The original test case emitted by Csmith was 94 KB—clearly much too large to be included in any reasonable bug report. C-Reduce's median run time when combined with Frama-C is seven minutes; with KCC it is 72 minutes.

In some cases, Berkeley delta or C-Reduce when combined with KCC produces different final output than the same tool combined with Frama-C. This happens when KCC and Frama-C disagree about the definedness of one or more variants. Often, the disagreement is due to a tool timing out; we killed either tool whenever it took more than three seconds longer to analyze a variant than it took to analyze the original, unreduced version of the program being reduced. However, there are also real differences between the sets of programs that these tools consider to be well-defined. We investigated these issues and found three classes of root causes. First, differential testing of KCC and Frama-C revealed a small number of bugs in the tools. (These bugs did not affect the numbers that we report, because we fixed them before running our experiments.) Second, C is a language with many extensions and dialects, and sometimes these tools' differing goals caused them to differently accept non-standard inputs. For example, Frama-C aims for pragmatic compatibility with existing C code, and so it accepts GCC's extended ternary operator which permits the second operand to be omitted: e.g., `x?:y`. On the other hand, KCC aims for strict standards compliance and rejects this construct. The third class of differences we found results from genuine corner cases in the standard; we were not always able to resolve these issues even after talking to experts. For example, the C99 standard is not entirely clear about the definedness of the expression `(s.f1=0) + (s.f2=0)` when `f1` and `f2` are bitfields that may occupy the same byte of storage.

7.4 Analysis of Compiler-Crash Bug Results

The general relationships between the reducers for wrong-code bugs (Table 1) also hold for compiler-crash bugs (Table 2). In terms of size of final output, Seq-Reduce and Fast-Reduce are worst, Berkeley delta is better, and C-Reduce is best.

Relative to the reducers' performance on test cases that trigger wrong-code bugs, test-case reduction for compiler-crash bugs is faster (C-Reduce, for example, always finished in less than 20 minutes) and the reduced test cases are generally smaller. The speed-up is partly due to not having to run the expensive validity checkers for undefined behavior (Section 5.2.4). Also, when the requirement to have a complete test case (including `main`) is relaxed, test cases can be made smaller, reducing the size of the search space.

For our corpus of test cases that trigger compiler-crash bugs, Listing 4 shows the median-sized reduced test case output by C-Reduce. The reduced test case is reportable as-is, whereas the corresponding original test case (C28) was 72 KB.

ID	Compiler	Flags	Original Size	Berkeley delta Size	Berkeley delta Time	Seq-Reduce Size	Seq-Reduce Time	Fast-Reduce Size	Fast-Reduce Time	C-Reduce Size	C-Reduce Time	Crash String
C1	Clang 2.6	–O0	102,012	696	0	1,320	20	98,543	0	101	1	Assertion 'RD->hasFlexibleArrayMember() && "Must have flexible arra...
C2	Clang 2.6	–O2	130,931	8,334	7	40,062	20	123,293	0	103	4	Assertion 'isa<X>(Val) && "cast<Ty>() argument of incompatible type...
C3	Clang 2.6	–O2	211,187	14,168	3	166,729	20	213,718	0	123	3	Assertion 'S < E && "Cannot create empty or backwards range"' failed.
C4	Clang 2.6	–O3	303,869	14,460	23	67,678	20	307,931	10	314	18	Assertion 'ConstantVal == V && "Marking constant with different val...
C5	Clang 2.6	–O2	41,049	41,189	0	11,548	20	35,505	0	810	3	Assertion 'getTypeSizeInBits(Op->getType()) > getTypeSizeInBits(Ty)...
C6	Clang 2.6	–O0	43,267	725	0	1,792	20	34,669	0	142	0	Assertion 'width > BitWidth && "Invalid APInt ZeroExtend request"' ...
C7	Clang 2.6	–O1	43,396	3,465	1	20,091	20	33,675	0	178	1	Assertion '(isa<PHINode>(GlobalUser) || isa<SelectInst>(GlobalUser)...
C8	Clang 2.6	–O1	65,657	954	0	1,565	20	62,804	0	104	1	Assertion 'NextFieldOffsetInBytes <= FieldOffsetInBytes && "Field o...
C9	Clang 2.6	–O2	76,960	14,397	3	52,627	20	70,416	0	261	6	Assertion 'SortedPos == AllNodes.end() && "Topological sort incompl...
C10	Clang 2.6	–O1	84,345	11,152	4	20,741	20	74,056	0	301	3	Assertion 'N->getOpcode() != ISD::DELETED_NODE && RV.getNode()->get...
C11	Clang 2.7	–O1	43,396	3,465	1	17,410	20	33,675	0	178	1	Assertion '(isa<PHINode>(GlobalUser) || isa<SelectInst>(GlobalUser)...
C12	Clang 2.7	–O0	55,234	5,479	0	14,129	20	46,145	0	65	1	Assertion 'unsignedRange.NonNegative && "unsigned range includes ne...
C13	Clang 2.7	–O2	82,690	12,682	3	38,030	20	73,032	0	119	4	Assertion '(!From->hasAnyUseOfValue(i) || From->getValueType(i) == ...
C14	GCC 3.2.0	–O1	105,197	8,942	3	13,382	20	9,757	1	101	2	Internal compiler error in fixup_var_refs_1, at function.c:1964
C15	GCC 3.2.0	–O3	118,289	11,063	2	16,622	20	11,036	0	339	4	unable to find a register to spill in class 'DREG'
C16	GCC 3.2.0	–O3	141,198	17,409	3	19,211	20	26,818	11	146	4	unable to find a register to spill in class 'AREG'
C17	GCC 3.2.0	–O2	44,047	7,371	1	6,779	20	6,584	0	97	1	Internal compiler error in extract_insn, at recog.c:2148
C18	GCC 3.2.0	–O1	53,948	5,828	1	6,629	20	2,501	0	55	1	Internal compiler error in do_SUBST, at combine.c:439
C19	GCC 3.2.0	–O3	60,878	10,539	2	11,953	20	58,479	0	177	2	Internal compiler error in print_reg, at config/i386/i386.c:5640
C20	GCC 3.3.0	–O3	66,580	7,930	1	26,282	20	6,659	1	233	3	internal compiler error: in print_reg, at config/i386/i386.c:6558
C21	GCC 3.4.0	–O3	148,886	28,554	3	30,883	20	147,895	1	125	11	internal compiler error: in output_211, at insn-output.c:1995
C22	GCC 3.4.0	–O3	66,580	8,131	2	26,028	20	6,198	1	210	3	internal compiler error: in print_reg, at config/i386/i386.c:7052
C23	GCC 4.0.0	–O2	105,843	2,965	4	85,245	20	949	0	74	2	internal compiler error: in get_indirect_ref_operands, at tree-ssa-...
C24	GCC 4.0.0	–O2	118,305	5,024	4	36,478	20	6,879	0	65	3	internal compiler error: in make_decl_rtl, at varasm.c:868
C25	GCC 4.0.0	–O0	194,529	5,629	1	17,182	20	23,291	10	71	1	internal compiler error: in c_common_type, at c-typeck.c:529
C26	GCC 4.0.0	–O1	253,152	28,222	10	33,443	20	254,373	1	124	10	internal compiler error: in expand_shift, at expmed.c:2297
C27	GCC 4.0.0	–O0	66,195	6,196	1	5,423	20	5,933	10	66	1	internal compiler error: in c_common_type, at c-typeck.c:531
C28	GCC 4.0.0	–O2	73,913	11,012	2	24,729	20	13,933	0	124	3	internal compiler error: in var_ann, at tree-flow-inline.h:34
C29	GCC 4.1.0	–O1	105,843	7,951	4	58,947	20	949	0	83	2	internal compiler error: in get_indirect_ref_operands, at tree-ssa-...
C30	GCC 4.1.0	–O1	137,615	18,096	7	29,013	21	141,423	1	133	4	internal compiler error: Segmentation fault
C31	GCC 4.1.0	–O2	190,613	16,178	6	47,255	20	186,777	0	89	5	internal compiler error: in compare_name_with_value, at tree-vrp.c:...
C32	GCC 4.1.0	–O1	60,756	8,758	2	31,582	20	3,811	0	95	2	internal compiler error: in simplify_cond_and_lookup_avail_expr, at...
C33	GCC 4.1.0	–O1	63,426	455	0	1,040	20	518	0	68	0	internal compiler error: in reg_or_subregno, at jump.c:2011
C34	GCC 4.1.0	–O3	70,438	6,913	3	24,780	20	10,737	0	154	3	fatal error: internal consistency failure
C35	GCC 4.2.0	–O1	105,843	7,983	4	85,270	20	949	0	83	2	internal compiler error: in get_indirect_ref_operands, at tree-ssa-...
C36	GCC 4.2.0	–O1	149,664	586	1	1,497	20	450	3	107	1	internal compiler error: in reg_or_subregno, at jump.c:2010
C37	GCC 4.3.0	–O1	138,798	8,843	8	103,928	20	4,460	2	164	6	internal compiler error: in set_lattice_value, at tree-ssa-ccp.c:486
C38	GCC 4.3.0	–O2	149,664	586	1	1,589	21	450	2	107	2	internal compiler error: in reg_or_subregno, at jump.c:1728
C39	GCC 4.3.0	–O3	155,051	20,084	7	18,071	20	16,732	1	128	5	internal compiler error: in vect_update_ivs_after_vectorizer, at tr...
C40	GCC 4.3.0	–O1	161,834	7,031	9	15,047	20	7,115	1	66	8	internal compiler error: in get_addr_dereference_operands, at tree-...
C41	GCC 4.3.0	–O3	218,114	38,941	22	52,361	20	219,872	0	203	19	Segmentation fault (program cc1)
C42	Intel CC 12.0.5	–O1	74,396	4,980	2	975	20	1,597	1	98	3	internal error: backend signals
C43	Open64 4.2.4	–O3	131,526	8,509	3	12,088	20	17,584	1	129	4	Assertion failure at line 2279 of lnoutils.cxx:
C44	Open64 4.2.4	–O3	202,966	26,531	18	44,403	20	24,116	10	64	13	Assertion failure at line 2088 of cgemit.cxx:
C45	Open64 4.2.4	–O3	262,005	11,513	7	68,541	28	17,417	2	57	5	Assertion failure at line 5450 of whirl2ops.cxx:
C46	Open64 4.2.4	–O2	52,497	8,541	2	8,585	20	48,185	0	233	4	Signal: Segmentation fault in Global Optimization -- Dead Code Elim...
C47	Open64 4.2.4	–O3	57,427	9,809	2	6,661	20	53,327	0	142	2	Signal: Segmentation fault in Global Optimization -- Create AUX Sym...
C48	Open64 4.2.4	–O3	66,890	3,721	1	9,994	20	2,873	0	161	2	Signal: Segmentation fault in CGLOOP phase.
C49	Open64 4.2.4	–O3	73,892	8,144	3	13,127	20	5,361	0	185	3	Assertion failure at line 2295 of lnoutils.cxx:
C50	Sun CC 5.11	–xO4	109,440	10,506	3	10,322	20	13,986	11	158	3	Fatal error in /home/regehr/z/SolarisStudio12.2-linux-x86-tar-ML/so...
C51	Sun CC 5.11	–fast	114,928	11,906	3	37,986	20	111,111	0	116	6	(iropt) error: IR_OP is not a reduction op!
C52	Sun CC 5.11	–xO4	130,691	8,554	2	80,198	20	125,552	0	152	2	(iropt) error: leaf_lookup_expr: bad leaf (tag=0)
C53	Sun CC 5.11	–fast	41,183	3,679	1	17,002	20	31,887	0	131	1	assertion failed in function node_approx() @ forward.c:291
C54	Sun CC 5.11	–xO0	51,049	272	0	1,579	20	1,226	0	65	0	internal compiler error: confused cg_inflush()
C55	Sun CC 5.11	–xO3	68,396	19,001	4	39,925	20	63,364	0	161	3	assertion failed in function cfg_process_loops() @ cfg.c:7146
C56	Sun CC 5.11	–xO4	71,941	13,204	2	2,340	20	6,362	0	122	2	Assertion 'new_childAddr.offset >= 0 && new_childAddr.offset < new_...
C57	Sun CC 5.11	–fast	72,249	5,935	2	44,507	20	67,569	0	325	3	assertion failed in function gra_biased_select() @ gra.c:10418
		Mean	108,608	10,407	4	29,519	20	52,184	2	151	4	
		Median	84,345	8,509	2	19,211	20	23,291	0	124	3	

Table 2. Compiler bugs used in the "crash" part of our evaluation. Program sizes are in bytes, and reduction times are in minutes.

```
int **a[][0];
static int ***const b = &a[0][1];
void fn1 ();
int
fn2 () {
  return ***b;
  fn1 ();
}
void
fn1 () {
  **b;
}
```

Listing 4. The median-sized reduced test case output by C-Reduce for compiler-crash bugs. GCC 4.0.0 for x86-64 crashes at –O2. This is C28 in Table 2.

File	Orig. Size (Tokens)	Reduced Test-Case Size (Tokens)		
		HDD*	Berkeley delta	C-Reduce
bug.c	277	51	61	41
boom7.c	420	19	256	20
cache.c	25,011	58	124	42

Table 3. Comparing HDD*, Berkeley delta, and C-Reduce

7.5 Detecting Invalid Variants

Our claim is that naïve reducers tend to introduce problematic undefined and unspecified behaviors. In the experiments we performed with our corpus, during every wrong-code reduction run using Berkeley delta and C-Reduce, the reducers encountered variants with undefined behavior that could not be detected using compiler warnings, LLVM/Clang's static analyzer, or Valgrind. However, these undefined variants were detected by KCC and Frama-C.

We performed another experiment in which we reduced the wrong-code test cases utilizing compiler warnings, the LLVM/Clang static analyzer, and Valgrind to detect invalid variants, but *not* using KCC or Frama-C. In this experiment, 12 of the 41 reduced test cases (29%) dynamically executed an undefined behavior that would have rendered the test case inappropriate for use in a bug report. This ratio is unacceptably high. In our experience with compiler-bug reporting, we believe that a compiler team would learn to mistrust and ignore a bug submitter after fewer than 12 invalid bug reports.

7.6 Comparison with Hierarchical Delta Debugging

Although source code for HDD is available, we were not able to obtain code for its C front end. Therefore we were not able to include HDD in our experiments that compare reducers over our corpus of inputs that trigger compiler-crash bugs and wrong-code bugs. We did, however, perform a small experiment to compare C-Reduce with previously reported HDD results.

We compared Berkeley delta and C-Reduce with the results reported by Misherghi and Su [13] for reducing three test cases that cause GCC 2.95.2 to crash. (We could not find source code for a fourth test case used in their paper.) In particular, we compared Berkeley delta and C-Reduce with the results reported for HDD*, which is the particular algorithm by Misherghi and Su that yields the best results for the three test cases. As in our previous experiments with crash bugs, we did not use KCC or Frama-C to check for undefined behavior in reduced test cases. This configuration also creates a fair comparison, since HDD* itself does not check for undefined behavior in test cases.

Table 3 shows the results. For two of the cases, C-Reduce produces smaller output. For `boom7.c`, C-Reduce's output is one token larger. A previous version of C-Reduce produced an 18-token output for this case, two smaller than the current version. Our experience is that incidental phase-ordering issues in the reducer (not unlike similar issues seen in compilers) can easily cause the final reduced output to be a few tokens larger or smaller. We did not compare the execution times of C-Reduce and HDD, but it is safe to assume that the brute-force C-Reduce is considerably slower.

7.7 When Does Reduction Fail?

Non-deterministic execution of the system under test can cause test-case reduction to fail. In our experience, the most common sources of non-determinism are memory-safety bugs interacting with ASLR and resource-exhaustion conditions such as timeouts and memory limits. However, even deterministic bugs can be resistant to reduction, particularly when these bugs stem from internal resource limits in a compiler. For example, a bug in register-spilling logic may simply require a large amount of code before it is triggered.

Reduction can fail in a different sense if the original and reduced test cases trigger different bugs. For crash bugs, we robustly avoid this problem by looking for the specific error string that characterizes the compiler crash. Examining the crash string is part of the process of disambiguating successful and unsuccessful variants. In contrast to compiler-crash bugs, wrong-code bugs have no obvious fingerprint. A pragmatic approach is to fix whatever bug happens to be triggered by the reduced test case, and then to check if the original test case still triggers a miscompilation.

8. Related Work

Previous work has sought to reduce C programs in order to track down compiler defects. Caron and Darnell [3] developed Bugfind, a tool that narrows wrong-code bug triggers down to a single C file and finds the lowest optimization level that triggers miscompilation. Whalley's tool, vpoiso [15], is primarily concerned with isolating the transformation that generates wrong code. However, it also includes functionality to narrow miscompilations down to a single function in the source program. McKeeman presented a random C program generator for testing C compilers [11], including a test-case reduction tool that operates at a finer granularity than Bugfind or vpoiso. McKeeman's tool appears to be similar to C-Reduce's peephole passes. An important difference between previous program reducers and ours is that our reducers address the test-case validity problem. To the best of our knowledge, the problem of maintaining the semantic validity of test cases during reduction has not been previously identified or solved.

Our new C program reducers are instances of generalized delta debugging algorithms. Zeller and Hildebrandt [18] developed delta debugging in 2002 and instantiated it in the *dd* and *ddmin* algorithms. Their main contribution was to abstract the test-case minimization problem away from any specific domain. McPeak and Wilkerson's version of *ddmin*, "Berkeley delta" [12], reduces test cases at line granularity. For appropriately structured inputs, this technique can be more efficient than character-based *ddmin*. By allowing only whole-line deletions, Berkeley delta reduces the size of the search space; if most lines are semantically independent from each other, variants are also likely to be valid test cases. Subsequently, Misherghi and Su [13] developed Hierarchical Delta Debugging (HDD), which reduces tree-structured test cases. Berkeley delta can also reduce tree-structured inputs with the help of its *topformflat* utility, which reformats block-structured text to match Berkeley delta's line-oriented strategy for producing variants. Permitting a delta debugger to exploit the natural hierarchical structure found in some domains leads to much faster reduction times and also to better results. Our new program reducers embody new techniques for generating variants, including random perturbation of a program generator's state (Seq-Reduce), run-time feedback (Fast-Reduce), and pluggable, non-localized program transformations (C-Reduce). In contrast to previous delta-debugging algorithms, Fast-Reduce and C-Reduce implement transformations that may increase the textual size of a test case (e.g., inlining), toward the goal of enabling subsequent reductions.

Our Fast-Reduce reducer utilizes run-time feedback, whereas our Seq-Reduce and C-Reduce implement "brute-force" techniques to generate variants. A third approach to program reduction is static analysis. Leitner et al. [9] combined static backward program slicing with delta debugging to reduce test cases that were randomly generated for unit testing Eiffel classes. Program slicing is used as the first step to narrow down instructions that are responsible for reaching the failure state. This greatly improves the scalability and efficiency of subsequent delta debugging.

9. Conclusion

Our goal was to take large C programs that trigger compiler bugs and automatically reduce them to test cases that are small enough to be directly inserted into compiler bug reports. Previous program reducers based on delta debugging failed to produce sufficiently small test cases. Moreover, they frequently produced invalid test cases that rely on undefined or unspecified behavior. We developed three new reducers based on a generalized notion of delta debugging, and we evaluated them on a corpus of 98 randomly generated C programs that trigger bugs in production compilers. Over this corpus, our best reduction algorithm achieves the goal of producing reportable and valid test cases automatically.

Our future plans include the automatic production of additional elements of a compiler bug report. Besides the information described in Section 2, it would be useful to automatically determine the first broken revision of the compiler and a minimized collection of compiler flags triggering the problem. Better yet, fault-localization techniques could be used to give compiler developers an idea about where in the compiler the bug is likely to be found.

Beyond the evaluation of new reduction techniques for C, our work provides insights into the nature of test-case reduction. First, we observed that highly structured inputs make reduction difficult; we claim that navigating complex input spaces requires rich and domain-specific transformations that are beyond the capabilities of basic delta-debugging searches. Second, we showed that it can be useful to structure a test-case reducer as a collection of modular reduction transformations whose execution is orchestrated by a fixpoint computation. Finally, we identified the *test-case validity problem*, which must be addressed in testing any system that admits undefined or unspecified behaviors.

Software Our new reducers are open-source software, available for download at `http://embed.cs.utah.edu/creduce/`.

Acknowledgments

We thank Alastair Reid and the anonymous PLDI '12 reviewers for their comments on drafts of this paper. Some of our experiments were run on machines provided by the Utah Emulab testbed [16]. This research was supported, in part, by an award from DARPA's Computer Science Study Group. Pascal Cuoq was supported in part by the ANR-funded U3CAT project. Chucky Ellison was supported in part by NSA contract H98230–10–C–0294.

References

[1] Bruno Blanchet, Patrick Cousot, Radhia Cousot, Jérôme Feret, Laurent Mauborgne, Antoine Miné, David Monniaux, and Xavier Rival. A static analyzer for large safety-critical software. In *Proc. of the ACM SIGPLAN 2003 Conf. on Programming Language Design and Implementation (PLDI)*, pages 196–207, San Diego, CA, June 2003.

[2] Géraud Canet, Pascal Cuoq, and Benjamin Monate. A value analysis for C programs. In *Proc. of the 9th IEEE Intl. Working Conf. on Source Code Analysis and Manipulation*, pages 123–124, Edmonton, Alberta, Canada, September 2009.

[3] Jacqueline M. Caron and Peter A. Darnell. Bugfind: A tool for debugging optimizing compilers. *SIGPLAN Notices*, 25(1):17–22, January 1990.

[4] Pascal Cuoq, Benjamin Monate, Anne Pacalet, Virgile Prevosto, John Regehr, Boris Yakobowski, and Xuejun Yang. Testing static analyzers with randomly generated programs. In *Proc. of the 4th NASA Formal Methods Symposium (NFM 2012)*, Norfolk, VA, April 2012.

[5] Pascal Cuoq, Julien Signoles, Patrick Baudin, Richard Bonichon, Géraud Canet, Loïc Correnson, Benjamin Monate, Virgile Prevosto, and Armand Puccetti. Experience report: OCaml for an industrial-strength static analysis framework. In *Proc. of the 14th ACM SIGPLAN Intl. Conf. on Functional Programming (ICFP)*, pages 281–286, Edinburgh, Scotland, 2009.

[6] Chucky Ellison and Grigore Roşu. An executable formal semantics of C with applications. In *Proc. of the 39th Symp. on Principles of Programming Languages (POPL)*, pages 533–544, Philadelphia, PA, January 2012.

[7] International Organization for Standardization. *ISO/IEC 9899:TC3: Programming Languages—C*, 2007. `http://www.open-std.org/jtc1/sc22/wg14/www/docs/n1256.pdf`.

[8] Rajeev Joshi, Greg Nelson, and Yunhong Zhou. Denali: A practical algorithm for generating optimal code. *ACM Transactions on Programming Languages and Systems*, 28(6):967–989, November 2006.

[9] Andreas Leitner, Manuel Oriol, Andreas Zeller, Ilinca Ciupa, and Bertrand Meyer. Efficient unit test case minimization. In *Proc. of the 22nd Intl. Conf. on Automated Software Engineering (ASE)*, pages 417–420, Atlanta, GA, November 2007.

[10] MathWorks. Polyspace server 8.1 for C/C++, product brochure, 2010. `http://www.mathworks.com/products/datasheets/pdf/polyspace-server-for-c-c++.pdf`.

[11] William M. McKeeman. Differential testing for software. *Digital Technical Journal*, 10(1):100–107, December 1998.

[12] Scott McPeak and Daniel S. Wilkerson. Delta, 2003. `http://delta.tigris.org/`.

[13] Ghassan Misherghi and Zhendong Su. HDD: Hierarchical delta debugging. In *Proc. of the 28th Intl. Conf. on Software Engineering (ICSE)*, pages 142–151, Shanghai, China, May 2006.

[14] James W. Moore. ISO/IEC JTC 1/SC 22/WG 23: Programming language vulnerabilities. `http://grouper.ieee.org/groups/plv/`.

[15] David B. Whalley. Automatic isolation of compiler errors. *ACM Transactions on Programming Languages and Systems*, 16(5):1648–1659, September 1994.

[16] Brian White, Jay Lepreau, Leigh Stoller, Robert Ricci, Shashi Guruprasad, Mac Newbold, Mike Hibler, Chad Barb, and Abhijeet Joglekar. An integrated experimental environment for distributed systems and networks. In *Proc. of the 5th Symp. on Operating Systems Design and Implementation (OSDI)*, pages 255–270, Boston, MA, December 2002.

[17] Xuejun Yang, Yang Chen, Eric Eide, and John Regehr. Finding and understanding bugs in C compilers. In *Proc. of the ACM SIGPLAN 2011 Conf. on Programming Language Design and Implementation (PLDI)*, pages 283–294, San Jose, CA, June 2011.

[18] Andreas Zeller and Ralf Hildebrandt. Simplifying and isolating failure-inducing input. *IEEE Transactions on Software Engineering*, 28(2):183–200, February 2002.

A Compiler Framework for Extracting Superword Level Parallelism

Jun Liu, Yuanrui Zhang, Ohyoung Jang, Wei Ding, Mahmut Kandemir
The Pennsylvania State University, University Park, PA 16802, USA
{jxl1036, yuazhang, oyj5007, wzd109, kandemir}@cse.psu.edu

Abstract

SIMD (single-instruction multiple-data) instruction set extensions are quite common today in both high performance and embedded microprocessors, and enable the exploitation of a specific type of data parallelism called SLP (Superword Level Parallelism). While prior research shows that significant performance savings are possible when SLP is exploited, placing SIMD instructions in an application code manually can be very difficult and error prone. In this paper, we propose a novel automated compiler framework for improving superword level parallelism exploitation. The key part of our framework consists of two stages: superword statement generation and data layout optimization. The first stage is our main contribution and has two phases, statement grouping and statement scheduling, of which the primary goals are to increase SIMD parallelism and, more importantly, capture more superword reuses among the superword statements through global data access and reuse pattern analysis. Further, as a complementary optimization, our data layout optimization organizes data in memory space such that the price of memory operations for SLP is minimized. The results from our compiler implementation and tests on two systems indicate performance improvements as high as 15.2% over a state-of-the-art SLP optimization algorithm.

Categories and Subject Descriptors D.3.4 [*Processors*]: Code Generation, Compilers, Optimization

General Terms Design, Algorithms, Languages, Experimentation, Performance

Keywords SLP, SIMD, Scheduling, Data Layout, Compiler

1. Introduction

As a response to demands from the application side, many microprocessors today employ multimedia extensions/support. While the implementation details of this support vary from one architecture to another, it generally comes in form of vector/SIMD (single-instruction multiple-data) instructions, which provide a mechanism to accelerate the performance of various application programs. The most popular commercial multimedia extensions include Intel's MMX/SSE/SSE2/SSE3/SSE4 [1, 14], AMD's 3DNow! [23], and IBM's VMX/Altivec [13].

PLDI'12, June 11–16, 2012, Beijing, China.

While earlier multimedia extensions supported only small data types, these newer extensions can operate on 128-bit superwords, leading to a new type of data parallelism, called the *Superword Level Parallelism* (SLP) [17]. Specifically, data can be packed in superwords and operated using SIMD instructions, as illustrated in Figure 1. It needs to be noted that SLP is different from well-known vector level parallelism [9, 21, 22, 29] in that the latter can only be applied to certain array-based codes where large amounts of parallelism exists. By contrast, SLP can be applicable even if small to moderate levels of parallelism is available in the application code. While a knowledgeable programmer can exploit SLP by manually transforming his/her code to short SIMD form, this is not a very desirable option due to its difficulty and error-proneness. More specifically, many data access patterns do not easily lend themselves to this transformation, and, in most cases, performing such code modifications requires an in-depth understanding of the data dependences and data reuse patterns.

In this work, we propose and evaluate a novel compiler support for improving SLP exploitation. In contrast to the prior efforts on this topic [17, 25–28, 30, 31], we employ a holistic approach from two perspectives. First, instead of depending on local heuristics that can result in poor solutions in terms of parallelism and superword access overheads, we take a more *global* view of the target application code when capturing the data reuse patterns before committing to optimization decisions. Second, we combine our main optimization, i.e., *superword statement generation*, with a *data layout optimization* stage to achieve further improvements.

Specifically, this paper makes the following contributions:

- We propose a compiler framework for SLP exploitation that accommodates two stages, namely, *superword statement generation* and *data layout optimization*, to achieve auto-detection and optimization of SLP. The superword statement generation is our main contribution and can be divided into two phases, i.e., *statement grouping* and *statement scheduling*. The first phase determines how statements are grouped for short SIMD operations, with the goal of increasing SIMD parallelism and, more importantly, capturing more superword reuses among the groups. The second phase decides the execution sequence of the groups, as well as the order of the statements within each individual group, in order to reduce the vector register permutation overheads. Further, as a complementary optimization, our data layout optimization analyzes the data access patterns after the first stage, and re-organizes data in memory space such that the price of memory operations for SLP is minimized.
- We implemented our framework in a compiler [33] and performed experiments using 16 application programs on two different commercial systems. Our experimental results indicate that the proposed SLP framework performs better than an existing SLP scheduling algorithm [17], and generates as much as 15.2% improvement over it.

The remainder of this paper is organized as follows. The next section explains SLP, goes over the prior work, and introduces the motivation for this work. Section 3 gives an overview of our compiler framework. Section 4 presents our main optimization, i.e., superword statement generation. Section 5 describes our data layout optimization strategy. Section 6 uses an example to illustrate how our approach is applied. Section 7 discusses the experimental results, and Section 8 concludes the paper.

2. Superword Level Parallelism

Most modern commercial microprocessors add support for multimedia extensions [1, 13, 14, 23] to meet the demands of computation-intensive multimedia applications. The core of these extensions is a set of SIMD instructions that can operate on aggregate data objects larger than a machine word, i.e., superwords, in the vector registers in parallel. The newer extensions can now operate on superwords of 128 bits, and the width of the SIMD data path is expected to keep increasing.

One critical issue regarding the efficient utilization of multimedia extensions is the compiler support to release the programmer from the burden of inserting short SIMD inline assembly routines manually. However, traditional compiler techniques for automatic parallelization on vector machines [6, 8–10, 12, 15, 18, 19, 24, 32, 34] can be efficient only when the applications expose large amounts of data parallelism. They also rely on complex high-level loop transformations and cannot deal with applications that are not vectorizable, e.g., codes that have mostly scalar data.

To solve the above problem, Larsen and Amarasinghe [17] proposed a new type of parallelism called the Superword Level Parallelism (SLP), targeting multimedia extensions. Different from vector parallelism, SLP exploits fine-grained parallelism from basic blocks rather than from loop nests. In [17], they first try to identify isomorphic statements, which are statements with the same operations in corresponding positions. The operations in all isomorphic statements should be in the same order, and the operands in the corresponding positions should have the same data type. They then group the isomorphic statements together as a superword statement for concurrent execution. In Figure 1 for example, statements S_1 and S_2 are isomorphic and can be put together as a superword statement $< S_1, S_2 >$ for SIMD operation. An important advantage of SLP is that it enables efficient utilization of multimedia extensions even if the parallelism available in the application code is small or moderate. Shin et al [26, 27] developed a strategy to manage the vector register file as a compiler-controlled cache in order to improve data locality when exploiting SLP [17]. In addition, they [25, 28] derived large basic blocks using instruction prediction in the presence of control flow to identify more superword level parallelism. Their studies are orthogonal to our approach proposed in this paper. Tenllado et al [30, 31] presented techniques to efficiently exploit SLP in applications where inner loops carry dependences. Nuzman et al [22] investigated a compiler technique that supports effective vectorization in the presence of interleaved data. Nuzman and Zaks [21] also revisited outer-loop vectorization techniques for short SIMD architectures. Barik et al [5] proposed to enable automatic vectorization on a low-level IR closer to the machine-level, and targeted at achieving compile time efficiency during dynamic compilation. As opposed to the prior work, which are built upon the original SLP algorithm [17], we propose an entirely different strategy for extracting SLP.

A critical requirement in exploiting SLP is that the operands in the superword statement need to be put together in a desired order as superwords in vector registers for short SIMD operations. If, however, the source operands in a superword are not available in the vector register, expensive memory accesses and additional vector register reshuffling/permutation instructions are needed to bring the data from memory and to rearrange them on demand in the vector register. This process is referred to as *superword packing*. Similar overheads can be incurred during the process of scattering the target operands in the superword for later uses, which is referred to as *superword unpacking*. Prior studies [17, 25] show that the superword packing/unpacking overheads can be so high that can even offset the potential performance gains brought by SLP.

Therefore, it is of great importance to reduce the packing/unpacking overheads as much as possible when exploiting SLP. One important observation is that, if the superword used in a superword statement already exists in the vector register, accessing its operands is almost free, without the need for expensive memory accesses or any register reshuffling/permutation instruction. For example, in Figure 1, the superword $< V_1, V_2 >$ used in the superword statement $< S_3, S_4 >$ can be obtained by directly reusing it from $< S_1, S_2 >$. Or, in some other cases, even if a direct reuse of superword is not possible but two superwords access the same data with different orderings, we can still save memory access overhead by only introducing the vector register permutation instructions. For example, in Figure 1, the superword $< V_2, V_1 >$ used in $< S_5, S_6 >$ can reuse the operands in $< V_1, V_2 >$ of $< S_3, S_4 >$ by interchanging the positions of V_1 and V_2. Hence, it is critical to locate and expose such reuses as much as possible when generating SIMD codes.

The greedy algorithm proposed by Larsen and Amarasinghe [17] and also employed in other related work [28, 31] tries to achieve superword reuses based on local heuristics. The algorithm targets basic blocks and starts by identifying isomorphic statement pairs with adjacent memory accesses as the *seed* superword statements. It then groups more isomorphic statements by following the *def-use* and *use-def* chains so that reuses may be caught between the newly generated superwords and the existing ones. The main problem with this algorithm is that the decision made at each step to generate new superword statements highly depends on the existing grouping decisions and the def-use/use-def chains, being oblivious to the rest of the statements. In other words, this approach does not have a global perspective. As a result, it is unable to fully utilize the potential superword reuse opportunities available in the input basic blocks. To address this problem, we introduce a new SLP algorithm, of which the basic idea is to keep a global (an entire basic block wide) view of *all* the statements regarding data access and reuse patterns at each step when constructing new superword statements. Thus, the grouping decisions made to increase superword reuses in our algorithm are based on a larger scope. To our knowledge, this is the first work to introduce the concept of global superword reuse optimization for exploiting SLP.

Though efficient exploitation of superword reuses is our main optimization and can greatly reduce the number of packing/unpacking operations as will be shown later, sometimes these operations are still required, e.g., when a superword is referred for the first time in a basic block. The mandatory packing operations can be costly and may reduce the potential performance benefits. To alleviate this problem, it is desirable to have those operands stored in an aligned and consecutive fashion in memory space so that the number of memory operations could be minimized during packing/unpacking. Prior work [17, 28] addressed this issue by choosing some statements with contiguous memory accesses as the seed superword statements. However, this can lead to poor solutions in terms of superword reuses. In addition, this strategy highly depends on the existing data layout of the data accessed. By contrast, we believe that the data layout optimization fits better when solving this issue in the sense that it has much less negative effect on the exploration of superword reuses and, above all, it can derive better access patterns from an SLP perspective. Henretty et al [11] proposed a data layout transformation to avoid stream align-

```
S1:  V1 = V3 + V5;
S2:  V2 = V4 + V6;
S3:  ... = V1 × ...;
S4:  ... = V2 × ...;
S5:  ... = V2 ;
S6:  ... = V1 ;
```

Figure 1. An example exploiting superword level parallelism.

```
S1:  V1 = V3;
S2:  V2 = V5;
S3:  V5 = V7;
S4:  V3 = V1 + V1;
S5:  V5 = V2 + V5;
```

Figure 2. An example basic block.

ment conflict on processors with SIMD capabilities. However, they specifically target stencil computations. In our compiler framework, we explore a much more general data layout modification as a post optimization to gain further benefits. To our knowledge, this is also the first work that combines superword statement generation with general data layout optimization to improve SLP exploitation.

3. Framework Overview

The input to our compiler framework is a set of basic blocks of a program. For loop-intensive applications, loop unrolling can be used to reveal more opportunities for short SIMD operations and to fully utilize the superword datapath available in the underlying architecture. Overall, there are three main goals that we want to achieve in order to exploit SLP more efficiently: (1) increasing parallelism by generating more superword statements; (2) reducing the number of superword packing/unpacking operations by achieving more superword reuses; and (3) reducing the overhead of mandatory packing/unpacking operations by employing data layout optimization.

Figure 3 gives an overview of the proposed compiler framework, which mainly accommodates three modules: *pre-processing*, *holistic SLP optimizer*, and *post-processing*. Taking the program source code as input, the pre-processing module first applies transformations including loop unrolling and alignment analysis, with the objective of exposing more opportunities for SLP exploitation. Next, our holistic SLP optimizer performs a set of SLP optimizations and generates vectorized code. Finally, the post-processing module performs register allocation and other low-level optimizations, and outputs executable. As the main contribution of this work, the holistic SLP optimizer adopts a two-stage strategy: superword statement generation and data layout optimization. At the first stage, the statement grouping determines how to group statements together for superword operations without fixing the ordering of the statements in each superword statement, aiming at identifying more (statement) groups as well as increasing the superword reuses among the groups. On the other hand, the statement scheduling decides the scheduling sequence of the groups and the order of the statements within each group, in order to minimize the number of vector register reshuffling/permutation instructions. To further increase improvements, at the second stage, the data layout optimization changes the memory layout of the data accessed in the superword statements, in an attempt to reduce the overhead of mandatory packing/unpacking operations. It is to be noted that while the first stage focuses on reducing the occurrences of packing/unpacking operations, the second stage aims at reducing the number of memory operations and vector register reshuffling/permutation instructions involved in these operations.

4. Superword Statement Generation

As shown in Figure 3, the superword statement generation includes two major phases: grouping and scheduling. Before going into the

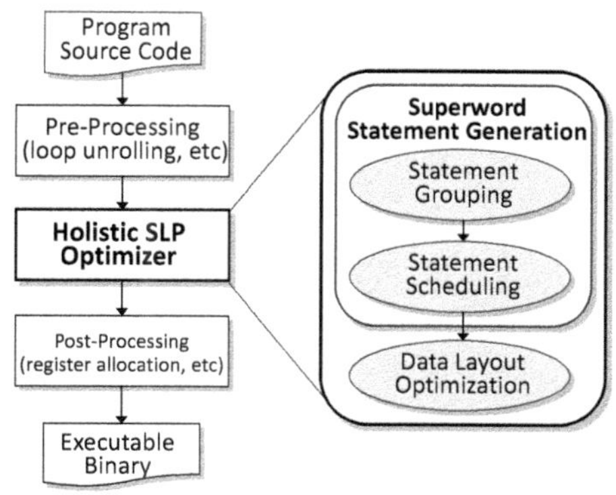

Figure 3. Overview of our framework.

detailed descriptions of these two phases, we first give a formal definition of the problem we are trying to solve in this section.

4.1 Problem Definition

Our SLP optimizer takes a set of basic blocks of an application program code as the input. Each basic block consists of a sequence of statements $S =< S_1, S_2, S_3, ..., S_n >$, where S_i represents a single statement. Given an SIMD datapath width supported by the target architecture, our goal at this stage is to find a scheduling of these statements for each basic block, represented by $D =< D_1, D_2, D_3, ..., D_m >$, such that the performance of the basic block is maximized. Here, D_i denotes either a single statement from S, or a superword statement that contains multiple statements. A scheduling D is said to be *valid*, if and only if it satisfies the following four constraints:

1. There is no dependence between the statements in each superword statement: $\forall D_i$, if D_i is a superword statement, then $\forall S_p, S_q \in D_i$, S_p and S_q are dependence free.
2. The dependences between the statements in the sequence S are preserved in D: if $S_p\ \delta\ S_q$, and $S_p \in D_i$, $S_q \in D_j$, then $D_i\ \delta\ D_j$, where δ stands for a dependence relationship between a source (single statement or superword statement, i.e., S_p or D_i), and a target (single statement or superword statement, i.e., S_q or D_j).
3. The statements within each superword statement are *isomorphic*, i.e., they contain the same operations in the same order.
4. The data width of the potential superword operation should not exceed the datapath width supported by the underlying architecture.

These constraints are necessary to guarantee the correctness of program execution (i.e., preserve the original semantics) when exploiting SIMD opportunities in the basic blocks.

We want to emphasize that, two schedulings D and D' for a basic block are identical, if and only if (1) they contain the same set of SIMD groups (the concept of SIMD group is similar to that of superword statement except that its statements are not ordered), (2) the sequence of the single statements and SIMD groups in both schedulings are the same, and (3) the ordering of the statements in their corresponding superword statements are the same. The first condition is crucial in that it determines how many SIMD instructions are produced and more importantly, how many superword reuses are generated. The second condition is used to help maintain the dependences in the original program code and bring superword reuses as closer as possible. The third condition can affect the number of vector register permutation instructions needed to reuse the superwords.

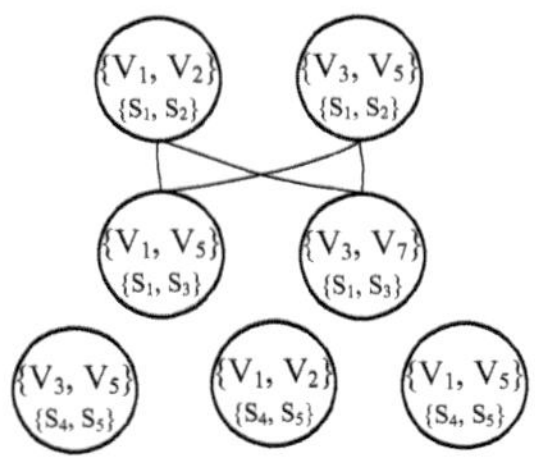

Figure 4. The variable pack conflicting graph of the example code in Figure 2.

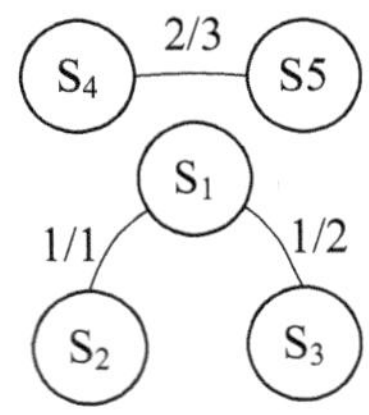

Figure 5. The statement grouping graph of the example code in Figure 2.

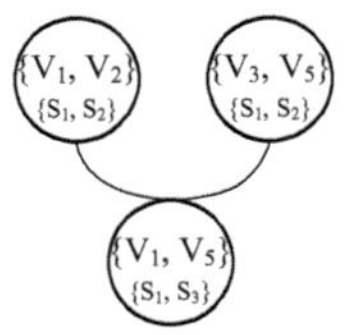

Figure 6. The auxiliary graph for calculating the weight of the candidate group $\{S_4, S_5\}$.

4.2 Grouping

We employ an iterative process to perform statement grouping. This approach first uses a *basic grouping algorithm* to find groups of size two, and then treats the groups already found as atomic statements, and applies the basic grouping algorithm again to obtain groups of larger sizes, until the target SIMD datapath is fully utilized. Thus, we are able to cope with processors with wider SIMD devices. In particular, in the basic grouping algorithm, we identify all possible statement groups and evaluate their "quality" (i.e., how much benefit a statement group can potentially bring to the the final SIMD code generated for an entire basic block) in order to decide which groups will be chosen. In other words, each group decision is made based on the global data access and reuse pattern analysis regarding the superword reuses, instead of employing local/greedy heuristics. Note that, in this phase, a superword is said to be *reused*, if the data it contains are used more than once in the code, even for the case with different orderings. The reason why we consider the latter case also as a reuse is because it does not require expensive memory operations between two usages, though it still needs vector register permutation instructions.

4.2.1 The Basic Grouping Algorithm

To facilitate our explanation, we use the first-round grouping, together with an example (a basic block), shown in Figure 2, to describe the basic grouping algorithm, where we try to obtain SIMD groups of size 2 (i.e., two statements).

The first step of our basic grouping algorithm is to **identify the candidate groups**. A candidate group refers to a potential SIMD group that contains two isomorphic statements $\{S_i, S_j\}$, where $S_i, S_j \in S$. According to the scheduling constraints listed above, there should be no dependence between these two statements, and the superword size of the candidate group should not exceed the target SIMD datapath width. Note that, there is no ordering between S_i and S_j in the candidate group. In other words, the ordering of the statements inside each group is ignored at this phase. Let $\mathcal{C} = \{C_1, C_2, \cdots, C_t\}$ denote the set of all t candidate groups identified in the basic block. Two candidate groups C_1 and C_2 from $\mathcal{C}$ are said to be conflicting with each other, if they have a common statement, e.g., $C_1 = \{S_p, S_q\}$ and $C_2 = \{S_p, S_r\}$, or there exists a dependence cycle between these two groups, e.g., $C_1\ \delta\ C_2$ and $C_2\ \delta\ C_1$, because of the dependences between their member statements. We can see that, in either case, conflicting candidate groups cannot coexist; otherwise, it would lead to incorrect execution. For example, the candidate group set for the code shown in Figure 2 is $\mathcal{C} = \{\{S_1, S_2\}, \{S_1, S_3\}, \{S_4, S_5\}\}$.

Based on the candidate group set, the second step **builds a variable pack conflicting graph**. A *variable pack* refers to a set of variables coming from the same position of different isomorphic statements in a candidate group, e.g., $\{V_1, V_2\}$ and $\{V_3, V_5\}$ from candidate group $\{S_1, S_2\}$ in the example code (Figure 2), which are expected to form superwords. Note that the variable packs are brought about by the statement grouping. Similar to statement grouping, we do not consider the ordering of the variables in a variable pack at this step. The purpose of building the variable pack conflicting graph is to capture all the conflicts between the candidate groups in $\mathcal{C}$, but at a finer granularity using variable packs. In this way, we can later refer to this graph for an accurate analysis of the reuse information of variable packs (or superwords). The variable pack conflicting graph $VP = (V, T)$ is constructed as follows: we go over all the candidate groups in $\mathcal{C}$ one-by-one; for each candidate group $\{S_p, S_q\}$, we create a new set of nodes representing all the variable packs generated from its statements. In addition, we insert edges between these newly-built nodes and the nodes already in the graph which were generated from candidate groups that conflict with $\{S_p, S_q\}$. It is to be noted that each node with variable pack $\{V_i, V_j\}$ is also tagged with its associated candidate group information, i.e., $\{V_i, V_j\}_{\text{-}\{S_p,S_q\}}$. Therefore, there may exist multiple nodes containing the same set of variables, but they are generated from different candidate groups. And, we distinguish them from one another in the graph. Most importantly, if such nodes do not have any edge among them, it means that the corresponding variable packs can coexist in the transformed code with SIMD operations. Thus, the number of such nodes in fact gives us the reuse information of the corresponding superword, e.g., $\{V_i, V_j\}$. Figure 4 illustrates a variable pack conflicting graph built from the candidate group set of the example code shown in Figure 2.

Our third step is to **build a statement grouping graph** $SG = (V', T')$, using both the candidate groups identified earlier and the variable pack conflicting graph obtained in the previous step. Each node ($\in V'$) in this graph denotes a statement S_p from the basic block, and each edge ($\in T'$) represents a candidate group between two statements. That is, if two statements belong to the same candidate group, there is an edge connecting them, e.g., S_1 and S_2 as shown in Figure 5. Moreover, the statement grouping graph is a weighted graph, where the weight of each edge represents an estimation of the "benefit", i.e., the variable pack (superword) reuses, that each candidate group can potentially bring to the entire code. To calculate the weight of an edge between two statements S_p and S_q from the candidate group $\{S_p, S_q\}$, we first construct an auxiliary graph by extracting all packs (nodes) from the variable packing graph VP, which are the same as those variable packs appearing in $\{S_p, S_q\}$ but do not conflict with them. Also, all the edges among the extracted nodes in VP are maintained in SG. For example, suppose we are calculating the weight of the edge between statements S_4 and S_5 in Figure 5. The auxiliary graph we construct is depicted in Figure 6. It includes all nodes in Figure 4 that are the same as the variable packs of $\{S_4, S_5\}$ and can also coexist with them. However, in the auxiliary graph, there may still exist edges among the nodes, which indicates that the extracted nodes cannot be used together in any scheduling. We introduce a greedy strategy to eliminate these conflicts: at each step, we select a node that has the highest degree (i.e., one with the largest number of edges connected to it), and remove

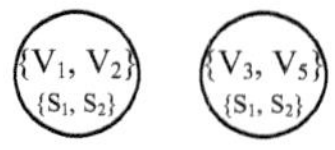

Figure 7. The updated auxiliary graph after conflict elimination from Figure 6.

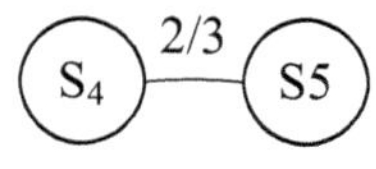

Figure 8. The updated statement graph after the first grouping decision $\{S_1, S_2\}$.

Figure 9. The updated variable pack conflicting graph after the first grouping decision $\{S_1, S_2\}$.

this node as well as all the edges associated with it. We repeat this procedure until no edge is left in the auxiliary graph, e.g., as shown in Figure 7. Now, by combining the remaining nodes in the auxiliary graph, e.g., $\{V_1, V_2\}_{\text{-}\{S_1,S_2\}}$ and $\{V_3, V_5\}_{\text{-}\{S_1,S_2\}}$, and the variable packs from $\{S_p, S_q\}$ in VP, e.g., $\{V_3, V_5\}_{\text{-}\{S_4,S_5\}}$, $\{V_1, V_2\}_{\text{-}\{S_4,S_5\}}$ and $\{V_1, V_5\}_{\text{-}\{S_4,S_5\}}$, we can obtain an average reuse of the variable packs (superwords) from $\{S_p, S_q\}$ in the entire basic block, e.g., $2/3$ for $\{S_4, S_5\}$. This reuse value is assigned as the *weight* of the edge between statements S_p and S_q in SG. Therefore, the weight between two statements provides an estimate of the potential benefit (in terms of superword reuses) for the entire basic block (global effect), brought by grouping them together as a superword statement in the final code.

The fourth step **makes grouping decisions** based on the statement grouping graph SG constructed in the previous step. Specifically, we first sort all the edges in SG in a non-increasing order according to their weights, and then select an edge that has the highest weight. The two statements connected by this edge are then decided to be grouped as a superword statement, e.g., $\{S_1, S_2\}$ in Figure 5. Note that, if two edges have the same weight, we randomly choose one. Once a decision is made, we update the two graphs, namely, SG and VP, as follows. In SG, we delete the nodes that represent the two statements in the SIMD group just found, as well as all the nodes connected to them (i.e., the conflicting statements), e.g., as shown in Figure 8. Similarly, in VP, we delete the nodes that represent the variable packs generated from the newly decided SIMD group, as well as all the nodes connected to them (i.e., the conflicting variable packs), e.g., as displayed in Figure 9. We then recalculate the weights of all retained edges in SG. We want to emphasize that, at this point, when we evaluate the global benefits (superword reuses) of a candidate group, we take into account *all* the variable packs that are the same as those of the SIMD groups determined so far. For example, when calculating the weight for the candidate group $\{S_4, S_5\}$ in Figure 8, we need to consider $\{S_4, S_5\}$ and the already-decided group $\{S_1, S_2\}$ together when building the auxiliary graph. This process continues until no edge is left in the statement graph SG, which means that we have exploited all the opportunities for SIMD operations.

As stated earlier in Section 2, the essential difference between our work and the original SLP algorithm [17] is that we take a global (an entire basic block wide) view when exploiting superword reuses during grouping, instead of employing a local/greedy heuristic. This is clearly reflected in the four steps involved in the basic grouping algorithm described above. Especially, the first step (identifying the candidate groups) provides all the grouping possibilities before making any decision; the second step (building the variable pack conflicting graph) retrieves information on the whole set of possible superwords resulting from grouping, taking into account the conflicts among them; the third step (building the statement grouping graph) then evaluates the benefits brought by each candidate group to the whole basic block, by extracting data access and reuse patterns from the variable pack conflicting graph; finally, the fourth step (making grouping decisions) selects the most beneficial one as the current grouping decision, which increases superword reuses across the basic block.

4.2.2 Iterative Grouping

In the basic grouping algorithm described above, the size of a generated SIMD group (superword statement) is two. If we simply use the output of the first-round grouping to generate the final superword statements, the SIMD datapath width available in the underlying architecture may be underutilized. To solve this problem, we extend our basic grouping algorithm using an iterative process to obtain SIMD groups with larger sizes. The basic idea is that, after the first-round grouping, we treat each SIMD group $\{S_p, S_q\}$ as a new single statement, and each variable pack as a new single variable. The original statement set of the input basic block is then updated by adding these new statements. Next we apply the basic grouping algorithm on the input basic block again, but with the updated statement set. Note that some SIMD groups may not be considered for further grouping because they already can fill the SIMD datapath width. We iteratively employ this strategy until the finally generated superword statements are able to exploit the SIMD datapath width to the largest extent possible. Therefore, our framework will be able to efficiently utilize the SIMD devices even when/if datapath widths increase in the future.

4.3 Scheduling

The first phase (grouping) described above solves the problem of grouping statements together as superword statements, and we focus on reducing expensive memory operations between two usages by achieving more superword reuses. However, additional vector register permutation instructions may still be needed if the same data are arranged in different sequences in two superwords. In this phase (scheduling), we try to solve two issues: (1) obtain a valid execution sequence for all statements (including single statements and superword statements) in the basic block and bring the superword reuses in the superword statements as close as possible; (2) fix the ordering of the statements within each superword statement to reduce the number of permutation operations as much as possible. In particular, we are more concerned about the ordering between superword statements and the statement ordering within each superword statement, than the sequence between single statements or between single statements and superword statements, as the former has an impact on the number of vector reshuffling/permutation operations needed, while the latter can be handled and optimized by instruction scheduling to be invoked later.

We start by building a dependence graph among the generated superword statements, based upon the execution sequence of the original single statements in the input basic block. In this graph, each node denotes a superword statement, and each directed edge indicates a dependence between the two connected superword statements. Since the grouping phase already excludes the existence of any cyclic dependence, we are guaranteed to have at least one valid scheduling for all superword statements, without eliminating any of them. For this reason, as compared to [17], our framework can retain more superword statements for SIMD operations. Note that, in reality, this dependence graph can provide more than one possibility of scheduling the superword statements. Thus we are able to take advantage of this flexibility to bring more benefits.

Based on the dependence graph, we schedule the superword statements and decide the ordering of the statements within each of them. We define a *live superword* set as a set of superwords that are most likely in vector registers currently. Note that, in the live superword set, the ordering of the statements of each superword is determined. Initially, the live superword set is set as empty. We then fetch from the dependence graph the ready superword statements, of which all the dependencies have been resolved. These statements are the candidates to be considered to be added into the target statement execution sequence. Next, we calculate the number of reuses between the superwords in each candidate superword statement and the ones in the live superword set. The candidate statement with the largest number of reuses is then selected as the next one to run, resulting in closer superword reuses and higher probability of reuses in the vector registers. We next decide an ordering for the statements of the superword statement just chosen. Given a superword statement of size N, there could be $N!$ different orderings. Yet we can reduce this number by testing only those orderings that lead to at least one direct superword reuse (i.e., reuse without any permutation operation). In other words, to improve efficiency, we don't employ exhaustive search across all valid orderings. Among the tested orderings, we choose the one that needs the smallest number of permutation operations for all the superword reuses in the considered superword statement. Meanwhile, we update the live superword set by inserting into it the newly ordered superwords and removing from it those existing superwords that access the same data. We then continue with our scheduling by fetching new ready superword statements and repeating the above steps until all the nodes in the dependence graph are processed.

It is to be noted that, by isolating the determination of the ordering of the statements in each superword statement from the grouping phase and postponing it to scheduling phase, our framework is able to fully exploit both the direct and indirect superword reuses. The latter is crucial as it can save expensive memory operations by introducing only register permutation instructions, which is neglected in the original SLP algorithm [17]. In addition, when determining the sequence for all statements (including single statements and superword statements) in the basic block, we not only obtain a valid scheduling, but also try to bring the superword reuses as close as possible, which helps transform the reuses into data locality in the vector register file.

After performing grouping and scheduling on the basic block, we employ a similar cost model used in [16] to estimate the potential speed-ups brought by the transformed code, taking into account all the important factors, e.g., the number of SIMD instructions, the number of memory operations and the number of vector register reshuffling/permutation instructions. If we realize that our transformation could potentially degrade the performance, we choose not to apply it. Specifically, even though we are able to increase parallelism by introducing SIMD operations, the overheads (memory access latencies/instructions, vector register instructions) brought by packing/unpacking operations, could be so high that it may take longer for the transformed code to finish. In this case, we skip the current basic block and move on to the next one.

4.4 Pseudo Code

The pseudo-code of our basic grouping algorithm is given in Figure 10. In this algorithm, line 1 identifies the candidate statement groups. Lines 2-11 build the variable pack conflicting graph, while lines 12-18 initialize the statement grouping graph. As the key part of our algorithm, Lines 21-42 make grouping decisions one by one. More specifically, lines 22-30 construct an auxiliary graph for weight calculation, based on current candidate group and the decided groups. The conflicts in the auxiliary graph are resolved in line 31, after which lines 32-38 calculate the weight (average superword reuse). Lines 40-41 choose the edge with the largest weight as the current grouping decision, and update the variable pack conflicting graph as well as the statement grouping graph. Lines 21-42 repeat until all groups are identified. The complexity of our basic grouping algorithm is $O(E_{SG}^2 \times N_{VP})$, where E_{SG} is the number of edges in the statement grouping graph and N_{VP} is the number of nodes in the variable packing conflict graph.

The second phase of our algorithm (scheduling), is given in Figure 11. Specifically, lines 1-9 form the dependence graph using the detected groups, from which lines 10-13 initialize the set of ready superword statements. Lines 15-18 select the superword statement that has the highest number of superword reuses with the current live superword set, as the next one in the statement execution sequence. Lines 19-27 determine the ordering of the statements in the selected superword statement, aiming at reducing permutation operations as much as possible. Finally, lines 28-35 update the live superword set, the dependence graph, and the set of ready superword statements. The algorithm then moves on to decide the next superword statement to put into the statement execution sequence.

5. Data Layout Optimization

The optimizations applied in previous section can reduce the number of packing/unpacking operations but cannot completely eliminate them. In fact, once a packing operation is required, its overhead can be significant if the data it accesses are not aligned and stored in memory in a contiguous fashion. The previously proposed SLP algorithm [17] handles this issue by grouping together some statements with contiguous memory accesses. However, this approach can lead to poor solutions in terms of superword reuses as we have discussed in the previous sections, and more importantly, it highly relies on the existing data layout. For this reason, in this section, we introduce an additional step, called data layout optimization, to further our benefits by reducing the number of memory operations and register instructions involved in the mandatory packing/unpacking operations.

The basic idea behind our data layout optimization is to organize the superwords in the memory in a way such that the overhead involved in loading them into vector registers (or writing them back to memory from vector register) could be minimized. For example, in Figure 13, assume the width of the SIMD datapath can hold two basic data types and we decide to group statements S_1 and S_2 together after the first stage which yields two superwords: $< a, b >$ and $< A[4i], A[4i+3] >$. Assume further that these two superwords are currently not in vector registers during execution. Thus, they need to be packed/unpacked into/from the vector registers before/after the SIMD operation. In this case, if variables a and b are already contiguous and aligned in the memory, we only need one memory operation to write $< a, b >$ back. For the same reason, it is also desirable to make the data accessed by $A[4i]$ and $A[4i+3]$ be contiguous and aligned in the memory space. In this work, we mainly target at optimizing the data layout for two classes of superwords, namely, *scalar superword* and *array reference superword.* In the scalar superword, all involved variables are scalar, whereas the array reference superword contains only array references. We treat these two classes of superwords separately when applying our data layout optimization. Specifically, we employ address assignment for scalar superwords, while applying array transformation and replication for the array reference superwords.

5.1 Optimization for Scalar Superword

We try to solve the problem of layout optimization for scalar superwords by applying a similar strategy used in the offset assignment problem in DSP code generation [20]. However, the difference is that, in our case, the desired layout of the variables is determined by our statement scheduling for SLP (i.e., superword statement generation) in the first stage. Specifically, our algorithm is an iterative process and works as follows. We first sort all the scalar superwords

Input: A sequence of statements of a basic block, $S =< S_1, S_2, S_3, ..., S_n >$
Output: A set of decided statement groups $\mathcal{D}$

Identify candidate statement group set $\mathcal{G}$;
Initialize VP; //VP: variable pack conflicting graph.
for $\{S_i, S_j\} \in \mathcal{G}$ **do**
  for $\{V_i, V_j\}, V_i \in S_i.\mathcal{V}$ *and* $V_j \in S_j.\mathcal{V}$ **do**
    $VP.\mathcal{V} \leftarrow VP.\mathcal{V} \cup \{\{V_i, V_j\}_{\text{-}\{S_i,S_j\}}\}$;
    for $\{V_q, V_r\}_{\text{-}\{S_q,S_r\}}$ and $\{S_q, S_r\} \cap \{S_i, S_j\} \neq \emptyset$ **do**
      $VP.\mathcal{E} \leftarrow VP.\mathcal{E} \cup$
      $\{\{V_i, V_j\}_{\text{-}\{S_i,S_j\}}, \{V_q, V_r\}_{\text{-}\{S_q,S_r\}}\}$;
    end for
  end for
end for
Initialize SG; //SG: statement grouping graph.
for $\{S_i, S_j\} \in \mathcal{G}$ **do**
  for $S \in \{S_i, S_j\}$ and $S \notin SG.\mathcal{V}$ **do**
    $SG.\mathcal{V} \leftarrow SG.\mathcal{V} \cup \{S\}$;
  end for
  $SG.\mathcal{E} \leftarrow SG.\mathcal{E} \cup \{\{S_i, S_j\}\}$;
end for
$\mathcal{D} \leftarrow \emptyset$;
while $SG.\mathcal{E} \neq \emptyset$ **do**
  for $\{S_i, S_j\} \in SG.\mathcal{E}$ **do**
    Initialize AG; //AG: auxiliary graph.
    for $\{V_i, V_j\}_{\text{-}\{S_q,S_r\}} \in VP.\mathcal{V}$ **do**
      if $\{V_i, V_j\}_{\text{-}\{S_i,S_j\}} \in VP.\mathcal{V}$ and $\{S_q, S_r\} \neq \{S_i, S_j\}$ and $\{\{V_i, V_j\}_{\text{-}\{S_q,S_r\}}, \{V_i, V_j\}_{\text{-}\{S_i,S_j\}}\} \notin VP.\mathcal{V}$ **then**
        $AG.\mathcal{V} \leftarrow AG.\mathcal{V} \cup \{\{V_i, V_j\}_{\text{-}\{S_q,S_r\}}\}$;
      end if
    end for
    for $P_m, P_n \in AG.\mathcal{V}$ and $\{P_m, P_n\} \in VP.\mathcal{E}$ **do**
      $AG.\mathcal{E} \leftarrow AG.\mathcal{E} \cup \{\{P_m, P_n\}\}$;
    end for
    Resolve conflicts in AG;
    //Calculate reuses for $\{S_i, S_j\}$.
    $r \leftarrow 0$;
    for $\{V_i, V_j\}$ appear in $AG.\mathcal{V}$ or $\mathcal{D} \cup \{\{S_i, S_j\}\}$ **do**
      $r \leftarrow r + (N_{\text{-}\{V_i,V_j\}} - 1)$; //$N_{\text{-}\{V_i,V_j\}}$: the number of occurence of $\{V_i, V_j\}$.
    end for
    $W_{\text{-}\{S_i,S_j\}} = r/N_t$; //$N_t$: the number of pack types in $\mathcal{D} \cup \{\{S_i, S_j\}\}$.
    $SG.\mathcal{W} \leftarrow SG.\mathcal{W} \cup \{W_{\text{-}\{S_i,S_j\}}\}$;
  end for
  $\mathcal{D} \leftarrow \mathcal{D} \cup \{S_i, S_j\}$; // $W_{\text{-}\{S_i,S_j\}} = MAX(SG.\mathcal{W})$.
  Update VP and SG;
  $SG.\mathcal{W} \leftarrow \emptyset$;
end while

Figure 10. Pseudo code for the basic *grouping* phase.

Input: A set of decided statement groups $\mathcal{D}$
Output: The ordering of the groups in $\mathcal{D}$ and the sequence Q of the statements in each group $D \in \mathcal{D}$

Initialize DG; //DG: group dependence graph DG.
for $D \in \mathcal{D}$ **do**
  $GDG.\mathcal{V} \leftarrow GDG.\mathcal{V} \cup \{D\}$;
end for
for $D_i, D_j \in GDG.\mathcal{V}$ **do**
  if D_i depends on D_j **then**
    $GDG.\mathcal{E} \leftarrow GDG.\mathcal{E} \cup < D_i, D_j >$;
  end if
end for
Initialize $\mathcal{LP}$ and $\mathcal{RD}$; //$\mathcal{LP}$: set of live packs. $\mathcal{RD}$: set of ready groups.
for $D_i \in GDG.\mathcal{V}$ and $not \exists < D_j, D_i > \in GDG.\mathcal{E}$ **do**
  $\mathcal{RD} \leftarrow \mathcal{RD} \cup \{D_i\}$;
end for
while $\mathcal{RD} = \emptyset$ **do**
  for $D \in \mathcal{RD}$ **do**
    $N_r = NumberOfReuses(D, \mathcal{LP})$;
  end for
  Choose D with largest N_r;
  //Decide the sequence for statements in D_i.
  $\mathcal{Q} \leftarrow \emptyset$; $\mathcal{Q}$: the candidate sequence set for D.
  for each sequence Q of D, such that D can directly reuse one pack in $\mathcal{LP}$ **do**
    $\mathcal{Q} \leftarrow \mathcal{Q} \cup \{Q\}$;
  end for
  for $Q \in \mathcal{Q}$ **do**
    $N_r = NumberOfPermutations(D, Q, \mathcal{LP})$;
  end for
  Choose Q of D with smallest N_p;
  for each pack $< V_i, V_j >$ from D in the order Q **do**
    $\mathcal{LP} \leftarrow \mathcal{LP} \cup < V_i, V_j >$;
    if $< V_q, V_r > \in \mathcal{LP}$ and $\{V_q, V_r\} = \{V_i, V_j\}$ **then**
      $\mathcal{LP} \leftarrow \mathcal{LP} - \{< V_q, V_r >\}$;
    end if
  end for
  Update GDG;
  Update RD;
end while

Figure 11. Pseudo code for the *scheduling* phase.

Input: A set of superwords, $\mathcal{P}$
Output: Data layout for $\mathcal{P}' \subseteq \mathcal{P}$

Initialize $\mathcal{C}$; //$\mathcal{C}$: set of scalar superwords;
Initialize $\mathcal{Y}$; //$\mathcal{Y}$: set of array reference superwords;
for $P \in \mathcal{P}$ **do**
  if $\forall V \in P, V$ is scalar **then**
    $\mathcal{C} \leftarrow \mathcal{C} \cup \{P\}$;
  else if $\forall V \in P, V$ is read-only reference to the same array **then**
    $\mathcal{Y} \leftarrow \mathcal{Y} \cup \{P\}$;
  end if
end for
//Layout optimization for scalar superwords.
while $\mathcal{C} \neq \emptyset$ **do**
  Sort $\mathcal{C}$ based on the occurences;
  Select $C \in \mathcal{C}$ with the largest number of occurences;
  Assign aligned memory slots to variables in C in the same order;
  for $C' \in \mathcal{C}$ **do**
    if $C' \cap C \neq \emptyset$ **then**
      $\mathcal{C} \leftarrow \mathcal{C} - \{C'\}$;
    end if
  end for
  $\mathcal{C} \leftarrow \mathcal{C} - \{C\}$;
  $\mathcal{P}' \leftarrow \mathcal{P}' \cup \{C\}$;
end while
//Layout optimization for array reference superwords.
while $\mathcal{Y} \neq \emptyset$ **do**
  Sort $\mathcal{Y}$ based on the occurrences;
  Select $Y \in \mathcal{Y}$ with the largest number of occurences;
  R is a reference in Y;
  for $R \in Y$ **do**
    $\vec{r}$ is the memory access vector of R;
    $\vec{r} \leftarrow \mathbf{Q}\vec{i} + \vec{O}$;
    //Apply the first layout transformation for spatial locality.
    Obtain a transformation matrix $\mathbf{M}$;
    $\vec{r_1} \leftarrow \mathbf{Q_1}\vec{i} + \vec{O_1}$; //$\mathbf{Q_1} = \mathbf{MQ}$ and $\vec{O_1} = \mathbf{M}\vec{O}$.
    //Apply mapping/replication of data access by $\vec{d}$ from A to B.
    $f(\vec{d}) \leftarrow (f'(\vec{d'}), \frac{q_{m,n} - O'_n - f'(\vec{d'})(q_{n,1}, ..., q_{n,m-1})^T}{q_{n,m}} L + p)$; L: the number of references in Y; p: the position of R in Y;
  end for
  $\mathcal{Y} \leftarrow \mathcal{Y} - \{Y\}$;
  $\mathcal{P}' \leftarrow \mathcal{P}' \cup \{Y\}$;
end while

Figure 12. Pseudo code for the data layout optimization.

```
S1:  a  =  A[4i];
S2:  b  =  A[4i+3];
```

Figure 13. An example that benefits from data layout optimization.

by their occurrences, followed by selecting the scalar superword with the largest number of occurrences as the current one to apply layout optimization. The scalars in the selected superword are then assigned consecutive memory locations in which the variables are organized in the same order as they appear in the superword. After that, we skip all the scalar superwords that share variable(s) with the current one and thus have conflicting layout requirements. We repeat the above process until all scalar superwords are processed. It needs to be noted that, our data layout optimization may not be able to handle all scalar superwords because of the existing conflicts among them. However, we ensure that those with higher access frequencies are handled with priority, as they are likely to incur more packing/unpacking operations.

5.2 Optimization for Array Reference Superword

Within a loop nest, an array reference can access different data elements in different iterations, which prevents us from treating it simply as a scalar when applying layout optimization. One alternative is to take advantage of the access patterns of array references to achieve the desired data layout. In this work, we focus on loop nests in which the loop bounds and array references are affine functions of the enclosing loop indices and loop independent variables. As a result, we are able to utilize existing polyhedral model [7] for our data layout optimization. In the polyhedral model, the memory access pattern of an array reference is represented as a memory access vector $\vec{r}$:

$$\vec{r} = \mathbf{Q}\vec{i} + \vec{O}, \tag{1}$$

in which $\vec{i}$ is the iteration vector, $\mathbf{Q}$ is the memory access matrix of size $m \times n$, and $\vec{O}$ is the access offset vector. Based on the access patterns of the variables in the array reference superwords, we combine two different optimizations together when solving the data layout optimization problem, i.e., *affine transformation* and *selective mapping/replication*. It is to be noted that two constraints need to be satisfied here. First, all references in the superword are intra-array references, i.e., accessing the same array. Second, since we use data replication and a given data element may appear in two different memory locations, it can only be applied to read-only array references. The problem of data layout optimization for array reference superword can then be expressed as follows. Given an array reference superword $P_A =< A(\vec{a_1}), ..., A(\vec{a_k}), ..., A(\vec{a_n}) >$ that accesses only array A, our goal is to obtain a new array B from A such that the references in P_A now access array B and the data accessed are arranged contiguously in the memory in the same order as they appear in P_A.

Figure 14 gives an example that illustrates the basic idea of this optimization. It assumes a SIMD datapath width of 2, and the array reference superword is $< A[4i], A[4i+3] >$. We can see that the access patterns of references $A[4i]$ and $A[4i+3]$ on array A require two register loads and additional register reshuffling/permutation operations to pack them in a superword. By contrast, if we can map the elements of array A to array B as illustrated in the example, and at the same time, change the original references to $< B[2i], B[2i+1] >$, we need only one register load to pack them. As a whole, the two references in the superword can now access the new array B in an interleaved fashion.

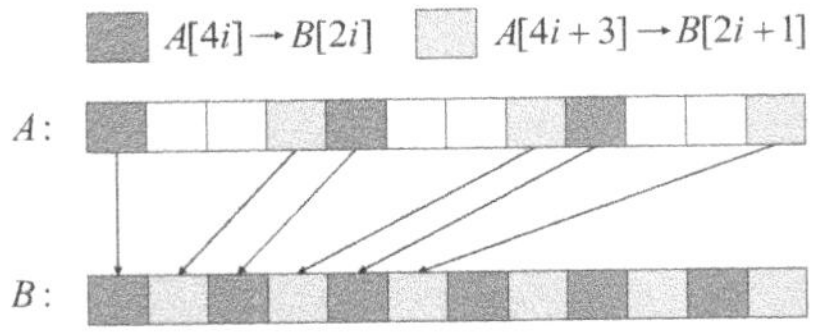

Figure 14. Example layout optimization for array reference pack $< A[4i], A[4i+3] >$.

To put it in a more general way, after the optimization, the access pattern of each individual reference to the new array is a strided pattern. The stride lengths of all the references are the same as the size of the superword, though the starting offsets of the references can vary depending on their respective positions within the superword. Therefore, the data transformation and replication for all the references can be conducted in a uniform fashion. We assume that the access pattern of a reference R to array A can be described as an access vector $\vec{r}$, as shown in Expression (1). Besides, we assume that the default layout $L_{default}$ adopted by the compiler is row major. Our optimization then consists of two steps: (1) affine transformation and (2) mapping to new array.

The first step is similar to data layout transformation for achieving spatial locality. Specifically, we start by determining the data layout L_{opt} for reference R when considering only spatial locality in the loop nest, which largely depends on the innermost loop index. In other words, L_{opt} is a data layout which achieves contiguous data accesses in successive iterations of the innermost loop. Based on that, we obtain a transformation matrix $\mathbf{M}$ for array A by solving the following equation:

$$L_{default}\mathbf{M} = L_{opt}. \tag{2}$$

After the transformation, the new reference R_1 will access neighboring data elements (may not be direct neighbors) of the transformed array A in the innermost loop. The new memory access vector r_1 for R_1 is:

$$\vec{r_1} = \mathbf{Q_1}\vec{i} + \vec{O_1}, \tag{3}$$

where $\mathbf{Q_1} = \mathbf{MQ}$ and $\vec{O_1} = \mathbf{M}\vec{O}$. Since the default layout is assumed to be *row major*, the last column of the new memory access matrix $\mathbf{Q_1}$ that denotes the new access pattern in the innermost loop will be $\vec{c_n} = (0, 0, ..., 0, q_{m,n})^T$.

In the second step, our goal is to map/replicate the data in the transformed array A accessed by R_1 to a new array B, using non-affine transformations, so that the data elements accessed by R_1 are stored in a strided manner within array B. The stride length is equal to the length of the superword L, and the starting offset in B is equal to p, which is the offset of R_1 in the array reference superword. Considering a simple case, if A is a one dimensional array and $R_1 = A[ai+b]$, we map the data in index d accessed by R_1 in A to array B using the following function:

$$f(d) = \frac{d-b}{a}L + p. \tag{4}$$

It is straightforward to prove that the above formula can be used to express the mapping in the example in Figure 14. On the other hand, if A is a two dimensional array, let us assume that $Q_1 =$

(a)
```
S1:  a = A[i];
S2:  c = a × B[4i];
S3:  g = q × B[4i-2];
S4:  b = A[i+1];
S5:  d = b × B[4i+4];
S6:  h = r × B[4i+2];
S7:  A[2i] = d + a × c;
S8:  A[2i+2] = g + r × h;
```

① (a) → (b)

(b)
```
S1:  a = A[i];
S4:  b = A[i+1];
S2:  c = a × B[4i];
S5:  d = b × B[4i+4];
S3:  g = q × B[4i-2];
S6:  h = r × B[4i+2];
S7:  A[2i] = d + a × c;
S8:  A[2i+2] = g + r × h;
```

② (a) → (c)

(c)
```
S1:  a = A[i];
S4:  b = A[i+1];
S5:  d = b × B[4i+4];
S3:  g = q × B[4i-2];
S2:  c = a × B[4i];
S6:  h = r × B[4i+2];
S7:  A[2i]   = d + a × c;
S8:  A[2i+2] = g + r × h;
```

③ (c) → (d)

(d)
```
S1:  a = A[i];
S4:  b = A[i+1];
S5:  d = b × C[2i];
S3:  g = q × C[2i+1];
S2:  c = a × D[2i];
S6:  h = r × D[2i+1];
S7:  A[2i]   = d + a × c;
S8:  A[2i+2] = g + r × h;
```

Figure 15. Example application of our SLP optimization and comparison. (a) Input basic block; (b) Optimization with the original SLP algorithm [17]; (c) Optimization with our superword statement generation; (d) Result obtained using our data layout optimization.

$\begin{bmatrix} q_{11} & 0 \\ q_{21} & q_{22} \end{bmatrix}$ and $\vec{O_1} = (o_1, o_2)^T$. For a data access index $\vec{d} = (d_1, d_2)$ in array A accessed by R_1, we can apply the following mapping function:

$$f(\vec{d}) = (\frac{d_1 - o_1}{q_{11}}, \frac{d_2 - o_2 - q_{21}\frac{d_1 - o_1}{q_{11}}}{q_{22}}L + p). \tag{5}$$

We now discuss the general mapping/replication function for an array A of N dimensions. We first obtain a new equation from Equation (3) by removing the last dimension of vectors $\vec{r_1}$, $\vec{i}$ and $\vec{O_1}$, as well as the last row and the last column of $\mathbf{Q_1}$:

$$\vec{r_1'} = \mathbf{Q_1'}\vec{i'} + \vec{O_1'}, \tag{6}$$

where $\mathbf{Q_1'}$ is nonsingular. Given an array index $\vec{d} = (d_1, d_2, ..., d_N)$ in A accessed by R_1, we first obtain a mapping function for $\vec{d'} = (d_1, d_2, ..., d_{N-1})$:

$$f'(\vec{d'}) = \mathbf{Q_1'}^{-1}(\vec{d_1'} - \vec{O_1'}). \tag{7}$$

Next we obtain the final mapping/replication function for $\vec{d}$ to ensure strided accesses to the new array B in the innermost loop:

$$f(\vec{d}) = (f'(\vec{d'}), \frac{q_{m,n} - O_n' - f'(\vec{d'})(q_{n,1}, ..., q_{n,m-1})^T}{q_{n,m}}L + p). \tag{8}$$

As stated before, our data layout optimization for array reference superwords are limited to intra-array and read-only references in the affine loop nests. In addition, since we employ data mapping/replication, more memory space are needed to hold the replicated data. In case the input data sizes retrieved by static analysis are too large and/or the physical memory available is too small, we can skip the layout transformation for array reference superwords, and only perform layout optimization for scalar superwords.

The pseudo-code of our data layout optimization algorithm is given in Figure 12. Lines 1-9 retrieve the scalar superwords and array reference superwords, on which our algorithm is applicable. Lines 10-22 and 23-39 then apply layout transformation to the scalar superwords and array reference superwords, respectively.

6. An Example

Figure 15 gives an example that illustrates our SLP optimization on a basic block, and compares it with the original SLP algorithm [17]. We assume that one superword can hold two variables. The original input code is shown in Figure 15 (a).

In the figure, the first transformation is performed by the original SLP algorithm. It starts by identifying the set of isomorphic statements with contiguous memory accesses as the seed groups, which are $\{< S_1, S_4 >\}$. It then follows the def-use/use-def chains to obtain additional superword statements, i.e., $< S_2, S_5 >$, while achieving superword reuses, $< a, b >$. The final set of generated superword statements is $\{< S_1, S_4 >, < S_2, S_5 >, < S_3, S_6 >, < S_7, S_8 >\}$, as shown in Figure 15 (b). We can see that, in the optimized code, there is only one superword reuse that can help save one packing operation. That is, packing of $< a, b >$ in $< S_2, S_5 >$ can be saved by reusing it in $< S_1, S_4 >$.

The second transformation in the example applies our first optimization (superword statement generation) to the input code. Following the strategy described in Section 4 step by step, we obtain the optimized code shown in Figure 15 (c), with the set of generated superword statements $\{< S_1, S_4 >, < S_5, S_3 >, < S_2, S_6 >, < S_7, S_8 >\}$. The differences between Figure 15 (b) and Figure 15 (c) mainly result from the grouping decisions for statements $\{S_2, S_3, S_5, S_6\}$. Our framework chooses to group them as $\{< S_5, S_3 >, < S_2, S_6 >\}$, instead of $\{< S_2, S_5 >, < S_3, S_6 >\}$, as the former can bring more superword reuses to the whole basic block. This is achieved by taking a global view whenever a grouping decision is made. As a result, in the transformed code (Figure 15 (c)), we obtain three superword reuses ($< d, g >$, $< c, h >$, and $< a, r >$), compared to only one in Figure 15 (b). Thus, our approach can bring more packing/unpacking reductions.

The third transformation shown performs data layout transformation on the code in Figure 15 (c). Note that more packing/unpacking savings are obtained by optimizing the data layout for both scalar superwords ($< a, b >$, $< d, g >$ and $< c, h >$), and array reference superword ($< B[4i + 4], B[4i - 2] >$ and $< B[4i], B[4i + 2] >$), using the strategy discussed in Section 5. The generated code is given in Figure 15 (d), in which arrays C and D are constructed using data replication and renaming. The boxes that appear in (d) but not in (c) indicate additional benefits from layout optimization. For example, when applying SIMD to S1 and S4, (c) will introduce unpacking overhead for scalar references a and b. But (d) will not, since a and b are already adjacent in memory after the layout transformation and can be written back together from one vector register.

7. Experimental Evaluation

7.1 Implementation and Setup

We evaluated our compiler framework on two systems using 16 benchmarks. We implemented our SLP framework on top of the SUIF 2.0 compiler infrastructure [4, 33]. We also implemented an alternate algorithm proposed in [17] against which we compare our proposed optimizations. In our implementation of the algorithm in [17], we tried to optimize its performance as much as we could. In both the implementations (ours and [17]), we included pre-processing steps which perform alignment analysis and loop-unrolling, with the purpose of exposing more superword level parallelism to the compiler. In other words, both the implementations use exactly the same pre-processing steps. In addition, for both the implementations, we map the register reshuffling/permutation operations to native shuffling instruction set supported by the underlying architecture, rather than loading/storing from/to physical memory. In the following discussion, we refer to the first stage optimization in our SLP framework (superword statement generation) as Global, and the SLP algorithm proposed in [17] as SLP. The version obtained by combining Global with our data layout optimization (discussed in Section 5), is referred to as Global+Layout. Finally, on both the systems, the native compiler-generated version when SLP optimization is enabled is denoted as Native. In our experiments, we compared these four schemes with each other as well as the original applications that do not employ any SLP specific optimization (scalar code). In terms of compilation overhead, compared to the SLP version, our approach increased compilation time by 27% on average.

Table 1. Characteristics of the Intel Dunnington based machine.

Number of Cores	12 cores (2 sockets)
core Type	Xeon CPU E7450(clocked at 2.40GHz)
L1 Data	32KB/core; 8-way; 64-byte line size
L2	total 18MB (6 × 3MB); 12-way; 64-byte line size
L3	total 24MB (2 × 12MB); 12-way, 64-byte line size

Table 2. Characteristics of the AMD Phenom II based machine.

Number of Cores	4 cores
Core Type	AMD Phenom II ×4 (clocked at 3.00GHz)
L1 Data	64KB/core; 2-way; 64-byte line size
L2	total 2MB (4 × 512KB); 16-way; 64-byte line size
L3	total 6MB (1 × 6MB); 48-way, 64-byte line size

Table 3. Benchmark description.

SPEC2006 [3]	cactusADM	Solving the Einstein evolution equations
	soplex	Liner programming solver using simplex algorithm
	lbm	Lattice Boltzmann method
	milc	Simulations of 3-D SU(3) lattic gauge theory
	povray	Ray-tracing: a rendering technique
	gromacs	Performing molecular dynamics
	calculix	Setting up finite element equations and solves them
	dealII	Object oriented finite element software library
	wrf	Weather research and forecasting
	namd	Simulation of large biomolecular systems
NAS [2]	ua	Unstructured adaptive
	ft	3-D Fast fourier transform (FFT)
	bt	Block tridiagonal
	sp	Scalar pentadiagonal
	mg	Multigrid to solve the 3-D possion PDE
	cg	Conjugate gradient

Both the systems used in our experiments, Intel Dunnington based machine and AMD Phenom II based machine, support the SSE/SSE2 instruction set. They contain a set of 128-bit vector registers that enable two 64-bit, four 32-bit, eight 16-bit, or sixteen 8-bit operands to be processed concurrently. In particular, the Intel Dunnington based machine has a dual hexa-core with Intel Xeon CPU E7450 clocking at 2.40GHz, whereas the AMD Phenom II based machine has a quad-core with AMD Phenom II X4 945 operating at 3.00GHz. Table 1 and Table 2 give the detailed configurations of these two commercial machines.

The set of benchmark programs used in this study are listed in Table 3. We used all C and C++ floating-point benchmarks in SPEC2006 [3] as well as six NAS benchmarks [2]. Our applications exhibit diversity in terms of the types of inherent parallelism they contain. For each benchmark, we used the largest input size available. The results reported below represent average values across multiple runs with the same configuration, and collected using one core by default (we present multicore results later).

7.2 Results

Our first set of results present the execution time reductions (on the Intel architecture) brought by Global, SLP and Native, all normalized, for each benchmark, to the execution time observed when no SLP optimization is enabled (scalar code). In Figure 16, bench-

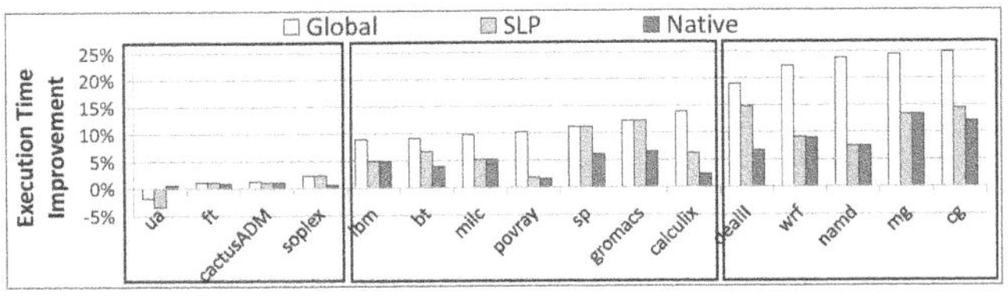

Figure 16. Performance improvements in terms of execution times on the Intel Dunnington based machine.

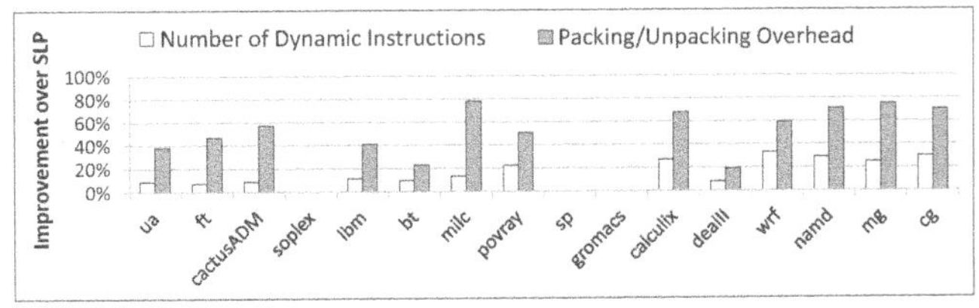

Figure 17. Percentage dynamic instruction and packing/unpacking overhead reductions brought by Global over SLP.

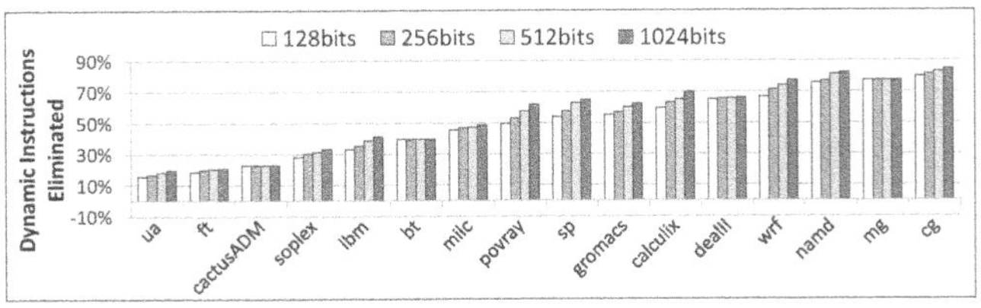

Figure 18. Percentage elimination of dynamic instructions under different datapath widths.

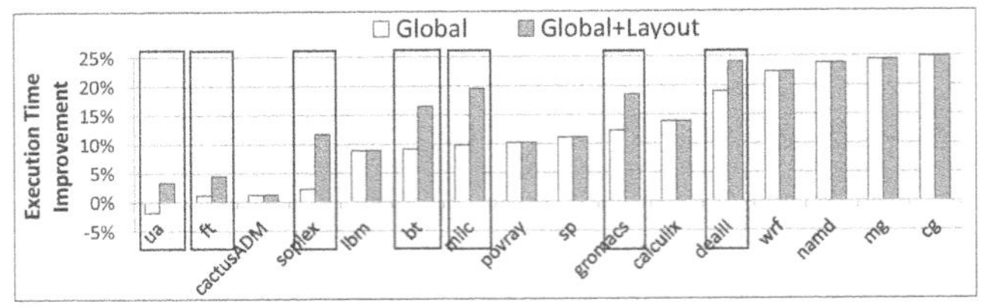

Figure 19. Performance improvements in terms of execution times with Global+Layout on the Intel Dunnington based machine.

marks on the x-axis are ordered from the one for which Global generates the least improvement, to the one it generates the highest improvement. Based on the improvements achieved by Global, we can divide our benchmarks into three categories (each category is marked by its own box in Figure 16). We further observe that our approach (Global) and SLP generate the same results in three of all the benchmarks tested; however, in all the other applications, Global consistently outperforms SLP. Our Global version performs better over SLP when there are more valid scheduling candidates and more potential superword reuses in a basic block. In addition, SLP and Native result in the same output code and performance in four applications.

To explain the performance difference between our approach (Global) and SLP, we present in Figure 17 the reductions brought by Global over SLP in terms of the dynamic instructions executed (excluding the packing/unpacking instructions) and the packing/unpacking overheads. It can be seen that our approach cuts dynamic instructions and packing/unpacking operations of SLP on average by 14.5% and 43.5%, respectively. In particular, we observe that Global achieves significant packing/unpacking instruction reductions for most benchmarks tested, which shows the advantage of our global strategy of extracting superword reuses.

We next study how close the results generated by our approach (Global) are to the optimal potential improvements, i.e., if superword level parallelism could be fully exploited. Figure 18 plots the percentage of dynamic instructions eliminated by Global over the scalar code for a variety of hypothetical datapath widths. Recall that both of our machines use superwords of 128 bits. When we look at the results of 128-bit superword, we observe that, on average, nearly 49.1% of the dynamic instructions of the original applications (without any SLP optimization) are eliminated by Global. Further, when we increase the datapath width to 1024 bits, this value climbs to 54.5%. Considering that future architectures may employ longer datapath widths, our approach can be more effective in the future.

Figure 19 gives the results (execution time reductions over the scalar code) of Global+Layout (results of Global are reproduced here for ease of comparison). We can observe that our data layout optimization brings additional benefits in seven of our benchmarks (those benchmarks are marked using rectangles). The reason why the layout optimization does not bring any benefit in the remaining benchmarks is because its application is restricted by certain constraints as discussed in Section 5. In particular, we employ data replication to optimize layout for the array reference superwords, which has a negative impact on the cache behavior. In order to achieve improvement, the benefit of layout optimization has to outweigh the cost. Otherwise, in our implementation, we skip the data optimization phase. It is to be noted that, when considering the results of the SLP version in Figure 16, the highest performance improvement Global+Layout brings over SLP is about 15.2%.

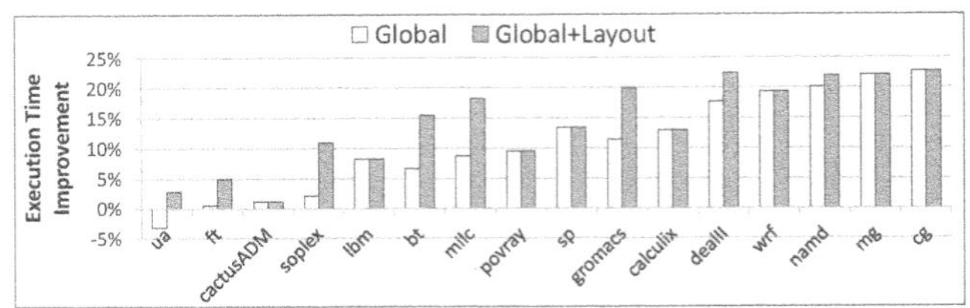

Figure 20. Performance improvements in terms of execution times with Global+Layout on the AMD Phenom II based machine.

We also present results collected on our AMD system. Figure 20 plots the execution time reductions brought by Global and Global+Layout over the scalar code, respectively. We see that, on average, Global and Global+Layout bring 10.8% and 14.1% improvements, which are similar to the average improvements we obtained on the Intel machine (12% and 14.9% for Global and Global+Layout, respectively). We believe that, in cases where savings are lower (compared to the Intel machine) on the AMD machine, the main factor is the higher packing/unpacking costs.

Finally, we evaluate the effectiveness of our compiler (both Global and Global+Layout) on multithreaded applications. For this evaluation, we focus on the NAS benchmarks in our experimental suite, and present the execution time reductions over the scalar code in Figure 21. These experiments are performed in our Intel Dunnington based machine (with a total core count of 12, distributed over two sockets). Note that, in these plots, the y-axis gives the execution time reductions brought by our approach over the original application, with both of them running on the same number of cores. We clearly see that both of our approaches, Global in Figure 21(a) and Global+Layout in Figure 21(b), bring consis-

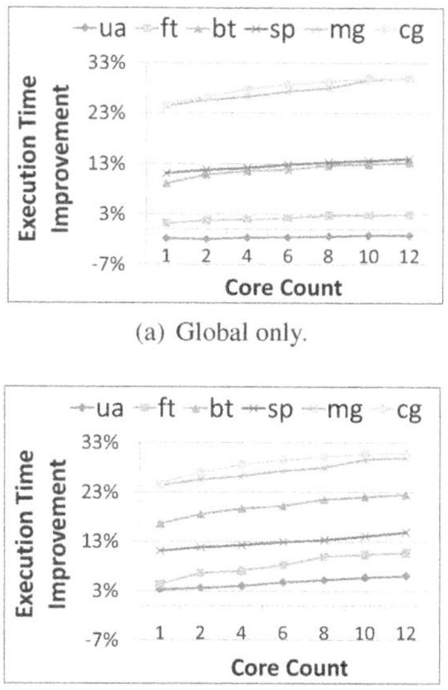

(a) Global only.

(b) Global+Layout.

Figure 21. Performance improvements in terms of execution times with different core counts (x-axis).

tent improvements across different core counts. The results become slightly better when we increase the number of cores, mostly due to the less-than-perfect scalability of the original applications.

8. Concluding Remarks

The main contribution of this paper is an automated compiler framework that detects and exploits superword level parallelism in application programs. We apply a two-stage strategy, namely, superword statement generation and data layout optimization, to increase SIMD level parallelism, reduce the number of superword packing/unpacking operations by extracting more superword reuses, and reduce the overhead of mandatory packing/unpacking operations by reorganizing data in the memory. The results collected on two commercial systems (Intel and AMD) indicate that the proposed SLP framework performs better than an existing SLP scheduling algorithm, bringing as much as 15.2% performance improvement.

Acknowledgments

This research is supported in part by NSF grants #1147388, #1152479, #1017882, #0963839, #0720645, #0811687, #0702519 and a grant from Microsoft Corporation.

References

[1] Pentium processor with MMX technology. `http://edc.intel.com/Platforms/Previous/Processors/Pentium-MMX/`.

[2] NAS parallel benchmark suite. `http://www.nas.nasa.gov/Resources/Software/npb.html`.

[3] Spec cpu2006. `http://www.spec.org/cpu2006/`.

[4] The SUIF 2 compiler system. `http://suif.stanford.edu/suif/suif2/`.

[5] R. Barik, J. Zhao, and V. Sarkar. Efficient selection of vector instructions using dynamic programming. *MICRO*, 2010.

[6] A. Bik, M. Girkar, P. Grey, and X. Tian. Automatic intra-register vectorization for the intel architecture. *IJPP*, 2002.

[7] U. Bondhugula, A. Hartono, J. Ramanujam, and P. Sadayappan. A practical automatic polyhedral parallelizer and locality optimizer. *Proc. of PLDI*, 2008.

[8] D. DeVries. A vectorizing SUIF compiler: Implementation and performance. *Master's Thesis*, 1997.

[9] A. Eichenberger, P. Wu, and K. O'Brien. Vectorization for SIMD architectures with alignment constraints. *PLDI*, 2004.

[10] R. Hanxleden and K. Kennedy. Relaxing SIMD control flow constraints using loop transformations. *PLDI*, 1992.

[11] T. Henretty, K. Stock, L. Pouchet, F. Franchetti, J. Ramanujam, and P. Sadayappan. Data layout transformation for stencil computations on short-vector SIMD architectures. *CC*, 2011.

[12] M. Hohenauer, F. Engel, R. Leupers, G. Ascheid, and H. Meyr. A SIMD optimization framework for retargetable compilers. *TACO*, 2009.

[13] IBM. PowerPC microprocessor family: Vector/SIMD multimedia extension technology programming environments manual. *IBM Systems and Technology Group*, 2005.

[14] Intel. IA-32 intel architecture optimization reference manual. 2005.

[15] A. Krall and S. Lelait. Compilation techniques for multimedia processors. *IJPP*, 2000.

[16] S. Larsen. Compilation techniques for short-vector instructions. *PhD Thesis*, 2006.

[17] S. Larsen and S. Amarasinghe. Exploiting superword level parallelism with multimedia instruction sets. *PLDI*, 2000.

[18] C. Lee and D. DeVries. Initial results on the performance and cost of vector microprocessors. *Micro*, 1997.

[19] C. Lee and M. Stoodley. Simple vector microprocessors for multimedia applications. *Micro*, 1998.

[20] R. Leupers and F. David. A uniform optimization technique for offset assignment problems. *ISSS*, 1998.

[21] D. Nuzman and A. Zaks. Outer-loop vectorization - revisited for short SIMD architectures. *PACT*, 2008.

[22] D. Nuzman, I. Rosen, and A. Zaks. Auto-vectorization of interleaved data for SIMD. *PLDI*, 2006.

[23] S. Oberman, G. Favor, and F. Weber. Amd 3dnow! technology: Architecture and implementations. *IEEE MICRO*, 1999.

[24] G. Ren, P. Wu, and D. Padua. Optimizing data permutations for simd devices. *PLDI*, 2006.

[25] J. Shin. Compiler optimizations for architectures supporting superword-level parallelism. *PhD Thesis*, 2005.

[26] J. Shin, J. Chame, and M. Hall. Compiler-controlled caching in superword register files for multimedia extension architectures. *PACT*, 2002.

[27] J. Shin, J. Chame, and M. Hall. Exploiting superword-level locality in multimedia extension architectures. *JILP*, 2003.

[28] J. Shin, M. Hall, and J. Chame. Superword-level parallelism in the presence of control flow. *CGO*, 2005.

[29] N. Sreraman and R. Govindarajan. A vectorizing compiler for multimedia extensions. *IJPP*, 2000.

[30] C. Tenllado, L. Pinuel, M. Prieto, and F. Catthoor. Pack transposition: Enhancing superword level parallelism exploitation. *PARCO*, 2005.

[31] C. Tenllado, L. P. M. Prieto, F. Tirado, and F. Catthoor. Improving superword level parallelism support in modern compilers. *CODES+ISSS*, 2005.

[32] M. Weiss. Strip-mining on SIMD architectures. *ICS*, 1991.

[33] R. Wilson, R. French, C. Wilson, S. Amarasinghe, J. Anderson, S. Tjiang, S. Liao, C. Tseng, M. Hall, M. Lam, and J. Hennessy. SUIF: An infrastructure for research on parallelizing and optimizing compilers. *ACM SIGPLAN Notices*, 1994.

[34] P. Wu, A. Eichenberger, and A. Wang. Efficient SIMD code generation for runtime alignment and length conversion. *CGO*, 2005.

Speculative Separation for Privatization and Reductions

Nick P. Johnson Hanjun Kim Prakash Prabhu Ayal Zaks† David I. August

Princeton University, Princeton, NJ
{npjohnso, hanjunk, pprabhu, august}@princeton.edu

†Intel Corporation, Haifa, Israel
ayal.zaks@intel.com

Abstract

Automatic parallelization is a promising strategy to improve application performance in the multicore era. However, common programming practices such as the reuse of data structures introduce artificial constraints that obstruct automatic parallelization. Privatization relieves these constraints by replicating data structures, thus enabling scalable parallelization. Prior privatization schemes are limited to arrays and scalar variables because they are sensitive to the layout of dynamic data structures. This work presents Privateer, the first fully automatic privatization system to handle dynamic and recursive data structures, even in languages with unrestricted pointers. To reduce sensitivity to memory layout, Privateer speculatively separates memory objects. Privateer's lightweight runtime system validates speculative separation and speculative privatization to ensure correct parallel execution. Privateer enables automatic parallelization of general-purpose C/C++ applications, yielding a geomean whole-program speedup of 11.4× over best sequential execution on 24 cores, while non-speculative parallelization yields only 0.93×.

Categories and Subject Descriptors D.1.3 [*Software*]: Concurrent Programming—Parallel Programming; D.3.4 [*Programming Languages*]: Processors—Compilers, Optimization

General Terms Languages, Performance, Design, Experimentation

Keywords Automatic parallelization, Separation, Speculation

1. Introduction

The microprocessor industry has committed to multicore architectures. These additional hardware resources, however, offer no benefit to sequential applications. Automatic parallelization is a promising approach to achieve performance on existing and new applications without additional programmer effort or application changes.

Yet automatic parallelization is not the norm. One limiting factor is the compiler's inability to distribute work across processors due to reuse of data structures. This reuse does not contribute to the constructive data flow of the program, but creates contention that prevents efficient parallel execution. A parallelizing compiler must either respect this contention by enforcing exclusivity on accesses to shared data structures, or ignore it and risk data races that change program behavior.

A compiler can remove contention by creating a *private* copy of the data structures for each worker process. Privatization eliminates contention and relaxes the program dependence structure by replicating the reused storage locations, producing multiple copies in memory that support independent, concurrent access. Similarly, reduction techniques relax ordering constraints on associative, commutative operators by replacing (or *expanding*) storage locations. Prior work [7, 21, 22, 29, 32] demonstrates that privatization and reductions are key enablers of parallelization.

Privatization Criterion	Memory Layout: Static	Memory Layout: Speculative
Speculative	LRPD [22] R-LRPD [7]	*Privateer (this work)*
Dynamic	PD [21]	
Static	Polaris [29] ASSA [14] Array Expansion [10] DSA [31] RSSA [23]	
Manual	Paralax [32]	STMs [8, 18]

Figure 1: Privatization Criterion and Memory Layout.

The applicability of privatization systems can be understood in two dimensions (Figure 1). A system uses the *Privatization Criterion* [21] to decide if replacing a shared data structure would change program behavior. To replicate object storage, a system determines *Memory Layout*: the base address and size of memory objects. Prior work assesses the privatization criterion statically [29], dynamically [21], or speculatively [7, 22].

However, prior work limits memory layout to arrays and scalar variables only and fails for programs that use linked or recursive data structures. The prevalent use of pointers and dynamic memory allocation creates a dichotomy between static accesses and objects. A pointer may refer to different objects of different sizes at different times, and static analysis usually fails to disambiguate these cases. As a result, it is difficult for a static compiler to decide *which objects* to duplicate, even when it can decide *which accesses* are private. Prior techniques are largely inapplicable to most C or C++ applications for this reason. Table 1 summarizes prior work.

This work proposes Privateer, the first fully automatic system capable of privatizing data structures in languages with pointers, type casts, and dynamic allocation. Instead of relying solely on static analysis to determine memory layout, Privateer employs profiling to characterize memory accesses at the granularity of memory objects. Using profiling information and static analysis, Privateer identifies accesses to memory objects that are expected to be iteration-private. Such objects are speculatively privatized, predicting that their accesses will remain iteration-private, thereby relaxing program dependence structure and enabling optimization and parallelization.

Privateer overcomes difficulties in memory layout while minimizing validation overheads. The loop's memory footprint is partitioned into several *logical heaps* according to observed access patterns. Privateer speculates that these heaps remain *separated* at runtime rather than speculating that individual memory access pairs are independent. Workers validate this separation property autonomously, requiring neither a log of accesses nor communication with other workers. This separation property is efficiently checked

PLDI'12, June 11–16, 2012, Beijing, China.

using compact metadata encoded in pointer *addresses*. Speculative separation reduces sensitivity to memory layout, thus allowing Privateer to extend an LRPD-style shadow memory test [22] to arbitrary objects. Privateer's robust, layout-insensitive privatization and reductions enable automatic parallelization of applications with linked and recursive data structures. This work contributes:

- the first **fully automatic** system to support privatization and reductions involving **pointers and dynamic allocation**;
- an efficient, scalable validation scheme for **speculative privatization and reductions** based on the **speculative separation** of logical heaps according to usage patterns; and,
- an application of this speculative privatization and reduction technique to the problem of **automatic parallelization**.

Privateer's transformations facilitate scalable automatic parallelization on commodity shared-memory machines. No programmer hints are used, nor are any hardware extensions assumed. We implement Privateer and evaluate it on a set of 5 programs. On a 24-core machine, results demonstrate a geomean whole-program speedup of 11.4× over best sequential execution. To achieve these results, Privateer privatized linked and recursive data structures which are beyond the abilities of prior work. Speculation via heap separation allows Privateer to extract scalable performance from general purpose, irregular applications.

2. Motivation

Automatic parallelization is sensitive to the dependences in a program. A single dependence may prevent a compiler from parallelizing an entire loop. Some dependences may never manifest, yet static analysis is unable to prove so. Speculation allows a compiler to overcome many of the limitations of static analysis. Instead of optimizing for a conservative worst case, a speculative compilation system assumes some common case of program behavior and optimizes accordingly [17, 19, 30]. A speculative system inserts code to validate these assumptions at runtime and recover when they fail. *Dependence speculation* is the application of speculative methods to remove those dependences which inhibit parallelization. However, dependence speculation is inappropriate for dependences which occur frequently. Privatization targets *false* (anti- and output-) dependences. Privatization succeeds even when false dependences are *frequent*, where dependence speculation fails.

Consider the code in Figure 2a (simplified from MiBench `dijkstra` [12]). Attempts to parallelize it are inhibited by frequent false dependences incident on reused data structures. The outer loop (Line 46) repeatedly performs Dijkstra's algorithm. However, the loop reuses two data structures across iterations: `Q`, a linked-list work queue (Line 5), and `pathcost`, an array of shortest path costs (Line 6). Although each iteration is conceptually independent, the reuse of `Q` and `pathcost` creates false dependences that impose an order on outer loop iterations, preventing parallelization.

These false dependences occur between every pair of iterations of the loop. If a naïve compiler were to speculate that these false dependences never manifest, the program would misspeculate on *every* iteration, and would fail to achieve scalable performance.

A privatization strategy is more appropriate for such cases. Privatization eliminates false dependences by creating a disjoint copy of the loop's memory footprint for each worker, enabling workers to proceed independently and without synchronization. Each worker operates on a different `Q` containing different linked list nodes and on different `pathcost` arrays. To prove the privatization criterion, the strategy must confirm the absence of a loop-carried flow dependence on every pointer load and store. This has been addressed using static analysis [29], dynamic tests [21], and speculation [7, 22] in prior work. To replace these data structures, the privatization strategy must also determine the memory layout.

Determining the memory layout entails identifying all private objects: `Q`, `pathcost`, and all linked list nodes. The memory layout enables the system to duplicate objects and re-route memory accesses so workers refer to their private copy. In the absence of pointers, a variable's source-level name uniquely identifies a memory object, allowing the compiler to determine the object's address and size. However, languages with pointers and dynamic allocation allow a many-to-many relationship between names and objects. Pointers refer to different objects at different times and allocation sites produce many objects, causing the code to exhibit different reuse patterns. Unlike related work, Privateer addresses the complications of pointers, type casts, and dynamic allocation.

Privateer speculatively separates the program state into several *logical heaps* according to the reuse patterns observed during profiling. The compiler indicates this separation to the runtime system, which in turn privatizes without concern for individual objects. By grouping objects, a logical heap can be privatized as a whole by adjusting virtual page tables, neither requiring complicated bookkeeping nor adjusting object addresses in a running program. All objects of each logical heap are placed within a fixed memory address range, allowing efficient validation of the separation property. In the example, `Q`, `pathcost`, and all linked list nodes are accessed privately whereas `adj` is only read; Privateer allocates them to distinct *logical heaps* of private objects and read-only objects at compile time, validating this separation at runtime.

Speculative separation greatly simplifies the memory layout problem, condensing unboundedly many objects into few heaps. This allows Privateer to apply a speculative privatization and reduction transformation on programs with pointers, dynamic allocation, and type casts. This removes false dependences, relaxing program constraints, and enables scalable automatic parallelization.

3. Design

Privateer is a combined compiler-runtime system that privatizes dynamic memory objects efficiently and addresses several challenges outlined in this section. The compiler system acts fully automatically without any guidance from the programmer. The compiler overcomes the limitations of static analysis by using profiling information to guide its transformations and produces code which interacts with the runtime system. The runtime system provides efficient mechanisms for replication of objects to support privatization and for recovery from misspeculation.

Privateer's privatization criterion, forbids cross-iteration flow dependences but, unlike [22], is not limited to arrays:

Privatization Criterion: *Let O be a memory object that is accessed in a loop L. O can be privatized if and only if no read from O returns a value written in an earlier iteration of L.*

Privateer also supports a related type of privatization that involves reduction operations with real flow dependences. The accumulator variable is expanded into multiple copies, each updated independently across iterations of the loop, after which all copies are merged to the final result. We list here our reduction criterion:

Reduction Criterion: *Let O be a memory object that is accessed in a loop L. O can be reduction-privatized if and only if all updates to O within L are performed by a single associative and commutative (reduction) operator, and no operation within L reads an intermediate value from O.*

The use of pointers and dynamic allocation in general purpose programs requires privatization and reduction systems to address:

1. *Rich Heap Model:* the solution needs to accurately distinguish among the many and diverse objects of the program, even when several objects are created by one static instruction.

Technique	Fully Automatic	Supports Pointers and Dynamic Allocation	Privatization			Reductions		
			Supported	Not limited by Static Analysis		Supported	Not limited by Static Analysis	
				Criterion	Memory Layout		Criterion	Memory Layout
Paralax [32]	×	-	✓	-	-	-	-	-
TL2 [8], Intel STM [18]	×	-	✓	-	-	-	-	-
PD [21], LRPD [22], R-LRPD [7]	✓	×	✓	✓	×	✓	✓	×
Hybrid Analysis [24]	✓	×	✓	✓	×	✓	✓	×
Array Expansion [10], ASSA [14], DSA [31]	✓	×	✓	×	×	×	-	-
STMLite+LLVM [17]	✓	✓	✓	✓	-	✓	×	×
CorD+Objects [27]	✓	✓	✓	×	×	✓	×	×
Privateer (this work)	✓	✓	✓	✓	✓	✓	✓	✓

Table 1: Comparison of Privateer with privatization and reduction schemes.

```
1  struct node {int vx; node *next}
2  struct queue {node *head,*tail}
3
5  queue Q;
6  int pathcost[N];
7  int adj[N][N];
8
9  void enqueueQ(int v) {
11  node* N = (node*)malloc(
12           sizeof(node));
13  N->vx = v;
16  N->next = Q.tail;
17  ...
20  Q.tail = N;
21 }
22
23 int dequeueQ(void) {
24  ...
27  qKill = Q.head;
30  v = qKill->vx;
33  Q.head = qKill->next;
35  free(qKill);
36  return v;
37 }
45 void hot_loop(int K) {
46  for (src=0; src < N; ++src) {
55   for (i=0; i < N; ++i)
56    pathcost[i] = infinity;
58
59   pathcost[src] = 0;
60   enqueueQ(src);
61
62   while (!emptyQ()) {
63    v = dequeueQ();
66    d = pathcost[v];
67    for (i=0; i < N; ++i) {
68     ncost = adj[v][i] + d;
69     if (pathcost[i] > ncost) {
73      pathcost[i] = ncost;
74      enqueueQ(i);
75     }
76    }
77   }
81  }
82 }
```

(a) Sequential `dijkstra` example.

```
1  struct node {int vx; node *next }
2  struct queue {node *head,*tail }
3
4  // Reallocation (Section 4.4)
5  queue *Q;
6  int *pathcost;
7  int **adj;
8
9  void enqueueQ(int v) {
10  // Reallocation (Section 4.4)
11  node* N = h_alloc(sizeof(node),
12                    SHORTLIVED);
13  N->vx = v;
14  // Privacy Check (Section 4.6)
15  private_read(&Q->tail, sizeof(node*));
16  N->next = Q->tail;
17  ...
18  // Privacy Check (Section 4.6)
19  private_write(&Q->tail, sizeof(node*));
20  Q->tail = N;
21 }
22
23 int dequeueQ(void) {
24  ...
25  // Privacy Check (Section 4.6)
26  private_read( &Q->head );
27  qKill = Q->head;
28  // Separation Check (Section 4.5)
29  check_heap( qKill, SHORTLIVED );
30  v = qKill->vx;
31  // Privacy Check (Section 4.6)
32  private_write( &Q->tail );
33  Q->head = qKill->next;
34  // Reallocation (Section 4.4)
35  h_dealloc(qKill, SHORTLIVED);
36  return v;
37 }
38
39 // Reallocation (Section 4.4)
40 void before_main(void) {
41  Q = h_alloc(sizeof(queue), PRIVATE);
42  pathcost = h_alloc(N*sizeof(int),PRIVATE);
43  adj = h_alloc(N*N*sizeof(int), READONLY);
44 }
45 void hot_loop(int K) {
46  for (src=0; src < N; ++src) {
47   // Privacy Check (Section 4.6)
48   private_write(&Q->head,sizeof(node*));
49   private_write(&Q->tail,sizeof(node*));
50   // Value prediction
51   Q->head = NULL;
52   Q->tail = NULL;
53   // Privacy Check (Section 4.6)
54   private_write(pathcost,N*sizeof(int));
55   for (i=0; i < N; ++i)
56    pathcost[i] = infinity;
57   // Privacy Check (Section 4.6)
58   private_write(&pathcost[src],sizeof(int));
59   pathcost[src] = 0;
60   enqueueQ(src);
61
62   while (!emptyQ()) {
63    v = dequeueQ();
64    // Privacy Check (Section 4.6)
65    private_read(&pathcost[v],sizeof(int));
66    d = pathcost[v];
67    for (i=0; i < N; ++i) {
68     ncost = adj[v][i] + d;
69     if (pathcost[i] > ncost) {
70      // Privacy Check (Section 4.6)
71      private_write( &pathcost[i],
72             sizeof(int) );
73      pathcost[i] = ncost;
74      enqueueQ(i);
75     }
76    }
77   }
78   // Value prediction
79   if( Q->head != NULL ) misspec();
80   if( Q->tail != NULL ) misspec();
81  }
82 }
```

(b) Speculatively privatized code, before parallelization. Changes are in grey.

Figure 2: Motivating example for Privateer. The original sequential application is on the left. The right shows the code after the speculative privatization transformation, before it is automatically parallelized. Unchanged lines are consistently numbered between (a) and (b).

2. *Robust Points-to Map:* Instructions manipulate pointers, yet privatization replicates memory objects. A robust mapping from pointers to objects is needed to consistently update both. In Figure 2, the system must determine the target object of pointers loaded from `queue` and `node` objects (Lines 27 and 33).

3. *Object Base, Size, Count:* The duplicated storage must be at least as large as the original. This also affects the allocation of metadata at per-object or per-byte resolution. In Figure 2, the system should know how many times, where, and how large it allocates before privatizing `node N` in Line 11.

4. *Replacement Transparency:* When replacing the storage in a running system, all pointers must remain valid. The system cannot *move* privatized storage as it cannot guarantee that all references will be updated. The system cannot even assume that pointer values are visible in the IR because of the possibility of "disguised" pointers [3].

Privateer overcomes these issues by speculating separation properties of the program. In this paper, we say that an *access path* is a sequence of operations which computes a pointer address, and that two access paths are *separated* if the sets of objects they name are disjoint. Separation is weaker than *points-to* information, since it does not enumerate the objects referenced by an access path. Separation is weaker than *alias* information, since it says nothing about two addresses within the same object. Yet separation information is strong enough to simplify memory layout. Further, separation can be validated at runtime without inter-worker communication.

3.1 Analysis and Transformation

The first task of the compiler is to recognize situations where privatization eliminates false dependences (and flow dependences for reductions), thereby enabling automatic parallelization. Privateer builds a representation of the dependence structure of the program's hot loops, and then employs memory and control profiling to remove rare and nonexistent dependences. This representation contains only frequently occurring dependences. Privateer interprets this as an optimistic view of the expected program dependences.

When the compiler discovers a hot loop that cannot be parallelized due to false or flow dependences, it investigates whether the privatization and reduction criteria apply. Privateer classifies every memory object according to its observed usage pattern within the loop. Based on this classification, the compiler decides if privatization is applicable and would enable parallelization.

The second task of the compiler is to perform the privatization transformation by inserting additional instructions to the program. These instructions interact with the runtime system to control the allocation of objects in memory and to validate that memory accesses match the expected patterns. The resulting speculatively privatized program is then amenable to automatic parallelization by parallelizing transformations such as DOALL.

3.2 Runtime Support System

Traditional privatization systems do not privatize many classes of dynamically allocated data structures since they are unable to determine the object sizes, number, and locations. Privateer takes a different approach. Privateer assigns each memory object to one of several *logical heaps*. At runtime, those objects are allocated within a known, fixed range for each logical heap. This simplifies the memory layout problem, since the runtime may treat each logical heap as a single object with known base and bound instead of many unknown objects. Privateer may test whether a pointer address falls within a given heap using only a few instructions. The system replaces object storage by manipulating page maps. Replacement transparency is satisfied since virtual addresses do not change.

Before or after the invocation of a parallel region, these logical heaps behave as *normal* program memory and support any form of access. During an invocation, Privateer changes the process' virtual page map, thus replacing the heaps' physical pages. This allows the runtime to replicate the storage for *all* objects in a heap, marking them with the copy-on-write page protection. Initially, values within the private heap appear identical to those from the sequential region. However, the OS traps updates to the private heap and silently duplicates those pages, thus isolating each worker's updates. The reduction heap is replaced and bytes within those pages are initialized with the identity value for the reduction operator.

Privateer validates most speculative properties with *instantaneous* checks—they can be determined at a point in the code and do not rely on history of previous operations. The speculative mapping of pointers to a particular heap can be checked by examining only the pointer address. The speculative restriction on the lifetime of short-lived objects can be checked at the end of each iteration. These properties are strong enough to provide the enabling benefits of speculation, yet induce only minimal runtime overhead.

Privacy validation is more complicated, requiring that we consider all operations that access a particular private object. A challenging aspect of privacy validation is allowing reads of values live-in to the loop. A worker who reads a live-in value must guarantee that no worker defined that value in an earlier iteration, requiring a flow of information among workers. The Privateer runtime system employs a two-phase approach to reduce the communication overhead of validation. The first phase occurs immediately, and detects several cases of privacy violation without any communication among the workers. The second phase completes the validation check by handling the cases of privacy violation that require communication. The second phase occurs during a checkpoint operation (see Section 5.2).

Upon entering the parallel region, the runtime also creates a *shadow* heap for each worker which has the same size as the private heap. Each byte of data within the private heap corresponds to a byte of metadata in the shadow heap. Privateer records metadata in the shadow heap about the history of accesses to private memory. This shadow heap is analogous to the shadow arrays in the LRPD technique [22]. Each byte of metadata contains a code indicating the history of that private byte given all information available to a worker. In particular, metadata contains enough information to determine whether a byte of private memory *may* contain a live-in value, or if it was necessarily defined during an earlier iteration of the parallel region. The interpretation of these codes is discussed in Section 5.1.

Since the compiler relies on profile driven speculative parallelization, the runtime system must support rollback and recovery in case of misspeculation. Privateer provides this via checkpointing. Speculative state is collected from all workers at regular intervals and validated for misspeculation. If no violations occur, then the checkpoint is marked non-speculative and used as a recovery point. Checkpoints are only collected and validated after a large number of iterations. This policy reduces checkpointing and validation overheads in the common case, but discards and recomputes a larger amount of work upon misspeculation.

4. The Privateer Analysis and Transformation

The Privateer system provides fully automatic analyses and transformations to privatize the data structures used by general purpose C and C++ applications. Figure 3 describes the compiler component. Each step is described in the following sections.

4.1 Profiling

The Privateer system uses a novel pointer-to-object profiler to connect dynamic pointer addresses with a set of object names. The profiler assigns static names to the memory objects of global or constant variables. The profiler names dynamic objects (e.g. `malloc` or `new`) or stack slots according to the instruction which allocates them and a *dynamic context*. The dynamic context distinguishes dynamic instances of a static instruction by listing the function and loop invocations which enclose that instruction.

The pointer-to-object profiler instruments the program to maintain a interval map from ranges of memory addresses to the name of the memory object which occupies that space, like [34]. This interval map enables the profiled program to determine the name of the object referenced by any pointer during a profiling run. The profiler instruments every pointer that cannot be mapped to a unique object at compile time. The profiler accumulates this information over program execution.

Finally, this profiler tracks the allocation and deallocation of memory objects with respect to dynamic contexts. This information allows the compiler to characterize the *lifetime* of objects and

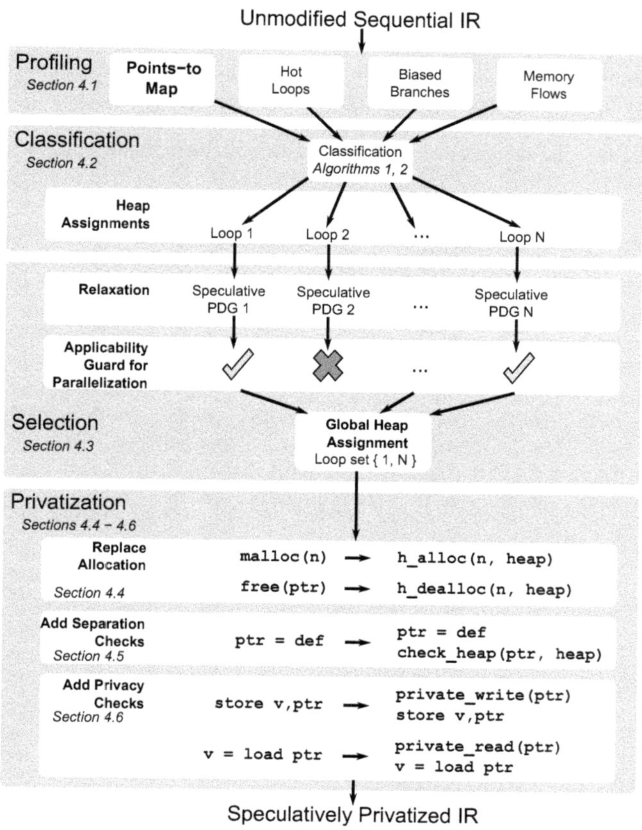

Figure 3: Structure of the Privateer Analysis and Transformation.

distinguish between short- and long-lived objects, supporting object lifetime speculation [13]. Short-lived objects exist only within a single iteration of a loop.

In Figure 2, the pointer-to-object map contains the following data. The pointer `qKill` on Line 27 always points to objects allocated by Line 11 in one of two contexts: either `enqueueQ` called at Line 60 or `enqueueQ` called at Line 74. All objects allocated on Line 11 are short-lived with respect to the loop on Line 46.

Privateer uses other profilers. A trip count profiler [15] identifies biased branches for control speculation (à la [5]). A memory flow dependence profiler similar to [4] augments static analysis. A value-prediction profiler guides value prediction speculation (à la [11]). Finally, an execution time profiler, similar to gprof [26], finds hot loops.

4.2 Classification

The hot loops access some objects in a restricted fashion. Using profile information, the system classifies each object as one of five access patterns: private, reduction, short-lived, read-only, and unrestricted. These labels are summarized in a *heap assignment*, which describes overall memory usage by mapping each object to one of the five heaps with restricted semantics.

Algorithm 1 determines a heap assignment for each loop. First, it calls `getFootprint` (Algorithm 2) to determine the read, write, and reduction footprints of the loop. These footprints are represented as sets of memory object names and may overlap. This function accumulates the objects written by a store operation or read by a load operation. The algorithm also identifies operation sequences which syntactically resemble an associative and commutative reduction operation. Limited profile *coverage* has minimal effect on Privateer's analyses, since such code is likely removed via control speculation.

Algorithm 1: *classify(L)*

let ShortLived = $\emptyset$; **let** Redux = $\emptyset$; **let** Unrestricted = $\emptyset$;
let Private = $\emptyset$; **let** ReadOnly = $\emptyset$;
let (ReadFootprint, WriteFootprint, ReduxFootprint) = getFootprint(L) ;
foreach *object* $o \in$ *WriteFootprint* $\cup$ *ReadFootprint* **do**
  if *Profile.isShortLived(o, L)* **then**
    ShortLived = ShortLived $\cup$ { o } ;
  end
end
foreach *object* $o \in$ *ReduxFootprint* **do**
  if *(o $\notin$ ReadFootprint)* **and** *(o $\notin$ WriteFootprint)* **then**
    Redux = Redux $\cup$ { o } ;
  end
end
let D = All cross-iteration memory flow dependences in L
  (assuming control and memory flow profiles)
foreach *dependence* $(a \rightarrow b) \in D$ **do**
  let (R_a, W_a, X_a) = getFootprint(a) ;
  let (R_b, W_b, X_b) = getFootprint(b) ;
  let F = $(W_a \cup X_a) \cap (R_b \cup X_b)$;
  Unrestricted = Unrestricted $\cup$ (F $\setminus$ ShortLived $\setminus$ Redux) ;
end
Private = WriteFootprint $\setminus$ ShortLived $\setminus$ Unrestricted $\setminus$ Redux;
ReadOnly = ReadFootprint $\setminus$ ShortLived $\setminus$ Unrestricted $\setminus$ Redux $\setminus$ Private;
return (ShortLived, Redux, Unrestricted, Private, ReadOnly);

In Figure 2a, Privateer computes the footprint of the hot loop (Line 46), as follows. The read set contains the global queue structure `Q`, the global arrays `pathcost` and `adj`, and all linked list nodes allocated by Line 11. The write set contains `Q`, `pathcost`, and all linked list nodes. The reduction set is empty.

Algorithm 2: *getFootprint(S)*

let ReadFootprint = $\emptyset$; **let** WriteFootprint = $\emptyset$; **let** ReduxFootprint = $\emptyset$;
foreach *instruction I in S* **do**
  if *I is of the form "r := load p"* **then**
    let O = Profile.mapPointerToObjects(p);
    if *(exists instruction of the form "store v, p")* **and**
      (exists instruction of the form "v := op r, x" where
      op is associative and commutative) **then**
      ReduxFootprint = ReduxFootprint $\cup$ O;
    else
      ReadFootprint = ReadFootprint $\cup$ O;
    end
  end
  if *I is of the form "store v, p"* **then**
    let O = Profile.mapPointerToObjects(p);
    if *(exists instruction of the form "r := load p")* **and**
      (exists instruction of the form "v := op r, x" where
      op is associative and commutative) **then**
      ReduxFootprint = ReduxFootprint $\cup$ O;
    else
      WriteFootprint = WriteFootprint $\cup$ O;
    end
  end
  if *I is of the form "r := call f(...)"* **then**
    recur on f;
  end
end
return (ReadFootprint, WriteFootprint, ReduxFootprint)

The classification algorithm (Algorithm 1) partitions the loop's memory footprint across the five heaps according to access patterns. If an object is allocated and freed within an iteration, classification assigns it to the short-lived heap. If the compiler does not expect an object in the reduction set to be accessed by loads or stores elsewhere in the loop, classification assigns it to the reduction heap. This indicates that the reduction criterion is expected to succeed, but will still be verified at runtime via separation checks (Section 5.1). The unrestricted heap contains objects which partake in a loop-carried dependence, unless those objects were already assigned to the short-lived or reduction heaps. The private

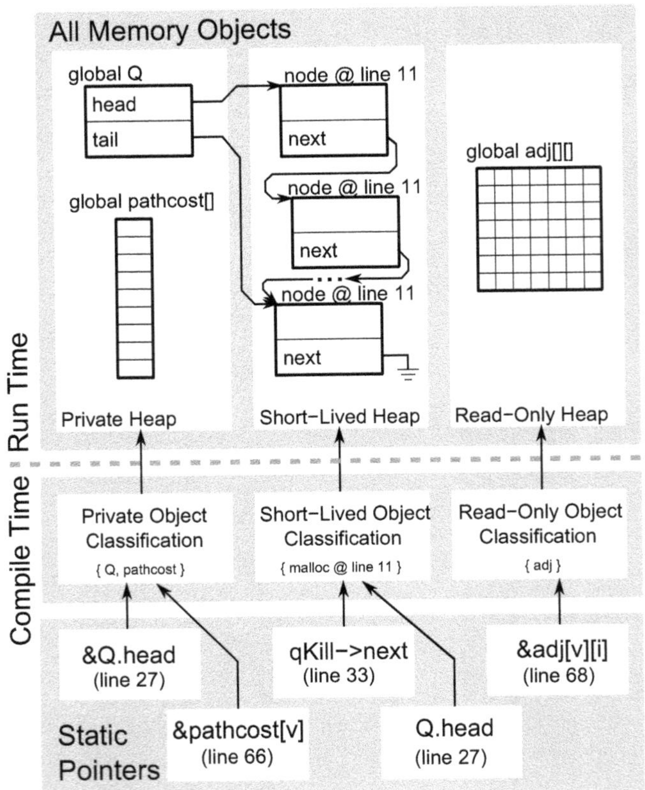

Figure 4: A heap assignment for Figure 2. Privateer speculatively separates objects into several classifications. Objects are allocated from *logical* heaps for efficient validation.

heap receives all other written objects. The read-only heap receives all other read objects. These five sets are collectively referred to as a *heap assignment*.

Figure 4 shows a heap assignment for the code in Figure 2a. The short-lived set contains all linked list nodes allocated at Line 11. The reduction and unrestricted sets are empty (and not shown). The private set contains the global queue structure `Q` and the global array `pathcost`. The read-only set contains the global array `adj`.

4.3 Selection

The compiler selects a subset of loops to parallelize from the set of hot loops with heap assignments. Program dependences are computed using static analysis and then refined according to the heap assignment:

- *The logical heaps are separated:* For a pair of operations o and p whose footprints are assigned to sets of heaps h_o and h_p respectively, if $h_o \cap h_p = \emptyset$ then remove all memory dependences $o \to p$ and $p \to o$.
- *The private, short-lived and reduction heaps eliminate loop-carried dependences:* For an operation o, if the footprint of o is contained in the private, short-lived, and/or reduction heaps, then for all operations x in the loop, remove all *loop-carried* memory dependences $o \to x$ and $x \to o$.

Additionally, dependences are refined with standard rules for value prediction, control speculation, and I/O deferral. The result is an optimistic view of program behavior in the expected case. This dependence structure is passed to parallelizing transformations to exclude inapplicable loops. The compiler selects the largest (by execution time) set of parallelizable loops subject to the following compatibility constraints. The compiler avoids nested parallelism: if the compiler finds (via static analysis or profiling results) that two loops may ever be simultaneously active, it marks the two loops incompatible. Second, two loops are incompatible if an object is assigned to different heaps for each loop. If two loops are incompatible, the compiler selects at most one of them. This selection process yields a single heap assignment for the set of selected hot loops.

4.4 Replace Allocation

Privateer replaces the allocation site for each object from the heap assignment. Storage for global objects is allocated from the appropriate heap during an initializer which runs before `main` (Lines 40–44), and is saved in a global variable (Lines 5–7). All uses of the addresses of such objects are replaced with loads from said global pointer. For stack allocations, the operation is replaced with an allocation from the appropriate heap and a corresponding deallocation is inserted at all function exits. Similarly, heap allocations and deallocations are replaced with the routines for the appropriate heap.

4.5 Add Separation Checks

The compiler inserts calls to trigger validation. To validate that a pointer refers only to objects within the correct heap, the compiler finds every static use of a pointer within the parallel region and traces back to the static definition of that pointer. It inserts calls to the `check_heap` function, which performs a separation check (see Section 5.1). Figure 2b shows a separation check on Line 29; other checks are proved successful at compile time and are elided.

4.6 Add Privacy Checks

To validate that private objects never partake in loop-carried flow dependences, the compiler finds every operation within the parallel region which accesses an object in the private heap. It inserts a call to `private_read` before loads, and a call to `private_write` before stores. These calls report address and access-size information to the runtime system, causing the runtime to validate privacy (see Section 5.1). In Figure 2b, Lines 15, 19 and 65 show privacy checks inserted by Privateer.

5. The Privateer Runtime Support System

The runtime support library serves several purposes. It manages the logical heaps and validates their speculative separation. It provides validation of speculative privacy. It coordinates periodic checkpoints and initiates recovery after a misspeculation. Parallel execution is governed by the parallelizing transformation applied to the program after privatization. In this investigation, the parallelizing transformation is DOALL.

Figure 5 shows a schematic time line of parallel execution with three workers. Speculative privatization does not add explicit communication between the workers, but requires periodic checkpoints, marked as CHKn. Additionally, each worker performs small inline misspeculation checks, denoted by grey bars. The figure shows a misspeculation at iteration $2k + 4$, followed by sequential, non-speculative recovery. Parallel execution resumes after recovery.

5.1 Runtime Validation of Speculation

Separate Heaps: The runtime system makes heavy use of the POSIX shared memory (shm) and memory map (mmap) facilities to achieve the desired separation model. Since workers must update their virtual memory maps independently, the Privateer runtime system uses processes and not threads. Heaps are created via `shm_open`. Each process maps them into its address space via `mmap` with read-only, read-write or copy-on-write protections.

The `mmap` facility allows the system to select a fixed, absolute virtual address for these heaps. Privateer exploits this feature by

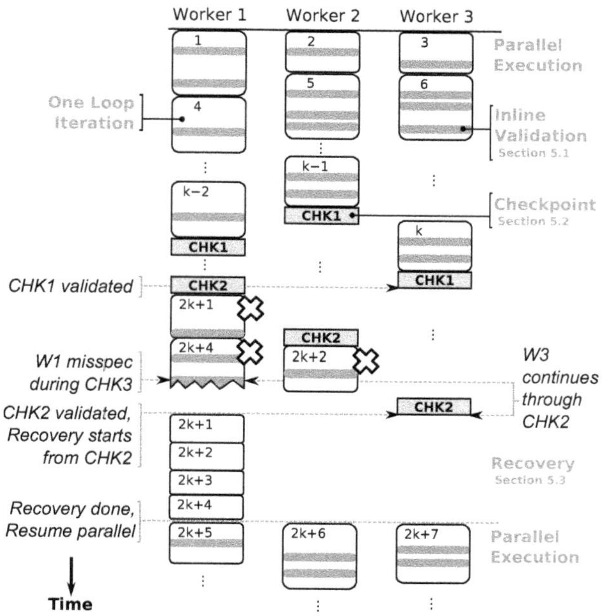

Figure 5: Example showing the worker processes during a parallel region. Iteration $2k+4$ misspeculates, triggering a recovery.

hiding a *heap tag* within the heaps' virtual addresses. Bits 44–46 of the address hold a 3-bit heap tag, allowing the runtime to quickly determine if a pointer references an address within the correct heap. As a heap is subdivided by allocations, all objects within that heap inherit its tag. This choice of bit location was selected for compatibility with common operating systems and hardware, and allows 16 terabytes of allocation within any heap.

The privatizing transformation inserts a heap check at each instruction which computes a pointer address in the parallel region. This check indicates an assumed target heap for that pointer. The runtime tests the pointer's heap tag via bit arithmetic, reporting misspeculation upon mismatch. The bit patterns for the private and shadow heaps are chosen so they differ by only one bit. For a byte at address p within the private heap, the system computes the address of the corresponding byte of metadata in the shadow heap with a single bit-wise OR instruction.

Validating Short-Lived Objects: Each worker counts the number of objects allocated and not freed from its short-lived heap. If any of these objects is live at the end of an iteration, then lifetime speculation is violated, and the worker reports misspeculation [13].

Validating Privacy: Privacy is validated in two phases. First, a worker employs a fast test upon each access to private memory. This test requires no communication with other workers, but may fail to catch some violations. A thorough check will catch remaining violations during the checkpoint operation (see Section 5.2).

Every byte of metadata contains one of four codes: *live-in* (0), *old-write* (1), *read-live-in* (2), or a timestamp $3+(i-i_0)$ encoding the iteration i after the most recent checkpoint i_0. Initially, the shadow heap contains all zero values (live-in). Privacy checks cause the runtime system to update metadata upon every private access. The transition rules for metadata are shown in Table 2. The simplest cases are the most common: a write to private memory updates the corresponding bytes of metadata with the current iteration timestamp; a read from private memory checks that the corresponding bytes of metadata match the current iteration timestamp. If the program ever reads a value that was defined by an earlier iteration, this can be detected by the fourth rule.

To support reading live-in values, the runtime marks a live-in byte with the code read-live-in. This indicates that a byte has been

Op.	Metadata Before	Metadata After	Comment
Read	0	2	Read a live-in value.
	1	misspec	Loop-carried flow dependence.
	2	2	Read a live-in value.
	$\alpha\ (2<\alpha<\beta)$	misspec	Loop-carried flow dependence.
	β	β	Intra-iteration (private) flow.
Write	0	β	Overwrite a live-in value.
	1	β	Overwrite an old write.
	2	misspec	Conservative false positive.
	$\alpha\ (2<\alpha\leq\beta)$	β	Overwrite a recent write.

Table 2: Metadata transitions on private accesses. β is the timestamp for the current iteration, and α is the timestamp for an earlier iteration.

read, and appears to be a live-in value, but that privacy cannot be guaranteed without communicating with other workers. Instead, this property will be checked at the next checkpoint. If such a byte is overwritten before the checkpoint occurs, the system will conservatively report a misspeculation. Such a misspeculation may represent a false-positive. We selected this design since tests without false positives require a separate read-iteration timestamp, doubling the size of metadata. We did not observe false positives in practice.

These metadata codes will eventually overflow a byte. A checkpoint resets the metadata range by replacing all writes before the checkpoint (metadata $\alpha\geq 3$) with old-write (1). Privateer triggers a checkpoint operation at least every 253 iterations.

5.2 Checkpoints

To support recovery, the speculative program periodically saves valid program state. The runtime selects a checkpoint period k before the parallel invocation. After every k-th iteration, worker processes copy their speculative state (the private, shadow, and reduction heaps) into a checkpoint object, as in Figure 5. This object is allocated by the first worker to reach that iteration and retired after the last worker reaches the iteration. The checkpoint system maintains an ordered list of checkpoint objects, each representing a distinct point in time, and allows arbitrarily many checkpoint objects. Workers acquire a lock on a single checkpoint object, not the whole checkpoint system, to avoid barrier penalties. This allows a fast worker to proceed to subsequent work units without waiting for slow worker processes to reach the checkpoint.

As mentioned in Section 5.1, privacy is validated by a two-phase approach. The runtime performs the *second* phase of validation as each worker adds its speculative state to the checkpoint object, using the same metadata transition rules as listed in Table 2. If misspeculation is detected while a worker is performing a checkpoint, that worker signals a misspeculation and aborts. Otherwise, that checkpoint object is marked non-speculative as soon as all workers have added their state to the checkpoint.

5.3 Recovery

If a worker detects misspeculation, it sets a global misspeculation flag and records the misspeculated iteration number. This worker terminates immediately, squashing all its speculative state created since its last checkpoint.

Since workers run at different speeds, it is possible that a remaining worker has not yet reached the checkpoint during which misspeculation occurred. Workers consult the global misspeculation flag after each iteration. If set, each worker compares its checkpoint ID $\lfloor i/k \rfloor$ against the ID of the checkpoint which misspeculated. If a worker has not yet reached the point of misspeculation, it continues execution; otherwise it terminates. This policy reduces wasted work upon misspeculation, as in Figure 5. If workers discover an *earlier* misspeculation before they terminate, they update the earliest iteration at which misspeculation occurs, and abort.

Once all worker processes have terminated, the main process begins non-speculative recovery. Using several calls to `mmap`, the main process replaces its heaps with those from the last valid checkpoint. The main process re-executes iterations non-speculatively until it has passed the iteration at which the earliest misspeculation occurred. Unless the program exits the loop during recovery, parallel execution resumes.

6. Evaluation

Privateer is evaluated on a shared-memory machine with four 6-core Intel Xeon® X7460 processors (24 cores total) running at 2.66 GHz with 24 GB of memory. Its operating system is 64-bit Ubuntu 9.10. The compiler is built on LLVM [15] revision 139148.

Privateer is evaluated with 5 programs that require speculative privatization for parallelization, as described in Table 3. Programs are selected from a set of C and C++ applications because their parallelization is limited by false dependences. We exclude many programs because they are parallelizable without Privateer. Some other programs feature data structures that Privateer can successfully privatize, but whose loops cannot be parallelized with DOALL because of real loop-carried flow dependences. We exclude those as well, since they are limited by DOALL, not by Privateer. More powerful parallelizing transformations, such as PS-DSWP [20] will be investigated in future work.

Specifically, we exclude `177.mesa` and `462.libquantum` since they can be parallelized without the aid of speculation, and thus we do not take credit for their performance. We exclude `164.gzip`, `256.bzip2`, and `456.hmmer` since the compiler cannot identify DOALL loops after Privateer's speculation has been applied. The compiler does not transform these codes.

Each benchmark is profiled with a training input (*train*). Performance evaluations are measured with a different testing input (*ref*). When we profile these with a third input (*alt*), the compiler generates identical code, suggesting that Privateer's analysis is reasonably stable with respect to profile input.

6.1 Parallel Performance Results

Figure 6 presents performance results generated by the fully automatic privatization and parallelization transform. These measurements are *whole application speedups* relative to the best sequential performance of the original application. The sequential applications are compiled with *clang -O3*.

These results indicate that privatization of data structures unlocks parallelization opportunities in these programs. Additionally, they indicate that Privateer's speculative separation is sufficiently powerful to reason about and operate on the dynamically allocated and irregular data structures present in these applications.

The `dijkstra` application from MiBench [12] reuses several data structures. It maintains a table of shortest paths and linked list of nodes whose shortest paths have changed—both as global variables. Successive iterations of the hot loop are synchronized by false dependences on these data structures. Privateer uses value prediction to speculate that the linked list is empty at the beginning of each iteration and privatizes the head node of the linked list and the shortest path table. The nodes within the linked list are assigned to the short-lived heap. Additionally, the hot loop includes calls to `printf` that are deferred into the speculative system, so that they may issue in any order yet commit in-order.

Privateer transforms the sequential version of the `swaptions` program from PARSEC [2]. It parallelizes the hot loop in the function `worker` by privatizing 17 memory objects, 15 of which are short-lived. The short-lived objects include a large number of vectors and matrices (arrays of pointers to row vectors) which

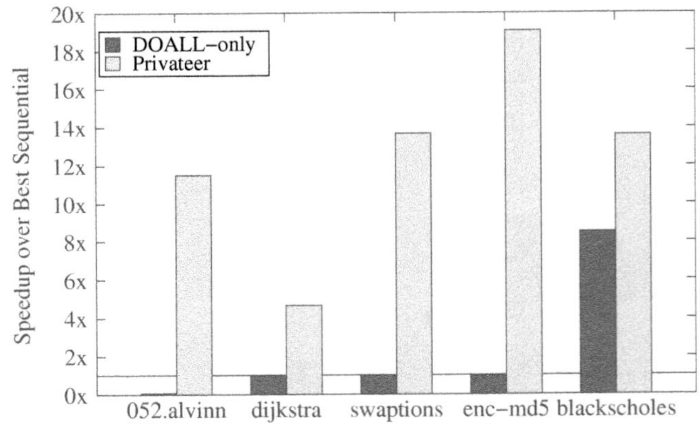

Figure 7: Enabling effect of Privateer at 24 worker processes.

are dynamically allocated at various points within `worker` and its callees, and passed around indirectly through other data structures. The LRPD-family techniques are inapplicable to this benchmark because of the linked matrix data structures.

The `052.alvinn` program is from SPEC [25]. To enable parallelization, Privateer privatizes four stack-allocated arrays. `052.alvinn` iterates over these arrays using pointer arithmetic and passes array references to callees, making static analysis difficult. Additionally, Privateer handles reductions on two global arrays and as well as a scalar local variable. At 8 cores, Privateer achieves a speedup of 5.66× on commodity hardware. OpenImpact [35] reports 6.44× with the help specialized hardware extensions. This compares favorably to STMLite+LLVM [17], which reports less than 2× in a software-only system with 8 cores.

The `enc-md5` program from Trimaran [28] computes message digests for a large number of data sets and prints each to standard output. Two factors limit parallelization of the programs outer loop: false dependences on the MD5 state object and digest buffer, and calls to `printf`. Privateer privatizes the state object and marks the digest buffer as short-lived. The side effects of stream output functions are issued through the checkpoint system and take effect only when the checkpoint is marked non-speculative.

Privateer transforms the sequential version of `blackscholes` from PARSEC [2]. In the hot loop-nest of this program, the inner loop is embarrassingly parallel. However, the outer loop cannot be parallelized directly because of output dependences on the pricing array, which is allocated in a different function. Privateer privatizes this array, allowing for parallel execution of the outer loop.

Figure 7 compares the performance of the DOALL transformation using 24 workers, with and without Privateer. "DOALL-only" refers to a non-speculative implementation which distributes loop iterations across worker threads, and thus does not incur checkpoint or validation overheads. Privateer enables parallelization of hotter loops. For `052.alvinn`, DOALL-only transforms a deeply nested inner loop. Performance gains do not outweigh the overhead of dispatching worker threads, and thus DOALL-only experiences slowdown. DOALL-only does not parallelize any loops in `dijkstra` or `enc-md5` because of real, frequent false dependences. The hot loop in `swaptions` is parallelizable but could not be proved parallelizable by our static analysis. DOALL-only parallelizes a hot inner loop in `blackscholes`; however, privatization allows the compiler to parallelize a hotter loop. Privatization enables the compiler to parallelize a single invocation, thus reducing spawn/join costs.

6.2 Overhead of the Runtime System

Privateer minimizes validation's runtime overhead. Figure 8 presents a breakdown of measured overheads for each program when using

Program	Dynamic				Replaced Static Allocation Sites					Extras
	Invoc	Checkpt	Priv R	Priv W	Private	Short-Lived	Read-Only	Redux	Unrestricted	
052.alvinn	200	2,600	8.2 GB	300 MB	4	0	4	3	0	-
dijkstra	1	5	84.9 GB	56.7 GB	10	3	11	0	0	Value, Control, I/O
blackscholes	1	5	0 B	4.0 GB	1	0	9	0	0	Value
swaptions	1	17	288 KB	169 KB	2	15	5	0	0	Value, Control
enc-md5	1	5	25.5 GB	30.8 GB	2	1	4	0	0	Control, I/O

Table 3: Details of privatized and parallelized programs, including number of invocations of the parallel region; total number of checkpoints constructed; total private bytes read and written; static number of objects assigned to each heap; and additional necessary transformation including value prediction speculation, control speculation, and deferral of I/O operations.

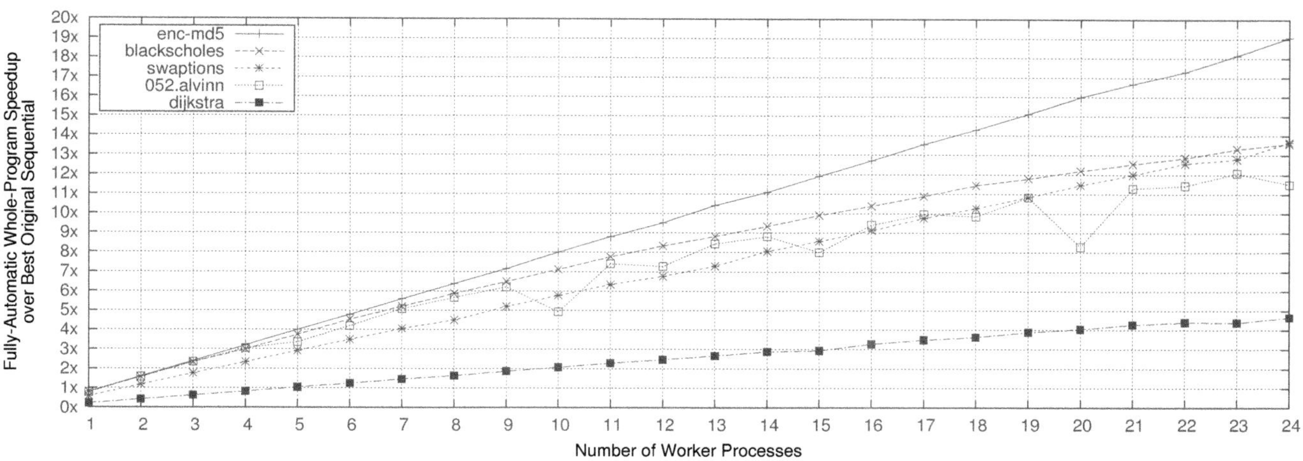

Figure 6: Whole program speedups of the fully automatically parallelized code, measured with respect to the best running time of the unmodified sequential application compiled with `clang -O3`. Each point is the average of three trials.

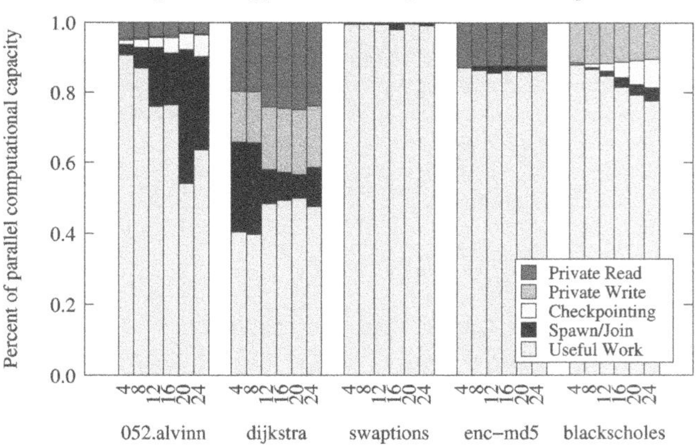

Figure 8: Breakdown of overheads on parallel performance.

4, 8, 12, 16, 20, and 24 worker processes. These numbers are normalized to the total computational capacity (CPU-seconds) of the parallel region: the number of processor cores times the duration of the parallel invocation. In these units, perfect utilization would be represented as 100% useful work. Overheads experienced during the parallel region subtract from utilization and prevent linear speedup. All times measure wall-clock time, not processor time: they include time spent blocking and context switching. If the parallel region invokes more than once, these numbers are the sum over all parallel invocations.

In the overheads figure, "Useful Work" refers to the portion of computational capacity spent executing instructions from the original sequential application. "Private Read" refers to the capacity spent updating metadata in response to a read from a private object. Similarly, "Private Write" refers to the bookkeeping for a write to a private object. "Checkpoint" refers to the capacity spent collecting, validating, and combining checkpoints.

Spawn refers to the unused capacity after a parallel invocation has begun, yet before the worker processes begin execution. This overhead is mostly determined by the latency of the operating system's implementation of `fork`. Join refers to the non-useful capacity after a worker process has finished its work units, yet before the parallel invocation has finished. This overhead is caused by four factors: imbalance among the workers, the latency of the worker-completed signal, the cost of installing the final non-committed state into the main process, and the cost of committing output operations that were issued during the parallel region. These two measurements are presented together as "Spawn/Join."

Results show that parallelized applications utilize most of the parallel resources for useful work. Both `052.alvinn` and `dijkstra` waste a significant amount of time joining their workers. This is caused by an imbalance in the latency of each worker, and a load balancing technique such as work stealing could potentially address this inefficiency. Validation of privacy is the next largest source of overhead. Percent of computational capacity used for privacy validation remained mostly constant as the number of workers increased, suggesting that the absolute amount of work for privacy validation grows with the number of workers.

6.3 Misspeculation Analysis

Privateer employs speculation to eliminate rare dependences and thus optimizes for the common case. To reduce the risk of misspeculation, Privateer interprets profiling results conservatively. No programs experienced misspeculation during evaluation. To better understand the effect of misspeculation, we inject artificial misspecu-

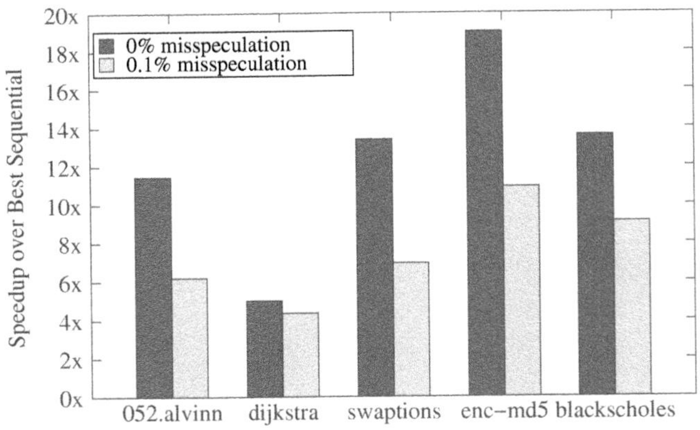

Figure 9: Performance degradation with misspeculation.

lation into the running application at fixed frequencies. The results of this experiment are shown in Figure 9. We present misspeculation rates as the percentage of *iterations* which misspeculate as opposed to *checkpoints*, since iterations are more standard. Privateer's recovery mechanism operates at the granularity of checkpoints (see Section 5.2). Thus, a misspeculation rate of 0.1% causes about one in four checkpoints to fail. For `blackscholes`, we increased the input size so that the hot loop executed at least 1,000 iterations.

For most programs, these results indicate that Privateer's performance benefits are sensitive to misspeculation. Four of five programs lose half of their speedup with a misspeculation rate of 0.1%. This suggests that Privateer requires high-confidence speculation for performance.

7. Related Work

Paralax [32] uses privatization to enable parallelization. The authors note that privatization analysis is difficult on C programs. They propose KILL annotations to assert the absence of flow dependences through a data structure, indirectly answering the privatization criterion. These annotations are applied to named objects or object referenced by a single pointer indirection. This prevents the application of KILL to recursive data structures.

Early works on privatization [16, 29] are limited by the strength of static analysis on the privatization criterion and memory layout problems. The PD Test [21] reduces reliance on static analysis by adding inspector loops to dynamically verify the privatization criterion at runtime. Similarly, Hybrid Analysis [24] uses a generalized representation for indirect array references to statically generate predicates, which are then resolved at runtime for dynamic privatization. The LRPD [22] and R-LRPD [7] Tests obviated the need for static analysis by evaluating the privatization criterion speculatively. All of these techniques are evaluated on array-based codes written in FORTRAN and cannot handle pointers, linked lists, and other dynamic data structures.

Array Static Single Assignment (ASSA) [14] extends Static Single-Assignment form [6] to arrays. ASSA requires that any named memory location has exactly one definition. Repeated updates are represented with new static names and joined via ϕ-nodes. In this form, false dependences do not exist, and a compiler may distribute operations across threads considering only flow dependences. However, pointer indirection allows for ambiguous updates and foils ASSA analysis. Array Expansion [10] and Dynamic Single Assignment (DSA) [31] are similar to ASSA. Instead of creating new names, these add a new dimension to arrays representing the new definition. Instead of inserting ϕ-nodes, DSA emits instructions to explicitly select the appropriate value at control join points. Region Array SSA [23] uses partial aggregation of array regions to reduce the runtime overhead of ASSA. These provide the same single-assignment semantics as ASSA, and suffer from the same applicability problems in light of unrestricted pointers and casts. A representative DSA [31] is inapplicable to loops which contain loads or stores from pointers.

Software Transactional Memory (STM) systems [8, 17, 18] provide isolation and consequently privatize data structures written during a transaction. To detect conflicts, these techniques keep a log of memory accesses for offline validation. STMLite integrates an automatic DOALL compiler featuring several enabling transformations [17] and implemented in LLVM [15]. STMLite's central commit process can quickly become an execution bottleneck. The other transactional systems are not evaluated in an automatic system; weak static analysis may cause a large volume of unnecessary validations, and it is unclear whether these systems scale to that volume. None of these STMs provide speculative reduction support, and so a compiler must rely on a static criterion.

The CorD+Objects [27] compiler and STM reduce copy overheads by tracking speculative state of *objects*. To address replacement transparency, the compiler transforms pointers into "double pointers" and the runtime maintains a map between copies of an object. This transformation assumes that all accesses conform to the object's declared type, but may fail due to reinterpretation casts. Static analysis cannot always determine whether an object is ever reinterpreted. The transformation also assumes that all pointer values are visible in the IR, but C's weak types allow "disguised" pointers, as discussed in [3]. Like STMs, CorD+Objects does not support speculative reductions. Since Privateer provides replacement transparency using virtual page mapping, its compiler has no need to identify or manipulate pointer values in the IR.

Several works modify the default process memory model by manipulating virtual memory maps. DoublePlay [33] employs the copy-on-write mechanism to isolate different epochs of a single process, providing a deterministic replay facility. Grace [1] implements a safe multithreading programming model to reduce development effort for parallel programs. Behavior oriented parallelization [9] provides a speculative execution model that resembles an STM and features an optimized value-based misspeculation detection system. These works are intended as programmer tools to aid the development of parallel applications, yet none automatically parallelize applications.

8. Conclusion

Automatic parallelization is a promising strategy to deliver scalable application performance on parallel architectures. Privateer enables a compiler to extract more parallelism by selectively privatizing data structures. Privateer's heap separation enables greater applicability than related techniques, and allows for efficient validation. Privateer's fully automatic privatization and parallelization delivers a geomean whole-program speedup of 11.4× over best sequential execution for 5 programs on a 24-core shared memory machine.

Acknowledgments

We thank the entire Liberty Research Group for their support and feedback during this work. We also thank the anonymous reviewers for their insightful comments. Additionally, we thank Andrew Appel, Gordon Stewart, Lennart Beringer, Jude Nelson and Daya Bill for commenting on early drafts. This material is based on work supported by National Science Foundation Grant 0964328 and DARPA contract FA8750-10-2-0253. Prakash Prabhu thanks Google, Inc. for fellowship support. This work was carried out while Ayal Zaks was visiting Princeton University, supported by the HiPEAC network of excellence, and on leave from IBM Haifa Research Lab.

References

[1] E. D. Berger, T. Yang, T. Liu, and G. Novark. Grace: safe multithreaded programming for C/C++. In *Annual ACM SIGPLAN Conference on Object-Oriented Programming Systems Languages and Applications*, 2009.

[2] C. Bienia, S. Kumar, J. P. Singh, and K. Li. The PARSEC benchmark suite: Characterization and architectural implications. In *Proceedings of the 17th International Conference on Parallel Architectures and Compilation Techniques*, 2008.

[3] H.-J. Boehm. Simple garbage-collector-safety. In *Proceedings of the ACM SIGPLAN 1996 conference on Programming Language Design and Implementation*, pages 89–98, New York, NY, 1996. ACM.

[4] T. Chen, J. Lin, X. Dai, W.-C. Hsu, and P.-C. Yew. Data dependence profiling for speculative optimizations. In E. Duesterwald, editor, *Compiler Construction*, volume 2985 of *Lecture Notes in Computer Science*, pages 2733–2733. Springer Berlin / Heidelberg, 2004.

[5] W. Y. Chen, S. A. Mahlke, and W. W. Hwu. Tolerating first level memory access latency in high-performance systems. In *Proceedings of the 1992 International Conference on Parallel Processing*, pages 36–43, Boca Raton, Florida, 1992. CRC Press.

[6] R. Cytron, J. Ferrante, B. K. Rosen, M. N. Wegman, and F. K. Zadeck. Efficiently computing static single assignment form and the control dependence graph. *ACM Transactions on Programming Languages and Systems*, 13(4):451–490, October 1991.

[7] F. H. Dang, H. Yu, and L. Rauchwerger. The R-LRPD test: Speculative parallelization of partially parallel loops. In *Proceedings of the 16th International Parallel and Distributed Processing Symposium*, pages 20–29, 2002.

[8] D. Dice, O. Shalev, and N. Shavit. Transactional locking II. In *Distributed Computing*, pages 194–208, 2006.

[9] C. Ding, X. Shen, K. Kelsey, C. Tice, R. Huang, and C. Zhang. Software behavior oriented parallelization. In *Proceedings of the 2007 ACM SIGPLAN Conference on Programming Language Design and Implementation*, pages 223–234, New York, NY, 2007. ACM.

[10] P. Feautrier. Array expansion. In *Proceedings of the 2nd International Conference on Supercomputing*, pages 429–441. ACM, 1988.

[11] F. Gabbay and A. Mendelson. Can program profiling support value prediction? In *Proceedings of the 30th annual ACM/IEEE International Symposium on Microarchitecture*, pages 270–280, Washington, DC, 1997. IEEE Computer Society.

[12] M. R. Guthaus, J. S. Ringenberg, D. Ernst, T. M. Austin, T. Mudge, and R. B. Brown. MiBench: A free, commercially representative embedded benchmark suite. In *Proceedings of the Workload Characterization, 2001. WWC-4. 2001 IEEE International Workshop*, pages 3–14, Washington, DC, 2001. IEEE Computer Society.

[13] H. Kim, N. P. Johnson, J. W. Lee, S. A. Mahlke, and D. I. August. Automatic speculative DOALL for clusters. *Proceedings of the 10th IEEE/ACM International Symposium on Code Generation and Optimization*, March 2012.

[14] K. Knobe and V. Sarkar. Array SSA form and its use in parallelization. In *Proceedings of the 25th ACM SIGPLAN-SIGACT Symposium on Principles of Programming Languages*, pages 107–120, 1998.

[15] C. Lattner and V. Adve. LLVM: A compilation framework for lifelong program analysis & transformation. In *Proceedings of the Annual International Symposium on Code Generation and Optimization*, pages 75–86, 2004.

[16] D. E. Maydan, S. P. Amarasinghe, and M. S. Lam. Array-data flow analysis and its use in array privatization. In *Proceedings of the 20th ACM SIGPLAN-SIGACT Symposium on Principles of Programming Languages*, pages 2–15, New York, NY, 1993. ACM.

[17] M. Mehrara, J. Hao, P.-C. Hsu, and S. Mahlke. Parallelizing sequential applications on commodity hardware using a low-cost software transactional memory. In *Proceedings of the 2009 ACM SIGPLAN Conference on Programming Language Design and Implementation*, 2009.

[18] Y. Ni, A. Welc, A.-R. Adl-Tabatabai, M. Bach, S. Berkowits, J. Cownie, R. Geva, S. Kozhukow, R. Narayanaswamy, J. Olivier, S. Preis, B. Saha, A. Tal, and X. Tian. Design and implementation of transactional constructs for C/C++. In *Annual ACM SIGPLAN Conference on Object-Oriented Programming Systems Languages and Applications*, pages 195–212, 2008.

[19] C. G. Quiñones, C. Madriles, J. Sánchez, P. Marcuello, A. González, and D. M. Tullsen. Mitosis compiler: an infrastructure for speculative threading based on pre-computation slices. In *Proceedings of the 2005 ACM SIGPLAN conference on Programming Language Design and Implementation*, pages 269–279, New York, NY, 2005. ACM.

[20] E. Raman, G. Ottoni, A. Raman, M. Bridges, and D. I. August. Parallel-stage decoupled software pipelining. In *Proceedings of the Annual International Symposium on Code Generation and Optimization*, 2008.

[21] L. Rauchwerger and D. Padua. The Privatizing DOALL test: A run-time technique for DOALL loop identification and array privatization. In *Proceedings of the 8th International Conference on Supercomputing*, pages 33–43, New York, NY, 1994. ACM.

[22] L. Rauchwerger and D. Padua. The LRPD test: speculative run-time parallelization of loops with privatization and reduction parallelization. *ACM SIGPLAN Notices*, 30(6):218–232, 1995.

[23] S. Rus, G. He, C. Alias, and L. Rauchwerger. Region Array SSA. In *Proceedings of the 15th International Conference on Parallel Architectures and Compilation Techniques*, pages 43–52. ACM, 2006.

[24] S. Rus, L. Rauchwerger, and J. Hoeflinger. Hybrid analysis: static & dynamic memory reference analysis. *International Journal of Parallel Programming*, 31:251–283, August 2003.

[25] Standard Performance Evaluation Corporation. http://spec.org.

[26] The GNU Project. GNU Binutils. http://gnu.org/software/binutils.

[27] C. Tian, M. Feng, and R. Gupta. Supporting Speculative Parallelization in the Presence of Dynamic Data Structures. In *ACM SIGPLAN Conference on Programming Language Design and Implementation*, 2010.

[28] Trimaran. Trimaran Benchmarks Packages. http://trimaran.org.

[29] P. Tu and D. A. Padua. Automatic array privatization. In *Proceedings of the 6th International Workshop on Languages and Compilers for Parallel Computing*, pages 500–521, 1994.

[30] N. Vachharajani, R. Rangan, E. Raman, M. J. Bridges, G. Ottoni, and D. I. August. Speculative decoupled software pipelining. In *Proceedings of the 16th International Conference on Parallel Architecture and Compilation Techniques*, pages 49–59, Washington, DC, 2007. IEEE Computer Society.

[31] P. Vanbroekhoven, G. Janssens, M. Bruynooghe, and F. Catthoor. A practical dynamic single assignment transformation. *ACM Transactions on Design Automation of Electronic Systems*, 12, September 2007.

[32] H. Vandierendonck, S. Rul, and K. De Bosschere. The Paralax infrastructure: Automatic parallelization with a helping hand. In *Proceedings of the 19th International Conference on Parallel Architecture and Compilation Techniques*.

[33] K. Veeraraghavan, D. Lee, B. Wester, J. Ouyang, P. M. Chen, J. Flinn, and S. Narayanasamy. Doubleplay: parallelizing sequential logging and replay. In *Proceedings of the 16th International Conference on Architectural Support for Programming Languages and Operating Systems*, pages 15–26, New York, NY, 2011. ACM.

[34] Q. Wu, A. Pyatakov, A. N. Spiridonov, E. Raman, D. W. Clark, and D. I. August. Exposing memory access regularities using object-relative memory profiling. In *Proceedings of the International Symposium on Code Generation and Optimization*. IEEE Computer Society, 2004.

[35] H. Zhong, M. Mehrara, S. Lieberman, and S. Mahlke. Uncovering hidden loop level parallelism in sequential applications. In *Proceedings of the 14th International Symposium on High-Performance Computer Architecture*, 2008.

Dynamic Trace-Based Analysis of Vectorization Potential of Applications

Justin Holewinski Ragavendar Ramamurthi Mahesh Ravishankar Naznin Fauzia
Louis-Noël Pouchet Atanas Rountev P. Sadayappan

Department of Computer Science and Engineering
The Ohio State University
{holewins,ramamurr,ravishan,fauzia,pouchet,rountev,saday}@cse.ohio-state.edu

Abstract

Recent hardware trends with GPUs and the increasing vector lengths of SSE-like ISA extensions for multicore CPUs imply that effective exploitation of SIMD parallelism is critical for achieving high performance on emerging and future architectures. A vast majority of existing applications were developed without any attention by their developers towards effective vectorizability of the codes. While developers of production compilers such as GNU gcc, Intel icc, PGI pgcc, and IBM xlc have invested considerable effort and made significant advances in enhancing automatic vectorization capabilities, these compilers still cannot effectively vectorize many existing scientific and engineering codes. It is therefore of considerable interest to analyze existing applications to assess the inherent latent potential for SIMD parallelism, exploitable through further compiler advances and/or via manual code changes.

In this paper we develop an approach to infer a program's SIMD parallelization potential by analyzing the dynamic data-dependence graph derived from a sequential execution trace. By considering only the observed run-time data dependences for the trace, and by relaxing the execution order of operations to allow any dependence-preserving reordering, we can detect potential SIMD parallelism that may otherwise be missed by more conservative compile-time analyses. We show that for several benchmarks our tool discovers regions of code within computationally-intensive loops that exhibit high potential for SIMD parallelism but are not vectorized by state-of-the-art compilers. We present several case studies of the use of the tool, both in identifying opportunities to enhance the transformation capabilities of vectorizing compilers, as well as in pointing to code regions to manually modify in order to enable auto-vectorization and performance improvement by existing compilers.

Categories and Subject Descriptors C.4 [*Performance of systems*]: Measurement techniques, Performance attributes; D.1.3 [*Programming techniques*]: Concurrent programming—Parallel programming; D.3.4 [*Programming Languages*]: Processors—Compilers, Optimization

General Terms Performance, Measurement, Algorithms

Keywords Performance analysis, dynamic analysis, vectorization

PLDI'12, June 11–16, 2012, Beijing, China.

1. Introduction

The SIMD vector units in modern multi-processors achieve very high performance by applying the same instruction to multiple data elements at once. As newer generations of multi-core processors and GPUs continue to extend the width of vector processors, the exploitation of vector instructions is of increasing importance. Unfortunately, many programs are written using structures, pointers, and other non-array constructs that prevent modern compilers from performing the analyses and transformations that are required to fully exploit these vector-processing resources. Even for programs that use arrays, vectorization potential that exists in the computation is often missed by compilers. Some typical reasons for this are (1) conservative dependence analysis, (2) conditional behavior for handling of boundary cases, which precludes the vectorization of the common case, and (3) data layouts that do not allow the contiguous memory accesses needed for efficient vector processing.

Given the sustained trend of increasingly-wide vector units, one key question is whether existing programs can take advantage of these hardware capabilities. The main contribution of our work is *an automatic approach to characterize the inherent vectorizability potential of existing applications* by analyzing information about run-time dependences and memory access patterns. The approach instruments the program to monitor and record instructions and their data accesses, and then analyzes the resulting trace to construct the dynamic dependence graph for the observed execution. Next, the graph is used to partition the dynamic instances of instructions into sets that are both independent and access the memory with a fixed stride. These sets represent instruction instances that can potentially utilize vector resources effectively.

Technical Challenges The identification of potentially vectorizable operations requires the discovery of fine-grained concurrency among operations that access contiguously located data elements. Although there has been considerable prior work (e.g., [2, 3, 8, 11, 12, 14, 16, 17, 19, 21, 23, 25, 28, 29, 33, 35, 39]) on using dynamic analysis for characterizing parallelism in applications, previously developed approaches have fundamental limitations for discovering potentially vectorizable operations. Existing work on using dynamic analysis to characterize potential parallelism in sequential programs falls broadly under two general categories: (1) generation of a parallelism profile and critical-path analysis of the directed acyclic graph (explicitly constructed or implicitly modeled) representing the run-time dependences of the computation, and (2) loop-level or region-level characterization of parallelism, where computations within the loop/region are constrained to execute in the original sequential order. An advantage of the former approach is that the generated parallelism profile implicitly models all possible dependence-preserving reordering of the operations since it performs critical-path analysis of the computation DAG. However, as discussed in the next section, a disadvantage is that independence and potential concurrency at the level of specific statements or expressions in a loop cannot be deduced. The significant advantage of the second approach is that such specific loop/region level concurrency information is extracted. But unlike the former type of analysis, this characterization may be constrained by the order of operations within the modeled region/loop that is imposed by the original program. Thus, the potential for increased parallelism via dependence-preserving reordering of operations is left unexplored. Finally, none of the previous approaches to dynamic analysis for characterizing parallelism consider the patterns of run-time memory accesses, which are critical in the characterization of vectorization potential.

Approach We develop *a new approach to analysis of the dynamic data dependence graph to characterize maximal concurrency per statement/operator under all possible dependence-preserving re-orderings of the computation, with further analysis of concurrent operations accessing contiguous or uniformly strided data.* The analysis is useful in a number of ways:

1. *Characterization of code bases:* An automated tool that can be run through large existing code bases to characterize the inherent vectorization potential of those programs can be valuable to multiple groups. First, ISVs (Independent Software Vendors) with large legacy software systems can assess which portions of the code may need complete algorithmic rewrite (if the tool shows no vectorizability) versus code changes without algorithm change (if the tool shows high vectorizability potential). The quantitative information on average vector lengths can be useful in assessing the potential benefit of converting the code to use GPUs (where much higher degree of SIMD parallelism is needed than with short-vector SIMD ISAs). Second, CPU/GPU designers can assess the potential future benefits of widened SIMD structures for important market segments by characterizing the inherent unexploited fine-grained parallelism available in widely-used software in different domains. In order to illustrate this use of the tool, we provide a characterization of the floating-point benchmarks of the SPEC 2006 benchmark suite.
2. *Aid in performance optimization:* Many existing applications contain hot loops with significant vectorization potential. While sometimes simple scanning of time-consuming loops by an application developer may reveal the potential for vectorization, this is non-trivial in many real codes due to multiple levels of function calls that must be analyzed. The automatic identification of code portions that exhibit inherent vectorizability potential can aid an applications expert who can then manually transform the code to enhance its vectorizability by compilers. We illustrate this use of the approach through several case studies.
3. *Aid to compiler writers:* Identification of potential vectorization (for existing programs) that is not exploited by current vectorizing compilers can lead to new insights for compiler writers, and eventually to new static analyses and transformations for state-of-the-art compiler technology. Further development (beyond the scope of this paper) to characterize patterns of statically-analyzable vectorization opportunities (i.e., no data-dependent conditions) missed by a vectorizing compiler can be helpful to compiler writers in enhancing auto-vectorization capabilities. We provide an illustration of this use case through a case study.

2. Background and Overview

The proposed approach is based on the following key observation: to identify and quantify the vectorization potential of a given program, the dynamic analysis needs to uncover *independent operations* that could be executed concurrently. Furthermore, these independent operations should exhibit a pattern of *contiguous access* to memory locations. The rest of this section provides high-level overview and examples to illustrate these two key issues. The specific details of the approach are elaborated later in the paper.

```
for(i = 1; i < N; ++i) {
  A[i] = 2.0 * A[i-1];                    // S1
}
for(i = 0; i < N; ++i) {
  for(j = 1; j < N; ++j) {
    B[j][i] = B[j-1][i] * A[i];           // S2
  }
}
```

Listing 1: Example 1 for dynamic parallelism analysis.

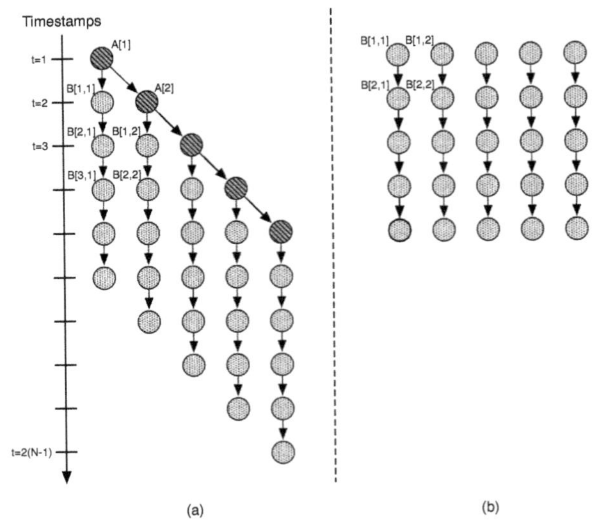

Figure 1: Dependences for Example 1.

2.1 Finding Independent Operations

Prior work on using dynamic analysis to characterize potential parallelism in sequential programs falls broadly under one of two general categories. One approach, exemplified by the early work of Kumar [11], performs timestamp-based analysis of instrumented statement-level execution of the sequential program, using shadow variables to maintain last-modify times for each variable. Each run-time instance of a statement is associated with a timestamp that is one greater than the largest of the last-modify times of all input operands of the statement. A histogram of the number of operations at each time value provides a fine-grained parallelism profile of the computation, and the maximal timestamp represents the critical path length for the entire computation.

In contrast to the above fine-grained approach, an alternate technique by Larus [14] performs analysis of loop-level parallelism at different levels of nested loops. Loop-level parallelism is measured by forcing a sequential order of execution of statements within each iteration of a loop being characterized, so that the only available concurrency is across different iterations of that loop.

To illustrate Kumar's approach, consider the code example in Listing 1. For explanation purposes, this example is extremely simple and is used only to highlight the parallelism characterization

```
for(i = 1; i < N; ++i) {
  A[i] = 2.0 * B[i-1];        // S1
  B[i] = 0.5 * C[i];          // S2
}
```

Listing 2: Example 2 for dynamic parallelism analysis.

from prior work. The run-time instances of the first statement form a chain of dependences of length $N-1$. The second statement has $N(N-1)$ run-time instances, with dependences as shown in the figure. The run-time statement instances and their dependences define a *dynamic data-dependence graph* (DDG), as shown in Fig. 1(a). The top row represents instances of statement S1 and the other nodes represent instances of statement S2. For ease of comprehension, a node may be labeled with the array element that is written by that node.

The analysis of potential parallelism computes a timestamp for each DDG node, representing the earliest time this node could be executed; these timestamps are also shown in Fig. 1(a). The largest timestamp, compared to the number of nodes, provides a characterization of the inherent fine-grain parallelism in the program; this largest timestamp gives the length of the *critical path* in the DDG. In essence, the timestamps implicitly model the best parallel execution of all possible dependence-preserving reorderings of the operations performed by the program. In the example from above, the critical path has length $2(N-1)$, and the overall parallelism is characterized by $(N+1)/2$, which is the ratio between the number $(N+1)(N-1)$ of DDG nodes and the length of the critical path.

All nodes with the same timestamp are independent and can be executed in parallel. However, this method for partitioning of DDG nodes cannot be used to uncover the groups of independent operations needed to characterize the vectorizability of the computation. Consider the example in Listing 1. Statement S2 has large vectorization potential: for a particular fixed value of `j`, all N run-time statement instances for various values of `i` are independent (and, as discussed later, they exhibit a pattern of contiguous access). However, if one were to consider the instances of S2 that are partitioned based on the same timestamp in Fig. 1(a), those partitions uncover *less parallelism* for S2 than what is truly available in the DDG: rather than having $N-1$ partitions of size N, we have a total of $2(N-1)$ partitions. Further, the operations in each partition do not access contiguous memory locations, i.e., are not potentially vectorizable.

As described later, we propose a new form of timestamp computation and critical path analysis that focuses on all instances *of a specific statement* (e.g., S2 in this example). This analysis considers whether two instances of the statement of interest are connected by a path in the DDG (with any instances of other statements along the path). If such a path exists, our algorithm guarantees that the timestamp of the first node is smaller than the timestamp of the second node (i.e., the two nodes will be placed in different partitions). Furthermore, each node is guaranteed to have the earliest possible timestamp. For the DDG from Fig. 1(a), our timestamps are shown in Fig. 1(b). Note that all instances of S2 for `j=1` are now given timestamp 1, because they do not depend on any other instances of S2. In general, all instances of S2 for a particular value of `j` have the same timestamp and form a partition. As described later, these partitions (containing independent operations) are then subjected to an analysis for contiguous memory access patterns.

The key problem in this example is that the parallelism analysis interleaves the instances of S1 and S2. An alternative approach could be to separately consider the loops in Listing 1, and perform loop-level parallelism analysis using an approach based on work by Larus [14]. This technique tracks inter-iteration dependences and

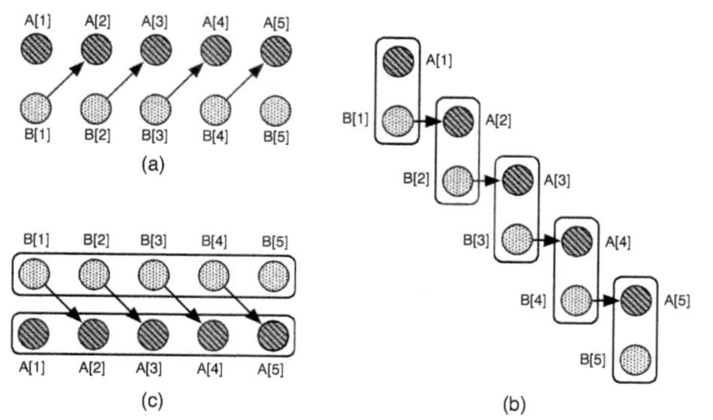

Figure 2: Dependences for Example 2.

computes timestamps for all statement instances in all loop iterations. Inside a loop iteration, the statement instances are executed sequentially. When a statement instance s in loop iteration i depends on a statement instance s' in another iteration, the execution of i stops upon reaching s, until s' is executed. With this approach, the second loop in Listing 1 will be considered independently, and the analysis will uncover that any two iterations of the `i` loop at line 4 are independent. In essence, this will create the parallel partitions shown in Fig. 1(b).

However, this approach for uncovering loop-level parallelism is also inappropriate for our target goal to discover independent operations that can be vectorized. The code in Listing 2 illustrates this point. There is a loop-carried dependence from S2 to S1, as illustrated in Fig. 2(a). As a result, the loop-level parallelism identified by the analysis would be of the form shown in Fig. 2(b). The resulting partitions do not expose the high vectorization potential of S1 (or S2). However, it is easy to see that the computation can be split into two separate loops: first, a loop that iterates over all instances of S2, followed by another loop that iterates over all instances of S1. The loop-level parallelism analysis can easily uncover that each loop (in this hypothetical transformed version) is fully parallel; in fact, each loop is fully vectorizable. However, since the unit of analysis is the original loop code, the potential for parallelism/vectorization is not discovered. Our approach, when analyzing the DDG in Fig. 2(a), will first consider all instances of S1, will discover that they are all independent, and will form a partition containing all of them. Similarly, all instances of S2 will be put in a single partition. The result of our technique is illustrated in Fig. 2(c). Comparing with Fig. 2(b), it is clear that we uncover more parallelism, which in turn leads to finding more potential vectorization.

To summarize, this technique characterizes the parallelism of an entire loop. However, this characterization is constrained by the order of operations within the loop body that is imposed by the sequential execution of the original program. Thus the potential for increased parallelism via dependence-preserving reordering of operations may be missed. Our approach considers all possible dependence-preserving reorderings of all run-time instances of a specific statement of interest, which exposes the necessary parallelism for the purposes of vectorization.

2.2 Finding Operations that Access Contiguously Located Data Elements

Consider again Example 1 from above, and specifically the timestamps shown in Fig. 1(b). Each timestamp defines a partition containing N instances of S2 that are independent of each other. Furthermore, all these instances access contiguous regions of memory.

For a fixed j and varying i, the triples of memory addresses corresponding to the triple of expressions (B[j][i], B[j − 1][i], A[i]) exhibit a pattern of contiguous memory access with the row-major data layout used for arrays in C. This makes the statement instances within each partition viable candidates for vectorization.

We propose *the first analysis* to analyze contiguous memory accesses of independent operations in order to characterize vectorization potential. As described later, the analysis considers all statement instances within a single parallel partition, and defines subpartitions such that within a subpartition, the tuples of memory accesses follow the same pattern of contiguous memory accesses. For example, tuple (B[j][i], B[j − 1][i], A[i]) for a fixed j and varying i will produce tuples of run-time addresses of the form $(c_1 + i \times d, c_2 + i \times d, c_3 + i \times d)$. Here d is the size an array element and $c_{1,2,3}$ are base addresses. These tuples represent accesses to contiguous memory, and together form one single subpartition (which covers the entire parallel partition defined by this particular value of j). One can imagine all statement instances in the subpartition being combined into a single vector operation $[c_1 : c_1+(N-1)\times d] = [c_2 : c_2+(N-1)\times d] \oplus [c_3 : c_3+(N-1)\times d]$ where $\oplus$ represents a vector operation on vectors of size N. Our analysis computes such subpartitions and uses them to characterize the vectorization potential of the analyzed statement.

3. Analyzing Dynamic Data-Dependence Graphs for Vectorization Potential

DDG Generation Generating a dynamic data-dependence graph (DDG) requires an execution trace of the program (or a contiguous subtrace), containing run-time instances of static instructions, including any relevant run-time data such as memory addresses for loads/stores, procedure calls, etc. Our implementation uses LLVM [15] to instrument arbitrary C/C++/Fortran code. The Clang [4] front-end is used to compile C/C++ code into LLVM IR, and the DragonEgg [5] GCC plugin is used to compile Fortran 77/90 code into LLVM IR. The LLVM IR is instrumented to generate a run-time trace to disk, and the instrumented code is compiled to native code.

Once an execution trace is available, the construction of the DDG creates a graph node for each dynamic instruction instance. Edges are created between pairs of dependent nodes (i.e., one instruction instance consumes a value produced by the other). In our implementation each graph node represents a dynamic instance of an LLVM IR instruction, and dependences are tracked through memory and LLVM virtual registers. To construct the graph edges, bookkeeping information for each memory/register remembers the graph node that performed the last write to this location. Note that the graph represents only flow dependences. Anti-dependences and output dependences are not considered, since they do not represent essential features of the computation, and could potentially be eliminated via transformations such as scalar/array expansion. Control dependences are also not considered, since our goal is to focus on the data flow and the optimization potential implied by it. It is straightforward to augment the DDG with additional categories of dependences, without having to modify in any way the subsequent graph analyses (described below).

One interesting case that arises in practice is due to reductions, for example, because of a statement s+=a[i] in an i-loop. The instances of such a statement would form a chain of dependences in the DDG. However, sometimes it is possible to vectorize reductions (e.g., by updating a vector sv instead of a scalar s). Our analysis currently does not consider the potential for such vectorization. A possible enhancement is to identify and remove dependence edges that are due to updates of reduction variables; detection of such

Algorithm 1: Timestamp computation.

```
Input: id: static instruction ID, graph: DDG
foreach Node node in TopologicalOrder(graph) do
    TS ← 0;
    foreach pred in Predecessors(graph, node) do
        TS ← Max(TS, GetTimeStamp(pred));
    end
    if GetInstructionID(node) == id then
        TS ← TS + 1;
    end
    AssignTimeStamp(node, TS);
end
```

dependences has already been used by prior work [22] in a different context.

Candidate Instructions The execution trace may contain many instructions that should not be analyzed for SIMD parallelism, such as integer operations for loop book-keeping. Hence, the analysis is restricted to instructions that involve floating-point addition, subtraction, multiplication, and division. These instructions correspond to the set of floating-point instructions that have vector counterparts in SIMD architectures. They are also of particular importance for optimization of certain computationally-intensive applications (as exemplified by the SPEC floating-point benchmarks). Of course, all other instructions that participate in dependences are taken into account by the analysis, but their potential SIMD parallelism is not characterized.

3.1 Generation of Parallel Partitions

To benefit from SIMD parallelism, an instruction must exhibit fine-grained parallelism. For a static instruction s that is being characterized, the potential parallelism of $\{s_1, s_2, \ldots\}$ (where s_k is the k-th run-time instance of s) can be uncovered by observing the data dependences from any s_i to any s_j for $j > i$. This is equivalent to identifying whether the DDG contains a path from the node for s_i to the node for s_j. Such a path exists if and only if the data produced by s_i is directly or indirectly used by s_j (i.e., s_i and s_j cannot be executed concurrently).

Each candidate static instruction s (as described earlier) is analyzed independently, using Algorithm 1. A unique ID for s is assigned at instrumentation time. A topological sort traversal of the DDG is performed and a timestamp is assigned to each node. For each visited node, the largest predecessor timestamp is determined. If the node is an instance of the static instruction s being analyzed, the timestamp is incremented by one; otherwise, it is not altered.

The generated timestamps are then used to construct partitions within the graph, by putting all instances of s with the same timestamp into the same partition. An example illustrating this approach was shown earlier in Section 2. Consider the DDG shown in Fig. 1(a). The nodes at the top of the DDG represent the run-time instances of S1, while the rest of the DDG nodes are instances of S2. Suppose we wanted to evaluate the potential vectorizability of S2. For this static instruction, the analysis will compute timestamps for S2 instances as shown in Fig. 1(b). Each timestamp value defines one partition of S2 instances.

PROPERTY 3.1. *Consider any DDG node s_i and a DDG path p ending at s_i. Let $s(p)$ be the number of nodes on p (excluding s_i) that are instances of the static instruction s being analyzed. The timestamp computed for s_i by Algorithm 1 is the largest value of $s(p)$ for all p leading to s_i.*

The proof is by induction on the length of p. This property has two implications. First, consider two instances s_i and s_j of s. If there exists a run-time dependence from s_i to s_j (either directly, or indirectly through instances of instructions other than s, or through other instances of s itself), then the timestamp of s_i is strictly smaller than the timestamp of s_j. Thus, all instances of s with the same timestamp (i.e., in the same partition) are independent of each other. Second, each s_i is assigned the smallest possible timestamp—that is, it is scheduled at the earliest possible time. Considering the average partition size as a metric of available parallelism for the instances of s, the following property can be proven easily.

PROPERTY 3.2. *Algorithm 1 finds the maximum available parallelism for each static instruction s.*

3.2 Partitioning for Contiguous Access

Algorithm 1 ensures that the instances of s within a partition are independent, but efficient SIMD parallelism also requires contiguous memory access. On most SIMD architectures, the cost of loading vector elements individually and shuffling them into a vector register offsets the benefit of exploiting the vector hardware.

Thus, the partitions must be further subdivided into units that exhibit parallelism *and* contiguous memory access. In general, we want to ensure unit-stride accesses—the distance in memory between consecutive memory accesses is equal to the size of the data type. We also allow zero-stride (i.e., the distance in memory between consecutive accesses is zero), since vector splats (copying a scalar value into all elements of a vector) are cheap for most SIMD architectures. Note that the zero-stride case also covers operations with constant operands.

To ensure unit-stride, the instruction instances within a parallel partition are sorted according to the memory addresses of their operands. For constants or values produced by other instructions but not saved to memory, an artificial address of zero is used. The sorted list is then scanned, ending the current subpartition (and starting a new one) when the stride is (1) non-zero and non-unit, or (2) different from the previously observed stride. The result is a (now potentially larger) set of subpartitions such that the dynamic instruction instances within a subpartition are independent, and exhibit uniform zero-stride or unit-stride accesses to memory. The average size of these subpartitions is a metric of the vectorization potential of the static instruction being characterized.

3.3 Non-Unit Constant Stride Access

The contiguous access check performed in the previous stage is important for discovering efficient vectorization potential, but a variation of the check can be used to explore the potential benefit of data layout transformations on the original code. It is not uncommon to find computations where fine-grained concurrency exists but the data accessed has a non-unit but constant stride. In the first loop in Listing 3 there is a loop-carried dependence along the inner j loop but the i loop is parallel. If the loops were permuted, we would have fine-grained parallelism in the inner loop for the instances of S1, but the access stride would be N. A data layout transformation to transpose the array (i.e., swap the first and second array dimensions) would enable unit-stride access and efficient vectorization. Listing 4 shows how the code could be transformed.

The second loop in Listing 3 illustrates a scenario with arrays of structures that results in fine-grained concurrent operations but non-unit access stride. The instances of S2 are all independent but they exhibit stride-2 access (e.g., 8 bytes if x and y are single-precision floating-point). The same is true for the instances of S3. In this case, changing the data structure from an array of structures to a structure of arrays would enable parallel, stride-1 access which could be automatically vectorized.

By relaxing the unit/zero-stride condition to instead check for any non-unit constant stride, we can detect cases such as the ones

```
for( i = 0 ; i < N ; i++ )
  for( j = 2 ; j < N ; j++ )
    A[i][j] = 2*A[i][j-1] - A[i][j-2]; // S1

for ( i = 0 ; i < N ; i++ ) {
  C[i].x = B[i].x + B[i].y;     // S2
  C[i].y = B[i].x - B[i].y;     // S3
}
```

Listing 3: Vectorization benefits of data layout transformations: stride-N column access and array-of-structures access.

```
// transposed declarations for A, B, and C
for( j = 2 ; j < N ; j++ )
  for( i = 0 ; i < N ; i++ )
    A[j][i] = 2*A[j-1][i] - A[j-2][i]; // S1

for ( i = 0 ; i < N ; i++ ) {
  C.x[i] = B.x[i] + B.y[i];     // S2
  C.y[i] = B.x[i] - B.y[i];     // S3
}
```

Listing 4: Loop transformations and data layout transformations applied to Listing 3.

illustrated in Listing 3. Given the partitions produced by Algorithm 1, we apply the unit-stride analysis from the previous subsection. At the end, any instruction instance that belongs to a subpartition of size one is identified. All such instances (of the same static instruction, and with the same timestamp) are then sorted and scanned. When the currently observed stride does not match the previously observed one, the instruction is put on a waitlist for future processing, and the scanning based on the current stride continues until the end of the list is reached; this results in one subpartition. Any waitlisted instructions are then traversed again, in sorted order, so that the next subpartition can be formed.

4. Evaluation

In this section we present a number of studies to illustrate the use of the dynamic analysis tool. Although the studies are restricted to analysis of sequential programs, the tool can also be used with parallel programs using Pthreads, OpenMP, MPI, etc.—the instrumentation and trace generation would be applied to one or more sequential processes or threads of the parallel program to assess the potential for SIMD vector parallelism within a process/thread. Further, although we only concentrate on characterizing floating-point operations (because they tend to be the focus of most SIMD optimization efforts), such analysis can be carried out for any type of operations, e.g., integer arithmetic.

The experiments were performed on a machine with an Intel Xeon E5630 processor and 12GB memory, running Linux 2.6.32. To obtain performance measurements, the Intel icc compiler (12.1.3) was used to compile the program code, at the O3 optimization level. Profiling data was obtained with HPCToolkit [10] version 5.2.1, at sampling period 500 thousand cycles. The instrumentation infrastructure was implemented in LLVM 3.0.

4.1 Characterization of Applications

We illustrate the use of the tool for characterizing software collections by applying it to the SPEC CFP2006 floating-point benchmarks, and kernels from the UTDSP benchmark suite [32]. We also include two stand-alone compute kernels: a 2-D Gauss-Seidel stencil code and a kernel from a 2-D PDE grid-based solver; they are elaborated upon later as case studies illustrating potential use of the analysis for performance optimization and compiler enhancement.

Benchmark	Loop	Percent Cycles	Percent Packed	Average Concur.	Unit Stride		Non-unit Stride	
					Percent Vec. Ops	Average Vec. Size	Percent Vec. Ops	Average Vec. Size
410.bwaves	block_solver.f : 55	79.2%	53.0%	39.9	97.5%	11.1	0.0%	–
	block_solver.f : 176	65.8%	66.4%	8.3	100.0%	5.0	0.0%	–
433.milc	gauge_stuff.c : 258	22.0%	0.0%	10453.4	36.2%	10427.4	49.7%	3.3
	path_product.c : 49	17.9%	0.0%	73316.6	36.4%	69441.5	63.6%	3.2
	quark_stuff.c : 566	15.2%	0.0%	23687.7	88.3%	11.4	7.5%	4.2
	quark_stuff.c : 960	44.9%	0.0%	11447.3	65.1%	15.5	18.7%	2.3
	quark_stuff.c : 973	35.0%	0.0%	61566.7	57.4%	13.8	32.9%	2.4
	quark_stuff.c : 1452	14.2%	0.0%	20736.0	36.4%	20736.0	63.6%	502.3
	quark_stuff.c : 1460	13.6%	0.0%	20736.0	36.4%	20736.0	63.6%	20736.0
	quark_stuff.c : 1523	15.4%	0.0%	2921.1	55.0%	2000.0	45.0%	4.2
434.zeusmp	advx3.f : 637	11.3%	35.0%	66613.9	74.3%	442.1	16.6%	16.0
435.gromacs	innerf.f : 3960	60.4%	4.4%	4.0	60.3%	12.0	21.5%	2.0
	ns.c : 1264	16.2%	3.8%	4.9	60.0%	42.0	20.9%	2.1
	ns.c : 1461	35.3%	3.3%	40.3	64.1%	31.0	35.1%	2.0
	ns.c : 1503	13.3%	0.0%	5.0	62.5%	5.0	30.0%	2.0
436.cactusADM	StaggeredLeapfrog2.F : 342	18.4%	100.0%	80.0	100.0%	80.0	0.0%	–
	StaggeredLeapfrog2.F : 366	81.1%	96.9%	78.0	100.0%	78.0	0.0%	–
437.leslie3d	tml.f : 522	15.6%	98.5%	8805.5	100.0%	158.3	0.0%	–
	tml.f : 889	13.4%	99.2%	7434.2	99.9%	178.4	0.0%	–
	tml.f : 1269	12.4%	99.2%	438.3	100.0%	22.0	0.0%	–
	tml.f : 3569	21.6%	98.6%	8100.0	100.0%	90.0	0.0%	–
444.namd	ComputeList.C : 71	33.2%	0.0%	130.2	86.0%	101.1	13.7%	11.4
	ComputeList.C : 75	66.4%	0.0%	313.3	93.3%	295.4	6.6%	7.8
	ComputeNonbondedBase.h : 321	12.9%	0.0%	15.6	85.9%	262.8	7.8%	5.4
447.dealII	mapping_q1.cc : 514	10.4%	0.0%	1.0	0.0%	–	0.0%	–
	step-14.cc : 715	16.2%	0.0%	130.9	75.6%	58.2	24.3%	24.9
	step-14.cc : 780	10.9%	0.0%	27.0	66.7%	27.0	33.3%	27.0
	step-14.cc : 3198	19.1%	3.1%	335.6	87.5%	12.5	12.5%	18.8
450.soplex	ssvector.cc : 983	10.6%	0.0%	373.0	32.2%	18.5	56.2%	18.2
	slufactor.cc : 839	12.5%	0.0%	59.7	43.2%	6.5	39.4%	2.0
	spxsolve.cc : 126	37.7%	0.0%	384.3	92.3%	25.6	3.5%	2.1
	spxsolve.cc : 200	58.5%	0.0%	361.6	88.2%	15.9	5.0%	2.1
	svector.h : 293	12.8%	0.0%	1.7	0.0%	–	40.0%	2.0
453.povray	bbox.cpp : 894	53.3%	0.2%	11.2	62.6%	14.8	27.3%	2.7
	csg.cpp : 248	58.6%	0.0%	4.3	35.5%	4.8	41.1%	2.0
	csg.cpp : 254	16.2%	0.2%	1.0	0.0%	–	0.0%	–
	lbuffer.cpp : 1373	23.0%	0.1%	14.8	63.8%	16.4	29.8%	2.9
	lighting.cpp : 600	66.9%	1.0%	13.1	65.4%	13.9	28.1%	2.0
	lighting.cpp : 938	27.1%	0.1%	13.7	63.3%	15.7	29.7%	2.8
	lighting.cpp : 2298	31.5%	1.0%	7.7	59.3%	16.2	26.5%	2.9
	lighting.cpp : 4120	41.7%	0.8%	11.4	64.8%	13.1	25.0%	2.1
454.calculix	Chv_update.c : 736	13.6%	91.5%	27.4	48.4%	15.0	51.6%	11.4
	e_c3d.f : 675	69.7%	0.1%	35.6	100.0%	12.3	0.0%	–
	FrontMtx_update.c : 207	16.4%	91.3%	774.0	96.4%	28.6	3.1%	9.4
	FrontMtx_update.c : 38	14.0%	91.2%	1116.3	96.7%	12.9	2.6%	4.7
	mafillsm.f : 144	74.7%	0.4%	6064.8	99.2%	136.9	0.8%	3.1
	Utilities_DV.c : 1241	11.4%	96.6%	2.0	50.0%	49.0	0.0%	–
459.GemsFDTD	NFT.F90 : 1068	17.4%	0.0%	24.2	69.9%	9.9	19.3%	2.1
	update.F90 : 108	17.3%	97.4%	201.0	100.0%	201.0	0.0%	–
	update.F90 : 242	17.1%	97.3%	200.0	100.0%	200.0	0.0%	–
465.tonto	mol.F90 : 5565	15.7%	80.4%	50779.4	99.2%	150.7	0.3%	2.4
	mol.F90 : 11659	59.0%	19.5%	266.6	97.2%	31.6	1.0%	4.4
470.lbm	lbm.c : 186	99.6%	100.0%	137487.0	61.6%	137487.0	38.4%	72.1
481.wrf	solve_em.F90 : 179	87.9%	79.1%	1198.6	97.4%	39.7	1.2%	15.1
	solve_em.F90 : 884	14.4%	89.3%	54721.8	99.8%	117.0	0.2%	29.1
	solve_em.F90 : 1258	14.8%	89.6%	9887.1	93.6%	89.1	6.4%	28.5
	solve_em.F90 : 1538	12.8%	87.4%	95531.4	95.4%	27.6	4.6%	7.6
482.sphinx3	approx_cont_mgau.c : 279	39.8%	68.1%	8949.0	75.2%	6886.1	24.8%	2.3
	cont_mgau.c : 652	17.0%	72.8%	3.7	75.0%	39.0	0.0%	–
	subvq.c : 456	30.8%	75.0%	19154.8	75.5%	15360.0	24.5%	2048.0
	vector.c : 521	25.9%	86.1%	3.3	75.0%	13.0	0.0%	–

Table 1: Analysis results for analyzed benchmark loops.

The stand-alone kernels and UTDSP benchmarks were directly analyzed by the tool and the results are shown in Tables 2 and 3. For full application codes, such as the SPEC CFP2006 floating-point benchmarks, the output produced by the dynamic analysis will be very extensive. Therefore, we only analyze and report characteristics for time-consuming loops identified via profiling by HPC-

Benchmark	Percent Packed	Average Concur.	Unit Stride Percent Vec. Ops	Unit Stride Average Vec. Size	Non-unit Stride Percent Vec. Ops	Non-unit Stride Average Vec. Size
2-D Gauss-Seidel Stencil	0.0%	226	22.2%	46.1	77.4%	9.3
2-D PDE Grid Solver	0.0%	231426	100.0%	820.8	0.0%	—

Table 2: Analysis results for computation kernels.

Benchmark	Type	Percent Packed	Average Concur.	Unit Stride Percent Vec. Ops	Unit Stride Average Vec. Size	Non-unit Stride Percent Vec. Ops	Non-unit Stride Average Vec. Size
FFT	Array	49.9%	568.9	79.3%	24.1	12.2%	2.0
	Pointer	0.0%	568.9	79.3%	24.1	12.2%	2.0
FIR	Array	99.8%	99.9	100.0%	57.4	0.0%	–
	Pointer	0.0%	99.9	100.0%	57.4	0.0%	–
IIR	Array	0.00%	43.6	64.8%	14.3	15.6%	8.9
	Pointer	0.00%	43.6	64.8%	14.3	15.6%	8.9
LATNRM	Array	7.8%	7.4	74.6%	23.9	0.0%	–
	Pointer	8.2%	7.4	74.6%	23.9	0.0%	–
LMSFIR	Array	0.0%	2.7	48.3%	22.1	16.5%	21.8
	Pointer	0.0%	2.8	49.4%	28.0	16.2%	21.9
MULT	Array	50.4%	181.9	100.0%	18.2	0.0%	–
	Pointer	0.00%	181.9	100.0%	18.2	0.0%	–

Table 3: Analysis results for UTDSP benchmark suite.

Toolkit, analyzing only loops that account for at least 10% of total execution cycles during a run of the benchmark using the SPEC reference data set (the 10% threshold was selected to reduce the amount of data presented; we also collected data at a threshold of 5%). To perform the DDG analysis for a particular loop, we collected several subtraces corresponding to separate instances of the loop (using the SPEC train data set, and for a few large loops the test data set). A subtrace was started upon loop entry and terminated upon loop exit and its DDG was constructed and analyzed. We randomly chose several instances of the loop, analyzed each corresponding subtrace to obtain the various metrics described later, and chose one representative subtrace to be included in the measurements presented in the paper.

The results of the analysis for SPEC CFP2006 are shown in Table 1. For each benchmark, we only show loops that account for at least 10% of total execution cycles. We start with all innermost loops, and only include a parent loop if the total percentage of execution cycles spent in it is at least 10 percentage points greater than the sum of the percentages for its inner loops. The `gamess` benchmark could not be compiled with LLVM and was not used in the experiments.

The *Percent Packed* metric shows the percentage of floating-point run-time operations that were executed using packed (i.e., vector) SSE instructions, as reported by HPCToolkit. This column provides information on the effectiveness of current compilers (we used Intel icc since we have found it to be superior to other production compilers in vectorization capability) in vectorizing each of the identified hot loops. A high value indicates that a significant fraction of the floating-point operations in that loop were executed via packed SIMD instructions. A zero value indicates that the compiler was unable to achieve any vectorization at all for the loop.

The *Average Concurrency* metric was computed by determining the average partition size across the collection of partitions for all floating-point instructions in the graph, where partitions were formed by considering only instruction independence (Sect. 3.1). For this metric, both singleton and non-singleton partitions were considered. From the non-singleton parallel partitions, subpartitions containing unit-stride operations were formed (as described in Sect. 3.2). The *Percent Vec. Ops* metric (i.e., potentially vectorizable run-time instructions) shows the number of operations that belong to non-singleton unit-stride subpartitions, as percent of the total number of operations in the graph. The *Average Vec. Size* metric represents the average size of these non-singleton vectorizable subpartitions. The general trend is that for most of the loops, many run-time instructions belong to partitions that exhibit both independence and contiguous memory access. Furthermore, the sizes of these partitions are large—in many cases, much larger than the vector sizes in existing and emerging architectures. Thus, the analysis indicates that the majority of the analyzed loops may have high vectorization potential.

The run-time instructions within a non-singleton parallel partition that did not belong in any unit-stride subpartition were further analyzed with the non-unit stride analysis described in Section 3.3. The analysis reported the number of such instructions that could be placed in subpartitions accessing data at some fixed non-unit stride. This number, as percent of the total number of all run-time instructions in the graph, is shown in column *Percent Vec. Ops*. The average size of such subpartitions is given in the last column. There are several examples where a significant number of independent instructions can be combined together using non-unit stride, and the sizes of the partitions are large as well. This indicates that data layout transformations may be beneficial in these cases.

There may be cases where the percentage of packed instructions observed via profiling exceeds the sum of the values in columns *Percent Vec. Ops* (e.g., `Utilities_DV.c:1241` in 454.calculix and `vector.c:521` in 482.sphinx3). This happens in the presence of a reduction (e.g., `s+=expr`): our analysis considers the chain of dependences and treats the computation as non-vectorizable. However, there exist approaches to vectorize reductions, and icc employs some of them. In future work, our approach could be extended to ignore dependences due to reductions, which would uncover these additional vectorization opportunities.

As is typical of other work on dynamic analysis of fine-grained dependences (e.g., [14, 36]), the instrumentation incurs an overhead of two to three orders of magnitude, relative to the execution time of the original unmodified code. The cost of DDG analysis depends on graph size and memory access patterns, and is typically of the order of tens to hundreds of microseconds per DDG node. Although we have not focused on tool optimization, the utility of the current unoptimized implementation of our prototype is not hampered for two reasons. First, the analysis is intended to be performed offline, e.g., during performance tuning. Many profiling analyses have been successfully used in this setting, and various existing techniques can be readily applied to reduce their cost (e.g., [36, 38]). Second, the instrumented code can be run with much smaller problem sizes than the "production" size: in our experience, although metrics such as average vector size can vary with problem size, the qualitative insights about potential vectorizability do not change.

4.2 Assisting Vectorization Experts

Many institutions possess large code bases that were largely developed before the recent emergence of SIMD parallelism in all CPUs/GPUs. When the original developers of the code are not available to adapt it for improved vectorization, an automated tool can be very valuable. For some loops, a quick scan of the code of a hot loop by a vectorization expert will immediately reveal the opportunities for enhancing vectorizability through code changes. But this is certainly not the norm, especially with C++ codes or C codes that make heavy use of pointers. An automated tool allows the vectorization expert to quickly eliminate loops with little to no vectorization potential, and concentrate on the loops with high potential. With these, some of the code structures involve multiple levels of function calls and the output from the tool is valuable input to the expert, indicating that the effort to unravel the code is likely worth it. As an example, the hot loops in `444.namd` are generated using C preprocessor macros and it is very difficult to get an understanding of the code just by scanning it. If we examine the HPCToolkit profile data, we know the loops are hot, but not whether or not we have any hope of vectorizing them. However, our analysis shows that there is a high potential for vectorization in this part of code, so it may be worth the time investment of a vectorization expert to carefully analyze these loops.

Another use case is for identifying missed opportunities in compiler test suites. Vendor compilers are typically tested against large amounts of code to gauge the performance of the compiler's vectorizer. It is easy to automate this testing to see how much of the code is vectorized, but for the remaining code, it is not clear whether the code is just not vectorizable, or if the compiler is missing an opportunity. It would take considerable effort for a vectorization expert to manually analyze all of the non-vectorized code. The analysis tool can help to automate the process and focus the expert's effort on identifying why code that has been identified as being potentially vectorizable is not actually being vectorized by the compiler.

4.3 Array-Based vs. Pointer-Based Code

Auto-vectorizing compilers are becoming increasingly good at vectorizing array-based code, but pointer-based code is often not vectorized due to the added complexities with pointer aliasing and the verification of contiguous access during the compiler's static analysis. A primary benefit of the proposed dynamic analysis technique is the ability to analyze pointer based code just as easily as array based code. Both versions of the same computation will provide the same analysis results, since the dynamic analysis considers IR-level arithmetic operations, and does not make a distinction between data that is read from arrays or pointer dereferencing.

To test this facet of our analysis, we used the UTDSP [32] benchmark suite, which contains both array- and pointer-based versions of several computation kernels for digital signal processors (DSP). The suite was created to evaluate the quality of code generated by a high-level language compiler (e.g., a C compiler) targeting a programmable DSP. Thus, each kernel was written in different styles, including an array-based version and a pointer-based version. Both versions provide identical functionality, except for the use of arrays or pointers to traverse the data structures.

Table 3 shows the results of this experiment. The measurements include the percentage of vectorizable operations found in the program, the average vector size, and the percentage of operations that are actually vectorized by the Intel icc compiler. We see that our analysis is invariant to the form of the code[1], but icc fails to vectorize some of the pointer-based code. Such knowledge would be very useful in optimizing certain applications, where a conversion from pointer-based code to array-based code may be worthwhile if the potential benefits are high. The dynamic analysis from our tool could be a valuable first step in the process.

		Original	Trans.	Speedup
2-D Seidel	Xeon E5630	0.228s	0.074s	3.086×
	Core i7 2600K	0.170s	0.083s	2.055×
	PhenomII 1100T	0.200s	0.068s	2.926×
2-D PDE	Xeon E5630	0.355s	0.185s	1.909×
	Core i7 2600K	0.198s	0.116s	1.699×
	PhenomII 1100T	0.722s	0.401s	1.799×
410.bwaves	Xeon E5630	2.42e-1s	1.88e-2s	1.284×
	Core i7 2600K	1.72e-1s	1.24e-1s	1.382×
	PhenomII 1100T	2.74e-1s	2.50e-1s	1.100×
433.milc	Xeon E5630	2.13e-2s	1.24e-2s	1.725×
	Core i7 2600K	9.10e-3s	7.30e-3s	1.245×
	Phenom II 1100T	3.05e-2s	1.99e-2	1.528×
435.gromacs	Xeon E5630	238.5s	149.4s	1.596×
	Core i7 2600K	163.6s	98.1s	1.667×
	Phenom II 1100T	210.3s	151.8s	1.386×

Table 4: Performance measurements for the case studies.

4.4 Case Studies

Based on the results from the previous subsections, some benchmarks were manually transformed to enable vectorization by icc. The targeted benchmarks were the Gauss-Seidel stencil, the PDE grid solver, and the 410.bwaves, 433.milc, and 435.gromacs benchmarks from SPEC CFP2006. A comparison of the performance of the original and modified versions is shown in Table 4. In addition to the Intel Xeon E5630 machine used for the measurements presented earlier, two other machines were used in these experiments: an Intel Core i7 2600K and an AMD PhenomII 1100T, both with the same icc configuration. For each benchmark, we show the total execution time for both versions, as well as the achieved speedup. When the target of the optimization is a particular loop (e.g., bwaves and gromacs), the measurements in the table are based on the total time spent in the loop. The reference data sets were used when running the SPEC benchmarks.

Gauss-Seidel In this case study we analyze the vectorization potential of a 9-point Gauss-Seidel stencil code. This code has been identified by our analysis as being not auto-vectorized by the vendor compiler, but possessing non-trivial vectorization potential (see Table 2). Listing 5 shows the original kernel. It has a loop-carried dependence in the innermost `j` loop, since the fourth operand `A[i][j-1]` is produced in the previous iteration of this loop. Similarly, the outer `i` loop also has loop-carried dependences. Due to the dependences, icc was unable to vectorize the code. This was not unexpected. However, what surprised us was that the dynamic analysis revealed vectorization potential for this code.

The analysis classified two out of the eight addition operations (`A[i-1][j-1]+A[i-1][j]+A[i-1][j+1]`) as vectorizable. This is because the operands were all produced in the previous iteration of the `i` loop. The only true dependence in the loop is

[1] The discrepancy in LMSFIR is due to a difference in the way the two versions are written, resulting in slightly different distributions of operations.

```
/* Original */
cnst = 1/9.0;
for(t=0; t<T ; t++)
  for(i=1; i<N-1; i++)
    for(j=1; j<N-1; j++)
      A[i][j] = (A[i-1][j-1] + A[i-1][j] +
                 A[i-1][j+1] + A[i][j-1] +
                 A[i][j]     + A[i][j+1] +
                 A[i+1][j-1] + A[i+1][j] +
                 A[i+1][j+1]) * cnst;
/* Transformed */
cnst = 1/9.0;
for(t=0; t<T; t++)
  for(i=1; i<N-1; i++) {
    for(j=1; j<N-1; j++)
      temp[j] = A[i-1][j-1] + A[i-1][j]   +
                A[i-1][j+1] + A[i][j]     +
                A[i][j+1]   + A[i+1][j-1] +
                A[i+1][j]   + A[i+1][j+1];

    for(j=1;j<N-1;j++)
       A[i][j] = cnst * (A[i][j-1] + temp[j]);
  }
```

Listing 5: Original and transformed Gauss-Seidel code.

due to `A[i][j-1]`. The operations involving elements from row `i+1`, and even the addition of `A[i][j]` and `A[i][j+1]`, could be performed in vectorized mode by splitting the loop into a sequence of two loops, as shown in Listing 5. The first `j` loop in the transformed code is now completely vectorized by icc, resulting in significant performance improvement (see the results in Table 4, obtained for $N = 1000$ and $T = 20$).

The extent of vectorizability of the Gauss-Seidel code was a surprise to us since our initial expectation was that the code would not exhibit vectorization potential due to loop-carried dependences. Closer examination of the dependences shows that all the information needed to transform the code is actually derivable from purely static analysis. However, to our knowledge, no research or production compiler can perform the transformation we performed manually. This example illustrates how the developed dynamic analysis can be valuable for compiler writers to identify scenarios where enhancements to static analysis and transformation capabilities can enable improved code transformations for vectorization.

2-D PDE Solver In this case study we analyze the core computation from a 2-D PDE grid-based solver. The code is from the examples included with PETSc [20] 3.1-p7 and solves the solid fuel ignition problem, modeled as a partial differential equation. The original source can be found under */src/snes/examples/tutorials/ex5.c* in the PETSc distribution. We see that this code is not auto-vectorized by icc, but our analysis shows very high vectorization potential. In this kernel, the 2-D computation grid is distributed onto a 2-D grid of blocks, where the computation is performed by iterating over every cell within every block. For our purposes, we consider only sequential execution of the program.

The per-block kernel code is shown in Listing 6. The `if` condition in the innermost loop is a boundary condition check that forces grid points on the boundary to follow a different path of execution as compared to the other interior points. The loop bounds for this loop nest, along with two of the four conditions that can trigger the `if` statement, are data dependent. As a result, compilers are forced to be conservative and assume that for each iteration of the loop, it is unknown whether the `then` or `else` clause will be executed. Due to this constraint, the vectorizability of this particular loop nest, as written, is very low. Further, without more constraints on the values within the `info` structure, static analysis cannot determine transformations that would enable vectorization.

```
/* Original */
for (j=info->ys; j<info->ys+info->ym; j++) {
  for (i=info->xs; i<info->xs+info->xm; i++) {
    if (i == 0 || j == 0 ||
        i == info->mx-1 || j == info->my-1) {
      f[j][i] = x[j][i];
    } else {
      u = x[j][i];
      uxx = (2.0*u-x[j][i-1]-x[j][i+1])*hydhx;
      uyy = (2.0*u-x[j-1][i]-x[j+1][i])*hxdhy;
      f[j][i] = uxx+uyy-sc*PetscExpScalar(u);
    }
  }
}
/* Transformed */
if(info->ys==0 || info->xs==0 ||
   (info->ys+info->ym)==my ||
   (info->xs+info->xm)==mx) {
  /* Same as lines 2-14 */
}
else {
  for(j=info->ys; j<info->ys+info->ym; j++) {
    for(i=info->xs; i<info->xs+info->xm; i++) {
      u = x[j][i];
      uxx = (2.0*u-x[j][i-1]-x[j][i+1])*hydhx;
      uyy = (2.0*u-x[j-1][i]-x[j+1][i])*hxdhy;
      f[j][i] = uxx+uyy-sc*PetscExpScalar(u);
    }
  }
}
```

Listing 6: Original and transformed 2-D PDE Solver.

However, the results of the dynamic analysis show a great potential for vectorizability within this code (see Table 2). Specifically, the `else` clause exhibits perfect vectorizability. To allow a compiler to vectorize this loop, we can rewrite the code to extract the `if/then/else` construct and then hoist an `if` to provide a vectorizable loop. The modified code is shown in Listing 6. The key to the vectorization-enabling transformation is the observation that cells which correspond to the boundary condition can only occur on boundary blocks. We observe that `i` and `j` cannot be zero except within blocks along the top or left edge of the grid, and cannot be equal to the maximum index value (`mx-1` and `my-1`) except within blocks along the right or bottom edge of the grid. Therefore, the kernel code can be split into two separate versions; one for boundary blocks and one for interior blocks, as shown in Listing 6. While this code should provide no speed-up for boundary blocks, it enables vectorization for interior blocks and provides an advantage when the blocks are in at least a 3×3 grid.

Table 4 shows the total execution time for the original and modified code for a case where the block size is 512×512 and blocks are in a grid of size 16×16. As shown in the table, the performance improvement is substantial.

410.bwaves In the 410.bwaves benchmark, one of the loops we analyzed in our extended study (at 5% threshold for hot loops) is at `jacobi_lam.f:30`. This loop exhibits a very low percentage of packed instructions, while the dynamic analysis shows that there are significant numbers of vectorizable operations at unit and non-unit stride. The result from the non-unit stride analysis suggests possible improvements through data layout transformation.

Listing 7 is representative of the computation within this loop. Arrays `je` and `jv` are of size `(5,5,nx,ny,nz)`, and array `q` is of size `(5,nx,ny,nz)` where `nx`, `ny` and `nz` are program constants. While there is no dependence between the iterations of the innermost loop `i`, there are two factors that hinder vectorization. First, there is no unit-stride data access pattern since `i` is used to access the third dimension of the arrays. Second, the use of `mod`

```
1  ish = 1
2  ksh = 1
3  jsh = 1
4  !! Original
5  do k = 1,nz
6     kp1 = mod(k,nz+1-ksh)+ksh
7     do j=1,ny
8        jp1=mod(j,ny+1-jsh)+jsh
9        do i=1,nx
10          ip1=mod(i,nx+1-ish)+ish
11          !! Some computation
12          je(1,1,i,j,k) = ...
13          je(1,2,i,j,k) = ...
14          ...
15          je(4,5,i,j,k) = ...
16          je(5,5,i,j,k) = ...
17          !! Some computation
18          ros = q(1,ip1,jp1,kp1)
19          !! Similar computation for jv as for je
20       enddo
21    enddo
22 enddo
23 !! Transformed
24 do k = 1,nz
25    kp1 = mod(k,nz+1-ksh)+ksh
26    do j=1,ny
27       jp1=mod(j,ny+1-jsh)+jsh
28       do i=1,nx-1
29          ip1=i+1
30          !! Some computation
31          je(i,1,1,j,k) = ...
32          je(i,1,2,j,k) = ...
33          ...
34          !! Some computation
35          ros = q(ip1,1,jp1,kp1)
36          !! Similar computation for jv as for je
37       enddo
38       i = nx
39       ip1 = 1
40       !! Inner loop computation (lines 11-19)
41    enddo
42 enddo
```

Listing 7: Original and transformed bwaves code.

operations to calculate the neighbor with wrap-around boundary conditions hampers the vectorization of accesses to array `q`.

To address these problems, a data layout transformation was performed on arrays `je`, `jv`, and `q`: the dimension which was originally accessed by `i` (and `ip1`) was moved to become the fastest varying dimension of the arrays. This transformation is shown in Listing 7. The modified code has a stride-1 data access pattern. The `mod` operations were removed by peeling the last iteration of the `i` loop, and introducing `ip1=i+1` within the loop. The value of `ip1` for the peeled iteration was set to 1. Table 4 shows the performance of the original and modified versions.

433.milc In this case study we explore the benefits of data layout transformations on the 433.milc benchmark. Specifically, we focus on one of the loops from Table 1. The loop starting at `quark_stuff.c`:1452 shows no automatic vectorization by the compiler. There is also limited potential for vectorization at unit stride. However, the non-unit stride analysis shows significant potential for vectorization, implying that a data layout transformation may speed up the computation.

This loop iterates over every point in a lattice, applying a matrix-vector multiplication operation at each point. The matrices are of size 3×3 and the vectors are of size 3, both containing complex numbers. The lattice itself holds a matrix at each point, and external arrays of vectors are used for the vector inputs and outputs. The matrix-vector multiplication is not vectorized by the compiler due to non-unit stride access (distribution of real/imaginary components) and a small inner loop trip count (3).

```
/* Original data layout */
typedef struct { double r, i; } complex;
typedef struct { complex c[3]; } su3_vector;
typedef struct { complex e[3][3]; } su3_matrix;
su3_matrix lattice[NUM_SITES];
su3_vector vec[NUM_SITES], out_vec[NUM_SITES];
/* Original computation */
for(s = 0; s < NUM_SITES; ++s) {
  for(i = 0; i < 3; ++i) {
    complex x = { 0.0, 0.0 };
    for(j = 0; j < 3; ++j) {
      complex y;
      y.r = lattice[s].e[i][j].r * vec[s].c[j].r -
            lattice[s].e[i][j].i * vec[s].c[j].i;
      y.i = lattice[s].e[i][j].r * vec[s].c[j].i +
            lattice[s].e[i][j].i * vec[s].c[j].r;
      x.r += y.r; x.i += y.i;
    }
    out_vec[s].c[i] = x;
  }
}
/* Transformed data layout */
typedef struct {
  double r[3][3][NUM_SITES];
  double i[3][3][NUM_SITES];
} lattice_dlt;
typedef struct {
  double r[3][NUM_SITES];
  double i[3][NUM_SITES];
} vec_dlt;
lattice_dlt lattice;
vec_dlt vec, out_vec;
/* Transformed computation */
/* Initialize the elements of out_vec to 0.0 */
for(i = 0; i < 3; ++i) {
  for(j = 0; j < 3; ++j) {
    for(s = 0; s < NUM_SITES; ++s) {
      double x_r, x_i;
      x_r = lattice.r[i][j][s] * vec.r[j][s] -
            lattice.i[i][j][s] * vec.i[j][s];
      x_i = lattice.r[i][j][s] * vec.i[j][s] +
            lattice.i[i][j][s] * vec.r[j][s];
      out_vec.r[i][s] += x_r;
      out_vec.i[i][s] += x_i;
    }
  }
}
```

Listing 8: Original and transformed milc code.

To help us isolate the required changes, we created a version of the benchmark that only contains the computation we identified. The full benchmark was too large to optimize manually without in-depth understanding of the entire application, and the smaller, kernel-ized version allowed us to show proof-of-concept benefits of a data layout transformation. To optimize this operation, the transformation was applied to the lattice data structure, where the lattice of matrices was converted to a matrix of lattices. This modification exposes unit-stride operations within the inner loop. The original and transformed code are shown in Listing 8. Table 4 demonstrates a significant speedup for the modified kernel.

435.gromacs For this case study we focus on the loop at line 3960 in `innerf.f` from 435.gromacs. While icc is not able to vectorize this loop in any significant manner, the dynamic analysis results indicate the existence of unit-stride operations. Lines 1–14 of Listing 9 represent the computation within the loop.

The value of `j3` is data dependent (based on the run-time values in indirection array `jjnr`) and is used to index into arrays `pos` and `faction`. The compiler has to assume that the loop is not parallel, in case two or more elements of `jjnr` have the same value and thus create a dependence through `faction(j3)`. Furthermore, the access patterns for `pos` and `faction` are not regular due to the arbitrary values of `j3`. Thus, the loop is not vectorized by icc.

```
1  !! Original
2  do k = nj0,nj1
3      jnr = jjnr(k)+1
4      j3  = 3*jnr-2
5      jx1 = pos(j3)
6      ...
7      tx11 = ...
8      fjx1 = faction(j3) - tx11
9      tx21 = ...
10     fjx1 = fjx1 - tx21
11     tx31 = ...
12     faction(j3) = fjx1 - tx31
13     ...
14 enddo
15 !! Transformed
16 do k = nj0,nj1,4
17     do k_vect = 1,4
18         jnr = jjnr(k+k_vect-1)+1
19         vect_j3(k_vect) = 3*jnr-2
20         vect_jx1(k_vect) = pos(vect_j3(k_vect))
21         ...
22         vect_fjx1(k_vect) = faction(vect_j3(k_vect))
23         ...
24     enddo
25     do k_vect = 1,4
26         tx11 = ...
27         vect_fjx1(k_vect) = vect_fjx1(k_vect) - tx11
28         tx21 = ...
29         vect_fjx1(k_vect) = vect_fjx1(k_vect) - tx21
30         tx31 = ...
31         vect_fjx1(k_vect) = vect_fjx1(k_vect) - tx31
32         ...
33     enddo
34     do k_vect = 1,4
35         faction(vect_j3(k_vect)) = vect_fjx1(k_vect)
36         ...
37     enddo
38 enddo
```

Listing 9: Original and transformed gromacs code.

When the dynamic analysis results were examined at the level of individual statements, it became clear that the loop is in fact parallel: the values in `jjnr` ensure that distinct elements of `faction` are accessed by each iteration. (The relatively low average concurrency in Table 1 is due to the small number of loop iterations and to a few chains of reductions.) Furthermore, although the accesses to `pos` and `faction` do not exhibit any patterns, the rest of the computation in the loop body is done through scalars and can be easily vectorized.

For better vectorization, the loop was strip-mined as shown in Lines 15–38 of Listing 9. (The cleanup loop is not shown.) Loop distribution of the inner `k_vect` loop was then applied to move all reads from `pos` and `faction` above the computation, and to move all writes to `faction` after the computation. Array expansion of temporary `j3` was also performed to hold the necessary indices of `faction`. The middle `k_vect` loop is now vectorized by icc. Table 4 shows the reduction in the total time spent in the loop due to the transformation.

Unlike in the earlier case studies, here the analysis results do not necessarily generalize to arbitrary input data. Specifically, the fact that all iterations of the loop were independent affects both the vectorization potential and the code modifications. As written, the transformed code in Listing 9 is not correct for all possible inputs. It becomes necessary to assert this correctness with the help of additional information—e.g., an expert's knowledge of certain properties of the problem domain, or some compiler analysis of the intra- and inter-procedural code context surrounding the loop.

Limitations Although these case studies demonstrate the usefulness of the analysis reports, the proposed technique has a number of limitations. For example, for the loop from 435.gromacs, the conclusions about vectorizability are dependent on properties of the input data. As another example, we investigated loop `bbox.cpp`:894 from 453.povray in greater depth. This benchmark is a ray-tracer, and the loop in question implements a work-list algorithm that intersects a ray with a tree of bounding boxes. The computation is driven by a priority queue. Each iteration of the loop removes a bounding box from the queue and, if necessary, adds other bounding boxes to the queue. Inside an iteration, what processing is performed on the current bounding box depends on whether it is an inner node or a leaf of the tree, and whether the ray intersects the boxes of its children. The overall structure of the computation is very irregular and heavily depends on the actual run-time data. As part of the intersection tests for boxes and the scene objects contained in them, some low-level operations (e.g., computing the angle between two vectors) occur repeatedly, with high concurrency and with some potential vectorizability for certain subcomputations. However, the highly-irregular structure of the control flow makes it extremely challenging to exploit the vectorization potential without significant changes to the code by a domain expert with a deep understanding of the algorithm.

An interesting direction for future work is to refine the dynamic analysis to distinguish computations with irregular data-dependent control flow from ones where the control flow is more structured and vectorization potential is more likely to be actually realizable through code transformations.

5. Related Work

A number of techniques have been proposed to measure the available parallelism at the statement or instruction level (e.g., [2, 8, 9, 11, 12, 16, 17, 21, 23–25, 28, 33]). Several approaches aim to characterize instruction-level parallelism (ILP) and how it is affected by hardware features and compiler optimizations (e.g., [12, 33]). Austin and Sohi [2] construct a dynamic dependence graph and use it to measure ILP for several configurations. Typically, in these and similar studies, a program execution trace is first created; next, possible parallel schedules are defined by taking into account the dependences between binary instructions in the trace, under various assumptions (e.g., anti and output dependences may be ignored). A notable exception is the work by Kumar [11], which does not create a trace and instead instruments the program to compute the parallel schedule online. Some generalizations of this approach have been proposed in recent work [8].

Researchers have also considered dynamic analysis of loop-level parallelism, where all iterations of a loop may run concurrently with each other. The approach by Larus [14] generates an execution trace and analyzes it to model the effects of loop-level parallelism. A related technique is applied in the context of speculative parallelization of loops, where shadow locations are used to track dynamic dependences across loop iterations [22]. Several other approaches of similar nature have been investigated in more recent work (e.g., [3, 19, 30, 31, 35, 39]).

The efficient collection of dynamic data-dependence information has also been explored by previous work. Tallam et al. use run-time control flow information to reconstruct significant portions of the dynamic data-dependence graph of the program run [26], and have proposed a technique for producing lightweight tracing of multi-threaded code [27]. Zhang et al. use an approach to collect compressed profiles from program executions, including data dependence information [37]; they also propose techniques to decrease the cost of maintaining a dynamic dependence graph in the context of dynamic slicing [36, 38].

Automatic parallelization is also closely related to the characterization of vectorization in programs. Techniques to automatically exploit fine-grained parallelism must first determine the dependences between instructions. There is a body of work on the characterization of dynamic data dependences in the context of speculative execution (e.g., [22, 30, 40]).

Automatic vectorization has been the subject of extensive study (e.g., [1, 6, 7, 13, 13, 18, 34]). These approaches use static dependence analysis and then convert scalar instructions to vector instructions, in cases when the conditions for efficient vectorization are met. To the best of our knowledge, no prior work has addressed the topic of this paper—the development of an approach for dynamic analysis of vectorizability of computations.

6. Conclusions

This paper presents a new dynamic analysis for the characterization of SIMD parallelism potential in programs. Existing methods for characterizing concurrency have fundamental limitations in discovering potentially vectorizable operations, but these problems are overcome by the newly developed approach. The use of the analysis is illustrated by characterizing several computationally-intensive loops in benchmarks. The results demonstrate that the approach can detect potential opportunities for vectorization that are missed by a state-of-the-art vectorizing compiler. In addition to its use in characterizing large software suites for vectorization potential, the proposed technique can assist vectorization experts in identifying potentially profitable code regions on which attention should be focused, as well as aid compiler experts by identifying potentially vectorizable code that the compiler's vectorizer misses.

Acknowledgments

We thank the PLDI reviewers for their valuable comments. This material is based upon work supported by the National Science Foundation under grants CCF-0811781, CCF-0926127, OCI-0904549, CCF-1017204, and by the Department of Energy's Office of Advanced Scientific Computing under grant DE-SC0005033.

References

[1] R. Allen and K. Kennedy. *Optimizing Compilers for Modern Architectures: A Dependence-based Approach.* Morgan Kaufmann, 2001.

[2] T. Austin and G. Sohi. Dynamic dependency analysis of ordinary programs. In *ISCA*, pages 342–351, 1992.

[3] M. Bridges, N. Vachharajani, Y. Zhang, T. Jablin, and D. August. Revisiting the sequential programming model for multi-core. In *MICRO*, pages 69–84, 2007.

[4] Clang. clang.llvm.org.

[5] DragonEgg. dragonegg.llvm.org.

[6] A. Eichenberger, P. Wu, and K. O'Brien. Vectorization for SIMD architectures with alignment constraints. In *PLDI*, pages 82–93, 2004.

[7] L. Fireman, E. Petrank, and A. Zaks. New algorithms for SIMD alignment. In *CC*, pages 1–15, 2007.

[8] S. Garcia, D. Jeon, C. M. Louie, and M. B. Taylor. Kremlin: Rethinking and rebooting gprof for the multicore age. In *PLDI*, pages 458–469, 2011.

[9] C. Hammacher, K. Streit, S. Hack, and A. Zeller. Profiling Java programs for parallelism. In *IWMSE*, pages 49–55, 2009.

[10] HPCToolkit. www.hpctoolkit.org.

[11] M. Kumar. Measuring parallelism in computation-intensive scientific/engineering applications. *IEEE TC*, 37(9):1088–1098, 1988.

[12] M. Lam and R. Wilson. Limits of control flow on parallelism. In *ISCA*, pages 46–57, 1992.

[13] S. Larsen and S. Amarasinghe. Exploiting superword level parallelism with multimedia instruction sets. In *PLDI*, pages 145–156, 2000.

[14] J. Larus. Loop-level parallelism in numeric and symbolic programs. *IEEE TPDS*, 4(1):812–826, 1993.

[15] C. Lattner and V. Adve. LLVM: A compilation framework for lifelong program analysis & transformation. In *CGO*, page 75, 2004.

[16] J. Mak and A. Mycroft. Limits of parallelism using dynamic dependency graphs. In *WODA*, pages 42–48, 2009.

[17] A. Nicolau and J. Fisher. Measuring the parallelism available for very long instruction word architectures. *IEEE TC*, 33(11):968–976, 1984.

[18] D. Nuzman, I. Rosen, and A. Zaks. Auto-vectorization of interleaved data for SIMD. In *PLDI*, pages 132–143, 2006.

[19] C. Oancea and A. Mycroft. Set-congruence dynamic analysis for thread-level speculation (TLS). In *LCPC*, pages 156–171, 2008.

[20] PETSc. www.mcs.anl.gov/petsc.

[21] M. Postiff, D. Greene, G. Tyson, and T. Mudge. The limits of instruction level parallelism in SPEC95 applications. *SIGARCH Computer Architecture News*, 27(1):31–34, 1999.

[22] L. Rauchwerger and D. Padua. The LRPD test: Speculative run-time parallelization of loops with privatization and reduction parallelization. In *PLDI*, pages 218–232, 1995.

[23] L. Rauchwerger, P. Dubey, and R. Nair. Measuring limits of parallelism and characterizing its vulnerability to resource constraints. In *MICRO*, pages 105–117, 1993.

[24] A. Rountev, K. Van Valkenburgh, D. Yan, and P. Sadayappan. Understanding parallelism-inhibiting dependences in sequential Java programs. In *ICSM*, page 9, 2010.

[25] D. Stefanović and M. Martonosi. Limits and graph structure of available instruction-level parallelism. In *Euro-Par*, pages 1018–1022, 2000.

[26] S. Tallam and R. Gupta. Unified control flow and data dependence traces. *ACM TACO*, 4(3):19, 2007.

[27] S. Tallam, C. Tian, R. Gupta, and X. Zhang. Enabling tracing of long-running multithreaded programs via dynamic execution reduction. In *ISSTA*, pages 207–218, 2007.

[28] K. Theobald, G. Gao, and L. Hendren. On the limits of program parallelism and its smoothability. In *MICRO*, pages 10–19, 1992.

[29] C. Tian, M. Feng, V. Nagarajan, and R. Gupta. Copy or discard execution model for speculative parallelization on multicores. In *MICRO*, pages 330–341, 2008.

[30] C. Tian, M. Feng, V. Nagarajan, and R. Gupta. Speculative parallelization of sequential loops on multicores. *JPP*, 37(5):508–535, 2009.

[31] G. Tournavitis, Z. Wang, Zheng, B. Franke, and M. O'Boyle. Towards a holistic approach to auto-parallelization. In *PLDI*, pages 177–187, 2009.

[32] UTDSP Benchmarks. www.eecg.toronto.edu/~corinna.

[33] D. Wall. Limits of instruction-level parallelism. In *ASPLOS*, pages 176–188, 1991.

[34] M. Wolfe. *High Performance Compilers For Parallel Computing*. Addison-Wesley, 1996.

[35] P. Wu, A. Kejariwal, and C. Caşcaval. Compiler-driven dependence profiling to guide program parallelization. In *LCPC*, pages 232–248, 2008.

[36] X. Zhang and R. Gupta. Cost effective dynamic program slicing. In *PLDI*, pages 94–106, 2004.

[37] X. Zhang and R. Gupta. Whole execution traces and their applications. *ACM TACO*, 2(3):301–334, 2005.

[38] X. Zhang, R. Gupta, and Y. Zhang. Cost and precision tradeoffs of dynamic data slicing algorithms. *ACM TOPLAS*, 27(4):631–661, 2005.

[39] H. Zhong, M. Mehrara, S. Lieberman, and S. Mahlke. Uncovering hidden loop level parallelism in sequential applications. In *HPCA*, pages 290–301, 2008.

[40] X. Zhuang, A. E. Eichenberger, Y. Luo, K. O'Brien, and K. O'Brien. Exploiting parallelism with dependence-aware scheduling. In *PACT*, pages 193–202, 2009.

Verifying GPU Kernels by Test Amplification *

Alan Leung Manish Gupta Yuvraj Agarwal Rajesh Gupta Ranjit Jhala Sorin Lerner
University of California, San Diego
{aleung,manishg,yuvraj,gupta,jhala,lerner}@cs.ucsd.edu

Abstract

We present a novel technique for verifying properties of data parallel GPU programs via *test amplification*. The key insight behind our work is that we can use the technique of static information flow to amplify the result of a single test execution over the set of all inputs and interleavings that affect the property being verified. We empirically demonstrate the effectiveness of test amplification for verifying race-freedom and determinism over a large number of standard GPU kernels, by showing that the result of verifying a single dynamic execution can be amplified over the massive space of possible data inputs and thread interleavings.

Categories and Subject Descriptors D.2.4 [*Software Engineering*]: Software/Program Verification – Validation; F.3.2 [*Semantics of Programming Languages*]: Semantics of Programming Languages – Program analysis

General Terms Languages, Reliability, Verification

Keywords Test Amplification, Determinism, GPU

1. Introduction

Despite its relative infancy, CUDA and related programming languages have already become one of the most widely used models for parallel programming. The appeal of this model is that it offers a way to exploit fine-grained data-parallelism within the comforts of C/C++ style imperative programming. The dramatic performance gains offered by the approach have led to its widespread use in a variety of domains including scientific computing, finance, and computational biology [29].

CUDA programs are very hard to get right, for all the usual reasons, and a few new ones. First, in the course of execution, a program can spawn millions of threads, which are clustered in multi-level hierarchies that mirror a multi-level shared memory hierarchy. Second, for performance reasons, well-weathered synchronization mechanisms like locks or transactions are eschewed in favor of barriers, and it is up to the programmer to make sure that concurrently executing threads do not conflict by ensuring that their algorithms make threads touch disjoint parts of memory. Third, a key source of efficiency is the extremely fine-grained memory sharing across threads. Memory bandwidth is maximized when threads with successive identifiers access, in lock-step, addresses that are physically adjacent in memory. This can lead to complex striding patterns of memory access that are hard to reason about.

An unfortunate consequence of these factors is that CUDA parallelism is difficult to analyze with existing static or dynamic approaches. Static techniques are thwarted by the complexity of the sharing patterns. A useful static analysis would have to find a succinct symbolic representation for the sets of addresses accessed by each thread. It is common for CUDA code to use modular arithmetic or bit-shifting to access memory indices according to complex linear or even non-linear patterns which makes such analyses difficult. Dynamic techniques are challenged by the combinatorial explosion of thread interleavings and space of possible data inputs: any reasonable number of tests would represent a small subset of the possible behaviors of the system. Finally, mechanisms for enforcing isolation at run-time are likely to impose unacceptable overheads, and would leave the developer the unenviable task of sifting through a huge execution trace to figure out what went wrong.

To attack these challenges, we employ *test amplification*, a general notion wherein a single dynamic run can be used to learn much more information about a program's behavior than is directly exhibited by that particular execution. Though this notion has been explored in many settings, we contribute a new formulation of test amplification specialized for verifying properties of CUDA kernels, which we call *flow-based test amplification*. Our technique skirts the limitations of existing static and dynamic approaches by combining their complementary strengths, as follows.

First, we run a dynamic analysis where we log the behavior of the kernel with some fixed test input and under a particular thread interleaving. Second, we use a static information flow analysis to compute the *property-integrity inputs*, namely, the input variables that actually flow-to, or affect the integrity of, the variables appearing in the property to be verified. Finally, we amplify the result of the test to hold over *all* the inputs that have the same values for the property-integrity inputs.

Of course, this approach would yield no mileage if all the inputs were property-integrity inputs. Our second contribution is to empirically demonstrate over a large number of CUDA benchmarks, that for key properties like race-freedom and determinism, the set of property-integrity inputs comprises just a small core of *configuration* inputs. These are typically parameters that describe the dimensions of the thread- and memory- hierarchies and dataset, and which are highly tuned for a given architecture and algorithm. Thus, test amplification allows us to use a single execution over the configuration to verify properties over the massive space of all possible *data inputs* (non-configuration inputs) and thread interleavings that constitute the behaviors of the kernel.

This simple insight ties together the complementary strengths of well-known static and dynamic approaches, yielding a clean way to analyze CUDA kernels. The static analysis is just a simple flows-to question that can be resolved via taint-propagation and

* This work was supported by NSF Expeditions in Computing grant CCF-1029783 and CAREER grants CCF-0644306 and CCF-0644361.

PLDI'12, June 11–16, 2012, Beijing, China.

an alias analysis. The dynamic analysis performs the difficult task of actually computing the sets of addresses that are accessed in complex striding patterns. Using the information flow, we can then generalize the dynamic analysis over all possible data inputs. In summary, we make the following contributions:

- We present *flow-based test amplification*, a hybrid technique specialized for analyzing GPU kernels which uses static information flow to generalize the result of a dynamic analysis over a large space of inputs (Section 3).
- We implement flow-based test amplification for CUDA using the LLVM framework, by implementing static taint-propagation and devising efficient ways to record and analyze traces of CUDA kernels (Section 4).
- We empirically demonstrate the effectiveness of flow-based test amplification for verifying race freedom and determinism of CUDA kernels, by conducting a systematic evaluation over the kernels available in the CUDA SDK [28] and demonstrating that the technique can be used for most kernels. Even when the technique does not apply, a kernel can often be slightly modified to fall under the scope of our analysis (Section 5). As a result, we believe test amplification can be a stepping stone to developing various safety and performance analyses for massively data-parallel programs.

2. Overview

We start with an overview of CUDA, and then motivate our technique with a textbook CUDA kernel.

2.1 CUDA Basics

To illustrate the CUDA programming model we use a simplified version of `scalarProd`, shown in Figure 1, a program from the CUDA SDK that performs a parallel dot product of two vectors. In a nutshell, the CUDA language is a variant of C++ extended with syntax to annotate parallel routines called *kernels*, and the shared data structures that the routines manipulate. The kernels execute on GPU hardware and must exploit the shared memory hierarchy in order to obtain maximum performance.

Thread Hierarchy A program written in CUDA decomposes parallel computation into a two-level geometric grid of `gridDim` *thread blocks*, where each block comprises `blockDim` threads, each performing a subset of the total workload. Due to hardware support, CUDA threads have much less overhead relative to CPU threads: a CUDA program might spawn more than one million threads in a single execution. The `gridDim` and `blockDim` configuration parameters are together called the *geometry* of the computation. (Although grids and thread blocks may be multi-dimensional, we omit finer grained $x-$ and $y-$ dimensions for clarity.)

Memory Hierarchy Threads communicate via a hierarchical memory model organized into three levels, in decreasing order of their thread visibility, size, and latency: *global memory* which is slowest and shared by all threads, *shared memory* which is faster but shared only by the threads within a particular block, and *registers* which are fastest but private to each thread. In our example, all threads belong to a single thread block, all with access to the shared array `accumRes` and the global arrays `d_A` and `d_B`.

Parallel Execution Threads are spawned and executed via *kernel calls*, which specify the kernel that is to be executed and the thread-geometry, *i.e.,* the delineation of threads into thread blocks. For example, a kernel call of the form

```
ScalarProd<<<1, 128>>>(d_C, d_A, d_B, 4096)
```

```
1: #define accumN 1024
2: void scalarProd( float *d_C
                  , float *d_A
                  , float *d_B
                  , int sizeN)
   {
3:   __shared__ float accumRes[accumN];

/*******************************************/
/********* Phase 1: Partial Sums ***********/
/*******************************************/

4:   for( int i = threadIdx
        ; i < accumN
        ; i += blockDim)
     {
5:     float sum = 0;
6:     for(int j = i; j < sizeN; j += accumN)
       {
7:       sum += d_A[j] * d_B[j];
       }
8:     accumRes[i] = sum;
     }

/*******************************************/
/********* Phase 2: Tree Reduction *********/
/*******************************************/

9:   for( int stride = accumN / 2
        ; stride > 0
        ; stride >>= 1)
     {
10:    __syncthreads();
11:    for( int i = threadIdx
          ; i < stride
          ; i += blockDim)
       {
12:      accumRes[i] += accumRes[stride + i];
       }
     }
13:  if(threadIdx == 0) *d_C = accumRes[0];
   }
```

Figure 1. `scalarProd` kernel

begins execution of a single block containing 128 threads, where each thread executes the code in the `scalarProd` routine from Figure 1. Although all threads execute the same kernel, each thread is distinguished by a unique identifier in the form of its coordinate within the grid, that is by the tuple of the variables `blockIdx` and `threadIdx` (and the elided x- and y- sub-dimensions.) Thus, a thread can use the values of its `blockIdx` and `threadIdx`, and the geometry variables `gridDim` and `blockDim`, to distinguish its portion of the workload from those of other threads.

Synchronization Threads synchronize via barriers: a thread that calls `__syncthreads()` will wait until all other threads in its thread block have also reached the barrier. No corresponding synchronization mechanism exists for threads in different thread blocks. (While one can encode synchronization mechanisms using global memory, such mechanisms are brittle and inefficient and hence discouraged.)

2.2 Scalar Dot Product

Now that we are equipped with a basic understanding of the CUDA model, let us turn our attention to the `scalarProd` benchmark provided with the CUDA SDK. The original program calculates the dot products of 256 pairs of vectors, each of length $\texttt{sizeN} = 4096$. To simplify exposition, we have reduced the example to calculate the dot product of a single pair of vectors of `sizeN` elements.

The example exhibits three characteristics of CUDA kernels optimized for performance: 1) Memory is accessed in strides in order to maximize memory bandwidth, 2) Shared memory is used to cache frequently accessed data, and 3) Threads cooperate to perform reductions with minimal synchronization and communication. The example also demonstrates that even a seemingly simple computation, an elementary linear algebra primitive, can require hard-to-analyze optimizations when adapted for parallelization via CUDA. The implementation uses a parallel algorithm separated into two phases, each with a different parallelization strategy, to increase performance.

Phase 1: Partial Products In the first phase (lines 4-8), each thread computes $\texttt{accumN}/\texttt{blockDim}$ (*i.e.,* 8) partial dot-products, of sub-vectors of size $\texttt{sizeN}/\texttt{accumN}$ (*i.e.,* 4), and stores these partial products into the array `accumRes`. This phase is implemented by the nested loops on lines 4 and 6. The outer loop on line 4 iterates `i` over

$$\begin{array}{l}\texttt{threadIdx} + 0 \times \texttt{blockDim},\\ \texttt{threadIdx} + 1 \times \texttt{blockDim},\\ \texttt{threadIdx} + 2 \times \texttt{blockDim}, \ldots\end{array}$$

and at each offset, uses the inner-loop on line 6 to compute the dot-product of the sub-vectors at indices

$$\begin{array}{l}\texttt{i} + 0 \times \texttt{accumN},\\ \texttt{i} + 1 \times \texttt{accumN},\\ \texttt{i} + 2 \times \texttt{accumN}, \ldots\end{array}$$

the result of which is stored in the shared `accumRes[i]` (line 8).

Note that the threads *do not* operate on contiguous vector elements but instead access elements with a stride of `accumN`. The strided access pattern is deliberate: we achieve maximum memory bandwidth when neighboring threads access consecutive elements in global memory because the hardware optimizes the accesses to occur in parallel. This feature is known as *memory coalescing*. If instead each thread accessed contiguous vector elements, the memory accesses would occur serially, thereby severely reducing performance. Note also that the partial dot products are stored in shared memory, not global memory, in order to exploit temporal locality of access to intermediate results when performing the subsequent reduction.

Phase 2: Tree Reduction In the second phase (lines 9-13), all threads cooperate to add up the partial products to a final value. A naïve implementation would assign a single thread to perform the entire sum, reverting to a sequential algorithm. Instead, we can view the reduction as follows: each partial product is a leaf in a binary tree, and each parent is the sum of its children. We iterate up the levels of the tree by calculating the parents' values until we reach the root of the tree. Recall that the the array `accumRes` contains the partial products. Thus, in each iteration, we simply overwrite the "left child" at index `i` with the sum of its own value, and that of the "right child" at index $\texttt{i} + \texttt{stride}$, thereby obtaining the "parent" value.

Each iteration is parallelized by using thread `threadIdx` to compute the "parent" values at indices

$$\begin{array}{l}\texttt{threadIdx} + 0 \times \texttt{blockDim},\\ \texttt{threadIdx} + 1 \times \texttt{blockDim},\\ \texttt{threadIdx} + 2 \times \texttt{blockDim}, \ldots\end{array}$$

as done in the inner-loop on lines 11-12. As before, this strided access pattern enables efficiency via parallel memory access.

We iterate up the levels of the tree using the outer loop on line 9 which shrinks `stride` by half at each iteration as the number of leaf nodes halves across each iteration. Note that the cells accessed by different threads overlap *across levels*. The `__syncthreads()` at line 10 ensures that a level has been completed before the computation proceeds to the next level, and thereby preventing memory conflicts between threads executing on different levels. When the iterations have all completed, thread 0 copies the final value from `accumRes[0]` into the destination `d_C` at line 13, and the kernel terminates.

2.3 Verification

Thus, the `scalarProd` kernel makes use of several sophisticated optimizations to squeeze performance out of the GPU hardware. Unfortunately, these optimizations are treacherous as it is easy enough for the usual sorts of concurrency-related errors to creep in. The GPU setting exacerbates matters, as dynamic monitoring and protection mechanisms would likely require expensive hardware support in order to be efficient. Even if such mechanisms could be implemented, errors would be difficult to debug due to the scale of the concurrency (millions of threads).

Property: Absence of Races Let us consider the concrete problem of verifying race freedom, *i.e.,* verifying that a given thread is not writing to a shared location at the same time that another is reading from the location. In the CUDA setting, the only synchronization primitive is the `__syncthreads()` barrier, and hence, the problem reduces to determining that the sets of memory locations read and written by different threads within matching barriers, are disjoint.

Difficulty of Static Verification Unfortunately, as the `scalarProd` example illustrates, existing static analyses are of little use in the face of the complex access patterns that are idiomatic in CUDA kernels. Aliasing-, Shape- or Escape- based approaches [30] can work for disjoint linked data structures, but are not precise enough to distinguish disjoint regions within shared arrays. More precise arithmetic abstractions for such regions, such as intervals, octagons, polyhedra and even interval congruences [26] would not suffice as the set of addresses accessed by each CUDA thread often follows complex patterns.

For example, in the first phase of `scalarProd` the thread `threadIdx` writes to the array `accumRes` at indices

$$\{\texttt{threadIdx} + m \times \texttt{blockDim} + n \times \texttt{accumN}\}$$

where m and n range over 0 and $\texttt{accumN}/\texttt{blockDim}$ and $\texttt{sizeN}/\texttt{accumN}$ respectively. The second phase is even more challenging, as in the kth iteration of the outer-loop, each thread reads the array `accumRes` at indices

$$\{\texttt{threadIdx} + m \times \texttt{blockDim} + \texttt{accumN}/2^k\}$$

where m ranges from 0 to $\texttt{accumN}/(\texttt{blockDim} \times 2^k)$.

2.4 Our Approach

Our solution skirts the limitations of current static verification techniques with a combination of dynamic race detection and static information flow analysis. Our dynamic analysis tests for races in a *single execution* by instrumenting the kernel to log memory accesses and verifying disjointness of read and write addresses. We then *amplify* the results of the dynamic analysis to apply to *all possible executions* of a configuration if we can verify that the kernel always performs the same memory accesses, regardless of the values of its data inputs, a property we call *access invariance*. Given that this property holds, we then know that a single execution's accesses are in fact representative for all the possible executions.

X	$\doteq$	threadIdx, x, y, ...	**Locals**
G	$\doteq$	g, h, ...	**Globals**
V	$\doteq$	$X \cup G$	**Variables**
e	::=		**Expressions**
	|	x	local-read
	|	n	constant
	|	$e_1 \oplus e_2$	binop
c	::=		**Commands**
	|	assume(e)	assume
	|	x = e	var-assignment
	|	x = g[x]	global-read
	|	g[x] = e	global-write
	|	$c; c$	sequence

Figure 2. Syntax

Putting it together, we can effectively guarantee that the kernel is race free and deterministic across *all data inputs*.

Dynamic Race Detection In addition to memory addresses we record the identity of the thread performing the access and the location of the barrier last encountered by that thread. To distinguish accesses to shared and global memory, we record the address and extent of each shared and global data structure.

We then check for races by verifying disjointness of write and read addresses between threads that can race to the same global or shared data structure. Given that the log demonstrates no such conflicting access, we provide the guarantee that the kernel is race free for the single instantiation of input values used for that execution. Because the analysis checks for the *possibility* of a race, not whether a destructive race has actually occurred, a kernel verified to be race free by this analysis is race free regardless of the particular interleaving exercised by the execution, once again for this single instantiation of input values. In addition, since the analysis verifies disjointness of accesses, we can also guarantee that the verified kernel executes deterministically on that input. However, note that this dynamic testing by itself can provide no guarantees about execution on any other instantiation of inputs.

Information Flow Although the guarantees provided by our dynamic race detector are desirable, they extend only to a single instantiation of inputs within an enormous universe of inputs, hence the need for a static analysis to amplify those guarantees further. In particular, we use a static information flow analysis that tracks flows from data inputs throughout the kernel. Intuitively, we apply a taint to data inputs values, track the flow of taint through program variables, then check that no tainted program variable is used as the address operand of a memory instruction. We additionally check that no memory access is control dependent on a tainted variable. If these two properties hold, we say that the kernel is *access invariant* and will exhibit the same memory accesses across all data inputs.

By itself, this property is interesting but not immediately useful. It is the combination of this property and the result of our dynamic analysis that produces a much more powerful guarantee: the verified kernel will exhibit no races in any execution, and so the kernel is deterministic.

3. Test Amplification via Information Flow

In this section we formalize a general framework for combining tests with information flow, and show how we instantiate it to verify CUDA kernels. We start by making precise the syntax and semantics of kernels, which enables us to define the ingredients of the main Theorem 1 which states how the results of a particular test can be amplified across different inputs via information flow. Next, we describe how the general framework is instantiated for the setting of CUDA kernels.

3.1 Syntax

Figure 2 summarizes the syntax of kernels. Informally, a kernel is a collection of concurrently executing threads which interact via shared memory.

Variables Our kernels include two kinds of variables: (thread)-local, denoted by x, y, *etc.* and global g, h, *etc.*. We write v, w to denote either local or global variables. We assume for simplicity that all global variables are arrays. Note that a scalar global is simply an array of size 1. For clarity, we abuse notation to omit the offset 0 when reading or writing such variables.

Expressions and Commands The set of kernel expressions includes reads of local variables, primitive constants (*e.g.*, $0, 1, 2, \ldots$) and binary operations over sub-expressions. Our language of expressions is side-effect free. The set of commands includes sequences of assume($\cdot$) (used to model branches), local assignment, and reads from and writes to global variables.

Reads and Writes A variable v is *read* in an expression if it appears in the expression. A variable is read in a command if the command contains an expression in which the variable is read. A variable v is written in a command if the command contains an assigment of the form v = e or v[x] = e.

Threads A *thread* t is a tuple (V_0, L, l_0, C), where V_0 is a set of *input variables*, L is a finite set of program locations, $l_0 \in L$ is a special *entry location*, and C is a *control flow map* from $L \times L$ to the set of commands. A variable is read (resp. written) on an edge if it is read (resp. written) on the command labelling the edge. A variable v is *immutable* in a thread if it is not written on any edge of the thread's control-flow map. We assume that V_0 includes any local or global variables that may be read before they are written. Finally, we assume that V_0 includes distinguished immutable local input variables **threadIdx** and **blockDim** that hold the (unique) identifier of the thread and the total number of threads, respectively.

Kernels A *kernel* is a pair of a set of *thread-identifiers* $Tid \subseteq \mathbb{N}$ and a thread. Intuitively, a kernel (Tid, V_0, L, l_0, C) has $|Tid|$ many distinct threads executing the same commands (given by C). However, the commands can inspect the value of the input **threadIdx**, and hence, different threads can behave differently.

Example Recall the **scalarProd** kernel from Figure 1. The body of the kernel can be mapped to a single thread's control-flow map, with locations corresponding to the program labels (3:, 4:, 5:, *etc.*.) in the standard way. The input variables of the thread are **d_A**, **d_B**, **d_C**, **sizeN**, the distinguished **threadIdx**, and **blockDim**.

3.2 Semantics

Next, we formalize the semantics via states and transitions.

Notation Let f map A to B. We write $f[a \mapsto b]$ for the map

$$\lambda x.\ \text{if } x = a \text{ then } b \text{ else } f\ x$$

Let A' be a subset of A. The *restriction* of f to A', is the map from A' to B that coincides with f on A'.

Kernel Transition $\boxed{P \vdash \sigma \hookrightarrow \sigma'}$

$$\frac{tid, C \vdash \sigma \hookrightarrow \sigma'}{(Tid, V_0, L, l_0, C) \vdash \sigma \hookrightarrow \sigma'} \ [\text{T-PGM}]$$

Thread Transition $\boxed{tid, C \vdash \sigma \hookrightarrow \sigma'}$

$$\frac{l = \sigma(tid) \qquad c = C(l, l') \qquad tid, c \vdash \sigma \hookrightarrow \sigma'}{tid, C \vdash \sigma \hookrightarrow \sigma'[tid \mapsto l']} \ [\text{T-THREAD}]$$

Command Transition $\boxed{tid, c \vdash \sigma \hookrightarrow \sigma'}$

$$\frac{tid, c_1 \vdash \sigma \hookrightarrow \sigma' \qquad tid, c_2 \vdash \sigma' \hookrightarrow \sigma''}{tid, c_1; c_2 \vdash \sigma \hookrightarrow \sigma''} \ [\text{T-SEQ}]$$

$$\frac{\sigma(tid)(e) = true}{tid, \texttt{assume}(e) \vdash \sigma \hookrightarrow \sigma} \ [\text{T-ASSUME}]$$

$$\frac{\sigma(e)(tid) = n}{tid, \texttt{x} = e \vdash \sigma \hookrightarrow \sigma[\texttt{x} \mapsto \sigma(\texttt{x})[tid \mapsto n]]} \ [\text{T-ASGN}]$$

$$\frac{\sigma(y)(tid) = n' \qquad \sigma(\texttt{g})(n') = n}{tid, x = \texttt{g}[y] \vdash \sigma \hookrightarrow \sigma[\texttt{x} \mapsto \sigma(\texttt{x})[tid \mapsto n]]} \ [\text{T-READ}]$$

$$\frac{\sigma(y)(tid) = n' \qquad \sigma(x)(tid) = n}{tid, \texttt{g}[y] = x \vdash \sigma \hookrightarrow \sigma[\texttt{g} \mapsto \sigma(\texttt{g})[n' \mapsto n]]} \ [\text{T-WRITE}]$$

Figure 3. Semantics

States A *state* σ is a map from $Tid \cup X \cup G$ to $L \cup (Tid \to \mathbb{N}) \cup (\mathbb{N} \to \mathbb{N})$, such that $\sigma(tid)$ is the program location of thread tid, $\sigma(\texttt{x})(tid)$ is the value of the local x in the thread tid, and $\sigma(\texttt{g})(n)$ is the value of the global array g at the index n. We write Σ for the set of all states.

Initial States A state σ is an initial state for kernel $P = (Tid, V_0, L, l_0, C)$ written $P \vdash \sigma$ if $\sigma(\texttt{blockDim}) = |Tid|$, and for each $tid \in Tid$, we have $\sigma(tid) = l_0$ and $\sigma(\texttt{threadIdx})(tid) = tid$.

Transitions The *transition* relation of a kernel is a subset of $\Sigma \times \Sigma$. We write $P \vdash \sigma \hookrightarrow \sigma'$ if the pair σ, σ' is in the transition relation of the kernel, defined formally in Figure 3. Intuitively, the transition relation is the union of the transition relations of the individual threads. Each thread transition atomically moves the thread from its current program location to a successor location, updating the locals of the thread and the globals whilst leaving the program locations and locals of all other threads untouched.

An assume transition [T-ASSUME] succeeds only if the condition holds, a local assignment [T-ASGN], [T-READ] updates the value of the local for the executing thread, and a write [T-WRITE] updates the global array at appropriate address. A command is a *sequence* of assignments and assumes, and [T-SEQ] ensures that the sequence executes atomically, thereby allowing us to construct higher level synchronization mechanisms as described later.

Branch Determinism We say a control flow map is *branch deterministic* if for any thread tid and state σ, there is at most a single σ' such that $tid, C \vdash \sigma \hookrightarrow \sigma'$. There is a simple sufficient condition for branch determinism, namely 1) the primitive operations $\oplus$ are deterministic, and 2) the program locations have at most two successor edges, 3) the nodes with multiple successor edges have edges labeled by $\texttt{assume}(e)$ and $\texttt{assume}(\neg e)$. The control flow maps compiled from standard structured languages are branch deterministic, so we will assume this property in the sequel.

Traces The *traces* of a kernel $\mathsf{Traces}(P)$ are finite sequences of of states $\tau = \sigma_0, \ldots, \sigma_n$ such that $P \vdash \sigma_0$ and $P \vdash \sigma_k \hookrightarrow \sigma_{k+1}$, for each $0 \le k < n$. We write $\tau(k)$ for the kth state in a trace.

3.3 Test Amplification

Now that we have formalized the semantics of kernels, we can describe what it means for a variable to flow-to another, and hence the notion of flow-based test amplification.

Projection and Equivalence Let Y be a set of variables. The *projection* of a state σ to Y, written $\sigma[Y]$ is the restriction of σ to the domain Y. We lift projection to sequences of states, *i.e.*, traces, in the natural way. A state σ is *equivalent over* Y to σ', written $\sigma \equiv_Y \sigma'$ if $\sigma[Y] = \sigma'[Y]$.

Information Flow A variable v *flows-to* w written $\texttt{v} \in \mathsf{FlowsTo}(P, \texttt{w})$ if there exist traces, τ and τ' in $\mathsf{Traces}(P)$ such that $\tau(0) \equiv_{V \setminus \texttt{v}} \tau'(0)$, and $\tau(k) \not\equiv_{\texttt{w}} \tau'(k)$ for some k. Intuitively, v flows-to w if there are two traces that agree on all variables *except* v at the beginning, but which differ on the value of w at some time k [18]. For a set of variables W we define

$$\mathsf{FlowsTo}(P, W) \doteq \cup_{\texttt{w} \in W} \mathsf{FlowsTo}(P, \texttt{w})$$

Thread Interleavings We say that a variable w is non-deterministically affected by thread interleavings if there exist traces $\tau, \tau' \in \mathsf{Traces}(P)$ such that $\tau(0) = \tau'(0)$ but for some k, $\tau(k)(\texttt{w}) \neq \tau'(k)(\texttt{w})$. We make the following observations:

1. If w is non-deterministically affected by interleavings then trivially, for all v we have $\texttt{v} \in \mathsf{FlowsTo}(P, \texttt{w})$.
2. If w is *not* non-deterministically affected by thread interleavings. Then $\texttt{v} \in \mathsf{FlowsTo}(P, \texttt{w})$ only if v is an input variable.

Properties A *property* Φ *over* V_Φ is a predicate over the (program) variables V_Φ. A state σ satisfies a property, written $\sigma \models \Phi$ if the predicate evaluates to true in σ. A trace τ satisfies a property, written $\tau \models \Phi$ if for each k, we have $\tau(k) \models \Phi$. The set $\mathsf{FlowsTo}(P, V_\Phi)$ is the set of *property-integrity inputs*, that is, the set of inputs that flow-to a variable in V_Φ.

THEOREM 1. **[Test Amplification]** *Let Φ be a property over V_Φ, and Y be a subset of the input variables. If*

- $\mathsf{FlowsTo}(P, V_\Phi) \subseteq Y$
- $\tau \in \mathsf{Traces}(P)$ *is such that* $\tau \models \Phi$

then $\forall \tau' \in \mathsf{Traces}(P).\ \tau(0) \equiv_Y \tau'(0)$ *implies* $\tau' \models \Phi$.

Informally, the theorem states that if Y contains the set of property-integrity inputs, then we can amplify the success of a *single* satisfying execution to conclude that all *all* executions that start with the same values for Y, regardless of the values of other inputs and thread scheduling, will also satisfy the property.

3.4 CUDA Verification

The conclusion of the test amplification theorem is trivial, and of little practical value if the set Y includes all the program variables. To analyze CUDA kernels, we must reduce Y to be as small as possible. We demonstrate that for verifying determinism of CUDA kernels, Y can be distilled down to a small core of *configuration* inputs that are highly tuned to a limited set of values for a given algorithm and architecture. Consequently, test amplification allows us to use a dynamic single execution over the configuration to verify properties over a massive space of possible data inputs and thread interleavings that constitute the behaviors of the kernel.

Thus, next, we describe how our framework can be instantiated to verify CUDA kernels. To do so, we need to: 1) encode CUDA semantics, in particular, barrier synchronization, 2) encode the properties that we wish to check, 3) describe the property variables V_Φ and configuration variables Y, 4) compute the set $\mathsf{FlowsTo}(P, V_\Phi)$.

Barriers CUDA includes a special barrier operation. Intuitively, when a thread reaches a barrier, it waits until all the other threads have reached the same barrier. We encode barriers by introducing two special variables `flag`, a local variable that has the value 1 iff the thread *tid* has reached a barrier, and `count`, a global variable (initialized to 0) which holds the number of threads that have reached the barrier. Now, a barrier operation between l and l' is a sequence of three CFG edges:

$$\begin{array}{lcl} C(l, l_{wait}) & \doteq & \texttt{assume}(\texttt{flag} = 0);\\ & & \texttt{flag} = 1;\\ & & \texttt{count} = \texttt{count} + 1\\ C(l_{wait}, l_{go}) & \doteq & \texttt{assume}(\texttt{count} = \texttt{blockDim})\\ C(l_{go}, l') & \doteq & \texttt{assume}(\texttt{threadIdx} = \texttt{count});\\ & & \texttt{flag} = 0;\\ & & \texttt{count} = \texttt{count} - 1 \end{array}$$

where l_{wait}, l_{go} are two distinct program locations introduced for each barrier operation.

Instrumentation: Recording Global Accesses To verify that the kernel is deterministic, we need to check in the trace that the set of global addresses written by a thread is disjoint from the addresses accessed by other threads. We need only perform this check on accesses within the same *barrier interval* because two accesses separated by a barrier cannot race [23]. Thus, we track both the set of addresses read or written by each thread, as well as timestamps uniquely identifying each barrier interval. We instrument the kernel to track this information as follows.

First, we introduce a special local variable `timestamp` (initialized to 0) which holds a logical timestamp for the current barrier interval. We instrument each barrier-wait $\texttt{assume}(\texttt{count} = \texttt{blockDim})$ to become

$$\texttt{assume}(\texttt{count} = \texttt{blockDim});$$
$$\texttt{timestamp} = \texttt{timestamp} + 1$$

We introduce a global array `log`, that maps Tid, to subsets of

$$\mathbb{N} \times \{\mathsf{Rd}, \mathsf{Wr}\} \times G \times \mathbb{N}$$

That is, each tuple consists of a barrier timestamp, access type, global array name, and array index, respectively. Next, we instrument each read and write command to record the access inside `log`. Global-reads `y = g[x]` become

$$\texttt{y} = \texttt{g}[\texttt{x}];$$
$$\texttt{log}[\texttt{threadIdx}] = \texttt{log}[\texttt{threadIdx}] \cup (\texttt{timestamp}, \mathsf{Rd}, \text{“g”}, \texttt{x})$$

and global-writes `g[x] = y` become

$$\texttt{log}[\texttt{threadIdx}] = \texttt{log}[\texttt{threadIdx}] \cup (\texttt{timestamp}, \mathsf{Wr}, \text{“g”}, \texttt{x});$$
$$\texttt{g}[\texttt{x}] = \texttt{y}$$

Property: Determinism Finally, to verify determinism we define the following property Φ_{Det}.

$$\forall t, i, i', \texttt{g}, n : (t, A, \text{“}g\text{”}, n) \in \texttt{log}[i] \wedge (t, A', \text{“}g\text{”}, n) \in \texttt{log}[i']$$
$$\Rightarrow i = i' \vee A = A' = \mathsf{Rd}$$

Intuitively, the property checks that within each barrier interval, the set of *writes* in the `log` of thread *tid* is disjoint from the set of *accesses* contained in the `log` of another thread *tid'*. As the instrumentation ensures that `log` contains all accesses, if the above sets are disjoint, then the sets of accesses of every two threads are disjoint, and the kernel is therefore deterministic [35].

Property and Configuration Variables The set of property variables is the singleton $\{\texttt{log}\}$ comprising the only variable inspected by Φ_{Det}. The configuration variables are those that describe the thread geometry of the given kernel, namely the number of threads `blockDim`, the thread identifier `threadIdx`, and algorithm- and architecture- specific parameters like the sizes of strides `accumN` and the global arrays `sizeN`. In general, the set of configuration variables depends heavily on the semantics of the kernel being analyzed and must be chosen based on domain knowledge.

Static Information Flow Analysis The last piece of the puzzle is the flow relation. Needless to say, the exact flows-to set for a set of property variables is not computable. We solve this problem, through a forwards taint-propagation based analysis that, given a kernel, a set of property variables V_Φ, and a set of configuration variables Y, checks whether $\mathsf{FlowsTo}(P, V_\Phi) \subseteq Y$. The analysis implements a form of taint-based integrity checking [15, 27].

We formalize the analysis as procedure $\mathsf{StaticFlowsTo}(P, V_\Phi, Y)$, which is implemented as follows. All the input variables *except* those in Y are tainted. The taints are propagated through assignments (data dependencies) and dominating assumes (control dependencies). Finally, we check whether any of the property variables V_Φ are tainted. If not, we can be sure that only the configuration variables flow to the property variables. As the procedure is flow-insensitive, it is sound in the face of multi-threading. Furthermore, as the kernels are branch deterministic, we can conclude that the statically computed flows-to relation is a conservative *overapproximation* of the actual flows-to relation.

PROPOSITION 1. **[Static Flows-To]** *For all branch-deterministic kernels P and variables V_Φ, Y, if* $\mathsf{StaticFlowsTo}(P, V_\Phi, Y)$ *then* $\mathsf{FlowsTo}(P, V_\Phi) \subseteq Y$.

Access Invariance and Determinism We say that a kernel P is *access invariant with respect to* Y if $\mathsf{StaticFlowsTo}(P, \{\texttt{log}\}, Y)$, that is, if only the configuration variables Y flow to the property variables. From the soundness of static flows-to, we get the following as an immediate corollary of Theorem 1.

PROPOSITION 2. **[CUDA Determinism]** *Let P be a* CUDA *kernel with configuration variables Y. If*

- *P is access invariant with respect to Y*
- *$\tau \in \mathsf{Traces}(P)$ is such that $\tau \models \Phi_{Det}$*

then forall $\tau' \in \mathsf{Traces}(P)$, if $\tau(0) \equiv_Y \tau'(0)$ then $\tau' \models \Phi_{Det}$.

Returning to the `scalarProd` example from Figure 1 we see that `log` has a data dependence on the indices `j`, `i`, `i` and `stride + i` which are used to access shared memory (at lines 7, 8, 12 and 12 respectively). The only inputs that flow to these expressions (i.e., the set of property-integrity inputs) are the parameters `threadIdx`, `accumN`, `sizeN`, and `blockDim`, which are a subset of the configuration variables, so the kernel is access invariant. Thus, a single trace that satisfies Φ_{Det} suffices to show that the kernel satisfies Φ_{Det} for all executions over the same configuration.

4. Implementation

We have implemented the analyses described in the previous section in the LLVM Compiler Infrastructure [22]. In particular, we have implemented a static taint-based information flow analysis that checks whether CUDA kernels are access invariant, and a dynamic instrumentation-based analysis that checks whether a kernel satisfies the determinism property Φ_{Det} for a particular execution. Though the formalism in the previous section presented a simplified, two-level memory model and one-dimensional thread geometry, our implementation handles the multi-dimensional thread geometries and three-layer memory hierarchy supported by CUDA. Next, we describe the static and dynamic analyses in greater detail.

4.1 Static Analysis

The static analysis proceeds via three LLVM passes. The first pass recursively inlines all function calls within a kernel, yielding a single call-free kernel. The second pass is a flow-insensitive intraprocedural pointer analysis based on Andersen's algorithm [1] that is used by the third pass, a static taint-based analysis that determines whether data inputs (that is, non-configuration input variables) flow to the property variables.

1. Kernel inlining For simplicity, our current implementation exploits the key restriction that CUDA kernels cannot be recursive or contain indirect functions calls. In particular, we fully inline functions called from kernels, so subsequent analyses can be intraprocedural without loss of precision, with one exception to deal with library functions – we analyze calls to CUDA library functions using specially crafted transfer functions (*i.e.,* summaries) as described below. (Recent NVIDIA cards do support recursion and function pointers. To handle such kernels we need only use interprocedural variants of our current analyses.)

2. Pointer analysis We use a pointer analysis to soundly propagate taints in the presence of aliasing. In particular, if a pointer refers to a tainted heap location, then the taints must be propagated to (dereferences of) all the aliases of the pointer. To this end we have implemented a flow-insensitive, intraprocedural variant of Andersen's algorithm. The precision lost by flow-insensitivity is mitigated by the fact that the LLVM intermediate representation is based on SSA, so the may-point-to set of most variables contain only a single element. In the CUDA setting, the following modifications allow us to further improve the precision of the pointer analysis.

- Our aggressive inlining step makes the analysis context sensitive. We inline all function calls with the exception of calls to CUDA library functions. To deal with those calls we include special transfer functions which account for the function's effects as specified in the documentation.
- Kernel formal parameters with pointer type are optimistically assumed to be *unique* upon entry to the function. That is, there are no other variables that refer to a block of memory pointed to by a formal parameter. Although this assumption is unsound in general, we have manually verified that it holds for all benchmarks in our evaluation. This simplification allows us to avoid making the conservative assumption that pointer function parameters may point to arbitrary memory locations.

3. Taint tracking The direct way to check the access invariance property is to implement $\mathsf{StaticFlowsTo}(P, \{\texttt{log}\}, Y)$ inside LLVM. Unfortunately, this would require us to rewrite the program to add `log` which we avoid for the reasons described in Section 4.2. Instead, we check that the access invariance property holds by statically verifying that the following two conditions hold. First, no address operand of a memory instruction may be affected by a data input. In other words the *flows-to* set of an address may contain only configuration inputs. Second, no memory instruction is control dependent on a tainted value. The latter is subtle and best explained by a small example:

```
if(taintedVar) { A[i] = e; } else { B[i] = e; }
```

Whether array `A` or `B` is written depends on the value of `taintedVar`, even though the array index `i` itself might not be tainted at all. Thus, with a different data input, the program may execute the other branch yielding a race (that does not occur on the test being amplified.) This condition is conservative, as it would flag a violation even when both sides of the branch perform identical accesses. (It is easy to check that these conditions are equivalent to the "direct" approach of checking whether non-configuration input variables flow-to the `log`.)

Our implementation verifies that both conditions are met using a standard worklist algorithm to perform forward taint propagation. We begin with an initial taint set consisting of the kernel's data inputs, then track the propagation of these taints through instructions. During propagation, if either condition is found to be violated, we terminate with the conclusion that the kernel is not access invariant. If instead we reach a fixpoint in which no new taints can be propagated and have not yet found a violation, we conclude that the kernel is access invariant.

There are two channels by which taint can propagate: explicit flow resulting from data dependences, and implicit flow resulting from control dependences. Explicit flow is handled in the straightforward way: we implement transfer functions for each class of instruction or CUDA library function to assign taint to the appropriate variables. For instance, we assign taint to the result of any arithmetic instruction with a tainted operand. We handle control dependences very conservatively by immediately flagging a violation of the access invariance property whenever a branch condition variable is tainted. This would flag an access invariance violation even if neither side of the branch performed any memory access at all, but is a straightforward and sound overapproximation. If no such control dependences exist, we can conclude that the second condition holds, and that no control dependences contribute to a violation of the first condition.

Finally, we must verify the first condition — that no addresses are tainted. LLVM programs calculate addresses with an explicit instruction called `getelementptr` that takes a base pointer and a variable number of operands representing offsets from the base. This instruction is designed to express arbitrary address arithmetic to compute the addresses of data structure elements. Whilst propagating taints, if we ever encounter a `getelementptr` with tainted operand, we conclude that the kernel is not access invariant.

4.2 Dynamic Analysis

The dynamic component of our analysis checks that a particular test execution satisfies the given property Φ_{Det}. Unfortunately, due to the sheer number of threads and frequency of accesses, it is impossible to hold the log in memory and check Φ_{Det} in an online manner. We get around this problem by logging all the accesses on disk and then checking offline that the trace satisfies Φ_{Det}.

Thus, our dynamic analysis consists of a single LLVM pass that instruments all memory accesses with extra instructions to log addresses and thread identifiers on disk. In order to distinguish accesses to global and shared data structures, all allocations and static array declarations for global and shared memory are instrumented to record base address and size. Finally, full 3D thread identifiers and 2D block identifiers are logged for each executing thread.

Barrier Interval Timestamps Recall that a problematic trace is one where different threads access the same shared location during the *same* barrier interval. Thus, in addition to the address and thread identifiers, we record for each access, the *barrier interval* number during which the access occurs, so that the offline check only compares accesses within the same interval. Although addresses and thread identifiers are readily accessible as variables in the uninstrumented code, barrier intervals are not explicitly labeled and must be dealt with specially. We maintain a shared table that contains one entry per thread to track the current barrier interval of each thread. Each element of the table corresponds to one thread's `timestamp` local variable as described in Section 3.4. Every call to `__syncthreads()` is replaced with an augmented version that additionally increments the thread's corresponding table entry. Thus, at any point during execution, the table contains a snapshot of the barrier interval in which each thread is executing. We simply look up the thread's entry in this table to determine the current barrier interval for logging. (The threads obey the barrier synchronization semantics; the intervals are logged solely to facilitate offline trace analysis.)

Determinism via Race Detection After generating a complete log by executing the instrumented kernel, we check that the trace satisfies the determinism property Φ_{Det}. In the presence of the three-level memory hierarchy, the property is satisfied if there are *no* global- or shared- memory races.

A global memory race occurs when a global data structure is written by one thread and accessed by another. Two threads in the same thread block may race only if executing in the same barrier interval. Two threads in different thread blocks cannot synchronize, so may race regardless of barrier interval.

A shared memory race occurs when two threads within the same thread block access a shared data structure within the same barrier interval, and at least one of the accesses is a write. Threads in different thread blocks cannot share the same shared data structure, and thus cannot conflict.

Offline Trace Analysis The sheer magnitude of the logs required that we devise non-trivial means for checking for races using a small memory footprint. Our implementation performs this check via a log postprocessing program that first translates raw addresses into array-offset pairs, then performs a sweep of the resulting log to check for conflicting accesses to each array. To perform the race checks efficiently, we first separate global and shared memory accesses into separate traces. Each trace is then *externally* sorted by address and barrier interval, which are the primary and secondary sort keys, respectively. Finally, a single linear sweep through the sorted traces checks for the aforementioned race conditions.

The above process only stores in memory a small window of the trace at any point: for global arrays, only those accesses to a single address at a time, and for shared arrays, only those accesses to a single address within a single barrier interval. These optimizations were essential in practice. Our initial naïve implementation, which attempted to detect races in unsorted traces, immediately ran into out-of-memory errors due to the size of the traces.

Limitations Our implementation does not currently handle several aspects of CUDA. First, the dynamic analyses are incompatible with programs using OpenGL because CUDA emulation does not support compilation of such programs. We resort to using CUDA emulation because we cannot perform logging when executing on real GPU hardware. Second, our analyses do not support code that uses the CUDA Driver API, a low-level framework above which the CUDA language and runtime are built, nor code that contains assembly instructions, atomic intrinsics, or warp voting functions. Third, our dynamic analysis does not track accesses to texture or constant memory, as they are strictly read-only during kernel execution and thus are not subject to races within the kernel. A final caveat is that we assume that conflicting accesses must be to the same exact address – our implementation has no notion of conflict between *unaligned* accesses, though presumably a higher-level type system could ensure the absence of such misaligned accesses.

5. Evaluation

Our goal is to evaluate the overall effectiveness of our approach in the setting of CUDA programs. To this end, we evaluate the effectiveness of our static invariance analysis (Section 5.2), the effectiveness of our dynamic analysis (Section 5.3), and the running-time of our approach (Section 5.4). Before presenting these results, we first describe our experimental setup (Section 5.1).

5.1 Experimental Setup

To evaluate our approach, we started with the 68 benchmarks in the NVIDIA CUDA SDK Version 3.0. Of these 68 benchmarks, 7 are small tutorial-like benchmarks with trivial kernels, and so we leave these out. Of the remaining benchmarks, 33 contain features which our analysis cannot run on, due to the limitations previously mentioned. We therefore omitted these as well, which leaves us with 28 benchmarks, for which we report results. These 28 benchmarks contain a total of 76 kernels.

The static analysis runs on one kernel at a time. We manually examined each kernel to determine the correct set of data inputs (non-configuration input variables) to supply the static analysis. We tried to minimize the set of configuration variables by manually examining code to determine the domain-specific interpretation of each input. The separation of data and configuration variables is usually quite immediate. As an example, for the `scalarProd` benchmark, the set of data input variables is `d_C`, `d_A`, and `d_B` (since these are the input vectors). Since `sizeN` represents the size of the data set, we consider it to be a configuration variable.

For the dynamic analysis, we run each benchmark containing access invariant kernels with instrumentation turned on. Benchmarks with multiple kernels will produce logs containing entries from several kernels. A postprocessing step separates the entries corresponding to each kernel. The logs can then be processed one kernel at a time.

5.2 Static Invariance Analysis

The results of our static invariance analysis are shown in Figure 4. Of the 76 kernels examined, 52 were shown to be access invariant by our static information flow analysis. These kernels are spread across a variety of benchmarks from different domains. Additionally, even benchmarks that demonstrated variance in some kernels often have at least one kernel that is in fact access invariant. For instance, although `histogram` contains 2 kernels that are not access invariant, it contains 2 that are. This aligns with the fact that CUDA algorithms are often implemented as multiple distinct kernels, each performing a different phase of the algorithm, some of which may be access invariant while others are not.

We have found three distinct patterns that cause a kernel to be access variant. For each pattern we provide an example from the benchmark suite.

Direct Flow The first pattern is the most direct: a memory access address is derived directly from an input value. This pattern is demonstrated by the `histogram` benchmark, which bins each byte of its input based on the value of its higher order bits. A straightforward sequential implementation of histogram is sketched in Figure 5. This implementation iterates over each element of `data`, uses the higher order bits to index into the array `bin` whose elements represent bin counts, then increments the indexed element. Although the parallel CUDA implementation is complicated by distribution of computation across multiple threads, the fundamental calculation is the same: the higher order bits of each byte are used to address into a shared array which contains the bin counts. The access variance of this kernel is a result of the fact that the bin address is derived directly from an input value.

Benchmark	LOC	#K	%I
reduction	695	7	100%
sortingNetworks*	571	6	100%
convolutionFFT2D	384	3	100%
fastWalshTransform	243	3	100%
convolutionSeparable	318	2	100%
convolutionTexture	314	2	100%
cppIntegration	125	2	100%
simplePitchLinearTexture	138	2	100%
transpose	146	2	100%
binomialOptions*	354	1	100%
BlackScholes*	276	1	100%
dwtHaar1D	266	1	100%
FDTD3d	818	1	100%
matrixMul	216	1	100%
scalarProd	136	1	100%
simpleCUFFT	137	1	100%
simpleTexture	121	1	100%
vectorAdd	92	1	100%
dct8x8	1402	8	87%
histogram	431	4	50%
lineOfSight	180	2	50%
radixSort	1894	10	30%
MonteCarlo	836	4	25%
eigenvalues	1901	4	0%
MersenneTwister	287	2	0%
quasiRandomGenerator	637	2	0%
clock	69	1	0%
dxtc	829	1	0%
28 Benchmarks	13816	76	68%

Figure 4. Static Analysis Results: **LOC**=Lines of Code, **#K**=Number of Kernels, **%I**=Percent Invariant Kernels, *modified as detailed in Section 5.2

```
void histogram(char *data, int *bin, int size) {
for(int i = 0, i < size, i++)
    bin[data[i] && 0x3FU]++;
}
```

Figure 5. Sequential Histogram

Indirect Flow The second pattern occurs in kernels in which a critical control flow statement depends on a condition derived from input. This is demonstrated by the `eigenvalues` benchmark. This benchmark calculates the eigenvalues of a matrix with an algorithm that subdivides intervals dependent on the values of the input matrix. This dependence is fundamental to the algorithm and cannot be removed.

Correctable Indirect Flow The `sortingNetworks` benchmark performs a bitonic sort, which is a sorting algorithm with the property that the comparisons it performs are independent of its input values. Whether elements are swapped, however, depends on the result of a comparison which ultimately derives from the magnitude of input values. Intuitively, it would seem that the kernel is *almost access invariant*, save for this conditional swap. It turns out that we can perform a simple rewrite, as shown in Figure 6, which effectively converts the control dependence into a data dependence. With this rewrite, `sortingNetworks` can be verified access invariant because we have removed a control dependence without introducing taint to the array indices. We have been able to perform similar transformations to the `binomialOptions` and `BlackScholes` kernels.

```
/** original version    **/
if(A[i] > A[j]) {
    t = A[i]; A[i] = A[j]; A[j] = t;
}

/** transformed version **/
bool cond = (A[i] > A[j]);
t    = A[i];
A[i] = cond * A[j] + (!cond) * A[i];
A[j] = cond * t    + (!cond) * A[j];
```

Figure 6. Removing a control dependence

Configuration Variable Selection The difference between a data input and a configuration variable is a semantic distinction that ultimately depends on the domain-specific meaning of each input to the kernel – it cannot be fully automated. In our experiments, we have manually examined kernels to extract this distinction.

However, the difference between a property-integrity input, and one which is not, is based on which inputs influence the access invariance property and which do not. This classification *can* be automated with our invariance analysis. We simply run our invariance analysis on each input in turn, and determine which inputs cause our analysis to report a violation of the access invariance property. The end result is that we have found a minimal set of property-integrity inputs.

For all kernels we have classified as access invariant, we would expect our set of manually chosen configuration variables to contain the set of property-integrity inputs. In addition, we would expect that for all variant kernels, at least one data input is in fact a property-integrity input. We have verified that both are true.

A final observation is that in cases where the set of property-integrity inputs is smaller than the set of chosen configuration variables, we can amplify our guarantees to an even larger set of inputs. We found this to be the case for `convolutionSeparable`, which contains two kernels, one which performs an image transform on the rows of the image, and another which acts on the columns. Both kernels take parameters `imageW` and `imageH` which indicate the height and width of the image being transformed, but the row- and column- transforming kernels are only variant with respect to the width and height parameters, respectively. Thus, although we manually specified both parameters to be configuration inputs, in fact we could have removed one and still maintained the access invariance property. In total, we have found that for 11 of the kernels the set of property-integrity inputs is in fact a subset of the set of configuration variables.

5.3 Dynamic Analysis

Our dynamic analysis found that most of the dynamic runs were race-free and deterministic. However, our analysis detected a race violation in the full implementation of `scalarProd`. The race was determined to be a result of a missing `__syncthreads()` call after a complete dot product had been calculated and stored into the output array, which corresponds to line 13 of Figure 1. Without this barrier, thread 0 might still be reading values from the `accumResult` array while its neighbors had already begun calculation on the next pair of vectors, potentially performing a destructive update before the previous result had been completed.

In practice, however, this race will not manifest itself due to the *warp-synchronous* nature of CUDA's execution model: neighboring threads are logically grouped into *warps* of 32 threads that execute synchronously on hardware. Thus, because threads 0 and 1 belong to the same warp, they will not exercise the race described.

Races were also detected in two other benchmarks, `histogram` and `reduction`. In both cases, the benchmarks once again relied on warp-synchronous execution to prevent races in the absence of explicit barrier synchronization. It is important to note, however, that warp-synchronous execution relies on the behavior of underlying hardware, which may change for future generations of GPUs or different target architectures, and cause these to become real errors.

5.4 Performance Evaluation

The running time of our static analysis was less than one second for most benchmarks, with none taking more than 10 seconds with two notable exceptions: `radixSort` which took 36m, and `reduction` which took 3.5m. The reason is that these benchmarks makes heavy use of C++-style templates. When compiled, each template specializes into multiple kernels, each of which is analyzed. `radixSort` instantiates 271 kernels, and our analysis takes an average of 8 seconds per instantiated kernel. Our analysis takes an average 1.6s on each of the 132 kernels instantiated by `reduction`.

To evaluate the performance penalty of our dynamic instrumentation and race detection, we measured running times for each benchmark with and without the analysis enabled. The geometric mean and median slowdown were 18X and 12X, respectively, while the total slowdown, measured by summing the running times of all benchmarks, was 310X. There were two benchmarks, `MonteCarlo` and `convolutionSeparable`, that had running times more than an order of magnitude higher than the others, at 2093X and 1324X, due to the size of their logs: `convolutionSeparable` in particular, produced a 508 GB log. We have found that slowdowns are highly correlated with the size of the memory traces, leading us to believe that the bottleneck in performance is disk I/O for writing log entries. This could be alleviated through the use of more sophisticated buffering techniques, but we leave this for future work.

6. Related Work

In this section we discuss the literature related to our work, which fall under two broad categories: race-freedom and determinism; and test amplification. The literature on enforcing race-freedom and determinism on shared memory multithreaded programs is enormous: we limit ourselves to work that studies problems similar to the domain of GPU programs, with massive, fine-grained data-sharing. Because test amplification is such a broad concept, it has appeared in many different forms in the literature. We present an indicative, albeit necessarily incomplete selection of work representative of the breadth of its application.

Race-Freedom and Determinism One closely related piece of work by Boyer et al. presents a dynamic analysis for detecting races in CUDA programs [4]. The work uses an instrumentation much like our own, to generate logs that can be used to dynamically detect races and barrier conflicts. Of course, without amplification, the results only hold for one run at a time, which is not likely to be very useful as the instrumentation imposes large overheads.

Our work is greatly inspired by PUG [23], a tool that analyzes CUDA programs via the machinery of symbolic execution. PUG logically encodes the program executions and uses an SMT solver to check whether different threads can race within a barrier interval. PUG has several optimizations that mitigate the explosion in thread interleavings. One of these is that it is limited to checking a program with just two threads. Similarly, Vechev et al. [35] use numeric abstract interpretation to compute the sets of indices used to access shared arrays. As both these techniques are fully static, they are limited to programs for which it can infer suitable simple (linear) loop invariants, which precludes usage on many CUDA kernels which often have complex, non-linear loop invariants computed with modular arithmetic and bitwise operations.

There is an enormous literature on dynamic and static race detection for general concurrent programs. Two classical examples include work by Dinning and Schonberg [8], and Savage et al. [32] that respectively pioneered the use of static and dynamic *locksets* in order to check for the absence of races. Several authors have built upon that line of work using types [11], dataflow analysis [10], and even greatly extended it to checking for higher level properties like atomicity [12, 13] and determinism [31]. Unfortunately, these methods don't apply in our setting as CUDA eschews lock-based synchronization.

Several authors have proposed dynamic mechanisms for enforcing determinism by constraining the scheduler. These include techniques that modify the language run-time [3, 25] or the OS [2]. Due to the run-time overheads, these methods are unlikely to apply in the GPU setting, where programs exhibit a high degree of fine-grained sharing, for example to maximize memory bandwidth.

The general idea of *non-interference* [18], in which static information flow has it roots, has been proposed as a means of formalizing correctness properties of multithreaded programs [9]. Previous work has also studied the connection between information flow and concurrency. In particular, Zdancewic and Myers [37] describe the notion of observational determinism wherein a program is secure iff its observable behaviors are independent of secure inputs and scheduling, and Terauchi [34] describes a type system for observational determinism. Our novel contribution is to demonstrate how of static information flow can be used to amplify the results of a single execution across all runs over the same configuration, thereby establishing the property for arbitrary thread interleavings and data values, and to empirically demonstrate the effectiveness of this technique for verifying CUDA programs.

Test Amplification Recent work on dynamic test generation has employed test amplification with the aim of increasing code coverage [5, 6, 16, 33]. Collectively dubbed *concolic testing*, these techniques use dynamic symbolic execution to collect logical constraints representing input-dependent control flow conditions, then solve the constraints to obtain inputs that steer execution along different paths. At a high level, all these techniques attempt to maximize code coverage by avoiding the generation of test inputs that redundantly follow the same paths. In this context, the identification of equivalence classes of inputs that exercise the same paths may be viewed as an instance of test amplification: a single input is amplified to *represent* its equivalence class of inputs.

Another form of test amplification has also been explored extensively in work on runtime fault monitoring [17, 19, 21]. By piggybacking symbolic execution on top of a dynamic run, these techniques are able to detect property violations across a much larger space of inputs than those exercised by a particular concrete execution. This method has been used to find buffer overflows [21], generalized to predict more generic property violations [19], and adapted to generate concrete test inputs that exercise those violations [17]. Because these techniques only check properties along the tested execution path, they rely on exhaustive path search to verify properties across all executions.

The described dynamic test generation and runtime monitoring techniques fall under what we call *symbolic-execution-based test amplification*, an umbrella term for techniques that employ symbolic execution to learn additional information from a concrete execution. Flow-based test amplification is potentially less precise than symbolic execution, but is also much cheaper, and as demonstrated by our evaluation, quite effective in the CUDA setting. Recent work on verifying memory-safety of programs with floating-point computation [15] has even combined dynamic symbolic execution with a static flow analysis which establishes that floating-point values do not interfere with non-floating point values, thereby allowing amplification of symbolic execution guarantees over floating point computations. The effectiveness of flow-based test amplification stems from the fact that programs in the domain isolate the *data* values being operated on (e.g. input arrays or floating point numbers) from those used to determine *control-flow* and *memory accesses*.

Finally, test amplification has also appeared in work on the analysis of general concurrent programs. Wang and Stoller [36] describe two dynamic analyses for detecting atomicity violations in concurrent Java programs: one that employs Lipton's theory of reduction [24] to reason about commutativity of concurrent events to infer atomicity, and another that searches for unserializable permutations of events to detect atomicity violations. Both analyses use test amplification in the sense that they examine a single execution but are capable of detecting violations occurring in other possible interleavings. A different instance of test amplification appears in work by Chen and Roşu [7], which proposes a relaxation of the classical happen-before causality partial order [14, 20] to admit a greater number of compatible interleavings. This relaxation amplifies the partial order to a larger space of possible executions, thus opening subsequent analyses to detect property violations in more interleavings. A key contribution of our work is to demonstrate that enumerating interleavings is simply unnecessary for many CUDA kernels: we can apply static information flow analysis to generalize our determinism guarantee to a massive space of interleavings from a single execution.

Acknowledgements

We wish to thank Mingxun Wang for his part in many fruitful discussions and his help on initial feasibility experiments. We are grateful to our shepherd, Patrice Godefroid, and the anonymous reviewers for their comments and feedback for improving the paper.

References

[1] L. Andersen. *Program analysis and specialization for the C programming language*. PhD thesis, 1994.

[2] A. Aviram, S.-C. Weng, S. Hu, and B. Ford. Efficient system-enforced deterministic parallelism. In *OSDI*, pages 193–206, 2010.

[3] T. Bergan, O. Anderson, J. Devietti, L. Ceze, and D. Grossman. CoreDet: a compiler and runtime system for deterministic multithreaded execution. In *ASPLOS*, pages 53–64, 2010.

[4] M. Boyer, K. Skadron, and W. Weimer. Automated dynamic analysis of CUDA programs. In *STMC*, 2008.

[5] C. Cadar, V. Ganesh, P. M. Pawlowski, D. L. Dill, and D. R. Engler. EXE: automatically generating inputs of death. In *CCS*, pages 322–335, 2006.

[6] C. Cadar, P. Godefroid, S. Khurshid, C. S. Păsăreanu, K. Sen, N. Tillmann, and W. Visser. Symbolic execution for software testing in practice: preliminary assessment. In *ICSE*, pages 1066–1071, 2011.

[7] F. Chen and G. Roşu. Parametric and sliced causality. In *CAV*, pages 240–253, 2007.

[8] A. Dinning and E. Schonberg. Detecting access anomalies in programs with critical sections. In *Workshop on Parallel and Distributed Debugging*, pages 85–96, 1991.

[9] P. A. Emrath and D. A. Padua. Automatic detection of nondeterminacy in parallel programs. In *PADD*, pages 89–99, 1988.

[10] D. Engler and K. Ashcraft. RacerX: Effective, static detection of race conditions and deadlocks. In *SOSP*, pages 237–252, 2003.

[11] C. Flanagan and S. Freund. Type-based race detection for Java. In *PLDI*, pages 219–232, 2000.

[12] C. Flanagan and S. N. Freund. Atomizer: a dynamic atomicity checker for multithreaded programs. In *POPL*, pages 256–267, 2004.

[13] C. Flanagan and S. Qadeer. A type and effect system for atomicity. In *PLDI*, pages 191–202, 2003.

[14] P. Godefroid. *Partial-Order Methods for the Verification of Concurrent Systems: An Approach to the State-Explosion Problem*. Springer-Verlag New York, Inc., Secaucus, NJ, USA, 1996.

[15] P. Godefroid and J. Kinder. Proving memory safety of floating-point computations by combining static and dynamic program analysis. In *ISSTA*, pages 1–12, 2010.

[16] P. Godefroid, N. Klarlund, and K. Sen. DART: directed automated random testing. In *PLDI*, pages 213–223, 2005.

[17] P. Godefroid, M. Y. Levin, and D. A. Molnar. Active property checking. In *EMSOFT*, pages 207–216, 2008.

[18] J. A. Goguen and J. Meseguer. Security policies and security models. *IEEE Symposium on Security and Privacy*, pages 11–20, 1982.

[19] P. Joshi, K. Sen, and M. Shlimovich. Predictive testing: amplifying the effectiveness of software testing. In *ESEC/FSE*, pages 561–564, 2007.

[20] L. Lamport. Time, clocks, and the ordering of events in a distributed system. *Commun. ACM*, 21(7):558–565, 1978.

[21] E. Larson and T. Austin. High coverage detection of input-related security faults. In *USENIX Security*, 2003.

[22] C. Lattner and V. Adve. LLVM: A compilation framework for lifelong program analysis & transformation. In *CGO*, 2004.

[23] G. Li and G. Gopalakrishnan. Scalable smt-based verification of gpu kernel functions. In *FSE*, pages 187–196, 2010.

[24] R. J. Lipton. Reduction: a method of proving properties of parallel programs. *Commun. ACM*, 18:717–721, December 1975.

[25] T. Liu, C. Curtsinger, and E. D. Berger. Dthreads: Efficient deterministic multithreading. In *SOSP*, pages 327–336, 2011.

[26] F. Masdupuy. Semantic analysis of interval congruences. In *Formal Methods in Programming and Their Applications*, LNCS 735. 1993.

[27] A. Myers. JFlow: Practical mostly-static information flow control. In *POPL*, pages 228–241, 1999.

[28] NVIDIA. CUDA toolkit 3.0. `http://developer.nvidia.com/cuda-toolkit-30-downloads`, 2010.

[29] NVIDIA. CUDA accelerated applications. `http://www.nvidia.com/object/cuda_app_tesla.html`, 2011.

[30] M. Raza, C. Calcagno, and P. Gardner. Automatic parallelization with separation logic. In *ESOP*, pages 348–362, 2009.

[31] C. Sadowski, S. N. Freund, and C. Flanagan. SingleTrack: A dynamic determinism checker for multithreaded programs. In *ESOP*, pages 394–409, 2009.

[32] S. Savage, M. Burrows, G. Nelson, P. Sobalvarro, and T. Anderson. Eraser: A dynamic data race detector for multi-threaded programs. *ACM Transactions on Computer Systems*, 15:391–411, 1997.

[33] K. Sen, D. Marinov, and G. Agha. CUTE: a concolic unit testing engine for c. In *ESEC/FSE*, pages 263–272, 2005.

[34] T. Terauchi. A type system for observational determinism. In *CSF*, pages 287–300, 2008.

[35] M. T. Vechev, E. Yahav, R. Raman, and V. Sarkar. Automatic verification of determinism for structured parallel programs. In *SAS*, pages 455–471, 2010.

[36] L. Wang and S. D. Stoller. Runtime analysis of atomicity for multithreaded programs. *IEEE Trans. Softw. Eng.*, 32:93–110, February 2006.

[37] S. Zdancewic and A. C. Myers. Observational determinism for concurrent program security. In *CSFW*, pages 29–43, 2003.

RockSalt: Better, Faster, Stronger SFI for the x86

Greg Morrisett *
Harvard University
greg@eecs.harvard.edu

Gang Tan
Lehigh University
gtan@cse.lehigh.edu

Joseph Tassarotti
Harvard University
tassarotti@college.harvard.edu

Jean-Baptiste Tristan
Harvard University
tristan@seas.harvard.edu

Edward Gan
Harvard University
egan@college.harvard.edu

Abstract

Software-based fault isolation (SFI), as used in Google's Native Client (NaCl), relies upon a conceptually simple machine-code analysis to enforce a security policy. But for complicated architectures such as the x86, it is all too easy to get the details of the analysis wrong. We have built a new checker that is smaller, faster, and has a much reduced trusted computing base when compared to Google's original analysis. The key to our approach is automatically generating the bulk of the analysis from a declarative description which we relate to a formal model of a subset of the x86 instruction set architecture. The x86 model, developed in Coq, is of independent interest and should be usable for a wide range of machine-level verification tasks.

Categories and Subject Descriptors D.2.4 [*Software Engineering*]: Software/Program Verification

General Terms security, verification

Keywords software fault isolation, domain-specific languages

1. Introduction

Native Client (NaCl) is a new service provided by Google's Chrome browser that allows native executable code to be run directly in the context of the browser [35]. To prevent buggy or malicious code from corrupting the browser's state, leaking information, or directly accessing system resources, the NaCl loader checks that the binary code respects a *sandbox* security policy. The sandbox policy is meant to ensure that, when loaded and executed, the untrusted code (a) will only read or write data in specified segments of memory, (b) will only execute code from a specified segment of memory, disjoint from the data segments, (c) will not execute a specific class of instructions (*e.g.*, system calls), and (d) will only communicate with the browser through a well-defined set of entry points.

Ensuring the correctness of the NaCl checker is crucial for preventing vulnerabilities, yet early versions had bugs that attackers could exploit, as demonstrated by a contest that Google ran [23]. A high-level goal of this work is to produce a high-assurance checker for the NaCl sandbox policy. Thus far, we have managed to construct a new NaCl checker for the 32-bit x86 (IA-32) processor (minus floating-point) which we call RockSalt. The RockSalt checker is smaller, marginally faster, and easier to modify than Google's original code. Furthermore, the core of RockSalt is automatically generated from a higher-level specification, and this generator has been proven correct with respect to a model of the x86 using the Coq proof assistant [8].

We are not the first to address assurance for SFI using formal methods. In particular, Zhao *et al.* [36] built a provably correct verifier for a sandbox policy similar to NaCl's. Specifically, building upon a model of the ARM processor in HOL [11], they constructed a program logic and a provably correct verification condition generator, which when coupled with an abstract interpretation, generates proofs that assembly code respects the policy.

Our work has two key differences: First, there is no formal model for the subset of x86 that NaCl supports. Consequently, we have constructed a new model for the x86 in Coq. We believe that this model is an important contribution of our work, as it can be used to validate reasoning about the behavior of x86 machine code in other contexts (*e.g.*, for verified compilers).

Second, Zhao *et al.*'s approach takes about 2.5 hours to check a 300 instruction program, whereas RockSalt checks roughly 1M instructions per second. Instead of a general-purpose theorem prover, RockSalt only relies upon a set of tables that encode a deterministic finite-state automaton (DFA) and a few tens of lines of (trusted) `C` code. Consequently, the checker is extremely fast, has a much smaller run-time trusted computing base, and can be easily integrated into the NaCl runtime.

1.1 Overview

This paper has two major parts: the first part describes our model of the x86 in Coq and the second describes the RockSalt NaCl checker and its proof of correctness with respect to the model.

The x86 architecture is notoriously complicated, and our fragment includes a parser for over 130 different instructions with se-

* This research was sponsored in part by NSF grants CCF-0915030, CCF-0915157, CNS-0910660, CCF-1149211, AFOSR MURI grant FA9550-09-1-0539, and a gift from Google.

PLDI'12, June 11–16, 2012, Beijing, China.

mantic definitions for over 70 instructions[1]. This includes support for operands that include byte and word immediates, registers, and complicated addressing modes (*e.g.*, scaled index plus offset). Furthermore, the x86 allows prefix bytes, such as operand size override, locking, and string repeat, that can be combined in many different ways to change the behavior of an instruction. Finally, the instruction set architecture is so complex, that it is unlikely that we can produce a faithful model from documentation, so we must be able to validate our model against implementations.

To address these issues, we have constructed a pair of domain-specific languages (DSLs), inspired by the work on SLED [28] and λ-RTL [27] (as well as more recent work [10, 17]), for specifying the semantics of machine architectures, and have embedded those languages within Coq. Our DSLs are declarative and reasonably high-level, yet we can use them to generate OCaml code that can be run as a simulator. Furthermore, the tools are architecture independent and can thus be re-used to specify the semantics of other machine architectures. For example, one of the undergraduate co-authors constructed a model of the MIPS architecture using our DSLs in just a few days.

The Decoder DSL provides support for specifying the translation from bits to abstract syntax in a declarative fashion. We were able to take the tables from Intel's manual [12] and use them to directly construct patterns for our decoder. Our embedding of the Decoder DSL includes both a denotational and operational semantics, and a proof of adequacy for the two interpretations. We use the denotational semantics for proving important properties about the decode stage of execution, and the operational semantics for execution validation.

The RTL (register transfer list) DSL is a small RISC-like core language parameterized by a notion of machine state. The RTL library includes an executable, small-step operational semantics. Each step in the semantics is specified as a (pure) function from machine states to machine states. We give meaning to x86 instructions by translating their abstract syntax to appropriate sequences of RTL instructions, similar to the way that a modern processor works. Reasoning about RTL is much easier than x86 code, as the number of instructions is smaller and orthogonal.

In what follows, we describe our DSLs and how they were used to construct the x86 model. We also describe our framework for validating the model against existing x86 implementations. We then describe the NaCl sandbox policy in detail, and the new RockSalt checker we have built to enforce it. Next, we describe the actual verification code and the proof of correctness. Finally, we close with a discussion of related work, future directions, and lessons learned.

2. A Coq Model of the x86

Our Coq model of the x86 instruction set architecture has three major stages: (1) a decoder that translates bytes into abstract syntax for instructions, (2) a compiler that translates abstract syntax into sequences of RTL instructions, (3) an interpreter for RTL instructions. The interface between the first two components is the definition of the abstract syntax, which is specified using a set of inductive datatype definitions that are informally sketched in Figure 1.

2.1 The Decoder Specification

The job of the x86 model's decoder is to translate bytes into abstract syntax. We specify the translation using generic grammars constructed in a domain-specific language, which is embedded into

[1] Some instructions have numerous encodings. For example, there are fourteen different opcode forms for the ADC instruction, but we count this as a single instruction.

Register	reg	::=	EAX | ECX | EDX | $\cdots$
Segment Reg.	$sreg$	::=	ES | CS | SS | $\cdots$
Scale	$scale$	::=	1 | 2 | 4 | 8

Operand

op ::= int_{32} | reg
  $int_{32} \times$ option $reg \times$ option($scale \times reg$)

Instruction

i ::= AAA | AAD | AAM | AAS | ADC(bool $\times\ op_1 \times op_2$)
  | ADD(bool $\times\ op_1 \times op_2$)
  | AND(bool $\times\ op_1 \times op_2$) | $\cdots$

Figure 1. Some Definitions for the x86 Abstract Syntax

```
Definition CALL_p : grammar instr :=
   "1110" $$ "1000" $$ word @
   (fun w => CALL true false (Imm_op w) None)
|| "1111" $$ "1111" $$ ext_op_modrm2 "010" @
   (fun op => CALL true true op None)
|| "1001" $$ "1010" $$ halfword $ word @
   (fun p => CALL false false (Imm_op (snd p))
             (Some (fst p)))
|| "1111" $$ "1111" $$ ext_op_modrm2 "011" @
   (fun op => CALL false true op None).
```

Figure 2. Parsing Specification for the CALL instruction

Coq. The language lets users specify a pattern and associated semantic actions for transforming input strings to outputs such as abstract syntax. Our pattern language is limited to regular expressions, but the semantic actions are arbitrary Coq functions.

Figure 2 gives an example parsing specification we use for the CALL instruction. At a high-level, this grammar specifies four alternatives that can build a CALL instruction. Each case includes a pattern specifying literal sequences of bits (*e.g.*, "1110"), followed by other components like word or modrm2 that are themselves grammars that compute values of an appropriate type. The "@" separates the pattern from a Coq function that can be used to transform the values returned from the pattern match. For example, in the first case, we take the word value and use it to build the abstract syntax for a version of the CALL instruction with an immediate operand.

We chose to specify patterns at the bit-level, instead of the byte-level, because this avoids the need to introduce or reason about shifts and masks in the semantic actions. Furthermore, we were able to take the tables from the Intel IA-32 instruction manual and translate them directly into appropriate patterns.

Our decoding specifications take advantage of Coq's notation mechanism, as well as some derived forms to make the grammar readable, but these are defined in terms of a small set of constructors given by the following type-indexed datatype:

```
Inductive grammar : Type → Type
| Char: char → grammar char
| Any: grammar char
| Eps: grammar unit
| Cat:∀T1 T2,grammar T1 → grammar T2 → grammar (T1*T2)
| Void: ∀T, grammar T
| Alt: ∀T, grammar T → grammar T → grammar T
| Star: ∀T, grammar T → grammar (list T)
| Map: ∀T1 T2, (T1 → T2) → grammar T1 → grammar T2
```

A value of type grammar T represents a relation between lists of chars[2] and semantic values of type T. Alternatively, we can think of the grammar as matching an input string and returning a set of associated semantic values. Formally, the denotation of a grammar

[2] Grammars are parameterized by the type char.

is the least relation over strings and values satisfying the following equations:

$$
\begin{array}{rcl}
[\![\texttt{Char}\ c]\!] & = & \{(c :: \texttt{nil}, c)\} \\
[\![\texttt{Any}]\!] & = & \bigcup_c \{(c :: \texttt{nil}, c)\} \\
[\![\texttt{Eps}]\!] & = & \{(\texttt{nil}, \texttt{tt})\} \\
[\![\texttt{Void}]\!] & = & \emptyset \\
[\![\texttt{Alt}\ g_1\ g_2]\!] & = & [\![g_1]\!] \cup [\![g_2]\!] \\
[\![\texttt{Cat}\ g_1\ g_2]\!] & = & \{((s_1 s_2), (v_1, v_2)) \mid (s_i, v_i) \in [\![g_i]\!]\} \\
[\![\texttt{Map}\ f\ g]\!] & = & \{(s, f(v)) \mid (s, v) \in [\![g]\!]\} \\
[\![\texttt{Star}\ g]\!] & = & [\![\texttt{Map}\ (\lambda\_.\, \texttt{nil})\ \texttt{Eps}]\!] \cup \\
 & & [\![\texttt{Map}\ (::)\ (\texttt{Cat}\ g\ (\texttt{Star}\ g))]\!]
\end{array}
$$

Thus, `Char c` matches strings containing only the character `c`, and returns that character as the semantic value. Similarly, `Any` matches a string containing any single character `c`, and returns `c`. `Eps` matches only the empty string and returns `tt` (Coq's unit). The grammar `Void` matches no strings and thus returns no values. When g_1 and g_2 are grammars that each return values of type T, then the grammar `Alt` $g_1\ g_2$ matches a string s if either g_1 matches s or g_2 matches s. It returns the union of the values that g_1 and g_2 associate with the string. `Cat` $g_1\ g_2$ matches a string if it can be broken into two pieces that match the sub-grammars. It returns a pair of the values computed by the grammars. `Star` matches zero or more occurrences of a pattern, returning the results as a list.

The last constructor, `Map`, is our constructor for semantic actions. When g is a grammar that returns T_1 values, and f is a function of type $T_1 \rightarrow T_2$, then `Map` $f\ g$ is the grammar that matches the same set of strings as g, but transforms the outputs from T_1 values to T_2 values using f. If a grammar forgoes the use of `Map`, then the semantic values represent a parse tree for the input. `Map` makes it possible to incrementally transform the parse tree into alternate semantic values, such as abstract syntax.

As noted above, we use Coq's notation mechanism to make the grammars more readable. In particular, the following table gives some definitions for the notation used here:

g_1 `||` g_2	:=	`Alt` $g_1\ g_2$	g_1 `$` g_2	:=	`Cat` $g_1\ g_2$
g `@` f	:=	`Map` $f\ g$	g_1 `$$` g_2	:=	(g_1 `$` g_2) `@ snd`

We encode the denotational semantics in Coq using an inductively defined predicate, which makes it easy to symbolically reason about grammars. For example, one of our key theorems shows that our top-level grammar, which includes all possible prefixes and all possible integer instructions, is deterministic:

$$(s, v_1) \in [\![\texttt{x86grammar}]\!] \wedge (s, v_2) \in [\![\texttt{x86grammar}]\!] \Longrightarrow v_1 = v_2$$

This helps provide some assurance that in transcribing the grammar from Intel's manual, we have not made a mistake. In fact, when we first tried to prove determinism, we failed because we had flipped a bit in an infrequently used encoding of the `MOV` instruction, causing it to overlap with another instruction.

2.2 The Decoder Implementation

While the denotational specification makes it easy to reason about grammars, it cannot be directly executed. Consequently, we define a parsing function which, when given a record representing a machine state, fetches bytes from the address specified by the program counter and attempts to match them against the grammar and build the appropriate instruction abstract syntax.

Our parsing function is defined by taking the *derivative* of the `x86grammar` with respect to the sequence of bits in each byte, and then checking to see if the resulting grammar accepts the empty string. The notion of derivatives is based on the ideas of Brzozowski [4] and more recently, Owens *et al.* [24] and Might *et al.* [22]. Reasoning about derivatives is much easier in Coq than attempting to transform grammars into the usual graph-based formalisms, as we need not worry about issues such as naming nodes, equivalence on graphs, or induction principles for graphs. Rather, all of our computation and reasoning can be done directly on the algebraic datatype of grammars.

Semantically, the derivative of a grammar g with respect to a character c is the relation:

$$\texttt{deriv}_c\ g = \{(s, v) \mid (c :: s, v) \in [\![g]\!]\}$$

That is, $\texttt{deriv}_c\ g$ matches the tail of any string that starts with c and matches g.

Fortunately, calculating the derivative, including the appropriate transformation on the semantic actions, can be written as a straightforward function:

$$
\begin{array}{rcll}
\texttt{deriv}_c\ \texttt{Any} & = & \texttt{Map}\ (\lambda\_.\, c)\ \texttt{Eps} & \\
\texttt{deriv}_c\ (\texttt{Char}\ c) & = & \texttt{Map}\ (\lambda\_.\, c)\ \texttt{Eps} & \\
\texttt{deriv}_c\ (\texttt{Alt}\ g_1\ g_2) & = & \texttt{Alt}\ (\texttt{deriv}_c\ g_1)\ (\texttt{deriv}_c\ g_2) & \\
\texttt{deriv}_c\ (\texttt{Star}\ g) & = & \texttt{Map}\ (::)\ (\texttt{Cat}(\texttt{deriv}_c\ g)\ (\texttt{Star}\ g)) & \\
\texttt{deriv}_c\ (\texttt{Cat}\ g_1\ g_2) & = & \texttt{Alt}(\texttt{Cat}\ (\texttt{deriv}_c\ g_1)\ g_2) & \\
 & & \quad (\texttt{Cat}\ (\texttt{null}\ g_1)\ (\texttt{deriv}_c\ g_2)) & \\
\texttt{deriv}_c\ (\texttt{Map}\ f\ g) & = & \texttt{Map}\ f\ (\texttt{deriv}_c\ g) & \\
\texttt{deriv}_c\ g & = & \texttt{Void} & \text{otherwise}
\end{array}
$$

where $\texttt{null}\ g$ is defined as:

$$
\begin{array}{rcll}
\texttt{null}\ \texttt{Eps} & = & \texttt{Eps} & \\
\texttt{null}\ (\texttt{Alt}\ g_1\ g_2) & = & \texttt{Alt}\ (\texttt{null}\ g_1)\ (\texttt{null}\ g_2) & \\
\texttt{null}\ (\texttt{Cat}\ g_1\ g_2) & = & \texttt{Cat}\ (\texttt{null}\ g_1)\ (\texttt{null}\ g_2) & \\
\texttt{null}\ (\texttt{Star}\ g) & = & \texttt{Map}\ (\lambda\_.\, \texttt{nil})\ \texttt{Eps} & \\
\texttt{null}\ (\texttt{Map}\ f\ g) & = & \texttt{Map}\ f\ (\texttt{null}\ g) & \\
\texttt{null}\ g & = & \texttt{Void} & \text{otherwise}
\end{array}
$$

Effectively, `deriv` strips off a leading pattern that matches c, and adjusts the grammar with a `Map` so that it continues to calculate the same set of values. If the grammar cannot match a string that starts with c, then the resulting grammar is `Void`. The `null` function returns a grammar equivalent to `Eps` when its argument accepts the empty string, and `Void` otherwise. It is used to calculate the derivative of a `Cat`, which is simply the chain-rule for derivatives.

Once we calculate the iterated derivative of the grammar with respect to a string of bits, we can extract the set of related semantic values by running the `extract` function, which returns those semantic values associated with the empty string:

$$
\begin{array}{rcll}
\texttt{extract Eps} & = & \{\texttt{tt}\} & \\
\texttt{extract}\ (\texttt{Star}\ g) & = & \{\texttt{nil}\} & \\
\texttt{extract}\ (\texttt{Alt}\ g_1\ g_2) & = & (\texttt{extract}\ g_1) \cup (\texttt{extract}\ g_2) & \\
\texttt{extract}\ (\texttt{Cat}\ g_1\ g_2) & = & \{(v_1, v_2) \mid v_i \in \texttt{extract}\ g_i\} & \\
\texttt{extract}\ (\texttt{Map}\ f\ g) & = & \{f(v) \mid v \in \texttt{extract}\ g\} & \\
\texttt{extract}\ g & = & \emptyset & \text{otherwise}
\end{array}
$$

To be reasonably efficient, it is important that we optimize the grammar as we calculate derivatives. In particular, when we build a grammar, we always use a set of "smart" constructors, which are functions that perform local reductions, including:

`Cat` g `Eps`	$\rightarrow$	g	`Cat Eps` g	$\rightarrow$	g
`Cat` g `Void`	$\rightarrow$	`Void`	`Cat Void` g	$\rightarrow$	`Void`
`Alt` g `Void`	$\rightarrow$	g	`Alt Void` g	$\rightarrow$	g
`Star (Star` g`)`	$\rightarrow$	`Star` g	`Alt` $g\ g$	$\rightarrow$	g

Of course, the optimizations must add appropriate `Map`s to adjust the semantic actions. Proving the optimizations correct is an easy exercise using the denotational semantics. Unfortunately, the last of these optimizations (`Alt` $g\ g \rightarrow g$) cannot be directly implemented as it demands a decidable notion of equality for grammars, yet our grammars include arbitrary Coq functions (and types). To work around these problems, we first translate grammars to an internal form, where all types and functions are replaced with a name that we can easily compare. An environment is used to track the

Machine locations
  loc ::= PC | EAX | ⋯ | CF | ⋯ | SS | ⋯
Local variables
  $x, y, z \in$ identifier
Arithmetic operators
  op ::= add | xor | shl | ⋯
Comparison operators
  cmp ::= lt | eq | gt
RTL instructions
  rt ::= x := y op z | x := y cmp z
    | x := imm | x := load loc
    | store loc x | x := Mem[y]
    | Mem[x] := y | x := choose | ⋯

Figure 3. The RTL Language

mapping from names back to their definitions, and is consulted in the `extract` function to build appropriate semantic values.

In the end, we get a reasonably efficient parser that we can extract to executable OCaml code. Furthermore, we prove that the parser, when given a grammar g and string s, produces a (finite) set of values $\{v_1, \cdots, v_n\}$ such that $(s, v_i) \in [\![g]\!]$. Since we have proven that our instruction grammar is deterministic, we know that in fact, we will get out at most one instruction for each sequence of bytes that we feed to the parser.

Finally, we note that calculating derivatives in this fashion corresponds to a lazy, on-line construction of a deterministic finite-state transducer. Our efficient NaCl checker, described in Section 3 is built from a deterministic finite-state automaton (DFA) generated off-line, re-using the definitions for the grammars, derivatives, *etc.* in the parsing library.

2.3 Translation To RTL

After parsing bytes into abstract syntax, we translate the corresponding instruction into a sequence of RTL (register transfer list) operations. RTL is a small RISC-like language for computing with bit-vectors. The language abstracts over an architecture's definition of machine state, which in the case of the x86 includes the various kinds of registers shown in Figure 1 as well as a memory, represented as a finite map from addresses to bytes. Internally, the language supports a countably infinite supply of local variables that can be used to hold intermediate bit-vector values.

The RTL instruction set is sketched in Figure 3 and includes standard arithmetic, logic, and comparison operations for bit vectors; operations to sign/zero-extend and truncate bit vectors; an operation to load an immediate value into a local variable; operations to load/store values in local variables from/to registers; operations to load and store bytes into memory; and a special operation for non-deterministically choosing a bit-vector value of a particular size. We use dependent types to embed the language into Coq and ensure that only bit-vectors of the appropriate size are used in instructions.

For each x86 constructor, we define a function that translates the abstract syntax into a sequence of RTL instructions. The translation is encapsulated in a monad that takes care of allocating fresh local variables, and that allows us to build higher-level operations out of sequences of RTL commands.

Figure 4 presents an excerpt of the translation of the `ADD` instruction. The `ADD` constructor is parameterized by a prefix record, a boolean mode, and two operands. The prefix record records modifiers including any segment, operand, or address override. The boolean mode is set when the default operand size is to be used

```
Definition conv_ADD prefix mode op1 op2 :=
  let load := load_op prefix mode in
  let set := set_op prefix mode in
  let seg := get_segment_op2 prefix DS op1 op2 in
  zero ← load_Z size1 0;
  up ← load_Z size1 1;
  p0 ← load seg op1;
  p1 ← load seg op2;
  p2 ← arith add p0 p1;
  set seg p2 op1;;
  b0 ← test lt zero p0;
  b1 ← test lt zero p1;
  b2 ← test lt zero p2;
  b3 ← arith xor b0 b1;
  b3 ← arith xor up b3;
  b4 ← arith xor b0 b2;
  b4 ← arith and b3 b4;
  set_flag OF b4;;
  ...
```

Figure 4. Translation Specification for the ADD instruction

(*i.e.*, 32-bits) and cleared when the operand size is set to a byte. The operands can be registers, immediate values, or effective addresses.

The first two local definitions specialize the load and store RTL to the given prefix and mode. The third definition selects the appropriate segment. Next, we load constant expressions 0 and 1 (of bit-size 1) into local variables `zero` and `up`. Then we fetch the bit-vector values from the operands and store them in local variables `p0` and `p1`. At this point, we actually add the two bit-vectors and place the result in local variable `p2`. Then we update the machine state at the location specified by the first operand. Afterwards, we set the various flag registers to hold the appropriate 1-bit value based on the outcome of the operation. Here, we have only shown the code needed to set the overflow (`OF`) flag.

Occasionally, the effect of an operation, particularly on flags, is under-specified or unclear. To over-approximate the set of possible behaviors, we use the `choose` operation, which non-deterministically selects a bit-vector value and stores this value in the appropriate location.

2.4 The RTL Interpreter

Once we have defined our decoder and translation to RTL, we need only give a semantics to the RTL instructions to complete the x86 model. One option would be to use a small-step operational semantics for modeling RTL execution, encoded as an inductive predicate. However, this would prevent us from extracting an executable interpreter which we need for validation.

Instead, we encode a step in the semantics as a function from RTL machine states to RTL machine states. RTL machine states record the values of the various x86 locations, the memory, and the values of the local variables. To support the non-determinism in the `choose` operation, the RTL machine state includes a stream of bits that serves as an *oracle*. Whenever we need to `choose` a new value, we simply pull bits from the oracle stream. Of course, when reasoning about the behavior of instructions, we must consider all possible oracle streams. This is a standard trick for turning a non-deterministic step relation into a function.

Most of the operations are simple bit-vector computations for which we use the CompCert integer bit-vector library [16]. Consequently, the definition of the interpreter is fairly straightforward and extracts to reasonable OCaml code that we can use for testing.

2.5 Model Validation

Any model of the x86 is complicated enough that it undoubtably has bugs. The only way we can gain any confidence is to test it against real x86 processors (and even they have bugs!). As described above, we have carefully engineered our model so that we can extract an executable OCaml simulator from our Coq definitions. We use this simulator to compare against an actual x86 processor.

One challenge in validating the simulator is extracting the machine state from the real processor. We use Intel's Pin tool [18] to insert dynamic instrumentation into a binary. The instrumentation dumps the values of the registers to a file after each instruction, and the values in memory after each system call. We then take the original binary and run it through our OCaml simulator, comparing the values of the registers after the RTL sequence for an instruction has been generated and interpreted. Unfortunately, this procedure sometimes generates false positives because of our occasional use of the oracle to handle undefined or under specified behaviors.

We use two different techniques to generate test cases to exercise the simulator. First, we generate small, random C programs using `Csmith` [34] and compile them using `GCC`. In this way, we simulated and verified over 10 million instruction instances in about 60 hours on an 8 core intel Xeon running at 2.6Ghz.

However, this technique does not exercise instructions that are avoided by compilers, and even some common instructions have encodings that are rarely emitted by assemblers. For example, our previously discussed bug in the encoding of the `MOV` instruction was not uncovered by such testing because it falls in this category.

A more thorough technique is to fuzz test our simulator by generating random sequences of bytes, which has previously proved effective in debugging CPU emulators [19]. Using our generative grammar, we randomly produce byte sequences that correspond to instructions we have specified. This lets us exercise unusual forms of all the instructions we define. For instance, an instruction like add with carry comes in fourteen different flavors, depending on the width and types of the operands, whether immediates are sign-extended, etc. Fuzzing such an instruction guarantees with some probability that all of these forms will be exercised.

3. The RockSalt NaCl Checker

Recall that our high level goal is to produce a checker for Native Client, which when given an x86 binary image, returns true only when the image respects the sandbox policy: when executed, the code will only read/write data from specified contiguous segments in memory, will not directly execute a particular set of instructions (*e.g.*, system calls), and will only transfer control within its own image or to a specified set of entry points in the NaCl run-time.

The 32-bit x86 version of NaCl takes advantage of the segment registers to enforce most aspects of this policy. In particular, by setting the `CS` (code), `DS` (data), `SS` (stack), and `GS` (thread-local) segment registers appropriately, the machine itself will ensure that data reads and writes are contained in the data segments, and that jumps are contained within the code segment. However, we must make sure that the untrusted instructions do not change the values of the segment registers, nor override the segments inappropriately.

At first glance, it appears sufficient to simply parse the binary into a sequence of instructions, and check that each instruction in the sequence preserves the values of the segment registers and does not override the segment registers with a prefix. Unfortunately, this simple strategy does not suffice. The problem is that, since the x86 has variable length instructions, we must not only consider the parse starting at the first byte, but all possible parses of the image. While most programs will respect the initial parse, a malicious or buggy program may not. For example, in a program that has a buffer overrun, a return address may be overwritten by a value that points into the middle of an instruction from the original parse.

To avoid this problem, NaCl provides a modified compiler that rewrites code to respect a stronger *alignment policy*, following the ideas of McCamant and Morrisett [20]. The alignment policy requires that all computed jumps (*i.e.*, jumps through a register) are aligned on a 32-byte boundary. This is ensured by inserting code to mask the target address with an appropriate constant, and by inserting no-ops so that potential jump targets are suitably aligned. In more detail, the aligned, sandbox policy requires that:

1. Starting with the first byte, the image parses into a legal sequence of instructions that preserve the segment registers;
2. Every 32nd byte is the beginning of an instruction in our parse;
3. Every indirect jump through a register r is immediately preceded by an instruction that masks r so that it is 32-byte aligned;
4. The masking operation and jump are both contained within a 32-byte-aligned block of instructions;
5. Each direct jump targets the beginning of an instruction and that instruction is not an indirect jump.

Requirements 4 and 5 are needed to ensure that the code cannot jump over the masking operation that protects an indirect jump.

3.1 Constructing a NaCl Checker

Google's NaCl checker is a hand-written `C` program that is intended to enforce the aligned, sandbox policy. Their checker partially decodes the binary, looking at fields such as the op-codes and mod/rm bits to determine whether the instruction is legal, and how long it is. Two auxiliary data structures are used: One is a bit-map that records which addresses are the starts of instructions. Each time an instruction is parsed, the corresponding bit for the address of the first byte is set. The other is an array of addresses for forward, direct jumps. After checking that the instructions are legal, the bit-map is checked to ensure that every 32nd byte is the start of an instruction. Then, the array of direct jump targets is checked to make sure they are valid according to the policy above.

There are two disadvantages with Google's checker: it is difficult to reason about because it is somewhat large (about 600 statements of code)[3] and the process of partial decoding is intertwined with policy enforcement. In particular, it is difficult to tell what instructions are supported and with what prefixes, and even more difficult to gain assurance that the resulting code enforces the appropriate sandbox policy. Furthermore, it is difficult to modify the code to *e.g.*, add new kinds of safe instructions or combinations of prefixes.

In contrast, the RockSalt checker we constructed and verified is relatively small, consisting of only about 80 lines of Coq code. This is because the checker uses table-driven DFA matching to handle the aspects of decoding, following an idea first proposed by Seaborn [31]. The basic idea is to break all instructions into four categories: (1) those that perform no control-flow, and are easily seen as okay; (2) those that perform a direct jump—we must check that the target is a valid instruction; (3) those that perform an indirect jump—we must check that the destination is appropriately masked; and (4) those instructions that should be rejected. Each of these classes, except the third one, can be described using a simple regular expression. The third class can be captured by a regular expression if we make the restriction that the masking operation must occur directly before the jump, which in practice is what the NaCl compiler does.

[3] To be fair, this includes CPU identification and support for floating-point and other instructions that we do not yet handle.

```
1. Bool verifier(DFA *NoControlFlow,
2.               DFA *DirectJump, DFA *MaskedJump,
3.               uint8_t *code, uint size)
4. {
5.   uint pos = 0, i, saved_pos;
6.   Bool b = TRUE;
7.   valid = (uint8_t *)calloc(size,sizeof(uint8_t));
8.   target = (uint8_t *)calloc(size,sizeof(uint8_t));
9.
10.  while (pos < size) {
11.    valid[pos] = TRUE;
12.    saved_pos = pos;
13.    if (match(MaskedJump,code,&pos,size)) continue;
14.    if (match(NoControlFlow,code,&pos,size)) continue;
15.    if (match(DirectJump,code,&pos,size) &&
16.        extract(code,saved_pos,pos,target)) continue;
17.    free(target); free(valid);
18.    return FALSE;
19.  }
20.
21.  for (i = 0; i < size; ++i)
22.    b = b && ( !(target[i]) || valid[i] ) &&
23.          ( i & 0x1F || valid[i] );
24.
25.  free(target); free(valid);
26.  return b;
27. }
```

Figure 5. Main Routine of our NaCl Checker

It is possible to extract OCaml code from our Coq definitions and use that as the core of the checker, but we elected to manually translate the code into C so that it would more easily integrate into the NaCl run-time. This avoids adding the OCaml compiler and run-time system to the trusted computing base, at the risk that our translation to C may have introduced an error. However, at under 100 lines of C code, we felt that this was a reasonable risk, since the vast majority of the information is contained in the DFA tables which are automatically generated and proven correct. Of course, one could try to use a verification tool, such as Frama-C/WP [9] or VCC [7], to prove the correctness of this version, in which case the functional code in Coq could serve as a specification.

Figure 5 shows the C code for the high-level verifier routine. This function relies upon two sub-routines, `match` and `extract` that we will explain later, but intuitively handle the aspects of decoding. Like Google's checker, the routine uses two auxiliary arrays: the `valid` array records those addresses in the code that are valid jump destinations, whereas the `target` array records those addresses that are jumped to by some direct control-flow operation. We used byte arrays instead of bit arrays to avoid having to reason about shifts and masks to read/write bits.

The main loop (line 10) iterates through the bytes in the `code` starting at position 0. This position is marked as `valid` and then we attempt to `match` the bytes at the current position against three patterns. The first pattern, `MaskedJump`, matches only when the bytes specify a mask of register r followed immediately by an indirect jump or call through r. Note that a successful match increments the position by `size` which records the length of the instruction(s), whereas a failure to match leaves the position unmodified. The second pattern, `NoControlFlow`, matches only when the bytes specify a legal NaCl instruction that does not affect control flow (*e.g.*, an arithmetic instruction). The third pattern, `DirectJump` matches only when the bytes specify a direct `JMP`, `Jcc` or `CALL` instruction. The routine `extract` then extracts the destination address of the jump, and marks that address in the `target` array. If none of these cases match, then the checker returns `FALSE` indicating that an illegal sequence of bytes was found in the code.

```
Bool match(DFA *A, uint8_t *code,
           uint *pos, uint size)
{
   uint8_t state = A->start;
   uint off = 0;

   while (*pos + off < size) {
     state = A->table[state][code[*pos + off]];
     off++;
     if (A->rejects[state]) break;
     if (A->accepts[state]) {
       *pos += off;
       return TRUE;
     }
   }
   return FALSE;
}
```

Figure 6. The DFA match routine

After the main loop terminates, we must check that (a) if an address is the target of a direct jump, then that address is the beginning of an instruction in our parse (line 22), and (b) if an address is aligned on a 32-byte boundary, then that address is the beginning of an instruction in our parse (line 23).

The process of matching a sequence of bytes against a pattern is handled by the routine `match` which is shown in Figure 6. The function simply executes the transitions of a DFA using the bytes at the current position in the code. The DFA has four fields: a starting state, a boolean array of accepting states, a boolean array of rejecting states, and a transition table that maps a state and byte to a new state.

3.2 DFA Generation

What we have yet to show are the definitions of the DFAs for the `MaskedJump`, `NoControlFlow`, and `DirectJump` patterns, and the correctness of our checker hinges crucially upon these definitions. These are generated from within Coq using higher-level specifications. In particular, for each of the patterns, we specify a grammar re-using the parsing DSL described in Section 2.1, and then compile that grammar to appropriate DFA tables. For example, the grammar for a `MaskedJump` is given below:

```
Definition nacl_MASK_p (r: register) :=
  "1000" $$ "0011" $$ "11" $$ "100"
  $$ bitslist (register_to_bools r)
  $  bitslist (int_to_bools safeMask).

Definition nacl_JMP_p  (r: register) :=
  "1111" $$ "1111" $$ "11" $$ "100"
  $$ bitslist (register_to_bools r).

Definition nacl_CALL_p (r: register) :=
  "1111" $$ "1111" $$ "11" $$ "010"
  $$ bitslist (register_to_bools r).

Definition nacljmp_p (r: register) :=
  nacl_MASK_p r $ (nacl_JMP_p r || nacl_CALL_p r).

Definition nacljmp_mask :=
  nacljmp_p EAX || nacljmp_p ECX || nacljmp_p EDX ||
  nacljmp_p EBX || nacljmp_p EBP || nacljmp_p ESI ||
  nacljmp_p EDI.
```

The `nacl_MASK_p` function takes a register name and generates a pattern for an "`AND` r, `safeMask`" instruction. The `nacl_JMP_p` and `nacl_CALL_p` functions take a register and generate patterns for a jump or call instruction (respectively) through that register. Thus, `nacljmp_mask` and the top-level grammar match any combination of a mask and jump through the same register (excluding `ESP`).

We compile grammars to DFAs from within Coq as follows: First, we strip off the semantic actions from the grammars so that we are left with a regular expression r_0. This regular expression corresponds to the starting state of the DFA. We use the `null` routine to check if this is an accepting state and a similar routine to check for rejection, and record this in a table. We then calculate the derivative of r_0 with respect to all 256 possible input bytes. This yields a set of regular expressions $\{r_1, r_2, \cdots, r_n\}$. Each r_i corresponds to a state in the DFA that is reachable from r_0. We assign each regular expression a state, and record whether that state is an accepting or rejecting state. We continue calculating derivatives of each of the r_i with respect to all possible inputs until we no longer create a new regular expression. The fact that there are a finite number of unique derivatives (up to the reductions performed by our smart constructors) was proven by Brzozowski [4] so we are ensured that the procedure terminates.

In practice, calculating a DFA in this fashion is almost as good as the usual construction [24], but avoids the need to formalize and reason about graphs. The degree to which we simplify regular expressions as we calculate derivatives determines how few states are left in the resulting DFA. In our case, the number of states is small enough (61 for the largest DFA) that we do not need to worry about further minimization.

3.3 Testing the C Checker

In the following section, we discuss the formal proof of correctness for the Coq version of the RockSalt checker. But as noted above, in practice we expect to use the C version, partially shown in figures 5 and 6. Although this code is a rather direct translation from the Coq code, to gain further assurance, we did extensive testing, comparing both positive and negative examples against Google's original checker.

For testing purposes, the `ncval` (Native Client Validator) command line tool was modified so that our verification routine can be used instead of Google's. We ensured that both verifiers reject a set of hand-crafted unsafe programs, and we also ensured that they both accept a set of benchmark programs once processed by the NaCl version of GCC which inserts appropriate no-ops and mask instructions. To work around the lack of floating-point support in our checker, we use the "-msoft-float" flag so that GCC avoids generating floating-point instructions. The benchmark programs were drawn from the same set as used in CompCert [16] and include an implementation of AES, SHA1, a virtual machine, fractal computation, a Perl interpreter, and 16 other programs representing more than 4,000 lines of code. We also used Csmith [34] to automatically generate C programs, and compiled them with NaCl's version of GCC. We then verified that our driver and Google's always agreed on a program's safety. Using this method we have verified over two thousand small C programs.

Finally, we measured the time it takes to check binaries using both our C checker and Google's original code. For the small benchmarks mentioned above, there was no measurable difference in checking times. However, on an artificially generated C program of about 200,000 lines of code, running on a 2.6 GHz Intel Xeon core, Google's checker took 0.90 seconds and our checker took 0.24 seconds (averaging over one hundred runs). Consequently, we believe that RockSalt is competitive with Google's approach.

4. Proof of Correctness for the Checker

After building and testing the checker, we wanted to prove its correctness with respect to the sandbox policy. That is, we wanted a proof that if the checker returns `TRUE` for a given input binary, and if that binary is loaded and executed in an appropriate environment (in particular, where the code and data segments are disjoint), then executing the binary would ensure that only the prescribed data segments are read and written, and control only transfers within the prescribed code segment.

At a high-level, our proof shows that at every step of the program execution, the values of the segment registers are the same as those in the initial state, and furthermore, that the bytes that make up the code-segment are the same bytes that were analyzed by the checker. These invariants are sufficient to show NaCl's sandbox policy is not violated. Furthermore, the checker should have ruled out system calls and other instructions that are not allowed. But of course, formalizing this argument requires a much more detailed set of invariants that connect the matching work done in the checker to the semantics, along with the issues of alignment, masking, and jump-destination checks.

We begin by defining the notion of an *appropriate* machine state:

DEFINITION 1. *A machine state is* appropriate *when:*

1. *the original data and code segments are disjoint,*
2. *the* `DS`, `SS`, *and* `GS` *segment registers point to their respective original segments,*
3. *the* `CS` *segment registers point to the original code segment,*
4. *the program counter points within the code segment, and*
5. *the original bytes of the program are stored in the code segment.*

Appropriateness captures the key data invariants that we need to maintain throughout execution of the program. We augment these data invariants with a predicate on the program counter to reach the definition of a *locally-safe* machine state:

DEFINITION 2. *A machine state is* locally-safe *when it is appropriate and the program counter holds an address corresponding to the start of an instruction that was matched by the* `verify` *process using one of the three generated DFAs.*

In other words, for a locally safe state, the `pc` is marked as `valid`.

We would like to argue that, starting from a locally-safe state, we can always execute an instruction and end up in a locally-safe state. This would imply that the segment registers have not changed, that the code has not changed, that any read or write done by the instruction would be limited to the original data segments, and that control remains within the original code segment.

Alas, we do not immediately reach a locally-safe state after executing one instruction. The problem is that our `MaskedJump` DFA operates over two instructions (the mask of the register, followed by the indirect jump). Thus, we introduce the notion of a *k-safe* state:

DEFINITION 3. *An appropriate state s is k-safe when $k > 0$ and, for any s' such that $s \longrightarrow s'$, either s' is locally-safe or s' is $(k-1)$-safe.*

With the definitions given above, it suffices to show that if a state is locally-safe, then it is also k-safe for some k (and in fact, k is either 1 or 2). Indeed, each locally-safe state s should be k-safe for some k: if $s \longrightarrow s'$ then either s' is locally-safe or we executed the mask of a `MaskedJump` and we should be in an appropriate state, ready to execute a branch instruction that will target a masked (and therefore valid) address. Then, assuming the computation starts in a locally-safe state (*e.g.*, with the `pc` at any valid address), it is easy to see that the code cannot step to a state where the segment registers have changed, or the bytes in the code segment have changed.

THEOREM 1. *If s is locally-safe, then it is also k-safe for some k.*

Since a locally-safe instruction has a program counter drawn from the set of `valid` instructions, and since the verifier did not return `FALSE`, we can conclude that a prefix of the bytes starting at this address matches one of the three DFAs. We must then argue that for each class of instructions that match the DFAs, after executing the instruction, we either end up in a locally-safe state or else after executing one more instruction, end up in a locally safe-state.

In the Section 4.1, we sketch the connection we formalized between the DFAs and a set of inversion principles that characterize the possible instructions that they can match. These principles allow us to do a case analysis on a subset of the possible instructions. For example, in the case that the `MaskedJump` DFA matches, we know that the bytes referenced by the program counter must decode into a masking operation on some register r, followed by bytes that decode into a jump or call to register r. The proof proceeds by case analysis for each of the three DFAs utilizing these inversion principles.

The easiest (though largest) case is when the `NoControlFlow` DFA has the successful match. We prove three properties for each non-control-flow instruction I that the inversion principle gives us:

(1) executing I does not modify segment registers;

(2) executing I modifies only the data segments' memory;

(3) after executing I, the new program counter is equal to the old program counter plus the length of I.

For the most part, arguing these cases is simple: For the first property, we simply iterate over the generated list of RTLs for I and ensure there are no writes to the segment registers. The second property follows from the inversion principles which forbid the use of a segment override prefix, and the third property follows from the semantics of non-control-flow instructions. From these three facts, it follows that after executing the instruction, we are immediately in a locally-safe state. That is, the original state was 1-safe.

In the case where I was matched by `DirectJump`, we must argue that the final loop in `verify` ensures that the target of the jump is `valid`. Of course, we must also show that the segment registers are preserved, the code is preserved, *etc.* But then we can again argue that the original state was 1-safe.

For the `MaskedJump` case, we must argue that the state is 2-safe. The inversion principle for the DFA restricts the first instruction to an `AND` of a particular register r with a constant that ensures after the step, the value of r is aligned on a 32-byte boundary, the segments are preserved, and the `pc` points to bytes within the code segment that decode into either a jump or call through r. We then argue that this state is 1-safe. Since the destination of the jump or call is 32-byte aligned, the final loop of the verifier has checked that this address is `valid`. Consequently, it is easy to show that we end up in a locally-safe state.

4.1 Inverting the DFAs

A critical piece in our proof of correctness is the relationship between the DFAs generated from the `NoControlFlow`, `DirectJump`, and `MaskedJump` regular expressions and our semantics for machine instructions. We sketch the key results that we have proven here.

One theorem specifies the connection between a regular expression, the DFA it generates, and the `match` procedure:

THEOREM 2. *If r is a regular expression, and D is the DFA generated from that regular expression, then executing* `match` *on D with a sequence of bytes $b_1, \ldots, b_n$ will return* `true` *if there is some $j \leq n$ such that the string $b_1, \ldots, b_j$ is in the denotation of r.*

The theorem requires proving that our DFA construction process, where we iteratively calculate all derivatives, produces a well-formed DFA with respect to r. Here, a well-formed DFA basically provides a mapping from states to derivatives of r that respect certain closure properties. Fortunately, the algebraic construction of the DFA makes proving this result relatively straightforward. The theorem also requires showing that running `match` on D with $b_1, \ldots, b_n$ is correct which entails, among other things, showing that the array accesses are in bounds, and that when we return `TRUE`, we are in a state that corresponds to the derivative of the regular expression with respect to the string $b_1, \ldots, b_j$.

Another key set of lemmas show that the languages accepted by the regular expressions are subsets of the languages accepted by our `x86grammar`. Additionally, we must prove an inversion principle for each regular expression that characterizes the possible abstract syntax we get when we run the semantics on the bytes. For example, we must show that `DirectJump` only matches bytes that when parsed, produce either (near) `JMP`, `Jcc`, or `CALL` instructions with an immediate operand. Fortunately, proving the language containment property and inversion principles is simple to do using the denotational semantics for grammars.

One of the most difficult properties to prove about the decoder was the uniqueness of parsing. In particular, we needed to show that each bit pattern corresponded to at most one instruction, and no instruction's bit pattern was a prefix of another instruction's bit pattern—*i.e.*, that our `x86grammar` was unambiguous. A naive approach, where we simply explore all possible bit patterns is obviously intractable, when there are instructions up to 15 bytes long. Another approach is to construct a DFA for the grammar and then show that each accepting state has at most one semantic value associated with it. While this is possible, the challenge is getting Coq to symbolically evaluate the DFA construction and reduce the semantic actions in a reasonable amount of time[4].

Consequently, we constructed a simple procedure that checks whether the intersection of two grammars is empty. The procedure, which only succeeds on star-free grammars (stripped of their semantic actions) works by generalizing the notion of a derivative from characters to star-free regular expressions:

$$
\begin{array}{rcl}
\texttt{Deriv}\ g\ \texttt{Eps} & = & g \\
\texttt{Deriv}\ g\ (\texttt{Char}\ c) & = & \texttt{deriv}_c\ g \\
\texttt{Deriv}\ g\ \texttt{Any} & = & \texttt{DrvAny}\ g \\
\texttt{Deriv}\ g\ \texttt{Void} & = & \texttt{Void} \\
\texttt{Deriv}\ g\ (\texttt{Alt}\ g_1\ g_2) & = & \texttt{Alt}\ (\texttt{Deriv}\ g\ g_1)\ (\texttt{Deriv}\ g\ g_2) \\
\texttt{Deriv}\ g\ (\texttt{Cat}\ g_1\ g_2) & = & \texttt{Deriv}\ (\texttt{Deriv}\ g\ g_1)\ g_2
\end{array}
$$

where

$$
\begin{array}{rcl}
\texttt{DrvAny}\ \texttt{Any} & = & \texttt{Eps} \\
\texttt{DrvAny}\ (\texttt{Char}\ c) & = & \texttt{Eps} \\
\texttt{DrvAny}\ \texttt{Eps} & = & \texttt{Void} \\
\texttt{DrvAny}\ \texttt{Void} & = & \texttt{Void} \\
\texttt{DrvAny}\ (\texttt{Alt}\ g_1\ g_2) & = & \texttt{Alt}\ (\texttt{DrvAny}\ g_1)\ (\texttt{DrvAny}\ g_2) \\
\texttt{DrvAny}\ (\texttt{Cat}\ g_1\ g_2) & = & \texttt{Alt}\ (\texttt{Cat}\ (\texttt{DrvAny}\ g_1)\ g_2) \\
& & \quad (\texttt{Cat}\ (\texttt{null}\ g_1)\ (\texttt{DrvAny}\ g_2))
\end{array}
$$

When it is defined, it is easy to show that:

$$\texttt{Deriv}\ g_1\ g_2 = \{s_2 \mid \exists s_1 . s_1 \in g_2 \wedge s_1 s_2 \in g_1\}$$

and thus, when $\texttt{Deriv}\ g_1\ g_2 \rightarrow \texttt{Void}$, we can conclude that there is no string in the intersection of the domains of g_1 and g_2, and furthermore, g_2's strings are not a prefix of those in g_1. This allowed us to easily prove (through Coq's symbolic evaluation) that the `x86grammar` is unambiguous: We simply recursively descend into the grammar, and each time we encounter an `Alt`, check that the intersection of the two sub-grammars is empty.

5. Related Work

With the growing interest in verification of software tools, formal models of processors that support machine-checked proofs have be-

[4] Recall that that the DFAs generated for the NaCl checker strip the semantic actions, so they do not need to worry about reducing semantic actions.

come a hot topic. Often, these models have limitations, not because of any inherent design flaw, but rather because they are meant only to prove specific properties. For example, work on formal verification of compilers [5, 16] only needs to consider the subset of the instructions that compilers use. Moreover, these compilers emit assembly instructions and do not prove semantics preservation all the way down to machine code, so their model leaves out the tricky problem of decoding. The same kinds of limitations exist for the processor models used in the formal verification of operating systems [6]. Some projects focus on one specific part of the model, for instance the media instructions [14], and some others [20] model just a few instructions mostly as a proof of concept. Even though we are focused here on NaCl verification, our long term goal is to develop a general model of the x86 so we have tried hard to achieve a more open and scalable design.

There are several projects focused on the development of general formal models of processors. Some projects have considered the formalizations of RISC processors [1, 11, 21]. As noted, developing a formal model for the x86 poses many new problems, partly because decoding is significantly more complex, but also for the definition and validation of such a vast number of instructions (over 1,000) with so many variations, from addressing modes to prefixes.

One model close in spirit to our own is the Y86 formalization in ACL2 by Ray [29]. Like our model, Ray's provides an executable simulator. However, the Y86 is a much smaller fragment (about 30 instructions), and has a much simpler instruction encoding (*e.g.*, no prefixes).

Perhaps the closest related research project, and the one from which we took much inspiration in our design, is the work on modeling x86 multi-processor memory models [25, 30, 32]. This work comes with a formal model of about 20 instructions, and we borrowed many of the ideas, such as the use of high-level grammars for specifying the decoder. However, their focus was on issues of non-determinism where it is seemingly more natural to use predicates to describe the possible behaviors of programs. The price paid is that validation requires symbolic evaluation and theorem proving to compare abstract machine states to concrete ones. Although this was largely automated, we believe that our functional approach provides a more scalable way to test the model. Indeed, we have been able to run three orders of magnitude more tests. On the other hand, it remains to be seen how effective our approach will be when we add support for concurrency.

Our decoder, formalized in Coq, uses parsers generated from regular expressions using the idea of derivatives. Others have formalized derivative-based regular expression *matching* [2] but not parsing. However, more general parser generators for algorithms such as SLR and LR have recently been formalized [3, 13].

The original idea for Software-based fault isolation (SFI) was introduced by Wahbe *et. al.* [33] in the context of a RISC machine. This work used an invariant on dedicated registers to ensure that all reads, writes, and jumps were appropriately isolated. Of course, parsing was not a problem because instructions had a uniform length. As noted earlier, McCamant and Morrisett [20] introduced the idea of the alignment constraint to handle variable-length instruction sets. In that paper, they formalized a small subset of the x86 (7 instructions) using ACL2 and proved that their high-level invariants were respected by those instructions, but did not prove the correctness of their checker. In fact, even with the small number of instructions, Kroll and Dean found a number of bugs in the decoder [15], which reinforces our argument that one should be wary of a trusted decoder or disassembler.

Pilkiewicz [26] developed a formally verified SFI checker in Coq for a simple assembly language.

6. Future work & Conclusions

We have presented a formal model for a significant subset of the x86, and a new formally verified checker for Native Client called RockSalt. The primary challenge in this work was building a model for an architecture as complicated as the x86. Although we only managed to model a small subset, we believe that the design is relatively robust thanks to our ability to extract and test executable code. The experience in using the model to reason about a simple but real policy such as NaCl's sandbox, provides some assurance that the model will be useful for reasoning in other contexts.

6.1 Future Work

As explained before, our x86 model is far from complete. We do not yet handle floating-point instructions, system programming instructions, nor any of the MMX, SSEn, 3dNow! or IA-64 instructions. On the other hand, we have managed to cover enough instructions that we can compile real applications and run them through the simulator. Moving forward, we would like to extend the model to cover at least those instructions that are used by compilers.

Our model of machine states is also overly simple. For example, we do not yet model concurrency, interrupts, or page tables. However, we believe that the use of RTL as a staging language makes it easier to add support for those features. For example, to model multiple processors and the total-store order (TSO) memory consistency model [32], we believe that it is sufficient to add a store buffer to the machine state for each processor. Of course, validating a concurrent model will present new challenges.

We believe that the use of domain-specific languages will further facilitate re-use and help to find and eliminate bugs. For example, one could imagine embedding these languages in other proof assistants (HOL, ACL2, *etc.*) to support portability of the specification across formal systems.

We would also like to close the gap on RockSalt so that the `C` code, derived from our verified Coq code, is itself verified and compiled with a proven-correct compiler such as CompCert. In fact, one fun idea is to simply bypass the compiler and write the checker directly in x86 assembly to see how easy it is to turn the process in on itself. Finally, there are richer classes of policies, such as XFI, for which we would like to write checkers and prove correctness.

6.2 Lessons Learned

The basic idea of using domain-specific languages to build a scalable semantics worked well for us. In our first iteration of the model, we tried to directly interpret x86 instructions, but soon realized that any reasoning work would be proportional to the number of distinct instructions. Compiling instructions to a small RISC-like core simplified our reasoning, and at the same time, made it easier to factor the model into smaller, more re-usable components.

One surprising aspect of the work was that the pressure to provide reasoning principles for parsers forced us to treat the problem more algebraically than is typically done. In particular, the use of derivatives, which operate directly on the abstract syntax of grammars, made our reasoning much simpler than it would be with graphs.

It goes without saying that constructing machine-checked proofs is still very hard. The definitions for our x86 model and NaCl checker are about 5,000 lines of heavily commented Coq code, but the RockSalt proofs are another 10,000 lines. Of course, many of these proofs will be useful in other settings (*e.g.*, that the decoder is unambiguous) but the ratio is still quite large. One reason for this is that reasoning about certain theories (*e.g.*, bit vectors) is still rather tedious in Coq, especially when compared to modern SAT or SMT solvers. Yet, the dependent types and higher-order features of the language were crucial for constructing the model, much less proving deep properties about it.

For us, another surprising aspect of the work was the difference that comes with scale. We have a fair amount of experience modeling simple abstract machines with proof assistants. Doing a case split on five or even ten instructions and manually discharging the cases is reasonable. But once you have hundreds of cases, any of which may change as you validate the model, such an approach is no longer tenable. Consequently, many of our proofs were actually done through some form of reflection. For example, to prove that the `x86grammar` is unambiguous, we constructed a computable function that tests for ambiguity and proved its correctness. In turn, this made it easier to add new instructions to the grammar. Frankly, we couldn't stomach the idea of proving the correctness of a hand-written x86 decoder, and so we were forced into finding a better solution. In short, when a mechanized development reaches a certain size, we are forced to develop more automated and robust proof techniques.

References

[1] J. Alglave, A. C. J. Fox, S. Ishtiaq, M. O. Myreen, S. Sarkar, P. Sewell, and F. Z. Nardelli. The semantics of Power and ARM multiprocessor machine code. In *Proc. of the Workshop on Declarative Aspects of Multicore Programming*, pages 13–24. ACM, 2009.

[2] J. B. Almeida, N. Moreira, D. Pereira, and S. M. de Sousa. Partial derivative automata formalized in Coq. In *Proc. of the 15th Intl. Conf. on Implementation and Application of Automata*, number 6482 in CIAA '10, pages 59–68. Springer-Verlag, Aug. 2010.

[3] A. Barthwal and M. Norrish. Verified, executable parsing. In *European Symp. on Programming*, ESOP '09, pages 160–174. LNCS, 2009.

[4] J. A. Brzozowski. Derivatives of regular expressions. *Journal of the ACM*, 11:481–494, 1964.

[5] A. Chlipala. A verified compiler for an impure functional language. In *Proc. of the 37th ACM SIGPLAN-SIGACT Symp. on Principles of Programming Languages*, pages 93–106. ACM, 2010.

[6] D. Cock. Lyrebird: assigning meanings to machines. In *Proc. of the 5th Intl. Conf. on Systems Software Verification*, SSV'10, pages 6–15. USENIX Association, 2010.

[7] E. Cohen, M. Dahlweid, M. Hillebrand, D. Leinenbach, M. Moskal, T. Santen, W. Schulte, and S. Tobies. VCC: A practical system for verifying concurrent C. In *Proc. of the 22nd Intl. Conf. on Theorem Proving in Higher Order Logics*, TPHOLs '09, pages 23–42. Springer-Verlag, 2009.

[8] Coq development team. The Coq proof assistant. `http://coq.inria.fr/`, 1989–2012.

[9] L. Correnson, Z. Dargaye, and A. Pacalet. *WP plug-in manual*. CEA LIST.

[10] J. Dias and N. Ramsey. Automatically generating instruction selectors using declarative machine descriptions. In *Proc. of the 37th ACM SIGPLAN-SIGACT Symp. on Principles of Programming Languages*, POPL '10, pages 403–416. ACM, 2010.

[11] A. C. J. Fox and M. O. Myreen. A trustworthy monadic formalization of the ARMv7 instruction set architecture. In *Interactive Theorem Proving*, volume 6172 of *LNCS*, pages 243–258. Springer, 2010.

[12] Intel Corporation. *Pentium Processor Family Developers Manual*, volume 3. Intel Corporation, 1996.

[13] J.-H. Jourdan, F. Pottier, and X. Leroy. Validating LR(1) parsers. In *European Symp. on Programming*, ESOP '12. Springer, 2012. To appear.

[14] W. A. H. Jr. and S. Swords. Centaur technology media unit verification. In *Computer Aided Verification, 21st Intl. Conf.*, volume 5643 of *LNCS*, pages 353–367. Springer, 2009.

[15] J. Kroll and D. Dean. BakerSFIeld: Bringing software fault isolation to x64. `http://www.cs.princeton.edu/~kroll/papers/bakersfield-sfi.pdf`.

[16] X. Leroy. Formal verification of a realistic compiler. *Commun. of the ACM*, 52(7):107–115, 2009.

[17] J. Lim. *Transformer Specification Language: A System for Generating Analyzers and its Applications*. PhD thesis, University of Wisconsin-Madison, May 2011.

[18] C.-K. Luk, R. Cohn, R. Muth, H. Patil, A. Klauser, G. Lowney, S. Wallace, V. J. Reddi, and K. Hazelwood. Pin: building customized program analysis tools with dynamic instrumentation. In *Proc. of the ACM SIGPLAN Conf. on Programming Language Design and Implementation*, PLDI '05, pages 190–200. ACM, 2005.

[19] L. Martignoni, R. Paleari, G. F. Roglia, and D. Bruschi. Testing CPU emulators. In *Proc. of the 18th Intl. Symp. on Software Testing and Analysis*, pages 261–272. ACM, 2009.

[20] S. McCamant and G. Morrisett. Evaluating SFI for a CISC architecture. In *Proc. of the 15th Conf. on USENIX Security Symp.*, pages 209–224. USENIX Association, 2006.

[21] N. G. Michael and A. W. Appel. Machine instruction syntax and semantics in higher order logic. In *Automated Deduction - CADE-17, 17th Intl. Conf. on Automated Deduction*, volume 1831 of *LNCS*, pages 7–24. Springer, 2000.

[22] M. Might, D. Darais, and D. Spiewak. Parsing with derivatives: a functional pearl. In *Proc. of the 16th ACM SIGPLAN Intl. Conf. on Functional Programming*, ICFP '11, pages 189–195. ACM, 2011.

[23] Native Client team. Native client security contest. `http://code.google.com/contests/nativeclient-security/index.html`, 2009.

[24] S. Owens, J. Reppy, and A. Turon. Regular-expression derivatives re-examined. *J. Funct. Program.*, 19:173–190, March 2009.

[25] S. Owens, P. Böhm, F. Z. Nardelli, and P. Sewell. Lem: A lightweight tool for heavyweight semantics. In *Interactive Theorem Proving*, volume 6898 of *LNCS*, pages 363–369. Springer, 2011.

[26] A. Pilkiewicz. A proved version of the inner sandbox. In *native-client-discuss mailing list*, April 2011.

[27] N. Ramsey and J. W. Davidson. Machine descriptions to build tools for embedded systems. In *Languages, Compilers, and Tools for Embedded Systems*, volume 1474 of *LNCS*, pages 176–192. Springer, 1998.

[28] N. Ramsey and M. F. Fernandez. Specifying representations of machine instructions. *ACM Trans. Program. Lang. Syst.*, 19(3):492–524, 1997.

[29] S. Ray. Towards a formalization of the X86 instruction set architecture. Technical Report TR-08-15, Department of Computer Science, University of Texas at Austin, March 2008.

[30] S. Sarkar, P. Sewell, F. Z. Nardelli, S. Owens, T. Ridge, T. Braibant, M. O. Myreen, and J. Alglave. The semantics of x86-CC multiprocessor machine code. In *Proc. of the 36th ACM SIGPLAN-SIGACT Symp. on Principles of Programming Languages*, pages 379–391. ACM, 2009.

[31] M. Seaborn. A DFA-based x86-32 validator for Native Client. In *native-client-discuss mailing list*, June 2011.

[32] P. Sewell, S. Sarkar, S. Owens, F. Z. Nardelli, and M. O. Myreen. x86-TSO: a rigorous and usable programmer's model for x86 multiprocessors. *Commun. ACM*, 53(7):89–97, 2010.

[33] R. Wahbe, S. Lucco, T. E. Anderson, and S. L. Graham. Efficient software-based fault isolation. In *Proc. of the 14th ACM Symp. on Operating Systems Principles*, SOSP '93, pages 203–216. ACM, 1993.

[34] X. Yang, Y. Chen, E. Eide, and J. Regehr. Finding and understanding bugs in C compilers. In *Proc. of the 32nd ACM SIGPLAN Conf. on Programming Language Design and Implementation*, PLDI '11, pages 283–294. ACM, 2011.

[35] B. Yee, D. Sehr, G. Dardyk, J. B. Chen, R. Muth, T. Ormandy, S. Okasaka, N. Narula, and N. Fullagar. Native Client: a sandbox for portable, untrusted x86 native code. *Commun. of the ACM*, 53(1):91–99, 2010.

[36] L. Zhao, G. Li, B. D. Sutter, and J. Regehr. Armor: Fully verified software fault isolation. In *11th Intl. Conf. on Embedded Software*. ACM, 2011.

Synthesizing Software Verifiers from Proof Rules

Sergey Grebenshchikov
Technische Universität München
grebensh@cs.tum.edu

Nuno P. Lopes
INESC-ID / IST - TU Lisbon
nuno.lopes@ist.utl.pt

Corneliu Popeea
Technische Universität München
popeea@model.in.tum.de

Andrey Rybalchenko
Technische Universität München
rybal@in.tum.de

Abstract

Automatically generated tools can significantly improve programmer productivity. For example, parsers and dataflow analyzers can be automatically generated from declarative specifications in the form of grammars, which tremendously simplifies the task of implementing a compiler. In this paper, we present a method for the automatic synthesis of software verification tools. Our synthesis procedure takes as input a description of the employed proof rule, e.g., program safety checking via inductive invariants, and produces a tool that automatically discovers the auxiliary assertions required by the proof rule, e.g., inductive loop invariants and procedure summaries. We rely on a (standard) representation of proof rules using recursive equations over the auxiliary assertions. The discovery of auxiliary assertions, i.e., solving the equations, is based on an iterative process that extrapolates solutions obtained for finitary unrollings of equations. We show how our method synthesizes automatic safety and liveness verifiers for programs with procedures, multi-threaded programs, and functional programs. Our experimental comparison of the resulting verifiers with existing state-of-the-art verification tools confirms the practicality of the approach.

Categories and Subject Descriptors D.2.4 [*Software Engineering*]: Software/Program Verification; D.4.5 [*Operating Systems*]: Reliability—Verification; F.3.1 [*Logics and Meanings of Programs*]: Specifying and Verifying and Reasoning about Programs

Keywords Proof rules, verification tool synthesis, software verification, software model checking

1. Introduction

Developing tools that deal with programs, e.g., parsers, compilers, analyzers, or verifiers, is a difficult yet necessary task for increasing programmer productivity. Programs are complex artifacts and their treatment within a tool requires careful consideration of various intricate aspects of program syntax and semantics. Tool synthesis offers an attractive alternative to manual tool development. Once a tool generator is developed for a given problem domain, it can be used to synthesize various tools that deal with particular problem instances in the given domain. For example, in the problem domain of parsing, a parser generator allows one to synthesize parsers for particular (programming) languages [1]. Each parser is synthesized by the generator from a language specification in the form of a grammar. Furthermore, static analyzers (including pointer alias analyzers) can be generated from attribute grammars [47], dataflow equations [29, 31], equations in the form of set constraints [2, 3, 27], or equations as Datalog rules [28, 34, 51]. These approaches take an analysis specification as a set of equations and produce an analyzer that infers program properties by solving the equations.

Recently, property verifiers became a target for automated tool construction. For example, the GETAFIX tool for checking Boolean programs was synthesized from a logical formula in μ-calculus using a BDD-based fixpoint solver [49]. Still, software verification tools such as SLAM [4], BLAST [20, 21], FSOFT [23], IMPACT [33], TERMINATOR [11], CPACHECKER [7], or DSOLVE [24, 43], are developed from the ground up in a complex manual effort that takes into account particularities of domain specific reasoning for the applied verification method. The development efforts may need to be repeated to a large extent once a different proof rule is employed, or programs in a different programming language are considered as input. This status quo hinders the advancement of the state-of-the-art in software verification, makes it prohibitively expensive to develop new verification methods and provide verification tools for the growing number of application domains. Without automatic tool support for the development of software verifiers, we cannot deliver required tools for improving software reliability and leave software developers alone in dealing with the increasing complexity of modern software systems.

In this paper we present a method for automating the development of software verification tools by providing the following key ingredients: a methodology for describing verification methods for reachability and termination properties as constraint solving problems, and an efficient solver for the resulting constraints. As a result, developing a new software verifier will become a two-step process: i) design and specification of a verification method in the form of constraints supported by our methodology, and ii) construction of a frontend that generates constraints from software source code. The main effort will be spent in the formulation of a suitable verification method, which is a creative activity that usually leverages existing methods and adapts them to new application domains. The frontend construction usually requires writing a translator from the compiler's intermediate representation into the language of constraints, which is a well-established routine. We be-

PLDI'12, June 11–16, 2012, Beijing, China.

```
    int sum(int n) {
      int s;
1:    if (n > 0) {
2:      s = sum(n-1);
3:      return s+n;
      } else {
4:      return 0;
      }
5: }
```

$$
\begin{aligned}
V &= (\mathtt{n}, \mathtt{s}, \mathtt{ret}, \mathtt{pc}) \\
\mathit{init}(V) &= (\mathtt{pc} = \ell_1) \\
\rho(V, V') &= (\mathtt{n} \geq 1 \wedge \mathit{move}(\ell_1, \ell_2) \wedge \mathit{skip}(\mathtt{n}, \mathtt{s}, \mathtt{ret})) \vee \\
&\quad\ (\mathtt{ret}' = \mathtt{s} + \mathtt{n} \wedge \mathit{move}(\ell_3, \ell_5) \wedge \mathit{skip}(\mathtt{n}, \mathtt{s})) \vee \\
&\quad\ (\mathtt{n} \leq 0 \wedge \mathit{move}(\ell_1, \ell_4) \wedge \mathit{skip}(\mathtt{n}, \mathtt{s}, \mathtt{ret})) \vee \\
&\quad\ (\mathtt{ret}' = 0 \wedge \mathit{move}(\ell_4, \ell_5) \wedge \mathit{skip}(\mathtt{n}, \mathtt{s})) \\
\mathit{call}(V, V') &= (\mathtt{n}' = \mathtt{n} - 1 \wedge \mathit{move}(\ell_2, \ell_1)) \\
\mathit{ret}(V, V') &= (\mathtt{s}' = \mathtt{ret} \wedge \mathit{move}(\ell_5, \ell_3)) \\
\mathit{loc}(V, V') &= (\mathit{skip}(\mathtt{n}, \mathtt{ret}) \wedge \mathit{move}(\ell_2, \ell_3))
\end{aligned}
$$

Figure 1. An example program and its representation as a transition system. $\mathit{skip}(v_1, \ldots, v_k)$ abbreviates the conjunction $v_1' = v_1 \wedge \cdots \wedge v_k' = v_k$. $\mathit{move}(\ell, \ell')$ abbreviates the conjunction $\mathtt{pc} = \ell \wedge \mathtt{pc}' = \ell'$.

lieve that our method offers promising potential to boost the development (and deployment) of software verifiers in the same way the parser generators paved the way to modern approaches to compiler construction.

Our method focuses on automatic construction of verification tools that implement proof rules for reachability and termination properties in the form of Horn(-like) clauses, see e.g. [30]. Proof rules in such form are shown to be sufficiently expressive and practically adequate for dealing with a wide range of programming languages (including sequential, concurrent, and functional programs), temporal specifications and verification techniques, see e.g. [13, 18, 19, 37, 42, 43]. We present an efficient algorithm for solving Horn-like clauses by generalizing state-of-the-art software verification algorithms, in particular counterexample guided abstraction and refinement schemes. To demonstrate the feasibility of our approach in practice, we apply our solving algorithm in combination with appropriate constraint generation frontends to develop a collection of verifiers for temporal properties of programs with procedures, multi-threaded programs, and functional programs.

This paper makes the following contributions.

- Conceptually, we identify a formulation of proof rules for reachability and termination properties in the form of Horn-like clauses suitable for automation using state-of-the-art techniques for software verification.
- Technically, we provide an algorithm for solving Horn-like clauses that is based on a generalization of the state-of-the-art counterexample guided abstraction refinement schemes.
- Practically, we present an implementation of our approach and its evaluation on important proof rules for the verification of transition systems, programs with procedures, multi-threaded programs, and functional programs.

2. Illustration

We illustrate our verification approach using a simple example for which we prove a safety and a termination property.

2.1 Verifying programs with procedures

See Figure 1 for an example program implementing a sum computation. The procedure `sum` takes an argument `n` and returns the sum of the numbers between 1 and `n`, or 0 if its argument `n` is not positive. We assume that the program state is given by a valuation of the program variables $V = (\mathtt{n}, \mathtt{s}, \mathtt{ret}, \mathtt{pc})$. The variable `ret` models return value passing, while `pc` is a procedure-local program counter variable that keeps track of the current control location. The initial states of the program are given as an assertion $\mathit{init}(V)$, where ℓ_1 indicates the program line labeled 1. We use assertions over a tuple of variables V and its primed version V' to model program statements as binary relations over states. In our program, $\rho(V, V')$ represents intra-procedural statements. $\mathit{call}(V, V')$ and $\mathit{ret}(V, V')$ model parameter and return value passing, respectively. The last assertion $\mathit{loc}(V, V')$ ensures that the caller's local data variables are unchanged during the callee's execution, while the caller's program counter moves over the call site. The set of local variables that are kept unchanged by the assertion $\mathit{loc}(V, V')$ excludes `s` , which is assigned by the call statement.

Proving safety We prove that `sum` always returns a non-negative value and formalize this property by the assertion $\mathit{error}(V) = (\mathtt{pc} = \ell_5 \wedge \mathtt{ret} < 0)$. To prove the property, we rely on a summarization proof rule for programs with procedures [42]. This proof rule requires the construction of an auxiliary assertion $\mathit{Summ}(V, V')$ that represents a binary relation between entry states of a procedure and their successors on the same level of recursion. The following constraints over $\mathit{Summ}(V, V')$ guarantee that all necessary pairs of states are captured.

$$
\begin{aligned}
&\mathit{init}(V) \wedge V = V' \rightarrow \mathit{Summ}(V, V') \\
&\mathit{Summ}(V, V') \wedge \rho(V', V'') \rightarrow \mathit{Summ}(V, V'') \\
&\mathit{Summ}(V, V') \wedge \mathit{call}(V', V'') \wedge V'' = V''' \rightarrow \mathit{Summ}(V'', V''') \\
&\mathit{Summ}(V, V') \wedge \mathit{call}(V', V'') \wedge \mathit{Summ}(V'', V''') \wedge \\
&\qquad \mathit{ret}(V''', V'''') \wedge \mathit{loc}(V', V'''') \rightarrow \mathit{Summ}(V, V'''')
\end{aligned}
$$

We obtain a correctness proof if we can find an instance of Summ that satisfies the above constraints together with the implication $\mathit{Summ}(V, V') \wedge \mathit{error}(V') \rightarrow \mathit{false}$. The following disjunction is a solution that is computed by our proposed Horn solving algorithm.

$$
\begin{aligned}
\mathit{Summ}(V, V') = {} & (\mathtt{pc} = \ell_1 \wedge \mathtt{pc}' \in \{\ell_1, \ell_4\}) \vee \\
& (\mathtt{pc} = \ell_1 \wedge \mathtt{pc}' = \ell_2 \wedge \mathtt{n}' \geq 1) \vee \\
& (\mathtt{pc} = \ell_1 \wedge \mathtt{pc}' = \ell_3 \wedge \mathtt{n}' + \mathtt{s}' \geq 1) \vee \\
& (\mathtt{pc} = \ell_1 \wedge \mathtt{pc}' = \ell_5 \wedge \mathtt{ret}' \geq 0)
\end{aligned}
$$

Note that the last disjunct ensures the non-negativeness of the return value.

Proving termination For proving that `sum` terminates on every input, we require that a so-called recursion relation between entry states of the caller and its immediate callee is well-founded, i.e., it does not admit infinite chains. We obtain the recursion relation by relational composition of the summary with the parameter passing relation. Hence, for proving termination, we need to find an assertion $\mathit{Summ}(V, V')$ that satisfies the above implications ensuring the summarization property and the following well-foundedness condition.

$$
\mathit{well\text{-}founded}(\mathit{Summ}(V, V') \wedge \mathit{call}(V', V''))
$$

To prove termination, our previous solution for $Summ(V, V')$ requires a strengthening $\texttt{n}' \leq \texttt{n}$ that keeps track of changes applied to n and guarantees that n never increases. Our solving algorithm computes the following solution.

$$\begin{aligned} Summ(V, V') = {} & (\texttt{pc} = \ell_1 \wedge \texttt{pc}' = \ell_1 \wedge \texttt{n} \geq \texttt{n}') \vee \\ & (\texttt{pc} = \ell_1 \wedge \texttt{pc}' = \ell_2 \wedge \texttt{n}' \geq 1 \wedge \texttt{n} \geq \texttt{n}') \vee \\ & (\texttt{pc} = \ell_1 \wedge \texttt{pc}' = \ell_3 \wedge \texttt{n}' + \texttt{s}' \geq 1) \vee \\ & (\texttt{pc} = \ell_1 \wedge \texttt{pc}' = \ell_4) \vee \\ & (\texttt{pc} = \ell_1 \wedge \texttt{pc}' = \ell_5 \wedge \texttt{ret}' \geq 0) \end{aligned}$$

The composition of the strengthened solution with the parameter passing relation is

$$(move(\ell_1, \ell_1) \wedge \texttt{n}' \geq 0 \wedge \texttt{n}' \leq \texttt{n} - 1) .$$

Its well-foundedness follows from the decrease of n at each step and its boundedness from below by $\texttt{n}' \geq 0$.

As our example illustrates, we consider proof rules that can be represented as a set of implication constraints over formulas representing the program and "unknown" formulas, e.g. $Summ(V, V')$. To provide a basis for efficient solving algorithms, our implication constraints resemble Horn clauses as they may have at most one unknown formula in the consequent part of a clause. We refer to such implications as Horn-*like* clauses, since we allow arbitrary disjunctions among "known" formulas.

2.2 Verifying functional programs

We represent the program from Figure 1 as a functional program.

```
let rec sum n =
  if n > 0 then let s = sum (n-1) in s+n
  else 0
```

For functional programs, typing constraints can be used to track value flow through program expressions. They relate refinement types [14, 26] that represent assertions over values of expressions and values of identifiers in scope. For example, the type of the above function sum can be represented as follows.

$$\texttt{sum} : (\texttt{n} : \{\nu : \texttt{int} \mid P_1(\nu)\} \rightarrow \{\nu : \texttt{int} \mid P_2(\texttt{n}, \nu)\})$$

Following recent work on refinement type inference, see e.g., [24, 48, 50], we embed the typing constraints into logical implications and obtain the following set of Horn-like clauses over $P_1(\nu)$ and $P_2(\texttt{n}, \nu)$.

$$\begin{aligned} & true \rightarrow P_1(\nu) \\ & P_1(\texttt{n}) \wedge \texttt{n} > 0 \wedge \nu = \texttt{n} - 1 \rightarrow P_1(\nu) \\ & P_1(\texttt{n}) \wedge \texttt{n} > 0 \wedge P_2(\texttt{n} - 1, \nu) \wedge \nu' = \texttt{n} + \nu \rightarrow P_2(\texttt{n}, \nu') \\ & P_1(\texttt{n}) \wedge \texttt{n} \leq 0 \wedge \nu = 0 \rightarrow P_2(\texttt{n}, \nu) \\ & P_2(\texttt{n}, \nu) \rightarrow \nu \geq 0 \end{aligned}$$

The first clause encodes that there is no restriction on the inputs to sum. The second and third clauses represent data flow if the branching condition succeeds. First, there is data flow due to the parameter passing, which is represented by the second clause. Then, the result of the recursive call is represented using the assertion $P_2(\texttt{n}-1, \nu)$. The sum of ν and n is the return value. The fourth clause encodes return value passing when the branching condition fails. The last clause represents the property that sum returns non-negative values. If there is a solution to the above clauses then sum satisfies the property.

Our solving algorithm computes solutions for $P_1(\nu)$ and $P_2(\texttt{n}, \nu)$, which yields the following type for sum.

$$\texttt{sum} : (\texttt{n} : \{\nu : \texttt{int} \mid true\} \rightarrow \{\nu : \texttt{int} \mid \nu \geq 0\}) .$$

3. Preliminaries

In this section we introduce preliminary definitions.

We write $\lambda x \in X.e$ to represent a definition that assigns to each $x \in X$ the value obtained by evaluating e. Given a function f, let $dom(f)$ denote the domain of f, i.e., the set of values for which f is defined. A binary relation is well-founded if it does not admit infinite chains. We write $well\text{-}founded(\varphi(v, v'))$ if $\varphi(v, v')$ is a well-founded relation, i.e., there is no infinite sequence $s_1, s_2, \dots$ such that $\varphi(s_i, s_{i+1})$ for all $i \geq 1$. Let ϵ denote the empty tuple. A relation $\varphi(v, v')$ is disjunctively well-founded if it is included in a finite union of well-founded relations, i.e., if there exist well-founded $\varphi_1(v, v'), \dots, \varphi_n(v, v')$ such that

$$\varphi(v, v') \models_{\mathcal{T}} \varphi_1(v, v') \vee \dots \vee \varphi_n(v, v').$$

For example, the relation $x \geq 0 \wedge x' \leq x - 1$ is well-founded, while the relation $x \geq 0 \wedge x' \leq x - 1 \vee y \leq 0 \wedge y' \geq y + 1$ is disjunctively well-founded.

Constraints Let $\mathcal{T}$ be a first-order theory in a given signature, $\mathcal{V}$ be a set of variables, and $\models_{\mathcal{T}}$ be the entailment relation with respect to $\mathcal{T}$. We write v to denote a non-empty tuple of variables, i.e., $v \in \mathcal{V}^+$. We refer to formulas in the given signature as constraints, and let $c(v)$ denote a constraint over the variables v. Let *false* denote an unsatisfiable constraint.

For example, let x, y, and z be variables. Then, $v = (x, y)$ and $w = (y, z)$ are tuples of variables. $x \leq 2$, $y \leq 1 \wedge x - y \leq 0$, and $f(x) + g(x, y) \leq 3 \vee z \leq 0$ are example constraints in the theory $\mathcal{T}$ of linear inequalities over rationals/reals and uninterpreted functions, where f and g are uninterpreted function symbols. The entailment $y \leq 1 \wedge x - y \leq 0 \models_{\mathcal{T}} x \leq 2$ is valid.

Queries and dwf-predicates We assume a set of uninterpreted predicate symbols $\mathcal{Q}$ that we refer to as query symbols. The arity of a query symbol is encoded in its name. We write q to denote a query symbol. Given q of a non-zero arity n and a tuple of variables v of length n, we define $q(v)$ to be a query. Furthermore, we introduce an interpreted predicate symbol dwf of arity one (dwf stands for disjunctive well-foundedness). Given a query $q(v, v')$ over tuples of variables with equal length, we refer to $dwf(q(v, v'))$ as a dwf-predicate.

For example, let $\mathcal{Q} = \{r, s\}$ be query symbols of arity one and two, respectively. Then, $r(x)$ and $s(x, y)$ are queries, and $dwf(s(x, y))$ is a dwf-predicate.

Horn-like clauses Let $h(v)$ range over queries and constraints with variables in v. We define a Horn-like clause to be either an implication

$$c(v_0) \wedge q_1(v_1) \wedge \dots \wedge q_n(v_n) \rightarrow h(v)$$

or a unit clause

$$dwf(q(v, v'))$$

which consists of a dwf-predicate. The left-hand side of the implication is called the body and the right-hand side is called the head. We use cl to denote a Horn-like clause.

The following set of clauses $\mathcal{C}$ illustrates our definition of Horn-like clauses.

$$\begin{aligned} \mathcal{C} = \{ & x \leq y \wedge y \leq -1 \rightarrow r(x), y = x + 1 \wedge r(x) \rightarrow s(x, y), \\ & r(x) \rightarrow x \leq 0, dwf(s(x, y))\} \end{aligned}$$

To support efficient verification, our Horn-like clauses slightly deviate from the standard notion of Horn clauses since constraints occurring in our clauses can contain disjunctions and conjunctions. For example, we admit clauses such as

$$(x \leq 0 \vee y \leq 0) \wedge s(x, y) \rightarrow s(x, y)$$

and

$$s(x,y) \to (x \le 0 \lor y \le 0).$$

While our presentation of the proposed method does not rely on the Boolean structure of constraints occurring in clauses, it is useful in practice to allow disjunction in constraints in order to keep the number of clauses small. (Note that the above two clauses can be translated into logically equivalent Horn clauses $x \le 0 \land s(x,y) \to s(x,y)$, $y \le 0 \land s(x,y) \to s(x,y)$ and $s(x,y) \land \neg(x \le 0) \to y \le 0$.) In contrast, we rely on the fact that there is at most one non-negated query in a clause.

Clauses in normal form Before formalizing the semantics of the clauses, we introduce assumptions on the syntax of Horn-like clauses that significantly simplify the presentation of the semantics without introducing any proper restrictions.

First, we assume that for each query symbol q there is a fixed tuple v of variables with the corresponding length and that each query with the symbol q is of the form $q(v)$. That is, each query has an *a priori* defined tuple of variables. Furthermore, we assume that all variables in v are pairwise distinct, i.e., for the tuple of variables $v = (x_1, \dots, x_n)$ we have x_i and x_j are different variables for all $1 \le i \ne j \le n$.

Second, we assume that in each clause a query symbol can occur at most once. Formally, for each clause $c(v_0) \land q_1(v_1) \land \dots \land q_n(v_n) \to h(v)$ we assume that q_i is different from q_j for all $1 \le i \ne j \le n$, and if the head $h(v)$ is a query $q(v)$ then q is different from each q_i for all $1 \le i \le n$.

The first assumption can be established by assigning tuples of variables to query symbols, and then translating queries into the desired form by adding corresponding equality constraints into the constraint of a clause. For example, for the query symbols r and s we assign variables $v_r = (x_r)$ and $v_s = (x_s, y_s)$, respectively. Then, a clause $x + y \le 0 \land r(x) \land s(x,x) \to y \le 0$ violates our first assumption but can be transformed to

$$\begin{aligned} &x = x_r \land x = x_s \land x = y_s \land \\ &\quad x + y \le 0 \land r(x_r) \land s(x_s, y_s) \to y \le 0. \end{aligned}$$

The first conjunct corresponds to the translation of the query $r(x)$, while the second and third conjuncts correspond to $s(x,x)$.

The second assumption can be established by introducing auxiliary queries and clauses each time there is a clause with multiple occurrences of some query. The violating clause is transformed by replacing the violating query occurrences in the clause body by the auxiliary queries.

For example, a clause $r(x_r) \land r(x_r) \to r(x_r)$ violates the second assumption due to the triple occurrence of $r(x_r)$. Hence, we introduce two auxiliary query symbols r_1 and r_2 of arity one together with the corresponding tuples of variables $v_{r_1} = (x_{r_1})$ and $v_{r_2} = (x_{r_2})$, respectively. Then, we express the relation between $r(x_r)$ and the introduced queries using the following auxiliary clauses: $x_r = x_{r_1} \land r(x_r) \to r_1(x_{r_1})$ and $x_r = x_{r_2} \land r(x_r) \to r_2(x_{r_2})$. Finally, we translate the original clause $r(x_r) \land r(x_r) \to r(x_r)$ to

$$x_r = x_{r_1} \land x_r = x_{r_2} \land r_1(x_{r_1}) \land r_2(x_{r_2}) \to r(x_r).$$

We refer to a set of Horn-like clauses that satisfies the above two conditions as clauses in normal form. In the rest of the paper, we assume that the clauses are Horn-like and in normal form.

For $\mathcal{C}$ defined above we obtain the following normal form $\mathcal{C}_{NF}$.

$$\begin{aligned} \{&x = x_r \land x \le y \land y \le -1 \to r(x_r), \\ &x = x_r \land x = x_s \land y = y_s \land y = x + 1 \land r(x_r) \to s(x_s, y_s), \\ &x = x_r \land r(x_r) \to x \le 0, \mathit{dwf}(s(x_s, y_s))\} \end{aligned}$$

Semantics of Horn-like clauses A set of clauses can be seen as an assertion over the queries that occur in the clauses.

We consider a function Σ that maps each query $q(v)$ occurring in a given set of clauses into a constraint over v. Such a function is called a solution if the following two conditions hold. First, for each clause $c(v_0) \land q_1(v_1) \land \dots \land q_n(v_n) \to h(v)$ from the given set we require:

$$c(v_0) \land \Sigma(q_1) \land \dots \land \Sigma(q_n) \models_{\mathcal{T}} \begin{cases} \Sigma(q) & \text{if } h(v) \text{ is } q(v), \\ c_h(v) & \text{if } h(v) \text{ is } c_h(v). \end{cases}$$

Second, for each clause $\mathit{dwf}(q(v,v'))$ in the input set we require that the relation $\Sigma(q)$ is disjunctively well-founded. Let $\models_{\mathcal{Q}}$ be the corresponding satisfaction relation, i.e., $\Sigma \models_{\mathcal{Q}} \mathcal{C}$ if Σ is a solution for $\mathcal{C}$.

For example, the previously defined set of clauses $\mathcal{C}_{NF}$ has a solution Σ such that

$$\begin{aligned} \Sigma(r) &= x_r \le -1, \\ \Sigma(s) &= x_s \le 0 \land y_s \ge x_s + 1. \end{aligned}$$

To check $\Sigma \models_{\mathcal{Q}} \mathcal{C}_{NF}$ we consider the validity of the entailments

$$\begin{aligned} &x = x_r \land x \le y \land y \le -1 \models_{\mathcal{T}} x_r \le -1, \\ &x = x_r \land x = x_s \land y = y_s \land y = x + 1 \land x_r \le -1 \\ &\quad \models_{\mathcal{T}} x_s \le 0 \land y_s \ge x_s + 1, \\ &x = x_r \land x_r \le -1 \models_{\mathcal{T}} x \le 0, \end{aligned}$$

and the fact that $\Sigma(s)$ is a (disjunctively) well-founded relation.

Dependency and recursion-free clauses For a clause cl such that

$$c(v_0) \land q_1(v_1) \land \dots \land q_n(v_n) \to h(v)$$

we define $\mathit{depends}(cl)$ to be the set of query symbols that appear in the body of cl, i.e., $\mathit{depends}(cl) = \{q_1, \dots, q_n\}$. A set of clauses defines a binary dependency relation on query symbols. Each clause cl that has a query $q(v)$ (rather than a constraint) in its head contributes the set of pairs $\{(q_i, q) \mid q_i \in \mathit{depends}(cl)\}$ to the dependency relation. We say that a set of clauses is recursion-free if the corresponding dependency relation is well-founded.

For example, the second clause in $\mathcal{C}$ depends on the set of query symbols $\{r\}$, and the entire set of clauses $\mathcal{C}$ defines the dependency relation $\{(r, s)\}$. This dependency relation is well-founded, hence $\mathcal{C}$ is recursion-free.

Solving recursion-free clauses We assume an algorithm for solving recursion-free clauses. This algorithm takes as input recursion-free clauses in the theory $\mathcal{T}$ and computes a solution Σ when it exists. There already exist such algorithms for the theory of linear arithmetic (see [19]) and linear arithmetic with uninterpreted functions (see [17]), which are based on extensions of interpolation algorithms [32, 46] to tree-like structures.

4. Algorithm HSF

In this section we present our algorithm HSF for finding solutions to recursive Horn-like clauses.

Let $\mathcal{C}$ be a finite set of clauses that is given as input to HSF. We partition $\mathcal{C}$ into inference clauses $\mathcal{I}$ and property clauses $\mathcal{P}$. Inference clauses contain queries in their heads, and property clauses contain the rest, i.e.,

$$\begin{aligned} \mathcal{I} &= \{cl \in \mathcal{C} \mid cl = (\ldots \to q(v))\}, \\ \mathcal{P} &= \mathcal{C} \setminus \mathcal{I}. \end{aligned}$$

Inference clauses impose a relationship between queries, while property clauses impose absolute assertions on queries.

HSF finds a solution by following an iterative, abstraction-based approach that relies on (spurious) counterexample derivations to refine the abstraction in case of imprecision. This approach is a generalization of the counterexample-guided abstraction refinement schemes for proving reachability and termination properties of software. Our generalization deals with Horn-like clauses (instead of transition systems/programs with procedures). Our approach inherits the advantages and disadvantages of the existing counterexample-guided abstraction refinement schemes: a sufficiently precise yet not overly detailed abstraction can be discovered automatically, however the abstraction discovery procedure may not terminate. In practice, the non-terminating behavior is sufficiently seldom.

The iteration proceeds in three main steps.

1. We find a solution for the inference clauses $\mathcal{I}$. At this step we perform logical inference and rely on abstraction to ensure termination in the presence of recursion and to ensure efficiency in the presence of large sets of clauses.
2. We check whether the computed solution satisfies the property clauses $\mathcal{P}$. If some property clause, say cl, is not satisfied then we proceed with the analysis of the inference tree computed in the first step. Otherwise, if all property clauses are satisfied, we return the solution.
3. We check whether the logical inference performed in the first step in the setting without any abstraction yields a solution that still violates the property clause cl. If the violation is present then we return the inference tree as a counterexample derivation. Otherwise we use the obtained solution to refine the abstraction function and go back to the first step.

The first step is implemented using a procedure INFERABST that applies ADDINFERRED to perform the necessary bookkeeping of the inference tree construction. MAKECEX extracts a relevant subtree of the inference tree in case a solution computed by INFERABST violates some property clause. We rely on existing procedures for the analysis of the obtained subtree. ADDPREDS converts solutions obtained by the successful subtree analysis into a refinement of the abstraction function. The procedure HSF puts the steps together in a loop (Figure 4).

Next we present the procedures that implement the three steps.

(Predicate) abstraction We use predicate abstraction as an approximation technique employed by HSF.

Let α be a function that takes as input a constraint $\varphi(v)$ together with a finite set $\{c_1(v), \dots, c_n(v)\}$ of predicates, i.e., atomic constraints, over v. The output is an over-approximation of $\varphi(v)$ that is constructed from the given predicates using Boolean operators. We use the following definition (which is called Cartesian abstraction in the literature [5]).

$$\alpha(\varphi(v), \{c_1(v), \dots, c_n(v)\}) = \bigwedge\{c_i(v) \mid i \in 1..n \wedge \varphi(v) \models_{\mathcal{T}} c_i(v)\}$$

For example, given the constraint $x \leq y \wedge y \leq z \wedge z \leq 0$ and the predicates $\{x \leq z, x \geq 0, x \leq 0\}$, the predicate abstraction function returns the conjunction $x \leq z \wedge x \leq 0$.

We rely on two properties of the abstraction function: over-approximation and monotonicity. That is, for each pair of constraints $\varphi(v)$, $\psi(v)$ and each set of predicates *Preds* we have i) $\varphi(v)$ entails $\alpha(\varphi(v), \mathit{Preds})$ and ii) if $\varphi(v)$ entails $\psi(v)$ then $\alpha(\varphi(v), \mathit{Preds})$ entails $\alpha(\psi(v), \mathit{Preds})$. The over-approximation will guarantee that combining logical inference with abstraction will yield solutions to inference clauses and the monotonicity will guarantee that such solutions can be computed using fixpoint iteration techniques.

Inference and abstraction Before presenting the procedure INFERABST, which performs logical inference, abstraction, and

$$\text{RINIT}\ \frac{c(v_0) \rightarrow q(v) \in \mathcal{I}}{\alpha(c(v_0), \mathit{Preds}(q)) \in \mathit{Inferred}(q)}$$

$$\text{RSTEP}\ \frac{\varphi_1(v_1) \in \mathit{Inferred}(q_1) \quad \dots \quad \varphi_n(v_n) \in \mathit{Inferred}(q_n) \qquad c(v_0) \wedge \bigwedge_{i=1}^{n} q_i(v_i) \rightarrow q(v) \in \mathcal{I}}{\alpha(c(v_0) \wedge \bigwedge_{i=1}^{n} \varphi_i(v_i), \mathit{Preds}(q)) \in \mathit{Inferred}(q)}$$

Figure 2. Abstract inference rules for a given set of clauses $\mathcal{I}$ and a predicate abstraction function with the set of predicates $\mathit{Preds}(q)$ for each query symbol q.

bookkeeping, we first present a characterization of what it computes in the form of inference rules.

See Figure 2. The presented rules RINIT and RSTEP define a relation between a possibly empty sequence of constraints in the premise and a constraint in the consequence such that the relation satisfies some inference clause from the input set $\mathcal{I}$.

We keep track of the inferred constraints in the set *Inferred* that we partition according to the query symbols of these constraints. The inference process applies the rules as long as the derived constraints are not subsumed by the previously derived ones. A constraint $\varphi(v)$ derived by applying a clause with the query $q(v)$ in its head is subsumed if there is a constraint $\psi(v)$ in $\mathit{Inferred}(q)$ such that $\varphi(v)$ entails $\psi(v)$. (This subsumption definition is called local entailment in the literature.)

We observe that the inference process terminates since the range of the abstraction function is finite, i.e., there are only finitely many different constraints that can be added to *Inferred*, and the abstraction function is monotonic. Furthermore, the resulting constraints yield a solution for the inference clauses. Formally, we define

$$\Sigma = \lambda q \in \mathit{dom}(\mathit{Inferred}). \bigvee \mathit{Inferred}(q)$$

and obtain $\Sigma \models_{\mathcal{Q}} \mathcal{I}$.

***Procedure* INFERABST** We turn the inference rules RINIT and RSTEP into a worklist-based iteration procedure INFERABST that also keeps track between inferred constraints and corresponding clauses. See Figure 3.

INFERABST takes as input the inference clauses $\mathcal{I}$ and a function *Preds* that assigns to each query symbol q (and the corresponding tuple of variables v) a finite set of predicates over v. The output of INFERABST consists of the inferred constraints *Inferred* and a function *Parent* that represent the bookkeeping results. *Parent* assigns to each inferred constraint $\varphi(v)$ a sequence of constraints and a clause that were used in the rule application that produced $\varphi(v)$. INFERABST maintains a worklist *WL* containing inference clauses that may infer new constraints.

The inference starts with applying all clauses that do not depend on any queries, and are hence applicable when no constraints are yet inferred. Each clause application follows the rule RINIT and applies ADDINFERRED to process the application result. Then, INFERABST iteratively applies the clauses from the worklist until no more non-subsumed constraints can be computed, i.e., until the worklist becomes empty. At every iteration step, INFERABST takes a clause from the worklist and exhaustively applies the clause following the rule RSTEP.

Example For the set of clauses $\mathcal{C}_{NF}$ defined in the previous section, we consider the predicates $\mathit{Preds}(r) = \{x_r \leq 0\}$ and $\mathit{Preds}(s) = \{x_s \leq y_s\}$. For brevity, we denote the four clauses from $\mathcal{C}_{NF}$ as cl_1 , cl_2 , cl_3, and cl_4 , respectively. Our algorithm initially processes the clauses that do not depend on any queries,

function INFERABST
input
$\mathcal{I}$ – inference clauses
Preds – predicate table
output
Inferred – inferred constraints
Parent – parent function for inferred constraints
vars
WL – worklist with clauses
procedure ADDINFERRED
input
$\varphi(v)$ – abstract relation
$\varphi_1(v_1), \ldots, \varphi_n(v_n)$ – parent abstract relations
$cl = (\ldots \to q(v))$ – parent clause with head $q(v)$
begin
1 **if** $\neg(\exists \psi(v) \in \mathit{Inferred}(q) : \varphi(v) \models_{\mathcal{T}} \psi(v))$ **then**
2 $\mathit{Inferred}(q) := \{\varphi(v)\} \cup \mathit{Inferred}(q)$
3 $\mathit{Parent}(\varphi(v)) := ((\varphi_1(v_1), \ldots, \varphi_n(v_n)), cl)$
4 $\mathit{WL} := \{cl' \in \mathcal{I} \mid q \in \mathit{depends}(cl')\} \cup \mathit{WL}$
end
begin
5 $\mathit{Inferred} := \lambda q \in \mathcal{Q}.\emptyset$
6 $\mathit{Parent} := \emptyset$
7 $\mathit{WL} := \emptyset$
8 **for** each $c(v_0) \to q(v) \in \mathcal{I}$ **do**
9 $\varphi(v) := \alpha(c(v_0), \mathit{Preds}(q))$
10 ADDINFERRED$(\varphi(v), \epsilon, c(v_0) \to q(v))$
11 **while** $\mathit{WL} \neq \emptyset$ **do**
12 $c(v_0) \wedge q_1(v_1) \wedge \cdots \wedge q_n(v_n) \to q(v)$:= take from WL
13 **for** each $i \in 1..n$ and $\varphi_i(v_i) \in \mathit{Inferred}(q_i)$ **do**
14 $\varphi(v) := \alpha(c(v_0) \wedge \varphi_1(v_1) \wedge \cdots \wedge \varphi_n(v_n), \mathit{Preds}(q))$
15 ADDINFERRED$(\varphi(v), (\varphi_1(v_1), \ldots, \varphi_n(v_n)),$
$c(v_0) \wedge q_1(v_1) \wedge \cdots \wedge q_n(v_n) \to q(v))$
16 **return** $(\mathit{Inferred}, \mathit{Parent})$
end

Figure 3. Abstract inference algorithm.

i.e., cl_1 (see lines 8–10 from Figure 3). The computation of a new constraint at line 9 proceeds as follows: $\varphi(x_r) = \alpha(x = x_r \wedge x \leq y \wedge y \leq -1, \{x_r \leq 0\}) = (x_r \leq 0)$. □

***Procedure* ADDINFERRED** The procedure ADDINFERRED is shown in Figure 3. Since ADDINFERRED is defined within INFERABST, *Inferred*, *Parent*, and *WL* are in scope of ADDINFERRED.

The input to ADDINFERRED is an inferred constraint $\varphi(v)$ that was computed by applying a clause cl with the head $q(v)$ on the possibly empty sequence of constraints $\varphi_1(v_1), \ldots, \varphi_n(v_n)$, i.e., n may be equal to zero. First, ADDINFERRED checks if $\varphi(v)$ is subsumed by already inferred constraints. If no subsumption takes place then we add it to the set of inferred constraints *Inferred*, extend *Parent* with a corresponding bookkeeping record, and add inference clauses that depend on q to the worklist.

Example (cont.) After computing the constraint $\varphi(x_r) = x_r \leq 0$, the inference algorithm calls ADDINFERRED$(x_r \leq 0, \epsilon, cl_1)$ (see line 10 of Figure 3) and records the information about the newly inferred constraint as follows:

$$\begin{aligned} \mathit{Inferred}(r) &= \{x_r \leq 0\} , \\ \mathit{Parent}(x_r \leq 0) &= (\epsilon, cl_1) , \\ \mathit{WL} &= \{cl_2\} . \end{aligned}$$

After adding the clause cl_2 to the worklist, it will be processed in the loop at lines 11–15 and a call ADDINFERRED$(x_s \leq y_s, (x_r \leq 0), cl_2)$ leads to a second inferred constraint as follows:

$$\begin{aligned} \mathit{Inferred}(s) &= \{x_s \leq y_s\} , \\ \mathit{Parent}(x_s \leq y_s) &= ((x_r \leq 0), cl_2) , \\ \mathit{WL} &= \emptyset . \end{aligned}$$

For the given sets of predicates, i.e., $\mathit{Preds}(r) = \{x_r \leq 0\}$ and $\mathit{Preds}(s) = \{x_s \leq y_s\}$, the computation of inferred constraints finishes here since the worklist is empty. □

***Procedure* HSF** The main procedure of our algorithm is HSF. It is shown in Figure 4. HSF takes as input a finite set of Horn-like clauses $\mathcal{C} = \mathcal{I} \uplus \mathcal{P}$ and iteratively computes a solution for the inference clauses $\mathcal{I}$ that also satisfies the property clauses $\mathcal{P}$.

HSF computes solution candidates from the constraints in *Inferred* that are inferred using INFERABST. The obtained candidate is guaranteed to satisfy $\mathcal{I}$, while satisfaction of $\mathcal{P}$ requires finding a sufficiently precise abstraction function. The abstraction function α is determined by a set of predicates *Preds* that is partitioned between query symbols.

A sufficiently precise abstraction function is computed by HSF iteratively by adding predicates to *Preds*, which is empty initially. For the given *Preds*, we first use INFERABST to compute inferred constraints *Inferred* and *Parent*. Then we check whether the solution for $\mathcal{I}$ defined by *Inferred* also satisfies $\mathcal{P}$. We distinguish between violation of a clause that has a constraint in its head from the violation of a clause consisting of a *dwf*-predicate.

If a clause $cl = c(v_0) \wedge q_1(v_1) \wedge \cdots \wedge q_n(v_n) \to c_h(v)$ is not satisfied by some sequence of inferred constraints, say $\varphi_1(v_1) \in \mathit{Inferred}(q_1), \ldots, \varphi_n(v_n) \in \mathit{Inferred}(q_n)$, then we check if repeating the same inference steps without applying the abstraction function computes a sequence of constraints that satisfies cl.

We reconstruct the inference steps that produced $\varphi_1(v_1), \ldots, \varphi_n(v_n)$ by using the procedure MAKECEX. The output of MAKECEX is a set of recursion-free clauses $\mathcal{X}$ whose queries correspond to the constraints that were involved, as recorded by *Parent*, in the computation of $\varphi_1(v_1), \ldots, \varphi_n(v_n)$. We record the correspondence using the function *Sym* that assigns query symbols of the involved constraints to the fresh query symbols that represent constraints derived without abstraction. We also include into $\mathcal{X}$ a clause imposing an assertion on the queries that correspond to $\varphi_1(v_1), \ldots, \varphi_n(v_n)$.

Now, we solve $\mathcal{X}$ using an existing tool for solving recursion-free clauses [17, 19]. If a solution exists then we use it to extract additional predicates for *Preds*. The function *Sym* translates query symbols from the domain of the solution into the query symbols in our clauses $\mathcal{C}$. In this case, after refining the abstraction we continue with another attempt to find a solution for $\mathcal{C}$. If a solution does not exist, we return the clauses $\mathcal{X}$ as a witness of the property violation.

Example (cont.) The set of clauses $\mathcal{C}_{NF}$ contains the property clause cl_3, i.e., $x = x_r \wedge r(x_r) \to x \leq 0$, which is satisfied by the candidate solution: $\mathit{Inferred}(r) = (x_r \leq 0)$. □

If a clause $\mathit{dwf}(q(v, v'))$ is not satisfied by some of the inferred constraints, say $\varphi(v, v') \in \mathit{Inferred}(q)$, then we proceed in a similar way as in the above case. First, we use MAKECEX to construct a set of recursion-free clauses $\mathcal{X}$ that reconstructs the inference steps leading to $\varphi(v, v')$. Then, we rely on an existing solver for recursion-free clauses to find a solution for $\mathcal{X}$ that assigns

function HSF
input
$\mathcal{I} \uplus \mathcal{P}$ – Horn-like inference and property clauses
vars
Preds – predicate table
Sym – definition of quoted query symbols
function MAKECEX
input
$\varphi(v)$ – inferred constraint
Parent – parent function
output
$\mathcal{X}$ – set of recursion-free clauses with root $\varphi(v)$
begin
1 $((\varphi_1(v_1), \dots, \varphi_n(v_n)),$
$c(v_0) \wedge \bigwedge_{i=1}^{n} q_i(v_i) \rightarrow h(v)) := \mathit{Parent}(\varphi(v))$
2 $\mathit{Sym} := \{\text{“}\varphi_1(v_1)\text{”} \mapsto q_1, \dots, \text{“}\varphi_n(v_n)\text{”} \mapsto q_n\} \cup \mathit{Sym}$
3 **return** $\{c(v_0) \wedge \bigwedge_{i=1}^{n} \text{“}\varphi_i(v_i)\text{”}(v_i) \rightarrow \text{“}\varphi(v)\text{”}(v)\} \cup$
4 $\bigcup_{i=1}^{n}$ MAKECEX$(\varphi_i(v_i), \mathit{Parent})$
end
procedure ADDPREDS
input
Σ – solution function
begin
5 **for** each $\text{“}\varphi(v)\text{”} \in \mathit{dom}(\Sigma)$ **do**
6 $q := \mathit{Sym}(\text{“}\varphi(v)\text{”})$
7 $\mathit{Preds}(q) := \Sigma(\text{“}\varphi(v)\text{”}) \cup \mathit{Preds}(q)$
end
begin
8 $\mathit{Preds} := \lambda q \in \mathcal{Q}.\emptyset$
9 **repeat**
10 $(\mathit{Inferred}, \mathit{Parent}) :=$ INFERABST$(\mathcal{I}, \mathit{Preds})$
11 **if** exist $c(v_0) \wedge \bigwedge_{i=1}^{n} q_i(v_i) \rightarrow c_h(v) \in \mathcal{P}$ and
$\varphi_i(v_i) \in \mathit{Inferred}(q_i)$ for each $i \in 1..n$ such that
12 $c(v_0) \wedge \bigwedge_{i=1}^{n} \varphi_i(v_i) \not\models_{\mathcal{T}} c_h(v)$ **then**
13 $\mathit{Sym} := \{\text{“}\varphi_1(v_1)\text{”} \mapsto q_1, \dots, \text{“}\varphi_n(v_n)\text{”} \mapsto q_n\}$
14 $\mathcal{X} := \{c(v_0) \wedge \bigwedge_{i=1}^{n} \text{“}\varphi_i(v_i)\text{”}(v_i) \rightarrow c_h(v)\} \cup$
15 $\bigcup_{i=1}^{n}$ MAKECEX$(\varphi_i(v_i), \mathit{Parent})$
16 **if** exists Σ such that $\Sigma \models_{\mathcal{Q}} \mathcal{X}$ **then**
17 ADDPREDS(Σ)
18 **else**
19 **return** “error derivation $\mathcal{X}$”
20 **else if** exist $\mathit{dwf}(q(v, v')) \in \mathcal{P}$ and $\varphi(v, v') \in \mathit{Inferred}(q)$
such that $\neg \mathit{well\text{-}founded}(\varphi(v, v'))$ **then**
21 $\mathit{Sym} := \{\text{“}\varphi(v, v')\text{”} \mapsto q\}$
22 $\mathcal{X} :=$ MAKECEX$(\varphi(v, v'), \mathit{Parent})$
23 **if** exists Σ such that $\Sigma \models_{\mathcal{Q}} \mathcal{X}$ and
$\mathit{well\text{-}founded}(\Sigma(\text{“}\varphi(v, v')\text{”}))$ **then**
24 ADDPREDS(Σ)
25 **else**
26 **return** “error derivation $\mathcal{X}$”
27 **else**
28 **return** “solution $\lambda q \in \mathit{dom}(\mathit{Inferred}). \bigvee \mathit{Inferred}(q)$”
end.

Figure 4. Abstract inference, checking, and refinement.

a well-founded relation to $q(v, v')$ [39]. If INFERABST infers a set of constraints *Inferred* that defines a solution for $\mathcal{P}$ then we return this solution.

Example (cont.) The set of clauses $\mathcal{C}_{NF}$ contains a second property clause, i.e., $\mathit{dwf}(s(x_s, y_s))$. The conditions at line 20 of Figure 4 are satisfied for the inferred constraint $x_s \leq y_s$: $\mathit{dwf}(s(x_s, y_s)) \in \mathcal{C}_{NF}$, $x_s \leq y_s \in \mathit{Inferred}(s)$ and $\neg \mathit{well\text{-}founded}(x_s \leq y_s)$. In this case, the inferred constraint does not correspond to a well-founded relation. □

***Procedure* MAKECEX** The procedure MAKECEX is shown in Figure 4. Its scope contains *Sym* and *Preds* from HSF. MAKECEX takes as input an inferred constraint $\varphi(v)$ and bookkeeping records *Parent* such that $\varphi(v) \in \mathit{dom}(\mathit{Parent})$.

Then, MAKECEX creates a clause that records the fact that $\varphi(v)$ was derived using the constraints and the clause in $\mathit{Parent}(\varphi(v))$. Let $\mathit{Parent}(\varphi(v))$ be the pair of $\varphi_1(v_1), \dots, \varphi_n(v_n)$ and $c(v_0) \wedge q_1(v_1) \wedge \dots \wedge q_n(v_n) \rightarrow h(v)$. This dependency is modeled by introducing auxiliary queries $\text{“}\varphi_1(v_1)\text{”}(v_1), \dots, \text{“}\varphi_n(v_n)\text{”}(v_n)$. These auxiliary queries stay in one-to-one correspondence with the constraints, i.e., $\text{“}\varphi_i(v_i)\text{”}(v_i)$ corresponds to q_i for all $1 \leq i \leq n$. This correspondence is established by applying a bijective quotation function “ · ” that translates a constraint into a query symbol. Finally, we recursively apply MAKECEX on the constraints that produced $\varphi(v)$ and return all constructed clauses.

Example (cont.) For the inferred constraint $s = x_s \leq y_s$, the procedure MAKECEX$(x_s \leq y_s, \mathit{Parent})$ is invoked at line 22 from Figure 4. As a result, a function *Sym* is constructed to keep track of the quoted query symbols: $\{\text{“}x_s \leq y_s\text{”} \mapsto s, \text{“}x_r \leq 0\text{”} \mapsto r\}$. Finally, the procedure MAKECEX returns the following set of recursion-free clauses:

$$\{x = x_r \wedge x = x_s \wedge y = y_s \wedge y = x + 1 \wedge \text{“}x_r \leq 0\text{”}(x_r) \rightarrow \text{“}x_s \leq y_s\text{”}(x_s, y_s),$$
$$x = x_r \wedge x \leq y \wedge y \leq -1 \rightarrow \text{“}x_r \leq 0\text{”}(x_r)\}$$

□

***Procedure* ADDPREDS** The procedure ADDPREDS is shown in Figure 4. It has *Sym* in scope and takes as input a solution function whose domain consists of quoted constraints. ADDPREDS uses *Sym* to translate quoted constraints into original query symbols and add the solution constraints into the corresponding partitions of *Preds*.

Example (cont.) Let us assume that the following solution Σ is returned at line 23 of Figure 4: $\{\text{“}x_r \leq 0\text{”}(x_r) \mapsto x_r \leq 0, \text{“}x_s \leq y_s\text{”}(x_s, y_s) \mapsto x_s < y_s\}$. The solution constraints are partitioned as follows: $\mathit{Preds}(r) = \{x_r \leq 0\}$ and $\mathit{Preds}(s) = \{x_s \leq y_s, x_s < y_s\}$. Given these predicates, the next iteration of the abstract inference algorithm computes abstract constraints precise enough to satisfy both property clauses cl_3 and cl_4 from our example.

$$\mathit{Inferred}(r) = \{x_r \leq 0\}$$
$$\mathit{Inferred}(s) = \{x_s \leq y_s \wedge x_s < y_s\}$$

□

Correctness Upon termination, the algorithm HSF computes a solution for the input clauses. The soundness of the approach is guaranteed by the fact that the abstraction function is over-approximating. Our abstraction refinement method guarantees that a set of counterexample clauses $\mathcal{X}$ is never analyzed twice, i.e., our refinement method satisfies the progress of refinement property. Such soundness and progress of refinement properties are standard for counterexample guided abstraction refinement schemes.

For assertions $\{T_f \text{ over } V_f \text{ and } V'_f \mid f \in Procs(P)\}$,

$$\begin{array}{lll}
\text{CP1}: init(V_{main}) \wedge V_{main} = V'_{main} & \rightarrow T_{main}(V_{main}, V'_{main}) & \\
\text{CP2}: T_f(V_f, V'_f) \wedge \rho_f(V'_f, V''_f) & \rightarrow T_f(V_f, V''_f) & \\
\text{CP3}: T_f(V_f, V'_f) \wedge call_{f,g}(V'_f, V''_g) \wedge V''_g = V'''_g & \rightarrow T_g(V''_g, V'''_g) & f, g \in Procs(P) \text{ such that } f \text{ calls } g \\
\text{CP4}: T_f(V_f, V'_f) \wedge call_{f,g}(V'_f, V''_g) \wedge T_g(V''_g, V'''_g) \wedge & & \\
\quad ret_{f,g}(V'''_g, V''''_f) \wedge loc_f(V'_f, V''''_f) & \rightarrow T_f(V_f, V''''_f) & f, g \in Procs(P) \text{ such that } f \text{ calls } g \\
\text{CP5}: T_f(V_f, V'_f) \wedge error(V'_f) & \rightarrow false & \\
\hline
& \text{program } P \text{ is safe} &
\end{array}$$

Figure 5. Summarization rule for programs with procedures.

Alternative solving methods In this paper we use predicate abstraction and refinement to solve Horn-like clauses. Predicate abstraction allows us to formulate a practical algorithm, yet the presented formulation is sufficiently general such that a different approximation techniques can be employed instead without any significant changes to HSF. For example, abstract domains based on widening can be used to compute a solution to inference clauses, by choosing the corresponding abstraction function for INFER-ABST. Alternatively, we could use model checking techniques, e.g., bounded model checking, to explore the clauses up to a finite bound. Usually, predicates are atomic constraints; however recent approaches to predicate abstraction show that predicates containing Boolean operators can be useful [7].

5. Proof rules as Horn-like clauses

In this section, we show a collection of proof rules that can be automated using our verification approach.

5.1 Transition systems

We consider a transition system with variables V, a set of initial states $init(V)$, a transition relation $\rho(V, V')$, and a standard semantics.

Safety Let $error(V)$ represent a set of error states. To verify safety the transition system, we use an invariance proof rule with conditions over a query $R(V)$ that characterizes reachable states as follows.

For assertion R over V ,

$$\begin{array}{lll}
\text{CR1}: & init(V) & \rightarrow R(V) \\
\text{CR2}: & R(V) \wedge \rho(V, V') & \rightarrow R(V') \\
\text{CR3}: & R(V) \wedge error(V) & \rightarrow false \\
\hline
& \text{transition system } P \text{ is safe} &
\end{array}$$

Condition CR1 requires that all initial states are present in $R(V)$. Condition CR2 states that a program transition starting from a state in $R(V)$ ends in a state that is in $R(V')$. Finally, CR3 states that the intersection of reachable and error states is empty. Our algorithm HSF finds a solution for the query $R(V)$.

Termination To reason about termination properties of transition systems, we use a proof rule based on transition invariants [37]. The assertion T represents a transition invariant, which is a superset of the transitive closure of the transition relation ρ .

For assertion R over V that satisfies CR1 and CR2 and assertion T over V and V' ,

$$\begin{array}{lll}
\text{CT1}: & R(V) \wedge \rho(V, V') & \rightarrow T(V, V') \\
\text{CT2}: & T(V, V') \wedge \rho(V', V'') & \rightarrow T(V, V'') \\
\text{CT3}: & dwf(T(V, V')) & \\
\hline
& \text{transition system } P \text{ terminates} &
\end{array}$$

We restrict the assertion $T(V, V')$ to states that are reachable using CT1, CT2 and two clauses from the invariance proof rule, CR1 and CR2 . The last clause, CT3, uses a predicate symbol dwf of arity one that requires a disjunctive well-founded argument $T(V, V')$. The existence of a (disjunctive well-founded) transition invariant guarantees program termination, cf. [37].

5.2 Programs with procedures

We consider programs with a set of recursive procedures $Procs(P)$. Let $main \in Procs(P)$ be the procedure that starts the program execution. For each $f \in Procs(P)$, let V_f the set of variables that are in scope, $\rho_f(V_f, V'_f)$ be the intra-procedural transition relation. If f calls a procedure $g \in Procs(P)$, then let $call_{f,g}(V_f, V'_g)$ and $ret_{f,g}(V_f, V'_g)$ be parameter and return value passing relations, respectively. The relation $loc_f(V_f, V'_f)$ states which local variables of f are not modified during a call to g.

Safety We prove safety properties of procedural programs using a rule based on context-free language reachability [42]. See Figure 5 for the proof rule that consists of constraints over assertions T_f , one for each program procedure. A query $T_f(V_f, V'_f)$ represents a summary of the procedure f, which is a binary relation between entry states of f and their successors on the same level of recursion. For simplicity, our formulation does not adopt the common distinction between path edges and summaries, see, e.g., [42].

The first condition CP1 of the proof rule requires that the initial states constraint implies the query corresponding to the entry procedure $main$. The condition CP2 extends a query $T_f(V_f, V'_f)$ with a transition relation from the same procedure. The third and fourth conditions handle procedure calls. In CP3, given a query $T_f(V_f, V'_f)$ of the caller and the calling context passed from the variables V'_f to V''_g, the result is used to seed the summary of the callee procedure g . The condition CP4 is the most complex clause of the proof rule and ensures procedure-modular reasoning. It uses a query from the caller $T_f(V_f, V'_f)$, links the calling context with the parameter passing relation $call_{f,g}(V'_f, V''_g)$, uses the summary of the callee $T_g(V''_g, V'''_g)$, passes the return value back in the scope of the caller with $ret_{f,g}(V'''_g, V''''_f)$ and links local variables not affected by the call with $loc_f(V'_f, V''''_f)$. Finally, the condition CP5 requires that states reachable at an arbitrary location in some procedure f do not intersect error states.

Termination For proving termination properties, we use the proof rule from Figure 5 with an additional well-foundedness condition that no infinite recursion is feasible. This condition is imposed on a transition relation that describes recursive descent by composing procedure summaries with call relations following [12]. Let $V_P = \bigcup_{f \in Procs(P)} V_f$ be the set of variables that occur in all procedures. The technique of [12] constructs an assertion $Descent(V_P, V'_P)$ such that the program P terminates if and only if $Descent(V_P, V'_P)$ is well-founded. By taking a transitive closure of $Descent(V_P, V'_P)$ as described above, we can replace well-foundedness condition by a disjunctive well-foundedness condition.

5.3 Multi-threaded programs

We consider a multi-threaded program that consists of N threads as a tuple $(V, init, \rho_1, \ldots, \rho_N)$, where ρ_i is the transition relation of the thread i. The transition relation of the program ρ is the disjoint union of the N transition relations of the threads.

Owicki-Gries rule for proving safety Based on Owicki-Gries method [36], we present the following proof rule for verifying safety of multi-threaded programs. This proof rule lists conditions over N query symbols R_i that characterize reachable states for each thread $i \in 1..N$.

For assertions $R_1, \ldots, R_N$ over V,

$$\begin{array}{ll}
\text{CO1}: init(V) & \rightarrow R_i(V) \\
\text{CO2}: R_i(V) \wedge \rho_i(V, V') & \rightarrow R_i(V') \\
\text{CO3}: R_i(V) \wedge (\bigvee_{i \in 1..N \setminus \{j\}} R_j(V) \wedge \rho_j(V, V')) & \rightarrow R_i(V') \\
\text{CO4}: R_1(V) \wedge \ldots R_N(V) \wedge error(V) & \rightarrow false \\
\hline
\multicolumn{2}{c}{\text{multi-threaded program } P \text{ is safe}}
\end{array}$$

The conditions CO1, CO2 and CO4 resemble those from the invariance proof rule, while the additional condition CO3 ensures that the query $R_i(V, V')$ corresponding to thread i is free from interference from the transitions of other threads j. The presence of distinct query symbols for the reachable states of each thread allows our HSF algorithm to perform abstraction at the thread boundaries and leads to more scalable verification compared to the monolithic proof rule.

Rely-guarantee rule for proving safety As an alternative to the above proof rule, we can use a proof rule based on rely-guarantee reasoning method [25]. The proof rule uses assertions R_i and E_i that characterize reachable states of each thread $i \in 1..N$ and environment transitions of each thread $i \in 1..N$, respectively, following [19].

Each assertion $R_i(V)$ includes the initial states due to CM1. States reachable after executing a transition of thread i or an environment transition $E_i(V, V')$ are in $R_i(V')$ due to CM2 and CM4, where $\rho_i^=$ requires that the local variables of thread i do not change during an environment step of thread i. CM3 requires that every step of thread i starting from a reachable state is captured by the environment transitions of each other thread j. CM5 ensures that the intersection of reachable states and error states is empty.

For assertions $R_1, \ldots, R_N$ over V and $E_1, \ldots, E_N$ over V, V',

$$\begin{array}{lll}
\text{CM1}: & init(V) & \rightarrow R_i(V) \\
\text{CM2}: & R_i(V) \wedge \rho_i(V, V') & \rightarrow R_i(V') \\
\text{CM3}: & (\bigvee_{i \in 1..N \setminus \{j\}} R_i(V) \wedge \rho_i(V, V')) & \rightarrow E_j(V, V') \\
\text{CM4}: & R_i(V) \wedge E_i(V, V') \wedge \rho_i^=(V, V') & \rightarrow R_i(V') \\
\text{CM5}: & R_1(V) \wedge \cdots \wedge R_N(V) \wedge error(V) & \rightarrow false \\
\hline
\multicolumn{3}{c}{\text{multi-threaded program } P \text{ is safe}}
\end{array}$$

Rely-guarantee rule for proving termination Rely-guarantee reasoning [25] can be combined with the transition invariance proof rule [37] to prove termination properties of multi-threaded programs. The proof rule uses assertions T_i for transition invariants and E_i for environment transitions [39].

For assertions $T_1, \ldots, T_N$ and $E_1, \ldots, E_N$ over V, V',

$$\begin{array}{ll}
\text{CG1}: init(V) \wedge \rho_i(V, V') & \rightarrow T_i(V, V') \\
\text{CG2}: T_i(V, V') \wedge \rho_i(V', V'') & \rightarrow T_i(V', V'') \\
\text{CG3}: T_i(V, V') \wedge \rho_i(V', V'') & \rightarrow T_i(V, V'') \\
\text{CG4}: (\bigvee_{j \in 1..N \setminus \{i\}} init(V) \wedge \rho_j(V, V')) & \rightarrow E_i(V, V') \\
\text{CG5}: (\bigvee_{j \in 1..N \setminus \{i\}} T_i(V, V') \wedge \rho_j(V', V'')) & \rightarrow E_i(V', V'') \\
\text{CG6}: init(V) \wedge E_i(V, V') \wedge \rho_i^=(V, V') & \rightarrow T_i(V, V') \\
\text{CG7}: T_i(V, V') \wedge E_i(V', V'') \wedge \rho_i^=(V, V') & \rightarrow T_i(V', V'') \\
\text{CG8}: T_i(V, V') \wedge E_i(V', V'') \wedge \rho_i^=(V, V') & \rightarrow T_i(V, V'') \\
\text{CG9}: dwf(T_1(V, V') \wedge \cdots \wedge T_N(V, V')) & \\
\hline
\multicolumn{2}{c}{\text{multi-threaded program } P \text{ terminates}}
\end{array}$$

The conditions CG1 and CG2 require that T_i over-approximates the transition relation of the thread i restricted to initial states and to arbitrary reachable states. The condition CG3 extends T_i with a relation from ρ_i. The conditions CG4 and CG5 populate the environment transitions of thread i with steps of all threads other than i. The three conditions CG6, CG7 and CG8 are similar to the first three conditions except local transitions from ρ_i are replaced by environment transitions $E_i \wedge \rho_i^=$. As before, $\rho_i^=$ requires that the local variables of thread i do not change during an environment step of thread i. The final condition CG9 ensures that the conjunction of the transition invariant queries, $T_1(V, V') \wedge \cdots \wedge T_N(V, V')$, is disjunctively well-founded.

6. Experiments

In this section we present an experimental comparison between verifiers developed using our HSF algorithm and state-of-the-art verification tools developed using traditional methods.

Our tool HSF is implemented in Prolog and compiled with the SICStus Prolog 4.2.0 compiler. The implementation relies on a built-in constraint solver for linear arithmetic. For C programs, we use the CIL library [35] and an additional frontend step that produces clauses for various proof rules. For verifying OCaml programs, we use DSolve [43] to generate automatically subtyping constraints and then our code translates these constraints to Horn-like clauses.

Benchmarks We used several sets of benchmarks for our experiments.

Program	BLAST	CPAchecker	HSF
Numerical Recipes			
amebsa	FAIL	T/O	**0.2s**
amotsa	FAIL	2.3s	**0.2s**
bandec	T/O	T/O	T/O
choldc	14.1s	2.7s	**2.6s**
crank	6.0s	1.9s	**0.9s**
cyclic	FAIL	T/O	**2.2s**
four1	FAIL	T/O	T/O
lop	FAIL	FAIL	**0.7s**
pzextr	11.2s	FAIL	**0.1s**
qrdcmp	75.2s	T/O	**12.2s**
qrsolv	FAIL	3.3s	**0.1s**
rsolv	T/O	33.6s	**0.2s**
spline	FAIL	1.6s	**0.3s**
tridag	4.1s	1.5s	**0.3s**
ntdrivers			
cdaudio_simpl1	64.8s	**24.9s**	393s
diskperf_simpl1	41.9s	**21.1s**	213s
floppy_simpl3	30.9s	**10.3s**	67s
floppy_simpl4	50.1s	**16.3s**	139s
kbfiltr_simpl1	3.7s	**2.7s**	3.2s
kbfiltr_simpl2	5.5s	**4.0s**	7.2s
cdaudio_simpl1_BUG	29.3s	**12.3s**	351s
floppy_simpl3_BUG	**1.5s**	7.5s	96s
floppy_simpl4_BUG	**1.5s**	12.9s	135s
kbfiltr_simpl2_BUG	**3.1s**	3.2s	14.7s
ssh-simplified			
s3_clnt_1	103s	8.0s	**7.4s**
s3_clnt_2	147s	59s	**4.2s**
s3_clnt_3	FAIL	7.4s	**7.3s**
s3_clnt_4	80s	9.7s	**6.6s**
s3_srvr_1	FAIL	23.2s	**9.8s**
s3_srvr_2	FAIL	40.0s	**10.1s**
s3_srvr_3	FAIL	**9.9s**	36.1s
s3_srvr_4	FAIL	11.3s	**8.9s**
s3_srvr_6	110s	**41.9s**	49.5s
s3_srvr_7	FAIL	**14.0s**	133s
s3_srvr_8	41.5s	**11.1s**	23.1s
s3_clnt_1_BUG	4.5s	3.0s	**1.3s**
s3_clnt_2_BUG	4.9s	2.6s	**1.4s**
s3_clnt_3_BUG	4.9s	2.9s	**1.3s**
s3_clnt_4_BUG	4.6s	3.0s	**1.4s**
s3_srvr_1_BUG	FAIL	**2.6s**	3.1s
s3_srvr_2_BUG	66s	2.5s	**2.2s**

Program	Threader	HSF
Multi-threaded programs		
Fig2-cex-BUG	0.2s	**0.1s**
Fig2-fixed	0.8s	**0.7s**
Fig4-cex-BUG	4.5s	**0.5s**
Fig4-fixed	1.5s	**0.5s**
Bluetooth2	29.1s	**12.9s**
Bluetooth2-fixed	3.7s	**0.2s**
Bluetooth3-fixed	135s	**18.6s**
Scull	129s	**11.6s**
Dekker	11.1s	**4.0s**
Peterson	4.7s	**3.7s**
Readers-writer-lock	0.2s	**0.1s**
Time varying mutex	11.8s	**9.8s**
Szymanski	32s	**8.7s**
NaiveBakery	**2.5s**	2.6s
Bakery	105s	**32.4s**
Lamport	121s	**30.5s**
QRCU	34.5s	**15.4s**

Program	HMC	HSF
OCaml programs (correct / buggy)		
na_dotprod-m	**0.04s / 0.04s**	0.11s / 0.06s
na_arraymax-m	0.32s / **0.05s**	**0.05s** / 0.07s
na_bcopy-m	0.09s / 5.94s	**0.06s / 0.07s**
na_bsearch-m	0.91s / 0.10s	**0.03s / 0.02s**
na_insertsort-m	**0.03s / 0.03s**	1.78s / 0.04s
mult-cps-m	**0.03s / 0.03s**	**0.03s / 0.03s**
mult-all-m	0.03s / 0.03s	**0.01s / 0.01s**
sum-all-m	0.03s / 0.03s	**0.01s / 0.01s**
sum-acm-m	0.04s / 0.03s	**0.01s / 0.01s**

Program	HSF
Terminating loops	
broydn (33 cutpoints)	591s
elmhes (9 cutpoints)	23.0s
jacobi (15 cutpoints)	16.0s
ludcmp (11 cutpoints)	4.2s
qrdcmp (9 cutpoints)	189s
rlft3 (7 cutpoints)	16.1s
spctrm (14 cutpoints)	86s

Table 1. Timings for the benchmarks. The left-side of the page shows statistics for sequential programs, with multi-threaded programs, functional programs and terminating loops on the right-side of the page. "T/O" stands for time out after 10 minutes, while "FAIL" indicates that the tool failed to return a verification result.

For verification of sequential programs, we used a set of programs from the Numerical Recipes book [40], with array bound checking being the safety property to verify. This set of benchmarks includes simulated annealing (amebsa), evaluate a trial point using simulated annealing (amotsa), fast fourier transform (four1), or polynomial extrapolation (pzextr). We also used two sets of benchmarks (ntdrivers and ssh-simplified) from the test suite of CPAchecker [7].

We collected multi-threaded and functional programs from the test suites of specialized verification tools, i.e., Threader [18] and HMC [24]. For termination checking, we used a set of programs from the Numerical Recipes book, including a secant method program (broydn), and a program to reduce a matrix to the Hessenberg form (elmhes).

Our benchmark suite includes both safe and non-safe programs. Non-safe programs have the word "BUG" attached to their name. For termination checking, all the benchmarks are terminating and we report the number of cutpoints as a measure for the effort to verify program termination.

Evaluation Our experiments were run on an Intel Core 2 Duo machine, clocked at 3.0 GHz, with 4 GB of RAM, and running Linux 2.6.38. See Table 1 for the results.

For the first three categories of benchmarks (Numerical Recipes, ntdrivers and ssh-simplified), we used HSF with the summarization proof rule described in Section 2. For the verification of these sequential C programs, we compare HSF with BLAST [20, 21] and CPAchecker [7]. For ntdrivers and ssh-simplified, we used BLAST 2.5 with the MathSat solver [9] and the following standard options: `-craig 2 -dfs -predH 7 -nosimplemem -alias ""`, as suggested by the tool's authors. The use of the MathSat solver led to Blast failing all the Numerical Recipes benchmarks, so instead we report statistics using the latest publicly available version of Blast that uses the Simplify solver. For CPAchecker, we used the revision r3842 from the tool repository and used the predicate abstraction with large block encoding configuration as suggested by the tool's authors.

For verification of multi-threaded programs, we used HSF with a proof rule based on rely-guarantee reasoning [25]. We compare HSF with Threader using a reasoning style that is equivalent to the proof rule mentioned above.

For the verification of functional OCaml programs, we compare HSF with HMC [24]. The techniques used in HMC extend a liquid type system (i.e., [43] that requires user-provided logical qualifiers) to enable automatic verification of OCaml programs.

We used HSF with a termination proof rule for the programs from the last table, Terminating loops. We do not have access to any public tool that can handle termination properties for these C benchmarks.

In general, HSF is comparable and sometimes significantly faster than state-of-the-art tools specialized to a particular verification proof rule. For all our experiments, the verification tools (including HSF) were run starting with an empty set of predicates, i.e., all predicates needed for verification were discovered automatically. Two limitations of our implementation lead to HSF being slower for the ntdrivers benchmarks: no direct support for equality predicates and the program representation with the transition relation in disjunctive normal form. For example, instead of a single equality predicate (say $x = y$), HSF tracks two predicates, i.e., $x \geq y$ and $x \leq y$, both during abstraction and refinement. We plan to implement heuristics to handle the high level of branching present in this set of benchmarks. On the other hand, we leverage the uniform representation of the Horn clauses for simplification and inlining steps before the start of the verification process. These transformations lead to substantial savings that are particularly effective in the Numerical Recipes, multi-threaded, and OCaml benchmarks. In total, HSF took approximately 48 minutes to analyze 35 kloc (we exclude the lines of code for the two programs on which HSF timed out).

We applied our tool on benchmarks from various classes of verification problems, which are usually approached using specialized tools.

Verification competition HSF(C) is a verifier for C programs developed using the HSF algorithm and based on the summarization proof rule. HSF(C) participated in the TACAS2012 software verification competition [6] and reached the 3rd place in the largest category ControlFlowInteger and it competed with recent implementations of Blast, CPAchecker and 6 more verification tools. (HSF(C) did not participate in the other categories that required bit-precise reasoning or pointer analysis features not supported by our CIL frontend.)

For the ControlFlowInteger category, HSF(C) analyzed 96 benchmarks from five groups: locks, ntdrivers, ntdrivers-simplified, ssh and ssh-simplified. Each of these benchmarks consists of a C program and a safety property, which may or may not hold. HSF timed out on 2 of these programs, verifying and finding counterexamples correctly for all the others, in total 207.2 kloc analyzed in 80 minutes. More details about HSF(C) can be found in the related competition report [16].

7. Related work

Section 1 points to existing approaches to generate various analyses based on dataflow domains that led to powerful program analysis frameworks [3, 27–29, 31, 34, 47, 51].

Verifiers have also been a target for automated tool construction. XSB [41] is a programmable fixed-point engine used for implementing model checkers for a concurrent language based on CCS with properties specified in a fragment of mu-calculus. Model checkers have been generated from algebraic specifications of a source language and various fragments of temporal logic [45]. More recently, verifier generators have been developed for Boolean programs (GETAFIX [49]) and programs for which Datalog style bottom up inference terminates (μZ [22]). For programs with unbounded data domains, MatchC [44] provides a verifier based on matching logic specifications that directly build upon the operational semantics of the source language. The verification is facilitated by (pattern) loop invariants provided by the programmer. In comparison, our approach adds an abstraction refinement loop, which is crucial for handling unbounded datatypes, and allows automation of proof rules for termination and liveness properties.

HSF synthesizes verifiers that are competitive with state-of-the-art tools from a recent verification competition, while benefiting from a series of verification algorithms. We build upon predicate abstraction [15], counterexample guided abstraction refinement [10], interpolation [32], ranking function generation [8, 38], and constraint solvers for recursion-free Horn clauses [17, 19, 39].

Our work provides an intermediate representation for verification tasks in the form of Horn-like clauses with the support for a dwf-predicate. This representation was inspired by the usage of Horn clauses for the inference of environment assumptions of multi-threaded programs [19]. Boogie provides a different intermediate representation for procedural and object-oriented programs. Boogie represents programs and therefore it requires an intermediate step to generate verification conditions, while Horn clauses encode verification tasks directly as constraints. We believe that generation of Horn clauses from Boogie programs will yield yet another verification tool for Boogie and all of its input languages.

8. Conclusion

We presented a next logical step towards the automatic generation of software verification tools. Our verifier generator takes as input a proof rule written as Horn-like clauses and produces a verifier that automates the proof rule. The experimental evaluation shows that automatically generated verifiers are competitive with existing state-of-the-art verification tools that are manually developed and tuned.

Acknowledgments

We thank Jasmin Blanchette for comments and suggestions.

References

[1] A. V. Aho, M. S. Lam, R. Sethi, and J. D. Ullman. *Compilers: Principles, Techniques, and Tools*. Pearson, 2006.

[2] A. Aiken. Introduction to set constraint-based program analysis. *Sci. Comput. Program.*, 35(2), 1999.

[3] A. Aiken, M. Fähndrich, J. S. Foster, and Z. Su. A toolkit for constructing type- and constraint-based program analyses. In *Types in Compilation*, 1998.

[4] T. Ball and S. K. Rajamani. The SLAM project: debugging system software via static analysis. In *POPL*, 2002.

[5] T. Ball, A. Podelski, and S. K. Rajamani. Boolean and cartesian abstraction for model checking C programs. In *TACAS*, 2001.

[6] D. Beyer. Competition on software verification - (SV-COMP). In *TACAS*, 2012.

[7] D. Beyer and M. E. Keremoglu. CPAchecker: A tool for configurable software verification. In *CAV*, 2011.

[8] A. R. Bradley, Z. Manna, and H. B. Sipma. Linear ranking with reachability. In *CAV*, 2005.

[9] R. Bruttomesso, A. Cimatti, A. Franzén, A. Griggio, and R. Sebastiani. The MathSAT 4SMT solver. In *CAV*, 2008.

[10] E. M. Clarke, O. Grumberg, S. Jha, Y. Lu, and H. Veith. Counterexample-guided abstraction refinement. In *CAV*, 2000.

[11] B. Cook, A. Podelski, and A. Rybalchenko. Termination proofs for systems code. In *PLDI*, 2006.

[12] B. Cook, A. Podelski, and A. Rybalchenko. Summarization for termination: no return! *Formal Methods in System Design*, 35(3), 2009.

[13] C. Flanagan and S. Qadeer. Thread-modular model checking. In *SPIN*, 2003.

[14] T. Freeman and F. Pfenning. Refinement types for ML. In *PLDI*, 1991.

[15] S. Graf and H. Saïdi. Construction of abstract state graphs with PVS. In *CAV*, 1997.

[16] S. Grebenshchikov, A. Gupta, N. P. Lopes, C. Popeea, and A. Rybalchenko. HSF(C): A software verifier based on Horn clauses - (competition contribution). In *TACAS*, 2012.

[17] A. Gupta, C. Popeea, and A. Rybalchenko. Solving recursion-free horn clauses over LI+UIF. In *APLAS*, 2011.

[18] A. Gupta, C. Popeea, and A. Rybalchenko. Threader: A constraint-based verifier for multi-threaded programs. In *CAV*, 2011.

[19] A. Gupta, C. Popeea, and A. Rybalchenko. Predicate abstraction and refinement for verifying multi-threaded programs. In *POPL*, 2011.

[20] T. A. Henzinger, R. Jhala, R. Majumdar, and G. Sutre. Lazy abstraction. In *POPL*, 2002.

[21] T. A. Henzinger, R. Jhala, R. Majumdar, and K. L. McMillan. Abstractions from proofs. In *POPL*, 2004.

[22] K. Hoder, N. Bjørner, and L. de Moura. μZ- an efficient engine for fixed points with constraints. In *CAV*, 2011.

[23] F. Ivancic, Z. Yang, M. K. Ganai, A. Gupta, I. Shlyakhter, and P. Ashar. F-Soft: Software verification platform. In *CAV*, 2005.

[24] R. Jhala, R. Majumdar, and A. Rybalchenko. HMC: Verifying functional programs using abstract interpreters. In *CAV*, 2011.

[25] C. B. Jones. Tentative steps toward a development method for interfering programs. *ACM Trans. Program. Lang. Syst.*, 5(4), 1983.

[26] K. W. Knowles and C. Flanagan. Type reconstruction for general refinement types. In *ESOP*, 2007.

[27] J. Kodumal and A. Aiken. Banshee: A scalable constraint-based analysis toolkit. In *SAS*, 2005.

[28] M. S. Lam, J. Whaley, V. B. Livshits, M. C. Martin, D. Avots, M. Carbin, and C. Unkel. Context-sensitive program analysis as database queries. In *PODS*, 2005.

[29] S. Lerner, T. D. Millstein, E. Rice, and C. Chambers. Automated soundness proofs for dataflow analyses and transformations via local rules. In *POPL*, 2005.

[30] Z. Manna and A. Pnueli. *Temporal verification of reactive systems: safety*. 1995.

[31] F. Martin. PAG – An efficient program analyzer generator. *STTT*, 2 (1), 1998.

[32] K. L. McMillan. An interpolating theorem prover. *TCS*, 2005.

[33] K. L. McMillan. Lazy abstraction with interpolants. In *CAV*, 2006.

[34] M. Naik, A. Aiken, and J. Whaley. Effective static race detection for Java. In *PLDI*, 2006.

[35] G. C. Necula, S. McPeak, S. P. Rahul, and W. Weimer. CIL: Intermediate language and tools for analysis and transformation of C programs. In *CC*, 2002.

[36] S. S. Owicki and D. Gries. An axiomatic proof technique for parallel programs I. *Acta Inf.*, 6, 1976.

[37] A. Podelski and A. Rybalchenko. Transition invariants. In *LICS*, 2004.

[38] A. Podelski and A. Rybalchenko. A complete method for the synthesis of linear ranking functions. In *VMCAI*, 2004.

[39] C. Popeea and A. Rybalchenko. Compositional termination proofs for multi-threaded programs. In *TACAS*, 2012.

[40] W. H. Press, B. P. Flannery, S. A. Teukolsky, and W. T. Vetterling. *Numerical Recipes in C: The Art of Scientific Computing*. 1992.

[41] Y. S. Ramakrishna, C. R. Ramakrishnan, I. V. Ramakrishnan, S. A. Smolka, T. Swift, and D. S. Warren. Efficient model checking using tabled resolution. In *CAV*, 1997.

[42] T. W. Reps, S. Horwitz, and S. Sagiv. Precise interprocedural dataflow analysis via graph reachability. In *POPL*, 1995.

[43] P. M. Rondon, M. Kawaguchi, and R. Jhala. Liquid types. In *PLDI*, 2008.

[44] G. Rosu and A. Stefanescu. Matching logic: a new program verification approach. In *ICSE*, 2011.

[45] T. Rus, E. V. Wyk, and T. Halverson. Generating model checkers from algebraic specifications. *Formal Methods in System Design*, 20(3), 2002.

[46] A. Rybalchenko and V. Sofronie-Stokkermans. Constraint solving for interpolation. In *VMCAI*, 2007.

[47] M. Sagiv. *High Level Formalisms for Program Flow Analysis and their use in Compiling*. PhD thesis, Technion, 1991.

[48] T. Terauchi. Dependent types from counterexamples. In *POPL*, 2010.

[49] S. L. Torre, P. Madhusudan, and G. Parlato. Analyzing recursive programs using a fixed-point calculus. In *PLDI*, 2009.

[50] H. Unno and N. Kobayashi. Dependent type inference with interpolants. In *PPDP*, 2009.

[51] J. Whaley and M. S. Lam. Cloning-based context-sensitive pointer alias analysis using binary decision diagrams. In *PLDI*, 2004.

Concurrent Data Representation Synthesis

Peter Hawkins
Computer Science Department, Stanford University
hawkinsp@cs.stanford.edu

Alex Aiken *
Computer Science Department, Stanford University
aiken@cs.stanford.edu

Kathleen Fisher †
Computer Science Department, Tufts University
kfisher@eecs.tufts.edu

Martin Rinard
MIT Computer Science and Artificial Intelligence Laboratory
rinard@csail.mit.edu

Mooly Sagiv
Tel-Aviv University
msagiv@post.tau.ac.il

Abstract

We describe an approach for synthesizing data representations for concurrent programs. Our compiler takes as input a program written using *concurrent relations* and synthesizes a representation of the relations as sets of cooperating data structures as well as the placement and acquisition of locks to synchronize concurrent access to those data structures. The resulting code is correct by construction: individual relational operations are implemented correctly and the aggregate set of operations is serializable and deadlock free. The relational specification also permits a high-level optimizer to choose the best performing of many possible legal data representations and locking strategies, which we demonstrate with an experiment autotuning a graph benchmark.

Categories and Subject Descriptors D.3.3 [*Programming Languages*]: Language Constructs and Features—Abstract data types, Concurrent programming structures, Data types and structures; E.2 [*Data Storage Representations*]

Keywords Synthesis, Lock Placement

1. Introduction

Consider the problem of implementing concurrent operations on a directed graph. We must decide how to represent the graph as a collection of data structures, perhaps using a lookup table mapping each node to the set of its adjacent nodes. We will need to pick concrete representations for both the lookup table (e.g., a concurrent hashmap) and the adjacency sets (e.g., linked lists). We must also decide how concurrency will be realized. We could add our own synchronization using locks and/or we could use a concurrent container data structure to implement the lookup table, the sets of adjacent nodes, or both.

Assume for the moment that we decide both containers will be concurrent. We must of course ensure there is enough synchronization to avoid harmful races, but not so much that we either limit scalability or introduce deadlocks. Using off-the-shelf concurrent containers can simplify this task, but even using concurrent containers for both data structures does not automatically imply that high-level graph operations that touch both structures (such as inserting or removing an edge from the graph) are correct. In fact, recent work in bug detection for concurrent programs has shown that programmers frequently fail to use standard concurrent containers correctly, especially when they must compose multiple concurrent operations [20].

On the other hand, it may be more efficient to have only the top-level lookup table be concurrent and use non-concurrent data structures for the sets of adjacent nodes—if it is very infrequent that threads try to access the same node simultaneously the extra overhead of a concurrent data structure for the adjacency sets won't be worthwhile. This design has different correctness requirements and would likely result in a different choice of where to place any needed synchronization to guarantee correctness. The right answer to the decision of whether to use a concurrent or non-concurrent data structure for the adjacency sets likely depends on the typical workload and it will be difficult to modify the interlinked synchronization and data structures if we decide later that the graph should be implemented differently.

In this paper we present an approach to synthesizing concurrent data representations, meaning that from a high-level specification of data we produce both the concrete data structures and the corresponding synchronization to implement the specification. In our approach, programs are written using *concurrent relations* (Section 2), a generalization of standard concurrent collections to relations with a concurrent interface to perform insertions, deletions, and lookups of tuples. Our compiler automatically synthesizes all aspects of the data representation, including the choice of data structures and how they interact, the number and placement of locks to guard access to those data structures (including, for example, whether locking should be fine-grain or coarse-grain), an order in which locks can be acquired to guarantee deadlock freedom, and all of the code to correctly manage the interplay of the data structures and synchronization.

* This work was supported by NSF Grant CCF-0702681 and Stanford's Army High Performance Research Center.

† The views expressed are those of the author and do not reflect the official policy or position of the Department of Defense or U.S. Government. Distribution Statement A (Approved for Public Release, Distribution Unlimited)

PLDI'12, June 11–16, 2012, Beijing, China.

By specifying a program's access to data using concurrent relations and avoiding a premature commitment to a particular representation, much of the low-level detail of programs is removed, making them easier to read and maintain, while simultaneously making it much easier to change the implementation if desired. Furthermore, concurrent relations give a high-level and pointer-free specification of data, which is good for compilers, because the compiler is now free to choose the concrete representation of the data without the usual requirement that it first perform a complex and usually brittle pointer analysis. Programs written using relational data specifications are simpler, correct by construction, and can be automatically optimized in ways that are out of reach of compilers for languages with traditional data structure definitions.

Beginning with Cohen and Campbell [5] researchers have investigated how to compile programs written using relations as the main (and sometimes only) aggregate form of data into low-level data representations. Our method builds on two recent results (Section 4): we use the *decompositions* of Hawkins et al. [12] to describe how relations can be decomposed into a set of cooperating data structures, and we use the theory of *lock placements* [13] to describe the space of possible locking strategies. Our specific contributions are:

- We introduce *concurrent relations*, a generalization of standard concurrent container data structures to containers of tuples, with concurrent operations to insert, remove, and query relations (Section 2).
- The selection of data structures is subtler than in the non-concurrent case, because there is the added dimension of using concurrent container structures, which may or may not require additional synchronization depending on the relational specification, and, in addition, different concurrent containers provide varying guarantees about the safety of concurrent access. We give a taxonomy of containers and their properties relevant to concurrent data representation synthesis (Section 3).
- We extend the relational decomposition language [12] to support concurrent relations. Just as the original decomposition language describes how to assemble a representation of a relation from a library of container data structures, concurrent decompositions describe how to compose concurrent and non-concurrent data structures together with locks to implement a concurrent relation primitive (Section 4.1).
- We show how to integrate *lock placements* [13], which describe a space of possible locking strategies on data structures, with the problem of selecting the data structures themselves. The choice of data structures and lock placements is done in such a way that the resulting code is guaranteed to ensure the serializability of relational operations (Section 4.2).
- We adapt and generalize the problem of selecting a good implementation of the relational primitives, called *query planning*, to concurrent relations (Section 5). One of the major issues is ensuring deadlock freedom, which we accomplish by selecting a global lock ordering that all relational operations obey by construction. Deadlock is not addressed in the previous work on lock placements [13].
- The optimal decomposition depends on the usage patterns of the data structure and the target machine. We present results from a full implementation, which includes an autotuner that allows us to discover a good combination of both locks and container data structures automatically for a training workload. We perform an evaluation of a concurrent graph benchmark, showing that the best data representation varies with the workload, and thus it is important to have the flexibility to easily alter the representation of concurrent data (Section 6).

2. Concurrent Relations

We advocate a view in which programmers write programs that operate on relations and a compiler selects the concrete representation of the relations. A *relational specification* is a set of column names C together with a set of *functional dependencies* Δ. Functional dependencies (FDs) specify which columns are uniquely determined by other columns. For example, we can represent the edges of a directed graph as a relation with three columns: src (source node), dst (destination node), and weight, together with a functional dependency src, dst $\to$ weight, which specifies that every edge of the graph has a unique weight. The relational specification is a contract between the client of our compiler and the generated code: If the client obeys the functional dependencies, then the compiler guarantees that the generated code preserves the semantics of the relational operations.

Values, Tuples, Relations We assume a set of untyped values v drawn from a universe $\mathbb{V}$ that includes the integers ($\mathbb{Z} \subseteq \mathbb{V}$). A *tuple* $t = \langle c_1\colon v_1, c_2\colon v_2, \dots\rangle$ maps a set of *columns* $\{c_1, c_2, \dots\}$ to values drawn from $\mathbb{V}$. We write $\operatorname{dom} t$ for the columns of t. A tuple t is a *valuation* for a set of columns C if $\operatorname{dom} t = C$. A *relation* r is a set of tuples $\{t_1, t_2, \dots\}$ over identical columns C. We write $t(c)$ for the value of column c in tuple t. We write $t \supseteq s$ if the tuple t *extends* tuple s, that is $t(c) = s(c)$ for all c in $\operatorname{dom} s$. We say tuple t *matches* tuple s, written $t \sim s$, if the tuples are equal on all common columns. Tuple t matches a relation r, written $t \sim r$, if t matches every tuple in r. A tuple t is a *key* for a relation r if the columns $\operatorname{dom} t$ functionally determine all columns of r.

We use the standard notation of relational algebra. Union ($\cup$), intersection ($\cap$), set difference ($\setminus$) have their usual meanings. The operator $\pi_C\, r$ projects relation r onto a set of columns C. A relation r has a *functional dependency* (FD) $C_1 \to C_2$ if any pair of tuples in r that are equal on columns C_1 are also equal on columns C_2.

Relational Operations We provide four atomic operations for creating and manipulating *concurrent relations*. In the following specification we represent relations as ML-style references to a set of tuples: ref x creates a new reference to x, $!x$ retrieves the current value of x, and $x \leftarrow y$ sets the current value of x to y.

$$\begin{aligned}
\mathsf{empty}\ () &= \mathsf{ref}\ \emptyset\\
\mathsf{remove}\ r\ s &= r \leftarrow !r \setminus \{t \in !r \mid t \supseteq s\}\\
\mathsf{query}\ r\ s\ C &= \pi_C\{t \in !r \mid t \supseteq s\}\\
\mathsf{insert}\ r\ s\ t &= \mathsf{if}\ \nexists u.\ u \in !r \wedge s \subseteq u\ \mathsf{then}\ r \leftarrow !r \cup \{s \cup t\}
\end{aligned}$$

Informally, empty () creates a new empty relation. Operation remove r s removes tuples matching s; in practice, our implementation requires that s is a key for the relation. Operation query r s C returns columns C of all tuples in r matching tuple s.

The most interesting operation is insert r s t, which inserts a new tuple x, where x is the union of the columns of tuples s and t, into a relation r, provided there is no existing tuple in r matching s. We require that s and t have disjoint domains. Insert generalizes the put-if-absent operation provided by standard concurrent key-value maps: *put-if-absent(k,v)* inserts value v into the map if no other value is already associated with key k, and would be written

$$\mathsf{insert}\ r\ \langle \mathrm{key}\colon k\rangle\ \langle \mathrm{value}\colon v\rangle$$

Insert operations may violate functional dependencies, and it is the client's obligation to ensure functional dependencies are observed. The form of the insert operation allows clients to test whether functional dependencies will be satisfied by a new tuple even in the presence of concurrent updates.

The relational compiler ensures that the implementations of the relational operations are *linearizable* [15] (equivalently *serializable*, since the relational operations are single operation transactions on a single object). Operations on an object are *linearizable* if every

Data Structure	Concurrency-safety			
	L/L L/S S/S	L/W	S/W	W/W
`HashMap`	yes	no	no	no
`TreeMap`	yes	no	no	no
`ConcurrentHashMap`	yes	yes	weak	yes
`ConcurrentSkipListMap`	yes	yes	weak	yes
`CopyOnWriteArrayList`	yes	yes	yes	yes

Figure 1. Concurrency safety properties of selected containers from the JDK. Possible operations are lookup (L), scan (S), or write (W). For an operation pair α/β, concurrently executing operations α and β on a container is either unsafe ("no"), safe but only weakly consistent ("weak"), or both safe and linearizable ("yes").

operation appears to take place atomically at a single point in time in between its invocation and response.

Continuing with our graph example, we create a new, empty graph relation r_0 using the empty () operation. Inserting an edge

$$\text{insert } r_0 \ \langle \text{src}\colon 1, \text{dst}\colon 2\rangle \ \langle \text{weight}\colon 42\rangle$$

results in a new relation $r_1 = \{\langle \text{src}\colon 1, \text{dst}\colon 2, \text{weight}\colon 42\rangle\}$. A subsequent insertion

$$\text{insert } r_1 \ \langle \text{src}\colon 1, \text{dst}\colon 2\rangle \ \langle \text{weight}\colon 101\rangle$$

leaves the relation unchanged, because relation r_1 already contains an edge with the same src and dst fields.

We can retrieve the dst and weight fields corresponding to the successors of node 1 in a relation r using the operation query r $\langle \text{src}\colon 1\rangle$ $\{\text{dst}, \text{weight}\}$, and finally we can delete edges with a dst of 2 using the operation remove r $\langle \text{dst}\colon 2\rangle$.

3. A Taxonomy of Concurrent Containers

Decompositions describe how to implement concurrent relations as a combination of both concurrent and non-concurrent data structures. Before diving into the details of the decomposition language (Section 4), we first describe the concurrency properties of the container data structures found in the wild, which form the building blocks of concurrent decompositions.

Container Interface A *container* is a data structure that implements an associative key-value map interface consisting of *read operations* lookup(k) and scan(f), and a *write operation* write(k, v).

- The *lookup* operation lookup(k) returns the value associated with a key k, if any.
- The *scan* operation scan(f) iterates over the map, and invokes the function $f(k, v)$ once for each key k and its associated value v in the map. A scan may or may not return the entries of the map in sorted order.
- The *write* operation write(k, v) sets the value associated with a key k to v. Here v is an optional value, in the style of ML. If v is Some w, then the operation updates the value associated with key k to w, whereas if v is None, representing the absence of a value, then any existing value associated with k is removed. The write operation subsumes operations to insert, update, and remove entries from a map.

3.1 Concurrency Safety and Consistency

We next discuss two related properties of containers, *concurrency safety*, which describes whether it is safe for two operations to occur in parallel, and *consistency*, which characterizes what a container guarantees about the possible orders of events in a concurrent execution. Figure 1 lists the concurrency safety and consistency properties of a selection of Java containers from the JDK; as we show, containers differ greatly in their support for concurrency.

Concurrency Safety For a given data structure, we say a pair of operations α/β is *concurrency-safe* if two threads may safely execute operations α and β in parallel with no external synchronization. A container is *concurrency-safe* if all pairs of operations are concurrency-safe. Concurrency safety is strictly a statement about the correct usage of the interface of a data structure; it is irrelevant how the data structure guarantees safety internally, whether by locks, atomic instructions, or by some other means.

Consider the data structures described in Figure 1. Almost all data structures support parallel read operations; for example concurrent threads may safely read or iterate over a Java `HashMap` in parallel without synchronization. Exceptions exist; for example, it would not be safe for threads to perform concurrent reads of a splay tree because splay tree read operations rebalance the tree.

Only a few containers permit write operations in parallel with other operations. For example, it is unsafe to read from or write to a `HashMap` object while another thread is writing to the same `HashMap`. By contrast a `ConcurrentHashMap` or a `CopyOnWriteArrayList` allow concurrent lookup and write operations, or pairs of concurrent write operations. On a concurrency-safe container, such as a `ConcurrentHashMap`, the lookup and write operations are linearizable even in the absence of any external concurrency control. For concurrency-unsafe operations, such as reading a splay tree, linearizability is the responsibility of an external concurrency control primitive, such as a lock.

The scan operation, however, behaves differently. Even many containers that allow iteration in parallel with mutation do not guarantee that iteration is linearizable. We identify two different possibilities. Some containers, such as `ConcurrentHashMap` provide *weakly consistent* concurrent iteration; that is, concurrent iteration is safe, but may or may not reflect inserts and removals that occur in parallel with the iteration. Iteration over a weakly-consistent container may not be linearizable, that is, the result of the iteration may not correspond to the set of entries present in the container at any instant in time. Conversely for containers that provide *snapshot iteration*, such as a `CopyOnWriteArrayList`, iteration behaves as if it operated over a linearizable snapshot of the container.

4. Concurrent Decompositions

The concurrent decomposition language describes how to assemble container data structures into representations of relations that support concurrent serializable transactions that implement the various relational operations. By combining concurrent and non-concurrent data structures with locks we can build a representation of a relation with strong concurrency guarantees, even if the constituent data structures themselves have limited support for concurrency.

We extend the relational decomposition language [12] to support concurrent operations from multiple threads. Two key ideas underlie safe and scalable concurrent decompositions: leveraging existing concurrent containers (Section 4.1) to the full extent possible, and supplementing containers with locks as necessary to ensure the safety and serializability of concurrent transactions over the complete decomposition (Section 4.2).

As a focus of this paper is extending decompositions to support concurrency, we first review the definition of decompositions.

4.1 Decompositions

A *decomposition* describes how to represent a relation as a combination of primitive container data structures. A decomposition is a static description of the heap, similar to a type. We use a graphical notation for decompositions isomorphic to the let-binding notation in the literature [12]. Figure 2(a) shows a decomposition of a filesystem directory tree relation, based on the directory entry cache in the Linux kernel. The relation has three columns parent, name, and child and obeys a functional dependency parent, name $\to$ child. Each 'parent' directory entry has zero or more 'child' directory entries, each with a distinct file 'name'.

Formally, a decomposition $\hat{d}$ is a rooted, directed acyclic graph, consisting of a set of vertices $V = \{u, v, \dots\}$ and a set of edges drawn from $V \times V$. A decomposition has a unique *source* vertex ρ with no incoming edges. All vertices must be reachable from the source vertex.

Each node v of a decomposition has an associated "type" $A \rhd B$, written $v\colon A \rhd B$. Intuitively, A is the set of columns whose representation is specified by paths from the root node to v, and B is the residual set of columns represented by the subgraph reachable from v. Each edge uv of the decomposition has an associated set of columns $\mathsf{cols}(uv)$, and a choice of container $\mathsf{ds}(uv)$ the compiler should use to implement the edge.

In Figure 2(a), the edge ρx from the root indicates that the relation is implemented by a `TreeMap` from each parent value to the residual relation of all (name, child) pairs for that parent. Recursively, this subrelation is implemented by another `TreeMap` from name to the child directory (edge xy). Finally, the functional dependency guarantees that the child directory is a singleton tuple and is implemented by its single value (edge yz). This structure (a map from parents to the set of child directory names) enables efficient iteration over the children of a directory, which is useful when, for example, unmounting a filesystem. To enable efficient directory lookup the decomposition also includes a global hashtable mapping (parent, name) pairs to child objects (edge ρy).

We assume that decompositions are *adequate* [12], that is decompositions are capable of representing all relations satisfying the relational specification. The adequacy conditions imply that for every edge uv where $u\colon A \rhd B$ and $v\colon C \rhd D$ we have $C \supseteq A \cup \mathsf{cols}(uv)$.

Decomposition Instances The run-time (dynamic) counterpart of a decomposition $\hat{d}$ is a *decomposition instance* d, which represents a particular concrete relation. Each node $v\colon A \rhd B$ in a decomposition $\hat{d}$ has a set of instances $\{v_t\}$ where $\mathrm{dom}\, t = A$, each corresponding to an object in memory. Each edge uv of a decomposition has a set of edge instances $\{uv_t\}$, where if $u\colon A \rhd B$ then $\mathrm{dom}\, t = A \cup \mathsf{cols}(uv)$. If $u\colon A \rhd B$ and $\mathrm{dom}\, t \supset A$, we write u_t to denote the node instance $u_{\pi_A t}$; similarly if $\mathrm{dom}\, t \supset A \cup \mathsf{cols}(uv)$ we write uv_t to denote $uv_{\pi_{A \cup \mathsf{cols}(uv)}\, t}$. A formal characterization of *well-formed* decomposition instances and an *abstraction function* that maps well-formed decomposition instances back to the relations they represent can be found in the literature [12].

Figure 2(b) depicts an instance of the decomposition of Figure 2(a) representing the relation containing 3 directory entries:

$$\{\, \langle \text{parent}: 1,\ \text{name}: \text{'a'},\ \text{child}: 2 \rangle\,,\ \langle \text{parent}: 2,\ \text{name}: \text{'b'},\ \text{child}: 3 \rangle\,,\ \langle \text{parent}: 2,\ \text{name}: \text{'c'},\ \text{child}: 4 \rangle \,\}.$$

4.2 Logical Locks, Transactions, and Serializability

Locks Given a decomposition d, we compile each relational operation into a transaction tailored to d. For safety and consistency transactions must acquire locks that protect the invariants upon which a transaction relies. By "lock" we mean a class of pessimistic synchronization primitives that may be held by a transaction in either of two different *modes*, namely *shared* or *exclusive*. A lock may, but need not, permit multiple transactions to hold shared access simultaneously; however if a transaction holds exclusive access to a lock the lock must not allow any other transaction to hold either shared or exclusive access.

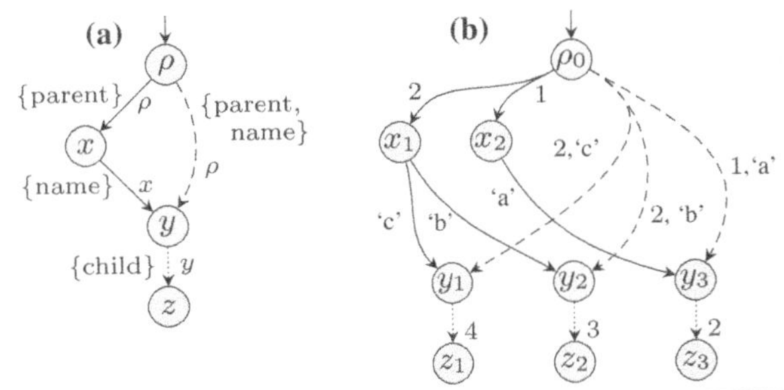

Figure 2. (a): A decomposition representing a directory tree relation with three columns {parent, name, child} and **(b)**: an instance of decomposition (a). Each edge of the decomposition is labeled with a set of columns $\{\cdots\}$, together with the label of the node whose lock protects instances of that edge (Section 4.3). Each edge of the instance is labeled with a valuation for the corresponding decomposition edge's columns. Solid edges indicate a `TreeMap`, dashed edges represent a `ConcurrentHashMap`, and dotted edges represent singleton tuples.

Logical Locks To ensure that transactions are serializable, the data in decomposition instances are protected by *logical locks*. We associate a distinct logical lock with every edge uv_t of a decomposition instance. Logical locks protect the state, either presence or absence, of an edge instance. If a transaction observes the presence or absence of an edge it must hold shared access to the corresponding logical lock, and if a transaction adds or removes an edge it must hold exclusive access to the corresponding logical lock. Logical locks are defined for every possible edge instance, irrespective of whether the edge is actually present in a particular decomposition instance or not.

For now, we leave the implementation of each logical lock uv_t abstract. In Section 4.3, we implement logical locks using a smaller set of *physical locks* attached to the nodes of a decomposition instance. By placing restrictions on the possible mappings from logical locks to physical locks we can ensure that containers (concurrent or not) and compositions of containers are used safely.

Two-Phase Locking Protocol Each transaction consists of a sequence of locks, reads, writes, and unlocks of the edges of a decomposition instance. The purpose of introducing logical locks is that by having a distinct lock for every edge (including edges that are absent) we are able to state a very simple and obviously correct protocol for transactions on decomposition instances. To ensure consistency of transactions, we use a standard two-phase locking protocol on logical locks:

- Transaction operations must be *logically well-locked*; that is, if a transaction observes the state (either present or absent) of an edge instance uv_t via a lookup or scan operation then it must hold shared access to the logical lock of uv_t, and if a transaction adds, removes, or updates an instance edge uv_t via a write operation then it must hold exclusive access to the logical lock of uv_t.
- Transactions must be *logically two-phase*, that is, transactions must be divided into a *growing* phase during which logical locks are acquired and a *shrinking* phase during which logical locks are released. All lock acquisitions must precede all lock releases.

It is a classic result that well-locked and two-phase transactions are serializable [10].

4.3 Physical Locks and Lock Placements

By associating a unique logical lock with every edge instance we can use a simple two-phase locking protocol to ensure that transactions are serializable. Such an approach would be impractical, however.

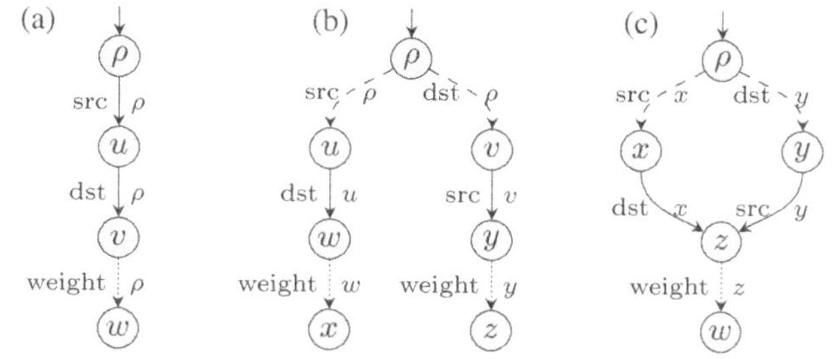

Figure 3. Three concurrent decompositions for a directed graph relation: (a) a "stick", with a single coarse lock around non-concurrent data structures, (b) a "split" decomposition, with locks at different granularities, and (c) a "diamond", with a mixture of speculatively-locked concurrent data structures and non-concurrent data structures. Solid edges indicate `TreeMap` containers, dashed edges represent `ConcurrentHashMap` containers, and dotted edges represent singleton tuples. Each edge is labeled with a set of columns on the left and the associated lock placement on the right.

Each edge instance corresponds to a entry in a container in the heap, and it would often be too slow to actually use locks at such a fine granularity, not to mention the practical problem that there are infinitely many logical locks defined for container entries that are absent. Further, as shown in Figure 1, in practice different containers have different levels of support for safe concurrency, and so while we must use locks to protect some containers from all concurrent accesses, in other cases we can rely on the container to mediate concurrent access. Finally, since we treat container implementations as black boxes, we have no way to attach locks to the edge instances directly.

Instead of literally maintaining one lock for every possible edge instance, we implement logical locks using a smaller set of *physical locks* attached to instances of nodes in a decomposition. We describe the correspondence between logical and physical locks using a *lock placement* [13], which is a mapping from the set of logical locks onto the set of physical locks. Many logical locks may map onto the same physical lock, and acquiring a physical lock corresponds to taking all of the corresponding logical locks. By choosing different lock placements we can describe different granularities of locking. Since physical locks are attached to node instances, in general there may be an unbounded number of physical locks.

Physical Locks To each node v in a decomposition we attach a set of physical locks $\{v^0, v^1, \dots\}$. If there is only a single physical lock attached to a node we simply write v for both the node and its unique physical lock.

Lock Placements A *lock placement* ψ is a function mapping the logical lock associated with each edge onto a physical lock on a node that implements it. We define lock placements on the (static) decomposition which we extend to (dynamic) decomposition instances in the obvious way; if a lock placement ψ maps the logical lock on edge e to the physical lock on node v, then at runtime the compiler maps the logical lock on edge instance e_t onto the physical lock on node instance v_t.

Recall the directed graph example from Section 2. The relation in question has three columns $\{\text{src}, \text{dst}, \text{weight}\}$ related via the functional dependency $\text{src}, \text{dst} \to \text{weight}$. Figure 3 shows three possible decompositions, each with a different choice of data structures and lock placements.

Figure 3(a) uses a coarse-grain lock placement

$$\psi_1(e) = \rho \text{ for all edges } e,$$

which protects all edges of the decomposition using a single lock at the root ρ. Since there is only one instance of the root node ρ in any decomposition instance, the same lock is used to protect everything. Further, since the logical locks of all edge instances are mapped to the same physical lock ρ, the lock serializes access to the entire decomposition data structure, ensuring that each (non-concurrent) `TreeMap` is only accessed by one transaction at a time.

Figure 3(b) depicts a fine-grain locking strategy decomposition in which each edge is protected by a lock at its head (i.e., objects in a container are protected by a single lock on the container itself), using the lock placement

$$\psi_2(\alpha\beta) = \alpha \text{ for all edges } \alpha\beta.$$

Edges ρu and ρv are protected by a lock at ρ, whereas edges uw, vy, wx and yz are protected by locks at u, v, w and y, respectively.

Both of the example lock placements described so far use a single lock to protect all the entries in each container. Figure 3(c) makes use of *speculative locking* (Section 4.5), one of two extensions which allow different dynamic instances of an edge in the same container to be protected by different locks. We defer further discussion of this example to Section 4.5.

Well-Formed Lock Placements We require that all lock placements satisfy the following conditions:

- The lock placement $\psi(uv)$ of each edge uv either must dominate the edge's source vertex u or be equal to v. (The latter case occurs in the speculatively-placed locks of Section 4.5.) By definition this condition ensures that the lock placement for an edge lies on every path from the root of the decomposition including that edge. This condition ensures the instance of the node $\psi(uv)$ named by the lock placement is unique for each edge instance uv_t. The domination requirement also simplifies query planning (Section 5), since it ensures that a query plan will always encounter the necessary locks for each edge no matter how the edge is reached.
- All edges between an edge and its lock placement share the same placement. That is, fix any edge uv and take any edge xy in a path in the decomposition from $\psi(uv)$ to u. Then we have $\psi(xy) = \psi(uv)$. This requirement ensures that if a lock protects an edge, then the lock also protects the path from the lock to that edge, thereby ensuring that if we hold a lock then the set of edges protected by that lock cannot change.

Logical Lock Implication Since we implement logical locks by mapping them onto a smaller set of physical locks, a transaction cannot acquire logical locks directly. Instead, a transaction must acquire physical locks that *imply* access to the logical locks that the transaction requires.

We say that a set of physical locks P held by a transaction *imply* exclusive or shared access, respectively, to the logical lock of edge instance uv_t under lock placement ψ if:

- the transaction holds exclusive or shared access, respectively, to the corresponding physical lock, that is, $\psi(uv)_t \in P$, and
- the mapping between the logical lock to the corresponding physical lock is stable, that is, there exists a path $\mathbf{w}_t$ from the root of the decomposition instance to u_t such that the transaction holds shared access to every edge in $\mathbf{w}_t$.

The stability criterion means that a physical lock only covers a logical lock if the transaction also holds locks that guarantee that the logical lock does in fact correspond to that physical lock; if not, a concurrent transaction might alter the heap and change the association between logical and physical locks. For example, consider a concurrent hashtable where the elements of each hash bucket are guarded by a lock. If a transaction moves an element v from bucket b_1 to bucket b_2 the lock guarding access to v changes, and any transaction that was concurrently accessing v by acquiring the lock on b_1 no longer holds the correct lock for v for the lock placement. Thus, in the presence of updates that can change the structure of the heap, it is not sufficient to just hold the locks L guarding access to the particular data, but it is also necessary to hold locks on whatever portion of the heap structure guarantees that L remains the correct set of locks to hold!

Since lock placements are defined using a decomposition structure, for locking using a placement to be well-defined we must ensure that transactions always yield heap states that are valid instances of the corresponding decomposition. One of the benefits of data representation synthesis is that we are guaranteed that the operations emitted by the compiler preserve the decomposition structure by construction.

4.4 Lock Striping

Lock striping is a technique for boosting the throughput of a transaction by using a set of locks instead of a single lock. Consider again the decomposition of Figure 3(b), in which the lock placement maps the logical lock on each edge to a physical lock at the source of the edge. While this lock placement ensures safe and consistent transactions, by protecting each container with a single lock we serialize access to containers, and hence we cannot make effective use of concurrent containers such as `ConcurrentHashMap`. To leverage concurrent containers we can partition the elements of the container into a number of *stripes*, each with its own lock.

For example, in Figure 3(b), rather than mapping all instances of edges ρu and ρv to a single physical lock at node ρ, we can use k physical locks $\rho^0, \ldots \rho^{k-1}$. We then use a lock placement that stripes the logical locks attached to instances of ρu and ρv across the k physical locks:

$$\psi_3(e,t) = \begin{cases} \rho^i & \text{if } e = \rho u,\ i = t(\text{src}) \bmod k \\ \rho^i & \text{if } e = \rho v,\ i = t(\text{dst}) \bmod k \\ \alpha_t & \text{otherwise, where } e = \alpha\beta \end{cases} \tag{1}$$

The lock placement takes as input an edge e annotated with a tuple t; the fields of tuple t are used to select one of the k physical locks at ρ. If we do not know the relevant tuple fields in advance, for example if we want to iterate over the container, we can always conservatively take all k locks.

Lock striping is only applicable for containers that are concurrency-safe. For a concurrency-unsafe container, such as a `TreeMap`, we are limited to at most one lock for the entire container to ensure that no two threads access the container concurrently.

By increasing the value k we can reduce lock contention to arbitrarily low levels, at the cost of making operations such as iteration that access the entire container more expensive.

4.5 Speculative Lock Placements

When striping logical locks across physical locks, as the number of physical locks k increases in the limit each container entry has its own individual lock. Rather than preallocating locks for an unbounded number of objects, we can achieve this limiting case more efficiently by using a technique called *speculative locking* [13], motivated by transactional predication [3]. Speculative locking lazily constructs a unique physical lock for each logical lock.

The key to speculative locking is the identity of the lock that protects an edge instance depends on the state of the edge instance itself. We map the logical lock to a distinct physical lock for each edge instance present in a container by placing the lock in the node that is the target of the edge instance. For serializability the lock placement must also be defined for edge instances that are absent from the decomposition, not just those edges that are present. Since we cannot place locks for non-existent edge instances at the target of the edge, instead we map the logical locks for absent edges onto physical locks at the edge's source.

Up to this point, we have required that the lock guarding an edge e appear on all paths from the root before e is reached. For speculative locks, this invariant does not hold—we do not know what lock to acquire until we have reached the object we wish to protect. The key is that it is safe to perform unlocked reads of a concurrency-safe container to guess the identity of the lock that we should acquire. Since the container is concurrency-safe, reading without holding a lock is safe, however we have no guarantees that any information that we read will remain stable. Once we have guessed and acquired a lock, we can check to see if our guess was correct. There are two possibilities — either we guessed correctly, in which case we already held the lock that protects the edge and our read was stable, or we guessed incorrectly, in which case the edge must point somewhere else. In the latter case we can release the lock we guessed and try again. While speculatively acquiring a lock is not physically two-phase, a transaction can be viewed as acquiring logical locks in a two phase manner [13].

Speculative lock acquisition differs from the well-known but broken double-checked locking idiom in two key ways—firstly, we always acquire a lock and recheck reads under that lock, and secondly we require that concurrent containers are linearizable, that is, with semantics analogous to a Java volatile field.

For example, the decomposition depicted in Figure 3(c) uses a mixture of both speculative and non-speculative locking — in particular, the locks that protect edges ρx and ρy are placed at the target of each edge on nodes x and y respectively. To take a lock on an edge instance ρx_t a transaction must first speculatively lookup entry t in the map without locking, acquire the lock on ρ or x_t if the edge instance is absent or present, respectively, and then verify that the correct lock was taken. The data structure implementing edge ρx is a `ConcurrentHashMap`, which is concurrency-safe, so it is safe to speculatively read an edge without holding its lock.

$$\psi_4(e,t) = \begin{cases} u_t & \text{if } e = \rho u,\ e_t \text{ is present} \\ \rho^i & \text{if } e = \rho u,\ e_t \text{ is not present},\ i = t(\text{src}) \bmod k \\ v_t & \text{if } e = \rho v,\ e_t \text{ is present} \\ \rho^i & \text{if } e = \rho v,\ e_t \text{ is not present},\ i = t(\text{dst}) \bmod k \\ \alpha_t & \text{otherwise, where } e = \alpha\beta \end{cases}$$

5. Query Planning and Lock Ordering

In Section 4 we introduced concurrent decompositions, which describe a relational specification using both concurrent and non-concurrent containers in combination with locks. In this section we show how to compile the relational operations of Section 2 into code tailored to a particular concurrent decomposition.

Existing work [12] described how to compile relational operations in a non-concurrent context. There are two additional complications we must deal with when generating concurrent implementations of relational operations—we must ensure that a transaction takes the locks that protect the decomposition edges it touches, and we must ensure that transactions are deadlock-free.

5.1 Deadlock-Freedom and Lock Ordering

A common strategy for ensuring that a set of concurrent transactions is deadlock-free is to impose a total order on locks. If all transactions acquire locks in ascending lock order, then we are guaranteed that concurrent transactions are deadlock-free.

We ensure deadlock-freedom for concurrent decomposition operations by imposing a total lock order on the physical locks of a decomposition; it is the responsibility of the query planner to generate code that respects this order.

$q ::= x \mid \text{let } x = q_1 \text{ in } q_2 \mid \text{lock}(q, v) \mid$ expressions
$\text{unlock}(q, v) \mid \text{scan}(q, uv) \mid \text{lookup}(q, uv)$

Figure 4. Concurrent query language. We only show the fragment necessary for implementing query operations.

All query plans must obey a single static order on all possible physical locks of a decomposition. The precise set of physical locks in existence may change as we allocate and deallocate node instances, but the relative order of any given pair of physical locks never changes during runtime. We order physical locks firstly on a topological sort of the decomposition nodes to which they belong. We order different instances of the same node lexicographically on the values of the key columns. Finally, we order the physical locks attached to each node instance by number.

For example, consider the decomposition of Figure 3(c). We fix a topological order of the nodes, say

$$\rho < x < y < z < w;$$

meaning that all locks attached to ρ are ordered before all locks attached to instances of x, and so on. We lift the topological order on nodes to a total order on node instances

$$\rho < x_{s_0} < x_{s_1} < \cdots < y_{t_0} < y_{t_1} < \cdots,$$

where the tuple sequences (s_i) and (t_i) are in lexicographic order. Finally, since there may be more than one physical lock per node due to lock striping, we lift the total order on node instances to a total order on physical locks:

$$\rho^0 < \rho^1 < \cdots < x^0_{s0} < x^1_{s0} < \cdots < x^0_{s1} < x^1_{s1} \cdots.$$

As an aside, it is necessary that we totally order the physical locks of a decomposition, not the logical locks; a query only acquires physical locks directly and it is the order of those physical locks that is pertinent to deadlock.

5.2 Query Language

Once we have fixed a total order on the physical locks of a decomposition, the query planner must generate well-locked, two-phase code that respects the lock order for each possible query.

A key requirement of a query plan is that it must make explicit which locks to acquire and in which order. The query trees in the literature [12] are not suitable for reasoning about locks since they have no notion of sequencing of expressions.

In the concurrent setting, we extend query trees to a fragment of a strict, impure functional language, shown in Figure 4. The let-binding construct of the concurrent query language can describe the order of execution of operations with side-effects, in particular lock and unlock operations. A query expression q is one of: a variable reference x, let-binding let $x = q_1$ in q_2, a lock acquisition lock(q, v), a lock release unlock(q, v), an edge lookup lookup(q, v), or an edge iteration scan(q, v). We discuss the semantics of expressions shortly.

Query States Evaluating any expression in the query language yields a set of *query states*. A *query state* is a pair (t, m) of a tuple t containing a subset of the relation's columns, together with a mapping m from decomposition nodes v to the corresponding node instance v_t. If a vertex v with type $v\colon A \triangleright B$ appears in the domain of m, tuple t must contain sufficient columns such that v_t is uniquely defined, that is, $A \subseteq \operatorname{dom} t$.

Query Expressions We now describe the semantics of each query expression. Variable lookup and variable binding are standard. Let bindings also allow us to sequence operations with side effects, such as locks; we use a don't-care variable let _ $= q_1$ in q_2 to denote executing q_1 just for its side effects, discarding its return value, and then executing q_2.

A lock acquisition lock(q, v) acquires the physical locks associated with the instance of node v in each query state in set q. Like all expressions in the query language, lock acts on a set of query states q, locking the instance of physical lock v in each element of the set. The lock operation must acquire locks in accordance with the lock order. While the query planner always produces the query plans with lock expressions in correct node order, the lock operator must sort node instances into the correct lexicographic order before acquiring locks. The counterpart unlock(q, v) unlocks the instances of node v in the set q; unlike the lock operation the unlock operation does not need to enforce sorted order on its arguments.

Recall that for each node instance u_t an edge uv in a decomposition corresponds to a container data structure that maps a set of key columns cols(uv) to a set of node instances of $v_{t'}$. The operation scan(q, uv) iterates over the contents of the container, returning the natural join of the input query states q together with the entries of the map. If the query states in q contain a superset of the key columns cols(uv), we can instead use the more efficient operation lookup(q, uv), which looks up the particular entry v_t in the container. Both the lookup and scan operations require that the input query states contain an instance of the source vertex u.

For example, suppose we wanted to iterate over all of the tuples of a directory entry relation represented using the decomposition of Figure 2(a) under a coarse lock placement which places all locks at the root node ($\psi(e) = \rho$ for all e). One possible query plan is:

$$\begin{array}{l} 1\colon \text{let } \_ = \text{lock}(a, \rho) \text{ in} \\ 2\colon \text{let } b = \text{scan}(\text{scan}(a, \rho y), yz) \text{ in} \\ 3\colon \text{let } \_ = \text{unlock}(a, \rho) \text{ in} \\ 4\colon b \end{array} \tag{2}$$

The query plan takes as input a variable a, consisting of a singleton query state containing the location of the decomposition root ρ. The query plan first locks the unique instance of the root vertex ρ in set a (line 1), and then iterates over instances of the edge ρy from the root vertex in set a (line 2, scan$(a, \rho y)$); the iteration yields a set of query states that contain instances of node y together with valuations of the parent and name fields. For each such query state, we then iterate over the singleton instances of edge yz (line 2, scan$(\cdots, yz)$), yielding a valuation for the child field; we store the resulting set of query states as a set b. We release the acquired locks (line 3), and return our final query states b (line 4).

To make the execution concrete, suppose we execute the query plan (2) on the decomposition instance of Figure 2(b). The query plan receives the input query state $a = \{(\langle\rangle, \{\rho \mapsto \rho_0\})\}$ as input, which contains the location of the decomposition root but no valuations for relation columns. The lock statement acquires the lock attached to ρ_0, which is the unique instance of ρ in set a. Evaluation of the expression scan$(a, \rho y)$ in line 2 yields states

$$\begin{array}{l} \{(\langle \text{parent: } 1,\ \text{name: `a'}\rangle, \{\rho \mapsto \rho_0,\ y \mapsto y_3\}) \\ \quad (\langle \text{parent: } 2,\ \text{name: `b'}\rangle, \{\rho \mapsto \rho_0,\ y \mapsto y_2\}) \\ \quad (\langle \text{parent: } 2,\ \text{name: `c'}\rangle, \{\rho \mapsto \rho_0,\ y \mapsto y_1\})\}. \end{array}$$

Applying the expression scan$(\cdots, yz)$ in line 2 yields the states

$$\begin{array}{l} \{(\langle \text{parent: } 1,\ \text{name: `a'},\ \text{child: } 2\rangle, \{\rho \mapsto \rho_0,\ y \mapsto y_3\ z \mapsto z_3\}) \\ \quad (\langle \text{parent: } 2,\ \text{name: `b'},\ \text{child: } 3\rangle, \{\rho \mapsto \rho_0,\ y \mapsto y_2\ z \mapsto z_2\}) \\ \quad (\langle \text{parent: } 2,\ \text{name: `c'},\ \text{child: } 4\rangle, \{\rho \mapsto \rho_0,\ y \mapsto y_1\ z \mapsto z_1\})\} \end{array}$$

which we store as set b. Finally, we unlock the lock at ρ_0 and return the entries of b as the query result.

Query plan (2) was not the only possible query plan, even under the same decomposition and lock placement. Another possible query plan uses edges ρx and xy instead of the edge ρy.

$$
\begin{array}{l}
1\!: \mathsf{let}\ \_ = \mathsf{lock}(a, \rho)\ \mathsf{in} \\
2\!: \mathsf{let}\ b = \mathsf{scan}(\mathsf{scan}(\mathsf{scan}(a, \rho x), xy), yz)\ \mathsf{in} \\
3\!: \mathsf{let}\ \_ = \mathsf{unlock}(a, \rho)\ \mathsf{in} \\
4\!: b
\end{array} \tag{3}
$$

Now suppose we want to make the same query on the same decomposition, under the lock placement shown in Figure 2(a), in which a lock on every node protects the edges with their source at that node. The equivalent of query plan (3) under the new finer-grained lock placement is:

$$
\begin{array}{l}
1\!: \mathsf{let}\ \_ = \mathsf{lock}(a, \rho)\ \mathsf{in} \\
2\!: \mathsf{let}\ b = \mathsf{scan}(a, \rho x)\ \mathsf{in} \\
3\!: \mathsf{let}\ \_ = \mathsf{lock}(b, x)\ \mathsf{in} \\
4\!: \mathsf{let}\ c = \mathsf{scan}(b, xy)\ \mathsf{in} \\
5\!: \mathsf{let}\ \_ = \mathsf{lock}(c, y)\ \mathsf{in} \\
6\!: \mathsf{let}\ d = \mathsf{scan}(c, yz)\ \mathsf{in} \\
7\!: \mathsf{let}\ \_ = \mathsf{unlock}(c, y)\ \mathsf{in} \\
8\!: \mathsf{let}\ \_ = \mathsf{unlock}(b, x)\ \mathsf{in} \\
9\!: \mathsf{let}\ \_ = \mathsf{unlock}(a, \rho)\ \mathsf{in} \\
10\!: d
\end{array} \tag{4}
$$

Query Planner To pick a good implementation for each query, the compiler uses a query planner that finds the query plan with the lowest cost as measured by a heuristic cost estimation function. The concurrent query planner is based on the non-concurrent query planner described in the literature [12]; like the non-concurrent query planner, the concurrent query planner enumerates valid query plans and chooses the plan with the lowest cost estimate.

The main extension for concurrency is the query planner must only permit queries that acquire and hold the right locks in the right order. Internally the query planner only considers plans with two phases, a growing phase consisting of a sequence of lock, scan, and lookup statements, and a shrinking phase containing a matching sequence of unlock statements in reverse order; such plans are trivially two-phase. To ensure that queries acquire the correct locks in the correct order, we extend the definition of query validity to require that lock statements in a query plan appear in the decomposition node lock order, and that lookup and scan operations must be preceded by a lock of the corresponding physical lock.

As in the non-concurrent case, we reuse the query planning infrastructure to compile mutation operations. Code for mutations is generated by first constructing a concurrent query plan that locates and locks all of the edges that require updating; the code generator then emits code that uses the query results to perform the required updates, just as in the non-concurrent case, sandwiched between the growing and shrinking phases of the query plan.

Query Expression Compilation Each query expression evaluates to a set of query states. Internally we compile each query expression into an iterator over query states. We compile let-bindings by evaluating the right-hand side of the binding and storing the results into a temporary set of query states; subsequent references to a bound variable compile to iterations over the stored state set.

In general the lock statement must sort the locks that it acquires. However, in some cases the set of locks may already be in the correct order, so it is superfluous to sort them. For example, consider the acquisition of the locks on node b in query 4 (line 3). Edge ρx is represented by a `TreeMap` in the decomposition, which stores its entries in sorted order; a scan over the edge will therefore yield entries in sorted order, which coincides with the correct lock order. Conversely, if edge was represented using a `HashMap` then iteration would return entries in an unpredictable order, so the code would have to sort the locks before acquiring them. The compiler uses a simple static analysis to detect lock statements where it can avoid sorting.

6. Experimental Evaluation

We have developed a prototype implementation of concurrent data representation synthesis, targeted at the Java virtual machine. The prototype is implemented as a Scala [18] compiler plugin; relations and relational operations are translated into Scala ASTs, which the Scala compiler backend converts to JVM bytecode. In this section we evaluate the performance of the resulting implementation.

6.1 Autotuner

A programmer may not know the best possible representation for a concurrent relation. To help find an optimal decomposition for a particular relational specification, we have implemented an autotuner which, given a concurrent benchmark, automatically discovers the best combination of decomposition structure, container data structures, and choice of lock placement.

Existing work [12] described an autotuner capable of identifying a good decomposition in the absence of concurrency. We extend the idea of autotuning to a concurrent setting.

To enumerate decompositions, the autotuner first chooses an adequate decomposition structure, exactly as for the non-concurrent case [12]. Next, the autotuner chooses a well-formed lock placement; every edge of a decomposition needs a corresponding physical lock. Finally the autotuner chooses a data structure implementation for each edge. If the chosen lock placement serializes access to an edge, the autotuner picks a non-concurrent container, whereas if concurrent access to a container is permitted by the lock placement then the autotuner chooses a concurrency-safe container.

6.2 Evaluation

We evaluate the generated code using a synthetic benchmark modeled after the methodology of Herlihy et. al [14] for comparing concurrent map implementations, extended to the more general context of a relation. We fix a particular relational specification, together with a set of relational operations. For any given choice of decomposition, the benchmark uses k identical threads that operate on a single shared relation. Starting from an initially empty relation, each thread executes 5×10^5 randomly chosen operations. We plot the total throughput of all threads in operations per second against the number of threads to obtain a throughput-scalability curve. By varying the distribution of relational operations we can evaluate the performance of the relation under different workloads.

For our benchmarks we use the directed graph relation described in Section 4.3, together with four relational operations, namely find successors, find predecessors, insert edge, and remove edge. The find successor operation chooses a random src value and queries the relation for the set of all dst, weight pairs corresponding to that src. The find predecessor operation is similar but chooses a random dst and queries for src, weight pairs. The insert edge operation chooses a random src, dst, weight triple to insert into the relation; to ensure that the relation's functional dependency is not violated we use the compare-and-set functionality of the insert operation to check that no existing edge shares the same src, dst parameters. Finally the remove operation chooses a random (src, dst) tuple and removes the corresponding edge, if present.

We performed our experiments on a machine with two six-core 3.33Ghz Intel X5680 Xeon CPUs, each with 12Mb of L3 cache, and 48Gb memory in total. Hyperthreading was enabled for a total of 24 hardware thread contexts. All benchmarks were run on a OpenJDK 6b20 Java virtual machine in server mode, with a 4Gb initial and maximum heap size. We repeated each experiment 8 times within the same process, with a full garbage collection between runs. We discarded the results of the first 3 runs to allow the JIT compiler time to warm up; the reported values are the average of the last 5 runs.

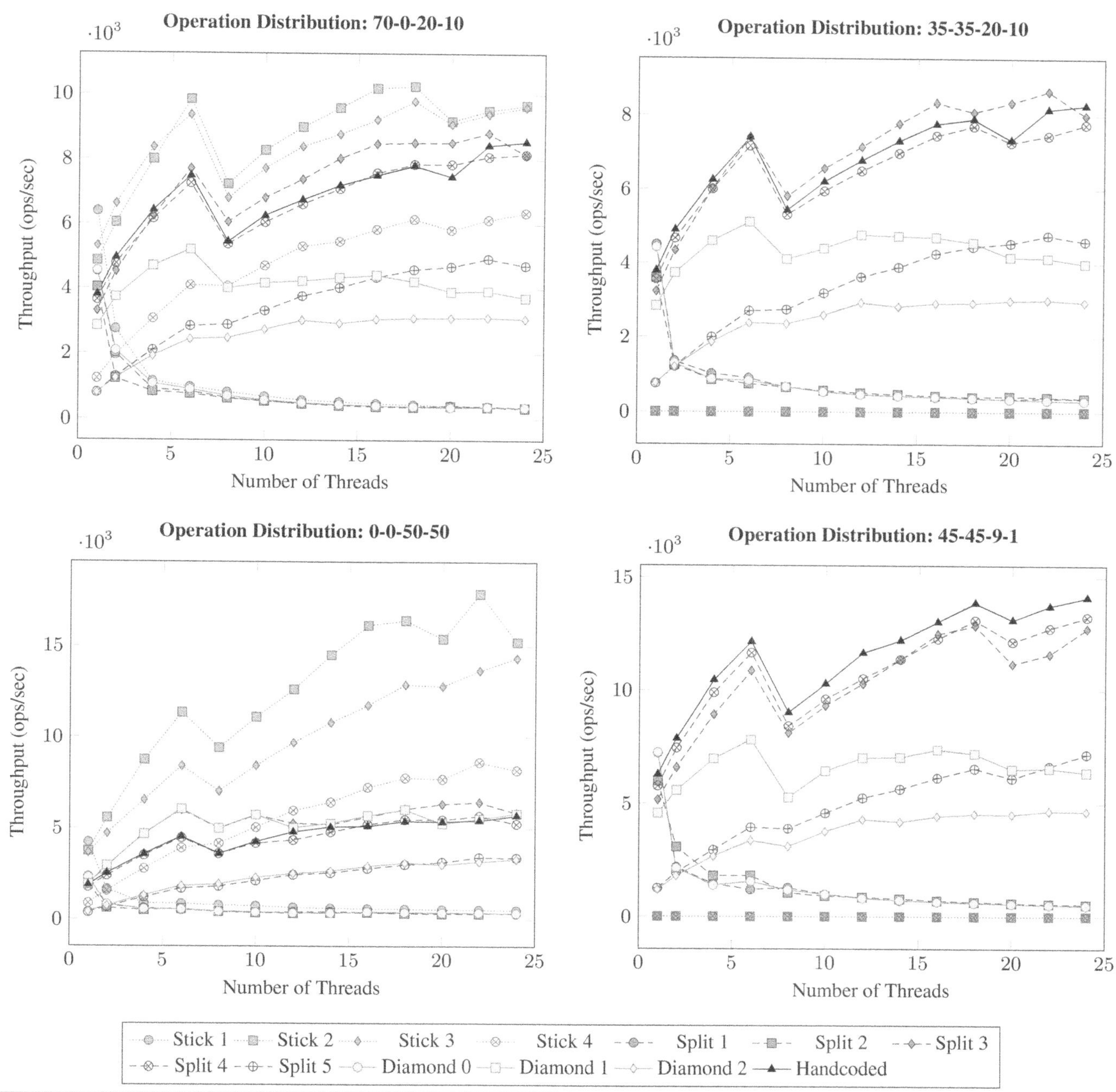

Figure 5. Throughput/scalability curves for a selection of decompositions. Each thread performs 5×10^5 random graph operations. Each graph is labeled x-y-z-w, denoting a distribution of $x\%$ successors, $y\%$ predecessors, $z\%$ inserts, and $w\%$ removes. "Stick" decompositions are structurally isomorphic to Figure 3(a) but have different choices of data structures and lock placements, similarly "split" to Figure 3(b), and "diamond" to Figure 3(c).

Figure 5 presents throughput-scalability curves for a selection of decompositions. We generated 448 variants of the three decomposition structures shown in Figure 3 using the autotuner, varying the choice of lock placement, lock striping factor (chosen for simplicity to be either 1 or 1024), and selection of containers from the options `ConcurrentHashMap`, `ConcurrentSkipListMap`, `HashMap`, and `TreeMap`. For clarity of presentation we selected 12 representative decompositions that cover a spectrum of different performance levels across the 4 benchmarks; we compare the performance of both the automatically generated implementations and a hand-written implementation.

One obvious feature of the results is that the "stick" decompositions, which are variants of the decomposition shown in Figure 3(a), perform relatively well for the two workloads (70-0-20-10 and 0-0-50-50) that consist only of successor, insert, and remove operations. For the workloads that include finding predecessors (35-35-20-10 and 45-45-9-1), "split" (Figure 3(b)) and "diamond" (Figure 3(c)) perform far better. Finding successors in a stick decomposition is much more efficient than finding predecessors, which requires iterating over all edges in the graph.

Coarsely-locked data structures scale poorly; three of the decompositions shown in the graph (Stick 1, Split 1, Diamond 1) use a single coarse lock to protect the entire decomposition; each container uses a coarsely locked `HashMap` to represent the top level of edges in the decomposition, and a `TreeMap` to represent the second level of edges. Another decomposition (Split 2) uses striped locks and concurrent maps on the left side of the decomposition (ρu, uw, wx), but uses a single coarse lock to protect the other edges of the graph, leading to similarly poor performance.

Sticks 2, 3, 4 use a striped lock at the root to protect a `ConcurrentHashMap` of `HashMap` containers, a `ConcurrentHashMap` of `TreeMap` containers, and a `ConcurrentSkipListMap` of `HashMap` containers, respectively; all scale much better than the coarsely-locked data structures.

Decompositions which do not share nodes between the two sides of the decomposition outperform decompositions that do. For example, Split 3 and Diamond 1 both use `ConcurrentHashMap` containers to represent the top-level edges and `HashMap` containers to represent the second level edges, differing only in the sharing structure of the decomposition; the split decomposition performs better in most cases. Split 4 is a variant of Split 3 with `TreeMap` containers in place of the `HashMap` containers. Interestingly, there is a small but consistent effect where Split 3 is the best choice for the 35-35-20-10 workload and Split 4 is better for the 45-45-9-1 workload. Split 5 and Diamond 2 are also similar to Split 3 and Diamond 2, except with `ConcurrentSkipListMap` containers in place of `ConcurrentHashMap` containers; once again, the split decomposition outperforms the diamond decomposition.

The handcoded implementation (which was written before the automated experiments) is essentially Split 4, and produces almost identical results; the difference in performance between the two is probably due to extra boxing in the generated code that could be eliminated with improvements to the code generator. But clearly the automatically generated code is competitive with the hand-written code but requires much less programmer effort, and unless one was willing to write many different hand-coded versions, the autotuner will be able to find variants that outperform any single hand-written code for particular workload characteristics.

It is interesting to note that diamond decompositions outperformed split decompositions in the non-concurrent case [12]; the result here is reversed for two reasons. The split decomposition produces less lock contention, since a pair of transactions may query for successors and predecessors in parallel without interfering with one another. Much of the benefit for sharing in the non-concurrent case came from the fact that it is possible to remove an object from the middle of an intrusive doubly-linked list in constant time. Since it is impossible to write such intrusive containers in a generic fashion in the Java type system, we do not gain the advantage of more efficient removals from shared nodes.

The prominent decrease in throughput evident in Figure 5 when increasing from 6 to 8 threads is an artifact of the thread scheduler and the memory hierarchy of the test machine. The test machine has two six-core CPUs, each with two hardware contexts per core. The benchmark harness schedules up to the first six threads on different cores of the same CPU, sharing a common on-chip L3 cache. The harness schedules the next six threads on the second CPU; when threads are split across two CPUs they must communicate via the processor interconnect, rather than via a shared on-chip cache. Communication off-chip is substantially slower than on-chip communication, producing the "notch" in the graph.

Overall the experiments show the benefits of automatic synthesis of both data structures and synchronization: sophisticated implementations competitive with hand written code can be produced at much lower cost in programmer effort, while at the same time providing guarantees about the correctness of the implementation of the high-level concurrent relational program.

7. Discussion and Related Work

Our results touch upon a great deal of previous work in several distinct domains. For space reasons our survey is necessarily brief.

We build upon previous work in data representation synthesis for sequential data structures [12] and the general theory of lock placements [13]. Our contributions beyond previous works include the extension of the programming interface to concurrent relations, the integration of different kinds of concurrent and non-concurrent data structures as building blocks, the extensions needed to integrate decompositions and lock placements, the redesign of query planning in the concurrent setting including guaranteeing deadlock freedom, and a complete implementation and experiments.

As mentioned in Section 1, the idea of compiling programs that work on relations into specialized data structures originated with [5], and its various developments [1, 2, 22]. Earlier work explored data structure selection for sets in SETL [7, 19]. Neither line of work addresses the synthesis of concurrent data representations.

The closest to our work in spirit is Paraglider [23], which provides semi-automatic assistance in synthesizing low-level concurrent algorithms and data structures. Paraglider focuses on the correct implementation of a single concurrent data structure, while our work is about assembling multiple concurrent and non-concurrent data structures into more complex abstractions. Thus, Paraglider is complementary to our approach, and we could extend our menu of concurrent building blocks with Paraglider-generated components.

Various authors have investigated techniques for inferring locks to implement atomic sections [4, 6, 9, 11, 16, 17, 24]. A related problem is automatically optimizing programs with explicit locking by combining multiple locks into one [8]. A key part of this class of work is constructing a mapping from program objects to the locks that protect them, which is similar to, but more specialized than, lock placements. This body of work also takes the data structures as fixed and attempts to infer the needed locks, while we consider the possible data representations and lock placements simultaneously.

Our system can be viewed as implementing a pessimistic software transactional memory [21]. Future extensions of our work could synthesize optimistic concurrency control primitives in addition to pessimistic locks. Unlike traditional software transactional memory systems, which perform on-line dynamic analysis to determine the read and write sets of transactions, our system performs much of the same analysis statically, resulting in run-time code with considerably lower overhead. Furthermore, our approach is able to automatically change the data structures and granularity of locking used to improve overall performance. It is also worth noting that speculative locking was first introduced in the context of advanced software transactional memory systems [3].

Finally the original paper on two-phase locking made explicit the idea of locking not just objects, but program predicates [10]. Logical locks are such predicates, which we realize in practice by mapping logical locks onto physical locks using a lock placement.

8. Conclusion

We have described an approach for synthesizing data representations for concurrent programs. Beginning with a program written using high-level concurrent relations, our system automatically selects the decomposition of the relation into a set of subrelations, chooses concrete data structures for the sub-relations, and selects a locking strategy that guarantees all relational operations are both serializable and deadlock free for the chosen representation. Because the high-level description admits multiple choices for each of these dimensions (subject to correctness constraints that rule out some possibilities), programs written in this style describe a space of possible implementations, a fact that we are able to exploit by using a combination of static and dynamic techniques to search this space to find a high-performance implementation. We have described an extensive experiment on a concurrent graph benchmark, demonstrating the wide range of possible implementations and their trade-offs.

References

[1] Don Batory and Jeff Thomas. P2: A lightweight DBMS generator. *Journal of Intelligent Information Systems*, 9:107–123, 1997. ISSN 0925-9902. doi: 10.1023/A:1008617930959.

[2] Don Batory, Gang Chen, Eric Robertson, and Tao Wang. Design wizards and visual programming environments for GenVoca generators. *IEEE Transactions on Software Engineering*, 26(5):441–452, May 2000. ISSN 0098-5589. doi: 10.1109/32.846301.

[3] Nathan G. Bronson, Jared Casper, Hassan Chafi, and Kunle Olukotun. Transactional predication: high-performance concurrent sets and maps for stm. In *Proceeding of the 29th ACM SIGACT-SIGOPS Symposium on Principles of Distributed Computing*, PODC '10, pages 6–15, New York, NY, USA, 2010. ACM. ISBN 978-1-60558-888-9. doi: 10.1145/1835698.1835703.

[4] Sigmund Cherem, Trishul Chilimbi, and Sumit Gulwani. Inferring locks for atomic sections. In *Proceedings of the ACM SIGPLAN conference on Programming Language Design and Implementation*, pages 304–315, New York, NY, USA, 2008. ACM. ISBN 978-1-59593-860-2. doi: 10.1145/1375581.1375619.

[5] Donald Cohen and Neil Campbell. Automating relational operations on data structures. *IEEE Software*, 10(3):53–60, May 1993. doi: 10.1109/52.210604.

[6] Dave Cunningham, Khilan Gudka, and Susan Eisenbach. Keep off the grass: Locking the right path for atomicity. In Laurie Hendren, editor, *Compiler Construction*, volume 4959 of *Lecture Notes in Computer Science*, pages 276–290. Springer Berlin / Heidelberg, 2008. ISBN 978-3-540-78790-7. doi: 10.1007/978-3-540-78791-4_19.

[7] Robert B. K. Dewar, Arthur Grand, Ssu-Cheng Liu, Jacob T. Schwartz, and Edmond Schonberg. Programming by refinement, as exemplified by the SETL representation sublanguage. *ACM Transactions on Programming Languages and Systems (TOPLAS)*, 1(1):27–49, January 1979. ISSN 0164-0925. doi: 10.1145/357062.357064.

[8] Pedro C. Diniz and Martin C. Rinard. Lock coarsening: Eliminating lock overhead in automatically parallelized object-based programs. *Journal of Parallel and Distributed Computing*, 49(2):218–244, 1998. ISSN 0743-7315. doi: 10.1006/jpdc.1998.1441.

[9] Michael Emmi, Jeffrey S. Fischer, Ranjit Jhala, and Rupak Majumdar. Lock allocation. In *Proceedings of the 34th annual ACM SIGPLAN-SIGACT symposium on Principles of Programming Languages (POPL)*, pages 291–296, New York, NY, USA, 2007. ACM. ISBN 1-59593-575-4. doi: 10.1145/1190216.1190260.

[10] K. P. Eswaran, J. N. Gray, R. A. Lorie, and I. L. Traiger. The notions of consistency and predicate locks in a database system. *Communications of the ACM*, 19:624–633, November 1976. ISSN 0001-0782. doi: 10.1145/360363.360369.

[11] Richard L. Halpert, Christopher J. F. Pickett, and Clark Verbrugge. Component-based lock allocation. In *Proceedings of the 16th International Conference on Parallel Architecture and Compilation Techniques*, PACT '07, pages 353–364, Washington, DC, USA, 2007. IEEE Computer Society. ISBN 0-7695-2944-5. doi: 10.1109/PACT.2007.23.

[12] Peter Hawkins, Alex Aiken, Kathleen Fisher, Martin Rinard, and Mooly Sagiv. Data representation synthesis. In *Proceedings of the 32nd ACM SIGPLAN Conference on Programming Language Design and Implementation (PLDI)*, pages 38–49, New York, NY, USA, 2011. ACM. ISBN 978-1-4503-0663-8. doi: 10.1145/1993498.1993504.

[13] Peter Hawkins, Alex Aiken, Kathleen Fisher, Martin Rinard, and Mooly Sagiv. Reasoning about lock placements. In *Proceedings of the European Symposium on Programming (ESOP)*, LNCS. Springer Berlin / Heidelberg, 2012. To appear.

[14] Maurice Herlihy, Yossi Lev, Victor Luchangco, and Nir Shavit. A provably correct scalable concurrent skip list. In *Conference On Principles of Distributed Systems (OPODIS)*, 2006.

[15] Maurice P. Herlihy and Jeannette M. Wing. Linearizability: a correctness condition for concurrent objects. *ACM Trans. Program. Lang. Syst.*, 12:463–492, July 1990. ISSN 0164-0925. doi: 10.1145/78969.78972.

[16] Michael Hicks, Jeffrey S. Foster, and Polyvios Pratikakis. Lock inference for atomic sections. In *Workshop on Languages, Compilers and Hardware Support for Transactional Computing*, 2006.

[17] Bill McCloskey, Feng Zhou, David Gay, and Eric Brewer. Autolocker: Synchronization inference for atomic sections. In *Proceedings of the 33rd ACM SIGPLAN-SIGACT Symposium on Principles of Programming Languages (POPL)*, pages 346–358, New York, NY, USA, 2006. ACM. ISBN 1-59593-027-2. doi: 10.1145/1111037.1111068.

[18] Martin Odersky, Philippe Altherr, Vincent Cremet, Iulian Dragos, Gilles Dubochet, Burak Emir, Sean McDirmid, Stéphane Micheloud, Nikolay Mihaylov, Michel Schinz, Erik Stenman, Lex Spoon, and Matthias Zenger. An Overview of the Scala Programming Language, second edition. Technical Report LAMP-REPORT-2006-001, École Polytechnique Fédérale de Lausanne (EPFL), Lausanne, Switzerland, 2006.

[19] Edmond Schonberg, Jacob T. Schwartz, and Micha Sharir. Automatic data structure selection in SETL. In *Proceedings of the ACM SIGPLAN-SIGACT Symposium on Principles of Programming Languages (POPL)*, pages 197–210, New York, NY, USA, 1979. ACM. doi: 10.1145/567752.567771.

[20] Ohad Shacham, Nathan Bronson, Alex Aiken, Mooly Sagiv, Martin Vechev, and Eran Yahav. Testing atomicity of composed concurrent operations. In *Proceedings of the ACM International Conference on Object Oriented Programming Systems Languages and Applications (OOPSLA)*, pages 51–64, New York, NY, USA, 2011. ACM. ISBN 978-1-4503-0940-0. doi: 10.1145/2048066.2048073.

[21] Nir Shavit and Dan Touitou. Software transactional memory. *Distributed Computing*, 10:99–116, 1997. ISSN 0178-2770. doi: 10.1007/s004460050028.

[22] Yannis Smaragdakis and Don Batory. DiSTiL: A transformation library for data structures. In *Conference on Domain-Specific Languages*, pages 257–271, October 1997.

[23] Martin Vechev and Eran Yahav. Deriving linearizable fine-grained concurrent objects. In *Proceedings of the ACM SIGPLAN conference on Programming Language Design and Implementation (PLDI)*, pages 125–135, New York, NY, USA, 2008. ACM. ISBN 978-1-59593-860-2. doi: 10.1145/1375581.1375598.

[24] Yuan Zhang, Vugranam Sreedhar, Weirong Zhu, Vivek Sarkar, and Guang Gao. Minimum lock assignment: A method for exploiting concurrency among critical sections. In *Languages and Compilers for Parallel Computing*, volume 5335 of *Lecture Notes in Computer Science*, pages 141–155. Springer Berlin / Heidelberg, 2008. ISBN 978-3-540-89739-2. doi: 10.1007/978-3-540-89740-8_10.

Dynamic Synthesis for Relaxed Memory Models

Feng Liu
Princeton University
fengliu@princeton.edu

Nayden Nedev
Princeton University
nnedev@princeton.edu

Nedyalko Prisadnikov
Sofia University
nedy88@gmail.com

Martin Vechev
ETH Zürich
martin.vechev@inf.ethz.ch

Eran Yahav *
Technion
yahave@cs.technion.ac.il

Abstract

Modern architectures implement relaxed memory models which may reorder memory operations or execute them non-atomically. Special instructions called *memory fences* are provided, allowing control of this behavior.

To implement a concurrent algorithm for a modern architecture, the programmer is forced to manually reason about subtle relaxed behaviors and figure out ways to control these behaviors by adding fences to the program. Not only is this process time consuming and error-prone, but it has to be repeated every time the implementation is ported to a different architecture.

In this paper, we present the first scalable framework for handling real-world concurrent algorithms running on relaxed architectures. Given a concurrent C program, a safety specification, and a description of the memory model, our framework tests the program on the memory model to expose violations of the specification, and synthesizes a set of necessary ordering constraints that prevent these violations. The ordering constraints are then realized as additional fences in the program.

We implemented our approach in a tool called DFENCE based on LLVM and used it to infer fences in a number of concurrent algorithms. Using DFENCE, we perform the first in-depth study of the interaction between fences in real-world concurrent C programs, correctness criteria such as sequential consistency and linearizability, and memory models such as TSO and PSO, yielding many interesting observations. We believe that this is the first tool that can handle programs at the scale and complexity of a lock-free memory allocator.

Categories and Subject Descriptors D.1.3 [*Concurrent Programming*]; D.2.4 [*Program Verification*]

General Terms Algorithms, Verification

Keywords Concurrency, Synthesis, Relaxed Memory Models, Weak Memory Models

* Deloro Fellow

1. Introduction

Modern architectures use relaxed memory models in which memory operations may be reordered and executed non-atomically [2]. These models enable improved hardware performance but pose a burden on the programmer, forcing her to understand the effect that the memory model has on their implementation. To allow programmer control over those executions, processors provide special *memory fence* instructions.

As multicore processors increasingly dominate the market, highly-concurrent algorithms become critical components of many systems [28]. Highly-concurrent algorithms are notoriously hard to get right [22] and often rely on subtle ordering of events, which may be violated under relaxed memory models [14, Ch.7].

Placing Memory Fences Manually reasoning where to place fences in a concurrent program running on a relaxed architecture is a challenging task. Using too many fences (over-fencing) hinders performance, while missing necessary fences (under-fencing) permits illegal executions. Manually balancing between over- and under- fencing is very difficult, time-consuming and error-prone [4, 14]. Furthermore, the process of placing fences is repeated whenever the algorithm changes, and whenever it is ported to a different architecture.

Our goal is to automate the task of fence placement and free the programmer to focus on the algorithmic details of her work. Automatic fence placement is important for expert designers of concurrent algorithms, as it lets the designer quickly prototype with different algorithmic choices. Automatic fence placement is also important for any programmer trying to implement a concurrent algorithm as published in the literature. Because fence placement depend on the specific architecture, concurrent algorithms are usually published without a detailed fence placements for different architectures. This presents a nontrivial challenge to any programmer trying to implement an algorithm from the literature on relaxed architectures.

Dynamic Synthesis Existing approaches to automatic fence inference are either overly conservative [26], resulting in over-fencing, or have severely limited scalability [17, 18]. The main idea in this paper is to break the scalability barrier of static approaches by performing the synthesis based on *dynamic executions*. To identify illegal executions, we introduce a *flush-delaying* demonic scheduler that is effective in exposing illegal executions under relaxed memory models.

Given a program P, a specification S, and a description of the memory model M, guided execution (using the flush-based scheduler) of P under M can be used to identify a set of illegal execu-

```
1   void put(int task) {
2    t = T;
3    items[t] = task;
4    fence(st-st); //F2
5    T = t + 1;
6    fence(st-st); //F3
7   }
```

```
1   int steal() {
2    while (true) {
3     h = H;
4     t = T;
5     if (h >= t)
6      return EMPTY;
7     task = items[h];
8     if(!cas32(&H,h,h+1))
9      continue;
10   return task;
11   }
12  }
```

```
1   int take() {
2    while (true) {
3     t = T - 1;
4     T = t;
5     fence(st-ld); //F1
6     h = H;
7     if (t < h) {
8      T = h;
9      return EMPTY;
10    }
11    task = items[t];
12    if (t > h)
13     return task;
14    T = h + 1;
15    if(!cas(&H,h,h+1))
16     continue;
17    return task;
18   }
19  }
```

Figure 1: Simplified version of the Chase-Lev work-stealing queue. Here, store-load fence F1 prevents the non-SC scenario of Fig. 2a under TSO; F1 combined with store-store fence F2 prevents the non-SC scenario of Fig. 2b under PSO. F1, F2 and store-store fence F3 prevent the linearizability violation of Fig. 2c under PSO.

tions (violating S). The tool will then automatically synthesize a program P' that avoids the observed illegal executions (under M), but still permits as many legal executions as possible.

Evaluation Enabled by our tool, we perform the first in-depth study of the subtle interaction between: i) required fences in a number of real-world concurrent `C` algorithms (including a lock-free memory allocator), ii) correctness criteria such as linearizabiltiy and (operation-level) sequential consistency [14], and iii) relaxed memory models such as TSO and PSO.

Main Contributions The main contributions of this paper are:

- A novel framework for dynamic synthesis of synchronization under relaxed memory models. The framework breaks the scalability barrier of static synthesis approaches by performing the synthesis based on dynamic executions.
- A flush-delaying demonic scheduler which delays the effect of global stores on shared memory and attempts to expose illegal executions under relaxed memory models.
- An implementation of our tool in LLVM. The implementation required a number of extensions of the LLVM interpreter (e.g. adding support for multi-threading) which are useful for general concurrency analysis and for plugging-in new memory models.
- An evaluation on a range of real world concurrent `C` algorithms, including work-stealing queues and a lock-free memory allocator. We believe this to be the first tool that can handle algorithms at the scale of a lock-free memory allocator.
- An in-depth study on the connection between: i) relaxed memory models such as TSO and PSO, ii) required fences in practical concurrent algorithms, and iii) correctness criteria such as linearizabiltiy and (operation-level) sequential consistency. Our results yield a number of insights, useful in understanding the interplay between relaxed memory models and concurrency.

2. Overview

In this section, we show how different synchronization requirements arise for different memory models and specifications. We use a practical work-stealing queue algorithm as an example.

Motivating Example Fig. 1 shows a pseudo-code of the Chase-Lev work-stealing queue [7] (note that our implementation handle the complete `C` code). A work-stealing queue is a special kind of double-ended queue that provides three operations: `put`, `take`, and `steal`. A single owner thread can `put` and `take` an item from the tail of the queue, and multiple thief threads can `steal` an item from the head of the queue.

In the implementation of Fig. 1, `H` and `T` are global shared variables storing head and tail indices of the valid section of the array `items` in the queue. The operations `put` and `take` operate on one end of the array, and `steal` operates on the other end.

The `put` operation takes a task as parameter, and adds it to the tail of the queue by storing it in `items[t]` and incrementing the tail index `T`. The `take` operation uses optimistic synchronization, repeatedly trying to remove an item from the tail of the queue, potentially restarting if the tail and the head refer to the same item. `take` works by first decrementing the tail index, and comparing the new value with the head index. There are three possible cases:

- new tail index is smaller than head index, meaning that the queue is empty. In this case, the original value of tail index is restored and the `take` returns `EMPTY` (line 9).
- new tail index is larger than head index, `take` then uses it to read and return the item from the array.
- new tail index equals to head index, in which case, the only item in the queue may be potentially stolen by a concurrent `steal` operation. A compare-and-swap (CAS) instruction is used to check whether the head has changed since we read it into `h`. If the head has not changed, then there is no concurrent steal, and the single item in the queue can be returned, while the head is updated to the new value `h+1`. If the value of head has changed, `take` restarts by going to the next loop iteration.

Similarly, the implementation of `steal` reads the head and tail indexes of the array first, and if the head index is larger or equal to the tail index, either the queue is empty or the only item is taken by the owner, and the thief returns `EMPTY`. Otherwise, it can read the items pointed by the head. In case no other thieves are stealing the same element, a CAS instruction is used to update the head index atomically. If the CAS succeeds, the item can be returned, otherwise, the `steal` function needs to retry.

Correctness Criteria and Terminology The implementation of Fig. 1 works correctly on an ideal processor without memory model effects. Under this ideal processor, the two CAS instructions in the algorithm are sufficient for correctly updating the head index `H`.

In this work, we focus on two important specifications: (operation-level) sequential consistency and linearizability. Note that the term operation-level sequential consistency refers to the behavior of the algorithm and *not* to the memory model itself. Precise definitions and extensive discussion comparing (operation-level) sequential consistency and linearizability can be found in [14, Ch. 3.4-3.5]. As we focus on relaxed memory models, in the rest of the paper we use the term sequential consistency to mean operation-level sequential consistency (and not hardware-level sequential consistency). Informally, both, (operation-level) sequential consistency and linearizability can be expressed as follows:

- Sequential consistency requires that for each concurrent execution, there exists a serial execution that yields the same result.
- Linearizability requires that for each concurrent execution, there exists a serial execution that yields the same result and maintains the ordering between non-overlapping operations in the concurrent execution.

We believe this work is the first detailed comparison between linearizability and sequential consistency specifications for real concurrent algorithms.

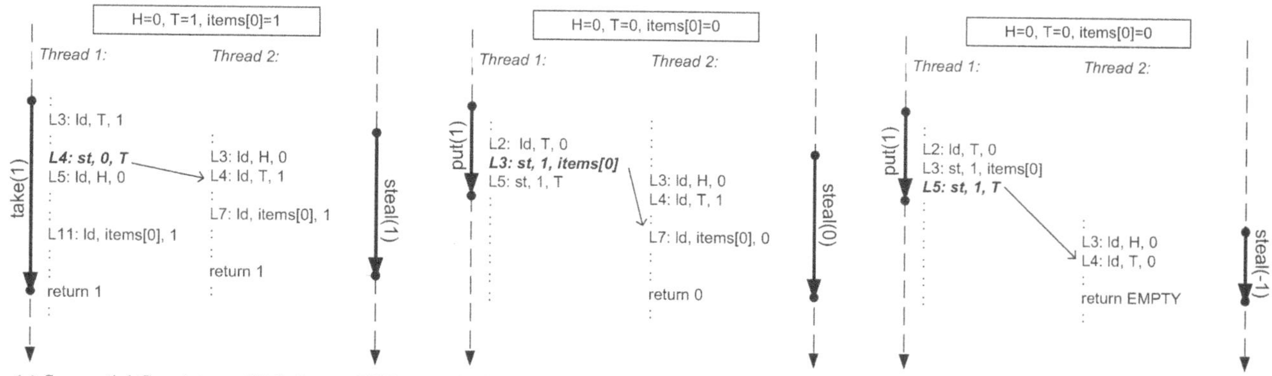

(a) Sequential Consistency Violation on TSO

(b) Sequential Consistency Violation on PSO

(c) Linearizability Violation on TSO/PSO. Note that the execution satisfies Sequential Consistency

Figure 2: Executions of a work-stealing queue violating different specifications under different memory models. Arguments of `take` and `steal` are the return values of the operations.

Returning to our algorithm, unfortunately, a relaxed memory model may reorder accesses to shared variables, leading to unexpected results. For example, in the total store order (TSO) memory model, loads can bypass earlier stores in the same thread, thus another thread can load an inconsistent value and produce an incorrect result. In the partial store order (PSO) memory model, both loads and stores can bypass earlier stores.

Correctness under TSO Fig. 2a shows an execution of the Chase-Lev queue under the TSO memory model violating sequential consistency. In this execution, thread 1 performs a `take(1)` operation, and thread 2 performs `steal(1)`, trying to steal the same item. Thread 1 first updates the tail index of the queue to 0, and then loads 1 from the head index. For thread 1, the head equals to the tail, and it takes the first element of the queue, 1, successfully. However, since the update of the tail index by thread 1 is buffered (noted in boldface), thread 2 can only load the original 1 from the tail index, and returns the same item 1. The same element is popped by two different threads, and we cannot find a serial execution that has the same result. The original implementation violates the sequential consistency on TSO memory model. To fix this problem, we need to guarantee that the buffered store of the tail index in thread 1 is committed to main memory and visible to other threads before the head index is loaded. This can be accomplished by inserting a memory fence after the store (F1 in Fig. 1), which enforces a flush of the buffered store to main memory.

Correctness under PSO Unfortunately, fence F1 is not sufficient when running the algorithm on the PSO memory model. Under PSO, a possible store-store reordering can still lead to violation of sequential consistency as shown in Fig. 2b. In this execution, thread 1 performs `put(1)` and thread 2 performs `steal(1)`. Thread 1 tries to store the item 1 in the first position of the queue and updates the tail index in main memory. Concurrently, thread 2 loads the new tail index, finds there is a single item in the queue and loads the item. However, the real value of the item is buffered by thread 1, and thread 2 *reads an uninitialized value* 0. For this execution, we cannot find a serial execution that can fetch an item which has not been put by any of the threads. To fix this problem, before thread 1 updates the tail index, we need to ensure that the corresponding item is updated first. Thus a memory fence F2 is added after the item store instruction. In general, this store-store reordering can also lead to a memory safety violation if for instance we use the value to index some array.

$load(x, r)$	load contents of global variable x into local variable r.
$store(r, x)$	store value of local variable r into global variable x.
$cas(x, r, s, q)$	an atomic compare-and-swap action. If the value in global variable x is as same as that in local variable r, then store in x the value in local variable s and set local variable q to $true$. Otherwise, do nothing and set q to $false$.
$call(f, \vec{a})$	function call of f with argument list $\vec{a}$.
$return(f, r)$	return from a function f with value r.
$fork(t, l)$	create a new thread t to execute statement starting at label l.
$join(t, u)$	thread t joins to thread u.
$fence$	memory fence instruction.
$self()$	return the id of the calling thread.
$flush(x)$	flush the value of shared variable x to main memory (specific to a given memory model, defined later). This statement is inserted by the scheduler, and we use it to model the relaxed memory model effect.

Table 1: Basic statements of our language.

Linearizability Linearizability is stricter than sequential consistency. Linearizability requires at least one additional fence in this algorithm.

Fig. 2c shows an execution of the implementation that satisfies SC under PSO (Fig. 2b), and shows that it violates linearizability. The schedule is similar to the one of Fig. 2b: thread 1 executes `put(1)`, and thread 2 executes `steal(-1)` after thread 1 finishes `put(1)`. Even though the store to the first item by thread 1 is committed to main memory before the tail index is updated, thread 2 can load an incorrect value of the tail index due to the buffering in thread 1, resulting in an empty steal. Because `put(1)` of thread 1 and `steal(-1)` of thread 2 are non-overlapping, we cannot find a serial execution where the thief fails to steal from a queue that is non-empty. The violation occurs because the update to tail is not committed to main memory. To flush the value of the tail index to main memory, another fence (F3 in Fig. 1) needs to be inserted before the method returns. This violation can also occur under TSO, and a memory fence is required there as well.

3. Language

In this section, we present the syntax of our language and the semantics of the two memory models used in the paper: Total Store Order (TSO) and Partial Store Order (PSO).

Syntax We consider a basic concurrent programming language augmented with procedure calls, where the basic statements are listed in Tab. 1. We denote the set of statements by $Stmt$. Given a program, we use $Label$ to denote the set of program labels. We also use the special labels $Inactive$ and $Finished$ to denote that a thread has not yet started or has completed execution. Statements in the program are uniquely labeled and for a label $l \in Label$, we use $stmt(l)$ to denote its corresponding statement in the program.

Semantics 1 Operational semantics under PSO.

$$\frac{stmt(pc) = load(x, r) \quad B(x) = \epsilon \quad G(x) = v}{L'(r) = v \quad pc' = n(pc)} \text{(LOAD-G)}$$

$$\frac{stmt(pc) = load(x, r) \quad B(x) = b \cdot v}{L'(r) = v \quad pc' = n(pc)} \text{(LOAD-B)}$$

$$\frac{stmt(pc) = store(r, x) \quad B(x) = b \quad L(r) = v}{B'(x) = b \cdot v \quad pc' = n(pc)} \text{(STORE)}$$

$$\frac{B(x) = v \cdot b}{B'(x) = b \quad G'(x) = v} \text{(FLUSH)}$$

$$\frac{stmt(pc) = fence \quad \forall x.B(x) = \epsilon}{pc' = n(pc)} \text{(FENCE)}$$

$$\frac{\begin{array}{c} stmt(pc) = cas(x, r, s, q) \\ G(x) = L(r) \quad L(s) = v \quad B(x) = \epsilon \end{array}}{G'(x) = v \quad L'(q) = true \quad pc' = n(pc)} \text{(CAS-T)}$$

$$\frac{stmt(pc) = cas(x, r, s, q) \quad G(x) \neq L(r) \quad B(x) = \epsilon}{L'(q) = false \quad pc' = n(pc)} \text{(CAS-F)}$$

$$\frac{stmt(pc) = fork(t, l) \quad pc(t) = Inactive}{\forall x.B(t, x) = \epsilon \quad pc(t) = l \quad \forall l.L(t, l) = 0 \quad pc' = n(pc)} \text{(FORK)}$$

$$\frac{\begin{array}{c} stmt(pc) = join(t, u) \\ pc(u) = Finished \quad \forall x.B(u, x) = \epsilon \end{array}}{pc' = n(pc)} \text{(JOIN)}$$

Semantics We use $Thread$ to denote a finite set of thread identifiers and $tid \in Thread$ to denote a thread identifier. A transition system is a tuple $\langle s_0, \Sigma, T \rangle$, where Σ is the set of program states, $s_0 \in \Sigma$ is the initial program state, and T is the transition relation: $T \subseteq \Sigma \times Thread \times Stmt \times \Sigma$.

A transition $s \xrightarrow{tid\,:\,stmt} s' \in T$ holds if $s, s' \in \Sigma$ and if executing statement $stmt$ in state s by thread tid results in state s'. For a transition t, we use $tr(t)$ to denote its executing thread, $label(t)$ for the label whose statement was executed, and $stmt(t)$ (overloaded) to obtain the statement.

A finite execution π is a sequence of transitions starting from the initial state:

$$\pi = s_0 \xrightarrow{tid_1\,:\,stmt_1} s_1 \xrightarrow{tid_2\,:\,stmt_2} \ldots \xrightarrow{tid_n\,:\,stmt_n} s_n.$$

A program state s is defined as a tuple $\langle pc, L, G \rangle$, where:

- $pc \in PC$, where $PC = Thread \rightarrow Label$ is a map of threads to program labels.
- $L \in Env$ where $Env = Thread \rightarrow Local \rightarrow D$ is a map from threads to local variables to values.
- $G \in GVar$ where $GVar = Shared \rightarrow D$ is a map from global shared variables to values.

Here D represents the domain from which the program variables take values. When updating mappings, we use $M'(x) = v$ as a shorthand for $M' = M[x \mapsto v]$. Given a function $pc \in PC$, if the thread tid is clear from the context, we use pc for $pc(tid)$, $stmt(pc)$ to denote the statement at pc, and $n(pc)$ to denote the statement following pc.

Semantics under Memory Models The full small-step (interleaving) transition semantics on sequentially consistent machines is standard. Here, we only give semantics for the statements affected by the memory model: TSO and PSO. To accomplish that, we augment the program state with a store buffer B, which is used to model the memory model effects:

- PSO: $B \in Thread \rightarrow Shared \rightarrow D^*$. That is, we keep a buffer of values for each (thread, shared variable) pair.
- TSO: $B \in Thread \rightarrow (Shared \times D)^*$. That is, we keep a single buffer of values for all variables in a thread.

The semantics of the relevant statements for PSO are given in Semantics 1. The semantics of TSO are the same except that we work with the per-thread buffer, and so they are more restrictive. For instance, in the global load rule LOAD-G, instead of checking that $B(x) = \epsilon$, we will check that $\forall (y, d) \in B.y \neq x$.

Given a program P and memory model M, we use $[\![P]\!]_M$ to denote the set of all possible program executions starting from the initial state.

4. Dynamic Synthesis

In this section, we discuss the algorithm for dynamically synthesizing memory fences. This algorithm can be combined with any demonic scheduler that tries to expose violating executions. The basic idea is to repair the program iteratively: whenever bad executions are encountered, they are repaired so that new executions cannot repeat the same errors.

The high level dynamic synthesis approach is shown in Algorithm 1. The input to the algorithm is a concurrent program P, a memory model M and a specification S. First, the algorithm attempts to trigger an execution that violates the specification. If such an execution is found, then the function $avoid$ computes all possible ways to avoid the execution and adds that to the formula φ. Next, we have a non-deterministic choice "*?*" between enforcing the possible solutions from φ into the program or choosing to accumulate repairs from more violating executions. In practice, "*?*" can be determined in various ways: user-specified bound, dynamically computed value, a heuristic, and so on. When the algorithm finds no violating execution, it aborts with the program P' (and if necessary, enforces any outstanding constraints left in φ). Next, we elaborate on the details of $avoid$ and $enforce$.

Algorithm 1: Dynamic Synchronization Synthesis

Input: Program P, Specification S, Memory Model M
Output: Program P' with restricted synchronization

```
P' = P;
φ = true;
while true do
    select π ∈ [[P']]_M such that π ⊭ S
    if no such π exists then
        return enforce(φ, P')
    δ = avoid(π, M)
    if δ = false then
        abort "cannot be fixed"
    φ = φ ∧ δ
    if ? then
        P' = enforce(φ, P')
        φ = true;
```

Semantics 2 Instrumented semantics under PSO.

$$\frac{stmt(pc) = load(x, r) \qquad \psi = v}{\psi' = v \vee \bigvee\{[l_y \prec pc] \mid y \neq x \wedge B^{\natural}(y) \neq \epsilon \wedge l_y \in B^{\natural}(y)\}} \text{ (LOAD-G)}$$

$$\frac{stmt(pc) = store(r, x) \qquad B^{\natural}(x) = l \qquad \psi = v}{\psi' = v \vee \bigvee\{[l_y \prec pc] \mid y \neq x \wedge B^{\natural}(y) \neq \epsilon \wedge l_y \in B^{\natural}(y)\}) \quad B'^{\natural}(x) = l \cdot pc} \text{ (STORE)}$$

$$\frac{B^{\natural}(x) = l \cdot b}{B'^{\natural}(x) = b} \text{ (FLUSH)}$$

$$\frac{stmt(pc) = fence}{\forall x. B'^{\natural}(x) = \epsilon} \text{ (FENCE)}$$

$$\frac{stmt(pc) = cas\ x, r, s, q \qquad B^{\natural}(x) = l \qquad \psi = v}{\psi' = v \vee \bigvee\{[l_y \prec pc] \mid y \neq x \wedge B^{\natural}(y) \neq \epsilon \wedge l_y \in B^{\natural}(y)\}) \quad B'^{\natural}(x) = \epsilon} \text{ (CAS)}$$

4.1 Avoiding Executions

When avoiding an execution, we would like to build all of the possible ways of repairing it. To accomplish that, we first define an ordering predicate that captures one way to repair an execution.

Ordering Predicates Given a pair of program labels l and k (in the same thread), we use $[l \prec k]$ to denote an ordering predicate. Informally, the intended meaning of $[l \prec k]$ is that in any execution involving these two labels, the statement at label l should have a visible effect before the statement at label k. Next we define what it means for an execution π to violate an ordering predicate $[l \prec k]$, denoted as $\pi \not\models [l \prec k]$.

An execution $\pi \not\models [l \prec k]$ if and only if: $\exists i, j.\ 0 \leq i < j < |\pi|$ such that:

1. $label(\pi_i) = l$, $label(\pi_j) = k$ and $tr(\pi_i) = tr(\pi_j)$.
2. $stmt(l) = store(r, x)$ and $stmt(k) \in \{store(p, y), load(y, p)\}$
3. $x \neq y$.
4. $\forall f.\ i < f < j$: $stmt(\pi_f) \neq flush(x)$, and $tr(\pi_f) = tr(\pi_i)$.

Informally, if we have an execution where a store is followed by some later store or a load (all by the same thread), where there is no flush of the first store to main memory in between the two operations, then the execution violates the predicate. The intuition is as follows: if the second operation is a read, then the read took effect before the first store became visible; if the second operation is a store, then, because flush can trigger at any point in an execution, it is possible to perform a flush of the second store immediately after the second store and make it visible before the first store is made visible. The above is a formulation for PSO. For TSO, we only need to change the second point to $stmt(k) \in \{load(y, p))\}$.

If π does not violate $[l \prec k]$, we say that π satisfies $[l \prec k]$, and write $\pi \models [l \prec k]$.

Computing a Repair for an Execution Given an execution, we would like to compute all possible ways to avoid it. We accomplish this by defining the instrumented semantics of Semantics 2 (here, we show the semantics for PSO, the semantics for TSO are similar). The semantics update an auxiliary map $B^{\natural}$ which records the program labels of statements accessing the buffer:

$$B^{\natural} \in Thread \rightarrow Shared \rightarrow Label^*$$

In the initial state, the buffers are empty, i.e. $\forall x. B^{\natural}(x) = \epsilon$, and $\psi = false$. Let us look at the STORE rule. The premise says that if the (auxiliary) buffer contains the sequence l, then (i) the program counter pc will be appended to the buffer, and (ii) we will create an ordering predicates between pc and each label belonging to other buffers with the same thread: the idea is that if there are pending stores in the other buffers (i.e. their labels are in their respective auxiliary buffer), then we can repair the current execution by ordering any of those stores before pc. The reason that we use $\vee$ when building ψ is that any of the enumerated ordering predicate is sufficient to repair the execution.

We note that even though in this work we only apply this repair procedure, by *avoid* function in the algorithm, for a violating execution (under some specification), the procedure is independent of whether the execution is violating or not. Hence, we can easily use this procedure as-is for any execution. For instance, recent work has shown that it may be interesting to repair correct executions [31].

Computing a Repair for a Set of Executions Finally, in Algorithm 1, we combine repairs for each execution into a global repair formula φ. The reason we use $\wedge$ when combining individual avoid predicates is because we need to make sure that each execution is eliminated. When the algorithm terminates, the formula φ will contain all of the possible ways to repair all of the (violating) executions seen during this algorithm invocation. Next, we discuss how to enforce the formula φ into the program.

4.2 Enforcing Constraints

Given the repair formula φ, a satisfying assignment of the formula is a set of truth assignments to ordering predicates. Such an assignment represents a potential solution for all of the violating executions that contributed to the formula. There are various ways to enforce such an assignment in the program.

Enforce with Fences In this work, we chose to enforce the assignment $[l \prec k]$: $true$ by inserting a memory fence between the labels l and k. This prohibits the reordering of the memory accesses at these two labels. Algorithm 2 takes in a formula φ and a program, finds a minimal satisfying assignment to the formula and enforces the predicates with a fence. In practice, we insert a more specific fence (store-load or store-store) depending on whether the statement at k is a load or a store.

Enforce with Atomicity We can enforce $[l \prec k]$: $true$ as an atomic section that includes both labels l and k. Such an atomicity constraint (that may require more than two shared accesses) can be realized in various ways: with locks, or with hardware transaction memory (HTM) mechanisms [9] (HTM is especially suitable if the number of shared locations is bounded).

Enforce with CAS On TSO, we can enforce the fence with CAS to a dummy location. That is, we can use $cas(dummy, r, s, q)$, where $dummy$ is a location not used by the program (similarly r, s and q are never read in the thread). Regardless of whether such a CAS fails or succeeds on the dummy location, in order to proceed, it requires that the buffer is flushed (similarly to a fence). On PSO, it is also possible to use CAS to enforce the predicate, by having a CAS on the *same* location as the first store in the predicate, i.e., $cas(x, r, s, q)$. However, we would need to make sure that the CAS always fails (so does not modify x). Hence, enforcing order using CAS on PSO will only work when the contents of x and r are provably different.

5. Implementation

5.1 Architecture

Our framework is based on the LLVM infrastructure. To support our dynamic analysis and synthesis framework, we extended the LLVM interpreter (called *lli*) with the following features, not supported by the original LLVM framework:

Algorithm 2: $enforce(\varphi, P)$

Input: Formula φ, Program P
Output: Program P' with fences that ensure an assignment satisfying φ

if $\varphi = true$ **then return** P
$I = \{[l_1 \prec k_1]...[l_n \prec k_n]\}$ be an assignment to predicates such that $I \models \varphi$ and I is a minimal satisfying assignment of φ.
$P' = P$
foreach $[l \prec k] \in I$ **do**
  insert a $fence$ statement right after label l in P'
return P'

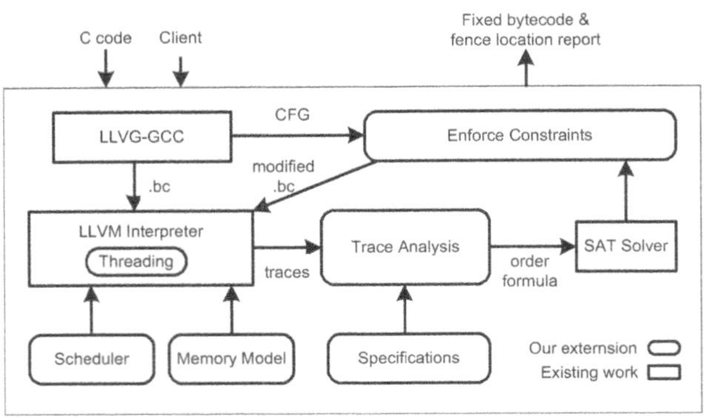

Figure 3: Schematic view of the structure of our tool. Rectangles denote existing work, while oval shapes denote our work.

- *Multi-Threading*: we added support for user-level threads. This includes support for statements *fork* and *join* as outlined in Section 3 as well as the *self* statement and per-thread local execution contexts.
- *Relaxed Memory Models*: we added support for both TSO and PSO memory models. This includes the relevant write buffers (outlined earlier), and extending LLVM intermediate instructions (e.g., stores and loads) to work with the memory model. We also support compare-and-swap (CAS) instructions, often used to implement locks and concurrent algorithms.
- *Scheduler*: we added scheduling support allowing us to plug-in different (demonic) schedulers for controlling the actions of the memory system (i.e., flushing) and thread operations.
- *Specifications*: we added support for checking memory safety errors such as array out of bounds and null dereferencing. We also added support for checking conditions such as linearizability and sequential consistency [14] (this required us to write a number of executable (sequential) specifications for all of the concurrent algorithms we analyzed).
- *Synthesis*: to repair a violating execution, we recorded all shared memory accesses in the violating execution. The resulting access history will be used to build a repair formula ψ as outlined in Semantics 2.

We believe that these extensions are of wide interest: for instance, we can use the framework for testing sequential programs for memory safety errors. Our extensions are parametric and the user simply selects the relevant parameters (e.g., which memory model, what properties to test) and runs their concurrent program with our version of the LLVM interpreter *lli*.

Figure 3 shows the overall structure of our synthesis framework. The input to DFENCE is a concurrent C algorithm and a (concurrent) client that calls the methods of the algorithm. LLVM-gcc then compiles both into a single bytecode file. Then, the interpreter can exercise the program with the given scheduler and memory model. The sequence of calls and returns that appear in the execution is collected, and is then checked against the given specification (e.g., linearizability). If the execution violates the specification, a repair for this single execution is calculated. A global repair for a set of violating executions can be calculated via a SAT solver and enforced into the given bytecode by inserting fences, producing a new bytecode representation. The new bytecode is fed back to the interpreter and the process repeats until no more violations are found or a user-specified timeout (or other bound e.g., number of times the program has run) is reached. All the phases of the flow in Figure 3 are completed by the framework automatically.

5.2 Extensions

The following provides additional details on each extension.

Multi-Threaded Support Supporting user level threads requires handling `fork`, `join`, and `self`. As outlined in Section 3, `fork` creates a new thread, `join` is used to wait for a thread to complete before proceeding and `self` returns the thread identifier of the caller. The reason we added `fork` and `join` is for handling clients that exercise concurrent algorithms. The reason we added `self` was because some concurrent algorithms require this method.

In the interpreter, we added a new map data structure, called *ThreadStacks* that maps a thread identifier to a list of execution contexts (stack frames). When the thread terminates, the vector becomes empty.

When `fork` is encountered, a new thread ID and a list of execution contexts is created in *ThreadStacks*. The execution of normal bytecodes proceed as-is (they access the particular execution context), and when a new function is called, a new execution context will be created. The call to `join` completes only if the target thread has finished, that is, its execution context list is empty, otherwise, the caller will block.

We added a function called *GetEnabledThreads* which returns the set of enabled threads. A thread is enabled if its list of execution contexts is not empty. This function is typically used by the scheduler to decide which thread to schedule next.

Relaxed Memory Model Support We maintain a write buffer for each thread (TSO) or each shared variable (PSO). The write buffer is simulated with a FIFO queue. The write buffers are managed by a dynamic map, and a new write buffer will be created when the memory address is *visited* for the first time. In this "lazy" approach, we do not need to change the functions that allocate memory such as `malloc` and `mmap`. Note that functions which deallocate memory, such as `free` and `munmap`, do not flush the write buffers.

Write buffers are only assigned to shared variables and thread-local variables access the memory directly. The implementation of shared variable accesses follows closely Semantics 1. To handle programs with locks, we implement lock acquire as a loop calling a CAS instruction to write 1 to the lock variable, and the function returns when CAS succeeds. Lock release writes 0 to the lock variable and returns. Both functions are wrapped with memory fences before and after the bodies, simulating the volatile feature of the lock variable.

Scheduler Support In our framework, the scheduler is designed as a plug-in, and is relatively independent of the interpreter. This allows experimenting with different schedulers for exposing violations.

To control scheduling, the probability of stores being delayed in the write buffer is gated by a parameter we call *flush probability*. The scheduler considers this parameter when deciding on the next step. At each step in the execution, based on the flush probability, the scheduler can decide which thread will take a step or which flushing action should be performed (for instance, for PSO, it can chose to flush only values for a particular variable):

- To reduce scheduling overhead, we use a form of partial-order reduction where a thread is not context switched if it keeps accessing local memory (thread-local variables).
- At each scheduling point, an enabled thread is selected randomly, and execution proceeds with the selected thread.
- Once a thread is selected, if its write buffers are empty, the thread makes a step. Otherwise, the scheduler randomly decides (with a user-provided flush probability) whether to flush the write buffer or proceed to the next step.

In our work, we found this strategy to be effective in exposing violations, but the framework allows the user to try out other scheduling strategies.

Specifications DFENCE supports both checking for memory safety properties such as array out of bounds, and null de-referencing, as well as properties such as linearizability and sequential consistency.

For space reasons, we do not elaborate on the precise definition of sequential consistency and linearizability. These, as well as extensive discussion comparing the two can be found in [14, Ch. 3.4-3.5]. Here we only discuss the essence of these conditions. Given a program execution, both of these criteria require us to first obtain a history (call it H) by extracting the sequence of calls and returns that appear in the execution. To check whether H is sequentially consistent, we compute two items: (i) sequentialization of H, call it $seq(H)$, and (ii) a witness history W that simply executes the relevant specification on the sequence of method calls appearing in $seq(H)$. If we find a sequentialization of H, where $W = seq(H)$, then we say that H is sequentially consistent, otherwise, if we cannot find any sequentialization of H which matches a witness, we say that H is not sequentially consistent. Linearizability is a more restricted variant of sequential consistency: it restricts how $seq(H)$ is computed. However, linearizability is compositional, while sequential consistency is not.

There are three key points to take away:

- Checking linearizability or sequential consistency requires a *semantic sequential specification* of the algorithm, e.g., specifying how the $push$ method of a stack behaves sequentially. Indeed, we had to provide such specifications for our experiments. The specifications are reusable for analyzing other concurrent algorithms: for instance, once we have the specification of a queue, we can use it to analyze any concurrent queue algorithm.
- Linearizability is a more restricted property than sequential consistency and is the one commonly used in the literature for concurrent algorithms. However, the interplay between sequential consistency, linearizability and relaxed memory models has not yet been well studied, and as we will see, interestingly, there are algorithms that look to be sequentially consistent, yet are non-lineraizable under relaxed memory models. The advantage of such algorithms is that they require less synchronization.
- Checking both of these properties requires computing all $seq(H)$'s of a history H, an operation clearly exponential in the length of H.

To check for linearizability and sequential consistency, the tool records a concurrent history and checks whether the concurrent history has a witness sequential history, as discussed above.

To detect memory safety violations, we keep auxiliary information such as the starting address and length, for global and heap memory units. For globals, this can be obtained by scanning the global segment of the intermediate bytecode. For heap, we can obtain the information from calls to `malloc` and `mmap` (the auxiliary state is deleted upon calling `free` or `munmap`).

When a load or a flush instruction occurs, the analysis checks whether the (to be) accessed address is within the current available memory (by checking in the auxiliary state). To reduce the overhead of the checking, we record each memory unit in a self balanced binary tree with the starting addresses as the keys. If we find that the target address is not inside any memory units, then a memory safety violation is triggered.

Synthesis Following Algorithm 1 from Section 4, once a violating execution π is discovered, the global avoid formula φ is updated to take avoiding π into account. In Algorithm 1, "?" indicates the non-deterministic choice of when the enforce procedure is invoked to produce a new program with a fix covering all violating executions accumulated so far. In DFENCE, we realized "?" as an iteration count, counting up to a user-defined threshold. To reduce overhead, DFENCE only records the relevant (shared memory accessing) instructions and not the whole execution.

To compute a satisfying assignment for the boolean formula φ, we use the off-the shelf MiniSAT [10] solver. Each (non-repeated) clause in the formula is assigned a unique integer. The satisfying assignment produced by MiniSAT has no guarantee of minimality. To obtain (all) minimal solutions, we call MiniSAT repeatedly to find out all solutions (when we find a solution, we adjust the formula to exclude that solution), and then we select the minimal ones.

Enforcing Once a minimal solution is selected, the labels in the ordering predicates are used to index the instruction pointers in the LLVM IR. The synchronization (e.g., fences) is then inserted into the IR by calling LLVM's instruction manipulation methods. The new IR is well-formed and is used for the next synthesis iteration. We optimize the insertion further by applying a merge phase which combines certain redundant fences: we apply a simple static analysis which eliminates a fence if it can prove that it always follows a previous fence statement in program order, with no store statements on shared variables occurring in between.

6. Evaluation

In this section, we evaluate the effectiveness of DFENCE in automatically inferring fences for realistic concurrent algorithms.

We used LLVM-GCC version 4.2 for compiling C programs into LLVM bytecode and LLVM runtime version 2.7 [19] for our implementation. Our implementation is designed to hook at the relevant places in LLVM and hence we expect it to be portable to newer versions. We used the open-source MiniSAT [10] solver.

6.1 Methodology

We applied DFENCE to a number of challenging concurrent C algorithms under different settings by varying four dimensions: (i) the memory model (TSO, PSO) (ii) the specification (memory safety, sequential consistency, and linearizability) (iii) the clients, and (iv) scheduler parameters.

In the first part of the evaluation, we evaluate the quality of fence inference under different choices along these four dimensions. Many of the algorithms used in our experiments have already been extensively tested on one memory model, usually TSO (x86). In this case, we first removed the fences from the algorithms and then ran DFENCE to see if it could infer them automatically. When we did not have the available fences for a given model, say PSO, we ran our tool and inspected the results manually to make sure the inferred fences were really required.

In the second part of our evaluation, we explore some of the connections between the different dimensions. In particular, we set out to answer the following questions:

1. **Memory Model:** How does the choice of memory model affect the choice of scheduler used to expose violations? How does it affect the choice of clients?
2. **Client:** How does the choice of client affect the ability to expose a violation, and how does it relate to the choice of specification and memory model?
3. **Specification:** How does the choice of specification affect the resulting fence placements?

6.2 Benchmarks

For our experiments, we used 13 concurrent C algorithms described in Tab. 2: five work-stealing queues (*WSQs*), three idempotent work-stealing queues (*iWSQ*'s), two queue algorithms, two set algorithms, and one lock-free concurrent memory allocator. All eight of the work-stealing queues share the same operations: `put`, `take` and `steal`. The Chase-Lev *WSQ* example has already been discussed in Section 2.

We chose *WSQ*s because they are a key technique for sharing work and are at the heart of many runtimes. We are not aware of any previous study which discusses extensive analysis or inference for *WSQ*s. Further, we believe that this is the first study to analyze and infer fences for Michael's lock-free memory allocator, arguably one of the largest and most complex concurrent C algorithms available. DFENCE consumes the C code directly and handles all low-level features of the implementation.

6.3 Results

Tab. 3 summarizes our results. Under each of the three specifications, we show the fences that DFENCE synthesized for a given memory model (we note that memory safety checking is always on, hence, Linearizability and Sequential Consistency columns include fences inferred due to memory safety violations). We describe each fence with the triple $(m, line1 : line2)$ to mean that we discovered the need for a fence in method m between lines $line1$ and $line2$. We use "−" to indicate the end of the method in the triple.

For *Chase-Lev's WSQ*, we use the locations indicated in Fig. 1. For *Cilk's THE WSQ*, the line numbers correspond to our C implementation. For all *WSQ* and *iWSQ*, the line numbers are the same as those found in [24]. Similarly for the rest of the algorithms.

For all *iWSQ* algorithms, the "Memory Safety" column also includes the "no garbage tasks returned" specification. Analysis of *iWSQ* algorithms under Linearizability or SC requires more involved sequential specifications and is left as future work.

The last column shows the number of locations where a fence can be potentially inserted — this corresponds to the total number of store instructions in the LLVM bytecode. Note that this number is an order of magnitude greater than the actual number of inferred fences, meaning that without any help from the tool, we would need to manually examine an exponential number of location combinations. By Source Lines of Code (LOC), we mean the actual C code and by Bytecode LOC we mean the LLVM bytecode (which is a much larger number).

6.3.1 Additional and Redundant Fences

The *iWSQ* algorithms of [24] are designed to not require store-load fences in the owner's operations (on TSO). Our experimental results support this claim: the tool did not find the need for store-load fences on both TSO and PSO.

On PSO, for all three *iWSQ*'s, our tool finds the need for an additional "inter-operation" fence (store-store) at the end of `take`. In addition, for *FIFO iWSQ*, the tool suggests an additional "inter-operation" fence at the end of `put`. We call these fences "inter-operation" as they appear at the end of operations (and can even be placed right outside the end of a method return). These "inter-operation" fences are not mentioned in [24] and the C code was only tested on TSO. Also, for the C implementation of the *THE* algorithm, our tool discovered a redundant (store-load) fence in the `take` operation. We believe these results suggest that the tool may be helpful to a designer in porting concurrent algorithms to different memory models.

6.3.2 Number of Executions

In Algorithm 1, we used "?" to denote a non-deterministic choice of when to stop gathering violating executions and implement their repair. This lets us control the number of executions (say K) we gather before performing a repair on the incorrect subset of those executions. We refer to each repair phase as a round. Our analysis terminates whenever we see K executions and in those K executions there are no incorrect executions. For example, one scenario with $K = 1000$ per round can be:

- Round 1: run the program with 1000 executions, discover 500 bad executions and repair them using 2 fences.
- Round 2: run the new program again for 1000 executions, discover 100 bad execution and repair them using 1 fence.
- Round 3: run the new program again for 1000 executions and discover no bad executions. The analysis terminates (having introduced a total of three fences to repair the observed executions).

Fig. 4 shows how the number of executions per round affects the synthesis results of *Cilk's THE* algorithm with sequential consistency specification on the PSO memory model (the x-axis is log). The "multiple rounds" points should be interpreted as follows:

- Take a value on the x-axis, say K. This value stands for the number of executions per round.
- Take the corresponding value on the y-axis, say F. This value stands for the number of inferred fences. The number of rounds is always less than $F + 1$. The "+1" is to account for the last round which does not find any violations and verifies the fixing.
- For example, if we take $K = 1000$, the corresponding y-axis value is $F = 3$. Hence, the number of rounds is certainly ≤ 4.

We observe that with about 1000 executions per round, and with *at most* four rounds, we can infer all three of the required fences.

Alternatively, we can try to gather as many executions as possible and repair them all at once. In that experiment we set the number of rounds to one. The results are the "one round" points in the figure. These results indicate that we will need at least 200,000 executions to infer all of the three fences, an increase of about 65x in the number of executions one needs to consider!

The intuition is that once we find some violations and repair them, we eliminate many executions that need not be inspected further. If we do not eliminate violating executions relatively quickly, then we can keep seeing the same executions for a while (or executions caused by the same missing fence(s)), and it may take significanly longer to find all distinct violating executions. Therefore, DFENCE invokes the repair procedure after examining a (relatively) small number of executions.

6.4 Client

The choice of client is an important factor in our experiments. If the client cannot exercise the inputs which could trigger violations, even an ideal scheduler would be unable to expose errors.

Client vs. Specification The worst case time required for checking linearizability or sequential consistency of an execution is exponential in the length of the execution.

Algorithm	Description
Chase-Lev's WSQ [7]	`put`, `take` operate on the same end of the queue, `steal` works at the opposite end. Both `take` and `steal` implemented using CAS.
Cilk's THE WSQ [12]	`put` and `take` operate on the same end of the queue, `steal` works at the opposite end. Both `take` and `steal` use locks. This is the core algorithm used in the MIT's Cilk runtime.
LIFO iWSQ (Fig.1, [24])	`put`, `take` and `steal` operate on the same end of the queue. Only `steal` uses CAS.
FIFO iWSQ (Fig.2, [24])	`put` operates on one end of the queue, `take` and `steal` work at the opposite end. Only `steal` uses CAS.
Anchor iWSQ (Fig.3 [24])	`put` and `take` operate on the same end of the queue, `steal` works at the opposite end. Only `steal` uses CAS.
LIFO WSQ	same as *LIFO iWSQ* except that all operations use CAS.
FIFO WSQ	same as *FIFO iWSQ* except that `take` uses CAS to update the `head` variable.
Anchor WSQ	same as *Anchor iWSQ* except that all operations use CAS.
MS2 Queue [23]	`enqueue` and `dequeue` operate at different ends of a linked list. Both use locks.
MSN Queue [23]	`enqueue` and `dequeue` operate at different ends of a linked list. Both use CAS.
LazyList Set [13]	`add`, `contains` and `remove` operate on a sorted linked list. All three use locks.
Harris's Set [8]	`add`, `contains` and `remove` operate on a sorted linked list. All three are implemented with CAS.
Michael's Allocator [21]	The `C` lock-free memory allocator exports two functions: `malloc` and `free`. These operations use CAS.

Table 2: Algorithms used in our experiments. We use *iWSQ* as a shortcut for idempotent work stealing queues.

Benchmark	Memory Safety		Sequential Consistency		Linearizability		Source LOC	Bytecode LOC	Insertion Points
	TSO	PSO	TSO	PSO	TSO	PSO			
Chase-Lev's WSQ	0	0	F1	F1, F2	F1, F2	F1, F2, F3	150	696	96
Cilk's THE WSQ	0	0	(put, 11:13) (take, 5:7)	(put, 11:13) (take, 5:7) (steal, 6:8)	-	-	167	778	105
FIFO iWSQ	0	(put, 4:5) (put, 5:-) (take, 5:-)	-	-	-	-	149	686	102
LIFO iWSQ	0	(put, 3:4) (take, 4:-)	-	-	-	-	152	702	101
Anchor iWSQ	0	(put, 3:4) (take, 4:-)	-	-	-	-	162	843	107
FIFO WSQ	0	0	0	(put, 4:5) (put, 5:-)	(put, 4:5)	(put, 4:5) (put, 5:-)	143	789	91
LIFO WSQ	0	0	0	(put, 3:4)	0	(put, 3:4)	136	693	92
Anchor WSQ	0	0	0	(put, 3:4)	0	(put, 3:4)	152	863	101
MS2 Queue	0	0	0	0	0	0	62	351	46
MSN Queue	0	0	0	(enqueue, E3:E4)	0	(enqueue,E3:E4)	81	426	43
LazyList Set	0	0	0	0	0	0	121	613	68
Harris's Set	0	0	0	(insert, 8:9)	0	(insert, 8:9)	155	695	86
Michael's Memory Allocator	0	(MFNSB, 11:13) (DescAlloc, 5:8) (DescRetire, 2:4)	0	(MFNSB, 11:13) (DescAlloc, 5:8) (DescRetire, 2:4) (free, 16:18)	0	(MFNSB, 11:13) (DescAlloc, 5:8) (DescRetire, 2:4) (free, 16:18)	771	2699	244

Table 3: Fences inferred for each algorithm under different specifications and memory models. The table also shows the size of each algorithm in terms of Source LOC, LOC in bytecode, and insertion points. MFNSB stands for MallocFromNewSB. "0" in the table means that the tool did not find any fences; "-" means "cannot satisfy the property (like *Cilk's THE WSQ*)" or that "a specification is not yet available". For *WSQ*'s and *iWSQ*'s, the numbers do *not* include fences in the `expand` function.

For linearizability, the complexity can be reduced to linear if the programmer provides linearization points, as commonly required in verification [29]. However, for many algorithms finding linearization points is very difficult. Further, for properties such as sequential consistency, the concept of a linearization point is not applicable. This means that when we are checking these two properties, it is important to have the client produce relatively short executions, yet rich enough to expose violations.

Client vs. Coverage A good client should achieve good coverage, at the least, it would allow for all program points in each method to be visited. For example, in the case of a *WSQ*, it is important to explore schedules where concurrent threads interact in a queue that is sometimes empty and sometimes not. This is because different violations can occur in both cases. Thus it is important that a client can generate both cases.

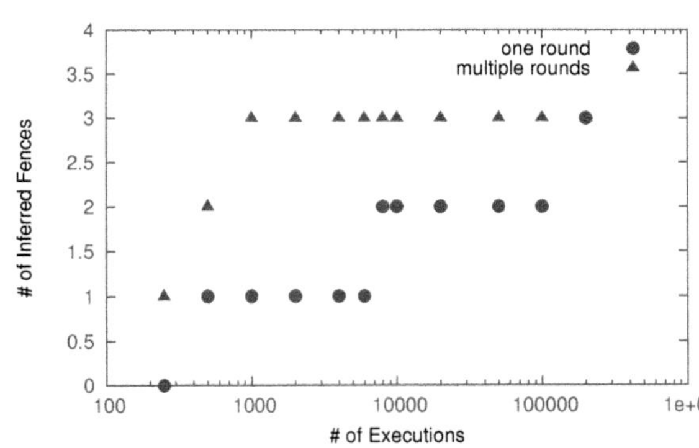

Figure 4: Number of Inferred Fences vs. Number of Rounds/Executions-per-Round.

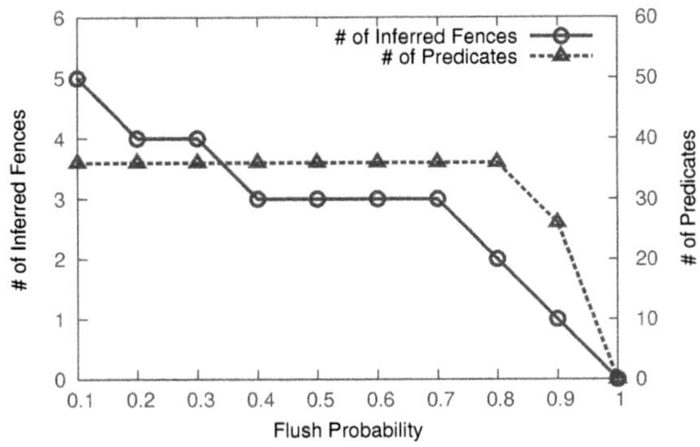

Figure 5: Effect of Flush Probability for Cilk's THE WSQ on PSO.

6.5 Scheduler vs. Memory Model

We find that setting the right flush probability (described in Sec. 5.2) is a key parameter for effectively triggering violations. With small values for the flush probability, meaning less flushing of the write buffers, we expose more violations and hence synthesize more missing fences, than we do with greater values. If the flush probability is too high, then the behavior of the program becomes as if the memory model is sequentially consistent (the intuition is that we are flushing more frequently, so the buffers are mostly empty), and hence it is more difficult to find violations.

Fig. 5 illustrates how the number of synthesized fences correlates with the flush probability for *Cilk's THE WSQ* under PSO with $K = 1000$. We can observe two tendencies:

- When the flush probability is large, i.e., greater than 0.8, the number of discovered ordering predicates decreases. With fewer predicates, some required fences cannot be inferred.
- When the flush probability is small, i.e., less than 0.4, the same unnecessary predicates may appear in most buggy executions, causing redundant fences. Thus the number of redundant fences is increased.

There are two ways to eliminate redundant fences. First, we can increase the flush probability. Second, we can collect more violating executions by increasing the execution number per round. If one of the violating executions does not contain the reordering which caused the generation of a redundant fence, then the redundant fence will not be inferred.

Flush Probability vs. PSO For PSO, we found that a flush probability around 0.5 is suitable for optimal inference for all benchmarks and specifications. With this value, the number of executions should be set high enough to collect sufficient predicates. For an accurate inference, we find that the number of collected violating executions should be around 10 times greater than the maximum number of possible predicates collected for the program. This maximum number can be obtained by testing executions with a low flush probability, and in Fig. 5 this number is 36.

Flush Probability vs. TSO Interestingly, we find that the optimal flush probability for the same program on TSO can be quite a bit smaller than the value used for PSO. In our experiments, the flush probability for TSO is usually set to 0.1. The intuition is that for the same program, the number of write buffers in TSO is usually much smaller than the number of buffers in PSO. This means that with the same flush probability, the chance that a buffer is flushed in TSO is higher than in PSO. It follows that if we use too high of a flush probability for write buffers, we are less likely to find violations caused by memory model reorderings.

We find that for the same specification, under PSO, the program requires more fences than under TSO. This is reasonable, since PSO allows both store-store and store-load reordering, while TSO only allows a store-load reordering.

6.6 Fences vs. Specification

Memory Safety is Ineffective As we see in the table of results, and perhaps counter-intuitively, we find that memory safety specifications are almost always not sufficiently strong to trigger violations. For instance, with *WSQ*'s, this is because a violating execution is more often exhibited in the form of losing an item or in returning duplicate items, rather than in accessing out of bounds memory. We note that one trick that may make memory safety more effective in triggering violations is to use a specific client: instead of elements of a primitive type, one stores pointers to newly allocated memory in the queue. Then, the client frees the pointer immediately after it has fetched it from the queue. In that way, one may be able to detect duplicate items. We leave this experiment as future work.

We find that safety specifications are useful for the memory allocator as there are many pointer dereferences performed in the code, and the buffering of an updated pointer value can cause a dereference of `NULL` pointer in another thread.

Linearizability vs. Sequential Consistency Another interesting point is that for the same memory model, linearizability generally requires more fences than sequential consistency. On one side, this can be expected as linearizability is a stronger property, but on the other, it is not obvious that by slightly weakening linearizability to sequential consistency, one does not end up with a completely "incorrect" algorithm (in the sense of losing items for *WSQ*'s or violating memory safety). For the four *WSQ*'s (excluding *THE*), the fence added to guarantee linearizability is used to trigger the flushing at the linearization point.

Algorithm without fences on TSO Interestingly, by weakening the correctness criteria from linearizability to sequential consistency, we obtain an algorithm, *FIFO WSQ* on TSO, for which the tool does not find any fences (except the slow path `expand` function). Note that unlike *iWSQ* algorithms, we did not weaken the actual specification of *FIFO*, that is, we did not need an idempotent variant of *FIFO*. Our finding is also inline with a recent result which shows that it is impossible to eliminate certain orders with linearizability [3], but by slightly weakening it, that may be possible.

Cilk's THE *is not linearizable* As our tool can check properties without any relaxed memory model effects, we were able to detect that *Cilk's THE WSQ* is not linearizable with a deterministic sequential specification (even without any relaxed memory model effects). However, the tool indicates that the algorithm is sequentially consistent and is indeed accepted to be correct [1]. DFENCE infers the necessary fences under the sequential consistency specification.

6.7 Memory Allocator

For the memory allocator, we used the client sequence *mmmfff* | *mfmf*, where *m* stands for malloc and *f* stands for free. In this sequence, the free function always frees up the oldest memory unit allocated by the same thread. As far as we know, no previous work can synthesize synchronization for concurrent algorithms of this scale. For the allocator, we found that three fences were required to satisfy the memory safety property, i.e., running to termination without segmentation fault. If we specified the additional criteria such as sequential consistency or linearizability, one additional fence in the `free` function is inferred. All four of the fences that our tool inferred are discussed in the paper which describes the memory allocator algorithm [21]. The `C` implementation of the allocator has 11 store-store memory fences and DFENCE was able to infer only 4 of them. The problem of how to uncover the other 7 fences is left as future work.

7. Related Work

Exhaustive Approaches for Relaxed Memory Models The works in [16, 25] describe explicit-state model checking for the Sparc RMO model, but neither of these approaches perform fence inference. The work in [15] describes an explicit-state model checker and a simple inference technique for the .NET memory model. Recent work [17, 18] focuses on fence inference based on model checking (with abstraction). In [4], a different approach is taken where instead of working with explicit state, they convert programs into a form that can be checked against an axiomatic model specification. Collectively, the fundamental limitation of these exhaustive approaches is that they are not inherently scalable for larger concurrent programs and often require manual intervention (to specify abstractions or a model of the program). In contrast, our focus is squarely on handling large concurrent C implementations, which in turn dictates our dynamic synthesis approach.

Delay Set Analysis A number of works on fence inference [11, 20, 27] rely on concepts such as delay sets and conflict graphs [26]. Particularly, the Pensieve project implements fence inference based on delay set analysis. This kind of analysis is necessarily more conservative than ours for two reasons: first, it is static in nature, and second, the correctness criteria are more restrictive than the ones used in this work. For instance, their criteria would prevent behaviors that are linearizable and should be allowed.

Other Approaches The works in [5, 6] present algorithms that find violations under the TSO and PSO memory models based on correctness criteria similar to the ones used in the delay set analysis approaches mentioned above, meaning that [5, 6] can be needlessly conservative. Further, both of these works do not support fence inference. In [30], the authors propose algorithms that automatically infer synchronization constructs such as atomic sections. Their work does not deal with relaxed memory models.

8. Conclusion

We introduced dynamic synthesis for concurrent programs running on relaxed memory models. The key idea is to break the scalability barrier of standard synthesis approaches by instead focusing on dynamic executions: when a set of violating executions is discovered, the program is automatically repaired to avoid these executions, and the synthesis procedure continues with the repaired program.

We implemented our techniques in LLVM and evaluated its effectiveness on a comprehensive list of concurrent C algorithms including a complex lock-free memory allocator. Each algorithm was evaluated with two memory models (TSO and PSO), three specifications (linearizability, sequential consistency and memory safety), various repair strategies, and different scheduling parameters (e.g. flush probability). We demonstrated the effectiveness of our approach by automatically synthesizing necessary fences for each of the concurrent algorithms.

As future work, we plan to extend our tool with more advanced demonic schedulers to discover violations even quicker. We also plan to add support for other memory models and to evaluate our tool on a wider set of concurrent C programs.

References

[1] Personal Communication with the Cilk Team, 2011.

[2] ADVE, S. V., AND GHARACHORLOO, K. Shared memory consistency models: A tutorial. *IEEE Computer 29* (1995), 66–76.

[3] ATTIYA, H., GUERRAOUI, R., HENDLER, D., KUZNETSOV, P., MICHAEL, M. M., AND VECHEV, M. Laws of order: expensive synchronization in concurrent algorithms cannot be eliminated. In *POPL'11* (New York, NY, USA), ACM, pp. 487–498.

[4] BURCKHARDT, S., ALUR, R., AND MARTIN, M. M. K. Check-Fence: checking consistency of concurrent data types on relaxed memory models. In *PLDI* (2007), pp. 12–21.

[5] BURCKHARDT, S., AND MUSUVATHI, M. Effective program verification for relaxed memory models. In *CAV* (2008), pp. 107–120.

[6] BURNIM, J., SEN, K., AND STERGIOU, C. Testing concurrent programs on relaxed memory models. In *ISSTA* (2011), pp. 122–132.

[7] CHASE, D., AND LEV, Y. Dynamic circular work-stealing deque. In *SPAA* (2005), pp. 21–28.

[8] DETLEFS, D. L., FLOOD, C. H., GARTHWAITE, A. T., GARTHWAITE, E. T., MARTIN, P. A., SHAVIT, N. N., JR., AND STEELE, G. L. Even better dcas-based concurrent deques. In *DISC'00*.

[9] DICE, D., LEV, Y., MARATHE, V. J., MOIR, M., NUSSBAUM, D., AND OLESZEWSKI, M. Simplifying concurrent algorithms by exploiting hardware transactional memory. In *SPAA'10*, ACM, pp. 325–334.

[10] EÉN, N., AND SÖRENSSON, N. An extensible sat-solver. In *SAT* (2003), pp. 502–518.

[11] FANG, X., LEE, J., AND MIDKIFF, S. P. Automatic fence insertion for shared memory multiprocessing. In *ICS* (2003), pp. 285–294.

[12] FRIGO, M., LEISERSON, C. E., AND RANDALL, K. H. The implementation of the cilk-5 multithreaded language. In *PLDI '98*.

[13] HELLER, S., HERLIHY, M., LUCHANGCO, V., MOIR, M., SCHERER, W., AND SHAVIT, N. A lazy concurrent list-based set algorithm. In *OPODIS '05*, pp. 3–16.

[14] HERLIHY, M., AND SHAVIT, N. *The Art of Multiprocessor Programming*. Morgan Kaufmann, Apr. 2008.

[15] HUYNH, T. Q., AND ROYCHOUDHURY, A. Memory model sensitive bytecode verification. *Form. Methods Syst. Des. 31*, 3 (2007).

[16] JONSSON, B. State-space exploration for concurrent algorithms under weak memory orderings. *SIGARCH Comput. Archit. News 36*, 5 (2008), 65–71.

[17] KUPERSTEIN, M., VECHEV, M., AND YAHAV, E. Automatic inference of memory fences. In *FMCAD'10*.

[18] KUPERSTEIN, M., VECHEV, M., AND YAHAV, E. Partial-coherence abstractions for relaxed memory models. In *PLDI'11*, pp. 187–198.

[19] LATTNER, C., AND ADVE, V. LLVM: A Compilation Framework for Lifelong Program Analysis & Transformation. In *CGO'04*, pp. 75–87.

[20] LEE, J., AND PADUA, D. A. Hiding relaxed memory consistency with a compiler. *IEEE Trans. Comput. 50*, 8 (2001), 824–833.

[21] MICHAEL, M. M. Scalable lock-free dynamic memory allocation. In *PLDI '04* (2004), pp. 35–46.

[22] MICHAEL, M. M., AND SCOTT, M. L. Correction of a memory management method for lock-free data structures. Tech. rep., 1995.

[23] MICHAEL, M. M., AND SCOTT, M. L. Simple, fast, and practical non-blocking and blocking concurrent queue algorithms. In *PODC* (1996), pp. 267–275.

[24] MICHAEL, M. M., VECHEV, M. T., AND SARASWAT, V. A. Idempotent work stealing. In *PPoPP* (2009), pp. 45–54.

[25] PARK, S., AND DILL, D. L. An executable specification and verifier for relaxed memory order. *IEEE Trans. on Computers 48* (1999).

[26] SHASHA, D., AND SNIR, M. Efficient and correct execution of parallel programs that share memory. *ACM Trans. Program. Lang. Syst. 10*, 2 (1988), 282–312.

[27] SURA, Z., WONG, C., FANG, X., LEE, J., MIDKIFF, S., AND PADUA, D. Automatic implementation of programming language consistency models. *LNCS 2481* (2005), 172.

[28] SUTTER, H., AND LARUS, J. Software and the concurrency revolution. *Queue 3*, 7 (2005), 54–62.

[29] VECHEV, M., YAHAV, E., AND YORSH, G. Experience with model checking linearizability. In *SPIN'09*, pp. 261–278.

[30] VECHEV, M., YAHAV, E., AND YORSH, G. Abstraction-guided synthesis of synchronization. In *POPL* (2010).

[31] WEERATUNGE, D., ZHANG, X., AND JAGANATHAN, S. Accentuating the positive: atomicity inference and enforcement using correct executions. In *OOPSLA'11*, pp. 19–34.

Automated Synthesis of Symbolic Instruction Encodings from I/O Samples

Patrice Godefroid
Microsoft Research
pg@microsoft.com

Ankur Taly *
Stanford University
ataly@stanford.edu

Abstract

Symbolic execution is a key component of precise binary program analysis tools. We discuss how to automatically boot-strap the construction of a symbolic execution engine for a processor instruction set such as x86, x64 or ARM. We show how to automatically synthesize symbolic representations of individual processor instructions from input/output examples and express them as bit-vector constraints. We present and compare various synthesis algorithms and instruction sampling strategies. We introduce a new synthesis algorithm based on *smart sampling* which we show is one to two orders of magnitude faster than previous synthesis algorithms in our context. With this new algorithm, we can automatically synthesize bit-vector circuits for over 500 x86 instructions (8/16/32-bits, outputs, EFLAGS) using only 6 synthesis templates and in less than two hours using the Z3 SMT solver on a regular machine. During this work, we also discovered several inconsistencies across x86 processors, errors in the x86 Intel spec, and several bugs in previous manually-written x86 instruction handlers.

Categories and Subject Descriptors D.2.3 [*Software Engineering*]: Coding Tools and Techniques; D.2.4 [*Software Engineering*]: Software/Program Verification; D.2.5 [*Software Engineering*]: Testing and Debugging; F.3.1 [*Logics and Meanings of Programs*]: Specifying and Verifying and Reasoning about Programs

General Terms Languages, Verification

Keywords Program Synthesis, Symbolic Execution, x86

1. Introduction

Symbolic execution is a key component of precise binary program analysis tools, for test generation [6, 17], program verification [2, 20], malware analysis [1, 23], and other applications. Symbolic execution engines are traditionally written by hand [1, 2, 6, 17, 20, 23]: the effect of executing each individual instruction is described by a symbolic constraint, called *symbolic instruction encoding*, written manually and derived by reading the processor instruction manual. Unfortunately, the semantics of the instruction set of general-purpose processors such as x86, x64 or ARM is very complex. For instance, x86 includes hundreds of instructions whose semantics is described in more than 2,000 pages divided in 3 volumes. This complexity makes the manual development of symbolic-execution engines tedious (many instructions), error-prone (many corner cases), partial (not all instructions are usually covered) and imprecise (approximations are often used). Moreover, the official reference manual is often under-specified and may itself contain errors.

In this work, we explore a radically different approach to developing symbolic-execution engines: what if most symbolic instruction encodings could be *synthesized automatically*?

To do this, we study how to adapt and extend recent advances on *automatic program synthesis*. Given a functional *specification* and a set of building blocks, called *components*, possibly combined together as described in a solution *template* or program sketch (i.e., a program with holes), automatic program synthesis consists of searching the space of all possible template completions for a fully-defined program (i.e., with no holes left) that satisfies the specification. In our context, we do not have access to a full functional specification of individual processor instructions — such a specification is precisely what we want to infer. But we have access to a cheap and fast *specification oracle*: we can execute instructions on a processor and observe their input/output behaviors.

Program synthesis from I/O samples has been recently investigated in [13]. There, an I/O *oracle-guided* synthesis algorithm is presented for loop-free programs. This algorithm consists of computing a set of I/O samples, then synthesizing a candidate program that satisfies those samples (to check whether such a program exists), then computing a *distinguishing input* that distinguishes this candidate program P from some other non-equivalent candidate program P' (to check whether P is unique), and if such an input exists, then query the I/O oracle with this distinguishing input to eliminate either P or P' as a possible solution. This *counter-example-guided iterative synthesis* process is repeated until one unique solution remains, or no solution exists if the synthesis template is too constrained. The algorithm assumes the existence of a *verification oracle* which can determine whether a solution is "correct".

In our context, we do not have access to such a verification oracle. For instructions with small I/O signatures, such as 8-bit instructions, exhaustive testing can provide a verification oracle, but exhaustive testing does not scale to 16-bit or 32-bit instructions. Another practical hurdle is that the counter-example-guided iterative synthesis algorithm of [13] can be very expensive when many iterations are needed, as we will show with results of experiments in Section 6.

To improve on this, we propose a new synthesis algorithm based on *smart sampling* which we show is one to two orders of magnitude faster than previous synthesis algorithms in our context. Given a specific template, the main idea is to generate upfront a set of distinguishing inputs which uniquely determine each possible so-

* The work of this author was done mostly while visiting Microsoft.

PLDI'12, June 11–16, 2012, Beijing, China.

lution refining the template. This way, our new synthesis algorithm converges faster to the unique solution, without requiring any additional expensive synthesis-refinement steps. Synthesis with smart sampling is more efficient when a template is repeatedly used for many instructions, as is the case in our context.

In this work, we want to *automatically* generate *concise* yet *precise* symbolic instruction encodings that can be used for bit-precise symbolic execution of large programs and long execution paths. Conciseness is important for scalability, while precision is key to detect subtle program bugs (for instance due to integer overflows). For these reasons, we adopt *bit-vector constraints* supported by SMT solvers as synthesis components.

For automatic synthesis to be practical, synthesis templates should be constrained enough to define a tractable search space, yet abstract enough to allow a simple representation of many possible solutions. Perhaps surprisingly, we show that the I/O behavior of over 500 x86 instructions (8/16/32-bits, outputs, EFLAGS) can be precisely captured with only 6 synthesis templates. Using these templates and our new smart sampling synthesis algorithm, we can automatically synthesize bit-vector circuits for all those 500+ instructions in less than two hours using the Z3 SMT solver on a regular x86 machine. Moreover, the size of the synthesized circuits is either constant or linear in the number of input/output bits, satisfying our conciseness requirement.

This paper is organized as follows. In Section 2, we precisely define the problem addressed in this work. Then, we review in Section 3 existing automatic synthesis approaches and discuss their applicability to our context. We introduce in Section 4 our new synthesis algorithm based on smart sampling. In Section 5, we present 6 synthesis templates that together abstract the semantics of over 500 x86 instructions, and we discuss properties of those templates. Next, we compare in Section 6 the performance of several synthesis algorithms with those templates. We discuss our overall results for x86, lessons learned and limitations in Section 7. We then discuss other related work in Section 8, and conclude in Section 9.

2. Problem Definition

We consider a *processor* which can execute a set of *instructions*. In this work, we focus on ALU instructions and will not consider floating point and SIMD instructions. We will also ignore specific addressing modes and assume that an instruction has some inputs and outputs, but we will not distinguish where those inputs or outputs are being stored, e.g., in a register or a memory location. However, we do consider the sizes of the input and output arguments of an instruction, which we assume are known (i.e., are not inferred automatically).

Formally, we define an instruction instance I as a *function* that takes a known fixed ordered set $\vec{i}$ of *inputs*, each of a known fixed size, which may be read during the execution of the instruction, and returns a known fixed ordered set $\vec{o}$ of *outputs*, each of a known fixed size, which may be written during the execution of the instruction. We thus assume that the execution of each instruction instance is *deterministic* and always terminates. In what follows, we will treat each output o in $\vec{o}$ separately, abuse notation by writing $o = f(\vec{i})$, and calling such a function an *instruction instance*.

For instance, SHL is an x86 instruction, while SHL8 is an instruction instance that takes two 8-bit values as inputs and returns an 8-bit value as output representing the main result, and $\texttt{SHL8}^{\texttt{CF}}$ is another instruction instance that takes again two 8-bit values as inputs but returns a boolean value representing the value of the CF flag (part of the x86 "EFLAGS") after executing the instruction.

The problem we consider in this work is to automatically synthesize a (concise and precise) representation of function f for a given instruction instance. We call such a representation a *symbolic representation*, or *symbolic encoding*, or *instruction handler*.

However, function f is unknown. All we are given to learn about f is a processor $\mathcal{P}$ implementing the instruction instance, which we can *sample* by providing some input values, executing the instruction instance, and then observing the output value. In other words, processor $\mathcal{P}$ is a *black-box input/output oracle* for instruction instance I. This oracle is denoted $\Phi(\mathcal{P}, I)$ in what follows.

Because we want to generate concise and precise symbolic representations, we will represent inputs and outputs by bit-vectors, and functions by logic expressions using the theory of bit-vectors as defined by modern SMT solvers. We will sometimes call such function representations *circuits*. If $\vec{i}$ represents two inputs i_1 and i_2, each of size s, we will write $i_1[j]$ with $0 \leq j < s$ to denote the jth bit of i_1.

In summary, the problem considered in this work is:

> Given a black-box processor $\mathcal{P}$ and an instruction instance I, how to automatically synthesize a function f that is semantically equivalent to the oracle $\Phi(\mathcal{P}, I)$?

3. Synthesis Procedures

In this section, we review prior synthesis approaches to the function synthesis problem given a black-box I/O oracle $\phi = \Phi(\mathcal{P}, I)$. We present two procedures `ExhaustVal` and `DInputVal` and discuss their correctness and scalability.

Both procedures involve three stages: a *sampling* stage, a *synthesis* stage, and a *verification* stage. In the sampling stage, the I/O oracle is queried on an initial set of inputs and a set of I/O samples $\mathcal{S}$ is obtained. In the synthesis stage, a function is synthesized whose behavior respects the samples $\mathcal{S}$. This is done by using a *template-based approach* (see below) to find a function f that satisfies $\bigwedge_{\vec{i},o\in\mathcal{S}} f(\vec{i}) = o$. The synthesized function f is then passed to the verification stage to check whether it matches the I/O oracle on other samples outside $\mathcal{S}$. Samples that fail the verification check are sent back to the synthesis stage, and the procedure is repeated until the verification check succeeds.The two procedures differ in the specific verification checks used.

Before presenting the two procedures in more details, we review the motivation for template-based synthesis.

3.1 Template-Based Synthesis

A direct approach for synthesizing a function f satisfying the samples $\mathcal{S}$ is to check the satisfiability of the formula

$$\exists f : \bigwedge_{\vec{i},o\in\mathcal{S}} f(\vec{i}) = o$$

Unfortunately, this second-order logic formula can be expensive or even impossible to check. A common approach to get rid of the quantification over functions is to use a *function template*. Informally, a function template T is a function with some free variables $\vec{c}$ called *coefficients*. Instantiating the coefficients with concrete values defines a closed (i.e., fully-defined) function $T(\vec{c})$, called *concretization*. The set $\gamma(T)$ of all possible concretizations of a template T is thus defined as the set $\{C \mid \exists\vec{c} : C = T(\vec{c})\}$. By replacing the function f in the synthesis formula above by a function template T and by existentially quantifying its coefficients, the synthesis problem is reduced to satisfiability checking of a first-order logic formula

$$\texttt{SYN}_{T,\mathcal{S}}(\vec{c}) := \exists\vec{c}: \bigwedge_{\vec{i},o\in\mathcal{S}} T(\vec{c},\vec{i}) = o$$

where $T(\vec{c},\vec{i})$ denotes application of function $T(\vec{c})$ with inputs $\vec{i}$.

$\texttt{ExhaustVal}(\phi, T, n_{syn})$

1. $\mathcal{I} := n_{syn}$ valid inputs for ϕ picked randomly
2. $\mathcal{I}_{ex} :=$ All valid inputs for ϕ
3. $\mathcal{S} := \texttt{Sample}(\mathcal{I}, \phi)$
4. $\mathcal{S}_{ex} := \texttt{Sample}(\mathcal{I}_{ex}, \phi)$
5. $\vec{\alpha} := \texttt{SAT}(\texttt{SYN}_{T,\mathcal{S}}(\vec{c}))$ // returns $\perp$ if UNSAT
6. **if** $(\vec{\alpha} = \perp)$ **return** "Insufficient Template"
7. $C := T(\vec{\alpha})$
8. $\mathcal{S}_{fail} := \texttt{Verify}(C, \mathcal{S}_{ex})$
9. **if** $(\mathcal{S}_{fail} == \emptyset)$ **return** C
10. $\mathcal{S} := \mathcal{S} \cup \mathcal{S}_{fail}$
11. **goto** step 5

Figure 1. Procedure ExhaustVal: Exhaustive Validation

If the template T is expressed as a quantifier-free formula using the theory of bit-vectors and if the set of possible values for the coefficients is finite, checking the satisfiability of the formula $\texttt{SYN}_{T,\mathcal{S}}(\vec{c})$ is decidable.

If the above formula is unsatisfiable, then the template cannot be used to synthesize a function that satisfies the samples $\mathcal{S}$. We define this property of *template sufficiency* as follows.

DEFINITION 1. [Template Sufficiency] A template T is *sufficient* for abstracting a function C if $C \in \gamma(T)$. ■

We now describe the two procedures ExhaustVal and DInputVal for efficiently solving the template-based synthesis problem. In what follows, $\texttt{Sample}(\mathcal{I}, \phi)$ for a set of inputs $\mathcal{I}$ and an I/O oracle $\phi = \Phi(\mathcal{P}, I)$ denotes the set $\{(\vec{\alpha}, \phi(\vec{\alpha})) \mid \vec{\alpha} \in \mathcal{I}\}$ of samples (I/O pairs) obtained by executing each input by the oracle. Moreover, $\texttt{Verify}(C, \mathcal{S})$ for a function C and a set of samples $\mathcal{S}$ denotes the set $\{(\vec{i}, o) \in \mathcal{S} \mid C(\vec{i}) \neq o\}$ of samples which do not agree with C (if any).

3.2 Procedure ExhaustVal

The procedure ExhaustVal is described in Figure 1. It takes as input an I/O oracle ϕ, a template T and a number of synthesis samples n_{syn}.

During the sampling stage (lines $1-4$), n_{syn} valid inputs are chosen randomly to define the set $\mathcal{I}$, while the set $\mathcal{I}_{ex}$ contains all possible valid inputs. Next, two sets $\mathcal{S}$ and $\mathcal{S}_{ex}$ of I/O samples are constructed by querying the oracle ϕ on inputs in $\mathcal{I}$ and $\mathcal{I}_{ex}$ respectively.

During the synthesis stage (lines $5-8$), the synthesis formula $\texttt{SYN}_{T,\mathcal{S}}(\vec{c})$ is checked for satisfiability. If the formula is unsatisfiable then the procedure returns "Insufficient Template", otherwise the satisfying assignment $\vec{\alpha}$ for all the template coefficients is used to construct the function $C := T(\vec{\alpha})$.

The verification stage (lines $9-11$) checks whether the synthesized function C agrees with all possible I/O samples $\mathcal{S}_{ex}$ using the procedure Verify. The procedure returns the set $\mathcal{S}_{fail}$ of all samples that fail. If $\mathcal{S}_{fail} = \emptyset$ then the function C is returned, else the set of failed samples $\mathcal{S}_{fail}$ are added to the set of synthesis samples $\mathcal{S}$ and the procedure loops back to the synthesis stage (line 3).

Note that the synthesis stage is more expensive (NP-hard) than the verification stage (linear in the size of each sample), which explains why the procedure ExhaustVal does not consider immediately the $\mathcal{S}_{ex}$ in its synthesis stage. We now state the main properties of the procedure ExhaustVal.

$\texttt{DInputVal}(\phi, T, n_{syn}, n_{ver})$

1. $\mathcal{I} := n_{syn}$ valid inputs for ϕ picked randomly
2. $\mathcal{S} := \texttt{Sample}(\mathcal{I}, \phi)$
3. $\vec{\alpha} := \texttt{SAT}(\texttt{SYN}_{T,\mathcal{S}}(\vec{c}))$ // returns $\perp$ if UNSAT
4. **if** $(\vec{\alpha} = \perp)$ **return** "Insufficient Template"
5. $C := T(\vec{\alpha})$
6. $\mathcal{I}_{ver} := n_{ver}$ valid inputs for ϕ picked randomly
7. $\mathcal{S}_{ver} := \texttt{Sample}(\mathcal{I}_{ver}, \phi)$
8. $\mathcal{S}_{fail} := \texttt{Verify}(C, \mathcal{S}_{ver})$
9. **if** $(\mathcal{S}_{fail} == \emptyset)$
10. $\quad \vec{i} := \texttt{SAT}(\texttt{DISTINCT}_{T,C,\mathcal{S}}(\vec{i}))$
11. $\quad$ **if** $(\vec{i} = \perp)$ **return** C
12. $\quad \mathcal{S} := \mathcal{S} \cup \texttt{Sample}(\{\vec{i}\}, \phi)$
13. $\quad$ **goto** step 3
14. $\mathcal{S} := \mathcal{S} \cup \mathcal{S}_{fail}$
15. **goto** step 3

Figure 2. Procedure DInputVal: Distinguishing-Input based Validation

THEOREM 1. *Given a template T, an oracle ϕ, and any $n_{syn} > 0$, the following holds:*

1. *If the template T is sufficient for abstracting the oracle ϕ, then the procedure $\texttt{ExhaustVal}(\phi, T, n_{syn})$ returns a function semantically equivalent to ϕ;*
2. *Else the procedure returns "Insufficient Template".*

In other words, procedure ExhaustVal is both sound and complete, thanks to its exhaustive validation. Unfortunately, exhaustive validation does not scale to large inputs, such as 16-bit and 32-bit instructions. For instance, any 16-bit instruction instance with two 16-bit inputs requires an exhaustive sample set of 2^{32} samples, that is, more than a billion samples to verify.

3.3 Procedure DInputVal

We now present the procedure DInputVal, described in Figure 2 which offers weaker verification guarantees but scales to larger input signatures. Besides an I/O oracle ϕ and a template T, this procedure takes two additional inputs n_{syn} and n_{ver} denoting the number of synthesis and verification samples, respectively.

This procedure *assumes* that the input template T is sufficient for abstracting the I/O oracle ϕ. Its goal is to search through all functions abstracted by the template and to return one that is semantically equivalent to the oracle. If this assumption is right, the procedure returns a correct function. But if the assumption is wrong, it may either detect that the template is not sufficient, or return a wrong function.

Similarly to the procedure ExhaustVal, the sampling stage (lines $1-2$) computes a set of synthesis samples $\mathcal{S}$ by querying the oracle ϕ on a set $\mathcal{I}$ of n_{syn} inputs chosen randomly. The synthesis stage (lines $3-5$) checks for a satisfying assignment for the formula $\texttt{SYN}_{T,\mathcal{S}}(\vec{c})$. If the formula is unsatisfiable then the procedure returns "Insufficient Template", otherwise the satisfying assignment $\vec{\alpha}$ for all the template coefficients is used to construct the function $C := T(\vec{\alpha})$. The procedure differs from ExhaustVal in its verification stage (lines $6-15$). We explain the main idea first and then present the details.

Intuitively, if we assume that the template T is sufficient for abstracting the oracle ϕ, and if we can show that all the concretization functions for T that satisfy samples $\mathcal{S}$ are all semantically equivalent, then the synthesized function C is semantically equivalent to the oracle. In order to show this, we make use of the *distinguishing input* check, introduced in [13]. A distinguishing input $\texttt{DISTINCT}_{T,C,\mathcal{S}}(\vec{i})$ for a function C, a template T and a set $\mathcal{S}$ of samples is an input $\vec{i}$ that can be used to distinguish C from another function that also concretizes the template and satisfies all the samples in $\mathcal{S}$. Formally, we define $\texttt{DISTINCT}_{T,C,\mathcal{S}}(\vec{i})$ as

$$\exists \vec{c} : (\bigwedge_{\vec{j},o \in \mathcal{S}} T(\vec{c}, \vec{j}) = o) \wedge T(\vec{c}, \vec{i}) \neq C(\vec{i})$$

If an input $\vec{i}$ satisfies the above formula, then there are at least two non-equivalent functions that concretize the template and satisfy the samples in $\mathcal{S}$; therefore, by querying the oracle with $\vec{i}$ and adding the resulting I/O sample to $\mathcal{S}$, we can strictly reduce the number of non-equivalent functions that concretize the template and satisfy all previous samples. Otherwise, if the formula is unsatisfiable, then C is guaranteed to be equivalent to all other functions that concretize the template and satisfy all previous samples.

We now describe the pseudo-code for the validation stage. The first step (lines 6 – 8) is to sample n_{ver} inputs at random and query the oracle on them, thereby building the set of I/O samples $\mathcal{S}_{ver}$. Next the synthesized function C is verified against the samples $\mathcal{S}_{ver}$, and the samples that fail are collected in the set $\mathcal{S}_{fail}$. If $\mathcal{S}_{fail} \neq \emptyset$, then the samples are added (line 14) to the set of synthesis samples $\mathcal{S}$ and the procedure loops back to the synthesis stage (line 3). If $\mathcal{S}_{fail} = \emptyset$, then the formula $\texttt{DISTINCT}_{T,C,\mathcal{S}}(\vec{i})$ is checked for satisfiability. If it is unsatisfiable, then the function C is returned; otherwise, the oracle is queried with the satisfying assignment $\vec{i}$, the sample $\texttt{Sample}(\{\vec{i}\}, \phi)$ is added to the set of synthesis samples $\mathcal{S}$, and the procedure then loops back to the synthesis stage.

The reason for the verification stage with the samples $\mathcal{S}_{ver}$ is to reduce the number of expensive satisfiability checks of formulas $\texttt{DISTINCT}_{T,C,\mathcal{S}}(\vec{i})$. If the template is sufficient for abstracting the oracle, any input that distinguishes the synthesized function C from the oracle is also a distinguishing input. Thus, checking C against a set of randomly chosen samples provides a cheap way of searching for distinguishing inputs. We now state the main property of the procedure `DInputVal`.

THEOREM 2. *Given a template T, an oracle ϕ, and any n_{syn}, $n_{ver} > 0$, if T is sufficient for abstracting ϕ, then the procedure $\texttt{DInputVal}(\phi, T, n_{syn}, n_{ver})$ returns a function C semantically equivalent to ϕ.*

A useful corollary is that, if the procedure `DInputVal` returns "Insufficient Template" for any n_{syn}, n_{ver}, then the template T is indeed insufficient for abstracting ϕ. However, this theorem is weaker than Theorem 1 as it does not guarantee that the procedure returns "Insufficient Template" *whenever* the template is insufficient.

Just like procedure `ExhaustVal`, `DInputVal` provides a satisfactory solution to the instruction handler synthesis problem provided we can find a template that is sufficient for abstracting the oracle $\Phi(\mathcal{P}, I)$. Although the procedure `DInputVal` scales to instruction instances with large inputs, the running time can still be very long for some templates, as we will see in Section 6. The most expensive step in the procedure is checking the satisfiability of formulas $\texttt{DISTINCT}_{T,C,\mathcal{S}}(\vec{i})$. Since the satisfiability of each such formula depends on a set $\mathcal{S}$ of random samples, the running time of the procedure can vary significantly across various invocations. In the next section, we present a new synthesis procedure that provides the same correctness guarantee as the procedure `DInputVal`, but alleviates the above limitations.

4. Smart Sampling

In this section, we present a new template-based synthesis procedure `SmartVal` that provides the same correctness guarantee as procedure `DInputVal` but does not require any distinguishing input check. As a result, the procedure has a significantly better and more predictable running time than the procedure `DInputVal`. As with procedure `DInputVal`, the procedure `SmartVal` also assumes that the given template is sufficient for abstracting the given I/O oracle.

Given a specific template, the main idea is to generate upfront a set of distinguishing inputs which uniquely determine each possible solution refining the template. This way, the new synthesis algorithm converges directly to the unique solution, without requiring any other expensive synthesis-iteration and distinguishing-input steps.

Recall from section 3.3 that the distinguishing input check is performed to guarantee that for a template T and a set of synthesis samples $\mathcal{S}$, the synthesized function C is semantically equivalent to all functions that concretize template T and satisfy all the samples in $\mathcal{S}$. In order to avoid the distinguishing input check, we want to run a (unique) synthesis step with a set of samples obtained with an input set $\mathcal{I}$ such that all the functions that concretize template T and satisfy all the samples in $\texttt{Sample}(\mathcal{I}, \phi)$, are all semantically equivalent. We call such an input set $\mathcal{I}$ *smart* for the template T and oracle ϕ. Formally, we have the following.

DEFINITION 2. [Smart Inputs] A set $\mathcal{I}$ of inputs is *smart* for a template T and an oracle ϕ if

$$\forall \vec{c} : (\bigwedge_{\vec{j},o \in \mathcal{S}} T(\vec{c}, \vec{j}) = o) \Rightarrow \neg\, \texttt{DISTINCT}_{T,T(\vec{c}),\mathcal{S}}(\vec{i})$$

with $\mathcal{S} = \texttt{Sample}(\mathcal{I}, \phi)$. ■

When a set $\mathcal{I}$ of inputs is smart for a template T and an oracle ϕ, we write $\texttt{Smart}_{T,\phi}(\mathcal{I})$.

The previous definition depends on a specific oracle ϕ. We can generalize it and define a stronger property on input sets, which we call *universal smartness* for a template T *independently* of any specific oracle ϕ. A set $\mathcal{I}$ of inputs is universally smart for a template T if any two functions that concretize the template and agree on all the inputs in $\mathcal{I}$ are semantically equivalent. Formally, we have the following.

DEFINITION 3. [Universally Smart Inputs] A set $\mathcal{I}$ of inputs is *universally smart* for a template T, denoted by $\texttt{USmart}_T(\mathcal{I})$, if

$$\forall \vec{c}, \vec{d}, \vec{i} : (\textstyle\bigwedge_{\vec{j} \in \mathcal{I}} T(\vec{c}, \vec{j}) = T(\vec{d}, \vec{j})) \Rightarrow T(\vec{c}, \vec{i}) = T(\vec{d}, \vec{i}) \ ■$$

By definition, a universally smart input set for a template is also smart for the template and any possible oracle ϕ.

LEMMA 3. $\texttt{USmart}_T(\mathcal{I}) \Rightarrow \forall \phi : \texttt{Smart}_{T,\phi}(\mathcal{I})$

Thus, for a fixed template, and given a set of universally smart inputs for that template, we are then guaranteed that, irrespective of the oracle, all functions synthesized by sampling those inputs do not require any distinguishing input check.

The procedure `SmartVal` is described in Figure 3. It takes as input an I/O oracle ϕ, a template T and a set $\mathcal{I}$ of inputs such as $\texttt{Smart}_{T,\phi}(\mathcal{I})$. The procedure has only one sampling and one synthesis stage. The sampling stage (lines 1) computes a set of samples for the smart set of inputs $\mathcal{I}$ by querying the oracle ϕ. The synthesis stage (lines 2 – 4) checks the formula $\texttt{SYN}_{T,\mathcal{S}}(\vec{c})$ for satisfiability. If the formula is unsatisfiable, then the procedure returns "Insufficient Template"; otherwise, the satisfying assignment $\vec{\alpha}$ defines

$\texttt{SmartVal}(\phi, T, \mathcal{I})$

1. $\mathcal{S} := \texttt{Sample}(\mathcal{I}, \phi)$
2. $\vec{\alpha} := \texttt{SAT}(\texttt{SYN}_{T,\mathcal{S}}(\vec{c}))$ // returns $\perp$ if UNSAT
3. **if** $(\vec{\alpha} = \perp)$ **return** "Insufficient Template"
4. **return** $T(\vec{\alpha})$

Figure 3. Procedure SmartVal

the concrete function $T(\vec{\alpha})$, which is then returned. We prove the following.

THEOREM 4. *Given a template T, an I/O oracle ϕ and a smart set $\mathcal{I}$ of inputs for T and ϕ, if T is sufficient for abstracting ϕ, then the procedure SmartVal$(\phi, T, \mathcal{I})$ returns a function C semantically equivalent to ϕ.*

Like procedure **DInputVal**, **SmartVal** is guaranteed to return a function semantically equivalent to the oracle ϕ only if the template T is sufficient for abstracting ϕ; if this assumption is wrong, it may either detect that the template is not sufficient, or return a wrong function. As will be shown in Section 6, **SmartVal** can be much faster than **DInputVal**. But it also requires a set of smart inputs.

We now discuss several approaches to compute smart or universally smart inputs. Trivially, the set of all possible inputs is universally smart for any template, but we want smart input sets to be as small as possible so that the synthesis step is fast.

Brute-force approach. Using Definition 3 for $\texttt{USmart}_T(\mathcal{I})$, we can compute a set $\mathcal{I}$ by checking the satisfiability of the formula

$$\exists \mathcal{I} : \forall \vec{c}, \vec{d}, \vec{i} : (\bigwedge_{\vec{j} \in \mathcal{I}} T(\vec{c}, \vec{j}) = T(\vec{d}, \vec{j})) \Rightarrow T(\vec{c}, \vec{i}) = T(\vec{d}, \vec{i})$$

If such a set $\mathcal{I}$ exists, then it is universally smart for T, by definition. Therefore, a straightforward procedure for synthesizing universally smart inputs is to check the satisfiability of the above formula for any set $\mathcal{I}$ of size 1, then 2, then 3, and so on. This approach can return a universally smart input set of minimum cardinality. Its drawback is that checking satisfiability of a $\exists \forall$ formula can be expensive.

Greedy approach. Here is a straightforward greedy procedure for constructing a universally smart set of inputs:

1. $\mathcal{I} := \emptyset$
2. If $\texttt{USmart}_T(\mathcal{I})$ holds then return $\mathcal{I}$
3. Else there exist coefficients $\vec{c}, \vec{d}$ and an input $\vec{i}$ such that $(\bigwedge_{\vec{j} \in \mathcal{I}} T(\vec{c}, \vec{j}) = T(\vec{d}, \vec{j})) \wedge T(\vec{c}, \vec{i}) \neq T(\vec{d}, \vec{i})$
   Add $\vec{i}$ to the set $\mathcal{I}$ and go to step (2)

Unlike the brute-force approach, this approach may not return a universally smart input set of minimum cardinality. But checking the validity of $\texttt{USmart}_T(\mathcal{I})$ can be cheaper because it avoids the existential quantifier on $\mathcal{I}$.

Manual approach. Universally smart input sets can be inferred from the structure of a template. Therefore, they can also be defined manually while designing the template. A manually defined set $\mathcal{I}$ can be verified for universal smartness using the predicate $\texttt{USmart}_T(\mathcal{I})$ and an SMT solver. If the verification fails, then the set can be used as the initial set for the greedy approach described above, which would then iteratively enlarge it and eventually return a universally smart input set.

Note that universally smart input sets need to be constructed only once for each template, and can then be re-used for all the instruction instances (oracles) covered by each template. Synthesis with smart sampling is thus especially attractive when a template is repeatedly used for many instructions instances, as is the case in our context.

5. Synthesis Templates for x86

We discuss in this section how to partially automate the construction of a symbolic execution engine for the x86 processor instruction set using the synthesis techniques described in the previous sections. Specifically, we present 6 synthesis templates that together abstract the semantics of over 500 x86 instruction instances. These templates are expressed using bit-vector constraints for the conciseness and precision requirements discussed in Section 2.

The x86 processor has a complex instruction set architecture (CISC) with 8, 16 and 32 bit instructions. The instructions can be divided into three broad groups: ALU instructions, floating-point instructions and SIMD instructions. In this work, we only focus on ALU instructions since modern SMT solvers supporting the theory of bit-vectors provide the required building-blocks for expressing their semantics (concisely and precisely). Each x86 ALU instruction takes from 0 to 3 inputs and has 0 to 2 outputs, all being stored in either registers or memory locations. The size of the register and memory locations determines the size of the individual inputs and outputs. Typically, most instructions are "overloaded" and can be executed with 8, 16 or 32 bit inputs. Moreover, the execution of each instruction can also set or reset special boolean flags, called EFLAGS. In this work, we consider the 5 most commonly used flags: the carry flag CF, the overflow flag OF, the zero flag ZF, the sign flag SF, and the parity flag PF.

As explained in Section 2, when defining instruction instances, we ignore where the inputs and outputs are stored, and only consider their sizes. For any instruction instance, all its inputs are of size either 8, 16 or 32 bits. The output of each instruction instance is either one of the *main outputs*, whose size is either 8, 16 or 32 bits, or one of the *flag outputs*, which are all 1-bit in size. As an example, the instruction SHL corresponds to $3 \times 6 = 18$ instruction instances: for each size of 8, 16 and 32 bits, there are 6 instances, 1 for the main output and 5 for each of the flag outputs.

In order to define a few tractable synthesis templates that are abstract enough to cover the semantics of many x86 ALU instructions, we first consulted the Intel x86 instruction set reference manual. Based on a preliminary study, we partitioned the ALU instructions into 3 groups, based on similarities in their execution semantics.

1. *Bit-wise group* (BW) contains instructions that perform bit-wise operations, such as AND, OR, and XOR.
2. *Arithmetic group* (ARI) includes instructions that perform arithmetic operations, such as ADD, SUB, and MUL.
3. *Bit-Shift group* (BS) contains instructions that perform shift, rotate and bit-flip operations, such as SHL, ROL, and BTS.

For each instruction group, we define two templates: one for the main output instruction instances, called the *main template*, and the other for the flag output instruction instances, called the *flag template*. Since, for a particular instruction, there are different instruction instances for the different sizes of inputs and outputs, we define synthesis templates that are parametric on the input and output size. From the Intel x86 specification, we learn that the flag outputs of an instruction often depend on the main output. For example, the zero flag is often set when the main output is zero. For this reason, we define each flag template as an extension of the main template for the corresponding instruction group: the flag template for an instruction is defined using a symbolic instruction encoding (a circuit) C_{main} for the main output of the same instruction, and this circuit C_{main} is synthesized first.

We now present the 6 templates. Throughout the description, we use i_1, i_2, i_3 to denote inputs, and o_{main}, o_{flag} to denote the main and flag outputs, respectively. To simplify the presentation, each template T is specified as a relation over the coefficients, inputs and output. In each case, the output is a (deterministic) function of the other parameters.

5.1 Templates for BW instruction instances

We now describe the main and flag templates for instruction instances in the BW group, which is the simplest of all 3 groups. The main and flag outputs depend only on two inputs i_1, i_2, which are both of the same size s. The main output o_{main} is also always of size s.

Main template. For all BW instructions, we "guess" that the ith bit of the main output is the result of a certain bit-wise operation performed on the ith bits of the two inputs. Since there are at most 16 different bit-wise operations, i.e., 16 possible functions from 2-bit inputs to 1-bit output, the search space is small. For a given size s, each of the 16 bit-wise operations can be expressed as functions in the theory of bit-vectors, which we denote by $\texttt{BW}_0[s], \ldots, \texttt{BW}_{15}[s]$. Thus, we design the main template such that its concretizations are exactly the set $\{\texttt{BW}_0[s], \ldots, \texttt{BW}_{15}[s]\}$ of functions. The template formula $T\text{-}BW^{main}(c, i_1, i_2, o)$ is formally defined as

$$\bigvee_{0 \leq \alpha \leq 15} (c = \alpha \wedge o_{main} = \texttt{BW}_\alpha[s](i_1, i_2))$$

It has one coefficient c which ranges over $\{0, \ldots, 15\}$. When $c = \alpha$, the template behaves as the concrete function $\texttt{BW}_\alpha[s]$. The coefficient c can thus be viewed as a "non-deterministic" choice; once the value of c is fixed, the nondeterminism disappears.

Note that we first "guessed" the above template from a superficial (i.e., non detailed) reading of the Intel x86 spec. Later, the application of the synthesis algorithms discussed in the previous sections, including their sampling stages, confirmed in an automated way (see Sections 6 and 7) that the above template was indeed sufficient to abstract BW instructions.

Flag template. We now define the flag template using the circuit C_{main} previously synthesized for the main output. From the specification manual, we learn that the flag output depends on the truth value of certain predicates over the inputs i_1, i_2 and the main output $o_{main} = C_{main}(i_1, i_2)$. We call each such predicate a *factor*. An example of a factor is $\texttt{msb}(i_1) = 0$ which denotes that the most significant bit of the first input i_1 is 0.

Given all the factors $\vec{F} := F_1, \ldots, F_n$, the flag circuit is essentially some function from the truth values of some of the factors to the set $\{0, 1\}$. Thus, we define the flag template such that its concretizations are all the possible functions from the truth values of the factors to the set $\{0, 1\}$. A general definition of such a template for the flag output o_{flag} and coefficients $\vec{c} := c_0, \ldots, c_{N-1}$, where $N = 2^n$, is given by the formula $\texttt{ENUM}(\vec{c}, \vec{F}, o_{flag})$, defined as

$$\begin{aligned}
&(\neg F_1 \wedge \ldots \wedge \neg F_n \wedge o_{flag} = c_0) \\
\vee\ &(\neg F_1 \wedge \ldots \wedge \neg F_{n-1} \wedge F_n \wedge o_{flag} = c_1) \\
\vee\ &(\neg F_1 \wedge \ldots \wedge F_{n-1} \wedge \neg F_n \wedge o_{flag} = c_2) \\
\vee\ &\ldots \\
\vee\ &(F_1 \wedge \ldots \wedge F_n \wedge o_{flag} = c_{N-1})
\end{aligned}$$

We now define the factors $\vec{F}_{\text{BW}} := F_1, \ldots, F_3$ used in defining the flag template $T\text{-}BW^{flag}$ for BW instructions.

$$\begin{aligned}
F_1 &:= \texttt{msb}(C_{main}(i_1, i_2)) = 1 \\
F_2 &:= C_{main}(i_1, i_2) = 0 \\
F_3 &:= \texttt{parity}(C_{main}(i_1, i_2)) = 1
\end{aligned}$$

Here $\texttt{msb}$ and $\texttt{parity}$ are the *most-significant-bit* and *parity* operators provided by the theory of bit-vectors. The template formula $T\text{-}BW^{flag}(\vec{c}, i_1, i_2)$ is formally defined as $\texttt{ENUM}(\vec{c}, \vec{F}_{\text{BW}}, o_{flag})$ and makes use of $2^3 = 8$ coefficients ranging over $\{0, 1\}$.

5.2 Templates for ARI instruction instances

We now describe the main and flag templates for instruction instances in the set ARI. The main and flag outputs for these instructions only depend on the first two inputs i_1, i_2, which could be of different sizes, denoted by s_1, s_2 respectively. We use s_o for the size of the main output. The flag outputs of ARI instructions not only depend on the main output but also on an internally computed overflow output, which gets discarded at the end of the computation. For instance, the carry flag after executing an `ADD` instruction is set whenever the overflow output is strictly greater than zero. We use o_{of} to denote the overflow output, whose size is also s_o.

In order to define the flag template, we design our main template such that for each concrete value of the coefficients, we synthesize two functions C_{main} and C_{of} for the main and overflow outputs respectively. This is done by first extending the inputs to size $s_{max} := 2max(s_1, s_2, s_o)$ and then applying them to some arithmetic operation (depending on the coefficients), as discussed below. This generates an output of size s_{max}, whose bits 0 to $s_o - 1$ are considered as the main output while bits s_o to $2s_o - 1$ define the overflow output.

Main template. All ARI instructions perform standard arithmetic operations: addition, subtraction, multiplication and division. However, they differ in whether the inputs are considered signed or unsigned. We design the main template $T\text{-}ARI^{main}$ such that its concretizations cover all these possibilities.

The template has 5 coefficients denoted by $\vec{c} := c_0, \ldots, c_4$. Coefficients c_0 and c_1 range over $\{1, 2, 3\}$ and determine whether the inputs i_1, i_2 respectively must be sign-extended (case 1), zero-extended (case 2) or replaced with a constant (case 3). The constants used for the third case are the values of the coefficients c_2 and c_3, which both range over $\{0, \ldots, 2^{s_{max}} - 1\}$. The extended value of inputs i_1, i_2 are given by the expressions i_1^{ext}, i_2^{ext} defined as

$$\begin{aligned}
i_1^{ext} &:= \texttt{ITE}(c_0 = 1, \texttt{zExt}(i_1, s_{max}), \\
&\qquad \texttt{ITE}(c_0 = 2, \texttt{sExt}(i_1, s_{max}), c_2)) \\
i_2^{ext} &:= \texttt{ITE}(c_1 = 1, \texttt{zExt}(i_2, s_{max}), \\
&\qquad \texttt{ITE}(c_1 = 2, \texttt{sExt}(i_2, s_{max}), c_3))
\end{aligned}$$

Here `ITE`, `zExt` and `sExt` are, respectively, the *if-then-else*, *zero-extend* and *sign-extend* operators provided by the theory of bit-vectors.

Coefficient c_4 ranges over $\{1, \ldots, 7\}$ and determines the arithmetic operation that must be applied to the two inputs. The operations provided by the theory of bit-vectors are: addition `bvadd` (case 1), subtraction `bvsub` (case 2), multiplication `bvmul` (case 3), unsigned division `bvudiv` (case 4), unsigned remainder `bvurem` (case 5), signed division `bvsdiv` (case 6), and signed remainder `bvsrem` (case 7). For convenience, we write $\texttt{ARI}_1, \ldots, \texttt{ARI}_7$ to refer to these operations. If $c_4 = k$, then operation $\texttt{ARI}_k$ is applied to the extended inputs, and bits 0 to $s_o - 1$ of the output are considered as the main output of the instance. Thus, in summary, the template $T\text{-}ARI^{main}(\vec{c}, i_1, i_2, o_{main})$ is defined as

$$\bigvee_{1 \leq \alpha \leq 7} c_4 = \alpha \ \wedge \ o_{main} = \texttt{ARI}_\alpha(i_1^{ext}, i_2^{ext})[0, s_o - 1]$$

Once the coefficients $\vec{c}$ for the main template have been synthesized, we define the function for the overflow output as

$$C_{of}(i_1, i_2) := \texttt{ARI}_\alpha(i_1^{ext}, i_2^{ext})[s_o, 2s_o - 1]$$

Here α is the value of coefficient c_4 in $\vec{c}$, and i_1^{ext}, i_2^{ext} are obtained by instantiating the concrete values of the coefficients $c_0, \ldots, c_3$ fixed in $\vec{c}$.

Flag template. As mentioned earlier, the flag template is built upon the circuits C_{main} and C_{of} for the main and overflow output respectively. Like $T\text{-}BW^{flag}$, the flag outputs for ARI instructions also depend on the truth value of certain factors defined over the inputs i_1, i_2, the main output $o_{main} = C_{main}(i_1, i_2)$ and overflow output $o_{of} = C_{of}(i_1, i_2)$. We therefore make use of the construction $\texttt{ENUM}(\vec{c}, \vec{F}, o_{flag})$ defined for flag output of BW instructions. The factors $\vec{F}_{\text{ARI}} := F_1, \ldots, F_7$ used in defining the flag template $T\text{-}ARI^{flag}$ for ARI instructions are defined as follows:

$$
\begin{aligned}
F_1 &:= \texttt{msb}(i_1) = 1\\
F_2 &:= \texttt{msb}(i_2) = 1\\
F_3 &:= \texttt{msb}(C_{main}(i_1, i_2)) = 1\\
F_4 &:= \texttt{parity}(C_{main}(i_1, i_2)) = 1\\
F_5 &:= C_{main}(i_1, i_2) = 0\\
F_6 &:= C_{of}(i_1, i_2) = 0\\
F_7 &:= C_{of}(i_1, i_2) = 2^{s_o} - 1
\end{aligned}
$$

The template $T\text{-}ARI^{flag}(\vec{c}, i_1, i_2)$ is formally defined as $\texttt{ENUM}(\vec{c}, \vec{F}_{\text{ARI}}, o_{flag})$ and makes use of $2^7 = 128$ coefficients ranging over $\{0, 1\}$.

5.3 Templates for BS instruction instances

We now describe the main and flag templates for BS instructions. The main and flag outputs for these instructions depend on all three inputs i_1, i_2, i_3. While describing BS instructions we will call the inputs i_1, i_2 as the *shift inputs* and i_3 as the *count input*. The size of the shift inputs and the main outputs is the same and is denoted by s. The size of the count input is always 8 bits.

Main template. From the specification manual, we learn that the execution of all BS instruction instances share the following common properties. First, the count input is always used after bit-masking to the lower 5 bits (equivalent to a modulo(%) 32 operation). Second, for a fixed value of the count input, each bit of the main output is either fixed to 0 or 1, or is a specific bit of one of the two shift inputs. We use these two properties to design the main template $T\text{-}BS^{main}$. The main idea is to case split on the count input i_3 bit-masked to the lower 5 bits and then, for each value $\alpha \in \{0, \ldots, 31\}$, use coefficients $\vec{c}_\alpha := c_{\alpha,0}, \ldots, c_{\alpha,s-1}$, each ranging over $\{0, \ldots, 2s+1\}$, to determine the mapping between each of the s bits of the output and the bits of the shift inputs. For a fixed value α of the (bit-masked) count input, the mapping is given by the relation $P_\alpha(\vec{c}_\alpha, i_1, i_2, o_m)$ defined below

$$
\bigvee_{0 \le \beta \le s-1} \left\{
\begin{array}{ll}
\vee & (0 \le c_{\alpha,\beta} \le s-1 \;\wedge\; o_m[\beta] = i_1[c_{\alpha,\beta}])\\
\vee & (s \le c_{\alpha,\beta} \le 2s-1 \;\wedge\; o_m[\beta] = i_2[c_{\alpha,\beta} - s])\\
\vee & (c_{\alpha,\beta} = 2s \;\wedge\; o_m[\beta] = 0)\\
\vee & (c_{\alpha,\beta} = 2s+1 \;\wedge\; o_m[\beta] = 1)
\end{array}
\right\}
$$

Template $T\text{-}BS^{main}(\vec{c}, i_1, i_2, i_3, o_m)$ is formally defined as

$$
\bigvee_{0 \le \alpha \le 31} i_3\%32 = \alpha \;\wedge\; P_\alpha(\vec{c}_\alpha, i_1, i_2, o_m)
$$

It uses $32s$ coefficients, each ranging over $\{0, \ldots, 2s+1\}$.

Flag template. We now define the flag template using the circuit C_{main} for the main output. From the specification manual, we learn that all the BS instructions set the flag output in a similar way: for a fixed count input value, the flag output is either a specific bit of one of the shift inputs, or is set based on the *parity* or *zeroness* of the main output, or the xor of the most-significant bits of the first shift input and the main output, or is one of the constants 0 or 1. Thus we define the flag template $T\text{-}BS^{flag}$ such that its concretizations cover all the above cases.

For a fixed value α of the (bit-masked) count input, the template uses a coefficient c_α ranging over $\{0, \ldots, 2s+4\}$, to define the mapping between the shift inputs i_1, i_2 and the flag output o_{flag}. This mapping is given by the relation $P^{flag}_\alpha(c_\alpha, i_1, i_2, o_{flag})$ defined as

$$
\begin{aligned}
& 0 \le c_\alpha \le s-1 \;\wedge\; o_{flag} = i_1[c_\alpha]\\
\vee\; & s \le c_\alpha \le 2s-1 \;\wedge\; o_{flag} = i_2[c_\alpha]\\
\vee\; & c_\alpha = 2s \;\wedge\; (o_{flag} = 1 \Leftrightarrow C_{main}(i_1, i_2) = 0)\\
\vee\; & c_\alpha = 2s+1 \;\wedge\; (o_{flag} = 1 \Leftrightarrow \texttt{parity}(C_{main}(i_1, i_2)) = 1)\\
\vee\; & c_\alpha = 2s+2 \;\wedge\; (o_{flag} = 1 \Leftrightarrow (\texttt{msb}(i_1) \oplus \texttt{msb}(C_{main}(i_1, i_2)))\\
\vee\; & c_\alpha = 2s+3 \;\wedge\; o_{flag} = 0\\
\vee\; & c_\alpha = 2s+4 \;\wedge\; o_{flag} = 1
\end{aligned}
$$

The template formula $T\text{-}BS^{flag}(\vec{c}, i_1, i_2, i_3, o_{flag})$ is formally defined as

$$
\bigvee_{0 \le \alpha \le 31} i_3\%32 = \alpha \;\wedge\; P^{flag}_\alpha(c_\alpha, i_1, i_2, o_{flag})
$$

Altogether, the template uses 32 coefficients $\vec{c} := c_0, \ldots, c_{31}$, ranging over $\{0, \ldots, 2s+4\}$.

5.4 Smart Inputs and Summary

We presented 6 templates (3 for main outputs and 3 for flag outputs) which abstract the semantics of a large number of x86 ALU instructions. In this section, we discuss some key properties of these templates. We start by discussing universally smart input sets, followed by a summary of the *search space* (size of the concretization set) and the *circuit size* (size of the circuits generated) for each template.

Smart inputs. We now present universally smart inputs for the main templates $T\text{-}BW^{main}$ and $T\text{-}BS^{main}$, and smart inputs for the main template $T\text{-}ARI^{main}$ and a large subset of ARI instructions. Those input sets were inferred manually from the structure of the corresponding template. As will be discussed in the next two sections, experiments with the procedure `DInputVal` show that this procedure performs reasonably well on all the flag templates, even for instructions with large (32 bits) input sizes, because of the structural simplicity (DNF formulas with few disjuncts) of the flag templates; therefore, we do not discuss smart inputs for those. In contrast, the procedure `DInputVal` has the worst performance on the $T\text{-}BS^{main}$ template, for which the use of smart inputs is much more important. As an illustration, we explain the methodology used for arriving at a (single!) universally smart input for the template $T\text{-}BW^{main}$. The methodology for the other templates is similar.

As discussed in Section 5.1, the concretizations of the template $T\text{-}BW^{main}$ are all the 16 possible bit-wise operations $\texttt{BW}_i$, which each take two bits as inputs and return one bit as output. How many inputs are needed to uniquely identify any of those 16 $\texttt{BW}_i$ functions? The answer is 4 provided the 4 inputs cover all four possible combinations of 0 and 1, namely is the set $\{(0,0), (0,1), (1,0), (1,1)\}$. Therefore, if a single pair of (bit-vector) inputs i_1, i_2, each of size s, for the template $T\text{-}BW^{main}$ covers these 4 boolean combinations, this single input pair (i_1, i_2) is universally smart for the template. A sufficient condition for finding such an input pair is that there exist bit indices k_1, k_2, k_3, k_4 such that the set of bit pairs $\{(i_1[k_1], i_2[k_1]), \ldots, (i_1[k_4], i_2[k_4])\}$ is equal to the set $\{(0,0), (0,1), (1,0), (1,1)\}$. A pair of inputs that satisfies the above condition is $i_1 = 12, i_2 = 10$. Indeed, the bit-vector representations of these decimal numbers are $i_1 = 12 = 0\ldots01100$, $i_2 = 10 = 0\ldots01010$, for any input size $s > 4$. Clearly the condition above is satisfied by the bit indices $0, \ldots, 3$. Thus, the input set $\mathcal{I}_{\text{BW}} := \{(10, 12)\}$ is universally smart for the template $T\text{-}BW^{main}$.

We now give a set of universally smart inputs for the template $T\text{-}BS^{main}$. For brevity, we only give the input set $\mathcal{I}_{\text{BS}_8}$ for the template instantiated with size 8 bits. Recall from Section 5.3 that BS instructions take 3 inputs and therefore the set $\mathcal{I}_{\text{BS}_8}$ is a set of

Template	Search space	Circuit size
$T\text{-}BW^{main}$	16	$O(1)$
$T\text{-}BW^{flag}$	2^8	$O(1)$
$T\text{-}ARI^{main}$	21×2^{2s}	$O(1)$
$T\text{-}ARI^{flag}$	2^{128}	$O(1)$
$T\text{-}BS^{main}$	$(2s+2)^{32s}$	$O(s)$
$T\text{-}BS^{flag}$	$(2s+5)^{32}$	$O(1)$

Figure 4. Templates summary

triples (i_1, i_2, i_3). It is defined as follows:

$$\begin{array}{ll} & \{(255,0,\alpha) \mid 0 \leq \alpha \leq 31\} \\ \cup & \{(1,1,\alpha) \mid 0 \leq \alpha \leq 31\} \\ \cup & \{(170,170,\alpha) \mid 0 \leq \alpha \leq 31\} \\ \cup & \{(204,204,\alpha) \mid 0 \leq \alpha \leq 31\} \\ \cup & \{(240,240,\alpha) \mid 0 \leq \alpha \leq 31\} \end{array}$$

The total number of inputs in the set $\mathcal{I}_{\text{BS}_8}$ is $32 \times 5 = 160$. In general for size parameter s, we define a universally smart set of inputs of size $32 \times (log(s) + 2)$.

For the template $T\text{-}ARI^{main}$, we define a set $\mathcal{I}_{\text{ARI}}$ of inputs which is smart for a large subset of ARI instructions. The set $\mathcal{I}_{\text{ARI}}$ is defined as

$$\{(17,5), (200,59), (170,-59)\}$$

This set is not universally smart for the template $T\text{-}ARI^{main}$ because the set was designed for an earlier version of the template which did *not* use the operations `bvsdiv` and `bvsrem`, which since then have been added and are currently handled by the values 6 and 7 of coefficient c_4. The earlier template was extended so that it could cover the main output of the instruction `IDIV` and a few other instructions. For the current template, we verified by running the smart inputs check (Definition 2) that the set $\mathcal{I}_{\text{ARI}}$ is still smart for the current template and all ARI instructions except `IDIV`, `DIV`,`CWD`, `CWDE`, `CDQ`. In practice, as validated by our experiments, the set $\mathcal{I}_{\text{ARI}}$ is a good initial set for seeding the `DInputVal` procedure for those remaining instructions, and sufficient for our purposes (see Section 7).

We also performed preliminary experiments to automatically generate sets of universally smart inputs. For instance, the set $\mathcal{I}_{\text{ARI}}$ can be augmented to a universally smart input set using the "greedy" approach described in Section 4: in the 8-bit case, this results in a (not necessarily minimal) set of 10 universally smart inputs obtained in 8 secs. In contrast, generating universally smart input sets with the "brute-force" approach (see Section 4) is much more computationally expensive. This topic should be investigated further in future work (see also the discussion in Section 8 on related work in machine learning).

Template summary. In Figure 4, we present a summary of the *Search space* and *Circuit size* for all the templates. The values for each of these properties are expressed as functions of the size s.

For the main template $T\text{-}BW^{main}$, the size of the search space is 16, which is the number of possible bit-wise operations, and the circuits generated are always of constant size as they are just one of the bit-wise operations. The flag template $T\text{-}BW^{flag}$ has a search space of size 2^8, which is the number of functions from 3 bits (from the 3 factors) to 1 bit. The circuits generated are again of constant size, in particular equal to the size of the formula $\texttt{ENUM}(\vec{c}, \vec{F}_{\text{BW}}, o_{flag})$. The main template $T\text{-}ARI^{main}$ has a search space of size 21×2^{2s}, the 2^{2s} factor comes from the third and fourth coefficients which vary over $\{0, \ldots, 2^s - 1\}$. The circuits generated are of constant size. The flag template $T\text{-}ARI^{flag}$ has a search space of 2^8, which is the number of functions from 7 bits (from the 7 factors) to 1 bit, and the circuits generated are again of constant size. The main template $T\text{-}BS^{main}$ has a search space of size $(2s+2)^{32s}$, since it has $32s$ coefficients ranging over $\{0, \ldots, 2s+1\}$. The circuits generated are of size $O(s)$ as each bit of the output is described individually using a separate circuit. The flag template $T\text{-}BS^{flag}$ has a search space of size $(2s+5)^{32}$, as there are 32 coefficients ranging over $\{0, \ldots, 2s+4\}$, and the circuits generated are of constant size.

Instr	n_{syn}	S-Iters	Time (ms)
AND8	10	1	26,808
AND8	10^2	1	**26,478**
AND8	10^3	1	26,692
MUL8	10	1	**32,462**
MUL8	10^2	1	33,581
MUL8	10^3	1	40,730
SHL8	10	41	1,171,060
SHL8	10^2	18	542,963
SHL8	10^3	1	**181,857**

Figure 5. Synthesis using Procedure `ExhaustVal`

6. Experimental Results

We report results of experiments performed with the synthesis algorithms and templates presented in the previous sections. All experiments were performed on a x86 HP xw4400 PC with a 32-bit 2.4GHz Intel Core2 processor, 2Gb of RAM and running Windows Vista. We used the Z3 [3] SMT solver for implementing all the synthesis algorithms.

We present results of detailed experiments for 3 instructions, each covered by a different synthesis template: `AND` with template $T\text{-}BW^{main}$, `MUL` with template $T\text{-}ARI^{main}$, and `SHL` with template $T\text{-}BS^{main}$. For each instruction, we consider their 8-bit, 16-bit and 32-bit versions to measure the impact of I/O sizes. In all the following experiments, the maximum number of failed verification samples (i.e., $|\mathcal{S}_{fail}|$ in Figure 1) is set to 10: when 10 samples have failed to be verified, the verification stage stops and those samples are fed back to the synthesis stage.

Figure 5 presents results obtained using the synthesis algorithm `ExhaustVal` and for various synthesis sample set sizes n_{syn} as defined in Figure 1. The exhaustive verification part of Procedure `ExhaustVal` does not scale to the 16-bit and 32-bit versions of those instructions (which each take two inputs of that size), so no results are presented for those cases. The number **S-Iters** of synthesis iterations is given in the third column. The overall time (in msecs) required to synthesize a verified circuit is given in the last column. The best runtime for an instruction is highlighted in boldface.

For `MUL8`, the best runtime is obtained with $n_{syn} = 10$ as 10 random synthesis samples are sufficient to identify the correct circuit, so more samples are not necessary. For `SHL8`, starting with 10 or 100 random synthesis samples requires several expensive synthesis iterations, while $n_{syn} = 10^3$ converges faster to the correct circuit. For `AND8`, all the runtimes are very close, and the differences are insignificant with respect to the overall runtime.

Figure 6 presents results obtained with the Procedure `DInputVal` of Section 3.3, for various numbers of synthesis samples n_{syn} and verification samples n_{ver}. The number of distinguishing-input checks is given under the column **D-Iters**. The best overall time for any given instruction is again highlighted in boldface.

For `AND` and `MUL`, a small set of 10 random synthesis samples is sufficient to synthesize the correct circuit in one iteration (**S-Iters**=1) with a single passing distinguishing-input check (**D-**

Instr	n_{syn}	n_{ver}	S-Iters	D-Iters	Time (ms)
AND8	10	10^2	1	1	**48**
AND8	10	10^3	1	1	414
AND8	10	10^4	1	1	4,007
AND8	10^2	10^2	1	1	68
AND8	10^2	10^3	1	1	429
AND8	10^2	10^4	1	1	4,023
AND8	10^3	10^2	1	1	273
AND8	10^3	10^3	1	1	637
AND8	10^3	10^4	1	1	4,206
AND16	10	10^2	1	1	**55**
AND16	10	10^3	1	1	484
AND16	10	10^4	1	1	4,791
AND16	10^2	10^2	1	1	79
AND16	10^2	10^3	1	1	509
AND16	10^2	10^4	1	1	4,813
AND16	10^3	10^2	1	1	338
AND16	10^3	10^3	1	1	760
AND16	10^3	10^4	1	1	5,040
AND32	10	10^2	1	1	**71**
AND32	10	10^3	1	1	619
AND32	10	10^4	1	1	6,497
AND32	10^2	10^2	1	1	98
AND32	10^2	10^3	1	1	642
AND32	10^2	10^4	1	1	6,124
AND32	10^3	10^2	1	1	411
AND32	10^3	10^3	1	1	963
AND32	10^3	10^4	1	1	6,451

Instr	n_{syn}	n_{ver}	S-Iters	D-Iters	Time (ms)
MUL8	10	10^2	1	1	**189**
MUL8	10	10^3	1	1	637
MUL8	10	10^4	1	1	4,996
MUL8	10^2	10^2	1	1	1,781
MUL8	10^2	10^3	1	1	1,686
MUL8	10^2	10^4	1	1	6,659
MUL8	10^3	10^2	1	1	8,805
MUL8	10^3	10^3	1	1	13,365
MUL8	10^3	10^4	1	1	14,692
MUL16	10	10^2	1	1	**609**
MUL16	10	10^3	1	1	1,070
MUL16	10	10^4	1	1	6,179
MUL16	10^2	10^2	1	1	2,864
MUL16	10^2	10^3	1	1	3,729
MUL16	10^2	10^4	1	1	8,363
MUL16	10^3	10^2	-	-	OOM
MUL16	10^3	10^3	-	-	OOM
MUL16	10^3	10^4	-	-	OOM
MUL32	10	10^2	1	1	**1,997**
MUL32	10	10^3	1	1	2,437
MUL32	10	10^4	1	1	9,133
MUL32	10^2	10^2	1	1	5,469
MUL32	10^2	10^3	1	1	5,008
MUL32	10^2	10^4	1	1	11,587
MUL32	10^3	10^2	-	-	OOM
MUL32	10^3	10^3	-	-	OOM
MUL32	10^3	10^4	-	-	OOM

Instr	n_{syn}	n_{ver}	S-Iters	D-Iters	Time (ms)
SHL8	10	10^2	14	4	82,184
SHL8	10	10^3	16	3	62,569
SHL8	10	10^4	13	1	60,730
SHL8	10^2	10^2	8	2	41,690
SHL8	10^2	10^3	9	1	38,691
SHL8	10^2	10^4	8	1	58,968
SHL8	10^3	10^2	1	1	**21,501**
SHL8	10^3	10^3	1	1	23,045
SHL8	10^3	10^4	1	1	49,105
SHL8	10^4	10^2	1	1	78,391
SHL8	10^4	10^3	1	1	84,433
SHL8	10^4	10^4	1	1	103,264
SHL16	10	10^2	20	3	938,122
SHL16	10	10^3	22	1	485,531
SHL16	10	10^4	20	3	1,019,270
SHL16	10^2	10^2	13	3	795,375
SHL16	10^2	10^3	12	2	678,463
SHL16	10^2	10^4	11	1	457,520
SHL16	10^3	10^2	1	1	**250,105**
SHL16	10^3	10^3	1	1	301,424
SHL16	10^3	10^4	1	1	291,452
SHL16	10^4	10^2	1	1	967,358
SHL16	10^4	10^3	1	1	1,064,090
SHL16	10^4	10^4	1	1	1,046,099
SHL32	10	10^2	31	4	24,168,853
SHL32	10	10^3	31	3	20,107,259
SHL32	10	10^4	31	1	11,754,805
SHL32	10^2	10^2	21	3	16,877,223
SHL32	10^2	10^3	22	3	17,577,444
SHL32	10^2	10^4	20	4	21,620,686
SHL32	10^3	10^2	1	1	**4,382,472**
SHL32	10^3	10^3	1	1	4,456,942
SHL32	10^3	10^4	1	1	4,707,855
SHL32	10^4	10^2	-	-	OOM
SHL32	10^4	10^3	-	-	OOM
SHL32	10^4	10^4	-	-	OOM

Figure 6. Synthesis using Procedure `DInputVal`

Iters=1), and the fastest runtime is achieved with the fewest verification samples ($n_{ver} = 10^2$). Note that for MUL16 and MUL32 with $n_{syn} = 10^3$, the synthesis algorithm runs out of memory (denoted by "OOM") and is unable to generate a circuit.

For SHL, the best times are achieved with $n_{syn} = 10^3$ and the smallest number of verification samples ($n_{ver} = 100$) we consider. For smaller numbers of synthesis samples, the `DInputVal` synthesis algorithm requires several synthesis stages and sometimes feedback from several distinguishing-input checks, which are expensive and increase overall runtime. (As an extreme example not shown in the figure, with $n_{syn} = 0$ and $n_{ver} = 100$, the `DInputVal` algorithm times out after 12h for SHL32.) With a larger set of synthesis samples ($n_{syn} = 10^4$), the `DInputVal` algorithm takes more time, or runs out of memory in the SHL32 case.

Figure 7 presents in its last column the runtimes obtained with the smart sampling synthesis algorithm `SmartVal` of Section 4. These results are compared to the best times obtained with the two other algorithms as reported in Figures 5 and 6. The speed-up obtained by an algorithm compared to the one to the immediate left is indicated by the symbol $\div$. In our experiments, the `SmartVal` algorithm is between 11 to 68 times faster than the best time obtained with the `DInputVal` algorithm, which is itself between 9 to 551 times faster than the `ExhaustVal` algorithm when the latter is applicable (i.e., in the 8-bit case only).

7. Overall Results, Lessons Learned, Limitations

Using the 6 templates presented in Section 4 and their associated smart inputs, we can automatically synthesize bit-vector circuits for 534 x86 instruction instances (8/16/32-bits, outputs, EFLAGS) in less than two hours on the regular machine described in the previous section (2Gb of RAM, 2.4GHz processor). We used the `SmartVal` algorithm whenever possible, i.e., whenever a set of universally smart inputs is available, and used the `DInputVal` algorithm otherwise (e.g., for all EFLAG circuits) still seeded with the smart inputs defined for that instruction family. We also used a verification stage with 1000 random verification samples for each circuit.

Instr	Exhaust	DInput	Smart Sampl
AND8	26,478	48 ($\div$551)	3 ($\div$16)
AND16	-	55	4 ($\div$14)
AND32	-	71	4 ($\div$18)
MUL8	32,462	189 ($\div$172)	17 ($\div$11)
MUL16	-	609	20 ($\div$30)
MUL32	-	1,997	29 ($\div$68)
SHL8	181,857	21,501 ($\div$9)	867 ($\div$25)
SHL16	-	250,105	8,064 ($\div$31)
SHL32	-	4,382,472	303,970 ($\div$14)

Figure 7. Synthesis using Procedure `SmartVal`: runtime (in msecs) and comparison

Instructions covered include `SHL, SHR, SAR, SAL, SHLD, SHRD, ROL, ROR, RCL, RCR, BT, BTR, BTS, BSWAP, AND, OR, XOR, TEST, NOT, NEG, XADD, ADD, SUB, INC, DEC, MUL, IMUL, DIV, IDIV, CWD, CWDE, CDQ, CBW, MOVZX, MOVSX, CMPXCHG`.

During the course of this work, we discovered several interesting and sometimes surprising details about the semantics of x86 instructions.

The Intel x86 reference manual often defines the semantics of x86 instructions *partially*, leaving some corner cases "undefined". In contrast, our automatic synthesis approach gives a precise semantics to all x86 instructions on the processor which is sampled, uncovering sometimes seemingly bizarre behaviors. As an example, the Intel specification says that the carry flag `CF` is undefined after a `ROR8` instruction when the count argument modulo 8 is 0; on an Intel XEON3.7 processor, the CF flag is actually set to 0 when the count argument is 0, and to 1 when the count argument is 16, 24 or 32. As another example, the Intel spec says that the OF flag of an ADD instruction is set "according to the result" (i.e., the output); however, on an Intel XEON3.7 processor, the OF flag is 1 only when the XOR of the most-significant bit of the *two inputs* is the negation of the most-significant bit of the output.

We also discovered cases where observed behaviors contradicts the x86 reference manual (which is unsurprising given the size and complexity of the spec). For instance, we discovered while debugging our template $T\text{-}ARI^{main}$ that the overflow OF flag should be set to 0 after executing IMUL8 with 65 and 254 as inputs according to the Intel spec, while the OF flag is actually set to 1 after the execution of this instruction with those inputs on an Intel XEON3.7 processor.

Moreover, we discovered that the semantics of instructions varies across Intel processors. For instance, on an Intel XEON3.7 or Core2 or i7 M620 processors and in accordance with the x86 spec, executing instructions ROL, SHL or SHR does not set the overflow OF flag if the count argument is not 1. However, on an Intel i7-2620M processor (HP EliteBook 2760p, 2.7Ghz, 8Gb RAM, 64-bit) processor, the OF flag is set to 1 even for certain cases when the count argument is greater than 1. Our template $T\text{-}BS^{flag}$ is actually unable to capture this behavior, which is why we detected these corner cases.

Finally, and unsurprisingly, we also discovered several errors in previous manually-written x86 instruction handlers used in the whitebox fuzzer SAGE [6].

Our current implementation has several limitations. First, instructions like DIV crash (trigger an error) on certain inputs, for instance when the quotient is larger than the output range. Currently, we use manually-written input preconditions to prevent such cases from occurring during synthesis. Such preconditions should be used as "active checkers" [5] during symbolic execution to check whether those error cases can be triggered during program analysis. In the future, those preconditions could be synthesized automatically by generating a special additional ERROR output. Second, instructions like SHL leave the flags ZF, PF and SF "unchanged" when the count operand is 0, therefore those flags should also be considered as inputs in those cases. This is not currently handled by our template $T\text{-}BS^{flag}$.

8. Other Related Work

Synthesizing transfer functions for embedded processors. The closest work to our work is [19] which presents a system for automatically synthesizing transfer functions for embedded processor instructions, which can be used for static analysis of embedded object code. This prior work synthesizes transfer functions in a given abstract domain (like intervals or bit-wise domain) and therefore performs a sound over-approximation of the concrete semantics. In contrast, our goal is to automatically synthesize a bit-precise symbolic representation of the concrete semantics. The approach used in [19] involves building a complete truth table by exhaustively sampling the processor, lifting the table to the abstract domain and then encoding it using BDDs. Due to the exhaustive sampling, this approach does not scale beyond 8-bit instructions. Moreover, the BDD encodings are often too large (several Kbs) to satisfy our conciseness requirement, which is imperative in our context to allow for bit-precise symbolic execution of long program execution traces as is needed for whitebox fuzzing [6]. In follow-up work, [18] develops another technique that assumes a structural constraint on the function being synthesized (analogous to template-based synthesis) and scales to larger instructions. However, the synthesized functions are again for certain abstract domains. Another difference with our work is that [18] generates abstract transfer functions using a simple custom brute-force solver, whereas we encode our templates as logic formulas in the theory of bit-vectors and carry out the search using an SMT solver.

Connection to machine learning. There is a close connection between the notion of universally smart inputs for a template and the notion of "teaching dimension for a concept class" [7]. Informally, the teaching dimension of a concept class (consisting of classifiers) is the minimum number of samples that a teacher must reveal in order to uniquely identify *any* concept in the class. The paper [7] investigates upper and lower bounds on the teaching dimension and its relation to structural properties of a concept class. Function templates can essentially be thought of as concept classes (concepts being the functions represented as relations over inputs and outputs). These results on teaching dimension shed light on the connection between templates and the set of universally smart inputs, and on the complexity of automatically synthesizing the smallest set of universally smart inputs. Another interesting (and related) connection that we plan to explore further in the future is that between the descriptive complexity [11] of a template and the size of the smallest set of universally smart inputs.

Template-based synthesis. In the last few years, there has been a large amount of work on automated synthesis using deductive techniques. A central theme of all these techniques is to express the synthesis problem as a search problem over a restricted space. The restricted space is defined either using a template [24, 25], or using a sketch [21, 22], or using a set of building blocks [9, 13], or using a restricted language [8, 12]. The synthesis techniques used in this paper are inspired from and build upon this prior work. The unique challenges associated with our specific application domain were the lack of an initial specification and the lack of a final verification oracle.

Black-box analysis of processors/assemblers. Another area of recent related work is work on designing and testing CPU emulators [14–16], especially for x86 processors. The goal of this work is to test whether an emulator faithfully mimics all aspects of the processor, including various addressing modes, privilege levels and clock cycles per instruction. [14] uses the architecture specification as the starting point for determining what instruction operand combinations are valid, and then intelligently modifying and testing each combination with various possible "edge case" values. On the other hand, [15] uses the CPU as the oracle to determine what byte sequences represent valid instructions and how instructions are encoded. The valid byte sequences are then run with various memory and register states. In the same spirit, [10] presents a technique for testing and reverse engineering assemblers for a given architecture, by testing them with permutations of assembly code and then decoding the output. The main relation with our work is the idea of analyzing a black-box system by strategically testing its interface and then inferring internal properties of the system from the outputs.

9. Conclusion

We showed that automatic synthesis of precise and concise symbolic representations of individual processor instructions is possible for a complex processor like x86. The main practical advantage of automatic synthesis is the gain in manual labor: instead of defining manually (probably incomplete and incorrect) detailed instruction handlers for 534 x86 ALU instruction instances, synthesis allowed us to define only 6 abstract instruction handlers (templates), from which 534 correct and precise instruction handlers were generated automatically, from input/output examples and expressed concisely as bit-vector constraints.

In this work, we focused on ALU instructions since those are used in virtually all programs. When symbolically executing a program, each instruction is executed symbolically using the corresponding symbolic instruction handler. Sequences of instructions are handled by combining the symbolic encodings (circuits) of individual instructions. Conditional statements (jumps) are handled using the flag circuits. For instance, a `jz <addr>` jump instruction is simply mapped to a constraint ZF $==$ 1 where ZF is the zero-flag circuit synthesized for the instruction immediately prior to the jump insturction. The circuit for regular memory operations such as `ld` (load), `mov` (move), etc. is simply the identity function. Handling all those operations (ALU, conditional jumps and regular memory operations) is already useful for (partial) symbolic execution of many applications, like whitebox fuzzing of file and packet parsers [6].

We believe our templates could be extended to cover x86 SIMD instructions, since they are essentially ALU instructions applied to vectors of registers. In contrast, extending our approach to floating-point instructions seems more challenging since most SMT solvers do not currently handle floating-point arithmetic. Fortunately, for the purpose of whitebox fuzzing, precise symbolic execution of floating-point instructions can often be avoided [4].

It would be interesting to design instruction templates for other processors such as x64 or ARM. Our general synthesis-based approach should be applicable to those processors as well, but details of the templates for those could be significantly different.

Acknowledgments

We thank David Molnar for suggesting the problem addressed in this work, Sumit Gulwani for helpful comments on program synthesis, and Ella Bounimova for interesting discussions on x86 semantics. We also thank the anonymous reviewers for their constructive comments to improve the presentation.

References

[1] D. Brumley, I. Jager, Th. Avgerinos, and E. J. Schwartz. BAP: A Binary Analysis Platform. In *CAV'2011*, July 2011.

[2] A. Chlipala. Modular Development of Certified Program Verifiers with a Proof Assistant. In *ICFP'2006*, September 2006.

[3] L. de Moura and N. Bjorner. Z3: An Efficient SMT Solver. In *TACAS'2008*, April 2008.

[4] P. Godefroid and J. Kinder. Proving Memory Safety of Floating-Point Computations by Combining Static and Dynamic Program Analysis. In *ISSTA'2010*, July 2010.

[5] P. Godefroid, M.Y. Levin, and D. Molnar. Active Property Checking. In *EMSOFT'2008*, October 2008.

[6] P. Godefroid, M.Y. Levin, and D. Molnar. Automated Whitebox Fuzz Testing. In *NDSS'2008*, February 2008.

[7] S. A. Goldman and M. J. Kearns. On the Complexity of Teaching. *Journal of Computer and System Sciences*, 50:303–314, 1992.

[8] S. Gulwani. Automating String Processing in Spreadsheets using Input-Output Examples. In *POPL'2011*, January 2011.

[9] S. Gulwani, V. A. Korthikanti, and A. Tiwari. Synthesizing Geometry Constructions. In *PLDI'2011*, May 2011.

[10] W. C. Hsieh, D. R. Engler, and G. Back. Reverse-Engineering Instruction Encodings. In *USENIX'2001*, June 2001.

[11] N. Immerman. *Descriptive complexity*. Springer, 1999.

[12] S. Itzhaky, S. Gulwani, N. Immerman, and M. Sagiv. A Simple Inductive Synthesis Methodology and its Applications. In *OOPSLA'2010*, October 2010.

[13] S. Jha, S. Gulwani, S. A. Seshia, and A. Tiwari. Oracle-Guided Component-Based Program Synthesis. In *ICSE'2010*, May 2010.

[14] W. Ma, A. Forin, and J. Liu. Rapid Prototyping and Compact Testing of CPU Emulators. In *Proceedings of the 21st IEEE International Symposium on Rapid System Prototyping*, June 2010.

[15] L. Martignoni, R. Paleari, G. Fresi Roglia, and D. Bruschi. Testing CPU Emulators. In *ISSTA'2009*, July 2009.

[16] L. Martignoni, R. Paleari, G. Fresi Roglia, and D. Bruschi. Testing System Virtual Machines. In *ISSTA'2010*, July 2010.

[17] D. Molnar, X. C. Li, and D. Wagner. Dynamic Test Generation To Find Integer Bugs in x86 Binary Linux Programs. In *Proc. of the 18th Usenix Security Symposium*, August 2009.

[18] J. Regehr and U. Duongsaa. Deriving Abstract Transfer Functions for Analyzing Embedded Software. In *LCTES'2006*, 2006.

[19] J. Regehr and A. Reid. HOIST: A System for Automatically Deriving Static Analyzers for Embedded Systems. In *ASPLOS'2004*, 2004.

[20] S. Sarkar, P. Sewell, F. Zappa Nardelli, S. Owens, T. Ridge, Th. Braibant, M. O. Myreen, and J. Aglave. The Semantics of x86-CC Multiprocessor Machine Code. In *POPL'2009*, January 2009.

[21] A. Solar-Lezama, R. M. Rabbah, R. Bodík, and K. Ebcioglu. Programming by Sketching for Bit-Streaming Programs. In *PLDI'2005*, May 2005.

[22] A. Solar-Lezama, L. Tancau, R. Bodík, S. A. Seshia, and V. A. Saraswat. Combinatorial Sketching for Finite Programs. In *ASPLOS'2006*, 2006.

[23] D. Song, D. Brumley, H. Yin, J. Caballero, I. Jager, M. G. Kang, Z. Liang, J. Newsome, P. Poosankam, and P. Saxena. BitBlaze: A New Approach to Computer Security via Binary Analysis. In *ICISS'2008*, December 2008.

[24] A. Taly, S. Gulwani, and A. Tiwari. Synthesizing Switching Logic Using Constraint Solving. In *VMCAI'2009*, January 2009.

[25] A. Taly and A. Tiwari. Switching Logic Synthesis for Reachability. In *EMSOFT'2010*, October 2010.

A Dynamic Program Analysis to find Floating-Point Accuracy Problems

Florian Benz
Saarland University
fbenz@stud.uni-saarland.de

Andreas Hildebrandt
Johannes-Gutenberg Universität Mainz
andreas.hildebrandt@uni-mainz.de

Sebastian Hack
Saarland University
hack@cs.uni-saarland.de

Abstract

Programs using floating-point arithmetic are prone to accuracy problems caused by rounding and catastrophic cancellation. These phenomena provoke bugs that are notoriously hard to track down: the program does not necessarily crash and the results are not necessarily obviously wrong, but often subtly inaccurate. Further use of these values can lead to catastrophic errors.

In this paper, we present a dynamic program analysis that supports the programmer in finding accuracy problems. Our analysis uses binary translation to perform every floating-point computation side by side in higher precision. Furthermore, we use a lightweight slicing approach to track the evolution of errors.

We evaluate our analysis by demonstrating that it catches well-known floating-point accuracy problems and by analyzing the Spec CFP2006 floating-point benchmark. In the latter, we show how our tool tracks down a catastrophic cancellation that causes a complete loss of accuracy leading to a meaningless program result. Finally, we apply our program to a complex, real-world bioinformatics application in which our program detected a serious cancellation. Correcting the instability led not only to improved quality of the result, but also to an improvement of the program's run time.

Categories and Subject Descriptors G.1.0 [*Numerical Analysis*]: General—Computer arithmetic, Error analysis, Multiple precision arithmetic

Keywords Dynamic program analysis, program instrumentation, floating-point accuracy

1. Introduction

Floating-point numbers are almost always mere approximations of the "true" real numbers: there is an uncountably infinite number of real values in any open interval on the real line, but any digital computer provides only finite storage for their representation. Due to this approximation, floating-point arithmetic is prone to accuracy problems caused by insufficient precision, rounding errors, and catastrophic cancellation. In fact, writing a *numerically stable* program is challenging. However, few programmers are aware of the intricacies that come with floating-point arithmetic. And even if a programmer is familiar with the problem per se, he will often be unable to detect or even prevent it: theoretical results often allow only a worst-case analysis that soon becomes overly pessimistic for complex cases. We lack the proper tools to support the programmers in efficiently and effectively finding floating-point problems at runtime. In the past, floating-point accuracy problems caused program failures that cost millions of dollars or even human life. And even if a numerical inaccuracy does not result in such catastrophic events, it can cause serious harm if it remains undetected: in many application scenarios, correct results can hardly be distinguished from incorrect ones. In such cases, an undetected numerical inaccuracy in a popular application can lead to countless flawed results.

One of the best-studied examples of an undetected accumulation of rounding errors was the failure of the MIM-104 Patriot air defense system in the Gulf War. As a result 28 US Army soldiers were killed by an Iraqi Scud missile on February 25, 1991. A government investigation [18] revealed that the system's internal clock had drifted by 0.3 seconds after operating for 100 hours. This was due to a rounding error when converting integer values to floating-point values.

Another well-studied example occurred at the Vancouver Stock Exchange. As reported by the Wall Street Journal [20], the index of the Stock Exchange was initialized at 1000 points in January 1982.

For each trade, the index was updated by first adding the weighted stock price to the previous index and then truncating the result to three decimal places. This operation occurred about 3000 times a day and the accumulated truncations led to a loss of around one point per day. The error remained undiscovered for 22 months. After the discovery, the index was corrected from 524.811 to 1098.892 points. The calculation of the index was then changed from truncating to rounding.

Both examples drastically demonstrate that floating-point issues can have dramatic consequences. However, there is only a surprisingly little number of tools that assist the programmers (who are usually totally unaware of the intricacies of floating-point arithmetic) in tracking down these problems *although* the need for easily usable tools for the dynamic analysis of numeric stability has been recognized in the literature and cast in the form of demands (e.g. by Kahan [12]). In the past, both static and dynamic program analyses have been proposed. Static analyses like Fluctuat [5] provide sound over-approximations of floating-point problems such as rounding errors. However, they suffer from imprecision and are heavily dependent on other analyses (e.g. pointer analyses) to disambiguate the data flow of a program. Therefore, static techniques work exceptionally well in special domains like embedded systems where the code does usually not exhibit complex and dynamic data structures. For large, possibly object-oriented programs, however, they are less suitable. In contrast, the dynamic program analyses proposed in the past [1, 2, 13] do either not scale to large-scale systems or make compromises in their analysis power to achieve scalability.

In this paper, we bridge this gap by proposing a dynamic program analysis that detects strictly more problems than previous

PLDI'12, June 11–16, 2012, Beijing, China.

approaches and scales to relevant real-world applications. In summary, we make the following contributions:

- Our analysis simulates real arithmetic by performing each floating-point computation in higher precision side by side to the original calculation. For every floating-point variable in the program, we introduce a *shadow variable* in higher precision. We use those shadow values to detect catastrophic cancellations and rounding errors. In contrast to a static analysis, we do not detect all such errors but, because of the higher precision of the shadow values, we detect significantly more than all previous dynamic analyses. For the sake of precision, we formally describe our dynamic program analysis by means of an operational semantics.
- In addition to the shadow value, we collect additional data for every floating-point operation. This information is used by a light-weight slicing technique which helps the programmer to reconstruct the path of operations along which an error propagated after the program run. This helps in localizing the source of inaccuracies that propagated to other program points where they were actually detected.
- We implemented the presented analysis in the Valgrind [16] binary instrumentation framework. We evaluate the effectiveness of our tool on pathological floating-point accuracy problems from the literature as well as on large-scale real-world programs: the SPEC CFP2006 benchmark suite of floating-point programs, the Biochemical Algorithms Library (BALL), and the GNU linear programming kit (GLPK). In all investigated programs, our program detects accuracy problems with various consequences, ranging from unnecessarily slow convergence to meaningless output. We are not aware of any previous *automated* study of floating-point accuracy problems on programs of that scale. Finally, we also present experiments that show the limits of our approach.

The rest of this paper is structured as follows: The next section summarizes the foundations of floating-point arithmetic relevant for this paper and gives an overview of several important classes of accuracy problems. Section 3 outlines the concepts of the analysis, Section 4 presents how the programmer interacts with the analysis, and Section 5 discusses issues of a concrete implementation of the analysis. Finally, in Section 6 we present an extensive case study of our analysis.

2. Foundations

We briefly repeat the necessary foundations of IEEE 754 floating-point arithmetic in this section. We follow the notation and terminology of Goldberg [8] and Higham [10]. The interested reader is referred to these publications for more detail.

2.1 The IEEE 754 Standard

A floating-point number has the form

$$x = \pm s \times \beta^e$$

where for each value, the sign, the significant s (also called mantissa), and the exponent e are stored. IEEE 754-1985, the arguably most important floating point standard, uses $\beta = 2$. The *precision* is the maximum number of digits which can be represented with the significant. IEEE 754-1985 defines four precisions: single, single-extended, double, and double-extended. Here we only consider single and double precision since these are the most common in today's programming languages.

As the representation uses only a finite number of bits, an error due to the approximation is unavoidable. Denoting the evaluation of an expression in floating-point arithmetic by the function fl, rounding can be represented by the transformation $x \mapsto fl\,(x)$. Rounding to the nearest representable number is the default and the only rounding mode considered here. In case of a tie, it is rounded to the nearest even number. The unit roundoff u, also called the machine epsilon, is defined as the largest positive number such that

$$fl\,(1+u) = 1$$

The unit roundoff depends on the base β and the precision p:

$$u = \beta/2 \cdot \beta^{-p}$$

Let $\mathbb{F} \subset \mathbb{R}$ be the set of numbers which can be exactly represented by floating-point arithmetic. If $x \in \mathbb{R}$ lies in the range of $\mathbb{F}$, then

$$fl\,(x) \quad = \quad x\,(1+\varepsilon) \quad |\varepsilon| < u$$

For all $a, b \in \mathbb{F}$, the following properties hold

$$\begin{array}{lcll} fl\,(a \circ b) & = & (a \circ b)\,(1+\varepsilon) \quad |\varepsilon| \leqslant u & \circ \in \{+,-,\times,/\} \\ fl\,(a \circ b) & = & fl\,(a \circ b) & \circ \in \{+,\times\} \end{array}$$

The standard requires that all basic operations are computed as if done exactly and rounded afterwards. This is stronger than the properties above as it requires $\varepsilon = 0$ if $a \circ b \in \mathbb{F}$. In floating-point arithmetic, addition and multiplication are commutative but no operation is associative.

2.2 Error Sources

The errors sources can be separated into three groups: rounding, data uncertainty, and truncation.

Rounding errors are unavoidable due to the finite precision. *Uncertainty* in the data comes from the initial input or the result of a previous computation. Input data from measurements or estimations is usually only accurate to a few digits. *Truncation* arises when a numerical algorithm approximates a mathematical function. Many numerical methods take finitely many terms of a Taylor-, Laurent-, or Fourier series; the terms omitted constitute the truncation error. A truncation error can only be analyzed with knowledge about the function the algorithm computes. Therefore, a tool working on the program as is can only track rounding errors and uncertainty from previous computations.

Usually, the discrepancy between a floating-point number and the corresponding exact number is measured as a relative error. Throughout this paper, the following definition is used

$$\text{relative error} = \left| \frac{\text{exact value} - \text{approximate value}}{\text{exact value}} \right|$$

Note that if the exact value is 0, the relative error is ∞.

2.2.1 Error Accumulation

A good example for a number which cannot be exactly represented in floating-point arithmetic is the decimal number 0.1, which is periodical in the binary system

$$(0.1)_{10} = \left(0.000\overline{1100}\right)_2$$

The relative error of 0.1 in single precision is close to the unit roundoff of 2^{-24} ($\approx 5.96 \times 10^{-8}$)

$$\left| \frac{(0.1)_{10} - (0.1)_{sp}}{(0.1)_{10}} \right| \approx 5.94 \times 10^{-8}$$

The error introduced by an approximate representation of a constant is in the same range as the rounding error after a computation. This error cannot be avoided because a representation of a real number with a finite number of bits can never be exact for all numbers.

Figure 1 shows a C program with large error accumulation. In the end, the value of `time` is 1999.6588. Thus, `time` has a

```
float time = 0.0f;
int i;
for (i = 0; i < 20000; i++) {
  time += 0.1f;
}
```

Figure 1. C program with large error accumulation

relative error of 1.7×10^{-4}. This is significantly higher than the error of the constant `0.1f`. If the same program is run with `time` in double precision and the constant is still represented in single precision (i.e. only replacing `float` with `double`) the relative error of `time` decreases to 1.5×10^{-8}. If, in addition to the double precision variable `time`, the constant is also represented in double precision (i.e. removing the `f` behind the constant) the relative error is reduced to 3.6×10^{-13}.

In general, an error introduced by a constant limits the accuracy of the result. The actual influence depends on the precision and the numerical stability of the algorithm. An algorithm is *numerically stable* if the influence of rounding errors to the result is provably always small. Thus, numerical stability is a property of an algorithm. A similar property, called the condition, describes the problem the algorithm tries to solve. The condition is independent from the algorithm and describes the dependency between the input and the output of a problem. The *condition number* is a measurement for the asymptotically worst case of how strongly changes in the input can influence the output. If small changes in the input lead to large changes in the output, the condition number is large. Thus, it is easier to design algorithms for problems with low condition numbers. In the example above, it does not matter if the error comes from a constant, because always adding the same number with an error tends to accumulate the error. Large errors usually occur due to the insidious growth of just a few rounding errors and it is hard to find their origins.

2.2.2 Insufficient Precision

The precision used in a program is usually a trade-off between performance and sufficient accuracy. The example program in Figure 2 uses a constant which is slightly smaller than the unit roundoff.

```
/* float unit roundoff is 0.00000006f */
float e = 0.00000005f;
float sum = 1.0f;
int i;
for (i = 0; i < 5; i++) {
  sum += e;
}
```

Figure 2. C program with an error due to insufficient precision

In the end, the value of `sum` is 1.0. Thus, the relative error of `sum` is 2.5×10^{-7}. Any precision slightly higher than single precision leads to a correct result. Insufficient precision is usually hard to discover manually because the error introduced by a single operation is small. However, large errors can occur due to error accumulation. Often, double precision is thus used to alleviate these problems. However, while double precision indeed suffices for many application scenarios, it can still be insufficient, depending on the details of the problem.

2.2.3 Catastrophic Cancellation

If two nearby quantities are subtracted, the most significant digits match and cancel each other. This effect is called cancellation and can be *catastrophic* or *benign*. A cancellation is catastrophic if at least one operand is subject to rounding. Otherwise, if both quantities are exactly known, the cancellation is benign. A cancellation can occur when subtracting or adding two numbers because both operands can be positive or negative. An example for a cancellation is the following computation

$$1.002 \times 10^3 - 1.000 \times 10^3 = 2.000 \times 10^0$$

This cancellation is catastrophic if the digit 2 in the first operand is the result of an error and benign otherwise. An operation with a cancellation can expose an error introduced by an earlier computation, but the same operation can be exact if no error has been introduced before. Some formulas can be rearranged to replace a catastrophic cancellation with a benign one, but only within the scope of the particular formula, i.e., this cannot guard against rounding errors present in the input. One example is the expression $x^2 - y^2$, where x^2 and y^2 are likely to be subject to rounding. In this case, a more accurate formula would be $(x - y)(x + y)$, because here, the subtraction is done directly on the variables x and y. Assuming that x and y are exactly known, a possible cancellation is thus guaranteed to be benign in the second variant.

The number of canceled digits can be calculated with the following formula

$$\max\{\text{exponent}(op_1), \text{exponent}(op_2)\} - \text{exponent}(res)$$

where op_1 and op_2 are the operands, and res the result. A cancellation has happened if the number of canceled digits is greater than zero. To conclude, for the analysis of floating-point software, it is crucial to decide whether a cancellation is catastrophic or benign.

2.3 Cancellation of Rounding Errors

Inaccurate intermediate results can still lead to an accurate final result. Therefore, not all inaccurate values indicate a problem.

One example from Higham [10] for a calculation where more inaccurate intermediate results lead to a more accurate final result is the calculation of $(e^x - 1)/x$ with a unit roundoff $u = 2^{-24}$. To obtain a more accurate result, it is better to compute $(e^x - 1)/\ln(e^x)$. For $x = 9 \times 10^{-8}$ the exact result is 1.00000005. The following calculations show that the second formula has more inaccurate intermediate results but the final result has a relative error that is 1.92×10^7 times lower than the error of the first formula

$$\begin{aligned} fl\left(\frac{e^x-1}{x}\right) &= fl\left(\frac{1.19209290\times10^{-7}}{9.00000000\times10^{-8}}\right) &= 1.32454766 \\ fl\left(\frac{e^x-1}{\ln(e^x)}\right) &= fl\left(\frac{1.19109290\times10^{-7}}{1.19209282\times10^{-7}}\right) &= 1.00000006 \end{aligned}$$

2.4 Summary

The dynamic program analysis we present in this paper addresses all issues discussed in this section:

- Error accumulation and insufficient precision is detected by our analysis by following values through the whole program with a side-by-side computation in higher precision. In the end, the accumulation and insufficient precision can be detected by comparing the original and the shadow value. Of course, our analysis is not correct in the sense that we pretend that the shadow values in higher precision are perfect substitutes for the exact real values. However, our experience shows that side-by-side calculation in higher precision helps in detecting severe accuracy problems.
- Our analysis detects catastrophic cancellations by calculating the canceled bits and the bits that are still exact for every floating-point addition and subtraction. This is explained in Section 3.1.
- The cancellation of rounding errors can lead to false positives in intermediate results. Our analysis addresses this problem by determining variables that are likely the final result and thus

helps the user to determine if the final result is affected. Error traces created by the analysis can then reveal that the inaccurate intermediate results led to an accurate final result. The error trace is explained in Section 3.2.

3. The Analysis

In the following, we describe a dynamic program analysis which assists the programmer in finding accuracy problems. The analysis' main ingredient is a side-by-side computation done with an arbitrary but fixed precision[1] which is higher than the precision used in the client program. The analysis tracks two kinds of information: For every *original value* that is computed by the program (this comprises variables which are written to memory as well as temporary results kept in registers), it stores a *shadow value* which consists of several components among which is a counterpart of the original value in higher precision. Additionally, we compute analysis information for every executed floating-point instruction. Our analysis essentially tracks the difference of a floating-point value in the client program and its corresponding shadow value. If this difference becomes too large, it is likely that the client program suffers from accuracy problems. The exact composition of the analysis information is shown in the first section of Figure 6.

We use two different sets of information (per variable, per instruction) because they are both relevant: Accuracy problems usually materialize as inaccurate contents of variables. From there, it is helpful to find the instructions that cause the problem and potentially reconstruct how the error propagated to that variable.

An important detail is that the side-by-side computation in our analysis does not affect the semantics of the program: For example, a comparison which decides whether a branch is taken can have a different outcome in higher precision than in the original precision. We would detect the accuracy problem but still follow the branch based on the result of the computation in original precision. As a consequence, the result of the analysis is *not* equal to the result of the program as if it would have been executed in higher precision. This is the desired behavior, because we want to track down problems in the program running in the original precision.

The results of the side-by-side computation are leveraged in two ways (further detailed in the following sections): By treating the shadow values as a potentially better approximation to the exact real value, we compute the relative error and the cancellation badness of every instruction. The latter detects catastrophic cancellations *and* indicates how much more precise a value would have to be for the cancellation to be benign (see Section 3.1). Furthermore, we use the shadow values to calculate the relative error on every instruction and original value. This information can be used to find the cause of the accuracy problem (see Section 3.2).

Finally, we want to stress that a dynamic program analysis is never complete. The capability of the presented analysis to detect floating-point accuracy problems is based on the assumption that the shadow values are a substitute for the real exact values.

3.1 Cancellation Detection

Because cancellations occur often and benign cancellations have no impact on the accuracy, it is important to detect if a cancellation is catastrophic or benign. To this end, we define *cancellation badness* as an indicator for catastrophic cancellations. The cancellation badness relates the number of bits canceled by an operation to the bits that where exact *before* the operation. The exact bits of a floating-point variable v are determined with respect to the "exact value" $\tilde{v}$ which is in our analysis stored in the shadow value of v as a floating-point number in higher precision[2]:

$$\mathrm{ebits}(\tilde{v}, v) := \begin{cases} p & \text{if } \tilde{v} = v \\ 0 & \text{if } \mathrm{exponent}(\tilde{v}) \neq \mathrm{exponent}(v) \\ \mathrm{ebits}'(\tilde{v}, v) & \text{otherwise} \end{cases}$$

with

$$\mathrm{ebits}'(\tilde{v}, v) := \min\{p, |\,\mathrm{exponent}(\tilde{v}) - \mathrm{exponent}(\tilde{v} - v)|\}$$

Consider an instruction $v' \leftarrow v_1 \diamondsuit v_2$. The number of bits canceled by executing the instruction is calculated by

$$cbits := \max\{\mathrm{exponent}(v_1), \mathrm{exponent}(v_2)\} - \mathrm{exponent}(v')$$

The cancellation badness $cbad$ now relates the least number of exact bits of the operands to the number of canceled bits:

$$cbad := \max\{0, 1 + cbits - \min\{\mathrm{ebits}(\tilde{v}_1, v_1), \mathrm{ebits}(\tilde{v}_2, v_2)\}\}$$

If the badness is greater than zero, a catastrophic cancellation happened. The value of $cbad$ itself indicates how much more precise the operands would have to be for the cancellation to not be catastrophic. If the badness is 0, the cancellation was benign.

Consider the following example:

$$1.379 - 1.375 = 0.004$$

Here, three digits are canceled. Assuming that the first operand has four exact digits and the second operand has three exact digits, the cancellation badness is one. Therefore, the cancellation is catastrophic and the result is completely inaccurate. If the same calculation is done with a second operand with four exact digits, the cancellation badness is zero and thus the cancellation is benign. Assuming that the exact fourth digit is 8, the accurate result

$$1.379 - 1.378 = 0.001$$

has only the exponent in common with the inaccurate result above.

For every instruction the sum of the cancellation badness of every execution of that instruction (field scb in an instruction's analysis information in Figure 6) and the maximum cancellation badness (mcb) that occurred over all executions of that instruction are maintained. Each shadow value tracks the maximum cancellation badness that occurred in the corresponding original value (field mcb in an shadow value's analysis information in Figure 6) and a pointer to the instruction where this maximum occurred (mcb_src).

3.2 Finding Operations that Cause Errors

Consider the pathological example in Figure 3. Naïvely, we would

```
1  float e = 0.00000006f;
2  float x = 0.5f;
3  float y = 1.0f + x;
4  float more = y + e;
5  float diff_e = more - y;
6  float diff_0 = diff_e - e;
7  float zero = diff_0 + diff_0;
8  float result = 2 * zero;
```

Figure 3. A program with insufficient precision and catastrophic cancellation.

expect `result` to be `0.0` after executing line 8. However, the operations in line 5 and 6 cause catastrophic cancellations which render the computed values inexact. This error propagates into variable `result` which is not `0.0` at the end. However, the operation on which `result` depends, the addition in line 7, does not contribute to this inaccuracy. All exact bits of `diff_0` are preserved. Hence, the programmer here wants to find the operations in line 5 and 6. Of

[1] The precision can be specified by the user before the analysis starts.

[2] In the following, the tilde stands for operations and numbers (and sets thereof) in higher precision.

course, in large programs, the operations contributing to the problem can be spread over several modules. Thus, it is hard to pinpoint the problem by just looking at the source code.

A dynamic slice (a data dependence graph of the execution) of the execution would help the programmer to locate this problem. However, recording the trace of the whole program execution and computing the relative errors afterwards can drastically slow down the analysis, because the result of every operation has to be written to disk. Instead, we pursue a more light-weight approach: For every instruction in the program, we maintain two values: The sum of the relative error of every execution (*sre* in Figure 6) of that instruction and the maximum relative error (mre) that occurred over all executions of that instruction.

Please note that for a shadow value of zero, the concept of a relative deviation becomes meaningless. To guard against such cases, our implementation allows the user to specify a threshold t_0 such that

$$\text{relative error} = \frac{|\text{shadow value} - \text{original value}|}{\max\left(|\text{shadow value}|, |t_0|\right)}$$

The sum over all relative errors is used to compute an average of the relative errors. If an instruction has a small average relative error, it is usually unlikely that this instruction is involved in significant accuracy problems. Hence, this value is used when the analysis results are presented to the user: Instructions with a comparably high average relative error are listed before instructions with a lower average relative error.

The maximum relative error is used to enable a light-weight slicing approach: Whenever the maximum relative error of an instructions changes, i.e. the instruction is executed again with a relative error that is higher than all the relative errors seen in previous executions, we store the instructions which computed the arguments to that instruction (field mre_src in an instruction's analysis information in Figure 6). In this way, we obtain insight into the origins of the values causing the maximum error. After the analysis run, this information is used to reconstruct a slice along which the maximum error propagated.

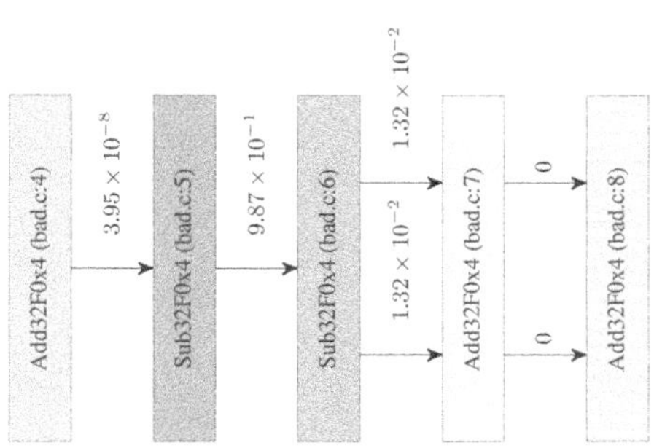

Figure 4. Error trace for the variable `result` in the truncated C program on the left which suffers from insufficient precision in line 4 and catastrophic cancellations in lines 5 and 6. The edges are labeled with the introduced error of the operation they flow out of.

To reveal the origins of an error, one has to find the operations which are the cause. Therefore, after the analysis run, the contribution of an operation to the maximum relative error is calculated. The contribution is called the *introduced error* of an operation. The introduced error is calculated as the smallest difference of the maximum error of the operation itself and the maximum error of one of the operations which is a direct predecessor in the error trace. Special cases occur when an operation is its own predecessor or when an operation has no predecessor. In these cases, the maximum error of the operation itself is taken instead of the difference.

Note that the introduced error can be negative, because errors can be canceled. Figure 4 shows an error trace for the example above. The edges in the graph are labeled with the introduced error of the operation producing the value that flows on the edge. One can directly see that the subtraction in line 5 introduces a large error of 9.87×10^{-1}.

Note that the error trace is not necessarily a part of the dynamic data-dependence graph of the program run. This is because the maximum relative errors of the instructions in the error trace might be observed at *different* instances of the instructions. Hence, the data flow suggested in the error trace might not have taken place in the execution of the program, since we only update the source of the error when the maximum relative error changes (see Figure 6). However, in our experiments we made the experience that the error trace very often resembles the actual data flow and is thus very helpful for getting a first impression on how an error propagates through a program.

3.3 Operational Semantics

In this section, we formally describe our analysis using a structural operational semantics. We base our formalization on Valgrind's VEX intermediate representation language, mainly because the tool implementing our analysis is implemented in Valgrind. However, the subset of VEX we use here is so generic that it does not affect the applicability of our analysis in other frameworks. Figure 5 shows the excerpt of the VEX grammar relevant for our analysis.

const	::=	constant
temp	::=	temporary variable
exp	::=	temp | const
stmt	::=	temp := load(exp) | store(exp, exp)
		| temp := get(exp) | put(exp, exp)
		| temp := exp | tmp := $\diamondsuit_u$ exp
		| temp := exp $\diamondsuit_b$ exp
program	::=	stmt*

Figure 5. Simplified grammar of the VEX intermediate representation used in Valgrind. Load and store describe memory accesses whereas put and get are for accessing registers.

The VEX intermediate representation consists of a sequence of numbered statements. Valgrind flattens the intermediate representation to simplify the instrumentation. As a result, an expression is only a temporary variable or a constant and can not be a tree of expressions. Statements consist of memory and register writes, and assignments. The right side of an assignment can be a memory read, register read, temporary variable, constant, unary operation, or binary operation.

Figure 6 summarizes the formalization of our analysis. Its first section shows the analysis information for instructions and variables. Elements of analysis information are stored in various maps: μ_t (μ_m) implements the store that maps temporaries (memory addresses) to original values. Δ_t (Δ_m) implements the store that maps temporaries (memory addresses) to shadow values. Ω maps addresses of instructions to elements of instruction analysis information. The notation $A[x \leftarrow y]$ stands for $\lambda w.w = x\ ?\ y : A(w)$.

In the inference rule section, we only show the rules for load, store, and the binary operation. Each inference rule is of the form:

$$\frac{\text{side-by-side computation} \quad \text{original computation}}{\langle\text{configuration}\rangle \text{ instruction} \rightsquigarrow \langle\text{configuration}'\rangle \text{ instruction}'}$$

The rules for put and get are purely technical and do mostly resemble the ones for load and store. Most interesting is the rule for the binary operator and the computation of the various analysis information components outlined in the last section of the figure. For

Analysis information tuple I for an instruction:

Name	Domain	Description
sre	$\widetilde{\mathbb{F}}$	Sum of relative errors
mre	$\widetilde{\mathbb{F}}$	Maximum relative error
mre_src	$\mathbb{N} \times \mathbb{N}$	Pair of instruction addresses that point to the instructions that computed the operands that caused the maximum relative error
scb	$\mathbb{N}$	Sum of cancellation badnesses
mcb	$\mathbb{N}$	Maximum cancellation badness

Shadow value tuple S for a variable:

Name	Domain	Description
val	$\widetilde{\mathbb{F}}$	Value in higher precision
td	$\mathbb{N}$	Depth of the computation tree
pc	$\mathbb{N}$	Address of the instruction that wrote to the variable lastly
mcb	$\mathbb{N}$	Maximum cancellation badness
mcb_src	$\mathbb{N}$	Instruction that caused maximum cancellation badness

Σ	:	$Addr \to Instr$	Maps an address to an instruction
μ_m	:	$Addr \to \mathbb{F}$	Maps an address to an original value
μ_t	:	$Temp \to \mathbb{F}$	Maps a temporary to an original value
Ω	:	$Addr \to I$	Maps an address to an instruction analysis information
Δ_m	:	$Addr \to S$	Maps an address to a shadow value
Δ_t	:	$Temp \to S$	Maps a temporary to a shadow value

$$\frac{\begin{array}{c} s = \Delta_m[a] \quad \Delta_t{}' = \Delta_t[n' \leftarrow s] \\ a = \mu_t[n] \quad v = \mu_m[a] \quad \mu_t{}' = \mu_t[n' \leftarrow v] \quad \iota = \Sigma[pc+1] \end{array}}{\langle \mu_t, \mu_m, \Delta_t, \Delta_m, \Sigma, pc \rangle\ n' := \text{load}(n) \rightsquigarrow \langle \mu_t{}', \mu_m, \Delta_t{}', \Delta_m, \Sigma, pc+1 \rangle\ \iota} \ \text{F-LOAD}$$

$$\frac{\begin{array}{c} s = \Delta_t[n_2] \quad \Delta_m{}' = \Delta_m[a \leftarrow s] \\ a = \mu_t[n_1] \quad v = \mu_t[n_2] \quad \mu_m{}' = \mu_m[a \leftarrow v] \quad \iota = \Sigma[pc+1] \end{array}}{\langle \mu_t, \mu_m, \Delta_t, \Delta_m, \Sigma, pc \rangle\ \text{store}(n_1, n_2) \rightsquigarrow \langle \mu_t, \mu_m{}', \Delta_t, \Delta_m{}', \Sigma, pc+1 \rangle\ \iota} \ \text{F-STORE}$$

$$\frac{\begin{array}{c} \Delta_t{}' = \Delta_t[n' \leftarrow s'] \quad \Omega' = \Omega[pc \leftarrow o'] \\ v_1 = \mu_t[n_1] \quad v_2 = \mu_t[n_2] \quad v' = v_1 \diamondsuit v_2 \quad \mu_t{}' = \mu_t[n' \leftarrow v'] \quad \iota = \Sigma[pc+1] \end{array}}{\langle \mu_t, \mu_m, \Delta_t, \Delta_m, \Sigma, pc \rangle\ n' := n_1 \diamondsuit n_2 \rightsquigarrow \langle \mu_t{}', \mu_m, \Delta_t{}', \Delta_m, \Sigma, pc+1 \rangle\ \iota} \ \text{F-BINOP}$$

Abbreviations used:

$$\begin{array}{rcl} \text{rel. error } rerr & := & |(s'.val - v')/d| \\ d & := & s'.val \neq 0\ ?\ s'.val : t_0 \\ \text{lookup}(n, v) & := & \exists w.\ (n, w) \in \Delta_t\ ?\ \Delta_t[n] : init \\ init & := & (v, 0, -, 0, -) \end{array}$$

Analysis information update for an instruction:

$$\begin{array}{rcl} o & = & \Omega[pc] \\ o'.sre & = & o.sre + rerr \\ o'.mre & = & \max\{o.mre, rerr\} \\ o'.mre\_src & = & rerr > o.mre\ ?\ (s_1.pc, s_2.pc) \\ & & : o.mre\_src \\ o'.scb & = & o.scb + cbad \\ o'.mcb & = & \max\{o.mcb, cbad\} \end{array}$$

Shadow value of the result of a binary operator:

$$\begin{array}{rcl} s_1 & = & \text{lookup}(n_1, v_1) \\ s_2 & = & \text{lookup}(n_2, v_2) \\ s'.pc & = & pc \\ s'.val & = & s_1.val\ \widetilde{\diamondsuit}\ s_2.val \\ s'.td & = & 1 + \max\{s_1.td, s_2.td\} \\ s'.mcb & = & \max\{s.mcb, cbad\} \\ s'.mcb\_src & = & cbad > s.mcb\ ?\ pc : s.mcb\_src \end{array}$$

Figure 6. Structural operational semantics for the original and the side-by-side computation

the sake of brevity, we also omit the unary operator. Conceptually, it equals the binary operator. However, computations that involve both operands of a binary operator (such as the calculation of the maximum cancellation badness) have to be adapted accordingly.

4. User Interface

Our tool can automatically collect information for the whole execution of a client program. Thereby all floating-point instructions and variables are analyzed and variables are determined that are likely the final result by the depth of the execution tree leading to them (field *td* in an shadow value's analysis information in Figure 6).

In addition, our implementation enables the user to perform a more targeted analysis by adding client requests to the source code of the analyzed program; client request are instructions that are only interpreted by our analysis and ignored in an execution without Valgrind.

With the client request, the user can exclude parts of the program from the analysis or can run the analysis only on specified parts. This not only allows to specify which parts are to be analyzed, but also grants access to the information gathered by the analysis during execution. Thus, via client requests, the relative error of a variable can be accessed and the error trace of a variable can be constructed at every point in the program where the variable is present.

Furthermore, an original value can be replaced with its shadow value, so that the user can correct a value without fixing all the code leading to this value in the client program. Thus, the user is given a simple way to check whether the correction of a value influences the result of a program.

Another powerful instrument are stages (originally proposed by Kahan [12]). The basic idea behind this concept is to add break points, called "stages", into a program, to observe the errors at each break point, and to complain if two consecutive stages differ too much. This is a semi-automatic technique that assumes that the programmer has an idea where interesting stages are located. In practice, interesting stages almost always correspond to loop iterations. Using our tool, the programmer can define multiple sets of stages that are analyzed independently. An example where stages prove to be useful is presented in Section 6.1. This example shows that stages help finding accuracy problems even if the shadow values on their own fail to do so because of their finite precision.

5. Implementation Details

The analysis presented in Section 3 instruments every floating-point machine instruction in the program. However, our early experiments showed that this is not sufficient. The basic reason is that on the assembly level, strict typing is no longer present. As a result, the types used by Valgrind do not necessarily match the type used in the source code of the client program. An example is shown in Figure 7. There, the compiler chose to load the bit pattern representing a floating-point constant into an integer register whose contents is then stored to memory. Later on, that memory cell is read into an SSE register and a floating-point operation is performed on the loaded value.

This means that the type with which constants are stored in memory does not have to match the type with which they are loaded. A naïve implementation would not only instrument the floating-point but also all integer instructions. However, this would result in a slow and error-prone implementation with a large memory overhead.

Instead, we start the instrumentation as late as possible. As a result, a floating-point variable is tracked from the point where it

```
movl $0x3356bf95, %eax          movl $0x3356bf95, %eax
movl %eax, -4(%rbp)             movl %eax, -4(%rbp)
...                             ...
addss -4(%rbp), %xmm0           fadds -4(%rbp)
```

Figure 7. Extracts from the assembly code for a SSE addition (left) and a x87 FPU addition (right) of two floating-point numbers. There are no indications that the loaded values are used in floating-point instructions later on.

is the result of a floating-point operation. For a constant or a value given as an input to the program there is no need for a shadow value as the shadow value would be exactly the same. In the operational semantics in Figure 6 this is expressed by the function lookup. Furthermore, we use copy propagation to avoid instrumentation of instructions that do not affect shadow values such as type cast operations. However, all reads and writes to the main memory have to be instrumented as in each such operation a floating-point value could be involved.

This scheme has the advantage that it does not only simplify instrumentation and increases the efficiency of the analysis but it also makes the analysis more robust. Floating-point operations which are not yet instrumented can only lead to undetected errors but do not affect the correctness of our analysis. This is due to the fallback to the original value if no shadow value exits.

6. Evaluation

The capabilities and the performance of the tool are evaluated in this section. Unless stated otherwise, all analyses are performed on an x86-64 system with a shadow value precision of 120 bit.

6.1 Wrong Limit of Convergent Sequence

The sequence u_n converges to 6, but if computed with any finite precision it converges to 100. The sequence is defined as

$$u_n = \begin{cases} 2 & \text{if } n = 0 \\ -4 & \text{if } n = 1 \\ 111 - \frac{1130}{u_{n-1}} + \frac{3000}{u_{n-1}u_{n-2}} & \text{if } n > 1 \end{cases}$$

This sequence has been analyzed by Kahan [12] and Muller et al. [15]. The strange behavior can be explained with the solution of the recurrence

$$u_n = \frac{\alpha \cdot 100^{n+1} + \beta \cdot 6^{n+1} + \gamma \cdot 5^{n+1}}{\alpha \cdot 100^n + \beta \cdot 6^n + \gamma \cdot 5^n}$$

where α, β, and γ depend on u_0 and u_1. For $u_0 = 2$ and $u_1 = -4$ one gets $\alpha = 0$, $\beta = -3$, and $\gamma = 4$. However, if computed with finite precision, roundoff errors cannot be avoided and result in an α that is not exactly zero. This leads to the different limits.

```
double u = 2, v = -4, w;
for (int i = 3; i <= 100; i++)
{
  FPDEBUG_BEGIN_STAGE(0);

  w = 111. - 1130./v + 3000./(v*u);
  u = v;
  v = w;
  printf("u%d = %1.17g\n", i, v);

  FPDEBUG_END_STAGE(0);
}
FPDEBUG_PRINT_ERROR(&"u_100", &v);
```

Figure 8. C code which tries to compute the sequence u_n

Therefore, it is clear that after analyzing the computation of u_n in Figure 8, no error can be observed because the shadow value is also 100. However, both values converge at a different rate which can be observed with stages. The stage report in Figure 9 reveals that the relative error grows faster than linear in the iterations 4, 18 and in all iterations in between. Thus, the stage concept allows the detection of this strange behavior which would otherwise have gone unnoticed.

```
Stage 0:

(0)   0x7ff000200 (15)
      executions: [4, 18]
      origin: 0x40089A
```

Figure 9. The stage report for the code in Listing 8 reveals problems starting in iteration 4 and ending in iteration 18. As 15 problems are reported, all iterations between 4 and 18 are affected.

6.2 Walker's Floating-Point Benchmarks

Walker [19] provides two floating-point benchmarks called fbench and ffbench.

The program *fbench* is an implementation of a complete optical design ray tracing algorithm. The largest relative error discovered is 9×10^{-13}. Thus, the algorithm used in fbench does not suffer from accuracy problems for the sample data. The program comes with its own version of the trigonometric functions used, but there is no difference in stability if the program is run with the trigonometric functions from the C library.

The second benchmark, *ffbench*, performs a two-dimensional Fast Fourier transform. Only 4 out of 131,089 shadow values have an error. The largest relative error is 9.6×10^{-2}. Two additions produce inaccuracies due to catastrophic cancellation. However, the inaccuracy stays local and has no influence on the final result.

A program where more than 99% of the variables are accurate is rare. Even considering that ffbench computes and then inverts a Fast Fourier transform, so that the program should result in the same value as the initial one, it requires that no significant digits are lost in between. Therefore, it depends on the numerical stability of the algorithm and on the initial values.

6.3 Analysis of expf

Let us now give an example of the limitations of our approach: The function `expf` from the GNU C Library computes e^x in single precision. The implementation of the function analyzed here is from `sysdeps/ieee754/flt-32/e_expf.c` (GNU C Library 2.12.2). Executing the function `expf` in higher precision leads to more inaccurate results because the algorithm used is designed for single precision and uses precomputed values.

The function is based on Gal's accurate tables method [6]. First, n, t, and y are computed such that x can be expressed as

$$x = n \cdot \ln(2) + \frac{t}{512} + \text{delta}[t] + y$$

and then e^x can be approximated as

$$e^x \approx 2^n e^{\frac{t}{512} + \text{delta}[t]} \cdot (1 + \text{p}(y + \text{delta}[t] + n \cdot \ln(2)))$$

where p is a second-degree polynomial approximating $e^x - 1$ and delta $[t]$ and $e^{\frac{t}{512} + \text{delta}[t]}$ are obtained from tables.

The problem arises when computing n and t. The value of n is computed with

$$n = x \cdot \frac{1}{\ln(2)} + \text{THREEp22} - \text{THREEp22}$$

where THREEp22 $= 12582912.0$ is a single precision constant and the operations are performed with single precision.

The remaining part dx of x is computed with

$$dx = x - n \cdot \ln(2)$$

One would expect $n \cdot \ln(2)$ to be equal to x. But for $x = 0.09$ the value of n is 0 because the large value of THREEp22 leaves no significant digits of x when added. This results in $dx = x = 0.09$ but the shadow value is 1.27×10^{-9}. The shadow value is not exactly 0 because $\frac{1}{\ln(2)} \cdot \ln(2)$ is not exactly 1 as the first factor is a single precision constant and the second factor a double precision one. The value of t is computed with

$$\frac{t}{512} = dx + \text{THREEp42} - \text{THREEp42}$$

where THREEp42 = 13194139533312.0 is a single precision constant but the operations are performed with double precision.

With the previous value of dx, one gets $\frac{t}{512} \approx x$ for the original value but $\frac{t}{512} = 0$ for the shadow value. Thus, t converted to an integer is 46 in the original program but 0 in the side-by-side computation.

Because of these differences the values taken from the precomputed table do not fit for the shadow value. For $x = 0.09$ this results in a relative error between the original and the shadow value of 1.56×10^{-4}. However, the original value only has a relative error of 2.18×10^{-8} compared to the exact result. This relative error is smaller than the single precision unit roundoff and thus cannot be more accurate.

6.4 SPECfp2006

SPECfp2006 is the floating-point component of the SPEC CPU2006 benchmark suite [3]. Most of the floating-point benchmarks from SPECfp2006 can be analyzed with our tool. The only exceptions are `zeusmp` which fails because Valgrind does not support data segments bigger than 1 GB, and `dealII` which does not terminate because it relies on the internal 80-bit representation of the x87 FPU. Valgrind however behaves IEEE 754 compliant and only works with 64 bits for double precision even if it is an x87 FPU instruction. The reasons for the problems were discovered by Weaver [21].

SPECfp2006 comes with three data sets for each benchmark: train, test, and ref. The "ref" data sets are the largest. Because of the slowdown caused by the instrumentation overhead, we focus on the "test" dataset.

All benchmarks were performed on a quad-core AMD Opteron processor with 2.5 GHz and 64 GB of RAM. Figure 10 shows the results for all SPECfp2006 benchmarks we executed. The side-by-side computation ran with a precision of 120 bit.

Benchmark	Original	Analyzed	Slowdown
bwaves	47.5 s	7920 s	167 x
gamess	0.7 s	381 s	544 x
milc	30.9 s	7860 s	224 x
gromacs	2.1 s	991 s	472 x
cactusADM	4.7 s	4777 s	1016 x
leslie3d	59.8 s	17467 s	292 x
namd	19.8 s	18952 s	957 x
soplex	0.027 s	5.0 s	185 x
povray	0.9 s	400.0 s	444 x
calculix	0.07 s	17.1 s	244 x
GemsFDTD	5.5 s	1146 s	208 x
tonto	1.26 s	404 s	321 x
lbm	9.55 s	2893 s	303 x
wrf	7.68 s	2623 s	342 x
sphinx3	4.41 s	938 s	213 x

Figure 10. Results of the SPECfp2006 benchmarks with the "test" data sets

6.4.1 Analysis of CalculiX

During our benchmarking, we observed a potential loss of accuracy in the benchmark CalculiX. Figure 11 shows the first entry of the mean error file which is sorted by the introduced error. This entry led to a deeper analysis of DVdot, a function in SPOOLES, a linear equation solver used by CalculiX, to compute the dot product of two vectors. As it turns out, it is not the multiplication which causes large inaccuracies, but rather the addition in this line. This shows that a globally computed introduced error is not a perfect indicator for the real origin of the problem. Computed only with knowledge about the function DVdot, the introduced errors reveal the real origin.

```
DVdot (Utilities_DV.c:245) Mul64F0x2 (116,010)
  avg error:   1.70635239241881 * 10^1
  max error:   1.55742240304371 * 10^6
  cancellation badness - max: 0, avg: 0.00
  introduced error (max path):   1.55.. * 10^6
```

Figure 11. Information about the operation with the largest introduced error in CalculiX. The output contains information about the function name, the place in the source code, the VEX IR operation name, the execution count, the average and the maximum relative error and average and maximum cancellation badness of all executions of the operation in comparison to the side-by-side computation, and the introduced error computed with the preceding operations.

After spotting a potential problem, we manually modified the function `DVdot` in SPOOLES to print out input causing large inaccuracies and to see if the insertion of a more accurate value influences the final result (see in Figure 12). The reset causes the deletion of all shadow values and thus, no previous inaccuracies influence the observation. If one starts the tool with the analysis disabled, then the begin and end client requests cause that only DVdot is observed and one obtains a good output of the mean errors of the operations in DVdot. After the computation of `sum`, the error of the variable is checked against the error bound of 10^{-2}. If the error is greater, the error and the content of the arrays are printed. At the end of the function, the variable `sum` is set to the shadow value. As the shadow value provides a significantly better result, this is a correction of the value of `sum`.

```
double DVdot(int size, double y[], double x[]) {
  FPDEBUG_RESET();
  FPDEBUG_BEGIN();

  double sum = 0.0;
  for (int i = 0; i < size; i++) {
    sum += y[i] * x[i];
  }

  double errorBound = 1e-2;
  if (FPDEBUG_ERROR_GREATER(&sum, &errorBound)) {
    FPDEBUG_PRINT_ERROR(&"sum", &sum);
    for (int j = 0; j < size; j++) {
      printf("x[%d] = %.20g\n", j, x[j]);
      printf("y[%d] = %.20g\n", j, y[j]);
    }
  }
  FPDEBUG_INSERT_SHADOW(&sum);
  FPDEBUG_END();

  return sum;
}
```

Figure 12. Shortened DVdot function with error detection and correction

During a run with the provided "test" data set, the function `DVdot` produces a relative error greater than 10^{-2} in 28 cases. In three of these cases the relative error is even greater than 10^{-1}. This means that in the worst case, no digit is correct. In that case, the original and the shadow value differ by a factor of nearly 1.76.

The error correction influences 8.5% of the floating-point numbers in the output of CalculiX. Some of the numbers differ in every digit. The "test" data set describes a cantilever beam under shear forces. The correction does not affect the computed stresses but the computed displacements. However, all of the influenced displacements are smaller than 10^{-10}; therefore, the influence may be negligible for this simulation. Nevertheless, one sees that the naïve implementation of an inconspicuous mathematical function can have an impact on the accuracy of a whole computation.

The whole mean error file, sorted by the introduced error, is shown in Figure 13. The multiplication only has operands which are seen as "exact" and thus only produces a relative error smaller than the double precision unit roundoff of 2^{-53} ($\approx 1.11 \times 10^{-16}$). Whereas the addition receives the results of the multiplications as an input and produces large errors due to catastrophic cancellation.

```
DVdot (Utilities_DV.c:248) Add64F0x2 (116,010)
  avg error:   2.72694149800805 * 10^-4
  max error:   1.61405640329709 * 10^0
  cancellation badness - max: 3, avg: 0.01
  introduced error (max path):   1.61.. * 10^0

DVdot (Utilities_DV.c:248) Mul64F0x2 (116,010)
  avg error:   3.96985521613801 * 10^-17
  max error:   1.10661002489201 * 10^-16
  cancellation badness - max: 0, avg: 0.00
  introduced error (max path):   1.10.. * 10^-16
```

Figure 13. Mean errors of floating-point operations in DVdot

The average relative error of the addition is large because a difference between the original and the shadow value can be introduced by a single addition but is considered by every addition later on.

6.5 BALL

Our original motivation for developing a dynamic analysis framework for numerical stability came from the field of structural bioinformatics, where huge amounts of often noisy data are routinely analyzed using highly complex numerical methods. In this section, we present our first application of the developed tool to a subset of the Biochemical Algorithms Library (BALL) [11], a rapid application development framework for structural bioinformatics.

Our first experiments were performed on version 1.4 of BALL and were focused on the optimization of molecular structures against the Amber force field. To this end, we used the program `add_hydrogens` which is distributed along with BALL's source code. First, `add_hydrogens` reads a molecular input structure from a PDB-file, performs a number of required pre-processing steps (such as normalization of atom names and types, inference of missing bonds and of missing atoms). It then sets up one of currently three force fields (we used the default, Amber96) and minimizes the potential energy with respect to the atomic coordinates of the newly added atoms (in a typical use-case, these will mostly be hydrogens) using one of a number of configurable optimizers (we kept the default conjugate gradient for 500 optimization steps).

A global analysis of `add_hydrogens` reports several potential problematic areas in BALL's functionality for structure optimization, i.e., in the Amber implementation and the molecular optimizer. These areas have been analyzed in-depth, but only one area has an accuracy problem that verifiably influences the final result. However, this area includes calls to methods which are reported as potentially problematic but are not problematic if analyzed alone.

The main problem encountered is a catastrophic cancellation in a double precision subtraction. In the worst case, 23 bits are canceled. While this number would be relatively unproblematic at double precision with 53 bit, the operands here are both results of single precision computations and thus can have at most 24 exact bits. Therefore, it is not surprising that the cancellation badness is greater than zero.

The inaccuracy affects the computation of the conjugate gradient computation, i.e., the search for a descent direction, in computing the minimum energy conformation of a molecular system. If the inaccuracy is fixed by computing the numbers used in the subtraction in double precision, the run-time for minimizing the energy of the protein 2PTH with an upper bound of iterations is reduced by 28% and – much more importantly – the result is closer to the optimum.

Thus, with minimal effort in the application of our novel tool, we have been able to identify a problematic situation in a framework that has been in use since 1996, have been able to rectify it using higher precision, and have not only succeeded in improving the quality of the computation, but surprisingly also reduced the runtime.

6.6 GLPK

Linear programming solvers are prone to rounding errors and therefore are interesting targets for an analysis. We performed an analysis of the GNU Linear Programming Kit (GLPK) [7] with an integer linear problem mentioned by Neumaier and Shcherbina [17]

$$\begin{array}{ll}
\text{min} & -x_{20} \\
\text{s.t.} & (s+1)\,x_1 - x_2 \geqslant s-1, \\
& -sx_{i-1} + (s+1)\,x_i - x_{i+1} \geqslant (-1)^i\,(s+1) \\
& \quad \text{for } i = 2:19, \\
& -sx_{18} - (3s-1)\,x_{19} + 3x_{20} \geqslant -(5s-7)\,, \\
& 0 \leqslant x_i \leqslant 10 \text{ for } i = 1:13, \\
& 0 \leqslant x_i \leqslant 10^6 \text{ for } i = 14:20, \\
& \text{all } x_i \text{ integers,}
\end{array}$$

The problem consists of 20 integer variables. For $s = 6$, the problem is solvable, but several solvers are unable to find the solution

$$x = (1, 2, 1, 2, \ldots, 1, 2)^T$$

GLPK in version 4.47 reports that the "problem has no integer feasible solution". The important constraint is

$$0 \leqslant x_i \leqslant 10^6 \text{ for } i = 14:20$$

For GLPK we found that the problem is solvable if 10^6 is replaced by a number between 2 and 21871. Therefore, we analyzed and compared the runs for the upper bounds 21871 and 21872.

For the upper bound 21871, our analysis reveals that -21871 is stored in a double precision value and occurs correctly in operations that are influenced by a tree of preceding operations with depth 159. As the largest tree of preceding operations measured has also a depth of 159, it is likely that this operation has an influence on the final result.

Increasing the upper bound by one to 21872 leads to noticeable changes in the result of the analysis. As before, -21872 is also stored in a double precision value and occurs in a operation that is influenced by a tree of depth 161. Here, 161 is the maximum depth of a tree of preceding operations. However, the original value is 0 and the shadow value is exactly -21872.

This shows that floating-point issues detected by our analysis lead to the wrong result of GLPK. Our analysis gives more details on the highly inaccurate value and automatically outputs an error trace for it, but a deeper analysis is beyond the scope of this paper.

7. Related Work

A manual rounding error analysis is one of the best ways to prove the stability of algorithms and to find errors because it works with a mathematical model of floating-point arithmetic. But because it has to be done by a human expert, it is only feasible for small programs.

Surprisingly few tools have been developed to assist the programmer in locating floating-point accuracy problems. Recent approaches are based on a static analysis (e.g. Fluctuat [9]) or try to dynamically detect or correct errors (e.g. automated error correction by Langlois [14]). A static analysis has the advantage that properties can be proven, however, often only with large error bounds. Furthermore, static approaches suffer from the incapability of disambiguating heap accesses as common in static analyses. Hence, such approaches only work well on scalar computations.

Brown et al. [2] designed an analysis to determine if floating-point operations can be optimized by going to a lower precision or by replacing floating-point with fixed-point arithmetic. This is of interest e.g. for synthesizing FPGAs. Their tool FloatWatch also builds on Valgrind. To employ fixed-point arithmetic, they track the overall range of all floating-point values. In addition, they track the maximum difference between single and double precision computations by performing all double precision operations side by side in single precision.

An et al. [1] present a dynamic binary analysis called FPInst based on DynInst to calculate errors side by side. In contrast to our analysis, the shadow values do not contain values in higher precision but an absolute error in double precision. Their functions for computing the error of instructions are derived from work by Dekker [4]. The formulas from Dekker enable higher precision floating-point arithmetic on top of lower precision arithmetic, but here the formulas are used to track the error throughout a program. Applied to the simple error accumulation shown in Section 2.2.2, the functions presented by An et al. give an error that alternates and does not monotonously increase like the real error. This shows that Dekker's formulas can not always be used to compute error accumulation and also explains the large discrepancies between the computed error and the real error in their examples.

Lam et al. [13] present a dynamic binary analysis based on DynInst to find floating-point operations where digits are canceled. This work can be seen as the one most similar to ours. Their analysis works by tracking all cancellations and reporting them. To minimize the output, the number of reports for the same instruction is decreased logarithmically. Finally, the number of cancellations per instruction and the average number of canceled bits per instruction are computed. However, the approach does not distinguish between benign and catastrophic cancellations, reducing its applicability in practice. Because most cancellations are benign, the user is left with many false positives.

8. Conclusions

In this paper, we presented a dynamic program analysis to detect floating-point accuracy problems. To our knowledge, it is the first dynamic analysis that detects catastrophic cancellations and uses a light-weight slicing approach at tracing accuracy problems through the program. We implemented our analysis in the Valgrind dynamic binary instrumentation framework and exercise it on large-scale benchmark programs in all of which we detect accuracy problems of varying severity: one problem slows down the convergence of an algorithm, other ones cause catastrophic cancellation leading to totally insignificant output of the problem. We showed how our analysis helps in tracking down and successfully fixing the causes of these issues.

9. Acknowledgments

This work is partly supported by the Intel Visual Computing Institute in Saarbrücken.

References

[1] D. An, R. Blue, M. Lam, S. Piper, and G. Stoker. FPInst: Floating point error analysis using dyninst, 2008. http://www.freearrow.com/downloads/files/fpinst.pdf.

[2] A. W. Brown, P. H. J. Kelly, and W. Luk. Profiling floating point value ranges for reconfigurable implementation. In *Proceedings of the 1st HiPEAC Workshop on Reconfigurable Computing*, pages 6–16, 2007.

[3] S. P. E. Corporation. SPEC CPU2006 benchmarks. http://www.spec.org/cpu2006/.

[4] T. J. Dekker. A floating-point technique for extending the available precision. *Numerische Mathematik*, 18:224–242, 1971. 10.1007/BF01397083.

[5] D. Delmas, E. Goubault, S. Putot, J. Souyris, K. Tekkal, and F. Védrine. Towards an industrial use of FLUCTUAT on safety-critical avionics software. In *FMICS '09*, pages 53–69. Springer-Verlag, 2009.

[6] S. Gal. An accurate elementary mathematical library for the IEEE floating point standard. *ACM Trans. Math. Softw.*, 17:26–45, March 1991.

[7] GNU Linear Programming Kit, ver. 4.47. http://www.gnu.org/software/glpk/.

[8] D. Goldberg. What every computer scientist should know about floating-point arithmetic. *ACM Comput. Surv.*, 23:5–48, 1991.

[9] E. Goubault and S. Putot. Static analysis of finite precision computations. In *VMCAI'11*, pages 232–247, Berlin, Heidelberg, 2011. Springer-Verlag.

[10] N. J. Higham. *Accuracy and Stability of Numerical Algorithms*. Society for Industrial and Applied Mathematics, Philadelphia, PA, USA, second edition edition, 2002.

[11] A. Hildebrandt, A. K. Dehof, A. Rurainski, A. Bertsch, M. Schumann, N. Toussaint, A. Moll, D. Stockel, S. Nickels, S. Mueller, H.-P. Lenhof, and O. Kohlbacher. BALL - biochemical algorithms library 1.3. *BMC Bioinformatics*, 11(1):531, 2010.

[12] W. Kahan. How futile are mindless assessments of roundoff in floating-point computation?, 2006. http://www.cs.berkeley.edu/ wkahan/Mindless.pdf.

[13] M. O. Lam, J. K. Hollingsworth, and G. W. Stewart. Dynamic floating-point cancellation detection. In *WHIST 11*, 2011.

[14] P. Langlois. Automatic linear correction of rounding errors. *BIT Numerical Mathematics*, 41:515–539, 2001.

[15] J.-M. Muller, N. Brisebarre, F. de Dinechin, C.-P. Jeannerod, V. Lefèvre, G. Melquiond, N. Revol, D. Stehlé, and S. Torres. *Handbook of Floating-Point Arithmetic*. Birkhäuser Boston, 2010.

[16] N. Nethercote and J. Seward. Valgrind: a framework for heavyweight dynamic binary instrumentation. In *PLDI '07*, pages 89–100. ACM, 2007.

[17] A. Neumaier and O. Shcherbina. Safe bounds in linear and mixed-integer linear programming. *Mathematical Programming*, 99:283–296, 2004. 10.1007/s10107-003-0433-3.

[18] U. G. A. Office. Patriot missile defense: Software problem led to system failure at Dhahran, Saudi Arabia, GAO report IMTEC 92-26, 1992. http://www.gao.gov/products/IMTEC-92-26/.

[19] J. Walker. Floating-point benchmarks. http://www.fourmilab.ch/fbench/, retrieved on 2011-03-03.

[20] The Wall Street Journal November 8, 1983, p.37.

[21] V. Weaver. SPEC CPU2006 problems of Valgrind. http://thread.gmane.org/gmane.comp.debugging.valgrind.devel/1488/, retrieved on 2011-03-03.

Chimera: Hybrid Program Analysis for Determinism

Dongyoon Lee Peter M. Chen Jason Flinn Satish Narayanasamy
University of Michigan
{dongyoon,pmchen,jflinn,nsatish}@umich.edu

Abstract

Chimera[1] uses a new hybrid program analysis to provide deterministic replay for commodity multiprocessor systems. Chimera leverages the insight that it is easy to provide deterministic multiprocessor replay for data-race-free programs (one can just record non-deterministic inputs and the order of synchronization operations), so if we can somehow transform an arbitrary program to be data-race-free, then we can provide deterministic replay cheaply for that program. To perform this transformation, Chimera uses a sound static data-race detector to find all potential data-races. It then instruments pairs of potentially racing instructions with a *weak-lock*, which provides sufficient guarantees to allow deterministic replay but does not guarantee mutual exclusion.

Unsurprisingly, a large fraction of data-races found by the static tool are false data-races, and instrumenting them each of them with a weak-lock results in prohibitively high overhead. Chimera drastically reduces this cost from 53x to 1.39x by increasing the granularity of weak-locks without significantly compromising on parallelism. This is achieved by employing a combination of profiling and symbolic analysis techniques that target the sources of imprecision in the static data-race detector. We find that performance overhead for deterministic recording is 2.4% on average for Apache and desktop applications and about 86% for scientific applications.

Categories and Subject Descriptors D.2.5 [*Software Engineering*]: Testing and Debugging; D.4.5 [*Operating Systems*]: Reliability

General Terms Design, Performance, Reliability

Keywords Determinism, Replay, Data-race detection, Static analysis, Profiling, Symbolic range analysis

1. Introduction

A shared-memory multithreaded program is not guaranteed to produce the same output across different executions even if the input is guaranteed to be the same. Lack of determinism significantly impairs a programmer's ability to reason about an execution and understand the root causes of program failure. This problem can be addressed by constructing multiprocessor systems that guarantee that every execution for a given input produces the same output [14]. Another approach is to record the non-deterministic thread interleavings and enable a programmer to deterministically replay and understand an execution [28]. In this paper, we focus on solving the latter replay problem for multithreaded programs, but the principles discussed here could be applied to build a deterministic multiprocessor system as well.

The ability to faithfully reproduce an execution has proven useful in many areas, including debugging [27, 47], fault tolerance [11], computer forensics [16], dynamic analysis [13, 36], and workload capture [34]. However, past solutions to deterministic replay for shared-memory multiprocessor systems have been unsatisfactory either due to performance costs [17, 29, 49], reliance on custom hardware [24, 32, 33, 54], or lack of sufficiently strong determinism guarantees [2, 38, 51, 56].

Uniprocessor replay is relatively easy. During a recording phase, non-deterministic events (e.g., interrupts and data read from input devices) are logged. If the program is multithreaded, then thread schedules (e.g., the instructions at which each thread is preempted) must also be logged and replayed [43]. Previous studies have shown that logging these non-deterministic events adds little overhead [55].

Efficient multiprocessor replay, however, remains an open problem. The fundamental challenge comes from recording the non-deterministic interleaving among threads, a property that is necessary to deterministically replay programs that contain data-races. Recording and replaying the frequent interactions among thread accesses to shared data can slow execution by an order of magnitude or more. However, if one could somehow statically guarantee that a program is data-race-free, then it is not necessary to record thread interactions — past research has shown that recording and replaying the happens-before order of synchronization operations is sufficient to ensure deterministic replay [40]. In most applications, synchronization operations are relatively infrequent compared to memory accesses, and therefore logging them is relatively cheap. Many uses of deterministic replay, including program debugging, reproducing errors encountered in the field in a test environment, replication for fault tolerance, and forensics following a computer intrusion, are especially useful for programs with bugs, so working only for bug-free programs (i.e., programs without data-races) is not a viable option.

Unfortunately, statically proving the absence of data-races in a program without rejecting data-race-free programs is hard. If there is a chance that a program contains a data-race, then one must record the order of potentially racing operations in order to guarantee that the recorded program can be replayed deterministically. One could discover such operations with a dynamic data-race detector. However, despite significant advances, dynamic data-race detection in software slows program execution by nearly 8x [20] for state-of-the-art detectors. Thus, logging the order of potentially

[1] Chimera is a mythological hybrid animal composed of parts of a lion, a goat and a snake.

PLDI'12, June 11–16, 2012, Beijing, China.

racing instructions is no less of a problem than detecting a data race.

In this paper we discuss Chimera, a deterministic replay system that employs a new hybrid program analysis to handle programs with data races. Chimera combines static data race analysis with off-line profiling and targeted, dynamic checks to provide deterministic replay efficiently.

Chimera instruments a program to log all non-deterministic inputs (e.g., system call results), the thread schedule on each processor core, and the happens-before relationships due to synchronization operations. This information is sufficient to guarantee that the program can later be replayed deterministically, provided the program contains no data-races.

To provide replay for racy programs, Chimera uses a sound but imprecise static data-race detector (RELAY [50]) to find potential data-races. Every memory instruction that potentially races with another instruction is placed inside a code region protected by a *weak-lock*. Chimera records all happens-before relationships due to weak-locks in addition to the relationships due to the original program synchronization. Thus, Chimera guarantees deterministic replay for all programs.

We use weak-locks instead of traditional locks in order to be conservative and avoid introducing artificial deadlocks. A weak-lock is essentially a time-out lock, where mutual exclusion is compromised if the weak-lock is not acquired in reasonable amount of time. In the rare case when a weak-lock times out, Chimera deterministically preempts the thread that currently holds the weak-lock and forces it to yield the weak-lock to the thread that timed out on the weak-lock; the original holder of the weak-lock must reacquire the weak-lock before resuming its execution. This approach splits the code region protected by the weak-lock into two regions across the preemption. Because this timeout mechanism enables Chimera to preserve the invariant that only one thread holds a given weak-lock at any given time, Chimera can support deterministic replay by reproducing the order of weak-locks at the same preemption point.

Unsurprisingly, we find that a sound data-race detector reports a large number of false data-races, and thus adding a weak-lock for every reported data-race results in prohibitively high overhead. Chimera employs two critical optimizations to drastically reduce this cost.

Both optimizations attempt to increase the granularity of a weak-lock, in terms of the size of the locked code region and the amount of data the lock protects. Coarser weak-locks reduce the cost of instrumentation but may serialize threads unnecessarily and compromise parallelism. Chimera's optimizations navigate this performance trade-off by targeting the main sources of imprecision in a static data-race detector [50].

The first optimization is based on the observation that a large fraction of false data-race reports are due to the inability of the static data-race detector to account for the happens-before relations due to synchronization operations other than locks. One example of this is that a number of data-races are reported between initialization code and the rest of the program because the static tool does not account for the happens-before relation due to fork-join synchronization. To address this problem, we profile the program offline over a variety of inputs. If the code regions containing potentially racing instructions are non-concurrent in all profile runs, Chimera increases the granularity of the weak-lock to protect the entire code region instead of just one instruction. Chimera currently treats functions as code regions. This optimization reduces the number of times weak-locks are acquired and released during a function's execution.

The second optimization pertains to the remaining set of false racy pairs that are part of function pairs that ran concurrently in at least one profile run. This optimization targets the inaccuracy caused by the conservative points-to analysis [3, 45] on which RELAY is based. Due to this analysis, RELAY overestimates the set of shared objects that could be accessed by a memory instruction and also underestimates the set of locks that could be acquired. We observe that while the numeric values for the address bounds of an object accessed by a memory instruction are generally hard to determine precisely during static analysis, one can often estimate reasonable bounds in the form of a symbolic expression [42].

Therefore, in our implementation, we compute symbolic address bounds of objects that can be accessed by a racing instruction within a loop. Using this information, we increase the granularity of the weak-lock to the entire loop containing the race, such that it protects the loop for the data variables specified by the loop's symbolic address bounds. This avoids the cost of instrumentation for every iteration of the loop.

Our evaluation shows that Chimera is more efficient than the state-of-the-art software solutions that guarantee multiprocessor replay [49]. We show that recording a set of server (e.g., Apache) and desktop (e.g., pbzip, aget) applications incurs only about 2.4% performance overhead, and recording a set of memory-intensive scientific applications (SPLASH [53] incurs about 86%. Replay overhead is also similar to that of recording. We find that our two optimizations play a significant role in bringing the average overhead from 53x (when all races are naively instrumented) to 1.39x.

Programs transformed by Chimera are data-race-free under the new set of synchronization operations. Though our immediate motive for this transformation is to provide deterministic record and replay, we envision that future work may be able to leverage the data-race-freedom provided by Chimera to provide stronger guarantees such as sequential consistency and deterministic execution [37], since these properties are much easier to guarantee in the absence of data-races.

The primary contributions of this paper are as follows:

- We discuss Chimera, a new deterministic replay system for commodity multiprocessors based on a static data-race detector.
- We discuss two optimizations that employ profiling and symbolic bounds analysis to drastically reduce the overhead of a naive method that instruments all false data-races.
- Our experimental study shows that the performance overhead is about 40% on average, which is less than the state-of-the-art software solutions for multiprocessor replay.

2. Design Overview

This section provides a design overview of the Chimera multiprocessor replay system.

2.1 Background

A program is said to be data-race-free if none of its executions exhibit a data-race. Two memory instructions are said to be *racy* if at least one of them is a write, and there is at least one execution where the two are executed in different threads and not ordered by any happens-before relation due to synchronization operations. For clarity, we define a few terms that we use in this paper. A race-pair is a pair of static memory instructions that are racy. The two functions (or loops) that contains the race-pair are referred to as a racy-function-pair (or a racy-loop-pair).

Chimera records non-deterministic input (e.g., interrupts and file reads) and happens-before relations due to synchronization accesses in a program. This is sufficient to later provide deterministic replay for data-race-free programs because all memory instructions are ordered by some happens-before relation [40]. However, it is

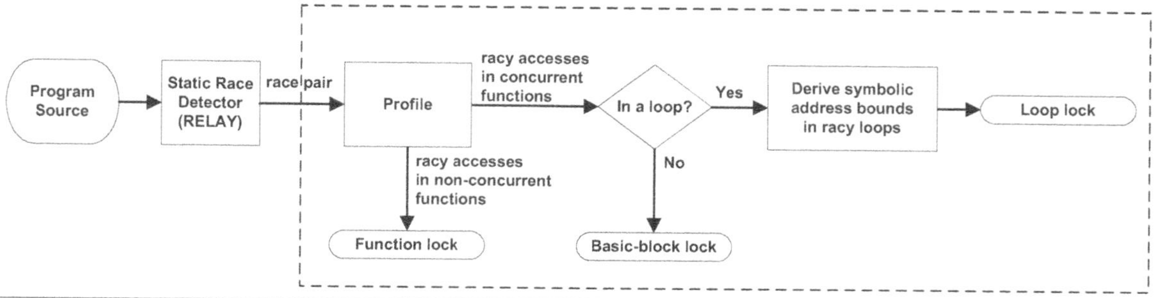

Figure 1. Chimera Overview

insufficient to later provide deterministic replay for programs that contain data-races.

2.2 Design Overview

Figure 1 presents an overview of how Chimera transforms a potentially racy program to a data-race-free program by adding additional synchronization and runtime constraints. Chimera's transformation does not attempt to correct a given program, it simply makes it easier to deterministically record and replay the program's execution.

Chimera analyzes a given program using the RELAY [50] static data-race detector. RELAY is sound, except for two corner cases (assembly instructions and pointer arithmetic). However, the unsoundness is modularized and can be addressed using additional analysis [5, 52] (Section 3.2).

In the simplest implementation of Chimera, each race-pair is placed inside a code section protected by an unique weak-lock w. Recording and replaying the happens-before relation due to weak-locks enables Chimera to record and replay the order of all racy accesses and thus guarantee deterministic replay for all programs.

A sound static data-race detector is imprecise as it has to make very conservative assumptions. This results in a huge number of false data-races, and naively recording all those races results in high overhead. The insight of this paper is that by employing a combination of profiling, symbolic address bounds analysis and dynamic checks, the overhead is significantly reduced to the point where deterministic record and replay is viable even for production systems.

We discuss two specific optimizations. The first optimization is based on our observation that for many false race-pairs, the code regions containing them are almost never executed concurrently. One main cause for this imprecision is the static data-race detector's inability to account for non-mutex synchronization operations. Chimera learns which code regions are almost always non-concurrent by profiling executions with a set of representative inputs. It uses profile information to increase the granularity of weak-locks, both in terms of size of the code region and the amount of shared objects they protect, which reduces the number of weak-lock operations at runtime. Chimera's profiler treats every function as a code region, though other granularities could be considered. As shown in Figure 1, racy-pairs in non-concurrent functions are handled using weak-locks instrumented at the granularity of a function (referred to as *function-locks*).

Not all false data-races are part of non-concurrent code regions. Two code regions can overlap in time, but still may not exhibit a data race if they access different sets of shared objects. However, a static data-race detector may not always be able to prove that the set of shared objects accessed in concurrently executed code regions are disjoint due to imprecise pointer analysis. While it is hard to accurately compute the numeric values for address bounds statically for a code region, it is often possible to derive a symbolic expression for the upper and lower bounds of an object that will be accessed within a code region [42].

For data-races that are not found to be part of non-concurrent functions, Chimera checks if they are part of a loop. If a data-race is not part of any loop, then Chimera simply instruments a weak-lock at the granularity of a basic block (referred to as a *basic block lock*). In case the basic block has a function call, Chimera instruments a weak-lock at the granularity of an instruction (referred to as an *instruction lock*).

If a data-race is part of a loop, Chimera derives a symbolic address bound for the range of addresses that a racy instruction can access within the loop. A race-pair is then guarded by instrumenting a loop-lock. The loop-lock is also a weak-lock, but it protects a range of addresses, which are computed at runtime using the symbolic expression derived statically. If the symbolic bounds expression is too imprecise (e.g., one of the bounds is infinity), and if the loop body is reasonably large in size, then Chimera instruments at the granularity of a basic block. In this manner, Chimera avoids the risk of over-serializing the execution of loops.

2.3 Weak-Lock Design

Chimera ensures that the instrumented weak-locks do not introduce a deadlock. Chimera orders the set of weak-locks constructed for each granularity of a code region (basic block, loop, and function) and ensures that they are always acquired in the same order. When a program has nested code regions (e.g., a function calling a function, a loop calling a function, etc.), an outer region releases all its weak-locks before starting the inner region, and acquires the weak-locks back after exiting the inner region. The order in which weak-locks of different granularities are acquired is also consistent. Function-locks are always acquired before loop and basic-block locks. Loop-locks are always acquired before basic-block locks. Hence, there cannot be a deadlock between weak-locks.

Chimera avoids deadlocks that may happen when a weak-lock protected code region contains a programmer specified synchronization wait. The "weak" part of the weak-lock is meant for handling such deadlocks. If a weak-lock is stalled for more than a threshold period of time, the stalled weak-lock invokes a special system call to handle the potential deadlock. The system call handler identifies the thread that currently owns the stalled weak-lock by examining the log files used to record the order of weak-lock acquires and releases. The kernel preempts the current owner, and forces it to release and reacquire the weak-lock that timed-out. This allows the stalled thread to acquire the weak-lock and proceed with its execution.

Though the above mechanism may compromise the atomicity of a weak-lock protected code region, we always preserve the invariant that only one thread holds a given weak-lock at any given time. Thus, recording and replaying the exact order of forced weak-lock release and reacquire operations with respect to instrumented weak-lock operations is sufficient to guarantee deterministic replay.

This requires that Chimera record and replay the exact instance when a thread is preempted and forced to release its weak-locks. For this purpose, we plan to use a mechanism from the Double-Play replay system [49] in which the kernel records the instruction pointer and the branch count (measured via hardware performance counters) at the point of preemption. We have not yet ported this implementation to the Chimera infrastructure as none of our benchmarks have exhibited a weak-lock timeout.

2.4 Discussion

Any data-race that exists in the original program can manifest in the transformed program. However, Chimera now records the order between the racing instructions. Increasing the granularity of weak-lock (e.g., to a basic-block) would make it less likely for instructions from two racy basic-blocks to interleave. If there is only one race between two racy basic-blocks, then all thread interleavings in the original program can manifest at approximately the same probability in the transformed program. However, if there is more than one race between two basic blocks, then Chimera's weak-locks will try to serialize them. While preventing fine-grained interleaving of smaller code regions may be beneficial for masking certain atomicity violations in production systems [31], a programmer trying to record and debug a test run might consider this to be a limitation of Chimera's optimizations.

3. Static Data-Race Detection

Chimera uses the RELAY [50] static data-race detector to identify potential data-races. In this section, we briefly summarize the RELAY detection algorithm, and then we discuss soundness and completeness of RELAY.

3.1 RELAY

RELAY is a lockset-based static race detection tool that scales to millions lines of code. A `lockset` for a program point is the set of locks held at that point. A lockset-based analysis assumes that for every shared object there is at least one common lock that is held whenever that object is accessed. The tool reports a race if a pair of memory accesses in different threads could access the same shared object, the intersection of their locksets is empty, and at least one of the accesses is a write.

We briefly summarize RELAY's analysis, but details can be found in the original paper [50]. RELAY starts by analyzing every leaf function in the static call graph ignoring the calling context. For each leaf function, it computes a summary. A function's summary soundly approximates the effect of the function on the set of locks held before the function execution. Also, it includes a summary of the set of shared objects accessed in the function and the lockset held during each of its accesses. For example, a summary of a function `bar(void *b)` may say that a write to the field `b->bob` can happen while holding a lock `b->lock`, and that the function releases the lock `b->lock` before returning. RELAY composes function summaries in a bottom-up manner over the call graph by plugging in the summaries of the callee functions to compute the summaries of the callers.

Thus, RELAY performs a bottom-up calling-context-sensitive analysis on the call graph to compute the access summaries for all functions that are thread entry points. This is done using a combination of flow-insensitive points-to [3, 45] and symbolic analysis.

3.2 Soundness

Chimera only instruments data-races found by the static data-race detector. Therefore, its deterministic replay guarantees are based on the soundness of the static data-race detector it uses.

RELAY has three potential sources of unsoundness, but they are modularized and each one can be addressed separately using known techniques. First, RELAY ignores memory operations that occur inside blocks of assembly code when calculating lockset summaries. However, this issue could be addressed with additional engineering that integrates memory access analysis for assembly instructions [5] with RELAY, or via manual annotations.

Second, the points-to analysis [3, 45] used by RELAY does not handle pointer arithmetic. RELAY's pointer analysis assumes that after any arithmetic operation on a pointer, the pointer still points to the same object. When this assumption does not hold true, the pointer analysis is not guaranteed to be sound. As a result, we can guarantee replay for an execution only until the first buffer overflow. However, this does not fundamentally affect Chimera's analysis. Enhancing pointer analysis to handle pointer arithmetic [52], or ensuring language safety would address this problem.

Finally, RELAY post-processes data-race warnings using unsound filters, but we do not use them.

3.3 False Positives

To provide soundness, RELAY makes conservative assumptions, resulting in its reporting a high number of false data-races. Instrumenting weak-locks for every false data-race results in prohibitively high overhead.

There are two main sources of false positives. First, RELAY accounts for lock synchronizations, but ignores happens-before relationships due to non-mutex synchronization operations such as fork/join, barriers, and conditional variables. As a result, RELAY may report a data-race between memory operations that can never execute concurrently. The second main source of false positives is due to the conservative pointer analysis it uses [3, 45]. Conservative pointer analysis would cause RELAY to underestimate the lockset held by a code region and overestimate the variables that could be accessed by a memory instruction.

Our experimental results in Section 7 show that RELAY reported data-race warnings on about 14% of memory operations in a dynamic execution. Instrumenting them with weak-locks to record the order of those potential data-races incurs an approximately 53x slowdown. We next discuss two important optimizations based on profiling (Section 4) and symbolic bounds analysis (Section 5) that significantly reduce this cost.

4. Profiling Non-Concurrent Functions

A static data-race detector may report races between code regions that are never executed concurrently. One reason for this is the inadequacy of the static analysis in accounting for non-mutex synchronization operations. To address this issue, Chimera uses a profile-guided analysis to determine code regions that are likely to never execute concurrently and use that information to increase the granularity of weak-locks without compromising an application's parallelism.

4.1 Overview

One important limitation of lockset based static data-race detectors, including RELAY, is that they account only for locks, but ignore happens-before relations due to non-mutex synchronization operations. Many false data-races may be reported due to this limitation. Figure 2(a) illustrates a false data-race reported for `water`. The data-race is false because the two supposedly racy functions are never executed concurrently due to a barrier synchronization. We also find that a number of false data-races are reported between initialization code and the rest of the code regions, as RELAY does not account for fork-join synchronization. Another source of false data-races, unrelated to non-mutex synchronizations, is the lack of static knowledge of control dependencies. For example, we found

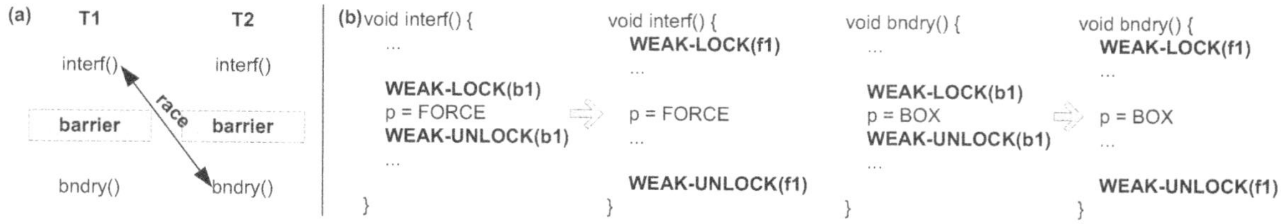

Figure 2. (a) A false data-race reported for `water` application from the SPLASH benchmark [53]. Functions `bndry()` and `interf()` are never executed concurrently due to the barrier synchronization, which is not accounted for in RELAY. (b) The granularity of weak-locks is increased to function level in the two potentially racy functions because Chimera's profiler finds them to be non-concurrent.

instances where a set of code regions are executed in only one thread, but RELAY reported false races among them. In all these cases, the two code regions containing the race-pair reported by RELAY are never executed concurrently.

We observe that such cases can be determined by profiling with a set of representative inputs. If a pair of potentially racy code regions are never executed concurrently in any of the profile runs, then there is sufficient confidence that they are likely to be *non-concurrent* in another execution. Profiling cannot guarantee that they will be non-concurrent in all executions. Nevertheless, we can take advantage of profiled information to increase the granularity of weak-locks to larger code regions and reduce the dynamic number of weak-lock operations.

If a pair of code regions containing a potential race-pair is likely to be non-concurrent, then Chimera increases the granularity of the weak-lock to protect the entire code region instead of just the basic blocks containing the race-pair. Figure 2(b) shows how this optimization affects the weak-lock instrumented to handle the false data-race that we discussed for `water` (Figure 2(a)). In this study, we consider functions as code regions while performing non-concurrent region profiling, but our method could be applied for other region granularities as well. We refer to a weak-lock that protects a function as a *function-lock*.

By increasing the granularity of the weak-lock to the function-level, Chimera reduces the dynamic number of operations on that lock. Increasing the granularity in terms of the code region size for a weak-lock also creates the opportunity to use a single weak-lock to guard multiple potential data-races. The next section discusses an optimization that exploits this opportunity.

4.2 Clique analysis

We propose a clique analysis to determine which racy function-pairs can share the same function-lock. Sharing a function-lock reduces the cost of instrumentation.

Figure 3(a) shows a graph with a node for every function that contains at least one potential data-race. A dotted edge connects a pair of functions that could potentially race. A solid edge connects a pair of functions that are found to be non-concurrent in all of the profile runs. For example, `alice` is potentially racy and non-concurrent with `bob` and `carol`. Functions `bob` and `carol` are non-concurrent, but are proven to be race-free with each other. Functions `bob` and `dave` are racy and have also been found to be concurrent in some profile run.

One simple algorithm would be to assign a unique weak-lock for every racy-function-pair. If the race-function pair is also non-concurrent, then we can use a function-level lock as shown in Figure 3(a). Note that `bob` and `dave` could run concurrently, and so we do not use function-level weak-locks to guard potential races between them, as that could serialize those the two concurrent functions and compromise on parallelism. Instead, a weak-lock is instrumented at the basic-block granularity.

The above algorithm requires that `alice` acquires and releases two function-level weak-locks (`f1 and f2`) every time it is executed. However, `alice`, `bob`, and `carol` are potentially non-concurrent with each other. Therefore, the two potential races could be guarded using a single function-lock `f0` as shown in Figure 3(b). This optimization would reduce the number of weak-lock operations.

To identify a group of functions which are mutually non-concurrent, we construct maximal cliques using a greedy algorithm in a graph of potentially non-concurrent functions (determined through profiling). A clique of an undirected graph is a subset of nodes where every node is connected to every other node. A maximal clique is a clique that cannot be extended by including one more adjacent node. Figure 3(c) shows a graph of potentially non-concurrent functions with two cliques, {`alice,bob,carol`} and {`carol,dave`}.

Once cliques are identified in a graph of non-concurrent functions, Chimera assigns function-locks as follows. For each race-pair, it checks if its racy functions are non-concurrent. If they are, then it finds the clique that the racy-function-pair is part of in the graph of non-concurrent functions. Chimera assigns the function-lock corresponding to that clique to both racy functions. For example in Figure 3(b), racy-function pairs {`alice,carol`} and {`alice,bob`} are both assigned a single function-lock `f0`. Notice that this weak-lock assignment is efficient for `alice` as it now has to acquire only one weak-lock as opposed to two. However, `bob` and `carol` are unnecessarily serialized (as they do not race with each other), which is still acceptable as they are also found to be non-concurrent during profiling.

It is possible that a racy-function-pair is part of two cliques. In that case, we use a greedy algorithm that chooses the weak-lock corresponding to the clique that contains the most number of racy-function-pairs.

5. Symbolic Bounds Analysis for Loops

Chimera's second optimization targets race-pairs that remain after applying the profile-based analysis described in the previous section. This optimization is based on symbolic address bounds analysis. It addresses the imprecision of the conservative but sound pointer analysis used in a static data-race detector.

5.1 Overview

Static data-race detectors [26, 50] use pointer analysis to determine the set of objects a memory instruction can access and also to determine the lockset at a program point. RELAY uses a combination of Steensgaard [45] and Andersen [3] flow-insensitive and context-insensitive pointer analysis, which are used in many static tools because they scale well to large programs. However, because these analyses are very conservative, RELAY overestimates the range of addresses that a memory instruction can access and underestimates the set of locks held at a program point, both of which cause it to report a number of false data races.

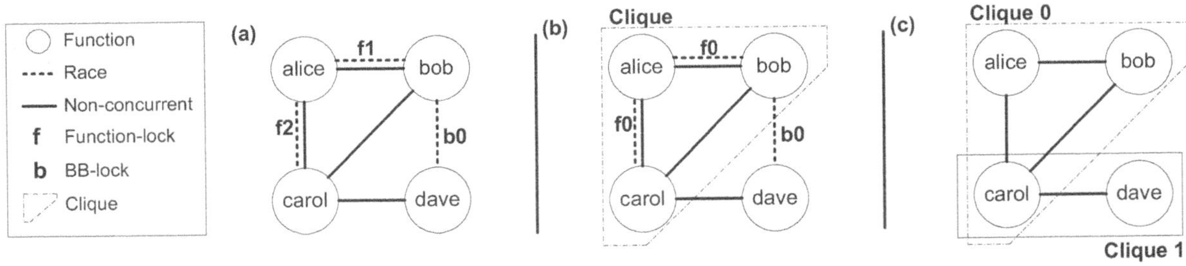

Figure 3. (a) One weak-lock is instrumented for each race-pair. If a racy function-pair is non-concurrent, a function-level weak-lock (`f1`, `f2`) is used. Otherwise, a basic-block level weak-lock is used (`b0`). (b) Two potential data-races in a clique in a graph of non-concurrent function share one function-lock (`f0`). (c) Cliques in a graph representing non-concurrent functions.

```
1:  for( i = 0 ; i < max_digits ; i ++ ) {
2:      WEAK-LOCK (&rank[0] to &rank[radix-1]);
3:      for ( j = 0 ; j < radix ; j++ ){
4:          rank[ j ] = 0;
5:      }
6:      WEAK-UNLOCK (&rank[0] to &rank[radix-1]);
7:
8:      WEAK-LOCK (-INF to +INF);
9:      for ( j = start ; j < stop ; j ++ ) {
10:         my_key = key_from[ j ] & bb;
11:         rank[ my_key ]++;
12:     }
13:     WEAK-UNLOCK (-INF to +INF);
14: }
```

Figure 4. Instrumenting weak-locks for a loop in the function `slave_sort` in `radix` using symbolic bounds.

For example, we find a number of false data-races between two functions executed concurrently in different threads. This often happens when a programmer partitions work between threads, but the static analysis is unable to determine that the function will access different parts of a data structure. Figure 4 shows an example. RELAY reports a false data-race on the `rank` array in line 4 and 11, and also on `key_from` array in line 10. However, `radix` divides a large array into multiple portions and assigns different portions to concurrent threads to process them in parallel. Therefore, the base address of `rank` and `key_from` are different for each worker thread, and hence the threads do not access the same entry in those arrays concurrently.

It is hard to statically determine the absolute values of address bounds of an object accessed by memory operations in a code region. However, it has been shown that the lower and upper bounds in the form of a symbolic expression can often be derived statically [41, 42] with much better accuracy. Chimera uses this information to increase the granularity of weak-locks that it must instrument for race-pairs in concurrent code regions. The weak-lock is constructed in such a way that it protects a code region for a range of addresses specified by a symbolic expression. Thus, two potentially racy code regions can execute concurrently (provided our symbolic bounds are accurate enough). At the same time, Chimera can protect the regions with weak-locks instrumented at larger granularities to reduce the number of operations.

Figure 4 shows an example. RELAY reports that `line 4` could race with itself. Instrumenting a weak-lock inside the loop would be very expensive. Instead, Chimera instruments a weak-lock that provides mutual exclusion for the entire loop (lines 3-5) only for the address range from `&rank[0]` to `&rank[radix-1]`. This range is computed by a sound static symbolic address bounds analysis, which we discuss in the next section.

5.2 Symbolic Bounds Analysis

We implemented our symbolic bounds analysis based on the algorithm proposed by Rugina and Rinard [41, 42]. The goal of this analysis is to determine the symbolic expressions that specify the upper and lower bounds for a pointer or array index variable at a program point that is found to be potentially racy by the static data race detector. For the example in Figure 4, the analysis determines that the symbolic lower bound of j of the first inner loop (line 4-7) is 0 and the upper bound is the initial value of radix $radix_0 - 1$. It also finds that `line 4` can access a memory region from `&rank[0]` to `&rank[radix-1]`. Details about the algorithm are discussed by Rugina and Rinard [42].

The effectiveness of our optimization depends on the accuracy of the lower and upper bounds. The analysis we use is sound, but imprecise. If the bounds are too conservative, we may serialize concurrent code regions unnecessarily. There are two main sources of imprecision. The first case is when the address of the racy object is based on the value of a variable that cannot be determined outside the code region. For example, precise symbolic bounds for the `rank` array accesses in the second inner loop (line 9-12) cannot be determined. The value of the index variable my_key cannot be computed outside the loop as it depends on the value read from another array key_from inside the loop (line 11). However, we can derive the symbolic bounds for the array key_from accurately. The second source of inaccuracy is when the racy object's bounds depends on an arithmetic operation (e.g., the modulo operation or logical AND/OR) not supported in the analysis.

5.3 Choosing the Granularity for Code Region

Rugina and Rinard's analysis [41, 42] describes a generic algorithm for larger code regions including inter-procedural analysis, but, as a first step, we applied their technique only for loops with no function calls in the loop body. As a result, our current implementation may not exploit all opportunities for optimization.

If the symbolic bounds are too imprecise, care must be taken to ensure that we do not over-serialize loops. If the derived symbolic expression for an address range is from negative infinity to positive infinity, we consider it to be *too imprecise* to be useful. Otherwise, we consider it to be *precise enough*. In that case, we balance the number of weak-lock operations with the loop serialization cost.

If the symbolic bounds of a racy loop is precise enough, we assign a weak-lock at the loop granularity (the first inner loop in Figure 4). If the bounds are too imprecise, we estimate via profiling the average number of instructions executed by a loop iteration. If the estimate is less than a `loop-body-threshold`, we still instrument at the loop granularity because the cost of operations on the weak-lock does not warrant exposing parallelism in the loop. Otherwise, we instrument a basic-block lock inside the loop body.

If a loop is nested, we select the outermost loop with precise enough bounds.

6. Implementation

This section presents the implementation details of the Chimera record and replay system.

6.1 Analysis, Instrumentation, and Runtime System

Our analysis and instrumentation framework is implemented in OCaml, using CIL [35] as a front end. To profile concurrent function pairs (Section 4), we instrumented the entry and exit of each function using CIL's source-to-source translation. To statically derive symbolic bounds of racy loops (Section 5), we also performed data flow analysis on a racy loop and produced linear programming constraints using CIL. Then, we used `lpsolve` [1], a mixed integer linear programming solver, to find a solution for static bounds that a racy loop may access. Finally, based on the results of the above static analysis, we used CIL to instrument weak-locks at the function, loop, basic block, or instruction granularity.

We modified the Linux kernel to record and replay non-deterministic input from system calls and signals. We also modified GNU pthread library version 2.5.1 to log the happens-before order of the original synchronization operations and the weak-locks added by Chimera.

6.2 Static Analysis and Source code

We used RELAY [50] to perform pointer analysis and to collect a set of potential data-races. We applied Andersen's inclusion-based pointer analysis [3] to resolve function pointers, and Steensgaard's unification-based approach [45] to perform alias analysis between lvalues. While performing pointer analysis, RELAY first translates function local arrays and address-taken variables to heap variables (making them global) in order to derive pointer constraints in a unified manner. RELAY performs static analysis on this modified source code. This can lead to unnecessary false data-races on local variables. To resolve this, we filtered out race warnings on a 'heapified' local variable that did not escape its function.

To perform sound static analysis, we made sure that all library source code (except for `apache` and `pbzip2`) are included in our static analysis. For the standard C library, we used uClibc [48] which is smaller and easier to analyze than the GNU glibc library, as it is developed for embedded Linux systems. The uClibc library involves all the necessary functions such as `libc` and `libm`.

For `apache`, we did not include libraries such as `gdbm`, `sqlite3`, etc., because they do not contain code that gets executed for the input we use in our study. It is possible that the source code of a third party library may not be available for static analysis. When any part of the source code of a library used by a program is not analyzed, the soundness of static analysis may be compromised. One solution is to ask library builders to provide annotation (lockset summaries) for their library functions so that it can be fed into RELAY to perform a sound data-race analysis. Developing such annotations would be an one-time cost for library builders, and it would not place any burden on software developers that use those libraries. Another possible solution is to assume that a library function will only access the set of objects pointed to by the parameters passed as function arguments without acquring any new locks. However, this approach is not guaranteed to be sound, because a library could retain pointers passed to previous calls to the same library. Also, instructions in a library's function can have a data-race on some shared-variable that is internal to the library. We employed the latter approach for `pbzip2` (we excluded the `libbz2` library used by `pbzip2`)

We also converted the C++ `pbzip2` program into ANSI-C code by replacing the vector STL container with a linked-list-based C library, because our instrumentation framework, CIL [35], can only handle C programs, but not C++ constructs.

7. Results

This section evaluates Chimera's recording and replaying overhead and demonstrates the effectiveness of the profiling and symbolic bounds optimizations.

7.1 Methodology

We evaluated our system using three sets of benchmarks which are listed in Table 1. The first set consists of three desktop applications: `aget`, `pfscan`, and `pbzip2`. The second set has two web sever programs: `knot` and `apache`, which are evaluated using the ApacheBench (ab) client. The final set contains four scientific programs from SPLASH-2 [53]: `ocean`, `water`, `fft`, and `radix`. To collect a set of concurrent function pairs for clique analysis (Section 4.2), we profiled each program 20 times with various inputs. The inputs used for profiling are significantly different from the input used for our performance evaluation.

Chimera is scalable to large programs. It is built on RELAY [50], which has been shown to scale to very large programs (e.g., Linux with 4.5 million lines of code). Chimera also uses static analysis to derive symbolic bounds, but it is a scalable intra-procedural analysis. Our benchmark set includes some fairly large programs. Table 1 provides the number of lines (LOC) of our benchmarks in their CIL representation. It does not account for the size of library code: libc(41.7K) and libm(3.6K).

Presence of assembly code and buffer overflow may compromise the soundness of static data-race analysis (Section 3.2). However, the programs we evaluated do not contain assembly code, except for a few library functions. Also, we are not aware of any buffer overflow bugs in our benchmarks. Also, we did not observe any weak-lock timeouts (Section 2.3) in any of our experiments.

We ran our experiments on a 2.66 GHz 8-core Xeon processor with 4 GB of RAM running CentOS Linux version 5.3. We modified Linux 2.6.26 kernel and GNU `pthread` library version 2.5.1 to support Chimera's record and replay features. All results are the mean of five trials with 4 worker threads (excluding main or control threads). Section 7.2 presents scalability results for which we used 2, 4, and 8 threads.

7.2 Record and replay performance

Table 2 shows Chimera's record and replay performance when all the optimizations (function, loop, and basic-block level weak-lock optimizations) are enabled. The first set of columns quantifies the number of logs generated for recording program input (read through systems calls) and the happens-before order of synchronization operations. These logs are sufficient to guarantee replay for data-race-free (DRF) programs. The second set of columns quantifies the number of logs due to various types of weak-locks. The next set of columns presents the performance overhead. The last set of columns quantifies the `gzip` compressed log sizes for recording the program input and the order of all synchronization operations (including weak-locks).

Chimera incurs negligible overhead for desktop and server applications. For scientific applications (with high frequency of accesses to shared variables) the overhead is relatively high. On average, our system incurs 40% performance overhead to record an execution with four worker threads. Replay overhead is similar to that of recording overhead for most applications, except for I/O intensive applications. Network intensive applications such as `aget`, `knot`, and `apache` replay much faster as we feed the recorded input directly to the replayed process without waiting for the network response. Chimera's performance overhead is an order of magnitude

application		LOC	profile environment	evaluation environment
desktop	aget	1.2K	2 workers, download a 29KB file from local network	2,4,8 workers, download a 10MB file from http://ftp.gnu.org
	pfscan	2.1K	2 workers, scan 236 KB of small 22 files	2,4,8 workers, scan 952 MB of 8 log files
	pbzip2	4.8K	2 workers, compress a 219 KB file, output to stdout	2,4,8 workers, compress 16 MB file, output to file
server	knot	1.3K	2 workers, 4 clients, 100 requests, 29KB file	2,4,8 workers, 16 clients, 1000 requests, 390KB file
	apache	99K	2 workers, 4 clients, 100 requests, 29KB file	2,4,8 workers, 16 clients, 1000 requests, 390KB file
scientific	ocean	5.3K	2 workers, 130*130 grid, 1e-01 error tolerance	2,4,8 workers, 1026*1026 grid, 1e-07 error tolerance
	water	2.5K	2 workers, 64 molecules, 5 steps	2,4,8 workers, 1000 molecules, 10 steps
	fft	1.4K	2 workers, 2^4 matrix , no inverse FFT check	2,4,8 workers, 2^{20} matrix, with inverse FFT check
	radix	1.3K	2 workers, 2^8 keys , no sanity check	2,4,8 workers, 2^{14} keys, with sanity check

Table 1. Benchmarks and input used for profiling and evaluating Chimera. The number of lines in the source program (LOC) is measured for the CIL representation. It does not include the size of library code: libc(41.7K) and libm(3.6K).

application		DRF Logs		logging order of potential data-races				performance				log size	
		system calls	synch. ops.	instr. log	basic blk. log	loop log	func. log	original time(ms)	record time(ms)	recording overhead	replay overhead	input log(KB)	order log (KB)
desktop	aget	16604	8424	28876	5191	15939	32416	5058	5114	1.01	0.06	20072	361
	pfscan	109	879	8	0	39	347	848	881	1.04	1.02	2	3
	pbzip2	592	2491	2621	81	1177	1540	1343	1371	1.02	1.03	1989	26
server	knot	8056	32	5136	0	251	2257	7137	7176	1.01	0.01	84	23
	apache	18301	36812	798891	266956	565863	1123337	18668	19376	1.04	0.02	178	6469
scientific	ocean	2750	9978	6237	8233	287642	37655	2328	5585	2.40	2.24	16	727
	water	10295	67202	21838	1409884	198993	1112798	1665	2820	1.69	1.75	101	12744
	fft	113	193	1843	38	49718	11595	586	1249	2.13	2.23	2	107
	radix	102	312	3	13	344	393	1599	1939	1.21	1.20	1	3

Table 2. Chimera record and replay performance. The results are the mean of five trials with 4 worker threads.

improvement over the state-of-the art software solutions that guarantee multiprocessor replay [49].

Log sizes of Chimera are within acceptable limits for various uses of replay. `aget` produces large logs because the contents of all the downloaded files are in the log. `water` also produces a large log size because of frequent user specified synchronizations and weak-locks.

7.3 Effectiveness of Optimizations

We analyzed the effect of different optimizations on recorder's overhead. Fine grained weak-locks (instruction and basic-block level weak-locks) enable higher concurrency, but they increase the number of program points instrumented resulting in higher performance and log size overhead. The opposite is true for coarser grained weak-locks such as function and loop level weak-locks. We use function-level weak-locks if two functions are likely to be non-concurrent (Section 4). We use loop-level weak-locks with runtime bounds checks if our static analysis can derive precise enough symbolic bounds (Section 5).

Figure 5 shows the performance overhead of Chimera's recorder with different sets of optimizations normalized to native execution time. As expected, instrumenting every potential data-race at the granularity of a source line (labeled as 'instr') incurs 53x slowdown. However, when we apply the profile-based optimization to increase the granularity of some weak-locks to function level ('inst+func') the overhead drops to 27x. If we use only symbolic analysis to coarsen the granularity of some weak-locks to loop level results in 33x overhead. However, when we employ all the optimizations together ('inst+bb+loop+func'), including basic block level weak-locks, the average overhead drops significantly to 1.39x.

Applications such as `pfscan` and `water` benefit significantly from function-level locks. In these applications, most data-races are in function-pairs ordered by some non-mutex synchronization operations that our static analysis could not account for. For applications such as `apache`, `ocean`, `fft`, and `radix`, loop-level locks reduce the recording overhead drastically. For example, in `apache`, RELAY reports a false data-race between memory operations within a hot loop in the `memset` library function that iterates approximately over 6 million times in our experiments. Function-level weak-lock is ineffective in this case, because two threads may execute the `memset` concurrently. However, our static analysis determines the bounds of addresses accessed within the hot loops of `memset` fairly accurately, which enabled us to use loop-level weak-locks effectively. We also observe noticeable benefits in coarsening weak-locks from instruction-level to basic-blocks (e.g., `water`).

Finally, for network applications like `aget`, `knot`, and `apache`, recording cost overlaps with I/O wait resulting in negligible overhead. Chimera could be used even in production systems for such applications.

Figure 6 shows the proportion of dynamic number of weak-lock operations with respect to the total number of dynamic memory operations. A naive dynamic data-race detector would have to instrument 100% of memory operations. This result shows the advantage of static data-race analysis and our optimizations in terms of reducing the number of instrumented points in the program. In general, results in Figure 6 for different optimizations are consistent with the recording overhead in Figure 5. This indicates that the savings obtained from coarser weak-locks was not overshadowed by any loss in parallelism.

On average, naively monitoring all data-races reported by the static data-race detector requires us to instrument about 14% of all dynamic memory operations. By increasing the weak-lock granularity to function, loop, and basic block levels, we can reduce the proportion of weak-lock operations with respect to memory accesses down to 0.02% on average. In general, this result shows that

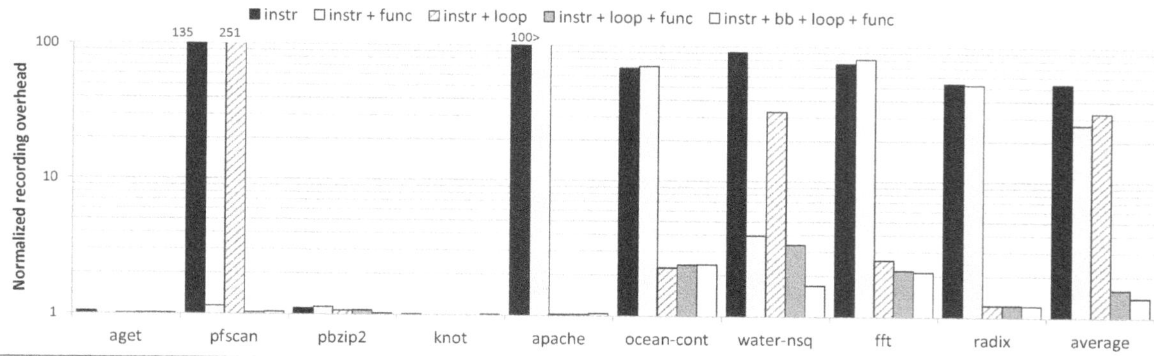

Figure 5. Normalized recording overhead for Chimera with different sets of optimizations

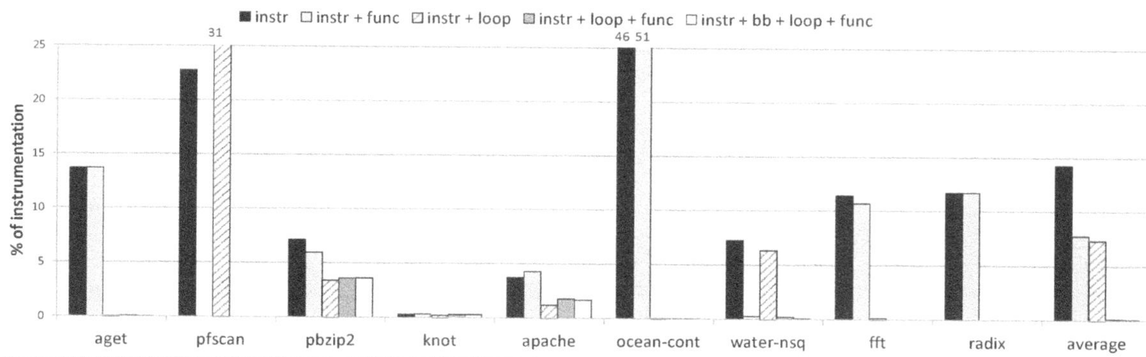

Figure 6. Proportion of instrumentation points for different logging schemes

increasing the granularity of weak-locks reduces the instrumentation cost.

However, in some fairly rare cases, increasing the locking granularity from instruction to loop-level may increase the frequency of weak-lock operations. The reason is due to control flow dependencies. In `pfscan`, there is a racy instruction inside a hot loop that is guarded by an `if` statement. If we use loop-level weak-lock, Chimera has to always perform weak-lock operations when the loop is executed. But if we use instruction-level weak-lock, the instrumented code will be executed only when the `if` condition gets satisfied.

In `apache` the number of weak-lock operations increase when we go from instruction-level to function-level granularity. The reason for this is behavior is best explained using a contrived example. Assume that RELAY finds a data-race between each of the functions `foo`, `bar`, and `qux`. Also, assume that all these functions are non-concurrent with each other, except for the function-pair `bar` and `qux`. For this example, Chimera will assign two different function level weak-locks (one for `foo-bar` and another for `foo-qux`). This allows `bar` and `qux` to run concurrently. As a result, `foo` is instrumented with two function-level locks, which may be more costlier than using one instruction-level lock if there is only one racy instruction inside `foo`.

We also studied the sensitivity of our profile-based non-concurrent function analysis to the number of profile runs. We did this study only for `pfscan` and `water-nsq`, because other applications shows little performance benefit from function-level logging (Figure 5). For these two applications, the number of concurrent function pairs observed quickly saturates after a small number of profile runs (five for `pfscan` and three for `water-nsq`).

7.4 Sources of Overhead and Scalability

Figure 7 provides a breakdown of the remaining sources of performance overhead in the Chimera recorder that incorporates all of our optimizations ('inst+bb+loop+func'). The results are normalized to the native execution time. We measure the performance of our system by instrumenting each type of weak-lock one by one. The performance overhead due to a weak-lock type is further broken down into the cost of logging the weak-lock operations and the cost due to weak-lock contention. To measure the time lost due to weak-lock contention, we subtracted the execution time of a program execution in which a weak-lock acquire operation always succeeds without waiting from the execution time of a program execution in which the weak-locks semantics are obeyed.

Contention for loop-level weak-locks dominate the overhead for scientific applications such as `ocean` and `fft`. The reason is that our static symbolic bounds analysis is not very precise for some performance critical loops in these programs because they tend to execute irregular array accesses and unmodeled arithmetic operations (Section 5.2). As a result, the bounds checks performed as part of loop-lock acquire operation over-serializes the execution. We also fail to use loop-level lock and resort to instruction-level logging (e.g., `water`), if the loop body contains a function call, because our symbolic analysis in intra-procedural.

Contention between loop-level weak-locks is the for increase in performance overhead as the number of threads increases for some applications (Figure 8). We believe that source-level inlining for small functions or inter-procedural symbolic bounds analysis could help reduce this overhead. Nevertheless, as we discussed earlier (Section 7.3), our current analysis already provides significant benefits with loop-level locks for many applications (e.g., `ocean`).

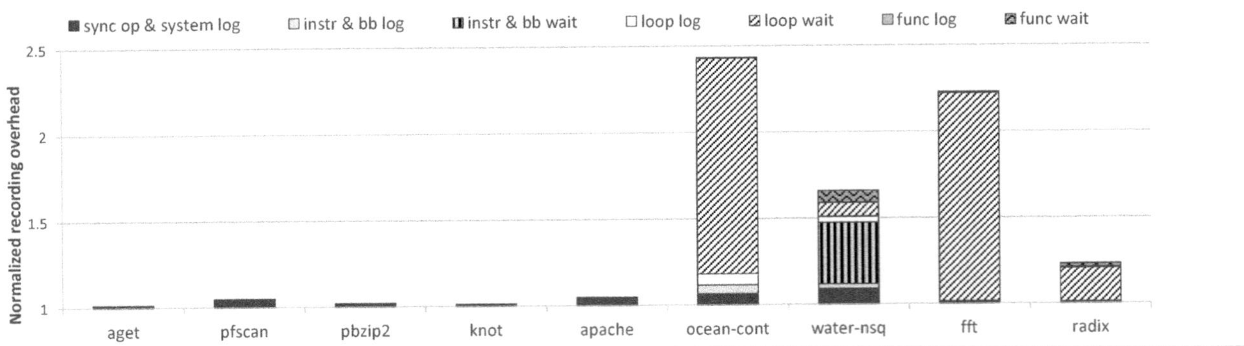

Figure 7. Sources of recording overhead

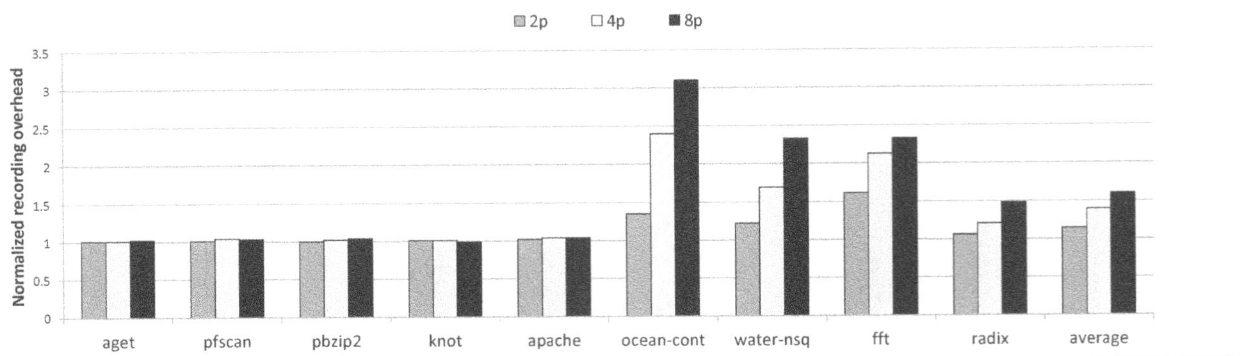

Figure 8. Scalability results on 2,4,and 8 processor executions

8. Related Work

Chimera is related to three distinct areas of prior work: deterministic record-and-replay, deterministic execution, and hybrid data-race detection.

Deterministic Replay. Support for checkpointing and logging non-deterministic input (interrupts, DMA, I/O, etc.) is sufficient to guarantee deterministic replay for single-threaded programs [44]. Deterministic replay for multithreaded programs running on a uniprocessor also can be provided at low cost by recording thread schedules [16]. However, multiprocessor replay remains an open challenge due to difficulties in detecting and logging shared memory dependencies. The earliest work in this area either incurred prohibitive performance overhead due to the cost of monitoring memory operations [8, 17, 34], supported deterministic record and replay only for data-race-free programs [40], or relied on custom hardware support [33, 54].

State-of-the-art software solutions mainly take two approaches: search or redundancy. PRES [38] and ODR [2] are offline search based replay systems. Instead of detecting and recording shared memory dependencies at runtime, they perform offline search to reconstruct thread interleavings. This class of systems show notable performance improvement during recording, but the offline search is not guaranteed to succeed in a bounded amount of time (failing to find a solution in some experiments). In some cases, the first deterministic replay may take prohibitively long time when the search does not scale. However, subsequent replays have low overhead, because a solution has been previously found. Alternatively, Respec [29] and DoublePlay [49] use redundant execution to detect data-races during recording that could compromise deterministic replay. While the record and replay latency overhead is low when spare cores are available to run an additional replica, these systems impose a minimum of a 2x CPU throughput overhead to run an additional replica.

LEAP [25] uses static escape analysis to provide efficient multiprocessor replay. LEAP improves the efficiency of a recorder by instrumenting accesses to only shared variables that are determined using a static escape analysis. LEAP also ignores accesses to variables that are immutable after initialization to improve efficiency. Monitoring and logging accesses to all mutable shared variables determined using a conservative static analysis can be quite expensive at runtime. LEAP can slowdown a program by more than 2x in the average case and 6x in the worst case [25].

In contrast to these prior systems, Chimera uses a sound static data race analysis and a series of optimizations to build the most efficient software replay solution for commodity multiprocessors to date.

Deterministic Execution. Deterministic execution systems help programmers reproduce a multiprocessor execution by ensuring that the thread interleaving observed is always the same for a given program and an input [14]. This approach obviates the need for recording the order of shared-memory accesses, but must still record any non-deterministic program input to provide deterministic replay. While deterministic execution can be supported fairly efficiently for programs without data-races [9, 37], current software-only solutions for racy programs incur high overhead [6]. Efficiency can be improved by using custom hardware [14, 15, 23], by restricting the class of programs supported to fork-join parallelism [7] or shared-nothing address spaces [4], or by allowing executions that are not consistent with the processor's memory consistency model [30]. Chimera transforms a program into an equivalent data-race-free program under the new set of synchronization operations. Future work can leverage this property to design an efficient software only solution for deterministic execution.

Data-Race Detection. There is a large body of work that uses locksets to perform static data-race detection for C/C++ programs [19, 26, 39, 46]. Type systems have been used to improve static data-race analysis [10, 21, 22]. We used lockset based RELAY [50] to build Chimera, but future advancements in this area could help us further reduce the overhead of our replay system.

Perhaps the most closely related study is the work on hybrid data-race detectors that used static analysis to eliminate runtime checks for memory operations that are proven to be data-race-free [12, 18]. Unlike Chimera, they check all suspected racy accesses at the instruction granularity, which we show could lead to a high runtime overhead. To reduce this overhead, Choi et al. [12] discuss unsound optimizations that may not find more than one data-race per memory location. Such weaker guarantees may be acceptable for detecting concurrency bugs, but are not sufficient to guarantee deterministic replay.

9. Conclusion

Non-determinism has been one of the thorny issues in shared-memory multithreaded programming. An efficient deterministic replay system can help solve this problem by empowering programmers with the ability to reproduce and understand a program's execution. This is critical in many stages of the software development process, including debugging, testing, reproducing problems from the field, and forensic analysis.

Chimera is the first software system for multiprocessors that leverages a static data-race detector tool to provide a low overhead replay solution. However, an efficient solution would not have been possible without the two critical optimizations that we employed to drastically reduce the overhead of recording all the data-races reported by a conservative, but sound static analysis tool.

Chimera's transformations ensure that the resultant code is data-race-free when instrumented with the new set of synchronization operations. We believe that this technique could also prove quite useful for enabling stronger semantics for concurrent languages such as sequential consistency and for enabling deterministic execution.

Acknowledgments

This work was funded in part by NSF with grants CCF-0916770, CNS-0905149, a Microsoft gift and an equipment grant from Intel.

References

[1] lpsolve, mixed integer linear programming solver. http://lpsolve.sourceforge.net/5.5.

[2] G. Altekar and I. Stoica. ODR: Output-deterministic replay for multicore debugging. In *Proceedings of the 22nd ACM Symposium on Operating Systems Principles*, pages 193–206, October 2009.

[3] L. O. Andersen. Program analysis and specialization for the c programming language. In *PhD thesis, DIKU, University of Copenhagen*, 1994.

[4] A. Aviram, S.-C. Weng, S. Hu, and B. Ford. Efficient system-enforced deterministic parallelism. In *Proceedings of the 9th Symposium on Operating Systems Design and Implementation*, Vancouver, BC, 2010.

[5] G. Balakrishnan and T. Reps. Analyzing memory accesses in x86 executables. In *In CC*, pages 5–23. Springer-Verlag, 2004.

[6] T. Bergan, O. Anderson, J. Devietti, L. Ceze, and D. Grossman. Coredet: a compiler and runtime system for deterministic multithreaded execution. In *Proceedings of the 15th International Conference on Architectural Support for Programming Languages and Operating Systems*, pages 53–64, Pittsburgh, PA, 2010.

[7] E. D. Berger, T. Yang, T. Liu, and G. Novark. Grace: Safe multithreaded programming for C/C++. In *Proceedings of the International Conference on Object Oriented Programming Systems, Languages, and Applications*, pages 81–96, Orlando, FL, October 2009.

[8] S. Bhansali, W. Chen, S. de Jong, A. Edwards, and M. Drinic. Framework for instruction-level tracing and analysis of programs. In *Second International Conference on Virtual Execution Environments*, pages 154–163, June 2006.

[9] R. L. Bocchino, Jr., V. S. Adve, D. Dig, S. V. Adve, S. Heumann, R. Komuravelli, J. Overbey, P. Simmons, H. Sung, and M. Vakilian. A type and effect system for deterministic parallel Java. In *Proceedings of the International Conference on Object Oriented Programming Systems, Languages, and Applications*, pages 97–116, Orlando, FL, October 2009.

[10] C. Boyapati and M. Rinard. A parameterized type system for race-free java programs. In *Proceedings of the 16th ACM SIGPLAN conference on Object-oriented programming, systems, languages, and applications*, OOPSLA '01, pages 56–69, New York, NY, USA, 2001.

[11] T. C. Bressoud and F. B. Schneider. Hypervisor-based fault tolerance. *ACM Transactions on Computer Systems*, 14(1):80–107, February 1996.

[12] J.-D. Choi, K. Lee, A. Loginov, R. O'Callahan, V. Sarkar, and M. Sridharan. Efficient and precise datarace detection for multithreaded object-oriented programs. In *Proceedings of the ACM SIGPLAN 2002 Conference on Programming Language Design and Implementation*, Berlin, Germany, June 2002.

[13] J. Chow, T. Garfinkel, and P. M. Chen. Decoupling dynamic program analysis from execution in virtual environments. In *Proceedings of the 2008 USENIX Technical Conference*, pages 1–14, June 2008.

[14] J. Devietti, B. Lucia, L. Ceze, and M. Oskin. DMP: Deterministic shared memory multiprocessing. In *Proceedings of the 2009 International Conference on Architectural Support for Programming Languages and Operating Systems (ASPLOS)*, pages 85–96, March 2009.

[15] J. Devietti, J. Nelson, T. Bergan, L. Ceze, and D. Grossman. Rcdc: a relaxed consistency deterministic computer. In *Proceedings of the sixteenth international conference on Architectural support for programming languages and operating systems*, pages 67–78, 2011.

[16] G. W. Dunlap, S. T. King, S. Cinar, M. A. Basrai, and P. M. Chen. ReVirt: Enabling intrusion analysis through virtual-machine logging and replay. In *Proceedings of the 5th Symposium on Operating Systems Design and Implementation*, pages 211–224, Boston, MA, December 2002.

[17] G. W. Dunlap, D. G. Lucchetti, M. Fetterman, and P. M. Chen. Execution replay on multiprocessor virtual machines. In *Proceedings of the 2008 ACM SIGPLAN/SIGOPS International Conference on Virtual Execution Environments (VEE)*, pages 121–130, March 2008.

[18] T. Elmas, S. Qadeer, and S. Tasiran. Goldilocks: A race and transaction-aware Java runtime. In *PLDI*, pages 245–255, 2007.

[19] D. Engler and K. Ashcraft. RacerX: Efficient static detection of race conditions and deadlocks. In *Proceedings of the 19th ACM Symposium on Operating Systems Principles*, pages 237–252, Bolton Landing, NY, 2003.

[20] C. Flanagan and S. Freund. FastTrack: Efficient and precise dynamic race detection. In *Proceedings of the ACM SIGPLAN 2009 Conference on Programming Language Design and Implementation*, pages 121–133, Dublin, Ireland, June 2009.

[21] C. Flanagan and S. N. Freund. Type-based race detection for java. In *Proceedings of the ACM SIGPLAN conference on Programming language design and implementation*, pages 219–232, Vancouver, British Columbia, Canada, 2000.

[22] D. Grossman. Type-safe multithreading in cyclone. In *Proceedings of the 2003 ACM SIGPLAN international workshop on Types in languages design and implementation*, TLDI '03, pages 13–25, New York, NY, USA, 2003.

[23] D. Hower, P. Dudnik, M. D. Hill, and D. A. Wood. Calvin: Deterministic or not? free will to choose. In *17th International Conference on High-Performance Computer Architecture*, February .

[24] D. R. Hower and M. D. Hill. Rerun: Exploiting episodes for lightweight memory race recording. In *Proceedings of the 2008 Inter-*

national Symposium on Computer Architecture, pages 265–276, June 2008.

[25] R. Huang, D. Y. Den, and G. E. Suh. Orthrus: Efficient software integrity protection on multi-cores. In *Proceedings of the 15th International Conference on Architectural Support for Programming Languages and Operating Systems*, pages 371–383, Pittsburgh, PA, March 2010.

[26] V. Kahlon, N. Sinha, E. Kruus, and Y. Zhang. Static data race detection for concurrent programs with asynchronous calls. In *Proceedings of the the 7th joint meeting of the European software engineering conference and the ACM SIGSOFT symposium on The foundations of software engineering*, ESEC/FSE '09, pages 13–22, New York, NY, USA, 2009.

[27] S. T. King, G. W. Dunlap, and P. M. Chen. Debugging operating systems with time-traveling virtual machines. In *Proceedings of the 2005 USENIX Technical Conference*, pages 1–15, April 2005.

[28] T. J. LeBlanc and J. M. Mellor-Crummey. Debugging parallel programs with instant replay. *IEEE Transaction on Computers*, 36(4): 471–482, 1987.

[29] D. Lee, B. Wester, K. Veeraraghavan, P. M. Chen, J. Flinn, and S. Narayanasamy. Respec: Efficient online multiprocessor replay via speculation and external determinism. In *Proceedings of the 15th International Conference on Architectural Support for Programming Languages and Operating Systems*, pages 77–89, Pittsburgh, PA, March 2010.

[30] T. Liu, C. Curtsinger, and E. D. Berger. Dthreads: efficient deterministic multithreading. In *Proceedings of the Twenty-Third ACM Symposium on Operating Systems Principles*, pages 327–336, 2011.

[31] B. Lucia, J. Devietti, K. Strauss, and L. Ceze. Atom-aid: Detecting and surviving atomicity violations. In *Proceedings of the 35th Annual International Symposium on Computer Architecture*, pages 277–288, Beijing, China, 2008.

[32] P. Montesinos, L. Ceze, and J. Torrellas. DeLorean: Recording and deterministically replaying shared-memory multiprocessor execution efficiently. In *Proceedings of the 2008 International Symposium on Computer Architecture*, pages 289–300, June 2008.

[33] S. Narayanasamy, C. Pereira, and B. Calder. Recording shared memory dependencies using Strata. In *ASPLOS-XII: Proceedings of the 12th International Conference on Architectural Support for Programming Languages and Operating Systems*, pages 229–240, 2006.

[34] S. Narayanasamy, C. Pereira, H. Patil, R. Cohn, and B. Calder. Automatic logging of operating system effects to guide application-level architecture simulation. In *International Conference on Measurements and Modeling of Computer Systems (SIGMETRICS)*, pages 216–227, June 2006.

[35] G. C. Necula, S. McPeak, S. P. Rahul, and W. Weimer. Cil: Intermediate language and tools for analysis and transformation of c programs. In *Proceedings of the 11th International Conference on Compiler Construction*, CC '02, pages 213–228, 2002.

[36] E. B. Nightingale, D. Peek, P. M. Chen, and J. Flinn. Parallelizing security checks on commodity hardware. In *Proceedings of the 13th International Conference on Architectural Support for Programming Languages and Operating Systems*, pages 308–318, Seattle, WA, March 2008.

[37] M. Olszewski, J. Ansel, and S. Amarasinghe. Kendo: efficient deterministic multithreading in software. In *Proceedings of the 2009 International Conference on Architectural Support for Programming Languages and Operating Systems (ASPLOS)*, pages 97–108, March 2009.

[38] S. Park, Y. Zhou, W. Xiong, Z. Yin, R. Kaushik, K. H. Lee, and S. Lu. PRES: Probabilistic replay with execution sketching on multiprocessors. In *Proceedings of the 22nd SOSP*, pages 177–191, October 2009.

[39] P. Pratikakis, J. S. Foster, and M. Hicks. Locksmith: Practical static race detection for c. *ACM Trans. Program. Lang. Syst.*, 33:3:1–3:55, January 2011.

[40] M. Ronsse and K. De Bosschere. RecPlay: A fully integrated practical record/replay system. *ACM Transactions on Computer Systems*, 17 (2):133–152, May 1999.

[41] R. Rugina and M. Rinard. Symbolic bounds analysis of pointers, array indices, and accessed memory regions. In *Proceedings of the ACM SIGPLAN 2000 conference on Programming language design and implementation*, PLDI '00, pages 182–195, New York, NY, USA, 2000.

[42] R. Rugina and M. C. Rinard. Symbolic bounds analysis of pointers, array indices, and accessed memory regions. *ACM Trans. Program. Lang. Syst.*, 27:185–235, March 2005.

[43] M. Russinovich and B. Cogswell. Replay for concurrent nondeterministic shared-memory applications. In *Proceedings of the ACM SIGPLAN 1996 Conference on Programming Language Design and Implementation*, pages 258–266, 1996.

[44] S. Srinivasan, C. Andrews, S. Kandula, and Y. Zhou. Flashback: A light-weight extension for rollback and deterministic replay for software debugging. In *Proceedings of the 2004 USENIX Technical Conference*, pages 29–44, Boston, MA, June 2004.

[45] B. Steensgaard. Points-to analysis in almost linear time. In *Proceedings of the 23rd ACM SIGPLAN-SIGACT symposium on Principles of programming languages*, POPL '96, pages 32–41, New York, NY, USA, 1996.

[46] N. Sterling. Warlock: A static data race analysis tool. pages 97–106, 1993.

[47] J. Tucek, S. Lu, C. Huang, S. Xanthos, and Y. Zhou. Triage: Diagnosing production run failures at the user's site. In *Proceedings of the 21st ACM Symposium on Operating Systems Principles*, pages 131–144, October 2007.

[48] uclib.org. uClibc, a C library for embedded Linux. `http://uClibc.org`.

[49] K. Veeraraghavan, D. Lee, B. Wester, J. Ouyang, P. M. Chen, J. Flinn, and S. Narayanasamy. DoublePlay: Parallelizing sequential logging and replay. In *Proceedings of the 16th International Conference on Architectural Support for Programming Languages and Operating Systems*, Long Beach, CA, March 2011.

[50] J. W. Voung, R. Jhala, and S. Lerner. Relay: static race detection on millions of lines of code. In *Proceedings of the the 6th joint meeting of the European software engineering conference and the ACM SIGSOFT symposium on The foundations of software engineering*, pages 205–214, Dubrovnik, Croatia, 2007.

[51] D. Weeratunge, X. Zhang, and S. Jagannathan. Analyzing multicore dumps to facilitate concurrency bug reproduction. In *Proceedings of the 2010 International Conference on Architectural Support for Programming Languages and Operating Systems (ASPLOS)*, pages 155–166, March 2010.

[52] R. P. Wilson and M. S. Lam. Efficient context-sensitive pointer analysis for c programs. In *Proceedings of the ACM SIGPLAN 1995 conference on Programming language design and implementation*, PLDI '95, pages 1–12, New York, NY, USA, 1995.

[53] S. C. Woo, M. Ohara, E. Torrie, J. P. Singh, and A. Gupta. The SPLASH-2 programs: Characterization and methodological considerations. In *Proceedings of the 22nd International Symposium on Computer Architecture*, pages 24–36, June 1995.

[54] M. Xu, R. Bodik, and M. D. Hill. A "flight data recorder" for enabling full-system multiprocessor deterministic replay. In *Proceedings of the 2003 International Symposium on Computer Architecture*, pages 122–135, June 2003.

[55] M. Xu, V. Malyugin, J. Sheldon, G. Venkitachalam, and B. Weissman. ReTrace: Collecting execution trace with virtual machine deterministic replay. In *Proceedings of the 2007 Workshop on Modeling, Benchmarking and Simulation (MoBS)*, June 2007.

[56] C. Zamfir and G. Candea. Execution synthesis: A technique for automated software debugging. In *Proceedings of the European Conference on Computer Systems*, pages 321–334, April 2010.

Static Analysis and Compiler Design for Idempotent Processing

Marc de Kruijf Karthikeyan Sankaralingam Somesh Jha
University of Wisconsin – Madison
{dekruijf,karu,jha}@cs.wisc.edu

Abstract

Recovery functionality has many applications in computing systems, from speculation recovery in modern microprocessors to fault recovery in high-reliability systems. Modern systems commonly recover using checkpoints. However, checkpoints introduce overheads, add complexity, and often save more state than necessary.

This paper develops a novel compiler technique to recover program state without the overheads of explicit checkpoints. The technique breaks programs into *idempotent regions*—regions that can be freely re-executed—which allows recovery without checkpointed state. Leveraging the property of idempotence, recovery can be obtained by simple re-execution. We develop static analysis techniques to construct these regions and demonstrate low overheads and large region sizes for an LLVM-based implementation. Across a set of diverse benchmark suites, we construct idempotent regions close in size to those that could be obtained with perfect runtime information. Although the resulting code runs more slowly, typical performance overheads are in the range of just 2-12%.

The paradigm of executing entire programs as a series of idempotent regions we call *idempotent processing*, and it has many applications in computer systems. As a concrete example, we demonstrate it applied to the problem of compiler-automated hardware fault recovery. In comparison to two other state-of-the-art techniques, redundant execution and checkpoint-logging, our idempotent processing technique outperforms both by over 15%.

Categories and Subject Descriptors D.3.4 [*Programming Languages*]: Processors—code generation, compilers

General Terms Algorithms, Design, Performance, Reliability

Keywords Idempotent processing, idempotent regions

1. Introduction

Recovery capability is a fundamental component of modern computer systems. It is used to recover from branch misprediction and out-of-order execution [33, 38], hardware faults [32, 34], speculative memory-reordering in VLIW machines [13, 18], optimistic dynamic binary translation and code optimization [11, 14], and transactional memory [17, 28]. In each of these cases, recovery is used to repair the state of the program in the rare event that an execution failure (i.e. a fault or mis-speculation) occurs.

Checkpoints provide a conceptually simple solution, and have strong commercial precedent [11, 32, 37]. However, checkpoints are problematic for several reasons. First, software checkpoints often have high performance overhead and hence, to maintain reasonable performance, hardware support is often necessary. This hardware support, however, forces interdependencies between processor structures, occupies space on the chip, and entails recurring energy expenditure regardless of failure occurrence. Particularly for emerging massively parallel and mobile processor designs, the per-core hardware support comes at a premium, while the recovery support may be desirable only under specific or rare circumstances. Hardware checkpointing resources are also rarely exposed to software, and are even less often configurable in terms of their checkpointing granularity, limiting their wider applicability. Finally, checkpoints have limited application visibility and are often overly aggressive in saving more state than is required by the application [9, 27].

To combat these difficulties, *idempotence*—the property that re-execution is free of side-effects—has been previously proposed as an alternative to checkpoints. In contrast to explicit checkpoints, idempotence allows the architecture state at the beginning of a code region to be used as an implicit checkpoint that is never explicitly saved or restored. In the event of an execution failure, idempotence is used to correct the state of the system by simple re-execution.

Over the years, idempotence has been both explicitly and implicitly employed as an alternative to checkpoints. Table 1 classifies prior work in terms of its application domain and the level at which idempotence is used and identified [2, 9, 10, 12, 16, 19, 21, 23, 25, 31, 36]. One of the earliest uses is by Mahlke *et al.* in using restartable instruction sequences for exception recovery in speculative processors [23]. More recently, Hampton and Asanović apply idempotence to support virtual memory on vector machines [16], Tseng and Tullsen apply idempotence to support data-triggered parallel thread execution [36], and Feng *et al.* leverage idempotence for low-cost hardware fault recovery [12]. As the table shows, idempotence has historically been applied only under specific domains such as exception recovery and multithreading, often only under restricted program scope, and often using only limited or no static analysis.

In this paper, we develop an analysis framework to enable each of the above uses (and others yet to be invented), irrespective of their application domain and their underlying purpose, and across entire programs. In particular, we develop static analysis techniques and a compilation strategy to statically partition programs into large idempotent regions. We develop a provably correct region partitioning algorithm, demonstrate a working compiler implementation, and demonstrate application to at least one specific problem domain. We bring together the somewhat disparate uses listed in

PLDI'12, June 11–16, 2012, Beijing, China.

Technique name	Application domain	Program scope	Idempotence discovery technique
Sentinel scheduling [23]	Speculative memory re-ordering	Speculative code regions	Register-level compiler analysis
Fast mutual exclusion [2]	Uniprocessor mutual exclusion	Atomicity primitives	Programmer inspection
Multi-instruction retry [21]	Branch mispredictions and faults	Whole program	Compiler antidependence analysis
Atomic heap transactions [31]	Memory allocation	Garbage collector	Programmer inspection
Reference idempotency [19]	Reducing speculative storage	Non-parallelizable code	Memory-level compiler analysis
Restart markers [16]	Virtual memory in vector machines	Loops and vector code	Compiler loop analysis
Relax [9]	Hardware fault recovery	Selected code regions	Programmer inspection
Data-triggered threads [36]	Data-triggered multi-threading	Selected code regions	Programmer inspection
Idempotent processors [10]	Processor simplification	Whole program	Unspecified compiler analysis
Encore [12]	Hardware fault recovery	Selected code regions	Compiler interval analysis
iGPU [25]	GPU exceptions and speculation	Whole GPU program	PTX-specific compiler analysis

Table 1. Uses of fine-grained idempotence in hardware and software design (in chronological order).

Table 1 and unify them under a single paradigm we call *idempotent processing*, which allows the synthesis of multiple such uses in a single system or implementation artifact.

In brief, our approach operates as follows. First, we note that using a conventional compiler, idempotent regions are typically small. Our static analysis eliminates the compilation artifacts responsible for these small idempotent region sizes by identifying regions in a function that are *semantically* idempotent. These regions are then compiled in such a way that no artifacts are introduced and the idempotence property is preserved throughout code generation. To do this, the compiler limits register and stack memory re-use, which reduces locality and thereby introduces runtime overhead. However, typical overheads are in the range of just 2-12%.

In exchange for these overheads, our analysis partitions a function into regions that are close in size to the largest regions that would be constructed given near-perfect runtime information. We show that the problem of finding very large idempotent regions can be cast as a vertex multicut problem, a problem known to be NP-complete in the general case. We apply an approximation algorithm and a heuristic that incorporates loop information to optimize for dynamic behavior and find that overall region sizes are in most cases close to ideal. Overall, we make the following contributions:

- We perform a detailed analysis of idempotent regions in conventional programs and quantitatively demonstrate that conventional compilers artificially inhibit the sizes of the idempotent regions in programs, severely limiting their usefulness.
- We develop static analysis and compiler techniques to preserve the inherent idempotence in applications and construct large idempotent regions. We formulate the problem of finding idempotent regions as a graph cutting (vertex multicut) problem and optimize for runtime behavior using a heuristic that incorporates loop information.
- We present a detailed characterization of our idempotent regions, which can be applied in the context of the various uses previously proposed in the literature.
- We demonstrate our idempotent processing solution applied to the problem of recovery from transient faults in microprocessors. Our idempotence-based recovery implementation performs over 15% better than two competing state-of-the-art compiler-automated recovery techniques.

The remainder of this paper is organized as follows. Section 2 gives a complete overview of this paper. Section 3 presents a quantitative study of idempotent regions as they exist inherently in application programs. Section 4 presents our idempotent region construction algorithm. Section 5 gives details of our compiler implementation. Section 6 presents our quantitative evaluation. Section 7 presents related work. Finally, Section 8 concludes.

2. Overview

This section provides a complete overview of this paper. We define idempotence in terms of data dependences and present a motivating example that illustrates how data dependences can inhibit idempotence. We show how these data dependences can be manipulated to grow the sizes of idempotent regions and give an overview of our partitioning algorithm that attempts to maximize the sizes of these regions. Finally, we describe how statically-identified idempotence can be used to recover from a range of dynamic execution failures.

2.1 Identifying Idempotent Regions

A region of code (assume a linear sequence of instructions for now) is idempotent if the effect of executing the region multiple times is identical to executing it only a single time. Intuitively, this behavior is achieved if the region does not overwrite its inputs. With the same inputs, the region will produce the same outputs. If a region overwrites its inputs, it reads the overwritten values when it re-executes, changing its behavior.

A variable is an input to a region if it is *live-in* to the region. Such a variable has a definition that reaches the region's entry point and has a corresponding use of that definition after the region entry point. Below, we use this observation to derive a precise definition of idempotence in terms of data dependences. We use the term *flow dependence* to refer to a read-after-write (RAW) dependence and the term *antidependence* to refer to a write-after-read (WAR) dependence.

By definition, a live-in variable has a flow dependence that spans the region's entry point. Because the variable's definition must come before the entry to the region, the definition is not inside the region, and hence there is no definition that precedes the first use of that variable inside the region. Hence, *a live-in has no flow dependence before the first use of that variable inside the region.* Since a live-in has no flow dependence, overwriting a live-in must occur after the point of the use. Thus, *an overwritten live-in has an antidependence after the absence of a flow dependence.* It follows that a region of code is idempotent *if it contains no antidependences not preceded by a flow dependence.*

The table below shows three statement sequences involving a variable x and uses the above definition to identify whether the sequences are idempotent or not:

	RAW	RAW→WAR	WAR
Sequence	**x** = 5 y = **x**	**x** = 5 y = **x** **x** = 8	y = **x** **x** = 8
Idempotent?	Yes	Yes	*No*

The antidependence after no flow dependence chain that breaks the idempotence property as shown on the right we call a *clobber*

```
1  typedef struct {
2    int *buf;  // buffer
3    int  size; // num elements
4    int  cap;  // capacity
5  } list_t;
6
7  extern list_t *other_list;
8
9  void list_push(list_t *list,
10                int      elem)
11 {
12   // check for overflow
13   int overflow =
14       (list->size == list->cap);
15
16   // if overflow use other list
17   if (overflow)
18     list = other_list;
19
20   // insert at end of list
21   list->buf[list->size] = elem;
22   list->size++;
23
24   return;
25 }
```

(a) A non-idempotent C function

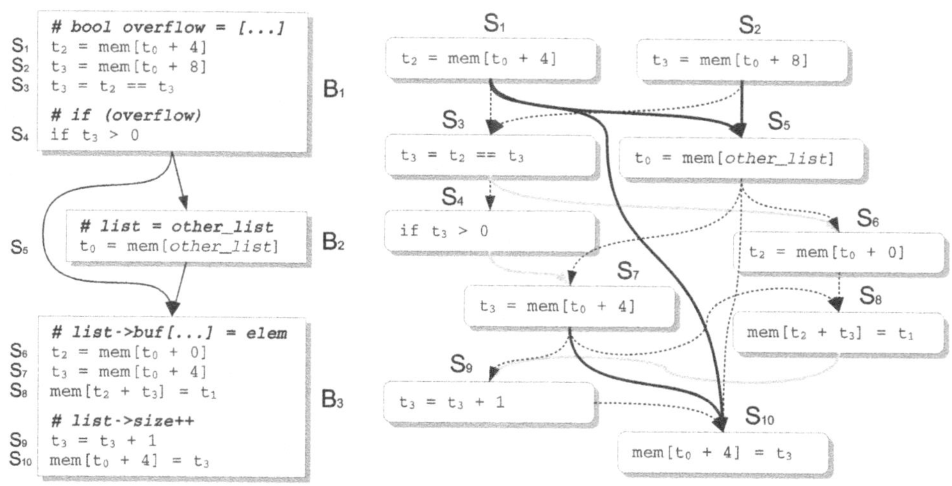

(b) The control flow graph and compiler intermediate code

(c) A subset of the data dependence graph, showing flow dependences (dashed), clobber antidependences (solid dark), and non-clobber antidependences (solid light)

Figure 1. An example illustrating how clobber antidependences inhibit idempotence.

antidependence. Some clobber antidependences are strictly necessary according to program semantics. These clobber antidependences we label *semantic* clobber antidependences. The other clobber antidependences we label *artificial* clobber antidependences. The following example demonstrates semantic and artificial clobber antidependences.

A motivating example. For the remainder of this section, we use the C function shown in Figure 1(a) as a running example. The function, `list_push`, checks a list for overflow and then pushes an integer element onto the end of the list. The semantics of the function clearly preclude idempotence: even if there is no overflow, re-executing the function will put the element onto the end of the already-modified list, after the copy that was pushed during the original execution. As we will show, the source of the non-idempotence is the increment of the input variable `list->size` on line 22: without this increment, re-execution would simply cause the value that was written during the initial execution to be safely overwritten with the same value.

Figure 1(b) shows the function compiled to a load-store intermediate representation. The figure shows the control flow graph of the function, which contains three basic blocks B_1, B_2, and B_3. Inside each block are shown the basic operations, S_i, and the use of pseudoregisters, t_i, to hold operands and read and write values to and from memory. Figure 1(c) shows the program dependence graph of the function focusing only on flow dependences (dashed) and antidependences (solid). The antidependences are further distinguished as clobber antidependences (dark) and not clobber antidependences (light)[1]. The figure shows four clobber antidependences: $S_1 \rightarrow S_5$, $S_2 \rightarrow S_5$, $S_1 \rightarrow S_{10}$, and $S_7 \rightarrow S_{10}$. The first two clobber antidependences depend on S_5, which overwrites the pseudoregister t_0, and the second two depend on S_{10}, which overwrites the memory location at $t_0 + 4$.

The two clobber antidependences that depend on S_5 are unnecessary: they are *artificial* clobber antidependences. We can eliminate these clobber antidependences simply by writing to a different pseudoregister. Figure 2 shows the effect of replacing t_0 in S_5

[1] For simplicity, we assume the pointer argument `list`, the global `other_list`, and their respective buffer arrays are known not to alias.

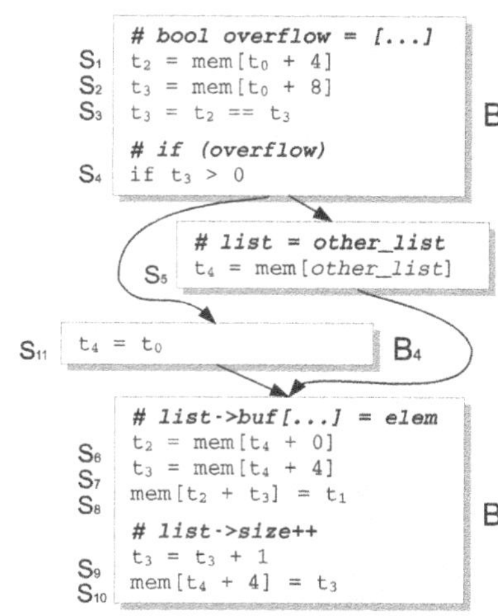

Figure 2. Renaming t_0 in S_5 to t_4.

with a new pseudoregister t_4. All uses of t_0 subsequent to S_5 are renamed to use t_4 as well, and a new statement S_{11} is inserted that moves t_0 into t_4 along the path where S_5 is not executed. S_{11} is placed inside a new basic block B_4 which bridges B_1 and B_3. A compiler can then permanently eliminate these artificial clobber antidependences by ensuring that t_4 and t_0 are not assigned to the same physical register or the stack slot during register allocation. If they are, then t_4 will overwrite t_0 and the two clobber antidependences will simply re-emerge. To do this, the register allocator can be constrained such that all pseudoregisters that are live-in to the region are also marked as live-out to the region. This enables idempotence in exchange for some additional register pressure.

The final two clobber antidependences write to the memory location $t_0 + 4$ in S_{10}, which corresponds with the store of the `list->size` increment on line 22 of Figure 1(a). Unfortunately, the destination of this store is fixed by the semantics of the program: if we didn't increment this variable, then the function would not increase the size of the list, which would violate the semantics of the function. Because we cannot legally rename the store destination, we label these clobber antidependences *semantic* clobber antidependences.

Summary. Table 2 summarizes the differences between semantic and artificial clobber antidependences. Semantic clobber antidependences act on heap, global, and non-local stack memory, which we hereafter often refer to as just "memory". These memory locations are not under the control of the compiler; they are specified in the program itself and cannot be re-assigned. In contrast, artificial clobber antidependences act on "pseudoregister" locations: registers and local stack memory. These resources are compiler controlled, and assuming effectively infinite stack memory, can be arbitrarily re-assigned. While in practice stack memory is limited, our compiler does not grow the size of the stack significantly and we have no size-related difficulties compiling any benchmarks.

2.2 Constructing Idempotent Regions

Assuming we can eliminate all artificial clobber antidependences, we show in Section 3 that the idempotent regions that exist in application programs are potentially very large. However, the problem of statically constructing large idempotent regions remains surprisingly non-trivial. In principle, the problem should be as simple as merely identifying and constructing regions that contain no semantic clobber antidependences. However, this solution is circularly dependent on itself: identifying semantic clobber antidependences requires identification of region live-in variables, which in turn requires identification of the regions. This circular dependence is illustrated below:

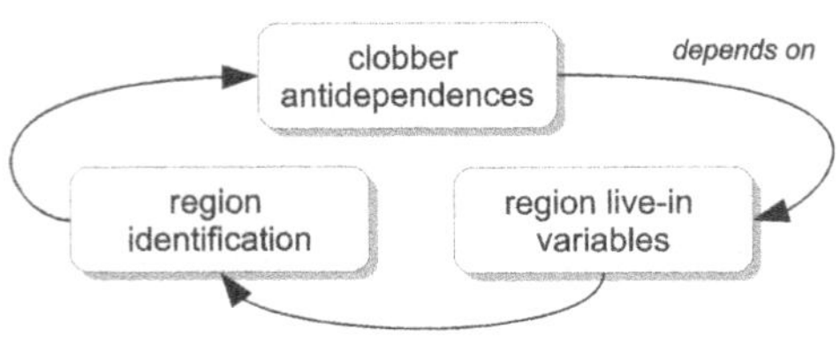

Our solution to this problem is to transform the function so that, with the exception of self-dependent pseudoregister antidependences[2], *all antidependences are necessarily semantic clobber antidependences.* We then construct idempotent regions by identifying regions that contain no antidependences. Antidependence information does not depend on region live-in information, and hence the circular dependence chain is broken. During this process, self-dependent pseudoregister antidependences are optimistically assumed not to emerge as clobber antidependences; those that would emerge as clobber antidependences after the region construction are patched in a subsequent refinement step.

Considering only antidependence information, we show that the problem of partitioning the program into idempotent regions is equivalent to the problem of "cutting" the antidependences, such that a cut before statement S starts a new region at S. In this manner, no single region contains both ends of an antidependence and hence the regions are idempotent. To maximize the region sizes, we cast the problem in terms of the NP-complete vertex multicut problem and use an approximation algorithm to find the minimum set of cuts, which finds the minimum set of regions. This maximizes the average static region size, and we then employ heuristics to maximize the sizes of regions as they occur dynamically at runtime. We refer to the overall algorithm as our *idempotent region construction algorithm.* In Section 4 we describe the algorithm in detail and in Section 5 we discuss the specifics of our implementation.

[2] These are antidependences that occur across loop iterations and have assignments of the form $t_i = f(t_i)$).

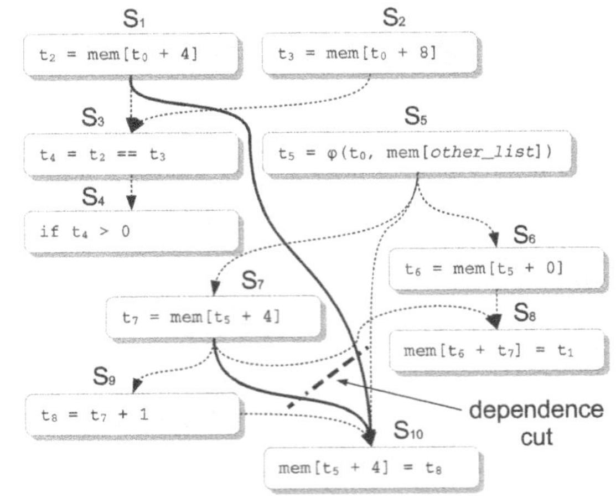

Figure 3. The data dependence graph in SSA form.

Figure 3 shows our algorithm applied to our running example. The initial step in the process is the conversion of all pseudoregister assignments to static single assignment (SSA) form [8]. The figure shows the dependence graph of Figure 1(c) simplified by the SSA transformation. The code structure is the same as in Figure 1(b) except that an SSA ϕ-node is placed at the head of B_3. The ϕ-node we label S_5 and we fold the original S_5 into it. Under SSA, the artificial clobber antidependences disappear and the semantic ones remain. Both semantic clobber antidependences write to memory location mem[t_5 + 4] in statement S_{10}, one with a may-alias read in statement S_1 and the other with a must-alias read in statement S_7. In general, the problem of finding the best places to cut the antidependences is NP-complete. However, for this simple example the solution is straightforward: it is possible to place a single cut that cuts both antidependences. The cut can be placed before S_8, S_9, or S_{10}. Regardless of where the cut is placed, the function is ultimately divided into three idempotent regions in total: under our initial definition of a region as a linear instruction sequence, depending on the outcome of the control decision inside the function, two linear sequences exist up to the point of the cut, and after the cut there is one additional sequence.

2.3 Using Idempotence for Recovery

In this section, we address how statically-identified idempotence can be used to recover from dynamic execution failures. This is not obvious because an execution failure may have side-effects that can corrupt arbitrary state. For instance, as a result of microprocessor branch misprediction or due to a hardware soft error, a region's inputs may be accidentally modified, or state that is outside the scope of the current region may be modified (resulting in problems for other regions).

Tolerating control flow errors. We first consider the possibility of incorrect control flow, which can arise due to e.g. a branch misprediction and can cause an incorrectly executed region to overwrite an input of the correct region or its succeeding regions.

Fortunately, tolerating control flow errors is relatively straightforward with our method of placing region boundaries using cuts. First, we observe that each control flow path from a given cut C to any subsequent cut constitutes an idempotent region, and hence any incorrect execution *belongs to an idempotent region with the same entry point at C as the region of the correct execution.* Hence, by compiling in such a way that the inputs of *all* regions starting at C are preserved between C and all subsequent cut points, execution can be made idempotent regardless of control flow.

Type of Clobber Antidependence	Storage Resources
Semantic clobber antidependence	Heap, global, non-local stack memory ("memory")
Artifial clobber antidependence	Registers and local stack memory ("pseudoregisters")

Table 2. Semantic and artificial clobber antidependences and the resources on which they operate.

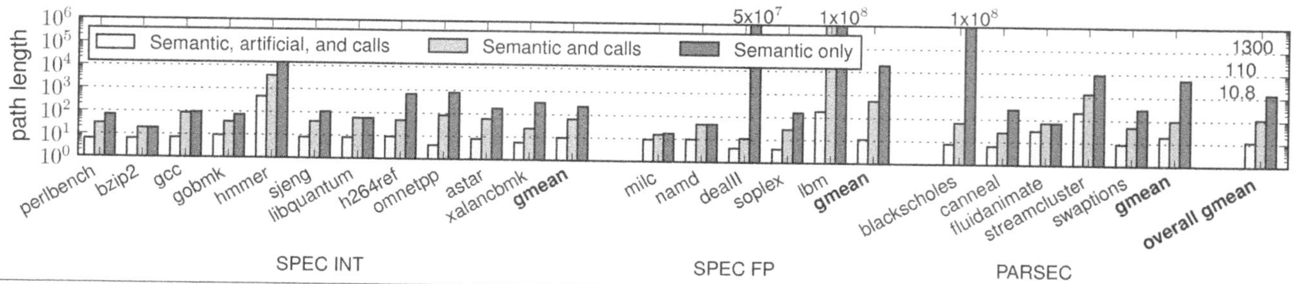

Figure 4. Average dynamic idempotent region sizes in the limit (y-axis is log-scale).

At this point, we rework our definition of idempotent region to achieve this property. Our previous definition of a region as an instruction sequence we now label more precisely as an *idempotent path*, and we redefine an idempotent region as a collection of idempotent paths that share the same entry point. (Thus, a *region* is a subset of a program's control flow graph with a single unique entry point and multiple possible exit points, and a *path* is a trace of instructions from such a region's entry point to one of its exit points.) An idempotent region preserves idempotence regardless of control flow by considering as inputs the collective inputs of all its containing paths. Unfortunately, however, it is now no longer possible to say that an input is necessarily overwritten only after the point of a read, as in the definition of idempotence in terms of a clobber antidependences; with this definition of region, a live-in may be written before it is read along an incorrect control flow path. This forces a more conservative compiler analysis.

For registers and stack memory, the impact of this conservative analysis is manageable and the static analysis and compiler implementation we describe in this paper preserves pseudoregister inputs regardless of control flow. However, for other types of storage—namely, heap, global, and non-local stack memory—we find the compiler's limited control over these resources too constricting. In particular, with the possibility for differing control flow on re-execution, an idempotent region would not be able to contain a store to a given address unless such a store occurred along all paths through the region. Thus, for memory we assume that stores are buffered and not released until control flow has been verified. We propose to re-use the store buffer that already exists in modern processors for this purpose. This allows us to reason about inputs from non-local memory more optimistically in terms of clobber antidependences, considering separately each path through an idempotent region. Considering our modified definition of a region, the first two idempotent paths (formerly, "regions") in the example of Figure 1 merge as one idempotent region.

Tolerating arbitrary errors. While the situation with hardware soft errors may appear much more dire, in practice techniques like error-correcting codes (ECC) can effectively protect existing memory and register state, leaving instruction execution itself as the only possible source of error. Since idempotence already precludes overwriting input state, regardless of whether the value written is corrupted or not, only three additional requirements are needed: (1) instructions must write to the correct register destinations, (2) execution must follow the program's static control flow edges, and (3) as with branch misprediction, stores must be buffered until they are verified. Altogether, these four total mechanisms—ECC, register destination verification, control flow verification, and store verification—are widely assumed in prior work on error recovery in software [6, 9, 21], and a variety of compatible hardware and software techniques have been previously developed [5, 24, 29, 30].

Recovering non-idempotent instructions. Finally, we note that some instructions such as certain memory-mapped I/O operations and some types of synchronization instructions are inherently non-idempotent. In this work, we consider such non-idempotent instructions as single-instruction idempotent regions that either terminate correctly or have no side-effects that make it unsafe for them to be re-executed for recovery.

3. Exploring the Potential: A Limit Study

To understand how much artificial clobber antidependences inhibit idempotent region sizes, we performed a limit study to ascertain the nature of the clobber dependences that emerge during program execution. Our goal is to understand the extent to which it would be possible to construct idempotent regions given perfect runtime information.

Methodology. We used the gem5 simulator [4] to measure the lengths of the idempotent paths that dynamically execute through a region across a range of benchmarks compiled for the ARMv7 instruction set. For each benchmark, we measured the distribution of path lengths occurring over a 100 million instruction period starting after the setup phase of the application. We evaluated two benchmark suites: SPEC 2006 [35], a suite targeted at conventional single-threaded workloads, and PARSEC [3], a suite targeted at emerging multi-threaded workloads.

We use a conventional optimizing compiler to generate program binaries, and measure idempotent path length optimistically as the number of instructions between dynamic occurrences of clobber antidependences. This optimistic (dynamic) measurement is used in the absence of explicit (static) region markings in these conventionally-generated binaries. We study idempotent regions divided by three different categories of clobber antidependences: (1) only semantic clobber antidependences, (2) only semantic clobber antidependences with regions split at function call boundaries, and (3) both semantic and artificial clobber antidependences with regions split at function call boundaries.

We consider as artificial clobber antidependences all clobber antidependences on registers and those with writes relative to the stack pointer, which are universally register spills for our compiler.

These are the clobber antidependences that can generally be eliminated by renaming pseudoregisters and careful register and stack slot allocation. We assume the remaining clobber antidependences are all semantic. We consider separately regions divided by semantic clobber antidependences that cross function call boundaries to understand the potential improvements of an inter-procedural compiler analysis over an intra-procedural one. To explore what is achievable in the inter-procedural case, we optimistically assume that call frames do not overwrite previous call frames. We also optimistically ignore antidependences that necessarily arise due to the calling convention (e.g. overwriting the stack pointer) and assume the calling convention can be redefined or very aggressive inlining can be performed such that this obstacle is weakened or removed.

Results and conclusions. Our experimental results, shown in Figure 4, identify three clear trends. First, we see that regions divided by both artificial and semantic clobber antidependences are much smaller than those divided by semantic clobber antidependences alone. The geometric mean path length considering both types is 10.8 instructions, while the length considering just semantic clobber antidependences is 110 instructions intra-procedurally (a 10x gain) and 1300 inter-procedurally (a 120x gain).

The second trend is a substantial gain (more than 10x) from allowing idempotent regions divided by semantic clobber antidependences to cross function boundaries. However, the gains are not reliably as large as the 10x gain achieved by removing the artificial clobber antidependences alone: the difference drops to only 4x when we drop the two outliers dealII and blackscholes.

The third and final trend is that path lengths tend to be larger for PARSEC and SPEC FP than for SPEC INT. PARSEC and SPEC FP benchmarks tend to overwrite their inputs relatively infrequently due to their memory streaming and compute-intensive nature.

Overall, we find that (1) there is a lot of opportunity to grow idempotent region sizes by eliminating artificial clobber antidependences, (2) an intra-procedural static analysis is a good starting point for constructing large idempotent regions, and (3) the greatest opportunity appears to lie with streaming and compute-intensive applications.

4. Region Construction Algorithm

In this section, we describe our idempotent region construction algorithm. The algorithm is an intra-procedural compiler algorithm that divides a function into idempotent regions. First, we describe the transformations that allow us to cast the problem of constructing idempotent regions in terms of cutting antidependences. Second, we describe the core static analysis technique for cutting antidependences, including optimizations for dynamic behavior. Finally, we describe our register and stack slot allocation to preserve the idempotence of our identified regions through code generation.

4.1 Program Transformation

Before we apply our static analysis, we first perform two code transformations to maximize the efficacy of the analysis. The two transformations are (1) the conversion of all pseudoregister assignments to static single assignment (SSA) form, and (2) the elimination of all memory antidependences that are not clobber antidependences. The details on why and how are given below.

The first transformation converts all pseudoregister assignments to SSA form. After this transformation, each pseudoregister is only assigned once and all artificial clobber antidependences are effectively eliminated (self-dependent artificial clobber antidependences, which manifest in SSA through ϕ-nodes at the head of loops, still remain, but it is safe to ignore them for now). The intent of this transformation is to expose primarily the semantic antidependences to the compiler. Unfortunately, among these antidependences we still do not know which are clobber antidependences and which are not, since, as explained in Section 2.2, this determination is circularly dependent on the region construction we are trying to achieve. Without knowing which antidependences will emerge as clobber antidependences, we do not know which antidependences must be cut to form the regions. Hence, we attempt to refine things further.

before	*after*
`1. mem[x] = a`	`1. mem[x] = a`
`2. b = mem[x]`	`2. b = a`
`3. mem[x] = c`	`3. mem[x] = c`

Figure 5. Eliminating non-clobber memory antidependences.

After the SSA transformation, it follows that the remaining antidependences are either self-dependent antidependences on pseudoregisters or antidependences on memory locations. For those on memory locations, we employ a transformation that resolves the aforementioned ambiguity regarding clobber antidependences. The transformation is a simple redundancy-elimination transformation illustrated by Figure 5. The sequence on the left has an antidependence on memory location x that is not a clobber antidependence because the antidependence is preceded by a flow dependence. Observe that in all such cases the antidependence is made redundant by the flow dependence: assuming both the initial store and the load of x "must alias" (if they only "may alias" we must conservatively assume a clobber antidependence) then there is no reason to reload the stored value since there is an existing pseudoregister that already holds the value. The redundant load is eliminated as shown on the right of the figure: the use of memory location x is replaced by the use of pseudoregister a and the antidependence disappears.

Unfortunately, there is no program transformation that resolves the uncertainty for self-dependent pseudoregister antidependences. In the following section, we initially assume that these antidependences can be register allocated such that they do not become clobber antidependences (i.e. we can precede the antidependence with a flow dependence on its assigned physical register or stack slot). Hence, we construct regions around them, considering only the known, memory-level clobber antidependences. After the construction is complete, we check to see if our assumption holds. If not, we insert additional region cuts as necessary.

4.2 Static Analysis

After our program transformations, our static analysis constructs idempotent regions by "cutting" all potential clobber antidependences in a function. The analysis consists of two parts. First, we construct regions based on semantic antidependence information by cutting memory-level antidependences and placing region boundaries at the site of the cuts. Second, we further divide loop-level regions as needed to accommodate the remaining self-dependent pseudoregister clobber antidependences.

4.2.1 Cutting Memory-Level Antidependences

To ensure that a memory-level antidependence is not contained inside a region, it must be split across the boundaries between regions. Our algorithm finds the set of splits, or "cuts", that creates the smallest number of these regions. In this section, we derive our algorithm as follows:

1. We define our problem as a graph decomposition that must satisfy certain conditions.
2. We reduce the problem of finding an optimal graph decomposition to the minimum vertex multicut problem.

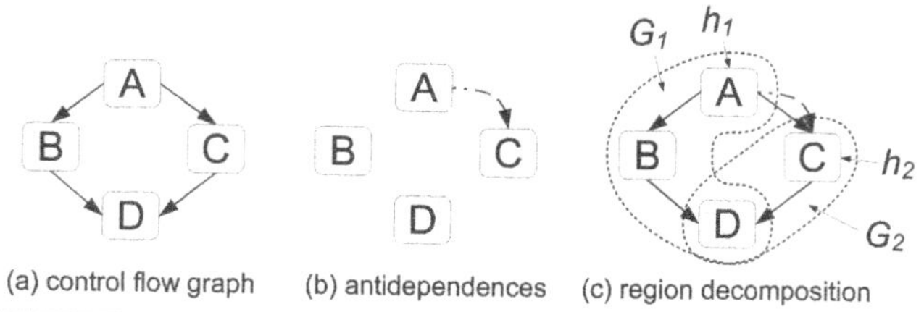

Figure 6. An example region decomposition.

3. To generate a solution, we formulate the problem in terms of the hitting set problem.
4. We observe that a near-optimal hitting set can be found efficiently using an approximation algorithm.

Problem definition. For a control flow graph $G = (V, E)$ we define a region as a sub-graph $G_i = (V_i, E_i, h_i)$ of G, where $h_i \in V_i$ and all nodes in V_i are reachable from h_i through edges in E_i. We call h_i the *header node*[3] of G_i. A *region decomposition* of the graph G is a set of sub-graphs $\{G_1, \cdots, G_k\}$ that satisfies the following conditions:

- each node $v \in V$ is in at least one sub-graph G_i,
- the header nodes for the sub-graph are distinct (for $i \neq j$, $h_i \neq h_j$), and
- no antidependence edge is contained in a sub-graph G_i for $1 \leq i \leq k$.[4]

Our problem is to decompose G into the smallest set of sub-graphs $\{G_1, \cdots, G_k\}$. Figure 6 gives an example. Figure 6(a) shows a control flow graph G and 6(b) shows the set of antidependence edges in G. Figure 6(c) shows a possible region decomposition for G. The shown region decomposition happens to be optimal; that is, it contains the fewest possible number of regions.

Reduction to vertex multicut. We now reduce the problem of finding an optimal region decomposition with the problem of finding a minimum vertex multicut.

Definition 1. (Vertex multicut) Let $G = (V, E)$ be a directed graph with set of vertices V and edges E. Assume that we are given pairs of vertices $A \subseteq V \times V$. A subset of vertices $H \subseteq V$ is called a *vertex multicut* for A if in the subgraph G' of G where the vertices from H are removed, for all ordered pairs $(a, b) \in A$ there does not exist a path from a to b in G'.

Let $G = (V, E)$ be our control flow graph, A the set of antidependence edge pairs in G, and H a vertex multicut for A. Each $h_i \in H$ implicitly corresponds to a region G_i as follows:

- The set of nodes V_i of G_i consists of all nodes $v \in V$ such that there exists a path from h_i to v that *does not* pass through a node in $H - \{h_i\}$.
- The set of edges E_i is $E \cap (V_i \times V_i)$.

It follows that a *minimum* vertex multicut $H = \{h_1, \cdots, h_k\}$ directly corresponds to an optimal region decomposition $\{G_1, \cdots, G_k\}$ of G over the set of antidependence edge pairs A in G.

[3] Note that, while we use the term *header node*, we do not require that a header node h_i dominates all nodes in V_i as defined in other contexts [1].

[4] This condition is stricter than necessary. In particular, an antidependence edge in G_i *with no path connecting the edge nodes*—implying that the the antidependence is formed over a loop revisiting G_i—is safely contained in G_i. However, determining the absence of such a path requires a path-sensitive analysis. We limit our solution space to path-insensitive analyses.

Solution using hitting set. The vertex multicut problem is NP-complete for general directed graphs [15]. To solve it, we reduce it to the hitting set problem, which is also NP-complete, but for which good approximation algorithms are known [7].

Definition 2. (Hitting set) Given a collection of sets $C = \{S_1, \cdots, S_m\}$, a *minimum hitting set* for C is the smallest set H such that, for all $S_i \in C$, $H \cap S_i \neq \emptyset$.

Note that we seek a set $H \subseteq V$ such that, for all $(a_i, b_i) \in A$, all paths π from a_i to b_i have a vertex in H (in other words, H is a "hitting set" of $\Pi = \cup_{(a_i,b_i)\in A}\pi_i$, where π_i is the set of paths from a_i to b_i). This formulation is not computationally tractable, however, as the number of paths between any pair (a_i, b_i) can be exponential in the size of the graph. Instead, for each $(a_i, b_i) \in A$, we associate a single set $S_i \subseteq V$ that consists of the set of nodes that dominate b_i but do not dominate a_i. We then compute a hitting set H over $C = \{S_i | S_i \text{ for } (a_i, b_i) \in A\}$. Using Lemma 1 it is easy to see that for all antidependence edges $(a_i, b_i) \in A$, every path from a_i to b_i passes through a vertex in H. Hence, H is both a hitting set for C and a vertex multicut for A.

We use a greedy approximation algorithm for the hitting set problem that runs in time $O(\sum_{S_i \in C} |S_i|)$. This algorithm chooses at each stage the vertex that intersects the most sets not already intersected. This simple greedy heuristic has a logarithmic approximation ratio [7] and is known to produce good quality results.

Lemma 1. Let $G = (V, E, s)$ be a directed graph with entry node $s \in V$ and (a, b) be a pair of vertices. If $x \in V$ dominates b but does not dominate a, then every path from a to b passes through x.

Proof: We assume that a pair of vertices (a, b) are both reachable from the entry node s. Let the following conditions be true.

- **Condition 1:** There exists a path from (a, b) that does not pass through the node x.
- **Condition 2:** There exists a path from s to a that does not pass through x.

If conditions 1 and 2 are true, then there exists a path from s to b that does not pass through x. This means x cannot dominate b. In other words, conditions 1 and 2 imply that x cannot dominate b.

Given that x dominates b, one of the conditions 1 and 2 must be false. If condition 1 is false, we are done. If condition 2 is false, then x dominates a, which leads to a contradiction. □

4.2.2 Cutting Self-Dependent Pseudoregister Antidependences

After memory antidependences have been cut, we have a preliminary region decomposition over the function. From here, we consider the remaining category of clobber antidependences—the self-dependent pseudoregister antidependences—and allocate them in such a way that they do not emerge as clobber antidependences.

In SSA form, a self-dependent pseudoregister antidependence manifests as a write occurring at the point of a ϕ-node assignment, with one of the ϕ-node's arguments data-dependent on the assigned pseudoregister itself. Due to SSA's dominance properties, such self-dependent pseudoregister assignments alway occur at the head of loops. Figure 7(a) provides a very simple example. Note that in the example the self-dependent "antidependence" is actually two antidependences, $S_1 \rightarrow S_2$ and $S_2 \rightarrow S_1$. We refer to it as only a single antidependence for ease of explanation.

To prevent self-dependent pseudoregister antidependences from emerging as clobber antidependences, the invariant we must enforce is that a loop containing such an antidependence either contains no cuts or contains at least two cuts along all paths through the loop body. If either of these conditions is already true, no modi-

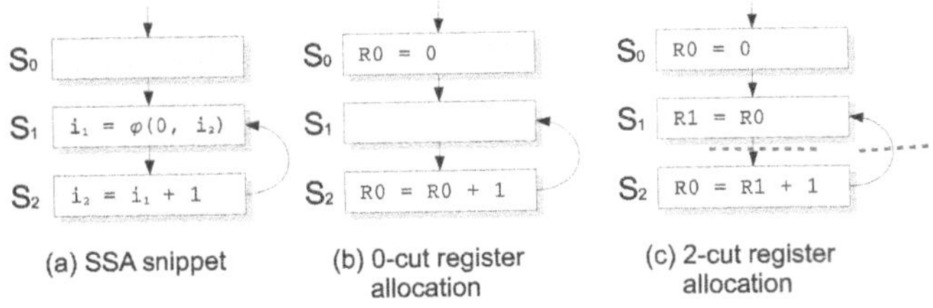

Figure 7. Clobber-free allocation of self-dependent pseudoregister antidependences.

fication to the preliminary region decomposition is necessary. Otherwise, we insert additional cuts such that the second condition becomes true. The details on why and how are provided below.

Case 1: A loop with no cuts. Consider the self-dependent antidependence shown in Figure 7(a). For a loop that contains no cuts, this antidependence can be trivially register allocated as shown in Figure 7(b). In the figure, we define the register (which could also be a stack slot if registers are scarce) of the antidependence outside the loop and hence across all loop iterations all instances of the antidependence are preceded by a flow dependence.

Case 2: A loop with at least 2 cuts. A self-dependent antidependence for a loop that contains at least two cuts can also be trivially-register allocated as shown in Figure 7(c). Here the antidependence is manipulated into two antidependences, one on R0 and one on R1, and the antidependences are placed so that they straddle region boundaries. Note that, for this to work, at least two cuts must exist along *all paths* through the loop body. This is obviously true in Figure 7(c) but in the general case it may not be.

Case 3: Neither case 1 or 2. In the remaining case, the self-dependent antidependence is in a loop that contains at least one cut but there exist one or more paths through the loop body that do not cross at least two cuts. In this case, we know of no way to register allocate the antidependence such that it does not emerge as a clobber antidependence. Hence, we resign ourselves to cutting the antidependence so that we have at least two cuts along all paths in the loop body, as in Case 2. This produces a final region decomposition resembling Figure 7(c).

4.3 Optimizing for Dynamic Behavior

Our static analysis algorithm optimizes for static region sizes. However, when considering loops, we know that loops tend to execute multiple times. We can harness this information to grow the sizes of the dynamic paths that execute through our regions at runtime.

We account for loop information by incorporating a simple heuristic into the hitting set algorithm from Section 4.2.1. In particular, we adjust the algorithm to greedily choose cuts at nodes from the outermost loop nesting depth first. We then break ties by choosing a node with the most sets not already intersected as normal. This improves the path lengths substantially in general, although there are cases where it reduces them. A better heuristic most likely weighs both loop nesting depth and intersecting set information more evenly, rather than unilaterally favoring one. Better heuristics are a topic for future work.

4.4 Code Generation

With the idempotent regions constructed, the final challenge is to code generate—specifically, register and stack allocate—the function so that artificial clobber antidependences are not re-introduced.

To do this, we constrain the register and stack memory allocators such that all pseudoregisters that are live-in to a region are also live-out to the region. This ensures that all registers and stack slots that contain input are not overwritten and hence no new clobber antidependences emerge.

5. Compiler Implementation

We implemented the region construction algorithm of Section 4 using LLVM [20]. Each phase of the algorithm is implemented as described below.

Code transformation. Of the two transformations described in Section 4.1, the SSA code transformation is automatic as the LLVM intermediate representation itself is in SSA form. We implement the other transformation, which removes all non-clobber memory antidependences, using an existing LLVM redundancy elimination transformation pass.

Cutting memory-level antidependences. We gather memory antidependence information using LLVM's "basic" alias analysis infrastructure. The antidependence cutting is implemented exactly as described in Section 4.2.1.

Cutting self-dependent pseudoregister antidependences. We handle self-dependent register antidependences as in Section 4.2.2 with one small enhancement: before inserting cuts, we attempt to unroll the containing loop once if possible. The reason is that inserting cuts increases the number of idempotent regions and thereby reduces the size of the loop regions. By unrolling the loop once, we can place the second necessary cut in the unrolled iteration. This effectively preserves region sizes on average. It also improves the performance of the register allocator by not requiring the insertion of extra copy operations between loop iterations (enabling a form of double buffering).

Optimizations for dynamic behavior. We optimize for dynamic behavior exactly as described in Section 4.3.

Code generation. We extend LLVM's register allocation passes to generate machine code as described in Section 4.4. To maintain the calling convention, functions that contain only a single region are split into two regions to allow parameter values to be overwritten by return values as necessary.

6. Evaluation

For evaluation, we first present the characteristics (region sizes and runtime overhead) produced by our idempotent region construction across a range of applications. We then present results evaluating our technique for recovery from transient hardware faults.

6.1 Methodology

We evaluate benchmarks from the SPEC 2006 [35] and PARSEC [3] benchmark suites. We compile each benchmark to two different binary versions: an *idempotent binary*, compiled using our idempotent region construction implemented in LLVM; and an *original binary*, generated using the regular optimized LLVM compiler flow.

Our performance results are obtained for the ARMv7 instruction set simulating a modern two-issue processor using the gem5 simulator [4]. To account for the differences in instruction count between the idempotent and original binary versions, simulation length is measured in terms of the number of functions executed, which is constant between the two versions. All benchmarks are fast-forwarded the number of function calls needed to execute at least 5 billion instructions on the original binary, and execution is then simulated for the number of function calls needed to execute 100 million additional instructions on the original binary.

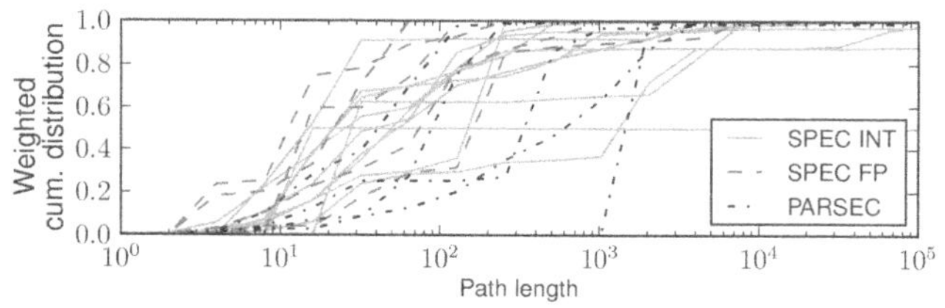

Figure 8. Distribution of idempotent path lengths.

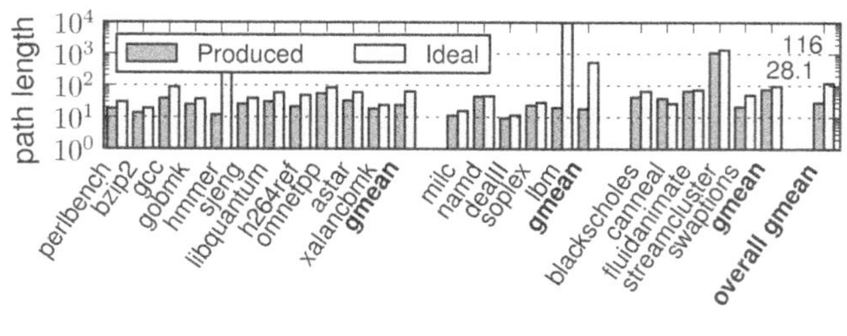

Figure 9. Average idempotent path lengths.

6.2 Idempotent Region Characteristics

Region sizes and path lengths. An important characteristic of our region construction is the size of the idempotent regions it statically produces. More important, however, is the length of the paths that dynamically execute through the idempotent regions at runtime. In general, longer path lengths are better for two reasons. The first has to do with runtime overhead: in the limit as path length approaches infinity, the relative cost to preserve a region's live-in state approaches zero. In the worst case, all live state must be pushed to the stack before the region's start, and this fixed maximum cost is amortized over the region's execution. The second reason has to do with detection latencies: longer path lengths allow execution to proceed speculatively for longer amounts of time while potential (but presumably unlikely) execution failures remain undetected.

In practice, however, optimal path length (and hence, region size) depends on a variety of factors. These factors include the effects of register pressure, aggravated by divergent control flow as regions grow beyond a small set of basic blocks (for reasons relating to potentially incorrect control flow as described in Section 2.3). Hence, larger regions are not always better. Additionally, while longer path lengths better tolerate long detection latencies, minimizing the recovery re-execution cost favors shorter path lengths. This is important particularly when failures are relatively frequent, as with e.g. branch prediction. In future work, we plan to explore this optimization space in detail. For this work, we aim to produce the longest possible paths, observing that path lengths are often easily reduced as needed to suit application demands.

Figure 8 plots the cumulative distribution (weighted by execution time) of the dynamic path lengths executed through our idempotent regions across the SPEC and PARSEC benchmark suites (in the interest of space, applications from the same suite are not individually labeled). The figure shows, for instance, that most applications spend less than 20% of their execution time executing paths of length 10 instructions or less. The figure also shows that path length distributions are highly application dependent. Generally, the PARSEC applications tend to have a wider, more heavy-tailed distribution, while SPEC FP applications have a narrower, more regular distribution. SPEC INT has applications in both categories.

Figure 9 shows the average length of our idempotent paths compared to those measured as ideal in the limit study from Section 3 (the ideal measurement is for "semantic and calls"—intra-procedural regions divided by dynamic semantic clobber antidependences). Our geometric mean path length across all benchmarks is roughly 4x less than the ideal (28.1 vs. 116). Two benchmarks, hmmer and lbm, have much longer path lengths in the ideal case. This is due to limited aliasing information in the region construction algorithm; with small modifications to the source code that improve aliasing knowledge, longer path lengths can be achieved. If we ignore these two outliers, the difference narrows to roughly 1.5x (30.2 vs. 44.9; not shown).

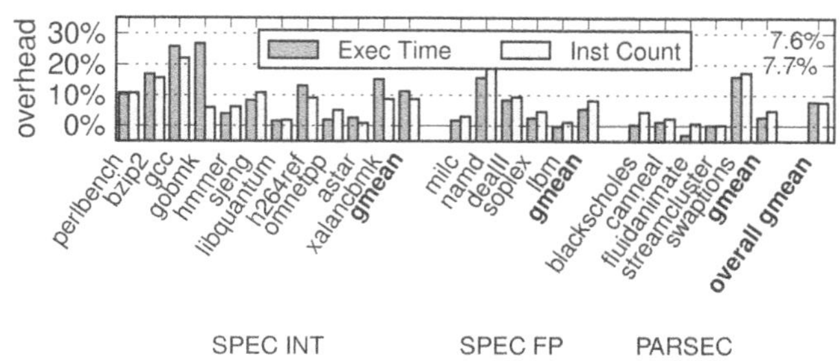

Figure 10. Execution time and instruction count overheads.

Runtime overheads. Forcing the register allocator to preserve input state across an idempotent region adds overhead because the allocator may not re-use live-in register or stack memory resources. Instead, it may need to allocate additional stack slots and spill more registers than might otherwise be necessary.

Figure 10 shows the percentage execution time and dynamic instruction count overheads. Across the SPEC INT, SPEC FP, and PARSEC benchmarks the geometric mean execution time overheads are 11.2%, 5.4%, and 2.7%, respectively (7.7% overall), These overheads are closely tracked by the increase in the dynamic instruction count: 8.7%, 8.2%, and 4.8% for SPEC INT, SPEC FP, and PARSEC, respectively (7.6% overall).

The one case where execution time overhead and instruction count overhead are substantially different is for gobmk, which has a 26.7% execution time overhead but only a 5.9% instruction count overhead. For this particular benchmark, some code sequences that were previously efficiently expressed using ARM predicated execution transform to regular control flow due to liveness constraints, resulting in more control flow sensitivity. Additionally, most of the added instructions are load and store (spill and refill) instructions, which have longer latency than regular move instructions.

For other applications, the differences mostly trend along the nature of the fundamental data type—floating point or integer. Integer applications such as those from SPEC INT tend to have higher execution time overheads because ARM has fewer general purpose registers than floating point registers (16 vs. 32). Hence, these applications are more reliant on register spills and refills to preserve liveness. In contrast, floating point benchmarks such as SPEC FP and PARSEC have many more available registers. Additionally, the comparatively long path lengths of PARSEC benchmarks tend to allow better register re-use since the cost of pushing live-ins to the stack is amortized over a longer period of time.

6.3 Idempotence-Based Recovery

Our compiler implementation and static analysis are general and span entire programs, and hence they can be used in the context of prior works using idempotence such as those presented in Table 1. As a concrete example, however, we consider the case for software-only recovery from transient hardware faults (soft errors). We evaluate against two other compiler-based recovery techniques, and for all techniques assume compiler-based error detection using

DMR Baseline

```
check(r0 != r0')
ld  r1  = [r0]
ld  r1' = [r0]
add r2  = r3 , r4
add r2' = r3', r4'
check(r1 != r1')
check(r2 != r2')
st [r1] = r2
```

INSTRUCTION-TMR

```
majority(r0, r0', r0'')
ld  r1   = [r0]
ld  r1'  = [r0]
ld  r1'' = [r0]
add r2   = r3  , r4
add r2'  = r3' , r4'
add r2'' = r3'', r4''
majority(r1, r1', r1'')
majority(r2, r2', r2'')
st [r1] = r2
```

CHECKPOINT-AND-LOG

```
br recvr, r0 != r0'
ld  r1  = [r0]
ld  r1' = [r0]
add r2  = r3 , r4
add r2' = r3', r4'
br recvr, r1 != r1'
br recvr, r2 != r2'
ld  tmp  = [r1]
ld  tmp' = [r1]
br recvr, tmp != tmp'
br recvr, lp  != lp'
st [lp] = tmp
st [lp + 8] = r1
add lp  = lp  + 16
add lp' = lp' + 16
st [r1] = r2
```

load old value at destination address

store old value and address to log

advance log pointer

IDEMPOTENCE

```
retry:
 mov rp = {retry}
 ...
 jmp rp, r0 != r0'
 ld  r1  = [r0]
 ld  r1' = [r0]
 add r2  = r3 , r4
 add r2' = r3', r4'
 jmp rp, r1 != r1'
 jmp rp, r2 != r2'
 st [r1] = r2
```

Figure 11. Three software recovery techniques on top of instruction-level DMR. Changes over original load-add-store sequence in bold.

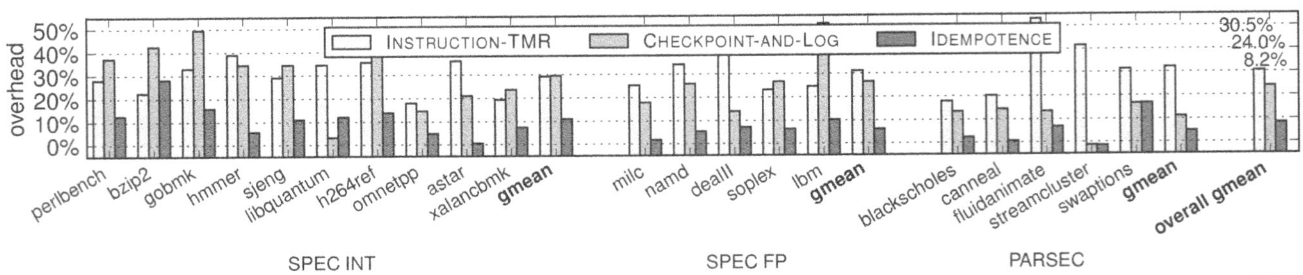

Figure 12. Overhead of three software recovery techniques relative to the DMR baseline.

instruction-level dual-modular redundancy (DMR). The DMR uses detection at load, store, and control flow boundaries, as previously proposed by Reis *et al.* [29] and Oh *et al.* [26]. We assume registers and memory are protected by ECC; thus, errors arise through instruction execution alone. Figure 11 illustrates the behavior of each recovery alternative.

The first recovery technique, INSTRUCTION-TMR, implements TMR at the instruction level. Our implementation attempts to replicate the work of Chang *et al.* [6], which adds a third copy of each non-memory instruction and use majority voting before load and store instructions to detect and correct failures. We support the majority voting as a single-cycle operation.

The second technique, CHECKPOINT-AND-LOG, is an implementation of software logging similar to logging in software transactional memory systems [17]. Before every store instruction, the value to be overwritten is loaded and written to a log along with the store address, and the pointer into the log (assigned a dedicated register, `lp`) is incremented. In our implementation, as the log fills, the log is reset and a register checkpoint is taken, which starts a new checkpointing interval. We assume a 16KB log size (1K stores per checkpoint interval) with intelligent periodic polling for log overflow using a technique similar to that proposed by Li and Fuchs [22]. In our simulations, all log traffic writes through the L1 cache, and we optimistically assume that both the register checkpointing and periodic polling contribute no runtime overhead.

The final technique, IDEMPOTENCE, is our idempotence-based recovery technique. Here, as each idempotent region boundary is encountered, its address is written to the register `rp`. In the event that a fault is detected, execution jumps to the address contained in `rp` (the use of a register to hold the restart address is necessary to handle potentially overlapping control flow between regions).

Results. Figure 12 presents results comparing the overhead of the three techniques relative to performance of the underlying DMR. Across all benchmarks, INSTRUCTION-TMR performs worst with 30.5% geometric mean performance overhead, CHECKPOINT-AND-LOG has 24.0% overhead, and IDEMPOTENCE performs best with only 8.2% overhead.

Compared to INSTRUCTION-TMR, CHECKPOINT-AND-LOG performs worse for applications with frequent memory interactions, such as several SPEC INT applications, but better for all other applications where its per-instruction overheads are lower. Overall, IDEMPOTENCE outperforms both techniques by a significant margin. It avoids the redundant operations added by INSTRUCTION-TMR to correct values in-place, and avoids the overheads associated with unnecessary logging in CHECKPOINT-AND-LOG. In particular, when logging only the first memory value written to a particular memory location is required to be logged. However, under CHECKPOINT-AND-LOG the occurrence of the first write is not statically known and cannot be efficiently computed at runtime. IDEMPOTENCE also preserves local stack memory more efficiently with its fully-integrated compile-time approach.

7. Related Work

The application of idempotence in compiler-based recovery has been previously explored, primarily in the context of exceptions and also hardware fault recovery. For exception recovery, Hampton and Asanović explore the use of idempotent regions for exception recovery in vector processors [16], De Kruijf and Sankaralingam use them for exception recovery in general purpose processors [10], and Mahlke *et al.* propose restartable (idempotent) instruction sequences under sentinel scheduling for exception recovery in VLIW processors [23]. For fault recovery, Feng *et al.* and De Kruijf *et al.* both explore mechanisms to opportunistically employ idempotence over code regions that together cover large parts—but not all parts—of a program. While De Kruijf *et al.* manually identify idempotent regions, Feng *et al.* identify them using a compiler interval analysis. We build upon this prior work and make several additional contributions: we develop a compiler analysis to uncover the minimal set of *semantically* idempotent regions across *entire* programs, we describe the algorithmic challenges in compiling for these regions, and we explore how they can be used to recover across a range of different types of execution failures.

In other related work, Shivers *et al.* [31] and Bershad [2] both explore using idempotence to achieve atomicity on uniprocessors. The work of Li *et al.* on compiler-based multiple instruction retry is also similar in that they breaks antidependences to create recoverable code regions [21]. However, they do so over a sliding window of the last N instructions rather than over static program regions. As such, they do not distinguish between clobber antidependences and other antidependences; all antidependences must be considered clobber antidependences over a sliding window since any flow dependence preceding an antidependence will eventually lie outside the window. Our use of static program regions allows for the construction of large recoverable regions with low overheads.

More general work on compiler-based recovery includes the work of Chang *et al.* on recovery of hardware transient faults at the granularity of single instructions using TMR on top of DMR [6]. Chang *et al.* also explore two partial recovery techniques in addition to TMR. However, for full recovery functionality, the overheads remain effectively the same as TMR, and our results show that idempotence-based recovery has potentially better performance than TMR. Finally, compilers have been proposed for coarse-grained, checkpoint-based recovery as well. Li and Fuchs study techniques for dynamic checkpoint insertion using a compiler [22]. To maintain the desired checkpoint interval, they periodically poll a clock to decide if a checkpoint should be taken.

8. Conclusion

The capability for fast and efficient recovery has applications in many domains, including microprocessor speculation, compiler speculation, and hardware reliability. Unfortunately, most prior software-based solutions typically have high performance overheads, particularly for fine-grained recovery, while hardware-based solutions involve substantial power and complexity overheads.

In this paper, we identified idempotence as a basic program property that can be used for general and efficient recovery in software. While it is intuitive that idempotence can be used to recover from execution failures with no visible side-effects (e.g. hardware exceptions), we showed how failures resulting in only incorrect control flow (e.g. branch misprediction) can also be supported in a straightforward manner. Additionally, we described how failures involving a wider range of side-effects (e.g. soft errors) can be recovered with a relatively small set of supporting mechanisms.

We demonstrated the potential for idempotence-based recovery by building a compiler that partitions programs into idempotent regions, enabling the paradigm of *idempotent processing*—execution in sequences of idempotent regions. We presented a static analysis that partitions applications into *semantically* idempotent regions and showed a compiler that generates code preserving the idempotence of these regions with low performance overhead (commonly less than 10%). As an example, we showed how our analysis and compiler can be used to recover from hardware transient faults efficiently, purely in software. However, our technique is general and applies to many other uses of idempotence as well.

While we demonstrated idempotence as a powerful primitive for program recovery, several questions remain for future research. First, while we showed that idempotent regions can be large, limited program knowledge sometimes inhibits region sizes unnecessarily. Better programmer aliasing information and/or the use of more declarative programming styles may allow the construction of much larger idempotent regions. Second, while we constructed these large regions in part as a first-order approximation towards minimizing performance overheads, in practice optimal region size depends on a variety of factors. An important topic of future work is to characterize the performance overheads based on such factors. Finally, future work exploring the applicability of idempotence with respect to specific failure scenarios will further help in understanding its full potential. Regardless of the outcomes to these questions, however, idempotent processing and the concept of semantic idempotence are likely to remain as valuable building blocks for use in future research on low-overhead software recovery solutions.

Acknowledgements

We thank the anonymous reviewers for comments and the Wisconsin Condor project and UW CSL for their assistance. Support for this research was provided by NSF under the following grant: CCF-0845751. Any opinions, findings, and conclusions or recommendations expressed in this material are those of the authors and do not necessarily reflect the views of NSF or other institutions.

References

[1] A. V. Aho, M. S. Lam, R. Sethi, and J. D. Ullman. *Compilers: Principles, Techniques, and Tools.* Addison Wesley, 2nd edition, 2007.

[2] B. N. Bershad, D. D. Redell, and J. R. Ellis. Fast mutual exclusion for uniprocessors. In *ASPLOS '92.*

[3] C. Bienia, S. Kumar, J. P. Singh, and K. Li. The PARSEC benchmark suite: Characterization and architectural implications. In *PACT '08.*

[4] N. Binkert, B. Beckmann, G. Black, S. K. Reinhardt, A. Saidi, A. Basu, J. Hestness, D. R. Hower, T. Krishna, S. Sardashti, R. Sen, K. Sewell, M. Shoaib, N. Vaish, M. D. Hill, and D. A. Wood. The gem5 simulator. *SIGARCH Comput. Archit. News*, 39:1–7, Aug. 2011.

[5] E. Borin, C. Wang, Y. Wu, and G. Araujo. Software-based transparent and comprehensive control-flow error detection. In *CGO '06.*

[6] J. Chang, G. A. Reis, and D. I. August. Automatic instruction-level software-only recovery. In *DSN '06.*

[7] T. H. Cormen, C. E. Leiserson, R. L. Rivest, and C. Stein. *Introduction to Algorithms.* The MIT Press, 2nd edition, 2001.

[8] R. Cytron, J. Ferrante, B. K. Rosen, M. N. Wegman, and F. K. Zadeck. An efficient method of computing static single assignment form. POPL '89.

[9] M. de Kruijf, S. Nomura, and K. Sankaralingam. Relax: An architectural framework for software recovery of hardware faults. In *ISCA '10*, 2010.

[10] M. de Kruijf and K. Sankaralingam. Idempotent processor architecture. In *MICRO '11.*

[11] J. C. Dehnert, B. K. Grant, J. P. Banning, R. Johnson, T. Kistler, A. Klaiber, and J. Mattson. The Transmeta code morphing software: Using speculation, recovery, and adaptive retranslation to address real-life challenges. In *CGO '03.*

[12] S. Feng, S. Gupta, A. Ansari, S. Mahlke, and D. August. Encore: Low-cost, fine-grained transient fault recovery. In *MICRO '11.*

[13] D. M. Gallagher, W. Y. Chen, S. A. Mahlke, J. C. Gyllenhaal, and W.-m. W. Hwu. Dynamic memory disambiguation using the memory conflict buffer. In *ASPLOS '94.*

[14] M. Gschwind and E. R. Altman. Precise exception semantics in dynamic compilation. In *CC '02.*

[15] J. Guo, F. HÃijffner, E. Kenar, R. Niedermeier, and J. Uhlmann. Complexity and exact algorithms for vertex multicut in interval and bounded treewidth graphs. *European Journal of Operational Research*, 186(2):542 – 553, 2008.

[16] M. Hampton and K. Asanović. Implementing virtual memory in a vector processor with software restart markers. In *ICS '06.*

[17] T. Harris, J. R. Larus, and R. Rajwar. *Transactional Memory.* Morgan & Claypool, 2nd edition, 2010.

[18] Intel. *Itanium Architecture Software Developer's Manual Rev. 2.3.* http://www.intel.com/design/itanium/manuals/iiasdmanual.htm.

[19] S. W. Kim, C.-L. Ooi, R. Eigenmann, B. Falsafi, and T. N. Vijaykumar. Exploiting reference idempotency to reduce speculative storage overflow. *ACM Trans. Program. Lang. Syst.*, 28:942–965, September 2006.

[20] C. Lattner and V. Adve. LLVM: A compilation framework for lifelong program analysis & transformation. In *CGO '04*.

[21] C.-C. J. Li, S.-K. Chen, W. K. Fuchs, and W.-M. W. Hwu. Compiler-based multiple instruction retry. *IEEE Transactions on Computers*, 44(1):35–46, 1995.

[22] C.-C. J. Li and W. K. Fuchs. CATCH – Compiler-assisted techniques for checkpointing. In *FTCS '90*.

[23] S. A. Mahlke, W. Y. Chen, W.-m. W. Hwu, B. R. Rau, and M. S. Schlansker. Sentinel scheduling for VLIW and superscalar processors. In *ASPLOS '92*.

[24] A. Meixner, M. E. Bauer, and D. J. Sorin. Argus: Low-cost comprehensive error detection in simple cores. *IEEE Micro*, 28(1):52–59, 2008.

[25] J. Menon, M. de Kruijf, and K. Sankaralingam. iGPU: exception support and speculative execution on GPUs. In *ISCA '12*, 2012.

[26] N. Oh, P. Shirvani, and E. McCluskey. Error detection by duplicated instructions in super-scalar processors. *Reliability, IEEE Transactions on*, 51(1):63 –75, March 2002.

[27] J. S. Plank, Y. Chen, K. Li, M. Beck, and G. Kingsley. Memory exclusion: Optimizing the performance of checkpointing systems. *Software – Practice & Experience*, 29(2):125–142, 1999.

[28] R. Rajwar and J. R. Goodman. Speculative lock elision: enabling highly concurrent multithreaded execution. In *MICRO '01*.

[29] G. Reis, J. Chang, N. Vachharajani, R. Rangan, and D. August. Swift: software implemented fault tolerance. In *CGO '05*.

[30] G. A. Reis, J. Chang, N. Vachharajani, R. Rangan, D. I. August, and S. S. Mukherjee. Design and evaluation of hybrid fault-detection systems. In *ISCA '05*, pages 148–159.

[31] O. Shivers, J. W. Clark, and R. McGrath. Atomic heap transactions and fine-grain interrupts. In *ICFP '99*.

[32] T. J. Slegel et al. IBM's S/390 G5 microprocessor design. *IEEE Micro*, 19(2):12–23, 1999.

[33] J. E. Smith and A. R. Pleszkun. Implementing precise interrupts in pipelined processors. *IEEE Transactions on Computers*, 37:562–573, May 1988.

[34] D. J. Sorin. *Fault Tolerant Computer Architecture*. Morgan & Claypool, 2009.

[35] Standard Performance Evaluation Corporation. *SPEC CPU2006*, 2006.

[36] H.-W. Tseng and D. Tullsen. Data-triggered threads: Eliminating redundant computation. In *HPCA '11*.

[37] K. C. Yeager. The MIPS R10000 superscalar microprocessor. *IEEE Micro*, 16(2):28–40, 1996.

[38] T.-Y. Yeh and Y. N. Patt. Two-level adaptive training branch prediction. In *MICRO '91*.

Effective Parallelization of Loops in the Presence of I/O Operations

Min Feng Rajiv Gupta Iulian Neamtiu

Department of Computer Science and Engineering
University of California, Riverside
{mfeng,gupta,neamtiu}@cs.ucr.edu

Abstract

Software-based thread-level parallelization has been widely studied for exploiting data parallelism in purely computational loops to improve program performance on multiprocessors. However, none of the previous efforts deal with efficient parallelization of *hybrid loops*, i.e., loops that contain a mix of computation and I/O operations. In this paper, we propose a set of techniques for efficiently parallelizing hybrid loops. Our techniques apply DOALL parallelism to hybrid loops by breaking the cross-iteration dependences caused by I/O operations. We also support speculative execution of I/O operations to enable speculative parallelization of hybrid loops. Helper threading is used to reduce the I/O bus contention caused by the improved parallelism. We provide an easy-to-use programming model for exploiting parallelism in loops with I/O operations. Parallelizing hybrid loops using our model requires few modifications to the code. We have developed a prototype implementation of our programming model. We have evaluated our implementation on a 24-core machine using eight applications, including a widely-used genomic sequence assembler and a multi-player game server, and others from PARSEC and SPEC CPU2000 benchmark suites. The hybrid loops in these applications take 23%–99% of the total execution time on our 24-core machine. The parallelized applications achieve speedups of 3.0x–12.8x with hybrid loop parallelization over the sequential versions of the same applications. Compared to the versions of applications where only computation loops are parallelized, hybrid loop parallelization improves the application performance by 68% on average.

Categories and Subject Descriptors D.3.2 [*Programming Languages*]: Language Constructs and Features – Concurrent programming structures

General Terms Languages, Performance

Keywords DOALL Parallelization, Speculative Parallelization, Helper Threading, I/O contention

1. Introduction

Uncovering parallelism is crucial for improving an application's performance on shared memory multiprocessors. Software-based thread-level parallelization has been widely studied for exploiting parallelism on multiprocessors. Many parallel programming models have been proposed to facilitate the development of parallel applications on shared memory multiprocessors. The shared-memory paradigm used by these programming models makes them easy-to-use for the programmer.

A majority of the parallel programming models (e.g., Threading Building Blocks [20], OpenMP [8], Galois [14], SpiceC [10]) focus on exploiting data parallelism in loops including DOALL, DOACROSS, pipelined, and speculatively parallelized loops. However, these programming models only target loops that contain pure computations, i.e., they are free of I/O operations. Since many applications contain loops with I/O operations, they fail to yield much speedup due to these loops still being sequential. Therefore, it is highly desirable to support parallel programming models which allow parallel execution of *hybrid loops*, i.e., loops with both computation and I/O operations. For example, `Velvet` [30] is a popular bioinformatics application. In its version 1.1 (i.e., the latest version when we conducted this work), 18 pure computation loops have been parallelized using OpenMP. However, since OpenMP lacks support for parallelizing loops with I/O operations, none of the hybrid loops in `Velvet` have been parallelized. Actually, `Velvet` has 39 hybrid loops, out of which 26 loops can be parallelized by the approach presented in this paper. These hybrid loops take a significant portion (27%–53%) of the total execution time in our experiments on a 24-core machine. Therefore, to further improve the performance of `Velvet`, developers must exploit the parallelism in hybrid loops. Interestingly, while we were writing this paper, the developers of `Velvet` were working independently on manually parallelizing the hybrid loops, which only confirms our observation of the need to parallelize hybrid loops.

In a few of the previous efforts [10, 26] where hybrid loops are parallelized, DOACROSS parallelism is used (i.e., synchronization is imposed to deal with cross-iteration dependences) even if the computation part of the loop can be performed using DOALL (i.e., no cross-iteration dependence in the computation part). However, DOACROSS execution is not as efficient as DOALL. Because DOACROSS execution assigns only one iteration per scheduling step, it results in significant synchronization and scheduling overhead. In addition, the speculation-based loop parallelization techniques proposed in these works are not applicable when the loop contains I/O operations. While the work on parallel I/O [22, 24, 25] provides a set of low-level techniques that change the I/O subsystem to improve the performance of multiple simultaneous I/O operations, it does not provide any means for programmers to parallelize hybrid loops.

In this paper, we propose compiler techniques for efficiently parallelizing *hybrid loops*, i.e., loops that contain I/O operations in addition to computation. Our techniques break the cross-iteration

PLDI'12, June 11–16, 2012, Beijing, China.

dependences involving I/O operations. Therefore, we are able to employ DOALL parallelism whenever there is no cross-iteration dependence in the computation part of the loop. Our techniques also support speculative execution of I/O operations to enable speculative parallelization of hybrid loops. We observe increased I/O bus contention with aggressive parallelization of hybrid loops. For performance scalability, we propose the use of helper threading to reduce the I/O bus contention. The helper thread enables the working threads to refill their input buffers and flush their output buffers so that the I/O traffic is spread out and not bursty. Unlike Parallel I/O work, our techniques do not require changes in the I/O subsystem.

We provide an easy-to-use programming model for exploiting parallelism in hybrid loops. The programming model contains two I/O related pragmas. Programmers can parallelize hybrid loops by merely inserting the pragmas preceding the loops in sequential code. Similarly, to enable speculative parallelization of hybrid loops, programmers just need to use one of the proposed pragmas at the beginning of the loop. Employing helper threading in parallel loops simply requires calling helper threading APIs preceding the loops.

We have developed a prototype implementation of our programming model. The core components of the implementation consist of a source-to-source translator and a user-level runtime library. We evaluate our implementation on a 24-core Dell PowerEdge R905 server using eight benchmarks from PARSEC [3] and SPEC CPU2000 benchmark suites, and two real applications. These benchmarks are parallelized via DOALL and speculative parallelism. Our implementation achieves 3.0x–12.8x speedup in these benchmarks. In comparison to the parallelized versions of benchmarks without hybrid loop parallelization, our technique improves the performance by 30% to 272%.

The rest of the paper is organized as follows. Section 2 illustrates our approach to parallelizing hybrid loops. Section 3 presents our programming model and its implementation. Section 4 presents the evaluation. Section 5 discusses related work and Section 6 concludes this paper.

2. Parallelizing Hybrid Loops

We begin by discussing the challenges in parallelizing hybrid loops and then describe our approach to overcoming these challenges. First, we discuss why existing techniques for DOALL parallelization and speculative loop parallelization cannot be directly applied if a loop also contains I/O operations. Our goal is to generalize these techniques so that they can be applied to hybrid loops. Second, we show that parallelization of hybrid loops can lead to I/O contention which must be effectively handled to realize the full benefits of parallelization.

Enabling DOALL Parallelization of Hybrid Loops. Figure 1(a) shows a typical loop with I/O operations that can be found in many applications (e.g., bzip2, parser [12], and stream encoder/decoder). Each loop iteration first checks if the end of the input file has been reached. If not, data is read from the file, computation on the data is performed, and finally results are written to the output file. When the computation within a loop does not involve cross-iteration dependences, maximum parallelism can be exploited via DOALL parallelization where all loop iterations can be executed in parallel. However, in a hybrid loop, even when the computation does not involve cross-iteration dependences, DOALL parallelization is not possible because the file read/write operations introduce cross-iteration dependences due to the movement (in our example, advancement) of the file pointer. In prior work, e.g., [10], such loops are parallelized using DOACROSS parallelism which incurs high scheduling and synchronization overhead—see Figure 1(b) for DOACROSS loop execution.

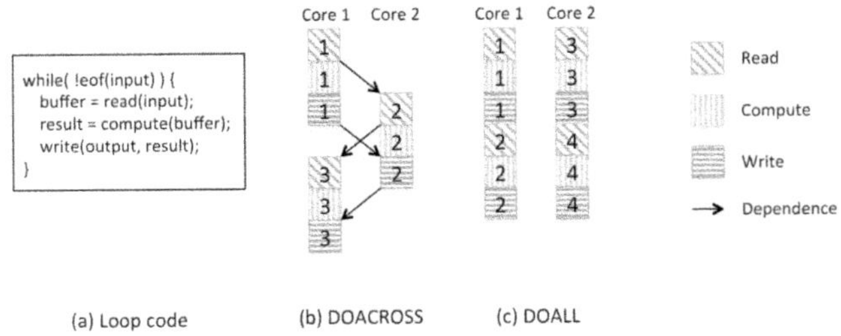

Figure 1. Execution of the loop example.

To fully exploit the parallelism in the loop, we need to find a way to break the cross-iteration dependences due to I/O operations. In this paper we develop solutions to enable DOALL parallelization which leads to the execution shown in Figure 1(c). With DOALL parallelization we can eliminate the synchronization between consecutive iterations and employ more efficient scheduling polices such as Guided Self Scheduling [17]. Figure 2 compares the performance of DOACROSS with the performance of DOALL on a microbenchmark constructed based on the example loop type. In the microbenchmark, the *compute* function is composed of a loop. We can adjust the ratio of I/O workload vs. computation workload by varying the loop size. The figure shows the performance comparison for both I/O-dominant workload and computation-dominant workload. In the I/O-dominant workload, the I/O calls take around 75% of the execution time of the sequential loop while in the computation-dominant workload the I/O calls take only 25% of the loop execution time. In both cases, DOALL performs better than DOACROSS, especially with large number of parallel threads. *Therefore, the first challenge addressed in this work is to efficiently parallelize hybrid loops by enabling DOALL parallelization.*

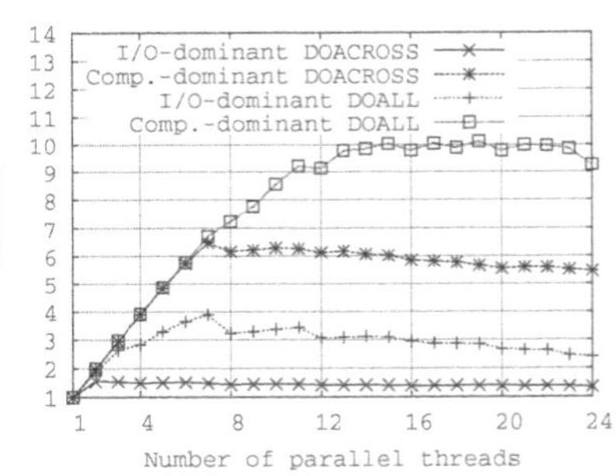

Figure 2. Performance comparison of DOACROSS and DOALL on the example loop.

Performing Speculative Parallelization of Hybrid Loops. Now let us consider the situation in which cross-iteration dependences exist in the computation part of the loop. We cannot perform DOALL parallelization of such loops even if we break the dependences introduced by I/O operations. Recent works have shown that an effective approach to handling cross-iteration dependences in the computation part is to employ speculative parallelization of loops. This approach is very effective when the cross-iteration dependences manifest themselves infrequently. Previous works [9, 26] have shown that speculative parallelization works better than non-speculative DOACROSS parallelization; however, these works also assume that the loops do not contain I/O operations. To apply speculative parallelization to the loops with I/O operations, we need to enable the speculative execution of the I/O

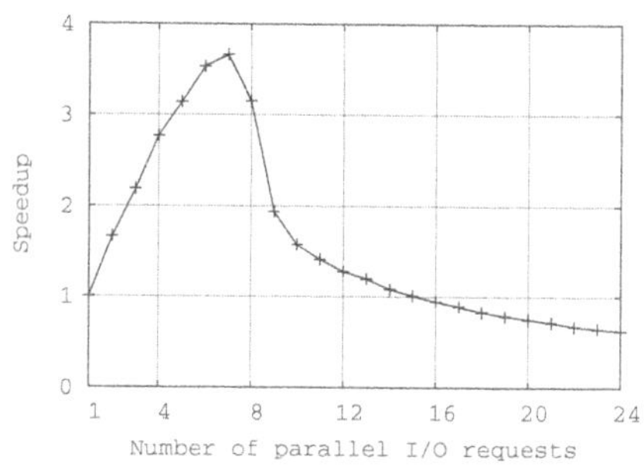

Figure 3. Performance of reading a 1 GB file using different numbers of parallel I/O requests.

operations. *Therefore, the second challenge of efficiently parallelizing hybrid loops is to develop solutions for speculative execution of I/O operations.*

I/O Contention due to Parallelization. Once DOALL and speculative parallelization of hybrid loops have been achieved, we are faced with yet another challenge. By increasing parallelism we also increase I/O bus contention. Figure 3 shows the performance of a microbenchmark that reads a 1 GB file from the disk. The microbenchmark creates multiple parallel threads, each of which then sends an I/O request to read a portion of the file. We varied the number of parallel threads (i.e., number of parallel I/O requests) to examine the impact of I/O bus contention. We can see that the I/O performance degrades quickly with more than 7 parallel I/O requests due to the I/O bus contention. With more than 16 parallel I/O requests, we actually get a slowdown compared to the performance with just one I/O request. Figure 2 also shows that the DOALL performance of the example loop degrades slightly with large number of parallel threads. *Therefore, to effectively parallelize hybrid loops, we must develop techniques for reducing I/O bus contention.*

2.1 DOALL Parallelization of Hybrid Loops

To apply DOALL parallelization to a hybrid loop we need to break the cross-iteration dependences introduced by the I/O operations in the loop. Our dependence-breaking strategies for input operations differ from those for output operations. Thus, we discuss them separately below.

Cross-iteration dependences caused by the input operations. These dependences arise because the starting file position for an iteration depends on the input operations performed in the previous iteration. The DOALL parallelization assigns each parallel thread a chunk of consecutive iterations for execution. Therefore to break the dependences we identify the starting file position corresponding to each parallel thread by directly calculating it before the execution of the loop. The method for computing the starting file positions depends upon the file access pattern used in the loop. Our examination of `Velvet` [30] and the programs in two benchmark suites, SPEC CPU 2000 and PARSEC [3], has identified three commonly-used file access patterns which are described next.

FSB: Fixed Size Blocks. The first access pattern, shown in Figure 4(a), is called the fixed-size blocks pattern as in this pattern each loop iteration reads a fixed-size block of data. The stride of the file pointer is equal to the size of the data block read by each iteration. Since we know the stride of the file pointer before entering the loop, we can easily calculate the size of data to be read by each parallel thread. Thus the starting file position of a parallel thread can be calculated by summing up the size of data to be read by previous parallel threads. Given the starting file position of each parallel thread, the time complexity of moving the file pointer to the starting file position via a *seek* operation is O(1).

FLS: Fixed Loop Size. In the second pattern, as shown in Figure 4(b), the loop first reads the total number of blocks from the file and then accesses one delimited block during each loop iteration. Since the blocks are of variable size, delimiters are used to separate them (e.g., in a text file, the delimiter is '\n'). From the total number of blocks, we can calculate the number of blocks, n, to be read by each parallel thread. Using a *scan* operation, we can locate the starting file position of parallel thread i by skipping $n * i$ occurrences of the delimiter. The time complexity is O(N), where N is the file size. This strategy is slow because it requires a *scan* as opposed to a *seek*.

FCS: Fixed Cumulative Size. In the third pattern, shown in Figure 4(c), each loop iteration accesses one delimited block that is encountered after skipping data blocks whose cumulative size reaches a given number. Because the data blocks are of variable size, delimiters are used to separate them. Since we know the total size of data to be read by the loop and the total number of parallel threads (T), we can locate the starting file position of parallel thread i by first skipping the i/T fraction of the data and then looking for the first occurrence of the delimiter. In this case, we actually assign equal amount of data instead of equal number of iterations to each parallel thread, which is different from typical DOALL parallelization. This strategy requires two operations—a *seek* and a *scan*. This *scan* is faster than the scan performed in *FLS* since it only scans to the first occurrence of the delimiter. The time complexity of this strategy is O(L), where L is the maximum length of a data block. This time complexity is much lower than that of assigning equal number of iterations to every thread—O(N), where N is the file size.

Cross-iteration dependences caused by the output operations. Simply computing the starting file position cannot help break cross-iteration dependences caused by output operations. This is because the calculated file position does not exist until all previous output operations have completed. Therefore, to break these dependences, we propose a different approach. We create an output buffer for each parallel thread. Each thread writes the outputs into its output buffer during the parallel execution of the loop. As a result, the output operations in one thread no longer depend on those in other threads. Flushing these buffers can be performed in parallel with the sequential code following the loop, as shown in Figure 5(a).

2.2 Speculative Parallelization of Hybrid Loops

Speculative parallelization is a way to efficiently exploit potential, but not guaranteed, parallelism in loops. Software speculative execution of non-I/O code has been studied in previous work [9, 26]. However, I/O operations cannot be executed speculatively in the same way because they use system calls. The code executed by the system calls is hidden from the compiler and runtime library, which thus cannot monitor the execution of system calls. Moreover, the results of I/O operations cannot be simply reversed once they are done. Therefore, to efficiently parallelize loops with I/O operations using speculative parallelism, we need support for speculative execution of I/O operations.

Speculative execution of input operations. Speculative execution of the input operations in each iteration is enabled by creating a copy of the file pointer at the start of each iteration and then using the copy to perform all input operations in the iteration. If speculation succeeds, the original file pointer is discarded and the copy is used in the subsequent iterations. If speculation fails, we simply discard the copy. One way of creating the copy is to instantiate a new file pointer and then *seek* to the current file position.

Speculative execution of output operations. Speculative execution of a loop iteration that contains output operations should satisfy the atomicity semantics, i.e., either all output operations occur or none occur. Therefore, the output operations in the loop iteration should not actually write to the file since that cannot be

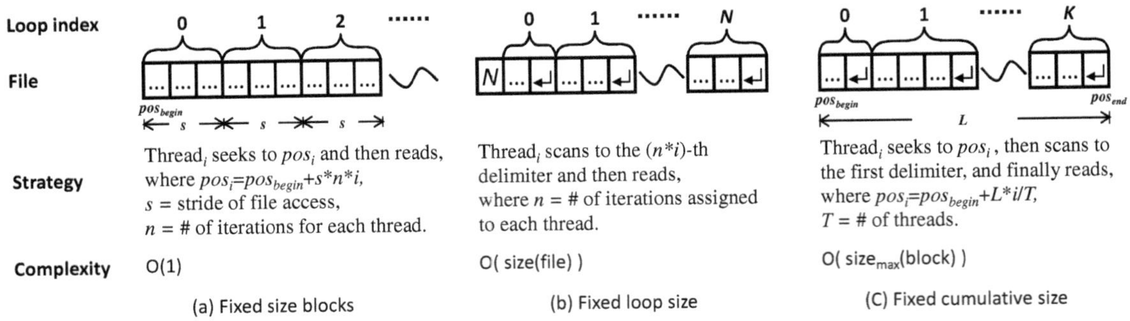

Figure 4. Commonly used file access patterns of loops and strategies for locating the starting file position for each parallel thread.

Programming constructs	Description
#pragma SpiceC parallel doall|doacross|pipelining	specify a parallel loop and the form of parallelism in which the loop is to be executed
#pragma SpiceC subregion [regionname] [after(iteration, region)]	specify a subregion in the parallel loop that is executed under the order specification
#pragma SpiceC commit [atomicity] [after(iteration, region)]	perform a commit operation with specified atomicity check and execution order

Table 1. SpiceC programming constructs.

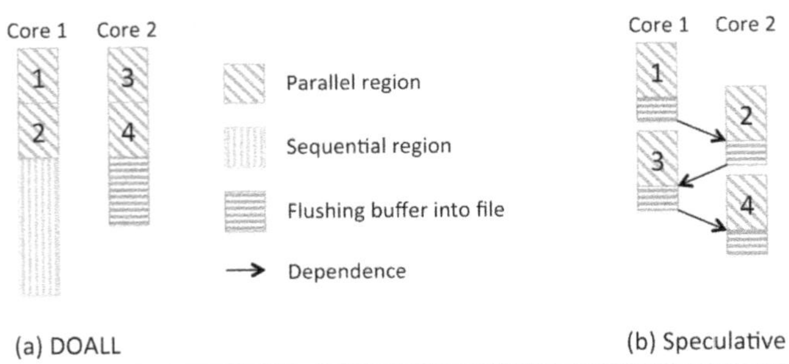

Figure 5. Strategies for flushing the output buffer.

reversed. Speculative execution of the output operations in an iteration can be realized by using the output buffering described in the previous section. If speculation succeeds, we keep the buffered output. If speculation fails, we simply discard the buffered output. We flush the output buffer at the end of each iteration as shown in Figure 5(b). Flushing the buffer at the end of each iteration requires small amount of memory since the buffer does not need to hold the outputs from the entire loop, but it incurs synchronization overhead because the flush operations need to be performed sequentially. The flush operation in an iteration needs to wait for the completion of the flush operation in the previous iteration as shown in Figure 5(b).

2.3 I/O Contention Reduction via Helper Threading

Parallelizing hybrid loops can lead to increased contention on the I/O bus. We propose the use of helper threading to reduce this I/O contention. Before entering a hybrid loop, we create a helper thread which monitors the file buffers of the associated file pointers and performs the following tasks. For an input file pointer, the helper thread refills the file buffer when the size of remaining data in the buffer is less than a predefined threshold. For an output file pointer, it flushes the file buffer when the size of buffered output is larger than a predefined threshold. The use of a helper thread actually causes the I/O requests sent to the I/O bus to be serialized. Therefore, it eliminates the slowdown caused by the bursty nature of I/O requests. Moreover, since the parallel threads only access the buffer in the memory instead of the file on the disk, the I/O latency is also hidden by the helper thread. The helper threading can also be used in sequential loops to reduce I/O latency.

3. Our System for Parallelizing Hybrid Loops

The strategies described to enable parallelization of hybrid loops have been incorporated into the SpiceC [10] system. We chose SpiceC because it already supports programming constructs, in the form of compiler directives, that can be used to express DOALL, DOACROSS, pipelining, and speculative parallelism. We have extended the SpiceC programming model to allow parallelization of hybrid loops. This section first presents our approach to programming parallel loops in the presence of I/O and illustrate it using several examples from real applications. Next we describe our implementation of the programming model.

3.1 Programming Parallel Hybrid Loops

Let us first consider our programming model for parallelizing hybrid loops. We show how parallel hybrid loops are programmed and describe the use of I/O helper threads to boost the I/O performance on multicores. We use the C standard I/O library (`stdio`) for illustrating our programming model. All the proposed APIs can be used for other I/O libraries, e.g., the C++ I/O library (`iostream`). The SpiceC [10] programming constructs used to express parallelism in this section are summarized in Table 1.

3.1.1 Parallelizing Loops with Input Operations

To enable DOALL parallelization of loops with input operations, we introduce the *pinput* clause:

```
#pragma SpiceC parallel doall \
        pinput(file, stride, start, end)
```

The *pinput* clause is designed to be used with the SpiceC DOALL construct. To parallelize a loop with input operations, programmers just need to insert the DOALL construct combined with the *pinput* clause. The *pinput* clause has four parameters: *file*, *stride*, *start*, and *end*. Parameter *file* is the input file pointer that causes cross-iteration dependences. Parameter *stride* gives the stride of *file* in the loop; it can be either the size of data block read by each iteration or the delimiter between data blocks. We distinguish between them based on the parameter's type. Parameter *start* is the initial position of *file* at the beginning of the loop. By default (i.e., when this parameter is empty), the current position pointed by *file* is used as the initial position. Parameter *end* is the ending position that *file* will reach at the end of the loop. The *end* should be left empty if the ending position of *file* is unknown before entering the loop (e.g., the FLS file access pattern shown in Figure 4(b)). Given these parameters, the compiler can then calculate the starting file position for each parallel thread using the strategies described in Section 2.1.

Pattern	Pragma Example
FSB	pinput(file, size, 0, EOF)
FCS	pinput(file, delimiter, 0, EOF)
FSB	pinput(file, size)
FLS	pinput(file, delimiter)

Table 2. Examples of the *pinput* clause.

Table 2 shows four examples of the *pinput* clause covering four different file input patterns. In the first two examples, the loop reads the whole file. We use 0 as the initial file position so that the compiler knows that the file pointer starts from the beginning of the file. The use of *EOF* as the ending file position tells the compiler that the file pointer will reach the end of the file. In the last two examples, the loop reads a fixed number of data blocks from the current file position. The initial file position is not given in the *pinput* clause since the current file position is used as the initial position. The ending file position is left empty because it is unknown. The first and third examples exhibit the FSB pattern (as shown in Figure 4(a)) since they use a constant block size as the stride of the file pointer. In the second example, a delimiter is used as the stride and the total data size read by the loop can be calculated by the initial and ending file position. Therefore, it exhibits the FCS pattern (as shown in Figure 4(c)). The last example exhibits the FLS pattern (as shown in Figure 4(b)) since a delimiter is used as the stride and the loop size is fixed.

```
file=fopen("input", "r");
fscanf(file, "%d", &ntuples);
#pragma SpiceC parallel doall pinput(file, "\n") {
  for( i=0; i<ntuples; i++) {
    fgets(line, maxsize, file);
    read_line(line, &index, &x, &y);
    tuples[index] = create_tuple(x,y,0);
  }
}
```

Figure 6. An input loop of benchmark *DelaunayRefinement*.

Figure 6 shows a real example of DOALL input loop that is similar to the fourth case given in Table 2. The original input loop is from the *DelaunayRefinement* benchmark [16]. Although the computation part of this benchmark has been parallelized in various ways [14, 21], its input loop, which contains I/O, has never been parallelized. The input loop reads an array of *ntuples* tuples from the file. Each iteration reads a line from the file and then creates a tuple structure from the input. In the example, the pragmas inserted to parallelize the loop are highlighted in bold. The SpiceC DOALL construct is used to identify the parallel region and type of parallelism. The *pinput* clause is used to specify the file input pattern. Since each iteration reads one line from the file, we give "\n" as the delimiter in the *pinput* clause.

3.1.2 Parallelizing Loops with Output Operations

To parallelize a loop with output operations using DOALL parallelism, we need to buffer the output of each iteration. Programmers can achieve this by using the *boutput* clause with the SpiceC DOALL construct as follows.

```
#pragma SpiceC parallel doall \
        boutput(file, isparallel)
```

The *boutput* clause tells the compiler that the output to *file* in the loop is written into its buffer. The buffer will not be flushed until the end of the loop, as shown in Figure 5(a). The *boutput* clause has two parameters: *file* and *isparallel*. Parameter *file* is the file pointer whose output needs to be buffered. Parameter *isparallel* specifies whether buffer flushing is performed in parallel with the computation threads or in a sequential fashion.

```
#pragma SpiceC parallel doall boutput(outfile, true) {
  for (index = 0; index<length; index++) {
    nucleotide = getNucleotide(descriptor, index);
    switch (nucleotide) {
      case ADENINE:
        fprintf(outfile, "A");
        break;
      case CYTOSINE:
        fprintf(outfile, "C");
        break;
      ...
    }
  }
}
```

Figure 7. An output loop of bioinformatics application `Velvet`.

Figure 7 shows an output loop of `Velvet` [30], a widely-used bioinformatics application (genomic sequence assembler). Although the computationally-intensive part of `Velvet` has recently been parallelized with OpenMP, its hybrid loops have not been parallelized. In the original output loop, each iteration of the loop gets a nucleotide from the descriptor and outputs a character based on the type of the nucleotide. The pragmas used to parallelize the loop are highlighted in bold. The SpiceC pragma is used to mark the parallel region and the *boutput* clause is used to buffer all outputs of *fprintf* so that the output operations do not cause any cross-iteration dependence on the file pointer. Buffer flushing is programmed to be performed in parallel with the sequential code after the loop.

The *boutput* clause can also be used to program DOACROSS loops with output operations. For DOACROSS parallelism, the buffer is flushed at the end of each iteration, as shown in Figure 5(b). Figure 8 shows the kernel of the benchmark *Parser*. Each iteration first reads a line from *stdin* and then parses the line. Because of the cross-iteration dependences in the *parse* portion of the loop, the loop cannot be parallelized using DOALL parallelism. However, since these dependences rarely manifest themselves at runtime, the loop can be parallelized using speculative DOACROSS parallelism. Because the *parse* portion of the loop calls *printf* to output the results, programmers need the *boutput* clause when applying speculative execution to the *parse* portion. In the figure, the pragmas inserted to speculatively parallelize the loop are highlighted in bold. The first SpiceC pragma is used to identify the parallel region and type of parallelism. The loop is divided into two subregions by the rest of the SpiceC pragmas. The first subregion, *READ*, performs the input operations. The *pinput* clause is used at the beginning of the loop to tell the compiler the file input pattern.

```
#pragma SpiceC parallel doacross \
   pinput(infile, "\n", 0, EOF) boutput(stdout, false) {
   for(index=0; !feof(infile); index++) {
      #pragma SpiceC subregion READ {
         fgets(line, max_line, infile); }
      #pragma SpiceC subregion PARSE {
         if ( special_command(line) ) continue;
         first_prepare_to_parse(1);
         while ( !success ) {
            /* parser code here */
            printf(" Linkage %d", index+1);
            /* parser code here */
         }
         #pragma SpiceC commit atomicity \
            after(ITER-1, PARSE)
      }
   }
}
```

Figure 8. Speculative parallelization of a kernel from *Parser*.

The compiler can then calculate the starting position of *infile* for each iteration and break the cross-iteration dependences introduced by *fgets*. The second subregion, *PARSE*, parses the input; it is executed speculatively as specified by the *commit* pragma at the end of the *PARSE* subregion. Since *printf* cannot be executed speculatively, the *boutput* clause is used with the DOACROSS construct to buffer the outputs to stdout in the loop. This enables speculative execution. Buffer flushing is performed at the end of each iteration in sequential order, as specified by parameter *isparallel* in the *boutput* clause.

3.1.3 Programming I/O Helper Threads

We use helper threading to reduce the I/O contention caused by the hybrid loop parallelization. Table 3 summarizes our API for programming I/O helper threads. Function *inithelper* is used to create a new I/O helper thread; it returns the handle of the created helper thread which can then be bound to a file pointer using the function *sethelper*. Once bound to a file pointer, the helper thread continues to monitor the buffer corresponding to that file pointer.

API	Description
inithelper()	initialize a I/O helper thread
sethelper(file, helper)	bind a helper thread to a file pointer

Table 3. APIs for programming I/O helper thread.

Figure 9 shows an example of using I/O helper threading in a parallel loop taken from *DelaunayRefinement* as shown in Figure 6. We create a helper thread and bind it to the input file pointer before entering the loop. Upon entering the parallel thread, the helper thread will automatically monitor the buffer corresponding to the file pointer copy in each parallel thread. Programmers do not need to code the binding of the helper thread to each copy of the file pointer.

I/O helper threading can also be used in sequential loops to reduce the I/O latency. Similar to the example of parallel loop, use of I/O helper thread in sequential loops is straightforward: programmers just need to call *inithelper* and *sethelper* before entering the loop.

3.2 Implementation

Figure 10 presents the overview of our implementation of the programming model. The core components of the implementation

```
file=fopen("input", "r");
fscanf(file, "%d", &ntuples);
helper = inithelper();
sethelper(file, helper);
#pragma SpiceC parallel doall pinput(file, "\n") {
   for( i=0; i<ntuples; i++) {
      fgets(line, maxsize, file);
      read_line(line, &index, &x, &y);
      tuples[index] = create_tuple(x,y,0);
   }
}
```

Figure 9. Example of using I/O helper threads.

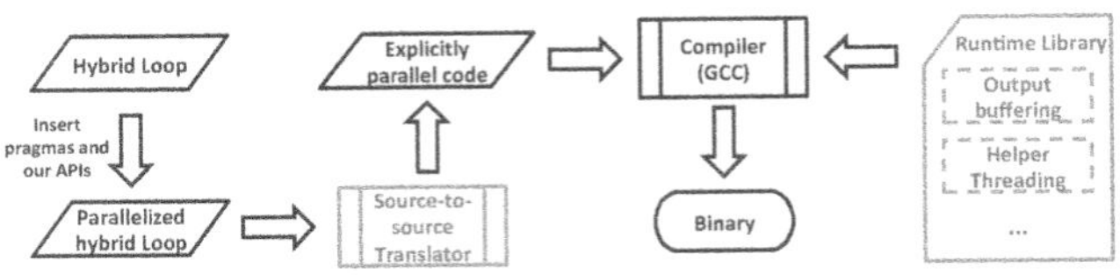

Figure 10. Implementation overview.

consist of a source-to-source translator and a user-level runtime library. The translator analyzes the hybrid loops parallelized with SpiceC directives and our APIs and translates them into explicitly parallel C/C++ code. We implemented the analysis by extending ROSE [18], a compiler infrastructure to build source-to-source code translators. The explicitly parallel code is compiled by the GCC compiler and linked with our runtime library. The runtime library implements output buffering and helper threading. Next, we describe the code transformation performed by the source-to-source translator and then elaborate how output buffering and helper threading are implemented.

3.2.1 Loop Transformation

API	Description
bwrite(index, data, size, file)	write *data* of *size* into the buffer of *file* in iteration *index*
bputs(index, string, file)	write *string* into the buffer of *file* in iteration *index*
bprintf(index, file, format, ...)	write formatted data into the buffer of *file* in iteration *index*
bflush(file, ALL/index, ispar)	flush the buffer of *file* using a separate thread or not

Table 4. Low-level functions for buffering outputs.

The code transformation from DOALL hybrid loops to C/C++ code is done automatically in our implementation. Figure 11 shows an example of the code transformation. Figure 11(a) shows a DOALL hybrid loop parallelized by our extended SpiceC directives. Each iteration of the loop reads 100 bytes from the input file, then processes them, and finally outputs them into the output file. Figure 11(b) shows the transformed main program. We insert initialization of the parallel threads at the beginning of the program and close the parallel threads at the end of the program. The DOALL loop is outlined into function *wrapper*. All variables used in the DOALL loop are wrapped into a structure which is then passed as a parameter to the outlined loop. We call function *start_doall* to execute the outlined loop in the parallel threads. Function *join_doall* is a synchronization method that waits until all parallel threads finish their work. Function *bflush* is called after the loop to flush the buffer of file pointer *out*. Figure 11(c) shows the

```
...
in = fopen("input", "r");
out = fopen("output", "w");
#pragma SpiceC parallel doall \
   pinput(in, 100, 0, EOF) boutput(out, true) {
   for( ; !feof(in); )
      fread(buf, 1, 100, in);
      process(buf);
      fputs(buf, out);
}
...
```

(a) Original code with SpiceC pragmas

```
init_parallel_threads();
...
in = fopen("input", "r");
out = fopen("output", "w");
args->in = in;
args->out = out;
start_doall(wrapper, args);
join_doall();
bflush(out, ALL, true);
...
close_parallel_threads();
```

(b) Transformed main program

```
void wrapper(void* args) {
   in = args->in;
   out = args->out;
   tid = get_thread_id();
   f = local_start(tid, in, 100, 0, EOF);
   c = local_count(tid, in, 100, 0, EOF);
   for( i=0; i<c; i++ )
      fread(buf, 1, 100, f);
      process(buf);
      bputs(i, buf, out);
}
```

(c) Transformed parallel loop

Figure 11. Example of code transformation.

outlined loop. Before the loop, three functions are called to prepare the workload for the current thread. Function *get_thread_id* is used to get the ID of the current thread. Function *local_start* is called to calculate the starting file position of the current thread. Function *local_count* is called to calculate the number of iterations to be performed in the current thread. Function *fputs* is replaced with our function *bputs* for buffering the outputs. Table 4 lists our substitute for the C standard I/O functions. They are designed to buffer and flush the outputs for breaking the cross-iteration dependences introduced by the output operations.

3.2.2 Output Buffering

To enable output buffering (e.g., *bputs*, *bflush*), we create an output buffer for each parallel thread. The structure of each output buffer is a linked list, as shown in Figure 12. Each node in the linked list is a buffer of predefined length which can typically hold the output from several iterations. Once a node is full, a new node is created and appended to the linked list.

Flushing the output buffers takes $O(n)$ time, where n is the total size of all output buffers. Figure 12(a) shows the data layout of the output buffers for a DOALL loop with two parallel threads. The output buffer of thread 1 stores the output from iteration 1 to 6 and the output buffer of thread 2 stores the rest. It is straightforward to flush the output buffers with this data layout. We can flush the output buffers starting from the first thread and ending with the last thread, which takes $O(n)$ time. Figure 12(b) shows the data layout of the output buffers for a DOACROSS loop. The output buffer of thread 1 stores the output from odd iterations and the output buffer of thread 1 stores the output from even iterations. In this case, we can flush the output buffers in a round-robin manner, which also takes $O(n)$ time. The output of the current iteration in a DOACROSS loop can be flushed efficiently (as shown in Figure 8) since the output of the current iteration is always pointed to by the tail pointer of the output buffer.

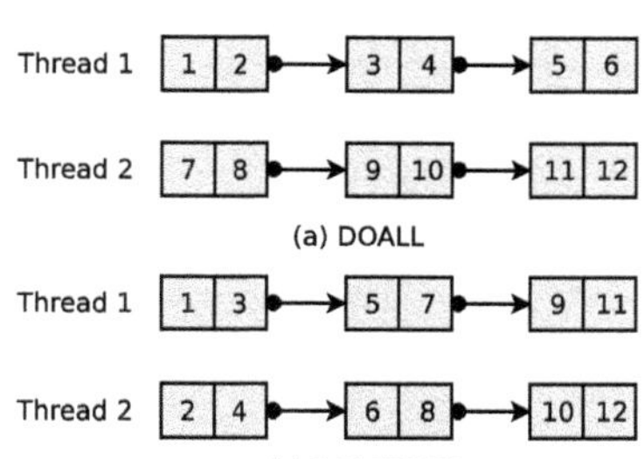

Figure 12. Buffer layout.

3.2.3 I/O Helper Threading

To enable I/O helper threading, our runtime library implements an extended version of the standard file pointer by dividing the file buffer into two parts of equal size: the f-buffer and the h-buffer, where the f-buffer is used as the file buffer directly accessed by the I/O operations and the h-buffer is the helper buffer used by the helper thread.

For input file pointers, all input operations read data from the f-buffer. Once the f-buffer is empty, it is switched with the h-buffer. The helper thread keeps monitoring the h-buffer. If the h-buffer is empty, it refills it by calling I/O system calls. Output file pointers work in a similar way.

In our implementation, we typically do not put the helper thread to sleep to minimize the refilling latency. However, when the number of parallel threads is equal to the number of processor cores in the system, the helper thread will compete with the parallel threads for CPU resources. Therefore in this case, instead of busy idling the helper thread, we put the helper thread to sleep when it does not find any buffer that needs refilling. The helper thread is then woken when an f-buffer is switched with the h-buffer in a buffer pair.

4. Evaluation

This section evaluates the prototype implementation of our programming model. The experiments were conducted on a 24-core DELL PowerEdge R905 machine. Table 5 lists the machine details.

Processors	4×6-core 64-bit AMD Opteron 8431 Processor (2.4GHz)
L1 cache	Private, 128KB for each core
L2 cache	Private, 512KB for each core
L3 cache	Shared among 6 cores, 6144KB
Memory	32GB RAM
OS	Ubuntu server, Linux kernel version 2.6.32

Table 5. Dell PowerEdge R905 machine details.

4.1 Benchmarks

Our programming model was applied to eight applications. Two are real-world applications, while the others are from the PARSEC [3] and SPEC CPU2000 suites. We selected these applications using the following criteria: (1) the applications must have at least one hybrid loop that can be efficiently parallelized (i.e., there is no frequent cross-iteration dependence in the computation part); and (2) the hybrid loop(s) must take a significant portion of execution time. Applying our techniques on applications that do not satisfy these criteria would diminish our capacity to measure and evaluate our approach. We applied DOALL parallelism to the hybrid loops

Name	Source	Loops	Input	Output?	Speculation?	Helper?	% runtime	# stmts
velveth	real application	8	FCS	Yes	No	Yes	53%	18
velvetg	real application	18	FCS	Yes	No	Yes	27%	46
spacetyrant	real application	4	–	Yes	No	No	95%	8
DelaunayRefinement	lonestar	3	FLS	No	No	Yes	23%	7
bzip2	SPEC CPU2000	1	FSB	Yes	No	Yes	99%	13
parser	SPEC CPU2000	1	FCS	Yes	Yes	No	99%	8
blackscholes	PARSEC	1	FLS	No	No	Yes	45%	6
fluidanimate	PARSEC	3	FLS	Yes	No	Yes	36%	10

Table 6. Benchmark summary. From left to right: benchmark name, source of the benchmark, number of parallelized hybrid loops, input file access pattern, whether output buffering is used, whether speculative parallelization is used, whether helper threading is used, percentage of total execution time taken by the hybrid loops, number of statements added or modified for parallelization.

in seven applications except `parser` (speculative parallelism was required to parallelize `parser`). Table 6 shows the details of the benchmarks.

`Velvet` [30] is a popular genomic sequence assembler. It contains two applications—`velveth` and `velvetg`. `Velveth` constructs the dataset and calculates what each input sequence represents. `Velvetg` manipulates the de Bruijn graph that is built on the dataset. 18 computation loops in `velveth` and `velvetg` have already been parallelized using OpenMP. In the experiment, we parallelized the hybrid loops in them. All parallelized input loops have the FCS pattern. We use output buffering to parallelize the loops that contain output operations. We used nucleotide sequence *SRR027005* [1] as input. `SpaceTyrant` [2] is an online multi-player game server. We parallelized its *backup* thread which executes the *backupdata* function to backup game data. The *backupdata* function has 4 output loops for storing different types of data. Output buffering was used to parallelize these loops. In the experiments, we assume that every data block is dirty and needs to be written to the file. `DelaunayRefinement` [16] is a meshing algorithm for two-dimensional quality mesh generation, originally written in JAVA; we ported it to C++. Its computation loop has been parallelized in previous work [14]. We parallelized the three input loops in the *read* function. The three loops read different aspects of the input graph. They all have the FLS pattern. We applied DOALL parallelism to them by breaking the I/O dependences. `Bzip2` is a tool used for data compression and decompression. In the experiments, we parallelized its compression loop using DOALL. There are many superfluous cross-iteration dependences on global variables in `bzip2`. To remove these dependences, we replicated buffers for each iteration and made many global variables local to each iteration. Some of the local variables are summarized into global variables after the loop. `Parser` is a syntactic parser for English. We used speculative parallelism to parallelize its *batch_process* function which reads and parses the sentences in the input filed. The function contains a FCS loop. We broke the I/O dependences by calculating the starting file position for each iteration and using output buffering. We need to speculate on dependences for control variables which may be altered by the special commands in the input file. `Blackscholes` is a computational finance application. We parallelized the input loop in the *main* function. The loop is a FLS loop that contains only input operations. `Fluidanimate` is designed to simulate an incompressible fluid in parallel. In its original *Parsec* version, the number of threads supplied by users must be a power of 2. We modified the workload partitioning to enable an arbitrary number of threads. For the PARSEC benchmarks used in the experiments, we use their pthread-based parallel versions.

4.2 Performance

Figure 13 shows the absolute speedup of the parallelized applications over their sequential versions for varying number of parallel threads. Figure 13(a) shows the speedup when applying our hybrid loop parallelization techniques—we achieve 3.0x–12.8x speedup. On average, we improve the performance of these applications by 6.6x on the 24-core machine. For some benchmarks, the performance degrades with 24 parallel threads. This is caused by the contention between the helper thread and parallel threads. `Fluidanimate` has unstable performance across varying the number of parallel threads because its workload cannot be evenly partitioned with certain numbers of threads. The performance of `SpaceTyrant` goes down with larger number of threads. This is caused by the dynamic memory allocation for output buffering. For comparison, Figure 13(b) shows the speedup of these parallelized applications without hybrid loop parallelization. The speedup of `SpaceTyrant` is always 1 since its backup thread cannot be parallelized without hybrid loop parallelization. The speedup of these applications without hybrid loop parallelization is between 2.3x–8.8x which is significantly lower than the speedups with hybrid loop parallelization.

Figure 14(a) shows the relative speedup of hybrid loops with parallelization vs. without parallelization. For seven applications, hybrid loop parallelization improves the hybrid loop performance by factors greater than 5x. On average, hybrid loop parallelization improves the loop performance by a factor of 7.54x. Figure 14(b) shows the relative parallelized full application speedups with hybrid loop parallelization vs. without hybrid loop parallelization. On average, hybrid loop parallelization improves the application performance by 68%.

4.3 Impact of Helper Threading

Figure 15 shows the impact of I/O helper threading. On average, I/O helper threading improves the performance of parallelized hybrid loops by 11.9%. I/O helper threading usually provides more benefit with larger number of threads except 24 parallel threads where the I/O parallel thread competes with the parallel threads for processing resources. Figure 16 shows the impact of the buffer size of the helper thread in two applications—`velveth` and `DelaunayRefinement`. I/O helper threading achieves higher speedup with larger buffer sizes.

The buffer size is a critical factor that determines whether a helper thread can efficiently load data for multiple threads. We use the following example to show how we set the proper buffer size for a helper thread. Figure 17 compares the computation time with the data load time for different numbers of iterations in *DelaunayRefinement*. The trend of the curves is similar for hybrid loops in other applications. We define tc_k as the computation time of k iterations and tl_k as the time of loading data for k iterations. From the figure, tc_k increases much more quickly than tl_k with the increase of k.

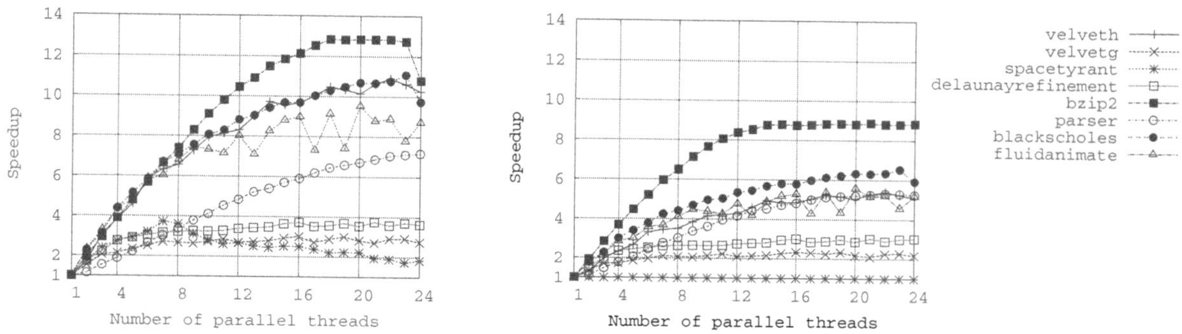

(a) With Hybrid Loop Parallelization

(b) Without Hybrid Loop Parallelization

Figure 13. Absolute parallelized application speedup over sequential programs.

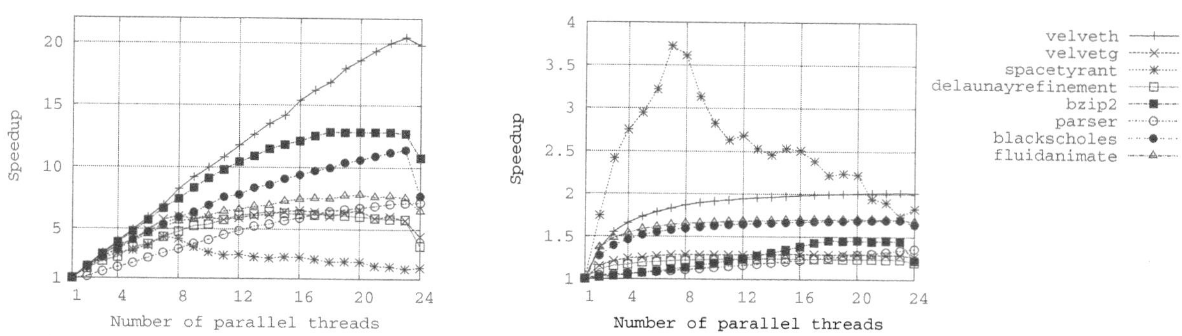

(a) Parallelized hybrid loops speedup

(b) Parallelized full application speedup

Figure 14. Relative speedup: with hybrid loop parallelization vs. without hybrid loop parallelization.

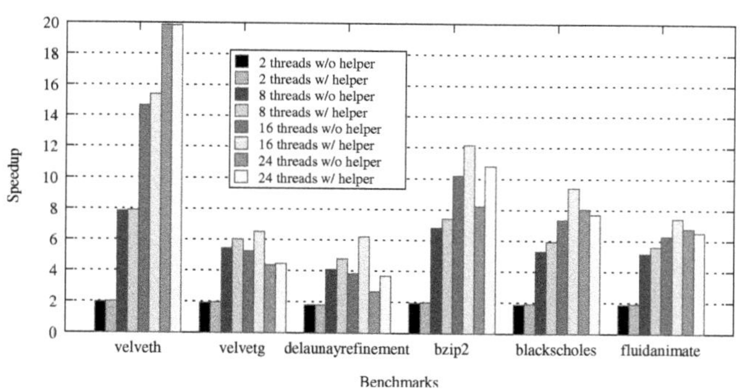

Figure 15. Impact of helper threading.

For a helper thread that loads data for p parallel threads, its buffer for each parallel thread should be able to hold data for n iterations where $tc_n > p * tl_n$ since loading data should be finished before the data in the buffer is used up. Since tc_k increases much more quickly than tl_k, there always exists n satisfying $tc_n > p * tl_n$.

4.4 Overhead

Figure 18 shows the breakdown of the hybrid loop execution time for the parallelized applications. The time is divided into four categories: computation, I/O, speculation, and synchronization. For 5 out of 8 applications, most time is spent on the computation. `SpaceTyrant` and `Blackscholes` spend most time on I/O operations since their hybrid loops contain very little computation. Since most loops are parallelized using DOALL parallelism, very little synchronization overhead was introduced. `Parser` has the highest synchronization overhead since it is parallelized speculatively. I/O operations take a higher percentage of execution time with larger number of parallel threads due to I/O bus contention. Figure 19 shows the memory overhead incurred by hybrid loop parallelization. For 5 out of 8 benchmarks, the memory overhead is smaller than 10MB. `Velveth` and `velvetg` have high memory overhead since their output, which needs to be buffered in the memory during loop execution, is large.

5. Related Work

Parallel programming models. Many programming models have been proposed to enable exploitation of data parallelism in sequential programs on shared memory multiprocessors. OpenMP [8] is a widely used programming model that provides a set of compiler directives for parallelizing sequential programs on shared-memory systems. Threading Building Blocks (TBB) [20] is a programming model that provides a set of thread-safe containers and algorithms for expressing parallelism on shared-memory systems. Single Program Multiple Data (SPMD) is another category of programming models and the message passing interface (MPI) [11] is currently the de facto standard for SPMD. Partitioned global address space (PGAS) [6, 7] is a set of parallel programming models which aim to combine the performance advantage of MPI with the programmability of a shared-memory model. Galois [14, 15] introduces a programming model to exploit the data parallelism in irregular applications. SpiceC [10] is a recently proposed parallel programming model for both multicores and manycores. SpiceC can be used to express multiple forms of parallelisms, including DOALL, DOACROSS, pipelining and speculative parallelism. Fi-

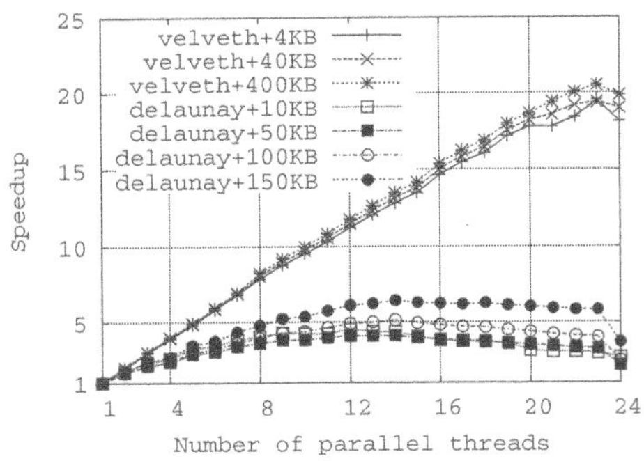

Figure 16. Speedup by varying buffer size.

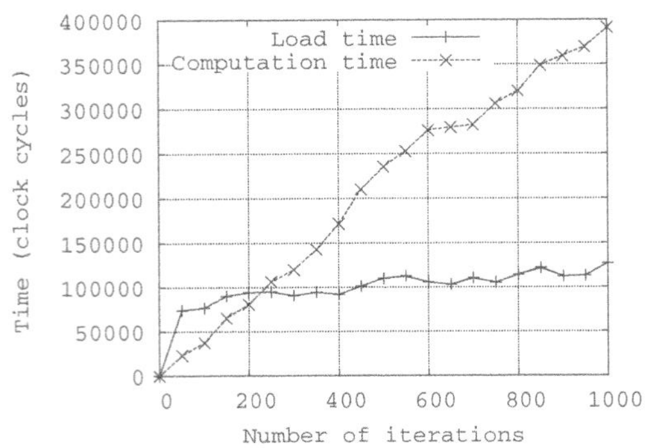

Figure 17. Computation time vs. data load time of benchmark *DelaunayRefinement*.

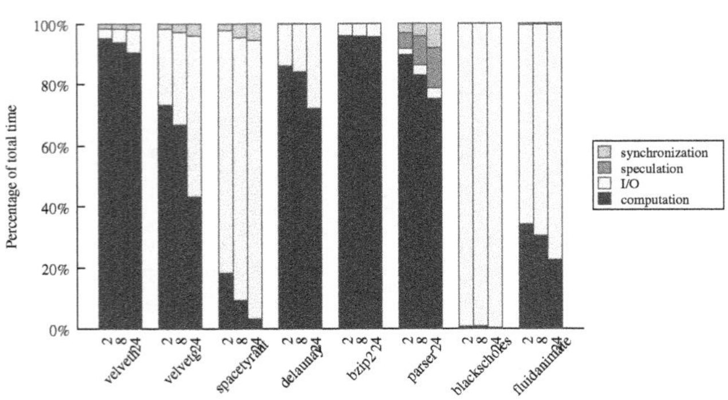

Figure 18. Breakdown of hybrid loop execution time.

nally, software-based thread level speculation (TLS) techniques have been proposed for automatically parallelizing sequential programs [9, 13, 26–28]. They are all based on state separation, i.e., the results of speculative computations are stored in a separate space from the non-speculative state space. Speculative Decoupled Software Pipelining (Spec-DSWP) [29] is another series of TLS works. Software multithreaded transactional memory system [19] has been developed to optimize the performance of Spec-DSWP.

None of the above programming models and techniques provide support for efficiently parallelizing hybrid loops. They cannot break the cross-iteration dependences caused by I/O operations. Therefore, they cannot perform the I/O part of loops in parallel. In addition, the TLS techniques that focus on speculative execution of data computation do not provide any rollback mechanism for I/O operations in case of misspeculation.

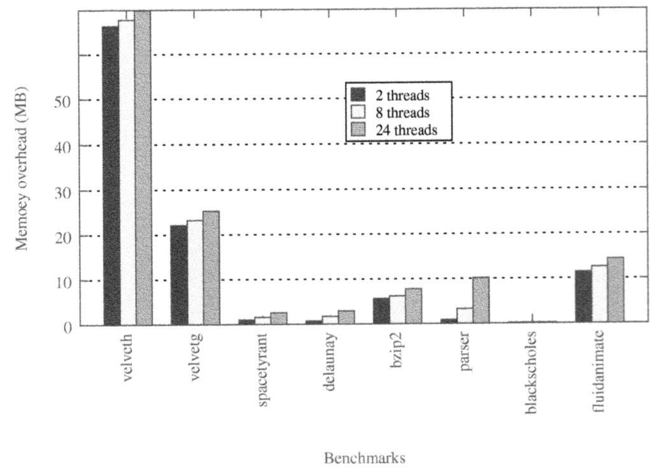

Figure 19. Memory overhead.

Parallel I/O. Parallel I/O has been proposed to improve the performance of multiple I/O operations at the same time. It is mostly designed to deal with massive amounts of data on distributed systems. Research work in parallel I/O can be mainly divided into two different groups: parallel file systems and parallel I/O libraries. Parallel file systems [22] usually spread data over multiple servers for high performance. They allow shared accesses to files from multiple processes. Parallel I/O libraries such as ROMIO [24] are APIs designed to access parallel file systems. Collective I/O [25] has been proposed to optimize non-contiguous I/O requests from multiple processes; it coordinates accesses to files by a group of processes in which collective I/O functions are called.

Our techniques are orthogonal to parallel I/O. Parallel I/O provides lower-level programming constructs designed to improve the I/O throughput of large-scale systems. However, when using parallel I/O, programmers must be highly skilled in order to express, and make efficient use of, parallel I/O operations. We make it easy for programmers to parallelize hybrid loops by providing a higher-level programming model. Our compiler techniques are designed to support our programming model and optimize the performance of hybrid loops written in our model.

More specifically, our approach differs in two ways. First, to parallelize a loop with operations using MPI I/O, programmers must write code to calculate the starting and ending offset for each thread and explicitly set the offset using the MPI I/O APIs. Programmers also need to take care of synchronization, scheduling, load balancing, etc. Using our programming model, programmers just need to insert a few pragmas. Second, Parallel I/O, such as MPI I/O, does not provide any support for speculative parallelization, while our techniques do.

I/O support for transactional memory. Unrestricted transactional memory [4] is a hardware transactional memory technique that has been proposed to support I/O calls in transactions. Transactions usually cannot contain I/O calls because these operations cannot easily be rolled back. Unrestricted transactional memory gives up some concurrency in exchange for gaining the ability to perform I/O calls within transactions by allowing only a single overflowed transaction per application.

I/O prefetching. Helper threading has been used in software-guided prefetching to hide I/O latency [5, 23]. To minimize I/O latency, these techniques require timely prefetching. They rely on the profiler or operating system to insert prefetching calls. Our helper threading technique is designed to reduce contention on the I/O bus instead of hiding the I/O latency. Therefore, we only require data residing in main memories (i.e., off-chip memories) instead of caches (i.e., on-chip memories) when they are read. Since main memories have very large capacity nowadays, we do not require very timely prefetching. Moreover, our helper threading is specially designed for loops with contiguous I/O accesses. Therefore, we do not require any support from a profiler or the operating system.

6. Conclusions

In this paper, we identified the opportunity to parallelize hybrid loops, i.e., loops with computation and I/O operations. We presented several techniques for efficiently parallelizing hybrid loops. We proposed an easy-to-use programming model for exploiting parallelism in hybrid loops. Parallelizing hybrid loops using our model requires few modifications to the code. We developed a prototype implementation of our programming model. The implementation was evaluated on a 24-core machine using eight applications, from PARSEC and SPEC CPU2000 benchmark suites, and real-world applications. The applications with hybrid loop parallelization achieve 3.0x–12.8x speedup while in comparison 2.3x–8.8x speedup was observed without hybrid loop parallelization.

Acknowledgments

We thank Stefano Lonardi for suggesting Velvet as an application. This research is supported by the National Science Foundation grants CCF-0963996 and CCF-0905509 to the University of California, Riverside.

References

[1] DDBJ sequence read archive. http://trace.ddbj.nig.ac.jp/dra/index_e.shtml.

[2] Space tyrant. http://spacetyrant.com/st.c.

[3] C. Bienia, S. Kumar, J. P. Singh, and K. Li. The PARSEC benchmark suite: Characterization and architectural implications. In *Proceedings of the International Conference on Parallel Architectures and Compilation Techniques (PACT)*, pages 72–81, 2008.

[4] C. Blundell, E. C. Lewis, and M. M. K. Martin. Unrestricted transactional memory: Supporting I/O and system calls within transactions. Technical Report TR-CIS-06-09, University of Pennsylvania, 2006.

[5] A. D. Brown, T. C. Mowry, and O. Krieger. Compiler-based I/O prefetching for out-of-core applications. *ACM Transactions on Computer Systems*, 19:111–170, May 2001.

[6] P. Charles, C. Grothoff, V. Saraswat, C. Donawa, A. Kielstra, K. Ebcioglu, C. von Praun, and V. Sarkar. X10: an object-oriented approach to non-uniform cluster computing. In *Proceedings of the ACM SIGPLAN Conference on Object-Oriented Programming, Systems, Languages & Applications (OOPSLA)*, pages 519–538, 2005.

[7] U. Consortium. UPC language specifications, v1.2. *Berkeley Lab Technical Report LBNL-59208*, 2005.

[8] L. Dagum and R. Menon. Openmp: An industry-standard api for shared-memory programming. *IEEE computational science & engineering*, 5(1):46–55, 1998.

[9] C. Ding, X. Shen, K. Kelsey, C. Tice, R. Huang, and C. Zhang. Software behavior oriented parallelization. In *Proceedings of the ACM SIGPLAN conference on Programming Language Design and Implementation (PLDI)*, pages 223–234, 2007.

[10] M. Feng, R. Gupta, and Y. Hu. SpiceC: scalable parallelism via implicit copying and explicit commit. In *Proceedings of the ACM SIGPLAN Symposium on Principles and Practice of Parallel Programming (PPoPP)*, pages 69–80, 2011.

[11] W. Gropp, E. Lusk, and A. Skjellum. *Using MPI: Portable Parallel Programming with the Message Passing Interface*. The MIT Press, 1994.

[12] J. L. Henning. SPEC CPU2000: Measuring cpu performance in the new millennium. *Computer*, 33:28–35, July 2000.

[13] K. Kelsey, T. Bai, C. Ding, and C. Zhang. Fast track: A software system for speculative program optimization. In *Proceedings of the International Symposium on Code Generation and Optimization (CGO)*, pages 157–168, 2009.

[14] M. Kulkarni, K. Pingali, B. Walter, G. Ramanarayanan, K. Bala, and L. P. Chew. Optimistic parallelism requires abstractions. In *Proceedings of the ACM SIGPLAN conference on Programming Language Design and Implementation (PLDI)*, pages 211–222, 2007.

[15] M. Kulkarni, K. Pingali, G. Ramanarayanan, B. Walter, K. Bala, and L. P. Chew. Optimistic parallelism benefits from data partitioning. In *Proceedings of the International Conference on Architectural Support for Programming Languages and Operating Systems (ASPLOS)*, pages 233–243, 2008.

[16] M. Kulkarni, M. Burtscher, C. Cascaval, and K. Pingali. Lonestar: A suite of parallel irregular programs. In *Proceedings of the IEEE International Symposium on Performance Analysis of Systems and Software (ISPASS)*, pages 65–76, 2009.

[17] C. D. Polychronopoulos and D. J. Kuck. Guided self-scheduling: A practical scheduling scheme for parallel supercomputers. *IEEE Transactions on Computers*, 36:1425–1439, 1987.

[18] D. Quinlan. Rose: Compiler support for object-oriented framework. In *Proceedings of the Workshop on Compilers for Parallel Computers (CPC)*, 2000.

[19] A. Raman, H. Kim, T. R. Mason, T. B. Jablin, and D. I. August. Speculative parallelization using software multi-threaded transactions. In *Proceedings of the International Conference on Architectural Support for Programming Languages and Operating Systems (ASPLOS)*, pages 65–76, 2010.

[20] J. Reinders. *Intel threading building blocks*. O'Reilly Media, 2007.

[21] M. Scott, M. F. Spear, L. Dalessandro, and V. J. Marathe. Delaunay triangulation with transactions and barriers. In *Proceedings of the IEEE International Symposium on Workload Characterization (IISWC)*, 2007.

[22] A. Silberschatz, P. B. Galvin, and G. Gagne. *Operating System Concepts*. Wiley Publishing, 2008.

[23] S. W. Son, S. P. Muralidhara, O. Ozturk, M. Kandemir, I. Kolcu, and M. Karakoy. Profiler and compiler assisted adaptive I/O prefetching for shared storage caches. In *Proceedings of the International Conference on Parallel Architectures and Compilation Techniques (PACT)*, pages 112–121, 2008.

[24] R. Thakur, W. Gropp, and E. Lusk. An abstract-device interface for implementing portable parallel-I/O interfaces. In *Proceedings of the Symposium on the Frontiers of Massively Parallel Computation (FRONTIERS)*, pages 180–187, 1996.

[25] R. Thakur, W. Gropp, and E. Lusk. Data sieving and collective I/O in ROMIO. In *Proceedings of the Symposium on the Frontiers of Massively Parallel Computation (FRONTIERS)*, pages 182–191, 1999.

[26] C. Tian, M. Feng, and R. Gupta. Copy or discard execution model for speculative parallelization on multicores. In *Proceedings of the Annual IEEE/ACM International Symposium on Microarchitecture (MICRO)*, pages 330–341, 2008.

[27] C. Tian, M. Feng, and R. Gupta. Supporting speculative parallelization in the presence of dynamic data structures. In *Proceedings of the ACM SIGPLAN conference on Programming Language Design and Implementation (PLDI)*, pages 62–73, 2010.

[28] C. Tian, C. Lin, M. Feng, and R. Gupta. Enhanced speculative parallelization via incremental recovery. In *Proceedings of the ACM SIGPLAN Symposium on Principles and Practice of Parallel Programming (PPoPP)*, pages 189–200, 2011.

[29] N. Vachharajani, R. Rangan, E. Raman, M. J. Bridges, G. Ottoni, and D. I. August. Speculative decoupled software pipelining. In *Proceedings of the International Conference on Parallel Architectures and Compilation Techniques (PACT)*, pages 49–59, 2007.

[30] D. R. Zerbino and E. Birney. Velvet: algorithms for de novo short read assembly using de bruijn graphs. *Genome Research*, 18:821–829, 2008.

Polyhedra Scanning Revisited

Chun Chen

University of Utah

Abstract

This paper presents a new polyhedra scanning system called CodeGen+ to address the challenge of generating high-performance code for complex iteration spaces resulting from compiler optimization and autotuning systems. The strength of our approach lies in two new algorithms. First, a loop overhead removal algorithm provides precise control of trade-offs between loop overhead and code size based on actual loop nesting depth. Second, an if-statement simplification algorithm further reduces the number of comparisons in the code. These algorithms combined with the expressive power of Presburger arithmetic enable CodeGen+ to support complex optimization strategies expressed in iteration spaces. We compare with the state-of-the-art polyhedra scanning tool CLooG on five loop nest computations, demonstrating that CodeGen+ generates code that is simpler and up to 1.15x faster.

Categories and Subject Descriptors D.3.4 [*Processors*]: Code generation, Compilers, Optimization

General Terms Performance, Algorithms

Keywords polyhedra scanning, polyhedral transformations

1. Introduction

The polyhedral model has long been considered a powerful tool in loop nest optimization. In contrast, ad-hoc loop transformation techniques typically apply one loop transformation at a time and have to switch back to a loop's syntactic form again for the next loop transformation. Subsequent transformations have to deal with increasingly complex loop structures, severely limiting the optimization strategy a compiler can apply. A polyhedral model represents each statement's execution in the loop nest as a lattice point in the space constrained by loop bounds, known as the iteration space. Then a loop transformation can be simply viewed as mapping from one iteration space to another, and various transformations can be composed. This enables reasoning about complex optimization strategies.

In a polyhedral model, polyhedra scanning is used to generate optimized code. The polyhedra representing the iteration spaces of an optimized loop nest are scanned from the first dimension to the last to generate the corresponding output nested loop structure. The quality of generated code directly affects the transformed code's performance. For example, unnecessary control flow in an innermost loop would most likely severely degrade performance on today's architectures. Expensive arithmetic operations such as modulo that result from polyhedra scanning can also degrade performance.

Polyhedra scanning has been studied by researchers since the early 1990s. Generating code from unimodular and non-unimodular transformations [6, 14, 20, 28–30] can be thought of as a polyhedra scanning problem. Ancourt and Irigoin [1] are among the first researchers to propose an algorithm to systematically scan polyhedra to generate loop code. However this method only deals with a single polyhedron. In a general polyhedral framework, statements may have different iteration spaces from each other. Kelly et al. [12] describe a polyhedra scanning system for a set of polyhedra. Their algorithms remove loop overhead from inner loops iteratively from the most compact code generated. Quillere et al. [18] argue that the iterative algorithms in [12] are inefficient, and instead split overlapping polyhedra at each dimension during the scanning process without iterating. However, the method in [18] still requires backtracking to remove dead code. In practice, removing overhead indiscriminately might unnecessarily cause code explosion with little benefit in performance. This might be a particular concern when generating codes for embedded systems where limiting code size is also important. Sometimes removing overhead from just the innermost loop may be a better choice in balancing code size and performance, as it is typically the structure of the inner loop body that directly affects instruction scheduling.

More recently, CLooG [2, 26] tries to overcome the above mentioned problem in Quillere et al.'s method. Conceptually, its algorithm can be thought of as the reverse of Kelly et al.'s method by reducing code size from a starting point of maximal overhead removal. However, we observe that CLooG's code compacting process does not follow the lexicographical order of iteration spaces. One could argue that this reordering might be beneficial to providing flexibility in overhead removal, but it also might result in incorrect code when there is a data dependence preventing such statement reordering.

CodeGen+ uses the same basic concept of Kelly et al.'s method, but its algorithms are completely reworked. Our goal is to produce high-performance code that is competitive with manually-tuned code, so efficiency of generated code is paramount. As context for this work, CodeGen+ has been used extensively as part of an *autotuning* compiler system, whereby the compiler generates a set of parameterized variants of a computation, and employs empirical techniques to find the best variant and associated set of optimization parameter values [25]. The variants represent different optimization strategies, while the optimization parameters are discrete values that govern code generation such as tile size or un-

This research was funded in part by the U.S. Government. The views and conclusions contained in this document are those of the authors and should not be interpreted as representing the official policies, either expressed or implied, of the U.S. Government.

roll factor. Due to its mathematical foundations, the polyhedral model is a powerful underlying technology for an autotuning compiler because it can generate correct code under different parameter values and complex optimization strategies. The code resulting from this system has been shown to achieve performance that is comparable and sometimes better than manually-tuned libraries such as ATLAS, Goto, ACML, Cray Scientific Library, PETSc and CUBLAS [3, 13, 19, 21, 23], and manually-tuned code written by programmers targeting supercomputers [19, 22, 24].

Considering the optimization strategies used in hand-tuned codes such as, for example, BLAS linear algebra libraries, to achieve comparable performance polyhedral frameworks must be able to compose a large collection of transformations, such as tiling, permutation, iteration-space splitting, shifting, and unroll-and-jam. Such complex optimization strategies result in correspondingly complex iteration spaces. Parallel code introduces additional transformations such as strip mining across threads, resulting in non-convex iteration spaces, which further increases complexity. Autotuning additionally introduces non-trivial parameter combinations during the search that lead to significant clean-up code and elaborate loop bound calculations.

To summarize, the requirements for polyhedral compilers targeting modern memory hierarchies, multi-core and heterogeneous systems pose significant challenges for polyhedra scanning algorithms, particularly when the goal is to achieve very high levels of performance. We describe in this paper algorithms in CodeGen+ that play an important role in meeting this goal. The main contributions of this paper are: (1) a new loop overhead removal algorithm that can handle complex constraint relationships from Presburger arithmetic among different polyhedra, and provides precise control of trade-offs between loop overhead and code size based on actual loop nesting depth; and, (2) a new algorithm to further simplify if-statements for the code after trade-offs. Since CLooG has recently been extended to use full Presburger arithmetic by integrating with ISL [27], we will provide direct comparisons on five loop nest computations for identical iteration spaces. These experiments demonstrate that our bottom-up algorithms built with mathematical rigor provide a better control of trade-offs between loop overhead and code size and are capable of generating better quality code.

This paper is organized as follows. Section 2 introduces the polyhedral model and the underlying mathematical model. Section 3 describes our polyhedra scanning algorithms and code generation process. In Section 4, we explain the design features and code quality improvements under the perspective of polyhedral framework. Finally, Section 5 summarizes the related work, and Section 6 concludes the paper.

2. Background

We first give a brief introduction of the polyhedral model for loop transformations. Polyhedra scanning is part of this complete solution, and its various design decisions must be considered in this greater context. As a prerequisite for the polyhedral model, we assume that loop nests have affine loop bounds, and there is no control dependence for statements inside the loop nest. We also explain essential functions from the underlying mathematical system that are critical to understand the polyhedra scanning algorithms described in this paper.

2.1 Polyhedral Model

Statements inside a loop nest can be viewed as lattice points in a polyhedron. Executing the loop nest sequentially is equivalent to enumerating those lattice points in lexicographical order. This conceptualization allows the compiler to reason about loop transformations as manipulating iteration spaces of loop nests. For example, consider the following loop nest:

```
      for (i=0;i<n;i++)
        for (j=0;j<i;j++)
s0:       a[i][j]=b[i][j]
```

Statement `s0`'s iteration space is

$$\{[i,j] : 0 \leq i < n \wedge 0 \leq j < i\}.$$

Dimension i in this iteration space corresponds to outer loop `i` in the above loop nest and dimension j corresponds to inner loop `j`. A reordering of a statement's execution order is valid as long as it preserves all data dependences, i.e., the source is always executed before the sink after transformation for any data dependence. Viewing a loop nest by its iteration spaces give us a powerful abstraction to transform a loop nest without being restricted to the original loop structure. Thus, a loop transformation can be represented by a mapping function from one space to the other and their dimensionality does not need to be the same. A mapping must be invertible to guarantee that the same amount of work is done before and after transformation, i.e., a *reordering transformation*. For example, applying mapping function $\{[i,j] \rightarrow [i',j'] : i' = j \wedge j' = i\}$ to the above iteration space would result in

$$\{[i',j'] : 0 \leq j' < i' < n\},$$

which represents the iteration space of the interchanged loop nest.

Thus, after a loop nest has been transformed in the polyhedral model, the new iteration spaces (set of polyhedra) must be converted back to their syntactic format as nested loops to produce code. This code generation is performed using polyhedra scanning. For a single polyhedron, it simply scans from the first dimension to the last while generating the loop bounds and step size for each dimension. Any other constraints that cannot be enforced by loops are represented by if-statements, e.g., a guard to only execute a statement on a subset of iterations of a loop. For example, the above iteration space after loop interchange generates the following code from polyhedra scanning:

```
      for (t1=0;t1<=n-2;t1++)
        for (t2=t1+1;t2<=n-1;t2++)
s0:       a[t2][t1]=b[t2][t1]
```

Further challenges come from scanning a set of polyhedra and allowing more complex constraints such as modulo constraints to be described in iteration spaces. Different polyhedra may overlap with each other with nontrivial constraint relationships. Polyhedra scanning needs to generate concise loop bounds and optimally place additional guard conditions, taking into account trade-offs between loop overhead and code size.

2.2 Integer Linear Arithmetic

CodeGen+ depends on Omega+ (Presburger arithmetic) to manipulate a system of integer equations and inequalities. Omega+ is an updated Omega library [11] which uses enhanced Fourier-Motzkin elimination as its core algorithm [15–17]. Omega+ further extends the Omega library to better support integer modulo constraints in various functions. This enables CodeGen+ to generate efficient codes when iteration spaces do not have unit stride. In this section, we describe a few high-level functions that provide key underlying support in designing polyhedra scanning algorithms. These are *Project*, *Gist* and *Hull*.

Project To project a variable from a polyhedron, the variable is eliminated from all equations and inequalities from a linear system. For example,

$$\text{Project}(\{1 \leq y \leq x \leq 100\}, x) = \{1 \leq y \leq 100\}.$$

In some cases, Project will generate additional constraints if necessary:

$$\text{Project}(\{1 \le x \le 100 \land y = 2x\}, x) = \{2 \le y \le 200 \land \exists\alpha(y = 2\alpha)\}.$$

Gist Gist is a unique function implemented in the Omega library. It takes two relations and the result must satisfy the following condition:

$$\text{Gist}(A, B) \land B = A \land B.$$

The function can be interpreted as this: given that we know B, what is the extra knowledge in A that has not been known in B. The following illustrates the behavior of this function.

$$\text{Gist}(\{i > 10 \land j > 10\}, \{j > 10\}) = \{i > 10\},$$
$$\text{Gist}(\{1 \le i \le 100\}, \{i > 10\}) = \{i \le 100\}.$$

A new enhancement in Omega+ enables Gist to reduce the strength of modulo constraints. For example,

$$\text{Gist}(\{\exists\alpha(i = 6\alpha)\}, \{\exists\alpha(i = 2\alpha)\}) = \{\exists\alpha(i = 3\alpha)\}.$$

The above result can be proved correct using the Chinese remainder theorem. Intuitively speaking, if we already know i is an even number, the extra information included in the fact that i is a multiple of 6 is that i must be a multiple of 3.

Hull Hull of a set of polyhedra returns a single polyhedron that must include all points in the original set of polyhedra. Algebraically, the result of Hull must be a conjunction of constraints. Although a convex hull is the minimal polyhedron that encloses all input polyhedra, it can be very expensive to compute in some cases. Our experience so far is that absolute tight bounds are not necessary when dealing with real application code. Instead, Hull is an approximation algorithm in finding the enclosing polyhedron. A new enhancement in Omega+ makes Hull handle stride conditions and find the lattice when input polyhedra have different modulo constraints. Below is a simple example illustrating Hull's behavior:

$$\begin{aligned}\text{Hull}(&\{1 \le i, j \le 100 \land \exists\alpha(j = i + 4\alpha)\} \cup \\ &\{1 \le i \le 50 \land 1 \le j \le 200 \land \exists\alpha(j = i + 6\alpha)\}) \\ = &\{1 \le i \le 100 \land 1 \le j \le 200 \land \exists\alpha(j = i + 2\alpha)\}.\end{aligned}$$

It should be pointed out that different mathematical frameworks other than Omega+ can be used as long as the same functionality is provided. The generated code quality may differ due to different capability implemented in each framework.

3. Polyhedra Scanning and Code Generation

In this section we describe our improved polyhedra scanning algorithms, including the ones for the *loop overhead removal* with code size trade-off control and the subsequent *if-statement simplification*. These optimizations are becoming increasingly important for generating high quality code, as optimization strategies become more sophisticated in response to the growing complexity of microprocessors and many-core architectures.

To simplify the discussion, we assume that each polyhedron to be scanned is the end result of applying a mapping function to the original iteration space. The mapping function only affects the variable substitution during the code generation process, which we assume will be properly handled by the system. Also keep in mind that CodeGen+ treats every dimension in the polyhedra during scanning the same way without exception. This allows a clean and consistent strategy for loop overhead optimization and provides a predictable behavior to higher-level polyhedral transformation frameworks.

split: node
  set active;
  (relation, node)* (restriction, body)[];

loop: node	**leaf: node**
set active;	*set* active;
int level;	*relation* known;
relation known;	*relation* guards[];
relation restriction;	
relation bounds;	
relation guard;	
*node** body;	

Figure 1. AST node structure.

3.1 AST Structure

CodeGen+ relies on an abstract syntax tree (AST) to track the breakdown of a conjunction of unordered constraints in iteration spaces into levels of constraints, where constraints at each level can only use loop variables of this level and the levels above. Our AST is the same as [12] with only minor reinterpretation. There are three types of nodes: *split*, *loop* and *leaf*. Figure 1 shows the structures of these node types. Note the common active field which includes statements that will be executed within the node or its subtree. In addition, all the fields with an Omega+ relation type must be a single conjunct, which is guaranteed after disjoint iteration spaces are preprocessed to be split into separate ones. Below are detailed descriptions of each node type.

Split A split node has as its fields an array of restrictions and associated subtrees (called body). The order of subtrees is important as it represents the lexicographical order of the scanning result. For each *body* node, the corresponding *restriction*, as its name implies, restricts the iteration space of any node in the subtree. Unlike the other two node types, a split node does not correspond to any actual code when converting from the AST to actual code. It only helps to separate disjoint iteration spaces at the designated level.

Loop The loop node is the core part of the AST. Each loop node corresponds to one loop level. Its *known* and *restriction* fields are for bookkeeping information calculated from its ancestor nodes. Known refers to what constraints have been enforced by the code enclosing this loop, and restriction indicates the restricted iteration space for this node. They are not necessarily the same since not all constraints in the restricted iteration spaces can be enforced by loop nodes seen so far from the top down. Thus, known must be a subset of restriction, a property maintained throughout AST restructuring. Two other fields, *bounds* and *guard*, correspond to actual code that will be generated. Bounds is the condition that can be represented by a loop structure, namely lower and upper bounds for this loop variable and one stride condition for a constant step size. Guard is a conjunction of those extra constraints that cannot be represented by a loop structure as they are too complicated and must be enforced by a separate if-statement. The logical relationship here is that guard is placed outside the loop structure that enforces bounds, and so constraints in guard cannot reference this loop variable.

Leaf A leaf node represents those statements that will be executed at the iteration space restricted by all its parent split nodes. Each statement has an array *guards* field which represents the remaining constraints in the restricted iteration spaces that cannot be enforced by any parent loop nodes and require additional if-statements to enforce. Unlike the split node, there is no or-

```
initAST(level, active, restriction)
input: level: current loop level;
        active: set of active statements;
        restriction: condition to restrict polyhedra;
output: root of AST

if (level > max_level)
   new leaf_node with active;
   return leaf_node;
if (single statement in active)
   child = initAST(level + 1, active, restriction);
   new loop_node with level and body = child;
   return loop_node;
for (each statement s ∈ active)
   /* In the following statement,
        IS_s is the iteration space of the transformed statement.   */
   /* Approximate is an existing Omega operation to simplify the
        iteration space representation.                              */
   R_s = Approximate(restriction ∩ Project(IS_s,
      l_(level+1) ··· l_max_level)); /* no existentials */
for (each statement s ∈ active)
   for (each constraint c ∈ R_s involving loop variable l_level)
      if (c splits R_s∈active into disjoint sets active1 and active2)
         WLOG assume l_level is smaller in the partition
         constrained by c than the one constrained by c̄
         child1 = initAST(level, active1, restriction ∩ c);
         child2 = initAST(level, active2, restriction ∩ c̄);
         new split_node with (c, child1) and (c̄, child2);
         return split_node;
child = initAST(level + 1, active, restriction);
new loop_node with level and body = child;
return loop_node;
```

Figure 2. Algorithm to initialize AST.

der requirement for statements active at this location as they all have the same lexicographical order.

3.2 Manipulating the AST

We first build an initial AST from a set of polyhedra as the basis for further optimization. As a preprocessing step, each statement's iteration space is split into a disjoint set of polyhedra. In addition, all polyhedra are extended to the same dimensionality of the maximum one, with constant values for additional dimensions. The extra dimensions are conveniently ignored when generating code, and since they are constant values no extra complexity is introduced. For completeness of discussion, Figure 2 shows the algorithm to build the initial AST, which is essentially the same as the one used by [12]. It is invoked initially with `initAST`(1, {all stmts}, { $\langle l_1$, *TRUE* $\rangle$, ..., $\langle l_{max\_level}$, *TRUE* $\rangle$ }), which invokes the algorithm on all statements in the loop nest, starting at the outermost loop and with no restrictions on the loop indices. The algorithm uses a simple strategy in that at any dimension, if there is an overlap between polyhedra, they are enclosed in the same loop node. Otherwise, several loop nodes with disjoint spaces to a common parent split node are created. This approach represents minimal code size from polyhedra scanning.

3.2.1 Computing Node Properties

After executing the algorithm in Figure 2, we still must initialize other fields such as bounds and guards for loop nodes and guards for leaf nodes. Figure 3 shows the algorithm to compute these node properties, starting at the root of the AST. The algorithm will also be invoked whenever the AST is updated due to a newly inserted split node. There are several key points in the algorithm that are important to overhead optimization and code generation. First, the bounds selected for a loop node are represented directly in a loop

```
node.recompute(parent_active, known, restriction)
input: parent_active: set of active statements in parent node;
        known: known condition for this node;
        restriction: restriction condition for this node;
output: root of new AST

active = active ∩ parent_active;
node.known = known;
node.restrictions = restrictions;
if (node is split node)
   for (each restriction and child pair (r, c) in node)
      c = c.recompute(active, known, restriction ∩ r);
elseif (node is loop node)
   for (every statement s ∈ active)
      R_s = Project(IS_s, l_(level+1) ··· l_max_level) ∩
         restriction;
      if (R_s == ∅)
         active = active - {s};
   hull = Hull(R_s∈active);
   let i be the index for the loop at level
   if (i is degenerate)
      bounds = i's equality constraint in hull;
      guard = TRUE;
   else
      bounds = i's lower and upper bounds and single
         modulo constraint with unit coefficient in hull;
      guard = Gist(Project(hull, i), known ∩ bounds);
   endif
   body = body.recompute(active, known ∩ bounds ∩
      guard, restriction ∩ bounds ∩ guard);
   if (body == NULL)
      delete node;
      return NULL;
   else return node;
elseif (node is leaf node)
   for (each statement s ∈ active)
      guards[s] = Gist(IS_s ∩ restriction, known);
      if (guards[s] == FALSE)
         active = active - {s};
   if (active == ∅)
      delete node;
      return NULL;
   else return node;
```

Figure 3. Algorithm to compute AST node properties.

structure. This guarantees that overhead optimization decisions described in the next algorithm are indeed based on the actual output loop nesting structure. Second, for a loop level with a single iteration (called *degenerate loops*), its guard condition is always set to true. This strategy postpones the extra constraints that cannot be enforced at this loop level into lower level (inner loop) nodes. Because there is an inherent comparison operation for each loop, by pushing the constraints inward, we avoid redundant checking by the guard at this level and an inner loop nest encountered in the subtree.

3.2.2 Loop Overhead Removal

Figure 4 shows the algorithm to lift overheads out of inner loops by duplicating the code. The level of code duplication is controlled by parameter d which is the loop nesting depth. The loop nesting depth can be calculated from the previous computed AST using a recursive function. The leaf node has a nesting depth zero. The nesting depth for other nodes is based on the maximum nesting depth, *max_depth*, among its children. For non-degenerate loop nodes, nesting depth is *max_depth+1*, and it is *max_depth* for all other node types. The `liftOverhead` algorithm also takes another parameter *propagate_up* as a flag to tell whether it is currently working on a node that is inside the subloop with a nesting depth $\leq d$.

Loop overheads arise from non-tautology guard conditions in loop and leaf nodes. They correspond to if-statements in a loop nest. In our algorithm, a single overhead condition selected to be lifted out of the current position corresponds to a constraint or a combination of constraints whose complement is a single conjunct. For example,

$$i \leq 5$$

can be one selected overhead condition. And

$$\exists \alpha(5\alpha \leq i \leq 5\alpha + 2)$$

can also be lifted out as a whole since its complement

$$\exists \alpha(5\alpha + 3 \leq i \leq 5\alpha + 4)$$

is a single conjunct. This requirement allows a single split node to partition the space into two disjoint subspaces each constrained by a single conjunct.

The algorithm begins at the root of the AST with *propagate_up* set to *FALSE*, and descends the AST recursively. The main part of the algorithm deals with loop nodes with a nesting depth $\leq d$, and thus it will be explained in more detail. When a suitable overhead to be optimized is located, it is propagated up the tree to the highest level possible. The highest level is the loop node such that one of the following conditions is satisfied: (1) the required nesting depth is reached; (2) for constraint(s) with existential variables, the maximum loop level of variables appearing inside is this loop level minus one; or, (3) for constraints without existential variables, the maximum loop level of variables appearing inside is this loop level. The reason for (1) is straightforward since that is the intended place to lift the overhead. Further up will cause more code duplication than required. The reason for (2) and (3) is that this overhead cannot be propagated higher since otherwise it will cause a referenced variable to be projected away.

At this point, the algorithm has identified the location in the AST for inserting a split node for the overhead condition to be lifted. A new split node is inserted at this location and the original subAST is duplicated and reinserted as two children to this newly created split node, one constrained by satisfying the overhead condition and the other by its complement. The order of these two subtrees follows the lexicographical order. Both subASTs are then recomputed for node properties since they are under different restricted spaces now. The algorithm `liftOverhead` is then recursively invoked on this new split node. This process stops when all candidate overhead conditions have been lifted.

Currently we do not treat min/max bounds in a loop nest as overhead since we have not found the run-time costs of such operations to be significant. Nevertheless, if desired, min/max bounds can be easily added into the algorithm and controlled by a different nesting depth parameter if needed. The constraint type is much simpler than those that would appear in the guard condition, and thus the implementation is straightforward.

3.2.3 If-statement Simplification

Our previous algorithm for lifting loop overhead only deals with trade-offs between loop overhead and code size. It is possible that guard conditions from loop nodes of the same level at different subASTs use the same constraint or they contradict each other. This gives us the opportunity to further reduce the control overhead without any negative impact on code size by constructing if-then-else subtrees (represented by IF nodes in the algorithm) and avoiding unnecessary conditionals. This algorithm is invoked for a set of adjacent nodes at the same nesting depth, with *postponed_guard* set to NULL, and *known_guard* representing the context in which the nodes are nested.

```
node.liftOverhead(d, propagate_up)
input: d: loop nesting depth counted from innermost;
       propagate_up: flag whether inside a loop nest of
           nesting depth ≤ d;
output: (overhead constraint, root of new AST)

if (node is split node)
  for (each restriction and child pair (r, c) in node)
    (r2, c2) = c.liftOverhead(d, propagate_up);
    (r, c) = (r, c2);
    if (r2 ≠ TRUE)
      return (r2, node);
  return (TRUE, node);
elseif (node is loop node)
  if (nestingDepth(node) > d)
    (r, c) = body.liftOverhead(d, FALSE);
    body = c;
    return (TRUE, node);
  else
    if (propagate_up)
      pick one guard r with single conjunct complement;
      if (r ≠ TRUE)
        return (r, node);
    if (propagate_up || bounds is not an equality)
      (r, c) = body.liftOverhead(d, TRUE);
    else
      (r, c) = body.liftOverhead(d, FALSE);
    body = c;
    if (r == TRUE)
      return (TRUE, node);
    if (bounds is an equality)
      substitute l_level in r using the equation;
    if (!propagate_up || (r has existential variables and
      the maximum level of loop variables used is level − 1) ||
      (r has no existential variables and the maximum level of
      loop variables used is level))
      WLOG assume l_level is smaller in the partition satisfying r;
      new split_node with (r, node) and (r̄, node);
      split_node.recompute(active, known, restriction);
      return split_node.liftOverhead(d, propagate_up);
    else
      return (r, node);
elseif (node is leaf node)
  for (each statement s ∈ active)
    if (guards[s] ≠ ∅)
      pick one constraint r from guards[s] with single
      conjunct complement;
      if (r ≠ TRUE)
        return (r, node);
  return (TRUE, node);
```

Figure 4. Algorithm to lift loop overhead.

There are two scenarios for if-statement simplification. For loop nodes, only guard conditions from neighboring nodes can be considered for merging since the generated code must follow the lexicographical order. On the other hand, for statements in a leaf node, since they all have the exact same lexicographical order, simplifying if-statements can be done in any order and this provides more flexibility in reducing the number of comparisons. Figure 5 shows the algorithm `mergeIfInOrder` to merge if-conditions in order. Merging if-conditions out-of-order can be done in a similar fashion, and it is omitted here due to space limitations.

The algorithm in Figure 5 takes the input of an array of contiguous loop nodes of the same level. It also takes two additional parameters: one tracks those constraints yet to be enforced, and one tracks constraints already generated. The basic idea of the algorithm is to test if a constraint from the guard condition in the first node matches the constraint appearing in the immediately following ones. For the remaining nodes, the algorithm tests if the guards contradict. This partitions the nodes into three contiguous parts with regard to the if-statement for this particular constraint: the first and second part are the then and else part of the if-statement respectively, and the third part follows this if-statement. Then the algorithm recursively works on each group until all constraints are processed. Note that simply comparing the constraints in isolation is not optimal in reducing the number of comparisons. These constraints have additional known conditions guarding execution of the code at this point, and there is no need to retest these conditions. Instead, the algorithm tests whether they are equivalent and complementary given the known condition using the *Gist* function. For example, as shown later in Figure 8(f), if we already know variable i is an even number from its enclosing loops, then the constraint $\exists\alpha(i = 4\alpha)$ is the exact complement of constraint $\exists\alpha(i = 4\alpha + 2)$. We can then put the statements guarded by $\exists\alpha(i = 4\alpha + 2)$ into the else part of the if-statement with condition $(mod(i, 4) == 0)$.

However, recall that in the algorithm to compute node properties (Figure 3), we postpone the computation of guard conditions for those loop nodes which are assignments (degenerate loops). This will cause a problem here in that now the guard conditions at the different loop levels in the AST might actually be translated to neighboring if-statements in the generated code if intermediate loop nodes are all degenerate. As a preprocessing step, we conceptually propagate guard conditions in the child loop nodes into upper level loop nodes if loop nodes between them are all degenerate, with variable substitutions according to those assignments. Such propagation may involve multiple levels of degenerate loop nodes or multiple split nodes if necessary. Figure 6 illustrates this behavior using one AST snippet as an example. Guard conditions in nodes C, D, E and F are translated to neighboring if-statements in the actual code. Thus in our preprocessing step, the guard condition in node C is propagated to node A, and the guard condition in node F is propagated to node E. Finally, node A, D, E and G with updated guard conditions are the first parameters to the algorithm in Figure 5.

3.3 Code Generation

Once the AST is constructed and subsequently optimized, it corresponds to a compiler's high-level intermediate representation (IR) AST if all split nodes are ignored. Thus code generation is a straightforward process that follows from scanning the AST. Some details of converting constraints to code are presented here.

For a loop node with unit stride, lower and upper bounds come from inequalities in bounds conditions, with min/max added if there are multiple such inequalities. For non-unit stride, CodeGen+ must know whether the lower bounds always satisfy the stride condition. Suppose K is the intersection of the known condition and bounds condition for this loop node. First, we create a relation with a modulo constraint for this loop variable with the same stride but starting at a lower bound and test whether there is new knowledge in this relation given K. If not, we further test whether there is new knowledge in the stride condition when this loop variable is set to the lower bound in K. Both tests are done by the Gist function and if both results are a tautology, we can safely use this lower bound; otherwise, we generate a remainder expression to be added to the lower bound.

For degenerate loop nodes (single iteration loops), we either generate assignment code directly or substitute every appearance of this loop variable in its child AST with a substitution expression. The choice depends on how complex the expression is, and whether it can be adjusted by a parameter. Additional consideration is needed when the coefficient c for this loop variable is not a unit; that is, when $|c| \neq 1$. We must test if the right hand side of the assignment without dividing by the c part is always a multiple of c using the Gist function given the known condition when code reaches here. If not, an if-statement with condition (mod(RHS, $|c|$) $== 0$) must be created to guard the assignment and the code from the child AST, where RHS is the right hand side of the assignment without dividing by the c part.

Here are a few examples where constraints in the guard conditions have existential variables:

$$\exists\alpha(4i = 5j + 4\alpha) \rightarrow mod(4 * i - 5 * j), 4) == 0,$$
$$\exists\alpha(4\alpha \leq i \leq 5\alpha) \rightarrow ceil(i, 5) <= floor(i, 4).$$

Our implementation also tries to recognize floor definitions from constraints and generate clean code whenever possible. For exam-

```
mergeIfInOrder(nodes[], postponed_guard, known_guard)
input: nodes[]: neighboring nodes for their guard conditions;
        postponed_guard: guard conditions yet to be enforced;
        known_guard: guard conditions already considered;
output: if-then-else tree

/* for convenience of illustration, assume parameter nodes always
   indexed from 1 to n */
if (nodes == ∅)
  return NULL;
r = Gist(nodes[1].guard, known_guard);
if ((nodes[1].known ∩ known_guard) ⊆ r)
  for (i in 2..n)
    if (Gist(nodes[i].guard, known_guard) ≠ TRUE)
      break;
  s1 = code for nodes[1..(i − 1)] without their guard condition;
  s2 = mergeIfInOrder(nodes[i..n], NULL, known_guard);
  s3 = concatenate s1 and s2 in this order;
  if (postponed_guard ≠ ∅)
    return new IF(postponed_guard, s3, NULL);
  else
    return s3;
else
  c = select a constraint from nodes[1].guard that maximizes
    the contiguous region of nodes starting from 2 to satisfy it;
  Let c partition nodes into three contiguous regions nodes1,
  nodes2 and nodes3 in this order where nodes1 satisfies c,
  nodes2 satisfies c̄ and nodes3 remaining nodes in the end;
  if (nodes2 == ∅ ∧ nodes3 == ∅)
    return mergeIfInOrder(nodes1, postponed_guard ∩ c,
      known_guard ∩ c);
  elseif (nodes2 == ∅)
    s1 = mergeIfInOrder(nodes1, c, known_guard ∩ c);
    s2 = mergeIfInOrder(nodes3, NULL, known_guard);
    s3 = concatenate s1 and s2 in this order;
    if (postponed_guard ≠ ∅)
      return new IF(postponed_guard, s3, NULL);
    else
      return s3;
  else
    s1 = mergeIfInOrder(nodes1, NULL, known_guard ∩ c);
    s2 = mergeIfInOrder(nodes2, NULL, known_guard ∩ c̄);
    s3 = mergeIfInOrder(nodes3, NULL, known_guard);
    s4 = new IF(c, s1, s2);
    s5 = concatenate s4 and s3 in this order;
    if (postponed_guard ≠ ∅)
      return new IF(postponed_guard, s5, NULL);
    else
      return s5;
```

Figure 5. Algorithm to merge neighboring if-conditions in order.

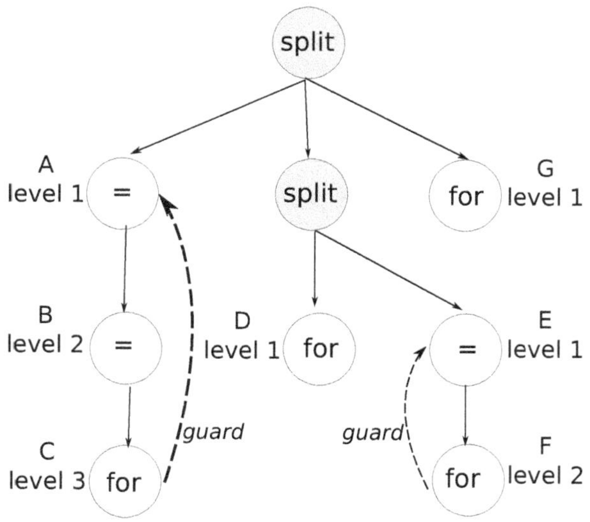

Figure 6. Propagate guard conditions up through degenerate loop nodes (marked by "=").

ple, with α defined by $\lfloor \frac{m}{4} \rfloor$ in the following relation,

$$\{[i] : \exists \alpha(m - 4 < 4\alpha <= m \wedge 4\alpha <= i <= n)\},$$

the generated lower bound for i is $4 * floor(m, 4)$. Thus there is no if-statement needed for the generated loop code from this polyhedron.

4. Experiments

With precise control of trade-offs between loop overhead and code size and reduction of if-conditions, while at the same time preserving the lexicographical order among statements represented in the input iteration spaces, CodeGen+ provides a clean interface and predictable behavior for high-level polyhedral loop transformation frameworks. In this section, we examine the quality of code generated by CodeGen+ after composing a sequence of transformations in a polyhedral framework for a set of loop nest computations. We will compare CodeGen+ with the state-of-the-art polyhedra scanning tool CLooG using examples to illustrate the improvements resulting from our new algorithms.

For the generated codes in this section, we use CLooG 0.16.3 and CodeGen+ 2.2.3. For code compilation and performance, we use gcc 4.6.1 with -O3 flag. For performance measurements, the target architecture is a single core of a 2.8GHz Intel Core i7 930 with 2GBytes memory. We first consider a set of simple code examples shown in Figures 7 and 8 to illustrate the differences resulting from the algorithms in the previous section. Subsequently, we examine a set of kernel computations, shown in Table 1. The code inputs are standard hand written kernels (e.g., a simple 3-deep loop nest for `gemm`) to which transformations are applied using the CHiLL transformation and code generation system [4]. While CHiLL can invoke CodeGen+ internally, we instead capture the iteration spaces of the transformed statements. Then, identical iteration spaces are input to both Codegen+ and to CLooG (via the iscc frontend to ISL in Barvinok) [27]. The output code from both are compared to produce the results in the table.

4.1 Control of Trade-offs

Precise control of trade-offs between loop overhead and code size is important in tailoring the output of polyhedra scanning. For example, in optimizing for high performance, code generation of an innermost loop impacts instruction-level parallelism or SIMD execution in multimedia extensions, which are critical for overall performance. Thus removing loop overhead from innermost loops is usually the best choice in balancing loop overhead and code size. For other situations, a different choice might be selected. As examples, we might not want to lift any overhead to avoid code growth in an embedded system, or we might want to remove as much control flow as possible from loops for the highest performance.

Figure 7(b-d) shows the three variations of generated code from iteration spaces in (a) with different trade-offs of removing loop overhead from subloops of depth 0, 1 and 2, respectively. Note that statement `s0` is enclosed in loop `t1` which itself is a loop nest of depth 2. Thus when removing loop overhead from nesting depth 0 and 1, its enclosing if-condition `(n>=2)` is not moved out of the `t1` loop. Only when removing loop overhead from all subloops of depth 2 is it moved out of the `t1` loop; no more if-conditions remain inside any loop in the generated code (Figure 7(d)). CLooG generates almost identical code to Figure 7(d), which follows the lexicographical order. However, it does not provide such a guarantee when generating codes for other trade-off points using the -f or -l flags, which move conditions based on the first or last loop's nesting depth, respectively.

4.2 If-condition Overhead

The algorithms presented in this paper can reduce the number of unnecessary if-conditions in the generated codes, especially in some difficult situations. Figure 8 shows two examples to compare number of if-conditions in the codes generated from CLooG and CodeGen+. For the iteration space in Figure 8(a), the output of CLooG in Figure 8(b) contains redundant modulo checking in the innermost loop, but this is removed by CodeGen+ as shown in Figure 8(c). Consider the iteration space of Figure 8(d) and the output of CLooG in Figure 8(e). Given that $c1$ is even, based on loop bounds, the condition $((c1 + 2)\%4 == 0)$ can be determined statically to be the complement of condition $(c1\%4 == 0)$. Thus, the mod operation occurs just once in the CodeGen+ code of Figure 8(f), and the outermost condition on variable `n` is not generated since the first loop encountered will check the same condition again as part of its standard bounds checking.

4.3 Application to Code Optimization

We now demonstrate that the improvements in the polyhedra scanning algorithms indeed make a significant impact on generating high-quality codes when complex optimization strategies are applied in polyhedral frameworks. Table 1 shows our comparison result with CLooG using the same iteration spaces generated from CHiLL [4] for three programs generated from scripts in CHiLL's example directory, matrix-vector multiply (`gemv`), matrix-matrix multiply (`gemm`) and LU factorization (`lu`), and two codes `qr` and `swim` taken from CLooG [26]. These examples illustrate the effect of complexity of iteration spaces on generated code. The kernel `gemv` is the simplest, followed by `qr`, `swim` and `gemm`. Iteration spaces for `lu` are by far the most complex.

For `gemv`'s simple unroll-and-jam optimization, both CLooG and CodeGen+ take roughly the same amount of time generating the codes, and the resulting codes have the same performance although the code generated by CLooG is somewhat larger because it generates extra if-conditions corresponding to modulo constraints. The optimization strategy for `qr` involves peeling, shifting and fusion; the resulting code is larger using CLooG which increases code generation and compile time, but performance is comparable for the two systems. For `swim`, the optimization strategy is very close to that of [8], employing peeling, shifting, and fusion. While the transformations are similar to what was used in `qr`, the iteration space complexity grows because there are three loop nests that all must be peeled and shifted different amounts to enable fusion. The

$s0 : \{[i] : 1 \leq i \leq 100 \wedge n > 1\};$
$s1 : \{[i,j] : 1 \leq i,j \leq 100 \wedge n > 1\};$
$s2 : \{[i,j] : 1 \leq i,j \leq 100\};$
(a) iteration spaces

```
for (t1=1;t1<=100;t1++)
  if (n>=2)
    s0(t1);
  for (t2=1;t2<=100;t2++)
    s2(t1,t2);
    if (n>=2)
      s1(t1,t2);
```

(b) no loop overhead removal (depth 0)

```
for (t1=1;t1<=100;t1++)
  if (n>=2)
    s0(t1);
    for (t2=1;t2<=100;t2++)
      s1(t1,t2);
      s2(t1,t2);
  else
    for (t2=1;t2<=100;t2++)
      s2(t1,t2);
```

(c) remove overhead from depth 1 loops (default)

```
if (n>=2)
  for(t1=1;t1<=100;t1++)
    s0(t1);
    for (t2=1;t2<=100;t2++)
      s1(t1,t2);
      s2(t1,t2);
else
  for (t1=1;t1<=100;t1++)
    for (t2=1;t2<=100;t2++)
      s2(t1,t2);
```

(d) remove overhead from depth 2 loops

Figure 7. Different trade-offs between loop overhead and code size in CodeGen+.

$$s0 : \{[i,j] : 1 \leq i \leq n \wedge i \leq j \leq n \wedge \exists\alpha, \beta(i = 1 + 4\alpha \wedge j = i + 3\beta)\};$$

(a) single iteration space with complex stride conditions

```
if (n>=1)
  for (i=1;i<=n;i+=4)
    for (j=i;j<=n;j+=3)
      if ((11*i+4*j+9)%12 == 0)
        s0(i,j);
```

(b) CLooG output from (a)

```
for (t1=1;t1<=n;t1+=4)
  for (t2=t1;t2<=n;t2+=3)
    s0(t1,t2);
```

(c) CodeGen+ output from (a)

$$s0 : \{[i] : 1 \leq i \leq n \wedge \exists\alpha(i = 4\alpha)\}; \quad s1 : \{[i] : 1 \leq i \leq n \wedge \exists\alpha(i = 4\alpha + 2)\};$$

(d) two iteration spaces with complex relationship with each other

```
if (n>=2)
  for (c1=2;c1<=n;c1+=2)
    if (c1%4==0)
      s0(c1);
    if ((c1+2)%4==0)
      s1(c1);
```

(e) CLooG output from (d)

```
for (t1=2;t1<=n;t1+=2)
  if (intMod(t1,4)==0)
    s0(t1);
  else
    s1(t1);
```

(f) CodeGen+ output from (d)

Figure 8. Comparison of number of if-conditions in the generated codes.

code generated by CLooG is more than four times larger than that generated by CodeGen+, and code generation time and compile time are consequently increased. `Swim` achieves CodeGen+'s highest execution-time speedup over CLooG of 1.15x. To consider a very different optimization strategy, both `gemm` and `lu` require multiple levels of tiling and result in many statements generated for the final set of iteration spaces. In addition, `lu` requires extensive splitting of the iteration spaces, for example to separate the computation into a mini-LU, triangular solve and matrix-matrix multiply as in highly-tuned implementations [10]. CodeGen+ generates significantly less lines of code for `gemm` and `lu` as compared with CLooG, a reduction of over 8x and 24x, respectively, while the resulting code performs 1.12x faster than the CLooG output for both. Moreover, code generation time and compilation time have up to an order of magnitude speedup; for example, 25x and 34x reductions, respectively, for `lu`.

Overall, the combined effect of lifting control overhead from innermost loops and if simplification in CodeGen+ results in simpler code with less branching than that generated by CLooG for identical iteration spaces. This simpler code takes less time to generate and compile. For the more complex examples, where tiling or unrolling is used resulting in modulo constraints, or where peeling and shifting causes additional control flow, the code generated by CodeGen+ also performs better, up to 1.15x faster. This performance difference is very significant in the high-performance computing community, where programmers are willing to expend significant extra effort to increase utilization of precious supercomputing resources. As future architectures become more complex, we anticipate the compiler transformation strategies must also increase in complexity, so that this gap in generated code quality is likely to grow.

5. Related Work

Early work on polyhedra scanning focuses on how to generate code for a single polyhedron. Ancourt and Irigoin [1] use Fourier-Motzkin elimination to find loop bounds for unimodular transformations. Their method is improved later by Le Fur; however only transformed iteration spaces without holes are considered [7]. Other research [6, 14, 20, 30] expands the mapping function to allow non-unimodular transformations. Hermite Normal Form is used to find loop strides. Besides using Fourier-Motzkin elimination to extract loop bounds from a system of linear inequalities, different mathematical solutions are pursued. Collard et al. [5] use a dual simplex method. Chernikova's algorithm is another geometric approach to simplify a set of linear inequalities. It is used by Quillere et al. [18] which will be mentioned later in this section.

Kelly et al. [12] are among the first to address the problem of code generation for a set of polyhedra. Moreover, their system is built on a systematic approach to integer linear systems, implemented as part of the Omega library [15–17]. However, loop overhead trade-off decisions are based on static loop levels, without taking into account that modern polyhedral frameworks often rely on additional auxiliary dimensions, some of which are constants, to manage complicated optimization strategies. Moreover, flaws in its code generation logic will cause suboptimal or incorrect code to be generated in some difficult cases.

Griebl et al. [9] also present their code generation solution for multiple polyhedra, which allows non-unimodular transformations.

	lines of generated code			code generation time			gcc compile time			code performance		
	CLooG	CodeGen+	Reduction	CLooG	CodeGen+	Speedup	CLooG	CodeGen+	Speedup	CLooG	CodeGen+	Speedup
gemv	39	24	1.70x	0.151s	0.132s	1.14x	0.095s	0.071s	1.34x	0.091s	0.091s	1.00x
qr	88	35	2.51x	0.316s	0.104s	3.04x	0.115s	0.057s	2.02x	4.255s	4.254s	1.00x
swim	501	107	4.68x	0.622s	0.251s	2.49x	2.767s	0.590s	4.69x	0.599s	0.522s	1.15x
gemm	373	42	8.88x	6.552s	1.082s	6.06x	0.364s	0.086s	4.23x	136.667s	121.736s	1.12x
lu	2635	106	24.86x	106.984s	4.170s	25.66x	7.360s	0.211s	34.88x	49.973s	44.551s	1.12x

Table 1. Comparison of code generation performance using iteration spaces representing real optimization strategies.

Their approach can generate two flavors of code from polyhedra scanning: a run-time solution and a compile-time solution, which loosely correspond to minimal code size and minimal overhead versions, respectively. Their method in reducing overhead would result in $N!$ possibilities in loop bounds for N parameters, which can be handled by Omega code generation [12] with proper min/max bounds with significantly fewer loops. One innovation of Griebl et al.'s approach is that it allows non-invertible mapping by expanding the matrix to an invertible one, filling in unit vectors, during polyhedra scanning. However, this may not be necessary if higher-level tools can select missing dimensions using better knowledge of intended transformations.

Quillere et al. [18] propose that by splitting overlapping iteration spaces at any dimension during the process of scanning polyhedra, they can generate minimum loop overhead code without the iterative method used by [12]. However, this method can easily cause code explosion and provides no control of trade-offs between loop overhead and code size. CLooG [2, 26] uses the same approach of Quillere et al., but it tries to overcome its code explosion limitation. After initial processing, the algorithm will try to reduce the number of polyhedra previously split. However, CLooG does not provide a guarantee of generating code respecting the lexicographical order in iteration spaces during its trade-offs other than the default choice.

6. Conclusion

This paper describes a polyhedra scanning system that can meet the challenge of supporting sophisticated polyhedral frameworks combined with autotuning to generate high-performance code. The algorithms are based on a strict mathematical foundation and are designed to handle complex constraint relationships among a set of polyhedra, with precise control of trade-offs between loop overhead and code size. We compare with the state-of-the-art polyhedra scanning tool CLooG on five loop nest computations, demonstrating that CodeGen+ generates code that is simpler and up to 1.15x faster. We believe that such a system is critical to expand the applicability of polyhedral frameworks and enable compilers to close or significantly narrow the performance gap between compiler-optimized loop nests and hand-tuned code, including domain-specific performance libraries such as BLAS.

Editorial Note. Author Chun Chen passed away shortly after submission of this manuscript. Anand Venkat, Protonu Basu and Mary Hall made minor editing changes to the document to respond to reviewer requests and improve readability, and most significantly, added experimental results for two additional benchmarks, `qr` and `swim`. Questions about the contents of the paper can be directed to {anandv,protonu,mhall}@cs.utah.edu.

Acknowledgments

This research was funded in part by DARPA contract HR0011-10-9-0008, National Science Foundation award CCF-1018881, and Department of Energy Office of Science awards DE-SC0003777 and DE-SC0003520.

References

[1] Corinne Ancourt and François Irigoin. Scanning polyhedra with DO loops. In *Proceedings of ACM SIGPLAN Symposium on Principles and Practice of Parallel Programming*, April 1991.

[2] Cédric Bastoul. Code generation in the polyhedral model is easier than you think. In *Proceedings of the International Conference on Parallel Architectures and Compilation Techniques*, October 2004.

[3] C. Chen, J. Shin, S. Kintali, J. Chame, and M. Hall. Model-guided empirical optimization for multimedia extension architecture s: A case study. In *Proceedings of the Workshop on Performance Optimization for High-Level Languages and Libraries (POHLL 2007)*, May 2007.

[4] Chun Chen, Jacqueline Chame, and Mary W. Hall. CHiLL: A framework for composing high-level loop transformations. Technical Report 08-897, University of Southern California, Jun 2008.

[5] Jean-François Collard, Tanguy Risset, and Paul Feautrier. Construction of DO loops from systems of affine constraints. *Parallel Processing Letters*, 5(3):421–436, 1995.

[6] Agustín Fernández, José M. Llabería, and Miguel Valero-García. Loop transformation using nonumimodular matrices. *IEEE Transactions on Parallel and Distributed Systems*, 6(8):832–840, August 1995.

[7] Marc Le Fur. Scanning parameterized polyhedron using Fourier-Motzkin elimination. *Concurrency: Practice and Experience*, 8(6):445–460, 1996.

[8] Sylvain Girbal, Nicolas Vasilache, Cédric Bastoul, Albert Cohen, David Parello, Marc Sigler, and Olivier Temam. Semi-automatic composition of loop transformations for deep parallelism and memory hierarchies. *International Journal of Parallel Programming*, 34(3):261–317, June 2006.

[9] Martin Griebl, Christian Lengauer, and Sabine Wetzel. Code generation in the polytope model. In *Proceedings of the International Conference on Parallel Architectures and Compilation Techniques*, October 1998.

[10] Mary Hall, Jacqueline Chame, Jaewook Shin, Chun Chen, Gabe Rudy, and Malik Murtaza Khan. Loop transformation recipes for code generation and auto-tuning. In *LCPC*, October, 2009.

[11] Wayne Kelly, Vadim Maslov, William Pugh, Evan Rosser, Tatiana Shpeisman, and David Wonnacott. The Omega Library interface guide. Technical Report CS-TR-3445, University of Maryland at College Park, March 1995.

[12] Wayne Kelly, William Pugh, and Evan Rosser. Code generation for multiple mappings. In *Proceedings of the 5th Symposium on the Frontiers of Massively Parallel Computation*, February 1995.

[13] Malik Khan. *Autotuning, code generation and optimizing compiler technology for GPUs*. PhD thesis, University of Southern California, May 2012.

[14] Wei Li and Keshav Pingali. A singular loop transformation framework based on non-singular matrices. In *Proceedings of the 5th International Workshop on Languages and Compilers for Parallel Computing*, August 1992.

[15] William Pugh. The Omega test: A practical algorithm for exact array dependence analysis. *Communications of the ACM*, 35(8):102–114, August 1992.

[16] William Pugh and David Wonnacott. An exact method for analysis of value-based array data dependences. In *Proceedings of the 6th International Workshop on Languages and Compilers for Parallel Computing*, August 1993.

[17] William Pugh and David Wonnacott. Experiences with constraint-based array dependence analysis. In *Proceedings of the Second International Workshop on Principles and Practice of Constraint Programming*, May 1994.

[18] Fabien Quilleré, Sanjay Rajopadhye, and Doran Wilde. Generation of efficient nested loops from polyhedra. *International Journal of Parallel Programming*, 28(5):469–498, October 2000.

[19] Shreyas Ramalingam, Mary Hall, and Chun Chen. Improving high-performance sparse libraries using compiler-assisted specialization : A PETSc case study. In *Proceedings of the Workshop on High-Level Parallel Programming Models and Supportive Environments (HIPS 2012)*, May 2012.

[20] J. Ramanujam. Beyond unimodular transformations. *The Journal of Supercomputing*, 9(4):365–389, February 1995.

[21] Gabe Rudy, Malik Murtaza Khan, Mary Hall, Chun Chen, and Cha Jacqueline. A programming language interface to describe transformations and code generation. In *Proceedings of the 23rd international conference on Languages and compilers for parallel computing*, pages 136–150. Springer-Verlag, 2011.

[22] Jaewook Shin, Mary W. Hall, Jacqueline Chame, Chun Chen, Paul F. Fischer, and Paul D. Hovland. Speeding up nek5000 with autotuning and specialization. In *Proceedings of the 24th ACM International Conference on Supercomputing*, ICS '10, pages 253–262, 2010.

[23] Jaewook Shin, Mary W. Hall, Jacqueline Chame, Chun Chen, and Paul D. Hovland. Transformation recipes for code generation and auto-tuning. In *The Fourth International Workshop on Automatic Performance Tuning*, October 2009.

[24] A. Tiwari, J. K. Hollingsworth, C. Chen, M. Hall, C. Liao, D. J. Quinlan, and J. Chame. Auto-tuning full applications: A case study. *International Journal of High Performance Computing Applications*, pages 286–294, August 2011.

[25] Ananta Tiwari, Chun Chen, Jacqueline Chame, Mary Hall, and Jeffrey K. Hollingsworth. A scalable autotuning framework for compiler optimization. In *IPDPS*, Rome, Italy, May 2009.

[26] Nicolas Vasilache, Cédric Bastoul, and Albert Cohen. Polyhedral code generation in the real world. In *Proceedings of the International Conference on Compiler Construction*, March 2006.

[27] Sven Verdoolaege. isl: An integer set library for the polyhedral model. In *International Congress on Mathematical Software*, September 2010.

[28] Michael E. Wolf and Monica S. Lam. A data locality optimizing algorithm. In *Proceedings of ACM SIGPLAN Conference on Programming Language Design and Implementation*, June 1991.

[29] Michael E. Wolf and Monica S. Lam. A loop transformation theory and an algorithm to maximize parallelism. *IEEE Transactions on Parallel and Distributed Systems*, 2(4):452–471, October 1991.

[30] Jingling Xue. Automating non-unimodular loop transformations for massive parallelism. *Parallel Computing*, 20(5):711–728, May 1994.

Logical Inference Techniques for Loop Parallelization

Cosmin E. Oancea
HIPERFIT, Department of Computer Science
University of Copenhagen, cosmin.oancea@diku.dk

Lawrence Rauchwerger
Parasol Lab, Texas A&M University
rwerger@cse.tamu.edu

Abstract

This paper presents a fully automatic approach to loop parallelization that integrates the use of static and run-time analysis and thus overcomes many known difficulties such as nonlinear and indirect array indexing and complex control flow. Our hybrid analysis framework validates the parallelization transformation by verifying the independence of the loop's memory references. To this end it represents array references using the USR (uniform set representation) language and expresses the independence condition as an equation, $S = \emptyset$, where S is a set expression representing array indexes. Using a language instead of an array-abstraction representation for S results in a smaller number of conservative approximations but exhibits a potentially-high runtime cost. To alleviate this cost we introduce a language translation $\mathcal{F}$ from the USR set-expression language to an equally rich language of predicates ($\mathcal{F}(S) \Rightarrow S = \emptyset$). Loop parallelization is then validated using a novel logic inference algorithm that factorizes the obtained complex predicates ($\mathcal{F}(S)$) into a sequence of sufficient-independence conditions that are evaluated first statically and, when needed, dynamically, in increasing order of their estimated complexities. We evaluate our automated solution on 26 benchmarks from PERFECT-CLUB and SPEC suites and show that our approach is effective in parallelizing large, complex loops and obtains much better full program speedups than the Intel and IBM Fortran compilers.

Categories and Subject Descriptors D.1.3 [*Concurrent Programming*]: Parallel Programming; D.3.4 [*Processors*]: Compiler

General Terms Performance, Design, Algorithms

Keywords auto-parallelization, USR, independence predicates.

1. Introduction

Automatic loop parallelization requires the analysis of memory references for the purpose of establishing their data independence. For array references, compilers have used data dependence analysis which has historically taken two distinct directions: Static (compile time) analysis and run-time (dynamic) analysis.

Static dependence analysis, first proposed by [2, 4, 12, 22], analyzes an entire loop nest by modeling the data dependencies between any pair of read/write accesses. While this technique can also drive powerful code transformations such as loop interchange, skewing, etc., they are typically limited to the affine array subscript domain and their effectiveness [21] is limited to relatively-small loop nests. However, in the more general case, there are many obstacles to loop parallelization such as difficult to analyze symbolic constants, complex control flow, array-reshaping at call sites, quadratic array indexing, induction variables with no closed-form solutions [6, 13, 20]. Various techniques have been proposed to partially address some of these difficulties. For example, a class of index-array and stack-like accesses may be disambiguated via access pattern-matching techniques [15, 16] and some monotonic accesses (e.g., quadratic indexing) can be disambiguated via non-affine dependency tests [7]. Similarly, Presburger arithmetic can be extended to the non-affine domain [24] to solve a class of irregular accesses and control-flow. The next step has been to extend analysis to program level by summarizing accesses interprocedurally, where an array abstraction is used to represent a (regular) set of memory references either via systems of affine constraints [13], or linear-memory-access descriptors [20], respectively. Loop independence has been modeled typically via an equation on summaries of shape $S = \emptyset$. To improve precision, summaries are paired with predicates [14, 18] that guard (otherwise unsafe) simplifications in the array-abstraction domain or predicate the summary existence (i.e., control-flow conditions).

Run-time analysis is necessary and useful when static analysis alone cannot decide whether a loop is independent or not and thus needs to make the conservative choice, i.e., not parallel. Run-time analysis can always resolve static ambiguities because it can use instances of symbols and thus produce accurate results. Historically, dynamic dependence analysis has been performed by tracing and analyzing a loop's relevant memory references by executing an inspector loop (inspector/executor model [26]), or by tracing and analyzing a speculative parallel execution of the loop as it is done in thread-level speculation [25]. Such approaches typically extract maximal parallelism, at the cost of significant overhead, usually proportional to the number of traced dynamic memory references.

In order to attain our goal of effectively parallelizing a large number of codes automatically we have devised a hybrid compiler technology that can extract maximum static information so that the overhead of the dynamic analysis is reduced to a minimum.

1.1 Static Analysis with Light Weight Dynamic Complement

Summary based static analysis based on the array abstraction has been shown by previous research to be more scalable and useful for loop parallelization. However, from our experience we have found that its main source of inaccuracy lies in the fact that the array abstraction does not form a closed algebra under the required set operations: (recurrence) union, intersection, subtraction, gates, call sites. This shortcoming results in the necessity of conservative approximations during early construction stages, both at the array-abstraction and its associated-predicate levels. Thus either fewer loops are qualified as parallel or more dynamic analysis is needed. To mitigate this lack of scalability we have adopted a more expressive, higher level intermediate representation language. We are using the USR(Uniform Set Representation) [28], a composable language that subsumes both the array abstraction as well as the

PLDI'12, June 11–16, 2012, Beijing, China.

```
SUBROUTINE solvh(HE,XE,IA,IB)
  DIMENSION  HE(32, *), XE(*)
  READ(*,*) SYM, NS, NP, N
  CCC    SOLVH_do20
  DO i = 1, N, 1
    DO k = 1, IA(i), 1
      id = IB(i) + k - 1
      CALL geteu    (XE, SYM,  NP)
      CALL matmult(HE(1,id),XE,NS)
      CALL solvhe   (HE(1,id), NP)
    ENDDO
ENDDO END

SUBROUTINE matmult(HE,XE,NS)
  DIMENSION HE(*), XE(*)

  DO j = 1, NS, 1
    HE(j) = XE(j)
    XE(j) = ...
ENDDO END
```

```
SUBROUTINE geteu(XE,SYM,NP)
  DIMENSION  XE(16,*)

  IF (SYM .NE. 1) THEN
    DO i = 1, NP, 1
      DO j = 1, 16, 1
        XE(j, i) = ...
      ENDDO
    ENDDO
  ENDIF
END

SUBROUTINE solvhe(HE,NP)
  DIMENSION  HE(8, *)

  DO j = 1, 3, 1
    DO i = 1, NP, 1
      HE(j, i)=HE(j, i)+..
    ENDDO
ENDDO END
```

Figure 1. Simplified Loop SOLVH_DO20 from DYFESM Bench.

control flow. It includes in the language results of operations previously deemed outside the array-abstraction domain. Thus we can express the loop data independence summary equation as a the set equation $S = \emptyset$. Sometimes this equation is easy to prove statically. However, usually for real codes, the USR which needs to proven empty is very complex. Furthermore, for outer loops, the set expressions become very long and cumbersome to deal with during compilation.

To deal with this problem in a scalable manner, i.e., for outer, program level loops, we define an equally-rich language of predicates (PDAG) and an effective rule-based translation between the two languages, such that the result predicate p is a sufficient condition for loop independence: $p \Rightarrow \{S = \emptyset\}$. This transformation shifts the effort of proving loop independence from manipulating set expressions to that of handling logical expressions. Our translation scheme is general, allows (later) expansion and builds a less-constrained *predicate program* with fewer conservative approximations than those of related approaches (e.g., p's input symbols need not be read-only). Finally, we have developed a powerful and extensible logical inference based factorization algorithm that generates a set of sufficient conditions for parallelism. Some of these factors can be disambiguated statically and others need to be evaluated dynamically if aggressive parallelization is to be achieved. The generated sufficient run-time tests are ordered based on their estimated complexity and/or probability of success. Depending on the level of risk desired, the run-time complexity of the dynamic tests can be upper bounded during compilation.

1.2 A Simple Code Example

Figure 1 shows the simplified version of loop SOLVH_DO20 from the **dyfesm** benchmark. We will now analyze the references to arrays **XE** and **HE** to establish loop independence. If we consider **XE** and **HE** as unidimensional arrays, we can observe that **XE** is written in subroutine **geteu** on all indexes belonging to interval **[1,16*NP]** whenever **SYM.NE.1** holds, and is read in **matmult** on indexes in **[1,NS]**. Similarly, **HE** is written in **matmult** on all indexes in interval **[**τ**+1,**τ**+NS]**, and is read and written in **solvhe** on a subset of indexes in interval **[**τ**+1,**τ**+8*NP-5]**, where τ**=32*(id-1)** is the array offset of parameter **HE(1,id)**.

Flow independence of the outermost loop is established by showing that the per-iteration read sets of **XE** and **HE** are covered by their respective per-iteration write sets. This corresponds to solving equations **[1,NS]**$\subseteq$**[1,16*NP]** and **[**τ**+1,**τ**+8*NP-5]**$\subseteq$**[**τ**+1,**τ**+NS]** that result in the independence predicates **SYM.NE.1** $\wedge$ **NS**$\leq$**16*NP** and **8*NP<NS+6** for arrays **XE** and **HE**, respectively.

Examining *output independence*, we observe that the per-iteration write set of array **XE** is invariant to the outermost loop, hence **XE** can be privatized and updated with the values written by the last iteration (i.e., static-last value SLV). As discussed in Section 3.3, a successful predicate that proves that the per-iteration writes of **HE** do not overlap across iterations, hence **HE**'s output independence, is: $\wedge_{i=1}^{N-1}$**NS**$\leq$**32*(IB(i+1)-IA(i)-IB(i)+1)**.

Finally, proving **solveh_do20** independent requires predicates derived from both summary equations, such as NS≤16*NP, and control flow, such as **SYM.NE.1**. Also **HE**'s output independence predicate requires a recurrence-based formula. The overhead represented by the dynamic predicate evaluation is negligible: $O(1)$ and $O(N)$, respectively, compared with the loop's $O(N^2)$ complexity.

Our set to predicate translation and predicate factorization approach can be applied beyond parallelization to optimize problems such as last-value assignment and reduction parallelization. Furthermore, our design is open ended because it can readily accept more rules for translation and factorization. The monotonicity-based techniques in Section 3.3 represent such an extension example which has been well integrated in our framework.

1.3 Main Contributions

The main contributions of this paper are:

- A compiler framework that integrates a language translation $\mathcal{F}$ from the USR set-expression language to a rich language of predicates ($\mathcal{F}(S) \Rightarrow S = \emptyset$).
- A novel and extensible logic inference algorithm that factorizes complex predicates ($\mathcal{F}(S)$) into a sequence of sufficient-independence conditions which can be evaluated statically and, when necessary, dynamically.
- an experimental evaluation on twenty six **Fortran** benchmarks from PERFECT-CLUB, SPEC92, 2000, and 2006 suites.

The experimental evaluation demonstrates that: (i) the extracted predicates are successful (accurate) in most cases, (ii) the runtime overhead of these predicates is negligible, i.e., under 1% of the parallel runtime, while the other parallelism-enabling techniques show scalable speedup, and that (iii) we obtain speedups as high as 4.5x and 8.4x and on average 2.4x and 5.4x on four and eight processors, respectively, which are superior to those obtained by INTEL's **ifort** and IBM's **xlf_r** commercial compilers.

Compared with results reported in the literature, the evaluation shows that (i) our novel factorization scheme parallelized a number of previously unreported benchmarks via light-weight predicates, (ii) our unified framework solves a class of non-affine loops that have been previously analyzed with a number of different techniques, and that (iii) we match previous results obtained by SUIF [13] and POLARIS [5] on the statically-analyzable codes.

2. Preliminary Concepts: Summary Construction

Our solution to automatic, run-time parallelization builds on Rus, Pennings and Rauchwerger's hybrid analysis [28] which we briefly review. The main idea is to summarize accesses into read-only (RO), write-first (WF), and read-write (RW) abstract sets [14]. This is achieved by constructing summaries via interprocedural, structural data-flow analysis and representing them accurately in a scoped, closed-under-composition language, named unified set reference (USR). In this setting, the loop independence is derived from examining whether an summaries equation ($S = \emptyset$) holds.

2.1 Unified Set Reference (USR) Construction

Summaries are constructed during a bottom-up parse of the call and control dependency graphs (CDG) of a structured program in SSA representation, where within a CDG region nodes are traversed in

COMPOSE $(REG_1; REG_2)$

$(WF_1, RO_1, RW_1) \leftarrow REG_1$

$(WF_2, RO_2, RW_2) \leftarrow REG_2$

$WF = WF_1 \cup (WF_2 - (RO_1 \cup RW_1))$

$RO = (RO_1 - (WF_2 \cup RW_2)) \cup (RO_2 - (WF_1 \cup RW_1))$

$RW = RW_1 \cup (RW_2 - WF_1) \cup (RO_1 \cap WF_2)$

RETURN (WF, RO, RW)

(a) Consecutive Region Composition

AGGREGATE $(REG_i, i = 1, N)$

$(WF_i, RO_i, RW_i) \leftarrow REG_i$

$WF = \bigcup_{i=1}^{N} (WF_i - \bigcup_{k=1}^{i-1} (RO_k \cup RW_k))$

$RO = \bigcup_{i=1}^{N} RO_i - \bigcup_{i=1}^{N} (WF_i \cup RW_i)$

$RW = \bigcup_{i=1}^{N} (RO_i \cup RW_i) - (WF \cup RO)$

RETURN (WF, RO, RW)

(b) Loop Aggregation

Figure 2. Data-Flow Equations Used in USR Construction.

program order. In this pass, data-flow equations dictate how summaries are initialized at statement level, merged across branches, translated across call sites, composed between consecutive regions, and aggregated across loops. The latter two cases are illustrated in Figures 2(a) and 2(b). For example, the composition of a read-only region S_1 with a write-first region S_2 gives $RO = S_1 - S_2$ (i.e., S_2 cannot contribute to the RO result since it corresponds to a write access), and similarly, $WF = S_2 - S_1$ and $RW = S1 \cap S2$.

Summaries use a directed-acyclic-graph (DAG) representation, named USR, in which *leafs* are sets of linear memory access descriptors [20] (LMAD). LMADs define an algebra for aggregating index sets over quasi-affine patterns. For example a sequence of array accesses of stride δ with offset τ and bounded by (span) σ leads to the index set $\{\tau + i * \delta | \ 0 \leq i * \delta \leq \sigma\}$. In a straightforward generalization, an LMAD describes an arbitrary number of such access sequences into an unidimensional (unified) set of indexes:

$$\{\tau + i_1 * \delta_1 + ... + i_M * \delta_M \mid 0 \leq i_k * \delta_k \leq \sigma_k, k \in [1, M]\} \quad (1)$$

denoted by $[\delta_1, ..., \delta_M] \vee [\sigma_1, ..., \sigma_M] + \tau$, where strides δ_k and spans σ_k model "virtual" multi-dimensional accesses.

For example, the WF summaries for the write access to A at each level of the loop nest below are presented on the right-hand side:

```
Lo  DO i = 1, N, 1     [k,N]∨[k(M-1),N(N-1)] + k-1
Li    DO j = 1, M, 1     [k]∨[k(M-1)] + (i-1)N+k-1
St      A[i*N+j*k] = ...      []∨[] + (i-1)*N+jk-1
    ENDDO ENDDO
```

At statement St the summary is a point; aggregating the accesses over loop L_i, creates an 1D-LMAD of stride $\delta_{L_i} = \tau_{j \leftarrow j+1} - \tau = \mathtt{k}$ and span $\sigma_{L_i} = \tau_{j \leftarrow M} - \tau_{j \leftarrow 1} = \mathtt{k(M-1)}$, etc. Note that an LMAD is transparent to the dimensionality of its corresponding array, and it does not guarantee that its dimensions do not overlap; this can be verified [14] via $\sum_{j=1}^{k-1} \sigma_j < \delta_k$ (i.e., N>k(M-1) in our example).

We found LMADs well suited for our representation because: (i) they support transparent array reshaping at call sites, as they are by definition a set of unidimensional points, and (ii) they provide better symbolic support, e.g., symbolic (constant) strides, are not affine constraints in Presburger arithmetic.

USR's *internal nodes* represent operations that cannot be accurately expressed in the LMAD domain: (i) irreducible set operations, such as union, intersection, subtraction ($\cup$, $\cap$, $-$), or (ii) control flow: gates predicating summary's existence, call sites across which summaries cannot be translated, or total ($\cup_{i=1}^{N}$) and partial ($\cup_{k=1}^{i-1}$) recurrences that fail exact aggregation. For example, with the USR in Figure 3(c), the set subtraction between LMADs $[1] \vee [\mathtt{NS} - 1] + 0$ and $[1] \vee [16 * \mathtt{NP} - 1] + 0$ cannot be represented in the symbolic LMAD domain, hence a subtraction USR node ($-$) was introduced. Moreover, the resulting (subtraction) set is part of the result *iff* gate SYM.NE.1 holds, etc. We note that resorting to conservative approximation instead of introducing the subtraction node, would *miss* the

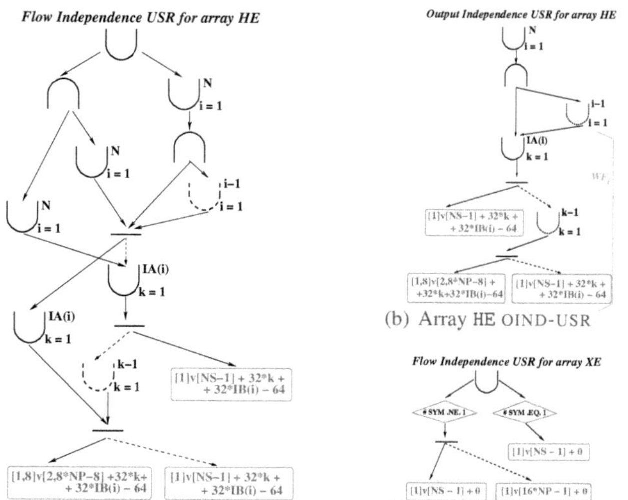

(a) Array HE FIND-USR (b) Array HE OIND-USR (c) Array XE FIND-USR

Figure 3. Flow/Output Independence USRs for HE, XE in Figure 1. Corresponding F/O-IND Predicates are: (c) SYM.NE.1∧NS≤16NP, (a) 8*NP<NS+6, (b) $\wedge_{i=1}^{N-1}$NS≤32*(IB(i+1)-IA(i)-IB(i)+1). Dotted line points to the subtracted part; dotted $\cup_{i=1}^{i-1}$ denotes partial recurrence under a fresh variable that ranges from 1 to $i - 1$.

condition under which the loop is provably *independent*. Similar arguments can be made for the USRs in Figures 3(a) and 3(c).

2.2 Loop Independence as USR Equations (IND-USR)

Having summarized accesses at loop level, answering loop independence reduces to establishing the satisfiability of an independence equation in the USR domain. Denoting by (WF_i, RO_i, RW_i) the per-iteration write-first, read-only and read-write summaries of array X in loop L, where L's iterations range from 1 to N, the output independence of array X in L is represented via equation:

$$\{\cup_{i=1}^{N} (WF_i \cap (\cup_{k=1}^{i-1} WF_k))\} = \emptyset \quad (2)$$

Equation 2 states that if for any i, the write-first set of iteration i does not overlap with the write-first set of any iteration preceding i, then no two different iterations write the same location, hence no cross-iteration dependency exists. We name the left-hand side of equation 2 the output-independence USR (OIND-USR) of X in L.

Similarly, flow-anti independence is established via equation:

$$\{(\cup_{i=1}^{N} WF_i) \cap (\cup_{i=1}^{N} RO_i)\} \cup \{(\cup_{i=1}^{N} WF_i) \cap (\cup_{i=1}^{N} RW_i)\} \cup \{(\cup_{i=1}^{N} RO_i) \cap (\cup_{i=1}^{N} RW_i)\} \cup \{\cup_{i=1}^{N} (RW_i \cap (\cup_{k=1}^{i-1} RW_k))\} = \emptyset \quad (3)$$

where we denote the left-hand side via FIND-USR. Figure3 depicts the independence USRs of our running example, where LMAD leafs were seen as intervals in Section 1.2.

When the independence USR (IND-USR) is definitely empty or non-empty the loop can be classified statically as independent or dependent, respectively. In numerous cases, however, independence is either statically undecidable, for example because certain variables are input dependent, or too complex to analyze with the current compiler infrastructure. In principle, a solution would be to directly evaluate IND-USR at run-time, and to implement conditional loop parallelization based on the independence result.

This technique works well in some special instances: (i) when IND-USR has $O(1)$ runtime complexity, as with the USR in Figure 3(c), or (ii) when its evaluation is amortized over many executions of the loop, i.e., USR evaluation has been safely hoisted out-

$g_1 = \texttt{SYM.NE.1} \quad S_1 = \texttt{[0,NS-1]} - \texttt{[0,16*NP-1]} \quad A = g_1 \# S_1$

$g_2 = \texttt{SYM.EQ.1} \quad S_2 = \texttt{[0,NS-1]} \quad B = g_2 \# S_2$

Translate $A \cup B$ i.e., $A \cup B = \emptyset \Leftarrow \mathcal{F}(A \cup B)$

$A \cup B = \emptyset \Leftarrow \mathcal{F}(A) \wedge \mathcal{F}(B)$

$A = \emptyset \Leftarrow \overline{g_1} \vee \mathcal{F}(S_1) = \texttt{SYM.EQ.1} \vee \mathcal{F}(S_1)$

$S_1 = \emptyset \Leftarrow \texttt{[0,NS-1]} \subseteq \texttt{[0,16*NP-1]} \Leftarrow \texttt{NS} \leq 16 * \texttt{NP}$

Hence $\mathcal{F}(A) = \texttt{SYM.EQ.1} \vee \texttt{NS} \leq 16 * \texttt{NP}$

$B = \emptyset \Leftarrow \overline{g_2} \vee \mathcal{F}(S_2) = \texttt{SYM.NE.1} \vee \mathcal{F}(S_2)$

$S_2 = \emptyset \Leftarrow \texttt{[0, NS-1]} \subseteq \emptyset \Leftarrow \mathit{false}$

Hence $\mathcal{F}(B) = \texttt{SYM.NE.1}$

Finally, $\mathcal{F}(A \cup B) = \texttt{NS} \leq 16 * \texttt{NP} \wedge \texttt{SYM.NE.1}$

Figure 4. Deriving the predicate program corresponding to the simple F-IND summary in Figure 3(c) via translation scheme $\mathcal{F}$.

side at least one outer loop. In the general case, however, we have found that runtime USR evaluation generates very high overhead, when compared with our technique.

3. Summary to Predicate Language Translation

IND-USR runtime evaluation is an expensive technique because it computes all the memory locations involved in potential cross-iteration dependencies, and as such, solves a more difficult problem than loop independence, which only requires classifying IND-USR as empty or non-empty. In contrast, our approach is to define an effective translation scheme $\mathcal{F}$ from USR to an equally expressive, closed-under-composition language of predicates, named PDAG: $\mathcal{F}$: USR $\rightarrow$ PDAG, $\mathcal{F}(S) \Rightarrow S = \emptyset$.

While the *predicate program* is just a sufficient condition for loop independence, it is less constrained than the flattened predicates of related approaches, e.g., it's input symbols need not be read-only, and it is also less conservative as a consequence of being constructed from non-trivial inference rules that pattern match the shape of an accurate independence summary (IND-USR). Finally, redundancy is removed by hoisting invariant terms outside loop-conjunction nodes, and the simplified predicate is factored into a sequence of sufficient conditions for loop independence, which are tested at runtime in the order of their estimated complexity.

This section is organized as follows: Section 3.1 presents at a high-level the language-translation scheme, implemented via a factorization algorithm. Section 3.2 describes how leaf predicates are extracted from operations in the LMAD domain. For completeness, Section 3.3 briefly explains more complex translation rules that naturally extend and are well integrated in our framework. Section 3.4 discusses two USR-reshaping transformations that enhance the resulting predicate accuracy. Finally, Section 3.5 explains how the result program is separated into a cascade of increasingly-complex predicates, and Section 3.6 discusses the asymptotic compile and run time complexity and the limitations of our framework.

3.1 Factorization Algorithm

Figure 4 demonstrates the gist of the language translation $\mathcal{F}$ on the simple IND-USR of Figure 3(c): A sufficient condition for the input USR, which is a union of two terms, to be empty is that each term is empty. Recursively, term A corresponds to a gated node, which exhibits a boolean expression g_1 under which summary S_1 exists. A sufficient condition for A to be empty is thus that either g_1 does not hold, or S_1 is empty. Finally, S_1 is the difference between two LMADS, seen for simplicity as intervals. If the first interval is included in the second then the difference is empty. The predicate corresponding to A is thus: `SYM.EQ.1` $\vee$ `NS` $\leq$ `16*NP`, and B is derived in the same manner. We note that, similarly to USR, the

PDAG **FACTOR**(S : USR)
// ***Output:*** P s.t. $P \Rightarrow (S = \emptyset)$
P = .FALSE.
CASE S ***OF***:
$q\#S_1$: $P = \overline{q} \vee$ **FACTOR**(S_1)
$S_1 \cup S_2$: $P =$ **FACTOR**(S_1) $\wedge$ **FACTOR**(S_2)
$S_1 - S_2$: $P =$ **FACTOR**(S_1) $\vee$ **INCLUDED**(S_1,S_2)
$S_1 \cap S_2$: $P =$ **FACTOR**(S_1) $\vee$ **FACTOR**(S_2) $\vee$ **DISJOINT**(S_1,S_2)
$\bigcup_{i=1}^{N}(S_i)$:
$P = \bigwedge_{i=1}^{N}$ **FACTOR**(S_i)
$S_1 \bowtie$ *CallSite*:
$P =$ **FACTOR**(S_1)$\bowtie$*CallSite*

PDAG **DISJOINT**(S_1, S_2 : USR)
// ***Output:*** $P \Rightarrow (S_1 \cap S_2 = \emptyset)$
IF ($S_1 = \bigcup_{i=1}^{N}(S_i^1)$ ***and*** $S_2 = \bigcup_{i=1}^{N}(S_i^2)$)
$(S_1^{\texttt{inv}}, S_2^{\texttt{inv}}) \leftarrow$ invariant overestimates of (S_i^1, S_i^2)
(1) $P =$ **DISJOINT**($S_1^{\texttt{inv}}$, $S_2^{\texttt{inv}}$)
ELSE
$P =$ **DISJOINT_H**(S_1, S_2) $\vee$ **DISJOINT_H**(S_2, S_1) $\vee$ **DISJOINT_APP**(S_1, S_2)

PDAG **DISJOINT_H**(U, S : USR)
// ***Output:*** $P \Rightarrow (U \cap S = \emptyset)$
CASE U ***OF***:
$q\#S_1$: $P = \overline{q} \vee$ **DISJOINT**(S_1, S)
$S_1 \cup S_2$:
$P =$ **DISJOINT**(S_1, S) $\wedge$ **DISJOINT**(S_2, S)
(2) $S_1 - S_2$:
$P =$ **DISJOINT**(S_1, S) $\vee$ **INCLUDED**(S, S_2)
$S_1 \cap S_2$:
$P =$ **DISJOINT**(S_1, S) $\vee$ **DISJOINT**(S_2, S)

(a) Factorizing IND-USR.

PDAG **INCLUDED**(S_1, S_2 : USR)
// ***Output:*** P s.t. $P \Rightarrow (S_1 \subseteq S_2)$
IF ($S_1 = \bigcup_{i=1}^{N} S_i^1$ ***and*** $S_2 = \bigcup_{i=1}^{N} S_i^2$)
(3) $P_1 = \wedge_{i=1}^{N}$ **INCLUDED**(S_i^1, S_i^2)
ELSE $P_1 =$ **INCLUDED_H**(S_1, S_2)
$P = P_1 \vee$ **INCLUDED_APP**(S_1, S_2)

PDAG **INCLUDED_H**(S, U : USR)
// ***Output:*** P s.t. $P \Rightarrow (S \subseteq U)$
$P = P_1 = P_2 =$ .FALSE.
CASE U ***OF***:
$q\#S_1$: $P_1 = q \wedge$ **INCLUDED**(S, S_1)
$S_1 \cup S_2$: $P_1 =$ **INCLUDED**(S, S_1) $\vee$ **INCLUDED**(S, S_2)
(4) $S_1 - S_2$: $P_1 =$ **INCLUDED**(S, S_1) $\wedge$ **DISJOINT**(S,S_2)
$S_1 \cap S_2$: $P_1 =$ **INCLUDED**(S, S_1) $\wedge$ **INCLUDED**(S, S_2)
(5) LMAD(L): $P_1 =$ **FILLS_ARR**(L)
CASE S ***OF***:
$q\#S_1$: $P_2 = \overline{q} \vee$ **INCLUDED**(S_1, U)
$S_1 \cup S_2$: $P_2 =$ **INCLUDED**(S_1, U) $\wedge$ **INCLUDED**(S_2, U)
$S_1 - S_2$: $P_2 =$ **INCLUDED**(S_1, U)
$S_1 \cap S_2$: $P_2 =$ **INCLUDED**(S_1, U) $\vee$ **INCLUDED**(S_2, U)
$P = P_1 \vee P_2$

PDAG **INCLUDED_APP**(C, D : USR)
$((P_C, \lceil C \rceil), (P_D, \lfloor D \rfloor)) \leftarrow$ condit. LMAD over/under-estim. of C, D
$P = P_C \vee (P_D \wedge$ **INCLUDED_LMADS**($\lceil C \rceil$, $\lfloor D \rfloor$))

PDAG **DISJOINT_APP**(C, D : USR)
$((P_C, \lceil C \rceil), (P_D, \lceil D \rceil)) \leftarrow$ condit. cond. LMAD overestim. of C, D
$P = P_C \vee P_D \vee$ **DISJOINT_LMADS**($\lceil C \rceil$, $\lceil D \rceil$)

(b) Helper Functions.

Figure 5. Logical Inference Rules of The Factorization Algorithm.

predicate language has a DAG representation in which leaves are boolean expressions, while internal nodes represent either logical `and`, `or` operators ($\wedge$, $\vee$), or control-flow: untranslatable call sites ($\bowtie$*Call Site*), or irreducible loop-level conjunctions ($\wedge_{i=1}^{N} P_i$).

Figure 5 presents the *factorization algorithm* (`FACTOR`), which implements the translation scheme $\mathcal{F}$. Inference on set-algebra properties guides a recursive construction of a predicate program via a top-down traversal of the input summary. For example, a subtraction between two summaries is empty if the first operand is either empty or is included in the second operand, and similarly an intersection is empty if any operand is empty or the two operands are disjoint. In such cases `INCLUDED` and `DISJOINT` are called, respectively, to add add more specialized factors to the result:

A summary S is *included* in the difference of other two summaries $S_1 - S_2$ if, as in rule (4), S is included in S_1 and disjoint with S_2: $S \subseteq S_1 - S_2 \Leftarrow \mathcal{F}(S - S_1) \wedge \mathcal{F}(S \cap S_2)$. Two recurrence-union summaries over the same loop are in an include relation if, as in rule (3), the iteration-based summaries are in an include relation: $(\cup_{i=1}^{N} S_i^1) \subseteq (\cup_{i=1}^{N} S_i^2) \Leftarrow \wedge_{i=1}^{N} \mathcal{F}(S_i^1 - S_i^2)$. Finally, rule (5) extracts via `FILLS_ARR` the predicate under which an LMAD L fully covers the maximal (declared) dimension of its corresponding array; this predicate guarantees that any summary is included in L.

Similarly, a summary S is *disjoint* from the difference between two summaries $S_1 - S_2$ if, as in rule (2), either S is disjoint with S_1 or is included in S_2, since in the latter case S cannot be part of the subtraction result: $S \cap (S_1 - S_2) = \emptyset \Leftarrow \mathcal{F}(S \cap S_1) \vee \mathcal{F}(S - S_2)$.

However, disjointness of per-iteration summaries of the same loop does not imply that the recurrence-union summaries are disjoint: $(\cup_{i=1}^{N} S_i^1) \cap (\cup_{i=1}^{N} S_i^2) = \emptyset \not\Leftarrow \wedge_{i=1}^{N} \mathcal{F}(S_i^1 \cap S_i^2)$. In this case, rule (1) of Figure 5 attempts to find loop-invariant overestimates for S_i^1 and S_i^2, denote them S_{inv}^1 and S_{inv}^2, for example by filtering out loop-variant gates. The disjointness of the overestimates is now a sufficient condition for the disjointness of the two recurrence-union summaries[1]: $(\cup_{i=1}^{N} S_i^1) \cap (\cup_{i=1}^{N} S_i^2) = \emptyset \Leftarrow \mathcal{F}(S_{inv}^1 \cap S_{inv}^2)$.

A powerful inference rule that solves a large class of nonlinear accesses refers to the pattern $\cup_{i=1}^{N} (S_i \cap \cup_{k=1}^{i-1} S_k) = \emptyset$, which is satisfied under predicate $\wedge_{i=1}^{N} \texttt{MONOTON}(S_i)$. While this rather complex rule [19] is briefly demonstrated in Section 3.3, the intuition is that S_i monotonicity, e.g., the maximal element of S_i being smaller than the minimal element of S_{i+1} is a sufficient condition for the targeted summary equation to hold.

3.2 Extracting Predicates from LMAD Operations

When the factorization algorithm reaches LMAD leafs or encounters summaries of shapes that are not covered by any rules, INCLUDED_APP and DISJOINT_APP conservatively flatten the problem to the LMAD domain. We first show how flattening is achieved and then describe an algebra under which leaf predicates are extracted from comparing LMADs for inclusion and disjointness; the generalization to sets of LMADs being straightforward[2].

We have found most useful to represent an overestimate of summary C as a pair $(P_C, \lceil C \rceil)$, where P_C is a predicate under which C is empty, while $\lceil C \rceil$ is a set of LMADs that overestimates C. The latter is computed via a recursively defined operator on the USR domain, which, (i) on the top-down parse disregards node B in terms such as $C - B$, $C \cap B$, and (ii) on the bottom-up parse it translates, aggregates and unions the encountered LMAD leafs over call site, recurrence, and $\cup$ nodes, respectively. Similarly, D is underestimated via $(P_D, \lfloor D \rfloor)$, where $\lfloor D \rfloor$ is a (maximal) LMAD-set-underestimate of D when predicate P_D holds.

We recall from Section 2.1 that an LMAD is denoted by $[\delta_1, ..., \delta_M] \vee [\sigma_1, ..., \sigma_M] + \tau$ and represents the set of indexes $\{\tau + i_1 * \delta_1 + ... + i_M * \delta_M \mid 0 \leq i_k * \delta_k \leq \sigma_k, k \in [1, M]\}$. Also, under the simplifying assumption that all LMAD strides are positive ($\delta_k > 0$), one can observe that the interval $[\tau, \tau + \sigma_1 + .. + \sigma_M]$ overestimates its corresponding LMAD.

We first treat the case of *uni-dimensional* LMADs: Two 1D-LMADs can be proved disjoint in two scenarios: (i) they either correspond to an interleaved, but non-overlapping sequence of accesses, e.g., LMADs $A_1 = [2] \vee [99] + 0 \equiv \{0, 2, .., 98\}$ and $A_2 = [2] \vee [99] + 1 \equiv \{1, 3, .., 99\}$ are disjoint, or (ii) they can be overestimated by disjoint intervals, e.g., $A_1 = [2] \vee [49] + 0 \subseteq [0, 49]$ and $A_2 = [2] \vee [49] + 50 \subseteq [50, 99]$.

Formally, a sufficient predicate for $A_1 = [\delta_1] \text{v} [\sigma_1] + \tau_1$ and $A_2 = [\delta_2] \text{v} [\sigma_2] + \tau_2$ to be *disjoint* is: $gcd(\delta_1, \delta_2) \not| (\tau_1 - \tau_2) \vee (\tau_1 > \tau_2 + \sigma_2 \ \vee \ \tau_2 > \tau_1 + \sigma_1)$, where the first and second term satisfy the interleaved-access and disjoint-intervals scenarios, respectively. Similarly, using the same notations, one can observe that a sufficient predicate for A_1 to be *included* in A_2 is: $(\delta_2 \mid \delta_1) \wedge (\delta_2 \mid \tau_1 - \tau_2) \wedge (\tau_1 \geq \tau_2) \wedge (\tau_1 + \sigma_1 \leq \tau_2 + \sigma_2)$.

For example, in loop CORREC_DO711 from the bdna benchmark, loop independence requires to establish that [1]$\vee$[0]+IX(2)+i-2 and [1]$\vee$[i-2]+IX(1)-1 are disjoint (the loop index is i $\in$ [1,NOP]).

---

[1] This rule solves several important loops from zeusmp, see Figure 9(b).

[2] The set of LMADs S_1 is disjoint from (included in) the set of LMADs S_2 if any LMAD in S_1 is disjoint to any (included in at least one) LMAD in S_2.

```
PDAG DISJOINT_LMAD(A, B : LMAD)
 //Input: P s.t. P ⇒ (A ∩ B = ∅)
 IF( A and B unidimensional LMADs)
   P = DISJOINT_LMAD_1D(A,B)
 ELSE
   (A^1d,B^1d) ← FLATTEN_LMADS(A,B)
   P_flat = DISJOINT_LMAD_1D(A^1d,B^1d)
   (C,D) ← UNIFY_LMAD_DIMS(A,B)
   (P_C^wf,C^in,C^out)←PROJ_OUTER_DIM(C)
   (P_D^wf,D^in,D^out)←PROJ_OUTER_DIM(D)
   P_d^out = DISJOINT_LMAD_1D(C^out, D^out)
   P_d^in = DISJOINT_LMAD    (C^in, D^in)
   P = P_flat ∨ (P_C^wf ∧ P_D^wf ∧ (P_d^out ∨ P_d^in))
```

(a) Predicate for Disjoint LMADs.

```
SE REDUCE_GT_0( expr )
 //Input:  an int-type expression
 //Output: P s.t. P ⇒ (expr > 0)
  (a, b, i, L, U, err) =
      FIND_SYMBOL(expr);
  // expr = a*i+b, L ≤ i ≤ U, i ∉ b
  // P = (a ≥ 0 ∧ a*L+b>0) ∨
  //     (a < 0 ∧ a*U+b>0)
  IF ( err ) RETURN (expr > 0);
  ELSE RETURN
      [ REDUCE_GT_0(a+1) ∧
      REDUCE_GT_0(a*L+b) ] ∨
      [ REDUCE_GT_0(−a)  ∧
      REDUCE_GT_0(a*U+b) ];
```

(b) Symbolic Fourier-Motzkin

Figure 6. Algorithm for Characterizing LMAD Disjointness.

Noting that the interleaved-access term evaluates to false (because 1 divides everything), the rules above yield predicate: IX(1)+1-IX(2)-i>0 $\vee$ IX(1)$\leq$IX(2).

To eliminate loop index i from term IX(1)+1-IX(2)-i>0, we use a Fourier-Motzkin-like algorithm, depicted in Figure 6(b). The algorithm receives a symbolic expression expr and returns a sufficient predicate for expr > 0 to hold. First, a scalar symbol i of known upper and lower bounds is picked from expr, and expr is re-written as a*i+b, where i does not appear in b. If no suitable i is found, the result is expr>0. Finally, when a$\geq$0 or a<0, i is replaced with its lower or upper bound, respectively, to give sufficient conditions for the inequation expr>0. Note that this leads to solving four subproblems of necessarily smaller exponent of i, which ensures that the recursion eventually terminates (in exponential time). In our example, the elimination of i yields term IX(2)+NOP$\leq$IX(1), and the overall $O(1)$ predicate for loop CORREC_DO711 becomes IX(2)+NOP$\leq$IX(1) $\vee$ IX(1)$\leq$IX(2).

In general, *multi-dimensional* LMADs present two difficulties: first, an LMAD dimensions may overlap, and second, since there is no relation between the LMAD dimensionality and that of its corresponding array, we may have to compare LMADs that exhibit a different number of dimensions. We address this via a heuristic that unifies the LMADs dimensions, projects and compares a dimension at a time, and joins the result. In addition, predicates are extracted to guard the safety of the projection (i.e., the non-overlap invariant).

We demonstrate the approach, sketched in Figure 6(a), on bdna's loop CORREC_DO900, which requires to prove LMADs [M]$\vee$[2*M]+j-1+2*M and [1,M]$\vee$[j-2,2*M]+2*M disjoint, where the loop index j is in 1..N. The first step is to flatten the input to 1D-LMADs and to extract a predicate $P_{\texttt{flat}}$ as discussed before. The second step is to unify LMAD dimensions, e.g., the 1D-LMAD is padded with an empty dimension of stride 1 and span 0 giving: [1,M]$\vee$[0,2*M]+j-1+2*M. Next, if both LMADs have equal outer strides, PROJ_OUTER_DIM(C) separates the outer dimension of C, returning a well-formedness predicate $P_C^{\texttt{wf}}$, together with LMADs C^{out} and C^{in} that correspond to the last and remaining dimensions.

With our example, C=[1,M]$\vee$[0,2*M]+j-1+2*M splits into $C^{\texttt{in}}$=[1]$\vee$[0]+j-1 and C^{out}=[M]$\vee$[2*M]+2*M. $P_C^{\texttt{wf}}$=(j-1<M) verifies that the separated dimensions do not overlap – i.e. the range of the inner LMAD is less than the outer stride. Fourier-Motzkin simplification gives $P_C^{\texttt{wf}}$=(N$\leq$M). Similarly, D=[1,M]$\vee$[j-2,2*M]+2*M is split into $D^{\texttt{in}}$=[1]$\vee$[j-2]+0, and D^{out}=[M]$\vee$[2*M]+2*M, where $P_D^{\texttt{wf}}$=(N-1$\leq$M). Recursively testing disjointness of the inner and outer LMADs gives predicates: $P_d^{\texttt{out}}$=false, since C^{out}=$D^{\texttt{out}}$, and $P_d^{\texttt{in}}$=true, since [j-1,j-1]$\cap$[0,j-2]=$\emptyset$. The independence predicate for CORREC_DO900 is thus $P_{\texttt{flat}} \vee$ (N $\leq$ M).

```
// Estimate ∪_{i=1}^{NRI}(WF_i)=
//    ∪_{i=1}^{NRI}([1]∨[2]+3*SHIFT(n))
(lower, upper) ← (⌈INT⌉,⌊INT⌋)
REDUCTION(MAX:upper)
REDUCTION(MIN:lower)
PRIVATE(tmp_lub,n)
DOALL n=1,NRI
  tmp_lub(1)=1+3*SHIFT(n)
  tmp_lub(2)=3+3*SHIFT(n)
  lower = MIN(tmp_lub(1), lower)
  upper = MAX(tmp_lub(2), upper)
ENDDOALL
```

(a) Estimating the size of FSHIFT in gromacs's loop INL_DO1130.

```
CIV@1 = Q
DO i = 1, N, 1
  CIV@2 = γ(i.EQ.1, CIV@1,CIV@4)
  cond = X(i+M).NE.1 .AND. NSP(i).GT.0
  IF (cond) THEN
    DO j = 1, NSP(i), 1
      IF(0.NE.IA(1,i)) X(j+CIV@2 )=..
    ENDDO
    CIV@3 = NSP(i) + CIV@2
  ENDIF
  CIV@4 = γ(cond, CIV@3, CIV@2)
ENDDO
CIV@5 = γ(N.GE.1, CIV@4, CIV@1)
```

(b) CIV_{agg} example for loop CORREC_DO401 of bdna.

Figure 7. (a) Optimizing Reduction and (b) CIV Aggregation

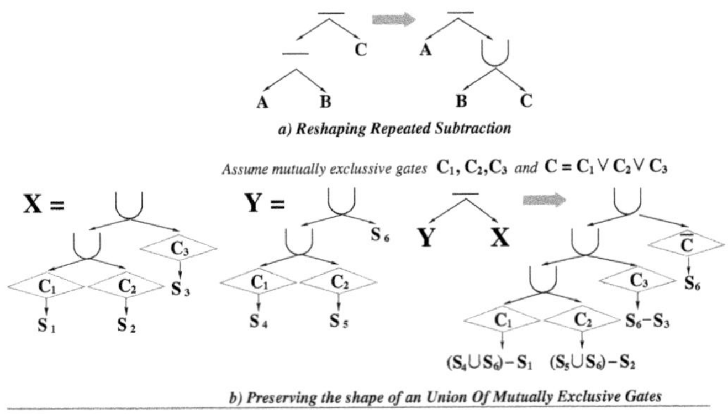

Figure 8. USR Reshaping Transformations.

3.3 Proving Non-Linear Access Independent

For completeness, this section sketches how our framework handles a class of non-linear accesses, such as those exhibiting array indexing or induction variables without closed-form solutions.

The first difficulty corresponds to quadratic or array indexing, which either appears directly in the code, e.g., sparse-matrix implementation uses index arrays, or as artifacts of transformations such as induction-variable substitution, e.g., quadratic indexes.

The intuition is that solving such accesses corresponds to a rather-complex rule, described in detail elsewhere [19], that translates equations of shape: $\cup_{i=1}^{N}(S_i \cap \cup_{k=1}^{i-1}(S_k))=\emptyset$ to the predicate domain. If S_i are seen as intervals, we can observe that if they form a monotonic sequence, e.g., the lower bound of the interval corresponding to iteration $i+1$ is always greater than the upper bound of that of iteration i – then the summaries S_i of any two consecutive iterations do not overlap, and by induction, any two summaries of distinct iterations do not overlap, hence the above equation is satisfied. Figure 3(b) shows such an example, where S_i =$\texttt{WF}_i$ is overestimated to interval `[32*(IB(i)-1),32*(IB(i)+IA(i)-2)+NS-1]`. Imposing the above strictly-increasing-monotonicity assumption results in predicate $\wedge_{i=1}^{N-1}$`NS`$\leq$`32*(IB(i+1)-IA(i)-IB(i)+1)` that verifies output independence under $O(N)$-runtime complexity.

The second difficulty corresponds to the use of induction variables that are conditionally incremented (CIV), such as `CIV` in Figure 7(b). The solution is to devise a flow-sensitive USR-aggregation technique that succeeds in summarizing CIV accesses at iteration and loop level. For example, on the CFG path that takes the `if` branch (and contains the inner loop), an overestimate of the per-iteration write access to `X`, denoted W_i, is interval `[CIV@2+1,CIV@2+NSP(i)]`, which can be rewritten as `[CIV@2+1,CIV@4]` (since `CIV@4=CIV@3=CIV@2+NSP(i)`).

On the other path, W_i is the empty set, which can also be written as `[CIV@2+1,CIV@4]`, since the interval's upper bound `CIV@4=CIV@2` is less then its lower bound `CIV@2+1`. Hence the interval overestimate $\lceil W_i \rceil$=`[CIV@2+1,CIV@4]` holds on all paths. One can compute overestimates: $\lceil \cup_{k=1}^{i-1} W_k \rceil$=`[Q+1,CIV@2]`, and $\lceil \cup_{i=1}^{N} W_i \rceil$=`[Q+1,CIV@5]` in a similar fashion. Output independence is proven statically since `[Q+1,CIV@2]`$\cap$`[CIV@2+1,CIV@4]` gives the empty interval. Observing that the read access to `X` can be overestimated via interval `[M,M+N]`, the flow independence predicate `Q`$\geq$`M+N` $\vee$ `M>CIV@5` is extracted from the requirement that the loop summaries for the write and read accesses are disjoint (i.e., `[M,M+N]`$\cap$`[Q+1,CIV@5]`=$\emptyset$). Finally, predicate evaluation and parallel execution of the loop requires that the CIV values at the beginning of each iteration are precomputed via a loop slice that is also executed in parallel to ensure scalable speedup.

3.4 Enabling USR Transformation for Predicate Extraction

Predicates are constructed by pattern matching the shape of the input summary, and as such, semantically equivalent summaries may translate to predicates of varying accuracy. Figure 8 depicts two high-level USR reshaping rules that we have found to improve predicates' quality in a significant number of (important) loops.

The first rule says that a repeated (irreducible) subtraction from a summary should be reorganized as one subtraction between that summary and the union of the subtracted terms[3]. In Figure 8 we show intuitively that when A is included in neither B nor C, perhaps the union of B and C can simplify to a larger set in the array-abstraction domain which includes A, thus enabling the extraction of a more meaningful predicate. Note that related approaches would likely miss this opportunity because in the absence of a language, subtractions are performed in order, and the irreducible $A - B$ would have already been treated conservatively.

The second rule refers to preserving the shape of a *union of mutually exclusive gates* (UMEG) when subtracting, intersecting and uniting summaries of compatible-UMEG shapes, i.e, to distribute the operation inside each mutually exclusive gate, where by compatible shapes we mean that the gates of one summary are either a subset or match those of the other summary. The motivation is similar to the one for the first rule; the missing step in the figure being that, before the rule fires, Y is (semantically) normalized to: $(C_1\#(S_4 \cup S_6)) \cup (C_2\#(S_5 \cup S_6)) \cup (C_3\#S_6) \cup (\overline{C}\#S_6)$.

The first transformation was useful in numerous loops, while the second was instrumental in parallelizing the larger SPEC2006 benchmarks ZEUSMP and CALCULIX. Figure 9(b) shows the *simplest* FIND-USR obtained via UMEG-preserving transformations for ZEUSMP's loop TRANX2_DO2100. Since C_i^{inv} and D_i^{inv} are loop-invariant overestimates for the two same-loop nodes of index k, `FACTOR` calls `DISJOINT(`C_i^{inv}`,`D_i^{inv}`)` which derives the independence predicate that succeeds at runtime:
`(jbeg.EQ.js)` $\vee$ `(jbeg.NE.js` $\wedge$ `jend<133` $\wedge$ `M<135)`, where the last two terms represent well-formedness predicates corresponding to separating the outer dimensions when comparing multi-dimensional LMADs (see Section 3.2). Without UMEG-preserving transformations, the FIND-USR is too large to be presented and none of the extracting predicates succeed at runtime.

3.5 Predicate Simplifications

The predicate program built under the language-translation scheme can be significantly optimized by (i) hoisting the loop-invariant terms outside loop nodes, and (i) by removing redundancy. The

[3] This resembles strength-reduction optimization, where addition is preferred to the more inexact subtraction operation.

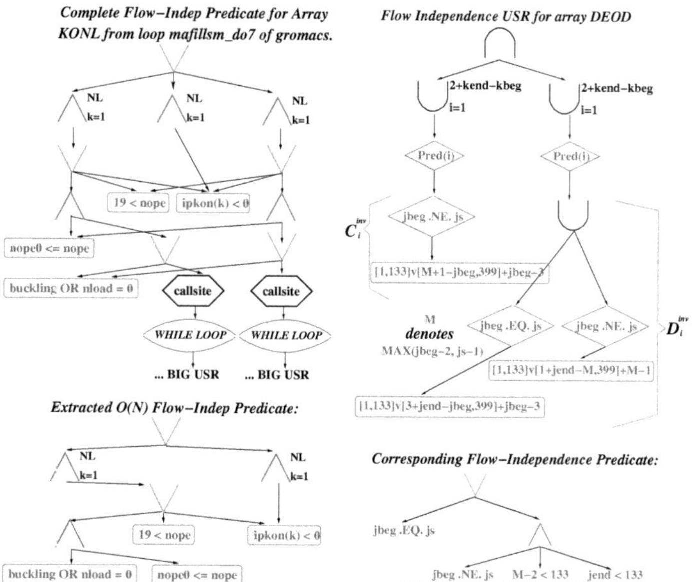

(a) Separating an $O(N)$ Predicate for loop MAFILLSM_DO7 of calculix.

(b) Demonstrating UMEG on zeusmp's TRANX2_DO2100.

Figure 9. Predicate-Separation & USR-Transformation Examples.

former transformation is essential in improving the accuracy of each term of the cascade of (partial) independence predicates.

For example *invariant hoisting* identifies loop-invariant children of a n-ary $\vee/\wedge$ node and hoists them outside the loop node, e.g., $\wedge_{i=1}^{N}(\vee(A_1^{\text{inv}},..,A_r^{\text{inv}},B_1^{\text{var}},..,B_p^{\text{var}})) \rightarrow \vee(A_1^{\text{inv}},..,A_r^{\text{inv}}) \vee \wedge_{i=1}^{N}(\vee(B_1^{\text{var}},..,B_p^{\text{var}}))$. Hoisting is mainly enabled by two transformations: First, $\vee/\wedge$ flattening merges repeated compositions of the same $\vee$ or $\wedge$ operator into one n-ary $\vee$ or $\wedge$ node, e.g., $(A_1 \vee A_2) \vee (A_3 \vee A_4) \rightarrow \vee(A_1, A_2, A_3, A_4)$, Second, common factor extraction, e.g., $\wedge(B_1 \vee A,..,B_p \vee A) \rightarrow \wedge(B_1,..,B_p) \vee A$, beside reducing redundancy, would allow now the loop-invariant predicate A to be hoisted outside the hypothetical loop node.

For example, running our algorithm on FIND-USR of Figure 3(a) identifies that a sufficient independence condition is that the bottom node[4] - `([1,8]`$\vee$`[2,8*NP-8]+`τ`)`$-$`([1]`$\vee$`[NS-1]+`τ`)` - is empty, where τ`=32*(k-2+IB(i))`. This reduces to satisfying the interval inclusion `[`τ`,`τ`+8*NP-6]`$\subseteq$`[`τ`,`τ`+NS-1]`, which gives predicate $P_{\texttt{leaf}}$ = `8*NP<NS+6`. However, even though $P_{\texttt{leaf}}$ is invariant to loops of indexes `k` and `i`, the algorithm bottom-up pass still wraps it inside loop nodes, giving $\wedge_{i=1}^{N}(\wedge_{k=1}^{\texttt{IA(i)}}\texttt{8*NP<NS+6})$. Applying the above simplifications moves $P_{\texttt{leaf}}$ outside both loop nodes and removes the now empty loops, giving the $O(1)$ predicate `8*NP<NS+6`.

Finally, the predicate is factored into terms of increasing runtime complexity, typically $O(1)$ and $O(N)$, where code is generated to implement these tests and to cascade them to implement conditional parallelization, privatization, etc. Separating $O(1)$ predicates applies more aggressive rules to extract invariant factors, e.g., $\wedge_{i=1}^{N}(\wedge(A_1^{\text{inv}} \vee B_1^{\text{var}},..,A_p^{\text{inv}} \vee B_p^{\text{var}})) \rightarrow \wedge(A_1^{\text{inv}},..,A_p^{\text{inv}})$.

Separating $O(N)$ predicates is obtained by replacing any inner-loop node (i.e., nest depth > 1) in the original predicate via `false` and simplifying the result. Figure 9(a) demonstrates this technique: removing the two `while`-loop nodes in the complete predicate results in the much simpler $O(N)$ counterpart that succeeds at runtime, where scalars `nope` and `nope0` are loop variant.

[4] Note that a conservative approximation at that point in the summary construction would miss on extracting the relevant independence predicate.

3.6 Asymptotic Complexity and Limitations Discussion

With respect to the compile-time complexity, we note that the Fourier-Motzkin-like elimination is (only) exponential in the number of eliminated symbols. The typical case is that we eliminate only the outermost loop index via Fourier-Motzkin. Hence, we expect $O(1)$ overhead, where the inner-loop indexes are eliminated by LMAD-level aggregation. Furthermore, while the factorization algorithm has worst-case exponential complexity, the typical USR input exhibits a sparse structure in the operations that cause the exponential behavior. This means that, in practice, the compile time is dominated by the quadratic time of building USRs [28].

We model a predicate's runtime complexity after the loop-nest depth exhibited by its implementation, where we bound a potential explosion in predicate size via a convenient constant factor. We generate the entire cascade of predicates, noting that we have not yet encountered a first-successful predicate of complexity greater than $O(N)$, where N is the number of iterations of the targeted loop. The last test is always an exact one, i.e., implemented either as USR evaluation or by means of thread-level speculation.

There several possible avenues for future investigation such as: More aggressive rules to the translation, e.g., nonlinear accesses, currently disambiguated by checking their monotonicity, could be more accurately modeled if existential quantifiers would be part of the predicate language. Furthermore, we could enhance the precision of the LMAD-level comparison, which currently results in only sufficient conditions even in the case of unidimensional LMADs.

4. Other Uses of the Infrastructure

The factorization algorithm extracts predicates that satisfy an arbitrary equation in the USR domain, and as such, its applicability goes beyond proving loop independence. For example, one can disambiguate at runtime whether a symbol requires only static, rather than dynamic last value computation. Static last value (SLV), can be represented via USR equation $\cup_{i=1}^{N}(\texttt{WF}_i) \subseteq \texttt{WF}_{i \leftarrow N}$, which says that the whole write-first set of the loop of index $i \in [1, N]$ is included in the write-first set of the last iteration. Array `array_psi` of loop EMIT_DO5 of SPEC89's `nasa7` benchmark is such a case, where the SLV successful predicate is: $\wedge_{i=1}^{N-1}$`(arrays_nwall(`i`)`$\leq$`arrays_nwall(`N`))`.

Similarly, we apply runtime tests to optimize and extend the applicability of reduction parallelization. Consider the simple loop:

```
      DO i = 1, N, 1
S1 :     A(i) = ...
S2 :     A(B(i)) = A(B(i)) + ...
      ENDDO
```

First, disregarding statement S_1, we observe that S_2 matches the reduction pattern and the loop can always be parallelized by computing the changes to `A` locally for each processor, and by merging (adding) them in parallel at the end of the loop. However, if B is injective, this treatment is unnecessary because each iteration reads/writes a distinct element of `A`, and thus every processor can work safely, directly with the shared array `A`. The predicate[5] obtained from solving equation $\cup_{i=1}^{N}(\texttt{RW}_i \cap \cup_{k=1}^{i-1}(\texttt{RW}_k))=\emptyset$ is a sufficient condition for the access to be independent, and thus will guard a conditional application of *reduction* at *runtime* (RRED).

Second, considering now S_1, one can observe that while S_1 and S_2 do not form a reduction group [17] (i.e., S_1 is not a reduction), one can still parallelize the loop by treating S_2 as a reduction *if* `A`'s index sets for statements S_1 and S_2 do not overlap (e.g., predicate $\wedge_{i=1}^{N} N < B(i)$). We name this case *extended reduction* (EXT-

[5] With our framework we obtain predicate $\wedge_{i=1}^{N-1} B(i) < B(i+1)$ extracted by the monotonicity rule.

RRED), where we allow A to be written outside reduction statements as long as these writes do not precede, on any path, any reduction statement. One can observe that EXT-RRED instances will have non-empty write-first and read-write sets, corresponding to statements such as S_1 and S_2, respectively, and a necessarily empty read-only set. Enabling parallelism in this case requires proving (i) flow independence, i.e., $\cup_{i=1}^{N}(\texttt{WF}_i) \cap \cup_{i=1}^{N}(\texttt{RW}_i)=\emptyset$, and either (ii) output independence, i.e., $\cup_{i=1}^{N}(\texttt{WF}_i \cap \cup_{k=1}^{i-1}(\texttt{WF}_k))=\emptyset$ or (iii) computing the last value of the write-first set (e.g., the last value corresponds to the last iteration if $\cup_{i=1}^{N}(\texttt{WF}_i) \subseteq \texttt{WF}_{i\leftarrow N}$). Loops MXMULT_DO10 and FORMR_DO20 that cover almost 55% of `dyfesm`'s sequential runtime, exhibit the EXT-RRED pattern.

Finally, in some cases such as `gromacs` and `calculix` benchmarks, the reduction is statically recognized but the bounds of the reduction array cannot be estimated at compile time because, for example, the array is passed as a parameter of assumed size to a Fortran subroutine called from C.

Our solution, shown in Figure 7(a) on the simplest example we encountered, is to compute at runtime the upper and lower bounds of the array indexes touched in the loop. This is achieved via overestimating $\cup_{i=1}^{N}(\texttt{RW}_i)$ by removing terms B from nodes such as $A-B$, $A\cap B$, etc., such that the resulting USR exhibits only $\cup$, call site and recurrence nodes. In contrast to USR's exact evaluation, our lightweight USR-*bounds estimation*, named BOUNDS-COMP, allows parallel evaluation, where the `lower` and `upper` bounds are MIN/MAX-reduced across iterations. On `gromacs` we are 1.66x faster than IBM's `xlf_r` compiler, which, in the absence of array-bounds information, appears to parallelize the loop by executing its reduction statements atomically causing frequent cross-processor conflicts.

While the example of Figure 7(a) is trivial, a challenging application for BOUNDS-COMP are arrays such as `AUB` from `calculix`'s `mafillsm_do7`, where $\texttt{RW}_i$ is complex and prohibitively expensive to compute via exact USR evaluation. Still, BOUNDS-COMP's overhead is less than 9% of the parallel runtime and scales well.

5. Code Generation: Putting Everything Together

The factorization analysis is implemented in a variant of the `Polaris` research compiler [5] for `Fortran77` and is applied on a control-flow-structured program under SSA representation. First, accesses are summarized via read-only, write-first and read-write USRs, and flow and anti independence USRs are computed for each symbol in the targeted loop. If IND-USR is decidable to be empty for all symbols or non-empty for at least one symbol then the loop is statically recognized independent or dependent, respectively. Exceptions are the cases when the symbol access is in a reduction pattern or when output dependencies can be fixed via the application of privatization and static last value. Next, a sequence of flow and output independence predicates is extracted for each unresolved symbol, where a `true` predicate still classifies independence statically.

Predicate code generation first extracts the loop slice that corresponds to the CDG-transitive closure of all statements that are necessary to compute the symbols appearing in the target predicate, where the non read-only symbols are privatized and copied in, if necessary. Next, one can observe that the definitions of the symbols appearing in a leaf node are necessarily on the same CFG path, hence the code for the leaf-node is placed immediately after the definition of the last symbol; we denote it the most dominated definition (MDD). Composition nodes, such as $\vee/\wedge$ are placed at the immediate common post-dominator of its child nodes, etc.

Predicates of non-constant complexity are evaluated in parallel, where we use `and/or` reduction to merge boolean results across iterations. Redundancy is further reduced by hoisting the calls to these predicates interprocedurally at the highest loop-dominator point where all predicate's input values are available (i.e., the MDD of its input values). It follows that all symbols' predicates are called on one CFG path, hence predicates can be cascaded (i.e., the first successful predicate disables the evaluation of the rest).

If all predicates fail, then we apply an exact, albeit potentially expensive, runtime test. If we can amortize the cost of the exact test against many execution of the loop (i.e., via hoisting), then we use direct evaluation of IND-USR, otherwise we use TLS [25].

Finally, we optimize parallelism by implementing conditional privatization, reduction or static-last value, where loop parallelization uses OpenMP directives. For example, code generation for an array `X` that requires the EXT-RRED of Section 4 uses a private copy of `X`, `X1`. Prior to (parallel) loop execution the reduction part of `X1`, i.e., $\cup_{i=1}^{N}(\texttt{RW}_i)$ is zeroed out. Next, each iteration computes its $\texttt{WF}_i$ set, and writes back to X the locations in $\texttt{WF}_i$ at iteration's end. After loop termination, the locations involved in reduction statements, i.e., $\cup_{i=1}^{N}(\texttt{RW}_i)$, are reduced across the `X1`'s copies and `X` is accordingly updated. If the access is proven independent at runtime, then none of the above are necessary and the code uses shared-array `X` instead of its private copies `X1`.

6. Experimental Results

This section evaluates our auto-parallelizing approach on 26 benchmarks from the PERFECT-CLUB, SPEC1992, 2000 and 2006 suites. Tables 1, 2 and 3 characterize each benchmark as a whole, named in column one, and several of its representative loops, where columns three and four show the loop name and its contribution to sequential coverage (LSC) as percentage of the sequential runtime, respectively. Column five shows how loops have been classified: whether the loop has been proven sequential/parallel statically[6](STATIC-PAR/SEQ), or it uses predicates to prove flow/output independence (F/OI), and the complexity of the runtime test (O(1)/O(N)), where N refers to the number of iterations of the outermost loop.

Finally, column two characterizes the benchmark as a whole: (i) the sequential coverage (SC) and the corresponding number of measured loops (NL_{sc}), but also the total number of analyzed loops (NL_{tot}) when different than NL_{sc}, (ii) the sequential coverage of the loops that require runtime independence tests (SC_{rt}), and the overhead of these tests (RT_{ov}) represented as percentage of the parallel runtime, and (iii) the parallelization techniques used: privatization (PRIV), static/dynamic last value (SLV/DLV), static/runtime/extended reduction (SRED/RRED/EXT-RRED/BOUNDS-COMP), as presented in Section 4.

Additionally, (i) UMEG refers to the transformation of Section 3.4 that preserves the USR particular shape of an union of mutually exclusive gates, (ii) MON signals the use of monotonicity tests, and CIV_{agg} and CIV-COMP refer to the summarization refinement in the presence of *conditional induction variables* (CIV) and to the parallel pre-computation of their iteration-wise values, as summarized in Section 3.3, and (iii) HOIST-USR means that independence was proven via runtime USR evaluation, where the USR has been successfully hoisted outside at least one loop, i.e., the overhead was amortized across the many loop executions.

Our compiler generates OpenMP-annotated Fortran source code. PERFECT-CLUB and SPEC92 benchmarks were compiled (`-O2 -ipo`) and compared with INTEL's `ifort` compiler version 11.1 (`-O2 -ipo -parallel`) on a commodity INTEL quad-core `Q9550@2.83GHz` machine with `8Gb` memory. The larger SPEC2000/2006 benchmarks were compiled (`-O4`) and compared with IBM's `xlf` compiler version 13 (`-O4 -qsmp=auto`) on a 8 dual-core POWER5+`@1.9GHz`, `32Gb`-memory machine. Benchmarks were run three times and the average was taken; This was

[6] In some cases the static decision refers to extracting a `true` predicate.

PERFECT CLUB Suite					
BENCH	BENCH PROPERTIES	SELECTED LOOPS	LSC %	GR ms	PAR/SEQ/ RT TEST
FLO52	SC=95%,NL_{sc}=30	PSMOO_do40	19.5%	.04	STATIC-PAR
	SC_{rt}=.3%, RT_{ov}=0%	DFLUX_do30	9.6%	.08	STATIC-PAR
	PRIV,SRED,SLV	EFLUX_do10	8.2%	.02	STATIC-PAR
	RRED,NL_{tot}=199	DFLUX_do40	0.3%	.01	OI O(1)
BDNA	SC=94%,NL_{sc}=6	ACTFOR_do500	59.5%	69	STATIC-PAR
	SC_{rt}=0%, RT_{ov}=0%	ACTFOR_do240	31.5%	36	CIV_{agg}
	PRIV,S/RRED,CIV_{agg}	RESTAR_do15	4.8%	28	STATIC-PAR
	NL_{tot}=272	ACTFOR_do320	1.8%	.1	STATIC-PAR
ARC2D	SC=97%,NL_{sc}=34	STEPFX_do210	16.3%	.8	STATIC-PAR
	SC_{rt}=20%, RT_{ov}=.2%	STEPFX_do230	11.9%	.6	STATIC-PAR
	PRIV,SLV,MON	XPENT2_do11,etc	10.7%	.002	FI O(1)
	NL_{tot}=207	FILERX_do15	9.0%	1.3	FI O(1)
DYFESM	SC=97%,NL_{sc}=10	MXMULT_do10	43.9%	.006	FI HOIST-USR
	SC_{rt}=96%,				OI O(N)
	RT_{ov}=.3%	SOLXDD_do10/4	27.3%	.007	OI O(N)
	PRIV,EXT-RRED	SOLVH_do20	14.2%	.03	F/OI O(1)/O(N)
	HOIST-USR,MON	FORMR_do20	10.5%	.02	FI HOIST-USR
	NL_{tot}=195				OI O(N)
MDG	SC=99%,NL_{sc}=12	INTERF_do1000	92%	24	STATIC-PAR
	SC_{rt}=0%, RT_{ov}=0%	POTENG_do2000	7.2%	19	STATIC-PAR
	PRIV,RRED,NL_{tot}=59	CORREC_do1000	0.1%	.04	STATIC-PAR
TRFD	SC=99%,NL_{sc}=4	OLDA_do100	63.7%	18	STATIC-PAR
	SC_{rt}=34.8%, RT_{ov}=0%	OLDA_do300	30.9%	9	FI O(1)
	PRIV,SLV,MON	INTGRL_do140	3.9%	2	OI O(N)
	NL_{tot}=44	INTGRL_do20	0.1%	.006	STATIC-PAR
TRACK	SC=97%,NL_{sc}=3	EXTEND_do400	49.2%	117	CIV-COMP
	SC_{rt}=97%, RT_{ov}=47%	FPTRAK_do300	47.7%	121	CIV-COMP
	PRIV,CIV_{agg},NL_{tot}=88	NLFILT_do300$3	1.2%	3.6	TLS
SPEC77	SC=76%,NL_{sc}=4	GLOOP_do1000	57.1%	31	STATIC-PAR
	SC_{rt}=11%, RT_{ov}=0%	GWATER_do190	16.5%	9.5	TLS
	PRIV,SRED,SLV	SICDKD_do1000	2.6%	1.3	FI O(1)
OCEAN	SC=65%,NL_{sc}=14	FTRVMT_do109	45.4%	.01	FI O(1)
	SC_{rt}=45%, RT_{ov}=.1%	CSR_do20	5.2%	.04	STATIC-PAR
	PRIV,SLV,MON	SCSC_do30/40	3.8%	.03	STATIC-PAR
	NL_{tot}=134	RCS_do20	1.8%	.04	STATIC-PAR
QCD	SC=99%,NL_{sc}=6	UPDATE_do1	31.9%	22	STATIC-SEQ
	SC_{rt}=1%, RT_{ov}=0%	UPDATE_do2	31.6%	22	STATIC-SEQ ..
	NL_{tot}=113	INIT_do2	1%	1.5	OI O(1)

Table 1. Properties of the PERFECT CLUB suite.
The layout of this table is explained in the beginning of Section 6

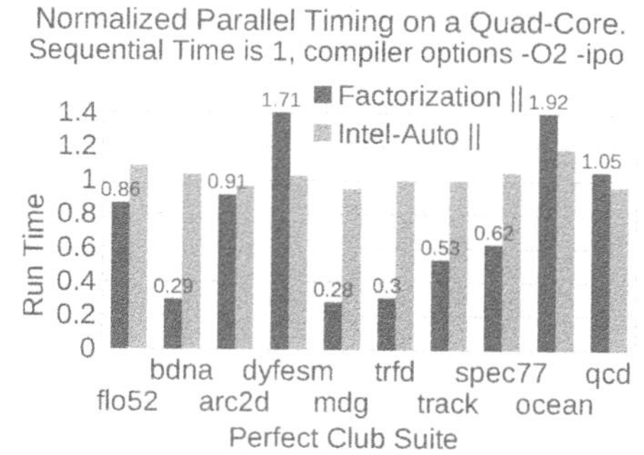

Figure 10. Timing Results for PERFECT-CLUB Suite.

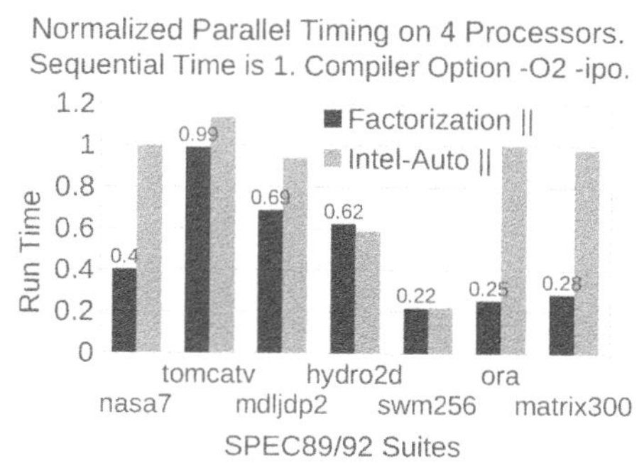

Figure 11. Timing Results for SPEC89/92 Suite.

deemed sufficient because their runtime typically exhibited negligible standard deviation.

6.1 Results Summary

Examining Figures 10, 11, 12 and 13, one can draw several high-level observations: First, the speedups achieved via our factorization approach are superior to the ones of INTEL's `ifort` and IBM's `xlf_r` compilers in all but four cases: `dyfesm`, `ocean`, `hydro2d`, and `qcd`. With `qcd` the results are close, and neither approach extracts significant parallelism. In the other cases, our approach successfully parallelizes a number of small-granularity loops which results in slowdown compared to sequential execution, while `ifort/xlf_r` fails to prove those loops parallel, hence executes them sequentially.

Second, the gains mainly reflect the commercial-compiler inability to parallelize the important loops of the corresponding benchmarks: (i) either because it lacks interprocedural dependence analysis, e.g., the benchmarks that were statically parallelized by SUIF a decade ago, or (ii) because it lacks extensive use of runtime-validation of parallelization (conditional parallelization, inspector/executor, speculative parallelization).

Third, the overhead of our techniques that enable parallelism at runtime is negligible in most cases, i.e., less than 1% of the parallel timing; the notable exceptions of `track`, `gromacs`, `calculix`, which still exhibit scalable speedup, will be discussed separately.

Fourth, we have classified parallelism exhaustively on a number of benchmarks, indicated via a large NL_{tot}, and the results support the feasibility of exploiting nested parallelism (e.g., `bdna` and `apsi` exhibit many inner loops that are solved via light predicates).

Finally, there are only two loops that require thread-level speculation (TLS): NLFILT_DO300 of `track` and GWATER_DO190 of `spec77`, and only one notable example where independence is proven via hoistable-USR evaluation: `apsi`'s RUN_DO20/40/etc.

6.2 PERFECT CLUB Suite Results

While being the oldest, PERFECT-CLUB suite is the most difficult to parallelize: `arc2d`, `dyfesm`, `trfd`, `ocean` and `bdna` all exhibit an abundance of flow and output independence predicates of $O(1)$ and $O(N)$ runtime complexity. Loops MXMULT_DO10 and FORMR_DO20 of `dyfesm` use the extended treatment for reduction of Section 4, while `trfd` and `dyfesm` are rich in the monotonicity predicates of Section 3.3.

Furthermore, `bdna`, but especially `track` use the CIV-aggregation refinement (CIV_{agg}) of Section 3.3. In `track`'s case, two while loops sum up to 97% of the sequential coverage. Parallelizing the two `while` loops requires (pre)computing the number of iterations of the loops, together with the per-iteration CIV values (CIV-COMP). The corresponding loop slice is almost as expensive as the loop, hence the runtime overhead is 47% of the total parallel timing. However, tested on extended datasets, parallelism scales well up to at least 16 processors (7.3x speedup).

Figure 10 shows the parallel timings under normal `-O2 -ipo` compilation. Unfortunately, PERFECT-CLUB uses (outdated) small datasets, which, in the cases of `flo52`, `arc2d`, `dyfesm`, and `ocean` results in loop granularities in the range of tens of microseconds, which are simply too small to amortize the thread-spawning overhead. However, extended datasets would likely enable scalable speedups on all four benchmarks; for example artificially increasing granularity by compiling under option `O0` results in speedups: 2.6x, 2.1x, 2.2x and 1.6x, respectively. The modest speedup of `ocean` is mainly due a sequential coverage of only 65%, because some parallel loops (`in,out`) with prohibitively small granularities (in the range of one microsecond) have not been considered. We have encountered similar problems in the `spec77` and `qcd` codes.

SPEC89 and SPEC92 Suites					
BENCH	BENCH PROPERTIES	SELECTED LOOPS	LSC %	GR ms	PAR/SEQ/ RT TEST
MATRIX300	SC=100%,NL_{sc}=9	SGEMM_do160	30.2%	160	STATIC-PAR
	SC_{rt}=26%	SGEMM_do120	30%	159	STATIC-PAR
	RT_{ov}=0%	SGEMM_do20/40	12.8%	34	OI O(1)
	PRIV,RRED	SGEMM_do60/100	12.8%	34	OI O(1)
SWM256	SC=99%,NL_{sc}=18	CALC2_do200	40.6%	.7	STATIC-PAR
	SC_{rt}=0% PRIV	CALC3_do300	29.7%	.5	STATIC-PAR
	RT_{ov}=0% SRED	CALC1_do100	27.8%	.5	STATIC-PAR
ORA	SC=100%,NL_{sc}=4	MAIN_do9999	99.9%	999	STATIC-PAR
	SC_{rt}=0% PRIV, SLV	MAIN_do25	0%	0	STATIC-PAR
	RT_{ov}=0% SRED	MAIN_do412	0%	0	STATIC-PAR
NASA7	SC=90%,NL_{sc}=9	GMTTST_do120	21.1%	980	FI O(1)
	SC_{rt}=43.6%	EMIT_do5	13.2%	61	SLV O(N)
	RT_{ov}=.03% PRIV				CIV-COMP
	SLV, SRED, CIV_{agg}	BTRTST_do120	9.4%	436	FI O(1)
TOMCATV	SC=100%,NL_{sc}=9	MAIN_do60	37.8%	7	STATIC-PAR
	SC_{rt}=0%	MAIN_do100$2	26.6%	.01	STATIC-PAR
	RT_{ov}=0%	MAIN_do120$2	10.9%	.01	STATIC-PAR
	PRIV,SLV,SRED	MAIN_do80	10.8%	2	STATIC-PAR
MDLJDP2	SC=87%,NL_{sc}=6	FRCUSE_do20	82.4%	.9	STATIC-PAR
	SC_{rt}=0%	POSTFR_do20	1.6%	.02	STATIC-PAR
	RT_{ov}=0%	PREFOR_do60	1.5%	.02	STATIC-PAR
	PRIV,S/RRED	POSTFR_do60	1.1%	.01	STATIC-PAR
HYDRO2D	SC=92%,NL_{sc}=58	TISTEP_do400	17.6%	1.2	STATIC-PAR
	SC_{rt}=0%	FILTER_do300	14.2%	.1	STATIC-PAR
	RT_{ov}=0% PRIV	T1_do10	7.5%	.07	STATIC-PAR

Table 2. Properties of the SPEC89 and SPEC92 suites.
The layout of this table is explained in the beginning of Section 6

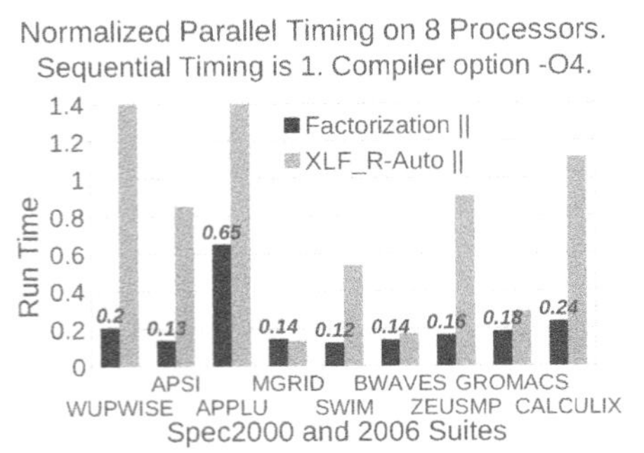

Figure 12. Timing Results for SPEC2000/2006 Suite.

6.3 SPEC89 and SPEC92 Suites Results

Figure 11 shows four-processor timings for several benchmarks in SPEC92 suite, from which **nasa7** uses independence predicates and CIV aggregation. While predicate overheads are negligible, **nasa7** obtains only 2.5x speedup because loops GMTTST_DO120 and EMIT_DO5 have 2 and 5 iterations, respectively. As with PERFECT-CLUB, we observe that our speedups are superior to the ones of **ifort**, and our lower speedups correspond to benchmarks that exhibit small loop granularity: **mdljdp**, **hydro2d** and **tomcatv**.

Tomcatv shows the need for further transformations in order to take advantage of parallelization. Loops MAIN_DO100$2 AND 120$2 exhibit too small granularities, to benefit from parallelization (in fact they suffer a slowdown). However the speedup increases to 2 on 8 procesors when the granularity is increased via loop interchange (though loosing locality). We expect loop tiling [27] (not implemented) to improve matters further.

6.4 SPEC2000 and SPEC2006 Suites Results

Figure 12 compares the parallel execution time of our approach against the one **xlf_r** on eight processors and shows that our speed-up is superior in most cases. Figure 13 shows our scalability speedups up to sixteen processors. Benchmark **gamess**, not measured, is notoriously difficult to parallelize [3] and we disambiguated only small-granularities loops that do not exhibit speedup, while **applu** exhibits two sequential loops that sum-up to 56% of sequential coverage and contain only sequential or small-granularity inner loops, which do not contribute to speedup.

SPEC2000 and SPEC2006 Suites					
BENCH	BENCH PROPERTIES	SELECTED LOOPS	LSC %	GR ms	PAR/SEQ/ RT TEST
WUPWISE	SC=93%,NL_{sc}=4	MULDEO_do100	20.6%	206	F/OI O(1)
	SC_{rt}=93%	MULDEO_do200	25.8%	258	F/OI O(1)
	RT_{ov}=0%, PRIV	MULDOE_do100	20.7%	207	F/OI O(1)
	RRED,SLV	MULDOE_do200	25.9%	259	F/OI O(1)
APSI	SC=99%,NL_{sc}=25	RUN_do20/30/40	17.6%	176	FI HOIST-USR
	SC_{rt}=28% RT_{ov}=.2%	RUN_do50/60/70	10.4%	122	FI HOIST-USR
	HOIST-USR,PRIV,SRED	WCONT_do40	11%	330	STATIC-PAR
	SLV, NL_{tot}=252	DVDTZ_do40	10.3%	314	STATIC-PAR
APPLU	SC=98%,NL_{sc}=9	BLTS_do10	28.4%	119	STATIC-SEQ
	SC_{rt}=0%	BUTS_do1	28.1%	117	STATIC-SEQ
	RT_{ov}=0%	JACLD_do1	14.1%	59	STATIC-PAR
	PRIV,S/RRED,SLV	JACU_do1	10%	314	STATIC-PAR
MGRID	SC=100%,NL_{sc}=12	RESID_do600	51.5%	42	STATIC-PAR
	SC_{rt}=0%	PSINV_do600	28.9%	7	STATIC-PAR
	RT_{ov}=0%	INTERP_do800	4.9%	2	STATIC-PAR
	PRIV	RPRJ3_do100	4.5%	2	STATIC-PAR
SWIM	SC=100%,NL_{sc}=18	SHALOW_do3500	44.8%	116	STATIC-PAR
	SC_{rt}=0%	CALC2_do200	20.5%	53	STATIC-PAR
	RT_{ov}=0%, PRIV	CALC1_do100	18%	47	STATIC-PAR
	SRED, NL_{tot}=252	CALC3_do300	15.4%	40	STATIC-PAR
BWAVES	SC=100%,NL_{sc}=20	MAT*VEC_do1	75.1%	206	STATIC-PAR
	SC_{rt}=0%,PRIV,SLV	FLUX_do2	5.8%	236	STATIC-PAR
	SRED,NL_{tot}=85	SHELL_do5$2	4.2%	509	STATIC-PAR
ZEUSMP	SC=99%,NL_{sc}=51	HSMOC_do360	10.3%	783	STATIC-PAR
	SC_{rt}=10%,RT_{ov}=.01%	MOMX3_do3000	5.1%	13	STATIC-PAR
	PRIV,SLV	TRANX2/3_do2100	7.6%	24	F/OI O(1)
	UMEG	TRANX1_do100	2.4%	26	OI O(1)
GROMACS	SC=90%,NL_{sc}=4	INL1130_do1	84.8%	33	BOUNDS-COMP
	SC_{rt}=90%,RT_{ov}=3.4%	INL1100_do1	2.2%	5	BOUNDS-COMP
	PRIV,RRED	INL1000_do1	1.9%	4	BOUNDS-COMP
	BOUNDS-COMP	INL0100_do1	0.8%	1	BOUNDS-COMP
CALCULIX	SC=74%,NL_{sc}=1	MAFILLSM_do7	73.7%	14s	BOUNDS-COMP
	SC_{rt}=74%,RT_{ov}=8.5%				F/OI O(N)
	SRED,PRIV,UMEG				F/OI O(1)
	BOUNDS-COMP				
GAMESS	SC=32%,NL_{sc}=2	DIRFCK_do300	18%	.04	STATIC-PAR
	SC_{rt}=0% PRIV,RRED	GENR70_do170	14.4%	.03	STATIC-PAR

Table 3. Properties of the SPEC2000 and SPEC2006 suites.
The layout of this table is explained in the beginning of Section 6

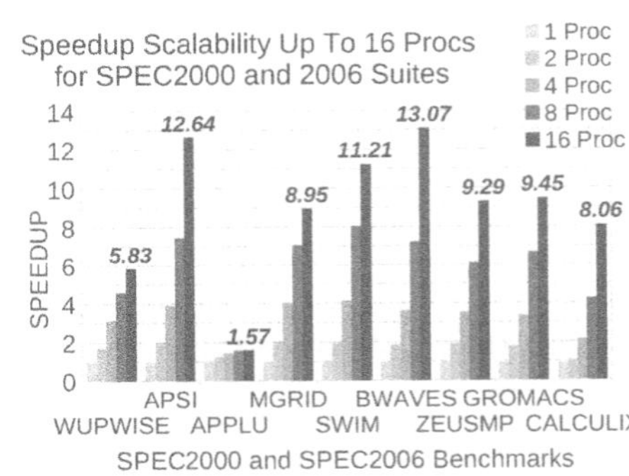

Figure 13. Scalability Results for Spec2006 Suite. Only the Fortran Parts of **gromacs** and **calculix** are measured.

We observe that speedups do not scale well between 8 to 16 processors; this is likely because the machine has eight dual-core processors, and executing on both cores decreases the per-core bandwidth. Benchmarks **mgrid**, **swim** and **bwaves** show good speedups, extracted statically. Both **calculix** and **gromacs** are written in a mixture of **C** and **Fortran**, from which we have analyzed and measured only the **Fortran** part, which shows a sequential coverage of 74% and 90% respectively. We remark that our speed-ups are superior to those of IBM's **xlf_r** compiler.

Half of the benchmarks use runtime parallelization techniques: **wupwise**, **zeusmp** and **calculix** use $O(1)$ and $O(N)$ flow and output independence tests, while **apsi** proves flow independence of loops such as RUN_DO20 via hoistable-USR evaluation. Both **gromacs** and **calculix** use reductions, where the target array is allocated in the **C** part and used in **Fortran** as an assumed-size-array parameter. Typical reduction implementation (e.g. OpenMP) requires to know the upper and lower bounds of the target array.

Our bounds-estimation technique, BOUNDS-COMP, described in Section 4, is responsible for the overheads $RT_{ov} = 3.4\%$ and 8.5%

of the parallel runtime of `gromacs` and `calculix`, respectively. BOUNDS-COMP's overhead (i) slightly increases for `gromacs` from normalized runtime .01 on one processor to .02 on 16 processors, due to the small granularity of the BOUNDS-COMP loop, but (ii) it scales perfectly with parallelism for `calculix`: from .16 on one processor to .01 on 16 processors. We note that our technique results in a parallel runtime about 1.66x faster than the one of `xlf_r` on `gromacs`, where `xlf_r`, in the absence of bounds information, appears to be wrapping reduction statements into atomic blocks (another `xlf` version exhibits slowdown).

7. Related Work

Solutions based on Presburger arithmetic [12, 22] analyze an entire loop nest at a time, albeit in the narrower affine domain where subscripts, loop bounds, `if` conditions are affine expressions of loop indexes. Both the memory dependencies and the flow of values between every pair of read-write accesses are accurately modeled via systems of affine inequations, which are solved by gaussian-like elimination. These solutions drive powerful code transformations to optimize and enable parallelism [21], but they are most effective when applied on relatively-small, intra-procedural loop nests exhibiting simple control flow. In comparison, our technique is better suited to parallelize larger loops, but is less effective in driving code transformations such as loop interchange, skewing, tiling, etc.

Pugh and Wonnacott are the first to show how to interpret irreducible Presburger formulas as simple predicates that can be verified either by the user or at runtime. The approach, named conditional dependency analysis [24], existentially quantifies the variables that correspond to the loop index in the Presburger formula of the flow dependence and computes the "gist" of the obtained formula, by removing false-alarm terms. Analysis is extended with uninterpreted-symbol functions [23] to model non-affine terms and a limited notion of control flow, where inductive simplification derives simpler, (only) sufficient conditions for independence.

To extend analysis to program level, several solutions have been proposed that (i) summarize accesses via an array abstraction, as dictated by (structural) data-flow analysis, and (ii) model loop independence via equations on these summaries. These approaches typically perform conservative approximations to keep the (successive) summary results within the array abstraction domain, e.g., they fail to disambiguate some more complicated cases of coupled subscripts, but they accommodate better more-complex control flow. For example, the simple loop [24]:

```
DO i = 1, N, 1
   IF(p[i] > 0) THEN A = ...
   ELSE              A = ... ENDIF
ENDDO
... = A
```

produces an inexact flow-dependence result for scalar `A` under Pugh and Wonnacott's approach: $\{[] \mid \nexists i\ s.th.\ 1 \le i \le n \wedge p(i) > 0\}$, but the `IF`-data-flow equation of a summary-based solution would identify that both mutually exclusive branches guard the same summary, hence the non-affine gate (`p[i]`) can be safely discarded.

Hoeflinger *et* al. use the LMAD [20] array abstraction to summarize accesses into read-only, write-first and read-write sets. The ART test [14] builds iteration-level summaries and aggregates them over the targeted loop. If this aggregation creates a new LMAD dimension that does not overlap with the existent dimensions, then a monotonicity-based argument establishes that independence holds.

Hall *et* al. organize summaries as systems of affine inequations and analyze the read, write and exposed-read abstract sets to establish loop independence [13]. In both approaches summaries are paired with predicates, typically extracted from control flow, that guard the summary existence. In addition, Moon and Hall also extract predicates that guard (otherwise unsafe) simplifications in the array abstraction domain, and use invariants synthetized from branch conditions to enhance the precision of the summary [18].

Adve and Mellor-Crummey present an interesting instance of an equational system, where summaries are represented via Presburger formula, and summary equations model computation partitioning and communication analysis for data-parallel programs [1]. The system defines a rich compositional algebra that starts from a set of user-define inputs, such as the alignment of an array with a template and the home of certain statements, and computes the set of locations that need to be sent/received to/from other processors. This formalism drives several important optimizations, such as message vectorization, in-place communication and in-place splitting. Whenever the result summary falls outside the affine domain, inspector/executor techniques are used to verify the desired invariant.

In comparison, rather than requiring constraints to be affine or resorting to conservative approximations, we build on Rus *et* al.'s language of USRs [28], recalled in Section 2, to construct exact read-only, read-write, and write-first summaries. Since runtime evaluation of USRs exhibits in many cases unacceptably-large overheads, we define a *language translation* scheme to an equally expressive language of *predicates*.

The obtained predicate program is less constrained than the ones of related solutions, and its construction typically involves less conservative approximations. For example, when predicate symbols are mutable we use a program slice to compute them. We improve both qualitatively and quantitatively on Rus *et* al. work [28, 29] in that: we define a complex system of inference rules, which are used more aggressively to derive predicates, and we show that predicates can disambiguate many loops that were either unreported or previously solved via the more expensive USR evaluation. Finally, we present the compiler infrastructure for improving predicates' accuracy (e.g., USR reshaping rules), for factorizing and cascading the predicate program into a set of increasingly-complex conditions for independence, and for implementing conditional reduction, etc.

A significant amount of work was aimed at disambiguating a class of irregular subscripts exhibiting quadratic or array indexing or induction variables without closed-form solutions. One direction was to enhance the mathematical support with more accurate symbolic ranges [8, 10], or more encompassing algebras, such as representing induction-variables via chains of recurrence [9]. For example, Blume and Eigenmann's Range Test [7] uses the extended range support and exploits the monotonicity of read-write accesses to disambiguate a class of quadratic or coupled indexing (e.g., loops `olda_do100/300` from `trfd` or `ocean`'s `ftrvmt_do109`).

Lin and Padua extend the library of recognizable access patterns to solve: (i) stack/queue-access patterns [16] (e.g., loops from `bdna`, `p3m` and `tree`, but not `track`), and (ii) index-array accesses [15]. The latter extends the applicability of the Range Test to cover array indexing, for the cases when the index-array value properties assumed by pattern recognition can be statically verified (e.g. loops from `trfd` and `dyfesm`, but not `solvh_do20`).

Pugh and Wonnacott extension of Presburger arithmetic [23] also solves a number of loops that would fall outside the traditional affine domain: for example some tricky cases of coupled subscripts, or the indirect array pattern of loop `intgrl_do540` from `trfd` or the non-trivial control flow of `mdg`'s `interf_do1000` and `poteng_do2000`, or the quasi-affine pattern of loop `filerx_do290` from `arc2d`. However, loops `olda_do100/300` from `trfd` are only recognized to form a monotonic indexing sequence before induction variable substitution, while loops `actfor_do240` and `extend_do400` from `bdna` and `track` are not disambiguated.

Finally, the ART test [14] of Hoeflinger *et* al. disambiguates a class of coupled subscripts and exponential indexing.

In comparison, we present a *unified framework* that parallelizes a large class of loops that have been previously analyzed with a number of different techniques: for example we match the results reported by SUIF [13] on a number of statically analyzable benchmarks (e.g., `mdg`, `ora`, `swim`, `applu`, `mgrid`, `hydro2d` etc.), and also solve most of the non-affine benchmarks that require conditional analysis. The latter corresponds in part to a complex translation rule [19] that exploits the monotonicity of a summary of a particular shape (see Section 3.3). Notable exceptions are the stack-access pattern of benchmark `p3m`, and several loops exhibiting exponential indexing and tricky instances of coupled subscripts. We solve loop `run_do20` from `apsi` via expensive USR evaluation, but which still results in negligible overhead due to the use of memoization. In addition we parallelize a number of previously unreported benchmarks using our minimal-weight predicates (e.g., `calculix`, `zeusmp`, `wupwise`, `nasa`, `track`, `gromacs`).

The other main direction of approaching autoparallelization has been to analyze memory references at run-time, either via inspector/executor [26], or via TLS techniques [25], or via faster but less scalable techniques [30]. These techniques have overhead proportional to the number of the original-loop accesses, and hence we use then only as last resort, once all the lighter predicates failed.

8. Conclusions

In this paper we presented a fully automatic approach to loop parallelization that integrates the use of static and run-time analysis and thus overcomes many previously known difficulties. Starting from our rich array reference representation, the USR language, we expressed the independence condition as an equation, $S = \emptyset$, where S is a set expression representing array indexes. We introduced a language translation $\mathcal{F}$ from the USR set-expression language to a language of predicates ($\mathcal{F}(S) \Rightarrow S = \emptyset$). Loop parallelization is then validated using a novel logic inference algorithm that factorizes the obtained complex predicates ($\mathcal{F}(S)$) into a sequence of sufficient-independence conditions which are evaluated first statically and, when necessary, at run-time, in increasing order of their estimated complexities. The experimental evaluation on 26 benchmarks from PERFECT-CLUB and SPEC suites and show speedups as high as 4.5x and 8.4x and on average 2.4x and 5.4x on four and eight processors, respectively, which are superior to the ones of INTEL's `ifort` and IBM's `xlf_r` commercial compilers. Our translation technique from set to predicate language and our factorization algorithm are extensible and can be applied to a variety of conditional optimizations. It is powerful because it can make use of dynamic information very efficiently.

Acknowledgments

This work was supported in part by NSF awards CRI-0551685, CCF-0833199, CCF-0830753, IIS-0917266, NSF/DNDO award 2008-DN-077-ARI018-02, by the DOE NNSA PSAAP grant DE-FC52-08NA28616, IBM, Intel, Oracle/Sun and Award KUS-C1-016-04, made by King Abdullah University of Science and Technology (KAUST). Since November 2011 Cosmin Oancea was supported by Danish Strategic Research Council, for the HIPERFIT research center under contract 10-092299.

References

[1] V. Adve and J. Mellor-Crummey. Using Integer Sets for Data-Parallel Program Analysis and Optimization. In *Procs. Int. Conf. Prog. Lang. Design and Implementation*, 1998.

[2] R. Allen and K. Kennedy. *Optimizing Compilers for Modern Architectures*. Morgan Kaufmann, 2002. ISBN 1-55860-286-0.

[3] B. Armstrong and R. Eigenmann. Application of Automatic Parallelization to Modern Challenges of Scientific Computing Industries. In *Int. Conf. Parallel Proc.* , pages 279–286, 2008.

[4] U. Banerjee. Speedup of Ordinary Programs. *Ph.D. Thesis, Univ. of Illinois at Urbana-Champaign*, Report No. 79-989, 1988.

[5] W. Blume *et* al. Parallel Programming with Polaris. *Computer*, 29(12), 1996.

[6] W. Blume and R. Eigenmann. Performance Analysis of Parallelizing Compilers on the Perfect Benchmarks Programs. *IEEE Transactions on Parallel and Distributed Systems*, 3:643–656, 1992.

[7] W. Blume and R. Eigenmann. The Range Test: A Dependence Test for Symbolic, Non-Linear Expressions. In *Procs. Int. Conf. on Supercomp*, pages 528–537, 1994.

[8] W. Blume and R. Eigenmann. Demand-Driven,Symbolic Range Propagation. In *Procs. Int. Lang. Comp. Par. Comp.* , 1995.

[9] R. A. V. Engelen. A unified framework for nonlinear dependence testing and symbolic analysis. In *Procs. Int. Conf.on Supercomp*, pages 106–115, 2004.

[10] T. Fahringer. Efficient Symbolic Analysis for Parallelizing Compilers and Performance Estimator. *Journal of Supercomp*,12:227–252,1997.

[11] P. Feautrier. Parametric Integer Programming. *Operations Research*, 22(3):243–268, 1988.

[12] P. Feautrier. Dataflow Analysis of Array and Scalar References. *Int. Journal of Par. Prog*, 20(1):23–54, 1991.

[13] M. W. Hall, S. P. Amarasinghe, B. R. Murphy, S.-W. Liao, and M. S. Lam. Interprocedural Parallelization Analysis in SUIF. *Trans. on Prog. Lang. and Sys.*, 27(4):662–731, 2005.

[14] J. Hoeflinger, Y. Paek, and K. Yi. Unified Interprocedural Parallelism Detection. *Int. Journal of Par. Prog*, 29(2):185–215, 2001.

[15] Y. Lin and D. Padua. Demand-Driven Interprocedural Array Property Analysis. In *Procs. Int. Lang. Comp. Par. Comp.*, 1999.

[16] Y. Lin and D. Padua. Analysis of Irregular Single-Indexed Arrays and its Applications in Compiler Optimizations. In *Procs. Int. Conf. on Compiler Construction*, pages 202–218, 2000.

[17] B. Lu and J. Mellor-Crummey. Compiler Optimization of Implicit Reductions for Distributed Memory Multiprocessors In *Int. Par. Proc. Symp.*, 1998

[18] S. Moon and M. W. Hall. Evaluation of Predicated Array Data-Flow Analysis for Automatic Parallelization. In *Proc. of Principles and Practice of Parallel Programming*, pages 84–95, 1999.

[19] C. E. Oancea and L. Rauchwerger. A Hybrid Approach to Proving Memory Reference Monotonicity. In *Procs. Int. Lang. Comp. Par. Comp.*, 2011.

[20] Y. Paek, J. Hoeflinger, and D. Padua. Efficient and Precise Array Access Analysis. *Trans. on Prog. Lang. and Sys.*, 24(1):65–109, 2002.

[21] L.N. Pouchet, et al. Loop Transformations: Convexity, Pruning and Optimization. In *Procs. of Princ. of Prog. Lang.*, 2011.

[22] W. Pugh. The Omega Test: a Fast and Practical Integer Programming Algorithm for Dependence Analysis. *Com. of the ACM*, 8:4–13, 1992.

[23] W. Pugh and D. Wonnacott. Nonlinear Array Dependence Analysis. In *Proc. Lang. Comp. Run-Time Support Scal. Sys.*, 1995.

[24] W. Pugh and D. Wonnacott. Constraint-Based Array Dependence Analysis. In *Trans. on Prog. Lang. and Sys.* , 20(3), 635–678, 1998.

[25] L. Rauchwerger and D. Padua. The LRPD Test: Speculative Run-Time Parallelization of Loops with Privatization and Reduction Parallelization. *IEEE Trans. Par. Distrib. Sys*, 10(2):160–199, 1999.

[26] L. Rauchwerger, N. Amato, and D. Padua. A Scalable Method for Run Time Loop Parallelization. *Int. Journal of Par. Prog*,26:26–6,1995.

[27] L. Renganarayanan, et. al. Parameterized Tiled Loops for Free. In *Int. Conf. Prog. Lang. Design and Implementation.*, 2007.

[28] S. Rus, J. Hoeflinger, and L. Rauchwerger. Hybrid analysis: Static & dynamic memory reference analysis. *Int. Journal of Par. Prog*, 31(3): 251–283, 2003.

[29] S. Rus, M. Pennings, and L. Rauchwerger. Sensitivity Analysis for Automatic Parallelization on Multi-Cores. In *Procs. Int. Conf. on Supercomp*, pages 263–273, 2007.

[30] X. Zhuang, et. al. Exploiting Parallelism with Dependence-Aware Scheduling. In *Int. Conf. Par. Arch. Compilation Tech.*, 2009.

Fully Automatic and Precise Detection of Thread Safety Violations

Michael Pradel
Department of Computer Science
ETH Zurich

Thomas R. Gross
Department of Computer Science
ETH Zurich

Abstract

Concurrent, object-oriented programs often use thread-safe library classes. Existing techniques for testing a thread-safe class either rely on tests using the class, on formal specifications, or on both. Unfortunately, these techniques often are not fully automatic as they involve the user in analyzing the output. This paper presents an automatic testing technique that reveals concurrency bugs in supposedly thread-safe classes. The analysis requires as input only the class under test and reports only true positives. The key idea is to generate tests in which multiple threads call methods on a shared instance of the tested class. If a concurrent test exhibits an exception or a deadlock that cannot be triggered in any linearized execution of the test, the analysis reports a thread safety violation. The approach is easily applicable, because it is independent of hand-written tests and explicit specifications. The analysis finds 15 concurrency bugs in popular Java libraries, including two previously unknown bugs in the Java standard library.

Categories and Subject Descriptors D.1.3 [*Programming Techniques*]: Concurrent Programming; D.1.3 [*Programming Techniques*]: Object-oriented Programming; D.2.5 [*Software Engineering*]: Testing and Debugging

General Terms Languages, Reliability, Algorithms

Keywords Thread safety, Testing, Concurrent test generation

1. Introduction

Writing correct concurrent programs is hard for many reasons. Developers tend to think think sequentially, making concurrent programs hard to write and understand because of their non-deterministic and parallel nature. Furthermore, testing techniques for concurrent programs have not yet reached the sophistication of techniques for sequential programs.

In this paper, we address the problem of testing concurrent programs. Ideally, a testing technique requires a single input—a piece of software to analyze—and produces a single output—true positive reports of concurrency bugs in the tested software. Existing techniques do not meet this requirement, because they either require additional input, produce undesirable additional output, or both. As an additional input besides the software to analyze, dynamic approaches need tests that execute the software. Writing tests is often neglected due to time constraints. Furthermore, writing effective concurrent tests is difficult, because they should lead the program to sharing state between concurrently executing threads and should trigger many different execution paths. Another additional input that many static and dynamic analyses rely on are explicit, formal specifications, which must be developed in addition to the program itself. Unfortunately, few programs provide such specifications. As an additional output besides true positive bug reports, many existing approaches produce false positives. They reduce the usability of a bug finding technique and can even make it unusable in practice [3].

This paper presents an automatic testing technique to detect concurrency bugs in thread-safe classes. We consider a class to be *thread-safe* if it "behaves correctly when accessed from multiple threads, regardless of the scheduling or interleaving of the execution of those threads by the runtime environment, and with no additional synchronization or coordination on the part of the calling code" [20]. We say that a class is *thread-unsafe* otherwise. Our approach requires a single input, a program or library containing the class under test (CUT), possibly accompanied by third-party libraries that the program depends on, and produces a single output, true positive reports about concurrency bugs in the CUT. The analysis reports problems that result in an exception or a deadlock. As both are obvious signs of misbehavior, the analysis reports only true positives. Each bug report contains an executable, concurrent test that exposes the problem.

As a motivating example, consider a previously unknown bug that our approach detected in the `StringBuffer` class of Sun's Java standard library in versions 1.6 and 1.7.[1] `StringBuffer` is documented as thread-safe and tries to synchronize all accesses to its internal data by locking on the `StringBuffer` instance (Figure 1a). Our analysis generates tests that use `StringBuffers` concurrently. For example, the test in Figure 1b creates a `StringBuffer` and uses it in two concurrent threads. Executing the test leads to an exception because `insert()` retrieves the length of `s`, a parameter of type `CharSequence`, before acquiring the lock. The documentation states: "This class synchronizes only on the string buffer performing the operation, not on the source." This behavior is fatal if the passed source is the `StringBuffer` itself, a case the developers of the class apparently forgot to consider. In this case, retrieving the size of the `StringBuffer` is non-atomic with the consecutive update, leading to a potential boundary error caused by an interleaved update. Our analysis detects this bug with no input but the `StringBuffer` class and producing no output but this bug report.

[1] We reported the problem and the developers acknowledged it as a bug. See entry 7100996 in Sun's bug database.

PLDI'12, June 11–16, 2012, Beijing, China.

```
class StringBuffer {
  StringBuffer(String s) {
    // initialize with the given String
  }
  synchronized void deleteCharAt(int index) {
    // modify while holding the lock
  }
  void insert(int dstOffset, CharSequence s) {
    int l = s.length();
    // BUG: l may change
    this.insert(dstOffset, s, 0, l);
  }
  synchronized void insert(int dstOffset,
      CharSequence s, int start, int end) {
    // modify while holding the lock
  }
}
```

(a) Supposedly thread-safe class.

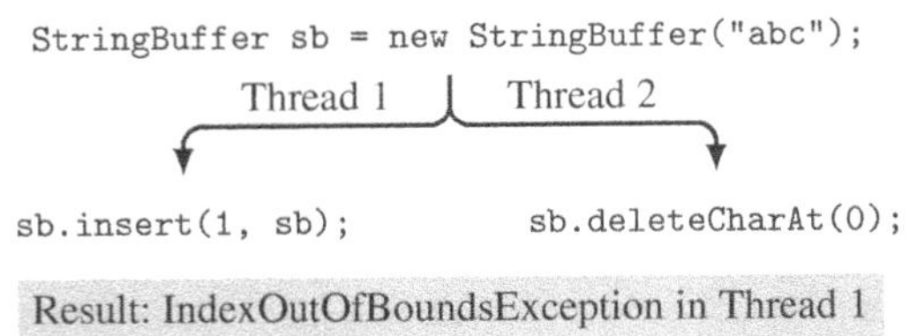

(b) Execution of a generated concurrent test exposing a thread-safety bug.

Figure 1: `StringBuffer` and a test execution exposing a thread-safety bug.

Our approach is enabled by the combination of two contributions. The first contribution is a test generation technique that creates input to exercise the methods of a CUT from multiple threads. Each generated test consists of a sequential part that instantiates the CUT and a concurrent part in which multiple threads call supposedly thread-safe methods on the CUT instance. The technique enhances existing techniques to generate sequential tests [11, 37] by adapting them to a concurrent setting. Simply running generated sequential tests in parallel is very unlikely to result in shared state and to expose concurrency bugs. Instead, our technique generates tests that share a single CUT instance between multiple threads and that expose concurrency bugs by using the instance concurrently.

Some existing bug finding techniques use a manually written test harness that, given a set of calls with concrete parameters, randomly selects and executes calls [5, 21]. Our test generation technique advances upon this approach in two ways. First, it relieves developers from providing calls and from finding appropriate parameters for these calls. The test generator creates parameters by instantiating other classes and by calling methods of other classes. Second, and even more important, an automated approach produces more diverse tests because it tries to combine many different methods, parameters, and receiver objects. As a result, generated tests include usage scenarios that a human may not come up with. For example, the test in Figure 1b triggers a bug by passing a `StringBuffer` to itself, a situation that apparently remained untested for several years.

The second contribution is a test oracle, called the *thread safety oracle*, that determines whether a concurrent test execution exposes a thread safety problem. The oracle classifies a concurrent execution as erroneous if the execution leads to an exception or to a deadlock *and* if this exception or deadlock cannot be triggered by any linearization of the calls in the concurrent execution. A linearization maps all calls of a concurrent test into a single thread while preserving the order of calls made by individual threads. The oracle assumes that sequential executions are deterministic. The thread safety oracle is generic, precise, and practical. It is generic, because it can detect different kinds of concurrency bugs, including data races, atomicity violations, and deadlocks, given that the bug eventually causes an exception or deadlock. A study of 105 real-world concurrency bugs found that 62% of all bugs lead to a crash or a deadlock [30], suggesting that the thread safety oracle addresses a significant problem. The oracle is precise, because it guarantees that each reported problem is a real bug, since exceptions and deadlocks are certainly undesired behavior. Finally, the oracle is practical, because it does not require any explicit specification to come with the CUT and instead leverages generic and implicit indicators of incorrectness.

The thread safety oracle relates to seminal work on linearizability as correctness criterion [22] and its recent adaption to object-oriented programs in Line-Up [5]. In contrast to Line-Up, our oracle is more effective and more efficient. It is more effective, because each test execution that fails according to the oracle is a true positive. In contrast, the Line-Up oracle classifies 426 of 1,800 test executions as failing, which—after manual inspection—contain seven bugs [5]. This high violations-to-bugs ratio is due to benign linearizability violations and to multiple violations caused by the same bug. Our oracle is more efficient, because it only runs linearizations of a concurrent test if the concurrent test leads to an exception or a deadlock. Instead, Line-Up explores all linearizations before running a concurrent test.[2]

We implement our approach as a prototype tool for Java and apply it to six popular code bases, including the Java standard library and Apache Commons Database Connection Pools (DBCP). The analysis detects six previously unknown bugs, for example, two problems in supposedly thread-safe classes, `ConcurrentHashMap` and `StringBuffer`, of the most recent version of the Java standard library. In total, our implementation successfully reveals 15 bugs in the analyzed code bases. Twelve of them are exposed through a deadlock or an exception thrown by the virtual machine or the Java standard library, that is, not relying on the use of exceptions in the CUT itself.

In summary, this paper makes the following contributions:

- A technique to generate concurrent tests that exercise a CUT from multiple threads.
- A generic test oracle that finds concurrent executions that expose thread safety bugs in the CUT.
- Empirical evidence that combining concurrent test generation with the thread safety oracle is effective in automatically finding concurrency bugs.

2. Overview

We presents a dynamic analysis to detect concurrency bugs in thread-safe classes. This section explains the key ideas of the analysis; Sections 3 and 4 fill in the details.

There are three requirements for detecting a thread safety bug with a dynamic analysis. First, a test that drives the CUT to a state exposing the bug. Second, an execution environment that exposes the bug when executing the test. Third, an oracle that recognizes the execution as erroneous. Various approaches addressing the second requirement have been proposed [6, 10, 12, 33, 43]. This work focuses on the first and the third requirement. We address the first requirement by generating tests that drive a CUT (Section 3). Using automatically generated tests instead of relying on existing

[2] A direct comparison of our results with Line-Up is not possible as the details about the classes under test [5], as well as the specific bugs found, are no longer available [4].

tests has two benefits: (1) it makes our approach easy to use and (2) it provides a large range of different inputs that can expose bugs not triggered by manually written tests. We address the third requirement with an oracle that determines whether a concurrent execution exposes a thread safety problem (Section 4).

Our analysis consists of three iteratively performed steps, which correspond to the three requirements. At first, a generator of concurrent tests creates a test that sets up an instance of the CUT and that calls methods on this instance from multiple threads. Next, we execute the generated test. Since the class is supposed to be thread-safe, it should synchronize concurrent calls on the shared instance as needed. As a result, the methods should "behave as if they occur in some serial order that is consistent with the order of the method calls made by each of the individual threads involved" [1]. The third step of our analysis checks whether the CUT behaves as expected. If the analysis finds that the concurrent execution shows behavior not possible in any linearization of calls, it reports a bug and terminates. Otherwise, the analysis goes back to the first step and continues until a stopping criterion, such as a timeout or a specified maximum number of generated tests, is reached.

3. Generating Concurrent Tests

This section presents a technique to generate concurrent tests that exercise a CUT from multiple threads. The input to the test generator is a class C and, optionally, a set of auxiliary classes $\mathcal{A}$ that C depends on. The generator creates *call sequences*. Each call c_i in a call sequence $(c_1, \ldots, c_n)$ consists of a method signature, a possibly empty list of input variables, and an optional output variable. The input variables of a call represent parameters passed to the method. For an instance call, the first input variable is the receiver of the call. The output variable of a call represents its return value. We model constructor invocations as calls where the output variable represents the new object. Similarly, we model field accesses as calls where the underlying object is the only input variable and where the output variable represents the field value. We say that a call sequence is *well-defined* if each input variable of a call c_j is the output variable of a call c_i with $i < j$, that is, if each call uses only variables defined on prior calls.

A *test* consists of a prefix and a set of suffixes. The *prefix* is a call sequence supposed to be executed in a single thread. The prefix instantiates the CUT and calls methods on the CUT instance to "grow" the object, that is, to bring it into a state that may allow the suffixes to trigger a bug. A *suffix* is a call sequence supposed to be executed concurrently with other suffixes after executing the prefix. All suffixes share the output variables of the prefix and can use them as input variables for suffix calls. In particular, all suffixes share the CUT instance created in the prefix. While our general approach is independent of the number of suffixes, we focus on two suffixes per test, so that a test is a triple (p, s_1, s_2) where p is the prefix and s_1, s_2 are suffixes. The rationale for this choice is that most real-world concurrency bugs involve no more than two threads [30].

Figure 1b is a very simple example for a test. The prefix is a single call to the constructor of `StringBuffer`, which returns the CUT instance `sb`. Each of the two suffixes calls a single method using the shared CUT instance `sb` as the receiver. In practice, effective concurrent tests are not always that simple. Calling a method often requires providing parameters of a particular type, which in turn may require calling other methods. Furthermore, triggering a bug often requires to bring the CUT instance in a particular state, for example, by calling setter methods.

3.1 Tasks

To automatically generate concurrent tests, we divide the generation of a test into simpler tasks, which build and extend call sequences. Each task takes a call sequence $s_{in} = (c_1, \ldots, c_i)$ and returns a new sequence $s_{out} = (c_1, \ldots, c_i, c_j, \ldots, c_n)$ that appends $n - j + 1$ additional calls to s_{in}. The additional calls can use output variables of previous calls as their input variables. We use three kinds of tasks:

- $instantiateCUTTask$, which appends a call to create a new instance of the CUT.
- $callCUTTask$, which appends a call to the CUT instance.
- $parameterTask$, which makes a parameter of a particular type available by choosing an output variable of a previous call or by appending a call that returns an object of the required type.

A task succeeds if it extends s_{in} with additional calls in such a way that s_{out} is well-defined and that s_{out} executes in a single thread without throwing an uncaught exception. The latter requirement adapts an idea from sequential test generation [37], namely to use the result of executing call sequences for selecting which sequences to extend further. Generated call sequences that result in an exception typically contain an illegal call, for example, a call that violates the precondition for calling the method. Although focusing on non-exceptional call sequences does not guarantee that each call is legal, it ensures that extending a sequence will eventually lead to executing more calls without reaching an obviously illegal state.

To successfully accomplish a task, the test generator extends s_{in} into *candidates* for s_{out} until a candidate is found that is well-defined and that executes without an exception. If after creating a specified number of candidates no candidate has fulfilled these conditions, the test generator gives up on this task and the task fails. For example, the $callCUTTask$ may fail if the CUT instance is in a state that does not allow calling any of the CUT methods.

3.2 Test Generation Algorithm

Algorithm 1 describes how our analysis generates a concurrent test. There are three global variables, which maintain their values over multiple invocations of the algorithm: the set $\mathcal{P}$ of prefixes, the map $\mathcal{M}$ assigning a prefix to its set of suffixes, and the set $\mathcal{T}$ of already generated but not yet returned tests.

The algorithm has three main steps. At first, it creates a new prefix or chooses a previously created prefix (lines 6 to 20). Then, it creates a new suffix for the prefix (lines 21 to 26). Finally, the algorithm creates tests by combining the new suffix with each existing suffix (lines 27 to 29). To create prefixes and suffixes, the algorithm invokes tasks. The functions $randTake$ and $randRemove$ randomly select an element of a set with a uniform probability distribution, and the $randRemove$ function also removes the selected element from the set.

Creating Prefixes During the first step (lines 6 to 20), the algorithm creates a new prefix unless $maxPrefixes$ (discussed in Section 5) have already been created. The reason for limiting the number of prefixes is that we require multiple suffixes for each prefix to test different concurrent usages of a CUT instance. To create a new prefix, the algorithm invokes the $instantiateCUTTask$. This task randomly chooses a method m from all methods in C and $\mathcal{A}$ that have C or a subtype of C as return type. If calling m requires parameters, the task invokes $parameterTask$s to make these parameters available. The $instantiateCUTTask$ returns a call sequence that creates all required parameters, stores them into output variables, and calls m. If the test generator cannot instantiate the CUT, for example, because there is no public constructor, the algorithm fails. For Figure 1b, the $instantiateCUTTask$ chose the `StringBuffer` constructor as m and obtains a string literal as parameter from $parameterTask$ (literals are passed without storing them into a variable).

Algorithm 1 Returns a concurrent test (p, s_1, s_2)

1: $\mathcal{P}$: set of prefixes ▷ global variables
2: $\mathcal{M}$: maps a prefix to suffixes
3: $\mathcal{T}$: set of ready-to-use tests
4: **if** $|\mathcal{T}| > 0$ **then**
5:    **return** $randRemove(\mathcal{T})$
6: **if** $|\mathcal{P}| < maxPrefixes$ **then** ▷ create a new prefix
7:    $p \leftarrow instantiateCUTTask$(empty call sequence)
8:    **if** $p = failed$ **then**
9:       **if** $\mathcal{P} = \emptyset$ **then**
10:          $fail$("cannot instantiate CUT")
11:       **else**
12:          $p \leftarrow randTake(\mathcal{P})$
13:    **else**
14:       **for** $i \leftarrow 1, maxStateChangerTries$ **do**
15:          $p_{ext} \leftarrow callCUTTask(p)$
16:          **if** $p_{ext} \neq failed$ **then**
17:             $p \leftarrow p_{ext}$
18:    $\mathcal{P} \leftarrow \mathcal{P} \cup \{p\}$
19: **else**
20:    $p \leftarrow randTake(\mathcal{P})$
21: $s_1 \leftarrow$ empty call sequence ▷ create a new suffix
22: **for** $i \leftarrow 1, maxCUTCallTries$ **do**
23:    $s_{1,ext} \leftarrow callCUTTask(s_1, p)$
24:    **if** $s_{1,ext} \neq failed$ **then**
25:       $s_1 \leftarrow s_{1,ext}$
26: $\mathcal{M}(p) \leftarrow \mathcal{M}(p) \cup \{s_1\}$
27: **for all** $s_2 \in \mathcal{M}(p)$ **do** ▷ one test for each pair of suffixes
28:    $\mathcal{T} \leftarrow \mathcal{T} \cup \{(p, s_1, s_2)\}$
29: **return** $randRemove(\mathcal{T})$

After instantiating the CUT, the algorithm tries to invoke methods on the CUT instance to change the state of the CUT instance. The $callCUTTask$ randomly chooses a method among all methods of C and invokes the $parameterTask$ for each required parameter. The prefix in Figure 1b contains no state changing call. Alternatively to the shown prefix, the test generator could have created the call sequence

```
StringBuffer sb = new StringBuffer();
sb.append("abc");
```

where the second call is a state changing call.

Creating Suffixes During the second step (lines 21 to 26), the algorithm creates a new suffix for the prefix p. Therefore, it repeatedly invokes the $callCUTTask$. In addition to the suffix, the call in line 23 passes the prefix to the task to allow for using output variables from the prefix as input variables in the suffix. After appending calls to the CUT instance, the new suffix is added to the set of suffixes for the prefix p.

All tasks that append method calls depend on the $parameterTask$. This task uses three strategies to make a parameter of a particular type t available. If the given call sequence already has one or more output variables of type t or a subtype of t, the task randomly chooses between reusing a variable and creating a fresh variable. The rationale for creating fresh variables is to diversify the generated tests instead of passing the same parameters again and again. To reuse a variable, the task randomly chooses from all available variables with matching type. To create a fresh variable, the behavior depends on the type t. If t is a primitive type or `String`, the task returns a randomly created literal. Otherwise, the tasks randomly chooses a method from all methods in C and $\mathcal{A}$ returning t or a subtype of t. If calling this method requires parameters, the task recursively invokes itself. We limit the number of recursions to avoid infinite loops and fail the task if the limit is reached. If there is no method providing t, the $parameterTask$ returns `null`. Using `null` as a parameter may be illegal. In this case, executing the sequence can result in an exception, for example, a `NullPointerException`, so that the candidate is rejected.

Creating Tests The third step of the algorithm (lines 27 to 29) combines the new suffix with each existing suffix for the prefix into a test. The algorithm stores the created tests in $\mathcal{T}$ and on further invocations returns a randomly selected test from $\mathcal{T}$ until $\mathcal{T}$ becomes empty.

3.3 Beyond This Work

The tests generated by Algorithm 1 provide input to exercise a class without any human effort, and hence, increase the usefulness of existing dynamic analyses. For example, executions of generated tests can be analyzed by existing detectors of data races [15, 32, 42, 44] or atomicity violations [16, 21, 28, 38, 45]. Without generated tests, these analyses are limited to manually created tests and the bugs exposed by these tests.

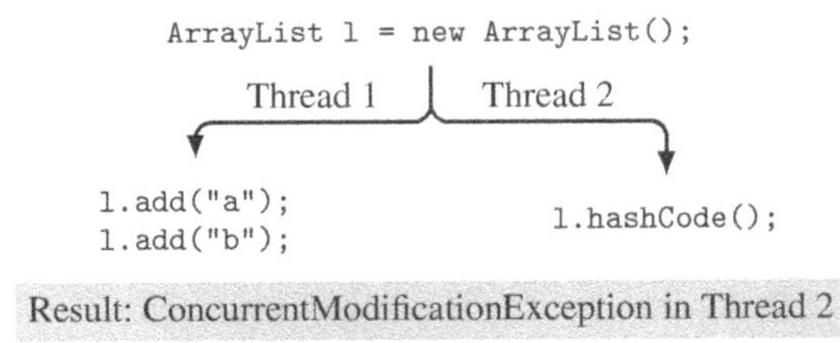

Figure 2: Test execution using a thread-unsafe class.

4. Thread Safety Oracle

This section presents an automatic technique to determine whether the execution of a concurrent test exposes a thread safety bug.

4.1 Thread Safety

A class is said to be thread-safe if multiple threads can use it without synchronization *and* if the behavior observed by each thread is equivalent to a linearization of all calls that maintains the order of calls in each thread [1, 20]. Saying that a class is thread-safe means that all its methods are thread-safe. Our approach can also deal with classes that guarantee thread safety for a subset of all methods by excluding the unsafe methods when generating suffixes for a test.

Figure 2 is an example for a thread-unsafe class and a test execution that exposes this property. The concurrent use of `ArrayList` from `java.util` results in an exception that does not occur in any of the three possible linearizations of the calls:

`add` → `add` → `hashCode`
`add` → `hashCode` → `add`
`hashCode` → `add` → `add`

Therefore, the execution in Figure 2 shows that `ArrayList` is thread-unsafe, as expected.

A property related to thread safety is atomicity, that is, the guarantee that a sequence of operations performed by a thread appears to execute without interleaved operations by other threads. One way to make a class thread-safe is to guarantee that each call to one of its methods appears to be atomic for the calling thread. However, a thread-safe class does *not* guarantee that multiple calls to a shared instance of the class are executed atomically [45]. For example, consider the use of the thread-safe class `java.util.concurrent.CopyOnWriteArrayList` in Figure 3. Executing the concurrent test has three possible outputs. For all three,

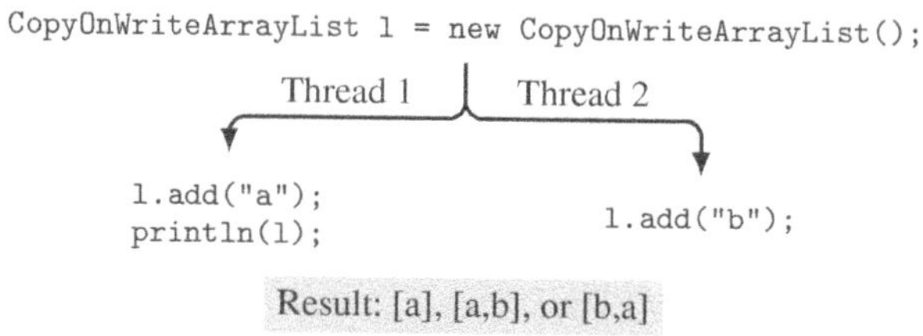

Figure 3: Test execution using a thread-safe class.

there is a linearization of calls that provides the same result, so the test execution does not expose a thread safety problem:

```
add("a") → println() → add("b")   gives [a]
add("a") → add("b") → println()   gives [a,b]
add("b") → add("a") → println()   gives [b,a]
```

4.2 Definitions

The thread safety oracle answers the question whether a concurrent test execution exposes a thread safety problem by comparing the concurrent execution to executions of linearizations of the test. We use $\oplus$ to concatenate sequences, and $c \rightarrow_s c'$ indicates that call c comes before call c' in a call sequence s.

Definition 1 (Linearization). *For a test (p, s_1, s_2), let $\mathcal{P}_{12}$ be the set of all permutations of the call sequence $s_1 \oplus s_2$. The set of linearizations of the test is:*

$$\mathcal{L}_{(p,s_1,s_2)} = \{p \oplus s_{12} \mid s_{12} \in \mathcal{P}_{12} \wedge (\forall c, c' \; (c \rightarrow_{s_1} c' \Rightarrow c \rightarrow_{s_{12}} c') \wedge (c \rightarrow_{s_2} c' \Rightarrow c \rightarrow_{s_{12}} c'))\}$$

That is, a linearization of a test (p, s_1, s_2) appends to p all calls from s_1 and from s_2 in a way that preserves the order of calls in s_1 and s_2.

Definition 2 (Execution). *For a test (p, s_1, s_2), we denote the set of all distinguishable executions of this test as $\mathcal{E}_{(p,s_1,s_2)}$. Each $e_{(p,s_1,s_2)} \in \mathcal{E}_{(p,s_1,s_2)}$ represents the sequential execution of p followed by a concurrent execution of s_1 and s_2. Likewise, we denote the sequential execution of a call sequence s as e_s.*

A single test can have multiple distinguishable executions because of the non-determinism of concurrent executions.

The following definition of thread safety refers to the equivalence $e_1 \cong e_2$ of two executions e_1 and e_2. We discuss in Section 4.3 how our oracle decides whether two executions are equivalent.

Definition 3 (Thread safety). *Let $\mathcal{T}_C$ be the set of all possible tests for a class C. C is thread-safe if and only if:*

$$\forall (p, s_1, s_2) \in \mathcal{T}_C \;\; \forall e_{(p,s_1,s_2)} \in \mathcal{E}_{(p,s_1,s_2)} \;\; \exists l \in \mathcal{L}_{(p,s_1,s_2)} \text{ so that } e_{(p,s_1,s_2)} \cong e_l$$

That is, a class is thread-safe if each concurrent test execution has an equivalent linearization.

4.3 The Test Oracle

Showing that a class is thread-safe according to Definition 3 is difficult in practice, because all possible tests and all possible executions of these tests would have to be considered. However, the thread safety oracle can show that a class C is thread-unsafe by showing:

$$\exists (p, s_1, s_2) \in \mathcal{T}_C \;\; \exists e_{(p,s_1,s_2)} \in \mathcal{E}_{(p,s_1,s_2)} \text{ so that } \forall l \in \mathcal{L}_{(p,s_1,s_2)} \;\; e_{(p,s_1,s_2)} \ncong e_l$$

Algorithm 2 Checks whether a test (p, s_1, s_2) exposes a thread safety bug

```
repeat
  e_(p,s1,s2) ← execute(p, s1, s2)
  if failed(e_(p,s1,s2)) then
    seqFailed ← false
    for all l ∈ L(p, s1, s2) do
      if seqFailed = false then
        e_l ← execute(l)
        if failed(e_l) ∧ sameFailure(e_(p,s1,s2), e_l) then
          seqFailed ← true
    if seqFailed = false then
      report bug e_(p,s1,s2) and exit
until maxConcExecs reached
```

That is, the thread safety oracle tries to find a test that exposes behavior not possible with any linearization of the test. To decide whether two executions are equivalent, the oracle compares the exceptions and deadlocks caused by the executions.

Definition 4 (Equivalence of executions). *Two executions e_1 and e_2 are equivalent if*

- *neither e_1 nor e_2 results in an exception or a deadlock, or*
- *both e_1 and e_2 fail for the same reason (that is, the same type of exception is thrown or both executions end with a deadlock).*

Although this abstraction ignores many potential differences between executions, such as different return values of method calls, it is crucial to ensure that the analysis only reports a class as thread-unsafe if this is definitely true.

Algorithm 2 shows how the analysis checks whether a test (p, s_1, s_2) exposes a thread safety problem. The algorithm repeatedly executes the test until a maximum number of concurrent executions is reached, or until a bug is found. If the test fails, that is, it throws an exception or results in a deadlock, the algorithm executes all linearizations of the test to check whether the same failure occurs during a sequential execution of the same calls. If no linearization exposes the same failure, the algorithm reports a bug because the CUT is thread-unsafe.

The thread safety oracle is sound but incomplete.[3] Every execution for which the oracle reports a bug is guaranteed to expose a real thread safety problem according to Definition 3, but the oracle may classify an execution as correct even though it exposes a thread safety problem. The soundness of the oracle ensures that our approach detects concurrency bugs without reporting false positives.

We build upon two assumptions, which we find true for most real-world classes during our evaluation. First, we assume that uncaught exceptions and deadlocks that occur in a concurrent usage of a class but not in a sequential usage are considered a problem. This assumption is in line with the commonly accepted definition of thread safety [1, 20]. Second, we assume that sequential executions of a call sequence behave deterministically. Sequentially non-deterministic methods, for example, methods that depend on the current system time, should be excluded from our analysis. Alternatively, our analysis can be combined with a runtime environment that ensures deterministic sequential execution [40].

[3] We mean soundness and completeness regarding incorrectness [47]. In other communities, such as type systems, the terms are typically used with respect to correctness, that is, inverse to the usage here.

5. Implementation

We implement the test generator and the thread safety oracle into an automatic bug detection tool for thread-safe Java classes. This section presents several challenges faced by the implementation and how we address them.

The test generator executes many call sequences and must do so both efficiently and without interference between different executions. To execute sequences efficiently we take a reflection-based approach similar to the sequential test generator Randoop [37]. A problem not addressed by Randoop is that different call sequences may interfere because of static state. For example, a call sequence s_1 may assign a value to a static field and a call sequence s_2 may read the static field. As a result, the outcome of executing s_2 may vary depending on whether s_1 is executed before s_2. This problem is independent of concurrency. We address the problem by resetting all static state to the state of the freshly loaded classes before each execution of a call sequence. For this purpose, our implementation instruments classes so that all modifications of static state are recorded and can be reset. Csallner and Smaragdakis describe a similar approach for a sequential test generator [11].

The test generator takes a random seed as an input, which allows for precise replay of the test generation process, as long as the tested classes behave deterministically in sequential executions. Experience with sequential, random test generation shows that short runs with many different seeds trigger bugs faster than few runs with a small number of seeds [9]. Our initial experiments confirmed this observation, so we run the analysis in multiple rounds that each use a different random seed. The first rounds stop after trying a small number of suffixes (ten) for a single prefix. Later rounds gradually raise the maximum number of generated prefixes ($maxPrefixes$) to 25 and the maximum number of generated suffixes to 500. The values of other parameters used in Algorithm 1 are $maxStateChangerTries = 5$, $maxConcExecs = 100$, and $maxCUTCallTries = 2$.

To detect deadlocks, we use the management interface for the thread system of the Java virtual machine. A daemon thread periodically queries this interface and notifies the thread safety oracle in case of a deadlock.

Although being a prototype, the performance of our tool is acceptable for a testing tool (details in Section 6). The by far most important bottleneck of our implementation is the repeated concurrent execution of tests. For example, for the CUT taking the longest to analyze, 99.5% of the time is spent with concurrent executions. We see two ways to address this issue. First, the analysis can exploit multiple cores by exploring different concurrent executions of the same test in parallel. Second, our analysis can be easily combined with existing techniques to increase the probability of hitting a bug by controlling or perturbing the scheduler [6, 10, 12, 33, 43]. Our current implementation executes tests with the standard Java thread scheduler. To plug a more sophisticated scheduling technique into our approach, one can redefine the $execute$ function of Algorithm 2.

6. Evaluation

We evaluate our approach by applying the prototype implementation to Java classes from six popular code bases: the Java standard library shipped with Sun's JDK, the database connection pool library Apache Commons DBCP, the serialization library XStream, the text processing toolkit LingPipe, the chart library JFreeChart, and Joda-Time, a library to handle data and time.

6.1 Experimental Setup

All experiments are done on an eight-core machine with 3GHz Intel Xeon processors and 8GB memory running 32-bit Ubuntu Linux and the Java Hotspot VM version 1.6.0_27, giving 2GB memory to the VM. We run experiments with different CUTs in parallel but run at most four tests at a time to reserve a core for each concurrent thread exercising the CUT. We repeat each experiment ten times with different random seeds [37].

To analyze a CUT, the test generator uses all other public classes from the code base and common classes from the Java standard library as auxiliary classes.

```
class ConcurrentHashMap {
  void clear() {
    final Segment[] segments = this.segments;
    for (int j = 0; j < segments.length; ++j) {
      Segment s = segmentAt(segments, j);
      if (s != null)
        s.clear(); // locks the segment
    }
  }
  void putAll(Map m) {
    for (Map.Entry e : m.entrySet())
      // BUG: m's entries may change
      put(e.getKey(), e.getValue());
  }
  Object put(Object key, Object value) {
    Segment s = /* get segment in a thread-safe way */;
    return s.put(key, value); // locks the segment
  }
}
```

(a) Supposedly thread-safe class.

```
ConcurrentHashMap map = new ConcurrentHashMap();
map.put("a", "b");
```

Thread 1	Thread 2
`map.clear();` `map.hashCode();`	`map.putAll(map);`

Result: StackOverflowError in Thread 1

(b) Execution of a generated concurrent test exposing a thread-safety bug.

Figure 4: Concurrency bug in `ConcurrentHashMap`.

6.2 Bugs Found

The analysis found 15 bugs in supposedly thread-safe classes, six of them previously unknown. Each bug can cause concurrency bugs in clients relying on thread-safe classes. Table 1 lists all bugs along with the reason for failing. The last column indicates whether the reason is a deadlock or an exception thrown implicitly by the virtual machine or by the Java standard library, or if triggering the bug requires an explicitly thrown exception in the analyzed code base. For twelve of 15 bugs, an implicit exception is sufficient to reveal the bug. That is, our approach reveals most bugs without any requirement on the analyzed classes, such as throwing an exception if an unsafe state is reached.

The analysis reveals two previously unknown bugs in the Java standard library, one of them shown as the motivating example in the introduction (Figure 1). The other new bug in the Java standard library is illustrated in Figure 4. The class `ConcurrentHashMap` is part of the `java.util.concurrent` package, which provides thread-safe collection classes. For better scalability, the class divides the map into segments that are locked independently of each other, instead of relying on a single exclusion lock. Unfortunately, `putAll()` does not consider the case where the passed map is the same as the receiver object of the call. The method retrieves the entries of the passed map without any synchronization and then passes each el-

ID	Code base	Class	Declared thread-safe	Found unsafe	Reason for failing	Implicit
Previously unknown bugs:						
(1)	JDK 1.6.0_27 and 1.7.0	StringBuffer	yes	yes	IndexOutOfBoundsException	yes
(2)	JDK 1.6.0_27 and 1.7.0	ConcurrentHashMap	yes	yes	StackOverflowError	yes
(3)	Commons DBCP 1.4	SharedPoolDataSource	yes	yes	ConcurrentModificationException	yes
(4)	Commons DBCP 1.4	PerUserPoolDataSource	yes	yes	ConcurrentModificationException	yes
(5)	XStream 1.4.1	XStream	yes	yes	NullPointerException	yes
(6)	LingPipe 4.1.0	MedlineSentenceModel	yes	yes	IllegalStateException	no
Known bugs:						
(7)	JDK 1.1	BufferedInputStream	yes	yes	NullPointerException	yes
(8)	JDK 1.4.1	Logger	yes	yes	NullPointerException	yes
(9)	JDK 1.4.2	SynchronizedMap	yes	yes	Deadlock	yes
(10)	JFreeChart 0.9.8	TimeSeries	yes	yes	NullPointerException	yes
(11)	JFreeChart 0.9.8	XYSeries	yes	yes	ConcurrentModificationException	yes
(12)	JFreeChart 0.9.12	NumberAxis	yes	yes	IllegalArgumentException	no
(13)	JFreeChart 1.0.1	PeriodAxis	yes	yes	IllegalArgumentException	no
(14)	JFreeChart 1.0.9	XYPlot	yes	yes	ConcurrentModificationException	yes
(15)	JFreeChart 1.0.13	Day	yes	yes	NumberFormatException	yes
Automatic classification of classes as thread-unsafe:						
(16)	Joda-Time 2.0	DateTimeFormatterBuilder	no	yes	IndexOutOfBoundsException (10x)	yes
(17)	Joda-Time 2.0	DateTimeParserBucket	no	yes	IllegalArgumentException (9x)	no
					NullPointerException (1x)	yes
(18)	Joda-Time 2.0	DateTimeZoneBuilder	no	yes	NullPointerException (6x)	yes
					ArrayIndexOutOfBoundsException (2x)	yes
					IllegalFieldValueException (2x)	yes
(19)	Joda-Time 2.0	MutableDateTime	no	yes	IllegalFieldValueException (9x)	no
					ArithmeticException (1x)	yes
(20)	Joda-Time 2.0	MutableInterval	no	yes	IllegalArgumentException (10x)	no
(21)	Joda-Time 2.0	MutablePeriod	no	yes	ArithmeticException (10x)	yes
(22)	Joda-Time 2.0	PeriodFormatterBuilder	no	yes	ConcurrentModificationException (5x)	yes
					IndexOutOfBoundsException (4x)	yes
					IllegalStateException (1x)	no
	Joda-Time 2.0	ZoneInfoCompiler	no	no	(stopped after 24h)	–

Table 1: Summary of results. The last column indicates whether the reason for failing is implicit in the Java runtime environment or explicitly specified in the code base under test.

ement to the correctly synchronized `put()`. As a result, a call to `map.putAll(map)` can undo changes done by a concurrently executing thread that also modifies the map—a clear thread safety bug. Our analysis generates the test in Figure 4b, which exposes the problem. Calling `hashCode()` results in a stack overflow for self-referential collections, because the method recursively calls itself (this is documented behavior). If `ConcurrentHashMap` were thread-safe, this behavior should not be triggered by the test, because all three possible linearizations of the calls in Figure 4b call `clear()` before calling `hashCode()`. However, the test fails with a `StackOverflowError`, because `putAll()` undoes the effects of the concurrently executed `clear()`.

Figure 5 is a previously unknown bug that our analysis detects in Apache Commons DBCP. The supposedly thread-safe class `SharedPoolDataSource` provides two methods `setDataSourceName()` and `close()` that register and unregister the data source via static methods of `InstanceKeyObjectFactory`, respectively. The factory class maintains a thread-unsafe `HashMap` assigning names to data sources. Although registering new instances is synchronized to avoid concurrent accesses to the `HashMap`, unregistering instances is not synchronized. The generated test in Figure 5b shows that this lack of synchronization leads to an exception when calling `setDataSourceName()` and `close()` concurrently.

To allow for reproducing our results, all analyzed classes, descriptions of the bugs, and a generated test to trigger each bug are available at **http://mp.binaervarianz.de/pldi2012**.

6.3 Annotating Classes as Thread-unsafe

Beyond finding bugs, our analysis can be used to analyze classes having no documentation on their thread safety and to automatically annotate these classes as thread-unsafe where appropriate. In a preliminary study for this work, we found that one of the most common concurrency-related questions of Java developers is whether a particular library class is thread-safe. Few libraries come with precise documentation to answer this question. To address this lack of documentation, our analysis can automatically annotate classes as thread-unsafe. Since the oracle is sound, these annotations are guaranteed to be correct.

To evaluate this usage scenario, we run our analysis on a library that specifies for each class whether it is thread-safe or not. The library (Joda-Time) contains 41 classes, of which 33 are documented as thread-safe and eight are documented as thread-unsafe. The lower part of Table 1 summarizes the results. For seven of the eight thread-unsafe classes, our analysis detects a thread safety problem. The missing class, `ZoneInfoCompiler`, reads files from the file system, transforms them, and writes other files as output.

```
class SharedPoolDataSource {
  void setDataSourceName(String v) {
    key = InstanceKeyObjectFactory
                .registerNewInstance(this);
  }
  void close() {
    InstanceKeyObjectFactory.removeInstance(key);
  }
}

class InstanceKeyObjectFactory {
  static final Map instanceMap = new HashMap();
  synchronized static String
      registerNewInstance(SharedPoolDataSource ds) {
    // iterate over instanceMap
  }
  static void removeInstance(String key) {
    // BUG: unsynchronized access to instanceMap
    instanceMap.remove(key);
  }
}
```

(a) Supposedly thread-safe class.

```
SharedPoolDataSource ds1 = new SharedPoolDataSource();
ds1.setConnectionPoolDataSource(null);
```

Thread 1 | Thread 2

```
dataSource.setDataSourceName("a");      dataSource.close();
```

Result: ConcurrentModificationException in Thread 1

(b) Execution of a generated concurrent test exposing a thread-safety bug.

Figure 5: Concurrency bug in Apache Commons DBCP.

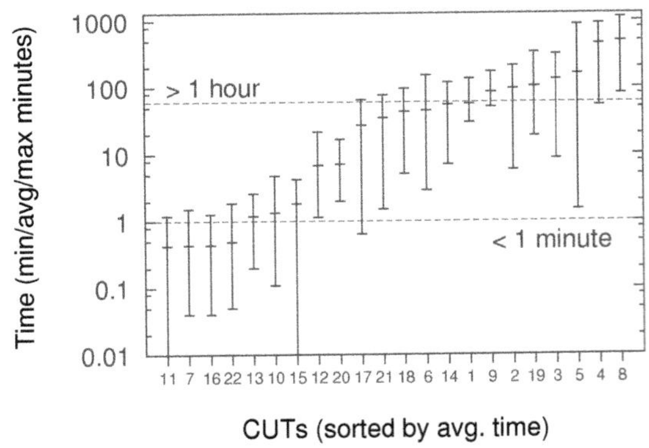

(a) Time to trigger a thread-safety problem.

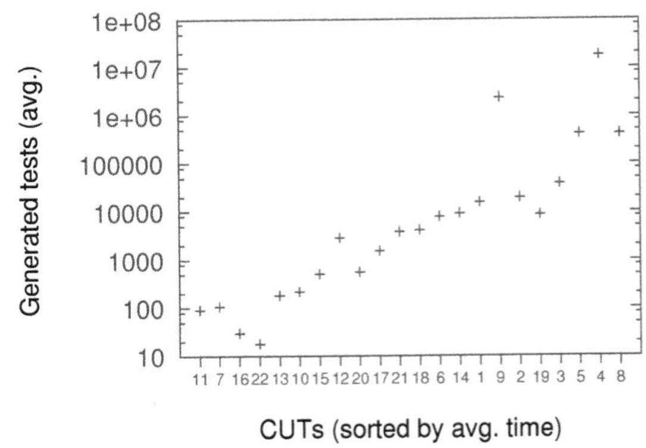

(b) Tests generated before triggering a thread-safety problem.

Figure 6: Effort required to trigger a thread-safety problem.

Since the thread-safety oracle does not check the integrity of such files, it cannot detect problems caused by concurrent usages of the class. For the 33 classes that are documented as thread-safe, no problems are found after running the analysis for 24 hours.

6.4 Effort of Using the Analysis

Using our approach involves minimal human effort, because the analysis requires the source code or byte code of the classes under test as only input and produces true positives as only output. Experience from applying automated bug finding techniques in industry shows that both properties are important [3].

The computational effort of our implementation is acceptable for an automatic testing tool. Figure 6a shows how long the analysis takes to trigger the problems from Table 1. The horizontal axis shows the IDs from Table 1, sorting the classes by the average time required to find the problem. The vertical axis gives the minimum, average, and maximum time taken to find the problem over ten runs. Most of the problems are found within one hour. For several problems, the analysis takes only a few seconds. Other classes require several hours of computation time, with up to 8.2 hours for bug 8 (JDK's `Logger`). Given that the bug remained unnoticed for several years in one of the most popular Java libraries, we consider this time to be still acceptable. Section 5 outlines ways to reduce the running time of our implementation with additional engineering effort. The approach has very moderate memory requirements. The test generator selects methods randomly and therefore does not maintain significant amounts of state. If executing a generated call sequence exceeds the available memory, an exception is thrown and the sequence is not extended.

A question related to running time is how many tests the analysis generates and executes before hitting a bug. Figure 6b shows the average number of generated tests for each bug, listing the bugs in the same order as in Figure 6a. For some bugs, a small number of tests (several hundreds or even less than hundred) suffices to expose the problem. Other bugs require more tests, up to 17 million for bug 4. A manual inspection of bugs requiring many tests suggests that the task of executing a bug-exposing test with the "right" thread interleaving dominates over the task of generating a bug-exposing test. Combining our work with techniques to control scheduling may reduce the number of tests for hitting a bug.

7. Limitations

First, the approach assumes that exceptions and deadlocks are undesirable. We found this "implicit specification" to be true in practice, but in principle a class could throw exceptions as part of its legal, concurrent behavior. Second, the approach has limited support for multi-object bugs. Although the generated tests combine multiple classes and objects, they only reveal bugs triggered by concurrent calls to the same object. Third, the approach is limited to bugs that manifest through an exception or deadlock, and therefore it may miss more subtle problems leading to incorrect but not obviously wrong results.

8. Related Work

8.1 Finding Concurrency Bugs

Table 2 compares this work with other bug finding techniques based on four criteria: whether static or dynamic analysis is used, the

Approach		Input			Output		Correctness criterion				
		P	PT	PTS	B	BF	DR	Atom	DL	Crash	Other
[15, 32, 36, 42, 49]	D	○	●	○	○	●	●	○	○	○	○
[8]	SD	○	●	○	○	●	●	○	○	○	○
[44]	D	○	●	○	●	○	●	○	○	●	○
[2, 14, 21, 29, 39, 48]	D	○	●	○	○	●	○	●	○	○	○
[16, 45]	D	○	○	●	●	○	○	●	○	○	○
[28, 38]	D	○	○	●	●	○	○	●	○	●	○
[34]	S	○	●	○	○	●	○	○	●	○	○
[25]	D	○	●	○	●	○	○	○	●	○	○
[26]	D	○	○	●	○	●	○	○	●	○	○
[51]	D	○	●	○	●	○	○	○	○	●	○
[13, 18]	D	○	○	●	●	○	○	○	○	○	●
[5, 24, 31]	D	○	●	○	○	●	○	○	○	○	●
[7, 17]	D	○	○	●	○	●	○	○	○	○	●
[52]	SD	○	●	○	○	●	○	○	○	○	●
This work	D	●	○	○	●	○	○	○	●	●	○

Table 2: Comparison with existing static (S) and dynamic (D) approaches. Input: program (P), program and tests (PT), or program, tests, and specifications (PTS). Output: bugs (B) or bugs and false positives (BF). Correctness criterion: data race (DR), atomicity violations (Atom), deadlock (DL), crash, or other.

input and output of the analysis, and the correctness criterion. The unique feature of our work is to require only a program as input.

Data Races Dynamic data race detectors search for unsynchronized, conflicting accesses to shared data by analyzing happens-before relations [15, 32], by checking whether the program follows a locking discipline [42, 49], or by a combination of both techniques [36]. Our approach detects data races, if they manifest through an exception or a deadlock.

Atomicity Violations Analyses for finding atomicity violations rely on specifications of atomic blocks or of sets of atomic variable accesses, provided manually [16, 38, 45] or inferred heuristically [2, 14, 21]. Inference causes false positives when violating source code is not supposed to be atomic. Our analysis detects atomicity violations, if they lead to an exception or a deadlock.

Deadlocks Naik et al. [34] search deadlocks statically but require tests. Joshi et al. [26] model check a reduced program and rely on annotations of condition variables. Both analyses report false positives. Our analysis finds deadlocks triggered by generated tests.

Active Testing To avoid false positives, active testing validates potential bugs by controlling the scheduler to provoke an exception or a deadlock. The approach has been applied to data races [44], atomicity violations [28, 38], deadlocks [25], and memory-related concurrency bugs [51]. Our approach shares the idea of reporting problems only if a certainly undesired situation occurs but does not rely on manually written tests.

Linearizability Herlihy and Wing introduce linearizability as a correctness criterion for concurrent objects [22]. Line-Up [5] checks the linearizability of calls but requires manually specified method parameters. As shown in Figure 1, unusual parameters that a human may miss can trigger long-standing bugs. Line-Up executes all linearizations before running a concurrent test, whereas our oracle analyzes linearizations only if the test fails. Elmas et al. [13] and Fonseca et al. [17] propose linearizability-based analyses that require specifications to abstract the state of a component.

Other Correctness Criteria Gao et al. [18] search for typestate errors in multi-threaded programs and rely on typestate specifications. Joshi et al. [27] filter false warnings from verifying concurrent programs by using a sequential version of a program as an oracle for the concurrent program. The approach relies on formal specifications and tests. Other approaches check for violations of inferred invariants [24, 31, 46] or unusual orderings [52]. The price paid for not relying on explicit specifications are false positives.

8.2 Support for Finding Concurrency Bugs

Several techniques control the thread scheduling when running a concurrent program repeatedly, for example, based on model checking [10, 33], random scheduling [6, 43], or artificial delays [12]. These techniques reduce the time to trigger a bug and could enhance the performance of our analysis. Pugh and Ayewah [41] and Jagannath et al. [23] address the problem of manually writing concurrent unit tests. Our work is orthogonal to theirs, because we generate tests automatically.

8.3 Test Generation

This work is inspired by techniques to generate sequential tests, such as [11, 19, 37]. In contrast to them, our test generator creates concurrent tests. Integrating more elaborate test generation techniques, such as learning from observed call sequences [50], into our approach could help to detect complex bugs faster.

Ballerina [35] generates efficient multi-threaded tests, showing that two threads, each with a single call, can trigger many concurrency bugs. The test generator described here is directed towards generating objects of required types and aims to generate (prefix, suffix, suffix) triples to expose concurrency problems. In addition, Ballerina checks test executions for linearizability (similar to [5]) and therefore produces false positives.

9. Conclusions

We present an automatic testing technique to reveal severe bugs in thread-safe classes. Using our approach involves very little human effort because it requires neither tests nor explicit specifications for the classes under test, and because it produces only true positive bug reports. The analysis is enabled by two contributions: (1) a technique for generating tests that exercise a thread-safe class from multiple threads, and (2) an oracle that reports a bug when a concurrent test execution results in an exception or a deadlock that cannot occur in any linearized execution of the test. We validate our claims by applying the analysis to six popular Java libraries. The analysis reveals 15 bugs in supposedly thread-safe classes, including two previously unknown bugs in the Java standard library.

Our technique for generating concurrent tests provides input that can drive other dynamic analyses, which traditionally rely on manually written tests. Generated tests not only add diversity to otherwise available tests but also allow for dynamically analyzing classes that have no tests at all.

Acknowledgments

Thanks to Zoltán Majó, Albert Noll, Faheem Ullah, and the anonymous reviewers for their valuable comments. The work presented in this paper was partially supported by the Swiss National Science Foundation under grant number 200021-134453.

References

[1] API documentation of *java.lang.StringBuffer* (Java platform standard edition 6), 2011.

[2] C. Artho, K. Havelund, and A. Biere. High-level data races. *Softw Test Verif Rel*, 13(4):207–227, 2003.

[3] A. Bessey, K. Block, B. Chelf, A. Chou, B. Fulton, S. Hallem, C. Henri-Gros, A. Kamsky, S. McPeak, and D. R. Engler. A few billion lines of code later: Using static analysis to find bugs in the real world. *Commun ACM*, 53(2):66–75, 2010.

[4] S. Burckhardt and R. Tan. Private communication, August 2011.

[5] S. Burckhardt, C. Dern, M. Musuvathi, and R. Tan. Line-Up: a complete and automatic linearizability checker. In *PLDI*, pages 330–340, 2010.

[6] S. Burckhardt, P. Kothari, M. Musuvathi, and S. Nagarakatte. A randomized scheduler with probabilistic guarantees of finding bugs. In *ASPLOS*, pages 167–178, 2010.

[7] J. Burnim, T. Elmas, G. C. Necula, and K. Sen. NDSeq: runtime checking for nondeterministic sequential specifications of parallel correctness. In *PLDI*, pages 401–414, 2011.

[8] J.-D. Choi, K. Lee, A. Loginov, R. O'Callahan, V. Sarkar, and M. Sridharan. Efficient and precise datarace detection for multithreaded object-oriented programs. In *PLDI*, pages 258–269, 2002.

[9] I. Ciupa, A. Pretschner, A. Leitner, M. Oriol, and B. Meyer. On the predictability of random tests for object-oriented software. In *ICST*, pages 72–81, 2008.

[10] K. E. Coons, S. Burckhardt, and M. Musuvathi. GAMBIT: effective unit testing for concurrency libraries. In *PPOPP*, pages 15–24, 2010.

[11] C. Csallner and Y. Smaragdakis. JCrasher: an automatic robustness tester for Java. *Software Pract Exper*, 34(11):1025–1050, Sept. 2004.

[12] O. Edelstein, E. Farchi, Y. Nir, G. Ratsaby, and S. Ur. Multithreaded Java program test generation. *IBM Syst J*, 41(1):111–125, 2002.

[13] T. Elmas, S. Tasiran, and S. Qadeer. VYRD: verifying concurrent programs by runtime refinement-violation detection. In *PLDI*, pages 27–37, 2005.

[14] C. Flanagan and S. N. Freund. Atomizer: a dynamic atomicity checker for multithreaded programs. In *POPL*, pages 256–267, 2004.

[15] C. Flanagan and S. N. Freund. FastTrack: efficient and precise dynamic race detection. In *PLDI*, pages 121–133, 2009.

[16] C. Flanagan, S. N. Freund, and J. Yi. Velodrome: a sound and complete dynamic atomicity checker for multithreaded programs. In *PLDI*, pages 293–303, 2008.

[17] P. Fonseca, C. Li, and R. Rodrigues. Finding complex concurrency bugs in large multi-threaded applications. In *EuroSys*, pages 215–228, 2011.

[18] Q. Gao, W. Zhang, Z. Chen, M. Zheng, and F. Qin. 2ndstrike: toward manifesting hidden concurrency typestate bugs. In *ASPLOS*, pages 239–250, 2011.

[19] P. Godefroid, N. Klarlund, and K. Sen. DART: directed automated random testing. In *PLDI*, pages 213–223, 2005.

[20] B. Goetz, T. Peierls, J. Bloch, J. Bowbeer, D. Holmes, and D. Lea. *Java Concurrency in Practice*. 2006.

[21] C. Hammer, J. Dolby, M. Vaziri, and F. Tip. Dynamic detection of atomic-set-serializability violations. In *ICSE*, pages 231–240, 2008.

[22] M. Herlihy and J. M. Wing. Linearizability: A correctness condition for concurrent objects. *ACM T Progr Lang Sys*, 12(3):463–492, 1990.

[23] V. Jagannath, M. Gligoric, D. Jin, Q. Luo, G. Rosu, and D. Marinov. Improved multithreaded unit testing. In *ESEC/FSE*, pages 223–233, 2011.

[24] G. Jin, A. V. Thakur, B. Liblit, and S. Lu. Instrumentation and sampling strategies for cooperative concurrency bug isolation. In *OOPSLA*, pages 241–255, 2010.

[25] P. Joshi, C.-S. Park, K. Sen, and M. Naik. A randomized dynamic program analysis technique for detecting real deadlocks. In *PLDI*, pages 110–120, 2009.

[26] P. Joshi, M. Naik, K. Sen, and D. Gay. An effective dynamic analysis for detecting generalized deadlocks. In *FSE*, pages 327–336, 2010.

[27] S. Joshi, S. K. Lahiri, and A. Lal. Underspecified harnesses and interleaved bugs. In *POPL*, pages 19–30, 2012.

[28] Z. Lai, S.-C. Cheung, and W. K. Chan. Detecting atomic-set serializability violations in multithreaded programs through active randomized testing. In *ICSE*, pages 235–244, 2010.

[29] S. Lu, J. Tucek, F. Qin, and Y. Zhou. AVIO: detecting atomicity violations via access interleaving invariants. In *ASPLOS*, pages 37–48, 2006.

[30] S. Lu, S. Park, E. Seo, and Y. Zhou. Learning from mistakes: a comprehensive study on real world concurrency bug characteristics. In *ASPLOS*, pages 329–339, 2008.

[31] B. Lucia and L. Ceze. Finding concurrency bugs with context-aware communication graphs. In *MICRO*, pages 553–563, 2009.

[32] D. Marino, M. Musuvathi, and S. Narayanasamy. LiteRace: effective sampling for lightweight data-race detection. In *PLDI*, pages 134–143, 2009.

[33] M. Musuvathi, S. Qadeer, T. Ball, G. Basler, P. A. Nainar, and I. Neamtiu. Finding and reproducing Heisenbugs in concurrent programs. In *OSDI*, pages 267–280, 2008.

[34] M. Naik, C.-S. Park, K. Sen, and D. Gay. Effective static deadlock detection. In *ICSE*, pages 386–396, 2009.

[35] A. Nistor, Q. Luo, M. Pradel, T. R. Gross, and D. Marinov. Ballerina: Automatic generation and clustering of efficient random unit tests for multithreaded code. In *ICSE*, 2012.

[36] R. O'Callahan and J.-D. Choi. Hybrid dynamic data race detection. In *PPOPP*, pages 167–178, 2003.

[37] C. Pacheco, S. K. Lahiri, M. D. Ernst, and T. Ball. Feedback-directed random test generation. In *ICSE*, pages 75–84, 2007.

[38] C.-S. Park and K. Sen. Randomized active atomicity violation detection in concurrent programs. In *FSE*, pages 135–145, 2008.

[39] S. Park, S. Lu, and Y. Zhou. CTrigger: exposing atomicity violation bugs from their hiding places. In *ASPLOS*, pages 25–36, 2009.

[40] H. Patil, C. Pereira, M. Stallcup, G. Lueck, and J. Cownie. PinPlay: a framework for deterministic replay and reproducible analysis of parallel programs. In *CGO*, pages 2–11, 2010.

[41] W. Pugh and N. Ayewah. Unit testing concurrent software. In *ASE*, pages 513–516, 2007.

[42] S. Savage, M. Burrows, G. Nelson, P. Sobalvarro, and T. E. Anderson. Eraser: A dynamic data race detector for multithreaded programs. *ACM T Comput Syst*, 15(4):391–411, 1997.

[43] K. Sen. Effective random testing of concurrent programs. In *ASE*, pages 323–332, 2007.

[44] K. Sen. Race directed random testing of concurrent programs. In *PLDI*, pages 11–21, 2008.

[45] O. Shacham, N. Bronson, A. Aiken, M. Sagiv, M. Vechev, and E. Yahav. Testing atomicity of composed concurrent operations. In *OOPSLA*, pages 51–64, 2011.

[46] Y. Shi, S. Park, Z. Yin, S. Lu, Y. Zhou, W. Chen, and W. Zheng. Do I use the wrong definition?: Defuse: definition-use invariants for detecting concurrency and sequential bugs. In *OOPSLA*, pages 160–174, 2010.

[47] Y. Smaragdakis and C. Csallner. Combining static and dynamic reasoning for bug detection. In *TAP*, pages 1–16, 2007.

[48] F. Sorrentino, A. Farzan, and P. Madhusudan. PENELOPE: weaving threads to expose atomicity violations. In *FSE*, pages 37–46, 2010.

[49] C. von Praun and T. R. Gross. Object race detection. In *OOPSLA*, pages 70–82, 2001.

[50] S. Zhang, D. Saff, Y. Bu, and M. D. Ernst. Combined static and dynamic automated test generation. In *ISSTA*, pages 353–363, 2011.

[51] W. Zhang, C. Sun, and S. Lu. ConMem: detecting severe concurrency bugs through an effect-oriented approach. In *ASPLOS*, pages 179–192, 2010.

[52] W. Zhang, J. Lim, R. Olichandran, J. Scherpelz, G. Jin, S. Lu, and T. W. Reps. ConSeq: detecting concurrency bugs through sequential errors. In *ASPLOS*, pages 251–264, 2011.

Scalable and Precise Dynamic Datarace Detection for Structured Parallelism

Raghavan Raman
Rice University
raghav@rice.edu

Jisheng Zhao
Rice University
jisheng.zhao@rice.edu

Vivek Sarkar
Rice University
vsarkar@rice.edu

Martin Vechev
ETH Zürich
martin.vechev@inf.ethz.ch

Eran Yahav *
Technion
yahave@cs.technion.ac.il

Abstract

Existing dynamic race detectors suffer from at least one of the following three limitations:

(i) *space overhead* per memory location grows linearly with the number of parallel threads [13], severely limiting the parallelism that the algorithm can handle.

(ii) *sequentialization*: the parallel program must be processed in a sequential order, usually depth-first [12, 24]. This prevents the analysis from scaling with available hardware parallelism, inherently limiting its performance.

(iii) *inefficiency*: even though race detectors with good theoretical complexity exist, they do not admit efficient implementations and are unsuitable for practical use [4, 18].

We present a new precise dynamic race detector that leverages structured parallelism in order to address these limitations. Our algorithm requires constant space per memory location, works in parallel, and is efficient in practice. We implemented and evaluated our algorithm on a set of 15 benchmarks. Our experimental results indicate an average (geometric mean) slowdown of 2.78× on a 16-core SMP system.

Categories and Subject Descriptors D.2.4 [*Software Engineering*]: Software/Program Verification—reliability, validation; D.2.5 [*Software Engineering*]: Testing and Debugging—monitors, testing tools; D.3.4 [*Programming Languages*]: Processors—debuggers; F.3.2 [*Logics and Meanings of Programs*]: Semantics of Programming Languages—program analysis

General Terms Algorithms, Languages, Verification

Keywords Parallelism, Program Analysis, Data Races

* Deloro Fellow

PLDI'12, June 11–16, 2012, Beijing, China.

1. Introduction

Data races are a major source of errors in parallel programs. Complicating matters, data races may occur only in few of the possible schedules of a parallel program, thereby making them extremely hard to detect and reproduce. The importance of detecting races has motivated significant work in the area. We briefly summarize existing race detectors and the main contributions of our approach below.

Existing Race Detectors FastTrack is a state-of-the art parallel race detection algorithm which handles classic unstructured fork-join programs with locks [13]. While versatile, a key drawback of FastTrack is its worst-case space overhead of $O(n)$ per instrumented memory location, where n is the number of threads in the program. This space overhead implies that the algorithm can typically only be used with a small number of parallel threads. Increasing the number of threads can quickly cause space overheads and slowdowns that render the algorithm impractical. FastTrack applies some optimizations to reduce the overhead, but even for locations that are read shared, the algorithm maintains $O(n)$ space. Unfortunately, in domains where structured parallelism dominates, programs typically use a massive number of lightweight tasks (e.g. consider a parallel-for loop on a GPU) and often the parallel tasks share read-only data.

There have been various proposals for race detectors targeting structured parallel languages, notably SP-bags [12] and All-Sets [8] for Cilk and its extension ESP-bags [24] for subsets of X10 [7] and Habanero-Java (HJ) [6]. The SP-bags, All-Sets, and ESP-bags algorithms only need $O(1)$ space per instrumented memory location but are limited in that they must always process the parallel program in a depth-first sequential manner. This means that the algorithms cannot utilize and scale with the available hardware parallelism. The SP-hybrid algorithm for Cilk [4] is an attempt to address the sequentialization limitation of the SP-bags algorithm. However, despite its good theoretical bounds, the SP-hybrid algorithm is very complex and incurs significant inefficiencies in practice. The original paper on SP-hybrid [4] provides no evaluation and subsequent evaluation of an incomplete implementation of SP-hybrid [18] was done only for a small number of processors; a complete empirical study for SP-hybrid has never been done. However, the inefficiency is clear from the fact that the CilkScreen race detector used in Intel Cilk++ [1] has chosen to use the sequential All-Sets algorithm over the parallel but inefficient SP-hybrid. Further, the SP-hybrid algorithm depends on a particular scheduling technique (i.e. a work-stealing scheduler).

Collectively, these three limitations raise the following question: *Is there a precise dynamic race detector that works in parallel, uses O(1) space per memory location, and is suitable for practical use?* In this paper we introduce such dynamic race detector targeting structured parallel languages such as Cilk [5], OpenMP 3.0 [23], X10 [7], and Habanero Java (HJ) [6]. Our algorithm runs in parallel, uses O(1) space per memory location, and performs well in practice.

Structured Parallelism Structured parallel programming simplifies the task of writing correct and efficient parallel programs in two ways. First, a wide range of parallel programs can be succinctly expressed with a few well-chosen and powerful structured parallel constructs. Second, the structure of the parallel program can be exploited to provide better performance, for instance, via better scheduling algorithms. Third, structured parallelism often provides guarantees of deadlock-freedom. Examples of languages and frameworks with structured parallelism include Cilk [5], X10 [7], and Habanero Java (HJ) [3].

Our Approach A key idea is to leverage the structured parallelism to efficiently determine whether conflicting memory accesses can execute in parallel. Towards that end, we present a new data structure called the Dynamic Program Structure Tree (DPST). With our algorithm, the time overhead for every monitoring operation is independent of the number of tasks and worker threads executing the program. Similarly to FastTrack, SP-bags and ESP-bags, our algorithm is sound and precise for a given input: if the algorithm does not report a race for a given execution, it means that no execution with the same input can trigger a race (i.e. there are no false negatives). Conversely, if a race is reported, then the race really exists (i.e. there are no false positives). These properties are particularly attractive when testing parallel programs as it implies that for a given input, we can study an arbitrary program schedule to reason about races that may occur in other schedules. As we will demonstrate later, our algorithm is efficient in practice and significantly outperforms existing algorithms.

Main Contributions The main contributions of this paper are:

- A dynamic data race detection algorithm for structured parallelism with the following properties:
  - works in parallel.
  - uses only constant space per monitored memory location.
  - is sound and precise for a given input.
- A data structure called the Dynamic Program Structure Tree (DPST) that keeps track of relationships between tasks and can be accessed and modified concurrently.
- An efficient implementation of the algorithm together with a set of static optimizations used to reduce the overhead of the implementation.
- An evaluation on a suite of 15 benchmarks indicating an average (geometric mean) slowdown of 2.78× on a 16-core SMP system.

The rest of the paper is organized as follows: Section 2 discusses the structured parallel setting, Section 3 presents the dynamic program structure tree (DPST), Section 4 introduces our new race detection algorithm, Section 5 presents the details of the implementation of our algorithm and the optimizations that we used to reduce the overhead, Section 6 discusses our experimental results, Section 7 discusses related work and Section 8 concludes the paper.

2. Background

In this section, we give a brief overview of the structured parallel model targeted by this paper. We focus on the async/finish structured parallelism constructs used in X10 [7] and Habanero Java (HJ) [6]. The async/finish constructs generalize the traditional spawn/sync constructs used in the Cilk programming system [5] since they can express a broader set of computation graphs than those expressible with the spawn/sync constructs used in Cilk [15].

While X10 and HJ include other synchronization techniques such as futures, clocks/phasers, and Cilk even includes locks, the core task creation and termination primitives in these languages are fundamentally based on the async/finish and spawn/sync constructs. The underlying complexity of a dynamic analysis algorithm is determined by these core constructs. Once a dynamic analysis algorithm for the core constructs is developed, subsequent extensions can be built on top of the core algorithm. To underscore the importance of studying the core portions of these languages, a calculus called Featherweight X10 (FX10) was proposed [20]. Also, the SP-bags algorithm [12] for Cilk was presented for the core spawn/sync constructs (the algorithm was later extended to handle accumulators and locks [8]).

The algorithm presented in this paper is applicable to async/finish constructs (which means it also handles spawn/sync constructs). The algorithm is independent of the sequential portions of the language, meaning that one can apply it to any language where the parallelism is expressed using the async/finish constructs. For example, the sequential portion of the language can be based on the sequential portions of Java as in HJ or C/C++ as in Cilk [15], Cilk++ [1], OpenMP 3.0 [23], and Habanero-C [9]. Next, we informally describe the semantics of the core async/finish constructs. A formal operational semantics can be found in [20].

Informal Semantics The statement `async { s }` causes the parent task to create a new child task to execute `s` *asynchronously* (i.e., before, after, or in parallel) with the remainder of the parent task. The statement `finish { s }` causes the parent task to execute `s` and then wait until all async tasks created within `s` have completed, including the transitively spawned tasks. Each dynamic instance T_A of an `async` task has a unique *Immediately Enclosing Finish* (IEF) instance F of a finish statement during program execution, where F is the innermost dynamic `finish` scope containing T_A. There is an implicit `finish` scope surrounding the body of *main()* so program execution will only end after all `async` tasks have completed.

The `finish` statement is a restricted join: while in the general unstructured fork-join case, a task can join with any other task, with the `finish` statement, a task can only join on tasks that are created in the enclosed statement. This is a fundamental difference between arbitrary unstructured fork-join and the async/finish (or spawn/sync) constructs. It is such restrictions on the join that make it possible to prove the absence of deadlocks for any program in the language [20], and provide an opportunity for discovering analysis algorithms that are more efficient than those for the general unstructured fork-join case.

As mentioned earlier, async/finish constructs can express a broader set of computation graphs than Cilk's spawn/sync constructs. The key relaxation in async/finish over spawn/sync is the way a task is allowed to join with other tasks as well as dropping the requirement that a parent task must wait for all of its child tasks to terminate. With spawn/sync, at any given sync point in a task execution, the task must join with *all* of its descendant tasks (and all recursive descendant tasks, by transitivity) created in between the start of the task and the join point. In contrast, with async/finish it is possible for a task to join with *some* rather than all of its descendant tasks: at the end of a finish block, the task only waits until the

```
finish { // F1
  S1;  } step1
  S2;  }
  async { // A1
    S3; }
    S4; } step2
    S5; }
    async { // A2
      S6; } step3
    } // async A2
    S7; } step4
    S8; }
  } // async A1
  S9;  }
  S10; } step5
  S11; }
  async { // A3
    S12; } step6
    S13; }
  } // async A3
} // finish F1
```

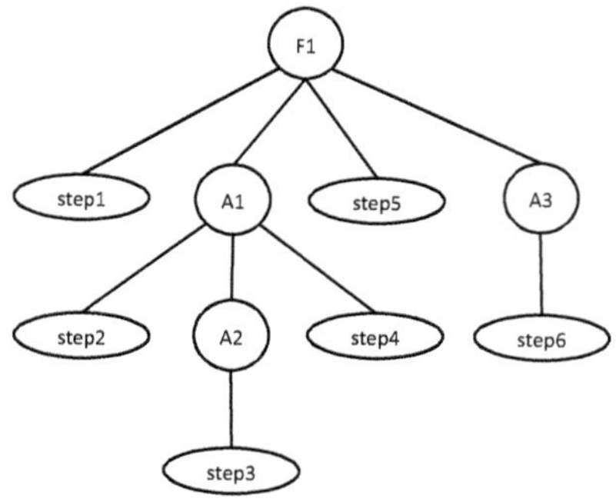

Figure 1. An example async/finish program and its final DPST.

descendant tasks created inside the finish scope have completed. More details comparing spawn/sync and async/finish can be found in [16].

Example Consider the example in Figure 1. For now, ignore the tree on the right and the step annotations, both of which are discussed in the next section. Initially, the main task begins execution with the main finish statement, labeled F1. It executes the first two statements S1 and S2 and then forks a new task A1 using the async statement. In turn, A1 executes statements S3, S4, S5 and forks task A2 which executes statement S6. Note that statement S6 (in task A2) and statements S7 and S8 in task A1 can execute in parallel. After forking A1, the main task can proceed to execute statements S9, S10 and S11 that follow A1. The main task then forks task A3 which executes statements S12 and S13. Note that the statement S11 (in the main task) and statements S12, S13 (in task A3) cannot execute in parallel because the task A3 will be forked only after the completion of S11. After forking A3, the main task has to wait until A1, A2, and A3 have terminated. Only after all these descendant tasks complete, the main task can exit past the end of finish F1.

3. Dynamic Program Structure Tree

Any dynamic data race detection algorithm needs to provide mechanisms that answer two questions: for any pair of memory accesses (with at least one write): (i) determine whether the accesses can execute in parallel, and (ii) determine whether they access the same location. In this section, we introduce the Dynamic Program Structure Tree (DPST), a data structure which can be used to answer the first question.

The DPST is an ordered rooted tree that is built at runtime to capture parent-child relationships among async, finish, and step (defined below) instances of a program. The internal nodes of a DPST represent async and finish instances. The leaf nodes of a DPST represent the steps of the program. The DPST can also be used to support dynamic analysis of structured parallel programs written in languages such as Cilk and OpenMP 3.0.

We assume standard operational semantics of async/finish constructs as defined in FX10 [20]. The semantics of statements and expressions other than async/finish is standard [30]. That is, each transition represents either a basic statement, an expression evaluation or the execution of an async or a finish statement. For our purposes, given a trace, we assume that the execution of each statement is uniquely identified (if a statement executes multiple times, each dynamic instance is uniquely identified). We refer to an execution of a statement as a dynamic statement instance. We say that a statement instance is an async instance if the statement performs an async operation. Similarly for finish instances.

Definition 1 (Step). *A step is a maximal sequence of statement instances such that no statement instance in the sequence includes an async or a finish operation.*

Definition 2 (DPST). *The Dynamic Program Structure Tree (DPST) for a given execution is a tree in which all leaves are steps, and all interior nodes are async and finish instances. The parent relation is defined as follows:*

- *Async instance A is the parent of all async, finish, and step instances directly executed within A.*
- *Finish instance F is the parent of all async, finish, and step instances directly executed within F.*

There is a left-to-right ordering of all DPST siblings that reflects the left-to-right sequencing of computations belonging to their common parent task. Further, the tree has a single root that corresponds to the implicit top-level finish construct in the main program.

3.1 Building a DPST

Next we discuss how to build the DPST during program execution. When the main task begins, the DPST will contain a root finish node F and a step node S that is the child of F. F corresponds to the implicit finish enclosing the body of the main function in the program and S represents the starting computation in the main task.

Task creation When a task T performs an async operation and creates a new task T_{child}:

1. An async node A_{child} is created for task T_{child}. If the immediately enclosing finish (IEF) F of T_{child} exists within task T, then A_{child} is added as the rightmost child of F. Otherwise, A_{child} is added as the rightmost child node of (the async) node corresponding to task T.
2. A step node representing the starting computations in task T_{child} is added as the child of A_{child}.
3. A step node representing the computations that follow task T_{child} in task T is added as the right sibling of A_{child}.

Note that there is no explicit node in a DPST for the main task because everything done by the main task will be within the implicit finish in the main function of the program and hence all of the corresponding nodes in a DPST will be under the root finish node.

Start Finish When a task T starts a finish instance F:

1. A finish node F_n is created for F. If the immediately enclosing finish F' of F exists within task T (with corresponding finish node F'_n in the DPST), then F_n is added as the rightmost child of F'_n. Otherwise, F_n is added as the rightmost child of the (async) node corresponding to task T.
2. A step node representing the starting computations in F is added as the child of F_n.

End Finish When a task T ends a finish instance F, a step node representing the computations that follow F in task T is added as the right sibling of the node that represents F in the DPST.

Note that the DPST operations described thus far only take $O(1)$ time. Thus, the DPST for a given program run grows monotonically as program execution progresses and new async, finish, and step instances are added to the DPST. Note that since all data accesses occur in steps, it follows that all tests for whether two accesses may happen in parallel will only take place between two leaves in a DPST.

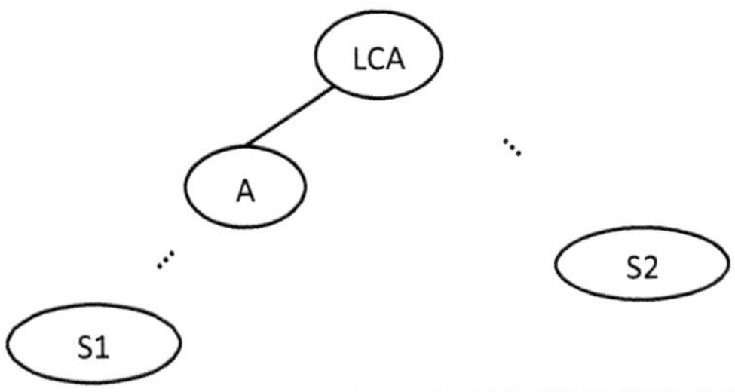

Figure 2. A part of a DPST. LCA is the Lowest Common Ancestor of steps S1 and S2. A is the DPST ancestor of S1 which is the child of LCA. S1 and S2 can execute in parallel if and only if A is an async node.

Example We can now return to the example program in Figure 1 and study its steps and final DPST. Note the way statement instances are grouped into steps. When the main task starts executing finish F1, a node corresponding to F1 is added as the root node of the DPST, and a step node step1 is added as the child of F1; step1 represents the starting computations in F1, i.e., instances of statements S1 and S2. When the main task forks the task A1, an async node corresponding to A1 is added as the right-most child of F1 (since the immediately enclosing finish of A1 is F1 and it is within the main task), a step node step2 is added as the child of A1, and a step node step5 is added as the right sibling of A1. step2 represents the starting computations in A1 (i.e., instance of statements S3, S4, and S5) and step5 represents the computation that follows A1 in the main task (i.e., instances of statements S9, S10, and S11). After this point, the main task and the task A1 can execute in parallel. Eventually, the DPST grows to the form shown in the figure.

3.2 Properties of a DPST

In this section, we briefly summarize some key properties of a DPST. The proofs of these properties have been omitted due to space limitations, but can be found in [25].

- For a given input that leads to a data-race-free execution of a given async-finish parallel program, all executions of that program with the same input will result in the same DPST.
- Let F be the DPST root (finish) node. Each non-root node n_0 is uniquely identified by a finite path from n_0 to F:

$$n_0 \xrightarrow{r_0} n_1 \xrightarrow{r_1} n_2 \xrightarrow{r_2} \ldots \xrightarrow{r_{k-1}} n_k$$

  where $k \geq 1$, $n_k = F$, and for each $0 \leq i < k$, n_i is the r_i^{th} child of node n_{i+1}. The path from n_0 to F stays invariant as the tree grows. For a given statement instance, its path to the root is unique regardless of which execution is explored (as long as the executions start with the same state). This property holds up to the point that a data race (if any) is detected.
- The DPST is amenable to efficient implementations in which nodes can be added to the DPST in parallel without any synchronization in O(1) time. One such implementation is described in Section 5.

Definition 3. *A node A is said to be to the left of a node B in a DPST if A appears before B in the depth first traversal of the tree.*

As mentioned above, even though the DPST changes during program execution, the path from a node to the root does not change and the left-to-right ordering of siblings does not change. Hence, even though the depth first traversal of the DPST is not fully specified during program execution, the *left* relation between any two nodes in the current DPST is well-defined.

Definition 4. *Two steps, S_1 and S_2, in a DPST Γ that corresponds to a program P with input ψ, may execute in parallel if and only if there exists at least one schedule δ of P with input ψ in which S_1 executes in parallel with S_2.*

The predicate *DMHP(S_1, S_2)* evaluates to *true* if steps S_1 and S_2 can execute in parallel in at least one schedule of a program and to *false* otherwise (*DMHP* stands for "Dynamic May Happen in Parallel" to distinguish it from the MHP relation used by static analyses). We now state a key theorem that will be important in enabling our approach to data race detection.

Theorem 1. *Consider two leaf nodes (steps) S1 and S2 in a DPST, where S1 $\neq$ S2 and S1 is to the left of S2 as shown in Figure 2. Let LCA be the node denoting the least common ancestor of S1 and S2. Let node A be the ancestor of S1 that is the child of LCA. Then, S1 and S2 can execute in parallel if and only if A is an async node.*

Proof. Please refer to [25]. □

Example Let us now look at the *DMHP* relation for some pairs of steps in the example program in Figure 1. First, let us consider *DMHP(step2, step5)*. Here *step2* is to the left of *step5*, since *step2* will appear before *step5* in the depth first traversal of the DPST. The lowest common ancestor of *step2* and *step5* is the node F1. The node A1 is the ancestor of *step2* (the left node) that is the child of F1. Since A1 is an async node, *DMHP(step2, step5)* will evaluate to *true* indicating that *step2* and *step5* can execute in parallel. This is indeed *true* for this program: *step2* is within A1, while *step5* follows A1 and is within A1's immediately enclosing finish.

Now, let us consider *DMHP(step6, step5)*. Here *step5* is to the left of *step6*, since *step5* will appear before *step6* in the depth first traversal of the DPST. Their lowest common ancestor is F1, and the ancestor of *step5* which is the child of F1 is *step5* itself. Since *step5* is not an async instance, *DMHP(step6, step5)* evaluates to *false*. This is consistent with the program because *step6* is in task A3 and A3 is created only after *step5* completes.

4. Race Detection Algorithm

Our race detection algorithm involves executing the given program with a given input and monitoring every dynamic memory access in the program for potential data races. The algorithm maintains a DPST as described in the previous section, as well as the relevant access history for each shared memory location. The algorithm performs two types of actions:

- Task actions: these involve updating the DPST with a new node for each async, finish, and step instance.
- Memory actions: on every shared memory access, the algorithm checks if the access conflicts with the access history for the relevant memory location. If a conflict is detected, the algorithm reports a race and halts. Otherwise, the memory location is updated to include the memory access in its access history.

A key novelty of our algorithm is that it requires constant space to store the access history of a memory location, while still guaranteeing that no data races are missed. We next describe the shadow memory mechanism that supports this constant space guarantee.

4.1 Shadow Memory

Our algorithm maintains a shadow memory M_s for every monitored memory location M. M_s is designed to store the relevant parts of the access history to M. It contains the following three fields, which are all initialized to null:

- w : a reference to a step that wrote M.
- r_1 : a reference to a step that read M.

- r_2 : a reference to another step that read M.

The following invariants are maintained throughout the execution of the program until the first data race is detected.

- $M_s.w$ refers to the step that last wrote M.
- $M_s.r_1$ & $M_s.r_2$ refer to the steps that last read M. All the steps $(a_1, a_2, ..., a_k)$ that have read M since the last synchronization are in the subtree rooted at *LCA($M_s.r_1$, $M_s.r_2$)*.

The fields of the shadow memory M_s are updated *atomically* by different tasks that access M.

4.2 Algorithm

The most important aspect of our algorithm is that it stores only three fields for every monitored memory location irrespective of the number of steps that access that memory location. The intuition behind this is as follows: it is only necessary to store the last write to a memory location because all the writes before the last one must have completed at the end of the last synchronization. This is assuming no data races have been observed yet during the execution. Note that though synchronization due to finish may not be global, two writes to a memory location have to be ordered by some synchronization to avoid constituting a data race. Among the reads to a memory location, $(a_1, a_2, ..., a_k)$, since the last synchronization, it is only necessary to store two reads, a_i, a_j, such that the subtree under *LCA(a_i, a_j)* includes all the reads $(a_1, a_2, ..., a_k)$. This is because every future read, a_n, which is in parallel with any discarded step will also be in parallel with at least one of a_i or a_j. Thus, the algorithm will not miss any data race by discarding these steps.

Definition 5. *In a DPST, a node n_1 is dpst-greater than a node n_2, denoted by $n_1 >_{dpst} n_2$, if n_1 is an ancestor of n_2 in the DPST. Note that, in this case, n_1 is higher in the DPST (closer to the root) than n_2.*

Algorithm 1: Write Check

Input: Memory location M, Step S that writes to M
if *DMHP($M_s.r_1$, S)* **then**
  Report a read-write race between $M_s.r_1$ and S
end
if *DMHP($M_s.r_2$, S)* **then**
  Report a read-write race between $M_s.r_2$ and S
end
if *DMHP($M_s.w$, S)* **then**
  Report a write-write race between $M_s.w$ and S
else
  $M_s.w \leftarrow S$
end

Algorithms 1 and 2 show the checking that needs to be performed on write and read accesses to monitored memory locations. When a step S writes to a memory location M, Algorithm 1 checks if S may execute in parallel with the reader in $M_s.r_1$ by computing *DMHP(S, $M_s.r_1$)*. If they can execute in parallel, the algorithm reports a read-write data race between $M_s.r_1$ and S. Similarly, the algorithm reports a read-write data race between $M_s.r_2$ and S if these two steps can execute in parallel. Then, Algorithm 1 reports a write-write data race between $M_s.w$ and S, if these two steps can execute in parallel. Finally, it updates the writer field, $M_s.w$, with the current step S indicating the latest write to M. Note that this happens only when the write to M by S does not result in data race with any previous access to M.

Algorithm 2: Read Check

Input: Memory location M, Step S that reads M
if *DMHP($M_s.w$, S)* **then**
  Report a write-read data race between $M_s.w$ and S
end
if $\neg$*DMHP($M_s.r_1$, S)* $\wedge$ $\neg$*DMHP($M_s.r_2$, S)* **then**
  $M_s.r_1 \leftarrow S$
  $M_s.r_2 \leftarrow null$
else if *DMHP($M_s.r_1$, S)* $\wedge$ *DMHP($M_s.r_2$, S)* **then**
  $lca_{12} \leftarrow$ LCA($M_s.r_1$, $M_s.r_2$)
  $lca_{1s} \leftarrow$ LCA($M_s.r_1$, S)
  $lca_{2s} \leftarrow$ LCA($M_s.r_2$, S)
  if $lca_{1s} >_{dpst} lca_{12} \vee lca_{2s} >_{dpst} lca_{12}$ **then**
    $M_s.r_1 \leftarrow S$
  end
end

When a step S reads a memory location M, Algorithm 2 reports a write-read data race between $M_s.w$ and S if these two steps can execute in parallel. Then, it updates the reader fields of M_s as follows: if S can never execute in parallel with either of the two readers, $M_s.r_1$ and $M_s.r_2$, then both these readers are discarded and $M_s.r_1$ is set to S. If S can execute in parallel with both the readers, $M_s.r_1$ and $M_s.r_2$, then the algorithm stores two of the these three steps, whose *LCA* is the highest in the DPST, i.e., if *LCA($M_s.r_1$, S)* or *LCA($M_s.r_2$, S)* is dpst-greater than *LCA($M_s.r_1$, $M_s.r_2$)*, then $M_s.r_1$ is set to S. Note that in this case S is outside the subtree under *LCA($M_s.r_1$, $M_s.r_2$)* and hence, *LCA($M_s.r_1$, S)* will be the same as *LCA($M_s.r_2$, S)*.

If S can execute in parallel with one of the two readers and not the other, then the algorithm does not update the readers because, in that case, S is guaranteed to be within the subtree under the *LCA($M_s.r_1$, $M_s.r_2$)*.

The *DMHP($M_s.r_2$, S)* can be computed from *DMHP($M_s.r_1$, S)* in some cases. This can be used to further optimize Algorithms 1 and 2. We do not present the details of this optimization here.

Atomicity Requirements A memory action for an access to a memory location M involves reading the fields of M_s, checking the predicates, and possibly updating the fields of M_s. Every such memory action has to execute atomically with respect to other memory actions for accesses to the same memory location.

Theorem 2. *If Algorithms 1 and 2 do not report any data race in some execution of a program P with input ψ, then no execution of P with ψ will have a data race on any memory location M.*

Proof. Please refer to [25]. □

Theorem 3. *If Algorithm 1 or 2 reports a data race on a memory location M during an execution of a program P with input ψ, then there exists at least one execution of P with ψ in which this race exists.*

Proof. Please refer to [25]. □

Theorem 4. *The race detection algorithm is sound and precise for a given input.*

Proof. From Theorem 2 it follows that our race detection algorithm is sound for a given input. From Theorem 3 it follows that our race detection algorithm is precise for a given input. □

5. Implementation and Optimizations

This section describes the implementation of the different parts of our race detection algorithm.

5.1 DPST

The DPST of the program being executed is built to maintain the parent-child relationship of asyncs, finishes and steps in the program. Every node in the DPST consists of the following 4 fields:

- *parent*: the DPST node which is the parent of this node.
- *depth*: an integer that stores the depth of this node. The root node of the DPST has depth 0. Every other node in the DPST has depth one greater than its parent. This field is immutable.
- *num_children*: number of children of this node currently in the DPST. This field is initialized to 0 and incremented when child nodes are added.
- *seq_no*: an integer that stores the ordering of this node among the children of its parent, i.e., among its siblings. Every node's children are ordered from left to right. They are assigned sequence numbers starting from 1 to indicate this order. This field is also immutable.

The use of depth for nodes in the DPST leads to a lowest common ancestor (LCA) algorithm with better complexity (than if we had not used this field). The use of sequence numbers to maintain the ordering of a node's children makes it easier to check for may happen in parallel given two steps in the program.

Note that all the fields of a node in the DPST can be initialized/updated without any synchronization: the *parent* field initialization is trivial because there are no competing writes to that field; the *depth* field of a node is written only on initialization, is never updated, and is read only after the node is created; the *num_children* field is incremented whenever a child node is added, but for a given node, its children are always added sequentially in order from left to right; the *seq_no* field is written only on initialization, is never updated, and is read only after the node is created.

5.2 Computing *DMHP*

A large part of the data race detection algorithm involves checking *DMHP* for two steps in the program. This requires computing the Lowest Common Ancestor (LCA) of two nodes in a tree. The function $LCA(\Gamma, S_1, S_2)$ returns the lowest common ancestor of the nodes S_1 and S_2 in the DPST Γ. This is implemented by starting from the node with the greater depth (say S_1) and traversing up Γ until a node with the depth same as S_2 is reached. From that point, Γ is traversed along both the paths until a common node is reached. This common node is the lowest common ancestor of S_1 and S_2. The time overhead of this algorithm is linear in the length of the longer of the two paths, $S_1 \rightarrow L$ and $S_2 \rightarrow L$.

Algorithm 3 computes *DMHP* relation between two steps S_1 and S_2. Algorithm 3 returns *true* if the given two steps S_1 and S_2 may happen in parallel and *false* otherwise. This algorithm first computes the lowest common ancestor L of the given two steps using the *LCA* function. If the step S_1 is to the left of S_2, then the algorithm returns *true* if the ancestor of S_1 (which is the child of L) is an async and *false* otherwise. If the step S_2 is to the left of S_1, then the algorithm returns *true* if the ancestor of S_2 which is the child of L is an async and *false* otherwise. The time overhead of this algorithm is same as that of the *LCA* function, since it only takes constant time to find the node which is the ancestor of the left step that is the child of *LCA* node and then check if that node is an async.

Algorithm 3: Dynamic May Happen in Parallel (*DMHP*)

Input: DPST Γ, Step S_1, Step S_2
Output: true/false

N_{lca} = LCA(Γ, S_1, S_2)
A_1 = Ancestor of S_1 in Γ which is the child of N_{lca}
A_2 = Ancestor of S_2 in Γ which is the child of N_{lca}
if *A_1 is to the left of A_2 in Γ* **then**
    if *A_1 is an Async* **then**
        return true
    else
        return false // S_1 happens before S_2
    end
else
    if *A_2 is an Async* **then**
        return true
    else
        return false // S_2 happens before S_1
    end
end

5.3 Space and Time Overhead

The size of the DPST will be $O(n)$, where n is the number of tasks in the program. More precisely, the total number of nodes in the DPST will be $3 * (a + f) - 1$, where a is the number of async instances and f is the number of finish instances in the program. This is because a program with just one finish node will have just one step node inside the finish of its DPST. When an async or a finish node is subsequently added to the DPST, it will result in adding 2 steps nodes, one as the child of the new node and the other as its sibling. The space overhead for every memory location is O(1), since we only need to store a writer step and two reader steps in the shadow memory of every memory location.

The time overhead at task boundaries is O(1), which is the time needed to add/update a node in the DPST. The worst case time overhead on every memory access is same as that of Algorithm 3.

Note that the time overhead is not proportional to the number of processors (underlying worker threads) that the program runs on. Hence, the overhead is not expected to scale as we increase the number of processors on which the program executes. This is an important property as future hardware will likely have many cores.

5.4 Relaxing the Atomicity Requirement

A memory action for an access to a memory location M involves reading the fields of its shadow memory location M_s, computing the necessary *DMHP* information and checking appropriate predicates, and possibly updating the fields of M_s. Let us refer to these three stages as *read*, *compute*, and *update* of a memory action.

In our algorithm, every memory action on a shadow memory M_s has to execute atomically relative to other memory actions on M_s. When there are parallel reads to a memory location, this atomicity requirement effectively serializes the memory actions due to these reads. Hence this atomicity requirement induces a bottleneck in our algorithm when the program is executed on a large number of threads. Note that the atomicity requirement does not result in a bottleneck in the case of writes to a memory location because the memory actions due to writes have no contention in data race free programs. (In a data race free program, there is a happens-before ordering between a write and every other access to a memory location.)

We now present our implementation strategy to overcome this atomicity requirement without sacrificing the correctness of our algorithm. This implementation strategy is based on the solution to the reader-writer problem proposed by Leslie Lamport in [19].

Our implementation allows multiple memory actions on the same shadow memory to proceed in parallel. This is done by adding two atomic integers to every shadow memory, i.e., M_s contains the following two additional fields:

- *startVersion*: an atomic integer that denotes the version number of M_s
- *endVersion*: an atomic integer that denotes the version number of M_s.

Both *startVersion* and *endVersion* are initialized to zero. Every time any of the fields $M_s.w$, $M_s.r_1$, or $M_s.r_2$ is updated, M_s.*startVersion* and M_s.*endVersion* are incremented by one. The following invariant is maintained on every shadow memory M_s during the execution of our algorithm: *any consistent snapshot of M_s will have the same version number in both startVersion and endVersion.* Now, we show how the read, compute, and update stages of a memory action on M_s are performed. Note that these rules use a *CompareAndSet (CAS)* primitive which is *atomic* relative to every operation on the same memory location.

Read:

- Read the version number in M_s.*startVersion* into a local variable, X.
- Read the fields $M_s.w$, $M_s.r_1$, and $M_s.r_2$ into local variables, W, R_1, and R_2.
- Perform a *fence* to ensure that all operations above are complete.
- Read the version number in M_s.*endVersion* into a local variable, Y.
- If X is not the same as Y, restart the *read* stage.

Compute:

- Perform the computation on the local variables, W, R_1, and R_2.

Update:

- Do the following steps if an update to any of the fields $M_s.w$, $M_s.r_1$, or $M_s.r_2$ is necessary.
- Perform a *CAS* on the version number in M_s.*endVersion* looking for the value X and updating it with an increment of one.
- If the above *CAS* fails, restart the memory action from the beginning of *read* stage.
- Write to the required fields of M_s.
- Write the incremented version number to M_s.*startVersion*.

When a memory action on M_s completes the *read* stage, the above rules ensure that a consistent snapshot of M_s was captured. This is because the *read* stage completes only when the same version number is seen in both M_s.*startVersion* and M_s.*endVersion*.

The *CAS* in the *update* stage of the memory action on M_s succeeds only when M_s.*endVersion* has the version number that was found in the *read* stage earlier. The *update* stage completes by writing to the reader and writer fields of M_s as necessary, followed by incrementing the version number in M_s.*startVersion*. When the *update* stage completes, both M_s.*startVersion* and M_s.*endVersion* will have the same version number and thus, the fields of M_s are retained in a consistent state.

The *CAS* in the *update* stage of a memory action α on M_s also ensures that the fields of M_s are updated only if it has not already been updated by any memory action on M_s, since the *read* stage of α. If this *CAS* fails, then there has been some update to M_s since the *read* stage and hence, the computations are discarded and the memory action is restarted from the beginning of the *read* stage. Thus, the memory actions are guaranteed to be atomic relative to other memory actions on the same memory location.

The main advantage of this implementation is that it allows multiple memory actions on the same shadow memory M_s to proceed in parallel. But if more than one of them needs to update the fields of M_s, then only one of them is guaranteed to succeed while the others repeat the action. This is especially beneficial when there are multiple parallel accesses to M whose memory actions do not update the fields of M_s. In our algorithm, this occurs when there are reads by step S such that S is in the subtree rooted at *LCA*($M_s.r_1$, $M_s.r_2$). These cases occur frequently in practice thereby emphasizing the importance of relaxing the atomicity requirement.

Our algorithm is implemented in Java and we use the *AtomicInteger* from Java Concurrency Utilities for the version numbers. The *CAS* on *Atomic Integer* is guaranteed to execute atomically with respect to other operations on the same location. Also, the *CAS* acts as a barrier for the memory effects of the instructions on its either side, i.e., all the instructions above it are guaranteed to complete before it executes and no instructions below it will execute before it completes. This is the same as the memory effects of the *fence* that is used in the read stage. The read of an *AtomicInteger* has the memory effects of the read of a volatile in Java. Hence, it does not allow any instruction after it to execute until it completes. Similarly, the write to an *AtomicInteger* has the memory effects of the write to a volatile in Java. Hence, it does not execute until all the instructions before it complete.

5.5 Optimizations

In the implementation of our algorithm, we also include the static optimizations that were described in [24]. These optimizations eliminate redundant updates to the shadow memory location due to redundant reads and writes to the corresponding memory location with a single step. These are static optimizations that perform data flow analysis on the input program to identify redundant shadow memory updates. The optimizations include: main-task check elimination, read-only check elimination, escape analysis to eliminate task-local checks, loop-invariant check optimizations, and read-/write check elimination. We note that these optimizations can be used to improve the performance of any race detection algorithm. We have also identified a number of dynamic optimizations that can reduce the space and time overhead of the *DMHP* algorithm even further. We leave those as future work.

6. Experimental Results

In this section, we present experimental results for our algorithm, which for convenience we refer to as *SPD3* (Scalable Precise Dynamic Datarace Detection). The algorithm was implemented as a Java library for detecting data races in HJ programs containing async and finish constructs [6]. Shadow locations were implemented by extending the `hj.lang.Object` class with shadow fields, and by using *array views* [6, 24] as anchors for shadow arrays. Programs were instrumented for race detection during a bytecode-level transformation pass implemented on HJ's Parallel Intermediate Representation (PIR) [31]. The PIR is an intermediate representation that extends Soot's Jimple IR [29] with parallel constructs such as async and finish. The instrumentation pass adds the necessary calls to our race detector library at async and finish boundaries and on reads and writes to shared memory locations.

We also compare *SPD3* with some race detectors from past work, namely Eraser [26], FastTrack [13], and ESP-bags [24]. For Eraser and FastTrack, we use the implementations included in the RoadRunner tool [14]. Since the performance of the FastTrack implementation available in the public RoadRunner download yielded worse results than those described in [13], we communicated with

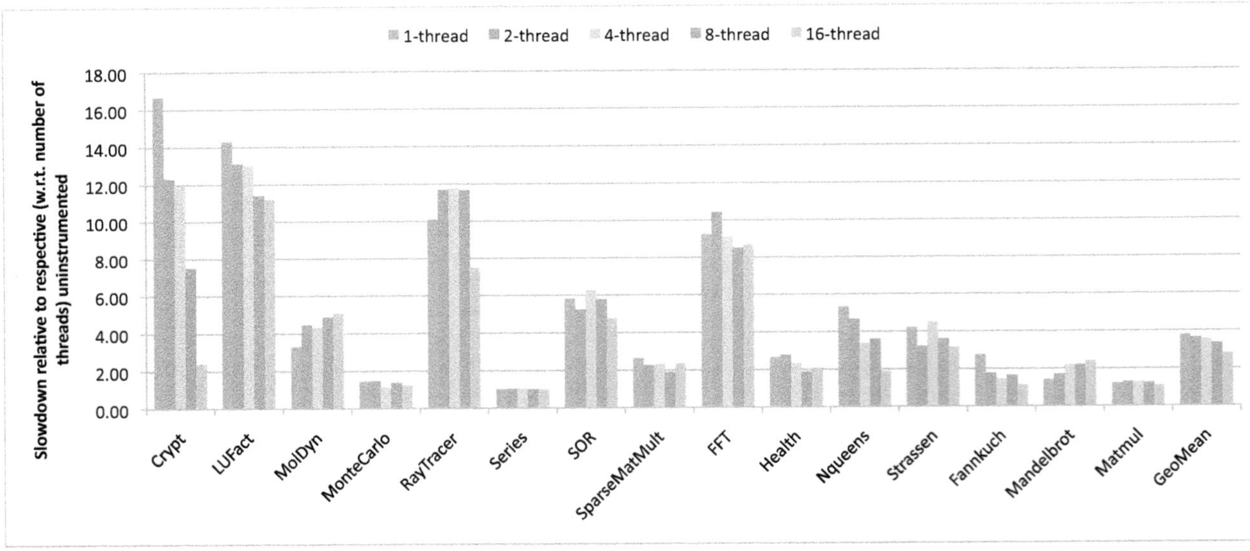

Figure 3. Relative slowdown of *SPD3* for all benchmarks on 1, 2, 4, 8, and 16 threads. Relative slowdown on n threads refers to the slowdown of the *SPD3* version on n threads compared to the HJ-Base version on n threads.

Table 1. List of Benchmarks Evaluated

Source	Benchmark	Description
JGF (Section 2)	Series (C)	Fourier coefficient analysis
	LUFact (C)	LU Factorisation
	SOR (C)	Successive over-relaxation
	Crypt (C)	IDEA encryption
	Sparse (C)	Sparse Matrix multiplication
JGF (Section 3)	MolDyn (B)	Molecular Dynamics simulation
	MonteCarlo (B)	Monte Carlo simulation
	RayTracer (B)	3D Ray Tracer
Bots	FFT (large)	Fast Fourier Transformation
	Health (large)	Simulates a country health system
	NQueens (14)	N Queens problem
	Strassen (large)	Matrix Multiply with Strassen's method
Shootout	Fannkuch (10M)	Indexed-access to tiny integer-sequence
	Mandelbrot (8000)	Generate Mandelbrot set portable bitmap
EC2	Matmul (1000^2)	Matrix Multiplication (Iterative)

the implementers and received an improved implementation of FastTrack which was used to obtain the results reported in this paper. For ESP-bags, we used the same implementation that was used in [24].

Our experiments were conducted on a 16-core (quad-socket, quad-core per socket) Intel Xeon 2.4GHz system with 30 GB memory, running Red Hat Linux (RHEL 5), and Sun Hotspot JDK 1.6. To reduce the impact of JIT compilation, garbage collection and other JVM services, we report the smallest time measured in 3 runs repeated in the same JVM instance for each data point. HJ tasks are scheduled on a fixed number of worker threads using a work-stealing scheduler with an adaptive policy [17]

6.1 Evaluation of *SPD3*

We evaluated *SPD3* on a suite of 15 task-parallel benchmarks listed in Table 1. It includes eight Java Grande Forum benchmarks (JGF) [28], four Barcelona OpenMP Task Suites benchmarks (BOTS) [11], two Shootout benchmarks [2], and one EC2 challenge benchmark.

All benchmarks were written using only finish and async constructs for parallelism, with fine grained one-async-per-iteration parallelism for parallel loops. As discussed later, the original version of the JGF benchmarks contained "chunked" parallel loops with programmer-specified decomposition into coarse grained one-chunk-per-thread parallelism. The fine grained task-parallel versions of the JGF benchmarks used for the evaluation in this section were obtained by rewriting the chunked loops into "unchunked" parallel loops. In addition, barrier operations in the JGF benchmarks were replaced by appropriate finish constructs.

HJ-Base refers to the uninstrumented baseline version of each of these benchmarks. All the JGF benchmarks were configured to run with the largest available input size. All input sizes are shown in Table 1.

No data race was expected in these 15 programs, and *SPD3* found only one data race which turned out to be a benign race. This was due to repeated parallel assignments of the same value to the same location in the async-finish version of the MonteCarlo benchmark, which was corrected by removing the redundant assignments. After that, all the benchmarks used in this section were observed to be data-race-free for the inputs used.

Figure 3 shows the relative slowdown of *SPD3* for all benchmarks when executed with 1, 2, 4, 8, and 16 worker threads. (Recall that these benchmarks create many more async tasks than the number of worker threads.) The relative slowdown on n threads refer to the slowdown of the *SPD3* instrumented version of the benchmark executing on n threads compared with the HJ-Base version executing on n threads. Ideally, a scalable race detector should have a constant relative slowdown as the number of worker threads increases. As evident from Figure 3, the slowdown for many of the benchmarks decrease as the number of worker threads increases from 1 to 16. The geometric mean of the slowdowns for all the benchmarks on 16 threads is 2.78×.

Though the geometric mean is below 3×, four of the 15 benchmarks (Crypt, LUFact, RayTracer, and FFT) exhibited a slowdown around 10× for worker threads from 1 to 16. This is because these benchmarks contain larger numbers of shared locations that need to be monitored for race detection. As discussed later, other race detection algorithms exhibit much larger slowdowns for these examples than *SPD3*. Note that even in these cases the slowdowns are similar across 1 to 16 threads. This clearly shows that *SPD3* scales well.

The slowdown for 1-thread is higher than that for all other threads in many benchmarks. This is because our implementation

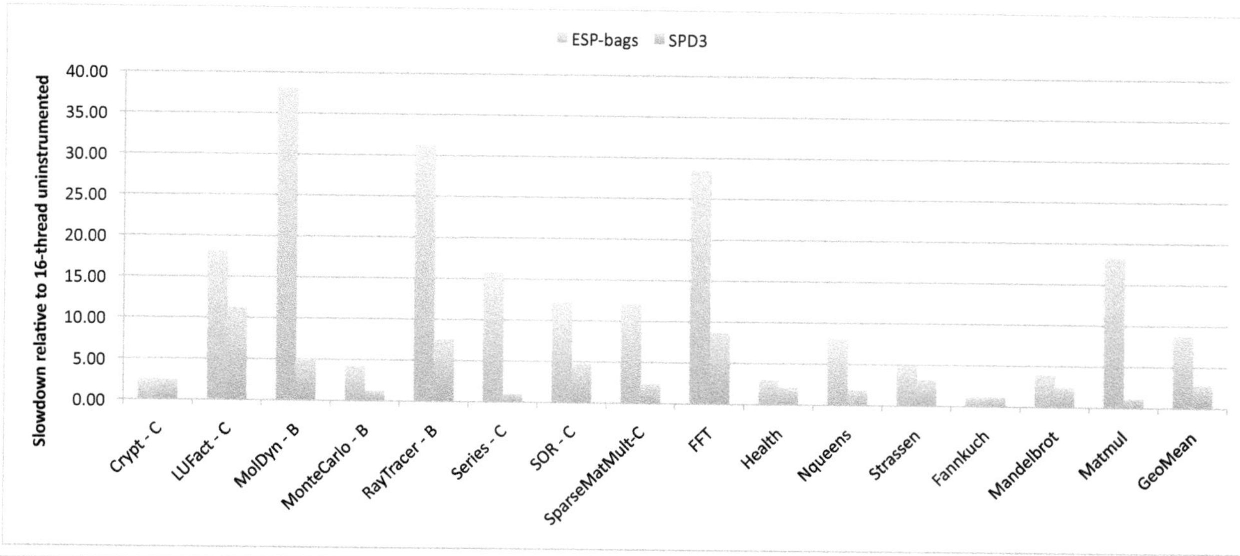

Figure 4. Slowdown of ESP-bags and *SPD3* relative to 16-thread HJ-Base version for all benchmarks. Note that the ESP-bags version runs on 1-thread while the *SPD3* version runs on 16-threads.

uses *compareAndSet* operations on atomic variables. These operations are not optimized for the no contention scenario as with 1-thread. Instead, if we use a lock that is optimized for no contention scenario, the slowdown for 1-thread cases would have been a lot lower. But that implementation does not scale well for larger numbers of threads. For example, the lock based implementation is $1.8\times$ slower (on average) than the *compareAndSet* implementation when running on 16-threads. While the two implementations are close for many benchmarks (within a factor of 2), there is a difference of upto $7\times$ for some benchmarks, when running on 16-threads. The *compareAndSet* implementation is always faster than the lock based implementation for larger numbers of threads. Since our aim was to make the algorithm scalable, we chose the *compareAndSet* approach.

6.2 Comparison with ESP-bags algorithm

In this section, we compare the performance of *SPD3* with ESP-bags [24]. Figure 4 shows the slowdown of ESP-bags and *SPD3* for all the benchmarks, relative to the execution time of the 16-thread HJ-Base version. Note that the ESP-bags version runs on 1-thread (because it is a sequential algorithm) while the *SPD3* version runs on 16-threads.

This comparison underscores the fact that the slowdown for a sequential approach to datarace detection can be significantly larger than that of parallel approaches, when running on a parallel machine. For example, the slowdown is reduced by more than a $15\times$ factor when moving from ESP-bags to *SPD3* for Series and MatMul benchmarks and by more than a $5\times$ factor for benchmarks like MolDyn and SparseMatMult that scale well. On the other hand, the slowdown for Crypt is similar for ESP-bags and *SPD3* because the uninstrumented async-finish version of Crypt does not scale well. On average, *SPD3* is $3.2\times$ faster than ESP-bags on our 16-way system. This gap is expected to further increase on systems with larger numbers of cores.

6.3 Comparison with Eraser and FastTrack

We only use the JGF benchmarks for comparisons with other algorithms since those are the only common benchmarks with past work on Eraser and FastTrack. However, since Eraser and FastTrack work on multithreaded Java programs rather than task-parallel variants like HJ, they used the original coarse-grained one-chunk-per-thread approach to loop parallelism in the JGF benchmarks with one thread per core. Converting these programs to fine-grained parallel versions using Java threads was not feasible since creating large numbers of threads quickly leads to OutOfMemoryError's. Further, it would also make the size of the vector clocks prohibitively large in the program in order to provide the same soundness and completeness guarantees as *SPD3*.

So, to enable an apples-to-apples comparison in this section, we created coarse-grained async-finish versions of the JGF benchmarks with chunked loops for the HJ versions. Since Eraser and FastTrack were implemented in RoadRunner, we used the execution of the Java versions of these benchmarks on RoadRunner without instrumentation (RR-Base) as the baseline for calculating the slowdowns for Eraser and FastTrack. The differences between RR-Base and HJ-Base arise from the use of array views in the HJ version, and from the use of finish operations instead of barriers as discussed below.

Our first observation when running *SPD3* on the coarse grained HJ versions of the eight JGF benchmarks was that data races were reported for four of the benchmarks: LUFact, MolDyn, RayTracer, and SOR. The data race reports pointed to races in shared arrays that were used by the programmer to implement custom barriers. However, all the custom barrier implementations were incorrect because they involved unsynchronized spin loops on shared array elements. Even though the programmer declared the array references as volatile, the volatile declaration does not apply to the elements of the array. (In all fairness to the programmer, the JGF benchmarks were written in the late 1990's when many Java practitioners were unaware of the implications of the Java memory model.)

Our second observation is that the default Eraser and FastTrack tools in the RoadRunner implementation did not report most of these data races. The only race reported was by FastTrack for SOR. After communication with the implementers of RoadRunner, we recently learned that RoadRunner recognizes a number of common barrier class implementations by default and generates special Barrier Enter and Barrier Exit events for them which in turn enables Eraser and FastTrack to take the barriers into account for race detection (even though the barriers are technically buggy). Further a "-nobarrier" option can be used to suppress this barrier detection.

We confirmed that all races were reported with the "-nobarrier" option. However, all RoadRunner performance measurements reported in this paper were obtained with default settings i.e., without the "-nobarrier" option.

Our third observation is that Eraser reported false data races for many benchmarks. This is not surprising since Eraser is known to not be a precise datarace detection algorithm.

To undertake a performance comparison, we converted the four benchmarks to race-free HJ programs by replacing the buggy barriers by finish operations. In some cases, this caused the HJ-base version to be slower than the RR-base version as a result (since RR-base measures the performance of the unmodified JGF benchmarks with custom barriers). Before we present the comparison, it is also worth noting that the implementation of Eraser and FastTrack in RoadRunner include some optimizations that are orthogonal to the race detection algorithm used [14]. Similarly, the static optimizations from [24] included in our implementation of *SPD3* are also orthogonal to the race detection algorithm. Both these sets of optimizations could be performed on any race detection algorithm to improve its performance.

Table 2. Relative slowdown of *Eraser*, *FastTrack* and *SPD3* for JGF benchmarks on 16 threads. The slowdown of Eraser and FastTrack was calculated over their baseline RR-Base while the slowdown of *SPD3* was calculated over its baseline HJ-Base. For benchmarks marked with *, race-free versions were used for *SPD3* but the original versions were used for Eraser and FastTrack.

Benchmark	RR-Base Time(s)	Eraser Slowdown	FastTrack Slowdown	HJ-Base Time(s)	*SPD3* Slowdown
Crypt	0.362	122.40	133.24	0.585	1.84
LUFact*	1.47	17.95	26.41	5.411	1.08
MolDyn*	16.185	8.39	9.59	3.750	13.56
MonteCarlo	2.878	10.95	13.54	5.605	1.86
RayTracer*	2.186	20.23	17.45	19.974	5.84
Series	112.515	1.00	1.00	88.768	1.00
SOR*	0.914	4.26	8.36	2.604	4.53
Sparse	2.746	14.29	20.59	4.607	1.72
GeoMean	-	11.21	13.87	-	2.63

Table 2 shows the slowdowns of Eraser, FastTrack, and *SPD3* for all the JGF benchmarks on 16 threads. Note that the slowdown of Eraser and FastTrack were calculated relative to RR-Base (with 16 threads), and the slowdown of *SPD3* was calculated over HJ-Base (with 16 threads). For benchmarks marked with *, race-free versions were used for *SPD3* but the original versions were used for Eraser and FastTrack; this accounts for differences in the execution times of RR-Base and HJ-Base for some benchmarks since the async-finish versions include more synchronization to correct the bugs in the original Java versions.

Table 2 shows that the relative slowdowns for Eraser and FastTrack are much larger than those for *SPD3*. On average (geometric mean), the slowdown for *SPD3* relative to HJ-base is 2.70× while that for Eraser and FastTrack are 11.21× and 13.87× respectively relative to RR-base. There is also a large variation. While the slowdowns are within a factor of 2 for SOR, there is more than a 60× gap in slowdowns for Crypt and quite a significant difference for LUFact, MonteCarlo, and SparseMatMult as well. The slowdown for *SPD3* on MolDyn is larger than the slowdowns for Eraser and FastTrack because the baseline for *SPD3* is more than 4× faster than the baseline for Eraser and FastTrack. For FastTrack, these slowdowns are consistent with the fact that certain data access patterns (notably, shared reads) can lead to large overheads because they prevent the use of optimized versions of vector clocks.

For the case with the largest gap in Table 2 (Crypt), Figure 5 shows the slowdown (scaled execution time) of RR-Base, Eraser, FastTrack, HJ-Base, and *SPD3* for the chunked version of the

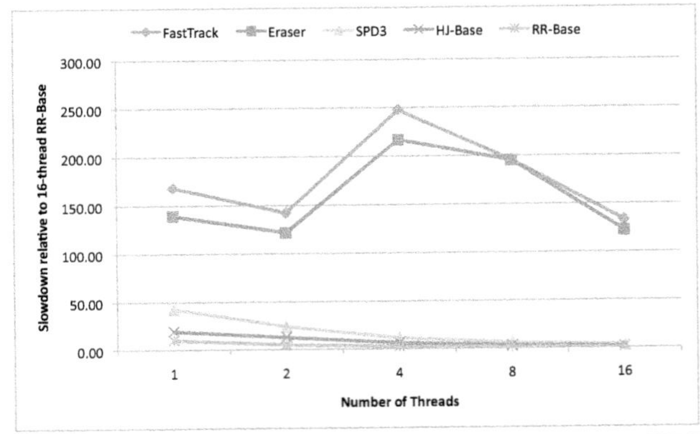

Figure 5. Slowdown (relative to 16-threads RR-Base) of RR-Base, Eraser, FastTrack, HJ-Base, and *SPD3* for Crypt benchmark (chunked version) on 1-16 threads

Crypt benchmark on 1-16 threads relative to the 16-thread RR-Base execution time. In this benchmark, RR-Base is the fastest for 16 threads as expected. The execution time of HJ-Base is 1.9× slower than RR-Base in the 1-thread case and 1.6× slower than RR-Base in the 16-thread case. Similarly, the execution time of *SPD3* version is also very close; it is 4.2× slower in the 1-thread case and 3× slower in the 16-thread case. The execution time of Eraser and FastTrack are 13.7× and 16.6× slower than RR-Base in the 1-thread case but they increase to more than 100× for 8-threads and 16-threads. This example shows that for some programs the performance overheads for Eraser and FastTrack can increase dramatically with the number of threads (cores).

6.4 Memory Overhead

We now compare the memory overheads of the Eraser, FastTrack and *SPD3* algorithms on the coarse-grained JGF benchmarks. Again, the baseline for Eraser and FastTrack was RR-Base and the baseline for *SPD3* was HJ-Base. To obtain a coarse estimation of the memory used, we used the *-verbose:gc* option in the JVM and picked the maximum heap memory used over all the GC executions in a single JVM instance. All three instrumented versions trigger GC frequently, so this is a reasonable estimate of the memory overhead.

Table 3. Peak heap memory usage of RR-Base, Eraser, FastTrack, HJ-Base, and *SPD3* for JGF benchmarks on 16 threads. For benchmarks marked with *, race-free versions were used for *SPD3* but the original versions were used for Eraser and FastTrack.

Benchmark	Memory (in MB)				
	RR-Base	Eraser	FastTrack	HJ-Base	*SPD3*
Crypt	209	8539	8535	149	6009
LUFact	80	1790	2455	47	203
MolDyn	382	1048	1040	9	35
MonteCarlo	1771	9316	9292	557	584
RayTracer	1106	4475	4466	43	88
Series	80	1067	1062	162	177
SOR	81	1161	1551	47	202
Sparse	225	2120	2171	88	714

Table 3 shows the estimated memory usage of these three algorithms and their baselines for JGF benchmarks on 16 threads. The table shows that the memory usage of HJ-Base is lower than that of RR-Base in all the benchmarks except Series. In all cases, the memory usage is lower for *SPD3*, compared to Eraser and FastTrack with significant variation in the gaps. The memory usage of Crypt with *SPD3* is quite high because the benchmark has arrays

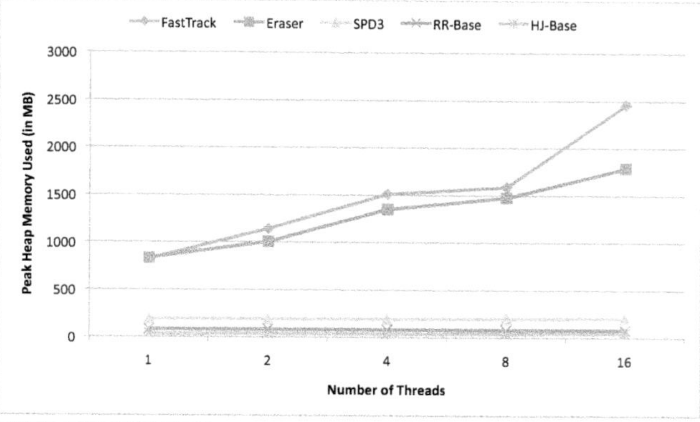

Figure 6. Estimated heap memory usage (in MB) of RR-Base, Eraser, FastTrack, HJ-Base, and *SPD3* for LUFact benchmark

of size 20 million and our algorithm maintains shadow locations for all elements of these arrays. But the memory used by *SPD3* for Crypt is still less than that of Eraser and FastTrack. The high memory usage for Eraser and FastTrack is not surprising because Eraser has to maintain all the locks held while accessing a particular location, and FastTrack's vector clocks may grow linearly in the number of threads in the worst case.

For one of the benchmarks in Table 3 (LUFact), Figure 6 shows the estimated memory usage of the three algorithms and their baselines as a function of the number of threads/cores used. Note that both the baselines (RR-Base and HJ-Base) are very close. While the estimated heap usage of RR-Base remains constant at $80M$, the estimated usage of HJ-Base varies from $33M$ to $47M$ as we go from 1 thread to 16 threads. The estimated heap usage of *SPD3* is about $6\times$ larger than HJ-Base: it varies between $192M$ and $203M$ across 16 threads. The estimated heap usage of Eraser increases from $833M$ for 1 thread to $1790M$ for 16 threads ($2.1\times$ increase). Similarly, the estimated heap usage of FastTrack increases from $825M$ for 1 thread to $2455M$ for 16 threads ($3\times$ increase). This clearly shows the increase in the memory usage for Eraser and FastTrack as we increase the number of threads for this benchmark.

7. Related Work

In the introduction, we outlined the key differences between our algorithm and FastTrack. In summary, on one hand, our algorithm uses $O(1)$ space per memory location, while in the worst-case, FastTrack uses $O(n)$. On the other, FastTrack handles more general computation graphs than those supported by our model. The time overhead of our algorithm is characteristic of the application, since it depends on the height of the LCA nodes in the DPST. It is independent of the number of threads (processors) the program executes on. On the other hand, FastTrack's worst-case time overhead is linear in the number of threads, which can grow very large with increasing numbers of cores.

Schonberg [27] presented one of the earliest dynamic data race detection algorithm for nested fork-join and synchronization operations. In this algorithm, a shared variable set is associated with each sequential block in every task. There is also a concurrency list associated with each shared variable set which keeps track of the concurrent shared variable sets that will complete at a later time. The algorithm detects anomalies by comparing complete concurrent shared variable sets at each time step. This algorithm applies only to a single execution instance of a program, as mentioned in [27]. The space required to store read information in the shared variable sets is bounded by $V \times N$, where V is the number of variables being monitored and N is the number of execution threads [1]. This space requirement increases with an increase in the number of threads the program is executed on, whereas our algorithm's space requirement is independent of the number of threads the program is executed on. A limitation of this work is that since access anomalies are detected at synchronization points, it does not identify the actual read and write operations involved in the data races.

Offset-Span (OS) labeling [21] is an optimized version of the English-Hebrew (EH) labeling technique [10] for detecting data races. The idea behind both these techniques is to attach a label to every thread in the program and use these labels to check if two threads can execute concurrently. They also maintain the access history for every shared variable that is monitored which is then used to check for conflicts. The length of the labels associated with each thread can grow arbitrarily long in EH labeling[2], whereas the length of the labels in OS labeling is bounded by the maximum nesting depth of fork-join in the program. While the EH labeling technique needs an access history of size equal to the number of threads for every monitored variable in the program, the OS labeling technique only needs constant size to store access history. While OS labeling algorithm supports only nested fork-join constructs, our algorithm supports a more general set of dynamic graphs. Further, though the OS labeling algorithm can execute the input program in parallel, it has been evaluated in a sequential setting only [22]. The effectiveness of this algorithm in a parallel implementation is not clear.

A related work on data race detection for structured parallel programs was done as part of the Cilk project [4]. This work gives an algorithm called SP-hybrid, which detects races in the program with a constant space and time overhead. Their algorithm has the best possible theoretical overheads for both space and time. However, despite its good theoretical bounds, the SP-hybrid algorithm is very complex and incurs significant inefficiencies in practice. The original paper on SP-hybrid [4] provides no evaluation and subsequent evaluation of an incomplete implementation of SP-hybrid [18] was done only for a small number of processors. One indicator of the inefficiency of SP-hybrid can be seen in the fact that the CilkScreen race detector used in Intel Cilk++ [1] uses the sequential All-Sets algorithm [8] rather than the parallel SP-hybrid algorithm. Another drawback of their algorithm is that it is tightly coupled with Cilk's work-stealing scheduler. Hence, their algorithm cannot be applied directly to other schedulers. In contrast, our algorithm is amenable to an efficient implementation, performs very well in practice, supports a more general set of computation graphs than Cilk's spawn/sync and is also independent of the underlying scheduler.

There has also been work on data race detection algorithms for spawn/sync [12] and async/finish models [24]. While they require only $O(1)$ space overhead per memory location, these algorithms must process the program in a sequential depth-first manner, fundamentally limiting the scalability of these approaches. In contrast, the algorithm presented in this work can process the program during parallel execution, while still requiring only $O(1)$ space per memory location.

[1] If N refers to the maximum number of threads possible in all executions of a program for a given input, then this algorithm can guarantee data race freedom for all executions of the program for that input. If not, then this guarantee will not hold.

[2] Note that the length of the labels is bounded by the maximum nesting level of fork-join in EH labeling in the presence of an effective heuristic as reported in [10]

8. Conclusion and Future Work

In this work, we presented a new dynamic data race detection algorithm for structured parallel programs. The algorithm can process the program in parallel, uses $O(1)$ space per memory location and admits an efficient implementation. The algorithm tracks what can happen in parallel via a new data structure called the dynamic program structure tree (DPST), and maintains two readers and a writer for each shared memory location in order to track potential conflicts between different tasks. We implemented the algorithm and demonstrated its effectiveness on a range of benchmarks. In future, it could be interesting to extend the algorithm to other structured parallel constructs such as HJ's phaser construct [6].

Acknowledgments

We are grateful to the authors of the RoadRunner tool [14], Cormac Flanagan and Stephen Freund, for sharing their implementation of FastTrack that was used to obtain the results reported in [13], and for answering our questions related to both FastTrack and RoadRunner. We would also like to thank John Mellor-Crummey from Rice University for his feedback and suggestions on this work. This work was supported in part by the U.S. National Science Foundation through awards 0926127 and 0964520. We also thank the US-Israel Binational Foundation (BSF) for their support.

References

[1] Intel Cilk++ Programmer's Guide. http://software.intel.com/en-us/articles/download-intel-cilk-sdk/.

[2] The Computer Language Benchmarks Game. http://shootout.alioth.debian.org/.

[3] BARIK, R., ET AL. The habanero multicore software research project. In *Proceeding of the 24th ACM SIGPLAN conference companion on Object oriented programming systems languages and applications* (2009), ACM, pp. 735–736.

[4] BENDER, M. A., ET AL. On-the-fly maintenance of series-parallel relationships in fork-join multithreaded programs. In *SPAA'04* (Barcelona, Spain, June27–30 2004), pp. 133–144.

[5] BLUMOFE, R. D., ET AL. Cilk: an efficient multithreaded runtime system. In *PPoPP'95* (Oct. 1995), pp. 207–216.

[6] CAVE, V., ZHAO, J., SHIRAKO, J., AND SARKAR, V. Habanero-java: the new adventures of old x10. In *PPPJ'11* (2011).

[7] CHARLES, P., ET AL. X10: An object-oriented approach to non-uniform cluster computing. In *OOPSLA 2005 Onward! Track* (2005).

[8] CHENG, G.-I., FENG, M., LEISERSON, C. E., RANDALL, K. H., AND STARK, A. F. Detecting data races in cilk programs that use locks. In *SPAA'98* (1998), pp. 298–309.

[9] CONG, J., SARKAR, V., REINMAN, G., AND BUI, A. Customizable Domain-Specific Computing. *IEEE Design and Test*, 2:28 (Mar 2011), 6–15.

[10] DINNING, A., AND SCHONBERG, E. An empirical comparison of monitoring algorithms for access anomaly detection. In *PPoPP'90* (1990), ACM, pp. 1–10.

[11] DURAN, A., ET AL. Barcelona OpenMP tasks suite: A set of benchmarks targeting the exploitation of task parallelism in openmp. In *ICPP'09* (2009), pp. 124–131.

[12] FENG, M., AND LEISERSON, C. E. Efficient detection of determinacy races in cilk programs. In *SPAA'97* (1997), ACM, pp. 1–11.

[13] FLANAGAN, C., AND FREUND, S. N. FastTrack: efficient and precise dynamic race detection. In *PLDI '09* (2009), ACM, pp. 121–133.

[14] FLANAGAN, C., AND FREUND, S. N. The roadrunner dynamic analysis framework for concurrent programs. In *PASTE'10* (2010), ACM, pp. 1–8.

[15] FRIGO, M., LEISERSON, C. E., AND RANDALL, K. H. The implementation of the cilk-5 multithreaded language. In *PLDI'98* (1998), ACM, pp. 212–223.

[16] GUO, Y., ET AL. Work-first and help-first scheduling policies for async-finish task parallelism. In *IPDPS'09* (2009), IEEE Computer Society, pp. 1–12.

[17] GUO, Y., ZHAO, J., CAVÉ, V., AND SARKAR, V. Slaw: A scalable locality-aware adaptive work-stealing scheduler. In *IPDPS* (2010).

[18] KARUNARATNA, T. C. Nondeterminator-3: A provably good data-race detector that runs in parallel. Master's thesis, Department of Electrical Engineering and Computer Science, MIT,, Sept. 2005.

[19] LAMPORT, L. Concurrent reading and writing. *Commun. ACM 20* (November 1977), 806–811.

[20] LEE, J. K., AND PALSBERG, J. Featherweight x10: a core calculus for async-finish parallelism. In *PPoPP'10* (2010), ACM, pp. 25–36.

[21] MELLOR-CRUMMEY, J. On-the-fly detection of data races for programs with nested fork-join parallelism. In *Supercomputing'91* (1991), ACM, pp. 24–33.

[22] MELLOR-CRUMMEY, J. Compile-time support for efficient data race detection in shared-memory parallel programs. In *PADD '93: Proceedings of the ACM/ONR workshop on Parallel and distributed debugging* (1993), ACM, pp. 129–139.

[23] OpenMP Application Program Interface v 3.0, 2008.

[24] RAMAN, R., ET AL. Efficient data race detection for async-finish parallelism. In *RV'10* (2010), Springer-Verlag, pp. 368–383.

[25] RAMAN, R., ZHAO, J., SARKAR, V., VECHEV, M., AND YAHAV, E. Scalable and precise dynamic datarace detection for structured parallelism. Tech. Rep. TR12-01, Department of Computer Science, Rice University, Houston, TX, 2012.

[26] SAVAGE, S., ET AL. Eraser: a dynamic data race detector for multi-threaded programs. *ACM Trans. Comput. Syst. 15*, 4 (1997), 391–411.

[27] SCHONBERG, E. On-the-fly detection of access anomalies. In *PLDI'98* (1998), pp. 285–297.

[28] SMITH, L. A., AND BULL, J. M. A Parallel Java Grande Benchmark Suite. In *In Supercomputing'01* (2001), ACM Press, p. 8.

[29] VALLÉE-RAI, R., ET AL. Soot - a Java Optimization Framework. In *Proceedings of CASCON 1999* (1999), pp. 125–135.

[30] WINSKEL, G. *The Formal Semantics of Programming Languages*. MIT Press, 1993.

[31] ZHAO, J., AND SARKAR, V. Intermediate language extensions for parallelism. In *VMIL'11* (2011), pp. 333–334.

Multicore Acceleration of Priority-Based Schedulers for Concurrency Bug Detection

Santosh Nagarakatte
University of Pennsylvania
santoshn@cis.upenn.edu

Sebastian Burckhardt
Microsoft Research
sburckha@microsoft.com

Milo M. K. Martin
University of Pennsylvania
milom@cis.upenn.edu

Madanlal Musuvathi
Microsoft Research
madanm@microsoft.com

Abstract

Testing multithreaded programs is difficult as threads can interleave in a nondeterministic fashion. Untested interleavings can cause failures, but testing all interleavings is infeasible. Many interleaving exploration strategies for bug detection have been proposed, but their relative effectiveness and performance remains unclear as they often lack publicly available implementations and have not been evaluated using common benchmarks. We describe NeedlePoint, an open-source framework that allows selection and comparison of a wide range of interleaving exploration policies for bug detection proposed by prior work.

Our experience with NeedlePoint indicates that priority-based probabilistic concurrency testing (the PCT algorithm) finds bugs quickly, but it runs only one thread at a time, which destroys parallelism by serializing executions. To address this problem we propose a parallel version of the PCT algorithm (PPCT). We show that the new algorithm outperforms the original by a factor of 5× when testing parallel programs on an eight-core machine. We formally prove that parallel PCT provides the same probabilistic coverage guarantees as PCT. Moreover, PPCT is the first algorithm that runs multiple threads while providing coverage guarantees.

Categories and Subject Descriptors D.2.5 [*Software Engineering*]: Testing and Debugging

General Terms Algorithms, Reliability, Verification

Keywords Concurrency, priority-based scheduling, multithreading, probabilistic concurrency testing, parallel testing

1. Introduction

Multithreaded programs are difficult to test and debug because their behavior depends on the specific interleaving of shared memory accesses, which in turn depends on how the threads are interleaved by multicore hardware and thread scheduling software. Because thread interleaving is non-deterministic and largely unpredictable, an astronomical number of interleavings is possible even for small programs. However, due to the statistical nature of the interleavings, repeatedly testing the program on the same platform results in redundant exploration of similar interleavings. The untested uncommon interleavings can have *concurrency bugs* that escape the testing process but manifest in deployed systems, especially if differences in the deployed system's hardware or software influence observed interleavings.

One way to address this problem is to increase the coverage achieved during testing by steering executions towards uncommon schedules. We classify prior proposals for such controlled scheduling into two categories. *Best-effort* tools insert explicit thread yields at selected points at runtime [7, 11, 12, 22–25]. The strategies for inserting yield points vary, ranging from random selection [7, 24] to heuristics based on identifying symptomatic bug patterns in the code, such as data races [25], potential atomicity violations [22, 23], and potential deadlocks [12]. On the other hand, *guaranteed-coverage* tools such as CHESS [21] and PCT [5] provide provable guarantees of the schedule coverage achieved during concurrency testing. To provide such coverage guarantees, both these tools require absolute control of the thread scheduling achieved by running the threads serially one at a time. Although coverage guarantees are appealing in practice, the serial execution limits the applicability of these tools, a disadvantage not shared by best-effort approaches.

To better understand the relative effectiveness and performance of prior best-effort and guaranteed-coverage tools, we set out to reproduce and compare prior research proposals by reimplementing several published algorithms. In this process, we identified a common set of mechanisms required by a wide range of bug detection techniques. These mechanisms include instrumenting synchronization accesses, identifying blocked threads, and handling starvation. A systematic approach to providing these mechanisms is useful because manual instrumentation or annotations become quickly impractical when controlling schedules of large applications.

Motivated by this observation, we developed NeedlePoint, a unified framework for implementing a wide range of controlled scheduling approaches — ranging from simple random sleeps to prioritized scheduling. The framework separates the mechanisms required to implement the various scheduling policies from the policies themselves. This separation allowed us to implement several previously proposed approaches as policies that plug into the framework. In particular, we reimplemented the following strategies: (1) a randomized version of preemption bounding [19], (2) AtomFuzzer [22], (3) simple random sleeps, and (4) probabilistic concurrency testing (PCT) [5].

We then used Needlepoint to test a collection of multithreaded programs containing known concurrency bugs and also benchmarks from the SPLASH and Parsec suites. Our experience with NeedlePoint shows empirically that PCT is highly effective at finding bugs. However, it also reveals that PCT's performance suffers significantly from its inherent restriction of scheduling only one thread at a time. Although running one thread is good enough for running small unit tests, it becomes a problem and causes significant slowdowns when testing large programs with a large number of threads or when testing highly parallel benchmarks.

PLDI'12, June 11–16, 2012, Beijing, China.

To alleviate this problem, we propose a new testing algorithm called PPCT (parallel PCT). Like best-effort tools, PPCT can schedule multiple threads at a time, thereby making better use of hardware parallelism. At the same time, PPCT provides the same coverage guarantees as PCT. To the best of our knowledge, PPCT is the first algorithm to provide coverage guarantees without requiring serial execution of threads.

We provide a brief overview of the PCT algorithm [5] before explaining our improvement. PCT assigns thread priorities chosen uniformly randomly at the beginning of the program. At every step of the algorithm, PCT schedules the unblocked thread with the highest priority. The scheduled thread executes instructions up to the next synchronization event before yielding the control back to the scheduler. During this execution, PCT performs a small number of priority changes at steps chosen uniformly randomly at the beginning of the execution. The guarantees provided by PCT depend on the *depth* of a concurrency bug, which is the number of scheduling constraints sufficient to trigger the buggy interleaving. For instance, ordering violations have a depth 1 and atomicity violations have a depth 2. Given a program with n threads that executes a maximum of k instructions, PCT triggers a bug of depth d with probability at least $\frac{1}{nk^{d-1}}$. For instance, PCT can find ordering violations with probability at least $\frac{1}{n}$.

The key intuition behind PPCT is that when searching for bugs of depth d, it is necessary to control the scheduling of only d threads. In particular, PPCT schedules *all* unblocked threads with a priority greater than d at every step of the algorithm. In the rare case when all unblocked threads have a priority smaller than or equal to d, PPCT resorts to serial scheduling and schedules the unblocked thread with the highest priority. We adapt the formal proof of PCT to show that PPCT provides the same coverage guarantees as PCT.

Empirically, our experiments confirm that PPCT detects bugs with either the same or higher rate when compared to PCT. Compared to PCT, however, PPCT provides significant speedups both on multi-core and single-core machines. PPCT provides speedups over PCT even on a single-core machine by providing more flexibility to the operating system scheduler to schedule a thread from a larger pool of enabled threads. On a multi-core machine with eight cores, replacing PCT by PPCT reduces the overhead of executing the program from 34× to just 6× on an average. Unlike a slowdown of 34×, a slowdown of 6× is still tolerable for testing interactive applications, and it enabled us to run priority based exploration with the Chrome web browser and other applications.

2. Background on Controlled Scheduling

This section provides background on the problem of schedule selection when testing multithreaded programs and the use of controlled scheduling to address the problem.

2.1 Schedule Selection

Of the many aspects of testing multithreaded programs, this paper focuses on the *schedule selection* problem, which involves effectively finding, among an astronomical number of possible thread schedules, those schedules that drive a program to an error. To this effect, we assume the existence of a test harness that provides necessary inputs to a multithreaded program and a test mechanism that determines a test failure, such as a program crash, an assertion violation, or an incorrect output.

Data-race detection is related to and is different from the schedule selection problem. A data race occurs when two threads concurrently access the same shared variable without appropriate synchronization, such as a missing lock. Although they are indications of erroneous programming, a data race is neither necessary or sufficient for a concurrency error [8, 14].[1] Schedule selection may also help data race detectors to uncover additional races.

2.2 Controlled Scheduling

Controlled scheduling techniques attempt to steer the program towards less common interleavings. This is typically accomplished by controlling the scheduling of threads and by allowing exactly one thread to execute at a given time. These techniques can systematically explore all possible interleavings (for smaller codes) or use various heuristics to guide which interleavings are explored (for larger codes). Further, they can provide repeatability by enforcing the same thread scheduling decisions, which aids debugging.

To control the order in which operations from various threads are executed, such systems typically use OS-level threads but control the execution in user mode by preventing all but one thread from making progress at a given time. A *scheduling policy* determines the thread that makes progress. A running thread invokes the user-level scheduler at each *scheduling point*. Scheduling points occur at thread creation, synchronization operations, and thread termination. To achieve full coverage of sequentially consistent behaviors, one also needs to insert scheduling points at certain shared-memory accesses, such as accesses to `volatile` variables (in Java), `atomic` variables (in C++), and variables participating in a data race. Instrumenting such shared-memory accesses, however, incurs additional overhead, requiring the tool designer to make an explicit overhead versus coverage tradeoff.

Controlled scheduling allows the user-level scheduler to determine the running/not-running status of each thread at each scheduling point. The status of each thread is maintained in shared memory. When the main thread spawns a thread, the newly created thread's status defaults to *not-running*. Whenever the running thread encounters a scheduling point, it invokes the scheduling policy which can then either (1) decide to execute the currently running thread or (2) choose another thread to execute, in which case the scheduling policy sets the other thread's status to *running* and sets the current thread's status to *not-running*. Inactive threads (ones that are marked as *not-running* by the user-level scheduler) check their status whenever scheduled by the OS-level scheduler, either discovering they have become the new active thread or yielding otherwise. To ensure forward progress for busy-waiting and other non-trivial synchronization idioms, the inactive threads also periodically invoke the scheduling policy

Lock-based synchronization can potentially block, *e.g.*, if the lock is held by some other thread. A controlled scheduling system must identify the threads that are blocked and should not schedule blocked threads, as doing so can cause the system to livelock. For simple locks, a controlled scheduling system can maintain a hashtable of all acquired locks with information about threads acquiring them. On a lock acquire operation, if the lock is already held by some other thread, then (1) the thread's status is changed to *blocked*, (2) the thread is added to the list of threads waiting for the lock, and (3) the scheduling policy is invoked as described above, which chooses one of the non-blocked threads. On a successful lock acquire, the hashtable is also updated with the information about the acquired lock and the acquiring thread. On a lock release, the scheduler changes the state of all blocked threads on the released lock from *blocked* to *not-running*.

2.3 Challenges with Controlled Scheduling

Implementing controlled scheduling is conceptually simple, but challenging in practice due to the following two reasons. First, real world programs use a plethora of synchronization primitives. Many programs define custom synchronization using the atomic primi-

[1] Here, we explicitly ignore weak-memory-model issues issues [3, 18]

tives provided by the hardware or use adhoc synchronization [26]. Accurately interpreting and handling all these synchronization operations in a controlled scheduling system is difficult and infeasible in practice. Further, even minor mistakes in interpreting synchronization operations can lead to erroneous livelocks in the controlled scheduling system and/or missed bugs. Second, the scheduling decisions made by the underlying scheduling policy to steer the multi-threaded program towards unexplored and buggy interleavings can have pathological interactions with the synchronization operations in the program. For example, scheduling a thread that is executing busy-wait synchronization operations or arbitrary spin loops to completion with preemption bounded exploration or priority based scheduling can cause starvation. These problems make interleaving exploration of real world programs with controlled scheduling challenging.

3. NeedlePoint Scheduling Framework

Although a large number of concurrency bug detection techniques have been proposed to address the schedule selection problem [8, 13, 15, 16, 23], publicly available concurrency bug detectors are primarily data race detectors such as Helgrind [1] and Intel Thread Checker [2]. Thus, the efficacy of the various previously proposed concurrency bug detectors with respect to each other is unknown.

To address this problem, we present NeedlePoint, a unified framework for implementing a wide range of controlled scheduling approaches — ranging from simple sleep insertions to randomized prioritization — with support for repeatable execution. NeedlePoint has two overall goals. First, the NeedlePoint framework is designed to handle the real-world complexities of instrumentation for inserting scheduling points and interpreting full-fledged synchronization libraries, resulting in a tool robust enough for use in testing real-world concurrent software with state-of-the-art controlled scheduling policies. Second, NeedlePoint aims to provide researchers in concurrency bug detection a framework to build upon when designing and evaluating new scheduling policies.

3.1 Mechanisms

NeedlePoint's key contribution is the separation of mechanisms required to implement the various scheduling policies from the scheduling policies themselves. This separation of concerns between the mechanisms required to implement controlled scheduling and the scheduling policies enabled us to implement many previously proposed controlled scheduling techniques and test real-world programs with them. We identified three key mechanisms for building a wide range of concurrency bug detectors: (1) instrumenting synchronization operations, (2) identifying blocked threads, and (3) ensuring starvation freedom.

3.1.1 Instrumenting Synchronization Operations

NeedlePoint invokes the underlying scheduling policy at every dynamic program point where threads can interleave. We name these dynamic program points as schedule points. NeedlePoint uses binary instrumentation to identify such schedule points, namely all synchronization operations, atomic operations, and user specified synchronization operations. Furthermore, to detect bugs with data races, NeedlePoint can be configured to instrument every memory access and invoke the scheduling policy on such accesses. We have built NeedlePoint using the Pin [17] dynamic binary instrumentation framework running on a x86 Linux machine. Pin enables NeedlePoint to identify synchronization operations (POSIX threads API by default), atomic operations (x86 instructions with a lock prefix), and memory operations. NeedlePoint uses Pin to insert a call to the scheduling framework at these scheduling points.

3.1.2 Blocking Information

Accurately interpreting all synchronization operations becomes impractical in the presence of wide range of synchronization primitives and adhoc synchronizations [26] used by real world programs. Rather than interpreting the blocking semantics of each synchronization operation, we decided to infer the blocked status. NeedlePoint lets the synchronization operation execute and infers whether it is blocked based on the number of yields performed by other threads spin-waiting to be scheduled. This scheme is based on the following intuition: a thread executing a synchronization operation that did not block will subsequently encounter another scheduling point. In contrast, a thread trying to acquire a lock that is already held will block and thus not encounter another scheduling point. NeedlePoint counts the number of yields performed by the threads waiting to be scheduled. When this count exceeds a threshold, NeedlePoint infers that the running thread is actually blocked on a synchronization operation. This threshold is parameterizable. Setting a smaller threshold can result in an unblocked thread being erroneously considered as blocked by NeedlePoint, which can hurt repeatability. In contrast, larger thresholds cause slowdowns in the execution of the program. In our experiments, a threshold of ten yields was sufficient to ensure repeatability (for serial scheduling policies).

3.1.3 Fairness and Starvation Freedom

We found that many programs use busy wait synchronization (*e.g.* waiting for a queue to become empty and sleeping, spinning, barriers, spin loops, and others) and adhoc synchronization [26]. Scheduling a thread to completion (as in preemption bounding or as in priority based scheduling) without inducing preemptions or thread switches may cause starvation resulting in program livelocks. To avoid such starvation, NeedlePoint must choose some other thread to be scheduled. However, making a large number of such choices arbitrarily in the presence of busy wait synchronization can cause the tool to miss bugs losing the benefits of controlled scheduling. To address this problem of starvation, we make the following observation inspired from prior work on a fair scheduler [20]: a program performing busy wait synchronization will encounter numerous scheduling points, which inturn invoke the scheduling policy. Hence, if we override the default scheduling policy with a small probability, starvation will be avoided. Thus, the NeedlePoint framework overrides the scheduling policy with a small probability for a single scheduling point thereby ensuring starvation freedom. As these starvation freedom mechanisms are invoked uniformly for each schedule point rather than invoking them based on the amount of time spent waiting, NeedlePoint ensures repeatability using the same random seed.

3.2 Policies

We implemented five previously proposed concurrency bug detectors using the NeedlePoint mechanisms.

- ***Random sleep (RS)***: The random sleep policy runs more than one unblocked thread at any point in time. At every schedule point, this policy introduces a small delay with an OS sleep call with a small probability. We used a probability of 1/30 to peform the sleep as it performed well in our experiments.
- ***Preemption always (PA)***: This policy runs one thread at a time and attempts to introduce a preemption at every schedule point. At every schedule point, the scheduler performs a preemption switching the current running thread to a randomly chosen non-blocked thread.
- ***Preemption bounding (PB) [19]***: This policy performs an exploration with a predetermined number of preemptions by run-

Program	Lines of code	Schedule points	Threads	Bug type	Bug depth
Pbzip2	15,188	1210	3	Ordering violation	2
Memc	11,182	845	4	Atomicity violation	2
t+15		2300			
t+25		3400			
t+35		3900			
am		79132			
WSQ-1	541	1916	4	Atomicity violation	3
WSQ-2		1086			2
WSQ-3		1717			2
Trans	33,622	38118	2	Ordering violation	1
NSPR	1,100	5361	3	Deadlock	2

Table 1. Concurrency bugs used for NeedlePoint's evaluation that we obtained from prior research [5, 10, 16, 27, 28]. WSQ is an implementation of the work stealing queue with lock free data structures. WSQ-1, WSQ-2, and WSQ-3 are the three distinct concurrency bugs in the WSQ implementation. Memc is the memcached daemon. Trans is the Transmission BitTorrent client.

ning one thread at a time. At the beginning of the program, few scheduling points are chosen as the preemption points using a distribution. When a pre-determined preemption point is encountered, a forced preemption is induced and a non-blocked thread is chosen to become the running thread. Unlike prior research [19] that used a round robin scheme to select the next running thread when a thread is blocked, this policy chooses a random thread because we found it to be more effective at detecting bugs.

- ***AtomFuzzer (AF) [22]***: This policy directs the search to find atomicity violations by running one thread at a time. At every schedule point, if the thread attempts to acquire a lock that was previously acquired by the same thread, then it pauses the thread and schedules another thread in an effort to trigger an atomicity violation.
- ***PCT [5]***: Our prior work uses priorities to make a few random choices at the beginning of the program and direct the search. The policy assigns priorities to the thread before execution. It runs the highest priority thread that is non-blocked at every step. At predetermined schedule points, the priority of the executing thread is changed to a predetermined priority.

The NeedlePoint framework is around 6K lines of C++ code. The individual policies that implement random sleeps, preemption always, randomized version of preemption bounding [19], AtomFuzzer [24], and PCT [5] are 75, 125, 221, 208 and 258 lines of C++ code respectively, signifying the ease of writing a custom scheduler with NeedlePoint. As a proof of concept, we have tested large multi-threaded programs including the Chrome web browser with various scheduling policies in the NeedlePoint framework.

4. Evaluation of Previous Techniques

This section provides an evaluation of previously proposed techniques using the NeedlePoint framework on a common set of concurrency bugs.

4.1 Concurrency Bugs

We evaluate the effectiveness of various scheduling policies with the previously known bugs listed in Table 1. These bugs have been widely used in prior research in this area [5, 10, 16, 27, 28]. Although many bug reports provided test cases or patches that introduce sleeps at appropriate places to trigger the bug, we did not patch or modify the application to increase the likelihood of finding bugs. For the memcached bug, we designed a test harness and created various instances of the memcached bug by varying the number of memcached operations performed before performing the increment operation that has the atomicity violation. These instances are listed as $t+x$ in Table 1. We also created an instance of memcached bug where NeedlePoint introduces a schedule point before every memory access and it is listed `am` in Table 1.

4.2 Comparison of Various Scheduling Policies

To compare the bug detection abilities of various scheduling policies in Section 3.2, we ran each application listed in Table 1 with each scheduling policy 100,000 times. We checked each run to see if the bug was triggered. Figure 1 reports the number of executions in which the bug was triggered. Similarly, Figure 2 reports the number of executions that triggered the bug with the different instances of the memcached configurations created by our test harness with the various scheduling policies. Both the graphs have five bars for each bug where each individual bar represents the number of buggy executions.

The bug detection efficacy of the scheduling policies varies with the bug. Simple choices such as random sleep and preemption always are effective for some bugs. From Figure 1, we observe that the random sleep policy performs reasonably well with the memcached bug but does not detect other bugs. We found that random sleep policy works best when the test case is small and the bugs are localized. Further Figure 2 shows that the random sleep policy's bug detection ability decreases with the increase in the amount of work done before the buggy access for the memcached bug.

Figure 1 and Figure 2 show that preemption bounding is reasonably effective in triggering most of the bugs except the Pbzip bug. Preemption bounding requires more executions to trigger some bugs as they execute a large number of schedule points. Figure 1 also shows that AtomFuzzer, which is directed to find atomicity violations, performs better than preemption bounding for many of the atomicity violations.

Our prior work PCT triggers all these bugs with similar or better efficacy than other scheduling policies. Only PCT detected the Pbzip bug. Pbzip uses adhoc synchronization with spin loops to signal when the compression is over. The program crashes with a segmentation fault when the main thread frees a synchronization variable that is later used by one of the other threads. In the presence of such adhoc synchronization, the threads need to be scheduled with a few random choices to trigger the bug. A combination of priority based scheduling with a robust starvation freedom mechanisms enable PCT to trigger the Pbzip bug effectively. Table 2 summarizes the ability of the scheduling policies to trigger the bug at least once in 1000 executions on average. We observe that our prior work PCT triggers all these bugs at least once within the 1000 runs.

4.3 Deficiencies of PCT

As a result of running one thread at a time, PCT suffers from two major problems in testing long running parallel applications. First, running one thread at at time cannot leverage multicores to speedup each execution. Further even on a single core, pathological interactions with PCT scheduling decisions and the OS scheduling decisions can cause significant performance slowdowns. Second, many multithreaded applications that use adhoc synchronization and busy-wait synchronization incur large slowdowns. PCT, which uses priority based scheduling with only one thread executing at any time, causes starvation in the presence of such synchronization idioms. PCT relies NeedlePoint's starvation freedom mechanisms to make progress thereby incurring large slowdowns that effectively

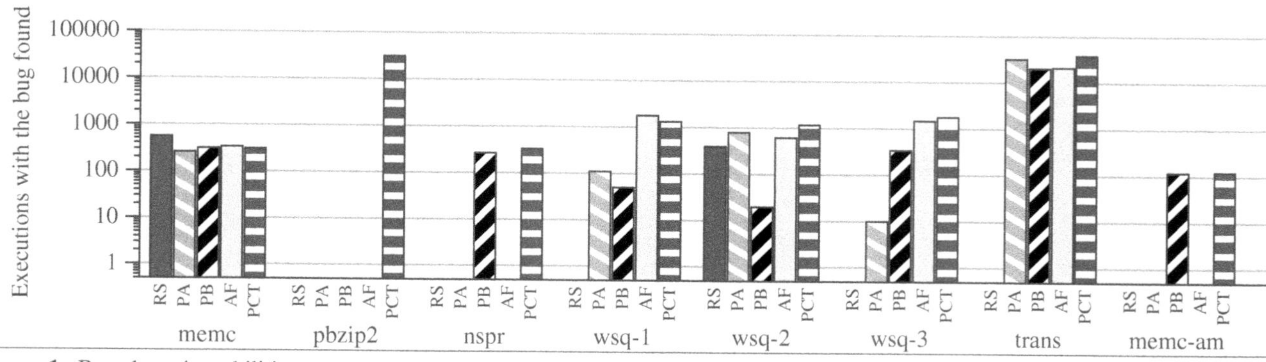

Figure 1. Bug detection abilities on common concurrency bugs for five different scheduling policies described in Section 3.2: Random Sleep (RS), Preemption Always (PA), Preemption Bounding (PB), AtomFuzzer (AF), and Probabilistic Concurrency Testing (PCT).

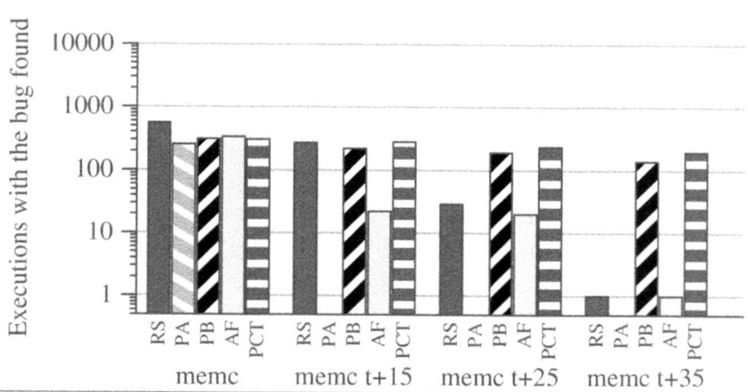

Figure 2. Bug detection ability of various scheduling policies with the variants of the memcached bug generated by the test harness.

Program	Random Sleep	Preemption Always	Preemption Bound	Atom Fuzzer	PCT
Memc	Yes	Yes	Yes	Yes	Yes
Pbzip2	No	No	No	No	Yes
NSPR	No	No	Yes	No	Yes
WSQ-1	No	Yes	No	Yes	Yes
WSQ-2	Yes	Yes	No	Yes	Yes
WSQ-3	No	No	Yes	Yes	Yes
Trans	No	Yes	Yes	Yes	Yes
Memc-am	No	No	Yes	No	Yes

Table 2. Do they trigger the bugs in 1000 runs?

prohibit the usage of PCT to test such applications. To enable testing of large parallel programs with large inputs rather than unit tests, we pursued parallelization of PCT. The key contribution of our parallelization effort is that our parallel PCT (PPCT) algorithm runs multiple threads while retaining the same probabilistic guarantee of PCT running one thread at at time.

5. Parallel PCT (PPCT)

In this section we provide background on the *bug depth* metric defined by PCT and used by our PPCT algorithm to classify concurrency bugs. We subsequently provide the PPCT algorithm for a particular bug depth.

5.1 Background on PCT's Bug Depth

Concurrency bugs in multithreaded software occur when instructions are scheduled in an order not envisioned by the programmer. *Bug depth* is defined as the minimum set of these ordering constraints between instructions from different threads that are sufficient to trigger the bug. It is possible for different sets of ordering constraints to trigger the same bug. In such a case, we focus on the set with the fewest constraints. For bugs of greater depth, more orderings need to enforced by the scheduler to trigger the bug, increasing the hardness of finding it. Figure 3 shows examples of common concurrency errors with ordering constraints, represented by arrows, that are sufficient to trigger the bug. Any schedule that satisfies these ordering constraints is guaranteed to trigger the bug irrespective of how it schedules instructions not relevant to the bug. For the examples in Figure 3 the depth respectively is 1, 2, and 2. In practice, we have found that many concurrency bugs to have small depths [5].

5.2 Intuition Behind the PPCT Algorithm

Both the original PCT algorithm and the PPCT algorithm use thread priorities to probabilistically enforce ordering constraints that drive the program to an error. The key difference between the two algorithms is the number of choices they provide to the adversary, which in our case is the underlying operating system scheduler, to schedule threads at each step.

The PCT algorithm allows the adversary exactly one thread, the highest priority thread, to schedule at each step. In contrast, the PPCT algorithm maintains two sets of threads, a higher priority set and a lower priority set. At each step, the adversary is allowed to pick *any* thread in the higher priority set. If this set is empty, then the adversary is required to pick the highest priority thread in the lower priority set.

In other words, while PCT serializes the execution of all threads, PPCT serializes the execution only of the threads in the lower-priority set. The threads in the higher-priority set can be executed in parallel. Importantly, the PPCT algorithm guarantees that the number of threads in the lower priority set is bounded by the parameter d, the depth of the bug the algorithm is attempting to trigger. Thus, any implementation of the algorithm is required to control the scheduling of only at most d threads, while the operating system is freely allowed to schedule the remaining threads on multiple cores as it deems fit.

Apart from the crucial difference above, the PPCT algorithm functions exactly like the PCT algorithm, assigns random priorities to the threads and changes priorities at randomly chosen points in the execution. We start with an informal description of the PPCT algorithm in the next subsection, before giving precise pseudocode and a proof of the guarantees in Section 6.

5.3 Informal Description of the PPCT Algorithm

Given inputs: number of threads n, total number of dynamic instructions k and the depth of the bug being explored d, PPCT works as follows.

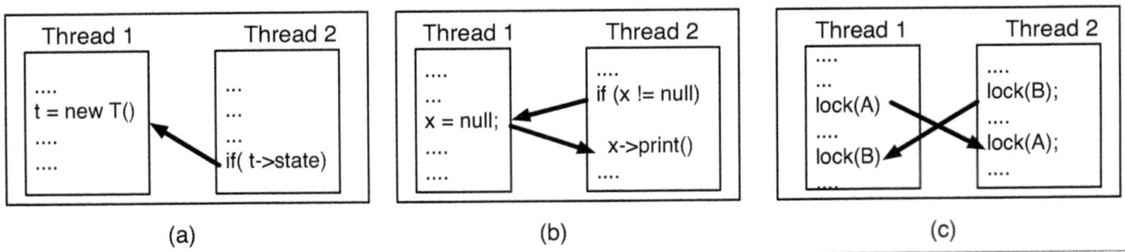

Figure 3. Three typical concurrency bugs and ordering edges sufficient to find each. (A) This ordering bug manifests whenever the test by thread 2 is executed before the initialization by thread 1. (B) This atomicity violation manifests whenever the test by thread 2 executed before the assignment by thread 1, and the latter is executed before the method call by thread 2. (C) This deadlock manifests whenever thread 1 locks A before thread 2, and thread 2 locks B before thread 1.

- **Pick a random low priority thread:** At the beginning of the program, pick a thread uniformly at random and assign it a priority d. In addition, insert this thread into the lower priority set L. Insert all other threads into the higher priority set H.
- **Pick random priority change points:** At the beginning of the program, pick $d-1$ priority change points $k_1, ..., k_{d-1}$ in the range $[1,k]$. Each k_i has an associated priority value of i.
- **Scheduler choice:** At each step, the scheduler picks any non-blocked thread in H to schedule. If H is empty or if all threads in H are blocked, the scheduler picks the highest priority thread in L.
- **Priority change:** After a step, increment a step counter. If the step counter matches k_i for some i, change the priority of the just executed thread to i and insert it into L.

5.4 Coverage Guarantees of PPCT

Given a program with n threads that executes at most k steps, the PPCT algorithm described above finds every bug of depth d with probability at least $\frac{1}{nk^{d-1}}$ in every run of the algorithm. This probabilistic guarantee exactly matches the original PCT algorithm, despite allowing more parallelism. We explain and prove this probabilistic bound in Section 6 below.

5.5 Starvation and Priority Based Scheduling

Not allowing a lower priority thread to execute can cause starvation. In the presence of starvation, to make progress, a lower priority thread must be scheduled for a single step. We randomly choose a thread with priority lower than d to run for a single step (execute one schedule point) by bumping its priority to the highest priority in the system and reverting back the priority of the thread to the original priority when it completes executing the step. We use the mechanisms provided by NeedlePoint to identify when we should make the policy decision to avoid starvation.

6. Proof of PPCT's Probabilistic Guarantees

In this section, we give a detailed description of PPCT and present a proof of its probabilistic guarantee. We start with a high-level informal description of the proof strategy and the differences between PPCT and PCT. We then walk through the proof in detail and fully formalize all concepts (bugs, programs, schedules) in the process.

6.1 Overview

The basic idea is to find bugs by guessing a *directive* that leads to the bug. A directive is essentially a sequence of program points. We say a directive finds a bug if all schedules that follow the directive's sequencing points trigger the bug. Directives exist for all bugs (because if we restrict the scheduler enough, we can guarantee that it finds the bug). The size of the directive (i.e. the number of sequencing points it contains) reflects how hard it is to trigger the bug. We call the size of the smallest directive that can find a given concurrency bug the *depth* of that bug. As explained in Section 5.1, our intuition about typical concurrency bugs suggests that many bugs have a relatively small depth and can thus benefit from a scheduler that is tuned to do well at covering small depths.

Although we know that a directive of size d exists for all bugs of depth d (by definition), in the concurrency testing scenario we do of course not know the actual bugs and which directives will find them. It turns out, however, that PPCT has a reasonable probability of just *guessing* the directive.

In the remainder of this section, we formalize and prove this claim. The basic proof strategy is to construct and compare two schedulers:

- A randomized scheduler that schedules the program under test based on a few random choices. This scheduler has no knowledge about the structure of the program under test or the bug we are targeting.
- A directed scheduler that schedules the program under test based on an explictly supplied directive. This directive identifies points of interest in the program under test, and it prescribes an order in which they should be executed. Note that we did not actually implement such a directed scheduler: its only purpose is to construct a proof.

We then show that given a directive of size d, the randomized scheduler and the directed scheduler produce the same schedule with probability at least $\frac{1}{nk^{d-1}}$ (where n is the number of threads and k is the number of schedule points in the program). This implies that the randomized scheduler finds any bug of depth d with probability at least $\frac{1}{nk^{d-1}}$, without any knowledge about the program or the bug.

6.2 PPCT vs. PCT

Once we understood in what way PCT does in fact require serial execution (it needs to execute the sequencing points of the directive in order) and in what way it does not (threads that are not at a sequencing point can be executed in any order and in parallel), we were able to leave the original algorithm and proof almost completely intact.

Thus the presented algorithms for the randomized and the directed scheduler are exactly the same as in [5] except for one line, where the scheduler is now allowed to pick from more threads. The proof of the probabilistic guarantees is also exactly the same, except for the proof of Lemma 12, which shows that the scheduling restrictions we removed (by providing more choices to the scheduler) do not compromise the invariants of the original algorithm.

Although these changes are few in number and localized, they are difficult to understand out of context. Thus we reproduce the complete proof here.

Require: program P, $d \geq 0$
Require: $n \geq maxthreads(P)$, $k \geq maxsteps(P)$
Require: **random variables** $k_1, \ldots, k_{d-1} \in \{1, \ldots, k\}$
Require: **random variable** $\pi \in Permutations(n)$

1: **procedure** $RandS(n,k,d)$ **begin**
2: **var** S : schedule
3: **var** p : **array**[n] **of** $\mathbb{N}$
4: $S \leftarrow \varepsilon$
// set initial priorities
5: **for all** $t \in \{1, \ldots, n\}$ **do**
6: $p[t] \leftarrow d + \pi(t) - 1$
7: **end for**
8: **while** $en_P(S) \neq \emptyset$ **do**
9: /* schedule thread of admissible priority */
10: $t \leftarrow$ element of $en_P(S)$ such that $p[t] > d$ or $p[t]$ maximal
11: $S \leftarrow S\,t$
/* are we at priority change point? */
12: **for all** $i \in \{1, \ldots, d-1\}$ **do**
13: **if** $length(S) = k_i$ **then**
14: $p[t] = d - i$
15: **end if**
16: **end for**
17: **end while**
18: **return** S
19: **end**

Figure 4. The PPCT randomized scheduler.

6.3 Definitions

We briefly recount some standard notation for operations on sequences. Let T be any set. Define T^* to be the set of finite sequences of elements from T. For a sequence $S \in T^*$, define $length(S)$ to be the length of the sequence. We let ε denote the sequence of length 0. For a sequence $S \in T^*$ and a number n such that $0 \leq n < length(S)$, let $S[n]$ be the n-th element of S (where counting starts with 0). For $t \in T$ and $S \in T^*$, we write $t \in S$ as a shorthand for $\exists m : S[m] = t$. For any $S \subset T^*$ and for any n, m such that $0 \leq n \leq m \leq length(S)$, let $S[n,m]$ be the contiguous subsequence of S starting at position n and ending at (and including) position m. For two sequences $S_1, S_2 \in T^*$, we let $S_1 S_2$ denote the concatenation as usual. We do not distinguish between sequences of length one and the respective element. We call a sequence $S_1 \in T^*$ a *prefix* of a sequence $S \in T^*$ if there exists a sequence $S_2 \in T^*$ such that $S = S_1 S_2$. A set of sequences $P \subseteq T^*$ is called *prefix-closed* if for any $S \in P$, all prefixes of S are also in P.

DEFINITION 1. *Define $T = \mathbb{N}$ to be the set of thread identifiers. Define $Sched = T^*$ to be the set of all schedules. Define a* program *to be a prefix-closed subset of Sched. For a given program $P \subseteq Sched$, we say a schedule $S \in P$ is* complete *if it is not the prefix of any schedule in P other than itself, and* partial *otherwise.*

Thus, we represent a program abstractly by its schedules, and each schedule is simply a sequence of thread identifiers. For example, the sequence 1221 represents the schedule where thread 1 takes one step, followed by two steps by thread 2, followed by another step of thread 1. We think of schedules as an abstract representation of the program state. Not all threads can be scheduled from all states, as they may be blocked. We say a thread is enabled in a state if it can be scheduled from that state.

DEFINITION 2. *Let $P \subseteq Sched$ be a program. For a schedule $S \in P$, define $en_P(S)$ to be the set $\{t \in T \mid St \in P\}$. Define $maxsteps(P) = \max\{length(S) \mid S \in P\}$ and $maxthreads(P) = \max\{S[i] \mid S \in P\}$ (or ∞ if unbounded).*

Finally, we represent a concurrency bug abstractly as the set of schedules that find it:

DEFINITION 3. *Let $P \subseteq Sched$ be a program. Define a* bug *B of P to be a subset $B \subset P$.*

6.4 The Algorithm

We now introduce the PPCT randomized scheduler (Fig. 4), which is identical to the original PCT scheduler [5] except for line 10, in which the scheduler now has more choice when picking the next thread to schedule.

As in the original algorithm, we expect $RandS(n,k,d)$ to be called with a conservative estimate for n (number of threads) and k (number of steps). During the progress of the algorithm, we store the current schedule in the variable S, and the current thread priorities in an array p of size n. The thread priorities are initially assigned random values (chosen by the random permutation π).

In each iteration, we pick an admissible thread for scheduling. As in the original PCT algorithm, we can always pick the enabled thread of maximal priority to execute next. In addition, however, we also allow any thread to be picked whose priority is larger than d. [2] Once we have (nondeterministically) picked a thread t, we execute it for one step. Then we check if we have reached a priority change point (determined by the random values k_i), and if so, we change the priority of t accordingly. This process repeats until no more threads are enabled (that is, we have reached a deadlock or the program has terminated).

6.5 Probabilistic Coverage Guarantee

In this section, we precisely state and then prove the probabilistic coverage guarantees for our randomized scheduler, in three steps. First, we introduce a general mechanism for identifying dynamic events in threads, which is a necessary prerequisite for defining ordering constraints on such events. Next, we build on that basis to define the depth of a bug as the minimum number of ordering constraints on thread events that will reliably reveal the bug. Finally, we state and prove the core theorem.

6.5.1 Event Labeling

The first problem is to clarify how we define the events that participate in the ordering constraints. For this purpose, we introduce a general definition of event labeling. Event labels must be unique within each execution, but may vary across executions. Essentially, an event labeling E defines a set of labels L_E (where each label $a \in L_E$ belongs to a particular thread $thread_E(a)$) and a function $next_E(S,t)$ that tells us what label (if any) the thread t is going to emit if scheduled next after schedule S. More formally, we define:

DEFINITION 4. *Let P be a program. An* event labeling *E is a triple $(L_E, thread_E, next_E)$ where L_E is a set of labels, $thread_E$ is a function $L_E \rightarrow T$, and $next_E$ is a function $P \times T \rightarrow (L_E \cup \{\perp\})$, such that the following conditions are satisfied:*

1. *(Affinity) If $next_E(S,t) = a$ for some $a \in L_E$, then $thread_E(a) = t$.*
2. *(Stability) If $next_E(S_1,t) \neq next_E(S_1 S_2,t)$, then $t \in S_2$.*
3. *(Uniqueness) If $next_E(S_1,t) = next_E(S_1 S_2,t) = a$ for some $a \in L_E$, then $t \notin S_2$.*
4. *(NotFirst) $next_E(\varepsilon,t) = \perp$ for all $t \in T$.*

Sometimes, we would like to talk about labels that have already been emitted in a schedule. For this purpose we define the auxiliary

[2] This scheduling policy corresponds precisely to the informal description in Section 5.3, where (1) all threads with priority larger than d are in the high priority set and (2) all other threads are in the low priority set.

functions $label_E$ and $labels_E$ as follows. For $S \in P$ and $0 \leq m < length(S)$, we define $label_E(S,m) = a$ if the label a is being emitted at position m, and we define $labels_E(S)$ to be the set of all labels emitted in S (more formally, $label_E(S,m) = a$ if $next_E(S[0,m-1],S[m]) = a$, and $label_E(S,m) = \perp$ otherwise; and $labels_E(S) = \{label_E(S,m) \mid 0 \leq m < length(S)\}$).

6.5.2 Bug Depth

We now formalize the notion of ordering constraints and bug depth that we motivated earlier. Compared to our informal introduction from Section 5.1, there are two variations worth mentioning. First, we generalize each edge constraint (a,b) (where a and b are event labels) to allow multiple sources (A,b), where A is a set of labels all of which have to be scheduled before b to satisfy the constraint. Second, because we are using dynamically generated labels as our events, we require that the ordering constraints are sufficient to guide the scheduler to the bug without needing to know about additional constraints implied by the program structure (as motivated by the example in Fig. 3).

We formulate the notion of a *directive* D of size d, which consists of a labeling and d constraints. The idea is that a directive can guide a schedule towards a bug, and that the depth of a bug is defined as the minimal size of a directive that is guaranteed to find it.

DEFINITION 5. *For some $d \geq 1$, a directive D for a program P is a tuple $(E,A_1,b_1,A_2,b_2,\ldots,A_d,b_d)$ where E is an event labeling for P, where $A_1,\ldots,A_d \subseteq L_E$ are sets of labels, and where $b_1,\ldots b_d \in L_E$ are labels that are pairwise distinct ($b_i \neq b_j$ for $i \neq j$). The size of D is d and is denoted by $size(D)$.*

DEFINITION 6. *Let P be a program and let D be a directive for P. We say a schedule $S \in P$* violates *the directive D if either (1) there exists an $i \in \{1,\ldots,d\}$ and an $a \in A_i$ such that $b_i \in labels_E(S)$, but $a \notin labels_E(S)$, or (2) there exist $1 \leq i < j \leq d$ such that $b_j \in labels_E(S)$, but $b_i \notin labels_E(S)$. We say a schedule $S \in P$* satisfies *D if it does not violate D, and if $b_i \in labels_E(S)$ for all $1 \leq i \leq d$.*

DEFINITION 7. *Let P be a program, B be a bug of P, and D be a directive for P. We say D* guarantees *B if and only if the following conditions are satisfied:*

1. *For any partial schedule $S \in P$ that does not violate D, there exists a thread $t \in en_P(S)$ such that St does not violate D.*
2. *Any complete schedule S that does not violate D does satisfy D and is in B.*

DEFINITION 8. *Let P be a program, and let B be a bug of P. Then we define the* depth *of B to be*

$$depth(B) = \min\{size(D) \mid D \text{ guarantees } B\}$$

6.5.3 Coverage Theorem

The following theorem states the key guarantee: the probability that one invocation $RandS(n,k,d)$ of our randomized scheduler (Fig. 4) detects a bug of depth d is at least $\frac{1}{nk^{d-1}}$.

THEOREM 9. *Let P be a program with a bug B of depth d, let $n \geq maxthreads(P)$, and let $k \geq maxsteps(P)$. Then*

$$\mathbf{Pr}[RandS(n,k,d) \in B] \;\geq\; \frac{1}{nk^{d-1}}$$

PROOF. Because B has depth d, we know there exists a directive D for B of size d. Of course, in any real situation, we do not know D, but by Def. 8 we know that it exists, so we can use it for the purposes of this proof. Essentially, we show that even without knowing D, here is a relatively high probability that $RandS(n,k,d)$ follows the directive D by pure chance. To prove that, we first construct an

```
Require: program P, d ≥ 0
Require: n >= maxthreads(P)
Require: k_1,...,k_{d-1} ≥ 1
Require: π ∈ Permutations(n)
Require: random variables k_1,...,k_{d-1} ∈ {1,...,k}
Require: random variable π ∈ Permutations(n)
Require: bug B
Require: directive D = (E, A_1, b_1, ..., A_d, b_d) for B

 1: procedure DirS(n,k,d,D) begin
 2:   var S : schedule
 3:   var p : array[n] of ℕ
 4:   S ← ε
      // set initial priorities
 5:   for all t ∈ {1,...,n} do
 6:     p[t] ← d + π(t) − 1
 7:   end for
 8:   [ assert: p[thread_E(b_1)] = d ]
 9:   while en_P(S) ≠ ∅ do
        /* schedule thread of admissible priority */
10:     t ← element of en_P(S) such that p[t] > d or p[t] maximal
11:     S ← S t
        /* change priority first time we peek a b-label */
12:     for all i ∈ {1,...,d−1} do
13:       if next_E(S,t) = b_{i+1} and p[t] ≠ d − i then
14:         p[t] = d − i
15:         [ assert: length(S) = k_i ]
16:       end if
17:     end for
18:   end while
19:   return S
20: end
```

Figure 5. The directed scheduler.

auxiliary algorithm $DirS(n,k,d,D)$ (Fig. 5) that uses the same random variables as *RandS*, but has knowledge of D and constructs its schedule accordingly.

Comparing the two programs, we see two differences. First, Line 13 uses a condition based on D to decide when to change priorities. In fact, this is where we make sure the call to $DirS(n,k,d,D)$ is following the directive D: whenever we catch a glimpse of thread t executing one of the labels b_i (for $i > 1$), we change the priority of t accordingly. Second, *DirS* has assertions which are not present in *RandS*. We use these assertions for this proof to reason about the probability that *DirS* guesses the right random choices. The intended behavior is that *DirS* fails (terminating immediately) if it executes a failing assertion.

The following three lemmas are key to our proof construction. The proofs of these lemmas are unchanged from the original proofs [5] except for Lemma 12, and the proofs of these lemmas are included in the subsections 6.5.4 through 6.5.7 below.

LEMMA 10. *The probability that $DirS(n,k,d,D)$ succeeds is at least $\frac{1}{nk^{d-1}}$.*

LEMMA 11. *If $DirS(n,k,d,D)$ succeeds, then*

$$RandS(P,n,d) = DirS(n,k,d,D).$$

LEMMA 12. *If $DirS(n,k,d,D)$ succeeds, it returns a schedule that finds the bug.*

We can formally assemble these lemmas into a proof as follows. Our sample space consists of all valuations of the random variables π and $k_1,\ldots,k_{d-1}$. By construction, each variable is distributed uniformly and independently (thus, the probability of each valuation is equal to $n!k^{d-1}$). Define $\mathcal{S}$ to be the event (that is, set of all valuations) such that $DirS(n,k,d,D)$ succeeds, and let $\overline{\mathcal{S}}$ be its complement.

$$
\begin{aligned}
&\mathbf{Pr}[RandS(n,k,d) \in B] \\
&= \mathbf{Pr}[RandS(n,k,d) \in B \mid \mathcal{S}] \cdot \mathbf{Pr}[\mathcal{S}] \\
&\quad + \mathbf{Pr}[RandS(n,k,d) \in B \mid \overline{\mathcal{S}}] \cdot \mathbf{Pr}[\overline{\mathcal{S}}] \\
&\geq \mathbf{Pr}[RandS(n,k,d) \in B \mid \mathcal{S}] \cdot \mathbf{Pr}[\mathcal{S}] \\
&= \mathbf{Pr}[DirS(n,k,d,D) \in B \mid \mathcal{S}] \cdot \mathbf{Pr}[\mathcal{S}] && \text{(by Lemma 11)} \\
&= 1 \cdot \mathbf{Pr}[\mathcal{S}] && \text{(by Lemma 12)} \\
&\geq \frac{1}{nk^{d-1}} && \text{(by Lemma 10)}
\end{aligned}
$$

□

6.5.4 Auxiliary Lemmas

To prepare for proving the three core lemmas used in the proof above, we state and prove the following four auxiliary lemmas.

LEMMA 13. *If $next_E(S,t) = b_j$ right before executing line 11 of $DirS(n,k,d,D)$, and if S does not violate D, then $p[t] = d-j+1$.*

PROOF. Distinguish cases $j > 1$ and $j = 1$.

Case $j > 1$. Def. 4 implies that the first action by any thread is not labeled, so our assumption $next_E(S,t) = b_j$ implies that there is a $m < length(S)$ such that $S[m] = t$. Choose a maximal such m. Then we know $next_E(S[0,m],t) = b_j$ (because Def. 4 implies that the next label does not change if other threads are scheduled). Thus, in the iteration that added $S[m]$ to the schedule, the test $next_E(S[0,m],t) = b_{i+1}$ on line 13 must have evaluated to true for $i = j-1$ (and for no other i, because the b_i are pairwise distinct by Def. 4). So we must have assigned $p[t] \leftarrow d-j+1$ on line 14. Because we chose m maximal, t was never scheduled after that, so its priority did not change and must thus still be $p[t] = d-j+1$.

Case $j = 1$. If we are about to execute line 11, then the assertion on line 8 must have succeeded, so at that time it was the case that $p[t] = d-j+1$. After that, $p[t]$ could not have changed: suppose line 14 was executed at some point to change $p[t]$. Say the value of variable S at that point was $S[0,m]$. Then the condition $next_E(S[0,m],t) = b_{i+1}$ on line 13 must have evaluated to true for some i. Now, because we know $next_E(S,t) = b_j$ and because $b_j \neq b_{i+1}$ (by Def. 4), there must exist a $m' > m$ such that $S[m'] = t$ (by Def. 4). But that implies $label_E(S,m') = b_{i+1}$, and since $b_j \notin labels_E(S)$, S violates D which contradicts the assumption. □

LEMMA 14. *Let $1 \leq t' \leq n$, and let $p[t'] = d-j+1$ for some $j \geq 2$ at the time line 10 is executed. Then either $b_j \in labels_E(S)$, or $next_E(S,t') = b_j$.*

PROOF. The only way to assign priorities less than d is through the assignment $p[t] = d-i$ on line 14. So this line must have executed with $t = t'$ and $i = j-1$. Thus, the condition $next_E(S,t) = b_{i+1}$ was true at that point, which is identical to $next_E(S,t') = b_j$. If t' is not scheduled after that point, this condition is still true; conversely, if t' is scheduled, then it must execute the label b_j, implying $b_j \in labels_E(S)$. □

LEMMA 15. *During the execution of $DirS(n,k,d,D)$ the assertion on line 15 is executed at most once for each $i \in \{1,\ldots,d-1\}$.*

PROOF. Consider the first time the assertion $length(S) = k_i$ on line 15 is executed for a given i. Then it must the case that $next_E(S,t) = b_{i+1}$. Because labels don't repeat, the only chance for this condition to be true again is for the same i (because the b_i are pairwise distinct) during the immediately following iterations of the while loop, and only if threads other than t are scheduled. But in that scenario, the priority $p[t]$ does not change, so the second part $p[t] \neq d-i$ of the condition on line 13 can not be satisfied. □

LEMMA 16. *If $DirS(n,k,d,D)$ succeeds, it executes the assertion $length(S) = k_i$ on line 15 at least once for each $i \in \{1,\ldots,d-1\}$.*

PROOF. Because $DirS(n,k,d,D)$ succeeds, it produces a complete schedule S which does not violate D. Thus, $b_i \in labels_E(S)$ for all $i \in \{1,\ldots,d\}$. Thus, for each $i \in \{2,\ldots,d\}$, there must be an m such that $S[0,m], thread_E(b_i)) = b_i$. Thus, the condition on line 13 must be satisfied at least once for each $i \in \{1,\ldots,d-1\}$, so we know the assertion $length(S) = k_i$ on line 15 gets executed for each $i \in \{1,\ldots,d-1\}$. □

6.5.5 Proof of Lemma 11

To prove the claim, we now show that the two respective conditions on lines 13

$$length(S) = k_i \tag{1}$$

$$next_E(S,t) = b_{i+1} \text{ and } p[t] \neq d-i \tag{2}$$

evaluate the same way, for any given iteration of the while and for loops (identified by current values of S and i, respectively). Clearly, if (2) evaluates to true for some S and i, $DirS$ executes the assertion on line 15, thus guaranteeing that (1) also evaluates to true. Conversely, if (1) evaluates to true for some S and i, consider that $DirS$ must execute an assertion of the form $length(S') = k_i$ at some point (by Lemma 16); but it turns out that this must happen in the very same iteration because the length of S uniquely identifies the iteration of the while loop, so the condition (2) must be satisfied.

6.5.6 Proof of Lemma 10

$DirS(n,k,d,D)$ succeeds if and only if if (1) the assertion $p[thread_E(b_1)] = d$ on line 8 passes, and (2) the assertion $length(S) = k_i$ on line 15 passes every time it is executed. The probability of the former passing is $1/n$ (because a random permutation assigns the lowest priority to any given thread with probability $1/n$), while the probability of each latter passing is $1/k$ (because the random variables k_i range over $\{1,\ldots,k\}$). By Lemma 15, the assertions $length(S) = k_i$ are executed at most once for each i. Thus, all of the assertions involve independent random variables, so we can multiply the individual success probabilities to obtain a total success probability for $DirS$ of at least $(1/n) \cdot (1/k)^{d-1}$.

6.5.7 Proof of Lemma 12

To prove the lemma, we will first prove that the following invariant holds during the execution of $DirS(n,k,d,D)$:

the variable S is a schedule that does not violate D.

Clearly, this invariant implies the claim of the lemma (the schedule returned in the end finds the bug), because if the while-loop terminates, S is a complete schedule, and by Def. 6, any complete schedule that does not violate D is in B.

Proving this invariant for PPCT is slightly harder than for PCT, since the scheduler can pick any thread with priority larger than d, not just the highest priority thread. However, it turns out that this has no ill effect since only threads of priority d or lower are capable of breaking the invariant!

More formally, we can prove the invariant as follows, proceeding indirectly. If S violates D, the first moment it does so must be right after executing $S \leftarrow St$ on line 11. Now, consider the state right before that. S does not violate D, but St does, so by Def. 5, there exists an i such that $next_E(S,t) = b_i$. By Lemma 13 this implies that $p[t] = d - i + 1$. Now, by Def. 6 there must exist an alternate choice $t' \in en_P(S)$ such that St' does not violate D. However, the scheduler did not pick t', but t, and t has priority at most d, so t' must have priority less than d. Therefore $p[t'] = d - j + 1$ for some $j > i$. By Lemma 14, that implies that either $b_j \in labels_E(S)$ or $b_j \in next_E(S,t')$. But both of these lead to a contradiction: $b_j \in labels_E(S)$ means that S violates D (because $b_i \notin labels_E(S)$), and $b_j \in next_E(S,t')$ means that St' violates D.

7. Experimental Evaluation of PPCT

The goal of the experimental evaluation of PPCT is to (1) evaluate the effectiveness of PPCT with respect to bug finding and (2) understand and evaluate the runtime speedups with PPCT algorithm compared to PCT. We implemented PPCT using the NeedlePoint framework. The PPCT scheduling policy obtains the set of non-blocked threads from NeedlePoint and chooses the thread to be scheduled at any given time. PPCT ensures starvation freedom by scheduling one of the lower priority threads for a single schedule point when indicated by the NeedlePoint starvation freedom policy. Using NeedlePoint, implementing a complete PPCT scheduling policy is just 230 lines of C++ code.

7.1 Effectiveness in Finding Bugs

Figure 7.2 shows the effectiveness of PPCT in comparison to PCT in terms of finding concurrency bugs in Table 1. The left and right bars show the number of executions in which the bug was detected by PPCT and PCT respectively. The graph shows us that PPCT finds concurrency bugs either as effectively as PCT and in many cases better than PCT. This empirically validates the fact that parallel bug exploration with PPCT still retains the detection guarantees formally proved in Section 6.

We found two new bugs when we were testing multithreaded applications with PPCT. During our experimentation with Parsec benchmarks, we found a concurrency bug in the Parsec 2.0 benchmark Streamcluster. The root cause of the bug was a missing barrier that caused non-deterministic outputs. This bug was simultaneously discovered by others resulting in a patch that is distributed with the latest Parsec versions. We also found a new bug in the Transmission BitTorrent client in which a platform specific robustness assert was triggered.

7.2 Performance Evaluation

To evaluate the execution time performance overhead of testing parallel applications, we use benchmarks from the Parsec benchmark suite [4]. We also added the Pbzip2 that performs parallel compression as it is included in our bug benchmarks. We use the native inputs to run the Parsec benchmarks. We performed all the experiments on a quad-core dual-socket Intel Core 2 machine (eight cores total). In our performance experiments with multiple cores, we restrict the number of threads to be equal to the number of cores in the system.

There are three sources of runtime overhead incurred when running any scheduling policy with NeedlePoint: (1) binary instrumentation overhead, (2) overhead due to NeedlePoint's mechanism to identify blocked threads, and (3) overhead due to serializations caused by the underlying scheduling policy. Introducing a schedule point using Pin before synchronization operations and atomic operations without doing anything at these schedule points slows down the program by 2× compared to native execution on eight cores. Further, introducing a schedule point at every memory access along with the synchronization accesses introduces another 5× slowdown. These represent the overhead of performing binary instrumentation.

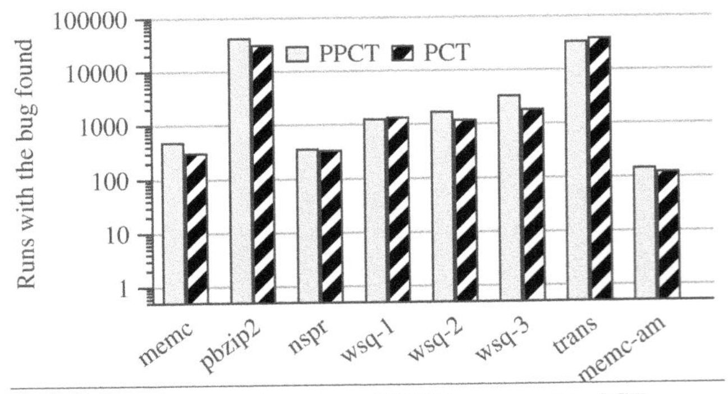

Figure 6. Bug detection of PPCT compared to PCT.

The overheads due to NeedlePoint's mechanisms for identifying blocked threads and scheduling policy serializations are dependent on the individual scheduling policies. Further, NeedlePoint mechanism's overhead for identifying blocked threads can be reduced in the presence of more information about synchronization operations. Reducing the serializations in the scheduling policy will reduce the third source of overhead. PPCT runs multiple threads and reduces the overhead due to serializations with PCT.

Figure 7 presents the execution time overhead of running PCT and PPCT over native execution on eight cores (smaller bars are better as they represent lower runtime overheads). The graph contains three bars for each benchmark. The height of the leftmost bar represents the overhead of running PCT on eight cores. On an average, the slowdown with PCT is 34× compared to the native execution on eight cores.

The height of the middle bar represents the overhead of running PPCT on a single core (which we performed by pinning all the threads in the process to a single core). It shows that running PPCT even on a single core reduces a significant portion of the overhead with PCT. This reduction is attributed to two reasons: (1) real programs have busy wait synchronization and in the presence of such constructs, the programs makes slow progress while running one thread at a time and (2) the underlying operating system scheduler has more flexibility to choose among the enabled threads to be run with PPCT when compared to PCT. On an average, PPCT on a single core incurs an overhead of 11× on a average compared to native execution on eight cores. The height of the rightmost bar in Figure 7 presents the overhead of PPCT running on eight cores. On an average, the slowdown with PPCT is 6× compared to native execution on eight cores.

PPCT serializes at most d threads when performing an exploration to trigger a bug of depth d. In contrast, PCT serializes all the threads. Figure 8 reports the speedup obtained with PPCT when compared to PCT for executions with various bug depths running on eight cores. There are four bars for each benchmark representing speedups over PCT exploration for bug depths from 1 to 4. On an average, PPCT provides 439%, 353%, 278% and 168% speedups on eight cores when compared to PCT for executions with bug depths 1, 2, 3 and 4 respectively. These results show that PPCT can provide significant speedups over PCT even for higher bug depth explorations. This speedup likely encourages the testing of long running parallel programs with PPCT even in the late stages of testing.

7.3 Testing with Real World Applications

Our goal is to enable controlled scheduling to be applied to real-world applications. However, we found PCT suffers debilitating slowdowns as a result of running one thread at a time, which prevented us from testing large real-world applications such as the Chrome web browser, the Intel Thread Building Blocks (TBB) test

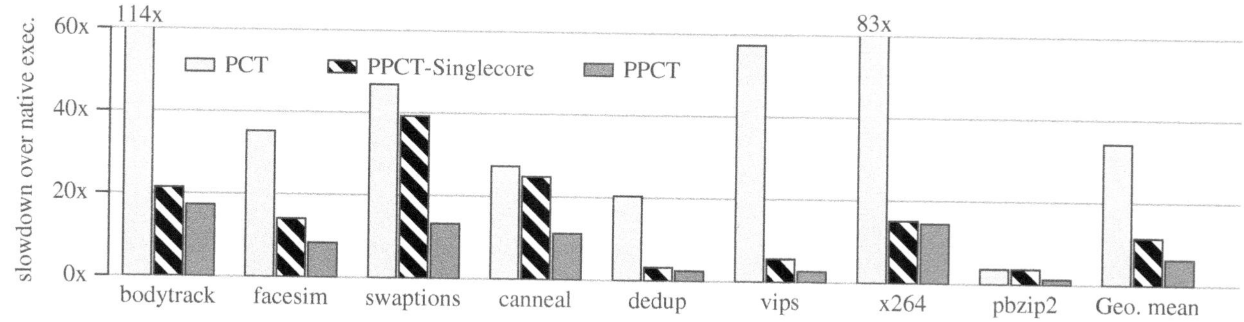

Figure 7. Runtime slowdown of PCT, PPCT on a single core and PPCT when compared to native multithreaded execution.

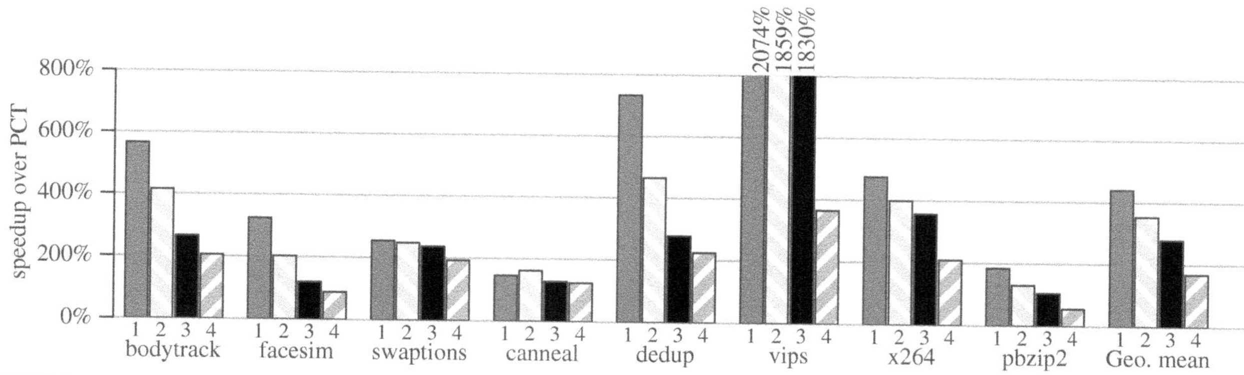

Figure 8. PPCT speedup over PCT that on a multicore machine for explorations with various bug depths. Bug depth of each PPCT exploration is indicated at the bottom of the bar.

suite, and applications using the LevelDB key value store. While experimenting with the Chrome browser, we found that Chrome creates approximately 30 threads in the single process mode, and PCT was executing the operations extremely slowly running one thread at a time. Further inspection revealed that starvation with PCT in the presence of busy-waiting synchronization also added additional slowdowns. These slowdowns resulted in browser warnings and prevented us from successfully applying PCT to Chrome. In contrast, PPCT's ability to execute multiple threads reduces the performance overhead significantly, enabling us to successfully test the Chrome web browser with PPCT without triggering browser warnings.

8. Related Work

Existing work on concurrency bug detection widely falls into best effort detection and detection with coverage guarantees. A commonly used best effort technique is stress testing where a program is run multiple times under heavy loads to trigger crashes. To introduce scheduling variety, researchers have proposed various heuristics to (1) detect suspicious activity in a program (such as variable access patterns that indicate potential atomicity violations [15, 16, 23], typestate errors [8], crashes [28] or lock acquisition orderings that indicate potential deadlocks [12]) and (2) direct the schedule towards suspected bugs [11, 22].

Other approaches such model checking [6] systematically enumerate the possible schedules either exhaustively or within some bound, such as the bound on the length of the execution [9] or the number of preemptions [21] and provide mathematical guarantees. Burckhardt et. al [5] proposed a randomized algorithm for schedule selection providing probabilistic guarantees of finding a bug in every run of the algorithm. All these prior techniques that provide guarantees run one thread at a time making them impractical for testing highly parallel applications and require mechanisms to carefully prevent starvation. PPCT is primarily motivated by the need to achieve the scalability of the stress and heuristic-directed testing without losing the ability to provide coverage guarantees.

9. Conclusion

This paper compared several previously proposed techniques for concurrency bug detection using a common set of concurrency bugs on a common framework. We found that simple policies do work well for concurrency bugs that are localized but not so well for hidden bugs. For hidden bugs, we propose PPCT, that not only detects these bugs but also detects them while running programs more than fives times faster than the serial PCT while retaining the mathematical coverage guarantees. Together, NeedlePoint and PPCT provide a framework and a scheduling policy for testing large real-world programs.

Acknowledgments

The authors thank Nicholas Jalbert and Jie Yu for providing information about RADBench and sharing the concurrency bugs respectively. We also thank the reviewers for their feedback on the paper. This paper is based upon work supported by the National Science Foundation (NSF) under Grant No. CCF-0644197 and CCF-0905464. Any opinions, findings and conclusions or recommendations expressed in this paper are those of the authors and do not necessarily reflect the views of NSF.

References

[1] Helgrind: A Thread Error Detector. `http://valgrind.org/docs/manual/hg-manual.html`.

[2] Intel Thread Checker. `http://software.intel.com/en-us/articles/intel-thread-checker-documentation/`.

[3] S. Adve and K. Gharachorloo. Shared Memory Consistency Models: A Tutorial. *Computer*, 29(12):66–76, 1996.

[4] C. Bienia. *Benchmarking Modern Multiprocessors*. PhD thesis, Princeton University, January 2011.

[5] S. Burckhardt, P. Kothari, M. Musuvathi, and S. Nagarakatte. A Randomized Scheduler with Probabilistic Guarantees of Finding Bugs. In *Proceedings of the 15th International Conference on Architectural Support for Programming Languages and Operating Systems (ASPLOS)*, 2010.

[6] E. Clarke, O. Grumberg, and D. Peled. *Model Checking*. MIT Press, 1999.

[7] O. Edelstein, E. Farchi, E. Goldin, Y. Nir, G. Ratsaby, and S. Ur. Framework for testing multi-threaded Java programs. *Concurrency and Computation: Practice and Experience*, 15(3–5):485–499, 2003.

[8] Q. Gao, W. Zhang, Z. Chen, M. Zheng, and F. Qin. 2ndStrike: Toward Manifesting Hidden Concurrency Typestate Bugs. In *Proceedings of the 16th International Conference on Architectural Support for Programming Languages and Operating Systems (ASPLOS)*, 2011.

[9] P. Godefroid. Model Checking for Programming Languages using VeriSoft. In *Proceedings of the 24th ACM Symposium on Principles of Programming Languages (POPL)*, 1997.

[10] N. Jalbert, C. Pereira, G. Pokam, and K. Sen. RADBench: A Concurrency Bug Benchmark Suite. In *Proceedings of the 3rd USENIX Conference on Hot Topics in Parallelism (HotPar)*, 2011.

[11] P. Joshi, M. Naik, C.-S. Park, and K. Sen. CalFuzzer: An Extensible Active Testing Framework for Concurrent Programs. In *Proceedings of the 21st International Conference on Computer Aided Verification (CAV)*, 2009.

[12] P. Joshi, C.-S. Park, K. Sen, and M. Naik. A Randomized Dynamic Program Analysis Technique for Detecting Real Deadlocks. In *Proceedings of the ACM SIGPLAN 2009 Conference on Programming Language Design and Implementation (PLDI)*, 2009.

[13] H. Jula, D. Tralamazza, C. Zamfir, and G. Candea. Deadlock Immunity: Enabling Systems to Defend Against Deadlocks. In *Proceedings of the 8th USENIX Symposium on Operating Systems Design and Implementation (OSDI)*, 2008.

[14] S. Lu, S. Park, E. Seo, and Y. Zhou. Learning from Mistakes: A Comprehensive Study on Real World Concurrency Bug Characteristics. In *Proceedings of the 13th International Conference on Architectural Support for Programming Languages and Operating Systems (ASPLOS)*, 2008.

[15] S. Lu, J. Tucek, F. Qin, and Y. Zhou. AVIO: Detecting Atomicity Violations via Access Interleaving Invariants. In *Proceedings of the 12th International Conference on Architectural Support for Programming Languages and Operating Systems (ASPLOS)*, 2006.

[16] B. Lucia and L. Ceze. Finding Concurrency Bugs with Context-Aware Communication Graphs. In *Proceedings of the 42nd Annual IEEE/ACM International Symposium on Microarchitecture (MICRO)*, 2009.

[17] C.-K. Luk, R. Cohn, R. Muth, H. Patil, A. Klauser, G. Lowney, S. Wallace, V. J. Reddi, and K. Hazelwood. Pin: Building Customized Program Analysis Tools with Dynamic Instrumentation. In *Proceedings of the ACM SIGPLAN 2005 Conference on Programming Language Design and Implementation (PLDI)*, 2005.

[18] J. Manson, W. Pugh, and S. Adve. The Java Memory Model. In *Proceedings of The 32nd ACM SIGPLAN/SIGACT Symposium on Principles of Programming Languages (POPL)*, 2005.

[19] M. Musuvathi and S. Qadeer. Iterative Context Bounding for Systematic Testing of Multithreaded Programs. In *Proceedings of the ACM SIGPLAN 2007 Conference on Programming Language Design and Implementation (PLDI)*, 2007.

[20] M. Musuvathi and S. Qadeer. Fair Stateless Model Checking. In *Proceedings of the ACM SIGPLAN 2008 Conference on Programming Language Design and Implementation (PLDI)*, 2008.

[21] M. Musuvathi, S. Qadeer, T. Ball, G. Basler, P. A. Nainar, and I. Neamtiu. Finding and Reproducing Heisenbugs in Concurrent Programs. In *Proceedings of the 8th USENIX Symposium on Operating Systems Design and Implementation (OSDI)*, 2008.

[22] C.-S. Park and K. Sen. Randomized Active Atomicity Violation Detection in Concurrent Programs. In *Proceedings of the 16th ACM SIGSOFT International Symposium on the Foundations of Software Engineering (FSE)*, 2008.

[23] S. Park, S. Lu, and Y. Zhou. CTrigger: Exposing Atomicity Violation Bugs from their Hiding Places. In *Proceedings of the 14th International Conference on Architectural Support for Programming Languages and Operating Systems (ASPLOS)*, 2009.

[24] K. Sen. Effective Random Testing of Concurrent Programs. In *Proceedings of 22nd IEEE/ACM International Conference on Automated Software Engineering (ASE)*, 2007.

[25] K. Sen. Race Directed Random Testing of Concurrent Programs. In *SIGPLAN Conference on Programming Language Design and Implementation (PLDI)*, 2008.

[26] W. Xiong, S. Park, J. Zhang, Y. Zhou, and Z. Ma. Ad Hoc Synchronization Considered Harmful. In *Proceedings of the 9th USENIX Symposium on Operating Systems Design and Implementation (OSDI)*, 2010.

[27] J. Yu and S. Narayanasamy. A Case for an Interleaving Constrained Shared-Memory Multi-Processor. In *Proceedings of the 36th Annual International Symposium on Computer Architecture (ISCA)*, 2009.

[28] W. Zhang, C. Sun, and S. Lu. ConMem: Detecting Severe Concurrency Bugs through an Effect-Oriented Approach. In *Proceedings of the 15th International Conference on Architectural Support for Programming Languages and Operating Systems (ASPLOS)*, 2010.

Author Index

NOTES

www.ingramcontent.com/pod-product-compliance
Ingram Content Group UK Ltd.
Pitfield, Milton Keynes, MK11 3LW, UK
UKHW051241300926
15471UKWH00015B/1638

9 781450 312059